# Introduction

The *Cambridge Learner's Dictionary* is a completely new dictionary for students and users of English throughout the world.

It has been written by a team of dictionary writers with a strong background in English language teaching, who really understand the needs of learners and the best way to explain what words mean and how they are used.

While writing this dictionary, we have spoken to hundreds of teachers and students in many different countries, asking them what they need, what they would like, and how they would like it presented. This has helped us to develop a style which is easy to understand while giving enough detail to help students understand and use English with confidence.

One way that teachers and students helped us was in choosing the words we used in our explanations. We already used a strictly controlled list of meanings, but as a result of our research we cut out even more words, so now we can be sure that we only use words that students are really likely to know.

This dictionary was written using the *Cambridge International Corpus*, a computerized collection of over 300 million words from a huge range of sources, both written and spoken, British and American. Our aim has been to include as many words and phrases as possible, while keeping a clear and attractive page. The corpus helps us to decide which are the most important words and meanings, and to find the most common patterns in which they are used. This means we do not waste space on rare words that students are less likely to need. The corpus also helps us find natural and typical examples to show how words and phrases are used.

Another extremely valuable tool we have is the *Cambridge Learners' Corpus*, several million words written by learners of English. This corpus shows which words cause the greatest problems for learners. We used it to help us to decide which words should have usage notes and which subjects to cover in our Study Section in the centre of the book. In other words, the information we show is there to deal with *real* problems met by *real* learners.

The *Cambridge Learner's Dictionary* is available with or without a CD-ROM which contains everything that is in the dictionary as well as some great extra features such as spoken pronunciations in British and American accents, and a unique thesaurus search feature so that you can search for words by meaning.

We hope you enjoy using the *Cambridge Learner's Dictionary*. If you have any comments about it, we would like to hear from you. Our dictionaries are all available for you to search online on our website:

http://dictionary.cambridge.org

# How to use this dictionary

Each word has a part of speech label (e.g. noun, verb, adj). For a list of the parts of speech, see inside the front cover.

Where a word has more than one meaning, the most common meaning is shown first.

Each entry begins with the base form of the word in blue.

**charity** /'tʃærɪti/ *noun* **1** ORGANIZATION [C, U] an official organization that gives money, food, or help to people who need it *The raffle will raise money for charity.* • *A percentage of the company's profits go to charity.* **2** MONEY/HELP [U] money, food, or other help that is given to people *I won't accept charity.* **3** KINDNESS [U] kindness towards other people *an act of charity*

**charity shop** *UK* (*US* **thrift shop**) *noun* [C] a shop which sells goods given by the public, especially clothes, to make money for a particular charity

Words which have several meanings have GUIDEWORDS to help you find the meaning you are looking for.

Some words (compounds) are made of two or more separate words. They are found in alphabetical order, ignoring the spaces between words. The stress pattern (= which part of the word you should emphasize when you say it) is shown on the word.

When two words have the same spelling but different parts of speech (e.g. a noun and a verb) they have separate entries.

**promise¹** /'prɒmɪs/ *verb* **1** [I, T] to say that you will certainly do something or that something will certainly happen [+ to do sth] *She promised to write to me every week.* • [+ (that)] *Paul promised me that he'd cook dinner tonight.* **2** [+ two objects] to say that you will certainly give something to someone *They promised us a reward.* • *Grandma's ring was promised to me.* **3 promise to be sth** If something promises to be good, exciting, etc, people expect that it will be good, exciting, etc. *It promises to be a really exciting game.*

### USAGE

**promise**

When you use the expression **promise someone something**, no preposition is needed after the verb.

*He promised his mum that he would clean his room.*

~~He promised to his mum that he would clean his room.~~

Grammar labels tell you how a word is used. There is an explanation of all the grammar codes on page 8.

Usage notes based on the Cambridge Learner Corpus give extra information about words which often cause problems for learners.

This symbol shows very common words which are important to learn.

**promise²** /'prɒmɪs/ *noun* **1** [C] when you say that you will certainly do something *I'm not sure I can do it so I won't **make** any **promises**.* **2 keep/break a promise** to do/not do what you said that you would do **3 show promise** If someone or something shows promise, they are likely to be successful. *As a child, he showed great promise as an athlete.*

Some words are used as part of a phrase. This is shown clearly at the start of the definition.

# Cambridge
# Learner's
# Dictionary

CAMBRIDGE
UNIVERSITY PRESS

PUBLISHED BY THE PRESS SYNDICATE OF THE UNIVERSITY OF CAMBRIDGE
The Pitt Building, Trumpington Street, Cambridge, United Kingdom

CAMBRIDGE UNIVERSITY PRESS
The Edinburgh Building, Cambridge CB2 2RU, UK
40 West 20th Street New York NY 10011–4211, USA
10 Stamford Road, Oakleigh, Melbourne 3166, Australia
Ruiz de Alarcón 13, 28014 Madrid, Spain
Dock House, The Waterfront, Cape Town, South Africa

http://www.cambridge.org

First published 2001

Printed in the United Kingdom at Omnia Books Ltd

*Typefaces* Monotype Nimrod and Adobe Frutiger    *System* QuarkXpress ®    [UPH]

*A catalogue record is available for this book from the British Library*

*Library of Congress Cataloguing in Publication data applied for*

ISBN  0 521 66366 0  paperback
ISBN  0 521 79955 4  paperback + CD-ROM
ISBN  3 12 517941 6  Klett paperback
ISBN  3 12 517942 4  Klett paperback + CD-ROM

# Contents

# Cambridge Learner's Dictionary

**Senior Commissioning Editor**
Patrick Gillard

**Managing Editor**
Elizabeth Walter

**Senior Lexicographer**
Kate Woodford

**Lexicographers**
Diane Cranz
Guy Jackson
Virginia Klein
Kerry Maxwell
Clea McEnery
Julie Moore
Martine Walsh
Sally Webber

**Systems Development Manager**
Andrew Harley

**Software Development**
Dominic Glennon
Richard Eradus
Robert Fairchild
Richard Matsen

**Corpus Development**
Ann Fiddes
Anne Finell
Marie Allan
Michael Stevens

**Design and Production**
Andrew Robinson
Samantha Dumiak
Peter Burgess
Cambridge Publishing Management

**Illustrators**
Corinne Burrows
Ray Burrows
Eikon Illustrators Ltd

Thanks are also due to the following people for their
lexicographic and editorial contributions:

Margit Aufterbeck, Jane Bottomley, Pat Bulhosen, Rebecca
Campbell, Carol Cassidy, Eric Fixmer, Lucy Hollingworth,
Tess Kaunhoven, Geraldine Mark, Mairi MacDonald,
Kate Mohideen, Diane Nichols, Elizabeth Potter, Glennis Pye,
Mira Shapur, Penny Stock, Alison Tunley, Laura Wedgeworth,
Susannah Wintersgill

Irregular inflections of words are clearly shown. There is a list of irregular verb inflections on page 748 and an explanation of regular inflections on page 12.

o–**buy¹** /baɪ/ *verb* [T] *past* **bought** to get something by paying money for it *I went to the shop to buy some milk.* • *They* **bought** *their house* **for** *£14,000.* • [+ two objects] *He bought me a camera for my birthday.*
**buy sb/sth out** to buy part of a company or building from someone else so that you own all of it *He bought out his partner for £3 million.*
**buy sth up** to quickly buy a lot of something, often all that is available *Most of the land in the area has been bought up by property developers.*
buy² /baɪ/ *noun* **a good buy** when you buy something good at a cheap price *This coat was a really good buy.*
buyer /ˈbaɪəʳ/ *noun* [C] someone who buys something
buyout /ˈbaɪaʊt/ *noun* [C] when a group of people buy the company that they work for

Phrasal verbs come after the entry for the verb. If there is more than one, they are in alphabetical order. There is a Study Page on phrasal verbs on centre page 34.

Words which are often used together (collocations) are shown in dark type in examples.

Example sentences, based on the Cambridge International Corpus, show how words are used in typical situations.

Pronunciations use the International Phonetic Alphabet. There is a list of these symbols inside the back cover of the dictionary. The most difficult symbols are also explained at the bottom of each page. There is an explanation of the pronunciation system on page 11.

o–**ice¹** /aɪs/ *noun* [U] **1** water that has frozen and become solid *Gerry slipped on the ice and broke his arm.* • *I've put a couple of bottles of champagne* **on ice** (= in a bucket of ice to get cold). **2** **break the ice** to make people who have not met before feel relaxed with each other, often by starting a conversation
ice² /aɪs/ (*also US* **frost**) *verb* [T] to cover a cake with icing (= sweet mixture used to cover cakes) *an iced bun*
iceberg /ˈaɪsbɜːɡ/ *noun* [C] a very large piece of ice that floats in the sea ⊃ *See also:* be the **tip¹** of the iceberg.

Some words are used as part of an idiom. These are shown at the end of the entry. There is a Study Page on idioms on p. centre 26.

All our explanations use very simple words. Where we have had to use a more difficult word than usual, that word is explained in brackets.

Cross references show you where you can find related information such as opposites, pictures, study pages, and idioms.

When a word can be spelled another way, or when there is another word for it, this is shown.

These labels show you when a word is used in British English or American English. There is an explanation of these labels on page 10.

**skive** /skaɪv/ (*also* **skive off**) *verb* [I, T] *UK* to not go to school or work when you should, or to leave school or work earlier than you should
• skiver *noun* [C] *UK informal* someone who skives

Some words which are formed from the main word are shown at the end of an entry. If a word is not formed with a regular pattern, or if its meaning is not easy to guess, it has its own explanation. There is a section on Word beginnings and endings on page 751.

These labels tell you how formal, informal, etc a word is. There is an explanation of all these labels on page 10.

# More information on using the dictionary

## Grammar labels

When a word must *always* be used in a particular grammatical form, that form is shown at the beginning of the entry or the beginning of the meaning. Patterns which are common and typical, but are not *always* used, are given next to example sentences showing how they are used.

### Nouns

| | | |
|---|---|---|
| C | countable noun | pencil, friend, house |
| U | uncountable noun, does not have a plural | water, advice, health |
| C, U | noun which can be countable or uncountable | ability, quantity, exercise<br>▶ *You should take some exercise.*<br>▶ *I do my exercises every morning.* |
| ⟳ | see also Study Page **Countable and uncountable nouns**, on p. centre 22. | |
| group | noun which refers to a group of people or things and can be used with either a singular or a plural verb | government, class, team<br>▶ *The French team are European champions.*<br>▶ *His team is top of the league.* |
| plural | plural noun, used with a plural verb | trousers, scissors, pliers |
| no plural | noun which can be used with **a** and **an**, but does not have a plural | rush, vicious circle, wait<br>▶ *Sorry, I'm in a rush.* |
| usually plural | noun usually used in the plural form | statistics, resources, regulations |
| usually singular | noun usually used in the singular form | mess, range, world |

### Verbs

| | | |
|---|---|---|
| I | intransitive verb, does not have an object | sleep, glance, fall<br>▶ *Anna's sleeping.* |
| T | transitive verb, must have an object | cure, hit, catch<br>▶ *Fiona hit her sister.* |
| I, T | verb that can be intransitive or transitive | sing, explain, drive<br>▶ *I always sing in the bath.*<br>▶ *He sang a love song.* |
| + two objects | ditransitive verb, that has two objects | give, send, lend<br>▶ *She gave me the keys.* |

| | | |
|---|---|---|
| often passive | verb often used in the passive | allow<br>▶ *Smoking is not allowed in the restaurant.* |
| often reflexive | verb often used with a reflexive pronoun (myself, yourself, herself, etc) | defend<br>▶ *He can defend himself.* |

If a verb or a meaning of a verb is *always* **passive** (e.g. inundate, demote, affiliate) or *always* **reflexive** (e.g. brace, ingratiate, steel), the whole grammar pattern is shown at the beginning of the entry.

Some verb or meanings of verbs are **always followed by an adverb or preposition** (e.g. creep, flick, trickle). When this happens, common examples of adverbs and prepositions used are shown at the beginning of the entry or the meaning.

↻ see also Study Page **Verb patterns**, on p. centre 42

## Adjectives

| | | |
|---|---|---|
| always before noun | attributive adjective, always comes before the noun | major, basic, staunch |
| never before noun | predicative adjective, used with verbs such as **be, seem, feel** | afraid, ready, done<br>▶ *She's afraid of water.* |
| always after noun | adjective always used directly after the noun | galore, proper, incarnate<br>▶ *The devil incarnate.* |

## Other grammar patterns

The following patterns can refer to nouns, adjectives, and verbs:

| | | |
|---|---|---|
| + that | the word is followed by a **that clause**, and the word **that** must be included | boast, assertion, evident<br>▶ *It was evident from her voice that she was upset.* |
| + (that) | the word is followed by a **that clause** but the word **that** does not have to be used | hope, amazed, doubt<br>▶ *I hope that the bus won't be late.*<br>*I hope the bus won't be late.* |
| + doing sth | the word is followed by a verb in the –ing form | enjoy, busy, difficulty<br>▶ *I enjoy going to the beach.* |
| + to do sth | the word is followed by a verb in the infinitive | confidence, careful, decide<br>▶ *I didn't have the confidence to speak up.* |
| + for/of, etc<br>+ doing sth | the word is followed by a preposition (e.g. for/of) and then a verb in the –ing form | apologize, idea, guilty<br>▶ *She apologized for being late.* |
| + question word | the word is followed by a question word (e.g. who, what, how) | ask, certain, clue<br>▶ *I'm not certain who to ask.* |
| used in questions and negatives | the word is used in questions and negative sentences | mind, much, yet<br>▶ *Do you mind if I come in?*<br>*I haven't seen him yet.* |

## Usage labels

| | | |
|---|---|---|
| *informal* | used when you are speaking, or communicating with people you know but not normally in serious writing | brainy, freebie, goalie |
| *formal* | used in serious writing or for communicating with people about things like law or business | examination, moreover, purchase |
| *very informal* | used when you are talking to people you know well, and not usually in writing. Some of these words may offend people, and this is explained in the entry. | prat, barf, crap |
| *spoken* | a way of writing a word which is used in conversation | yeah, hey, eh |
| *humorous* | used in order to be funny or to make a joke | couch potato, snail mail |
| *literary* | used in books and poems, not in ordinary conversation | beloved, slumber, weep |
| *old-fashioned* | not used in modern English – you might find these words in books, used by older people, or used in order to be funny | gramophone, spectacles, farewell |
| *trademark* | the name of a product that is made by one company, but which has become used as a general word | Coke, Hoover, Sellotape |

## UK/US labels

The spelling used in definitions and examples in this dictionary is British English. However, American English is also explained clearly, and where there is a difference between British and American English, this is shown.

| | | |
|---|---|---|
| *UK* | only used in British English | pavement, petrol station |
| *US* | only used in American English | sidewalk, gas station |
| *mainly UK* | mainly used in British English, but sometimes in American English | lecturer, rubbish, nightdress |
| *mainly US* | mainly used in American English, but sometimes in British English | movie, apartment, semester |
| *also UK* | another word that can also be used in British English | truck (*also UK* lorry) ▪ **truck** is used in Britain and America **lorry** is also used in Britain |

*also US*   another word that can also be used in American English

railway (*also US* railroad)
■ **railway** is used in Britain and America
**railroad** is also used in America

⊃ see also Study Page **UK and US English**, on p. centre 41

## Pronunciation

All pronunciations use the International Phonetic Alphabet. There is a complete list of phonetic symbols inside the back cover.

Many phonetic symbols, e.g. /p/, /s/, /k/, sound exactly like the most common pronunciation of the letter they look like. Those that do not are explained at the bottom of every page of the dictionary.

Where more than one pronunciation is shown, the more common one is first, but both are often used.

### British and American pronunciation

Most words are given only one pronunciation, which is acceptable in British and American English. There are some regular differences between British and American English which are not shown for every word.

The main ones are:

1   In American English, the **r** in words such as **hard** or **teacher** is pronounced, and in British English it is silent.

2   In American English, **t** and **tt** in words such as **later** and **butter**, are pronounced in a soft way, almost like a /d/ sound.

Where there is a big difference between British and American pronunciation, both forms are shown. The symbol ⓤⓢ is shown before an American pronunciation, e.g. **schedule** /'ʃedjuːl ⓤⓢ 'skedʒuːl/

### Stress patterns

Stress patterns show you which parts of the word you should emphasize when you say them.

/'/ shows the main emphasis on a word. For example, in the word **picture** /'pɪktʃər/, you should emphasize the first part, and in the word **deny** /dɪ'naɪ/ you should emphasize the second part.

/ˌ/ shows the second most important emphasis on the word. For example, in the word **submarine** /ˌsʌbmərˈiːn/, the main emphasis is on the last part of the word, but you should also emphasize the first part of the word slightly.

Compound words (words made of two or more separate words) have their stress patterns shown on them. For example in the word **casˈsette reˌcorder**, the main emphasis is on the second part of the first word, but you should also emphasize the second part of the second word slightly.

### Strong forms and weak forms

Some common words (e.g. and, them, of) have strong forms and weak forms. The weak forms are more common.

For example, in the sentence '*I saw them leave.*', the weak form /ðəm/ would be used.

The strong form is used when you want to emphasize the word. For instance, in the sentence '*They said they saw me, but I didn't see them.*', the strong form /ðem/ would be used.

## Regular inflections

All inflections (e.g. plurals, past tenses) that are not regular (= are not formed in the usual way) are shown at the entry for the word. The regular way of forming inflections is shown below.

### Nouns

Most nouns form their plurals by adding –s
▶ *chair, chairs*     ▶ *plate, plates*

Nouns which end in –s, –ss, –ch, –x, and –z, make their plurals by adding –es
▶ *mass, masses*     ▶ *match, matches*

Nouns which end in a consonant (e.g. m, t, p) + –y, form their plurals by taking away the –y and adding –ies
▶ *baby, babies*     ▶ *university, universities*

### Adjectives

↻ see also Study Page **Adjectives,** on p. centre 18

The comparative form of adjectives is used to show that someone or something has more of a particular quality than someone or something else. To make the regular comparative form, you either add –er to the end of the adjective, or use the word **more** before it.

The superlative form of adjectives is used to show that someone or something has more of a particular quality than anyone or anything else. To make the regular superlative form, you either add –est to the end of the adjective, or use the word **most** before it.

One-syllable adjectives usually form their comparative and superlative with –er and –est
▶ *small, smaller, smallest*

Two-syllable adjectives can all form their comparative and superlative with **more** and **most.**
▶ *complex, more complex, most complex*

Some two-syllable adjectives can use –er and –est too. The most common of these are:
■ adjectives ending in –y and –ow,
  ▶ *happy, noisy, shallow*
■ adjectives ending in –le,
  ▶ *able, noble, simple*
■ some other common two-syllable adjectives,
  ▶ *common, cruel, handsome, pleasant, polite, quiet, solid, wicked*

Three-syllable adjectives usually form their comparative and superlative with **more** and **most**
▶ *beautiful, more beautiful, most beautiful*

When you are using the –er, –est forms, if the adjective ends in –e, take away the –e before adding the ending
▶ *pale, paler, palest*

If the adjective ends in –y, change this to –i before adding the ending
▶ *happy, happier, happiest*

### Verbs

Regular verbs add the following endings:

for the 3rd **person singular** add –s, or –es to verbs that end in –s, –ss, –ch, –x, and –z

for the **present participle** add –ing

for the **past tense** and the **past participle** add –ed
▶ *pack, packs, packing, packed*

For verbs ending in –e, take away the –e before adding the present participle, past tense, and past participle endings.
▶ *hate, hates, hating, hated*

For verbs ending in –y, for the third person singular take away the –y and add –ies, and for the past tense and past participle take away the –y and add –ied.
▶ *cry, cries, crying, cried*

**A, a** /eɪ/ the first letter of the alphabet

o┅**a** (also **an**) strong form /eɪ/ weak form /ə/ determiner **1** BEFORE NOUN used before a noun to refer to a single thing or person but not a particular thing or person or not one that you have referred to before I need a new car. • I bought a nice coat yesterday. • I saw a woman speaking to him. **2** ONE one a hundred dollars • a dozen eggs **3** EVERY/EACH every or each A child needs love. • Take one tablet three times a (= each) day. **4** TYPE used to say what type of thing or person something or someone is It's a guinea-pig. • She's a doctor. **5** AN ACTION used before some action nouns when referring to one example of the action I'm just going to have a wash. • Take a look at this. **6** TWO NOUNS used before the first of two nouns that are often used together a cup and saucer **7** AMOUNTS used before some phrases saying how much of something there is a few days • a bit of sugar **8** NAME used before a person's name when referring to someone you do not know There's a Ms Leeming to see you.

### USAGE

**a or an?**

Remember to use **an** in front of words which begin with a vowel sound. These are words which start with the letters a, e, i, o, u, or a sound like those letters.

a car, an orange, an hour

**aback** /ə'bæk/ adv **be taken aback** to be very surprised or shocked I was rather taken aback by her honesty.

**abacus** /'æbəkəs/ noun [C] a square object with small balls on wires, used for counting

**abandon** /ə'bændən/ verb [T] **1** to leave someone or something somewhere, sometimes not returning to get them They were forced to abandon the car. • He was abandoned by his mother as a baby. **2** to stop doing something before it is finished, or to stop following a plan, idea, etc The match was abandoned because of rain. • abandoned adj • abandonment noun [U]

**abate** /ə'beɪt/ verb [I] formal to become less strong By the weekend, the storms had abated.

**abattoir** /'æbətwɑːʳ/ UK (UK/US **slaughterhouse**) noun [C] a place where animals are killed for meat

**abbey** /'æbi/ noun [C] a group of buildings that is or was a home for monks or nuns (= religious men or women who live separately from other people)

**abbreviate** /ə'briːvieɪt/ verb [T] to make a word or phrase shorter The word 'street' is often abbreviated to 'St'.

**abbreviation** /ə,briːvi'eɪʃᵊn/ noun [C] a shorter form of a word or phrase, especially used in writing A doctor is often called a 'GP', an abbreviation for 'general practitioner'.

**abdicate** /'æbdɪkeɪt/ verb **1** [I] If a king or queen abdicates, they choose to stop being king or queen. **2 abdicate responsibility** formal to decide not to be responsible for something any more • abdication /,æbdɪ'keɪʃᵊn/ noun [C, U]

**abdomen** /'æbdəmən/ noun [C] formal the lower part of a person or animal's body, containing the stomach and other organs • abdominal /æb'dɒmɪnᵊl/ adj abdominal pains

**abduct** /əb'dʌkt/ verb [T] to take someone away illegally He was abducted and murdered by a terrorist group. • abduction /əb'dʌkʃᵊn/ noun [C, U]

**aberration** /,æbə'reɪʃᵊn/ noun [C] formal a temporary change from what usually happens

**abet** /ə'bet/ verb **abetting**, past **abetted** ⊃ See aid.

**abhor** /əb'hɔːʳ/ verb [T] abhorring, past abhorred formal to hate something or someone very much • abhorrence /əb'hɒrᵊns/ noun [U] formal

**abhorrent** /əb'hɒrᵊnt/ adj formal morally very bad an abhorrent crime

**abide** /ə'baɪd/ verb **can't abide sb/sth** to strongly dislike someone or something I can't abide rudeness.

**abide by sth** to obey a rule Staff who refused to abide by the rules were fired.

**abiding** /ə'baɪdɪŋ/ adj [always before noun] An abiding feeling or memory is one that you have for a long time. My abiding memory is of him watering his plants in the garden. ⊃ See also: law-abiding.

o┅**ability** /ə'bɪləti/ noun [C, U] the physical or mental skill or qualities that you need to do something athletic/academic ability • [+ to do sth] He **had the ability** to explain things clearly and concisely. • The report questions the technical ability of some of the staff. ⊃ Compare disability, ⊃ Opposite inability.

**abject** /'æbdʒekt/ adj **1 abject misery/poverty/terror**, etc when someone is extremely unhappy, poor, afraid, etc **2** showing that you are very ashamed of what you have done an abject apology

**ablaze** /ə'bleɪz/ adj [never before noun] burning strongly

o┅**able** /'eɪbl/ adj **1 be able to do sth** to have the ability to do something or the possibility of doing something He'll be able to help you. • I wouldn't be able to come at that time anyway. ⊃ Opposite unable **2** clever or good at doing something Even the most able students found the test difficult. • ably adv Robson, ably assisted by Anderson, has completely rebuilt the team.

**able-bodied** /,eɪbl'bɒdɪd/ adj having all the physical abilities that most people have

**abnormal** /æb'nɔːmᵊl/ adj different from what is normal or usual, in a way which is strange or dangerous abnormal behaviour/weather • They found abnormal levels of lead in the water. • abnormally adv abnormally high temperatures

**abnormality** /,æbnɔː'mæləti/ noun [C, U] something abnormal, usually in the body a genetic abnormality

**aboard** /ə'bɔːd/ adv, preposition on or onto a plane, ship, bus, or train Welcome aboard flight BA109 to Paris.

**abode** /əˈbəʊd/ noun [C] formal a home

**abolish** /əˈbɒlɪʃ/ verb [T] to officially end something, especially a law or system *National Service was abolished in Britain in 1962.* • abolition /ˌæbəˈlɪʃⁿn/ noun [U] *the abolition of slavery*

**abominable** /əˈbɒmɪnəbl/ adj extremely bad *abominable behaviour/conditions* • abominably adv

**Aboriginal** /ˌæbəˈrɪdʒⁿnⁿl/ adj relating or belonging to the original race of people who lived in Australia • Aborigine /ˌæbəˈrɪdʒⁿni/ noun [C] an Aboriginal person

**abort** /əˈbɔːt/ verb [T] 1 to stop a process before it has finished *The take-off was aborted due to bad weather.* 2 to end a pregnancy that is not wanted using a medical operation

**abortion** /əˈbɔːʃⁿn/ noun [C, U] a medical operation to end a pregnancy when the baby is still too small to live *to have an abortion*

**abortive** /əˈbɔːtɪv/ adj [always before noun] An abortive attempt or plan fails before it is complete.

**abound** /əˈbaʊnd/ verb [I] formal to exist in large numbers *Rumours abound about a possible change of leadership.*

o⊶**about¹** /əˈbaʊt/ preposition 1 relating to a particular subject or person *a book about the Spanish Civil War* • *What was she talking about?* 2 UK (US **around**) to or in different parts of a place, often without purpose or order *They were creeping about the garden.* • *We heard someone moving about outside.* 3 **what/how about ...?** a used to make a suggestion *How about France for a holiday?* b used to ask for someone's opinion on a particular subject *What about Ann – is she nice?*

o⊶**about²** /əˈbaʊt/ adv 1 APPROXIMATELY used before a number or amount to mean approximately *It happened about two months ago.* 2 DIRECTION UK (US **around**) to or in different parts of a place, often without purpose or order *She's always leaving her clothes lying about.* 3 NEAR UK informal (US **around**) If someone or something is about, they are near to the place where you are now. *Is Kate about?* 4 **be about to do sth** to be going to do something very soon *I stopped her just as she was about to leave.*

o⊶**above¹** /əˈbʌv/ adv, preposition 1 HIGHER POSITION in or to a higher position than something else *There's a mirror above the washbasin.* • *I could hear music coming from the room above.* 2 MORE more than an amount or level *It says on the box it's for children aged three and above.* • *Rates of pay are above average.* 3 RANK in a more important or advanced position than someone else *Sally's a grade above me.* 4 TOO IMPORTANT too good or important for something *No one is above suspicion in this matter.* 5 **above all** most importantly *Above all, I'd like to thank everyone.*

**above²** /əˈbʌv/ adj, adv higher on the same page *the above diagram* • *the address shown above*

**above board** adj [never before noun] honest and legal *We hired a lawyer to make sure the agreement was all above board.*

**abrasive** /əˈbreɪsɪv/ adj 1 An abrasive substance is rough and can be used for rubbing surfaces, to make them clean or smooth. 2 speaking or behaving in a rude and unpleasant way *an abrasive manner*

**abreast** /əˈbrest/ adv 1 **keep (sb) abreast of sth** to make sure you or someone else knows about the most recent changes in a subject or situation *I'll keep you abreast of any developments.* 2 **two/three/four, etc abreast** If people who are moving are two/three, etc abreast, that number of people are next to each other, side by side. *They were cycling four abreast, completely blocking the road.*

**abridged** /əˈbrɪdʒd/ adj An abridged book or other piece of writing has been made shorter. ➔ Opposite **unabridged**. • abridge /əˈbrɪdʒ/ verb [T]

o⊶**abroad** /əˈbrɔːd/ adv in or to a foreign country *He goes abroad a lot with his job.*

**abrupt** /əˈbrʌpt/ adj 1 sudden and not expected *Our conversation came to an abrupt end because Jean was called away.* 2 dealing with people in a quick way that is unfriendly or rude *She has a rather abrupt manner.* • abruptly adv

**abscess** /ˈæbses/ noun [C] a painful, swollen area on the body which contains a yellow liquid

**abscond** /əbˈskɒnd/ verb [I] formal to leave somewhere suddenly without permission because you want to escape, or because you have stolen something

**absence** /ˈæbsⁿns/ noun 1 [C, U] a time when you are not in a particular place *Lisa will be acting as manager in Phil's absence* (= while Phil is not here). • *A large number of absences from work are caused by back problems.* 2 [U] when something does not exist *In the absence of any proof, it is impossible to accuse her.*

**absent** /ˈæbsⁿnt/ adj not in the place where you are expected to be, especially at school or work *He has been absent from school all week.*

**absentee** /ˌæbsⁿnˈtiː/ noun [C] someone who is not in a place where they should be • absenteeism noun [U] when someone is often absent from work or school

**absently** /ˈæbsⁿntli/ adv without thinking about what you are doing *He stared absently at the television screen.*

**absent-minded** /ˌæbsⁿntˈmaɪndɪd/ adj often forgetting things • absent-mindedly adv • absent-mindedness noun [U]

**absolute** /ˈæbsəluːt/ adj [always before noun] 1 complete *absolute power/control* • *The party was an absolute disaster.* 2 definite *There was no absolute proof of fraud.*

o⊶**absolutely** /ˌæbsəˈluːtli/ adv 1 completely *The food was absolutely delicious.* • *She absolutely hated the place.* • *There's absolutely nothing* (= nothing at all) *left.* 2 **Absolutely.** used to strongly agree with someone *"Do you think it helped his career?" "Absolutely."* 3 **Absolutely not.** used to strongly disagree with someone or to agree with something negative *"Are you suggesting that we should just ignore the problem?" "No, absolutely not."*

**absolve** /əbˈzɒlv/ verb [T] formal to formally say that someone is not guilty of something, or to forgive someone

**absorb** /əbˈzɔːb/ *verb* [T] **1** LIQUID If a substance absorbs a liquid, it takes it in through its surface and holds it. *The fabric absorbs all the moisture, keeping your skin dry.* **2 be absorbed in sth** to give all your attention to something that you are doing *Simon was so absorbed in his computer game, he didn't notice me come in.* **3** REMEMBER to understand and remember facts that you read or hear *It's hard to absorb so much information.* **4** BECOME PART OF If something is absorbed into something else, it becomes part of it. *The drug is quickly **absorbed into** the bloodstream.*

**absorbent** /əbˈzɔːbənt/ *adj* An absorbent substance can take liquids in through its surface and hold them.

**absorbing** /əbˈzɔːbɪŋ/ *adj* very interesting *an absorbing book/game*

**abstain** /əbˈsteɪn/ *verb* [I] **1** *formal* to not do something that you enjoy because it is bad or unhealthy *The doctor suggested that he **abstain from** alcohol.* **2** to choose not to vote for or against something *63 members voted in favour, 39 opposed and 5 abstained.* • abstention /əbˈstenʃ°n/ *noun* [C, U]

**abstinence** /ˈæbstɪnəns/ *noun* [U] *formal* when you do not do something that you enjoy because it is bad or unhealthy

**abstract** /ˈæbstrækt/ *adj* **1** relating to ideas and not real things *an abstract concept* **2** Abstract art involves shapes and colours and not images of real things or people.

**absurd** /əbˈzɜːd/ *adj* very silly *an absurd situation/suggestion* • absurdity *noun* [C, U] • absurdly *adv*

**abundance** /əˈbʌndəns/ *noun* [U, no plural] *formal* a lot of something *an abundance of flowers* • *There was food **in abundance** (= a lot of food).*

**abundant** /əˈbʌndənt/ *adj* existing in large quantities *an abundant supply of food* • abundantly *adv*

**abuse¹** /əˈbjuːs/ *noun* **1** WRONG USE [C, U] when something is used for the wrong purpose in a way that is harmful or morally wrong *drug/alcohol abuse* • *abuse of public money* **2** VIOLENCE [U] violent, cruel treatment of someone *child abuse* • *sexual abuse* **3** LANGUAGE [U] rude and offensive words said to another person *Rival fans shouted abuse at each other.*

**abuse²** /əˈbjuːz/ *verb* [T] **1** VIOLENCE to treat someone cruelly and violently *He was physically abused by his alcoholic father.* **2** WRONG USE to use something for the wrong purpose in a way that is harmful or morally wrong *to abuse alcohol* **3** LANGUAGE to say rude and offensive words to someone *The crowd started abusing him.* • abuser *noun* [C]

**abusive** /əˈbjuːsɪv/ *adj* saying rude and offensive words to someone *an abusive phone call* • *He was drunk and abusive.*

**abysmal** /əˈbɪzm°l/ *adj* very bad, especially of bad quality *the team's abysmal performance last season* • abysmally *adv*

**abyss** /əˈbɪs/ *noun* [C] **1** a very bad situation which will not improve [usually singular] *The country is sinking into an abyss of violence and bloodshed.* **2** *literary* a very deep hole

**academia** /ˌækəˈdiːmiə/ *noun* [U] the people and organizations, especially universities, involved in studying

**academic¹** /ˌækəˈdemɪk/ *adj* **1** EDUCATION related to education, schools, universities, etc *academic ability/standards* • *It's the start of the **academic year**.* **2** SUBJECTS related to subjects which involve thinking and studying and not technical or practical skills *academic subjects* **3** CLEVER clever and good at studying **4** NOT REAL If what someone says is academic, it has no purpose because it relates to a situation that does not exist. *The whole discussion is academic since management won't even listen to us.* • academically *adv*

**academic²** /ˌækəˈdemɪk/ *noun* [C] someone who teaches at a university or college or is paid to study there

**academy** /əˈkædəmi/ *noun* [C] **1** a college which teaches people the skills needed for a particular job *a military academy* **2** an organization whose purpose is to encourage and develop an art, science, language, etc *the Royal Academy of Music*

**accelerate** /əkˈseləreɪt/ *verb* **1** [I] to start to drive faster **2** [I, T] to start to happen more quickly, or to make something start to happen more quickly *Inflation is likely to accelerate this year.* • acceleration /əkˌseləˈreɪʃ°n/ *noun* [U]

**accelerator** /əkˈseləreɪtəʳ/ (*also US* **gas pedal**) *noun* [C] the part of a car which you push with your foot to make it go faster ⊃ *See colour picture* **Car** *on page Centre 3.*

**accent** /ˈæks°nt/ *noun* [C] **1** PRONUNCIATION the way in which someone pronounces words, influenced by the country or area they come from, or their social class *an American accent* • *a French accent* • *He speaks with a strong northern accent.* **2** WRITTEN MARK a mark above a letter to show you how to pronounce it, for example (â) and (é) **3** WORD EMPHASIS the word or part of a word that you emphasize when you are speaking *In the word 'impossible' the accent is on the second syllable.* **4 the accent on sth** particular importance or attention that you give to something *a wonderful menu with the accent on fresh fish*

**accentuate** /əkˈsentʃueɪt/ *verb* [T] to emphasize something so that people notice it *make-up to accentuate the eyes*

o—accept /əkˈsept/ *verb* **1** AGREE [I, T] to agree to take something that is offered to you *to accept an invitation/offer* • *to accept a job* • *He won't accept advice from anyone.* • *Do you accept credit cards?* **2** ADMIT [T] to admit that something is true, often something unpleasant [+ (that)] *He refuses to accept that he's made a mistake.* **3** ALLOW TO JOIN [T] to allow someone to join an organization or become part of a group *She's been accepted by two universities.* • *Many of the refugees have now been accepted into the local community.* **4 accept responsibility/blame** to admit that you caused something bad that happened *The company has now accepted responsibility for the accident.* **5** UNDERSTAND [T] to understand that you cannot change a very sad or unpleasant situation *The hardest part is accepting the fact that you'll never see that person again.*

| j yes | k cat | ʃ she | ʒ decision | θ thin | ð this | ŋ ring | tʃ chip | dʒ jar | æ cat | ɑː arm | e bed | eə hair | ə ago | ɜː her | ɪ sit | i cosy |

---

### USAGE

**accept** or **agree**?

When you accept an invitation, job, or offer, you say yes to something which is offered. **Accept** is never followed by another verb.

*They offered me the job and I've accepted it.*

~~They offered me the job and I've accepted to take it.~~

When you **agree** to do something, you say that you will do something which someone asks you to do.

*They offered me the job and I agreed to take it.*

---

o━**acceptable** /ək'septəbl/ *adj* **1** good enough work of an acceptable standard • *We still hope to find a solution which is acceptable to both sides.* **2** allowed or approved of *Smoking is less and less socially acceptable.* ⊃ *Opposite* **unacceptable.** • acceptability /ək,septə'bɪləti/ *noun* [U]

**acceptance** /ək'septəns/ *noun* [C, U] when you accept something *his acceptance of the award* • *There is a growing public acceptance of alternative medicine.*

**accepted** /ək'septɪd/ *adj* agreed or approved by most people *an accepted spelling*

**access**[1] /'ækses/ *noun* [U] **1** when you have the right or opportunity to use or see something *I don't have access to that kind of information.* • *Do you have Internet access?* **2** the way in which you can enter a place or get to a place *The only access to the village is by boat.* • *better access for the disabled*

**access**[2] /'ækses/ *verb* [T] to find or see information, especially using a computer *You can access the files over the Internet.*

**accessible** /ək'sesəbl/ *adj* **1** easy to find or reach *Information such as this is freely accessible to the public.* • *The hotel is in a quiet but easily accessible part of the resort.* ⊃ *Opposite* **inaccessible. 2** easy to understand *They are attempting to make opera accessible to a wider audience.* • accessibility /ək,sesə'bɪləti/ *noun* [U]

**accessory** /ək'sesəri/ *noun* [C] **1** something extra which is not necessary but is attractive or useful [usually plural] *They sell belts and scarves and other fashion accessories.* • *bathroom accessories* • *computer accessories* **2** *formal* someone who helps a criminal to commit a crime *an accessory to murder*

o━**accident** /'æksɪdənt/ *noun* [C] **1** something bad which happens that is not intended and which causes injury or damage *a car/traffic accident* • *(UK) He was involved in a road accident a month ago.* • *She had an accident in the kitchen.* • *I didn't mean to spill his drink. It was an accident.* **2 by accident** without being intended *I deleted the wrong file by accident.*

**accidental** /,æksɪ'dentəl/ *adj* not intended *accidental damage* • accidentally *adv She accidentally knocked over a glass of red wine.*

**accident-prone** /'æksɪdənt,prəʊn/ *adj* Someone who is accident-prone often has accidents.

**acclaim** /ə'kleɪm/ *noun* [U] praise from a lot of people *international/public acclaim*

**acclaimed** /ə'kleɪmd/ *adj* praised by a lot of people *the acclaimed singer and songwriter*

**acclimatize** (*also UK* **-ise**) /ə'klaɪmətaɪz/ *verb* [I, T] to start to feel happy with the weather, the way of life, etc in a new place, or to make someone do this • acclimatization /ə,klaɪmətaɪ'zeɪʃən/ *noun* [U]

**accolade** /'ækəleɪd/ *noun* [C] *formal* a prize or praise given to someone because they are very good at something

**accommodate** /ə'kɒmədeɪt/ *verb* [T] **1** HAVE SPACE FOR to have enough space or room for a number of things or people *We need more roads to accommodate the increase in traffic.* **2** HELP to do what someone wants, often by providing them with something *He requires special equipment and, where possible, we've accommodated those needs.* **3** GIVE A HOME to provide someone with a place to live or stay *The athletes will be accommodated in a special Olympic village.*

**accommodating** /ə'kɒmədeɪtɪŋ/ *adj* willing to change your plans in order to help people

o━**accommodation** /ə,kɒmə'deɪʃən/ *noun* [U] (*also US* **accommodations** [plural]) a place where you live or stay *rented accommodation* • *The price includes travel and accommodation.*

**accompaniment** /ə'kʌmpənimənt/ *noun* **1** [C] *formal* something that is nice to eat or drink with a particular food or drink *salmon with an accompaniment of green salad* **2** [C, U] music that is played with the main instrument or with a singing voice *a song with piano accompaniment*

**accompany** /ə'kʌmpəni/ *verb* [T] **1** GO WITH *formal* to go somewhere with someone *We accompanied her back to her hotel.* **2** HAPPEN TOGETHER to happen or exist at the same time as something else *The teachers' book is accompanied by a video cassette.* **3** MUSIC to play a musical instrument with someone else who is playing or singing

**accomplice** /ə'kʌmplɪs/ *noun* [C] someone who helps a criminal to commit a crime

**accomplish** /ə'kʌmplɪʃ/ *verb* [T] to succeed in doing something good *I feel as if I've accomplished nothing all day.*

**accomplished** /ə'kʌmplɪʃt/ *adj* having a lot of skill in art, music, writing, etc *an accomplished musician/painter*

**accomplishment** /ə'kʌmplɪʃmənt/ *noun* **1** [U] when you succeed in doing something good *Finishing the course gave me a great sense of accomplishment.* **2** [C] *formal* a skill in art, music, writing, etc

**accord**[1] /ə'kɔːd/ *noun* **1 of your own accord** If you do something of your own accord, you choose to do it and no one else forces you. *Luckily, she left of her own accord.* **2** [C] an official agreement, especially between countries *a peace/trade accord*

**accord**[2] /ə'kɔːd/ *verb* [T] *formal* to treat someone specially, usually by showing respect *the respect accorded to doctors*

**accordance** /ə'kɔːdəns/ *noun formal* **in accordance with sth** agreeing with a rule, law, or wish *Both companies have insisted that they were acting in accordance with the law.*

**accordingly** /ə'kɔːdɪŋli/ *adv* in a way that is suitable *We'll wait until we hear the decision and act accordingly.*

o→**according to** /ə'kɔːdɪŋtuː/ *preposition* **1** as said by someone or shown by something *According to Susie, he didn't even have a girlfriend.* • *According to our records, she was absent last Friday.* **2** based on a particular system or plan *Children are allocated to schools according to the area in which they live.*

**accordion** /ə'kɔːdiən/ *noun* [C] a musical instrument with a folding centre part and keyboards at both ends which you play by pushing the two ends together

**accost** /ə'kɒst/ *verb* [T] If someone you do not know accosts you, they move towards you and start talking to you in an unfriendly way.

**account¹** /ə'kaʊnt/ *noun* [C] **1** REPORT a written or spoken description of something that has happened *They gave conflicting accounts of the events.* • *The documents provide a detailed account of the town's early history.* **2** BANK (*also* **bank account**) an arrangement with a bank to keep your money there and to let you take it out when you need to *I paid the money into my account this morning.* **3** SHOP an agreement with a shop or company that allows you to buy things and pay for them later **4 take sth into account/take account of sth** to consider something when judging a situation *You have to take into account the fact that he is less experienced when judging his performance.* **5 on account of sth** *formal* because of something *He doesn't drink alcohol on account of his health.* **6 by all accounts** as said by a lot of people *The party was, by all accounts, a great success.* **7 on my account** just for or because of me *Please don't change your plans on my account.* **8 on no account/not on any account** *UK* not for any reason or in any situation *On no account must these records be changed.* ➔ *See also:* **checking account**, **current account**, **deposit account**.

**account²** /ə'kaʊnt/ *verb*
**account for sth 1** to be part of a total number of something *Oil accounts for 40% of Norway's exports.* **2** to be the reason for something, or to explain the reason for something *He'd had an argument with Caroline, which accounts for his bad mood this morning.* • *She was asked to account for the missing money.*

**accountable** /ə'kaʊntəbl/ *adj* [never before noun] having to be responsible for what you do and able to explain your actions *Hospitals must be held **accountable** for their mistakes.* • *Politicians should be **accountable to** the public that elects them.* ➔ *Opposite* **unaccountable**. • **accountability** /ə,kaʊntə'bɪləti/ *noun* [U]

**accountancy** /ə'kaʊntənsi/ *UK* (*US* **accounting**) *noun* [U] the job of being an accountant

**accountant** /ə'kaʊntənt/ *noun* [C] someone whose job is to keep or examine the financial records of a company or organization

**accounts** /ə'kaʊnts/ *noun* [plural] an official record of all the money a company or organization has received or paid

**accreditation** /ə,kredɪ'teɪʃᵊn/ *noun* [U] official approval of an organization • **accredited** /ə'kredɪtɪd/ *adj* officially approved

**accumulate** /ə'kjuːmjəleɪt/ *verb* [I, T] to increase in amount over a period of time, or to make something increase over a period of

time *The chemicals accumulate in your body.* • *to accumulate wealth/debts* • **accumulation** /ə,kjuːmjə'leɪʃᵊn/ *noun* [U]

**accuracy** /'ækjərəsi/ *noun* [U] how correct or exact something is *The new system should help to improve the accuracy of weather forecasts.*

o→**accurate** /'ækjərət/ *adj* correct or exact *accurate information/measurements* • *She was able to give police a fairly accurate description of the man.* ➔ *Opposite* **inaccurate**. • **accurately** *adv*

**accusation** /,ækju'zeɪʃᵊn/ *noun* [C] when you say that someone has done something bad *He **made** a number of **accusations against** his former colleagues.*

o→**accuse** /ə'kjuːz/ *verb* [T] to say that someone has done something bad *He was falsely **accused of** murder.* • [+ of + doing sth] *She accused Andrew of lying to her.* • **accuser** *noun* [C]

**the accused** /ə'kjuːzd/ *noun formal* the person or people who are accused of a crime in a court of law

**accusing** /ə'kjuːzɪŋ/ *adj* showing that you think someone is responsible for something bad *Why are you giving me that accusing look?*

**accustom** /ə'kʌstəm/ *verb*
**accustom yourself to sth/doing sth** to experience something often enough for it to seem normal to you

**accustomed** /ə'kʌstəmd/ *adj* **accustomed to sth/doing sth** If you are accustomed to something, you have experienced it often enough for it to seem normal to you. *I've worked nights for years now so I've **grown accustomed to** it.* • *She isn't accustomed to dealing with so much media attention.*

**ace¹** /eɪs/ *noun* [C] **1** a playing card with one symbol on it, that has the highest or lowest value in many games **2** when the first shot by a tennis player is too good for the other player to hit back

**ace²** /eɪs/ *adj informal* very good

**ache¹** /eɪk/ *noun* [C] a feeling of pain over an area of your body which continues for a long time *There's a dull ache in my right shoulder.* ➔ *See also:* **stomach ache**.

**ache²** /eɪk/ *verb* [I] If a part of your body aches, it is painful. *My legs are aching after all that exercise.*

o→**achieve** /ə'tʃiːv/ *verb* [T] to succeed in doing something good, usually by working hard *to achieve an ambition* • *I've been working all day but I feel I've achieved nothing.* • **achievable** *adj* possible to achieve *achievable goals* • **achiever** *noun* [C] *He's from a family of high achievers* (= very successful people).

o→**achievement** /ə'tʃiːvmənt/ *noun* **1** [C] something good that you achieve *This film is his greatest achievement to date.* **2** [U] when you succeed in doing something good, usually by working hard *You get such a **sense of achievement** when you finish the course.*

**acid¹** /'æsɪd/ *noun* [C, U] one of several liquid substances which react with other substances, often burning or dissolving them *hydrochloric acid* • **acidity** /ə'sɪdəti/ *noun* [U]

**acid²** /'æsɪd/ *adj* **1** (*also* **acidic** /ə'sɪdɪk/) containing acid, or having similar qualities to an acid *acid soil* • *an acid smell/taste* **2 acid remark/**

**comment, etc** an unkind remark that criticizes someone

,acid 'rain *noun* [U] rain that contains chemicals from pollution and damages plants, etc

acknowledge /ək'nɒlɪdʒ/ *verb* [T] 1 ACCEPT to accept that something is true or exists [+ (that)] *At least he acknowledged that there was a problem.* 2 LETTER to tell someone, usually in a letter, that you have received something they sent you *They sent a letter acknowledging receipt of my application.* 3 SAY HELLO to let someone know that you have seen them, usually by saying hello *She didn't even acknowledge my presence.*

acknowledgement (*also* **acknowledgment**) /ək'nɒlɪdʒmənt/ *noun* 1 ACCEPT [C, U] when you accept that something is true or exists *There was no acknowledgement of the extent of the problem.* 2 LETTER [C] a letter telling you that someone has received something that you sent them 3 BOOK [C] something written at the front of a book by the author to thank people who have helped them [usually plural] *His name appears in the acknowledgements.*

acne /'ækni/ *noun* [U] a skin problem that young people often have that causes spots on the face

acorn /'eɪkɔːn/ *noun* [C] an oval nut which grows on oak trees

acoustic /ə'kuːstɪk/ *adj* 1 [always before noun] An acoustic musical instrument does not use electricity. *an acoustic guitar* 2 relating to sound and hearing

acoustics /ə'kuːstɪks/ *noun* [plural] the way in which the shape of a room affects the quality of sound *The acoustics of the hall were terrible.*

acquaintance /ə'kweɪntᵊns/ *noun* [C] someone who you know but do not know well *He's just a business acquaintance.*

acquainted /ə'kweɪntɪd/ *adj* [never before noun] *formal* 1 If you are acquainted with someone, you have met them but do not know them well. *We're already acquainted – we met at Elaine's party.* 2 **be acquainted with sth** to know about something *I'm afraid I'm not yet acquainted with the system.*

acquiesce /ˌækwi'es/ *verb* [I] *formal* to agree to something, often when you do not want to ● acquiescence *noun* [U] *formal*

acquire /ə'kwaɪəʳ/ *verb* [T] 1 to get something *I managed to acquire a copy of the report.* ● *His family acquired (= bought) the property in 1985.* 2 to learn something *to acquire knowledge/skills*

acquisition /ˌækwɪ'zɪʃᵊn/ *noun* 1 [U] the process of learning or getting something *children's acquisition of language* 2 [C] something that you get, usually by buying it *And the hat – is that a recent acquisition?*

acquit /ə'kwɪt/ *verb* [T] **acquitting**, *past* **acquitted** If someone is acquitted of a crime, a court of law decides that they are not guilty. [often passive] *Both men were acquitted of murder.*

acquittal /ə'kwɪtᵊl/ *noun* [C, U] when a court of law decides that someone is not guilty of a crime

acre /'eɪkəʳ/ *noun* [C] a unit for measuring area, equal to 4047 square metres

acrid /'ækrɪd/ *adj* An acrid smell is unpleasant and causes a burning feeling in your throat.

acrimonious /ˌækrɪ'məʊniəs/ *adj* involving a lot of anger, disagreement, and bad feelings *an acrimonious debate/divorce* ● acrimony /'ækrɪməni/ *noun* [U] angry, bad feelings between people

acrobat /'ækrəbæt/ *noun* [C] someone who entertains people by performing difficult physical acts, such as walking on a wire high above the ground ● acrobatic /ˌækrə'bætɪk/ *adj* ● acrobatics /ˌækrə'bætɪks/ *noun* [plural] the actions of an acrobat

acronym /'ækrəʊnɪm/ *noun* [C] a word made from the first letters of other words *AIDS is the acronym for 'acquired immune deficiency syndrome'.*

o-across /ə'krɒs/ *adv, preposition* 1 SIDES from one side of something to the other *I was walking across the road.* ● *They've built a new bridge across the river.* 2 OPPOSITE on the opposite side of *There's a library just across the street.* 3 MEASURE used after a measurement to show how wide something is *The window measures two metres across.*

acrylic /ə'krɪlɪk/ *adj* made of a material produced by a chemical process *acrylic paint* ● *an acrylic sweater*

o-act¹ /ækt/ *verb* 1 BEHAVE [I] to behave in a particular way *to act responsibly* ● *Jeff's been acting strangely recently.* ● *Stop acting like a child!* 2 DO SOMETHING [I] to do something, especially in order to solve a problem *We have to act now to stop the spread of this disease.* 3 PERFORM [I, T] to perform in a play or film *He's acted in a number of successful Hollywood films.*

**act as sth** to do a particular job, especially one you do not normally do *He was asked to act as an adviser on the project.* 2 to have a particular effect *Caffeine acts as a stimulant.*

**act sth out** to perform the actions and words of a situation or story *The children acted out a verse from their favourite poem.*

**act up** If someone, especially a child, acts up, they behave badly.

act² /ækt/ *noun* 1 DO [C] something that someone does *an act of terrorism/kindness* 2 LAW [C] a law made by a government *an act of Congress/Parliament* 3 THEATRE [C] one of the parts a play is divided into *Her character doesn't appear until Act 2.* 4 PERFORMERS [C] one or several performers who perform for a short while in a show *a comedy double act* 5 FALSE BEHAVIOUR [no plural] behaviour which hides your real feelings or intentions *Was she really upset or was that just an act?* 6 **in the act (of doing sth)** doing something wrong *I caught him in the act of opening one of my letters.* 7 **get your act together** *informal* to organize your activities so that you can make progress 8 **get in on the act** *informal* to become involved in something successful that someone else has started

acting¹ /'æktɪŋ/ *adj* **acting chairman/director, etc** someone who does a job for a short time while the person who usually does it is not there

acting² /'æktɪŋ/ *noun* [U] the job of performing in plays and films *He's trying to get into acting.*

O━**action** /'ækʃ°n/ *noun* **1** DO [C, U] something that you do *She has to accept the consequences of her actions.* • *We must take action* (= do something) *before the problem gets worse.* • *So what do you think is the best course of action* (= way of dealing with the situation)? • *It was the first time I'd seen firemen in action* (= doing a particular activity). **2** ACTIVITY [U] things which are happening, especially exciting or important things *He likes films with a lot of action.* ➔ *Opposite* **inaction. 3 out of action** damaged or hurt and not able to operate or play sports *I'm afraid my car's out of action.* • *They've got three players out of action.* **4 legal action** a legal process in a court *They are planning to take legal action against the company.* **5** FIGHTING [U] fighting in a war *He was killed in action* (= while fighting). **6** PROCESS [no plural] a movement or natural process *The rocks are smoothed by the action of water.* ➔ *See also:* **industrial action**, be all **talk²** and no action.

**action-packed** /'ækʃ°n,pækt/ *adj* An action-packed film or story has a lot of exciting events.

,**action 'replay** *UK* (*US* **instant replay**) *noun* [C] when part of a film of a sporting event is shown again, often more slowly

**activate** /'æktıveıt/ *verb* [T] to make something start working *The alarm can be activated by a laser beam.*

O━**active** /'æktıv/ *adj* **1** INVOLVED very involved in an organization or planned activity *an active member of the church* • *He played an active role in the campaign.* **2** BUSY doing a lot of things, or moving around a lot *Even at the age of 80 she's still very active.* ➔ *Opposite* **inactive. 3** GRAMMAR An active verb or sentence is one in which the subject of the verb is the person or thing doing the action. For example 'Andy drove the car.' is an active sentence. ➔ *Compare* **passive. 4** VOLCANO An active volcano could throw out rocks, fire, etc at any time.

**actively** /'æktıvli/ *adv* in a way that causes something to happen *He actively encourages me to spend money.*

**activist** /'æktıvıst/ *noun* [C] someone who tries to cause social or political change *a political activist* • **activism** *noun* [U]

O━**activity** /æk'tıvəti/ *noun* **1** EVENTS [C] things which you do for enjoyment, especially organized events *The centre offers a range of activities, such as cycling, swimming, and tennis.* **2** WORK [C, U] the work of a group or organization to achieve an aim *criminal/terrorist activities* **3** MOVEMENT [U] when a lot of things are happening or people are moving around *There was a sudden flurry of activity* (= short period of activity) *at the back of the hall.* ➔ *Opposite* **inactivity.**

O━**actor** /'æktər/ *noun* [C] someone, especially a man, whose job is to perform in plays and films

O━**actress** /'æktrəs/ *noun* [C] a woman whose job is to perform in plays and films

O━**actual** /'æktʃuəl/ *adj* **1** real, not guessed or imagined *We were expecting about fifty people, though the actual number was a lot higher.* **2 in actual fact** *UK* really *It was due to start at ten, but in actual fact, it didn't begin until nearly eleven.*

O━**actually** /'æktʃuəli/ *adv* **1** TRUTH used when you are saying what is the truth of a situation *He didn't actually say anything important.* • *So what actually happened?* **2** SURPRISE used when you are saying something surprising *She sounds English but she's actually Spanish.* **3** MISTAKE *mainly UK* used when you are disagreeing with someone or saying no to a request *"You didn't tell me." "Actually, I did."* • *"Do you mind if I smoke?" "Actually, I'd rather you didn't."*

**acumen** /'ækjʊmən/ *noun* [U] the ability to make good judgments and decisions *business/political acumen*

**acupuncture** /'ækjʊpʌŋktʃər/ *noun* [U] a way of treating pain or illness by putting thin needles into different parts of the body

**acute** /ə'kjuːt/ *adj* **1** EXTREME An acute problem or negative feeling is extreme. *There's an acute shortage of medical staff.* • *acute pain* • *acute embarrassment/anxiety* **2** ANGLE An acute angle is less than 90 degrees. **3** QUICK TO NOTICE quick to notice or understand things *an acute mind* • *Dogs rely on their acute sense of smell.*

**acutely** /ə'kjuːtli/ *adv* very strongly *I was acutely aware of how Alex felt about the matter.*

**AD** /,eı'diː/ *abbreviation for* Anno Domini: used to show that a particular year came after the birth of Christ *1066 AD*

**ad** /æd/ *noun* [C] an advertisement ➔ *See also:* **classified ad.**

**adamant** /'ædəmənt/ *adj* very sure of what you think and not willing to change your opinion *They are adamant that they have not broken any rules.* • **adamantly** *adv*

**Adam's apple** /,ædəmz'æpl/ *noun* [C] the lump in a man's throat that you can see moving up and down when he speaks or swallows

**adapt** /ə'dæpt/ *verb* **1** CHANGE BEHAVIOUR [I] to change your behaviour so that it is suitable for a new situation *It takes time to adapt to a new working environment.* **2** CHANGE SOMETHING [T] to change something so that it is suitable for a different use or situation *Courses have to be adapted for different markets.* **3** BOOK [T] to change a book or play so that it can be made into a film or television programme *Both novels have been adapted for television.*

**adaptable** /ə'dæptəbl/ *adj* able to change to suit different situations or uses • **adaptability** /ə,dæptə'bıləti/ *noun* [U]

**adaptation** /,ædæp'teıʃ°n/ *noun* **1** [C] a film, television programme, or play which has been made from a book **2** [C, U] the process or act of

A

changing to suit a new situation *Evolution occurs as a result of **adaptation to new environments**.*

**adapter** (*also* **adaptor**) /ə'dæptər/ *noun* [C] something that is used for connecting two or more pieces of electrical equipment to an electrical supply

o━**add** /æd/ *verb* **1** PUT WITH [T] to put something with something else *Add the eggs to the cream.* • *Could you add apples to your shopping list?* **2** INCREASE [I, T] to increase an amount or level *Then there's the service charge which **adds** another ten percent to the bill.* • *His voice just **adds** to his appeal.* **3** SAY MORE [T] to say another thing [+ that] *She said she liked him but added that he was difficult to work with.* **4** CALCULATE [T] to put two or more numbers or amounts together to get a total ⊃ *See also:* add **insult**² to injury.

**add (sth) up** to put numbers together in order to reach a total *When you add up everything we've spent, it's cost well over £200.*

**not add up** *informal* If something does not add up, you cannot believe it is true. *She gave me an explanation but somehow it doesn't add up.*

**adder** /'ædər/ *noun* [C] a small, poisonous snake

**addict** /'ædɪkt/ *noun* [C] **1** someone who cannot stop taking a drug *a heroin/drug addict* **2** *informal* someone who likes something very much and does it or has it very often *a TV/computer game addict*

**addicted** /ə'dɪktɪd/ *adj* **1** not able to stop taking a drug *He later became **addicted to** heroin.* **2** *informal* liking something very much and doing or having it too often *He's **addicted to** chocolate/football.*

**addiction** /ə'dɪkʃn/ *noun* [C, U] when you cannot stop doing or taking something because you are addicted to it

**addictive** /ə'dɪktɪv/ *adj* If something is addictive, it makes you want more of it so that you become addicted. *Tobacco is highly addictive.*

**addition** /ə'dɪʃn/ *noun* **1 in addition (to sth)** added to what already exists or happens, or more than you already do or have *In addition to teaching, she works as a nurse in the holidays.* **2** [U] the process of adding numbers or amounts together in order to get a total **3** [C] a new or extra thing which is added to something *Defender Matt Smith is the latest **addition** to the team.*

**additional** /ə'dɪʃnəl/ *adj* extra to what already exists *We plan to take on an additional ten employees over the next year.* • **additionally** *adv*

**additive** /'ædɪtɪv/ *noun* [C] a chemical which is added to food in order to make it taste or look better or to keep it fresh

o━**address**¹ /ə'dres US 'ædres/ *noun* [C] **1** OF BUILDING the details of where a building is, including the building number, road name, town, etc **2** ELECTRONIC a series of letters, signs, or numbers used to send email to someone or to reach a page of information on the Internet *an email/web address* **3** SPEECH a formal speech to a group of people ⊃ *See also:* **forwarding address, public address system.**

**address**² /ə'dres/ *verb* [T] **1** BUILDING DETAILS to write a name or address on an envelope or

parcel *A parcel arrived **addressed to** Emma.* **2** DEAL WITH to deal with a problem *We have to address the problem before it gets worse.* **3** SPEAK *formal* to speak to someone, or to give a speech to an audience *Today she will be addressing a major conference in London.* **4 address sb as sth** *formal* to give someone a particular name or title when you speak or write to them *Do you think I should address him as 'Mr Benson' or 'Albert'?*

**adept** /'ædept/ *adj* good at doing something difficult *She's very **adept at** dealing with the media.*

**adequate** /'ædɪkwət/ *adj* **1** enough *I didn't have adequate time to prepare.* **2** good enough, but not very good *The sound quality isn't exceptional but it's **adequate for** everyday use.* ⊃ *Opposite* **inadequate.** • **adequately** *adv Make sure you are adequately equipped for the journey.*

**adhere** /əd'hɪər/ *verb* [I] *formal* to stick to a surface

**adhere to sth** to obey a rule or principle *We always adhere strictly to the guidelines.*

**adherence** /əd'hɪərəns/ *noun* [U] *formal* when someone obeys a set of rules or principles • **adherent** *noun* [C] *formal* someone who obeys a particular set of rules, principles, etc

**adhesive** /əd'hiːsɪv/ *noun* [C] a substance used for sticking things together • **adhesive** *adj*

**ad hoc** /,æd'hɒk/ *adj* not regular or planned, but happening only when necessary *We meet **on an ad hoc basis.***

**adjacent** /ə'dʒeɪsənt/ *adj formal* If two things are adjacent, they are next to each other. *The fire started in an adjacent building.* • *They live in a house **adjacent to** the railway.*

o━**adjective** /'ædʒɪktɪv/ *noun* [C] a word that describes a noun or pronoun. The words 'big', 'boring', 'purple', and 'obvious' are all adjectives. • **adjectival** /,ædʒɪk'taɪvəl/ *adj* containing or used like an adjective *an adjectival phrase*

**adjoining** /ə'dʒɔɪnɪŋ/ *adj* next to and joined to something *an adjoining room*

**adjourn** /ə'dʒɜːn/ *verb* [I, T] *formal* to stop a meeting, especially a legal process, for a period of time or until a later date *The judge adjourned the case until March 31.* • **adjournment** *noun* [C]

**adjudicate** /ə'dʒuːdɪkeɪt/ *verb* [I, T] *formal* to make an official judgment or decision about a competition or disagreement *Occasionally, he has to **adjudicate on** a pensions matter.* • **adjudication** /ə,dʒuːdɪ'keɪʃn/ *noun* [U] • **adjudicator** *noun* [C]

**adjust** /ə'dʒʌst/ *verb* **1** [T] to change something slightly so that it works better, fits better, or is more suitable *You can adjust the heat using this switch here.* • *She adjusted her hat in the mirror.* • *The figures need to be adjusted for inflation.* **2** [I] to change the way you behave or think in order to suit a new situation *They found it hard **adjusting to** life in a new country.*

**adjustable** /ə'dʒʌstəbl/ *adj* able to be changed slightly in order to suit different people or situations *an adjustable seat*

**adjustment** /ə'dʒʌstmənt/ *noun* [C, U] a slight change that you make to something so that it

A

works better, fits better, or is more suitable *We've* **made** *a few* **adjustments** *to the schedule.*

**ad lib** /ˌæd'lɪb/ *verb* [I, T] to speak in public without having planned what to say *I had no script so I had to ad lib.*

**admin** /'ædmɪn/ *noun* [U] *UK short for* administration

**administer** /əd'mɪnɪstəʳ/ *verb* [T] **1** to organize or arrange something *to administer a programme/test* • *The fund is administered by the Economic Development Agency.* **2** *formal* to give medicine or medical help to someone *to administer first aid*

**administration** /əd,mɪnɪ'streɪʃᵊn/ *noun* **1** [U] the work of organizing and arranging the operation of something, such as a company *The job involves a lot of administration.* **2** [C] *mainly US* the President and politicians who govern a country at a particular time, or a period of government *the Clinton administration*

**administrative** /əd'mɪnɪstrətɪv/ *adj* relating to the organization and management of something *The work is largely administrative.*

**administrator** /əd'mɪnɪstreɪtəʳ/ *noun* [C] someone who helps to manage an organization

**admirable** /'ædmᵊrəbl/ *adj* If something is admirable, you respect or approve of it. *He has many admirable qualities.* • admirably *adv*

**admiral** /'ædmᵊrəl/ *noun* [C] an officer of very high rank in the navy

O⊶**admiration** /ˌædmə'reɪʃᵊn/ *noun* [U] when you admire someone or something *My* **admiration** *for him grows daily.*

O⊶**admire** /əd'maɪəʳ/ *verb* [T] **1** to respect or approve of someone or something *You have to* **admire** *him for being so determined.* • *I really admire people who can go out and work in such difficult conditions.* **2** to look at something or someone, thinking how attractive they are *We stood for a few minutes, admiring the view.* • *I was just admiring your shirt.* • admirer *noun* [C]

**admissible** /əd'mɪsəbl/ *adj formal* allowed or acceptable, especially in a court of law *admissible evidence*

**admission** /əd'mɪʃᵊn/ *noun* **1** MONEY [U] the money that you pay to enter a place *Art exhibition – admission free.* **2** TRUTH [C] when you agree that you did something bad, or that something bad is true *She is, by her own* **admission**, *lazy.* • *His departure was seen by many as an* **admission** *of guilt.* **3** PERMISSION [C, U] when someone is given permission to enter somewhere or to become a member of a club, university, etc *She's applied for* **admission to** *law school.*

O⊶**admit** /əd'mɪt/ *verb* **admitting**, *past* **admitted** **1** [I, T] to agree that you did something bad, or that something bad is true [+ doing sth] *Both men admitted taking illegal drugs.* • [+ to + doing sth] *She* **admitted** *to stealing the keys.* • *I was wrong – I admit it.* • [+ (that)] *He finally admitted that he couldn't cope.* **2** [T] to allow someone to enter somewhere, especially to take someone who is ill into hospital *(UK) to be* **admitted to** *hospital/(US) to be* **admitted to** *the hospital* • *It says on the ticket 'admits 2'.*

**admittance** /əd'mɪtᵊns/ *noun* [U] permission to enter a place

**admittedly** /əd'mɪtɪdli/ *adv* used when you are agreeing that something is true although you do not want to *Admittedly I was partly to blame but it wasn't all my fault.*

**admonish** /əd'mɒnɪʃ/ *verb* [T] *formal* to gently tell someone that they have done something wrong

**ado** /ə'duː/ *noun* **without further/more ado** without waiting any more

**adolescence** /ˌædᵊl'esᵊns/ *noun* [U] the period of time in someone's life between being a child and an adult

**adolescent** /ˌædᵊl'esᵊnt/ *noun* [C] a young person who is between being a child and an adult • adolescent *adj*

**adopt** /ə'dɒpt/ *verb* **1** [I, T] to legally become the parents of someone else's child **2** [T] to accept or start using something new *I soon adopted the Mediterranean habit of taking a siesta after lunch.* • adopted *adj an adopted son* • adoption /ə'dɒpʃᵊn/ *noun* [C, U]

**adorable** /ə'dɔːrəbl/ *adj* very attractive, often because of being small *They have an adorable little boy.*

**adore** /ə'dɔːʳ/ *verb* [T] **1** to love someone and have a very good opinion of them *Sarah adored her father.* **2** to like something very much *I adore travelling.* • adoration /ˌædə'reɪʃᵊn/ *noun* [U]

**adorn** /ə'dɔːn/ *verb* [T] *formal* to decorate something *The room was* **adorned with** *flowers.* • adornment *noun* [C, U]

**adrenalin** (*also* **adrenaline**) /ə'drenᵊlɪn/ *noun* [U] a substance that your body produces when you are angry, excited, or frightened which makes your heart beat faster

**adrift** /ə'drɪft/ *adj* **1** [never before noun] If a boat is adrift, it floats around in the water and is not tied to anything. *The engine failed, leaving the boat adrift a long way off shore.* **2** **come adrift** to become loose and not joined to anything *A few bricks in the garden wall had come adrift.*

**adulation** /ˌædjʊ'leɪʃᵊn/ *noun* [U] great praise and admiration for someone, often which they do not deserve

O⊶**adult¹** /'ædʌlt, ə'dʌlt/ *noun* [C] a person or animal that has finished growing and is not now a child

**adult²** /'ædʌlt, ə'dʌlt/ *adj* **1** NOT A CHILD having finished growing *an adult male rat* **2** RELATING TO ADULTS [always before noun] for or relating to adults *adult education* • *adult life* **3** SEXUAL *Adult books, films, etc show naked people or sexual acts and are not for children.*

**adultery** /ə'dʌltᵊri/ *noun* [U] sex between a married person and someone who is not their husband or wife • adulterous *adj an adulterous affair*

**adulthood** /'ædʌlthʊd ⓊⓈ ə'dʌlthʊd/ *noun* [U] the part of your life when you are an adult

**advance¹** /əd'vɑːns/ *noun* **1 in advance** before a particular time *You need to book your ticket at least 14 days in advance.* **2** PROGRESS [C, U] new discoveries and inventions *technological/*

*scientific advances* **3** MONEY [C] a payment given to someone before work has been completed, or before the usual time **4** FORWARD [C] a movement forward, especially by an army

**advance²** /əd'vɑːns/ *verb* **1** [I, T] to develop or progress, or to make something develop or progress *He moved to New York with hopes of advancing his career.* • *Research has advanced our understanding of the virus.* **2** [I] to move forward to a new position, especially while fighting *Rebel soldiers advanced on the capital.*

**advance³** /əd'vɑːns/ *adj* [always before noun] happening or ready before an event *advance planning/warning* • *an advance booking*

**advanced** /əd'vɑːnst/ *adj* **1** having developed or progressed to a late stage *advanced technology* • *The disease was at an advanced stage.* **2** at a higher, more difficult level *an advanced English course*

**advancement** /əd'vɑːnsmənt/ *noun* [C, U] progress *career advancement* • *technological advancements*

**advances** /əd'vɑːnsɪz/ *noun* **sb's advances** things that someone says and does to try to start a sexual relationship with someone

o⬧**advantage** /əd'vɑːntɪdʒ/ *noun* [C, U] **1** something good about a situation that helps you *One of the advantages of living in town is having the shops so near.* **2** something that will help you to succeed *These new routes will give the airline a considerable advantage over its competitors.* • *By half time we had a 2–0 advantage* (= were winning by two points). • *If we could start early it would be to our advantage* (= help us to succeed). ⊃ *Opposite* **disadvantage**. **3 take advantage of sth** to use the good things in a situation *I thought I'd take advantage of the sports facilities while I'm here.* **4 take advantage of sb/sth** to treat someone badly in order to get what you want

**advantageous** /ˌædvən'teɪdʒəs/ *adj* helping to make you more successful

**advent** /'ædvent/ *noun* **1 the advent of sth** the start or arrival of something new *the advent of the Internet* **2 Advent** the religious period before Christmas (= a Christian holiday) in the Christian year

o⬧**adventure** /əd'ventʃəʳ/ *noun* [C, U] an exciting and sometimes dangerous experience *It's a film about the adventures of two friends travelling across Africa.* • **adventurer** *noun* [C]

**adventurous** /əd'ventʃ°rəs/ *adj* **1** willing to try new and often difficult things *I'm trying to be more adventurous with my cooking.* **2** exciting and often dangerous *He led an adventurous life.*

o⬧**adverb** /'ædvɜːb/ *noun* [C] a word that describes or gives more information about a verb, adjective, phrase, or other adverb. In the sentences 'He ate quickly.' and 'It was extremely good.', 'quickly' and 'extremely' are both adverbs.

**adversary** /'ædvəs°ri/ *noun* [C] *formal* someone who you are fighting or competing against

**adverse** /'ædvɜːs/ *adj formal* **1 adverse conditions/effects/impact** things that cause problems or danger *adverse weather conditions*

• *Pollution levels like these will certainly have an adverse effect on health.* **2 adverse comment/publicity/reaction, etc** something negative that is said or written about someone or something • **adversely** *adv*

**adversity** /əd'vɜːsəti/ *noun* [C, U] *formal* an extremely difficult situation *She showed a great deal of courage in adversity.*

**advert** /'ædvɜːt/ *noun* [C] *UK* an advertisement

**advertise** /'ædvətaɪz/ *verb* **1** [I, T] to tell people about a product or service, for example in newspapers or on television, in order to persuade them to buy it *Companies are not allowed to advertise cigarettes on television any more.* **2** [I] to put information in a newspaper or on the Internet, asking for someone or something that you need *The university is advertising for administrative staff.* • **advertiser** [C] a company that advertises things

**advertisement** /əd'vɜːtɪsmənt/ US /ˌædvər'taɪzmənt/ *noun* [C] a picture, short film, song, etc which tries to persuade people to buy a product or service *a newspaper/television advertisement*

o⬧**advertising** /'ædvətaɪzɪŋ/ *noun* [U] the business of trying to persuade people to buy products or services *an advertising agency/campaign* • *She works in advertising.*

o⬧**advice** /əd'vaɪs/ *noun* [U] suggestions about what you think someone should do or how they should do something *She asked me for advice about writing a book.* • *There's a booklet giving advice on how to set up your own club.* • *I took your advice* (= did what you suggested) *and went home early.* • *Can I give you a piece of advice?*

**advisable** /əd'vaɪzəbl/ *adj* [never before noun] If something is advisable, it will avoid problems if you do it. *It is advisable to book seats at least a week in advance.*

o⬧**advise** /əd'vaɪz/ *verb* **1** [I, T] to make a suggestion about what you think someone should do or how they should do something [+ to do sth] *His doctor advised him to take time off work.* • *They advise the government on environmental matters.* • *The government is advising against travelling in the area.* • [+ that] *They're* *advising that children be kept out of the sun altogether.* **2** [T] *formal* to give someone official information about something *They were advised of their rights.*

**adviser** (*also* **advisor**) /əd'vaɪzəʳ/ *noun* [C] someone whose job is to give advice about a subject *a financial adviser*

**advisory¹** /əd'vaɪzʳri/ *adj* **advisory committee/panel/board, etc** a group of people whose purpose is to give advice

**advisory²** /əd'vaɪzʳri/ *noun* [C] *US* an official announcement that contains advice, information, or a warning [usually plural] *weather/travel advisories*

**advocate¹** /'ædvəkeɪt/ *verb* [T] to express support for a particular idea or way of doing things *I certainly wouldn't advocate the use of violence.* • advocacy /'ædvəkəsi/ *noun* [U] when someone advocates something

**advocate²** /'ædvəkət/ *noun* [C] **1** someone who supports a particular idea or way of doing things *He has always been an advocate of stricter gun controls.* **2** *UK* a lawyer who defends someone in court

**aerial¹** /'eəriəl/ *UK* (*US* **antenna**) *noun* [C] a piece of metal that is used for receiving television or radio signals ⟹ *See colour picture* **Car** *on page Centre 3.*

**aerial²** /'eəriəl/ *adj* [always before noun] in or from the air, especially from an aircraft *an aerial photograph/view*

**aerobic** /eə'rəʊbɪk/ *adj* Aerobic exercise is intended to make your heart stronger.

**aerobics** /eə'rəʊbɪks/ *noun* [U] physical exercises that you do to music, especially in a class *She goes to aerobics* (= to aerobics classes).

**aerodynamic** /ˌeərəʊdaɪ'næmɪk/ *adj* having a shape that moves quickly through the air • aerodynamics *noun* [U] the study of how objects move through the air

**aeroplane** /'eərəpleɪn/ *UK* (*US* **airplane**) *noun* [C] a vehicle that flies and has an engine and wings

**aeroplane** *UK*, **airplane** *US*

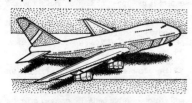

cockpit      cabin

**aerosol** /'eərəsɒl/ *noun* [C] a metal container that forces a liquid out in small drops when you press a button

**aerosol**

**aerospace** /'eərəʊspeɪs/ *noun* [U] the design and production of aircraft *an aerospace engineer*

**aesthetic** (*also US* **esthetic**) /es'θetɪk/ *adj* relating to beauty and the way something looks *the aesthetic appeal of cats* • aesthetically *adv*

**aesthetics** (*also US* **esthetics**) /es'θetɪks/ *noun* [U] the study of beauty, especially in art

**afar** /ə'fɑːʳ/ *adv literary* **from afar** from a long distance *He had admired her from afar.*

**affable** /'æfəbl/ *adj* pleasant and friendly

**affair** /ə'feəʳ/ *noun* **1** [C] a situation or set of related events, especially bad ones *The government's handling of the affair has been widely criticized.* **2** [C] a sexual relationship between two people when one or both of them is married to someone else *He's been having an affair with a woman at work.* **3 be sb's affair** If something is your affair, it is private and you do not want anyone else to be involved or know about it. ⟹ *See also:* **love affair**.

**affairs** /ə'feəz/ *noun* [plural] situations or subjects that involve you *He refused to discuss his financial affairs.* ⟹ *See also:* **current affairs**, **state of affairs**.

o— **affect** /ə'fekt/ *verb* [T] **1** to influence someone or something, or cause them to change *It's a disease which affects many older people.* • *The building was badly affected by the fire.* **2** to cause a strong emotion, especially sadness [often passive] *I was deeply affected by the film.* ⟹ *See usage note at* **effect**.

**affectation** /ˌæfek'teɪʃʳn/ *noun* [C, U] a way of speaking or behaving that is not natural to someone

**affected** /ə'fektɪd/ *adj* behaving or speaking in a way that is not natural or sincere

**affection** /ə'fekʃʳn/ *noun* [C, U] a feeling of liking or loving someone *Ann's affection for her grandfather was obvious.*

**affectionate** /ə'fekʃʳnət/ *adj* showing that you like or love someone *an affectionate little girl* • *He's very affectionate.* • affectionately *adv*

**affiliate** /ə'fɪlieɪt/ *verb* **be affiliated to/with sth** to be officially connected to, or a member of, a larger organization *a college affiliated to*

**A**

the University of London • affiliation /ə,fɪli'eɪʃ°n/ noun [C, U]

**affinity** /ə'fɪnəti/ noun **1** [no plural] a feeling that you like and understand someone or something *She seems to have a natural **affinity** for/with water.* **2** [C, U] a similarity *There are **affinities** between this poem and some of his earlier work.*

**affirm** /ə'fɜːm/ verb [T] formal to say that something is true *He gave a speech affirming the government's commitment to education.* • affirmation /,æfə'meɪʃ°n/ noun [C, U]

**affirmative** /ə'fɜːmətɪv/ adj formal In language, an affirmative word or phrase Iexpresses the meaning 'yes'. *an affirmative answer*

**affix** /'æfɪks/ noun [C] a group of letters that you add to the beginning or the end of a word to make another word. In the word 'non-alcoholic', 'non-' is an affix. ⊃ Compare **prefix**, **suffix**.

**afflict** /ə'flɪkt/ verb [T] formal If an illness or problem afflicts you, it makes you suffer. [often passive] *a country afflicted by civil war* • *It is an illness that afflicts women more than men.* • affliction /ə'flɪkʃ°n/ noun [C, U] something that makes you suffer

**affluent** /'æfluənt/ adj having a lot of money *affluent families/neighbourhoods* • affluence /'æfluəns/ noun [U]

⊶**afford** /ə'fɔːd/ verb [T] **1 can afford** to have enough money to buy something or enough time to do something *I can't afford a new computer.* • [+ to do sth] *Can we afford to go away?* • *I'd love to come out but I can't afford the time.* **2 can afford to do sth** If you can afford to do something, it is possible for you to do it without causing problems. *We can't afford to take that risk.*

**USAGE**

**afford to do** something

When **afford** is followed by a verb, it is always in the to + infinitive form.

*We can't afford to go on holiday this year.*

~~We can't afford going on holiday this year.~~

**affordable** /ə'fɔːdəbl/ adj cheap enough for most people *affordable housing/prices*

**affront** /ə'frʌnt/ noun [C] something that is offensive or insulting to someone *He regarded the comments as an **affront** to his dignity.*

**afield** /ə'fiːld/ adv mainly UK **far/further afield** away from the place where you are *We hired a car so we could travel further afield.*

**afloat** /ə'fləʊt/ adj **1** floating on water **2 stay afloat** to have enough money to continue a business *Many small business are struggling to stay afloat.*

**afoot** /ə'fʊt/ adj [never before noun] being planned, or happening now *There are plans afoot to launch a new radio station.*

⊶**afraid** /ə'freɪd/ adj [never before noun] **1 I'm afraid** used to politely tell someone bad news or to politely disagree with someone *We haven't got any tickets left, I'm afraid.* • [+ (that)]

*I'm afraid that I've broken your vase.* **2** frightened *She's **afraid of** water.* **3** worried that something bad might happen [+ (that)] *Many people are afraid that they might lose their jobs.* • [+ of + doing sth] *He was **afraid of** upsetting Clare.*

**afresh** /ə'freʃ/ adv If you do something afresh, you do it again in a different way. *Juan tore up the letter he was writing and started afresh.*

**African** /'æfrɪkən/ adj relating or belonging to Africa *African art/music* • African noun [C] someone from Africa

**African-American** /,æfrɪkənə'merɪkən/ (also **Afro-American** /,æfrəʊə'merɪkən/) adj relating or belonging to American people whose families came from Africa in the past *the African-American community* • African-American (also **Afro-American**) noun [C] *a 25-year-old African-American*

**Afro-Caribbean** /,æfrəʊkærɪ'biːən/ adj UK relating or belonging to the countries of Africa and the Caribbean *Afro-Caribbean art/music*

⊶**after¹** /'ɑːftə'/ preposition **1** TIME/EVENT when a time or event has happened *We went swimming after lunch.* • *I'm seeing her the day after tomorrow.* • *Let's get the shopping. After that, we can have coffee.* **2** LIST following in order *H comes after G in the alphabet.* **3** TIME US (UK/US **past**) used to say how many minutes past the hour it is *It's five after three.* **4** BECAUSE OF because of something that happened *I'll never trust her again after what she did to me.* **5** DESPITE despite *I can't believe he was so unpleasant after you gave him so much help.* **6** FOLLOW following someone or something *We ran after him, but he escaped.* **7 after 5 minutes/2 weeks, etc** when five minutes, two weeks, etc have passed *The bus arrived after twenty minutes.* **8 day after day/year after year, etc** continuing for a long time, or happening many times *I'm bored with going to school day after day.* **9** NAMED FOR used when giving someone or something the same name as another person or thing *It was called the Biko building, after the famous South African.* **10 after all a** NOT EXPECTED used to say that something happened or was true although you did not expect it to happen or be true *Helen couldn't come to the party after all.* **b** EMPHASIZE TRUTH used to add information that shows that what you have just said is true *You can't expect to be perfect – after all, it was only your first lesson.* **11 be after sth** informal to be trying to get something *What type of job are you after?* **12 be after sb** informal to be looking for someone *The police are after him.*

⊶**after²** /'ɑːftə'/ conjunction at a later time than something else happens *We arrived after the game had started.* • *My computer went wrong a week after I bought it.* • *After further discussion, we decided to call the police.*

**after³** /'ɑːftə'/ adv later than someone or something else *He had the operation on Monday and I saw him the day after.*

**aftermath** /'ɑːftəmɑːθ/ noun [no plural] a situation that is the result of an accident, crime, or other violent event *There are calls for tighter airport security **in the aftermath of** last week's bombing.*

⊶**afternoon** /ˌɑːftəˈnuːn/ noun **1** [C, U] the time between the middle of the day, and the evening *I played tennis on Saturday afternoon.* • *The train arrives at 3 o'clock in the afternoon.* • *What are you doing this afternoon* (= today in the afternoon)*?* **2 (Good) afternoon.** used to say hello to someone in the afternoon

### USAGE

#### afternoon

If you talk about what happens during the afternoon, use the preposition in.

*In the afternoon I phoned my girlfriend.*

~~At the afternoon I phoned my girlfriend.~~

If you say a day of the week before 'afternoon', use the preposition on.

*I'm going to the dentist on Tuesday afternoon.*

**aftershave** /ˈɑːftəʃeɪv/ noun [C, U] a liquid with a pleasant smell that men put on their faces after shaving (= removing hair)

**aftertaste** /ˈɑːftəteɪst/ noun [C] the taste that a food or drink leaves in your mouth [usually singular] *a bitter/sweet aftertaste*

**afterthought** /ˈɑːftəθɔːt/ noun [C] something that you say or do later [usually singular] *She only asked me to the party as an afterthought.*

**afterwards** /ˈɑːftəwədz/ (*also US* **afterward**) *adv* at a later time, after something else has happened *I did my homework and went swimming afterwards.*

⊶**again** /əˈgen/ *adv* **1** once more *I'll ask her again.* • *I'll see you again next week.* **2** as before *Get some rest and you'll soon be well again.* **3 again and again** many times *He played the same song again and again.* **4 all over again** repeated from the beginning *We had to start all over again.* **5 then/there again** used when adding a fact to something you have just said *I failed my history test – but then again, I didn't do much studying for it.*

⊶**against** /əˈgenst/ *preposition* **1** NOT AGREE disagreeing with a plan or activity *Andrew wants to change offices but I'm against it.* • *There were 70 votes for the new proposal and 30 against.* **2** COMPETE competing with or opposing someone or something *Liverpool is playing against AC Milan.* • *the fight against racism* **3** TOUCH touching something *Push the bed against the wall.* **4** PROTECT protecting you from something bad *Fresh fruit in the diet may protect against cancer.* **5** OPPOSITE DIRECTION in the opposite direction to the way something is moving *I was cycling against the wind.* **6 against the law/the rules** forbidden by a law or by rules *It's against the law to leave young children alone in the house.* **7 against sb's advice/wishes, etc** If you do something against someone's advice, wishes, etc, you do it although they have said you should not or must not. *He flew there against his doctor's advice.* **8 have sth against sb/sth** to have a reason not to like someone or something *I've got nothing against him personally, I just don't think he's the right man for the job.*

⊶**age**[1] /eɪdʒ/ noun **1** HOW OLD [C, U] the number of years that someone has lived, or that something has existed *The show appeals to people of all ages.* • *She left India at the age of 12.* • *Children under 10 years of age must be accompanied by an adult.* • *She's about your age* (= the same age as you)*.* ➡ *See usage note at* **year.** **2** HISTORY [C] a period of history *the Ice Age* • *We're living in the age of electronic communication.* **3** OLD [U] when something is old *Some wines improve with age.* **4 under age** too young to do something legally ➡ *See also:* **the Middle Ages, old age**

**age**[2] /eɪdʒ/ *verb* [I, T] *UK* **ageing** *US* **aging,** *past* **aged** to become older or to make someone seem older *Dad has aged a lot recently.*

**aged**[1] /eɪdʒd/ *adj* having a particular age *They have one daughter, aged three.* ➡ *See also:* **middle-aged.**

**aged**[2] /ˈeɪdʒɪd/ *adj* old *an aged dog* • *improved health care for the aged*

**'age ˌgroup** noun [C] people of a particular age *job training for people in the 16–24 age group*

**ageing**[1] *UK* (*US* **aging**) /ˈeɪdʒɪŋ/ *adj* becoming older *an ageing population*

**ageing**[2] *UK* (*US* **aging**) /ˈeɪdʒɪŋ/ noun [U] the process of becoming older *the ageing process*

**agency** /ˈeɪdʒ⁰nsi/ noun [C] **1** a business that provides a service *an advertising agency* **2** an international organization or government department *an international development agency* ➡ *See also:* **travel agency.**

**agenda** /əˈdʒendə/ noun [C] **1** a list of subjects that people will discuss at a meeting *There are several items on the agenda.* **2** important subjects that have to be dealt with *The issue of rail safety is back on the political agenda.* • *The government has put education at the top of its agenda* (= considers it most important)*.*

**agent** /ˈeɪdʒ⁰nt/ noun [C] **1** someone whose job is to deal with business for someone else *The company has agents all over the world.* • *a literary agent* **2** (*also* **secret agent**) someone who tries to find out secret information, especially about another country ➡ *See also:* **estate agent** *UK,* **real estate agent** *US,* **travel agent.**

**ages** /ˈeɪdʒɪz/ noun [plural] *informal* a very long time *I've been waiting here for ages.* • *It takes ages to cook.*

**aggravate** /ˈægrəveɪt/ *verb* [T] **1** to make a situation or condition worse *His comments only aggravated the problem.* **2** to annoy someone *She's starting to really aggravate me.* • **aggravating** *adj* • **aggravation** /ˌægrəˈveɪʃ⁰n/ noun [C, U]

**aggregate** /ˈægrɪgət/ noun [C, U] a total *(UK) Liverpool won 2–0 on aggregate* (= in total)*.*

**aggression** /əˈgreʃ⁰n/ noun [U] angry or violent behaviour towards someone *an act of aggression*

**aggressive** /əˈgresɪv/ *adj* **1** behaving in an angry and violent way towards another person *He was drunk and aggressive.* • *aggressive behaviour* **2** using forceful methods and determined to succeed *an aggressive marketing campaign* • **aggressively** *adv*

**aggressor** /əˈgresə⁰/ noun [C] someone who starts a fight or war with someone else

A

**aggrieved** /ə'gri:vd/ *adj* upset or angry because someone has treated you unfairly

**aghast** /ə'gɑ:st/ *adj* [never before noun] very shocked *She looked at him aghast.*

**agile** /'ædʒaɪl ⑥ 'ædʒ³l/ *adj* **1** able to move your whole body easily and quickly **2** able to think quickly in an intelligent way *an agile mind*
• **agility** /ə'dʒɪləti/ *noun* [U]

**aging** /'eɪdʒɪŋ/ *adj, noun* US spelling of ageing

**agitate** /'ædʒɪteɪt/ *verb* [I] to argue strongly about something in order to achieve social or political changes *They continued to **agitate for** changes to the legal system.* • **agitator** *noun* [C]

**agitated** /'ædʒɪteɪtɪd/ *adj* very anxious or upset *He seemed agitated, as if something was worrying him.* • **agitation** /,ædʒɪ'teɪʃ³n/ *noun* [U]

**agnostic** /æg'nɒstɪk/ *noun* [C] someone who believes that we cannot know if God exists or not • **agnostic** *adj*

○⃒**ago** /ə'gəʊ/ *adv* **ten minutes/six years/a long time ago** used to refer to a time in the past *They moved to London ten years ago.* • *I went to China a long time ago.*

**agonize** (also UK **-ise**) /'ægənaɪz/ *verb* [I] to spend a lot of time worrying about a decision *Lee **agonized** over what to buy his girlfriend.*

**agonizing** (also UK **-ising**) /'ægənaɪzɪŋ/ *adj* causing you a lot of pain or worry *an agonizing choice*

**agony** /'ægəni/ *noun* [C, U] extreme suffering, either physical or mental *She lay on the bed **in agony**.*

**'agony ,aunt** *noun* [C] UK someone who gives advice on personal problems, in a newspaper or magazine

○⃒**agree** /ə'gri:/ *verb* **agreeing**, *past* **agreed** **1** [SAME OPINION] [I, T] to have the same opinion as someone *I **agree with** you.* • *"She's definitely the right person for the job." "I agree."* • [+ (that)] *We all agreed that mistakes had been made.* • *We **agree about** most things.* **2** [SAY YES] [I] to say you will do something that someone asks you to do [+ to do sth] *She agreed to help him.* ➔ *See usage note at* **accept**. **3** [DECIDE] [I, T] to decide something with someone *We couldn't **agree on** what to buy.* • [+ to do sth] *They agreed to meet on Sunday.* • [+ (that)] *We agreed that they would deliver the sofa in the morning.* **4** [DESCRIPTION] [I] If two descriptions agree, they are the same. ➔ *Opposite* **disagree**.

**agree with sth** to think that something is morally acceptable *I don't agree with hunting.*

**agreeable** /ə'gri:əbl/ *adj formal* **1** pleasant or nice *an agreeable young man* ➔ *Opposite* **disagreeable**. **2 be agreeable to sth** to be willing to do or accept something *If Harvey is agreeable to the proposal, we'll go ahead.*
• **agreeably** *adv*

○⃒**agreement** /ə'gri:mənt/ *noun* **1** [C] a promise or decision made between two or more people *an international agreement* • *It was difficult to **reach an agreement**.* **2** [U] when people have the same opinion as each other *Not everyone was **in agreement**.* ➔ *Opposite* **disagreement**.

**agriculture** /'ægrɪkʌltʃər/ *noun* [U] the work and methods of growing crops and looking after animals which are then used for food
• **agricultural** /,ægrɪ'kʌltʃ³r³l/ *adj*

**aground** /ə'graʊnd/ *adv* **run aground** If a ship runs aground, it cannot move because the water is not deep enough.

**ah** /ɑ:/ *exclamation* **1** used to show sympathy or to show pleasure at seeing a baby or attractive animal *Ah, you poor thing!* • *Ah, look at that little kitten!* **2** used to show that you have just understood something *Ah, now I see what you're saying!*

**aha** /ɑ:'hɑ:/ *exclamation* used when you suddenly understand or find something *Aha! That's where I left my keys!*

○⃒**ahead** /ə'hed/ *adj, adv* **1** [IN FRONT] in front *The road ahead is very busy.* • *Rick walked **ahead** of us.* **2** [FUTURE] in the future *She has a difficult time ahead of her.* **3** [MORE POINTS] having more points than someone else in a competition *Barcelona was ahead after ten minutes.* **4** [MORE PROGRESS] making more progress than someone or something else *Sue is **ahead** of everyone else in French.* **5 go ahead** *informal* used to allow someone to do something *"Can I use your phone?" "Sure, go ahead."* **6 ahead of time/schedule** before the time that was planned *We finished the project ahead of schedule.* ➔ *See also:* be one **step¹** ahead (of sb), be streets (**street**) ahead (of sb/sth), be ahead of your **time¹**.

**aid¹** /eɪd/ *noun* **1** [U] money, food, or equipment that is given to help a country or group of people *Emergency aid was sent to the flood victims.* • *aid workers* **2 in aid of sb/sth** UK in order to collect money for a group of people who need it *a concert in aid of famine relief* **3 with the aid of sth** using something to help you *She can walk with the aid of a stick.* **4 come/go to sb's aid** to go to someone and help them *Luckily a policeman came to my aid.* **5** [C] a piece of equipment that helps you to do something *teaching aids such as books and videos* ➔ *See also:* **Band-Aid**, **first aid**, **visual aid**.

**aid²** /eɪd/ *verb formal* **1** [T] to help someone **2 aid and abet (sb)** in law, to help someone do something that is illegal

**aide** /eɪd/ *noun* [C] someone whose job is to help someone important, especially in the government *a former aide to the President*

**AIDS, aids** /eɪdz/ *noun* [U] *abbreviation for* acquired immune deficiency syndrome: a serious disease that destroys the body's ability to fight infection ➔ *Compare* **HIV**.

**ailing** /'eɪlɪŋ/ *adj* weak or ill *an ailing company/economy* • *I'm going to visit my ailing father.*

**ailment** /'eɪlmənt/ *noun* [C] an illness *Treat minor ailments yourself.*

○⃒**aim¹** /eɪm/ *noun* **1** [C] the purpose of doing something, and what you hope to achieve *The **aim of** the film was to make people laugh.* • [+ of + doing sth] *He went to Paris **with the aim** of improving his French.* **2 sb's aim** someone's ability to hit an object by throwing something or shooting at something **3 take aim** to point a weapon towards someone or something

○⃒**aim²** /eɪm/ *verb* **1 aim for/at sth; aim to do sth** to intend to achieve something *I aim to arrive at three o'clock.* • *We're aiming for a 10%*

*increase in sales.* **2 be aimed at sb** to be intended to influence or affect a particular person or group *advertising aimed at students* • *His comment was aimed at Lesley.* **3 be aimed at doing sth** to be intended to achieve a particular thing *a plan aimed at reducing traffic* **4** [I, T] to point a weapon towards someone or something *He aimed the gun at the lion.*

**aimless** /'eɪmləs/ *adj* with no purpose • **aimlessly** *adv*

**ain't** /eɪnt/ *informal short for* am not, is not, are not, have not, or has not. This word is not considered correct by most people. *"Is Terry here?" "No, I ain't seen him all day."*

O→**air¹** /eəʳ/ *noun* **1** [GAS] [U] the mixture of gases around the Earth which we breathe *air pollution* • *He went outside to get some **fresh air** (=* clean, cool air). **2 the air** the space above and around things *He fired his gun into the air.* **3** [TRAVEL] [U] travel in an aircraft *I like travelling by air.* • *air safety* **4** [QUALITY] [no plural] a particular appearance or quality *He has **an air of authority.*** **5 be on air** to be broadcasting on television or radio **6 clear the air** If an argument or discussion clears the air, people feel less angry or upset after it. **7 disappear/ vanish into thin air** to suddenly disappear in a mysterious way **8 be up in the air** If something is up in the air, no decision has been made. *Our plans for the summer are still up in the air.* ➔ *See also:* a **breath** of fresh air, **mid-air**

**air²** /eəʳ/ *verb* **1** [BROADCAST] [T] to broadcast something on radio or television **2 air your opinions/views, etc** to say what your opinions are *The meeting will give everyone a chance to air their views.* **3** [ROOM] [T] to make a room smell better by opening a door or window **4** [CLOTHES] [I,T] If clothes air, or if you air them, you hang them up with a lot of air around them.

**airbag** /'eəbæg/ *noun* [C] a bag in the front of a car that protects people in an accident by filling with air *passenger/twin airbags*

**airbase** /'eəbeɪs/ *noun* [C] a military airport

**airborne** /'eəbɔːn/ *adj* moving in, or carried by the air *airborne troops* • *an airborne virus*

**'air con,ditioner** *noun* [C] a machine that keeps the air cool in a building or a car

**'air con,ditioning** *noun* [U] a system that keeps the air cool in a building or car • **air-conditioned** /'eəkən,dɪʃənd/ *adj* having air conditioning *an air-conditioned office*

**aircraft** /'eəkrɑːft/ *noun* [C] *plural* **aircraft** a vehicle that can fly

**'aircraft ,carrier** *noun* [C] a ship on which aircraft can take off and land

**airfare** /'eəfeəʳ/ *noun* [C] the cost of a ticket to fly somewhere

**airfield** /'eəfiːld/ *noun* [C] a place where small or military aircraft can take off and land

**'air ,force** *noun* [C] the part of a country's military organization that uses aircraft to fight wars

**'air ho,stess** *UK (UK/US* **flight attendant)** *noun* [C] someone whose job is to serve passengers on an aircraft and to make sure that safety rules are obeyed

**'airing ,cupboard** *noun* [C] *UK* a warm cupboard where you keep sheets, clean clothes, etc

**airless** /'eələs/ *adj* An airless room does not have enough fresh air.

**airlift** /'eəlɪft/ *noun* [C] when people or things are moved by aircraft because it is too difficult or too slow to travel by road *an airlift of medical supplies* • **airlift** *verb* [T] [often passive] *Three small children were airlifted to safety.*

**airline** /'eəlaɪn/ *noun* [C] a company that provides regular flights to places

**airliner** /'eəlaɪnəʳ/ *noun* [C] a large plane for carrying people

**airmail** /'eəmeɪl/ *noun* [U] the sending of letters or parcels by plane *an airmail letter*

**airman** /'eəmən/ *noun* [C] *plural* **airmen** a man who flies an aircraft in a country's air force

**airplane** /'eəpleɪn/ *US (UK* **aeroplane)** *noun* [C] a vehicle that flies and has an engine and wings ➔ *See picture at* **aeroplane.**

O→**airport** /'eəpɔːt/ *noun* [C] a place where planes take off and land, with buildings for passengers to wait in

**'air ,raid** *noun* [C] an attack by military planes

**airspace** /'eəspeɪs/ *noun* [U] the sky above a country that belongs to that country

**airstrike** /'eəstraɪk/ *noun* [C] an attack by military planes

**airtight** /'eətaɪt/ *adj* An airtight container does not allow air in or out.

**airy** /'eəri/ *adj* An airy room or building is pleasant because it has a lot of space and air.

**aisle** /aɪl/ *noun* [C] a passage between the lines of seats or goods in a plane, church, supermarket, etc

**aisle**

**ajar** /ə'dʒɑːʳ/ *adj* [never before noun] If a door is ajar, it is slightly open.

**aka** /,eɪkeɪ'eɪ/ *adv abbreviation for* also known as: used when giving the name that a person is generally known by, after giving their real name *Peter Parker, aka Spiderman*

**akin** /ə'kɪn/ *adj formal* **be akin to sth** to be similar to something

**à la carte** /,ælə'kɑːt/ *adj, adv* choosing food as separate items from a menu (= list of food), not as a meal with a fixed price

**alacrity** /ə'lækrəti/ *noun* [U] *formal* If you do something with alacrity, you do it in a very quick and willing way.

**alarm**[1] /ə'lɑːm/ *noun* **1** WARNING [C] a loud noise that warns you of danger *a fire alarm* • *to set off an alarm* **2** CLOCK [C] (*also* **alarm clock**) a clock that makes a noise to wake you **3** WORRY [U] a sudden feeling of fear or worry that something bad might happen *There's no need for alarm – it is completely safe.* **4 raise the alarm** to warn someone of a dangerous situation *Her parents raised the alarm when she failed to return home.* ⊃ *See also:* **burglar alarm, false alarm.**

**alarm**[2] /ə'lɑːm/ *verb* [T] to make someone worried or frightened *I don't want to alarm you but he really should be here by now.*

**a'larm ,clock** *noun* [C] a clock that makes a noise to wake you *I've set the alarm clock for six.*

**alarmed** /ə'lɑːmd/ *adj* worried or frightened by something *I was a bit alarmed at the number of people in the audience.*

**alarming** /ə'lɑːmɪŋ/ *adj* making you feel worried or frightened *alarming news*

**alas** /ə'læs/ *exclamation literary* used to show sadness

**albeit** /ɔːl'biːɪt/ *conjunction formal* although *He tried, albeit without success.*

**albino** /æl'biːnəʊ ⑤ æl'baɪnəʊ/ *noun* [C] a person or animal with white skin, white hair or fur, and pink eyes

**album** /'ælbəm/ *noun* [C] **1** several songs or pieces of music on a CD, etc *Have you heard their new album?* **2** a book in which you keep photographs, stamps, etc

**alcohol** /'ælkəhɒl/ *noun* [U] **1** drinks such as wine and beer that can make you drunk **2** a liquid that has no colour and is in drinks that make you drunk

**alcoholic**[1] /ˌælkə'hɒlɪk/ *noun* [C] someone who regularly drinks too much alcohol and cannot stop the habit

**alcoholic**[2] /ˌælkə'hɒlɪk/ *adj* **1** containing alcohol *alcoholic drinks* **2** [always before noun] regularly drinking too much alcohol and unable to stop the habit *She lived with her alcoholic father.*

**alcoholism** /'ælkəhɒlɪzᵊm/ *noun* [U] the condition of being an alcoholic

**alcove** /'ælkəʊv/ *noun* [C] a part of a wall in a room that is further back than the rest of the wall

**ale** /eɪl/ *noun* [C, U] a type of beer

**alert**[1] /ə'lɜːt/ *adj* quick to notice and react to things around you *A young dog should be alert and playful.* • *Teachers need to be alert to sudden changes in students' behaviour.* • **alertness** *noun* [U]

**alert**[2] /ə'lɜːt/ *verb* [T] to warn someone of a possibly dangerous situation *Six hours later she still wasn't home so they alerted the police.*

**alert**[3] /ə'lɜːt/ *noun* [C] a warning about a possibly dangerous situation *a bomb alert* **2 be on full/red alert** to be expecting problems and ready to deal with them *Police in the region were on full alert against further attacks.*

**'A ,level** *noun* [C] in England and Wales, an exam taken at the age of eighteen, or the qualification itself

**algae** /'ældʒiː/ *noun* [U, group] a plant with no stem or leaves that grows in or near water

**algebra** /'ældʒɪbrə/ *noun* [U] a type of mathematics in which numbers and amounts are shown by letters and symbols

**alias**[1] /'eɪliəs/ *noun* [C] a false name, especially one used by a criminal

**alias**[2] /'eɪliəs/ *preposition* used when giving the name that a person is generally known by, after giving their real name *Grace Kelly, alias Princess Grace of Monaco*

**alibi** /'ælɪbaɪ/ *noun* [C] proof that someone was not in the place where a crime happened and so cannot be guilty

**alien**[1] /'eɪliən/ *adj* **1** strange and not familiar *The custom was totally alien to her.* **2** [always before noun] relating to creatures from another planet *an alien spacecraft*

**alien**[2] /'eɪliən/ *noun* [C] **1** a creature from another planet **2** *formal* someone who does not legally belong to the country where they live or work

**alienate** /'eɪliəneɪt/ *verb* [T] **1** to make someone stop supporting and liking you *The government's comments have alienated many teachers.* **2** to make someone feel that they are different and do not belong to a group *Disagreements can alienate teenagers from their families.* • **alienation** /ˌeɪliə'neɪʃᵊn/ *noun* [U]

**alight**[1] /ə'laɪt/ *adj* [never before noun] *mainly UK* burning *Vandals set the car alight* (= made it burn).

**alight**[2] /ə'laɪt/ *verb* [I] *formal* to get out of a bus, train, etc *He alighted from the taxi.*

**align** /ə'laɪn/ *verb* [T] **1** to put things in an exact line or make them parallel **2 align yourself with sb; be aligned with sb** to support the opinions of a political group, country, etc *Many voters are not aligned with any party.* • **alignment** *noun* [C, U]

**alike**[1] /ə'laɪk/ *adj* [never before noun] similar *The children look so alike.*

**alike**[2] /ə'laɪk/ *adv* **1** in a similar way *We think alike.* **2** used to say that two people or groups are included *It is a disease which affects men and women alike.*

**alimony** /'ælɪməni/ *noun* [U] money that someone must pay regularly to their wife or husband after the marriage has ended

o─**alive** /ə'laɪv/ *adj* [never before noun] **1** NOT DEAD living, not dead *Are your grandparents still alive?* **2** PLACE full of activity and excitement *The bar was alive with the sound of laughter.* • *The city comes alive at night.* **3** CONTINUING continuing to exist *Local people are fighting to keep the language alive.* **4 be alive and kicking/well** to continue to be popular or successful *Despite rumours to the contrary, feminism is alive and kicking.*

o─**all**[1] /ɔːl/ *pronoun, determiner* **1** EVERY ONE every person or thing in a group *We were all dancing.* • *I've watched all of the programmes in the series.* **2** WHOLE AMOUNT the whole amount of something *Who's eaten all the cake?* • *He spends all of his money on clothes.* **3** WHOLE TIME the whole of a period of time *all week/month/year* • *He's been studying all day.* **4** ONLY THING the only thing *All I remember is waking up in hospital.* • *I'm sorry, this is all I can offer you.* **5 at all** [used in questions and negatives] in any way *He hasn't changed at all.* • *(UK) Can I help at all?* **6 in all** in total *There were twenty people at the meeting in all.*

**USAGE**

**all + period of time**

You do not say 'the' when you use **all** + a period of time.

*all day/morning/week/year/summer*

~~all the day/morning/week/year/summer~~

O⇥**all²** /ɔːl/ *adv* **1** completely or very *You're all wet!* • *I'm all excited now.* **2 all over a** in every place *Lee has travelled all over the world.* **b** finished *It was all over very quickly.* **3 2/5/8, etc all** used to say that two players or teams have the same number of points in a game *It was 3 all at half time.* **4 all along** from the beginning of a period of time *I said all along that it was a mistake.* **5 all but** almost *The film was all but over by the time we arrived.* **6 all the better/easier/more exciting, etc** much better, easier, etc *The journey was all the more dangerous because of the bad weather.* **7 all in all** considering everything *All in all, I think she did very well.*

**Allah** /ˈælə/ *noun* the Muslim name for God

**allay** /əˈleɪ/ *verb formal* **allay sb's concerns/ fears/suspicions, etc** to make someone feel less worried or frightened, etc *I tried to allay his fears about the interview.*

**allegation** /ˌælɪˈɡeɪʃⁿn/ *noun* [C] when you say that someone has done something wrong or illegal, without proof that this is true *allegations of corruption* • [+ that] *He denied allegations that he had cheated.*

**allege** /əˈledʒ/ *verb* [T] to say that someone has done something wrong or illegal, but not prove it [often passive] *The teacher is alleged to have hit a student.* • [+ (that)] *He alleges that Bates attacked him.*

**alleged** /əˈledʒd/ *adj* [always before noun] believed to be true, but not proved *an alleged attack* • **allegedly** /əˈledʒɪdli/ *adv He was arrested for allegedly stealing a car.*

**allegiance** /əˈliːdʒⁿns/ *noun* [U] loyalty and support *To become a citizen, you have to **pledge/swear allegiance to** (= say you will be loyal to) the United States.*

**allegory** /ˈælɪɡəri/ *noun* [C, U] a story, poem, or painting that has a hidden meaning, especially a moral one • **allegorical** /ˌælɪˈɡɒrɪkəl/ *adj*

**allergic** /əˈlɜːdʒɪk/ *adj* **1** [never before noun] having an allergy *I'm **allergic to** eggs.* **2** [always before noun] caused by an allergy *an allergic reaction*

**allergy** /ˈælədʒi/ *noun* [C] a medical condition in which your body reacts badly to something that you eat, breathe, or touch *an allergy to dogs*

**alleviate** /əˈliːvieɪt/ *verb* [T] to make problems or suffering less extreme *She's been given some tablets to alleviate the pain.* • **alleviation** /əˌliːviˈeɪʃⁿn/ *noun* [U]

**alley** /ˈæli/ (*also* **alleyway** /ˈæliweɪ/) *noun* [C] **1** a narrow road between buildings **2 be right up sb's alley** *US informal* (*UK* **be right up sb's**

street) to be exactly the type of thing that someone knows about or likes to do *I've got a question here which should be right up your alley.*

**alliance** /əˈlaɪəns/ *noun* [C] an agreement between countries or political parties to work together to achieve something *an alliance between France and Britain*

**allied** /ˈælaɪd/ *adj* **1** [always before noun] joined by a formal agreement *the allied powers* **2 be allied to/with sth** to be related to something *a group closely allied with the Green Party*

**alligator** /ˈælɪɡeɪtə⁻/ *noun* [C] a big reptile with a long mouth and sharp teeth, that lives in lakes and rivers

alligator

**allocate** /ˈæləkeɪt/ *verb* [T] to give some time, money, space, etc to be used for a particular purpose *The government has promised to allocate extra money for health care.* • *More police time should be allocated to crime prevention.*

**allocation** /ˌæləˈkeɪʃⁿn/ *noun* **1** [C] an amount of money, time, space, etc that is allocated **2** [U] when money, time, space, etc is allocated *the allocation of money*

**allot** /əˈlɒt/ *verb* [T] **allotting**, *past* **allotted** to give someone a particular amount of something [often passive] *They were allotted seats on the front row.*

**allotment** /əˈlɒtmənt/ *noun* **1** [C] in Britain, a small area of land that people rent and grow vegetables and flowers on **2** [C, U] the process of sharing something, or the amount that you get

**all-out** /ˈɔːlˌaʊt/ *adj* [always before noun] complete and with as much effort as possible *an all-out battle/effort*

O⇥**allow** /əˈlaʊ/ *verb* [T] **1** GIVE PERMISSION to give someone permission for something [often passive] *Smoking is not allowed in the restaurant.* • *Are dogs allowed in the hotel?* • [+ to do sth] *You are not allowed to use calculators in the exam.* • [+ two objects] *Patients are not allowed visitors after nine o'clock.* **2** NOT PREVENT to not prevent something from happening [+ to do sth] *They have allowed the problem to get much worse.* **3** MAKE POSSIBLE to make it possible for someone to do something [+ to do sth] *The extra money will allow me to upgrade my computer.* **4** TIME/MONEY to plan to use a particular amount of money, time, etc for something *Allow three hours for the whole journey.*

**USAGE**

**allow or let?**

Allow and let have similar meanings.

Allow is used in more formal or official situations, especially when talking about rules and laws.

**A**

Verb patterns – **allow someone to do something/ allow something to happen**

*The new legislation allows companies to charge for this service.*

*We can't allow this situation to continue.*

Let is used in more informal and spoken situations.

Verb patterns – **let someone do something /let something happen**

*Dad never lets anyone else drive his car.*

*She let her hair grow longer.*

**allow for sth** to consider or include something when you are making plans *The journey should take about two hours, allowing for delays.*

**allowance** /ə'laʊəns/ *noun* [C] **1** money that you are given regularly, especially to pay for a particular thing *a clothing allowance* **2** an amount of something that you are allowed *The luggage allowance is 25 kilos.* **3 make allowances for sb/sth** to remember that someone has a disadvantage which is not their fault when you are judging their behaviour or work *They made allowances for the fact that he had been ill.*

**alloy** /'ælɔɪ/ *noun* [C] a metal that is a mixture of two or more metals

,**all 'right**[1] (*also* **alright**) *adj, adv* [never before noun] **1** good enough, although not very good *The hotel wasn't brilliant but it was all right.* ● *It's a cheap wine but it tastes all right.* **2** safe or well *I'm all right thanks. How are you?* ● *Did you get home all right last night?* **3 that's all right a** used as an answer when someone thanks you *"Thanks for cleaning the kitchen." "That's all right."* **b** something you say when someone says sorry to show that you are not angry *"I'm sorry – I forgot all about it." "That's all right."*

,**all 'right**[2] (*also* **alright**) *exclamation* used to agree to a suggestion or request *"How about going out for dinner?" "All right."*

**allude** /ə'luːd/ *verb*
**allude to sb/sth** *formal* to refer to someone or something but not directly

**allure** /ə'ljʊəʳ/ *noun* [U] an attractive or exciting quality *the allure of the city* ● **alluring** *adj* attractive or exciting *an alluring image*

**allusion** /ə'luːʒən/ *noun* [C, U] *formal* when you refer to someone or something but not directly *a play full of allusions to Shakespeare*

**ally**[1] /'ælaɪ/ *noun* [C] **1** someone who supports you, especially when other people are against you **2** a country that has agreed to help another country, especially in a war

**ally**[2] /ə'laɪ/ *verb*
**ally yourself to/with sb** to join someone and support them

**almighty** /ɔːl'maɪti/ *adj* **1** [always before noun] very strong or forceful *All of a sudden I heard an almighty bang in the kitchen.* **2** having the power to do everything, like a god *Almighty God*

**almond** /'ɑːmənd/ *noun* [C,U] a flat, oval nut, often used in cooking

○━**almost** /'ɔːlməʊst/ *adv* **1** If something almost happens, it does not happen but it is very

close to happening. *I almost missed the bus.* **2 almost always/everyone/half, etc** not always/everyone/half, etc but very close to it *He's almost always late.* ● *Almost everyone I know likes chocolate.*

○━**alone** /ə'ləʊn/ *adj, adv* **1** [never before noun] without other people *She lives alone.* ● *We're all alone.* **2** [always after noun] used to emphasize that only one person or thing is involved *Last year alone the company made a million dollars.* ● *You alone know how you feel.* **3 leave sb alone** to stop talking to someone or annoying them *Leave him alone, he's tired.* **4 leave sth alone** to stop touching something *Leave your hair alone!* ⊃ *See also:* **let** alone.

**USAGE**

**alone** or **lonely**?

Alone means without other people. If you feel sad because you are alone, you are **lonely**.

*Sometimes I like to be alone to think.*

*She has been very lonely since her husband died.*

○━**along**[1] /ə'lɒŋ/ *preposition* **1** DIRECTION from one part of a road, river, etc to another *a romantic walk along the beach* **2** NEXT TO in a line next to something long *a row of new houses along the river* **3** PARTICULAR PLACE at a particular place on a road, river, etc *Somewhere along this road there's a garage.*

○━**along**[2] /ə'lɒŋ/ *adv* **1** forward *We were just walking along, chatting.* **2 be/come along** to arrive somewhere *You wait ages for a bus and then three come along at once.* **3 bring/take sb along** to take someone with you to a place *She asked if she could bring some friends along to the party.* **4 along with sb/sth** in addition to someone or something else *California along with Florida is probably the most popular American holiday destination.*

**alongside** /ə,lɒŋ'saɪd/ *adv, preposition* **1** next to someone or something *A car pulled up alongside ours.* **2** together with someone *She enjoyed working alongside such famous actors.*

**aloof** /ə'luːf/ *adj* **1** not friendly, especially because you think you are better than other people *He seems arrogant and aloof.* **2** not involved in something *He tried to remain aloof from family arguments.*

**aloud** /ə'laʊd/ *adv* in a way that other people can hear *to laugh aloud* ● *The author read aloud from his new book.*

**alphabet** /'ælfəbet/ *noun* [C] a set of letters used for writing a language *The English alphabet starts at A and ends at Z.*

**alphabetical** /,ælfə'betɪkəl/ *adj* arranged in the same order as the letters of the alphabet *Put the names in alphabetical order.* ● **alphabetically** *adv*

**alpine** /'ælpaɪn/ *adj* [always before noun] existing in, or relating to high mountains *an alpine village*

○━**already** /ɔːl'redi/ *adv* **1** before now, or before a particular time in the past *I've already told him.* ● *By the time we arrived, he'd already left.* **2** used to say that something has happened earlier than you expected *I'm already full and I've only eaten one course.*

alright /ɔːlˈraɪt/ *adj, adv, exclamation* another spelling of **all right**

o–∗**also** /ˈɔːlsəʊ/ *adv* in addition *She speaks French and also a little Spanish.* • *The book also has a chapter on grammar.*

altar /ˈɔːltəʳ/ *noun* [C] a table used for religious ceremonies, especially in a Christian church

alter /ˈɔːltəʳ/ *verb* [I, T] to change, or to make someone or something change *We've had to alter our plans.* • *Your life alters completely when you have kids.*

alteration /ˌɔːltəˈreɪʃʳn/ *noun* [C, U] a change, or the process of changing something *We've made a few alterations to the kitchen.*

alternate¹ /ɔːlˈtɜːnət/ *adj* **1** **alternate days/weeks/years, etc** one out of every two days, weeks, years, etc *I work alternate Saturdays.* **2** with first one thing, then another thing, and then the first thing again, etc *a dessert with alternate layers of chocolate and cream* **3** [always before noun] *US* An alternate plan, method, etc is one that you can use if you do not want to use another one. • alternately *adv*

alternate² /ˈɔːltəneɪt/ *verb* **1** [I] If two things alternate, one thing happens, then the other thing happens, then the first thing happens again, etc. *She alternates between cheerfulness and deep despair.* **2** **alternate sth with sth** to use or do one thing then another thing and then the first thing again, etc *They alternate classical pieces with more modern works.* • alternating *adj alternating moods of anger and sadness*

o–∗**alternative¹** /ɔːlˈtɜːnətɪv/ *noun* [C] one of two or more things that you can choose between *a low-fat alternative to butter* • *After the public protests the government had no alternative but to change its policy.*

alternative² /ɔːlˈtɜːnətɪv/ *adj* [always before noun] **1** (*also US* alternate) An alternative plan, method, etc is one that you can use if you do not want to use another one. *We can make alternative arrangements if necessary.* **2** different to what is usual or traditional *alternative comedy/medicine*

alternatively /ɔːlˈtɜːnətɪvli/ *adv* used to give a second possibility *We could go there by train or, alternatively, I could drive us.*

o–∗**although** /ɔːlˈðəʊ/ *conjunction* **1** despite the fact that *She walked home by herself, although she knew it was dangerous.* **2** but *He's coming this evening, although I don't know exactly when.*

altitude /ˈæltɪtjuːd/ *noun* [C, U] the height of something above sea level *flying at an altitude of 8000 metres.*

alto /ˈæltəʊ/ *noun* [C] a woman or boy with a low singing voice

o–∗**altogether** /ˌɔːltəˈgeðəʳ/ *adv* **1** [COMPLETELY] completely *The train slowed down and then stopped altogether.* • *I'm not altogether sure about the idea.* **2** [TOTAL] in total *There were twenty people there altogether.* **3** [GENERALLY] when you consider everything *Altogether, I'd say the party was a great success.*

aluminium /ˌæljəˈmɪniəm/ *UK* (*US* **aluminum** /əˈluːmɪnəm/) *noun* [U] a light, silver-coloured metal used for making containers, cooking equipment, and aircraft parts *aluminium cans/foil*

o–∗**always** /ˈɔːlweɪz/ *adv* **1** [EVERY TIME] every time, or at all times *Diane is always so cheerful.* • *I always walk to work.* **2** [UNTIL NOW] at all times in the past *We've always lived here.* **3** [FOREVER] forever *I will always remember you.* **4** [MANY TIMES] again and again, usually in an annoying way [+ doing sth] *He's always losing his keys.* **5** **can/could always do sth** used to suggest something *You can always stay with us if you miss your train.*

o–∗**a.m.** (*also* **am**) /ˌeɪˈem/ used to refer to a time between 12 o'clock in the night and 12 o'clock in the day *We're open from 9 a.m. to 5 p.m. daily.*

am *strong form* /æm/ *weak forms* /əm, m/ *present simple I of* **be**

amalgamate /əˈmælgəmeɪt/ *verb* [I, T] If two or more organizations amalgamate, they join to become one, and if you amalgamate them, you make them do this. *a decision to amalgamate with another school* • amalgamation /əˌmælgəˈmeɪʃʳn/ *noun* [C, U]

amass /əˈmæs/ *verb* [T] *formal* to get a lot of money or information over a period of time *He amassed a fortune in the diamond trade.*

amateur¹ /ˈæmətəʳ/ *adj* doing something as a hobby and not as your job *an amateur photographer*

amateur² /ˈæmətəʳ/ *noun* [C] **1** someone who does something as a hobby and not as their job **2** someone who is not good at what they do *I won't be giving them any more work – they're a bunch of amateurs.*

amateurish /ˈæmətʳrɪʃ (US) ˌæməˈtɜːrɪʃ/ *adj* done without skill or attention

amaze /əˈmeɪz/ *verb* [T] to make someone very surprised *It amazes me how much energy that woman has.*

amazed /əˈmeɪzd/ *adj* extremely surprised *I was amazed at the price.* • [+ (that)] *I was amazed that Paul recognized me.*

amazement /əˈmeɪzmənt/ *noun* [U] extreme surprise *Jana looked at him in amazement.* • *To his amazement they offered him the job.*

o–∗**amazing** /əˈmeɪzɪŋ/ *adj* very surprising [+ question word] *It's amazing how many people can't read.* • amazingly *adv She looked amazingly well.*

ambassador /æmˈbæsədəʳ/ *noun* [C] the main official sent by the government of a country to represent it in another country *the French ambassador to Britain*

amber /ˈæmbəʳ/ *noun* [U] **1** a colour between yellow and orange **2** a hard, clear yellowish-brown substance, used for making jewellery • amber *adj an amber traffic light*

ambience (*also* **ambiance**) /ˈæmbiəns/ *noun* [U, no plural] the qualities of a place and the way it makes you feel *Lighting adds a lot to the ambience of a room.*

ambiguity /ˌæmbɪˈgjuːəti/ *noun* [C, U] when something has more than one possible meaning *Legal documents must be free of ambiguity.*

# A

**ambiguous** /æm'bɪgjuəs/ *adj* having more than one possible meaning *an ambiguous statement* • ambiguously *adv*

o⸳**ambition** /æm'bɪʃᵊn/ *noun* **1** [C] something you want to achieve in your life *My ambition is to retire at forty.* **2** [U] a strong feeling that you want to be successful or powerful *My sister always had more ambition than me.*

**ambitious** /æm'bɪʃəs/ *adj* **1** wanting to be successful or powerful *an ambitious young lawyer* **2** An ambitious plan will need a lot of work and will be difficult to achieve. *This is our most ambitious project so far.*

**ambivalent** /æm'bɪvələnt/ *adj* having two different feelings about something *He was **ambivalent about** moving to London.* • ambivalence /æm'bɪvᵊləns/ *noun* [U]

**amble** /'æmbl/ *verb* **amble along/around/ through, etc** to walk somewhere in a slow and relaxed way *We ambled home across the fields.*

**ambulance** /'æmbjələns/ *noun* [C] a vehicle that takes people to hospital when they are ill or hurt

**ambush** /'æmbʊʃ/ *verb* [T] to attack a person or vehicle after hiding somewhere and waiting for them to arrive [often passive] *The bus was ambushed by a gang of youths.* • ambush *noun* [C] *Two policemen were killed in a terrorist ambush.*

**ambush**

**ameliorate** /ə'miːliᵊreɪt/ *verb* [T] *formal* to make a bad situation better

**amen** /ˌɑː'men/ *exclamation* something that Christians say at the end of a prayer

**amenable** /ə'miːnəbl/ *adj* willing to do or accept something *She may be more **amenable to** the idea now.*

**amend** /ə'mend/ *verb* [T] to slightly change the words of a document [often passive] *The contract has now been amended.*

**amendment** /ə'mendmənt/ *noun* [C, U] a change in the words of a document, or the process of doing this *to make an amendment to the human rights law*

**amends** /ə'mendz/ *noun* **make amends** to do something nice for someone to show that you are sorry for something that you have done *I want to **make amends for** the worry I've caused you.*

**amenity** /ə'miːnəti ⓤⓢ ə'menəti/ *noun* [C] a building, piece of equipment, or service that is provided for people's comfort or enjoyment [usually plural] *The campsite's amenities include a pool and three restaurants.*

**American** /ə'merɪkən/ *adj* **1** relating to the United States of America *an American accent* **2 North/South American** relating to one or more of the countries of North/South America *the North American Free Trade agreement* • American *noun* [C] someone who comes from the United States of America ⊃ *See also:* **Native American**.

**American 'football** UK (US **football**) *noun* [U] a game for two teams of eleven players in which each team tries to kick, run with, or throw an oval ball across the opposing team's goal line ⊃ *See colour picture* **Sports 2** *on page Centre 16.*

**American 'Indian** *adj* relating or belonging to the original race of people who lived in North America • American Indian *noun* [C]

**amiable** /'eɪmiəbl/ *adj* pleasant and friendly *an amiable young man* • amiably *adv*

**amicable** /'æmɪkəbl/ *adj formal* done in a friendly way, without arguments *an amicable agreement/divorce* • amicably *adv*

**amid** /ə'mɪd/ (*also* **amidst** /ə'mɪdst/) *preposition formal* **1** while something else is happening *Security was increased amid fears of further terrorist attacks.* **2** among *a village set amid the hills*

**amiss**[1] /ə'mɪs/ *adj* [never before noun] If something is amiss, there is something wrong. *I knew something was amiss when he didn't answer the door.*

**amiss**[2] /ə'mɪs/ *adv* **1 would not go amiss** UK If something would not go amiss, it would be useful or nice in a particular situation. *A cup of coffee wouldn't go amiss.* **2 take it amiss** UK to feel upset by what someone says or does *I think she might take it amiss if I left early.*

**ammonia** /ə'məʊniə/ *noun* [U] a liquid or gas with a strong smell, used in cleaning substances

**ammunition** /ˌæmjə'nɪʃᵊn/ *noun* [U] **1** a supply of bullets and bombs to be fired from guns **2** facts that you can use to criticize someone

**amnesia** /æm'niːʒə/ *noun* [U] a medical condition that makes you forget things

**amnesty** /'æmnəsti/ *noun* **1** [C, U] a time when a government allows political prisoners to go free **2** [C] a time when people can give weapons or drugs to the police, or admit that they have done something illegal, without being punished

o⸳**among** /ə'mʌŋ/ (*also* **amongst** /ə'mʌŋst/) *preposition* **1** IN THE MIDDLE in the middle of something *He disappeared among the crowd.* **2** IN A GROUP in a particular group *The decision will not be popular among students.* • *I'm going to give you a minute to talk **amongst yourselves** (= talk to each other).* **3** ONE OF A GROUP to be one of a small group *He is among the top five tennis players in the country.* **4** DIVIDE to each one in a group *She divided the cake among the children.*

**amoral** /ˌeɪ'mɒrəl/ *adj* not caring if what you are doing is morally wrong *an amoral person/act*

**amorous** /'æmᵊrəs/ *adj* full of love and sexual excitement *amorous adventures*

o⸳**amount**[1] /ə'maʊnt/ *noun* [C] how much there is of something *The project will take a huge **amount of** time and money.*

USAGE

**amount of** or **number of**?

Amount of is used with uncountable nouns.

*I should reduce the amount of coffee I drink.*

*Did you use the right amount of flour?*

Number of is used with countable nouns.

*We don't know the number of people involved yet.*

*They received a large number of complaints.*

**amount²** /ə'maʊnt/ *verb*
**amount to sth 1** to be the same as something, or to have the same effect as something *He gave what amounted to an apology on behalf of the company.* **2** to have a particular total *goods amounting to $800*

**amp** /æmp/ (*also* **ampere** /'æmpeər/) *noun* [C] a unit for measuring the strength of an electric current

**ample** /'æmpl/ *adj* **1** enough, or more than enough *She's had ample time to get the work done.* **2** large *her ample bosom/stomach* • **amply** *adv*

**amplifier** /'æmplɪfaɪər/ *noun* [C] a piece of electronic equipment that makes sounds louder

**amplify** /'æmplɪfaɪ/ *verb* [T] **1** to make a sound louder using electronic equipment **2** *formal* to make a feeling or opinion stronger or clearer • amplification /ˌæmplɪfɪ'keɪʃən/ *noun* [U]

**amputate** /'æmpjəteɪt/ *verb* [I, T] to cut off someone's leg, arm, finger, etc in a medical operation *His leg was amputated at the knee.* • amputation /ˌæmpjə'teɪʃən/ *noun* [C, U]

**amuse** /ə'mjuːz/ *verb* [T] **1** to make someone smile or laugh *I took him an article that I thought might amuse him.* **2** to keep someone interested and help them to have an enjoyable time [**often reflexive**] *I bought a magazine to amuse myself while I was on the train.*

**amused** /ə'mjuːzd/ *adj* **1** showing that you think something is funny *an amused smile* • *She was very **amused by/at** your comments.* **2 keep sb amused** to keep someone interested and help them to have an enjoyable time *How do you keep an eight-year-old boy amused?*

**amusement** /ə'mjuːzmənt/ *noun* **1** [U] the feeling that you have when something makes you smile or laugh *I watched the performance **with great amusement**.* • *To our amusement the tent collapsed on top of them.* **2** [C, U] an enjoyable way of spending your time *I play the piano but just for my own amusement.*

**a'musement ˌpark** *noun* [C] a large park where you can ride on exciting machines

**amusing** /ə'mjuːzɪŋ/ *adj* making you laugh or smile *an amusing letter*

**O—an** *strong form* /æn/ *weak form* /ən/ *determiner* used instead of 'a' when the next word starts with a vowel sound *an apple* • *an hour* ⊃ *See usage note at* **a**.

**anaemia** UK (US **anemia**) /ə'niːmiə/ *noun* [U] a medical condition in which your blood does not contain enough red cells • anaemic UK (US **anemic**) /ə'niːmɪk/ *adj*

**anaesthetic** UK (US **anesthetic**) /ˌænəs'θetɪk/ *noun* [C, U] a drug that makes you unable to feel pain during an operation *The operation is done **under anaesthetic** (= using anaesthetic).* ⊃ *See also:* **general anaesthetic**, **local anaesthetic**.

**anaesthetist** UK (US **anesthetist**) /ə'niːsθətɪst (US) ə'nesθətɪst/ *noun* [C] a doctor in a hospital who gives anaesthetics to people

**anagram** /'ænəgræm/ *noun* [C] a word or phrase made by putting the letters of another word or phrase in a different order *'Team' is an anagram of 'meat'.*

**anal** /'eɪnəl/ *adj* relating to the anus (= hole where solid waste comes out of the body)

**analogous** /ə'næləgəs/ *adj formal* similar in some ways *It's often said that life is **analogous** to a journey.*

**analogy** /ə'nælədʒi/ *noun* [C, U] a comparison that shows how two things are similar *She **draws an analogy between** life's events and a game of chance.*

**analyse** UK (US **analyze**) /'ænəlaɪz/ *verb* [T] to examine the details of something carefully, in order to understand or explain it *to analyse information* • *Blood samples were analysed in the laboratory.*

**analysis** /ə'næləsɪs/ *noun* [C, U] *plural* **analyses** /ə'næləsiːz/ the process of analysing something *a detailed analysis* • *A sample of soil was sent for analysis.*

**analyst** /'ænəlɪst/ *noun* [C] someone whose job is to examine the details of a situation carefully, and give their opinion about it *a financial/political analyst*

**analytical** /ˌænə'lɪtɪkəl/ (*also* **analytic**) *adj* examining the details of something carefully, in order to understand or explain it *analytical skills* • *an analytical mind*

**analyze** /'ænəlaɪz/ *verb* [T] US *spelling of* analyse

**anarchist** /'ænəkɪst/ *noun* [C] someone who thinks that society should not be controlled by a government and laws

**anarchy** /'ænəki/ *noun* [U] when there is no law or government, or when people ignore them • anarchic /æn'ɑːkɪk/ *adj*

**anatomy** /ə'nætəmi/ *noun* **1** [U] the scientific study of the body and how its parts are arranged **2** [C] the body of a person or living thing [**usually singular**] *the female anatomy* • anatomical /ˌænə'tɒmɪkəl/ *adj*

**ancestor** /'ænsestər/ *noun* [C] a relative who lived a long time ago *My ancestors came from Ireland.* • ancestral /æn'sestrəl/ *adj*

**ancestry** /'ænsestri/ *noun* [C, U] your relatives who lived a long time ago, or the origin of your family *Americans of Japanese ancestry*

**anchor¹** /'æŋkər/ *noun* [C] **1** a heavy, metal object that is dropped into water to stop a boat from moving **2** US

**anchor**

**A**

someone who reads the news and announcements on a television or radio programme

**anchor²** /'æŋkə'/ verb **1** BOAT [I, T] to stop a boat from moving by dropping a heavy metal object into the water **2** FASTEN [T] to make something or someone stay in one position by fastening them firmly *We anchored ourselves to the rocks with a rope.* **3** PROGRAMME [T] *US* to read the news or announcements on television or radio as your job

**ancient** /'eɪnʃ°nt/ adj [always before noun] from a long time ago *ancient Greece/Rome* • *an ancient building* **2** *humorous* very old *This computer is ancient.*

o━**and** *strong form* /ænd/ *weak forms* /ənd, ən/ conjunction **1** JOIN used to join two words or two parts of a sentence *tea and coffee* • *We were tired and hungry.* • *Tim lives in Brighton and Anne in Oxford.* **2** AFTER used to say that one thing happens after another thing *I got dressed and had my breakfast.* **3** SO so *The car wouldn't start and I had to get a taxi.* **4** AFTER VERB *mainly UK* used instead of 'to' after some verbs, such as 'try' and 'go' *Try and eat something.* **5** NUMBERS used when saying or adding numbers *It cost a hundred and twenty pounds.* • *(UK) Two and three equals five.* **6** EMPHASIZE used between two words that are the same to make their meaning stronger *The sound grew louder and louder.*

**anecdote** /'ænɪkdəʊt/ noun [C] a short story that you tell someone about something that happened to you or someone else *a speech full of anecdotes* • anecdotal /,ænɪk'dəʊt°l/ adj consisting of things that people have said, and not facts *anecdotal evidence*

**anemia** /ə'ni:miə/ noun [U] *US spelling of* anaemia (= a medical condition in which your blood does not contain enough red cells)

**anemic** /ə'ni:mɪk/ adj *US spelling of* anaemic

**anesthetic** /,ænəs'θetɪk/ noun [C, U] *US spelling of* anaesthetic (= a drug that makes you unable to feel pain during an operation)

**anesthetist** /ə'nesθətɪst/ noun [C] *US spelling of* anaesthetist (= a doctor who gives anaesthetics to people)

**anew** /ə'nju:/ adv *literary* If you do something anew, you do it again in a different way. *Moving to another city gave me the chance to start anew.*

**angel** /'eɪndʒ°l/ noun [C] **1** a spiritual creature like a human with wings, who some people believe lives with God in heaven **2** a very good, kind person *Be an angel and get me a drink.* • angelic /æn'dʒelɪk/ adj very beautiful or good *an angelic child*

o━**anger¹** /'æŋgə'/ noun [U] a strong feeling against someone who has behaved badly, making you want to shout at them or hurt them *public anger at the terrorist killings* • *He never once raised his voice in anger.*

**anger²** /'æŋgə'/ verb [T] to make someone angry [often passive] *Students were angered by the college's decision.*

**angle¹** /'æŋgl/ noun [C] **1** SPACE a space between two lines or surfaces that meet at one point, which you measure in degrees *an angle of 90 degrees* **2 at an angle** not horizontal or vertical, but sloping *He wore his hat at an*

*angle.* **3** WAY OF THINKING the way you think about a situation *Try looking at the problem from my angle.* **4** DIRECTION the direction from which you look at something *This is the same building photographed from different angles.* ⊃ *See also:* **right angle.**

**angle** 

**angle²** /'æŋgl/ verb [T] to aim or turn something in a direction that is not horizontal or vertical *She angled a shot into the corner of the court.*

**be angling for sth** to try to get something without asking for it in a direct way *Is he angling for an invitation?*

**angler** /'æŋglə'/ noun [C] someone who catches fish as a hobby or sport

**Anglican** /'æŋglɪkən/ adj belonging or relating to the Church of England (= the official church in England) • Anglican noun [C]

**angling** /'æŋglɪŋ/ noun [U] the sport or hobby of catching fish

o━**angry** /'æŋgri/ adj having a strong feeling against someone who has behaved badly, making you want to shout at them or hurt them *He's really angry at/with me for upsetting Sophie.* • *I don't understand what he's angry about.* • angrily adv

**angst** /æŋst/ noun [U] a strong feeling of worry and unhappiness *teenage angst*

**anguish** /'æŋgwɪʃ/ noun [U] extreme suffering, especially mental suffering *It's the anguish of knowing that I can do nothing to help.* • anguished adj [always before noun] *anguished parents*

**angular** /'æŋgjʊlə'/ adj An angular shape or object has a lot of straight lines and sharp points. *an angular face*

o━**animal¹** /'ænɪm°l/ noun [C] **1** NOT A HUMAN something that lives and moves but is not a person, bird, fish, or insect *a wild animal* • *She's a real animal lover.* **2** NOT A PLANT anything that lives and moves, including people, birds, etc *Are humans the only animals to use language?* **3** CRUEL PERSON *informal* a very cruel and violent person

**animal²** /'ænɪm°l/ adj [always before noun] Animal qualities and feelings relate to your basic physical needs. *animal passion*

**animate** /'ænɪmət/ adj *formal* alive ⊃ *Opposite* **inanimate.**

**animated** /'ænɪmeɪtɪd/ adj **1** showing a lot of interest and excitement *an animated conversation* **2** An animated film is one in which drawings and models seem to move.

**animation** /,ænɪ'meɪʃ°n/ noun **1** [U] interest and excitement *She spoke with great animation.* **2** [C, U] an animated film, or the process of making animated films *computer animation*

**animosity** /,ænɪ'mɒsəti/ noun [C, U] when someone hates or feels angry towards someone else *There is no **animosity between** the two teams.*

**ankle** /'æŋkl/ *noun* [C] the part of your leg that is just above your foot ➜ *See colour picture* **The Body** *on page Centre 2.*

**annex**[1] /ə'neks/ *verb* [T] to start to rule or control an area or country next to your own • annexation /ˌænek'seɪʃʰn/ *noun* [C, U]

**annex**[2] (*also UK* **annexe**) /'æneks/ *noun* [C] a building that is joined to a larger one

**annihilate** /ə'naɪɪleɪt/ *verb* [T] **1** to destroy something completely *a city annihilated by an atomic bomb* **2** *informal* to defeat someone very easily • annihilation /ˌə,naɪɪ'leɪʃʰn/ *noun* [U]

**anniversary** /ˌænɪ'vɜːsʰri/ *noun* [C] a date on which you remember or celebrate something that happened on that date one or more years ago *a wedding anniversary* • *the 30th anniversary of Kennedy's death* ➜ *See also:* **silver wedding anniversary**.

O─**announce** /ə'naʊns/ *verb* [T] to tell people about something officially or with force or confidence *The company has announced plans to open six new stores.* • [+ (that)] *Halfway through dinner, he announced that he was going out.*

**announcement** /ə'naʊnsmənt/ *noun* **1** [C] something that someone says officially, giving information about something *The Prime Minister **made** an unexpected **announcement** this morning.* **2** [no plural] when someone announces something

**announcer** /ə'naʊnsə<sup>r</sup>/ *noun* [C] someone who introduces programmes on the radio or television

**annoy** /ə'nɔɪ/ *verb* [T] to make someone slightly angry *He's always late and it's starting to annoy me.* • *I'm sorry – is my cough annoying you?*

**annoyance** /ə'nɔɪəns/ *noun* [U] the feeling of being annoyed *He kept losing his keys, **much to the annoyance of** (= which annoyed) his wife.*

**annoyed** /ə'nɔɪd/ *adj* slightly angry *I was a bit **annoyed with/at** Kathy for not phoning to tell us she'd be late.*

**annoying** /ə'nɔɪɪŋ/ *adj* making you feel annoyed *an annoying habit/cough*

**annual**[1] /'ænjuəl/ *adj* **1** happening or produced once a year *an annual meeting/report* **2** measured over a period of one year *annual rainfall* • annually *adv*

**annual**[2] /'ænjuəl/ *noun* [C] **1** a plant which grows, produces seed, and dies within one year **2** a book produced every year containing new information about the same subject

**annulment** /ə'nʌlmənt/ *noun* [C, U] *formal* when a court says officially that a marriage or agreement does not now exist and was never legal

**anomaly** /ə'nɒməli/ *noun* [C] *formal* something that is unusual or that does not seem right *There are some anomalies in the data.*

**anonymity** /ˌænə'nɪməti/ *noun* [U] when someone's name is not given or known *She agreed to speak to a journalist but **requested anonymity.***

**anonymous** /ə'nɒnɪməs/ *adj* not giving a name *an anonymous phone call* • *The winner has asked to **remain anonymous.*** • anonymously *adv*

**anorak** /'ænʰræk/ *noun* [C] *UK* a jacket with a hood (= part that covers your head) that protects you from rain and cold

**anorexia** /ˌænʰr'eksiə/ (*also* **anorexia nervosa** /ˌænʰr,eksiənʰ'vəʊsə/) *noun* [U] a mental illness in which someone refuses to eat and becomes very thin

**anorexic** /ˌænʰr'eksɪk/ *adj* having the illness anorexia

O─**another** /ə'nʌðə<sup>r</sup>/ *pronoun, determiner* **1** one more person or thing, or an additional amount *Would you like another piece of cake?* • *We can fit another person in my car.* • *For another £30 you can get a better model.* **2** a different person or thing *I'm going to look for another job.* • *This one's slightly damaged – I'll get you another.*

USAGE

**another** or **other**?

Another means 'one other' and is used with a singular noun. It is written as one word.

*Would you like another cup of coffee?*

~~Would you like other cup of coffee?~~

Other is used with a plural noun and means different things or people than the ones you are talking about.

*She had other ambitions.*

~~She had another ambitions.~~

O─**answer**[1] /'ɑːnsə<sup>r</sup>/ *verb* **1** WORDS [I, T] to speak or write back to someone who has asked you a question or spoken to you *I asked when she was leaving but she didn't answer.* • *You still haven't answered my question.* • *I must answer his letter.* **2** DOOR [I, T] to open the door when someone has knocked on it or rung a bell *I knocked several times but no one answered.* **3** TELEPHONE [I, T] to pick up the telephone receiver (= part that you hold to your ear) when it rings *Could someone answer the phone?* **4** TEST [T] to write or say something as a reply to a question in a test or competition

**answer (sb) back** If a child answers back, they reply rudely to an adult. *Dad told me off for answering back.*

**answer for sth 1** to be responsible for something, or punished for something *Do you think parents should have to answer for their children's behaviour?* **2 have a lot to answer for** to be the main cause of something bad which has happened *"Why is violent crime on the increase?" "Well, I think television has a lot to answer for."*

O─**answer**[2] /'ɑːnsə<sup>r</sup>/ *noun* [C] **1** WORDS what you say or write back to someone who has asked you a question or spoken to you *I asked him if he was going but I didn't hear his answer.* • *Please give me your **answer** by next week.* **2** DOOR/TELEPHONE when someone answers the telephone or the door [usually singular] *I rang the bell but there was no answer.* **3** SOLUTION a way of solving a problem *It's a difficult situation and I don't know what the answer is.* **4** TEST the correct number or information given as a reply to a question in a test or competition *Did you get the answer to Question 6?*

# A

**answerphone** /'ɑːnsəfəʊn/ UK (UK/US **answering machine**) noun [C] a machine that records your message if you telephone someone and they do not answer *I left a message on her answerphone.*

**ant** /ænt/ noun [C] a small, black or red insect that lives in groups on the ground ➔ *See picture at* **insect**.

**antagonism** /æn'tæɡ°nɪz°m/ noun [U] feelings of strong disagreement or hate *There's a history of antagonism between the two teams.*

**antagonistic** /æn,tæɡ°n'ɪstɪk/ adj strongly disagreeing with someone or something

**antagonize** (also UK **-ise**) /æn'tæɡ°naɪz/ verb [T] to make someone angry or unfriendly towards you *He's antagonized colleagues by making changes without discussing them.*

**the Antarctic** /æn'tɑːktɪk/ noun the very cold area around the South Pole • **antarctic** adj [always before noun] *antarctic wildlife*

**antelope** /'æntɪləʊp/ noun [C] an animal like a large deer with long horns

**antenatal** /,æntɪ'neɪt°l/ UK (US **prenatal**) adj [always before noun] relating to pregnant women before their babies are born *an antenatal class* • *antenatal care*

**antenna** /æn'tenə/ noun [C] **1** plural **antennae** one of two long, thin parts on the head of an insect or sea creature, used for feeling things **2** plural **antennae** or **antennas** US (UK **aerial**) a piece of metal that is used for receiving television or radio signals ➔ *See colour picture* **Car** on page Centre 3.

**anthem** /'ænθəm/ noun [C] a song chosen by a country or organization to be sung on special occasions ➔ *See also:* **national anthem**.

**anthology** /æn'θɒlədʒi/ noun [C] a book which includes stories or poems written by different people

**anthropology** /,ænθrə'pɒlədʒi/ noun [U] the scientific study of human development and society or different societies • **anthropologist** /,ænθrə'pɒlədʒɪst/ noun [C] • **anthropological** /,ænθrəpə'lɒdʒɪk°l/ adj

**antibiotic** /,æntɪbaɪ'ɒtɪk/ noun [C] a medicine which cures infections by destroying harmful bacteria [usually plural] *He is taking antibiotics for an ear infection.*

**antibody** /'æntɪ,bɒdi/ noun [C] a substance produced in your blood to fight disease

**anticipate** /æn'tɪsɪpeɪt/ verb [T] to expect something, or to prepare for something before it happens *to anticipate a problem/question* • [+ that] *We anticipate that prices will fall next year.*

**anticipation** /æn,tɪsɪ'peɪʃ°n/ noun [U] **1** when you are waiting for something to happen, usually with excitement *The children were breathless with anticipation.* **2 in anticipation (of)** in preparation for something happening *She's even decorated the spare room in anticipation of your visit.*

**anticlimax** /,æntɪ'klaɪmæks/ noun [C, U] a disappointing experience, often one that you thought would be exciting before it happened or one that comes after a more exciting experience *After so much preparation, the party was a bit of an anticlimax.*

**anti-clockwise** /,æntɪ'klɒkwaɪz/ UK (US **coun-**
**terclockwise**) adj, adv in the opposite direction to the way the hands (= parts that point to the numbers) of a clock move *Turn the knob anti-clockwise.* • *an anti-clockwise direction* ➔ *See picture at* **clockwise**.

**antics** /'æntɪks/ noun [plural] unusual or bad behaviour that entertains or annoys people *He's well known for his antics on and off the tennis court.*

**anti-depressant** /,æntɪdɪ'pres°nt/ noun [C] a medicine for people who are depressed (= severely unhappy)

**antidote** /'æntɪdəʊt/ noun [C] **1 antidote to sth** an activity that stops something bad from harming you *Exercise is the best antidote to stress.* **2** a substance that stops another substance from damaging your body *a deadly poison with no antidote*

**antipathy** /æn'tɪpəθi/ noun [U] formal a strong feeling of dislike for someone *He is a private man with a deep antipathy to/towards the press.*

**antiperspirant** /,æntɪ'pɜːspʰrənt/ noun [C, U] a substance that prevents you from becoming wet under your arms when you are hot

**antiquated** /'æntɪkweɪtɪd/ adj very old and not modern enough *an antiquated system*

**antique** /æn'tiːk/ noun [C] an object that is old and often rare or beautiful *His home is full of valuable antiques.* • *an antique shop* • **antique** adj *antique furniture/china*

**antiquity** /æn'tɪkwəti/ noun **1** [U] formal the ancient past *the writers of antiquity* **2** [C] an ancient object [usually plural] *priceless Egyptian antiquities*

**anti-Semitism** /,æntɪ'semɪtɪz°m/ noun [U] when someone hates Jewish people, or treats them in a cruel or unfair way • **anti-Semitic** /,æntɪsɪ'mɪtɪk/ adj

**antiseptic** /,æntɪ'septɪk/ noun [C, U] a substance that you put on an injury to prevent infection • **antiseptic** adj *antiseptic cream*

**anti-social** /,æntɪ'səʊʃ°l/ adj **1** Anti-social behaviour harms or upsets the people around you. *Increasingly, smoking is regarded as an anti-social habit.* **2** An anti-social person does not like being with other people. *I don't answer the phone when I'm feeling anti-social.*

**antithesis** /æn'tɪθəsɪs/ noun [C] plural **antitheses** /æn'tɪθəsiːz/ formal the exact opposite [usually singular] *She is slim and shy – the antithesis of her sister.*

**antler** /'æntlə°/ noun [C] a horn that looks like branches on the head of a male deer

**anus** /'eɪnəs/ noun [C] a hole where solid waste comes out of the body

**anxiety** /æŋ'zaɪəti/ noun [C, U] the feeling of being very worried *That explains his anxiety about her health.*

**anxious** /'æŋkʃəs/ adj **1** worried and nervous *She's very anxious about her exams.* • *I saw his anxious face at the window.* **2** wanting to do something or wanting something to happen [+ to do sth] *He's anxious to get home.* • [+ that] *I was anxious that no one else should know.* • **anxiously** adv *We waited anxiously by the phone.*

◦▪**any**[1] strong form /,eni/ weak form /əni/ pronoun, determiner **1** used in questions and negatives to mean 'some' *Is there any of that lemon cake left?* • *I haven't seen any of his films.* • *I asked Andrew for some change but he hasn't got any.* ➔ *See usage note at* **some**. **2** one of or each of a particular kind of person or thing when it is not important which *Can you pass me a spoon? Any will do.* • *Any advice that you can give me would be greatly appreciated.* • *Any of those shirts would be fine.*

o⃰**any²** *strong form* /'eni/ *weak form* /əni/ *adv* used in questions and negatives to emphasize a comparative adjective or adverb *Do you feel any better?* • *I can't walk any faster.* • *She couldn't wait* **any longer.**

o⃰**anybody** /'eni,bɒdi/ *pronoun another word for* anyone

**anyhow** /'enihaʊ/ (*also* **anyway**) *adv* **1** MORE IMPORTANTLY used to give a more important reason for something that you are saying *I don't need a car and I can't afford one anyhow.* **2** DESPITE despite that *He hates carrots but he ate them anyhow.* **3** IN CONVERSATION used when you are returning to an earlier subject *Anyhow, as I said, I'll be away next week.* **4** CHANGING STATEMENT used when you want to slightly change something that you have just said *Boys aren't horrible – not all of them anyhow!*

,any 'more (*also* **anymore**) *adv* If you do not do something or something does not happen any more, you have stopped doing it or it does not now happen. *This coat doesn't fit me any more.* • *Don't you eat meat any more?*

o⃰**anyone** /'eniwʌn/ (*also* **anybody**) *pronoun* **1** used in questions and negatives to mean 'a person or people' *I didn't know anyone at the party.* • *Does anyone else* (= another person/ other people) *want to come?* **2** any person or any people *Anyone can go – you don't have to be invited.*

**anyplace** /'enipleɪs/ *adv US* anywhere

o⃰**anything** /'eniθɪŋ/ *pronoun* **1** used in questions and negatives to mean 'something' *I haven't got anything to wear.* • *Can I get you anything?* • *Was there anything else* (= another thing) *you wanted to say?* **2** any object, event, or situation *We can do anything you like.* • *Tom will eat anything.* **3** **anything like** used in questions and negatives to mean 'at all similar to' *Does he look anything like his brother?*

o⃰**anyway** /'eniweɪ/ (*also* **anyhow**) (*also US* **anyways** /'eniweɪz/) *adv* **1** MORE IMPORTANTLY used to give a more important reason for something that you are saying *I don't need a car and I can't afford one anyway.* • *We can drive you to the station – we go that way anyway.* **2** DESPITE despite that *He hates carrots but he ate them anyway.* **3** IN CONVERSATION used when you are returning to an earlier subject *Anyway, as I said, I'll be away next week.* **4** CHANGING STATEMENT used when you want to slightly change something that you have just said *Boys aren't horrible – not all of them anyway!*

o⃰**anywhere** /'eniweəʳ/ (*also US* **anyplace**) *adv* **1** in or to any place *Just sit anywhere.* • *I couldn't find a post office anywhere.* **2** used in questions and negatives to mean 'a place' *He doesn't have anywhere to stay.* • *Can you find anywhere*

to hang your coat? • *Is there anywhere else you'd like to visit while you're here?* **3** **anywhere near sth** used in questions and negatives to mean 'close to being or doing something' *The house isn't anywhere near ready.* **4** **not get anywhere** *informal* to not make any progress *I tried discussing the problem with her but I didn't get anywhere.*

o⃰**apart** /ə'pɑːt/ *adv* **1** separated by a space or period of time *Stand with your feet wide apart.* • *Our kids were born just eighteen months apart.* **2** into separate, smaller pieces *My jacket is coming/falling apart.* **3** **apart from a** except for *Apart from Jodie, who hurt her leg, all the children were fine.* **b** in addition to *He works a ten-hour day and that's apart from the work he does at the weekend.*

**apartheid** /ə'pɑːtaɪt/ *noun* [U] in the past in South Africa, a political system in which white people had power over black people and made them live separately

o⃰**apartment** /ə'pɑːtmənt/ *noun* [C] *mainly US* a set of rooms for someone to live in on one level of a building or house

a'partment ,building *noun* [C] *US* a building which is divided into apartments

**apathetic** /,æpə'θetɪk/ *adj* not interested in anything or willing to change things *Young people today are so apathetic about politics.*

**apathy** /'æpəθi/ *noun* [U] when someone is not interested in anything or willing to change things

**ape** /eɪp/ *noun* [C] a hairy animal like a monkey but with no tail and long arms

**aperitif** /ə,perə'tiːf/ *noun* [C] a small alcoholic drink before a meal

**aperture** /'æpətʃəʳ/ *noun* [C] a small hole, especially one that allows light into a camera

**apex** /'eɪpeks/ *noun* [C] the highest part of a shape *the apex of a pyramid*

**apiece** /ə'piːs/ *adv* each *Dolls from this period sell for £300 apiece.*

the **apocalypse** /ə'pɒkəlɪps/ *noun* in some religions, the final destruction of the world

**apocalyptic** /ə,pɒkə'lɪptɪk/ *adj* showing or describing the destruction of the world *an apocalyptic vision of the future*

**apologetic** /ə,pɒlə'dʒetɪk/ *adj* showing or saying that you are sorry about something *an apologetic smile* • *She was very apologetic about missing the meeting.*

**apologize** (*also UK* **-ise**) /ə'pɒlədʒaɪz/ *verb* [I] to tell someone that you are sorry about something you have done *The bank apologized for the error.* • *The pilot apologized to passengers for the delay.*

**apology** /ə'pɒlədʒi/ *noun* [C, U] something you say or write to say that you are sorry about something you have done *I have an apology to make to you – I opened your letter by mistake.* • *a letter of apology*

**apostle** /ə'pɒsl/ *noun* [C] one of the twelve men chosen by Jesus Christ to teach people about Christianity

**apostrophe** /ə'pɒstrəfi/ *noun* [C] **1** a mark (') used to show that letters or numbers are absent *I'm* (= I am) *hungry.* • *I graduated in '98* (= 1998). **2** a punctuation mark (') used before

**A**

the letter 's' to show that something belongs to someone or something *I drove my brother's car.* ➔ *See study section* **Punctuation** *on page Centre 37.*

**appal** UK (US **appall**) /əˈpɔːl/ *verb* [T] **appalling**, *past* **appalled** to make someone extremely shocked or upset *The amount of violence on television appals me.* • *We were **appalled at/by** her behaviour.* • appalled *adj*

**appalling** /əˈpɔːlɪŋ/ *adj* **1** shocking and very unpleasant *Many live in appalling conditions.* • *appalling injuries* **2** very bad *appalling behaviour/weather* • appallingly *adv*

**apparatus** /ˌæpərˈeɪtəs (US) ˌæpəˈrætəs/ *noun* [C, U] a set of equipment or tools used for a particular purpose *The diver was wearing breathing apparatus.*

**apparel** /əˈpærəl/ *noun* [U] mainly US clothes *children's/women's apparel*

**apparent** /əˈpærənt/ *adj* **1** obvious or easy to notice [+ that] *It soon became apparent that she had lost interest in the project.* • *Suddenly, for **no apparent reason** (= without a reason) he started screaming and shouting.* **2** [always before noun] seeming to exist or be true *I was a little surprised by her apparent lack of interest.*

⚬━**apparently** /əˈpærəntli/ *adv* **1** used to say that you have read or been told something although you are not certain it is true *Apparently it's going to rain today.* **2** used to say that something seems to be true, although it is not certain *There were two apparently unrelated deaths.*

**apparition** /ˌæpərˈɪʃən/ *noun* [C] literary a ghost

⚬━**appeal**[1] /əˈpiːl/ *noun* **1** [REQUEST] [C] when a lot of people are asked to give money, information, or help *The appeal raised over £2 million for AIDS research.* **2** [QUALITY] [U] the quality in someone or something that makes them attractive or enjoyable *I've never understood the appeal of skiing.* **3** [LAW] [C] a request to a court of law to change a previous legal decision *He won his **appeal against** his jail sentence.*

**appeal**[2] /əˈpiːl/ *verb* [I] **1** [REQUEST] to strongly request something, often publicly *The police have **appealed for** more information.* • *They **appealed to** the commission to keep the hospital open.* **2** [ATTRACT] to attract or interest someone *Cycling has never **appealed to** me.* **3** [FORMALLY ASK] to formally ask someone to change an official or legal decision *He is **appealing against** a ten year prison sentence.*

**appealing** /əˈpiːlɪŋ/ *adj* attractive or interesting *The idea of living in Paris is very appealing.* • appealingly *adv*

⚬━**appear** /əˈpɪər/ *verb* [I] **1** [SEEM] to seem to be a particular thing or have a particular quality *He appeared calm and relaxed.* • *She **appeared to be** crying.* • [+ (that)] *It appears that we were wrong about him.* **2** [BE SEEN] to start to be seen *He suddenly appeared in the doorway.* • *Then a bright light appeared in the sky.* ➔ *Opposite* **disappear**. **3** [BECOME AVAILABLE] to start to exist or become available *Laptop computers first appeared in the 1990s.* • *The story appeared in all the major newspapers.* **4** **appear in/at/on, etc** to perform in a film, play, etc, or be seen in public *She appears briefly in the new Bond film.* • *The Princess hasn't appeared in public since her divorce was announced.*

⚬━**appearance** /əˈpɪərəns/ *noun* **1** [IN PUBLIC] [C] an occasion when someone appears in public *a television/public appearance* • *He made two appearances during his brief visit.* **2** [WAY YOU LOOK] [no plural] the way a person or thing looks *She's very concerned with her appearance.* **3** [ARRIVAL] [no plural] when you arrive somewhere or can be seen somewhere *Her appearance at the party was a surprise.* ➔ *Opposite* **disappearance**. **4** [BECOMING AVAILABLE] [no plural] when something starts to exist or becomes available *The appearance of new products on the market has increased competition.*

**appease** /əˈpiːz/ *verb* [T] to avoid more arguments by doing what someone wants • appeasement *noun* [U]

**appendicitis** /əˌpendɪˈsaɪtɪs/ *noun* [U] an illness in which your appendix becomes larger than usual and painful

**appendix** /əˈpendɪks/ *noun* [C] **1** *plural* **appendixes** a small tube-shaped part inside the body below the stomach **2** *plural* **appendices** a separate part at the end of a book, article, etc which contains extra information

**appetite** /ˈæpɪtaɪt/ *noun* [C, U] **1** the feeling that makes you want to eat *All that walking has given me an appetite.* **2** **an appetite for sth** when you want something very much *his appetite for adventure* **3** **whet sb's appetite** to make someone want more of something

**appetizer** /ˈæpɪtaɪzər/ US (UK **starter**) *noun* [C] something that you eat as the first part of a meal

**appetizing** (also UK **-ising**) /ˈæpɪtaɪzɪŋ/ *adj* If food is appetizing, it looks or smells as if it will taste good.

**applaud** /əˈplɔːd/ *verb* **1** [I, T] to clap your hands to show that you have enjoyed a performance, talk, etc *The audience applauded loudly.* **2** [T] formal to approve of or admire something *It is thought that most people will applaud the decision.*

**applause** /əˈplɔːz/ *noun* [U] when people make a noise by clapping their hands to show they have enjoyed or approve of something *There was loud applause at the end of her speech.*

⚬━**apple** /ˈæpl/ *noun* [C] a hard, round fruit with a green or red skin ➔ *See also:* **Adam's apple**, ➔ *See colour picture* **Fruit and Vegetables** *on page Centre 8.*

**appliance** /əˈplaɪəns/ *noun* [C] a piece of electrical equipment with a particular purpose in the home *fridges, radios, and other electrical appliances*

**applicable** /əˈplɪkəbl/ *adj* affecting or relating to a person or situation *This law is only applicable to people living in Europe.*

**applicant** /ˈæplɪkənt/ *noun* [C] someone who asks for something officially, often by writing *There were over fifty applicants for the job.*

**application** /ˌæplɪˈkeɪʃən/ *noun* **1** [REQUEST] [C] an official request for something, usually in writing *an application for a bank loan* **2** [USE] [C, U] a way in which something can be used for a particular purpose *This technology has many practical applications.* **3** [COMPUTER PROGRAM] [C] a computer program designed for a particular purpose

**appli'cation ,form** noun [C] a form that you use to officially ask for something, for example a job

**applied** /ə'plaɪd/ adj **applied mathematics/ science, etc** mathematics, science, or another subject which is studied for a practical use

o─**apply** /ə'plaɪ/ verb 1 ASK [I] to ask officially for something, often by writing I've **applied for** a job/grant/visa. • He has **applied to** several companies. 2 AFFECT [I] to affect or relate to a particular person or situation This law only **applies to** married people. 3 USE [T] to use something in a particular situation The same method can be applied to other situations. 4 ON SURFACE [T] to spread a substance on a surface Apply the cream daily until the symptoms disappear. 5 **apply yourself** to work hard If he doesn't apply himself, he'll never pass his exams.

**appoint** /ə'pɔɪnt/ verb [T] to officially choose someone for a job He was **appointed as** company director last year.

**appointed** /ə'pɔɪntɪd/ adj **appointed date/ time/place, etc** the date, time, place, etc that has been chosen for something to happen

**appointment** /ə'pɔɪntmənt/ noun 1 [C] a time you have arranged to meet someone or go somewhere a doctor's/dental appointment • I **made** an **appointment** with my hairdresser for next Monday. 2 [C, U] when you officially choose someone for an important job, or the job itself the appointment of three new teachers • a temporary appointment

**apportion** /ə'pɔːʃən/ verb [T] formal 1 to choose how much of something a person or each person should have 2 **apportion blame/ responsibility** to say who was responsible for something bad that happened

**appraisal** /ə'preɪzᵊl/ noun [C, U] when you examine someone or something and judge how good or successful they are a critical appraisal

**appraise** /ə'preɪz/ verb [T] to examine something and judge it We need to stop and appraise the situation.

**appreciable** /ə'priːʃəbl/ adj formal large or important enough to be noticed There's an appreciable difference in temperatures between the two regions.

o─**appreciate** /ə'priːʃieɪt/ verb 1 VALUE [T] to understand how good something or someone is and be able to enjoy them There's no point buying him expensive wines – he doesn't appreciate them. 2 GRATEFUL [T] to feel grateful for something I'd really appreciate your help. 3 UNDERSTAND [T] to understand something about a situation, especially that it is complicated or difficult [+ (that)] I appreciate that it is a difficult decision for you to make. 4 INCREASE [I] formal to increase in value Houses and antiques generally appreciate with time.

**appreciation** /ə,priːʃi'eɪʃᵊn/ noun [U] 1 VALUE when you understand how good something or someone is and are able to enjoy them His **appreciation of** art increased as he grew older. 2 FEEL GRATEFUL when you feel grateful for something To show our appreciation, we've bought you a little gift. 3 UNDERSTANDING when you understand something about a situation,

especially that it is complicated or difficult He has no **appreciation of** the size of the problem. 4 INCREASE formal an increase in value

**appreciative** /ə'priːʃiətɪv/ adj showing that you understand how good something is, or are grateful for something an appreciative audience

**apprehend** /,æprɪ'hend/ verb [T] formal If the police apprehend someone, they catch them and take them away to ask them about a crime which they might have committed.

**apprehension** /,æprɪ'henʃᵊn/ noun [U] an anxious feeling about something that you are going to do It's normal to feel a little apprehension before starting a new job.

**apprehensive** /,æprɪ'hensɪv/ adj feeling anxious about something that you are going to do He's a bit **apprehensive about** living away from home.

**apprentice** /ə'prentɪs/ noun [C] a person who is learning a job by working for someone who already has skills and experience

**apprenticeship** /ə'prentɪʃɪp/ noun [C, U] when someone learns the skills needed to do a job by working for someone who already has skills and experience

o─**approach¹** /ə'prəʊtʃ/ noun 1 METHOD [C] a way of doing something Liam has a different **approach to** the problem. • We've decided to **adopt/take** a new **approach**. 2 ASKING [C] when you speak or write to someone, often asking to buy something or offering them work 3 COMING CLOSER [U] when something or someone gets nearer, in distance or time the approach of winter 4 PATH [C] a path or route that leads to a place

o─**approach²** /ə'prəʊtʃ/ verb 1 COME CLOSE [I, T] to come close in distance or time The train now approaching platform 2 is the 5.35 to London, Kings Cross. • Christmas is fast approaching. 2 DEAL WITH [T] to deal with something I'm not sure how to approach the problem. 3 SPEAK TO SOMEONE [T] to speak or write to someone, often asking to buy something or offering them work She's been approached by a modelling agency.

**USAGE**

**approach**

The verb **approach** is not normally followed by a preposition.

He approached the door.

He approached to the door.

**approachable** /ə'prəʊtʃəbl/ adj friendly and easy to talk to

o─**appropriate¹** /ə'prəʊpriət/ adj suitable or right for a particular situation or person Is this film **appropriate for** young children? ➔ Opposite **inappropriate**. • **appropriately** adv appropriately dressed

**appropriate²** /ə'prəʊprieɪt/ verb [T] formal to take or steal something

**approval** /ə'pruːvᵊl/ noun [U] 1 when you think that something or someone is good or right I don't need his approval. ➔ Opposite **disapproval**. 2 official permission The project has now received approval from the government.

**A**

o╌**approve** /ə'pruːv/ verb **1** [T] to allow or officially agree to something *The council has approved plans for a new shopping centre.* **2** [I] to think that something is good or right *I don't **approve** of smoking.* ➔ *Opposite* **disapprove**.

**approving** /ə'pruːvɪŋ/ adj showing that you think something is good or right *an approving smile* ➔ *Opposite* **disapproving**. • approvingly adv

**approx** written abbreviation for approximately

**approximate**¹ /ə'prɒksɪmət/ adj not completely accurate but close *Do you have an approximate idea of when he's arriving?*

**approximate**² /ə'prɒksɪmeɪt/ (also **approximate to**) verb [T] formal to be almost the same as something • approximation /ə,prɒksɪ'meɪʃᵊn/ noun [C, U]

o╌**approximately** /ə'prɒksɪmətli/ adv close to a particular number or time although not exactly that number or time *The college has approximately 700 students.*

**Apr** written abbreviation for April

**apricot** /'eɪprɪkɒt/ noun [C] a small, soft, orange fruit

**April** /'eɪprᵊl/ (written abbreviation **Apr**) noun [C, U] the fourth month of the year

**April 'Fool's Day** noun 1 April, a day when people play tricks on people, then say 'April fool!'

**apron** /'eɪprən/ noun [C] a piece of clothing you wear when cooking to keep your clothes clean

**apt** /æpt/ adj **1** suitable for a particular situation *an apt description* **2 be apt to do sth** to often do something *He's apt to forget his keys.* • aptly adv

**aptitude** /'æptɪtjuːd/ noun [C, U] a natural skill or an ability to do something well *He has an **aptitude** for learning languages.* • an aptitude test

**aquarium** /ə'kweəriəm/ noun [C] **1** a building where fish and other water animals are kept for people to visit **2** a glass container filled with water that fish are kept in

**Aquarius** /ə'kweəriəs/ noun [C, U] the sign of the zodiac which relates to the period of 21 January – 19 February, or a person born during this period ➔ *See picture at* **zodiac**.

**aquatic** /ə'kwætɪk/ adj living or growing in water, or related to water *aquatic animals/plants*

**Arab** /'ærəb/ adj relating or belonging to the people of the Middle East or North Africa whose families came from Arabia in the past *Arab countries* • Arab noun [C] an Arab person

**Arabic** /'ærəbɪk/ noun [U] the language used by Arab peoples • Arabic adj

**arable** /'ærəbl/ adj suitable for or used for growing crops *arable land/farming*

**arbiter** /'ɑːbɪtəʳ/ noun [C] **1** someone who judges what is right or helps to solve an argument **2 arbiter of fashion/style/taste, etc** someone who decides what is beautiful or stylish

**arbitrary** /'ɑːbɪtrᵊri/ adj not based on a system or principles and often seeming unfair *an arbitrary decision/rule* • arbitrarily /,ɑːbɪ'treᵊrᵊli/ adv

**arbitrate** /'ɑːbɪtreɪt/ verb [I, T] to officially help to solve an argument between two people or groups • arbitrator noun [C]

**arbitration** /,ɑːbɪ'treɪʃᵊn/ noun [U] the process of solving an argument between people by helping them to agree to an acceptable solution

**arc** /ɑːk/ noun [C] a curved line that looks like part of a circle

**arcade** /ɑː'keɪd/ noun [C] **1** a place where you can pay to play games on machines *an amusement arcade* **2** a passage, especially between shops, that is covered by a roof *a shopping arcade*

**arch**¹ /ɑːtʃ/ noun [C] **1** a curved structure that usually supports something, for example a bridge or wall **2** the curved, middle part of your foot that does not touch the ground

**arch**

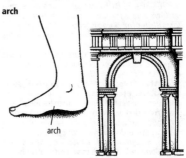

arch

**arch**² /ɑːtʃ/ verb [I, T] to be a curved shape or make something become a curved shape *The bridge arched over the river.* • *She arched her back.*

**archaeologist** (also US **archeologist**) /,ɑːki'ɒlədʒɪst/ noun [C] someone who studies archaeology

**archaeology** (also US **archeology**) /,ɑːki'ɒlədʒi/ noun [U] the study of ancient cultures by looking for and examining their buildings, tools, and other objects • archaeological (also US **archeological**) /,ɑːkiə'lɒdʒɪkᵊl/ adj *He is on an archaeological dig in Egypt.*

**archaic** /ɑː'keɪɪk/ adj very old and often not suitable for today *an archaic law*

**archbishop** /,ɑːtʃ'bɪʃəp/ noun [C] a priest of the highest rank in some Christian churches, responsible for a very large area *Archbishop Desmond Tutu*

**archeologist** /,ɑːki'ɒlədʒɪst/ noun [C] another US spelling of archaeologist

**archeology** /,ɑːki'ɒlədʒi/ noun [U] another US spelling of archaeology

**archery** /'ɑːtʃᵊri/ noun [U] a sport in which you shoot arrows

**architect** /'ɑːkɪtekt/ noun [C] someone who designs buildings

**architecture** /'ɑːkɪtektʃəʳ/ noun [U] **1** the design and style of buildings *modern architecture* **2** the skill of designing buildings *He studied architecture at university.* • architectural /,ɑːkɪ'tektʃᵊrᵊl/ adj

**archive** /'ɑːkaɪv/ noun [C] a collection of historical documents that provides information about the past, or a place where they are kept *the national archives*

**the Arctic** /'ɑːktɪk/ noun the very cold area

around the North Pole • arctic *adj* arctic *temperatures*

**ardent** /'ɑ:dᵊnt/ *adj* [always before noun] enthusiastic or showing strong feelings *an ardent supporter of Arsenal* • **ardently** *adv*

**arduous** /'ɑ:djuəs/ *adj* needing a lot of effort to do *an arduous journey/task*

**are** *strong form* /ɑ:ʳ/ *weak form* /əʳ/ *present simple you/we/they of* be

o—**area** /'eəriə/ *noun* **1** REGION [C] a region of a country or city *an industrial area* • *a mountainous area* • *the London area* **2** PART [C] a part of a building or piece of land used for a particular purpose *a play/picnic area* **3** SUBJECT [C] a part of a subject or activity *Software is not really my area of expertise.* **4** SIZE [C, U] the size of a flat surface calculated by multiplying its width by its length ⊃ *See also:* **catchment area, no-go area**.

'**area ˌcode** *noun* [C] a set of numbers used at the beginning of all the telephone numbers in a particular area

**arena** /ə'ri:nə/ *noun* [C] **1** a flat area with seats around where you can watch sports and other entertainments *an Olympic/sports arena* **2 in the political/public, etc arena** involved in politics/the government, etc *He thought he could do more good in the political arena.*

**aren't** /ɑ:nt/ **1** *short for* are not *We aren't going to the party.* **2 aren't I?** *short for* am I not? *I am invited, aren't I?*

**arguable** /'ɑ:gjuəbl/ *adj* **1 It is arguable that** it is possibly true that *It is arguable that the government has failed in this respect.* **2** If something is arguable, it is not certain if it is true. *It is arguable whether this method would even have succeeded.*

**arguably** /'ɑ:gjuəbli/ *adv* possibly *He's arguably the greatest footballer in the world.*

o—**argue** /'ɑ:gju:/ *verb* **arguing,** *past* **argued 1** [I] to speak angrily to someone, telling them that you disagree with them *My parents are always **arguing** about money.* • *Kids, will you stop **arguing with** each other?* **2** [I, T] to give reasons to support or oppose an idea, action, etc [+ that] *He argued that cuts in military spending were necessary.* • *She argued for/against tax cuts.*

o—**argument** /'ɑ:gjəmənt/ *noun* [C] **1** an angry discussion with someone in which you both disagree *They **had an argument** about who should do the cleaning.* **2** a reason or reasons why you support or oppose an idea, action, etc *There are many **arguments for/against** nuclear energy.*

**argumentative** /,ɑ:gjə'mentətɪv/ *adj* often arguing or wanting to argue

**aria** /'ɑ:riə/ *noun* [C] a song that one person sings in an opera

**arid** /'ærɪd/ *adj* very dry and without enough rain for plants *an arid region/climate*

**Aries** /'eəri:z/ *noun* [C, U] the sign of the zodiac which relates to the period of 21 March – 20 April, or a person born during this period ⊃ *See picture at* **zodiac**.

**arise** /ə'raɪz/ *verb* [I] *past t* **arose,** *past p* **arisen 1** If a problem arises, it starts to happen. *The whole problem **arose from** a lack of communication.* **2** *literary* to get up, usually from a bed

**aristocracy** /,ærɪ'stɒkrəsi/ *noun* [group] the highest social class, usually in countries which have or had a royal family

**aristocrat** /'ærɪstəkræt/ *noun* [C] a member of the highest social class • **aristocratic** /,ærɪstə'krætɪk/ *adj an aristocratic family*

**arithmetic** /ə'rɪθmətɪk/ *noun* [U] when you calculate numbers, for example by multiplying or adding

o—**arm¹** /ɑ:m/ *noun* [C] **1** BODY PART the long part at each side of the human body, ending in a hand *She held the tiny baby in her arms.* • *He put his arms around her.* • *She was standing with her arms folded* (= with one arm crossed over the other). ⊃ *See colour picture* **The Body** *on page Centre 2.* **2 arm in arm** with your arm gently supporting or being supported by someone else's arm *They walked through the park, arm in arm.* **3** CLOTHES the part of a piece of clothing that you put your arm in **4** CHAIR the part of a chair where your arm rests **5 twist sb's arm** *informal* to persuade someone to do something *If Sam can't take me to the airport I might twist Andy's arm.* ⊃ *See also:* **arms**.

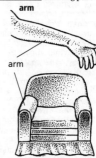
arm

arm

**arm²** /ɑ:m/ *verb* [T] to give weapons to someone *The terrorists had **armed** themselves **with** automatic rifles.* ⊃ *Opposite* **disarm**.

**armaments** /'ɑ:məmənts/ *noun* [plural] military weapons and equipment *nuclear armaments*

**armband** /'ɑ:mbænd/ *noun* [C] **1** a strip of material worn around your upper arm *a black/reflective armband* **2 armbands** *UK* two plastic tubes that you fill with air and wear round the top of your arms when you are learning to swim

**armchair** /'ɑ:m,tʃeəʳ/ *noun* [C] a comfortable chair with sides that support your arms ⊃ *See colour picture* **The Living Room** *on page Centre 11.*

**armed** /ɑ:md/ *adj* **1** carrying or using weapons *armed guards/police* • *an armed robbery* (= robbery where guns are used) ⊃ *Opposite* **unarmed**. **2 armed with sth** carrying or knowing something that will be useful *I like to go to a meeting armed with the relevant facts.*

**the ˌarmed 'forces** (*also* **the ˌarmed 'services**) *noun* [plural] a country's military forces, for example the army and the navy

**armful** /'ɑ:mfʊl/ *noun* [C] the amount that you can carry in your arms *an armful of books*

**armistice** /'ɑ:mɪstɪs/ *noun* [C] an agreement to stop fighting that is made between two countries

**armour** *UK* (*US* **armor**) /'ɑ:məʳ/ *noun* [U] metal clothing which soldiers wore in the past to protect them when fighting *a suit of armour*

**armoured** *UK* (*US* **armored**) /'ɑ:məd/ *adj* covered with a protective layer of metal *an armoured vehicle*

**armpit** /'ɑ:mpɪt/ *noun* [C] the part of your body

under your arm, where your arm meets your shoulder ⊃ *See colour picture* **The Body** *on page Centre 2.*

**arms** /ɑːmz/ *noun* [plural] **1** weapons *the sale of arms* **2 be up in arms** to be very upset and angry about something *Local residents are up in arms over plans to close the swimming pool.*

○⊶**army** /ˈɑːmi/ *noun* [C] **1** a military force that fights wars on the ground *the British Army* • *an army officer/base* **2** a group of people that is organized to do the same job *an army of cleaners/helpers*

**aroma** /əˈrəʊmə/ *noun* [C] a nice smell that usually comes from food or drink *the aroma of freshly baked bread* • aromatic /ˌærəʊˈmætɪk/ *adj* having a nice smell

**arose** /əˈrəʊz/ *past tense of* arise

○⊶**around** /əˈraʊnd/ *adv, preposition* **1** IN A CIRCLE (*also UK* **round**) on all sides of something *They sat around the table.* • *He put his arms around her waist.* **2** DIRECTION (*also UK* **round**) to the opposite direction *He turned around and looked at her.* **3** CIRCULAR MOVEMENT (*also UK* **round**) in a circular movement *This lever turns the wheels around.* **4** ALONG OUTSIDE (*also UK* **round**) along the outside of something, not through it *You have to walk around the house to get to the garden.* **5** TO A PLACE (*also UK* **round**) to or in different parts of a place *She showed me around the museum.* • *I spent a year travelling around Australia.* **6** SEVERAL PLACES (*also UK* **round**) from one place or person to another *She passed a plate of biscuits around.* • *There's a virus going around the school.* **7** HERE here, or near this place *Is Roger around?* **8** EXISTING present or available *Mobile phones have been around for years now.* **9** APPROXIMATELY used before a number or amount to mean 'approximately' *around twenty thousand pounds* ⊃ *See also:* throw your **weight** around.

**arousal** /əˈraʊzəl/ *noun* [U] when someone is sexually excited

**arouse** /əˈraʊz/ *verb* [T] **1** to make someone have a particular feeling or reaction *It's a subject which has aroused a lot of interest.* **2** to make someone sexually excited

○⊶**arrange** /əˈreɪndʒ/ *verb* [T] **1** to make the necessary plans and preparations for something to happen *to arrange a meeting* • *I'll arrange for a car to come and pick you up.* • [+ to do sth] *We've arranged to visit the house on Saturday afternoon.* **2** to put objects in a particular order or position *The books are arranged alphabetically by author.* • *We arranged the chairs in a circle.*

○⊶**arrangement** /əˈreɪndʒmənt/ *noun* **1** PLANS [C] plans for how something will happen [usually plural] *We're meeting tomorrow to discuss arrangements for the competition.* • [+ to do sth] *I've made arrangements to go home this weekend.* **2** AGREEMENT [C, U] an agreement between two people or groups *We have an arrangement whereby we share the child-care.* • *Viewing is by prior arrangement.* **3** POSITION [C] a group of objects in a particular order or position *a flower arrangement*

**array** /əˈreɪ/ *noun* [C] a large number of different things [usually singular] *There is a vast array of books on the subject.*

**arrears** /əˈrɪəz/ *noun* [plural] money that is owed and should have been paid before *mortgage/rent arrears* • *He is already in arrears with the rent.*

**arrest**[1] /əˈrest/ *verb* [T] If the police arrest someone, they take them away to ask them about a crime which they might have committed. *He was arrested for possession of illegal drugs.*

**arrest**[2] /əˈrest/ *noun* [C, U] when the police take someone away to ask them about a crime which they might have committed *Police made 20 arrests at yesterday's demonstration.* • *He's under arrest* (= has been arrested). ⊃ *See also:* **house arrest.**

**arrival** /əˈraɪvəl/ *noun* **1** ARRIVING [U] when someone or something arrives somewhere *He first met Panos soon after his arrival in Greece.* • *There was a car waiting for him on arrival.* **2** BECOME AVAILABLE [U] when something new is discovered or created or becomes available *The town grew rapidly with the arrival of the railway.* **3** NEW PERSON/THING [C] a new thing or person that has arrived *Two teachers were there to greet the new arrivals.*

○⊶**arrive** /əˈraɪv/ *verb* [I] **1** to get to a place *When he first arrived in New York, he didn't speak a word of English.* • *We were the last to arrive at the station.* • *A letter arrived for you this morning.* **2 arrive at an answer/decision/conclusion, etc** to find an answer to a problem or make a decision after a lot of discussion *We didn't arrive at any firm conclusions.* **3** to happen or start to exist *Summer had finally arrived.*

---

### USAGE

**arrive somewhere**

Be careful to choose the correct preposition after **arrive**.

You **arrive at** a place such as a building.

*We arrived at the hotel just after 12 o'clock.*

You **arrive in** a town, city or country.

*They arrived in Tokyo on Wednesday.*

*When did David arrive in Australia?*

You **arrive** home, here, or there. You do not use a preposition when **arrive** is used before these words.

*We arrived home yesterday.*

*I had a lot of problems when I first arrived here.*

---

**arrogant** /ˈærəgənt/ *adj* believing that you are better or more important than other people *I found him arrogant and rude.* • arrogance /ˈærəgəns/ *noun* [U] • arrogantly *adv*

**arrow** /ˈærəʊ/ *noun* [C] **1** a symbol used on signs to show a direction **2** a long, thin stick with a sharp point at one end which is fired

arrow

arrow

from a bow (= curved piece of wood with a tight string fixed at both ends)

**arse** /ɑːs/ *UK very informal* (*US* **ass**) *noun* [C] a person's bottom

**arsenal** /ˈɑːsᵊnᵊl/ *noun* [C] a large collection of weapons

**arsenic** /ˈɑːsᵊnɪk/ *noun* [U] a chemical element that is a very strong poison

**arson** /ˈɑːsᵊn/ *noun* [U] the crime of intentionally burning something, such as a building ● arsonist *noun* [C] someone who commits arson

o━**art** /ɑːt/ *noun* **1** [U] the making or study of paintings, drawings, etc, or the objects created *fine/modern art* ● *an art exhibition/gallery* **2** [C, U] a skill in a particular activity *the art of conversation* ⊃ *See also:* **martial art**, **work of art**.

**artefact** *UK* (*US* **artifact**) /ˈɑːtɪfækt/ *noun* [C] an object, especially something very old of historical interest

**artery** /ˈɑːtᵊri/ *noun* [C] **1** one of the tubes in your body that carries blood from your heart **2** an important route for traffic

**artful** /ˈɑːtfᵊl/ *adj* [always before noun] showing skill *an artful use of colour* ● artfully *adv*

**arthritis** /ɑːˈθraɪtɪs/ *noun* [U] an illness which causes the parts of the body where bones meet to become painful and often big ● arthritic /ɑːˈθrɪtɪk/ *adj an arthritic hip/knee*

**artichoke** /ˈɑːtɪʃəʊk/ *noun* [C, U] a round, green vegetable with thick, pointed leaves covering the outside

**article** /ˈɑːtɪkl/ *noun* [C] **1** WRITING a piece of writing in a magazine, newspaper, etc **2** OBJECT an object, especially one of many *an article of clothing/furniture* **3** GRAMMAR in grammar, used to mean the words 'the', 'a', or 'an' ⊃ *See also:* **definite article**, **indefinite article**.

**articulate**[1] /ɑːˈtɪkjələt/ *adj* able to express ideas and feelings clearly in words *She's an intelligent and highly articulate young woman.* ⊃ *Opposite* **inarticulate**.

**articulate**[2] /ɑːˈtɪkjəleɪt/ *verb* [T] *formal* to express ideas or feelings in words *He articulates the views and concerns of the local community.* ● articulation /ɑːˌtɪkjəˈleɪʃᵊn/ *noun* [U]

**articulated** /ɑːˈtɪkjəleɪtɪd/ *adj* [always before noun] *mainly UK* An articulated vehicle is long and has two parts which are joined together to help it turn corners. *an articulated lorry*

**artifact** /ˈɑːtɪfækt/ *noun* [C] *US spelling of* artefact

o━**artificial** /ˌɑːtɪˈfɪʃᵊl/ *adj* **1** not natural, but made by people *an artificial flower/lake* ● *an artificial heart* **2** not sincere ● artificially *adv*

**artificial intelligence** *UK* (*US* **arti,ficial in'telligence**) *noun* [U] the study and development of computer systems which do jobs that previously needed human intelligence

**artillery** /ɑːˈtɪlᵊri/ *noun* [U] large guns, especially those fixed on wheels used by an army

**artisan** /ˌɑːtɪˈzæn ⓤS ˈɑːrtəzᵊn/ *noun* [C] *old-fashioned* someone who does skilled work with their hands

o━**artist** /ˈɑːtɪst/ *noun* [C] someone who creates art, especially paintings and drawings

**artistic** /ɑːˈtɪstɪk/ *adj* **1** showing skill and imag-

ination in creating things, especially in painting, drawing, etc *artistic talent* **2** [always before noun] relating to art *the artistic director of the theatre* ● artistically *adv*

**artistry** /ˈɑːtɪstri/ *noun* [U] great skill in creating or performing something, such as in writing, music, sport, etc

**arts** /ɑːts/ *noun* **1** [plural] (*also US* **liberal arts**) subjects of study which are not science, such as history, languages, etc *an arts subject/degree* **2** **the arts** activities such as painting, music, film, dance, and literature *public interest in the arts* ⊃ *See also:* **the performing arts**.

**artwork** /ˈɑːtwɜːk/ *noun* [U] the pictures or patterns in a book, magazine, CD cover, etc

**arty** /ˈɑːti/ (*also US* **artsy** /ˈɑːtsi/) *adj* knowing a lot about art, or wanting to appear as if you do

o━**as** *strong form* /æz/ *weak form* /əz/ *preposition, conjunction* **1** **as .... as** used to compare two things, people, amounts, etc *He's not as tall as his brother.* ● *She earns three times as much as I do.* **2** WHILE used to describe two things happening at the same time or something happening at a particular time *He was shot in the back as he tried to escape.* ● *I think your opinions change as you get older.* **3** FOR THIS PURPOSE used to describe the purpose, job, or appearance of something or someone *She works as a waitress.* ● *It could be used as evidence against him.* **4** LIKE in the same way *This year, as in previous years, tickets sold very quickly.* **5** IN THIS WAY used to describe the way in which people see or think of something or someone *She was regarded as a great beauty in her day.* ● *Most people think of nursing as a female occupation.* **6** BECAUSE because *You can go first as you're the oldest.* ● *As I'd never been to Poland before, I bought a guidebook.* **7** **as if/as though** used to describe how a situation seems to be *It looks as if it might rain.* **8** **as for** used to talk about how another person or thing is affected by something *I was pleased. As for Emily, well, who cares what she thinks.* **9** **as from/as of** *formal* starting from a particular time, date, etc *The new conditions are effective as of 15 May.* **10** **as to** *formal* about *There's no decision as to when the work might start.*

**asap** /ˌeɪeseɪˈpiː/ *abbreviation for* as soon as possible

**asbestos** /æsˈbestɒs/ *noun* [U] a soft grey-white material which does not burn easily, once used in building

**ascend** /əˈsend/ *verb* [I, T] *formal* to move up or to a higher position

**ascendancy** (*also* **ascendency**) /əˈsendᵊnsi/ *noun* [U] *formal* a position of power, strength, or success

**ascending** /əˈsendɪŋ/ *adj* [always before noun] starting with the lowest or smallest and becoming greater or higher *They announced the results in ascending order.*

**ascent** /əˈsent/ *noun* **1** CLIMB [C] when someone climbs or moves up *his first ascent of the mountain* **2** BECOMING SUCCESSFUL [no plural] when someone starts to become successful *The book describes his rapid ascent from truck driver to film star.* **3** PATH UP [C] a path or road which goes up a hill or mountain *We struggled up a steep ascent.*

**ascertain** /,æsə'teɪn/ *verb* [T] *formal* to discover something [+ question word] *We are still trying to ascertain whether the fire was started deliberately.*

**ascribe** /ə'skraɪb/ *verb*
**ascribe sth to sth** *formal* to say that something is caused by something else *She ascribes her success to hard work.*

**ash** /æʃ/ *noun* **1** [U] the soft, grey powder which remains when something has burnt *cigarette ash* **2** [C] a forest tree

o⟶**ashamed** /ə'ʃeɪmd/ *adj* **1** feeling guilty or embarrassed about something you have done *You've got nothing to be **ashamed of**.* • [+ to do sth] *He was ashamed to admit his mistake.* **2 be ashamed of sb** to be angry and disappointed with a family member or friend because they have behaved badly *He was so rude to Phil – I was ashamed of him.*

**ashes** /'æʃɪz/ *noun* **sb's ashes** the powder that remains when a dead person's body has been burnt

**ashore** /ə'ʃɔːr/ *adv* onto land from the sea, a river, a lake, etc *We swam ashore.*

**ashtray** /'æʃ,treɪ/ *noun* [C] a small, open container used to put cigarette ash and finished cigarettes in

**Asian** /'eɪʒən/ *adj* relating or belonging to Asia *Asian culture* • **Asian** *noun* [C] someone from Asia

**aside¹** /ə'saɪd/ *adv* **1** in a direction to one side *I gave her a plate of food but she pushed it aside.* **2** If you put or set something aside, you do not use it now, but keep it to use later. *We've put some money aside to pay for the children's education.* **3 aside from** except for

**aside²** /ə'saɪd/ *noun* [C] something which you say quietly so that not everyone can hear it, often something funny

o⟶**ask** /ɑːsk/ *verb* **1** QUESTION [I, T] to say something to someone as a question which you want them to answer [+ two objects] *Can I **ask** you a few questions?* • *I asked him about his hobbies.* • [+ question word] *I asked why the plane was so late.* ➙ *See usage note at* **question**. **2** WANT SOMETHING [I, T] to say something to someone because you want them to give you something *He's **asked** for a bike for his birthday.* **3** REQUEST [I, T] to say something to someone because you want them to do something [+ to do sth] *They've asked me to look after their dog while they're away.* **4** INVITE [T] to invite someone to do something *She **asked** him out to lunch the next day.* **5** WANT PERMISSION [I, T] to say something to someone because you want to know if you can do something *Bruce asked if he could stay with us for a few days.* • [+ to do sth] *She asked to leave early.* **6** PRICE [T] to want a particular amount of money for something which you sell *How much are you **asking for** it?* **7 ask yourself sth** to think about something carefully *You've got to ask yourself whether it's what you really want.* **8 ask for it/trouble** *informal* to behave in a way that is likely to make something unpleasant happen to you or to cause you problems *His wife left him, but it seems to me he was asking for it.* • *Drinking and driving is asking for trouble.*

**ask** or **demand**?

**Ask** is the usual word for questions in English.

*She asked her secretary to arrange an appointment.*

*"How much would that cost?" he asked.*

**Demand** is not as polite as **ask**. It is usually used when someone is angry.

*He demanded to know where his money had gone.*

*The hijackers have demanded a million dollars.*

**askew** /ə'skjuː/ *adj* [never before noun] not straight *The picture was slightly askew.*

o⟶**asleep** /ə'sliːp/ *adj* **1 be asleep** to be sleeping *The children are asleep.* • *I was **fast/sound asleep** (= sleeping deeply).* **2 fall asleep** to start sleeping *He fell asleep in front of the TV.*

**asparagus** /ə'spærəgəs/ *noun* [U] a vegetable consisting of a long, green stem with a pointed end

**aspect** /'æspekt/ *noun* [C] one part of a situation, problem, subject, etc *His illness affects almost every aspect of his life.*

**asphalt** /'æsfælt/ *noun* [U] a hard, black substance used to make roads and paths

**asphyxiate** /əs'fɪksieɪt/ *verb* **be asphyxiated** to die because you cannot breathe • **asphyxiation** /əs,fɪksi'eɪʃən/ *noun* [U]

**aspiration** /,æspər'eɪʃən/ *noun* [C, U] something you hope to achieve [usually plural] *The story is about the lives and aspirations of the Irish working classes.*

**aspire** /ə'spaɪər/ *verb* **aspire to sth; aspire to do sth** to hope to achieve something *Unlike so many men, he has never aspired to a position of power.*

**aspirin** /'æspərɪn/ *noun* [C, U] *plural* **aspirin** or **aspirins** a common drug used to reduce pain and fever

**aspiring** /ə'spaɪərɪŋ/ *adj* **an aspiring actor/ politician/writer, etc** someone who is trying to become a successful actor/politician/writer, etc

**ass** /æs/ *noun* [C] **1** BOTTOM *US very informal* (*UK* **arse**) a person's bottom **2** PERSON *informal* a stupid person **3** ANIMAL *old-fashioned* a donkey (= animal like a small horse)

**assailant** /ə'seɪlənt/ *noun* [C] *formal* a person who attacks someone *Can you describe your assailant?*

**assassin** /ə'sæsɪn/ *noun* [C] a person who kills someone important or famous, often for money

**assassinate** /ə'sæsɪneɪt/ *verb* [T] to kill someone important or famous • **assassination** /ə,sæsɪ'neɪʃən/ *noun* [C, U]

**assault** /ə'sɔːlt/ *noun* [C, U] an attack *an **assault** on a police officer* • *He was accused of sexual assault.* • **assault** *verb* [T]

**assemble** /ə'sembl/ *verb* **1** [I, T] to join other people somewhere to make a group, or to bring people together into a group *They assembled in the meeting room after lunch.* **2** [T] to build something by joining parts together

**assembly** /ə'sembli/ *noun* **1** SCHOOL [C, U] *UK* a regular meeting of all the students and

teachers at a school *morning assembly*
**2** GROUP [C] a group of people, such as a government, who meet to make decisions, laws, etc *the national assembly* **3** BUILD [U] when you build something by joining parts together

**assent** /əˈsent/ *noun* [U] *formal* agreement or approval • assent *verb* [I] *formal* to agree to something

**assert** /əˈsɜːt/ *verb* **1 assert yourself** to behave or speak in a strong, confident way **2 assert your authority/control/independence, etc** to do something to show other people that you have power **3** *formal* [T] to say that something is certainly true [+ that] *He asserts that she stole money from him.*

**assertion** /əˈsɜːʃən/ *noun* [C, U] *formal* when you say that something is certainly true [+ that] *I don't agree with his assertion that men are safer drivers than women.*

**assertive** /əˈsɜːtɪv/ *adj* behaving or speaking in a strong, confident way *You need to be much more assertive.* • assertively *adv* • assertiveness *noun* [U]

**assess** /əˈses/ *verb* [T] to make a judgment about the quality, size, value, etc of something *The tests are designed to assess a child's reading skills.* • assessment *noun* [C, U]

**asset** /ˈæset/ *noun* [C] **1** a person, skill, or quality which is useful or helps you to succeed *He'll be a great asset to the team.* **2** something which a person or company owns which has a value [usually plural] *The company has $70 billion in assets.*

**assiduous** /əˈsɪdjuəs/ *adj formal* showing a lot of effort and determination • assiduously *adv*

**assign** /əˈsaɪn/ *verb* [T] to give someone a particular job or responsibility [+ two objects] *UN troops were assigned the task of rebuilding the hospital.* • [often passive] *The case has been assigned to our most senior officer.*
**assign sb to sth** to give someone a particular job or place to work [often passive] *Which police officer has been assigned to this case?*

**assignment** /əˈsaɪnmənt/ *noun* [C, U] a piece of work or job that you are given to do *a written assignment* • *He's on assignment in Brazil.*

**assimilate** /əˈsɪmɪleɪt/ *verb formal* **1** [T] to understand and remember new information **2** [I, T] to become part of a group, society, etc, or to make someone or something become part of a group, society, etc *The refugees have now assimilated into the local community.* • assimilation /əˌsɪmɪˈleɪʃən/ *noun* [U]

**assist** /əˈsɪst/ *verb* [I, T] to help *The army arrived to assist in the search.* • *He's assisting the police with their investigation.*

**assistance** /əˈsɪstəns/ *noun* [U] *formal* help *financial/medical assistance* • *Can I be of any assistance?* (= Can I help you?)

**assistant** /əˈsɪstənt/ *noun* [C] **1** someone whose job is to help a person who has a more important job *an administrative assistant* • *assistant manager* **2** a **sales/shop assistant** *mainly UK* someone who helps customers in a shop

**associate¹** /əˈsəʊʃieɪt/ *verb* [T] to relate two things, people etc in your mind *Most people associate this brand with good quality.*
**associate with sb** *formal* to spend time with someone

**be associated with sth** to be related to something or caused by something *There are many risks associated with smoking.*

**associate²** /əˈsəʊʃiət/ *noun* [C] someone who you know because of work or business *She's a business associate of mine.*

**associate³** /əˈsəʊʃiət/ *adj* **associate director/editor/producer, etc** someone in a slightly less important position than the main person

**association** /əˌsəʊsiˈeɪʃən/ *noun* **1** [C] an organization of people with the same interests or with a particular purpose *the Football Association* **2** [C, U] a connection or relationship between two things or people **3 in association with** working together with *The event was organized in association with the Sports Council.* ➔ *See also:* **savings and loan association.**

**assorted** /əˈsɔːtɪd/ *adj* of different types *a box of assorted chocolates*

**assortment** /əˈsɔːtmənt/ *noun* [C] a group of different types of something *an assortment of vegetables*

**assuage** /əˈsweɪdʒ/ *verb* [T] *formal* to make unpleasant feelings less strong *The government tried to assuage the public's fears.*

o-ᴙ**assume** /əˈsjuːm/ *verb* [T] **1** to think that something is likely to be true, although you have no proof [+ (that)] *Everything was quiet when I got home so I assumed that you had gone out.* **2 assume control/power/responsibility, etc** to take a position of control/power/responsibility, etc *He has assumed the role of spokesman for the group.* **3 assume an air/expression, etc** *formal* to pretend to have a feeling that you do not have **4 assume a false identity/name, etc** to pretend to be someone else *an assumed name*

**assumption** /əˈsʌmpʃən/ *noun* [C] **1** something that you think is true without having any proof *People tend to make assumptions about you when you have a disability.* • *These calculations are based on the assumption that prices will continue to rise.* **2 the assumption of power/responsibility, etc** when someone takes a position of power, responsibility, etc

**assurance** /əˈʃʊərəns/ *noun* **1** [C] a promise [+ that] *He gave us an assurance that it would not happen again.* **2** [U] confidence *He spoke with calm assurance.*

**assure** /əˈʃɔː/ *verb* [T] **1** to tell someone that something is certainly true, especially so that they do not worry [+ (that)] *She assured them that she would be all right.* **2** to make something certain to happen *This loan should assure the company's future.*

**assured** /əˈʃʊəd/ *adj* **1** showing skill and confidence *an assured performance* **2 be assured of sth** to be certain to get or achieve something in the future *They are now assured of a place in the final.* ➔ *See also:* **self-assured.**

**asterisk** /ˈæstərɪsk/ *noun* [C] a written symbol in the shape of a star (*), often used to mark a particular word, phrase, etc

**asthma** /ˈæsmə/ *noun* [U] an illness which makes it difficult to breathe *She had an asthma attack.* • asthmatic /æsˈmætɪk/ *adj an asthmatic child*

**astonish** /ə'stɒnɪʃ/ *verb* [T] to make someone very surprised *Her quick recovery has astonished doctors.*

**astonished** /ə'stɒnɪʃt/ *adj* very surprised *He was astonished at her behaviour.*

**astonishing** /ə'stɒnɪʃɪŋ/ *adj* very surprising *It's astonishing that so many people believed his story.* • astonishingly *adv*

**astonishment** /ə'stɒnɪʃmənt/ *noun* [U] extreme surprise *The others stared at him in astonishment.* • *To my astonishment, he started laughing.*

**astound** /ə'staʊnd/ *verb* [T] to make someone very surprised *The speed of her recovery has astounded doctors.*

**astounded** /ə'staʊndɪd/ *adj* very surprised *I'm astounded at/by these prices.*

**astounding** /ə'staʊndɪŋ/ *adj* very surprising *an astounding success* • astoundingly *adv*

**astray** /ə'streɪ/ *adv* 1 go astray to get lost or go in the wrong direction *One of my bags went astray at the airport.* 2 lead sb astray to encourage someone to do bad things that they should not do *He was led astray by his friends.*

**astride** /ə'straɪd/ *adv* If you sit or stand astride something, you have one foot on each side of it.

**astrology** /ə'strɒlədʒi/ *noun* [U] the study of the positions and movements of stars and planets to say how they might influence people's lives • astrologer *noun* [C] someone who studies astrology • astrological /,æstrə'lɒdʒɪkəl/ *adj*

**astronaut** /'æstrənɔːt/ *noun* [C] someone who travels into space

**astronomical** /,æstrə'nɒmɪkəl/ *adj* 1 An astronomical amount is extremely large. *astronomical prices* 2 relating to astronomy • astronomically *adv*

**astronomy** /ə'strɒnəmi/ *noun* [U] the scientific study of stars and planets • astronomer *noun* [C] a scientist who studies astronomy

**astute** /ə'stjuːt/ *adj* good at judging situations and making decisions which give you an advantage *an astute businesswoman* • politically astute • astutely *adv*

**asylum** /ə'saɪləm/ *noun* 1 [U] when someone is allowed to stay somewhere because they are escaping danger in another country 2 [C] *old-fashioned* a hospital for people with a mental illness Ɔ *See also:* political asylum.

**asymmetrical** /,eɪsɪ'metrɪkəl/ *adj* not being exactly the same shape and size on both sides • asymmetry /eɪ'sɪmɪtri/ *noun* [U]

o⟶**at** *strong form* /æt/ *weak form* /ət/ *preposition* 1 PLACE used to show the place or position of something or someone *We met at the station.* • *She was sitting at the table.* • *She's at the library.* 2 TIME used to show the time something happens *The meeting starts at three.* 3 DIRECTION towards or in the direction of *She threw the ball at him.* • *He's always shouting at the children.* 4 ABILITY used after an adjective to show a person's ability to do something *He's good at making friends.* • *I've always been useless at tennis.* 5 CAUSE used to show the cause of something, especially a feeling *We were surprised at the news.* 6 AMOUNT used to show the price, speed, level, etc of something *He denied driving at 120 miles per hour.*

7 ACTIVITY used to show a state or activity *She was hard at work when I arrived.* • *a country at war* 8 INTERNET the @ symbol, used in email addresses to separate the name of a person, department, etc from the name of the organization or company

**ate** /eɪt, et/ *past tense of* eat

**atheist** /'eɪθiɪst/ *noun* [C] someone who believes that there is no god • atheism *noun* [U]

**athlete** /'æθliːt/ *noun* [C] someone who is very good at a sport and who competes with others in organized events

**athletic** /æθ'letɪk/ *adj* 1 strong, healthy, and good at sports 2 [always before noun] relating to athletes or to the sport of athletics

**athletics** /æθ'letɪks/ *UK* (*US* track and field) *noun* [U] the sports which include running, jumping, and throwing Ɔ *See colour picture* **Sports 1** *on page Centre 15.*

**atlas** /'ætləs/ *noun* [C] a book of maps *a road atlas* • *a world atlas*

**ATM** /,eɪtiː'em/ *noun* [C] *mainly US abbreviation for* automated teller machine: a machine that you get money from using a plastic card

o⟶**atmosphere** /'ætməsfɪə/ *noun* 1 [U] the feeling which exists in a place or situation *a relaxed/tense atmosphere* 2 the atmosphere the layer of gases around the Earth 3 [no plural] the air inside a room or other place *a smoky atmosphere*

**atmospheric** /,ætməs'ferɪk/ *adj* 1 [always before noun] relating to the air or to the atmosphere *atmospheric conditions/pressure* 2 creating a special feeling, such as mystery or romance *atmospheric music/lighting*

**atom** /'ætəm/ *noun* [C] the smallest unit that an element can be divided into

**atomic** /ə'tɒmɪk/ *adj* 1 [always before noun] relating to atoms *an atomic particle* 2 using the energy created when an atom is divided *atomic power/weapons*

**a,tomic 'bomb** (*also* 'atom ,bomb) *noun* [C] a very powerful bomb which uses the energy created when an atom is divided

**a,tomic 'energy** *noun* [U] energy which is produced by dividing atoms

**atop** /ə'tɒp/ *preposition US* on the top of

**atrium** /'eɪtriəm/ *noun* [C] a large, central room with a glass roof in an office building, restaurant, etc

**atrocious** /ə'trəʊʃəs/ *adj* 1 extremely bad *atrocious weather* 2 violent and shocking *an atrocious crime*

**atrocity** /ə'trɒsəti/ *noun* [C, U] when someone does something extremely bad and shocking *Soldiers have been committing atrocities against civilians.*

o⟶**attach** /ə'tætʃ/ *verb* [T] 1 to join or fix one thing to another *She attached a photograph to her letter.* 2 attach importance/value, etc to sb/sth to think that someone or something has importance/value, etc *You attach too much importance to money.* 3 to include something as part of something else *There were too many conditions attached to the deal.* Ɔ *See also:* no strings (string¹) attached.

**attached** /ə'tætʃt/ *adj* be attached to sb/sth to like someone or something very much *I've*

A

*become rather attached to my old car.*

**attachment** /ə'tætʃmənt/ *noun* **1** [FEELING] [C, U] a feeling of love or strong connection to someone or something **2** [EMAIL] [C] a computer file which is sent together with an email message *I wasn't able to open that attachment.* **3** [EQUIPMENT] [C] an extra part which can be added to a piece of equipment *There's a special attachment for cleaning in the corners.*

o-**attack**¹ /ə'tæk/ *noun* **1** [VIOLENCE] [C, U] a violent act intended to hurt or damage someone or something *a terrorist attack on the capital* **2** [CRITICISM] [C, U] when you say something to strongly criticize someone or something *a scathing attack on the president* **3** [ILLNESS] [C] a sudden, short illness *a nasty attack of flu* **4** [SPORT] [C, U] in games such as football, when the players in a team try to score points, goals, etc ⊃ *See also:* **counter-attack**.

o-**attack**² /ə'tæk/ *verb* **1** [VIOLENCE] [I, T] to use violence to hurt or damage someone or something *He was attacked and seriously injured by a gang of youths.* **2** [CRITICIZE] [T] to strongly criticize someone or something *She attacked the government's new education policy.* **3** [DISEASE] [T] If a disease, chemical, etc attacks someone or something, it damages them. *The virus attacks the central nervous system.* **4** [SPORT] [I, T] If players in a team attack, they move forward to try to score points, goals, etc.

**attacker** /ə'tækə<sup>r</sup>/ *noun* [C] a person who uses violence to hurt someone *The police think she must have known her attackers.*

**attain** /ə'teɪn/ *verb* [T] to achieve something, especially after a lot of work *She's attained a high level of fitness.* • **attainable** *adj* possible to achieve • **attainment** *noun* [C, U] when you achieve something

o-**attempt**¹ /ə'tempt/ *noun* [C] **1** when you try to do something *This is his second attempt at the exam.* • [+ to do sth] *They closed the road in an attempt to reduce traffic in the city.* • *She made no attempt* (= did not try) *to be sociable.* **2 an attempt on sb's life** when someone tries to kill someone

o-**attempt**² /ə'tempt/ *verb* [T] to try to do something, especially something difficult [+ to do sth] *He attempted to escape through a window.*

**attempted** /ə'temptɪd/ *adj* **attempted murder/robbery, etc** when someone tries to commit a crime but does not succeed

**attend** /ə'tend/ *verb* [I, T] *formal* **1** to go to an event *to attend a concert/meeting* **2 attend a church/school, etc** to go regularly to a particular church/school, etc

**attend to sb/sth** *formal* to deal with something or help someone

**attendance** /ə'tendəns/ *noun* [C, U] **1** the number of people who go to an event, meeting, etc *falling attendance* **2** when you go somewhere such as a church, school, etc regularly *His attendance at school is very poor.* **3 in attendance** *formal* present at an event *They have doctors in attendance at every match.*

**attendant** /ə'tendənt/ *noun* [C] someone whose job is to help the public in a particular place *a parking attendant* ⊃ *See also:* **flight attendant**.

o-**attention** /ə'tenʃən/ *noun* [U] **1** when you watch, listen to, or think about something carefully or with interest *Ladies and gentlemen, could I have your attention, please?* • *I was watching TV so you didn't have my full attention.* **2 pay attention (to sth)** to watch, listen to, or think about something carefully or with interest *You weren't paying attention to what I was saying.* **3 bring/draw (sb's) attention to sth/sb** to make someone notice something or someone *If I could just draw your attention to the second paragraph.* • *She's always trying to draw attention to herself.* **4 attract/get (sb's) attention** to make someone notice you *I waved at him to get his attention.* **5** treatment to deal with a problem *medical attention* • *This old engine needs a lot of attention.*

USAGE

**attention**

Attention is usually followed by the preposition to.

*You should pay attention to what she tells you.*

*We want to draw people's attention to the risks involved.*

**attentive** /ə'tentɪv/ *adj* listening or watching carefully and showing that you are interested *an attentive student* • **attentively** *adv*

**attest** /ə'test/ *verb* [I, T] *formal* to show or prove that something is true

**attic** /'ætɪk/ *noun* [C] a room at the top of a house under the roof

**attire** /ə'taɪə<sup>r</sup>/ *noun* [U] *old-fashioned* the clothes that you wear • **attired** *adj* dressed in a particular way *suitably attired*

o-**attitude** /'ætɪtjuːd/ *noun* [C, U] how you think or feel about something and how this makes you behave *a positive attitude* • *He has a very bad attitude to/towards work.*

**attorney** /ə'tɜːni/ *noun* [C] *US* a lawyer *a defense attorney* ⊃ *See also:* **district attorney**, ⊃ *See usage note at* **lawyer**.

o-**attract** /ə'trækt/ *verb* [T] **1** to make people come to a place or do a particular thing by being interesting, enjoyable, etc *The castle attracts more than 300,000 visitors a year.* • *We need to attract more science graduates to teaching.* **2 attract attention/interest, etc** to cause people to pay attention/be interested, etc **3 be attracted to sb** to like someone, especially sexually, because of the way they look or behave *I was attracted to him straight away.* **4** If something attracts a substance or object, it causes it to move towards it. *Magnets attract metal.*

**attraction** /ə'trækʃən/ *noun* **1** [C] something that makes people come to a place or want to do a particular thing *a tourist attraction* • *The opportunity to travel is one of the main attractions of this job.* **2** [U] when you like someone, especially sexually, because of the way they look or behave *physical attraction*

o-**attractive** /ə'træktɪv/ *adj* **1** beautiful or pleasant to look at *an attractive woman* • *I find him very attractive.* **2** interesting or useful *a very attractive offer* • *We want to make the club attractive to a wider range of people.* ⊃ *Opposite* **unattractive.** • **attractively** *adv* • **attractiveness** *noun* [U]

**attributable** /əˈtrɪbjətəbl/ *adj* **attributable to sth** caused by something *A lot of crime is attributable to the use of drugs.*

**attribute¹** /əˈtrɪbjuːt/ *verb*
**attribute sth to sth** to say that something is caused by something else *He attributes his success to hard work.*
**attribute sth to sb** to say that someone wrote, said, or made something *This drawing has been attributed to Picasso.*

**attribute²** /ˈætrɪbjuːt/ *noun* [C] a quality or characteristic that someone or something has *Her hair is her best attribute.*

**attributive** /əˈtrɪbjətɪv/ *adj* An attributive adjective comes before the noun it describes. ➲ *Compare* **predicative**.

**aubergine** /ˈəʊbəʒiːn/ *UK* (*US* **eggplant**) *noun* [C, U] an oval, purple vegetable that is white inside ➲ *See colour picture* **Fruit and Vegetables** *on page Centre 8.*

**auburn** /ˈɔːbən/ *adj* Auburn hair is red-brown.

**auction** /ˈɔːkʃən/ *noun* [C, U] a sale in which things are sold to the person who offers the most money • auction (*also* **auction off**) *verb* [T] to sell something at an auction

**auctioneer** /ˌɔːkʃənˈɪər/ *noun* [C] the person who is in charge of an auction

**audacity** /ɔːˈdæsəti/ *noun* [U] when someone shows too much confidence in their behaviour in a way that other people find shocking or rude *And then he had the audacity to blame me for his mistake!* • audacious /ɔːˈdeɪʃəs/ *adj*

**audible** /ˈɔːdəbl/ *adj* If something is audible, you can hear it. *His voice was barely audible.* ➲ *Opposite* **inaudible**. • audibly *adv*

☀**audience** /ˈɔːdiəns/ *noun* **1** GROUP [group] the people who sit and watch a performance at a theatre, cinema, etc *There were a lot of children in the audience.* **2** TYPE [group] the type of people who watch a particular TV show, read a particular book, etc *This magazine is aimed at a teenage audience.* **3** MEETING [C] *formal* a formal meeting with an important person *an audience with the Queen*

**audio** /ˈɔːdiəʊ/ *adj* relating to the recording or playing of sound *audio equipment*

**audit** /ˈɔːdɪt/ *noun* [C] when an independent person examines all the financial records of a company to produce a report • audit *verb* [T] • auditor *noun* [C]

**audition** /ɔːˈdɪʃən/ *noun* [C] when someone does a short performance to try to get a job as an actor, singer, etc • audition *verb* [I]

**auditorium** /ˌɔːdɪˈtɔːriəm/ *noun* [C] the part of a theatre, hall, etc where people sit to watch a performance

**Aug** *written abbreviation for* August

**augment** /ɔːgˈment/ *verb* [T] *formal* to increase the size or value of something by adding something to it

**August** /ˈɔːgəst/ (*written abbreviation* **Aug**) *noun* [C, U] the eighth month of the year

☀**aunt** /ɑːnt/ (*also* **auntie, aunty** /ˈɑːnti/) *noun* [C] the sister of your mother or father, or the wife of your uncle ➲ *See also:* **agony aunt.**

**au pair** /ˌəʊˈpeər/ *noun* [C] a young person who goes to live with a family in another country

and looks after their children, does work in their house, etc

**aura** /ˈɔːrə/ *noun* [C] a feeling which a person or place seems to have *an aura of mystery*

**aural** /ˈɔːrəl/ *adj* relating to hearing

**auspices** /ˈɔːspɪsɪz/ *noun* **under the auspices of sb/sth** *formal* with the help or support of a person or organization *The conference was held under the auspices of the Red Cross.*

**auspicious** /ɔːˈspɪʃəs/ *adj* If an event or time is auspicious, it makes you believe that something will be successful in the future. *an auspicious start*

**austere** /ɒsˈtɪər/ *adj* **1** plain, simple, and without unnecessary decorations or luxuries *an austere room* **2** strict or severe *an austere woman* • austerity /ɒsˈterəti/ *noun* [U]

**authentic** /ɔːˈθentɪk/ *adj* If something is authentic, it is real, true, or what people say it is. *an authentic painting* • authentically *adv* • authenticity /ˌɔːθenˈtɪsəti/ *noun* [U]

**author** /ˈɔːθər/ *noun* [C] someone who writes a book, article, etc *a popular author of children's fiction*

**authoritarian** /ˌɔːθɒrɪˈteəriən/ *adj* very strict and not allowing people freedom to do what they want *an authoritarian leader/regime*

**authoritative** /ɔːˈθɒrɪtətɪv/ *adj* **1** An authoritative book, report, etc is respected and considered to be accurate. *an authoritative guide* **2** confident and seeming to be in control of a situation *an authoritative manner/voice*

☀**authority** /ɔːˈθɒrəti/ *noun* **1** POWER [U] the official power to make decisions or to control other people *a position of authority* • [+ to do sth] *The investigators have the authority to examine all the company's records.* • *We need the support of someone in authority.* **2** OFFICIAL GROUP [C] an official group or government department with power to control particular public services *the local housing authority* **3** QUALITY [U] the quality of being confident and being able to control people *She has an air of authority.* **4 an authority on sth** someone who has a lot of knowledge about a particular subject *She is an authority on seventeenth-century English literature.* ➲ *See also:* **local authority.**

**authorize** (*also UK* **-ise**) /ˈɔːθəraɪz/ *verb* [T] **1** to give official permission for something **2 be authorized to do sth** to be officially allowed to do something *Only managers are authorized to sign expense forms.* • authorization /ˌɔːθəraɪˈzeɪʃən/ *noun* [U]

**autistic** /ɔːˈtɪstɪk/ *adj* Autistic children have a mental illness which causes problems with communicating and forming relationships. • autism /ˈɔːtɪzəm/ *noun* [U]

**auto-** /ɔːtəʊ-/ *prefix* used at the beginning of words to mean 'operating automatically or independently' *an autofocus camera*

**autobiography** /ˌɔːtəʊbaɪˈɒgrəfi/ *noun* [C] a book written by someone about their own life • autobiographical /ˌɔːtəʊbaɪəʊˈgræfɪkəl/ *adj*

**autograph** /ˈɔːtəgrɑːf/ *noun* [C] a famous person's name, written by that person • autograph *verb* [T] *an autographed photo*

**automate** /'ɔːtəmeɪt/ *verb* [T] to control something using machines and not people ● automated *adj a fully automated system* ● automation /,ɔːtə'meɪʃ°n/ *noun* [U]

**automatic¹** /,ɔːtə'mætɪk/ *adj* **1** MACHINE An automatic machine works by itself or with little human control. *automatic doors* **2** CERTAIN certain to happen as part of the normal process or system *You get an automatic promotion after two years.* **3** REACTION done as a natural reaction without thinking *My automatic response was to pull my hand away.* ● automatically *adv*

**automatic²** /,ɔːtə'mætɪk/ *noun* [C] a car in which you do not have to change the gears (= parts that control how fast the wheels turn)

**automobile** /'ɔːtəməubiːl/ *noun* [C] *US* a car *the automobile industry*

**automotive** /,ɔːtə'məutɪv/ *adj* [always before noun] relating to cars and car production *the automotive industry*

**autonomous** /ɔː'tɒnəməs/ *adj* independent and having the power to make your own decisions *an autonomous region/state*

**autonomy** /ɔː'tɒnəmi/ *noun* [U] the right of a country or group of people to govern itself *The government wants to give local councils more autonomy.*

**autopsy** /'ɔːtɒpsi/ *noun* [C] a medical examination of a dead body to discover the exact cause of death

O─**autumn** /'ɔːtəm/ (*also US* **fall**) *noun* [C, U] the season of the year between summer and winter, when leaves fall from the trees *I'm starting a new job* **in the autumn.** ● *autumn leaves* ● autumnal /ɔː'tʌmn°l/ *adj* typical of autumn

**auxiliary** /ɔːg'zɪli°ri/ *adj* providing extra help or support *an auxiliary nurse*

**au,xiliary 'verb** *noun* [C] a verb which is used with another verb to form tenses, negatives, and questions. In English the auxiliary verbs are 'be', 'have', and 'do'.

**avail** /ə'veɪl/ *noun* **to no avail** without success, especially after a lot of effort *She sent more than 50 letters, but to no avail.*

O─**available** /ə'veɪləbl/ *adj* **1** If something is available, you can use it or get it. *This information is available free on the Internet.* ● *The new drug is not yet* **available to** *the public.* **2** If someone is available, they are not busy and so are able to do something. *No one from the company was available to comment on the accident.* ➔ *Opposite* **unavailable.** ● availability /ə,veɪlə'bɪləti/ *noun* [U]

**avalanche** /'æv°lɑːnʃ/ *noun* [C] **1** when a large amount of snow falls down the side of a mountain **2 an avalanche of sth** a sudden, large amount of something, usually more than you can deal with *an avalanche of mail*

**avalanche**

**avant-garde** /,ævɒŋ'gɑːd/ *adj* If art, music, etc, is avant-garde, it is new and unusual in style.

**avarice** /'æv°rɪs/ *noun* [U] *formal* a strong feeling that you want a lot of money and possessions

**Ave** *written abbreviation for* avenue *132, Gainsborough Ave*

**avenge** /ə'vendʒ/ *verb* [T] *literary* to punish someone for doing something bad to you, your family, etc *He swore he would avenge his brother's death.*

**avenue** /'æv°njuː/ *noun* [C] **1** (*written abbreviation* **Ave**) a wide road in a town or city, often with trees along it **2** a possible way of doing or achieving something *We have exhausted all other avenues of treatment.*

O─**average¹** /'æv°rɪdʒ/ *adj* **1** USUAL usual and like the most common type *an average person* ● *an average day* **2** AMOUNT [always before noun] An average amount is calculated by adding some amounts together and then dividing by the number of amounts. *an average age/temperature* **3** NOT EXCELLENT not excellent, although not bad *The food was pretty average.*

O─**average²** /'æv°rɪdʒ/ *noun* **1** [C] an amount calculated by adding some amounts together and then dividing by the number of amounts *They work an average of 30.5 hours per week.* **2** [C, U] the usual or typical amount *well above/below average* **3 on average** usually, or based on an average *Female workers earn, on average, a third less than men.*

**average³** /'æv°rɪdʒ/ *verb* [T] to reach a particular amount as an average *He averages about 20 points a game.*

**averse** /ə'vɜːs/ *adj* **1 not be averse to sth** *UK humorous* to be happy or willing to do or have something *She's not averse to the occasional glass of champagne.* **2 be averse to sth** *formal* to strongly dislike something

**aversion** /ə'vɜːʒ°n/ *noun* **an aversion to sth** when you strongly dislike something

**avert** /ə'vɜːt/ *verb* **1 avert a crisis/disaster/ war, etc** to prevent something bad from happening **2 avert your eyes/face/gaze** to turn your head away so that you do not see something

**aviary** /'eɪvi°ri/ *noun* [C] a large cage for birds

**aviation** /,eɪvi'eɪʃ°n/ *noun* [U] flying aircraft or producing aircraft *the aviation industry*

**avid** /'ævɪd/ *adj* very interested and enthusiastic *an avid football fan* ● *an avid reader* ● avidly *adv*

**avocado** /,ævə'kɑːdəu/ *noun* [C, U] a dark green, oval fruit which is pale green inside and is not sweet

O─**avoid** /ə'vɔɪd/ *verb* [T] **1** to stay away from a person, place, situation, etc *He's been avoiding me all week.* ● *Try to avoid the city centre.* **2** to prevent something from happening *Book early to avoid disappointment.* **3 avoid doing sth** to intentionally not do something *She managed to avoid answering my question.* ● avoidable *adj* possible to avoid ➔ *Opposite* **unavoidable.** ● avoidance *noun* [U] when you avoid something

USAGE

**avoid doing** something

When **avoid** is followed by a verb, the verb is always in the -ing form.

*I avoided seeing him for several days.*

~~I avoided to see him for several days.~~

**await** /əˈweɪt/ *verb* [T] *formal* **1** to wait for something *We are awaiting the results of the tests.* **2** If something awaits you, you will experience it in the future. *A surprise awaits her when she gets home.*

o⟶**awake¹** /əˈweɪk/ *adj* **1 be/lie/stay, etc awake** to not be sleeping *Is Tom awake yet?* • *I'm going to watch the late film if I can stay awake.* • *The noise from the party kept me **awake** all night.* **2 be wide awake** to be completely awake

**awake²** /əˈweɪk/ *verb* [I, T] *past t* **awoke**, *past p* **awoken** *literary* to wake up, or make someone wake up

**awaken** /əˈweɪk³n/ *verb* **1** [T] *formal* to cause an emotion, feeling, etc *The song awakened painful memories.* **2** [I, T] *literary* to wake up, or make someone wake up

**awakening** /əˈweɪkənɪŋ/ *noun* [no plural] **1** when you start to be aware of something or feel something **2 a rude awakening** If you have a rude awakening, you have a shock when you discover the truth about a situation.

**award¹** /əˈwɔːd/ *noun* [C] **1** a prize given to someone for something they have achieved *the award for best actress* • *to receive/win an award* **2** money given to someone because of a legal decision

**award²** /əˈwɔːd/ *verb* [T] to officially give someone something such as a prize or an amount of money [+ two objects, often passive] *He was awarded the Nobel Prize for Physics.*

o⟶**aware** /əˈweə³/ *adj* **1 be aware of/that** to know about something *Are you aware of the risks involved?* • *She was well aware that he was married.* ⊃*Opposite* **unaware**. **2** interested in and knowing a lot about a particular subject *politically/socially aware* • awareness *noun* [U]

**awash** /əˈwɒʃ/ *adj* **be awash with sth** *UK* (*US* **be awash in sth**) to have a lot of something, often too much *The sport is awash with money.*

o⟶**away¹** /əˈweɪ/ *adv* **1** DIRECTION to or in a different place or situation *Go away and leave me alone.* • *Fish and chips to take away, please.* • *We'd like to move **away from** the town centre.* **2** DISTANCE FROM at a particular distance from a place *The nearest town was ten miles away.* • *How far away is the station?* **3** NOT THERE not at the place where someone usually lives or works *Shirley's feeding the cat while we're away.* **4** SAFE PLACE into a usual or safe place *Can you put everything away when you've finished?*

**5 two weeks/five hours, etc away** at a particular time in the future *My exam's only a week away now.* **6** CONTINUOUS ACTION used after a verb to mean 'continuously or repeatedly' *Chris was hammering away in the garden all day.* **7** GRADUALLY gradually disappearing until almost or completely gone *The snow has melted away.* **8** SPORT *UK* If a sports team is playing away, the game is at the place where the other team usually plays. ⊃*See also:* take your **breath** away, give the **game¹** away.

**away²** /əˈweɪ/ *adj* [always before noun] *UK* In sports, an away game is played at the place where the other team usually plays.

**awe** /ɔː/ *noun* [U] **1** a feeling of great respect and sometimes fear *I was filled with awe at the sheer size of the building.* **2 be in awe of sb** to feel great respect for someone *As children we were rather in awe of our grandfather.*

**awe-inspiring** /ˈɔːɪnspaɪərɪŋ/ *adj* causing people to feel great respect or admiration

**awesome** /ˈɔːsəm/ *adj* very great, large, or special and making you feel respect and sometimes fear *an awesome challenge/responsibility* • *The scenery was awesome.*

o⟶**awful** /ˈɔːf³l/ *adj* **1** very bad, of low quality, or unpleasant *an awful place* • *The film was absolutely awful.* **2 an awful lot (of sth)** *informal* a large amount *It cost an awful lot of money.*

**awfully** /ˈɔːf³li/ *adv* very *awfully difficult/good*

**awhile** /əˈwaɪl/ *adv* *US* for a short time *Let's wait awhile and see what happens.*

o⟶**awkward** /ˈɔːkwəd/ *adj* **1** DIFFICULT difficult or causing problems *an awkward customer* • *an awkward question* **2** EMBARRASSING embarrassing and not relaxed *an awkward pause/silence* • *I found myself in an awkward situation.* **3** NOT ATTRACTIVE moving in a way that is not attractive *His movements were slow and awkward.* • awkwardly *adv* • awkwardness *noun* [U]

**awoke** /əˈwəʊk/ *past tense of* awake

**awoken** /əˈwəʊk³n/ *past participle of* awake

**awry** /əˈraɪ/ *adv* **go awry** to not happen in the correct way *Suddenly everything started to go awry.*

**axe¹** (*also US* **ax**) /æks/ *noun* [C] a tool consisting of a wooden handle with a sharp piece of metal at one end, used for cutting trees or wood

**axe²** (*also US* **ax**) /æks/ *verb* [T] to get rid of something or someone suddenly *The company has announced plans to axe 500 jobs.*

**axes** /ˈæksiːz/ *plural of* axis

**axis** /ˈæksɪs/ *noun* [C] *plural* **axes** /ˈæksiːz/ **1** an imaginary, central line around which an object turns **2** a line at the side or bottom of a graph (= picture showing measurements)

**axle** /ˈæksl/ *noun* [C] a long metal bar which connects two wheels on a vehicle

**aye** /aɪ/ *exclamation informal* yes, used especially in Scotland and the North of England

# B

**B, b** /biː/ the second letter of the alphabet

**BA** /ˌbiːˈeɪ/ noun [C] abbreviation for Bachelor of Arts: a university or college qualification in an arts (= not science) subject which usually takes 3 or 4 years of study *I've got a BA in English literature from Liverpool University.*

**baa** /baː/ noun [C] the sound that a sheep makes

**babble** /ˈbæbl/ verb [I] to talk quickly in a way which is confused, silly, or has no meaning
• **babble** noun [U] *the babble of voices*

**babe** /beɪb/ noun [C] **1** very informal a young, attractive woman **2** literary a baby

o➤**baby** /ˈbeɪbi/ noun [C] **1** a very young child *a baby girl/boy* • *baby clothes/food* • *Liz has had a baby.* • *Maria's expecting a baby* (= she is pregnant). **2** a very young animal *a baby bird/rabbit*

**'baby ,boom** noun [C] a time when a lot of babies are born in a particular area *the postwar baby boom*

**'baby ,carriage** noun [C] US a small vehicle with four wheels for carrying a baby

**babyish** /ˈbeɪbiɪʃ/ adj Babyish behaviour is silly, like the behaviour of a young child.

**babysit** /ˈbeɪbisɪt/ verb [I, T] **babysitting**, past **babysat** to look after children while their parents are not at home • **babysitter** noun [C] *We'd like to come, but we can't get a babysitter.*
• **babysitting** noun [U]

**bachelor** /ˈbætʃələr/ noun [C] **1** a man who is not married **2 Bachelor of Arts/Science/ Education, etc** a university or college qualification which usually takes 3 or 4 years of study, or a person who has this qualification

o➤**back¹** /bæk/ adv **1** RETURNING where someone or something was before *I'll be back in Sydney on the 20th.* • *When do you go back to college?* • *I put it back in the cupboard.* **2** BEHIND in a direction behind you *Anna stepped back.* • *Flint leaned back in his chair.* **3** REPLY as a reply or reaction to something *(UK) to ring back/(US) to call back* • *I signalled to her and she waved back.* **4** STATE to the state something or someone was in before *Hopefully things will get back to normal again now.* • *I'm sure we can put it back together again* (= repair it). • *Try to go back to sleep.* **5** EARLIER at or to an earlier time *We first met back in 1973.* • *Looking back, I think we did the right thing.* **6** AWAY FROM in a direction away from something *He pulled back the curtain.* • *The house was a short distance back from the road.* **7 back and forth** (also UK **backwards and forwards**) in one direction, then the opposite way, then in the original direction again many times *He has to travel back and forth between London and Paris every week.*

o➤**back²** /bæk/ noun [C] **1** NOT FRONT the part of something that is furthest from the front or in the opposite direction to the front *He wrote his number down on the back of an envelope.* • *We*

were sitting near the back and couldn't see much. • *I always keep a blanket in the back of the car.* **2** BODY the part of your body from your shoulders to your bottom *back injuries/pain* • *He was lying on his back.* ➔ See colour picture **The Body** on page Centre 2. **3** SEAT the part of a seat that you lean against when you are sitting *the back of a chair/sofa* **4 back to front** UK with the back part of something where the front should be *You've got your trousers on back to front.* **5 in back of** US behind *They sat in back of us on the plane.* **6 at/in the back of your mind** If you have a thought or idea at the back of your mind, you are always thinking about it. **7 behind sb's back** If you do something behind someone's back, you do it without them knowing, often in an unfair way. *Have they been saying things about me behind my back?* **8 be glad/happy, etc to see the back of sb/sth** UK to be pleased when someone leaves or something ends because you did not like them **9 be on sb's back** to remind someone again and again to do something, or to criticize someone in an annoying way **10 turn your back on sb/sth** to decide to stop having contact with someone or something, or to refuse to help someone *She turned her back on Hollywood and went to live in Florida.* ➔ See also: a **pat²** on the back, be (like) **water¹** off a duck's back

**back³** /bæk/ verb **1** [T] to give support or help to a person, plan, or idea *He backed Mr Clark in the recent election.* • *Parents backed the idea by more than two to one.* **2** [T] to risk money by saying that you think a horse, team, etc will win a race, game, or competition in order to win more money if they do *Many people are backing Holyfield to win the fight.* **3 back (sth) away/into/out, etc** to move backwards or drive backwards *She saw he had a gun and backed away.* • *He backed into a wall when he was trying to park.*

**back away** to show that you do not support a plan or idea any more and do not want to be involved with it *The government has backed away from plans to increase taxes.*

**back down** to admit that you were wrong or agree not to do something *The council **backed down** over rent increases.*

**back off 1** to move away from someone, usually because you are afraid *I saw the knife and backed off.* **2** mainly US to stop supporting a plan *The president has **backed off from** a threat to expel U.N. soldiers.*

**back out** to decide not to do something you had planned or agreed to do *Nigel backed out at the last minute, so we had a spare ticket.*

**back sb up 1** to support or help someone *My family backed me up in my fight for compensation.* **2** to say that someone is telling the truth *Honestly, that's exactly what happened – Claire'll back me up.*

**back sth up 1** to prove that something is true [often passive] *His claims are backed up by recent research.* **2** to make an extra copy of computer information

**back (sth) up** to drive backwards

o➤**back⁴** /bæk/ adj **1** [always before noun] at or near

the back of something *back door/garden/page* • *I put it in the back pocket of my jeans.* **2 back road/street** a very small road or street that goes behind or between buildings ⮕ *See also:* put sth on the back **burner**.

**backbench** /,bæk'bentʃ/ *adj UK* **a backbench MP/politician, etc** a member of the government who does not have an important position • backbencher *noun* [C] a backbench politician

**the backbenches** /,bæk'bentʃɪz/ *noun* [plural] *UK* the place where backbench politicians sit *He prefers to remain on the backbenches.*

**backboard** /'bækbɔːd/ *noun* [C] in basketball (= a sport), a board behind the metal ring that you have to throw the ball through to score ⮕ *See colour picture* **Sports 2** *on page Centre 16.*

**backbone** /'bækbəʊn/ *noun* [C] **1** the main or strongest part of something *The car industry remains the backbone of the area's economy.* **2** the line of bones down the centre of your back

**backdrop** /'bækdrɒp/ *noun* [C] **1** the situation that an event happens in [usually singular] *The attack took place against a backdrop of rising tensions between the two communities.* **2** the painted cloth at the back of a stage in a theatre

**backer** /'bækər/ *noun* [C] someone who supports a person or plan, especially by giving them money

**backfire** /,bæk'faɪər/ *verb* [I] If something that you do backfires, it has the opposite result of what you wanted.

o━**background** /'bækɡraʊnd/ *noun* **1** SOUND [no plural] Sounds in the background are not the main sounds you can hear. *background music/noise* • *I could hear a baby crying in the background.* **2** PERSON [C] a person's education, family, and experience of life *She came from a middle-class background.* **3** PICTURE [C, U] the parts at the back of a picture, view, etc which are not the main things you look at *gold stars on a black background* **4** SITUATION [C] the situation that an event happens in, or things which have happened in the past which affect it [usually singular] *The talks are taking place against a background of economic uncertainty.* **5 in the background** If a person stays in the background, they try not to be noticed.

**backhand** /'bækhænd/ *noun* [C] when you hit a ball with your arm across your body, in sports such as tennis

**backing** /'bækɪŋ/ *noun* [U] support, especially money, for a person or plan *financial backing* • *The proposal has the full backing of the government.*

**backlash** /'bæklæʃ/ *noun* [C] when people react against an idea which was previously popular [usually singular] *a backlash against the royal family*

**backlog** /'bæklɒɡ/ *noun* [C] work that should have been done earlier

**backpack** /'bækpæk/ *noun* [C] a bag that you carry on your back ⮕ *See picture at* **luggage**. • backpacking *noun* [U] *to go backpacking* • backpacker *noun* [C]

**backside** /,bæk'saɪd/ ⓤ̄ˢ 'bæk,saɪd/ *noun* [C] *informal* the part of your body that you sit on

**backstage** /,bæk'steɪdʒ/ *adv* in the area behind the stage in a theatre where performers get ready

**backstroke** /'bækstrəʊk/ *noun* [U] a style of swimming on your back

**back-to-back** /,bæktə'bæk/ *adj, adv* **1** If two people or things are back-to-back, their backs are touching or facing each other. *They stood back-to-back.* **2** If two things happen back-to-back, one happens after the other without a pause. *back-to-back interviews*

**backtrack** /'bæktræk/ *verb* [I] to say that you did not mean something you said earlier *The government has backtracked on promises to pensioners.*

**backup** /'bækʌp/ *noun* **1** [C, U] extra help, support, or equipment which is available if you need it *Medical staff are on call to provide backup in case of an emergency.* **2** [C] an extra copy of computer information *to make a backup*

**backward** /'bækwəd/ *adj* **1** [always before noun] in the direction behind you *a backward glance* **2** less developed or slower to develop than normal *a backward country*

o━**backwards** /'bækwədz/ (*also* **backward**) *adv* **1** DIRECTION towards the direction behind you *She took a couple of steps backwards.* • *He fell backwards off the stool.* **2** EARLIER towards an earlier time or an earlier stage of development *Let's start with your most recent job and work backwards.* **3** OPPOSITE ORDER in the opposite order to what is usual *"Erehwon" is "nowhere" spelled backwards.* **4** WRONG WAY (*also UK* **back to front**) with the part that is usually at the front at the back *You've got your skirt on backwards.* **5 backwards and forwards** *UK* (*UK/US* **back and forth**) in one direction then the opposite way and back again many times *I have to drive backwards and forwards between here and Ipswich every day.* **6 bend over backwards** to try extremely hard to help or to please someone [+ to do sth] *She bent over backwards to help him.*

**backyard** /,bæk'jɑːd/ *noun* [C] *US* the area behind a house

**bacon** /'beɪkən/ *noun* [U] meat from a pig cut into long thin slices

**bacteria** /bæk'tɪəriə/ *noun* [plural] very small living things that sometimes cause disease • bacterial *adj* made from or caused by bacteria *bacterial infections*

o━**bad** /bæd/ *adj* **worse, worst 1** NOT PLEASANT not pleasant *bad weather* • *bad news* • *a bad dream* • *My phone bill was even worse than I'd expected.* • *He's in a bad mood today.* **2** LOW QUALITY of low quality *bad behaviour/manners* • *The service was really bad.* • *He's always been bad at maths.* **3** SEVERE very serious or severe *a bad injury* • *the worst flooding for years* **4** NOT LUCKY not lucky, not convenient, or not happening how you would like *It was just bad luck that she heard us.* • *Is this a bad time to ask?* **5 not bad** satisfactory *"There are about 10 people in a group." "Oh well, that's not bad."* • *That's not bad for such a small company.* **6 be bad for sb/sth** to be harmful for someone or something *Looking at a computer screen for too long can be bad for* your eyes. • *The negative publicity has been bad for business.* **7 feel bad about sth/doing sth** to feel guilty or sorry about something that has happened *I felt bad about letting her down.* **8 too bad** a *mainly US informal* used to say that you are sorry about a situation *"He didn't get the job." "Oh, that's too bad."* **b** *informal* used to say that nothing can be done to change a situation *I know you don't want to go but it's too bad, we have to.* **9** EVIL evil *She's a really bad person.* **10** NOT FRESH Bad food is not fresh and cannot be eaten. **11** PAINFUL [always before noun] If you have a bad arm, leg, heart, etc, there is something wrong with it and it is painful. **⊃** *See also:* bad **blood**, be in sb's bad books (**book¹**).

**baddie** /'bædi/ *noun* [C] *mainly UK informal* a bad person in a film, book, etc

**bade** /bæd/ *past tense of* bid³

**badge** /bædʒ/ *noun* [C] **1** a piece of plastic, metal, etc which you wear on your clothes showing your name or the organization you work for **2** *UK* (*US* **button**) a piece of plastic, metal, etc with words or pictures on it that you wear on your clothes for decoration

**badger** /'bædʒəʳ/ *noun* [C] a wild animal with thick black and white fur that lives under the ground and comes out at night

○━**badly** /'bædli/ *adv* **worse**, **worst 1** very seriously *badly damaged/injured* **2** in a way that is of low quality or in an unpleasant way *to behave badly* • *Some of the animals were very badly treated.* • *They played badly in the first half.*

**badminton** /'bædmɪntən/ *noun* [U] a sport for two or four people in which you hit a shuttlecock (= a light object with feathers) over a net

**baffle** /'bæfl/ *verb* [T] If something baffles you, you cannot understand it at all. [often passive] *The police were baffled by his disappearance.* • *I found his explanation baffling.*

○━**bag¹** /bæg/ *noun* [C] **1** CONTAINER a container made of paper, plastic, etc, used for carrying things *a paper/plastic bag* • *He packed his bags and left.* **2** FOR WOMAN (*also* **handbag**) *mainly UK* a bag with handles in which a woman carries her money, keys, etc **3** AMOUNT the amount a bag contains *It doesn't weigh more than a couple of bags of sugar.* **4 bags of sth** *mainly UK informal* a large amount of something *There's bags of room.* **5 bags** Bags

**bag**

handbag

rucksack *UK*,
backpack *US*

carrier bag *UK*
grocery bag *US*

briefcase

under your eyes are areas of loose or dark skin. **⊃** *See also:* **carrier bag**, let the **cat** out of the bag, **shoulder bag**, **sleeping bag**, **tote bag**.

**bag²** /bæg/ *verb* [T] **bagging**, *past* **bagged** *informal* to get something, especially before other people have a chance to take it *Bag us some decent seats.*

**bagel** /'beɪgəl/ *noun* [C] a type of bread made in the shape of a ring **⊃** *See picture at* **bread**.

**baggage** /'bægɪdʒ/ *noun* [U] **1** all the cases and bags that you take with you when you travel *baggage reclaim* **2** feelings and experiences from the past that influence how you think and behave now *emotional baggage*

**baggy** /'bægi/ *adj* Baggy clothes are big and loose.

**bagpipes** /'bægpaɪps/ *noun* [plural] a Scottish musical instrument that is played by blowing air into a bag and forcing it through pipes

**bail¹** /beɪl/ *noun* [U] when money is paid to a court so that someone can be released from prison until their trial *He was released on bail.* • *She was granted bail.*

**bail²** /beɪl/ *verb* **be bailed** If someone is bailed until a particular time, they can leave prison until then if they pay money to the court.

**bail sb out 1** to help a person or organization by giving them money *Companies can't expect the government to keep bailing them out.* **2** to pay money to a court so that someone can be released from prison until their trial

**bailiff** /'beɪlɪf/ *noun* [C] **1** *UK* someone whose job is to take away things people own when they owe money **2** *US* someone whose job is to guard prisoners in a court

**bait¹** /beɪt/ *noun* [U, no plural] **1** food that is used to try to attract fish or animals so that you can catch them **2** something that you use to persuade someone to do something

**bait²** /beɪt/ *verb* [T] **1** to put food in or on something to try to catch fish or animals *a mouse trap baited with cheese* **2** to try to make someone angry by laughing at them or criticizing them

**bake** /beɪk/ *verb* [I, T] to cook something such as bread or a cake with dry heat in an oven *a baked potato* **⊃** *See picture at* **cook**.

**baked 'beans** *noun* [plural] beans cooked in a tomato (= soft, round, red fruit used like a vegetable) sauce and sold in tins (= metal containers)

**baker** /'beɪkəʳ/ *noun* [C] someone who makes and sells bread, cakes, etc *Can you call at the baker's and get a loaf of bread?*

**bakery** /'beɪkᵊri/ *noun* [C] a shop where you can buy bread, cakes, etc

**baking** /'beɪkɪŋ/ *adj informal* Baking weather is very hot.

○━**balance¹** /'bæləns/ *noun* **1** WEIGHT [U] when the weight of someone or something is spread in such a way that they do not fall over *I lost my balance and fell off the bike.* • *The force of the explosion threw him off balance* (= it was difficult for him to stay standing). **2** EQUAL [U, no plural] when the correct amount of importance is given to each thing so that a situation is successful *We hope to strike a balance between police powers and the protection of citizens.*

B

- *The new factory will destroy the ecological balance in the area.* ⊃ *Opposite* **imbalance**. **3** [FAIR] [U] when you consider all the facts in a fair way *I felt his report lacked balance.* **4 on balance** used to give your opinion after you have considered all the facts about something *On balance, I'd prefer a woman dentist to a man.* **5** [MONEY] [C] the amount of money that you still have to pay, or that you have left to use [usually singular] *I always pay off the balance on my credit card each month.* **6 be/hang in the balance** If something hangs in the balance, nobody knows if it will continue to exist in the future or what will happen to it. *After a bad year, Judd's career hung in the balance.*

o━**balance²** /ˈbæləns/ *verb* **1** [I, T] to be in a position where you will not fall to either side, or to put something in this position *She was trying to balance a book on her head.* **2** [T] to give the correct amount of importance to each thing so that a situation is successful *I struggle to balance work and family commitments.* **3 balance the books/budget** to make sure that you do not spend more money than you get **balance sth against sth** to compare the advantages and disadvantages of something *The ecological effects of the factory need to be balanced against the employment it provides.*

**balanced** /ˈbælənst/ *adj* **1** considering all the facts in a fair way *a balanced discussion of his work* **2 a balanced diet/meal** a healthy mixture of different kinds of food ⊃ *See also:* **well-balanced**.

,**balance of 'payments** *noun* [no plural] *mainly UK* the difference between how much a country earns by selling things to other countries and how much it spends buying things from them

,**balance of 'power** *noun* [no plural] the way in which power is divided between different people or groups *maintaining the balance of power in the European Union*

'**balance ,sheet** *noun* [C] a document that shows what a company has earned and what it has spent

**balcony** /ˈbælkəni/ *noun* [C] **1** a small area joined to the wall outside a room on a high level where you can stand or sit **2** the seats in an upper area of a theatre

**bald** /bɔːld/ *adj* **1** with little or no hair *John started to go bald at an early age.* • *I've got a bald patch.* **2** [always before noun] Bald facts or ways of saying things are very clear and are not intended to comfort you.

• **baldness** *noun* [U]

**balding** /ˈbɔːldɪŋ/ *adj* becoming bald

**baldly** /ˈbɔːldli/ *adv* If you say something baldly, you say it in a very clear way which may upset the person you are speaking to. *"I don't love you any more," he said baldly.*

**bald**

**bale** /beɪl/ *noun* [C] a large amount of something such as paper, cloth, or hay (= dried grass), that is tied together so that it can be stored or moved

**baleful** /ˈbeɪlfʰl/ *adj formal* evil or angry *a baleful look*

**balk** (*also UK* **baulk**) /bɔːlk US bɔːk/ *verb* [I] to not want to do something that is unpleasant or difficult *Most people balk at paying these kind of prices for clothes.*

o━**ball** /bɔːl/ *noun* [C] **1** a round object that you throw, kick, or hit in a game, or something with this shape *a tennis ball* • *a ball of string* • *The cat curled itself into a ball.* **2** a large formal occasion where people dance **3 have a ball** *informal* to enjoy yourself very much *We had a ball in Miami.* **4 be on the ball** *informal* to be quick to understand and react to things **5 set/start the ball rolling** to begin an activity that involves a group of people *I've started the ball rolling by setting up a series of meetings.* ⊃ *See also:* **ball game**, **crystal ball**.

**ball**

**ballad** /ˈbæləd/ *noun* [C] a song that tells a story, especially about love

**ballerina** /ˌbæləˈriːnə/ *noun* [C] a female ballet dancer

**ballet** /ˈbæleɪ US bælˈeɪ/ *noun* **1** [DANCING] [U] a type of dancing that is done in a theatre and tells a story, usually with music **2** [PERFORMANCE] [C] a particular story or performance of ballet dancing *Mary's favourite ballet was 'Giselle'.* **3** [DANCERS] [C] a group of ballet dancers who work together *the Royal Ballet*

'**ball ,game** *noun* [C] **1** *US* a game of baseball (= where teams hit a ball and run round four fixed points), basketball (= where teams throw a ball through a high net), or American football *Hey, kids, let's go to a ball game tonight.* **2 a whole new ball game** *informal* (*also* **a different ball game**) a completely different situation from how things were before *We'd been climbing in Scotland, but the Himalayas were a whole new ball game.*

**ballistic** /bəˈlɪstɪk/ *adj* **go ballistic** *informal* to suddenly become very angry

**balloon¹** /bəˈluːn/ *noun* [C] a small coloured rubber bag that you fill with air to play with or to use as a decoration *Could you help me to*

**balloon**

hot-air
balloon

*blow up* some *balloons?* ⊃ *See also:* **hot-air balloon**.

**balloon²** /bəˈluːn/ *verb* [I] to suddenly become much larger *I ballooned to 14 stone when I had my second baby.*

**ballot¹** /ˈbælət/ *noun* [C, U] a secret written vote *to hold a ballot* • *She was the only candidate on the ballot* (= available to vote for). • *(UK) ballot papers* • *a ballot box* (= box where votes are collected)

**ballot²** /ˈbælət/ *verb* [T] *mainly UK* to ask people to vote in a ballot so that you can find out their opinion about something *In July he will ballot his members on how they want to proceed.*

**ballpark** /ˈbɔːlpɑːk/ *noun* **1** [C] *US* a place where baseball (= game where teams hit a ball and run round four fixed points) is played and watched **2 ballpark estimate/figure** a number or amount that is not exact but should be near the correct number or amount *$3 million would be a ballpark figure for sales next year.*

**ballpoint pen** /ˌbɔːlpɔɪntˈpen/ *noun* [C] a pen with a very small ball in the end that rolls ink onto the paper

**ballroom** /ˈbɔːlruːm/ *noun* [C] a large room where dances are held

**bamboo** /bæmˈbuː/ *noun* [C, U] a tall plant with hard hollow stems, often used for making furniture

**ban¹** /bæn/ *verb* [T] **banning,** *past* **banned** to officially say that someone must not do something *A lot of people think boxing should be banned.* • [+ from + doing sth] *Ian's been banned from driving for 2 years.*

**ban²** /bæn/ *noun* [C] an official rule that people must not do or use something *There is a **ban on** developing land around the city.*

**banal** /bəˈnɑːl/ *adj* ordinary and not exciting *banal pop songs*

**banana** /bəˈnɑːnə/ *noun* [C, U] a long, curved fruit with a yellow skin ⊃ *See colour picture* **Fruit and Vegetables** *on page Centre 8.*

⊶**band¹** /bænd/ *noun* [C] **1** MUSIC a group of musicians who play modern music together *a jazz band* **2** LINE a line of a different colour or design *The band of lighter coloured soil marks*

the position of the fort. **3** CIRCLE a piece of material put around something *an elastic band* **4** PEOPLE a group of people who do something together *the Cathedral's band of regular worshippers* **5** PART *UK* one of the groups that something is divided into *the 20–25 age band* ⊃ *See also:* **elastic band, rubber band**.

**band²** /bænd/ *verb*
**band together** to work with other people in order to achieve something *Companies banded together to keep prices high.* ⊃ *Opposite* **disband**.

**bandage¹** /ˈbændɪdʒ/ *noun* [C] a long piece of soft cloth that you tie around a wound or injury

**bandage**

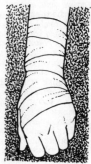

**bandage²** /ˈbændɪdʒ/ *verb* [T] to put a bandage around a wound or injury

**Band-Aid** /ˈbændeɪd/ *US trademark* (*UK* **plaster**) *noun* [C] a small piece of cloth or plastic that sticks to your skin to cover and protect a small wound

**bandit** /ˈbændɪt/ *noun* [C] a thief who attacks people who are travelling in a wild place

**bandwagon** /ˈbændˌwægən/ *noun* **get/jump on the bandwagon** to become involved in an activity which is successful so that you can get the advantages of it yourself *Publishers are rushing to get on the CD-ROM bandwagon.*

**bang¹** /bæŋ/ *noun* [C] **1** a sudden loud noise *The door slammed with a deafening bang.* **2** when you suddenly hit part of your body on something hard *a nasty bang on the head* **3 go out with a bang** *informal* If someone or something goes out with a bang, they stop existing or doing something in an exciting way.

**bang²** /bæŋ/ *verb* [I, T] **1** to make a loud noise, especially by hitting something against something hard *We heard the door bang.* • *Ben banged his fist on the desk.* **2** to hit part of your body against something hard *Ted fell and banged his head.* ⊃ *See also:* be banging your **head¹** against a brick wall.

**bang³** /bæŋ/ *adv UK informal* exactly *The books were piled up **slap bang** in the middle of the kitchen table.* • *The curtain rose **bang on** time.*

**banger** /ˈbæŋər/ *noun* [C] *UK informal* **1** an old car that is in a bad condition **2** a sausage (= tube of meat and spices)

**bangs** /bæŋz/ *noun* [plural] *US* (*UK* **fringe** [C]) hair that is cut short and straight at the top of someone's face ⊃ *See colour picture* **Hair** *on page Centre 9.*

**banish** /ˈbænɪʃ/ *verb* [T] **1** to send someone away from a place, often as a punishment [often passive] *He was **banished to** a remote Alaskan island.* • *Smokers were banished to the garden.* **2** to make yourself stop thinking about something or feeling a particular way *Banish winter blues with a holiday in the sun!*

**banister** /'bænɪstə<sup>r</sup>/ *noun* [C] a long piece of wood that you can hold as you go up or down stairs

**banjo** /'bændʒəʊ/ *noun* [C] a musical instrument like a guitar with a round body

o━**bank**¹ /bæŋk/ *noun* [C] **1** MONEY an organization or place where you can borrow money, save money, etc *Most banks are reluctant to lend money to new businesses.* • *I must remember to go to the bank on my way home.* **2** RIVER the land along the side of a river *We found a shady spot on the river bank.* **3** STORE a place where a supply of something can be kept until it is needed *a blood bank* **4** PILE a large pile of snow, sand, or earth ➔ *See also:* **bottle bank**, **merchant bank**, **piggy bank**

**bank**² /bæŋk/ *verb* **1** [I, T] to put or keep money in a bank *to bank a cheque* • *Who do you bank with?* • *I bank at the First National Bank.* **2** [I] When a plane banks, it flies with one wing higher than the other when turning.

**bank on sb/sth** to depend on someone doing something or something happening *Chrissie might arrive on time, but I wouldn't bank on it.*

'**bank a,ccount** *noun* [C] an arrangement with a bank to keep your money there and take it out when you need to

**banker** /'bæŋkə<sup>r</sup>/ *noun* [C] someone who has an important job in a bank

,**bank 'holiday** *noun* [C] *UK* an official holiday when all banks and most shops and offices are closed *Spring bank holiday*

**banking** /'bæŋkɪŋ/ *noun* [U] the business of operating a bank

**banknote** /'bæŋknəʊt/ *mainly UK* (*US* **bill**) *noun* [C] a piece of paper money

**bankrupt**¹ /'bæŋkrʌpt/ *adj* unable to continue in business because you cannot pay your debts *He went bankrupt after only a year in business.*

**bankrupt**² /'bæŋkrʌpt/ *verb* [T] to make someone bankrupt

**bankruptcy** /'bæŋkrəptsi/ *noun* [C, U] when a person or organization becomes bankrupt *Factories that continue to make losses could soon face bankruptcy.*

'**bank ,statement** *noun* [C] a piece of paper that shows how much money you have put into your bank account and how much you have taken out

**banner** /'bænə<sup>r</sup>/ *noun* [C] a long piece of cloth, often stretched between poles, with words or a sign written on it

**banquet** /'bæŋkwɪt/ *noun* [C] a large formal dinner for a lot of people

**banter** /'bæntə<sup>r</sup>/ *noun* [U] conversation which is funny and not serious

**baptism** /'bæptɪz²m/ *noun* [C, U] a Christian ceremony in which water is put on someone to show that they are a member of the Church

**Baptist** /'bæptɪst/ *adj* belonging or relating to a Christian group which only believes in baptism for people who are old enough to understand what it means *the Baptist Church* • **Baptist** *noun* [C]

**baptize** (*also UK* **-ise**) /bæp'taɪz/ (US) /'bæptaɪz/ *verb* [T] to perform a baptism ceremony for someone

o━**bar**¹ /bɑː<sup>r</sup>/ *noun* [C] **1** DRINKING a place where

alcoholic drinks are sold and drunk, or the area behind the person serving the drinks *I met him in a bar in Soho.* **2** BLOCK a small block of something solid *a chocolate bar* • *gold bars* ➔ *See colour picture* **Quantities** *on page Centre 14.* **3** LONG PIECE a long, thin piece of metal or wood *There were bars on the downstairs windows.* **4** PREVENTING SUCCESS *UK* something that prevents you doing something or having something *Lack of money should not be **a bar to** a good education.* **5** MUSIC one of the short, equal groups of notes that a piece of music is divided into *The band played the first few bars.* **6** **the bar** lawyers (= people whose job is to know about the law and deal with legal situations) thought of as a group *Haughey was **called to** the bar* (= became a lawyer) *in 1949.* **7** **behind bars** in prison

**bar**² /bɑː<sup>r</sup>/ *verb* [T] **barring**, *past* **barred** **1** PREVENT to officially prevent someone doing something or going somewhere, or to prevent something happening [+ from + doing sth] *The court barred him from contacting his former wife.* • *The government barred demonstrations during the state visit.* **2** KEEP OUT to stop someone going into a place *A line of policemen barred the entrance to the camp.* **3** CLOSE to close and lock a door or gate

**bar**³ /bɑː<sup>r</sup>/ *preposition* **1** except *I've read all her books, bar one.* **2** **bar none** used to emphasize that someone or something is the best *the best suspense writer going, bar none*

**barbarian** /bɑː'beəriən/ *noun* [C] someone who behaves in a way which shows they are not well educated and do not care about the feelings of others

**barbaric** /bɑː'bærɪk/ *adj* violent and cruel *a barbaric act of violence* • **barbarically** *adv*

**barbecue**¹ /'bɑːbɪkjuː/ *noun* [C] **1** a party at which you cook food over a fire outdoors **2** a metal frame for cooking food over a fire outdoors

**barbecue**² /'bɑːbɪkjuː/ *verb* [I, T] **barbecuing**, *past* **barbecued** to cook food on a barbecue *barbecued chicken wings*

**barbed wire** /,bɑːbd'waɪə<sup>r</sup>/ *noun* [U] strong wire with short, sharp points on it to keep people out of a place *a barbed wire fence*

**barber** /'bɑːbə<sup>r</sup>/ *noun* [C] someone whose job is to cut men's hair *Dad goes to **the barber's** (= the barber's shop) once a month.*

'**bar ,code** *noun* [C] a row of black lines on something you buy, that a computer reads to find the price

**bare**¹ /beə<sup>r</sup>/ *adj* **1** NO CLOTHES not covered by clothes *a bare chest* • *She ran out into the road in her bare feet.* **2** NOT COVERED not covered by anything *bare floorboards* **3** EMPTY empty *a bare room* • *The cupboard was bare.* **4** BASIC including only the smallest amount that you need of something *The report just gave us the barest facts about the accident.* • *Tony's salary only covers **the bare essentials** for the family.* ➔ *See also:* with your bare hands (**hand**¹)

**bare**² /beə<sup>r</sup>/ *verb* [T] to take away the thing that is covering something so that it can be seen *He bared his chest.* • *The dog bared its teeth.*

**barefoot** /beəˈfʊt/ *adj, adv* not wearing any shoes or socks *They ran barefoot along the wet beach.*

**barely** /ˈbeəli/ *adv* only just *He was barely alive when they found him.* • *Barely 18, Lee was sent out to fight in the Gulf.*

**barf** /bɑːf/ *verb* [I] *US very informal* to vomit • barf *noun* [U]

**bargain¹** /ˈbɑːgɪn/ *noun* [C] **1** something that is sold for less than its usual price or its real value *At $8.95, it's a bargain.* **2** when you agree to something someone else wants so that they will agree to something you want *They were prepared to strike a bargain to avoid more fighting.* **3 into the bargain** mainly UK as well as everything else *Caffeine has no good effects on health and is mildly addictive into the bargain.*

**bargain²** /ˈbɑːgɪn/ *verb* [I] to try to make someone agree to something better for you *Do not hesitate to bargain over the price.*

**bargain for/on sth** to expect or be prepared for something *We hadn't bargained on such a long wait.* • *The stormy weather proved to be more than anybody bargained for.*

**barge¹** /bɑːdʒ/ *noun* [C] a long, narrow boat with a flat bottom that is used to carry goods

**barge²** /bɑːdʒ/ *verb informal* **barge past/through/ahead, etc** to walk somewhere quickly, pushing people or things out of the way *Fred barged through the crowd.*

**barge in/barge into sth** to walk into a room quickly and without being invited

**baritone** /ˈbærɪtəʊn/ *noun* [C] a man who sings in a voice that is quite low

**bark¹** /bɑːk/ *noun* **1** [U] the hard substance that covers the surface of a tree **2** [C] the sound that a dog makes

**bark²** /bɑːk/ *verb* **1** [I] If a dog barks, it makes loud, short sounds. **2** [I, T] to say something loudly and quickly *I'm sorry, I had no right to bark at you like that.*

**barley** /ˈbɑːli/ *noun* [U] a type of grain used for making food and alcoholic drinks

**barmaid** /ˈbɑːmeɪd/ *UK* (*US* **bartender**) *noun* [C] a woman who serves drinks in a bar

**barman** /ˈbɑːmən/ *UK* (*US* **bartender**) *noun* [C] *plural* **barmen** a man who serves drinks in a bar

**barmy** /ˈbɑːmi/ *adj UK informal* crazy or silly *What a barmy idea!* • *That bloke must have thought you were barmy!*

**barn** /bɑːn/ *noun* [C] a large building on a farm where crops or animals can be kept

**barometer** /bəˈrɒmɪtəʳ/ *noun* [C] **1** a way of showing what people think or what the quality of something is *Car sales are viewed as a barometer of consumer confidence.* **2** a piece of equipment that measures air pressure (= the force of the air) and shows when the weather will change

**baron** /ˈbær⁰n/ *noun* [C] **1** a man of high social rank in the UK and other parts of Europe *Baron Thyssen* **2** a man who owns or controls a lot of a particular industry *a wealthy media baron*

**baroness** /ˈbærⁿnes/ *noun* [C] a woman of the same rank as a baron or married to a baron, or a title given to a woman in the UK who has earned official respect *Baroness Thatcher*

**baroque** /bəˈrɒk/ *adj* relating to the style of art, building, and music that was popular in Europe in the 17th and early 18th century, and which had a lot of decoration

**barracks** /ˈbærəks/ *noun* [C] *plural* **barracks** a group of buildings where soldiers live

**barrage** /ˈbærɑːdʒ/ ⑤ bəˈrɑːdʒ/ *noun* **1 a barrage of sth** a lot of questions, complaints, or criticisms *He faced a barrage of questions about his decision to leave the show.* **2** [C] a continuous attack with several big guns

**barrel** /ˈbærⁿl/ *noun* [C] **1** a large, round container for storing liquids such as oil or wine **2** the tube in a gun that the bullet shoots out of

**barren** /ˈbærⁿn/ *adj* **1** Land that is barren does not produce crops. **2** *old-fashioned* A woman who is barren cannot have children. • barrenness *noun* [U]

**barricade¹** /ˌbærɪˈkeɪd/ *noun* [C] something that is quickly put across a road or entrance to prevent people from going past

**barricade²** /ˌbærɪˈkeɪd/ *verb* [T] to build a barricade somewhere [often reflexive] *They barricaded themselves in the building* (= built a barricade so that nobody could get to them).

**barrier** /ˈbæriəʳ/ *noun* [C] **1** a type of fence that prevents people from going into an area *Police erected barriers to hold back the crowd.* **2** something that prevents people from doing what they want to do *Kim is taking Spanish lessons in an attempt to overcome the language barrier.* • *Shyness is a big barrier to making friends.* ⊃ *See also:* **crash barrier**.

**barring** /ˈbɑːrɪŋ/ *preposition* if something does not happen *We should arrive at about five o'clock, barring accidents.*

**barrister** /ˈbærɪstəʳ/ *noun* [C] in the UK, a lawyer (= someone whose job is to know about the law and deal with legal situations) who can work in the highest courts ⊃ *See usage note at* **lawyer**.

**barrow** /ˈbærəʊ/ *UK* (*UK/US* **wheelbarrow**) a big, open container with a wheel at the front and handles that is used to move things, especially around in a garden

**bartender** /ˈbɑːˌtendəʳ/ *US* (*UK* **barman/barmaid**) *noun* [C] someone who serves drinks in a bar

**barter** /ˈbɑːtəʳ/ *verb* [I, T] to exchange goods or services for other goods or services, without using money

**base¹** /beɪs/ *noun* [C] **1** BOTTOM the bottom part of something, or the part something rests on *It's quite easy to fasten the monitor onto the base.* • *I felt a sharp pain at the base of my thumb.* **2** MAIN PART the most important part of something, from which other things can develop *a solid economic base* **3** PLACE the main place where a person lives or works, or from where they do things *Keswick is an excellent base for exploring the Lake District.* **4** ARMY a place where people in the army or navy live and work *an American Air Force base* **5** ORGANIZATION the place where the main work of an organization is done *The company's European base is in Frankfurt.* **6** SUBSTANCE the main substance in a mixture *paints with an oil base* **7** BASEBALL one of the four places in baseball that a player must run to in order to win a point **8 be off base** *US informal* to be wrong *In 1893, many of the forecasts about 1993 were way off base.* **9 touch/cover all the bases** *mainly US* to deal with every part of a situation or activity *We need to make sure that we are covering all the bases in our campaign.*

o⊶**base²** /beɪs/ *verb* **be based at/in, etc** If you are based at/in, etc a particular place, that is the main place where you live or work. *The company is based in Geneva.*

**base sth on/upon sth** If you base something on facts or ideas, you use those facts or ideas to develop it. *Her latest TV serial is based on a true story.*

o⊶**baseball** /'beɪsbɔːl/ *noun* **1** [U] a game in which two teams try to win points by hitting a ball and running around four fixed points **2** [C] the ball used in this game ➲ *See colour picture* **Sports 2** *on page Centre 16.*

'**base ,camp** *noun* [C] the place from which people go to climb mountains

**basement** /'beɪsmənt/ *noun* [C] a room or set of rooms that is below ground level in a building *The kitchen department is in the basement.*

**bases** /'beɪsiːz/ *plural of* basis

**bash¹** /bæʃ/ *verb* [T] *informal* **1** to hit someone or something hard *I bashed my arm on the car door as I got out.* **2** immigrant-bashing/lawyer-bashing/union-bashing, etc when particular groups are criticized strongly and unfairly

**bash²** /bæʃ/ *noun* [C] *informal* **1** a party **2** a hard hit on something *a bash on the nose* **3 have a bash (at sth)** *UK informal* to try to do something *I've never been water-skiing but I'd love to have a bash at it.*

**bashful** /'bæʃfəl/ *adj* shy and easily embarrassed • **bashfully** *adv*

o⊶**basic** /'beɪsɪk/ *adj* **1** [MAIN] [always before noun] being the main or most important part of something *basic ideas/principles* • *The basic problem is very simple.* **2** [NECESSARY] including or providing only the things that are most necessary *basic training/services/skills* **3** [SIMPLE] very simple, with nothing special added *My software is pretty basic.*

o⊶**basically** /'beɪsɪkəli/ *adv* **1** in the most important ways *Frazier's films are basically documentaries.* • *The two PCs are basically the same.* **2** used to introduce a short explanation about something *Basically, what he's saying is that we need more time.*

**the basics** /'beɪsɪks/ *noun* the most important facts, skills, or needs *the basics of computer technology*

**basil** /'bæzəl/ (US) 'beɪzəl/ *noun* [U] a herb with a sweet smell

**basin** /'beɪsən/ *noun* [C] **1** [BOWL] *mainly UK* a bowl for liquids or food *a basin of water* **2** [BATHROOM] *UK* (*UK/US* **sink**) the bowl that is fixed to the wall in a bathroom, where you can wash your hands and face **3** [LAND] a low area of land from which water flows into a river

o⊶**basis** /'beɪsɪs/ *noun* [C] *plural* **bases** /'beɪsiːz/ **1 on a daily/monthly/regular, etc basis** how often something happens or is done *Meetings are held on a weekly basis.* **2 on a commercial/**

**full-time/percentage, etc basis** the way something happens or is organized *We will consider claims for asylum on a case by case basis.* **3** the reason for something *Marks are awarded on the basis of progress and performance.* • *There is no legal basis for his claim.* **4** a situation, fact, or idea from which something can develop *Dani's essay can serve as a basis for our discussion.*

**bask** /bɑːsk/ *verb* [I] to sit or lie in a place that is warm *Seals basked on the rocks.*

**bask in sth** to enjoy the way other people admire you *They basked in the glory victory had brought them.*

o⊶**basket** /'bɑːskɪt/ *noun* [C] **1** a container with a handle made of thin pieces of wood, wire, plastic, etc *a shopping basket* **2** when a player throws the ball through the net in basketball ➲ *See also:* **wastepaper basket**

**basketball** /'bɑːskɪtbɔːl/ *noun* **1** [U] a game in which two teams try to win points by throwing a ball through a high net **2** [C] the large ball used in the game of basketball ➲ *See colour picture* **Sports 2** *on page Centre 16.*

**bass** /beɪs/ *noun* **1** [VOICE] [C] a man who sings with a very low voice **2** [MUSIC] [U] the lower half of the set of musical notes **3** [INSTRUMENT] [C, U] (*also* **double bass**) a large, wooden musical instrument with four strings that you play while standing up or sitting on a high chair **4** [GUITAR] [C, U] (*also* ,bass gui'tar) an electric guitar that makes a low sound

**bassoon** /bə'suːn/ *noun* [C] a long, wooden musical instrument that you blow through to make a low sound

**bastard** /'bɑːstəd/ *noun* [C] **1** an offensive word for a man you do not like **2** *old-fashioned* an offensive word for a child whose parents are not married

**bastion** /'bæstiən/ *noun* [C] a place, organization, etc where particular ideas or ways of doing things are protected *the last bastion of male chauvinism*

**bat¹** /bæt/ *noun* [C] **1** a piece of wood used to hit the ball in some sports **2** a small animal like a mouse with wings that flies at night

**bat²** /bæt/ *verb* [I] **batting**, *past* **batted** to try to hit a ball with a bat *Rimmer batted well for Oxford.* ➲ *See also:* not bat an **eyelid**.

**batch** /bætʃ/ *noun* [C] a group of things or people that are dealt with at the same time or are similar in some way *the university's first batch of students* • *Fry the aubergines in batches.*

**bated** /'beɪtɪd/ *adj* ➲ *See* with bated **breath**.

o⊶**bath¹** /bɑːθ/ *noun* [C] **1** *UK* (*US* **bathtub**) the container that you sit or lie in to wash your body ➲ *See colour picture* **The Bathroom** *on page Centre 1.* **2** when you wash your body in a bath, or the water in the bath [usually singular] *I'll just have a quick bath.* • *(UK) She ran herself a bath* (= filled a bath with water).

**bath²** /bɑːθ/ *verb* [I, T] *UK* to wash yourself or someone else in a bath *Emma usually baths the kids about seven o'clock.*

**bathe** /beɪð/ *verb* **1** [WASH YOURSELF] [I, T] to wash yourself or someone else in a bath *As a rule, I bathe every day.* **2** [PART OF BODY] [T] to wash part of someone's body, often because it is hurt

*Bathe your eye with cool salty water.* **3** SWIM [I] *old-fashioned* to swim **4 be bathed in light** to look attractive in a beautiful light *The mountain was bathed in red-gold light from the setting sun.*

**'bathing ,suit** *noun* [C] a piece of clothing that you wear to swim in

**bathrobe** /'bɑːθrəʊb/ *noun* [C] a soft coat that you wear before or after a bath

⚬ᐟ**bathroom** /'bɑːθruːm/ *noun* [C] **1** a room with a bath, sink (= bowl for washing), and often a toilet ➪ *See colour picture* **The Bathroom** *on page Centre 1.* **2 go to the bathroom** *US* to use the toilet ➪ *See usage note at* **toilet**.

**bathtub** /'bɑːθtʌb/ *US* (*UK* **bath**) *noun* [C] the container that you sit or lie in to wash your body

**baton** /'bætᵊn ⓤ bə'tɑːn/ *noun* [C] **1** STICK a thin stick used to control the rhythm of a group of musicians **2** POLICE a thick stick that a police officer uses as a weapon **3** RACE a stick that a runner passes to the next person in a race

**batsman** /'bætsmən/ *noun* [C] *plural* **batsmen** *UK* the person who is trying to hit the ball in cricket ➪ *See colour picture* **Sports 2** *on page Centre 16.*

**battalion** /bə'tæliən/ *noun* [C] a large group of soldiers made from several smaller groups

**batter**[1] /'bætəʳ/ *noun* **1** [U] a mixture of flour, milk, and often eggs used to make cakes and pancakes (= thin fried cakes), and to cover fish, etc before it is fried **2** [C] the person who is trying to hit the ball in baseball ➪ *See colour picture* **Sports 2** *on page Centre 16.*

**batter**[2] /'bætəʳ/ *verb* [I, T] to hit someone or something repeatedly very hard *If you don't open up we'll **batter** the door **down.*** • *Waves **battered against** the rocks.* • *battered wives/women*

**battered** /'bætəd/ *adj* old and not in very good condition *a battered copy of her favourite novel*

**battering** /'bætərɪŋ/ *noun* [C] when someone or something is hit repeatedly, criticized strongly, or damaged badly [usually singular] *The prime minister has **taken** quite **a battering** this week.*

⚬ᐟ**battery** /'bætᵊri/ *noun* **1** [C] an object that provides electricity for things such as radios, toys, or cars *Are there any spare batteries for my tape recorder?* • *My car has got **a flat battery** (= one that has no electricity left).* **2** [U] the crime of hitting someone *assault and battery*

**battle**[1] /'bætl/ *noun* **1** WAR [C, U] a fight between two armies in a war *the Battle of Waterloo* • *Her grandfather was killed **in battle** (= while fighting).* **2** POWER [C] when two people or groups compete against each other or have an argument about something *a battle for control in the boardroom* **3** PROBLEMS/ILLNESS [C] a fight against something that is hurting or destroying you *a long battle against cancer* **4 fight a losing battle** to try hard to do something when there is no chance that you will succeed *I try to control what my children watch on TV, but I think I'm fighting a losing battle.*

**battle**[2] /'bætl/ *verb* [I] to try very hard to do something that is difficult *Both teams **are battling for** a place in the Premier League.* • *Throughout the campaign Johnson was **battling against** severe health problems.*

**baulk** /bɔːk, bɔːlk/ *UK* (*UK/US* **balk**) *verb* [I] to not want to do something that is unpleasant or difficult *Most people would **baulk at** paying these kind of prices for clothes.*

**bawl** /bɔːl/ *verb* [I, T] *informal* to shout or cry loudly

**bay** /beɪ/ *noun* **1** [C] an area of coast where the land curves in *a sandy bay* **2** [C] a part of a building or place that is used for a particular purpose *the school sick bay* • *a parking bay* **3 keep/hold sth at bay** to prevent something unpleasant from coming near you or from happening *Gunmen kept police at bay for almost four hours.*

**bayonet** /'beɪənət/ *noun* [C] a knife that is fastened onto the end of a long gun

**bazaar** /bə'zɑːʳ/ *noun* [C] **1** a market in Eastern countries **2** a sale where goods are sold to raise money for a school, church, etc

**B&B** /,biːən'biː/ *noun* [C] *abbreviation for* bed and breakfast (= a small hotel or private house where you pay for a room to sleep in for the night and a meal in the morning)

**BBC** /,biːbiː'siː/ *noun abbreviation for* British Broadcasting Corporation: one of the main television and radio companies in the United Kingdom *a cookery programme on BBC2*

**BC** /biː'siː/ *abbreviation for* Before Christ: used to show that a particular year came before the birth of Christ *331 BC*

⚬ᐟ**be**[1] *strong form* /biː/ *weak forms* /bi, bɪ/ *verb* **1** used to describe or give information about someone or something *I'm sixteen.* • *I'm Andy.* • *Her mother is a teacher.* • *He's German.* • *They were very upset.* • *He was very ill last year.* • *I'm sorry I'm late.* • *They've been unlucky.* • *Be quiet!* **2 there is/there are/there was, etc** used to show that someone or something exists *There were about fifty people at the party.* • *Is there a bank near here?* **3** used to show the position of someone or something *It's been in the cupboard for months.* • *She's in the kitchen.* **4 it is/it was, etc** used to give a fact or your opinion about something *It's not surprising that she left him.* • *It's a good idea to keep a spare key somewhere safe.*

---

**USAGE**

**be**

| present tense | past tense |
|---|---|
| *I am (I'm)* | *I was* |
| *you are (you're)* | *you were* |
| *he/she/it is (he's/she's/it's)* | *he/she/it was* |
| *we are (we're)* | *we were* |
| *you are (you're)* | *you were* |
| *they are (they're)* | *they were* |

past participle

| *been* | *I have been on holiday.* |
|---|---|

present participle

| *being* | *He's being silly.* |
|---|---|

short negative forms

| *aren't* | *isn't* | *wasn't* | *weren't* |
|---|---|---|---|

*Aren't you hot in that thick coat?*

---

**B**

**be²** *strong form* /biː/ *weak forms* /bi, bɪ/ *auxiliary verb* **1** used with the present participle of other verbs to describe actions that are or were still continuing *Where are you going?* • *How long have you been sitting there?* • *He was standing by the window.* • *He's working at the moment.* **2** used with the present participle of other verbs, and sometimes after a modal verb, to describe actions that will happen in the future *I'm coming back on Tuesday.* • *I'll be coming back on Tuesday.* **3** used with the past participle of other verbs to form the passive *He was injured in a car crash.* • *The results will be announced next week.* **4** used in conditional sentences to say what might happen *If he were to offer me the job, I'd take it.* **5** used to say that someone must or should do something *You are not to see him again.* **6** *formal* used to show that something has been organized *They are to stay with us when they arrive.*

○━**beach** /biːtʃ/ *noun* [C] an area of sand or rocks next to the sea

**beacon** /ˈbiːkᵊn/ *noun* [C] a light on a hill or in a tower that warns people of something or is a signal or guide

**bead** /biːd/ *noun* [C] **1** a small, round ball of glass, plastic, or wood that is used for making jewellery *a necklace of coloured glass beads* **2** a small drop of liquid on a surface *beads of sweat*

**beak** /biːk/ *noun* [C] the hard part of a bird's mouth

**beaker** /ˈbiːkər/ *noun* [C] *UK* a tall cup without a handle, usually made of plastic

**beam¹** /biːm/ *noun* [C] **1** LIGHT a line of light shining from something *a laser beam* ➋ *See picture at* **light**. **2** WOOD a long, thick piece of wood, metal, or concrete that is used to support weight in a building or other structure **3** SMILE *UK* a big smile

**beam²** /biːm/ *verb* **1** SMILE [I] to smile very happily *The baby beamed at me.* **2** SEND [T] to send a television or radio signal [often passive] *The match was beamed live by satellite around the world.* **3** SHINE [I] If the sun or the moon beams, it shines brightly.

**bean** /biːn/ *noun* [C] **1** SEED a seed of some climbing plants, that is used as food *soya beans* **2** VEGETABLE a seed case of some climbing plants that is eaten as a vegetable *green beans* **3** COFFEE/CHOCOLATE plant seeds used to make coffee and chocolate *coffee beans* ➋ *See also:* **baked beans, runner bean**

○━**bear¹** /beər/ *verb* [T] *past t* **bore**, *past p* **borne** **1** ACCEPT to accept someone or something unpleasant *She couldn't bear the thought of him suffering.* • *I like her, but I can't bear her friends.* • [+ to do sth] *How can you bear to watch?* • *The pain was too much to bear.* **2** **bear a resemblance/relation, etc to sb/sth** to be similar to someone or something *He bears a striking resemblance to his father.* **3** CARRY *formal* to carry something *He came in, bearing*

*a tray of drinks.* **4** WEIGHT to support the weight of something *I don't think that chair will bear his weight.* **5** **bear the responsibility/cost, etc** to accept that you are responsible for something, you should pay for something, etc *He must bear some responsibility for the appalling conditions in the prison.* **6** FEELING to continue to have a bad feeling towards someone *They were rude to her in the past, but she's not the kind of woman who bears grudges* (= continues to be angry). **7** HAVE CHILD *formal* to give birth to a child *She has been told that she will never bear children.* **8** NAME to have or show a particular name, picture, or symbol *The shop bore his family name.* **9** **bear left/right** to turn left or right *Bear right at the next set of traffic lights.* ➋ *See also:* **bear fruit, grin and bear it.**

**bear sb/sth out** to prove that someone is right or that something is true *The facts do not bear out his claims.*

**bear with sb** to be patient and wait while someone does something *If you'll bear with me for a moment, I'll just find your details.*

**bear²** /beər/ *noun* [C] a large, strong, wild animal with thick fur ➋ *See also:* **polar bear, teddy bear**.

**bear**

**bearable** /ˈbeərəbl/ *adj* If an unpleasant situation is bearable, you can accept or deal with it. *Having her there made life at home more bearable for me.* ➋ *Opposite* **unbearable**.

**beard** /bɪəd/ *noun* [C] the hair that grows on a man's chin (= the bottom of his face) ➋ *See colour picture* **Hair** *on page Centre 9.* • **bearded** *adj* with a beard

**bearer** /ˈbeərər/ *noun* [C] a person who brings or carries something *I am sorry to be the bearer of bad news.*

**bearing** /ˈbeərɪŋ/ *noun* **have a bearing on sth** to have an influence on something or a relationship to something *What you decide now could have a considerable bearing on your future.*

**bearings** /ˈbeərɪŋz/ *noun* **1** **get/find your bearings a** to find out where you are *She looked at the sun to find her bearings.* **b** to become confident in a new situation *When you start a new job, it can take some time to get your bearings.* **2** **lose your bearings** to become confused about where you are

**beast** /biːst/ *noun* [C] **1** *formal* an animal, especially a large or wild one **2** *old-fashioned* an annoying or cruel person

**beastly** /ˈbiːstli/ *adj old-fashioned* unkind or unpleasant

○━**beat¹** /biːt/ *verb past t* **beat**, *past p* **beaten** *also US* **beat 1** DEFEAT [T] to defeat someone in a competition *Our team beat Germany 3–1.* ➋ *See usage note at* **win.** **2** HIT [I, T] to hit a person or animal hard many times *She beat the dog with a stick.* ● *She was beaten to death.* **3** SOUND [I, T] to hit against something hard, making a continuous or regular sound *soldiers beating drums* ● *We could hear the pigeons beating their wings.* ● *Rain beat against the windows.* **4** GET RID OF [T] to get rid of something bad *measures to beat crime* ● *I'm determined to beat this illness.* **5** HEART [I] When your heart beats, it makes regular movements and sounds. *By the time the doctor arrived, his heart had stopped beating.* **6** BE BETTER [T] to be better than something [+ doing sth] *Being at the youth club beats sitting at home.* **7 you can't beat sth** used to emphasize that something is best *You can't beat Pedro's for a great pizza.* **8 take a lot of/some, etc beating** to be so good or enjoyable that it is hard to find anything better *This ice cream takes some beating.* **9** FOOD [T] to mix food using hard, quick movements *Beat the egg whites until they are stiff.* **10 It beats me** *informal* something that you say when you do not understand a situation or someone's behaviour *It beats me why she goes out with him.* ⊃ *See also:* beat about the **bush**, beat the (living) **daylights** out of sb, off the beaten **track¹**.

**beat down** If the sun beats down, it is very hot and bright.

**beat sb down** *UK* to persuade someone to charge you less for something

**beat sb/sth off** to manage to defeat someone who is attacking you

**beat sb to sth** to do something before someone else does it *I was going to ask her to the party, but you beat me to it.*

**beat sb up** to attack someone by hitting or kicking them many times *He beat up one of the other prisoners.*

**beat²** /biːt/ *noun* [C] **1** REGULAR SOUND a regular sound that is made by your heart or by something hitting a surface *a heart beat* ● *the beat of a drum* **2** RHYTHM the main rhythm of a piece of music *loud music with a repetitive beat* **3** AREA the area of a town or city that a police officer walks around regularly *Having more police officers on the beat* (= walking around their beat) *should help to reduce crime.*

**beating** /'biːtɪŋ/ *noun* **1** [C] when someone hits another person hard many times **2 take a beating** to be defeated, criticized, or damaged *Our team took a severe beating in the tournament.*

**beautician** /bjuː'tɪʃən/ *noun* [C] someone whose job is to improve people's appearance by treatments to their hair, skin, etc

O━**beautiful** /'bjuːtɪfəl/ *adj* **1** very attractive *a beautiful woman* ● *beautiful scenery* **2** very pleasant *beautiful music* ● *It's a beautiful day* (= the sun is shining). ● **beautifully** *adv* *a beautifully illustrated book* ● *She sings beautifully.*

O━**beauty** /'bjuːti/ *noun* **1** QUALITY [U] the quality of being beautiful *The whole area is famous for its natural beauty.* ● *a beauty contest* (= competition to find the most beautiful woman) **2 the beauty of sth** the quality that makes something especially good or attractive *The beauty of the plan is that it won't cost anything.* **3 a**

**beauty product/treatment** a product or treatment to make you more beautiful **4** EXCELLENT THING [C] *informal* something that is an excellent example of its type *That last goal was a beauty.* **5** WOMAN [C] *old-fashioned* a beautiful woman

'**beauty ,salon** (*also US* '**beauty ,parlor**) *noun* [C] a place where you can have beauty treatments

'**beauty ,spot** *noun* [C] **1** *UK* a place in the countryside that is very beautiful **2** a small dark mark on someone's face

**beaver** /'biːvər/ *noun* [C] an animal with brown fur, a long, flat tail, and sharp teeth, which builds dams (= walls made of pieces of wood) across rivers

**became** /bɪ'keɪm/ *past tense of* become

O━**because** /bɪ'kɒz, bɪ'kəz/ *conjunction* used to give a reason for something *I phoned because I needed to talk to you.* ● *I can't come out tonight because I've got too much homework.*

O━**because of** /bɪ'kɒzəv, bɪ'kəzəv/ *preposition* as a result of someone or something *We got into all this trouble because of you.*

**beck** /bek/ *noun* **be at sb's beck and call** to be always ready and willing to do what someone wants

**beckon** /'bekən/ *verb* **1** WAVE [I, T] to move your hand, head, etc to show someone that you would like them to come nearer *She beckoned to the waiter.* **2** BE LIKELY [I] to seem very likely to happen *A career as a lead guitarist beckoned.* **3** BE ATTRACTIVE [I] If a place beckons, it is very attractive to you, and you want to go there. *The bright lights of London beckoned.*

O━**become** /bɪ'kʌm/ *verb past t* **became,** *past p* **become 1 become available/rich/a writer, etc** to begin to be something *They became great friends.* ● *She wants to become a teacher when she leaves school.* ● *This style of skirt is becoming fashionable.* **2 what/whatever became of sb/sth** something you say when you want to know what has happened to someone *Whatever became of your friend Harry?*

O━**bed¹** /bed/ *noun* **1** FURNITURE [C, U] a piece of furniture that you sleep on *a single/double bed* ● *What time did you go to bed last night?* ● *She was lying in bed when I arrived.* ● *He had only just got out of bed.* ● *Have you made the bed* (= tidied the bed after you have slept in it)? **2** GROUND [C] a piece of ground that is used for growing plants, especially flowers *a flower bed* **3** BOTTOM [C] the ground at the bottom of the sea, a river, etc *the sea bed* ⊃ *See also:* **bunk beds.**

,**bed and 'breakfast** *noun* [C] a small hotel or private house where you pay for a room to sleep in for the night and a meal in the morning

**bedclothes** /'bedkləʊðz/ *noun* [plural] the sheets and other pieces of cloth that cover you and keep you warm in bed

**bedding** /'bedɪŋ/ *noun* [U] **1** the sheets and other pieces of cloth that cover you and keep you warm in bed **2** material such as hay (= dried grass) that animals sleep on

**bedraggled** /bɪ'dræɡld/ *adj* untidy, and often wet and dirty

---

**bedrock** /'bedrɒk/ *noun* [U] *formal* a situation, idea, or principle that provides a strong base for something *Family life is **the bedrock** of a stable society.*

o–⊷**bedroom** /'bedruːm/ *noun* [C] a room used for sleeping in

**bedside** /'bedsaɪd/ *noun* [no plural] **1** the area at the side of a bed *He was at her bedside in the hospital.* • *a bedside table/lamp* **2 bedside manner** a doctor's ability to make the people they are treating feel comfortable *My surgeon has a wonderful bedside manner.*

**bedsit** /'bedsɪt/ *noun* [C] *UK* a rented room where you live, sleep, and cook your meals

**bedspread** /'bedspred/ *noun* [C] a cloth cover that is put over a bed

**bedtime** /'bedtaɪm/ *noun* [C, U] the time that you usually go to bed

**bee** /biː/ *noun* [C] a flying insect that has a yellow and black body and makes honey (= sweet, sticky food) *the queen bee*

**beech** /biːtʃ/ *noun* [C, U] a large tree with a smooth grey trunk (= main, vertical part) that produces small nuts

**beef**[1] /biːf/ *noun* [U] the meat of a cow *roast beef* ⊃ *See also:* **ground beef**.

**beef**[2] /biːf/ *verb*
**beef sth up** to make something stronger or more important *The company wants to beef up its sales force by employing new graduates.*

**beefburger** /'biːf,bɜːɡəʳ/ *UK* (*UK/US* **hamburger**) *noun* [C] very small pieces of meat that are pressed together into a round flat shape, cooked, and eaten between bread

**beehive** /'biːhaɪv/ (*also* **hive**) *noun* [C] a special container where people keep bees

**been** /biːn, bɪn/ *verb* **have been to** to have gone to a place and come back *Have you ever been to Thailand?* ⊃ *Inflection of* **be**.

**beep** /biːp/ *verb* **1** [I] If a machine beeps, it makes a short, high noise. **2** [I, T] If a car horn (= part you press to make a warning sound) beeps or if you beep it, it makes a loud noise. *Beep the horn to let me know that you're here.*
• **beep** *noun* [C]

**beeper** /'biːpəʳ/ *noun* [C] a small piece of electronic equipment that you carry which makes a short high sound when someone wants to talk to you

o–⊷**beer** /bɪəʳ/ *noun* [C, U] an alcoholic drink made from grain, or a glass or container of this drink *a pint of beer*

**beet** /biːt/ *US* (*UK* **beetroot**) *noun* [C, U] a round, dark red vegetable, that is usually cooked and eaten cold

**beetle** /'biːtl/ *noun* [C] an insect with a hard, usually black, shiny body

**beetroot** /'biːtruːt/ *UK* (*US* **beet**) *noun* [C, U] a round, dark red vegetable, that is usually cooked and eaten cold

**befall** /bɪ'fɔːl/ *verb* [T] *past t* **befell**, *past p* **befallen** *formal* If something bad befalls you, it happens to you. *A dreadful misfortune has befallen the family.*

**befit** /bɪ'fɪt/ *verb* [T] **befitting**, *past* **befitted** *formal* to be suitable or right for someone or something *He was given a huge welcome, as befits such a hero.*

o–⊷**before**[1] /bɪ'fɔːʳ/ *preposition* **1** EARLIER earlier than something or someone *a week before Christmas* • *She arrived before me.* • [+ doing sth] *Think hard before accepting the offer.* **2** IN FRONT OF in a position in front of someone or something *I've never performed this before an audience.* • *He stood before her, shaking.* **3** PLACE at a place that you arrive at first when travelling towards another place *The hospital is just before the bridge.* **4** IN ORDER in front of someone or something in an order or a list *P comes before Q in the alphabet.* **5** IMPORTANCE treated as more important than someone or something *They always put the children's needs before their own.* **6** EXAMINATION being formally examined or considered by a group *the proposal before the committee* • *He appeared before the court dressed in jeans.*

o–⊷**before**[2] /bɪ'fɔːʳ/ *conjunction* **1** EARLIER earlier than the time when something happens *He was a teacher before he became famous.* • *It was dark before we found him.* • *Before I could warn him, he had fallen.* **2** TO AVOID STH in order to avoid something bad happening *Put that stick down before you hurt someone.* **3** UNTIL until *It took a few moments before I realized that he was lying.*

o–⊷**before**[3] /bɪ'fɔːʳ/ *adv* at an earlier time, or on a previous occasion *I've never seen her before.* • *We had spoken on the phone a few days before.*

**beforehand** /bɪ'fɔːhænd/ *adv* before a particular time or event *Did you know beforehand what they had planned to do?*

**befriend** /bɪ'frend/ *verb* [T] *formal* to be friendly to someone, especially someone who needs support or help

**beg** /beɡ/ *verb* **begging**, *past* **begged** **1** [I] to ask someone for food or money, because you do not have any *Young children were begging on the streets.* **2** [I, T] to make a very strong and urgent request *She begged him for help.* • [+ to do sth] *I begged her not to go.* ⊃ *See also:* **I beg your pardon**[2].

**began** /bɪ'ɡæn/ *past tense of* begin

**beggar** /'beɡəʳ/ *noun* [C] a poor person who lives by asking other people for money and food

o–⊷**begin** /bɪ'ɡɪn/ *verb* **beginning**, *past t* **began**, *past p* **begun** **1** [I, T] to start to do something [+ to do sth] *The children began to cry.* • [+ doing sth] *Have they begun building the wall yet?* • *She began her career as a journalist on a local newspaper.* **2** [I] to start to happen *What time does the film begin?* • *The war began at the end of August.* **3 begin with sth** to have something at the start *Local phone numbers begin with 018.* **4 to begin with a** at the start of a situation *To begin with, the two girls got on well.* **b** used to give the first important reason for something *To begin with, we can't leave the children alone.*

**beginner** /bɪ'ɡɪnəʳ/ *noun* [C] someone who is starting to learn something for the first time *I'm a complete beginner at yoga.*

o–⊷**beginning** /bɪ'ɡɪnɪŋ/ *noun* [C] the first part of something or the start of something [usually singular] *We met at the beginning of 1998.* • *Things went well in the beginning.*

**begrudge** /bɪ'ɡrʌdʒ/ *verb* [T] **1** to feel upset

because someone has something that you would like [+ two objects] *I don't begrudge him his success.* **2** to feel upset because you have to spend money on something or spend time doing something *They begrudge every penny that they have to spend on him.*

**beguile** /bɪˈgaɪl/ *verb* [T] *formal* to attract someone very much, sometimes in order to deceive them [often passive] *I can see how people are beguiled by his charm.* ● *a beguiling smile/argument*

**begun** /bɪˈgʌn/ *past participle of* begin

**behalf** /bɪˈhɑːf/ *noun* **on sb's behalf** If you do something on someone's behalf, you do it for them or instead of them. *We are campaigning on behalf of thousands of refugees.* ● *Will you accept the prize on my behalf?*

○━**behave** /bɪˈheɪv/ *verb* [I] **1** to do or say things in a particular way *to behave badly/stupidly* ● *They are behaving like children.* **2** (*also* **behave yourself**) to be polite and not make a situation difficult *Try to behave.* ● *The children can only come if they promise to behave themselves.* ➔ *Opposite* **misbehave**.

**-behaved** /bɪˈheɪvd/ *suffix* used after a word describing how someone behaves *a badly-behaved child* ➔ *See also:* **well-behaved**.

○━**behaviour** UK (*US* **behavior**) /bɪˈheɪvjəʳ/ *noun* [U] the way that you behave *good/bad behaviour* ● *Did you notice anything odd about his behaviour?*

**behavioural** UK (*US* **behavioral**) /bɪˈheɪvjərəl/ *adj* relating to behaviour *behavioural changes/problems*

**behead** /bɪˈhed/ *verb* [T] to cut someone's head off

**beheld** /bɪˈheld/ *past of* behold

○━**behind**[1] /bɪˈhaɪnd/ *preposition* **1** ⟨BACK⟩ at or to the back of someone or something *Close the door behind you.* ● *The pub is behind the train station.* ● *The letter had fallen behind the desk.* **2** ⟨LESS SUCCESSFUL⟩ slower or less successful than someone or something *Our team is 3 points behind the winners.* ● *The building work is already behind schedule* (= late). **3** ⟨CAUSING⟩ causing something, or responsible for something *What was the reason behind her decision to leave?* **4** ⟨SUPPORTING⟩ giving your help or support to someone *The group is 100 percent behind her.* **5** ⟨NOT AFFECTING⟩ If a bad experience or your own bad behaviour is behind you, it does not exist or affect your life now. *He's put his criminal past behind him.*

○━**behind**[2] /bɪˈhaɪnd/ *adv* **1** ⟨BACK⟩ at or to the back of someone or something *Somebody grabbed me from behind.* **2** ⟨SLOWER⟩ slower or later than someone else, or than you should be *She's behind with the rent* (= is late to pay it). **3** ⟨PLACE⟩ in the place where someone or something was before *You go on ahead. I'll stay behind and tidy up.* ● *When we got to the restaurant, I realized that I had left my purse behind.*

**behind**[3] /bɪˈhaɪnd/ *noun* [C] *informal* the part of your body that you sit on

**behold** /bɪˈhəʊld/ *verb* [T] *past* **beheld** *literary* to see something

**beige** /beɪʒ/ *noun* [U] a pale brown colour ● *beige adj* ➔ *See colour picture* **Colours** *on page Centre 6.*

**being**[1] /ˈbiːɪŋ/ *noun* **1** [C] a living person or imaginary creature *human beings* **2** **come into being** to start to exist *The new law comes into being next month.* ➔ *See also:* **well-being**.

**being**[2] /ˈbiːɪŋ/ *present participle of* be

**belated** /bɪˈleɪtɪd/ *adj* coming late, or later than expected *a belated attempt to win votes* ● **belatedly** *adv Supermarkets have belatedly realized the purchasing power of mothers.*

**belch**[1] /beltʃ/ *verb* **1** [I] to make a sudden noise as air from your stomach comes out through your mouth **2** [T] (*also* **belch out**) to produce a lot of smoke, fire, gas, etc *tall chimneys belching smoke*

**belch**[2] /beltʃ/ *noun* [C] the noise you make when you belch

**beleaguered** /bɪˈliːgəd/ *adj formal* having a lot of problems *the beleaguered farming industry*

**belfry** /ˈbelfri/ *noun* [C] the tower of a church where the bells are hung

**belie** /bɪˈlaɪ/ *verb* [T] **belying**, *past* **belied** *formal* to give a wrong idea about something *His shy manner belied his very sharp mind.*

○━**belief** /bɪˈliːf/ *noun* **1** ⟨TRUE⟩ [U, no plural] when you believe that something is true or real *It is a widely-held belief that smoking helps you lose weight.* ● *She married him in the belief that he would change.* ➔ *Opposite* **disbelief**. **2** ⟨IDEA⟩ [C, U] an idea that you are certain is true *religious/political beliefs* **3** ⟨EFFECTIVE⟩ [U, no plural] the feeling that someone or something is effective or right *a belief in social justice* **4** **beyond belief** too bad, good, difficult, etc to be imagined *The evil of this man is beyond belief.*

**believable** /bɪˈliːvəbl/ *adj* If something is believable, you can believe that it could be true or real. ➔ *Opposite* **unbelievable**.

○━**believe** /bɪˈliːv/ *verb* **1** ⟨TRUE⟩ [T] to think that something is true, or that what someone says is true [+ (that)] *They believe that their health has suffered because of the chemicals.* ● *Do you believe him?* ● *I can't believe that she wants to go out with me.* ➔ *Opposite* **disbelieve**. **2** ⟨THINK⟩ [T] to think something, without being completely sure *"Is he coming home tonight?" "I believe so."* ● *The murderer is believed to be in his thirties.* **3** ⟨RELIGION⟩ [I] to have religious beliefs **4** **not believe your eyes/ears** to be very surprised when you see someone or something, or when you hear what someone says *I couldn't believe my ears when Dan said they were getting married.* **5** **believe it or not** used to say that something is true although it seems surprising *He even remembered my birthday, believe it or not.*

**believe in sth** to be certain that something exists *I believe in life after death.*

**believe in sth/doing sth** to be confident that something is effective or right *He believes in saying what he thinks.*

**believer** /bɪˈliːvəʳ/ *noun* [C] **1** a person who has a religious belief **2** **a firm/great/strong, etc believer in sth/doing sth** someone who has confidence in a particular idea or way of doing things *She's a firm believer in freedom of speech.*

**belittle** /bɪˈlɪtl/ *verb* [T] *formal* to say that someone or something is not very important or not very good

**B**

○⚬**bell** /bel/ *noun* [C] **1** a hollow, metal object, shaped like a cup, that makes a ringing sound when you hit it *the sound of church bells ringing* **2** an electrical object that makes a ringing sound when you press a switch *Please ring the bell for attention.* **3 give sb a bell** *UK informal* to telephone someone **4 ring a bell** If a word, especially a name, rings a bell, you think you have heard it before.

**bell**

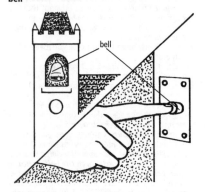

bell

**belligerent** /bə'lɪdʒ°rənt/ *adj* wanting to fight or argue

**bellow** /'beləʊ/ *verb* [I, T] to shout something in a loud voice • **bellow** *noun* [C]

**belly** /'beli/ *noun* [C] *informal* your stomach (= organ where food is digested), or the front part of your body between your chest and your legs

'**belly ,button** *noun* [C] *informal* the small, round, and usually hollow place on your stomach, where you were connected to your mother before birth

○⚬**belong** /bɪ'lɒŋ/ *verb* **1 belong in/on/there, etc** to be in the right place *That chair belongs in the dining room.* **2** [I] to feel happy and comfortable in a place or with a group of people *I never felt that I belonged there.*

**belong to sb** If something belongs to you, you own it. *This necklace belonged to my grandmother.*

**belong to sth** to be a member of a group or organization *We belong to the same youth club.*

**belongings** /bɪ'lɒŋɪŋz/ *noun* [plural] the things that you own *I took a few personal belongings with me.*

**beloved** /bɪ'lʌvɪd/ *adj literary* very much loved *in memory of our beloved son*

○⚬**below** /bɪ'ləʊ/ *adv, preposition* **1** POSITION in a lower position than someone or something else *He could hear people shouting below his window.* • *Send your answers to the address below* (= lower on the page or on a later page). **2** LESS less than an amount or level *The temperature there rarely drops below 22°C.* • *His work is below average.* **3** RANK lower in rank *Monica is a grade below me.*

○⚬**belt**[1] /belt/ *noun* [C] **1** WAIST a long, thin piece of

leather, cloth, or plastic that you wear around your waist ➔ *See colour picture* **Clothes** *on page Centre 5.* **2** AREA an area of a particular type of land, or an area where a particular group of people live *the commuter belt* • *a narrow belt of trees* **3** MACHINE part of a machine that moves in a circle to carry objects or to make a machine work *The car needs a new fan belt.* **4 have sth under your belt** to have already achieved, learnt, or done something important *At 18, she already has several victories under her belt.* **5 tighten your belt** to try to spend less money ➔ *See also:* **conveyor belt**, **green belt**, **safety belt**, **seat belt**.

**belt**[2] /belt/ *verb informal* **1 belt along/down/ through, etc** *UK* to move very fast *He came belting down the street.* **2** [T] to hit someone or something very hard

**belt sth out** to sing something very loudly

**belt up** *UK informal* used to tell someone to stop talking or making a noise *Just belt up, would you? I'm trying to concentrate.*

**belying** /bɪ'laɪɪŋ/ *present participle of* belie

**bemused** /bɪ'mjuːzd/ *adj* slightly confused *He seemed bemused by all the attention.*

**bench** /benʃ/ *noun* [C] **1** a long seat for two or more people, usually made of wood or metal *a park bench* **2 the bench a** in some sports, a place where players sit when they are not playing **b** a judge in court, or judges as a group *Please address your comments to the bench.*

**benchmark** /'benʃmɑːk/ *noun* [C] a level of quality with which other things of the same type can be compared *Her performance set a new benchmark for ballet dancing.*

○⚬**bend**[1] /bend/ *verb* [I, T] *past* **bent 1** to move your body or part of your body so that it is not straight *He was bending over to tie his shoelaces.* • *Bend your knees when lifting heavy objects.* **2** to become curved, or to make something become curved *The trees were bending in the wind.* • *The road bent sharply to the left.* ➔ *See also:* bend over **backwards**, bend the rules (**rule**[1]).

**bend**[2] /bend/ *noun* [C] **1** a curved part of something *a bend in the road/river* **2 drive/send sb round the bend** *informal* to make someone very angry, especially by continuing to do something annoying ➔ *See also:* **hairpin bend**.

**beneath**[1] /bɪ'niːθ/ *adv, preposition* **1** under something, or in a lower position than something *He hid the letter beneath a pile of papers.* • *She looked out of the window at the children playing beneath.* **2** If someone or something is beneath you, you think they are not good enough for you. *He thinks housework is beneath him.*

**benefactor** /'benɪfæktər/ *noun* [C] someone who gives money to help an organization or person

**beneficial** /ˌbenɪ'fɪʃ°l/ *adj* helpful or useful *Exercise is beneficial to almost everyone.*

**beneficiary** /ˌbenɪ'fɪʃ°ri/ *noun* [C] *formal* someone who receives money, help, etc from something or someone else *They were the beneficiaries of free education.*

○⚬**benefit**[1] /'benɪfɪt/ *noun* [C, U] **1** something that helps you or gives you an advantage *I've had* *the benefit of a happy childhood.* **2** money that the government gives to people who are ill, poor, not working, etc *unemployment benefit* **3 for sb's benefit** in order to help someone *We bought the piano for the children's benefit.* **4 give sb the benefit of the doubt** to choose to believe what someone tells you even though it may be wrong or a lie ⊃ *See also:* **child benefit**, **fringe benefit**.

**benefit²** /'benɪfɪt/ *verb* **benefiting**, *past* **benefited 1** [I] to be helped by something *The film benefited from the excellent acting by its stars.* **2** [T] to help someone *The charity supports activities that directly benefit children.*

**benevolent** /bɪ'nevᵊlᵊnt/ *adj formal* kind, generous, and helpful • benevolence /bɪ'nevᵊlᵊns/ *noun* [U]

**benign** /bɪ'naɪn/ *adj* **1** not likely to kill you *a benign tumour* **2** kind, or not intending to harm anyone *a benign ruler*

**bent¹** /bent/ *adj* **1** curved and not now straight or flat *The metal bars were bent and twisted.* **2 bent on sth/doing sth** determined to do something or get something *Both parties are bent on destroying each other's chances of winning.* **3** *UK informal* not honest *a bent policeman*

**bent²** /bent/ *past of* bend

**bequeath** /bɪ'kwiːð/ *verb* [+ two objects] *formal* to formally arrange to give someone something after you die *He bequeathed his art collection to the city of Glasgow.*

**bequest** /bɪ'kwest/ *noun* [C] *formal* money or property that you have arranged for someone to get after you die

**berate** /bɪ'reɪt/ *verb* [T] *formal* to speak angrily to someone *She berated him for being late.*

**bereaved** /bɪ'riːvd/ *adj* If you have been bereaved, someone you loved has died. *bereaved parents* • *The minister spoke quietly with the bereaved.* • bereavement *noun* [C, U] *formal*

**bereft** /bɪ'reft/ *adj formal* **1 bereft of sth** completely without something *They were bereft of new ideas.* **2** [never before noun] alone and extremely sad *She was left bereft by his death.*

**beret** /'bereɪ ⑮ bə'reɪ/ *noun* [C] a round, flat hat made of soft material ⊃ *See colour picture* **Clothes** *on page Centre 5.*

**berry** /'beri/ *noun* [C] a small, round fruit on some plants and trees

**berserk** /bə'zɜːk/ *adj* **go berserk** *informal* to become extremely angry or violent

**berth** /bɜːθ/ *noun* [C] **1** a bed on a boat or train **2** a place for a boat to stay in a port

**beset** /bɪ'set/ *verb* [T] *formal* If problems beset you, they cause you continuing difficulties. [often passive] *The project has been beset by problems from the start.*

o—**beside** /bɪ'saɪd/ *preposition* **1** next to someone or something, or very near them *She knelt beside his bed.* **2 be beside yourself (with sth)** to experience a powerful emotion *He was beside himself with rage.*

**besides¹** /bɪ'saɪdz/ *preposition* in addition to something or someone *Do you play any other sports besides football?*

**besides²** /bɪ'saɪdz/ *adv* **1** used to give another

reason for something *She won't mind if you're late – besides, it's not your fault.* **2** in addition to *Besides looking after the children, she also runs a successful business.*

**besiege** /bɪ'siːdʒ/ *verb* **1 be besieged by/with sb** to have lots of people asking you questions or making demands *The president was besieged by reporters.* **2 be besieged by/with sth** to receive many demands or criticisms *The radio station was besieged with calls from angry listeners.* **3** [T] to surround a place with an army in order to attack it

o—**best¹** /best/ *adj* (*superlative of* good) better than any other *She's one of our best students.* • *Give her my best wishes.* • *Susie's my best friend* (= the friend I like more than any other). • *What's the best way to get to Manchester from here?* ⊃ *See also:* **second best**, the best **thing** since sliced bread.

o—**best²** /best/ *adv* (*superlative of* well) **1** most, or more than any other *Which of the songs did you like best?* **2** in the most suitable or satisfactory way *I sleep best with the windows open.*

**best³** /best/ *noun* **1 the best** someone or something that is better than any other *He's the best of the new players.* **2 at best** used to show that the most positive way of considering something is still not good *At best, only 50 per cent of babies born at 24 weeks will survive.* **3 at his/its, etc best** at the highest level of achievement or quality *The article is an example of journalism at its best.* **4 do/try your best** to make the greatest effort possible *I did my best to persuade him.* **5 bring out the best in sb** to cause someone's best qualities to show **6 make the best of sth** to try to be positive about a situation you do not like but cannot change *Our hotel room is rather small, but we'll just have to make the best of it.* **7 for the best** If something is for the best, it seems unpleasant now, but will improve a situation in the future. *Divorce is always painful, but it really was for the best.* **8 at the best of times** used to show that something is not good when it is the best it can be *He's not exactly patient at the best of times.* **9 have the best of both worlds** to have the advantages of two different situations *Living in the country and working in the city you have the best of both worlds.*

,best 'man *noun* [no plural] a man who stands next to the man who is getting married at the marriage ceremony and helps him

**bestow** /bɪ'stəʊ/ *verb* [T] *formal* to give someone an important present or a public reward for their achievements *He won the Nobel Peace Prize, an honour also bestowed on his colleague.*

**bestseller** /ˌbest'selər/ *noun* [C] a very popular book that many people have bought • bestselling *adj* [always before noun] *best-selling authors*

o—**bet¹** /bet/ *verb* [I, T] **betting**, *past* **bet 1** to risk money on the result of a game, competition, etc *He lost all his money betting on horses.* • [+ two objects + (that)] *I bet him a dollar that I was right.* **2 I bet** *informal* something that you say to show that you believe that something is true or will happen [+ (that)] *I bet that he's forgotten my* birthday again. **3 You bet!** *mainly US informal* used to say that you will do something with enthusiasm *"Are you going to Pam's party?" "You bet!"*

**bet**[2] /bet/ *noun* [C] **1** when you risk money on the result of a game, competition, etc *She won her bet.* • *He* **put a bet** *on Manchester United winning on Saturday.* **2 a good bet** something that would be useful, clever, or enjoyable to do *Putting your savings in a high-interest account would be a good bet.* **3 your best bet** the best decision or choice *Your best bet in terms of value would be the Regent Hotel.* **4 hedge your bets** to avoid choosing one particular thing or action when it is not certain which is the right choice *Journalists are hedging their bets on the likely outcome of the election.* **5 a safe bet** something that you are certain will happen *Wheeler is a safe bet for a place on the team.*

**betray** /bɪ'treɪ/ *verb* [T] **1** PERSON to behave in a dishonest or cruel way to someone who trusts you *When I heard what he had said about me, I felt betrayed.* **2** SECRETS If you betray your country or an organization, you give secret information to its enemies or to other organizations. **3** EMOTION to show an emotion that you were trying to hide *Her face was calm, but her hands betrayed her nervousness.*

**betrayal** /bɪ'treɪəl/ *noun* [C, U] when you betray someone *a betrayal of trust*

o━**better**[1] /'betər/ *adj* **1** (*comparative of* good) of a higher quality, more effective, or more enjoyable than something or someone else *Jeff's been offered a better job in the States.* • *The sales figures were* **better than** *expected.* • *Her English has* **got** *a lot* **better** (= improved) *recently.* • *It would have been better to have discussed the problem first.* **2** healthy, or less ill than before *I feel much better.* • *I hope you get better soon.* **3 the bigger/brighter/hotter, etc the better** used to say that the bigger, brighter, hotter, etc something is, the more pleased they will be

o━**better**[2] /'betər/ *adv* **1** (*comparative of* well) to a greater degree, or in a more successful or effective way *I'd like to get to know you better.* • *Helen did much* **better than** *me in the exam.* **2 he/you, etc had better do sth** used in order to say what you think someone should do *You'd better hurry or you'll miss the train.* **3 know better** to have enough experience not to do something stupid or something that will not achieve anything *I thought she'd listen to me – I should have known better.*

**better**[3] /'betər/ *noun* **1 for the better** If a situation changes for the better, it improves. *Their relationship has changed for the better.* **2 get the better of sb** If a feeling gets the better of you, it becomes too strong to control. *Curiosity finally got the better of her and she opened the letter.*

**better**[4] /'betər/ *verb* [T] to do something better than it has been done before *He bettered his previous best time for a marathon.*

‚**better 'off** *adj* [never before noun] **1** richer *We're a lot better off now that Jane's started work again.* **2** in a better situation *Simon's such an idiot – you'd be better off without him.* **3 you're**

**better off doing sth** used to give advice *You're better off getting a taxi.*

o━**between**[1] /bɪ'twiːn/ *preposition* **1** SPACE in the space that separates two places, people, or things *The town lies halfway between Florence and Rome.* • *A narrow path runs between the two houses.* **2** TIME in the period of time that separates two events or times *The shop is closed for lunch between 12.30 and 1.30.* **3** INVOLVE involving two or more groups of people *Tonight's game is between the New Orleans Saints and the Los Angeles Rams.* **4** AMOUNT used to show the largest and smallest amount or level of something *Between 50 and 100 people will lose their jobs.* **5** CONNECT connecting two or more places or things *There is a regular train service between Glasgow and Edinburgh.* **6** SEPARATE separating two or more things or people *the gap between rich and poor* • *What's the* **difference between** *these two cameras?* **7** SHARE shared by a particular number of people *We drank two bottles of wine between four of us.* **8** AMOUNT If something is between two amounts, it is larger than the first amount but smaller than the second. *The temperature will be between 20 and 25 degrees today.* **9** CHOOSE If you choose between two things, you choose one thing or the other.

o━**between**[2] /bɪ'twiːn/ *adv* (*also* **in between**) **1** in the space that separates two places, people, or things *The wood is in neat piles with newspaper placed between.* **2** in the period of time that separates two events or times *There's a train at 6.15 and one at 10.30 but nothing in between.*

**beverage** /'bevərɪdʒ/ *noun* [C] *formal* a drink

**beware** /bɪ'weər/ *verb* [I] used in order to warn someone to be careful *Beware of the dog.* • [+ of + doing sth] *You should beware of spending too long in the sun.*

**USAGE**

**beware**

You can only use this verb in the imperative or infinitive form.

**bewildered** /bɪ'wɪldəd/ *adj* very confused and not sure what to do *She looked bewildered.* • **bewilderment** *noun* [U] *He stared at me in bewilderment.*

**bewildering** /bɪ'wɪldərɪŋ/ *adj* making you feel confused *There was a bewildering range of subjects to choose from.*

**bewitch** /bɪ'wɪtʃ/ *verb* [T] If someone or something bewitches you, you find them extremely attractive and interesting. *a bewitching smile*

**beyond**[1] /bi'ɒnd/ *preposition* **1** DISTANCE on the other side of something *Our house is just beyond the bridge.* **2** TIME continuing after a particular time or date *A lot of people now live beyond the age of 80.* **3 beyond belief/repair/ recognition, etc** impossible to believe/repair/ recognize, etc *Steven had changed beyond all recognition.* **4** NOT UNDERSTAND *informal* If something is beyond you, you cannot understand it. *Computer studies is completely beyond me.* • *It's beyond me why anyone would want to*

B

*buy that house.* **5** EXCEPT except for *She said very little beyond the occasional 'yes' and 'no'.* **6** INVOLVING OTHERS involving or affecting other things or people than the ones you have talked about *You should try to develop interests beyond the family.*

**beyond²** /bi'ɒnd/ *adv* **1** on the other side of something *From the top of the hill, we could see our house and the woods beyond.* **2** continuing after a particular time or date *The strike looks set to continue into March and beyond.*

**biannual** /baɪˈænjuəl/ *adj* happening twice a year ➔ *Compare* **biennial**.

**bias** /ˈbaɪəs/ *noun* [C, U] when you support or oppose someone or something in an unfair way because you are influenced by your personal opinions *a bias towards/against private education* ● *The news channel has been accused of bias in favour of the government.*

**biased** /ˈbaɪəst/ *adj* showing unfair support for or opposition to someone or something because of your personal opinions *to be biased against/towards younger workers*

**bib** /bɪb/ *noun* [C] a piece of cloth or plastic that is worn by young children when they are eating in order to stop their clothes getting dirty

**bible** /ˈbaɪbl/ *noun* **1 the Bible** the holy book of the Christian and Jewish religions **2** [C] a copy of this book **3** [C] a book or magazine that gives important information and advice about a particular subject *'Vogue' was regarded as the fashion student's bible.*

**biblical** /ˈbɪblɪkəl/ *adj* relating to the Bible

**bibliography** /ˌbɪbliˈɒɡrəfi/ *noun* [C] a list of books and articles on a particular subject

**bicentenary** /ˌbaɪsenˈtiːnəri/ *UK* (*US* **bicentennial** /ˌbaɪsenˈteniəl/) *noun* [C] the day or year that is 200 years after an important event *the bicentenary of Schubert's birth* ● *bicentennial celebrations*

**biceps** /ˈbaɪseps/ *noun* [C] *plural* **biceps** the large muscle at the front of your upper arm

**bicker** /ˈbɪkər/ *verb* [I] to argue about something that is not very important *They were bickering over which channel to watch.*

o⇥**bicycle** /ˈbaɪsɪkl/ *noun* [C] a vehicle with two wheels that you sit on and move by turning the two pedals (= parts you press with your feet) ➔ *See colour picture* **Sports 2** *on page Centre 16.*

**bid¹** /bɪd/ *noun* [C] **1** ATTEMPT an attempt to achieve something *a successful bid for re-election* ● [+ to do sth] *The council has banned cars from the city centre in a bid to reduce pollution.* **2** BUY an offer to pay a particular amount of money for something *I made a bid of $150 for the painting.* **3** WORK an offer to do work for someone for a particular amount of money *We put in a bid for the stadium contract.*

**bid²** /bɪd/ *verb* **bidding,** *past* **bid 1** [I, T] to offer to pay an amount of money for something *They bid $500 million for the company.* **2 bid for sth; bid to do sth** to try to do or obtain something *Five firms have bid for the contract.*

**bid³** /bɪd/ *verb* **bidding,** *past t* **bid** or **bade,** *past p* **bid** or **bidden bid sb farewell/goodbye/ good night, etc** *literary* to say goodbye, good night (= goodbye at night), etc *She bade her guests good night.*

**bidder** /ˈbɪdər/ *noun* [C] someone who offers to pay a particular amount of money for something *The house will be sold to the highest bidder* (= the person who offers to pay the most).

**bidding** /ˈbɪdɪŋ/ *noun* [U] **1** when people offer to pay a particular amount of money for something **2 do sb's bidding** *literary* to do what someone tells you to do

**bide** /baɪd/ *verb* ➔ *See* bide your **time¹**.

**biennial** /baɪˈeniəl/ *adj* happening every two years ➔ *Compare* **biannual**.

o⇥**big** /bɪɡ/ *adj* **bigger, biggest 1** SIZE large in size or amount *I come from a big family.* ● *We're looking for a bigger house.* **2** IMPORTANT important or serious *Tonight's big game is between Real Madrid and Manchester United.* ● *Buying that car was a big mistake.* **3 your big brother/ sister** *informal* your older brother/sister **4** SUCCESSFUL *informal* successful or popular *The programme's been a big hit* (= very popular) *with young children.* **5 make it big** *informal* to become very successful or famous

**big business** *noun* [U] **1** an activity that makes a lot of money *Football has become big business.* **2** large, powerful businesses

**bigot** /ˈbɪɡət/ *noun* [C] a bigoted person

**bigoted** /ˈbɪɡətɪd/ *adj* A bigoted person has very strong, unfair opinions and refuses to consider different opinions. ● **bigotry** /ˈbɪɡətri/ *noun* [U] when someone is bigoted

**big-ticket** /ˈbɪɡˌtɪkɪt/ *adj* [always before noun] *US* Big-ticket items are expensive things to buy, such as cars or furniture.

o⇥**bike** /baɪk/ *noun* [C] **1** *informal short for* bicycle **2** *informal short for* motorbike/motorcycle (= vehicle with two wheels and an engine)

**biker** /ˈbaɪkər/ *noun* [C] someone who rides a motorbike (= vehicle with two wheels and an engine)

**bikini** /bɪˈkiːni/ *noun* [C] a piece of clothing with two parts that women wear for swimming ➔ *See colour picture* **Clothes** *on page Centre 5.*

**bilateral** /baɪˈlætərəl/ *adj* involving two groups or countries *bilateral talks/agreements/trade*

**bile** /baɪl/ *noun* [U] a bitter liquid made and stored in the body that helps to digest fat

**bilingual** /baɪˈlɪŋɡwəl/ *adj* using or able to speak two languages *a bilingual dictionary* ● *She's bilingual.*

o⇥**bill¹** /bɪl/ *noun* [C] **1** PAYMENT a piece of paper that tells you how much you must pay for something you have bought or for a service you have used *Have you paid the electricity bill?* **2** LAW a written plan for a law *Parliament will vote today on whether to pass the reform bill.* **3** MONEY *US* (*UK* **note**) a piece of paper money *a five dollar bill* **4** ENTERTAINMENT *UK* what is on at a cinema or theatre **5** BEAK a bird's beak

**bill²** /bɪl/ *verb* **1 be billed as sth** to be advertised with a particular description *The film was billed as a romantic comedy.* **2** [T] to give or send someone a bill asking for money that they owe for a product or service *He billed us for the materials.*

**billboard** /ˈbɪlbɔːd/ (*also UK* **hoarding**) *noun* [C] a large board used for advertising, especially by the side of a road

**billfold** /ˈbɪlfəʊld/ *US (UK/US* **wallet***) noun* [C] a small, flat container for carrying paper money and credit cards (= plastic cards used for paying with)

**billiards** /ˈbɪliədz/ *noun* [U] a game in which two people try to hit coloured balls into holes around the edge of a table using long, thin sticks

**billing** /ˈbɪlɪŋ/ *noun* [U] **1** when people are sent letters to ask for payments **2 star/top billing** when a particular performer is shown as the most important person in a performance

**billion** /ˈbɪljən/ the number 1,000,000,000

**billow** /ˈbɪləʊ/ *verb* [I] to be moved and spread out by a current of air *Smoke billowed out of the building.*

**bimbo** /ˈbɪmbəʊ/ *noun* [C] *very informal* a young woman who is attractive but not intelligent

o━**bin** /bɪn/ *noun* [C] **1** *UK (US* **trash can***)* a container that is used to put waste in *a rubbish/wastepaper bin* • *I threw it in the bin.* ➔ *See colour picture* **The Office** *on page Centre 12.* **2** a container for storing things *a storage bin*

**binary** /ˈbaɪnᵊri/ *adj* The binary system expresses numbers using only 1 and 0, and is especially used for computers.

**bind¹** /baɪnd/ *verb* [T] *past* **bound 1** TIE to tie something together with string, rope, etc *His hands were bound behind his back.* **2** KEEP PROMISE to force someone to keep a promise *His contract binds him to working a six-day week.* **3** UNITE to unite people *Culture and language bind people together.* **4** BOOK to fasten together pages to make a book *The book was printed and bound in New York.*

**bind²** /baɪnd/ *noun* [no plural] *informal* **1** a difficult or unpleasant situation *a financial bind* **2** *UK* a job which uses a lot of your time *Cleaning the bathroom is a bind.*

**binder** /ˈbaɪndəʳ/ *noun* [C] a strong cover for holding together pieces of paper

**binding** /ˈbaɪndɪŋ/ *adj* A binding agreement, promise, etc cannot be broken or changed. *a legally binding contract*

**binge¹** /bɪndʒ/ *noun* [C] when you eat or drink too much or spend too much money in shops *to go on a drinking binge*

**binge²** /bɪndʒ/ *verb* [I] **binging** or **bingeing** to eat too much food at one time *I've been bingeing on chocolate.*

**bingo** /ˈbɪŋgəʊ/ *noun* [U] a game in which people mark numbers on a card as they are called, and the person whose numbers are called first is the winner

**binoculars** /bɪˈnɒkjələz/ *noun* [plural] a piece of equipment for looking at things that are far away, made from two tubes with glass at the ends *a pair of binoculars*

**biochemical** /ˌbaɪəʊˈkemɪkᵊl/ *adj* relating to the chemistry of living things

**biochemistry** /ˌbaɪəʊˈkemɪstri/ *noun* [U] the study of the chemistry of living things such as plants, animals, or people • **biochemist** *noun* [C] a scientist who studies biochemistry

**biodegradable** /ˌbaɪəʊdɪˈgreɪdəbl/ *adj* Biodegradable substances decay naturally without damaging the environment.

**biographer** /baɪˈɒgrəfəʳ/ *noun* [C] someone who writes the story of a particular person's life

**biography** /baɪˈɒgrəfi/ *noun* [C] the story of a person's life written by another person • **biographical** /ˌbaɪəʊˈgræfɪkəl/ *adj* about someone's life *biographical information*

**biological** /ˌbaɪəˈlɒdʒɪkᵊl/ *adj* **1** relating to the study of living things such as plants and animals *biological sciences* **2** using living things or poisons made from living things *biological weapons* • **biologically** *adv*

**biology** /baɪˈɒlədʒi/ *noun* [U] the study of living things • **biologist** *noun* [C] a scientist who studies biology

**biopsy** /ˈbaɪɒpsi/ *noun* [C] when a small number of cells are taken from a part of the body and examined to see if there is a disease

**biotechnology** /ˌbaɪəʊtekˈnɒlədʒi/ *noun* [U] the use of living cells and bacteria in chemical processes, especially in the food and medical industries

**bipartisan** /baɪˈpɑːtɪzæn/ *adj* involving two political parties *a bipartisan agreement*

**birch** /bɜːtʃ/ *noun* [C, U] a tree that has thin, smooth branches

o━**bird** /bɜːd/ *noun* [C] an animal that has wings and feathers and is usually able to fly

**birdie** /ˈbɜːdi/ *US (UK* **shuttlecock***) noun* [C] a small object with feathers that is used like a ball in badminton (= a sport like tennis)

**bird of ˈprey** *noun* [C] *plural* **birds of prey** a large bird that kills smaller animals for food

**bird-watching** /ˈbɜːdˌwɒtʃɪŋ/ *noun* [U] the hobby of looking at birds

**biro** /ˈbaɪərəʊ/ *noun* [C, U] *UK trademark* a type of pen that has a very small metal ball at its end and a thin tube of ink inside

o━**birth** /bɜːθ/ *noun* **1 give birth** When a woman or an animal gives birth, she produces a baby from her body. *She gave birth to twins.* **2** [C, U] the time when a baby is born *a difficult birth* • *Write your date of birth* (= the date when you were born) *here.* **3** [U] *literary* the beginning of something *the birth of modern science* **4 American/Italian, etc by birth** born in a particular place or having parents with a particular nationality

**ˈbirth cerˌtificate** *noun* [C] an official document that records when and where a person was born

**ˈbirth conˌtrol** *noun* [U] methods of limiting the number of children you have

o━**birthday** /ˈbɜːθdeɪ/ *noun* [C] the day on which someone was born, or the same date each year *She is celebrating her seventieth birthday.* • *Happy Birthday!* • *a birthday cake/party*

**birthmark** /ˈbɜːθmɑːk/ *noun* [C] a mark on someone's skin that has been there since they were born

**birthplace** /ˈbɜːθpleɪs/ *noun* [C] the place where someone was born

**ˈbirth ˌrate** *noun* [C] a measurement of the number of babies born in a particular period

o━**biscuit** /ˈbɪskɪt/ *noun* [C] **1** *UK (US* **cookie***)* a thin, flat cake that is dry and usually sweet ➔ *See colour picture* **Food** *on page Centre 7.* **2** *US* a small, soft, round bread

**bisexual** /baɪˈsekʃʊəl/ *adj* sexually attracted to both men and women

**bishop** /ˈbɪʃəp/ *noun* [C] a priest of high rank in some Christian churches *the Bishop of Oxford*

**bison** /ˈbaɪsᵊn/ *noun* [C] *plural* **bison** a large, wild animal similar to a cow with long hair

o━**bit**¹ /bɪt/ *noun* [C] **1** [SMALL AMOUNT] a small amount or piece of something *I wrote it down on a bit of paper.* • *There's a little bit more pasta left.* • *My favourite bit of the film is right at the end.* • *The books are falling to bits* (= into separate parts). **2 a bit a** slightly *It's a bit cold in here.* • *It was a bit too expensive.* **b** *informal* a short time *I'll see you in a bit.* • *She lived in Italy for a bit.* **3 a bit of a change/fool/problem, etc** a change, fool (= stupid person), problem, etc, but not an important or serious one *I am a bit of a romantic.* • *It was a bit of a shock.* **4 quite a bit** *informal* a lot *He does quite a bit of travelling.* • *She is quite a bit older than him.* **5 a bit much** *informal* more than is fair, or more than you can deal with *It's a bit much to expect me to tidy up their mess.* **6 bit by bit** gradually *She saved up the money, bit by bit.* **7 every bit as** used to emphasize that one thing is equally good, important, etc as something else *The gardens are every bit as impressive as the castle itself.* **8 bits and pieces** small things or jobs which are not connected or not very important *We've packed most of it up now, there are just a few bits and pieces left.* **9** [COMPUTER] a unit of information in a computer **10** [HORSE] a piece of metal which goes in the mouth of a horse to control it

**bit²** /bɪt/ *past tense of* bite

**bitch¹** /bɪtʃ/ *noun* [C] **1** *very informal* an offensive name for an unpleasant woman **2** a female dog

**bitch²** /bɪtʃ/ *verb* [I] *very informal* to talk in an unkind way about people *She's always **bitching about** her boss.*

**bitchy** /ˈbɪtʃi/ *adj* If someone is bitchy, they often say unkind things about people. *a bitchy comment*

o━**bite¹** /baɪt/ *verb past t* **bit**, *past p* **bitten 1** [I, T] to cut something using your teeth *She bit into an apple.* • *He bites his fingernails.* • *He was bitten by a dog.* **2** [I] to begin to have a bad effect *Higher mortgage rates are beginning to bite.* ➔ *See also:* bite the **bullet**, bite the **dust**¹.

**bite²** /baɪt/ *noun* **1** [C] a piece taken from food when you bite it *She **took a bite** from her pizza.* **2** [C] an injury caused when an animal or insect bites you *mosquito bites* **3 a bite** a small meal *I just want to grab a bite to eat.*

**biting** /ˈbaɪtɪŋ/ *adj* A biting wind or biting cold is extremely cold and hurts your skin.

**bitten** /ˈbɪtən/ *past participle of* bite

**bitter¹** /ˈbɪtər/ *adj* **1** [ANGRY] angry and upset because of something bad which has happened that you cannot forget *I feel very **bitter about** my childhood.* **2** [HATE] full of hate or anger *a bitter argument/dispute* **3** [SOUR] having a strong, sour, usually unpleasant taste **4** [COLD] extremely cold *a bitter wind* **5 to/until the bitter end** until something is completely finished, usually something unpleasant *He was determined to stay right to the bitter end.* **6** [DIS-APPOINTED] making you feel very disappointed *Losing the championship was a bitter disappointment.* • **bitterness** *noun* [U]

**bitter²** /ˈbɪtər/ *noun* [U] *UK* a type of beer with a bitter taste

**bitterly** /ˈbɪtᵊli/ *adv* **1** in a way which shows strong negative emotion such as anger or disappointment *We were bitterly disappointed about the decision.* • *Greg complained bitterly about the conditions.* **2** If it is bitterly cold, the weather is extremely and unpleasantly cold.

**bizarre** /bɪˈzɑːr/ *adj* very strange and surprising *bizarre behaviour* • bizarrely *adv*

o━**black¹** /blæk/ *adj* **1** [COLOUR] being the colour of coal or of the sky on a very dark night *a black jacket* ➔ *See colour picture* **Colours** *on page Centre 6.* **2** [PERSON] Someone who is black has the dark skin typical of people from Africa. *black athletes/Americans* **3** [OF BLACK PEOPLE] relating to black people *the black community* **4** [DRINK] Black tea or coffee has no milk or cream added to it. **5** [HUMOUR] funny about unpleasant or frightening subjects *black comedy* **6** [ANGRY] angry *He gave her a black look.* **7** [SITUATION] If your situation or future is black, it is very bad. **8 black and blue** covered with bruises (= marks on your skin from being hit) **9 black and white** very clear or simple *The issue of nuclear weapons is not black and white.* • blackness *noun* [U] ➔ *See also:* **jet-black**, **pitch-black**.

o━**black²** /blæk/ *noun* **1** [C, U] the colour of coal or of the sky on a very dark night *She always dresses in black* (= in black clothes). ➔ *See colour picture* **Colours** *on page Centre 6.* **2** [C] a black person **3 in the black** If your bank account is in the black, it contains some money. **4 in black and white a** printed in a book, newspaper, or official document *Look at the contract – it's all there in black and white.* **b** using or seeing no colours, but only black, white, and grey *I saw the original film in black and white.* ➔ *See also:* **jet-black**.

**black³** /blæk/ *verb*

**black out** *informal* to suddenly become unconscious

**blackberry** /ˈblækbᵊri/ *noun* [C] a small, soft, dark purple fruit with seeds

**blackbird** /ˈblækbɜːd/ *noun* [C] a bird with black feathers and a yellow beak

**blackboard** /ˈblækbɔːd/ (*also US* **chalkboard**) *noun* [C] a large board with a dark surface that teachers write on with chalk (= soft, white rock) ➔ *See colour picture* **Classroom** *on page Centre 4.*

**blackcurrant** /ˌblækˈkʌrᵊnt/ (US) ˈblæk,kɜːrᵊnt/ *noun* [C] *UK* a very small, round, sour, dark purple fruit *blackcurrant juice/jelly*

**blacken** /ˈblækᵊn/ *verb* **1** [I, T] to become black or to make something become black *Storm clouds blackened the sky.* **2** [T] If you blacken someone's name, you say bad things about them.

,**black 'eye** *noun* [C] an eye that has a dark circle around it because it has been hit

,**black 'hole** *noun* [C] an area in outer space that sucks material and light into it from which it cannot escape

**blacklist** /ˈblæklɪst/ *verb* [T] to include someone on a list of people you think are bad or you will not deal with [often passive] *He was blacklisted by the banks and credit card companies.*

,**black 'magic** *noun* [U] magic used for evil

**blackmail** /'blækmeɪl/ *noun* [U] when someone forces you to do something, or to pay them money, by saying they will tell another person something that you want to keep secret • black-mail *verb* [T] [+ into + doing sth] *They used the photographs to blackmail her into spying for them.* • blackmailer *noun* [C]

,**black 'market** *noun* [C] illegal trading of goods that are not allowed to be bought and sold or that there are not enough of for everyone who wants them *the black market in heroin*

**blackout** /'blækaʊt/ *noun* [C] **1** UNCONSCIOUS when someone suddenly becomes unconscious **2** NO INFORMATION when information is kept from people [usually singular] *a media/news blackout* **3** NO ELECTRICITY a failure in the supply of electricity **4** NO LIGHTS a period during a war when no lights must show at night

**blacksmith** /'blæksmɪθ/ *noun* [C] someone whose job is to make things from metal, especially shoes for horses

**bladder** /'blædə/ *noun* [C] the organ where waste liquid is stored before it leaves your body ⟳ *See also:* **gall bladder**.

**blade** /bleɪd/ *noun* [C] **1** the flat, sharp, metal part of a knife, tool, or weapon **2** a long, narrow leaf of grass or a similar plant *a blade of grass* ⟳ *See also:* **razor blade**, **shoulder blade**.

o⁻ᵏ**blame**[1] /bleɪm/ *verb* [T] **1** to say or think that someone or something is responsible for something bad which has happened *Many people blame him for Tony's death.* • *Poor housing is to blame for many of their health problems.* • *They apologized for the delay and blamed it on technical problems.* **2 I don't blame him/them/you, etc** used to say that you understand and accept the reason for what someone is doing *"I think I'll go home early." "I don't blame you – you look really tired."*

o⁻ᵏ**blame**[2] /bleɪm/ *noun* [U] when people say that someone or something is responsible for something bad *The manager should take the blame for the team's defeat.* • *They put the blame on faulty equipment.*

**blameless** /'bleɪmləs/ *adj* not responsible for anything bad *They concluded that Lucy was entirely blameless.*

**bland** /blænd/ *adj* **1** not interesting or exciting *bland statements* **2** If food is bland, it does not have much taste.

**blank**[1] /blæŋk/ *adj* **1** with no writing, pictures, or sound *a blank page* • *a blank tape* • *The space for the date was left blank.* **2 go blank** If your mind goes blank, you suddenly cannot remember or think of something. **3** showing no feeling or understanding *a blank expression* ⟳ *See also:* **point-blank**.

**blank**[2] /blæŋk/ *noun* **1** [C] an empty space on a piece of paper or form where information can be given *Just fill in the blanks.* **2 draw a blank** to be unable to get information, think of something, or achieve something *All their investigations have drawn a blank so far.*

,**blank 'cheque** UK (*mainly US* ,**blank 'check**) *noun* [C] If you give someone a blank cheque,

you allow them as much money as they want or need to do something.

**blanket**[1] /'blæŋkɪt/ *noun* [C] **1** a thick, warm cover that you sleep under **2** a thick layer of something *a blanket of cloud/snow*

**blanket**[2] /'blæŋkɪt/ *adj* [always before noun] including or affecting everything *a blanket ban*

**blanket**[3] /'blæŋkɪt/ *verb* [T] to completely cover something *The ground was blanketed with snow.*

**blankly** /'blæŋkli/ *adv* without showing any emotion or understanding *She just stared at me blankly.*

**blare** /bleə/ (*also* **blare out**) *verb* [I] to make a very loud noise *There was music blaring from his room.*

**blasphemy** /'blæsfəmi/ *noun* [U] something which you say or do that shows you do not respect God or a religion • blasphemous /'blæsfəməs/ *adj* expressing blasphemy

**blast**[1] /blɑːst/ *noun* **1** EXPLOSION [C] an explosion *a bomb blast* **2** AIR [C] a sudden strong movement of air *a blast of cold air/heat* **3 full blast** If something is happening or working full blast, it is at its loudest, strongest, or fastest level. *The heating was on full blast.* **4** NOISE [C] a sudden loud noise *a blast on the trumpet* **5** ENJOYMENT [no plural] *US very informal* an exciting and enjoyable experience *Eric's party was a blast.*

**blast**[2] /blɑːst/ *verb* **1** NOISE [I, T] (*also* **blast out**) to make a very loud noise *rock music blasting from a stereo* **2** MOVE [I, T] to move through something or to hit something with force *Dixon blasted the ball past the goalkeeper.* **3** EXPLODE [T] to break through rock using explosives *They blasted a hole in the rock face.* **4** GUNS [T] to destroy a person or place with guns or bombs **blast off** When a spacecraft blasts off, it leaves the ground to go into space.

**blast**[3] /blɑːst/ *exclamation UK* used when you are annoyed at something *Blast! I forgot my keys.*

**blast-off** /'blɑːstɒf/ *noun* [U] when a spacecraft leaves the ground

**blatant** /'bleɪt²nt/ *adj* very obvious, with no attempt to be honest or behave well *blatant lies/racism* • blatantly *adv*

**blaze**[1] /bleɪz/ *verb* [I] to burn or shine very brightly or strongly *The sun blazed down on the dry countryside.*

**blaze**[2] /bleɪz/ *noun* [C] **1** a large, strong fire *The blaze started in the hall.* **2 a blaze of colour/lights, etc** very bright colour, lights, etc *The tulips provided a blaze of colour outside her window.* **3 a blaze of glory/publicity** a lot of public attention for a short time

**blazer** /'bleɪzə/ *noun* [C] a type of jacket, often worn as part of a school uniform

**blazing** /'bleɪzɪŋ/ *adj* [always before noun] **1** very hot *a blazing log fire* **2** UK very angry *a blazing row*

**bleach**[1] /bliːtʃ/ *noun* [U] a strong chemical used for cleaning things or removing colour from things

**bleach**[2] /bliːtʃ/ *verb* [T] to remove the colour

B

from something or make it lighter using chemicals *She's bleached her hair.*

**bleak** /bliːk/ *adj* **1** If a situation is bleak, there is little or no hope for the future. *The future is looking bleak for small clubs struggling with debts.* **2** If a place is bleak, it is cold, empty and not attractive. *a bleak landscape* • **bleakness** *noun* [U]

**bleary** /ˈblɪəri/ *adj* If you have bleary eyes, you cannot see clearly because you are tired or have just woken up.

**bleat** /bliːt/ *verb* [I] **1** to make the noise of a sheep or goat **2** to speak or complain in a weak and annoying way *She keeps bleating about her lack of money.* • **bleat** *noun* [C]

**bled** /bled/ *past of* bleed

**bleed** /bliːd/ *verb* [I] *past* **bled** to have blood coming from a cut in your body • **bleeding** *noun* [U] *Try to stop the bleeding.*

**bleep** /bliːp/ *noun* [C] a short, high electronic noise • **bleep** *verb* [I]

**bleeper** /ˈbliːpəʳ/ *UK* (*UK/US* **beeper**) *noun* [C] a small piece of electronic equipment which you carry that makes a sound when someone wants to speak to you

**blemish** /ˈblemɪʃ/ *noun* [C] a mark which spoils the appearance of someone or something

**blend¹** /blend/ *verb* **1** [T] to mix two or more things together completely *Blend the ingredients into a smooth paste.* **2** [I, T] to combine two or more things *The team blends new, young players with more mature, experienced ones.*

**blend in** If something or someone blends in, they look or seem the same as the people or things around them and so are not easily noticed. *Their uniform is designed so that they blend in with the background.*

**blend²** /blend/ *noun* [C] a combination of two or more things *Their music is a blend of jazz and African rhythms.*

**blender** /ˈblendəʳ/ *noun* [C] an electric machine for making soft foods into a smooth liquid ➔ *See colour picture* **Kitchen** *on page Centre 10.*

**bless** /bles/ *verb* [T] **1** to ask God to help or protect someone or something, or to make it holy *The priest blessed their marriage.* **2** **be blessed with sth** to be lucky enough to have something good *He's blessed with a wonderful singing voice.* **3** **bless you!** something you say when someone sneezes • **bless her/him/them, etc** *informal* used to show your affection for the person you are talking about *Peter, bless him, slept all the way through it.*

**blessed** /ˈblesɪd/ *adj* [always before noun] **1** pleasant and wanted very much *The rain was a blessed relief.* **2** holy *the Blessed Virgin Mary*

**blessing** /ˈblesɪŋ/ *noun* **1** LUCK [C] something which is lucky or makes you happy *It is a blessing that no one was hurt.* **2** APPROVAL [U] approval that someone gives to a plan or action *Mr Newton has given his blessing for the plan.* **3** RELIGION [C, U] protection or help from God, or a prayer to ask for this **4 a blessing in disguise** something that has a good effect, although at first it seemed that it would be bad **5 a mixed blessing** something which has both good and bad effects

**blew** /bluː/ *past tense of* blow

**blight** /blaɪt/ *noun* [no plural] something which has a very bad effect on something, often for a long time *the blight of poverty/unemployment* • **blight** *verb* [T] to cause damage to or have a bad effect on something *Injury has blighted his career.*

o—←**blind¹** /blaɪnd/ *adj* **1** not able to see *She went blind after an accident.* • *This project provides guide dogs for the blind.* **2 be blind to sth** to not notice something, or not want to notice something *Drivers who speed are often blind to the risks they cause.* **3 blind panic/rage/trust, etc** an extremely strong feeling that makes you do things without thinking **4 a blind corner/bend** *UK* a bend or corner on a road that is dangerous because you cannot see cars coming around it • **blindness** *noun* [U] ➔ *See also:* **colour-blind,** turn a blind **eye¹** (to sth).

**blind²** /blaɪnd/ *verb* **1** [T] to make someone blind, either for always or for a short time [often passive] *I was blinded by the car headlights.* **2 blind sb to sth** to make someone unable to understand the truth about someone or something *Love blinded her to all his faults.*

**blind³** /blaɪnd/ *noun* [C] a cover that you pull down over a window ➔ *See also:* **venetian blind.**

**blind 'date** *noun* [C] a romantic meeting between a man and a woman who have not met before

**blindfold** /ˈblaɪndfəʊld/ *noun* [C] a piece of cloth that you put over someone's eyes so they cannot see • **blindfold** *verb* [T] to put a blindfold on someone

**blinding** /ˈblaɪndɪŋ/ *adj* **1** A blinding light is extremely bright. **2** A blinding headache (= pain in the head) is extremely painful.

**blindly** /ˈblaɪndli/ *adv* **1** not able to see or not noticing what is around you *Carly reached blindly for the light switch.* **2** not thinking about what you are doing *They just blindly followed orders.*

**'blind ,spot** *noun* [C] **1** a difficulty in accepting or understanding a particular thing *She has a complete blind spot where relations with the press are concerned.* **2** the part of the road just behind you, that you cannot see when you are driving

**blink** /blɪŋk/ *verb* **1** [I, T] to open and close both of your eyes quickly **2** [I] If a light blinks, it goes on and off quickly. • **blink** *noun* [C]

**blinkered** /ˈblɪŋkəd/ *adj* not willing to consider new or different ideas *a blinkered attitude*

**blip** /blɪp/ *noun* [C] **1** a small, temporary, and usually negative change from what usually happens *The rise in unemployment may just be a blip.* **2** a small spot of light on an electronic screen, sometimes with a short, high sound

**bliss** /blɪs/ *noun* [U] complete happiness *My idea of bliss is lying on a sunny beach.* • **blissful** *adj* making you feel very happy *a blissful childhood* • **blissfully** *adv* She seemed blissfully unaware of the chaos she had caused.

**blister¹** /ˈblɪstəʳ/ *noun* [C] a painful, raised area of skin with liquid inside, that you get if your skin has been rubbed or burned, or a similar area on a painted surface

**blister²** /ˈblɪstəʳ/ *verb* [I, T] to get or cause blisters

**blistering** /ˈblɪstərɪŋ/ *adj* **1** CRITICISM using

very strong criticism *a blistering attack* **2** HEAT extremely hot *blistering sunshine* **3** SPEED extremely fast *The economy has grown at a blistering pace.*

**blithely** /'blaɪðli/ *adv* without thinking about what might happen *People were blithely ignoring warnings not to swim in the river.*

**blitz¹** /blɪts/ *noun* [C] **1** a lot of activity to achieve something in a short time *We had a cleaning blitz before my parents came home.* **2 the Blitz** bomb attacks on British cities during the Second World War

**blitz²** /blɪts/ *verb* [T] **1** to defeat someone or something completely **2** to drop bombs on something

**blizzard** /'blɪzəd/ *noun* [C] a storm with strong winds and snow

**bloated** /'bləʊtɪd/ *adj* **1** swollen because of air or liquid inside **2** feeling uncomfortable because you have eaten too much

**blob** /blɒb/ *noun* [C] a small amount of a thick liquid *a blob of cream/glue* ➜ *See colour picture* **Quantities** *on page Centre 14.*

**bloc** /blɒk/ *noun* [C] a group of countries with similar political ideas, who work together *the communist bloc*

**block¹** /blɒk/ *noun* [C] **1** PIECE a solid piece of something, usually in the shape of a square or rectangle *a block of ice/stone/wood* **2** DISTANCE *US* the distance along a street from where one road crosses it to the place where the next road crosses it *They only live two blocks away from the school.* **3** BUILDING a large building containing many apartments or offices *(UK) a block of flats* **4** GROUP OF BUILDINGS a square group of buildings or houses with roads on each side *Omar took the dog for a walk **round the block.*** **5** CANNOT THINK If you have a block about something, you cannot understand it or remember it. *I had a complete **mental block** about his name.* **6** STOP PROGRESS something that makes it difficult to move or make progress **7** AMOUNT an amount or group of something that is considered together *This block of seats is reserved.* ➜ *See also:* be a **chip¹** off the old block, **stumbling block**, **tower block**.

**block**

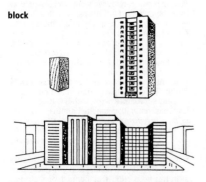

o⚫**block²** /blɒk/ *verb* [T] **1** CANNOT PASS *(also block up)* to prevent anyone or anything from passing through a place *A fallen tree blocked*

the road. • *The sink is blocked up.* • *a blocked drain* **2** STOP PROGRESS to stop something from happening or making progress *The council's blocked plans for a new supermarket.* **3** CANNOT SEE to be between someone and the thing they are looking at, so that they cannot see *A pillar was blocking my view.*

**block sth off** to close a road, path, or entrance so that people cannot use it *Police blocked off the road where the body was found.*

**block sth out 1** to try to stop yourself thinking about something unpleasant *I've blocked out memories of the accident.* **2** to stop light or noise passing through something *Most sunscreens block out ultraviolet B radiation.*

**blockade** /blɒk'eɪd/ *noun* [C] when a government or soldiers stop goods or people from entering or leaving a place *The government **imposed a blockade on** oil trading.* • blockade *verb* [T]

**blockage** /'blɒkɪdʒ/ *noun* [C] something that stops something else passing through *His death was caused by a blockage in his arteries.*

**blockbuster** /'blɒk,bʌstə'/ *noun* [C] *informal* a book, film, etc that is very popular and successful *a new blockbuster movie*

**block 'capitals** *noun* [plural] letters in the form A, B, C, not a, b, c

**bloke** /bləʊk/ *noun* [C] *UK informal* a man *Jake's a nice bloke.*

**blonde¹** (*also blond*) /blɒnd/ *adj* **1** Blonde hair is pale yellow. ➜ *See colour picture* **Hair** *on page Centre 9.* **2** Someone who is blonde has pale yellow hair.

**blonde²** (*also blond*) /blɒnd/ *noun* [C] someone, especially a woman, who has pale yellow hair

o⚫**blood** /blʌd/ *noun* [U] **1** the red liquid that flows around your body *a blood test/sample* **2** the family or place that you come from *I've got some Spanish blood in me.* **3 be in your blood** If something is in your blood, you and other people in your family are interested in it or good at it. *Sailing is in my blood.* **4 bad blood** feelings of hate between people because of things that have happened in the past *There's been bad blood between them for years.* **5 in cold blood** in a cruel way, without showing any emotion *He shot three policemen in cold blood.* **6 new blood** new people in an organization who will provide new ideas and energy ➜ *See also:* your own **flesh** and blood.

**bloodbath** /'blʌdbɑːθ/ *noun* [no plural] an extremely violent event in which many people are killed

**blood-curdling** /'blʌd,kɜːdlɪŋ/ *adj* extremely frightening *a blood-curdling scream*

**'blood ,donor** *noun* [C] someone who gives some of their blood for ill people who need it

**'blood ,group** *UK* (*UK/US* **blood type**) *noun* [C] one of the groups that human blood is divided into

**bloodless** /'blʌdləs/ *adj* achieved without killing or violence *a bloodless coup*

**'blood ,pressure** *noun* [U] the force with which blood flows around your body *high/low blood pressure*

**bloodshed** /'blʌdʃed/ *noun* [U] when people are killed or injured in fighting *Peace talks have failed to end the bloodshed in the region.*

**B**

**bloodshot** /'blʌdʃɒt/ *adj* Bloodshot eyes are red in the part that should be white.

'blood ˌsport *noun* [C] a sport in which animals are killed

**bloodstained** /'blʌdsteɪnd/ *adj* Something that is bloodstained has blood on it.

**bloodstream** /'blʌdstriːm/ *noun* [no plural] the flow of blood around your body *The dead driver had very high levels of alcohol in his bloodstream.*

**bloodthirsty** /'blʌd,θɜːsti/ *adj* enjoying using or watching violence

'blood transˌfusion *noun* [C] when blood is put into someone's body

'blood ˌtype (*also UK* **blood group**) *noun* [C] one of the groups that human blood is divided into

'blood ˌvessel *noun* [C] one of the small tubes that blood flows through in your body

**bloody**[1] /'blʌdi/ *adj* **1** covered in blood *bloody hands* **2** violent and involving a lot of blood and injuries *a bloody war*

**bloody**[2] /'blʌdi/ *adj, adv UK very informal* used to show anger or to emphasize what you are saying in a slightly rude way *I can't find my bloody keys.* • *We were bloody lucky to win.*

**bloom**[1] /bluːm/ *noun* **1** [C] a flower *beautiful, pink blooms* **2** **in bloom** with flowers that are open *In June the roses are in bloom.*

**bloom**[2] /bluːm/ *verb* [I] **1** If a plant blooms, its flowers open. **2** to develop and become successful, happy, or healthy *Their romance bloomed while they were in Paris.*

**blossom**[1] /'blɒsᵊm/ *noun* [C, U] a small flower, or the small flowers on a tree or plant *cherry blossom*

**blossom**[2] /'blɒsᵊm/ *verb* [I] **1** If a tree blossoms, it produces flowers. **2** to develop and become successful or beautiful *She has blossomed into a world champion.*

**blot**[1] /blɒt/ *verb* [T] **blotting**, *past* **blotted** to dry wet marks using soft paper or a cloth

**blot sth out** **1** to stop yourself from thinking about something unpleasant *I've tried to blot out memories of my relationship with Dieter.* **2** If smoke or cloud blots out the sun, it prevents it from being seen.

**blot**[2] /blɒt/ *noun* **1** [C] a mark on something, made by ink or paint falling on it **2** **a blot on sth** something that spoils something else *The financial scandal was a blot on his reputation.*

**blotch** /blɒtʃ/ *noun* [C] a mark on something, especially your skin • **blotchy** (*also* **blotched**) *adj* having blotches

'blotting ˌpaper *noun* [U] thick paper used for drying wet ink

**blouse** /blaʊz ⑮ blaʊs/ *noun* [C] a piece of clothing like a shirt that women wear

o▬**blow**[1] /bləʊ/ *verb past t* **blew**, *past p* **blown** **1** WIND [I] If the wind blows, it moves and makes currents of air. *A cool sea breeze was blowing.* **2** PERSON [I] to force air out through your mouth *She blew on her coffee before taking a sip.* **3** **blow sth down/across/off, etc** If the wind blows something somewhere, it makes it move in that direction. *The storm blew trees across the road.* **4** MOVE [I] to move in the wind *branches blowing in the breeze* **5** INSTRUMENT [I, T] to make a sound by forcing air out of your mouth and

through an instrument *Ann blew a few notes on the trumpet.* **6** MAKE [T] to make shapes out of something by blowing it *to blow bubbles* **7** SPEND [T] *informal* to spend a lot of money quickly and without considering it seriously *Lou blew all her prize money on a diamond necklace.* **8** **blow it/your chance(s)** *informal* If you blow it or blow your chance, you lose an opportunity to do something by doing or saying the wrong thing. *I blew it when I criticized the way she ran the office.* • *Tom blew his chances of getting the job by arriving late for the interview.* **9** **blow your nose** to clear your nose by forcing air through it into a handkerchief (= piece of cloth or soft paper) **10** ELECTRICITY [I, T] If a piece of electrical equipment blows, it suddenly stops working because the electric current is too strong. ➔ *See also:* blow your **mind**[1], blow sth out of **proportion**.

**blow sb away** *mainly US informal* to surprise or please someone very much *a movie that will blow you away.*

**blow (sth) out** If a flame blows out, or if you blow it out, it stops burning because you or the wind have blown it. *Emma blew out the candle.*

**blow over** If a storm or an argument blows over, it ends.

**blow (sb/sth) up** to destroy something or kill someone with a bomb, or to be destroyed by a bomb *Terrorists blew up an office building in the city.*

**blow sth up** to fill something with air *blow up a balloon*

**blow up** **1** If a storm or an argument blows up, it starts suddenly. **2** *informal* to suddenly become very angry *My Dad blew up at me when I told him what had happened.*

**blow**[2] /bləʊ/ *noun* [C] **1** DISAPPOINTMENT a shock or disappointment *Losing his job was a terrible blow to him.* **2** HIT a hard hit with a hand or heavy object *He suffered serious blows to the head during the attack.* **3** INSTRUMENT when you blow something or blow into an instrument or other object *a blow on the whistle* **4** **come to blows** to fight or argue

**blow-by-blow** /ˌbləʊbaɪ'bləʊ/ *adj* **a blow-by-blow account/description** a description of an event that gives all the details in the exact order that they happened

**blow-dry** /'bləʊdraɪ/ *verb* [T] to dry your hair in a particular style using a hairdryer (= electrical equipment for drying hair) • **blow-dry** *noun* [no plural] *I had a cut and blow-dry.*

**blown** /bləʊn/ *past participle of* blow

**blowout** /'bləʊaʊt/ *noun* [C] **1** TYRE when a tyre suddenly explodes while a vehicle is still moving **2** MEAL/PARTY *informal* an expensive meal or a big party **3** SPORT *US informal* when one team or player beats another easily in a sport

**bludgeon** /'blʌdʒᵊn/ *verb* [T] to hit someone several times with a heavy object [often passive] *She was bludgeoned to death with a hammer.*

o▬**blue**[1] /bluː/ *adj* **1** COLOUR being the same colour as the sky when there are no clouds *a dark blue jacket* ➔ *See colour picture* **Colours** *on page Centre 6.* **2** SAD *informal* sad **3** SEX *about sex a blue joke/movie* ➔ *See also:* **black**[1] and blue, once in a blue **moon**.

o━**blue²** /bluː/ *noun* **1** [C, U] the colour of the sky when there are no clouds ⊃ *See colour picture* **Colours** *on page Centre 6*. **2 out of the blue** If something happens out of the blue, you did not expect it. *One day, completely out of the blue, I had a letter from her.*

**bluebell** /'bluːbel/ *noun* [C] a plant with small, blue flowers shaped like bells

**blueberry** /'bluːbᵊri/ *noun* [C] a small, sweet, dark blue fruit that grows on bushes

**blue-chip** /ˌbluːˈtʃɪp/ *adj* [always before noun] A blue-chip company or investment is considered certain to make a profit.

**blue-collar** /ˌbluːˈkɒləʳ/ *adj* [always before noun] A blue-collar worker does physical work, especially in a factory.

**blueprint** /'bluːprɪnt/ *noun* [C] a plan that shows how someone will design, build, or achieve something *a blueprint for political reform*

**blues** /bluːz/ *noun* [plural] **1** a type of slow, sad music that was developed by African-Americans *jazz and blues* **2 have/get the blues** *informal* to feel or become sad

**bluff¹** /blʌf/ *verb* [I, T] to pretend you will do something or that you have knowledge, in order to force someone to do something *He won't really leave her – he's only bluffing.*

**bluff²** /blʌf/ *noun* **1** [C] an attempt to bluff **2 call sb's bluff** to tell someone to do the thing they say they will do, because you do not think they will do it

**blunder¹** /'blʌndəʳ/ *noun* [C] a serious and often stupid mistake *a series of financial blunders*

**blunder²** /'blʌndəʳ/ *verb* **1** [I] to make a serious mistake **2 blunder around/into, etc** to move somewhere in a heavy way, as if you cannot see well *He blundered around, looking for the light switch.*

**blunt¹** /blʌnt/ *adj* **1** not sharp *a blunt knife* **2** saying exactly what you think without caring about people's feelings *a blunt letter* • **bluntness** *noun* [U]

**blunt²** /blʌnt/ *verb* [T] **1** to make a feeling less strong *Mario's comments blunted everyone's enthusiasm.* **2** to make something less sharp

**bluntly** /'blʌntli/ *adv* saying exactly what you think without caring about people's feelings *"I don't believe a word you're saying," she replied bluntly.*

**blur¹** /blɜːʳ/ *verb* [I, T] **blurring**, *past* **blurred** **1** to make the difference between two things less clear, or to make it difficult to see the exact truth about something *a book that blurs the distinction between reality and fiction* **2** to become difficult to see clearly, or to make something become difficult to see clearly *soft sunlight that blurred the edges of the mountains*

**blur**

**blur²** /blɜːʳ/ *noun* [no plural] something that you cannot see

or remember clearly *The accident happened so quickly that it's all a blur.*

**blurb** /blɜːb/ *noun* [C] a short description to advertise a product, especially a book

**blurred** /blɜːd/ *adj* **1** (*also* **blurry** /'blɜːri/) not clear *a blurred photograph* • *blurred memories* **2** If your sight is blurred, you cannot see clearly. *blurred vision*

**blurt** /blɜːt/ (*also* **blurt out**) *verb* [T] to say something suddenly and without thinking, especially because you are excited or nervous *"Will you marry me?" he blurted.*

**blush** /blʌʃ/ *verb* [I] If you blush, your face becomes red, especially because you are embarrassed. *He blushed with shame.* • **blush** *noun* [C]

**blusher** /'blʌʃəʳ/ *UK* (*US* **blush**) *noun* [U] red powder or cream that women put on their faces in order to make them more attractive ⊃ *See picture at* **make up.**

**bluster** /'blʌstəʳ/ *verb* [I, T] to speak in a loud and angry way, often with little effect • **bluster** *noun* [U]

**blustery** /'blʌstᵊri/ *adj* very windy *a cold, blustery day*

**boar** /bɔːʳ/ *noun* [C] **1** a male pig **2** (*also* **wild boar**) a wild pig

**board¹** /bɔːd/ *noun* **1** ⟨WOOD⟩ [C] a long, thin, flat piece of wood *He nailed some boards across the broken window.* **2** ⟨SURFACE⟩ [C] a flat piece of wood, plastic, etc used for a particular purpose *an ironing board* • *a chopping board* **3** ⟨INFORMATION⟩ [C] a piece of wood, plastic, etc on a wall, where information can be put *Have you seen the poster on the board?* **4** ⟨SCHOOL ROOM⟩ [C] a surface on the wall of a school room that the teacher writes on *Copy down the sentences from the board.* **5** ⟨GAMES⟩ [C] a piece of wood, cardboard, etc for playing games on *a chess board* **6** ⟨ORGANIZATION⟩ [group] a group of people who officially control a company or organization, or a particular type of business activity *The board approved the sales plan.* • *the Gas/Tourist Board* **7 on board** on a boat, train, aircraft, etc **8** ⟨MEALS⟩ [U] meals that are provided when you stay in a hotel *bed and board* • *How much is a single room with full board* (= all meals)? **9 across the board** affecting everyone or every part of something *Jobs are likely to be lost across the board.*, ⊃ *See*

**board**

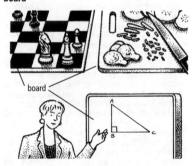

board

*also:* **bulletin board**, **diving board**, **drawing board**, **full board**, **half board**, **ironing board**.

**board²** /bɔːd/ *verb* **1** [I, T] to get on a bus, boat, aircraft, etc *He boarded the train to London.* **2** [I] If an aircraft, train, etc is boarding, passengers are getting onto it. *The plane is now boarding at gate 26.*

**board sth up** to cover a door or window with wooden boards

**boarder** /'bɔːdəʳ/ *noun* [C] **1** STUDENT UK a student who lives at school **2** PERSON US (UK **lodger**) someone who pays for a place to sleep and meals in someone else's house **3** SPORT someone who goes snowboarding (= sport where you stand on a board to move over snow)

'**board ,game** *noun* [C] a game such as chess that is played on a board

'**boarding ,house** *noun* [C] a house where you pay for a room and meals

'**boarding ,pass** (*also* '**boarding ,card**) *noun* [C] a piece of paper you must show to get on an aircraft

'**boarding ,school** *noun* [C] a school where students live and study

**boardroom** /'bɔːdruːm/ *noun* [C] a room where the people who control a company or organization have meetings

**boast¹** /bəʊst/ *verb* **1** [I, T] to talk with too much pride about what you have done or what you own *I wish she would stop boasting about her exam results.* • [+ that] *Liam boasted that he owned two sports cars.* **2** [T] If a place boasts something good, it has it. *New York boasts some of the best museums in the world.*

**boast²** /bəʊst/ *noun* [C] something you are proud of and like to tell people about

**boastful** /'bəʊstfʊl/ *adj* talking with too much pride *boastful remarks*

o-=**boat** /bəʊt/ *noun* **1** [C] a vehicle for travelling on water *a fishing/sailing boat* **2 be in the same boat** to be in the same unpleasant situation as other people *She complains that she doesn't have enough money, but we're all in the same boat.* **3 miss the boat** to be too late to get what you want *I'm afraid you've missed the boat. All the tickets have been sold.* **4 push the boat out** UK to spend a lot of money, especially when you are celebrating **5 rock the boat** to do or say something that changes a situation in a way that causes problems ➜ *See also:* **rowing boat**.

**bob** /bɒb/ *verb* [I] **bobbing**, *past* **bobbed** to move up and down quickly and gently *boats bobbing in the harbour*

**bobby** /'bɒbi/ *noun* [C] UK informal old-fashioned a police officer

'**bobby ,pin** US (UK **hairgrip**) *noun* [C] a small, thin piece of metal, used to fasten a woman's hair in position

**bode** /bəʊd/ *verb literary* **bode ill/well** to be a bad or good sign for the future *These religious differences do not bode well for their marriage.*

**bodily¹** /'bɒdɪli/ *adj* [always before noun] relating to a person's body *bodily strength*

**bodily²** /'bɒdɪli/ *adv* If you move someone bodily, you lift or push them. *He carried her bodily out of the room.*

o-=**body** /'bɒdi/ *noun* **1** PERSON [C] the whole physical structure of a person or animal *the human body* • *They covered their bodies with mud.* ➜ *See colour picture* **The Body** *on page Centre 2.* **2** DEAD [C] a dead person *Police found the body in a field.* **3** NOT ARMS/LEGS [C] the main part of a person or animal's body, not the head, arms, or legs *a dog with a thin body and short legs* **4** GROUP [group] an official group of people who work together *the sport's regulatory body* **5** MAIN PART [no plural] the main part of something *The body of the book is about his childhood.* **6** AMOUNT [no plural] a large amount of information *a body of research into AIDS* **7** VEHICLE [C] the main part of a vehicle *The body of the ship was not damaged.*

**bodybuilding** /'bɒdibɪldɪŋ/ *noun* [U] doing exercises with heavy weights to make your muscles big • **bodybuilder** *noun* [C]

**bodyguard** /'bɒdigɑːd/ *noun* [C] someone whose job is to protect someone

'**body ,language** *noun* [U] the way you move your body, that shows people what you are feeling

**bog¹** /bɒg/ *noun* [C, U] an area of soft, wet ground

**bog²** /bɒg/ *verb*

**be bogged down** to become so involved in something that you cannot do anything else *Try not to get too bogged down in details.*

**boggle** /'bɒgl/ *verb* **the mind boggles** UK informal (US informal **it boggles the mind**) something you say if something is difficult for you to accept, imagine, or understand *The mind boggles at the stupidity of some people.* ➜ *See also:* **mind-boggling**.

**bogus** /'bəʊgəs/ *adj* pretending to be real *a bogus doctor* • *bogus documents*

**bohemian** /bəʊ'hiːmiən/ *adj* typical of artists, musicians, etc, who live in a more informal way than most people

o-=**boil¹** /bɔɪl/ *verb* [I, T] **1** LIQUID If a liquid boils, or if you boil it, it reaches the temperature where bubbles rise up in it and it produces steam. *I'll boil some water for a cup of tea.* • *boiling water* **2** CONTAINER If a container of liquid boils, or if you boil it, the liquid inside it reaches the temperature where bubbles rise up in it and it produces steam. *I've boiled the kettle.* **3** COOK to cook food in water that is boiling *Boil the pasta for 10 minutes.* ➜ *See picture at* **cook**.

**boil down to sth** If a situation or problem boils down to something, that is the main reason for it. *The problem boils down to one thing – lack of money.*

**boil over 1** If a liquid that is being heated boils over, it flows over the side of the pan. **2** If a difficult situation or bad emotion boils over, it cannot be controlled any more and people start to argue or fight. *Finally her anger boiled over and she started hitting him.*

**boil²** /bɔɪl/ *noun* **1 bring sth to the boil** to heat something until it starts to produce bubbles and steam *Bring the water to the boil, then add the rice.* **2** [C] a red swollen area on the skin that is infected

**boiler** /'bɔɪləʳ/ *noun* [C] a piece of equipment that provides hot water for a house

B

**boiling** /ˈbɔɪlɪŋ/ (also **boiling ˈhot**) adj informal very hot *It's boiling in here!*

**ˈboiling ˌpoint** noun [C] the temperature that a liquid boils at

**boisterous** /ˈbɔɪstᵊrəs/ adj noisy and full of energy *a boisterous child* • boisterously adv

**bold** /bəʊld/ adj 1 not frightened of taking risks *It was a bold decision to go and live abroad.* 2 strong in colour or shape *bold colours* • *a bold design* • boldly adv • boldness noun [U]

**bollard** /ˈbɒlɑːd/ noun [C] UK a short thick post in a road, used to stop cars driving somewhere

**bolster** /ˈbəʊlstəʳ/ verb [T] to make something stronger by supporting or encouraging it *Strong sales and high profits are bolstering the economy.*

**bolt¹** /bəʊlt/ noun [C] 1 a metal bar that you push across a door or window to lock it 2 a small piece of metal that is used with a nut (= metal piece with a hole in the middle) to fasten pieces of wood or metal together ⊃ *See picture at* **tool.** ⊃ *See also:* the nuts (**nut**) and bolts.

**bolt²** /bəʊlt/ verb 1 [FASTEN] to fasten two things together with a bolt *The seats in the cinema were bolted to the floor.* 2 [LOCK] to lock a door or window with a bolt *I bolted the door before going to bed.* 3 **bolt down/out/through, etc** to move suddenly and quickly *The cat bolted out of the door when it saw the dog.* 4 [EAT] (also **bolt down**) to eat something very quickly

**ˌbolt ˈupright** adv sitting or standing with your back very straight

○-**bomb¹** /bɒm/ noun [C] a weapon that explodes and causes damage *The bomb destroyed several office buildings in the city.* ⊃ *See also:* **atomic bomb.**

**bomb²** /bɒm/ verb 1 [T] to attack a place using bombs *The factories were bombed during the war.* 2 **bomb along/down/through, etc** UK informal to move very quickly *A car came bombing down the road.*

**bombard** /bɒmˈbɑːd/ verb [T] to continuously attack a place using guns and bombs • bombardment noun [C, U] an aerial bombardment **bombard sb with sth** to give someone so much information, ask them so many questions, etc that it is difficult for them to deal with

**bomber** /ˈbɒməʳ/ noun [C] 1 an aircraft that drops bombs 2 someone who puts a bomb somewhere

**bombshell** /ˈbɒmʃel/ noun [C] informal a piece of usually bad news that surprises you very much *He dropped a bombshell by announcing that he was quitting the sport.*

**bona fide** /ˌbəʊnəˈfaɪdi/ adj real and honest *Make sure you are dealing with a bona fide company.*

**bonanza** /bəˈnænzə/ noun [C] a situation in which many people are successful and get a lot of money *The Internet is a bonanza for the computer industry.*

**bond¹** /bɒnd/ noun [C] 1 an interest, experience, or feeling that makes two people feel connected *A love of opera created a bond between them.* 2 an official document from a government or company to show that you have given them money that they will pay back with a certain amount of extra money

**bond²** /bɒnd/ verb 1 [I, T] If two things bond, they stick together, or if you bond them, you make them stick together. *This glue bonds wood and metal in seconds.* 2 [I] to develop a strong relationship with someone *Physical contact helps a mother bond with her baby.*

**bondage** /ˈbɒndɪdʒ/ noun [U] when someone is completely controlled by something or is a slave (= owned by the person they work for)

○-**bone¹** /bəʊn/ noun 1 [C, U] one of the hard pieces that make the structure inside a person or animal *He broke a bone in his hand.* 2 **a bone of contention** something that people argue about 3 **have a bone to pick with sb** informal to want to talk to someone because you are annoyed about something they have done 4 **make no bones about sth/ doing sth** to say what you think or feel, with-out being embarrassed *She made no bones about her reluctance to work with me.*

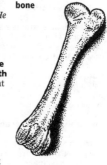

bone

**bone²** /bəʊn/ verb [T] to remove the bones from meat or fish

**ˈbone ˌmarrow** noun [U] the soft substance inside bones

**bonfire** /ˈbɒnfaɪəʳ/ noun [C] a large fire outside, often used for burning waste

**bonkers** /ˈbɒŋkəz/ adj informal crazy

**bonnet** /ˈbɒnɪt/ noun [C] 1 UK (US **hood**) the metal cover of a car's engine ⊃ *See colour picture* **Car** *on page Centre 3.* 2 a hat that you tie under your face

**bonus** /ˈbəʊnəs/ noun [C] 1 an extra amount of money that you are given, especially because you have worked hard *All employees received a bonus of £500.* 2 another pleasant thing in addition to something you were expecting *The sunny weather was an added bonus.*

**bony** /ˈbəʊni/ adj very thin, so that you can see or feel bones *bony elbows*

**boo** /buː/ verb [I, T] booing, past booed to shout the word "boo" to show that you do not like a speech, performance, etc • boo noun [C]

**boob** /buːb/ noun [C] informal 1 a woman's breast 2 a silly mistake

**booby prize** /ˈbuːbiˌpraɪz/ noun [C] a prize that you get if you finish last in a competition

**booby trap** /ˈbuːbiˌtræp/ noun [C] something dangerous, especially a bomb, that is hidden somewhere that looks safe • booby-trap verb [T] [often passive] *His car was booby-trapped.*

○-**book¹** /bʊk/ noun 1 [C] a set of pages fastened together in a cover for people to read *a book about animals* • *Please open your books.* 2 **a book of stamps/tickets, etc** a set of stamps, tickets, etc that are fastened together inside a cover 3 [C] a set of pages fastened together in a cover and used for writing on *an address book* 4 **do sth by the book** to do something exactly as the rules tell you **5 be in sb's good/bad books** *UK informal* If you are in someone's good books, they are pleased with you, and if you are in their bad books, they are angry with you. ➲ *See also:* **cookery book**, take a **leaf**[1] out of sb's book, **phone book**, **reference book**.

o━**book**[2] /bʊk/ *verb* **1** ARRANGE [I, T] to arrange to use or do something at a particular time in the future *to book a ticket/hotel room* • *We've booked a trip to Spain for next month.* • *Sorry, the hotel is fully booked* (= has no more rooms). **2** CRIME [T] to officially accuse someone of a crime *Detectives booked him for resisting arrest.* **3** SPORT [T] If a sports official books you, they write an official record of something you have done wrong. *The referee booked two players for fighting during the game.*

**book in/book into sth** *UK* to say that you have arrived when you get to a hotel

**book sb in/book sb into sth** *mainly UK* to arrange for someone to stay at a hotel

**bookcase** /'bʊkkeɪs/ *noun* [C] a piece of furniture with shelves for putting books on ➲ *See colour picture* **The Living Room** *on page Centre 11.*

**bookie** /'bʊki/ *noun* [C] *informal* someone whose job is to take and pay out money that people risk trying to guess the result of horse races, sports events, etc

**booking** /'bʊkɪŋ/ *noun* [C, U] *mainly UK* an arrangement you make to have a hotel room, tickets, etc at a particular time in the future *Many hotels won't accept bookings for less than two nights.* • *advance booking*

**bookkeeping** /'bʊkˌkiːpɪŋ/ *noun* [U] recording the money that an organization or business spends and receives • **bookkeeper** *noun* [C]

**booklet** /'bʊklət/ *noun* [C] a small, thin book that contains information *The tourist office has booklets about the area.*

**bookmaker** /'bʊkˌmeɪkəʳ/ *noun* [C] a bookie

**bookmark** /'bʊkmɑːk/ *noun* [C] **1** something you put in a book so you can find the page you want **2** a record of an address on the Internet so that you can quickly find something again *Add this website to your bookmarks.*

**books** /bʊks/ *noun* [plural] the written financial records of a business or organization

**bookseller** /'bʊkˌseləʳ/ *noun* [C] a person or company that sells books

**bookshop** /'bʊkʃɒp/ *UK* (*US* **bookstore** /'bʊkstɔːʳ/) *noun* [C] a shop that sells books

**bookworm** /'bʊkwɜːm/ *noun* [C] *informal* someone who enjoys reading very much

**boom**[1] /buːm/ *noun* [C] **1** a period when there is a big increase in sales or profits *an economic boom* • *The 1990's saw a boom in computer sales.* **2** a loud, deep sound ➲ *See also:* **baby boom**.

**boom**[2] /buːm/ *verb* [I] **1** If something is booming, it is increasing or becoming more successful or popular very quickly. *House prices are booming.* **2** to make a loud, deep sound, or to speak in a loud, deep voice

**boomerang** /'buːməˈræŋ/ *noun* [C] a curved piece of wood that comes back to you when you throw it

**boon** /buːn/ *noun* [C] something helpful that improves your life [usually singular] *Microwaves are a boon for busy people.*

**boost**[1] /buːst/ *noun* [C] something that makes you feel more confident and happy, or that helps something increase or improve *Increased tourism was a major boost to the local economy.*

**boost**[2] /buːst/ *verb* [T] to increase or improve something *Getting the job has boosted my confidence.*

**booster** /'buːstəʳ/ *noun* **1 a confidence/morale, etc booster** something that makes you feel happier or more confident **2** [C] an engine on a spacecraft that gives extra power for the first part of a flight

**boot**[1] /buːt/ *noun* [C] **1** a strong shoe that covers your foot and part of your leg *a pair of boots* ➲ *See colour picture* **Clothes** *on page Centre 5.* **2** *UK* (*US* **trunk**) a closed space at the back of a car for storing things in ➲ *See colour picture* **Car** *on page Centre 3.* **3 get/be given the boot** *informal* to be told that you must leave your job **4 too big for your boots** *UK informal* (*US* **too big for your britches** *informal*) behaving as if you are more important or more clever than you really are ➲ *See also:* **car boot sale**.

**boot**[2] /buːt/ *verb* [T] *informal* to kick someone or something

**boot sb out** *informal* to make someone leave a place or job

**booth** /buːð/ *noun* [C] a small area that is separated from a larger public area, especially used for doing something privately *a telephone booth*

**booty** /'buːti/ *noun* [U] valuable things stolen by thieves or by an army in a war

**booze**[1] /buːz/ *noun* [U] *informal* alcoholic drinks

**booze**[2] /buːz/ *verb* [I] *informal* to drink alcohol

o━**border**[1] /'bɔːdəʳ/ *noun* [C] **1** the line that separates two countries or states *the border between France and Spain* • *We crossed the border from Canada into the US.* **2** a strip around the edge of something for decoration *white plates with a blue border*

**border**[2] /'bɔːdəʳ/ *verb* [T] **1** to form a line around the edge of something [often passive] *The fields are bordered by tall trees.* **2** to have a border with another country [often passive] *Spain is bordered by France and Portugal.*

**border on sth** to almost be a more extreme thing *Her anger bordered on aggression.*

**borderline**[1] /'bɔːdᵊlaɪn/ *adj* If something or someone is borderline, it is not clear if they are good enough or if they will succeed. *Borderline cases should take the exam again.*

**borderline**[2] /'bɔːdᵊlaɪn/ *noun* [no plural] the point where one feeling, quality, level, etc ends and another one begins *My work was on the borderline between two grades.*

**bore**[1] /bɔːʳ/ *verb* **1** [T] to make someone feel bored *His war stories really bore me.* **2** [I, T] to make a hole in something hard with a tool

**bore**[2] /bɔːʳ/ *noun* **1** [C] someone who talks too much about things that are not interesting **2** [no plural] a situation or job that annoys you because it causes difficulties or is not interesting *It's a real bore not having a car.*

**bore**[3] /bɔːʳ/ *past tense of* bear

o━**bored** /bɔːd/ *adj* feeling tired and unhappy because something is not interesting or because you have nothing to do *I'm **bored with** doing homework.* • *We were **bored stiff** (= extremely bored) in her lessons.* • boredom /'bɔːdəm/ *noun* [U] when you are bored *I nearly died of boredom.*

○━**boring** /'bɔːrɪŋ/ *adj* not interesting or exciting *a boring job* • *The film was so boring, I fell asleep.*

---

**USAGE**

**bored** or **boring**?

**Bored** is used to describe how someone feels about something.

*He didn't enjoy the lesson because he was bored.*

~~He didn't enjoy the lesson because he was boring.~~

If something or someone is **boring**, they make you feel bored.

*The book was long and boring.*

---

○━**born¹** /bɔːn/ *verb* **be born 1** When a person or animal is born, they come out of their mother's body and start to exist. *She was born in London in 1973.* • *an American-born writer* (= born in America) **2** If an idea is born, it starts to exist.

**born²** /bɔːn/ *adj* **a born actor/leader/teacher, etc** someone who has a natural ability to act, lead, teach, etc

**born-again** /ˌbɔːnə'gen/ *adj* **a born-again Christian** someone who has become a very enthusiastic member of the Christian religion

**borne** /bɔːn/ *past participle of* bear

**borough** /'bʌrə ⑮ 'bɜːrəʊ/ *noun* [C] a town or part of a city

○━**borrow** /'bɒrəʊ/ *verb* **1** USE [T] to use something that belongs to someone else and give it back later *Can I borrow a pen please?* • *I borrowed the book from my sister.* **2** MONEY [I, T] to take money from a bank or financial organization and pay it back over a period of time **3** IDEA [T] to take and use a word or idea *The English word 'rucksack' is borrowed from German.*

**borrower** /'bɒrəʊəʳ/ *noun* [C] someone who borrows money

**bosom** /'bʊzᵊm/ *noun* **1** [C] a woman's breasts **2 a bosom buddy/pal, etc** a very good friend

**boss¹** /bɒs/ *noun* [C] someone who is responsible for employees and tells them what to do *I'll ask my boss if I can leave work early tomorrow.*

**boss²** /bɒs/ (*also* **boss about/around**) *verb* [T] to tell someone what they should do all the time *My older brother is always bossing me about.*

**bossy** /'bɒsi/ *adj* always telling other people what to do • bossiness *noun* [U]

**botanist** /'bɒtᵊnɪst/ *noun* [C] someone who studies plants

**botany** /'bɒtᵊni/ *noun* [U] the scientific study of plants • botanic /bə'tænɪkəl/ (*also* **botanic** /bə'tænɪk/) *adj* relating to botany

**botch** /bɒtʃ/ (*also* **botch up**) *verb* [T] to spoil something by doing it badly *a botched robbery*

○━**both** /bəʊθ/ *pronoun, determiner, quantifier* **1** used to talk about two people or things *The children both have red hair.* • *Both her parents*

are dead. • ***Both of** my sisters are teachers.* • *Would you like cream, ice cream, or both?* **2 both...and...** used to emphasize that you are talking about two people or things *Both Jack and his wife are keen chess players.* ➔ *See also:* have the **best³** of both worlds.

○━**bother¹** /'bɒðəʳ/ *verb* **1** ANNOY [T] to annoy someone by trying to get their attention when they do not want to see you or talk to you *Don't bother your father when he's working.* • *Sorry to bother you, but could you spare any change?* **2** WORRY [T] to make someone feel worried or upset *Living on my own doesn't bother me at all.* **3** DO [I, T] to make the effort to do something [+ doing sth] *Don't bother making the bed – I'll do it later.* • [+ to do sth] *He didn't even bother to call.* **4 can't be bothered** *informal* If you can't be bothered to do something, you are too lazy or tired to do it. [+ to do sth] *I can't be bothered to iron my clothes.* **5 not bothered** *UK informal* If you are not bothered about something, it is not important to you and does not worry you. *"Do you want tea or coffee?" "Either, I'm not bothered."* • *I'm not bothered whether I win or lose.*

**bother²** /'bɒðəʳ/ *noun* [U] trouble or problems *"Are you sure you don't mind taking me?" "No, it's no bother, really!"*

**bothered** /'bɒðəd/ *adj* [never before noun] If you are bothered about something, it is important to you and you are worried about it. *He's very **bothered about** what other people think.*

○━**bottle¹** /'bɒtl/ *noun* [C] a container for liquids, usually made of glass or plastic, with a narrow top *an empty bottle* • *a bottle of wine* ➔ *See also:* **hot-water bottle**.

**bottle²** /'bɒtl/ *verb* [T] to put liquid into a bottle [often passive] *This wine was bottled in France.* • *bottled beer/water*

**bottle sth up** to not allow yourself to show or talk about your feelings

'**bottle ˌbank** *noun* [C] *UK* a large container outside, where you can put empty bottles so that the glass can be used again

**bottleneck** /'bɒtlnek/ *noun* [C] **1** something that causes a process to happen more slowly than it should **2** a narrow part of a road where traffic moves slowly

○━**bottom¹** /'bɒtəm/ *noun* **1** LOWEST PART [C] the lowest part of something [usually singular] *Click on the icon **at the bottom** of the page.* **2** FLAT SURFACE [C] the flat surface on the lowest side of something [usually singular] *There was a price tag on **the bottom** of the box.* **3** LOWEST POSITION [no plural] the lowest position in a group, organization, etc *He got bad exam marks and is **at the bottom** of the class.* **4** SEA/RIVER ETC [no plural] the ground under a river, lake, or sea *Divers found the wreck on the **bottom** of the ocean.* **5** FURTHEST PART [no plural] the part of a road or area of land that is furthest from where you are *Go to the bottom of the road and turn left.* **6** PART OF THE BODY [C] the part of your body that you sit on **7 be at the bottom of sth** to be the cause of a problem or situation **8 get to the bottom of sth** to discover the truth about a situation ➔ *See also:* **rock bottom**, from **top¹** to bottom.

**bottom²** /'bɒtəm/ *adj* [always before noun] in the lowest position *the bottom drawer*

**bottomless** /'bɒtəmləs/ *adj* **a bottomless pit** a supply, especially of money, that has no limit

**the ˌbottom 'line** *noun* the most important fact in a situation *The bottom line is that if you don't work, you'll fail the test.*

**bough** /baʊ/ *noun* [C] *literary* a large branch on a tree

**bought** /bɔːt/ *past of* buy

**boulder** /'bəʊldə'/ *noun* [C] a very large rock

**boulevard** /'buːləvɑːd/ *noun* [C] a wide road in a city, usually with trees along it

**bounce¹** /baʊns/ *verb* **1** BALL [I, T] to hit a surface and then move quickly away, or to make something do this *The ball bounced high into the air.* **2** JUMP [I] to jump up and down several times on a soft surface *The children loved bouncing on the bed.* **3 bounce along/ around/into, etc** to move somewhere in a happy and energetic way *Sarah bounced into the room with a big smile on her face.* **4** NOT PAY [I, T] If a cheque (= piece of printed paper you write on to pay for things) bounces, or a bank bounces it, the bank will not pay it because there is not enough money in the account.

**bounce back** to be successful or happy again after a failure, disappointment, etc *After a terrible start the team bounced back and won the game.*

**bounce²** /baʊns/ *noun* [C, U] when something bounces, or the quality that makes something able to bounce

**bouncer** /'baʊnsə'/ *noun* [C] someone whose job is to stand at the door of a bar, party, etc and keep out people who are not wanted

**bouncy** /'baʊnsi/ *adj* **1** happy and full of energy *She's very bouncy and confident.* **2** able to bounce *bouncy balls*

**bound¹** /baʊnd/ *adj* **1 bound to do sth** certain to do something, or certain to happen *You're bound to feel nervous before your driving test.* **2 bound up with sth** closely connected with something *A country's culture is bound up with its language and history.* **3** [never before noun] having a moral or legal duty to do something *The witness was bound by an oath to tell the truth.* **4** [never before noun] travelling towards a particular place *He was on a train bound for Berlin.*

**bound²** /baʊnd/ *verb* **bound across/down/ into, etc** to move quickly with large steps or jumps *Guy bounded across the room to answer the phone.*

**bound³** /baʊnd/ *noun* [C] a big jump ⊃ *See also:* by/in leaps (**leap²**) and bounds.

**bound⁴** /baʊnd/ *past of* bind

**boundary** /'baʊndᵊri/ *noun* [C] **1** a line that divides two areas or forms an edge around an area *The mountains mark the **boundary** between the two countries.* **2** a limit *Such violence is beyond the boundaries of civilized conduct.*

**boundless** /'baʊndləs/ *adj* having no limit *boundless energy/enthusiasm*

**bounds** /baʊndz/ *noun* **1** [plural] legal or social limits *They have overstepped the bounds of good taste.* **2 out of bounds** If a place is out of

bounds, you are not allowed to go there. *The staff room is out of bounds to students.*

**bounty** /'baʊnti/ *noun* **1** [C, U] a large or generous amount of something **2** [C] an amount of money paid as a reward

**bouquet** /bʊ'keɪ/ *noun* [C] flowers that are tied together in an attractive way

**bourbon** /'bɜːbən/ *noun* [C, U] a type of American whisky (= strong alcoholic drink)

**bourgeois** /'bɔːʒwɑː/ *adj* typical of middle class people who are too interested in money and correct social behaviour *bourgeois values*
• **the bourgeoisie** /ˌbɔːʒwɑː'ziː/ *noun* [group] the middle class, that owns most of society's money

**bout** /baʊt/ *noun* [C] **1** a short period of activity or illness *a bout of depression* **2** a fight in boxing

**boutique** /buː'tiːk/ *noun* [C] a small shop that sells fashionable clothes

**bovine** /'bəʊvaɪn/ *adj* relating to cows

**bow¹** /baʊ/ *verb* [I, T] to bend your head or body forward in order to show respect or to thank an audience *The actors all bowed after the performance.* • *We **bowed** our **heads** in prayer.*

**bow out** to leave a job or stop doing an activity, usually after a long time *He **bowed** out of politics at the age of 70.*

**bow to sth/sb** to do what someone else wants you to do *The government are refusing to bow to public pressure.*

**bow²** /baʊ/ *noun* [C] **1** when you bow *The actors came back on stage and **took a bow**.* **2** the front part of a ship

**bow³** /bəʊ/ *noun* [C] **1** KNOT a knot with two curved parts and two loose ends, that is used to tie shoes or as decoration **2** MUSIC a long, thin piece of wood with hair stretched between the ends, used to play some musical instruments **3** WEAPON a piece of curved wood with string fixed to both ends, used for shooting arrows

**bowel** /baʊəl/ *noun* [C] the long tube that carries solid waste from your stomach out of your body [usually plural] *He's got trouble with his bowels.*

o─ᴗ**bowl¹** /bəʊl/ *noun* [C] a round, deep dish used for holding soup and other food *a bowl of rice/soup*

**bowl²** /bəʊl/ *verb* [I, T] **1** to roll a ball along a surface as part of a game **2** in cricket, to throw a ball to the person who has to hit it

**bowler** /'bəʊlə'/ *noun* [C] in cricket, the player who throws the ball so someone can hit it ⊃ *See colour picture* **Sports 2** *on page Centre 16.*

**ˌbowler 'hat** *UK* (*US* **derby**) *noun* [C] a round, hard, black hat worn by men, especially in the past

**bowling** /'bəʊlɪŋ/ *noun* [U] a game in which you roll a large ball along a wooden track in order to knock down bottle-shaped objects

**bowls** /bəʊlz/ *noun* [U] *UK* a game in which you roll large balls as close as possible to a smaller ball

**ˌbow 'tie** *noun* [C] a piece of cloth around the neck in the shape of a bow that men sometimes wear, especially at formal events ⊃ *See colour picture* **Clothes** *on page Centre 5.*

o─ᴗ**box¹** /bɒks/ *noun* **1** CONTAINER [C] a square or

**box** 80 o━ Important words to learn

**B**

rectangular container *a cardboard box* • *a box of chocolates/matches* ➔ *See picture at* **container**. **2** [SQUARE SPACE] [C] a small square on a page that gives you information or where you write information *Tick the box if you would like more details*. **3** [SMALL PLACE] [C] a small area of a theatre, court, etc that is separate from where other people are sitting **4 the box** *informal* the television *What's on the box tonight?* ➔ *See also:* **phone box, post box, witness box**.

**box²** /bɒks/ *verb* **1** [I, T] to do the sport of boxing **2** [T] (*also* **box up**) to put something in a box *We boxed up the old books and put them in the attic.*
**box sb/sth in** to move so close to someone or something that they cannot move [often passive] *When I returned I found that my car had been boxed in.*

**boxer** /'bɒksər/ *noun* [C] someone who does the sport of boxing

**'boxer ,shorts** *noun* [plural] loose underwear worn by men ➔ *See colour picture* **Clothes** *on page Centre 5*.

**boxing** /'bɒksɪŋ/ *noun* [U] a sport in which two people hit each other while wearing big, leather gloves (= pieces of clothing for your hands) ➔ *See colour picture* **Sports 1** *on page Centre 15*.

**'Boxing ,Day** *noun* [C, U] 26 December, a public holiday in Britain and Canada

**'box ,office** *noun* [C] the place in a theatre, cinema, etc where you buy tickets

o━**boy¹** /bɔɪ/ *noun* **1** [C] a male child or young man *We've got three children – a boy and two girls.* **2 the boys** *informal* a group of male friends *Steve's gone out with the boys.*

**boy²** /bɔɪ/ (*also* **oh boy**) *exclamation* used when you are excited or pleased *Boy, that was good!*

**boycott** /'bɔɪkɒt/ *noun* [C] when someone refuses to buy, use, or do something because they do not approve of it *Environmental groups have called for a boycott of the company's products.* • **boycott** *verb* [T] *Several countries boycotted the international peace talks.*

o━**boyfriend** /'bɔɪfrend/ *noun* [C] a man or boy who someone is having a romantic relationship with

**boyhood** /'bɔɪhʊd/ *noun* [U] the part of a male's life when they are a boy

**boyish** /'bɔɪɪʃ/ *adj* like a boy *boyish charm* • *a boyish face*

**,Boy 'Scout** *UK* (*US* **'Boy ,Scout**) *noun* [C] a boy who belongs to an organization that teaches boys practical skills

**bra** /brɑː/ *noun* [C] a piece of woman's underwear that supports the breasts ➔ *See colour picture* **Clothes** *on page Centre 5*.

**brace¹** /breɪs/ *verb* **brace yourself** to prepare for something difficult or unpleasant *I braced myself for bad news.*

**brace²** /breɪs/ *noun* [C] **1** something that supports or holds something in the correct position *He wore a neck brace for months after the accident.* **2** a wire object that some children wear to make their teeth straight

**bracelet** /'breɪslət/ *noun* [C] a piece of jewellery that you wear around your wrist ➔ *See picture at* **jewellery**.

**braces** /'breɪsɪz/ *UK* (*US* **suspenders**) *noun* [plural] two straps fixed to a pair of trousers that go over your shoulders and stop the trousers from falling down

**bracing** /'breɪsɪŋ/ *adj* Bracing weather or a bracing activity makes you feel cold but healthy and full of energy. *bracing sea air* • *a bracing walk*

**bracket¹** /'brækɪt/ *noun* [C] **1** a group of people whose ages, taxes, etc are between two limits *Most heart attack victims are in the 45–65 age bracket.* **2** a piece of metal, wood, etc, that is fixed to a wall to support something, especially a shelf

**bracket²** /'brækɪt/ *verb* [T] **1** to put curved lines ( ) around words, phrases, numbers, etc to make them separate **2** to consider two or more people or things to be similar [often passive] *Canadian accents are often bracketed with American accents.*

**brackets** /'brækɪts/ (*also* **parentheses**) *noun* [plural] *UK* two curved lines ( ) used around extra information or information that should be considered as separate from the main part

**brag** /bræg/ *verb* [I] **bragging**, *past* **bragged** to talk with too much pride about what you have done or what you own *He's always bragging about how much money he earns.*

**braid¹** /breɪd/ *noun* **1** [C] *US* (*UK* **plait**) a single piece of hair made by twisting three thinner pieces over and under each other ➔ *See colour picture* **Hair** *on page Centre 9*. **2** [U] a thin piece of cloth or twisted threads used for decorating clothes

**braid²** /breɪd/ *US* (*UK* **plait**) *verb* [T] to twist three pieces of hair over and under each other

**braille** /breɪl/ *noun* [U] a system of printing for blind people, using raised patterns that they read by touching

o━**brain** /breɪn/ *noun* **1** [C] the organ inside your head that controls your thoughts, feelings, and movements *brain damage* **2** [C] *informal* an extremely intelligent person [usually plural] *This university attracts some of the best brains in the country.* **3 brains** intelligence *He has brains and good looks.* **4 have sth on the brain** *informal* to think or talk about something all the time *You've got football on the brain!* **5 the brains behind sth** *informal* the person who has planned and organized something successful *Anthony is the brains behind the project.*

**brainchild** /'breɪntʃaɪld/ *noun* **the brainchild of sb** someone's new and clever idea or invention *The project is the brainchild of a Japanese designer.*

**brainstorm** /'breɪnstɔːm/ *US* (*UK* **brainwave**) *noun* [C] a sudden, clever idea

**brainstorming** /'breɪnˌstɔːmɪŋ/ *noun* [U] when a group of people meet to develop new ideas *a brainstorming session*

**brainwash** /'breɪnwɒʃ/ *verb* [T] to make someone believe something by telling them that it is true many times [+ into + doing sth] *Advertising often brainwashes people into buying things they do not really need.* • **brainwashing** *noun* [U]

**brainwave** /'breɪnweɪv/ *UK* (*US* **brainstorm**) *noun* [C] a sudden, clever idea

**B**

**brainy** /'breɪni/ adj informal clever

**brake¹** /breɪk/ noun [C] **1** the part of a vehicle that makes it stop or go more slowly **2** something that stops or slows the progress of something High inflation has **put the brakes on** economic growth.

**brake²** /breɪk/ verb [I] to make a vehicle stop or move more slowly, using its brake Pierre braked to avoid hitting the dog.

'**brake ˌpedal** noun [C] the part of a car which you push with your foot to make it go more slowly ➔ See colour picture **Car** on page Centre 3.

o─**branch¹** /brɑːnʃ/ noun [C] **1** TREE one of the many parts of a tree that grows out from its trunk (= main, vertical part) ➔ See picture at **tree. 2** BUSINESS one of several shops, offices, etc that are part of a company or organization a bank with branches all over the country **3** SUBJECT a part of a subject Neurology is a branch of medicine.

**branch²** /brɑːnʃ/ (also **branch off**) verb [I] If a road, path, etc branches, it separates into two or more roads, paths, etc.

**branch out** to start to do something different from what you usually do, especially in your job After working in publishing, she **branched out into** journalism.

**brand¹** /brænd/ noun [C] **1** a product that is made by a particular company Which brand of toothpaste do you use? **2** a particular type of something a team that plays a distinctive brand of football

**brand²** /brænd/ verb [T] **1** to describe someone or something in a way that makes them seem bad The media branded him a liar. **2** to burn a mark on an animal to show who owns it

**brandish** /'brændɪʃ/ verb [T] to wave something in the air, especially a weapon He came running into the room, brandishing a gun.

'**brand ˌname** noun [C] the special name that a company gives to a product

ˌbrand '**new** adj completely new

**brandy** /'brændi/ noun [C, U] a strong alcoholic drink made from wine

**brash** /bræʃ/ adj too confident a brash young businessman

**brass** /brɑːs/ noun [U] **1** a shiny yellow metal a door with a brass handle **2** the group of musical instruments made from brass a brass band

**brat** /bræt/ noun [C] a child who behaves badly a spoilt brat

**bravado** /brə'vɑːdəʊ/ noun [U] behaviour that is intended to make people admire you for your bravery and confidence

o─**brave¹** /breɪv/ adj showing no fear of dangerous or difficult situations He died after a brave fight against cancer. • **bravely** adv

**brave²** /breɪv/ verb [T] to deal with a dangerous or unpleasant situation in a brave way Crowds braved the cold weather to watch the game.

**bravery** /'breɪvəri/ noun [U] when someone is brave

**bravo** /brɑː'vəʊ/ exclamation something you shout to show that you approve of something, for example a performance

**brawl** /brɔːl/ noun [C] a noisy fight, usually in public a drunken brawl in a bar • brawl verb [I]

**brazen** /'breɪz²n/ adj not feeling at all ashamed about your bad behaviour a brazen cheat • **brazenly** adv

**breach¹** /briːtʃ/ noun **1** [C, U] when someone breaks a rule, agreement, or law a policy that is in breach of international law • He was sued for **breach of** contract. **2** [C] formal a serious disagreement between two groups, countries, etc

**breach²** /briːtʃ/ verb [T] to break a rule, law, or agreement

o─**bread** /bred/ noun [U] a basic food made by mixing and baking flour, water, and sometimes yeast (= substance that makes it rise) a slice of bread • a loaf of white bread ➔ See also: the best/greatest **thing** since sliced bread.

**bread**

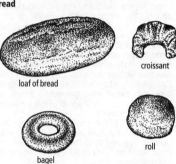

croissant

loaf of bread

roll

bagel

**breadcrumbs** /'bredkrʌmz/ noun [plural] very small pieces of dry bread, used in cooking

**breadth** /bretθ/ noun [U, no plural] **1** the distance from one side of something to the other side a swimming pool with a breadth of 10 metres and a length of 50 metres **2** sb's **breadth of experience/knowledge/interest,** etc the great number of different things that someone has done, knows, is interested in, etc ➔ See also: the **length** and breadth of sth.

**breadwinner** /'bred,wɪnər/ noun [C] the person who earns the money in a family

o─**break¹** /breɪk/ verb past t **broke,** past p **broken** **1** SEPARATE [I, T] to separate into two or more pieces, or to make something separate into two or more pieces The vase fell on the floor and broke. • They had to break a window to get in. **2 break your arm/leg,** etc to damage a bone in your arm/leg, etc Carolyn broke her leg in a skiing accident. **3** NOT WORK [I, T] If you break a machine, object, etc, or if it breaks, it stops working because it is damaged. Who broke the video? **4 break an agreement/promise/rule,** etc to not do what you should according to an agreement/promise/rule, etc Police stopped him for breaking the speed limit. **5 break the law** to do something illegal **6 break the news to sb** to tell someone about something unpleasant that has happened Who's going to break the news to his wife? **7 break the silence** to make a noise, speak, etc and end a period of silence The silence was broken by a sudden knock at the door. **8 break a habit/routine,** etc to stop doing something that you usually do **9 break a record** to do something faster, better, etc than anyone else *He broke the world record for the 200m.* **10** REST [I, T] to stop the activity you are doing to have a short rest *Let's break for five minutes and have a drink.* **11** BECOME KNOWN [I, T] If news or a story breaks, or if someone breaks it, it becomes known by the public for the first time. **12** WEATHER [I] *UK* If the weather breaks, it changes suddenly, and usually becomes worse. **13** VOICE [I] When a boy's voice breaks, it becomes deeper and sounds like a man's voice. **14** WAVE [I] When a wave breaks, it reaches its highest point as it moves towards the land, and then becomes flat and white. **15** STORM [I] If a storm breaks, it starts suddenly. **16 break even** to not make money but also not lose money *The company only managed to break even this year.* **17 break free/loose** to suddenly escape or become separate from something *The prisoner broke free while the guards weren't looking.* **18 dawn/day breaks** When dawn (= early morning)/day breaks, the sky becomes lighter because the sun is rising. *Dawn was breaking and the birds were singing.* ⊃ *See also:* break new **ground¹**, break sb's **heart**, to break the **ice¹**, break the **mould¹**, break ranks (**rank¹**)

**break away 1** to suddenly leave or escape from someone who is holding you **2** to stop being part of a group because you disagree with them *Some members broke away to form a new political party.*

**break down 1** MACHINE If a machine or vehicle breaks down, it stops working. *My car broke down on the way to work.* **2** COMMUNICATION If a system, relationship, or discussion breaks down, it fails because there is a problem or disagreement. *Their marriage broke down after only two years.* **3** CRY to become very upset and start crying

**break sth down** to divide something into smaller, simpler parts

**break in** to get into a building or car using force, usually to steal something

**break sth in** to wear something new, usually shoes, for short periods of time to make them more comfortable

**break into sth 1** to get into a building or car using force, usually to steal something *The office has been broken into twice since Christmas.* **2** to suddenly start doing something *The crowd broke into a cheer when he came on stage.*

**break (sth) off** to separate a part from a larger piece, or to become separate from something *He broke off a piece of chocolate.*

**break off** to suddenly stop speaking or doing something *She broke off in the middle of a sentence.*

**break sth off** to end a relationship *She broke off the engagement just two weeks before the wedding.*

**break out 1** If a fire, war, disease, etc breaks out, it starts suddenly. *A fight broke out among the crowd.* **2** to escape from prison *to break out of jail* **3 break out in a rash/sweat, etc** to suddenly have spots or sweat (= salty liquid) appear on your skin.

**break through sth** to force your way through something that is holding you back *Protesters broke through the barriers.*

**break (sth) up** to divide into many pieces, or to divide something into many pieces *The company has been broken up and sold.*

**break up 1** If people break up, they stop having a relationship or stop working together. *He's just broken up with his girlfriend.* **2** *UK* When schools or colleges break up, the classes end and the holidays begin.

**break**

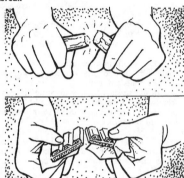

⊶**break²** /breɪk/ *noun* [C] **1** STOP when you stop an activity for a short time, usually to rest or to eat *a coffee/tea break* • *Take a break and come back after lunch.* **2** HOLIDAY a holiday or period of time away from work, school, etc *the spring break* • *a weekend break to Paris* **3** OPPORTUNITY a lucky opportunity *His big break came when he was offered a part in a TV series.* **4** DAMAGE where something has separated in an accident *a break in the bone* **5 a break with sth** when you end a relationship, connection, or way of doing something *a break with tradition*

**breakage** /ˈbreɪkɪdʒ/ *noun* [C, U] when something has been broken *The delivery company must pay for any breakages.*

**breakaway** /ˈbreɪkəweɪ/ *adj* **a breakaway group/republic/region, etc** a group/region, etc that has separated itself from a larger group or region because of a disagreement

**breakdown** /ˈbreɪkdaʊn/ *noun* [C] **1** ILLNESS (*also* **nervous breakdown**) a short period of mental illness when people are too ill to continue with their normal lives *to have a breakdown* **2** FAILURE when something such as communication or a relationship fails or ends *a breakdown in the peace talks* **3** EXPLANATION a short explanation of the details of something *I need a breakdown of the costs involved.* **4** NOT WORKING when a vehicle or machine stops working for a period of time

⊶**breakfast** /ˈbrekfəst/ *noun* [C] the food you eat in the morning after you wake up *She had breakfast in bed this morning.* • breakfast *verb* [I]

**B**

➔ *See also:* **English breakfast, bed and breakfast, continental breakfast.**

**break-in** /'breɪkɪn/ *noun* [C] when someone forces their way into a building or car, usually to steal something *There has been another break-in at the office.*

'**breaking ,point** *noun* [U] when a situation has become so bad that it cannot continue *Things had become so bad at work they'd almost reached breaking point.*

**breakneck** /'breɪknek/ *adj* **breakneck speed/ growth, etc** dangerously fast speed/growth, etc

**breakout** /'breɪkaʊt/ *noun* [C] an escape, usually from prison

**breakthrough** /'breɪkθruː/ *noun* [C] an important discovery or development that helps solve a problem *a major breakthrough in the fight against cancer*

**break-up** /'breɪkʌp/ *noun* [C] **1** when a close relationship ends *He moved away after the break-up of his marriage.* **2** when a country, group, etc separates into several smaller parts

**breast** /brest/ *noun* **1** [C] one of the two soft, round parts on a woman's chest **2** [C, U] the front part of a bird's body, or the meat from this area *chicken breast*

**breast-feed** /'brestfiːd/ *verb* [I, T] *past* **breast-fed** If a woman breast-feeds, she gives a baby milk from her breast. • **breast-feeding** *noun* [U]

**breaststroke** /'breststrəʊk/ *noun* [U] a way of swimming in which you push your arms forward and then to the side, while you kick your legs backwards

**breath** /breθ/ *noun* **1** [U] the air that comes out of your lungs *His breath smells of garlic.* **2** [C] when air goes into or out of your lungs *She took a deep breath before she started.* **3 be out of breath** to be breathing quickly because you have been running, walking fast, etc **4 catch your breath; get your breath back** to rest for a short time until you can breathe regularly again **5 under your breath** If you say something under your breath, you say it very quietly so that other people cannot hear it. **6 hold your breath** to keep air in your lungs and not let it out *How long can you hold your breath under water?* **7 don't hold your breath** *humorous* something that you say in order to tell someone that an event is not likely to happen *He said he'd phone, but don't hold your breath.* **8 a breath of fresh air** someone or something that is new, different, and exciting **9 take your breath away** If something takes your breath away, you feel surprise and admiration because it is so beautiful or exciting. *The view from the window took my breath away.* **10 with bated breath** in an excited or anxious way *I waited with bated breath as the results were read out.*

**breathalyser** /'breθəlaɪzəʳ/ *noun* [C] *UK* a piece of equipment that tests your breath to measure how much alcohol you have had • **breathalyse** *verb* [T] *UK* to measure the alcohol in someone's body using a breathalyser

o-**breathe** /briːð/ *verb* [I, T] to take air into and out of your lungs *breathe in/out* • **breathe deeply** • *Doctors gave him oxygen to help him breathe.*

➔ *See also:* be breathing down sb's **neck**, not breathe a **word**¹.

**breather** /'briːðəʳ/ *noun* [C] *informal* a short rest *If you start to feel tired, take a breather.*

**breathing** /'briːðɪŋ/ *noun* [U] when you take air into and out of your lungs *The doctor listened to my breathing.*

'**breathing ,space** *noun* [U] an opportunity to stop, relax, or think about things

**breathless** /'breθləs/ *adj* not able to breathe enough • **breathlessly** *adv*

**breathtaking** /'breθ,teɪkɪŋ/ *adj* very beautiful or surprising *breathtaking views* • **breathtakingly** *adv*

**bred** /bred/ *past of* breed

**breed**¹ /briːd/ *noun* [C] **1** a type of dog, sheep, pig, etc *a rare breed of cattle* **2** a type of person or thing *a new breed of bank*

**breed**² /briːd/ *verb past* **bred** /bred/ **1** [I] If animals breed, they produce young animals. **2 breed chickens/horses/rabbits, etc** to keep animals in order to produce young animals **3 breed contempt/ignorance, etc** to cause something to develop, especially something bad

**breeder** /'briːdəʳ/ *noun* [C] someone who keeps animals in order to produce young animals *a dog/horse breeder*

**breeding** /'briːdɪŋ/ *noun* [U] **1** when animals produce young animals *the breeding season* **2** when someone keeps animals in order to produce young animals *horse breeding*

'**breeding ,ground** *noun* [C] **1** a place where something develops quickly, especially something bad *This estate is a breeding ground for crime.* **2** a place where animals breed

**breeze**¹ /briːz/ *noun* [C] a gentle wind *a cool breeze*

**breeze**² /briːz/ *verb informal* **breeze along/ into/through, etc** to move somewhere quickly in a confident way and without worrying

**breezy** /'briːzi/ *adj* **1** with a slight wind *a cool, breezy day* **2** happy, confident, and enthusiastic *a cheerful, breezy style* • **breezily** *adv*

**brethren** /'breðrən/ *noun* [plural] members of an organized group, especially a religious group of men

**brevity** /'brevəti/ *noun* [U] *formal* **1** when speech or writing is short and contains few words **2** when something lasts for a short time

**brew**¹ /bruː/ *verb* **1** [T] to make beer **2** [I, T] If you brew tea or coffee, you make it by adding hot water, and if it brews, it gradually develops flavour in hot water. **3 be brewing** If something bad is brewing, it is beginning to develop. *There is a row brewing over the plans.*

**brew**² /bruː/ *noun* [C] *informal* a drink made by brewing, such as beer or tea

**brewer** /'bruːəʳ/ *noun* [C] a person or organization that makes beer

**brewery** /'bruːʳri/ *noun* [C] a company that makes beer

**bribe** /braɪb/ *noun* [C] money or a present given to someone so that they will do something for you, usually something dishonest *The politician was accused of accepting bribes from businessmen.* • **bribe** *verb* [T] [+ to do sth] *He was bribed to give false evidence at the trial.*

**bribery** /'braɪbªri/ *noun* [U] when someone is offered money or a present so that they will do something, usually something dishonest *bribery and corruption*

**bric-a-brac** /'brɪkə,bræk/ *noun* [U] a collection of small, decorative objects that have little value

**brick** /brɪk/ *noun* [C] a small, hard, rectangular block used for building walls, houses, etc *a brick wall* ⊃ *See also:* be banging your **head¹** against a brick wall.

**bricklayer** /'brɪk,leɪªr/ *noun* [C] someone whose job is to build houses, walls, etc with bricks

**bridal** /'braɪdªl/ *adj* [always before noun] relating to a woman who is getting married, or relating to a wedding *a bridal gown*

**bride** /braɪd/ *noun* [C] a woman who is getting married *the bride and groom*

**bridegroom** /'braɪdgruːm/ (*also* **groom**) *noun* [C] a man who is getting married

**bridesmaid** /'braɪdzmeɪd/ *noun* [C] a woman or girl who helps the bride on her wedding day

o─**bridge¹** /brɪdʒ/ *noun* **1** [STRUCTURE] [C] a structure that is built over a river, road, etc so that people or vehicles can go across it *to go across/over a bridge* • *Brooklyn Bridge* **2** [CONNECTION] [C] something that connects two groups, organizations, etc and improves the relationship between them *After the war they tried to build bridges with neighbouring countries.* **3 the bridge of your nose** the hard part of your nose between your eyes **4 the bridge** the raised area of a ship where the controls are **5** [GAME] [U] a card game for four players **6 I'll/We'll cross that bridge when I/we come to it.** something you say when you do not intend to worry about a possible problem now, but will deal with it if or when it happens

**bridge²** /brɪdʒ/ *verb* **bridge the gap/gulf, etc** to make the difference between two things smaller *This course is designed to **bridge the gap between** school and work.*

**bridle** /'braɪdl/ *noun* [C] a set of straps that you put on a horse's head to control it

o─**brief¹** /briːf/ *adj* **1** lasting only for a short time *a brief visit* **2** using only a few words *a brief description/statement* **3 in brief** using only a few words *world news in brief* • **briefly** *adv They discussed the matter briefly.*

**brief²** /briːf/ *verb* [T] to give someone instructions or information [often passive] *At the meeting reporters were **briefed on** the plans.*

**brief³** /briːf/ *noun* [C] a set of instructions or information [+ to do sth] *My brief was to improve the image of the city.*

**briefcase** /'briːfkeɪs/ *noun* [C] a flat, rectangular case with a handle for carrying documents, books, etc ⊃ *See picture at* **bag**.

**briefing** /'briːfɪŋ/ *noun* [C, U] a meeting when people are given instructions or information *a press briefing*

**briefs** /briːfs/ *noun* [plural] underwear that you wear on your bottom *a pair of briefs*

**brigade** /brɪ'geɪd/ *noun* [C] **1** a large group of soldiers **2** *UK humorous* a group of people with a particular characteristic or interest *the anti-smoking brigade* ⊃ *See also:* **fire brigade**.

**brigadier** /,brɪgə'dɪªr/ *noun* [C] a British army officer of high rank

o─**bright** /braɪt/ *adj* **1** [COLOUR] having a strong, light colour *bright yellow/blue* **2** [LIGHT] full of light or shining strongly *bright sunshine* • *The room is small but bright.* **3** [INTELLIGENT] intelligent *He's a bright boy.* **4** [HAPPY] happy or full of hope *She's always so bright and cheerful.* • **brightly** *adv brightly coloured flowers* • **brightness** *noun* [U]

**brighten** /'braɪtªn/ (*also* **brighten up**) *verb* [I, T] **1** to become lighter or more colourful, or to make something become lighter or more colourful *A picture or two would brighten up the room.* **2** to become happier, or to make someone become happier *She brightened up when she saw him.*

**brilliant** /'brɪliənt/ *adj* **1** [GOOD] *UK* very good *We saw a brilliant film.* **2** [CLEVER] extremely clever *a brilliant scholar* **3** [LIGHT] full of light or colour *The sky was a brilliant blue.* • **brilliantly** *adv* • **brilliance** /'brɪliəns/ *noun* [U]

**brim¹** /brɪm/ *verb* **brimming,** *past* **brimmed be brimming with sth** to be full of something *Her eyes were brimming with tears.*

**brim²** /brɪm/ *noun* [C] **1** the flat part around the bottom of a hat **2** the top edge of a container *He filled my glass to the brim.*

**brine** /braɪn/ *noun* [U] salty water, often used for keeping food from decaying *olives in brine*

o─**bring** /brɪŋ/ *verb* [T] *past* **brought 1** to take someone or something with you when you go somewhere *Did you bring an umbrella with you?* • [+ two objects] *He brought me some flowers.* **2 bring happiness/peace/shame, etc** to cause happiness/peace/shame, etc *Money does not always bring happiness.* **3 can not bring yourself to do sth** to not be willing to do something because it is so unpleasant *He couldn't bring himself to talk to her.* ⊃ *See also:* bring sb/sth to their knees (**knee**), bring sth to **light¹**.

**USAGE**

**bring** or **take?**

Use **bring** to talk about moving something or someone towards the speaker or towards the place where you are now.

*Did you bring any money?*

*I've brought you a present.*

Use **take** to talk about moving something or someone away from the speaker or away from the place where you are now.

*I can take you to the station.*

*Don't forget to take your umbrella.*

**bring sth about** to make something happen *The Internet has brought about big changes in the way we work.*

**bring sth back 1** to return from somewhere with something [+ two objects] *Can you bring me back some milk from the shop, please?* **2** to make someone think about something from the past *The photos brought back some wonderful memories.*

**bring sb down** to cause someone in a position of

B

power to lose their job *This scandal could bring down the government.*

**bring sth down** to reduce the level of something *to bring down prices*

**bring sth forward** to change the date or time of an event so that it happens earlier than planned *I've brought forward the meeting to this week.*

**bring sth in 1** to introduce something new, usually a product or a law *New safety regulations were brought in last year.* **2** to earn or make money *The film has brought in millions of dollars.*

**bring sb in** to ask someone to do a particular job *We need to bring in an expert to sort out this problem.*

**bring sth off** to succeed in doing something difficult *How did he manage to bring that off?*

**bring sth on** to make something happen, usually something bad [often passive] *Headaches are often brought on by stress.*

**bring sth out 1** to produce something to sell to the public *They have just brought out a new, smaller phone.* **2** to make a particular quality or detail noticeable *Salt can help to bring out the flavour of food.*

**bring sb together** to cause people to be friendly with each other *The disaster brought the community closer together.*

**bring sb up** to look after a child and teach them until they are old enough to look after themselves *She was brought up by her grandparents.*

**bring sth up 1** to start to talk about a particular subject *There are several points I'd like to bring up at tomorrow's meeting.* **2** UK to vomit something

**brink** /brɪŋk/ *noun* **be on the brink of sth** to be in a situation where something bad is going to happen very soon *The two countries are on the brink of war.*

**brisk** /brɪsk/ *adj* quick and energetic *a brisk walk* ● **briskly** *adv*

**bristle¹** /'brɪsl/ *verb* [I] to show that you are annoyed about something *She bristled at the suggestion that it was her fault.*

**bristle²** /'brɪsl/ *noun* [C, U] a short, stiff hair ● **bristly** *adj*

**Brit** /brɪt/ *noun* [C] *informal* someone who comes from Great Britain

**British** /'brɪtɪʃ/ *adj* relating to Great Britain or the United Kingdom

**the British** /'brɪtɪʃ/ *noun* [plural] the people of Great Britain or the United Kingdom

**Briton** /'brɪtən/ *noun* [C] someone who comes from Great Britain

**brittle** /'brɪtl/ *adj* hard but able to be broken easily *brittle bones*

**broach** /brəʊtʃ/ *verb* **broach an idea/subject/topic, etc** to begin to talk about something, usually something difficult or embarrassing *I don't know how to broach the subject of money with him.*

o━**broad** /brɔːd/ *adj* **1** wide *broad shoulders* ● *a broad smile* **2** **a broad range/variety, etc** a group that includes many different things or people *a broad range of subjects* **3** **a broad outline/picture, etc** a general description,

without detail *This is just a broad outline of the proposal.* **4** A broad accent (= way of speaking from a region) is very noticeable. *a broad Irish accent* **5** **in broad daylight** during the day when it is light and people can see *He was attacked in broad daylight.*

**broadcast¹** /'brɔːdkɑːst/ *noun* [C] a television or radio programme *a news broadcast* ● **broadcast** *adj* [always before noun] relating to television or radio *broadcast news*

**broadcast²** /'brɔːdkɑːst/ *verb* [I, T] *past* **broadcast** *also US* **broadcasted** to send out a programme on television or radio [often passive] *The concert will be broadcast live next week.* ● **broadcaster** *noun* [C] someone who speaks on radio or television as a job ● **broadcasting** *noun* [U]

**broaden** /'brɔːdən/ *verb* [I, T] **1** to increase or make something increase and include more things or people *We need to broaden the range of services that we offer.* ● *Travel broadens your mind.* **2** to become wider or make something become wider *Her smile broadened and she began to laugh.*

**broadly** /'brɔːdli/ *adv* in a general way and not including everything or everyone *The plans have been broadly accepted.*

**broadsheet** /'brɔːdʃiːt/ *noun* [C] UK a large newspaper, usually considered to be more serious than smaller newspapers

**broccoli** /'brɒkəli/ *noun* [U] a green vegetable with a thick stem

**brochure** /'brəʊʃəʳ* (ⓤ) *brəʊ'ʃʊr/ *noun* [C] a thin book with pictures and information, usually advertising something *a holiday/travel brochure*

**broil** /brɔɪl/ *US (UK/US* **grill***) verb* [T] to cook food using direct heat

**broiler** /'brɔɪləʳ/ *US (UK/US* **grill***) noun* [C] a piece of equipment used for cooking food under direct heat

**broke¹** /brəʊk/ *adj informal* **1 be broke** to not have any money *I can't afford it – I'm broke.* **2 go broke** to lose all your money and have to end your business

**broke²** /brəʊk/ *past tense of* break

o━**broken¹** /'brəʊkən/ *adj* **1** damaged and separated into pieces *broken glass* ⊃ *Opposite* **unbroken.** **2** **a broken arm/leg, etc** an arm/leg, etc with a damaged bone **3** If a machine or piece of equipment is broken, it is not working. *The video's broken.* **4** **a broken heart** when you are very sad because someone you love has ended a relationship with you **5** **a broken home** a family in which the parents do not now live together **6** **a broken promise** a promise that has not been kept **7** **broken English/Spanish, etc** English/Spanish, etc that is spoken slowly and has a lot of mistakes in it

**broken²** /'brəʊkən/ *past participle of* break

**broken-down** /ˌbrəʊkən'daʊn/ *adj* not working or in bad condition *a broken-down vehicle*

**broken-hearted** /ˌbrəʊkən'hɑːtɪd/ *adj* very sad because someone you love has ended a relationship with you

**broker¹** /'brəʊkəʳ/ *noun* [C] **1** (*also* **stockbroker**) someone whose job is to buy and sell shares (= equal parts of a company's total value) **2 an**

**insurance/mortgage, etc broker** someone who makes other people's financial arrangements for them

**broker**[2] /'brəʊkəʳ/ *verb* [T] to arrange an agreement *The peace deal was brokered by the US.*

**bronchitis** /brɒŋ'kaɪtɪs/ *noun* [U] an illness in your lungs which makes you cough and have problems breathing

**bronze**[1] /brɒnz/ *noun* **1** METAL [U] a shiny orange-brown metal **2** COLOUR [U] an orange-brown colour **3** PRIZE [C] a bronze medal (= a small, round disc given to someone for finishing third in a competition) *He won a bronze in the 200m.*

**bronze**[2] /brɒnz/ *adj* **1** made of bronze *a bronze statue* **2** being the colour of bronze

,bronze 'medal *noun* [C] a small, round disc given to someone for finishing third in a race or competition

**brooch** /brəʊtʃ/ *noun* [C] a piece of jewellery for women which is fastened onto clothes with a pin *a diamond brooch*

**brood**[1] /bruːd/ *noun* [C] a family of young birds or animals, all born at the same time

**brood**[2] /bruːd/ *verb* [I] to think for a long time about things that make you sad or angry *I wish he'd stop **brooding about** the past.*

**brook** /brʊk/ *noun* [C] a small stream

**broom** /bruːm/ *noun* [C] a brush with a long handle used for cleaning the floor ➔ *See picture at* **brush**.

**broth** /brɒθ/ *noun* [U] soup, usually made with meat *chicken broth*

**brothel** /'brɒθ°l/ *noun* [C] a building where prostitutes (= people who have sex for money) work

o━**brother** /'brʌðəʳ/ *noun* [C] **1** a boy or man who has the same parents as you *an older/younger brother • my big/little brother* **2** MEMBER a man who is a member of the same race, religious group, organization, etc **3** RELIGION (*also* **Brother**) a monk (= man who lives in a male religious group) *Brother Paul*

**brotherhood** /'brʌðəhʊd/ *noun* **1** [C] a group of men who have the same purpose or religious beliefs **2** [U] friendship and loyalty, like the relationship between brothers

**brother-in-law** /'brʌðərɪnlɔː/ *noun* [C] *plural* **brothers-in-law** the man married to your sister, or the brother of your husband or wife

**brotherly** /'brʌð°li/ *adj* [always before noun] relating to or typical of brothers *brotherly love*

**brought** /brɔːt/ *past of* **bring**

**brow** /braʊ/ *noun* [C] **1** the front part of your head between your eyes and your hair *He wiped the sweat from his brow.* **2 brow of a hill/slope** *UK* the top part of a hill or slope

o━**brown** /braʊn/ *adj* **1** being the same colour as chocolate or soil *a brown leather bag • dark brown hair/eyes* ➔ *See colour picture* **Colours** *on page Centre 6.* **2** having darker skin because you have been in the sun *You're really brown – you must have had good weather.* • **brown** *noun* [C, U] the colour brown

**brownie** /'braʊni/ *noun* [C] a small, square cake made with chocolate and nuts

**browse** /braʊz/ *verb* **1** INTERNET [I, T] to look at information on the Internet *to browse the Internet/Web* **2** READ [I] to read a book, magazine, etc in a relaxed way and not in detail *She **browsed through** some travel brochures looking for ideas.* **3** SHOP [I] to walk around a shop and look at things without buying anything *I love **browsing around** bookshops.*

**browser** /'braʊzəʳ/ *noun* [C] **1** a computer program which allows you to look at pages on the Internet **2** someone who browses

**bruise** /bruːz/ *noun* [C] a dark area on your skin where you have been hurt *He suffered cuts and bruises after falling off his bike.* • **bruise** *verb* [T] to cause someone or something to have a bruise [often passive] *He was badly bruised in the accident.* • **bruising** *noun* [U] *He suffered serious bruising in the attack.*

**brunette** /bruː'net/ *noun* [C] a white woman with dark brown hair

**brunt** /brʌnt/ *noun* **bear/feel/take the brunt of sth** to experience the worst part of something *He took the brunt of the criticism.*

**brush**[1] /brʌʃ/ *noun* **1** [C] an object made of short, thin pieces of plastic, wire, etc fixed to a handle and used to tidy hair, to clean, to paint, etc *a stiff wire brush* **2** [no plural] the action of using a brush *I need to **give** my hair a quick **brush**.* **3 the brush of sth** when something touches you lightly *She felt the brush of his lips against her cheek.* **4 a brush with sth** when you experience something, or almost experience something, especially something unpleasant *a brush with death*

**brush**

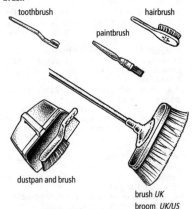

toothbrush         hairbrush

paintbrush

dustpan and brush

brush *UK*
broom *UK/US*

**brush**[2] /brʌʃ/ *verb* [T] **1** to use a brush to clean or tidy something *to brush your hair/teeth* **2 brush sth away/off, etc** to move something somewhere using a brush or your hand *He brushed the snow off his coat.* **3 brush against/past sb/sth** to lightly touch someone or something as you move past *He brushed past me as he went up the stairs.*

**brush sth aside/off** to refuse to think about something seriously *He brushed aside her suggestion.*

**brush up (on) sth** to improve your skills in something *I'm trying to brush up on my French before I go to Paris.*

**brush-off** /'brʌʃɒf/ *noun informal* **give sb the brush-off** to be unfriendly to someone by not talking to them

**brusque** /bruːsk/ ⑤ brʌsk/ *adj* dealing with people in a quick way that is unfriendly or rude *a brusque manner/reply* • brusquely *adv*

**brussel sprout** /ˌbrʌsᵊl'spraʊt ⑤ 'brʌsᵊlˌspraʊt/ *noun* [C] a small, green vegetable which is round and made of leaves

**brutal** /'bruːtᵊl/ *adj* very violent or cruel *a brutal murder* • brutally *adv* **brutally murdered** • *brutally honest* • brutality /bruː'tæləti/ *noun* [C, U]

**brute¹** /bruːt/ *noun* [C] someone who behaves in a very violent and cruel way • brutish /'bruːtɪʃ/ *adj* like a brute

**brute²** /bruːt/ *adj* **brute force/strength** great force or strength

**BSc** /ˌbiːes'siː/ *UK* (*US* **BS** /biː'es/) *noun* [C] *abbreviation for* Bachelor of Science: a university or college qualification in a science subject which usually takes 3 or 4 years of study *He has a BSc in computer science.*

**BSE** /ˌbiːes'iː/ *noun* [U] *abbreviation for* bovine spongiform encephalopathy: a disease that kills cows by destroying their brains

**bubble¹** /'bʌbl/ *noun* [C] a ball of air or gas with liquid around it *an air bubble*

**bubble²** /'bʌbl/ *verb* [I] **1** If a liquid bubbles, balls of air or gas rise to its surface. *The soup was bubbling on the stove.* **2 bubble (over) with confidence/enthusiasm, etc** to be full of a positive emotion or quality

**'bubble ˌgum** *noun* [U] a sweet that you chew and blow into a bubble

**bubbly** /'bʌbli/ *adj* **1** happy and enthusiastic *a bubbly personality* **2** full of bubbles

**buck¹** /bʌk/ *noun* [C] **1** *US informal* a dollar (= US unit of money) *It cost me twenty bucks to get a new bike lock.* **2** a male rabbit or deer **3 pass the buck** to blame someone or to make them responsible for a problem that you should deal with yourself

**buck²** /bʌk/ *verb* [I] If a horse bucks, it kicks its back legs into the air.

**bucket** /'bʌkɪt/ *noun* [C] a round, open container with a handle used for carrying liquids *a bucket of water*

**buckle¹** /'bʌkl/ *noun* [C] a metal object used to fasten the ends of a belt or strap *a silver buckle* ➔ *See colour picture* **Clothes** *on page Centre 5.*

**buckle²** /'bʌkl/ *verb* **1** FASTEN [I, T] to fasten a belt or strap with a buckle **2** BEND [I, T] to bend, or to cause something to bend because of too much weight, heat, etc *His legs buckled as he reached the finishing line.* **3** SUFFER [I] to suffer and stop working effectively because of too many problems or too much work

**buckle down** to start working hard *I must buckle down to some work this afternoon.*

**bud** /bʌd/ *noun* [C] **1** a part of a plant that develops into a leaf or a flower *In spring the trees are covered in buds.* **2 nip sth in the bud** to stop a small problem from getting worse by stopping it soon after it starts ➔ *See also:* **taste buds.**

**Buddha** /'bʊdə ⑤ 'buːdə/ *noun* the Indian holy man on whose life and teachings Buddhism is based

**Buddhism** /'bʊdɪzᵊm ⑤ 'buːdɪzᵊm/ *noun* [U] a religion based on the teachings of Buddha

**Buddhist** /'bʊdɪst ⑤ 'buːdɪst/ *noun* [C] someone who believes in Buddhism • Buddhist *adj a Buddhist temple*

**budding** /'bʌdɪŋ/ *adj* [always before noun] starting to develop well *a budding romance* • *a budding young actor*

**buddy** /'bʌdi/ *noun* [C] *informal* a friend *my best buddy*

**budge** /bʌdʒ/ *verb* [I, T] **1** If something will not budge, or you cannot budge it, it will not move. *I've tried to open the window, but it won't budge.* **2** If someone will not budge, or you cannot budge them, they will not change their opinion.

**budgerigar** /'bʌdʒᵊrɪgɑːʳ/ *noun* [C] *UK* a budgie

**budget¹** /'bʌdʒɪt/ *noun* [C] **1** a plan that shows how much money you have and how you will spend it **2** the amount of money you have for something *an annual budget of £30 million* **3 the Budget** in the UK, when the government officially tells the public about its plans for taxes and spending • budgetary *adj* [always before noun] relating to a budget

**budget²** /'bʌdʒɪt/ *verb* [I, T] to plan how much money you will spend on something *An extra £20 million has been budgeted for schools this year.*

**budget³** /'bʌdʒɪt/ *adj* **a budget hotel/price, etc** a very cheap hotel, price, etc

**budgie** /'bʌdʒi/ *noun* [C] *UK* a small, brightly coloured bird often kept as a pet

**buff** /bʌf/ *noun* [C] **a computer/film/wine, etc buff** someone who knows a lot about computers/films/wine, etc

**buffalo** /'bʌfᵊləʊ/ *noun* [C] *plural* **buffaloes** or **buffalo** a large, wild animal, like a cow with horns *a herd of wild buffalo*

**buffer** /'bʌfəʳ/ *noun* [C] something that helps protect someone or something from harm *I have some money saved to act as* **a buffer against** *unexpected bills.*

**'buffer ˌzone** *noun* [C] an area created to separate two countries that are fighting

**buffet¹** /'bʊfeɪ ⑤ bə'feɪ/ *noun* [C] a meal in which dishes of food are arranged on a table and you serve yourself *a cold buffet* • *a buffet lunch*

**buffet²** /'bʌfɪt/ *verb* [T] If something is buffeted by the weather, sea, etc, it is hit repeatedly and with force. [often passive] *The little boat was buffeted by the waves.*

**'buffet ˌcar** *noun* [C] *UK* the part of a train where you can buy something to eat or drink

**buffoon** /bə'fuːn/ *noun* [C] *old-fashioned* someone who does silly things

**bug¹** /bʌg/ *noun* [C] **1** ILLNESS a bacteria or

virus, or the illness that it causes *a flu/stomach bug* **2** COMPUTER a mistake in a computer program *This program is full of bugs.* **3** INSECT a small insect **4** EQUIPMENT a small, electronic piece of equipment used to secretly listen to people talking **5 be bitten by the bug/get the bug** *informal* to develop a strong interest or enthusiasm for a particular activity *He's been bitten by the tennis bug.*

**bug²** /bʌg/ *verb* **bugging**, *past* **bugged 1** to hide a piece of equipment somewhere in order to secretly listen to people talking [often passive] *Their hotel room had been bugged.* **2** *informal* to annoy someone *He's been bugging me all morning.*

**buggy** /ˈbʌgi/ *noun* [C] **1** *UK* (*US* **stroller**) a chair on wheels which is used to move small children **2** a vehicle with two wheels that is pulled by a horse, especially in the past

**bugle** /ˈbjuːgl/ *noun* [C] a small, metal musical instrument that you play by blowing into it

o→ **build¹** /bɪld/ *verb past* **built 1** [I, T] to make something by putting materials and parts together *build a house/wall* • *The bridge is built of steel and aluminium.* • *They're starting to build on that stretch of land.* **2** [T] to create and develop something over a long time *They have built a solid friendship over the years.*

**build sth into sth** to make something a part of something else *There are video screens built into the back of the seats.*

**build on sth** to use a success or achievement as a base from which to achieve more success

**build (sth) up** to increase or develop, or to make something increase or develop *This will help to build up his confidence.* • *Traffic usually builds up in the late afternoon.*

**build²** /bɪld/ *noun* [C, U] the size and shape of a person's body *He's of medium build with short brown hair.*

**builder** /ˈbɪldəʳ/ *noun* [C] someone who makes or repairs buildings as a job

o→ **building** /ˈbɪldɪŋ/ *noun* **1** [C] a structure with walls and a roof, such as a house, school, etc *an office building* **2** [U] the activity of putting together materials and parts to make structures *building materials* ⊃ *See also:* **apartment building**.

**'building so,ciety** *UK* (*US* **savings and loan association**) *noun* [C] an organization similar to a bank which lends you money to buy a house

**build-up** /ˈbɪldʌp/ *noun* [U] **1** when something slowly increases [usually singular] *the build-up of traffic* **2 the build-up to sth** *UK* the period of preparation before something happens *There was a lot of excitement in the build-up to the Olympics.*

**built** /bɪlt/ *past of* build

**built-in** /ˌbɪlt'ɪn/ *adj* [always before noun] included as part of the main structure of something *a computer with a built-in modem*

**built-up** /ˌbɪlt'ʌp/ *adj* a built-up area has a lot of buildings

**bulb** /bʌlb/ *noun* [C] **1** (*also* **light bulb**) a glass object containing a wire which produces light from electricity *an electric light bulb* **2** a round root that some plants grow from *daffodil bulbs*

**bulbous** /ˈbʌlbəs/ *adj* large and round in an unattractive way *a bulbous nose*

**bulge¹** /bʌldʒ/ *verb* [I] to look larger and rounder or fuller than normal *Her bags were bulging with shopping.*

**bulge²** /bʌldʒ/ *noun* [C] a round, raised area on a surface

**bulimia** /buˈlɪmiə/ *noun* [U] a mental illness in which someone eats too much and then forces themselves to vomit • **bulimic** *noun* [C], *adj*

**bulk** /bʌlk/ *noun* **1 in bulk** in large amounts *to buy in bulk* **2 the bulk of sth** the largest part or most of something *He spends the bulk of his money on rent.* **3** [no plural] the large size of something or someone

**bulky** /ˈbʌlki/ *adj* too big and taking up too much space

**bull** /bʊl/ *noun* [C] a male cow ⊃ *See also:* be like a red **rag** to a bull.

**bulldog** /ˈbʊldɒg/ *noun* [C] a short, strong dog with a large head and neck

**bulldozer** /ˈbʊlˌdəʊzəʳ/ *noun* [C] a heavy vehicle used to destroy buildings and make the ground flat • **bulldoze** *verb* [T]

o→ **bullet** /ˈbʊlɪt/ *noun* **1** [C] a small, metal object that is fired from a gun *a bullet wound* **2 bite the bullet** to make yourself do something or accept something difficult or unpleasant *I'm going to bite the bullet and ask my boss for a pay rise.*

**bulletin** /ˈbʊlətɪn/ *noun* [C] **1** a short news programme on television or radio *the evening news bulletin* **2** a regular newspaper or report containing news about an organization

**'bulletin ,board** *noun* [C] **1** a computer which you can connect to directly using a telephone line and where you can store or read messages about a particular subject **2** *US* (*UK* **noticeboard**) a board on a wall where you put advertisements and announcements ⊃ *See colour picture* **Classroom** *on page Centre 4.*

**bulletproof** /ˈbʊlɪtpruːf/ *adj* made of material that a bullet cannot go through *bulletproof vests*

**bullion** /ˈbʊliən/ *noun* [U] blocks of gold or silver

**bullock** /ˈbʊlək/ *noun* [C] a young bull (= male cow)

**bully¹** /ˈbʊli/ *verb* [T] to intentionally frighten someone who is smaller or weaker than you *He was bullied at school by some older boys.* • [+ into + doing sth] *She was bullied into leaving.* • **bullying** *noun* [U] *Bullying is a problem in many schools.*

**bully²** /ˈbʊli/ *noun* [C] someone who intentionally frightens a person who is smaller or weaker than them

**bum¹** /bʌm/ *noun* [C] **1** *UK informal* your bottom **2** *US informal* someone who has no home and no money

**bum²** /bʌm/ *verb* [T] **bumming**, *past* **bummed** *very informal* to ask someone for something, such as money or cigarettes, without intending to pay for them *Hey, could I bum a cigarette?*

**bum around** *informal* to spend time being lazy and doing very little

**bum around sth** *informal* to travel to different places and not do any work

**bumbag** /ˈbʌmbæg/ *UK* (*US* **fanny pack**) *noun* [C]

a small bag fixed to a belt that you wear around your waist

**bumblebee** /'bʌmblbiː/ *noun* [C] a large, hairy bee (= flying insect)

**bumbling** /'bʌmblɪŋ/ *adj* [always before noun] confused and showing no skill *a bumbling idiot*

**bummer** /'bʌmə'/ *noun* **a bummer** *informal* something unpleasant or annoying *That last exam was a real bummer.*

**bump¹** /bʌmp/ *verb* **1** [T] to hurt part of your body by hitting it against something hard *I bumped my head on the door.* **2 bump into/against sth** to hit your body, your car, etc against something by accident *He kept falling over and bumping into things.* **3 bump along/over sth** to move in a vehicle over a surface that is not smooth *The bus bumped along the country road.*

**bump into sb** *informal* to meet someone you know when you have not planned to meet them *I bumped into an old school friend in town today.*

**bump sb off** *informal* to murder someone *The film's about a guy who tries to bump off his wife.*

**bump²** /bʌmp/ *noun* [C] **1** SURFACE a round, raised area on a surface *My bike hit a bump in the road.* **2** BODY a raised area on your body where it has been hurt by hitting something hard *a nasty bump on the head* **3** MOVEMENT when something hits something hard *I heard a bump upstairs.*

**bumper¹** /'bʌmpə'/ *noun* [C] a bar fixed along the front or back of a vehicle to protect it in an accident *a front/rear bumper*

**bumper²** /'bʌmpə'/ *adj* [always before noun] bigger or better than usual *bumper profits* ● *a bumper year*

**bumper ,sticker** *noun* [C] a sign that you stick on a car, often with a funny message on it

**bumpy** /'bʌmpi/ *adj* **1** SURFACE A bumpy road or surface is not smooth but has raised areas on it. **2** JOURNEY A bumpy journey is uncomfortable because the vehicle moves around a lot. **3** SITUATION full of problems or sudden changes *We had a bumpy start.*

**bun** /bʌn/ *noun* [C] **1** CAKE a small, round cake *an iced bun* **2** BREAD a small, round piece of bread *a hamburger/hot cross bun* **3** HAIR a hairstyle in which the hair is arranged in a small, round shape on the back of the head

**bunch¹** /bʌnʃ/ *noun* **1** [C] a number of things of the same type which are joined or held together *He handed me a bunch of flowers.* ⊃ *See colour picture* **Quantities** *on page Centre 14.* **2** [C] *informal* a group of people [usually singular] *His friends are a nice bunch.* **3 a bunch of sth** *US informal* a large amount or number of something *There's a whole bunch of places I'd like to visit.*

**bunch²** /bʌnʃ/ *verb*

**bunch (sb/sth) together/up** to move close together so that you make a tight group, or to make someone or something do this [often passive] *We were all bunched up at the back of the room.*

**bunch (sth) up** If material bunches up, or if someone bunches it up, it moves into tight folds. [often passive] *My shirt's all bunched up at*

*the back.*

**bunches** /'bʌntʃɪz/ *noun* [plural] *UK* a hairstyle in which the hair is tied together in two parts, one on each side of the head

**bundle¹** /'bʌndl/ *noun* **1** [C] a number of things that are tied together *a bundle of letters/clothes* **2 a bundle of energy/nerves** *informal* a very energetic or nervous person

**bundle²** /'bʌndl/ *verb* **bundle sb into/out of/through sth** to push or carry someone somewhere quickly and roughly *He was bundled into the back of a car and driven away.*
**bundle sth up** to tie a number of things together
**bundle (sb) up** to put warm clothes on yourself or someone else

**bung** /bʌŋ/ *verb* **bung sth in/on, etc** *UK informal* to put something somewhere in a quick, careless way *Shall I bung a chicken in the oven for dinner?*
**bung sth up** *UK informal* to cause something to be blocked so that it does not work in the way it should [often passive] *The toilet was bunged up with paper.*

**bungalow** /'bʌŋgələʊ/ *noun* [C] a house that has all its rooms on the ground floor

**bungle** /'bʌŋgl/ *verb* [T] to do something wrong in a very careless or stupid way *a bungled robbery* ● **bungling** *noun* [U]

**bunk** /bʌŋk/ *noun* [C] a narrow bed in a ship, train, etc

**bunk ,beds** *noun* [plural] two beds fixed together with one on top of the other

**bunker** /'bʌŋkə'/ *noun* [C] **1** an underground room where people go to be protected, especially from bombs **2** in golf, a hollow area filled with sand

**bunny** /'bʌni/ (*also* **bunny ,rabbit**) *noun* [C] a child's word for 'rabbit'

**buoy¹** /bɔɪ/ *noun* [C] a floating object used in water to mark dangerous areas for boats

**buoy²** /bɔɪ/ *verb* **be buoyed (up) by sth** to feel happy or confident because of something *The team was buoyed up by their win last week.*

**buoyant** /'bɔɪənt/ *adj* **1** CONFIDENT happy and confident *in a buoyant mood* **2** BUSINESS successful or making a profit *a buoyant economy* **3** FLOATING floating or able to float ● **buoyancy** /'bɔɪənsi/ *noun* [U]

**burden** /'bɜːdən/ *noun* [C] something difficult or unpleasant that you have to deal with or worry about *the burden of responsibility* ● *I'd hate to be a burden to you when I'm older.* ● **burden** *verb* [T] to give someone something difficult or unpleasant to deal with or worry about *Sorry to burden you with my problems.* ● **burdensome** *adj*

**bureau** /'bjʊərəʊ/ *noun* [C] *plural* **bureaux** *US* **bureaus 1** OFFICE a department or office **2** WRITING *UK* a piece of furniture with drawers and a sloping top used for writing **3** CLOTHES *US* (*UK* **chest of drawers**) a piece of furniture with drawers for keeping clothes in

**bureaucracy** /bjʊə'rɒkrəsi/ *noun* **1** [U] complicated rules and processes used by an organization, especially when they do not seem necessary *government bureaucracy* **2** [C, U] a government or organization in which there are

**B**

a lot of officials in a lot of departments • **bureaucrat** /'bjʊərəʊkræt/ *noun* [C] someone working in a bureaucracy • **bureaucratic** /ˌbjʊərəʊ'krætɪk/ *adj*

**burgeoning** /'bɜːdʒ°nɪŋ/ *adj* growing very quickly *a burgeoning population*

**burger** /'bɜːɡəʳ/ *noun* [C] a flat, round piece of food, usually made of meat, that is fried and served between pieces of bread *burger and fries* • *a veggie burger*

**burglar** /'bɜːɡləʳ/ *noun* [C] someone who gets into buildings illegally and steals things

'**burglar aˌlarm** *noun* [C] something that makes a noise if someone tries to get into a building illegally

**burglarize** /'bɜːɡləraɪz/ *verb US* burgle

**burglary** /'bɜːɡl°ri/ *noun* [C, U] when someone gets into a building illegally and steals things

**burgle** /'bɜːɡl/ *UK* (*US* **burglarize**) *verb* [T] to get into a building illegally and steal things [often passive] *They've been burgled twice recently.*

**burial** /'beriəl/ *noun* [C, U] when a dead body is put into the ground

**burly** /'bɜːli/ *adj* A burly man is large and strong.

o━**burn¹** /bɜːn/ *verb past* **burnt** or **burned** **1** DESTROY [I, T] to destroy something with fire, or to be destroyed by fire *I burnt all his letters.* • *The factory burned to the ground.* • *He dropped his cigarette and burnt a hole in his jacket.* **2** FLAMES [I] to produce flames *The fire's burning well.* **3** COOK TOO MUCH [I, T] If you burn something that you are cooking, you cook it too much and if something you are cooking burns, it cooks too much. *Check the pizza – I think it's burning!* **4** **burn yourself/your fingers, etc** to be hurt by fire or heat *He burned his hand on the kettle.* **5** ENERGY [T] (*also* **burn up**) to use fuel to produce heat or energy *to burn calories/fuel* **6** SKIN [I] to be very hot or sore *Her cheeks were burning.* **7** **burn with anger/hatred, etc** to feel an emotion very strongly

**burn (sth) down** to destroy something, especially a building, by fire, or to be destroyed by fire *Their house burnt down while they were away on holiday.*

**burn out** If a fire burns out, it stops producing flames because nothing remains that can burn.

**burn (sth) up** to destroy something completely, or to be destroyed completely by fire or heat *The satellite will burn up when it enters the atmosphere.*

**burn²** /bɜːn/ *noun* [C] a place where fire or heat has damaged or hurt something *She has a nasty burn on her arm.*

**burner** /'bɜːnəʳ/ *noun* **1** [C] a piece of equipment used to burn or heat something **2** **put sth on the back burner** to not deal with something now, but intend to deal with it at a later time

**burning** /'bɜːnɪŋ/ *adj* **1** very hot *the burning heat of the midday sun* **2** **burning ambition/desire, etc** a very strong need to do something *a burning issue/question* **3** **a burning issue/question** a subject or question that must be dealt with or answered quickly

**burnt¹** /bɜːnt/ *adj* destroyed or made black by fire or heat *burnt toast*

**burnt²** /bɜːnt/ *past of* burn

**burnt-out** /ˌbɜːnt'aʊt/ (*also* **burned-out** /bɜːnd'aʊt/) *adj* **1** A burnt-out car or building has been almost completely destroyed by fire. **2** *informal* tired and without enthusiasm because you have worked too hard *a burnt-out teacher*

**burp** /bɜːp/ *verb* [I] to let air from your stomach come out of your mouth in a noisy way • **burp** *noun* [C]

**burrow¹** /'bʌrəʊ/ *verb* [I] When an animal burrows, it digs a hole or passage in the ground to live in. *There are rabbits burrowing under the building.*

**burrow²** /'bʌrəʊ/ *noun* [C] a hole or passage in the ground dug by an animal to live in

o━**burst¹** /bɜːst/ *verb past* **burst** **1** [I, T] If a container bursts, or if you burst it, it breaks suddenly, so that what is inside it comes out. *A water pipe burst and flooded the cellar.* **2** **burst in/out/through, etc** to move somewhere suddenly and forcefully *Three masked men burst into the shop.* **3** **burst into flames** to suddenly start burning **4** **burst into laughter/tears, etc** to suddenly start laughing/crying, etc *She burst into tears and ran away.* **5** **burst open** to open suddenly and with force **6** **be bursting with confidence/joy, etc** to be full of an emotion or quality *She was bursting with pride.* **7** **be bursting to do sth** *informal* to want to do something very much *I was bursting to tell him about the party.*

**burst out 1** to suddenly say something loudly *'Don't go!' he burst out.* **2** **burst out laughing/crying** to suddenly start laughing/crying *I walked in and everyone burst out laughing.*

**burst²** /bɜːst/ *noun* **1** **a burst of sth** a sudden large amount of noise, activity, etc *a burst of applause/laughter* **2** [C] when something breaks open and what is inside it comes out

o━**bury** /'beri/ *verb* [T] **1** to put a dead body into the ground [often passive] *He was buried next to his wife.* **2** to hide something in the ground or under something *buried treasure* • [often passive] *Two climbers were buried in the snow.* **3** **bury your face/head in sth** to move your face/head somewhere where it is hidden *She buried her face in her hands.* **4** **bury yourself in sth** to give all your attention to something *He buried himself in his work.* ➔ *See also:* bury the **hatchet**.

o━**bus** /bʌs/ *noun* [C] *plural* **buses** a large vehicle that carries passengers by road, usually along a fixed route *a school bus* • *I'll go home by bus.* • **bus** *verb* [T] *UK* bussing, *past* bussed, *US* busing, *past* bused to take a group of people somewhere in a bus ➔ *See picture at* **vehicle**.

**bush** /bʊʃ/ *noun* **1** [C] a short, thick plant with a lot of branches *a rose bush* • *There was someone hiding in the bushes.* **2** **the bush** wild parts of Australia or Africa where very few people live **3** **beat about the bush** to avoid talking about something difficult or embarrassing

**bushy** /'bʊʃi/ *adj* If hair or a plant is bushy, it has grown very thick. *bushy eyebrows*

**busily** /'bɪzɪli/ *adv* in a busy, active way *He was busily writing notes.*

**bush**

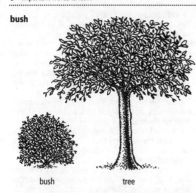

bush                    tree

o→**business** /ˈbɪznɪs/ *noun* **1** TRADE [U] the buying and selling of goods or services *The shop closed last year, but now they're back in business.* • *We do a lot of business with China.* • *His company has gone out of business* (= failed). **2** ORGANIZATION [C] an organization that sells goods or services *My uncle runs a small decorating business.* **3** WORK [U] work that you do to earn money *She's in Vienna on business* (= working). **4 a nasty/strange, etc business** an unpleasant/strange, etc situation **5 be sb's (own) business** to be something private that other people do not need to know *What he does in his own home is his business.* **6 be none of sb's business** If something is none of someone's business, they do not need to know about it, although they want to, because it does not affect them. **7 mind your own business** used to tell someone in a rude way that you do not want them to ask about something private ⊃ *See also:* **big business, show business**.

**businesslike** /ˈbɪznɪslaɪk/ *adj* working in a serious and effective way *a businesslike manner*

**businessman, businesswoman** /ˈbɪznɪsmən, ˈbɪznɪsˌwʊmən/ *noun* [C] *plural* **businessmen, businesswomen** someone who works in business, usually in a high position in a company

**busk** /bʌsk/ *verb* [I] *UK* to perform music in a public place to get money from people walking past • **busker** *noun* [C]

'**bus ˌstation** (*also UK* **coach station**) *noun* [C] a building where a bus starts or ends its journey

'**bus ˌstop** *noun* [C] a place where buses stop to let passengers get on or off *I saw her waiting at the bus stop.* ⊃ *See usage note at* **station**.

**bust¹** /bʌst/ *verb* [T] *past* **bust** *US* **busted** *informal* **1** to break or damage something *The cops had to bust the door down to get in.* **2** If the police bust someone, they catch them and accuse them of a crime. [often passive] *He was busted for selling drugs.*

**bust²** /bʌst/ *noun* [C] **1** a woman's breasts, or their size in relation to clothing *a 36-inch bust* **2** a model of someone's head and shoulders *a bronze bust of the Queen* **3 a drug bust** when the police catch people selling or using illegal drugs *Officers arrested two men in a major drug bust last night.*

**bust³** /bʌst/ *adj* **1 go bust** If a business goes

bust, it stops trading because it does not have enough money. *His company went bust, leaving huge debts.* **2** *UK informal* (*US* **busted** /ˈbʌstɪd/) broken *My phone's bust – can I use yours?*

**bustle¹** /ˈbʌsl/ *verb* **1 bustle about/around/in, etc** to move around and do things in a quick, busy way *There were lots of shoppers bustling about.* **2 bustle with sth** to be full of people or activity *The town centre was bustling with people.*

**bustle²** /ˈbʌsl/ *noun* [U] people and activity *We left the bustle of the city behind us.*

**bustling** /ˈbʌslɪŋ/ *adj* full of people and activity *a bustling city/street*

**bust-up** /ˈbʌstʌp/ *noun* [C] *UK informal* a serious disagreement *He left home after a big bust-up with his dad.*

o→**busy¹** /ˈbɪzi/ *adj* **1** PERSON If you are busy, you are working hard, or giving your attention to a particular activity. *Mum was busy in the kitchen.* • [+ doing sth] *I was busy mowing the lawn.* • *I've got plenty of jobs to keep you busy.* • *He was too busy talking to notice us come in.* **2** PLACE A busy place is full of activity or people. *a busy restaurant/road* **3** TIME In a busy period you have a lot of things to do. *I've had a very busy week.* **4** TELEPHONE *US* (*UK* **engaged**) If a telephone line is busy, someone is using it.

**busy²** /ˈbɪzi/ *verb* **busy yourself** to spend time working or doing something *We busied ourselves in the kitchen preparing dinner.*

o→**but¹** *strong form* /bʌt/ *weak form* /bət/ *conjunction* **1** OPPOSITE INFORMATION used to introduce something new that you say, especially something which is different or the opposite from what you have just said *I'd drive you there, but I haven't got my car.* • *The tickets were expensive, but the kids really enjoyed it.* **2** EXPLAINING WHY used before you say why something did not happen or is not true *I was going to go to his party, but I was ill.* **3** SHOWING SURPRISE used to show that you are surprised about what someone has just said *'Tim is leaving.' 'But why?'* **4** CONNECTING PHRASES used to connect 'excuse me' or 'I'm sorry' with what you say next *Excuse me, but would you mind shutting the door?*

o→**but²** *strong form* /bʌt/ *weak form* /bət/ *preposition* except *Everyone but Andrew knows.* • *Can you buy me a sandwich? Anything but ham.* • *This is the last programme but one* (= the programme before the last).

o→**but³** *strong form* /bʌt/ *weak form* /bət/ *adv formal* only *We can but try.*

**butcher¹** /ˈbʊtʃəʳ/ *noun* [C] someone who prepares and sells meat

**butcher²** /ˈbʊtʃəʳ/ *verb* [T] **1** to kill someone in a very violent way **2** to cut an animal into pieces of meat

**butcher's** /ˈbʊtʃəz/ *UK* (*US* '**butcher ˌshop**) *noun* [C] a shop that prepares and sells meat *I went to the butcher's to buy some sausages.*

**butler** /ˈbʌtləʳ/ *noun* [C] a man who opens the door, serves dinner, etc in a large house as a job

**butt¹** /bʌt/ *noun* **1** BOTTOM [C] *US informal* your bottom *He just sits on his butt all day long.* **2** CIGARETTE [C] the end of a cigarette that is left after it is smoked *There were cigarette butts all over the floor.* **3** GUN [C] the end of the handle of a gun *the butt of a rifle* **4 a head butt** when you hit someone with the top, front part of your head **5 kick sb's butt** *US informal* to punish someone or defeat someone with a lot of force

**butt²** /bʌt/ *verb* [T] to hit something with the top, front part of your head *He butted me in the stomach.*

**butt in** to interrupt or join in a conversation or activity when the other people do not want you to *The interviewer kept butting in and wouldn't let me answer the question.*

⚬⃥**butter¹** /'bʌtəʳ/ *noun* **1** [U] a soft, pale yellow food made from cream that you put on bread and use in cooking ➔ *See colour picture* **Food** *on page Centre 7.* **2 butter wouldn't melt in sb's mouth** used to say that someone looks as if they would never do anything wrong ➔ *See also:* **peanut butter**.

**butter²** /'bʌtəʳ/ *verb* [T] to put a layer of butter on something *hot buttered toast*

**butter sb up** *informal* to be very nice to someone so that they will do what you want them to do

**buttercup** /'bʌtəkʌp/ *noun* [C] a small, bright yellow flower

**butterfly** /'bʌtəflaɪ/ *noun* **1** [C] an insect with large, patterned wings ➔ *See picture at* **insect**. **2 have butterflies (in your stomach)** to feel very nervous about something that you are going to do *She had butterflies in her stomach as she walked out onto the stage.*

**buttock** /'bʌtək/ *noun* [C] one of the two sides of your bottom

**button¹** /'bʌtⁿn/ *noun* [C] **1** a small, round object that you push through a hole to fasten clothing *to do up/undo your buttons* **2** a switch that you press to control a piece of equipment *Press the play button to listen to your recording.* ➔ *See also:* **belly button**.

**button²** /'bʌtⁿn/ (*also* **button up**) *verb* [T] to fasten a piece of clothing with buttons *Jack buttoned up his jacket.* ➔ *Opposite* **unbutton**.

**buttonhole** /'bʌtⁿnhəʊl/ *noun* [C] **1** a hole that you push a button through on a piece of clothing **2** *UK* a flower worn on a jacket or coat for a special occasion

**buxom** /'bʌksəm/ *adj* A buxom woman has large breasts.

⚬⃥**buy¹** /baɪ/ *verb* [T] *past* **bought** to get something by paying money for it *I went to the shop to buy some milk.* • *They* **bought** *their house for £14,000.* • [+ two objects] *He bought me a camera for my birthday.*

**buy sb/sth out** to buy part of a company or building from someone else so that you own all of it *He bought out his partner for £3 million.*

**buy sth up** to quickly buy a lot of something, often all that is available *Most of the land in the area has been bought up by property developers.*

**buy²** /baɪ/ *noun* **a good buy** when you buy something good for a cheap price *This coat was a really good buy.*

**buyer** /'baɪəʳ/ *noun* [C] someone who buys something

**buyout** /'baɪaʊt/ *noun* [C] when a group of people buy the company that they work for

**buzz¹** /bʌz/ *noun* **1** [no plural] *informal* a feeling of excitement, energy, or pleasure *He gets a real buzz from going to the gym.* **2** [C] a continuous sound like a bee makes

**buzz²** /bʌz/ *verb* [I] **1** to make a continuous sound like a bee *I can hear something buzzing.* **2** to be full of activity or excitement *The crowd was buzzing with excitement.* **3 buzz about/ around, etc** to move around in a quick and busy way

**buzzer** /'bʌzəʳ/ *noun* [C] a piece of electronic equipment that makes a long sound as a signal *to press the buzzer*

**buzzword** /'bʌzwɜːd/ *noun* [C] a word or expression that has become fashionable, usually in a particular subject or group of people *a new political buzzword*

⚬⃥**by¹** *strong form* /baɪ/ *weak forms* /bɪ, bə/ *preposition* **1** DO used to show the person or thing that does something *She was examined by a doctor.* • *The building had been destroyed by fire.* • *a painting by Van Gogh* **2** HOW through doing or using something *Can I pay by cheque?* • *I sent it by email.* • *We'll get there by car.* • [+ doing sth] *Open the file by clicking on the icon.* **3** HOLDING holding a particular part of someone or something *She grabbed me by the arm.* **4** NEAR near or next to something or someone *I'll meet you by the post office.* • *A small child stood by her side.* **5** NOT LATER not later than a particular time or date *Applications have to be in by the 31st.* **6** ACCORDING TO according to *By law you must be eighteen to purchase alcohol.* **7** PAST past *He sped by me on a motorcycle.* **8** AMOUNT used to show measurements or amounts *twelve by ten metres of floor space* • *Interest rates have been increased by 0.25%.* • *I'm paid by the hour.* • *Copies have sold by the million.* **9 by accident/chance/mistake, etc** as a result of an accident, chance, mistake, etc *I went to the wrong room by mistake.* **10 by day/night** during the day/night **11 day by day/little by little/one by one, etc** used in particular phrases to mean 'gradually' or 'in units of' *Day by day he grew stronger.*

⚬⃥**by²** /baɪ/ *adv* past *A motorcycle sped by.*

⚬⃥**bye** /baɪ/ (*also* **bye-bye**) *exclamation* goodbye *Bye, see you tomorrow.*

**by-election** /'baɪɪlekʃⁿn/ *noun* [C] an election in the UK to choose a new member of parliament for an area because the old one has left or died

**bygone** /'baɪgɒn/ *adj literary* **bygone age/ days/era, etc** a time in the past

**bygones** /'baɪgɒnz/ *noun* **let bygones be bygones** something that you say to tell someone to forget about the unpleasant things in the past

**bypass¹** /'baɪpɑːs/ *noun* [C] **1** a road that goes around a town and not through it **2** a medical operation to make blood flow along a different route and avoid a damaged part of the heart *a coronary/heart bypass*

**bypass²** /'baɪpɑːs/ *verb* [T] **1** to go around a place or thing and not through it *I was hoping to bypass the city centre.* **2** to avoid dealing with someone or something by dealing directly with someone or something else *They bypassed him and went straight to his manager.*

**by-product** /ˈbaɪˌprɒdʌkt/ *noun* [C] something that is produced when you are making or doing something else *Carbon monoxide is a by-product of burning.*

**bystander** /ˈbaɪˌstændə/ *noun* [C] someone who is near the place where an event happens, but not directly involved in it *The gunman began firing at innocent bystanders.*

**byte** /baɪt/ *noun* [C] a unit for measuring the amount of information a computer can store, equal to 8 bits (= smallest unit of computer information)

# C

**C, c** /siː/ the third letter of the alphabet

**C** *abbreviation for* Celsius or centigrade: measurements of temperature *30°C*

**c** *written abbreviation for* circa (= used before a number or date to show that it is not exact) *c. 1900*

**cab** /kæb/ *noun* [C] **1** *informal* a taxi (= car that you pay to travel in) *We **took a cab** to the theatre.* • *a cab driver* **2** the front part of a truck where the driver sits

**cabaret** /'kæbəreɪ/ *noun* [C, U] when someone entertains people with songs, jokes, etc in a bar or restaurant *He's appearing **in cabaret** at the Cafe Royal.*

**cabbage** /'kæbɪdʒ/ *noun* [C, U] a large, round vegetable that consists of a lot of thick leaves *boiled cabbage*

**cabbie** /'kæbi/ *noun* [C] *informal* someone who drives a taxi (= car that you pay to travel in)

**cabin** /'kæbɪn/ *noun* [C] **1** HOUSE a small, simple house made of wood *a log cabin* **2** SHIP a small room to sleep in on a ship **3** AIRCRAFT the area where passengers sit on an aircraft

**cabinet** /'kæbɪnət/ *noun* **1 the Cabinet** a group of people in a government who are chosen by and who advise the highest leader *a Cabinet minister/member* **2** [C] a cupboard with shelves or drawers to store or show things in *a bathroom/medicine cabinet* ⊃ *See also:* **filing cabinet**.

**cable¹** /'keɪbl/ *noun* **1** WIRE [C, U] a wire covered by plastic that carries electricity, telephone signals, etc *overhead power cables* **2** ROPE [C, U] thick wire twisted into a rope **3** SYSTEM [U] the system of sending television programmes or telephone signals along wires under the ground *cable TV* • *This channel is only available **on cable**.*

**'cable ,car** *noun* [C] a vehicle that hangs from thick cables and carries people up hills and mountains

**cache** /kæʃ/ *noun* [C] a secret supply of something *a cache of weapons*

**cachet** /'kæʃeɪ ⓊⓈ kæʃ'eɪ/ *noun* [U] when something is admired or respected

**cacophony** /kə'kɒfəni/ *noun* [no plural] a loud, unpleasant mixture of sounds *a cacophony of voices*

**cactus** /'kæktəs/ *noun* [C] *plural* **cacti** /'kæktaɪ/ or **cactuses** a plant with thick leaves for storing water and often sharp points that grows in deserts

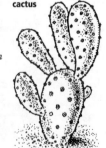
cactus

**caddie** /'kædi/ *noun* [C] someone who carries the equipment for someone playing golf ⊃ *See colour picture* **Sports 2** *on page Centre 16.* • **caddie** *verb* [I] **caddying**, *past* **caddied** to be a caddie for someone

**cadet** /kə'det/ *noun* [C] a young person who is training to be in a military organization, the police, etc *an army cadet*

**caesarean** (*also US* **cesarean**) /sɪ'zeəriən/ *noun* [C] an operation in which a baby is taken out of a woman through a cut in the front of her body

**cafe** (*also* **café**) /'kæfeɪ ⓊⓈ kæ'feɪ/ *noun* [C] a small restaurant where you can buy drinks and small meals

**cafeteria** /,kæfə'tɪəriə/ *noun* [C] a restaurant where you collect and pay for your food and drink before you eat it *a school cafeteria*

**caffeine** /'kæfiːn/ *noun* [U] a chemical in coffee, tea, etc that makes you feel more awake

**cage** /keɪdʒ/ *noun* [C] a container made of wire or metal bars used for keeping birds or animals in *a bird cage* ⊃ *See also:* **rib cage**.

**cagey** /'keɪdʒi/ *adj* If someone is cagey, they are not very willing to give information, and you may think they are not honest. *He's very **cagey about** his past.*

**cajole** /kə'dʒəʊl/ *verb* [I, T] to persuade someone to do something by being friendly or by promising them something [+ into + doing sth] *She cajoled me into helping with the dinner.*

○= **cake** /keɪk/ *noun* [C, U] **1** a sweet food made from flour, butter, sugar, and eggs mixed together and baked *a chocolate/fruit cake* • *a piece/slice of cake* • *to bake/make a cake* ⊃ *See colour picture* **Food** *on page Centre 7.* **2 have your cake and eat it** to have or do two things that it is usually impossible to have or do at the same time ⊃ *See also:* the **icing** on the cake, be a **piece¹** of cake.

**caked** /keɪkt/ *adj* **be caked in/with sth** to be covered with a thick, dry layer of something *His boots were caked in mud.*

**calamity** /kə'læməti/ *noun* [C] a sudden, bad event that causes a lot of damage or unhappiness

**calcium** /'kælsiəm/ *noun* [U] a chemical element in teeth, bones, and chalk (= a soft, white rock)

○= **calculate** /'kælkjəleɪt/ *verb* [T] **1** to discover an amount or number using mathematics *to calculate a cost/percentage* **2 be calculated to do sth** to be intended to have a particular effect *His comments were calculated to embarrass the prime minister.*

**calculated** /'kælkjəleɪtɪd/ *adj* based on careful thought or planning, not on emotion *a calculated risk/decision*

**calculating** /'kælkjəleɪtɪŋ/ *adj* Calculating people try to get what they want by thinking carefully and without emotion, and not caring about other people. *a cold, calculating criminal*

○= **calculation** /,kælkjə'leɪʃⁿn/ *noun* **1** [C, U] when you use mathematics to discover a number or amount *I **did** some quick **calculations** to see if I could afford to buy it.* **2** [U] when someone thinks very carefully about something without any emotion

**calculator** /'kælkjəleɪtəʳ/ *noun* [C] an electronic device that you use to do mathematical calculations

**calendar** /'kæləndə$^r$/ *noun* **1** [C] something that shows all the days, weeks, and months of the year **2 the Christian/Jewish/Western, etc calendar** the system used to measure and arrange the days, weeks, months and special events of the year according to Christian/ Jewish/Western, etc tradition **3 the political/ school/sporting, etc calendar** the events that are arranged during the year for a particular activity or organization

**calf** /kɑːf/ *noun* [C] *plural* **calves** /kɑːvz/ **1** a young cow **2** the back of your leg below your knee ➲ *See colour picture* **The Body** *on page Centre 2.*

**calibre** *UK* (*US* **caliber**) /'kælɪbə$^r$/ *noun* [U] **1** the quality or level of ability of someone or something *The calibre of applicants was very high.* **2** the measurement across the inside of a gun, or across a bullet

o⇠**call¹** /kɔːl/ *verb* **1 be called sth** to have a particular name *a man called John* • *What's your dog called?* • *Their latest record is called "Ecstasy".* **2** GIVE NAME [+ two objects] to give someone or something a particular name *I want to call the baby Alex.* **3** DESCRIBE [+ two objects] to describe someone or something in a particular way *She called him a liar.* • *Doctors are calling it an epidemic.* **4** ASK TO COME [T] to ask someone to come somewhere *She called me into her office.* • *He was called to an emergency meeting.* **5** SHOUT [I, T] (*also* **call out**) to shout or say something in a loud voice *I thought I heard someone calling my name.* **6** TELEPHONE [I, T] to telephone someone *He called me every night while he was away.* • *Has anyone called the police?* ➲ *See usage note at* **phone**. **7** VISIT [I] (*also* **call by/in/round**) *UK* to visit someone for a short time *John called round earlier.* **8 call an election/meeting, etc** to arrange for an election/meeting, etc to happen *The chairman has called an emergency meeting.* ➲ *See also:* call sb's **bluff²**, call it a **day**

**call back** *UK* to go back to a place in order to see someone or collect something *I'll call back later to pick up the books.*

**call (sb) back** to telephone someone again, or to telephone someone who telephoned you earlier *I can't talk now – I'll call you back in ten minutes.*

**call for sth 1** to demand that something happens *to call for a ban on guns* **2** to need or deserve a particular action or quality *You passed your test? This calls for a celebration!*

**call for sb** to go to a place in order to collect someone *I'll call for you at eight.*

**call sth off 1** to decide that a planned event or activity will not happen because it is not possible, useful, or wanted now *The game has been called off because of the weather.* **2** to decide to stop an activity *Police have called off the search.*

**call on sb to do sth** to ask someone in a formal way to do something *He called on the rebels to stop fighting.*

**be called up** to be ordered to join a military organization or asked to join an official team *He was called up soon after the war started.*

**call (sb) up** *mainly US* to telephone someone *My dad called me up to tell me the good news.*

**call sth up** to find and show information on a computer screen *I'll just call up your account details.*

o⇠**call²** /kɔːl/ *noun* [C] **1** TELEPHONE (*also* **phone call**) when you use the telephone *Give me a call at the weekend.* • *I got a call from Sue this morning.* **2 a call for sth** a demand for something to happen *a call for action/peace* **3** VISIT a short visit *I thought I'd pay Gary a call.* **4** SHOUT when someone shouts something **5** BIRD a sound made by a bird or other animal **6 sb's call** *mainly US informal* when someone can decide something *I don't mind what we do – it's your call.* **7 call for sth** when people want or need a particular thing *There's not much call for interior designers round here.* **8 be on call** to be ready to go to work if you are needed, as part of your job **9 a close call** when something you do not want to happen nearly happens ➲ *See also:* be at sb's **beck** and call, **wake-up call**.

**caller** /'kɔːlə$^r$/ *noun* [C] **1** someone who makes a telephone call *an anonymous caller* **2** *mainly UK* someone who visits for a short time

**call-in** /'kɔːlɪn/ *US* (*UK* **phone-in**) *noun* [C] a television or radio programme in which the public can ask questions or give opinions over the telephone

**calling** /'kɔːlɪŋ/ *noun* [C] a strong feeling that you should do a particular type of work *She found her true calling in teaching.*

**callous** /'kæləs/ *adj* cruel and not caring about other people *a callous remark* • *callously adv*

o⇠**calm¹** /kɑːm/ *adj* **1** PERSON relaxed and not worried, frightened, or excited *a calm voice/manner* • *Try to stay calm – the doctor will be here soon.* **2** SEA If the sea is calm, it is still and has no large waves. **3** WEATHER If the weather is calm, there are no storms or wind. • *calmness noun* [U]

**calm²** /kɑːm/ *noun* [U] when people or conditions are calm

**calm³** /kɑːm/ *verb* [T] to make someone stop feeling upset, angry, or excited *The police tried to calm the crowd.* • *a calming effect*

**calm (sb) down** to stop feeling upset, angry, or excited, or to make someone stop feeling this way *Calm down and tell me what's wrong.*

**calmly** /'kɑːmli/ *adv* in a relaxed way *He spoke slowly and calmly.*

**calorie** /'kæl$^ə$ri/ *noun* [C] a unit for measuring the amount of energy food provides *I try to eat about 2000 calories a day.*

**calves** /kɑːvz/ *plural of* calf

**camaraderie** /,kæmə'rɑːd$^ə$ri/ *noun* [U] special friendship felt by people who work together or experience something together

**camcorder** /'kæm,kɔːdə$^r$/ *noun* [C] a camera that you can hold in your hand and that takes moving pictures

**came** /keɪm/ *past tense of* come

**camel** /'kæm$^ə$l/ *noun* [C] a large animal that lives in the desert and has one or two humps (= raised parts on its back)

**cameo** /'kæmiəʊ/ *noun* [C] when someone famous appears for a short time in a film or play *a cameo role*

o⇠**camera** /'kæm$^ə$rə/ *noun* [C] a piece of equipment

used to take photographs or to make films *a digital camera* • *a television camera*

**cameraman** /'kæmˈrəmæn/ *noun* [C] *plural* **cameramen** someone who operates a television camera or film camera as their job

**camouflage** /'kæməflɑːʒ/ *noun* [U] when the colour or pattern on something is similar to the area around it making it difficult to see *a camouflage jacket* • camouflage *verb* [T]

**camp**[1] /kæmp/ *noun* **1** [C] an area where people stay in tents for a short time, usually for a holiday **2 an army/prison/refugee, etc camp** an area containing temporary buildings or tents used for soldiers/prisoners/refugees (= people forced to leave their home), etc ➔ *See also:* **base camp, concentration camp.**

**camp**[2] /kæmp/ (*also* **camp out**) *verb* [I] to stay in a tent or temporary shelter *We camped on the beach for two nights.*

**campaign**[1] /kæm'peɪn/ *noun* [C] **1** a series of organized activities or events intended to achieve a result *an advertising/election campaign* **2** a series of military attacks *a bombing campaign*

**campaign**[2] /kæm'peɪn/ *verb* [I] to organize a series of activities to try to achieve something *to campaign against/for something* • campaigner *noun* [C] *an animal rights campaigner*

**camper** /'kæmpər/ *noun* [C] **1** someone who stays in a tent on holiday **2** (*also* **'camper ,van**) a vehicle containing a bed, kitchen equipment, etc that you can live in

**camping** /'kæmpɪŋ/ *noun* [U] when you stay in a tent for a holiday *We're going camping in France this summer.* • *a camping trip*

**campsite** /'kæmpsaɪt/ (*also US* **campground** /'kæmpgraʊnd/) *noun* [C] an area where people can stay in tents for a holiday

**campus** /'kæmpəs/ *noun* [C, U] the land and buildings belonging to a college or university *I lived on campus in my first year.*

⊶**can**[1] *strong form* /kæn/ *weak forms* /kən, kn/ *modal verb past* **could 1** ⁅ABILITY⁆ to be able to do something *Anna can speak four languages.* • *We can't pay the rent.* • *Can you drive?* **2** ⁅PERMISSION⁆ to be allowed to do something *You can't park here.* • *Can I go now?* **3** ⁅ASK⁆ used to ask someone to do or provide something *Can you tell me the way out there?* • *Can I have a drink of water?* **4** ⁅OFFER⁆ used to politely offer to do something *Can I carry those bags for you?* **5** ⁅POSSIBLE⁆ used to talk about what is possible *You can buy stamps from the shop on the corner.* • *Smoking can cause cancer.* **6** ⁅TYPICAL⁆ used to talk about how someone often behaves or what something is often like *She can be really rude at times.* • *This area can be dangerous at night.* **7** ⁅SURPRISE⁆ [used in questions and negatives] used to show surprise or lack of belief *You can't possibly be hungry already!* • ➔ *See study section* **Modal verbs** *on page Centre 31.*

**can**[2] /kæn/ *noun* [C] **1** a closed, metal container for food or liquids *a can of soup/beans* • *a can of paint* ➔ *See picture at* **container. 2 a can of worms** a situation which causes a lot of trouble for you when you start to deal with it ➔ *See also:* **trash can, watering can.**

**can**[3] /kæn/ *verb* [T] **canning**, *past* **canned** to put

food or drink into metal containers in a factory *canned tomatoes*

**Canadian** /kə'neɪdiən/ *adj* relating to Canada • Canadian *noun* [C] someone who comes from Canada

**canal** /kə'næl/ *noun* [C] an artificial river built for boats to travel along or to take water where it is needed

**canary** /kə'neəri/ *noun* [C] a small, yellow bird that sings

⊶**cancel** /'kænsᵊl/ *verb* [T] *UK* **cancelling**, *past* **cancelled**, *US* **canceling**, *past* **canceled 1** to say that an organized event will not now happen [often passive] *The meeting has been cancelled.* **2** to stop an order for goods or services that you do not now want

**cancel sth out** If something cancels out another thing, it stops it from having any effect.

**cancellation** /ˌkænsᵊl'eɪʃᵊn/ *noun* [C, U] when someone decides that an event will not now happen or stops an order for something *a last-minute cancellation*

**Cancer** /'kænsər/ *noun* [C, U] the sign of the zodiac which relates to the period of 22 June – 22 July, or a person born during this period ➔ *See picture at* **zodiac.**

**cancer** /'kænsər/ *noun* [C, U] a serious disease that is caused when cells in the body grow in a way that is uncontrolled and not normal *breast/lung cancer* • *His wife died of cancer.* • cancerous *adj a cancerous growth*

**candid** /'kændɪd/ *adj* honest, especially about something that is unpleasant or embarrassing *She was very candid about her personal life in the interview.* • candidly *adv*

**candidacy** /'kændɪdəsi/ *noun* [U] when someone is a candidate in an election

**candidate** /'kændɪdət/ *noun* [C] **1** one of the people taking part in an election or trying to get a job *a presidential candidate* **2** *UK* someone who is taking an exam

**candle** /'kændl/ *noun* [C] a stick of wax with string going through it that you burn to produce light ➔ *See colour picture* **The Living Room** *on page Centre 11.*

**candlelight** /'kændllaɪt/ *noun* [U] light produced by a candle *We ate dinner by candlelight.*

**candlestick** /'kændlstɪk/ *noun* [C] an object that holds a candle

**can-do** /'kæn,duː/ *adj informal* determined to deal with problems and achieve results *I really admire her can-do attitude.*

**candour** *UK* (*US* **candor**) /'kændər/ *noun* [U] when you speak honestly, especially about something that is unpleasant or embarrassing

**candy** /'kændi/ *noun* [C, U] *US* a small piece of sweet food made from sugar, chocolate, etc *a box of candy* • *a candy bar*

**cane**[1] /keɪn/ *noun* **1** ⁅STEM⁆ [C, U] the long, hard, hollow stem of some plants, sometimes used to make furniture **2** ⁅WALK⁆ [C] a long stick used by people to help them walk **3** ⁅PUNISH⁆ [C] *UK* a long stick used in the past to hit children at school

**cane**[2] /keɪn/ *verb* [T] *UK* to hit someone, especially a school student, with a stick as a punishment

**canine** /'keɪnaɪn/ adj relating to dogs

**canister** /'kænɪstəʳ/ noun [C] a metal container for gases or dry things *a gas canister*

**cannabis** /'kænəbɪs/ *mainly UK* (*mainly US* **marijuana**) *noun* [U] a drug that some people smoke for pleasure and that is illegal in many countries

**canned** /kænd/ (*also UK* **tinned**) *adj* Canned food is sold in metal containers.

**cannibal** /'kænɪbᵊl/ noun [C] someone who eats human flesh ● **cannibalism** *noun* [U]

**cannon** /'kænən/ noun [C] a very large gun, in the past one that was on wheels

**cannot** /'kænɒt/ *modal verb* the negative form of 'can' *I cannot predict what will happen.*

**canny** /'kæni/ adj clever and able to think quickly, especially about money or business *a canny businessman*

**canoe** /kə'nuː/ noun [C] a small, narrow boat with pointed ends that you move using a paddle (= stick with a wide, flat part) ● **canoeing** *noun* [U] the activity of travelling in a canoe

**canon** /'kænən/ noun [C] a Christian priest who works in a cathedral (= large, important church) *Canon of Westminster*

**'can ˌopener** (*also UK* **tin opener**) *noun* [C] a piece of kitchen equipment for opening metal food containers ➔ *See colour picture* **Kitchen** *on page Centre 10.*

**canopy** /'kænəpi/ noun [C] a cover or type of roof for protection or decoration

**can't** /kɑːnt/ *modal verb* **1** short for cannot *I can't find my keys.* **2** used to suggest that someone should do something *Can't you ask Jonathan to help?*

**canteen** /kæn'tiːn/ noun [C] a restaurant in an office, factory, or school

**canter** /'kæntəʳ/ verb [I] When a horse canters, it runs quite fast. ● **canter** *noun* [no plural]

**canvas** /'kænvəs/ noun **1** [U] strong cloth used for making sails, tents, etc **2** [C] a piece of canvas used for a painting

**canvass** /'kænvəs/ verb **1** [I, T] to try to persuade people to vote for someone in an election *He's canvassing for the Labour party.* **2** [T] to ask people their opinion about something *The study canvassed the views of over 9000 people.*

**canyon** /'kænjən/ noun [C] a deep valley with very steep sides

**cap¹** /kæp/ noun [C] **1** a hat with a flat, curved part at the front *a baseball cap* ➔ *See colour picture* **Clothes** *on page Centre 5.* **2** a small lid that covers the top or end of something ➔ *See also:* **skull cap.**

**cap²** /kæp/ verb [T] **capping,** *past* **capped 1** END to be the last and the best or worst event in a series of events *The party capped a wonderful week.* **2** LIMIT to put a limit on an amount of money that can be borrowed, charged, etc [often passive] *The interest rate has been capped at 5%.* **3** COVER to cover the top of something [often passive] *The mountains were capped with snow.*

**capability** /ˌkeɪpə'bɪləti/ noun [C, U] the ability or power to do something [+ to do sth] *Both players have the capability to win this match.*

**o—̅capable** /'keɪpəbl/ adj **1** able to do things effectively and achieve results *She's a very capable young woman.* **2** **capable of sth/doing sth**

having the ability or qualities to be able to do something *He's capable of doing much better than this.* ● *She was capable of great cruelty.* ➔ *Opposite* **incapable.**

**capacity** /kə'pæsəti/ noun **1** CONTAIN [C, U] the largest amount or number that a container, building, etc can hold *The restaurant has a capacity of about 200.* ● *The stadium was filled to capacity* (= completely full). **2** PRODUCE [U] the amount that a factory or machine can produce *The factory is operating at full capacity* (= producing as much as possible). **3** ABILITY [C] the ability to do, experience, or understand something *She has a great capacity for love.* **4** JOB [C] a position or job *He attended over 100 events last year in his capacity as mayor.*

**cape** /keɪp/ noun [C] **1** a loose coat without any sleeves that is fastened at the neck **2** a large area of land that goes out into the sea

**caper** /'keɪpəʳ/ noun [C] something that is done as a joke, or intended to entertain people *His new movie is a comic caper.*

**capillary** /kə'pɪlᵊri ⓤⓢ 'kæpəleri/ noun [C] a very thin tube that carries blood around the body

**o—̅capital¹** /'kæpɪtᵊl/ noun **1** CITY [C] the most important city in a country or state, where the government is based *Paris is the capital of France.* **2** MONEY [U] an amount of money that you can use to start a business or to make more money **3** LETTER [C] (*also* ˌcapital 'letter) a large letter of the alphabet used at the beginning of sentences and names ➔ *See study section* **Punctuation** *on page Centre 37.* ➔ *See also:* **block capitals.**

**capital²** /'kæpɪtᵊl/ adj **a capital crime/offence** a crime that can be punished by death

**capitalism** /'kæpɪtᵊlɪzᵊm/ noun [U] a political and economic system in which industry is owned privately for profit and not by the state

**capitalist** /'kæpɪtᵊlɪst/ noun [C] someone who supports capitalism ● **capitalist** *adj a capitalist society*

**capitalize** (*also UK* **-ise**) /'kæpɪtᵊlaɪz/ verb [T] to write something using capital letters, or starting with a capital letter

**capitalize on sth** to use a situation to achieve something good for yourself *He failed to capitalize on his earlier success.*

**ˌcapital 'punishment** *noun* [U] when someone is killed by the state for committing a serious crime

**capitulate** /kə'pɪtjʊleɪt/ verb [I] to stop disagreeing or fighting with someone and agree to what they want ● **capitulation** /kəˌpɪtjʊ'leɪʃᵊn/ *noun* [C, U]

**cappuccino** /ˌkæpʊ'tʃiːnəʊ/ noun [C, U] coffee made with milk that has been heated with steam to produce a lot of small bubbles

**capricious** /kə'prɪʃəs/ adj likely to suddenly change your ideas or behaviour

**Capricorn** /'kæprɪkɔːn/ noun [C, U] the sign of the zodiac which relates to the period of 23 December – 20 January, or a person born during this period ➔ *See picture at* **zodiac.**

**capsize** /kæp'saɪz/ verb [I, T] If a boat capsizes, or if it is capsized, it turns over in the water.

**capsule** /'kæpsjuːl/ noun [C] **1** a small container

with medicine inside that you swallow **2** the part of a spacecraft that people live in

**captain**[1] /ˈkæptɪn/ *noun* [C] **1** SHIP the person in control of a ship or aircraft **2** ARMY an officer of middle rank in the army, navy, or air force **3** SPORT the leader of a team

**captain**[2] /ˈkæptɪn/ *verb* [T] to be the captain of a team, ship, or aircraft *He has captained the England cricket team three times.*

**captaincy** /ˈkæptɪnsi/ *noun* [U] when someone is the captain of a team

**caption** /ˈkæpʃᵊn/ *noun* [C] words written under a picture to explain it

**captivate** /ˈkæptɪveɪt/ *verb* [T] to interest or attract someone very much *She captivated film audiences with her beauty and charm.* • captivating *adj a captivating performance*

**captive**[1] /ˈkæptɪv/ *adj* **1** A captive person or animal is being kept somewhere and is not allowed to leave. **2 a captive audience/market** a group of people who have to watch something or have to buy something because they do not have a choice **3 hold/take sb captive** to keep someone as a prisoner or make someone a prisoner *They were held captive by rebels for 32 days.*

**captive**[2] /ˈkæptɪv/ *noun* [C] someone who is kept as a prisoner

**captivity** /kæpˈtɪvəti/ *noun* [U] when a person or animal is kept somewhere and is not allowed to leave *lion cubs born in captivity*

**capture**[1] /ˈkæptʃəʳ/ *verb* [T] **1** PRISONER to catch someone and make them your prisoner *Two soldiers were captured by the enemy.* **2** CONTROL to get control of a place with force *Rebel troops have captured the city.* **3** GET to succeed in getting something when you are competing against other people *The Green Party has captured 12% of the vote.* **4** DESCRIBE to show or describe something successfully using words or pictures *His book really captures the spirit of the place.* **5 capture sb/sth on camera/film, etc** to record someone or something on camera/film, etc **6 capture sb's attention/imagination** to make someone very interested or excited *The campaign has really captured the public's imagination.* **7 capture sb's heart** to make someone love you *She captured the hearts of the nation.*

**capture**[2] /ˈkæptʃəʳ/ *noun* [U] **1** when someone is caught and made a prisoner *He shot himself to avoid capture.* **2** when someone gets control of a place with force *the capture of the city by foreign troops*

o⊸**car** /kɑːʳ/ *noun* [C] **1** a vehicle with an engine, four wheels, and seats for a small number of passengers *She goes to work by car.* • *Where did you park your car?* ➔ *See colour picture* **Car** *on page Centre 3.* **2** *US* a part of a train in which passengers sit, eat, sleep, etc *the dining car* ➔ *See also:* **buffet car**, **cable car**, **estate car**, **sports car**.

**caramel** /ˈkærəmᵊl/ *noun* [U] sugar that has been heated until it turns brown and that is used to add colour and flavour to food, or a sweet made from sugar, milk, and butter

**carat** (*also US* **karat**) /ˈkærət/ *noun* [C] a unit for measuring how pure gold is, or how much jewels (= valuable stones) weigh *22 carat gold*

**caravan** /ˈkærəvæn/ *noun* [C] **1** *UK* a vehicle which people can live in on holiday and which is pulled by a car *a caravan site* **2** a group of people with animals or vehicles who travel together across a desert

**carbohydrate** /ˌkɑːbəʊˈhaɪdreɪt/ *noun* [C, U] a substance in food such as sugar, potatoes, etc that gives your body energy

**carbon** /ˈkɑːbᵊn/ *noun* [U] a chemical element present in all animals and plants and in coal and oil

**carbonated** /ˈkɑːbəneɪtɪd/ *adj* Carbonated drinks contain a lot of small bubbles.

ˌ**carbon ˈcopy** *noun* [C] **1** a copy of a written document that is made using carbon paper (= thin paper covered in carbon) **2** an exact copy of something *He's a carbon copy of his father.*

**carbon dioxide** /ˌkɑːbᵊndaɪˈɒksaɪd/ *noun* [U] a gas that is produced when people and animals breathe out, or when carbon is burned

**carbon monoxide** /ˌkɑːbᵊnməˈnɒksaɪd/ *noun* [U] a poisonous gas that is produced by burning some types of fuel, especially petrol (= fuel for cars)

ˈ**carbon ˌpaper** *noun* [U] thin paper that is covered on one side with carbon (= a black substance) and is used for making copies of written documents

ˌ**car ˈboot sale** *noun* [C] *UK* an event where people sell things they no longer want from the backs of their cars

**carburettor** *UK* (*US* **carburetor** /ˈkɑːrbəreɪtər/) /ˌkɑːbəˈretəʳ ⓊⓈ /ˈkɑːbəreɪtər/ *noun* [C] the part of an engine that mixes fuel and air which are then burned to provide power

**carcass** /ˈkɑːkəs/ *noun* [C] the body of a dead animal

**carcinogen** /kɑːˈsɪnədʒᵊn/ *noun* [C] a substance that can cause cancer (= a disease when cells in your body grow in an uncontrolled way) • carcinogenic /ˌkɑːsɪnəʊˈdʒenɪk/ *adj carcinogenic chemicals*

o⊸**card** /kɑːd/ *noun* **1** MESSAGE [C] a folded piece of stiff paper with a picture on the front and a message inside that you send to someone on a special occasion *a birthday card* **2** INFORMATION [C] a piece of stiff paper or plastic that has information printed on it *a library card* • *This phone accepts coins and cards.* **3** GAME [C] (*also* **playing card**) one of a set of 52 pieces of stiff paper with numbers and pictures used for playing games (*UK*) *a pack of cards*/(*US*) *a deck of cards* • *We spent the evening playing cards* (= playing games using cards). **4** PAPER [U] *UK* thick, stiff paper **5** WITHOUT ENVELOPE [C] a postcard (= card with a picture on one side that you send without an envelope) **6 be on the cards** *UK* (*US* **be in the cards**) to be likely to happen *Do you think marriage is on the cards?* **7 put/lay your cards on the table** to tell someone honestly what you think or plan to do ➔ *See also:* **Christmas card**, **cash card**, **charge card**, **credit card**, **debit card**, **phone card**, **smart card**, **swipe card**, **trump card**, **wild card**.

**cardboard** /ˈkɑːdbɔːd/ *noun* [U] thick, stiff paper that is used for making boxes

**cardiac** /'kɑːdiæk/ *adj* [always before noun] relating to the heart *cardiac surgery* • *cardiac arrest* (= when the heart stops beating)

**cardigan** /'kɑːdɪɡən/ *noun* [C] a piece of clothing, often made of wool, that covers the top part of your body and fastens at the front ➔ *See colour picture* **Clothes** *on page Centre 5.*

**cardinal¹** /'kɑːdɪnᵊl/ *noun* [C] a priest with a high rank in the Catholic Church *Cardinal Basil Hume*

**cardinal²** /'kɑːdɪnᵊl/ *adj* [always before noun] *formal* extremely important or serious *One of the **cardinal rules** of business is know what your customer wants.*

,cardinal 'number (*also* **cardinal**) *noun* [C] a number such as 1, 2, 3, etc that shows the quantity of something

o-** care¹ /keᵊ/ *verb* 1 [I, T] to think that something is important and to feel interested in it or worried about it *He **cares** deeply **about** the environment.* • [+ question word] *I don't care how long it takes – just get the job done.* 2 [I] to love someone *Your parents are only doing this because they **care about** you.* • *I knew that Amy still **cared for** me.* 3 **I/he, etc couldn't care less** *informal* used to emphasize that someone is not interested in or worried about something or someone [+ question word] *I couldn't care less what people think.* 4 **Who cares?** *informal* used to emphasize that you do not think something is important *"Manchester United will be in the final if they win this match." "Who cares?"* 5 **Would you care for sth/to do sth?** *formal* used to ask someone if they want something or want to do something *Would you care for a drink?* • *Would you care to join us for dinner?* **care for sb/sth** to look after someone or something, especially someone who is young, old, or ill *The children are being cared for by a relative.* **not care for sth/sb** *formal* to not like something or someone *I don't care for shellfish.*

o-** care² /keᵊ/ *noun* 1 PROTECTION [U] the process of looking after something or someone, especially someone who is young, old, or ill *skin/hair care* • *A small baby requires constant care.* 2 ATTENTION [U] If you do something with care, you give a lot of attention to it so that you do not make a mistake or damage anything. *She planned the trip with great care.* • *Fragile – please handle with care.* 3 **take care** to give a lot of attention to what you are doing so that you do not have an accident or make a mistake *The roads are very icy so take care when you drive home.* 4 **Take care!** *informal* used when saying goodbye to someone *See you soon, Bob – take care!* 5 WORRY [C] a feeling of worry *He was sixteen years old and **didn't have a care in the world*** (= had no worries). 6 **in care** *UK* Children who are in care are looked after by government organizations because their parents cannot look after them. *She was put/taken into care at the age of twelve.* 7 **take care of sb/sth** to look after someone or something *My parents are going to take care of the house while we're away.* 8 **take care of sth/doing sth** to be responsible for dealing with something *I did the cooking while Guy took care of the washing up.* ➔ *See also:* **intensive care**.

o-** career¹ /kəˈrɪəʳ/ *noun* [C] 1 a job that you do for a long period of your life and that gives you the chance to move to a higher position and earn more money *a successful career in marketing* 2 the time that you spend doing a particular job *She began her acting career in TV commercials.* ➔ *See usage note at* **work**.

**career²** /kəˈrɪəʳ/ *verb* **career down/into/off, etc** *UK* to move quickly and in an uncontrolled way *The train careered off a bridge and plunged into the river.*

**carefree** /'keəfriː/ *adj* without any worries or problems *a carefree childhood*

o-** careful /'keəfᵊl/ *adj* giving a lot of attention to what you are doing so that you do not have an accident, make a mistake, or damage something *careful planning/consideration* • *Be careful, Michael – that knife's very sharp.* • [+ to do sth] *We were careful to avoid the midday sun.* • **carefully** *adv a carefully prepared speech*

**caregiver** /'keə,ɡɪvəʳ/ *US* (*UK* **carer**) *noun* [C] someone who looks after a person who is young, old, or ill

**careless** /'keələs/ *adj* not giving enough attention to what you are doing *It was very **careless** of you to forget your passport.* • *He was fined £250 for careless driving.* • **carelessly** *adv* • **carelessness** *noun* [U]

**carer** /'keərəʳ/ *UK* (*US* **caregiver**) *noun* [C] someone who looks after a person who is young, old, or ill

**caress** /kəˈres/ *verb* [T] to touch someone in a gentle way that shows that you love them *He caressed the back of her neck.* • **caress** *noun* [C]

**caretaker** /'keə,teɪkəʳ/ *noun* [C] 1 someone whose job is to look after a large building, such as a school 2 *US* someone who looks after a person who is young, old, or ill

**cargo** /'kɑːɡəʊ/ *noun* [C, U] *plural* **cargoes** goods that are carried in a vehicle *a cargo of oil* • *a cargo ship/plane*

**caricature** /'kærɪkətʃʊəʳ/ *noun* [C] a funny drawing or description of someone, especially someone famous, which makes part of their appearance or character more noticeable than it really is • **caricature** *verb* [T]

**caring** /'keərɪŋ/ *adj* kind and supporting other people *She's a very caring person.*

**carjacking** /'kɑː,dʒækɪŋ/ *noun* [C, U] the crime of attacking someone who is driving and stealing their car • **carjacker** *noun* [C] someone who commits the crime of carjacking

**carnage** /'kɑːnɪdʒ/ *noun* [U] *formal* when a lot of people are violently killed or injured

**carnation** /kɑːˈneɪʃᵊn/ *noun* [C] a small flower with a sweet smell that is usually white, pink, or red

**carnival** /'kɑːnɪvᵊl/ *noun* [C] 1 a public celebration where people wear special clothes and dance and play music in the roads 2 *US* a place of outside entertainment where there are machines you can ride on and games that can be played for prizes

**carnivore** /'kɑːnɪvɔːʳ/ *noun* [C] an animal that eats meat • **carnivorous** /kɑːˈnɪvᵊrəs/ *adj* eating meat

**carol** /'kærᵊl/ (*also* **Christmas carol**) *noun* [C] a song that people sing at Christmas

**carousel** /ˌkærəˈsel/ noun [C] **1** a moving strip where passengers collect their bags at an airport **2** *mainly US* a machine that goes round and round and has toy animals or cars for children to ride on

**carp**[1] /kɑːp/ noun [C, U] *plural* **carp** or **carps** a large fish that lives in lakes and rivers, or the meat of this fish

**carp**[2] /kɑːp/ verb [I] to complain continually about things that are not important *He's always **carping about** how badly organized the office is.*

'**car ˌpark** *UK* (*US* **parking lot**) noun [C] a place where vehicles can be parked

**carpenter** /ˈkɑːpᵊntəʳ/ noun [C] a person whose job is making and repairing wooden objects

**carpentry** /ˈkɑːpᵊntri/ noun [U] making and repairing wooden objects

**carpet** /ˈkɑːpɪt/ noun **1** [C, U] thick material for covering floors, often made of wool *a new living room carpet* ● (*UK*) *fitted carpets* (= carpets that cover floors from wall to wall) **2 a carpet of sth** a thick layer of something that covers the ground *a carpet of snow* ● **carpet** verb [T] to put carpet on the floor of a room *The stairs were carpeted.* ➔ *See also:* **the red carpet**.

**carriage** /ˈkærɪdʒ/ noun **1** TRAIN [C] *UK* one of the separate parts of a train where the passengers sit *The front carriage of the train is for first-class passengers only.* **2** WITH HORSE [C] a vehicle with wheels that is pulled by a horse **3** GOODS [U] *UK* the cost of transporting goods ➔ *See also:* **baby carriage**.

**carriageway** /ˈkærɪdʒweɪ/ noun [C] *UK* one of the two sides of a motorway or main road *the southbound carriageway* ➔ *See also:* **dual carriageway.**

**carrier** /ˈkæriəʳ/ noun [C] **1** TRANSPORT a person, vehicle, or machine that transports things from one place to another **2** DISEASE a person who has a disease that they can give to other people without suffering from it themselves **3** COMPANY a company that operates aircraft ➔ *See also:* **aircraft carrier**, **letter carrier**.

'**carrier ˌbag** noun [C] *UK* a large paper or plastic bag with handles that you are given in a shop to carry the things you have bought ➔ *See picture at* **bag.**

**carrot** /ˈkærət/ noun **1** [C, U] an orange-coloured vegetable that is long and thin and grows in the ground ➔ *See colour picture* **Fruit and Vegetables** *on page Centre 8.* **2** [C] *informal* something that is offered to someone in order to encourage them to do something **3 carrot and stick** If you use a carrot-and-stick method, you offer someone rewards if they do something and say you will punish them if they do not.

○━**carry** /ˈkæri/ verb **1** HOLD [T] to hold something or someone with your hands, arms, or on your back and take them from one place to another *He was carrying my bags.* ● *She picked up the child and carried him down the stairs.* **2** TRANSPORT [T] to move someone or something from one place to another *The plane was carrying 30 passengers.* ● *Underground cables carry electricity to all parts of the building.* ● *Strong currents carried them out to sea.* **3** HAVE WITH YOU [T] to have

something with you in a pocket, bag, etc *She still carries his photo in her purse.* **4** DISEASE [T] to have a disease that you might give to someone else *Mosquitoes carry malaria and other infectious diseases.* **5** PART [T] to have something as a part or a result of something *All cigarette advertising must carry a government health warning.* ● *Murder still carries the death penalty there.* **6** SOUND [I] If a sound or someone's voice carries, it can be heard a long way away. **7** SUPPORT [T] to support the weight of something *Is the ice thick enough to carry my weight?* **8** DEVELOP [T] to develop something in a particular way *She carried her diet to extremes.* **9 be carried** to be formally accepted by people voting at a meeting *The **motion was carried** by 210 votes to 160.* ➔ *See also:* carry **weight.**

**be carried away** to be so excited about something that you do not control what you say or do *There's far too much food – I'm afraid I got a bit carried away.*

**carry sth off** to succeed in doing or achieving something difficult *It's not an easy part to act but he carried it off brilliantly.*

**carry on** to continue doing something [+ doing sth] *The doctors have warned him but he just carries on drinking.* ● *Carry on with your work while I'm gone.*

**carry out sth** to do or complete something, especially something that you have said you would do or that you have been told to do *I was only carrying out orders.*

**carryall** /ˈkæriɔːl/ *US* (*UK* **holdall**) noun [C] a large bag for carrying clothes ➔ *See picture at* **luggage.**

**cart**[1] /kɑːt/ noun [C] **1** a vehicle with two or four wheels that is pulled by an animal and used for carrying goods **2** *US* (*UK* **trolley**) a metal structure on wheels that is used for carrying things ➔ *See picture at* **trolley.** ➔ *See also:* **go-cart.**

**cart**[2] /kɑːt/ verb *informal* **cart sb/sth around/ away/off, etc** to take someone or something somewhere *I've had to cart the kids around with me all day.*

**carte blanche** /ˌkɑːtˈblɑːnʃ/ noun [U] complete freedom to do what you want [+ to do sth] *She was **given carte blanche** to make whatever changes she wanted.*

**cartel** /kɑːˈtel/ noun [C] a group of companies who join together to control prices and limit competition

**cartilage** /ˈkɑːtɪlɪdʒ/ noun [C, U] a strong elastic substance found where two bones connect in the human body *a torn cartilage in his right knee*

**carton** /ˈkɑːtᵊn/ noun [C] a container for food and drink that is made from strong, stiff paper or plastic *a carton of milk/fruit juice* ➔ *See picture at* **container.**

**cartoon** /kɑːˈtuːn/ noun [C] **1** a film made using characters that are drawn and not real *Mickey Mouse and other famous cartoon characters* **2** a funny drawing, especially in a newspaper or magazine ● **cartoonist** noun [C] someone whose job is to draw cartoons

**cartridge** /ˈkɑːtrɪdʒ/ noun [C] **1** a small container that is used in a larger piece of

**cartoon**

equipment and can be easily replaced *an ink cartridge* **2** a tube containing an explosive substance and a bullet for use in a gun

**carve** /kɑːv/ *verb* [I, T] **1** to make an object, a shape, or a pattern by cutting wood, stone, etc *The statue was **carved out of** stone.* ● *They had **carved** their initials **into** the tree.* **2** to cut a large piece of cooked meat into smaller pieces **3 carve (out) a niche/career/role, etc for yourself** to be successful in a particular job or activity

**carve sth up** to divide something into smaller parts, in a way that people do not approve of *The countryside has been carved up and sold to property developers.*

**carving** /ˈkɑːvɪŋ/ *noun* **1** [C] an object or a pattern that has been carved **2** [U] the activity of carving an object or pattern *wood carving*

**cascade** /kæsˈkeɪd/ *verb* [I] to fall quickly and in large amounts *Water cascaded from the rocks above.* ● *cascade noun* [C] *literary* a large amount of something, especially something falling or hanging *a cascade of golden hair*

o▬**case** /keɪs/ *noun* **1** SITUATION [C] a particular situation or example of something *People were imprisoned, and, in some cases, killed for their beliefs.* ● *We usually ask for references, but in your case it will not be necessary.* ● *The whole film is based on **a case** of mistaken identity.* **2** COURT OF LAW [C] something that is decided in a court of law *a libel/criminal/divorce case* ● *He lost his case.* **3** CRIME [C] a crime that police are trying to solve *a murder case* ● *Police in the town have investigated 50 cases of burglary in the past month.* **4** ILLNESS [C] an illness, or somebody with an illness *4,000 new cases of the disease are diagnosed every year.* **5 be the case** to be true *Bad diet can cause tiredness, but I don't think that's the case here.* **6** REASONS [C] facts or reasons that prove a particular opinion [usually singular] *There is **a strong case for/against** bringing in the new legislation.* ● *mainly UK He **put the case for** more funding very convincingly.* **7** CONTAINER [C] a container for storing or protecting something *a pencil case* ● *a cigarette case* ● *The statues are kept in a glass case.* **8** BAG [C] *UK* another word for suit-

case (= a rectangular bag or container with a handle which you use for carrying clothes in when you are travelling) **9 (just) in case** because something might happen, or might have happened *I don't think that it's going to rain, but I'll bring a raincoat just in case.* **10 in any case** used to give another reason for something that you are saying, or that you have done *I don't want to go skiing and, in any case, I can't afford it.* **11 in that case/in which case** because that is the situation/if that is the situation *"Peter's coming tonight." "Oh, in that case, I'll stay in."* **12 be a case of doing sth** to be necessary to do something *We know that we're right. It's just a case of proving it.* **13 in case of sth** *formal* when something happens, or in preparation for when something happens *We keep a bucket of water backstage, in case of fire.* **14 a case in point** a good example of something *Supermarkets often charge too much for goods. Bananas are a case in point.* **15 be/get on sb's case** *informal* to criticize someone in an annoying way because of something that they have done *She's always on my case about something.* **16 be on the case** *UK informal* to be doing what needs to be done ⊃ *See also:* **lower case, upper case.**

,case 'history *noun* [C] a record of what happens to a particular person *The study used case histories from 500 teenage boys.*

'case ,study *noun* [C] a report about a particular person or thing, to show an example of a general principle

o▬**cash**[1] /kæʃ/ *noun* [U] **1** money in the form of coins or notes (= paper money) *I'm taking £50 in cash.* ● *Are you paying by cheque or by cash?* **2** *informal* money in any form *She's a bit short of cash at the moment.* ● *a cash prize* ⊃ *See also:* **e-cash, hard cash.**

**cash**[2] /kæʃ/ *verb* **cash a cheque** to exchange a cheque (= piece of paper printed by a bank and used to pay for things) for coins or paper money *Where can I cash our traveller's cheques?*

**cash in on sth** to get money or another advantage from an event or a situation, often in an unfair way *Her family have been accused of cashing in on her death.*

'cash ,card *noun* [C] *UK* a plastic card that you use to get money from a machine

'cash ,crop *noun* [C] a crop that is grown to be sold

'cash ,desk *noun* [C] *UK* the place in a shop where you pay for the things that you buy

**cashew** /ˈkæʃuː, kəˈʃuː/ (*also* 'cashew ˌnut) *noun* [C] a curved nut that you can eat

**cashflow** /ˈkæʃfləʊ/ *noun* [U] the movement of money in and out of a business or bank account

**cashier** /kæʃˈɪə/ *noun* [C] someone whose job is to receive and pay out money in a shop, bank, etc

'cash maˌchine (*also UK* **cashpoint**) *noun* [C] a machine, usually in a wall outside a bank, that you can get money from using a plastic card

**cashmere** /ˈkæʃmɪə/ ⓤⓢ /ˈkæʒmɪr/ *noun* [U] a type of very soft, expensive wool

**cashpoint** /ˈkæʃpɔɪnt/ *UK* (*UK/US* **cash machine**)

*noun* [C] a machine, usually in a wall outside a bank, that you can get money from using a plastic card

'cash ,register *noun* [C] a machine that is used in shops for keeping money in, and for recording everything that is sold

casino /kə'si:nəʊ/ *noun* [C] a place where card games and other games of risk are played for money

cask /kɑːsk/ *noun* [C] a strong, round, wooden container that is used for storing alcoholic drinks

casket /'kɑːskɪt/ *noun* [C] **1** *UK* a small, decorated box that is used for keeping valuable objects **2** *US* (*UK/US* **coffin**) a box in which a dead body is buried

casserole /'kæsᵊrəʊl/ *noun* **1** [C, U] a mixture of meat or beans with liquid and vegetables cooked for a long time in the oven **2** [C] (*also* 'casserole ,dish) a large, heavy container with a lid, that is used for cooking casseroles

cassette /kə'set/ *noun* [C] a flat, plastic case containing a long piece of magnetic material that is used to record and play sound or pictures *a video cassette* • *The album is available on CD or cassette.*

ca'ssette ,player *noun* [C] a machine that plays cassettes of music or sound

ca'ssette re,corder *noun* [C] a machine that is used for playing cassettes of music or sound and for recording music or sound onto cassettes

cast¹ /kɑːst/ *verb* [T] *past* **cast 1** ACTOR to choose an actor for a particular part in a film or play [often passive] *Why am I always* **cast as** *the villain?* **2** THROW *literary* to throw something **3** LIGHT *literary* to send light or shadow (= dark shapes) in a particular direction *The moon cast a white light into the room.* **4 cast doubt/suspicion on sb/sth** to make people feel less sure about or have less trust in someone or something *A leading scientist has cast doubts on government claims that the drug is safe.* **5 cast a/your vote** to vote **6 cast a spell on sb a** to seem to use magic to attract someone *The city had cast a spell on me and I never wanted to leave.* **b** to use magic to make something happen to someone **7** METAL to make an object by pouring hot metal into a container of a particular shape ➔ *See also:* cast your/an **eye¹** over sth, cast **light¹** on sth, cast a **pall²** over sth, cast a **shadow¹** over sth.

**cast off** If a boat casts off, it leaves.

cast² /kɑːst/ *noun* **1** [group] all the actors in a film or play *The cast are in rehearsal at the moment.* **2** [C] a hard cover used to keep a broken bone in the correct position until it gets better

castaway /'kɑːstəweɪ/ *noun* [C] someone who is left on an island, or in a place where there are few or no other people, after their ship has sunk

caste /kɑːst/ *noun* [C, U] a system of dividing Hindu society into social groups, or one of these groups *the caste system*

castigate /'kæstɪɡeɪt/ *verb* [T] *formal* to criticize someone severely

cast-iron /'kɑːst,aɪən/ *adj* **1** [always before noun]

able to be trusted completely, or impossible to doubt *I need a cast-iron guarantee that the work will be finished on time.* **2** made of cast iron

,cast 'iron *noun* [U] a type of very hard iron

castle /'kɑːsl/ *noun* [C] a large, strong building with towers and high walls, that was built in the past to protect the people inside from being attacked

castle

cast-off /'kɑːstɒf/ *noun* [C] a piece of clothing or other item that you give to someone because you do not want it any more [usually plural] *This dress is another of my sister's cast-offs.*

castrate /kæs'treɪt/ ⓤⓢ 'kæstreɪt/ *verb* [T] to remove the testicles (= organs that produce sperm) of a man or male animal • castration /kæs'treɪʃᵊn/ *noun* [U]

casual /'kæʒjuəl/ *adj* **1** NOT PLANNED [always before noun] not planned, or without particular meaning or importance *a casual remark/ acquaintance/meeting* • *He was bored with casual affairs and wanted a proper relationship.* **2** RELAXED relaxed and not seeming very interested in someone or something *a casual manner/approach* • *She's much too casual about her work.* **3** CLOTHING Casual clothing is comfortable and not suitable for formal occasions. **4** WORK [always before noun] *mainly UK* Casual work is not regular or fixed. *casual labour/workers/jobs*

casually /'kæʒjuəli/ *adv* **1** in a relaxed way, or not seeming to be interested in someone or something *I asked as casually as I could if she was going to be at the party.* **2** If you dress casually, you do not dress in a formal way.

casualty /'kæʒjuəlti/ *noun* **1** INJURED [C] someone who is injured or killed in an accident or war *Both sides in the conflict have promised to try to avoid civilian casualties.* **2** BADLY AFFECTED [C] someone or something that is badly affected by something that happens *The health service has been the biggest casualty of government cuts.* **3** HOSPITAL [U] *UK* (*US* **emergency room**) the part of a hospital where people go when they have been injured or have urgent illnesses so that they can be treated immediately

○━cat /kæt/ *noun* [C] **1** a small animal with fur, four legs and a tail that is kept as a pet **2** a large, wild animal that is related to the cat, such as the lion **3 let the cat out of the bag** to tell people secret information, often without intending to

cataclysmic /,kætə'klɪzmɪk/ *adj* sudden, shocking, and violent *cataclysmic changes/events*

catalogue¹ (*also US* **catalog**) /'kætᵊlɒɡ/ *noun* [C] **1** a book with a list of all the goods that you can buy from a shop, or of all the books, paintings, etc that you can find in a place *a clothing catalogue* **2 a catalogue of disasters/errors/ failures, etc** a series of bad events

**catalogue²** (*also US* **catalog**) /'kæt²lɒg/ *verb* [T] **cataloguing**, *past* **catalogued** to make a list of things, especially in order to put it in a catalogue

**catalyst** /'kæt²lɪst/ *noun* [C] someone or something that causes change *Recent riots and suicides have acted as a catalyst for change in the prison system.*

**catapult¹** /'kætəpʌlt/ *verb* **1 catapult sb/sth into/out/through, etc** to make someone or something move through the air very quickly and with great force [often passive] *When the two cars collided, he was catapulted out of his seat.* **2 catapult sb to stardom/into the lead, etc** to make someone suddenly very famous, successful, etc

**catapult²** /'kætəpʌlt/ *UK* (*US* **slingshot**) *noun* [C] a Y-shaped object with a piece of elastic used by children to shoot small stones

**cataract** /'kæt²rækt/ *noun* [C] an area of someone's eye with a disease that gradually prevents them from seeing correctly

**catarrh** /kə'tɑːr/ *noun* [U] *UK* the thick substance that is produced in your nose and throat when you have a cold

**catastrophe** /kə'tæstrəfi/ *noun* [C, U] an extremely bad event that causes a lot of suffering or destruction *After the drought, the country is facing environmental catastrophe.*

**catastrophic** /ˌkæt²'strɒfɪk/ *adj* causing a lot of suffering or destruction

O━**catch¹** /kætʃ/ *verb past* **caught 1** [GET HOLD] [T] to stop someone or something that is moving through the air by getting hold of it *Try to catch the ball.* • *She fell backwards but he caught her in his arms.* **2** [STOP ESCAPING] [T] to find and stop a person or animal who is trying to escape *He ran after his attacker but couldn't catch him.* • *Did you catch many fish today?* **3** [CRIMINAL] [T] If the police catch a criminal, they find them and take them away. *These terrorists must be caught.* **4** [ILLNESS] [T] to get an illness or disease *I think I've caught a cold.* **5** [TRANSPORT] [T] to get on a bus, train, etc in order to travel somewhere *You can catch the bus from the top of the hill.* **6** [DISCOVER] [T] to discover someone who is doing something wrong or something secret [+ doing sth] *I caught her listening outside the door.* • *informal You won't catch me wearing* (= I never wear) *a tie.* **7** [STICK] [I, T] to stick somewhere, or to make something stick somewhere *My dress caught on the door handle as I was leaving.* **8** [COLLECT] [T] to collect something that is falling *I used a bucket to catch the drips.* **9** [BE IN TIME] [T] to manage to be in time to see or do something *I only caught the end of the programme.* **10** [HEAR] [T] to hear or understand something correctly *I'm sorry. I didn't catch your name.* **11 catch fire** to start burning **12 be/get caught** to be unable to avoid something unpleasant *I got caught in the rain.* **13 catch the sun** *UK* to burn your skin in the sun *You've caught the sun on your shoulders.* **14 catch sight of sth** to see something suddenly, often only for a short time *He caught sight of himself in the mirror.* **15** [HIT] [T] *UK* to hit something or someone *The ball flew across the garden, and caught me on*

the chin. ➔ *See also:* catch sb's **eye¹**, catch sb off **guard¹**.

**catch on 1** to become popular *I wonder if the game will catch on with young people?* **2** *informal* to understand something, especially after a long time *It took him a while to catch on to what we meant.*

**catch sb out** *UK* to trick someone so that they make a mistake

**catch (sb/sth) up 1** to reach someone or something that is in front of you, by going faster than them *We soon caught up with the car in front.* **2** to reach the same level or quality as someone or something else *She's doing extra work to catch up with the rest of the class.*

**catch up** to learn or discuss the most recent news *Let's meet for a chat – I need to catch up on all the gossip.*

**be/get caught up in sth** to become involved in a situation, often without wanting to *How did the paper get caught up in a legal dispute?*

**catch up on/with sth** to do something that you did not have time to do earlier *After the exams, I need to catch up on some sleep.*

**catch up with sb** If something bad that you have done or that has been happening to you catches up with you, it begins to cause problems for you. *I can feel the stress of the last few weeks beginning to catch up with me.*

**catch²** /kætʃ/ *noun* [C] **1** [WITH HANDS] when someone catches something that is moving through the air *a brilliant catch* **2** [FISH] the amount of fish that someone has caught **3** [PROBLEM] a hidden problem or difficulty with something *He's offering us a free flight? There must be a catch.* **4** [LOCK] a part on something that fastens it and keeps it closed *a safety catch*

**catching** /'kætʃɪŋ/ *adj* [never before noun] If an illness or a mood is catching, other people can get it from you.

**catchment area** /'kætʃmənt,eəriə/ *noun* [C] *UK* the area around a school or a hospital, where most of the students or patients come from

**catchphrase** /'kætʃfreɪz/ *noun* [C] a phrase which is often repeated by a particular organization or person, and becomes connected with them

**catchy** /'kætʃi/ *adj* A catchy song, tune, or phrase is easy to remember.

**categorical** /ˌkætə'gɒrɪk²l/ *adj* If someone is categorical about what they say, they say it with force and are completely certain about it. *a categorical assurance/denial* • **categorically** *adv They have denied categorically that they were involved in the conspiracy.*

**categorize** (*also UK* **-ise**) /'kætəg²raɪz/ *verb* [T] to divide people or things into groups of similar types *The books are categorized according to subject.*

O━**category** /'kætəg²ri/ *noun* [C] a group of people or things of a similar type *Our customers fall into two main categories: retired people and housewives.*

**cater** /'keɪtər/ *verb* [I, T] to provide and often serve food and drinks for a particular event *How many are we catering for at the wedding reception?*

**cater for sb/sth** *mainly UK* to provide what is

wanted or needed by a particular group of people *The club caters for children between the ages of 4 and 12.*
**cater to sb/sth** to give people exactly what they want, usually something that people think is wrong *This legislation simply caters to unacceptable racist opinions.*

**caterer** /ˈkeɪtᵊrəʳ/ *noun* [C] a person or company that provides food and drinks for particular events, or for an organization

**catering** /ˈkeɪtərɪŋ/ *noun* [U] providing food and drinks for people *Who **did the catering** for the party?*

**caterpillar** /ˈkætəpɪləʳ/ *noun* [C] a small, long animal with many legs that eats leaves

**caterpillar**

**cathartic** /kəˈθɑːtɪk/ *adj* A cathartic experience or event helps you to express and get rid of strong emotions.

**cathedral** /kəˈθiːdrᵊl/ *noun* [C] the largest and most important church in a particular area

**Catholic** /ˈkæθᵊlɪk/ (*also* **Roman Catholic**) *adj* belonging or relating to the part of the Christian religion that has the Pope (= a very important priest) as its leader *a Catholic priest/school* • Catholic *noun* [C] *I think he's a Catholic.*

**the ˌCatholic ˈChurch** *noun* the Catholic religion and all the people who believe in it

**Catholicism** /kəˈθɒlɪsɪzᵊm/ (*also* ˌRoman Caˈtholicism**) *noun* [U] the beliefs of the Catholic religion

**catsup** /ˈkætsəp/ *noun* [U] *another US spelling of* ketchup (= a thick, red sauce that is eaten cold with food)

**cattle** /ˈkætl/ *noun* [plural] male and female cows, kept on a farm for their milk and meat *beef/dairy cattle*

**catty** /ˈkæti/ *adj informal* intending to hurt someone by saying unkind things *catty remarks*

**catwalk** /ˈkætwɔːk/ *noun* [C] the narrow, raised path that people walk along in a fashion show

**Caucasian** /kɔːˈkeɪzən/ *adj* belonging to a race of people with white or pale skin • Caucasian *noun* [C] a Caucasian person

**caught** /kɔːt/ *past of* catch

**cauldron** /ˈkɔːldrᵊn/ *noun* [C] *literary* a large, round metal pot that is used for cooking over a fire

**cauliflower** /ˈkɒlɪˌflaʊəʳ/ *noun* [C, U] a large, round, white vegetable with thick, green leaves around the outside ➔ *See colour picture* **Fruit and Vegetables** *on page Centre 8.*

**o→cause¹** /kɔːz/ *noun* **1** MAKES HAPPEN [C] someone or something that makes something happen *The police are still trying to establish the cause of the fire.* • *She died of natural causes.* **2** REASON [U] a reason to feel something or to behave in a particular way *He's never

given me any **cause for** concern.* **3** PRINCIPLE [C] a principle or aim that a group of people support or fight for *The money will all go to a good cause.* • *He fought for the Republican cause in the war.*

**o→cause²** /kɔːz/ *verb* [T] to make something happen *The hurricane caused widespread damage.* • *Most heart attacks are **caused by** blood clots.* • [+ two objects] *I hope the children haven't caused you too much trouble.* • [+ to do sth] *What caused the washing machine to blow up?*

**causeway** /ˈkɔːzweɪ/ *noun* [C] a raised path or road over a wet area

**caustic** /ˈkɔːstɪk/ *adj* **1** A caustic remark is extremely unkind and intended to upset or criticize someone. **2** Caustic chemicals can burn things.

**caution¹** /ˈkɔːʃᵊn/ *noun* **1** [U] great care and attention not to take risks or get into danger *Travellers have been advised to exercise great caution when passing through the region.* • *I would **treat** anything he says **with** extreme caution* (= not be too quick to believe it). **2** [C] *UK* when a police officer or other person in authority warns you that you will be punished if you do something bad again **3 throw caution to the wind** to take a risk ➔ *See also:* err on the **side¹** of caution.

**caution²** /ˈkɔːʃᵊn/ *verb* **1** [I, T] *formal* to warn someone of something [often passive] *They were cautioned against buying shares in the company.* **2** [T] *UK* If police caution people, they are given a spoken warning that they will be punished next time.

**cautionary** /ˈkɔːʃᵊnᵊri/ *adj* intended to warn or advise someone *a cautionary tale*

**cautious** /ˈkɔːʃəs/ *adj* taking care to avoid risks or danger *She is cautious about lending money to anyone.* • cautiously *adv He crept cautiously towards the door.*

**cavalier** /ˌkævᵊlˈɪəʳ/ *adj formal* without caring about other people or about a dangerous or serious situation *a cavalier attitude*

**the cavalry** /ˈkævᵊlri/ *noun* [U, group] soldiers who fight on horses

**cave¹** /keɪv/ *noun* [C] a large hole in the side of a cliff (= straight, high rock next to the sea), mountain, or under the ground

**cave²** /keɪv/ *verb*
**cave in 1** If a ceiling, roof, or other structure caves in, it breaks and falls into the space below. **2** to agree to something that you were against before, after someone has persuaded you or made you afraid *The company has finally caved in to the demands of the unions.*

**caveat** /ˈkæviæt/ *noun* [C] *formal* something you say which warns that there is a limit on a general announcement made earlier

**cavern** /ˈkævᵊn/ *noun* [C] a large cave

**caviar** (*also* **caviare**) /ˈkæviɑːʳ/ *noun* [U] the eggs of a large fish, eaten as a food and usually very expensive

**cavity** /ˈkævəti/ *noun* [C] **1** a hole or a space inside something solid or between two surfaces **2** a hole in a tooth

**cavort** /kəˈvɔːt/ *verb* [I] to jump, dance, or move about in an excited way

---

**cc** /ˌsiː'siː/ **1** *abbreviation for* carbon copy: used on a letter to show that you are sending a copy to other people **2** *abbreviation for* cubic centimetre: a unit for measuring the volume of something *a 750cc motorcycle*

o—ᴸ **CD** /ˌsiː'diː/ *noun* [C] *abbreviation for* compact disc: a small disc on which music or information is recorded ⊃ *See colour picture* **The Office** *on page Centre 12.*

ˌ**C'D** ˌ**player** *noun* [C] a machine that is used for playing music CDs

**CD-ROM** /ˌsiːdiː'rɒm/ *noun* [C] *abbreviation for* compact disc read-only memory: a CD that holds large amounts of information that can be read by a computer

**cease** /siːs/ *verb* [I, T] *formal* to stop [+ doing sth] *He ordered his men to cease firing.* ● [+ to do sth] *Her behaviour never ceases to amaze me.*

**ceasefire** /'siːsfaɪəʳ/ *noun* [C] an agreement between two armies or groups to stop fighting

**ceaseless** /'siːsləs/ *adj formal* continuous *the ceaseless movement of the sea* ● **ceaselessly** *adv*

**cedar** /'siːdəʳ/ *noun* [C, U] a tall, evergreen (= with leaves that do not fall off in winter) tree, or the red wood of this tree

**cede** /siːd/ *verb* [T] *formal* to give something such as land or power to another country or person, especially because you are forced to

**ceiling** /'siːlɪŋ/ *noun* [C] **1** the surface of a room which you can see when you look above you **2** a limit on the amount that can be paid for something *They have set a ceiling on pay rises.*

o—ᴸ **celebrate** /'seləbreɪt/ *verb* [I, T] to do something enjoyable because it is a special day, or because something good has happened *Do you celebrate Christmas in your country?*

**celebrated** /'seləbreɪtɪd/ *adj* famous for a special ability or quality *She is celebrated for her wit.*

**celebration** /ˌselə'breɪʃᵊn/ *noun* [C, U] when you celebrate a special day or event *Let's buy some champagne in celebration of her safe arrival.* ● *You've passed? This calls for a celebration.*

**celebratory** /ˌselə'breɪtᵊri/ ⑤ 'seləbrətɔːri/ *adj* done to celebrate something or wanting to celebrate something *a celebratory dinner* ● *in a celebratory mood*

**celebrity** /sə'lebrəti/ *noun* [C] a famous person

**celery** /'selᵊri/ *noun* [U] a vegetable with long, pale green stems, often eaten in salads ⊃ *See colour picture* **Fruit and Vegetables** *on page Centre 8.*

**celestial** /sə'lestiəl/ *adj literary* relating to heaven or the sky

**celibate** /'seləbət/ *adj* Someone who is celibate does not have sex. ● **celibacy** /'seləbəsi/ *noun* [U] when you do not have sex

**cell** /sel/ *noun* [C] **1** the smallest living part of an animal or a plant *brain/cancer cells* **2** a small room in a prison or police station where a prisoner is kept

**cellar** /'seləʳ/ *noun* [C] a room under the floor of a building ⊃ *See also:* **salt cellar**.

**cellist** /'tʃelɪst/ *noun* [C] someone who plays the cello

**cello** /'tʃeləʊ/ *noun* [C] a large, wooden musical instrument with four strings that you hold between your knees to play

**Cellophane** /'seləfeɪn/ *noun* [U] *trademark* thin, transparent material that is used for wrapping goods, especially flowers and food

**cellular** /'seljələʳ/ *adj* **1** relating to animal or plant cells *cellular damage* **2** [always before noun] relating to cellular phones *cellular companies/communications*

ˈ**cellular** ˌ**phone** (*also* **cellphone** /'selfəʊn/) *noun* [C] a mobile phone (= telephone that you can carry everywhere with you) ⊃ *See picture at* **telephone**.

**cellulite** /'seljəlaɪt/ *noun* [U] fat that looks like small lumps below the skin, especially on the upper legs *I can't seem to get rid of my cellulite.*

**cellulose** /'seljələʊs/ *noun* [U] a substance in plants that is used to make some paper and plastics

**Celsius** /'selsiəs/ (*abbreviation* **C**) *noun* [U] a measurement of temperature in which water freezes at 0° and boils at 100°

**Celtic** /'keltɪk/ *adj* relating to the people of Ireland, Scotland, and Wales *Celtic art/music/literature*

**cement**[1] /sɪ'ment/ *noun* [U] a grey powder used in building which is mixed with water and sand or stones to make a hard substance

**cement**[2] /sɪ'ment/ *verb* [T] **1** to make something such as a relationship, a belief, or a position stronger *It was the holiday that really cemented our friendship.* **2** (*also* **cement over**) to cover something with cement

**cemetery** /'semətri/ *noun* [C] a place where dead people are buried

**censor** /'sensəʳ/ *verb* [T] to examine books, documents, or films and remove parts of them that are offensive or not allowed by rules [often passive] *The book was heavily censored before publication.* ● **censor** *noun* [C] *The film was banned by censors.*

**censorship** /'sensəʃɪp/ *noun* [U] when a book, film, newspaper, or other information is censored *political/state censorship*

**censure** /'sensjəʳ/ *verb* [T] *formal* to criticize someone formally for something that they have done *She was censured by the medical board for revealing details about her patient's condition.* ● **censure** *noun* [U] *formal*

**census** /'sensəs/ *noun* [C] when people in a country are officially counted and information is taken about them

o—ᴸ **cent** /sent/ *noun* [C] a coin or unit of money with a value of 1/100 of a dollar (= US unit of money); ¢ *The newspaper costs sixty-five cents.*

**centenary** /sen'tiːnᵊri/ ⑤ 'sentᵊneri/ (*also US* **centennial** /sen'teniəl/) *noun* [C] the day or year that is 100 years after an important event *This year, there will be many concerts to mark the centenary of the composer's death.*

o—ᴸ **center** /'sentəʳ/ *noun, verb US spelling of* centre

**centerpiece** /'sentəpiːs/ *noun* [C] *US spelling of* centrepiece

**centigrade** /'sentɪgreɪd/ (*abbreviation* **C**) *noun* [U] a measurement of temperature in which water freezes at 0° and boils at 100°

**centilitre** /'sentɪˌliːtəʳ/ *UK* (*US* **centiliter**) (*written abbreviation* **cl**) *noun* [C] a unit for measuring liquid, equal to 0.01 litres

**centimetre** *UK* (*US* **centimeter**) (*written abbreviation* **cm**) /'senti,mi:tər/ *noun* [C] a unit for measuring length, equal to 0.01 metres

⊶**central** /'sentr<sup>ə</sup>l/ *adj* **1** POSITION in or near the centre of a place or object *central Africa/ America* • *The roof is supported by a central column.* **2** ORGANIZATION [always before noun] controlled or organized in one main place *central authorities/government* • *the US central bank* • *central control/planning* **3** IMPORTANT main or most important *a central character/ figure* • *the central argument of the book* • *Her role is central to the film.* **4** CITY in the main part of a town or city *Our offices are very central.* • **centrally** *adv*

,central 'heating *noun* [U] a system of heating a building by warming air or water in one place and carrying it to different rooms in pipes

**centralize** (*also UK* **-ise**) /'sentr<sup>ə</sup>laɪz/ *verb* [T] If a country or organization is centralized, it is controlled from one place. [often passive] *centralized control/government* • *We are centralizing our pricing systems.* • **centralization** /,sentr<sup>ə</sup>laɪ'zeɪʃ<sup>ə</sup>n/ *noun* [U]

⊶**centre¹** *UK* (*US* **center**) /'sentər/ *noun* **1** MIDDLE [C] the middle point or part of something *She stood in the centre of the room.* • *Cars are not allowed in the town centre.* **2** PLACE [C] a place or a building used for a particular activity *a health/advice centre* • *a centre for the homeless* **3** BUSINESS [C] a place where a lot of a particular activity or business takes place *an industrial centre* **4** POLITICAL [no plural] (*also the* **centre**) a political position with opinions that are not extreme *His political views are left of centre.* **5 be the centre of attention** to receive more attention than anyone or anything else ➔ *See also:* **community centre, garden centre, shopping centre.**

**centre²** *UK* (*US* **center**) /'sentər/ *verb* [T] to put something in the middle of an area

**centre around/on sb/sth** to have someone or something as the main part of a discussion or activity *The dispute centres on racial issues.*

,centre of 'gravity *noun* [C] *plural* **centres of gravity** the point in an object where its weight is balanced

**centrepiece** *UK* (*US* **centerpiece**) /'sentəpi:s/ *noun* [C] **1** the most important or attractive part of something *The employment programme is the centrepiece of the government's economic strategy.* **2** a decoration that is put in the middle of a dinner table

⊶**century** /'senʃ<sup>ə</sup>ri/ *noun* [C] a period of 100 years, especially used in giving dates *the twentieth century*

**ceramics** /sə'ræmɪks/ *noun* [plural] objects that are made by shaping and heating clay • **ceramic** *adj* made by shaping and heating clay *a ceramic pot*

**cereal** /'sɪəriəl/ *noun* [C, U] **1** a plant that is grown to produce grain for food *cereal crops* **2** a food that is made from grain and eaten with milk, especially in the morning *breakfast cereals* ➔ *See colour picture* **Food** *on page Centre 7.*

**cerebral** /'serəbr<sup>ə</sup>l/ *adj formal* **1** Cerebral films, books, etc need a lot of thought to understand

them, and cerebral people think a lot. **2** [always before noun] relating to the brain *cerebral arteries*

**ceremonial** /,serɪ'məʊniəl/ *adj* relating to a ceremony *The soldiers were in full ceremonial dress.* • **ceremonially** *adv*

**ceremony** /'serɪməni/ *noun* **1** [C] a formal event that is performed on important social or religious occasions *a wedding/marriage ceremony* • *an award ceremony* **2** [U] formal behaviour, words, and actions that are part of a ceremony

⊶**certain** /'sɜːt<sup>ə</sup>n/ *adj* **1** NO DOUBT [never before noun] completely sure of something, or knowing without doubt that something is true [+ (that)] *I feel absolutely certain that you're doing the right thing.* • [+ question word] *Nobody was certain how the accident had happened.* • *He was quite* **certain about/of** *the thief's identity.* ➔ *Opposite* **uncertain**. **2 know/say for certain** to know something without doubt *We don't know for certain whether she's coming.* **3** SURE TO HAPPEN sure to happen, to do something, or to be true [+ (that)] *It now looks certain that she will resign.* • [+ to do sth] *She is certain to do well in the exams.* • *How can we* **make certain that** (= do something to be sure that) *she sees the note?* • *One thing is certain. Her attacker knew where she lived.* **4** PARTICULAR [always before noun] used to refer to a particular person or thing without naming or describing them exactly *The museum is only open at certain times of the day.* • *Certain people react badly to these drugs.* **5 a certain** used before a noun to mean existing, but difficult to describe the exact quality or amount *He's got a certain charm.* • *You have to have a certain amount of courage to perform in public.* **6 certain of** *formal* used to refer to some of a group of people or things *Certain of you already know the news.*

⊶**certainly** /'sɜːt<sup>ə</sup>nli/ *adv* **1** used to emphasize something and show that there is no doubt about it *Their team certainly deserved to win.* • *"Are your parents paying for dinner?" "I certainly hope so."* • *She may never find out. I'm certainly not going to tell her.* • *"Do you regret what you said?" "Certainly not!"* **2** used to agree to a request *"Could you pass the salt, please?" "Certainly."*

**certainty** /'sɜːt<sup>ə</sup>nti/ *noun* **1** [U] when you are completely sure about something *I can't say* **with** *any* **certainty** *what time she left.* **2** [C] something that is very likely to happen or cannot be doubted *There are no absolute certainties in life.*

**certificate** /sə'tɪfɪkət/ *noun* [C] an official document that gives details to show that something is true *a death/marriage certificate* • *an exam certificate* ➔ *See also:* **birth certificate.**

**certify** /'sɜːtɪfaɪ/ *verb* [T] **1** TRUTH *formal* to say in a formal or official way that something is true or correct [+ (that)] *I certify that the information I have given is true.* • *She was* **certified dead** *on arrival at the hospital.* **2** CERTIFICATE to give someone a certificate to say that they have completed a course of study *a certified accountant* **3** HEALTH to say officially that someone has a mental illness

**certitude** /'sɜːtɪtjuːd/ *noun* [U] *formal* when you feel certain about something

**cervix** /'sɜːvɪks/ *noun* [C] the narrow entrance to a woman's womb • cervical /sə'vaɪkᵊl, 'sɜːvɪkᵊl/ *adj cervical cancer*

**cesarean** /sɪ'zeəriən/ *noun* [C] *US spelling of* caesarean

**cessation** /ses'eɪʃᵊn/ *noun* [C, U] *formal* when something, especially violence, stops *the cessation of hostilities*

**cf** used in writing when you want the reader to make a comparison between the subject being discussed and something else

**CFC** /ˌsiːef'siː/ *noun* [C] *abbreviation for* chlorofluorocarbon: a type of gas used in fridges (= containers for keeping food cold) and aerosols (= containers for making liquids come out in small drops), which damages the layer of gases around the Earth

**chafe** /tʃeɪf/ *verb* **1** [I] to feel angry because of rules and limits *He **chafed against/at** the narrow academic approach of his school*. **2** [I, T] to make part of the body painful by rubbing, or to become painful because of being rubbed

**chagrin** /'ʃæɡrɪn ⓤ ʃə'ɡrɪn/ *noun* [U] anger or disappointment caused by something that does not happen the way you wanted it *To his parents **chagrin**, he had no intention of becoming a lawyer*.

**chain¹** /tʃeɪn/ *noun* **1** METAL RINGS [C, U] a line of metal rings connected together *a bicycle chain* • *She wore a gold chain around her neck*. • *The hostages were kept **in chains***. **2** BUSINESS [C] a number of similar shops, restaurants, etc owned by the same company *a chain of hotels/supermarkets* **3** EVENTS [C] a series of things that happen one after the other *His arrival set off a surprising **chain of events***.

**chain**

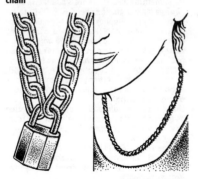

**chain²** /tʃeɪn/ (*also* **chain up**) *verb* [T] to fasten someone or something to someone or something else using a chain *I **chained** my bike **to** a lamppost*. • *You shouldn't keep a dog chained up like that*.

**ˌchain reˈaction** *noun* [C] a series of events where each one causes the next one to happen

**chain-smoke** /'tʃeɪnsməʊk/ *verb* [I, T] to smoke cigarettes one after another • 'chain ˌsmoker *noun* [C]

**ˈchain ˌstore** *noun* [C] one of a group of similar shops owned by the same company

o⟀**chair¹** /tʃeəʳ/ *noun* [C] **1** FURNITURE a seat for one person, with a back, usually four legs, and sometimes two arms ➔ *See colour picture* **The Office** *on page Centre 12*. **2** MEETING someone who controls a meeting or organization [usually singular] *All questions should be addressed to the chair*. **3** UNIVERSITY a very important position in a university department, or the person who has this position ➔ *See also:* **the electric chair**.

**chair²** /tʃeəʳ/ *verb* [T] to control a meeting or organization *I've been asked to chair the committee*.

**chairman,** **chairwoman** /'tʃeəmən, 'tʃeəˌwʊmən/ *noun* [C] *plural* **chairmen, chairwomen** a man/woman who controls a meeting, company, or other organization

**chairperson** /'tʃeəˌpɜːsᵊn/ *noun* [C] someone who controls a meeting, company, or other organization

**chalet** /'ʃæleɪ ⓤ ʃæl'eɪ/ *noun* [C] a small wooden house, often in a mountain area, or for people who are on holiday

**chalk¹** /tʃɔːk/ *noun* **1** [U] a type of soft, white rock **2** [C, U] a small stick of chalk that is used for writing and drawing *a piece of chalk* ➔ *See colour picture* **Classroom** *on page Centre 4*. **3** **be like chalk and cheese** *UK* If two people are like chalk and cheese, they are completely different from each other.

**chalk²** /tʃɔːk/ *verb* [T] *UK* to write something with a piece of chalk

**chalk sth up** to achieve something *She's chalked up five goals this season*.

**chalkboard** /'tʃɔːkbɔːd/ *US* (*UK/US* **blackboard**) *noun* [C] a large board with a dark surface that teachers write on with chalk

**chalky** /'tʃɔːki/ *adj* made of chalk, or similar to chalk

o⟀**challenge¹** /'tʃælɪndʒ/ *noun* **1** DIFFICULT [C, U] something that is difficult and that tests someone's ability or determination *Finding a decision that pleases everyone is the **challenge** which now **faces** the committee*. • *It was the element of challenge which attracted me to the job*. **2** INVITATION [C] an invitation to compete in a game or a fight *I'm sure Paul will race you. He never refuses a challenge*. **3** DISAGREEMENT [C] an expression of disagreement with ideas, rules, or someone's authority *a challenge to the authority of the President*

**challenge²** /'tʃælɪndʒ/ *verb* [T] **1** to express disagreement with ideas, rules, or someone's authority *The election results are being challenged*. **2** to invite someone to compete in a game or fight *He **challenged** Smith **to** a fight*.

**challenger** /'tʃælændʒəʳ/ *noun* [C] someone who competes in a game, competition, or election, often to win a position that someone else has *There are five challengers for the title*.

**challenging** /'tʃælɪndʒɪŋ/ *adj* difficult to do in a way that tests your ability or determination *This has been a challenging time for us all*.

**chamber** /'tʃeɪmbəʳ/ *noun* [C] **1** ROOM a room used for an official or special purpose *a debating chamber* • *a burial chamber* **2** PARLIAMENT one of the groups that a parliament is divided into *the upper/lower chamber* **3** MACHINE/BODY a closed space in a machine or in your body *the*

**C**

*left chamber of the heart* ⊃ *See also:* **gas chamber**.

**chambermaid** /'tʃeɪmbəmeɪd/ *noun* [C] a woman whose job is to clean and tidy hotel bedrooms

**chamber music** *noun* [U] music that is written for a small group of musicians

**chamber of commerce** *noun* [C] *plural* **chambers of commerce** an organization of business people who work together to improve business in their local area

**champ** /tʃæmp/ *noun* [C] *informal short for* champion

**champagne** /ʃæm'peɪn/ *noun* [U] French white wine with lots of bubbles in it which people often drink to celebrate something

**champion¹** /'tʃæmpiən/ *noun* [C] **1** a person, animal, or team that wins a competition *a boxing champion* • *the world champions* **2** someone who supports, defends, or fights for a person, belief, or principle *a champion of human rights* ⊃ *See also:* **reigning champion**.

**champion²** /'tʃæmpiən/ *verb* [T] to support, defend, or fight for a person, belief, or principle *She championed the cause of free speech.*

**championship** /'tʃæmpiənʃɪp/ *noun* [C] **1** a competition to find the best team or player in a particular game or sport *The world championship will be held in this country next year.* **2** the position of being a champion *She is current holder of our tennis championship.*

o⤐**chance¹** /tʃɑːns/ *noun* **1** POSSIBILITY [C, U] the possibility that something will happen [+ (that)] *There's a chance that she'll still be there.* • *She has little chance of passing the exam.* • *Is there any chance of a drink?* • *She's ruined my chances of getting the job.* **2** OPPORTUNITY [C] the opportunity to do something [+ to do sth] *I didn't get a chance to speak to you at the party.* • *I hope you've had the chance to look around the exhibition.* • *Give me a chance to prove that I can do the work.* • *Going on a world cruise is the chance of a lifetime* (= an opportunity which only comes once in your life). **3** LUCK [U] when something happens because of luck, or without being planned *I saw her by chance in the shop.* • *a game of chance* **4** RISK [C] a risk *I'm delivering my work by hand. I'm not taking any chances.* **5 by any chance** used to ask in a polite way whether something is possible or true *You're not Spanish by any chance, are you?* **6 stand a chance** to have a chance of success or of achieving something *He stands a good chance of winning the election.* **7 chances are** it is likely [+ (that)] *Chances are that he'll refuse.* **8 No chance!/Not a chance!** used to emphasize that there is no possibility of something happening *"Do you think she'd go out with me?" "No chance!"* **9 fat chance** *informal* used to say that you do not think that something is likely to happen *"Do you think we'll win?" "Fat chance."* ⊃ *See also:* **off-chance**, **outside chance**.

**chance²** /tʃɑːns/ *verb* [T] *informal* to take a risk by doing something *He'd probably never find out if I did go to the party, but I can't afford to chance it.*

**chance³** /tʃɑːns/ *adj* [always before noun] A chance

event is not planned or expected. *a chance meeting*

**chancellor** /'tʃɑːnsᵊlər/ *noun* [C] **1** GOVERNMENT the leader of the government in some countries *the German chancellor* **2** UNIVERSITY the person with the highest position in some universities **3** MONEY (*also* **Chancellor of the Exchequer**) *UK* the person in the British government who makes decisions about taxes and government spending

**chandelier** /ˌʃændə'lɪər/ *noun* [C] a large light that hangs from the ceiling that is made of many small lights or candles and small pieces of glass

o⤐**change¹** /tʃeɪndʒ/ *verb* **1** DIFFERENT [I, T] to become different, or to make someone or something become different *I hadn't seen her for twenty years, but she hadn't changed a bit.* • *The course changed my life.* • *She's changed from being a happy, healthy child to being ill all the time.* • *Since he met her, he's a changed man.* • *changing attitudes* **2** FROM ONE THING TO ANOTHER [I, T] to stop having or using one thing and start having or using another *The doctor has recommended changing my diet.* • *I'll have to ask them if they can change the time of my interview.* • *You'll have to change gear to go up the hill.* **3** CLOTHES [I, T] to take off your clothes and put on different ones *He changed out of his school uniform into jeans and a T-shirt.* • *Is there somewhere I can get changed?* **4** JOURNEY [I, T] to get off a bus, plane, etc and catch another, in order to continue a journey *I have to change trains at Bristol.* • *Is there a direct service, or do we have to change?* **5** IN SHOP [T] *UK* to take something you have bought back to a shop and exchange it for something else *If the dress doesn't fit, can I change it for a smaller one?* **6** MONEY [T] to get or give someone money in exchange for money of a different type *Where can I change my dollars?* • *Can you change a £20 note for two tens?* **7** BED [T] to take dirty sheets off a bed and put on clean ones *to change the bed/sheets* **8** BABY [T] to put a clean nappy (= thick cloth worn on a baby's bottom) on a baby ⊃ *See also:* **chop¹** and change, change hands (**hand¹**), change your **tune¹**.

**change sth around/round** to move objects such as furniture into different positions *The room looks very different since you've changed the furniture around.*

**change over** *UK* to stop using or having one thing and start using or having something else *We've just changed over from gas central heating to electric.*

o⤐**change²** /tʃeɪndʒ/ *noun* **1** DIFFERENCE [C, U] when something becomes different, or the result of something becoming different *We need to make a few changes to the design.* • *There is no change in the patient's condition* (= the illness has not got better or worse). • *How can we bring about social change?* **2** FROM ONE THING TO ANOTHER [C, U] when you stop having or using one thing and start having or using another *This country needs a change of government.* • *I've notified the school of our change of address.* **3** NEW EXPERIENCE [C] something that you enjoy because it is a new experience [usually singular] *Going abroad for our anniversary would make a lovely change.* • *It's nice to eat together as a family for a change.* **4** [MONEY] [U] the money that you get back when you pay more for something than it costs *There's your receipt and £3 change.* **5** [COINS] [U] coins, not paper money *Have you got any change for the parking meter?* • *Have you got change for £5* (= can you give me £5 in coins in return for paper money)? **6 a change of clothes** a set of clean clothes that you can put on if you need to take off the ones you are wearing **7 a change of heart** If you have a change of heart, you change your opinion or feelings about something. ➲ *See also:* **small change**.

**changeable** /ˈtʃeɪndʒəbl/ *adj* often changing, or likely to change *The weather was very changeable last summer.*

**changeover** /ˈtʃeɪndʒ,əʊvəʳ/ *noun* [C] a change from one system or situation to another [usually singular] *the changeover from the old computer system to the new one*

**'changing ,room** *noun* [C] *UK* a room in a shop where you can try clothes, or a room where you change into clothes to do sport

o-►**channel¹** /ˈtʃænᵊl/ *noun* [C] **1** [TELEVISION] a television or radio station (= broadcasting company) **2** [PASSAGE] a long, narrow passage for water or other liquids to flow along *an irrigation channel* **3** [COMMUNICATION] a way of communicating with people or getting something done *a channel of communication* • *Please make your request through the proper channels.* **4 the Channel** (*also* **the ,English 'Channel**) the narrow area of water between England and France **5** [RIVER] a part of a river or sea that is deep and wide enough for ships to travel along *a navigable channel*

**channel²** /ˈtʃænᵊl/ *verb* [T] *UK* **channelling**, *past* **channelled**, *US* **channeling**, *past* **channeled 1** to direct water along a particular route *The waste water is channelled through this pipe.* **2** to use money or energy for a particular purpose *We've channelled all our resources into this project.*

**chant¹** /tʃɑːnt/ *verb* [I, T] **1** to repeat or sing a word or phrase many times, often shouting *The demonstrators chanted anti-racist slogans.* **2** to sing a religious song or prayer using a very simple tune

**chant²** /tʃɑːnt/ *noun* [C] **1** a word or phrase that is repeated many times **2** a religious song or prayer that is sung using a very simple tune

**chaos** /ˈkeɪɒs/ *noun* [U] a situation where there is no order at all and everyone is confused *The country's at war and everything is in chaos.*

**chaotic** /keɪˈɒtɪk/ *adj* in a state of chaos *a chaotic situation*

**chap** /tʃæp/ *noun* [C] *UK informal* a man

**chapel** /ˈtʃæpᵊl/ *noun* [C] a small church, or a room used as a church in a building

**chaperone¹** (*also* **chaperon**) /ˈʃæpᵊrəʊn/ *noun* [C] an older person who goes somewhere with a younger person in order to make sure they behave well, especially a woman in the past who went with a younger woman who was not married

**chaperone²** (*also* **chaperon**) /ˈʃæpᵊrəʊn/ *verb* [T] to go somewhere with someone as their chaperone

**chaplain** /ˈtʃæplɪn/ *noun* [C] a priest in the army, a school, a hospital, or a prison

**chapter** /ˈtʃæptəʳ/ *noun* [C] **1** one of the parts that a book is divided into **2** a period of time when something happens in history or in someone's life *an interesting chapter in Spanish history*

o-►**character** /ˈkærəktəʳ/ *noun* **1** [QUALITIES] [C, U] the combination of qualities and personality that makes one person or thing different from others *It's not in her character to be jealous* (= she would not usually be jealous). • *It would be very out of character* (= not typical) *of her to lie.* • *The character of the village has changed since the road was built.* **2** [STORY] [C] a person in a book, film, etc *a cartoon character* **3** [GOOD QUALITIES] [U] qualities that are interesting or unusual *a hotel of character* **4** [PERSON] [C] *informal* a particular kind of person *an unpleasant character* **5** [INTERESTING PERSON] [C] an interesting or funny person whose behaviour is different from most people's *Your granny's a real character.* **6** [WRITING] [C] a letter, sign, or number that you use when you are writing or printing *Chinese characters*

**characteristic¹** /,kærəktəˈrɪstɪk/ *noun* [C] a typical or obvious quality that makes one person or thing different from others *a national characteristic* • *Does he have any distinguishing physical characteristics?*

**characteristic²** /,kærəktəˈrɪstɪk/ *adj* typical of someone or something *Grey stone is characteristic of buildings in that area.* • *With characteristic generosity, she offered to pay for us all.* ➲ *Opposite* **uncharacteristic**. • **characteristically** *adv All through his time in hospital, he was characteristically brave and good-humoured.*

**characterization** (*also UK* **-isation**) /,kærəktᵊraɪˈzeɪʃᵊn/ *noun* [U] the way that people are described in a play, book, etc

**characterize** (*also UK* **-ise**) /ˈkærəktᵊraɪz/ *verb* [T] **1** to be typical of someone or something [often passive] *Her behaviour in class has been characterized by rudeness and laziness.* **2** to describe or show someone or something in a particular way *Historians have characterized the age as a period of great change.*

**charade** /ʃəˈrɑːd ⓤ͡s ʃəˈreɪd/ *noun* [C] a situation which is clearly false, but where people behave as if it is true or serious *The interview was just a charade.*

**charcoal** /ˈtʃɑːkəʊl/ *noun* [U] a hard, black substance that is produced by burning wood without much air, and that is used as fuel or for drawing

o-►**charge¹** /tʃɑːdʒ/ *noun* **1** [MONEY] [C, U] the amount of money that you have to pay for something, especially for an activity or a service *bank charges* • *There's no charge for children under 14.* • *He repaired the computer free of charge* (= it did not cost anything). **2 be in charge** to be the person who has control of or is responsible for someone or something *She's in charge of a team of 20 people.* • *Who's in* *charge of organizing the music for the party?* **3 take charge** to take control of or make yourself responsible for something *I was happy to let her take charge of paying all the bills.* **4** CRIME [C] a formal police statement saying that someone is accused of a crime *to bring/press charges* ● *She was arrested on charges of theft and forgery.* **5** ACCUSE [C] when you accuse someone of something *This is a serious charge to make against your colleagues.* **6** ATTACK [C] an attack in which people or animals run forward suddenly **7 reverse the charges** *UK* (*US* **call collect**) to make a telephone call that is paid for by the person who receives it ➔ *See also:* **service charge**.

○━**charge²** /tʃɑːdʒ/ *verb* **1** ASK TO PAY [I, T] to ask someone to pay an amount of money for something, especially for an activity or a service [+ two objects] *They are going to charge motorists a tax to drive into the city centre.* ● *How much do you charge for delivery?* **2** ACCUSE [T] If the police charge someone, they accuse them officially of a crime. [often passive] *He was charged with assault.* **3** ATTACK [I, T] to attack someone or something by moving forward quickly *The bull looked as if it was about to charge.* **4 charge around/into/through, etc** to run from one place to another *The children charged around the house.* **5** ELECTRICITY [I, T] to put electricity into something

'**charge ,card** *noun* [C] a small plastic card that allows you to buy something and pay for it at a particular date in the future

**charged** /tʃɑːdʒd/ *adj* A situation or a subject that is charged causes strong feelings or arguments. *a highly charged debate*

**chariot** /'tʃæriət/ *noun* [C] a vehicle with two wheels that was used in races and fights in ancient times and was pulled by a horse

**charisma** /kə'rɪzmə/ *noun* [U] a natural power which some people have to influence or attract people ● **charismatic** /ˌkærɪz'mætɪk/ *adj*

**charitable** /'tʃærɪtəbl/ *adj* **1** [always before noun] A charitable event, activity, or organization gives money, food, or help to people who need it. **2** kind, and not judging other people in a severe way ● **charitably** *adv*

**charity** /'tʃærɪti/ *noun* **1** ORGANIZATION [C, U] an official organization that gives money, food, or help to people who need it *The raffle will raise money for charity.* ● *A percentage of the company's profits go to charity.* **2** MONEY/HELP [U] money, food, or other help that is given to people *I won't accept charity.* **3** KINDNESS [U] kindness towards other people *an act of charity*

'**charity ,shop** *UK* (*US* **thrift shop**) *noun* [C] a shop which sells goods given by the public, especially clothes, to make money for a particular charity

**charlatan** /'ʃɑːlətᵊn/ *noun* [C] someone who pretends to have skills or knowledge that they do not have

**charm¹** /tʃɑːm/ *noun* **1** [C, U] a quality that makes you like someone or something *The building had a certain charm.* **2** [C] an object that you keep or wear because you believe that it is lucky *a lucky charm*

**charm²** /tʃɑːm/ *verb* [T] to attract someone or persuade someone to do something because of your charm [often passive] *We were charmed by his boyish manner.*

**charmed** /tʃɑːmd/ *adj* very lucky, or managing to avoid danger *The young boy had led **a charmed life.***

**charmer** /'tʃɑːmə*/ *noun* [C] *informal* someone who knows how to be charming in order to attract people or persuade them to do things

**charming** /'tʃɑːmɪŋ/ *adj* pleasant or attractive *a charming smile/place* ● **charmingly** *adv*

**charred** /tʃɑːd/ *adj* black from having been burned *charred wreckage*

**chart¹** /tʃɑːt/ *noun* **1** [C] a drawing which shows information in a simple way, often using lines and curves to show amounts *a sales chart* **2 the charts** an official list of the most popular songs each week *This song entered the charts at number 8.* **3** [C] a map of the sea or the sky

**chart²** /tʃɑːt/ *verb* [T] **1** to watch and record information about something over a period of time *The documentary charted the progress of the war.* **2** to make a map of an area of land, sea, or sky

**charter¹** /'tʃɑːtə*/ *noun* [C] a formal, written description of the principles, activities, and purpose of an organization *a UN charter for international peace*

**charter²** /'tʃɑːtə*/ *verb* [T] to rent a vehicle, especially an aircraft *The holiday company chartered a plane to fly us all home.*

**charter³** /'tʃɑːtə*/ *adj* **a charter flight/company/plane, etc** using aircraft paid for by travel companies for their customers

**chartered** /'tʃɑːtəd/ *adj* [always before noun] *UK* having the necessary qualifications to work in a particular profession *a chartered accountant/surveyor*

○━**chase¹** /tʃeɪs/ *verb* **1** [I, T] to run after someone or something in order to catch them *The dog was chasing a rabbit.* **2 chase sb/sth away/off/out, etc** to run after a person or animal to make them leave a place *I chased the cat away.* **3** [T] *UK* to try very hard to get something *There are hundreds of graduates chasing very few jobs.*

**chase**

**chase²** /tʃeɪs/ *noun* **1** [C] when you go after someone or something quickly in order to catch them *a high speed car chase* **2 give chase**

to go after someone or something quickly in order to catch them

**chasm** /'kæzᵊm/ *noun* [C] **1** a long, deep, narrow hole in rock or ice **2** a very large difference between two opinions or two groups of people

**chassis** /'ʃæsi/ *noun* [C] *plural* **chassis** /'ʃæsiz/ the structure of a vehicle that the outer metal is fixed onto

**chaste** /tʃeɪst/ *adj* not having had sex, or without sexual thoughts or intentions *a chaste relationship*

**chasten** /'tʃeɪsᵊn/ *verb* [T] *formal* to make someone feel ashamed by making them understand that they have failed or done something wrong [often passive] *The team were chastened by their defeat.* • **chastening** *adj*

**chastise** /tʃæs'taɪz/ *verb* [T] *formal* to criticize or punish someone

**chastity** /'tʃæstəti/ *noun* [U] when someone does not have sex

**chat¹** /tʃæt/ *verb* [I] **chatting**, *past* **chatted** to talk with someone in a friendly and informal way *I wanted to chat to you about the party on Saturday.*

**chat sb up** *UK informal* to talk to someone in a way that shows them that you are sexually attracted to them

**chat²** /tʃæt/ *noun* [C, U] a friendly, informal conversation

**chateau** /'ʃætəʊ/ Ⓤ Ⓢ ʃæ'təʊ/ *noun* [C] *plural* **chateaux** a large house or castle in France

'**chat ,room** *noun* [C] a place on the Internet where you can use email for discussions with other people

'**chat ,show** *UK* (*US* **talk show**) *noun* [C] a television or radio programme where people are asked questions about themselves

**chatter** /'tʃætəʳ/ *verb* [I] **1** to talk for a long time about things that are not important **2** If your teeth chatter, they knock together because you are cold or frightened. • **chatter** *noun* [U]

**chatty** /'tʃæti/ *adj* **1** liking to talk **2** A piece of writing that is chatty has a friendly and informal style. *a chatty letter/style*

**chauffeur** /'ʃəʊfəʳ Ⓤ Ⓢ ʃəʊ'fɜːr/ *noun* [C] someone whose job is to drive a car for someone else • **chauffeur** *verb* [T]

**chauvinist** /'ʃəʊvənɪst/ *noun* [C] **1** (*also* **male chauvinist**) a man who believes that men are better or more important than women **2** someone who believes that their country or race is better or more important than other countries or races • **chauvinism** *noun* [U] the beliefs and behaviour of chauvinists

o-**cheap¹** /tʃiːp/ *adj* **1** NOT EXPENSIVE not expensive, or costing less than usual *I got a cheap flight to Spain at the last minute.* • *It will be a lot cheaper to go by bus.* **2** PAY LESS where you have to pay less than usual or less than you expect *Are there any cheap restaurants around here?* **3** LOW QUALITY low in price and quality *cheap perfume* **4** PERSON *US* not willing to spend money

**cheap²** /tʃiːp/ *adv informal* **1** for a low price *You'll get the table cheap if you buy the chairs too.* **2** be going cheap *UK* to be offered for sale for less money than is usual **3** not come cheap to be expensive *Good carpets don't come cheap.*

**cheaply** /'tʃiːpli/ *adv* for a low price *You can buy some goods more cheaply in America.*

**cheat¹** /tʃiːt/ *verb* [I, T] to behave in a way that is not honest or fair in order to win something or to get something *She was caught (UK) cheating in her French exam/(US) cheating on her French exam.* • *He cheats at cards.*

**cheat on sb** to have a secret sexual relationship with someone who is not your usual sexual partner

**cheat sb out of sth** to get something that belongs to someone else by deceiving them *He claimed that his brother had cheated him out of his inheritance.*

**cheat²** /tʃiːt/ *noun* [C] someone who cheats

o-**check¹** /tʃek/ *verb* **1** EXAMINE [I, T] to examine something in order to make sure that it is correct or the way it should be [+ (that)] *I went to check that I'd locked the door.* • *Have you checked your facts?* • *I knelt down beside the body and checked for a pulse.* • *I haven't had my eyes checked recently.* **2** FIND OUT [I, T] to find out about something [+ question word] *I'll check whether Peter knows about the party.* **3** ASK [I] to ask someone for permission to do something *I'd like to stay overnight, but I need to check with my parents.* **4** STOP [T] to stop something bad from increasing or continuing *The government needs to find a way to check rising inflation.* **5** MARK [T] *US* (*UK* **tick**) to put a mark by an answer to show that it is correct, or by an item on a list to show that you have dealt with it **6** LEAVE [T] *US* to leave your coat, bags, or other possessions temporarily in someone's care *Passengers on this flight will be allowed one carry-on bag, and will have to check any additional bags.* ⊃ *See also:* **double-check**.

**check in 1** to go to the desk at an airport in order to say that you have arrived and to get the number of your seat *We have to check in three hours before the flight leaves.* **2** to go to the desk at a hotel in order to say that you have arrived and to get the key to your room

**check sth off** *US* (*UK* **tick sth off**) to put a mark next to a name or an item on a list to show that it is correct, or that it has been dealt with

**check (up) on sb/sth** to try to discover how something is progressing or whether someone

**check in**

is doing what they should be doing *My boss is always checking up on me.*

**check out** to leave a hotel after paying your bill

**check sth out 1** [INFORMATION] *informal* to examine something or get more information about it in order to be certain that it is true, safe, or suitable *We'll need to check out his story.* **2** [GO TO SEE] *informal* to go to a place in order to see what it is like *Let's check out that new dance club.* **3** [BOOKS] *mainly US* to borrow books from a library

**check²** /tʃek/ *noun* **1** [EXAMINATION] [C] an examination of something in order to make sure that it is correct or the way it should be *We do safety checks on all our equipment.* **2** [BANK] [C] *US* spelling of cheque (= a piece of paper printed by a bank that you use to pay for things) **3** [RESTAURANT] [C] *US* (*UK* **bill**) a list that you are given in a restaurant showing how much your meal costs **4** [MARK] [C] *US* (*UK* **tick**) a mark (✓) that shows that an answer is correct, or that you have dealt with something on a list **5** [PATTERN] [C, U] a pattern of squares of different colours **6 hold/keep sth in check** to control something that could increase too quickly or become too large or powerful *We need to keep our spending in check.* ⊃ *See also:* **rain check.**

**checkbook** /'tʃekbʊk/ *noun* [C] *US* spelling of chequebook (= a book of papers printed by a bank that you use to pay for things)

**checked** /tʃekt/ *adj* with a pattern of squares of different colours *a checked shirt/tablecloth*

**checkers** /'tʃekəz/ *US* (*UK* **draughts**) *noun* [U] a game that two people play by moving flat, round objects around on a board of black and white squares

**check-in** /'tʃekɪn/ *noun* [C] the place at an airport where you go to say that you have arrived for your flight, or the act of going to the check-in to say that you have arrived for your flight *a check-in counter/desk*

'**checking ac,count** *US* (*UK* **current account**) *noun* [C] a bank account which you can take money out of at any time

**checklist** /'tʃeklɪst/ *noun* [C] a list of things that you should think about, or that you must do

**checkmate** /'tʃekmeɪt/ *noun* [U] the final position in the game of chess when your king cannot escape and you have lost the game

**checkout** /'tʃekaʊt/ (*also US* '**checkout ,counter**) *noun* [C] the place in a large shop, especially a food shop, where you pay for your goods *a supermarket checkout*

**checkpoint** /'tʃekpɔɪnt/ *noun* [C] a place where people and vehicles are stopped and examined *a military/police checkpoint*

**check-up** /'tʃekʌp/ *noun* [C] a general medical examination to see if you are healthy *I'm going to the doctor for a check-up.*

**cheddar** /'tʃedə'/ *noun* [U] a type of hard, yellow cheese

**cheek** /tʃiːk/ *noun* **1** [C] the soft part of your face below your eye *Tears ran down his cheeks.* ⊃ *See colour picture* **The Body** *on page Centre 2.* **2** [U, no plural] *mainly UK* rude behaviour that shows that you do not respect someone [+ to do sth] *She had the cheek to ask me to pay for her!*

**cheekbone** /'tʃiːkbəʊn/ *noun* [C] one of the two bones below your eyes

**cheeky** /'tʃiːki/ *adj UK* slightly rude or behaving without respect, but often in a funny way *He's got such a cheeky grin.* • **cheekily** *adv*

**cheer¹** /tʃɪə'/ *verb* **1** [I, T] to shout loudly in order to show your approval or to encourage someone *The crowd stood up and cheered at the end of the concert.* **2 be cheered by sth** to feel happier or encouraged because of something

**cheer sb on** to shout loudly in order to encourage someone in a competition

**cheer (sb) up** to stop feeling sad, or to make someone feel happier *Cheer up. It's not the end of the world.* • *Let's send her some chocolates to cheer her up.*

**cheer sth up** to make a place look brighter or more attractive

**cheer²** /tʃɪə'/ *noun* [C] a shout of approval or encouragement

**cheerful** /'tʃɪəf°l/ *adj* **1** happy *I'm not feeling very cheerful today.* **2** bright and pleasant to look at *a bright and cheerful room* • **cheerfully** *adv He sang cheerfully as he worked.* • **cheerfulness** *noun* [U]

**cheering¹** /'tʃɪərɪŋ/ *noun* [U] shouts of encouragement and approval

**cheering²** /'tʃɪərɪŋ/ *adj* Something cheering encourages you and makes you feel happier. *We received some cheering news.*

**cheerleader** /'tʃɪə,liːdə'/ *noun* [C] a girl, especially in the United States, who leads the crowd in shouting encouragement to a team who are playing a sport

**cheers** /tʃɪəz/ *exclamation* **1** something friendly that you say before you start to drink alcohol with someone **2** *UK informal* thank you

**cheery** /'tʃɪəri/ *adj* bright and happy *a cheery wave/smile* • **cheerily** *adv*

o━**cheese** /tʃiːz/ *noun* **1** [C, U] a food that is made from milk, is usually white or yellow, and can be either hard or soft *a cheese sandwich* ⊃ *See colour picture* **Food** *on page Centre 7.* **2 Say cheese!** something that you say to make someone smile when you are taking their photograph ⊃ *See also:* be like **chalk¹** and cheese, **cottage cheese, cream cheese.**

**cheesecake** /'tʃiːzkeɪk/ *noun* [C, U] a sweet cake made with soft, white cheese on a biscuit base

**cheesy** /'tʃiːzi/ *adj informal* **1** not fashionable and of low quality *cheesy music* **2 a cheesy grin** a wide smile that is not always sincere

**cheetah** /'tʃiːtə/ *noun* [C] a large, wild cat that has black spots and can run very fast

**chef** /ʃef/ *noun* [C] someone who is the main cook (= person who cooks) in a hotel or a restaurant

**chemical¹** /'kemɪk°l/ *adj* relating to chemistry or chemicals *a chemical reaction* • *chemical weapons* • **chemically** *adv*

o━**chemical²** /'kemɪk°l/ *noun* [C] a basic substance that is used in chemistry or produced by chemistry

**chemist** /'kemɪst/ *noun* [C] **1** *UK* (*US* **pharmacist**) someone whose job is to prepare and sell drugs in a shop **2** a scientist who does work involving chemistry

**chemistry** /'kemɪstri/ *noun* [U] the scientific study of substances and how they change when they combine

**chemist's** /'kemɪsts/ *UK* (*US* **drugstore**) *noun* [C] a shop where you can buy drugs, soap, beauty products, etc

o—ᴧ**cheque** (*US* **check**) /tʃek/ *noun* [C] a piece of paper printed by a bank that you use to pay for things *a cheque for £1500* • *Are you **paying by cheque**?* ➲ *See also:* **blank cheque**, **traveller's cheque**.

**chequebook** *UK* (*US* **checkbook**) /'tʃekbʊk/ *noun* [C] a book of cheques

**cherish** /'tʃerɪʃ/ *verb* [T] **1** to love someone or something very much and take care of them **2** If you cherish an idea, hope, memory, etc, it is very important to you.

**cherry** /'tʃeri/ *noun* [C] a small, round red or black fruit with a large seed inside

**cherub** /'tʃerəb/ *noun* [C] a small child with a beautiful, round face and wings who appears in religious paintings

**chess** /tʃes/ *noun* [U] a game that two people play by moving differently shaped pieces around a board of black and white squares *a chess set*

**chest** /tʃest/ *noun* [C] **1** the front of your body between your neck and your waist *a hairy chest* • *chest pains* ➲ *See colour picture* **The Body** *on page Centre 2.* **2** a strong, usually wooden, container with a lid, used for keeping things in *a treasure chest* **3 get sth off your chest** *informal* to tell someone about something that you have been worried or angry about for a long time

**chestnut** /'tʃesnʌt/ *noun* **1** [C] a nut that has a shiny, red-brown surface and is white inside, or the tree that produces these nuts *roasted chestnuts* **2** [C, U] a dark red-brown colour ➲ *See also:* **horse chestnut**.

,**chest of 'drawers** *UK* (*US* **bureau**) *noun* [C] a piece of furniture with drawers for keeping clothes in

**chew** /tʃuː/ *verb* [I, T] **1** to crush food between your teeth before you swallow it *This meat is difficult to chew.* **2** to repeatedly bite something without swallowing it *to chew gum*

**chew sth over** to think carefully about something, or to discuss it *We've been chewing over the possibility of moving house.*

'**chewing ,gum** *noun* [U] a sweet substance that you chew but do not swallow *a stick of chewing gum*

**chewy** /'tʃuːi/ *adj* Chewy food needs to be chewed a lot before you can swallow it.

**chic** /ʃiːk/ *adj* fashionable and attractive *a chic restaurant*

**chick** /tʃɪk/ *noun* [C] a baby bird, especially a baby chicken

**chicken¹** /'tʃɪkɪn/ *noun* **1** [C] a bird kept on a farm for its meat and eggs **2** [U] the meat of a chicken *a chicken sandwich*

**chicken²** /'tʃɪkɪn/ *verb*

**chicken out** *informal* to decide not to do something because you are too nervous *I was going to ask Mitsuko for a date, but I chickened out.*

'**chicken ,pox** *noun* [U] a children's disease that causes a fever and red spots on the skin

**chief¹** /tʃiːf/ *adj* [always before noun] **1** most

important *The wonderful weather was our chief reason for coming here.* **2** highest in rank *chief economic adviser to the government*

**chief²** /tʃiːf/ *noun* [C] **1** the leader of a group of people *tribal chiefs* **2** a person who controls other people in an organization *police chiefs*

**chiefly** /'tʃiːfli/ *adv* mainly *magazines intended chiefly for teenagers*

**chieftain** /'tʃiːftən/ *noun* [C] the leader of a tribe (= group of people with the same language and customs)

**chiffon** /'ʃɪfɒn ⑤ ʃɪ'fɑːn/ *noun* [U] a soft, thin cloth used for making women's clothes

o—ᴧ**child** /tʃaɪld/ *noun* [C] *plural* **children** **1** a young person who is not yet an adult *an eight-year-old child* • *How many children are there in your class?* **2** someone's son or daughter, also when they are adults *Both our children have grown up and moved away.* ➲ *See also:* **only child**.

,**child 'benefit** *noun* [U] money that the British government pays every week to families with children

**childbirth** /'tʃaɪldbɜːθ/ *noun* [U] the process during which a baby is born *His mother died in childbirth.*

**childcare** /'tʃaɪldkeəʳ/ *noun* [U] when someone looks after children while their parents are working

**childhood** /'tʃaɪldhʊd/ *noun* [C, U] the part of your life when you are a child *an unhappy childhood*

**childish** /'tʃaɪldɪʃ/ *adj* **1** Childish behaviour is silly, like that of a small child. *Don't be so childish!* **2** typical of a child *childish handwriting* • **childishly** *adv* • **childishness** *noun* [U]

**childless** /'tʃaɪldləs/ *adj* A childless person has no children.

**childlike** /'tʃaɪldlaɪk/ *adj* Childlike people are like children in some ways, such as trusting people or behaving in a natural way. *a childlike enthusiasm for life*

**childminder** /'tʃaɪld,maɪndəʳ/ *noun* [C] *UK* someone whose job is to look after children while their parents are working

'**child ,support** *noun* [U] money that someone gives the mother or father of their children when they do not live with them

**chili** /'tʃɪli/ *noun US spelling of* chilli

**chill¹** /tʃɪl/ *verb* [I, T] to become cold, or to make someone or something become cold *Chill the wine before serving.*

**chill out** *very informal* to relax completely, or not allow things to upset you *Chill out, Dad – if we miss this train there's always another one.*

**chill²** /tʃɪl/ *noun* **1** COLD [no plural] a cold feeling *There is a definite chill in the air.* **2** FEAR [C] a sudden frightened feeling *The scream sent a chill down my spine.* **3** ILLNESS [C] *UK* a cold (= common illness that makes you sneeze) that is not very bad

**chilli** *UK* (*US* **chili**) /'tʃɪli/ *noun plural* **chillies** **1** [C, U] a small, thin, red or green vegetable that tastes very hot *chilli powder* **2** [U] a spicy dish of beans, meat, and chillies

**chilling** /'tʃɪlɪŋ/ *adj* very frightening *a chilling tale*

**chilly** /'tʃɪli/ *adj* **1** unpleasantly cold *a chilly evening* **2** unfriendly *He gave me a chilly look.*

---

**chime** /tʃaɪm/ *verb* [I, T] If a bell or clock chimes, it rings. ● **chime** *noun* [C]
**chime in** to suddenly say something in order to add your opinion to a conversation *"Quite right too!" Tony chimed in.*

**chimney** /'tʃɪmni/ *noun* [C] a wide pipe that allows smoke from a fire to go out through the roof

**chimney**

**'chimney ,sweep** *noun* [C] someone whose job is to clean inside a chimney, using long brushes

**chimpanzee** /,tʃɪmpᵊn'ziː/ (*also* **chimp** /tʃɪmp/ *informal*) *noun* [C] an African animal like a large monkey

**chin** /tʃɪn/ *noun* [C] the bottom part of your face, below your mouth ➾ *See colour picture* **The Body** *on page Centre 2.*

**china** /'tʃaɪnə/ *noun* [U] **1** the hard substance that plates, cups, bowls, etc are made from *a china teapot* **2** cups, plates, bowls, etc that are made from china *My parents only use the best china when we have visitors.*

**chink** /tʃɪŋk/ *noun* [C] **1** a small, narrow opening in something **2** a short ringing sound that is made when glass or metal objects touch each other

**chip¹** /tʃɪp/ *noun* [C] **1** POTATO (*US* **french fry**) a long, thin piece of potato that is cooked in oil [usually plural] *fish and chips* ➾ *See colour picture* **Food** *on page Centre 7.* **2** IN BAG *US* (*UK* **crisp**) a very thin, dry, fried slice of potato [usually plural] *barbecue flavoured potato chips* ➾ *See colour picture* **Food** *on page Centre 7.* **3** COMPUTER a microchip (= very small part of a computer that stores information) **4** SMALL PIECE a small piece that has broken off something *wood chips* **5** HOLE a place where a small piece has broken off something *This cup has a chip in it.* **6 be a chip off the old block** *informal* to be very similar to your mother or father **7 have a chip on your shoulder** *informal* to blame other people for something bad that has happened to you and continue to feel angry about it *She's always had a real chip on her shoulder because she didn't go to university.*

**chip²** /tʃɪp/ *verb* [T] **chipping**, *past* **chipped** to break a small piece off something *Becker may have chipped a bone in his wrist.* ● *a chipped plate*
**chip in** *informal* to interrupt a conversation in order to say something *I'll start and you can all chip in with your comments.*
**chip in (sth)** If several people chip in, they each give money to buy something together. *We all chipped in to buy our teacher a present.*

**chiropodist** /kɪ'rɒpədɪst/ *UK* (*US* **podiatrist**) *noun* [C] someone whose job is to treat problems with people's feet

**chirp** /tʃɜːp/ *verb* [I] If birds or insects chirp, they make short, high sounds. ● **chirp** *noun* [C]

**chirpy** /'tʃɜːpi/ *adj UK informal* happy and active *Why's Ben so chirpy this morning?*

**chisel** /'tʃɪzᵊl/ *noun* [C] a tool with a sharp end that you use for cutting and shaping wood or stone ➾ *See picture at* **tool**.

**chivalrous** /'ʃɪvᵊlrəs/ *adj* A chivalrous man behaves very politely towards women. ● **chivalry** *noun* [U] polite behaviour towards women

**chives** /tʃaɪvz/ *noun* [plural] a plant with long, thin leaves used in cooking to give a flavour similar to onions

**chlorine** /'klɔːriːn/ *noun* [U] a gas with a strong smell, used to make water safe to drink and swim in

◑━**chocolate** /'tʃɒkᵊlət/ *noun* **1** SUBSTANCE [U] a sweet, brown food that is usually sold in a block *a bar of chocolate* ● *milk chocolate* ● *a chocolate cake* **2** SWEET [C] a small piece of sweet food covered in chocolate *a box of chocolates* **3** DRINK [C, U] a sweet drink made with chocolate and hot milk

◑━**choice¹** /tʃɔɪs/ *noun* **1** RIGHT [U, no plural] when you can choose between two or more things *If I had a choice, I'd give up work.* ● *He had no choice but to accept their offer.* ● *I'm single by choice* (= because I want to be). **2** DECISION [C] the decision to choose one thing or person and not someone or something else *In the past women had to make a choice between a career or marriage.* **3** THINGS TO CHOOSE FROM [U, no plural] the things or people you can choose from *The dress is available in a choice of colours.* ● *The evening menu offers a wide choice of dishes.* **4** CHOSEN ONE [C] the person or thing that someone has chosen [usually singular] *Harvard was not his first choice.* ● *The winner got £1000 to give to the charity of her choice.* ➾ *See also:* **multiple choice**.

**choice²** /tʃɔɪs/ *adj* [always before noun] of very good quality *the choicest cuts of meat*

**choir** /kwaɪəʳ/ *noun* [group] a group of people who sing together *a school/church choir*

**choke¹** /tʃəʊk/ *verb* **1** [I, T] If you choke, or if something chokes you, you stop breathing because something is blocking your throat. *Children can choke on peanuts.* **2** [T] (*also* **choke up**) to fill something such as a road or pipe so that nothing can pass through [often passive] *The roads were choked with traffic.*
**choke sth back** to try not to show how angry or upset you are *She ran to the door, choking back the tears.*
**choke (sb) up** to become unable to speak because you are starting to cry *I can't watch that movie without choking up.*

**choke²** /tʃəʊk/ *noun* [C] a piece of equipment that controls the amount of air going into a car engine

**cholera** /'kɒlᵊrə/ *noun* [U] a serious disease that affects the stomach and bowels, usually caused by dirty water or food

**cholesterol** /kə'lestᵊrɒl/ *noun* [U] a type of fat in your body that can cause heart disease if you have too much

◑━**choose** /tʃuːz/ *verb past t* **chose**, *past p* **chosen** **1** [I, T] to decide which thing you want *I helped my sister choose a name for her baby.* ● *They* have to **choose between** earning a living or getting an education. • There were lots of books to **choose from**. • [+ question word] How did you choose which school to go to? • Adam was **chosen as** team captain. **2 choose to do sth** to decide to do something Manuela chose to take a job in Paris.

**choosy** /'tʃuːzi/ adj difficult to please because of being very exact about what you like a choosy customer

**chop¹** /tʃɒp/ verb **chopping**, past **chopped 1** [T] (also **chop up**) to cut something into small pieces Chop an onion finely. **2 chop and change** UK informal to keep changing your opinions, activities, or job

**chop sth down** to cut through something to make it fall down

**chop sth off** to cut off part of something with a sharp tool

chop

**chop²** /tʃɒp/ noun [C] **1** a flat piece of meat with a bone in it a lamb chop **2** a quick, hard hit with a sharp tool or with the side of your hand

**chopper** /'tʃɒpər/ noun [C] **1** informal a helicopter (= aircraft with turning parts on top) **2** a heavy tool with a sharp edge for cutting wood, meat, etc

**choppy** /'tʃɒpi/ adj Choppy water has a lot of small waves.

**chopsticks** /'tʃɒpstɪks/ noun [plural] thin sticks used for eating food in East Asia

**choral** /'kɔːrəl/ adj Choral music is written for a choir (= group of people who sing).

**chord** /kɔːd/ noun **1** [C] two or more musical notes that are played at the same time **2 strike a chord (with sb)** If something strikes a chord with you, you like it or are interested in it because it is connected with your own life or opinions. ⊃ See also: **vocal chords**.

**chore** /tʃɔːr/ noun [C] a boring job that you must do I find cooking a real chore.

**choreograph** /'kɒriəɡrɑːf/ verb [T] **1** to arrange an event or series of events carefully a carefully choreographed publicity stunt **2** to design the dances for a performance • choreographer /ˌkɒriˈɒɡrəfər/ noun [C]

**choreography** /ˌkɒriˈɒɡrəfi/ noun [U] the process of designing dances for a performance

**chorus¹** /'kɔːrəs/ noun **1** [SONG] [C] the part of a song that is repeated several times **2** [SINGING GROUP] [group] a large group of people who sing together **3** [IN A SHOW] [group] a group of dancers and singers in a show who do not have the main parts **4 a chorus of approval/demands/protest, etc** something that a lot of people say at the same time

**chorus²** /'kɔːrəs/ verb [T] UK If two or more people chorus something, they say it at the same time.

**chose** /tʃəʊz/ past tense of choose

**chosen** /'tʃəʊzən/ past participle of choose

**Christ** /kraɪst/ (also **Jesus Christ**) noun the Jewish holy man believed by Christians to be the Son of God, and on whose life and teachings Christianity is based

**christen** /'krɪsən/ verb [T] to give a baby a name at a Christian ceremony and make them a member of the Christian Church [often passive] She's being christened in June.

**christening** /'krɪsənɪŋ/ noun [C] a ceremony where someone is christened

**Christian** /'krɪstʃən/ noun [C] someone who believes in Christianity • Christian adj a Christian charity/organization

**Christianity** /ˌkrɪstiˈænəti/ noun [U] a religion based on belief in God and the life and teachings of Jesus Christ, and on the Bible

**'Christian ˌname** noun [C] your first name, not your family name

**Christmas** /'krɪsməs/ noun [C, U] the Christian period of celebration around 25 December, when Christians celebrate the birth of Jesus Christ and people give each other presents, or the day itself We're going to my mother's for Christmas. • Merry Christmas! • Christmas dinner ⊃ See also: **Father Christmas**.

**'Christmas ˌcard** noun [C] a decorated card that you send to someone at Christmas

**ˌChristmas 'carol** UK (US **'Christmas ˌcarol**) noun [C] a song that people sing at Christmas

**ˌChristmas 'cracker** noun [C] a coloured paper tube with a small toy inside, that people in the UK pull open at Christmas

**ˌChristmas 'Day** noun [C, U] 25 December, the day on which Christians celebrate the birth of Jesus Christ

**ˌChristmas 'Eve** noun [C, U] the day before Christmas Day

**'Christmas ˌtree** noun [C] a real or artificial tree that people decorate inside their home for Christmas

**chrome** /krəʊm/ noun [U] a hard, shiny metal that is used to cover objects chrome bath taps

**chromosome** /'krəʊməsəʊm/ noun [C] the part of a cell that controls what an animal or plant is like

**chronic** /'krɒnɪk/ adj A chronic illness or problem continues for a long time. a chronic shortage of nurses • chronic back pain • chronically adv

**chronicle¹** /'krɒnɪkl/ noun [C] a written record of things that happened in the past

**chronicle²** /'krɒnɪkl/ verb [T] to make a record of something, or give details of something The book chronicles his life as an actor.

**chronological** /ˌkrɒnəˈlɒdʒɪkəl/ adj arranged

in the order in which events happened
• **chronologically** *adv*

**chubby** /'tʃʌbi/ *adj* pleasantly fat *the baby's chubby legs*

**chuck** /tʃʌk/ *verb* [T] *informal* to throw something *Don't just chuck your coat on the floor!*
**chuck sth away/out** *informal* to throw something away *I chucked out all my old clothes.*
**chuck sth in** *UK informal* to stop doing something because it is boring *Paul's chucked his history course in.*
**chuck sb out** *informal* to force someone to leave a place

**chuckle** /'tʃʌkl/ *verb* [I] to laugh quietly
• **chuckle** *noun* [C]

**chug** /tʃʌg/ *verb* **chugging**, *past* **chugged chug across/along/up, etc** If a vehicle chugs somewhere, it moves slowly, making a low, regular noise with its engine. *a boat chugging across the lake*

**chum** /tʃʌm/ *noun* [C] *informal* a friend
• **chummy** *adj* friendly

**chunk** /tʃʌŋk/ *noun* [C] **1** a large piece of something *a chunk of cheese* ➔ *See colour picture* **Quantities** *on page Centre 14.* **2** a large part of something *I spend a big chunk of my money on clothes.*

**chunky** /'tʃʌŋki/ *adj* **1** A chunky person is short and heavy. **2** big, thick, and heavy *chunky shoes*

◦•**church** /tʃɜːtʃ/ *noun* **1** [C, U] a building where Christians go to worship God *We used to go to church every Sunday morning.* **2** [C] (*also* **Church**) one of the different groups that make up the Christian religion *the Anglican Church* ➔ *See also:* **the Catholic Church**.

**churchgoer** /'tʃɜːtʃˌgəʊəʳ/ *noun* [C] someone who goes to church regularly

**churchyard** /'tʃɜːtʃjɑːd/ *noun* [C] the land around a church, often where people are buried

**churn**[1] /tʃɜːn/ *verb* **1** SURFACE [T] (*also* **churn up**) to mix something, especially liquids, with great force *The sea was churned up by heavy winds.* **2** STOMACH [I] If your stomach is churning, you feel sick, usually because you are nervous. **3** BUTTER [T] to mix milk until it becomes butter
**churn sth out** *informal* to produce large quantities of something very quickly *The factory churns out thousands of pairs of shoes every week.*

**churn**[2] /tʃɜːn/ *noun* [C] **1** a container that you fill with milk and mix to make butter **2** *UK* a tall metal container for storing and transporting milk

**chute** /ʃuːt/ *noun* [C] **1** a long thin structure that people or things can slide down *a water chute* **2** *informal short for* parachute

**chutney** /'tʃʌtni/ *noun* [U] a mixture of fruit, vegetables, sugar, and vinegar that you eat with meat or cheese

**the CIA** /ˌsiːaɪˈeɪ/ *noun abbreviation for* Central Intelligence Agency: the department of the US government that collects secret information about people and organizations

**the CID** /ˌsiːaɪˈdiː/ *noun abbreviation for* Criminal Investigation Department: the part of the British police force that deals with serious crimes

**cider** /'saɪdəʳ/ *noun* [C, U] **1** *UK* a drink made from apples that contains alcohol **2** *US* a drink made from apples that contains no alcohol

**cigar** /sɪˈgɑːʳ/ *noun* [C] a thick tube made from rolled tobacco leaves, that people smoke

◦•**cigarette** /ˌsɪgəˈret/ *noun* [C] a thin tube of paper filled with tobacco, that people smoke

**cilantro** /sɪˈlæntrəʊ/ *US* (*UK/US* **coriander**) *noun* [U] a herb that is used in cooking

**cinder** /'sɪndəʳ/ *noun* [C] a small piece of coal, wood, etc that has been burned

◦•**cinema** /'sɪnəmə/ *noun* **1** [C] *UK* (*US* **movie theater**) a building where you go to watch films **2** [U] the art or business of making films *an article about French cinema*

**cinnamon** /'sɪnəmən/ *noun* [U] a brown spice that is used in cooking

**circa** /'sɜːkə/ *formal* (*written abbreviation* **c**) *preposition* used before a date to show that something happened at about that time *Gainsborough's painting 'The Cottage Door' (circa 1780)*

◦•**circle**[1] /'sɜːkl/ *noun* **1** [C] a round, flat shape like the letter O, or a group of people or things arranged in this shape *We all sat on the floor in a circle.* ➔ *See picture at* **shape**. **2** [C] a group of people with family, work, or social connections *a close circle of friends* • *It's a technical term used in medical circles.* **3** **the circle** *UK* the seats in the upper area of a theatre ➔ *See also:* **inner circle, traffic circle, vicious circle.**

**circle**[2] /'sɜːkl/ *verb* **1** [I, T] to move in a circle, often around something *Birds circled above the trees.* **2** [T] to draw a circle around something *Circle the answer you think is correct.*

**circuit** /'sɜːkɪt/ *noun* [C] **1** TRACK a path, route, or sports track that is shaped like a circle **2** ELECTRIC a complete circle that an electric current travels around **3** EVENTS a regular series of places or events that people involved in a particular activity go to [usually singular] *the tennis circuit* ➔ *See also:* **short-circuit.**

**circular**[1] /'sɜːkjələʳ/ *adj* **1** shaped like a circle *a circular rug* **2** A circular journey takes you around in a circle, back to the place where you started. *a circular walk*

**circular**[2] /'sɜːkjələʳ/ *noun* [C] a letter or advertisement that is sent to a lot of people at the same time

**circulate** /'sɜːkjəleɪt/ *verb* **1** INFORMATION [I] If information circulates, a lot of people hear about it. *Rumours are circulating that the mayor is going to resign.* **2** SEND INFORMATION [T] to give or send information to a group of people *A copy of the report was circulated to each director.* **3** MOVE [I, T] to move around or through something, or to make something move around or through something *Hot water circulates through the pipes.*

**circulation** /ˌsɜːkjəˈleɪʃʰn/ *noun* **1** BLOOD [U] the movement of blood around your body *Exercise improves your circulation.* **2** INFORMATION [U] when something such as information, money, or goods pass from one person to another *Police have warned there are a lot of fake £50 notes in circulation.* **3** NEWSPAPERS [no plural] the number of copies of a newspaper or magazine that are sold each day, week, etc

**circumcise** /'sɜːkəmsaɪz/ *verb* [T] to cut off the skin at the end of a boy's or man's penis, or cut off part of a girl's sex organs • circumcision /ˌsɜːkəm'sɪʒ°n/ *noun* [C, U] when someone is circumcised

**circumference** /sə'kʌmf°r°ns/ *noun* [C, U] the distance around the edge of a circle or round object *The lake is 250km in circumference.*

**circumspect** /'sɜːkəmspekt/ *adj formal* careful about things you do or say

**circumstances** /'sɜːkəmstænsɪz/ *noun* [plural] **1** facts or events that make a situation the way it is *I think they coped very well under the circumstances.* • *We oppose capital punishment in/under any circumstances.* **2 under no circumstances** used to say that something must never happen *Under no circumstances should you approach the man.*

**circumstantial** /ˌsɜːkəm'stænʃ°l/ *adj* **circumstantial evidence** information about a crime that makes you believe that something is true, but does not prove it

**circumvent** /ˌsɜːkəm'vent/ *verb* [T] *formal* to find a way of avoiding something, especially a law or rule

**circus** /'sɜːkəs/ *noun* [C] a show in which a group of people and animals perform in a large tent

**cistern** /'sɪstən/ *noun* [C] a large container to store water, especially one that supplies water to a toilet ➔ *See colour picture* **The Bathroom** *on page Centre 1.*

**citadel** /'sɪtəd°l/ *noun* [C] a strong castle that was used in the past to protect people when their city was attacked

**cite** /saɪt/ *verb* [T] *formal* **1** to mention something as an example or proof of something else *The doctor cited the case of a woman who had died after taking the drug.* **2** *US* to order someone to go to court because they have done something wrong [often passive] *A local farmer was cited for breaking environmental standards.*

**citizen** /'sɪtɪz°n/ *noun* [C] **1** someone who lives in a particular town or city *the citizens of Berlin* **2** someone who has a legal right to live in a particular country *My husband became a British citizen in 1984.* ➔ *See also:* **senior citizen.**

**citizenship** /'sɪtɪz°nʃɪp/ *noun* [U] the legal right to be a citizen of a particular country *British/French citizenship*

**citrus fruit** /'sɪtrəsˌfruːt/ *noun* [C, U] an orange, lemon, or similar fruit

**o━city** /'sɪti/ *noun* **1** [C] a large town *the city of Boston* • *the city centre* **2 the City** *UK* the part of London where the large financial organizations have their offices ➔ *See also:* **inner city.**

**civic** /'sɪvɪk/ *adj* [always before noun] relating to a city or town and the people who live there *civic leaders* • *The opera house was a source of great civic pride* (= people in the city were proud of it).

**civil** /'sɪv°l/ *adj* **1** [PEOPLE] [always before noun] relating to the ordinary people or things in a country and not to military or religious organizations *They married in a civil ceremony.* **2** [LAW] [always before noun] relating to private arguments between people and not criminal cases *a civil court* **3** [POLITE] polite in a formal way *He and his ex-wife can't even have a civil conversation.*

**civil engi'neering** *noun* [U] the planning and building of roads, bridges, and public buildings

**civilian** /sɪ'vɪliən/ *noun* [C] someone who is not a member of a military organization or the police

**civility** /sɪ'vɪləti/ *noun* [U] polite behaviour

**civilization** (*also UK* **-isation**) /ˌsɪv°laɪ'zeɪʃ°n/ *noun* **1** [C, U] human society with its developed social organizations, or the culture and way of life of a society at a particular period of time *ancient civilizations* • *Nuclear war could mean the end of civilization.* **2** [U] when people have an advanced and comfortable way of life *modern civilization*

**civilize** (*also UK* **-ise**) /'sɪv°laɪz/ *verb* [T] to educate a society so that it becomes more advanced and organized

**civilized** (*also UK* **-ised**) /'sɪvəlaɪzd/ *adj* **1** A civilized society is advanced and has well-developed laws and customs. *A fair justice system is an important part of civilized society.* **2** polite and calm *Let's discuss this in a civilized manner.*

**civil 'liberties** *noun* [plural] the freedom people have to do, think, and say what they want

**civil 'rights** *noun* [plural] the rights that everyone in a country has

**civil 'servant** *noun* [C] someone who works in the Civil Service

**the ˌCivil 'Service** *noun* the government departments and the people who work in them

**civil 'war** *noun* [C, U] a war between groups of people who live in the same country

**cl** *written abbreviation for* centilitre (= unit for measuring liquid) *a 75 cl bottle of wine*

**clad** /klæd/ *adj literary* covered or dressed in something *He came to the door clad only in a towel.*

**o━claim¹** /kleɪm/ *verb* **1** [SAY] [T] to say that something is true, although you have not proved it [+ (that)] *She claimed that the dog attacked her.* • [+ to do sth] *He claims to have seen a ghost.* **2 claim credit/responsibility/success, etc** to say that you have done or achieved something *No one has claimed responsibility for yesterday's bomb attack.* ➔ *Opposite* **disclaim.** **3** [DEMAND] [I, T] to ask for something because it belongs to you or you have the right to have it *She claimed $2,500 in travel expenses.* • *If no one claims the watch, then you can keep it.* **4** [KILL] [T] If an accident, war, etc claims lives, people are killed because of it. *The floods claimed over 200 lives.*

**claim²** /kleɪm/ *noun* [C] **1** [ANNOUNCEMENT] when someone says that something is true, although it has not been proved [+ (that)] *She rejected claims that she had lied.* **2** [DEMAND] an official demand for something you think you have a right to *a claim for compensation* **3** [RIGHT] a right to have something *You don't have any claim to the land.* **4 lay claim to sth** *formal* to say that something is yours or that you have done something **5 sb's/sth's claim to fame** a reason why someone or something is known *My main claim to fame is meeting the President.*

**clam¹** /klæm/ *noun* [C] a small sea creature with a shell in two parts, that you can eat

**clam²** /klæm/ *verb*
**clam up** *informal* to suddenly stop talking, usually because you are embarrassed or nervous *He was afraid he would clam up in front of the television camera.*

**clamber** /ˈklæmbər/ *verb* **clamber into/over/ up, etc** to climb somewhere with difficulty, especially using your hands and feet *The children clambered into the boat.*

**clammy** /ˈklæmi/ *adj* unpleasantly wet and sticky *clammy hands*

**clamour¹** UK (US **clamor**) /ˈklæmər/ *verb* **clamour for sth; clamour to do sth** to ask for something continuously in a loud or angry way *Fans were clamouring for their autographs.*

**clamour²** UK (US **clamor**) /ˈklæmər/ *noun* [no plural] **1** a demand for something, or a complaint about something that is made by a lot of people *the public's clamour for organic food* **2** a loud, continuous noise made by people talking or shouting *We heard the clamour of voices in the street outside.*

**clamp¹** /klæmp/ *noun* [C] **1** a piece of equipment that is used for holding things together tightly **2** UK a metal cover that is put on the wheel of a car so you cannot move it if you have parked in an illegal place

**clamp²** /klæmp/ *verb* **1 clamp sth around/ over/to, etc** to put something in a particular position and hold it there tightly *He clamped his hand over her mouth.* **2 clamp sth onto/ to/together, etc** to fasten two things together using a clamp **3** [T] UK to fasten a metal cover on the wheel of a car to stop it moving because it has been parked in an illegal place
**clamp down** to do something strict to try to stop or limit an activity *Local police have clamped down on teenage drinking.*

**clampdown** /ˈklæmpdaʊn/ *noun* [C] a strict attempt to stop or limit an activity [usually singular] *a clampdown on inner city pollution*

**clan** /klæn/ *noun* [C] a large group of families who are all related to each other, especially in Scotland

**clandestine** /klænˈdestɪn/ *adj formal* secret and often illegal *a clandestine meeting*

**clang** /klæŋ/ *verb* [I, T] If something metal clangs, it makes a loud ringing sound, or if you clang it, you make it do this. *The gate clanged shut behind me.* • **clang** *noun* [C]

**clank** /klæŋk/ *verb* [I] If metal objects clank, they make a low noise when they hit each other. *The bracelets on her arm clanked as she moved.* • **clank** *noun* [C]

**clap¹** /klæp/ *verb* **clapping**, *past* **clapped 1** [I, T] to hit your hands together, often repeatedly, especially in order to show that you enjoyed a performance *The crowd clapped and cheered for more.* **2 clap sb on the back/shoulder** to hit someone on the back or shoulder in a friendly way **3** [T] to put something somewhere suddenly *She clapped her hands over her ears and refused to listen.*

**clap²** /klæp/ *noun* **1** [no plural] when you hit your hands together, often repeatedly *Let's give our*

**clap**

*winning contestant a big clap.* **2 a clap of thunder** a sudden, loud sound that is made by thunder

**claret** /ˈklærət/ *noun* [U] UK red wine from the area of France around Bordeaux

**clarify** /ˈklærɪfaɪ/ *verb* [T] to make something easier to understand by explaining it *The law aims to clarify building regulations.* • **clarification** /ˌklærɪfɪˈkeɪʃən/ *noun* [C, U]

**clarinet** /ˌklærɪˈnet/ *noun* [C] a musical instrument like a long, black tube, that you play by blowing into it and pressing metal keys

**clarity** /ˈklærəti/ *noun* [U] the quality of being clear and easy to understand *She described the process with great clarity.*

**clash¹** /klæʃ/ *verb* **1** FIGHT [I] to fight or argue *Government troops clashed with rebel soldiers.* • *Many young people clash with their parents over what time they must be home at night.* **2** COLOUR [I] If colours or styles clash, they do not look good together. *You can't wear pink lipstick – it clashes with your dress.* **3** EVENT [I] UK If two events clash, they happen at the same time so that you cannot go to them both. *Emma's party clashes with my brother's wedding.* **4** NOISE [I, T] to make a loud noise by hitting metal objects together

**clash²** /klæʃ/ *noun* [C] **1** FIGHT a fight or argument *There were violent clashes between the police and demonstrators.* **2** DIFFERENCE when ideas or qualities are very different, and this causes problems *a clash of personalities* **3** SOUND a loud sound that is made when metal objects hit each other *the clash of pans in the sink*

**clasp¹** /klɑːsp/ *verb* [T] to hold something or someone tightly *He clasped his daughter in his arms.*

**clasp²** /klɑːsp/ *noun* **1** [C] a small metal object that is used to fasten a bag, belt, or piece of jewellery **2** [no plural] a tight hold

**class¹** /klɑːs/ *noun* **1** STUDENTS [C] a group of students who have lessons together *Katie and Sarah are in the same class at school.* **2** LESSON [C, U] a period of time in which students are taught something *My first class starts at 8.30.* • *He was told off for talking in class* (= during the lesson). **3** SOCIAL GROUP [C, U] one of the groups in a society with the same social and economic position, or the system of dividing people into these groups *People are still very conscious of class in British society.* • *She's from a working-class background.* **4** QUALITY [C] a group into which people or things are put according to their quality *When it comes to mathematics, he's in a different class to his peers.* • *second-class mail* **5** SIMILARITY [C] a group of similar or related things, especially plants and animals **6** STYLE [U] *informal* the quality of being stylish or fashionable *a player with real class* ⊃ *See also:* **middle class**, **upper class**, **working class**.

---

**USAGE**

**class** or **classroom**?

A **class** is a group of students who have lessons together.

*The whole class arrived late.*

A **classroom** is a room where lessons happen.

*There is a TV and video in every classroom.*

---

**class²** /klɑːs/ *verb* **class sb/sth as sth** to put someone or something in a particular group according to their qualities *The tower is classed as a historic monument.*

**classic¹** /ˈklæsɪk/ *adj* **1** POPULAR A classic book, film, etc is one that has been popular for a long time and is considered to be of a high quality. *the classic film 'Gone with the Wind'* **2** TRADITIONAL having a traditional style that is always fashionable *a classic black jacket* **3** TYPICAL typical *Dan's a classic example of a child who's clever but lazy.*

**classic²** /ˈklæsɪk/ *noun* [C] a classic book, film, etc

**classical** /ˈklæsɪkᵊl/ *adj* **1** **classical music** serious music by people like Mozart and Stravinsky *Do you prefer classical music or pop music?* **2** traditional in style *classical and modern dance* **3** relating to ancient Greece and Rome *classical literature*

**classically** /ˈklæsɪkᵊli/ *adv* **1** in a traditional style *a classically trained actor* **2** in a typical style *a classically English tea room*

**classics** /ˈklæsɪks/ *noun* [U] the study of ancient Greece and Rome, especially the language, literature, and history

**classification** /ˌklæsɪfɪˈkeɪʃᵊn/ *noun* [C, U] the process of putting people or things into groups by their type, size, etc, or one of these groups *the classification of plants*

**classified** /ˈklæsɪfaɪd/ *adj* Classified information is officially kept secret by a government. *classified documents/material*

**classified 'ad** *noun* [C] a small advertisement that you put in a newspaper if you want to buy or sell something

**classify** /ˈklæsɪfaɪ/ *verb* [T] to put people or things into groups by their type, size, etc [often passive] *A third of the population has been classified as poor.* • *The books are classified by subject.*

**classmate** /ˈklɑːsmeɪt/ *noun* [C] someone who is in your class at school or college

**o—ᴴclassroom** /ˈklɑːsruːm/ *noun* [C] a room in a school where students have lessons ⊃ *See colour picture* **Classroom** *on page Centre 4.*

**classy** /ˈklɑːsi/ *adj informal* stylish and fashionable

**clatter** /ˈklætəʳ/ *verb* **1** [I] If something clatters, it makes a lot of noise when it hits something hard. **2 clatter about/around/down, etc** to move somewhere in a very noisy way *I could hear Sue clattering about upstairs.* • **clatter** *noun* [no plural] *He dropped his spoon with a clatter.*

**clause** /klɔːz/ *noun* [C] **1** a part of a legal document *a clause in a contract* **2** a group of words containing a subject and a verb, that is usually only part of a sentence ⊃ *See also:* **relative clause**, **subordinate clause**.

**claustrophobia** /ˌklɒstrəˈfəʊbiə/ *noun* [U] fear of being in a small or crowded place

**claustrophobic** /ˌklɒstrəˈfəʊbɪk/ *adj* **1** feeling very anxious when you are in a small or crowded place **2** A claustrophobic place makes you feel anxious because it is very small or crowded. *a claustrophobic room*

**claw¹** /klɔː/ *noun* [C] one of the sharp, curved nails on the feet of some animals and birds

**claw²** /klɔː/ *verb* [I, T] If a person or animal claws something, they try to get hold of it or damage it with their nails or claws. *He clawed at the rope, trying to free himself.*

**claw sth back** *mainly UK* to try to get back something that you had before *The party is desperately trying to claw back support.*

**clay** /kleɪ/ *noun* [U] a type of heavy soil that becomes hard when dry, used for making things such as bricks and containers *a clay pot*

**o—ᴴclean¹** /kliːn/ *adj* **1** NOT DIRTY not dirty *clean hands* • *clean clothes* • *You should try to keep the kitchen a bit cleaner.* **2** NO SEX not about sex *a clean joke* **3** NO CRIME showing that you have not done anything illegal *a clean driving licence/record* **4** FAIR fair and honest *a clean election/fight* **5 come clean** *informal* to tell the truth about something that you have been keeping secret *The boys decided to come clean about crashing the car.*

**o—ᴴclean²** /kliːn/ *verb* [I, T] to remove the dirt from something *I spent the morning cleaning the house.* • *Clean the wound with soap and water.* ⊃ *See also:* **dry clean**, **spring clean**.

**clean sth out 1** to take everything out of a room, car, container, etc and clean the inside of it **2** *informal* to steal everything from a place *Her apartment had been cleaned out by burglars.*

**clean (sb/sth) up** to make a person or place clean and tidy *We have to clean up before we leave.*

**clean³** /kliːn/ *adv informal* used to emphasize that something is done completely *The bullet went clean through his head.*

**clean-cut** /ˌkliːnˈkʌt/ *adj* Someone who is clean-cut has a tidy appearance.

**cleaner** /ˈkliːnəʳ/ *noun* **1** [C] someone whose job is to clean houses, offices, public places, etc **2** [C, U] a substance used for cleaning things *carpet/oven cleaner* **3 the cleaner's** a shop where clothes are cleaned with chemicals ⊃ *See also:* **vacuum cleaner**.

---

| j yes | k cat | ʃ she | ʒ decision | θ thin | ð this | ŋ ring | tʃ chip | dʒ jar | æ cat | ɑː arm | e bed | eə hair | ə ago | ɜː her | ɪ sit | i cosy |

**cleanliness** /'klenlınəs/ *noun* [U] the state of being clean, or the practice of keeping things clean *a hotel with high standards of cleanliness*

**cleanly** /'kliːnli/ *adv* in a quick and tidy way *The branch broke cleanly away from the tree.*

**cleanse** /klenz/ *verb* [T] to clean your face or an injured part of your body

**cleanser** /'klenzəʳ/ *noun* [C, U] a substance for cleaning, especially your face

o━**clear¹** /klɪəʳ/ *adj* **1** UNDERSTAND easy to understand *clear instructions* **2** HEAR/SEE easy to hear, read, or see *These photos are very clear.* • *Can we make the sound any clearer?* **3** NO DOUBT not possible to doubt *The evidence against him was clear.* • [+ (that)] *It was clear that Leif was angry.* • *Ella made it clear that she didn't like James.* **4** CERTAIN [never before noun] certain about something *Are you clear about how to get there?* • [+ question word] *I'm not very clear why she phoned.* **5** NOT BLOCKED not covered or blocked by anything *a clear road* • *a clear desk* **6** WITHOUT CLOUDS A clear sky does not have any clouds. **7** TRANSPARENT easy to see through *clear water* • *clear glass* ⊃ *See also:* the **coast¹** is clear, **crystal clear**.

o━**clear²** /klɪəʳ/ *verb* **1** EMPTY [T] to remove all the objects or people from a place *clear a room/shelf* • *Police cleared the building because of a bomb threat.* **2** WEATHER [I] If the sky or weather clears, the clouds and rain disappear. **3** NOT GUILTY [T] to prove that someone is not guilty of something that they were accused of *The jury cleared him of murder.* **4** MONEY [I] If a cheque (= printed paper used to pay for things) clears, the money goes from one person's bank account to another person's bank account. **5** GO OVER [T] to jump over something without touching it *The horse easily cleared the fence.* **6** GIVE PERMISSION [T] to give or get permission to do something *The plane is cleared for take-off.* • *You have to clear it with the headteacher if you want a day off school.* ⊃ *See also:* clear the **air¹**.

**clear sth away** to make a place tidy by removing things from it, or putting them where they should be *The children are not very good at clearing away their toys.*

**clear off** *UK informal* used to tell someone to go away immediately *Just clear off and leave me alone!*

**clear sth out** to tidy a place by getting rid of things that you do not want

**clear (sth) up 1** *mainly UK* to make a place tidy by removing things from it, or putting them where they should be *Dad was clearing up in the kitchen.* **2** to make an illness better *Antibiotics will clear up the infection.*

**clear sth up** to give an explanation for something, or to deal with a problem or argument *Before we sign the contract, there are a few points we should clear up.*

**clear up** *informal* If the weather clears up, the cloud and rain disappears.

**clear³** /klɪəʳ/ *adv* **1** away from something so that you are not touching it *Stand clear of the doors, please.* **2** steer clear of sb/sth to avoid someone or something because they are

unpleasant or dangerous *Steer clear of Tony this morning – he's in a bad mood.*

**clear⁴** /klɪəʳ/ *noun* **in the clear** *informal* **1** not responsible for a mistake or crime **2** *UK* not in a difficult situation or having problems any more *We have had money problems but we should be in the clear by next year.*

**clearance** /'klɪərᵊns/ *noun* [C, U] **1** PERMISSION permission from someone in authority *The company needs to get government clearance for the deal.* **2** DISTANCE the distance that is needed for one thing to avoid touching another thing **3** REMOVING THINGS when waste or things you do not want are removed from a place *Demolition and clearance of the site will take two weeks.*

**clear-cut** /,klɪəˈkʌt/ *adj* very certain or obvious *The issue is not very clear-cut.*

**clearing** /'klɪərɪŋ/ *noun* [C] a small area in the middle of a forest, where there are no trees

o━**clearly** /'klɪəli/ *adv* **1** EASY in a way that is easy to see, hear, read, or understand *He spoke very clearly.* **2** CERTAIN used to show that you think something is obvious or certain *Clearly he's very talented.* **3** NOT CONFUSED If you think clearly, you are not confused.

**cleavage** /'kliːvɪdʒ/ *noun* [C, U] the area between a woman's breasts

**cleaver** /'kliːvəʳ/ *noun* [C] a heavy knife with a large, square blade *a meat cleaver*

**clef** /klef/ *noun* [C] a sign written at the beginning of a line of music, that shows how high or low the notes are

**clemency** /'klemənsi/ *noun* [U] *formal* when a judge, king, etc decides not to punish someone severely although they have committed a crime

**clench** /klenʃ/ *verb* [T] to close your hands or teeth very tightly, or to hold something tightly *Dan clenched his fists.*

**clergy** /'klɜːdʒi/ *noun* [plural] priests or religious leaders *a member of the clergy*

**clergyman** /'klɜːdʒɪmən/ *noun* [C] *plural* **clergymen** a man who is a member of the clergy

**cleric** /'klerɪk/ *noun* [C] a member of the clergy

**clerical** /'klerɪkᵊl/ *adj* **1** relating to work done in an office *a clerical assistant* **2** relating to priests or religious leaders

**clerk** /klɑːk/ ⑥ klɜːrk/ *noun* [C] **1** someone who works in an office or bank, keeping records and doing general office work *a bank clerk* **2** *US* someone who sells things in a shop *a store/sales clerk*

o━**clever** /'klevəʳ/ *adj* **1** able to learn and understand things quickly and easily *a clever student* **2** designed in an effective and intelligent way *a clever idea* • *a clever tool* • **cleverly** *adv* a cleverly designed toy* • **cleverness** *noun* [U]

**cliché** /'kliːʃeɪ/ ⑥ kliːˈʃeɪ/ *noun* [C] something that people have said or done so much that it has become boring or has no real meaning

**click¹** /klɪk/ *verb* **1** SOUND [I, T] to make a short, sharp sound, or to use something to make this sound *The door clicked shut behind him.* **2** COMPUTER [I, T] to press on part of a computer mouse (= small computer control) to make the computer do something *To start the program, click on its icon.* **3** PEOPLE [I] *informal* If two

people click, they like each other immediately.
**4** [IDEA] [I] *informal* to suddenly understand
something *Suddenly everything clicked and I
realized where I'd met him.* ➔ *See also:* **double-
click**, click your fingers (**finger¹**).

**click²** /klɪk/ *noun* [C] a short, sharp sound *the
click of a switch*

**client** /ˈklaɪənt/ *noun* [C] someone who pays
someone else for services or advice *a lawyer
with a lot of famous clients*

**clientele** /ˌkliːɒnˈtel/ *noun* [group, no plural] the
regular customers of a business *The new bar
aims to attract a younger clientele.*

**cliff** /klɪf/ *noun* [C] an area of high, steep rocks
beside the sea

**climactic**
/klaɪˈmæktɪk/ *adj*
[always before noun]
*literary* A climactic
event or time is one
in which important
or exciting things
happen. *a climactic
moment in history*

**climate** /ˈklaɪmət/
*noun* **1** [C, U] the
weather conditions
that an area usually
has *a hot, dry
climate* **2** [C] the
situation, feelings,
and opinions that

**cliff**

exist at a particular time [usually singular] *the
political/ social climate* • *Terrorism **creates a
climate** of fear.*

**climatic** /klaɪˈmætɪk/ *adj formal* relating to the
weather conditions that an area usually has
*climatic change*

**climax¹** /ˈklaɪmæks/ *noun* [C] the most exciting
or important part of something [usually singular]
*The **climax of** her career was winning a gold
medal.* ➔ *Opposite* **anticlimax**.

**climax²** /ˈklaɪmæks/ *verb* [I, T] to reach the most
important or exciting part *The festival cli-
maxed with/ in a huge fireworks display.*

o━**climb** /klaɪm/ *verb* **1** [PERSON] [I, T] (*also* **climb up**)
to go up something, or onto the top of some-
thing *climb a ladder/tree/mountain* • *He
climbed up on a chair to change the light bulb.*
• *My grandfather finds it difficult to climb
stairs now.* **2** **climb into/out of/through, etc**
to move somewhere using your hands and legs
*The child climbed into the back of the car.*
**3** [NUMBER] [I] If a price, number, or amount
climbs, it increases. *Profits climbed 11% last
quarter.* **4** [MOVE HIGHER] [I] to move to a higher
position *The road climbs quite steeply.* • *climb
noun* [C] *a long/steep/uphill climb*

**climb down** *UK informal* to change your
opinion or admit that you are wrong *The government has been forced to **climb down** over the
issue of increased taxes.*

**climbdown** /ˈklaɪmdaʊn/ *noun* [C] *UK* when
someone admits that they were wrong about
something or have changed their opinion *an
embarrassing climbdown by the government*

**climber** /ˈklaɪmə/ *noun* [C] someone who climbs
mountains, hills, or rocks as a sport

**climb**

He climbed a tree.      They went climbing.

**climbing** /ˈklaɪmɪŋ/ *noun* [U] the sport of climbing mountains, hills, or rocks *rock/mountain
climbing* • *climbing boots*

**clinch** /klɪnʃ/ *verb* [T] *informal* **1** to finally get or
win something *clinch a deal* **2** **clinch it** *informal* to make someone finally decide what to do
*When he said the job was in Paris, that clinched
it for me.*

**cling** /klɪŋ/ *verb* [I] *past* **clung** **1** to hold someone
or something tightly, especially because you
are frightened *She was found **clinging to** the
ledge.* • *I **clung on to** his hand in the dark.* **2** to
stick to something *His damp hair **clung to** his
forehead.*

**cling (on) to sth** to try very hard to keep something *He clung on to power for ten more years.*

**cling to sth** to refuse to stop believing or hoping
for something *He clung to the belief that his
family were alive.*

**clingfilm** /ˈklɪŋfɪlm/ *UK trademark* (*US* **plastic
wrap**) *noun* [U] thin, transparent plastic used
for wrapping or covering food

**clingy** /ˈklɪŋi/ *adj mainly UK* always wanting to
be with someone and not wanting to do things
alone *a clingy child*

**clinic** /ˈklɪnɪk/ *noun* [C] a place where people go
for medical treatment or advice *an eye/skin
clinic*

**clinical** /ˈklɪnɪkᵊl/ *adj* [always before noun] relating to medical treatment and tests *clinical
trials/research* **2** only considering facts and
not influenced by feelings or emotions *a clinical approach/attitude* • clinically *adv*

**clinician** /klɪˈnɪʃᵊn/ *noun* [C] a doctor who treats
ill people and does not just study diseases

**clink** /klɪŋk/ *verb* [I, T] If pieces of glass or metal
clink, they make a short ringing sound when
they touch, and if you clink them, you make
them do this. • clink *noun* [C]

**clip¹** /klɪp/ *noun* [C] **1** a small metal or plastic
object used for holding things together **2** a
short part of a film or television programme
that is shown at a different time *They showed
clips from Spielberg's new movie.* **3 a clip round
the ear/earhole** *UK informal* a quick hit on the
side of someone's head ➔ *See also:* **paper clip**.

**clip²** /klɪp/ *verb* **clipping**, *past* **clipped 1** FASTEN [I, T] to fasten things together with a clip, or to be fastened in this way *Clip the microphone to the collar of your jacket.* **2** CUT [T] to cut small pieces from something *Jamie was outside clipping the hedge.* **3** HIT [T] to hit something quickly and lightly *The plane clipped a telephone line and crashed.*

**clipped** /klɪpt/ *adj* If someone speaks in a clipped voice, their words sound quick, short, and not friendly.

**clippers** /'klɪpəz/ *noun* [plural] a tool used to cut small pieces off something *hedge clippers*

**clipping** /'klɪpɪŋ/ *noun* [C] **1** (*also UK* **cutting**) an article or picture that has been cut out of a newspaper or magazine *a collection of newspaper clippings about the princess* **2** a small piece that has been cut off something [usually plural] *grass clippings*

**clique** /kliːk/ *noun* [C] a small group of people who spend a lot of time together and are unfriendly to people who are not in the group

**cloak** /kləʊk/ *noun* **1** [C] a loose coat without sleeves that hangs down from your shoulders **2 a cloak of sth** *literary* something that is intended to cover or hide the truth of something else *a cloak of secrecy/mystery*

**cloakroom** /'kləʊkruːm/ *noun* [C] **1** a room where you leave your coat at a theatre, school, etc **2** *UK old-fashioned* a toilet in a public building

**clobber** /'klɒbə'/ *verb* [T] *informal* **1** to hit someone **2** to affect someone very badly *a policy that has clobbered people on low incomes*

○━**clock¹** /klɒk/ *noun* [C] **1** a piece of equipment that shows you what time it is, usually in a house or on a building *She could hear the hall clock ticking.* ➔ *See colour picture* **The Living Room** *on page Centre 11.* **2** *UK* a piece of equipment in a vehicle for measuring how far it has travelled *a car with 63,000 kilometres on the clock* **3 around/round the clock** all day and all night *Rescue teams are working round the clock to search for survivors of the earthquake.* **4 race/work against the clock** to do something as fast as you can in order to finish before a particular time **5 turn/put the clock back** *UK* to make a situation the same as it was at an earlier time *I wish I could turn the clock back.* ➔ *See also:* **alarm clock**, **grandfather clock**

**clock²** /klɒk/ *verb*

**clock sth up** to achieve a particular number or amount of something *Yuri has clocked up 5,500 flying hours.*

**clockwise** /'klɒkwaɪz/ *adj, adv* in the same direction as the hands (= parts that point to the numbers) on a clock move ➔ *Opposite* **anti-clockwise** *UK*, **counterclockwise** *US*.

**clockwork** /'klɒkwɜːk/ *noun* **1** [U] a system of machinery that starts when you turn a handle or key *a clockwork radio/toy* **2 (as) regular as clockwork** extremely regularly *The bell rang at 8 a.m., regular as clockwork.* **3 run/go like clockwork** to happen exactly as planned, with no problems *an event that went like clockwork*

**clog** /klɒg/ (*also* **clog up**) *verb* [I, T] **clogging**, *past* **clogged** to fill something so that nothing can pass through it, or to be filled in this way [often passive] *The plughole was clogged with hair.* • *If you eat too much fat, your arteries will clog up.*

**clogs** /klɒgz/ *noun* [plural] shoes made from wood, or shoes with a wooden sole (= bottom part)

**cloister** /'klɔɪstə'/ *noun* [C] a covered stone passage around the edges of a garden in a church or religious building

**clone¹** /kləʊn/ *noun* [C] **1** an exact copy of a plant or animal that scientists make by removing one of its cells **2** *informal* someone or something that is very similar to someone or something else

**clone²** /kləʊn/ *verb* [T] to create a clone of a plant or animal *Scientists have already cloned a sheep.* • **cloning** *noun* [U] *animal/human cloning*

○━**close¹** /kləʊz/ *verb* [I, T] **1** DOOR/WINDOW ETC If something closes, it moves so that it is not open, and if you close something, you make it move so that it is not open. *Jane closed the window.* • *Lie down and close your eyes.* • *Suddenly the door closed.* **2** PUBLIC PLACE If a shop, restaurant, public place, etc closes, people cannot go in it. *The supermarket closes at 8 p.m.* **3** ORGANIZATION (*also* **close down**) If a business or organization closes, or if someone or something closes it, it stops operating. *Many factories have closed in the last ten years.* **4** END to end, or to end something *She closed the meeting with a short speech.* ➔ *See usage note at* **open**.

**close (sth) down** If a business or organization closes down, or if someone or something closes it down, it stops operating.

**close in** If people close in, they gradually get nearer to someone, usually in order to attack them or stop them escaping. *Police closed in on the demonstrators.*

**close sth off** to put something across the entrance to a place in order to stop people entering it *Police quickly closed off the area.*

○━**close²** /kləʊs/ *adj* **1** DISTANCE near in distance *His house is close to the sea.* **2** TIME near in time *It was close to lunchtime when we arrived.* **3** FRIENDLY If people are close, they know each other very well and like each other a lot. *close friends* • *I'm very close to my brother.* **4** RELATIVE [always before noun] A close relative is someone who is directly related to you, for example your mother, father, or brother. **5** RELATIONSHIP seeing or talking with someone a lot *Our school has close links with a school in China.* • *I'm still in close contact with my school friends.* **6 be/come close to doing**

clockwise        anti-clockwise *UK*,
                 counter-clockwise *US*

**sth** to almost achieve or do something *We are close to reaching an agreement.* **7 be close to sth** If someone or something is close to a particular state, they are almost in that state. *She was close to death/tears.* **8** COMPETITION A close game, competition, etc is one in which people's scores are nearly the same. **9** CAREFUL [always before noun] looking at or listening to someone or something very carefully *On close inspection, you could see that the painting was a fake.* • *Keep a close watch on the children* (= watch them carefully). **10** WEATHER Close weather is too warm and there is not enough fresh air. • **closeness** noun [U] ⊃ *See also:* a close **call²**, a close **shave²**.

o—ᵏ**close³** /kləʊs/ *adv* **1** near in distance *He stayed close to his mother.* • *Come a bit closer.* • *We walked close behind them.* • *There's a great beach close by* (= near). • *He held me close.* **2** near in time *The time for change is coming closer.*

**close⁴** /kləʊz/ *noun* **1** [no plural] the end of something *They finally reached an agreement at the close of a week of negotiations.* • *The year was drawing to a close.* **2** [C] (*also* **Close**) used in the name of a road that cars can only enter from one end *They live at 7 Kingswear Close.*

o—ᵏ**closed** /kləʊzd/ *adj* **1** BUSINESS/SHOP not open for business *We went to the library but it was closed.* **2** NOT OPEN not open *The door was closed.* • *Her eyes were closed.* **3** NOT ACCEPTING IDEAS not wanting to accept new ideas, people, customs, etc *a closed mind* ⊃ *See usage note at* **open**.

,**closed-circuit 'television** *noun* [C, U] a system of hidden cameras that take pictures of people in public places, used to help prevent crime

**close-knit** /ˌkləʊsˈnɪt/ *adj* A close-knit group of people is one in which everyone helps and supports each other. *a close-knit community/family*

**closely** /ˈkləʊsli/ *adv* **1** CAREFULLY If you look at or listen to something closely, you look at it or listen to it very carefully. **2** CONNECTED If two things are closely connected, related, etc, they are very similar to each other or there is a relationship between them. *The two languages are closely related.* • *I saw a cat that closely resembles ours.* **3** VERY NEAR in a way that is very near in distance or time *Elke came into the room, closely followed by her children.* **4** WORK If you work closely with someone, you work together a lot. *Nurses work closely with other medical staff.*

**closet¹** /ˈklɒzɪt/ *US* (*UK* **wardrobe**) *noun* [C] a large cupboard for keeping clothes in ⊃ *See also:* have a **skeleton** in the closet.

**closet²** /ˈklɒzɪt/ *adj* a **closet intellectual/liberal/socialist, etc** someone who hides their true opinions or way of life

**close-up** /ˈkləʊsʌp/ *noun* [C] a photograph of someone or something that is taken by standing very close to them

**closing** /ˈkləʊzɪŋ/ *adj* [always before noun] The closing part of an event or period of time is the final part of it. *Owen scored a goal in the closing minutes of the game.*

**closure** /ˈkləʊʒər/ *noun* [C, U] when a business, organization, etc stops operating *factory closures* • *The company announced the closure of its Paris office.*

**clot¹** /klɒt/ *noun* [C] **1** a lump that forms when a liquid, especially blood, becomes almost solid **2** *UK informal* a stupid person

**clot²** /klɒt/ *verb* [I, T] **clotting**, *past* **clotted** to form clots, or to make clots form

**cloth** /klɒθ/ *noun* **1** [U] material made from cotton, wool, etc, and used, for example, to make clothes or curtains *a piece of cloth* **2** [C] a piece of cloth used for cleaning or drying things

**clothe** /kləʊð/ *verb* [T] to supply clothes for someone *Aid agencies will feed and clothe the refugees.*

**clothed** /kləʊðd/ *adj* wearing clothes *fully clothed*

o—ᵏ**clothes** /kləʊðz/ *noun* [plural] items such as shirts and trousers that you wear on your body *She was wearing her sister's clothes.* • *to put on/take off your clothes* ⊃ *See colour picture* **Clothes** *on page Centre 5.*

**clothes**

Remember that **clothes** is plural. If you want to talk about one particular thing that you wear, use the expression **piece/item of clothing**.

*I need some new clothes.*

*He bought two or three pieces of clothing.*

**clothesline** /ˈkləʊðzlaɪn/ *noun* [C] a rope for hanging wet clothes on until they dry

'**clothes ,peg** *UK* (*US* **clothespin** /ˈkləʊðzpɪn/) *noun* [C] a short piece of wood or plastic that is used to hold clothes on a rope while they dry

**clothing** /ˈkləʊðɪŋ/ *noun* [U] clothes, especially of a particular type *outdoor/protective clothing*

**cloud¹** /klaʊd/ *noun* **1** [C, U] a white or grey mass that floats in the sky, made of small water drops *rain/storm clouds* • *The entire region is covered in thick cloud.* **2** [C] a mass of gas or very small pieces of something floating in the air *a cloud of dust/smoke* **3 be under a cloud** If someone is under a cloud, they are not trusted or not popular because people think they have done something bad. *It is sad that he must end his career under a cloud.* • **cloudless** *adj* without clouds

**cloud²** /klaʊd/ *verb* **1** [T] to make someone confused, or make something harder to understand *to cloud someone's judgment/vision* **2** [I, T] If something transparent clouds, it becomes hard to see through, and if something clouds it, it makes it hard to see through.

**cloud over** to become covered with clouds

**cloudy** /ˈklaʊdi/ *adj* **1** When it is cloudy, there are clouds in the sky. **2** A cloudy liquid is not transparent. *cloudy water*

**clout** /klaʊt/ *noun* **1** [U] power and influence over other people *As mayor, he has political clout.* **2** [C] *UK informal* a heavy blow made with the hand

**clove** /kləʊv/ *noun* [C] **1** a small, dark-brown, dried flower that is used as a spice **2** one separate part in a root of garlic (= plant with a strong taste used in cooking)

**clover** /'kləʊvər/ *noun* [U] a small plant that has three round leaves and round flowers

**clown**[1] /klaʊn/ *noun* [C] **1** a performer who has special clothes and a painted face and makes people laugh **2** a silly person

**clown**[2] /klaʊn/ (*also* **clown around**) *verb* [I] to behave in a silly way in order to make people laugh

o━**club**[1] /klʌb/ *noun* [C] **1** ORGANIZATION an organization for people who want to take part in a sport or social activity together, or the building they use for this *a fitness/football club* **2** GOLF (*also* **golf club**) a long, thin stick used to hit the ball in golf ➜ *See colour picture* **Sports 2** *on page Centre 16.* **3** WEAPON a heavy stick used as a weapon **4** DANCE a place open late at night where people can dance **5** **clubs** playing cards with black shapes like three leaves on them *the ten of clubs* ➜ *See also:* **fan club.**

**club**[2] /klʌb/ *verb* **clubbing**, *past* **clubbed** [T] to hit a person or animal with a heavy stick **2** **go clubbing** *mainly UK* to go to clubs where there is music and dancing

**club together** If a group of people club together to buy something, they share the cost of it.

**clubhouse** /'klʌbhaʊs/ *noun* [C] a building that the members of a club use for social activities or for changing their clothes

**cluck** /klʌk/ *verb* [I] to make the sound that a chicken makes ● **cluck** *noun* [C]

o━**clue** /kluː/ *noun* [C] **1** a sign or a piece of information that helps you to solve a problem or answer a question *Police are searching the area for* **clues** *to the murder.* ● *I can't remember who wrote it.* **Give me a clue. 2 not have a clue** *informal* to be completely unable to guess, understand, or deal with something [+ question word] *I haven't a clue what you're talking about.*

**clued 'up** *adj UK* knowing all the most important information about something *He's very* **clued up on** *the law.*

**clueless** /'kluːləs/ *adj informal* A clueless person does not know anything about a particular subject.

**clump** /klʌmp/ *noun* [C] a group of plants growing closely together *a clump of grass*

**clumsy** /'klʌmzi/ *adj* **1** PERSON Clumsy people move in a way that is not controlled or careful enough, and often knock or damage things. **2** BEHAVIOUR If you behave in a clumsy way, you upset people because you are not careful about their feelings. *a clumsy attempt to be friendly* **3** OBJECT Clumsy objects are large, not attractive, and often difficult to use. ● **clumsily** *adv* ● **clumsiness** *noun* [U]

**clung** /klʌŋ/ *past of* **cling**

**cluster**[1] /'klʌstər/ *noun* a group of similar things that are close together *a cluster of galaxies*

**cluster**[2] /'klʌstər/ *verb* **cluster around/round/ together, etc** to form a close group *Photographers clustered round the film star.*

**clutch**[1] /klʌtʃ/ *verb* [T] to hold something tightly *She clutched a coin.*

**clutch at sth** to try very hard to hold something *She clutched wildly at the branch.*

**clutch**[2] /klʌtʃ/ *noun* **1** [U] the part of a car or truck that you press with your foot when you change gear (= part that controls how fast the wheels turn) ➜ *See colour picture* **Car** *on page Centre 3.* **2** [C, U] when someone holds or tries to hold something tightly **3 sb's clutches** If you are in someone's clutches, they control you, often in an evil way.

**clutter**[1] /'klʌtər/ (*also* **clutter up**) *verb* [T] to cover a surface, or to fill a place with things that are not tidy or well organized [often passive] *Every shelf is* **cluttered with** *ornaments.*

**clutter**[2] /'klʌtər/ *noun* [U] a lot of objects that are not tidy or well organized *I've got too much clutter on my desk.*

**cm** *written abbreviation for* centimetre (= a unit for measuring length)

**c/o** *written abbreviation for* care of: used when you send a letter to someone who will give it to the person you are writing to

**Co 1** *written abbreviation for* Company (= name of business) *Williams & Co* **2** *written abbreviation for* County (= area with own local government) *Co. Wexford*

o━**coach**[1] /kəʊtʃ/ *noun* [C] **1** BUS *UK* a comfortable bus used to take groups of people on long journeys *a coach trip* **2** PERSON someone whose job is to teach people to improve at a sport, skill, or school subject *a football/tennis coach* **3** OLD VEHICLE a vehicle with wheels that is pulled by horses

**coach**[2] /kəʊtʃ/ *verb* [T] to teach someone so they improve at a sport, skill, or in a school subject ● **coaching** *noun* [U]

**'coach ,station** *UK* (*UK/US* **bus station**) *noun* [C] a building where a bus starts or ends its journey

**coal** /kəʊl/ *noun* **1** [U] a hard, black substance that is dug from under the ground and burnt as fuel *a lump of coal* **2** **coals** pieces of coal, usually burning

**coalition** /ˌkəʊə'lɪʃən/ *noun* [C] two or more political parties that have joined together, usually to govern a country *to form a coalition* ● *a coalition government*

**'coal ,mine** *noun* [C] (*also UK* **colliery**) a place where people work digging coal from under the ground

**coarse** /kɔːs/ *adj* **1** rough and thick, or not in very small pieces *coarse breadcrumbs* **2** not polite *coarse language* ● **coarsely** *adv*

o━**coast**[1] /kəʊst/ *noun* [C, U] **1** the land beside the sea *The island lies* **off** *the North African coast* (= in the sea near North Africa). ● *They live* **on** *the east coast of Scotland.* **2 coast to coast** from one side of a country to the other **3 the coast is clear** If the coast is clear, you can do something or go somewhere because there is nobody who might see you.

**coast**[2] /kəʊst/ *verb* [I] **1** to progress or succeed without any effort or difficulty *Pakistan* **coasted** *to a four-wicket victory over Australia.* **2** to move forward in a vehicle without using the engine, usually down a hill

**coastal** /'kəʊstəl/ *adj* situated on or relating to the coast *a coastal town/resort* ● *coastal waters*

**coastguard** /'kəʊstɡɑːd/ *noun* [C] a person or the organization responsible for preventing accidents and illegal activities in the sea near a coast

**coastline** /'kəustlaın/ noun [C, U] the part of the land along the edge of the sea *a rocky coastline*

o⊶**coat¹** /kəut/ noun [C] **1** CLOTHES a piece of clothing with sleeves that you wear over your other clothes, especially when you go outside *a fur/winter coat* ⊃ *See colour picture* **Clothes** *on page Centre 5.* **2** FUR the fur that covers an animal's body **3** LAYER a layer of a substance such as paint *a coat of paint/varnish*

**coat²** /kəut/ verb [T] to cover something with a thin layer of something *Stir the rice until it is coated with butter.*

'coat ,hanger noun [C] a wire, wooden, or plastic object for hanging clothes on

**coating** /'kəutıŋ/ noun [C] a thin layer that covers the surface of something *a protective/non-stick coating*

**coax** /kəuks/ verb [T] to persuade someone in a gentle way [+ into + doing sth] *She coaxed me into joining the group.*

**cobble¹** /'kɒbl/ verb
**cobble sth together** to make something quickly and not very carefully

**cobble²** /'kɒbl/ noun [C] a rounded stone used on the surface of an old-fashioned road
• **cobbled** adj made with cobbles *cobbled streets*

**cobbler** /'kɒblə/ noun [C] mainly UK old-fashioned someone whose job is to make or repair shoes

**cobblestone** /'kɒblstəun/ noun [C] a rounded stone that is used on the surface of an old-fashioned road

**cobra** /'kəubrə/ noun [C] a poisonous snake that makes the skin of its neck wide and flat when it is going to attack

**cobweb** /'kɒbweb/ noun [C] a structure of fine threads made by a spider (= insect with eight legs) to catch insects

**Coca Cola** /ˌkəukə'kəulə/ noun [U] trademark a sweet, dark-brown drink with lots of bubbles

**cocaine** /kəu'keın/ noun [U] an illegal drug, often used in the form of white powder

**cock¹** /kɒk/ noun [C] an adult male chicken

**cock²** /kɒk/ verb [T] to move part of the body up or to the side *to cock an ear/eyebrow*
**cock sth up** UK informal to do something wrong or badly *I really cocked up my exams.*

**cockerel** /'kɒkᵊrᵊl/ noun [C] UK a young male chicken

**cockney** /'kɒkni/ noun **1** [U] a type of English spoken in East London **2** [C] someone who speaks Cockney

**cockpit** /'kɒkpıt/ noun [C] the part of an aircraft or racing car that contains the controls

**cockroach** /'kɒkrəutʃ/ noun [C] a large, brown or black insect that can live in houses and places where food is prepared

**cocktail** /'kɒkteıl/ noun **1** MIXTURE [C] a mixture of powerful substances *a cocktail of drugs/chemicals* **2** DRINK [C] an alcoholic drink made from two or more kinds of drink mixed together *a cocktail bar/party* **3** DISH [C, U] a cold dish containing small pieces of food mixed together *a prawn cocktail* • *fruit cocktail*

**cock-up** /'kɒkʌp/ noun [C] UK informal a stupid mistake or failure

**cocky** /'kɒki/ adj confident in an annoying way

**cocoa** /'kəukəu/ noun [U] **1** a dark-brown powder produced from a type of bean, used to make chocolate **2** a drink made by mixing cocoa powder with hot milk

**coconut** /'kəukənʌt/ noun [C] a very large nut with a hard, hairy shell, a white part that you eat, and liquid in the centre

**cocoon** /kə'ku:n/ noun [C] a cover that protects some insects as they develop into adults

**cod** /kɒd/ noun [C, U] plural **cod** a large sea fish which can be eaten as food

**code** /kəud/ noun **1** SECRET MESSAGE [C, U] a set of letters, numbers, or signs that are used instead of ordinary words to keep a message secret *It was written in code.* • *They were trying to break* (= understand) *the enemy's code.* **2** TELEPHONE [C] UK (UK/US **area code**) a set of numbers used at the beginning of all the telephone numbers in a particular area **3** RULES [C] a set of rules on how to behave or how to do things *a code of conduct/practice* • *The club has a strict dress code* (= rules about what you wear). ⊃ *See also:* **bar code**, **zip code**

**coded** /'kəudıd/ adj written or sent in code *a coded message/warning*

**codeine** /'kəudi:n/ noun [U] a medicine used to reduce pain

**co-ed** /ˌkəu'ed ⓤⓢ 'kəuˌed/ adj with both male and female students

**coerce** /kəu'ɜ:s/ verb [T] formal to make someone do something that they do not want to do [+ into + doing sth] *Employees said they were coerced into signing the agreement.* • coercion /kəu'ɜ:ʃᵊn/ noun [U] *They accused the police of coercion.*

**coexist** /ˌkəuıg'zıst/ verb [I] If two things or groups coexist, they exist at the same time or together, although they may be very different. *Can science and religion coexist?* • coexistence noun [U]

o⊶**coffee** /'kɒfi/ noun **1** [C, U] a hot drink made from dark beans which are made into a powder, or a cup of this drink *Do you want a cup of coffee?* **2** [U] the beans from which coffee is made, or the powder made from these beans *instant coffee*

'coffee ,table noun [C] a low table in a room where people sit ⊃ *See colour picture* **The Living Room** *on page Centre 11.*

**coffers** /'kɒfəz/ noun [plural] a supply of money that a group or organization has and can spend *government/party coffers*

**coffin** /'kɒfın/ noun [C] (also US **casket**) a box in which a dead body is buried ⊃ *See also:* the final **nail¹** in the coffin.

**cog** /kɒg/ noun [C] a part shaped like a tooth on the edge of a wheel in a machine, that makes another wheel turn

**cogent** /'kəudʒᵊnt/ adj A cogent argument, reason, or explanation is one which people will believe because it is clear and careful.

**cognac** /'kɒnjæk/ noun [U] good quality French brandy (= strong alcoholic drink)

**cognitive** /'kɒgnətıv/ adj [always before noun] formal relating to how people think, understand, and learn

**cohabit** /kəu'hæbıt/ verb [I] formal If two people

cohabit, they live together and are sexual partners but are not married. • cohabitation /kəʊ,hæbɪ'teɪʃ°n/ *noun* [U]

**coherent** /kəʊ'hɪərªnt/ *adj* **1** A coherent argument, plan, etc is clear, and each part of it has been carefully considered. **2** If someone is coherent, you can understand what they say. ⊃ *Opposite* **incoherent**. • coherence /kəʊ'hɪərªns/ *noun* [U] • coherently *adv*

**cohesion** /kəʊ'hiːʒ°n/ *noun* [U] when the members of a group or society are united *The country needs greater social cohesion.* • cohesive /kəʊ'hiːsɪv/ *adj* united and working together effectively *a cohesive unit/group*

**cohort** /'kəʊhɔːt/ *noun* [C] someone who supports someone else, especially a political leader *the prime minister's cohorts*

**coil**[1] /kɔɪl/ *noun* [C] a long piece of wire, rope, etc curled into several circles *a coil of rope*

**coil**[2] /kɔɪl/ (*also* **coil up**) *verb* [I, T] to twist something into circles, or to become twisted into circles *Her hair was coiled in a bun on top of her head.*

**coin**[1] /kɔɪn/ *noun* **1** [C] a flat, usually round, piece of metal used as money *a pound coin* **2 toss a coin** to throw a coin into the air so that it turns over several times, and see which side it lands on, in order to make a decision

**coin**[2] /kɔɪn/ *verb* [T] **1** to be the first person who uses a new word or phrase *The Czech playwright, Capek, coined the word 'robot'.* **2 to coin a phrase** something you say before using a common expression *Still, to coin a phrase, there is light at the end of the tunnel.*

**coincide** /,kəʊɪn'saɪd/ *verb* [I] **1** to happen at the same time as something else *The band's American tour coincided with the release of their second album.* **2** When people's opinions or ideas coincide, they are the same.

**coincidence** /kəʊ'ɪnsɪdªns/ *noun* [C, U] when two very similar things happen at the same time but there is no reason for it *an amazing/ strange coincidence* • *It was pure coincidence that we both married dentists.* • coincidental /kəʊ,ɪnsɪ'dentªl/ *adj* happening by coincidence *The similarities are coincidental.* • coincidentally /kəʊ,ɪnsɪ'dentªli/ *adv*

**Coke** /kəʊk/ *noun* [C, U] *trademark short for* Coca Cola (= a sweet, dark-brown drink with lots of bubbles)

**Col** *written abbreviation for* Colonel (= an officer of high rank in the army or air force)

**cola** /'kəʊlə/ *noun* [U] a sweet, dark-brown drink with lots of bubbles ⊃ *See also:* **Coca Cola**.

**colander** /'kɒləndəʳ/ *noun* [C] a bowl with small holes in it used for washing food or separating water from food after cooking ⊃ *See colour picture* **Kitchen** *on page Centre 10.*

o━**cold**[1] /kəʊld/ *adj* **1** TEMPERATURE having a low temperature *cold water/weather* • *This soup has gone cold.* • *The nights are getting colder now.* • *My hands are getting cold.* **2** UNFRIENDLY unfriendly or showing no emotion *a cold stare/voice* • *She became quite cold and distant with me.* **3** FOOD served cold *cold roast beef* • coldness *noun* [U] ⊃ *See also:* in cold **blood**, get cold feet (**foot**[1]).

**cold**[2] /kəʊld/ *noun* **1** [C] a common illness which

makes you sneeze and makes your nose produce liquid *I've got a cold.* • *He **caught a bad cold** at school.* **2** [C] the cold weather or temperatures *She was shivering from the cold.* **3 leave sb out in the cold** to not allow someone to be part of a group or activity *Women's football teams feel they are left out in the cold as far as media coverage is concerned.*

**cold**[3] /kəʊld/ *adv* **1 be out cold** *informal* to be unconscious *I hit my head and was out cold for two minutes.* **2** completely and immediately *I offered him £10 but he turned me down cold.*

**cold-blooded** /,kəʊld'blʌdɪd/ *adj* showing no emotion or sympathy *a cold-blooded killer*

**cold-hearted** /,kəʊld'hɑːtɪd/ *adj* feeling no kindness or sympathy towards other people

**coldly** /'kəʊldli/ *adv* in a way that is not friendly or emotional *He looked at me coldly.*

**colic** /'kɒlɪk/ *noun* [U] When a baby has colic, it has a bad pain in the stomach.

**collaborate** /kə'læbªreɪt/ *verb* [I] **1** When two or more people collaborate, they work together to create or achieve the same thing. *Didn't you collaborate with him on one of your books?* **2** to help people who are an enemy of your country or government *He was accused of collaborating with the enemy.* • collaborator *noun* [C]

**collaboration** /kə,læbªª'reɪʃ°n/ *noun* **1** [C, U] when two or more people work together to create or achieve the same thing, or a product of this *The show was a result of collaboration between several museums.* **2** [U] when someone helps an enemy country or government

**collage** /kɒl'ɑːʒ/ *noun* [C, U] a picture made by sticking small pieces of paper or other materials onto a surface, or the process of making pictures like this

**collapse**[1] /kə'læps/ *verb* **1** FALL [I] When someone collapses, they fall down, usually because they are ill or weak. *He collapsed and died of a heart attack.* **2** OBJECT [I, T] to fall down or towards the inside, or to make a structure or object fall down or towards its inside *The roof collapsed under the weight of snow.* **3** FAIL [I] to fail to work or succeed *The peace talks have collapsed.*

**collapse**[2] /kə'læps/ *noun* [C, U] **1** the sudden failure of a system, organization, business, etc **2** when a person or structure becomes too weak to stand and suddenly falls

**collapsible** /kə'læpsɪbl/ *adj* able to be folded or made flat in order to be stored or carried *a collapsible table/boat*

**collar**[1] /'kɒləʳ/ *noun* [C] **1** the part of a shirt, coat, etc that is usually folded over and goes round your neck *a shirt collar* ⊃ *See picture at* **jacket**. **2** a narrow piece of leather or plastic that you fasten round the neck of an animal

**collar**[2] /'kɒləʳ/ *verb* [T] *informal* to find someone and stop them going somewhere, often so that you can talk to them about something *On my way to the meeting, Jack collared me about his new proposal.*

**collarbone** /'kɒləbəʊn/ *noun* [C] a bone between the base of your neck and your shoulder

**collateral** /kə'lætªrªl/ *noun* [U] things that you agree to give someone if you are not able pay back money you have borrowed from them *I used my car **as collateral** for a loan.*

◦━**colleague** /'kɒliːg/ *noun* [C] someone that you work with

◦━**collect¹** /kə'lekt/ *verb* **1** BRING TOGETHER [T] to get things from different places and bring them together *Police collected a good deal of information during the investigation.* • *Would you collect up the books please, Joanne?* **2** KEEP [T] to get and keep things of one type such as stamps or coins as a hobby *She collects dolls.* **3** GO TO GET [T] *UK* to go to a place and bring someone or something away from it *She collects Anna from school at three o'clock.* **4** MONEY [I, T] to ask people to give you money for something, for example a charity (= organization that helps people) *I'm collecting on behalf of Oxfam.* **5** RECEIVE [T] to receive money that you are owed *You can begin to collect a pension at age 62.* **6** COME TOGETHER [I] to come together in a single place *Journalists collected outside the palace.* **7 collect yourself/your thoughts** to get control over your feelings and thoughts

**collect²** /kə'lekt/ *adj, adv US* When you telephone collect or make a collect telephone call, the person you telephone pays for the call. *She called me collect.*

**collected** /kə'lektɪd/ *adj* **1** [always before noun] brought together in one book or series of books *His collected poems were published in 1928.* **2** showing control over your feelings *Jane was very **calm and collected**.*

◦━**collection** /kə'lekʃ°n/ *noun* **1** OBJECTS [C] a group of objects of the same type that have been collected by one person or in one place *a private art collection* **2** TAKING AWAY [U] when something is taken away from a place *rubbish collection* **3** MONEY [C] an amount of money collected from several people *We had a collection for Emily's gift.* **4** GROUP [C] a group of things or people *There's quite a collection of toothbrushes in the bathroom.*

**collective¹** /kə'lektɪv/ *adj* involving, felt by, or owned by everyone in a group *collective responsibility*

**collective²** /kə'lektɪv/ *noun* [C] a business that is owned and controlled by the people who work in it

**collectively** /kə'lektɪvli/ *adv* as a group *She has a staff of four who collectively earn almost $200,000.*

**collector** /kə'lektər/ *noun* [C] **1** someone whose job is to collect tickets or money from people *a tax collector* **2** someone who collects objects because they are interesting or beautiful *a collector of modern art*

◦━**college** /'kɒlɪdʒ/ *noun* **1** EDUCATION [C, U] *UK* a place where students are educated when they are between 16 and 18 years old, or after they have finished school *a sixth-form college* • *teacher-training college* **2** UNIVERSITY [C, U] *US* a university **3** PART OF UNIVERSITY [C] a part of a university that has its own teachers and students *Cambridge/Oxford colleges* ➔ See also: **community college**, **junior college**.

**collegiate** /kə'liːdʒiət/ *adj* relating to or belonging to a college or its students *collegiate sports*

**collide** /kə'laɪd/ *verb* [I] When two objects collide, they hit each other with force, usually while moving. *The car **collided with** a van.*

**colliery** /'kɒljəri/ *UK* (*UK/US* **coal mine**) *noun* [C] a place where people work digging coal from under the ground

**collision** /kə'lɪʒ°n/ *noun* **1** [C] an accident that happens when two vehicles hit each other with force **2 be on a collision course** If two people or groups are on a collision course, they are doing or saying things that are certain to cause a serious disagreement or fight between them.

**colloquial** /kə'ləʊkwiəl/ *adj* Colloquial words or expressions are informal. *colloquial speech* • colloquially *adv*

**collude** /kə'luːd/ *verb* [I] *formal* to do something secretly with another person or group, in order to deceive or cheat others *The company colluded with competitors to fix prices.* • collusion /kə'luːʒ°n/ *noun* [U] *He was accused of being in collusion with the terrorists.*

**colon** /'kəʊlɒn/ *noun* [C] **1** a mark (:) used before a list, an example, an explanation, etc ➔ See study section **Punctuation** *on page Centre 37.* **2** the lower part of a person's bowels

**colonel** /'kɜːn°l/ *noun* [C] an officer of high rank in the army or air force

**colonial** /kə'ləʊniəl/ *adj* [always before noun] relating to colonialism or a colony (= country controlled by another country) *colonial rule/government*

**colonialism** /kə'ləʊniəlɪz°m/ *noun* [U] the system in which powerful countries control other countries

**colonize** (*also UK* **-ise**) /'kɒlənaɪz/ *verb* [T] **1** to send people to live in and govern another country [often passive] *Burundi was first colonized by the Germans.* **2** to start growing or living in large numbers in a place *Weeds quickly colonize areas of cleared ground.* • colonist /'kɒlənɪst/ *noun* [C] someone who goes to colonize a country • colonization /ˌkɒlənaɪˈzeɪʃ°n/ *noun* [U]

**colony** /'kɒləni/ *noun* [C] **1** COUNTRY a country or area controlled in an official, political way by a more powerful country *a French/British colony* **2** GROUP a group of the same type of animals, insects, or plants living together in a particular place *a colony of ants* **3** PEOPLE a group of people with the same interests or job who live together *an artists' colony*

◦━**color** /'kʌlər/ *noun, verb US spelling of* colour

**colored** /'kʌləd/ *adj US spelling of* coloured

**colorful** /'kʌləfəl/ *adj US spelling of* colourful

**coloring** /'kʌlərɪŋ/ *noun* [U] *US spelling of* colouring

**colorless** /'kʌlələs/ *adj US spelling of* colourless

**colossal** /kə'lɒs°l/ *adj* extremely large *colossal amounts of money*

◦━**colour¹** *UK* (*US* **color**) /'kʌlər/ *noun* **1** RED/BLUE ETC [C, U] red, blue, green, yellow, etc *She dressed in bright colours.* • *Green is my favourite colour.* • *What colour shall I paint the kitchen?* ➔ See colour picture **Colours** *on page Centre 6.* **2** FILM/TV ETC [U] using or showing all the colours, not only black and white *Why didn't he shoot the film in colour?* **3** SKIN [U] the colour of a person's skin, which shows their

**C**

race **4** FACE [U] healthy pink skin on someone's face *The colour drained from her cheeks.* **5** INTEREST [U] interesting or exciting qualities or parts *We added your story for a bit of local colour.* **6 with flying colours** with a very high score or with great success *He passed the entrance exam with flying colours.* ➔ See also: **primary colour**.

**colour²** *UK* (*US* **color**) /'kʌləʳ/ *verb* **1** [I, T] to become a particular colour, or to make something a particular colour *He drew a heart and coloured it red.* • *Fry the onions until they start to colour.* **2** [T] to affect what someone does, says, or feels [often passive] *Her views are coloured by her own bad experiences.*

**colour sth in** to fill an area with colour using paint, pens, etc

**colour-blind** *UK* (*US* **color-blind**) /'kʌləblaɪnd/ *adj* unable to see the difference between particular colours

**coloured** *UK* (*US* **colored**) /'kʌləd/ *adj* **1** having or producing a colour or colours *coloured lights/cloth* **2** an old-fashioned way of describing someone from a race with dark skin that is now considered offensive

**colourful** *UK* (*US* **colorful**) /'kʌləfˀl/ *adj* **1** having bright colours *a colourful painting* **2** interesting and unusual *a colourful character*

**colouring** *UK* (*US* **coloring**) /'kʌlərɪŋ/ *noun* [U] **1** the colour of something, especially an animal or person's skin, hair, and eyes *The boys have their father's colouring.* **2** a substance that is used to colour something *food/artificial colouring*

**colourless** (*US* **colorless**) /'kʌlələs/ *adj* **1** without any colour *a colourless liquid* **2** without the qualities that make someone or something interesting and unusual *a colourless account of his time in parliament*

**colt** /kəʊlt/ *noun* [C] a young male horse

**column** /'kɒləm/ *noun* [C] **1** TALL POST a tall, solid, usually stone post which is used to support a roof or as decoration in a building *a stone/marble column* **2** NEWSPAPER a regular article in a newspaper or magazine on a particular subject or by the same writer **3** PRINT one of the blocks of print into which a page of a newspaper, magazine, or dictionary is divided **4** NUMBERS ETC any block of numbers or words written one under the other **5 a column of sth** something with a tall, narrow shape *A column*

column

of smoke rose from the chimney. **6** PEOPLE MOVING a long line of moving people or vehicles *a column of refugees* ➔ See also: **gossip column**.

**columnist** /'kɒləmnɪst/ *noun* [C] someone who writes a regular article for a newspaper or magazine *a sports/gossip columnist*

**coma** /'kəʊmə/ *noun* [C] when someone is not conscious for a long time [usually singular] *She has been in a coma for over a week.*

**comb¹** /kəʊm/ *noun* [C] a flat piece of metal or plastic with a row of long, narrow parts along one side, that you use to tidy your hair

**comb²** /kəʊm/ *verb* [T] **1** to tidy your hair using a comb **2** to search a place very carefully *Investigators combed through the wreckage.*

**combat¹** /'kɒmbæt/ *noun* [C, U] a fight, especially during a war *The aircraft was shot down in combat.*

**combat²** /'kɒmbæt/ *verb* [T] to try to stop something unpleasant or harmful from happening or increasing *new measures to combat the rise in crime*

**combatant** /'kɒmbətˀnt/ *noun* [C] *formal* someone who fights in a war

**combative** /'kɒmbətɪv/ *adj* *formal* eager to fight or argue

○━**combination** /ˌkɒmbɪ'neɪʃˀn/ *noun* **1** [C, U] a mixture of different people or things *Strawberries and cream – a perfect combination!* • *We won through a combination of luck and skill.* • *This drug can be safely used in combination with other medicines.* **2** [C] a set of numbers or letters in a particular order which is needed to open some types of locks *a combination lock*

○━**combine** /kəm'baɪn/ *verb* **1** [I, T] to become mixed or joined, or to mix or join things together *My wages combined with your savings should just pay for it.* • *The band combines jazz rhythms and romantic lyrics.* **2** [T] to do two or more activities at the same time *I don't know how she combines working with studying.*

**combined** /kəm'baɪnd/ *adj* [always before noun] joined together *the combined effects of poverty and disease*

**combine harvester** /ˌkɒmbaɪn'hɑːvɪstəʳ/ (*also* **combine**) *noun* [C] a large farm machine which cuts a crop and separates the grain from the stem

**combustion** /kəm'bʌstʃˀn/ *noun* [U] the process of burning

○━**come** /kʌm/ *verb* past t **came**, past p **come** **1** MOVE TOWARDS [I] to move or travel towards a person who is speaking or towards the place that they are speaking about *Come and see what I've done.* • *Can you come to my party?* • *She came in the evening.* • *The rain came down heavily.* • *Here comes Adam* (= Adam is coming). **2** ARRIVE [I] to arrive somewhere, or go to a place *I'll come and see you later.* • [+ to do sth] *I've come to see Mr Curtis.* • *I've come about the job.* • *Has the paper come yet?* • *Dad will come for you at six.* • *We came to a crossroads.* **3** GO WITH SOMEONE [I] to go somewhere with the person who is speaking *Come for a walk with us.* • *We're going to the cinema. Do you* _want to come?_ **4 come after/first/last, etc** to have or achieve a particular position in a race, competition, list, etc _Our team came third._ • _Sunday comes after Saturday._ **5 come past/to/up to, etc** to reach a particular length, height, or depth _The water came up to my waist._ **6 come apart/off, etc** to become separated or removed from something _The book came apart in my hands._ • _The handle **came off**._ • _My shoelaces have **come undone**._ • _The door came open._ **7 come easily/easy/naturally** to be very easy for someone _Singing came naturally to Louise._ **8** BE HAPPEN [I] to happen _Spring has come early._ • _The worst problems are still **to come**._ • _I've finished cleaning the bathroom. What comes next?_ **9 how come** _informal_ used to ask why or how something has happened _How come you didn't go to the party?_ **10 come and go** to exist or happen somewhere for a short time and then go away _The feeling of nausea comes and goes._ **11** BE AVAILABLE [I] to be available in a particular size, colour, etc _The table comes in three different sizes._ • _Furniture like this doesn't **come cheap**._ **12 come to do sth** to start to do something _I have come to rely on acupuncture._ • _This place has come to be known as 'Pheasant Corner'._ **13 when it comes to sth/doing sth** used to introduce a new idea that you want to say something about _When it comes to baking cakes, she's an expert._ **14 come to think of it** used to say that you have just thought of something _Come to think of it, I've got two batteries that you can have upstairs._ **15 Come off it!** _informal_ used to tell someone that you do not believe them or that you disagree with them ⊃ _See also:_ come to blows (**blow²**), I'll/We'll cross that **bridge¹** when I/we come to it., come **clean¹**, if/when it comes to the **crunch¹**, come (back) down to **earth**, come under **fire¹**, come up with the **goods**, come to **grief**, come to grips (**grip¹**) with sth, come to **light¹**, come into your/its **own¹**, not come up to **scratch²**, come to your senses (**sense¹**), come up trumps (**trump¹**).

**come about** to happen, or start to happen _How did the idea for an arts festival come about?_

**come across sb/sth** to meet someone or discover something by chance _I came across a lovely little restaurant in the village._

**come across 1** to seem to be a particular type of person _He came across as shy._ **2** If an idea or emotion comes across, it is expressed clearly and people understand it. _His bitterness comes across in his poetry._

**come along 1** ARRIVE to arrive or appear at a place _A taxi never comes along when you need one._ **2** GO WITH SOMEONE to go somewhere with someone _We're going to the cinema. Do you want to come along?_ **3** EXIST to start to exist _I gave up climbing when my first child came along._ **4 be coming along** to be developing or making progress _Hassan's English is coming along well._

**come around 1** VISIT to visit someone at their house **2** AGREE to change your opinion about something, or agree to an idea or a plan that you were against _I'm sure she'll **come around** to our view eventually._ **3** EVENT If an event that

happens regularly comes around, it happens, or is going to happen soon. _Thanksgiving has come around again._ **4** BECOME CONSCIOUS to become conscious again after an accident or medical operation

**come back 1** to return to a place _I've just come back from the dentist's._ **2** If a style or a fashion comes back, it becomes popular again. _Miniskirts are coming back into fashion._

**come back to sb** If something comes back to you, you remember it. _Suddenly, the horror of the accident came back to me._

**come between sb** to harm the relationship between two or more people _I won't let anything come between me and my children._

**come by sth** to get something, especially something that is unusual or difficult to find _Cheap organic food is still difficult to come by._

**come down 1** to break and fall to the ground _A lot of trees came down in the storm._ **2** If a price or a level comes down, it becomes lower. _Prices always come down after Christmas._ **3** to decide that you support a particular person or side in an argument, etc _The government has **come down on the side of** military action._

**come down on sb** to punish or criticize someone _The police are **coming down hard on** people for not paying parking fines._

**come down to sth/doing sth** If a situation, problem, decision, etc comes down to something, then that is the thing that will influence it most.

**come down with sth** _informal_ to get an illness _I came down with the flu at Christmas._

**come forward** to offer to help someone or to give information _We need witnesses to **come forward with** information about the attack._

**come from sth** to be born, obtained from, or made somewhere _She comes from Poland._ • _Milk comes from cows._ • _Where did that radio come from?_ (= where did you get it?)

**come from sth/doing sth** to be caused by something _"I feel awful." "That comes from eating too many sweets."_

**come in 1** ENTER to enter a room or building _Do you want to come in for a cup of tea?_ **2** FASHION If a fashion or a product comes in, it becomes available or becomes popular. _Flared trousers came in during the seventies._ **3** BE RECEIVED If news, information, a report, etc comes in, it is received. _News is just coming in about the explosion._ **4 come in first/second, etc** to finish a race or a competition in first/second, etc position **5** SEA If the tide (= regular change in the level of the sea) comes in, the sea moves towards the beach or coast. **6** BE INVOLVED _informal_ used to describe how someone is involved in a situation, story, or plan _We need people to help clean up, and that's where you come in._

**come in for sth** If someone comes in for criticism, praise, etc, they are criticized, praised, etc.

**come into sth 1** to get money from someone who has died _Just after I left university, I came into a bit of money._ **2 come into it** _UK informal_ to influence a situation _Money doesn't come into it._

**come of sth/doing sth** [used in questions and negatives] to happen as a result of something *Did anything come of all those job applications?*

**come off 1** to happen successfully *His attempt to impress us all didn't quite come off.* **2 come off badly/best/well, etc** to be in a bad or good position at the end of a fight, argument, etc *She usually comes off best in an argument.* **3 Come off it!** *informal* used to tell someone that you do not agree with them or do not believe them *Oh, come off it! I saw you take it!*

**come on 1** START to start to happen or work *The heating comes on at six in the morning.* • *I've got a cold coming on.* **2** MAKE PROGRESS to make progress *How's your new novel coming on?* **3 Come on!** *informal* **a** ENCOURAGEMENT used to encourage someone to do something, to hurry, to try harder, etc *Come on! We're going to be late.* **b** DISAGREEMENT used to tell someone that you do not agree with them, do not believe them, etc *Come on Bob! You made the same excuse last week.*

**come out 1** BECOME AVAILABLE If a book, record, film, etc comes out, it becomes available for people to buy or see. *When does their new album come out?* **2** SUN If the sun, the moon, or a star comes out, it appears in the sky. **3** BECOME KNOWN to become known *The truth about him will come out in the end.* **4** SOCIAL EVENT *UK* to go somewhere with someone for a social event *Would you like to come out for a drink?* **5** RESULT If you describe how something comes out at the end of a process or activity, you say what it is like. *How did your chocolate cake come out?* **6** INFORMATION If results or information come out, they are given to people. *The exam results come out in August.* **7** BE REMOVED If dirt or a mark comes out of something, it disappears when you clean it. *Will this red wine stain come out?* **8** PHOTOGRAPH If a photograph comes out, the picture can be seen clearly. *The photos didn't come out very well.* **9** BE SAID If something that you say comes out in a particular way, you say it in that way. *I wanted to tell her that I loved her, but it came out all wrong.* **10** TELL to tell people that you are homosexual (= sexually attracted to people of the same sex) **11 come out against/in favour of sth** to say publicly that you oppose or support something

**come out in sth** If you come out in a skin disease, it appears on your skin. *When I eat cheese, I come out in a rash.*

**come out of sth** If something comes out of a process or event, it is one of the results. *I hope something good can come out of this mess.*

**come out with sth** to say something suddenly that is not expected *She came straight out with it and accused him of lying.*

**come over 1** to come to a place, move from one place to another, or move towards someone *Come over here and I'll do your hair for you.* • *Are your family coming over from Greece for the wedding?* **2** to seem to be a particular type of person *Henry came over as a real enthusiast.*

**come over sb** If a feeling comes over you, you suddenly experience it. *I don't usually get so angry. I don't know what came over me.*

**come round** *UK* **1** VISIT to visit someone at their house *You must come round to the flat for dinner some time.* **2** AGREE to change your opinion about something, or agree to an idea or a plan that you were against *I know Debby doesn't like you borrowing her car but she'll soon come round.* **3** EVENT If an event that happens regularly comes round, it happens, or is going to happen soon. *I can't believe that winter has come round already.* **4** BECOME CONSCIOUS to become conscious again after an accident or medical operation

**come through 1** If information or a result comes through, you receive it. *Have the results of the tests come through yet?* **2** If an emotion comes through, other people can notice it. *His nervousness came through when he spoke.*

**come through (sth)** to manage to get to the end of a difficult or dangerous situation *We've had some hard times, but we've come through them.*

**come to** to become conscious again after an accident or medical operation *Has he come to yet?*

**come to sb** If a thought or idea comes to you, you suddenly remember it or start to think about it. *I can't remember his name but it will come to me in a minute.*

**come to sth 1** to be a particular total when numbers or amounts are added together *That comes to £50, please.* **2 come to a decision/conclusion/arrangement, etc** to make a decision or decide what to think about something **3** to reach a particular state or situation, especially a bad one *You won't come to any harm.*

**come under sth 1 come under attack/criticism/scrutiny, etc** to be attacked, criticized, examined, etc **2** to be controlled or dealt with by a particular authority *Water rates come under local government control.* **3** to be in a particular part of a book, list, etc *Hairdressers come under 'beauty salons' in the Yellow Pages.*

**come up 1** MOVE TOWARDS to move towards someone *After the concert, he came up to me to ask for my autograph.* **2** BE DISCUSSED to be discussed or suggested *The issue of security came up at the meeting yesterday.* **3** OPPORTUNITY If a job or opportunity comes up, it becomes available. **4** PROBLEM If a problem or difficult situation comes up, it happens. **5 be coming up** to be happening soon *My exams are coming up next month.* **6** SUN OR MOON If the sun or the moon comes up, it rises. **7** COMPUTER If information comes up on a computer screen, it appears there.

**come up against sth/sb** to have to deal with a problem or difficulty *She came up against a lot of sexism in her first engineering job.*

**come up to sth** to reach the usual or necessary standard *This essay doesn't come up to your usual standards.*

**come up with sth** to think of a plan, an idea, or a solution to a problem *We need to come up with a good scheme to make money.*

**comeback** /'kʌmbæk/ *noun* [C] a successful attempt to become powerful, important, or famous again *She's made a comeback with her first new album for twenty years.*

**comedian** /kə'miːdiən/ *noun* [C] someone who entertains people by telling jokes

**comedown** /'kʌmdaʊn/ noun [C] informal a situation that is not as good as one you were in before [usually singular] Cleaning windows is a bit of a comedown after his last job.

◻**comedy** /'kɒmədi/ noun [C, U] entertainment such as a film, play, etc which is funny The film is a romantic comedy.

**comet** /'kɒmɪt/ noun [C] an object in space that leaves a bright line behind it in the sky

**comfort¹** /'kʌmfət/ noun 1 NO PAIN [U] a pleasant feeling of being relaxed and free from pain The car has been designed for practicality, safety, and comfort. ● Now you can watch the latest films in the comfort of your sitting room. 2 FOR SADNESS [U] when you feel better after being worried or sad What she said brought me great comfort. 3 ENOUGH MONEY [U] when you have a pleasant life with enough money for everything that you need He can afford to retire and live in comfort for the rest of his life. 4 a comfort to sb someone or something that helps you when you are anxious or sad The children have been a great comfort to me since his death. 5 PLEASANT THING [C] something that makes your life easy and pleasant [usually plural] Good chocolate is one of life's little comforts. ➔ Opposite **discomfort**.

**comfort²** /'kʌmfət/ verb [T] to make someone feel better when they are anxious or sad The family of the dead were being comforted by friends. ● comforting adj He said a few comforting words.

◻**comfortable** /'kʌmftəbl/ adj 1 NOT CAUSING PAIN Comfortable furniture, clothes, rooms, etc make you feel relaxed and do not cause any pain. comfortable shoes ● We had a comfortable journey. 2 PERSON If you are comfortable, you are relaxed and have no pain. Make yourself comfortable while I fetch you a drink. ● I don't feel comfortable in high heels. ➔ Opposite **uncomfortable**. 3 WITHOUT WORRIES If you are comfortable in a situation, you do not have any worries about it. I don't feel comfortable about leaving the children here alone. 4 MONEY having enough money for everything that you need a comfortable retirement 5 WIN If you win a game or competition by a comfortable amount, you win easily. a comfortable lead/ victory ● comfortably adv

**comforter** /'kʌmfətəʳ/ US (UK duvet) noun [C] a cover filled with feathers or warm material, that you sleep under

**comfy** /'kʌmfi/ adj informal comfortable

**comic¹** /'kɒmɪk/ adj funny a comic actor

**comic²** /'kɒmɪk/ noun [C] 1 (also 'comic ,book) a magazine with stories told in pictures 2 someone who entertains people by telling jokes

**comical** /'kɒmɪkəl/ adj funny in a strange or silly way You look comical in those big shoes. ● comically adv

'**comic ,strip** noun [C] a set of pictures telling a story, usually in a newspaper

**coming¹** /'kʌmɪŋ/ noun 1 the coming of sth the arrival of something the coming of spring 2 comings and goings people's movements to and from a particular place over a period of time

**coming²** /'kʌmɪŋ/ adj [always before noun] a coming time or event will come or happen soon the coming elections ➔ See also: **up-and-coming**.

**comma** /'kɒmə/ noun [C] a mark (,) used to separate parts of a sentence, or to separate the items in a list ➔ See study section **Punctuation** on page Centre 37. ➔ See also: **inverted commas**.

**command¹** /kə'mɑːnd/ noun 1 CONTROL [U] control over someone or something and responsibility for them The soldiers were under the command of a tough sergeant-major. ● Jones was in command (= the leader). 2 ORDER [C] an order to do something 3 KNOWLEDGE [no plural] knowledge of a subject, especially a language She had a good command of French. 4 be at sb's command to be ready to obey someone's orders 5 COMPUTER [C] an instruction to a computer

**command²** /kə'mɑːnd/ verb formal 1 [T] to control someone or something and tell them what to do He commanded the armed forces. 2 [I, T] to order someone to do something [+ to do sth] The officer commanded his men to shoot. 3 command attention/loyalty/respect, etc to deserve and get attention, loyalty, respect, etc from other people

**commandeer** /,kɒmən'dɪəʳ/ verb [T] formal to take something, especially for military use The ships were commandeered as naval vessels.

**commander** /kə'mɑːndəʳ/ noun [C] an officer who is in charge of a military operation, or an officer of middle rank in the navy

**commanding** /kə'mɑːndɪŋ/ adj [always before noun] in a very successful position and likely to win or succeed He has a commanding lead in the championships.

**commandment** /kə'mɑːndmənt/ noun [C] one of the ten important rules of behaviour given by God in the Bible

**commando** /kə'mɑːndəʊ/ noun [C] a soldier who is part of a small group who make surprise attacks

**commemorate** /kə'meməreɪt/ verb [T] to do something to show you remember an important person or event in the past with respect a ceremony to commemorate the battle ● commemoration /kə,memə'reɪʃᵊn/ noun [U] a march in commemoration of the war of independence

**commemorative** /kə'memᵊrətɪv/ adj intended to commemorate a person or event a commemorative coin

**commence** /kə'mens/ verb [I, T] formal to begin something ● commencement noun [C, U] formal the beginning of something

**commend** /kə'mend/ verb [T] formal to praise someone or something [often passive] His courage was commended by the report. ● commendation /,kɒmen'deɪʃᵊn/ noun [C, U]

**commendable** /kə'mendəbl/ adj deserving praise She showed commendable modesty.

◻**comment¹** /'kɒment/ noun [C, U] 1 something that you say or write that shows what you think about something He made negative comments to the press. 2 No comment. used to say that you do not want to answer someone's question

◻**comment²** /'kɒment/ verb [I, T] to make a comment My mum always comments on what

**C**

*I'm wearing.* • [+ that] *He commented that the two essays were very similar.*

**commentary** /'kɒmənt³ri/ *noun* **1** [C, U] a spoken description of an event on the radio or television while the event is happening *the football commentary* **2** [U, no plural] a discussion or explanation of something *a commentary on American culture*

**commentator** /'kɒmənteɪtə³/ *noun* [C] someone who describes an event on the radio or television while it is happening *a sports commentator*

**commerce** /'kɒmɜːs/ *noun* [U] the activities involved in buying and selling things ➋ *See also:* **chamber of commerce, e-commerce.**

**commercial**[1] /kə'mɜːʃ³l/ *adj* **1** relating to buying and selling things **2** intended to make a profit *commercial television* • **commercially** *adv*

**commercial**[2] /kə'mɜːʃ³l/ *noun* [C] an advertisement on the radio or television

**commercialism** /kə'mɜːʃ³lɪz³m/ *noun* [U] when making money is the most important aim of an activity

**commercialized** (*also UK* **-ised**) /kə'mɜːʃ³laɪzd/ *adj* organized to make profits *Christmas has become so commercialized.* • **commercialization** /kə'mɜːʃ³laɪˈzeɪʃ³n/ *noun* [U]

**commiserate** /kə'mɪz³reɪt/ *verb* [I] to express sympathy to someone who is sad or has had bad luck

**commission**[1] /kə'mɪʃ³n/ *noun* **1** GROUP OF PEOPLE [group] an official group of people who have been chosen to find out about something and say what they think should be done about it **2** PIECE OF WORK [C, U] when you arrange for someone to do a piece of work for you such as painting, writing, or making something **3** MONEY [C, U] money given to someone when they sell something *The staff receive 5% commission on everything that they sell.* • *Many salesmen work on commission.*

**commission**[2] /kə'mɪʃ³n/ *verb* [T] to arrange for someone to do a piece of work [+ to do sth] *I've been commissioned to write a song for their wedding.*

**commissioner** /kə'mɪʃ³nə³/ *noun* [C] a member of a commission or someone with an important government job in a particular area

⊶**commit** /kə'mɪt/ *verb* [T] **committing**, *past* **committed 1** CRIME to do something that is considered wrong, or that is illegal *He was sent to prison for a crime that he didn't commit.* • *to commit suicide/adultery* **2** DECISION to make a firm decision that you will do something *He committed himself to helping others.* **3** **not commit yourself** to refuse to express an opinion about a particular subject **4** MONEY/TIME If you commit money, time, energy, etc to something, you use it to try to achieve something. *The government has committed thousands of pounds to the research.*

⊶**commitment** /kə'mɪtmənt/ *noun* **1** PROMISE [C] a promise or firm decision to do something *Players must make a commitment to daily training.* **2** LOYALTY [U] when you are willing to give your time and energy to something that you believe in *We are looking for someone with talent, enthusiasm, and commitment.* **3** ACTIVITY [C] something that you must do that takes your

time *I've got too many commitments at the moment.*

**committed** /kə'mɪtɪd/ *adj* loyal and willing to give your time and energy to something that you believe in *a committed Christian* • *She's committed to the job.*

**committee** /kə'mɪti/ *noun* [group] a group of people who have been chosen to represent a larger organization and make decisions for it

**commodity** /kə'mɒdəti/ *noun* [C] a product that you can buy or sell

⊶**common**[1] /'kɒmən/ *adj* **1** USUAL happening often or existing in large numbers *Injuries are common in sports such as hockey.* ➋ *Opposite* **uncommon**. **2** SHARED belonging to or shared by two or more people or things *a common goal/interest* • *English has some features common to many languages.* **3** **common knowledge** something that a lot of people know [+ that] *It's common knowledge that he spent time in jail.* **4** ORDINARY [always before noun] not special in any way *The herbs all have common names and Latin names.* **5** LOW CLASS *UK* typical of a low social class *My mum thinks dyed blonde hair is really common.*

**common**[2] /'kɒmən/ *noun* **1** **have sth in common** to share interests, experiences, or other characteristics with someone or something *Sue and I don't have much in common.* **2** **in common with sb/sth** in the same way as someone or something *In common with many working mothers, she feels guilty towards her children.* **3** [C] a large area of grass in a town or village which everyone is allowed to use

**common ground** *noun* [U] shared interests, beliefs, or ideas *It's difficult for me to find any common ground with my dad.*

**common-law** /ˌkɒmən'lɔː/ *adj* [always before noun] A common-law wife or husband is someone who is not married, but has lived with their partner for a long time as if they were married.

**commonly** /'kɒmənli/ *adv* often or usually *These caterpillars are commonly found on nettles.*

**commonplace** /'kɒmənpleɪs/ *adj* [never before noun] happening often or existing in large numbers, and so not considered special or unusual *Mobile phones have become commonplace in recent years.*

**the Commons** /'kɒmənz/ (*also* **the House of Commons**) *noun* one of the two parts of the British parliament, with elected members who make laws

**common sense** *noun* [U] the natural ability to be practical and to make good decisions *The children shouldn't be in any danger as long as they use their common sense.*

**the Commonwealth** /'kɒmənwelθ/ *noun* Britain and the group of countries that used to be in the British Empire (= ruled by Britain)

**commotion** /kə'məʊʃ³n/ *noun* [U, no plural] a sudden period of noise and confused or excited movement *He looked up to see what all the commotion was about.*

**communal** /'kɒmjʊn³l/ ⑮ kə'mjuːn³l/ *adj* belonging to or used by a group of people *a communal changing room*

**commune** /'kɒmju:n/ noun [C] a group of people who live together, sharing the work and the things they own

o⌐**communicate** /kə'mju:nɪkeɪt/ verb [I, T] **1** to share information with others by speaking, writing, moving your body, or using other signals *We can now communicate instantly with people on the other side of the world.* ● *Has the news been communicated to the staff yet?* **2** to talk about your thoughts and feelings, and help other people to understand them *He can't communicate with his parents.*

o⌐**communication** /kə,mju:nɪ'keɪʃᵃn/ noun **1** [U] the act of communicating with other people *The school is improving communication between teachers and parents.* ● *We are in direct communication with Moscow.* **2** [C] *formal* a message sent to someone by letter, telephone, etc

**communications** /kə,mju:nɪ'keɪʃᵃnz/ noun [plural] the different ways of sending information between people and places, such as post, telephones, computers, and radio *the communications industry*

**communicative** /kə'mju:nɪkətɪv/ adj willing to talk to people and give them information

**communion** /kə'mju:niən/ noun [U] (also **Communion**) the Christian ceremony in which people eat bread and drink wine, as symbols of Christ's body and blood

**communiqué** /kə'mju:nɪkeɪ/ ⑤ kə,mju:nɪ'keɪ/ noun [C] an official announcement

**communism, Communism** /'kɒmjənɪzᵃm/ noun [U] a political system in which the government controls the production of all goods, and where everyone is treated equally

**communist, Communist** /'kɒmjənɪst/ noun [C] someone who supports communism ● communist adj *a communist country/leader*

**community** /kə'mju:nəti/ noun **1** [C] the people living in a particular area *a rural/small community* **2** [group] a group of people with the same interests, nationality, job, etc *the business/Chinese community*

**com'munity ,centre** UK (US **community center**) noun [C] a place where people who live in an area can meet together to play sport, go to classes, etc

**com,munity 'college** noun [C, U] US a two-year college where students can learn a skill or prepare to enter a university

**com,munity 'service** noun [U] work that someone who has committed a crime does to help other people instead of going to prison

**commute** /kə'mju:t/ verb [I] to regularly travel between work and home ● commuter noun [C]

**compact¹** /kəm'pækt/ adj small and including many things in a small space

**compact²** /kəm'pækt/ verb [T] to press something together so that it becomes tight or solid

**,compact 'disc** noun [C] a CD (= a disc for recorded music or information)

**companion** /kəm'pænjən/ noun [C] someone who you spend a lot of time with or go somewhere with *a travelling companion*

**companionship** /kəm'pænjənʃɪp/ noun [U] the feeling of having friends around you

o⌐**company** /'kʌmpəni/ noun **1** [BUSINESS] [C] an organization which sells goods or services *a software/telephone company* **2** [PEOPLE] [U] when you have a person or people with you *I enjoy his company.* ● *I didn't realize that you had company.* **3 keep sb company** to stay with someone so that they are not alone **4 be good company** to be a pleasant or interesting person to spend time with **5** [PERFORMERS] [C] a group of performers such as actors or dancers *the Royal Shakespeare Company* ➔ *See also:* **limited company**.

**comparable** /'kɒmpᵃrəbl/ adj similar in size, amount, or quality to something else *Our prices are comparable to those in other shops. The two experiences are not comparable.*

**comparative¹** /kəm'pærətɪv/ adj **1 comparative comfort/freedom/silence, etc** a situation which is comfortable/free/silent, etc when compared to another situation or to what is usual *I enjoyed the comparative calm of his flat after the busy office.* **2** comparing similar things *a comparative study of two poems*

**comparative²** /kəm'pærətɪv/ noun [C] the form of an adjective or adverb that is used to show that someone or something has more of a particular quality than someone or something else. For example 'better' is the comparative of 'good' and 'smaller' is the comparative of 'small'. ➔ *Compare* **superlative**.

**comparatively** /kəm'pærətɪvli/ adv **comparatively cheap/easy/little, etc** cheap/easy/little, etc when compared to something else or to what is usual

o⌐**compare** /kəm'peᵃʳ/ verb **1** [T] to examine the ways in which two people or things are different or similar *The teachers are always comparing me with/to my sister.* **2** [I] to be as good as something else *This product compares well with more expensive brands.* **3 compared to/with sb/sth** used when saying how one person or thing is different from another *This room is very tidy compared to mine.* ➔ *See also:* compare notes (**note¹**).

**compare sb/sth to sb/sth** to say that someone or something is similar to someone or something else *Some people have compared him to Elvis.*

o⌐**comparison** /kəm'pærɪsᵃn/ noun [C, U] **1** when you compare two or more people or things *They published a comparison of schools in the area.* ● *She's so tall that he looks tiny by/in comparison.* **2 There's no comparison.** used to say that someone or something is much better than someone or something else

**compartment** /kəm'pɑ:tmənt/ noun [C] **1** one of the separate areas inside a vehicle, especially of a train *The first class compartment is at the front of the train.* **2** a separate part of a container, bag, etc *a fridge with a small freezer compartment*

**compass**

**compass** /'kʌmpəs/ noun [C] a piece of equipment which shows you which direction you are going in

**compasses** /'kʌmpəsɪz/ *noun* [plural] *UK* (*US* **compass** [C]) a piece of equipment which is used for drawing circles *a pair of compasses*

**compassion** /kəm'pæʃ°n/ *noun* [U] a feeling of sympathy for people who are suffering

**compassionate** /kəm'pæʃ°nət/ *adj* showing compassion

**compatible** /kəm'pætɪbl/ *adj* **1** [EQUIPMENT] compatible equipment can be used together *This keyboard is compatible with all of our computers.* **2** [PEOPLE] If people are compatible, they like each other and are happy to spend time together. **3** [IDEAS] *formal* compatible ideas or situations can exist together *Such policies are not compatible with democratic government.* • compatibility /kəm,pætə'bɪləti/ *noun* [U]

**compatriot** /kəm'pætriət/ *noun* [C] *formal* someone who comes from the same country

**compel** /kəm'pel/ *verb* **compelling**, *past* **compelled** *formal* **compel sb to do sth** to force someone to do something [often passive] *He felt compelled to resign from his job.*

**compelling** /kəm'pelɪŋ/ *adj* **1** very exciting or interesting and making you want to watch, listen, etc *a compelling story* **2** If a reason, argument, etc is compelling, it makes you believe it or accept it because it is so strong. *compelling evidence*

**compensate** /'kɒmpənseɪt/ *verb* **1** [T] to pay someone money because you are responsible for injuring them or damaging something *Victims of the crash will be compensated for their injuries.* **2** [I, T] to reduce the bad effect of something, or make something bad become something good *Nothing will ever compensate for his lost childhood.*

**compensation** /,kɒmpən'seɪʃ°n/ *noun* **1** [U] money that you pay to someone because you are responsible for injuring them or damaging something *Most of the workers have won compensation for losing their jobs.* **2** [C, U] something you get to make you feel better when you have suffered something bad *Free food was no compensation for a very boring evening.*

**compère** /'kɒmpeə'/ *noun* [C] *UK* someone whose job is to introduce performers on television, radio, or in a theatre

o⁻**compete** /kəm'piːt/ *verb* [I] **1** to take part in a race or competition *She's competing for a place in next year's Olympics.* **2** to try to be more successful than someone or something else *It's difficult for small shops to compete with/against the big supermarkets.*

**competent** /'kɒmpɪt°nt/ *adj* able to do something well *a competent swimmer/teacher* • competence /'kɒmpɪt°ns/ *noun* [U] the ability to do something well • competently *adv*

o⁻**competition** /,kɒmpə'tɪʃ°n/ *noun* **1** [C] an organized event in which people try to win a prize by being the best, fastest, etc *to enter a competition* **2** [U] when someone is trying to win something or be more successful than someone else *There's a lot of competition between computer companies.* • *Applicants face stiff competition for university places this year.* **3** the competition people you are competing against, especially in business

**competitive** /kəm'petɪtɪv/ *adj* **1** [SITUATION] involving competition *competitive sports* • *a highly competitive industry* **2** [PERSON] wanting to win or to be more successful than other people *She's very competitive.* **3** [PRICES/SERVICES] Competitive prices, services, etc are as good as or better than other prices, services, etc. • competitively *adv* • competitiveness *noun* [U]

**competitor** /kəm'petɪtə'/ *noun* [C] a person, team, or company that is competing with others *Their prices are better than any of their competitors.*

**compilation** /,kɒmpɪ'leɪʃ°n/ *noun* [C] a recording, book, or film containing a collection of things from many different recordings, books, or films

**compile** /kəm'paɪl/ *verb* [T] to collect information and arrange it in a book, report, or list

**complacent** /kəm'pleɪs°nt/ *adj* feeling so satisfied with your own abilities or situation that you do not feel that you need to try any harder *We can't afford to become too complacent about our work.* • complacency *noun* [U] when someone is complacent • complacently *adv*

o⁻**complain** /kəm'pleɪn/ *verb* [I] to say that something is wrong or that you are annoyed about something *Lots of people have complained about the noise.* • [+ that] *He's always complaining that nobody listens to him.*

**complain about** something

Be careful to choose the correct preposition after complain.

*I am writing to* **complain about** *the trip.*

~~I am writing to complain for the trip.~~

~~I am writing to complain on the trip.~~

**complain of sth** to tell other people that something is making you feel ill *She's been complaining of a headache all day.*

o⁻**complaint** /kəm'pleɪnt/ *noun* **1** [NOT SATISFACTORY] [C, U] when someone says that something is wrong or not satisfactory *a letter of complaint* • *I wish to make a complaint.* • *We received several complaints about the noise.* **2** [ANNOYING THING] [C] something that makes you complain *My only complaint was the lack of refreshments.* **3** [ILLNESS] [C] an illness *a stomach complaint*

**complement¹** /'kɒmplɪmənt/ *noun* [C] **1** [MAKE GOOD] something that makes something else seem good, attractive, or complete *This wine is the perfect complement to the meal.* **2** [TOTAL NUMBER] the total amount or number of something that is needed to complete a group *Do we have a full complement of players for Saturday's match?* **3** [GRAMMAR] a word or phrase which comes after the verb and gives more information about the subject of the verb

**complement²** /'kɒmplɪment/ *verb* [T] to make something else seem good or attractive *The music complements her voice perfectly.*

**complementary** /,kɒmplɪ'ment°ri/ *adj*

**1** Things which are complementary are good or attractive together. *complementary colours/flavours* **2 complementary medicine/treatment, etc** ways of treating medical problems which people use instead of or in addition to ordinary medicine *The clinic offers complementary therapies such as homeopathy.*

o➤**complete**¹ /kəm'pliːt/ *adj* **1** ⎡WHOLE⎤ with all parts *the complete works of Oscar Wilde* ● *The report comes **complete with** (= including) diagrams and colour photographs.* **2** ⎡TOTAL⎤ [always before noun] used to emphasize what you are saying *a complete waste of time* ● *a complete idiot* **3** ⎡FINISHED⎤ finished *Our report is almost complete.*

o➤**complete**² /kəm'pliːt/ *verb* [T] **1** ⎡FINISH⎤ to finish doing or making something *The palace took 15 years to complete.* ● *She will complete her studies in France.* **2** ⎡MAKE STH WHOLE⎤ to provide the last part needed to make something whole *Complete the sentence with one of the adjectives provided.* **3** ⎡WRITE⎤ to write all the details asked for on a form or other document

o➤**completely** /kəm'pliːtli/ *adv* in every way or as much as possible *I completely forgot that you were coming.* ● *The two sisters are completely different from each other.*

**completion** /kəm'pliːʃən/ *noun* [U] when something that you are doing or making is finished *The stadium is due for completion in 2008.* ● *They will be paid **on completion of** the job.*

o➤**complex**¹ /'kɒmpleks, kəm'pleks/ *adj* involving a lot of different but connected parts in a way that is difficult to understand *complex details/issues* ● *The situation is very complex.*
● **complexity** /kəm'pleksəti/ *noun* [C, U] when something is complex *the complexities of life*

**complex**² /'kɒmpleks/ *noun* [C] **1** a group of buildings or rooms that are used for a particular purpose *a sports/housing complex* **2** a mental problem which makes someone anxious or frightened about something *an inferiority complex*

**complexion** /kəm'plekʃən/ *noun* [C] **1** the colour and appearance of the skin on someone's face *a clear complexion* **2** the way something seems to be *This new information **puts a** completely different **complexion on** the situation.*

**compliance** /kəm'plaɪəns/ *noun* [U] *formal* when people obey an order, rule, or request *The work was done **in compliance with** planning regulations.*

**compliant** /kəm'plaɪənt/ *adj* Compliant people are willing to do what other people want them to.

**complicate** /'kɒmplɪkeɪt/ *verb* [T] to make something more difficult to deal with or understand *These new regulations just complicate matters further.*

o➤**complicated** /'kɒmplɪkeɪtɪd/ *adj* involving a lot of different parts, in a way that is difficult to understand *a complicated problem/process* ● *The instructions were too complicated for me.*

**complication** /ˌkɒmplɪ'keɪʃən/ *noun* [C] **1** something which makes a situation more difficult **2** a new medical problem that develops when you are already ill *Eye problems can be a complication of diabetes.*

**complicity** /kəm'plɪsəti/ *noun* [U] *formal* when someone is involved in doing something wrong

**compliment**¹ /'kɒmplɪmənt/ *noun* **1** [C] something that you say or do to show praise or admiration for someone *She was always **paying** him **compliments**.* **2 with the compliments of sb** *formal* used by someone to express good wishes when they give you something free, for example in a restaurant *Please accept this champagne with the compliments of the manager.*

**compliment**² /'kɒmplɪment/ *verb* [T] to praise or express admiration for someone *He **complimented** me **on** my writing.*

**complimentary** /ˌkɒmplɪ'mentˀri/ *adj* **1** praising or expressing admiration for someone *a complimentary report* **2** given free, especially by a business *a complimentary glass of wine*

**comply** /kəm'plaɪ/ *verb* [I] to obey an order, rule, or request *The pilot **complied with** instructions to descend.*

**component** /kəm'pəʊnənt/ *noun* [C] one of the parts of something, especially a machine

**compose** /kəm'pəʊz/ *verb* **1** ⎡PARTS⎤ [T] to be the parts that something consists of [often passive] *The committee **was composed** of elected leaders and citizens.* **2** ⎡MUSIC⎤ [I, T] to write a piece of music **3 compose yourself** to make yourself calm again after being angry or upset *He needed some time to compose himself.* **4** ⎡WRITING⎤ [T] to write a speech, letter, etc, thinking carefully about the words to use *Laura was composing a letter of sympathy.*

**composed** /kəm'pəʊzd/ *adj* calm and in control of your emotions

**composer** /kəm'pəʊzəʳ/ *noun* [C] someone who writes music

**composite** /'kɒmpəzɪt/ *adj* consisting of several different parts *a composite image of the killer*

**composition** /ˌkɒmpə'zɪʃən/ *noun* **1** ⎡PARTS⎤ [U] the parts, substances, etc that something consists of *the composition of the atmosphere* **2** ⎡MUSIC⎤ [C] a piece of music that someone has written *The children played their own compositions in the concert.* **3** ⎡WRITING MUSIC⎤ [U] the process or skill of writing music *He taught composition at Yale.* **4** ⎡WRITING⎤ [C, U] a short piece of writing about a particular subject, done by a student **5** ⎡ARRANGEMENT⎤ [U] the way that people or things are arranged in a painting or photograph

**compost** /'kɒmpɒst/ *noun* [U] a mixture of decayed leaves and plants that is added to the soil to improve its quality *a compost heap*

**composure** /kəm'pəʊʒəʳ/ *noun* [U] when you feel or look calm and confident *to keep/lose your composure*

**compound**¹ /'kɒmpaʊnd/ *noun* [C] **1** ⎡MIXTURE⎤ a substance that is a combination of two or more elements *Water is a compound of hydrogen and oxygen.* **2** ⎡AREA⎤ an area of land with a group of buildings surrounded by a fence or wall *a prison compound* **3** ⎡GRAMMAR⎤ (*also* **compound noun/verb/adjective**) a noun, verb, or adjective that is made by two or more words used together. For example, 'golf club' is a compound.

**compound²** /kəm'paʊnd/ verb [T] to make a problem or difficult situation worse *Severe drought has compounded food shortages in the region.*

**comprehend** /ˌkɒmprɪ'hend/ verb [I, T] formal to understand *I was too young to comprehend what was happening.*

**comprehensible** /ˌkɒmprɪ'hensəbl/ adj easy to understand *Computer manuals should be easily comprehensible.*

**comprehension** /ˌkɒmprɪ'henʃᵊn/ noun **1** [U] the ability to understand something *It's beyond my comprehension* (= I can't understand) *how anyone could be so cruel.* **2** [C, U] UK a test to see how well students understand written or spoken language *a reading comprehension*

**comprehensive¹** /ˌkɒmprɪ'hensɪv/ adj including everything *a comprehensive study of the subject* • **comprehensively** adv completely *We were comprehensively beaten in the finals.*

**comprehensive²** /ˌkɒmprɪ'hensɪv/ (also **compre'hensive ˌschool**) noun [C] a school in Britain for students aged 11 to 18 of all levels of ability

**compress** /kəm'pres/ verb [T] to make something smaller, especially by pressing it, so that it uses less space or time *compressed air* • *The course compresses two years' training into six months.* • **compression** /kəm'preʃᵊn/ noun [U]

**comprise** /kəm'praɪz/ verb [T] formal **1** to consist of particular parts or members *The orchestra was comprised of amateur and professional musicians.* **2** to form part of something, especially a larger group *Women comprise 15% of the police force.*

**compromise¹** /'kɒmprəmaɪz/ noun [C, U] when you agree to something which is not exactly what you want *We need to reach a compromise over this issue.* • *Decorating is usually a compromise between taste and cost.*

**compromise²** /'kɒmprəmaɪz/ verb **1** AGREE [I] to agree to something that is not exactly what you want *The president may be willing to compromise in order to pass the bill.* • *I never compromise on fresh ingredients.* **2 compromise yourself** to do something dishonest or embarrassing that makes people stop admiring you **3** BELIEFS [T] to do something that does not agree with what you believe in *I refuse to compromise my principles.* **4** HARM [T] formal to have a harmful effect on something *The trial has been seriously compromised by sensational media coverage.*

**compromising** /'kɒmprəmaɪzɪŋ/ adj A compromising situation, photograph, etc makes people think you have done something wrong. *The press printed compromising photographs of the princess and her bodyguard.*

**compulsion** /kəm'pʌlʃᵊn/ noun **1** [C] a strong wish to do something, often something that you should not do **2** [U] when you are forced to do something *We were under no compulsion to attend.*

**compulsive** /kəm'pʌlsɪv/ adj **1** A compulsive habit is something that you do a lot because you want to so much that you cannot control yourself. *a compulsive eating disorder* **2** a **compulsive eater/gambler/liar, etc** someone who is unable to stop eating, lying, etc, despite

knowing that they should stop **3** so interesting or exciting that you cannot stop reading, playing, or watching it *This documentary about life in prison makes compulsive viewing.* • **compulsively** adv

**compulsory** /kəm'pʌlsᵊri/ adj If something is compulsory, you must do it because of a rule or law.

○⁻**computer** /kəm'pjuːtəʳ/ noun [C] an electronic machine that can store and arrange large amounts of information *We've put all our records on computer.* • *computer software* • *computer games*

**computerize** (also UK **-ise**) /kəm'pjuːtᵊraɪz/ verb [T] to use a computer to do something that was done by people or other machines before *a computerized accounts system* • **computerization** /kəmˌpjuːtᵊraɪ'zeɪʃᵊn/ noun [U]

**computing** /kəm'pjuːtɪŋ/ noun [U] the study or use of computers *a degree in computing*

**comrade** /'kɒmreɪd ⑤ 'kɑːmræd/ noun [C] **1** literary a friend, especially someone who fights with you in a war **2** a word used by some members of trade unions (= organizations which represent people who do a particular job) or other Socialist organizations to talk to or about each other

**comradeship** /'kɒmreɪdʃɪp/ noun [U] the feeling of friendship between people who live or work together, especially in a difficult situation

**con¹** /kɒn/ verb [T] **conning,** past **conned** informal to trick someone, especially in order to take money from them *Thieves conned him out of his life savings.* • *She felt she had been conned into buying the car.*

**con²** /kɒn/ noun [C] informal a trick to get someone's money, or make them do what you want

**'con ˌartist** noun [C] someone who tricks people into giving them money or valuable things

**concave** /'kɒnkeɪv/ adj A concave surface curves inwards. *a concave lens*

**conceal** /kən'siːl/ verb [T] to hide something *The listening device was concealed in a pen.* • *She could barely conceal her irritation.* • **concealment** noun [U] when something is hidden

**concede** /kən'siːd/ verb **1** [T] to admit that something is true, even though you do not want to [+ (that)] *Even the company chairman concedes that the results are disappointing.* **2** [I, T] to allow someone to have something, even though you do not want to *We must try not to concede any more points to the opposition.* • *The government will not concede to rebel demands.* **3 concede defeat** to admit that you have lost a fight, argument, game, etc *The senator conceded defeat after the first few results were announced.*

**conceit** /kən'siːt/ noun [U] when you are too proud of yourself and your actions

**conceited** /kən'siːtɪd/ adj too proud of yourself and your actions • **conceitedly** adv

**conceivable** /kən'siːvəbl/ adj possible to imagine or to believe *every conceivable kind of fruit* • [+ (that)] *It is just conceivable that the hospital made a mistake.* • **conceivably** adv *Her story could, conceivably, be true.*

**conceive** /kən'si:v/ *verb* **1** BABY [I, T] to become pregnant **2** IMAGINE [I, T] to be able to imagine something *I cannot conceive of anything more horrible.* **3** IDEA [T] to think of an idea or plan *The original idea for the novel was conceived in Rome.*

O━**concentrate** /'kɒnsᵊntreɪt/ *verb* **1** [I] to think very carefully about something you are doing and nothing else *Be quiet – I'm trying to concentrate.* • *I can't concentrate on my work. It's too noisy here.* **2 be concentrated around/in/on, etc** to be present in large numbers or amounts in a particular area *Most of the fighting was concentrated in the mountains.*

**concentrate on sth** to use most of your time and effort to do something *She gave up her job to concentrate on writing a novel.*

**concentrated** /'kɒnsəntreɪtɪd/ *adj* **1** [always before noun] using a lot of effort to succeed at one particular thing *a concentrated effort to finish the work* **2** A concentrated liquid has had most of the water removed. *concentrated tomato puree*

**concentration** /ˌkɒnsᵊn'treɪʃᵊn/ *noun* **1** [U] the ability to think carefully about something you are doing and nothing else **2** [C, U] a large number or amount of something in the same place *high concentrations of minerals*

**concen'tration ˌcamp** *noun* [C] a prison where large numbers of people are kept in very bad conditions, especially for political reasons

**concentric** /kən'sentrɪk/ *adj* Concentric circles have the same centre but are different sizes.

O━**concept** /'kɒnsept/ *noun* [C] an idea or principle *the concept of free speech*

**conception** /kən'sepʃᵊn/ *noun* **1** [C, U] an idea about what something is like or a way of understanding something **2** [U] when a woman or animal becomes pregnant

**conceptual** /kən'septʃuəl/ *adj formal* based on ideas *a conceptual model*

O━**concern¹** /kən'sɜːn/ *verb* **1** INVOLVE to involve someone or be important to them *Environmental issues concern us all.* • *He's more concerned about profits than the safety of his employees.* **2** WORRY to worry or upset someone *What really concerns me is her lack of experience.* **3** BE ABOUT If a story, film, etc concerns a particular subject, it is about that subject. **4 concern yourself** to become involved with doing something *You needn't concern yourself with the travel arrangements.*

**concern²** /kən'sɜːn/ *noun* **1** WORRY [C, U] a feeling of worry about something, or the thing that is worrying you *I have concerns about his health.* **2** IMPORTANT THING [C, U] something that involves or affects you or is important to you *Our primary concern is safety.* **3** BUSINESS [C] a company or business *The perfume factory was a family concern.*

O━**concerned** /kən'sɜːnd/ *adj* **1** worried [+ that] *I am very concerned that class sizes seem to be growing.* • *People are becoming more concerned about what they eat.* ⊃ *Opposite* **unconcerned.** **2** [never before noun] involved in something or affected by it *A letter will be sent out to everyone concerned.* **3 as far as sb is**

**concerned** used to show what someone thinks about something *As far as our customers are concerned, price is the main consideration.* **4 as far as sth is concerned** used to tell someone what you are talking about *As far as college is concerned, everything is fine.*

O━**concerning** /kən'sɜːnɪŋ/ *preposition* about something *I've had a letter concerning my tax payments.*

O━**concert** /'kɒnsət/ *noun* [C] a performance of music and singing *a pop concert*

**concerted** /kən'sɜːtɪd/ *adj* [always before noun] done with a lot of effort, often by a group of people working together *Iceland has made a concerted effort to boost tourism.*

**concerto** /kən'tʃeətəʊ/ *noun* [C] a piece of music for one main instrument and an orchestra (= large group of musicians) *a piano concerto*

**concession** /kən'seʃᵊn/ *noun* **1** AGREEMENT [C, U] something that you agree to do or give to someone in order to end an argument *Both sides will have to make concessions.* **2** BUSINESS [C] a special right to use buildings or land or to sell a product in a particular area *a concession to develop oil fields in the north* **3** LOW PRICE [C] *UK* a reduction in the price of a ticket for a particular group of people such as students, people without a job, or old people

**conciliation** /kənˌsɪli'eɪʃᵊn/ *noun* [U] *formal* the process of trying to end an argument

**conciliatory** /kən'sɪliətᵊri/ *adj formal* If people behave in a conciliatory manner, they try to make people stop being angry with them. *a conciliatory approach*

**concise** /kən'saɪs/ *adj* **1** giving a lot of information clearly in a few words **2** A concise book is small. *a concise history of France* • concisely *adv* • conciseness *noun* [U]

**conclude** /kən'kluːd/ *verb* **1** END [I, T] *formal* to end something such as a meeting, speech, or piece of writing by doing or saying one last thing *The concert concluded with a firework display.* • *I would like to conclude by thanking you all for attending.* **2** DECIDE [T] to decide something after studying all the information about it very carefully [+ that] *The report concluded that the drug was safe.* **3** COMPLETE [T] to complete something, especially an agreement or a business arrangement *talks aimed at concluding the peace treaty*

**concluding** /kən'kluːdɪŋ/ *adj* [always before noun] last in a series of things *Don't miss tonight's concluding episode.*

O━**conclusion** /kən'kluːʒᵊn/ *noun* **1** OPINION [C] the opinion you have after considering all the information about something *I've come to the conclusion that we'll have to sell the car.* **2** END [C] the final part of something *the dramatic conclusion of the film* • *The case should finally be brought to a conclusion* (= end) *this week.* **3 in conclusion** used to introduce the last part of a speech or piece of writing *In conclusion, I would like to thank our guest speaker.* **4** ARRANGEMENT [U] when something is arranged or agreed formally *the conclusion of peace talks* **5 jump to conclusions** to guess the facts about a situation without having enough information *You shouldn't jump to conclusions* *just because they were holding hands.* ➔ *See also:* **foregone conclusion**.

**conclusive** /kən'kluːsɪv/ *adj* proving that something is true *conclusive evidence/proof* • **conclusively** *adv* *Tests have proved conclusively that the drugs are effective.*

**concoct** /kən'kɒkt/ *verb* [T] **1** to invent a story or explanation in order to deceive someone *He had concocted a web of lies.* **2** to make something unusual, especially food, by mixing things together • **concoction** /kən'kɒkʃ³n/ *noun* [C] *a concoction of meringue, ice cream, and fresh strawberries*

**concourse** /'kɒŋkɔːs/ *noun* [C] a large room or open area inside a building such as an airport or station

**concrete¹** /'kɒŋkriːt/ *noun* [U] a hard substance that is used in building and is made by mixing sand, water, small stones, and cement (= grey powder that is mixed with water and becomes hard when it dries) *concrete blocks*

**concrete²** /'kɒŋkriːt/ *adj* **1** certain or based on facts *concrete evidence/proof* **2** existing in a real form that can be seen or felt *concrete achievements/actions* • *concrete objects*

**concrete³** /'kɒŋkriːt/ *verb* [T] UK to cover something with concrete

**concur** /kən'kɜː/ *verb* [I] **concurring,** *past* **concurred** *formal* to agree *The new report concurs with previous findings.*

**concurrent** /kən'kʌrənt/ *adj* happening or existing at the same time *three concurrent prison sentences* • **concurrently** *adv*

**concussed** /kən'kʌst/ *adj* [never before noun] If someone is concussed, they are suffering from concussion.

**concussion** /kən'kʌʃ³n/ *noun* [C, U] a slight injury to the brain that is caused by being hit on the head and makes you feel tired or sick *mild concussion*

**condemn** /kən'dem/ *verb* [T] **1** to say very strongly that you think something is wrong or very bad *The Prime Minister was quick to condemn the terrorists.* **2** to say that a building must be destroyed because it is not safe enough for people to use

**condemn sb to sth 1** to say what the punishment of someone who is guilty of a serious crime will be *He was condemned to death.* **2** to make someone suffer in a particular way *Poor education condemns many young people to low-paid jobs.*

**condemnation** /ˌkɒndem'neɪʃ³n/ *noun* [C, U] when you say very strongly that you think something is wrong or very bad *widespread condemnation of the war*

**condensation** /ˌkɒnden'seɪʃ³n/ *noun* [U] small drops of water that form when warm air touches a cold surface

**condense** /kən'dens/ *verb* **1** AIR [I, T] If hot air or a gas condenses, it changes into a liquid as it becomes colder. **2** WORDS [T] to make something such as a speech or piece of writing shorter *You need to condense your conclusion into a single paragraph.* **3** LIQUID [T] to make a liquid thicker by taking some of the water out of it *condensed milk*

**condescend** /ˌkɒndɪ'send/ *verb* **condescend to**

**do sth** *humorous* to agree to do something even though you think you are too important to do it *I wonder if Michael will condescend to visit us?*

**condescend to sb** to treat someone as though you are better or more important than them *He knows how to explain things without condescending to his audience.*

**condescending** /ˌkɒndɪ'sendɪŋ/ *adj* showing that you think that you are better or more important than someone else *a condescending smile* • **condescendingly** *adv*

**condescension** /ˌkɒndɪ'senʃ³n/ *noun* [U] when you behave as though you are better or more important than someone else

o— **condition¹** /kən'dɪʃ³n/ *noun* **1** STATE [U, no plural] the state that something or someone is in *My bike's a few years old but it's in really good condition.* • *He's in no condition* (= not well enough) *to travel.* **2** AGREEMENT [C] something that must happen or be agreed before something else can happen *One of the conditions of the contract is that we can't keep pets.* **3 on condition that** only if *Visitors are allowed in the gardens on condition that they don't touch the plants.* **4** ILLNESS [C] an illness *a serious heart condition* **5 conditions** the physical situation that people are in *working/living conditions* • *severe weather conditions*

**condition²** /kən'dɪʃ³n/ *verb* [T] **1** to make a person or animal behave in a particular way by influencing the way they think [often passive + to do sth] *The boys were conditioned to be aggressive.* **2** to put a special liquid on your hair to make it soft and healthy

**conditional** /kən'dɪʃ³n³l/ *adj* **1** If an offer or agreement is conditional, it will only happen if something else is done first. *Their fee is conditional on the work being completed by January.* ➔ *Opposite* **unconditional**. **2** A conditional sentence usually begins with 'if' and says that something must be true or happen before something else can be true or happen.

**conditioner** /kən'dɪʃ³nə/ *noun* [C] a liquid that you use when you wash your hair to make it soft

**conditioning** /kən'dɪʃ³nɪŋ/ *noun* [U] when a person or animal is made to behave in a particular way *social/physical conditioning* ➔ *See also:* **air conditioning**.

**condo** /'kɒndəʊ/ *noun* [C] US informal short for condominium

**condolence** /kən'dəʊləns/ *noun* [C, U] formal sympathy for the family or friends of a person who has recently died *Please offer my condolences to your father.*

**condom** /'kɒndɒm (US) 'kɑːndəm/ *noun* [C] a thin rubber covering that a man wears on his penis during sex to stop a woman becoming pregnant, or to protect against diseases

**condominium** /ˌkɒndə'mɪniəm/ *noun* [C] US a building containing apartments which are owned by the people living in them, or one of these apartments

**condone** /kən'dəʊn/ *verb* [T] to accept or allow behaviour that is wrong *His comments appeared to condone drug abuse.*

**conducive** /kən'djuːsɪv/ *adj* making something

possible or likely to happen *Such a noisy environment was not* **conducive to** *a good night's sleep.*

**conduct**[1] /'kɒndʌkt/ *noun* **1** [U] the way someone behaves *a code of* **conduct** (= rules about how to behave) **2** **conduct of sth** the way someone organizes or does something *He was criticized for his conduct of the inquiry.*

**conduct**[2] /kən'dʌkt/ *verb* **1** DO [T] to organize or do something *They're conducting a survey.* **2** MUSIC [I, T] to stand in front of a group of musicians and control their performance **3** HEAT [T] If a substance conducts electricity or heat, it allows electricity or heat to go through it. **4** **conduct yourself** to behave in a particular way *She conducted herself with great dignity.* **5** LEAD [T] *formal* to lead someone to a place *I was conducted to a side room.*

**conductor** /kən'dʌktər/ *noun* [C] **1** MUSIC someone who stands in front of a group of musicians or singers and controls their performance **2** BUS *UK* someone whose job is to sell or check tickets on a bus, train, etc **3** TRAIN *US* (*UK* **guard**) someone whose job is to be responsible for a train and the people who work on it **4** HEAT a substance that allows electricity or heat to go through it

**cone** /kəʊn/ *noun* [C] **1** a solid shape with a round or oval base which narrows to a point, or an object which has this shape *a row of traffic cones* **2** a container for ice cream (= sweet, frozen food) that you can eat

**confectionery** /kən'fekʃənəri/ *noun* [U] *mainly UK* sweet food like sweets and chocolate

**confederacy** /kən'fedərəsi/ (*also* **confederation** /kən,fedə'reɪʃən/) *noun* [C] an organization of smaller groups who have joined together for business or political purposes

**confer** /kən'fɜːr/ *verb* **conferring**, *past* **conferred** **1** [I] to discuss something with other people before making a decision *I'll need to* **confer** **with** *my lawyers.* **2** [T] *formal* to give someone something, especially an official title, an honour, or an advantage

**conference** /'kɒnfərəns/ *noun* [C] **1** a large, formal meeting, often lasting a few days, where people discuss their work, politics, subjects they are studying, etc *the annual sales conference* **2** a small, private meeting for discussion of a particular subject ⊃ *See also:* **press conference**.

**confess** /kən'fes/ *verb* [I, T] **1** to admit that you have done something wrong or something that you feel guilty about [+ to + doing sth] *The man has confessed to stealing the painting.* • *Rawlinson finally confessed to the murder.* **2** to tell a priest or God about all the wrong things that you have done

**confession** /kən'feʃən/ *noun* [C, U] **1** when you admit that you have done something wrong or illegal *Sutcliffe has* **made** *a full* **confession to** *the police.* **2** when someone tells a priest all the wrong things they have done *to go to confession*

**confetti** /kən'feti/ *noun* [U] small pieces of coloured paper that you throw when celebrating something such as a marriage

**confidant, confidante** /'kɒnfɪdænt/ *noun* [C]

a person you can talk to about your feelings and secrets

**confide** /kən'faɪd/ *verb* [I, T] to tell a secret to someone who you trust not to tell anyone else [+ that] *Holly confided to me that she was ill.* **confide in sb** to tell someone who you trust about things that are secret or personal

o—**confidence** /'kɒnfɪdəns/ *noun* **1** ABILITY [U] when you are certain of your ability to do things well *He's a good student, but he* **lacks** **confidence**. • [+ to do sth] *His training has given him the confidence to deal with any problem that arises.* **2** TRUST [U] trusting someone's ability or believing that something will produce good results *Kate's new to the job, but I've got* **every** **confidence in** *her.* **3** SECRET [C] something secret that you tell someone *to exchange confidences* **4 in confidence** If you tell something to someone in confidence, you do not want them to tell anyone else.

o—**confident** /'kɒnfɪdənt/ *adj* **1** certain about your ability to do things well *a confident grin* • *He feels* **confident of** *winning.* **2** being certain that something will happen [+ (that)] *Doctors are confident that she'll recover.* • **confidently** *adv* ⊃ *See also:* **self-confident**.

**confidential** /ˌkɒnfɪ'denʃəl/ *adj* secret, especially in an official situation *These documents are strictly confidential.* • **confidentially** *adv* • **confidentiality** /ˌkɒnfɪdenʃi'æləti/ *noun* [U]

**confine** /kən'faɪn/ *verb* [T] to prevent someone from leaving a place, or to prevent something from spreading [often passive] *He was* **confined** *to a prison cell for several days.* **be confined to sth/sb** to only exist in a particular area or group of people *The flooding was confined to the basement.* **confine sb/sth to sth** to limit an activity *Please confine your discussion to the topic.*

**confined** /kən'faɪnd/ *adj* [always before noun] A confined space is very small.

**confinement** /kən'faɪnmənt/ *noun* [U] when someone is kept in a room or area, usually by force ⊃ *See also:* **solitary confinement**.

**confines** /'kɒnfaɪnz/ *noun* [plural] the outer limits or edges of something

**confirm** /kən'fɜːm/ *verb* [T] **1** to say or show that something is true *The report could not be confirmed independently.* • [+ (that)] *His wife confirmed that he'd left the house at 8.* **2** to make an arrangement certain *Flights should be confirmed 48 hours before departure.* **3 be confirmed** to become a member of the Christian Church at a special ceremony

**confirmation** /ˌkɒnfə'meɪʃən/ *noun* [C, U] **1** an announcement or proof that something is true or certain *You'll receive* **written confirmation of** *your reservation within five days.* **2** a special ceremony in which someone becomes a full member of the Christian Church

**confirmed** /kən'fɜːmd/ *adj* **a confirmed atheist/bachelor/pessimist, etc** someone who has behaved in a particular way for a long time and is not likely to change

**confiscate** /'kɒnfɪskeɪt/ *verb* [T] to take something away from someone, especially as a punishment • **confiscation** /ˌkɒnfɪ'skeɪʃən/ *noun* [C, U] *the confiscation of illegal weapons*

**conflict¹** /'kɒnflɪkt/ noun [C, U] **1** DISAGREEMENT serious disagreement *The Government was in conflict with the unions over pay.* • *The peasants often came into conflict with the landowners.* **2** FIGHTING fighting between groups or countries *armed conflict* **3** DIFFERENCE when two or more different things cannot easily exist together *the conflict between science and religion* **4 a conflict of interest** a situation where someone cannot make fair decisions because they are influenced by something

**conflict²** /kən'flɪkt/ verb [I] If things such as beliefs, needs, or facts conflict, they are very different and cannot easily exist together or both be true. *Her views on raising children conflict with mine.* • *There were conflicting accounts of how the fight started.*

**conform** /kən'fɔːm/ verb [I] to behave in the way that most other people behave

**conform to/with sth** to obey a rule or to do things in a traditional way *Women must conform to a strict dress code.* • *All our toys conform with safety standards.*

**conformity** /kən'fɔːməti/ noun [U] **1** behaving in the way that most other people behave **2 conformity to/with sth** *formal* following rules or traditional ways of doing things

**confound** /kən'faʊnd/ verb [T] If something confounds someone, it makes them surprised and confused, because they cannot explain it. *The growth in the economy continues to confound the experts.*

**confront** /kən'frʌnt/ verb [T] **1** ACCUSE to tell someone something, or show them something to try to make them admit they have done something wrong *Confronted with the evidence, she broke down and confessed.* **2 be confronted by/with sth** to be in a difficult situation, or to be shown something which may cause difficulties *We are confronted by the possibility of war.* **3** FRIGHTEN to stand in front of someone in a frightening way *He was confronted by two masked men.* **4** DEAL WITH to see that a problem exists and try to deal with it *First, they must confront their addiction.*

**confrontation** /ˌkɒnfrʌn'teɪʃᵃn/ noun [C, U] a fight or argument

**confrontational** /ˌkɒnfrʌn'teɪʃᵃnᵃl/ adj intentionally causing fighting or an argument *a confrontational style of management*

⊶**confuse** /kən'fjuːz/ verb [T] **1** to make someone unable to think clearly or understand something *These advertisements simply confused the public.* **2** to think that one person or thing is another person or thing *I don't see how anyone could confuse me with my mother!* • *Students sometimes confuse these two verbs.*

**confused** /kən'fjuːzd/ adj **1** unable to think clearly or to understand something *Sorry, I'm completely confused.* • *The politicians themselves are confused about what to do.* **2** not clear *The witnesses gave confused accounts of what happened.*

**confusing** /kən'fjuːzɪŋ/ adj difficult to understand *I found the instructions very confusing.*

⊶**confusion** /kən'fjuːʒᵃn/ noun **1** NOT UNDERSTAND [C, U] when people do not understand what is happening or what they should

do *There was a lot of confusion about what was actually going on.* **2** THOUGHT [U] a feeling of not being able to think clearly *He could see the confusion on Marion's face.* **3** BETWEEN SIMILAR THINGS [U] when you think that one person or thing is another **4** SITUATION [U] a situation which is confusing because there is a lot of noise and activity *In the confusion, several prisoners tried to escape.*

**congeal** /kən'dʒiːl/ verb [I] If a liquid congeals, it becomes thick and almost solid. *congealed fat*

**congenial** /kən'dʒiːniəl/ adj formal pleasant and friendly *congenial company*

**congenital** /kən'dʒenɪtᵃl/ adj Congenital diseases or problems are ones that people have from when they are born. *congenital heart defects*

**congested** /kən'dʒestɪd/ adj full or blocked, especially with traffic *The roads are very congested.*

**congestion** /kən'dʒestʃᵃn/ noun [U] when something is full or blocked, especially with traffic *traffic congestion*

**conglomerate** /kən'glɒmᵃrət/ noun [C] a large company that is made up of several smaller companies

**congratulate** /kən'grætʃuleɪt/ verb [T] to tell someone that you are happy because they have done something good or something good has happened to them *Did you congratulate Cathy on her engagement?*

**congratulations** /kənˌgrætʃu'leɪʃᵃnz/ exclamation something that you say when you want to congratulate someone *Congratulations on doing an outstanding job.* • *I hear you're getting married. Congratulations!*

**congregate** /'kɒŋgrɪgeɪt/ verb [I] to come together in a group *Young people congregated on street corners.*

**congregation** /ˌkɒŋgrɪ'geɪʃᵃn/ noun [group] a group of people meeting to worship in church

**congress** /'kɒŋgres/ noun **1** [C] a large meeting of the members of one or more organizations *an international congress on art history* **2 Congress** the group of people who make laws in the United States. Congress consists of the Senate and the House of Representatives.

**congressional** /kən'greʃᵃnᵃl/ adj [always before noun] relating to the United States Congress *a congressional committee* • *congressional elections*

**congressman, congresswoman** /'kɒŋgresˌmən, 'kɒŋgresˌwʊmən/ noun [C] plural **congressmen, congresswomen** a man or woman who is a member of the United States Congress

**conical** /'kɒnɪkᵃl/ adj Conical objects have a wide, round base, sloping sides and a pointed top.

**conifer** /'kɒnɪfəʳ/ noun [C] a tree with cones (= hard, brown, oval objects) and thin green leaves that stay green all winter

**conjecture** /kən'dʒektʃəʳ/ noun [C, U] formal guessing about something without real evidence *Exactly what happened that night is still a matter for conjecture.* • **conjecture** verb [I, T] formal [+ (that)] *Some people conjectured that it was an attempt to save money.*

**conjugal** /'kɒndʒʊgəl/ *adj formal* relating to marriage

**conjugate** /'kɒndʒʊgeɪt/ *verb* [T] to add different endings to a verb in order to produce all its different forms • conjugation /,kɒndʒʊ'geɪʃən/ *noun* [C, U]

**conjunction** /kən'dʒʌŋkʃən/ *noun* **1** [C] a word that is used to connect phrases or parts of a sentence. For example the words 'and', 'because', and 'although' are conjunctions. **2 in conjunction with sth/sb** working, used, or happening with something or someone else *Our librarians use their knowledge in conjunction with the computer network.*

**conjure** /'kʌndʒəʳ/ *verb*

**conjure sth up 1** to make a picture or idea appear in someone's mind *Familiar tunes can help us conjure up memories of the past.* **2** to make something in a quick and clever way, especially food

**conjurer** /'kʌndʒərər/ *noun* [C] *another spelling of* conjuror

**conjuring** /'kʌndʒərɪŋ/ *noun* [U] performing magic to entertain people *a conjuring trick*

**conjuror** /'kʌndʒərər/ *noun* [C] a person who performs magic to entertain people

**conman** /'kɒnmæn/ *noun* [C] a man who tricks people into giving him money or valuable things

o—**connect** /kə'nekt/ *verb* **1** JOIN [I, T] to join two things or places together *A small bridge connects the two parts of the building.* • *Ferries connect the mainland with the islands.* • *Connect up the printer to your computer.* **2** INVOLVE [T] to see or show that two or more people or things are involved with each other *There is no evidence to connect him with the crime.* **3** TRAVEL [I] If buses, trains, aircraft, etc connect, they arrive at a particular time so that passengers can get off one and onto another. *Can you get me a connecting flight?* **4** TELEPHONE [T] to make it possible for two people to talk to each other on the telephone *I'll try to connect you.* ➲ *Opposite* disconnect.

**connected** /kə'nektɪd/ *adj* **1** If people or things are connected, there is a relationship between them. *a series of loosely connected stories* • *The hospital is connected to the University of Rochester.* • *He remained closely connected with the museum until his death.* ➲ *Opposite* unconnected. **2** If two things are connected, they are joined together. *The Red Sea is connected to the Mediterranean by the Suez Canal.* ➲ *Opposite* disconnected. ➲ *See also:* well-connected.

o—**connection** /kə'nekʃən/ *noun* **1** RELATIONSHIP [C, U] a relationship between people or things *The connection between smoking and heart disease is well known.* • *He denied having any connection with the terrorists.* **2** JOINING THINGS [C, U] something that joins things together *Many companies now offer free connection to the Internet.* **3** TRAVEL [C] a train, bus, or aircraft that leaves a short time after another arrives, so that people can continue their journey *The train was half an hour late and I missed my connection.* **4 in connection with** used to say what something is about *A man has been arrested in connection with the murder.*

**connections** /kə'nekʃənz/ *noun* [plural] important or powerful people who you know and who will help you *He has connections in Washington.*

**connive** /kə'naɪv/ *verb* [I] to work secretly to do something wrong or illegal, or to allow something wrong or illegal to happen *They accused the government of conniving in drug smuggling.*

**connoisseur** /,kɒnə'sɜːʳ/ *noun* [C] someone who knows a lot about and enjoys good food, wine, art, etc

**connotation** /,kɒnəʊ'teɪʃən/ *noun* [C, U] the feelings or ideas that words give in addition to their meanings *The word 'second-hand' has connotations of poor quality.*

**conquer** /'kɒŋkəʳ/ *verb* **1** [I, T] to take control of a country, or to defeat people by war *Peru was conquered by the Spanish in 1532.* **2** [T] to succeed in stopping or dealing with a bad feeling or a difficult problem *He has finally conquered his fear of spiders.*

**conqueror** /'kɒŋkərəʳ/ *noun* [C] someone who has conquered a country or its people

**conquest** /'kɒŋkwest/ *noun* [C, U] when someone takes control of a country, area, or situation *the Roman conquest of Britain* • *man's conquest of nature*

o—**conscience** /'kɒnʃəns/ *noun* **1** [C, U] the part of you that makes you feel guilty when you have behaved badly *a guilty conscience* • *My conscience is clear* (= I do not feel guilty) *because I've done nothing wrong.* **2 be on your conscience** If something is on your conscience, it is making you feel guilty. *I don't want to have someone's death on my conscience.*

**conscientious** /,kɒnʃi'enʃəs/ *adj* always doing your work with a lot of care *a conscientious student* • conscientiously *adv*

**conscientious objector** /kɒnʃi,entʃəs əb'sʒektəʳ/ *noun* [C] someone who refuses to work in the armed forces because they think war is wrong

o—**conscious** /'kɒnʃəs/ *adj* **1 be conscious of/that** to know that something is present or that something is happening *She became conscious of his stare.* • *I'm very conscious that a lot of people disagree with me.* **2 a conscious decision/choice/effort, etc** a decision, choice, effort, etc that you make intentionally *Did you make a conscious decision to lose weight?* ➲ *Opposite* subconscious. **3** awake and able to think and notice things *He's still conscious but he's very badly injured.* ➲ *Opposite* unconscious. • consciously *adv More and more people are consciously trying to improve their health.* ➲ *See also:* self-conscious.

**-conscious** /'kɒnʃəs/ *suffix* used at the end of words to mean 'thinking that something is important' *a safety-conscious mother* • *fashion-conscious teenagers*

**consciousness** /'kɒnʃəsnəs/ *noun* **1** [U] when someone is awake and can think and notice things *He lost consciousness* (= stopped being conscious) *for several minutes.* • *I want to be here when she regains consciousness* (= becomes conscious again). **2** [no plural] when someone knows about something *There's a* *growing consciousness about environmental issues among young people.*

**conscript**[1] /'kɒnskrɪpt/ *noun* [C] someone who has been made to join the army

**conscript**[2] /kən'skrɪpt/ *verb* [T] to make someone join the army [often passive] *During World War I, he was conscripted into the Russian army.*

**conscription** /kən'skrɪpʃ°n/ *noun* [U] a system in which people are made to join the army

**consecrate** /'kɒnsɪkreɪt/ *verb* [T] to make a place or object holy in a religious ceremony ● consecration /,kɒnsɪ'kreɪʃ°n/ *noun* [U] *a consecration ceremony*

**consecutive** /kən'sekjʊtɪv/ *adj* Consecutive events, numbers, or periods of time come one after the other. *the third consecutive day of rain* ● consecutively *adv Tickets are numbered consecutively from 1 to 100.*

**consensus** /kən'sensəs/ *noun* [U, no plural] when all the people in a group agree about something *to reach a consensus* ● *The general consensus is that we should wait and see what happens.*

**consent**[1] /kən'sent/ *noun* [U] 1 permission for someone to do something *You can't come without your parents' consent.* 2 **by common consent** *UK* used to say that everyone agrees about something *He is, by common consent, the most talented actor in Hollywood.*

**consent**[2] /kən'sent/ *verb* [I] to agree to do something, or to allow someone to do something [+ to do sth] *They eventually consented to let us enter.*

○━**consequence** /'kɒnsɪkwəns/ *noun* 1 [C] the result of an action or situation, especially a bad result *The ship capsized, with disastrous consequences.* ● *If you make him angry, you'll have to suffer the consequences.* 2 **of little/no consequence** *formal* not important *The money was of little consequence to Tony.*

**consequent** /'kɒnsɪkwənt/ *adj* [always before noun] *formal* happening as a result of something *the closure of the factory and the consequent loss of 400 jobs*

**consequently** /'kɒnsɪkwəntli/ *adv* as a result *She was the child of two models and, consequently, she was very tall.*

**conservation** /,kɒnsə'veɪʃ°n/ *noun* [U] 1 the protection of nature *wildlife conservation* ● *conservation groups* 2 when you are careful not to waste energy, water, etc

**conservationist** /,kɒnsə'veɪʃ°nɪst/ *noun* [C] someone who believes that people should protect nature

**conservatism** /kən'sɜːvətɪz°m/ *noun* [U] conservative actions and beliefs

**conservative** /kən'sɜːvətɪv/ *adj* 1 not trusting sudden changes or new ideas *Older people tend to be very conservative.* 2 **a conservative estimate/guess** a guess about a number or amount that is probably lower than the true number or amount *At a conservative guess, I'd say there were about 100 people there.*

**Conservative** /kən'sɜːvətɪv/ *noun* [C] someone who supports the Conservative Party in the UK *the Conservative candidate/MP*

**the Con'servative ,Party** *noun* [group] one of the three main political parties in the UK

**conservatory** /kən'sɜːvətri/ *noun* [C] a room

attached to a house that has windows all around it and a glass roof

**conserve** /kən'sɜːv/ *verb* [T] 1 to use something in a way that does not waste it *Insulating the walls will help to conserve heat.* 2 to prevent harm or damage to animals or places

○━**consider** /kən'sɪdəʳ/ *verb* 1 [T] to think carefully about a decision or something you might do *Have you considered surgery?* ● [+ doing sth] *We're considering buying a new car.* 2 [T] to think about particular facts when you are making a decision about something *If you buy an old house, you have to consider the cost of repairs.* 3 **consider sb/sth (to be) sth; consider that** to have a particular opinion about someone or something [often reflexive] *I don't consider myself to be a great athlete.* ● *They don't consider that he did anything wrong.*

**considerable** /kən'sɪdºrəbl/ *adj* large or important enough to have an effect *a considerable amount of money* ● *The damage has been considerable.* ● considerably *adv Rates of pay vary considerably.*

**considerate** /kən'sɪdºrət/ *adj* kind and helpful *a polite and considerate child* ⊃ *Opposite* **inconsiderate**.

**consideration** /kən,sɪdºr'eɪʃ°n/ *noun* 1 IMPORTANT FACT [C] something that you have to think about when you make decisions or plans *Safety is our main consideration.* 2 CAREFUL THOUGHT [U] when you think about something very carefully *After careful consideration, we have decided to offer you the job.* ● *Several options are under consideration* (= being considered). 3 KINDNESS [U] when you are kind to people or think about their feelings *They always treated me with consideration.* 4 **take sth into consideration** to think about something when you make a decision or plan

**considered** /kən'sɪdəd/ *adj* 1 [always before noun] A considered opinion or decision is based on careful thought. *It is our considered opinion that he should resign.* 2 **all things considered** used when you are giving your opinion about something after thinking carefully about all the facts *All things considered, I think we made the right choice.*

**considering** /kən'sɪdərɪŋ/ *preposition, conjunction* used for saying that you have a particular opinion about something, because of a particular fact about it *She's fairly fit considering her age.* ● *Considering she'd only been there once before, she did well to find the way.*

**consign** /kən'saɪn/ *verb*
**consign sb/sth to sth** *formal* to get rid of someone or something or to put them in an unpleasant place or situation *They were consigned to a life of poverty.*

**consignment** /kən'saɪnmənt/ *noun* [C] an amount of goods that is being sent somewhere *a ship carrying a small consignment of rice*

○━**consist** /kən'sɪst/ *verb*
**consist of sth** to be formed or made from two or more things *a dessert consisting of fruit and cream*

**consistency** /kən'sɪstənsi/ *noun* 1 [U] when someone always behaves or performs in a similar way or when something always happens in a similar way *The team has won a few matches but lacks consistency.* **2** [C, U] how thick or smooth a liquid is *Beat the mixture to a smooth consistency.*

**consistent** /kən'sɪstᵊnt/ *adj* **1** always behaving or happening in a similar, usually positive, way *consistent effort/improvement* **2** **consistent with sth** *formal* having the same principles as something else, or agreeing with other facts *His account of events is entirely consistent with the video evidence.* • **consistently** *adv The President has consistently denied the rumours.*

**consolation** /ˌkɒnsə'leɪʃᵊn/ *noun* [C, U] something that makes you feel better about a bad situation *If it's any consolation, I failed my driving test too.*

**console¹** /kən'səʊl/ *verb* [T] to make someone who is sad feel better *I tried to console her but she just kept crying.*

**console²** /'kɒnsəʊl/ *noun* [C] an object that contains the controls for a piece of equipment *a video game console*

**consolidate** /kən'sɒlɪdeɪt/ *verb* **1** [I, T] to make sure that you become more powerful, or that success and achievements continue strongly *It will take him some time to consolidate his position in the banking world.* **2** [T] to combine several things, especially businesses, so that they become more effective, or to be combined in this way *He consolidated his businesses into one large company.* • **consolidation** /kənˌsɒlɪ'deɪʃᵊn/ *noun* [U]

**consonant** /'kɒnsᵊnənt/ *noun* [C] a letter of the alphabet that is not a vowel

**consort** /kən'sɔːt/ *verb*
**consort with sb** to spend time with a bad person *They claimed he had been consorting with drug dealers.*

**consortium** /kən'sɔːtiəm/ *noun* [C] *plural* **consortiums** or **consortia** an organization consisting of several businesses or banks *an international consortium of airlines*

**conspicuous** /kən'spɪkjuəs/ *adj* very easy to notice *His army uniform made him very conspicuous.* • **conspicuously** *adv His wife was conspicuously absent.*

**conspiracy** /kən'spɪrəsi/ *noun* [C, U] when a group of people secretly plan to do something bad or illegal [+ to do sth] *a conspiracy to overthrow the government*

**conspirator** /kən'spɪrətəʳ/ *noun* [C] someone who secretly plans with other people to do something bad or illegal

**conspire** /kən'spaɪəʳ/ *verb* **1** [I] to join with other people to secretly plan to do something bad or illegal [+ to do sth] *He was convicted of conspiring to blow up the World Trade Center.* • *The king accused his advisers of **conspiring against** him.* **2** **conspire against sb; conspire to do sth** If events or a situation conspire against you, they cause problems for you. *Circumstances had conspired to ruin her plans.*

**constable** /'kʌnstəbl/ *noun* [C] a British police officer of the lowest rank

**constant** /'kɒnstənt/ *adj* **1** happening a lot or all the time *machines that are in constant use* • *She's in constant pain.* **2** staying at the same level *The temperature remained constant.*

• **constantly** *adv He's constantly changing his mind.*

**constellation** /ˌkɒnstə'leɪʃᵊn/ *noun* [C] a group of stars

**consternation** /ˌkɒnstə'neɪʃᵊn/ *noun* [U] a feeling of shock or worry

**constipated** /'kɒnstɪpeɪtɪd/ *adj* unable to empty your bowels as often as you should

**constipation** /ˌkɒnstɪ'peɪʃᵊn/ *noun* [U] when you are constipated

**constituency** /kən'stɪtjuənsi/ *noun* [C] an area of a country which elects someone to represent it in the government, or the people who live there

**constituent** /kən'stɪtjuənt/ *noun* [C] **1** one of the parts or substances that something is made of *Methane is the main **constituent** of natural gas.* **2** someone who lives in a particular constituency

**constitute** /'kɒnstɪtjuːt/ *verb* [T] to be or form something *This defeat constitutes a real setback for their championship hopes.*

**constitution** /ˌkɒnstɪ'tjuːʃᵊn/ *noun* [C] **1** the set of laws and principles that a country's government must obey *the US Constitution* **2** the state of someone's health *a strong/weak constitution*

**constitutional** /ˌkɒnstɪ'tjuːʃᵊnᵊl/ *adj* relating to the constitution of a country *a constitutional crisis*

**constrain** /kən'streɪn/ *verb* [T] to control something by limiting it *regulations that constrain industry* • [often passive] *I'm constrained by decisions made in the past.*

**constraint** /kən'streɪnt/ *noun* [C] something that limits what you can do *budget constraints* • *There are **constraints on** the medicines doctors can prescribe.*

**constrict** /kən'strɪkt/ *verb* **1** [T] to limit someone's freedom to do what they want to or be the way they want to *His creativity was constricted by the political regime he lived under.* **2** [I, T] to become narrower or tighter, or to make something narrower or tighter *The blood vessels constricted.* • **constriction** /kən'strɪkʃᵊn/ *noun* [U]

**construct** /kən'strʌkt/ *verb* [T] to build something from several parts *The building was constructed in 1930.*

**construction** /kən'strʌkʃᵊn/ *noun* **1** [BUILDING WORK] [U] the work of building houses, offices, bridges, etc *railway construction* • *construction work* **2** [LARGE BUILDING] [C] something large that is built *a large steel construction* **3** [WORDS] [C] The construction of a sentence or phrase is the way the words are arranged.

**constructive** /kən'strʌktɪv/ *adj* helpful or useful *constructive advice/criticism* • **constructively** *adv*

**construe** /kən'struː/ *verb* [T] **construing**, *past* **construed** to understand something in a particular way *Her comments could be **construed as** patronizing.*

**consul** /'kɒnsᵊl/ *noun* [C] someone whose job is to work in a foreign country taking care of the people from their own country who go or live there

**consular** /'kɒnsjʊləʳ/ *adj* [always before noun]

C

relating to a consul or a consulate *consular officials*

**consulate** /ˈkɒnsjʊlət/ *noun* [C] the offices where a consul works *the Cuban consulate in Mexico City*

**consult** /kənˈsʌlt/ *verb* [T] **1** to go to a particular person or book to get information or advice *For more information, consult your travel agent.* **2** to discuss something with someone before you make a decision *Why didn't you consult me about this?*

**consultancy** /kənˈsʌltᵊnsi/ *noun* **1** [C] a company that gives advice on subjects it knows a lot about *a management/recruitment consultancy* **2** [U] the activity of giving advice on a particular subject

**consultant** /kənˈsʌltᵊnt/ *noun* [C] **1** someone who advises people about a particular subject *a tax consultant* **2** UK a hospital doctor who is an expert in a particular area of medicine

**consultation** /ˌkɒnsᵊlˈteɪʃᵊn/ *noun* **1** [C] a meeting to discuss something or to get advice *a medical consultation* **2** [U] when you discuss something with someone in order to get their advice or opinion about it *After consultation with his lawyers, he decided to abandon the case.*

**consultative** /kənˈsʌltətɪv/ *adj* A consultative group or document gives advice about something.

**consume** /kənˈsjuːm/ *verb* [T] **1** USE to use something such as a product, energy, or fuel *These lights don't consume much electricity.* **2** EAT OR DRINK *formal* to eat or drink something **3** be consumed with/by sth to have so much of a feeling that it affects everything you do *a dancer consumed by ambition* **4** FIRE If fire consumes something, it completely destroys it.

**consumer** /kənˈsjuːməʳ/ *noun* [C] someone who buys or uses goods or services *These price cuts are good news for consumers.*

**consumerism** /kənˈsjuːmərɪzᵊm/ *noun* [U] buying and selling things, especially when this is an important part of a society's activities

**consummate**[1] /ˈkɒnsəmeɪt/ *verb* [T] to make a marriage or relationship complete by having sex ● consummation /ˌkɒnsəˈmeɪʃᵊn/ *noun* [U]

**consummate**[2] /kənˈsʌmət, ˈkɒnsəmət/ *adj* [always before noun] *formal* having great skill *a consummate professional* ● *consummate ease/skill*

**consumption** /kənˈsʌmpʃᵊn/ *noun* [U] **1** the amount of something that someone uses, eats, or drinks *China's total energy consumption* **2** when someone uses, eats, or drinks something *products sold for personal consumption*

**contact**[1] /ˈkɒntækt/ *noun* **1** COMMUNICATION [U] when you communicate with someone, especially by speaking to them *We keep in close contact with our grandparents.* ● *Jo and I are determined not to lose contact.* **2** TOUCH [U] when two people or things are touching each other *She dislikes any kind of physical contact.* ● *Wash your hands if they come into contact with chemicals.* **3** PERSON [C] someone you know who may be able to help you because of their job or position *business contacts* **4** EYE [C]

(*also* **contact lens**) a small piece of plastic that you put on your eye to make you see more clearly ➲ *See also:* **eye contact**.

**contact**[2] /ˈkɒntækt/ *verb* [T] to telephone someone or write to them *I've been trying to contact you for days.*

**'contact ˌlens** UK (US ˌcontact 'lens) *noun* [C] a small piece of plastic that you put on your eye to make you see more clearly

**contagious** /kənˈteɪdʒəs/ *adj* **1** A contagious disease is one that you can get if you touch someone who has it. **2** A contagious feeling spreads quickly amongst people. *Her excitement was contagious.*

**contain** /kənˈteɪn/ *verb* [T] **1** INSIDE If one thing contains another, it has it inside it. *a box containing a diamond ring* **2** PART to have something as a part *Does this drink contain alcohol?* **3** CONTROL to control something by stopping it from spreading *The police were unable to contain the fighting.* **4** EMOTION to control your emotions *He could barely contain his anger.* ● [often reflexive] *I could not contain myself any longer.*

**contain** or **include**?

Use **contain** to talk about objects which have something else inside them.

*This folder contains important letters.*

*This soup contains garlic and onions.*

Use **include** to say that something or someone is a part of something else.

*The team includes two new players.*

*The price of the ticket includes insurance and tax.*

**container** /kənˈteɪnəʳ/ *noun* [C] an object such as a box or a bottle that is used for holding something

**contaminate** /kənˈtæmɪneɪt/ *verb* [T] to make something dirty or poisonous *contaminated drinking water* ● contamination /kənˌtæmɪˈneɪʃᵊn/ *noun* [U]

**contemplate** /ˈkɒntəmpleɪt/ *verb* [T] to think about something for a long time or in a serious way [+ doing sth] *I'm contemplating changing my name.* ● *He even contemplated suicide.* ● contemplation /ˌkɒntəmˈpleɪʃᵊn/ *noun* [U]

**contemporary**[1] /kənˈtempᵊrᵊri, kənˈtempəri/ *adj* **1** of the present time *contemporary music* **2** [always before noun] existing or happening at the same time as something *Most contemporary accounts of the event have been destroyed.*

**contemporary**[2] /kənˈtempᵊrᵊri, kənˈtempəri/ *noun* [C] Someone's contemporaries are the people who live at the same time as them. *Shakespeare and his contemporaries* ● *a contemporary of Beethoven*

**contempt** /kənˈtempt/ *noun* **1** [U] a strong feeling that you do not respect someone or something *He has utter contempt for anyone with power.* **2** contempt of court behaviour that is illegal because it does not obey the rules of a law court

**container**

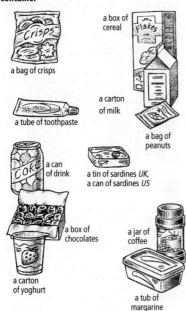

a bag of crisps

a box of cereal

a tube of toothpaste

a carton of milk

a can of drink

a bag of peanuts

a tin of sardines UK, a can of sardines US

a box of chocolates

a jar of coffee

a carton of yoghurt

a tub of margarine

**contemptible** /kən'temptəbl/ adj extremely bad, because of being dishonest or cruel

**contemptuous** /kən'temptʃuəs/ adj showing contempt • contemptuously adv

**contend** /kən'tend/ verb 1 [T] formal to say that something is true [+ (that)] His lawyers contend that he is telling the truth. 2 [I] to compete with someone to try to win something one of the groups contending for power
**contend with sth** to have to deal with a difficult or unpleasant situation I have enough problems of my own to contend with.

**contender** /kən'tendə'/ noun [C] someone who competes with other people to try to win something a leading contender for an Oscar

**content¹** /'kɒntent/ noun [no plural] 1 the information or ideas that are talked about in a book, speech, film, etc The content of the article was controversial. 2 the amount of a particular substance that something contains Most soft drinks have a high sugar content.

**content²** /kən'tent/ adj happy or satisfied Not content with second place, Jeff played only to win. • [+ to do sth] I was content to stay home and read.

**content³** /kən'tent/ verb
**content yourself with sth** to do something or have something although it is not exactly what you want Since it rained we had to content ourselves with playing cards.

**contented** /kən'tentɪd/ adj satisfied, or making you feel satisfied ⊃ Opposite **discontented**.
• contentedly adv

**contention** /kən'tenʃ°n/ noun 1 OPINION [C] formal a belief or opinion There's a general contention that too much violence is shown on TV. 2 COMPETITION [U] when people or groups compete for something Johnson is back in contention for the championships. 3 DISAGREEMENT [U] arguments and disagreements ⊃ See also: a **bone¹** of contention.

**contentious** /kən'tenʃəs/ adj likely to make people argue a contentious issue

**contentment** /kən'tentmənt/ noun [U] the feeling of being happy or satisfied

o-=**contents** /'kɒntents/ noun [plural] 1 THINGS INSIDE all of the things that are contained inside something Please empty out the contents of your pockets. 2 INFORMATION the information or ideas that are written in a book, letter, document, etc the contents of his will 3 BOOK a list in a book that tells you what different parts the book contains a table of contents

**contest¹** /'kɒntest/ noun [C] a competition or election

**contest²** /kən'test/ verb [T] 1 to say formally that something is wrong or unfair and try to have it changed Mr Hughes went back to court to contest the verdict. 2 to compete for something

**contestant** /kən'test°nt/ noun [C] someone who competes in a contest

**context** /'kɒntekst/ noun [C, U] 1 all the facts, opinions, situations, etc relating to a particular thing or event This small battle is important in the context of Scottish history. 2 other words that were said or written at the same time as the word or words you are talking about Taken out of context, her remark sounded like an insult.

o-=**continent** /'kɒntɪnənt/ noun [C] one of the seven main areas of land on the Earth, such as Asia, Africa, or Europe

**the Continent** /'kɒntɪnənt/ noun UK the main part of land in Europe, not including Britain

**continental** /,kɒntɪ'nent°l/ adj relating to a continent the continental US

**Continental** /,kɒntɪ'nent°l/ adj mainly UK relating to Europe, but not Britain

,continental 'breakfast noun [C] a breakfast (= morning meal) consisting of fruit juice, coffee, and bread

**contingency** /kən'tɪndʒənsi/ noun [C] 1 an event or situation that might happen in the future, especially one which could cause problems a contingency fund/plan (= money or a plan that can be used if there are problems) 2 a contingency fee money that lawyers (= people who advise people about the law and deal with legal situations) charge, which is a share of what the person they represent has won

**contingent¹** /kən'tɪndʒ°nt/ noun [group] 1 a group of people from the same country, organization, etc who are part of a much larger group 2 a group of soldiers who are part of a larger military group

**contingent²** /kən'tɪndʒ°nt/ adj **contingent on sth** depending on something else in order to happen Buying the new house was contingent on selling the old one.

**continual** /kən'tɪnjuəl/ *adj* happening again and again over a long period of time *I can't work with these continual interruptions.* • **continually** *adv Dad continually complains about money.*

**continuation** /kən,tɪnju'eɪʃᵊn/ *noun* **1** [C] something that comes after an event, situation, or thing to make it continue or go further *Today's meeting will be a continuation of yesterday's talks.* **2** [U, no plural] when something continues to exist, happen, or be used *the continuation of their partnership*

○⊷**continue** /kən'tɪnjuː/ *verb* **continuing**, *past* **continued 1** [I, T] to keep happening, existing, or doing something [+ **to do sth**] *It continued to snow heavily for three days.* • [+ **doing sth**] *Ann continued working part-time until June.* **2** [T] to start doing or saying something again, after stopping for a short period *We'll have to continue this discussion tomorrow.* • *"Ever since then," he continued, "I've been afraid of heights."* **3 continue along/down/up, etc** to go further in a particular direction *Continue down the road until you reach Walnut Street.*

**continued** /kən'tɪnjuːd/ *adj* [always before noun] still happening, existing, or done *his continued success*

**continuity** /,kɒntɪ'njuːəti/ *noun* [U] the state of continuing for a long period of time without being changed or stopped

○⊷**continuous¹** /kən'tɪnjuəs/ *adj* **1** happening or existing without stopping *continuous pain* • *ten years of continuous service in the army* **2** The continuous form of a verb is used to show that an action is continuing to happen. The sentence 'He was eating lunch.' is in the continuous form. • **continuously** *adv Their baby cried continuously all afternoon.*

**the continuous** /kən'tɪnjuəs/ *noun* the continuous form of the verb

**contort** /kən'tɔːt/ *verb* [I, T] If your face or body contorts, or you contort it, you twist it into a different shape, often because you are experiencing a strong emotion. *His face was contorted with pain.*

**contour** /'kɒntʊəʳ/ *noun* [C] **1** the shape of the outer edge of something *the contours of her body* **2** (*also* '**contour ,line**) a line on a map joining places that are at the same height

**contraband** /'kɒntrəbænd/ *noun* [U] goods that are brought into or taken out of a country illegally

**contraception** /,kɒntrə'sepʃᵊn/ *noun* [U] methods that prevent a woman from becoming pregnant *What form of contraception do you use?*

**contraceptive** /,kɒntrə'septɪv/ *noun* [C] a drug or object that prevents a woman from becoming pregnant

○⊷**contract¹** /'kɒntrækt/ *noun* [C] a legal agreement between two people or organizations, especially one that involves doing work for a particular amount of money

**contract²** /kən'trækt/ *verb* **1** REDUCE [I, T] to become smaller or shorter, or to make something do this *The wood contracts in dry weather.* **2** DISEASE [T] *formal* to get a serious disease *She contracted malaria while living abroad.*

**3** AGREEMENT [I, T] to make a legal agreement with someone to do work or to have work done for you [+ **to do sth**] *He's been contracted to perform in five shows.*

**contract out sth** to make a formal arrangement for other people to do work that you are responsible for *They've contracted out the cleaning to a private firm.*

**contraction** /kən'trækʃᵊn/ *noun* **1** MUSCLE [C] a strong, painful movement of the muscles that a woman has when she is having a baby *She was having contractions every ten minutes.* **2** WORD [C] a short form of a word or group of words *'Won't' is a contraction of 'will not'.* **3** REDUCTION [U] when something becomes smaller or shorter

**contractor** /kən'træktəʳ/ *noun* [C] a person or company that supplies goods or does work for other people

**contractual** /kən'træktʃuəl/ *adj* relating to or stated in a contract (= legal agreement) *a contractual dispute*

**contradict** /,kɒntrə'dɪkt/ *verb* **1** [T] If two things that are said or written about something contradict each other, they are so different that they cannot both be true. *His account of the accident contradicts the official government report.* **2** [I, T] to say that what someone else has just said is wrong *He said we were all happy at work, and nobody dared to contradict him.*

**contradiction** /,kɒntrə'dɪkʃᵊn/ *noun* **1** [C] a big difference between two things that are said or written about the same subject, or between what someone says and what they do *There is a clear contradiction between what she says and what she does.* **2** [U] when you say that what someone has just said is wrong **3 a contradiction in terms** a phrase that is confusing because it contains words that seem to have opposite meanings *An honest politician – isn't that a contradiction in terms?*

**contradictory** /,kɒntrə'dɪktᵊri/ *adj* If two statements about the same subject or two actions by the same person are contradictory, they are very different.

**contraption** /kən'træpʃᵊn/ *noun* [C] a machine or object that looks strange or complicated

**contrary¹** /'kɒntrᵊri/ *noun* **1 to the contrary** saying or showing the opposite *She claimed she hadn't been involved, despite evidence to the contrary.* **2 on the contrary** used to show that the opposite of what has just been said is true *"You're a vegetarian, aren't you?" "On the contrary, I love meat."*

**contrary²** /'kɒntrᵊri/ *adj* **1** opposite or very different *a contrary opinion/view* **2 contrary to sth a** opposite to what someone said or thought *Contrary to popular belief, bottled water is not always better than tap water.* **b** If something is contrary to a rule, it does not obey that rule. *Her actions are contrary to the teachings of the church.*

○⊷**contrast¹** /'kɒntrɑːst/ *noun* [C, U] **1** an obvious difference between two people or things *The contrast between their lifestyles couldn't be greater.* • *The busy north coast of the island is in sharp contrast to the peaceful south.* **2 by/in**

**contrast** used to show that someone or something is completely different from someone or something else *She's quite petite, in contrast with her tall sister.*

**contrast²** /kən'trɑːst/ *verb* **1** [T] to compare two people or things in order to show the differences between them *If you contrast his early novels with his later work, you can see how his writing has developed.* **2** [I] If one thing contrasts with another, it is very different from it. *The sharpness of the lemons contrasts with the sweetness of the honey.*

**contrasting** /kən'trɑːstɪŋ/ *adj* very different *contrasting colours/styles*

**contravene** /ˌkɒntrə'viːn/ *verb* [T] *formal* to do something that is forbidden by a law or rule ● **contravention** /ˌkɒntrə'venʃən/ *noun* [C, U] *By accepting the money, she was in contravention of company rules.*

o-◄**contribute** /kən'trɪbjuːt, 'kɒntrɪbjuːt/ *verb* [I, T] **1** to give something, especially money, in order to provide or achieve something together with other people *I contributed $20 towards Andrea's present.* **2** to write articles for a newspaper, magazine, or book *She contributes to several magazines.*

**contribute to sth** to be one of the causes of an event or a situation *Smoking contributed to his early death.*

o-◄**contribution** /ˌkɒntrɪ'bjuːʃən/ *noun* [C] **1** something that you do to help produce or develop something, or to help make something successful *She has made a major contribution to our work.* **2** an amount of money that is given to help pay for something *a generous contribution to charity*

**contributor** /kən'trɪbjutər/ *noun* [C] **1** ARTICLE someone who writes articles for a newspaper, magazine, or book **2** MONEY someone who gives something, especially money, together with other people **3** CAUSE one of the causes of something *Speeding is a major contributor to road accidents.*

**contributory** /kən'trɪbjutəri/ *adj* helping to cause something

**contrive** /kən'traɪv/ *verb* [T] *formal* to manage to do something difficult, or to make something happen, by using your intelligence or by tricking people [+ to do sth] *They contrived to meet in secret.*

**contrived** /kən'traɪvd/ *adj* Something that is contrived seems false and not natural.

o-◄**control¹** /kən'trəʊl/ *noun* **1** POWER [U] the power to make a person, organization, or object do what you want *The new teacher has no control over the class.* ● *The police are in control of the situation.* ● *The place was in chaos, and nobody seemed to be in control.* ● *He lost control of the vehicle.* **2** RULE [U] the power to rule or govern an area *Soldiers took control of the airport.* **3 under control** being dealt with successfully *Don't worry – everything's under control.* ● *I couldn't keep my drinking under control.* **4 out of control** If something or someone is out of control, you cannot influence, limit, or direct them. *The mob was completely out of control.* **5** RULE [C, U] a rule or law that limits something *The government has*

*introduced tighter immigration controls.* **6** CALM [U] the ability to be calm *It took a lot of control to stop myself hitting him.* **7** EQUIPMENT [C] a switch or piece of equipment that you use to operate a machine or vehicle *Where's the volume control on your stereo?* **8** OFFICIAL PLACE [C, U] a place where something official, usually a document, is checked *passport/immigration control* ➔ *See also:* **birth control, remote control, self-control.**

o-◄**control²** /kən'trəʊl/ *verb* [T] **controlling,** *past* **controlled 1** MAKE SB DO STH to make a person, organization, or object do what you want *A board of directors controls the company.* ● *This switch controls the temperature.* ● *Can't you control your dogs?* **2** LIMIT to limit the number, amount, or increase of something *Fire crews struggled to control the blaze.* **3** RULE to rule or govern an area *The whole area is controlled by rebel forces.* **4** EMOTION to stop yourself expressing strong emotions or behaving in a silly way *He can't control his temper.* ● [often reflexive] *Please try to control yourself – you're upsetting everyone.*

**controller** /kən'trəʊlər/ *noun* [C] someone who directs the work of other people *a marketing controller*

**controversial** /ˌkɒntrə'vɜːʃəl/ *adj* causing a lot of disagreement or argument *a controversial decision/issue*

**controversy** /'kɒntrəvɜːsi/ *noun* [C, U] a lot of disagreement and argument about something *There is a lot of controversy over mobile phone towers.*

**conundrum** /kə'nʌndrəm/ *noun* [C] a problem or question that is difficult to solve

**convalescence** /ˌkɒnvə'lesəns/ *noun* [U] the period of time when you rest and get better after a serious illness ● **convalesce** *verb* [I]

**convene** /kən'viːn/ *verb* [I, T] *formal* to arrange a meeting, or to meet for a meeting *The committee convenes three times a year.*

**convenience** /kən'viːniəns/ *noun* **1** [U] when something is easy to use and suitable for what you want to do *the convenience of credit cards* **2** [C] something that makes life easier *Fortunately, the house has every modern convenience.*

**con'venience ˌstore** *noun* [C] *mainly US* a shop that sells food, drinks, etc, and is usually open late

o-◄**convenient** /kən'viːniənt/ *adj* **1** easy to use, or suiting your plans well *When would be a convenient time to meet?* **2** near or easy to get to *The new supermarket is very convenient for me.* ● **conveniently** *adv*

**convent** /'kɒnvənt/ *noun* [C] a building where nuns (= religious women) live and pray together

**convention** /kən'venʃən/ *noun* **1** MEETING [C] a large formal meeting of people with the same interest or work *the Democratic Party convention* **2** CUSTOM [C, U] a usual and accepted way of behaving or doing something *In many countries it is the convention to wear black at funerals.* **3** AGREEMENT [C] a formal agreement between countries *an international convention on human rights*

# conventional

**conventional** /kən'venʃⁿnⁿl/ *adj* **1** Conventional people are traditional and not willing to try new ideas. **2** Conventional objects or ways of doing things are the usual ones which have been used for a long time. *conventional farming/medicine* **3** **conventional arms/ forces/warfare, etc** not involving the use of nuclear weapons **4 conventional wisdom** what most people believe ➔ *Opposite* **unconventional**.

**conventionally** /kən'venʃⁿnⁿli/ *adv* in a traditional way *He dressed conventionally in a suit and tie.*

**converge** /kən'vɜːdʒ/ *verb* [I] **1** COME TOGETHER If lines, roads, or rivers converge, they meet at a particular point. **2** FORM GROUP to move towards a particular point and form a group there *The protesters converged on the town square.* **3** BECOME SIMILAR If ideas, interests, or systems converge, they become more similar to one another. • **convergence** *noun* [U]

○━**conversation** /ˌkɒnvə'seɪʃⁿn/ *noun* [C, U] a talk between two or more people, usually an informal one *a telephone conversation* • We **had a conversation** about football. • **conversational** *adj* relating to or like a conversation *a conversational style*

**converse** /kən'vɜːs/ *verb* [I] *formal* to talk with someone

**conversely** /'kɒnvɜːsli/ *adv* used to introduce something that is different to something you have just said *Dark lipsticks make your mouth look smaller. Conversely, light shades make it larger.*

**conversion** /kən'vɜːʒⁿn/ *noun* [C, U] **1** when the appearance, form, or purpose of something is changed *the country's conversion to democracy* **2** when someone changes to a new religion or belief *her conversion to Christianity*

**convert¹** /kən'vɜːt/ *verb* **1** [I, T] to change the appearance, form, or purpose of something *The old warehouse was converted into offices.* • *How do you convert miles into kilometres?* **2** [I, T] to change to a new religion, belief, etc, or to make someone do this *When did he convert to Islam?*

**convert²** /'kɒnvɜːt/ *noun* [C] someone who has been persuaded to change to a different religion or belief *a Catholic convert*

**convertible¹** /kən'vɜːtⁿbl/ *adj* able to be converted

**convertible²** /kən'vɜːtⁿbl/ *noun* [C] a car with a folding roof

**convex** /kɒn'veks/ *adj* A convex surface curves out. *a convex mirror/lens*

**convey** /kən'veɪ/ *verb* [T] **1** to communicate information, feelings, or images to someone *She always conveys a sense of enthusiasm for her work.* **2** to transport something or someone to a particular place

**conveyor belt** /kən'veɪəˌbelt/ *noun* [C] a continuous moving piece of rubber or metal used to transport objects from one place to another

**convict¹** /kən'vɪkt/ *verb* [T] to decide officially in a court of law that someone is guilty of a particular crime [often passive] *He was convicted of murder.* • *a convicted criminal*

**convict²** /'kɒnvɪkt/ *noun* [C] someone who is in

prison because they are guilty of a particular crime

**conviction** /kən'vɪkʃⁿn/ *noun* **1** [C] when someone is officially found to be guilty of a particular crime *He already had two convictions for burglary.* **2** [C, U] a strong opinion or belief *religious/moral convictions*

○━**convince** /kən'vɪns/ *verb* [T] **1** to make someone believe that something is true [+ that] *He tried to convince me that I needed a new car.* • *She convinced the jury of her innocence.* **2** to persuade someone to do something [+ to do sth] *I convinced her to go to the doctor's.*

**convinced** /kən'vɪnst/ *adj* completely certain about something [+ (that)] *I'm convinced that he's made a mistake.*

**convincing** /kən'vɪnsɪŋ/ *adj* **1** able to make you believe that something is true or right *a convincing argument* **2 a convincing win/victory** a win or victory where the person or team that wins is much better than the people they are competing against • **convincingly** *adv*

**convoluted** /'kɒnvəluːtɪd/ *adj* *formal* extremely complicated and difficult to understand *a convoluted argument/story*

**convoy** /'kɒnvɔɪ/ *noun* [C] a group of vehicles or ships that travel together

**convulsion** /kən'vʌlʃⁿn/ *noun* [C] a sudden uncontrollable movement of muscles in your body, caused by illness or drugs [usually plural] *The venom causes fever and convulsions.*

**coo** /kuː/ *verb* [I] **cooing,** *past* **cooed 1** to make a soft, low sound, like a pigeon (= large, grey bird) **2** to speak in a soft, low voice

○━**cook¹** /kʊk/ *verb* **1** [I, T] to prepare food and usually heat it *Who's cooking this evening?* • *She cooked the meat in oil and spices.* **2** [I] If food cooks, it is heated until it is ready to eat. *The rice is cooking.* • **cooked** *adj* not raw

**cook sth up** *informal* to invent a story, plan, etc, usually dishonestly *He arrived late and cooked up some excuse about the bus being late.*

**cook**

bake / fry / boil / grill / roast

**cook²** /kʊk/ *noun* [C] someone who prepares and cooks food

**cookbook** /'kʊkbʊk/ (*also UK* **cookery book**) *noun* [C] a book containing instructions for preparing food

**cooker** /'kukə'/ *UK* (*UK/US* **stove**) *noun* [C] a piece of equipment used to cook food *an electric cooker* ➜ *See also:* **pressure cooker**.

**cookery** /'kuk°ri/ *noun* [U] *UK* preparing or cooking food

'**cookery ,book** *UK* (*UK/US* **cookbook**) *noun* [C] a book containing instructions for preparing food

**cookie** /'kuki/ *US* (*also UK* **biscuit**) *noun* [C] a thin, flat cake that is dry and usually sweet ➜ *See colour picture* **Food** *on page Centre 7*.

O─**cooking** /'kukɪŋ/ *noun* [U] **1** preparing or cooking food *I do most of the cooking.* **2** a style of preparing food *vegetarian/French cooking* • cooking *adj* [always before noun] suitable to cook with *cooking oil/apples*

O─**cool¹** /ku:l/ *adj* **1** COLD slightly cold, but not too cold *a cool breeze/day* • *cool water* **2** GOOD *informal* good, stylish, or fashionable *He looks really cool in those sunglasses.* **3** CALM calm and not emotional *She seemed cool and confident.* **4** UNFRIENDLY unfriendly • coolness *noun* [U]

**cool²** /ku:l/ *verb* [I, T] **1** to become less hot, or make something become less hot *Allow the bread to cool before slicing it.* **2** If emotions or relationships cool, or if something cools them, they become less strong.

**cool (sb/sth) down/off 1** to become less hot, or to make someone or something become less hot *We went for a swim to cool off.* **2** To become calmer, or to make someone become calmer *Leave her to cool off and then talk to her.*

**cool³** /ku:l/ *noun* **1 the cool** a cool temperature *the cool of the early morning* **2 keep your cool** to remain calm **3 lose your cool** to suddenly become very angry

**cool⁴** /ku:l/ *exclamation informal* used when you like something or agree to something

**coolly** /'ku:lli/ *adv* without showing emotion or interest *Her colleagues reacted coolly to the idea.*

**coop¹** /ku:p/ *noun* [C] a cage for birds such as chickens

**coop²** /ku:p/ *verb*
**coop sb up** to keep a person or animal in a small area [often passive] *We've been cooped up in a plane all day.*

**co-op** /'kəʊɒp/ *noun* [C] *informal short for* cooperative²

**cooperate** (*also UK* **co-operate**) /kəʊ'ɒp°reɪt/ *verb* [I] **1** to work together with someone in order to achieve the same aim *Witnesses are cooperating with detectives.* • *Several countries are cooperating in the relief effort.* **2** to help someone or do what they ask *We can get there early as long as the children will cooperate.*

**cooperation** (*also UK* **co-operation**) /kəʊˌɒp°'reɪʃ°n/ *noun* [U] when you work together with someone or do what they ask you *international cooperation* • *The clubs work in close cooperation with the Football Association.*

**cooperative¹** (*also UK* **co-operative**) /kəʊ'ɒp°rətɪv/ *adj* **1** willing to help or do what people ask *a cooperative and polite employee* **2** involving people working together to achieve the same aim *a cooperative relationship* • cooperatively *adv*

**cooperative²** (*also UK* **co-operative**) /kəʊ'ɒp°rətɪv/ *noun* [C] a business or organization owned and managed by the people who work in it

**coordinate** (*also UK* **co-ordinate**) /kəʊ'ɔːdɪneɪt/ *verb* [T] to make different people or things work together effectively, or to organize all the different parts of an activity *My manager is coordinating the new project.*

**coordination** (*also UK* **co-ordination**) /kəʊˌɔːdɪ'neɪʃ°n/ *noun* [U] **1** when you organize the different parts of an activity or make people or things work together effectively *The President called for closer coordination between business and government.* **2** the ability to make different parts of your body move together in a controlled way *Dancing helps develop balance and coordination.*

**coordinator** (*also UK* **co-ordinator**) /kəʊ'ɔːdɪneɪtə'/ *noun* [C] someone who organizes the different parts of an activity or makes people or things work together effectively

**cop** /kɒp/ *noun* [C] *mainly US informal* a police officer

O─**cope** /kəʊp/ *verb* [I] to deal quite successfully with a difficult situation *How do you cope with stress?*

**copier** /'kɒpiə'/ *mainly US* (*UK/US* **photocopier**) *noun* [C] a machine which produces copies of documents by photographing them

**copious** /'kəʊpiəs/ *adj* [always before noun] in large amounts *They drank copious amounts of wine.* • copiously *adv*

**copper** /'kɒpə'/ *noun* **1** METAL [U] a soft, red-brown metal, used in electrical equipment and to make coins, etc *copper wire* **2** MONEY [C] *UK* a brown coin with a low value **3** POLICE [C] *UK informal* a police officer

O─**copy¹** /'kɒpi/ *noun* [C] **1** something that is made to look exactly like something else *Always make copies of important documents.* **2** a single book, newspaper, etc of which many have been produced *a copy of the New York Times* • *Four million copies of the book were sold in the first year.* ➜ *See also:* **carbon copy**.

O─**copy²** /'kɒpi/ *verb* **1** PRODUCE [T] to produce something that is similar or exactly the same as something else *Copy the file onto disk.* • *The design was copied from the American model.* **2** BEHAVE [T] to behave like someone else *He likes to copy his older brother.* **3** CHEAT [I, T] to cheat by looking at and using someone else's work *She copied his answers.*
**copy sth out** *UK* If you copy out a piece of writing, you write it again on a piece of paper.

**copyright** /'kɒpiraɪt/ *noun* [C, U] the legal right to control the use of an original piece of work such as a book, play, or song *The book is protected by copyright.*

**coral** /'kɒrəl/ *noun* [U] a hard, usually pink or white substance produced by a type of very small sea animal *a coral reef*

**cord** /kɔːd/ *noun* [C, U] **1** thick string, or a piece of this **2** (*also UK* **flex**) a piece of wire covered in plastic, used to connect electrical equipment to a power supply *an electrical cord* • *a telephone cord* ➜ *See also:* **umbilical cord**.

C

**cordial** /ˈkɔːdiəl/ *adj* polite and friendly *a cordial invitation* • **cordially** *adv*

**cordless** /ˈkɔːdləs/ *adj* able to operate without an electrical cord *a cordless phone*

**cordon¹** /ˈkɔːdᵊn/ *noun* [C] a line of police, soldiers, vehicles, etc around an area, protecting it or keeping people out

**cordon²** /ˈkɔːdᵊn/ *verb*

**cordon sth off** If the police, army, etc cordon off an area, they stop people from entering it.

**cords** /kɔːdz/ *noun* [plural] *informal* trousers made from corduroy

**corduroy** /ˈkɔːdərɔɪ/ *noun* [U] thick, cotton cloth with raised parallel lines on the outside *a corduroy jacket*

**core** /kɔːʳ/ *noun* **1** IMPORTANT PART [no plural] the most important part of a system or principle *core values* • *Better health care was **at the core of** the senator's campaign.* **2** FRUIT [C] the hard, central part of certain fruits, such as apples, which contains the seeds **3** PLANET [no plural] the centre of a planet *the Earth's core* ➲ *See also:* **hard core**.

**coriander** /ˌkɒriˈændəʳ/ (*also US* **cilantro**) *noun* [U] a herb that is used in cooking

**cork** /kɔːk/ *noun* **1** [U] a light material obtained from the bark (= outer layer) of a particular type of tree **2** [C] a small cylindrical piece of this material put in the top of a bottle, especially a wine bottle, to close it

**corkscrew** /ˈkɔːkskruː/ *noun* [C] a piece of equipment used for pulling corks out of wine bottles

**corn** /kɔːn/ *noun* [U] **1** *mainly UK* a crop of grain, or the seed from this crop used to make flour or feed animals *fields of corn* **2** *US* (*UK* **sweetcorn**) a tall plant with yellow seeds that are cooked and eaten as a vegetable ➲ *See colour picture* **Fruit and Vegetables** *on page Centre 8.*

**corner¹** /ˈkɔːnəʳ/ *noun* [C] **1** POINT the point or area where two lines, walls, or roads meet *the corner of the table* • *There was a television **in the corner** of the room.* • *The pub is **on/at the corner** of Ross Street and Mill Road.* • *Write your name in the top right-hand corner of the answer sheet.* **2** PLACE a part of a larger area, often somewhere quiet or far away *He lives in a beautiful corner of northern California.* **3** FOOTBALL a kick or hit taken from the corner of the field in some games, especially football **4 from/out of the corner of your eye** If you see something out of the corner of your eye, you just see it, but do not look at it directly. **5 around/round the corner** going to happen soon *Christmas is round the corner and I still haven't bought any presents.* **6 cut corners** to do something in the quickest or cheapest way, often harming the quality of your work

**corner²** /ˈkɔːnəʳ/ *verb* **1** [T] to force a person or animal into a situation or place from which it is hard to escape *His attackers cornered him in a dark alley.* **2 corner the market** to become so successful at selling or making a particular product that almost no one else sells or makes it

**cornerstone** /ˈkɔːnəstəʊn/ *noun* [C] something very important that something else depends on *Freedom of speech is the cornerstone of democracy.*

**cornflakes** /ˈkɔːnfleɪks/ *noun* [plural] a food made from corn (= grain) and eaten with milk for breakfast (= morning meal)

**corny** /ˈkɔːni/ *adj informal* repeated too often to be interesting or funny *a corny joke/film*

**coronary¹** /ˈkɒrənᵊri/ *adj* relating to the heart *coronary heart disease*

**coronary²** /ˈkɒrənᵊri/ *noun* [C] a heart attack (= when the heart stops working normally)

**coronation** /ˌkɒrəˈneɪʃᵊn/ *noun* [C] a ceremony at which someone is officially made king or queen

**coroner** /ˈkɒrənəʳ/ *noun* [C] an official who examines the causes of someone's death, usually if it was violent or sudden

**Corp** *noun* [C] *written abbreviation for* corporation (= used after the name of a large company in the United States)

**corporal** /ˈkɔːpᵊrᵊl/ *noun* [C] a soldier of low rank in the army or air force

**ˌcorporal ˈpunishment** *noun* [U] physical punishment, especially of children, usually by hitting with the hand or a stick

**corporate** /ˈkɔːpᵊrət/ *adj* [always before noun] relating to a large company or group *corporate finance*

**corporation** /ˌkɔːpᵊrˈeɪʃᵊn/ *noun* [C] a large company or group of companies

**corps** /kɔːʳ/ *noun* [C] *plural* **corps 1** a group of people involved in the same job *the press/diplomatic corps* **2** a special part of a military force *the Air Corps*

**corpse** /kɔːps/ *noun* [C] a dead person's body

**correct¹** /kəˈrekt/ *adj* **1** accurate, or having no mistakes *Check that you have the correct information.* • *Was that the correct answer?* **2** suitable for a particular situation *correct behaviour* • *Have you got the correct number of players for the match?* • **correctly** *adv* • **correctness** *noun* [U] ➲ *See also:* **politically correct**.

**USAGE**

**correct** or **right?**

**Correct** means 'accurate' or 'without mistakes'.

*All the details were correct.*

**Right** is another word for 'correct'. It also means 'suitable' or 'morally acceptable'.

*Be careful to choose the right word.*

*I don't think it's right for parents to hit their children.*

Remember that **correct** does not mean 'good'.

*The hotel was cheap but good.*

~~*The hotel was cheap but correct.*~~

**correct²** /kəˈrekt/ *verb* [T] **1** MAKE RIGHT to make a mistake or problem right or better *The new software finds and corrects any errors on the hard disk.* **2** IMPROVE to improve the quality of something *These contact lenses will help to correct your vision.* **3** SHOW MISTAKE to show someone the mistakes in something they have said or written *Our teacher normally corrects our pronunciation.*

**correction** /kəˈrekʃᵊn/ *noun* [C, U] a change to

make something right or better, or when you make such a change *She made some corrections before handing in the essay.*

**corrective** /kə'rektɪv/ *adj formal* intended to improve or correct something *corrective surgery/lenses*

**correlate** /'kɒrəleɪt/ *verb* [I, T] If facts or pieces of information correlate, they are connected to each other and influence each other, and if you correlate them, you show their connections.

**correlation** /,kɒrə'leɪʃᵊn/ *noun* [C] a connection between two or more things, usually where one causes or influences the other *The research showed a close **correlation between** smoking and lung cancer.*

**correspond** /,kɒrɪ'spɒnd/ *verb* [I] **1** to be the same or very similar *The newspaper story does not **correspond with/to** what really happened.* **2** to communicate with someone by writing letters

**correspondence** /,kɒrɪ'spɒndəns/ *noun* **1** [U] letters from one person to another, or the activity of writing and receiving letters *business correspondence* **2** [C, U] when there is a connection or similarity between two or more things

**correspondent** /,kɒrɪ'spɒndᵊnt/ *noun* [C] **1** someone who reports news for newspapers, television, or radio, usually from another country *a correspondent for the New York Times* **2** someone who writes letters, usually regularly

**corresponding** /,kɒrɪ'spɒndɪŋ/ *adj* [always before noun] similar or related *Draw a line between the words with corresponding meanings.*

**corridor** /'kɒrɪdɔːʳ/ *noun* [C] a passage in a building or train with rooms on one or both sides

**corroborate** /kə'rɒbᵊreɪt/ *verb* [T] *formal* to say something or provide information that supports what someone says *A witness corroborated his account of the accident.* ● **corroboration** /kə,rɒbə'reɪʃᵊn/ *noun* [U]

**corrode** /kə'rəʊd/ *verb* **1** [I, T] If metal corrodes, or rain or chemicals corrode it, it is slowly damaged by them. *Rain corroded the metal pipes.* **2** [T] to slowly damage someone or something *He was corroded by guilt.* ● **corrosion** /kə'rəʊʒᵊn/ *noun* [U] ● **corrosive** /kə'rəʊsɪv/ *adj Acid rain is highly corrosive.*

**corrugated** /'kɒrəgeɪtɪd/ *adj* [always before noun] Corrugated metal or cardboard has parallel rows of folds that look like waves. *a corrugated iron roof*

o—ₐ**corrupt¹** /kə'rʌpt/ *adj* **1** dishonest or illegal *a corrupt government* **2** If information on a computer is corrupt, it has been damaged or spoiled. *corrupt files*

**corrupt²** /kə'rʌpt/ *verb* [T] **1** to make someone or something become dishonest or immoral [often passive] *He became corrupted by power and money.* **2** to damage information on a computer

**corruption** /kə'rʌpʃᵊn/ *noun* [U] **1** dishonest or immoral behaviour, usually by people in positions of power *He was arrested for corruption and bribery.* **2** when you cause someone or something to become dishonest or immoral *the corruption of innocent young children*

**corset** /'kɔːsət/ *noun* [C] a tight piece of under-wear worn by women to make themselves look thinner, especially in the past

**cosmetic** /kɒz'metɪk/ *adj* **1** intended to improve your appearance *cosmetic surgery* **2** involving only small changes or improvements that will not solve a problem *Critics claimed that the changes were only cosmetic.*

**cosmetics** /kɒz'metɪks/ *noun* [plural] substances that you put on your face or body to improve your appearance

**cosmic** /'kɒzmɪk/ *adj* relating to the whole universe *cosmic rays*

**cosmopolitan** /,kɒzmə'pɒlɪtᵊn/ *adj* **1** consisting of people and things from many different countries *London is a very cosmopolitan city.* **2** having experience of many different countries or cultures *a dynamic, cosmopolitan businesswoman*

**the cosmos** /'kɒzmɒs/ *noun* the whole universe

o—ₐ**cost¹** /kɒst/ *noun* **1** [C, U] the amount of money that you need to buy or do something *The cruise ship was built at a cost of $400 million.* ● *Software is included at no extra cost.* ● *The cost of living* (= the cost of food, clothes, etc) *has increased.* **2** [no plural] something that you give or lose, in order to get or achieve something else *He rescued four people at the cost of his own life.* **3 at all costs** If something must be done at all costs, it is very important that it is done. *We have to succeed at all costs.* **4 to your cost** UK because of a bad experience you have had *An ankle injury can last a long time, as I know to my cost.*

o—ₐ**cost²** /kɒst/ *verb past* **cost 1** [T] If something costs a particular amount of money, you have to pay that in order to buy or do it. *How much do these shoes cost?* ● [+ to do sth] *It costs $5 to send the package by airmail.* ● [+ two objects] *It's going to cost me a lot of money to buy a new car.* **2** [+ two objects] to make someone lose something *His lazy attitude cost him his job.*

**cost³** /kɒst/ *verb* [T] to calculate the amount of money needed to do or make something *The building work has been costed at $30,000.*

**co-star¹** /'kəʊstɑːʳ/ *noun* [C] one of two famous actors who both have important parts in a particular film

**co-star²** /kəʊ'stɑːʳ US 'kəʊstɑːr/ *verb* **co-starring**, *past* **co-starred 1** [T] If a film, play, etc co-stars two or more famous actors, they are in it. **2** [I] to be in a film, play, etc with another famous actor *Hugh Grant co-stars with Julia Roberts in 'Notting Hill'.*

**costly** /'kɒstli/ *adj* **1** expensive [+ to do sth] *It would be too costly to build a swimming pool.* **2** causing a lot of problems, or causing you to lose something important *a costly mistake*

**costume** /'kɒstjuːm/ *noun* **1** [C, U] a set of clothes that someone wears to make them look like someone or something else, for example in a play *actors in costume* ● *He arrived at the party dressed in a gorilla costume.* **2** [U] a set of clothes that are typical of a particular country or time in history *Japanese national costume*. ➋ *See also:* **swimming costume**.

**cosy** UK (US **cozy**) /'kəʊzi/ *adj* comfortable and warm

**cot** /kɒt/ *UK (US crib) noun* [C] a bed with high sides for a baby

**cottage** /ˈkɒtɪdʒ/ *noun* [C] a small house, usually in the countryside

**cottage 'cheese** *noun* [U] a soft, white cheese with small lumps in it

**cotton**[1] /ˈkɒt²n/ *noun* [U] **1** CLOTH cloth or thread that is produced from the cotton plant *a cotton shirt/dress* **2** PLANT a plant that produces a soft, white substance used for making thread and cloth **3** FOR CLEANING *US* (*UK* **cotton wool**) a soft mass of cotton, usually used for cleaning your skin

**cotton 'wool** *UK (US* **cotton***) noun* [U] a soft mass of cotton, usually used for cleaning your skin ➔ *See colour picture* **The Bathroom** *on page Centre 1.*

**couch**[1] /kaʊtʃ/ *noun* [C] a long, comfortable piece of furniture that two or more people can sit on

**couch**[2] /kaʊtʃ/ *verb* **be couched in/as sth** to be expressed in a particular way *His explanation was couched in technical language.*

**'couch po,tato** *noun* [C] *UK humorous* a person who is not active and spends a lot of time watching television

o┅**cough**[1] /kɒf/ *verb* [I] to make air come out of your throat with a short sound *Paul has been coughing and sneezing all day.*

**cough sth up** to make something come out of your lungs or throat by coughing *Doctors were worried when she started coughing up blood.*

**cough (sth) up** *informal* to give money to someone although you do not want to *It's your turn to buy the drinks – come on, cough up!*

**cough**[2] /kɒf/ *noun* [C] **1** when you cough, or the sound this makes **2** an illness that makes you cough a lot *Uwe has a nasty cough.* ➔ *See also:* **whooping cough.**

o┅**could** *strong form* /kʊd/ *weak form* /kəd/ *modal verb* **1** CAN used as the past form of 'can' to talk about what someone or something was able or allowed to do *I couldn't see what he was doing.* ● *You said we could watch television when we'd finished our homework.* **2** POSSIBLE used to talk about what is possible or might happen *The baby could arrive any day now.* ● *This kind of crime could easily be prevented.* ● *She could have* (= might have) *been seriously injured.* **3** ASK used to ask someone politely to do or provide something *Could you lend me £5?* ● *Could I have another drink?* **4** ASK PERMISSION used to ask politely for permission to do something *Could I speak to Mr Davis, please?* **5** SUGGEST used to make a suggestion *You could try painting it a different colour.* **6 I could (have)** used when you feel so happy, sad, angry, etc that you would like to do something *I was so grateful I could have kissed her!* ➔ *See study section* **Modal verbs** *on page Centre 31.*

**couldn't** /ˈkʊd²nt/ *short for* could not *I couldn't understand what he was saying.*

**could've** /ˈkʊdəv/ *short for* could have *It could've been much worse.*

**council, Council** /ˈkaʊns²l/ *noun* [C] **1** a group of people who are elected to control a town, city, or area *Edinburgh City Council* ● *a council meeting* **2** a group of people who are elected or

chosen to give advice or make decisions *the Medical Research Council* **3 a council house/ flat** in the UK a house or flat that is owned by a city or town council and rented to people

**councillor** *UK (US* **councilor***) /ˈkaʊns²lər/ *noun* [C] a member of a town, city, or area council

**counsel**[1] /ˈkaʊns²l/ *noun* **1** [C] a lawyer (= someone who advises people about the law and deals with legal situations) who speaks for someone in court **2** [U] *literary* advice

**counsel**[2] /ˈkaʊns²l/ *verb* [T] *UK* **counselling**, *past* **counselled**, *US* **counseling**, *past* **counseled** **1** *formal* to advise someone to do something [+ to do sth] *Lawyers had counselled him not to say anything.* **2** to give advice to someone who has problems

**counselling** *UK (US* **counseling***) /ˈkaʊnsəlɪŋ/ *noun* [U] the job or process of listening to someone and giving them advice about their problems *a counselling service*

**counsellor** *UK (US* **counselor***) /ˈkaʊnsələr/ *noun* [C] someone whose job is to listen to people and give them advice about their problems

o┅**count**[1] /kaʊnt/ *verb* **1** CALCULATE [T] to see how many people or things there are *She began to count the students to make sure everyone was there.* ● *I counted the money on the table.* **2** SAY NUMBERS [I] to say numbers in their correct order *Can you count to twenty in French?* **3** CONSIDER [T] to think of someone or something in a particular way *She counted Tim as her closest friend.* ● *You should count yourself lucky you weren't hurt.* **4** IMPORTANT [I] to be important *I believe that health and happiness count more than money.* ● *Doesn't my opinion count for anything?* **5** INCLUDE [T] to include something or someone in a calculation *There are 1500 people at my school, counting teachers.* **6** BE ACCEPTED [I] to be accepted or allowed as part of something *I've been to sixteen different countries, but I only spent half an hour in Luxembourg, so that doesn't really count.*

**count against sb/sth** to make someone or something more likely to fail *She's got the qualifications for the job, but her lack of experience will count against her.*

**count sb in** to include someone in an activity *If you're going for a pizza, you can count me in.*

**count on sb** to be confident that you can depend on someone *I can always count on my parents to help me.*

**count on sth** to expect something to happen and make plans based on it *I didn't count on so many people coming to the party.*

**count sth out** to count coins or pieces of paper money one by one as you put them down *She counted out five crisp $20 bills.*

**count sb out** to not include someone in an activity

**count towards sth** to be part of what is needed to complete something or achieve something *This essay counts towards my exam result.*

**count up sb/sth** to add together all the people or things in a group

**count**[2] /kaʊnt/ *noun* **1** NUMBER [C] when you count something, or the total number you get after counting [usually singular] *At the last count* *there were 410 club members.* **2 lose count** to forget how many of something there is *I've **lost count of** the number of times she's arrived late.* **3 on all/both/several, etc counts** in all, both, several, etc parts of a situation, argument, etc *I had been wrong **on both counts.*** **4** RANK [C] (*also* **Count**) a man of high social rank in some European countries **5** CRIME [C] one of the times that someone has been accused of a particular crime *He was charged with two counts of assault.* ➔ *See also:* **pollen count.**

**countable noun** /ˌkaʊntəbᵊlˈnaʊn/ (*also* **'count ˌnoun**) *noun* [C] a noun that has both plural and singular forms ➔ *See study section* **Countable and uncountable nouns** *on page Centre 22.*

**countdown** /ˈkaʊntdaʊn/ *noun* [C] the time just before an important event when people are counting the time until it happens [usually singular] *The **countdown** to the Olympics has begun.*

**countenance¹** /ˈkaʊntᵊnəns/ *noun* [C] *literary* the appearance or expression of someone's face

**countenance²** /ˈkaʊntᵊnəns/ *verb* [T] to accept that something should happen *They will not countenance building a new airport.*

**counter¹** /ˈkaʊntər/ *noun* [C] **1** IN A SHOP the place in a shop, bank, etc, where people are served *The woman behind the counter took his money.* **2** SURFACE *US* a flat surface in a kitchen on which food can be prepared **3** DISC a small disc used in some games that are played on a board

**counter²** /ˈkaʊntər/ *verb* [T] **1** to prevent something or reduce the bad effect that it has *This skin cream claims to counter the effects of sun damage.* **2** to say something to show that what someone has just said is not true *"Of course I love him," Clare countered.*

**counter³** /ˈkaʊntər/ *adv* **be/run counter to sth** to have the opposite effect to something else *The new road plans run counter to the government's aim of reducing pollution.*

**counteract** /ˌkaʊntᵊrˈækt/ *verb* [T] to reduce the bad effect that something else has *drugs that counteract the side effects of sea sickness*

**counter-attack** /ˈkaʊntərəˌtæk/ *noun* [C] an attack that you make against someone who has attacked you in a sport, war, or argument
• counter-attack *verb* [I, T]

**counterclockwise** /ˌkaʊntəˈklɒkwaɪz/ *US* (*UK* **anti-clockwise**) *adj, adv* in the opposite direction to the way the hands (= parts that point to the numbers) of a clock move ➔ *See picture at* **clockwise.**

**counterfeit** /ˈkaʊntəfɪt/ *adj* made to look like the real thing, in order to trick people *counterfeit money/jewellery*

**counterpart** /ˈkaʊntəpɑːt/ *noun* [C] someone or something that has the same job or position as someone or something in a different place or organization

**counterproductive** /ˌkaʊntəprəˈdʌktɪv/ *adj* having the opposite effect from the one you want

**countess** /ˈkaʊntɪs/ *noun* [C] a woman who has a high social rank in some European countries, especially the wife of an earl or count (= man of high social rank) *the Countess of Abingdon*

**countless** /ˈkaʊntləs/ *adj* [always before noun] very many *The song has been played countless times on the radio.*

○━**country¹** /ˈkʌntri/ *noun* **1** [C] an area of land that has its own government, army, etc *European countries* **2 the country a** the areas that are away from towns and cities **b** the people who live in a country *The country was shocked by the President's decision.*

**USAGE**

**country, land, nation,** or **state?**

**Country** is the most general word which means 'an area of land'. It usually means an area of land with its own government and people.

*China, Japan, and other countries in Asia*

**Nation** is used to talk about a country, especially when you mean the people or the culture of that country.

*The nation celebrated the 100th anniversary of independence.*

**State** is used to talk about a country as a political or official area. Some countries are divided into political units that are also called **states.**

*Belgium became an independent state in 1830.*

*America is divided into 50 states.*

*the State of Florida*

**Land** means an area of ground, not an area with its own government.

*We bought some land to build a house on.*

**country²** /ˈkʌntri/ *adj* [always before noun] in or relating to the areas that are away from towns and cities *country roads/hotels*

**countryman** /ˈkʌntrimən/ *noun* [C] *plural* **countrymen** someone from the same country as you

**ˌcountry 'music** (*also* ˌcountry and 'western) *noun* [U] a style of popular music from the southern and western US

○━**countryside** /ˈkʌntrɪsaɪd/ *noun* [U] land that is not in towns or cities and has farms, fields, forests, etc ➔ *See usage note at* **nature.**

**county** /ˈkaʊnti/ *noun* [C] an area of Britain, Ireland, or the US that has its own local government

**coup** /kuː/ *noun* [C] **1** (*also* **coup d'état** /ˌkuːdeɪˈtɑː/) when a group of people suddenly takes control of a country using force *a military coup* **2** an important achievement, often one that was not expected *The award is a major coup for the university.*

○━**couple¹** /ˈkʌpl/ *noun* **1** [no plural] two or a few *I went to New York with **a couple of** friends.*
• *The weather has improved over the last couple of weeks.* **2** [C] two people who are married or having a romantic relationship *a married couple*

**couple²** /ˈkʌpl/ *verb* **coupled with sth** combined with something else *Concern about farming methods, coupled with health awareness, have led to a fall in meat consumption.*

**coupon** /ˈkuːpɒn/ *noun* [C] **1** a piece of printed paper that you can use to buy something at a cheaper price or to get something free *Collect 10 coupons to get a free meal.* **2** a printed form in a magazine or newspaper, that you use to send for information, enter a competition, etc

**courage** /'kʌrɪdʒ/ *noun* [U] **1** the ability to deal with dangerous or difficult situations without being frightened *The soldiers fought with great courage.* • [+ to do sth] *She didn't have the courage to tell him the truth.* **2 pluck up the courage (to do sth)** to decide to do something that you were too frightened to do before *Gerhard finally plucked up the courage to ask Nicole for a date.*

**courageous** /kə'reɪdʒəs/ *adj* brave • **courageously** *adv*

**courgette** /kɔː'ʒet/ *UK* (*US* **zucchini**) *noun* [C, U] a long, green vegetable which is white inside

**courier** /'kʊriəʳ/ *noun* [C] **1** someone whose job is to take and deliver documents and parcels **2** *UK* someone whose job is to look after people who are on holiday

○⚹**course** /kɔːs/ *noun* **1 of course a** used to say 'yes' and emphasize your answer *"Can you help me?" "Of course!"* **b** used to show that what you are saying is obvious or already known *The rain meant, of course, that the barbecue was cancelled.* • *Of course, the Olympics are not just about money.* **2 of course not** used to say 'no' and emphasize your answer *"Do you mind if I borrow your pen?" "Of course not."* **3** LESSONS [C] a series of lessons about a particular subject *She did a ten-week course in computing.* **4** PART OF MEAL [C] a part of a meal *a three-course dinner* **5** SPORT [C] an area used for horse races or playing golf *a golf course* **6** MEDICINE [C] *mainly UK* a fixed number of regular medical treatments *a course of antibiotics* **7** ROUTE [C, U] the direction in which a ship, aircraft, etc is moving *During the storm, the boat was blown off course* (= in the wrong direction). **8** ACTION [C] (*also* **course of** '**action**) something that you can do in a particular situation *I think the best course of action would be to write to him.* **9 during/in/over the course of sth** during a particular time or activity *In the course of the interview she mentioned her previous experience.* **10 in due course** at a suitable time in the future *The results will be sent to you in due course.* **11** DEVELOPMENT [no plural] the way something develops, usually over a long time *Nuclear weapons have changed the course of modern history.* **12 in the course of time** *UK* gradually, or over a period of time *His English will improve in the course of time.* **13 be on course for sth/to do sth** *UK* to be very likely to succeed at something **14 run its course** If something runs its course, it continues naturally until it has finished. ⊃ *See also:* be on a **collision** course, **crash course**, be **par** for the course.

**coursebook** /'kɔːsbʊk/ *noun* [C] *UK* a book used by students when they do a particular course of study

**coursework** /'kɔːswɜːk/ *noun* [U] *UK* work done by students as part of their course of study

○⚹**court¹** /kɔːt/ *noun* [C, U] **1** LAW the place where a judge decides whether someone is guilty of a crime *The suspect appeared in court charged with robbery.* • *You can take them to court* (= make them be judged in court) *if they don't pay.* **2 the court** the judge and group of people at a trial who decide whether someone is guilty of a crime *She told the court what happened on the night of the murder.* **3** SPORT an area for playing particular sports *a tennis/basketball court* **4** ROYAL HOUSE the official home of a king or queen and the people who live with them ⊃ *See also:* **High Court**, **the supreme court**.

**court²** /kɔːt/ *verb* **1** PLEASE [T] to try to please someone because you want them to support you or join you *Adams is being courted by several football clubs.* **2** TRY TO GET [T] to try to get or achieve something *to court investment/publicity* **3** RELATIONSHIP [I, T] *old-fashioned* to have a romantic relationship with someone you hope to marry *They courted for two years before getting married.* **4 court controversy/danger/disaster, etc** to behave in a way that risks bad results

**courteous** /'kɜːtiəs/ *adj* polite and showing respect • **courteously** *adv*

**courtesy** /'kɜːtəsi/ *noun* **1** [U] behaviour that is polite and shows respect, or a polite action or remark *The hotel treats all guests with courtesy.* • [+ to do sth] *He didn't even have the courtesy to thank me.* **2 (by) courtesy of sb/sth** If you have something courtesy of someone, they have allowed you to have it. *The photograph is courtesy of the Natural History Museum.*

**courthouse** /'kɔːthaʊs/ *noun* [C] *plural* **courthouses** /'kɔːthaʊzɪz/ *mainly US* a building with law courts inside it

**courtier** /'kɔːtiəʳ/ *noun* [C] someone who spent a lot of time in the home of a king or queen in the past

**court-martial¹** /ˌkɔːt'mɑːʃəl/ *noun* [C] a military court, or a trial in a military court

**court-martial²** /ˌkɔːt'mɑːʃəl/ *verb* [T] to judge someone in a military court

**courtroom** /'kɔːtrʊm/ *noun* [C] the room where a judge and other people decide whether someone is guilty of a crime

**courtship** /'kɔːtʃɪp/ *noun* [C, U] *formal* the time when people have a romantic relationship with the intention of getting married

**courtyard** /'kɔːtjɑːd/ *noun* [C] an open area by a building with walls or buildings around it

○⚹**cousin** /'kʌzⁿn/ *noun* [C] the child of your aunt or uncle

**couture** /kuː'tjʊəʳ/ *noun* [U] the design, making, and selling of expensive and fashionable clothes

**cove** /kəʊv/ *noun* [C] a place on the coast where the land curves in

**covenant** /'kʌvⁿnənt/ *noun* [C] a formal written agreement

○⚹**cover¹** /'kʌvəʳ/ *verb* [T] **1** PUT to put something over something else, in order to protect or hide it *They covered him with a blanket.* • *He covered his face with his hands.* ⊃ *Opposite* **uncover**. **2** LAYER to form a layer on the surface of something *Snow covered the trees.* • *My legs were covered in/with mud.* **3** DISTANCE to travel a particular distance *We covered 700 kilometres* *in four days.* **4** AREA to be a particular size or area *The town covers an area of 10 square miles.* **5** INCLUDE to include or deal with a subject or piece of information *The book covers European history from 1789–1914.* **6** REPORT to report on an event for a newspaper, television programme, etc *Dave was asked to cover the Olympics.* **7** MONEY to be enough money to pay for something *£100 should cover the cost of the repairs.* **8** FINANCIAL PROTECTION to provide financial protection if something bad happens *travel insurance that covers accident and injury* ➜ *See also:* cover all the bases (**base¹**)

**cover sth up** to put something over something else, in order to protect or hide it *We used a picture to cover up a hole in the wall.*

**cover (sth) up** to stop people from discovering the truth about something bad *She tried to cover up her mistakes.*

o—**cover²** /'kʌvəʳ/ *noun* **1** BOOK [C] the outer part of a book, magazine, etc, that protects the pages *Her picture was on the cover of 'Vogue' magazine.* **2** PROTECTION [C] something you put over something else, usually to protect it *an ironing board cover* • *a lens cover* **3** FINANCIAL [U] financial protection so that you get money if something bad happens *The policy provides £50,000 accidental damage cover.* **4** FROM WEATHER/ATTACK [U] protection from bad weather or an attack *They took cover under some trees until the rain stopped.* **5** FOR ILLEGAL ACTIVITY [C] something used to hide a secret or illegal activity *The club is used as a cover for a gang of car thieves.*

**coverage** /'kʌvərɪdʒ/ *noun* [U] **1** the way a newspaper, television programme, etc reports an event or subject *There is live coverage of the game on cable TV.* **2** mainly US financial protection so that you get money if something bad happens

**coveralls** /'kʌvərɔːlz/ *US* (*UK* **overalls**) *noun* [plural] a piece of clothing that you wear over your clothes to keep them clean while you are working

**covering** /'kʌvərɪŋ/ *noun* [C] a layer that covers something *a thick covering of snow*

**covering 'letter** *UK* (*US* '**cover** ,**letter**) *noun* [C] a letter that you send with something to explain what it is or to give more information about it

**covers** /'kʌvəz/ *noun* [plural] the sheets and other layers of cloth on your bed that keep you warm

**covert** /'kəʊvɜːt/ *adj* done in a secret way *covert police operations* • *covertly adv*

**cover-up** /'kʌvərʌp/ *noun* [C] an attempt to prevent people finding out the truth about a crime or a mistake *Police denied accusations of a cover-up.*

**covet** /'kʌvɪt/ *verb* [T] *formal* to want something very much, especially something that someone else has

o—**cow** /kaʊ/ *noun* [C] **1** a large farm animal kept for milk or meat **2** *UK informal* an offensive word for a woman

**coward** /kaʊəd/ *noun* [C] someone who is not brave and tries to avoid dangerous or difficult situations

**cowardice** /'kaʊədɪs/ *noun* [U] behaviour that shows that someone is not brave

**cowardly** /'kaʊədli/ *adj* behaving in a way that shows you are not brave

**cowboy** /'kaʊbɔɪ/ *noun* [C] **1** a man whose job is to look after cattle (= animals such as cows) in the US, and who usually rides a horse **2** *UK informal* someone who does their job badly or who is dishonest in business *cowboy builders*

**cower** /kaʊəʳ/ *verb* [I] to bend down or move back because you are frightened

**co-worker** /ˌkəʊˈwɜːkəʳ/ *noun* [C] *mainly US* someone that you work with

**coy** /kɔɪ/ *adj* **1** not wanting to give people information about something *Nigel's very coy about how much he earns.* **2** pretending to be shy *a coy look* • *coyly adv*

**coyote** /kaɪˈəʊti/ *noun* [C] a wild animal similar to a dog, that lives in North America

**cozy** /'kəʊzi/ *adj US spelling of* cosy

**crab** /kræb/ *noun* [C, U] a sea creature with ten legs and a round, flat body covered by a shell, or the meat from this animal

**crack¹** /kræk/ *verb* **1** BREAK [I, T] to break something so that it does not separate, but very thin lines appear on its surface, or to become broken in this way *Linda cracked her tooth when she fell.* • *The concrete had started to crack.* • *cracked dishes* **2** EGG/NUT [T] to open an egg or nut by breaking its shell **3** HIT [T] to hit a part of your body against something hard, by accident *He cracked his head on the cupboard door.* **4** SOLVE [T] *informal* to solve a difficult problem *It took three months to crack the enemy's code.* **5 get cracking** *informal* to start doing something quickly *Let's get cracking! We've only got two days to finish.* **6** LOSE CONTROL [I] to lose control of your emotions and be unable to deal with a situation *He finally cracked after years of stress and long working hours.* **7** NOISE [I, T] to make a sudden, short noise, or to cause something to make this noise **8 crack a joke** to tell a joke **9 not all it's cracked up to be** (*also* **not as good as it's cracked up to be**) *informal* not as good as people think or say *Being an actor isn't all it's cracked up to be.*

**crack down** to start dealing with bad or illegal behaviour in a more severe way *Police are cracking down on crime in the area.*

**crack up** *informal* to become mentally ill

**crack (sb) up** *informal* to suddenly laugh a lot, or to make someone suddenly laugh a lot *I just cracked up when I saw her in that hat.*

**crack²** /kræk/ *noun* **1** LINE [C] a line on the surface of something that is damaged *Several cups had cracks in them.* **2** NARROW SPACE [C] a narrow space between two parts of something or between two things *I could see sunlight through a crack in the curtains.* **3** DRUG [U] an illegal drug that is very harmful **4** NOISE [C] a sudden, short noise *a crack of thunder* **5** JOKE [C] an unkind joke or remark *He was always making cracks about my weight.* **6 have/take a crack at sth** *informal* to try to do something *I've never put up shelves before, but I'll have a crack at it.* **7 the crack of dawn** very early in the morning *He gets up at the crack of dawn.*

**crack³** /kræk/ *adj* [always before noun] of the highest quality *a crack regiment*

**crackdown** /'krækdaʊn/ *noun* [C] when bad or illegal behaviour is dealt with in a very severe way, in order to stop it happening *The police are having a crackdown on speeding.*

**cracker** /'krækəʳ/ *noun* **1** [FOOD] [C] a dry biscuit that you eat with cheese **2** [CHRISTMAS] [C] (*also* **Christmas cracker**) a coloured paper tube with a small toy inside, that people pull open at Christmas (= a Christian holiday) in the UK **3** [GOOD] [no plural] *UK informal* someone or something that is very good

**crackle** /'krækl/ *verb* [I] to make a lot of short, dry noises *A fire crackled in the hearth.* ● **crackle** *noun* [no plural]

**cradle¹** /'kreɪdl/ *noun* **1** [C] a baby's bed, especially one that swings from side to side **2 the cradle of sth** the place where something started *Massachusetts, the cradle of the American Revolution*

**cradle²** /'kreɪdl/ *verb* [T] to hold someone or something in a careful, gentle way *He cradled her in his arms.*

**craft¹** /krɑːft/ *noun* **1** [C, U] an activity in which you make something using a lot of skill, especially with your hands *traditional crafts such as weaving* **2** [C] *plural* **craft** a boat

**craft²** /krɑːft/ *verb* [T] to make something using a lot of skill [often passive] *a bowl that was beautifully crafted from wood*

**craftsman** /'krɑːftsmən/ *noun* [C] *plural* **craftsmen** someone who uses special skill to make things, especially with their hands ● craftsmanship *noun* [U] skill at making things

**crafty** /'krɑːfti/ *adj* clever at getting what you want, especially by deceiving people ● craftily *adv*

**crag** /kræg/ *noun* [C] a high, rough mass of rock that sticks up from the land around it

**cram** /kræm/ *verb* **cramming**, *past* **crammed** **1 cram sth between/in/into, etc** to force things into a small space *The refugees were crammed into the truck.* **2** [I] to study a lot before an exam

**crammed** /kræmd/ *adj* completely full of people or things *crammed commuter trains* ● *The room was crammed with boxes.*

**cramp¹** /kræmp/ *noun* [C, U] a sudden, strong pain in a muscle that makes it difficult to move *I've got cramp in my legs.*

**cramp²** /kræmp/ *verb* ⊃ *See* cramp sb's **style¹**.

**cramped** /kræmpt/ *adj* A cramped room, building, etc is unpleasant because it is not big enough.

**cranberry** /'krænbªri/ *noun* [C] a small, red berry (= soft fruit) with a sour taste

**crane¹** /kreɪn/ *noun* [C] **1** a large machine used for lifting and moving heavy things **2** a bird with long legs and a long neck

**crane²** /kreɪn/ *verb* [I, T] to stretch your neck, in order to see or hear something

**crank** /kræŋk/ *noun* [C] **1** *informal* someone with strange ideas or behaviour **2** a handle that you turn to make a machine work

**cranny** /'kræni/ *noun* ⊃ *See* every **nook** and cranny.

**crap¹** /kræp/ *noun* [U] *very informal* a very impo-lite word for something that you think is wrong or bad *He was talking a lot of crap!*

**crap²** /kræp/ *UK* (*UK/US* **crappy** /'kræpi/) *adj very informal* a very impolite word for describing things that are very bad in quality *a crap car/job*

**crash¹** /kræʃ/ *noun* [C] **1** [VEHICLE] an accident in which a vehicle hits something *a car/plane crash* **2** [NOISE] a sudden, loud noise made when something falls or breaks *I heard a crash and hurried into the kitchen.* **3** [COMPUTER] when a computer or computer system suddenly stops working **4** [BUSINESS] when the value of a country's businesses suddenly falls by a large amount *He lost a lot of money in the stock market crash of 1929.*

**crash²** /kræʃ/ *verb* **1** [VEHICLE] [I, T] If a vehicle crashes, it hits something by accident, and if you crash a vehicle, you make it hit something by accident. *The van skidded and crashed into a tree.* ● *Rick crashed his dad's car.* **2** [COMPUTER] [I] If a computer or computer system crashes, it suddenly stops working. **3 crash against/on/ through, etc** to hit something and make a loud noise *The waves crashed against the rocks.* **4** [LOUD NOISE] [I] to make a sudden, loud noise *Thunder crashed overhead.* **5** [MONEY] [I] If a financial market crashes, prices suddenly fall by a large amount.

**'crash ,barrier** *noun* [C] *UK* a fence along the middle or edge of a road for preventing accidents

**'crash ,course** *UK* (*US* **,crash 'course**) *noun* [C] a course that teaches you a lot of basic facts in a very short time

**'crash ,helmet** *noun* [C] a hard hat that protects your head when you ride a motorcycle

**crass** /kræs/ *adj* showing that you do not understand or care about other people's feelings *a crass remark*

**crate** /kreɪt/ *noun* [C] a large box used for carrying or storing things

**crater** /'kreɪtəʳ/ *noun* [C] **1** the round, open part at the top of a volcano **2** a big hole in the ground *The explosion left a crater in the road.*

**crave** /kreɪv/ *verb* [T] to want something very much *a child who craves affection* ● craving *noun* [C] a strong feeling that you want or need a particular thing *She had a craving for chocolate.*

**crawl¹** /krɔːl/ *verb* **1** [PERSON] [I] to move on your hands and knees *I crawled under the desk to plug the lamp in.* **2** [ANIMAL] [I] If an insect crawls, it uses its legs to move. *There's an ant crawling up your leg.* **3** [TRAFFIC] [I] If traffic crawls, it moves extremely slowly. *We were crawling along at 10 miles per hour.* **4** [TRY TO PLEASE] [I] *UK informal* to try to please someone because you want them to like you or help you *My brother is always crawling to Mum.* **5 be crawling with sb/sth** to be full of insects or people in a way that is unpleasant *The kitchen's crawling with ants.*

**crawl²** /krɔːl/ *noun* **1** [no plural] a very slow speed *Traffic slowed to a crawl.* **2** [U] a style of swimming in which you move your arms over your head and kick with straight legs

**crayon** /'kreɪɒn/ *noun* [C] a stick of coloured wax used for drawing

---

| iː see | ɒ hot | ɔː saw | ʌ run | ʊ put | uː too | aɪ my | aʊ how | eɪ day | əʊ no | ɪə near | ɔɪ boy | ʊə poor | aɪə fire | aʊə sour |

**craze** /kreɪz/ *noun* [C] something that is very popular for a short time

**crazed** /kreɪzd/ *adj* behaving in a dangerous and uncontrolled way *a crazed gunman*

o--**crazy** /'kreɪzi/ *adj* **1** stupid or strange *a crazy idea* • *I was crazy not to take that job.* **2** annoyed or angry *The children are driving me crazy* (= making me annoyed). • *Dad went crazy when I told him what had happened.* **3 be crazy about sb/sth** to love someone very much, or to be very interested in something *Mia's crazy about baseball.* **4 go crazy** to become very excited about something *When he came on stage the audience went crazy.* **5 like crazy** *informal* If you do something like crazy, you do a lot of it, or do it very quickly. *We worked like crazy to get everything finished.* • crazily *adv* • craziness *noun* [U]

**creak** /kriːk/ *verb* [I] If something such as a door or a piece of wood creaks, it makes a long noise when it moves. *creaking floorboards* • creak *noun* [C] • creaky *adj* A creaky door, stair, etc creaks.

**cream¹** /kriːm/ *noun* **1** FOOD [U] a thick, yellowish-white liquid that is taken from milk *raspberries and cream* **2** FOR SKIN [C, U] a soft substance that you rub into your skin to make it softer or less painful *face/hand cream* **3** COLOUR [U] a yellowish-white colour **4 the cream of sth** the best people or things in a particular group *the cream of Milan's designers* ⊃ *See also:* **ice cream**.

**cream²** /kriːm/ *adj* being a yellowish-white colour

**cream³** /kriːm/ *verb*
**cream sth/sb off** *UK* to take away the best part of something, or the best people in a group, and use them for your own advantage *Football clubs like to cream off schoolchildren with talent.*

,**cream 'cheese** *noun* [U] smooth, soft, white cheese

**creamy** /'kriːmi/ *adj* like cream or containing cream *creamy sauce/soup*

**crease¹** /kriːs/ *noun* [C] a line on cloth or paper where it has been folded or crushed

**crease²** /kriːs/ *verb* [I, T] If cloth, paper, etc creases, or if you crease it, it gets a line in it where it has been folded or crushed. *Cotton creases very easily.*

o--**create** /kri'eɪt/ *verb* [T] to make something happen or exist *The project will create more than 500 jobs.* • *The snow created further problems.*

**creation** /kri'eɪʃ⁰n/ *noun* **1** PROCESS [U] when someone makes something happen or exist *the creation of a new political party* **2** PRODUCT [C] something that someone has made *The museum contains some of his best creations.* **3** UNIVERSE [U] (*also* **Creation**) in many religions, when God made the universe and everything in it

**creative** /kri'eɪtɪv/ *adj* good at thinking of new ideas or using imagination to create new and unusual things *Her book is full of creative ways to decorate your home.* • creatively *adv* • creativity /ˌkriːeɪ'tɪvəti/ *noun* [U] the ability to produce new ideas or things using skill and imagination

**creator** /kri'eɪtə/ *noun* **1** [C] someone who invents or makes something **2 the Creator** God

o--**creature** /'kriːtʃə/ *noun* [C] anything that lives but is not a plant *Dolphins are intelligent creatures.*

**creche** /kreʃ/ *noun* [C] *UK* a place where babies and young children are looked after while their parents do something else

**credence** /'kriːd⁰ns/ *noun* **add/give/lend credence to sth** to make a story, theory, etc seem more likely to be true *The letters lend credence to the idea that he had an unhappy life.*

**credentials** /krɪ'denʃlz/ *noun* [plural] **1** skills and experience that show you are suitable for a particular job or activity *academic credentials* **2** documents that prove who you are

**credibility** /ˌkredə'bɪləti/ *noun* [U] when someone can be believed and trusted *This decision has damaged the President's credibility.*

**credible** /'kredəbl/ *adj* able to be trusted or believed *credible evidence*

**credit¹** /'kredɪt/ *noun* **1** PAYMENT [U] a way of buying something in which you arrange to pay for it at a later time *We offer interest-free credit on all new cars.* • *He bought most of the furniture on credit.* **2** PRAISE [U] praise that is given to someone for something they have done *I did most of the work but Dan got all the credit!* • *We should give her credit for her honesty.* • *I can't take full credit for this meal – Sam helped.* **3 be a credit to sb/sth** to do something that makes a person or organization proud of you *Giorgio is a credit to his family.* **4 to sb's credit** If something is to someone's credit, they deserve praise for it. *To his credit, Bill never blamed her for the incident.* **5 have sth to your credit** to have achieved something *By the age of 25, she had five novels to her credit.* **6 in credit** having money in your bank account **7** MONEY [C] an amount of money that you put into your bank account ⊃ *Opposite* **debit**. **8** COURSE [C] a unit that shows you have completed part of a college course

**credit²** /'kredɪt/ *verb* [T] **1** to add money to someone's bank account **2** to believe that something is true *Dean's getting married! Who would have credited it?*
**credit sth to sb** to say that someone is responsible for something good *an idea credited to Isaac Newton*
**credit sb with sth** to believe that someone has a particular quality *Credit me with some intelligence!*
**credit sb with sth/doing sth** to say that someone is responsible for something good *She is credited with making the business a success.*

**creditable** /'kredɪtəbl/ *adj* Something that is creditable deserves praise. *a creditable performance*

'**credit ,card** *noun* [C] a small plastic card that allows you to buy something and pay for it later *He paid by credit card.*

**creditor** /'kredɪtə/ *noun* [C] a person or organization that someone owes money to

**the credits** /'kredɪts/ *noun* [plural] a list of people who made a film or television programme

**creed** /kriːd/ *noun* [C] a set of beliefs, especially religious beliefs that influence your life

**creek** /kriːk/ *noun* [C] **1** *UK* a narrow area of water that flows into the land from a sea or river **2** *mainly US* a stream or narrow river

**creep¹** /kriːp/ *verb past* **crept 1** MOVE QUIETLY **creep along/in/out, etc** to move very quietly and carefully *I crept out of the room.* **2** START TO APPEAR **creep across/in/into, etc** to gradually start to exist or appear *Problems were beginning to creep into their relationship.* **3** MOVE SLOWLY **creep along/down/through, etc** to move somewhere very slowly *The convoy crept along in the darkness.*

**creep up on sb 1** to surprise someone by moving closer to them from behind *Don't creep up on me like that!* **2** If a feeling or state creeps up on you, it happens gradually so that you do not notice it. *Old age just creeps up on you.*

**creep²** /kriːp/ *noun* [C] **1** *UK* someone who you do not like because they are nice to people in a way that is not sincere **2** someone who you think is unpleasant

**creeps** /kriːps/ *noun* **give sb the creeps** *informal* to make someone feel frightened or nervous *These old buildings give me the creeps.*

**creepy** /ˈkriːpi/ *adj informal* strange and frightening *a creepy story/person*

**cremate** /krɪˈmeɪt/ *verb* [T] to burn a dead body • **cremation** /krɪˈmeɪʃ³n/ *noun* [C, U] the ceremony where someone is cremated

**crematorium** /ˌkreməˈtɔːriəm/ (*also US* **crematory** /ˈkriːmətɔːri/) *noun* [C] a place where people are cremated

**crept** /krept/ *past of* creep

**crescendo** /krɪˈʃendəʊ/ *noun* [C] when a noise or piece of music gradually gets louder

**crescent** /ˈkres³nt/ *noun* **1** [C] a curved shape that is narrow at each end and wider in the middle *the pale crescent of the moon* **2** **Crescent** used in the names of streets that have a curved shape *Her address was 57 Park Crescent.*

**crest** /krest/ *noun* [C] **1** TOP the highest part of a hill or wave **2** FEATHERS the feathers that point upwards on a bird's head **3** DESIGN a design used as the symbol of a school, important family, etc

**crestfallen** /ˈkrest,fɔːl³n/ *adj* disappointed or sad

**crevasse** /krɪˈvæs/ *noun* [C] a deep, wide crack, especially in ice

**crevice** /ˈkrevɪs/ *noun* [C] a small, narrow crack, especially in a rock

**crew** /kruː/ *noun* [group] **1** the people who work together on a ship, aircraft, or train *a crew member* **2** a team of people with special skills who work together *Fire and ambulance crews were at the scene.*

**crewman** /ˈkruːmæn/ *noun* [C] *plural* **crewmen** a member of the crew of a ship or aircraft

**crib** /krɪb/ *US* (*UK* **cot**) *noun* [C] a bed with high sides for a baby

**cricket** /ˈkrɪkɪt/ *noun* **1** [U] a game in which two teams of eleven people try to score points by hitting a ball and running between two wickets (= sets of three wooden sticks) *a cricket ball/bat* ➔ *See colour picture* **Sports 2** *on page Centre 16.* **2** [C] an insect that jumps and makes a noise by rubbing its wings together

**cricketer** /ˈkrɪkɪtə²/ *noun* [C] someone who plays cricket, especially as their job

o━**crime** /kraɪm/ *noun* **1** [U] illegal activities *violent crime* • *tough new measures to fight crime* **2** [C] something someone does that is illegal *He committed a serious crime.* ➔ *See also:* **war crime.**

**criminal¹** /ˈkrɪmɪn³l/ *adj* **1** [always before noun] relating to crime *criminal activity* • *He has a criminal record* (= the police have an official record of his crimes). **2** *informal* very bad or morally wrong *It's criminal that people are having to wait so long for hospital treatment.* • **criminally** *adv*

o━**criminal²** /ˈkrɪmɪn³l/ *noun* [C] someone who has committed a crime *a dangerous/violent criminal*

**criminologist** /ˌkrɪmɪˈnɒlədʒɪst/ *noun* [C] someone who studies crime and criminals

**crimson** /ˈkrɪmz³n/ *noun* [U] a dark red colour • **crimson** *adj*

**cringe** /krɪndʒ/ *verb* [I] **1** to feel very embarrassed about something *Jan cringed at the sight of her father dancing.* **2** to move away from something because you are frightened

**crinkle** /ˈkrɪŋkl/ *verb* [I, T] to become covered in small lines or folds, or to make something become covered in small lines or folds • **crinkly** *adj* Something that is crinkly has crinkles in it.

**cripple¹** /ˈkrɪpl/ *verb* [T] **1** to injure someone so that they cannot use their arms or legs [often passive] *His son was crippled by a riding accident.* **2** to damage something very badly and make it weak or not effective [often passive] *a country crippled by war*

**cripple²** /ˈkrɪpl/ *noun* [C] *old-fashioned* an offensive word for someone who cannot use their legs or arms in a normal way

**crippling** /ˈkrɪplɪŋ/ *adj* **1** [always before noun] A crippling illness makes someone unable to use their arms or legs in a normal way. **2** causing great damage

**crisis** /ˈkraɪsɪs/ *noun* [C, U] *plural* **crises** /ˈkraɪsiːz/ a situation or time that is extremely dangerous or difficult *an economic/financial crisis* • *The country's leadership is in crisis.* ➔ *See also:* **midlife crisis.**

**crisp¹** /krɪsp/ *adj* **1** FOOD Crisp food is pleasantly hard. *a crisp apple* • *crisp pastry* **2** MATERIAL Crisp cloth or paper money is clean and looks new, with no folds. *a crisp linen shirt* **3** WEATHER Crisp weather is pleasantly cold and dry. *a crisp autumn day* **4** QUICK A crisp way of talking or behaving is quick and confident. **5** IMAGE A crisp image is very clear.

**crisp²** /krɪsp/ *UK* (*US* **chip**) *noun* [C] a very thin slice of potato that has been cooked in oil and is eaten cold [usually plural] *a packet of crisps* ➔ *See colour picture* **Food** *on page Centre 7.*

**crispy** /ˈkrɪspi/ *adj* Crispy food is pleasantly hard and easy to bite through. *crispy bacon*

**criss-cross** /ˈkrɪskrɒs/ *verb* [I, T] If something criss-crosses an area, it crosses it several times in different directions. [often passive] *The forest is criss-crossed with paths and tracks.*

**criterion** /kraɪ'tɪəriən/ *noun* [C] *plural* **criteria** a fact or level of quality that you use when making a choice or decision [+ **for** + doing sth] *We have strict criteria for deciding which students will receive a grant.*

**critic** /'krɪtɪk/ *noun* [C] **1** someone who says that they do not approve of someone or something *an outspoken critic of the government* **2** someone whose job is to give their opinion of a book, play, film, etc *a theatre/film critic*

O━**critical** /'krɪtɪkᵊl/ *adj* **1** NOT PLEASED saying that someone or something is bad or wrong *a critical report* ● *He is very **critical** of the way I work.* **2** IMPORTANT very important for the way things will happen in the future *a critical decision* **3** SERIOUS extremely serious or dangerous *The doctors said her condition was critical and she might not survive.* **4** OPINIONS giving judgments and opinions on books, plays, films, etc *a critical study of Tennyson's work* ● critically *adv*

O━**criticism** /'krɪtɪsɪzᵊm/ *noun* **1** [C, U] when you say that something or someone is bad *Plans to close the hospital attracted strong public criticism.* **2** [U] when someone gives their judgments and opinions on books, plays, films, etc *literary criticism*

O━**criticize** (*also UK* **-ise**) /'krɪtɪsaɪz/ *verb* [I, T] to say that something or someone is bad [often passive, + **for** + doing sth] *The film was criticized for being too violent.*

**critique** /krɪ'tiːk/ *noun* [C] a report that says what is good and bad about something

**croak** /krəʊk/ *verb* **1** [I, T] to talk or say something in a low, rough voice *"I don't feel well," he croaked.* **2** [I] If a bird or frog (= green jumping animal) croaks, it makes a deep, low sound.

**crochet** /'krəʊʃeɪ ⓤⓢ krəʊ'ʃeɪ/ *verb* [I, T] to make clothes and other items using wool and a special needle with a hook at one end

**crockery** /'krɒkᵊri/ *noun* [U] plates, cups, and other dishes, especially those made from clay

**crocodile** /'krɒkədaɪl/ *noun* [C] a big reptile with a long mouth and sharp teeth, that lives in lakes and rivers

**crocus** /'krəʊkəs/ *noun* [C] a small yellow, purple, or white spring flower

**croissant** /'kwæsɒŋ ⓤⓢ kwɑː'sɒŋ/ *noun* [C] a soft, curved piece of bread, eaten for breakfast ⊃ *See picture at* **bread**.

**crony** /'krəʊni/ *noun* [C] *informal* one of a group of friends who help each other, especially in a way that is not fair [usually plural] *He gave his cronies all the best jobs.*

**crook** /krʊk/ *noun* **1** [C] *informal* a criminal or someone who cheats people **2 the crook of your arm** the inside part of your arm where it bends

**crooked** /'krʊkɪd/ *adj* **1** not straight *crooked teeth* **2** *informal* not honest *a crooked politician*

**croon** /kruːn/ *verb* [I, T] to sing in a soft, low, romantic voice

O━**crop¹** /krɒp/ *noun* **1** [C] a plant such as a grain, fruit, or vegetable that is grown in large amounts by farmers **2** [C] the amount of plants of a particular type that are produced at one time *We had a record crop of grapes this year.*

**3 a crop of sth** a group of the same type of things or people that exist at the same time *He's one of the current crop of young Italian artists.* ⊃ *See also:* **cash crop**.

**crop²** /krɒp/ *verb* **cropping**, *past* **cropped 1** [T] to cut something so that it is short **2** [I] *UK* If a plant crops, it produces fruit, flowers, etc.
 **crop up** to happen or appear suddenly *The same old problems kept cropping up.*

**cropper** /'krɒpəʳ/ *noun* **come a cropper** *UK* **1** to fall over *The horse came a cropper at the first fence.* **2** to fail in an embarrassing way, or to make an embarrassing mistake *He came a cropper because he'd forgotten to bring the notes for his speech.*

**croquet** /'krəʊkeɪ ⓤⓢ krəʊ'keɪ/ *noun* [U] a game played on grass, in which you hit a ball with a wooden hammer through curved wires pushed into the ground

O━**cross¹** /krɒs/ *verb* **1** FROM ONE SIDE TO ANOTHER [I, T] to go from one side of something to the other side *It's not a good place to cross the road.* **2** LINE/BORDER [I, T] to travel over a border or line into a different area, country, etc *They crossed from Albania into Greece.* **3** MEET AND GO ACROSS [I, T] If two lines, roads, etc cross, they go over or across each other. **4 cross your arms/fingers/legs** to put one of your arms, fingers, or legs over the top of the other **5 cross yourself** to touch your head, chest, and both shoulders as a sign to God **6** ANIMAL/PLANT [T] to mix two breeds of animal or plant to produce a new breed **7** MAKE SOMEONE ANGRY [T] to make someone angry by refusing to do what they want you to do ⊃ *See also:* I'll/We'll cross that **bridge¹** when I/we come to it., **criss-cross**, **double-cross**, keep your fingers (**finger¹**) crossed, cross your **mind¹**.
 **cross sth off (sth)** to remove a word from a list by drawing a line through it *Did you cross her name off the guest list?*
 **cross sth out** to draw a line through something that you have written, usually because it is wrong *Cross out that last sentence.*

O━**cross²** /krɒs/ *noun* **1** WOOD [C] two pieces of wood that cross each other, on which people were left to die as a punishment in the past **2** SYMBOL [C] an object in the shape of a cross, used as a symbol of the Christian religion **3** MARK [C] a written mark (x), used for showing where something is, or that something that has been written is wrong **4 a cross between sth and sth** a mixture of two different things or people *The dog is a cross between a terrier and a rottweiler.* **5** SPORT [C] when someone kicks or hits the ball across the field in sport, especially football

**cross³** /krɒs/ *adj* annoyed or angry *Don't be cross with me!*

**crossbar** /'krɒsbɑːʳ/ *noun* [C] **1** the post at the top of a goal in games such as football **2** the metal tube that joins the front and back of a bicycle

**cross-border** /'krɒs,bɔːdəʳ/ *adj* [always before noun] between different countries, or involving people from different countries *cross-border trade*

**cross-Channel** /ˌkrɒsˈtʃænᵊl/ adj [always before noun] connecting or happening between England and France *a cross-Channel ferry/route*

**cross-country** /ˌkrɒsˈkʌntri/ adj [always before noun], adv **1** across fields and countryside *cross-country running/skiing* • *He prefers skiing cross-country.* **2** from one side of a country to the other side *Airlines are cutting cross-country fares.*

**cross-examine** /ˌkrɒsɪɡˈzæmɪn/ verb [T] to ask someone a lot of questions about something they have said, in order to discover if it is true, especially in a court of law • cross-examination /ˌkrɒsɪɡˌzæmɪˈneɪʃᵊn/ noun [U]

**cross-eyed** /krɒsˈaɪd/ adj A cross-eyed person has both eyes looking in towards their nose.

**crossfire** /ˈkrɒsfaɪə/ noun **1** [U] bullets fired towards you from different directions *Civilians died when a bus was caught in the crossfire between government and rebel troops.* **2 be caught in the crossfire** to be involved in a situation where people around you are arguing *Several people were caught in the political crossfire.*

**crossing** /ˈkrɒsɪŋ/ noun [C] **1** WHERE PEOPLE CROSS a place where people can go across a road, river, etc **2** SEA JOURNEY a journey across water *regular ferry crossings from Tenerife to Gran Canaria* **3** WHERE LINES CROSS a place where roads, railways, etc cross each other ⊃ *See also:* **grade crossing**, **level crossing**, **zebra crossing**.

**cross-legged** /ˌkrɒsˈleɡɪd/ adv **sit cross-legged** to sit on the floor with your knees wide apart and one foot over the other foot

**cross 'purposes** noun **at cross purposes** If two people are at cross purposes, they do not understand each other because they are talking about different things but do not know this.

**cross 'reference** noun [C] a note in a book that tells you to look somewhere else in the book for more information about something

**crossroads** /ˈkrɒsrəʊdz/ noun [C] plural **crossroads 1** a place where two roads cross each other **2** a time when you have to make an important decision that will affect your future life *I felt I was at a crossroads in my life.*

**cross-section** /ˈkrɒssekʃᵊn/ noun [C] **1** a small group of people or things that represents all the different types in a larger group *a cross-section of society* **2** something that has been cut in half so that you can see the inside, or a picture of this *a cross-section of a human heart*

**crosswalk** /ˈkrɒswɔːk/ US (UK **pedestrian crossing**) noun [C] a special place on a road where traffic must stop if people want to cross

**crossword** /ˈkrɒswɜːd/ (also **'crossword ˌpuzzle**) noun [C] a game in which you write words which are the answers to questions in a pattern of black and white squares

**crotch** /krɒtʃ/ (also UK **crutch**) noun [C] the part of your body between the tops of your legs, or the part of a piece of clothing that covers this area

**crouch** /kraʊtʃ/ (also **crouch down**) verb [I] to move your body close to the ground by bending your knees *I crouched behind the chair to avoid being seen.*

**crow¹** /krəʊ/ noun **1** [C] a large black bird that makes a loud noise **2 as the crow flies** when measured in a straight line *It's about 50 miles from London to Cambridge as the crow flies.*

**crow²** /krəʊ/ verb [I] **1** to talk in a proud and annoying way about something you have done *Donald wouldn't stop crowing about his exam results.* **2** If a cock (= male chicken) crows, it makes a loud noise, usually in the early morning.

o‑ **crowd¹** /kraʊd/ noun **1** [C] a large group of people who are together in one place *A large crowd had gathered to wait for the princess.* • *Shop early and avoid the crowds.* **2** [no plural] informal a group of friends or people with similar interests *the art/theatre crowd* • *I don't know many people in Ellen's crowd.*

**crowd²** /kraʊd/ verb [T] **1** to stand together in large numbers *Protesters crowded the streets.* **2** to stand too close to someone *Don't crowd me!*

**crowd around/round (sb/sth)** If a group of people crowd around or crowd around someone or something, they stand very close all around them. *Everyone crowded around my desk.*

**crowd in/crowd (sb) into sth** If a large group of people crowd into somewhere, they all go there and fill the place.

**crowd sb out** to prevent someone or something from succeeding or existing by being much more successful than them or by being present in much larger numbers *Large national companies often crowd out smaller local businesses.*

o‑ **crowded** /ˈkraʊdɪd/ adj very full of people *a crowded room/train*

**crown¹** /kraʊn/ noun **1** KING/QUEEN [C] a round object made of gold and jewels (= valuable stones) that a king or queen wears on their head **2** TOP [C] the top of a hat, head, or hill **3 the Crown** used to refer to the power or government of a king or queen *All this land belongs to the Crown.* **4** TOOTH [C] an artificial top that is put on a damaged tooth

**crown²** /kraʊn/ verb [T] **1** MAKE KING/QUEEN to put a crown on someone's head in an official ceremony that makes them a king or queen [often passive] *Queen Elizabeth II of England was crowned in 1952.* **2** ON TOP literary to be on top of something else *A large domed ceiling crowns the main hall.* **3** BEST PART to be the best or most successful part of something *a book that crowned his successful writing career*

**crowning** /ˈkraʊnɪŋ/ adj [always before noun] more important, beautiful, etc than anything else *It was the crowning achievement of his political career.*

**crucial** /ˈkruːʃᵊl/ adj extremely important or necessary *a crucial decision/question* • *Her work has been crucial to the project's success.* • crucially adv

**crucifix** /ˈkruːsɪfɪks/ noun [C] a model of a cross with Jesus Christ on it

**crucifixion** /ˌkruːsəˈfɪkʃᵊn/ noun [C, U] in the past, when someone was fastened to a cross and left to die *the crucifixion of Christ*

**crucify** /ˈkruːsɪfaɪ/ verb [T] **1** in the past, to

fasten someone to a cross and leave them to die **2** *informal* to criticize someone or something in a cruel and damaging way [often passive] *The film has been crucified by the media.*

**crude** /kru:d/ *adj* **1** made or done in a simple way and without much skill *a crude device/ weapon* **2** rude and offensive *a crude comment/ remark* • **crudely** *adv*

,crude 'oil (*also* **crude**) *noun* [U] oil in its natural state before it has been treated

o━**cruel** /'kru:əl/ *adj* **crueller, cruellest** or **crueler, cruelest** extremely unkind, or causing people or animals to suffer *a cruel joke* • *Many people think hunting is cruel to animals.* • **cruelly** *adv*

**cruelty** /'kru:əlti/ *noun* [C, U] cruel behaviour or a cruel action *laws against cruelty to animals*

**cruise¹** /kru:z/ *noun* [C] a holiday on a ship, sailing from place to place

**cruise²** /kru:z/ *verb* **1** [I] to move in a vehicle at a speed that does not change *The plane is cruising at 500 miles per hour.* **2** [I] to go on a cruise **3 cruise to success/victory, etc** *informal* to win a competition easily *Johnson cruised to an easy victory in the final.*

,cruise 'missile *UK* (*US* 'cruise ,missile) *noun* [C] a weapon that flies through the air, and which often carries nuclear weapons

**cruiser** /'kru:zəʳ/ *noun* [C] **1** a large military ship used in wars **2** (*also* 'cabin ,cruiser) a motor boat with a room for people to sleep in

'cruise ,ship (*also* 'cruise ,liner) *noun* [C] a large ship like a hotel, which people travel on for pleasure

**crumb** /krʌm/ *noun* **1** [C] a very small piece of bread, cake, etc ➾ *See colour picture* **Quantities** *on page Centre 14.* **2 a crumb of sth** a very small amount of something

**crumble** /'krʌmbl/ *verb* **1** [I, T] to break into small pieces, or to make something break into small pieces *Buildings crumbled as the earth-quake struck.* **2** [I] If a relationship, system, or feeling crumbles, it fails or ends. *His first mar-riage crumbled after only a year.*

**crummy** /'krʌmi/ *adj informal* unpleasant, or of bad quality *a crummy job* • *a crummy hotel*

**crumple** /'krʌmpl/ *verb* **1** [I, T] If something such as paper or cloth crumples, it becomes crushed, and if you crumple it, you crush it until it is full of folds. *a crumpled shirt* **2** [I] If someone's face crumples, they suddenly look very sad or disappointed.
**crumple sth up** to crush a piece of paper until it is full of folds

**crunch¹** /krʌnʃ/ *noun* **1** [C] the sound of some-thing being crushed [usually singular] *the crunch of dried leaves under our feet* **2 if/when it comes to the crunch** if/when a situation becomes serious or you have to make an impor-tant decision *When it came to the crunch, I was too nervous to ask her for a date.*

**crunch²** /krʌnʃ/ *verb* **1** [I, T] to make a noise by chewing hard food *She was crunching on an apple.* **2** [I] to make a sound as if something is being crushed *The gravel crunched under our feet.*

**crunchy** /'krʌntʃi/ *adj* Crunchy food is hard and makes a noise when you eat it.

**crusade** /kru:'seɪd/ *noun* [C] a determined

attempt to change or achieve something that you believe in strongly • **crusader** *noun* [C] someone who is involved in a crusade

**crush¹** /krʌʃ/ *verb* [T] **1** to press something so hard that it is made flat or broken into pieces *Her car was crushed by a falling tree.* **2** to defeat someone or something completely *government attempts to crush protests* • *a crushing defeat*

**crush²** /krʌʃ/ *noun* **1** [no plural] a crowd of people forced to stand close together because there is not enough room *Many people fell over in the crush.* **2** [C] *informal* a strong temporary feeling of love for someone *Tim has a crush on Jennifer.*

**crust** /krʌst/ *noun* [C, U] **1** the hard outer surface of bread or other baked foods **2** a hard, dry layer on the surface of something

**crusty** /'krʌsti/ *adj* **1** unfriendly and becoming annoyed very easily **2** Something that is crusty has a hard outer layer. *crusty bread*

**crutch** /krʌtʃ/ *noun* [C] **1** a stick that you put under your arm to help you walk if you have injured your leg or foot [usually plural] *Charles was on crutches* (= walking with crutches) *for six weeks.* **2** *UK* (*UK/US* **crotch**) the part of your body between the tops of your legs, or the part of a piece of clothing that covers this area

**crux** /krʌks/ *noun* **the crux (of sth)** the main or most important part of a problem, argument, etc

o━**cry¹** /kraɪ/ *verb* **1** [I] to produce tears from your eyes, usually because you are sad, angry, or hurt *I could see that she'd been crying.* • *My baby brother cries all the time.* **2** [I, T] to speak or say something loudly *"Look at this!" cried Raj.* ➾ *See also:* **cry your eyes out (eye¹), a shoulder¹** to cry on.
**be crying out for sth** *informal* to need some-thing very much *a school that's crying out for more money*
**cry out (sth)** to shout or make a loud noise because you are frightened, hurt, etc *She cried out in terror.*

o━**cry²** /kraɪ/ *noun* **1** [C] a shout, especially one that shows that someone is fright-ened, hurt, etc *a cry of horror/joy/pain* • *I could hear the cries of children playing in the street.* **2** [C] a sound that a particular animal or bird makes *an eagle's cry* **3 have a cry** to produce tears from your eyes, usually because you are sad, angry, or hurt *Isabel went home and had a good cry.* **4 be a far cry from sth** to be very different from something *Her luxury mansion is a far cry from the house she grew up in.*

**cry**

**crying** /'kraɪɪŋ/ *adj* **1 a crying need for sth** *mainly UK* a need that is very urgent *There's a crying need for more nurses.* **2 it's a crying shame** used to say that you think a situation is very wrong

**crypt** /krɪpt/ *noun* [C] a room under a church, especially one where people are buried

**cryptic** /'krɪptɪk/ *adj* mysterious and difficult to understand *a cryptic comment/message* ● cryptically *adv*

**crystal** /'krɪstəl/ *noun* **1** ROCK [C, U] a type of transparent rock **2** GLASS [U] a type of high quality glass *a crystal vase* **3** SHAPE [C] a piece of a substance that has become solid, with a regular shape *ice crystals*

,**crystal 'ball** *noun* [C] a large, glass ball that some people believe you can look into to see what will happen in the future

,**crystal 'clear** *adj* very obvious and easy to understand *She made her feelings crystal clear to me.*

**cub** /kʌb/ *noun* [C] a young bear, fox, lion, etc

**cube**[1] /kjuːb/ *noun* **1** [C] a solid object with six square sides of the same size *Cut the cheese into small cubes.* ➔ *See picture at* **shape. 2 the cube of sth** the number you get when you multiply a particular number by itself twice *The cube of 3 is 27.* ➔ *See also:* **ice cube.**

**cube**[2] /kjuːb/ *verb* [T] **1** to multiply a particular number by itself twice *5 cubed is 125.* **2** to cut something into cubes

**cubic** /'kjuːbɪk/ *adj* **cubic centimetre/inch/ metre, etc** a unit of measurement that shows the volume (= length×width×height) of something *a reservoir that holds 22 million cubic metres of water*

**cubicle** /'kjuːbɪkl/ *noun* [C] a small space with walls around it, that is separate from the rest of a room *a shower cubicle*

**cuckoo** /'kʊkuː/ *noun* [C] a small bird that makes a sound like its name and puts its eggs into other birds' nests

**cucumber** /'kjuːkʌmbə[r]/ *noun* [C, U] a long, green vegetable that you eat raw in salads ➔ *See colour picture* **Fruit and Vegetables** *on page Centre 8.*

**cuddle** /'kʌdl/ *verb* [I, T] to put your arms around someone to show them that you love them *Her mother cuddled her until she stopped crying.* ● cuddle *noun* [C]

**cuddle up** to sit or lie very close to someone *The children cuddled up to me to keep warm.*

**cuddly** /'kʌdli/ *adj* soft and pleasant to hold close to you

**cue** /kjuː/ *noun* **1** ACTION/EVENT [C] an action or event that is a sign that something should happen *The final goal was the cue for celebration.* **2** SIGNAL [C] a signal that tells someone to start speaking or doing something when acting in a play, film, etc **3 on cue** If something happens on cue, it happens at exactly the right time. *Then, right on cue, Andrew appeared at the door.* **4 take your cue from sb/sth** to copy what someone else does *I took my cue from the others and left.* **5** STICK [C] a long, straight stick used to hit the balls in games like snooker (= a game played with small coloured balls on a table)

**cuff** /kʌf/ *noun* [C] **1** the bottom part of a sleeve that goes around your wrist ➔ *See picture at* **jacket. 2 off the cuff** If you speak off the cuff, you do it without having planned what you will say. *She wasn't expecting to give a speech, and just said a few things off the cuff.*

**cuisine** /kwɪˈziːn/ *noun* [U] a style of cooking *French/international cuisine* ➔ *See usage note at* **kitchen.**

**cul-de-sac** /'kʌldəsæk/ *noun* [C] a short road with houses which is blocked at one end

**culinary** /'kʌlɪnəri/ *adj* [always before noun] *formal* related to food and cooking *culinary equipment*

**cull** /kʌl/ *verb* [T] to kill some of the animals in a group, especially the weakest ones, to limit their numbers ● cull *noun* [C]

**cull sth from sth** to collect ideas or information from several different places [often passive] *The book is culled from over 800 pages of his diaries.*

**culminate** /'kʌlmɪneɪt/ *verb formal* **1 culminate in/with sth** to finish with a particular event, or reach a final result after gradual development and often a lot of effort *The course culminates in a series of written exams.* ● *His career culminated with the post of ambassador to NATO.* **2** [T] *US* to be the final thing in a series of events *The discovery of a body culminated two days of desperate searching.* ● culmination /,kʌlmɪˈneɪʃən/ *noun* [no plural] *This discovery is the culmination of years of research.*

**culpable** /'kʌlpəbl/ *adj formal* deserving to be blamed for something bad ● culpability /,kʌlpəˈbɪləti/ *noun* [U]

**culprit** /'kʌlprɪt/ *noun* [C] **1** someone who has done something wrong *If caught, the culprit could face up to five years in jail.* **2** something that is responsible for a bad situation *In many of these illnesses, stress is the main culprit.*

**cult** /kʌlt/ *noun* [C] **1** someone or something which has become very popular with a particular group of people *a cult figure/movie* **2** a religious group whose ideas are considered strange by many people

**cultivate** /'kʌltɪveɪt/ *verb* [T] **1** to prepare land and grow crops on it *This shrub is cultivated in Europe as a culinary herb.* **2** to try to develop or improve something *She has cultivated an image as a tough negotiator.* ● cultivation /,kʌltɪˈveɪʃən/ *noun* [U]

**cultivated** /'kʌltɪveɪtɪd/ *adj* A cultivated person has had a good education and knows a lot about art, books, music, etc.

**cultural** /'kʌltʃərəl/ *adj* **1** relating to the habits, traditions and beliefs of a society *cultural diversity/identity* **2** relating to music, art, theatre, literature, etc *cultural events* ● culturally *adv*

⚬ **culture** /'kʌltʃə[r]/ *noun* **1** SOCIETY [C, U] the habits, traditions, and beliefs of a country, society, or group of people *American/Japanese culture* ● *It's a good opportunity for children to learn about other cultures.* **2** ARTS [U] music, art, theatre, literature, etc *popular culture* **3** BIOLOGY [C, U] the process of growing things, especially bacteria (= very small living things that can cause disease), for scientific purposes, or the bacteria produced by this process

**cultured** /'kʌltʃəd/ *adj* A cultured person knows a lot about music, art, theatre, etc. *She described him as a well-educated, cultured, young man.*

'**culture ,shock** *noun* [U] the feeling of confusion someone has when they go to a new and very different place

---

**-cum-** /kʌm/ used between two nouns to describe something which combines the two things *a kitchen-cum-dining room* (= room which is used as a kitchen and a dining room)

**cumbersome** /ˈkʌmbəsəm/ *adj* **1** large and difficult to move or use *cumbersome safety equipment* **2** slow and not effective *cumbersome bureaucracy*

**cumulative** /ˈkjuːmjələtɪv/ *adj* reached by gradually adding one thing after another *a cumulative score*

**cunning** /ˈkʌnɪŋ/ *adj* clever at getting what you want, especially by tricking people *a cunning plan/ploy* • cunning *noun* [U] • cunningly *adv*

o-=**cup**[1] /kʌp/ *noun* [C] **1** CONTAINER a small, round container with a handle on the side, used to drink from *a cup of tea/coffee* **2** SPORT a prize given to the winner of a competition, or the name of the competition *the World Cup* **3** COOKING mainly US a measurement of amounts of food used in cooking **⊃** *See also:* **egg cup**.

**cup**[2] /kʌp/ *verb* [T] **cupping**, *past* **cupped** to make your hands into the shape of a cup, or to hold something with your hands in this shape

o-=**cupboard** /ˈkʌbəd/ *noun* [C] a piece of furniture with a door on the front and shelves inside, used for storing things **⊃** *See colour picture* **Kitchen** *on page Centre 10* **⊃** *See also:* have a **skeleton** in the cupboard.

**curate** /ˈkjʊərət/ *noun* [C] a person who works for the Church of England and whose job is to help the vicar (= priest in a particular area)

**curator** /kjʊəˈreɪtəʳ/ *noun* [C] a person who is in charge of a museum (= a building where you can look at objects, such as art or old things)

**curb**[1] /kɜːb/ *verb* [T] to limit or control something *to curb crime/inflation*

**curb**[2] /kɜːb/ *noun* [C] **1** something which limits or controls something *They are proposing a curb on tobacco advertising.* **2** US spelling of kerb (= the line of stones at the edge of a path next to the road)

**curdle** /ˈkɜːdl/ *verb* [I, T] If a liquid curdles, or if you curdle it, it gets thicker and develops lumps. *Heat the sauce slowly or it will curdle.*

**cure**[1] /kjʊəʳ/ *noun* [C] **1** something that makes someone with an illness healthy again *They are trying to find a cure for cancer.* **2** a solution to a problem

o-=**cure**[2] /kjʊəʳ/ *verb* [T] **1** to make someone with an illness healthy again *Getting a better chair completely cured my back problems.* **2** to solve a problem *the fight to cure social inequality*

**curfew** /ˈkɜːfjuː/ *noun* [C] a time, especially at night, when people are not allowed to leave their homes

**curiosity** /ˌkjʊəriˈɒsəti/ *noun* **1** [U] the feeling of wanting to know or learn about something *My curiosity got the better of me and I opened the envelope.* • *Just out of curiosity, how did you get my address?* **2** [C] something strange or unusual

**curious** /ˈkjʊəriəs/ *adj* **1** wanting to know or learn about something *I was curious about his life in India.* • *I was curious to know what would happen next.* **2** strange or unusual *The house was decorated in a curious style.* • curiously *adv* *She looked at him curiously.*

**curl**[1] /kɜːl/ *noun* [C] something with a small, curved shape, especially a piece of hair *a child with blonde curls*

**curl**[2] /kɜːl/ *verb* [I, T] to make something into the shape of a curl, or to be this shape *The cat curled its tail around its body.*
**curl up 1** to sit or lie in a position with your arms and legs close to your body *She curled up and went to sleep.* **2** If something flat, such as a piece of paper, curls up, the edges start to curve up.

**curly** /ˈkɜːli/ *adj* shaped like a curl, or with many curls *curly hair* **⊃** *See colour picture* **Hair** *on page Centre 9.*

**currant** /ˈkʌrᵊnt/ *noun* [C] a small, black dried fruit used in cooking, especially in cakes

**currency** /ˈkʌrᵊnsi/ *noun* **1** [C, U] the units of money used in a particular country *foreign currency* **2** [U] when an idea is believed or accepted by many people *This view is gaining currency within the government.* **⊃** *See also:* **hard currency**.

o-=**current**[1] /ˈkʌrᵊnt/ *adj* happening or existing now *What is your current address?* • *the current issue of Newsweek magazine* **⊃** *See usage note at* **actual**. • currently *adv* *The factory currently employs 750 people.*

**current**[2] /ˈkʌrᵊnt/ *noun* **1** [C] the natural flow of air or water in one direction *a current of air* • *dangerous/strong currents* **2** [C, U] the flow of electricity through a wire *an electrical current*

**current ac'count** UK (US **checking account**) *noun* [C] a bank account which you can take money out of at any time

**current af'fairs** UK (US **,current e'vents**) *noun* [plural] important political or social events which are happening in the world at the present time

**curriculum** /kəˈrɪkjələm/ *noun* [C] *plural* **curricula** or **curriculums** all the subjects taught in a school, college, etc or on an educational course *the school curriculum*

**curry** /ˈkʌri/ *noun* [C, U] a type of food from India, made of vegetables or meat cooked with hot spices

**curse**[1] /kɜːs/ *noun* [C] **1** MAGIC magic words which are intended to bring bad luck to someone *to put a curse on someone* **2** RUDE WORDS a rude or offensive word or phrase **3** PROBLEM something that causes harm or unhappiness, often over a long period of time *Traffic is one of the curses of modern living.*

**curse**[2] /kɜːs/ *verb* **1** [I] to use rude or offensive words *He cursed angrily under his breath.* **2** [T] to express anger towards someone or something *He cursed himself for not telling David about it earlier.* **3** be cursed by/with sth to have something which causes problems over a long period of time *I am cursed with an interfering family.*

**cursor** /ˈkɜːsəʳ/ *noun* [C] a symbol on a computer screen which shows the place where you are working

**cursory** /ˈkɜːsᵊri/ *adj* [always before noun] *formal* done quickly and without much care *a cursory glance*

**curt** /kɜːt/ *adj* If something you say or write is curt, it is short and not very polite. • curtly *adv*

C

**curtail** /kɜː'teɪl/ *verb* [T] *formal* to reduce, limit, or stop something *to curtail spending* • **curtailment** *noun* [U]

**curtain** /'kɜːtᵊn/ *noun* [C] a piece of material which hangs down to cover a window, stage, etc *to draw the curtains* (= open or close them) • *The curtain goes up* (= the performance starts) *at 8 o'clock* . ➔ *See colour picture* **The Living Room** *on page Centre* 11.

**curtsey** (*also* **curtsy**) /'kɜːtsi/ *noun* [C] a movement where a girl or woman puts one foot behind the other and bends her knees, especially to show respect to a king or queen • **curtsey** *verb* [I]

o⇤**curve**[1] /kɜːv/ *noun* [C] a line which bends round like part of a circle *a road with gentle curves*

**curve**[2] /kɜːv/ *verb* [I, T] to move in a curve, form a curve, or make something into the shape of a curve *The road curves to the left.* • *a chair with a curved back* ➔ *See picture at* **flat**.

**cushion**[1] /'kʊʃᵊn/ *noun* [C] **1** a cloth bag filled with something soft which you sit on or lean against to make you comfortable ➔ *See colour picture* **The Living Room** *on page Centre* 11. **2** something which protects you from possible problems *Overseas savings provide **a cushion against** tax rises at home.*

**cushion**[2] /'kʊʃᵊn/ *verb* [T] **1** to reduce the bad effects of something *attempts to cushion the impact of unemployment* **2** to protect something, especially part of the body, with something soft *Soft grass cushioned his fall.*

**cushy** /'kʊʃi/ *adj informal* very easy *a cushy job*

**custard** /'kʌstəd/ *noun* **1** [U] a sweet, yellow sauce made from milk and eggs, usually eaten hot with sweet food *apple pie and custard* **2** [C, U] a soft baked mixture made from milk, eggs, and sugar *a custard pie/tart*

**custodial** /kʌs'təʊdiəl/ *adj* If someone is given a custodial sentence (= punishment), they are sent to prison.

**custodian** /kʌs'təʊdiən/ *noun* [C] **1** *formal* a person who takes care of something valuable or important *He's the grandson of Oscar Wilde and custodian of his private papers.* **2** *US* someone whose job is to look after a building, especially a school

**custody** /'kʌstədi/ *noun* [U] **1** the legal right to look after a child, especially when parents separate *When they divorced, it was Nicola who **won custody** of their two children.* **2** when someone is kept in prison, usually while they are waiting for a trial in court *He is being **held in custody** in Los Angeles charged with assault.* • *He was **taken into custody** by Mexican authorities.*

o⇤**custom** /'kʌstəm/ *noun* **1** [C, U] a habit or tradition **2** [U] when people buy things from shops or businesses *Free gifts are a good way of attracting custom.*

**custom-** /'kʌstəm/ *prefix* used before another word to mean 'specially designed for a particular person or purpose' *custom-built* • *custom-designed*

**customary** /'kʌstəmᵊri/ *adj* normal or expected for a particular person, situation, or society [+ to do sth] *It is **customary for** the chairman to make the opening speech.* • **customarily** /ˌkʌstə'merᵊli/ *adv*

o⇤**customer** /'kʌstəmər/ *noun* [C] a person or organization that buys goods or services from a shop or business

**customise** *UK* (*US* **customize**) /'kʌstəmaɪz/ *verb* [T] to change something to make it suitable for a particular person or purpose *Our language courses are customised to each student.*

**customs** /'kʌstəmz/ *noun* [U] the place where your bags are examined when you are going into a country, to make sure you are not carrying anything illegal *customs officials* • *to go through customs*

o⇤**cut**[1] /kʌt/ *verb* cutting, past cut **1** KNIFE [I, T] to use a knife or other sharp tool to divide something, remove part of something, or make a hole in something *Use a pair of scissors to cut the paper.* • *Cut the meat into small pieces.* • *He cut the piece of wood in half.* • *I had my hair cut last week.* • *Surgeons cut out the tumour.* • *She cut off all the diseased buds.* • *These old scissors don't cut very well.* **2** REDUCE [T] to reduce the size or amount of something *Prices have been cut by 25%.* • *The company is cutting 50 jobs.* **3** INJURE [T] to injure yourself on a sharp object which makes you bleed *She cut her finger on a broken glass.* **4** REMOVE [T] to remove part of a film or piece of writing *The film was too long so they cut some scenes.* ➔ *See also:* cut corners (**corner**[1]), cut it/things **fine**[2], have your **work**[2] cut out.

**cut across sth 1** to go from one side of an area to the other instead of going round it *If we cut across this field, it will save time.* **2** If a problem or subject cuts across different groups of people, all of those groups are affected by it or interested in it. *Interest in the Internet cuts across all age groups.*

**cut back (sth)** to reduce the amount of money being spent on something *We have had to **cut back on** training this year.*

**cut sth down** to make a tree or other plant fall to the ground by cutting it near the bottom

**cut down (sth)** to eat or drink less of something, or to reduce the amount or number of something *My doctor says I should cut down on cigarettes.*

**cut sb off** to stop someone speaking by interrupting them or putting the telephone down *She cut me off in the middle of our conversation.*

**cut sb/sth off 1** to prevent people from reaching or leaving a place, or to separate them from other people [often passive] *The whole village was cut off by flooding.* • *She lives abroad and feels very **cut off from** her family.* **2** to stop providing something such as electricity or food supplies [often passive] *If we don't pay the gas bill, we'll be cut off.*

**cut sth out 1** to remove something or form a shape by cutting, usually something made of paper or cloth *She cut out his picture from the magazine.* **2** to stop eating or drinking something, usually to improve your health *I've cut out red meat from my diet.* **3 Cut it out!** *informal* something you say to tell someone to stop doing something annoying *Cut it out! Can't you see I'm trying to work?* **4 not be cut out to be sth/not be cut out for sth** to not have the right qualities for something *I'm not really cut out to be a nurse.*

**cut out** If an engine, machine, or piece of equipment cuts out, it suddenly stops working.

**cut sth/sb out** to not let someone share something or be included in something *They cut me out of the conversation and ignored me completely.*

**cut sth up 1** to cut something into pieces **2 be cut up** *UK informal* to be very upset about something *He was very cut up when his brother died.*

**cut**

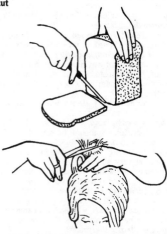

**cut²** /kʌt/ *noun* [C] **1** INJURY an injury made when the skin is cut with something sharp *He suffered cuts and bruises in the accident.* **2** OPENING an opening made with a sharp tool *She made a cut in the material.* **3** REDUCTION a reduction in the number or amount of something *tax/job cuts* • *The workers were angry about the cut in pay.* **4** MEAT a piece of meat from a particular part of an animal *an expensive cut of beef* **5** SHARE a share of something, usually money *My family owns the company, so we get a cut of the profits.* **6 an electricity/ power, etc cut** when the supply of something is stopped **7** HAIR (*also* **haircut**) the style in which your hair has been cut つ *See also:* **shortcut**.

,**cut and** '**paste** *verb* [I, T] **cutting and pasting**, *past* **cut and pasted** to move words or pictures from one place to another in a computer document

**cutback** /'kʌtbæk/ *noun* [C] a reduction of something, usually to save money *The company has made cutbacks and closed one of its factories.*

**cute** /kjuːt/ *adj* **1** attractive *a cute baby* **2** *US informal* clever in a way that is annoying or rude *He thinks it's cute to tell dirty jokes.*

**cutlery** /'kʌtləri/ *UK* (*US* **silverware**) *noun* [U] knives, forks, and spoons

**cutlet** /'kʌtlət/ *noun* [C] a small piece of meat still joined to the bone *a lamb cutlet*

**cut-price** /'kʌt,praɪs/ *mainly UK* (*US* **cut-rate**) *adj* [always before noun] cheaper than usual *cut-price tickets*

**cutters** /'kʌtəz/ *noun* [plural] a tool for cutting something *wire cutters*

**cut-throat** *mainly UK* (*also US* **cutthroat**) /'kʌtθrəʊt/ *adj* a cut-throat business or other situation is where people will do anything to succeed and do not care if they hurt others *the cut-throat world of journalism*

**cutting¹** /'kʌtɪŋ/ *noun* [C] **1** a piece cut from a plant and used to grow a new plant **2** *UK* (*UK/US* **clipping**) an article or picture that has been cut out of a newspaper or magazine

**cutting²** /'kʌtɪŋ/ *adj* If something you say or write is cutting, it is unkind. *a cutting remark/ comment*

**cutting-edge** /,kʌtɪŋ'edʒ/ *adj* very modern and with all the newest developments *cutting-edge design/technology*

**CV** /,siː'viː/ *UK* (*US* **résumé**) *noun* [C] a document which describes your qualifications and the jobs you have done, which you send to an employer that you want to work for

**cwt** *written abbreviation for* hundredweight (= a unit for measuring weight, equal to 50.8 kilograms in the UK and 45.36 kilograms in the US)

**cyanide** /'saɪənaɪd/ *noun* [U] a very strong poison

**cybercafe** /'saɪbə,kæfeɪ/ *noun* [C] a place where customers can buy food and drink and use computers to search for information on the Internet

**cyberspace** /'saɪbə,speɪs/ *noun* [U] the Internet, considered as an imaginary area where you can communicate with people and find information

**cycle¹** /'saɪkl/ *noun* [C] **1** a series of events which happen in a particular order and are often repeated *the life cycle of a moth* **2** a bicycle つ *See also:* **life cycle**.

**cycle²** /'saɪkl/ *verb* [I] to ride a bicycle • **cycling** *noun* [U] つ *See colour picture* **Sports 2** *on page Centre 16.* • **cyclist** *noun* [C] someone who rides a bicycle

**cyclical** /'sɪklɪkl/ *adj* happening in a regular and repeated pattern *the cyclical nature of the country's history*

**cyclone** /'saɪkləʊn/ *noun* [C] a violent storm with very strong winds which move in a circle

**cylinder** /'sɪlɪndər/ *noun* [C] **1** a shape with circular ends and long, straight sides, or a container or object shaped like this *an oxygen cylinder* つ *See picture at* **shape. 2** a part in a car or machine's engine which is shaped like a tube, and where another part moves up and down

**cylindrical** /sə'lɪndrɪkl/ *adj* having the shape of a cylinder

**cymbal** /'sɪmbl/ *noun* [C] a musical instrument like a metal plate which is played by being hit with a stick or another cymbal

**cynic** /'sɪnɪk/ *noun* [C] a cynical person

**cynical** /'sɪnɪkl/ *adj* believing that people are only interested in themselves and are not sincere *Many people have become cynical about politicians.* • **cynically** *adv* • **cynicism** /'sɪnɪsɪzəm/ *noun* [U] cynical beliefs

**cyst** /sɪst/ *noun* [C] a small lump containing liquid that can grow under your skin

**cystic fibrosis** /,sɪstɪkfaɪ'brəʊsɪs/ *noun* [U] a serious disease which causes the lungs and other organs to become blocked

**czar** (*also UK* **tsar**) /zɑːr/ *noun* [C] **1** a male Russian ruler before 1917 **2** *informal* a powerful official who makes important decisions for the government about a particular activity *a drugs czar*

# D

**D, d** /diː/ the fourth letter of the alphabet

**dab** /dæb/ *verb* [I, T] **dabbing**, *past* **dabbed** to touch something with quick, light touches, or to put a substance on something with quick, light touches *She **dabbed at** her eyes with a tissue.* • *She dabbed a drop of perfume behind her ears.* • **dab** *noun* [C] a small amount of something *a dab of lipstick*

**dabble** /'dæbl/ *verb* [I] to try something or take part in an activity in a way that is not serious *I only **dabble in** politics.* • *He **dabbled with** drugs at university.*

o-¤**dad** /dæd/ *noun* [C] *informal* father *My dad and I have the same curly brown hair.* • *Can I go to the park, Dad?*

**daddy** /'dædi/ *noun* [C] a word for 'father', used especially by children

**daffodil** /'dæfədɪl/ *noun* [C] a yellow flower that usually grows in spring

**daft** /dɑːft/ *adj UK informal* silly *That's a daft idea.*

**dagger** /'dægəʳ/ *noun* [C] a short knife, used as a weapon

**daily**[1] /'deɪli/ *adj* [always before noun], *adv* **1** happening or produced every day or once a day *a daily newspaper* • *He exercises daily.* • *The shop is open daily from 8 a.m. to 6 p.m.* **2** relating to one single day *They are paid on a daily basis.* **3 daily life** the usual things that happen to you every day *Shootings are part of daily life in the region.*

**daily**[2] /'deɪli/ *noun* [C] a newspaper that is published every day except Sunday

**dainty** /'deɪnti/ *adj* small, attractive, and delicate *dainty feet* • **daintily** *adv*

**dairy**[1] /'deəri/ *noun* [C] **1** a place where milk is stored and cream and cheese are made **2** a company which sells milk and products made of milk

**dairy**[2] /'deəri/ *adj* [always before noun] relating to milk or products made using milk *dairy products* • *dairy cattle*

**daisy** /'deɪzi/ *noun* [C] a small flower with white petals and a yellow centre that often grows in grass

**dam** /dæm/ *noun* [C] a strong wall built across a river to stop the water and make a lake • **dam** *verb* [T] **damming**, *past* **dammed** to build a dam across a river

o-¤**damage**[1] /'dæmɪdʒ/ *noun* [U] harm or injury *He suffered brain damage in the car crash.* • *The strong wind caused serious **damage to** the roof.*

o-¤**damage**[2] /'dæmɪdʒ/ *verb* [T] to harm or break something *Many buildings were damaged in the storm.* • *Smoking can seriously damage your health.* • **damaging** *adj* harmful *the damaging effects of pollution*

**damages** /'dæmɪdʒɪz/ *noun* [plural] money that a person or organization pays to someone because they have harmed something or something

that belongs to them *She was awarded £400 **in damages.***

**dame** /deɪm/ *noun* [C] **1** a title used in the UK before the name of a woman who has been officially respected *Dame Agatha Christie* **2** *US informal, old-fashioned* a woman

**damn**[1] /dæm/ (*also* **damned** /dæmd/) *adj* [always before noun] *informal* used to express anger *He didn't listen to a damn thing I said.* • *That dog's a damned nuisance.*

**damn**[2] /dæm/ (*also* **damn it**) *exclamation* used to express anger or disappointment *Damn! I've forgotten the tickets.*

**damn**[3] /dæm/ (*also* **damned** /dæmd/) *adv informal* very *He worked damn hard to pass that exam.* • *It was a damn good film.*

**damn**[4] /dæm/ *noun* **not give a damn** *informal* to not be interested in or worried about someone or something *I don't give a damn what people think.*

**damn**[5] /dæm/ *verb* **1 damn him/it/you, etc** used to express anger about someone or something *Stop complaining, damn you!* **2** [T] to strongly criticize someone or something *He was damned by the media.*

**damning** /'dæmɪŋ/ *adj* criticizing someone or something very strongly, or showing clearly that someone is guilty *damning evidence* • *a damning report on education standards*

**damp** /dæmp/ *adj* slightly wet, usually in an unpleasant way *damp clothes/grass* • *It was cold and damp outside.* • **damp** (*also* **dampness**) *noun* [U] when something is slightly wet *She hated the damp of the tropics.*

**dampen** /'dæmpən/ (*also* **damp**) *verb* [T] **1** to make something less strong *Nothing you can say will dampen her enthusiasm.* **2** to make something slightly wet

**damper** /'dæmpəʳ/ *noun* **put a damper on sth** to stop an occasion from being enjoyable *The accident put a damper on their holiday.*

o-¤**dance**[1] /dɑːns/ *verb* [I, T] to move your feet and body to the rhythm of music *She's dancing with Steven.* • *Can you dance the tango?* • **dancer** *noun* [C] • **dancing** *noun* [U]

o-¤**dance**[2] /dɑːns/ *noun* **1** [MOVING] [C] when you move your feet and body to music *I had a dance with my dad.* **2** [STEPS] [C] a particular set of steps or movements to music *My favourite dance is the tango.* **3** [EVENT] [C] a social event where people dance to music **4** [ACTIVITY] [U] the activity or skill of dancing *a dance school*

**dandelion** /'dændɪlaɪən/ *noun* [C] a yellow wild flower

**dandruff** /'dændrʌf/ *noun* [U] small pieces of dead skin in someone's hair or on their clothes

o-¤**danger** /'deɪndʒəʳ/ *noun* **1** [C, U] the possibility that someone or something will be harmed or killed, or that something bad will happen *the dangers of rock climbing* • *The soldiers were **in** serious **danger**.* • *We were **in danger of** missing our flight.* **2** [C] something or someone that may harm you *Icy roads are a **danger to** drivers.*

o-¤**dangerous** /'deɪndʒ°rəs/ *adj* If someone or something is dangerous, they could harm you. *a dangerous chemical* • *It's dangerous to ride a motorcycle without a helmet.* • **dangerously** *adv* *dangerously close to the edge*

**dangle** /'dæŋgl/ *verb* **1** [I, T] to hang loosely, or to hold something so that it hangs loosely *Electrical wires were **dangling** from the ceiling.* **2** [T] to offer someone something they want in order to persuade them to do something *They dangled the possibility of a job in Paris in front of him.*

**dank** /dæŋk/ *adj* wet, cold, and unpleasant *a dark, dank basement*

**dapper** /'dæpər/ *adj* A dapper man looks stylish and tidy.

**o–⚬dare¹** /deər/ *verb* **1 dare (to) do sth** to be brave enough to do something *I didn't dare tell Dad that I'd scratched his car.* **2 dare sb to do sth** to try to make someone do something dangerous *She dared her friend to climb onto the roof.* **3 Don't you dare** *informal* used to tell someone angrily not to do something *Don't you dare hit your sister!* **4 How dare she/you, etc!** used to express anger about something someone has done *How dare you talk to me like that!* **5 I dare say** (*also* **I daresay**) used when you think that something is probably true or will probably happen *I dare say she'll change her mind.*

**dare²** /deər/ *noun* [C] something that you do to prove that you are not afraid [usually singular] *She climbed down the cliff for a dare.*

**daredevil** /'deə,devəl/ *noun* [C] someone who enjoys doing dangerous things

**daren't** /deənt/ *UK short for* dare not *I daren't tell my wife how much it cost.*

**daring** /'deəriŋ/ *adj* brave and taking risks *a daring escape* • **daring** *noun* [U]

**o–⚬dark¹** /dɑːk/ *adj* **1** NO LIGHT with no light or not much light *It's a bit dark in here. Can you turn the light on please?* • *It doesn't get dark until 9 o'clock in the evening.* **2** NOT PALE nearer to black than white in colour *dark blue/green* • *dark clouds* • *He's got dark hair and blue eyes.* ➔ *See colour picture* **Hair** *on page Centre 9.* **3** PERSON having black or brown hair or brown skin *a short, dark woman with glasses* **4** BAD frightening or unpleasant *a dark period in human history*

**o–⚬dark²** /dɑːk/ *noun* **1 the dark** when there is no light somewhere *I don't like going out alone in the dark.* • *He's scared of the dark.* **2 before/after dark** before/after it becomes night *She doesn't let her children out after dark.* **3 be in the dark** to not know about something that other people know about *I'm completely in the dark about all this.* ➔ *See also:* **a shot¹** in the dark.

**darken** /'dɑːkən/ *verb* [I, T] **1** to become dark or make something dark *the darkening sky* • *a darkened room* **2** If someone's mood darkens, or if something darkens it, they suddenly feel less happy.

**darkly** /'dɑːkli/ *adv* in a frightening or mysterious way *"He might not be what he seems," she said darkly.*

**darkness** /'dɑːknəs/ *noun* [U] when there is little or no light *He stumbled around in the darkness looking for the light switch.* • *There was a power cut and the house was **in darkness**.*

**darling¹** /'dɑːliŋ/ *noun* [C] used when you speak to someone you love *Would you like a drink, darling?*

**darling²** /'dɑːliŋ/ *adj* [always before noun] loved very much *my darling daughter*

**darn¹** /dɑːn/ *US informal* (*also* **darned** /dɑːnd/) *adj* [always before noun], *adv* used to emphasize what you are saying, or to show that you are annoyed *I'm too darn tired to care.*

**darn²** /dɑːn/ *verb* [I, T] to repair a piece of clothing by sewing across a hole with thread *to darn socks*

**dart¹** /dɑːt/ *noun* [C] a small arrow used in the game of darts or as a weapon *a tranquilizer dart*

**dart²** /dɑːt/ *verb* **dart between/in/out, etc** to run or move somewhere quickly and suddenly *A cat darted across the street.*

**darts** /dɑːts/ *noun* [U] a game played by throwing small arrows at a round board

**darts**

**dash¹** /dæʃ/ *verb* **1** [I] to go somewhere quickly *She dashed downstairs when she heard the phone.* • *I must dash. I've got to be home by 7 p.m.* **2 dash sb's hopes** to destroy someone's hopes *Saturday's 2–0 defeat dashed their hopes of reaching the final.* **3 dash (sth) against/on, etc** *literary* to hit or throw something with great force, usually causing damage *Waves dashed against the cliffs.*

**dash sth off** *UK* to write something very quickly *She dashed off a letter to her solicitor.*

**dash²** /dæʃ/ *noun* **1** RUN [no plural] when you run somewhere very quickly *As the rain started, we **made a dash for** shelter.* **2** AMOUNT [C] a small amount of something, often food *Add a dash of milk to the sauce.* **3** MARK [C] a mark (-) used to separate parts of sentences

**dashboard** /'dæʃbɔːd/ *noun* [C] the part facing the driver at the front of a car with controls and equipment to show things such as speed and temperature ➔ *See colour picture* **Car** *on page Centre 3.*

**dashing** /'dæʃiŋ/ *adj* A dashing man is attractive in a confident and exciting way.

**o–⚬data** /'deɪtə/ *noun* [U] **1** information or facts about something *financial data* **2** information in the form of text, numbers, or symbols that can be used by or stored in a computer

**database** /'deɪtəbeɪs/ *noun* [C] information stored in a computer in an organized structure so that it can be searched in different ways *a national database of missing people*

**D**

o━**date**[1] /deɪt/ *noun* [C] **1** PARTICULAR DAY a particular day of the month or year *"What's the date today?" "It's the fifth."* • *Please give your name, address and date of birth.* **2** ARRANGED TIME a time when something has been arranged to happen *Let's make a date to have lunch.* • *We agreed to finish the report at a later date.* **3 to date** *formal* up to the present time *This novel is his best work to date.* **4** GOING OUT a romantic meeting when two people go out somewhere, such as to a restaurant or to see a film *He's asked her out on a date.* **5** PERSON someone who you are having a romantic meeting with *Who's your date for the prom?* **6** FRUIT a sticky brown fruit with a long seed inside ➜ *See also:* **blind date, sell-by date.**

**date**[2] /deɪt/ *verb* **1** MEET [I, T] to regularly spend time with someone you have a romantic relationship with *We've been dating for six months.* **2** WRITE [T] to write the day's date on something *a letter dated March 13th* **3** TIME [T] to say how long something has existed or when it was made *Scientists have dated the bones to 10,000 BC.* **4** NOT MODERN [I, T] to stop seeming modern, or to make something not seem modern *Clothes like these date really quickly.*

**date back** to have existed a particular length of time or since a particular time *This house dates back to 1650.*

**date from sth** to have existed since a particular time *The castle dates from the 11th century.*

**dated** /ˈdeɪtɪd/ *adj* not modern *This film seems a bit dated today.*

**daub** /dɔːb/ *verb* [T] to put a lot of a substance like paint on a surface in a careless way, often to write words or draw pictures *The walls have been daubed with graffiti.*

o━**daughter** /ˈdɔːtəʳ/ *noun* [C] your female child

**daughter-in-law** /ˈdɔːtərɪnlɔː/ *noun* [C] *plural* **daughters-in-law** your son's wife

**daunt** /dɔːnt/ *verb* [T] If someone is daunted by something, they are worried because it is difficult or frightening. [often passive] *I was a bit daunted by the idea of cooking for so many people.*

**daunting** /ˈdɔːntɪŋ/ *adj* If something is daunting, it makes you worried because it is difficult or frightening. *a daunting challenge/task*

**dawdle** /ˈdɔːdl/ *verb* [I] to walk very slowly, or do something very slowly in a way that wastes time *Stop dawdling! You'll be late for school!*

**dawn**[1] /dɔːn/ *noun* [U] **1** the early morning when light first appears in the sky *We woke at dawn.* **2 the dawn of sth** *literary* the time when something began *the dawn of civilization* ➜ *See also:* the **crack**[2] of dawn.

**dawn**[2] /dɔːn/ *verb* [I] If a day or a period of time dawns, it begins. *The day of her party dawned at last.*

**dawn on sb** If a fact dawns on you, you become aware of it after a period of not being aware of it. [+ that] *It suddenly dawned on them that Mary had been lying.*

o━**day** /deɪ/ *noun* **1** 24 HOURS [C] a period of 24 hours *the days of the week* • *January has 31 days.* • *Matthew runs five miles every day.* • *I saw her the day before yesterday.* **2** LIGHT HOURS [C, U] the period during the day when there is

light from the sun *a bright, sunny day* • *We've been travelling all day.* • *These animals sleep during the day and hunt at night.* **3** WORK HOURS [C] the time that you usually spend at work or school *She's had a very busy day at the office.* **4 the other day** a few days ago *I saw Terry the other day.* **5 day after day** every day for a long period of time *Day after day they marched through the mountains.* **6 one day** used to talk about something that happened in the past *One day, I came home to find my windows smashed.* **7 one day/some day/one of these days** used to talk about something you think will happen in the future *One of these days I'll tell her what really happened.* **8 days a** used to talk about a particular period of time when something happened or existed *in my younger days* • *This book was written before the days of computers.* **b** a long time *I haven't seen Jack for days.* **9 these days** used to talk about the present time *I don't go out much these days.* **10 in those days** used to talk about a period in the past *In those days, boys used to wear short trousers.* **11 the old days** a period in the past **12 call it a day** *informal* to stop doing something, especially working *It's almost midnight – let's call it a day.* **13 it's early days** *UK* something that you say when it is too early to know what will happen *Both teams are at the bottom of the league, but it's early days yet.* **14 make sb's day** to make someone very happy *Go on, ask him to dance – it'll make his day!* **15 save the day** to do something that solves a serious problem *My neighbour saved the day by agreeing to babysit at the last moment.* ➜ *See also:* **April Fool's Day, Boxing Day, Christmas Day, Independence Day, Mother's Day, New Year's Day, Valentine's Day,** at the **end**[1] of the day, **field day, open day, polling day.**

**daybreak** /ˈdeɪbreɪk/ *noun* [U] the time in the morning when light first appears in the sky

**daycare** /ˈdeɪkeəʳ/ *noun* [U] care provided during the day for people who cannot look after themselves, especially young children or old people *a daycare centre*

**daydream** /ˈdeɪdriːm/ *verb* [I] to have pleasant thoughts about something you would like to happen • **daydream** *noun* [C]

**daylight** /ˈdeɪlaɪt/ *noun* **1** [U] the natural light from the sun **2 in broad daylight** used to emphasize that something happens when it is light and people can see *He was attacked in broad daylight.*

**daylights** /ˈdeɪlaɪts/ *noun* **1 beat/knock the (living) daylights out of sb** *informal* to hit someone very hard many times **2 scare/frighten the (living) daylights out of sb** *informal* to frighten someone very much

ˌ**day reˈturn** *noun* [C] *UK* a ticket for a bus or train when you go somewhere and come back on the same day *a day return to Norwich*

**daytime** /ˈdeɪtaɪm/ *noun* [U] the period of the day when there is light from the sun, or the period when most people are at work *daytime television* • *a daytime telephone number*

**day-to-day** /ˌdeɪtəˈdeɪ/ *adj* [always before noun]

happening every day as a regular part of your job or your life *day-to-day activities/problems*

**daze** /deɪz/ *noun* **in a daze** when you cannot think clearly because you are shocked or have hit your head *The survivors were walking around in a daze.*

**dazed** /deɪzd/ *adj* not able to think clearly because you are shocked or have hit your head *a dazed expression*

**dazzle** /'dæzl/ *verb* [T] **1** If you are dazzled by someone or something, you think they are extremely good and exciting. [often passive] *I was dazzled by his intelligence and good looks.* **2** If light dazzles someone, it makes them unable to see for a short time.

**dazzling** /'dæzlɪŋ/ *adj* **1** extremely good and exciting *a dazzling display/performance* **2** A dazzling light is so bright that you cannot see for a short time after looking at it. *a dazzling white light*

**deacon** /'diːkən/ *noun* [C] an official in some Christian churches

o--◦**dead¹** /ded/ *adj* **1** NOT ALIVE not now alive *She's been dead for 20 years now.* • *He was shot dead by a masked intruder.* • *There were three children among the dead.* ➔ *See usage note at* **die**. **2** EQUIPMENT If a piece of equipment is dead, it is not working. *a dead battery* • *The phone suddenly went dead.* **3** QUIET *informal* If a place is dead, it is too quiet and nothing interesting is happening there. **4** COMPLETE [always before noun] complete *We waited in dead silence as the votes were counted.* **5** BODY *mainly UK* If part of your body is dead, you cannot feel it. *My arm's gone dead.* **6** **wouldn't be caught/ seen dead** *informal* If someone wouldn't be caught dead in a place or doing something, they would never go there or do it, usually because it would be too embarrassing. [+ doing sth] *I wouldn't be caught dead wearing a bikini.* **7 drop dead** *informal* to die very suddenly

**dead²** /ded/ *adv* **1** *informal* extremely or completely *(UK) The exam was dead easy.* • *(US) His advice was dead wrong.* **2 be dead set against sth/doing sth** to oppose something strongly *My parents were dead set against us getting married.* **3 stop dead** to suddenly stop moving or doing something

**dead³** /ded/ *noun* **the dead of night/winter** the middle of the night/winter

**deadbeat** /'dedbiːt/ *noun* [C] *US informal* someone who does not pay their debts *a dead-beat dad*

**deaden** /'dedⁿn/ *verb* [T] to make something less painful or less strong *She gave me an injection to deaden the pain.*

,**dead 'end** *noun* [C] **1** a road which is closed at one end **2** a situation in which it is impossible to make progress *The peace talks have reached a dead end.* • dead-end /,ded'end/ *adj* *a dead-end job/relationship* • *a dead-end street*

,**dead 'heat** *noun* [C] when two people finish a race at exactly the same time

**deadline** /'dedlaɪn/ *noun* [C] a time by which something must be done *to meet/miss a deadline* • *The deadline for entering the competition is tomorrow.*

**deadlock** /'dedlɒk/ *noun* [U] a situation in which it is impossible to make progress or to reach a decision *The talks have reached dead-lock.* • *There have been several attempts to break the deadlock.* • deadlocked *adj*

**deadly¹** /'dedli/ *adj* likely to cause death *a deadly virus* • *a deadly weapon*

**deadly²** /'dedli/ *adv* **deadly dull/serious, etc** extremely dull/serious, etc

**deadpan** /'dedpæn/ *adj* looking or sounding serious when you are telling a joke *a deadpan expression*

**deaf** /def/ *adj* **1** unable to hear *Many deaf people learn to lip read.* • *He goes to a school for the deaf.* **2 be deaf to sth** to refuse to listen to something • deafness *noun* [U] ➔ *See also:* fall on deaf ears (**ear**), **tone-deaf**.

**deafening** /'defⁿnɪŋ/ *adj* extremely loud *a deaf-ening noise*

**deal¹** /diːl/ *noun* **1** [C] an arrangement or an agreement, especially in business *a business deal* • *The police refused to do/make/strike a deal with the terrorists.* **2** [C] the price you pay for something, and what you get for your money *I got a really good deal on my new car.* **3 a good/great deal** a lot *A great deal of time and effort went into arranging this party.* • *I paid a good deal less than it was worth.*

o--◦**deal²** /diːl/ *verb* [I, T] *past* **dealt** to give cards to players in a game *Whose turn is it to deal?*

**deal in sth** to buy and sell particular goods as a business *a shop dealing in rare books*

**deal with sth 1** to take action in order to achieve something or to solve a problem *Can you deal with this gentleman's complaint?* • *The government must deal with unemployment.* **2** to be about a particular subject *The programme dealt with teenage pregnancy.*

**deal with sb/sth** to do business with a person or organization *I usually deal with the accounts department.*

**deal with sb** to meet or talk to someone, especially as part of your job *She's used to dealing with foreign customers.*

**dealer** /'diːlə/ *noun* [C] **1** a person or company that buys and sells things for profit *a car dealer* • *a drug dealer* **2** a person who gives out cards to players in a game

**dealership** /'diːlə∫ɪp/ *noun* [C] a business that sells cars, usually cars made by a particular company *a Ford/Toyota dealership*

**dealings** /'diːlɪŋz/ *noun* [plural] activities involving other people, especially in business *Have you had any dealings with their London office?*

**dealt** /delt/ *past of* deal

**dean** /diːn/ *noun* [C] **1** an official in a college or university **2** an official in charge of a large church or group of churches

o--◦**dear¹** /dɪə/ *adj* **1** IN LETTERS used at the beginning of a letter, before the name of the person you are writing to *Dear Amy* • *Dear Mrs Simpson* • *Dear Sir/Madam* **2** LIKED [always before noun] A dear person is someone who you know and like very much. *my dear Peter* • *He's one of my dearest friends.* **3** EXPENSIVE *UK* expensive *I wouldn't buy anything there, it's far too dear.* **4 dear to sb/sb's heart** If something is dear to someone or dear to their heart, it is

D

very important to them. *The charity was very dear to his heart.*

**dear²** /dɪəʳ/ *exclamation* **oh dear** used to express surprise and disappointment *Oh dear! I forgot my keys!*

**dear³** /dɪəʳ/ *noun* [C] used to address someone in a friendly way, especially a child or someone you love *Don't cry, my dear.* • *Yes, dear?*

**dearly** /ˈdɪəli/ *adv* very much *I would dearly love to visit Rome again.*

**dearth** /dɜːθ/ *noun formal* **a dearth of sth** when there are not many or not enough of something available *a dearth of new homes*

○⚫**death** /deθ/ *noun* **1** [C, U] the end of life *Do you believe in life after death?* • *We need to reduce the number of deaths from heart attacks.* • *a death threat* **2 to death** until you die *He was beaten to death by a gang of youths.* **3 put sb to death** to kill someone as a punishment [often passive] *She was put to death for her beliefs.* **4 frightened/bored, etc to death** *informal* extremely frightened/bored, etc *She's scared to death of dogs.*

**deathbed** /ˈdeθbed/ *noun* **on your deathbed** very ill and going to die soon

**deathly** /ˈdeθli/ *adj, adv* extreme in a way which is unpleasant *a deathly silence* • *Her face turned deathly pale.*

**'death ˌpenalty** *noun* [C] the legal punishment of death for a crime

**ˌdeath 'row** *noun* **on death row** in prison and waiting to be killed as a punishment for a crime

**'death ˌtoll** *noun* [C] the number of people who die because of an event such as a war or an accident *The death toll from the earthquake has risen to 1500.*

**debase** /dɪˈbeɪs/ *verb* [T] *formal* to reduce the value or quality of something *They argue that money has debased football.*

**debatable** /dɪˈbeɪtəbl/ *adj* If something is debatable, it is not certain if it is true or not. *It's debatable whether a university degree will help you in this job.*

**debate¹** /dɪˈbeɪt/ *noun* [C, U] discussion or argument about a subject *a political debate* • *There has been a lot of public **debate on** the safety of food.*

**debate²** /dɪˈbeɪt/ *verb* **1** [I, T] to discuss a subject in a formal way *These issues need to be debated openly.* **2** [T] to try to make a decision about something [+ question word] *I'm still debating whether to go out tonight or not.*

**debilitating** /dɪˈbɪlɪteɪtɪŋ/ *adj formal* A debilitating illness or problem makes you weak and unable to do what you want to do. *the debilitating effects of flu*

**debit¹** /ˈdebɪt/ *noun* [C] money taken out of a bank account, or a record of this ⊃ *Opposite* **credit**, ⊃ *See also:* **direct debit**.

**debit²** /ˈdebɪt/ *verb* [T] to take money out of a bank account as a payment for something *Twenty pounds has been debited from my account.*

**'debit ˌcard** *noun* [C] a plastic card used to pay for things directly from your bank account

**debris** /ˈdebriː/ ⓊⓈ də'briː/ *noun* [U] broken pieces of something *Debris from the aircraft was scattered over a wide area.*

○⚫**debt** /det/ *noun* **1** [C] an amount of money that you owe someone *She's working in a bar to try to **pay off** her debts.* **2** [U] when you owe money to someone *We don't want to **get into** debt.* • *He's heavily **in debt**.* **3 be in sb's debt** to feel grateful to someone who has helped you or given you something *I shall forever be in your debt.*

**debtor** /ˈdetəʳ/ *noun* [C] someone who owes money

**debut** /ˈdeɪbjuː/ ⓊⓈ deɪ'bjuː/ *noun* [C] when someone performs or presents something to the public for the first time *She **made her debut** as a pianist in 1975.* • *This is the band's debut album.*

**Dec** *written abbreviation for* December

○⚫**decade** /ˈdekeɪd/ *noun* [C] a period of ten years

**decadence** /ˈdekəd°ns/ *noun* [U] when you do or have things only for your own pleasure or behave in an immoral way • **decadent** *adj a decadent lifestyle*

**decaf** /ˈdiːkæf/ *noun* [C, U] *informal short for* decaffeinated coffee

**decaffeinated** /dɪˈkæfɪneɪtɪd/ *adj* Decaffeinated tea or coffee is made by removing the caffeine (= chemical which makes you feel more awake).

**decay** /dɪˈkeɪ/ *verb* [I] to gradually become bad or weak or be destroyed, often because of natural causes like bacteria or age *decaying leaves* • *Sugar makes your teeth decay.* • **decay** *noun* [U] when something decays *tooth decay* • *Many of the buildings had **fallen into decay**.*

**deceased** /dɪˈsiːst/ *adj formal* **1** dead *the deceased man's belongings* **2 the deceased** someone who has died *The police have not yet informed the family of the deceased.*

**deceit** /dɪˈsiːt/ *noun* [U] when someone tries to make someone believe something that is not true • **deceitful** *adj deceitful behaviour*

○⚫**deceive** /dɪˈsiːv/ *verb* [T] to make someone believe something that is not true *The company deceived customers by selling old computers as new ones.*

**December** /dɪˈsembəʳ/ *(written abbreviation* **Dec)** *noun* [C, U] the twelfth month of the year

**decency** /ˈdiːs°nsi/ *noun* [U] behaviour that is good, moral, and acceptable in society *a sense of decency* • *She didn't even **have the decency to** tell me she wasn't coming.*

**decent** /ˈdiːs°nt/ *adj* **1** SATISFACTORY of a satisfactory quality or level *He earns a decent salary.* • *I haven't had a decent cup of coffee since I've been here.* **2** HONEST honest and morally good *Decent people have had their lives ruined by his behaviour.* • *She should do the decent thing and apologize.* **3** CLOTHES [never before noun] wearing clothes *Can I come in? Are you decent?* • **decently** *adv*

**decentralize** *(also UK* **-ise**) /diːˈsentrəlaɪz/ *verb* [T] to move the control of an organization or a government from a single place to several smaller places • **decentralization** /diːˌsentrəlaɪˈzeɪʃ°n/ *noun* [U]

**deception** /dɪˈsepʃ°n/ *noun* [C, U] when someone makes someone believe something that is not true *He was found guilty of obtaining money by deception.*

**deceptive** /dɪˈseptɪv/ *adj* If something is deceptive, it makes you believe something that is not true. *Appearances can be deceptive.* • **deceptively** *adv*

**decibel** /ˈdesɪbel/ *noun* [C] a unit for measuring how loud a sound is

o-* **decide** /dɪˈsaɪd/ *verb* **1** [I, T] to choose something after thinking about several possibilities [+ question word] *I haven't decided whether or not to tell him.* • [+ to do sth] *She's decided to take the job.* • [+ (that)] *The teachers decided that the school would take part in the competition.* **2** [T] to be the reason or situation that makes a particular result happen *This match will decide the tournament.* **3 deciding factor** the thing that helps to make the final decision

**decide on sth/sb** to choose something or someone after thinking carefully *I've decided on blue walls for the bathroom.*

**decided** /dɪˈsaɪdɪd/ *adj* [always before noun] certain, obvious, or easy to notice *She had a decided advantage over her opponent.* • **decidedly** *adv That exam was decidedly more difficult than the last one.*

**deciduous** /dɪˈsɪdjuəs/ *adj* A deciduous tree has leaves that drop off every autumn.

**decimal**¹ /ˈdesɪməl/ *adj* involving counting in units of 10 *a decimal system*

**decimal**² /ˈdesɪməl/ *noun* [C] a number less than one that is written as one or more numbers after a point *The decimal 0.5 is the same as the fraction 1/2.*

,**decimal 'place** UK (US **'decimal ,place**) *noun* [C] the position of a number after a decimal point *The number is accurate to three decimal places.*

,**decimal 'point** UK (US **'decimal ,point**) *noun* [C] the point (.) that is used to separate a whole number and a decimal

**decimate** /ˈdesɪmeɪt/ *verb* [T] *formal* to destroy large numbers of people or things *Populations of endangered animals have been decimated.*

**decipher** /dɪˈsaɪfər/ *verb* [T] to discover what something says or means *It's sometimes difficult to decipher his handwriting.*

o-* **decision** /dɪˈsɪʒən/ *noun* [C] a choice that you make about something after thinking about several possibilities *She has had to **make** some very difficult **decisions**.* • [+ to do sth] *It was his decision to leave.* • *The committee should **come to/reach a** final **decision** by next week.*

**decisive** /dɪˈsaɪsɪv/ *adj* **1** strongly affecting how a situation will progress or end *a decisive goal/victory* • *Seeing that advertisement was a decisive moment in my life.* **2** making decisions quickly and easily *You need to be more decisive.* Ɔ *Opposite* **indecisive.** • **decisively** *adv We must act quickly and decisively to stop the spread of the disease.* • **decisiveness** *noun* [U]

**deck**¹ /dek/ *noun* [C] SHIP/BUS/PLANE one of the floors of a ship, bus, or aircraft *The children like to sit on the top deck of the bus.* **2 on deck** on the top floor of a ship that is not covered **3** CARDS *US* (*UK* **pack**) a collection of cards that you use to play a game **4** MACHINE a machine that you use to play records or tapes (= plastic cases containing magnetic material used to record sounds) *a tape deck*

**deck**² /dek/ *verb*
**be decked out** to be decorated with something, or dressed in something special *The bar was decked out with red and yellow flags.*

**deckchair** /ˈdektʃeər/ *noun* [C] a folding chair that you use outside

**declaration** /ˌdekləˈreɪʃən/ *noun* [C] an announcement, often one that is written and official *a declaration of independence*

**declare** /dɪˈkleər/ *verb* [T] **1** to announce something publicly or officially *to declare war* • [+ that] *Scientists have declared that this meat is safe to eat.* **2** to officially tell someone the value of goods you have bought, or the amount of money you have earned because you might have to pay tax *Have you got anything to declare?*

**decline**¹ /dɪˈklaɪn/ *noun* [C, U] when something becomes less in amount, importance, quality, or strength *a steady decline in sales/standards*

**decline**² /dɪˈklaɪn/ *verb* **1** [I, T] *formal* If you decline something, you refuse it politely. *She declined his offer of a lift.* • [+ to do sth] *He declined to comment.* **2** [I] to become less in amount, importance, quality, or strength *Sales of records have declined steadily.*

**decode** /ˌdiːˈkəʊd/ *verb* [T] to discover the meaning of a message that is in code (= secret system of communication)

**decoder** /diːˈkəʊdər/ *noun* [C] a piece of equipment that allows you to receive particular television signals *You need a decoder to get these channels.*

**decompose** /ˌdiːkəmˈpəʊz/ *verb* [I] If a dead person, animal, or plant decomposes, it decays and is gradually destroyed. *a decomposing body*

**decor** /ˈdeɪkɔːr/ ⑤ deɪˈkɔːr/ *noun* [U, no plural] the style of decoration and furniture in a room or building

o-* **decorate** /ˈdekəreɪt/ *verb* **1** [T] to make something look more attractive by putting things on it or around it *They decorated the room with balloons for her party.* **2** [I, T] to put paint or paper on the walls or other surfaces of a room or building *The whole house needs decorating.*

**decorate**

D

**3 be decorated** to be given a medal (= small, metal disc) as official respect for military action *He was decorated for bravery.*

**decoration** /,dekə'reɪʃən/ *noun* **1** ATTRACTIVE THING [C, U] when you make something look more attractive by putting things on it or around it, or something that you use to do this *Christmas decorations* • *She hung some pictures around the room for decoration.* **2** PAINT [U] when the walls or other surfaces of rooms or buildings are covered with paint or paper *This place is badly in need of decoration.* **3** OFFICIAL RESPECT [C] an official sign of respect such as a medal (= small, metal disc)

**decorative** /'dekərətɪv/ *adj* making something or someone look more attractive *decorative objects*

**decorator** /'dekəreɪtər/ *noun* [C] **1** *UK* someone whose job is to put paint or paper on the walls and other surfaces of rooms or buildings **2** *US* someone whose job is to design the appearance of rooms in houses and buildings

**decorum** /dɪ'kɔːrəm/ *noun* [U] *formal* behaviour which is considered to be polite and correct

**decoy** /'diːkɔɪ/ *noun* [C] someone or something used to lead a person or animal to a place so that they can be caught

**decrease** /dɪ'kriːs/ *verb* [I, T] to become less, or to make something become less *During the summer months, rainfall decreases.* • decrease /'diːkriːs/ *noun* [C, U] *There has been a decrease in the number of violent crimes.* ⊃ Opposite **increase**.

**decree** /dɪ'kriː/ *noun* [C] an official order or decision from a government or leader *a presidential/royal decree* • decree *verb* [T] **decreeing**, *past* **decreed**

**decrepit** /dɪ'krepɪt/ *adj* old and in very bad condition *a decrepit building*

**dedicate** /'dedɪkeɪt/ *verb* **1 dedicate your life/yourself to sth** to give most of your energy and time to something *She has dedicated her life to helping others.* **2 dedicate sth to sb** to say that something you have made or done is to show your love or respect for someone [often passive] *This book is dedicated to my daughter.*

**dedicated** /'dedɪkeɪtɪd/ *adj* **1** believing that something is very important and giving a lot of time and energy to it *a dedicated teacher* **2** designed to be used for a particular purpose *a dedicated word processor*

**dedication** /,dedɪ'keɪʃən/ *noun* **1** [U] when you are willing to give a lot of time and energy to something because you believe it is very important *She thanked the staff for their dedication and enthusiasm.* **2** [C] when someone says that something has been made or done to show love and respect for someone else *a dedication to the poet's mother*

**deduce** /dɪ'djuːs/ *verb* [T] to decide that something is true using the available information [+ (that)] *From the contents of his shopping basket, I deduced that he was single.*

**deduct** /dɪ'dʌkt/ *verb* [T] to take an amount or a part of something away from a total *The*

*company will deduct tax from your earnings.* • *Marks are deducted for spelling mistakes.*

**deduction** /dɪ'dʌkʃən/ *noun* [C, U] **1** when an amount or a part of something is taken away from a total, or the amount that is taken *tax deductions* **2** when you decide that something is true using the available information

**deed** /diːd/ *noun* [C] **1** *formal* something that you do *good deeds* • *I judge a person by their deeds, not their words.* **2** a legal document recording an agreement, especially saying who owns something [usually plural] *Where do you keep the deeds to the house?*

**deem** /diːm/ *verb* [T] *formal* to judge or consider something in a particular way *The book was deemed to be unsuitable for children.*

o━**deep¹** /diːp/ *adj* **1** TOP TO BOTTOM having a long distance from the top to the bottom *The water is a lot deeper than it seems.* **2** FRONT TO BACK having a long distance from the front to the back *How deep are the shelves?* **3 one metre/6ft, etc deep** one metre/6 ft, etc from the top to the bottom, or from the front the back *This end of the pool is two metres deep.* **4** FEELING A deep feeling is very strong. *deep affection/regret* **6** SOUND A deep sound is low. *a deep voice* **7** SERIOUS serious and difficult for most people to understand *a deep and meaningful conversation* **8 a deep sleep** when someone is sleeping in a way that makes it difficult to wake them up **9** COLOUR A deep colour is strong and dark. *deep brown eyes* **10 take a deep breath** to fill your lungs with air *Take a deep breath and relax.* **11 deep in thought/conversation** giving all of your attention to what you are thinking or talking about, and not noticing anything else ⊃ See also: throw sb in at the deep **end¹**, be in deep **water¹**.

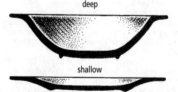

deep

shallow

**deep²** /diːp/ *adv* **1** a long way into something from the top or outside *They travelled deep into the forest.* • *She pushed her hands deep into her pockets.* **2 deep down** If you know or feel something deep down, you are certain that it is true, or you feel it strongly although you do not admit it or show it. *Deep down, I knew that I was right.* **3 go/run deep** If a feeling or a problem goes deep, it is very strong or serious and has existed for a long time.

**deepen** /'diːpən/ *verb* [I, T] **1** to become deeper, or to make something become deeper *The sky deepened to a rich, dark blue.* **2** to become worse, or to make something become worse *a deepening crisis*

,deep 'freeze *UK* (*US* ,deep ,freeze) *noun* [C] another word for freezer (= a large container in which food can be frozen and stored)

**deep-fried** /ˌdiːpˈfraɪd/ *adj* fried in a lot of oil

**deeply** /ˈdiːpli/ *adv* **1** very much *I have fallen deeply in love with her.* **2 breathe deeply** to fill your lungs with air

**deep-seated** /ˌdiːpˈsiːtɪd/ (*also* **deep-rooted**) *adj* strongly felt or believed and difficult to change *deep-seated fears/problems*

**deer** /dɪə<sup>r</sup>/ *noun* [C] *plural* **deer** a large, wild animal that is sometimes hunted for food and which has antlers (= long horns) if it is male

deer

**deface** /dɪˈfeɪs/ *verb* [T] to spoil the appearance of something, especially by writing or painting on it *Several posters have been defaced with political slogans.*

**default**<sup>1</sup> /dɪˈfɔːlt/ *noun* **1** [no plural] what exists or happens usually if no changes are made **2 by default** If something happens by default, it happens only because something else does not happen. *No one else stood in the election, so he won by default.* • default *adj* [always before noun] *The default font size is 10.*

**default**<sup>2</sup> /dɪˈfɔːlt/ *verb* [I] to not do what you have made an agreement to do, especially paying back money you have borrowed *They have **defaulted on** their debt repayments.*

o━**defeat**<sup>1</sup> /dɪˈfiːt/ *verb* [T] **1** to win against someone in a fight or competition *She was defeated by an Australian player in the first round of the tournament.* **2** to make someone or something fail *The bill was narrowly defeated in parliament.*

o━**defeat**<sup>2</sup> /dɪˈfiːt/ *noun* **1** [C, U] when someone loses against someone else in a fight or competition *The Chicago Cubs have suffered their worst defeat of the season.* **2** [no plural] when someone or something is made to fail *the defeat of apartheid*

**defeatism** /dɪˈfiːtɪz<sup>ə</sup>m/ *noun* [U] behaviour or thoughts that show that you do not expect to be successful

**defeatist** /dɪˈfiːtɪst/ *adj* behaving in a way that shows that you do not expect to be successful *a defeatist attitude* • defeatist *noun* [C]

**defect**<sup>1</sup> /ˈdiːfekt/ *noun* [C] a fault or problem with someone or something *a birth defect* • *A mechanical defect caused the plane to crash.* • defective /dɪˈfektɪv/ *adj* having a fault or problem *defective goods*

**defect**<sup>2</sup> /dɪˈfekt/ *verb* [I] to leave your country or organization and go to join an enemy country

or competing organization *He defected to the West.* • defection /dɪˈfekʃ<sup>ə</sup>n/ *noun* [C, U] when someone defects • defector *noun* [C]

o━**defence** *UK* (*US* **defense**) /dɪˈfens/ *noun* **1** MILITARY [U] the weapons and military forces that a country uses to protect itself against attack *Government spending on defence is increasing.* • *the defence minister/industry* **2** PROTECTION [C, U] protection, or something that provides protection against attack or criticism *the body's defences against infection* • *She argued strongly **in defence of** her actions.* **3 come to sb's defence** to support someone when they are being criticized **4 the defence** [group] the lawyers in a court who work in support of the person who is accused of a crime *He was cross-examined by the defence.* • *a defence lawyer* **5** SPORT [C, U] the part of a sports team which tries to prevent the other team from scoring points *Our team has a very strong defence.* ➔ *See also:* **self-defence**.

**defenceless** *UK* (*US* **defenseless**) /dɪˈfensləs/ *adj* weak and unable to protect yourself from attack *a small, defenceless child*

o━**defend** /dɪˈfend/ *verb* **1** PROTECT [T] to protect someone or something from being attacked, especially by fighting *The army was sent in to **defend** the country **against** enemy attack.* • [often reflexive] *She tried to defend herself with a knife.* **2** SUPPORT [T] to support someone or something that is being criticized *The newspaper's editor defended his decision to publish the photos.* **3** LAW [T] to try to show in a court that someone is not guilty of a crime *He has hired two lawyers to defend him in court.* **4** SPORT [I, T] to try to stop the other sports team from scoring points **5 defend a championship/title, etc** to try to win a match or competition that you have won before *She will be defending her title for the third year running.* • defender *noun* [C]

**defendant** /dɪˈfendənt/ *noun* [C] the person in a court who is accused of a crime

o━**defense** /dɪˈfens/ *noun* *US spelling of* defence

**defenseless** /dɪˈfensləs/ *adj* *US spelling of* defenceless

**defensive**<sup>1</sup> /dɪˈfensɪv/ *adj* **1** CRITICISM quick to protect yourself from being criticized *He's very **defensive about** his weight.* **2** SPORT *mainly US* A defensive player in a sports team tries to stop the other team scoring points. **3** ATTACK done or used to protect someone or something from attack • defensively *adv* "I wasn't even there," she said defensively.

**defensive**<sup>2</sup> /dɪˈfensɪv/ *noun* **on the defensive** ready to protect yourself because you are expecting to be criticized or attacked

**defer** /dɪˈfɜː<sup>r</sup>/ *verb* [T] **deferring**, *past* **deferred** to arrange for something to happen at a later time *The payments can be deferred for three months.*

**deference** /ˈdef<sup>ə</sup>rəns/ *noun* [U] polite behaviour that shows that you respect someone or something • deferential /ˌdef<sup>ə</sup>ˈrenʃ<sup>ə</sup>l/ *adj*

**defiance** /dɪˈfaɪəns/ *noun* [U] when you refuse to obey someone or something *an act of defiance*

**defiant** /dɪˈfaɪənt/ *adj* refusing to obey someone or something *a defiant child* • defiantly *adv*

D

**deficiency** /dɪˈfɪʃ°nsi/ *noun* [C, U] **1** when you do not have enough of something *a vitamin deficiency* **2** a mistake or fault in something so that it is not good enough *Parents are complaining of serious deficiencies in the education system.*

**deficient** /dɪˈfɪʃ°nt/ *adj* **1** not having enough of something *If you have poor night vision you may be deficient in vitamin A.* **2** not good enough *His theory is deficient in several respects.*

**deficit** /ˈdefɪsɪt/ *noun* [C] the amount by which the money that you spend is more than the money that you receive *a budget deficit*

**defile** /dɪˈfaɪl/ *verb* [T] *formal* to spoil someone or something that is pure, holy, or beautiful

**define** /dɪˈfaɪn/ *verb* [T] **1** to say exactly what something means, or what someone or something is like *Your duties are clearly defined in the contract.* • *Can you define what it means to be an American?* **2** to show the outer edges or shape of something *It has sharply defined edges.*

○⚬**definite** /ˈdefɪnət/ *adj* **1** certain, fixed, and not likely to change *We need a definite answer by tomorrow.* **2** clear and obvious *There has been a definite improvement in her behaviour.*

ˌ**definite ˈarticle** *noun* [C] in grammar, used to mean the word 'the' ⊃ *Compare* **indefinite article**.

○⚬**definitely** /ˈdefɪnətli/ *adv* without any doubt *This book is definitely worth reading.* • *"Do you want to come?" "Yes, definitely."*

**definition** /ˌdefɪˈnɪʃ°n/ *noun* **1** [C] an explanation of the meaning of a word or phrase *a dictionary definition* **2** [U] how clear an image of something is in a photograph or on a screen

**definitive** /dɪˈfɪnətɪv/ *adj* **1** certain, clear, and not likely to change *a definitive answer* **2** A definitive book or piece of work is the best of its type. *the definitive guide to London* • **definitively** *adv*

**deflate** /dɪˈfleɪt/ *verb* **1** [I, T] to let all the air or gas out of something, or to become emptied of air or gas *to deflate a balloon/tyre* **2** [T] to make someone lose confidence or feel less important [often passive] *They were totally deflated by losing the match.*

**deflect** /dɪˈflekt/ *verb* **1** [I, T] to make something change direction by hitting or touching it, or to change direction after hitting something *The ball was deflected into the corner of the net.* **2** **deflect attention/blame/criticism, etc** to cause attention/blame/criticism, etc to be directed away from you • **deflection** /dɪˈflekʃ°n/ *noun* [C, U]

**deforestation** /diːˌfɒrɪˈsteɪʃ°n/ *noun* [U] when all the trees in a large area are cut down

**deformed** /dɪˈfɔːmd/ *adj* with a shape that has not developed normally *deformed hands* • **deform** /dɪˈfɔːm/ *verb* [T]

**deformity** /dɪˈfɔːməti/ *noun* [C, U] when a part of the body has not developed in the normal way or with the normal shape

**defraud** /dɪˈfrɔːd/ *verb* [T] to obtain money from someone illegally by being dishonest

**defrost** /ˌdiːˈfrɒst/ *verb* [I, T] **1** If food defrosts, it becomes warmer after being frozen, and if you defrost it, you make it become warmer after

being frozen. *You need to defrost the fish before you can cook it.* **2** If you defrost a fridge or freezer (= machines that keep food cold), you make them warmer and remove the ice, and if they defrost, they become warmer and the ice melts.

**deft** /deft/ *adj* quick and showing great skill *a deft movement/touch* • **deftly** *adv formal*

**defunct** /dɪˈfʌŋkt/ *adj* not working or existing now

**defuse** /ˌdiːˈfjuːz/ *verb* [T] **1** to make a difficult or dangerous situation calmer *He made a joke to defuse the tension.* **2** to prevent a bomb from exploding by removing the fuse (= part that starts the explosion)

**defy** /dɪˈfaɪ/ *verb* **1** [T] to refuse to obey someone or something *Some of these children openly defy their teachers.* **2** **defy belief/description/ explanation, etc** to be impossible to believe, describe, explain, etc *His attitude defies belief.* **3 defy sb to do sth** to tell someone to do something that you think will be impossible *I defy you to prove that I'm wrong.*

**degenerate¹** /dɪˈdʒen°reɪt/ *verb* [I] to become worse *The protest soon degenerated into violence.* • **degeneration** /dɪˌdʒenəˈreɪʃ°n/ *noun* [U]

**degenerate²** /dɪˈdʒen°rət/ *adj* having low moral principles

**degrade** /dɪˈɡreɪd/ *verb* [T] **1** to treat someone without respect and as if they have no value *They think the advert degrades women.* **2** to damage the quality or condition of something • **degradation** /ˌdeɡrəˈdeɪʃ°n/ *noun* [U]

**degrading** /dɪˈɡreɪdɪŋ/ *adj* treating people without respect and as if they have no value *degrading work*

○⚬**degree** /dɪˈɡriː/ *noun* **1** TEMPERATURE [C] a unit for measuring temperature, shown by the symbol (°) written after a number **2** ANGLE [C] a unit for measuring angles, shown by the symbol ° written after a number **3** QUALIFICATION [C] a qualification given for completing a university course *She has a degree in physics.* **4** AMOUNT [C, U] an amount or level of something *They had a certain degree of success.* • *I agree with you to a degree* (= in some ways but not completely). ⊃ *See also:* Master's (**master¹**) degree

**dehydrated** /ˌdiːhaɪˈdreɪtɪd/ *adj* not having enough water in your body *If you don't drink in this heat, you'll get dehydrated.*

**dehydration** /ˌdiːhaɪˈdreɪʃ°n/ *noun* [U] when you do not have enough water in your body

**deign** /deɪn/ *verb* **deign to do sth** to do something that you think you are too important to do

**deity** /ˈdeɪɪti ⓤⓈ ˈdiːəti/ *noun* [C] *formal* a god or goddess (= female god)

**deja vu** /ˌdeɪʒɑːˈvuː/ *noun* [U] a feeling that you have already experienced exactly what is happening now *She suddenly had a strong sense of deja vu.*

**dejected** /dɪˈdʒektɪd/ *adj* unhappy and disappointed *He looked tired and dejected.* • **dejection** /dɪˈdʒekʃ°n/ *noun* [U]

○⚬**delay¹** /dɪˈleɪ/ *verb* **1** [I, T] to make something happen at a later time than originally planned or expected *Can you delay your departure until next week?* **2** [T] to cause someone or something to be slow or late [often passive] *I was delayed by traffic.*

o━**delay²** /dɪ'leɪ/ *noun* [C, U] when you have to wait longer than expected for something to happen, or the time that you have to wait *An accident caused long delays on the motorway.*

**delectable** /dɪ'lektəbl/ *adj formal* extremely nice, especially to eat

**delegate¹** /'delɪgət/ *noun* [C] someone who is sent somewhere to represent a group of people, especially at a meeting

**delegate²** /'delɪgeɪt/ *verb* [I, T] to give someone else part of your work or some of your responsibilities *He needs to learn to delegate or he'll never get everything done.*

**delegation** /,delɪ'geɪʃ°n/ *noun* **1** [C] a group of people who have been chosen to represent a much larger group of people *a delegation of Chinese officials* **2** [U] when you give someone else part of your work or some of your responsibilities

**delete** /dɪ'liːt/ *verb* [T] to remove something, especially from a computer's memory *All names have been deleted from the report.* • deletion /dɪ'liːʃ°n/ *noun* [C, U]

**deli** /'deli/ *noun* [C] *short for* delicatessen

**deliberate¹** /dɪ'lɪb°rət/ *adj* **1** done intentionally, or planned *This was a deliberate attempt by them to deceive us.* **2** careful and without hurry *Her movements were calm and deliberate.*

**deliberate²** /dɪ'lɪb°reɪt/ *verb* [I, T] to consider something carefully before making a decision *They deliberated for ten hours before reaching a decision.*

o━**deliberately** /dɪ'lɪb°rətli/ *adv* intentionally, having planned to do something *He deliberately lied to the police.*

**deliberation** /dɪ,lɪbə'reɪʃ°n/ *noun* [C, U] careful thought or talk about a subject before a decision is made *The jury began deliberations on Thursday.*

**delicacy** /'delɪkəsi/ *noun* **1** FOOD [C] a special food, usually something rare or expensive **2** GENTLE QUALITY [U] the quality of being soft, light, or gentle **3** EASY TO DAMAGE [U] when something is easy to damage or break **4** NEEDING CARE [U] when something needs to be treated very carefully *You need to be very tactful because of the delicacy of the situation.* **5** ATTRACTIVE [U] when something has a thin, attractive shape

o━**delicate** /'delɪkət/ *adj* **1** GENTLE soft, light, or gentle *a delicate flavour* • *a delicate shade of pink* **2** EASY TO DAMAGE easy to damage or break *a delicate china cup* **3** NEEDING CARE needing to be dealt with very carefully *I need to discuss a very delicate matter with you.* **4** ATTRACTIVE having a thin, attractive shape *delicate hands* • delicately *adv*

**delicatessen** /,delɪkə'tes°n/ *noun* [C] a shop, or a part of a shop which sells cheeses, cooked meats, salads, etc

**delicious** /dɪ'lɪʃəs/ *adj* If food or drink is delicious, it smells or tastes extremely good. *This soup is absolutely delicious.* • deliciously *adv* *a deliciously fruity drink*

**delight¹** /dɪ'laɪt/ *noun* **1** [U] happiness and excited pleasure *The children screamed with*

delight. **2** [C] someone or something that gives you pleasure *She is a delight to have around.*

**delight²** /dɪ'laɪt/ *verb* [T] to make someone feel very pleased and happy *The new discovery has delighted scientists everywhere.*

**delight in sth/doing sth** to get a lot of pleasure from something, especially something unpleasant *She seems to delight in making him look stupid.*

**delighted** /dɪ'laɪtɪd/ *adj* very pleased [+ to do sth] *I'd be delighted to accept your invitation.* • *They are **delighted with** their new car.*

**delightful** /dɪ'laɪtf°l/ *adj* very pleasant, attractive, or enjoyable *We had a delightful evening.* • delightfully *adv*

**delinquency** /dɪ'lɪŋkwənsi/ *noun* [U] criminal or bad behaviour, especially by young people

**delinquent** /dɪ'lɪŋkwənt/ *noun* [C] a young person who behaves badly, usually by committing crimes • delinquent *adj delinquent behaviour*

**delirious** /dɪ'lɪriəs/ *adj* **1** speaking or thinking in a confused way, often because of a fever or drugs **2** extremely happy *delirious fans* • deliriously *adv*

o━**deliver** /dɪ'lɪvə'/ *verb* **1** [I, T] to take things such as letters, parcels, or goods to a person or place *They can deliver the sofa on Wednesday.* **2** [I, T] to achieve or do something that you have promised to do, or that people expect you to do *The company failed to deliver the high quality service that we expect.* **3 deliver a speech/talk, etc** to speak formally to a group of people *She delivered the speech on national TV.* **4 deliver a baby** to help take a baby out of its mother when it is being born ➲ *See also:* deliver the **goods**.

**delivery** /dɪ'lɪv°ri/ *noun* [C, U] **1** when someone takes things such as letters, parcels, or goods to a person or place *Is there a charge for delivery?* **2** when a baby is born and comes out of its mother *Her husband was present at the delivery.*

**delta** /'deltə/ *noun* [C] a low, flat area of land where a river divides into smaller rivers and goes into the sea *the Nile delta*

**delude** /dɪ'luːd/ *verb* [T] to make someone believe something that is not real or true [often reflexive, + into + doing sth] *She deluded herself into thinking she could win.* • deluded *adj* believing things that are not real or true

**deluge¹** /'deljuːdʒ/ *noun* [C] **1** a very large amount of something that suddenly arrives *They have received a deluge of complaints.* **2** a sudden, large amount of rain, or a flood

**deluge²** /'deljuːdʒ/ *verb* **be deluged with/by sth** to receive very large amounts of something suddenly *Our switchboard was deluged with calls last night.*

**delusion** /dɪ'luːʒ°n/ *noun* [C, U] when someone believes something that is not true [+ (that)] *She is **under the delusion** that her debts will just go away.*

**deluxe** /də'lʌks/ *adj* luxurious and of very high quality *a deluxe hotel*

**delve** /delv/ *verb* **delve in/into/inside, etc** to search in a container to try to find something *He delved in his pocket and pulled out a pen.*

**delve into sth** to examine something carefully

in order to discover more information about someone or something *I don't like to delve too deeply into his past.*

**demand**[1] /dɪˈmɑːnd/ *noun* **1** [U, no plural] a need for something to be sold or supplied *There's an increasing **demand for** cheap housing.* **2** [C] a strong request *They received a final **demand** for payment.* **3 in demand** wanted or needed in large numbers *Good teachers are always in demand.*

○⊷**demand**[2] /dɪˈmɑːnd/ *verb* [T] **1** to ask for something in a way that shows that you do not expect to be refused *I demanded an explanation.* ● [+ that] *The survivors are demanding that the airline pays them compensation.* ➜ See usage note at **ask**. **2** to need something such as time or effort *This job demands a high level of concentration.*

**demanding** /dɪˈmɑːndɪŋ/ *adj* needing a lot of your time, attention, or effort *a very demanding job*

**demands** /dɪˈmɑːndz/ *noun* [plural] the difficult things that you have to do *the demands of modern life* ● *His new job **makes** a lot of **demands on** him* (= he has to work very hard).

**demeaning** /dɪˈmiːnɪŋ/ *adj* If something is demeaning, it makes you feel that you are not respected. *Some people consider beauty competitions demeaning to women.*

**demeanour** *UK* (*US* **demeanor**) /dɪˈmiːnəʳ/ *noun* [C] the way that someone looks, seems, and behaves *a quiet, serious demeanour*

**demented** /dɪˈmentɪd/ *adj* mentally ill, or behaving in a very strange way without any control

**dementia** /dɪˈmenʃə/ *noun* [U] a mental illness suffered especially by old people

**demise** /dɪˈmaɪz/ *noun* **1** [no plural] when something ends, usually because it has stopped being popular or successful *the demise of apartheid* **2 sb's demise** someone's death

**demo** /ˈdeməʊ/ *noun* [C] **1** an example of a product, given or shown to someone to try to make them buy it *a software demo* **2** *UK* short for demonstration (= political march) *a student demo*

○⊷**democracy** /dɪˈmɒkrəsi/ *noun* [C, U] a system of government in which people elect their leaders, or a country with this system

**democrat** /ˈdeməkræt/ *noun* [C] **1** someone who supports democracy **2 Democrat** someone who supports the Democratic Party in the US *the Democrat candidate* ➜ See also: **Liberal Democrat**.

**democratic** /ˌdeməˈkrætɪk/ *adj* **1** following or supporting the political system of democracy *a democratic society/government* **2** where everyone has equal rights and can help to make decisions *a democratic discussion/debate* ● democratically *adv* *a democratically elected government*

**the De'mocratic ˌParty** *noun* [group] one of the two main political parties in the US

**demolish** /dɪˈmɒlɪʃ/ *verb* [T] **1** to destroy something such as a building *The factory is dangerous, and will have to be demolished.* **2** to show that an idea or argument is wrong *He completely demolished my argument.*

**demolition** /ˌdeməˈlɪʃ°n/ *noun* [C, U] when something such as a building is destroyed *the demolition of dangerous buildings*

**demon** /ˈdiːmən/ *noun* [C] an evil spirit

**demonic** /dɪˈmɒnɪk/ *adj* evil

**demonstrable** /dɪˈmɒnstrəbl/ *adj* Something that is demonstrable can be shown to exist or be true. *a demonstrable fact* ● demonstrably *adv*

○⊷**demonstrate** /ˈdemənstreɪt/ *verb* **1** PROVE [T] to show or prove that something exists or is true [+ that] *The survey clearly demonstrates that tourism can have positive benefits.* ● *These problems demonstrate the importance of planning.* **2** SHOW HOW [T] to show someone how to do something, or how something works *She demonstrated how to use the new software.* **3** EXPRESS [T] to express or show that you have a feeling, quality, or ability *He has demonstrated a genuine interest in the project.* **4** MARCH [I] to march or stand with a group of people to show that you disagree with or support someone or something *Thousands of people gathered to **demonstrate against** the new proposals.*

**demonstration** /ˌdemənˈstreɪʃ°n/ *noun* **1** MARCH [C] when a group of people march or stand together to show that they disagree with or support someone or something *They're taking part in a **demonstration against** nuclear weapons.* **2** SHOWING HOW [C, U] showing how to do something, or how something works *We asked the sales assistant to give us a demonstration.* **3** PROOF [C, U] proof that something exists or is true *This disaster is a clear demonstration of the need for tighter controls.*

**demonstrative** /dɪˈmɒnstrətɪv/ *adj* willing to show your feelings, especially your affection

**demonstrator** /ˈdemənstreɪtəʳ/ *noun* [C] a person who marches or stands with a group of people to show that they disagree with or support someone or something

**demoralized** (*also UK* **-ised**) /dɪˈmɒrəlaɪzd/ *adj* having lost your confidence, and hope *After the match, the players were tired and demoralized.* ● demoralizing *adj* making you lose your confidence, enthusiasm, and hope *a demoralizing defeat* ● demoralize /dɪˈmɒrəlaɪz/ *verb* [T]

**demote** /dɪˈməʊt/ *verb* **be demoted** to be moved to a less important job or position, especially as a punishment ● demotion /dɪˈməʊʃ°n/ *noun* [C, U]

**demotivated** /ˌdiːˈməʊtɪveɪtɪd/ *adj* not having any enthusiasm for your work

**demure** /dɪˈmjʊəʳ/ *adj* If a young woman is demure, she is quiet and shy. ● demurely *adv*

**den** /den/ *noun* [C] **1** ANIMAL'S HOME the home of some wild animals *a lions' den* **2** ILLEGAL ACTIVITY a place where secret and illegal activity happens *a gambling den* **3** ROOM mainly *US* a room in your home where you relax, read, watch television, etc

**denial** /dɪˈnaɪəl/ *noun* **1** [C, U] when you say that something is not true *a denial of his guilt* **2** [U] not allowing someone to have or do something *the denial of medical treatment*

**denigrate** /ˈdenɪgreɪt/ *verb* [T] to criticize and

not show much respect for someone or something

**denim** /'denɪm/ *noun* [U] thick, strong, cotton cloth, usually blue, which is used to make clothes *denim jeans*

**denomination** /dɪ,nɒmɪ'neɪʃən/ *noun* [C] **1** a religious group which has slightly different beliefs from other groups which share the same religion **2** the value of a particular coin, piece of paper money, or stamp

**denote** /dɪ'nəʊt/ *verb* [T] to be a sign of something *The colour red is used to denote passion or danger.*

**denounce** /dɪ'naʊns/ *verb* [T] to publicly criticize someone or something, or to publicly accuse someone of something *They've been **denounced as** terrorists.*

**dense** /dens/ *adj* **1** with a lot of people or things close together *dense forest* **2** If cloud, smoke, etc is dense, it is thick and difficult to see through. *dense fog* • densely *adv a densely populated area*

**density** /'densɪti/ *noun* [C, U] **1** the number of people or things in a place when compared with the size of the place *The area has a high population density.* **2** the relationship between the weight of a substance and its size *bone density*

**dent**[1] /dent/ *noun* [C] **1** a hollow area in a hard surface where it has been hit *The car door had a dent in it.* **2** a reduction in something *The cost of repairs made a serious dent in my savings.*

**dent**[2] /dent/ *verb* [T] **1** to create a hollow area in the hard surface of something by hitting it *The side of the car was dented in the accident.* **2** to reduce someone's confidence or positive feelings about something *The defeat did little to dent her enthusiasm.*

**dental** /'dentəl/ *adj* relating to teeth *dental treatment*

**dentist** /'dentɪst/ *noun* [C] someone who examines and repairs teeth *I've got an appointment at the dentist's* (= where the dentist works) *tomorrow.* • dentistry *noun* [U] the subject or job of examining and repairing teeth

**dentures** /'dentʃəz/ *noun* [plural] false teeth

**denunciation** /dɪ,nʌnsi'eɪʃən/ *noun* [C, U] when you publicly criticize someone or something, or publicly accuse someone of something

○━**deny** /dɪ'naɪ/ *verb* [T] **1** to say that something is not true, especially something that you are accused of *She denies any involvement in the attack.* • [+ (that)] *He never denied that he said those things.* • [+ doing sth] *He denies murdering his father.* **2** to not allow someone to have or do something [often passive] *These children are being denied access to education.*

**deodorant** /di'əʊdərənt/ *noun* [C, U] a substance that you put on your body to prevent or hide unpleasant smells

**depart** /dɪ'pɑːt/ *verb* [I] *formal* to leave a place, especially to start a journey to another place *The train to Lincoln will depart from platform 9.* • *He departed for Paris on Tuesday.*

○━**department** /dɪ'pɑːtmənt/ *noun* [C] a part of an organization such as a school, business, or government which deals with a particular area of work *the sales department* • *head of the*

*English department* ➲ *See also:* **police department**.

**departmental** /,diːpɑːt'mentəl/ *adj* relating to a department *the departmental budget*

**de'partment ,store** *noun* [C] a large shop divided into several different parts which sell different types of things

**departure** /dɪ'pɑːtʃə/ *noun* [C, U] **1** when someone or something leaves a place, especially to start a journey to another place *the departure of flight BA117* • *This fare is valid for weekday departures from Manchester.* **2** a change from what is expected, or from what has happened before *This film is a major departure from his previous work.*

○━**depend** /dɪ'pend/ *verb* **it/that depends** used to say that you are not certain about something because other things affect your answer [+ question word] *"Are you coming out tonight?" "It depends where you're going."*

**depend on/upon sb/sth 1** NEED to need the help of someone or something in order to exist or continue as before *She depends on her son for everything.* • *The city's economy depends largely on the car industry.* **2** BE INFLUENCED BY If something depends on someone or something, it is influenced by them, or changes because of them. [+ question word] *The choice depends on what you're willing to spend.* **3** TRUST to be able to trust someone or something to help, or to do what you expect [+ to do sth] *You can always depend on Andy to keep his promises.*

**dependable** /dɪ'pendəbl/ *adj* able to be trusted and very likely to do what you expect *the team's most dependable player*

**dependant** UK (US **dependent**) /dɪ'pendənt/ *noun* [C] someone, usually a child, who depends on you for financial support *The pension provides for him and all his dependants.*

**dependence** /dɪ'pendəns/ (also **dependency** /dɪ'pendənsi/) *noun* [U] when you need someone or something all the time in order to exist or continue as before *Our society needs to reduce its dependence on the car.*

**dependent**[1] /dɪ'pendənt/ *adj* **1** needing the help of someone or something in order to exist or continue as before *She's completely dependent on her parents for money.* **2** dependent on/upon sth influenced by or decided by something *The amount of tax you pay is dependent on how much you earn.*

**dependent**[2] /dɪ'pendənt/ *noun* [C] US spelling of dependant

**depict** /dɪ'pɪkt/ *verb* [T] to represent someone or something in a picture or story *The cartoon* *depicts* the president *as* a vampire. • depiction /dɪˈpɪkʃᵊn/ *noun* [C, U]

**deplete** /dɪˈpliːt/ *verb* [T] to reduce the amount of something, especially a natural supply *Alcohol depletes the body of B vitamins.* • depletion /dɪˈpliːʃᵊn/ *noun* [U] *the depletion of the ozone layer*

**deplorable** /dɪˈplɔːrəbl/ *adj* very bad or morally wrong *Your son's behaviour is absolutely deplorable.*

**deplore** /dɪˈplɔːr/ *verb* [T] *formal* to feel or express strong disapproval of something *We deeply deplore the loss of life.*

**deploy** /dɪˈplɔɪ/ *verb* [T] to move soldiers or equipment to a place where they can be used when they are needed • deployment *noun* [U] *the deployment of nuclear weapons*

**deport** /dɪˈpɔːt/ *verb* [T] to force a foreign person to leave a country *Thousands of illegal immigrants are **deported from** the US every year.* • deportation /ˌdiːpɔːˈteɪʃᵊn/ *noun* [C, U] *He now faces deportation back to his native country.*

**depose** /dɪˈpəʊz/ *verb* [T] to remove a ruler or leader from their position of power • deposed *adj the deposed president*

**deposit¹** /dɪˈpɒzɪt/ *noun* [C] **1** BUYING a payment that you make immediately when you decide to buy something, as proof that you will really buy it *They've put down a **deposit on** a house.* **2** BANK an amount of money that you pay into a bank *to make a deposit* **3** SUBSTANCE a layer of a substance that has developed from a natural or chemical process *deposits of iron ore* **4** RENT an amount of money that you pay when you rent something, and that is given back to you when you return it without any damage

**deposit²** /dɪˈpɒzɪt/ *verb* [T] **1** PUT DOWN to put something down somewhere *He deposited his books on the table.* **2** MONEY to put money into a bank or valuable things into a safe place *She deposited $150,000 in a Swiss bank account.* **3** SUBSTANCE to leave something lying on a surface, as a result of a natural or chemical process

**deˈposit acˌcount** *noun* [C] *UK* a bank account that pays interest on the money you put into it and that you use for saving

**depot** /ˈdepəʊ/ *noun* [C] **1** VEHICLES a place where trains, trucks, or buses are kept **2** GOODS a building where supplies of goods are stored **3** STATION *US* a small bus or train station

**depraved** /dɪˈpreɪvd/ *adj* morally bad • depravity /dɪˈprævəti/ *noun* [U]

**depreciate** /dɪˈpriːʃieɪt/ *verb* [I] to lose value over a period of time *New computers depreciate in value very quickly.* • depreciation /dɪˌpriːʃiˈeɪʃᵊn/ *noun* [U]

**depress** /dɪˈpres/ *verb* [T] **1** to make someone feel very unhappy, especially about the future *This place really depresses me.* **2** to reduce the value or level of something, especially in business *Competition between stores has depressed prices.*

**depressed** /dɪˈprest/ *adj* **1** very unhappy, often for a long time *She has been feeling very depressed since her marriage broke up.* **2** A depressed country, area, or economy does not have enough jobs or business activity. *an economically depressed area*

**depressing** /dɪˈpresɪŋ/ *adj* making you feel unhappy and without any hope for the future *The news is very depressing.*

**depression** /dɪˈpreʃᵊn/ *noun* [C, U] **1** when you feel very unhappy, or a mental illness that makes you feel very unhappy *Nearly three million people suffer from depression every year.* **2** a time when there is not much business activity *The stock market crash marked the start of a severe depression.*

**deprive** /dɪˈpraɪv/ *verb*
**deprive sb/sth of sth** to take something important or necessary away from someone or something *They were deprived of food for long periods.* • deprivation /ˌdeprɪˈveɪʃᵊn/ *noun* [C, U] *sleep deprivation*

**deprived** /dɪˈpraɪvd/ *adj* not having enough food, money, and the things that you need to have a normal life *children from deprived backgrounds*

**dept** *written abbreviation for* department (= a part of an organization or government)

◦━**depth** /depθ/ *noun* **1** TOP TO BOTTOM [C, U] the distance from the top of something to the bottom *The lake reaches a maximum **depth** of 292 metres.* • *Dig a hole 10 cm **in depth**.* ⊃ *See picture at* **length**. **2** FRONT TO BACK [C, U] the distance from the front to the back of something **3** AMOUNT [U] how much someone knows or feels about something *She was amazed at the depth of his knowledge.* **4 in depth** giving all the details *With access to the Internet, students can do their homework in greater depth.* **5 be out of your depth** to not have the knowledge, experience or skills to deal with a particular subject or situation

**depths** /depθs/ *noun* [plural] **1** a position far below the surface or far into something *the depths of the forest* **2** the worst period of something *the depths of despair*

**deputy** /ˈdepjəti/ *noun* [C] someone who has the second most important job in an organization *the deputy Prime Minister*

**derail** /dɪˈreɪl/ *verb* **1** [I, T] If a train derails, or is derailed, it comes off the railway tracks. **2** [T] If you derail plans, you prevent them from happening. • derailment *noun* [C, U]

**deranged** /dɪˈreɪndʒd/ *adj* behaving in a way that is not normal, especially when suffering from a mental illness *He was shot by a deranged fan.*

**derby** /ˈdɑːbi ⑥ ˈdɜːrbi/ *noun* [C] **1** *mainly UK* a type of sports competition *a fishing/motorcycle derby* **2 Derby** a type of horse race **3** *US* (*UK* **bowler hat**) a round, hard, black hat worn by men, especially in the past

**deregulate** /ˌdiːˈregjəleɪt/ *verb* [T] to remove national or local government controls from a business *The government plans to deregulate banking.* • deregulation /ˌdiːregjəˈleɪʃᵊn/ *noun* [U]

**derelict** /ˈderəlɪkt/ *adj* A derelict building or piece of land is not used any more and is in a bad condition. *a derelict house*

**deride** /dɪˈraɪd/ *verb* [T] *formal* to talk about someone or something as if they are ridiculous and do not deserve any respect *This building, once derided by critics, is now a major tourist attraction.*

**derision** /dɪˈrɪʒ°n/ *noun* [U] when you talk about someone or something as if they are ridiculous and do not deserve respect *The novel was greeted with derision in the UK, but praised in the US.*

**derisive** /dɪˈraɪsɪv/ *adj* showing derision towards someone or something

**derisory** /dɪˈraɪs°ri/ *adj* **1** so small that it seems ridiculous *a derisory sum of money* **2** cruel and making someone feel stupid *derisory remarks*

**derivation** /ˌderɪˈveɪʃ°n/ *noun* [C, U] the origin of something, such as a word, from which another form has developed, or the new form itself

**derivative** /dɪˈrɪvətɪv/ *noun* [C] a form of something, such as a word, that has developed from another form

**derive** /dɪˈraɪv/ *verb*
**derive (sth) from sth 1** to come from or be developed from something *The name derives from Latin.* **2 derive comfort/pleasure, etc from sth** to get a positive feeling or advantage from someone or something *I derive great pleasure from gardening.*

**dermatitis** /ˌdɜːməˈtaɪtɪs/ *noun* [U] a condition which makes your skin red and painful

**derogatory** /dɪˈrɒgət°ri/ *adj* showing strong disapproval and not showing any respect for someone *derogatory comments/remarks*

**descend** /dɪˈsend/ *verb* [I, T] *formal* to move or go down *We descended four flights of stairs.*
**be descended from sb/sth** to be related to a person or creature that lived a long time ago *Her father is descended from Greek royalty.*

**descendant** /dɪˈsendənt/ *noun* [C] someone who is related to someone who lived a long time ago *She is a descendant of Queen Victoria.*

**descent** /dɪˈsent/ *noun* [C, U] **1** a movement down *The plane began its descent from a height of 10,000 metres.* **2 of Irish/French, etc descent** being related to people who lived in the past in Ireland/France, etc *Most of the workers were of Spanish descent.*

o╍**describe** /dɪˈskraɪb/ *verb* [T] to say what someone or something is like *She was able to describe her attacker to the police.* • *Neighbours described her as a shy, quiet girl.* • [+ question word] *I tried to describe what I had seen.*

o╍**description** /dɪˈskrɪpʃ°n/ *noun* **1** [C, U] something that tells you what someone or something is like *I gave the police a description of the stolen jewellery.* **2 of any/every/some description** of any/every/some type *They sell plants of every description.*

**descriptive** /dɪˈskrɪptɪv/ *adj* describing something, especially in a detailed, interesting way *descriptive passages*

**desert¹** /ˈdezət/ *noun* [C, U] a large, hot, dry area of land with very few plants *the Sahara Desert*

**desert²** /dɪˈzɜːt/ *verb* **1** PERSON [T] to leave someone and never come back *He deserted his wife and children.* **2** PLACE [T] to leave a place, so that it is empty *Young people are deserting the countryside to work in towns.* **3** ARMY [I, T] to leave the army without permission • **desertion** /dɪˈzɜːʃ°n/ *noun* [U]

**deserted** /dɪˈzɜːtɪd/ *adj* If a place is deserted, it has no people in it. *a deserted street*

**deserter** /dɪˈzɜːtər/ *noun* [C] someone who leaves the army without permission

**desert island** *noun* [C] a tropical island where no one lives, far from any other places

o╍**deserve** /dɪˈzɜːv/ *verb* [T] If you deserve something good or bad, it should happen to you because of the way you have behaved. *The school deserves praise for the way it has raised standards.* • [+ to do sth] *He deserves to be locked up for life.* • **deservedly** *adv The film deservedly won an Oscar.*

**deserving** /dɪˈzɜːvɪŋ/ *adj* If something or someone is deserving, people should help or support them. *The children's charity is a deserving cause.*

o╍**design¹** /dɪˈzaɪn/ *noun* **1** PLANNING [U] the way in which something is planned and made *There was a fault in the design of the aircraft.* **2** DRAWING [C] a drawing which shows how an object, machine, or building will be made *Production engineers are working on the new designs.* **3** DECORATION [C] a pattern or decoration *a design of fish and sea shells* **4** PROCESS [U] the process of making drawings to show how something will be made *a course in art and design* ➔ *See also:* **interior design**.

o╍**design²** /dɪˈzaɪn/ *verb* [T] **1** to draw or plan something before making it *She designs furniture.* **2 be designed to do sth** to have been planned or done for a particular purpose *The new law is designed to protect children.*

**designate** /ˈdezɪgneɪt/ *verb* [T] *formal* to choose someone or something for a particular purpose or duty *The area has been designated as a nature reserve.* • **designation** /ˌdezɪgˈneɪʃ°n/ *noun* [C, U]

**designer¹** /dɪˈzaɪnər/ *noun* [C] someone who draws and plans how something will be made *a fashion designer*

**designer²** /dɪˈzaɪnər/ *adj* **designer jeans/sunglasses, etc** clothes or objects made by a fashionable designer

**desirable** /dɪˈzaɪərəbl/ *adj* If something is desirable, it is very good or attractive and most people would want it. *A good education is highly desirable.* ➔ *Opposite* **undesirable**.

o╍**desire¹** /dɪˈzaɪər/ *noun* **1** [C, U] a strong feeling that you want something [+ to do sth] *I have no desire to have children.* • *There is a strong desire for peace among the people.* **2** [U] when you are sexually attracted to someone

**desire²** /dɪˈzaɪər/ *verb* [T] *formal* to want something *You can have whatever you desire.*

**desired** /dɪˈzaɪəd/ *adj* **the desired effect/result/shape, etc** the effect/result/shape, etc that is wanted *Her medicine seems to have had the desired effect.*

o╍**desk** /desk/ *noun* [C] a table that you sit at to write or work, often with drawers ➔ *See colour picture* **The Office** *on page Centre 12,* ➔ *See also:* **cash desk**.

**desktop** /ˈdesktɒp/ *adj* [always before noun] **1** desktop computer equipment is small enough to fit on a desk (= office table) **2 desktop publishing** producing finished designs for pages of books or documents using a small computer and printer (= machine for printing)

**desolate** /'des³lət/ *adj* **1** A desolate place is empty and makes you feel sad. *a desolate landscape* **2** lonely and unhappy *She felt desolate when he left.* • desolation /,des³'leɪʃ³n/ *noun* [U]

**despair¹** /dɪ'speə³/ *noun* a feeling of having no hope *She shook her head in despair.*

**despair²** /dɪ'speə³/ *verb* [I] to feel that you have no hope *Don't despair – things will improve.* • [+ of + doing sth] *He had begun to despair of ever finding a job.* • despairing *adj*

**despatch¹** *UK (UK/US* **dispatch**) /dɪ'spætʃ/ *verb* [T] *formal* to send someone or something somewhere *They despatched a police car to arrest him.*

**despatch²** *UK (UK/US* **dispatch**) /dɪ'spætʃ/ *noun* **1** [U] when someone or something is sent somewhere *the despatch of troops* **2** [C] an official report that someone in a foreign country sends to their organization

**desperate** /'desp³rət/ *adj* **1** WITHOUT HOPE feeling that you have no hope and are ready to do anything to change the situation you are in *He was absolutely desperate and would have tried anything to get her back.* **2** NEEDING SOMETHING needing or wanting something very much *By two o'clock I was desperate for something to eat.* **3** BAD A desperate situation is very bad or serious. *The economy is in a really desperate situation.* • desperately *adv* • desperation /,desp³'reɪʃ³n/ *noun* [U]

**despicable** /dɪ'spɪkəbl/ *adj* very unpleasant or cruel *a despicable act/crime*

**despise** /dɪ'spaɪz/ *verb* [T] to hate someone or something and have no respect for them *The two groups despise each other.*

o⚬**despite** /dɪ'spaɪt/ *preposition* **1** used to say that something happened or is true, although something else makes this seem not probable *I'm still pleased with the house despite all the problems we've had.* • [+ doing sth] *He managed to eat lunch despite having had an enormous breakfast.* **2 despite yourself** If you do something despite yourself, you do it although you did not intend to.

**despondent** /dɪ'spɒndənt/ *adj* unhappy and having no enthusiasm *She was feeling a bit despondent after losing the match.* • despondency *noun* [U]

**despot** /'despɒt/ *noun* [C] a very powerful person, especially someone who treats people cruelly

**dessert** /dɪ'zɜːt/ *noun* [C, U] sweet food that is eaten after the main part of a meal *We had ice cream for dessert.*

**dessertspoon** /dɪ'zɜːtspuːn/ *noun* [C] *UK* a medium-sized spoon used for eating or measuring food, or the amount this spoon can hold *Add one dessertspoon of sugar.*

**destabilize** (*also UK* **-ise**) /,diː'steɪb³laɪz/ *verb* [T] to cause change in a country or government so that it loses its power or control *a plot to destabilize the government*

**destination** /,destɪ'neɪʃ³n/ *noun* [C] the place where someone or something is going *Spain is a very popular holiday destination.*

**destined** /'destɪnd/ *adj* **be destined for sth; be destined to do sth** to be certain to be some-

thing or do something in the future *She was destined for a brilliant future.*

**destiny** /'destɪni/ *noun* **1** [C] the things that will happen to someone in the future *At last she feels in control of her own destiny.* **2** [U] a power that some people believe controls what will happen in the future *Nick said it was destiny that we met.*

**destitute** /'destɪtjuːt/ *adj* so poor that you do not have the basic things you need to live, such as food, clothes, or money • destitution /,destɪ'tjuːʃ³n/ *noun* [U]

o⚬**destroy** /dɪ'strɔɪ/ *verb* [T] to damage something so badly that it does not exist or cannot be used *Many works of art were destroyed in the fire.*

**destroyer** /dɪ'strɔɪə³/ *noun* [C] a small, fast ship that is used in a war

**destruction** /dɪ'strʌkʃ³n/ *noun* [U] when something is destroyed *We are all responsible for the destruction of the forest.* • destructive /dɪ'strʌktɪv/ *adj* causing a lot of damage *the destructive power of nuclear weapons* ➔ *See also:* **self-destructive**.

**detach** /dɪ'tætʃ/ *verb* [T] to take a part of something off so that it is separate *Please complete and detach the form below and return it to the school.* • detachable *adj*

**detached** /dɪ'tætʃt/ *adj* **1** *UK* A detached building is not joined to another building. **2** If someone is detached, they do not feel involved with someone or emotional about something. *He seemed cool and detached.* ➔ *See also:* **semi-detached**.

**detachment** /dɪ'tætʃmənt/ *noun* **1** [U] when someone does not feel involved in a situation *He spoke with cool detachment.* **2** [C] a small group of soldiers with a particular job to do

o⚬**detail¹** /'diːteɪl/ *noun* [C, U] **1** a fact or piece of information about something *Please send me details of your training courses.* • *She didn't include very much detail in her report.* **2 in detail** including every part of something *He explained it all in great detail.* **3 go into detail** to include all the facts about something

**detail²** /'diːteɪl/ *verb* [T] to describe something completely, giving all the facts *She wrote a book detailing her experiences in prison.*

**detailed** /'diːteɪld/ *adj* giving a lot of information *a detailed account/description*

**detain** /dɪ'teɪn/ *verb* [T] to keep someone some-

**dessert**

where and not allow them to leave, especially in order to ask them about a crime *Three men were detained by police for questioning.*

**detect** /dɪ'tekt/ *verb* [T] to discover or notice something, especially something that is difficult to see, hear, smell, etc *This special camera can detect bodies by their heat.* • *I thought I detected a smile in his eyes.*

**detection** /dɪ'tekʃ°n/ *noun* [U] **1** when someone notices or discovers something *the early detection of cancer* **2** when the police discover information about a crime

**detective** /dɪ'tektɪv/ *noun* [C] someone, especially a police officer, whose job is to discover information about a crime

**detector** /dɪ'tektəʳ/ *noun* [C] a piece of equipment used to discover something, especially something that is difficult to see, hear, smell, etc *a smoke detector*

**detente** /ˌdeɪ'tɒnt/ *noun* [U] *formal* when countries become friendly with each other after a period of not being friendly

**detention** /dɪ'tenʃ°n/ *noun* **1** [U] when someone is officially kept somewhere and not allowed to leave **2** [C, U] when a student is kept in school after the other students leave, as a punishment

**deter** /dɪ'tɜːʳ/ *verb* [T] **deterring**, *past* **deterred** to make someone less likely to do something, or to make something less likely to happen *We have introduced new security measures to deter shoplifters.* • [+ from + doing sth] *Higher fuel costs could deter people from driving their cars.*

**detergent** /dɪ'tɜːdʒ°nt/ *noun* [C, U] a liquid or powder that is used to clean things

**deteriorate** /dɪ'tɪəriəʳeɪt/ *verb* [I] to become worse *Her condition deteriorated rapidly.* • deterioration /dɪˌtɪəriə'reɪʃ°n/ *noun* [U]

**determination** /dɪˌtɜːmɪ'neɪʃ°n/ *noun* [U] when someone continues trying to do something, although it is very difficult *He'll need great determination and skill to win this match.*

**determine** /dɪ'tɜːmɪn/ *verb* [T] **1** to discover the facts or truth about something [+ question word] *The doctors are still unable to determine what is wrong.* **2** to decide what will happen [+ question word] *Her exam results will determine which university she goes to.*

○━**determined** /dɪ'tɜːmɪnd/ *adj* wanting to do something very much, and not letting anyone stop you [+ to do sth] *He's determined to win this match.*

**determiner** /dɪ'tɜːmɪnəʳ/ *noun* [C] a word that is used before a noun or adjective to show which person or thing you are referring to. For example 'my' in 'my old car' and 'that' in 'that man' are determiners.

**deterrent** /dɪ'ter°nt/ *noun* [C] something that stops people doing something because they are afraid of what will happen if they do *They've installed a security camera as a deterrent to thieves.* • deterrent *adj a deterrent effect*

**detest** /dɪ'test/ *verb* [T] to hate someone or something very much *They used to be friends, but now they absolutely detest each other.*

**detonate** /'det°neɪt/ *verb* [I, T] to explode or make something explode *The bomb was detonated safely by army officers and no one was hurt.* • detonation /ˌdet°n'eɪʃ°n/ *noun* [C, U]

**detonator** /'det°neɪtəʳ/ *noun* [C] a piece of equipment that makes a bomb explode

**detour** /'diːtʊəʳ/ *noun* [C] a different, longer route to a place that is used to avoid something or to visit something *Several roads were closed, so we had to **take a detour**.*

**detox** /'diːtɒks/ *noun* [U] *informal* treatment to clean out your blood, stomach, etc and get rid of bad substances such as drugs

**detract** /dɪ'trækt/ *verb*
**detract from sth** to make something seem less good than it really is, or than it was thought to be

**detriment** /'detrɪmənt/ *noun* **to the detriment of sth** causing damage to something *He was working very long hours, to the detriment of his health.* • detrimental /ˌdetrɪ'ment°l/ *adj a detrimental effect*

**devaluation** /ˌdiːvæljuˈeɪʃ°n/ *noun* [C, U] when the value of something is reduced *the devaluation of the dollar*

**devalue** /ˌdiː'væljuː/ *verb* [T] **devaluing**, *past* **devalued** **1** to make something less valuable, especially a country's money *to devalue the pound* **2** to make someone or something seem less important than they really are

**devastate** /'devəsteɪt/ *verb* [T] to destroy or damage something very badly *A recent hurricane devastated the city.* • devastation /ˌdevə'steɪʃ°n/ *noun* [U]

**devastated** /'devəsteɪtɪd/ *adj* **1** very shocked and upset *She was devastated when her husband died.* **2** completely destroyed

**devastating** /'devəsteɪtɪŋ/ *adj* **1** making someone very shocked and upset *Despite the devastating news, no one is giving up hope.* **2** causing a lot of damage or destruction *The fire has had a devastating effect on the local wildlife.*

**devastatingly** /'devəsteɪtɪŋli/ *adv* extremely *devastatingly funny/handsome*

○━**develop** /dɪ'veləp/ *verb* **1** CHANGE [I, T] to grow or change and become more advanced, or to make someone or something do this *The baby develops inside the mother for nine months.* • *She's taking a course to develop her computer skills.* • *He's **developing into** a very good tennis player.* **2** MAKE [T] to make something new such as a product *Scientists are developing new drugs all the time.* **3** ILLNESS [T] to start to have something, such as an illness, problem, or feeling *Shortly after take-off the plane developed engine trouble.* • *He's recently developed an interest in football.* **4** HAPPEN [I] to start to happen or exist *Further problems may develop if you do not deal with this now.* **5** FILM [T] to use special chemicals on a piece of film to make photographs appear *I need to get my holiday photos developed.* **6** BUILD [T] to build houses, factories, shops, etc on a piece of land

**developed** /dɪ'veləpt/ *adj* **a developed country/nation, etc** a country with an advanced level of technology, industry, etc ➜ *Opposite* **undeveloped**.

**developer** /dɪ'veləpəʳ/ *noun* [C] a person or company that buys land and builds houses, factories, shops, etc

o━**development** /dɪ'veləpmənt/ *noun* **1** CHANGE [C, U] when someone or something grows or changes and becomes more advanced *The nurse will do some tests to check on your child's development.* • *There have been some major developments in technology recently.* **2** MAKE [C, U] when something new is made *the development of new drugs* **3** START [U] when something starts to happen or exist *Smoking encourages the development of cancer.* **4** BUILD [U] when new houses, factories, shops, etc, are built on an area of land *land suitable for development* **5** BUILDINGS [C] an area of land with new houses, factories, shops, etc on it *a new housing development* **6** EVENT [C] something new that happens and changes a situation *Have there been any more developments since I left?* **7** PHOTOGRAPH [U] when someone makes photographs from a film

**deviant** /'di:viənt/ *adj* different to what most people think is normal or acceptable, usually relating to sexual behaviour • deviant *noun* [C]

**deviate** /'di:vieɪt/ *verb* [I] to do something in a different way from what is usual or expected *The aircraft deviated from its original flight plan.*

**deviation** /ˌdiːvi'eɪʃən/ *noun* [C, U] when something is different to what is usual, expected, or accepted by most people *sexual deviation*

**device** /dɪ'vaɪs/ *noun* **1** [C] a piece of equipment that is used for a particular purpose *A pager is a small, electronic device for sending messages.* **2 leave someone to their own devices** to leave someone to do what they want to do *With both parents out at work, the kids were often left to their own devices.*

**devil** /'devəl/ *noun* **1 the Devil** the most powerful evil spirit, according to the Christian and Jewish religions **2** [C] an evil spirit **3** [C] *informal* someone who behaves badly **4 lucky/poor, etc devil** *informal* used to describe a person **5 speak/talk of the devil** *informal* something that you say when someone you have been talking about suddenly appears

**devilish** /'devəlɪʃ/ *adj* evil or bad *a devilish smile* • devilishly *adv* very *devilishly difficult*

**devious** /'di:viəs/ *adj* clever in a way that is bad and not honest *a devious mind*

**devise** /dɪ'vaɪz/ *verb* [T] to design or invent something such as a system, plan, or piece of equipment

**devoid** /dɪ'vɔɪd/ *adj* **devoid of sth** *formal* completely without a quality

**devolution** /ˌdiːvə'luːʃən/ *noun* [U] when power moves from a central government to local governments

**devolve** /dɪ'vɒlv/ *verb*
**devolve sth to sb/sth** *formal* to give power or responsibility to a person or organization at a lower or more local level

**devote** /dɪ'vəʊt/ *verb*
**devote sth to sb/sth 1** to use time, energy, etc for a particular purpose *She devotes most of her free time to charity work.* **2** to use a space or area for a particular purpose [often passive] *Most of the magazine was devoted to coverage of the royal wedding.*

**devoted** /dɪ'vəʊtɪd/ *adj* loving or caring very much about someone or something *She's*

*absolutely devoted to her grandchildren.* • devotedly *adv*

**devotee** /ˌdevəʊ'tiː/ *noun* [C] someone who likes something or someone very much *a devotee of classical music*

**devotion** /dɪ'vəʊʃən/ *noun* [U] **1** great love or loyalty for someone or something *She will always be remembered for her devotion to her family.* **2** strong religious belief or behaviour

**devour** /dɪ'vaʊə²/ *verb* [T] **1** to eat something quickly because you are very hungry *I watched him devour a whole packet of biscuits.* **2** to read something quickly and enthusiastically

**devout** /dɪ'vaʊt/ *adj* extremely religious *a devout Catholic/Muslim* • devoutly *adv*

**dew** /djuː/ *noun* [U] drops of water that form on surfaces outside during the night

**dexterity** /dek'sterəti/ *noun* [U] skill at doing something, especially using your hands *manual dexterity*

**diabetes** /ˌdaɪə'biːtiːz/ *noun* [U] a serious medical condition in which your body cannot control the level of sugar in your blood • diabetic /ˌdaɪə'betɪk/ *adj* • diabetic /ˌdaɪə'betɪk/ *noun* [C] someone who has diabetes

**diabolical** /ˌdaɪə'bɒlɪkəl/ *adj* extremely bad

**diagnose** /'daɪəgnəʊz/ *verb* [T] to say what is wrong with someone who is ill [often passive] *She was diagnosed with/as having cancer last year.*

**diagnosis** /ˌdaɪəg'nəʊsɪs/ *noun* [C, U] *plural* **diagnoses** when a doctor says what is wrong with someone who is ill

**diagnostic** /ˌdaɪəg'nɒstɪk/ *adj* **diagnostic methods/tests, etc** methods/tests, etc that help you discover what is wrong with someone or something

**diagonal** /daɪ'ægənəl/ *adj* **1** A diagonal line is straight and sloping and not horizontal or vertical. *a tie with diagonal stripes* **2** going from the top corner of a square to the bottom corner on the other side • diagonally *adv*

**diagram** /'daɪəgræm/ *noun* [C] a simple picture showing what something looks like, or explaining how something works

**dial**¹ /daɪəl/ *noun* [C] **1** TIME/MEASUREMENT the round part of a clock, watch, or machine that shows you the time or other measurement **2** BUTTON a round part on a piece of equipment such as a television or radio that you turn to operate it, make it louder, etc **3** TELEPHONE the ring of holes with numbers that you turn on the front of an old telephone

**dial**² /daɪəl/ *verb* [I, T] *UK* **dialling**, *past* **dialled**, *US* **dialing**, *past* **dialed** to make a telephone call to a particular number *Dial 0 for the operator.*

**dialect** /'daɪəlekt/ *noun* [C, U] a form of a language that people speak in a particular part of a country

**dialogue** (*also US* **dialog**) /'daɪəlɒg/ *noun* [C, U] **1** the talking in a book, play, or film **2** a formal discussion between countries or groups of people

**diameter** /daɪ'æmɪtə²/ *noun* [C, U] a straight line that goes from one side of a circle to the other side and through the centre, or the length of this line *The cake was about 30 centimetres in diameter.*

D

**diamond** /'daɪəmənd/ noun **1** [STONE] [C, U] a very hard, transparent stone that is extremely valuable and is often used in jewellery *a diamond ring* **2** [SHAPE] [C] a shape with four straight sides of equal length that join to form two large angles and two small angles **3** [BASEBALL] [C] the field where baseball is played **4 diamonds** playing cards with red, diamond shapes on them *the queen of diamonds*

**diamond**

**diaper** /'daɪəpə<sup>r</sup>/ US (UK **nappy**) noun [C] a thick piece of paper or cloth worn by a baby on its bottom

**diaphragm** /'daɪəfræm/ noun [C] the large muscle between your lungs and your stomach

**diarrhoea** UK (US **diarrhea**) /ˌdaɪə'rɪə/ noun [U] an illness in which your solid waste is more liquid than usual, and comes out of your body more often

**diary** /'daɪəri/ noun [C] **1** a book containing spaces for all the days and months of the year, in which you write meetings and other things that you must remember *According to my diary, I've got two meetings on Monday.* **2** a book in which you write each day about your personal thoughts and experiences *She kept a diary of her trip to Egypt.*

**dice¹** /daɪs/ noun [C] *plural* **dice** a small object with six equal square sides, each with between one and six spots on it, used in games *Roll the dice to see who starts the game.*

**dice²** /daɪs/ verb [T] to cut food into small, square pieces *diced onions*

**dicey** /'daɪsi/ adj *informal* possibly dangerous or involving a risk

**dichotomy** /daɪ'kɒtəmi/ noun [C] *formal* the difference between two completely opposite ideas or things *the dichotomy between good and evil*

**dictate** /dɪk'teɪt/ verb **1** [I, T] to say or read something for someone to write down *Tony was busy dictating letters to his secretary.* **2** [T] to decide or control what happens [+ question word] *The weather will dictate where we hold the party.*
**dictate to sb** to tell someone what to do, often in a way that annoys them *I'm 15 years old – you can't dictate to me any more.*

**dictation** /dɪk'teɪʃ<sup>ə</sup>n/ noun **1** [U] when someone speaks or reads something for someone else to write down **2** [C, U] when a teacher says or reads something for students to write down as a test

**dictator** /dɪk'teɪtə<sup>r</sup>/ noun [C] a leader who has complete power in a country and has not been elected by the people ● dictatorial /ˌdɪktə'tɔ:riəl/ adj

**dictatorship** /dɪk'teɪtəʃɪp/ noun [C, U] a country or system of government with a dictator as leader

**dictionary** /'dɪkʃ<sup>ə</sup>n°ri/ noun [C] a book that contains a list of words in alphabetical order with their meanings explained or written in another language *Use your dictionaries to look up any words you don't understand.*

**did** /dɪd/ *past tense of* do

**didn't** /'dɪd<sup>ə</sup>nt/ *short for* did not

o—►**die** /daɪ/ verb **dying**, *past* **died 1** [I] to stop living *At least 3,000 people have died in the earthquake.* ● *Many of the refugees* **died** *of hunger.* ● *She* **died from** *brain injuries after a road accident.* **2 be dying for sth; be dying to do sth** *informal* to very much want to have, eat, drink, or do something *I'm dying for a drink.* ● *Sit down, I'm dying to hear all about it.* **3 to die for** *informal* If something is to die for, it is extremely good. ⊃ *See also:* die **hard²**.

**die**

Be careful to choose the correct preposition.

*He* died *of a heart attack.*

~~He died by a heart attack.~~

**died** or **dead**?

Be careful not to confuse the verb and adjective forms of these words. **Died** is the past of the verb 'to die', which means 'to stop living'.

*My cat died last week.*

**Dead** is an adjective and is used to talk about people or things which are not alive.

*My cat is dead.*

**die away** If something, especially a sound, dies away, it gradually becomes less strong and then stops.

**die down** If something, especially noise or excitement, dies down, it gradually becomes less loud or strong until it stops. *She waited for the laughter to die down before she spoke.*

**die off** If a group of plants, animals, or people dies off, all of that group dies over a period of time.

**die out** to become more and more rare and then disappear completely *Dinosaurs died out about 65 million years ago.*

**diehard** /'daɪhɑ:d/ adj [always before noun] supporting something in a very determined way and refusing to change *a diehard fan*

**diesel** /'di:z<sup>ə</sup>l/ noun **1** [U] fuel used in the engines of some vehicles, especially buses and trucks **2** [C] a vehicle that uses diesel in its engine

o—►**diet¹** /daɪət/ noun **1** [C, U] the type of food that someone usually eats *His diet isn't very healthy.* **2** [C] when someone eats less food, or only particular types of food, because they want to become thinner, or because they are ill *No cake for me, thanks – I'm* **on a diet**.

**diet²** /daɪət/ verb [I] to eat less food so that you become thinner *I've been dieting for a week, and I still haven't lost any weight.*

**differ** /'dɪfə/ *verb* [I] **1** to be different *How does the book differ from the film?* • *These computers differ quite a lot in price.* **2** to have a different opinion *Economists differ on the cause of inflation.*

○━**difference** /'dɪfᵊrᵊns/ *noun* **1** WAY [C, U] the way in which two people or things are not the same *What's the difference between an ape and a monkey?* **2** QUALITY [U] when two people or things are not the same **3** AMOUNT [C, U] the amount by which one thing or person is different from another *There's a big difference in age between them.* **4** DISAGREEMENT [C] a disagreement or different opinion *They must try to resolve their differences peacefully.* **5 make a/any difference** to have an effect on a situation *Painting the walls white has made a big difference to this room.* • *Do what you like, it makes no difference to me.*

---
**USAGE**

**difference**

Be careful to use the correct preposition.

You talk about the **difference between** two things when you are comparing them.

*What's the difference between a cup and a mug?*

You talk about the **difference in** something or someone when you want to say how something or someone has changed.

*Have you noticed a difference in him since last year?*

---

○━**different** /'dɪfᵊrᵊnt/ *adj* **1** not the same as someone or something else *Jo's very different from her sister, isn't she?* • *(UK) The house is different to how I expected it to be.* **2** [always before noun] used to talk about separate things or people of the same type *I had to go to three different shops to find the book she wanted.* • differently *adv* **Ɔ** *See also:* a different **ball game**.

---
**USAGE**

**different**

**Different** is usually followed by the preposition **from**. In British English people also use **to**.

*Anne is very different from her younger sister.*

In American English people also use **than**, but teachers prefer students to use **from**.

---

**differential** /,dɪfᵊ'renʃᵊl/ *noun* [C] a difference between amounts of things *differentials in pay/wealth*

**differentiate** /,dɪfᵊ'renʃieɪt/ *verb* **1** [I, T] to understand or notice how two things or people are different from each other *He can't differentiate between blue and green.* **2** [T] to make someone or something different *We need to differentiate ourselves from the competition.* • differentiation /,dɪfᵊrenʃi'eɪʃᵊn/ *noun* [U]

○━**difficult** /'dɪfɪkᵊlt/ *adj* **1** not easy and needing skill or effort to do or understand *Japanese is a difficult language for Europeans to learn.* • *This game is too difficult for me.* • [+ to do sth] *It's difficult to think with all that noise.* **2** not

friendly or easy to deal with *a difficult teenager*

○━**difficulty** /'dɪfɪkᵊlti/ *noun* **1** [U] when something is not easy to do or understand [+ in + doing sth] *He was having difficulty in breathing because of the smoke.* • [+ doing sth] *I had difficulty finding somewhere to park.* • *She had twisted her ankle and was walking with difficulty.* **2** [C] something that is not easy to deal with *The company is having some financial difficulties at the moment.*

---
**USAGE**

**have difficulty doing** something

You can say you **have difficulty doing** something or **have difficulty in doing** something.

*She has difficulty walking.*

*She has difficulty in walking.*

~~I have difficulty to walk.~~

---

**diffident** /'dɪfɪdᵊnt/ *adj* shy and without any confidence *a diffident young man* • diffidence /'dɪfɪdᵊns/ *noun* [U]

**diffuse** /dɪ'fjuːz/ *verb* [I, T] to spread, or to make something spread over a large area, or to a large number of people

○━**dig¹** /dɪg/ *verb* **digging**, *past* **dug** **1** [I, T] to break or move the ground with a tool, machine, etc *Digging the garden is good exercise.* **2 dig a hole/ tunnel, etc** to make a hole in the ground by moving some of the ground or soil away *They've dug a huge hole in the road.* **Ɔ** *See also:* dig the/up **dirt¹** on sb.

dig

**dig in/dig into sth** *informal* to start eating food *Dig in, there's plenty for everyone.*

**dig (sth) into sb/sth** to press or push hard into someone or something, or to press something hard into someone or something *She dug her fingernails into my wrist.* • *A stone was digging into my heel.*

**dig sb/sth out** to get someone or something out of somewhere by digging.

**dig sth out** to find something that you have not seen or used for a long time *Mum dug out some old family photographs to show me*

**dig sth up 1** TAKE OUT to take something out of the ground by digging *Could you dig up a few potatoes for dinner?* **2** BREAK GROUND to break the ground or make a hole in the ground with a tool, machine, etc *They're digging up the road outside my house.* **3** INFORMATION to discover information that is secret or forgotten by searching very carefully *See if you can dig up anything interesting about his past.*

---

**dig²** /dɪg/ *noun* **1** [REMARK] [C] something that you say to annoy or criticize someone *He was having a dig at me.* **2** [PLACE] [C] a place where people are digging in the ground looking for ancient things to study *an archaeological dig* **3** [PUSH] [no plural] *informal* a quick, hard push *a dig in the ribs*

**digest** /daɪ'dʒest/ *verb* [T] **1** to change food in your stomach into substances that your body can use *Your stomach contains acid to help you digest your food.* **2** to read and understand new information *You need to give me time to digest this report.* • **digestible** *adj* easy to digest

**digestion** /daɪ'dʒestʃ°n/ *noun* [U] when your body changes food in your stomach into substances that it can use

**digestive** /daɪ'dʒestɪv/ *adj* [always before noun] relating to digestion *the digestive system*

**digger** /'dɪgə°/ *noun* [C] a large machine that is used to lift and move soil, or a person who digs

**digit** /'dɪdʒɪt/ *noun* [C] any of the numbers from 0 to 9, especially when they form part of a longer number *a seven digit telephone number*

**digital** /'dɪdʒɪt°l/ *adj* **1** using an electronic system that changes sounds or images into signals in the form of numbers before it stores them or sends them *digital television* • *a digital camera* **2** A digital clock or watch shows the time in the form of numbers.

**dignified** /'dɪgnɪfaɪd/ *adj* calm, serious and behaving in a way that makes people respect you *a quiet, dignified woman*

**dignitary** /'dɪgnɪt°ri/ *noun* [C] someone with an important, official position *a group of visiting dignitaries*

**dignity** /'dɪgnəti/ *noun* [U] calm and serious behaviour that makes people respect you *He behaved with great dignity and courage.*

**digress** /daɪ'gres/ *verb* [I] to start talking about something that is not related to what you were talking about before • **digression** /daɪ'greʃ°n/ *noun* [C, U]

**digs** /dɪgz/ *noun* [plural] *UK informal* a room in someone's house that you pay rent to live in

**dike** (*also* **dyke**) /daɪk/ *noun* **1** a wall built to stop water from a sea or river going onto the land **2** *UK* a passage that has been dug to take water away from fields

**dilapidated** /dɪ'læpɪdeɪtɪd/ *adj* A dilapidated building or vehicle is old and in bad condition. • **dilapidation** /dɪ,læpɪ'deɪʃ°n/ *noun* [U]

**dilate** /daɪ'leɪt/ *verb* [I, T] If a part of your body dilates, or if you dilate it, it becomes wider or more open. *The drug causes your pupils to dilate.* • **dilation** /daɪ'leɪʃ°n/ *noun* [U]

**dilemma** /dɪ'lemə/ *noun* [C] when you have to make a difficult choice between two things you could do *She's still in a dilemma about whether she should go or not.*

**diligence** /'dɪlɪdʒ°ns/ *noun* [U] when you work hard with care and effort

**diligent** /'dɪlɪdʒ°nt/ *adj* working hard with care and effort *a diligent student* • **diligently** *adv*

**dilute** /daɪ'luːt/ *verb* [T] to make a liquid thinner or weaker by adding water or another liquid to it *You need to dilute this before you drink it.* • **dilute** *adj*

**dim¹** /dɪm/ *adj* **dimmer, dimmest 1** not bright or clear *He could hardly see her in the dim light.* **2 a dim memory/recollection, etc** when you can remember something slightly, but not very well **3** *UK informal* stupid *He's nice, but a bit dim.* • **dimly** *adv a dimly lit room*

**dim²** /dɪm/ *verb* [I, T] **dimming**, *past* **dimmed** to become less bright, or to make something become less bright *He dimmed the lights and turned up the music.*

**dime** /daɪm/ *noun* [C] **1** a US or Canadian coin with a value of 10 cents **2 a dime a dozen** *mainly US informal* easy to find and very ordinary *Millionaires are now a dime a dozen.*

**dimension** /,daɪ'menʃ°n/ *noun* [C] **1** a particular part of a situation, especially something that affects how you think or feel *Music has added a new dimension to my life.* **2** a measurement of the length, width, or height of something [usually plural] *We need to know the exact dimensions* (= size) *of the room.*

**diminish** /dɪ'mɪnɪʃ/ *verb* [I, T] to become less, or to make something become less *Your pain should diminish gradually after taking these tablets.*

**diminutive** /dɪ'mɪnjətɪv/ *adj formal* extremely small *a diminutive figure*

**dimple** /'dɪmpl/ *noun* [C] a small hollow place on your skin, often one that appears on your face when you smile • **dimpled** *adj*

**din** /dɪn/ *noun* [no plural] a lot of loud, unpleasant noise *The children were making a terrible din upstairs.*

**dine** /daɪn/ *verb* [I] *formal* to eat dinner *On Saturday we dined with friends.*

**dine out** *formal* to eat your evening meal in a restaurant

**diner** /'daɪnə°/ *noun* [C] **1** someone who is eating in a restaurant **2** *mainly US* a small, informal restaurant

**dinghy** /'dɪŋi/ *noun* [C] a small boat *an inflatable dinghy*

**dingy** /'dɪndʒi/ *adj* dirty and not bright *a dingy basement*

**'dining ,room** *noun* [C] a room where you eat your meals in a house or hotel

O⃞ **dinner** /'dɪnə°/ *noun* [C, U] the main meal of the day that people usually eat in the evening *What's for dinner tonight?*

**'dinner ,jacket** *UK* (*US* **tuxedo**) *noun* [C] a black or white jacket that a man wears on a very formal occasion

dinner jacket *UK*, tuxedo *US*

**dinosaur** /'daɪnəsɔː°/ *noun* [C] a very large animal that used to live millions of years ago

**diocese** /'daɪəsɪs/ *noun* [C] the area controlled by a bishop (= an important Christian official)

**dip¹** /dɪp/ *noun* **1** [FOOD] [C, U] a thick sauce that you can

**dinosaur**

put pieces of food into before you eat them *a blue cheese dip* **2** [SURFACE] [C] a lower area on a surface *a sudden dip in the road* **3** [AMOUNT] [C] a sudden fall in the level or amount of something *a dip in profits* **4** [SWIM] [C] *informal* a short swim *Let's have a quick dip in the pool before breakfast.*

**dip²** /dɪp/ *verb* dipping, *past* dipped **1** [T] to put something into a liquid for a short time *She dipped the brush into the paint.* **2** [I] to become lower in level or amount *The number of students taking sciences has dipped sharply.*

**dip into sth 1** *UK* to read small parts of a book or magazine *It's the sort of book you can dip into now and then.* **2** to spend part of a supply of money that you have been keeping *I had to dip into my savings to pay for the repairs.*

**diphtheria** /dɪpˈθɪəriə/ *noun* [U] a very serious disease of the throat

**diphthong** /ˈdɪfθɒŋ/ *noun* [C] a sound made by two vowels which are said together

**diploma** /dɪˈpləʊmə/ *noun* [C] a qualification from a school, college, or university, or an official document showing that someone has completed a course of study *a diploma in art and design*

**diplomacy** /dɪˈpləʊməsi/ *noun* [U] **1** dealing with the relationships between governments *international diplomacy* **2** skill in dealing with people well and not upsetting them *She showed great tact and diplomacy in the meeting.*

**diplomat** /ˈdɪpləmæt/ *noun* [C] someone whose job is to live in another country and to keep a good relationship between their government and that country's government

**diplomatic** /ˌdɪpləˈmætɪk/ *adj* **1** [always before noun] relating to diplomacy or diplomats *diplomatic relations* **2** good at dealing with people without upsetting them *That's a very diplomatic answer.* • diplomatically *adv*

**dire** /daɪəʳ/ *adj* very serious or bad *He's in dire need of help.*

o—ᴹ **direct¹** /dɪˈrekt, daɪˈrekt/ *adj* **1** [STRAIGHT] going straight from one place to another without turning or stopping *We went by the most direct route.* **2** [NOTHING BETWEEN] with no other person or thing involved or between *There is a direct link between smoking and cancer.* **3** [CLEAR] saying clearly and honestly what you think *a direct answer* ↪ *Opposite* **indirect**.

**direct²** /dɪˈrekt, daɪˈrekt/ *adv* going straight from one place to another without turning or stopping *Several airlines now fly direct to Vancouver.*

o—ᴹ **direct³** /dɪˈrekt, daɪˈrekt/ *verb* **1** [FILM/PLAY] [T] to tell the actors in a film or play what to do *a film directed by Alfred Hitchcock* **2** direct sth against/at/towards, etc sb/sth to aim something at someone or something *The demonstrators' anger was directed at the police.* **3** [ROUTE] [T] to show or tell someone how to get to a place *Can you direct me to the manager's office please?* **4** [ORGANIZE] [T] to organize and control the way something is done *He directed the building of the new art gallery.* **5** direct sb to do sth *formal* to officially order someone to do something *They directed us not to discuss the matter.*

**direct 'debit** *noun* [C, U] an arrangement that allows an organization to take money from your bank account at regular times to pay for goods or services *I pay my council tax by direct debit.*

o—ᴹ **direction** /dɪˈrekʃən/ *noun* **1** [WAY] [C] the way that someone or something is going or facing *The car sped away in the direction of the airport.* • *I think we're going in the wrong direction.* **2** in sb's direction towards someone *She keeps looking in my direction.* **3** [DEVELOPMENT] [C] the way that someone or something changes or develops *Our careers have gone in very different directions.* **4** [CONTROL] [U] control or instructions *Under his direction the company has doubled its profits.* **5** [PURPOSE] [U] knowing what you want to do *According to his teachers, he lacks direction.*

**directions** /dɪˈrekʃənz/ *noun* [plural] instructions that tell you how to get to a place, or how to do something *We stopped to ask for directions.* • *Just follow the directions on the label.*

**directive** /dɪˈrektɪv/ *noun* [C] *formal* an official instruction *The government has issued new directives on food hygiene.*

**directly** /dɪˈrektli/ *adv* **1** with no other person or thing involved or between *Why don't you speak to him directly?* **2** directly after/behind/opposite, etc exactly or immediately after/behind/opposite, etc *She was sitting directly opposite me.* **3** clearly and honestly *Let me answer that question directly.*

**directness** /dɪˈrektnəs/ *noun* [U] when someone is clear and honest in their speech or behaviour *He liked her directness and simplicity.*

**direct 'object** *noun* [C] the direct object of a transitive verb is the person or thing that is affected by the action of the verb. In the sentence 'I bought a new car yesterday.', 'a new car' is the direct object. ↪ *Compare* **indirect object**.

o—ᴹ **director** /dɪˈrektəʳ/ *noun* [C] **1** an important manager in an organization or company *Meet the new sales director.* **2** someone who tells the actors in a film or play what to do *the famous film director, Alfred Hitchcock* ↪ *See also:* **funeral director, managing director**.

**directorate** /dɪˈrektərət/ *noun* [C] a part of a government or other organization with responsibility for a particular activity

**directory** /dɪ'rekt°ri/ *noun* [C] a book or list of names, numbers, or other facts ⊃ *See also:* **telephone directory**.

**dirt¹** /dɜːt/ *noun* [U] **1** an unpleasant substance that makes something not clean *You've got some dirt on your trousers.* **2** soil or rough ground *a dirt road/track* **3 dig the/up dirt on sb** *informal* to try to discover bad things about someone to stop other people admiring them

**dirt²** /dɜːt/ *adj* **dirt cheap/poor** extremely cheap/poor

○━**dirty¹** /'dɜːti/ *adj* **1** NOT CLEAN not clean *dirty clothes* • *dirty dishes* **2** OFFENSIVE talking about sex in a way that some people find offensive *dirty books/jokes* **3** DISHONEST dishonest or unfair *a dirty business* ⊃ *See also:* do sb's dirty **work²**.

**dirty²** /'dɜːti/ *verb* [T] to make something dirty

**disability** /,dɪsə'bɪləti/ *noun* [C, U] an illness, injury, or condition that makes it difficult for someone to do the things that other people do *They need to improve access for people with disabilities.*

**disable** /dɪ'seɪbl/ *verb* [T] **1** If someone is disabled by an illness or injury, it makes it difficult for them to live in the way that most other people do. [often passive] *Some children were permanently disabled by the bomb.* **2** to stop a piece of equipment from working *The thieves must have disabled the alarm system.*

○━**disabled** /dɪ'seɪbld/ *adj* having an illness, injury, or condition that makes it difficult to do the things that other people do *They are demanding equal rights for the disabled.*

**disadvantage** /,dɪsəd'vɑːntɪdʒ/ *noun* **1** [C] something which makes a situation more difficult, or makes you less likely to succeed *One disadvantage of living in the country is the lack of public transport.* **2 at a disadvantage** having problems that other people do not have *Being shy puts him at a disadvantage.*

**disadvantaged** /,dɪsəd'vɑːntɪdʒd/ *adj* Disadvantaged people are poor and do not have many opportunities. *disadvantaged children*

**disaffected** /,dɪsə'fektɪd/ *adj* disappointed with someone or something and not supporting them as you did before *disaffected voters* • disaffection /,dɪsə'fekʃ°n/ *noun* [U]

○━**disagree** /,dɪsə'griː/ *verb* [I] **disagreeing**, *past* **disagreed** to have a different opinion from someone else about something *I disagree with most of what he said.* • *Experts disagree about/ on the causes of the disease.*

**disagreeable** /,dɪsə'griːəbl/ *adj formal* unpleasant *a disagreeable old man*

**disagreement** /,dɪsə'griːm°nt/ *noun* [C, U] when people have a different opinion about something or have an argument *They had a disagreement about/over money.* • *There is a lot of disagreement among doctors on this matter.*

**disallow** /,dɪsə'laʊ/ *verb* [T] to officially refuse to accept something because the rules have been broken *The goal was disallowed by the referee.*

○━**disappear** /,dɪsə'pɪəʳ/ *verb* [I] **1** NOT SEE to become impossible to see *She watched him disappear into the crowd.* **2** GO to suddenly go somewhere else and become impossible to find *Her husband disappeared in 1991.*

**3** STOP EXISTING to stop existing *These flowers are disappearing from our countryside.* • disappearance /,dɪsə'pɪər°ns/ *noun* [C, U] *Police are investigating the girl's disappearance.* ⊃ *See also:* disappear into thin **air¹**.

**disappoint** /,dɪsə'pɔɪnt/ *verb* [T] to make someone feel unhappy because someone or something was not as good as they had expected *We don't want to disappoint the fans.*

○━**disappointed** /,dɪsə'pɔɪntɪd/ *adj* unhappy because someone or something was not as good as you hoped or expected, or because something did not happen [+ (that)] *I was very disappointed that he didn't come.* • *I'm really disappointed in you.*

**disappointing** /,dɪsə'pɔɪntɪŋ/ *adj* making you feel disappointed *a disappointing performance/result*

**disappointment** /,dɪsə'pɔɪntm°nt/ *noun* **1** [U] the feeling of being disappointed *She couldn't hide her disappointment when she lost.* **2** [C] someone or something that disappoints you *I'm sorry I'm such a disappointment to you.*

**disapproval** /,dɪsə'pruːv°l/ *noun* [U] when you think that someone or something is bad or wrong

**disapprove** /,dɪsə'pruːv/ *verb* [I] to think that someone or something is bad or wrong *Her family disapproved of the marriage.* • disapproving *adj* showing that you think someone or something is bad or wrong *a disapproving look*

**disarm** /dɪs'ɑːm/ *verb* **1** [I, T] to give up your weapons, or to take away someone else's weapons *Both sides have agreed to disarm.* **2** [T] to make someone feel less angry *His smile disarmed her.*

**disarmament** /dɪs'ɑːməmənt/ *noun* [U] when a country or group gets rid of some or all of its weapons *nuclear disarmament*

**disarming** /dɪs'ɑːmɪŋ/ *adj* behaving in a way that stops people feeling angry with you or criticizing you *a disarming smile*

**disarray** /,dɪs°r'eɪ/ *noun* [U] when something is untidy and not organized *The house was in complete disarray.*

○━**disaster** /dɪ'zɑːstəʳ/ *noun* **1** DAMAGE [C] something that causes a lot of harm or damage *floods and other natural disasters* **2** FAILURE [C] a failure or something that has a very bad result *His idea was a total disaster.* **3** BAD SITUATION [U] an extremely bad situation *The holiday ended in disaster.*

**disastrous** /dɪ'zɑːstrəs/ *adj* extremely bad *disastrous consequences* • *a disastrous week*

**disband** /dɪs'bænd/ *verb* [I, T] *formal* to stop working together as a group, or to stop a group from working together

**disbelief** /,dɪsbɪ'liːf/ *noun* [U] when you do not believe that something is true or real *She shook her head in disbelief.*

**disbelieve** /,dɪsbɪ'liːv/ *verb* [T] to not believe someone or something *There was no reason to disbelieve him.*

**disc** (*also US* **disk**) /dɪsk/ *noun* [C] **1** SHAPE a flat, round shape or object **2** RECORDING a record or CD **3** BACK a piece of cartilage (= strong material in the body) between the bones in your back ⊃ *See also:* **compact disc**.

**discard** /dɪˈskɑːd/ *verb* [T] to throw something away *discarded food wrappers*

**discern** /dɪˈsɜːn/ *verb* [T] *formal* to see or recognize something • **discernible** *adj There was no discernible difference between them.*

**discerning** /dɪˈsɜːnɪŋ/ *adj* having or showing good judgment, especially about style and quality *a discerning customer/reader*

**discharge¹** /dɪsˈtʃɑːdʒ/ *verb* [T] **1** to allow someone to leave a hospital or prison, or to order or allow someone to leave an organization such as the army [often passive] *She was discharged from the army yesterday.* **2** If a liquid or gas is discharged from something, it comes out of it. *There is evidence that radioactive waste was discharged from the factory.*

**discharge²** /ˈdɪstʃɑːdʒ/ *noun* [C, U] **1** LEAVE when someone is officially allowed or ordered to leave somewhere such as a prison, hospital, or the army **2** COME OUT when a liquid or gas comes out of something *the discharge of carbon dioxide* **3** SUBSTANCE a liquid or gas that comes out of something

**disciple** /dɪˈsaɪpl/ *noun* [C] someone who follows the ideas and teaching of someone, especially of a religious leader

**disciplinarian** /ˌdɪsəplɪˈneəriən/ *noun* [C] someone who is very strict and gives punishments when people break rules

**disciplinary** /ˌdɪsəˈplɪnəri/ US /ˈdɪsəplɪˌneri/ *adj* [always before noun] relating to punishment for someone who has broken rules *disciplinary action*

o━**discipline¹** /ˈdɪsəplɪn/ *noun* **1** CONTROL [U] when people's behaviour is controlled using rules and punishments *There should be better discipline in schools.* **2** SELF CONTROL [U] when you can control your own behaviour carefully *I don't have enough discipline to save money.* **3** KNOWLEDGE [C] *formal* a particular subject of study *the scientific disciplines* ⊃ *See also:* **self-discipline**.

**discipline²** /ˈdɪsəplɪn/ *verb* [T] **1** to punish someone [often passive] *He was disciplined for missing a training session.* **2** to teach someone to behave in a controlled way [often reflexive] *You have to learn to discipline yourself.*

**disciplined** /ˈdɪsəplɪnd/ *adj* behaving in a very controlled way *the most disciplined army in the world*

**ˈdisc ˌjockey** (*also* **DJ**) *noun* [C] someone who plays music on the radio or at discos

**disclaim** /dɪsˈkleɪm/ *verb* [T] *formal* to say that you know nothing about something, or are not responsible for something *The terrorists disclaimed responsibility for the bomb.*

**disclaimer** /dɪsˈkleɪməʳ/ *noun* [C] when someone officially says that they are not responsible for something

**disclose** /dɪsˈkləuz/ *verb* [T] *formal* to give new or secret information to someone *He refused to disclose details of the report.*

**disclosure** /dɪsˈkləuʒəʳ/ *noun* [C, U] when someone gives people new or secret information

**disco** /ˈdɪskəu/ *noun* [C] a place or event where people dance to pop music

**discoloured** UK (US **discolored**) /dɪsˈkʌləd/ *adj* If something is discoloured, it has become a less attractive colour than it was originally. *discoloured teeth*

**discomfort** /dɪsˈkʌmfət/ *noun* **1** PAIN [U] slight pain *You may feel some discomfort for a few days.* **2** MENTAL FEELING [U] when you feel slightly embarrassed or anxious **3** SITUATION [C, U] a physically uncomfortable situation

**disconcert** /ˌdɪskənˈsɜːt/ *verb* [T] to make someone feel confused or anxious [often passive] *She was disconcerted by his questions.*

**disconcerting** /ˌdɪskənˈsɜːtɪŋ/ *adj* making you feel confused or anxious *a disconcerting silence* • **disconcertingly** *adv*

**disconnect** /ˌdɪskəˈnekt/ *verb* [T] to separate two things that are joined or connected, especially a piece of equipment and a power supply *Switch off the machine before **disconnecting** it **from** the power supply.*

**disconnected** /ˌdɪskəˈnektɪd/ *adj* not joined in any way *disconnected thoughts*

**discontent** /ˌdɪskənˈtent/ *noun* [U] unhappiness about a situation *There is growing **discontent with** this government.* • **discontented** *adj*

**discontinue** /ˌdɪskənˈtɪnjuː/ *verb* [T] **discontinuing**, *past* **discontinued** to stop producing or providing something such as a product or service [often passive] *I'm afraid this model has been discontinued.*

**discord** /ˈdɪskɔːd/ *noun* [U] disagreement between people

**discount¹** /ˈdɪskaunt/ *noun* [C, U] a reduction in price *They offer a 10 percent **discount on** rail travel for students.*

**discount²** /dɪˈskaunt/ *verb* [T] **1** to ignore something because you do not believe that it is true or that it will happen *You shouldn't discount the possibility of him coming back.* **2** to reduce the price of something *discounted goods/rates*

**discourage** /dɪˈskʌrɪdʒ/ *verb* **1 discourage sb from doing sth** to try to persuade someone not to do something *a campaign to discourage people from smoking* **2** [T] to try to prevent something from happening *a campaign to discourage smoking* **3** [T] to make someone less confident or enthusiastic about something *I didn't mean to discourage her.* • **discouragement** *noun* [U] ⊃ *Opposite* **encourage**.

**discouraged** /dɪˈskʌrɪdʒd/ *adj* having lost your confidence or enthusiasm for something

**discouraging** /dɪˈskʌrɪdʒɪŋ/ *adj* making you feel less enthusiastic or confident about something *discouraging results*

o━**discover** /dɪˈskʌvəʳ/ *verb* [T] **1** FIND to find something *They came to California hoping to discover gold.* • *The body was discovered in a ditch.* **2** FIRST to be the first person to find something important *Who discovered America?* **3** GET INFORMATION to get information about something for the first time [+ (that)] *She discovered that he had been married three times before.* • [+ question word] *Have they discovered what was causing your headaches?*

**discoverer** /dɪˈskʌvərəʳ/ *noun* [C] someone who is the first person to find something important

o━**discovery** /dɪˈskʌvəri/ *noun* [C, U] when someone discovers something *the discovery of bones in the garden* • *Scientists have **made*** *some important **discoveries** about genetics recently.* **2** [C] something or someone that is discovered

**discredit** /dɪ'skredɪt/ *verb* [T] to make someone or something appear bad and lose the respect of other people *They're always looking for ways to discredit her.*

**discreet** /dɪ'skriːt/ *adj* careful not to cause embarrassment or attract too much attention, especially by keeping something secret *Can I trust you to be discreet?* ➲ *Opposite* **indiscreet**. • **discreetly** *adv*

**discrepancy** /dɪ'skrepənsi/ *noun* [C, U] when two things that should be the same are different *There is a slight **discrepancy between** the two statements.*

**discrete** /dɪ'skriːt/ *adj* separate and different *a word that has two discrete meanings*

**discretion** /dɪ'skreʃən/ *noun* [U] **1** when someone is careful not to cause embarrassment or attract too much attention, especially by keeping something secret *You can rely on my discretion.* ➲ *Opposite* **indiscretion**. **2** the right to decide something *Students can be expelled **at the discretion of** the head teacher* (= if the head teacher decides it).

**discretionary** /dɪ'skreʃənəri/ *adj* decided by officials and not fixed by rules *Judges have great discretionary powers.*

**discriminate** /dɪ'skrɪmɪneɪt/ *verb* [I] **1** to treat someone unfairly because of their sex, race, religion, etc *The company was accused of **discriminating against** people on the basis of age.* **2** to notice a difference between two things *Police dogs are very good at **discriminating between** different smells.*

**discriminating** /dɪ'skrɪmɪneɪtɪŋ/ *adj* good at judging what is good quality *a discriminating shopper*

**discrimination** /dɪˌskrɪmɪ'neɪʃən/ *noun* [U] when someone is treated unfairly because of their sex, race, religion, etc *racial discrimination* • *discrimination against older workers*

**discus** /'dɪskəs/ *noun* [C] a round, flat, heavy object that people throw as a sport

o--**discuss** /dɪ'skʌs/ *verb* [T] to talk about something with someone and tell each other your ideas or opinions *Have you discussed this matter with anyone else?*

o--**discussion** /dɪ'skʌʃən/ *noun* [C, U] when people talk about something and tell each other their ideas or opinions *They were **having** a **discussion** about football.* • *Several ideas are still **under discussion** (= being discussed).*

**disdain** /dɪs'deɪn/ *noun* [U] when you dislike someone or something and think that they do not deserve any respect *His **disdain for** politicians is obvious.* • **disdainful** *adj* **disdainful** *remarks* • **disdainfully** *adv*

o--**disease** /dɪ'ziːz/ *noun* [C, U] an illness caused by an infection or by a failure of health and not by an accident *heart disease* • *an infectious disease* • **diseased** *adj* affected by a disease *a diseased lung*

**disembark** /ˌdɪsɪm'bɑːk/ *verb* [I] *formal* to leave a ship, boat, or aircraft *All passengers must disembark in Vancouver.* • **disembarkation** /ˌdɪsɪmbɑː'keɪʃən/ *noun* [U]

**disembodied** /ˌdɪsɪm'bɒdid/ *adj* seeming not to have a body or not to be connected to a body *a disembodied voice*

**disenchanted** /ˌdɪsɪn'tʃɑːntɪd/ *adj* disappointed with something that you thought was good in the past *He became **disenchanted with** politics.* • **disenchantment** *noun* [U]

**disengage** /ˌdɪsɪn'geɪdʒ/ *verb* [I, T] to become separated from something, or to make two things become separate from each other *He gently disengaged his hand from hers.*

**disentangle** /ˌdɪsɪn'tæŋgl/ *verb* [T] **1** to separate someone or something that is connected to something else in a complicated way *He **disentangled** himself **from** her arms.* **2** to separate things such as pieces of string, hair, or wire that have become twisted together *I tried to disentangle the wires under my desk.*

**disfigure** /dɪs'fɪgə/ *verb* [T] to spoil someone's or something's appearance [often passive] *Her face was disfigured by a huge scar.*

**disgrace**[1] /dɪs'greɪs/ *verb* [T] to make people stop respecting you or your family, team, etc by doing something very bad *You have disgraced us all with your behaviour.*

**disgrace**[2] /dɪs'greɪs/ *noun* [U] **1** when someone does something very bad that makes people stop respecting them or their family, team, etc *They were sent home **in disgrace**.* **2** **be a disgrace** to be very bad [+ that] *It's a disgrace that money is being wasted like this.* **3** **be a disgrace to sb/sth** to be so bad or unacceptable that you make people stop respecting a particular group, activity, etc *You are a disgrace to your profession.*

**disgraced** /dɪs'greɪst/ *adj* A disgraced person has lost other people's respect because they have done something very bad. *a disgraced politician*

**disgraceful** /dɪs'greɪsfəl/ *adj* very bad *disgraceful behaviour* • **disgracefully** *adv*

**disgruntled** /dɪs'grʌntld/ *adj* angry and upset *Disgruntled workers have decided to go on strike.*

**disguise**[1] /dɪs'gaɪz/ *noun* [C, U] clothes and other things that you wear to change the way you look so that people cannot recognize you *She usually goes out **in disguise** to avoid being bothered by the public.* ➲ *See also:* a **blessing** in disguise.

**disguise**[2] /dɪs'gaɪz/ *verb* **1** **disguise yourself/your voice, etc** to change your appearance/voice, etc so that people cannot recognize you *He managed to escape by **disguising** himself as a woman.* **2** **be disguised as sb/sth** to be wearing clothes and other things that

**D**

make you look like someone or something else **3** [T] to hide something such as a feeling or opinion *She couldn't disguise her disappointment.*

**disgust¹** /dɪsˈɡʌst/ *noun* [U] a very strong feeling of dislike or disapproval *She walked out in disgust.*

**disgust²** /dɪsˈɡʌst/ *verb* [T] If something disgusts you, it makes you feel extreme dislike or disapproval. *These pictures disgust me.*

**disgusted** /dɪsˈɡʌstɪd/ *adj* feeling extreme dislike or disapproval of something *I'm totally disgusted with your behaviour.*

**disgusting** /dɪsˈɡʌstɪŋ/ *adj* extremely unpleasant *What's that disgusting smell?*

o⚬**dish¹** /dɪʃ/ *noun* [C] **1** a curved container for eating or serving food from *a baking/serving dish* **2** food that is prepared in a particular way as part of a meal *a chicken/vegetarian dish* **3** the dishes dirty plates, bowls, and other objects for cooking or eating food *Who's going to wash the dishes?*

**dish²** /dɪʃ/ *verb*
**dish sth out** *informal* to give or say things to people without thinking about it carefully *She's always dishing out advice to someone.*

**dishcloth** /ˈdɪʃklɒθ/ *noun* [C] a cloth used for washing dirty dishes

**disheartened** /dɪsˈhɑːtᵊnd/ *adj* disappointed or without hope *She was very disheartened by the results of the test.*

**disheartening** /dɪsˈhɑːtᵊnɪŋ/ *adj* making you feel disappointed or without hope *a disheartening experience*

**dishevelled** UK (US **disheveled**) /dɪˈʃevᵊld/ *adj* very untidy *dishevelled hair*

**dishonest** /dɪˈsɒnɪst/ *adj* not honest and likely to lie or do something illegal • **dishonestly** *adv* • **dishonesty** *noun* [U] when someone is not honest

**dishonour¹** UK (US **dishonor**) /dɪˈsɒnəʳ/ *noun* [U] when people stop respecting you because you have done something bad *You have brought dishonour on your family.* • **dishonourable** *adj* bad or not deserving respect *dishonourable conduct*

**dishonour²** UK (US **dishonor**) /dɪˈsɒnəʳ/ *verb* [T] to show no respect for someone or something by behaving badly *He felt that he had dishonoured his country.*

**dishtowel** /ˈdɪʃtaʊəl/ US (UK **tea towel**) *noun* [C] a cloth that is used for drying plates, dishes, etc

**dishwasher** /ˈdɪʃˌwɒʃəʳ/ *noun* [C] a machine that washes plates, glasses and other kitchen equipment *I'll load the dishwasher.* ➔ *See colour picture* **Kitchen** *on page Centre 10.*

**disillusion** /ˌdɪsɪˈluːʒᵊn/ *verb* [T] to cause someone to discover that something they believed is not true

**disillusioned** /ˌdɪsɪˈluːʒᵊnd/ *adj* feeling disappointed because something is not as good as you thought it was *She says she's disillusioned with the music business.*

**disillusionment** /ˌdɪsɪˈluːʒᵊnmənt/ (also **disillusion**) *noun* [U] the disappointment someone feels when they discover something is not as good as they thought it was *There's growing disillusionment with the government.*

**disinfect** /ˌdɪsɪnˈfekt/ *verb* [T] to clean something with a chemical that destroys bacteria

**disinfectant** /ˌdɪsɪnˈfektənt/ *noun* [C, U] a chemical substance that destroys bacteria

**disintegrate** /dɪˈsɪntɪɡreɪt/ *verb* [I] **1** to break into a lot of small pieces **2** to become much worse *The situation is disintegrating into total chaos.* • **disintegration** /dɪˌsɪntɪˈɡreɪʃᵊn/ *noun* [U]

**disinterested** /dɪˈsɪntrəstɪd/ *adj* not involved in a situation and so able to judge it without supporting a particular side *a disinterested observer*

**disjointed** /dɪsˈdʒɔɪntɪd/ *adj* having words or ideas that are not in a clear order *a disjointed conversation*

o⚬**disk** /dɪsk/ *noun* [C] **1** another US spelling of disc **2** a piece of computer equipment that records and stores information electronically *How much disk space is there?* ➔ *See colour picture* **The Office** *on page Centre 12.* ➔ *See also:* **floppy disk**, **hard disk**.

**diskette** /dɪˈsket/ *noun* [C] a small, flat, plastic object that you put in your computer to record and store information electronically

**dislike¹** /dɪˈslaɪk/ *verb* [T] to not like someone or something *Why do you dislike her so much?* • [+ doing sth] *I dislike ironing intensely.*

**dislike²** /dɪˈslaɪk/ *noun* [C, U] when you do not like someone or something *a dislike of cold weather* • *I took an instant dislike to her* (= disliked her immediately).

**dislocate** /ˈdɪsləʊkeɪt/ *verb* [T] If you dislocate a part of your body, the bones move away from their correct position. *I think you've dislocated your shoulder.* • *a dislocated hip* • **dislocation** /ˌdɪsləʊˈkeɪʃᵊn/ *noun* [U]

**dislodge** /dɪˈslɒdʒ/ *verb* [T] to move something away from a fixed position

**disloyal** /dɪˈslɔɪəl/ *adj* not loyal or not supporting someone who you should support *I don't want to be disloyal to my friend.* • **disloyalty** *noun* [U] *They accused her of disloyalty.*

**dismal** /ˈdɪzməl/ *adj* very bad or unpleasant and making you feel unhappy *What dismal weather.* • *That was a dismal performance.* • **dismally** *adv* *I tried to cheer her up, but failed dismally* (= completely failed).

**dismantle** /dɪˈsmæntl/ *verb* [T] **1** to take something apart so that it is in several pieces *He's specially trained to dismantle bombs.* **2** to get rid of a system or organization

**dismay** /dɪˈsmeɪ/ *noun* [U] a feeling of unhappiness and disappointment *To our dismay, it started raining.*

**dismayed** /dɪˈsmeɪd/ *adj* unhappy and disappointed [+ to do sth] *I was dismayed to discover that he'd lied to me.*

**dismember** /dɪˈsmembəʳ/ *verb* [T] to cut the arms and legs off the body of a person or animal *a dismembered body*

**dismiss** /dɪˈsmɪs/ *verb* [T] **1** NOT CONSIDER to refuse to consider an idea or opinion *The committee dismissed the idea as rubbish.* **2** MAKE LEAVE to officially make someone leave their job [often passive] *Anyone who breaks company rules will be dismissed.* **3** ALLOW TO LEAVE to give someone official permission to leave *The bell rang and the teacher dismissed the class.*

**dismissal** /dɪˈsmɪsᵊl/ *noun* **1** [U] when someone refuses to consider an idea or opinion **2** [C, U] when an employer officially makes someone leave their job

**dismissive** /dɪˈsmɪsɪv/ *adj* treating something as if it is not important *a dismissive attitude* • *He's so **dismissive of** all my suggestions.* • **dismissively** *adv*

**dismount** /dɪˈsmaʊnt/ *verb* [I] *formal* to get off a horse or bicycle

**disobedience** /ˌdɪsəˈbiːdiəns/ *noun* [U] when someone refuses to do what someone in authority tells them to do

**disobedient** /ˌdɪsəˈbiːdiənt/ *adj* refusing to do what someone in authority tells you to do *a disobedient child*

**disobey** /ˌdɪsəˈbeɪ/ *verb* [T] to not do what you are told to do by someone in authority *How dare you disobey me!*

**disorder** /dɪˈsɔːdə⁰/ *noun* **1** [ILLNESS] [C] a disease or mental problem *a blood disorder* **2** [BAD BEHAVIOUR] [U] uncontrolled, bad behaviour, especially by large groups of people *crime and disorder* **3** [NOT ORGANIZED] [U] when things are untidy or confused and not organized *His financial affairs are in complete disorder.* ➔ *See also:* **eating disorder**.

**disordered** /dɪˈsɔːdəd/ *adj* confused and not organized *a disordered mind*

**disorderly** /dɪˈsɔːdᵊli/ *adj* **1** behaving badly by being noisy or violent *He was charged with being drunk and disorderly.* **2** untidy

**disorganized** (*also UK* **-ised**) /dɪˈsɔːɡənaɪzd/ *adj* **1** not planned or organized well *The competition was completely disorganized.* **2** not good at planning or organizing things *She's terribly disorganized.*

**disorient** /dɪˈsɔːriənt/ (*also UK* **disorientate** /dɪˈsɔːriənteɪt/) *verb* [T] to make someone not know where to go or what to do

**disoriented** /dɪˈsɔːriəntɪd/ (*also UK* **disorientated** /dɪˈsɔːriənteɪtɪd/) *adj* confused and not knowing where to go or what to do *Whales become disoriented in shallow water.*

**disown** /dɪˈsəʊn/ *verb* [T] to say that you do not want to have any involvement or connection with someone *Even his parents have disowned him.*

**disparage** /dɪˈspærɪdʒ/ *verb* [T] to say that you think someone or something is not very good [often passive] *He is often disparaged by the critics.*

**disparaging** /dɪˈspærɪdʒɪŋ/ *adj* criticizing someone or something *disparaging remarks*

**disparate** /ˈdɪspᵊrət/ *adj formal* completely different *people from disparate cultures*

**disparity** /dɪˈspærəti/ *noun* [C, U] *formal* difference, usually relating to the money people earn or their position

**dispatch¹** (*also UK* **despatch**) /dɪˈspætʃ/ *verb* [T] *formal* to send someone or something somewhere *They dispatched a police car to arrest him.*

**dispatch²** (*also UK* **despatch**) /dɪˈspætʃ/ *noun* **1** [U] when someone or something is sent somewhere *the dispatch of troops* **2** [C] an official

report that someone in a foreign country sends to their organization

**dispel** /dɪˈspel/ *verb* [T] **dispelling**, *past* **dispelled** to get rid of a feeling, thought, or belief *He appeared on TV to dispel rumours that he was dying.*

**dispensary** /dɪˈspensᵊri/ *noun* [C] a place where medicines are given out

**dispensation** /ˌdɪspenˈseɪʃᵊn/ *noun* [C, U] special permission to do something [+ to do sth] *The court would not grant him a dispensation to visit his children.*

**dispense** /dɪˈspens/ *verb* [T] to give something out *a machine that dispenses drinks and snacks* **dispense with sth/sb** to stop using something or someone, or to get rid of something or someone, usually because you do not need them

**dispenser** /dɪˈspensə⁰/ *noun* [C] a machine that you can get something from *a drink/soap dispenser*

**disperse** /dɪˈspɜːs/ *verb* [I, T] to separate and go in different directions, or to make something do this *We waited until the crowds had dispersed.* • **dispersal** *noun* [U]

**dispirited** /dɪˈspɪrɪtɪd/ *adj* unhappy and without hope

**displace** /dɪˈspleɪs/ *verb* [T] **1** to take the place of someone or something *Many of these workers will be displaced by modern technology.* **2** to make someone or something leave their usual place or position *The earthquake displaced thousands of people.* • **displacement** *noun* [U]

**display¹** /dɪˈspleɪ/ *noun* **1** [ARRANGEMENT] [C] a collection of objects or pictures arranged for people to look at *a display of children's paintings* **2 on display** If something is on display, it is there for people to look at. *Many old aircraft are on display at the museum.* **3** [SHOW] [C] a performance or show for people to watch *a firework display* **4** [ON SCREEN] [C, U] when something is shown electronically such as on a computer screen *The display problems might be due to a shortage of disk space.* **5 a display of affection/anger**, *etc* when someone behaves in a way that shows they have a particular feeling

**display²** /dɪˈspleɪ/ *verb* **1** [ARRANGE] [T] to arrange something somewhere so that people can see it *There were some family photographs displayed on his desk.* **2** [ON SCREEN] [I, T] to show something electronically such as on a computer screen *The text can be displayed and edited on screen.* **3** [FEELING] [T] to show how you feel by your expression or behaviour *He never displayed any interest in girls.*

**displease** /dɪˈspliːz/ *verb* [T] *formal* to make someone annoyed or unhappy *I don't want to do anything to displease him.* • **displeased** *adj*

**displeasure** /dɪˈspleʒə⁰/ *noun* [U] *formal* when someone is annoyed or unhappy about something *She expressed great displeasure at his behaviour.*

**disposable** /dɪˈspəʊzəbl/ *adj* intended to be used only once and then thrown away *a disposable camera/razor*

**disposable ˈincome** *UK* (*US* **dis,posable ˈincome**) *noun* [C, U] the amount of money that you have available to spend after tax, rent and other basic things that you must pay for

**disposal** /dɪˈspəʊz³l/ *noun* [U] **1** when you get rid of something, especially by throwing it away *waste disposal* • *the disposal of hazardous substances* **2 at sb's disposal** available for someone to use *We will have a car at our disposal for the whole trip.*

**dispose** /dɪˈspəʊz/ *verb*
**dispose of sth** to get rid of something, especially by throwing it away *How did they dispose of the body?*

**disposed** /dɪˈspəʊzd/ *adj formal* **1 be disposed to do sth** to be willing or likely to do something *I tried to tell her but she didn't seem disposed to listen.* **2 be favourably/well, etc disposed towards sth** to like or approve of something *She seems well disposed towards the idea.*

**disposition** /ˌdɪspəˈzɪʃ³n/ *noun* [C] the type of character someone has *a cheerful/nervous disposition*

**disproportionate** /ˌdɪsprəˈpɔːʃ³nət/ *adj* too large or small in comparison to something else *There are a disproportionate number of girls in the class.* • disproportionately *adv*

**disprove** /dɪˈspruːv/ *verb* [T] to prove that something is not true

**dispute¹** /ˈdɪspjuːt/ *noun* [C, U] a disagreement, especially one that lasts a long time *A man stabbed his neighbour in a dispute over noise.*

**dispute²** /dɪˈspjuːt/ *verb* [T] to disagree with something someone says [+ (that)] *I'm not disputing that the drug has benefits.*

**disqualify** /dɪˈskwɒlɪfaɪ/ *verb* [T] to stop someone from being in a competition or doing some other activity because they have done something wrong [often passive] *She was disqualified from the race after a drugs test.* • disqualification /dɪˌskwɒlɪfɪˈkeɪʃ³n/ *noun* [U]

**disquiet** /dɪˈskwaɪət/ *noun* [U] *formal* when people are anxious or worried about something

**disregard¹** /ˌdɪsrɪˈɡɑːd/ *noun* [U, no plural] when someone does not care about or show any interest in someone or something *His behaviour shows a total disregard for other people.*

**disregard²** /ˌdɪsrɪˈɡɑːd/ *verb* [T] to ignore something *She chose to disregard my advice.*

**disrepair** /ˌdɪsrɪˈpeə³/ *noun* [U] when a building is in a bad condition because someone has not taken care of it *The house has fallen into disrepair.*

**disreputable** /dɪsˈrepjətəbl/ *adj* not respected or trusted by people *a disreputable company*

**disrepute** /ˌdɪsrɪˈpjuːt/ *noun* **bring sb/sth into disrepute** *formal* to cause people not to respect or trust someone or something *Corrupt policemen are bringing the law into disrepute.*

**disrespect** /ˌdɪsrɪˈspekt/ *noun* [U] when someone does not show any respect or behave politely towards someone or something *a disrespect for authority*

**disrespectful** /ˌdɪsrɪˈspektf³l/ *adj* being rude and not showing any respect *Don't be disrespectful to your mother.* • disrespectfully *adv*

**disrupt** /dɪsˈrʌpt/ *verb* [T] to interrupt something and stop it continuing as it should *He dis-*

*turbs other children and disrupts the class.* • disruption /dɪsˈrʌpʃ³n/ *noun* [C, U] *the disruption of services* • disruptive *adj disruptive behaviour*

**dissatisfaction** /dɪsˌsætɪsˈfækʃ³n/ *noun* [U] when you are not pleased or happy with something *He expressed his dissatisfaction with the legal system.*

**dissatisfied** /dɪsˈsætɪsfaɪd/ *adj* not pleased or happy with something *a dissatisfied customer* • *Are you dissatisfied with our service?*

**dissect** /daɪˈsekt/ *verb* [T] to cut something into pieces for scientific study *We had to dissect a rat in biology.* • dissection /daɪˈsekʃ³n/ *noun* [U]

**disseminate** /dɪˈsemɪneɪt/ *verb* [T] to spread information or ideas *They are using their website to disseminate political propaganda.* • dissemination /dɪˌsemɪˈneɪʃ³n/ *noun* [U]

**dissent** /dɪˈsent/ *noun* [U] when someone does not agree with something *There is a lot of dissent within the Church about women priests.* • dissent *verb* [I] to not agree with other people about something • dissenter *noun* [C]

**dissertation** /ˌdɪsəˈteɪʃ³n/ *noun* [C] a very long piece of writing done as part of a course of study *She's writing a dissertation on American poetry.*

**disservice** /ˌdɪsˈsɜːvɪs/ *noun* [no plural] when something causes harm to someone or something *Bad teaching does a great disservice to children.*

**dissident** /ˈdɪsɪd³nt/ *noun* [C] someone who criticizes their government in a public way *political dissidents*

**dissimilar** /ˌdɪsˈsɪmɪlə³/ *adj* different *Her hair is not dissimilar to yours* (= is similar to yours).

**dissipate** /ˈdɪsɪpeɪt/ *verb* [I, T] to disappear, or to make something disappear *The heat gradually dissipates into the atmosphere.*

**dissociate** /dɪˈsəʊʃieɪt/ *verb* **dissociate yourself from sb/sth** to say that you do not have any connection or involvement with someone or something *He's trying to dissociate himself from his former friends.*

**dissolution** /ˌdɪsəˈluːʃ³n/ *noun* [U] when an organization or an official arrangement ends

**dissolve** /dɪˈzɒlv/ *verb* **1** [I, T] If a solid dissolves, it becomes part of a liquid, and if you dissolve it, you make it become part of a liquid. *These tablets dissolve in water.* **2** [T] to end an organization or official arrangement [often passive] *Their marriage was dissolved in 1996.* **3 dissolve into laughter/tears, etc** to suddenly start to laugh/cry, etc

**dissuade** /dɪˈsweɪd/ *verb* [T] to persuade someone not to do something [+ from + doing sth] *We tried to dissuade him from leaving.*

o━**distance¹** /ˈdɪst³ns/ *noun* **1** [C, U] the length of the space between two places or things *We're only a short distance from my house.* • *He calculated the distance between the Earth and the Sun.* • *Are the shops within walking distance?* **2** [no plural] somewhere that is far away, but close enough for you to see or hear the things that are there *I could see Mary in the distance.* • *From a distance, it sounded like a bell ringing.*

**distance²** /ˈdɪst³ns/ *verb* **distance yourself**

**from sb/sth** to say or show that you are not connected or involved with someone or something *She has tried to distance herself from the book.*

o━**distant** /'dɪstᵊnt/ *adj* **1** [FAR AWAY] far away in space or time *distant galaxies* • *the distant sound of traffic* • *We hope to see you in the not too distant future.* **2** [RELATIVE] A distant relative is not very closely related to you. *a distant cousin* **3** [NOT FRIENDLY] [never before noun] not friendly *She seemed cold and distant.* • distantly *adv distantly related*

**distaste** /dɪ'steɪst/ *noun* [U] when you dislike something and think it is unpleasant *I have developed a distaste for meat.*

**distasteful** /dɪ'steɪstfᵊl/ *adj* unpleasant or offensive *I find this advertisement extremely distasteful.* • distastefully *adv*

**distil** UK (US **distill**) /dɪ'stɪl/ *verb* [T] **distilling,** *past* **distilled** to make a liquid stronger or more pure by heating it until it changes into a gas and then changing it into a liquid again *distilled water* • distillation /,dɪstɪ'leɪʃᵊn/ *noun* [U] • distillery /dɪ'stɪlᵊri/ *noun* [C] a place where strong alcoholic drinks are produced

**distinct** /dɪ'stɪŋkt/ *adj* **1** [DIFFERENT] different and separate *This word has three distinct meanings.* **2** [HEAR/SEE] easy to hear, see, or smell *The voices gradually became louder and more distinct.* ➔ Opposite **indistinct. 3** [CLEAR] [always before noun] clear and certain *There's been a distinct improvement in your work.* • distinctly *adv*

**distinction** /dɪ'stɪŋkʃᵊn/ *noun* [C, U] **1** a difference between two similar things *the distinction between spoken and written language* **2** a quality or fact that makes someone or something special or different *wines of distinction* • *He has the distinction of being the youngest player in the World Cup finals.*

**distinctive** /dɪ'stɪŋktɪv/ *adj* Something that is distinctive is easy to recognize because it is different from other things. *a distinctive style of writing* • distinctively *adv*

**distinguish** /dɪ'stɪŋgwɪʃ/ *verb* **1** [RECOGNIZE DIFFERENCES] [I, T] to recognize the differences between two people, ideas, or things *Children must learn to distinguish between right and wrong.* • *People have difficulty distinguishing Tracy from her twin sister Mary.* **2** [SHOW DIFFERENCES] [T] to make one person or thing seem different from another *His great skill distinguishes him from the rest of the team.* **3** [SEE/HEAR] [T] to be able to see, hear, or understand something **4 distinguish yourself** to do something so well that people notice and admire you • distinguishable *adj*

**distinguished** /dɪ'stɪŋgwɪʃt/ *adj* famous, praised, or admired *a distinguished writer*

**distort** /dɪ'stɔːt/ *verb* [T] **1** to change the shape, sound, or appearance of something so that it seems strange *It's a bad recording – the microphone distorted our voices.* **2** to change information so that it is not true or realistic *Newspapers distorted the truth about their marriage.* • distorted *adj* • distortion /dɪ'stɔːʃᵊn/ *noun* [C, U] *a gross distortion of the facts*

**distract** /dɪ'strækt/ *verb* [T] to make someone stop giving their attention to something *Stop distracting me – I'm trying to finish my essay.*

**distracted** /dɪ'stræktɪd/ *adj* anxious and unable to think carefully

**distraction** /dɪ'strækʃᵊn/ *noun* **1** [C, U] something that makes you stop giving your attention to something else *The phone calls were a constant distraction.* **2 drive sb to distraction** *UK* to make someone very annoyed

**distraught** /dɪ'strɔːt/ *adj* extremely upset and unhappy

**distress¹** /dɪ'stres/ *noun* [U] **1** the feeling of being extremely upset or worried *The newspaper reports caused her a great deal of distress.* **2** when someone or something is in danger and needs help *an aircraft in distress*

**distress²** /dɪ'stres/ *verb* [T] to make someone feel upset or worried *It distressed me to see how ill she looked.* • distressing *adj a distressing experience*

**distribute** /dɪ'strɪbjuːt/ *verb* [T] **1** to give something out to people or places *The books will be distributed free to local schools.* **2** to supply goods to shops and companies *The company manufactures and distributes computer equipment worldwide.*

**distribution** /,dɪstrɪ'bjuːʃᵊn/ *noun* **1** [U] when something is supplied or given out to people or places *the sale and distribution of videos* **2** [U, no plural] the way something is divided and shared in a group or area *the distribution of wealth*

**distributor** /dɪ'strɪbjətəʳ/ *noun* [C] a person or organization that supplies goods to shops and companies

**district** /'dɪstrɪkt/ *noun* [C] a part of a city or country, either an official area or one that is known for having a particular characteristic or business *the fashion district of New York*

,**district at'torney** *noun* [C] *US* a lawyer who works for the government of a particular district

**distrust** /dɪ'strʌst/ *noun* [U] when you do not trust someone or something *He has a deep distrust of foreigners.* • distrust *verb* [T]

o━**disturb** /dɪ'stɜːb/ *verb* [T] **1** [INTERRUPT] to interrupt what someone is doing by making noise or annoying them *Don't disturb him, he needs to sleep.* **2** [UPSET] to make someone feel anxious or upset *Some scenes are violent and may disturb younger viewers.* **3** [CHANGE] to change something by touching it or moving it from its original position

**disturbance** /dɪ'stɜːbᵊns/ *noun* **1** [C, U] something that interrupts what you are doing, especially something loud or annoying **2** [C] when people fight or shout *A man was shot during a disturbance in King Street.*

**disturbed** /dɪ'stɜːbd/ *adj* not thinking or behaving normally because of mental or emotional problems

**disturbing** /dɪ'stɜːbɪŋ/ *adj* unpleasant in a way that makes people feel anxious or upset *disturbing images*

**disused** /dɪ'sjuːzd/ *adj* not used now *a disused warehouse* • disuse /dɪ'sjuːs/ *noun* [U] when something is not used *to fall into disuse*

**ditch¹** /dɪtʃ/ *noun* [C] a long, narrow hole in the ground next to a road or field, which water can

flow through

**ditch²** /dɪtʃ/ *verb* [T] *informal* to get rid of someone or something that you do not need or want now *He ditched his girlfriend when she got pregnant.*

**dither** /'dɪðəʳ/ *verb* [I] to spend too much time trying to make a decision *Stop dithering and tell me which one you want!*

**ditto¹** /'dɪtəʊ/ *adv* used to agree with something that has been said, or to avoid repeating something that has been said

**ditto²** /'dɪtəʊ/ *noun* [C] a mark (") used instead of words to show that you are repeating what is written above it

**ditty** /'dɪti/ *noun* [C] a short, simple song

**Divali** (*also* **Diwali**) /dɪ'væli/ *noun* [U] the Hindu period of religious celebration held in the autumn

**dive¹** /daɪv/ *verb* [I] *past t* **dived** *also US* **dove**, *past p* **dived 1** JUMP IN to jump into water with your head and arms going in first *He dived off the side of the boat into the sea.* **2** SWIM to swim under water, usually with breathing equipment **3 dive into/over/under, etc** to move somewhere quickly *He heard footsteps and dived under the table.* **4** FLY to fly down through the air very quickly *Suddenly the plane dived to the ground.* **5** VALUE If a value or price dives, it suddenly becomes less.

**dive²** /daɪv/ *noun* [C] **1** JUMP a jump into water

**dive**

with your arms and head going in first **2** MOVEMENT a quick movement somewhere **3** VALUE when the value or price of something suddenly becomes less *Share prices took a dive today.* **4** PLACE *informal* a place such as a bar which is considered to be dirty or of low quality

**diver** /'daɪvəʳ/ *noun* [C] someone who swims under water, usually with breathing equipment

**diverge** /daɪ'vɜːdʒ/ *verb* [I] to be different, or to go or develop in a different direction *Over the years our interests have diverged.* • **divergence** *noun* [C, U]

**diverse** /daɪ'vɜːs/ *adj* including many different

types *a diverse collection of music*

**diversify** /daɪ'vɜːsɪfaɪ/ *verb* [I, T] If a business diversifies, it starts making new products or offering new services. *Many designers are diversifying into casual wear.* • diversification /daɪ,vɜːsɪfɪ'keɪʃᵊn/ *noun* [U]

**diversion** /daɪ'vɜːʃᵊn/ *noun* **1** CHANGE [C, U] when something is sent somewhere different from where it was originally intended to go *the diversion of money to other projects* **2** ROUTE [C] *UK* (*US* **detour**) a different route that is used because a road is closed **3** ATTENTION [C] something that takes your attention away from something else *John created a diversion while the rest of us escaped.* **4** ENTERTAINMENT [C] an activity you do for entertainment or pleasure *Reading is a pleasant diversion.*

**diversity** /daɪ'vɜːsəti/ *noun* [U] when many different types of things or people are included in something *ethnic diversity*

**divert** /daɪ'vɜːt/ *verb* **1** [T] to send someone or something somewhere different from where they were expecting to go *The plane was diverted to Stansted because of engine trouble.* • *The police were diverting traffic away from the town.* **2 divert sb's attention/thoughts, etc** to take someone's attention away from something

o━**divide** /dɪ'vaɪd/ *verb* **1** SEPARATE [I, T] to separate into parts or groups, or to make something separate into parts or groups *We divided up into teams of six.* • *Each school year is divided into two semesters.* **2 divide sth (up) among/ between sb** to separate something into parts and give a part to each person in a group *The prize money will be divided equally among the winners.* **3** PLACE [T] to separate a place into two areas *An ancient wall divides the city.* **4** NUMBERS [I, T] to calculate how many times a number can go into another number *12 divided by 6 equals 2.* **5** DISAGREE [T] to cause people to disagree about something [*often* **passive**] *Council members were divided over plans to build a new stadium.*

**dividend** /'dɪvɪdend/ *noun* [C] an amount of money paid regularly to someone who owns shares in a company from the company's profits

**divine** /dɪ'vaɪn/ *adj* relating to or coming from God or a god

**diving** /'daɪvɪŋ/ *noun* [U] **1** the activity or sport of swimming under water, usually using special breathing equipment **2** the activity or sport of jumping into water with your arms and head going in first ➩ *See also:* **scuba diving**

**'diving ,board** *noun* [C] a raised board next to a swimming pool that you jump from into the water

**divisible** /dɪ'vɪzəbl/ *adj* **divisible by 2/7/50, etc** able to be divided by 2/7/50, etc

**division** /dɪ'vɪʒᵊn/ *noun* **1** SEPARATED [U] when something is separated into parts or groups, or the way that it is separated *the equal division of labour among workers* **2** ORGANIZATION [C] one of the groups in a business or organization *the sales division* **3** DISAGREEMENT [C, U] when people disagree about something *a division over* the issue of free medical care **4** CALCULATION [U] when you calculate how many times one number goes into another number

**divisive** /dɪˈvaɪsɪv/ adj causing disagreements between people a divisive issue

o━**divorce** /dɪˈvɔːs/ noun [C, U] when two people officially stop being married *My parents are getting a divorce.* • divorce verb [I, T] *She's divorcing her husband.*

**divorced** /dɪˈvɔːst/ adj **1** married before but not married now **2 get divorced** to officially stop being married *My parents got divorced when I was seven.* ➔ See usage note at **married**.

**divulge** /daɪˈvʌldʒ/ verb [T] to give secret or private information to someone *He would not divulge how much the house cost.*

**DIY** /ˌdiːaɪˈwaɪ/ noun for do it yourself: when you do building, decorating, or repairs in your own home

**dizzy** /ˈdɪzi/ adj feeling like everything is turning round, so that you feel ill or as if you might fall

**DJ** /ˈdiːˌdʒeɪ/ (also **disc jockey**) noun [C] someone who plays music on the radio or at discos

**DNA** /ˌdiːenˈeɪ/ noun [U] a chemical in the cells of living things which contains genetic information

**do¹** strong form /duː/ weak form /də/ auxiliary verb **1** QUESTIONS/NEGATIVES used with another verb to form questions and negative phrases *Do you need any help?* • *When does the next bus leave?* • *I don't know.* **2** MAKE QUESTION used in a phrase at the end of a sentence to make it into a question *Sarah lives near here, doesn't she?* • *That doesn't make any sense, does it?* **3** AVOID REPEATING used to avoid repeating a verb that has just been used *"I hate that song." "So do I."* • *My sister reads a lot more than I do.* **4** EMPHASIZE used to emphasize the main verb *He does like you, he's just shy.* • *Do come and visit us soon.*

**do**

| present tense | past tense |
|---|---|
| I do | I did |
| you do | you did |
| he/she/it does | he/she/it did |
| we do | we did |
| you do | you did |
| they do | they did |

past participle

| done | I have done my homework. |
|---|---|

present participle

| doing | I'm doing my homework. |
|---|---|

short negative forms

| don't | doesn't | didn't |
|---|---|---|

o━**do²** verb **1** ACTION/JOB [T] to perform an action or job *Go upstairs and do your homework.* • *What are you doing this weekend?* • *What does she do?* (= What is her job?) **2** MAKE [T] to make or prepare something *Our printer only*

does black and white copies. • *Max's Cafe does great sandwiches.* **3 do badly/well, etc** to be unsuccessful/successful, etc *Sam did very well in her exams.* **4 do biology/French/history, etc** UK to study biology/French/history, etc **5 do your hair/make-up, etc** to make your hair/make-up, etc look nice **6 do sb good** to have a good effect on someone *A holiday would do you good.* **7 do damage/harm, etc** to cause damage/harm, etc *Luckily the fire didn't do much damage.* **8 will do** to be satisfactory *You don't have to pay now, next week will do.* **9** SPEED [T] to travel at a particular speed *For most of the journey we were doing 70 miles an hour.*

**do** or **make?**

Do usually means to perform an activity or job.

*I should do more exercise.*

~~I should make more exercise.~~

Make usually means to create or produce something.

*Did you make the dress yourself?*

~~Did you do the dress yourself?~~

**do away with sth** to get rid of something, or to stop using something *We may do away with the school uniform soon.*

**do away with sb** informal to kill someone

**do sb in** informal **1** to make someone extremely tired *All that exercise has done me in.* **2** to attack or kill someone

**do sth over** US to do something again because you did not do it well the first time

**do sth up 1** mainly UK to fasten something *Do your coat up. It's cold outside.* **2** to repair or decorate a building so that it looks attractive

**do with sth** used to ask where someone put something *What did you do with my keys?*

**do with sb/sth 1 could do with sb/sth** to need or want someone or something *I could do with a few days off work.* **2 be/have to do with sb/sth** to be about or connected with someone or something *My question has to do with yesterday's homework.*

**do without (sb/sth)** to manage without having someone or something *Jack's the kind of player we can't do without.*

**do³** noun [C] UK informal a party *Are you going to the Christmas do?*

**docile** /ˈdəʊsaɪl/ ⑤ /ˈdɑːsəl/ adj A docile person or animal is quiet and easily controlled.

**dock¹** /dɒk/ noun **1** [C] the place where ships stop and goods are taken off or put on **2 the dock** UK (US **the stand**) the place in a law court where the person who is accused of a crime sits

**dock²** /dɒk/ verb **1** [I, T] If a ship docks, it arrives at a dock. **2 dock sb's pay/wages** to take away part of the money you pay someone, usually as a punishment

o━**doctor¹** /ˈdɒktəʳ/ noun **1** [C] a person whose job is to treat people who have an illness or injury *I have to go to the doctor's for a check-up.* • *He*

D

*went back to see Doctor Jones when the pain got worse.* • *Is it serious, Doctor?* **2 Doctor of Philosophy/Divinity, etc** someone who has the most advanced type of qualification from a university *a Doctor of Philosophy* ⊃ *See also:* **spin doctor**.

**doctor²** /'dɒktə'/ *verb* [T] to change something, usually in a dishonest way *The photo in his passport had been doctored.*

**doctorate** /'dɒktºrət/ *noun* [C] the most advanced type of qualification from a university *He has a doctorate in physics from Cambridge.*

**doctrine** /'dɒktrɪn/ *noun* [C, U] a belief or set of beliefs taught by a religious or political group *Christian doctrine*

○⌐**document** /'dɒkjəmənt/ *noun* [C] **1** a piece of paper with official information on it *Please sign and return the insurance documents enclosed.* **2** a piece of text produced electronically on a computer *How do I create a new document?*

**documentary** /,dɒkjə'mentºri/ *noun* [C] a film or television programme that gives facts about a real situation or real people *a TV documentary about the Russian Revolution*

**documentation** /,dɒkjəmen'teɪʃºn/ *noun* [U] **1** pieces of paper containing official information **2** the instructions written for a piece of computer software or equipment

**docusoap** /'dɒkju:səʊp/ *noun* [C] *UK* an entertaining television programme about the lives of real people who live in the same place or who do the same thing

**doddle** /'dɒdl/ *noun UK* **be a doddle** *informal* to be very easy *This computer's a doddle to use.*

**dodge¹** /dɒdʒ/ *verb* **1** [I, T] to move quickly to avoid someone or something *He managed to dodge past the security guard.* **2** [T] to avoid talking about something or doing something you should do *The minister dodged questions about his relationship with the actress.*

**dodge²** /dɒdʒ/ *noun* [C] when you avoid something, usually in a dishonest way *a tax dodge*

**dodgy** /'dɒdʒi/ *adj UK informal* bad, or not able to be trusted *His friend's a bit dodgy.*

**doe** /dəʊ/ *noun* [C] a female deer

**does** *strong form* /dʌz/ *weak form* /dəz/ *present simple he/she/it of* do

**doesn't** /'dʌzºnt/ *short for* does not *Keith doesn't like mushrooms or garlic.*

○⌐**dog¹** /dɒg/ *noun* [C] an animal with fur, four legs and a tail that is kept as a pet, or trained to guard buildings and guide blind people *Let's take the dog for a walk.* ⊃ *See also:* **guide dog**, **hot dog**.

**dog²** /dɒg/ *verb* [T] **dogging**, *past* **dogged** to cause someone or something trouble for a long time [often passive] *His football career has been dogged by injury.*

**dog-eared** /'dɒgɪəd/ *adj* If a piece of paper or a book is dog-eared, its corners are folded and torn from being touched a lot.

**dogged** /'dɒgɪd/ *adj* [always before noun] continuing to do or believe in something, although it is difficult *dogged determination* • **doggedly** *adv*

**doghouse** /'dɒghaʊs/ *noun plural* **doghouses 1** [C] *US* (*UK* **kennel**) a small building for a dog to sleep in **2 be in the doghouse** If you are in the doghouse, you have done something to make people angry or annoyed with you.

**dogma** /'dɒgmə/ *noun* [C, U] a belief or set of beliefs that people are expected to accept as the truth, without ever doubting them *political dogma*

**dogmatic** /dɒg'mætɪk/ *adj* not willing to accept other ideas or opinions because you think yours are right

**dogsbody** /'dɒgzbɒdi/ *noun* [C] *UK* someone who has to do boring jobs for someone else

**doing** /'du:ɪŋ/ *noun* **1 be sb's doing** to have been done or caused by someone *The problem is not all his doing.* **2 take some/a lot of doing** *informal* to be difficult to do *It took some doing to convince him to come.*

**doldrums** /'dɒldrəmz/ *noun* **in the doldrums 1** If a business or job is in the doldrums, it is not very successful and nothing new is happening in it. *After two years in the doldrums, profits are finally rising.* **2** *UK* sad and with no energy or enthusiasm

**the dole** /dəʊl/ *noun UK* money that the government gives someone when they are unemployed *He's been on the dole for years.*

**dole** /dəʊl/ *verb*
**dole sth out** to give something, especially money, to several people or in large amounts *My parents are always doling out money to my sisters.*

**doleful** /'dəʊlfºl/ *adj* very sad *doleful eyes*

**doll** /dɒl/ *noun* [C] a child's toy that looks like a small person

○⌐**dollar** /'dɒlə'/ *noun* [C] the unit of money used in the US, Canada, and some other countries; $ *a hundred dollars/$100* • *a dollar bill*

**dollop** /'dɒləp/ *noun* [C] a lump or mass of a soft substance, usually food *a dollop of cream*

**dolphin** /'dɒlfɪn/ *noun* [C] an intelligent animal that lives in the sea, breathes air, and looks like a large, smooth, grey fish

**domain** /dəʊ'meɪn/ *noun* [C] **1** a particular area, activity, or subject that someone controls or deals with *The garden is his domain.* • *This information should be in the public domain* (= known by the public). **2** an address on the Internet where email can be sent or documents shown *a domain name that ends with .com*

**dome** /dəʊm/ *noun* [C] a curved, round roof of a building • **domed** *adj a domed roof*

**domestic** /də'mestɪk/ *adj* **1** HOME relating to the home and family relationships *domestic violence* • *What are his domestic arrangements?* **2** COUNTRY inside one country and not international *a domestic flight* **3** ANIMAL A domestic animal is kept as a pet.

**domesticated** /də'mestɪkeɪtɪd/ *adj* **1** A domesticated animal is kept as a pet or lives on a farm. **2** A domesticated person is able or willing to do cleaning, cooking, and other jobs in the home.

**domesticity** /,dɒmes'tɪsəti/ *noun* [U] life at home looking after a house and family

**dominance** /'dɒmɪnəns/ *noun* [U] power, influence, and control *the company's dominance in the software industry*

**dominant** /'dɒmɪnənt/ *adj* **1** main or most important *Her mother was the dominant influence in her life.* **2** strongest and wanting to take control *a dominant older brother*

**dominate** /'dɒmɪneɪt/ *verb* [I, T] **1** to control or have power over someone or something *The US* *continues to dominate the world politically.* **2** to be the largest, most important, or most noticeable part of something *The cathedral dominates the skyline.*

**domination** /ˌdɒmɪˈneɪʃⁿn/ *noun* [U] great power and control over someone or something else *world domination*

**domineering** /ˌdɒmɪˈnɪərɪŋ/ *adj* trying to control people too much *a domineering mother*

**dominion** /dəˈmɪnjən/ *noun* [U] *formal* the power and right to control someone or something

**domino** /ˈdɒmɪnəʊ/ *noun* [C] *plural* **dominoes** a small, rectangular object that has spots on it, used in a game ● dominoes *noun* [U] a game played using dominoes *Do you want to play dominoes?*

**don** /dɒn/ *verb* [T] **donning,** *past* **donned** *formal* to put on a piece of clothing such as a coat or hat

**donate** /dəʊˈneɪt/ *verb* [T] **1** to give money or goods to a person or organization that needs help *Four hundred new computers were donated to the college.* **2** to allow some of your blood or part of your body to be used for medical purposes

**donation** /dəʊˈneɪʃⁿn/ *noun* [C, U] when money or goods are given to help a person or organization *Would you like to* **make a donation?**

**done¹** /dʌn/ *adj* **1** finished or completed *Did you get your essay done in time?* **2** cooked enough *The potatoes aren't quite done yet.* ➝ *See also:* easier **(easy²)** said than done, **well-done.**

**done²** /dʌn/ *exclamation* something that you say to show that you accept someone's offer *"I'll give you 50 pounds for the whole lot." "Done!"*

**done³** /dʌn/ *past participle of* do

**donkey** /ˈdɒŋki/ *noun* [C] **1** an animal that looks like a small horse with long ears **2 for donkey's years** *UK informal* for a long time *I haven't seen him for donkey's years.*

**'donkey ˌwork** *noun* [U] *UK informal* the most boring or difficult parts of a job *Poor George had to do all the donkey work.*

**donor** /ˈdəʊnəʳ/ *noun* [C] **1** someone who gives some of their blood or part of their body to be used for medical purposes **2** someone who gives money or goods to a person or organization that needs help *Ten thousand dollars was given by an anonymous donor.* ➝ *See also:* **blood donor.**

**don't** /dəʊnt/ *short for* do not *Please don't talk during the exam.*

**donut** /ˈdəʊnʌt/ *noun* [C] *another US spelling of* doughnut (= a small, round, fried cake)

**doodle** /ˈduːdl/ *verb* [I, T] to draw little pictures or patterns on something without thinking about it *She sat doodling in her notebook.* ● doodle *noun* [C]

**doom** /duːm/ *noun* [U] **1** death, destruction, and other

unpleasant events that cannot be avoided *a horrible sense of doom* **2 doom and gloom** unhappiness and feeling no hope for the future *Life's not all doom and gloom, you know.*

**doomed** /duːmd/ *adj* certain to fail, die, or have problems *Their marriage was doomed from the start.*

o⟶**door** /dɔːʳ/ *noun* [C] **1** the part of a building, room, vehicle, or piece of furniture that you open or close to get inside it or out of it *Please shut the door behind you.* ● *I can't open the door.* ● *There's someone* **at the door.** **2** the space in a wall where you enter a building or room *He led us through the door to the rear of the building.* **3 behind closed doors** privately and not in public *Most of the deals were done behind closed doors.* **4 two/three, etc doors away** in a place that is two/three, etc houses away *We live just a few doors away from the Smiths.* ➝ *See also:* **trap door.**

**doorbell** /ˈdɔːbel/ *noun* [C] a button that you press next to a door that makes a noise to let someone know that you are there

**doorknob** /ˈdɔːnɒb/ *noun* [C] a round object on a door that you hold and turn to open or close it

**doorman** /ˈdɔːmən/ *noun* [C] *plural* **doormen** a man who stands near the doors of a large building such as a hotel to watch and help the visitors

**doormat** /ˈdɔːmæt/ *noun* [C] **1** a piece of thick material on the floor by a door used to clean your shoes before entering a building **2** *informal* someone who allows other people to treat them very badly

**doorstep** /ˈdɔːstep/ *noun* [C] **1** a step in front of the door of a building **2 on your doorstep** very near to where you live *They have the Rocky Mountains on their doorstep.*

**door-to-door** /ˌdɔːtəˈdɔːʳ/ *adj* [always before noun], *adv* **1** going from one house or building to another *The hotel offers a door-to-door service to the airport.* **2** going to every house in an area *a door-to-door salesman*

**doorway** /ˈdɔːweɪ/ *noun* [C] an entrance to a building or room through a door *She waited in the doorway while I ran back inside.*

**dope¹** /dəʊp/ *noun informal* **1** [U] an illegal drug taken for pleasure, especially cannabis (= drug that you smoke) **2** [C] *US informal* a stupid or silly person

**dope²** /dəʊp/ *verb* **1** [T] to give a drug to a person or animal, usually so that they become sleepy **2 be doped up** to have a lot of a drug in your body affecting your behaviour

**dork** /dɔːk/ *noun* [C] *US informal* a stupid or silly person

**dormant** /ˈdɔːmənt/ *adj* not active or developing now, but possibly active in the future *a dormant volcano*

**dormitory** /ˈdɔːmɪtʳri/ (*also* **dorm** /ˈdɔːm/ *informal*) *noun* [C] **1** a large bedroom with a lot of beds, especially in a school **2** *US* (*UK* **hall of residence**) a large building at a college or university where students live

**dosage** /ˈdəʊsɪdʒ/ *noun* [C] how much medicine you should take and how often you should take it *the recommended daily dosage*

**dose** /dəʊs/ *noun* [C] **1** a measured amount of

**doodle**

medicine that is taken at one time or during a period of time *What is the recommended dose?* **2 a dose of sth** an amount of something, often something unpleasant *a dose of bad news* • **dose** *verb* [T] to give someone a drug or medicine

**doss** /dɒs/ (*also* **doss down**) *verb* [I] *UK informal* to sleep somewhere temporarily, such as on the floor *Can I doss at your house tonight?*

**doss about/around** *UK, informal* to spend your time doing very little

**dossier** /'dɒsieɪ/ *noun* [C] a set of documents that contain information about a particular person or subject *The officers compiled a dossier on the case.*

**dot**¹ /dɒt/ *noun* **1** [C] a small, round mark or spot *a pattern of blue and green dots* **2** [U] *spoken* the spoken form of '.' in an internet address *dot co dot uk* (= .co.uk) **3 on the dot** at that exact time *We have to leave at 7.30 on the dot.*

**dot**² /dɒt/ *verb* [T] **dotting**, *past* **dotted 1** to put a dot or dots on something **2** (*also* **dot around**) to be spread across an area *The company has 43 hotels dotted around the UK.*

**dote** /dəʊt/ *verb*

**dote on sb** to love someone completely and believe that they are perfect *She absolutely dotes on that little boy.*

**doting** /'dəʊtɪŋ/ *adj* [always before noun] extremely loving and caring *doting parents*

**dotted 'line** *noun* [C] a line of printed dots on a piece of paper **2 sign on the dotted line** to make an agreement official by writing your name on it

**dotty** /'dɒti/ *adj UK* slightly crazy *a dotty old woman*

✪**double**¹ /'dʌbl/ *adj* **1** TWO PARTS having two parts of the same type or size *double doors* • *My number is four, two, six, double two, five* (= 426225). **2** TWICE THE SIZE twice the amount, number, or size of something *a double vodka* • *a double hamburger* **3** FOR TWO made to be used by two people *a double bed/room*

✪**double**² /'dʌbl/ *verb* [I, T] to increase and become twice the original size or amount, or to make something do this *Our house has almost doubled in value.* • *They have managed to double their profits over the last year.*

**double (up) as sth** If something doubles up as something else, it also has the purpose of that thing. *The school's gymnasium doubles up as a dining room.*

**double back** to turn and go back in the direction that you have come from *When they realized they had taken the wrong road they had to double back.*

**double (sb) over/up** to suddenly bend your body forward, usually because of pain or laughter, or to make someone do this *We all doubled up with laughter when he walked in.*

**double**³ /'dʌbl/ *noun* **1** [C, U] something that is twice the usual amount, number, or size **2 sb's double** someone who looks exactly the same as someone else

**double**⁴ /'dʌbl/ *determiner* twice as much or as many *Our new house is double the size of our old one.*

**double-barrelled** *UK* (*US* **double-barreled**) /ˌdʌbl'bærᵊld/ *adj* **1** A double-barrelled gun has

two of the cylindrical parts that bullets come out of. **2** *UK* A double-barrelled name is two names joined together.

**double 'bass** *noun* [C] a wooden musical instrument with four strings, like a very large violin (= instrument you hold against your neck), that you play while standing up or sitting on a high chair

**double-breasted** /ˌdʌbl'brestɪd/ *adj* A double-breasted jacket or coat has two sets of buttons to fasten at the front.

**double-check** /ˌdʌbl'tʃek/ *verb* [I, T] to examine something again so that you are certain it is safe or correct *Always double-check your work before giving it to the teacher.*

**double-click** /ˌdʌbl'klɪk/ *verb* [I, T] to quickly press a button twice on a mouse (= small computer control) to make something happen on a computer screen *Double-click on the icon to start the program.*

**double-cross** /ˌdʌbl'krɒs/ *verb* [T] to deceive someone who you should be helping

**double-decker** /ˌdʌbl'dekə²/ *noun* [C] *UK* A tall bus with two levels *a double-decker bus*

**double-glazing** /ˌdʌbl'gleɪzɪŋ/ *noun* [U] *UK* windows that have two layers of glass to keep a building warm or quiet

**doubles** /'dʌblz/ *noun* [U] a game, especially tennis, in which two people play together against two other people

**double 'standard** *noun* [C] when people are given different treatment in an unfair way [usually plural] *Critics accused the government of double standards in its policies.*

**double 'take** *noun* [C] when you quickly look at someone or something a second time because you cannot believe you have seen something or heard something [usually singular] *He did a double take when he saw her.*

**doubly** /'dʌbli/ *adv* twice as much, or very much more *It is doubly important to drink plenty of water when it's hot.*

✪**doubt**¹ /daʊt/ *noun* **1** [C, U] when you are not certain about something, or do not trust someone or something *I have some doubts about his ability to do the job.* **2 have no doubt** to be certain [+ (that)] *I have no doubt that I made the right decision.* **3 there's no doubt** it is certain [+ (that)] *There is no doubt that he's a good player.* **4 be in doubt** to not be certain *The future of the project is in doubt.* **5 cast doubt on sth** to make something seem uncertain *Witnesses have cast doubt on the suspect's innocence.* **6 without (a) doubt** certainly *She is without doubt a great musician.* **7 no doubt** used to say that something is very likely *No doubt she'll spend the money on new clothes.* ➔ *See also:* give sb the **benefit**¹ of the doubt, beyond/without a **shadow**¹ of a doubt.

✪**doubt**² /daʊt/ *verb* [T] **1** to feel uncertain about something or think that something is not probable [+ (that)] *I doubt that I'll get the job.* • *I doubt if/whether he'll win.* **2** to not believe someone or something *Do you have any reason to doubt her?*

**doubtful** /'daʊtfᵊl/ *adj* **1** not probable *It's doubtful if/whether he'll be able to come.* • [+ (that)] *It's doubtful that anyone survived the fire.*

**2** not feeling certain about something *She's still doubtful about her decision.* ● doubtfully *adv*

**doubtless** /'daʊtləs/ *adv* probably *He will doubtless be criticized by journalists.*

**dough** /dəʊ/ *noun* [U] a thick mixture of flour and liquid used to make foods such as bread or pastry

**doughnut** (*also US* **donut**) /'dəʊnʌt/ *noun* [C] a small, round, fried cake, sometimes with a hole in the middle

**dour** /dʊəᵊ, daʊəᵊ/ *adj* unfriendly and serious *a dour expression*

**douse** /daʊs/ *verb* [T] **1** to pour a lot of liquid over someone or something *The dessert was doused with brandy and set alight.* **2** to stop a fire burning by putting a lot of water on it *to douse the flames/fire*

**dove¹** /dʌv/ *noun* [C] a white bird, sometimes used as a symbol of peace

**dove²** /dəʊv/ *US past tense of* dive

**dowdy** /'daʊdi/ *adj* plain and not fashionable *She looks a bit dowdy in that old dress.*

**O━down¹** /daʊn/ *adv, preposition* **1** LOWER PLACE towards or in a lower place *The kids ran down the hill to the gate.* ● *She tripped and fell down.* ● *I bent down to have a look.* **2** LEVEL/AMOUNT towards or at a lower level or amount *Can you turn the music down?* ● *Slow down so they can see us.* **3** SURFACE moving from above and onto a surface *I sat down and turned on the TV.* ● *Put that box down on the floor.* **4** DIRECTION in or towards a particular direction, usually south *Pete's moved down to London.* **5** **down the road/river, etc** along or further along the road/river, etc *There's another pub further down the street.* **6** **note/write, etc sth down** to write something on a piece of paper *Can I just take down your phone number?* **7** STOMACH inside your stomach *He's had food poisoning and can't keep anything down.* **8** **be down to sb** *UK* to be someone's responsibility or decision *I've done all I can now, the rest is down to you.* **9** **come/go down with sth** to become ill *The whole family came down with food poisoning.* **10** **down under** *informal* Australia, or in Australia

**down²** /daʊn/ *adj* [never before noun] **1** sad *What's the matter? You look a bit down today.* **2** If a computer or machine is down, it is temporarily not working. *The network was down all morning.*

**down³** /daʊn/ *noun* [U] soft feathers, often used as a warm filling for bed covers ➋ *See also:* **ups and downs**.

**down⁴** /daʊn/ *verb* [T] *informal* to drink something quickly *He was so thirsty, he downed two bottles of beer.*

**down-and-out** /,daʊnən'aʊt/ *adj* If someone is down-and-out, they have no money, possessions, or opportunities. ● down-and-out *noun* [C]

**downcast** /'daʊnkɑːst/ *adj* **1** sad or disappointed **2** If someone's eyes are downcast, they are looking down.

**downgrade** /,daʊn'greɪd/ *verb* [T] to move someone or something to a less important position

**downhearted** /,daʊn'hɑːtɪd/ *adj* sad or disappointed

**downhill¹** /,daʊn'hɪl/ *adv* **1** towards the bottom of a hill or slope *It's so much easier cycling downhill.* **2** **go downhill** to gradually become worse *After his wife died, his health started to go downhill.*

**downhill²** /,daʊn'hɪl/ *adj* **1** leading down towards the bottom of a hill or slope *downhill skiing* **2** **be all downhill; be downhill all the way** to be much easier *From now on it will be all downhill.*

**download** /,daʊn'ləʊd ⓤⓢ 'daʊn,ləʊd/ *verb* [T] to copy computer programs or information electronically, usually from a large computer to a small one *You can download this software free from their website.*

**downmarket** /,daʊn'mɑːkɪt/ *adj UK* cheap and low quality

**down payment** *noun* [C] the first amount of money that you pay when you buy something expensive and pay over a period of time *a down payment on a house*

**downplay** /,daʊn'pleɪ/ *verb* [T] to make something seem less important or bad than it really is *The report downplays the risks of nuclear power.*

**downpour** /'daʊnpɔːᵊ/ *noun* [C] when it suddenly rains a lot

**downright** /'daʊnraɪt/ *adv* **downright dangerous/rude/ugly, etc** extremely dangerous/rude/ugly, etc

**downside** /'daʊnsaɪd/ *noun* [no plural] the disadvantage of a situation *The downside of living in a city is all the pollution.*

**downsize** /'daʊn,saɪz/ *verb* [I, T] to make a company or organization smaller by reducing the number of people who work there ● downsizing *noun* [U]

**downstairs** /,daʊn'steəz/ *adv* on or to a lower level of a building *She went downstairs to see who was at the door.* ● downstairs *adj a downstairs bathroom*

**downstream** /,daʊn'striːm/ *adv* in the direction that the water in a river is moving in

**down-to-earth** /,daʊntu'ɜːθ/ *adj* practical and realistic

**downtown** /,daʊn'taʊn/ *adj* [always before noun], *adv US* in or to the central part or main business area of a city *downtown Chicago*

**downtrodden** /'daʊn,trɒdᵊn/ *adj* treated badly and without respect by other people *downtrodden workers*

**downturn** /'daʊntɜːn/ *noun* [C] when a business or economy becomes less successful *There has been a sharp downturn in sales.*

**downwards** (*also US* **downward**) /'daʊnwədz/ *adv* towards a lower place or level *The road slopes downwards to the river.* ● downward *adj* ➋ *See also:* a downward **spiral**.

**downwind** /,daʊn'wɪnd/ *adj, adv* in the direction that the wind is blowing

**dowry** /'daʊri/ *noun* [C] money that a woman's family gives to the man she is marrying in some cultures

**doze** /dəʊz/ *verb* [I] to sleep lightly *Grandma was dozing in front of the TV.*

**doze off** to gradually start sleeping, usually during the day *He dozed off during the film.*

**dozen** /'dʌzᵊn/ *noun, determiner* **1** twelve, or a group of twelve *There were about a dozen people at the party.* **2 dozens** *informal* a lot *She's got dozens of friends.* ⊃ *See also:* a **dime** a dozen.

**Dr** *written abbreviation for* doctor *Dr Paul Thomas*

**drab** /dræb/ *adj* without colour and boring to look at *drab, grey buildings*

**draconian** /drə'kəʊniən/ *adj* very severe *draconian laws*

**draft¹** /drɑːft/ *noun* **1** [C] a piece of writing or a plan that is not yet in its finished form *He made several changes to the first draft.* **2 the draft** *US* when people are told that they must join the armed forces **3** [C] *US spelling of* draught (= a current of cold air in a room)

**draft²** /drɑːft/ *verb* [T] **1** to produce a piece of writing or a plan that you intend to change later *to draft a letter* **2** to order someone to join the armed forces
**draft sb in/draft sb into sth** *UK* to bring someone somewhere to do a particular job *Extra police were drafted in to stop the demonstration.*

**draftsman** *US* (*UK* **draughtsman**) /'drɑːftsmən/ *noun* [C] *plural* **draftsmen** someone who draws detailed drawings as plans for something

**drafty** /'drɑːfti/ *adj US spelling of* draughty

**drag¹** /dræg/ *verb* **dragging,** *past* **dragged**
**1 drag sth/sb across/along/over, etc** to pull something or someone along the ground somewhere, usually with difficulty *The table was too heavy to lift, so we had to drag it across the room.* **2 drag sb along/out/to, etc** to make someone go somewhere they do not want to go *She dragged me to the mall to look at shoes.* • *I have to drag myself out of bed every morning.* **3** [T] to move something somewhere on a computer screen using a mouse (= small computer control) **4** [I] (*also* **drag on**) to continue for too much time in a boring way *The negotiations dragged on for months.* ⊃ *See also:* drag your feet (**foot¹**).
**drag sb down** *UK* If an unpleasant situation drags someone down, it makes them feel unhappy or ill.
**drag sb into sth** to force someone to become involved in an unpleasant or difficult situation *I don't want to be dragged into this argument.*
**drag sth out** to make something continue for more time than is necessary

**drag²** /dræg/ *noun* **1 in drag** *informal* If a man is in drag, he is wearing women's clothes. **2 be a drag** *informal* to be boring and unpleasant *Cleaning the house is such a drag.* **3** [C] when you breathe in smoke from a cigarette *He took a drag on his cigarette.*

**dragon** /'drægᵊn/ *noun* [C] a big, imaginary creature which breathes out fire

**dragonfly** /'drægᵊnflaɪ/ *noun* [C] an insect with long wings and a thin, colourful body, often seen flying near water ⊃ *See picture at* **insect**.

**drain¹** /dreɪn/ *verb* **1** [REMOVE LIQUID] [T] to remove the liquid from something, usually by pouring it away *Drain the pasta and add the tomatoes.* **2** [FLOW AWAY] [I] If something drains, liquid flows away or out of it. **3** [MAKE TIRED] [T]

to make someone very tired *The long journey drained him.* **4** [DRINK] [T] If you drain a glass or cup, you drink all the liquid in it.

**drain²** /dreɪn/ *noun* **1** [C] a pipe or hole that takes away waste liquids or water *She poured the dirty water down the drain.* **2 a drain on sth** something that uses or wastes a lot of money or energy *Keeping these people in prison is a huge drain on government finances.* **3 down the drain** *informal* If money or work goes down the drain, it is wasted. *If you leave the course now, all your hard work will go down the drain.*

**drainage** /'dreɪnɪdʒ/ *noun* [U] the system of water or waste liquids flowing away from somewhere into the ground or down pipes

**drained** /dreɪnd/ *adj* If someone is drained, they are extremely tired.

**drama** /'drɑːmə/ *noun* **1** [PLAY] [C] a play in a theatre or on television or radio *a historical drama* **2** [PLAYS/ACTING] [U] plays and acting generally *modern drama* • *She studied drama and English at college.* **3** [EXCITEMENT] [C, U] when something exciting happens *There was a lot of drama in the courtroom.*

**dramatic** /drə'mætɪk/ *adj* **1** [SUDDEN] very sudden or noticeable *a dramatic change/improvement* **2** [EXCITING] full of action and excitement *a dramatic rescue* **3** [THEATRE] [always before noun] relating to plays and acting **4** [BEHAVIOUR] showing your emotions in a very obvious way because you want other people to notice you *Stop being so dramatic!* • dramatically *adv*

**dramatist** /'dræmətɪst/ *noun* [C] someone who writes plays

**dramatize** (*also UK* **-ise**) /'dræmətaɪz/ *verb* [T]
**1** to make an event or situation seem more exciting than it really is *The media tends to dramatize things.* **2** to change a story so that it can be performed as a play • dramatization /ˌdræmətaɪ'zeɪʃᵊn/ *noun* [C, U]

**drank** /dræŋk/ *past tense of* drink

**drape** /dreɪp/ *verb* **1 drape sth across/on/over, etc** to put something such as cloth or a piece of clothing loosely over something *He draped his jacket over the chair and sat down to eat.* **2 be draped in/with sth** to be loosely covered with a cloth *The coffin was draped in a flag.*

**drapes** /dreɪps/ *noun* [plural] *mainly US* long, heavy curtains

**drastic** /'dræstɪk/ *adj* Drastic action or change is sudden and extreme. *drastic reductions in price* • drastically *adv*

**draught¹** *UK* (*US* **draft**) /drɑːft/ *noun* [C] a current of cold air in a room *There's a terrible draught coming from under the door.*

**draught²** *UK* (*US* **draft**) /drɑːft/ *adj* **draught beer/lager, etc** a drink that comes from a large container and not from a can or bottle

**draughts** /drɑːfts/ *UK* (*US* **checkers**) *noun* [U] a game that two people play by moving flat, round objects around on a board of black and white squares

**draughtsman** *UK* (*US* **draftsman**) /'drɑːftsmən/ *noun* [C] *plural* **draughtsmen** someone who draws detailed drawings as plans for something

**draughty** UK (US **drafty**) /'drɑːfti/ adj having currents of cold air blowing through *a draughty old building*

o⟶**draw¹** /drɔː/ verb past t **drew**, past p **drawn** **1** PICTURE [I, T] to produce a picture by making lines or marks, usually with a pen or pencil *She drew a picture of a tree.* **2 draw sth/sb across/back/over, etc** to pull something or someone gently in a particular direction *He took her hand and drew her towards him.* **3 draw into/out/away, etc** to move somewhere, usually in a vehicle *The train drew into the station.* **4 draw the curtains** to pull curtains open or closed **5 draw (sb's) attention to sth/sb** to make someone notice someone or something *I don't want to draw too much attention to myself.* **6** ATTRACT [T] to attract someone to a place or person *Thousands of tourists are drawn to the city every year.* **7** SPORT [I, T] UK to finish a game or competition with each team or player having the same score *England drew 2-2 against Italy.* **8** TAKE OUT [T] to take something out of a container or your pocket, especially a weapon *He drew a knife and started threatening me.* **9 draw near/close** to become nearer in space or time *Her birthday's drawing nearer every day.* **10 draw (a) breath** to breathe in air *She drew a deep breath and started her speech.* **11** MONEY [T] (*also* **draw out**) to take money from your bank account **12 draw to a close/end** to be almost finished **13 draw conclusions** to make judgments after considering a subject or situation *What conclusions should we draw from this report?* **14 draw a comparison/distinction** to say that there is a similarity or difference between two things ⊃ *See also:* draw a **blank²**, draw the **line¹** at sth, draw a **veil** over sth.

**draw back** to move away from someone or something, usually because you are surprised or frightened *She drew back in disgust when she saw the snake.*

**draw sb/sth into sth** to make someone or something become involved in a difficult or unpleasant situation *I'm not going to be drawn into this argument.*

**draw on sth** to use information or your knowledge or experience of something to help you do something *His novels draw heavily on his childhood.*

**draw sth up** to prepare something, usually a plan, list, or an official agreement, by writing it

**draw²** /drɔː/ noun [C] **1** mainly UK when a game or competition finishes with each player or team having the same score *The match ended in a draw.* **2** (*also US* **drawing**) a competition that is decided by choosing a particular ticket or number *the National Lottery draw* ⊃ *See also:* the **luck** of the draw.

**drawback** /'drɔːbæk/ noun [C] a problem or disadvantage *The only drawback with this camera is the price.*

**drawer** /drɔːʳ/ noun [C] a container like a box without a lid that is part of a piece of furniture and that slides in and out *She opened the drawer and took out a knife.* ⊃ *See also:* **chest of drawers**.

**drawing** /'drɔːɪŋ/ noun **1** PICTURE [C] a picture made with a pencil or pen *There were some children's drawings pinned up on the wall.* **2** ACTIVITY [U] the skill or activity of making pictures using a pencil or pen *Do you want to do some drawing?* **3** NUMBER/TICKET [C] US (UK/US **draw**) a competition that is decided by choosing a particular ticket or number

'**drawing ,board** noun **back to the drawing board** If you go back to the drawing board, you have to start planning a piece of work again because the first plan failed.

'**drawing ,pin** UK (US **thumbtack**) noun [C] a pin with a wide, flat top, used for fastening pieces of paper to a wall

'**drawing ,room** noun [C] old-fashioned a room in a large house used for sitting in and talking with guests

**drawl** /drɔːl/ noun [no plural] a lazy way of speaking that uses long vowel sounds • **drawl** verb [I]

**drawn¹** /drɔːn/ adj looking very tired or ill *She looked pale and drawn after the operation.* ⊃ *See also:* **horse-drawn**.

**drawn²** /drɔːn/ past participle of draw

**drawn-out** /,drɔːn'aʊt/ adj continuing for longer than you think is necessary *long, drawn-out negotiations*

**dread¹** /dred/ verb **1** [T] to feel worried or frightened about something that has not happened yet *I'm dreading the first day at my new school.* • [+ doing sth] *I dread seeing him again.* **2 I dread to think** UK used to say that you do not want to think about something because it is too worrying *I dread to think what could have happened if we hadn't been wearing seat belts.*

**dread²** /dred/ noun [U, no plural] a strong feeling of fear or worry [+ of + doing sth] *a dread of being lonely*

**dreadful** /'dredfʰl/ adj extremely bad or unpleasant *a dreadful mistake* • *a dreadful man*

**dreadfully** /'dredfəli/ adv **1** mainly UK formal very *I'm dreadfully sorry.* **2** very badly *The children behaved dreadfully.*

**dreadlocks** /'dredlɒks/ noun [plural] a hairstyle in which the hair is twisted together in lengths and is never brushed

o⟶**dream¹** /driːm/ noun **1** [C] a series of events and images that happen in your mind while you are sleeping *a bad dream* • *I had a very strange dream last night.* **2** [C] something that you want to happen although it is not very likely *It was his dream to become an actor.* **3 be in a dream** UK to not notice things that are around you because you are thinking about something else **4 beyond your wildest dreams** bigger or better than anything you could imagine or hope for **5 like a dream** If something or someone does something like a dream, they do it very well. *Our new dishwasher works like a dream.*

o⟶**dream²** /driːm/ verb past **dreamed** or **dreamt** **1** [I, T] to experience events and images in your mind while you are sleeping [+ (that)] *Last night I dreamed that I was flying.* **2** [I, T] to imagine something that you would like to happen [+ of + doing sth] *I dream of living on a desert island.* • [+ (that)] *He never dreamed that one day he* *would become President.* **3 wouldn't dream of doing sth** used to say that you would not do something because you think it is wrong or silly

**dream sth up** to think of an idea or plan, usually using a lot of imagination *Who dreams up these new designs?*

**dream³** /driːm/ *adj* **dream house/job/car, etc** the perfect house/job/car, etc

**dreamer** /ˈdriːmə<sup>r</sup>/ *noun* [C] someone who is not practical and thinks about things that are not likely to happen

**dreamy** /ˈdriːmi/ *adj* **1** seeming to be in a dream and thinking about pleasant things instead of what is happening around you *She had a dreamy look in her eyes.* **2** very pleasant *a dreamy dessert* • dreamily *adv*

**dreary** /ˈdrɪəri/ *adj* boring and making you feel unhappy *a rainy, dreary day* • *a dreary job*

**dredge** /dredʒ/ *verb* [T] to clean the bottom of a lake or river by removing dirt, plants, or rubbish

**dredge sth up** to talk about something bad or unpleasant that happened in the past *The newspapers dredged up details about the singer's unhappy childhood.*

**dregs** /dregz/ *noun* **1** [plural] the part of a drink at the bottom of a glass or other container that usually contains small solid bits **2 the dregs of society/humanity** people who you think are extremely bad or unimportant

**drench** /drenʃ/ *verb* [T] to make something or someone completely wet [often passive] *He was completely drenched by the time he got home.*

o⟶**dress¹** /dres/ *verb* **1** [I, T] to put clothes on yourself or someone else *I usually get dressed before having breakfast.* • *My husband usually dresses the children for school.* ⊃ *Opposite* **undress.** **2** [I] to wear a particular type, style, or colour of clothes *Ali always dresses smartly for work.* • [often passive] *She was dressed in black.* **3 dress a burn/cut/wound, etc** to clean an injury and put a covering over it to protect it

**USAGE**

**be/get dressed**

Be careful to use the correct preposition. You do not always need one.

*I got dressed and went to school.*

*Are you dressed yet?*

*He was dressed in a black suit.*

~~He was dressed with a black suit.~~

**dress up 1** to put on formal clothes for a special occasion *Weddings are a great opportunity to dress up.* **2** to wear special clothes in order to change your appearance, usually for a game or party *He dressed up as Superman for the party.*

o⟶**dress²** /dres/ *noun* **1** [C] a piece of clothing for women or girls which covers the top of the body and hangs down over the legs *She was wearing a short, black dress.* ⊃ *See colour picture* **Clothes** *on page Centre 5.* **2** [U] a particular style

of clothes *casual/formal dress* ⊃ *See also:* **fancy dress.**

**dresser** /ˈdresə<sup>r</sup>/ *noun* [C] **1** mainly US a piece of bedroom furniture with a mirror and drawers for keeping clothes in **2** UK a piece of furniture consisting of a cupboard with shelves above for keeping plates, cups, and other kitchen equipment

**dressing** /ˈdresɪŋ/ *noun* **1** [C, U] a sauce, especially a mixture of oil and vinegar for salad **2** [C] a covering that protects an injury

ˈ**dressing ˌgown** UK (US **robe**) *noun* [C] a piece of clothing, like a long coat, that you wear at home when you are not dressed

ˈ**dressing ˌroom** *noun* [C] a room where actors or sports teams get dressed before a performance or game

ˈ**dressing ˌtable** *noun* [C] mainly UK a piece of bedroom furniture like a table with a mirror and drawers

**dressy** /ˈdresi/ *adj* Dressy clothes are suitable for a formal occasion.

**drew** /druː/ *past tense of* draw

**dribble** /ˈdrɪbl/ *verb* **1** [MOUTH] [I] If someone dribbles, a small amount of liquid comes out of their mouth and goes down their face. *Babies dribble a lot.* **2** [LIQUID] [I, T] If a liquid dribbles, it falls slowly in small amounts, and if you dribble a liquid, you pour it so it falls slowly in small amounts. *Dribble some oil over the vegetables.* **3** [SPORT] [I, T] to move a ball along by using your hand to hit it against the ground or kicking it several times • dribble *noun* [C, U]

**dried** /draɪd/ *past of* dry

**drier** /ˈdraɪə<sup>r</sup>/ *noun* [C] *another spelling of* dryer (= a machine for drying wet things)

**drift¹** /drɪft/ *verb* **1 drift across/down/ towards, etc** to be moved slowly somewhere by currents of wind or water *Smoke drifted across the rooftops.* • *The boat drifted towards the beach.* **2 drift in/out/into, etc** to move somewhere slowly *Guests were drifting out onto the terrace.* **3** [I] to get into a situation or job without having any particular plan *He drifted into acting after university.* **4** [I] If snow or leaves drift, they are blown into piles by the wind.

**drift apart** If two people drift apart, they gradually become less friendly and the relationship ends.

**drift off** to gradually start to sleep *I drifted off during the lecture.*

**drift²** /drɪft/ *noun* **1** [C] slow, gradual movement from one place to another *the drift of people into Western Europe* **2 catch/get sb's drift** to understand the general meaning of what someone is saying **3** [C] a pile of snow or leaves that has been blown somewhere

**drill¹** /drɪl/ *noun* **1** [TOOL] [C] a tool or machine for making holes in a hard substance *an electric drill* ⊃ *See picture at* **tool.** **2** [FOR LEARNING] [C, U] a teaching method in which students repeat something several times to help them learn it *We do lots of drills to practise pronunciation.* **3 an emergency/fire, etc drill** when you practise what to do in an emergency/fire, etc **4** [SOLDIERS] [C, U] when soldiers do training for marching

**drill²** /drɪl/ *verb* **1** [I, T] to make a hole in a hard substance using a special tool *Billy drilled a hole in the wall.* • *The engineers were drilling for oil.* **2** [T] to make someone repeat something several times so that they learn it

**drily** /'draɪli/ *adv another spelling of* dryly (= in a serious voice but trying to be funny)

o-**drink¹** /drɪŋk/ *verb past t* **drank,** *past p* **drunk 1** [I, T] to put liquid into your mouth and swallow it *Would you like something to drink?* • *He was drinking a glass of milk.* **2** [I] to drink alcohol, usually regularly *She doesn't smoke or drink.*
**drink to sb/sth** to hold your glass up before drinking from it, in order to wish someone or something good luck or success
**drink (sth) up** to finish your drink completely *Drink up! We've got to leave soon.*

o-**drink²** /drɪŋk/ *noun* **1** [C] a liquid or an amount of liquid that you drink *a hot/cold drink* • *Can I have a drink of water please?* **2** [C, U] alcohol, or an alcoholic drink *Do you fancy a drink tonight to celebrate?* ➔ *See also:* **soft drink.**

**drinker** /'drɪŋkəʳ/ *noun* **1** [C] someone who regularly drinks alcohol *He's a heavy drinker* (= drinks a lot of alcohol). **2 a coffee/tea/wine, etc drinker** someone who regularly drinks a particular drink

**drinking** /'drɪŋkɪŋ/ *noun* [U] when someone drinks alcohol *Drinking and smoking are bad for your health.*

**'drinking ,water** *noun* [U] water that is safe for people to drink

**drip¹** /drɪp/ *verb* **dripping,** *past* **dripped 1** [I, T] If a liquid drips, it falls in drops, or you make it fall in drops. *There was water dripping from the ceiling.* **2** [I] to produce drops of liquid *The candle's dripping.*

**drip²** /drɪp/ *noun* **1** [DROP] [C] a drop of liquid that falls from something **2** [SOUND] [no plural] the sound or action of a liquid falling in drops **3** [MEDICAL] [C] *UK* (*US* **IV**) a piece of medical equipment used for putting liquids into your body *The doctor's put him on a drip.*

o-**drive¹** /draɪv/ *verb past t* **drove,** *past p* **driven 1** [CONTROL VEHICLE] [I, T] to make a car, bus, or train move, and control what it does *She's learning to drive.* • *He drives a red sports car.* **2** [TRAVEL] [I, T] to travel somewhere in a car, or to take someone somewhere in a car *We decided to drive to the airport.* • *My friend drove me home last night.* **3 drive sb out/away/from, etc** to force someone to leave a place *The supermarket has driven many small shops out of the area.* **4 drive sb crazy/mad/wild, etc** to make someone feel crazy, annoyed, or excited *That noise is driving me mad.* **5 drive sb to sth; drive sb to do sth** to make someone have a bad feeling or do something bad *The arguments and violence drove her to leave home.* **6 drive sth into/through/towards, etc** to push something somewhere by hitting it hard *He drove the nail into the wall with a hammer.* **7** [MAKE WORK] [T] to provide the power or energy that makes someone or something work [often passive] *She was driven by greed and ambition.* ➔ *See also:* drive sb round the **bend²,** drive sb up the **wall.**

USAGE

**drive** or **ride?**

You **drive** a car, truck, or bus.

*She drives an expensive sports car.*

You **ride** a bicycle, motorcycle, or horse.

*My brother is learning to ride a bicycle.*

~~My brother is learning to drive a bicycle.~~

**be driving at sth** used to ask what someone really means *Just what are you driving at?*
**drive off** to leave in a car

**drive²** /draɪv/ *noun* **1** [JOURNEY] [C] a journey in a car *The drive from Boston to New York took 4 hours.* **2** [GROUND] [C] the area of ground that you drive on to get from your house to the road *You can park on the drive.* **3** [COMPUTER] [C] a part of a computer that can read or store information *a DVD drive* • *Save your work on the C: drive.* **4** [EFFORT] [C] when someone makes a great effort to achieve something [+ to do sth] *The government started a drive to improve standards in schools.* **5** [ENERGY] [U] energy and determination to achieve things *She has drive and ambition.*

**drive-in** /'draɪvɪn/ *noun* [C] *mainly US* a cinema or restaurant that you can visit without getting out of your car

**drivel** /'drɪvəl/ *noun* [U] nonsense *He was talking complete drivel.*

**driven** /'drɪvən/ *past participle of* drive

o-**driver** /'draɪvəʳ/ *noun* [C] someone who drives a vehicle *a bus/train driver* ➔ *See also:* **engine driver.**

**'driver's ,license** *US* (*UK* **driving licence**) *noun* [C] an official document that allows you to drive a car

**drive-through** /'draɪvθruː/ *noun* [C] a place where you can get some type of service by driving through, without needing to get out of your car *a drive-through restaurant*

**driveway** /'draɪvweɪ/ *noun* [C] the area of ground that you drive on to get from your house to the road

**driving¹** /'draɪvɪŋ/ *noun* [U] when you drive a car, or the way someone drives *Peter's driving is very dangerous.*

**driving²** /'draɪvɪŋ/ *adj* **1 driving rain/snow** rain or snow that is falling very fast and being blown by the wind **2 the driving force** a person or thing that has a very strong effect and makes something happen *She was the driving force behind the project.*

**'driving ,licence** *UK* (*US* **driver's license**) *noun* [C] an official document that allows you to drive a car

**drizzle** /'drɪzl/ *noun* [U] light rain • drizzle *verb* [I]

**drone¹** /drəʊn/ *verb* [I] to make a continuous, low sound, like an engine *I could hear traffic droning in the distance.*
**drone on** to talk for a long time in a very boring way *I wish he'd stop droning on about school.*

**drool** /druːl/ *verb* [I] If a person or animal drools, liquid comes out of the side of their mouth. *Our dog starts drooling when he sees meat.*

**drool over sb/sth** to look at someone or something in a way that shows you think they are very attractive *The girls were drooling over the band's lead singer.*

**droop** /druːp/ *verb* [I] to hang down, often because of being weak, tired, or unhappy *He was tired and his eyelids were starting to droop.*

o⟶**drop**¹ /drɒp/ *verb* **dropping**, *past* **dropped**
**1** LET FALL [T] to let something you are carrying fall to the ground *She tripped and dropped the vase.* • *The dog dropped the stick at my feet.* **2** FALL [I] to fall *The ball dropped to the ground.* **3** BECOME LESS [I] If a level or amount drops, it becomes less. *Unemployment has dropped from 8% to 6% in the last year.* **4** TAKE [T] (*also* **drop off**) to take someone or something to a place, usually by car as you travel somewhere else *I can drop you at the station on my way to work.* **5** STOP ACTIVITY [T] If you drop a plan, activity, or idea, you stop doing or planning it. *Plans for a new supermarket have been dropped.* • *When we heard the news, we **dropped everything** (= stopped what we were doing) and rushed to the hospital.* **6** STOP INCLUDING [T] to decide to stop including someone in a group or team *The coach dropped me from the team.* **7** **drop it/the subject** to stop talking about something, especially because it is annoying or upsetting someone **8** VOICE [I, T] If your voice drops, or you drop your voice, you talk more quietly. ⊃ *See also:* be dropping like flies (**fly**²).

**drop by/in** to visit someone for a short time, usually without arranging it before *I **dropped in on** George on my way home from school.*

**drop sb/sth off** to take someone or something to a place, usually by car as you travel somewhere else

**drop off 1** *informal* to start to sleep *She dropped off in front of the TV.* **2** If the amount, number, or quality of something drops off, it becomes less. *The demand for mobile phones shows no signs of dropping off.*

**drop out** to stop doing something before you have completely finished *He **dropped out of** school at 14.*

o⟶**drop**² /drɒp/ *noun* **1** LIQUID [C] a small, round shaped amount of liquid *I felt a few drops of rain.* ⊃ *See colour picture* **Quantities** *on page Centre 14.* **2** REDUCTION [no plural] when the level or amount of something becomes less *There has been a **drop in** crime recently.* **3** SMALL AMOUNT [no plural] a small amount of a liquid you can drink *Would you like a drop more milk?* **4** DISTANCE [no plural] a vertical distance down from somewhere to the ground *It's a drop of about 50 metres from the top of the cliff.*

**dropout** /ˈdrɒpaʊt/ *noun* [C] **1** a student who

drop

leaves school or university before they have completely finished *a high-school dropout* **2** someone who does not want to have a job, possessions, etc because they do not want to be like everyone else

**droppings** /ˈdrɒpɪŋz/ *noun* [plural] solid waste from birds and some small animals *rabbit droppings*

**drought** /draʊt/ *noun* [C, U] a long period when there is no rain and people do not have enough water *A severe drought ruined the crops.*

**drove** /drəʊv/ *past tense of* drive

**droves** /drəʊvz/ *noun* **in droves** If people do something in droves, they do it in large numbers. *People came in droves to see the new bridge.*

**drown** /draʊn/ *verb* **1** [I, T] to die because you are under water and cannot breathe, or to kill someone in this way *Two people drowned in a boating accident yesterday.* **2** [T] (*also* **drown out**) If a loud noise drowns the sound of something else, it prevents that sound from being heard. *His voice was drowned out by the traffic.*

**drowning** /ˈdraʊnɪŋ/ *noun* [C, U] when someone dies because they are under water and cannot breathe

**drowsy** /ˈdraʊzi/ *adj* feeling tired and wanting to sleep *The sun was making me drowsy.* • **drowsily** *adv* • **drowsiness** *noun* [U]

**drudgery** /ˈdrʌdʒ³ri/ *noun* [U] work that is very boring

o⟶**drug**¹ /drʌg/ *noun* [C] **1** an illegal substance that people take to make them feel happy [usually plural] *He started **taking/using drugs** such as heroin and cocaine.* • *Greg is **on drugs** (= he uses drugs regularly).* • *a drug dealer* **2** a chemical substance used as a medicine *Scientists are developing a new drug to treat cancer.* ⊃ *See also:* **hard drugs**.

**drug**² /drʌg/ *verb* [T] **drugging**, *past* **drugged** to give someone a chemical substance that makes them sleep or stop feeling pain *He drugged his victims before robbing them.*

**'drug ,addict** *noun* [C] someone who cannot stop taking drugs

**drugstore** /ˈdrʌgstɔːʳ/ *US* (*UK* **chemist's**) *noun* [C] a shop that sells medicines and also things such as soap and beauty products

**drum**¹ /drʌm/ *noun* [C] **1** a round, hollow, musical instrument that you hit with your hands or with sticks *Anna **plays the drums**.* **2** a large, round container for holding substances such as oil or chemicals

**drum**² /drʌm/ *verb* [I, T] **drumming**, *past* **drummed** to hit something several times and make a sound like a drum, or to make something do this *the sound of rain drumming on the roof* • *She drummed her fingers nervously on the desk.*

**drum sth into sb** to make someone remember or believe an idea or fact by repeating it to them many times [often passive] *The importance of good manners was drummed into me by my father.*

**drum up sth** to increase interest in something or support for something *He was trying to drum up some enthusiasm for his idea.*

**drummer** /ˈdrʌmə³/ *noun* [C] someone who plays a drum

**D**

o-ᴗ**drunk¹** /drʌŋk/ *adj* unable to behave or speak normally because you have drunk too much alcohol *He usually **gets drunk** at parties.*

**drunk²** /drʌŋk/ *past participle of* drink

**drunken** /ˈdrʌŋkən/ *adj* [always before noun] drunk, or involving people who are drunk *a drunken man* • **drunkenly** *adv* • **drunkenness** *noun* [U]

o-ᴗ**dry¹** /draɪ/ *adj* **drier**, **driest** or **dryer**, **dryest** **1** [NOT WET] Something that is dry does not have water or liquid in it or on its surface. *dry paint* • *Is your hair dry yet?* **2** [NO RAIN] with no or not much rain *a dry summer* **3** [HAIR/SKIN] Dry skin or hair does not feel soft or smooth. *My lips feel really dry.* **4** [WINE] Dry wine is not sweet. **5** [BORING] If a book, talk, or subject is dry, it is not interesting. **6** [FUNNY] saying something in a serious way but trying to be funny *a dry sense of humour* • **dryness** /ˈdraɪnəs/ *noun* [U]

o-ᴗ**dry²** /draɪ/ *verb* [I, T] to become dry, or to make something become dry *He dried his hands on a towel.* • *She hung her clothes outside to dry.* ➔ *See also:* **blow-dry**.

**dry (sb/sth) off** to make someone or something dry, or to become dry, especially on the surface [often reflexive] *I dried myself off with a towel and got dressed.*

**dry (sth) out** to become dry, or to make something become dry

**dry (sth) up** *mainly UK* to make plates, cups, etc dry with a cloth after they have been washed

**dry up 1** If a supply of something dries up, it ends. *The work dried up and he went out of business.* **2** If a river or lake dries up, the water in it disappears.

,**dry 'clean** *verb* [T] to clean clothes using a special chemical and not with water • **dry cleaner's** *noun* [C] a shop where you can have your clothes cleaned this way • **dry cleaning** *noun* [U]

**dryer** (*also* **drier**) /ˈdraɪəʳ/ *noun* [C] a machine for drying wet things, usually clothes or hair ➔ *See also:* **tumble dryer**.

**dryly** (*also* **drily**) /ˈdraɪli/ *adv* If you say something dryly, you say it in a serious way but you are trying to be funny.

**dual** /ˈdjuːəl/ *adj* [always before noun] having two parts, or having two of something *dual nationality*

,**dual 'carriageway** *noun* [C] *UK* a road that consists of two parallel roads, so that traffic travelling in opposite directions is separated by a central strip of land

**dub** /dʌb/ *verb* [T] **dubbing**, *past* **dubbed 1** to give someone or something an unofficial or funny name [often passive] *He was dubbed 'Big Ears' by the media.* **2** to change the language in a film or television programme into a different language [often passive] *The film was **dubbed into** English.*

**dubious** /ˈdjuːbiəs/ *adj* **1** thought not to be completely true, honest, or legal *dubious evidence* • *a man with a dubious reputation* **2** not certain that something is good or true *He's **dubious about** the benefits of acupuncture.* • **dubiously** *adv*

**duchess** /ˈdʌtʃɪs/ *noun* [C] a woman of very high social rank in some European countries *the Duchess of Windsor*

**duck¹** /dʌk/ *noun* [C, U] a bird with short legs that lives in or near water, or the meat from this bird ➔ *See also:* be (like) **water¹** off a duck's back.

**duck**

**duck²** /dʌk/ *verb* **1** [I, T] to move your head or body down quickly to avoid being hit or seen *Billy ducked behind a car when he saw his teacher.* **2** [T] *informal* to avoid something that is difficult or unpleasant *He managed to duck the issue.*

**duck out of sth** to avoid doing something that other people are expecting you to do [+ doing sth] *She was trying to duck out of doing her homework.*

**duct** /dʌkt/ *noun* [C] **1** a tube in the body that a liquid substance can flow through *a tear duct* **2** a tube or passage for air or wires that is part of the structure of a building *a heating duct*

**dud** /dʌd/ *noun* [C] something that does not work correctly • **dud** *adj*

**dude** /duːd/ *noun* [C] *mainly US very informal* a man *a cool dude*

o-ᴗ**due¹** /djuː/ *adj* **1** [EVENT] [never before noun] expected or planned [+ to do sth] *He was due to fly back this morning.* • *Her book is due out* (= expected to be published) *next week.* • *When is the baby due* (= expected to be born)? **2** **due to sth** because of something *The train was late due to snow.* **3** [MONEY] [never before noun] Money that is due is owed to someone and must be paid. *The rent is due today.* **4** [DESERVE] Something that is due to you is something that is owed to you or something you deserve. *He didn't get the praise and recognition that was due to him.* **5** [BEHAVIOUR] [always before noun] *formal* correct and suitable *He was fined for driving without due care and attention.* ➔ *Opposite* **undue**. **6 be due for sth** If you are due for something, it should happen very soon. *I'm due for a check-up at the dentist's.*

**due²** /djuː/ *noun* **give sb their due** something that you say when you want to describe someone's good qualities after they have done something wrong or after you have criticized them *Joe's a bit slow but, to give him his due, he does work hard.*

**due³** /djuː/ *adv* **due east/north/south/west, etc** directly east/north/south/west, etc *sail/ fly due south*

**duel** /'dju:əl/ *noun* [C] **1** a type of fight in the past between two people with weapons, used as a way of deciding an argument **2** an argument or competition between two people or groups

**dues** /dju:z/ *noun* [plural] money that you must pay to be a member of an organization *annual dues*

**duet** /dju'et/ *noun* [C] a piece of music for two people to perform together

**dug** /dʌg/ *past of* dig

**duke** /dju:k/ *noun* [C] a man of very high social rank in some parts of Europe *the Duke of Beaufort*

**dull¹** /dʌl/ *adj* **1** BORING not interesting *a dull place* • *a dull person* **2** NOT BRIGHT not bright *dull colours* • *dull weather* **3** SOUND A dull sound is not loud or clear. *a dull thud* **4** PAIN [always before noun] A dull pain is not strong. *a dull ache* • **dullness** *noun* [U] • **dully** *adv*

**dull²** /dʌl/ *verb* [T] to make a feeling or quality become less strong *He's on morphine to dull the pain.*

**duly** /'dju:li/ *adv formal* at the correct time, in the correct way, or as you would expect *I ordered it over the Internet and within a few days, it duly arrived.* • *I was duly impressed.*

**dumb** /dʌm/ *adj* **1** *mainly US informal* stupid *a dumb idea/question* • *He's too dumb to understand.* **2** physically unable to talk **3 be struck dumb** to be unable to speak because you are so shocked or angry • **dumbly** *adv*

**dumbfounded** /ˌdʌm'faʊndɪd/ *adj* extremely surprised

**dummy¹** /'dʌmi/ *noun* [C] **1** BABY EQUIPMENT *UK* (*US* **pacifier**) a small, rubber object that a baby sucks to stop it crying **2** STUPID PERSON *mainly US informal* a stupid person *She's no dummy.* **3** MODEL a model of a person

**dummy²** /'dʌmi/ *adj* [always before noun] not real but made to look real *dummy weapons*

**dump¹** /dʌmp/ *verb* **1** [T] to put something somewhere to get rid of it, especially in a place where you should not put it *The company was fined for illegally dumping toxic chemicals.* **2 dump sth on/in/down, etc** to put something somewhere quickly and carelessly *Henri dumped his bag on the table and went upstairs.*

**dump²** /dʌmp/ (*also UK* **tip**) *noun* [C] **1** a place where people take things that they do not want *We took our old mattress to the dump.* **2** *informal* a place that is dirty and untidy *His room is a dump.*

**dumpling** /'dʌmplɪŋ/ *noun* [C] a round mixture of fat and flour that has been cooked in boiling liquid *stew and dumplings*

**dumps** /dʌmps/ *noun* **be down in the dumps** *informal* to be unhappy *He looks a bit down in the dumps.*

**Dumpster** /'dʌmpstər/ *US trademark* (*UK* **skip**) *noun* [C] a very large, metal container for big pieces of rubbish

**dumpy** /'dʌmpi/ *adj informal* short and fat

**dune** /dju:n/ (*also* **sand dune**) *noun* [C] a hill of sand in the desert or on the coast

**dung** /dʌŋ/ *noun* [U] solid waste from a large animal

**dungarees** /ˌdʌŋgə'ri:z/ *UK* (*US* **overalls**) *noun*

[plural] trousers with a part that covers your chest and straps that go over your shoulders

**dungeon** /'dʌndʒən/ *noun* [C] a dark, underground prison, used in the past

**dunk** /dʌŋk/ *verb* [T] to quickly put something into liquid and take it out again *He dunked the roll in his soup.*

**dunno** /də'nəʊ/ *informal short for* do not know.

**duo** /'dju:əʊ/ *noun* [C] two people who perform together *a comedy/pop duo*

**dupe** /dju:p/ *verb* [T] to trick someone [often passive, + into + doing sth] *He was duped into paying $4000 for a fake painting.*

**duplicate¹** /'dju:plɪkeɪt/ *verb* [T] **1** to make an exact copy of something *The document has been duplicated.* **2** to do something that has already been done, in exactly the same way *Ajax hope to duplicate last year's success.* • **duplication** /ˌdju:plɪ'keɪʃən/ *noun* [U]

**duplicate²** /'dju:plɪkət/ *noun* **1** [C] something that is an exact copy of something else *I lost my passport and had to get a duplicate.* **2 in duplicate** If a document is in duplicate, there are two copies of it. • **duplicate** *adj a duplicate key*

**duplicity** /dju'plɪsəti/ *noun* [U] when you dishonestly tell different people different things

**durable** /'djʊərəbl/ *adj* remaining in good condition for a long time *durable goods* • *a fabric that is comfortable and durable* • **durability** /ˌdjʊərə'bɪləti/ *noun* [U]

**duration** /djʊə'reɪʃən/ *noun* [U] *formal* the amount of time that something lasts *The singer remained in the hotel for the duration of his stay in the UK.*

**duress** /dju'res/ *noun formal* **under duress** If you do something under duress, you do it because someone is forcing you to. *a confession made under duress*

o–➤**during** /'djʊərɪŋ/ *preposition* **1** for the whole of a period of time *Emma's usually at home during the day.* **2** at a particular moment in a period of time *We'll arrange a meeting some time during the week.*

**USAGE**

**during** or **for**?

Use **during** to talk about a period of time when something happens.

*I'm at work during the day, so it's better to phone in the evening.*

*Please don't take photos during the performance.*

Use **for** to say how long something happens or continues, for example 'for two hours', 'for three days'.

*I've been in Cambridge for six months now.*

*We waited for an hour and then left.*

~~We waited during an hour and then left.~~

**dusk** /dʌsk/ *noun* [U] the time in the evening when it starts to become dark *As dusk fell, we headed back to the hotel.*

**dust¹** /dʌst/ *noun* [U] a powder of dirt or soil that you see on a surface or in the air *The shelves were covered in a thick layer of dust.*

• *He drove off in a cloud of dust.* **2 bite the dust** *informal* to die, fail, or stop existing **3 the dust settles** If the dust settles after an argument or big change, the situation becomes calmer. *Let the dust settle a bit before you make any decisions about the future.*

**dust²** /dʌst/ *verb* [I, T] to remove dust from something *I tidied and dusted the shelves.*

**dustbin** /'dʌstbɪn/ *UK* (*US* **garbage can**) *noun* [C] a large container for rubbish kept outside your house

**duster** /'dʌstə'/ *noun* [C] *UK* a cloth used for removing dust (= powder of dirt) from furniture and other objects

**dustman** /'dʌstmən/ *UK* (*US* **garbage man**) *noun* [C] *plural* **dustmen** someone whose job is to remove rubbish from containers outside people's houses

**dustpan** /'dʌstpæn/ *noun* [C] a flat container with a handle, used with a brush for removing dirt from a floor *Get the dustpan and brush and I'll sweep this up.* ⊃ *See picture at* **brush**.

**dusty** /'dʌsti/ *adj* covered with dust (= powder of dirt) *a dusty old chair* • *dusty streets*

**dutiful** /'dju:tɪfªl/ *adj* doing everything that you should do in your position or job *a dutiful son* • **dutifully** *adv*

o—ᴬ**duty** /'dju:ti/ *noun* [C, U] **1** RIGHT THING TO DO something you must do because it is morally or legally right *a moral duty* • [+ to do sth] *Rail companies* **have a duty** *to provide safe transport.* **2** JOB something you do as part of your job or because of your position *professional/official duties* **3 on/off duty** If a doctor, police officer, etc is on duty, they are working, and if they are off duty, they are not working. *I'm on duty tomorrow night.* **4** TAX tax that you pay on something you buy

**duty-free** /ˌdju:ti'fri:/ *adj* Duty-free goods are things that you can buy and bring into a country without paying tax.

**duvet** /'dju:veɪ ⓊⓈ du:'veɪ/ *UK* (*US* **comforter**) *noun* [C] a cover filled with feathers or warm material that you sleep under

**DVD** /ˌdi:vi:'di:/ *noun* [C] *abbreviation for* digital versatile disc: a small disc for storing music, films and information *a DVD player/drive* • *Is this film available on DVD?*

**dwarf¹** /dwɔ:f/ *noun* [C] **1** an imaginary creature like a little man, in children's stories *Snow White and the Seven Dwarves* **2** an offensive word for someone who is very short • **dwarf** *adj* A dwarf animal or plant is much smaller than the normal size.

**dwarf²** /dwɔ:f/ *verb* [T] If something dwarfs other things, it is very big and makes them seem small. [often passive] *The hotel is dwarfed by skyscrapers.*

**dwell** /dwel/ *verb* *past* **dwelt** or **dwelled**
**dwell in/among/with, etc** *literary* to live somewhere

**dwell on/upon sth** to keep thinking or talking about something, especially something bad or unpleasant *I don't want to dwell on the past.*

**dweller** /'dwelə'/ *noun* **an apartment/city/ country, etc dweller** someone who lives in an apartment/city/the country, etc

**dwelling** /'dwelɪŋ/ *noun* [C] *formal* a house or place to live in

**dwindle** /'dwɪndl/ *verb* [I] to become smaller or less *The number of students in the school has* **dwindled** *to 200.* • *Our savings slowly* **dwindled away.** • *dwindling supplies of oil*

**dye¹** /daɪ/ *noun* [C, U] a substance that is used to change the colour of something

**dye²** /daɪ/ *verb* [T] **dyeing**, *past* **dyed** to change the colour of something by using a dye *He dyed his hair pink last week.*

**dying** /'daɪɪŋ/ *present participle of* die

**dyke** (*also* **dike**) /daɪk/ *noun* [C] **1** a wall built to stop water from a sea or river going onto the land **2** *UK* a passage that has been dug to take water away from fields

**dynamic** /daɪ'næmɪk/ *adj* **1** ACTIVE full of ideas, energy, and enthusiasm *a dynamic, young teacher* • *dynamic leadership* **2** CHANGING continuously changing or moving *a dynamic economy* **3** PRODUCING MOVEMENT A dynamic force makes something move. • **dynamically** *adv*

**dynamics** /daɪ'næmɪks/ *noun* **1** [plural] the way that parts of a situation, group, or system affect each other *political dynamics* • *The* **dynamics** *of family life have changed greatly.* **2** [U] the scientific study of the movement of objects

**dynamism** /'daɪnəmɪzªm/ *noun* [U] the quality of being dynamic

**dynamite** /'daɪnəmaɪt/ *noun* [U] **1** a type of explosive *a stick of dynamite* **2** *informal* someone or something that is very exciting, powerful, or dangerous *an issue that is political dynamite*

**dynasty** /'dɪnəsti ⓊⓈ 'daɪnəsti/ *noun* [C] a series of rulers who are all from the same family *the Ming dynasty*

**dysentery** /'dɪsªntªri/ *noun* [U] an infectious disease which causes severe problems with the bowels, making solid waste become liquid

**dysfunctional** /dɪs'fʌŋkʃªnªl/ *adj* *formal* not behaving, working, or happening in the way that most people think is normal *a dysfunctional family/childhood*

**dyslexia** /dɪ'sleksiə/ *noun* [U] a condition affecting the brain that makes it difficult for someone to read and write • **dyslexic** /dɪ'sleksɪk/ *adj* having dyslexia

# E

**E, e** /iː/ the fifth letter of the alphabet

o⚡**each** /iːtʃ/ pronoun, determiner every one in a group of two or more things or people when they are considered separately *A player from each of the teams volunteered to be captain.* • *The bill is £36 between the four of us, that's £9 each.*

,**each 'other** pronoun used to show that each person in a group of two or more people does something to the others *The kids are always arguing with each other.*

**eager** /ˈiːgəʳ/ adj wanting to do or have something very much [+ to do sth] *Sam was eager to go home and play on his computer.* • **eagerly** adv *an eagerly awaited announcement* • **eagerness** noun [U]

**eagle** /ˈiːgl/ noun [C] a large, wild bird with a big, curved beak, that hunts smaller animals

**eagle**

o⚡**ear** /ɪəʳ/ noun **1** [C] one of the two organs on your head that you hear with *The child whispered something in her mother's ear.* ➔ *See colour picture* **The Body** *on page Centre 2.* **2** [C] the top part of some crop plants, which produces grain *an ear of wheat/corn* **3 have an ear for sth** to be good at hearing, repeating, or understanding a particular type of sound *He has no ear for music.* **4 fall on deaf ears** If advice or a request falls on deaf ears, people ignore it. **5 play it by ear** to decide how to deal with a situation as it develops *I'm not sure what to tell Dad – I'll just have to play it by ear.* **6 play sth by ear** to play a piece of music by remembering the notes

**earache** /ˈɪəreɪk/ noun [C, U] pain in your ear *I've got (UK) earache/(US) an earache.*

**eardrum** /ˈɪədrʌm/ noun [C] a part inside your ear made of thin, tight skin that allows you to hear sounds

**earl** /ɜːl/ noun [C] a man of high social rank in the UK *the Earl of Northumberland*

**earlobe** /ˈɪələʊb/ noun [C] the soft part at the bottom of your ear

o⚡**early** /ˈɜːli/ adj, adv **1** near the beginning of a period of time, process, etc *the early 1980s* • *It is too early to say whether he will recover completely.* **2** before the usual time or the time that was arranged *early retirement* • *The plane arrived ten minutes early.* **3 at the earliest** used after a time or date to show that something will not happen before then *Building will not begin until July at the earliest.* **4 early on** in the first stage or part of something *I lost interest quite early on in the book.* ➔ *See also:* it's early days (**day**).

**earmark** /ˈɪəmɑːk/ verb [T] to decide that something, especially money, will be used for a particular purpose [often passive] *More than $7 million has been earmarked for schools in the area.* • *The land is earmarked for development.*

o⚡**earn** /ɜːn/ verb **1** GET MONEY [I, T] to get money for doing work *She earns more than £40,000 a year.* **2 earn a/your living** to work to get money for the things you need **3** DESERVE [T] to get something that you deserve because of your work, qualities, etc *As a teacher you have to earn the respect of your students.* **4** PROFIT [T] to make a profit *an account that earns a high rate of interest*

**earner** /ˈɜːnəʳ/ noun [C] **1** someone who earns money *a high earner* **2** UK informal a product or service that earns you money *She has a nice little earner making curtains.*

**earnest** /ˈɜːnɪst/ adj **1** very serious and sincere *an earnest young man* • *an earnest effort* **2 in earnest** If something begins to happen in earnest, it really starts to happen in a serious way. *The research will begin in earnest early next year.* **3 be in earnest** to be very serious about something and mean what you are saying • **earnestly** adv • **earnestness** noun [U]

**earnings** /ˈɜːnɪŋz/ noun [plural] money that you get from working

**earphones** /ˈɪəfəʊnz/ noun [plural] a piece of electronic equipment that you put on your ears so that you can listen privately to radio, recorded music, etc

**earring** /ˈɪərɪŋ/ noun [C] a piece of jewellery that you wear on or through your ear [usually plural] *diamond earrings*

**earring**

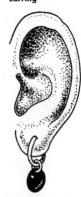

**earshot** /ˈɪəʃɒt/ noun **be out of/within earshot** If you are out of earshot, you are too far away to hear something, and if you are within earshot, you are close enough to hear something. *As soon as she was out of earshot, they started talking again.*

o⚡**earth** /ɜːθ/ noun **1** PLANET [no plural] (also **the Earth**) the planet that we live on **2** SUBSTANCE [U] soil or ground *a mound of earth* **3** ELECTRICAL WIRE [C] UK (US **ground**) a wire that makes electrical equipment safer **4 cost/charge, etc the earth** *UK informal* to cost/charge, etc an extremely large amount of money **5 come (back) down to earth** to start dealing with life and problems again after you have had a very exciting time *After our wedding, it took us a long time to come back down to earth again.* **6 how/what/why, etc on earth** *informal* used when you are extremely surprised, confused, or angry about something *Why on earth didn't you tell me before?*

**earthly** /'ɜːθli/ *adj* **1 no earthly doubt/ reason/use, etc** used to emphasize that there is not any doubt/reason/use, etc *There's no earthly reason why you should feel guilty.* **2** *literary* relating to this world and not any spiritual life *earthly powers*

**earthquake** /'ɜːθkweɪk/ *noun* [C] a sudden movement of the Earth's surface, often causing severe damage *A powerful **earthquake** struck eastern Turkey last night.*

**earthy** /'ɜːθi/ *adj* **1** referring to sex and the human body in a direct way *earthy jokes* **2** similar to soil in colour, smell, or taste

**earwig** /'ɪəwɪg/ *noun* [C] a small dark-brown insect with two curved parts on its tail

**ease**[1] /iːz/ *noun* **1** [U] If you do something with ease, it is very easy for you to do it. *Gary passed his exams **with ease**.* • *I'm amazed at the ease with which he learnt the language.* **2 at ease** feeling relaxed and comfortable *I felt completely at ease with him.* **3 ill at ease** feeling anxious

**ease**[2] /iːz/ *verb* **1** [I, T] to become less severe, or to make something become less severe *The new road should ease traffic problems in the village.* • *The pain eased after a few minutes.* **2 ease sb/sth back/out/up, etc** to move someone or something gradually and gently to another position [often reflexive] *Tom eased himself back in his chair.*

**ease off/up 1** [STOP] to gradually stop or become less *The storm is easing off.* **2** [WORK LESS] to start to work less or do things with less energy *As he got older, he started to ease up a little.* **3** [TREAT LESS SEVERELY] to start to treat someone less severely *I wish his supervisor would ease up on him a bit.*

**easel** /'iːzəl/ *noun* [C] something used to support a painting while you paint it

o─**easily** /'iːzɪli/ *adv* **1** with no difficulty *This diary fits easily into my bag.* • *She makes friends easily.* **2** used to emphasize that something is likely *A comment like that could easily be misunderstood.* **3 easily the best/worst/ biggest, etc** certainly the best/worst/biggest, etc

o─**east, East** /iːst/ *noun* **1** [U] the direction that you face to see the sun rise *Which way's east?* **2 the east** the part of an area that is further towards the east than the rest *This town is the largest in the east.* **3 the East** the countries of Asia, especially Japan and China • **east** *adj New York is east of Chicago.* • **east** *adv* towards the east *They sailed east.* ➔ *See also:* **the Middle East**.

**Easter** /'iːstər/ *noun* [C, U] the Christian period of celebration around Easter Sunday (= the special Sunday in March or April on which

Christians celebrate Jesus Christ's return to life) *the Easter holidays*

**'Easter ,egg** *noun* [C] a chocolate egg that people give and receive at Easter

**easterly** /'iːstəli/ *adj* **1** towards or in the east *The river flows in an easterly direction.* **2** An easterly wind comes from the east.

**eastern, Eastern** /'iːstən/ *adj* [always before noun] **1** in or from the east part of an area *eastern Europe* **2** in or from the countries of Asia *Eastern philosophy* • *an Eastern religion*

**easterner, Easterner** /'iːstənər/ *noun* [C] *mainly US* someone from the east part of a country or area

**,Easter 'Sunday** (*also* ,Easter 'Day) *noun* [C, U] the special Sunday in March or April on which Christians celebrate Jesus Christ's return to life

**eastward, eastwards** /'iːstwəd, 'iːstwədz/ *adv* towards the east • **eastward** *adj an eastward direction*

o─**easy**[1] /'iːzi/ *adj* **1** not difficult *an easy choice* • *He thought the exam was very easy.* • [+ to do sth] *It's easy to see why he's so popular.* **2** relaxed and comfortable *She has a very easy manner.* **3 I'm easy** *informal* used to say that you do not mind which choice is made *"Would you like pizza or curry?" "I'm easy. You choose."*

**easy**[2] /'iːzi/ *adv* **1 take it/things easy** to relax and not use too much energy *After his heart attack, he had to take things easy for a while.* **2 go easy on sb** *informal* to treat someone in a gentle way and not be so strict *Go easy on the boy – he's only young.* **3 go easy on sth** *informal* to not eat or use too much of something *Go easy on the chips, there aren't many left.* **4 easier said than done** used to say that something seems like a good idea but it would be difficult to do *I want to ask her out, but it's easier said than done.*

**easy-going** /,iːzi'gəʊɪŋ/ *adj* relaxed and not easily upset or worried

o─**eat** /iːt/ *verb past t* **ate**, *past p* **eaten 1** [I, T] to put food into your mouth and then swallow it *Who ate all the cake?* • *You should eat more slowly.* • *I haven't eaten since breakfast.* • *Let's have **something to eat** (= some food).* **2** [I] to eat a meal *We usually eat in the kitchen.* ➔ *See also:* have your **cake** and eat it.

**eat away at sb** If a memory or bad feeling eats away at someone, it makes them feel more and more unhappy.

**eat away at sth** to gradually damage or destroy something

**eat into sth** to use or take away a large part of something valuable, such as money or time

**eat out** to eat at a restaurant *Let's eat out tonight.* ⊃ *See colour picture* **Phrasal Verbs** *on page Centre 13.*

**eat (sth) up** to eat all the food you have been given *Be a good boy and eat up your spinach.*

**eat up sth** to use or take away a large part of something valuable, such as money or time *Cities are eating up more and more farmland.*

**eater** /'iːtə'/ *noun* **a big/fussy/meat, etc eater** someone who eats in a particular way or eats a particular food

**eatery** /'iːtəri/ *noun* [C] *informal* a restaurant

'**eating di,sorder** *noun* [C] a mental illness in which someone cannot eat normal amounts of food

**eaves** /iːvz/ *noun* [plural] the edges of a roof where it is wider than the walls

**eavesdrop** /'iːvzdrɒp/ *verb* [I] **eavesdropping**, *past* **eavesdropped** to secretly listen to a conversation *He stood outside the door eavesdropping on their conversation.* ● **eavesdropper** *noun* [C]

**ebb**[1] /eb/ *noun* **1 the ebb (tide)** when the sea flows away from the land **2 be at a low ebb** If someone's enthusiasm, confidence, etc is at a low ebb, it is much less than before. *Staff morale is at a low ebb.* **3 ebb and flow** the way in which the level of something regularly becomes higher or lower in a situation *the ebb and flow of the economy*

**ebb**[2] /eb/ *verb* [I] **1** (*also* **ebb away**) to gradually disappear *She watched her father's life slowly ebbing away.* **2** When the tide ebbs, the sea flows away from the land.

**ebony** /'ebᵊni/ *noun* [U] hard black wood

**ebullient** /ɪ'bʊliənt/ *adj* energetic, enthusiastic, and excited *an ebullient personality*

**e-cash** /'iːkæʃ/ *noun* [U] money in an electronic form, used for buying goods and services on the Internet

**eccentric**[1] /ɪk'sentrɪk/ *adj* behaving in a strange and unusual way *an eccentric professor* ● **eccentric behaviour** ● **eccentrically** *adv* ● **eccentricity** /ˌeksen'trɪsəti/ *noun* [U] when someone is eccentric

**eccentric**[2] /ɪk'sentrɪk/ *noun* [C] someone who is eccentric *a harmless eccentric*

**ecclesiastical** /ɪˌkliːzi'æstɪkᵊl/ *adj* relating to the Christian Church *ecclesiastical law/history*

**echelon** /'eʃəlɒn/ *noun formal* **the lower/ upper echelons** the people at the lower/upper level of a large organization or society *the upper echelons of government/management /society*

**echo**[1] /'ekəʊ/ *verb* **echoing**, *past* **echoed 1** [I] If a sound echoes, or a place echoes with a sound, you hear the sound again because you are in a large, empty space. *Their voices echoed around the room.* **2** [T] to repeat something that someone else has said because you agree with it *This report echoes some of the earlier research I've read.*

**echo**[2] /'ekəʊ/ *noun* [C] *plural* **echoes 1** a sound that you hear more than once because you are in a big, empty space **2** something that is very much like something else and makes you think of it [usually plural] *There are echoes of Shakespeare's work in the play.*

**eclectic** /ek'lektɪk/ *adj* including many different styles and types *an eclectic mix*

**eclipse**[1] /ɪ'klɪps/ *noun* [C] when the sun is covered by the moon, or the moon is covered by the Earth's shadow (= dark area) *a solar/lunar eclipse*

**eclipse**[2] /ɪ'klɪps/ *verb* [T] **1** to make another person or thing seem much less important, good, or famous [often passive] *Braque was somewhat eclipsed by Picasso.* **2** to make an eclipse of the moon or sun

**ecological** /ˌiːkə'lɒdʒɪkᵊl/ *adj* relating to ecology or to the environment *an ecological disaster* ● **ecologically** *adv*

**ecology** /i'kɒlədʒi/ *noun* [U, no plural] the relationship between living things and the environment, or the scientific study of this ● **ecologist** *noun* [C] someone who studies ecology

**e-commerce** /'iːˌkɒmɜːs/ *noun* [U] the buying and selling of goods and services on the Internet

○━**economic** /ˌiːkə'nɒmɪk, ˌekə'nɒmɪk/ *adj* **1** [always before noun] relating to trade, industry, and money *economic growth* ● *economic policies* **2** making a profit, or likely to make a profit *It's not economic to produce goods in small quantities.* ⊃ *Opposite* **uneconomic.** ● **economically** *adv The country would benefit economically.*

**economical** /ˌiːkə'nɒmɪkᵊl/ *adj* not using a lot of money, fuel, etc *I need a car that's economical and reliable.* ● **economically** *adv*

**economics** /ˌiːkə'nɒmɪks/ *noun* [U] the study of the way in which trade, industry, and money are organized ● **economist** /ɪ'kɒnəmɪst/ *noun* [C] someone who studies economics ⊃ *See also:* **home economics.**

**economize** (*also UK* **-ise**) /ɪ'kɒnəmaɪz/ *verb* [I] to use less of something because you want to save money

○━**economy** /ɪ'kɒnəmi/ *noun* **1** [C] the system by which a country produces and uses goods and money *the German/US economy* ● *a global economy* **2** [C, U] when someone or something does not use much money, fuel, etc *The car's design combines comfort with economy.* ● *(UK) We'll need to **make** some **economies** when I stop work.*

**ecosystem** /'iːkəʊˌsɪstəm/ *noun* [C] all the living things in an area and the way they affect each other and the environment *Tourism is damaging the fragile ecosystem of the reef.*

**ecstasy** /'ekstəsi/ *noun* **1** [U] a feeling of extreme happiness *She danced about in ecstasy.* **2 Ecstasy** an illegal drug that makes you feel happier and more active

**ecstatic** /ɪk'stætɪk/ *adj* extremely happy ● **ecstatically** *adv*

**ecumenical** /ˌekjʊ'menɪkᵊl/ *adj* encouraging different types of Christian churches to unite *an ecumenical service*

**eczema** /'eksɪmə/ *noun* [U] a medical condition which makes areas of skin become red and dry

○ᵂ**edge**[1] /edʒ/ noun **1** [C] the part around something that is furthest from the centre *Rick was sitting on the edge of the bed.* ● *She ran down to the water's edge.* **2** [C] the part of a blade of a knife or tool that cuts *a sharp/cutting edge* **3** have the edge on/over sb/sth to be slightly better than someone or something else **4** be on edge to be nervous or worried *Sorry for shouting – I'm a bit on edge today.* **5** take the edge off sth to make something unpleasant have less of an effect on someone *Have an apple – It'll take the edge off your hunger.*

**edge**[2] /edʒ/ verb **1** edge (sth) up/down/past, etc to move somewhere gradually, or to make something move somewhere gradually *She edged her way through the crowd of reporters.* **2** [T] to put something around the edge of something else as a decoration *The cloth was edged with gold.*

**edgeways** /'edʒweɪz/ UK (US **edgewise** /'edʒwaɪz/) adv with the narrowest part going first *We should be able to get the sofa through edgeways.* ⇒ *See also:* not get a **word**[1] in edgeways.

**edgy** /'edʒi/ adj nervous *David was starting to feel a bit edgy.*

**edible** /'edɪbl/ adj safe to eat and not harmful *edible berries* ⇒ *Compare* **inedible**.

**edict** /'iːdɪkt/ noun [C] formal an official order from someone in authority

**edifice** /'edɪfɪs/ noun [C] formal a very large building

**edit** /'edɪt/ verb [T] to prepare text, film, etc by deciding what to include and making mistakes correct

**edition** /ɪ'dɪʃ°n/ noun [C] **1** a book, newspaper, etc that is one of several that are the same and were produced at the same time *a new edition* ● *The paperback edition costs £7.95.* **2** a radio or television programme that is one of a series

**editor** /'edɪtə'/ noun [C] **1** someone whose job is to prepare text, film, etc by deciding what to include and making mistakes correct **2** someone who is in charge of a newspaper or magazine

**editorial**[1] /ˌedɪ'tɔːriəl/ adj [always before noun] **1** relating to editors or editing *editorial skills* **2** written by or expressing the opinions of a newspaper editor *editorial pages*

**editorial**[2] /ˌedɪ'tɔːriəl/ noun [C] an article in a newspaper expressing the editor's opinion

**educate** /'edʒukeɪt/ verb [T] **1** to teach someone at a school or college [often passive] *She was educated at the Perse School.* **2** to give people information about something so that they understand it better *This is part of a campaign to educate people about the dangers of smoking.*

**educated** /'edʒukeɪtɪd/ adj **1** Someone who is educated has learned a lot at school or university and has a good level of knowledge. **2** an educated guess a guess that is probably correct because you have enough knowledge about something ⇒ *See also:* **well-educated**.

○ᵂ**education** /ˌedʒu'keɪʃ°n/ noun [U, no plural] the process of teaching and learning in a school or college, or the knowledge that you get from this *More money should be spent on education.* ● *We expect a good standard of education for our*

children. ● **educational** adj providing education, or relating to education *the educational system* ● **educationally** adv ⇒ *See also:* **further education, higher education**.

**eel** /iːl/ noun [C] a long fish that looks like a snake

**eerie** /'ɪəri/ adj unusual and slightly frightening *an eerie silence* ● **eerily** adv ● **eeriness** noun [U]

○ᵂ**effect**[1] /ɪ'fekt/ noun **1** [C, U] a change, reaction, or result that is caused by something *The accident had a huge effect on her life.* ● *We don't know the long-term effects of this drug.* **2** in effect used to say what the real situation is *This means, in effect, that the plan has been scrapped.* **3** come/go into effect to start being used *New food safety rules come into effect on Monday.* **4** take effect to start to produce results or changes *The anaesthetic takes effect in about ten minutes.* **5** to that effect used to say that you are giving the general meaning of something but not the exact words *He said he was bored with school or something to that effect.* **6** a sound/special/visual, etc effect a sound, image, etc that is created artificially ⇒ *See also:* **side-effect**.

**affect** or **effect**?

Be careful not to confuse these two words.

Affect is a verb which means to cause a change.

*Pollution seriously affects the environment.*

Use the noun effect to talk about the change, reaction, or result caused by something.

*Global warming is one of the effects of pollution.*

**effect**[2] /ɪ'fekt/ verb [T] formal to make something happen *The civil rights movement effected a huge change in America.*

○ᵂ**effective** /ɪ'fektɪv/ adj **1** successful or achieving the result that you want *effective management* ● *What is the most effective way of teaching grammar?* **2** become/be effective If changes, laws, etc become effective, they officially start. *The new tax law becomes effective on Monday.* **3** [always before noun] used to say what the real situation is although officially it is different *She has effective control of the company.* ⇒ *Opposite* **ineffective**. ● **effectiveness** noun [U]

**effectively** /ɪ'fektɪvli/ adv **1** in a way that is successful and achieves what you want *Teachers need to be able to communicate ideas effectively.* **2** used when you describe what the real result of a situation is *His illness effectively ended his career.*

**effects** /ɪ'fekts/ noun [plural] formal possessions *my personal effects*

**effeminate** /ɪ'femɪnət/ adj An effeminate man behaves or looks like a woman.

**efficiency** /ɪ'fɪʃ°nsi/ noun [U] when someone or something uses time and energy well, without wasting any *fuel efficiency* ● *We must improve the efficiency of the industry.*

**efficient** /ɪ'fɪʃ°nt/ adj working well and not

wasting time or energy *an efficient person/organization* ● *Email is a quick and efficient way of contacting people.* ⊃ *Opposite* **inefficient**. ● **efficiently** *adv*

**effigy** /'efɪdʒi/ *noun* [C] a model of a person *Protesters burned effigies of the president.*

○━**effort** /'efət/ *noun* **1** [C, U] an attempt to do something [+ to do sth] *We huddled together in an effort to keep warm.* ● *He was making an effort to be sociable.* **2** [U] the energy that you need to do something *I put a lot of effort into organizing the party.* ● [+ to do sth] *It would take too much effort to tidy my bedroom.* **3** **be an effort** to be difficult or painful *After his accident, walking was an effort.*

**effortless** /'efətləs/ *adj* achieved without any special or obvious effort *effortless grace/style* ● **effortlessly** *adv*

**effusive** /ɪ'fjuːsɪv/ *adj* showing a lot of enthusiasm or approval for someone or something, often too much

**EFL** /ˌiːef'el/ *noun* [U] *abbreviation for* English as a Foreign Language: the teaching of English to students whose first language is not English

○━**e.g.** (*also* **eg**) /ˌiː'dʒiː/ used to give an example of what you mean *crime writers, e.g. Agatha Christie and Ruth Rendell*

**egalitarian** /ɪˌɡælɪ'teəriən/ *adj formal* believing that everyone should have the same freedom and opportunities

○━**egg**[1] /eg/ *noun* **1** FOOD [C, U] an oval object produced by a female chicken, that you eat as food *a boiled/fried egg* ⊃ *See colour picture* **Food** *on page Centre 7.* **2** BABY [C] an oval object with a hard shell that contains a baby bird, insect, or other creature *The bird lays* (= produces) *its eggs in a nest.* **3** FEMALE CELL [C] a cell inside a female person or animal that can develop into a baby **4 have egg on your face** to seem stupid because of something you have done *You'll be the one who has egg on your face if it goes wrong.* ⊃ *See also:* **Easter egg**, **scrambled eggs**.

**egg**[2] /eg/ *verb*
**egg sb on** to encourage someone to do something, usually something that is wrong, stupid, or dangerous *Two girls were fighting outside the club, egged on by a group of friends.*

'**egg ˌcup** *noun* [C] a small container for holding a boiled egg while you eat it

**eggplant** /'egplɑːnt/ *US* (*UK* **aubergine**) *noun* [C, U] an oval, purple vegetable that is white inside ⊃ *See colour picture* **Fruit and Vegetables** *on page Centre 8.*

**ego** /'iːɡəʊ, 'eɡəʊ/ *noun* [C] your opinion of yourself *He has a huge ego.*

**egocentric** /ˌiːɡəʊ'sentrɪk/ *adj* interested only in yourself

**egotism** /'iːɡəʊtɪz³m/ (*also* **egoism** /'iːɡəʊɪz³m/) *noun* [U] when someone thinks that they are very important and is not interested in other people ● **egotist** *noun* [C] ● **egotistic** /ˌiːɡəʊ'tɪstɪk/ (*also* **egotistical** /ˌiːɡəʊ'tɪstɪk³l/) *adj*

**egregious** /ɪ'ɡriːdʒəs/ *adj formal* extremely bad or shocking in an obvious way *an egregious example of racism*

**eh?** /eɪ/ *exclamation UK informal spoken* **1** used to ask someone to repeat something because

you did not hear or understand it *"You're looking tired." "Eh?" "I said, you're looking tired."* **2** used to show interest or surprise at something *Sue's had a baby girl, eh?*

**eight** /eɪt/ the number 8

**eighteen** /ˌeɪ'tiːn/ the number 18 ● **eighteenth** 18th written as a word

**eighth**[1] /eɪtθ/ 8th written as a word

**eighth**[2] /eɪtθ/ *noun* [C] one of eight equal parts of something; 1/8

**eighty** /'eɪti/ **1** the number 80 **2 the eighties** the years from 1980–1989 **3 be in your eighties** to be aged between 80 and 89 ● **eightieth** 80th written as a word

**either**[1] /'aɪðə², 'iːðə²/ *conjunction* **either...or** used when you are giving a choice of two or more things *Either call me tonight or I'll speak to you tomorrow.* ● *There's either mashed, boiled, or baked potatoes.*

○━**either**[2] /'aɪðə², 'iːðə²/ *pronoun, determiner* **1** one of two people or things when it is not important which *"Would you like red or white wine?" – "Oh, either."* ● *Ask Dom or Andrew, either of them will help you.* **2** both *People were smoking on either side* (= at both sides) *of me.* ● *You can use the train or the bus, either way it'll take an hour.*

○━**either**[3] /'aɪðə², 'iːðə²/ *adv* used in negative sentences to mean that something else is also true *The menu is boring and it's not cheap either.* ● *I don't eat meat and Sam doesn't either.* ⊃ *See usage note at* **not**.

**eject** /ɪ'dʒekt/ *verb* **1** LEAVE PLACE [T] *formal* to make someone leave a place, usually using force [**often passive**] *He was ejected from the courtroom for shouting.* **2** LEAVE MACHINE [I, T] to come out of a machine when a button is pressed, or to make something do this *How do you eject the tape?* **3** LEAVE AIRCRAFT [I] to leave an aircraft in an emergency by being pushed out while still in your seat

**eke** /iːk/ *verb*
**eke sth out 1** to use something slowly or carefully because you only have a small amount of it **2 eke out a living/existence** to earn only just enough money to pay for things you need *He ekes out a living by cleaning windows.*

**elaborate**[1] /ɪ'læb³rət/ *adj* complicated, detailed, or made carefully from many parts *an elaborate system/scheme* ● *an elaborate design* ● **elaborately** *adv*

**elaborate**[2] /ɪ'læb³reɪt/ *verb* [I, T] to explain something and give more details *He wouldn't elaborate on the details.* ● **elaboration** /ɪˌlæbə'reɪʃ³n/ *noun* [U]

**elapse** /ɪ'læps/ *verb* [I] *formal* If time elapses, it passes. *Two years have elapsed since the attack.*

**elastic**[1] /ɪ'læstɪk/ *adj* Something that is elastic can stretch and return to its original size. *Your skin is more elastic when you are young.* ● **elasticity** /ˌiːlæs'tɪsəti/ *noun* [U] the quality of being elastic

**elastic**[2] /ɪ'læstɪk/ *noun* [U] a type of rubber that returns to its original size and shape after you stretch it

**e,lastic 'band** *UK* (*UK/US* **rubber band**) *noun* [C] a thin circle of rubber used to hold things together

**elated** /ɪˈleɪtɪd/ *adj* extremely happy and excited *We were **elated by/at** the news.*
• **elation** /ɪˈleɪʃᵊn/ *noun* [U]

**elbow¹** /ˈelbəʊ/ *noun* [C] the part in the middle of your arm where it bends ➜ *See colour picture* **The Body** *on page Centre 2.*

**elbow²** /ˈelbəʊ/ *verb* [T] to push someone with your elbow, especially so you can move past them *He **elbowed his way through** the crowds of shoppers.*

ˈ**elbow ˌroom** *noun* [U] space to move easily

**elder¹** /ˈeldəʳ/ *adj* **elder brother/daughter/ sister, etc** the oldest of two brothers/daughters/sisters, etc *Their elder daughter lives in South America.* ➜ *See usage note at* **old**.

**elder²** /ˈeldəʳ/ *noun* **1 the elder** the oldest of two people *He's the elder of two sons.* **2 your elders** people older than you *I was taught to respect my elders.* **3** [C] an important, respected, older member of a group

**elderly** /ˈeldᵊli/ *adj* a more polite word for 'old', used to describe people *an elderly man* • *Children should show respect for the elderly.*

**eldest** /ˈeldɪst/ *adj* **eldest child/daughter/ brother, etc** the oldest child/daughter/brother, etc *My eldest brother is a doctor.* • *Susan is **the eldest** of three sisters.*

**elect** /ɪˈlekt/ *verb* **1** [T] to choose someone for a particular job or position by voting [often passive] *She was **elected to** the US Senate in 1984.* • *He was elected president in 1997.* **2 elect to do sth** *formal* to choose to do something *The child elected to stay with his mother.* ➜ *See also:* **re-elect.**

o─**election** /ɪˈlekʃᵊn/ *noun* [C, U] a time when people vote in order to choose someone for a political or official job *a presidential election* • *Who do you think will win the election?* • *Will you **stand/run for election** again this year?* ➜ *See also:* **by-election, general election, re-election.**

eˈ**lection ˌday** *US* (*UK* **polling day**) *noun* [C] the day when people vote in an election

**electoral** /ɪˈlektᵊrᵊl/ *adj* [always before noun] relating to elections *the electoral system* • *electoral reform*

**electorate** /ɪˈlektᵊrət/ *noun* [group] the people who are allowed to vote in an election *the British electorate*

o─**electric** /ɪˈlektrɪk/ *adj* **1** EQUIPMENT Electric lights, tools, etc work using electricity. *an electric light/heater* **2** SUPPLY supplying electricity *an electric socket* • *electric current* **3** EXCITING full of excitement and emotion *The atmosphere backstage was electric.*

o─**electrical** /ɪˈlektrɪkᵊl/ *adj* **1** Electrical goods or equipment work using electricity. *electrical appliances/goods* **2** relating to the production and supply of electricity *an electrical engineer*

**the eˌlectric ˈchair** *noun* a chair used in parts of the US to kill a criminal using electricity

**electrician** /ɪˌlekˈtrɪʃᵊn/ *noun* [C] someone whose job is to put in, check, or repair electrical wires and equipment

o─**electricity** /ɪˌlekˈtrɪsəti/ *noun* [U] a type of energy that can produce light and heat, or make machines work *The electricity has been turned off.* • *an electricity bill*

eˌ**lectric ˈshock** *noun* [C] a sudden, painful feeling that you get when electricity flows through your body

**electrify** /ɪˈlektrɪfaɪ/ *verb* [T] **1** to make people who are watching something feel very excited *She electrified the crowd with her fantastic performance.* **2** to supply something with electricity *an electrified railway*

**electrocute** /ɪˈlektrəkjuːt/ *verb* [T] to kill someone by causing electricity to flow through their body [often passive] *He was electrocuted while playing on a railway line.* • **electrocution** /ɪˌlektrəˈkjuːʃᵊn/ *noun* [U]

**electrode** /ɪˈlektrəʊd/ *noun* [C] the point where an electric current enters or leaves something such as a battery (= object which provides electricity)

**electron** /ɪˈlektrɒn/ *noun* [C] an extremely small piece of an atom with a negative electrical charge

o─**electronic** /ɪˌlekˈtrɒnɪk/ *adj* **1** Electronic equipment consists of things such as computers, televisions, and radios. **2** Electronic music, games, etc use electronic equipment. • **electronically** *adv electronically controlled gates*

**electronics** /ɪˌlekˈtrɒnɪks/ *noun* [U] the science of making electronic equipment *the electronics industry*

**elegance** /ˈelɪgᵊns/ *noun* [U] when someone or something is stylish or attractive in their appearance or behaviour

**elegant** /ˈelɪgᵊnt/ *adj* stylish or attractive in appearance or behaviour *an elegant dining room* • *She's a very elegant woman.* • **elegantly** *adv*

**element** /ˈelɪmənt/ *noun* **1** PART [C] a part of something *This book has all the elements of a good detective story.* **2 an element of sth** a small amount of an emotion or quality *There's an element of truth in what she says.* **3** PEOPLE [C] a group of people of a particular type *The disruptive element on the committee voted against the proposal.* **4** SIMPLE SUBSTANCE [C] a simple substance which cannot be reduced to smaller chemical parts *Iron is one of the elements of the Earth's crust.* **5** HEAT [C] the part of a piece of electrical equipment which produces heat **6 be in your element** to be happy because you are doing what you like doing and what you are good at *I'm in my element at a children's party.*

**elementary** /ˌelɪˈmentᵊri/ *adj* **1** basic *I only have an elementary knowledge of physics.* • *an elementary mistake* **2** relating to the early stages of studying a subject *students at elementary level*

eleˈmentary ˌschool *US* (*UK* **primary school**) *noun* [C] a school for children from the ages of five to eleven

**elements** /ˈelɪmənts/ *noun* **the elements** the weather, especially bad weather *Shall we brave the elements and go out for a walk?*

**elephant** /ˈelɪfənt/ *noun* [C] a very large, grey animal with big ears and a very long nose

**elevate** /ˈelɪveɪt/ *verb formal* **1 be elevated to sth** to be given a more important position *She has been elevated to deputy manager.* • *an elevated position* **2** [T] to move something to a

**elephant**

higher level or height *High stress levels elevate blood pressure.* • *Try to keep your leg elevated.*

**elevation** /ˌelɪ'veɪʃᵊn/ *noun* **1** [C] the height of a place above the level of the sea *The hotel is situated at an elevation of 1000m.* **2** [U] *formal* when someone or something is given a more important position *his sudden elevation to stardom*

**elevator** /'elɪveɪtᵊr/ *US* (*UK* **lift**) *noun* [C] a machine that carries people up and down in tall buildings

**eleven** /ɪ'levᵊn/ the number 11 • **eleventh** 11th written as a word

**elf** /elf/ *noun* [C] *plural* **elves** a small person with pointed ears who has magic powers in children's stories

**elicit** /ɪ'lɪsɪt/ *verb* [T] *formal* to get information or a reaction from someone *You have to ask the right questions to elicit the information you want.*

**eligible** /'elɪdʒəbl/ *adj* **1** If you are eligible to do something, you can do it because you are in the right situation. [+ to do sth] *Only people over 18 are eligible to vote.* • *You might be eligible for a grant for your studies.* ⊃ *Opposite* **ineligible**. **2** If someone who is not married is eligible, they would be a good husband or wife because they are rich, attractive, etc. *an eligible young bachelor* • **eligibility** /ˌelɪdʒə'bɪləti/ *noun* [U]

**eliminate** /ɪ'lɪmɪneɪt/ *verb* [T] **1** to remove something from something, or get rid of something *The doctor advised me to eliminate salt from my diet.* **2** to defeat someone so that they cannot go any further in a competition [often passive] *She was eliminated after the first round of the tournament.*

**elimination** /ɪˌlɪmɪ'neɪʃᵊn/ *noun* **1** [U] when you eliminate someone or something **2 a process of elimination** when you remove all possible answers to something until only one remains *We arrived at this result by a process of elimination.*

**elite** /ɪ'liːt/ *noun* [group] the richest, most powerful, or best educated group in a society *a member of the elite* • *an elite group*

**elitism** /ɪ'liːtɪzᵊm/ *noun* [U] when a small group of rich, powerful, or educated people are given an advantage in a situation • **elitist** *adj* elitist attitudes

**elm** /elm/ *noun* [C, U] a large tree which loses its leaves in winter

**elocution** /ˌelə'kjuːʃᵊn/ *noun* [U] the skill of speaking in a careful, clear way

**elongated** /'iːlɒŋgeɪtɪd/ *US* iː'lɒŋgeɪtɪd/ *adj* longer and thinner than usual

**elope** /ɪ'ləʊp/ *verb* [I] to leave home secretly with someone in order to get married

**eloquent** /'eləkwənt/ *adj* expressing ideas clearly and in a way that influences people *the most eloquent speaker at the conference* • **eloquence** /'eləkwəns/ *noun* [U] when someone or something is eloquent • **eloquently** *adv*

o━**else** /els/ *adv* **1** [IN ADDITION] in addition to someone or something *Would you like anything else to eat?* • *What else did he say?* **2** [DIFFERENT] different from someone or something *I don't like it here. Let's go somewhere else.* • *I didn't say that. It must have been someone else.* **3** [OTHER] other things or people *I forgot my toothbrush, but I remembered everything else.* **4 or else a** used to compare two different things or situations *He talks to her all the time, or else he completely ignores her.* **b** used to say what will happen if another thing does not happen *We must be there by six, or else we'll miss the beginning.* **5 if all else fails** if no other plan is successful *If all else fails, you're welcome to stay at our house.*

**elsewhere** /ˌels'weər/ *adv* in or to another place *The report studies economic growth in Europe and elsewhere.* • *If we can't find it here, we'll have to go elsewhere.*

**ELT** /ˌiːel'tiː/ *noun* [U] *abbreviation for* English Language Teaching: the teaching of English to students whose first language is not English

**elucidate** /ɪ'luːsɪdeɪt/ *verb* [T] *formal* to explain something, or make it clear

**elude** /ɪ'luːd/ *verb* [T] *formal* **1** [NOT ACHIEVE] If something that you want eludes you, you do not succeed in achieving it. *The gold medal continues to elude her.* **2** [NOT BE CAUGHT] to not be caught by someone *He eluded the police for years before he was arrested.* **3** [NOT REMEMBER] If a piece of information eludes you, you cannot remember it. *I know the man you mean, but his name eludes me.*

**elusive** /ɪ'luːsɪv/ *adj* difficult to describe, find, achieve, or remember *The answers to these questions remain as elusive as ever.*

**elves** /elvz/ *plural of* elf

**'em** /əm/ *informal spoken short for* them

**emaciated** /ɪ'meɪsieɪtɪd/ *adj* very thin and weak because of being ill or not eating enough food

**email** (*also* **e-mail**) /'iːmeɪl/ *noun* **1** [U] a system for sending messages electronically, especially from one computer to another using the Internet *You can contact me by email.* • *What's your email address?* **2** [C, U] a message sent electronically *I got an email from Danielle yesterday.* • **email** *verb* [T] to send a message using email

**emanate** /'eməneɪt/ *verb*

**emanate from sth** *formal* to come from something *Strange noises emanated from the room next door.*

**emancipate** /ɪ'mænsɪpeɪt/ *verb* [T] *formal* to give people more freedom or rights by removing social, legal, or political controls that limit

them *emancipated women* • **emancipation**
/ɪˌmænsɪˈpeɪʃᵊn/ *noun* [U]

**embalm** /ɪmˈbɑːm/ *verb* [T] to use oils and chemicals to prevent a dead body from decaying

**embankment** /ɪmˈbæŋkmənt/ *noun* [C] an artificial slope built from soil or stones to stop floods, or to support a road or railway *a railway embankment*

**embargo** /ɪmˈbɑːɡəʊ/ *noun* [C] *plural* **embargoes** an order by a government to stop trade with another country *an arms/oil embargo* • *We will not lift* (= stop) *the trade embargo until they end this war.*

**embark** /ɪmˈbɑːk/ *verb* [I] to get on a ship, boat, or aircraft to begin a journey ➔ *Opposite* **disembark**.
**embark on/upon sth** to start something new or important *You're never too old to embark on a new career.*

**embarrass** /ɪmˈbærəs/ *verb* [T] to make someone feel ashamed or shy *My dad's always embarrassing me in front of my friends.*

o▬**embarrassed** /ɪmˈbærəst/ *adj* feeling ashamed or shy *She felt embarrassed about undressing in front of the doctor.* • [+ to do sth] *I was too embarrassed to admit that I was scared.*

o▬**embarrassing** /ɪmˈbærəsɪŋ/ *adj* making you feel embarrassed *an embarrassing defeat* • *What has been your most embarrassing moment?* • **embarrassingly** *adv The play was embarrassingly bad.*

**embarrassment** /ɪmˈbærəsmənt/ *noun* **1** [U] when you feel embarrassed *He blushed with embarrassment.* • *Her behaviour has caused great embarrassment to her family.* **2** [C] something or someone that makes you feel embarrassed *He is becoming an embarrassment to the government.*

**embassy** /ˈembəsi/ *noun* [C] the official group of people who live in a foreign country and represent their government there, or the building where they work *When I lost my passport, I had to contact the British Embassy.*

**embedded** /ɪmˈbedɪd/ *adj* **1** fixed into the surface of something *A small piece of glass was embedded in his finger.* **2** If an emotion, attitude, etc is embedded in someone or something, it is a very strong and important part of them. *A sense of guilt was deeply embedded in my conscience.*

**embellish** /ɪmˈbelɪʃ/ *verb* [T] to make something more beautiful or interesting by adding something to it *He embellished the story with lots of dramatic detail.* • **embellishment** *noun* [C, U]

**embers** /ˈembəz/ *noun* [plural] pieces of wood or coal that continue to burn after a fire has no more flames

**embezzle** /ɪmˈbezl/ *verb* [T] to steal money that belongs to the company or organization that you work for • **embezzlement** *noun* [U]

**embittered** /ɪmˈbɪtəd/ *adj* very angry about unfair things that have happened to you

**emblazoned** /ɪmˈbleɪzᵊnd/ *adj* decorated in a very obvious way with something such as a name or a design *Her T-shirt was emblazoned with the company logo.*

**emblem** /ˈembləm/ *noun* [C] a picture, object, or symbol that is used to represent a person, group, or idea *The rose is the national emblem of England.*

**embodiment** /ɪmˈbɒdimənt/ *noun* **the embodiment of sth** If someone or something is the embodiment of a particular idea or quality, they express or represent it exactly. *The mother in the story is the embodiment of evil.*

**embody** /ɪmˈbɒdi/ *verb* [T] to represent an idea or quality exactly *He embodies the values of hard work and fair play.*

**embrace¹** /ɪmˈbreɪs/ *verb* **1** ‖HOLD‖ [I, T] If you embrace someone, you put your arms around them, and if two people embrace, they put their arms around each other. **2** ‖ACCEPT‖ [T] to accept new ideas, beliefs, methods, etc in an enthusiastic way *We are always eager to embrace the latest technology.* **3** ‖INCLUDE‖ [T] *formal* to include a number of things *The report embraces a wide range of opinions.*

**embrace²** /ɪmˈbreɪs/ *noun* [C] when you put your arms around someone *a passionate embrace*

**embroider** /ɪmˈbrɔɪdəʳ/ *verb* **1** [I, T] to decorate cloth by sewing small patterns or pictures onto it **2** [T] to add imaginary details to a story to make it more interesting *They accused him of embroidering the facts.*

**embroidery** /ɪmˈbrɔɪdᵊri/ *noun* [U] **1** the activity of sewing small patterns or pictures onto things *She is very good at embroidery.* **2** decoration on cloth made by sewing small patterns or pictures onto it

**embroil** /ɪmˈbrɔɪl/ *verb* *formal* **be embroiled in sth** to be involved in an argument or difficult situation *We don't want to become embroiled in a dispute over ownership.*

**embryo** /ˈembriəʊ/ *noun* [C] a human or an animal that is starting to develop in its mother's uterus

**embryonic** /ˌembriˈɒnɪk/ *adj formal* starting to develop *The project is still at an embryonic stage.*

**emerald** /ˈemᵊrᵊld/ *noun* **1** [C] a bright green stone used in jewellery **2** [U] (*also* ˌemerald ˈgreen) a bright green colour • **emerald** *adj*

**emerge** /ɪˈmɜːdʒ/ *verb* [I] **1** ‖COME OUT‖ to appear from somewhere or come out of somewhere *A figure emerged from the shadows.* **2** ‖BECOME KNOWN‖ to become known *It emerged that she had lied to her employers.* **3** ‖DIFFICULT SITUATION‖ to reach the end of a difficult situation *They emerged victorious from the fight.* • **emergence** *noun* [U]

o▬**emergency** /ɪˈmɜːdʒᵊnsi/ *noun* [C] a serious or dangerous situation that needs immediate action *You should only ring this number in an emergency.* • *an emergency exit*

e**ˈmergency ˌbrake** *US* (*UK* **handbrake**) *noun* [C] a stick inside a car that you can pull up to stop the car from moving ➔ *See colour picture* **Car** *on page Centre 3.*

e**ˈmergency ˌroom** *US* (*UK* **casualty**) *noun* [C] the part of a hospital where people go when they have been injured or have urgent illnesses so that they can be treated immediately

e**ˌmergency ˈservices** *noun* [plural] the

organizations who deal with accidents and urgent problems such as fire, illness, or crime

**emerging** /ɪˈmɜːdʒɪŋ/ adj [always before noun] starting to exist or develop *emerging economies/ markets*

**emigrant** /ˈemɪɡrənt/ noun [C] someone who leaves their own country to go and live in another one

**emigrate** /ˈemɪɡreɪt/ verb [I] to leave your own country to go and live in another one *We're thinking of emigrating to New Zealand.* • **emigration** /ˌemɪˈɡreɪʃ°n/ noun [U]

**eminent** /ˈemɪnənt/ adj famous, respected, or important *an eminent historian* • **eminence** /ˈemɪnəns/ noun [U] ➔ See also: **pre-eminent**.

**eminently** /ˈemɪnəntli/ adv formal very *He is eminently qualified for the job.*

**emission** /ɪˈmɪʃ°n/ noun [C, U] when gas, heat, light, etc is sent out into the air, or an amount of gas, heat, light, etc that is sent out *Carbon dioxide emissions will be reduced by 20%.*

**emit** /ɪˈmɪt/ verb [T] **emitting**, past **emitted** to send out gas, heat, light, etc into the air *The machine emits a high-pitched sound when you press the button.*

**emoticon** /ɪˈməʊtɪkɒn/ noun [C] an image such as :-) which looks like a face when you look at it from the side, made using keyboard symbols and used in emails to express emotions

○╼**emotion** /ɪˈməʊʃ°n/ noun [C, U] a strong feeling such as love or anger, or strong feelings in general *He finds it hard to express his emotions.* • *She was overcome with emotion and burst into tears.*

**emotional** /ɪˈməʊʃ°n°l/ adj 1 [EMOTIONS] relating to emotions *a child's emotional development* 2 [STRONG FEELINGS] showing strong feelings, or making people have strong feelings *an emotional speech* • *After the argument, I was feeling confused and emotional.* 3 [PERSON] An emotional person shows their emotions very easily or very often. • **emotionally** adv

**emotive** /ɪˈməʊtɪv/ adj making people feel strong emotions *Animal experimentation is a very emotive issue.*

**empathy** /ˈempəθi/ noun [U] the ability to imagine what it must be like to be in someone's situation • **empathize** (also UK **-ise**) /ˈempəθaɪz/ verb [I] to feel empathy with someone *I think people find it easy to empathize with the main character.*

**emperor** /ˈemp°rə°/ noun [C] the male ruler of an empire (= group of countries ruled by one person or government) *Emperor Charlemagne*

○╼**emphasis** /ˈemfəsɪs/ noun [C, U] plural **emphases** /ˈemfəsiːz/ 1 particular importance or attention that you give to something *Schools are starting to place/put greater emphasis on passing exams.* 2 the extra force that you give to a word or part of a word when you are saying it *The emphasis is on the final syllable.*

○╼**emphasize** (also UK **-ise**) /ˈemfəsaɪz/ verb [T] to show that something is especially important or needs special attention *The government is emphasizing the importance of voting in the election.* • [+ that] *He emphasized that the driver was not to blame for the accident.*

**emphatic** /ɪmˈfætɪk/ adj done or said in a strong way and without any doubt *an emphatic victory* • **emphatically** adv

**empire** /ˈempaɪə°/ noun [C] 1 a group of countries that is ruled by one person or government 2 a large group of businesses that is controlled by one person or company *a publishing empire*

**empirical** /ɪmˈpɪrɪk°l/ adj formal based on experience or scientific experiments and not only on ideas *empirical evidence* • **empirically** adv

○╼**employ** /ɪmˈplɔɪ/ verb [T] 1 If a person or company employs someone, they pay that person to work for them. *The company employs 2500 staff.* • [+ to do sth] *They employ her to look after their children.* 2 formal to use something *Companies employ clever tactics to persuade us to buy their products.*

**employee** /ɪmˈplɔɪiː/ noun [C] someone who is paid to work for a person or company *How many employees does the firm have?*

○╼**employer** /ɪmˈplɔɪə°/ noun [C] a person or company that pays people to work for them

○╼**employment** /ɪmˈplɔɪmənt/ noun [U] 1 when someone is paid to work for a person or company *full-time/part-time employment* • *It is not easy to find employment in the countryside.* • *employment opportunities/rights* ➔ Compare **unemployment**. 2 formal the use of something

**empower** /ɪmˈpaʊə°/ verb 1 [T] to give someone the confidence, skills, freedom, etc to do something [+ to do sth] *Education empowers people to take control of their lives.* 2 **be empowered to do sth** to have the legal or official right to do something *The court is empowered to take away your children.*

**empress** /ˈemprəs/ noun [C] the female ruler, or the wife of a male ruler, of an empire (= group of countries ruled by one person or government) *Empress Josephine*

○╼**empty**[1] /ˈempti/ adj 1 If something is empty, it does not contain any things or people. *an empty house/street* • *empty bottles/glasses* • *The train was completely empty when it reached London.* ➔ See picture at **full**. 2 having no meaning or value *an empty promise/threat* • **emptiness** noun [U]

**empty**[2] /ˈempti/ verb 1 [T] (also **empty out**) If you empty a container, or if you empty the things inside it, you remove everything from it. *Where can I empty this ashtray?* • *He emptied the dirty water into the sink.* 2 [I] to become empty *The room emptied rapidly when the fire started.*

**empty-handed** /ˌemptiˈhændɪd/ adj without bringing or taking anything *We can't go to the party empty-handed.*

**emulate** /ˈemjəleɪt/ verb [T] formal to try to be like someone or something that you admire or that is successful *They hope to emulate the success of other software companies.*

**emulsion** /ɪˈmʌlʃ°n/ noun [U] paint used to cover walls, ceilings, etc

○╼**enable** /ɪˈneɪbl/ verb [T] to make someone able to do something, or to make something possible [+ to do sth] *This money has enabled me to buy a new computer.*

**enact** /ɪˈnækt/ verb [T] 1 to make something into a law [often passive] *When was this legislation* *enacted?* **2** *formal* to perform a story or play • **enactment** *noun* [U]

**enamel** /ɪˈnæməl/ *noun* [U] **1** a hard, shiny substance that is used to decorate or protect metal or clay **2** the hard, white substance that covers your teeth

**enamoured** *UK formal* (*US* **enamored**) /ɪˈnæməd/ *adj* **be enamoured of/with sb/sth** to like someone or something very much

**enc** (*also* **encl**) *abbreviation for* enclosed: used at the end of a business letter to show that there is something else in the envelope

**encapsulate** /ɪnˈkæpsjəleɪt/ *verb* [T] to express or show the most important facts about something *The film encapsulates the essence of that period.*

**encase** /ɪnˈkeɪs/ *verb formal* **be encased in sth** to be completely covered in something *The outside walls are encased in concrete.*

**enchanted** /ɪnˈtʃɑːntɪd/ *adj* **1** If you are enchanted by something, you like it very much. *She was enchanted by the Scottish landscape.* **2** affected by magic *an enchanted forest*

**enchanting** /ɪnˈtʃɑːntɪŋ/ *adj* very nice *What an enchanting child!*

**encircle** /ɪnˈsɜːkl/ *verb* [T] *formal* to form a circle around something [often passive] *The house is encircled by a high fence.*

**enclave** /ˈenkleɪv/ *noun* [C] a place which is different from the area that is around it because its people have a different language or culture *an Italian enclave in Switzerland*

**enclose** /ɪnˈkləʊz/ *verb* [T] **1** to send something in the same envelope or parcel as something else *I enclose a map of the area.* **2** to be all around something and separate it from other things or places • **enclosed** *adj He doesn't like enclosed spaces.*

**enclosure** /ɪnˈkləʊʒəʳ/ *noun* [C] a small area of land that has a wall or fence around it

**encompass** /ɪnˈkʌmpəs/ *verb* [T] to include a lot of things, ideas, places, etc *Their albums encompass a wide range of music.*

**encore** /ˈɒŋkɔːʳ/ *noun* [C] an extra song or piece of music that is performed at the end of a show because the audience shout for it *She could hear the crowd screaming for an encore.*

**encounter**[1] /ɪnˈkaʊntəʳ/ *verb* [T] **1** to experience something unpleasant *We encountered quite a few problems at the beginning.* **2** *literary* to meet someone, especially when you do not expect it

**encounter**[2] /ɪnˈkaʊntəʳ/ *noun* [C] a meeting, especially one that happens by chance

o━**encourage** /ɪnˈkʌrɪdʒ/ *verb* [T] **1** to make someone more likely to do something, or make something more likely to happen [+ **to do sth**] *My parents encouraged me to try new things.* • *Cutting back plants will encourage growth.* **2** to give someone confidence or hope • *My parents encouraged me when things weren't going well at school.* ⊃ *Opposite* **discourage**. • **encouragement** *noun* [C, U] *Children need lots of encouragement from their parents.*

**encouraged** /ɪnˈkʌrɪdʒd/ *adj* having more confidence or hope about something *We were very encouraged by his exam results.*

**encouraging** /ɪnˈkʌrɪdʒɪŋ/ *adj* making you feel more hope and confidence *The team's performance was very encouraging.* ⊃ *Opposite* **discouraging**. • **encouragingly** *adv*

**encroach** /ɪnˈkrəʊtʃ/ *verb*

**encroach on/upon sth** to gradually take away someone's rights, power, etc, or get control of something, often without being noticed *Our cat will not let another cat encroach on her territory.* • *My job is starting to encroach on my family life.*

**encrusted** /ɪnˈkrʌstɪd/ *adj* covered with something hard, for example dirt or stones *My trousers were encrusted with mud.*

**encyclopedia** (*also* UK **encyclopaedia**) /ɪnˌsaɪkləˈpiːdiə/ *noun* [C] a book or a set of books containing facts about a lot of subjects

o━**end**[1] /end/ *noun* **1** [FINAL PART] [no plural] the final part of something such as a period of time, activity, or story *I'll pay you at the end of next month.* • *I didn't meet him until the end of the course.* • *a film with a twist at the end* **2** [FURTHEST PART] [C] the furthest part or final part of a place or thing *They live at the other end of the street.* • *They were standing at opposite ends of the room.* **3** [STOP] [C] when something stops happening [usually singular] *They are calling for **an end to** the violence.* **4 in the end** finally, after something has been thought about or discussed a lot *We thought we might go abroad for Christmas, but in the end we stayed at home.* **5 come to an end** to finish **6 put an end to sth** to make something stop happening or existing *He's determined to put an end to these rumours.* **7 bring sth to an end** to make something finish *The stories in the newspaper brought her career to a sudden end.* **8 no end** *informal* a lot *I've had **no end of** trouble finding a hotel room.* **9 for hours/days, etc on end** for days, hours, etc without stopping *He waited by the telephone for hours on end.* **10** [INTENTION] [C] an intention or purpose *She only has one end in mind.* **11 be at a loose end** to have nothing to do *Come and visit us if you're at a loose end over the weekend.* **12 at the end of the day** *UK* something that you say before you give the most important fact of a situation *At the end of the day, what matters is that you're safe.* **13 at the end of your tether** (*also US* **at the end of your rope**) so tired, annoyed, or worried by something that you do not feel that you can deal with it **14 get (hold of) the wrong end of the stick** to not understand a situation correctly *My mum got the wrong end of the stick and thought that Jim was my boyfriend.* **15 make ends meet** to have just enough money to pay for the things that you need *I've taken a second job in the evenings just to make ends meet.* **16 not be the end of the world** If something is not the end of the world, it will not cause very serious problems. *It won't be the end of the world if I don't get the job.* **17 be on/at the receiving end of sth** If you are on the receiving end of something, you suffer something unpleasant when you have done nothing to deserve it. *They are often on the receiving end of verbal abuse from angry customers.* **18 throw sb in at the deep end** to make someone start a new and difficult job or activity without helping them or preparing them for it ⮞ *See also:* **the West End, dead end, light¹** at the end of the tunnel, **odds** and ends, the **tail¹** end of sth, be at your **wits'** end.

o-¤**end²** /end/ *verb* [I, T] to finish or stop, or to make something finish or stop *What time does the concert end?* • *These talks do not look likely to end the war.*

**end in/with sth** to finish in a particular way *The evening ended in a big argument.*

**end up** to finally be in a particular place or situation *I never thought he'd end up in prison.* • [+ doing sth] *He always ends up doing what Alan wants to do.* • *She'll end up pregnant.*

**endanger** /ɪn'deɪndʒəʳ/ *verb* [T] to put someone or something in a situation where they might be harmed or seriously damaged *He would never do anything to endanger the children's lives.*

**endangered** /ɪn'deɪndʒəd/ *adj* **endangered birds/plants/species, etc** animals or plants which may soon not exist because there are very few now alive

**endear** /ɪn'dɪəʳ/ *verb*
**endear sb to sb** If a quality in someone's character, or their behaviour endears them to you, it makes you like them.

**endearing** /ɪn'dɪərɪŋ/ *adj* An endearing quality is one that makes people like you.

**endeavour** *UK formal* (*US* **endeavor**) /ɪn'devəʳ/ *verb* **endeavour to do sth** to try very hard to do something *I endeavoured to help her, but she wouldn't let me.* • **endeavour** *noun* [C, U] *human/ artistic endeavour*

**endemic** /en'demɪk/ *adj formal* If something unpleasant is endemic in a place or among a group of people, there is a lot of it there. *Corruption is endemic in some parts of the police force.*

**ending** /'endɪŋ/ *noun* [C] **1** the last part of a story *I hope this film has a happy ending.* **2** the part added to the end of a word *To make the plural of 'dog', you add the plural ending '-s'.*

**endive** /'endaɪv/ *noun* [C, U] a plant with bitter green leaves that are eaten in salads

**endless** /'endləs/ *adj* continuing for a long time and never finishing, or never seeming to finish *He seems to think that I have an endless supply of money.* • **endlessly** *adv*

**endorse** /ɪn'dɔːs/ *verb* [T] *formal* to say publicly that you support a person or action [often passive] *The idea was endorsed by a majority of members.* • **endorsement** *noun* [C, U]

**endow** /ɪn'daʊ/ *verb formal* **1 be endowed with sth** to have a particular quality or characteristic *The country is richly endowed with natural resources.* **2** [T] to give a large amount of money to a college, hospital, etc

**end-product** /'end,prɒdʌkt/ *noun* [C] the thing that you get at the end of a process or activity

**endurance** /ɪn'djʊərᵊns/ *noun* [U] the ability to keep doing something difficult, unpleasant, or painful for a long time *a race to test athletes' endurance*

**endure** /ɪn'djʊəʳ/ *verb* [T] *formal* to suffer something difficult, unpleasant, or painful *She's already had to endure three painful operations on her leg.*

**enduring** /ɪn'djʊərɪŋ/ *adj* existing for a long time *the enduring popularity of cartoons*

o-¤**enemy** /'enəmi/ *noun* **1** [C] a person who you dislike or oppose *I try not to make any enemies.* **2** [group] a country or army that your country or army is fighting against in a war *enemy forces/territory*

**energetic** /,enə'dʒetɪk/ *adj* having or involving a lot of energy *an energetic young woman* • *Aerobics is too energetic for me.* • **energetically** *adv*

o-¤**energy** /'enədʒi/ *noun* [C, U] **1** the power and ability to be very active without becoming tired *Looking after children takes up a lot of time and energy.* • [+ to do sth] *I didn't even have the energy to get out of bed.* **2** the power that comes from electricity, gas, etc *nuclear energy* • *energy conservation* ⮞ *See also:* **atomic energy**.

**enforce** /ɪn'fɔːs/ *verb* [T] **1** to make people obey a rule or law *It is the duty of the police to enforce the law.* **2** to make a particular situation happen, or to make people accept it *The new teacher failed to enforce discipline.* • **enforcement** *noun* [U] *law enforcement*

**engage** /ɪn'geɪdʒ/ *verb* [T] *formal* **1** to interest someone in something and keep them thinking about it *The debate about food safety has engaged the whole nation.* **2** to employ someone [+ to do sth] *I have engaged a secretary to deal with all my paperwork.*

**engage in sth** to take part in something

**engage sb in sth** If you engage someone in conversation, you start a conversation with them.

**engaged** /ɪn'geɪdʒd/ *adj* **1** If two people are engaged, they have formally agreed to marry each other. *When did they get engaged?* **2** *UK* If a telephone line or a toilet is engaged, it is already being used.

**engagement** /ɪn'geɪdʒmənt/ *noun* [C] **1** an agreement to get married to someone *an engagement ring* **2** an arrangement to meet someone or do something at a particular time

**engaging** /ɪn'geɪdʒɪŋ/ *adj* pleasant, interesting, or attractive *She has a very engaging personality.*

**engender** /ɪn'dʒendəʳ/ *verb* [T] *formal* to make people have a particular feeling or make a situation start to exist *We want to engender loyalty to our products.*

o-¤**engine** /'endʒɪn/ *noun* [C] **1** the part of a vehicle that uses energy from oil, electricity, or steam to make it move *a diesel/petrol engine* • *Please turn your engine off while waiting in the queue.* **2** the part of a train that pulls it along ⮞ *See also:* **fire engine, search engine**.

**'engine ,driver** *UK* (*US* **engineer**) *noun* [C] someone whose job is to drive a train

**engineer¹** /,endʒɪ'nɪəʳ/ *noun* [C] **1** someone whose job is to design, build, or repair machines, engines, roads, bridges, etc *a mechanical/structural engineer* • *a software engineer* **2** *US* someone whose job is to drive a train

**engineer²** /,endʒɪ'nɪəʳ/ *verb* [T] to arrange for something to happen, especially in a clever and secret way [often passive] *She was convinced that the accident had been engineered by his enemies.*

---

**engineering** /ˌendʒɪˈnɪərɪŋ/ *noun* [U] the work of an engineer, or the study of this work *She studied engineering at the University of Michigan.* ● *mechanical engineering* ➲ *See also:* **civil engineering**, **genetic engineering**.

**English¹** /ˈɪŋglɪʃ/ *noun* **1** [U] the language that is spoken in the UK, the US, and in many other countries *American/British English* ● *Do you speak English?* **2 the English** [plural] the people of England

**English²** /ˈɪŋglɪʃ/ *adj* **1** relating to the English language *an English teacher* **2** relating to England *English law*

ˌEnglish ˈbreakfast *noun* [C] *UK* a dish including cooked meat and eggs, eaten as the first meal of the day

ˌEnglish ˈmuffin *US* (*UK* muffin) *noun* [C] a small, round, flat bread that is often eaten hot with butter ➲ *See picture at* **muffin**.

**engrave** /ɪnˈgreɪv/ *verb* [T] to cut words or pictures into the surface of metal, stone, etc *He gave her a silver pen engraved with her name.* ● **engraver** *noun* [C]

**engraving** /ɪnˈgreɪvɪŋ/ *noun* [C] a picture printed from an engraved piece of metal or wood

**engrossed** /ɪnˈgrəʊst/ *adj* giving all your attention to something *He was so engrossed in what he was doing that he didn't hear the bell.*

**engrossing** /ɪnˈgrəʊsɪŋ/ *adj* very interesting, and needing all your attention *an engrossing book*

**engulf** /ɪnˈgʌlf/ *verb* [T] **1** to surround or cover someone or something completely [often passive] *The house was quickly engulfed in flames.* **2** to affect a place or a group of people quickly and strongly *Panic is threatening to engulf the country.*

**enhance** /ɪnˈhɑːns/ *verb* [T] *formal* to improve something *Winning that award greatly enhanced her reputation.* ● **enhancement** *noun* [C, U] when something is improved

**enigma** /ɪˈnɪgmə/ *noun* [C] someone or something that is mysterious and difficult to understand *She is a complete enigma to me.*

**enigmatic** /ˌenɪgˈmætɪk/ *adj* mysterious and impossible to understand completely

O─**enjoy** /ɪnˈdʒɔɪ/ *verb* [T] **1** If you enjoy something, it gives you pleasure. *I hope you enjoy your meal.* ● [+ doing sth] *I really enjoyed being with him.* **2 enjoy yourself** to get pleasure from something that you are doing *Everyone eventually relaxed and began to enjoy themselves.* **3** *formal* to have or experience something good such as success *His play enjoyed great success on Broadway.*

USAGE

**enjoy doing** something

When **enjoy** is followed by a verb, the verb must be in the -ing form.

*My parents enjoy walking in the mountains.*

~~My parents enjoy to walk in the mountains.~~

**enjoyable** /ɪnˈdʒɔɪəbl/ *adj* An enjoyable event or experience gives you pleasure. *We had a very enjoyable evening.*

**enjoyment** /ɪnˈdʒɔɪmənt/ *noun* [U] when you enjoy something *She gets a lot of enjoyment from music.*

**enlarge** /ɪnˈlɑːdʒ/ *verb* [I, T] to become bigger or to make something become bigger [often passive] *I want to get this photo enlarged.* ● *an enlarged liver*

**enlarge on/upon sth** *formal* to give more details about something that you have said or written

**enlargement** /ɪnˈlɑːdʒmənt/ *noun* [C, U] when something is enlarged, or something that has been enlarged *I'm going to get an enlargement of this wedding photo.*

**enlighten** /ɪnˈlaɪtⁿn/ *verb* [T] *formal* to give someone information about something, so that they understand a situation *He believes he has a duty to enlighten the public on these matters.*

**enlightened** /ɪnˈlaɪtⁿnd/ *adj* having practical, modern ideas and ways of dealing with things *an enlightened attitude*

**enlightening** /ɪnˈlaɪtⁿnɪŋ/ *adj* giving you more information and understanding about something *an enlightening book*

**enlist** /ɪnˈlɪst/ *verb* **1 enlist the help/support of sb** to ask for and get help or support from someone *They are hoping to enlist the support of local politicians.* **2** [I] to join the army, navy, etc

**enliven** /ɪnˈlaɪvⁿn/ *verb* [T] to make something more interesting *The children's arrival enlivened a boring evening.*

**en masse** /ɒnˈmæs/ *adv* If a group of people do something en masse, they do it together as a group. *They surrendered en masse.*

**enmity** /ˈenmɪti/ *noun* [U] *formal* a strong feeling of hate

**enormity** /ɪˈnɔːməti/ *noun* **the enormity of sth** how big or important something is *He hadn't realized the enormity of the problem.*

O─**enormous** /ɪˈnɔːməs/ *adj* extremely large *This living room is enormous.* ● *They spent an enormous amount of money on the project.* ● **enormously** *adv* extremely or very much *The show was enormously popular.*

O─**enough¹** /ɪˈnʌf/ *pronoun, quantifier* **1** as much as is necessary *They had enough fuel for one week.* ● [+ to do sth] *Have you had enough to eat?* **2** as much as or more than you want *I've got enough work at the moment, without being given any more.* **3 have had enough** to want something to stop because it is annoying you *I've had enough of your excuses.* **4 that's enough** used to tell someone to stop behaving badly

O─**enough²** /ɪˈnʌf/ *adv* **1** as much as is necessary [+ to do sth] *Are you old enough to vote?* ● *You're not going fast enough.* **2** slightly, but not very *He's nice enough, but I don't really want to go out with him.* **3 funnily/oddly/strangely enough** although it may seem strange *I was dreading the party, but I really enjoyed it, funnily enough.*

**enquire** *UK* (*UK/US* inquire) /ɪnˈkwaɪəʳ/ *verb* [I, T] to ask someone for information about something *"Are you staying long?" she enquired.* ● *I'm enquiring about dentists in the area.* ● **enquirer** *UK* (*UK/US* inquirer) *noun* [C] **enquire after sb** *UK formal* to ask someone for information about someone else's health and what they are doing, in order to be polite

**enquire into sth** *formal* to try to discover the facts about something

**enquiring** *UK* (*UK/US* **inquiring**) /ɪn'kwaɪərɪŋ/ *adj* [always before noun] **1** always wanting to learn new things *an enquiring mind* **2** an enquiring expression on your face shows that you want to know something.

**enquiry** *UK* (*UK/US* **inquiry**) /ɪn'kwaɪəri/ *noun* **1** QUESTION [C] *formal* a question that you ask when you want more information *We receive a lot of enquiries about tax issues.* **2** OFFICIAL PROCESS [C] an official process to discover the facts about something bad that has happened *The hospital is holding an enquiry into the accident.* **3** ASKING QUESTIONS [U] *formal* the process of asking questions in order to get information

**enrage** /ɪn'reɪdʒ/ *verb* [T] to make someone very angry [often passive] *Farmers are enraged by the government's refusal to help.*

**enrich** /ɪn'rɪtʃ/ *verb* [T] to improve the quality of something by adding something to it [often passive] *Our culture has been enriched by the many immigrants who live here.* • **enrichment** *noun* [U]

**enrol** *UK* (*US* **enroll**) /ɪn'rəʊl/ *verb* [I, T] **enrolling**, *past* **enrolled** to become or make someone become an official member of a course, college, or group *I've (UK) enrolled on/(US) enrolled in a creative writing course.* • **enrolment** *UK* (*US* **enrollment**) *noun* [C, U]

**en route** /ˌɒn'ruːt/ *adv* on the way to or from somewhere *We stopped in Monaco en route to Switzerland.*

**ensemble** /ɒn'sɒmbᵊl/ *noun* [C] a small group of musicians or actors who regularly play or perform together

**enshrined** /ɪn'ʃraɪnd/ *verb formal* **be enshrined in sth** If a political or social right is enshrined in something, it is protected by being included in it. *These fundamental human rights are enshrined in the constitution.*

**enslave** /ɪn'sleɪv/ *verb* [T] *formal* to control someone and keep them in a bad situation [often passive] *These workers are enslaved by poverty.*

**ensue** /ɪn'sjuː/ *verb* [I] **ensuing**, *past* **ensued** *formal* to happen after something, often as a result of it • **ensuing** *adj* [always before noun] *the ensuing hours/months*

**en suite** /ˌɒn'swiːt/ *adj UK* An en suite bathroom is directly connected to a bedroom.

**ensure** /ɪn'ʃɔːr/ *verb* [T] *formal* to make certain that something is done or happens [+ (that)] *Please ensure that all examination papers have your name at the top.*

**entail** /ɪn'teɪl/ *verb* [T] to involve something *What exactly does the job entail?*

**entangled** /ɪn'tæŋgld/ *adj* **1** involved with someone or something so that it is difficult to escape *I don't know how I ever got entangled in this relationship.* **2** caught in something such as a net or ropes *The dolphin had become entangled in the fishing net.*

◐⁺**enter** /'entər/ *verb* **1** PLACE [I, T] to come or go into a place *The police entered by the back door.*

• *She is accused of entering the country illegally.* **2** INFORMATION [T] to put information into a computer, book, or document *You have to enter a password to access this information.* **3** COMPETITION [I, T] to take part in a competition, race, or exam, or to arrange for someone else to do this *Are you going to enter the photography competition?* **4** ORGANIZATION [T] to become a member of a particular organization, or start working in a particular type of job *She didn't enter the legal profession until she was 40.* **5** PERIOD OF TIME [T] to begin a period of time *The violence is now entering its third week.*

---

**USAGE**

**enter** a place

You do not need to use a preposition after **enter**.

*I entered the classroom.*

~~I entered in the classroom.~~

Be careful not to use 'enter' with vehicles.

*The children got on the bus.*

~~The children entered the bus.~~

---

**enter into sth** to start to become involved in something, especially a discussion or agreement

**enterprise** /'entəpraɪz/ *noun* **1** BUSINESS [C] a business or organization *a state-owned enterprise* **2** PLAN [C] a difficult and important plan *Putting on the concert will be a joint enterprise between the two schools.* **3** QUALITY [U] when someone is enthusiastic and willing to do something new and clever, although there are risks involved *The scheme shows imagination and enterprise.* ➔ *See also:* **free enterprise**.

**enterprising** /'entəpraɪzɪŋ/ *adj* enthusiastic and willing to do something new, clever, and difficult *The film was made by an enterprising group of students.*

**entertain** /ˌentə'teɪn/ *verb* **1** INTEREST [T] to keep someone interested and help them to have an enjoyable time *We hired a clown to entertain the children.* **2** GUEST [I, T] to invite someone to be your guest and give them food, drink, etc *We don't entertain as much as we used to.* **3** THINK ABOUT [T] *formal* to consider or be willing to accept an idea or suggestion *He had never even entertained the idea of her returning.*

**entertainer** /ˌentə'teɪnər/ *noun* [C] someone whose job is to entertain people by singing, telling jokes, etc

**entertaining** /ˌentə'teɪnɪŋ/ *adj* interesting and helping someone to have an enjoyable time *an entertaining and informative book*

◐⁺**entertainment** /ˌentə'teɪnmənt/ *noun* [C, U] shows, films, television, or other performances or activities that entertain people *popular entertainment* • *There is live entertainment in the bar every night.*

**enthral** *UK* (*US* **enthrall**) /ɪn'θrɔːl/ *verb* [T] **enthralling**, *past* **enthralled** to keep someone's interest and attention completely [often passive] *The children were enthralled by the circus.*

• **enthralling** *adj* keeping someone's interest and attention completely

**enthuse** /ɪn'θjuːz/ *verb* [I] to express excitement about something or great interest in it *She couldn't stop enthusing about the film.*

**enthusiasm** /ɪn'θjuːziæzᵊm/ *noun* [U] when you feel very interested in something and would very much like to be involved in it *She has always had a lot of **enthusiasm for** her work.*

**enthusiast** /ɪn'θjuːziæst/ *noun* [C] someone who is very interested in and involved with a particular activity or subject *a sports enthusiast*

○⟶**enthusiastic** /ɪn,θjuːzi'æstɪk/ *adj* showing enthusiasm *enthusiastic support* • *The teacher was very **enthusiastic about** my project.* • **enthusiastically** *adv*

**entice** /ɪn'taɪs/ *verb* [T] to persuade someone to do something by offering them something pleasant [+ to do sth] *Supermarkets use all sorts of tricks to entice you to buy things.* • **enticing** *adj* Something which is enticing attracts you by offering you something pleasant.

**entire** /ɪn'taɪᵊr/ *adj* [always before noun] whole or complete *She spent her entire life caring for other people.*

**entirely** /ɪn'taɪəli/ *adv* completely *I'm not entirely convinced that it will work.*

**entirety** /ɪn'taɪərəti/ *noun* **in its entirety** with all parts included *This is the first time that the book has been published in its entirety.*

**entitle** /ɪn'taɪtl/ *verb* **1 entitle sb to (do) sth** to give someone the right to do or have something [often passive] *I'm entitled to apply for citizenship.* • *These vouchers entitle you to claim a free meal.* **2** [T] to give something a particular title *a lecture entitled "Language, Learning and Literacy"*

**entitlement** /ɪn'taɪtlmənt/ *noun* [C, U] when you have the right to do or have something

**entity** /'entɪti/ *noun* [C] something which exists apart from other things *They want the area recognized as a separate political entity.*

**entourage** /'ɒntʊrɑːʒ ⒰⒮ ɒntʊ'rɑːʒ/ *noun* [group] the group of people who travel with an important or famous person *She arrived with her usual entourage of dancers and musicians.*

○⟶**entrance** /'entrəns/ *noun* **1** [DOOR] [C] a door or other opening which you use to enter a building or place *They must have used the back **entrance to** the building.* • *I'll meet you **at the** main **entrance**.* **2** [COMING IN] [C] when someone comes into or goes into a place, especially in a way that makes people notice them *The whole room went quiet when he **made his entrance**.* **3** [RIGHT] [U] the right to enter a place or to join an organization, college, etc *Entrance is free, but you have to pay for your drinks.* • *an entrance examination*

**entranced** /ɪn'trɑːnst/ *adj* If you are entranced by someone or something, you cannot stop watching them because they are very interesting or very beautiful. *The children were entranced by the puppet show.*

**entrant** /'entrənt/ *noun* [C] someone who enters a competition, organization, or examination

**entreat** /ɪn'triːt/ *verb* [T] *formal* to try very hard to persuade someone to do something

**entrenched** /ɪn'trenʃt/ *adj* Entrenched ideas are so fixed or have existed for so long that they cannot be changed. *These attitudes are firmly entrenched in our culture.*

**entrepreneur** /,ɒntrəprə'nɜːʳ/ *noun* [C] someone who starts their own business, especially when this involves risks • **entrepreneurial** *adj*

**entrust** /ɪn'trʌst/ *verb* [T] to make someone responsible for doing something or looking after something [often passive] *I was entrusted **with** the task of organizing the party.*

○⟶**entry** /'entri/ *noun* **1** [COMING IN] [U] when you come into or go into a place *She was refused entry to the US.* • *Police gained entry by breaking a window.* **2** [JOINING/TAKING PART] [U] when you join an organization or take part in a competition *Are there lots of exams for **entry into** the legal profession?* • *an entry form* **3** [COMPETITION WORK] [C] a piece of work that you do to try to win a competition *The first ten correct entries will receive a prize.* **4** [PIECE OF INFORMATION] [C] one of the pieces of information or writing that is recorded in a book such as a dictionary, or in a computer system *a diary entry* **5** [ADDING INFORMATION] [U] when someone puts information into something such as a computer system *data entry*

**entwined** /ɪn'twaɪnd/ *adj* **1** twisted together or twisted around something *Their arms were entwined.* **2** unable to be separated *My fate is entwined with his.*

**enumerate** /ɪ'njuːmᵊreɪt/ *verb* [T] *formal* to name each thing on a list

**envelop** /ɪn'veləp/ *verb* [T] to completely cover something [often passive] *The farm was enveloped in fog.*

**envelope** /'envələʊp/ *noun* [C] a flat paper container for a letter ⊃ *See colour picture* **The Office** *on page Centre 12.*

**enviable** /'enviəbl/ *adj* If someone is in an enviable situation, you wish that you were also in that situation. *She's in the enviable position of being able to choose who she works for.*

**envious** /'enviəs/ *adj* wishing that you had what someone else has *She was **envious of** his successful career.* • **enviously** *adv*

○⟶**environment** /ɪn'vaɪᵊrᵊnmənt/ *noun* **1 the environment** the air, land, and water where people, animals, and plants live *The new road may cause damage to the environment.* ⊃ *See usage note at* **nature**. **2** [C] the situation that you live or work in, and how it influences how you feel *We are working in a very competitive environment.*

**environmental** /ɪn,vaɪᵊrᵊn'mentᵊl/ *adj* relating to the environment *environmental damage* • **environmentally** *adv environmentally damaging chemicals*

**environmentalist** /ɪn,vaɪᵊrᵊn'mentᵊlɪst/ *noun* [C] someone who tries to protect the natural environment from being damaged

**en,vironmentally 'friendly** *adj* not damaging the environment *environmentally-friendly washing powder* • *We only use products that are environmentally friendly.*

**envisage** /ɪn'vɪzɪdʒ/ *mainly UK* (*mainly US* **envision** /ɪn'vɪʒᵊn/) *verb* [T] to imagine something happening, or think that something is likely to happen *The police don't envisage any trouble at the festival.*

**envoy** /'envɔɪ/ *noun* [C] someone who is sent to represent their government in another country

**envy**[1] /'envi/ *noun* **1** [U] the feeling that you wish you had something that someone else has *I watched with envy as he climbed into his brand new sports car.* **2 be the envy of sb** to be liked and wanted by someone *Her new office was the envy of the whole company.*

**envy**[2] /'envi/ *verb* [T] to wish that you had something that someone else has *I envy her good looks.* • [+ two objects] *I don't envy him that job.*

**enzyme** /'enzaɪm/ *noun* [C] a chemical substance produced by living cells which makes particular chemical reactions happen in animals and plants

**ephemeral** /ɪ'femᵊrᵊl/ *adj* lasting for only a short time

**epic** /'epɪk/ *noun* [C] a story or film which is very long and contains a lot of action • **epic** *adj an epic journey*

**epidemic** /,epɪ'demɪk/ *noun* [C] when a large number of people get the same disease over the same period of time *the AIDS epidemic*

**epilepsy** /'epɪlepsi/ *noun* [U] a brain disease which can make someone become unconscious and have fits (= when you shake in an uncontrolled way)

**epileptic** /,epɪ'leptɪk/ *noun* [C] someone who suffers from epilepsy • **epileptic** *adj*

**epilogue** /'epɪlɒg/ *noun* [C] a speech or piece of writing that is added to the end of a play or book

**epiphany** /ɪ'pɪfᵊni/ *noun* [U] *literary* a moment when you suddenly understand or become aware of something

**episode** /'epɪsəʊd/ *noun* [C] **1** one programme of a series shown on television *Did you see last week's episode of The X-Files?* **2** a single event or period of time *an important episode in British history*

**epitaph** /'epɪtɑːf/ *noun* [C] words that are written to remember a dead person, usually on the stone where they are buried

**epitome** /ɪ'pɪtᵊmi/ *noun* **be the epitome of sth** to be a perfect example of a quality or type of thing *The hotel was the epitome of luxury.*

**epitomize** (*also UK* -**ise**) /ɪ'pɪtᵊmaɪz/ *verb* [T] to be a perfect example of a quality or type of thing *She epitomizes elegance and good taste.*

**epoch** /'iːpɒk/ ⓤⓢ /'epək/ *noun* [C] *plural* **epochs** a long period of time in history

**eponymous** /ɪ'pɒnɪməs/ *adj* [always before noun] *literary* An eponymous character in a play, book, etc, has the same name as the title. *He played the eponymous hero in the movie Rob Roy.*

o⤴**equal**[1] /'iːkwəl/ *adj* **1** the same in amount, number, or size *The sides are of equal length.* • *One metre is equal to 39.37 inches.* **2 equal opportunities/rights,** etc opportunities/ rights, etc that are the same for everyone without anyone having an unfair advantage ➌ *Opposite* **unequal**.

**equal**[2] /'iːkwəl/ *verb* [T] (*UK*) **equalling**, *past*

**equalled,** (*US*) **equaling,** *past* **equaled 1** to have the same value, size, etc as something else, often shown using a symbol (=) *Two plus two equals four.* **2** to be as good as someone or something else *She equalled her own world record in the race.*

**equal**[3] /'iːkwəl/ *noun* [C] someone who has the same ability, opportunities, or rights as someone else *The teacher treats us all as equals.*

**equality** /ɪ'kwɒləti/ *noun* [U] when everyone is equal and has the same opportunities, rights, etc *racial/sexual equality* • *equality between men and women* ➌ *Opposite* **inequality**.

**equalize** (*also UK* -**ise**) /'iːkwᵊlaɪz/ *verb* **1** [I] *UK* to get the point in a game or competition that makes your score the same as the other team or player *Liverpool equalized just before half time.* **2** [T] to make things or people equal

o⤴**equally** /'iːkwəli/ *adv* **1** [SAME DEGREE] to the same degree or level *an equally important question* • *She did equally well in the competition last year.* **2** [SAME AMOUNTS] into amounts or parts that are the same size *She shared the money equally between the four children.* **3** [SAME WAY] If you treat people equally, you treat everyone in the same way so that no one has an unfair advantage.

'**equal ,sign** (*also* '**equals ,sign**) *noun* [C] the symbol =, used to show that two things are the same in value, size, meaning, etc

**equanimity** /,ekwə'nɪməti/ *noun* [U] *formal* the ability to react calmly, especially in difficult situations

**equate** /ɪ'kweɪt/ *verb* [T] to consider one thing to be the same as or equal to another thing *Many people equate wealth with happiness.*

**equation** /ɪ'kweɪʒᵊn/ *noun* [C] when you show that two amounts are equal using mathematical symbols

**equator** /ɪ'kweɪtəʳ/ *noun* [U] the imaginary line around the Earth that divides it into equal north and south parts • **equatorial** /,ekwə'tɔːriəl/ *adj* relating to the equator

**equestrian** /ɪ'kwestriən/ *adj* relating to riding horses

**equip** /ɪ'kwɪp/ *verb* **equipping,** *past* **equipped 1 be equipped with sth** to include the things that are needed for a particular purpose *The new trains are equipped with all the latest technology.* **2** [T] to give someone the skills they need to do a particular thing [+ to do sth] *The course didn't really equip me to be a journalist.*

o⤴**equipment** /ɪ'kwɪpmənt/ *noun* **1** [U] the things that are used for a particular activity or purpose *kitchen/office equipment* • *electrical equipment* (= equipment that uses electricity) **2 a piece of equipment** a tool or object used for a particular activity or purpose

**equitable** /'ekwɪtəbl/ *adj formal* treating everyone in an equal way *a fair and equitable voting system* • **equitably** *adv*

**equity** /'ekwɪti/ *noun* [U] *formal* when everyone is treated fairly and equally *pay equity* ➌ *Compare* **inequity**.

**equivalent**[1] /ɪ'kwɪvᵊlənt/ *adj* equal in amount, value, importance, or meaning *The UK's Brit Awards are roughly equivalent to the Oscars.*

**equivalent**[2] /ɪ'kwɪvᵊlənt/ *noun* [C] something

that has the same value, importance, size, or meaning as something else *She won **the equivalent of** $5 million.*

**er** /ɜːʳ/ *exclamation UK spoken (US **uh**)* something that you say while you are thinking what to say next *Well, er, I'm not too sure about that.*

**ER** /ˌiːˈɑːʳ/ *noun* [C] *US abbreviation for* emergency room: the part of a hospital where people go when they have been injured or have urgent illnesses so that they can be treated immediately

**era** /ˈɪərə/ *noun* [C] a period of time in history that is special for a particular reason *the Victorian era* ● *a new era of peace*

**eradicate** /ɪˈrædɪkeɪt/ *verb* [T] *formal* to destroy or completely get rid of something such as a social problem or a disease ● **eradication** /ɪˌrædɪˈkeɪʃᵊn/ *noun* [U]

**erase** /ɪˈreɪz ⓊⓈ ɪˈreɪs/ *verb* [T] to completely remove words, music, pictures, etc that were written or stored on a computer or other piece of equipment *I accidentally erased the tape she lent me.*

**eraser** /ɪˈreɪzəʳ ⓊⓈ ɪˈreɪsər/ *US (UK **rubber**) noun* [C] **1** a small object which is used to remove pencil marks from paper **2** an object which is used to remove marks from a blackboard (= a large dark board that teachers write on) ➤ *See colour picture **Classroom** on page Centre 4.*

**erect¹** /ɪˈrekt/ *adj* straight and standing up *She stood very erect, with her hands behind her back.*

**erect²** /ɪˈrekt/ *verb* [T] *formal* to build or put up a structure *When was this building erected?* ● *The police erected barriers across the road.*

**erection** /ɪˈrekʃᵊn/ *noun* **1** [C] when a penis becomes harder and bigger than usual **2** [C, U] *formal* when a structure is built or put up, or the building itself

**erode** /ɪˈrəʊd/ *verb* **1** [I, T] If soil, stone, etc erodes or is eroded, it is gradually damaged and removed by the sea, rain, or wind. [often passive] *The coastline is slowly being eroded by the sea.* **2** [T] *formal* to gradually destroy a good quality or situation *Reports of corruption have eroded people's confidence in the police.* ● **erosion** /ɪˈrəʊʒᵊn/ *noun* [U] *soil erosion*

**erotic** /ɪˈrɒtɪk/ *adj* making you feel strong sexual feelings, or involving sexual love *an erotic film* ● **erotically** *adv*

**err** /ɜːʳ/ *verb* [I] *formal* to make a mistake or do something that is wrong ➤ *See also:* err on the **side¹** of caution.

**errand** /ˈerənd/ *noun* [C] a short journey in order to buy or do something for someone *I've got to **run** a few **errands** this morning before we go.*

**errant** /ˈerənt/ *adj* [always before noun] An errant person has behaved badly. *an errant husband*

**erratic** /ɪˈrætɪk/ *adj* often changing suddenly and not regular *His behaviour is becoming more and more erratic.* ● **erratically** *adv*

**erroneous** /ɪˈrəʊniəs/ *adj formal* not correct *an erroneous answer*

o━**error** /ˈerəʳ/ *noun* [C, U] a mistake, especially one that can cause problems *a computer error/ human error* ● *to make an error* ● *The documents were destroyed **in error** (= by mistake) by the police.*

**erupt** /ɪˈrʌpt/ *verb* [I] **1** VOLCANO If a volcano erupts, it suddenly throws out smoke, fire, and melted rocks. **2** HAPPEN to happen suddenly or violently *Violence erupted in the city on Friday night.* **3** PERSON to suddenly become very excited or angry, or start to shout *The whole stadium erupted when he scored the second goal.* ● **eruption** /ɪˈrʌpʃᵊn/ *noun* [C, U] *a volcanic eruption*

**escalate** /ˈeskəleɪt/ *verb* **1** [I, T] If a violent or bad situation escalates, or is escalated, it quickly becomes worse or more serious. *The fight quickly escalated into a riot.* **2** [I] to rise or increase quickly *Airline prices escalate during the holiday season.* ● **escalation** /ˌeskəˈleɪʃᵊn/ *noun* [C, U] *an escalation in violence*

**escalator** /ˈeskəleɪtəʳ/ *noun* [C] moving stairs that take people from one level of a building to another *We took the escalator down to the basement.*

**escapade** /ˌeskəˈpeɪd/ *noun* [C] an exciting and sometimes dangerous experience

o━**escape¹** /ɪˈskeɪp/ *verb* **1** GET AWAY [I] to succeed in getting away from a place where you do not want to be *The two killers **escaped from** prison last night.* **2** AVOID [I, T] to avoid a dangerous or unpleasant situation *to escape capture/injury* **3** FORGET [T] If something such as a name escapes you, you cannot remember it. *The name of her book escapes me at the moment.* **4** NOT NOTICE [T] If something escapes your notice or attention, you do not notice or see it. *Nothing that goes on in this office escapes her attention.* **5** GAS/LIQUID [I] If a gas or liquid escapes from a pipe or container, it comes out, especially when it should not. ● **escaped** *adj an escaped prisoner*

o━**escape²** /ɪˈskeɪp/ *noun* **1** [C, U] when someone succeeds in getting out of a place or a dangerous or bad situation *There was an escape from the prison last night.* **2 a narrow escape** when someone almost dies or almost has a very bad experience *They had a very narrow escape.* **3** [U, no plural] something that helps you to forget about your usual life or problems *I love old movies, they're such an **escape from** the real world.* ➤ *See also:* **fire escape.**

**escapism** /ɪˈskeɪpɪzᵊm/ *noun* [U] entertainment or imagination that helps you to forget about your work and your problems ● **escapist** *adj*

**escort¹** /ˈeskɔːt/ *noun* **1** [C, U] a person or vehicle that goes somewhere with someone to protect or guard them *She was driven to court **under** police escort.* **2** [C] a person who goes with someone else to a social event, sometimes for payment

**escort²** /ɪˈskɔːt/ *verb* [T] to go somewhere with someone, often to protect or guard them *He offered to escort me home.* ● *They were escorted off the premises by police.*

**Eskimo** /ˈeskɪməʊ/ *noun* [C, U] *plural **Eskimos** or **Eskimo** old-fashioned* another word for Inuit (= a group of people who live in the cold, northern areas of North America, Russia, and Greenland, or a member of this group) *an Eskimo village*

**ESL** /ˌiːesˈel/ *noun* [U] *abbreviation for* English as a Second Language: the teaching of English to students whose first language is not English, but who live in a country where it is the main language

⊶**especially** /ɪ'speʃ°li/ *adv* **1** more than other things or people, or much more than usual *He's always making comments about her appearance, especially her weight.* ● *She's especially interested in American poetry.* **2** for one particular person, purpose, or reason *I cooked this meal especially for you.* ⊃ *See usage note at* **specially**.

**espionage** /'espɪənɑːʒ/ *noun* [U] the activity of discovering secret information about a country or company that is fighting or competing against you *industrial espionage*

**espouse** /ɪ'spaʊz/ *verb* [T] *formal* to support a belief or way of life

**espresso** /es'presəʊ/ *noun* [C, U] strong, black coffee

⊶**essay** /'eseɪ/ *noun* [C] a short piece of writing about a particular subject, especially one written by a student *He wrote an essay on modern Japanese literature.*

**essence** /'es°ns/ *noun* **1** [U, no plural] the basic or most important idea or quality of something *The essence of his argument is that we should not eat meat.* **2** [C, U] a strong liquid, usually made from a plant or flower, that is used to add a flavour or smell to something *vanilla essence*

⊶**essential** /ɪ'senʃ°l/ *adj* **1** very important and necessary *Computers are an essential part of our lives.* ● *Fibre is essential for a healthy digestive system.* ● [+ to do sth] *It is essential to arrive early for the show.* ● [+ (that)] *It is absolutely essential that she gets this message.* **2** the most basic and important *There's one essential point I think you've forgotten.*

**essentially** /ɪ'senʃ°li/ *adv* used when you are emphasizing the basic facts about something *What he is saying is essentially true.*

**es,sential 'oil** *noun* [C, U] a strong oil made from a plant which contains its smell or other special qualities

**essentials** /ɪ'senʃ°lz/ *noun* [plural] the most important or necessary things

**establish** /ɪ'stæblɪʃ/ *verb* **1** START [T] to start a company or organization that will continue for a long time [often passive] *The brewery was established in 1822.* **2 establish sb/sth as sth** to put someone or something into a successful and lasting position [often reflexive] *He quickly established himself as a talented actor.* **3 establish communication/relations, etc** to start having a relationship or communicating with another company, country, or organization *The two countries have only recently established diplomatic relations.* **4** DECIDE [T] to decide something *Our first step must be to establish priorities for the weeks ahead.* **5** DISCOVER [T] to find out information or prove something [+ question word] *The police are trying to establish how he died.* ● **established** *adj*

**establishment** /ɪ'stæblɪʃmənt/ *noun* **1** [C] an organization or business **2** [U] when an organization, school, business, etc is started *the establishment of a new national bank* **3 the Establishment** the people and organizations that have most power and influence in a

country **4 the legal/medical, etc establishment** the group of people with most influence in a particular area of work or activity

**estate** /ɪ'steɪt/ *noun* [C] **1** LAND a large area of land in the countryside that is owned by one person or organization *a country estate* **2** BUILDINGS *UK* an area with a lot of buildings of the same type *an industrial estate* **3** POSSESSIONS the possessions and money that someone owns when they die *She left her entire estate to a charity for cats.* ⊃ *See also:* **housing estate, real estate**.

**es'tate ,agent** *UK* (*US* **real estate agent**) *noun* [C] someone who sells buildings and land as their job

**es'tate ,car** *UK* (*US* **station wagon**) *noun* [C] a big car with a large space for bags behind the back seat

**esteem** /ɪ'stiːm/ *noun* [U] *formal* respect and admiration for someone *My father was held in high esteem by everyone who knew him.* ⊃ *See also:* **self-esteem**.

**esteemed** /ɪ'stiːmd/ *adj formal* respected and admired *a highly esteemed professor*

**esthetic** /es'θetɪk/ *adj* another US spelling of aesthetic (= relating to beauty and the way something looks) ● **esthetically** *adv*

**esthetics** /es'θetɪks/ *noun* [U] another US spelling of aesthetics (= the study of beauty)

**estimate¹** /'estɪmət/ *noun* [C] **1** a guess of what a size, value, amount, etc might be *a rough estimate* **2** a written document saying how much it will probably cost to do a job *Can you give me an estimate for the work?*

⊶**estimate²** /'estɪmeɪt/ *verb* [T] to guess the cost, size, value, etc of something [+ that] *They estimate that a hundred people were killed in the accident.* ● *The number of dead is estimated at a hundred.* ● **estimated** *adj an estimated cost*

**estimation** /,estɪ'meɪʃ°n/ *noun* [U] your opinion of someone or something *He is a total genius, in my estimation.*

**estranged** /ɪ'streɪndʒd/ *adj formal* **1** not now communicating with a friend or a member of your family, because you have argued **2** not now living with your husband or wife *his estranged wife* ● **estrangement** *noun* [C, U]

**estrogen** /'iːstrədʒ°n/ US 'estrədʒ°n/ *noun* [U] *US* spelling of oestrogen (= a chemical substance in a woman's body)

**estuary** /'estjuəri/ *noun* [C] the wide part of a river where it goes into the sea

⊶**etc** /et'set°rə/ *abbreviation for* et cetera: used at the end of a list to show that other things or people could also be added to it

**etch** /etʃ/ *verb* [I, T] to cut lines on a hard surface to make a picture or words

**eternal** /ɪ'tɜːn°l/ *adj* continuing forever, or seeming to continue forever *eternal youth* ● **eternally** *adv I will be eternally grateful to you.*

**eternity** /ɪ'tɜːnəti/ *noun* **1** [U] time that continues forever, especially after death **2 an eternity** *informal* a very long time *It seemed like an eternity until she came back.*

**ethereal** /ɪ'θɪəriəl/ *adj* very delicate and light and almost seeming not to be from this world ● **ethereally** *adv*

**ethic** /'eθɪk/ *noun* [no plural] a belief or idea that influences the way you think or behave

**ethical** /'eθɪkəl/ *adj* **1** relating to what is right or wrong *The book raises some serious ethical questions.* **2** morally correct and good *He dealt with this case in a completely professional and ethical manner.* ➔ *Opposite* **unethical**. • **ethically** *adv*

**ethics** /'eθɪks/ *noun* [plural] ideas and beliefs about what type of behaviour is morally right and wrong *a code of ethics* • *the ethics of genetic engineering*

**ethnic** /'eθnɪk/ *adj* relating to a particular race of people *ethnic minorities*

**ethos** /'iːθɒs/ *noun* [no plural] the ideas and beliefs of a particular person or group

**etiquette** /'etɪket/ *noun* [U] rules about what is polite and correct behaviour

**etymology** /,etɪ'mɒlədʒi/ *noun* [U] the study of the history and origin of words and their meanings • **etymological** /,etɪmə'lɒdʒɪkəl/ *adj* • **etymologically** *adv*

**the EU** /,iː'juː/ *noun abbreviation for* the European Union: a European political and economic organization that encourages business and good relationships between the countries that are members

**euphemism** /'juːfəmɪzəm/ *noun* [C, U] a polite word or phrase that is used to avoid saying something embarrassing or offensive *'Passed away' is a euphemism for 'died'.* • **euphemistic** /,juːfə'mɪstɪk/ *adj* • **euphemistically** *adv*

**euphoria** /juː'fɔːriə/ *noun* [U] a feeling of extreme happiness and excitement • **euphoric** /juː'fɒrɪk/ *adj*

**euro** /'jʊərəʊ/ *noun* [C] a unit of money used in European countries that belong to the European Union (= a European political and economic organization)€

**European** /,jʊərə'piːən/ *adj* relating or belonging to Europe *European countries/languages* • *the European Parliament* • **European** *noun* [C] *Many Europeans speak English.*

**the ˌEuropean ˈUnion** (*also* **the EU**) *noun a* European political and economic organization that encourages business and good relationships between the countries that are members

**euthanasia** /,juːθə'neɪziə/ *noun* [U] when someone who is very old or very ill is killed so that they do not suffer any more *voluntary euthanasia*

**evacuate** /ɪ'vækjueɪt/ *verb* [T] to move people from a dangerous place to somewhere safer *The police quickly evacuated the area after the bomb threat.* • **evacuation** /ɪ,vækju'eɪʃən/ *noun* [C, U] *the evacuation of civilians from the war zone*

**evacuee** /ɪ,vækju'iː/ *noun* [C] someone who is evacuated from a place to somewhere safer

**evade** /ɪ'veɪd/ *verb* **1** [T] to avoid something or someone, especially in a dishonest way *to evade capture* • *to evade paying tax* • *He managed to evade the police.* **2 evade the issue/question, etc** to intentionally not talk about something or not answer something

**evaluate** /ɪ'væljueɪt/ *verb* [T] *formal* to consider or study something carefully and decide how good or bad it is • **evaluation** /ɪ,vælju'eɪʃən/ *noun* [C, U]

**evangelical** /,iːvæn'dʒelɪkəl/ *adj* Evangelical Christians believe that faith in Jesus Christ and studying the Bible are more important than religious ceremonies.

**evaporate** /ɪ'væpəreɪt/ *verb* **1** [I, T] If a liquid evaporates or is evaporated, it changes into steam. **2** [I] If feelings evaporate, they disappear. • **evaporation** /ɪ,væpə'reɪʃən/ *noun* [U]

**evasion** /ɪ'veɪʒən/ *noun* [C, U] when you avoid something, especially in a dishonest way *tax evasion*

**evasive** /ɪ'veɪsɪv/ *adj* **1** trying to avoid talking about something *He was very evasive about his past.* • *an evasive answer* **2 take evasive action** to do something to avoid an accident or bad situation • **evasively** *adv* • **evasiveness** *noun* [U]

**eve** /iːv/ *noun* **1 Christmas Eve/New Year's Eve** the day or night before Christmas Day/New Year's Day **2 the eve of sth** the time just before something important happens *They were married in Washington on the eve of the Second World War.*

**even**¹ /'iːvən/ *adj* **1** FLAT flat, level, or smooth *Find an even surface to work on.* ➔ *Opposite* **uneven**. **2** NOT CHANGING An even temperature or rate is regular and does not change very much. *Walking at an even pace, they covered about four miles in the first hour.* **3** NUMBER An even number is a number which can be exactly divided by two, for example four, six, or eight. ➔ *Opposite* **odd**. **4** MONEY *informal* not now owing someone money *If you pay for my cinema ticket, we'll be even.* **5** COMPETITION An even race or competition is one that both players, teams, or people involved have an equal chance of winning. **6 get even (with sb)** *informal* If you get even with someone who has done something bad to you, you do something bad to them.

o-* **even**² /'iːvən/ *adv* **1** used to emphasize something that is surprising *Everyone danced, even Mick.* • *I said hello, but he didn't even look at me.* **2 even better/faster/smaller, etc** used when comparing things, to emphasize the difference *I think Alex is going to be even taller than his father.* **3 even if** used to emphasize that a particular situation would not change what you have just said *I would never eat meat, even if I was really hungry.* **4 even though** although *He still smokes, even though he's got asthma.* **5 even so** used to emphasize that something surprising is true despite what you have just said *Car prices have gone down a lot, but even so, we couldn't afford to buy one.*

**even**³ /'iːvən/ *verb*

**even (sth) out** to become equal, or to make something equal *Sometimes I pay and sometimes Tom does – it usually evens out in the end.*

o-* **evening** /'iːvnɪŋ/ *noun* **1** [C, U] the part of the day between the afternoon and the night *Are you doing anything this evening?* • *I go to band practice on Monday evenings.* • *We usually eat our main meal in the evening.* **2 (Good) evening.** something that you say when you meet someone in the evening

**evenly** /'iːvənli/ *adv* **1** into equal amounts, or in a regular way *They decided to divide the prize* *money evenly between them.* **2 evenly matched** Two people or teams who are evenly matched are equally good, or have an equal chance of winning.

o→**event** /ɪ'vent/ *noun* [C] **1** something that happens, especially something important or unusual *Local people have been shocked by recent events in the town.* **2** a race, party, competition, etc that has been organized for a particular time *a social/sporting event* **3 in the event** *UK* used to emphasize what did happen when it was not what you had expected *In the event, we didn't need the extra money.* **4 in the event of sth** *formal* if something happens *An airbag could save your life in the event of an accident.* **5 in any event** whatever happens *I'm not sure if I'm coming on Friday, but in any event, I'll see you next week.* ⊃ *See also:* **non-event**.

**eventful** /ɪ'ventfᵊl/ *adj* full of interesting or important events *a very eventful day/journey*

**eventual** /ɪ'ventʃuəl/ *adj* [always before noun] happening or existing at the end of a process or period of time *the eventual winner of the competition*

o→**eventually** /ɪ'ventʃuəli/ *adv* in the end, especially after a long time *We all hope that an agreement can be reached eventually.*

o→**ever** /'evəʳ/ *adv* **1** at any time *Have you ever been skiing?* • *If you're ever in town, do come and see me.* • *No one ever calls me any more.* **2 better/faster/happier, etc than** ever better/faster/happier, etc than at any time before **3 hardly ever** almost never *We hardly ever go out these days.* **4 ever since** always since that time *We met at school and have been friends ever since.* **5 ever so/ever such a** *UK* very/a very *She's ever so pretty.* • *She's ever such a pretty girl.* **6 for ever** *UK (UK/US* **forever**) always in the future *I'm not going to live here for ever.* **7 ever-changing/growing/ increasing, etc** always changing/growing/ increasing, etc

**evergreen** /'evəgriːn/ *adj* An evergreen plant has green leaves that do not fall off in winter. • **evergreen** *noun* [C] a plant with leaves that do not fall off in winter

**everlasting** /ˌevə'lɑːstɪŋ/ *adj* continuing for a long time or always *everlasting love*

**evermore** /ˌevə'mɔːʳ/ *adv literary* always in the future

o→**every** /'evri/ *determiner* **1** EACH each one of a group of people or things *He knows the name of every child in the school.* • *Every one of the paintings was a fake.* **2** HOW OFTEN used to show that something is repeated regularly *He goes to Spain every summer.* • *Take the antibiotics every four hours.* **3** POSSIBLE as much as is possible *I'd like to wish you every success in your new job.* • *Every effort is being made to rectify the problem.* **4 every now and then/every so often** sometimes, but not often *We still meet up every now and then.* **5 one in every five/ten, etc** used to show how many people or things in a group are affected by or involved in something

**every**

When **every** is followed by **body, one, thing**, or **where**, you write the words together.

*Everybody needs to bring something to eat.*

*Can everyone see that?*

*Have you got everything you need?*

*I've looked everywhere for it.*

In other situations you use **every** as a separate word.

*You have to take your membership card every time you go.*

*Do you go jogging every morning?*

o→**everybody** /'evri,bɒdi/ *pronoun* another word for everyone

**everyday** /'evrideɪ/ *adj* [always before noun] normal, usual, or happening every day *Computers are now part of everyday life.*

o→**everyone** /'evriwʌn/ (*also* **everybody**) *pronoun* **1** every person *I've received a reply from everyone now.* • *Everyone agreed with the decision.* **2 everyone else** every other person *Everyone else was wearing jeans.*

**everyplace** /'evripleɪs/ *adv US* another word for everywhere

o→**everything** /'evriθɪŋ/ *pronoun* **1** all things or each thing *They lost everything in the fire.* • *You can't blame Tom for everything that goes wrong.* • *What's the matter Nick, is everything all right?* **2 everything else** all the other things *The meat tasted strange, but everything else was okay.* **3 be/mean everything** to be the most important part of someone's life *His children mean everything to him.* • *Money isn't everything.*

o→**everywhere** /'evriweəʳ/ *adv* in or to every place *I've looked everywhere, but I still can't find that letter.*

**evict** /ɪ'vɪkt/ *verb* [T] to legally force someone to leave the house they are living in *They were evicted after complaints from their neighbours.* • **eviction** /ɪ'vɪkʃᵊn/ *noun* [C, U]

o→**evidence** /'evɪdᵊns/ *noun* [U] **1** something that makes you believe that something is true or exists *evidence of global warming* • [+ that] *There is no scientific evidence that the drug is addictive.* **2** information that is given or objects that are shown in a court of law to help to prove if someone has committed a crime *He was arrested despite the lack of evidence against him.* **3 give evidence** *UK* to give information and answer questions in a court of law *She was called to give evidence at his trial.* **4 be in evidence** *formal* to be noticeable

**evident** /'evɪdᵊnt/ *adj formal* obvious to everyone and easy to see or understand [+ that] *It was evident from his voice that he was upset.* ⊃ *See also:* **self-evident**.

**evidently** /'evɪdᵊntli/ *adv* **1** used to say that something can easily be noticed *He evidently likes her.* **2** used to say that something seems probable from the information you have *The* *intruder evidently got in through an open window.*

**evil¹** /ˈiːvᵊl/ *adj* very cruel, bad, or harmful *an evil monster*

**evil²** /ˈiːvᵊl/ *noun* [C, U] something that is very bad and harmful *The theme of the play is the battle between good and evil.* • *the evils of drug and alcohol abuse* ⊃ *See also:* the **lesser** of two evils.

**evocative** /ɪˈvɒkətɪv/ *adj* making you remember or imagine something that is pleasant *evocative music* • *evocative of the sea*

**evoke** /ɪˈvəʊk/ *verb* [T] to make someone remember something or feel an emotion *The story evoked memories of my childhood.*

**evolution** /ˌiːvəˈluːʃᵊn/ *noun* [U] **1** the way in which living things gradually change and develop over millions of years *Darwin's theory of evolution* **2** a gradual process of change and development *the evolution of language* • **evolutionary** *adj*

**evolve** /ɪˈvɒlv/ *verb* **1** [I] to develop from other forms of life over millions of years **2** [I, T] to develop or make something develop, usually gradually *rapidly evolving technology*

**ewe** /juː/ *noun* [C] a female sheep

**ex** /eks/ *noun* [C] *informal* someone who used to be your husband, wife, or partner *My ex and his new wife live abroad.*

**exacerbate** /ɪɡˈzæsəbeɪt/ *verb* [T] to make something worse *Sunny weather exacerbates the effects of pollution.*

o⌐**exact¹** /ɪɡˈzækt/ *adj* completely correct in every detail *I'm afraid I can't give you the exact details of the show yet.* • *Are you quite sure of the exact time that you saw him?* • *They've lived here a long time – 25 years to be exact.* • **exactness** *noun* [U]

**exact²** /ɪɡˈzækt/ *verb* [T] *formal* to demand and get something from someone

**exacting** /ɪɡˈzæktɪŋ/ *adj* needing a lot of effort and attention *an exacting training schedule*

o⌐**exactly** /ɪɡˈzæktli/ *adv* [COMPLETELY CORRECT] used when you are giving or asking for information that is completely correct *What exactly seems to be the problem?* • *The train got in at exactly ten o'clock.* **2** [EMPHASIS] used to emphasize what you are saying *I found a dress that's exactly the same colour as my shoes.* **3** [AGREEMENT] something you say when you agree completely with someone *"Surely they should have told us about this problem sooner?" "Exactly."* **4 not exactly** used to say that something is not completely true *"Do you live here?" "Not exactly, I'm staying with friends."* **5 not exactly easy/new/clear, etc** *informal* used to say that a description is completely untrue *Let's face it, we're not exactly rich, are we?*

**exaggerate** /ɪɡˈzædʒəreɪt/ *verb* [I, T] to make something seem larger, better, worse, etc than it really is *Don't exaggerate – it didn't cost that much!*

**exaggeration** /ɪɡˌzædʒᵊrˈeɪʃᵊn/ *noun* [C, U] when you describe something as larger, better, worse, etc than it really is *a gross exaggeration of the facts*

**exalted** /ɪɡˈzɔːltɪd/ *adj formal* very highly respected, or with a very high position

o⌐**exam** /ɪɡˈzæm/ *noun* [C] **1** an official test of how much you know about something, or how well you can do something *a maths exam* • *to fail/pass an exam* • *(UK)* to sit/*(US/UK)* to take (= do) *an exam* **2** *US* a series of medical tests *an eye exam*

**USAGE**

**take/sit an exam**

To **take an exam** means to do an official test. 'Sit' is slightly more formal than 'take' in this phrase and is only used in the UK.

*We have to take an exam at the end of the course.*

~~We have to write an exam at the end of the course.~~

If you **pass an exam**, you are successful because you get a good mark. If you **fail an exam**, you are not successful because you get a bad mark.

**examination** /ɪɡˌzæmɪˈneɪʃᵊn/ *noun* **1** [C, U] when someone looks at something very carefully *a medical examination* • *a close examination of the facts* **2** [C] *formal* an exam

**examine** /ɪɡˈzæmɪn/ *verb* [T] **1** [LOOK AT] to look at someone or something very carefully, especially to try to discover something *She picked up the knife and examined it closely.* • *He was examined by a doctor as soon as he arrived.* **2** [TEST] *formal* to test someone to see how much they know or how well they can do something *You'll be examined in three main areas: speaking, listening, and reading comprehension.* **3** [CONSIDER] to consider a plan or an idea carefully *They have called a special meeting to examine the proposal.* ⊃ *See also:* **cross-examine**.

**examiner** /ɪɡˈzæmɪnəʳ/ *noun* [C] someone who tests how much you know about something, or how well you can do something

o⌐**example** /ɪɡˈzɑːmpl/ *noun* **1** [C] something that is typical of the group of things that you are talking about *This is a good example of medieval Chinese architecture.* **2 for example** used to give an example of what you are talking about *Some people, students for example, can get cheaper tickets.* **3** [C] someone or something that is very good and should be copied *He is a very good example to the rest of the class.* **4 set an example** to behave in a way that other people should copy

**exasperate** /ɪɡˈzæspᵊreɪt/ *verb* [T] to annoy someone a lot

**exasperated** /ɪɡˈzæspᵊreɪtɪd/ *adj* extremely annoyed *He's become increasingly exasperated with the situation.*

**exasperating** /ɪɡˈzæspᵊreɪtɪŋ/ *adj* extremely annoying *It's exasperating trying to explain anything to him.*

**exasperation** /ɪɡˌzæspəˈreɪʃᵊn/ *noun* [U] when you feel extremely annoyed with someone or something

**excavate** /ˈekskəveɪt/ *verb* [I, T] to dig in the ground, especially with a machine, or to look for objects from the past *These Roman coins were excavated from a site in Cambridge.* • **excavation** /ˌekskəˈveɪʃᵊn/ *noun* [C, U]

**exceed** /ɪkˈsiːd/ *verb* **1** [T] to be more than a

particular number or amount *Sales have exceeded $1 million so far this year.* **2 exceed the speed limit** to drive faster than you are allowed to according to the law

**exceedingly** /ɪkˈsiːdɪŋli/ *adv formal* very *He was clever, attractive, and exceedingly rich.*

**excel** /ɪkˈsel/ *verb* **excelling,** *past* **excelled** *formal* **1** [I] to be very good at something *Paula always excelled in languages at school.* **2 excel yourself** to do something better than you usually do *The British team have excelled themselves this year to reach the finals.*

○⁻**excellent** /ˈeksəlⁿnt/ *adj* very good, or of a very high quality *That was an excellent meal.* • **excellently** *adv Robert has behaved excellently this year.* • **excellence** /ˈeksəlⁿns/ *noun* [U]

○⁻**except** /ɪkˈsept/ *preposition, conjunction* not including a particular fact, thing, or person *The boat sails from Oban every day except Sunday.* • *Everyone passed the exam except for Rory.* • [+ (that)] *So nothing changed, except that Anna saw her son less and less.*

**excepted** /ɪkˈseptɪd/ *adj* [always after noun] *formal* not included *Everybody who was asked, myself excepted, said no.*

**excepting** /ɪkˈseptɪŋ/ *preposition* not including

**exception** /ɪkˈsepʃⁿn/ *noun* **1** [C, U] someone or something that is not included in a rule, group, or list *There are exceptions to every rule.* • *I like all kinds of movies,* **with the exception of** *horror films.* • *All our pupils,* **without exception,** *have access to the Internet.* • *Her films are always popular and this one is* **no exception.** **2 make an exception** to not treat someone or something according to the usual rules *They don't usually take cheques, but they said they'd make an exception in my case.* **3 take exception to sth** *formal* to be annoyed or insulted by something

**exceptional** /ɪkˈsepʃⁿnəl/ *adj* **1** extremely good *an exceptional student* **2** very unusual and not likely to happen very often *Visitors are only allowed in exceptional circumstances.* • **exceptionally** *adv an exceptionally gifted pianist*

**excerpt** /ˈeksɜːpt/ *noun* [C] a short piece from a book, film, piece of music, etc

**excess¹** /ɪkˈses/ *noun* **1** [U, no plural] more of something than is usual or needed *An excess of oil on the markets has caused prices to fall sharply.* **2 in excess of sth** more than a particular amount or level *He earns in excess of £60,000 a year.* **3 do sth to excess** to do something too much *He occasionally has a beer, but he never drinks to excess.*

**excess²** /ɪkˈses/ *adj* [always before noun] more than is usual or allowed *We had to pay £100 for excess baggage.*

**excesses** /ɪkˈsesɪz/ *noun* [plural] extreme, harmful, or immoral actions or behaviour

**excessive** /ɪkˈsesɪv/ *adj* more than is necessary or wanted *They accused the police of using excessive force.* • **excessively** *adv*

**exchange¹** /ɪksˈtʃeɪndʒ/ *noun* **1** GIVING [C, U] when you give something to someone and they give you something else *an exchange of ideas/information* • *They were given food and shelter* **in exchange for** *work.* **2** STUDENTS [C] an arrangement by which students and teach-

ers from one country go to stay with students and teachers in another *Janet has happy memories of going on an exchange to France.* **3** CONVERSATION [C] a short conversation or argument *There were angry exchanges between the police and demonstrators.* ⊃ *See also:* **the stock exchange.**

○⁻**exchange²** /ɪksˈtʃeɪndʒ/ *verb* **1** [T] to give something to someone and receive something similar from them *It's traditional for the two teams to exchange shirts after the game.* **2** [T] to take something back to the shop where you bought it and change it for something else *Could I exchange this shirt for a larger size?* **3 exchange looks/smiles/words, etc** If two people exchange looks, smiles, words, etc, they look at each other, smile at each other, talk to each other, etc. *The couple opposite us sat through the whole meal without exchanging a word.*

**exˈchange ˌrate** *noun* [C] the amount of another country's money that you can buy with a particular amount of your own country's money

**excise** /ˈeksaɪz/ *noun* [U] government taxes that must be paid on some things that are made or sold in a particular country

**excitable** /ɪkˈsaɪtəbl/ *adj* easily becoming excited *a very excitable child/puppy*

**excite** /ɪkˈsaɪt/ *verb* [T] **1** to make someone feel very happy and enthusiastic *Try not to excite the children too much.* **2** *formal* to cause a particular reaction in someone *This product has excited a great deal of interest.*

○⁻**excited** /ɪkˈsaɪtɪd/ *adj* feeling very happy and enthusiastic *happy, excited faces* • *The children are getting really* **excited about** *the party.* • **excitedly** *adv*

○⁻**excitement** /ɪkˈsaɪtmənt/ *noun* [U] when people feel very happy and enthusiastic *The competition is causing a lot of excitement.*

○⁻**exciting** /ɪkˈsaɪtɪŋ/ *adj* making you feel very happy and enthusiastic *an exciting football match* • *You're going to Africa? How exciting!*

**exclaim** /ɪksˈkleɪm/ *verb* [I, T] to say something suddenly and loudly because you are surprised, annoyed, excited, etc *"How terrible!" she exclaimed.*

**exclamation** /ˌekskləˈmeɪʃⁿn/ *noun* [C] something that you say loudly and suddenly because you are surprised, angry, excited, etc *an exclamation of delight*

**exclaˈmation ˌmark** (*also US* **exclaˈmation ˌpoint**) *noun* [C] a mark (!) used at the end of a sentence that expresses surprise, excitement, or shock, or that is a greeting or an order ⊃ *See study section* **Punctuation** *on page Centre 37.*

**exclude** /ɪksˈkluːd/ *verb* [T] **1** KEEP OUT to not allow someone or something to take part in an activity or enter a place [often passive] *Women are still* **excluded from** *the club.* **2** NOT INCLUDE to intentionally not include something *The insurance cover excludes particular medical conditions.* **3** POSSIBILITY to decide that something is certainly not true or possible *We can't exclude the possibility that he is dead.*

**excluding** /ɪksˈkluːdɪŋ/ *preposition* not including *That's $600 per person for seven days, excluding travel costs.*

**exclusion** /ɪksˈkluːʒ⁰n/ *noun* **1** [C, U] when someone or something is not allowed to take part in an activity or to enter a place *the exclusion of disruptive pupils* ➔ *Opposite* **inclusion**. **2 to the exclusion of sth** If you do something to the exclusion of something else, you do it so much that you have no time to do anything else.

**exclusive¹** /ɪksˈkluːsɪv/ *adj* **1** expensive and only for people who are rich or of a high social class *an exclusive private club • an apartment in a very exclusive part of town* **2 exclusive of sth** not including something *The price of the meal is exclusive of drinks.* ➔ *Opposite* **inclusive**. **3** not shared with another person, organization, newspaper, etc *an exclusive interview*

**exclusive²** /ɪksˈkluːsɪv/ *noun* [C] a news story that appears in only one newspaper or on one television programme

**exclusively** /ɪksˈkluːsɪvli/ *adv* only *an exclusively female audience*

**excrement** /ˈekskrəmənt/ *noun* [U] *formal* solid waste that comes out of the bottom of a person or animal

**excrete** /ɪkˈskriːt/ *verb* [I, T] to get rid of waste substances from the body • **excretion** /ɪkˈskriːʃ⁰n/ *noun* [C, U]

**excruciating** /ɪkˈskruːʃieɪtɪŋ/ *adj* very bad or painful *Her illness causes her excruciating pain.* • **excruciatingly** *adv an excruciatingly embarrassing situation*

**excursion** /ɪkˈskɜːʒ⁰n/ *noun* [C] a short journey made by a group of people for pleasure *We've booked to go on an excursion to Pompeii.*

**excusable** /ɪkˈskjuːzəbl/ *adj* easy to forgive ➔ *Opposite* **inexcusable**.

o--**excuse¹** /ɪkˈskjuːz/ *verb* [T] **1** FORGIVE to forgive someone for something that is not very serious *Please excuse my appearance, I've been painting.* • [+ for + doing sth] *She asked him to excuse her for being so rude.* **2** NOT DO to say that someone does not have to do something that they usually have to do *Could I be excused from football training today?* **3** EXPLAIN to be given as a reason for someone's bad behaviour, so that it does not seem so bad *Nothing can excuse what he did.* **4 excuse me a** used to politely get someone's attention *Excuse me, does this bus go to Oxford Street?* **b** used to say sorry for something that you do without intending to *Oh, excuse me, did I take your seat?* • **excusable** *adj*

o--**excuse²** /ɪkˈskjuːs/ *noun* [C] **1** a reason that you give to explain why you did something wrong [+ for + doing sth] *I hope he's got a good excuse for being so late.* **2** a false reason that you give to explain why you do something *Nick was just looking for an excuse to call her.*

**execute** /ˈeksɪkjuːt/ *verb* [T] **1** to kill someone as a legal punishment *He was executed for murder.* **2** *formal* to do something, such as follow a plan or order *to execute a deal/plan*

**execution** /ˌeksɪˈkjuːʃ⁰n/ *noun* **1** [C, U] when someone is killed as a legal punishment **2** [U] when you do something, such as follow a plan or order *He was killed in the execution of his duties as a soldier.*

**executioner** /ˌeksɪˈkjuːʃ⁰nəʳ/ *noun* [C] someone whose job is to execute criminals

**executive¹** /ɪgˈzekjətɪv/ *adj* [always before noun] **1** relating to making decisions and managing businesses *an executive director* **2** suitable for people who have important jobs in business *Peter always stays in the executive suite.*

**executive²** /ɪgˈzekjətɪv/ *noun* **1** [C] someone who has an important job in a business *a company executive* **2 the executive** *mainly UK* the people who have the power to make decisions in an organization

**exemplary** /ɪgˈzempl⁰ri/ *adj formal* very good and suitable to be copied by people *Sarah's behaviour is always exemplary.*

**exemplify** /ɪgˈzemplɪfaɪ/ *verb* [T] *formal* to be or give a typical example of something

**exempt¹** /ɪgˈzempt/ *adj* [never before noun] with special permission not to have to do something or pay something *The first £4,000 that you earn is exempt from tax.*

**exempt²** /ɪgˈzempt/ *verb* [T] *formal* to officially say that someone does not have to do something or pay for something [often passive] *Students are exempted from payment.* • **exemption** /ɪgˈzempʃ⁰n/ *noun* [C, U]

o--**exercise¹** /ˈeksəsaɪz/ *noun* **1** PHYSICAL ACTIVITY [C, U] physical activity that you do to make your body strong and healthy *Swimming is my favourite form of exercise.* • *Let's do some stretching exercises to start with.* **2** TEST [C] a piece of written work that helps you learn something *For your homework, please do exercise 3 on page 24.* **3** MILITARY [C] a set of actions that a group of soldiers do to practise their skills *The cadets are out on military exercises.* **4** USE [U] *formal* the use of something such as a power or right

**exercise**

**exercise²** /ˈeksəsaɪz/ *verb* **1** [I, T] to do physical activities to make your body strong and healthy *I try to exercise every day.* **2** [T] *formal* to use a power, right, or ability *You should always exercise your right to vote.*

**exert** /ɪgˈzɜːt/ *verb* **1** [T] to use something such as authority, power, influence, etc in order to make something happen *My parents exerted a lot of pressure on me to do well at school.*

**2 exert yourself** to use a lot of physical or mental energy to do something *She was too ill to exert herself much.*

**exertion** /ɪgˈzɜːʃən/ *noun* [C, U] when you use a lot of physical or mental energy to do something *I get out of breath with any kind of physical exertion.*

**exhale** /eksˈheɪl/ *verb* [I, T] *formal* to send air out of your lungs *Exhale slowly through your nose.* ⊃ *Opposite* **inhale**.

**exhaust**[1] /ɪgˈzɔːst/ *verb* [T] **1** SUPPLY to finish all of the supply of something *How long will it be before the world's fuel supplies are exhausted?* **2** TIRED to make someone very tired *The long journey exhausted me.* **3** SUBJECT to say everything possible about a subject *We seem to have exhausted that topic of conversation.*

**exhaust**[2] /ɪgˈzɔːst/ *noun* **1** [U] the waste gas from a vehicle's engine *exhaust fumes* **2** (*also* **exhaust pipe**) *mainly UK* the pipe that waste gas from a vehicle's engine flows through ⊃ *See colour picture* **Car** *on page Centre 3.*

**exhausted** /ɪgˈzɔːstɪd/ *adj* very tired *I'm too exhausted to take the dog for a walk tonight.*

**exhausting** /ɪgˈzɔːstɪŋ/ *adj* making you feel very tired *What an exhausting day!*

**exhaustion** /ɪgˈzɔːstʃən/ *noun* [U] when you are extremely tired *The tennis star was suffering from exhaustion.*

**exhaustive** /ɪgˈzɔːstɪv/ *adj* complete and including everything *an exhaustive account of the incident*

**exˈhaust ˌpipe** *mainly UK* (*also US* **tailpipe**) *noun* [C] the pipe that waste gas from a vehicle's engine flows through

**exhibit**[1] /ɪgˈzɪbɪt/ *verb* **1** [I, T] to show objects such as paintings to the public *She's exhibiting her roses at the local flower show.* **2** [T] *formal* to show a feeling, quality, or ability *The crew exhibited great courage when the plane crashed.*

**exhibit**[2] /ɪgˈzɪbɪt/ *noun* [C] an object such as a painting that is shown to the public *a museum exhibit* ● **exhibitor** *noun* [C] someone who shows something that they own or have made to the public

**exhibition** /ˌeksɪˈbɪʃən/ *noun* **1** [C, U] when objects such as paintings are shown to the public *There's a new **exhibition of** sculpture on at the city gallery.* ● *an exhibition centre* **2** [C] when someone shows a particular skill or quality that they have to the public

**exhibitionist** /ˌeksɪˈbɪʃənɪst/ *noun* [C] someone who tries to attract attention to themselves with their behaviour ● **exhibitionism** /ˌeksɪˈbɪʃənɪzəm/ *noun* [U] behaviour which tries to attract attention

**exhilarated** /ɪgˈzɪləreɪtɪd/ *adj* very excited and happy *We finally got home at 9 o'clock, exhausted but exhilarated.*

**exhilarating** /ɪgˈzɪləreɪtɪŋ/ *adj* making you feel very excited and happy *There's nothing more exhilarating than water-skiing.*

**exhilaration** /ɪgˌzɪləˈreɪʃən/ *noun* [U] when you feel very excited and happy

**exhort** /ɪgˈzɔːt/ *verb* [T] *formal* to strongly encourage someone to do something ● **exhortation** /ˌegzɔːˈteɪʃən/ *noun* [C, U]

**exile** /ˈeksaɪl, ˈegzaɪl/ *noun* **1** [U] when someone has to leave their home and live in another country, often for political reasons *He spent the war years **in exile** in New York.* ● *The King was forced **into exile**.* **2** [C] someone who is forced to live in another country *She lived the rest of her life as an exile in the UK.* ● **exile** *verb* [T] to force someone to leave their home and live in another country, often for political reasons ● **exiled** *adj*

o━**exist** /ɪgˈzɪst/ *verb* [I] **1** to be real or present *Do you think that fairies exist?* ● *Poverty still exists in this country.* **2** to live in difficult conditions *You can't exist without water for more than a week.*

**existence** /ɪgˈzɪstəns/ *noun* **1** [U] when something or someone exists *She never doubted **the existence of** God.* ● *The theatre company that we started is still **in existence** today.* ● *When did the Football League **come into existence** (= begin to exist)?* **2** [C] a particular way of life *We could have a much more peaceful existence in the countryside.*

**existing** /ɪgˈzɪstɪŋ/ *adj* [always before noun] which exist or are used at the present time *Existing schools will have to be expanded to accommodate the extra students.* ● *How many existing customers have you got?* ⊃ *See also:* **pre-existing**.

o━**exit**[1] /ˈeksɪt/ *noun* [C] **1** DOOR the door or gate which you use to leave a public building or place *a fire exit* ● *an emergency exit* **2** LEAVING when someone leaves a place *Sue **made** a quick exit when she saw Mick come in.* **3** ROAD a road which you use to leave a motorway (= wide, fast road) or roundabout (= place where three or more main roads meet) *Take the third exit at the next roundabout.*

**exit**[2] /ˈeksɪt/ *verb* [I, T] **1** to stop using a program on a computer *Press escape to exit the game.* **2** *formal* to leave a place or a competition

**exodus** /ˈeksədəs/ *noun* [no plural] when a large number of people all leave a place together *There has been **a mass exodus** of workers from the villages to the towns.*

**exonerate** /ɪgˈzɒnəreɪt/ *verb* [T] *formal* to say that someone is not guilty of doing something that they have been blamed for [often passive] *He was **exonerated of** all blame by the investigation.* ● **exoneration** /ɪgˌzɒnəˈreɪʃən/ *noun* [U]

**exorbitant** /ɪgˈzɔːbɪtənt/ *adj* Exorbitant prices or costs are much too high. *an exorbitant rate of interest*

**exorcism** /ˈeksɔːsɪzəm/ *noun* [C, U] when an evil spirit is exorcized

**exorcize** (*also UK* **-ise**) /ˈeksɔːsaɪz/ *verb* [T] **1** to make evil spirits leave a person or place by saying special prayers and having a special ceremony **2** to get rid of something such as a bad memory *She moved to Paris to try to exorcize the past.*

**exotic** /ɪgˈzɒtɪk/ *adj* unusual, interesting, and often foreign *exotic fruits*

**expand** /ɪkˈspænd/ *verb* [I, T] to increase in size or amount, or to make something increase *We are hoping to expand our range of products.* ● *Electronic services are rapidly expanding to meet demand.*

**expand on sth** to give more details about something that you have said or written *She mentioned a few ideas, but she didn't expand on them.*

**expanse** /ɪk'spæns/ *noun* [C] a large, open area of land, sea, or sky *a vast expanse of water*

**expansion** /ɪk'spænʃ°n/ *noun* [U] when something increases in size or amount *the rapid expansion of the software industry*

**expansive** /ɪk'spænsɪv/ *adj formal* very happy to talk to people in a friendly way *He was in an expansive mood on the night of the party.*

**expatriate** /ɪk'spætriət/ (*also UK* **expat** /ˌek'spæt/ *informal*) *noun* [C] someone who does not live in their own country ● **expatriate** *adj*

o→**expect** /ɪk'spekt/ *verb* **1** [T] to think that something will happen [+ to do sth] *He didn't expect to see me.* ● [+ (that)] *I expect that she'll be very angry about this.* **2 be expecting sb/sth** to be waiting for someone or something to arrive *We've been expecting you.* ● *I'm expecting a letter from my sister.* **3** [T] to think that someone should behave in a particular way or do a particular thing *I expect punctuality from my students.* ● [+ to do sth] *You will be expected to work some weekends.* **4 I expect** *mainly UK informal* used to show that you think that something is likely to be true *I expect Isabel's told you about me?* ● *"Will you be coming to the party?" "I expect so."* **5 be expecting** to be going to have a baby *I'm expecting my first baby in May.* ➔ *See usage note at* **wait**.

**expectancy** /ɪk'spekt°nsi/ *noun* [U] when you think that something pleasant or exciting is going to happen *An air of expectancy filled the room.* ➔ *See also:* **life expectancy**.

**expectant** /ɪk'spekt°nt/ *adj* **1** thinking that something pleasant or exciting is going to happen *the children's expectant faces* **2 an expectant mother/father, etc** someone who is going to have a baby soon ● **expectantly** *adv They looked at me expectantly.*

**expectation** /ˌekspek'teɪʃ°n/ *noun* **1** [C] when you expect good things to happen in the future [usually plural] *The holiday lived up to all our expectations* (= was as good as we expected). ● *My parents had high expectations for me* (= expected me to be successful). **2** [C, U] when you expect something to happen *He had gone away and there was no expectation of his return.*

**expedient**[1] /ɪk'spi:diənt/ *adj formal* An expedient action achieves a useful purpose, although it may not be moral. *It might be expedient not to pay him until the work is finished.* ● **expediency** /ɪk'spi:diənsi/ *noun* [U] when something is expedient *an issue of political expediency*

**expedient**[2] /ɪk'spi:diənt/ *noun* [C] *formal* a useful or clever action

**expedite** /'ekspɪdaɪt/ *verb* [T] *formal* to make an action or process happen more quickly

**expedition** /ˌekspɪ'dɪʃ°n/ *noun* [C] an organized journey, especially a long one for a particular purpose *Peary led the first expedition to the North Pole.* ● *a shopping expedition*

**expel** /ɪk'spel/ *verb* [T] **expelling**, *past* **expelled 1** to make someone leave a school, organization, or country because of their behaviour [often passive] *He was expelled from school for*

hitting another student. **2** *formal* to force air, gas, or liquid out of something *Slowly expel all the air from your lungs.*

**expend** /ɪk'spend/ *verb* [T] *formal* to use effort, time, or money to do something [+ doing sth] *You expend far too much energy doing things for other people.* ● *Governments* **expend** *a lot of resources* **on** *war.*

**expendable** /ɪk'spendəbl/ *adj* If someone or something is expendable, people can do something or deal with a situation without them. *He considers his staff as temporary and expendable.*

**expenditure** /ɪk'spendɪtʃər/ *noun* [U] *formal* **1** the total amount of money that a government or person spends *The government's annual expenditure on arms has been reduced.* **2** when you use energy, time, or money *There has not been enough expenditure of effort on this project.*

o→**expense** /ɪk'spens/ *noun* **1** [C, U] the money that you spend on something *You have to pay your own medical expenses.* ● *He eventually found her the car she wanted, at great expense* (= it cost him a lot of money). **2 at the expense of sth** If you do one thing at the expense of another, doing the first thing harms the second thing. *He spent a lot of time at work, at the expense of his marriage.* **3 at sb's expense a** If you do something at someone's expense, they pay for it. *We went on holiday at my father's expense.* **b** in order to make someone look stupid *Stop making jokes at my expense.*

**expenses** /ɪk'spensɪz/ *noun* [plural] money that you spend when you are doing your job, that your employer will pay back to you *travel expenses* ● *They pay us two hundred pounds a week, plus expenses.*

o→**expensive** /ɪk'spensɪv/ *adj* costing a lot of money *expensive jewellery* ● [+ to do sth] *It's too expensive to go out every night.* ➔ *Opposite* **inexpensive**. ● **expensively** *adv expensively dressed*

o→**experience**[1] /ɪk'spɪəriəns/ *noun* **1** [U] knowledge that you get from doing a job, or from doing, seeing, or feeling something *Do you have any experience of working with children?* ● *He knows from experience not to play with fire.* ● *In my experience, people smile back if you smile at them.* **2** [C] something that happens to you that affects how you feel *My trip to Australia was an experience I'll never forget.*

**experience**[2] /ɪk'spɪəriəns/ *verb* [T] If you experience something, it happens to you, or you feel it. *It was the worst pain I had ever experienced.* ● *We experienced a lot of difficulty in selling our house.*

o→**experienced** /ɪk'spɪəriənst/ *adj* having skill and knowledge because you have done something many times *Karsten's a very experienced ski instructor.* ➔ *Opposite* **inexperienced**.

o→**experiment**[1] /ɪk'sperɪmənt/ *noun* [C] a test, especially a scientific one, that you do in order to learn something or discover if something is true *to conduct/do/perform an experiment* ● *They're conducting experiments on hamster cells to test the effects of the drug.*

**experiment**[2] /ɪk'sperɪment/ *verb* [I] **1** to try something in order to discover what it is like

*Did he ever **experiment with** drugs?* **2** to do an experiment *Experimenting on mice can give us an idea of the effect of the disease in humans.* ● **experimentation** /ɪkˌsperɪmen'teɪʃ°n/ *noun* [U]

**experimental** /ɪkˌsperɪ'ment°l/ *adj* relating to tests, especially scientific ones *The two scientists used very different experimental methods.* ● **experimentally** *adv The theory has never been proved experimentally.*

o━ **expert¹** /'ekspɜːt/ *noun* [C] someone who has a lot of skill in something or a lot of knowledge about something *He's **an expert on** Japanese literature.* ● *Show me how to use this computer – You're the expert.*

**expert²** /'ekspɜːt/ *adj* [always before noun] having a lot of skill in something or knowing a lot about something *I need some expert advice on investments.* ● *What's your expert opinion?* ● **expertly** *adv He carved the roast expertly.*

**expertise** /ˌekspɜː'tiːz/ *noun* [U] skill *the technical expertise of the engineers*

**expire** /ɪk'spaɪə'/ *verb* [I] If a legal document or agreement expires, you can no longer use it. *Your contract expired six months ago.*

**expiry** /ɪk'spaɪəri/ *noun* [U] *UK* the end of a period when something can be used *What's **the expiry date** on your passport?*

o━ **explain** /ɪk'spleɪn/ *verb* [I, T] to make something clear or easy to understand by giving reasons for it or details about it [+ question word] *Can you explain why you did this?* ● *Can you explain to me how this mobile phone works?* ● [+ (that)] *He explained that he was going to stay with his sister.* ● *How do you explain her strange behaviour?* ● **explaining** *noun* [U] when you have to explain or give a good reason for your actions *You'll **have** a lot **of explaining to do** when dad finds out what happened.*

---

**USAGE**

**explain something**

Explain is followed by the thing you are explaining.

*I'll explain the situation.*

Remember to use the preposition to before a person.

*I'll explain the situation to my parents.*

~~I'll explain the situation my parents.~~

---

o━ **explanation** /ˌeksplə'neɪʃ°n/ *noun* [C, U] the details or reasons that someone gives to make something clear or easy to understand *What's your **explanation for** the team's poor performance?* ● *Could you give me a quick **explanation** of how it works?*

**explanatory** /ɪk'splænət°ri/ *adj* giving an explanation about something *There are explanatory notes with the diagram.* ➔ *See also:* **self-explanatory.**

**expletive** /ɪk'spliːtɪv/ (US) /'eksplətɪv/ *noun* [C] *formal* a swear word (= word which people think is rude or offensive)

**explicable** /ɪk'splɪkəbl/ *adj formal* Something that is explicable can be explained. ➔ *Opposite* **inexplicable.**

**explicit** /ɪk'splɪsɪt/ *adj* **1** clear and exact *She was very **explicit about** her plans.* ● *He made*

*no explicit references to Tess.* **2** showing or talking about sex or violence in a very detailed way *a sexually explicit film* ● **explicitly** *adv She explicitly stated that she did not want her name to be revealed.*

o━ **explode** /ɪk'spləʊd/ *verb* **1** [I, T] If something such as a bomb explodes, it bursts (= breaks suddenly from inside) with noise and force, and if you explode it, you make it burst with noise and force. *One of the bombs did not explode.* **2** [I] to suddenly start shouting because you are very angry *She exploded when he said he was going to the pub with his friends.*

**exploit¹** /ɪk'splɔɪt/ *verb* [T] **1** to not pay or reward someone enough for something [often passive] *I felt as though I was being exploited.* **2** to use or develop something for your advantage *We are not fully exploiting all the resources that we have.* ● **exploitation** /ˌeksplɔɪ'teɪʃ°n/ *noun* [U] *the exploitation of child workers*

**exploit²** /'eksplɔɪt/ *noun* [C] something unusual, brave, or interesting that someone has done [usually plural] *Have you heard about her amazing exploits travelling in Africa?*

**exploratory** /ɪk'splɒrət°ri/ *adj* done in order to discover or learn about something *an exploratory expedition* ● *an exploratory operation*

o━ **explore** /ɪk'splɔː'/ *verb* **1** [I, T] to go around a place where you have never been in order to find out what is there *The children love exploring.* ● *The best way to explore the countryside is on foot.* **2** [T] to think about something very carefully before you make a decision about it *We're exploring the possibility of buying a holiday home.* ● **exploration** /ˌeksplə'reɪʃ°n/ *noun* [C, U] *She's always loved travel and exploration.*

**explorer** /ɪk'splɔːrə'/ *noun* [C] someone who travels to places where no one has ever been in order to find out what is there

o━ **explosion** /ɪk'spləʊʒ°n/ *noun* [C] **1** when something such as a bomb explodes *Forty people were killed in the explosion.* **2** when something increases suddenly by a large amount *the recent population explosion*

**explosive¹** /ɪk'spləʊsɪv/ *adj* **1** An explosive substance or piece of equipment can cause explosions. *The explosive device was hidden in a suitcase.* ● *an explosive mixture of oil vapour and oxygen* **2** An explosive situation or subject causes strong feelings, and may make people angry or violent. *a highly explosive political issue*

**explosive²** /ɪk'spləʊsɪv/ *noun* [C] a substance or piece of equipment that can cause explosions

**exponent** /ɪk'spəʊnənt/ *noun* [C] someone who supports a particular idea or belief, or performs a particular activity *The early **exponents of** votes for women suffered greatly.*

**export¹** /'ekspɔːt/ *noun* **1** [C] a product that you sell in another country *Scottish beef exports to Japan* **2** [U] the business of sending goods to another country in order to sell them there *the export of industrial goods* ➔ *Opposite* **import.**

**export²** /ɪk'spɔːt/ *verb* [I, T] to send goods to another country in order to sell them there *Singapore exports large quantities of rubber.* ● *The company no longer exports to Europe.*

---

➔ *Opposite* **import**. • **exporter** *noun* [C] *Brazil is the world's largest exporter of coffee.*

**expose** /ɪkˈspəʊz/ *verb* [T] **1** HIDDEN THING to remove what is covering something so that it can be seen *He removed the bandage to expose the wound.* • *Our bodies need to be exposed to sunlight in order to make vitamin D.* **2** BAD THING to make public something bad or something that is not honest *The review exposed widespread corruption in the police force.* **3** be **exposed to sth** to experience something or be affected by something because you are in a particular situation or place *It was the first time I'd been exposed to violence.* **4** PHOTOGRAPHY to allow light to reach a piece of camera film in order to produce a photograph

**exposed** /ɪkˈspəʊzd/ *adj* having no protection from bad weather *an exposed cliff*

**exposure** /ɪkˈspəʊʒəʳ/ *noun* **1** EXPERIENCING [U] when someone experiences something or is affected by it because they are in a particular situation or place *There is a risk of **exposure to** radiation.* • *Many young children now have exposure to computers in the home.* **2** MAKING PUBLIC [C, U] when something bad that you have done is made public *She was threatened with exposure by a journalist.* **3** MEDICAL [U] a serious medical condition that is caused by being outside in very cold weather *He died of exposure while trying to climb Mount Everest.* **4** PHOTOGRAPH [C] a single photograph on a piece of film *This film has 24 exposures.*

**expound** /ɪkˈspaʊnd/ *verb* [I, T] *formal* to give a detailed explanation of something *He's always **expounding on** what's wrong with the world.* • *She uses her newspaper column to expound her views on environmental issues.*

O—¤ **express¹** /ɪkˈspres/ *verb* [T] to show what you think or how you feel using words or actions *I'm simply expressing my opinion.* • *These paintings express the terror of war.* • [often reflexive] *You're not expressing yourself* (= saying what you mean) *very clearly.*

**express²** /ɪkˈspres/ *adj* **1** an **express service/train, etc** a service, train, etc that is much faster than usual *an express train* • *an express service* **2** an **express aim/intention/ purpose, etc** a clear and certain aim, intention, purpose, etc *You came here with the express purpose of causing trouble.*

**express³** /ɪkˈspres/ (*also* **ex'press ,train**) *noun* [C] a fast train *I took the express to London.*

O—¤ **expression** /ɪkˈspreʃᵊn/ *noun* **1** LOOK [C] the look on someone's face showing what they feel or think *your facial expression* • *He had a sad expression on his face.* **2** PHRASE [C] a phrase that has a special meaning *'A can of worms' is an expression meaning a difficult situation.* **3** SHOWING THOUGHTS [C, U] when you say what you think or show how you feel using words or actions *As **an expression of** our disapproval, we will no longer use his shop.*

**expressive** /ɪkˈspresɪv/ *adj* showing your feelings *expressive language* • *a very expressive face*

**expressly** /ɪkˈspresli/ *adv formal* **1** If you say something expressly, you say it in a clear way, so that your meaning cannot be doubted. *I*

expressly stated that I did not want any visitors. **2** If something is expressly for a particular reason or person, it is for that reason or person only. *The picture was painted expressly for me.*

**expressway** /ɪkˈspresweɪ/ *US* (*UK* **motorway**) *noun* [C] a long, wide road, usually used by traffic travelling fast over long distances

**expulsion** /ɪkˈspʌlʃᵊn/ *noun* [C, U] when someone is made to leave their school, organization, or country because of their behaviour *They threatened him with **expulsion from** school.*

**exquisite** /ɪkˈskwɪzɪt/ *adj* very beautiful or perfect *a garden of exquisite flowers* • **exquisitely** *adv an exquisitely dressed woman*

**extend** /ɪkˈstend/ *verb* **1** MAKE BIGGER [T] to make something bigger or longer *We're going to extend our kitchen.* • *Can you extend the ladder a bit?* **2** MAKE LAST [T] to make an activity, agreement, etc last for a longer time *They have extended the deadline by one week.* **3** extend **from/into/over, etc** to continue or stretch over a particular area of land or period of time *a mountain range that extends down the Italian peninsula* • *Will the building work extend into next week?* **4** STRETCH OUT [T] to stretch out a part of your body *She smiled and extended her hand.* **5** extend an invitation/ thanks, etc to sb *formal* to give someone an invitation, thanks, etc *I'd like to extend a warm welcome to our guests.*

**extension** /ɪkˈstenʃᵊn/ *noun* [C] **1** PART OF A BUILDING a new room or rooms that are added to a building *You could build an extension onto the back of the house.* **2** EXTRA TIME extra time that you are given to do or use something *You might be able to get an extension on your visa.* **3** TELEPHONE a telephone that is connected to the main telephone in an office or other large building *Call me on extension 213.*

**extensive** /ɪkˈstensɪv/ *adj* large in amount or size *an extensive art collection* • *The hurricane caused extensive damage.* • **extensively** *adv I have travelled extensively in Europe.*

**extent** /ɪkˈstent/ *noun* **1** [no plural] the size or importance of something *They are just beginning to realize the full extent of the damage.* • *Her face was injured to such an extent* (= so much) *that he didn't recognize her.* **2** to some extent/to a certain extent in some ways *I was, to some extent, responsible for the accident.*

**exterior** /ɪkˈstɪəriəʳ/ *noun* [C] the outside part of something or someone [usually singular] *The exterior of the house was painted white.* • *Behind that cold exterior he is a very passionate man.* • **exterior** *adj* [always before noun] *an exterior wall* ➔ *Opposite* **interior**.

**exterminate** /ɪkˈstɜːmɪneɪt/ *verb* [T] to kill a large group of people or animals • **extermination** /ɪkˌstɜːmɪˈneɪʃᵊn/ *noun* [C, U]

**external** /ɪkˈstɜːnᵊl/ *adj* **1** relating to the outside part of something *the external walls of the house* • *The ointment is for external use only* (= it must not be put inside the body). **2** coming from or relating to another country, group, or organization *All exams are marked by an external examiner.* ➔ *Opposite* **internal**. • **externally** *adv*

**extinct** /ɪkˈstɪŋkt/ *adj* If a type of animal is extinct, it does not now exist.

**extinction** /ɪkˈstɪŋkʃ°n/ *noun* [U] when a type of animal no longer exists *Many species of animal are threatened with extinction.*

**extinguish** /ɪkˈstɪŋgwɪʃ/ *verb* [T] *formal* to stop something burning or giving out light *The fire took two hours to extinguish.*

**extinguisher** /ɪkˈstɪŋgwɪʃəʳ/ (*also* **fire extinguisher**) *noun* [C] a piece of equipment shaped like a tube, which is used to spread a substance onto a fire to stop it burning

**extol** /ɪkˈstəʊl/ *verb* [T] **extolling**, *past* **extolled** to say that you think that something is very good *He always extols the virtues of* (= praises) *French cooking.*

**extort** /ɪkˈstɔːt/ *verb* [T] to get money from someone by saying that you will harm them ● **extortion** /ɪkˈstɔːʃ°n/ *noun* [U]

**extortionate** /ɪkˈstɔːʃ°nət/ *adj* Extortionate prices or costs are very high. *You pay an extortionate amount for rented accommodation in the city centre.*

o━**extra**[1] /ˈekstrə/ *adj* more, or more than usual *Can I invite a few extra people?* ● *She's been babysitting to earn some extra cash.*

**extra**[2] /ˈekstrə/ *noun* [C] **1** something that costs more when you buy goods or pay for a service *The hi-fi comes with optional extras such as headphones and remote control.* **2** an actor in a film who does not have a main part and usually plays someone in a crowd

**extra**[3] /ˈekstrə/ *adv* more than usual *Do you get paid extra for working late?* ● *I worked extra hard on that essay.*

**extract**[1] /ɪkˈstrækt/ *verb* [T] **1** to take something out, especially using force *He's going to the dentist's to have a tooth extracted.* **2** to get the money, information, etc that you want from someone who does not want to give it to you *They were not able to extract a confession from her.*

**extract**[2] /ˈekstrækt/ *noun* [C] **1** a particular part of a book, poem, etc that is chosen so that it can be used in a discussion, article, etc *The teacher read out an extract from 'Brave New World'.* **2** a substance taken from a plant, flower, etc and used especially in food or medicine *pure vanilla extract*

**extraction** /ɪkˈstrækʃ°n/ *noun* **1** [C, U] when something is taken out, especially using force **2 of Chinese/Italian, etc extraction** having a family whose origin is Chinese, Italian, etc

**extradite** /ˈekstrədaɪt/ *verb* [T] to send someone back to the country where they are accused of a crime, so that a court there can decide if they are guilty [often passive] *The suspects were extradited to the UK.* ● **extradition** /ˌekstrəˈdɪʃ°n/ *noun* [C, U]

**extraneous** /ɪkˈstreɪniəs/ *adj* not directly connected to something *extraneous information/noise*

**extraordinary** /ɪkˈstrɔːd°n°ri/ *adj* very special, unusual, or strange *an extraordinary tale of courage* ● *She was an extraordinary young woman.* ● *How extraordinary that you should be here too!* ● **extraordinarily** *adv Their last album was extraordinarily successful.*

**extravagant** /ɪkˈstrævəgənt/ *adj* **1** costing too much or spending a lot more money than you need to *the extravagant lifestyle of a movie star* **2** too unusual and extreme to be believed or controlled *the extravagant claims made by cosmetics companies* ● **extravagance** /ɪkˈstrævəgəns/ *noun* [C, U] when someone or something is extravagant ● **extravagantly** *adv*

**extravaganza** /ɪkˌstrævəˈgænzə/ *noun* [C] a large, exciting, and expensive event or entertainment *a 3-hour extravaganza of country music*

o━**extreme**[1] /ɪkˈstriːm/ *adj* **1** SERIOUS the most unusual or most serious possible *extreme weather conditions* ● *In extreme cases, the disease can lead to blindness.* **2** VERY LARGE very large in amount or degree *extreme pain* ● *extreme wealth* **3** OPINIONS having such strong opinions or beliefs that most people cannot agree with you *extreme views* ● *the extreme right* **4** FURTHEST [always before noun] at the furthest point of something *in the extreme south of the island*

**extreme**[2] /ɪkˈstriːm/ *noun* [C] the largest possible amount or degree of something *Anna's moods went from one extreme to another* (= first she was very happy, then she was very unhappy). ● *Coach Wilson took our training to extremes* (= made us train extremely hard).

o━**extremely** /ɪkˈstriːmli/ *adv* very, or much more than usual *extremely beautiful* ● *We all studied extremely hard for the exam.*

**extremist** /ɪkˈstriːmɪst/ *noun* [C] someone who has such strong opinions or beliefs that most people cannot agree with them *religious extremists* ● **extremism** /ɪkˈstriːmɪz°m/ *noun* [U] ● **extremist** *adj*

**extremities** /ɪkˈstremətiz/ *noun* [plural] the end parts of your body such as your hands and feet

**extricate** /ˈekstrɪkeɪt/ *verb* **extricate yourself from sth** to get yourself out of a difficult situation or unpleasant place *I didn't know how to extricate myself from such an embarrassing situation.*

**extrovert** /ˈekstrəvɜːt/ *noun* [C] someone who is very confident and likes being with other people ⊃ *Opposite* **introvert**. ● **extrovert** *adj an extrovert personality* ⊃ *Opposite* **introverted**.

**exuberant** /ɪgˈzjuːb°rᵊnt/ *adj* full of happiness, excitement, and energy *a warm and exuberant personality* ● **exuberance** /ɪgˈzjuːb°rᵊns/ *noun* [U]

**exude** /ɪgˈzjuːd/ *verb* [T] If you exude love, confidence, pain, etc, you show that you have a lot of that feeling.

**exult** /ɪgˈzʌlt/ *verb* [I] to show great pleasure, especially at someone else's defeat or failure *She seems to exult in her power.* ● **exultation** /ˌegzʌlˈteɪʃ°n/ *noun* [U]

o━**eye**[1] /aɪ/ *noun* **1** [C] one of the two organs in your face, which you use to see with *Sara has black hair and brown eyes.* ● *She closed her eyes and fell off to sleep.* **2** [C] the small hole at the end of a needle, that you put the thread through **3 have an eye for sth** to be good at noticing a particular type of thing *Your son has a very good eye for detail.* **4 keep your/an eye on sb/sth** to watch or look after someone or something *Could you keep an eye on this pan*

*of soup for a moment?* **eye**
**5 have your eye on sth** *informal* to want something and intend to get it *Jane's got her eye on that new advertising job.*
**6 can't keep/take your eyes off sb/sth** to be unable to stop looking at someone

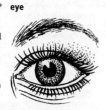

or something because they are so attractive or interesting *He couldn't take his eyes off her all night.* **7 lay/set eyes on sb/sth** to see someone or something for the first time *They fell in love the moment they laid eyes on each other.* **8 look sb in the eye/eyes** to look at someone in a direct way, without show-ing fear or shame *Look me in the eye and say that you didn't steal it.* **9 in sb's eyes** in some-one's opinion *In my parents' eyes, I'll always be a child.* **10 cast/run your/an eye over sth** *UK* to look at something quickly, often in order to give your opinion about it *Would you cast an eye over our work so far?* **11 catch sb's eye a** to get someone's attention by looking at them *I tried to catch her eye, but she had already turned away.* **b** to be attractive or different enough to be noticed by people *It was the colour of his jacket that caught my eye.* **12 cry your eyes out** If someone cries their eyes out, they cry a lot about a problem or situation. *She cried her eyes out when he left her for another girl.* **13 keep your eyes open/peeled (for sb/sth)** to watch carefully for someone or something *Keep your eyes peeled, he should be here any minute.* **14 keep an eye out for sb/sth** to watch carefully for someone or something to appear *Keep an eye out for the delivery van.* **15 see eye to eye (with sb)** If two people see eye to eye, they agree with each other. *Our teachers don't always see eye to eye with the headmaster.* **16 turn a blind eye (to sth)** to choose to ignore something that you know is wrong or illegal **17 with your eyes open** knowing about all of the problems that could happen if you do something *I went into this marriage with my eyes open.* ➔ *See also:* **black eye**.

**eye²** /aɪ/ *verb* [T] **eyeing** (*also US* **eying**), *past eyed* to look at someone or something with interest *The two women eyed each other suspiciously.*

**eyeball** /'aɪbɔːl/ *noun* [C] the whole of the eye, that has the shape of a small ball

**eyebrow** /'aɪbraʊ/ *noun* [C] the thin line of hair that is above each eye ➔ *See colour picture* **The Body** *on page Centre 2.*

**eye-catching** /'aɪˌkætʃɪŋ/ *adj* attractive, inter-esting, or different enough to be noticed *an eye-catching poster*

**'eye ˌcontact** *noun* [U] If two people make eye contact, they look at each other at the same time.

**-eyed** /aɪd/ *suffix* used at the end of a word describing a person's eyes *Both sisters are brown-eyed.* ➔ *See also:* **cross-eyed**, **wide-eyed**.

**eyelash** /'aɪlæʃ/ (*also* **lash**) *noun* [C] one of the short hairs that grow from the edge of your eyelids [usually plural] *false eyelashes*

**eyelid** /'aɪlɪd/ *noun* [C] **1** the piece of skin that covers your eyes when you close them **2 not bat an eyelid** to not react to something unusual

**eyeliner** /'aɪˌlaɪnə/ *noun* [C, U] a coloured sub-stance, usually contained in a pencil, which you put in a line above or below your eyes in order to make them more attractive ➔ *See picture at* **make up**.

**eye-opener** /'aɪˌəʊpᵊnə/ *noun* [C] something that surprises you and teaches you new facts about life, people, etc *Living in another country can be a real eye-opener.*

**eyeshadow** /'aɪʃædəʊ/ *noun* [C, U] a coloured cream or powder which you put above or around your eyes in order to make them more attractive

**eyesight** /'aɪsaɪt/ *noun* [U] the ability to see *My eyesight is getting worse.*

**eyesore** /'aɪsɔː/ *noun* [C] a building, area, etc that looks ugly compared to the things that are around it

**eyewitness** /ˌaɪ'wɪtnɪs/ (*also* **witness**) *noun* [C] someone who saw something such as a crime or an accident happen *Eyewitnesses saw two men running away from the bank.*

E

# F

**F, f** /ef/ the sixth letter of the alphabet

**F** *written abbreviation for* Fahrenheit (= a measurement of temperature) *a body temperature of 98.6 °F*

**FA** /,ef'eɪ/ *noun abbreviation for* Football Association: the national organization for football in England *the FA cup*

**fable** /'feɪbl/ *noun* [C] a short, traditional story, usually involving animals, which is intended to show people how to behave *Aesop's fables*

**fabric** /'fæbrɪk/ *noun* **1** [C, U] cloth *a light/woollen fabric* **2 the fabric of sth a** the basic way in which a society or other social group is organized *The family is part of the fabric of society.* **b** *UK* the walls, floor, and roof of a building

**fabricate** /'fæbrɪkeɪt/ *verb* [T] to invent facts, a story, etc in order to deceive someone *He claims that the police fabricated evidence against him.*
● fabrication /,fæbrɪ'keɪʃᵊn/ *noun* [C, U]

**fabulous** /'fæbjələs/ *adj* extremely good *They've got a fabulous house.* ● *We had an absolutely fabulous holiday.* ● fabulously *adv* extremely *Her family is fabulously wealthy.*

**facade** (*also* façade) /fə'sɑːd/ *noun* [C] **1** a false appearance *Behind that amiable facade, he's a deeply unpleasant man.* **2** the front of a large building *the gallery's elegant 18th century façade*

o⤸**face¹** /feɪs/ *noun* **1** [C] the front part of the head where the eyes, nose, and mouth are, or the expression on this part *She's got a long, thin face.* ● *I can't wait to see her face when she opens the present.* **2 make a face** (*also UK* **pull a face**) to show with your face that you do not like someone or something *The baby made a face every time I offered her some food.* **3 make faces** to make silly expressions with your face in order to try and make people laugh **4 sb's face falls/lights up** someone starts to look disappointed/happy *His face fell when I said that she wasn't coming.* **5 to sb's face** If you say something unpleasant to someone's face, you say it to them directly, when you are with them. *If you've got something to say, say it to my face.* **6** the front or surface of something *the north face of the cliff* ● *a clock face* **7 in the face of sth** while having to deal with a difficult situation or problem *She refused to leave him, in the face of increasing pressure from friends and family.* **8 on the face of it** used when you are describing how a situation seems on the surface *On the face of it, it seems like a bargain, but I bet there are hidden costs.* **9 keep a straight face** to manage to stop yourself from smiling or laughing *I can never play jokes on people because I can't keep a straight face.* **10 lose/save face** to do something so that people stop respecting you/still respect you *He seemed more interested in saving face than telling the truth.* ➔ *See also:* have **egg¹** on your face, a **slap²** in the face.

o⤸**face²** /feɪs/ *verb* [T] **1** DIRECTION to be or turn in a particular direction *The room faces south.* ● *She turned to face him.* ● *Could you face the front please, children?* **2** PROBLEM If you face a problem, or a problem faces you, you have to deal with it. [often passive] *This is one of the many problems faced by working mothers.* ● *Passengers could face long delays.* **3 can't face sth/doing sth** to not want to do something or deal with something because it is so unpleasant *I had intended to go for a run, but now I just can't face it.* **4** ACCEPT to accept that something unpleasant is true and start to deal with the situation *She's going to have to face the fact that he's not coming back to her.* **5 let's face it** something that you say before you say something that is unpleasant but true *Let's face it, none of us are getting any younger.* **6** PUNISHMENT If you face something unpleasant, especially a punishment, then it might happen to you. *If found guilty, the pair face fines of up to $40,000.* **7** DEAL WITH to deal with someone when the situation between you is difficult *How can I face him now that he knows what I've done?* **8** COMPETITION to play against another player or team in a competition, sport, etc *We face Spain in the semifinal.* ➔ *See also:* face the **music**.

**face up to sth** to accept that a difficult situation exists *You've got to face up to the truth sometime – he'll never marry you.*

**facelift** /'feɪslɪft/ *noun* [C] **1** medical treatment which makes the skin of your face tighter so that you look younger *She looks like she's had a facelift.* **2** when you improve a place and make it look more attractive *The council is planning a £6 million facelift for the old harbour area.*

**facet** /'fæsɪt/ *noun* [C] one part of a subject, situation, etc that has many parts *She has many facets to her personality.*

**facetious** /fə'siːʃəs/ *adj* trying to make a joke or a clever remark in a way that annoys people *He's sure to say something facetious when you tell him the news.*

**face-to-face** /,feɪstə'feɪs/ *adj, adv* directly, meeting someone in the same place *We need to talk face-to-face.* ● *She came face-to-face with the gunman as he strode into the playground.*

**face value** *noun* **take sth at face value** to accept the way that something first appears without thinking about what it really means *You can't just take everything you read in the papers at face value.*

**facial** /'feɪʃᵊl/ *adj* of or on the face *facial expressions/hair*

**facile** /'fæsaɪl/ ⓤⓢ /'fæsᵊl/ *adj formal* A facile remark is too simple and has not been thought about enough.

**facilitate** /fə'sɪlɪteɪt/ *verb* [T] *formal* to make something possible or easier *I will do everything in my power to facilitate the process.*

**facilities** /fə'sɪlətiz/ *noun* [plural] buildings, equipment, or services that are provided for a particular purpose *sports/washing facilities* ● *childcare facilities*

**facility** /fə'sɪləti/ *noun* [C] **1** a part of a system or machine which makes it possible to do something *This phone has a memory facility.* **2** a place where a particular activity happens *a new medical facility*

O━**fact** /fækt/ *noun* **1** [C] something that you know is true, exists, or has happened *I'm not angry that you drove my car, it's just the fact that you didn't ask me first.* ● *No decision will be made until we know all the facts.* ● *He knew for a fact* (= was certain) *that Natalie was lying.* **2** [U] real events and experiences, not things that are imagined *It's hard to separate fact from fiction in what she says.* **3 in fact/in actual fact/as a matter of fact a** used to emphasize what is really true *I was told there were some tickets left, but in actual fact they were sold out.* **b** used when giving more information about something *"Is Isabel coming?" "Yes. As a matter of fact, she should be here soon."* **4 the fact (of the matter) is** used to tell someone that something is the truth *I wouldn't usually ask for your help, but the fact is I'm desperate.* **5 the facts of life** details about sexual activity and the way that babies are born

**faction** /'fækʃ°n/ *noun* [C] a small group of people who are part of a larger group, and oppose the ideas of everyone else

**factor** /'fæktər/ *noun* [C] **1** one of the things that has an effect on a particular situation, decision, event, etc *Money was an important factor in their decision to move.* **2** a number that another larger number can be divided by exactly *5 is a factor of 10.*

O━**factory** /'fækt°ri/ *noun* [C] a building or group of buildings where large amounts of products are made or put together *a textile factory*

**factual** /'fæktʃuəl/ *adj* using or consisting of facts *There aren't enough factual programmes on television.* ● **factually** *adv factually correct/incorrect*

**faculty** /'fæk°lti/ *noun* **1** [C] a natural ability to hear, see, think, move, etc [usually plural] *After her stroke, my mother lost many of her faculties.* **2 the English/law/science, etc faculty** a particular department at a college or university, or the teachers in that department **3 the faculty** *US* all of the teachers at a school or college

**fad** /fæd/ *noun* [C] something that is fashionable to do, wear, say, etc for a short period of time *the latest health fad*

**fade** /feɪd/ *verb* **1** [I, T] If a colour or a sound fades, or if something fades it, it become less bright or strong. *The music began to fade.* ● *The walls had been faded by the sun.* **2** (*also* **fade away**) to slowly disappear, lose importance, or become weaker *With time, memories of that painful summer would fade away.*

**faeces** *UK* (*US* **feces**) /'fiːsiːz/ *noun* [plural] *formal* solid waste that comes out of the bottom of a person or animal

**fag** /fæg/ *noun* [C] *UK informal* a cigarette

**Fahrenheit** /'fær°nhaɪt/ (*written abbreviation* **F**) *noun* [U] a measurement of temperature in which water freezes at 32° and boils at 212°

O━**fail¹** /feɪl/ *verb* **1** NOT SUCCEED [I] to not be successful *Dad's business failed after just three years.* ● *She keeps failing in her attempt to lose weight.* **2 fail to do sth** to not do what is necessary or expected *John failed to turn up for foot-*

ball practice yesterday. **3** EXAM [I, T] to not pass a test or an exam, or to decide that someone has not passed *I'm worried about failing my driving test.* **4** STOP WORKING [I] to stop working normally, or to become weaker *Two of the plane's engines had failed.* ● *My eyesight's beginning to fail.* **5** NOT HELPING [T] to stop being helpful or useful to someone when they need you *The government is failing the poor and unemployed.* **6 I fail to see/understand** used to show that you do not accept something [+ question word] *I fail to see why you cannot work on a Sunday.*

**fail²** /feɪl/ *noun* **without fail** If you do something without fail, you always do it, also when it is difficult. *I go to the gym every Monday and Thursday without fail.*

**failing¹** /'feɪlɪŋ/ *noun* [C] a bad quality or fault that someone or something has *Despite one or two failings, he's basically a nice guy.*

**failing²** /'feɪlɪŋ/ *preposition* **failing that** if something is not possible or does not happen *Our goal is to move out by January, or failing that, by March.*

O━**failure** /'feɪljər/ *noun* **1** NO SUCCESS [U] when someone or something does not succeed *Their attempt to climb Everest ended in failure.* **2** PERSON/ACTION [C] someone or something that does not succeed *All my life I've felt like a failure.* **3 failure to do sth** when you do not do something that you must do or are expected to do *Failure to pay within 14 days will result in prosecution.* **4** NOT WORKING [C, U] when something does not work, or stops working as well as it should *heart failure* ● *All trains were delayed due to a power failure.*

**faint¹** /feɪnt/ *adj* **1** slight and not easy to notice, smell, hear, etc *a faint smell of smoke* ● *faint laughter coming from next door* **2 feel faint** to feel very weak and as if you might fall down *Seeing all the blood made me feel faint.* **3 faint hope/praise/chance, etc** very little hope, praise, chance, etc *a faint hope of winning the gold medal* **4 not have the faintest idea** used to emphasize that you do not know something [+ question word] *I haven't the faintest idea what you're talking about.*

**faint²** /feɪnt/ *verb* [I] to suddenly become unconscious for a short time, usually falling down onto the floor *She fainted with exhaustion.*

**faintly** /'feɪntli/ *adv* slightly *faintly embarrassed*

O━**fair¹** /feər/ *adj* **1** EQUAL treating everyone in the same way, so that no one has an advantage *a fair trial* ● *That's not fair. You always go first!* **2** RIGHT acceptable or right *a fair deal* ● *We'd like to move abroad, but it's just not fair on the children.* ➲ *Opposite* **unfair**. **3** HAIR/SKIN having pale skin or a light colour of hair *a boy with fair hair and blue eyes* ➲ *See colour picture* **Hair** *on page Centre 9.* **4 a fair amount/distance/size, etc** quite a large amount, distance, size, etc *There's still a fair bit of work to be done on the house.* **5** WEATHER sunny and not raining *Tomorrow will be fair, with some early morning frost.* **6** AVERAGE not very good but not very bad *He has a fair chance of winning.* **7 fair enough** *UK informal* used to say that you agree, or think that something is acceptable

*"He'll only work on Sunday if he gets paid extra." "Fair enough."* ➔ *See also:* fair **play²**, have your fair **share²** of sth.

**fair²** /feəʳ/ *noun* [C] **1** an event outside where you can ride large machines for pleasure and play games to win prizes **2** an event where people show and sell goods or services relating to a particular business or hobby *a trade fair*

fair

**fair³** /feəʳ/ *adv* **1 play fair** to do something in a fair and honest way **2 fair and square** in an honest way and without any doubt *We won the match fair and square.*

**fairground** /ˈfeəɡraʊnd/ *noun* [C] an outside area that is used for fairs

**fair-haired** /ˌfeəˈheəd/ *adj* having a light colour of hair *a fair-haired child*

o-**fairly** /ˈfeəli/ *adv* **1** more than average, but less than very *a fairly big family* • *fairly quickly* **2** in a fair way *treating people fairly*

**fairness** /ˈfeənəs/ *noun* [U] when you treat everyone in the same way, so that no one has an advantage *He believes in fairness and decency.*

**fairy** /ˈfeəri/ *noun* [C] a small, imaginary creature that looks like a person with wings, and has magic powers

**ˈfairy ˌtale** *noun* [C] a story told to children which involves magic, imaginary creatures and a happy ending

o-**faith** /feɪθ/ *noun* **1** TRUST [U] the belief that someone or something is good, right, and able to be trusted *Have faith in me. I won't let you down.* **2** STRONG BELIEF [U] strong belief in a god or gods *Throughout her illness, she never lost her faith in God.* **3** RELIGION [C] a religion *the Jewish and Christian faiths* **4 in good faith** If you act in good faith, you believe that what you are doing is good, honest, or legal. *Mr Daniels claims the money was given to him in good faith.*

**faithful** /ˈfeɪθfəl/ *adj* **1** RELATIONSHIP If your husband, wife, or partner is faithful, they do not have a sexual relationship with anyone else. *a faithful husband* • *They remained faithful to each other throughout their long marriage.* **2** LOYAL always loyal *his trusted and faithful servant* **3** NOT CHANGED not changing any of the original details, facts, style, etc *Does the film adaptation stay faithful to the novel?* ➔ *Opposite* **unfaithful.** • **faithfulness** *noun* [U]

**faithfully** /ˈfeɪθfəli/ *adv* **1** in a faithful way

**2 Yours faithfully** used to end a formal letter to someone whose name you do not know

**fake¹** /feɪk/ *adj* not real, but made to look or seem real *fake fur* • *a fake passport*

**fake²** /feɪk/ *noun* [C] **1** a copy of something that is intended to look real or valuable and deceive people *Experts say that the painting is a fake.* **2** someone who pretends to have particular skills or qualities so that they can deceive people or get their admiration

**fake³** /feɪk/ *verb* [T] **1** to copy something in order to deceive people *faked documents* **2** to pretend that you have a particular feeling or emotion *He said he was feeling sick, but he was just faking it.*

**falcon** /ˈfɔːlkən/ *noun* [C] a large bird that eats small animals and is often taught to hunt by people

o-**fall¹** /fɔːl/ *verb* [I] *past t* **fell**, *past p* **fallen 1** MOVE DOWN to move down towards the ground *Huge drops of rain were falling from the sky.* • *By winter, all the leaves had fallen off the trees.* **2** STOP STANDING to suddenly go down and hit the ground without intending to *She fell off her bike and broke her arm.* **3** BECOME LESS to become less in number or amount *Housing prices have fallen by 15% since last year.* • *Temperatures are expected to fall from 15°C to 9°C.* **4** BECOME WORSE to become worse, or start to be in a bad situation or condition *Education standards are continuing to fall.* • *Empty for 30 years, the building had fallen into ruin* (= become very damaged). **5 fall asleep/ill/still, etc** to start to sleep, become ill, become quiet, etc *I fell asleep on the sofa watching TV.* **6 darkness/night falls** *literary* used to say that it is becoming dark **7** LOSE POWER to lose power and start to be controlled by a different leader *In 1453 the city fell to the Turks.* **8** HANG DOWN to hang down *Her long blonde hair fell softly over her shoulders.* ➔ *See also:* fall on deaf ears **(ear)**, fall **flat³**, fall **foul¹** of sb/sth, fall to pieces **(piece¹)**, fall into **place¹**, fall **prey¹** to sth, fall by the **wayside**.

**fall apart 1** to break into pieces *My poor old boots are falling apart.* **2** to start having problems that you cannot deal with *Their relationship fell apart after they moved to Detroit.*

**fall back on sb/sth** to use someone or something when other things have failed, or when there are no other choices *We've been saving up the past few years, to have something to fall back on.*

**fall behind** to not do something fast enough, or

not do something by a particular time *Lucy's been falling behind in her homework again.*

**fall for sb** to suddenly have strong, romantic feelings about someone

**fall for sth** to be tricked into believing something that is not true *He told me he owned a mansion in Spain and I fell for it.*

**fall in** If a roof or ceiling falls in, it drops to the ground because it is damaged.

**fall off** If the amount, rate, or quality of something falls off, it becomes smaller or lower. *Demand for new cars is falling off.*

**fall on sth** to happen on a particular day or date *New Year's Day falls on a Tuesday this year.*

**fall out** *UK* to argue with someone and stop being friendly with them *Have you and Sam fallen out with each other again?*

**fall over** If someone or something falls over, they fall to the ground or onto their side. *Be careful! You're going to fall over!* • *The fence fell over in the wind.* ➔ *See colour picture* **Phrasal Verbs** *on page Centre 13.*

**fall through** If a plan or agreement falls through, it fails to happen.

o━**fall²** /fɔːl/ *noun* **1** AMOUNT [C] when the number or amount of something becomes smaller *There's been a sharp fall in prices.* **2** MOVEMENT [C] when someone or something moves down to the ground *a heavy fall of snow* • *The climbers were rushed to hospital after being injured in a fall.* **3** SEASON [C, U] *US (UK/US* **autumn**) the season of the year between summer and winter, when leaves fall from the trees *He started a new job in the fall.* **4** DEFEAT [no plural] when a city, government, leader, etc loses power or control *the fall of communism*

**fallacy** /'fæləsi/ *noun* [C, U] a belief that is not true or correct *It's a fallacy that problems will disappear if you ignore them.*

**fallen** /'fɔːlən/ *past participle of* fall

**fallible** /'fæləbl/ *adj* able to make mistakes *We place our trust in doctors, but even they are fallible.* ➔ *Opposite* **infallible**. • **fallibility** /,fælə'bɪləti/ *noun* [U]

**fallout** /'fɔːlaʊt/ *noun* [U] the radiation (= powerful and dangerous energy) from a nuclear explosion

**fallow** /'fæləʊ/ *adj* If land is left fallow, it is not planted with crops, in order to improve the quality of the soil.

o━**false** /fɔːls/ *adj* **1** NOT TRUE not true or correct *a false name* • *Many rumours about her life were later proved to be false.* **2** NOT REAL not real, but made to look or seem real *false teeth* • *false documents* **3** NOT SINCERE not sincere or expressing real emotions *false promises* • *I hate the way he smiles at everyone. It's so false.* • **falsely** *adv*

,**false a'larm** *noun* [C] an occasion when people believe that something dangerous is happening, but it is not *Fire engines rushed to the scene, but it was a false alarm.*

**falsehood** /'fɔːlshʊd/ *noun* [C] *formal* a lie

,**false 'start** *noun* [C] an occasion when you try to start an activity, event, or process, but fail and have to stop *The after-school club finally opened this term, after several false starts.*

**falsify** /'fɔːlsɪfaɪ/ *verb* [T] to change important

information, especially in documents, in order to deceive people

**falter** /'fɔːltəʳ/ *verb* [I] **1** to stop being confident, powerful, or successful *In the late 1980s his career began to falter.* **2** to pause, make mistakes, or seem weak when you are talking or moving *Her voice didn't falter once during the ceremony.* • *a few faltering steps*

**fame** /feɪm/ *noun* [U] when you are known by many people because of your achievements, skills, etc *fame and fortune* • *She first rose to fame as a pop star at the age of 16.* ➔ *See also:* sb's/sth's **claim²** to fame.

**famed** /feɪmd/ *adj* famous, especially for having particular qualities *It is a city famed for its ski slopes and casinos.*

o━**familiar** /fə'mɪliəʳ/ *adj* **1** easy to recognize because of being seen, met, heard, etc before *It's nice to see a few familiar faces* (= people that I recognize) *around here.* • *This street doesn't look familiar to me.* **2 be familiar with sth** to know about something or have experienced it many times before *Anyone who's familiar with his poetry will find the course easy.* ➔ *Opposite* **unfamiliar**. **3** friendly and very informal *He doesn't like to be too familiar with his staff.*

**familiarity** /fə,mɪli'ærəti/ *noun* [U] **1** a good knowledge of something, or experience of doing or using it *Her familiarity with computers is very impressive.* **2** friendly and informal behaviour *the growing familiarity between William and Jane*

**familiarize** (*also UK* **-ise**) /fə'mɪliəraɪz/ *verb* **familiarize sb/yourself with sth** to teach someone more about something new, or try to understand more about it yourself *We spent a few minutes familiarizing ourselves with the day's schedule.*

o━**family** /'fæmʲli/ *noun* **1** RELATED PEOPLE [group] a group of people who are related to each other, such as a mother, a father, and their children *Is your family coming to the graduation ceremony?* • *Her (UK) family are/(US) family is originally from Ireland.* • *a family business* **2** CHILDREN [C] the children in a family [usually singular] *Single parents have to raise a family on their own.* • *Paul and Alison are hoping to start a family soon.* **3** PLANTS/ANIMALS [C] a group of similar types of plants or animals that are related to each other

'**family ,name** *noun* [C] the name that is used by all the members of a family

,**family 'planning** *noun* [U] controlling how many children you have by using contraceptives (= pills or objects that prevent a woman from becoming pregnant)

,**family 'tree** *noun* [C] a drawing that shows the relationships between the different members of a family, especially over a long period of time

**famine** /'fæmɪn/ *noun* [C, U] when people living in a particular area do not have enough food for a long time causing suffering and death

o━**famous** /'feɪməs/ *adj* known or recognized by many people *a famous actress* • *New York is a city famous for its shopping and nightlife.* ➔ *See also:* **world-famous**.

**famously** /'feɪməsli/ *adv* **1 get on famously (with sb)** to have a very friendly relationship with someone **2** in a way that is famous

⚬━**fan¹** /fæn/ *noun* [C] **1** someone who admires and supports a famous person, sport, type of music, etc *More than 15,000 Liverpool fans attended Saturday's game.* • *He's a big fan of country music.* **2** something that is used to move the air around so that it feels cooler, such as a machine or an object that you wave with your hand *an electric fan*

**fan²** /fæn/ *verb* [T] **fanning**, *past* **fanned** to move the air around with a fan or something used like a fan, to make it feel cooler [often reflexive] *The spectators sat in the bright sun, fanning themselves with newspapers.*

**fan out** If a group of people fan out, they move out in different directions from a single point.

**fanatic** /fə'nætɪk/ *noun* [C] someone whose interest in something or enthusiasm for something is extreme *religious fanatics* • **fanatical** *adj* extremely enthusiastic about something *She's fanatical about football.* • **fanaticism** /fə'nætɪsɪzᵊm/ *noun* [U]

**fanciful** /'fænsɪfᵊl/ *adj* Something that is fanciful comes from someone's imagination and so is probably not true or real. *a fanciful story*

'**fan ,club** *noun* [C] an organization for the people who support and admire a particular singer, actor, sports team, etc *the Spice Girls' official fan club*

**fancy¹** /'fænsi/ *verb* [T] **1** WANT UK to want to have or do something *Do you fancy a drink?* • [+ doing sth] *We fancy going to the Caribbean for our holiday.* **2** PERSON UK informal to feel sexually attracted to someone *I fancied him the first time I saw him.* **3 fancy (that)!** UK informal used to show that you are surprised or shocked by something [+ doing sth] *Fancy seeing you here!* • *He's going out with Marie? Well fancy that!* **4** THINK formal to think that something is true [+ (that)] *I fancy that he was smiling, but I can't be sure.*

**fancy²** /'fænsi/ *adj* **1** Fancy things and places are expensive and fashionable. *a fancy restaurant* **2** with lots of decoration, or very complicated *fancy cakes*

**fancy³** /'fænsi/ *noun* **1 take a fancy to sb/sth** to start to like someone or something a lot *Marina had taken a fancy to her.* **2 take sb's fancy** If something or someone takes your fancy, you find them interesting or attractive. *We can go anywhere that takes your fancy.*

,**fancy 'dress** *noun* [U] UK special clothes that people wear for a party, which make them look like a different person *a fancy dress party*

**fanfare** /'fænfeəʳ/ *noun* [C] a short, loud tune played on a trumpet (= metal musical instrument) to announce an important person or event

**fang** /fæŋ/ *noun* [C] a long, sharp tooth of an animal such as a dog or a snake

'**fanny ,pack** US (UK **bumbag**) *noun* [C] a small bag fixed to a belt that you wear around your waist

**fantasize** (*also* UK **-ise**) /'fæntəsaɪz/ *verb* [I, T] to imagine something that you would like to happen, but is not likely to happen *We used to fantasize about becoming famous actresses.*

**fang**

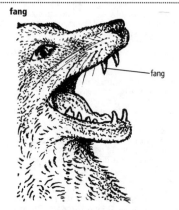

fang

**fantastic** /fæn'tæstɪk/ *adj* **1** GOOD *informal* very good *He looks fantastic in that suit.* • *I've had a fantastic time.* **2** LARGE *informal* A fantastic amount or number of something is very large. *They're making fantastic amounts of money.* **3** STRANGE very strange and probably not true *fantastic stories about monsters and witches*

**fantastically** /fæn'tæstɪkᵊli/ *adv* extremely *fantastically rich*

**fantasy** /'fæntəsi/ *noun* [C, U] a situation or event that you imagine, which is not real or true

**FAQ** /,efei'kjuː/ *noun* [C] *abbreviation for* frequently asked question: something that many people ask when they use the Internet or a computer program, or a file (= collection) of these questions with their answers

⚬━**far¹** /fɑːʳ/ *adv* **1** used to talk about how distant something is *It's the first time I've been so far away from home.* • *How far is it to the supermarket?* • *Bournemouth is not far from Poole.* • *In the summer the herds move farther north.* **2** a long time *How far back can you remember?* • *We need to plan further ahead.* **3 far better/ cheaper/more, etc** much better, cheaper, more, etc *Young people are far more independent these days.* **4 far too difficult/expensive/ late, etc** much too difficult, expensive, late, etc *His trousers were far too tight.* **5 as far as I know** *informal* used to say what you think is true, although you do not know all the facts *As far as I know, they haven't reached a decision yet.* **6 as far as sb is concerned** used to say what someone's opinion is *It's all over as far as I'm concerned.* **7 as far as sth is concerned** used to say what you are talking about *As far as sport's concerned, I like tennis and football.* **8 by far** used to emphasize that something is the biggest, the best, etc *This is his best film by far.* **9 far from sth** certainly not something *The situation is far from clear.* **10 far from doing sth** certainly not doing something *Far from being pleased, he was embarrassed by the praise.* **11 far from it** *informal* used to tell someone that something is certainly not true *He's not handsome – far from it.* **12 as far as**

**possible** as much as is possible *We try to buy organic food as far as possible.* **13 go so far as to do sth** to take the extreme action of doing something *He even went so far as to stop her using the telephone.* **14 go too far** to behave in a way that upsets or annoys other people *He's said some stupid things in the past, but this time he's gone too far.* **15 how far** used to talk about how true something is *How far do politicians represent the views of ordinary people?* **16 so far** until now *So far, we haven't made much progress.* **17 so far so good** *informal* used to say that something has gone well until now **18 not go (very) far** If something such as money does not go far, you cannot do very much with it. *£1 doesn't go very far these days.*

o—**far²** /fɑː/ *adj* **farther, farthest** or **further, furthest** **1** [always before noun] the part of something that is most distant from you or from the centre *His office is at the far end of the corridor.* • *They live in the far south of the country.* **2 the far left/right** used to describe political groups whose opinions are very extreme ➔ *See also:* be a far **cry²** from sth.

**faraway** /ˌfɑːrəˈweɪ/ *adj* **1** [always before noun] *literary* a long distance away *faraway places* **2 a faraway look/expression** an expression on someone's face that shows that they are not thinking about what is happening around them *He had a faraway look in his eyes.*

**farce** /fɑːs/ *noun* **1** [no plural] a serious event or situation that becomes ridiculous because it is so badly organized *The meeting was a complete farce.* **2** [C] a funny play in which a lot of silly things happen • *farcical* /ˈfɑːsɪkᵊl/ *adj* like a farce

o—**fare¹** /feəʳ/ *noun* [C] the price that you pay to travel on an aircraft, train, bus, etc *air/train fares*

**fare²** /feəʳ/ *verb formal* **fare well/badly/better, etc** used to say how well or badly someone or something does in a particular situation *All the children fared well in the exams.*

**farewell** /ˌfeəˈwel/ *exclamation, old-fashioned* goodbye • **farewell** *noun* [C] when someone says goodbye *a sad farewell* • *a farewell party*

**far-fetched** /ˌfɑːˈfetʃt/ *adj* difficult to believe and not likely to be true *The idea is not as far-fetched as it might sound.*

o—**farm¹** /fɑːm/ *noun* [C] an area of land with fields and buildings that is used for growing crops and keeping animals as a business *a dairy farm* • *farm animals/buildings*

**farm²** /fɑːm/ *verb* [I, T] to grow crops or keep animals as a business *Only 2% of the country's farmland is farmed organically.*

o—**farmer** /ˈfɑːməʳ/ *noun* [C] someone who owns or looks after a farm

**farmhouse** /ˈfɑːmhaʊs/ *noun* [C] *plural* **farmhouses** /ˈfɑːmhaʊzɪz/ the house on a farm where the farmer lives

**farming** /ˈfɑːmɪŋ/ *noun* [U] working on a farm or organizing the work there

**farmland** /ˈfɑːmlænd/ *noun* [U] land which is used for or suitable for farming

**farmyard** /ˈfɑːmjɑːd/ *noun* [C] an area of ground with farm buildings around it

**far-off** /ˌfɑːrˈɒf/ *adj literary* a long distance away or a long time in the past or future *far-off lands*

**far-reaching** /ˌfɑːˈriːtʃɪŋ/ *adj* Far-reaching acts, events, or ideas have very big effects. *far-reaching changes in the education system*

**farsighted** /ˈfɑːˌsaɪtɪd/ *US* (*UK* **long-sighted**) *adj* able to see objects which are far away, but not things which are near to you

**farther** /ˈfɑːðəʳ/ *adj, adv* (*comparative of* far) more distant *I couldn't walk any farther.* ➔ *See usage note at* **further**.

**farthest** /ˈfɑːðɪst/ *adj, adv* (*superlative of* far) most distant *They walked to the farthest edge of the garden.*

**fascinate** /ˈfæsɪneɪt/ *verb* [T] to interest someone a lot *Science has always fascinated me.*

**fascinated** /ˈfæsɪneɪtɪd/ *adj* extremely interested *They were absolutely fascinated by the game.*

**fascinating** /ˈfæsɪneɪtɪŋ/ *adj* extremely interesting *I found the movie fascinating.*

**fascination** /ˌfæsɪˈneɪʃᵊn/ *noun* [U, no plural] when you find someone or something fascinating *Her fascination with fashion started at an early age.*

**fascism, Fascism** /ˈfæʃɪzᵊm/ *noun* [U] a political system in which the government is extremely powerful and controls people's lives

**fascist** /ˈfæʃɪst/ *noun* [C] **1** (*also* **Fascist**) someone who supports fascism **2** someone who you do not like because they try to control other people's behaviour • *fascist adj a fascist dictator/regime*

o—**fashion¹** /ˈfæʃᵊn/ *noun* **1** STYLE [C, U] the most popular style of clothes, appearance, or behaviour at a particular time *Long hair is back in fashion for men.* • *Fur coats have gone out of fashion.* **2** BUSINESS [U] making and selling clothes *the fashion industry* **3** WAY [no plural] *formal* the way in which someone does something *He told the story in a very amusing fashion.*

**fashion²** /ˈfæʃᵊn/ *verb* [T] *formal* to make something *jewellery fashioned from recycled metal*

o—**fashionable** /ˈfæʃᵊnəbl/ *adj* popular at a particular time *fashionable clothes* • [+ to do sth] *It's no longer fashionable to smoke.* ➔ *Opposite* **unfashionable**. • *fashionably adv fashionably dressed*

**farm**

o➔**fast¹** /fɑːst/ *adj* **1** moving, happening, or doing something quickly *fast cars* • *a fast swimmer* • *Computers are getting faster all the time.* **2** [never before noun] If a clock or watch is fast, it shows a time that is later than the correct time. *My watch is five minutes fast.* ➔ *See also:* a fast **track¹** (to sth).

o➔**fast²** /fɑːst/ *adv* **1** moving or happening quickly *We ran as fast as we could.* • *You'll have to act fast.* **2 fast asleep** completely asleep (= sleeping) **3** in a firm or tight way *He tried to get away, but she held him fast.* ➔ *See also:* **thick¹** and fast.

**fast³** /fɑːst/ *verb* [I] to eat nothing, or much less than you usually eat for a period of time • fast *noun* [C]

o➔**fasten** /'fɑːsən/ *verb* **1** [I, T] to close or fix something together, or to become closed or fixed together *Fasten your seat belts.* • *This dress fastens at the side.* **2 fasten sth on/to/together, etc** to fix one thing to another *He fastened the rope to a tree.* ➔ *Opposite* **unfasten**.

**fastener** /'fɑːsənə/ *noun* [C] something that is used to close or fix things together

,**fast 'food** *noun* [U] hot food that can be served very quickly in a restaurant because it is already prepared *fast food restaurants*

**fast-forward** /,fɑːst'fɔːwəd/ *verb* [I, T] If you fast-forward a recording, or if it fast-forwards, you make it play at very high speed so that you get to the end more quickly. • fast-forward *noun* [U]

**fastidious** /fæs'tɪdiəs/ *adj* Someone who is fastidious wants every detail of something to be correct and perfect.

o➔**fat¹** /fæt/ *adj* **fatter**, **fattest 1** Someone who is fat weighs too much. *She eats all the time but never gets fat.* **2** thick or large *a fat book* ➔ *See also:* fat **chance¹**.

**fat²** /fæt/ *noun* **1** [U] the substance under the skin of people and animals that keeps them warm *body fat* **2** [C, U] a solid or liquid substance like oil that is taken from plants or animals and used in cooking *animal/vegetable fat* ➔ *See also:* **saturated fat**.

**fatal** /'feɪtᵊl/ *adj* **1** A fatal accident or illness causes death. *a fatal car crash* **2** Fatal actions have very bad effects. *a fatal error* • fatally *adv fatally injured*

**fatalism** /'feɪtᵊlɪzᵊm/ *noun* [U] the belief that people cannot change events, and that bad events cannot be avoided • fatalistic /,feɪtᵊl'ɪstɪk/ *adj*

**fatality** /fə'tæləti/ *noun* [C] *formal* the death of a person caused by violence or an accident

**fate** /feɪt/ *noun* **1** [C] what happens to someone, especially when it is something bad *His fate is now in the hands of the jury.* **2** [U] a power that some people believe decides what will happen *I believe it was fate that caused us to meet again.* ➔ *See also:* **quirk** of fate.

**fated** /'feɪtɪd/ *adj* [never before noun] If something that happens or someone's actions are fated, they are decided by a power that controls events, and cannot be avoided. [+ to do sth] *I seem fated to meet him wherever I go.* ➔ *See also:* **ill-fated**.

**fateful** /'feɪtfᵊl/ *adj* A fateful event has an

important and usually bad effect on the future. *a fateful decision*

o➔**father¹** /'fɑːðə/ *noun* **1** [C] your male parent **2 Father** the title of some Christian priests *Father O'Brian* **3 the father of sth** the man who invented or started something *Descartes is known as the father of modern philosophy.*

**father²** /'fɑːðə/ *verb* [T] *formal* to become a male parent *He fathered three children.*

,**Father 'Christmas** *noun* [no plural] *UK* a kind, fat, old man in red clothes who people say brings presents to children at Christmas

'**father ,figure** *noun* [C] an older man who gives you advice and support like a father

**fatherhood** /'fɑːðəhʊd/ *noun* [U] being a father

**father-in-law** /'fɑːðərɪnlɔː/ *noun* [C] *plural* **fathers-in-law** the father of your husband or wife

**fathom¹** /'fæðəm/ (*also UK* **fathom out**) *verb* [T] to be able to understand or started something after thinking about it a lot [+ question word] *No one could fathom why she had left so early.*

**fathom²** /'fæðəm/ *noun* [C] a unit for measuring the depth of water, equal to 1.8 metres

**fatigue** /fə'tiːg/ *noun* [U] when you feel very tired • fatigued *adj*

**fatigues** /fə'tiːgz/ *noun* [plural] special clothes that soldiers wear when they are fighting or working

**fatten** /'fætᵊn/ *verb* [T] to make animals fatter so that they can be eaten

**fatten sb/sth up** to give a thin person or animal lots of food so that they become fatter *I think my mum's trying to fatten me up.*

**fattening** /'fætᵊnɪŋ/ *adj* Fattening food can make you fat. *I don't eat chips, they're too fattening.*

**fatty** /'fæti/ *adj* Fatty foods contain a lot of fat.

**fatuous** /'fætjuəs/ *adj formal* very stupid and not deserving your attention or respect *a fatuous comment/remark*

**faucet** /'fɔːsɪt/ *US* (*UK/US* **tap**) *noun* [C] an object at the end of a pipe which you turn to control the flow of water ➔ *See picture at* **tap**.

o➔**fault¹** /fɔːlt/ *noun* **1 sb's fault** If something bad that has happened is someone's fault, they are responsible for it. *She believes it was the doctor's fault that Peter died.* **2 at fault** responsible for something bad that has happened *I was at fault and I would like to apologize.* **3** [C] something that is wrong with something or with someone's character *The car has a serious design fault.* • *One of his faults is that he's a bad loser.* **4 find fault with sb/sth** to criticize someone or something, especially without good reasons

---

**USAGE**

**fault** or **mistake**?

Use **fault** for explaining who is responsible when something bad happens.

*It's my fault that the car was stolen. I left the window open.*

~~It's my mistake the car was stolen. I left the window open.~~

Use **mistake** for talking about something that you did or

---

thought which was wrong.

*I still make lots of mistakes in my essays.*

~~I still make lots of faults in my essays.~~

**fault²** /fɔːlt/ *verb* [T] to find a reason to criticize someone or something *I can't fault the way that they dealt with the complaint.*

**faultless** /'fɔːltləs/ *adj* perfect, or without any mistakes *a faultless performance*

**faulty** /'fɔːlti/ *adj* not working correctly *faulty brakes/wiring*

**fauna** /'fɔːnə/ *noun* [group] all the animals that live in a particular area *the flora and fauna of the area*

**favour¹** UK (US **favor**) /'feɪvər/ *noun* **1** [C] something that you do to help someone *Could you do me a favour please?* • *I wanted to ask you a favour.* **2 be in favour of sth** to agree with or approve of a plan or idea *Most people are in favour of reducing traffic in cities.* **3 in favour of sb/sth** If you refuse or get rid of someone or something in favour of someone or something else, you choose them instead. *They dropped him from the team in favour of a much younger player.* **4 in sb's favour a** If something is in your favour, it helps you to win or succeed. *Both sides have strong arguments in their favour.* **b** If a game, vote, or judgement is in someone's favour, they win. *The final score was 16–10 in England's favour.* **5** [U] *formal* when people like something or someone *Her work never found favour among the critics.* **6 be in favour/out of favour** to be popular/unpopular *He has fallen out of favour recently.*

**favour²** UK (US **favor**) /'feɪvər/ *verb* [T] **1** to choose or prefer one possibility [often passive] *These are the running shoes favoured by marathon runners.* **2** to act unfairly by treating one person better than another *She always felt that her parents favoured her brother.*

**favourable** UK (US **favorable**) /'feɪvərəbl/ *adj* **1** showing that you like or approve of someone or something, or making you like or approve of them *His comments were highly favourable.* • *She made a very favourable impression on us.* **2** making something more likely to be successful *favourable weather conditions* ➔ *Opposite* **unfavourable**. • favourably UK (US **favorably**) *adv*

o⊸**favourite¹** UK (US **favorite**) /'feɪvərət/ *adj* [always before noun] Your favourite person or thing is the one that you like best. *What's your favourite band?*

**favourite²** UK (US **favorite**) /'feɪvərət/ *noun* [C] **1** a person or thing that you like more than all others *These chocolates are my favourites.* • *It was obvious which pupils were the teacher's favourites.* **2** the person or animal that is most likely to win a competition *The Dallas Cowboys are now favourites to win.*

**favouritism** UK (US **favoritism**) /'feɪvərətɪzᵊm/ *noun* [U] unfairly treating one person or group better than another

**fawn¹** /fɔːn/ *noun* **1** [C] a young deer **2** [U] a light brown colour

**fawn²** /fɔːn/ *verb*

   **fawn on/over sb** to praise someone or be nice to

someone in a way that is false in order to get something or to make them like you *The waiters fawned over them.*

**fax¹** /fæks/ *noun* **1** DOCUMENT [C] a document that is sent or received using a special machine and a telephone line *I got a fax from them this morning.* **2** SYSTEM [U] the system of sending or receiving documents using a special machine and a telephone line *Some products can be ordered by fax.* **3** MACHINE [C] (*also* '**fax ,machine**) a machine that is used to send and receive faxes ➔ *See colour picture* **The Office** *on page Centre 12.*

**fax²** /fæks/ *verb* [T] to send documents using a fax machine [+ **two objects**] *Can you fax me a price list?*

**the FBI** /,efbiː'aɪ/ *noun abbreviation for* the Federal Bureau of Investigation: one of the national police forces in the US that is controlled by the central government *He is wanted by the FBI for fraud.*

o⊸**fear¹** /fɪər/ *noun* **1** [C, U] a strong, unpleasant feeling that you get when you think that something bad, dangerous, or frightening might happen *She was trembling with fear.* • *Unlike the rest of us, Dave had no fear of snakes.* • [+ (that)] *There are fears that the disease will spread to other countries.* **2 for fear of sth/doing sth** because you are worried about something/doing something *I didn't want to move for fear of waking her up.*

**fear²** /fɪər/ *verb* [T] **1** to be worried or frightened that something bad might happen or might have happened [+ (that)] *Police fear that the couple may have drowned.* • *We huddled together, fearing we'd be killed.* **2** to be frightened of something or someone unpleasant *Most older employees fear unemployment.* **3 fear the worst** If you fear the worst, you are frightened that an unpleasant situation will become much worse. *When there was no sign of the children, rescuers feared the worst.*

   **fear for sth/sb** to be worried about something, or to be worried that someone is in danger *Her parents fear for her safety* (= worry that she may not be safe).

**fearful** /'fɪəfᵊl/ *adj formal* **1** frightened or worried [+ of + doing sth] *Many women are fearful of travelling alone.* **2** [always before noun] UK very bad *Nigel has a fearful temper.* • fearfully *adv*

**fearless** /'fɪələs/ *adj* not frightened of anything *a fearless fighter* • fearlessly *adv*

**fearsome** /'fɪəsəm/ *adj* very frightening *a fearsome opponent* • *Sharks are fearsome creatures.*

**feasible** /'fiːzəbl/ *adj* possible to do *a feasible plan* • [+ to do sth] *It may be feasible to clone human beings, but is it ethical?* • feasibility /,fiːzə'bɪləti/ *noun* [U]

**feast¹** /fiːst/ *noun* [C] a large meal, especially to celebrate something special *a wedding feast*

**feast²** /fiːst/ *verb*

   **feast on sth** to eat a lot of food and enjoy it very much *We feasted on fried chicken, ice cream, and chocolate cake.*

**feat** /fiːt/ *noun* **1** [C] an act or achievement that shows great skill or strength *The Eiffel Tower is a remarkable feat of engineering.* **2 be no**

**F**

**mean feat** used when you want to emphasize that an act or achievement is very difficult *Learning to ski at 60 is no mean feat!*

**feather** /'feðə<sup>r</sup>/ *noun* [C] one of the soft, light things that grow from and cover a bird's skin • **feathery** *adj* like feathers *feathery leaves*

○━**feature¹** /'fiːtʃə<sup>r</sup>/ *noun* [C] **1** PART a typical quality, or important part of something *The town's main features are its beautiful mosque and ancient marketplace.* • *This phone has several new features.* **2** FACE Someone's features are the parts of their face that you notice when you look at them. *His eyes are his best feature.* **3** NEWSPAPER a special article in a newspaper or magazine, or a special television programme *a double-page feature on global warming*

**feature²** /'fiːtʃə<sup>r</sup>/ *verb* [T] to include someone or something as an important part *a new movie featuring Bruce Willis* • *The CD will feature music from all over the world.*
**feature in sth** to be an important part of something

**'feature ˌfilm** *noun* [C] a film that is usually 90 or more minutes long *She's appeared in more than 20 feature films.*

**February** /'febru<sup>a</sup>ri/ *(written abbreviation **Feb**) noun* [C, U] the second month of the year

**feces** /'fiːsiːz/ *noun* [plural] *US spelling of* faeces (= solid body waste)

**feckless** /'fekləs/ *adj* A feckless person is not willing to work or take responsibility for their actions.

**fed** /fed/ *past of* feed

**federal** /'fed<sup>a</sup>r<sup>a</sup>l/ *adj* [always before noun] **1** relating to the central government, and not to the government of a region, of some countries such as the United States *the federal government* • *a federal agency/employee* **2** A federal system of government consists of a group of regions that is controlled by a central government.

**ˌfederal 'holiday** *US* (*UK/US* **national holiday**) *noun* [C] a day when most people in a country do not have to work

**federalism** /'fed<sup>a</sup>r<sup>a</sup>lɪz<sup>a</sup>m/ *noun* [U] a political system in which separate states are organized under a central government • **federalist** *noun* [C] someone who supports federalism *federalist principles*

**federation** /ˌfed<sup>a</sup>r'eɪʃ<sup>a</sup>n/ *noun* [C] a group of organizations, countries, regions, etc that have joined together to form a larger organization or government *the International Tennis Federation*

**ˌfed 'up** *adj informal* [never before noun] annoyed or bored by something that you have experienced for too long *I'm fed up with my job.*

**fee** /fiː/ *noun* [C] an amount of money that you pay to do something, to use something, or to get a service *an entrance fee* • *university fees* • *We couldn't afford to pay the lawyer's fee.*

**feeble** /'fiːbl/ *adj* **1** extremely weak *She became too feeble to get out of bed.* **2** not very good or effective *a feeble argument/excuse* • **feebly** *adv*

○━**feed¹** /fiːd/ *verb past* **fed 1** GIVE FOOD [T] to give food to a person, group, or animal *I fed Simone's cat while she was away.* • *Let's feed the children first, and then have our dinner.* **2** EAT FOOD [I] If an animal or a baby feeds, it eats. *The caterpillars feed on cabbage leaves.* **3** SUPPLY [T] to supply something such as information to a person or a machine, especially in a regular or continuous way *We fed them false information about our plans.* • *Nicola fed the pages into the photocopier.* ⊃ *See also:* **breast-feed**.

**feed²** /fiːd/ *noun* **1** [U] food for animals that are not kept as pets *cattle/chicken feed* **2** [C] *UK* (*US* **feeding**) a meal for a baby or an animal *He has three feeds during the night.*

**feedback** /'fiːdbæk/ *noun* [U] an opinion from someone about something that you have done or made *positive/negative feedback* • *We've had lots of **feedback on** these new products **from** our customers.*

○━**feel¹** /fiːl/ *verb past* **felt 1** EXPERIENCE [I, T] to experience an emotion or a physical feeling *You shouldn't feel embarrassed about making a mistake.* • *I felt a sharp pain in my side when I stood up.* • *"Are you feeling better?" "Yes, thanks, I feel fine now."* **2 feel better/ different/strange, etc; feel like/as if** If you describe the way a place, situation, or object feels, you say how it seems to you, or what your experience of it is like. *It felt strange to see him again after so long.* • *The house feels empty without the children.* • *This shirt feels tight under my arms.* • *I feel as if I've known you for ages.* **3 feel like sb/sth** to seem to be similar to a type of person, thing, or situation *My feet feel like blocks of ice.* • *I felt like a fool when I saw what everyone else was wearing.* **4** OPINION [I, T] to think something or have an opinion [+ (that)] *I feel that he's the best person for the job.* • *Do you feel strongly* (= have strong opinions) *about it?* • *She feels certain that she's right.* **5** TOUCH [I, T] to touch something, especially with your hands, in order to examine it *He felt her ankle to see if it was broken.* • *I felt for a pulse.* **6 feel like sth/doing sth** to want something, or want to do something *I feel like some chocolate.* • *Jane felt like crying.* **7** BE AWARE [T] to be aware of something *You could feel the tension in the room.* • *I could feel them watching me.* ⊃ *See usage note at* **fall.** ⊃ *See also:* feel **free¹**, feel the **pinch²**, be/feel under the **weather¹**.
**feel for sb** to feel sorry for someone because they are very unhappy, or in a difficult situation *I really feel for him, having to take the exam again.*

**feel²** /fiːl/ *noun* **1** [no plural] the way that something seems, or feels when you touch it *I love the feel of silk against my skin.* • *His art has a very modern feel to it.* **2 a feel for sth** *informal* the ability to do something or use something well *Once you get a feel for it, using the mouse is easy.* • *Claire has a feel for this kind of work.*

○━**feeling** /'fiːlɪŋ/ *noun* **1** EMOTION [C, U] emotion *guilty feelings* • *a feeling of joy/sadness* • *Her performance was completely lacking in feeling.* **2** PHYSICAL [C, U] when you feel something physical *I had a tingling feeling in my fingers.* • *Pablo lost all feeling* (= could not feel anything) *in his feet.* **3** OPINION [C] an opinion or belief *My feeling is that we should wait until* *they come back.* • *He has strong feelings about environmental issues.* **4 have/get a feeling (that)...** to think that something is likely *I had a feeling he'd be there.* • *I get the feeling that he doesn't like me.* **5 bad/ill feeling** when people are upset or angry with each other *I don't want to cause any bad feeling between us.*

**feelings** /'fiːlɪŋz/ *noun* **1** [plural] Your feelings are your beliefs and emotions. *You can't hide your feelings from me.* **2 hurt sb's feelings** to make someone feel unhappy *It hurt my feelings when he said I was ugly.*

**feet** /fiːt/ *plural of* foot

**feign** /feɪn/ *verb* [T] *formal* If you feign an emotion, illness, etc, you pretend to have it. *He feigned illness to avoid having to work.*

**feisty** /'faɪsti/ *adj* active, confident and determined *a feisty young woman*

**feline** /'fiːlaɪn/ *adj* relating to cats, or like a cat

**fell¹** /fel/ *verb* [T] **1** to cut down a tree **2** to knock someone down *He was felled with a single punch.*

**fell²** /fel/ *past tense of* fall

**fella** (*also* **feller**) /'felə/ *noun* [C] *informal* a man

**fellow¹** /'feləʊ/ *noun* [C] **1** [MAN] *old-fashioned* a man *a big fellow with broad shoulders* **2** [COLLEGE] someone whose job is to teach or study a particular subject at some colleges or universities *She's a research fellow at St Peter's college.* **3** [MEMBER] a member of an official organization for a particular subject or job

**fellow²** /'feləʊ/ *adj* **fellow countrymen/ students, etc** used to describe people who share your interests or situation *She's earned enormous respect from her fellow artists.*

**fellowship** /'feləʊʃɪp/ *noun* **1** [JOB] [C] a job teaching or studying a particular subject at some colleges or universities *a research fellowship at Harvard* **2** [FEELING] [U] a friendly feeling among people **3** [GROUP] [C] a group of people who share the same interests or beliefs

**felon** /'felən/ *noun* [C] someone who is guilty of a serious crime in the US *a convicted felon*

**felony** /'feləni/ *noun* [C, U] a serious crime in the US *to commit a felony*

**felt¹** /felt/ *noun* [U] a soft, thick cloth that is made from wool, hair, or fur that has been pressed together

**felt²** /felt/ *past of* feel

**felt-tip 'pen** *noun* [C] a pen with a point made of soft material, usually with brightly coloured ink for colouring pictures

o-◄**female¹** /'fiːmeɪl/ *adj* belonging to or relating to women, or to the sex that can produce eggs or have babies *a female athlete/employee* • *a female butterfly/elephant* • *Is it male or female?*

**female²** /'fiːmeɪl/ *noun* [C] a person or animal that belongs to the sex that can produce eggs or have babies *Our dog's just had puppies – three males and two females.*

**feminine** /'femɪnɪn/ *adj* **1** showing qualities that people generally think are typical of women *a feminine voice* • *feminine beauty* **2** in some languages, belonging to a group of nouns or adjectives that have the same grammatical behaviour. The other groups are 'masculine' and 'neuter'.

**femininity** /ˌfemɪ'nɪnəti/ *noun* [U] when

someone shows qualities that people generally think are typical of women

**feminism** /'femɪnɪzᵊm/ *noun* [U] the belief that women should have the same economic, social, and political rights as men • **feminist** *noun* [C] someone who supports feminism *a radical feminist* • **feminist** *adj* *feminist literature* • *a feminist writer*

**fence¹** /fens/ *noun* [C] **1** a wood, wire, or metal structure that divides or goes around an area *a garden/electric fence* **2 sit on the fence** to wait before you choose between two possibilities *The mayor is sitting on the fence, saying that he must remain neutral.* ➔ *See also:* **picket fence**.

**fence** 

**fence²** /fens/ *verb* [I] to take part in the sport of fencing

**fence sth in** to build a fence around an area *We'll have to fence in the garden if we get a dog.*

**fence sth off** to separate one area from another by building a fence [often passive] *The children's play area was fenced off from the rest of the park.*

**fencing** /'fensɪŋ/ *noun* [U] **1** the sport of fighting with thin swords (= weapons like long knives) **2** fences, or the material that is used to make them

**fend** /fend/ *verb*

**fend for yourself** to take care of yourself without help *When you go away to college, you have to learn to fend for yourself.*

**fend sb/sth off** to defend yourself against someone or something that is attacking you or annoying you *They managed to fend off their attackers with rocks and sticks.* • *She fended off questions about her marriage.*

**fender** /'fendə/ *noun* [C] **1** [CAR] *US* (*UK* **wing**) one of the parts at each corner of a car above the wheels **2** [BICYCLE] *US* (*UK* **mudguard**) a curved piece of metal or plastic fixed above a wheel of a bicycle or motorcycle to prevent water or dirt from hitting the legs of the person who is riding it **3** [FIREPLACE] *UK* a low, metal structure around an open fireplace which stops the coal or wood from falling out

**feng shui** /fʌŋ'ʃweɪ/ *noun* [U] an ancient Chinese belief that the way your house is built and the way that you arrange objects affects your success, health, and happiness

**fennel** /'fenᵊl/ *noun* [U] a plant whose base can be eaten, and whose leaves and seeds are used as a spice in cooking

**ferment¹** /fə'ment/ *verb* [I, T] If food or drink ferments, or if you ferment it, the sugar in it changes into alcohol because of a chemical process. *wine fermenting in barrels* • **fermentation** /ˌfɜːmen'teɪʃᵊn/ *noun* [U]

**ferment²** /'fɜːment/ *noun* [U] *formal* excitement or disagreement caused by change or a difficult situation

**F**

**fern** /fɜːn/ *noun* [C] a green plant with long stems, narrow leaves like feathers, and no flowers

**fern**

**ferocious** /fəˈrəʊʃəs/ *adj* extremely angry, violent, or forceful *a ferocious dog • a ferocious attack* • **ferociously** *adv*

**ferocity** /fəˈrɒsəti/ *noun* [U] extreme violence or force *a storm of incredible ferocity*

**ferret¹** /ˈferɪt/ *noun* [C] a small animal with a long, thin body that is sometimes used to hunt rabbits

**ferret²** /ˈferɪt/ *verb*
**ferret sth out** to find something after searching carefully for it *We managed to ferret out some information about her private life.*

**Ferris wheel** /ˈferɪsˌwiːl/ *noun* [C] an entertainment consisting of a large wheel that turns slowly with seats for people to sit in

**ferry¹** /ˈferi/ *noun* [C] a boat that regularly carries passengers and vehicles across an area of water *a car/passenger ferry*

**ferry²** /ˈferi/ *verb* [T] to regularly carry passengers or goods from one place to another in a vehicle *The space shuttle will ferry supplies to and from the new space station.*

**fertile** /ˈfɜːtaɪl/ ⓤⓢ /ˈfɜːrtᵊl/ *adj* **1** Fertile land or soil produces a lot of healthy plants. **2** If people or animals are fertile, they are able to have babies. **3 fertile ground (for sth)** a situation or place where an idea, activity, etc is likely to succeed **4 a fertile imagination** If someone has a fertile imagination, they have lots of interesting and unusual ideas. • **fertility** /fəˈtɪləti/ *noun* [U]

**fertilize** (*also UK* **-ise**) /ˈfɜːtɪlaɪz/ *verb* [T] **1** to cause an egg to start to develop into a young animal or baby by combining it with a male cell *Once an egg is fertilized it becomes an embryo.* **2** to put a natural or chemical substance on land in order to make plants grow well • **fertilization** /ˌfɜːtɪlaɪˈzeɪʃᵊn/ *noun* [U]

**fertilizer** (*also UK* **-iser**) /ˈfɜːtɪlaɪzəʳ/ *noun* [C, U] a natural or chemical substance that you put on land in order to make plants grow well

**fervent** /ˈfɜːvᵊnt/ *adj* showing sincere and enthusiastic beliefs or feelings *a fervent supporter of animal rights* • **fervently** *adv*

**fervour** *UK* (*US* **fervor**) /ˈfɜːrvəʳ/ *noun* [U] extremely strong beliefs or feelings *religious/patriotic fervour*

**fest** /fest/ *noun mainly US* **a beer/film/jazz, etc fest** a special event where people can enjoy a particular activity or thing

**fester** /ˈfestəʳ/ *verb* [I] **1** If a bad feeling or situation festers, it becomes worse over a period of time. *Hatred between the two groups has festered for years.* **2** If an injury festers, it becomes infected. *a festering wound*

**festival** /ˈfestɪvᵊl/ *noun* [C] **1** a series of special events, performances, etc that often takes place over several days *a dance/music festival • the Berlin Film Festival* **2** a special day or period when people celebrate something, especially a religious event *the Jewish festival of Hanukkah*

**festive** /ˈfestɪv/ *adj* happy and enjoyable because people are celebrating *a festive mood/occasion • What are you doing for the festive season* (= Christmas)*?* • **festivity** /fesˈtɪvəti/ *noun* [U] when people are happy and celebrating

**festivities** /fesˈtɪvətiz/ *noun* [plural] events that people organize in order to celebrate something *The evening's festivities included fireworks and a concert.*

**festoon** /fesˈtuːn/ *verb* [T] to cover something with objects, especially decorations [often passive] *The balcony was festooned with flags and ribbons.*

○━**fetch** /fetʃ/ *verb* [T] **1** to go to another place to get something or someone and bring them back *Can you fetch my glasses from the bedroom?* **2** If something fetches a particular amount of money, it is sold for that amount. *The painting is expected to fetch $50,000 in the auction.*

**fetching** /ˈfetʃɪŋ/ *adj* attractive *That scarf looks rather fetching on you.*

**fête** /feɪt/ *noun* [C] **1** *UK* an event that is held outside and includes competitions, games, and things for sale *a village fête* **2** *US* a special event to celebrate someone or something • **fête** *verb* [T] to publicly celebrate someone, often by having a special party [often passive] *She was fêted by audiences all over the world.*

**fetish** /ˈfetɪʃ/ *noun* [C] **1** a strong sexual interest in something unusual *a rubber fetish* **2** something that someone spends too much time thinking about or doing *a fetish for cleanliness*

**fetus** /ˈfiːtəs/ *noun* [C] *US spelling of* foetus (= a young human or animal that is still developing inside its mother) • **fetal** /ˈfiːtᵊl/ *adj US spelling of* foetal

**feud** /fjuːd/ *noun* [C] a serious and sometimes violent argument between two people or groups that continues for a long period • **feud** *verb* [I] *The families have been feuding for years.*

**feudal** /ˈfjuːdᵊl/ *adj* relating to a social system in the past in which people worked and fought for a lord (= a man of high rank) in exchange for land and protection • **feudalism** *noun* [U]

**fever** /ˈfiːvəʳ/ *noun* **1** [C, U] when someone's body temperature rises because they are ill *a high/slight fever* **2** [U] when people are very excited about something *Election fever has gripped the nation.* ➔ *See also:* **glandular fever**, **hay fever**.

**feverish** /ˈfiːvᵊrɪʃ/ *adj* **1** having a fever *I feel a bit feverish.* **2** Feverish activity is done quickly, often because of excitement or fear. *The rescuers worked at a feverish pace.* • **feverishly** *adv* *They worked feverishly to put out the fire.*

**'fever ˌpitch** *noun* **reach fever pitch** If emotions reach fever pitch, they become so strong that they are difficult to control. *Excitement in the crowd had reached fever pitch.*

○━**few** /fjuː/ *quantifier* **1 a few** some, or a small

number of *She's staying at the cottage for a few days.* • *It'll be here in a few minutes.* • *I met a few of the other employees at my interview.* **2 quite a few/a good few** quite a large number of *Quite a few people have had the same problem.* **3** not many, or only a small number of *We get few complaints.* • *Few of the children can read or write yet.* • *Very few people can afford to pay those prices.* ➔ *See usage note at* **less**. **4 few and far between** not happening or existing very often *Opportunities like this are few and far between.*

**fiancé** /fi'ɑːnseɪ/ *noun* [C] A woman's fiancé is the man that she has promised to marry.

**fiancée** /fi'ɑːnseɪ/ *noun* [C] A man's fiancée is the woman that he has promised to marry.

**fiasco** /fi'æskəʊ/ *noun* [C] a complete failure, especially one that embarrasses people *My last dinner party was a complete fiasco.*

**fib** /fɪb/ *noun* [C] *informal* a small lie that is not very important *Don't tell fibs.* • fib *verb* [I] **fibbing,** *past* **fibbed** to say something that is not true

**fibre** *UK* (*US* **fiber**) /'faɪbəʳ/ *noun* **1** [CLOTH] [C, U] cloth made from thin threads twisted together *Man-made fibres like nylon are easy to wash.* **2** [THIN THREAD] [C] one of the thin threads that forms a substance such as cloth *The fibres are woven into fabric.* **3** [FOOD] [U] the substance in plants which cannot be digested and helps food pass through your body *Broccoli is a good source of fibre.* **4** [BODY] [C] a structure like a thread in your body *muscle/nerve fibres*

**fibreglass** *UK* (*US* **fiberglass**) /'faɪbəglɑːs/ *noun* [U] a strong, light material made by twisting together glass or plastic threads

**fickle** /'fɪkl/ *adj* Someone who is fickle often changes their opinion about things.

O━**fiction** /'fɪkʃ°n/ *noun* **1** [U] literature and stories about imaginary people or events *What's the best-selling children's fiction title?* ➔ *Opposite* **nonfiction.** **2** [U, no plural] something that is not true or real *Nobody knows whether his statement is fact or fiction.* ➔ *See also:* **science fiction.**

**fictional** /'fɪkʃ°n°l/ *adj* existing only in fiction *a fictional character*

**fictitious** /fɪk'tɪʃəs/ *adj* invented and not real or true *a fictitious name*

**fiddle¹** /'fɪdl/ *verb* [T] *UK informal* to change something dishonestly in order to get money *She was fired for fiddling her travel expenses.* **fiddle (about/around) with sth 1** to touch or move things with your fingers because you are nervous or bored *Stop fiddling with your hair!* **2** to make small changes to something to try to make it work *He fiddled with the wires to get the radio working again.*

**fiddle²** /'fɪdl/ *noun* [C] **1** *informal* a violin (= a wooden musical instrument with strings) **2** *UK* a dishonest way to get money *a tax fiddle*

**fiddler** /'fɪdləʳ/ *noun* [C] someone who plays the violin (= a wooden musical instrument with strings)

**fiddly** /'fɪdli/ *adj UK* difficult to do because the parts involved are small *Repairing a watch is very fiddly.*

**fidelity** /fɪ'deləti/ *noun* [U] loyalty, especially to a sexual partner ➔ *Opposite* **infidelity.**

**fidget** /'fɪdʒɪt/ *verb* [I] to keep making small movements with your hands or feet because you are nervous or bored *She fidgeted all the way through the job interview.* • fidgety *adj*

O━**field¹** /'fiːld/ *noun* **1** [LAND] [C] an area of land used for growing crops or keeping animals *a wheat field* • *a field of cows* **2** [SPORT] [C] an area of grass where you can play a sport *a football field* **3** [AREA OF STUDY] [C] an area of study or activity *He's an expert in the field of biochemistry.* **4** [IN RACE/BUSINESS] [no plural] the people who are competing in a race, activity, or business *We lead the field in genetic research.* **5 a gas/oil field** an area of land containing gas or oil **6 a gravitational/magnetic field** an area affected by a particular physical force ➔ *See also:* **paddy field, playing field.**

**field²** /'fiːld/ *verb* **1** [I, T] to try to catch or stop a ball after it has been hit in a game such as cricket or baseball *Are we fielding or batting?* **2** [T] to send out a team or player to play in a game *Brazil fielded a strong team in the World Cup.* **3 field questions/telephone calls** to answer or deal with questions/telephone calls

'**field ,day** *noun* **have a field day** to have the opportunity to do a lot of something you want to do, especially to criticize someone *The press had a field day when they found out about the scandal.*

**fielder** /'fiːldəʳ/ *noun* [C] a player who tries to catch or stop the ball in games such as cricket or baseball

'**field ,hockey** *US* (*UK* **hockey**) *noun* [U] a team game played on grass where you hit a small ball with a long, curved stick

,**field 'marshal** *UK* (*US* '**field ,marshal**) *noun* [C] an officer of the highest rank in the British army

**fiend** /fiːnd/ *noun* [C] **1** an evil or cruel person **2** someone who is very interested in a particular thing

**fiendish** /'fiːndɪʃ/ *adj* **1** evil or cruel *a fiendish attack* **2** very difficult or complicated *a fiendish crossword* • fiendishly *adv mainly UK* extremely *fiendishly clever/difficult*

**fierce** /fɪəs/ *adj* **1** violent or angry *a fierce attack* • *a fierce dog* **2** very strong or powerful *fierce winds/storms* • *There is fierce competition between car manufacturers.* • fiercely *adv*

**fiery** /'faɪəri/ *adj* **1** showing strong emotion, especially anger *a fiery temper* **2** bright or burning like a fire *a fiery sunset*

**fifteen** /,fɪf'tiːn/ the number 15 • fifteenth 15th written as a word

**fifth¹** /fɪfθ/ 5th written as a word

**fifth²** /fɪfθ/ *noun* [C] one of five equal parts of something; 1/5

**fifty** /'fɪfti/ **1** the number 50 **2 the fifties** the years from 1950 to 1959 **3 be in your fifties** to be aged between 50 and 59 • fiftieth 50th written as a word

**fifty-fifty** /,fɪfti'fɪfti/ *adj, adv informal* **1** shared equally between two people *Let's divide the bill fifty-fifty.* **2 a fifty-fifty chance** If something has a fifty-fifty chance, it is equally likely to happen or not to happen. *We have a fifty-fifty chance of winning the match.*

**fig.** *written abbreviation for* figure (= a picture or drawing in a book or document, usually with a number) *See fig. 1.*

**fig** /fɪg/ *noun* [C] a dark, sweet fruit with lots of seeds, that is often eaten dried

○━**fight¹** /faɪt/ *verb past* **fought 1** USE FORCE [I, T] When people fight, they use physical force to try to defeat each other. *Two men were arrested for fighting outside a bar.* • *Sam's always fighting with his little brother.* **2** JOIN WAR [I, T] to take part in a war *Millions of young men fought in World War I.* **3** ARGUE [I] to argue *We've got to stop fighting in front of the children.* **4** TRY TO STOP [I, T] to try hard to stop something bad happening *He fought against racism.* • *New measures have been introduced to fight crime.* • *Aspirin and vitamin C help fight colds and flu.* **5** TRY TO ACHIEVE [I] to try hard to achieve something you want or think is right *They are fighting for their freedom.* • [+ to do sth] *He had to fight very hard to keep his job.* **6 be fighting for your life** to be trying very hard to stay alive when you are very ill or badly injured ➲ *See also:* fight a losing **battle¹**.

**fight back** to defend yourself when someone or something attacks you or causes problems for you

○━**fight²** /faɪt/ *noun* [C] **1** PHYSICAL FORCE when people use physical force to hurt or attack others *He's always getting into fights.* **2** EFFORT a determined effort to achieve or stop something *She was very active in the fight against drugs.* • *Join us in our fight for freedom!* • [+ to do sth] *This year has brought some good news in the fight to save the whales.* **3** ARGUMENT an argument *I don't want to have a fight over this.* **4** SPORT a boxing competition

**fighter** /'faɪtə'/ *noun* [C] **1** (*also* **'fighter ,plane**) a fast military aircraft that can attack other aircraft *a fighter pilot* **2** someone who fights in a war or as a sport

**fighting** /'faɪtɪŋ/ *noun* [U] when people fight, usually in a war *Thousands of civilians were killed in the fighting.*

**figment** /'fɪgmənt/ *noun* **a figment of sb's imagination** something that someone believes is real but that only exists in their imagination

**figurative** /'fɪgjᵊrətɪv/ *adj* **1** A figurative meaning of a word or phrase is a more imaginative meaning developed from the usual meaning. **2** Figurative art shows people, places, or things in a similar way to how they look in real life. • **figuratively** *adv*

○━**figure¹** /'fɪgə'/ *noun* [C] **1** SYMBOL a symbol for a number *Write down the amount in words and figures.* • *He's now being paid a six-figure salary.* **2 single/double, etc figures** numbers from 0 to 9/numbers from 10 to 99, etc **3** AMOUNT a number that expresses an amount, especially in official documents *Government figures show a rise in unemployment.* **4** TYPE OF PERSON a particular type of person, often someone important or famous *a mysterious figure* • *Lincoln was a major figure in American politics.* **5** PERSON a person that you cannot see clearly *I could see two figures in the distance.* **6** BODY SHAPE the shape of someone's

body, usually an attractive shape *She's got a good figure for her age.* **7** PICTURE (*written abbreviation* **fig.**) a picture or drawing in a book or document, usually with a number *Look at the graph shown in Figure 2.* ➲ *See also:* **father figure**.

**figure²** /'fɪgə'/ *verb* **1** [I] to be a part of something, or to appear in something *Love figures in most pop songs.* **2** [T] to decide something after thinking about it [+ (that)] *I figured that it was time to tell her the truth.* **3 that/it figures** *informal* something you say when you expected something to happen *"I've run out of money, mum." "That figures."*

**figure sth/sb out** to finally understand something or someone after a lot of thought [+ question word] *I never could figure out what she saw in him.*

**figurehead** /'fɪgəhed/ *noun* [C] a leader who has no real power

,**figure of 'speech** *noun* [C] *plural* **figures of speech** words that are used together in an imaginative way to mean something different from their usual meaning

○━**file¹** /faɪl/ *noun* **1** INFORMATION [C] a collection of information and documents about someone or something *The school keeps files on all its pupils.* **2** COMPUTER [C] a collection of information such as text, pictures, or computer programs stored together electronically with a single name *Do you want to download all these files?* **3** CONTAINER [C] a box or folded piece of thick paper used to put documents in *He keeps all his bank statements in a file.* ➲ *See colour picture* **Classroom** *on page Centre 4.* **4 on file** If information is on file, it is recorded and stored somewhere. *The police have kept all the details on file.* **5** TOOL [C] a small tool with a rough edge that is used to make a surface smooth *a nail file* **6 in single file** in a line with one person following the other ➲ *See also:* the **rank¹** and file.

**file²** /faɪl/ *verb* **1** PAPER [T] (*also* **file away**) to put documents into an ordered system of boxes or files where you can easily find them again *She filed all her tax returns under T.* **2** LAW [T] (*also* **file for**) to officially state that you are going to take someone to court *The police filed charges against the suspect.* • *His wife's filing for divorce.* **3** RUB [T] to rub something with a rough tool in order to make it smooth **4 file along/into/through, etc** to walk somewhere in a line, one behind the other *The audience slowly filed back to their seats.*

**filet** /fɪ'leɪ/ *noun* [C] *another US spelling of* fillet (= a piece of meat or fish with the bones taken out)

'**filing ,cabinet** (*also US* '**file ,cabinet**) *noun* [C] a piece of office furniture with deep drawers for storing documents ➲ *See colour picture* **The Office** *on page Centre 12.*

○━**fill¹** /fɪl/ *verb* **1** MAKE FULL [I, T] (*also* **fill up**) to make a container or space full, or to become full *He filled the bucket with water.* • *I made a drink while the bath was filling.* • *Her eyes filled up with tears when she heard the news.* **2** TAKE SPACE [T] If people or things fill a place, there are a lot of them in it. *The streets were*

*filled with* tourists. • *Dark clouds filled the sky.*
**3** BE NOTICEABLE [T] If light, sound, or a smell
fills a place, you can easily notice it. *The smell
of smoke filled the room.* **4 fill sb with anger/
joy/pride, etc** to make someone feel very
angry/happy/proud, etc *The thought of losing
him filled her with fear.* **5 fill a post/posi-
tion/vacancy** to take a new a job *They still
haven't found anyone to fill the vacancy.* **6 fill a
need/gap/demand** to provide something that
people need or want

**fill sth in/out** to write the necessary information on an official document *to fill in a
form/questionnaire*

**fill (sth) up** to become full, or to make something become full *Her eyes filled up with tears
when she heard the bad news.* • *The restaurant
soon filled up with people.*

**fill²** /fɪl/ *noun* **your fill** as much of something as
you want or need *I've **had my fill of** living in
the city.*

**fillet** (*also US* **filet**) /ˈfɪlɪt ⑤ fɪˈleɪ/ *noun* [C] a
piece of meat or fish with the bones taken out

**filling¹** /ˈfɪlɪŋ/ *noun* **1** [C, U] food that is put
inside things such as cakes, pastry, pieces of
bread, etc *What sort of filling do you want in
your sandwich?* **2** [C] a hard substance that fills
a hole in a tooth

**filling**

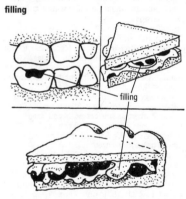

filling

**filling²** /ˈfɪlɪŋ/ *adj* Food that is filling makes
your stomach feel full. *This soup is very filling.*
**ˈfilling ˌstation** *noun* [C] a petrol station
(= place where you can buy fuel for your car)
o-·**film¹** /fɪlm/ *noun* **1** PICTURES [C] (*also US* **movie**)
a story shown in moving pictures, shown at the
cinema or on television *'Titanic' was one of the
most popular Hollywood films ever made.*
**2** MATERIAL [C, U] special thin plastic used for
making photographs or moving pictures, or a
length of this *I need to buy another **roll of film**.*
**3** LAYER [no plural] a thin layer of something on
a surface *A thick film of dust covered the furniture.*

**film²** /fɪlm/ *verb* [I, T] to record moving pictures
with a camera, usually to make a film for the
cinema or television *Most of the scenes were
filmed in a studio.* • *filming noun* [U]

**film-maker** *UK* (*US* **filmmaker**) /ˈfɪlmmeɪkə<sup>r</sup>/

*noun* [C] someone who makes films for the
cinema or television

**ˈfilm ˌstar** *noun* [C] a famous cinema actor or
actress

**filter¹** /ˈfɪltə<sup>r</sup>/ *verb* **1** [T] to pass a liquid or gas
through a piece of equipment in order to
remove solid pieces or other substances *The
water was filtered to remove any impurities.*
**2 filter down/in/ through, etc** to gradually
appear or become known *News is filtering in of
an earthquake in Mexico.* • *The sunlight filtered through the bedroom curtains.*

**filter sth out** to remove a particular substance
from a liquid or gas

**filter²** /ˈfɪltə<sup>r</sup>/ *noun* [C] a piece of equipment that
you pass a liquid or gas through in order to
remove particular substances *a coffee filter*

**filth** /fɪlθ/ *noun* [U] **1** thick and unpleasant dirt
*His clothes were covered in filth and mud.*
**2** offensive language or pictures, usually relating to sex *Many parents are shocked by the
amount of filth on television.*

**filthy** /ˈfɪlθi/ *adj* **1** extremely dirty *Wash your
hands, they're filthy!* **2** rude or offensive *filthy
language/jokes* • *Smoking is a filthy habit.*

**fin** /fɪn/ *noun* [C] a thin, triangular part on a fish,
which helps it to swim

o-·**final¹** /ˈfaɪn<sup>ə</sup>l/ *adj* **1** [always before noun] last in a
series or coming at the end of something *the
final paragraph* • *They scored a goal in the
final minute.* **2** If a decision, agreement, or
answer is final, it will not be changed or discussed any more. *The committee's decision is
final.* ⊃ See also: the final **nail¹** in the coffin, the
final **straw**.

**final²** /ˈfaɪn<sup>ə</sup>l/ *noun* **1** [C] the last part of a competition to decide which person or team will be
the winner *the European Cup Final* • *The
finals will be shown on TV.* **2 finals** exams
taken at the end of a university course

**finale** /fɪˈnɑːli/ *noun* [C] the last part of a show,
event, or piece of music

**finalist** /ˈfaɪn<sup>ə</sup>lɪst/ *noun* [C] a person or team in
the last part of a competition

**finalize** (*also UK* **-ise**) /ˈfaɪn<sup>ə</sup>laɪz/ *verb* [T] to
make a final and certain decision about a plan,
date, etc *to finalize arrangements/details*

o-·**finally** /ˈfaɪn<sup>ə</sup>li/ *adv* **1** AFTER A LONG TIME] after a
long time or some difficulty *We finally got home
just after midnight.* • *After months of looking,
he finally found a job.* **2** LAST POINT] used to
introduce the last point or idea *Finally, I'd like
to thank everyone for coming this evening.*
**3** CERTAINLY] in a way that will not be changed
*The date of the wedding hasn't been finally
decided yet.*

**finance¹** /ˈfaɪnæns/ *noun* **1** [U] the control of
how large amounts of money should be spent
**2** [U] the money that is needed to support a
business *Who put up the finance for the project?*
**3 sb's finances** the money which a person,
company, or country has *You must learn how to
manage your own finances.*

**finance²** /ˈfaɪnæns/ *verb* [T] to provide the
money needed to do something *Who's financ-
ing the project?*

o-·**financial** /faɪˈnænʃ<sup>ə</sup>l/ *adj* relating to money or
how money is managed *a financial adviser*

• She's having some financial difficulties at the moment. • financially adv Many students are still financially dependent on their parents.

**finch**¹ /fɪnʃ/ noun [C] a small singing bird with a short beak

◦⚊**find**¹ /faɪnd/ verb [T] past **found 1** ⌈DISCOVER WHEN SEARCHING⌉ to discover something or someone that you have been searching for I can't find my glasses and I've looked everywhere. • Police found the missing girl at a London railway station. • [+ two objects] Has he found himself a place to live yet? **2** ⌈DISCOVER BY CHANCE⌉ to discover something or someone by chance The body was found by a man walking his dog. • I found a $10 bill on the sidewalk. **3** ⌈BECOME AWARE⌉ to become aware that something exists, or has happened I came home to find that my cat had had kittens. • I found that I could easily swim a mile. **4 find the energy/money/time**, etc to have or get enough energy/money/time, etc to do something Where do you find the energy to do all these things? **5 find sb/sth easy/boring/funny**, etc to think or feel a particular way about someone or something I still find exams very stressful. **6 find yourself somewhere/doing sth** to become aware that you have gone somewhere or done something without intending to I suddenly found myself making everyone's lunch. **7 be found** to exist or be present somewhere Vitamin C is found in oranges and other citrus fruit. **8 find sb guilty/not guilty** to judge that someone is guilty or not guilty in a law court [often passive] She was found guilty of murder.
**find (sth) out** to get information about something, or to learn a fact for the first time I must find out the train times. • [+ question word] Peter was shocked when he found out what we had done. ➔ See usage note at **know**.

**find**² /faɪnd/ noun [C] something or someone valuable, interesting, or useful that you discover [usually singular] This hotel was a real find.

**finding** /'faɪndɪŋ/ noun [C] a piece of information that has been discovered as a result of an official study [usually plural] The findings of this research will be published next year.

◦⚊**fine**¹ /faɪn/ adj **1** ⌈WELL⌉ well, healthy, or happy "How are you?" "I'm fine thanks. And you?" • I had a cold last week, but I'm fine now. **2** ⌈GOOD⌉ good or good enough "Is the soup hot enough?" "Yes, it's fine." **3** ⌈EXCELLENT⌉ excellent, or of very good quality fine wines • He's a fine musician. **4 (that's) fine** used to agree with a suggestion, idea, decision, etc "Shall we meet at 8 o'clock?" "Yes, that's fine by me." **5** ⌈THIN⌉ thin or made of very small pieces fine, brown hair • fine sand **6** ⌈SUNNY⌉ mainly UK sunny and not raining If it's fine, we could have a picnic. **7 the finer details/points**, etc of sth the more detailed or more difficult parts of an argument, idea, etc

**fine**² /faɪn/ adv informal **1** very well or without any problems "How did your exam go?" "It went fine thanks." **2 cut it/things fine** to leave yourself only just enough time to do something Twenty minutes to get to the station? That's cutting it a bit fine!

**fine**³ /faɪn/ verb [T] to make someone pay an amount of money as a punishment for breaking a law or rule [often passive] He was fined £500 for dangerous driving.

**fine**⁴ /faɪn/ noun [C] an amount of money that you must pay for breaking a law or rule a parking fine • The court gave her two weeks to pay the fine.

**finely** /'faɪnli/ adv **1** into small pieces Finely chop the garlic. **2** very exactly a finely tuned machine

◦⚊**finger**¹ /'fɪŋɡər/ noun **1** [C] one of the five, long, separate parts at the end of your hand, including your thumb ➔ See colour picture **The Body** on page Centre 2. **2 have green fingers** UK (US **have a green thumb**) to be good at gardening and making plants grow well **3 keep your fingers crossed** informal to hope that things will happen in the way that you want them to Let's keep our fingers crossed that it doesn't rain. **4 not lift a finger** informal to not help someone do something, usually because you are too lazy He never lifts a finger to help with the housework. **5 put your finger on sth** to understand exactly why a situation is the way it is Something was wrong, but I couldn't put my finger on it. **6 snap your fingers** (also UK **click your fingers**) to press your thumb and middle finger together until the finger hits your hand and makes a short sound ➔ See also: **index finger**.

**finger**² /'fɪŋɡər/ verb [T] to touch or feel something with your fingers

**fingernail** /'fɪŋɡəneɪl/ noun [C] the hard, thin part on the top of the end of your finger

**fingerprint** /'fɪŋɡəprɪnt/ noun [C] the mark made on something by the pattern of curved lines on the end of someone's finger The police found fingerprints all over the murder weapon.

**fingertip** /'fɪŋɡətɪp/ noun **1** [C] the end of your finger **2 at your fingertips** If you have something at your fingertips, you can get it and use it very easily. He had all the information he needed at his fingertips.

◦⚊**finish**¹ /'fɪnɪʃ/ verb **1** ⌈COMPLETE⌉ [I, T] to complete something, or come to the end of an activity When I finish my homework, can I watch TV? • [+ doing sth] Have you finished reading that book yet? **2** ⌈END⌉ [I] to end The meeting should finish at five o'clock. **3** ⌈USE COMPLETELY⌉ [T] (also **finish off**) to eat, drink, or use something completely They finished their drinks and left the bar. **4 finish first/second**, etc to be in the first/second, etc winning position at the end of a race or competition
**finish sth off 1** to complete the last part of something that you are doing I have to finish off this report by Friday. **2** to eat, drink, or use the last part of something Would you like to finish off the pizza?
**finish up** mainly UK to finally be in a particular place, state, or situation, usually without having planned it I only went for two days, but I finished up staying for a week.
**finish with sth** to stop using or needing something Have you finished with the newspaper?
**finish with sb** UK to stop having a romantic relationship with someone

**finish²** /'fɪnɪʃ/ noun [C] **1** the end of a race, or the last part of something *a close/exciting finish* • *I enjoyed the film from start to finish.* **2** the way the surface of something feels or looks *The table has a smooth, shiny finish.*

**finished** /'fɪnɪʃt/ adj **1** completed *How much does the finished product cost?* ○ *Opposite* **unfinished. 2 be finished** If you are finished, you have completed something. *I hope I'll be finished before 5 p.m.*

**fir** /fɜːʳ/ (*also* 'fir ,tree) noun [C] a tree with thin, straight leaves shaped like needles that do not fall in winter

o→**fire¹** /faɪəʳ/ noun **1** FLAME [U] heat, light, and flames that are produced when something burns **2 catch fire** to start burning *The car crashed and caught fire.* **3 on fire** burning *That house is on fire.* **4 set fire to sth; set sth on fire** to make something start burning, usually to cause damage *Enemy troops set fire to the village.* **5** EVENT [C] when something burns in a way that causes damage and cannot be controlled *Three people were killed in the fire.* • *It took the firefighters two hours to put the fire out* (= stop it burning). **6** NATURAL HEAT [C] a pile of wood, coal, etc that is burning to produce heat *We sat by the fire.* • *They put up the tents and lit a fire.* **7 an electric/ gas fire** UK a piece of equipment that uses electricity or gas to heat a room **8** SHOOTING [U] the shooting of guns and other weapons *The soldiers opened fire* (= started shooting). **9 come under fire** to be criticized *The government has come under fire for closing the hospital.*

**fire**

o→**fire²** /faɪəʳ/ verb **1** [I, T] to shoot a bullet from a gun *She fired three shots at him.* **2** [T] *informal* to tell someone they must leave their job [often passive] *I was fired for being late.* **3 fire sb's imagination** to make someone very excited or interested in something **4 fire questions at sb** to ask someone questions quickly one after the other

**fire sb up** to make someone excited or angry *He always gets so fired up about politics.*

**firearm** /'faɪərɑːm/ noun [C] a gun that you can carry easily

'**fire bri,gade** UK (US '**fire de,partment**) noun [C] an organization of people whose job is to stop fires burning

'**fire ,engine** noun [C] a vehicle for carrying firefighters and equipment for stopping large fires

'**fire es,cape** noun [C] a set of metal stairs on the outside of a building which allows people to leave if there is an emergency

'**fire ex,tinguisher** noun [C] a piece of equipment kept inside buildings which is used to stop small fires

**firefighter** /'faɪəfaɪtəʳ/ noun [C] someone whose job is to stop fires burning

**fireman** /'faɪəmən/ noun [C] plural **firemen** a man whose job is to stop fires burning

**fire escape**

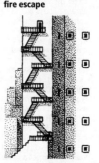

**fireplace** /'faɪəpleɪs/ noun [C] a space in the wall of a room where you can have a fire, or the structure around this space ○ *See colour picture* **The Living Room** *on page Centre 11.*

**fireside** /'faɪəsaɪd/ noun [U] the area next to a fireplace

'**fire ,station** noun [C] the building where fire engines are kept, and firefighters wait for emergencies

**firewood** /'faɪəwʊd/ noun [U] wood that is used for burning on a fire

**firework** /'faɪəwɜːk/ noun [C] a small object that explodes to produce a loud noise and bright colours and is often used to celebrate special events *a firework display*

'**firing ,squad** noun [C] a group of soldiers who are ordered to shoot and kill a prisoner

o→**firm¹** /fɜːm/ adj **1** NOT SOFT not soft, but not completely hard *A firm bed is better for your back.* **2** FIXED [always before noun] certain or fixed and not likely to change *We don't have any firm plans for the weekend yet.* • *I'm a firm believer in equal rights.* **3** STRONG strong and tight *a firm handshake/grip* **4** STRICT strict and making certain that people do what you want *You've got to be firm with children.* • **firmly** adv • **firmness** noun [U]

**firm²** /fɜːm/ noun [C] a company that sells goods or services *a law firm*

**first¹** /fɜːst/ adj **1** BEFORE coming before all others *Who was the first person to arrive at the party?* • *He was nervous on his first day at school.* • *Her first novel didn't sell very well.* • *They went abroad last year for the first time since having children.* **2** NUMBER 1st written as a word **3** IMPORTANT most important *Sheila won first prize in the photo competition.* ○ *See also:* in the first **place¹**.

o→**first²** /fɜːst/ adv **1** before everything or everyone else *I can go to the cinema, but I've got to do my homework first.* • *Jason came first in the 400 metres* (= he won). **2** for the first time *I first heard the song on the radio.* • *He first started playing the piano at school.* **3 at first** at the beginning of a situation or period of time *At first I thought she was unfriendly, but actually she is just shy.* **4 first/first of all a** used to introduce the first idea, reason, etc in a series *First, I think we have to change our marketing strategy.* **b** before doing anything else *First of all check you have all the correct ingredients.* **5 come first** to be the most important person or thing *Her career always comes first.* **6 put sb/sth first** to consider someone or something to be the most important thing *Most couples put their children first when sorting out their problems.* **7 First come, first served.** something you say when there is not enough of something for everyone and only the first people who ask for it will get it

**first³** /fɜːst/ *noun, pronoun* **1 the first** the first person, people, thing, or things *Hillary and Norgay were the first to climb Everest.* • *I enjoyed his second novel more than the first.* **2 be a first** to be something that has never happened before *Man walking on the moon was a first in space history.* **3** [C] the highest exam result that you can achieve at the end of a university course in the UK

,first 'aid *noun* [U] basic medical treatment that you give someone who is ill or injured in an emergency *The policeman **gave** him **first aid** before the ambulance arrived.*

**first-class** /ˌfɜːstˈklɑːs/ *adj* **1** relating to the best and most expensive available service, especially when travelling or sending something somewhere *a first-class ticket* • *a first-class stamp* **2** of very good quality *It was a first-class restaurant.* • first class *adv How much is it to send this letter first class?*

,first 'floor *noun* [no plural] **1** *UK* the level of a building directly above the ground level **2** *US* (*UK* **ground floor**) the level of a building on the same level as the ground

**firsthand** /ˌfɜːstˈhænd/ *adj, adv* experienced, seen, or learnt directly *Police heard firsthand accounts of the accident from witnesses.* • *The soldiers knew firsthand about the horrors of war.*

**firstly** /ˈfɜːstli/ *adv* used to introduce the first idea, reason, etc in a series *The aim of this activity is firstly to have a fun, and secondly to keep fit.*

'first ,name *noun* [C] the name that people who know you call you and that comes before your family name *My sister's first name is Claire.*

the ,first 'person *noun* the form of a verb or pronoun that is used when people are speaking or writing about themselves. For example, 'I' and 'we' are first person pronouns.

**first-rate** /ˌfɜːstˈreɪt/ *adj* extremely good *a first-rate team/writer*

**fiscal** /ˈfɪskəl/ *adj* relating to government money, especially taxes

○-**fish¹** /fɪʃ/ *noun plural* **fish** or **fishes** **1** [C] an animal that lives only in water and swims using its tail and fins (= thin, triangular parts) *Are there any fish in the pond?* **2** [U] fish eaten as food *fish and chips* ➔ *See colour picture* **Food** on *page Centre 7.*

**fish** or **fishes**?

Fish is the usual plural of fish.

*I caught six fish in the river.*

~~I caught six fishes in the river.~~

Fishes is sometimes used to talk about different types of fish.

**fish²** /fɪʃ/ *verb* [I] to try to catch fish *They're fishing for tuna.*

**fish sth out** *informal* to pull or take something out of a bag or pocket, especially after searching *He put his hand in his pocket and fished out his car keys.*

**fisherman** /ˈfɪʃəmən/ *noun* [C] *plural* **fishermen** someone who catches fish as a job or as a hobby

**fishing** /ˈfɪʃɪŋ/ *noun* [U] the sport or job of catching fish *Dad loves to **go fishing**.* • *fishing boats*

'fish ,slice *noun* [C] *UK* a kitchen tool with a wide, flat end used for lifting and serving food ➔ *See colour picture* **Kitchen** *on page Centre 10.*

**fishy** /ˈfɪʃi/ *adj* **1** smelling or tasting like fish **2** making you feel that someone is lying or something dishonest is happening *His story sounds a bit fishy to me.*

**fist** /fɪst/ *noun* [C] a hand closed into a ball with the fingers and thumb curled tightly together *He banged his fist down angrily on the table.*

**fist**

○-**fit¹** /fɪt/ *verb* **fitting**, *past* **fitted** **1** RIGHT SHAPE [I, T] to be the right shape or size for someone or something *These trousers don't fit any more.* • *I can't find a lid to fit this jar.* **2 fit (sth) in/ through/ under, etc** If people or things fit somewhere, or if you can fit them somewhere, that place is big enough for them. *How many people can you fit in your car?* • *This radio is small enough to fit into my pocket.* **3** PUT [T] *mainly UK* to put or fix something somewhere *You ought to fit a smoke alarm in the kitchen.* **4** SAME [I, T] to be the same as or like something *She seems to fit the police description.* **5** SUITABLE [T] to be suitable for something *The punishment should fit the crime.*

**fit** or **suit**?

Remember that the verb **fit** means to be the right shape or size.

*This jacket doesn't fit me. It's too tight.*

Use the verb **suit** when you want to say that something is right for someone or makes them look more attractive.

*That dress looks lovely. Red really suits you.*

*Life in the big city didn't suit him.*

~~Life in the big city didn't fit him.~~

**fit in** to feel that you belong to a particular group and are accepted by them *He doesn't **fit in with** the other pupils in his class.*

**fit sb/sth in** to find the time to see someone or do something *The dentist can fit you in on Tuesday morning.*

**fit in with sth** If one activity or event fits in

with another, they exist or happen together in a way that is convenient. *The party is in early June. How does that fit in with your holiday plans?*

**fit²** /fɪt/ *adj* **fitter, fittest 1** of a good enough quality or suitable type for a particular purpose [+ to do sth] *Is this water fit to drink?* • *She's not in a fit state to drive.* **2** healthy, especially because you exercise regularly *He's very fit for his age.* ➋ Opposite **unfit**. **3 do sth as you see/think fit** to do something that you feel is the right thing to do, although other people might disapprove *You must spend the money as you see fit.*

**fit³** /fɪt/ *noun* **1 a good/loose/tight, etc fit** when something fits someone or somewhere well, loosely, tightly, etc *These shoes are a perfect fit.* **2** [C] a sudden, uncontrolled period of doing something or feeling something *a coughing fit* • *I hit him in a fit of anger.* **3** [C] a short period of illness when someone cannot control their movements and becomes unconscious *to have an epileptic fit* **4 have a fit** *informal* to become extremely angry *Mum had a fit when she saw the mess we'd made.*

**fitful** /'fɪtfᵊl/ *adj* stopping and starting and not happening in a regular or continuous way *fitful sleep* • **fitfully** *adv*

**fitness** /'fɪtnəs/ *noun* [U] **1** the condition of being physically strong and healthy *physical fitness* **2** the quality of being suitable for a particular purpose, job, course of study, etc *The purpose of the exercise is to judge a soldier's fitness for combat.*

**fitted** /'fɪtɪd/ *adj* **1** *UK* made or cut to fill a particular space exactly *fitted carpets/kitchens* **2** Fitted clothes fit tightly to your body. *a fitted jacket*

**fitting** /'fɪtɪŋ/ *adj* suitable or right for a particular situation *The promotion was a fitting reward for all his hard work.*

**fittings** /'fɪtɪŋz/ *noun* [plural] *mainly UK* **1** parts that are fixed to a piece of furniture or equipment *a circular bath with gold fittings* **2** things that are fixed to the walls, floors, and ceilings inside a house but that can be moved *Does the price of the house include all the usual fittings?*

**five** /faɪv/ the number 5

**fiver** /'faɪvəʳ/ *noun* [C] *UK informal* a piece of paper money worth £5 *You owe me a fiver.*

o━**fix¹** /fɪks/ *verb* [T] **1** REPAIR to repair something *My watch is broken – can you fix it?* **2** DECIDE to decide a certain and exact date, price, plan, etc *Let's fix a day to have lunch together.* • *The price has been fixed at $10.* **3 fix sth onto/to/under, etc** to fasten something in a particular place *They fixed the bookcase to the wall.* **4** PREPARE to prepare a drink or meal [+ two objects] *I'll fix you a sandwich.* **5** CHEAT to do something dishonest to make certain that a competition, race, or election is won by a particular person [often passive] *People are saying that the elections were fixed.*

**fix sth up 1** *UK* to arrange a meeting, date, event, etc *Can we fix up a date for the next meeting?* **2** to repair or change something in order to improve it *Nick loves fixing up old cars.*

**fix sb up** to provide someone with something that they need *My uncle has fixed me up with a summer job.*

**fix²** /fɪks/ *noun* **1 a quick fix** a way of solving a problem easily *There is no quick fix for unemployment.* **2 be in a fix** to be in a difficult situation *I'm in a fix and need your help.* **3** [C] *informal* an amount of an illegal drug or something that you want very much *Cath needs her fix of chocolate every day.*

**fixation** /fɪk'seɪʃᵊn/ *noun* [C] an unnaturally strong interest in a particular person or thing *She's got an unhealthy fixation with her weight.*

**fixed** /fɪkst/ *adj* **1** decided already and not able to be changed *a fixed price* • *Is the date of the wedding fixed yet?* **2** fastened somewhere and not able to be moved

**fixture** /'fɪkstʃəʳ/ *noun* [C] **1** a piece of furniture or equipment that is fixed inside a house or building and is usually sold with it [usually plural] *It comes with the usual fixtures and fittings.* **2** *UK* a sports event that is arranged for a particular day

**fizz** /fɪz/ *noun* [U] bubbles of gas in a liquid or the sound that they make *This cola has lost its fizz.* • **fizz** *verb* [I]

**fizzle** /'fɪzl/ *verb*

**fizzle out** to gradually end in a disappointing way *Their relationship soon fizzled out when they got back from holiday.*

**fizzy** /'fɪzi/ *adj* A fizzy drink has lots of bubbles of gas in it.

**flabbergasted** /'flæbəgɑːstɪd/ *adj informal* extremely surprised

**flabby** /'flæbi/ *adj* having too much loose fat on your body *flabby arms/thighs*

**flag¹** /flæg/ *noun* [C] a piece of cloth with a special design and colours, that is fixed to a pole as the symbol of a country or group *the French flag* • *There was a flag flying above the castle.*

fizzy

**flag²** /flæg/ *verb* [I] **flagging, past flagged** to become tired or less interested in something *The players started to flag towards the end of the game.*

**flag sth down** to make a vehicle stop by waving at the driver

**flagrant** /'fleɪɡrənt/ *adj* shocking because of being so obviously wrong or bad *a flagrant disregard for the law* • **flagrantly** *adv*

**flagship** /'flæɡʃɪp/ *noun* [C] a product or service that is the best and most admired that a company has

**flail** /fleɪl/ (*also* **flail about/around**) *verb* [I, T] to wave or move your arms and legs about energetically and in an uncontrolled way *The wasp came towards us and Howard started flailing his arms around.*

**flair** /fleəʳ/ *noun* **1** [no plural] a natural ability to do something well *She has a **flair** for languages.* **2** [U] when you do something in an exciting and interesting way *He played with great imagination and flair.*

**flak** /flæk/ *noun* [U] *informal* criticism *The government took a lot of **flak** for breaking its election promises.*

**flake¹** /fleɪk/ *noun* [C] a small, flat, thin piece of something *flakes of paint/snow*

**flake²** /fleɪk/ *verb* [I] to come off in small, flat, thin pieces *The paint was flaking off the walls.* • **flaky** *adj* coming off easily in small, flat, thin pieces *dry, flaky skin*

flake off

**flamboyant** /flæm'bɔɪənt/ *adj* **1** A flamboyant person is loud, stylish, and confident. *a flamboyant pop star* **2** Flamboyant clothes or colours are very bright and noticeable. • **flamboyance** /flæm'bɔɪəns/ *noun* [U]

**flame** /fleɪm/ *noun* [C, U] hot, bright, burning gas produced by something on fire *Smoke and flames were pouring out of the burning factory.* • *The whole building was soon **in flames** (=* burning). • *The car crashed and **burst into flames** (=* suddenly started burning).

**flaming** /'fleɪmɪŋ/ *adj* [always before noun] **1** [BURNING] burning with a bright light *a flaming building* **2** [BRIGHT] very bright in colour or light *flaming red hair* **3** [ANNOYED] *UK informal* used to emphasize something when you are annoyed *What a flaming idiot!*

**flamingo** /flə'mɪŋgəʊ/ *noun* [C] a large bird with long, thin legs and pink feathers that lives near water in some hot countries

**flammable** /'flæməbl/ (*also* **inflammable**) *adj* Flammable liquids, gases, or materials burn very easily.

**flan** /flæn/ *noun* [C, U] a round, open pastry base filled with something such as fruit, or cheese and vegetables *cheese and onion flan*

**flank¹** /flæŋk/ *verb* **be flanked by sb/sth** to have someone or something at the side or at each side *The President was flanked by police officers.*

**flank²** /flæŋk/ *noun* [C] **1** the side of the body of an animal or person from the chest to the hips **2** the side of an army when it is ready to fight

**flannel** /'flænᵊl/ *noun* **1** [U] soft, warm cloth for making clothes *flannel pyjamas* **2** [C] *UK* (*US* **washcloth**) a small cloth that you use to wash your face and body ➔ *See colour picture* **The Bathroom** *on page Centre 1.*

**flap¹** /flæp/ *noun* **1** [C] a piece of cloth or material fixed along one edge to cover or close an opening **2** [C, U] *US* when someone is worried or excited, or a situation that causes them to feel this way *The President's remarks caused a huge flap.* **3** **be/get in a flap** *mainly UK informal* to be or become worried or excited *You shouldn't get in such a flap about things.*

**flap²** /flæp/ *verb* **flapping**, *past* **flapped** **1** [WINGS] [T] If a bird flaps its wings, it moves them up and down. **2** [MOVE] [I] If something such as cloth or paper flaps, the side that is not fixed to something moves around, especially in the wind. *The curtains were flapping around in the breeze.* **3** [WORRY] [I] *UK informal* to become worried or excited about something *Don't flap! We've got plenty of time to get to the airport.*

**flare¹** /fleə/ (*also* **flare up**) *verb* [I] **1** If something bad such as anger or pain flares or flares up, it suddenly starts or gets worse. *Violence flared up between football fans yesterday.* **2** to suddenly burn brightly, usually for a short time *The rocket flared in the sky and disappeared into space.*

**flare²** /fleə/ *noun* [C] **1** a piece of safety equipment that produces a bright signal when you are lost or injured **2** a sudden, bright light

**flash¹** /flæʃ/ *verb* **1** [I, T] to shine brightly and suddenly, or to make something shine in this way *The doctor flashed a light into my eye.* • *Lightning flashed across the sky.* **2** [I, T] (*also* **flash up**) to appear for a short time, or to make something appear for a short time *An icon flashed up on the screen.* **3** **flash by/past/through**, etc to move somewhere fast *The motorcycle flashed past us and around the corner.* **4** **flash (sb) a look/smile**, etc to look, smile, etc at someone quickly *She flashed him a smile as he came in.*

**flash back** If your mind or thoughts flash back to something that happened in the past, you suddenly remember it. *His mind flashed back to the night of the murder.*

**flash²** /flæʃ/ *noun* **1** [BRIGHT LIGHT] [C] a sudden bright light *The bomb exploded in a flash of yellow light.* **2** [CAMERA] [C, U] a piece of camera equipment that produces a bright light when you take a photograph in a dark place **3** [SUDDEN EXPERIENCE] [C] a sudden experience of something such as a feeling or idea *a flash of anger* • *I had a flash of inspiration.* **4** **in a flash** immediately, or very quickly *I'll be back in a flash.* **5** **a flash in the pan** a sudden success that does not continue

**flashback** /'flæʃbæk/ *noun* [C] **1** when you suddenly remember something that happened in the past, usually something bad **2** part of a film or book that goes back in time to something that happened before the main story began

**flashlight** /'flæʃlaɪt/ *US* (*UK* **torch**) *noun* [C] an electric light that you can hold in your hand

**flashy** /'flæʃi/ *adj* looking too bright, big, and expensive, in a way that is intended to get attention *flashy gold jewellery*

**flask** /flɑːsk/ *noun* [C] **1** [HOT DRINKS] *UK* (*UK/US* **Thermos**) a special container that keeps drinks hot or cold *a flask of coffee* **2** [ALCOHOL] a flat bottle that is used to carry alcohol in your pocket **3** [SCIENCE] a glass container with a wide base and a narrow opening used in science

○━**flat¹** /flæt/ *mainly UK* (*mainly US* **apartment**) *noun* [C] a set of rooms to live in, with all the rooms on one level of a building *a large block of flats*

**flask**

flask *UK*, Thermos *US*

flask

o⃗**flat²** /flæt/ *adj* **flatter, flattest 1** SMOOTH smooth and level, with no curved, high, or hollow parts *a flat surface* • *The countryside around here is very flat.* **2** WITHOUT EMOTION without any energy, interest, or emotion *Her voice sounded very flat.* **3** WITHOUT AIR If a tyre is flat, it does not contain enough air. **4** WITHOUT GAS If a drink is flat, it does not contain enough bubbles of gas. **5** WITHOUT POWER *UK* If a battery (= object which provides electricity) is flat, it does not contain any more electrical power. **6 a flat price/rate, etc** a price/rate, etc which is the same for everyone and does not change *He charges a flat rate of £15 an hour.* **7 B flat/E flat, etc** the musical note that is between the note B/E, etc and the note below it **8** TOO LOW A flat musical note sounds unpleasant because it is slightly lower than it should be. **9** LOW Flat shoes do not raise your feet far from the ground.

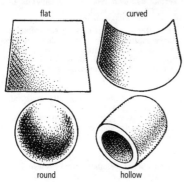

flat — curved
round — hollow

**flat³** /flæt/ *adv* **flatter, flattest 1** in a horizontal or level position on a surface *She spread the cloth flat across the kitchen table.* **2 flat out** using all your energy or effort *We've all been working flat out to finish the project on time.*

**3 in 5 minutes/30 seconds, etc flat** in exactly and only 5 minutes, 30 seconds, etc *He showered and got dressed in 10 minutes flat.* **4 fall flat** If an event or joke falls flat, it fails to have the effect that you wanted, such as making people laugh. *All the jokes in his speech fell flat.*

**flatly** /ˈflætli/ *adv* **1 flatly deny/refuse, etc** to say something in a direct and certain way *He flatly refused to answer our questions.* **2** without showing any emotion or interest *"He's gone," she said flatly.*

**flatmate** /ˈflætmeɪt/ *mainly UK* (*US* **roommate**) *noun* [C] someone who you share a flat with

**flatten** /ˈflætᵊn/ *verb* [I, T] to become flat or to make something become flat *Roll out the dough into balls and flatten them slightly.*

**flatter** /ˈflætəʳ/ *verb* **1** [T] to say nice things to someone in order to make them feel attractive or important, sometimes in a way that is not sincere *The interviewer flattered him about his recent work.* **2 be flattered** to feel very pleased and proud [+ to do sth] *I am flattered to have been given this award.* • *She was flattered by his attention.* **3** [T] to make someone look more attractive than usual *That new hairstyle really flatters you.* **4 flatter yourself** to believe something good about yourself, although it might not be true *He flatters himself that he's a good driver.*

**flattering** /ˈflætərɪŋ/ *adj* making you look more attractive than usual *a flattering picture*

**flattery** /ˈflætᵊri/ *noun* [U] when you say nice things to someone, often because you want something from that person

**flaunt** /flɔːnt/ *verb* [T] to make your success, money, beauty, etc very obvious so that people notice it and admire you *Although he's a millionaire, he doesn't flaunt his wealth.*

**flavour¹** *UK* (*US* **flavor**) /ˈfleɪvəʳ/ *noun* **1** [C, U] the taste of a particular type of food or drink *We sell 50 different flavours of ice cream.* • *Add some salt to give the soup more flavour.* **2** [no plural] a particular quality or style that something has *London has a very international flavour.*

**flavour²** *UK* (*US* **flavor**) /ˈfleɪvəʳ/ *verb* **1** [T] to give a particular taste to food or drink [often passive] *This sauce is flavoured with garlic and herbs.* **2 cheese/chocolate, etc -flavoured** tasting of cheese/chocolate, etc *lemon-flavoured sweets*

**flavouring** *UK* (*US* **flavoring**) /ˈfleɪvərɪŋ/ *noun* [C, U] something that is added to food or drink to give it a particular taste

**flaw** /flɔː/ *noun* [C] a mistake or bad characteristic that stops someone or something from being perfect *There's a flaw in your reasoning.* • **flawed** *adj* *a flawed argument*

**flawless** /ˈflɔːləs/ *adj* with no mistakes or bad characteristics *a flawless complexion* • **flawlessly** *adv* *Sarah played the piece flawlessly.*

**flea** /fliː/ *noun* [C] a small, jumping insect that lives on animals or people and drinks their blood

**'flea ,market** *noun* [C] a market where you can buy old or used things cheaply

**fleck** /flek/ *noun* [C] a mark, or a very small piece of something *His shirt was covered in flecks of paint.*

**F**

**fledgling** /'fledʒlɪŋ/ *adj* [always before noun] A fledgling company, country, or organization is new and not yet developed. *a fledgling democracy*

**flee** /fliː/ *verb* [I, T] **fleeing**, *past* **fled** to leave a place quickly because you are in danger or are afraid *Police think the suspect has now fled the country.*

**fleece** /fliːs/ *noun* [C, U] **1** a warm, soft, light jacket, or the material used to make it **2** the thick covering of wool on a sheep

**fleet** /fliːt/ *noun* [C] **1** a group of ships, or all of the ships in a country's navy **2** a group of vehicles that are owned and controlled by one person or organization *a fleet of aircraft/cars*

**flesh** /fleʃ/ *noun* [U] **1** the soft part of a person's or animal's body between the skin and bones **2 in the flesh** in real life and not on television or in a film *She looks much taller in the flesh.* **3** the soft part of a fruit or vegetable which you can eat **4 your own flesh and blood** a member of your family ● **fleshy** *adj* fat or thick, or with a lot of flesh

**flew** /fluː/ *past tense of* fly

**flex**[1] /fleks/ *verb* [T] to bend a part of your body so that the muscle becomes tight

**flex**[2] /fleks/ *UK* (*UK/US* **cord**) *noun* [C, U] a piece of wire covered in plastic, that is used to connect electrical equipment to a power supply

**flexible** /'fleksɪbl/ *adj* **1** able to change or be changed easily according to the situation *I'd like a job with more flexible working hours.* **2** A flexible substance can bend easily without breaking. ● **flexibility** /ˌfleksɪ'bɪləti/ *noun* [U]

**flick**[1] /flɪk/ *verb* **1 flick sth into/off/over, etc** to move something somewhere suddenly and quickly through the air, usually with your fingers *He quickly flicked the crumbs off the table.* **2 flick down/out/towards, etc** to make a sudden, quick movement somewhere *His eyes flicked between her and the door.* **3 flick a switch** to move a switch in order to make electrical equipment start or stop working

**flick sth on/off** to move a switch in order to make electrical equipment start/stop working

**flick through sth** to look quickly at the pages of a magazine, book, etc

**flick**[2] /flɪk/ *noun* [C] a sudden, quick movement *With a flick of her wrist, she threw the pebble into the water.*

**flicker**[1] /'flɪkəʳ/ *verb* [I] **1** to shine with a light that is sometimes bright and sometimes weak *a candle flickering in the window* **2** to appear for a short time or make a sudden movement somewhere *A smile flickered across her face.*

**flicker**[2] /'flɪkəʳ/ *noun* [no plural] **1** when a light is sometimes bright and sometimes weak *the soft flicker of candlelight* **2** a slight, brief feeling or expression of an emotion *a flicker of hope*

**flier** (*also* **flyer**) /'flaɪəʳ/ *noun* [C] **1** a small piece of paper advertising a business, show, event, etc **2** someone who flies, especially a passenger on an aircraft

**flies** /flaɪz/ *UK* (*UK/US* **fly**) *noun* [plural] the part where trousers open and close at the front

o━**flight** /flaɪt/ *noun* **1** JOURNEY [C] a journey in an aircraft *Have you booked your flight yet?* ● The

*flight to Chicago took 4 hours.* **2** AIRCRAFT [C] an aircraft that carries passengers from one place to another *Flight 102 is ready for boarding at Gate 3.* **3** MOVEMENT [U] when something flies or moves through the air *an eagle in flight* **4 a flight of stairs/steps** a set of stairs *The lift was broken so we had to climb six flights of stairs.*

'**flight at,tendant** *noun* [C] someone whose job is to look after passengers on an aircraft

**flimsy** /'flɪmzi/ *adj* **1** thin and not solid or strong *a flimsy cardboard box* ● *Aren't you cold in that flimsy dress?* **2** A flimsy argument, excuse, etc is weak and difficult to believe. *I'm sick of his flimsy excuses for being late.*

**flinch** /flɪnʃ/ *verb* [I] **1** to make a sudden movement backwards because you are afraid or in pain *She didn't flinch when the nurse cleaned the wound.* **2** to avoid doing something that is unpleasant *Nick never flinches from difficult decisions.*

**fling**[1] /flɪŋ/ *verb past* **flung** **fling sth around/across/down, etc** to throw or move something suddenly and with a lot of force *She flung her arms around his neck.* ● *He flung himself down on the sofa.*

**fling**[2] /flɪŋ/ *noun* [C] **1** a sexual relationship that is short and not serious *She had a fling with someone last summer.* **2** a short period of time when you have a lot of enjoyment or pleasure *This is my last fling before the exams.*

**flint** /flɪnt/ *noun* [C, U] a very hard, grey stone that can be used to produce a flame

**flip** /flɪp/ *verb* **flipping**, *past* **flipped** **1** [I, T] to turn or make something turn onto a different side, or so that it is the wrong way up *to flip a coin/pancake* ● *The boat flipped right over.* **2** [I] *informal* to become uncontrollably angry, crazy, or excited *Dad completely flipped when he saw the car.*

**flip through sth** to look quickly at the pages of a magazine, book, etc

**flippant** /'flɪpªnt/ *adj* without respect or not serious *a flippant remark* ● **flippantly** *adv* ● **flippancy** /'flɪpªnsi/ *noun* [U]

**flipper** /'flɪpəʳ/ *noun* [C] **1** a part like a wide, flat arm without fingers that some sea animals use for swimming **2** a long, flat, rubber shoe that you use when swimming underwater

**flipping** /'flɪpɪŋ/ *adj* [always before noun] *UK informal* used to emphasize something, or to show slight anger *Where are my flipping keys?*

**the** '**flip** ,**side** *noun* the opposite, less good, or less popular side of something

**flirt**[1] /flɜːt/ *verb* [I] to behave as if you are sexually attracted to someone, usually not in a very serious way *She was flirting with a guy at the bar.*

**flirt with sth 1** to be interested in an idea, activity, etc but not seriously, or for only a short time *He flirted with the idea of becoming a priest.* **2 flirt with danger/disaster, etc** to risk experiencing something bad ● **flirtation** /flɜː'teɪʃªn/ *noun* [C, U]

**flirt**[2] /flɜːt/ *noun* [C] someone who often flirts with people

**flirtatious** /flɜː'teɪʃəs/ *adj* behaving as if you

are sexually attracted to someone, usually not in a very serious way

**flit** /flɪt/ *verb* **flitting**, *past* **flitted flit about/ around/in and out, etc** to fly or move quickly from one place to another *Birds were flitting from tree to tree.*

o─**float¹** /fləʊt/ *verb* **1** LIQUID [I, T] to stay on the surface of a liquid instead of sinking, or to make something do this *I like floating on my back in the pool.* **2** AIR [I] to stay in the air, or move gently through the air *A balloon floated across the sky.* **3** BUSINESS [I, T] to start selling a company's shares to the public

float                        sink

**float²** /fləʊt/ *noun* [C] **1** VEHICLE a large, decorated vehicle that is used in public celebrations **2** WATER an object that floats on water, used in fishing or when learning to swim **3** BUSINESS when you float a business

**flock¹** /flɒk/ *noun* [group] **1** a group of birds or sheep *a flock of geese* **2** a group of people led by one person *a flock of children/visitors*

**flock²** /flɒk/ *verb* [I] to move or come together in large numbers *Tourists are **flocking to** the beaches.* • [+ to do sth] *People flocked to hear him speak.*

**flog** /flɒg/ *verb* [T] **flogging**, *past* **flogged 1** to hit someone repeatedly as a punishment with something such as a stick **2** *UK informal* to sell something quickly or cheaply *I had to flog the car to pay my bills.* • **flogging** *noun* [C, U]

**flood¹** /flʌd/ *verb* [I, T] **1** If a place floods or is flooded, it becomes covered in water. [often passive] *The town was flooded when the river burst its banks.* • *I left the taps running and flooded the bathroom.* **2** to fill or enter a place in large numbers or amounts *Light flooded the room.* • *Shoppers **flooded into** the store.* • **flooding** *noun* [U] *There is widespread flooding in the South.*

**be flooded with sth** to receive so many letters, telephone calls, etc that you cannot deal with them *We were flooded with calls from worried parents.*

o─**flood²** /flʌd/ *noun* **1** [C] when a lot of water covers an area that is usually dry, especially when a river becomes too full *The flood destroyed thousands of homes.* **2** [C] a large number or amount of things or people that

arrive at the same time *a flood of letters/calls* **3 in floods of tears** *UK* crying a lot *She collapsed in floods of tears.*

**flood**

**floodgates** /ˈflʌdgeɪts/ *noun* **open the floodgates** to make it possible for a lot of people to do something

**floodlights** /ˈflʌdlaɪts/ *noun* [plural] powerful lights used to light up sports fields or the outside of buildings at night • **floodlit** /ˈflʌdlɪt/ *adj* lit up by floodlights

o─**floor** /flɔːʳ/ *noun* **1** SURFACE [C] a surface that you walk on inside a building *a wooden/tiled floor* • *I must sweep the kitchen floor.* **2** BUILDING [C] a particular level of a building *the second/third floor* • *Which floor are we on?* **3** BOTTOM [no plural] the ground or surface at the bottom of something *the forest/sea floor* **4** AREA [C] an area where a particular activity happens *a dance floor* ⊃ *See also:* **first floor**, **ground floor**, **shop floor**.

**floorboard** /ˈflɔːbɔːd/ *noun* [C] a long, narrow, flat board that forms part of a wooden floor in a building

**flooring** /ˈflɔːrɪŋ/ *noun* [U] the material used to make or cover a floor *vinyl flooring*

**flop¹** /flɒp/ *verb* [I] **flopping**, *past* **flopped 1 flop down/into/onto, etc** to fall or sit somewhere suddenly in a heavy or relaxed way *He flopped down on the sofa.* **2** to hang loosely *Her hair kept flopping in her eyes.* **3** *informal* If a film, product, plan, etc flops, it is not successful.

**flop²** /flɒp/ *noun* [C] *informal* **1** something that is not a success *The party was a bit of a flop.* **2** a movement towards the ground, or the noise someone or something makes as they fall down *She fell onto the bed with a flop.*

**floppy** /ˈflɒpi/ *adj* soft and loose or hanging down loosely *floppy hair* • *a floppy hat*

**floppy 'disk** *noun* [C] a small disk inside a flat, square piece of plastic used for storing information electronically from a computer

**flora** /ˈflɔːrə/ *noun* [U, group] the plants that grow naturally in a particular area *Scotland's flora and fauna*

**floral** /ˈflɔːrəl/ *adj* [always before noun] made from flowers or relating to flowers *a floral arrangement/pattern*

**florist** /ˈflɒrɪst/ *noun* [C] **1** someone who sells and arranges flowers in a shop **2** (*also* **florist's**) a shop that sells flowers

**flotation** /fləʊ'teɪʃ³n/ *noun* **1** [C, U] when a company's shares are sold to the public for the first time **2** [U] when something or someone floats on or in liquid

**flounder** /'flaʊndə³/ *verb* [I] **1** MOVEMENT to make wild movements with your arms or body, especially because you are trying not to sink **2** NOT KNOW to not know what to do or say *When he resigned, the team was left floundering.* **3** FAIL If a relationship, organization, or plan flounders, it fails or begins to experience problems. *By 1993 his marriage was floundering.*

**flour** /flaʊə³/ *noun* [U] a powder made from grain that is used to make bread, cakes, and other food

**flourish¹** /'flʌrɪʃ/ *verb* **1** [I] to grow or develop well *The company soon began to flourish under his expert management.* ● *a flourishing tourist industry* **2** [T] to wave something around in the air

**flourish²** /'flʌrɪʃ/ *noun* [no plural] when someone does something in a special and noticeable way *The waiter handed me the menu with a flourish.*

**flout** /flaʊt/ *verb* [T] to intentionally not obey or accept something *to flout the law/rules*

**flow¹** /fləʊ/ *verb* [I] **1** If something such as a liquid flows, it moves somewhere in a smooth, continuous way. *The river flows from the Andes to the ocean.* ● *Electric current flows down this wire.* **2** If words, ideas, or conversations flow, they continue in an easy and relaxed way without stopping. *At dinner, the conversation flowed freely.*

**flow²** /fləʊ/ *noun* **1** [no plural] when something such as a liquid moves somewhere in a smooth, continuous way *the flow of blood* ● *the flow of information* **2 go with the flow** *informal* to do or accept what other people are doing because it is the easiest thing to do *Just relax and go with the flow!* ⊃ *See also:* **ebb¹** and flow.

o‒**flower¹** /flaʊə³/ *noun* **1** [C] the attractive, coloured part of a plant where the seeds grow *a bunch of flowers* **2** [C] a type of plant that produces flowers *spring/wild flowers* **3 be in flower** When plants are in flower, they have flowers on them. **4 the flower of sth** *literary* the best part of something *the flower of our nation's youth*

**flower²** /flaʊə³/ *verb* [I] to produce flowers *These pansies flower all summer.* ● *a flowering plant*

**'flower ,bed** *noun* [C] an area of soil in a garden that you grow flowers in

**flowery** /'flaʊəri/ *adj* **1** (*also* **flowered** /flaʊəd/) decorated with a pattern of flowers *a flowery dress* **2** Flowery language contains unnecessarily complicated and unusual words. *a flowery description*

**flowing** /'fləʊɪŋ/ *adj* **1** hanging down in a long, loose way *flowing robes/hair* **2** produced in a smooth, continuous, or relaxed style *flowing lines*

**flown** /fləʊn/ *past participle of* fly

**fl oz** *written abbreviation for* fluid ounce (= a unit for measuring liquid)

**flu** /fluː/ *noun* [U] an illness like a very bad cold, that makes you feel hot and weak *I had the flu last week.*

**fluctuate** /'flʌktʃueɪt/ *verb* [I] to keep changing, especially in level or amount *Oil prices have fluctuated wildly in recent weeks.* ● fluctuation /,flʌktʃu'eɪʃ³n/ *noun* [C, U] *fluctuations in house prices*

**fluent** /'fluːənt/ *adj* **1** able to use a language naturally without stopping or making mistakes *She is fluent in six languages.* **2** produced or done in a smooth, natural style *Hendrik speaks fluent English.* ● fluency /'fluːənsi/ *noun* [U] ● fluently *adv*

**fluff¹** /flʌf/ *noun* [U] small, loose bits of wool or other soft material *There's a piece of fluff on your jacket.*

**fluff²** /flʌf/ *verb* [T] *informal* to fail to do something successfully *I had a great chance to score but I fluffed it.*

**fluff sth out/up** to make something appear bigger or fuller by hitting or shaking it so that it contains more air *I'll fluff up your pillows for you.*

**fluffy** /'flʌfi/ *adj* made or covered with soft fur or cloth *a fluffy toy*

**fluid¹** /'fluːɪd/ *noun* [C, U] a liquid *cleaning fluid* ● *Drink plenty of fluids.*

**fluid²** /'fluːɪd/ *adj* **1** LIQUID able to flow easily like liquid **2** CHANGING likely or able to change *a fluid situation* **3** SMOOTH smooth and continuous *fluid movements*

**,fluid 'ounce** (*written abbreviation* **fl oz**) *noun* [C] a unit for measuring liquid, equal to 0.0284 litres in the UK and 0.0296 litres in the US

**fluke** /fluːk/ *noun* [C, U] something good that happens only because of luck or chance *That first goal was just a fluke.*

**flung** /flʌŋ/ *past of* fling

**fluorescent** /flɔː'res³nt/ *adj* **1** Fluorescent lights are very bright, tube-shaped, electric lights, often used in offices. **2** Fluorescent colours, clothes, etc are very bright and can be seen in the dark. *fluorescent pink* ● *a fluorescent jacket*

**fluoride** /'flɔːraɪd/ *noun* [U] a chemical that helps to prevent tooth decay *fluoride toothpaste*

**flurry** /'flʌri/ *noun* [C] **1** a sudden, short period of activity, interest, or excitement *a flurry of phone calls* **2** a sudden, short period of snow and wind

**flush¹** /flʌʃ/ *verb* **1** [I, T] If you flush a toilet, or if it flushes, its contents empty and it fills with water again. **2 flush sth away/down/out, etc** to get rid of something by pushing it somewhere with lots of water, such as down a toilet **3** [I] If you flush, your face becomes red and hot, usually because you are embarrassed or angry.

**flush sb/sth out** to force a person or animal to come out from where they are hiding

**flush²** /flʌʃ/ *noun* [C] **1** when your face becomes hot and red *a hot flush* **2 a flush of excitement/pleasure, etc** a sudden feeling of excitement/pleasure, etc

**flush³** /flʌʃ/ *adj* [never before noun] **1** at the same level as another surface *I want the door flush with the wall.* **2** *informal* rich *flush with cash*

**flustered** /'flʌstəd/ *adj* upset and confused *She arrived very late, looking flustered.*

**flute** /fluːt/ *noun* [C] a musical instrument in the

shape of a tube that is held out to the side and played by blowing across a hole near one end

**flutter¹** /'flʌtər/ verb **1** [I, T] to move quickly and gently up and down or from side to side in the air, or to make something move in this way *The flag was fluttering in the breeze.* **2 flutter about/around/down, etc** to move somewhere quickly and gently, usually without any particular purpose *There were several moths fluttering around the light.*

**flutter²** /'flʌtər/ noun [C] **1** MOVEMENT a quick, gentle movement *the flutter of wings* **2** EMOTION a state of excitement or worry *a flutter of excitement* **3** RISK MONEY *UK informal* when you risk money on the result of a game, competition, etc

**flux** /flʌks/ noun [U] continuous change *The housing market is still in a state of flux.*

o━**fly¹** /flaɪ/ verb past t **flew**, past p **flown 1** MOVE THROUGH AIR [I] When a bird, insect, aircraft, etc flies, it moves through the air. *The robin flew up into a tree.* • *The plane was flying at 5000 feet.* **2** TRAVEL [I] to travel through the air in an aircraft *I'm flying to Delhi tomorrow.* **3** CONTROL AIRCRAFT [I, T] to control an aircraft *She learned to fly at the age of 18.* **4** TAKE/SEND [T] to take or send people or goods somewhere by aircraft [often passive] *She was flown to hospital by helicopter.* **5 fly along/down/past, etc** to move somewhere very quickly *He grabbed some clothes and flew down the stairs.* **6 send sb/sth flying** to cause someone or something to move through the air suddenly, usually in an accident **7** LEAVE [I] *UK* to leave suddenly *I must fly – I'm late for work.* **8 let fly (at sb/sth)** *mainly UK informal* to start shouting angrily or attacking someone **9** TIME [I] If time flies, it passes very quickly. **10** FLAG [I, T] If you fly a flag, or a flag is flying, it is fixed to a rope or pole and raised in the air. • **flying** noun [U] *Ben's afraid of flying.* ⊃ *See also:* as the **crow¹** flies, fly off the **handle²**.

**fly about/around** If ideas or remarks are flying about, they are being passed quickly from one person to another and causing excitement. *All kinds of rumours are flying around about the school closing.*

**fly into a rage/temper** to suddenly become very angry

**fly²** /flaɪ/ noun **1** [C] a small insect with two wings *There was a fly buzzing around in the kitchen.* ⊃ *See picture at* **insect**. **2** [C] (*also UK* **flies** [plural]) the part where trousers open and close at the front *a button/zip fly* **3 fly on the wall** If you say that you would like to be a fly on the wall in a certain situation, you mean that you would like to be there secretly to see and hear what happens. **4 a fly-on-the-wall documentary/film** a television programme or film in which people do not act but are recorded in real situations, sometimes without knowing **5 be dropping like flies** to be dying or becoming ill in large numbers **6 wouldn't hurt a fly** If you say that someone wouldn't hurt a fly, you mean that they are very gentle and would never do anything to injure or upset anyone. *He looks big and tough but he wouldn't hurt a fly.*

**flyer** (*also* **flier**) /'flaɪər/ noun [C] **1** a small piece of paper advertising a business, show, event, etc *She's handing out flyers in the shopping centre.* **2** someone who flies, especially a passenger on an aircraft *a frequent flyer* ⊃ *See also:* **high-flyer**.

**flying** /'flaɪɪŋ/ adj [always before noun] **1** A flying creature or object moves or is able to move through the air. *flying ants* **2 a flying visit** *UK* a very brief visit *He paid them a flying visit on his way to the airport.* ⊃ *See also:* with flying colours (**colour¹**).

**flyover** /'flaɪ,əʊvər/ *UK* (*US* **overpass**) noun [C] a bridge that carries a road over another road

**FM** /,ef'em/ noun [U] a system of radio signals used for broadcasting programmes

**foal** /fəʊl/ noun [C] a young horse

**foam** /fəʊm/ noun [U] **1** BUBBLES a mass of small, white bubbles on the surface of a liquid **2** PRODUCT a thick substance of small, white bubbles used as a cleaning or beauty product *shaving foam* **3** FILLING a soft substance used to fill furniture and other objects

**focal point** /'fəʊkəl,pɔɪnt/ noun [no plural] the thing that attracts most of your attention or interest in a place, picture, etc *The fireplace is the focal point of the room.*

**focus¹** /'fəʊkəs/ verb **focusing**, *past* **focused 1** [T] If you focus a camera or something else that you look through, you make small changes to it until you can see something clearly. **2** [I, T] If you focus your eyes, or your eyes focus, they change so that you can see clearly. *Give your eyes time to focus in the darkness.*

**focus (sth) on sth** to give a lot of attention to one particular subject or thing *The research focused on men under thirty.*

**focus²** /'fəʊkəs/ noun **1 the focus of sth** the person or thing that is getting most attention in a situation or activity *the focus of our attention* • *He is the focus of a police investigation.* **2** [U] when you give special attention to something *Their main focus must be on reducing crime.* **3 in focus** If an image is in focus, you are able to see it clearly. **4 out of focus** If an image is out of focus, you are not able to see it clearly.

**'focus ,group** noun [group] a group of people who are brought together to discuss what they think about something such as a new product

**fodder** /'fɒdər/ noun [U] food such as dried grass for animals that are kept on farms *cattle fodder*

**foe** /fəʊ/ noun [C] *literary* an enemy

**foetus** *UK* (*US* **fetus**) /'fiːtəs/ noun [C] a young human or animal that is still developing inside its mother • **foetal** *UK* (*US* **fetal**) /'fiːtəl/ adj *foetal development*

**fog** /fɒg/ noun [U] thick cloud just above the ground or sea that makes it difficult to see

**foggy** /'fɒgi/ adj **1** with fog *a foggy day* **2 not have the foggiest (idea)** *informal* to not know anything about something [+ question word] *I haven't the foggiest idea what you're talking about.*

**foible** /'fɔɪbl/ noun [C] a slightly unusual or annoying habit [usually plural] *Married couples must learn to accept each other's little foibles.*

**foil¹** /fɔɪl/ noun **1** [U] metal made into very thin sheets like paper and used mainly for covering

food *(UK) aluminium foil/(US) aluminum foil*
**2 a foil for sb/sth** a person or thing that shows
or emphasizes how different someone or
something else is

**foil²** /fɔɪl/ *verb* [T] to stop a crime, plan, etc from
succeeding, or to stop someone doing what
they want to do [often passive] *The plot was foiled
by undercover police officers.* • *This device is
designed to foil car thieves.*

o—ᴑ**fold¹** /fəʊld/ [MATERIAL] [T] If you fold
paper, cloth, etc, you bend it so that one part of
it lies flat on top of another part. *Can you help
me fold the sheets?* • *He folded the letter in half.*
**2** [FURNITURE] [I, T] (*also* **fold up**) to make something such as a chair or table smaller or flatter
by closing it or bending it together *I folded up
the table and put it away.* • *a folding chair*
⊃ *Opposite* **unfold**. **3** [BUSINESS] [I] *informal* If a
business folds, it fails and is unable to continue. *The magazine folded last year.* **4 fold
your arms** to bend your arms across your
chest, with one crossing over the other *He sat
with his arms folded.*

**fold²** /fəʊld/ *noun* [C] **1** a line or mark where
paper, cloth, etc was or is folded *Make a fold
across the centre of the card.* **2** a thick part
where something folds or hangs over itself
[usually plural] *folds of skin/fabric*

**folder** /ˈfəʊldəʳ/ *noun* [C] **1** a piece of plastic or
thick paper folded down the middle and used to
store loose papers ⊃ *See colour picture* **The Office**
*on page Centre 12.* **2** a place on a computer where
particular files (= documents, pictures, etc) are
kept

**foliage** /ˈfəʊliːɪdʒ/ *noun* [U] the leaves on a plant

**folk¹** /fəʊk/ *noun* **1** [plural] *UK* (*US* **folks**) *informal* people *country folk* • *old folk* **2** sb's **folks**
someone's parents *We always spend Christmas
with my folks.* **3** [U] folk music

**folk²** /fəʊk/ *adj* **folk art/dancing, etc** the
traditional style of art, dancing, etc among a
particular group of people

'**folk ˌmusic** *noun* [U] music written and played
in a traditional style

o—ᴑ**follow** /ˈfɒləʊ/ *verb* **1** [GO] [I, T] to move behind
someone or something and go where they go,
sometimes secretly *She followed me into the
kitchen.* • *He employed a private detective to
follow his wife.* **2** [HAPPEN] [I, T] to happen or
come after something *The weeks that followed
were the happiest days of my life.* • *There was a
bang, followed by a cloud of smoke.* **3 follow a
path/road, etc** to travel along a path, road, etc
*Follow the main road down to the traffic lights.*
**4 follow instructions/orders/rules, etc** to do
what the instructions, orders, rules, etc say
you should do *I followed your advice and stayed
at home.* **5 follow sb's example/lead** to copy
someone's behaviour or ideas *You should
follow Meg's example and tidy your room.*
**6** [UNDERSTAND] [I, T] to understand something
*Could you say that again? I didn't quite follow.*
**7** [BE INTERESTED] [T] to be interested in an event
or activity *I followed the trial closely.* **8 as
follows** used to introduce a list or description
**9 it follows that** used to say that if one thing
is true, another thing will also be true *He's big,
but it doesn't follow that he's strong.* ⊃ *See also:*

follow in sb's footsteps (**footstep**), follow
**suit¹**.

**follow on** *mainly UK* to happen or exist as the
next part of something *This report follows on
from my earlier study.*

**follow sth through** to do something as the next
part of an activity or period of development,
usually to make certain that it is completed or
successful

**follow sth up** to discover more about a situation or take further action in connection with
it

**follower** /ˈfɒləʊəʳ/ *noun* [C] someone who
believes in a particular person or set of ideas *a
follower of Jesus*

**following¹** /ˈfɒləʊɪŋ/ *adj* **1 the following
day/morning, etc** the next day, morning, etc
**2 the following** what comes next, often used
to introduce a list, report, etc *The following is
an extract from her diary: Today I stayed in bed
all day.*

**following²** /ˈfɒləʊɪŋ/ *noun* [no plural] a group of
people who follow a leader, sport, etc, or admire
a particular performer *He has a large and loyal
following.*

**following³** /ˈfɒləʊɪŋ/ *preposition* after or as a
result of *He died on October 23rd, following
several years of illness.*

**follow-up** /ˈfɒləʊʌp/ *noun* [C] something that is
done to continue or complete something that
was done before *a follow-up meeting*

**fond** /fɒnd/ *adj* **1 be fond of sb/sth** to like
someone or something *to be fond of animals/
music* • [+ doing sth] *He's not very fond of
dancing.* **2** [always before noun] expressing or
causing happy feelings *fond memories* **3 a
fond hope/belief, etc** something that you
wish were true, but probably is not • *fondly adv*
• **fondness** *noun* [C, U] *We both have a fondness
for cricket.*

**fondle** /ˈfɒndl/ *verb* [T] to touch and rub part of
someone's body, in a loving or sexual way

**font** /fɒnt/ *noun* [C] **1** a set of letters and
symbols that are printed in a particular design
and size *What size font are you using?* **2** a container in a church which holds the water for a
baptism (= Christian ceremony)

o—ᴑ**food** /fuːd/ *noun* [C, U] something that people
and animals eat, or plants absorb, to keep them
alive *baby/dog food* • *His favourite food is
pizza.* ⊃ *See colour picture* **Food** *on page Centre 7*
⊃ *See also:* **fast food, junk food.**

'**food ˌpoisoning** *noun* [U] an illness caused
by eating food containing harmful bacteria

'**food ˌprocessor** *noun* [C] a piece of electrical
equipment with a sharp blade, for cutting and
mixing food ⊃ *See colour picture* **Kitchen** *on page
Centre 10.*

**foodstuff** /ˈfuːdstʌf/ *noun* [C] *formal* a substance used as food or to make food [usually
plural] *They need basic foodstuffs like rice and
corn.*

**fool¹** /fuːl/ *noun* **1** [C] a stupid person *I was a
fool to trust him.* **2 make a fool (out) of sb** to
try to make someone look stupid intentionally
*She was always trying to make a fool out of me
in front of my friends.* **3 make a fool of yourself** to behave in a silly or embarrassing way

*I got drunk and started singing and making a fool of myself.* **4 act/play the fool** *UK* to behave in a silly way, usually in order to make people laugh *Joe is always playing the fool in class.*

**fool²** /fuːl/ *verb* **1** [T] to trick someone *Don't be fooled by his appearance.* • [+ into + doing sth] *He fooled the old man into giving him the money.* **2 you could have fooled me** *informal* something that you say when you do not believe what someone says about something that you saw or experienced yourself *"I wasn't cross." "Really? You could have fooled me."*

**fool around/about** to behave in a silly way or have a good time *Stop fooling around – this is serious!*

**fool with sb/sth** *mainly US* to deal with someone or something that could be dangerous in a stupid or careless way

**foolhardy** /ˈfuːlˌhɑːdi/ *adj* taking or involving silly and unnecessary risks *a foolhardy decision*

**foolish** /ˈfuːlɪʃ/ *adj* silly and not wise *a foolish man/mistake* • [+ to do sth] *It would be foolish to ignore his advice.* • **foolishly** *adv* • **foolishness** *noun* [U]

**foolproof** /ˈfuːlpruːf/ *adj* A foolproof method, plan, or system is certain to succeed and not fail.

○━**foot¹** /fʊt/ *noun* **1** [C] *plural* **feet** one of the two flat parts on the ends of your legs that you stand on *bare feet* • *He stepped on my foot.* ⊃ *See colour picture* **The Body** *on page Centre 2.* **2** [C] *plural* **foot** or **feet** (*written abbreviation* **ft**) a unit for measuring length, equal to 0.3048 metres or 12 inches *Alex is about 6 feet tall.* • *an eight foot high wall* **3 the foot of sth** the bottom of something such as stairs, a hill, a bed, or a page *Put the notes at the foot of the page.* **4 on foot** If you go somewhere on foot, you walk there. ⊃ *See usage note at* **walk.** **5 be on your feet** to be standing and not sitting *I'm exhausted, I've been on my feet all day.* **6 put your feet up** to relax, especially by sitting with your feet supported above the ground *You put your feet up for half an hour before the kids get home.* **7 set foot in/on sth** to go into a place or onto a piece of land *He told me never to set foot in his house again.* **8 get/rise to your feet** to stand up after you have been sitting *The audience rose to their feet.* **9 drag your feet** to deal with something slowly because you do not really want to do it **10 get cold feet** to suddenly become too frightened to do what you had planned to do, especially something important *I tried to ask her out, but I got cold feet.* **11 get/start off on the wrong foot** to start a relationship or activity badly *He got off on the wrong foot with my parents by arriving late.* **12 not put a foot wrong** *UK* to not make any mistakes **13 put your foot down** to tell someone in a strong way that they must do something or must stop doing something **14 put your foot in it** *UK* (*US* **put your foot in your mouth**) to say something silly or embarrassing, without intending to **15 stand on your own two feet** to do things for yourself without wanting or needing anyone else to

help you *That son of hers should learn to stand on his own two feet.*

**foot²** /fʊt/ *verb* **foot the bill** to pay for something *Why should taxpayers have to foot the bill?*

**footage** /ˈfʊtɪdʒ/ *noun* [U] film of an event *news/TV footage*

○━**football** /ˈfʊtbɔːl/ *noun* **1** [UK GAME] [U] *UK* (*UK/ US* **soccer**) a game in which two teams of players kick a round ball and try to score goals *a game of football* • *a football match/team* ⊃ *See colour picture* **Sports 2** *on page Centre 16.* **2** [US GAME] [U] *US* (*UK* **American football**) a game in which two teams of players try to kick, run with, or throw an oval ball across each other's goal line **3** [BALL] [C] a large ball for kicking, especially in football • **footballer** *noun* [C] *UK* someone who plays football, especially as their job

**foothills** /ˈfʊthɪlz/ *noun* [plural] the lower hills next to a mountain or line of mountains

**foothold** /ˈfʊthəʊld/ *noun* [C] **1** a place where it is safe to put your foot when you are climbing **2** a safe position from which you can make more progress, for example in business *We are still trying to* **gain a foothold** *in the Japanese market.*

**footing** /ˈfʊtɪŋ/ *noun* **1** [no plural] when you are standing on a surface firmly *I lost my footing and fell.* **2 be on an equal/firm, etc footing** to be in an equal/safe, etc position or situation *When we're on a firmer financial footing we can employ more staff.*

**footnote** /ˈfʊtnəʊt/ *noun* [C] extra information that is printed at the bottom of a page

**footpath** /ˈfʊtpɑːθ/ *noun* [C] *mainly UK* a path or track for people to walk along, especially in the countryside *a public footpath*

**footprint** /ˈfʊtprɪnt/ *noun* [C] a mark made by a foot or shoe [usually plural] *The police found some footprints in the mud.*

**footstep** /ˈfʊtstep/ *noun* **1** [C] the sound of a foot hitting the ground when someone walks [usually plural] *I heard footsteps behind me and quickly turned round.* **2 follow in sb's footsteps** to do the same job or the same things in your life as someone else, especially a member of your family *He followed in his father's footsteps and became an actor.*

**footwear** /ˈfʊtweəʳ/ *noun* [U] shoes, boots, and other things that you wear on your feet *a footwear company*

○━**for** strong form /fɔːʳ/ weak form /fəʳ/ *preposition* **1** [GIVEN/USED] intended to be given to or used by someone or something *I've bought a few clothes for the new baby.* • *We need some curtains for the spare bedroom.* • *parking for residents only* **2** [PURPOSE] having a particular purpose *a cream for dry skin* • *What are those large scissors for?* **3** [BECAUSE OF] because of or as a result of something [+ doing sth] *I got fined for travelling without a ticket.* • *Scotland is famous for its spectacular countryside.* **4** [TIME/DISTANCE] used to show an amount of time or distance *We drove for miles before we found a phone box.* • *I've been living with my parents for a few months.* ⊃ *See usage note at* **during.** **5** [GET] in order to get or achieve something *I've sent off* *for an application form.* ● *We had to wait for a taxi.* **6** HELP in order to help someone *I'll carry those bags for you.* **7** OCCASION on the occasion of *We're having a party for Jim's 60th birthday.* **8** AT A TIME at a particular time *I've booked a table for 9 o'clock.* **9** IN EXCHANGE in exchange for something, especially an amount of money *How much did you pay for your computer?* ● *I'd like to change it for a smaller one.* **10** SUPPORT supporting or agreeing with someone or something *Who did you vote for?* ● *There were 16 people for the motion and 14 against.* **11** REPRE-SENT representing or working with a country, organization, etc *He plays football for Cambridge United.* ● *She works for a charity.* **12** TOWARDS towards or in the direction of *Just follow the signs for the airport.* **13** COMPARE when compared to a particular fact *She's quite tall for her age.* **14** MEANING meaning or representing something *What's the German word for 'cucumber'?* **15** RESPONSI-BILITY used to say whose responsibility something is *I can't tell you whether you should go or not – that's for you to decide.* **16 for all** despite *For all her qualifications, she's useless at the job.* **17 for all I care/know** used to say that a fact is not important to you *He could be married by now, for all I care.* **18 for now** used to say that something should happen or be done now but can be changed later *Just put everything on the table for now.* **19 be for it** UK *informal* (*UK/US* **be in for it**) to be in trouble *If Hilary finds out I'll be for it!*

**forage** /'fɒrɪdʒ/ *verb* [I] to move about searching for things you need, especially food *Chimpanzees spend most of the day foraging for fruit, leaves, and insects.*

**foray** /'fɒreɪ/ *noun* [C] when you try to do something that is not familiar to you, or go somewhere different, for a short time *In 1997, she made her first foray into politics.*

**forbid** /fə'bɪd/ *verb* [T] **forbidding**, *past t* **forbade**, *past p* **forbidden 1** to order someone not to do something, or to say that something must not happen [+ to do sth] *I forbid you to see that boy again.* ● [often passive + from + doing sth] *He is forbidden from leaving the country.* **2 God/ Heaven forbid!** something you say when you hope that something will not happen [+ (that)] *God forbid that he should die during the operation.* ● **forbidden** *adj* not allowed by an official rule *Smoking is strictly forbidden in this area.*

**forbidding** /fə'bɪdɪŋ/ *adj* looking unpleasant, unfriendly, or frightening *a cold and forbidding landscape*

○━**force**[1] /fɔːs/ *noun* **1** POWER [U] physical power or strength *The force of the explosion shattered every window in the street.* ● *The army has seized power by force.* **2** ORGANIZED GROUP [C] a group of people organized to work together for a particular purpose, for example in military service *the Royal Air Force* ● *a skilled work force* **3** INFLUENCE [C, U] power and influence, or a person or thing that has it *the forces of good/evil* **4 in/into force** If a law, rule, etc is in force, it is being used, and if it comes into force, it starts to be used. *The new law came into force in April.* **5 be out in force** to be somewhere in

large numbers *Photographers were out in force at the palace today.* **6 a force to be reckoned with** a very powerful person or organization **7 join forces** When two people or groups join forces, they act or work together. [+ to do sth] *She joined forces with her sister-in-law to set up a restaurant.* ⊃ *See also:* **air force, the armed forces, market forces, police force, task force.**

○━**force**[2] /fɔːs/ *verb* [T] **1** to make someone do something that they do not want to do [+ to do sth] *The hijacker forced the pilot to fly to New York.* ● [often passive] *She was forced out of the race by a knee injury.* **2** to make an object move or open by physical strength or effort *They had to force the lock.* ● *She forced the window open.*

**forceful** /'fɔːsfəl/ *adj* expressing opinions strongly and demanding attention or action *a forceful manner/personality* ● **forcefully** *adv* to argue forcefully

**forcible** /'fɔːsəbl/ *adj* A forcible action is done using force. *forcible entry/arrest* ● **forcibly** *adv* *Thousands of people were forcibly removed from their homes.*

**fore** /fɔːʳ/ *noun* **to the fore** in or to an important or popular position *The band first came to the fore in the late 1990s.*

**forearm** /'fɔːrɑːm/ *noun* [C] the lower part of your arm between your hand and your elbow (= the place where it bends)

**foreboding** /fɔː'bəʊdɪŋ/ *noun* [U, no plural] a feeling that something very bad is going to happen *a sense of foreboding*

**forecast**[1] /'fɔːkɑːst/ *noun* [C] a report saying what is likely to happen in the future *economic forecasts* ⊃ *See also:* **weather forecast.**

**forecast**[2] /'fɔːkɑːst/ *verb* [T] *past* **forecast** or **forecasted** to say what you expect to happen in the future *In 1990 a serious earthquake was forecast for the area.* ● **forecaster** *noun* [C] *a weather forecaster*

**forecourt** /'fɔːkɔːt/ *noun* [C] *UK* a large area with a hard surface at the front of a building *a garage forecourt*

**forefather** /'fɔːˌfɑːðəʳ/ *noun formal* **sb's fore-fathers** someone's relatives who lived a long time ago

**forefinger** /'fɔːˌfɪŋgəʳ/ *noun* [C] the finger next to your thumb

**forefront** /'fɔːfrʌnt/ *noun* **be at/in the fore-front of sth** to have an important position or job in an area of activity *The company is at the forefront of developing new technology.*

**forego** /fɔː'gəʊ/ *verb* [T] **foregoing**, *past t* **forewent**, *past p* **foregone** another spelling of forgo (= to decide not to have or do something you want)

**foregone con·clusion** *noun* [no plural] a result that is obvious before it happens [+ (that)] *It was a foregone conclusion that he'd go into politics.*

**the foreground** /'fɔːgraʊnd/ *noun* **1** the area of a view or picture which seems closest to you *There's a seated figure in the foreground of the painting.* **2** the subject or person that people give most attention to *Environmental issues have recently moved to the foreground.*

**forehand** /'fɔːhænd/ *noun* [C] when you hit the

ball in sports such as tennis with your arm held out on the side that you hold the racket (= object to hit balls with) *a forehand volley*

**forehead** /'fɔːhed/ *noun* [C] the part of your face between your eyes and your hair ➔ *See colour picture* **The Body** *on page Centre 2.*

o-ᴗ**foreign** /'fɒrɪn/ *adj* **1** belonging to or coming from another country, not your own *a foreign language/student* • *foreign cars/films* ➔ *See usage note at* **strange. 2** [always before noun] relating to or dealing with countries that are not your own *foreign policy* • *the Foreign Minister* **3 be foreign to sb** to be something you know nothing about or do not understand *The concept of loyalty is completely foreign to him.*

**foreigner** /'fɒrɪnə<sup>r</sup>/ *noun* [C] someone from another country

**foreman** /'fɔːmən/ *noun* [C] *plural* **foremen** someone who leads a group of workers *a factory foreman*

**foremost** /'fɔːməʊst/ *adj, adv formal* most important *He's one of the country's foremost experts on military law.*

**forename** /'fɔːneɪm/ *noun* [C] *UK formal* your first name, which comes before your family name

**forensic** /fə'rensɪk/ *adj* [always before noun] relating to scientific methods of solving crimes *forensic evidence* • *a forensic scientist*

**forerunner** /'fɔːˌrʌnə<sup>r</sup>/ *noun* [C] an earlier, less developed example *the forerunner of the modern car*

**foresee** /fɔː'siː/ *verb* [T] **foreseeing**, *past t* **foresaw**, *past p* **foreseen** to expect a future situation or event *I don't foresee any problems in the future.*

**foreseeable** /fɔː'siːəbl/ *adj* **for/in the foreseeable future** as far in the future as you can imagine *Prices will remain high for the foreseeable future.*

**foreshadow** /fɔː'ʃædəʊ/ *verb* [T] *formal* to show or warn that something bigger, worse, or more important is coming

**foresight** /'fɔːsaɪt/ *noun* [U] when you know or can judge what will happen or what you will need in the future *She had the foresight to book her flight early.*

**foreskin** /'fɔːskɪn/ *noun* [C, U] the loose skin that covers the end of a penis

o-ᴗ**forest** /'fɒrɪst/ *noun* [C, U] a large area of trees growing closely together *pine forest* • **forested** *adj* covered by forest *heavily forested areas*

**forestall** /fɔː'stɔːl/ *verb* [T] to prevent something from happening by taking action before it does *to forestall an attack/crisis*

**forestry** /'fɒrɪstri/ *noun* [U] the work of looking after or making forests

**foretell** /fɔː'tel/ *verb* [T] *past* **foretold**

**forest**

*formal* to say what is going to happen in the future

**forever** /fə'revə<sup>r</sup>/ *adv* **1** [IN FUTURE] for all time in the future *I'll love you forever.* **2** [A LONG TIME] *informal* used to emphasize that something takes a long time *The journey home took forever.* **3** [OFTEN] used to emphasize that something happens often *She is forever helping people.*

**foreword** /'fɔːwɜːd/ *noun* [C] a short piece of writing at the front of a book that introduces the book or its writer

**forfeit** /'fɔːfɪt/ *verb* [T] to lose the right to do something or have something because you have done something wrong *They have forfeited the right to live in society.*

**forgave** /fə'geɪv/ *past tense of* forgive

**forge¹** /fɔːdʒ/ *verb* [T] **1** to make an illegal copy of something in order to deceive people *a forged passport* **2** to develop a good relationship with someone or something *The group forged friendships that have lasted more than twenty years.*

**forge ahead** to suddenly make a lot of progress with something *The organizers are forging ahead with a programme of public events.*

**forge²** /fɔːdʒ/ *noun* [C] a place where metal objects are made by heating and shaping metal

**forgery** /'fɔːdʒəri/ *noun* **1** [C] an illegal copy of a document, painting, etc **2** [U] the crime of making an illegal copy of something *The doctor was convicted on two charges of forgery.*

o-ᴗ**forget** /fə'get/ *verb* **forgetting**, *past t* **forgot**, *past p* **forgotten 1** [NOT REMEMBER] [I, T] to be unable to remember a fact, something that happened, or how to do something *I've forgotten his name.* • [+ (that)] *Don't forget that Lucy and John are coming this weekend.* • *He'd completely forgotten about their quarrel.* • [+ question word] *You never forget how to ride a bike.* **2** [NOT DO] [I, T] to not remember to do something [+ to do sth] *Dad's always forgetting to take his pills.* **3** [NOT BRING] [T] to not bring something with you because you did not remember it *Oh no, I've forgotten my passport.* **4** [STOP THINKING] [T] (*also* **forget about**) to stop thinking about someone or something *I'll never forget him for as long as I live.* • *Let's try to forget about work and have a good time.* **5 forget it** used to tell someone not to worry about something as it is not important *"I'm sorry I missed your birthday." "Forget it, it doesn't matter."* **6 I forget** used instead of 'I have forgotten' *I forget when we last saw him.* **7 forget yourself** to do or say something that is not acceptable in a particular situation *She completely forgot herself and started screaming at him.*

**forgetful** /fə'getf<sup>ə</sup>l/ *adj* often forgetting things *She's 84 now and getting a bit forgetful.* • **forgetfulness** *noun* [U]

o-ᴗ**forgive** /fə'gɪv/ *verb* [I, T] *past t* **forgave**, *past p* **forgiven 1** to decide not to be angry with someone or not to punish them for something they have done *I've apologized, but I don't think she'll ever forgive me.* • [often reflexive] *Mike would never forgive himself if anything happened to the children.* • [+ for + doing sth] *Jane never forgave her mother for lying to her.*

**2 forgive me** used before you ask or say something that might seem rude *Forgive me for asking, but how much did you pay for your bag?*
**3 sb could be forgiven for doing sth** used to say that you can understand if someone might think, believe, or do something

**forgiveness** /fə'gɪvnəs/ *noun* [U] when you forgive someone for something they have done

**forgiving** /fə'gɪvɪŋ/ *adj* ready to forgive someone for something they have done *My father is the most forgiving man I know.*

**forgo** /fɔː'gəʊ/ *verb* [T] **forgoing**, *past t* **forwent**, *past p* **forgone** *formal* to decide not to have or do something, although you want to have it or do it *She had to forgo her early ambition to be a writer.*

**forgot** /fə'gɒt/ *past tense of* forget

**forgotten** /fə'gɒtən/ *past participle of* forget

o⸺**fork¹** /fɔːk/ *noun* [C] **1** FOOD a small object with three or four points and a handle, that you use to pick up food and eat with *a knife and fork* **2** DIGGING a tool with a long handle and three or four points, used for digging and breaking soil into pieces *a garden fork* **3** ROAD a place where a road or river divides into two parts *Turn right when you reach a fork in the road.*

**fork²** /fɔːk/ *verb* [I] If a road or river forks, it divides into two parts.

**fork sth out** UK (*US* **fork sth over**) *informal* to pay or give money for something, especially when you do not want to *So far they've forked out £500.*

**forlorn** /fə'lɔːn/ *adj* lonely and unhappy *The captured soldiers looked forlorn and helpless.*
● **forlornly** *adv*

o⸺**form¹** /fɔːm/ *noun* **1** TYPE [C] a type of something or way of doing something *Swimming is the best **form** of exercise.* **2** PAPER [C] a printed document with spaces for you to write information *Please **fill in/out the form** using black ink.* **3 the form of sth** the particular way in which something exists *The novel is written in **the form** of a series of letters.* ● *The medicine comes in the form of a liquid or pills.* **4** SPORT [U] In sport, someone's form is how well or badly they are performing. *The team seems to have **lost its form** lately.* **5 be in/on/off form** UK If someone is in form or on form, they are feeling or performing well, and if they are off form they are not feeling or performing well. *Harry was on good form last night.* **6** SCHOOL GROUP [C] UK (*US* **grade**) a school class or group of classes for students of the same age or ability *He's in the third form.* **7** SHAPE [C] the body or shape of someone or something **8** GRAMMAR [C] a way of writing or saying a word that shows if it is singular or plural, past or present, etc *The plural form of 'sheep' is 'sheep'.* ⊃ *See also:* **application form**, **sixth form.**

o⸺**form²** /fɔːm/ *verb* **1** BEGIN [I, T] to begin to exist, or to make something begin to exist [often passive] *We are learning more about how stars are formed.* ● *The trees form new leaves once the weather improves.* **2** SHAPE [I, T] to take, or to make something take a particular shape *Hold hands and form a circle.* ● *Form the dough into little balls.* **3** COMBINE [T] to make something by

combining different parts *In English you form the present participle by adding -ing to the verb.* **4** START [T] to start an organization or business *Brown formed her own company eleven years ago.* **5** BE [T] to be the thing talked about or be part of it *The Alps form a natural barrier between Italy and Switzerland.* ● *Her diary forms the basis of the book.* **6 form an opinion/impression, etc** to begin to have a particular opinion or idea about something because of the information you have

o⸺**formal** /'fɔːməl/ *adj* **1** SERIOUS used about clothes, language, and behaviour that are serious and not friendly or relaxed *a formal dinner party* **2** OFFICIAL [always before noun] public or official *a formal announcement/apology* **3** IN SCHOOL [always before noun] Formal education, training, etc happens in a school or college. *Tom had little formal schooling.*

**formality** /fɔː'mæləti/ *noun* **1** [C] something that the law or an official process says must be done *There are certain legal formalities to be completed.* **2** [U] formal and polite behaviour *the formality of a royal funeral*

**formally** /'fɔːməli/ *adv* **1** officially *The deal will be formally announced on Tuesday.* **2** in a polite way *They shook hands formally.*

**format¹** /'fɔːmæt/ *noun* [C] the way something is designed, arranged, or produced *This year's event will have a new format.*

**format²** /'fɔːmæt/ *verb* [T] **formatting**, *past* **formatted 1** to prepare a computer disk so that information can be stored on it **2** to organize and design the words on a page or document

**formation** /fɔː'meɪʃən/ *noun* **1** [U] the development of something into a particular thing or shape *the formation of a crystal* **2** [C, U] when something has a particular shape or things are arranged in a particular way *rock/cloud formations* ● *The planes flew overhead **in formation** (= in a pattern).*

**formative** /'fɔːmətɪv/ *adj* relating to the time when your character and opinions are developing *She spent **her formative years** in New York.*

**former** /'fɔːmə$^r$/ *adj* [always before noun] happening, existing, or true in the past but not now *the former Soviet Union* ● *the former president*

**the former** /'fɔːmə$^r$/ *noun* the first of two people or things that have just been talked about

**formerly** /'fɔːməli/ *adv* in the past *The European Union was formerly called the European Community.*

**formidable** /'fɔːmɪdəbl/ *adj* **1** Someone who is formidable is strong and a little frightening. *a formidable woman* **2** difficult and needing a lot of effort or thought *a formidable task*

**formula** /'fɔːmjələ/ *noun* [C] *plural* **formulas** or **formulae 1** METHOD a plan or method that is used to achieve something *There's no magic **formula** for success.* **2** RULE a set of letters, numbers, or symbols that are used to express a mathematical or scientific rule **3** LIST a list of the substances that something is made of

**formulate** /'fɔːmjəleɪt/ *verb* [T] **1** to develop all the details of a plan for doing something *They formulated a plan to save the company.* **2** to say what you think or feel after thinking carefully *to formulate an answer/reply* • formulation /ˌfɔːmjəˈleɪʃⁿn/ *noun* [C, U]

**forsake** /fəˈseɪk/ *verb* [T] *past t* **forsook**, *past p* **forsaken** *formal* **1** to leave someone, especially when they need you *He felt he couldn't forsake her when she was so ill.* **2** to stop doing or having something *He decided to forsake politics for journalism.*

**fort** /fɔːt/ *noun* [C] a strong building that soldiers use to defend a place

**forth** /fɔːθ/ *adv literary* out of a place or away from it *The knights rode forth into battle.*

**forthcoming** /ˌfɔːθˈkʌmɪŋ/ *adj* **1** [SOON] [always before noun] *formal* going to happen soon *the forthcoming election/visit* **2** [OFFERED] [never before noun] If money or help is forthcoming, it is offered or given. *He insisted that no more money would be forthcoming.* **3** [WILLING] [never before noun] willing to give information *Elaine wasn't very forthcoming about her love life.*

**forthright** /ˈfɔːθraɪt/ *adj* saying what you think honestly and clearly *They dealt with all our questions in a very forthright manner.*

**forthwith** /ˌfɔːθˈwɪθ/ *adv formal* immediately

**fortifications** /ˌfɔːtɪfɪˈkeɪʃⁿnz/ *noun* [plural] strong walls, towers, etc that are built to protect a place

**fortify** /ˈfɔːtɪfaɪ/ *verb* [T] **1** to build strong walls, towers, etc around a place to protect it *a fortified city/town* **2** to make someone feel stronger physically or mentally *She had a sandwich to fortify herself before going on.*

**fortitude** /ˈfɔːtɪtjuːd/ *noun* [U] *formal* when you are brave and do not complain about pain or problems

**fortnight** /ˈfɔːtnaɪt/ *noun* [C] *UK* two weeks [usually singular] *a fortnight's holiday* • *We usually get together about once a fortnight.* • fortnightly *adv UK* happening every two weeks *a fortnightly meeting*

**fortress** /ˈfɔːtrəs/ *noun* [C] a castle or other strong building built to defend a place

**fortunate** /ˈfɔːtʃⁿnət/ *adj* lucky [+ to do sth] *I'm very fortunate to be alive.* • [+ (that)] *It was fortunate that someone was available to take over.* ➔ *Opposite* **unfortunate**.

o-***fortunately** /ˈfɔːtʃⁿnətli/ *adv* happening because of good luck *Fortunately, no one was hurt in the accident.* ➔ *Opposite* **unfortunately**.

**fortune** /ˈfɔːtʃuːn/ *noun* **1** [C] a lot of money *She made a fortune selling her story to the newspapers.* • *Nick's new car must have cost a fortune!* **2** [C, U] the good or bad things that happen to you [usually plural] *The family's fortunes changed almost overnight.* **3 tell sb's fortune** to say what is going to happen to someone in the future *Have you ever had your fortune told?*

**fortune-teller** /ˈfɔːtʃuːnˌtelər/ *noun* [C] someone who tells you what will happen to you in the future

**forty** /ˈfɔːti/ the number 40 • fortieth 40th written as a word

**forum** /ˈfɔːrəm/ *noun* [C] a situation or meeting in which people can exchange ideas and discuss things *a forum for debate/discussion*

o-***forward**[1] /ˈfɔːwəd/ (*also* **forwards**) *adv* **1** [DIRECTION] towards the direction that is in front of you *She leaned forward to make sure I could hear her.* **2** [FUTURE] towards the future *I always look forward, not back.* **3** [PROGRESS] used to say that something is making good progress *This is a big step forward for democracy.*

**forward**[2] /ˈfɔːwəd/ *adj* **1 forward motion/ movement, etc** movement towards the direction that is in front of you **2 forward planning/thinking, etc** when you plan or think about something for the future **3** Someone who is forward is too confident or too friendly with people they do not know.

**forward**[3] /ˈfɔːwəd/ *verb* [T] to send a letter, email, etc that you have received to someone else *Could you forward my mail to me while I'm away?* ➔ *See also:* **fast-forward**.

**forward**[4] /ˈfɔːwəd/ *noun* [C] a player in a sport such as football who plays near the front and tries to score goals

**forwarding address** *noun* [C] a new address that letters and parcels should be sent to

**forward-looking** /ˈfɔːwədlʊkɪŋ/ *adj* planning for the future and using new ideas or technology *a forward-looking plan/policy*

**forwards** /ˈfɔːwədz/ *adv another word for* forward

**forwent** /fɔːˈwent/ *past participle of* forgo

**fossil** /ˈfɒsⁿl/ *noun* [C] part of an animal or plant from thousands of years ago, preserved in rock

**fossil fuel** *noun* [C, U] a fuel such as coal or oil that is obtained from under the ground

**foster**[1] /ˈfɒstər/ *verb* [T] **1** to encourage a particular feeling, situation, or idea to develop *The growth of the Internet could foster economic development worldwide.* **2** to look after a child as part of your family for a time, without becoming their legal parent

**foster**[2] /ˈfɒstər/ *adj* **1 foster home/mother/ parent, etc** the home where a child who is fostered lives, or the person or people who foster a child **2 foster child/daughter/son, etc** a child who is fostered

**fought** /fɔːt/ *past of* fight

**foul**[1] /faʊl/ *adj* **1** very dirty, or with an unpleasant smell *the foul smell of rotting fish* **2** very bad or unpleasant *foul weather* • *She's in a foul mood.* **3 foul language/words** very rude and offensive words **4 fall foul of sb/sth** *UK* to do something which causes you to be in trouble

**foul**[2] /faʊl/ *verb* **1** [T] to make something very dirty *The beaches had been fouled by dogs.* **2** [I, T] to do something that is against the rules in a sport *He was fouled as he was about to shoot at goal.*

**foul sth up** *informal* to spoil something completely *The travel company completely fouled up our holiday.*

**foul**[3] /faʊl/ *noun* [C] something that someone does in a sport that is not allowed by the rules

**foul play** *noun* [U] when someone's death is caused by a violent crime *Police do not suspect foul play at present.*

**found**[1] /faʊnd/ *verb* [T] **1** to start an organization, especially by providing money *The company was founded in 1861.* **2** to base something on a set of ideas or beliefs [often passive] *a society founded on principles of equality*

**found²** /faʊnd/ *past of* find

**foundation** /faʊnˈdeɪʃ⁰n/ *noun* **1** IDEA [C] the idea or principle that something is based on *Jefferson's document formed the foundation of a new nation.* **2** STARTING [U] when an organization, state, or country is established *the foundation of a new state* **3** ORGANIZATION [C] an organization that gives money for a particular purpose *the Mental Health Foundation* **4** **foundations** [plural] *UK* (*US* **foundation** [C]) the part of a building, road, bridge, etc that is under the ground and supports it *concrete foundations* **5** MAKE-UP [U] make-up that is worn all over the face to give it a smooth appearance **6 be without foundation; have no foundation** If something is without foundation, there is no proof that it is true. *The allegations are completely without foundation.* **7 lay the foundation(s) for/of sth** to provide the conditions that make it possible for something to happen *His reforms laid the foundation of future greatness.*

**founder** /ˈfaʊndə⁰/ *noun* [C] someone who establishes an organization

**foundry** /ˈfaʊndri/ *noun* [C] a place where metal or glass is melted and made into objects

**fountain** /ˈfaʊntɪn/ *noun* [C] a structure that forces water up into the air as a decoration

**'fountain ,pen** *noun* [C] a pen that you fill with ink

**four** /fɔːʳ/ the number 4

**fours** /fɔːz/ **on all fours** with your hands and knees on the ground *I got down on all fours and crawled over to the door.*

**foursome** /ˈfɔːsəm/ *noun* [C] a group of four people *We could go out as a foursome.*

**fourteen** /ˌfɔːˈtiːn/ the number 14 • **fourteenth** 14th written as a word

**fourth¹** /fɔːθ/ 4th written as a word

**fourth²** /fɔːθ/ *US* (*UK/US* **quarter**) *noun* [C] one of four equal parts of something; 1/4

**,Fourth of Ju'ly** (*also* **Independence Day**) *noun* [U] 4 July, a national holiday in the US to celebrate the country's freedom from Great Britain in 1776

**fowl** /faʊl/ *noun* [C] *plural* **fowl** or **fowls** a bird that is kept for its eggs and meat, especially a chicken

**fox** /fɒks/ *noun* [C] a wild animal like a dog with red-brown fur, a pointed nose, and a long thick tail

**foyer** /ˈfɔɪeɪ Ⓤ ˈfɔɪər/ *noun* [C] a room at the entrance of a hotel, theatre, cinema, etc

**fracas** /ˈfrækɑː Ⓤ ˈfreɪkəs/ *noun* [no plural] a noisy fight or argument

**fraction** /ˈfrækʃ⁰n/ *noun* [C] **1** a number less than 1, such as 1/2 or 3/4 **2** a very small number or amount *a fraction of a second* • **fractionally** *adv* by a very small amount *Harry is fractionally taller than Ben.*

**fracture** /ˈfræktʃəʳ/ *verb* [T] to break something hard such as a bone, or a piece of rock *She's fractured her ankle.* • **fracture** *noun* [C]

**fragile** /ˈfrædʒaɪl Ⓤ ˈfrædʒ⁰l/ *adj* **1** easily broken, damaged, or destroyed *a fragile china cup* • *a fragile economy* **2** physically or emotionally weak *a fragile little girl* • **fragility** /frəˈdʒɪləti/ *noun* [U]

**fragment¹** /ˈfrægmənt/ *noun* [C] a small piece of something *fragments of pottery*

**fragment²** /frægˈment/ *verb* [I, T] to break something into small parts, or to be broken in this way *The opposition has fragmented into a number of small groups.* • **fragmented** *adj* *a fragmented society*

**fragrance** /ˈfreɪgrəns/ *noun* [C, U] **1** a pleasant smell *the delicate fragrance of roses* **2** a substance which people put on their bodies to make themselves smell nice *a new fragrance for men*

**fragrant** /ˈfreɪgrənt/ *adj* with a pleasant smell *fragrant flowers*

**frail** /freɪl/ *adj* not strong or healthy *a frail old lady*

**frailty** /ˈfreɪlti/ *noun* [C, U] when someone is physically or morally weak

**frame¹** /freɪm/ *noun* [C] **1** PICTURE a structure that goes around the edge of something such as a door, picture, window, or mirror *a picture frame* • *a window frame* **2** STRUCTURE the basic structure of a building, vehicle, or piece of furniture that other parts are added onto *a bicycle frame* **3** BODY the shape of someone's body *his large/small frame* **4 frame of mind** the way someone feels at a particular time *She was in a much more positive frame of mind today.*

**frame**

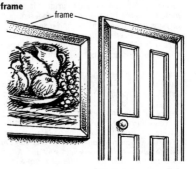

**frame²** /freɪm/ *verb* [T] **1** PICTURE to put something such as a picture into a frame *I'm going to frame this and put it on the wall.* **2** EDGE to form an edge to something in an attractive way *Dark hair framed her face.* **3** CRIME to intentionally make it seem as if someone is guilty of a crime [often passive] *He claimed he had been framed by the police.* **4** EXPRESS *formal* to express something choosing your words carefully *I tried to frame a suitable reply.*

**frames** /freɪmz/ *noun* [plural] the plastic or metal structure that holds together a pair of glasses

**framework** /ˈfreɪmwɜːk/ *noun* [C] **1** a system of rules, ideas, or beliefs that is used to plan or decide something *a legal framework for resolving disputes* **2** the basic structure that supports something such as a vehicle or building and gives it its shape

**franchise** /ˈfrænʃaɪz/ *noun* **1** [C] the right to sell a company's products or services in a particular area using the company's name *a fast food* *franchise* **2** [U] the legal right to vote in elections

**frank** /fræŋk/ *adj* speaking honestly and saying what you really think *a full and frank discussion* • ***To be frank**, I don't really want to see him.* • **frankness** *noun* [U]

**frankfurter** /ˈfræŋkfɜːtəʳ/ *noun* [C] a long, thin sausage (= tube of meat and spices), often eaten with bread

**frankly** /ˈfræŋkli/ *adv* in an honest and direct way *The children spoke frankly about the effects of the divorce.* • ***Quite frankly**, I think you're making a big mistake.*

**frantic** /ˈfræntɪk/ *adj* **1** done in a fast and excited way and not calm or organized *a frantic search* **2** very worried or frightened *frantic calls for help* • *I got home to find Joe **frantic with worry**.* • **frantically** *adv Laura was searching frantically for her keys.*

**fraternal** /frəˈtɜːnəl/ *adj* like or relating to a brother

**fraternity** /frəˈtɜːnəti/ *noun* **1** [U] a feeling of friendship between people **2** [C] in the US, a social organization of male college students

**fraud** /frɔːd/ *noun* **1** [U] when someone does something illegal in order to get money *credit card fraud* **2** [C] someone who deceives people by pretending to be someone or something that they are not

**fraudulent** /ˈfrɔːdjələnt/ *adj formal* dishonest and illegal *fraudulent insurance claims* • **fraudulently** *adv*

**fraught** /frɔːt/ *adj* **1 fraught with danger/difficulties, etc** full of danger/difficulties, etc *The present situation is fraught with danger.* **2** *mainly UK* causing worry, or feeling worried *a fraught silence* • *Is everything okay? You're looking a bit fraught.*

**fray[1]** /freɪ/ *verb* **1** [I, T] If material or clothing frays, or if it is frayed, the threads at the edge break and become loose. **2** [I] If your temper (= mood) frays or your nerves fray, you gradually become annoyed or upset. *After hours of waiting, tempers were beginning to fray.*

**fray[2]** /freɪ/ *noun* **enter/join, etc the fray** to start taking part in an argument or fight *The time had come for the US to enter the fray.*

**freak[1]** /friːk/ *noun* [C] **1** *informal* someone who is very interested in a particular subject or activity *My brother's a bit of a computer freak.* **2** someone who looks strange or behaves in a strange way *They made me feel like a freak.*

**freak[2]** /friːk/ *adj* **a freak accident/storm, etc** A freak event is one that is very unusual.

**freak[3]** /friːk/ (*also* **freak out**) *verb* [I, T] *informal* to suddenly become very angry, frightened, or surprised, or to make someone do this *I hated that film, it totally freaked me out.*

**freckle** /ˈfrekl/ *noun* [C] a very small, brown spot on your skin from the sun • **freckled** *adj*

o– **free[1]** /friː/ *adj* **1** NOT CONTROLLED able to live, happen, or exist without being controlled by anyone or anything *free trade* • *a free society* • [+ to do sth] *People should be free to say what they think.* **2** NO COST not costing any money *a free sample of perfume* • *Entry is free for children under 12.* • *The unemployed get their prescriptions **free of charge**.* **3** NOT A PRISONER not in prison or in a cage *He opened the cage and **set** the birds **free**.* **4** NOT BUSY not busy doing anything *Are you free this evening?* • *I don't have much **free time**.* **5** NOT USED not being used by anyone *Is this seat free?* **6 free from/of sth** not containing or having anything harmful or unpleasant *a life free from pain* **7 feel free** something that you say in order to tell someone that they are allowed to do something [+ to do sth] *Please feel free to ask questions.* ➲ *See also:* **duty-free**, a free **hand[1]**, free **rein**, **tax-free**, **toll-free**.

**free[2]** /friː/ *adv* **1** without cost or payment *Children under five travel free.* • *He offered to do it **for free**.* **2** in a way that is not tied, limited, or controlled *She **broke free** from his grasp and ran away.*

o– **free[3]** /friː/ *verb* [T] **freeing**, *past* **freed** **1** ALLOW TO LEAVE to allow someone to leave a prison or place where they have been kept *The last hostages were finally freed yesterday.* **2** GET OUT to get someone out of a situation or place that they cannot escape from *Firefighters worked for two hours to **free** the driver **from** the wreckage.* **3** TAKE AWAY to help someone by taking something unpleasant away from them *The book's success **freed** her **from** her financial worries.* **4** MAKE AVAILABLE (*also* **free up**) to make something available for someone to use *I need to free up some space for these files.*

**-free** /friː/ *suffix* used at the end of words to mean 'without' or 'not containing' *sugarfree gum* • *an interest-free loan*

**freebie** /ˈfriːbi/ *noun* [C] *informal* something that you are given, usually by a company, and do not have to pay for

o– **freedom** /ˈfriːdəm/ *noun* **1** [C, U] the right to live in the way you want, say what you think, and make your own decisions without being controlled by anyone else *religious freedom* • *freedom of choice/speech* • [+ to do sth] *You have the freedom to do what you want to do.* **2 freedom from sth** a situation in which you are not suffering because of something unpleasant or harmful *freedom from fear/poverty* **3** [U] when someone is no longer a prisoner

**ˌfree ˈenterprise** *noun* [U] when trade and business is allowed to operate without much control from the government

**ˌfree ˈkick** *noun* [C] a kick that a player in a football match is allowed to take after a player from the other team has broken the rules

**freelance** /ˈfriːlɑːns/ *adj, adv* working for several different organizations, and paid according to the hours you work *a freelance photographer* • *Most of our producers work freelance.* • **freelance** *verb* [I] *I've been freelancing for two years now.* • **freelancer** *noun* [C]

F

**freely** /'friːli/ adv **1** without being controlled or limited *For the first time in months she could move freely.* • *Exotic foods are freely available in supermarkets.* **2** If you freely admit something, you are very willing to agree that it is true. *I freely admit that I was wrong about him.*

,free 'market *noun* [no plural] when the government does not control prices and trade *a free-market economy*

**freephone** /'friːfəʊn/ UK (US **toll-free**) adj [always before noun] A freephone number is a telephone number that you can connect to without paying.

**free-range** /friː'reɪndʒ/ adj relating to or produced by farm animals that are allowed to move around outside and are not kept in cages *free-range eggs*

,free 'speech *noun* [U] the right to express your opinions in public

**freeware** /'friːweə/ *noun* [U] computer software that you do not have to pay for, for example from the Internet

**freeway** /'friːweɪ/ US (UK **motorway**) *noun* [C] a long, wide road, usually used by traffic travelling fast over long distances

,free 'will *noun* **1** [U] when people choose and decide what they want to do in their own lives **2 do sth of your own free will** to do something because you want to, not because someone forces you to *She had gone there of her own free will.*

⚬**freeze¹** /friːz/ *verb* past t **froze**, past p **frozen** **1** ICE [I, T] If something freezes or is frozen, it becomes hard and solid because it is very cold. *The river had frozen overnight.* • *Water freezes at 0° Celsius.* **2** FOOD [I, T] to make food last a long time by making it very cold and hard *You can freeze any cakes that you have left over.* **3** PERSON [I] to feel very cold *One of the climbers froze to death on the mountain.* **4** NOT MOVE [I] to suddenly stop moving, especially because you are frightened *She saw someone outside the window and froze.* **5** LEVEL [T] to fix the level of something such as a price or rate so that it does not increase

**freeze²** /friːz/ *noun* **1** LEVEL [C] when the level of something such as a price or rate is fixed so that it does not increase *a pay freeze* **2** PROCESS [C] when a process is stopped for a period of time *an immediate freeze on all new building in the city* **3** COLD [no plural] *informal* a period of extremely cold weather

**freezer** /'friːzə/ *noun* [C] a large container operated by electricity in which food can be frozen and stored ➔ *See colour picture* **Kitchen** *on page Centre 10.*

**freezing¹** /'friːzɪŋ/ adj *informal* very cold *It's absolutely freezing in here.*

**freezing²** /'friːzɪŋ/ *noun* [U] the temperature at which water freezes *It was five degrees below/above freezing.*

'freezing ,point *noun* [C, U] the temperature at which a liquid freezes

**freight** /freɪt/ *noun* [U] goods that are carried by trains, trucks, ships, or aircraft

**freighter** /'freɪtə/ *noun* [C] a large ship or aircraft that carries goods

'french ,fries US (UK **chips**) *noun* [plural] long,

thin pieces of potato that have been cooked in hot oil ➔ *See colour picture* **Food** *on page Centre 7.*

,French 'windows (also ,French 'doors) *noun* [plural] a pair of glass doors that usually open into a garden

**frenetic** /frə'netɪk/ adj fast and exciting in an uncontrolled way *a frenetic pace* • *frenetic activity*

**frenzied** /'frenzid/ adj wild and uncontrolled *a frenzied dance*

**frenzy** /'frenzi/ *noun* [U, no plural] when you are so excited, nervous, or anxious that you cannot control what you are doing *She hit him in a frenzy of rage.*

**frequency** /'friːkwənsi/ *noun* [C, U] **1** the number of times something happens in a particular period, or the fact that something happens often or a large number of times *The frequency of attacks seems to have increased recently.* **2** the rate at which a sound wave or radio wave is repeated *the very high frequencies of a television signal*

⚬**frequent¹** /'friːkwənt/ adj happening often *He is a frequent visitor to the US.*

**frequent²** /frɪ'kwent US 'friːkwent/ *verb* [T] to go to a place often *a bar frequented by criminals*

⚬**frequently** /'friːkwəntli/ adv *formal* often *a frequently asked question* • *I see him quite frequently.*

⚬**fresh** /freʃ/ adj **1** DIFFERENT new or different from what was there before *We're looking for fresh ideas.* • *They decided to move abroad and make a fresh start.* **2** NOT OLD Fresh food has been produced or collected recently and has not been frozen, dried, etc. *fresh fruit/vegetables* • *fresh bread* **3** CLEAN/COOL smelling clean or feeling pleasantly cool *a fresh breeze* • *a fresh smell* **4 fresh air** air outside buildings that is clean and cool *Let's go outside and get some fresh air.* **5 fresh water** water from lakes, rivers, etc that has no salt in it **6** NOT TIRED having a lot of energy and not feeling tired *We got up the next day feeling fresh and relaxed.* **7** SKIN Fresh skin looks healthy. *a fresh complexion* **8** RECENT recently made or done and not yet changed by time *The memory of the accident is still very fresh in my mind.* **9 fresh from/out of sth** having just left a place *The new French teacher's fresh out of college.* • **freshness** *noun* [U] ➔ *See also:* a **breath** of fresh air.

**freshen** /'freʃən/ *verb*

**freshen up** to quickly wash yourself so that you feel clean *Would you like to freshen up before dinner?*

**freshen sth up** to make something look cleaner and more attractive *A coat of paint would help to freshen this place up.*

**fresher** /'freʃə/ *noun* [C] UK *informal* a student in the first year of university

**freshly** /'freʃli/ adv recently *freshly baked bread*

**freshman** /'freʃmən/ *noun* [C] *plural* **freshmen** US a student in the first year of a course at a US college, university, or high school (= school for students aged 15 to 18)

**freshwater** /'freʃ,wɔːtə/ adj relating to water that is not salty *freshwater fish*

**fret** /fret/ verb [I] **fretting**, past **fretted** to be anxious or worried *There's no point in fretting about what you cannot change.* ● **fretful** adj anxious and unhappy

**Fri** written abbreviation for Friday

**friar** /fraɪəʳ/ noun [C] a member of a religious group of men

**friction** /'frɪkʃən/ noun [U] **1** when a surface rubs against something, often making movement more difficult *When you rub your hands together the friction produces heat.* **2** when people argue or disagree, often over a long period of time *There's a lot of friction between my wife and my mother.*

**Friday** /'fraɪdeɪ/ (written abbreviation **Fri**) noun [C, U] the day of the week after Thursday and before Saturday ⊃ See also: **Good Friday**.

**fridge** /frɪdʒ/ noun [C] a large container that uses electricity to keep food cold ⊃ See colour picture **Kitchen** on page Centre 10.

**fried** /fraɪd/ adj cooked in hot oil or fat *a fried egg* ⊃ See also: **deep-fried**.

o-■ **friend** /frend/ noun [C] **1** someone who you know well and like *Sarah's my best friend* (= the friend I like most). ● *Gordon is a friend of mine.* ● *I'm going to New York to visit some friends.* **2 an old friend** someone who you have known and liked for a long time **3 be friends (with sb)** to know and like someone *I have been friends with Jo for years.* **4 make friends (with sb)** to begin to know and like someone *He's shy and finds it difficult to make friends.*

o-■ **friendly**¹ /'frendli/ adj **1** behaving in a pleasant, kind way towards someone *a friendly face/smile* ● *The other students have been very friendly to us.* ⊃ Opposite **unfriendly**. **2 be friendly with sb** to know and like someone *Her brother is quite friendly with my brother.* ● **friendliness** noun [U]

**friendly**² /'frendli/ noun [C] UK a sports match that is not part of an official competition

**-friendly** /'frendli/ suffix **1** used at the end of words to mean 'not harmful' *environmentally-friendly detergent* **2** used at the end of words to mean 'suitable for particular people to use' *a family-friendly restaurant* ⊃ See also: **user-friendly**.

**friendship** /'frendʃɪp/ noun [C, U] when two people are friends *a close friendship*

**fries** /fraɪz/ mainly US (also UK **chips**) noun [plural] long, thin pieces of potato that have been cooked in hot oil *A hamburger and regular fries, please.*

**frieze** /friːz/ noun [C] an area of decoration along a wall

**frigate** /'frɪgət/ noun [C] a small, fast military ship

**fright** /fraɪt/ noun [U, no plural] a sudden feeling of shock and fear *That dog gave me a terrible fright.* ● *She screamed in fright when she saw him.*

o-■ **frighten** /'fraɪtən/ verb [T] to make someone afraid or nervous *It frightens me when he drives so fast.* ⊃ See also: frighten the (living) **daylights** out of sb, frighten sb out of their **wits**.

**frighten sb away/off** to make a person or animal afraid or nervous so that they go away

o-■ **frightened** /'fraɪtənd/ adj afraid or nervous *I've always been frightened of going to the dentist.* ● [+ (that)] *Gerry was frightened that people would laugh at him.*

o-■ **frightening** /'fraɪtənɪŋ/ adj making you feel afraid or nervous *a very frightening film* ● **frighteningly** adv

**frightful** /'fraɪtfəl/ adj UK old-fashioned very bad *The house was in a frightful mess.*

**frightfully** /'fraɪtfəli/ adv UK old-fashioned very *They're frightfully rich, you know.*

**frigid** /'frɪdʒɪd/ adj **1** not enjoying sexual activity, usually said about a woman **2** literary not friendly or emotional

**frill** /frɪl/ noun **1** [C] a strip of material with a lot of folds which is used to decorate the edge of cloth **2 frills** extra things that are added to something to make it nicer or more attractive, but that are not really necessary *a cheap, no frills airline service*

**frilly** /'frɪli/ adj with a lot of frills *a frilly dress*

**fringe**¹ /frɪndʒ/ noun [C] **1** HAIR UK (US **bangs** [plural]) hair that is cut short and straight at the top of someone's face ⊃ See colour picture **Hair** on page Centre 9. **2** DECORATION loose threads that hang along the edge of cloth as a decoration **3** EDGE the outside edge of an area, group, or subject and not the main part

**fringe**² /frɪndʒ/ verb **be fringed with sth** If a place or object is fringed with something, that thing forms a border along the edge. *The river is fringed with wild flowers.*

**fringe**³ /frɪndʒ/ adj [always before noun] not belonging to the main part of a group, activity, or subject *fringe politics/theatre*

**fringe 'benefit** noun [C] something extra that you get from your employer in addition to money [usually plural] *fringe benefits such as private health care*

**frisk** /frɪsk/ verb **1** [T] to move your hands over someone's body to discover if they are hiding something such as a weapon *There were guards frisking people as they went into the building.* **2** [I] to run and jump happily like a young animal

**frisky** /'frɪski/ adj energetic and wanting to be active or play *a frisky puppy*

**fritter** /'frɪtəʳ/ verb

**fritter sth away** to waste money or time on something that is not important *You mustn't fritter all your money away on lottery tickets.*

**frivolity** /frɪ'vɒləti/ noun [C, U] when people are being silly and not being serious

**frivolous** /'frɪvələs/ adj silly and not serious ● **frivolously** adv

**frizzy** /'frɪzi/ adj Frizzy hair has a lot of very small, tight curls.

**fro** /frəʊ/ adv ⊃ See **to**³ and fro.

**frog** /frɒg/ noun [C] a small, green animal with long back legs for jumping that lives in or near water

**frogman** /'frɒgmən/ noun [C] plural **frogmen** someone whose job is to swim under water wearing a rubber suit and using special breathing equipment *Police frogmen are searching the lake.*

o-■ **from** strong form /frɒm/ weak form /frəm/ preposition **1** STARTING PLACE used to show the place, time, or level that someone or something started at *Did you walk all the way from Bond Street?* • *The museum is open from 9.30 to 6.00, Tuesday to Sunday.* • *Prices start from £5,595.* **2** HOME used to say where someone was born, or where someone lives or works *His mother's originally from Poland.* • *Our speaker tonight is from the BBC.* **3** DISTANCE used to say how far away something is *Their holiday cottage is about 15 kilometres from the coast.* **4** GIVING used to say who gave or sent something to someone *Have you had a Christmas card from Faye yet?* • *What beautiful flowers! Who are they from?* **5** REMOVING If you take something from a person, place, or amount, you take it away. *Two from ten leaves eight.* • *We had to borrow some money from my father to pay the bill.* • *He took a knife from the drawer.* **6** PRODUCED used to say where something was produced or grown *These vegetables are fresh from the garden.* **7** MATERIAL used to say what something is made of *juice made from oranges* **8** AVOID used to show something that you want to avoid or prevent *There's a bar across the front to prevent you from falling out.* **9** POSITION used to show where you are when you look at something or how you see something *The view from the top was absolutely breathtaking.* • *From the company's point of view, this is an excellent opportunity.* **10** REASON used to say why you think or believe something *I guessed from her accent that she must be French.* • *From what I've heard, the new exam is going to be a lot more difficult.* **11** CAUSE used to say what causes something *Deaths from heart disease continue to rise every year.* • *He was rushed to hospital* ***suffering from*** *severe burns.* **12** COMPARE used when you are saying how similar or different two things, people, or places are *University is very different from school.* **13 a week/six months/ten years, etc from now** a week/six months/ten years, etc after the time when you are speaking *Who knows what we'll all be doing five years from now?* **14 from now/then, etc on** starting now/then, etc and continuing into the future *They were good friends from that day on.*

○━**front**[1] /frʌnt/ *noun* **1 the front a** the side of something that is most important or most often seen because it faces forward *You need to write the address clearly* ***on the front of*** *the envelope.* • *There was blood on the front of his shirt.* **b** the part of something that is furthest forward *We asked to sit* ***in the front of*** *the plane.* • *He was standing right* ***at the front****.* **2 in front a** FURTHER FORWARD further forward than someone or something else *The car in front stopped suddenly and I went straight into the back of it.* • *She started a conversation with the man sitting* ***in front of*** *her.* **b** WINNING winning in a game or competition *By half time the Italians were well* ***in front****.* **3 in front of a** close to the front part of something *He parked the car in front of the house.* **b** where someone can see or hear you *Please don't swear in front of the children.* **4** BEHAVIOUR [C] when someone behaves in a way that hides how they really feel [usually singular] *Many parents decide*

to stay together, putting up a front for the children's sake. **5** ILLEGAL ACTIVITY [C] an organization or activity that is used to hide a different, illegal activity [usually singular] *Police discovered the restaurant was just a front for a drugs operation.* **6 the front** an area of land where soldiers fight during a war *Thousands of young men were sent to the front to fight.* **7 on the business/jobs/politics, etc front** in a particular area of activity *How are things on the work front at the moment?* **8** WEATHER [C] a line where warm air meets cold air affecting the weather *A cold front is moving across the Atlantic.*

○━**front**[2] /frʌnt/ *adj* [always before noun] in or at the front of something *the front door/garden* • *the front page of the newspaper*

**frontal** /ˈfrʌntᵊl/ *adj* **1** relating to the front of something **2 a frontal attack/assault** when you criticize or attack someone or something in a very strong and direct way

**frontier** /frʌnˈtɪəʳ/ *noun* **1** [C] a line or border between two countries **2 the frontiers of sth** the limits of what is known or what has been done before in an area of knowledge or activity *the frontiers of science and technology*

**front 'line** *noun* **the front line 1** the place where soldiers fight in a war **2** a position of direct and important influence *doctors working in the front line of medicine* • front-line /ˈfrʌntlaɪn/ *adj* [always before noun] *front-line troops*

**front-page** /ˈfrʌntˌpeɪdʒ/ *adj* **front-page news/story, etc** news that is very important and suitable for the front page of a newspaper

**front-runner** /ˌfrʌntˈrʌnəʳ ⑤ ˈfrʌntˌrʌnəʳ/ *noun* [C] the person or organization that will most probably win something *She's the front-runner for the best actress award.*

**frost**[1] /frɒst/ *noun* **1** [U] a thin, white layer of ice that forms on surfaces, especially at night, when it is very cold **2** [C] when the temperature is cold and water freezes *We're expecting a hard frost tonight.*

**frost**[2] /frɒst/ *US* (*UK/US* **ice**) *verb* [T] to cover a cake with frosting (= sweet mixture used to cover cakes)

**frostbite** /ˈfrɒstbaɪt/ *noun* [U] when extreme cold injures your fingers and toes

**frosted** /ˈfrɒstɪd/ *adj* Frosted glass has a special surface so that you cannot see through it.

**frosting** /ˈfrɒstɪŋ/ *US* (*UK/US* **icing**) *noun* [U] a sweet mixture used to cover or fill cakes, made from sugar and water or sugar and butter

**frosty** /ˈfrɒsti/ *adj* **1** very cold, with a thin layer of white ice covering everything *a frosty morning* **2** not friendly *She gave me a very frosty look.*

**froth** /frɒθ/ *noun* [U] small, white bubbles such as on the surface of a liquid • froth *verb* [I] • frothy *adj frothy coffee*

**frown**[1] /fraʊn/ *verb* [I] to make your face show that you are annoyed or worried by moving your eyebrows (= lines of hair above your eyes) *She frowned when I mentioned his name.*

**frown on/upon sth** to think that something is wrong and that you should not do it [often passive] *Smoking is frowned upon in many public places.*

**frown²** /fraʊn/ *noun* [C] the expression on your face when you frown *He looked at me with a puzzled frown.*

**froze** /frəʊz/ *past tense of* freeze

**frozen¹** /'frəʊzən/ *adj* FOOD Frozen food has been made so that it will last a long time by freezing. *frozen peas* **2** WATER turned into ice *The pond was frozen and people were skating on it.* **3** PERSON *informal* extremely cold *Is there any heating in here? I'm frozen!*

**frozen²** /'frəʊzən/ *past participle of* freeze

**frugal** /'fruːgəl/ *adj* careful not to spend very much money

o━**fruit** /fruːt/ *noun* **1** [C, U] something such as an apple or orange that grows on a tree or a bush, contains seeds, and can be eaten as food *dried/fresh fruit* • *fruit juice* ➔ *See colour picture* **Fruit and Vegetables** *on page Centre 8.* **2 the fruit(s) of sth** the good result of someone's work or actions *This book is the fruit of 15 years' research.* **3 bear fruit** If something that someone does bears fruit, it produces successful results. *Our decision is just beginning to bear fruit.* ➔ *See also:* **citrus fruit**.

**fruitful** /'fruːtfəl/ *adj* producing good or useful results *We had a very fruitful discussion.*

**fruition** /fruˈɪʃən/ *noun* [U] when a plan or an idea really begins to happen, exist, or be successful *The plan never really came to fruition.*

**fruitless** /'fruːtləs/ *adj* not successful or achieving good results *a long and fruitless search*

**fruity** /'fruːti/ *adj* smelling or tasting of fruit *a fruity wine/taste*

**frustrate** /frʌsˈtreɪt/ US 'frʌstreɪt/ *verb* [T] **1** to make someone feel annoyed because things are not happening in the way that they want, or in the way that they should *It really frustrates me when she arrives late for meetings.* **2** to prevent someone from achieving something, or to prevent something from happening *They have frustrated all our attempts to find a solution to this problem.*

**frustrated** /frʌsˈtreɪtɪd/ US 'frʌstreɪtɪd/ *adj* annoyed because things are not happening in the way that you want, or in the way that they should *I'm very frustrated at/with my lack of progress.*

**frustrating** /frʌsˈtreɪtɪŋ/ US 'frʌstreɪtɪŋ/ *adj* making you feel frustrated *a frustrating situation* • *It's frustrating to see money going to waste like that.*

**frustration** /frʌsˈtreɪʃən/ *noun* [C, U] the feeling of being annoyed because things are not happening in the way that you want, or in the way that they should *I could sense his frustration at not being able to help.*

**fry** /fraɪ/ *verb* [I, T] to cook something in hot oil or fat or to be cooked in hot oil or fat *fried rice* • *Fry the onions in a little butter.* ➔ *See picture at* **cook**.

**'frying ,pan** *noun* [C] a flat, metal pan with a long handle that is used for frying food ➔ *See colour picture* **Kitchen** *on page Centre 10.*

**ft** *written abbreviation for* foot (= a unit for measuring length)

**fudge¹** /fʌdʒ/ *noun* [U] a soft sweet food made from butter, sugar, and milk

**fudge²** /fʌdʒ/ *verb informal* **1** [T] *UK* to avoid making a decision or giving a clear answer about something *The government continues to fudge the issue.* **2** [I, T] *US* to slightly cheat, often by not telling the exact truth *He fudged on his income tax return.*

o━**fuel¹** /'fjuːəl/ *noun* [C, U] a substance that is burned to provide heat or power *The plane ran out of fuel and had to land at sea.* • *fuel bills*

**fuel²** /'fjuːəl/ *verb* [T] *(UK)* **fuelling**, *past* **fuelled**, *(US)* **fueling**, *past* **fueled** to make people's ideas or feelings stronger, or to make a situation worse *an atmosphere of hatred fuelled by alcohol* • *Newspaper reports are fuelling fears about GM foods.*

**fugitive** /'fjuːdʒətɪv/ *noun* [C] someone who is escaping or hiding from the police or from a dangerous situation

**fulfil** *UK* (*US* **fulfill**) /fʊlˈfɪl/ *verb* **fulfilling**, *past* **fulfilled 1 fulfil a duty/promise/responsibility, etc** to do something that you have promised to do or that you are expected to do *He has failed to fulfil his duties as a father.* **2 fulfil an ambition/dream/goal, etc** to do something that you really wanted to do *She has finally fulfilled her childhood ambition to swim with dolphins.* **3 fulfil a function/need/role, etc** to do something that is necessary or useful *You seem to fulfil a very useful role in the organization.* **4 fulfil criteria/requirements/qualifications, etc** to have all the qualities that are wanted or needed for something *You have to fulfil certain requirements to qualify for the competition.*

**fulfilled** /fʊlˈfɪld/ *adj* feeling happy that you are receiving everything that you want from your life ➔ *Opposite* **unfulfilled**.

**fulfilling** /fʊlˈfɪlɪŋ/ *adj* If something is fulfilling, it satisfies you and makes you happy. *a fulfilling job*

**fulfilment** *UK* (*US* **fulfillment**) /fʊlˈfɪlmənt/ *noun* [U] **1** a feeling of pleasure because you are receiving or achieving what you want *I hope that you'll find happiness and fulfilment in your life together.* **2** when someone does something necessary or something that they have wanted or promised to do *Being here is the fulfilment of a lifelong ambition.*

o━**full¹** /fʊl/ *adj* **1** NO MORE POSSIBLE If a container or a space is full, it contains as many things or people as possible or as much of something as possible. *We couldn't get in, the cinema was full.* • *The shelves were full of books.* • *The bottle was still nearly full.* **2** A LOT containing a lot of things or people or a lot of something *The room was full of people.* • *His face was full of anger.* • *Don't speak with your mouth full.* **3** COMPLETE [always before noun] complete and including every part *Please give your full name and address.* • *I don't*

full          empty

think that we've heard the full story yet. **4 full speed/ strength/volume, etc** the greatest speed, strength, volume, etc possible *We were driving at full speed.* ● *She got full marks in the test.* **5 be full of yourself** to think that you are very important **6 be full of sth** to be talking or thinking a lot about a particular thing *He's full of stories about his holiday.* **7** FOOD *informal (also UK* **full up**) having eaten enough food *No more for me, thanks, I'm full.* **8 a full face/ figure** a face or body shape that is large and round ➔ *See also:* have your hands (**hand¹**) full, be in full **swing².**

**full²** /fʊl/ *noun* **1 in full** completely and with nothing missing *The speech will be published in full in tomorrow's newspaper.* ● *He paid the bill in full.* **2 to the full** *mainly UK* as much or as well as possible *She certainly lived life to the full.*

**full-blown** /ˌfʊlˈbləʊn/ *adj* completely developed *a full-blown crisis* ● *a full-blown disease*

ˌfull ˈboard *noun* [U] *UK* when all your meals are provided in a hotel

**full-fledged** /ˌfʊlˈfledʒd/ *US* (*UK* **fully-fledged**) *adj* [always before noun] having finished developing, studying, or establishing yourself

**full-grown** /ˌfʊlˈɡrəʊn/ *adj* A full-grown person, animal, or plant has developed completely, and is not expected to grow more. *a full-grown man*

ˌfull ˈhouse *noun* [C] when all the seats in a place such as a theatre or cinema are full *They performed to a full house on Saturday night.*

**full-length** /ˌfʊlˈleŋθ/ *adj* **1 a full-length book/film, etc** a book or film that is the usual length and not shorter *a full-length feature film* **2 a full-length mirror/photograph, etc** a mirror or image that shows a person's whole body from the head to the feet **3 a full-length coat/dress/skirt, etc** a long piece of clothing that reaches to your feet

ˌfull ˈmoon *noun* [no plural] the moon when it appears as a complete circle

**full-page** /ˌfʊlˈpeɪdʒ/ *adj* [always before noun] filling a complete page in a newspaper or magazine *a full-page ad*

**full-scale** /ˌfʊlˈskeɪl/ *adj* [always before noun] **1** very large or serious and involving everything that is possible or expected *a full-scale investigation* ● *The violence had developed into a full-scale war.* **2** A full-scale model is the same size as the original thing that it is representing.

ˌfull ˈstop *UK* (*US* **period**) *noun* [C] a mark (.) used at the end of a sentence, or to show that the letters before it are an abbreviation ➔ *See study section* **Punctuation** *on page Centre 37.*

**full-time** /ˌfʊlˈtaɪm/ *adj* happening or working for the whole of the working week and not only part of it *a full-time job/course* ● full-time *adv She works full-time for the council.*

⊶**fully** /ˈfʊli/ *adv* completely *The restaurant was fully booked.* ● *He is fully aware of the dangers involved.*

**fully-fledged** /ˌfʊliˈfledʒd/ *UK* (*US* **full-fledged**) *adj* [always before noun] having finished developing, studying, or establishing yourself *I won't be a fully-fledged doctor until after the exams.*

**fumble** /ˈfʌmbl/ *verb* [I] to use your hands with

difficulty to try to get hold of something or find something *She fumbled in her bag for her glasses.*

**fume** /fjuːm/ *verb* [I] to be extremely angry, especially in a quiet way *A week later, she was still fuming about his behaviour.*

**fumes** /fjuːmz/ *noun* [plural] strong, unpleasant, and often dangerous gas or smoke *car exhaust fumes*

⊶**fun¹** /fʌn/ *noun* [U] **1** enjoyment or pleasure, or something that gives you enjoyment or pleasure *You'll like it – it's good fun!* ● *She's great fun to be with.* ● *Have fun!* (= enjoy yourself) ● *It's no fun having to work late every night.* **2 for fun; for the fun of it** for pleasure and not for any other reason **3 make fun of sb/sth** to make a joke about someone or something in an unkind way *The other children at school used to make fun of his hair.*

**fun²** /fʌn/ *adj* enjoyable or entertaining *There are lots of fun things to do here.*

⊶**function¹** /ˈfʌŋkʃən/ *noun* [C] **1** the purpose of something or someone *Each button has a different function.* ● *I'm not quite sure what my function is within the company.* **2** a large, formal party or ceremony *a charity function*

**function²** /ˈfʌŋkʃən/ *verb* [I] to work or operate *The operation should help his lungs to function properly again.*

**function as sth** to have a particular purpose *The spare bedroom also functions as a study.*

**functional** /ˈfʌŋkʃənᵊl/ *adj* **1** designed to be practical or useful and not only attractive *functional clothing* **2** operating or working correctly *The system is not yet fully functional.*

⊶**fund¹** /fʌnd/ *noun* **1** [C] an amount of money collected, saved, or provided for a purpose *a pension fund* **2 funds** [plural] money needed or available to spend on something *The charity closed down due to lack of funds.* ● fund *verb* [T] to provide money for an event, activity, or organization *Who is the project funded by?*

**fundamental** /ˌfʌndəˈmentᵊl/ *adj* relating to the most important or main part of something *a fundamental change/difference* ● *Training is fundamental to success.* ● fundamentally *adv The world has changed fundamentally over the last century.*

**fundamentalism** /ˌfʌndəˈmentᵊlɪzᵊm/ *noun* [U] the belief that the traditions and rules of a religion should be followed exactly

**fundamentalist** /ˌfʌndəˈmentᵊlɪst/ *noun* [C] someone who believes that the rules of their religion should be followed exactly ● fundamentalist *adj*

**fundamentals** /ˌfʌndəˈmentᵊlz/ *noun* [plural] the main principles, or most important parts of something *All children should be taught the fundamentals of science.*

**funding** /ˈfʌndɪŋ/ *noun* [U] money given by a government or organization for an event or activity *They received state funding for the project.*

**fundraiser** /ˈfʌndˌreɪzəʳ/ *noun* [C] a person or an event that collects money for a particular purpose

**fundraising** /ˈfʌndˌreɪzɪŋ/ *noun* [U] when you collect money for a particular purpose *a fundraising event*

o-**funeral** /'fju:nᵊrᵊl/ *noun* [C] a ceremony for burying or burning the body of a dead person *The funeral will be held next Friday.*

'**funeral ,director** UK (US '**funeral di,rector**) *noun* [C] someone whose job is to organize funerals and prepare dead bodies to be buried or burned

**fungus** /'fʌŋgəs/ *noun* [C, U] *plural* **fungi** or **funguses** a type of plant without leaves and without green colouring which gets its food from other living or decaying things *This fungus attacks roses and causes black spots on their leaves.*

**funk** /fʌŋk/ *noun* [U] a style of popular music with a strong rhythm that is influenced by African and jazz music

**funky** /'fʌŋki/ *adj informal* **1** fashionable in an unusual and noticeable way *She's got some very funky clothes.* **2** Funky music has a strong rhythm, and is good to dance to.

**funnel** /'fʌnᵊl/ *noun* [C] **1** a tube with a wide part at the top that you use to pour liquid or powder into something that has a small opening **2** a metal pipe on the top of a ship or train which smoke comes out of

**funnel**

**funnily** /'fʌnɪli/ *adv*
*UK* **funnily enough** although it seems strange and surprising *Funnily enough, I was just thinking about you when you called.*

o-**funny** /'fʌni/ *adj*
**1** making you smile or laugh *a funny story* • *It's not funny. Don't laugh!* **2** strange or unusual and not what you expect *This chicken tastes a bit funny.* • *That's funny. I'm sure I locked that door.*

---

**USAGE**

**fun** or **funny**?

Use **fun** to talk about something which you enjoy doing.

*Going to the cinema is fun.*

Use **funny** to describe something which makes you laugh.

*The film was really funny.*

---

o-**fur** /fɜːʳ/ *noun* **1** [U] the thick hair that covers the bodies of some animals like cats and rabbits **2** [C, U] the skin of an animal covered in thick hair and used for making clothes, or a piece of clothing made from this *fake fur* • *a fur coat/hat*

**furious** /'fjʊəriəs/ *adj* **1** extremely angry *He's furious at the way he's been treated.* • *My boss was furious with me.* **2** very energetic or fast *a furious attack* • **furiously** *adv*

**furlong** /'fɜːlɒŋ/ *noun* [C] a unit of length used in horse races equal to 201 metres

**furnace** /'fɜːnɪs/ *noun* [C] a container which is heated to a very high temperature and used to heat buildings, melt metal, or burn things

**furnish** /'fɜːnɪʃ/ *verb* [T] to put furniture into a room or building *They have furnished the room very simply.*
**furnish sb with sth** *formal* to provide someone with something *Can you furnish me with any further information?*

**furnished** /'fɜːnɪʃt/ *adj* If a room or building is furnished, there is furniture in it. *He's renting a fully furnished apartment by the river.*

**furnishings** /'fɜːnɪʃɪŋz/ *noun* [plural] the furniture, curtains and other decorations in a room or building

o-**furniture** /'fɜːnɪtʃəʳ/ *noun* [U] objects such as chairs, tables, and beds that you put into a room or building *antique furniture* • *The only piece of furniture in their living room is a sofa.*

**furore** /fjʊəˈrɔːri/ *UK* (*US* **furor** /'fjʊrɔːr/) *noun* [no plural] a sudden, excited, or angry reaction to something by a lot of people *The book caused a furore when it was published.*

**furrow¹** /'fʌrəʊ/ *noun* [C] **1** a deep line cut into a field that seeds are planted in **2** a deep line on someone's face, especially above their eyes

**furrow²** /'fʌrəʊ/ *verb* **furrow your brow** to make deep lines appear on your face above your eyes *He furrowed his brow as he struggled to think of a solution.*

**furry** /'fɜːri/ *adj* covered with fur or with something that feels like fur

**further¹** /'fɜːðəʳ/ *adv* **1** more *He refused to discuss the matter further.* • *Are these prices likely to be reduced any further?* • *Have you got any further* (= achieved any more) *with your research?* **2** (*comparative of* far) at or to a place or time that is a longer distance away *Let's walk a bit further down the road.* • *I can't remember any further back than that.*

**further²** /'fɜːðəʳ/ *adj* [always before noun] more or extra *For further details about the offer, call this number.* • *We will let you know if there are any further developments.*

---

**USAGE**

**further** or **farther**?

**Further** means the same as **farther** when you are talking about distance.

*We walked further down the street.*

*We walked farther down the street.*

In all other situations you should use **further**.

*Petrol prices have increased further.*

*For further information contact our office.*

---

**further³** /'fɜːðəʳ/ *verb* [T] to make something develop or become more successful *He'll do anything to further his career.*

,**further edu'cation** *noun* [U] *UK* education at a college for people who have left school but are not at a university

**furthermore** /,fɜːðəˈmɔːʳ (US) 'fɜːrðərmɔːr/ *adv* in addition to what has just been said

**furthest** /'fɜːðɪst/ *adj, adv* (*superlative of* far)

most distant *What is the furthest distance you can run?*

**furtive** /'fɜːtɪv/ *adj* doing something secretly, or done secretly, so that people do not notice *He gave her a furtive glance as soon as his wife left the room.* • **furtively** *adv*

**fury** /'fjʊəri/ *noun* [U, no plural] extreme anger *He could hardly control his fury.*

**fuse**[1] /fjuːz/ *noun* [C] **1** a small object that stops electrical equipment working if there is too much electricity going through it *The fuse has blown. You'll have to change it.* • *a fuse box* **2** the part of a bomb or other explosive object that starts the explosion *Light the fuse, and then stand back.*

**fuse**[2] /fjuːz/ *verb* [I, T] **1** *UK* If a piece of electrical equipment fuses, or if you fuse it, it stops working because there is too much electricity going through it. *You've fused the lights.* **2** to join or become combined *The bones of the skull are not properly fused at birth.*

**fuselage** /'fjuːzəlɑːʒ/ *noun* [C] the main body of an aircraft

**fusion** /'fjuːʒᵊn/ *noun* [C, U] when two or more things join or become combined *nuclear fusion* • *She describes her music as a fusion of folk and rock.*

**fuss**[1] /fʌs/ *noun* **1** [U, no plural] when people become excited, annoyed, or anxious about something, especially about something unimportant *What's all the fuss about?* • *They were making a big fuss over nothing.* **2 kick up/ make a fuss** to complain about something *If they don't bring our food soon, I'll have to kick up a fuss.* **3 make a fuss of/over sb** to give someone a lot of attention and treat them well *My uncle always makes a big fuss of the children.*

**fuss**[2] /fʌs/ *verb* [I] to worry too much or get too excited, especially about unimportant things *Please don't fuss, Mum. Everything's under control.*

**fuss over sb/sth** to give someone or something too much attention because you want to show that you like them *I hate the way my grandparents fuss over me.*

**fussy** /'fʌsi/ *adj* **1** [NOT LIKING] only liking particular things and very difficult to please *She's a very fussy eater.* **2** [CAREFUL] too careful about unimportant details **3** [TOO COMPLICATED] If something is fussy, it is too complicated in design and has too many details.

**futile** /'fjuːtaɪl/ ⓤⓢ /'fjuːtəl/ *adj* certain not to have a successful effect or result *a futile attempt to escape* • **futility** /fjuː'tɪləti/ *noun* [U] when something is futile

**futon** /'fuːtɒn/ *noun* [C] a flat bed filled with soft material that can be used on the floor or on a wooden base, or folded into a seat

○━**future**[1] /'fjuːtʃər/ *noun* **1 the future a** the time which is to come *He likes to plan for the future.* • *They hope to get married in the near future* (= soon). **b** In grammar, the future is the form of the verb used to talk about something that will happen. **2 in future** *UK* (*mainly US* **in the future**) beginning from now *In future, I'll be more careful about who I lend my bike to.* **3** [C] what will happen to someone or something in the time which is to come *We need to discuss the future of the company.* **4** [U, no plural] the chance of continuing to exist or succeed *She's got a very promising future ahead of her.*

○━**future**[2] /'fjuːtʃər/ *adj* [always before noun] **1** happening or existing in the time which is to come *future plans* • *in future years* • *What will we leave for future generations?* **2 future tense** the form of the verb which is used to talk about something that will happen

**the ˌfuture ˈperfect** *noun* the form of the verb which is used to show that an action will have been completed before a particular time in the future. The sentence 'I'll probably have left by then.' is in the future perfect.

**futuristic** /ˌfjuːtʃə'rɪstɪk/ *adj* very modern and strange and seeming to come from some imagined time in the future *a futuristic steel building*

**fuzzy** /'fʌzi/ *adj* **1** confused and not clear *We could only get a fuzzy picture on the television.* **2** covered in soft, short hairs, or material like this *a fuzzy kitten* • *fuzzy slippers*

# G

**G, g** /dʒiː/ the seventh letter of the alphabet

**g** *written abbreviation for* gram (= a unit for measuring weight)

**gabble** /'gæbl/ *verb* [I, T] *UK informal* to talk quickly or in a way that people cannot understand *He gabbled something in Italian.*

**gable** /'geɪbl/ *noun* [C] the top end of a wall of a building where two sloping parts of a roof meet at a point

**gadget** /'gædʒɪt/ *noun* [C] a small piece of equipment that does a particular job, especially a new type *a kitchen gadget*

**Gaelic** /'geɪlɪk, 'gælɪk/ *noun* [U] a language spoken in parts of Scotland and Ireland • **Gaelic** *adj* relating to Gaelic or to the Gaelic culture of Scotland and Ireland

**gaffe** /gæf/ *noun* [C] when someone says or does something embarrassing without intending to *The minister has made a series of embarrassing gaffes.*

**gag**¹ /gæg/ *verb* **gagging**, *past* **gagged** **1** COVER MOUTH [T] to fasten something over someone's mouth so that they cannot speak *The owners of the house were found bound and gagged in the cellar.* **2** STOP INFORMATION [T] to prevent someone from giving their opinion or giving information about something *The government is trying to gag the press over the issue.* **3** ALMOST VOMIT [I] to feel that you are going to vomit *The sight of the body made him gag.*

**gag**² /gæg/ *noun* [C] **1** *informal* a joke or funny story **2** something that is fastened over someone's mouth to stop them speaking

**gaggle** /'gægl/ *noun* [C] a group of people, especially when they are noisy *a gaggle of newspaper reporters*

**gaiety** /'geɪəti/ *noun* [U] *old-fashioned* happiness or excitement

**gaily** /'geɪli/ *adv old-fashioned* in a happy way

o─**gain**¹ /geɪn/ *verb* **1** GET [T] to get something useful or positive *The country gained independence in 1948.* • *You'll gain a lot of experience working there.* **2 gain by/from sth** to get an advantage or something valuable from something *Who stands to gain from the will?* **3** INCREASE [T] to increase in something such as size, weight, or amount *He's gained a lot of weight in the last few months.* **4** CLOCK [I, T] If a clock or a watch gains, it works too quickly and shows a time that is later than the real time. ↪ *See also:* gain **ground**¹, gain the upper **hand**¹.

**gain on sb/sth** to get nearer to someone or something that you are chasing *Quick! They're gaining on us.*

**gain**² /geɪn/ *noun* [C, U] **1** when you get something useful or positive *financial gain* **2** an increase in something such as size, weight, or amount

**gait** /geɪt/ *noun* [C] someone's particular way of walking *I recognized his gait from a distance.*

**gala** /'gɑːlə US 'geɪlə/ *noun* [C] a special social event, performance, or sports competition *a gala concert*

**galaxy** /'gæləksi/ *noun* [C] a very large group of stars held together in the universe

**gale** /geɪl/ *noun* [C] a very strong wind

**gall**¹ /gɔːl/ *noun* **have the gall to do sth** to be rude enough to do something that is not considered acceptable *I can't believe he had the gall to complain.*

**gall**² /gɔːl/ *verb* [T] to annoy someone *What galls me is that he escaped without punishment.* • **galling** *adj* annoying *It's particularly galling for me that she gets paid more than I do.*

**gallant** /'gælənt/ *adj literary* **1** brave *a gallant attempt to rescue a drowning man* **2** polite and kind, especially to women • **gallantly** *adv* • **gallantry** *noun* [U] when someone is gallant

**'gall ˌbladder** *noun* [C] an organ in the body that contains a substance that helps to digest food

**gallery** /'gæl°ri/ *noun* [C] **1** a room or building that is used for showing paintings and other art to the public *a museum and art gallery* **2** a floor at a higher level that looks over a lower inside a large room or building *The courtroom has a public gallery.*

**galley** /'gæli/ *noun* [C] a kitchen in a ship or aircraft

**gallon** /'gælən/ *noun* [C] a unit for measuring liquid, equal to 4.546 litres in the UK and 3.785 litres in the US

**gallop** /'gæləp/ *verb* [I] If a horse gallops, it runs very fast. • **gallop** *noun* [no plural]

**gallows** /'gæləʊz/ *noun* [C] *plural* **gallows** a wooden structure used in the past to hang criminals from to kill them

**galore** /gə'lɔːʳ/ *adj* [always after noun] in large amounts or numbers *There are bargains galore at the new supermarket.*

**galvanize** (*also UK* **-ise**) /'gælvənaɪz/ *verb* [T] to make someone suddenly decide to do something *His words galvanized the team into action.*

**gamble**¹ /'gæmbl/ *verb* [I, T] to risk money on the result of a game, race, or competition *He gambled away all of our savings.* • **gambler** *noun* [C] • **gambling** *noun* [U]

**gamble on sth** to take a risk that something will happen

**gamble**² /'gæmbl/ *noun* [C] a risk that you take that something will succeed *Buying this place was a big gamble, but it seems to have paid off.*

o─**game**¹ /geɪm/ *noun* **1** ACTIVITY [C] an entertaining activity or sport that people play, usually needing some skill and played according to rules *a computer game* • *Football's an exciting game.* • *Do you want to play a different game?* **2** OCCASION [C] a particular competition, match, or occasion when people play a game *Would you like a game of chess?* • *Who won yesterday's game?* **3 games** *UK* organized sports that children do at school *I always hated games at school.* • *a games teacher* **4 the European/ Commonwealth, etc Games** a special event where there are lots of competitions for different sports **5** SECRET PLAN [C] *UK informal* a secret plan *What's your game?* **6** ANIMALS [U]

---

| j yes | k cat | ʃ she | ʒ decision | θ thin | ð this | ŋ ring | tʃ chip | dʒ jar | æ cat | ɑː arm | e bed | eə hair | ə ago | ɜː her | ɪ sit | i cosy |

wild animals and birds that are hunted for food or sport **7 give the game away** *UK* to spoil a surprise or joke by letting someone know something that should have been kept secret **8 play games** to not deal with a situation seriously or honestly *Someone's life is in danger here – we're not playing games.* ➔ *See also:* **the Olympic Games, ball game, board game, video game.**

**game²** /geɪm/ *adj* to be willing to do new things, or things that involve a risk *She's game for anything.*

**gamekeeper** /'geɪmˌkiːpəʳ/ *noun* [C] someone whose job is to look after wild animals and birds that are going to be hunted

**'game ˌshow** *noun* [C] a programme on television in which people play games to try to win prizes

**gammon** /'gæmən/ *noun* [U] *UK* a type of meat from a pig, usually cut in thick slices

**gamut** /'gæmət/ *noun* [no plural] the whole group of things that can be included in something *The film explores the whole gamut of emotions from despair to joy.*

**gang¹** /gæŋ/ *noun* [C] **1** YOUNG PEOPLE a group of young people who spend time together, usually fighting with other groups and behaving badly *a member of a gang* • *gang violence* **2** CRIMINALS a group of criminals who work together *a gang of armed robbers* **3** FRIENDS *informal* a group of young friends

**gang²** /gæŋ/ *verb*
**gang up against/on sb** to form a group to attack or criticize someone, usually unfairly *Some older girls have been ganging up on her at school.*

**gangly** /'gæŋgli/ (*also* **gangling**) *adj* tall and thin *a gangly youth*

**gangrene** /'gæŋgriːn/ *noun* [U] the death and decay of a part of the body because blood is not flowing through it

**gangster** /'gæŋstəʳ/ *noun* [C] a member of a group of violent criminals

**gangway** /'gæŋweɪ/ *noun* [C] **1** *UK* a space that people can walk down between two rows of seats in a vehicle or public place **2** a board or stairs for people to get on and off a ship

**gaol** /dʒeɪl/ *noun* [C, U] *another UK spelling of* jail (= a place where criminals are kept as a punishment)

o━**gap** /gæp/ *noun* [C] **1** SPACE an empty space or hole in the middle of something, or between two things *There's quite a big gap between the door and the floor.* • *The sun was shining through a gap in the curtains.* **2** DIFFERENCE a difference between two groups of people, two situations, etc *an age gap* • *This course bridges the gap between school and university.* **3** ABSENT THING something that is absent and stops something from being complete *There are huge gaps in my memory.* **4 a gap in the market** an opportunity for a product or service that does not already exist **5** TIME a period of time when nothing happens, or when you are doing something different from usual *I decided to go back to teaching after a gap of 10 years.* ➔ *See also:* **the generation gap.**

**gape** /geɪp/ *verb* [I] **1** to look at someone or

**gap**

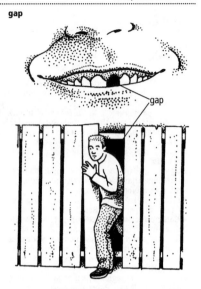

something with your mouth open because you are so surprised *We stood there **gaping** in wonder **at** the beautiful landscape.* **2** to be wide open

**gaping** /'geɪpɪŋ/ *adj* **a gaping hole/wound, etc** a hole/wound, etc that is open very wide

o━**garage** /'gærɑːʒ US gəˈrɑːʒ/ *noun* [C] **1** a small building, often built next to a house, that you can put a car in **2** a business that repairs or sells cars, and sometimes also sells fuel

**garbage** /'gɑːbɪdʒ/ *US* (*UK* **rubbish**) *noun* [U] **1** things that you throw away because you do not want them *Don't forget to take out the garbage.* **2** something that you think is nonsense, wrong, or very bad quality *How can you listen to that garbage on the radio!*

**'garbage ˌcan** *US* (*UK* **dustbin**) *noun* [C] a large container for waste kept outside your house

**'garbage colˌlector** *US* (*UK* **dustman**) *noun* [C] someone whose job is to remove the waste from containers left outside houses

**'garbage ˌman** *noun* [C] *US another word for* garbage collector

**garbled** /'gɑːbˀld/ *adj* Garbled words or messages are not clear and very difficult to understand.

o━**garden** /'gɑːdˀn/ *noun* **1** [C] *UK* (*US* **yard**) an area of ground belonging to a house, often containing grass, flowers, or trees *the front/back garden* • *Dad's outside in the garden.* **2 gardens** [plural] a park or large public area where plants and flowers are grown • **garden** *verb* [I] to work in a garden, growing plants and making it look attractive

**'garden ˌcentre** *noun* [C] *UK* a place that sells things for gardens such as plants and tools

**gardener** /'gɑːdˀnəʳ/ *noun* [C] someone who works in a garden, growing plants and making it look attractive

**gardening** /ˈgɑːdᵊnɪŋ/ *noun* [U] the job or activity of growing a garden and keeping it attractive

**gargle** /ˈgɑːgl/ *verb* [I] to move liquid or medicine around in your throat without swallowing, especially to clean it or stop it feeling painful

**garish** /ˈgeərɪʃ/ *adj* unpleasantly bright in colour, or decorated too much *a garish red jacket*

**garlic** /ˈgɑːlɪk/ *noun* [U] a vegetable like a small onion with a very strong taste and smell *a clove of garlic* ➔ *See colour picture* **Fruit and Vegetables** *on page Centre 8.*

**garment** /ˈgɑːmənt/ *noun* [C] *formal* a piece of clothing

**garnish** /ˈgɑːnɪʃ/ *verb* [T] to decorate food with something such as herbs or pieces of fruit *salmon garnished with herbs and lemon* ● **garnish** *noun* [C]

**garrison** /ˈgærɪsᵊn/ *noun* [C] a group of soldiers living in a particular area or building to defend it

**garter** /ˈgɑːtəʳ/ *noun* [C] a piece of elastic that holds a woman's stockings (= very thin pieces of clothing that cover a woman's foot and leg)

**gas¹** /gæs/ *noun* 1 [SUBSTANCE] [C, U] a substance in a form like air and not solid or liquid *poisonous gases* 2 [FUEL] [U] a substance in a form like air used as a fuel for heating and cooking *(UK) a gas cooker/(US) a gas stove* 3 [CAR FUEL] [U] *US* (*UK* **petrol**) a liquid fuel used in cars *half a tank of gas* 4 [STOMACH] [U] *US* (*UK* **wind**) gas or air in your stomach that makes you feel uncomfortable and sometimes makes noises 5 **the gas** *US informal* the part of a car which you push with your foot to make it go faster *We'd better step on the gas* (= drive faster). ➔ *See also:* **natural gas, tear gas**.

**gas²** /gæs/ *verb* [T] **gassing**, *past* **gassed** to poison or kill someone with gas

**'gas ˌchamber** *noun* [C] a room that is filled with poisonous gas to kill people

**gash** /gæʃ/ *noun* [C] a long, deep wound or cut *He has a nasty gash under his right eye.* ● **gash** *verb* [T]

**'gas ˌmask** *noun* [C] a cover you wear over your face to protect you from breathing poisonous gas

**gasoline** /ˈgæsᵊliːn/ *US* (*UK* **petrol**) *noun* [U] *another word for* gas (= a liquid fuel used in cars)

**gasp** /gɑːsp/ *verb* [I] 1 to make a noise by suddenly breathing in because you are shocked or surprised *She gasped in horror as the car spun out of control.* 2 to breathe loudly and with difficulty trying to get more air *He clutched his heart, gasping for breath.* ● **gasp** *noun* [C] *a gasp of surprise*

**'gas ˌpedal** *US* (*UK/US* **accelerator**) *noun* [C] the part of a car which you push with your foot to make it go faster

**'gas ˌstation** *US* (*UK* **petrol station**) *noun* [C] a place where you can buy petrol (= fuel for cars)

**gastric** /ˈgæstrɪk/ *adj* relating to the stomach

**gastronomic** /ˌgæstrəˈnɒmɪk/ *adj* relating to good food and cooking

**gate** /geɪt/ *noun* [C] 1 the part of a fence or outside wall that opens and closes like a door *Please shut the gate.* 2 the part of an airport where passengers get on or off an aircraft *The flight to Dublin is now boarding at gate 8.*

**gateau** /ˈgætəʊ/ *noun* [C, U] *UK plural* **gateaux** a large cake, usually filled and decorated with cream

**gatecrash** /ˈgeɪtkræʃ/ *verb* [I, T] to go to a party or private event without an invitation ● **gatecrasher** *noun* [C] someone who gatecrashes

**gateway** /ˈgeɪtweɪ/ *noun* 1 [C] an opening in a fence or outside wall that is closed with a gate 2 **the gateway to sth** the way to get into something or somewhere *the gateway to the North*

O━**gather** /ˈgæðəʳ/ *verb* 1 [MAKE A GROUP] [I, T] to join other people somewhere to make a group, or to bring people together into a group *Crowds of fans gathered at the stadium for the big match.* 2 [COLLECT] [T] to collect several things together, often from different places or people *They interviewed 1000 people to gather data on TV viewing habits.* ● *She gathered her things together and left.* 3 [THINK] [T] to think something is true because you have heard or seen information about it *From what I can gather, they haven't sold their house yet.* 4 **gather speed/strength/support, etc** to increase in speed/strength/support, etc

**gathering** /ˈgæðᵊrɪŋ/ *noun* [C] a party or a meeting when many people get together as a group *a family gathering*

**gaudy** /ˈgɔːdi/ *adj* unpleasantly bright in colour or decoration *a gaudy pink sweatshirt with gold embroidery*

**gauge¹** /geɪdʒ/ *verb* [T] 1 to make a judgment about a situation or about what someone thinks or feels [+ question word] *It's impossible to gauge what her reaction will be.* 2 to measure a distance, size, or amount

**gauge²** /geɪdʒ/ *noun* [C] 1 a way of judging something such as a situation or what someone thinks or feels *Street interviews aren't an accurate gauge of public opinion.* 2 a method or piece of equipment that you use to measure something *a fuel gauge*

**gaunt** /gɔːnt/ *adj* very thin, especially because of being ill or old *a pale, gaunt face*

**gauntlet** /ˈgɔːntlət/ *noun* 1 [C] a long, thick glove (= piece of clothing for your hand) 2 **run the gauntlet** to have to deal with a lot of people who are criticizing or attacking you 3 **throw down the gauntlet** to invite someone to argue, fight, or compete with you

**gauze** /gɔːz/ *noun* [U] thin, transparent cloth, especially used to cover injuries

**gave** /geɪv/ *past tense of* give

**gawp** /gɔːp/ *UK* (*US* **gawk** /gɔːk/) *verb* [I] to look at someone or something with your mouth open because you are shocked or surprised *He just stood there gawping at me.*

**gay¹** /geɪ/ *adj* 1 homosexual *Have you told your parents you're gay yet?* ● *a gay bar/club* 2 *old-fashioned* very happy and enjoying yourself

**gay²** /geɪ/ *noun* [C] someone who is homosexual, especially a man *equal rights for gays and lesbians*

**gaze** /geɪz/ *verb* **gaze at/into, etc** to look for a long time at someone or something or in a particular direction *They gazed into each other's eyes.* • **gaze** *noun* [no plural]

**GB** *written abbreviation for* gigabyte (= a unit for measuring the amount of information a computer can store) *a 4 GB hard drive*

**GCSE** /ˌdʒiːsiːesˈiː/ *noun* [C] *abbreviation for* General Certificate of Secondary Education: in the UK, an exam taken by students at the age of sixteen, or the qualification itself *Mary's got nine GCSEs.*

**gear¹** /gɪəʳ/ *noun* **1** [C] a set of parts in a motor vehicle or bicycle that control how fast the wheels turn [usually plural] *a mountain bike with 21 gears* • **to change gear** **2 first/second/third, etc gear** a particular position of the gears in a motor vehicle or bicycle that controls how fast the wheels turn *The lights turned green, but I couldn't* **get into** *first gear.* **3** [U] the clothes and equipment used for a particular purpose *sports/swimming gear* • *I've left all my gear at home.*

**gear²** /gɪəʳ/ *verb*
**gear sth to/towards sb/sth** to design or organize something so that it is suitable for a particular purpose, situation, or group of people [often passive] *These advertisements are geared towards a younger audience.*
**gear (sb/sth) up** to prepare for something that you have to do, or to prepare someone else for something [often reflexive] *I'm trying to* **gear** *myself up for the exams.*

**gearbox** /ˈgɪəbɒks/ *noun* [C] the set of gears in a motor vehicle and the metal box that contains them

**'gear ˌlever** UK (US **gearshift** /ˈgɪəʃɪft/) *noun* [C] a stick with a handle that you move to change gear in a vehicle ⊃ *See colour picture* **Car** *on page Centre 3.*

**gearstick** /ˈgɪəstɪk/ *noun* [C] UK *another word for* gear lever ⊃ *See colour picture* **Car** *on page Centre 3.*

**GED** /ˌdʒiːiːˈdiː/ *noun* [C] *abbreviation for* General Equivalency Diploma: an official document in the US that is given to someone who did not complete high school (= school for students aged 15 to 18) but who has passed a government exam instead

**geese** /giːs/ *plural of* goose

**geezer** /ˈgiːzəʳ/ *noun* [C] UK *very informal* a man

**gel** /dʒel/ *noun* [C, U] a thick, clear, liquid substance, especially a product used to style hair *hair gel* • *shower gel*

**gelatine** UK (US **gelatin** /ˈdʒelətɪn/) /ˈdʒelətiːn/ *noun* [U] a clear substance made from animal bones, often used to make food thicker

**gem** /dʒem/ *noun* [C] **1** a valuable stone, especially one that has been cut to be used in jewellery **2** *informal* someone or something that you like very much and think is very special *She's an absolute gem.*

**Gemini** /ˈdʒemɪnaɪ/ *noun* [C, U] the sign of the zodiac which relates to the period of 23 May – 21 June, or a person born during this period ⊃ *See picture at* **zodiac**.

**gender** /ˈdʒendəʳ/ *noun* [C, U] **1** the state of being male or female **2** the division of nouns, pro-

nouns and adjectives into masculine, feminine and neuter types

**gene** /dʒiːn/ *noun* [C] a part of a cell that is passed on from a parent to a child and that controls particular characteristics *Scientists have discovered the gene responsible for causing this disease.*

○⚬**general¹** /ˈdʒenʳrʳl/ *adj* **1** NOT DETAILED not detailed, but including the most basic or necessary information *These leaflets contain some general information about the school.* • *I've got a general idea of how it works.* **2** MOST PEOPLE [always before noun] relating to or involving all or most people, things, or places *There seems to be general agreement on this matter.* **3** NOT LIMITED [always before noun] including a lot of things or subjects and not limited to only one or a few *general knowledge* **4 in general a** considering the whole of someone or something, and not just a particular part of them *I still have a sore throat, but I feel much better in general.* **b** usually, or in most situations *In general, the weather here stays sunny.*

**general²** /ˈdʒenʳrʳl/ *noun* [C] an officer of very high rank in the army, navy, or air force

**ˌgeneral anaesˈthetic** UK (US **general anesthetic**) *noun* [C, U] a substance that is used to stop someone being conscious when they have an operation so that they do not feel any pain

**ˌgeneral eˈlection** *noun* [C] a big election in which the people living in a country vote to decide who will represent them in the government

**generalization** (*also* UK **-isation**) /ˌdʒenʳrʳlaɪˈzeɪʃʳn/ *noun* [C, U] when someone says something very basic that is often true but not always true

**generalize** (*also* UK **-ise**) /ˈdʒenʳrʳlaɪz/ *verb* [I] to say something very basic that is often true but not always true

○⚬**generally** /ˈdʒenʳrʳli/ *adv* **1** USUALLY usually, or in most situations *I generally wake up early.* **2** AS A WHOLE considering the whole of someone or something, and not just a particular part of them *The police said that the crowd was generally well-behaved.* **3** BY MOST PEOPLE by most people, or to most people *He is generally believed to be their best player.*

**ˌgeneral pracˈtitioner** (*also* **GP**) *noun* [C] a doctor who sees people in the local area and treats illnesses that do not need a hospital visit

**generate** /ˈdʒenʳreɪt/ *verb* [T] **1** to cause something to exist *to generate income/profit* • *This film has generated a lot of interest.* **2** to produce energy *Many countries use nuclear fuels to generate electricity.*

**generation** /ˌdʒenʳreɪʃʳn/ *noun* **1** PEOPLE [C] all the people in a society or family who are approximately the same age *the older/younger generation* • *This is the story of three generations of women.* **2** TIME [C] a period of about 25 to 30 years, the time it takes for a child to become an adult and take the place of their parents in society *Our family has lived in this village for generations.* **3** PRODUCT [C] a product when it is at a particular stage of development *a new generation of computers* **4** ENERGY [U] the production of energy *the generation of electricity*

the gener'ation ,gap *noun* when young people and old people do not understand each other because of their age difference

generator /'dʒenˀreɪtəʳ/ *noun* [C] a machine that produces electricity

generic /dʒə'nerɪk/ *adj* **1** relating to a whole group of things or type of thing **2** A generic product such as a drug is not sold with the name of the company that produced it.

generosity /,dʒenˀ'rɒsəti/ *noun* [U] the quality of being generous *I really appreciate all of your help and generosity.*

o—•**generous** /'dʒenˀrəs/ *adj* **1** giving other people a lot of money, presents, or time in a kind way *a very generous man* **2** larger than usual or than expected *a generous discount for students* • *a generous portion* • **generously** *adv*

genetic /dʒə'netɪk/ *adj* relating to genes *a rare genetic disorder* • *genetic research* • **genetically** *adv*

ge,netic engi'neering *noun* [U] when scientists change the genes in the cells of plants or animals

genetics /dʒə'netɪks/ *noun* [U] the scientific study of genes

genial /'dʒiːniəl/ *adj* kind and friendly

genitals /'dʒenɪtˀlz/ *noun* [plural] the sexual organs

genius /'dʒiːniəs/ *noun* **1** [C] someone who is extremely intelligent or extremely good at doing something *Einstein was a genius.* **2** [U] the quality of being extremely intelligent or extremely good at doing something *Einstein's genius*

genocide /'dʒenəsaɪd/ *noun* [U] the intentional killing of a large group of people who belong to a particular race or country

genre /'ʒɒnrə/ *noun* [C] a type of art or writing with a particular style *a literary/musical genre*

gent /dʒent/ *noun* [C] *informal short for* gentleman

genteel /dʒen'tiːl/ *adj* very polite, especially in an artificial way • **gentility** /,dʒen'tɪləti/ *noun* [U]

o—•**gentle** /'dʒentl/ *adj* **1** KIND kind and careful not to hurt or upset anyone or anything *My mother was such a gentle, loving person.* **2** NOT STRONG not strong or severe *a mild soap that is gentle on your skin* • *a gentle breeze* **3** SLOPE A gentle slope or climb is not steep. • **gently** *adv* *He kissed her gently on the cheek.* • **gentleness** *noun* [U]

gentleman /'dʒentlmən/ *noun* [C] *plural* **gentlemen** **1** a man who behaves politely and treats people with respect *He was a perfect gentleman.* **2** a polite word for 'man', used especially when talking to or about a man you do not know *There's a gentleman here to see you.*

the gents /dʒents/ *noun* [group] *UK informal* a toilet in a public place for men ➲ *See usage note at* **toilet**.

o—•**genuine** /'dʒenjuɪn/ *adj* **1** If a person or their feelings are genuine, they are sincere and honest. *He shows a genuine concern for the welfare of his students.* • *She's very genuine and friendly.* **2** If something is genuine, it is really what it seems to be. *a genuine gold necklace* • **genuinely** *adv*

genus /'dʒiːnəs, 'dʒenəs/ *noun* [C] *plural* **genera** a group of animals or plants that have the same characteristics

geography /dʒi'ɒɡrəfi/ *noun* [U] the study of all the countries of the world, and of the surface of the Earth such as the mountains and seas • **geographer** *noun* [C] someone who studies geography • **geographical** /,dʒiːəʊ'ɡræfɪkˀl/ (*also* **geographic** /dʒiːəʊ'ɡræfɪk/) *adj* • **geographically** *adv*

geology /dʒi'ɒlədʒi/ *noun* [U] the study of rocks and soil and the physical structure of the Earth • **geological** /,dʒiːəʊ'lɒdʒɪkəl/ *adj* • **geologist** *noun* [C] someone who studies geology

geometric /,dʒiːəʊ'metrɪk/ (*also* **geometrical**) *adj* **1** having a regular shape such as a circle or triangle, or having a pattern made of regular shapes **2** relating to geometry

geometry /dʒi'ɒmɪtri/ *noun* [U] a type of mathematics that deals with points, lines, angles and shapes

geriatric /,dʒeri'ætrɪk/ *adj* relating to very old people *geriatric patients* • *a geriatric hospital* • **geriatrics** *noun* [U] care and medical treatment for very old people

germ /dʒɜːm/ *noun* **1** [C] a very small living thing that causes disease *Wash your hands before cooking so that you don't spread germs.* **2 the germ of sth** the beginning of something *the germ of a brilliant idea*

,German 'measles (*also* **rubella**) *noun* [U] a disease which causes red spots on your skin

germinate /'dʒɜːmɪneɪt/ *verb* [I, T] If a seed germinates or is germinated, it begins to grow. • **germination** /,dʒɜːmɪ'neɪʃˀn/ *noun* [U]

gerund /'dʒerˀnd/ *noun* [C] a noun made from the form of a verb that ends with -ing, for example 'fishing' in 'John loves fishing.'

gesticulate /dʒes'tɪkjəleɪt/ *verb* [I] to move your hands and arms around to emphasize what you are saying or to express something

gesture¹ /'dʒestʃəʳ/ *noun* [C] **1** a movement you make with your hand, arm, or head to express what you are thinking or feeling *He made a rude gesture at the crowd.* **2** something you do to show people how you feel about a person or situation *It would be a nice gesture to invite her to dinner.*

gesture² /'dʒestʃəʳ/ *verb* [I] to point at something or express something using your hand, arm, or head *He gestured towards the window.*

get /ɡet/ *verb* **getting**, *past t* **got**, *past p* **got** (*US*) **gotten 1** OBTAIN [T] to obtain or buy something *Great shoes. Where did you get them?* • *I need to get some bread on the way home.* • [+ **two objects**] *I'll try to get you a ticket.* **2** BRING [T] to go somewhere and bring back something or someone *Wait here while I get the car.* **3** RECEIVE [T] to receive something or be given something *Did you get anything nice for your birthday?* • *Guy still hasn't got my email yet.* **4** UNDERSTAND [T] to understand something *He never gets any of my jokes.* **5 get into/off/through, etc** to move somewhere *Get over here right now!* **6 get sth into/down/out, etc** to move something somewhere *Could you get that bowl down from the shelf for me?* **7 get here/there/to the bank, etc** to arrive somewhere *What time do you normally* *get home from work?* **8 get sb/sth to do sth** to make someone or something do something *Sorry, I couldn't get the window to shut properly.* ● *We might be able to get dad to pay.* **9 get to do sth** to have an opportunity to do something *I never get to sit in the front seat.* **10 get ill/rich/wet, etc** to become ill/rich/wet, etc *We should go. It's getting late.* **11 get caught/killed/married, etc** to have something done to you **12 get sth painted/repaired, etc** to arrange for someone to do something for you, usually for money *I need to get my hair cut.* **13 get cancer/flu/malaria, etc** to become ill or develop an illness *I feel like I'm getting a cold.* **14 get a bus/train, etc** to travel somewhere on a bus/train, etc *Maybe we should get a taxi home.* **15 get the phone/door** *informal* to answer someone calling on the telephone or waiting at the door *Can you get the phone? I'm in the shower.*

**got** or **gotten?**

The past participle of the verb 'get' is **got** in British English and **gotten** in American English.

*Have you got my email yet? UK*

*Have you gotten my email yet? US*

**get about** *UK* (*US* **get around**) **1** TRAVEL to travel to a lot of places **2** MOVE to be able to go to different places without difficulty, especially if you are old or ill **3** INFORMATION If news or information gets about, a lot of people hear about it.

**get sth across** to successfully communicate information to other people *This is the message that we want to get across to the public.*

**get ahead** to be successful in the work that you do *It's tough for any woman who wants to get ahead in politics.*

**get along** *mainly US* (*mainly UK* **get on**) **1** If two or more people get along, they like each other and are friendly to each other. *I don't really get along with my sister's husband.* **2** to deal with a situation, especially successfully *I wonder how Michael's getting along in his new job?*

**get around sth** (*also UK* **get round sth**) to find a way of dealing with or avoiding a problem *Our lawyer found a way of getting around the adoption laws.*

**get around to sth** (*also UK* **get round to sth**) to do something that you have intended to do for a long time *I finally got around to calling her yesterday.*

**get at sb** *UK informal* to criticize someone in an unkind way

**be getting at sth** *informal* If you ask someone what they are getting at, you are asking them what they really mean. *What are you getting at, Andy?*

**get at sth** to be able to reach or get something

**get away 1** to leave or escape from a place or person, often when it is difficult to do this *We walked to the next beach to get away from the crowds.* **2** to go somewhere to have a holiday, especially because you need to rest *We decided*

*to go up to Scotland to get away from it all* (= have a relaxing holiday).

**get away with sth** to succeed in doing something bad or wrong without being punished or criticized *He shouldn't treat you like that. Don't let him get away with it.*

**get back** to return to a place after you have been somewhere else *By the time we got back to the hotel, Lydia had already left.*

**get sth back** If you get something back, something that you had before is given to you again. *I wouldn't lend him anything, you'll never get it back.*

**get sb back** *informal* to do something unpleasant to someone because they have done something unpleasant to you

**get back to sb** to talk to someone, usually on the telephone, to give them some information they have asked for or because you were not able to speak to them before

**get back to sth** to start doing or talking about something again *Anyway, I'd better get back to work.*

**get behind** If you get behind with work or payments, you have not done as much work or paid as much money as you should by a particular time.

**get by** to be able to live or deal with a situation with difficulty, usually by having just enough of something you need, such as money *I don't know how he gets by on so little money.*

**get sb down** to make someone feel unhappy *All this uncertainty is really getting me down.*

**get sth down** to write something, especially something that someone has said

**get down to sth** to start doing something seriously and with a lot of attention and effort *Before we get down to business, I'd like to thank you all for coming today.*

**get in 1** ENTER to succeed in entering a place, especially a building *They must have got in through the bathroom window.* **2** PERSON ARRIVING to arrive at your home or the place where you work *What time did you get in last night?* **3** VEHICLE ARRIVING If a train or other vehicle gets in at a particular time, that is when it arrives. *Our flight's getting in later than expected.* **4** BE CHOSEN to succeed in being chosen or elected for a position in a school or other organization *He wanted to go to Oxford but he didn't get in.*

**get into sth 1** to succeed in being chosen or elected for a position in a school or other organization **2** to become interested in an activity or subject, or start being involved in an activity *How did you get into journalism?*

**get into sb** If you do not know what has got into someone, you do not understand why they are behaving strangely. *I just can't understand what's got into him.*

**get off (sth) 1** to leave a bus, train, aircraft, or boat *We should get off at the next stop.* ⊃ See *colour picture* **Phrasal Verbs** *on page Centre 13.* **2** to leave the place where you work, usually at the end of the day *What time do you get off work?* **Get off!** *UK informal* something that you say in order to tell someone to stop touching someone or something

**get (sb) off (sth)** to avoid being punished for something you have done wrong, or to help someone avoid getting punished for something they have done wrong *He got off with a £20 fine.*

**get off on sth** *informal* If you get off on something, it makes you feel very excited, especially in a sexual way.

**get off with sb** *UK informal* to begin a sexual relationship with someone *She got off with some bloke at the party.*

**get on (sth)** to go onto a bus, train, aircraft, or boat *I think we got on the wrong bus.* ➋ *See colour picture* **Phrasal Verbs** *on page Centre 13.*

**be getting on** *informal* **1** to be old *How old's George, then? He must be getting on.* **2** *mainly UK* If time is getting on, it is becoming late.

**get on** *mainly UK* (*mainly US* **get along**) **1** If two or more people get on, they like each other and are friendly to each other. *I never knew that Karen didn't get on with Sue.* **2** to deal with a situation, especially successfully *How's Frank getting on in his new job?*

**get on with sth** to continue doing something, especially work *Get on with your homework.*

**get onto sth** to start talking about a subject after discussing something else *How did we get onto this subject?*

**get out 1** MOVE OUT to move out of something, especially a vehicle *I'll get out when you stop at the traffic lights.* **2** DIFFERENT PLACES to go out to different places and meet people in order to enjoy yourself *She doesn't get out so much now that she's got the baby.* **3** NEWS If news or information gets out, people hear about it although someone is trying to keep it secret.

**get (sb) out** to escape from or leave a place, or to help someone do this *I left the door open and the cat got out.*

**get out of sth** to avoid doing something that you should do, often by giving an excuse *You're just trying to get out of doing the housework!*

**get sth out of sb** to persuade or force someone to tell or give you something *He was determined to get the truth out of her.*

**get sth out of sth** to enjoy something or think that something is useful *It was an interesting course but I'm not sure I got much out of it.*

**get over sth 1** to begin to feel better after being unhappy or ill *It took her months to get over the shock of Richard leaving.* **2 can't/couldn't get over sth** *informal* to be very shocked or surprised about something *I can't get over how different you look with short hair.*

**get sth over with** to do and complete something difficult or unpleasant that must be done *I'll be glad to get these exams over with.*

**get round** *UK* (*US* **get around**) If news or information gets round, a lot of people hear about it.

**get round sth** *UK* (*US* **get around sth**) to find a way of dealing with or avoiding a problem

**get round sb** *UK* to persuade someone to do what you want by being kind to them

**get through** to manage to talk to someone on the telephone *I tried to ring earlier, but I couldn't get through.*

**get through sth 1** to deal with a difficult or unpleasant experience successfully, or to help someone do this *If I can just get through my exams I'll be so happy.* **2** *mainly UK* to finish doing or using something *We got through a whole jar of coffee last week.*

**get through to sb** to succeed in making someone understand or believe something *I just don't seem to be able to get through to him these days.*

**get to sb** *informal* to make someone feel upset or angry *I know he's annoying, but you shouldn't let him get to you.*

**get together 1** to meet in order to do something or spend time together *Jan and I are getting together next week for lunch.* **2** to begin a romantic relationship *She got together with Phil two years ago.*

**get (sb) up** to wake up and get out of bed, or to make someone do this *I had to get up at five o'clock this morning.* ➋ *See colour picture* **Phrasal Verbs** *on page Centre 13.*

**get up** to stand up *The whole audience got up and started clapping.*

**get up to sth** *UK* to do something, especially something that other people think is wrong *She's been getting up to all sorts of mischief lately.*

**getaway** /ˈgetəweɪ/ *noun* [C] when someone leaves a place quickly, especially after committing a crime *They had a car waiting outside so they could* **make** *a quick* **getaway.**

**get-together** /ˈgettəgeðə/ *noun* [C] an informal meeting or party *We have a big family get-together every year.*

**ghastly** /ˈgɑːstli/ *adj* very bad or unpleasant *a ghastly mistake* • *a ghastly man*

**ghetto** /ˈgetəʊ/ *noun* [C] *plural* **ghettos** or **ghettoes** an area of a city where people of a particular race or religion live, especially a poor area

**ghost** /gəʊst/ *noun* **1** [C] the spirit of a dead person which appears to people who are alive *Do you believe in ghosts?* • *a ghost story* **2 give up the ghost** *UK humorous* If a machine gives up the ghost, it stops working completely. *My car has given up the ghost.* • **ghostly** *adv a ghostly figure*

**'ghost ,town** *noun* [C] a town where few or no people now live

**ghoul** /guːl/ *noun* [C] an evil spirit

**GI** /ˌdʒiːˈaɪ/ *noun* [C] a soldier in the US army

**giant¹** /ˈdʒaɪənt/ *adj* [always before noun] extremely big, or much bigger than other similar things *a giant spider*

**giant²** /ˈdʒaɪənt/ *noun* [C] **1** an imaginary man who is much bigger and stronger than ordinary men **2** a very large and important company or organization *a media/software giant*

**gibberish** /ˈdʒɪbᵊrɪʃ/ *noun* [U] something that someone says that has no meaning or that cannot be understood

**gibe** /dʒaɪb/ *noun* [C] *another spelling of* jibe (= an insulting remark)

**giddy** /ˈgɪdi/ *adj* feeling as if you cannot balance and are going to fall

o—x**gift** /gɪft/ *noun* [C] **1** something that you give to someone, usually for a particular occasion *a birthday/wedding gift* **2** a natural ability or skill *She* **has a gift for** *design.*

**gift cer,tificate** *US* (*UK* **token**) *noun* [C] a piece of paper that you give someone which they can exchange for a book, CD, etc

**gifted** /'gɪftɪd/ *adj* A gifted person has a natural ability or is extremely intelligent. *a gifted athlete* • *a school for gifted children*

**gig** /gɪg/ *noun* [C] *informal* a performance of pop or rock music

**gigabyte** /'gɪgəbaɪt/ (*written abbreviation* **GB**) *noun* [C] a unit for measuring the amount of information a computer can store, equal to 1,000,000,000 bytes

**gigantic** /dʒaɪ'gæntɪk/ *adj* extremely big *a gigantic teddy bear*

**giggle** /'gɪgl/ *verb* [I] to laugh in a nervous or silly way *She started giggling and couldn't stop.* • **giggle** *noun* [C]

**gilded** /'gɪldɪd/ *adj* covered with a thin layer of gold or gold paint *a gilded frame/mirror*

**gill** /gɪl/ *noun* [C] an organ on each side of a fish or other water creature which it uses to breathe

**gilt** /gɪlt/ *noun* [U] a thin covering of gold or gold paint • **gilt** *adj*

**gimmick** /'gɪmɪk/ *noun* [C] something that is used only to get people's attention, especially to make them buy something *a marketing/publicity gimmick* • **gimmicky** *adj*

**gin** /dʒɪn/ *noun* [C, U] a strong alcoholic drink which has no colour

**ginger**[1] /'dʒɪndʒəʳ/ *noun* [U] a pale brown root with a strong taste used as a spice in cooking *ginger cake*

**ginger**[2] /'dʒɪndʒəʳ/ *adj UK* Ginger hair is an orange-brown colour. *She's got ginger hair and freckles.*

**gingerly** /'dʒɪndʒ³li/ *adv* slowly and carefully *He lowered himself gingerly into the water.*

**gipsy** /'dʒɪpsi/ *noun* [C] another UK spelling of gypsy (= a member of a race of people who travel from place to place, especially in Europe)

**giraffe** /dʒɪ'rɑːf/ *noun* [C] a large African animal with a very long neck and long, thin legs

giraffe

**girder** /'gɜːdəʳ/ *noun* [C] a long, thick piece of metal that is used to support bridges or large buildings

⦿ **girl** /gɜːl/ *noun* **1** [C] a female child or young woman *We have three children – a boy and two girls.* **2 the girls** a group of female friends *I'm going out with the girls tonight.*

⦿ **girlfriend** /'gɜːlfrend/ *noun* [C] **1** a woman or girl who someone is having a romantic relationship with *Have you met Steve's new girlfriend?* **2** a female friend, especially of a woman

**girth** /gɜːθ/ *noun* [C, U] the measurement around something round, such as someone's waist

**gist** /dʒɪst/ *noun* **the gist of sth** the main point or meaning of something without the details

⦿ **give**[1] /gɪv/ *verb past t* **gave**, *past p* **given**
**1** PROVIDE [+ two objects] to provide someone with something *Her parents gave her a car for her birthday.* • *Do you give money to charity?* • *Could you give me a lift to the station, please?*
**2** PUT NEAR [+ two objects] to put something near someone or in their hand so that they can use it or look at it *Can you give me that pen?* • *He poured a cup of coffee and gave it to Isabel.*
**3** ALLOW [+ two objects] to allow someone to have a right or an opportunity *We didn't really give him a chance to explain.* **4** TELL [T] to tell someone something *The woman refused to give her name.* • [+ two objects] *Can you give Jo a message?* **5** CAUSE [+ two objects] to cause someone to have or feel something *I hope he hasn't given you any trouble.* • *Smoking gives you cancer.* • *This news will give hope to thousands of sufferers.* **6** ALLOW TIME [+ two objects] to allow someone or something a particular amount of time *I'm nearly ready – just give me a few minutes.* **7** PAY MONEY [+ two objects] to pay someone a particular amount of money for something *I gave him £20 for his old camera.*
**8** DO [T] to perform an action *to give a cry/shout* • [+ two objects] *He gave her a kiss on the cheek.* **9 give sb a call/ring** to telephone someone *Why don't you just give him a call?*
**10 give a performance/speech, etc** to perform or speak in public *Tony gave a great speech.* **11 give a party** to have a party *Claire's giving a birthday party for Eric.* **12** MOVE [I] to bend, stretch, or break because of too much weight **13 give way** *UK* (*US* **yield**) to stop in order to allow other vehicles to go past before you drive onto a bigger road

**give sth away 1** to give something to someone without asking for any money *They're giving away a CD with this magazine.* **2** to let someone know a secret, often without intending to *The party was meant to be a surprise, but Caroline gave it away.*

**give sth back** to return something to the person who gave it to you *Has she given you those books back yet?*

**give in 1** to finally agree to what someone wants after a period when you refuse to agree *We will never give in to terrorists' demands.* **2** to accept that you have been beaten and agree to stop competing or fighting

**give sth in** *UK* to give a piece of written work or a document to someone for them to read, judge, or deal with *I have to give my essay in on Monday.*

**give off sth** to produce heat, light, a smell, or a gas *The fire was giving off a lot of smoke.*

**give sth out** to give something to a large number of people *He gave out copies of the report at the end of the meeting.*

**give out** If a machine or part of your body gives out, it stops working correctly. *She read until her eyes gave out.*

**give up (sth) 1** If you give up a habit such as smoking, or give up something unhealthy such as alcohol, you stop doing it or having it. *I gave up smoking two years ago.* **2** to stop doing something before you have completed it, usually because it is too difficult [+ doing sth] *I've given up trying to help her.*

**give up sth** to stop doing a regular activity or job *Are you going to give up work when you have your baby?*

**give up** to stop trying to think of the answer to a joke or question *Do you give up?*

**give yourself up** to allow the police or an enemy to catch you

**give up on sb** to stop hoping that someone will do what you want them to do *The doctors have given up on him.*

**give up on sth** to stop hoping that something will achieve what you want it to achieve

**give²** /gɪv/ *noun* **1** [U] when something can bend or move from its normal shape to take extra weight or size **2 give and take** when people reach agreement by letting each person have part of what they want

**giveaway** /'gɪvəweɪ/ *noun* **1** [C] something that is given to people free **2** [no plural] something that makes it easy for people to guess something

**given¹** /'gɪvᵊn/ *adj* **1** [always before noun] already arranged or agreed *They can only stay for a given amount of time.* **2 any given day/time/ week, etc** any day/time/week, etc *About 4 million women are pregnant in the US at any given time.*

**given²** /'gɪvᵊn/ *preposition* when you consider *Given the force of the explosion, it's a miracle they survived.*

**given³** /'gɪvᵊn/ *past participle of* give

**glacial** /'gleɪsiəl ⓤⓢ 'gleɪʃᵊl/ *adj* [always before noun] relating to glaciers or ice *glacial lakes*

**glacier** /'glæsiə ⓤⓢ 'gleɪʃər/ *noun* [C] a large mass of ice that moves very slowly, usually down a slope or valley

O➤**glad** /glæd/ *adj* [never before noun] **1** happy about something [+ (that)] *She's very glad that she left.* • [+ to do sth] *I'm so glad to see you.* **2** very willing to do something [+ to do sth] *She's always glad to help.* **3 be glad of sth** *formal* to be grateful for something *I was glad of a few days off before going back to work.*

**gladly** /'glædli/ *adv* willingly or happily *I would gladly pay extra for better service.*

**glamorize** (*also UK* **-ise**) /'glæmᵊraɪz/ *verb* [T] to make something seem glamorous

**glamorous** /'glæmᵊrəs/ *adj* attractive in an exciting and special way *a glamorous woman* • *a glamorous lifestyle*

**glamour** (*also US* **glamor**) /'glæmə/ *noun* [U] the quality of being attractive, exciting and special *the glamour of Hollywood*

**glance¹** /glɑːns/ *verb* **1 glance at/around/ towards, etc** to look somewhere for a short time *He glanced at his watch.* **2 glance at/ over/through, etc** to read something quickly *She glanced through the newspaper.*

**glance²** /glɑːns/ *noun* **1** [C] a quick look *She had a quick glance around the restaurant.* **2 at a glance** If you see something at a glance, you see it very quickly or immediately.

**gland** /glænd/ *noun* [C] an organ in the body that produces a particular chemical substance or liquid *The glands in my neck are a bit swollen.*

**glandular fever** /,glændjʊlə'fiːvə/ *UK* (*US* **mononucleosis**) *noun* [U] an infectious disease that makes your glands swell and makes you feel tired

**glare¹** /gleə/ *noun* **1** [U] strong, bright light that hurts your eyes *I get a lot of glare from my computer screen.* **2** [C] a long, angry look **3 the glare of publicity/the media, etc** when someone gets too much attention from newspapers and television

**glare²** /gleə/ *verb* [I] to look at someone in an angry way *She glared at him and stormed out of the room.*

**glaring** /'gleərɪŋ/ *adj* **1 a glaring error/ mistake/omission, etc** a very noticeable mistake or problem **2 glaring light/sun, etc** light which is too strong and bright

O➤**glass** /glɑːs/ *noun* **1** [U] a hard, transparent substance that objects such as windows and bottles are made of *broken glass* • *glass jars* **2** [C] a container made of glass that is used for drinking *I'll get you a clean glass.* • *Would you like a glass of water?* ➷ *See also:* **magnifying glass, stained glass**.

**glass**

The window is made of glass.

glass

glasses

**glasses** /'glɑːsɪz/ *noun* [plural] a piece of equipment with two transparent parts that you wear in front of your eyes to help you see better *a pair of glasses* • *She was wearing glasses.*

**glassy** /'glɑːsi/ *adj* **1** A glassy surface is smooth and shiny like glass. **2** Glassy eyes show no expression and seem not to see anything.

**glaze¹** /gleɪz/ *verb* **1** [EYES] [I] (*also* **glaze over**) If someone's eyes glaze or glaze over, they stop showing any interest or expression because they are bored or tired. **2** [CLAY] [T] to cover the surface of objects made of clay with a liquid that makes them hard and shiny when they are baked **3** [FOOD] [T] to put a liquid on food to make it shiny and more attractive **4** [GLASS] [T] to put glass in a window or door

**glaze²** /gleɪz/ *noun* [C, U] **1** a liquid that is put on objects made of clay to make them hard and shiny when they are baked **2** a liquid that is put on food to make it shiny and attractive

**gleam¹** /gliːm/ *verb* [I] to shine in a pleasant, soft way *Her eyes gleamed in the dark.* • *a gleaming new car*

**gleam²** /gliːm/ *noun* [no plural] **1** when something shines in a pleasant, soft way *the gleam of sunlight on the frozen lake* **2** an expression in someone's eyes *She had a strange gleam in her eye.*

**glean** /gliːn/ *verb* [T] to discover information slowly or with difficulty [often passive] *Some useful information can be gleaned from this study.*

**glee** /gliː/ *noun* [U] a feeling of great happiness, usually because of your good luck or someone else's bad luck *Rosa began laughing with glee.* • **gleeful** *adj* • **gleefully** *adv*

**glib** /glɪb/ *adj* using words in a way that is clever and confident, but not sincere

**glide** /glaɪd/ *verb* **glide along/into/over, etc** to move somewhere smoothly and quietly *The train slowly glided out of the station.*

**glider** /'glaɪdər/ *noun* [C] an aircraft that has no engine and flies on air currents • **gliding** *noun* [U] the activity of flying in a glider ➔ *See also:* **hang glider, hang gliding.**

**glimmer¹** /'glɪmər/ *noun* **1** a **glimmer of happiness/hope, etc** a small sign of something good **2** [C] when a light shines in a weak way

**glimmer²** /'glɪmər/ *verb* [I] to shine in a weak way

**glimpse** /glɪmps/ *noun* [C] when you see something or someone for a very short time *He caught/got a glimpse of her as she got into the car.* • **glimpse** *verb* [T] to see something or someone for a very short time *She glimpsed him out of the corner of her eye.*

**glint** /glɪnt/ *noun* [no plural] **1** when your eyes shine with excitement or because you are going to do something bad *She had a wicked glint in her eye.* **2** when something shines or reflects light for a short time • **glint** *verb* [I]

**glisten** /'glɪsᵊn/ *verb* [I] If something glistens, it shines, often because it is wet. *Their faces were glistening with sweat.*

**glitch** /glɪtʃ/ *noun* [C] *informal* a mistake or problem that stops something from working correctly *technical glitches*

**glitter¹** /'glɪtər/ *verb* [I] to shine with small flashes of light *Snow glittered on the mountains.*

**glitter²** /'glɪtər/ *noun* [U] **1** very small, shiny pieces of metal used for decoration **2** when something seems exciting and attractive

**glittering** /'glɪtᵊrɪŋ/ *adj* **1** shining with small flashes of light *glittering jewels* **2** successful and exciting *a glittering party/career*

**glitz** /glɪts/ *noun* [U] when something is attractive, exciting and shows money in an obvious way • **glitzy** *adj a glitzy nightclub*

**gloat** /gləʊt/ *verb* [I] to show pleasure at your success or at someone else's failure *His enemies were gloating over his defeat.*

**global** /'gləʊbᵊl/ *adj* relating to the whole world *the global problem of nuclear waste* • **globally** *adv*

**global warming** *noun* [U] when the air around the world becomes warmer because of pollution

**globe** /gləʊb/ *noun* **1 the globe** the world *This event is being watched by 200 million people around the globe.*

**2** [C] a model of the world shaped like a ball with a map of all the countries on it

**globule** /'glɒbjuːl/ *noun* [C] a small, round mass or lump of a liquid substance *a globule of oil*

**gloom** /gluːm/ *noun* [U] **1** a feeling of unhappiness and of not having any hope *an atmosphere of gloom* **2** when it is dark, but not completely dark

**gloomy** /'gluːmi/ *adj* **1** NEGATIVE very negative about a situation *a gloomy report* **2** DARK dark in an unpleasant way *a small, gloomy room* **3** UNHAPPY unhappy and without hope *a gloomy face* • **gloomily** *adv*

**glorify** /'glɔːrɪfaɪ/ *verb* [T] **1** to describe or represent something in a way that makes it seem better or more important than it really is *films that glorify violence* **2** to praise someone, especially God

**glorious** /'glɔːriəs/ *adj* **1** beautiful or wonderful *We had four days of glorious sunshine.* • **glorious colours 2** deserving praise and respect *a glorious career* • **gloriously** *adv*

**glory¹** /'glɔːri/ *noun* [U] **1** when people praise and respect you for achieving something important **2** great beauty *The castle has been restored to its former glory.*

**glory²** /'glɔːri/ *verb*

**glory in sth** to enjoy something and be very proud of it

**gloss¹** /glɒs/ *noun* **1** PAINT [U] paint that creates a shiny surface **2** SHINE [U] shine on a surface **3** EXPLANATION [C] a short explanation of a word or phrase in a text

**gloss²** /glɒs/ *verb* [T] to give a short explanation of a word or phrase

**gloss over sth** to avoid discussing something, or to discuss something without any details in order to make it seem unimportant

**glossary** /'glɒsᵊri/ *noun* [C] a list of difficult words with their meanings like a small dictionary, especially at the end of a book

**glossy** /'glɒsi/ *adj* **1** smooth and shiny *glossy hair* **2** Glossy magazines and pictures are printed on shiny paper. *a glossy brochure*

**glove** /glʌv/ *noun* [C] a piece of clothing which covers your fingers and hand *a pair of gloves*

**glow¹** /gləʊ/ *noun* [no plural] **1** a soft, warm light *the warm glow of the moon* **2** when your face feels or appears warm and healthy *Sam's face had lost its rosy glow.* **3 a glow of happiness/pride, etc** a strong feeling of being happy/proud, etc

**glow²** /gləʊ/ *verb* [I] **1** to produce a soft, warm light *toys which glow in the dark* **2** to have a warm and healthy appearance *Her eyes were bright and her cheeks were glowing.* **3 glow with happiness/pride, etc** to feel very happy, proud, etc *Glowing with pride, she showed me her painting.*

**glower** /glaʊər/ *verb* [I] to look at someone in a very angry way *The woman glowered at her husband.*

**glowing** /'gləʊɪŋ/ *adj* praising someone a lot *She got a glowing report from her teacher.*

**glucose** /'gluːkəʊs/ *noun* [U] a type of sugar

**glue¹** /gluː/ *noun* [U] a substance used to stick things together *Put a bit of glue on both edges*

globe

*and hold them together.* ⟳ *See colour picture* **Classroom** *on page Centre 4.*

**glue²** /gluː/ *verb* [T] **glueing** or **gluing**, *past* **glued** to stick something to something else with glue *Do you think you can* **glue** *this vase back together?*

**be glued to sth** to be watching something, especially television *The kids were glued to the TV all morning.*

**glum** /glʌm/ *adj* unhappy *Why are you looking so glum today?* • **glumly** *adv*

**glut** /glʌt/ *noun* [C] more of something than is needed [usually singular] *There is a glut of houses for sale in this area.*

**glutton** /'glʌtᵊn/ *noun* **1** [C] someone who eats too much **2 be a glutton for punishment** to enjoy doing things that are unpleasant or difficult

**gluttony** /'glʌtᵊni/ *noun* [U] when someone eats too much

**gm** *written abbreviation for* gram (= a unit for measuring weight)

**GM** *adj abbreviation for* genetically modified: changed by adding genes from another plant or animal *GM foods*

**GMT** /ˌdʒiːemˈtiː/ *noun* [U] *abbreviation for* Greenwich Mean Time: the time at Greenwich in London, which is used as an international measurement for time

**gnarled** /nɑːld/ *adj* rough and twisted, usually because of being old *a gnarled tree trunk*

**gnat** /næt/ *noun* [C] a small flying insect that can bite you

**gnaw** /nɔː/ *verb* [I, T] to bite something with a lot of small bites *He was gnawing on a bone.*

**gnaw at sb** to make someone feel more and more anxious or annoyed *Doubt kept gnawing at him.*

**gnome** /nəʊm/ *noun* [C] an imaginary little man with a pointed hat *a garden gnome*

**GNP** /ˌdʒiːenˈpiː/ *noun* [U] *abbreviation for* gross national product: the total value of goods and services produced in a country in a year, including the profits made in foreign countries

o━**go¹** /gəʊ/ *verb* [I] **1** MOVE to move or travel somewhere *I'd love to go to America.* • *We went into the house.* • *Are you* **going** *by train?* **2** DO SOMETHING to move or travel somewhere in order to do something *Let's go for a walk.* • [+ doing sth] *We're going camping tomorrow.* **3** DISAPPEAR to disappear or no longer exist *When I turned round the man had gone.* **4 go badly/well, etc** to develop in a particular way *My exams went really badly.* **5** CONTINUE to continue to be in a particular state *We won't let anyone go hungry.* **6** WORKING to work correctly *Did you manage to get the car going?* **7** STOP WORKING to stop working correctly *Her hearing is going, so speak loudly.* **8** MATCH If two things go, they match each other. *That jumper doesn't* **go with** *those trousers.* **9** TIME If time goes, it passes. *The day went very quickly.* **10** SONG to have a particular tune or words *I can't remember how it goes.* **11** SOUND/MOVEMENT to make a particular sound or movement *My dog goes like this when he wants some food.*

| j yes | k cat | ʃ she | ʒ decision | θ thin | ð this | ŋ ring | tʃ chip | dʒ jar | æ cat | ɑː arm | e bed | eə hair | ə ago | ɜː her | ɪ sit | i cosy |

---

**USAGE**

**go**

| present tense | past tense |
|---|---|
| I go | I went |
| you go | you went |
| he/she/it goes | he/she/it went |
| we go | we went |
| you go | you went |
| they go | they went |

| past participle | |
|---|---|
| gone | They have gone to the cinema. |

| present participle | |
|---|---|
| going | Where are you going? |

---

**USAGE**

**go, gone,** and **been**

**Gone** is the usual part participle of the verb **go.** Sometimes you use the past participle **been** when you want to say that you have gone somewhere and come back, or to say that you have visited somewhere.

*Paul has gone to the hospital this morning* (= he is still there).

*Paul has been to the hospital this morning* (= he went and has come back).

*He has gone to New York* (= he is still there).

*Have you ever been to New York?* (= Have you ever visited New York?)

---

**go about sth** to start to do something or deal with something *What's the best way to go about this?*

**go after sb** to chase or follow someone in order to catch them *He ran away, but the police went after him.*

**go against sth** If something goes against a rule or something you believe in, it does not obey it or agree with it. *It goes against my principles to lie.*

**go against sb** If a decision or vote goes against someone, they do not get the result that they needed. *The judge's decision went against us.*

**go ahead 1** to start to do something *We have permission to go ahead with the project.* **2** something that you say to someone to give them permission to do something *"Can I borrow your book?" "Yes, go ahead."*

**go along 1** *UK* to go to a place or event, usually without much planning *I might go along to the party after work.* **2** to continue doing something *I'll tell you the rules as we go along.*

**go along with sth/sb** to support an idea, or to agree with someone's opinion *She'll never go along with this idea.*

**go around** (*also UK* **go round**) **1** to be enough for everyone in a group *There aren't enough chairs to go around.* **2 go around doing sth** to spend your time behaving badly or doing something that is unpleasant for other people *She's been going around telling people I'm stupid.*

**go at sth** *UK informal* to start doing something

with a lot of energy and enthusiasm *There were a lot of dishes to wash so we went at it straight away.*

**go away 1** [LEAVE] to leave a place *Go away – I'm busy.* **2** [HOLIDAY] to leave your home in order to spend time in a different place, usually for a holiday *They're going away for a few weeks in the summer.* **3** [DISAPPEAR] to disappear *That smell seems to have gone away.*

**go back** to return to a place where you were or where you have been before *When are you going back to London?*

**go back on sth** to not do something that you promised you would do *I never go back on my word* (= not do what I said I would do).

**go back to sb** to start a relationship again with a person who you had a romantic relationship with in the past *Jim's gone back to his ex-wife.*

**go back to sth** to start doing something again that you were doing before *It's time to go back to work now.*

**go by 1** If time goes by, it passes. *The days went by really slowly.* **2** to move past *A green sports car went by.*

**go by sth** to use information about something to help you make a decision about the best thing to do *You can't go by anything she says.*

**go down 1** [BECOME LESS] to become lower in level *Interest rates are going down at the moment.* **2** [SUN] When the sun goes down, it moves down in the sky until it cannot be seen any more. **3** [COMPUTER] If a computer goes down, it stops working. **4** [REMEMBER] to be considered or remembered in a particular way *This will go down as one of the most exciting soccer matches ever played.* ● *(UK) I don't think my plan will go down well at all.*

**go down with sth** *UK informal* to become ill, usually with an illness that is not very serious *Our whole class went down with the flu.*

**go for sth 1** [CHOOSE] to choose something *What sort of printer are you going to go for?* **2** [HAVE] *informal* to try to have or achieve something *He'll be going for his third straight Olympic gold medal in the 200-meter dash.* ● *If you want it, go for it* (= do what you need to do in order to have or achieve it). **3** [GET] to try to get something *He tripped as he was going for the ball.* **4** [MONEY] If something goes for a particular amount of money, it is sold for that amount.

**go for sb** to attack someone *He suddenly went for me with a knife.*

**go in** to enter a place *I looked through the window, but I didn't actually go in.*

**go in for sth** to like a particular activity *I don't really go in for sports.*

**go into sth 1** [START] to start to do a particular type of work *What made you decide to go into politics?* **2** [DESCRIBE] to describe, discuss, or examine something in a detailed way *She didn't go into any detail about the job.* **3** [BE USED] If an amount of time, money, or effort goes into a product or activity, it is used or spent creating that product or doing that activity. *A lot of effort has gone into producing this play.*

**go off 1** [LEAVE] to leave a place and go somewhere else *She's gone off to the pub with Tony.*

**2** [FOOD] *UK informal* If food goes off, it is not good to eat any more because it is too old. **3** [STOP] If a light or machine goes off, it stops working. *The heating goes off at 10 o'clock.* **4** [EXPLODE] If a bomb or gun goes off, it explodes or fires. **5** [MAKE NOISE] If something that makes a noise goes off, it suddenly starts making a noise. *His car alarm goes off every time it rains.*

**go off sb/sth** *UK* to stop liking someone or something *I've gone off fish recently.*

**go on 1** [LAST] to last for a particular period of time *The film seemed to go on forever.* **2** [CONTINUE] to continue doing something [+ doing sth] *We can't go on living like this.* **3 go on to do sth** to do something else in the future *He went on to win the final.* **4** [HAPPEN] to happen *What's going on?* **5** [TALK] *UK* to talk in an annoying way about something for a long time *I wish she'd stop going on about her boyfriend.* **6** [TALK AGAIN] to start talking again after stopping for a short time *He paused and then went on with his story.* **7 Go on** *informal* something that you say to encourage someone to do something *Go on, what happened next?*

**go on sth** to use a piece of information to help you discover or understand something *Her first name was all we had to go on.*

**go out 1** [LEAVE] to leave a place in order to go somewhere else *Are you going out tonight?* **2** [LIGHT/FIRE] If a light or something that is burning goes out, it stops producing light or heat. *It took ages for the fire to go out.* **3** [RELATIONSHIP] If two people go out together, they have a romantic relationship with each other. *I've been going out with him for a year.*

**go over** *US* to be thought of in a particular way *I wonder how my speech will go over this afternoon.* ● *I don't think my comments went over well at all.*

**go over sth** to talk or think about something in order to explain it or make certain that it is correct *Let's go over the plan one more time.*

**go round** *UK (UK/US* **go around**) **1** to be enough for everyone in a group *There aren't enough chairs to go round.* **2 go round doing sth** to spend your time behaving badly or doing something that is unpleasant for other people *She's been going round telling people I'm stupid.*

**go through sth 1** [EXPERIENCE] to experience a difficult or unpleasant situation *She's going through a difficult time with her job.* **2** [EXAMINE] to carefully examine the contents of something or a collection of things in order to find something *A customs officer went through my suitcase.* **3** [USE] to use a lot of something *I've gone through two boxes of tissues this week.*

**go through** If a law, plan, or deal goes through, it is officially accepted or approved.

**go through with sth** to do something unpleasant or difficult that you have planned or promised to do *He was too scared to go through with the operation.*

**go under** If a company or business goes under, it fails financially.

**go up 1** [INCREASE] to become higher in level *House prices keep going up.* **2** [BE FIXED] If a building or sign goes up, it is fixed into position. **3** EXPLODE to suddenly explode *There was a loud bang, and then the building went up in flames.*

**go without (sth)** to not have something that you usually have *They went without food for four days.*

**go²** /gəʊ/ *noun* [C] *plural* **goes 1** *UK* when someone tries to do something *I had a go at catching a fish.* • *If you think you might like skiing, why don't you give it a go* (= try to do it)? **2** *mainly UK* someone's turn to do something *Throw the dice Jane, it's your go.* **3 have a go at sb** *UK* to criticize someone angrily *My mother's always having a go at me about my hair.* **4 make a go of sth** to try to make something succeed, usually by working hard *They're determined to make a go of their business.*

**goad** /gəʊd/ *verb* [T] to make someone angry or annoyed so that they react in the way that you want [+ into + doing sth] *They tried to goad us into attacking the police.*

o━**goal** /gəʊl/ *noun* [C] **1** POINT a point scored in sports such as football when a player sends a ball or other object into a particular area, such as between two posts *He scored two goals in the second half.* **2** AREA in some sports, the area between two posts where players try to send the ball ➔ *See colour picture* **Sports 2** *on page Centre 16.* **3** AIM something you want to do successfully in the future *Andy's goal is to run in the New York Marathon.*

**goalie** /'gəʊli/ *noun* [C] *informal short for* goalkeeper

**goalkeeper** /'gəʊl,kiːpəʳ/ (*also US* **goaltender** /'gəʊl,tendəʳ/) *noun* [C] the player in a sport such as football who tries to stop the ball going into the goal ➔ *See colour picture* **Sports 2** *on page Centre 16.*

**goalpost** /'gəʊlpəʊst/ *noun* [C] either of the two posts that are each side of the area where goals are scored in sports such as football ➔ *See colour picture* **Sports 2** *on page Centre 16.*

**goat** /gəʊt/ *noun* [C] an animal with horns which is kept for the milk it produces

**gobble** /'gɒbl/ (*also* **gobble up/down**) *verb* [T] *informal* to eat food very quickly

**gobbledygook** (*also* **gobbledegook**) /'gɒbldi,guːk/ *noun* [U] *informal* nonsense or very complicated language that you cannot understand

**go-between** /'gəʊbɪ,twiːn/ *noun* [C] someone who talks and gives messages to people who will not or cannot talk to each other

**goblin** /'gɒblɪn/ *noun* [C] a short, ugly, imaginary creature who behaves badly

**go-cart** (*also UK* **go-kart**) /'gəʊkɑːt/ *noun* [C] a small, low racing car with no roof or windows

o━**god** /gɒd/ *noun* **1 God** in Jewish, Christian, or Muslim belief, the spirit who created the universe and everything in it, and who rules over it *He prayed to God to make his mother well again.* **2** [C] a spirit, especially a male one, that people pray to and who has control over parts of the world or nature *the ancient Greek gods and goddesses* **3 (Oh) (my) God!** *informal* used to emphasize how surprised, angry, shocked, etc you are *Oh my God! The car has been stolen.* **4 thank God** *informal* something you say when you are happy because something bad did not happen *Thank God nobody was hurt in the accident.*

**godchild** /'gɒdtʃaɪld/ *noun* [C] *plural* **godchildren** a child who has godparents (= people who take responsibility for the child's moral and religious development)

**goddess** /'gɒdes/ *noun* [C] a female spirit that people pray to and who has control over parts of the world or nature *the ancient goddess of hunting*

**godfather** /'gɒdfɑːðəʳ/ *noun* [C] a man who is responsible for the moral and religious development of another person's child

**godforsaken** /'gɒdfə,seɪkⁿn/ *adj* [always before noun] *informal* A godforsaken place is very unpleasant and usually far from other places.

**godlike** /'gɒdlaɪk/ *adj* having qualities that make someone admired and respected as if they were a god or God

**godmother** /'gɒd,mʌðəʳ/ *noun* [C] a woman who is responsible for the moral and religious development of another person's child

**godparent** /'gɒd,peərⁿnt/ *noun* [C] a person who is responsible for the moral and religious development of another person's child

**godsend** /'gɒdsend/ *noun* [no plural] something good which happens unexpectedly, usually when you really need it *The lottery win was a godsend for her.*

**goes** /gəʊz/ *present simple he/she/it of* go

**goggles** /'gɒglz/ *noun* [plural] special glasses which fit close to your face to protect your eyes *a pair of goggles* ➔ *See colour picture* **Sports 1** *on page Centre 15.*

**going¹** /'gəʊɪŋ/ *noun* **1** DIFFICULTY [U] how easy or difficult something is *I found the exam quite hard going.* **2** GROUND [U] the condition of the ground for walking, riding, etc **3** LEAVING [no plural] when someone leaves somewhere *His going came as a big surprise.*

**going²** /'gəʊɪŋ/ *adj* **the going price/rate, etc** the usual amount of money you would expect to pay for something *What's the going rate for babysitting these days?* ➔ *See also:* **easy-going**.

**going³** /'gəʊɪŋ/ *present participle of* go

**goings-on** /,gəʊɪŋz'ɒn/ *noun* [plural] *informal* unusual events or activities *strange goings-on*

**go-kart** /'gəʊkɑːt/ *noun* [C] *another UK spelling of* go-cart (= a small, low racing car with no roof or windows)

**gold¹** /gəʊld/ *noun* **1** [U] a valuable, shiny, yellow metal used to make coins and jewellery **2** [C, U] a gold medal (= a small, round disc given to someone for winning a race or competition)

**gold²** /gəʊld/ *adj* **1** made of gold *gold coins* **2** being the colour of gold *gold paint*

**golden** /'gəʊldⁿn/ *adj* **1** being a bright yellow colour *bright golden hair* **2** *literary* made of gold or like gold *a golden ring* **3 a golden opportunity** a very exciting and valuable opportunity

**golden 'wedding** *noun* [C] the day when two people have been married for 50 years

**goldfish** /'gəʊldfɪʃ/ *noun* [C] *plural* **goldfish** or **goldfishes** a small, orange fish that is often kept as a pet

,**gold** '**medal** *noun* [C] a small, round disc given to someone for winning a race or competition *to win an Olympic gold medal*

'**gold** ,**mine** *noun* [C] **1** a place where gold is taken from the ground **2** something that provides you with a lot of money

**golf** /gɒlf/ *noun* [U] a game on grass where players try to hit a small ball into a series of holes using a long, thin stick • **golfer** *noun* [C] ➔ *See colour picture* **Sports 2** *on page Centre 16.*

'**golf** ,**club** *noun* [C] **1** a place where people can play golf **2** a long, thin stick used to play golf ➔ *See colour picture* **Sports 2** *on page Centre 16.*

**gone** /gɒn/ *past participle of* go

**gong** /gɒŋ/ *noun* [C] a metal disc which makes a loud sound when you hit it with a stick

**gonna** /ɡ²nə/ *informal short for* going to

**goo** /guː/ *noun* [U] a thick, sticky substance

o━**good**[1] /ɡʊd/ *adj* **better, best** **1** PLEASANT enjoyable, pleasant, or interesting *a good book* • *Did you have a good time at the party?* **2** HIGH QUALITY of a high quality or level *She speaks good French.* • *The food at this restaurant is very good.* **3** SUCCESSFUL successful, or able to do something well *Anne's a good cook.* • *She's very good at geography.* **4** KIND kind or helpful *a good friend* • *My granddaughter is very good to me.* **5** POSITIVE having a positive or useful effect *Exercise is good for you.* **6** SUITABLE suitable or satisfactory *When would be a good time to phone?* **7** BEHAVIOUR A good child or animal behaves well. **8** MORALLY RIGHT morally right *a good person* • *He sets a good example to the rest of the class.* **9** COMPLETE complete and detailed *She got a good look at the robbers.* **10** LARGE used to emphasize the number, amount, quality, etc of something *There's a good chance he'll pass the exam.* **11** SATISFACTION something you say when you are satisfied or pleased about something or when you agree with something *Oh good, he's arrived at last.* **12 Good God/grief/heavens!, etc** used to express surprise or shock *Good heavens! It's already 11 p.m.* **13 a good 20 minutes/30 miles, etc** not less than 20 minutes/30 miles, etc and probably a bit more ➔ *See also:* be in sb's good books (**book**[1]), it's good **job**, for good **measure**[2], stand sb in good **stead**.

---

**USAGE**

**good** or **well?**

Good is an adjective and is used to describe nouns.

*She's a **good** cook.*

*Her children had a **good** education.*

Well is an adverb and is used to describe verbs.

*She cooks **well**.*

*Her children were **well** educated.*

---

**good**[2] /ɡʊd/ *noun* **1** [U] something that is an advantage or help to a person or situation *It's hard work, but it's for your own good.* **2 be no good/not any good** to not be useful, helpful, or valuable *That diet is no good – you haven't lost any weight yet.* **3 do sb good** to be useful

or helpful to someone *A holiday will do you good.* **4** [U] what people think is morally right *Children don't always understand the difference between good and bad.* **5 for good** forever *When he was 20, he left home for good.* ➔ *See also:* do sb a/the **world**[1] of good.

,**good** **after**'**noon** *exclamation* something you say to greet someone when you meet them in the afternoon

o━**goodbye** /ɡʊd'baɪ/ *exclamation* something you say when you leave someone or when they leave you *She said goodbye to everyone.* • *Goodbye Vicki! See you next week.*

,**good** '**evening** *exclamation* something you say to greet someone in the evening

,**Good** '**Friday** *noun* [C, U] the Friday before Easter (= a Christian holiday), a day when Christians remember the death of Jesus Christ

**good-humoured** UK (US **good-humored**) /,ɡʊd'hjuːməd/ *adj* pleasant and friendly

**goodies** /'ɡʊdiz/ *noun* [plural] *informal* special or nice things that you will enjoy *She gave the children some sweets and other goodies.*

**good-looking** /,ɡʊd'lʊkɪŋ/ *adj* If someone is good-looking, they have an attractive face. *a good-looking woman*

,**good** '**looks** *noun* [plural] an attractive face

,**good** '**morning** *exclamation* something you say to greet someone when you meet them in the morning

**good-natured** /,ɡʊd'neɪtʃəd/ *adj* pleasant and friendly *a good-natured smile/crowd*

**goodness** /'ɡʊdnəs/ *noun* **1** [U] the quality of being good *She believes in the goodness of human nature.* **2 my goodness** *informal* something you say when you are surprised *My goodness, he's a big baby isn't he?* **3 thank goodness** *informal* something you say when you are happy because something bad did not happen *Thank goodness that dog didn't bite you.* **4 for goodness sake** used when you are annoyed or when you want something to happen quickly *For goodness sake, come in out of the rain.*

,**good** '**night** *exclamation* something you say when you leave someone or when they leave you in the evening or when someone is going to bed

o━**goods** /ɡʊdz/ *noun* **1** [plural] items which are made to be sold *radios, stereos and other electrical goods* **2 deliver/come up with the goods** If you deliver the goods, you do what people hope you will do. *Do you really think the England team can deliver the goods?*

**goodwill** /ɡʊd'wɪl/ *noun* [U] kind, friendly, or helpful feelings towards other people *He gave them a thousand pounds as a gesture of goodwill.*

**goody-goody** /'ɡʊdi,ɡʊdi/ *noun* [C] *informal* someone who tries too hard to be good, usually to parents or teachers

**gooey** /'ɡuːi/ *adj* soft and sticky *a sweet, gooey sauce*

**goof** /guːf/ (*also* **goof up**) *verb* [I] US *informal* to make a silly mistake

**goof around** US to spend your time doing silly or unimportant things

**goof off** US to avoid doing any work

**goofy** /'ɡuːfi/ *adj mainly US* silly *a goofy sense of humour*

**goose** /ɡuːs/ *noun* [C, U] *plural* **geese** a large water bird similar to a duck, or the meat from this bird

**gooseberry** /'ɡʊzbₐri ⓤⓢ 'ɡuːsberi/ *noun* [C] a small, sour, green fruit with a hairy skin

**'goose ˌpimples** (*also US* **'goose ˌbumps**) *noun* [plural] small, raised lumps that appear on your skin when you are cold or frightened

**gore¹** /ɡɔːʳ/ *noun* [U] blood, usually from a violent injury

**gore²** /ɡɔːʳ/ *verb* [T] If an animal gores someone, it injures them with its horn.

**gorge¹** /ɡɔːdʒ/ *noun* [C] a narrow and usually steep valley

**gorge²** /ɡɔːdʒ/ *verb* **gorge (yourself) on sth** to eat food until you cannot eat any more *She gorged herself on chocolate biscuits.*

**gorgeous** /'ɡɔːdʒəs/ *adj* very beautiful or pleasant *You look gorgeous in that dress.* • *What gorgeous flowers!*

**gorilla** /ɡə'rɪlə/ *noun* [C] a big, black, hairy animal, like a large monkey

**gorse** /ɡɔːs/ *noun* [U] a bush with yellow flowers and sharp, pointed leaves

**gory** /'ɡɔːri/ *adj* involving violence and blood *a gory murder*

**gosh** /ɡɒʃ/ *exclamation* used to express surprise or shock *Gosh! I didn't realize it was that late.*

**gosling** /'ɡɒzlɪŋ/ *noun* [C] a young goose (= large water bird)

**gospel** /'ɡɒspₐl/ *noun* **1** [TEACHING] [no plural] the teachings of Jesus Christ *to preach the gospel* **2** [BOOK] [C] one of the four books in the Bible that tells the life of Jesus Christ **3 the gospel truth** something that is completely true **4** [MUSIC] [U] a style of Christian music, originally sung by black Americans

**gossip¹** /'ɡɒsɪp/ *noun* **1** [U] conversation or reports about other people's private lives that might or might not be true *an interesting piece of gossip* **2** [C] someone who likes to talk about other people's private lives

**gossip²** /'ɡɒsɪp/ *verb* [I] to talk about other people's private lives *They were gossiping about her boss.*

**'gossip ˌcolumn** *noun* [C] an article appearing regularly in a newspaper giving information about famous people's private lives

**got** /ɡɒt/ *past of* get

**gotta** /'ɡɒtə/ *informal short for* got to

**gotten** /'ɡɒtⁿn/ *US past participle of* get

**gouge** /ɡaʊdʒ/ *verb* [T] to make a hole or long cut in something
**gouge sth out** to remove something by digging or cutting it out of a surface, often violently

**gourmet¹** /'ɡʊəmeɪ/ *noun* [C] someone who enjoys good food and drink and knows a lot about it

**gourmet²** /'ɡʊəmeɪ/ *adj* [always before noun] relating to good food and drink *a gourmet meal*

**govern** /'ɡʌvⁿn/ *verb* **1** [I, T] to officially control a country *The country is now governed by the Labour Party.* • *a governing body* **2** [T] to influence or control the way something happens or is done *There are rules that govern how teachers treat children.*

**governess** /'ɡʌvⁿnəs/ *noun* [C] a woman employed to teach the children in a family at home

o-= **government** /'ɡʌvⁿnmənt/ *noun* **1** [group] the group of people who officially control a country *The Government has cut taxes.* • *a government department* **2** [U] the method or process of governing a country *a new style of government* • **governmental** /ˌɡʌvⁿn'mentⁿl/ *adj* relating to government

**governor** /'ɡʌvⁿnəʳ/ *noun* [C] someone who is officially responsible for controlling a region, city, or organization *a prison/school governor* • *the Governor of Texas*

**gown** /ɡaʊn/ *noun* [C] **1** a woman's dress, usually worn on formal occasions *a silk gown* **2** a loose piece of clothing like a coat worn for a particular purpose *a hospital gown* ⊃ *See also:* **dressing gown**.

**GP** /ˌdʒiː'piː/ *noun* [C] *abbreviation for* general practitioner: a doctor who sees people in the local area and treats illnesses that do not need a hospital visit *If the fever and sore throat continue, go and see your GP.*

**grab¹** /ɡræb/ *verb* [T] **grabbing**, *past* **grabbed** **1** [TAKE SUDDENLY] to take hold of something or someone suddenly *He grabbed my arm and pulled me away.* **2** [DO QUICKLY] *informal* to eat, do, or get something quickly because you do not have much time *I grabbed a sandwich on the way to the station.* **3 grab sb's attention** *informal* to attract someone's attention *The advertisement is designed to grab people's attention.* **4** [TAKE OPPORTUNITY] If someone grabs a chance or opportunity, they take it quickly and with enthusiasm.
**grab at sb/sth** to try to get hold of someone or something quickly, with your hand

**grab²** /ɡræb/ *noun* **1 make a grab for sth/sb** to try to take hold of something or someone suddenly *He made a grab for the gun.* **2 up for grabs** *informal* If something is up for grabs, it is available to anyone who wants to try to get it. *Ten free concert tickets are up for grabs.*

**grace¹** /ɡreɪs/ *noun* [U] **1** [MOVEMENT] the quality of moving in a smooth, relaxed, and attractive way *She moved with grace and elegance.* **2** [POLITENESS] the quality of being pleasantly polite *He had the grace to apologize for his mistake the next day.* **3 with good grace** in a willing and happy way *He accepted the failure with good grace.* **4 a month's/week's, etc grace** an extra month/week, etc you are given before something must be paid or done **5** [PRAYER] a prayer of thanks said before or after a meal *to say grace*

**grace²** /ɡreɪs/ *verb* [T] When a person or object graces a place or thing, they make it more attractive. *Her face has graced the covers of magazines across the world.*

**graceful** /'ɡreɪsfⁿl/ *adj* **1** moving in a smooth, relaxed, and attractive way, or having a smooth, attractive shape *graceful movements* • *a graceful neck* **2** behaving in a polite and pleasant way • **gracefully** *adv*

**gracious** /'ɡreɪʃəs/ *adj* **1** behaving in a pleasant, polite, calm way *He was gracious enough to thank me.* **2** comfortable and with a good

G

appearance and quality *gracious homes/living*
**3 Good/Goodness gracious!** used to express
polite surprise ● **graciously** *adv*

**grade¹** /greɪd/ *noun* [C] **1** SCORE a number or
letter that shows how good someone's work or
performance is *Steve never studies, but he
always gets good grades.* ● *(UK) Carla got a
grade A in German.* **2** LEVEL a level of quality,
size, importance, etc *I applied for a position a
grade higher than my current job.* **3** SCHOOL
GROUP *US* (*UK* **form**) a school class or group of
classes for students of the same age or ability
*My son is in fifth grade.* **4 make the grade** to
perform well enough to succeed *He wanted to
get into the team but he didn't make the grade.*

**grade²** /greɪd/ *verb* [T] **1** to separate people or
things into different levels of quality, size,
importance, etc *The fruit is washed and then
graded by size.* **2** *US* (*UK* **mark**) to give a score to
a student's piece of work *to grade work/papers*

**'grade ,crossing** *US* (*UK* **level crossing**) *noun*
[C] a place where a railway crosses a road

**'grade ,school** *noun* [C, U] *US* a school for the
first six to eight years of a child's education

**gradient** /'greɪdiənt/ *noun* [C] how steep a slope
is *a steep/gentle gradient*

o▬**gradual** /'grædʒuəl/ *adj* happening slowly over a
period of time *a gradual change/improvement*

o▬**gradually** /'grædʒuəli/ *adv* slowly over a period
of time *Gradually he began to get better.*

**graduate¹** /'grædʒuət/ *noun* [C] **1** *UK* someone
who has studied for and received a degree
(= qualification) from a university *a science
graduate* **2** *US* someone who has studied for and
received a degree (= qualification) from a school,
college, or university *a high-school graduate*

**graduate²** /'grædjueɪt/ *verb* **1** [I] to complete
your education successfully at a university,
college, or, in the US, at school *He **graduated
from** Cambridge University in 1997.* **2 graduate to sth** to move up to something more
advanced or important

**graduated** /'grædjueɪtɪd/ *adj* divided into
levels or stages *a graduated scale*

**graduation** /,grædʒu'eɪʃ°n/ *noun* [C, U] when
you receive your degree (= qualification) for
completing your education or a course of study
*a graduation ceremony*

**graffiti** /grə'fiːti/ *noun* [U] writing or pictures
painted on walls and public places, usually illegally

**graffiti**

**graft¹** /grɑːft/ *noun* **1** SKIN/BONE [C] a piece of
skin or bone taken from one part of a body and
joined to another part *a skin/bone graft*
**2** PLANT [C] a piece cut from one plant and
joined onto another plant **3** WORK [U] *UK informal* work *hard graft*

**graft²** /grɑːft/ *verb* **1** SKIN/BONE [T] to join a
piece of skin or bone taken from one part of the
body to another part **2** PLANT [T] to join a piece
cut from one plant onto another plant **3** WORK
[I] *UK informal* to work hard

**grain** /greɪn/ *noun* **1** SEED [C, U] a seed or seeds
from types of grass which are eaten as food
*grains of wheat/rice* **2** PIECE [C] a very small
piece of something *a grain of sand/sugar*
**3** QUALITY [no plural] a very small amount of a
quality *There isn't a grain of truth in her story.*
**4 the grain** the natural direction and pattern
of lines which you can see in wood or material
*to cut something along/against the grain* **5 go
against the grain** If something goes against
the grain, you would not normally do it
because it would be unusual or morally wrong.
➔ *See also:* take sth with a grain of **salt¹**.

**gram** (*also UK* **gramme**) (*written abbreviation* **g,
gm**) /græm/ *noun* [C] a unit for measuring
weight, equal to 0.001 kilograms

**grammar** /'græmə/ *noun* **1** [U] the way you
combine words and change their form and
position in a sentence, or the rules or study of
this **2** [C] *mainly UK* a book of grammar rules

**'grammar ,school** *noun* [C, U] **1** in the UK, a
school which clever children over 11 years old
can go to if they pass a special exam **2** *US*
*another word for* elementary school (= a school
for children from the ages of five to eleven in
the US)

**grammatical** /grə'mætɪk°l/ *adj* relating to
grammar, or obeying the rules of grammar
*grammatical rules* ● *a grammatical sentence*
● **grammatically** *adv*

**gramme** /græm/ *noun* [C] *another UK spelling of*
gram

**gramophone** /'græməfəʊn/ *noun* [C] *old-fashioned* a machine for playing music

**gran** /græn/ *noun* [C] *UK informal short for*
grandmother

**grand¹** /grænd/ *adj* **1** LARGE very large and
special *a grand hotel* ● *the Grand Canal*
**2** IMPORTANT rich and important, or behaving
as if you are *a grand old lady* **3** GOOD *informal*
very good or enjoyable

**grand²** /grænd/ *noun* [C] *plural* **grand** *informal*
one thousand dollars or pounds *The holiday
cost me two grand.*

**grandad** /'grændæd/ *noun* [C] *another UK
spelling of* granddad

**grandchild** /'græntʃaɪld/ *noun* [C] *plural*
**grandchildren** the child of your son or daughter

**granddad** /'grændæd/ *noun* [C] *mainly UK informal* grandfather

**granddaughter** /'grænd,dɔːtə/ *noun* [C] the
daughter of your son or daughter

**grandeur** /'grændjə/ *noun* [U] the quality of
being very large and special or beautiful *the
grandeur of the hills*

o▬**grandfather** /'grænd,fɑːðə/ *noun* [C] the father
of your mother or father

,grandfather 'clock *noun* [C] a clock in a very tall, wooden case

grandiose /'grændiəus/ *adj* large or detailed and made to appear important, often in an unnecessary and annoying way *grandiose plans*

grandly /'grændli/ *adv* in a very important way, or as if you are very important

grandma /'grændmɑː/ *noun* [C] *informal another word for* grandmother

o⭐ grandmother /'grænd,mʌðəʳ/ *noun* [C] the mother of your mother or father

grandpa /'grændpɑː/ *noun* [C] *informal another word for* grandfather

grandparent /'grænd,peəʳ³nt/ *noun* [C] the parent of your mother or father

,grand pi'ano *noun* [C] a very large piano, usually used in public performances

,grand 'slam *noun* [C] when you win all the important competitions that are held in one year for a particular sport

grandson /'grændsʌn/ *noun* [C] the son of your son or daughter

grandstand /'grændstænd/ *noun* [C] a large, open structure containing rows of seats, used for watching sporting events

granite /'grænɪt/ *noun* [U] a type of very hard, grey rock

granny /'græni/ *noun* [C] *informal another word for* grandmother

grant¹ /grɑːnt/ *verb* **1** [T] *formal* to give or allow someone something, usually in an official way [+ two objects] *to grant someone a licence/visa* **2** [T] *formal* to admit or agree that something is true *She's a good-looking woman, I grant you.* **3 take sb/sth for granted** to not show that you are grateful for someone or something, and forget that you are lucky to have them *Most of us take our freedom for granted.* **4 take it for granted** to believe that something is true without checking or thinking about it [+ (that)] *I took it for granted that we'd be invited.*

grant² /grɑːnt/ *noun* [C] an amount of money provided by a government or organization for a special purpose *They received a research grant for the project.*

granule /'grænjuːl/ *noun* [C] a small, hard piece of a substance *coffee granules* • **granulated** /'grænjəleɪtɪd/ *adj granulated sugar*

grape /greɪp/ *noun* [C] a small, round, green or red fruit that grows in large, close groups and is often used to make wine *a bunch of grapes* ⊃ *See colour picture* **Fruit and Vegetables** *on page Centre 8.*

grapefruit /'greɪpfruːt/ *noun* [C, U] *plural* grapefruit *or* grapefruits a large, round, yellow fruit with a sour taste

grapevine /'greɪpvaɪn/ *noun* **hear sth on/through the grapevine** to hear news from someone who heard the news from someone else

graph /grɑːf/ *noun* [C] a picture with measurements marked on it as lines or curves, used to compare different things or show the development of something

graphic /'græfɪk/ *adj* A graphic description or image is extremely clear and detailed. *The film contains graphic violence.* • **graphically** *adv*

,graphic de'sign *noun* [U] the art of designing pictures and text for books, magazines, advertisements, etc

graphics /'græfɪks/ *noun* [plural] images shown on a computer screen

graphite /'græfaɪt/ *noun* [U] a soft, grey-black form of carbon used in pencils

grapple /'græpl/ *verb*

**grapple with sth** to try to deal with or understand something difficult

**grapple with sb** to hold onto someone and fight with them

grasp¹ /grɑːsp/ *verb* [T] **1** to take hold of something or someone firmly *He grasped my hand enthusiastically.* **2** to understand something *I find these mathematical problems difficult to grasp.*

**grasp at sth** to quickly try to get hold of something

grasp² /grɑːsp/ *noun* [no plural] **1** UNDERSTAND when you understand something *He has an excellent grasp of English.* **2** HOLD when you hold onto someone or something *I tried to pull him out but he slipped from my grasp.* **3** ABILITY the ability to obtain or achieve something *Victory is within our grasp.*

grasping /'grɑːspɪŋ/ *adj* wanting much more of something than you need, especially money *a grasping, greedy man*

o⭐ grass /grɑːs/ *noun* **1** [U] a common plant with narrow green leaves that grows close to the ground in gardens and fields *to mow/cut the grass* • *We lay on the grass in the sunshine.* **2** [C] a particular type of grass *ornamental grasses*

grasshopper /'grɑːs,hɒpəʳ/ *noun* [C] a green insect which jumps about using its long back legs

,grass 'roots *noun* [plural] ordinary people in a society or political organization and not the leaders

grassy /'grɑːsi/ *adj* covered with grass *a grassy slope/meadow*

grate¹ /greɪt/ *verb* **1** [T] to break food such as cheese into small, thin pieces by rubbing it against a grater (= kitchen tool with holes) *grated cheese/carrot* **2** [I] to make an unpleasant noise when rubbing against something *The chair grated against the floor.*

**grate on sb/sth** If someone's voice or behaviour grates on you, it annoys you. *Her voice really grates on me.*

grate² /greɪt/ *noun* [C] a metal structure for holding the wood or coal in a fireplace

o⭐ grateful /'greɪtf³l/ *adj* feeling or showing thanks *I'm really grateful to you for all your help.* ⊃ *Opposite* **ungrateful**. • **gratefully** *adv All donations gratefully received.*

grater /'greɪtəʳ/ *noun* [C] a kitchen tool with a surface full of holes with sharp edges, used to grate (= break into small pieces) foods such as cheese ⊃ *See colour picture* **Kitchen** *on page Centre 10.*

gratify /'grætɪfaɪ/ *verb* [T] *formal* to please someone or satisfy their wishes or needs *I was gratified by their decision.* • *a gratifying result* • **gratification** /,grætɪfɪ'keɪʃ³n/ *noun* [U]

grating /'greɪtɪŋ/ *noun* [C] a flat structure made of long, thin pieces of metal crossing each other over a hole in the ground or a window

**G**

**gratitude** /'grætɪtjuːd/ noun [U] the feeling or quality of being grateful *I would like to express my deep gratitude to all the hospital staff.*

**gratuitous** /grə'tjuːɪtəs/ adj unnecessary and done without a good reason *gratuitous violence*

**gratuity** /grə'tjuːəti/ noun [C] formal an extra amount of money given to someone to thank them for providing a service

○┅**grave¹** /greɪv/ noun [C] a place in the ground where a dead body is buried *She visits his grave every day.*

**grave²** /greɪv/ adj very serious *grave doubts* • *a grave mistake* • **gravely** adv

**gravel** /'grævəl/ noun [U] small pieces of stone used to make paths and road surfaces

**gravestone** /'greɪvstəʊn/ noun [C] a stone that shows the name of a dead person who is buried under it

**graveyard** /'greɪvjɑːd/ noun [C] an area of land where dead bodies are buried, usually next to a church

**gravitate** /'grævɪteɪt/ verb

**gravitate to/towards sth/sb** to be attracted to something or someone, or to move in the direction of something or someone *The best players always gravitate towards clubs which pay the best money.*

**gravitational** /ˌgrævɪ'teɪʃᵊnᵊl/ adj relating to gravity *gravitational force*

**gravity** /'grævəti/ noun [U] **1** the force that makes objects fall to the ground or that pulls objects towards a planet or other body *the laws of gravity* **2** formal when something is very serious *You don't seem to realize the gravity of the situation.* ➔ *See also:* **centre of gravity**.

**gravy** /'greɪvi/ noun [U] a warm, brown sauce made from the fat and liquid that comes from meat when it is being cooked

**gray** /greɪ/ noun [C, U], adj US spelling of grey

**graying** /'greɪɪŋ/ adj US spelling of greying (= having hair that is becoming grey or white)

**graze¹** /greɪz/ verb **1** [EAT] [I] When cows or other animals graze, they eat grass. *Cattle grazed in the meadow.* **2** [INJURE] [T] UK (UK/US **skin**) to injure your skin by rubbing it against something rough *I fell and grazed my knee.* **3** [TOUCH] [T] to touch or move lightly along the surface or edge of something *A bullet grazed his cheek.*

**graze²** /greɪz/ noun [C] mainly UK an injury on the surface of your skin caused by rubbing against something *She has a nasty graze on her elbow.*

**grease¹** /griːs/ noun [U] **1** a substance such as oil or fat **2** a substance like thick oil that is put on parts in an engine or machine to make them move more smoothly

**grease²** /griːs/ verb [T] to put fat or oil on or in something *Grease the pan before pouring in the cake mixture.*

**greasy** /'griːsi/ adj containing or covered with fat or oil *greasy food/fingers*

○┅**great** /greɪt/ adj **1** [EXCELLENT] very good *We had a great time.* • *I've had a great idea!* **2** [IMPORTANT] important or famous *a great statesman/novelist* **3** [LARGE] large in amount, size, or degree *a great crowd of people* **4** [EXTREME] extreme *great success/difficulty* **5** **great big/long, etc** very big/long, etc *I gave her a great big hug.* **6** a

**great many** a large number • **greatness** noun [U] ➔ *See also:* go to great lengths (**length**) to do sth, set great **store¹** by sth, the greatest **thing** since sliced bread.

**great-** /greɪt/ prefix **1** **great-grandfather/-grandmother** the father/mother of your grandfather or grandmother **2** **great-aunt/-uncle** the aunt/uncle of your mother or father **3** **great-grandchild/-granddaughter, etc** the child/daughter, etc of your grandson or granddaughter **4** **great-niece/-nephew** the daughter/son of your niece or nephew

**greatly** /'greɪtli/ adv very much *I greatly admire your paintings.* • *We will miss her greatly.*

**greed** /griːd/ noun [U] when you want a lot more food, money, etc, than you need

**greedy** /'griːdi/ adj wanting a lot more food, money, etc, than you need *greedy, selfish people* • *They were greedy for money.* • **greedily** adv • **greediness** noun [U]

**Greek** /griːk/ adj relating to the culture, language, or people of Greece or ancient Greece

○┅**green¹** /griːn/ adj **1** [COLOUR] being the same colour as grass *The traffic lights turned green.* ➔ *See colour picture* **Colours** *on page Centre 6.* **2** [ENVIRONMENT] [always before noun] relating to nature and protecting the environment *a green activist/campaigner* **3** [GRASS] covered with grass or other plants *green spaces* **4** [NOT EXPERIENCED] informal having little experience or understanding *I was very green when I joined the company.* **5** **be green with envy** to wish very much that you had something that another person has ➔ *See also:* have green fingers (**finger¹**), **green light**.

○┅**green²** /griːn/ noun **1** [COLOUR] [C, U] the colour of grass ➔ *See colour picture* **Colours** *on page Centre 6.* **2** [GOLF] [C] a special area of very short, smooth grass on a golf course *the 18th green* **3** [VILLAGE] [C] an area of grass in the middle of a village

**green belt** noun [C] an area of land around a city or town where no new building is allowed

**green card** noun [C] an official document allowing a foreigner to live and work in the US permanently

**greenery** /'griːnᵊri/ noun [U] green leaves, plants, or branches

**greengrocer** /'griːnˌgrəʊsəʳ/ noun [C] UK **1** **greengrocer's** a shop where you buy fruit and vegetables **2** someone who sells fruit and vegetables

**greenhouse** /'griːnhaʊs/ noun [C] plural **greenhouses** /'griːnhaʊzɪz/ a building made of glass for growing plants in

**the greenhouse ef,fect** noun the gradual warming of the Earth's surface caused by an increase in pollution and gases in the air

**green light** noun [no plural] permission to do something [+ to do sth] *They've been given the green light to build two new supermarkets.*

**the Green Party** noun [group] a political party whose main aim is to protect the environment

**greens** /griːnz/ noun [plural] green leaves that are cooked and eaten as a vegetable

**greet** /griːt/ verb [T] **1** to welcome someone *He greeted me at the door.* **2** to react to something in a particular way [often passive] *His story was* **greeted with** *shrieks of laughter.*

**greeting** /'griːtɪŋ/ *noun* [C] *formal* something friendly or polite that you say or do when you meet or welcome someone

**gregarious** /grɪˈɡeəriəs/ *adj* If you are gregarious, you enjoy being with other people.

**grenade** /grəˈneɪd/ *noun* [C] a small bomb that is thrown or fired from a weapon

**grew**[1] /gruː/ *past tense of* grow

**grey**[1] UK (US **gray**) /greɪ/ *adj* **1** COLOUR being a colour that is a mixture of black and white *grey clouds* ➔ *See colour picture* **Colours** *on page Centre 6.* **2** HAIR having hair that has become grey or white *She went grey in her thirties.* ➔ *See colour picture* **Hair** *on page Centre 9.* **3** WEATHER cloudy and not bright *a cold, grey morning* **4** BORING not interesting or attractive *Life was grey and tedious.* **5 grey area** something which people are not certain about, usually because there are no clear rules for it

**grey**[2] UK (US **gray**) /greɪ/ *noun* [C, U] a colour that is a mixture of black and white ➔ *See colour picture* **Colours** *on page Centre 6.*

**greyhound** /'greɪhaʊnd/ *noun* [C] a thin dog with short hair that runs very fast, sometimes in races

**greying** UK (US **graying**) /'greɪɪŋ/ *adj* having hair that is becoming grey or white

**grid** /grɪd/ *noun* **1** PATTERN [C] a pattern or structure made from horizontal and vertical lines crossing each other to form squares **2** POWER [no plural] a system of connected wires used to supply electrical power to a large area *the National Grid* **3** MAP [C] a pattern of squares with numbers or letters used to find places on a map

**gridlock** /'grɪdlɒk/ *noun* [U] when the traffic cannot move in any direction because all of the roads are blocked with cars

**grief** /griːf/ *noun* **1** [U] great sadness, especially caused by someone's death **2 Good grief!** *informal* something that you say when you are surprised or annoyed **3 come to grief** *informal* to suddenly fail or have an accident **4 cause/give sb grief** *informal* to annoy someone or cause trouble or problems for them

**grievance** /'griːvᵊns/ *noun* [C] *formal* a complaint, especially about unfair behaviour

**grieve** /griːv/ *verb* **1** [I] to feel or express great sadness, especially when someone dies *He is still **grieving for** his wife.* **2** [T] *formal* to make someone feel very sad

**grievous** /'griːvəs/ *adj formal* very serious *grievous injuries* • **grievously** *adv*

**grill**[1] /grɪl/ *noun* [C] **1** (*also US* **broiler**) a piece of equipment which cooks food using direct heat from above ➔ *See colour picture* **Kitchen** *on page Centre 10.* **2** a flat, metal structure used to cook food over a fire

**grill**[2] /grɪl/ *verb* [T] **1** (*also US* **broil**) to cook food using direct heat *Grill the fish for 2 to 3 minutes on each side.* ➔ *See picture at* **cook.** **2** to ask someone questions continuously and for a long time *I was grilled by the police for two days.*

**grille** /grɪl/ *noun* [C] a metal structure of bars built across something to protect it

**grim** /grɪm/ *adj* **grimmer, grimmest 1** BAD

worrying and bad *grim news* • *The future looks grim.* **2** SERIOUS sad and serious *a grim expression* **3** UNPLEASANT A grim place is ugly and unpleasant. • **grimly** *adv*

**grimace** /'grɪməs/ *verb* [I] to make your face show an expression of pain or unhappiness *He grimaced at the bitter taste.* • **grimace** *noun* [C]

**grime** /graɪm/ *noun* [U] dirt that covers a surface *The walls were covered in grime.* • **grimy** *adj* covered in dirt *grimy hands*

**grin** /grɪn/ *verb* **grinning, past grinned 1** [I] to smile a big smile *He **grinned at** me from the doorway.* **2 grin and bear it** to accept an unpleasant or difficult situation because there is nothing you can do to improve it *The noise and disruption is irritating, but I'll just have to grin and bear it.* • **grin** *noun* [C] *She had a big grin on her face.*

**grind**[1] /graɪnd/ *verb* [T] *past* **ground 1** to keep rubbing something between two rough, hard surfaces until it becomes a powder *to grind coffee* **2** to rub a blade against a hard surface to make it sharp **3 grind your teeth** to rub your teeth together, making an unpleasant sound **grind sb down** to gradually make someone lose hope, energy, or confidence *Living alone in London really ground me down.*

**grind**[2] /graɪnd/ *noun* [no plural] *informal* work or effort that is boring and unpleasant and makes you tired because it does not change *the daily grind*

**grinder** /'graɪndəʳ/ *noun* [C] a machine used to rub or press something until it becomes a powder *a coffee grinder*

**grip**[1] /grɪp/ *noun* [no plural] **1** when you hold something tightly *She tightened her **grip on** my arm.* **2** control over something or someone *He has a firm **grip** on the economy.* **3 come/get to grips with sth** to understand and deal with a problem or situation *It's a difficult subject to get to grips with.* **4 get a grip (on yourself)** to make an effort to control your emotions and behave more calmly *Stop panicking and get a grip on yourself!*

**grip**[2] /grɪp/ *verb* [T] **gripping, past gripped 1** HOLD to hold something tightly *She gripped his arm.* **2** INTEREST to keep someone's attention completely *This trial has gripped the whole nation.* **3** EMOTION When an emotion grips you, you feel it very strongly. [often passive] *He was gripped by fear.*

**gripe** /graɪp/ *verb* [I] *informal* to complain, often in an annoying way • **gripe** *noun* [C]

**gripping** /'grɪpɪŋ/ *adj* If something is gripping, it is so interesting that it holds your attention completely. *a gripping story*

**grisly** /'grɪzli/ *adj* very unpleasant, especially because death or blood is involved *a grisly murder*

**grit**[1] /grɪt/ *noun* [U] **1** very small pieces of stone or sand *I've got a bit of grit in my eye.* **2** the quality of being brave and determined

**grit**[2] /grɪt/ *verb* [T] **gritting, past gritted** to put grit onto a road surface when the road has ice on it ➔ *See also:* grit your teeth (**tooth**).

**gritty** /'grɪti/ *adj* **1** showing unpleasant details about a situation in a way that seems very real *a gritty drama* **2** brave and determined

**groan** /grəʊn/ *verb* [I] to make a long, low sound such as when expressing pain, unhappiness, etc *He collapsed, groaning with pain.* • **groan** *noun* [C]

**grocer** /ˈgrəʊsəʳ/ *noun* **1 grocer's** UK a shop that sells food and other products used in the home **2** [C] someone who owns or works in a grocer's

**groceries** /ˈgrəʊsʳriz/ *noun* [plural] goods bought to be used in the home such as food and cleaning products

**grocery** /ˈgrəʊsʳri/ (*also* US **'grocery ˌstore**) *noun* [C] a shop that sells food and products used in the home

**groggy** /ˈgrɒgi/ *adj informal* unable to think or act quickly because you have just woken up, been ill, etc *I felt a bit groggy after the operation.*

**groin** /grɔɪn/ *noun* [C] the area where the legs join the rest of the body near the sexual organs *He pulled a muscle in his groin.*

**groom¹** /gruːm/ *verb* [T] **1** to prepare someone carefully for a special position or job *He's being groomed for stardom.* **2** to clean and brush an animal's fur

**groom²** /gruːm/ *noun* [C] **1** (*also* **bridegroom**) a man who is getting married **2** someone who cleans and looks after horses

**groove** /gruːv/ *noun* [C] a long, narrow line that has been cut into a surface

**grope** /grəʊp/ *verb* **1** [I, T] to try to get hold of something with your hand, usually when you cannot see it *I groped in my bag for my keys.* **2 grope your way along/through, etc** to move somewhere with difficulty, feeling with your hands because you cannot see clearly *We groped our way through the smoke to the exit.* **grope for sth** to try to think of the right words or the right way to express something *He groped for the words to tell her.*

**gross¹** /grəʊs/ *adj* **1** TOTAL A gross amount of money has not had taxes or other costs taken from it. *gross earnings/profit* **2** SERIOUS [always before noun] *formal* very serious or unacceptable *gross misconduct* **3** UNPLEASANT *informal* very unpleasant *Oh, yuck. That's really gross.*

**gross²** /grəʊs/ *verb* [T] to earn a particular amount of money as a total before tax or other costs are taken from it *The film grossed $250 million.*

**grossly** /ˈgrəʊsli/ *adv* extremely *grossly unfair/ exaggerated*

**grotesque** /grəʊˈtesk/ *adj* strange and unpleasant, especially in a ridiculous or slightly frightening way *a grotesque image* • **grotesquely** *adv*

**grotto** /ˈgrɒtəʊ/ *noun* [C] a small cave

○┅**ground¹** /graʊnd/ *noun* **1 the ground** the surface of the Earth *I sat down on the ground.* **2** SOIL [U] the soil in an area *soft/stony ground* **3** AREA [C] an area of land used for a particular purpose or activity *a football ground* **4** KNOWLEDGE [U] an area of knowledge, information, interest, or experience *He had to go over the same ground several times before I understood it.* **5 break new ground** to do something that is different to anything that has been done before **6 gain/lose ground** to become more/ less popular and accepted *The idea is gradually gaining ground.* **7 get (sth) off the ground** If a plan or activity gets off the ground, or if you get it off the ground, it starts or succeeds. *He worked hard at getting the project off the ground.* **8 stand your ground** to refuse to change your opinion or move your position despite attempts to make you **9 suit sb down to the ground** UK to be exactly right or suitable for someone *That job would suit you down to the ground.* **10 be thin on the ground** UK to exist only in small numbers or amounts ⊃ *See also:* **breeding ground**, **common ground**.

**ground²** /graʊnd/ *verb* **1 be grounded** If a vehicle that travels on water or in the air is grounded, it cannot or may not leave the ground. *The aircraft was grounded by fog.* **2 be grounded in sth** *formal* to be based firmly on something *Fiction should be grounded in reality.*

**ground³** /graʊnd/ *past of* grind

**ˌground 'beef** US (UK **mince**) *noun* [U] beef (= meat from a cow) that has been cut into very small pieces by a machine

**groundbreaking** /ˈgraʊndˌbreɪkɪŋ/ *adj* based on or containing completely new ideas *ground-breaking research*

**ˌground 'floor** UK (US **first floor**) *noun* [C] the level of a building which is on the ground

**grounding** /ˈgraʊndɪŋ/ *noun* [no plural] knowledge of the basic facts and principles of a subject *The course gave me a good grounding in bookkeeping.*

**groundless** /ˈgraʊndləs/ *adj* Groundless fears, worries, etc have no reason or facts to support them.

**'ground ˌrules** *noun* [plural] the basic rules or principles for doing something *We need to set the ground rules for playing the game.*

**grounds** /graʊndz/ *noun* [plural] **1** the reason for doing or believing something *He resigned on medical grounds.* • *I refused on the grounds that* (= because) *it was too risky.* **2** the land around and belonging to a particular building or organization *We strolled around the hospital grounds.*

**groundwork** /ˈgraʊndwɜːk/ *noun* [U] work or events that prepare for something that will be done or produced in the future *The project is laying the groundwork for a new approach to research.*

○┅**group¹** /gruːp/ *noun* [C] **1** a number of people or things that are together in one place or are connected *She went camping with a small group of friends.* **2** a few musicians or singers who perform together, usually playing popular music *a pop group* ⊃ *See also:* **age group**, **blood group**, **focus group**, **peer group**, **pressure group**.

**group²** /gruːp/ *verb* [I, T] to form a group or put people or things into a group or groups *The children are grouped according to their ability.*

**grouping** /ˈgruːpɪŋ/ *noun* [C] a group of people or things that have the same aims or qualities *regional groupings*

**grouse¹** /graʊs/ *noun* [C] **1** *plural* **grouse** a small, fat, brown bird that some people hunt for food **2** a small complaint about something

**grouse²** /graʊs/ *verb* [I] to complain about something

**grove** /grəʊv/ *noun* [C] a small group of trees *an olive grove*

**grovel** /'grɒvᵊl/ *verb* [I] UK **grovelling**, *past* **grovelled**, US **groveling**, *past* **groveled 1** to try very hard to be nice to someone important so that they will be nice to you or forgive you *She grovelled to the producer to get that part.* **2** to move around on your hands and knees *He was grovelling around on the floor.*

O⊷ **grow** /grəʊ/ *verb past t* **grew**, *past p* **grown 1** DEVELOP [I] to develop and become bigger or taller as time passes *Children grow very quickly.* **2** PLANT [I, T] If a plant grows, or you grow it, it develops from a seed to a full plant. *These shrubs grow well in sandy soil.* **3** INCREASE [I] to increase *The number of people living alone grows each year.* **4 grow tired/old/calm, etc** to gradually become tired/old/calm, etc *He grew bored of the countryside.* • *The music grew louder and louder.* **5** HAIR [I, T] If your hair or nails grow, or if you grow them, they get longer. *Mandy wants to grow her hair long.*

**grow into sb/sth** to develop into a particular type of person or thing *In the last few years, he's grown into a fine, responsible young man.*

**grow into sth** If a child grows into clothes, they gradually become big enough to wear them.

**grow on sb** If someone or something grows on you, you start to like them. *I didn't like her at first but she's grown on me over the years.*

**grow out of sth 1** If children grow out of clothes, they gradually become too big to wear them. *Adam's grown out of his shoes.* **2** to stop doing something as you get older *He still bites his nails, but hopefully he'll grow out of it.*

**grow up 1** to become older or an adult *She grew up in New York.* **2** to develop or become bigger or stronger *A close friendship had grown up between them.*

**grower** /'grəʊəʳ/ *noun* [C] someone who grows fruit or vegetables to sell to people

**growing** /'grəʊɪŋ/ *adj* increasing *A growing number of people are choosing to live alone.*

**growl** /graʊl/ *verb* [I] If a dog or similar animal growls, it makes a deep, angry noise in its throat. • **growl** *noun* [C]

**grown¹** /grəʊn/ *adj* **a grown man/woman** an adult, used especially when they are not behaving like an adult

**grown²** /grəʊn/ *past participle of* grow

**grown-up¹** /'grəʊnʌp/ *noun* [C] an adult, used especially when talking to children *Ask a grown-up to cut the shape out for you.*

**grown-up²** /'grəʊn,ʌp/ *adj* with the physical and mental development of an adult *Jenny has a grown-up son of 24.*

O⊷ **growth** /grəʊθ/ *noun* **1** [U, no plural] when something grows, increases, or develops *population growth* • *A balanced diet is essential for healthy growth.* **2** [C] something that grows on your skin or inside your body, that should not be there

**grub** /grʌb/ *noun* **1** [U] *informal* food **2** [C] a young, developing insect which has a fat, white tube shape

**grubby** /'grʌbi/ *adj* quite dirty *a grubby little boy*

**grudge¹** /grʌdʒ/ *noun* [C] a feeling of dislike or anger towards someone because of something they have done in the past *He is not the type of person to **bear a grudge** against anyone.*

**grudge²** /grʌdʒ/ *verb* [T] to not want to spend time or money or to give something to someone *He grudged the time he spent in meetings.*

**grudging** /'grʌdʒɪŋ/ *adj* done against your will, in a way that shows you do not want to do it *He treated her with grudging respect.* • **grudgingly** *adv*

**gruelling** UK (US **grueling**) /'gruːᵊlɪŋ/ *adj* Gruelling activities are very difficult and make you very tired. *a gruelling bicycle race*

**gruesome** /'gruːsəm/ *adj* very unpleasant or violent, usually involving injury or death *a gruesome murder*

**gruff** /grʌf/ *adj* sounding unfriendly *a gruff voice* • **gruffly** *adv*

**grumble** /'grʌmbl/ *verb* [I] to complain about something in a quiet but angry way *She's always **grumbling about** something.* • **grumble** *noun* [C]

**grumpy** /'grʌmpi/ *adj* easily annoyed and often complaining *a grumpy old man* • **grumpily** *adv* • **grumpiness** *noun* [U]

**grunt** /grʌnt/ *verb* **1** [I, T] to make a short, low sound instead of speaking, usually when you are angry or in pain **2** [I] If a pig grunts, it makes short, low sounds. • **grunt** *noun* [C]

**guarantee¹** /,gærᵊn'tiː/ *verb* [T] **guaranteeing**, *past* **guaranteed 1** to promise that something is true or will happen *Every child is guaranteed a place at a local school.* • [+ (that)] *We can't guarantee that it will happen in time.* **2** If a company guarantees its products, it makes a written promise to repair them or give you a new one if they have a fault. *The repair is guaranteed for 6 months.*

**guarantee²** /,gærᵊn'tiː/ *noun* [C, U] **1** a written promise made by a company to repair one of its products or give you a new one if it has a fault *a three-year guarantee* • *I'm afraid this camera is no longer **under guarantee**.* **2** a promise that something will be done or will happen [+ (that)] *There's no guarantee that it actually works.*

**guard¹** /gɑːd/ *noun* **1** PROTECT [C] someone whose job is to make certain someone does not escape or to protect a place or another person *a security guard* • *prison guards* **2** SOLDIERS [no plural] a group of soldiers or police officers who are protecting a person or place **3** TRAIN [C] UK (US **conductor**) someone who is in charge of a train **4** THING [C] something that covers or protects someone or something *a fire guard* **5 be on guard; stand guard** to be responsible for protecting a place or a person *Armed police stood guard outside the house.* **6 be under guard** to be kept in a place by a group of people who have weapons *The suspect is now under guard in the local hospital.* **7 catch sb off guard** to surprise someone by doing something when they are not ready to deal with it **8 be on (your) guard** to be ready to deal with something difficult that might happen

*Companies were warned to be on their guard for suspicious packages.*

**guard²** /gɑːd/ *verb* [T] **1** to protect someone or something from being attacked or stolen *Soldiers guarded the main doors of the embassy.* **2** to watch someone and make certain that they do not escape from a place *Five prison officers guarded the prisoners.*

**guard against sth** to try to make certain that something does not happen by being very careful *Regular exercise helps guard against heart disease.*

**guarded** /ˈgɑːdɪd/ *adj* careful not to give too much information or show how you really feel *a guarded response* ● **guardedly** *adv*

**guardian** /ˈgɑːdɪən/ *noun* [C] **1** someone who is legally responsible for someone else's child *The consent form must be signed by the child's parent or guardian.* **2** a person or organization that protects laws, principles, etc ● **guardianship** *noun* [U]

**guerrilla** /gəˈrɪlə/ *noun* [C] a member of an unofficial group of soldiers fighting to achieve their political beliefs *guerrilla warfare*

○➔**guess¹** /ges/ *verb* **1** [I, T] to give an answer or opinion about something without having all the facts *Can you guess how old he is?* ● *I would say he probably works in the media, but I'm just guessing.* **2** [I, T] to give a correct answer without having all the facts *"You've got a promotion!" "Yes, how did you guess?"* ● [+ (that)] *I'd never have guessed that you two were related.* **3 I guess** used when you think that something is probably true or likely *I've known her for about 12 years, I guess.* **4 I guess so/not** used when you agree/disagree but are not completely certain about something **5 Guess what?** something you say when you have some surprising news for someone *Guess what? I'm pregnant.*

**guess²** /ges/ *noun* [C] **1** an attempt to give the right answer when you are not certain what it is *How old do you think John is? Go on, (UK) have a guess/(US) take a guess.* ● *At a guess, I'd say there were about 70 people there.* **2** an opinion that you have formed by guessing *My guess is they'll announce their engagement soon.* **3 be anybody's guess** *informal* to be something that no one can be certain about *What happens after the election is anybody's guess.*

**guesswork** /ˈgeswɜːk/ *noun* [U] when you try to find an answer by guessing

○➔**guest** /gest/ *noun* [C] **1** VISITOR someone who comes to visit you in your home, at a party, etc *We've got some guests coming this weekend.* **2** HOTEL someone who is staying in a hotel *The hotel has accommodation for 200 guests.* **3** TV a famous person who takes part in a television programme or other entertainment *Our special guest tonight is George Michael.* **4 Be my guest.** something you say when you give someone permission to use something or do something

**guidance** /ˈgaɪdᵊns/ *noun* [U] help or advice *Students make choices about their future, with the guidance of their teachers.*

**guide¹** /gaɪd/ *noun* [C] **1** PERSON someone whose job is to show interesting places to visitors, or to help people get somewhere *a tour*

**guide²** BOOK a book that gives information about something or tells you how to do something *a hotel/restaurant guide* ● *a user's guide* **3** PLAN something that helps you plan or decide what to do [usually singular] *Parents use this report as a guide when choosing schools for their children.* **4 Guide** (*also* ,Girl 'Guide) a girl who belongs to an organization in the UK that teaches practical things like living outside, and how to work as part of a team **5 the Guides** an organization in the UK that teaches girls practical skills and how to work as part of a team

**guide²** /gaɪd/ *verb* [T] **1** to help someone or something go somewhere *These missiles are guided by computers.* ● *He gently guided her back to her seat.* **2** to tell someone what they should do *She had no one to guide her as a teenager.*

**guidebook** /ˈgaɪdbʊk/ *noun* [C] a book that gives visitors information about a particular place

**'guide ,dog** (*also US* seeing eye dog) *noun* [C] a dog that is trained to help blind people

**guidelines** /ˈgaɪdlaɪnz/ *noun* [plural] advice about how to do something *government guidelines on tobacco advertising*

**guild** /gɪld/ *noun* [C] an organization of people who have the same job or interests *the Designers' Guild*

**guile** /gaɪl/ *noun* [U] *formal* clever but sometimes dishonest behaviour that you use to deceive someone

**guillotine** /ˈgɪlətiːn/ *noun* [C] a piece of equipment used to cut off criminals' heads in the past ● **guillotine** *verb* [T]

**guilt** /gɪlt/ *noun* **1** FEELING the strong feeling of shame that you feel when you have done something wrong *He was overcome with guilt over what he had done.* **2** ILLEGAL the fact that someone has done something illegal *The prosecution must convince the jury of his guilt.* **3** WRONG the responsibility for doing something bad

**guilt-ridden** /ˈgɪltrɪdᵊn/ *adj* feeling very guilty

○➔**guilty** /ˈgɪlti/ *adj* **1** ashamed because you have done something wrong [+ about + doing sth] *I feel so guilty about not going to see them.* **2** having broken a law *The jury found her guilty* (= decided that she was guilty of a crime). ● *They found him guilty of rape.* ● **guiltily** *adv* ● **guiltiness** *noun* [U]

**guinea pig** /ˈgɪni,pɪg/ *noun* [C] **1** a small animal with long fur and no tail that people sometimes keep as a pet **2** *informal* someone who is used in a test for something such as a new medicine or product

**guise** /gaɪz/ *noun* [C] *formal* what something seems to be, although it is not *Banks are facing new competition in the guise of supermarkets.*

**guitar** /gɪˈtɑːʳ/ *noun* [C] a musical instrument

**guitar**

with strings that you play by pulling the strings with your fingers or a piece of plastic *an electric guitar*

**guitarist** /gɪ'tɑːrɪst/ *noun* [C] someone who plays the guitar, especially as their job

**gulf** /gʌlf/ *noun* [C] **1** a large area of sea that has land almost all the way around it *the Arabian Gulf* **2** an important difference between the opinions or situations of two groups of people *There is a growing **gulf between** the rich and the poor.*

**gull** /gʌl/ (*also* **seagull**) *noun* [C] a white or grey bird that lives near the sea and has a loud cry

**gullible** /'gʌlɪbl/ *adj* Someone who is gullible is easily tricked because they trust people too much. *How could you be so gullible?*

**gully** /'gʌli/ *noun* [C] a narrow valley which is usually dry except after a lot of rain

**gulp** /gʌlp/ *verb* **1** DRINK/EAT [T] (*also* **gulp down**) to drink or eat something quickly *I just had time to gulp down a cup of coffee before I left.* **2** BREATHE [I, T] to breathe in large amounts of air **3** SWALLOW [I, T] to swallow suddenly, sometimes making a noise, because you are nervous or surprised *She gulped when she saw him coming towards her.* • **gulp** *noun* [C] *He took a large gulp of tea.*

**gum¹** /gʌm/ *noun* **1** MOUTH [C] the hard, pink part inside your mouth that your teeth grow out of [usually plural] *Protect your teeth and gums by visiting your dentist regularly.* • **gum disease** **2** SWEET [U] (*also* **chewing gum**) a sweet substance that you chew (= bite repeatedly) but do not swallow *a stick of gum* **3** STICKY [U] a sticky substance like glue, used for sticking papers together ⊃ *See also:* **bubble gum.**

**gum²** /gʌm/ *verb* [T] **gumming**, *past* **gummed** *UK* to stick things together using glue

O⅃**gun¹** /gʌn/ *noun* **1** [C] a weapon that you fire bullets out of **2 jump the gun** to do something too soon, before you have thought about it carefully *Don't you think you're jumping the gun a bit – you've only known him for six weeks!* **3 stick to your guns** *informal* to refuse to change your ideas although other people try to make you ⊃ *See also:* **machine gun.**

**gun²** /gʌn/ *verb* **gunning**, *past* **gunned**
**gun sb down** to shoot someone and kill them or injure them badly *He was gunned down in front of his house.*

**gunboat** /'gʌnbəut/ *noun* [C] a small ship used during a war

**gunfire** /'gʌnfaɪə'/ *noun* [U] when guns are fired, or the noise that this makes *Neighbours heard gunfire and called the police.*

**gunman** /'gʌnmən/ *noun* [C] *plural* **gunmen** a criminal with a gun

**gunner** /'gʌnə'/ *noun* [C] a soldier or sailor whose job is to fire a large gun

**gunpoint** /'gʌnpɔɪnt/ *noun* **at gunpoint** with someone aiming a gun towards you *The hostages are being held at gunpoint.*

**gunpowder** /'gʌn,paudə'/ *noun* [U] an explosive powder

**gunshot** /'gʌnʃɒt/ *noun* [C] when a gun is fired *I*
heard a gunshot and rushed into the street. • *gunshot wounds to the chest*

**gurgle** /'gɜːgl/ *verb* [I] to make a sound like bubbling liquid *The baby was gurgling happily.* • **gurgle** *noun* [C]

**guru** /'guːruː/ *noun* [C] **1** someone whose opinion you respect because they know a lot about a particular thing **2** a teacher or leader in the Hindu religion

**gush¹** /gʌʃ/ *verb* [I, T] **1** If liquid gushes from an opening, it comes out quickly and in large amounts. *He ran down the street, blood gushing from a wound in his neck.* **2** to praise someone so much that they do not believe you are sincere *"Darling! I'm so excited!" she gushed.*

**gush²** /gʌʃ/ *noun* [C] **1** a large amount of liquid or gas that flows quickly **2** a sudden feeling of a particular emotion

**gust** /gʌst/ *verb* [I] If winds gust, they blow strongly. *Winds gusting to 50 mph brought down power cables.* • **gust** *noun* [C] *a gust of air* • **gusty** *adj*

**gusto** /'gʌstəu/ *noun* **with gusto** with a lot of energy and enthusiasm *Everyone joined in the singing with great gusto.*

**gut¹** /gʌt/ *noun* [C] the tube in your body that takes food from your stomach to be passed out as waste

**gut²** /gʌt/ *adj* **gut reaction/feeling/instinct** a reaction, feeling, etc that you feel certain is right, although you have no reason to think so *I had a gut feeling that he was going to come back.*

**gut³** /gʌt/ *verb* [T] **gutting**, *past* **gutted 1** to remove the organs from inside a fish or other animal **2** to completely destroy or remove the inside of a building *A fire gutted the bookshop last week.*

**guts** /gʌts/ *noun* [plural] *informal* **1** the bravery and determination that is needed to do something difficult or unpleasant *It took guts to stand up and tell the boss how she felt.* **2** the organs inside a person or animal's body **3 hate sb's guts** *informal* to dislike someone very much

**gutsy** /'gʌtsi/ *adj* brave and determined *a gutsy performance*

**gutted** /'gʌtɪd/ *adj* *UK informal* very disappointed and upset [+ (that)] *Neil's absolutely gutted that he's been dropped from the team.*

**gutter** /'gʌtə'/ *noun* [C] **1** a long, open pipe that is fixed to the edge of a roof to carry water away **2** the edge of a road where water flows away

**guy** /gaɪ/ *noun informal* **1** [C] a man *What a nice guy!* **2 guys** used when you are talking to or about two or more people *Come on, you guys, let's go home.*

**guzzle** /'gʌzl/ *verb* [I, T] *informal* to eat or drink a lot of something quickly *Who's guzzled all the beer?*

**gym** /dʒɪm/ *noun* **1** [C] a building with equipment for doing exercises *Nick goes to the gym three times a week.* **2** [U] exercises done inside, especially as a school subject

**gymnasium** /dʒɪm'neɪziəm/ *noun* [C] a gym

**gymnast** /'dʒɪmnæst/ *noun* [C] someone who does gymnastics *an Olympic gymnast*

**G**

**gymnastics** /dʒɪm'næstɪks/ *noun* [U] a sport in which you do physical exercises on the floor and on different pieces of equipment, often in competitions

**gynaecologist** *UK* (*US* **gynecologist**) /ˌgaɪnə'kɒlədʒɪst/ *noun* [C] a doctor who treats medical conditions that only affect women

**gynaecology** *UK* (*US* **gynecology**) /ˌgaɪnə'kɒlədʒi/ *noun* [U] the study and treatment of diseases and medical conditions that only affect women
● **gynaecological** /ˌgaɪnəkə'lɒdʒɪkəl/ *adj*

**gypsy** (*also UK* **gipsy**) /'dʒɪpsi/ *noun* [C] a member of a race of people who travel from place to place, especially in Europe *a gypsy caravan*

**gymnastics**

**G**

**H, h** /eɪtʃ/ the eighth letter of the alphabet

**ha** /hɑː/ *exclamation* something you say when you are surprised or pleased

o━**habit** /ˈhæbɪt/ *noun* **1** REGULAR ACTIVITY [C, U] something that you do regularly, almost without thinking about it *He's just eating out of habit – he's not really hungry.* ● *We don't want the children to get into the habit of watching a lot of TV.* **3** BAD ACTIVITY [C, U] something that you often do that is bad for your health or is annoying *He has some really nasty habits.* ● *We offer help to alcoholics who want to kick the habit.* **4** CLOTHING [C] a long, loose piece of clothing worn by some religious groups *a monk's habit*

**habitable** /ˈhæbɪtəbl/ *adj* A habitable building is in good enough condition to live in.

**habitat** /ˈhæbɪtæt/ *noun* [C] the natural environment of an animal or plant

**habitation** /ˌhæbɪˈteɪʃᵊn/ *noun* [U] when people live in a place *This place is not fit for human habitation.*

**habitual** /həˈbɪtʃuəl/ *adj* **1** usual or typical *an habitual expression/gesture* **2** doing something often because it is a habit *a habitual drug user* ● **habitually** *adv*

**hack¹** /hæk/ *verb* [I, T] **1** to cut something roughly into pieces *The victim had been hacked to death.* **2** to use a computer to illegally get into someone else's computer system and read the information that is kept there *Two British youths were caught hacking into government computers.*

**hack²** /hæk/ *noun* [C] *informal* someone who produces low quality writing for books, newspapers, etc

**hacker** /ˈhækəʳ/ *noun* [C] someone who illegally gets into someone else's computer system

**had** *strong form* /hæd/ *weak forms* /həd, əd, d/ *verb* **1** *past of* have **2** **be had** *informal* to be tricked or made to look silly *I think I've been had – this camera doesn't work.*

**haddock** /ˈhædək/ *noun* [C, U] *plural* **haddock** a fish that lives in northern seas and is eaten as food

**hadn't** /ˈhædᵊnt/ *short for* had not *I hadn't seen Megan since college.*

**haemophilia** UK (US **hemophilia**) /ˌhiːməˈfɪliə/ *noun* [U] a serious disease in which the flow of blood from someone's body cannot be stopped when they are hurt ● **haemophiliac** UK (US **hemophiliac**) *noun* [C] someone who has haemophilia

**haemorrhage** UK (US **hemorrhage**) /ˈhemᵊrɪdʒ/ *noun* [C, U] when someone suddenly loses a lot of blood *a brain haemorrhage*

**haemorrhoids** UK (US **hemorrhoids**) /ˈhemərɔɪdz/ *noun* [plural] painful swollen tissue around the opening of a person's bottom

**haggard** /ˈhægəd/ *adj* Someone who is haggard has a thin face with dark marks around their eyes because they are ill or tired. *The poor doctor was looking thin and haggard.*

**haggle** /ˈhægl/ *verb* [I] to argue, especially about the price of something *I spent 20 minutes haggling over the price of a leather bag.*

**ha 'ha** *exclamation* used in writing to represent the sound someone makes when they laugh

**hail¹** /heɪl/ *noun* **1** [U] small, hard pieces of frozen rain that fall from the sky **2 a hail of bullets/stones/bottles, etc** a lot of bullets/stones/bottles, etc that are fired or thrown at the same time

**hail²** /heɪl/ *verb* **1** [T] to call or wave to someone to get their attention *She stepped into the road and hailed a taxi.* **2 it hails** If it hails, small, hard pieces of frozen rain fall from the sky. *Look! It's hailing!*
**hail sb/sth as sth** to say publicly and enthusiastically that someone or something is something very good *He was hailed as a hero for rescuing the three-year-old from her burning home.*
**hail from** to come from a particular place *Joe originally hails from Toronto.*

o━**hair** /heəʳ/ *noun* **1** [U] the thin, thread-like parts that grow on your head *a girl with long, fair hair* ➲ *See colour picture* **Hair** *on page Centre 9.* **2** [C] one of the thin thread-like parts that grow on a person's or animal's skin *My black skirt was covered in cat hairs.* **3 let your hair down** *informal* to relax and enjoy yourself *I'd love to see Clare let her hair down for once.* **4 pull/tear your hair out** to be very anxious about something *When they still weren't home by midnight, I was pulling my hair out.* **5 split hairs** to argue about small details that are not important ➲ *See also:* **pubic hair**.

**hairbrush** /ˈheəbrʌʃ/ *noun* [C] a brush that you use to make your hair look tidy ➲ *See picture at* **brush**.

**haircut** /ˈheəkʌt/ *noun* [C] **1** when someone cuts your hair *I really need a haircut.* **2** the style in which your hair has been cut *I like your new haircut.*

**hairdo** /ˈheəduː/ *noun* [C] *informal* the style in which someone arranges their hair

**hairdresser** /ˈheəˌdresəʳ/ *noun* **1** [C] someone whose job is to wash, cut, colour, etc people's hair **2 hairdresser's** the place where you go to have your hair washed, cut, coloured, etc

**hairdryer** /ˈheəˌdraɪəʳ/ *noun* [C] a piece of electrical equipment for drying your hair with hot air

**-haired** /-ˈheəd/ *suffix* used after a word describing someone's hair *a red-haired woman* ● *a short-haired cat* ➲ *See also:* **fair-haired**.

**hairgrip** /ˈheəgrɪp/ UK (US **bobby pin**) *noun* [C] a small, thin piece of metal, used to fasten a woman's hair in position

**hairline** /ˈheəlaɪn/ *noun* **1** [C] the place at the top of your face where your hair starts growing **2 a hairline crack/fracture** a very thin line where something hard such as a bone or cup is broken

**hairpin** /ˈheəpɪn/ *noun* [C] a piece of metal shaped like a U, used to fasten a woman's hair in position

,hairpin 'bend UK (US ,hairpin 'turn) noun [C] a bend shaped like a U on a steep road

hair-raising /'heə,reɪzɪŋ/ adj frightening but in an enjoyable way It was a rather hair-raising journey down the mountain road.

hairstyle /'heəstaɪl/ noun [C] the style in which someone arranges their hair Do you like my new hairstyle?

hairy /'heəri/ adj 1 covered in hair a hairy chest • hairy legs 2 informal frightening or dangerous There were some rather hairy moments during the race. • hairiness noun [U]

halal /hæl'æl/ adj Halal meat is prepared according to Islamic law.

hale /heɪl/ adj hale and hearty healthy and full of life

○━half¹ /hɑːf/ noun, determiner plural halves 1 [C, U] one of two equal parts of something; 1/2; Rice is eaten by half of the world's population. • Divide the lemons into halves. • It'll take half an hour to get there. • Jenny lived in Beijing for a year and a half. 2 break/cut/split sth in half to divide something into two equal parts Divide the dough in half and roll it out into two circles. 3 decrease/increase, etc sth by half to make something smaller/larger, etc by half its size The drug reduces the risk of stroke by half. 4 half past one/two/three, etc mainly UK 30 minutes past one o'clock/two o'clock/three o'clock, etc We got back to our hotel at half past seven. 5 half one/two/three, etc UK informal 30 minutes past one o'clock/ two o'clock/three o'clock, etc "What time does it start?" "About half six." 6 go halves with sb informal to divide the cost of something with someone Shall we go halves on a present for Laura? 7 half the fun/time/pleasure, etc informal a large part of the enjoyment/time, etc Kids today – parents don't know where they are half the time. 8 not half as good/bad/ exciting, etc informal to be much less good/ bad/exciting, etc than something else Her new book's not half as good as the last one.

half² /hɑːf/ adv partly, but not completely half empty/full • Sophia is half Greek and half Spanish (= she has one Greek parent and one Spanish parent). • She was only half aware of what was happening.

,half 'board noun [U] mainly UK the price for a room in a hotel, which includes breakfast and dinner

half-brother /'hɑːf,brʌðəʳ/ noun [C] a brother who is the son of only one of your parents

half-hearted /,hɑːf'hɑːtɪd/ adj without much effort or interest a half-hearted attempt • half-heartedly adv

half-sister /'hɑːf,sɪstəʳ/ noun [C] a sister who is the daughter of only one of your parents

half-term /hɑːf't3ːm/ noun [C, U] UK a short holiday in the middle of a school term (= one of the periods the school year is divided into)

half-time /,hɑːf'taɪm/ noun [U] a short period of rest between the two halves of a game

halfway /,hɑːf'weɪ/ adj, adv at an equal distance between two places, or in the middle of a period of time the halfway point • He was released halfway through his prison sentence.

○━hall /hɔːl/ noun [C] 1 (also hallway /'hɔːlweɪ/) a room or passage in a building, which leads to other rooms I left my coat and umbrella in the hall. 2 a large room or building where meetings, concerts, etc are held The Albert Hall • The disco will be held in the school hall. ➔ See also: town hall.

hallmark /'hɔːlmɑːk/ noun [C] 1 an official mark that is put on something made of silver or gold to prove that it is real 2 a quality or method that is typical of a particular type of person or thing Simplicity is a hallmark of his design.

hallo UK (UK/US hello) /hə'ləʊ/ exclamation 1 used to greet someone Hallo, Chris, how are things? 2 used to start a conversation on the telephone Hallo, this is Alex.

,hall of 'residence UK (US dormitory) noun [C] plural halls of residence a building where university or college students live

hallowed /'hæləʊd/ adj 1 respected and considered important a hallowed tradition 2 made holy by a priest the hallowed ground of the churchyard

Halloween /,hæləʊ'iːn/ noun [U] the night of 31 October when children dress in special clothes and people try to frighten each other

hallucinate /hə'luːsɪneɪt/ verb [I] to see things that are not really there, because you are ill or have taken an illegal drug

hallucination /hə,luːsɪ'neɪʃᵊn/ noun [C, U] when you see things that are not really there because you are ill or have taken an illegal drug A high temperature can cause hallucinations.

halo /'heɪləʊ/ noun [C] a gold circle of light that is shown around the head of a holy person in a painting

halt¹ /hɒlt/ noun 1 [no plural] when something stops moving or happening The car came to a halt just inches from the edge of the cliff. • News of the accident brought the party to a halt. 2 call a halt to sth to officially order something to stop The government has called a halt to all new building in the area.

halt² /hɒlt/ verb [I, T] formal to stop or make something stop The council ordered that work on the project should be halted immediately.

halting /'hɒltɪŋ/ adj stopping often while you are saying or doing something, especially because you are nervous He spoke quietly, in halting English.

halve /hɑːv/ verb 1 [T] to divide something into two equal parts Peel and halve the potatoes. 2 [I, T] If you halve something, or if it halves, it is reduced to half the size it was before. They have almost halved the price of flights to New York.

ham /hæm/ noun [C, U] meat from a pig's back or upper leg a ham sandwich

hamburger /'hæm,b3ːgəʳ/ noun 1 [C] a round, flat shape of meat which is cooked in hot oil and eaten between round pieces of bread a hamburger and fries 2 [U] US (UK mince) beef (= meat from a cow) that is cut into very small pieces

hamlet /'hæmlət/ noun [C] a very small village

hammer¹ /'hæməʳ/ noun [C] a tool with a heavy, metal part at the top that you use to hit nails into something ➔ See picture at tool.

hammer² /'hæmə'/ *verb* [I, T] to hit something with a hammer *Could you hammer a nail into the wall to hang this picture up?*

**hammer sth into sb** to repeat something to someone a lot of times until they remember it *I've never forgotten my Latin verbs – they were hammered into me when I was at school.*

**hammer on sth** to hit something many times, making a lot of noise *They were woken up by someone hammering on the door.*

**hammer sth out** to finally agree on a plan, business agreement, etc after arguing about the details for a long time

hammering /'hæmᵊrɪŋ/ *noun* **1** [U] the noise made by hitting something with a hammer or hitting something hard with your hands **2** [no plural] *UK informal* a very bad defeat

hammock /'hæmək/ *noun* [C] a large piece of cloth or strong net that you hang between two trees or poles to sleep on

hamper¹ /'hæmpə'/ *verb* [T] to make it difficult for someone to do something *The police investigation was hampered by a lack of help from the community.*

hamper² /'hæmpə'/ *noun* [C] a large basket (= container made of thin pieces of wood) with a lid

hamster /'hæmstə'/ *noun* [C] a small animal with soft fur and no tail that is often kept as a pet

hamstring¹ /'hæmstrɪŋ/ *noun* [C] a tendon (= part that connects a muscle to a bone) at the back of the upper part of your leg *a hamstring injury*

hamstring² /'hæmstrɪŋ/ *verb* [T] *past* **hamstrung** to make it difficult for a person, team, or organization to do something

-hand /hænd/ ⊃ *See* **left-hand**, **right-hand**, **second-hand**.

o—hand¹ /hænd/ *noun* **1** [ARM] [C] the part of your body on the end of your arm that has fingers and a thumb *Take your hands out of your pockets.* ⊃ *See colour picture* **The Body** *on page Centre 2.* **2 take sb by the hand** to get hold of someone's hand *Bill took her by the hand and led her into the garden.* **3 hand in hand** holding each other's hand *The young couple walked hand in hand by the lake.* **4 hold hands** to hold each other's hand **5 at hand** near in time or space *Teachers are always close at hand to give help to any child who needs it.* **6 by hand** done or made by a person instead of a machine *This sweater has to be washed by hand.* **7 in hand** being worked on or dealt with now *Despite the pressures we are determined to get on with the job in hand.* **8 be in sb's hands** to be in someone's control or care *The matter is now in the hands of my solicitor.* **9 on hand** (*also UK* **to hand**) near to someone or something, and ready to help or be used when necessary *Extra supplies will be on hand, should they be needed.* **10 at the hands of sb** If you suffer at the hands of someone, they hurt you or treat you badly. **11** [CLOCK] [C] one of the long, thin pieces that point to the numbers on a clock or watch **12** [CARDS] [C] the set of playing cards that one player has been given in a game **13 a hand** some help, especially to do something practical *Could you give me a hand*

*with these suitcases?* • *I think Matthew might need a hand with his homework.* **14 on the one hand ... on the other hand** used when you are comparing two different ideas or opinions *On the one hand, computer games develop many skills, but on the other, they mean kids don't get enough exercise.* **15 hands off** *informal* used to tell someone not to touch something *Hands off – that's mine!* **16 change hands** to be sold by someone and bought by someone else *The hotel has changed hands twice since 1982.* **17 a free hand** permission to make your own decisions about how you want to do something *The students were given a free hand as far as designing their product was concerned.* **18 get out of hand** to become difficult to control *It was the end of term and the children were getting a little out of hand.* **19 go hand in hand** If two things go hand in hand, they exist together and are connected with each other. **20 have your hands full** to be very busy *Shelley has her hands full with three kids under 5.* **21 get/lay your hands on sth** to find something **22 get/gain the upper hand** to get into a stronger position than someone else so that you are controlling a situation *Government troops are gradually gaining the upper hand over the rebels.* **23 with your bare hands** without using a weapon or tool **24 wring your hands** to press your hands together because you are upset or worried about something

o—hand² /hænd/ *verb* **1** [+ two objects] to give something to someone *Could you hand me that book, please?* **2 you have to hand it to sb** *informal* used when you want to show that you admire someone *You have to hand it to Mick, he's done a good job on that kitchen.*

**hand sth back** to return something to the person who gave it to you *I was absent when the teacher handed back our homework.*

**hand sth down 1** to give toys, clothes, books, etc to children who are younger than you in your family **2** to pass traditions from older people to younger ones *a custom handed down through the generations*

**hand sth in** to give something to someone in a position of authority *Have you handed your history essay in yet?*

**hand sth out** to give something to all the people in a group *A girl was handing out leaflets at the station.*

**hand sb/sth over** to give someone or something to someone else *The hijacker was handed over to the French police.*

handbag /'hændbæg/ *mainly UK* (*mainly US* **purse**) *noun* [C] a bag carried by a woman with her money, keys, etc inside ⊃ *See picture at* **bag.**

handbook /'hændbʊk/ *noun* [C] a book that contains information and advice about a particular subject *a teacher's handbook*

handbrake /'hændbreɪk/ *UK* (*US* **emergency brake**) *noun* [C] a stick inside a car that you can pull up to stop the car from moving ⊃ *See colour picture* **Car** *on page Centre 3.*

handcuffs /'hændkʌfs/ *noun* [plural] two metal rings that are joined by a chain and are put on a prisoner's wrists (= lower arm)

-handed /'hændɪd/ *suffix* ⊃ *See* **empty-**

H

**handed, heavy-handed, left-handed, red-handed, right-handed, single-handed**.

**handful** /ˈhændfʊl/ noun **1** [C] the amount of something that you can hold in one hand **2 a handful of sth** a small number of people or things *Only a handful of people came to the meeting.* **3 a handful** *informal* someone who is difficult to control, especially a child *Daisy's only three and she's quite a handful.*

**handgun** /ˈhændgʌn/ noun [C] a small gun that you can hold in one hand

**handicap** /ˈhændɪkæp/ noun [C] **1** something that is wrong with your mind or body permanently *a mental/physical handicap* **2** something that makes it more difficult for you to do something *I found not having a car quite a handicap in the countryside.*

**handicapped** /ˈhændɪkæpt/ adj not able to use part of your body or your mind because it has been damaged in some way *mentally/physically handicapped*

**handicraft** /ˈhændɪkrɑːft/ noun **1** [C] an activity that involves making things with your hands and that needs skill and artistic ability **2 handicrafts** things that people make with their hands *a sale of handicrafts*

**handiwork** /ˈhændɪwɜːk/ noun [U] something that someone makes or does *She put down the brush and stood back to admire her handiwork.*

**handkerchief** /ˈhæŋkətʃiːf/ noun [C] a small piece of cloth or soft paper that you use to dry your eyes or nose

o-ʷ**handle¹** /ˈhændl/ verb [T] **1** DEAL WITH to deal with something *He handled the situation very well.* • *This office handles thousands of enquiries every day.* **2** TOUCH to touch, hold, or pick up something *You must wash your hands before handling food.* **3** BUY to buy and sell goods *He's been charged with handling stolen goods.*

**handle²** /ˈhændl/ noun **1** [C] the part of something that you use to hold it or open it *a door handle* • *the handle on a suitcase* **2 fly off the handle** *informal* to suddenly become very angry

**handle**

handle

**handlebars** /ˈhændlbɑːz/ noun [plural] the metal bars at the front of a bicycle or motorcycle that you hold onto to control direction

**handler** /ˈhændlə/ noun [C] someone whose job is to deal with or control a particular type of thing *a police dog handler*

'**hand ˌluggage** noun [U] small bags that you can carry onto an aircraft with you when you travel

**handmade** /ˌhændˈmeɪd/ adj made by hand instead of by machine

**handout** /ˈhændaʊt/ noun [C] **1** money or food that is given to people who are poor *Increasing numbers of people are dependent on government handouts.* **2** a copy of a document that is given to all the people in a class or meeting

**handpicked** /ˌhændˈpɪkt/ adj carefully chosen for a particular purpose or job *a handpicked audience*

**handshake** /ˈhændʃeɪk/ noun [C] the action of taking someone's right hand and shaking it when you meet or leave each other

**handsome** /ˈhændsəm/ adj **1** A handsome man is attractive. *tall, dark and handsome* **2 a handsome profit/sum, etc** a large amount of money

**hands-on** /ˌhændzˈɒn/ adj physically doing something and not only studying it or watching someone else do it *hands-on experience*

**handwriting** /ˈhændˌraɪtɪŋ/ noun [U] the way that someone forms the letters when they write with a pen or pencil

**handwritten** /ˌhændˈrɪtʰn/ adj written with a pen or pencil *a handwritten letter*

**handy** /ˈhændi/ adj **1** useful or easy to use *a handy container/tool* **2 come in handy** *informal* to be useful at some time in the future *Don't throw those jars away – they might come in handy.* **3** *UK informal* near to a place *It's a nice house and it's handy for the station.* **4 be handy with sth** to be good at using something, usually a tool *He's very handy with a paintbrush.*

**handyman** /ˈhændimæn/ noun [C] plural **handymen** someone who is good at making things or repairing them

o-ʷ**hang¹** /hæŋ/ verb past hung or hanged **1** FASTEN [I, T] to fasten something so that the top part is fixed but the lower part is free to move, or to be fastened in this way *He hung his coat on the hook behind the door.* **2** KILL [I, T] to kill someone by putting a rope around their neck and making them drop, or to die in this way *The poor woman tried to hang herself with her sheet.* **3** IN AIR [I] to stay in the air for a long time *Thick fog hung over the town.* ⊃ *See also:* hang in the **balance¹**, hang your **head¹** (in shame).

**hang around** *informal* (also UK **hang about**) **1** to spend time somewhere, usually without doing very much *There's nowhere for teenagers to go, so they just hang around on street corners.* **2 hang around with sb** to spend time with someone *I got into drugs because I was hanging around with the wrong people.*

**hang on 1** *informal* to wait for a short time *Hang on – I'm almost finished.* **2** to hold something tightly *Hang on, we're going over a big bump here.*

**hang onto sth** *informal* to keep something *You should hang onto that – it might be worth something.*

**hang out** *informal* to spend a lot of time in a particular place or with a particular group of people

**hang up** to finish a conversation on the telephone by putting the phone down

**hang sth up** to put something such as a coat somewhere where it can hang *You can hang up your jacket over there.*

**hang²** /hæŋ/ *noun* **get the hang of sth** *informal* to gradually learn how to do or use something

**hangar** /'hæŋgəʳ/ *noun* [C] a large building where aircraft are kept

**hanger** /'hæŋəʳ/ (*also* **coat hanger**) *noun* [C] a wire, wooden, or plastic object for hanging clothes on

**'hang ,glider** *noun* [C] a structure covered in cloth that you hold onto and float through the air

**'hang ,gliding** *noun* [U] the sport of flying using a structure covered in cloth that you hang from

**hangover** /'hæŋəʊvəʳ/ *noun* [C] If you have a hangover, you feel ill because you drank too much alcohol the evening before.

**hanker** /'hæŋkəʳ/ *verb*

**hanker after/for sth** to want something very much, especially over a long period of time *I might buy him that CD player he's been hankering after.*

**hankie** (*also* **hanky**) /'hæŋki/ *noun* [C] *informal* short for handkerchief

**Hanukkah** /'hɒnəkə/ *noun* [U] the special Jewish period of celebration held in December

**haphazard** /ˌhæp'hæzəd/ *adj* not planned, organized, controlled, or done regularly *The whole examination process seemed completely haphazard.* • **haphazardly** *adv*

**hapless** /'hæpləs/ *adj literary* having bad luck

o⊸**happen** /'hæpʰn/ *verb* [I] **1** If an event or situation happens, it exists or starts to be done, usually by chance. *Were you anywhere nearby when the accident happened?* • *We can't let a mistake like this happen again.* **2** to be the result of an action, situation, or event that someone or something experiences *Did you hear what happened to Jamie last night?* • *What happens if we can't get enough tickets?* **3 happen to do sth** to do something by chance *If you happen to see Peter, say "hi" for me.* • *You don't happen to know her phone number, do you?* **4 as it happens; it so happens** something that you say in order to introduce a surprising fact *As it happens, her birthday is the day after mine.*

**happen on/upon sth/sb** to find something or meet someone without planning to *When clearing out my desk I happened upon an old photo of us.*

**happening** /'hæpʰnɪŋ/ *noun* [C] something that happens, often a strange event that is difficult to explain

**happily** /'hæpɪli/ *adv* **1** HAPPY in a happy way *happily married* **2** WILLING in a way that is very willing *I'd happily drive you to the airport.* **3** LUCKY having a good or lucky result *Happily, the operation was a complete success.*

**happiness** /'hæpɪnəs/ *noun* [U] the feeling of being happy *Your happiness is all that matters to me.*

o⊸**happy** /'hæpi/ *adj* **1** PLEASED pleased and in a good mood, especially because something good

has happened *I'm glad you've finally found someone who makes you happy.* • *Jean seems much happier now that she's moved out.* **2 happy to do sth** to be willing to do something *I'd be very happy to help, if you need a hand.* **3** SHOWING HAPPINESS making you feel happy, or expressing happiness *a big, happy smile* • *Did the book have a happy ending?* **4** SATISFIED satisfied and not worried *Are you **happy with** your exam results?* • *I'm not very **happy about** you travelling alone at night.* **5 Happy Birthday/ New Year, etc** something friendly that you say to someone on a special day or holiday *Happy Christmas!* ⊃ *Opposite* **unhappy**.

**happy-go-lucky** /ˌhæpɪgəʊ'lʌki/ *adj* not worried and not having any responsibilities

**harass** /'hærəs, hə'ræs/ *verb* [T] to continue to annoy or upset someone over a period of time *Stop harassing me!*

**harassed** /'hærəst/ *adj* tired and feeling anxious *harassed passengers*

**harassment** /'hærəsmənt/ *noun* [U] behaviour that annoys or upsets someone *sexual harassment*

**harbour¹** *UK* (*US* **harbor**) /'hɑːbəʳ/ *noun* [C] an area of water near the coast where ships are kept and are safe from the sea

**harbour²** *UK* (*US* **harbor**) /'hɑːbəʳ/ *verb* [T] **1** If you harbour doubts, hopes, thoughts, etc, you feel or think about them for a long time. *He harboured dreams of one day becoming a professional footballer.* **2** to hide someone or something bad *to harbour a criminal*

o⊸**hard¹** /hɑːd/ *adj* **1** FIRM firm and stiff, and not easy to press or bend *a hard surface* • *The seats in the waiting room were hard and uncomfortable.* **2** DIFFICULT difficult to do or understand [+ to do sth] *It must be hard to study with all this noise.* • *Actually, the exam wasn't that hard.* • *Quitting my job was the hardest decision I ever had to make.* **3** WITH EFFORT using or done with a lot of effort *the long, hard struggle* • *With a bit of hard work and determination we might still finish on time.* **4** UNPLEASANT full of problems and difficult to deal with *My grandparents had a very hard life.* • *The past few months must've been really hard for you.* **5** NOT KIND not gentle or kind *She had a cold, hard look in her eyes.* **6 be hard on sb** **a** to criticize someone too much or treat them unfairly *You shouldn't be so hard on yourself.* **b** to make someone unhappy by causing them problems *Our divorce has been particularly hard on the children.* **7 be hard on sth** to damage something or make it have problems *Stress can be hard on any relationship.* **8 do/learn sth the hard way** to do or learn something by experiencing a lot of problems or difficulty ⊃ *See also:* give sb a hard **time¹**.

o⊸**hard²** /hɑːd/ *adv* **1** with a lot of effort *She tried very hard but she wasn't quite fast enough.* • *You'll have to work harder, if you want to pass this exam.* **2** with a lot of force *It's been raining hard all day.* • *She kicked the ball as hard as she could.* **3 die hard** If a belief, custom, or habit dies hard, it is very difficult to change. *I'm afraid that old habits die hard.* **4 hit sb hard** *UK* If a situation or experience hits you hard, it makes you so upset that you have difficulty dealing with it. *Her death has hit us all very hard.*

**hardback** /'hɑːdbæk/ *noun* [C] a book that has a thick, stiff cover

**hard-boiled** /,hɑːd'bɔɪld/ *adj* A hard-boiled egg has been boiled with its shell on, until the inside is solid.

,**hard 'cash** *noun* [U] coins and paper money

,**hard 'copy** *UK* (*US* '**hard ,copy**) *noun* [C, U] information from a computer that has been printed on paper

**hardcore** (*also* **hard-core**) /'hɑːd,kɔː/ *adj* **1** extremely loyal to someone or something, and not willing to change *a hard-core following* **2** Hardcore magazines, films, etc show very active or offensive sexual acts. *hardcore pornography*

,**hard 'core** *noun* [no plural] a small group of people in society or an organization who are very active and determined not to change *a hard core of activists*

,**hard 'currency** *noun* [U] money that is valuable and can be exchanged easily because it comes from a powerful country

,**hard 'disk** *UK* (*US* '**hard ,disk**) (*also* '**hard ,drive**) *noun* [C] the part inside a computer that is not removed and stores very large amounts of information

,**hard 'drugs** *noun* [plural] very strong, illegal drugs

**harden** /'hɑːdᵊn/ *verb* [I, T] **1** to become hard and stiff, or to make something become hard and stiff *This island is formed from volcanic lava that has hardened into rock.* **2** to stop feeling emotions about someone or something, so that you seem less kind, gentle, or *hardened criminals*

**hard-headed** /,hɑːd'hedɪd/ *adj* very determined, and not willing to be influenced by your emotions *a hard-headed manager*

**hard-hearted** /,hɑːd'hɑːtɪd/ *adj* not caring how other people feel

**hard-hitting** /,hɑːd'hɪtɪŋ/ *adj* A hard-hitting speech, report, article, etc is very severe or criticizes someone or something a lot.

,**hard 'line** *noun* [no plural] when someone is very strict and severe *Judge Tucker has a reputation for **taking a hard line on** criminals.* • hardline /,hɑːd'laɪn/ *adj a hardline policy on illegal immigrants*

o★**hardly** /'hɑːdli/ *adv* **1** almost not, or only a very small amount *I was so tired that I could hardly walk.* • *We've **hardly** ever spoken to each other.* • *There's **hardly any** food left in the fridge.* **2** used to emphasize that you think something is not likely, true, possible, etc *I hardly think she'll want to talk to me now that I have a new girlfriend.*

**USAGE**

**hardly**

Remember not to use two negative words together. Hardly (= almost not) already has a negative meaning so you do not need 'not' in the same sentence.

*She could hardly speak.*

~~She couldn't hardly speak.~~

**hard-nosed** /,hɑːd'nəʊzd/ *adj* very determined, and not willing to be influenced by your emotions *a hard-nosed lawyer*

**hard-pressed** /,hɑːd'prest/ *adj* **1** **be hard-pressed to do sth** to not be able to do something, or have difficulty doing something *You'd be hard-pressed to find a better worker than Jeff.* **2** having problems because you are poor *hard-pressed farmers*

**hardship** /'hɑːdʃɪp/ *noun* [C, U] a problem or situation that makes you suffer a lot, especially because you are very poor *They have suffered years of financial hardship.*

,**hard 'shoulder** *UK* (*US* **shoulder**) *noun* [C] the area on the edge of a main road where a car can stop in an emergency

,**hard 'up** *adj informal* not having enough money

**hardware** /'hɑːdweəʳ/ *noun* [U] **1** the machines or equipment that your computer system is made from, not the programs **2** tools and strong equipment, such as those used in the home or garden

**hard-working** /,hɑːd'wɜːkɪŋ/ *adj* doing a job seriously and with a lot of effort *He's always been hard-working and conscientious.*

**hardy** /'hɑːdi/ *adj* strong enough to deal with bad conditions or difficult situations

**hare** /heəʳ/ *noun* [C] an animal like a large rabbit that can run very fast and has long ears

**harem** /'hɑːriːm ⓤⓢ 'herəm/ *noun* [C] a group of women who live with or are married to one man in some Muslim societies, or the place where these women live

o★**harm¹** /hɑːm/ *noun* **1** [U] hurt or damage *Smoking can cause serious harm to the lungs.* • *Alan would never **do** anyone any **harm**.* **2** **not come to any harm** to not be hurt or damaged **3** **not do any harm** to not be a bad thing to do and possibly be a good thing [+ to do sth] *It wouldn't do any harm to have another look.* **4** **there's no harm in doing sth** used to say that something is not a bad thing to do and could possibly have a good effect *I suppose there's no harm in trying.* **5** **not mean any harm** to not intend to hurt someone or damage something *I never meant him any harm, I just wanted him to leave me alone.* **6** **out of harm's way** safe from a dangerous place or situation

o★**harm²** /hɑːm/ *verb* [T] to hurt someone or damage something *Thankfully no one was harmed in the accident.*

**harmful** /'hɑːmfᵊl/ *adj* causing or likely to cause harm *Doctors believe that smoking is harmful to your health.*

**harmless** /'hɑːmləs/ *adj* **1** not able or not likely to cause any hurt or damage *Taken in small doses, this drug is completely harmless.* **2** not likely to shock or upset people *Their jokes seemed harmless enough.* • harmlessly *adv*

**harmonica** /hɑː'mɒnɪkə/ *noun* [C] a small musical instrument that you blow into as you move it across your mouth

**harmonious** /hɑː'məʊniəs/ *adj* **1** friendly and peaceful *a harmonious business relationship* **2** having or making a pleasant sound

**harmonize** (*also UK* -**ise**) /'hɑːmənaɪz/ *verb* [I, T] **1** to be suitable together, or to make different people, plans, situations, etc suitable for each other *The gardens had been designed to harmonize with the natural landscape.* **2** to sing or play music in harmony

**harmony** /'hɑːməni/ *noun* **1** [U] when people are peaceful and agree with each other, or when different things seem right or suitable together *living together in peace and harmony* **2** [C, U] a pleasant sound in music, made by playing or singing a group of different notes together

**harness¹** /'hɑːnɪs/ *noun* [C] **1** a set of straps fastened around a horse's body and connecting it to a vehicle that it will pull **2** a set of strong, flat ropes that fasten equipment to your body or fasten you to a vehicle to prevent you from moving too much *All climbers must wear safety harnesses and helmets.*

**harness²** /'hɑːnɪs/ *verb* [T] **1** to put a harness on a horse, or to connect a horse to a vehicle using a harness **2** to control something so that you can use its power or qualities for a particular purpose

**harp¹** /hɑːp/ *noun* [C] a large wooden musical instrument with many strings that you play with your fingers

**harp²** /hɑːp/ *verb*
**harp on (about sb/sth)** to talk about someone or something too much *I don't see why you have to keep harping on about money.*

**harpoon** /ˌhɑː'puːn/ *noun* [C] a weapon with a sharp point, used especially for hunting whales (= large sea animals)

**harrowing** /'hærəʊɪŋ/ *adj* making you feel extremely frightened or upset *a harrowing experience*

**harsh** /hɑːʃ/ *adj* **1** CRUEL cruel, unkind, or unpleasant in a way that seems unfair *harsh criticism/punishment* • *Taking him out of the game was bit harsh.* **2** DIFFICULT very cold, dangerous, or unpleasant and difficult to live in *harsh conditions* **3** STRONG too strong, bright, loud, etc *harsh chemicals* • *harsh lighting* • **harshly** *adv* • **harshness** *noun* [U]

**harvest¹** /'hɑːvɪst/ *noun* **1** [C, U] when crops are cut and collected from fields **2** [C] the quality or amount of crops that are collected

**harvest²** /'hɑːvɪst/ *verb* [I, T] to cut and collect crops when they are ready

**has** *strong form* /hæz/ *weak forms* /həz, əz, z/ *present simple he/she/it of* have

**has-been** /'hæzbiːn/ *noun* [C] *informal* someone who was famous or important in the past but is now ignored

**hash** /hæʃ/ *noun* **make a hash of sth** *UK informal* to do something very badly

**hashish** /hæʃ'iːʃ/ (*also* **hash**) *noun* [U] an illegal drug that is usually smoked for pleasure

**hasn't** /'hæzªnt/ *short for* has not *It hasn't rained for three weeks.*

**hassle¹** /'hæsl/ *noun* [C, U] **1** something that is annoying because it is difficult or unpleasant to do *I don't want to drive – it's such a hassle finding a place to park.* **2** an argument or fight *They aren't giving you any hassle, are they?*

**hassle²** /'hæsl/ *verb* [T] to annoy someone, especially by asking them something again and again *He's always hassling me about money.*

**haste** /heɪst/ *noun* [U] when you are in a hurry

and do something more quickly than you should *In their haste to escape, they left behind all their belongings.*

**hasten** /'heɪsªn/ *verb* **1** [T] to make something happen faster than usual **2 hasten to do sth** to hurry to do or say something *I was not, I hasten to add, the only male there.*

**hasty** /'heɪsti/ *adj* done very quickly, usually too quickly and without thinking enough *a hasty decision/remark* • **hastily** *adv*

o﹣**hat** /hæt/ *noun* [C] something you wear to cover your head, for fashion or protection *a cowboy hat* ➔ *See colour picture* **Clothes** *on page Centre 5.* ➔ *See also:* **bowler hat, top hat.**

**hatch¹** /hætʃ/ *verb* **1** [I, T] If an egg hatches or is hatched, it is broken open by a baby creature such as a bird, fish, or snake being born. **2 hatch a plan/plot, etc** to plan something secretly, especially something bad *He hatched a plot to kill his wife.*

**hatch²** /hætʃ/ *noun* [C] a small door or opening, especially in a ship, aircraft, or spacecraft *an escape hatch*

**hatchback** /'hætʃbæk/ *noun* [C] a car that has a large door at the back, which you lift up to open

**hatchet** /'hætʃɪt/ *noun* **1** [C] a small axe (= tool for cutting wood) **2 bury the hatchet** to forget about your arguments and become friends with someone again

o﹣**hate¹** /heɪt/ *verb* [T] **1** to dislike someone or something very much *They've hated each other since they were kids.* • [+ doing sth] *He hates going to the dentist's.* • [+ to do sth] *I hate to see you look so upset.* **2** used to emphasize that you are sorry you have to do something *I hate to interrupt, John, but we need to leave.* ➔ *See also:* **hate sb's guts.**

**hate²** /heɪt/ *noun* [U] when you dislike someone or something very much ➔ *See also:* **pet hate.**

**hateful** /'heɪtfªl/ *adj* extremely unpleasant or unkind *She called me the most hateful names.*

**hatred** /'heɪtrɪd/ *noun* [U] when you dislike someone or something very much *He developed an intense hatred of all women.*

**'hat ,trick** *noun* [C] when a player or team has three successes, one after the other, especially three goals in a game

**haughty** /'hɔːti/ *adj* showing that you think you are much better or more important than other people *a haughty young actress* • **haughtily** *adv*

**haul¹** /hɔːl/ *verb* [T] to pull something somewhere slowly and with difficulty *They hauled the piano into the living room.*

**haul²** /hɔːl/ *noun* **1** [C] an amount of something that has been stolen or that is owned illegally *a haul of arms/drugs* **2 be a long haul** to be difficult and take a long time *His return to health will be a long haul.*

**haulage** /'hɔːlɪdʒ/ *noun* [U] *UK* the business of moving things by road or railway *a road haulage firm*

**haunt¹** /hɔːnt/ *verb* [T] **1** If a ghost haunts a place, it appears there often. *a haunted house* **2** If an unpleasant memory or feeling haunts you, you think about or feel it often. [often passive] *He was haunted by memories of the war.*

**haunt²** /hɔːnt/ *noun* [C] a place that someone visits often *Regents Park is one of my favourite haunts in London.*

**haunting** /ˈhɔːntɪŋ/ *adj* beautiful, but in a sad way *the haunting beauty of Africa*

o━**have¹** *strong form* /hæv/ *weak forms* /həv, əv, v/ *auxiliary verb* used with the past participle of another verb to form the present and past perfect tenses *Have you seen Roz?* • *I've passed my test.* • *He hasn't visited London before.* • *It would have been better to tell the truth.* • *He's been working in France for two years now.* • *I had met his wife before.*

---

**USAGE**

**have**

| present tense | past tense |
|---|---|
| *I have (I've)* | *I had* |
| *you have (you've)* | *you had* |
| *he/she/it has (he's/she's/it's)* | *he/she/it had* |
| *we have (we've)* | *we had* |
| *you have (you've)* | *you had* |
| *they have (they've)* | *they had* |

past participle

| *had* | *He has had a bad car accident.* |
|---|---|

present participle

| *having* | *He is having some problems at school.* |
|---|---|

short negative forms

| *haven't* | *hasn't* | *hadn't* |
|---|---|---|

---

o━**have²** /hæv/ *modal verb* **have to do sth; have got to do sth 1** to need to do something or be forced to do something *I have to go to Manchester tomorrow.* • *Do we have to finish this today?* • *They've had to change their plans.* **2** used when you are telling someone how to do something *You've got to type in your name, then your password.* **3** used to say that you feel certain that something is true or will happen *Interest rates have to come down at some point.* • *There's* (= there has) *got to be a better way of doing this.* ⊃ *See study section* **Modal verbs** *on page Centre 31.*

o━**have³** *strong form* /hæv/ *weak forms* /həv, əv, v/ *verb* **1** OWN [T] (*also* **have got**) to own something *I have two horses.* • *Laura has got beautiful blue eyes.* **2** HOLD [T] used to say that someone is holding something, or that someone or something is with them *He had a pen in his hand.* • *She had a baby with her.* **3** BE ILL [T] (*also* **have got**) If you have a particular illness, you are suffering from it. *Have you ever had the measles?* **4** EAT/DRINK [T] to eat or drink something *We are having dinner at 7 o'clock.* • *Can I have a drink of water?* **5 have a bath/sleep/walk, etc** used with nouns to say that someone does something *Can I have a quick shower?* • *Let Mark have a try.* **6 have difficulty/fun/problems, etc** used with nouns to say that someone experiences something *We had a great time in Barcelona.* **7 have a baby** to give birth to a baby **8 have sth done** If you have something done, someone does it for you.

*I'm having my hair cut tomorrow.* • *We had the carpets cleaned.* **9 have had it** to be broken or not working well *I think the car engine's had it.* **10 have it in for sb** to be determined to harm or criticize someone **11 have it out (with sb)** to talk to someone about something they have done which makes you angry, in order to try to solve the problem

**have (got) sth on** to be wearing something *She only had a bikini on.*

**have sb on** *UK* to make someone think that something is true, as a joke *He's not really angry – he's just having you on.*

**have sth out** to have something removed from your body *I'm having two teeth out next week.*

**haven** /ˈheɪvən/ *noun* [C] a safe place *a haven for wildlife*

**haven't** /ˈhævənt/ *short for* have not *I haven't finished eating.*

**havoc** /ˈhævək/ *noun* [U] a very confused and possibly dangerous situation *The snow has caused havoc on Scotland's roads today.*

**hawk** /hɔːk/ *noun* [C] a large hunting bird

**hay** /heɪ/ *noun* [U] dried grass for animals to eat

**'hay ˌfever** *noun* [U] an illness caused by a bad reaction to plants that some people get in the summer, especially affecting the nose and eyes

**haystack** /ˈheɪstæk/ *noun* [C] a large pile of hay

**hazard¹** /ˈhæzəd/ *noun* **1** [C] something that is dangerous *a fire hazard* • *a health hazard* **2 an occupational hazard** something unpleasant that happens to people who do a particular job

**hazard²** /ˈhæzəd/ *verb* **hazard a guess** to risk guessing something *I don't know where he is, but I'd be willing to hazard a guess.*

**hazardous** /ˈhæzədəs/ *adj* dangerous *hazardous chemicals*

**haze** /heɪz/ *noun* [U] when the air is not very clear because of something such as heat or smoke, making it difficult to see well

**hazel** /ˈheɪzəl/ *adj* green-brown in colour *hazel eyes*

**hazy** /ˈheɪzi/ *adj* **1** If the air is hazy, it is not very clear because of something such as heat or smoke, making it difficult to see well. *a hazy day* **2** not remembering things clearly *He has only a hazy recollection of what happened.*

o━**he** *strong form* /hiː/ *weak form* /hi/ *pronoun* used as the subject of the verb when referring to someone male who has already been talked about *"When is Paul coming?" "He'll be here in a minute."*

o━**head¹** /hed/ *noun* [C] **1** BODY the part of your body above your neck which contains your brain, eyes, ears, mouth, nose, etc and on which your hair grows *He fell and hit his head on the table.* ⊃ *See colour picture* **The Body** *on page Centre 2.* **2** MIND your mind *All these thoughts were going round in my head.* **3** ORGANIZATION the person who is in charge of an organization *Her father is the head of an oil company.* **4** SCHOOL (*also* ˌhead **'teacher**) *UK* the person in charge of a school *You'll have to ask the head if you can have a day off school.* **5** FRONT/TOP the front or top part of something *Who is that at the head of the table?* **6 £10/$6, etc a head** costing £10/$6, etc for each person *The meal costs £20 a head.* **7 heads** the side of a coin that has a picture of someone's head on it *Heads or tails?* **8 be banging your head against a brick wall** to do, say, or ask for something repeatedly but to be unable to change a situation *I keep asking her not to park there, but it's like banging my head against a brick wall.* **9 come to a head** If a problem or disagreement comes to a head, it becomes so bad that you have to start dealing with it. **10 go over sb's head** to be too difficult for someone to understand *All this talk about philosophy went right over my head.* **11 go to your head** If something that you have achieved goes to your head, it makes you too proud. *Fame and fortune had gone to his head.* **12 hang your head (in shame)** to look ashamed or embarrassed **13 keep your head** to stay calm in a difficult situation **14 lose your head** to stop being calm in a difficult situation **15 raise/rear its ugly head** If a problem or something unpleasant raises its ugly head, it becomes a problem that people have to deal with. **16 laugh/shout/scream, etc your head off** to laugh/shout/scream, etc very much and very loudly ➲ *See also:* hit the **nail¹** on the head, a **roof** over your head, off the **top¹** of your head.

**head²** /hed/ *verb* **1 head back/down/towards, etc** to move in a particular direction *They headed back to the shore.* **2** [LEAD] [T] to lead an organization or group [often passive] *The company is headed by a young entrepreneur.* **3** [FRONT/TOP] [T] to be at the front or top of something *Jo headed a very short list of candidates.* **4** [HIT] [T] to hit a ball with your head *Owen headed the ball straight into the back of the net.*

**be heading for sth** to be likely to get or experience something soon *Those children are heading for trouble.*

**head off** to start a journey or leave a place *What time are you heading off?*

**headache** /'hedeɪk/ *noun* [C] pain inside your head *I've got a bad headache.* ➲ *See also:* **splitting headache**.

**heading** /'hedɪŋ/ *noun* [C] words at the top of a piece of writing that tell you what it is about

**headlight** /'hedlaɪt/ *noun* [C] one of the two large lights on the front of a car ➲ *See picture at* **light**.

**headline** /'hedlaɪn/ *noun* **1** [C] the title of a newspaper story that is printed in large letters above it *a front-page headline* **2 the headlines** the main stories in newspapers, on television, etc *That story made headlines all over the world.*

**headlong** /'hedlɒŋ/ *adv* quickly and directly *The plane plunged headlong into the sea.*

**headmaster** /ˌhed'mɑːstəʳ/ *UK* (*US* **principal**) *noun* [C] a man who is in charge of a school

**headmistress** /ˌhed'mɪstrəs/ *UK* (*US* **principal**) *noun* [C] a woman who is in charge of a school

**head 'on** *adv* **1** If two vehicles hit each other head on, the front parts hit each other as they are moving forward. **2** If you deal with something head on, you deal with it directly, although it is difficult. • **head-on** /ˌhed'ɒn/ *adj a head-on collision*

**headphones** /'hedfəʊnz/ *noun* [plural] a piece of equipment that you wear over your ears so that you can listen to music without anyone else hearing it *a pair of headphones*

**headphones**

**headquarters** /'hedˌkwɔːtəz/ *noun* [group] *plural* **headquarters** the place from where an organization is controlled *police headquarters*

**headstone** /'hedstəʊn/ *noun* [C] a stone that shows the name of a dead person who is buried under it

**headstrong** /'hedstrɒŋ/ *adj* extremely determined *a headstrong young girl*

**headteacher** /ˌhed'tiːtʃəʳ/ *UK* (*US* **principal**) *noun* [C] the person in charge of a school

**headway** /'hedweɪ/ *noun* **make headway** to make progress in what you are doing *The builders aren't making much headway with our new house.*

**heady** /'hedi/ *adj* having a powerful effect on the way you feel, for example by making you feel excited *a heady experience*

**heal** /hiːl/ (*also* **heal up**) *verb* [I, T] If a wound or broken bone heals, it becomes healthy again, and if something heals it, it makes it healthy again. *The wound on his head had begun to heal.* • **healer** *noun* [C] someone who makes ill people well again using something such as prayer or magic

o⟶ **health** /helθ/ *noun* [U] **1** the condition of your body *to be in good/poor health* • *Regular exercise is good for your health.* **2** how successful and strong something is *the financial health of the business* ➲ *See also:* **the National Health Service**.

**health-care** /'helθ,keəʳ/ *noun* [U] the set of services provided by a country or an organization for treating people who are ill

o⟶ **healthy** /'helθi/ *adj* **1** [PHYSICALLY STRONG] physically strong and well *Sue is a normal healthy child.* **2** [GOOD] good for your health *a healthy diet* **3** [SUCCESSFUL] successful and strong *a healthy economy* ➲ *Opposite* **unhealthy**.

**heap¹** /hiːp/ *noun* **1** [C] an untidy pile of things *a heap of rubbish* **2 heaps of sth** *informal* a lot of something *He's got heaps of money.*

**heap²** /hiːp/ *verb informal* **1** [T] to put things into an untidy pile *He heaped more food onto his plate.* **2 heap criticism/insults/praise, etc on sb** to criticize/insult/praise, etc someone a lot

o⟶ **hear** /hɪəʳ/ *verb past* **heard 1** [SOUND] [I, T] to be aware of a sound through your ears *I could hear his voice in the distance.* • *I can't hear – can you turn the sound up?* **2** [INFORMATION] [I, T] to be told some information *When did you first hear about this?* • *Have you heard the news? Jane's back.* • [+ (that)] *I hear that you're leaving.* **3** [LAW] [T] If a judge hears a case, they listen to it in a law court, to decide if someone is guilty or not.

**4 will not hear of sth** If someone will not hear of something, they will not allow it. *I wanted to pay for her meal but she wouldn't hear of it.*

**hear from sb** to receive a letter, telephone call, or other message from someone *Have you heard from Sue recently?*

**have heard of sb/sth** to know that someone or something exists *I've never heard of her.*

**hearing** /ˈhɪərɪŋ/ *noun* **1** [U] the ability to hear sounds *He lost his hearing when he was a child.* **2** [C] a meeting in a law court when a judge hears the facts of a case *The preliminary hearing will take place next week.* **3 a fair hearing** If you get a fair hearing, someone listens to your opinion. *He felt that his teachers did not give him a fair hearing.*

**hearsay** /ˈhɪəseɪ/ *noun* [U] things that people have told you and that may or may not be true *Everything we heard was based on hearsay and rumour.*

**hearse** /hɜːs/ *noun* [C] a large car that is used to take a dead body to a funeral

o━**heart** /hɑːt/ *noun* **1** ORGAN [C] the organ inside your chest that sends blood around your body *Isabel's heart was beating fast.* • *heart disease/failure* **2** CENTRE [no plural] the centre of something *Her office is in the heart of Tokyo.* **3 the heart of sth** the most important part of something *We need to get to the heart of the matter.* **4** FEELINGS [C, U] someone's deepest feelings and true character *She has a kind heart.* **5** SHAPE [C] a shape that is used to mean love ➲ *See picture at* **shape. 6 hearts** playing cards with red, heart shapes on them **7 at heart** used to say what someone is really like *I'm just a kid at heart.* **8 in your heart** used to say what you really think *In his heart he felt they were wrong.* **9 with all your heart** used to say that you feel something very strongly *I thank you with all my heart.* **10 not have the heart to do sth** to decide not to do something that would make someone unhappy **11 learn/know, etc sth by heart** to be able to remember all of something **12 break sb's heart** to make someone very unhappy **13 heart and soul** used to say that you give all your attention and enthusiasm to something *She threw herself into teaching heart and soul.* ➲ *See also:* a **change**² of heart.

**heartache** /ˈhɑːteɪk/ *noun* [C, U] extreme sadness

'**heart at,tack** *noun* [C] when someone's heart suddenly stops working correctly, sometimes causing death *I think he's had a heart attack.*

**heartbeat** /ˈhɑːtbiːt/ *noun* [C, U] the regular movement of the heart as it moves blood around the body

**heartbreaking** /ˈhɑːtˌbreɪkɪŋ/ *adj* causing extreme sadness *heartbreaking news*

**heartbroken** /ˈhɑːtˌbrəʊkən/ *adj* If you are heartbroken, you feel extremely sad about something that has happened.

**-hearted** /-ˈhɑːtɪd/ ➲ *See* **broken-hearted, cold-hearted, half-hearted, hard-hearted, light-hearted.**

**heartened** /ˈhɑːtənd/ *adj* feeling happier because of something *We all felt heartened by the news.* ➲ *Opposite* **disheartened.**

**heartening** /ˈhɑːtənɪŋ/ *adj* making you feel happier *heartening news* ➲ *Opposite* **disheartening.**

'**heart ,failure** *noun* [U] when someone's heart stops working, often causing death

**heartfelt** /ˈhɑːtfelt/ *adj* Heartfelt feelings and words are strong and sincere. *heartfelt thanks/gratitude*

**hearth** /hɑːθ/ *noun* [C] the floor around a fireplace

**heartily** /ˈhɑːtɪli/ *adv* **1** with a lot of enthusiasm *We all laughed heartily at the joke.* **2** completely or very much *I am heartily sick of the situation.*

**heartland** /ˈhɑːtlænd/ *noun* [C] the place where an activity or belief is strongest *the traditional heartland of the motor industry*

**heartless** /ˈhɑːtləs/ *adj* cruel and not caring about other people

**heart-to-heart** /ˌhɑːttəˈhɑːt/ *noun* [C] a serious conversation between two people in which they talk honestly about their feelings

**hearty** /ˈhɑːti/ *adj* **1** friendly and full of energy *a hearty laugh/welcome* **2** Hearty meals are large and satisfy you.

o━**heat**¹ /hiːt/ *noun* **1** HOT [U] the quality of being hot or warm *the heat of summer* **2 the heat** when it is very hot *I don't really like the heat.* **3** TEMPERATURE [U, no plural] the temperature of something *Cook on a low heat.* **4 the heat** US (UK **the heating**) the system that keeps a building warm *Could you turn the heat up a little.* **5** RACE [C] a competition, especially a race, which decides who will be in the final event **7 in the heat of the moment** If you do or say something in the heat of the moment, you do or say it without thinking because you are angry or excited. ➲ *See also:* **dead heat.**

**heat**² /hiːt/ (*also* **heat up**) *verb* [I, T] to make something become hot or warm, or to become hot or warm *I'll just heat up some soup.*

**heated** /ˈhiːtɪd/ *adj* **1** made warm or hot **2 a heated argument/debate, etc** an angry or excited argument

**heater** /ˈhiːtəʳ/ *noun* [C] a machine that heats air or water

**heath** /hiːθ/ *noun* [C] an open area of land covered with wild plants and rough grass

**heather** /ˈheðəʳ/ *noun* [C, U] a small plant with purple or white flowers that grows on hills

**heating** /ˈhiːtɪŋ/ UK (US **heat**) *noun* [U] the system that keeps a building warm ➲ *See also:* **central heating.**

**heave** /hiːv/ *verb* **1** [I, T] to move something heavy using a lot of effort *He heaved the bag on to his shoulder.* **2** [I] to move up and down *Her chest heaved as she started to cry.* **3 heave a sigh of relief** to breathe out loudly because you are pleased that something bad has not happened • heave *noun* [C]

**heaven** /ˈhevən/ *noun* [U] **1** according to some religions, the place where good people go when they die **2** *informal* something very nice that gives you great pleasure *This cake is absolute heaven.*

**heavenly** /ˈhevənli/ *adj* **1** [always before noun] relating to heaven *the heavenly kingdom* **2** *informal* very nice *a heavenly day*

**heavens** /ˈhevᵊnz/ noun **1 the heavens** literary the sky **2 (Good) Heavens!** used when you are surprised or annoyed Heavens, what's the matter?

**heavily** /ˈhevɪli/ adv **1** a lot or to a great degree She's heavily involved in politics. **2 drink/ smoke heavily** to drink/smoke a lot **3 rain/ snow heavily** to rain/snow a lot **4** using a lot of force to breathe heavily

o-**heavy** /ˈhevi/ adj **1** WEIGHING A LOT Heavy objects weigh a lot. heavy bags • heavy machinery/equipment **2** HOW MUCH used to say how much someone or something weighs How heavy are you? • Oxygen is sixteen times heavier than hydrogen. **3** A LOT large in amount or degree heavy traffic • heavy costs **4 a heavy drinker/smoker** someone who drinks/smokes a lot **5 heavy snow/rain** when a lot of snow/ rain falls **6** FORCE using a lot of force a heavy blow • heavy breathing **7** SERIOUS informal serious The discussion got a bit too heavy. **8 heavy going** mainly UK too serious or difficult I found the book very heavy going.

**heavy-handed** /ˌhevɪˈhændɪd/ adj using too much force in dealing with people

**heavy ˈmetal** noun [U] a type of very loud, modern music

**heavyweight** /ˈheviweɪt/ noun [C] **1** a fighter such as a boxer who is in the heaviest weight group the heavyweight champion of the world **2** someone who is powerful and important a political heavyweight

**Hebrew** /ˈhiːbruː/ noun [U] the language used in the Jewish religion and in Israel • Hebrew adj

**hectare** /ˈhekteəʳ/ noun [C] a unit for measuring area, equal to 10,000 square metres

**hectic** /ˈhektɪk/ adj extremely busy and full of activity a hectic day/week

**he'd** /hiːd/ **1** short for he had We knew he'd taken the money. **2** short for he would No one thought he'd get the job.

**hedge**¹ /hedʒ/ noun [C] a row of bushes growing close together, often used to divide land into separate areas

**hedge**² /hedʒ/ verb [I, T] to avoid giving a direct answer ⊃ See also: hedge your bets (**bet**²).

**hedgehog** /ˈhedʒhɒg/ noun [C] a small animal whose body is covered with sharp points

**hedgerow** /ˈhedʒrəʊ/ noun [C] UK a row of bushes and small trees along the edge of a field or road

**heed**¹ /hiːd/ verb [T] formal to pay attention to some advice or a warning Officials failed to heed his warning.

**heed**² /hiːd/ noun formal **take heed of sth** to pay attention to something, especially some advice or a warning

**heel** /hiːl/ noun [C] **1** the back part of your foot ⊃ See colour picture **The Body** on page Centre 2. **2** the part of a shoe that is under your heel high heels

**hefty** /ˈhefti/ adj informal very large a hefty bill/fine • a hefty woman with dyed hair

o-**height** /haɪt/ noun **1** HOW TALL [C, U] how tall or high something or someone is a man of average height • The tower measures 27.28 metres **in height**. **2** HOW FAR UP [C, U] how far above the ground something is The aircraft

was flying at a height of about 6000 metres. **3** TALL [U] being tall People always make comments about his height. **4 the height of sth** the strongest or most important part of something I met him when he was at the height of his fame.

**heighten** /ˈhaɪtᵊn/ verb [I, T] to increase or make something increase heightened awareness • [often passive] The book's success was heightened by the scandal.

**heights** /haɪts/ noun **1** [plural] high places I've always been afraid of heights. **2 new heights** when something is better or more successful than ever before Our athletes have reached new heights of sporting glory.

**heinous** /ˈheɪnəs/ adj formal very bad and shocking heinous crimes

**heir** /eəʳ/ noun [C] a person who will have the legal right to someone's money and possessions when they die He is the **heir to** a huge fortune.

**heiress** /ˈeəres/ noun [C] a woman who will have the legal right to someone's money and possessions when they die

**held** /held/ past of hold

**helicopter** /ˈhelɪkɒptəʳ/ noun [C] an aircraft which flies using long, thin parts on top of it that turn round and round very fast

**helicopter**

**helium** /ˈhiːliəm/ noun [U] a gas that is lighter than air and that will not burn a helium balloon

**he'll** /hiːl/ short for he will He'll be home soon.

o-**hell** /hel/ noun **1** [U] according to some religions, the place where bad people go when they die **2** [U] informal an experience that is very unpleasant It's been hell working with him. **3 the hell** informal used to emphasize something in a rude or angry way What the hell are you doing here? **4 a/one hell of a** informal used to say that someone or something is very good, big, etc a hell of a noise • He's one hell of a tennis player. **5 from hell** informal used to say that someone or something is extremely bad We had the holiday from hell. **6 like hell** informal very much It's raining like hell out there.

**hellish** /ˈhelɪʃ/ adj informal extremely bad or unpleasant a hellish place/journey

o-**hello** (also UK **hallo**) /helˈəʊ/ exclamation **1** used to greet someone Hello, Chris, how are

**H**

*things?* **2** used to start a conversation on the telephone *Hello, this is Alex.*

**helm** /helm/ *noun* **1** [C] the part that you use to direct a boat or ship **2 at the helm** controlling a group or organization *With Lewis at the helm we are certain of success.*

**helmet** /ˈhelmət/ *noun* [C] a hard hat that protects your head *a cycling helmet* ➔ *See colour picture* **Sports 2** *on page Centre 16.* ➔ *See also:* **crash helmet.**

o⤓**help¹** /help/ *verb* **1** [I, T] to make it easier for someone to do something *Thank you for helping.* • [+ (to) do sth] *Shall I help you to set the table?* • *Dad always **helps** me **with** my homework.* **2** [I, T] to make something easier or better [+ to do sth] *When you're nervous or frightened, it helps to breathe slowly and deeply.* • *The signals help aircraft pilots to navigate safely.* **3 can't/couldn't help sth** to be unable to stop yourself doing something or to stop something happening [+ doing sth] *I couldn't help thinking about what had happened.* • *He couldn't help it, he slipped.* **4 help yourself (to sth)** to take something, especially food or drink, without asking *Please help yourself to some coffee.*

**help (sb) out** to help someone, especially by giving them money or working for them *Carol's been helping out in the shop this week.* • *Mum said she'd help me out with buying the car.*

o⤓**help²** /help/ *noun* **1** [U] when someone helps another person *I was too embarrassed to ask for help.* • *Do you want any help?* **2** [no plural] something or someone that helps *Dave has been a great help to me.* **3 with the help of sth** using something *We assembled the computer with the help of the manual.*

**help³** /help/ *exclamation* something that you shout when you are in danger *Help! I'm drowning!*

**helper** /ˈhelpəʳ/ *noun* [C] someone who helps another person to do something

**helpful** /ˈhelpfᵊl/ *adj* **1** useful *helpful advice/ comments* **2** willing to help *The staff here are very helpful.* ➔ *Opposite* **unhelpful.** • helpfully *adv* • helpfulness *noun* [U]

**helping** /ˈhelpɪŋ/ *noun* [C] an amount of food given to one person at one time *She gave me a very large helping of pasta.*

**helpless** /ˈhelpləs/ *adj* not able to defend yourself or do things without help *a helpless animal/child* • helplessly *adv*

**hem** /hem/ *noun* [C] the edge of a piece of clothing or cloth that has been folded under and sewn • hem *verb* [T] **hemming,** *past* **hemmed** to sew a hem on a piece of clothing or cloth

**hem sb in** to prevent someone from moving, or from doing what they want to do

**hemisphere** /ˈhemɪsfɪəʳ/ *noun* [C] one half of the Earth *birds of the northern hemisphere*

**hemophilia** /ˌhiːməˈfɪliə/ *noun* [U] *US spelling of* haemophilia (= a serious disease in which the flow of blood from someone's body cannot be stopped when they are hurt)

**hemophiliac** /ˌhiːməˈfɪliæk/ *noun* [C] *US spelling of* haemophiliac (= someone who has haemophilia)

**hemorrhage** /ˈhemᵊrɪdʒ/ *noun* [C, U] *US spelling*

*of* haemorrhage (= when someone suddenly loses a lot of blood)

**hemorrhoids** /ˈhemərɔɪdz/ *noun* [plural] *US spelling of* haemorrhoids (= painful swollen tissue around the opening of a person's bottom)

**hemp** /hemp/ *noun* [U] a plant that is used for making rope, cloth, and the drug cannabis

**hen** /hen/ *noun* [C] a female bird, especially a chicken

**hence** /hens/ *adv* **1** for this reason *He's got an interview today, hence the suit.* **2 three weeks/two months, etc hence** *formal* three weeks/two months, etc from this time

**henceforth** /ˌhensˈfɔːθ/ *adv formal* from this time *Henceforth only English may be spoken in this classroom.*

**henchman** /ˈhenʃmən/ *noun* [C] *plural* **henchmen** someone who does unpleasant jobs for a powerful person

**hepatitis** /ˌhepəˈtaɪtɪs/ *noun* [U] a serious disease that affects your liver (= the organ that cleans your blood)

o⤓**her¹** *strong form* /hɜːʳ/ *weak forms* /həʳ, əʳ/ *pronoun* **1** used after a verb or preposition to refer to someone female who has already been talked about *Where's Kath – have you seen her?* **2** used to refer to a country or ship *God bless HMS Victoria and all who sail in her.*

o⤓**her²** *strong form* /hɜːʳ/ *weak form* /həʳ/ *determiner* belonging to or relating to someone female who has already been talked about *That's her house on the corner.* • *It's not her fault.*

**herald¹** /ˈherəld/ *verb* [T] to be a sign that a particular event will happen soon *Thick black clouds heralded rain.*

**herald²** /ˈherəld/ *noun* [C] a sign that a particular event will happen soon *A fall in unemployment was a **herald of** economic recovery.*

**herb** /hɜːb US ɜːrb/ *noun* [C] a plant that is used in cooking to add flavour to food or used in medicines • herbal /ˈhɜːbᵊl/ *adj herbal medicine*

**herd¹** /hɜːd/ *noun* [C] a large group of animals such as cows that live and eat together *a herd of cattle/deer*

**herd²** /hɜːd/ *verb* [T] If people or animals are herded somewhere, they are moved there in a group. [often passive] *The passengers were quickly herded onto a bus.*

o⤓**here** /hɪəʳ/ *adv* **1** IN THIS PLACE in the place where you are *Does Jane live near here?* • *Come here!* • *How long have you been here?* **2** GETTING ATTENTION used to bring someone's attention to someone or something *Look, here's our bus.* • *Here, put this on.* **3 here you are/ here he is, etc** used when you see someone or something you have been looking for or waiting for *Here she is at last.* • *Here we are, this is the place.* **4** GIVING used when you are giving someone something *Here's a present for you.* **5 Here you are.** used when you are giving someone something *"Have you got the paper?" "Here you are."* **6** AT THIS POINT at this point in a discussion *I don't have time here to go into all the arguments.* **7** ON THE TELEPHONE used when saying who you are on the telephone *Hello, it's Tim here.* **8 here and there** in several different places but without any pattern *Tall trees were growing here and there.*

**hereafter** /ˌhɪərˈɑːftəʳ/ *adv formal* from now or after this time

**hereby** /ˌhɪəˈbaɪ/ *adv formal* with these words or this action *I hereby declare you the winner.*

**hereditary** /hɪˈredɪtʳri/ *adj* **1** passed to a child from its parents before birth *Depression is often hereditary.* **2** passed from parent to child as a right *a hereditary title*

**heredity** /hɪˈredəti/ *noun* [U] the way in which mental or physical qualities pass from parent to child

**heresy** /ˈherəsi/ *noun* [C, U] a belief which is against what a group or society generally believe to be right or good

**heretic** /ˈherətɪk/ *noun* [C] someone with a belief which is against what a group or society generally believe to be right or good • heretical /həˈretɪkʳl/ *adj*

**heritage** /ˈherɪtɪdʒ/ *noun* [U] the buildings, paintings, customs, etc which are important in a culture or society because they have existed for a long time *our architectural/cultural heritage*

**hermit** /ˈhɜːmɪt/ *noun* [C] someone who chooses to live alone and away from other people

**hernia** /ˈhɜːniə/ *noun* [C] a medical condition in which an organ pushes through the muscle which is around it

**hero** /ˈhɪərəʊ/ *noun* [C] *plural* **heroes 1** someone who does something brave or good which people respect or admire them for *He became a national hero for his part in the revolution.* **2** the main male character in a book or film who is usually good *the hero of her new novel*

**heroic** /hɪˈrəʊɪk/ *adj* **1** very brave *a heroic figure* • *a heroic act/deed* **2** If someone makes a heroic effort to do something, they work very hard to try to do it. *In spite of England's heroic efforts, they lost the match.* • heroically *adv*

**heroics** /hɪˈrəʊɪks/ *noun* [plural] actions which seem brave but are stupid because they are dangerous *Any heroics, and I will kill your wife.*

**heroin** /ˈherəʊɪn/ *noun* [U] a very strong drug which some people use illegally for pleasure *a heroin addict*

**heroine** /ˈherəʊɪn/ *noun* [C] **1** the main female character in a book or film, who is usually good *the heroine of the film 'Alien'* **2** a woman who does something brave or good which people respect or admire her for

**heroism** /ˈherəʊɪzʳm/ *noun* [U] very brave behaviour *an act of heroism*

**herring** /ˈherɪŋ/ *noun* [C, U] a small, silver-coloured fish which lives in the sea and is eaten as food ➔ *See also:* **red herring**.

o-**hers** /hɜːz/ *pronoun* the things that belong or relate to someone female who has already been talked about *That's Ann's coat over there – at least I think it's hers.* • *I borrowed it from a friend of hers.*

o-**herself** /həˈself/ *pronoun* **1** the reflexive form of the pronoun 'she' *She kept telling herself that nothing was wrong.* **2** used to emphasize the pronoun 'she' or the particular female person you are referring to *She decorated the cake herself.* **3 (all) by herself** alone or without anyone else's help *She managed to put her shoes on all by herself.* **4 (all) to herself** for her

use only *Mum's got the house to herself this weekend.*

**hertz** /hɜːts/ *(written abbreviation* **Hz**) *noun* [C] *plural* **hertz** a unit for measuring the number of cycles (= events which are repeated) that happen every second, used especially in electronics

**he's** /hiːz/ **1** *short for* he is *He's my best friend.* **2** *short for* he has *Sam must be tired – he's been dancing all night!*

**hesitant** /ˈhezɪtʳnt/ *adj* If you are hesitant, you do not do something immediately or quickly because you are nervous or not certain. *She was hesitant about returning to her home town.* • hesitantly *adv* • hesitancy *noun* [U]

**hesitate** /ˈhezɪteɪt/ *verb* **1** [I] to pause before doing something, especially because you are nervous or not certain *Richard hesitated before answering.* **2 not hesitate to do sth** to be very willing to do something because you are certain it is right *They would not hesitate to call the police at the first sign of trouble.*

**hesitation** /ˌhezɪˈteɪʃʳn/ *noun* **1** [C, U] when you pause before doing something, especially because you are nervous or not certain *After a moment's hesitation, he unlocked the door.* **2 have no hesitation in doing sth** when you are very willing to do something because you know it is the right thing to do *He had no hesitation in signing for the team.*

**heterogeneous** /ˌhetʳrəʊˈdʒiːniəs/ *adj formal* consisting of parts or things of different types *a heterogeneous sample of people*

**heterosexual** /ˌhetʳrəʊˈsekʃuʳl/ *adj* sexually attracted to people of the opposite sex • heterosexual *noun* [C]

**het up** /ˌhetˈʌp/ *adj* [never before noun] *UK informal* worried and upset *Why are you getting so het up about this?*

**hexagon** /ˈheksəgən/ *noun* [C] a flat shape with six sides of the same length • hexagonal /hekˈsægʳnʳl/ *adj* shaped like a hexagon

**hey** /heɪ/ *exclamation spoken* used to get someone's attention or to show that you are interested, excited, angry, etc *Hey, Helen, look at this!* • *Hey, wait a minute!*

**heyday** /ˈheɪdeɪ/ *noun* [no plural] the time when something or someone was most successful or popular *In its heyday, the company employed over a thousand workers.*

**hi** /haɪ/ *exclamation* hello *Hi! How's it going?*

**hiatus** /haɪˈeɪtəs/ *noun* [no plural] *formal* a short pause in which nothing happens or is said

**hibernate** /ˈhaɪbəneɪt/ *verb* [I] If an animal hibernates, it goes to sleep for the winter. • hibernation /ˌhaɪbəˈneɪʃʳn/ *noun* [U]

**hiccup** *(also* **hiccough**) /ˈhɪkʌp/ *noun* [C] **1** a quick noise you make in your throat when a muscle in your chest moves suddenly [usually plural] *I got hiccups from drinking too quickly.* **2** a small, temporary problem *I'm afraid there's been a slight hiccup.*

o-**hide**[1] /haɪd/ *verb past t* **hid**, *past p* **hidden 1** THING [T] to put something in a place where it cannot be seen or found *I hid the money in a vase.* • [often passive] *She kept the diary hidden in a drawer.* **2** PERSON [I] *(also* **hide yourself**) to go to a place where you cannot be seen or found

*She ran off and hid behind a tree.*
**3** FEELING/INFORMATION [T] to keep a feeling or information secret *He couldn't hide his embarrassment.* • *There's something about her past that she's trying to* **hide** *from me.*

**hide**

**hide²** /haɪd/ *noun* [C, U] the skin of an animal which is used for making leather

**hide-and-seek** /ˌhaɪdən'siːk/ *noun* [U] a children's game in which one child hides and the others try to find them

**hideaway** /'haɪdəweɪ/ *noun* [C] a place where you go to hide or to be alone

**hideous** /'hɪdiəs/ *adj* very ugly *a hideous monster* • **hideously** *adv*

**hideout** /'haɪdaʊt/ *noun* [C] a place where you go to hide, especially from the police or if you are in danger

**hiding** /'haɪdɪŋ/ *noun* **be in hiding; go into hiding** to hide in a place, especially from the police or if you are in danger

**hierarchy** /'haɪərɑːki/ *noun* [C] a system or organization in which people or things are arranged according to their importance • **hierarchical** /ˌhaɪə'rɑːkɪkəl/ *adj a hierarchical structure*

**hieroglyphics** /ˌhaɪərəʊ'glɪfɪks/ *noun* [plural] a system of writing which uses pictures instead of words, especially used in ancient Egypt

**hi-fi** /'haɪfaɪ/ *noun* [C] a set of electronic equip-

ment for playing music, consisting of a CD player, radio, etc

o━**high¹** /haɪ/ *adj* **1** TALL having a large distance from the bottom to the top *a high building/ mountain* **2** ABOVE GROUND a large distance above the ground or the level of the sea *a high shelf/window* • *The village was* **high up** *in the mountains.* **3** MEASUREMENT used to say how big the distance is from the top of something to the bottom, or how far above the ground something is *How high is it?* • *It's ten metres high.* **4** AMOUNT great in amount, size, or level *a high temperature* • *high prices/costs* • *The car sped away* **at high speed.** **5** VERY GOOD very good *high standards/quality* **6** IMPORTANT important, powerful, or at the top level of something *a high rank* • *Safety is our highest priority.* **7** DRUGS If someone is high, they are behaving in an unusual way because they have taken an illegal drug. *The whole band seemed to be high on heroin.* **8** SOUND A high sound or note is near the top of the set of sounds that people can hear. **9 high in sth** If a food is high in something, it contains a lot of it. *Avoid foods that are high in salt.*

o━**high²** /haɪ/ *adv* **1** at or to a large distance above the ground *We flew high above the city.* • *He threw the ball high into the air.* **2** at or to a large amount or level *Temperatures rose as high as 40 degrees.*

**high³** /haɪ/ *noun* [C] **1** the top amount or level which something reaches *Computer ownership has reached an* **all-time high** (= more people own computers than ever before). **2** a feeling of excitement or happiness [usually singular] *The players are still* **on a high** *from their last match.*

**highbrow** /'haɪbraʊ/ *adj* A highbrow book, film, etc is serious and intended for very intelligent or well-educated people.

**high-class** /ˌhaɪ'klɑːs/ *adj* of very good quality *a high-class hotel*

**High 'Court** *noun* [C] the most important law court in some countries *a High Court judge*

**higher edu'cation** *noun* [U] education at a college or university

**high-flyer** (*also* **high-flier**) /ˌhaɪ'flaɪəʳ/ *noun* [C] someone who is very successful or who is likely to be very successful, especially in business • **high-flying** *adj*

**the 'high jump** *noun* a sports event in which people try to jump over a bar which gets higher and higher during the competition ➔ *See colour picture* **Sports 1** *on page Centre 15.*

**highlands** /'haɪləndz/ *noun* [plural] an area with a lot of mountains *the Scottish highlands* • **highland** /'haɪlənd/ *adj* in or relating to the highlands *a highland village*

**high-level** /ˌhaɪ'levəl/ *adj* involving important or powerful people *high-level meetings/talks*

**highlight¹** /'haɪlaɪt/ *verb* [T] **1** to emphasize something or make people notice something *to highlight a problem/danger* • *The report highlights the need for stricter regulations.* **2** to make something a different colour so that it is more easily noticed, especially written words

**highlight²** /'haɪlaɪt/ *noun* [C] the best or most important part of something *The boat trip was one of the* **highlights** *of the holiday.*

**highlighter** /'haɪ,laɪtəʳ/ *noun* [C] a pen with bright, transparent ink which is used to emphasize words in a book, article, etc ⊃ *See colour picture* **The Office** *on page Centre 12.*

O— **highly** /'haɪli/ *adv* **1** very or to a large degree *a highly effective treatment* • *It is highly unlikely that they will succeed.* **2** at a high level *a highly paid worker* **3** **to speak/think highly of sb/sth** to have or express a very good opinion of someone or something *The course is very highly thought of.*

**Highness** /'haɪnəs/ *noun* **Her/His/Your Highness** used when you are speaking to or about a royal person *Thank you, Your Highness.*

**high-powered** /,haɪ'paʊəd/ *adj* very important or responsible *a high-powered executive/job*

**high-profile** /,haɪ'prəʊfaɪl/ *adj* A high-profile person or event is known about by a lot of people and receives a lot of attention from television, newspapers, etc. *a high-profile campaign/case*

**high-rise** /'haɪ,raɪz/ *adj* A high-rise building is very tall and has a lot of floors.

'**high ,school** *noun* [C, U] a school in the US which children go to between the ages of 14 and 18 *I played violin when I was in high school.* • *a high-school student/teacher*

'**high ,street** *noun* [C] *UK* the main road in the centre of a town where there are a lot of shops

**high-tech** (*also UK* **hi-tech**) /,haɪ'tek/ *adj* using or involved with the most recent and advanced electronic machines, computers, etc *high-tech companies/industry*

**highway** /'haɪweɪ/ *noun* [C] *mainly US* a main road, especially between two towns or cities

**hijack** /'haɪdʒæk/ *verb* [T] to take control of an aircraft during a journey, especially using violence [often passive] *The plane was hijacked by terrorists.* • hijacker *noun* [C] • hijacking *noun* [C, U]

**hike**[1] /haɪk/ *noun* [C] a long walk, usually in the countryside

**hike**[2] /haɪk/ *verb* [I] to go for a long walk in the countryside • hiker *noun* [C] • hiking *noun* [U] *to go hiking in the mountains*

**hilarious** /hɪ'leəriəs/ *adj* extremely funny *They all thought the film was hilarious.* • hilariously *adv hilariously funny*

**hilarity** /hɪ'lærəti/ *noun* [U] when people laugh very loudly and think something is very funny

O— **hill** /hɪl/ *noun* [C] a raised area of land, smaller than a mountain *They climbed up the hill to get a better view.*

**hillside** /'hɪlsaɪd/ *noun* [C] the sloping side of a hill

**hilly** /'hɪli/ *adj* having a lot of hills *hilly countryside*

**hilt** /hɪlt/ *noun* **to the hilt** very much or as much as is possible *Mark borrowed to the hilt to pay for his new car.*

O— **him** *strong form* /hɪm/ *weak form* /ɪm/ *pronoun* used after a verb or preposition to refer to someone male who has already been talked about *Where's Serge – have you seen him?*

O— **himself** /hɪm'self/ *pronoun* **1** the reflexive form of the pronoun 'he' *John always cuts himself when he's shaving.* **2** used to emphasize the pronoun 'he' or the particular male person you are referring to *Do you want to speak to Dr Randall himself or his secretary?* • *He made the bookcase himself.* **3** **(all) by himself** alone or without anyone else's help *Joe made that snowman all by himself.* **4** **(all) to himself** for his use only *Tim wants a desk all to himself.*

**hind** /haɪnd/ *adj* **a hind foot/leg** a foot/leg at the back of an animal

**hinder** /'hɪndəʳ/ *verb* [T] to make it difficult to do something or for something to develop [often passive] *His performance at the Olympics was hindered by a knee injury.*

**hindrance** /'hɪndrəns/ *noun* [C] something or someone that makes it difficult for you to do something *Large class sizes are a hindrance to teachers.*

**hindsight** /'haɪndsaɪt/ *noun* [U] the ability to understand an event or situation only after it has happened *With hindsight, I should have taken the job.*

**Hindu** /'hɪnduː/ *noun* [C] someone who believes in Hinduism • Hindu *adj a Hindu temple*

**Hinduism** /'hɪnduːɪzᵊm/ *noun* [U] the main religion of India, based on belief in many gods and the belief that when someone dies their spirit returns to life in another body

**hinge**[1] /'hɪndʒ/ *noun* [C] a metal fastening that joins the edge of a door, window, or lid to something else and allows you to open or close it

**hinge**[2] /'hɪndʒ/ *verb*
**hinge on sth** to depend completely on something *Her career hinges on the success of this project.*

**hint**[1] /hɪnt/ *noun* **1** [C] when you say something that suggests what you think or want, but not in a direct way *He dropped* (= made) *several hints that he wanted a CD player for his birthday.* **2** [C] a small piece of advice *The magazine gives lots of useful hints on how to save money.* **3** **a hint of sth** a small amount of something *There was a hint of anger in her voice.*

**hint**[2] /hɪnt/ *verb* [I, T] to suggest something, but not in a direct way [+ (that)] *He hinted that he wants to retire next year.* • *She hinted at the possibility of moving to America.*

**hip**[1] /hɪp/ *noun* [C] one of the two parts of your body above your leg and below your waist *She stood waiting with her hands on her hips.* ⊃ *See colour picture* **The Body** *on page Centre 2.*

**hip**[2] /hɪp/ *adj informal* fashionable

**hippie** /'hɪpi/ (*also UK* **hippy**) *noun* [C] someone who believes in peace and love and has long hair, especially someone who was young in the 1960s

**hippo** /'hɪpəʊ/ *noun* [C] *short for* hippopotamus

**hippopotamus** /,hɪpə'pɒtəməs/ *noun* [C] *plural* **hippopotamuses** or **hippopotami** a very large animal with a thick skin that lives near water in parts of Africa

O— **hire**[1] /haɪəʳ/ *verb* [T] **1** *UK* (*US* **rent**) to pay money in order to use something for a short time *They hired a car for a few weeks.* ⊃ *See usage note at* **rent.** **2** to begin to employ someone *We hired a new secretary last week.*
**hire sth out** *UK* to allow someone to borrow something from you in exchange for money *The shop hires out electrical equipment.*

**hire²** /haɪəʳ/ *noun* [U] *UK* when you arrange to use something by paying for it *The price includes flights and car hire.* • *Do you have bikes for hire?*

o-**his¹** *strong form* /hɪz/ *weak form* /ɪz/ *determiner* belonging to or relating to someone male who has already been talked about *Alex is sitting over there with his daughter.* • *It's not his fault.*

o-**his²** /hɪz/ *pronoun* the things that belong or relate to someone male who has already been talked about *That's Frank's coat over there – at least I think it's his.* • *I borrowed them from a friend of his.*

**Hispanic** /hɪˈspænɪk/ *adj* relating or belonging to people whose families came from Spain or Latin America in the past • Hispanic *noun* [C] a Hispanic person

**hiss** /hɪs/ *verb* **1** [I] to make a long noise like the letter 's' *The gas hissed through the pipes.* **2** [T] to speak in an angry or urgent way *"Will you be quiet," she hissed.* • hiss *noun* [C] a sound like the letter 's'

**historian** /hɪˈstɔːriən/ *noun* [C] someone who studies or writes about history

**historic** /hɪˈstɒrɪk/ *adj* important in history or likely to be important in history *historic buildings* • *a historic day/moment*

**historical** /hɪˈstɒrɪkˀl/ *adj* relating to events or people in the past, or the study of history *a historical novel* • *historical documents* • historically *adv*

o-**history** /ˈhɪstˀri/ *noun* **1** [PAST] [U] the whole series of events in the past which relate to the development of a country, subject, or person *The Civil War was a terrible time in American history.* • *What do you know about the history of jazz?* **2** [SUBJECT] [U] the study of events in the past *He's very interested in modern European history.* • *a history book* **3** **a history of sth** If you have a history of a particular problem or illness, you have already suffered from it. *a man with a history of drug addiction* **4** [DESCRIPTION] [C] a description or record of events in the past relating to someone or something *The doctor read through his medical history.* ➔ *See also:* **case history**, **natural history**.

---

**USAGE**

**history** or **story?**

**History** is events that happened in the past.

*He's studying history at university.*

A **story** is a description of real or imaginary events, often told to entertain people.

*The story is about two friends travelling across India.*

---

o-**hit¹** /hɪt/ *verb* **hitting**, *past* **hit 1** [HAND] [T] to touch something quickly and with force using your hand or an object in your hand *She hit him on the head with her tennis racket.* **2** [TOUCH] [T] to touch someone or something quickly and with force, usually causing injury or damage *The car skidded and hit a wall.* • *As she fell, she hit her head on the pavement.* **3** [AFFECT] [I, T] to affect

something badly [often passive] *The economy has been hit by high unemployment.* **4** [REACH] [T] to reach a place, position, or state *Our profits have already hit $1 million.* **5** [THINK] [T] *informal* If an idea or thought hits you, you suddenly think of it. *The idea for the book hit me in the middle of the night.* **6** **hit it off** *informal* If people hit it off, they like each other and become friendly immediately. ➔ *See also:* hit sb **hard²**, hit the **jackpot**, hit the **nail¹** on the head, hit the **roof**.

**hit back** to criticize or attack someone who has criticized or attacked you *The President hit back at journalists who said he was a liar.*

**hit on/upon sth** to have a good idea, especially one which solves a problem *We hit upon the idea of writing to the mayor to ask for his help.*

**hit**

**hit²** /hɪt/ *noun* [C] **1** [SONG/FILM] a very successful song, film, book, etc *The film 'Titanic' was a big hit.* **2** [PERSON/THING] a popular person or thing *The chocolate cake was a big hit with the children.* **3** [TOUCH] when you touch something or when something touches you quickly and with force **4** [INTERNET] a request to see a document on the Internet that is then counted to calculate the number of people looking at the page

**hit-and-miss** /ˌhɪtˀnˈmɪs/ *UK* (*US* **hit or miss**) *adj* not planned, but happening by chance

**hit-and-run** /ˌhɪtˀnˈrʌn/ *adj* A hit-and-run accident is when the driver of a vehicle hits and injures someone, but then drives away without helping.

**hitch¹** /hɪtʃ/ *noun* [C] a small problem *The ceremony went without a hitch.*

**hitch²** /hɪtʃ/ *verb* **1** **hitch a lift/ride** to get a free ride in someone's vehicle, by standing next to the road and waiting for someone to pick you up **2** [T] (*also US* **hitch up**) to fasten something to an object or vehicle *They hitched the caravan to the car.*

**hitch sth up** to pull up a piece of clothing

**hitchhike** /ˈhɪtʃhaɪk/ *verb* [I] to get free rides in people's vehicles by standing next to the road and waiting for someone to pick you up • **hitch-hiker** *noun* [C]

**hi-tech** *UK* (*UK/US* **high-tech**) /ˌhaɪˈtek/ *adj* using or involved with the most recent and advanced electronic machines, computers, etc

**hitherto** /ˌhɪðəˈtuː/ *adv formal* until now, or until a particular point in time

**HIV** /ˌeɪtʃaɪˈviː/ *noun* [U] *abbreviation for* human immunodeficiency virus: a virus which causes AIDS (= a serious disease that destroys the body's ability to fight infection) *The blood tests show that she is HIV-positive* (= has the virus).

**hive** /haɪv/ *noun* **1** [C] (*also* **beehive**) a special container where people keep bees **2 a hive of activity** a place where people are busy and working hard

**hm** (*also* **hmm**) /həm/ *spoken* something you say when you pause while talking or when you are uncertain *"Which one do you like best?" "Hmm. I'm not sure."*

**hoard** /hɔːd/ *verb* [T] to collect and store a large supply of something, often secretly *He hoarded antique books in the attic.* • **hoard** *noun* [C] a large, secret supply or collection of something *Police found a hoard of stolen jewellery in the car.*

**hoarding** /ˈhɔːdɪŋ/ *UK* (*UK/US* **billboard**) *noun* [C] a large board used for advertising, especially by the side of a road

**hoarse** /hɔːs/ *adj* If you are hoarse, your voice sounds rough when you speak, often because you are ill. *The teacher was hoarse from shouting.* • **hoarsely** *adv*

**hoax** /həʊks/ *noun* [C] when someone tries to make people believe something which is not true *The police said the bomb threat was a hoax.*

**hob** /hɒb/ *noun* [C] *UK* the flat part on top of an oven where you heat food in pans ➔ *See colour picture* **Kitchen** *on page Centre 10.*

**hobble** /ˈhɒbl/ *verb* [I] to walk with small, uncomfortable steps, especially because your feet hurt

**hobby** /ˈhɒbi/ *noun* [C] an activity that you enjoy and do regularly when you are not working *Do you have any hobbies?*

**hockey** /ˈhɒki/ *noun* [U] **1** *UK* (*US* **field hockey**) a team game played on grass where you hit a small ball with a long, curved stick **2** *US* (*UK/US* **ice hockey**) a team game played on ice where you hit a small, hard object with a long, curved stick ➔ *See colour picture* **Sports 1** *on page Centre 15.*

**hoe** /həʊ/ *noun* [C] a garden tool with a long handle used for removing weeds (= plants you do not want)

**hog¹** /hɒg/ *noun* [C] *mainly US* a large pig

**hog²** /hɒg/ *verb* [T] **hogging**, *past* **hogged** *informal* to use or keep all of something for yourself *Stop hogging the newspaper! I want to read it too.*

**hoist** /hɔɪst/ *verb* [T] to raise something, sometimes using a rope or machine *They slowly hoisted the flag.*

o⫯**hold¹** /həʊld/ *verb* *past* **held** **1** IN HAND [T] to have something in your hand or arms *He was holding a glass of wine.* • *She held the baby in her arms.* • *They were holding hands and*

kissing. **2** KEEP IN POSITION [T] to keep something in a particular position *Can you hold the door open please?* • *Hold your hand up if you know the answer.* • *The frame was held together with screws.* • *They held a gun to his head.* **3** ORGANIZE [T] to organize an event *to hold talks/an election* **4** CONTAIN [T] to contain something or to be able to contain a particular amount of something *The bucket holds about 10 litres.* **5** JOB OR QUALIFICATION [T] to have a particular job, position, or qualification *She held the post of treasurer.* **6** COMPETITION [T] to have a particular position in a competition *to hold the world record* • *to hold the lead* **7** STORE [T] to store documents, information, etc in a particular place *The documents are held in the local library.* **8** PRISONER [T] to keep someone as a prisoner *Police held the suspect overnight.* • *The hijackers are **holding** them **hostage/prisoner**.* **9** ARMY [T] If soldiers hold a place, they control it. *Rebel troops held the village.* **10 hold an opinion/belief/view** to believe something *They held the view that corporal punishment was good for children.* **11 hold a conversation** to have a conversation **12 hold sb's attention/interest** to keep someone interested in something *The film held my attention from beginning to end.* **13** TELEPHONE [I, T] to wait on the telephone until someone can speak to you *Her line's busy. Would you like to hold?* • *Hold the line, please.* **14** NOT BREAK [I] to not break *The rope held.* **15 Hold it!** *informal* used to tell someone to wait or stop doing something *Hold it! I've forgotten my coat.* **16 hold shares** to own shares (= small, equal parts of the value of a company) **17 hold your breath a** to intentionally stop breathing for a time **b** to wait for something to happen, often feeling anxious **18 hold your nose** to close your nose with your fingers to avoid smelling something unpleasant ➔ *See also:* hold your own¹.

**hold sth against sb** to like someone less because they have done something wrong or behaved badly *It was his mistake, but I won't hold it against him.*

**hold sb/sth back 1** to prevent someone or something from moving forward *The police held back the protesters.* **2** to prevent someone or something from making progress *She felt that having children would hold her back.*

**hold sth back 1** to stop yourself showing an emotion *She couldn't hold back the tears.* **2** to not give information to someone

**hold sth/sb down 1** to stop someone moving or escaping *It took three officers to hold down the suspect.* **2** to keep the cost of something at a low level *to hold down prices/wages* **3 hold down a job** to keep a job *It's difficult for mothers to hold down a full-time job.*

**hold off (sth/doing sth)** to wait before doing something *They are holding off making a decision until next week.*

**hold on** *informal* **1** to wait *Hold on! I'll just check my diary.* **2** to hold something or someone firmly with your hands or arms *Hold on tight!*

**hold onto sth/sb** to hold something or someone

firmly with your hands or arms *Hold onto the rope and don't let go.*

**hold onto/on to sth** to keep something you have *It was a tough election, but they held onto their majority.*

**hold sth out** to move your hand or an object in your hand towards someone *She held out her glass for some more wine.*

**hold out 1** If a supply of food or money holds out, you have enough for a particular period of time. **2** to continue to defend yourself against an attack *The city is still **holding out against** rebel troops.*

**hold out for sth** to wait until you get what you want *I decided to hold out for a better offer.*

**hold sth up** to prevent something from falling down *The tent was held up by ropes.*

**hold sth/sb up** to make something or someone slow or late *Sorry I'm late. I got held up in traffic.*

**hold up sth** to try to steal money from a bank, shop, or vehicle using force

**hold**² /həʊld/ *noun* **1** [C] when you hold something or someone, or the way you do this *Keep a tight hold on your tickets.* **2 catch/grab/take, etc hold of sth/sb** to start holding something or someone *He tried to escape, but I grabbed hold of his jacket.* **3 get hold of sth/sb** to obtain something, or to manage to speak to someone *I got hold of a copy at the local library.* • *I rang three times, but couldn't get hold of her.* **4 on hold a** If a plan or activity is on hold, it will not be done until a later time. *The project is on hold until we get more money.* **b** waiting to speak to someone on the telephone *His secretary **put me on hold**.* **5 keep hold of sth** to keep something *Keep hold of this. You might need it later.* **6 hold on/over sth/sb** power or control over something or someone *Their company has a strong hold on the computer market.* **7** [C] an area on a ship or aircraft for storing things *a cargo hold* ➔ *See also:* get (hold of) the wrong **end¹** of the stick.

**holdall** /ˈhəʊldɔːl/ *UK* (*US* **carryall**) *noun* [C] a large bag for carrying clothes ➔ *See picture at* **luggage**.

**holder** /ˈhəʊldəʳ/ *noun* [C] someone who officially owns something *the world record holder* • *passport holders* ➔ *See also:* **title-holder**.

**holding** /ˈhəʊldɪŋ/ *noun* [C] part of a company which someone owns

**hold-up** *UK* (*US* **holdup**) /ˈhəʊldʌp/ *noun* [C] **1** something that slows you down or makes you late *There were several hold-ups on the motorway.* **2** when someone steals money from a bank, shop, or vehicle using force

○ᴹ**hole¹** /həʊl/ *noun* **1** [C] a hollow space in something, or an opening in a surface *a bullet hole* • *There's a **hole in the roof**.* • *We dug a hole to plant the tree.* **2 a rabbit/mouse, etc hole** a hollow space where a rabbit/mouse, etc lives **3** a small, hollow space in the ground that you try to hit a ball into in a game of golf

**hole²** /həʊl/ *verb*

**hole up** *informal* (*also* **be holed up**) to stay or hide somewhere *During the siege they were holed up in a hotel room.*

○ᴹ**holiday¹** /ˈhɒlədeɪ/ *noun* **1** ‖NO WORK‖ [C, U] *UK*

(*US* **vacation**) a time when you do not have to go to work or school *My aunt looks after us during the school holidays.* **2** ‖VISIT‖ [C, U] *UK* (*US* **vacation**) a long visit to a place away from where you live, for pleasure *a skiing/walking holiday* • *Are you **going on holiday** this year?* **3** ‖DAY‖ [C] an official day when you do not have to go to school or work *a public holiday* ➔ *See also:* **bank holiday, federal holiday, national holiday, package holiday**.

**holiday²** /ˈhɒlədeɪ/ *UK* (*US* **vacation**) *verb* [I] to have your holiday somewhere *We usually holiday in Spain.*

**holidaymaker** /ˈhɒlədeɪˌmeɪkəʳ/ *noun* [C] *UK* someone who is away from home on holiday

**holiness** /ˈhəʊlɪnəs/ *noun* [U] the quality of being holy

**holistic** /həʊˈlɪstɪk/ *adj* dealing with or treating the whole of something or someone and not just some parts

**holler** /ˈhɒləʳ/ *verb* [I] *US informal* to shout or call loudly • **holler** *noun* [C]

**hollow¹** /ˈhɒləʊ/ *adj* **1** having a hole or empty space inside *a hollow shell/tube* ➔ *See picture at* **flat²**. **2** without meaning or real feeling *a hollow victory* • *a hollow laugh* **3 hollow cheeks/eyes** If someone has hollow cheeks/eyes, their face seems to curve in around these areas.

**hollow²** /ˈhɒləʊ/ *noun* [C] a hole or empty space in something, or a low area in a surface

**hollow³** /ˈhɒləʊ/ *verb*

hollow

**hollow sth out** to make an empty space inside something

**holly** /ˈhɒli/ *noun* [U] a green bush with sharp, pointed leaves and small, red fruit

**holocaust** /ˈhɒləkɔːst/ *noun* [C] when a very large number of people are killed and things destroyed, such as in a war or fire *a nuclear holocaust*

**hologram** /ˈhɒləgræm/ *noun* [C] a photograph or image which appears to be solid and have depth when light shines on it in a particular way

**holster** /ˈhəʊlstəʳ/ *noun* [C] a leather container for carrying a gun on your body

**holy** /ˈhəʊli/ *adj* **1** relating to a religion or a god *the holy city of Jerusalem* **2** very religious or pure *a holy man*

**homage** /ˈhɒmɪdʒ/ *noun* **pay homage to sb** to show your respect for someone, especially by praising them in public *Fans paid homage to the actress who died yesterday.*

○ᴹ**home¹** /həʊm/ *noun* **1** [C, U] the place where you live or feel you belong *I tried to ring him, but he wasn't **at home**.* • *We sold our home in London and moved to Scotland.* • *He left home* (= stopped living with his family) *when he was eighteen.* **2** [C] a place where people who need special care live *a children's home* • *My grandmother lives in a home now.* **3 feel at home** to feel happy and confident in a place or situation *After a month she felt at home in her new job.* **4 make yourself at home** to behave in a relaxed way in a place, as if it was your own home *Take off your coat and make yourself at home.* **5 the home of sth/sb** the place where you usually find something or someone, or where they come from *France, the home of good food* ⊃ *See also:* **nursing home**, **stately home**.

### USAGE

#### home

When you use verbs of movement with **home**, for example 'go' or 'come', you do not need to use a preposition.

*What time did you go home?*

*I'll call you as soon as I get home.*

When you use the verbs **be** or **stay** with **home**, you can use the preposition **at**.

*I was at home all afternoon.*

*I'll stay at home to look after the children.*

*Let's stay home and watch a movie. (mainly US)*

o⊶**home²** /həʊm/ *adv* **1** to the place where you live *He didn't come home until midnight.* ● *I went home to visit my parents.* ● *I remembered on my way home.* **2** at or in the place someone lives *Will you be home tomorrow evening?*

**home³** /həʊm/ *adj* **1** sb's home address/phone number, etc an address/telephone number, etc for the place where someone lives **2** FOR/FROM HOME made or used in the place where someone lives *home cooking* ● *a home computer* **3** SPORT relating to the place where a sporting event happens *The home team won 2-0.* **4** COUNTRY relating to things in your own country *home affairs*

**home⁴** /həʊm/ *verb*

**home in on sth/sb** to give a lot of attention to something or someone *The report only homes in on the negative points.*

**homecoming** /ˈhəʊmˌkʌmɪŋ/ *noun* [C, U] when someone returns home, usually after being away for a long time

**home eco'nomics** *noun* [U] a school subject in which you learn how to cook and sew

**home-grown** /ˌhəʊmˈɡrəʊn/ *adj* **1** from your own garden *home-grown vegetables* **2** If someone or something is home-grown, they belong to or were developed in your own country. *Our football team has many home-grown players.*

**homeland** /ˈhəʊmlænd/ *noun* [C] the country where you were born

**homeless** /ˈhəʊmləs/ *adj* without a place to live *10,000 people were made homeless by the floods.* ● *They're opening a new shelter for **the home-less**.* ● **homelessness** *noun* [U]

**homely** /ˈhəʊmli/ *adj* **1** UK A homely place is simple, but comfortable and pleasant. *It's a small restaurant with a homely atmosphere.* **2** US Someone who is homely is not very attractive.

**homemade** (*also UK* **home-made**) /ˌhəʊmˈmeɪd/ *adj* made at home and not bought from a shop *homemade bread/cookies*

**homeopathy** /ˌhəʊmiˈɒpəθi/ *noun* [U] a way of treating illnesses using very small amounts of natural substances ● **homeopathic** /ˌhəʊmiəʊˈpæθɪk/ *adj a homeopathic remedy*

**homeowner** /ˈhəʊmˌəʊnəʳ/ *noun* [C] someone who owns the house that they live in

**'home ˌpage** *noun* [C] the first page that you see when you look at a website on the Internet

**homesick** /ˈhəʊmsɪk/ *adj* feeling sad because you are away from your home ● **homesickness** *noun* [U]

**homestead** /ˈhəʊmsted/ *noun* [C] *mainly US* a house and area of land usually used as a farm

**hometown** *US* (*UK/US* ˌhome 'town) /ˌhəʊmˈtaʊn/ *noun* [C] the town or city that you come from

**homeward** /ˈhəʊmwəd/ *adj, adv* towards home *the homeward journey*

o⊶**homework** /ˈhəʊmwɜːk/ *noun* [U] **1** work which teachers give students to do at home *Have you **done** your **homework** yet?* **2 do your homework** to prepare carefully for a situation *It was clear that she had done her homework before the meeting.*

**homicide** /ˈhɒmɪsaɪd/ *noun* [C, U] *US* the crime of killing someone *There were over 400 homicides in Chicago last year.* ● **homicidal** /ˌhɒmɪˈsaɪdˀl/ *adj* likely to murder someone *a homicidal maniac*

**homogeneous** /ˌhɒməˈdʒiːniəs, ˌhəʊməˈdʒiːniəs/ *adj formal* consisting of parts or members that are all the same *The village was a fairly homogeneous community.*

**homophobia** /ˌhəʊməˈfəʊbiə/ *noun* [U] hate of homosexual people ● **homophobic** *adj* hating homosexual people

**homosexual** /ˌhəʊməˈsekʃuˀl/ *adj* sexually attracted to people of the same sex *a homosexual couple* ● **homosexual** *noun* [C] someone who is homosexual ● **homosexuality** /ˌhəʊməʊˌsekʃuˈæləti/ *noun* [U] the quality of being homosexual

**hone** /həʊn/ *verb* [T] to improve something and make it perfect *an opportunity for you to hone your skills*

o⊶**honest** /ˈɒnɪst/ *adj* **1** sincere and telling the truth *If you want my honest opinion, I think your hair looks awful.* **2** not likely to lie, cheat, or steal *an honest man* ⊃ *Opposite* **dishonest**. **3 to be honest** *informal* used to express your real opinion *To be honest, I didn't really enjoy the party.*

**honestly** /ˈɒnɪstli/ *adv* **1** EMPHASIZE used to emphasize that you are telling the truth *Thanks, but I honestly couldn't eat another piece of cake.* **2** HONEST in an honest way **3** ANNOYED used to show that you are annoyed or do not approve of something *Honestly! He should have been here hours ago.*

**honesty** /ˈɒnɪsti/ *noun* **1** [U] the quality of being honest **2 in all honesty** used when you are saying what you really think or feel about something *In all honesty, I'd rather not go.* ⊃ *Opposite* **dishonesty**.

**honey** /ˈhʌni/ *noun* **1** [U] a sweet, sticky food

that is made by bees ⊃ *See colour picture* **Food** *on page Centre 7.* **2** [C] *mainly US* a name that you call someone you love or like very much

**honeymoon** /'hʌnimuːn/ *noun* [C] a holiday taken by two people who have just got married *We went to Paris on our honeymoon.* • honey-mooner *noun* [C]

**honk** /hɒŋk/ *verb* [I, T] to make a short sound with your car's horn (= part you press to make a warning noise) *The lorry driver honked his horn at me.*

**honor** /'ɒnəʳ/ *noun, verb US spelling of* honour

**honorable** /'ɒnʳəbl/ *adj US spelling of* honourable

**honorary** /'ɒnʳəri/ *adj* **1** given as a reward to show respect *He was given an honorary degree from Cambridge University.* **2** If you have an honorary job, you are not paid for it. *the honorary chairman*

**honour¹** *UK* (*US* **honor**) /'ɒnəʳ/ *noun* **1** RESPECT [U] when people respect you because you have done what you believe is honest and right, or the quality of doing this *a man of honour* • *The soldiers fought for the honour of their country.* ⊃ *Opposite* **dishonour**. **2 in honour of sb/sth** in order to celebrate or show great respect for someone or something *a banquet in honour of the President* **3** PRIDE [no plural] something which makes you feel proud and pleased [+ to do sth] *It's an honour to be team captain.* • [+ of + doing sth] *I had the great honour of meeting the King.* **4** REWARD [C] something that you give to someone in public to show respect for them and their achievements *She was granted the Order of Merit – one of the nation's highest honours.* **5 Her/His/Your Honour** used when you are speaking to or about a judge **6 honours** A qualification or university course with honours is of a very high level. *an honours degree*

**honour²** *UK* (*US* **honor**) /'ɒnəʳ/ *verb* **1** [T] to show great respect for someone or something, usually in public [often passive] *He was honoured for his bravery.* • *She was honoured with an Oscar.* **2 honour an agreement/contract/promise, etc** to do what you agreed or promised to do *The government failed to honour its promise to cut taxes.* ⊃ *Opposite* **dishonour**.

**honourable** /'ɒnʳəbl/ *adj UK* (*US* **honorable**) honest and fair, or deserving praise and respect *a decent, honourable man* ⊃ *Opposite* **dishonourable**. **2 the Honourable a** a title used before the name of some important government officials **b** a title used in the UK before the name of certain people of high social rank • honourably *adv*

**hood** /hʊd/ *noun* [C] **1** a part of a coat or jacket that covers your head and neck *a waterproof jacket with a hood* **2** *US* (*UK* **bonnet**) the metal part that covers a car engine ⊃ *See colour picture* **Car** *on page Centre 3.*

**hooded** /'hʊdɪd/ *adj* having or wearing a hood *a hooded sweatshirt* • hooded figures

**hoof** /huːf/ *noun* [C] *plural* **hooves** or **hoofs** the hard part on the foot of a horse and some other large animals

**hook¹** /hʊk/ *noun* **1** [C] a curved piece of metal or plastic used for hanging something on, or a

similar object used for catching fish *His coat was hanging from a hook on the door.* **2 off the hook** If a telephone is off the hook, the part you speak into is not in its correct position, so the telephone will not ring. **3 a left/right hook** when you hit someone hard with your left/right hand **4 get/let sb off the hook** *informal* to allow someone to escape from a difficult situation or to avoid doing something that they do not want to do

**hook²** /hʊk/ *verb* **1** [T] to fasten something with a hook, hang something on a hook, or catch something with a hook **2 be/get hooked on sth** *informal* **a** to like or start to like doing something very much and want to do it all the time *He's completely hooked on computer games.* **b** If you are hooked on a drug, you cannot stop taking it. • hooked *adj* shaped like a hook *a hooked nose*

**hook sth/sb up** to connect a machine to a power supply or to another machine, or to connect someone to a piece of medical equipment *Are you hooked up to the Internet yet?*

**hooligan** /'huːlɪgʰn/ *noun* [C] someone who behaves badly or violently and causes damage in a public place • hooliganism *noun* [U]

**hoop** /huːp/ *noun* [C] a ring made of metal, plastic, or wood

**hooray** (*also* **hurrah**) /hʊ'reɪ/ *exclamation* something that you shout when you are happy, excited, etc or when you approve of someone or something *Hip, hip, hooray!*

**hoot¹** /huːt/ *noun* **1** [C] a short sound made by an owl (= bird) or by a car horn (= warning equipment) **2 a hoot of laughter** when someone laughs loudly **3** [no plural] *informal* something or someone that is very funny *The film was an absolute hoot.*

**hoot²** /huːt/ *verb* **1** [I, T] *mainly UK* to make a short sound with your car's horn (= part you press to make a warning noise) *The van driver hooted his horn impatiently.* **2** [I] If an owl (= bird) hoots, it makes a low 'oo' sound. **3 hoot with laughter** to laugh a lot very loudly

**Hoover** /'huːvəʳ/ *mainly UK trademark* (*UK/US* **vacuum cleaner**) *noun* [C] an electric machine which cleans floors by sucking up dirt • hoover *verb* [I, T]

**hooves** /huːvz/ *plural of* hoof

**hop¹** /hɒp/ *verb* [I] **hopping**, *past* **hopped 1** ONE FOOT to jump on one foot or to move about in this way **2** ANIMAL If a small animal, bird, or insect hops, it moves by jumping on all of its feet at the same time. *Rabbits were hopping across the field.* **3** MOVE QUICKLY *informal* to go somewhere quickly or get into or out of a vehicle quickly *to hop on a plane/train*

**hop²** /hɒp/ *noun* **1** [C] a short jump, especially on one leg **2 a short hop** *informal* a short journey or distance *London to Paris is only a short hop by plane.*

o⤴**hope¹** /həʊp/ *verb* [I, T] to want something to happen or be true [+ (that)] *I hope that the bus won't be late.* • *We had hoped for better weather than this.* • *"Do you think it's going to rain?" "I hope not!"* • *"Is he coming?" "I hope so."* **2 hope to do sth** to intend to do something *Dad hopes to retire next year.*

o-**hope**² /həʊp/ *noun* **1** [C, U] a positive feeling about the future, or something that you want to happen *a message full of hope* • *What are your* **hopes** *and dreams for the future?* • *Don't give up hope – I'm sure he'll be fine.* • [+ of + doing sth] *Young people are growing up in our cities without any hope of getting a job.* **2 sb's best/last/only hope** the best/last/only person or thing that can help you and make you succeed *Doctors say his only hope is a transplant.* **3 in the hope of/that** because you want something good to happen [+ doing sth] *She went to Paris in the hope of improving her French.* • *They wrote to the Prime Minister in the hope that he would help.* **4 pin your hopes on sb/sth** to hope that someone or something will help you achieve what you want

**hopeful** /'həʊpf°l/ *adj* **1** feeling positive about a future event or situation *Many teenagers do not feel* **hopeful** *about the future.* • [+ (that)] *Police are still hopeful that they will find the missing family.* **2** If something is hopeful, it makes you feel that what you want to happen will happen. *There are hopeful signs that she will make a full recovery.* • hopefulness *noun* [U] • hopeful *noun* [C] someone who hopes to succeed, especially in the entertainment business *a young hopeful*

o-**hopefully** /'həʊpf°li/ *adv* **1** used, often at the start of a sentence, to express what you would like to happen *Hopefully it won't rain.* **2** in a hopeful way *"Are there any tickets left?" she asked hopefully.*

**hopeless** /'həʊpləs/ *adj* **1** VERY BAD very bad and not likely to succeed or improve *a hopeless situation* • *They searched for survivors, but it was hopeless.* **2** NOT ABLE very bad at a particular activity *Dad's a hopeless cook.* • *I'm hopeless at sports.* **3** NOT POSITIVE feeling no hope *She was depressed and felt totally hopeless about the future.* • hopelessness *noun* [U]

**hopelessly** /'həʊpləsli/ *adv* extremely, or in a way that makes you lose hope *hopelessly lost* • *They met at university and fell hopelessly in love.*

**hops** /hɒps/ *noun* [plural] the flowers of a plant that are used to make beer

**horde** /hɔːd/ *noun* [C] a large group of people *There was a* **horde** *of tourists outside Buckingham Palace.*

**horizon** /həˈraɪz°n/ *noun* **1** [C] the line in the distance where the sky seems to touch the land or sea **2 broaden/expand/widen your horizons** to increase the number of things that you know about, have experienced, or can do *Travelling certainly broadens your horizons.* **3 on the horizon** likely to happen soon *Economic recovery is on the horizon.*

**horizontal** /ˌhɒrɪˈzɒnt°l/ *adj* level and flat, or parallel to the ground or to the bottom of a page *a horizontal line/stripe* • horizontally *adv The lines run horizontally across the page.*

**hormone** /'hɔːməʊn/ *noun* [C] one of several chemicals produced in your body that influence its growth and development • hormonal /hɔːˈməʊn°l/ *adj a hormonal imbalance*

**horn** /hɔːn/ *noun* [C] **1** ANIMAL one of the two hard, pointed growths on the heads of cows, goats, and some other animals **2** EQUIPMENT a

**horizontal/vertical**

horizontal stripes

vertical stripes

piece of equipment used to make a loud sound as a warning or signal *a car horn* • *The taxi driver hooted his horn.* **3** MUSIC a curved musical instrument that you blow into to make a sound *the French horn*

**horoscope** /'hɒrəskəʊp/ *noun* [C] a description of what someone is like and what might happen to them in the future, based on the position of the stars and planets when they were born

**horrendous** /hɒrˈendəs/ *adj* extremely unpleasant or bad *She suffered horrendous injuries in the accident.* • horrendously *adv* extremely or extremely badly *horrendously expensive*

**horrible** /'hɒrəbl/ *adj* very unpleasant or bad *What's that horrible smell?* • *That was a horrible thing to say to your sister.* • horribly *adv* extremely, or in a very bad or unpleasant way *His plan went horribly wrong.*

**horrid** /'hɒrɪd/ *adj* very unpleasant or unkind *The other pupils were horrid to him.*

**horrific** /hɒrˈɪfɪk/ *adj* very bad and shocking *a horrific accident/crime* • *horrific injuries* • horrifically *adv*

**horrify** /'hɒrɪfaɪ/ *verb* [T] to make someone feel very shocked [often passive] *I was horrified to hear about your accident.* • horrifying *adj*

**horror** /'hɒrəʳ/ *noun* **1** [C, U] a strong feeling of shock or fear, or something that makes you feel shocked or afraid *She watched in horror as the car skidded across the road.* **2 a horror film/movie/story** a film or story that entertains people by shocking or frightening them

o-**horse** /hɔːs/ *noun* [C] a large animal with four legs, which people ride or use to pull heavy things

**horseback** /'hɔːsbæk/ *noun* **1 on horseback** riding a horse *police on horseback* **2 horseback riding** US (UK **horse riding**) the sport or activity of riding a horse ⊃ *See colour picture* **Sports 1** *on page Centre 15.*

ˌhorse ˈchestnut *noun* [C] a tree that produces shiny, brown nuts in thick green shells with sharp points, or one of these nuts

**horse-drawn** /'hɔːsdrɔːn/ *adj* [always before noun] A horse-drawn vehicle is pulled by a horse.

**horseman, horsewoman** /'hɔːsmən, 'hɔːs,wʊmən/ *noun* [C] *plural* **horsemen, horsewomen** a man/woman who rides horses well

**horsepower** /'hɔːs,pauəʳ/ (*written abbreviation* **hp**) *noun* [U] a unit for measuring the power of an engine

'horse ,racing *noun* [U] the sport where people race on horses, usually to win money

'horse ,riding *UK* (*US* 'horseback ,riding) *noun* [U] the sport or activity of riding a horse ➔ *See colour picture* **Sports 1** *on page Centre 15.*

**horseshoe** /'hɔːsʃuː/ *noun* [C] a U-shaped piece of metal that is nailed to a horse's foot

**horticulture** /'hɔːtɪkʌltʃəʳ/ *noun* [U] the study or activity of growing plants ● horticultural /,hɔːtɪ'kʌltʃʳrˡl/ *adj* relating to gardening

**hose** /həuz/ *noun* **1** [C] (*also UK* **hosepipe** /'həuzpaɪp/) a long pipe made of rubber or plastic and used for directing water somewhere, usually onto a garden or fire **2** [plural] (*also* **pantyhose**) *US* a piece of women's clothing made of very thin material that covers the legs and bottom

**hospice** /'hɒspɪs/ *noun* [C] a place where people who are dying live and are cared for

**hospitable** /hɒs'pɪtəbl/ *adj* A hospitable person or place is friendly, pleasant, and welcomes visitors.

○⁻**hospital** /'hɒspɪtˡl/ *noun* [C, U] a place where ill or injured people go to be treated by doctors and nurses *He was (UK)* **in hospital**/(US) **in the hospital** *for two weeks.*

**hospitalize** (*also UK* **-ise**) /'hɒspɪtˡlaɪz/ *verb* [T] to take someone to hospital and keep them there for treatment [often passive] *My wife was often hospitalized for depression.*

**host¹** /həust/ *noun* **1** PARTY [C] someone who organizes a party and invites the guests **2** TELEVISION [C] someone who introduces the guests on a radio or television programme *a talk show host* **3** PLACE [C] a country or city that provides the place and equipment for an organized event *Australia played host to the Olympics in 2000.* **4 a host of sth** a large number of people or things *I've got a whole host of questions to ask you.*

**host²** /həust/ *verb* [T] to be the host of an event *to host a party/dinner*

**hostage** /'hɒstɪdʒ/ *noun* **1** [C] someone who is kept as a prisoner and may be hurt or killed in order to force other people to do something **2 take/hold sb hostage** to catch or keep someone as a prisoner *Two tourists were held hostage by terrorists.*

**hostel** /'hɒstˡl/ *noun* [C] a place like a cheap hotel, where you can live when you are away from home or have no home *a hostel for the homeless* ● *a student hostel* ➔ *See also:* **youth hostel.**

**hostess** /'həustɪs/ *noun* [C] **1** a woman who organizes a party and invites the guests **2** a woman who introduces the guests on a television programme ➔ *See also:* **air hostess.**

**hostile** /'hɒstaɪl/ *adj* **1** unfriendly and not liking or agreeing with something *Some politicians were very hostile to the idea.* **2** unpleasant or not suitable for living or growing *a hostile climate*

**hostility** /hɒs'tɪləti/ *noun* **1** [U] unfriendly, angry behaviour that shows that you dislike someone *hostility towards outsiders* **2** [U] when

you strongly disagree with something or someone *There is still open* **hostility to** *the idea.* **3 hostilities** [plural] *formal* fighting in a war

○⁻**hot¹** /hɒt/ *adj* **hotter, hottest 1** VERY WARM having a high temperature *a hot summer's day* ● *a hot drink/meal* ● *I'm too hot in this jacket.* **2** SPICY Hot food contains strong spices which cause a burning feeling in your mouth. *Be careful. The chilli sauce is very hot.* **3** EXCITING *informal* exciting or interesting *Hollywood's hottest new actress* **4 a hot issue/topic** a subject which people discuss and have strong feelings about *The legalization of drugs is a hot topic.* ➔ *See also:* **piping hot, red-hot.**

**hot²** /hɒt/ *verb*

**hot up** *UK informal* If a situation or event hots up, it becomes more exciting and more things start to happen. *The competition is really hotting up now.*

**hot-'air bal,loon** *noun* [C] a very large balloon filled with hot air, that has a container below it where people can travel ➔ *See picture at* **balloon.**

**hotbed** /'hɒtbed/ *noun* [C] a place where there is a lot of a particular activity, usually something bad *The government was a hotbed of corruption.*

'hot ,dog *noun* [C] a cooked sausage (= tube of meat and spices) that you usually eat inside bread

○⁻**hotel** /həu'tel/ *noun* [C] a place where you pay to stay when you are away from home *We spent our honeymoon in a luxury hotel.* ● *a hotel room*

**hotelier** /həu'telieɪ/ ⓊⓈ həu'təljəʳ/ *noun* [C] someone who owns or is in charge of a hotel

**hotline** /'hɒtlaɪn/ *noun* [C] a telephone number that you can ring for help or information *Ring our 24-hour hotline for advice.*

**hotly** /'hɒtli/ *adv* **1** in an angry or excited way *He hotly denied the rumours.* **2 hotly contested** If a race, election, or other competition is hotly contested, everyone is trying very hard to win it.

,hot-'water bottle *noun* [C] a flat, rubber container that you fill with hot water to keep you warm

**hound¹** /haund/ *noun* [C] a dog that is used when people hunt animals

**hound²** /haund/ *verb* [T] to follow someone and annoy them by asking questions or taking photographs [often passive] *She is always being hounded by photographers.*

○⁻**hour** /auəʳ/ *noun* **1** [C] a period of time equal to 60 minutes *half an hour* ● *The store is open 24 hours a day.* ● *It's a six-hour flight.* ● *The job pays $5 an hour.* **2** [C] the period of time when a particular activity happens or when a shop or public building is open [usually plural] *working hours* ● *Our opening hours are from 8 to 6.* ● *I've got to go to the bank (UK) in my lunch hour/(US) on my lunch hour.* **3 hours** *informal* a long time *I spent hours doing my homework.* **4 the hour** the point when a new hour begins *The train leaves at two minutes past the hour.* ● *My watch beeps on the hour.* **5 all hours** very late at night, until early morning, or almost all the time *Our neighbours are up till all hours every night, playing loud music.* **6 the early/small**

**hours** the hours between midnight and the time that the sun rises ⊃ *See also:* **rush hour**.

USAGE

**hour** or **time?**

An **hour** is a period of 60 minutes.

*The journey takes about three hours.*

*We went for a 2-hour walk.*

**Time** is measured in hours and minutes. We use **time** to refer to a particular point during the day or night, or to say when something happens.

*What time do you get up in the morning?*

*There's only one bus at that time of night.*

Remember to use **time** not 'hour' when you are talking about what time it is.

*"What time is it?" "2 o'clock."*

~~"What hour is it?" "2 o'clock."~~

**hourly** /'auəli/ *adj, adv* **1** happening every hour *There is an hourly bus service.* **2** for each hour *an hourly rate/wage*

o-- **house¹** /haus/ *noun plural* **houses** /'hauzɪz/ **1** BUILDING [C] a building where people live, usually one family or group *a three-bedroomed house* ● *We went to my aunt's house for dinner.* **2** PEOPLE [no plural] the people who live in a house *The baby's screaming woke the whole house up.* **3** PLACE FOR ACTIVITY [C] the place where a particular business or activity happens *an opera house* ● *a publishing house* **4** **the House** a group of people which makes a country's laws, or the place where they meet *the House of Commons/Representatives* ● *The House voted on the proposals.* **5** THEATRE [C] the people watching a performance or the area where they sit [usually singular] *The actors played to a full house.* **6** **on the house** If food or drink is on the house in a bar or restaurant, it is free. ⊃ *See also:* **the White House, boarding house, full house, row house, terraced house**.

**house²** /hauz/ *verb* [T] **1** to give a person or animal a place to live *This development will house over 100 families.* **2** to provide space for something *The museum houses a huge collection of paintings.*

**house ar'rest** *noun* **under house arrest** when you are kept as a prisoner in your own home

**houseboat** /'hausbəut/ *noun* [C] a boat that people can live on

**housebound** /'hausbaund/ *adj* unable to leave your home because you are too ill or old

**household¹** /'haushəuld/ *noun* [C] a family or group of people who live together in a house *Many households own more than one television.*

**household²** /'haushəuld/ *adj* **1** [always before noun] connected with or belonging to a home *household bills/expenses* ● *household products/goods* **2** **a household name** someone or something that everyone knows *Her TV roles made her a household name in the UK.*

**householder** /'haushəuldə'/ *noun* [C] *UK* someone who owns or rents a house

**housekeeper** /'haus,ki:pə'/ *noun* [C] someone who is paid to clean and cook in someone else's house

**housekeeping** /'haus,ki:pɪŋ/ *noun* [U] the cleaning and cooking that you do in your home

**House of 'Commons** *noun* [no plural] one of the two parts of the British parliament, with elected members who make laws

**House of 'Lords** *noun* [no plural] one of the two parts of the British parliament, with members who are chosen by the government

**House of Repre'sentatives** *noun* [no plural] the group of politicians elected by people in the US to make laws

**Houses of 'Parliament** *noun* [plural] the House of Commons and the House of Lords, or the building in London where they meet

**'house ,warming** *noun* [C] a party to celebrate moving into a new house

**housewife** /'hauswaɪf/ *noun* [C] *plural* **housewives** /'hauswaɪvz/ a woman who stays at home to cook, clean, and take care of her family

**housework** /'hausw3ːk/ *noun* [U] the work that you do to keep your house clean *I can't stand doing housework.*

**housing** /'hauzɪŋ/ *noun* [U] buildings for people to live in *a shortage of local housing*

**'housing e,state** *UK* (*US* **'housing de,velopment**) *noun* [C] an area with a large number of houses that were built at the same time

**hover** /'hɒvə'/ *verb* [I] **1** to stay up in the air but without moving anywhere *A helicopter hovered overhead.* **2** If you hover, you stand and wait near someone or something. *A waiter hovered at the table ready to take our order.*

**hovercraft** /'hɒvəkrɑːft/ *noun* [C] a boat that moves across the surface of water or land supported by a large cushion (= soft container) of air

USAGE

**how** or **what?**

In these expressions we use **what**. Be careful not to use 'how'.

**what something is called**

*I don't know what it's called in English.*

~~I don't know how it's called in English.~~

**what something/someone looks like**

*I'd like to see what it looks like before I buy it.*

*What does your brother look like?*

o-- **how¹** /hau/ *adv* **1** WAY used to ask about the way something happens or is done *How did he die?* ● *How does she manage to keep the house so tidy?* **2** QUANTITY used to ask about quantity, size, or age *How big is the house?* ● *How old are they?* ● *How much* (= what price) *was that dress?* ● *How far is the next garage?* **3** EMPHASIZE used before an adjective or adverb to emphasize it *I was amazed at how quickly she finished.* **4** HEALTH used to ask about someone's health *How are you feeling today?* **5** SITUATION used to ask about the success or progress of a situation

*How's everything going?* • *How was the exam?* **6 How are you?** used to ask someone if they are well and happy *"How are you Jane?" "Oh, not so bad thanks."* **7 How about..?** used to make a suggestion *How about a drink?* • [+ doing sth] *How about going to the cinema?* **8 How come?** *informal* used to ask about the reason for something, especially when you feel surprised about it *"Kate's gone to the party on her own." "How come?"* ➔ *See also:* **know-how**.

**how²** /haʊ/ *conjunction* used to talk about the way that something happens or is done [+ to do sth] *I don't know how to turn the video on.*

o-ᴋ**however¹** /haʊˈevəʳ/ *adv* **1 however cold/ difficult/slowly, etc** used to say that it does not make any difference how cold/difficult/ slowly, etc *We're not going to get there in time, however fast we drive.* **2** used when you are about to say something which is surprising compared with what you have just said *He had always been a successful businessman. Recently, however, things have not been going well for him.* **3** *UK* used to ask about how something happened when the person asking feels surprised *However did you manage to persuade her?*

**however²** /haʊˈevəʳ/ *conjunction* in any way *However you look at it, it's still a mess.* • *You can do it however you like.*

**howl** /haʊl/ *verb* [I] **1** ANIMAL If a dog or wolf (= wild animal like a dog) howls, it makes a long, sad sound. **2** MAKE SOUND to make a loud sound, usually to express pain, sadness, or another strong emotion *He howled in pain.* • *The audience was howling with laughter.* **3** WIND If the wind howls, it blows hard and makes a lot of noise. *The wind was howling outside.* • howl *noun* [C]

**hp** *written abbreviation for* horsepower (= a unit for measuring the power of an engine)

**HQ** /ˌeɪtʃˈkjuː/ *noun* [C, U] *abbreviation for* headquarters (= the place from where an organization is controlled)

**hr** *written abbreviation for* hour

**HRH** /ˌeɪtʃɑːrˈeɪtʃ/ *abbreviation for* His/Her Royal Highness: used when speaking to or about a royal person

**http** /ˌeɪtʃtiːtiːˈpiː/ *abbreviation for* hypertext transfer protocol: a set of instructions made by a computer program that allows your computer to connect to an Internet document

**hub** /hʌb/ *noun* [C] **1** a place that is the centre of a particular activity [usually singular] *Silicon Valley has become the hub of the electronics industry.* **2** the round part in the centre of a wheel

**huddle¹** /ˈhʌdl/ (*also* **huddle together/up**) *verb* [I] to move closer to other people, or to hold your arms and legs close to your body, usually because you are cold or frightened *They huddled around the fire to keep warm.*

**huddle²** /ˈhʌdl/ *noun* [C] a group of people or things that are standing close together

**hue** /hjuː/ *noun* [C] *literary* a colour

**huff¹** /hʌf/ *verb* **huff and puff** *informal* to breathe loudly, especially because you have been exercising *Pam was huffing and puffing by the time she reached the top of the stairs.*

**huff²** /hʌf/ *noun* **in a huff** *informal* angry with someone *Mum's in a huff because I didn't call yesterday.*

**hug¹** /hʌg/ *verb* **hugging,** *past* **hugged 1** [I, T] to put your arms around someone and hold them tightly, usually because you love them *They hugged and kissed each other.* **2** [T] to stay very close to the edge of something *The road hugs the coast for several miles.*

**hug²** /hʌg/ *noun* [C] when you put your arms around someone and hold them tightly *She gave me a big hug before she left.*

o-ᴋ**huge** /hjuːdʒ/ *adj* extremely large *a huge house* • *a huge piece of cake*

**hugely** /ˈhjuːdʒli/ *adv* extremely *hugely popular/successful*

**huh** /hʌ/ *exclamation informal* used to ask a question, or to express surprise, anger, etc *So, you're leaving, huh?* • *Huh! What a waste of time.*

**hull** /hʌl/ *noun* [C] the main part of a ship that is mostly under water

**hullo** *UK* (*UK/US* **hello**) /həˈləʊ/ *exclamation* **1** used to greet someone *Hullo, Chris, how are things?* **2** used to start a conversation on the telephone *Hullo, this is Alex.*

**hum** /hʌm/ *verb* **humming,** *past* **hummed 1** [I, T] to sing without opening your mouth *She hummed to herself as she walked to school.* • *I've forgotten the tune. Can you hum it to me?* **2** [I] to make a continuous, low sound *The computers were humming in the background.* **3 be humming** If a place is humming, it is busy and full of activity. • hum *noun* [C] a low, continuous sound *the hum of traffic/voices*

o-ᴋ**human¹** /ˈhjuːmən/ *adj* **1** relating to people or their characteristics *the human body* • *human behaviour* • *The accident was caused by human error* (= a person's mistake). **2 be only human** to not be perfect *Of course Tom makes mistakes – he's only human.*

**human²** /ˈhjuːmən/ (*also* ˌhuman ˈbeing) *noun* [C] a man, woman, or child *The disease affects both humans and animals.*

**humane** /hjuːˈmeɪn/ *adj* kind, especially towards people or animals that are suffering *They fought for more humane treatment of prisoners of war.* ➔ *Opposite* **inhumane**. • humanely *adv*

**humanism** /ˈhjuːmənɪzᵊm/ *noun* [U] a belief system based on human needs and values and not on a god or religion • humanist *noun* [C] • humanistic /ˌhjuːməˈnɪstɪk/ *adj*

**humanitarian** /hjuːˌmænɪˈteəriən/ *adj* connected with improving people's lives and reducing suffering *The UN is sending humanitarian aid to the refugees.*

**humanities** /hjuːˈmænətiz/ *noun* [plural] subjects that you study which are not connected with science, such as literature and history

**humanity** /hjuːˈmænəti/ *noun* [U] **1** ALL PEOPLE all people *The massacre was a crime against humanity.* **2** KINDNESS kindness and sympathy towards others *Mother Teresa was famous for her compassion and humanity.* ➔ *Opposite* **inhumanity**. **3** BEING HUMAN the condition of being human

**humankind** /ˌhjuːmənˈkaɪnd/ *noun* [U] all the people in the world

**humanly** /'hju:mənli/ *adv* **humanly possible** able to be done by people *Doctors did everything humanly possible to save her life.*

,human 'nature *noun* [U] feelings, qualities, and behaviour that are typical of most people *It's human nature to want to be loved.*

the ,human 'race *noun* all the people in the world

,human re'sources *UK* (*US* ,human 'resources) *noun* [U] the department of an organization that deals with finding new people to work there, keeping records about all the organization's employees, and helping them with any problems

,human 'rights *noun* [plural] the basic rights that every person should have, such as justice and the freedom to say what you think *international laws protecting human rights* • *the human rights group Amnesty International*

**humble**¹ /'hʌmbl/ *adj* **1** not proud or not believing that you are important *He's very humble about his success.* **2** poor or of a low social rank *She rose from humble beginnings to become Prime Minister.* • **humbly** *adv*

**humble**² /'hʌmbl/ *verb* [T] to make someone understand that they are not as important or special as they think they are *She was humbled by the unexpected defeat.* • **humbling** *adj a humbling experience*

**humdrum** /'hʌmdrʌm/ *adj* boring and ordinary *a humdrum existence*

**humid** /'hju:mɪd/ *adj* Humid air or weather is hot and slightly wet. *a hot and humid climate*

**humidity** /hju:'mɪdəti/ *noun* [U] a measurement of how much water there is in the air

**humiliate** /hju:'mɪlieɪt/ *verb* [T] to make someone feel stupid or ashamed *How could you humiliate me in front of all my friends!* • **humiliated** *adj Sue felt completely humiliated.* • **humiliation** /hju:,mɪli'eɪʃən/ *noun* [C, U]

**humiliating** /hju:'mɪlieɪtɪŋ/ *adj* making you feel stupid or ashamed *a humiliating defeat*

**humility** /hju:'mɪləti/ *noun* [U] the quality of not being proud or not thinking that you are better than other people

**humor** /'hju:mə/ *noun, verb US spelling of* humour

**humorless** /'hju:mələs/ *adj US spelling of* humourless

**humorous** /'hju:m³rəs/ *adj* funny, or making you laugh *a humorous book* • **humorously** *adv*

**humour**¹ *UK* (*US* **humor**) /'hju:mə/ *noun* [U] **1** [ABILITY] the ability to laugh and recognize that something is funny *He's got a great sense of humour.* **2** [FUNNY QUALITY] the quality of being funny, or things that are funny *His speech was full of humour.* **3** [MOOD] *formal* the way you are feeling, or your mood *good humour*

**humour**² *UK* (*US* **humor**) /'hju:mə/ *verb* [T] to do what someone wants so that they do not become annoyed or upset *Carol applied for the job just to humour me.*

**humourless** *UK* (*US* **humorless**) /'hju:mələs/ *adj* unable to laugh and recognize when something is funny, or being without funny qualities

**hump** /hʌmp/ *noun* [C] **1** a round, raised area on a road or other surface **2** a round, hard part on an animal's or person's back *a camel's hump*

**hunch**¹ /hʌnʃ/ *noun* [C] a feeling or guess that something might be true, when there is no proof *My hunch is that he will resign.* • *I had a hunch that he would get the job.*

**hunch**² /hʌnʃ/ *verb* [I] to stand or sit with your shoulders and back curved forward *Sitting hunched over a computer all day can cause back problems.*

**hunchback** /'hʌnʃbæk/ *noun* [C] someone with a large lump on their back, which makes them lean forward

o—ᵃ**hundred** /'hʌndrəd/ **1** the number 100 **2** **hundreds** *informal* a lot *Hundreds of people wrote in to complain.*

**hundredth**¹ /'hʌndrədθ/ 100th written as a word

**hundredth**² /'hʌndrədθ/ *noun* [C] one of a hundred equal parts of something; 1/100; .01 *a hundredth of a second*

**hundredweight** /'hʌndrədweɪt/ (*written abbreviation* **cwt**) *noun* [C] *plural* **hundredweight** a unit for measuring weight, equal to 50.8 kilograms in the UK and 45.36 kilograms in the US

**hung** /hʌŋ/ *past of* hang

**hunger** /'hʌŋgə/ *noun* **1** [FEELING] [U] the feeling you have when you need to eat *The children were almost crying with hunger by the time we got home.* **2** [NOT ENOUGH FOOD] [U] when you do not have enough food *Many of the refugees **died of hunger**.* **3** [WISH] [no plural] a strong wish for something *a hunger for success/knowledge*

---

**USAGE**

**hunger** or **hungry**?

Remember that **hungry** describes someone who wants or needs food.

*I am hungry.*

~~I have hunger.~~

**Hunger** is the feeling or situation when you do not have food.

*Thousands died of hunger during the famine.*

---

'hunger ,strike *noun* [C, U] when someone refuses to eat in order to show that they strongly disagree with something *The prisoners went on hunger strike.*

**hungover** /,hʌŋ'əʊvə/ *adj* feeling ill after drinking too much alcohol the day before

o—ᵃ**hungry** /'hʌŋgri/ *adj* **1** wanting or needing food *I'm hungry. What's for supper?* • *If you get hungry, there's some food in the fridge.* **2** **go hungry** to not have enough food to eat *In an ideal world, nobody should go hungry.* **3** be **hungry for sth** to have a strong wish for something *The journalists were hungry for more details of the accident.* • **hungrily** *adv*

**hunk** /hʌŋk/ *noun* [C] **1** *informal* an attractive man who is often young and has a strong body **2** a piece of something, usually large and not flat or smooth *a hunk of bread*

**hunt**¹ /hʌnt/ *verb* [I, T] **1** to chase and kill wild animals *to hunt deer/rabbits* **2** to search for something *The children hunted for sea shells on the beach.* • **hunter** *noun* [C] a person who hunts wild animals

**hunt sb/sth down** to search everywhere for someone or something until you find them *The terrorists must be hunted down and brought to justice.*

**hunt²** /hʌnt/ *noun* [C] **1** a search for something or someone *a job hunt* • *The detective leading the hunt for the killer spoke at the news conference.* **2** when people chase and kill wild animals *a fox/deer hunt* ○ *See also:* **witch-hunt.**

**hunting** /'hʌntɪŋ/ *noun* [U] the sport of chasing and killing animals *fox-hunting*

**hurdle¹** /'hɜːdl/ *noun* [C] **1** a bar or fence that people or horses jump over in a race **2** a problem or difficulty that you have to deal with in order to be able to make progress *Getting a work permit was the first hurdle to overcome.*

**hurdle²** /'hɜːdl/ *verb* [I, T] to jump over something, such as a bar or a fence, when you are running • *hurdler noun* [C]

**hurl** /hɜːl/ *verb* **1** [T] to throw something with a lot of force, usually in an angry or violent way *The demonstrators hurled stones at police.* **2 hurl abuse/insults, etc at sb** to shout something at someone in a rude or angry way

**hurrah** (*also* **hooray**) /hə'rɑː/ *exclamation* something that you shout when you are happy, excited, etc, or when you approve of someone or something *Hurrah! Ian's won!*

**hurricane** /'hʌrɪkən/ *noun* [C] a violent storm with very strong winds

**hurried** /'hʌrid/ *adj* done more quickly than normal *a hurried explanation/meeting* • *hurriedly adv*

○━**hurry¹** /'hʌri/ *verb* [I, T] to move or do things more quickly than normal or to make someone do this *to hurry away/home* • *Please hurry, the train is about to leave.* • [+ to do sth] *We had to hurry to get there on time.*

**hurry up** to start moving or doing something more quickly *Hurry up! We're going to be late.*

**hurry²** /'hʌri/ *noun* **1 be in a hurry** If you are in a hurry, you want or need to do something quickly. *If you're in a hurry, it's better to take a taxi.* • *He left in a hurry and forgot his umbrella.* **2 be in no hurry; not be in any hurry** If you are in no hurry to do something, either you do not need to do it soon or you do not really want to do it . [+ to do sth] *They are in no hurry to sign a contract.*

○━**hurt¹** /hɜːt/ *verb past* **hurt 1** CAUSE PAIN [T] to cause someone pain or to injure them *Simon hurt his knee playing football.* • [often reflexive] *She hurt herself when she slipped on an icy step.* **2** BE PAINFUL [I] If a part of your body hurts, it is painful. *My eyes really hurt.* • *Where does it hurt ?* • [+ to do sth] *It hurts to walk on it.* **3** UPSET [I, T] to cause emotional pain to someone *Her comments about my work really hurt.* **4** AFFECT [T] to have a harmful effect on something *His chances of re-election were hurt by allegations of corruption.* **5 it won't/ wouldn't hurt (sb) to do sth** *informal* used to say that someone should do something *It wouldn't hurt to get there a bit earlier than usual.* ○ *See also:* wouldn't hurt a **fly².**

**hurt²** /hɜːt/ *adj* [never before noun] **1** injured or in pain *Several people were seriously hurt in the accident.* • *Put that knife away before someone*

*gets hurt.* **2** upset or unhappy *She was deeply hurt by what he said.*

**hurt³** /hɜːt/ *noun* [U] emotional pain *She has caused a lot of hurt.* • *hurtful adj* making someone feel upset *hurtful comments/remarks*

**hurtle** /'hɜːtl/ *verb* [I] to move very quickly in a way which is not controlled and may be dangerous *The explosion sent pieces of glass and metal hurtling through the air.*

○━**husband** /'hʌzbənd/ *noun* [C] the man you are married to *Janet's husband is in the Navy.*

**hush¹** /hʌʃ/ *exclamation* used to tell someone to be quiet, especially if they are crying *It's okay. Hush now and wipe your eyes.*

**hush²** /hʌʃ/ *noun* [no plural] a period of silence *A hush fell over the room.* • *hushed adj a hushed atmosphere/crowd*

**hush³** /hʌʃ/ *verb* [T] to make someone be quiet

**hush sth up** to keep something secret, especially from the public, because it could cause embarrassment or trouble *The whole affair was hushed up by the management.*

**hush-hush** /ˌhʌʃ'hʌʃ/ *adj informal* If something is hush-hush, it is kept secret. *The project's all very hush-hush.*

**husky¹** /'hʌski/ *adj* **1** A husky voice is low and rough but usually sounds attractive. **2** *US* A husky man or boy is big and strong.

**husky²** /'hʌski/ *noun* [C] a large, strong dog that is used to pull heavy things across snow

**hustle¹** /'hʌsl/ *verb* **1** [T] to make someone move somewhere, especially by pushing them quickly *The security men hustled him out of the back door.* **2** [I, T] *informal* to try to persuade someone, especially to buy something, often illegally *to hustle for business/customers*

**hustle²** /'hʌsl/ *noun* **hustle and bustle** busy movement and noise, especially where there are a lot of people *He wanted to escape the hustle and bustle of city life.*

**hustler** /'hʌslə²/ *noun* [C] someone who tries to persuade people to give them what they want, especially in order to make money illegally

**hut** /hʌt/ *noun* [C] a small, simple building, often made of wood *a mountain hut*

**hybrid** /'haɪbrɪd/ *noun* [C] **1** a plant or animal that is produced from two different types of plant or animal **2** something, for example a machine, which is made using ideas or parts from two different things • *hybrid adj*

**hydrant** /'haɪdrənt/ *noun* [C] a pipe, especially at the side of the road, which is connected to the water system and is used to get water to stop fires *a fire hydrant*

**hydraulic** /haɪ'drɔːlɪk/ *adj* operated using the force of water or another liquid

**hydroelectric** /ˌhaɪdrəʊɪ'lektrɪk/ *adj* using the force of water to create electricity *hydroelectric power*

**hydrogen** /'haɪdrədʒən/ *noun* [U] a gas that combines with oxygen to form water

**hygiene** /'haɪdʒiːn/ *noun* [U] the process of keeping things clean, especially to prevent disease *health and hygiene regulations* • *dental/personal hygiene* • *hygienic* /haɪ'dʒiːnɪk/ *adj* very clean, so that bacteria cannot spread

**hymn** /hɪm/ *noun* [C] a song sung by Christians in church to praise God

**hype¹** /haɪp/ noun [U] when people talk a lot about something, especially in newspapers, on television, etc, and make it seem more important or exciting than it really is *media hype* • *There's been a lot of hype about/surrounding his latest film.*

**hype²** /haɪp/ (*also* **hype up**) verb [T] to make something seem more important or exciting than it really is by talking about it a lot, especially in newspapers, on television, etc *It's being hyped as the musical event of the year.* • hyped *adj*

**hyper** /'haɪpər/ adj informal Someone who is hyper has more energy than is normal and is very excited.

**hyperactive** /ˌhaɪpər'æktɪv/ adj Someone who is hyperactive has more energy than is normal, gets excited easily, and cannot stay still or think about their work. *hyperactive children* • hyperactivity /ˌhaɪpərˈræktɪvəti/ noun [U]

**hyperbole** /haɪˈpɜːbəli/ noun [U] formal when you describe something as much better, more important, etc than it really is

**hyperlink** /'haɪpəlɪŋk/ noun [C] a connection that lets you move easily between two computer documents or two pages on the Internet

**hypertext** /'haɪpətekst/ noun [U] a way of joining a word or image to another page, document, etc on the Internet or in another computer program so that you can move from one to the other easily

**hyphen** /'haɪfᵊn/ noun [C] a mark (-) used to join two words together, or to show that a word has been divided and continues on the next line • hyphenated *adj* written with a hyphen

**hypnosis** /hɪpˈnəʊsɪs/ noun [U] a mental state like sleep, in which a person's thoughts can be easily influenced by someone else *Police placed witnesses under hypnosis in an effort to gain additional information.* • hypnotic /hɪpˈnɒtɪk/ adj

**hypnotize** (*also UK* **-ise**) /'hɪpnətaɪz/ verb [T] to place someone in a mental state like sleep, in which their thoughts can be easily influenced

• hypnotist *noun* [C] someone who hypnotizes people • hypnotism /'hɪpnətɪzᵊm/ noun [U] when someone is hypnotized

**hypochondriac** /ˌhaɪpəˈkɒndriæk/ noun [C] someone who worries about their health more than is normal, although they are not really ill • hypochondria /ˌhaɪpəʊˈkɒndriə/ noun [U]

**hypocrisy** /hɪˈpɒkrəsi/ noun [C, U] when someone pretends to believe something that they do not really believe or that is the opposite of what they do or say at another time

**hypocrite** /'hɪpəkrɪt/ noun [C] someone who pretends to believe something that they do not really believe or that is the opposite of what they do or say at another time • hypocritical /ˌhɪpəʊˈkrɪtɪkᵊl/ adj • hypocritically adv

**hypothermia** /ˌhaɪpəʊˈθɜːmiə/ noun [U] a serious illness caused by someone's body becoming too cold

**hypothesis** /haɪˈpɒθəsɪs/ noun [C] plural **hypotheses** /haɪˈpɒθəsiːz/ a suggested explanation for something which has not yet been proved to be true

**hypothetical** /ˌhaɪpəˈθetɪkᵊl/ adj A hypothetical situation or idea has been suggested but does not yet really exist or has not been proved to be true.

**hysteria** /hɪˈstɪəriə/ noun [U] extreme fear, excitement, anger, etc which cannot be controlled *mass hysteria*

**hysterical** /hɪˈsterɪkᵊl/ adj **1** If someone is hysterical, they cannot control their feelings or behaviour because they are extremely frightened, angry, excited, etc. *hysterical laughter* • *As soon as Wendy saw the blood, she became hysterical.* **2** informal extremely funny • hysterically adv *They all thought it was hysterically funny.*

**hysterics** /hɪˈsterɪks/ noun **1** [plural] uncontrolled behaviour **2 in hysterics** informal laughing so much that you cannot stop *Most of the audience was in hysterics by this time.*

**Hz** written abbreviation for hertz (= a unit of measurement used in electronics)

H

icon

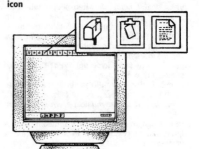

**I, i** /aɪ/ the ninth letter of the alphabet

o-**I** /aɪ/ *pronoun* used when the person speaking or writing is the subject of the verb *I had lunch with Glen yesterday.* • *Chris and I have been married for twelve years.* ⊃ *See usage note at* **me**.

o-**ice¹** /aɪs/ *noun* [U] **1** water that has frozen and become solid *Gerry slipped on the ice and broke his arm.* • *I've put a couple of bottles of champagne on ice* (= in a bucket of ice to get cold). **2 break the ice** to make people who have not met before feel relaxed with each other, often by starting a conversation

**ice²** /aɪs/ (*also US* **frost**) *verb* [T] to cover a cake with icing (= sweet mixture used to cover cakes) *an iced bun*

**iceberg** /'aɪsbɜːɡ/ *noun* [C] a very large piece of ice that floats in the sea ⊃ *See also:* be the **tip¹** of the iceberg.

**ice 'cream** *UK* (*US* '**ice ,cream**) *noun* [C, U] a sweet food made from frozen milk or cream and sugar *chocolate/vanilla ice cream*

'**ice ,cube** *noun* [C] a small block of ice that you put into drinks to make them cold

'**ice ,hockey** (*also US* **hockey**) *noun* [U] a game played on ice in which two teams try to hit a small hard object into a goal using long curved sticks ⊃ *See colour picture* **Sports 1** *on page Centre 15.*

'**ice ,rink** *noun* [C] an area of ice, usually inside a building, which is prepared for people to ice skate on

'**ice ,skate** *noun* [C] a boot with a metal part on the bottom, used for moving across ice • **ice skate** *verb* [I] to move across ice using ice skates • **ice skating** *noun* the activity or sport of moving across ice using ice skates ⊃ *See colour picture* **Sports 1** *on page Centre 15.*

**icicle** /'aɪsɪkl/ *noun* [C] a long, thin piece of ice that hangs down from something

**icing** /'aɪsɪŋ/ *noun* [U] **1** (*also US* **frosting**) a sweet mixture used to cover or fill cakes, made from sugar and water or sugar and butter *chocolate butter icing* **2 the icing on the cake** something that makes a good situation better *He was delighted to get the article published and the £100 payment was the icing on the cake.*

**icon** /'aɪkɒn/ *noun* [C] **1** a small picture on a computer screen that you choose in order to make the computer do something *Click on the print icon.* **2** a person or thing that is famous because it represents a particular idea or way of life *a cultural/feminist icon*

**icy** /'aɪsi/ *adj* **1** WITH ICE covered in ice *icy conditions/roads* **2** COLD extremely cold *an icy wind* • *icy water* **3** WITHOUT EMOTION without showing any emotion *an icy look/stare* • **icily** *adv*

**I'd** /aɪd/ **1** short for I had *Everyone thought I'd gone.* **2** short for I would *I'd like to buy some stamps, please.*

**ID** /ˌaɪ'diː/ *noun* [C, U] *abbreviation for* identification: an official document that shows or proves

who you are *You'll need to show some form of ID, such as a passport or driving licence.*

o-**idea** /aɪ'dɪə/ *noun* **1** SUGGESTION [C] a suggestion or plan *"Why don't we ask George?" "That's a good idea."* • [+ for + doing sth] *Stevens explained his ideas for improving production.* • [+ to do sth] *It was Kate's idea to hire a car.* **2** THOUGHT [U, no plural] an understanding, thought, or picture in your mind [+ of + doing sth] *Clive soon got used to the idea of having children around the house again.* • [+ (that)] *I don't want them to get the idea that we're not interested.* **3 have no idea** to not know *Beth had no idea where he'd gone.* **4** OPINION [C] an opinion or belief *My husband and I have very different ideas about school discipline.* **5** AIM [no plural] the aim or purpose of something *The idea is to give local people a chance to voice their opinions.* ⊃ *See also:* not have the foggiest (**foggy**) idea.

**ideal¹** /aɪ'dɪəl/ *adj* perfect, or the best possible *an ideal candidate/solution* • *The book is ideal for children aged 4 to 6.* • *In an ideal world, you wouldn't need to use a keyboard at all.*

**ideal²** /aɪ'dɪəl/ *noun* **1** [C] a belief about the way you think something should be *democratic ideals* • *They are committed to the ideal of equality.* **2** [no plural] a perfect thing or situation *The ideal would be to have a house in the country and a flat in the city too.*

**idealism** /aɪ'dɪəlɪzᵊm/ *noun* [U] the belief that your ideals can be achieved, often when this does not seem likely to others • **idealist** *noun* [C] a person who believes that it is possible to achieve your ideals • **idealistic** /aɪˌdɪə'lɪstɪk/ *adj*

**ideally** /aɪ'dɪəli/ *adv* **1** used to describe how something would be in a perfect situation *Ideally, I'd like to work at home.* **2** in a perfect way *She seemed ideally suited for the job.*

**identical** /aɪ'dentɪkᵊl/ *adj* exactly the same *The two rooms were almost/virtually identical.* • *She found a dress identical to the one in the picture.* • **identically** *adv*

**i,dentical 'twin** *noun* [C] one of two babies who are born at the same time from the same egg, and look exactly the same

**identifiable** /aɪˌdentɪ'faɪəbl/ *adj* If someone or something is identifiable, you can recognize them and say or prove who or what they are. *clearly/readily identifiable*

**identification** /aɪˌdentɪfɪˈkeɪʃən/ noun [U] **1** when you recognize and can name someone or something *Most of the bodies were badly burned, making identification almost impossible.* **2** an official document that shows or proves who you are *an identification card/number* • *The shop requires two forms of identification before you can borrow a video.*

O─┐**identify** /aɪˈdentɪfaɪ/ verb [T] **1** RECOGNIZE to recognize someone or something and say or prove who or what they are *The gunman in Wednesday's attack has been identified as Lee Giggs, an unemployed truck driver.* **2** NAME to tell people who someone is *My informant asked not to be identified.* **3** DISCOVER to find a particular thing or all the things of a particular group *You need to identify your priorities.*

**identify sb/sth with sb/sth** to connect one person or thing with another *As a politician he was identified with liberal causes.*

**identify with sb/sth** to feel that you are similar to someone, and can understand them or their situation because of this *I grew up on a farm too, so I can identify with his problems.*

**identity** /aɪˈdentəti/ noun [C, U] **1** who someone is *They promised to keep her identity secret.* • *Police are trying to establish the identity of a woman seen walking away from the accident.* **2** the things that make one person or group of people different from others *cultural/national identity*

**ideological** /ˌaɪdiəˈlɒdʒɪkəl/ adj based on or relating to a particular set of ideas or beliefs *ideological conflicts/disagreements* • ideologically adv

**ideology** /ˌaɪdiˈɒlədʒi/ noun [C, U] a set of ideas or beliefs, especially about politics *socialist ideology*

**idiom** /ˈɪdiəm/ noun [C] a group of words used together with a meaning that you cannot guess from the meanings of the separate words • idiomatic /ˌɪdiəˈmætɪk/ adj *idiomatic language*

**idiosyncratic** /ˌɪdiəʊsɪŋˈkrætɪk/ adj An idiosyncratic quality or way of behaving is typical of only one person and is often strange or unusual. • idiosyncrasy /ˌɪdiəʊˈsɪŋkrəsi/ noun [C] *an idiosyncratic habit or way of behaving*

**idiot** /ˈɪdiət/ noun [C] a stupid person or someone who is behaving in a stupid way *Like an idiot, I believed him.* • idiocy /ˈɪdiəsi/ noun [C, U] stupid behaviour • idiotic /ˌɪdiˈɒtɪk/ adj stupid *an idiotic grin/idea* • idiotically adv

**idle¹** /ˈaɪdl/ adj **1** NOT WORKING not working or being used *The factory has stood idle for over a year.* **2** NOT SERIOUS [always before noun] not serious or having no real purpose *idle gossip* • *This is no idle threat.* **3** LAZY lazy and not willing to work *He knows what has to be done, he's just bone idle* (= extremely lazy). • idleness noun [U] • idly adv *We cannot stand idly by* (= not do anything) *and let this plan go ahead.*

**idle²** /ˈaɪdl/ verb ENGINE [I] If an engine or machine idles, it runs slowly but does not move or do any work. *He left the engine idling and ran into the shop.* **2** STOP WORKING [T] US to stop someone or something working or being used, often because there is not enough work to do *The closure of the plant idled about 300 workers.* **3** TIME [I] to spend time doing nothing *We saw her idling in the school grounds.*

**idle sth away** to waste time doing nothing *I idled away a few hours watching TV.*

**idol** /ˈaɪdəl/ noun [C] **1** someone that you admire and respect very much *a pop/sporting idol* **2** a picture or object that people pray to as part of their religion • idolize (also UK -ise) verb [T] to admire and respect someone very much

**idyllic** /ɪˈdɪlɪk/ adj An idyllic place or experience is extremely pleasant, beautiful, or peaceful. *an idyllic childhood/summer*

**i.e.** (also **ie**) /ˌaɪˈiː/ used to explain exactly what you are referring to or what you mean *The price must be more realistic, i.e. lower.*

O─┐**if¹** /ɪf/ conjunction **1** DEPEND used to say that something will happen only after something else happens or is true *We'll have the party in the garden if the weather's good.* • *If you eat up all your dinner you can have some chocolate.* **2** MIGHT used to talk about something that might happen or be true *I'm sorry if I've offended you.* • *What will we do if this doesn't work?* **3** WHETHER whether *I wonder if he'll get the job.* • *Have you asked her if she'd like to come?* **4** ALWAYS used to mean always or every time *If you mention his mother, he always cries.*

**if²** /ɪf/ noun [C] informal something which is not certain or not yet decided *There are still a lot of ifs.* • *There are no ifs and buts* (= no doubts or excuses) *about it – we'll have to start again.*

**iffy** /ˈɪfi/ adj informal **1** not completely good, honest, or suitable *The milk smells a bit iffy.* **2** not certain or decided *Simon's still kind of iffy about going to Columbia.*

**igloo** /ˈɪɡluː/ noun [C] a house made of blocks of hard snow

**igloo**

**ignite** /ɪɡˈnaɪt/ verb formal **1** [I, T] to start to burn or make something start to burn *A spark ignited the fumes.* **2** [T] to start an argument or fight

**ignition** /ɪɡˈnɪʃən/ noun **1** [no plural] the part of a car that starts the engine *He turned the key in the ignition.* ➾ *See colour picture* **Car** *on page Centre 3.* **2** [U] formal when something makes something start to burn

**ignominious** /ˌɪɡnəˈmɪniəs/ adj formal making you feel embarrassed or ashamed *an ignominious defeat* • ignominiously adv

**ignorance** /ˈɪɡnərəns/ noun [U] when someone does not have enough knowledge, understanding, or information about something *There is still widespread **ignorance about** the disease.* • *I was shocked by her total **ignorance of** world history.*

**ignorant** /ˈɪɡnərənt/ adj **1** not having enough knowledge, understanding, or information about something *He was a newcomer to Formula One and **ignorant of** many of the* *circuits.* **2** *UK* not polite or showing respect *an ignorant lout*

o━ **ignore** /ɪɡˈnɔːʳ/ *verb* [T] to pay no attention to something or someone *They just ignored him and carried on with the game.* • *We cannot afford to ignore the fact that the world's population is increasing rapidly.*

o━ **ill**[1] /ɪl/ *adj* **1** not feeling well, or suffering from a disease *critically/seriously ill* • *Her mother was too ill to travel.* • *Mark had been feeling ill for a couple of days.* ➜ *See usage note at* **sick**. **2** [always before noun] *formal* bad *ill health* • *He suffered no ill effects from his fall.* ➜ *See also:* ill at **ease**[1].

**ill**[2] /ɪl/ *noun* [C] *formal* a problem [usually plural] *social and economic ills*

**ill**[3] /ɪl/ *adv formal* **1** badly *Many of the nurses were ill prepared to deal with such badly burned patients.* **2 can ill afford (to do) sth** If you can ill afford to do something, it is likely to make things difficult for you if you do it. *This is a match United can ill afford to lose.* **3 speak ill of sb** to say bad things about someone

**ill-advised** /ˌɪlədˈvaɪzd/ *adj* not wise, and likely to cause problems in the future

**ill-conceived** /ˌɪlkənˈsiːvd/ *adj* badly planned or not wise

o━ **illegal** /ɪˈliːɡ³l/ *adj* not allowed by law *illegal drugs/weapons* • [+ to do sth] *It is illegal to sell cigarettes to anyone under 16.* • **illegally** *adv an illegally parked car*

**il,legal 'immigrant** (*also US* **il,legal 'alien**) *noun* [C] someone who goes to live or work in another country when they do not have the legal right to

**illegible** /ɪˈledʒəbl/ *adj* Illegible writing is difficult or impossible to read.

**illegitimate** /ˌɪlɪˈdʒɪtəmət/ *adj* **1** An illegitimate child is born to parents who are not married to each other. **2** not legal, honest, or fair *an illegitimate use of council funds* • **illegitimacy** /ˌɪlɪˈdʒɪtəməsi/ *noun* [U]

**ill-equipped** /ˌɪlɪˈkwɪpt/ *adj* **1** not having the necessary equipment **2** not having the necessary ability or qualities to do something [+ to do sth] *These teachers were ill-equipped to deal with rowdy students.*

**ill-fated** /ˌɪlˈfeɪtɪd/ *adj* unlucky and often unsuccessful *an ill-fated expedition to the South Pole*

**ill-fitting** /ˌɪlˈfɪtɪŋ/ *adj* Ill-fitting clothes do not fit well.

**ill-gotten** /ˌɪlˈɡɒt³n/ *adj literary* obtained in a dishonest or illegal way *He deposited his ill-gotten gains in foreign bank accounts.*

**illicit** /ɪˈlɪsɪt/ *adj* not legal or not approved of by society *an illicit love affair*

**ill-informed** /ˌɪlɪnˈfɔːmd/ *adj* without enough knowledge or information *an ill-informed decision*

**illiterate** /ɪˈlɪt³rət/ *adj* not able to read or write

o━ **illness** /ˈɪlnəs/ *noun* **1** [C] a disease of the body or mind *a serious/terminal illness* • *He died at the age of 83 after a long illness.* **2** [U] when you are ill *Unfortunately I couldn't go because of illness.*

**illogical** /ɪˈlɒdʒɪk³l/ *adj* not based on careful thought *It would be illogical for them to stop at this stage.*

**illuminate** /ɪˈluːmɪneɪt/ *verb* [T] **1** to shine lights on something *The paintings and sculptures are illuminated by spotlights.* **2** to explain something clearly or make it easier to understand • **illumination** /ɪˌluːmɪˈneɪʃ³n/ *noun* [C, U] *formal*

**illuminating** /ɪˈluːmɪneɪtɪŋ/ *adj* giving you new information about something or making it easier to understand *a most illuminating discussion*

**illusion** /ɪˈluːʒ³n/ *noun* **1** [C, U] an idea or belief that is not true *He had no illusions about his talents as a singer.* • *We are not under any illusion – we know the work is dangerous.* **2** [C] something that is not really what it seems to be *There is a large mirror at one end to create the illusion of more space.* ➜ *See also:* **optical illusion**.

**illustrate** /ˈɪləstreɪt/ *verb* [T] **1** to give more information or examples to explain or prove something *to illustrate a point/problem* • [+ question word] *This new discovery illustrates how little we know about early human history.* **2** to draw pictures for a book, magazine, etc *an illustrated children's book*

**illustration** /ˌɪləˈstreɪʃ³n/ *noun* **1** [C] a picture in a book, magazine, etc *a full-page colour illustration* **2** [C, U] an example that explains or proves something *This is another illustration of the power of the media.*

**illustrator** /ˈɪləstreɪtəʳ/ *noun* [C] a person whose job is to draw or paint pictures for books

**illustrious** /ɪˈlʌstriəs/ *adj formal* famous and well respected *an illustrious career*

**,ill 'will** *noun* [U] bad feelings between people because of things that happened in the past

**I'm** /aɪm/ *short for* I am

o━ **image** /ˈɪmɪdʒ/ *noun* **1** PUBLIC [C, U] the way that other people think someone or something is *The aim is to improve the public image of the police.* **2** PICTURE [C] a picture, especially on film or television or in a mirror *television images of starving children* **3** IDEA [C] a picture in your mind or an idea of how someone or something is *I have an image in my mind of the way I want the garden to look.*

**imagery** /ˈɪmɪdʒ³ri/ *noun* [U] the use of words or pictures in books, films, paintings, etc to describe ideas or situations

**imaginable** /ɪˈmædʒɪnəbl/ *adj* possible to think of *ice cream of every imaginable flavour* ➜ *Opposite* **unimaginable**.

**imaginary** /ɪˈmædʒɪn³ri/ *adj* not real but imagined in your mind *The story takes place in an imaginary world.*

o━ **imagination** /ɪˌmædʒɪˈneɪʃ³n/ *noun* **1** [C] the part of your mind that creates ideas or pictures of things that are not real or that you have not seen [usually singular] *There's nothing out here – it's just your imagination.* **2** [U] the ability to create ideas or pictures in your mind *The job needs someone with creativity and imagination.* ➜ *See also:* not by any **stretch**[2] of the imagination.

**imaginative** /ɪˈmædʒɪnətɪv/ *adj* **1** Something which is imaginative is new or clever and often unusual. *an imaginative use of colour* **2** Someone who is imaginative is able to create new and interesting ideas or things. *a highly imaginative poet* • imaginatively *adv*

o—•**imagine** /ɪˈmædʒɪn/ *verb* [T] **1** CREATE to create an idea or picture of something in your mind [+ doing sth] *Imagine being able to do all your shopping from your armchair.* • [+ question word] *You can imagine how pleased I was when the letter arrived.* **2** BELIEVE to believe that something is probably true *I imagine he must be under a lot of pressure at the moment.* **3** NOT REAL to think that you hear or see something which does not really exist *I can't hear anything – you must be imagining it.*

**imaging** /ˈɪmɪdʒɪŋ/ *noun* [U] the process of producing an exact picture of something, especially on a computer screen *computer/digital imaging*

**imbalance** /ˌɪmˈbæləns/ *noun* [C] when two things which should be equal or are normally equal are not *There is a huge economic imbalance between the two countries.*

**imbue** /ɪmˈbjuː/ *verb* imbuing, *past* imbued **imbue sb/sth with sth** to fill someone or something with a particular feeling, quality, or idea *His poetry is imbued with deep religious feeling.*

**imitate** /ˈɪmɪteɪt/ *verb* [T] to copy the way someone or something looks, sounds, or behaves *She tried to imitate the way the models walked.* • imitator *noun* [C]

**imitation** /ˌɪmɪˈteɪʃᵊn/ *noun* **1** [C, U] when someone copies the way another person speaks or behaves *He does a very good imitation of the Prime Minister.* **2** [C] a copy of something that is made to look like the real thing *It wasn't a genuine Gucci handbag, just a cheap imitation.* • *imitation leather/fur*

**immaculate** /ɪˈmækjələt/ *adj* **1** perfectly clean and tidy or in perfect condition *an immaculate garden/room* **2** perfect and without any mistakes *an immaculate performance* • immaculately *adv*

**immaterial** /ˌɪməˈtɪəriəl/ *adj* If something is immaterial, it is not important because it does not affect a situation.

**immature** /ˌɪməˈtjʊəʳ/ *adj* **1** not behaving in a way which is as wise and calm as people expect from someone your age *Some of the boys are quite immature for their age.* **2** not completely developed *immature cells* • immaturity *noun* [U]

**immeasurable** /ɪˈmeʒᵊrəbl/ *adj* very large or extreme and so impossible to measure *the immeasurable pain of losing a child* • immeasurably *adv His confidence has grown immeasurably since he got the job.*

o—•**immediate** /ɪˈmiːdiət/ *adj* **1** WITHOUT WAITING happening or done without waiting or very soon after something else *The government has promised to take immediate action.* • *Her first novel was an immediate success.* • *The drugs will have an immediate effect.* **2** IMPORTANT NOW important now and needing attention *Our immediate concern is getting food and water to the refugees.* **3** CLOSEST [always before noun] closest to something or someone *Police cleared people from the immediate area following the bomb warning.* **4** **the immediate future** the period of time that is coming next **5** **sb's immediate family** someone's closest relatives, such

as their parents, children, husband, or wife

o—•**immediately**[1] /ɪˈmiːdiətli/ *adv* **1** now or without waiting or thinking about something *You have to come home immediately.* • *The cause of the problem wasn't immediately obvious.* **2** next to something, or close to something in time *There are fields immediately behind the house.* • *Cole scored again immediately after half-time.*

**immediately**[2] /ɪˈmiːdiətli/ *conjunction UK* as soon as *Immediately I saw her I knew something terrible had happened.*

**immense** /ɪˈmens/ *adj* extremely big *immense pressure/value* • *Health care costs the country an immense amount of money.*

**immensely** /ɪˈmensli/ *adv* extremely *immensely important/popular*

**immerse** /ɪˈmɜːs/ *verb* **1** **be immersed in sth; immerse yourself in sth** to be or become completely involved in something, so that you do not notice anything else *I didn't hear him come in because I was totally immersed in my book.* **2** [T] to put something in a liquid so that it is completely covered • immersion /ɪˈmɜːʃᵊn/ *noun* [U]

**immigrant** /ˈɪmɪgrənt/ *noun* [C] someone who comes to live in a different country ➋ *See also:* **illegal immigrant**.

**immigration** /ˌɪmɪˈɡreɪʃᵊn/ *noun* [U] **1** when someone comes to live in a different country *immigration policy* **2** the place where people's official documents are checked when they enter a country at an airport, port, border, etc *immigration control* • *an immigration official* • immigrate /ˈɪmɪɡreɪt/ *verb* [I] to come to live in a different country

**imminent** /ˈɪmɪnənt/ *adj* coming or happening very soon *imminent danger* • *An agreement looks imminent.*

**immobile** /ɪˈməʊbaɪl/ US /ɪˈməʊbᵊl/ *adj* not moving or not able to move • immobility /ˌɪməʊˈbɪləti/ *noun* [U]

**immoral** /ɪˈmɒrᵊl/ *adj* morally wrong *immoral behaviour* • immorality /ˌɪməˈræləti/ *noun* [U]

**immortal** /ɪˈmɔːtᵊl/ *adj* **1** living or lasting forever *an immortal soul/God* **2** famous or remembered for a very long time *Then he uttered the immortal line - "My name is Bond".* • immortality /ˌɪmɔːˈtæləti/ *noun* [U]

**immortalize** (*also UK* -ise) /ɪˈmɔːtᵊlaɪz/ *verb* [T] to make someone or something famous for a long time [often passive] *Their relationship was immortalized in a recent film.*

**immune** /ɪˈmjuːn/ *adj* **1** PROTECTED [never before noun] If you are immune to a disease, you will not get it. *Once you've had the virus, you are immune to it.* **2** BODY SYSTEM [always before noun] relating to the way your body fights disease *an immune deficiency/response* **3** NOT AFFECTED [never before noun] not affected by a particular type of behaviour or emotion *He is immune to flattery.* **4** NOT PUNISHED [never before noun] not able to be punished or damaged by something *His diplomatic passport makes him immune from prosecution.*

im'mune ˌsystem *noun* [C] the cells and tissues in your body that fight against infection [usually singular] *Vitamins help boost*

(= make stronger) *your **immune system**.*

**immunity** /ɪˈmjuːnəti/ *noun* [U] when you are immune, especially to disease or from legal action *diplomatic immunity* • *The vaccine gives you lifelong **immunity to** the virus.*

**immunize** (*also UK* **-ise**) /ˈɪmjənaɪz/ *verb* [T] to make a person or animal immune by giving them special medicine *He was **immunized against** measles as a child.* • immunization /ˌɪmjənaɪˈzeɪʃᵊn/ *noun* [C, U] *a programme of mass immunization*

**impact**[1] /ˈɪmpækt/ *noun* **1** [no plural] the effect that a person, event, or situation has on someone or something *Latino singers **have had** a major **impact on** pop music this year.* **2** [U] the force or action of one object hitting another *The impact of the collision threw her out of the van.* • *The missile explodes on **impact** (= when it hits another object).*

**impact**[2] /ɪmˈpækt/ (*also* **impact on/upon**) *verb* [T] *mainly US* to affect something or someone *Rising interest rates are sure to **impact on** the housing market.*

**impair** /ɪmˈpeəʳ/ *verb* [T] *formal* to harm something and make it less good [often passive] *When you're tired your judgment is impaired.* • impairment *noun* [C, U] when something is impaired *mental/physical impairment*

**impaired** /ɪmˈpeəd/ *adj* **visually/hearing impaired** unable to see or hear as well as most people

**impale** /ɪmˈpeɪl/ *verb* [T] to push a sharp object through something or someone

**impart** /ɪmˈpɑːt/ *verb* [T] *formal* **1** to communicate information or knowledge to someone *I have disappointing news to impart.* **2** to give something a particular feeling, quality, or taste *Preservatives can impart colour and flavour to a product.*

**impartial** /ɪmˈpɑːʃᵊl/ *adj* not supporting or preferring any person, group, plan, etc more than others *impartial advice* • *A trial must be fair and impartial.* • impartiality /ɪmˌpɑːʃiˈæləti/ *noun* [U] when someone or something is impartial

**impassable** /ɪmˈpɑːsəbl/ *adj* If roads or paths are impassable, vehicles cannot move along them.

**impasse** /ˈæmpæs ⓊⓈ ˈɪmpæs/ *noun* [U] a situation in which it is impossible to make any progress *He is determined to **break** (= end) **the impasse** in the peace process.*

**impassioned** /ɪmˈpæʃᵊnd/ *adj* showing and expressing strong emotion *an impassioned plea/speech*

**impassive** /ɪmˈpæsɪv/ *adj* An impassive person or face shows no emotion. • impassively *adv*

**impatience** /ɪmˈpeɪʃᵊns/ *noun* [U] when someone is impatient

**impatient** /ɪmˈpeɪʃᵊnt/ *adj* **1** easily annoyed by someone's mistakes or because you have to wait *I do get **impatient with** the children when they won't do their homework.* **2** [never before noun] wanting something to happen as soon as possible [+ to do sth] *We were up early, impatient to make a start.* • *People are increasingly **impatient for** change in this country.* • impatiently *adv We waited impatiently for the show to begin.*

**impeccable** /ɪmˈpekəbl/ *adj* perfect and with

no mistakes *She speaks impeccable English.* • *His manners were impeccable.* • impeccably *adv impeccably dressed*

**impede** /ɪmˈpiːd/ *verb* [T] *formal* to make it difficult or impossible for someone or something to move or make progress *A broken-down car is impeding the flow of traffic.*

**impediment** /ɪmˈpedɪmənt/ *noun* [C] **1** *formal* something that makes it difficult or impossible for someone or something to move or make progress *Cramped classrooms are an **impediment to** learning.* **2** a problem that makes speaking, hearing, or moving difficult *a speech impediment*

**impel** /ɪmˈpel/ *verb* [T] **impelling**, *past* **impelled** *formal* to make you feel that you must do something [+ to do sth] *Harry felt impelled to tell the truth.*

**impending** /ɪmˈpendɪŋ/ *adj* [always before noun] An impending event will happen soon and is usually bad or unpleasant. *impending disaster/doom* • *I've just heard about the impending departure of our chairman.*

**impenetrable** /ɪmˈpenɪtrəbl/ *adj* **1** impossible to understand *impenetrable jargon* **2** impossible to see through or go through *impenetrable fog*

**imperative**[1] /ɪmˈperətɪv/ *adj* **1** *formal* When an action or process is imperative, it is extremely important that it happens or is done. [+ (that)] *It is imperative that I speak with him at once.* **2** An imperative form of a verb is used to express an order. In the sentence 'Stop the machine!', the verb 'stop' is an imperative verb.

**imperative**[2] /ɪmˈperətɪv/ *noun* [C] **1** something that must happen, exist, or be done *a moral/political imperative* **2** the imperative form of a verb

**imperceptible** /ˌɪmpəˈseptəbl/ *adj* not able to be noticed or felt *She heard a faint, almost imperceptible cry.* • imperceptibly *adv*

**imperfect** /ɪmˈpɜːfɪkt/ *adj* not perfect and with some mistakes *an imperfect solution* • imperfectly *adv*

**the imperfect** /ɪmˈpɜːfɪkt/ (*also* **the im‚perfect 'tense**) *noun* The form of the verb that is used to show an action in the past which has not been completed. In the sentence 'We were crossing the road', 'were crossing' is in the imperfect.

**imperfection** /ˌɪmpəˈfekʃᵊn/ *noun* [C, U] something or someone is not perfect *Make-up can hide small skin imperfections.*

**imperial** /ɪmˈpɪəriəl/ *adj* **1** [always before noun] relating or belonging to an empire (= group of countries ruled by one person or government) or the person who rules it *imperial rule* • *the imperial family* **2** The imperial system of measurement uses units based on measurements such as inches, pints, and ounces.

**imperialism** /ɪmˈpɪəriəlɪzᵊm/ *noun* [U] **1** when one government or person rules a group of other countries *the age of imperialism* **2** when one country has a lot of power or influence over others *cultural/economic imperialism* • imperialist *adj* relating to imperialism

**imperil** /ɪmˈperᵊl/ *verb* [T] (*UK*) **imperilling**, *past*

**imperilled**, (US) **imperiling**, *past* **imperiled** *formal* to put someone or something in a dangerous situation *A police raid would imperil the lives of the hostages.*

**imperious** /ɪmˈpɪəriəs/ *adj formal* showing that you think that you are important and expect others to obey you *an imperious manner*

**impersonal** /ɪmˈpɜːsᵊnᵊl/ *adj* not being friendly towards people or showing any interest in them *a cold and impersonal letter*

**impersonate** /ɪmˈpɜːsᵊneɪt/ *verb* [T] to copy the way someone looks and behaves in order to pretend to be them or to make people laugh *Impersonating a police officer is a serious offence.* • impersonation /ɪmˌpɜːsᵊnˈeɪʃᵊn/ *noun* [C, U] *He did an impersonation of Bill Clinton.* • impersonator *noun* [C] *an Elvis impersonator*

**impertinent** /ɪmˈpɜːtɪnənt/ *adj formal* rude or not showing respect *an impertinent remark*

**impervious** /ɪmˈpɜːviəs/ *adj* **1** not affected by something *She was **impervious** to the pain.* **2** *formal* Impervious material does not let liquid into or through it. *impervious rock*

**impetuous** /ɪmˈpetʃuəs/ *adj* done or acting quickly and without thinking carefully *an impetuous outburst*

**impetus** /ˈɪmpɪtəs/ *noun* [U] **1** something that makes an activity or process happen or continue with more speed and energy *His visit gave new **impetus** to the peace process.* **2** a physical force that makes an object start or continue to move

**impinge** /ɪmˈpɪndʒ/ *verb formal*
**impinge on/upon sb/sth** to affect or limit someone or something *How does your religious commitment impinge upon your professional life?*

**implacable** /ɪmˈplækəbl/ *adj formal* determined not to change the strong feelings you have against someone or something *implacable opposition/hostility*

**implant¹** /ˈɪmplɑːnt/ *noun* [C] an object placed inside part of your body in an operation, to improve your appearance or treat a medical condition *breast implants*

**implant²** /ɪmˈplɑːnt/ *verb* [T] to place something into someone's body in a medical operation *Two embryos were implanted in her womb.*

**implausible** /ɪmˈplɔːzəbl/ *adj* difficult to believe or imagine *an implausible explanation*

**implement¹** /ˈɪmplɪment/ *verb* [T] *formal* to make a law, system, plan, etc start to happen or operate *Our new computerized system will soon be fully implemented.* • implementation /ˌɪmplɪmenˈteɪʃᵊn/ *noun* [U]

**implement²** /ˈɪmplɪmənt/ *noun* [C] a tool *a garden/farm implement*

**implicate** /ˈɪmplɪkeɪt/ *verb* [T] to show that someone or something is involved in something bad, especially a crime [often passive] *Two senior officers are implicated in the drugs scandal.*

**implication** /ˌɪmplɪˈkeɪʃᵊn/ *noun* **1** EFFECT [C] a result or effect that seems likely in the future [usually plural] *financial/health implications* • *This scheme **has** serious **implications for** the local economy.* **2** SUGGESTION [C, U] when you seem to suggest something without saying it

directly *The **implication** was that the school had to do much better or it would be closed.* **3** INVOLVEMENT [U] when something or someone is implicated in something bad

**implicit** /ɪmˈplɪsɪt/ *adj* **1** suggested but not stated directly *an implicit threat* • *We interpreted his silence as implicit agreement.* **2** complete *implicit faith/trust* • implicitly *adv* *I trust him implicitly.*

**implore** /ɪmˈplɔː/ *verb* [T] *literary* to ask for something in a serious and emotional way [+ to do sth] *I implored him to let the child go.*

**imply** /ɪmˈplaɪ/ *verb* [T] to suggest or show something, without saying it directly [+ (that)] *Are you implying that I'm fat?* • *an implied criticism*

**impolite** /ˌɪmpᵊlˈaɪt/ *adj formal* not polite

**import¹** /ɪmˈpɔːt/ *verb* [T] **1** to bring something into your country from another country for people to buy *We import about 20 percent of our food.* **2** to copy information from one computer or computer program to another *to import data* • *imported files* ➜ Opposite **export**. • importation /ˌɪmpɔːˈteɪʃᵊn/ *noun* [U] • importer *noun* [C]

**import²** /ˈɪmpɔːt/ *noun* **1** [C] a product which is imported from another country [usually plural] *Japanese/American imports* **2** [U] when you import goods *a ban on the import of beef* ➜ Opposite **export**.

o—ⱸ **importance** /ɪmˈpɔːtᵊns/ *noun* [U] how important someone or something is *He emphasized the **importance** of following safety procedures.* • *She **attaches** a lot of **importance to** personal possessions* (= she thinks they are important).

o—ⱸ **important** /ɪmˈpɔːtᵊnt/ *adj* **1** valuable, useful, or necessary *My family is very **important to** me.* • [+ to do sth] *Listen, Donna has something important to say.* **2** having a lot of power, influence, or effect *an important person/decision* ➜ Opposite **unimportant**. • importantly *adv* *They provided hot showers and, more importantly, clean clothes.*

**impose** /ɪmˈpəʊz/ *verb* [T] **1** to officially order that a rule, tax, punishment, etc will happen *to impose a ban/tax* • *The judge imposed the death penalty on both men.* **2** to force someone to accept a belief or way of living *I don't want them to **impose** their religious beliefs **on** my children.*
**impose on sb** to ask or expect someone to do something that may give them extra work or trouble *I hate to impose on you, but could I stay the night?*

**imposing** /ɪmˈpəʊzɪŋ/ *adj* looking big and important in a way that people admire *He was an imposing figure – tall and broad-chested.*

**imposition** /ˌɪmpəˈzɪʃᵊn/ *noun* **1** [U] when you impose something *the imposition of a fine* **2** [C] the cause of extra work or trouble for someone else *It's a bit of an imposition, but could you take me to the airport?*

o—ⱸ **impossible¹** /ɪmˈpɒsəbl/ *adj* **1** If an action or event is impossible, it cannot happen or be done. *an impossible task* • *He finds walking almost impossible.* • [+ to do sth] *It was impossible to sleep because of the noise.* **2** very difficult to deal with *You just can't reason with her, she's absolutely impossible.* • *You're putting me* *in an impossible position.* ● impossibility /ɪmˌpɒsə'bɪləti/ *noun* [C, U] when something is impossible [usually singular] *I can't do it – it's a physical impossibility.*

**the impossible** /ɪm'pɒsəbl/ *noun* something that it is not possible to have or achieve

**impossibly** /ɪm'pɒsəbli/ *adv* extremely, in a way that is very difficult to achieve or deal with *a picture of an impossibly pretty woman* ● *The documents were impossibly muddled.*

**impostor** (*also* **imposter**) /ɪm'pɒstə'/ *noun* [C] someone who pretends to be someone else in order to deceive people

**impotent** /'ɪmpətənt/ *adj* **1** An impotent man is unable to have sex because his penis does not become or stay hard. **2** not having the power or strength to do anything to change a situation *When your child is ill, you feel so impotent.* ● impotence /'ɪmpətəns/ *noun* [U]

**impound** /ɪm'paʊnd/ *verb* [T] If the police or someone in authority impounds something that belongs to you, for example your car, they take it away because you have broken the law.

**impoverished** /ɪm'pɒv²rɪʃt/ *adj formal* **1** poor or made poor *an impoverished country/family* **2** made worse or weaker *culturally/emotionally impoverished*

**impractical** /ɪm'præktɪk²l/ *adj* **1** METHOD/IDEA Impractical ideas, methods, etc cannot be used or done easily. **2** PERSON Impractical people are not good at making, repairing, or planning things. **3** MATERIAL/CLOTHING not suitable for using in normal situations *I love high heels but they're rather impractical.*

**imprecise** /ˌɪmprɪ'saɪs/ *adj* not accurate or exact *an imprecise description*

**impress** /ɪm'pres/ *verb* [T] to make someone admire or respect you *I was impressed by her professionalism.* ● *Sarah was hoping to **impress** him with her cooking.*

**impress sth on sb** to make someone understand the importance of something *He tried to impress the importance of hygiene on them.*

○━**impression** /ɪm'preʃ²n/ *noun* **1** OPINION [no plural] an idea, feeling, or opinion about something or someone [+ (that)] *I got/had the impression that he was bored.* ● *Monica gives the impression of being shy.* ● *Remember that it makes a bad impression if you're late.* ● *I think Mick was under the impression that* (= thought that) *we were married.* **2** COPY [C, U] when you copy the way a particular person or animal speaks or behaves, often to make people laugh *He does a brilliant impression of the president.* **3** MARK [C] a mark left when an object is pressed into something soft

**impressionable** /ɪm'preʃ²nəbl/ *adj* easy to influence *impressionable young people*

**impressive** /ɪm'presɪv/ *adj* Someone or something that is impressive makes you admire and respect them. *an impressive performance/view* ● impressively *adv*

**imprint** /'ɪmprɪnt/ *noun* **1** [C] a mark left when an object is pressed into something soft *The steps showed the imprint of his boots in the snow.* **2** [no plural] the effect that something leaves behind *Much of the house still bears the imprint of her personality.*

**imprison** /ɪm'prɪz²n/ *verb* [T] to put someone in prison or keep them as a prisoner [**often passive**] *Taylor was imprisoned in 1969 for burglary.* ● imprisonment *noun* [U]

**improbable** /ɪm'prɒbəbl/ *adj* **1** not likely to be true or to happen **2** surprising *Shirley seemed an improbable choice for a supermodel.* ● improbably *adv*

**impromptu** /ɪm'prɒmptjuː/ *adj, adv* not planned or prepared *an impromptu performance/party*

**improper** /ɪm'prɒpə'/ *adj formal* not correct, suitable, honest, or acceptable *improper conduct* ● improperly *adv The court ruled that he had acted improperly.*

**impropriety** /ˌɪmprə'praɪəti/ *noun* [U] *formal* behaviour that is not correct, suitable, or honest *The enquiry found no evidence of financial impropriety.*

○━**improve** /ɪm'pruːv/ *verb* [I, T] to get better or to make something better *Scott's behaviour has improved a lot lately.* ● *Every year thousands of students come to London to improve their English.* ● *improved earnings/productivity*

**improve on sth** to do something in a better way or with better results than before *I hope our team can improve on last Saturday's performance.*

○━**improvement** /ɪm'pruːvmənt/ *noun* [C, U] when something gets better or when you make it better *home improvements* ● *There's been a noticeable **improvement in** her work this term.* ● *He's a definite **improvement on** her last boyfriend.* ● *Sadly, her health has **shown** no improvement.*

**improvise** /'ɪmprəvaɪz/ *verb* [I, T] **1** to make or do something without any preparation, using only the things that are available *For a football, we improvised with some rolled-up socks.* **2** to play music or say words that you are inventing, not reading or remembering *The show is not scripted – the actors have to improvise.* ● improvisation /ˌɪmprəvaɪ'zeɪʃ²n/ *noun* [C, U]

**impulse** /'ɪmpʌls/ *noun* **1** [C] a sudden feeling that you must do something, without thinking about the results [usually singular] *Her first impulse was to run away.* **2 on impulse** suddenly and without thinking first *I tend to act on impulse.* **3** [C] a short signal that carries information through a system, for example an electrical system or the nerves in your body

**impulsive** /ɪm'pʌlsɪv/ *adj* Impulsive people do things suddenly, without planning or thinking carefully, but because they want to. ● impulsively *adv*

**impunity** /ɪm'pjuːnəti/ *noun formal* **with impunity** without being punished *Criminal gangs are terrorizing the city with apparent impunity.*

**impure** /ɪm'pjʊə'/ *adj* not pure, but mixed with other substances ● impurity *noun* [C, U] when something is impure or a substance that is impure

○━**in¹** /ɪn/ *preposition* **1** POSITION inside or towards the inside of a container, place, or area *There's milk in the fridge.* ● *a shop in South London* ● *He put his hand in his pocket.* **2** DURING

during part or all of a period of time *We're going to Italy in April.* • *I started working here in 1993.* • *The guinea pig lives inside in the winter.* **3** USING TIME needing or using no more than a particular amount of time *They managed to complete the work in two weeks.* • *I'll be ready in a few minutes.* **4** PART OF part of something *Who's the woman in the painting?* • *There's a few spelling mistakes in your essay.* **5** JOB involved in a particular kind of job *a career in publishing/politics* **6** SUBJECT connected with a particular subject *a degree in philosophy* • *advances in medical science* **7** WEARING wearing *Do you know that man in the grey suit?* **8** EXPRESSED expressed or written in a particular way *Complete the form in black ink.* • *She spoke to him in Russian.* **9** ARRANGED arranged in a particular way *We sat down in a circle.* • *Is this list in alphabetical order?* **10** EXPERIENCE experiencing an emotion or condition *We watched in horror as a body was pulled from the wreckage.* • *She's in a bad mood this morning.* • *The kitchen's in a terrible state.* **11 in all** used to show the total amount of something *Some of the children came, so there were 15 of us in all.*

o—ⁿ**in²** /ɪn/ *adv* **1** INTO A SPACE into an area or space from the outside of it *He rushed in halfway through the meeting.* • *Annie opened the car door and threw her luggage in.* **2** AT A PLACE at the place where a person usually lives or works *I phoned, but she wasn't in.* • *Could you ask him to ring me when he gets in?* **3** TRAIN/PLANE If a train, plane, etc is in, it has arrived at the place it was going to. *My train gets in at 17.54.* **4** SENT given or sent to someone official in order to be read *Applications must be in by 28th February.* **5** TOWARDS LAND used when the sea or a ship moves close to land *Let's go – the tide is coming in.* **6 be in for sth** *informal* If someone is in for a surprise, treat, shock, etc, it will happen to them soon. *If he thinks looking after a baby is easy, he's in for a shock.* **7 have it in for sb** *informal* to dislike and want to cause problems for someone *John's mother has really got it in for me!* **8 be in on sth** *informal* If you are in on something, you know about it or are involved in it. *Were you in on the surprise?* • *Please let me in on* (= tell me) *the secret.* **9** SPORT *UK* In cricket and similar sports, if a person or team is in, they are taking a turn to play. **10 be in for it** (*also UK* **be for it**) to be in trouble

**in³** /ɪn/ *adj informal* fashionable or popular *Luigi's Bar is the in place to go.* • *Pink is in this season.*

**in⁴** /ɪn/ *noun* **the ins and outs of sth** the details of a particular subject *the ins and outs of the legal system*

**in⁵** (*also* **in.**) *written abbreviation for* inch (= a unit for measuring length)

**inability** /ˌɪnəˈbɪləti/ *noun* [no plural] when you are unable to do something [+ to do sth] *I'm depressed by the police's inability to reduce street crime.*

**inaccessible** /ˌɪnəkˈsesəbl/ *adj* impossible or extremely difficult to get to *The plane crashed in a mountain area totally inaccessible to vehicles.*

**inaccurate** /ɪnˈækjərət/ *adj* not correct or exact *inaccurate information/figures* • *The newspaper story was very inaccurate.* • inaccuracy /ɪnˈækjərəsi/ *noun* [C, U] when something is not correct or exact *His book contains historical inaccuracies.*

**inaction** /ɪnˈækʃᵊn/ *noun* [U] when people do not take any action, especially about a problem *This announcement follows months of inaction and delay.*

**inactive** /ɪnˈæktɪv/ *adj* not active or working *Beetle grubs stay inactive underground until spring.* • inactivity /ˌɪnækˈtɪvəti/ *noun* [U] when something or someone is not active or working *a period of inactivity*

**inadequacy** /ɪˈnædɪkwəsi/ *noun* **1** [C, U] when something or someone is not good enough or not of a high enough quality *feelings of inadequacy* • *He pointed out several inadequacies in the present system.* **2** [U] when there is not enough of something *The basic problem is the inadequacy of our school budget.*

**inadequate** /ɪˈnædɪkwət/ *adj* **1** not good enough or too low in quality *inadequate facilities/training* • *Our equipment is totally inadequate for a job like this.* **2** not enough *inadequate funds* • inadequately *adv*

**inadvertent** /ˌɪnədˈvɜːtᵊnt/ *adj* not done intentionally *an inadvertent error* • inadvertently *adv I had inadvertently picked up the wrong keys.*

**inane** /ɪˈneɪn/ *adj* very silly and annoying *an inane question*

**inanimate** /ɪˈnænɪmət/ *adj* not alive *an inanimate object*

**inappropriate** /ˌɪnəˈprəʊpriət/ *adj* not suitable *inappropriate behaviour* • *It would be inappropriate for me to comment, without knowing the facts.* • inappropriately *adv*

**inarticulate** /ˌɪnɑːˈtɪkjələt/ *adj* unable to express clearly what you feel or mean in words

**inasmuch as** /ɪnəzˈmʌtʃˌəz/ *conjunction formal* used to introduce a phrase which explains the degree to which something you have just said is true *They were strict about our appearance inasmuch as we weren't allowed to wear jewellery or make-up.*

**inaudible** /ɪˈnɔːdəbl/ *adj* impossible to hear *His voice was almost inaudible.*

**inaugural** /ɪˈnɔːgjərᵊl/ *adj* [always before noun] An inaugural speech, meeting, etc is the first one of a new organization or leader. *the President's inaugural address*

**inaugurate** /ɪˈnɔːgjəreɪt/ *verb* [T] **1** to have a ceremony to celebrate an important person starting a new job, a new building opening, etc *Ronald Reagan was inaugurated in 1981.* **2** *formal* to start a new system or organization *He inaugurated a programme to fight tuberculosis.* • inauguration /ɪˌnɔːgjəˈreɪʃᵊn/ *noun* [C, U] *the inauguration of the Lord Mayor*

**Inc.** *written abbreviation for* incorporated (= used after the name of some companies) *Macmillan Inc.*

**incalculable** /ɪnˈkælkjələbl/ *adj* too big to measure *The cost in human terms is incalculable.*

**incapable** /ɪnˈkeɪpəbl/ *adj* **incapable of sth/doing sth** not able to do something or to feel a particular emotion *He's incapable of controlling his temper.* ● *I think she's incapable of love.*

**incapacitate** /ˌɪnkəˈpæsɪteɪt/ *verb* [T] *formal* to make someone too ill or weak to work or do things normally [often passive] *He was incapacitated by illness.* ● **incapacity** /ˌɪnkəˈpæsəti/ *noun* [U] when you cannot do something because you do not have the ability or you are too weak

**incarcerate** /ɪnˈkɑːsəreɪt/ *verb* [T] *formal* to put and keep someone in prison [often passive] *Marks was incarcerated for robbery.* ● **incarceration** /ɪnˌkɑːsəˈreɪʃən/ *noun* [U]

**incarnate** /ɪnˈkɑːnət/ *adj* [always after noun] in human form *He was acting like* ***the devil incarnate.***

**incarnation** /ˌɪnkɑːˈneɪʃən/ *noun* **1** [C] a particular form of something or someone that is changing or developing *In their new incarnation, the band have acquired a female singer.* **2 the incarnation of sth** the physical form of a god or quality *the incarnation of evil/freedom* **3** [C] a particular life, in religions which believe we have many lives

**incendiary** /ɪnˈsendiəri/ *adj* [always before noun] designed to cause a fire *an incendiary bomb/device*

**incense** /ˈɪnsens/ *noun* [U] a substance which burns with a strong, sweet smell, often used in religious ceremonies

**incensed** /ɪnˈsenst/ *adj* extremely angry

**incentive** /ɪnˈsentɪv/ *noun* [C, U] something that encourages you to act in a particular way *People had little* ***incentive*** *to save.* ● [+ to do sth] *The government should provide* ***incentives for*** *young people to stay in school.*

**inception** /ɪnˈsepʃən/ *noun* [no plural] *formal* the time when an organization or official activity began *He has directed the project since its inception.*

**incessant** /ɪnˈsesənt/ *adj* continuous, especially in a way that is annoying or unpleasant *incessant rain/noise* ● **incessantly** *adv The phone rang incessantly.*

**incest** /ˈɪnsest/ *noun* [U] sex that is illegal because it is between closely related people, for example a father and daughter

**incestuous** /ɪnˈsestjuəs/ *adj* **1** involving sex between people who are closely related **2** involving a group of people who are not interested in people or things outside the group *Universities can be very incestuous places.*

**inch¹** /ɪnʃ/ *noun* [C] **1** (*written abbreviation* **in.**) a unit for measuring length, equal to 2.54 centimetres **2 not budge/give an inch** *informal* to refuse to change your opinions **3 to be every inch sth** to be a particular kind of person in every way *He is* ***every inch*** *a gentleman.*

**inch²** /ɪnʃ/ *verb* **inch closer/forward/up, etc** to move somewhere slowly or by very small amounts *She began inching her way towards the door.*

**incidence** /ˈɪnsɪdəns/ *noun* [C] how often something happens, especially something bad [usually singular] *There's a* ***high incidence of*** *crime in the area.*

**incident** /ˈɪnsɪdənt/ *noun* [C] *formal* an event, especially one that is bad or unusual *Police are investigating the incident.*

**incidental** /ˌɪnsɪˈdentəl/ *adj* less important than the thing something is connected with or part of *The lyrics here are* ***incidental to*** *the music.*

**incidentally** /ˌɪnsɪˈdentəli/ *adv* used when you say something that is not as important as the main subject of conversation but is connected to it *Incidentally, talking of Stephen, have you met his girlfriend?*

**incinerator** /ɪnˈsɪnəreɪtər/ *noun* [C] a machine that is used to burn waste, especially harmful materials

**incipient** /ɪnˈsɪpiənt/ *adj* [always before noun] *formal* just beginning *incipient wrinkles*

**incision** /ɪnˈsɪʒən/ *noun* [C] *formal* an opening that is made in something with a sharp tool, especially in someone's body during an operation

**incisive** /ɪnˈsaɪsɪv/ *adj* showing an ability to think quickly and clearly and deal with situations effectively *incisive questions*

**incite** /ɪnˈsaɪt/ *verb* [T] to do or say something that encourages people to behave violently or illegally *They denied* ***inciting*** *the crowd to violence.* ● **incitement** *noun* [C, U] when someone does or says something that incites people

**incl** *written abbreviation for* including or inclusive

**inclination** /ˌɪnklɪˈneɪʃən/ *noun* [C, U] a feeling that you want to do something [+ to do sth] *She showed little inclination to leave.*

**incline¹** /ɪnˈklaɪn/ *verb* [T] *formal* If you incline your head, you bend your neck so that your face bends down.
**incline to/towards sth** *formal* to think that a belief or opinion is probably correct *I incline to the view that peace can be achieved.*

**incline²** /ˈɪnklaɪn/ *noun* [C] *formal* a slope *a steep/gentle incline*

**inclined** /ɪnˈklaɪnd/ *adj* [never before noun] **1 be inclined to think/believe/agree, etc** to have an opinion, but not a strong opinion *I'm inclined to agree with you.* **2 inclined to do sth a** often behaving in a particular way *Tom is inclined to be forgetful.* **b** wanting to do something *No one seemed inclined to help.* **3 artistically/technically, etc inclined** having natural artistic/technical, etc ability *She's very bright, but not academically inclined.*

○━**include** /ɪnˈkluːd/ *verb* [T] **1** to have something or someone as part of something larger or more general, such as a group, price, or process *His books include the best-selling novel 'The Foundling'.* ● *The price includes flights and three nights' accommodation.* ➔ *See usage note at* **contain**. **2** to allow someone to take part in an activity [often passive] *Local residents were* ***included in*** *the initial planning discussions.* ➔ *Opposite* **exclude**.

○━**including** /ɪnˈkluːdɪŋ/ *preposition* used to show that someone or something is part of a larger group, amount, or process *Fourteen people, including a prison warden, were killed.* ● *It's £24.99, including postage and packing.*

**inclusion** /ɪnˈkluːʒən/ *noun* [C, U] when you include someone or something, especially in a group, amount, or event *Her self-portrait was chosen for inclusion in the exhibition.* ➔ *Opposite* **exclusion**.

**inclusive** /ɪnˈkluːsɪv/ *adj* **1** COST An inclusive price or amount includes everything. *Prices are inclusive of flights and accommodation.* **2** NUMBERS [always after noun] including the first and last date or number stated *The course will run from October 19 to November 13, inclusive.* **3** PEOPLE Inclusive groups try to include many different types of people. *Our aim is to create a fairer, more inclusive society.* ➔ *Opposite* **exclusive**.

**incoherent** /ˌɪnkəʊˈhɪərənt/ *adj* not using clear words or ideas, and difficult to understand *His statement to the police was rambling and incoherent.* ● incoherence /ˌɪnkəʊˈhɪərəns/ *noun* [U]

o—**income** /ˈɪŋkʌm/ *noun* [C, U] money that you earn by working, investing, or producing goods *families on low incomes* ● *Tourism accounts for 25% of the country's national income.* ➔ *See usage note at* **pay**.

**'income sup,port** *noun* [U] in the UK, money that is paid by the government to people who have very little or no income

**'income ,tax** *noun* [C, U] tax that you have to pay on your income

**incoming** /ˈɪnˌkʌmɪŋ/ *adj* [always before noun] coming into a place or starting a job *incoming phone calls/mail* ● *the incoming government*

**incomparable** /ɪnˈkɒmpərəbl/ *adj* too good to be compared with anything or anyone else *incomparable beauty* ● *the incomparable Mohammed Ali*

**incompatible** /ˌɪnkəmˈpætəbl/ *adj* **1** too different to exist or live together *He regarded being a soldier as incompatible with his Christian faith.* **2** If equipment or software is incompatible with other equipment or software, it will not work with it. ● incompatibility /ˌɪnkəmˌpætəˈbɪləti/ *noun* [U] when two people or things are incompatible

**incompetent** /ɪnˈkɒmpɪtənt/ *adj* not able to do your job, or things that you are expected to do, successfully *incompetent managers* ● incompetence /ɪnˈkɒmpɪtəns/ *noun* [U]

**incomplete** /ˌɪnkəmˈpliːt/ *adj* not finished, or having one or more parts missing *'The Canterbury Tales' remained incomplete when Chaucer died in 1400.* ● *Decisions were made on the basis of incomplete information.* ● incompleteness *noun* [U]

**incomprehensible** /ɪnˌkɒmprɪˈhensəbl/ *adj* impossible to understand *The instructions are almost incomprehensible.* ● *His behaviour is quite incomprehensible to me.*

**incomprehension** /ɪnˌkɒmprɪˈhenʃən/ *noun* [U] *formal* when you do not understand something *She looked at him in total incomprehension.*

**inconceivable** /ˌɪnkənˈsiːvəbl/ *adj* impossible to imagine [+ that] *I find it inconceivable that she could be a killer.*

**inconclusive** /ˌɪnkənˈkluːsɪv/ *adj* not leading to a definite decision or result *inconclusive evidence/results* ● *The battle was inconclusive.*

**incongruous** /ɪnˈkɒŋgruəs/ *adj formal* strange or not suitable for a particular situation *Bill was an incongruous sight, standing on the beach in his suit.*

**inconsequential** /ɪnˌkɒnsɪˈkwenʃəl/ *adj formal* not important *inconsequential remarks*

**inconsiderate** /ˌɪnkənˈsɪdərət/ *adj* not caring about other people's situations or the way they feel *It was very inconsiderate of you to keep us all waiting.*

**inconsistency** /ˌɪnkənˈsɪstənsi/ *noun* [C, U] when something is inconsistent *The report was full of errors and inconsistencies.*

**inconsistent** /ˌɪnkənˈsɪstənt/ *adj* **1** not staying the same in quality or behaviour *His homework is very inconsistent.* **2** not having the same principles as something else, or not agreeing with other facts *The story Robert told his mother is totally inconsistent with what he told me.*

**inconspicuous** /ˌɪnkənˈspɪkjuəs/ *adj* not noticeable or attracting attention *Emma tried to make herself as inconspicuous as possible.*

**incontinent** /ɪnˈkɒntɪnənt/ *adj* not able to control when urine or faeces come out of your body

**incontrovertible** /ˌɪnˌkɒntrəˈvɜːtəbl/ *adj formal* certainly true *incontrovertible evidence/proof*

**inconvenience** /ˌɪnkənˈviːniəns/ *noun* [C, U] when something is inconvenient, or something that is inconvenient *The Director apologized for any inconvenience caused.* ● [usually singular] *Having to wait for ten minutes was a minor inconvenience.* ● inconvenience *verb* [T] *There were complaints from travellers inconvenienced by delays and cancellations.*

**inconvenient** /ˌɪnkənˈviːniənt/ *adj* involving or causing difficulty, such as unexpected changes or effort *It was very inconvenient for me not having the car.* ● *I'm sorry, I seem to have called at an inconvenient time.*

**incorporate** /ɪnˈkɔːpəreɪt/ *verb* [T] to include something as part of another thing *He began to incorporate dance and music into his plays.* ● incorporation /ɪnˌkɔːpərˈeɪʃən/ *noun* [U]

**Incorporated** /ɪnˈkɔːpəreɪtɪd/ (*written abbreviation* **Inc.**) *adj* used after the name of companies which have been organized in a particular legal way *They formed their own company, Broadcast Music Incorporated.*

**incorrect** /ˌɪnkəˈrekt/ *adj* not correct *His answers were incorrect.* ● incorrectly *adv My name is spelled incorrectly on your list.*

**incorrigible** /ɪnˈkɒrɪdʒəbl/ *adj* having particular faults and not likely ever to change

o—**increase**[1] /ɪnˈkriːs/ *verb* [I, T] to get bigger or to make something bigger in size or amount *Eating fatty food increases the risk of heart disease.* ● *Exports of computers have increased by 15% since January.* ● *increased demand/competition* ● *Her anxieties are shared by an increasing number of women.* ➔ *Opposite* **decrease**.

o—**increase**[2] /ˈɪnkriːs/ *noun* **1** [C, U] when the number, size, or amount of something gets bigger *a price/tax increase* ● *We are seeing an increase in standards of living.* **2** **on the increase** If something is on the increase, it is happening more often. *Violent crime is on the increase.* ➔ *Opposite* **decrease**.

**increase in** or **increase of?**

Use **increase in** before the thing which is increasing.

*an increase in profits/sales*

*an increase in the number of AIDS cases*

Use **increase of** before the size of the increase.

*an increase of 30%*

**increasingly** /ɪnˈkriːsɪŋli/ *adv* more and more *increasingly important* • *Increasingly, education is seen as a right, not a privilege.*

o⁻**incredible** /ɪnˈkredɪbl/ *adj* **1** *informal* very good, exciting, or large *We had an incredible time that summer.* • *an incredible noise* **2** too strange to be believed *an incredible story*

**incredibly** /ɪnˈkredɪbli/ *adv* **1** *informal* extremely *The team played incredibly well.* **2** in a way that is difficult to believe *Incredibly, no one was hurt.*

**incredulous** /ɪnˈkredjələs/ *adj* not able to believe something *He looked incredulous when I told him the results.* • incredulity /ˌɪnkrəˈdjuːləti/ *noun* [U] • incredulously *adv*

**increment** /ˈɪnkrəmənt/ *noun* [C] *formal* one of a series of increases *pay increments*

**incremental** /ˌɪnkrəˈmentᵊl/ *adj formal* increasing by small amounts *incremental changes*

**incriminate** /ɪnˈkrɪmɪneɪt/ *verb* [T] to make someone seem guilty of a crime or to show that they are guilty [often reflexive] *He refused to answer questions on the grounds that he might incriminate himself.*

**incriminating** /ɪnˈkrɪmɪneɪtɪŋ/ *adj* Something that is incriminating makes someone seem guilty of a crime. *incriminating evidence*

**incubator** /ˈɪŋkjubeɪtəʳ/ *noun* [C] a heated container that provides the right conditions for a baby born too early, or for very young birds, animals, or eggs

**incumbent¹** /ɪnˈkʌmbənt/ *noun* [C] *formal* someone who has an official job, especially a political one *the previous incumbent*

**incumbent²** /ɪnˈkʌmbənt/ *adj* **1 be incumbent on/upon sb to do sth** *formal* to be someone's duty or responsibility to do something **2** [always before noun] holding an official job, especially a political one *the incumbent president*

**incur** /ɪnˈkɜːʳ/ *verb* [T] **incurring**, *past* **incurred** *formal* to experience something unpleasant as a result of something you have done *to incur debts* • *I am sorry to have incurred his anger.*

**incurable** /ɪnˈkjuərəbl/ *adj* impossible to cure *an incurable disease*

**incursion** /ɪnˈkɜːʃᵊn/ *noun* [C] *formal* a sudden attack or entry into an area that belongs to other people *incursions into enemy territory*

**indebted** /ɪnˈdetɪd/ *adj* **1 be indebted to sb** to be very grateful to someone *I'm indebted to my parents for all their support.* **2** having a debt to pay *indebted countries* • indebtedness *noun* [U]

**indecent** /ɪnˈdiːsᵊnt/ *adj* showing or consisting of sexual behaviour, language, etc which is

unacceptable to most people *indecent photographs* • indecency /ɪnˈdiːsᵊnsi/ *noun* [U] indecent behaviour, or when something is indecent • indecently *adv*

**indecision** /ˌɪndɪˈsɪʒᵊn/ *noun* [U] when you cannot make a decision *a moment of indecision*

**indecisive** /ˌɪndɪˈsaɪsɪv/ *adj* not good at making decisions, or not producing a decision *She was weak and indecisive.*

**indeed** /ɪnˈdiːd/ *adv* **1** [EMPHASIS] used to add emphasis after 'very' followed by an adjective or adverb *For a four-year-old, her vocabulary is very good indeed.* • *Thank you very much indeed.* **2** [REACTION] used when someone has said something that surprises, interests, or annoys you *"She asked if you were married." "Did she, indeed?"* **3** [TRUE] used to emphasize that something is true or that you agree with it *"He sounds a very interesting man." "He is indeed."* **4** [MORE] *formal* used when you say more to support or develop what has already been said *For such creatures speed is not important, indeed it is counterproductive.*

**indefatigable** /ˌɪndɪˈfætɪgəbl/ *adj formal* never becoming tired *She was indefatigable in promoting her cause.*

**indefensible** /ˌɪndɪˈfensəbl/ *adj* completely wrong, and so impossible to defend or support *Racism is morally indefensible.*

**indefinable** /ˌɪndɪˈfaɪnəbl/ *adj* difficult to describe or explain *an indefinable atmosphere of tension*

**indefinite** /ɪnˈdefɪnət/ *adj* with no fixed time, size, end, or limit *an indefinite period/number*

**in,definite 'article** *noun* [C] in grammar, a phrase used to mean the words 'a' or 'an' ⊃ Compare **definite article**.

**indefinitely** /ɪnˈdefɪnətli/ *adv* for a period of time for which no end has been fixed *His visit has been postponed indefinitely.*

**indelible** /ɪnˈdeləbl/ *adj* **1** impossible to forget *an indelible impression/image* **2** impossible to wash away or remove *indelible ink*

**indemnity** /ɪnˈdemnəti/ *noun formal* **1** [U] protection against possible damage or punishment **2** [C, U] money paid or promised to you if something valuable to you is lost or damaged *indemnity insurance*

**indentation** /ˌɪndenˈteɪʃᵊn/ *noun* [C] a mark, cut, or hole in the surface of something

o⁻**independence** /ˌɪndɪˈpendəns/ *noun* [U] **1** when someone looks after themselves and does not need money, help, or permission from other people *My parents gave me a lot of independence.* • *Many old people are afraid of losing their independence.* **2** when a country has its own government and is not ruled by another country *Mexico gained its independence from Spain in l821.*

**Inde'pendence ,Day** (*also* **Fourth of July**) *noun* 4 July, a national holiday in the US to celebrate the country's freedom from Great Britain in 1776

o⁻**independent¹** /ˌɪndɪˈpendənt/ *adj* **1** [RULE] not controlled or ruled by anyone else *an independent state/company* • *The group is independent of any political party.* **2** [NEED] not wanting or needing anyone else to help you or do things for

you *She's a proud, independent woman.*
**3** INFLUENCE not influenced by anyone or anything else *an independent expert/study* • independently *adv to operate independently* • *She
can no longer live independently.*

**independent²** /ˌɪndɪ'pendənt/ *noun* [C] a politician who does not belong to a political party

**in-depth** /'ɪnˌdepθ/ *adj* [always before noun]
involving or considering all the details of
something *in-depth knowledge* • *an in-depth
study/interview*

**indescribable** /ˌɪndɪ'skraɪbəbl/ *adj* so good,
bad, large, etc that it is impossible to describe
*an indescribable feeling* • *indescribable agony*

**indestructible** /ˌɪndɪ'strʌktəbl/ *adj* impossible
to destroy or break *These toys are virtually
indestructible.*

**indeterminate** /ˌɪndɪ'tɜːmɪnət/ *adj* impossible
to know *a large woman of indeterminate age*

**index¹** /'ɪndeks/ *noun* [C] **1** LIST *plural* **indexes**
an alphabetical list of subjects or names at the
end of a book, showing on what page they are
found in the text *Look up 'heart disease' in the
index.* **2** INFORMATION *plural* **indexes** a collection of information stored on a computer or on
cards in alphabetical order **3** SYSTEM *plural*
**indices** *or* **indexes** a system for comparing different values and recording changes, especially in financial markets *the retail price index*

**index²** /'ɪndeks/ *verb* [T] to make an index for
text or information, or arrange it in an index

**'index ˌfinger** *noun* [C] the finger next to your
thumb

**Indian** /'ɪndiən/ *noun* [C] **1** someone from India
**2** an American Indian (= one of the original
race of people who lived in North America)
• Indian *adj* ⊃ *See also:* **West Indian.**

**indicate** /'ɪndɪkeɪt/ *verb* **1** SHOW [T] to show
that something exists or is likely to be true
[+ (that)] *Recent evidence indicates that the skeleton is about 3 million years old.* **2** SAY [T] to say
something or give a signal to show what you
mean or what you intend to do *He has indicated
his intention to resign.* • *She nodded to indicate
she was listening.* **3** POINT [T] to point to
someone or something *He indicated a man in a
dark coat.* **4** SIGNAL [I, T] UK to show that you
intend to turn left or right when you
are driving *The driver turned right without
indicating.*

**indication** /ˌɪndɪ'keɪʃ³n/ *noun* [C, U] **1** a sign
showing that something exists or is likely to be
true [+ (that)] *There are strong indications that
the case will be referred to the Court of Appeal.*
**2** a sign showing what someone means or
what they intend to do *Helen's face gave no
indication of what she was thinking.*

**indicative¹** /ɪn'dɪkətɪv/ *adj formal* **1** **be indicative of sth** to be a sign that something exists,
is true, or is likely to happen *These statistics
are indicative of a widespread problem.* **2** An
indicative form of a verb is used to express a
fact or action.

**indicative²** /ɪn'dɪkətɪv/ *noun* [no plural] the
indicative form of a verb

**indicator** /'ɪndɪkeɪtə³/ *noun* [C] **1** a fact, measurement, or condition that shows what something is like or how it is changing *With some

goods, cost is the most reliable indicator of
quality.* **2** UK (US **turn signal**) a light that
flashes on a vehicle to show that the driver
intends to turn right or left ⊃ *See colour picture*
**Car** *on page Centre 3.*

**indict** /ɪn'daɪt/ *verb* [T] *formal* to accuse
someone officially of a crime [often passive]
*Pound was indicted for treason.*

**indictment** /ɪn'daɪtmənt/ *noun* **1** [C] something
which shows the bad things which a person or
system is responsible for *The novel is a
scathing indictment of the slave trade.* **2** [C, U]
when someone is legally indicted, or the official document or process for doing this

**indie** /'ɪndi/ *noun* [C, U] *informal* a small independent music company or film producer *indie
music/bands*

**indifference** /ɪn'dɪf³r³ns/ *noun* [U] when you do
not care about something or have any particular opinions about it *an air of indifference*

**indifferent** /ɪn'dɪf³r³nt/ *adj* **1** not caring about
or interested in someone or something *They
are indifferent to the plight of the unemployed.*
**2** neither good nor bad *an indifferent performance* • *I buy wine without really knowing if it's
good, bad, or indifferent.*

**indigenous** /ɪn'dɪdʒɪnəs/ *adj* having always
lived or existed in a place *indigenous peoples*
• *The kangaroo is indigenous to Australia.*

**indigestion** /ˌɪndɪ'dʒestʃ³n/ *noun* [U] pain
which you feel when your stomach is unable to
digest food correctly

**indignant** /ɪn'dɪgnənt/ *adj* angry because you
have been treated badly or unfairly *Consumers
are indignant at/about the high prices
charged by car dealers.* • indignantly *adv*
*"That's not fair!" she said indignantly.*

**indignation** /ˌɪndɪg'neɪʃ³n/ *noun* [U] when
someone is indignant *His voice was trembling
with indignation.*

**indignity** /ɪn'dɪgnəti/ *noun* [C, U] a situation
which makes you lose respect or look silly, or
the feeling of shame and embarrassment it
gives you [+ of + doing sth] *They suffered the indignity of being searched like common criminals.*

**indigo** /'ɪndɪgəʊ/ *noun* [U] a blue-purple colour
• indigo *adj*

**indirect** /ˌɪndɪ'rekt/ *adj* **1** NOT CONNECTED not
directly caused by or connected with something *Indirect effects of the fighting include
disease and food shortages.* **2** NOT OBVIOUS
hidden, or not taken or given in a way that is
obvious *indirect taxes/costs* • *an indirect criticism* **3** NOT STRAIGHT not going straight from
one place or person to another *an indirect route*
• indirectly *adv*

**ˌindirect 'object** *noun* [C] the indirect object
of a verb with two objects is the person or thing
that is affected by the result of the action of the
verb. In the sentence 'Give Val some cake.',
'Val' is the indirect object. ⊃ *Compare* **direct
object.**

**indiscreet** /ˌɪndɪ'skriːt/ *adj* saying or doing
things which let people know things that
should be secret *indiscreet remarks* • indiscretion /ˌɪndɪ'skreʃ³n/ *noun* [C, U]

**indiscriminate** /ˌɪndɪ'skrɪmɪnət/ *adj* not
planned or controlled in a responsible or

careful way *the indiscriminate use of pesticides* • **indiscriminately** *adv The gunman fired indiscriminately into the crowd.*

**indispensable** /ˌɪndɪˈspensəbl/ *adj* completely necessary *an indispensable tool/guide* • *She quickly became indispensable to him.*

**indisputable** /ˌɪndɪˈspjuːtəbl/ *adj* obviously and certainly true *an indisputable fact*

**indistinct** /ˌɪndɪˈstɪŋkt/ *adj* not clear *His words became indistinct.*

**indistinguishable** /ˌɪndɪˈstɪŋgwɪʃəbl/ *adj* impossible to see or hear as different or separate *Many toy pistols are indistinguishable from real guns.* • *Their voices are virtually indistinguishable.*

**individual¹** /ˌɪndɪˈvɪdʒuəl/ *adj* **1** [always before noun] considered separately from other things in a group *Read out the individual letters of each word.* **2** given to or relating to one particular person or thing *We deal with each case on an individual basis.*

**individual²** /ˌɪndɪˈvɪdʒuəl/ *noun* [C] **1** a person, especially when considered separately and not as part of a group *We try to treat our students as individuals.* **2** *informal* a person with a special characteristic, usually one you dislike *a ruthless individual*

**individualism** /ˌɪndɪˈvɪdʒuəlɪzᵊm/ *noun* [U] the quality of being different from other people

**individualist** /ˌɪndɪˈvɪdʒuəlɪst/ *noun* [C] someone who likes to behave or do things differently from other people • **individualistic** /ˌɪndɪˌvɪdʒuəˈlɪstɪk/ *adj* behaving or doing things differently from other people *an individualistic approach*

**individuality** /ˌɪndɪˌvɪdʒuˈæləti/ *noun* [U] the quality of being different from others *The houses had no character and no individuality.*

**individually** /ˌɪndɪˈvɪdʒuəli/ *adv* separately and not as a group *Ask the students to work individually.* • *He apologized to each person individually.*

**indoctrinate** /ɪnˈdɒktrɪneɪt/ *verb* [T] to make someone accept your ideas and beliefs by repeating them so often that they do not consider any others *They try to indoctrinate young people with their religious beliefs.* • **indoctrination** /ɪnˌdɒktrɪˈneɪʃᵊn/ *noun* [U] *political indoctrination*

**indoor** /ˌɪnˈdɔːʳ/ *adj* [always before noun] happening, used, or existing in a building *an indoor swimming pool*

**indoors** /ˌɪnˈdɔːz/ *adv* into or inside a building *If you're feeling cold, we can go indoors.* • *Many ferns grow well indoors.*

**induce** /ɪnˈdjuːs/ *verb* [T] **1** [PERSUADE] *formal* to persuade someone do something [+ to do sth] *Nothing would induce me to marry that man!* **2** [CAUSE] *formal* to cause a particular condition *High doses of the drug may induce depression.* **3** [BABY] to give a woman a drug to make her have a baby earlier than she would naturally

**inducement** /ɪnˈdjuːsmənt/ *noun* [C, U] *formal* something that someone offers you to try to persuade you to do something *They offered me more money as an inducement to stay.*

**induct** /ɪnˈdʌkt/ *verb* [T] *formal* to accept someone officially as a member of an organization *He was inducted into the army in 1943.*

**induction** /ɪnˈdʌkʃᵊn/ *noun* [C, U] when someone is officially accepted into a new job or an organization *a two-week induction course*

**indulge** /ɪnˈdʌldʒ/ *verb* **1** [I, T] to let yourself do or have something that you enjoy but which may be bad for you *They indulged in a bit of gossip.* • [often reflexive] *Go on, indulge yourself! Have another chocolate.* **2** [T] to let someone do or have anything they want *Their children are dreadfully indulged.*

**indulgence** /ɪnˈdʌldʒəns/ *noun* **1** [U] when you eat or drink too much or do anything you want *I need to lose weight after all that indulgence on holiday.* **2** [C] something that you do or have because you want to, not because you need it *Silk sheets are one of my indulgences.*

**indulgent** /ɪnˈdʌldʒənt/ *adj* If you are indulgent to someone, you give them anything they want and do not mind if they behave badly. *an indulgent father* • **indulgently** *adv She smiled indulgently at her son.* ➔ *See also:* **self-indulgent**.

⊶**industrial** /ɪnˈdʌstriəl/ *adj* **1** connected with industry *industrial production/development* • *the industrial revolution* **2** with a lot of factories *an industrial city such as Sheffield*

**in,dustrial 'action** *noun* [U] *UK* when workers stop working or do less work because they want better pay or conditions

**in,dustrial es'tate** *UK* (*US* **industrial park**) *noun* [C] an area where there are a lot of factories and businesses

**industrialist** /ɪnˈdʌstriəlɪst/ *noun* [C] someone who owns or has an important position in a large industrial company

**industrialization** /ɪnˌdʌstriəlaɪˈzeɪʃᵊn/ *noun* [U] the process of developing industries in a country *Japan's rapid industrialization*

**industrialized** (*also UK* **-ised**) /ɪnˈdʌstriəlaɪzd/ *adj* Industrialized countries have a lot of industry. *the industrialized nations*

**in'dustrial ,park** *US* (*UK* **industrial estate**) *noun* [C] an area where there are a lot of factories and businesses

**in,dustrial tri'bunal** *noun* [C] in the UK, a type of law court that decides on disagreements between companies and their workers

**industrious** /ɪnˈdʌstriəs/ *adj formal* Industrious people work hard. • **industriously** *adv*

⊶**industry** /ˈɪndəstri/ *noun* **1** [U] the production of goods in factories *heavy industry* **2** [C] all the companies involved in a particular type of business *the entertainment industry*

**inedible** /ɪˈnedɪbl/ *adj* not suitable for eating *The meat was inedible.*

**ineffective** /ˌɪnɪˈfektɪv/ *adj* If something is ineffective, it does not work well. *Morphine is used only when other painkillers are ineffective.* • **ineffectively** *adv* • **ineffectiveness** *noun* [U]

**ineffectual** /ˌɪnɪˈfektʃuᵊl/ *adj* Ineffectual people or actions do not achieve much. *a weak and ineffectual president* • **ineffectually** *adv*

**inefficient** /ˌɪnɪˈfɪʃᵊnt/ *adj* Inefficient people or things waste time, money, or effort, and do not achieve as much as they should. *an inefficient heating system* • **inefficiently** *adv* • **inefficiency** /ˌɪnɪˈfɪʃᵊnsi/ *noun* [C, U]

**ineligible** /ɪˈnelɪdʒəbl/ *adj* not allowed to do something or have something [+ to do sth]

*Foreign residents are ineligible to vote.* • *Non-graduates are **ineligible for** this position.*
• ineligibility /ɪˌnelɪdʒəˈbɪləti/ *noun* [U]

**inept** /ɪˈnept/ *adj* unable to do something well *socially inept* • *She was totally **inept at** telling jokes.* • ineptly *adv* • ineptitude /ɪˈneptɪtjuːd/ *noun* [U]

**inequality** /ˌɪnɪˈkwɒləti/ *noun* [C, U] when some groups in a society have more advantages than others *inequality between the sexes*

**inequity** /ɪˈnekwəti/ *noun* [C, U] when something is unfair, or something that is unfair *inequities in the health care system*

**inert** /ɪˈnɜːt/ *adj formal* **1** Inert substances do not produce a chemical reaction when another substance is added. *inert gases* **2** not moving *Vanessa lay inert on the sofa.* • inertly *adv*

**inertia** /ɪˈnɜːʃə/ *noun* [U] **1** [NO CHANGE] when a situation remains the same or changes very slowly *the inertia of larger organizations* **2** [LAZY] when you are too lazy to do anything *International inertia could lead to a major disaster in the war zone.* **3** [FORCE] the physical force that keeps something in the same position or moving in the same direction

**inescapable** /ˌɪnɪˈskeɪpəbl/ *adj* An inescapable fact cannot be ignored. *Racial discrimination is an inescapable fact of life for some people.* • inescapably *adv*

**inevitable** /ɪˈnevɪtəbl/ *adj* **1** If something is inevitable, you cannot avoid or prevent it. [+ (that)] *It was inevitable that his crime would be discovered.* **2 the inevitable** something that cannot be prevented *Eventually the inevitable happened and he had a heart attack.* • inevitably *adv Inevitably, there was a certain amount of fighting between the groups.* • inevitability /ɪˌnevɪtəˈbɪləti/ *noun* [U]

**inexcusable** /ˌɪnɪkˈskjuːzəbl/ *adj* Inexcusable behaviour is too bad to be forgiven. *His rudeness was inexcusable.*

**inexhaustible** /ˌɪnɪɡˈzɔːstəbl/ *adj* existing in very large amounts that will never be finished *The Internet is an inexhaustible source of information.*

**inexorable** /ɪˈneksᵊrəbl/ *adj formal* continuing without any possibility of being stopped *the inexorable progress of civilization* • inexorably *adv These events led inexorably to war.*

**inexpensive** /ˌɪnɪkˈspensɪv/ *adj* cheap but of good quality *inexpensive children's clothes*

**inexperience** /ˌɪnɪkˈspɪəriəns/ *noun* [U] when you do not know how to do something because you have not done it or experienced it much before *The accident was probably caused by the driver's inexperience.*

**inexperienced** /ˌɪnɪkˈspɪəriənst/ *adj* without much experience or knowledge of something *Kennedy was young and inexperienced.*

**inexplicable** /ˌɪnɪkˈsplɪkəbl/ *adj* so strange or unusual that you cannot understand or explain it *To me his behaviour was quite inexplicable.* • inexplicably *adv*

**inextricably** /ˌɪnɪkˈstrɪkəbli/ *adv* If things are inextricably connected, they are so closely connected that you cannot separate them. *His story is **inextricably linked** with that of his brother.*

**infallible** /ɪnˈfæləbl/ *adj* always right, true, or correct *infallible evidence of guilt* • *They're experts, but they're not infallible.* • infallibility /ɪnˌfælə̍bɪləti/ *noun* [U]

**infamous** /ˈɪnfəməs/ *adj* famous for being bad *The area became infamous for its slums.*

**infancy** /ˈɪnfənsi/ *noun* **1** [U] when you are a baby or a very young child *Their fourth child died **in infancy**.* **2 in its infancy** Something that is in its infancy has only just begun to develop. *In the 1950s, space travel was in its infancy.*

**infant** /ˈɪnfənt/ *noun* [C] *formal* a baby or very young child

**infantile** /ˈɪnfəntaɪl/ *adj* behaving like a young child in a way that seems silly *Don't be so infantile.*

**infantry** /ˈɪnfəntri/ *noun* [U, group] soldiers who fight on foot

**infatuated** /ɪnˈfætjueɪtɪd/ *adj* If you are infatuated with someone, you feel extremely strongly attracted to them. *As the weeks passed he became totally **infatuated with** her.* • infatuation /ɪnˌfætjuˈeɪʃᵊn/ *noun* [C, U]

**infect** /ɪnˈfekt/ *verb* [T] **1** [DISEASE] to give someone a disease [often passive] *Thousands of people were infected with the virus.* **2** [PLACE/SUBSTANCE] If a place, wound, or substance is infected, it contains bacteria or other things that can cause disease. [often passive] *The wound became infected.* • *infected water/meat* ⊃ Compare **disinfect**. **3** [FEELING] to make other people feel the same way as you do [often passive] *They became infected by the general excitement.*

o━**infection** /ɪnˈfekʃᵊn/ *noun* [C, U] a disease in a part of your body that is caused by bacteria or a virus *an ear/throat infection*

**infectious** /ɪnˈfekʃəs/ *adj* **1** An infectious disease can be passed from one person to another. **2** Infectious laughter or feelings quickly spread from one person to another. *infectious enthusiasm*

**infer** /ɪnˈfɜːʳ/ *verb* [T] **inferring**, *past* **inferred** *formal* to guess that something is true because of the information that you have [+ (that)] *I **inferred from** the number of cups that he was expecting visitors.*

**inference** /ˈɪnfᵊrᵊns/ *noun* [C] *formal* a fact that you decide is true because of the information that you have *What inferences can we draw from this?*

**inferior¹** /ɪnˈfɪəriəʳ/ *adj* not good, or not so good as someone or something else *I've never felt **inferior to** anyone.* • *They're selling inferior products at inflated prices.* • inferiority /ɪnˌfɪəriˈɒrəti/ *noun* [U] when something is not as good as another thing, or when someone feels they are not as good as other people

**inferior²** /ɪnˈfɪəriəʳ/ *noun* [C] someone who is considered to be less important than other people

**inferno** /ɪnˈfɜːnəʊ/ *noun* [C] *literary* a very large hot fire

**infertile** /ɪnˈfɜːtaɪl ⑤ ɪnˈfɜːrtᵊl/ *adj* **1** An infertile person or animal cannot have babies. **2** Infertile land is not good enough for plants to grow well there. • infertility /ˌɪnfəˈtɪləti/ *noun* [U] when a person or piece of land is infertile *infertility treatment*

I

---

| j yes | k cat | ʃ she | ʒ decision | θ thin | ð this | ŋ ring | tʃ chip | dʒ jar | æ cat | ɑː arm | e bed | eə hair | ə ago | ɜː her | ɪ sit | i cosy |

**infest** /ɪnˈfest/ *verb* [T] If insects, animals, weeds (= plants you do not want), etc infest a place, they cause problems by being there in large numbers. [often passive] *The hotel was **infested with** cockroaches.*

**infidelity** /ˌɪnfɪˈdeləti/ *noun* [C, U] when someone who is married or in a relationship has sex with someone who is not their wife, husband, or regular partner

**infighting** /ˈɪnˌfaɪtɪŋ/ *noun* [U] arguments between the members of a group *political infighting*

**infiltrate** /ˈɪnfɪltreɪt/ *verb* [T] to secretly join a group or organization so that you can learn more about them *A journalist managed to infiltrate the gang of drug dealers.* ● infiltration /ˌɪnfɪlˈtreɪʃᵊn/ *noun* [C, U] ● infiltrator *noun* [C]

**infinite** /ˈɪnfɪnət/ *adj* **1** extremely large or great *She took infinite care with the painting.* **2** without limits or without an end *God's power is infinite.*

**infinitely** /ˈɪnfɪnətli/ *adv* very or very much *Travel is infinitely more comfortable now than it used to be.*

**infinitive** /ɪnˈfɪnətɪv/ *noun* [C] the basic form of a verb that usually follows 'to'. In the sentence 'She decided to leave.', 'to leave' is an infinitive.

**infinity** /ɪnˈfɪnəti/ *noun* [U] **1** time or space that has no end **2** a number that is larger than all other numbers

**infirm** /ɪnˈfɜːm/ *adj formal* weak or ill, especially because of being old

**infirmary** /ɪnˈfɜːmᵊri/ *noun* [C] **1** *UK formal* used in the name of some hospitals *Leicester Royal Infirmary* **2** *mainly US* a room in a school, prison, etc where people go when they are ill

**infirmity** /ɪnˈfɜːməti/ *noun* [C, U] *formal* when someone is weak and unhealthy, or the illness they have

**inflame** /ɪnˈfleɪm/ *verb* [T] to cause or increase strong emotions *These brutal attacks have inflamed passions in a peaceful country.*

**inflamed** /ɪnˈfleɪmd/ *adj* If part of your body is inflamed, it is red and often painful and swollen.

**inflammable** /ɪnˈflæməbl/ *adj* Inflammable liquids, gases, or materials burn very easily.

**inflammation** /ˌɪnfləˈmeɪʃᵊn/ *noun* [C, U] a red, painful, and often swollen area in or on a part of your body

**inflammatory** /ɪnˈflæmətᵊri/ *adj* intended or likely to cause anger or hate *inflammatory statements/speeches*

**inflatable** /ɪnˈfleɪtəbl/ *adj* An inflatable object has to be filled with air before you can use it. *an inflatable boat*

**inflate** /ɪnˈfleɪt/ *verb* **1** [I, T] to fill something with air or gas, or to become filled with air or gas *In the event of an accident, the airbag will inflate instantly.* **2** [T] to make something such as a number, price, etc larger

**inflated** /ɪnˈfleɪtɪd/ *adj* Inflated prices, costs, numbers, etc are higher than they should be.

o→**inflation** /ɪnˈfleɪʃᵊn/ *noun* [U] the rate at which prices increase, or a continuing increase in prices *low/rising inflation* ● *The inflation rate fell again last month.*

**inflationary** /ɪnˈfleɪʃᵊnᵊri/ *adj* likely to make prices rise

**inflection** /ɪnˈflekʃᵊn/ *noun* [C, U] **1** the way the end of a word changes to show tense, plural forms, etc **2** the way that your voice goes up and down when you speak, for example to show that you are asking a question

**inflexible** /ɪnˈfleksəbl/ *adj* **1** Inflexible rules, opinions, beliefs, etc do not change easily. *a cold and inflexible man* **2** Inflexible materials do not bend easily. ● inflexibility /ɪnˌfleksəˈbɪləti/ *noun* [U]

**inflict** /ɪnˈflɪkt/ *verb* [T] to make someone suffer by doing something unpleasant to them *I would never have inflicted such suffering on you.*

**in-flight** /ˈɪnˌflaɪt/ *adj* [always before noun] happening or available during a flight *in-flight entertainment*

o→**influence¹** /ˈɪnfluəns/ *noun* **1** [C, U] the power to affect how someone thinks or behaves, or how something develops *The drug companies have a lot of **influence on** doctors.* **2** [C] someone or something that has an effect on another person or thing *His grandfather was a strong **influence on** him.*

**influence²** /ˈɪnfluəns/ *verb* [T] to affect or change how someone or something develops, behaves, or thinks *Many factors influence a film's success.* ● [often passive] *Were you influenced by anybody when you were starting your career?*

**influential** /ˌɪnfluˈenʃᵊl/ *adj* having a lot of influence *an influential figure in modern jazz*

**influenza** /ˌɪnfluˈenzə/ *noun* [U] *formal* flu (= an illness like a very bad cold, that makes you feel hot and weak)

**influx** /ˈɪnflʌks/ *noun* [C] the arrival of a lot of people or things at the same time [usually singular] *The 1990s saw an **influx** of foreign players into British football.*

**info** /ˈɪnfəʊ/ *noun* [U] *informal short for* information

**inform** /ɪnˈfɔːm/ *verb* [T] **1** to tell someone about something *If he calls me again, I shall inform the police.* ● [+ (that)] *He informed us that we would have to leave.* **2** to give someone information about something [often passive] *Patients should be **informed about** the risks.* ● *He keeps his parents **informed** of his whereabouts.*

**inform against/on sb** to tell the police about something illegal that someone has done

**informal** /ɪnˈfɔːmᵊl/ *adj* **1** relaxed and friendly *an informal discussion/meeting* **2** suitable for normal situations *informal clothes* ● *informal language* ● informality /ˌɪnfɔːˈmæləti/ *noun* [U] ● informally *adv*

**informant** /ɪnˈfɔːmənt/ *noun* [C] someone who gives information to another person *Our survey is based on over 200 informants.*

o→**information** /ˌɪnfəˈmeɪʃᵊn/ *noun* [U] facts about a situation, person, event, etc *a vital piece of information* ● *Police are urging anyone with **information about** the crime to contact them.*

**information**

Remember you cannot make **information** plural. Do not say 'informations'.

*Could you send me some information about your courses?*

*For more information contact our office.*

*That's the only piece of information we've been able to find out.*

---

**infor‚mation tech'nology** *noun* [U] the use of computers and other electronic equipment to store and send information

**informative** /ɪnˈfɔːmətɪv/ *adj* containing a lot of useful facts *a very informative lecture*

**informed** /ɪnˈfɔːmd/ *adj* having a lot of information or knowledge about something *an informed choice/decision* ➲ *See also:* **well-informed**.

**informer** /ɪnˈfɔːmər/ *noun* [C] someone who secretly gives information to the police about a crime

**infraction** /ɪnˈfrækʃən/ *noun* [C, U] *formal* when someone breaks a rule or the law

**infrared** /ˌɪnfrəˈred/ *adj* Infrared light feels warm but cannot be seen.

**infrastructure** /ˈɪnfrəˌstrʌktʃər/ *noun* [C] the basic systems, such as transport and communication, that a country or organization uses in order to work effectively [usually singular] *The country's infrastructure is in ruins.*

**infrequent** /ɪnˈfriːkwənt/ *adj* not happening very often *Some students make very infrequent use of computers.* • infrequently *adv*

**infringe** /ɪnˈfrɪndʒ/ *verb* [T] **1** *formal* to break a law or rule *They infringed building regulations.* **2** (*also* **infringe on**) to limit someone's rights or freedom *This law infringes on a citizen's right to bear arms.* • infringement *noun* [C, U] *an infringement of copyright*

**infuriate** /ɪnˈfjʊərieɪt/ *verb* [T] to make someone very angry *What really infuriated me was the fact that he'd lied.* • infuriating *adj* extremely annoying

**infuse** /ɪnˈfjuːz/ *verb* **1** [T] *formal* to fill someone or something with a lot of a particular emotion or quality [often passive] *His work is infused with a love for tradition.* **2** [I, T] to put something into a liquid so that its taste goes into the liquid

**infusion** /ɪnˈfjuːʒən/ *noun* [C, U] *formal* when one thing is added to another thing to make it stronger or better *an infusion of cash*

**ingenious** /ɪnˈdʒiːniəs/ *adj* very clever and involving new ideas, equipment, or methods *an ingenious idea/scheme/solution* • *The film's plot is ingenious.* • ingeniously *adv*

**ingenuity** /ˌɪndʒɪˈnjuːəti/ *noun* [U] skill at inventing things or finding new ways to solve problems

**ingest** /ɪnˈdʒest/ *verb* [T] *formal* to eat or drink something • ingestion *noun* [U]

**ingrained** /ɪnˈɡreɪnd/ *adj* **1** Ingrained beliefs, behaviour, problems, etc have existed for a long time and are difficult to change. *For most of us, watching television is a deeply ingrained habit.* **2** Ingrained dirt has got under the surface of something and is difficult to remove.

**ingratiate** /ɪnˈɡreɪʃieɪt/ *verb* **ingratiate yourself (with sb)** to try to make people like you by doing things to please them • ingratiating *adj* Ingratiating behaviour is done to try to make people like you. *an ingratiating smile/manner*

**ingratitude** /ɪnˈɡrætɪtjuːd/ *noun* [U] when someone is not grateful for something

**ingredient** /ɪnˈɡriːdiənt/ *noun* [C] **1** one of the different foods that a particular type of food is made from **2** one of the parts of something successful *Trust is an essential ingredient in a successful marriage.*

**inhabit** /ɪnˈhæbɪt/ *verb* [T] *formal* to live in a place [often passive] *an area inhabited by artists and writers*

**inhabitant** /ɪnˈhæbɪtənt/ *noun* [C] someone who lives in a particular place *a city with 10 million inhabitants*

**inhabited** /ɪnˈhæbɪtɪd/ *adj* An inhabited place or building has people living in it. *Is the island inhabited?*

**inhale** /ɪnˈheɪl/ *verb* [I, T] *formal* to breathe air, smoke, or gas into your lungs *People who had inhaled the fumes were taken to hospital.*

**inherent** /ɪnˈherənt/ *adj* existing as a natural and basic part of something *The desire for freedom is inherent in all people.* • inherently *adv There's nothing inherently wrong with his ideas.*

**inherit** /ɪnˈherɪt/ *verb* [T] **1** FROM DEAD PERSON to receive possessions or money from someone who has died *In 1842 he inherited a small estate near Liverpool.* **2** QUALITY to have the same physical or mental characteristics as one of your parents or grandparents *Miranda has inherited her father's red hair.* **3** PROBLEM If you inherit a problem, situation, or belief, it is passed on to you by someone who had it before. *The mayor will inherit a city hopelessly in debt.*

**inheritance** /ɪnˈherɪtəns/ *noun* [C, U] money or possessions that someone gives you when they die *Nick has sold off much of his inheritance.*

**inhibit** /ɪnˈhɪbɪt/ *verb* [T] **1** to make the progress or growth of something slower *a product which inhibits the growth of harmful bacteria* **2** to make it more difficult for someone to do something *Their threats inhibited witnesses from giving evidence.*

**inhibited** /ɪnˈhɪbɪtɪd/ *adj* not confident enough to say or do what you want

**inhibition** /ˌɪnhɪˈbɪʃən/ *noun* [C, U] a feeling of embarrassment or worry that prevents you from saying or doing what you want *The whole point about dancing is to lose all your inhibitions.*

**inhospitable** /ˌɪnhɒsˈpɪtəbl/ *adj* **1** An inhospitable place is not pleasant or easy to live in because it is too hot, cold, etc. *the world's most inhospitable deserts* **2** not friendly towards people who are visiting you

**in-house** /ˌɪnˈhaʊs/ *adj, adv* done in the offices of a company or organization by employees of that company *in-house training of staff*

**inhuman** /ɪnˈhjuːmən/ *adj* extremely cruel *the inhuman treatment of prisoners*

**inhumane** /ˌɪnhjuːˈmeɪn/ *adj* treating people or animals in a cruel way *inhumane experiments on monkeys* • **inhumanely** *adv*

**inhumanity** /ˌɪnhjuːˈmænəti/ *noun* [U] extremely cruel behaviour *the inhumanity of war*

**initial¹** /ɪˈnɪʃəl/ *adj* [always before noun] first, or happening at the beginning *My initial reaction was one of anger.*

**initial²** /ɪˈnɪʃəl/ *noun* [C] the first letter of a name [usually plural] *His initials are S.G.M.*

**initial³** /ɪˈnɪʃəl/ *verb* [T] (*UK*) **initialling**, *past* **initialled**, (*US*) **initialing**, *past* **initialed** to write your initials on something *Could you just initial that change you made on your cheque?*

**initially** /ɪˈnɪʃəli/ *adv* at the beginning *The situation was worse than they initially thought.*

**initiate** /ɪˈnɪʃieɪt/ *verb* [T] **1** to make something begin [often passive] *The reforms were initiated by Gorbachev.* **2** to make someone a member of a group or organization in a special ceremony, or to show someone how to do an activity *At the age of 50, he was initiated into the priesthood.* • **initiation** /ɪˌnɪʃiˈeɪʃən/ *noun* [C, U]

**initiative** /ɪˈnɪʃətɪv/ *noun* **1** [C] a plan or activity that is done to solve a problem or improve a situation *a new government initiative to reduce crime* **2** [U] the ability to make decisions and do things without needing to be told what to do *We need someone who can work on their own initiative* (= without anyone telling them what to do). **3 take the initiative** to be the first person to do something that solves a problem or improves a situation *Jackson had taken the initiative and prepared a report.*

**inject** /ɪnˈdʒekt/ *verb* [T] **1** DRUG to put a drug into someone's body using a needle *Phil's diabetic and has to inject himself with insulin every day.* **2** IMPROVE to add a good quality to something *The new teacher has injected a bit of enthusiasm into the school.* **3** MONEY to provide a large amount of money for a plan, service, organization, etc *The government plans to inject £100 million into schools.*

**injection** /ɪnˈdʒekʃən/ *noun* **1** [C, U] when someone puts a drug into your body using a needle *an injection of insulin* **2** [C] when a large amount of money is provided for a plan, service, organization, etc *The university has welcomed the $5 million cash injection.*

**injection**

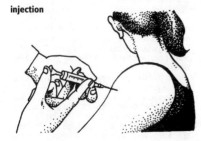

**injunction** /ɪnˈdʒʌŋkʃən/ *noun* [C] an official order from a court that prevents someone from

doing something *The courts have **issued an injunction** to prevent the book from being published.*

○—**injure** /ˈɪndʒər/ *verb* [T] to hurt a person, animal, or part of your body *She injured her ankle when she fell.*

**injured** /ˈɪndʒəd/ *adj* hurt *Fortunately, no one was seriously injured in the accident.*

○—**injury** /ˈɪndʒəri/ *noun* [C, U] damage to someone's body in an accident or attack *head injuries* • *The passenger in the car escaped with minor injuries.* ➔ *See also:* add **insult²** to injury.

**injustice** /ɪnˈdʒʌstɪs/ *noun* [C, U] a situation or action in which people are treated unfairly *the fight against racial injustice* • *the injustices of the legal system*

**ink** /ɪŋk/ *noun* [C, U] a coloured liquid that you use for writing, printing, or drawing

**inkling** /ˈɪŋklɪŋ/ *noun* **have an inkling** to think that something might be true or might happen *She had absolutely no inkling that we were planning the party.*

**inland¹** /ˈɪnlənd/ *adj* [always before noun] Inland areas, lakes, towns, etc are a long way from the coast.

**inland²** /ˈɪnlænd/ *adv* towards the middle of a country and away from the coast *The landscape changed as we drove further inland.*

**in-laws** /ˈɪnlɔːz/ *noun* [plural] *informal* the parents of your husband or wife, or other people in their family *My in-laws have invited us for dinner.*

**inlet** /ˈɪnlet/ *noun* [C] a narrow part of a sea, river, or lake where it flows into a curve in the land

**ˌin-line ˈskate** *noun* [C] (*also* **rollerblades** [plural]) a boot with a single line of wheels on the bottom, used for moving across the ground ➔ *See colour picture* **Sports 1** *on page Centre 15.*

**inmate** /ˈɪnmeɪt/ *noun* [C] someone who lives in a prison or in a hospital for people with mental illnesses

**inn** /ɪn/ *noun* [C] a small hotel in the countryside

**innate** /ɪˈneɪt/ *adj* An innate quality or ability is one that you were born with, not one you have learned. *He has an innate desire to win.* • **innately** *adv*

**inner** /ˈɪnər/ *adj* [always before noun] **1** on the inside, or near the middle of something *The monastery is built around an inner courtyard.* ➔ *Opposite* **outer**. **2** Inner feelings, thoughts, etc are ones that you do not show or tell other people. *a profound sense of inner peace*

**ˌinner ˈcircle** *noun* [C] the small group of people who control an organization, political party, etc *The statement was made by a member of the President's inner circle.*

**ˌinner ˈcity** *noun* [C] the part of a city that is closest to the centre, often where buildings are in a bad condition and there are social problems *a plan to tackle rising crime in inner cities* • **inner-city** /ˈɪnəˌsɪti/ *adj* [always before noun] *inner-city schools*

**innermost** /ˈɪnəməʊst/ *adj* [always before noun] **1** Your innermost feelings, thoughts, etc are the most private ones that you do not want other people to know about. **2** *formal* closest to the middle of something

**inning** /'ɪnɪŋ/ *noun* [C] one of the nine playing periods in a baseball game

**innings** /'ɪnɪŋz/ *noun* [C] *plural* **innings** the period of time in a game of cricket when one player or one team hits the ball

**innocence** /'ɪnəs²ns/ *noun* [U] **1** when someone is not guilty of a crime *She fought to prove her son's innocence.* **2** when someone does not have much experience of life and does not know about the bad things that happen *the innocence of childhood*

o-**innocent** /'ɪnəs²nt/ *adj* **1** NOT GUILTY not guilty of committing a crime *He claims to be innocent of the crime.* **2** NO EXPERIENCE not having much experience of life and not knowing about the bad things that happen *an innocent young woman* **3** NOT DESERVED used to emphasize that someone who was hurt had done nothing wrong *Several innocent civilians were killed in the bombing.* **4** NOT INTENDED TO HARM not intended to harm or upset anyone *It was an innocent mistake.* • innocently *adv*

**innocuous** /ɪ'nɒkjuəs/ *adj* not likely to upset or harm anyone *The parcel looked innocuous enough.* • innocuously *adv*

**innovation** /ˌɪnəʊ'veɪʃ²n/ *noun* [C, U] a new idea or method that is being tried for the first time, or the use of such ideas or methods *the latest innovations in education*

**innovative** /'ɪnəvətɪv ⑤ 'ɪnəveɪtɪv/ *adj* using new methods or ideas *an innovative approach to programme making*

**innovator** /'ɪnəveɪtə²/ *noun* [C] someone who uses or designs new methods or products

**innuendo** /ˌɪnju'endəʊ/ *noun* [C, U] *plural* **innuendoes** or **innuendos** a remark that intentionally suggests something about sex, or something unpleasant about someone, without saying it directly *The advertisement was criticized for its sexual innuendo.*

**innumerable** /ɪ'njuːm²rəbl/ *adj* very many, or too many to count *innumerable problems*

**inoffensive** /ˌɪnə'fensɪv/ *adj* not likely to upset anyone or make them angry *an inoffensive colour*

**inordinate** /ɪ'nɔːdɪnət/ *adj formal* much more than is usual or suitable *James seems to spend an inordinate amount of time on his computer.* • inordinately *adv*

**inorganic** /ˌɪnɔː'gænɪk/ *adj* not being or consisting of living things *inorganic waste*

**in-patient** /'ɪnˌpeɪʃ²nt/ *noun* [C] someone who stays in hospital for one or more nights while they are receiving treatment

**input¹** /'ɪnpʊt/ *noun* **1** IDEAS [C, U] ideas, money, effort, etc that you put into an activity or process in order to help it succeed *Input from students is used to develop new and exciting courses.* **2** ELECTRICAL [C, U] electrical energy that is put into a machine to make it work **3** COMPUTER [U] information that is put into a computer

**input²** /'ɪnpʊt/ *verb* [T] **inputting**, *past* **inputted** or **input** to put information into a computer

**inquest** /'ɪŋkwest/ *noun* [C] a legal process to discover the cause of an unexpected death *There will be an inquest into the deaths of the three men.*

**inquire** *formal* (*also UK* **enquire**) /ɪn'kwaɪə²/ *verb* [I, T] to ask someone for information about something *"Why do you want to see Thacker?" he inquired.* • *If you like languages, why don't you inquire about French classes in your area?* • [+ question word] *Vronsky inquired whether the picture was for sale.* • inquirer (*also UK* **enquirer**) *noun* [C]

**inquire after sb** *UK formal* to ask someone for information about someone else's health and what they are doing, in order to be polite *Jane inquired after your mother.*

**inquire into sth** *formal* to try to discover the facts about something *a report inquiring into the causes of the region's housing problem*

**inquiring** (*also UK* **enquiring**) /ɪn'kwaɪərɪŋ/ *adj* [always before noun] **1** always wanting to learn new things *an inquiring mind* **2** An inquiring expression on your face shows that you want to know something. • inquiringly *adv*

**inquiry** (*also UK* **enquiry**) /ɪn'kwaɪəri/ *noun* **1** QUESTION [C] *formal* a question that you ask when you want more information *The company has received a lot of inquiries about its new Internet service.* **2** OFFICIAL PROCESS [C] an official process to discover the facts about something bad that has happened *There will be an official inquiry into the train crash.* **3** ASKING QUESTIONS [U] *formal* the process of asking questions in order to get information

**inquisitive** /ɪn'kwɪzətɪv/ *adj* wanting to discover as much as you can about things *an inquisitive child* • inquisitively *adv* • inquisitiveness *noun* [U]

**inroads** /'ɪnrəʊdz/ *noun* **make inroads (into/on sth)** to start to become successful by getting sales, power, votes, etc that someone else had before *Women have made great inroads into the male-dominated legal profession.*

**the ˌins and 'outs** *noun* all the details and facts about something *Tolya is someone who knows the ins and outs of the music industry.*

**insane** /ɪn'seɪn/ *adj* **1** very silly or stupid *an insane decision* **2** seriously mentally ill *a hospital for the criminally insane* • insanely *adv*

**insanity** /ɪn'sænəti/ *noun* [U] **1** when someone is seriously mentally ill **2** when something is extremely stupid *It would be insanity to expand the business at the moment.*

**insatiable** /ɪn'seɪʃəbl/ *adj* always wanting more of something *There was an insatiable demand for pictures of Princess Diana.* • insatiably *adv*

**inscribe** /ɪn'skraɪb/ *verb* [T] *formal* to write words in a book or cut them on an object [often passive] *The child's bracelet was inscribed with the name 'Amy'.*

**inscription** /ɪn'skrɪpʃ²n/ *noun* [C, U] words that are written or cut in something *The inscription on the gravestone was almost illegible.*

o-**insect** /'ɪnsekt/ *noun* [C] a small creature with six legs, for example a bee or a fly

**insecticide** /ɪn'sektɪsaɪd/ *noun* [C, U] a chemical that is used for killing insects

**insecure** /ˌɪnsɪ'kjʊə²/ *adj* **1** having no confidence in yourself and what you can do *a shy, insecure*

insect

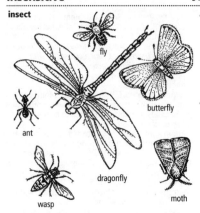

fly

butterfly

ant

dragonfly

wasp

moth

*teenager* **2** not safe or protected *Many of our staff are worried because their jobs are insecure.* ● insecurely *adv* ● insecurity /,ɪnsɪ'kjʊərəti/ *noun* [U]

**insensitive** /ɪn'sensətɪv/ *adj* **1** not noticing or not caring about other people's feelings *an insensitive remark* ● *He was completely insensitive to Maria's feelings.* **2** not able to feel something, or not affected by it *She was insensitive to the pain.* ● insensitively *adv* ● insensitivity /ɪn,sensə'tɪvəti/ *noun* [U]

**inseparable** /ɪn'sepʳrəbl/ *adj* **1** *formal* Two things that are inseparable are so closely connected that you cannot consider them separately. *Rossetti's work was inseparable from his life.* **2** People who are inseparable are always together because they are such good friends. *The two girls got on very well and soon became inseparable.* ● inseparably *adv*

**insert¹** /ɪn'sɜːt/ *verb* [T] *formal* **1** to put something into something else *Insert the coin in the slot.* **2** to add something to the middle of a document or piece of writing *He inserted a new paragraph.* ● insertion /ɪn'sɜːʃʳn/ *noun* [C, U]

**insert²** /'ɪnsɜːt/ *noun* [C] something that is made to go inside or into something else *The leaflet is designed as an insert for a magazine.*

**inshore** /,ɪn'ʃɔːʳ/ *adj, adv* near or towards the coast *inshore waters*

○⌐**inside¹** /,ɪn'saɪd/ *noun* **1 the inside** the part of something that is under its surface *I cleaned the inside of the oven.* ● *The door had been locked from the inside.* **2 inside out** If a piece of clothing is inside out, the part that is usually outside is on the inside. *Harry, you've got your sweater on inside out again.* **3 know sth inside out** to know everything about something *Let Meg drive – she knows these roads inside out.*

**inside²** /,ɪn'saɪd/ *adj* **1** [always before noun] in or on the part of something under its surface *Put your wallet in the inside pocket of your jacket.* **2 inside information/knowledge, etc** information that is only known by people who are part of an organization, group, etc *I needed someone with inside knowledge to back up my story.*

○⌐**inside³** /,ɪn'saɪd/ *preposition* **1** [CONTAINER] in or into a room, building, container, etc *There were some keys inside the box.* ● *Luckily, no one was inside the house when the fire started.* **2** [TIME] in less than a particular length of time *The doctor's promised to be here inside an hour.* **3** [ORGANIZATION] in an organization, group, etc and not known or happening outside it *rumours of disputes inside the company*

○⌐**inside⁴** /,ɪn'saɪd/ *adv* **1** [CONTAINER] in or into a room, building, container, etc *She opened the drawer and laid the scarf inside.* ● *I'm freezing, let's go back inside.* **2** [FEELING] If you have a feeling inside, people do not know about it if you do not tell them. *She looked calm but was feeling nervous inside.* **3** [PRISON] *informal* in prison

**insider** /ɪn'saɪdəʳ/ *noun* [C] someone who knows about a business or organization because they are part of it *Industry insiders say they are surprised by the company's success.* ⊃ *Compare* **outsider**.

**insides** /,ɪn'saɪdz/ *noun* [plural] *informal* your stomach

**insidious** /ɪn'sɪdiəs/ *adj* having harmful effects that happen gradually so you do not notice them for a long time *the insidious effects of pollution* ● insidiously *adv* ● insidiousness *noun* [U]

**insight** /'ɪnsaɪt/ *noun* [C, U] the ability to understand what something is really like, or an example of this *The book provides a fascinating insight into the world of art.*

**insignia** /ɪn'sɪgniə/ *noun* [C] *plural* **insignia** a piece of cloth or a symbol that shows someone's military rank or official position

**insignificant** /,ɪnsɪg'nɪfɪkʳnt/ *adj* not important or large enough to consider or worry about *insignificant differences* ● insignificance /,ɪnsɪg'nɪfɪkʳns/ *noun* [U] ● insignificantly *adv*

**insincere** /,ɪnsɪn'sɪəʳ/ *adj* pretending to feel something that you do not really feel, or not meaning what you say *an insincere apology* ● insincerely *adv* ● insincerity /,ɪnsɪn'serəti/ *noun* [U]

**insinuate** /ɪn'sɪnjueɪt/ *verb* [T] to suggest that something bad is true without saying it directly [+ that] *She insinuated that Perez had lied.* ● insinuation /ɪn,sɪnju'eɪʃʳn/ *noun* [C, U]

**insipid** /ɪn'sɪpɪd/ *adj* not interesting, exciting, or colourful *a dull, insipid man* ● *The soup was rather insipid.* ● insipidly *adv*

○⌐**insist** /ɪn'sɪst/ *verb* [I, T] **1** to say firmly that something is true, especially when other people do not believe you [+ (that)] *Mia insisted that she and Carlo were just friends.* **2** to demand that something must be done or that you must have a particular thing *The school insists on good behaviour from its students.* ● [+ on + doing sth] *Frank insisted on doing all the work himself.* ● [+ (that)] *Gerlinde insisted that I stay for dinner.*

**insistence** /ɪn'sɪstʳns/ *noun* [U] **1** when you demand that something must be done or that you must have a particular thing [+ that] *his insistence that his children should have a good education* ● *Clare's insistence on a vegetarian diet caused arguments with her mother.* **2** when you say firmly that something is true, especially when other people do not believe you [+ that] *Jane was in trouble despite her insistence that she had done nothing wrong.*

**insistent** /ɪnˈsɪstᵊnt/ *adj* firmly saying that something is true or must be done [+ that] *Pedro is absolutely insistent that Sinda should be invited too.* • insistently *adv*

**insofar as** /ɪnsəʊˈfɑːr.əz/ *conjunction formal* to the degree that *The story is based insofar as possible on notes made by Scott himself.*

**insolent** /ˈɪnsᵊlənt/ *adj formal* rude and not showing respect *an insolent reply* • insolence /ˈɪnsᵊləns/ *noun* [U] • insolently *adv*

**insoluble** /ɪnˈsɒljəbl/ *adj* **1** An insoluble problem, mystery, etc is impossible to solve. **2** An insoluble substance does not dissolve when you put it in liquid.

**insomnia** /ɪnˈsɒmniə/ *noun* [U] when you find it difficult to sleep *Many people suffer from insomnia.* • insomniac /ɪnˈsɒmniæk/ *noun* [C] someone who often finds it difficult to sleep

**inspect** /ɪnˈspekt/ *verb* [T] **1** to officially visit a building or organization, in order to check that everything is correct and legal *Schools will be inspected regularly to maintain standards.* **2** to look at something very carefully *Clara inspected her make-up in the mirror.*

**inspection** /ɪnˈspekʃᵊn/ *noun* [C, U] **1** an official visit to a building or organization to check that everything is correct and legal *Fire officers **carried out an inspection** of the building.* **2** when you look at something carefully *On **closer inspection** (= when looked at more carefully), the painting was discovered to be a fake.*

**inspector** /ɪnˈspektər/ *noun* [C] **1** someone whose job is to check that things are being done correctly *a factory inspector* **2** a police officer of middle rank

**inspiration** /ˌɪnspᵊrˈeɪʃᵊn/ *noun* **1** [C, U] someone or something that gives you ideas for doing something *Africa has long been a source of **inspiration for** his painting.* **2** [C] a sudden good idea about what you should do **3 be an inspiration to sb** to be so good that someone else admires you and is encouraged by your behaviour *The way she has dealt with her illness is an inspiration to us all.*

**inspire** /ɪnˈspaɪər/ *verb* [T] **1** ENCOURAGE to make someone feel that they want to do something and can do it [+ to do sth] *A drama teacher at school had inspired Sam to become an actor.* **2** FEELING to make someone have a particular feeling or reaction *Robson's first task will be to **inspire** his team **with** some confidence.* • *He **inspires** great loyalty **in** his staff.* **3** PROVIDE IDEA to give someone an idea for a book, play, painting, etc [often passive] *a television drama that was inspired by a true story* • inspiring *adj* giving you new ideas and making you feel you want to do something *an inspiring teacher* • *an inspiring book*

**inspired** /ɪnˈspaɪəd/ *adj* showing a lot of skill and good ideas *an inspired performance*

**instability** /ˌɪnstəˈbɪləti/ *noun* [U] when a situation or someone's behaviour changes a lot and you do not know what will happen next *political/mental instability*

**install** (*also UK* **instal**) /ɪnˈstɔːl/ *verb* [T]

**1** EQUIPMENT to put a piece of equipment somewhere and make it ready to use *The school has installed a burglar alarm.* **2** PERSON to give someone an important and powerful job *She will be installed as Managing Director in May.* **3** COMPUTER to put software onto a computer • installation /ˌɪnstəˈleɪʃᵊn/ *noun* [C, U]

**instalment** *UK* (*US* **installment**) /ɪnˈstɔːlmənt/ *noun* [C] **1** a regular payment that you make, for example each month, in order to pay for something *You can pay for your computer in six monthly **instalments.*** **2** one of the parts of a story that you can see every day or week in a magazine or on television *Don't miss next week's exciting instalment.*

**instance** /ˈɪnstəns/ *noun* **1 for instance** for example *Many teenagers earn money, for instance by babysitting or cleaning cars.* **2** [C] an example of a particular type of event, situation, or behaviour *There have been several **instances of** violence in the school.*

o— **instant¹** /ˈɪnstənt/ *adj* **1** happening immediately *The book was an instant success in the US.* **2** Instant food or drink is dried, usually in the form of a powder, and can be made quickly by adding hot water. *instant coffee* ⊃ See also: **instant replay.**

**instant²** /ˈɪnstənt/ *noun* [C] a moment *Take a seat, I'll be with you in an instant.* • *Stop that this instant!*

**instantaneous** /ˌɪnstənˈteɪniəs/ *adj* happening immediately *The Internet offers almost instantaneous access to vast amounts of information.* • instantaneously *adv*

**instantly** /ˈɪnstəntli/ *adv* immediately *A car hit them, killing them both instantly.*

**instant replay** *US* (*UK* **action replay**) *noun* [C] when part of a film of a sporting event is shown again, often more slowly

o— **instead** /ɪnˈsted/ *adv* in the place of someone or something else *If you don't want pizza, we can have pasta instead.* • *I'm going swimming on Monday **instead of** Friday now.* • [+ of + doing sth] *Why don't you help instead of just complaining?*

**instigate** /ˈɪnstɪgeɪt/ *verb* [T] *formal* to make something start to happen *Carolyn had instigated divorce proceedings.* • instigation /ˌɪnstɪˈgeɪʃᵊn/ *noun* [U] • instigator *noun* [C]

**instil** *UK* (*US* **instill**) /ɪnˈstɪl/ *verb* [T] **instilling,** *past* **instilled** to make someone have a particular feeling or idea *He's a manager with great skill at **instilling** confidence **in/into** his players.*

**instinct** /ˈɪnstɪŋkt/ *noun* [C, U] the way someone naturally reacts or behaves, without having to think or learn about it [+ to do sth] *a mother's instinct to protect her children*

**instinctive** /ɪnˈstɪŋktɪv/ *adj* behaving or reacting naturally and without thinking *Her instinctive response was to fight back.* • instinctively *adv* *Kate knew instinctively that something was wrong.*

**institute¹** /ˈɪnstɪtjuːt/ *noun* [C] an organization where people do a particular kind of scientific, educational, or social work *the Massachusetts Institute of Technology*

**institute²** /ˈɪnstɪtjuːt/ *verb* [T] *formal* to start a

plan, law, system, etc *Major reforms were instituted in the company's finance department.*

**institution** /ˌɪnstɪˈtjuːʃ°n/ *noun* [C] **1** ORGANIZATION a large and important organization, such as a university or bank *one of the country's top medical institutions* **2** PLACE a building where people are sent so they can be looked after, for example a prison or hospital **3** TRADITION a custom that has existed for a long time *the institution of marriage* • institutional *adj* relating to an institution

**instruct** /ɪnˈstrʌkt/ *verb* [T] **1** to officially tell someone to do something [+ to do sth] *Staff are instructed not to use the telephones for personal calls.* **2** *formal* to teach someone about something *She is there to instruct people in the safe use of the gym equipment.*

०ᐟ**instruction** /ɪnˈstrʌkʃ°n/ *noun* **1** [C] something that you have been told to do [+ to do sth] *I had strict instructions to call them as soon as I arrived home.* **2** [U] *formal* the activity of teaching or training someone, or the information you are being taught *religious instruction*

**instructions** /ɪnˈstrʌkʃ°nz/ *noun* [plural] information that explains how to do or use something *Are there any instructions on how to load the software?* • *I just followed the instructions.*

**instructive** /ɪnˈstrʌktɪv/ *adj* providing useful information *an instructive discussion* • instructively *adv*

**instructor** /ɪnˈstrʌktəʳ/ *noun* [C] someone who teaches a particular sport or activity *a driving instructor*

०ᐟ**instrument** /ˈɪnstrəmənt/ *noun* [C] **1** TOOL a tool that is used for doing something *scientific instruments* **2** MUSIC an object that is used for playing music, for example a piano or drum **3** EQUIPMENT a piece of equipment that is used for measuring speed, light, fuel level, etc **4** FOR ACHIEVING SOMETHING someone or something that is used for achieving something *The Internet is a very powerful instrument of communication.* ⊃ *See also:* **wind instrument**.

**instrumental** /ˌɪnstrəˈment°l/ *adj* **1** be instrumental in sth/doing sth to be one of the main people or things that make something happen *Mikan was instrumental in establishing professional basketball in the US.* **2** involving only musical instruments, and no singing

**insubordinate** /ˌɪnsəˈbɔːdᵊnət/ *adj* not willing to obey rules or people in authority • insubordination /ˌɪnsəˌbɔːdɪˈneɪʃ°n/ *noun* [U]

**insubstantial** /ˌɪnsəbˈstænʃ°l/ *adj* not very large, strong, or good *The meal was rather insubstantial.*

**insufferable** /ɪnˈsʌfᵊrəbl/ *adj* extremely annoying or unpleasant *insufferable arrogance* • insufferably *adv*

**insufficient** /ˌɪnsəˈfɪʃ°nt/ *adj* not enough *insufficient information* • [+ to do sth] *Her income is insufficient to support a family.* • insufficiently *adv*

**insular** /ˈɪnsjələʳ/ *adj* only interested in your own country, life, etc and not willing to accept new ideas or people • insularity /ˌɪnsjəˈlærəti/ *noun* [U]

**insulate** /ˈɪnsjəleɪt/ *verb* [T] **1** to cover something with a special material so that heat, electricity, or sound cannot escape through it **2** to protect someone from unpleasant experiences or bad influences *parents who want to insulate their children from real life*

**insulation** /ˌɪnsjəˈleɪʃ°n/ *noun* [U] **1** a special material used for insulating something such as a wall, roof, or building **2** when you insulate something, or when something is insulated

**insulin** /ˈɪnsjəlɪn/ *noun* [U] a substance produced by the body that controls the amount of sugar in your blood

**insult¹** /ɪnˈsʌlt/ *verb* [T] to say or do something to someone that is rude and offensive *How dare you insult me in front of my friends!* • insulting *adj* rude and offensive *an insulting remark*

**insult²** /ˈɪnsʌlt/ *noun* [C] **1** a rude and offensive remark or action *They were shouting insults at each other.* • *His comments are an insult to the victims of the war.* **2** add insult to injury to make someone's bad situation worse by doing something else to upset them

**insurance** /ɪnˈʃʊəʳ°ns/ *noun* [U] an agreement in which you pay a company money and they pay your costs if you have an accident, injury, etc *travel/car insurance* • *an insurance policy*

**insure** /ɪnˈʃʊəʳ/ *verb* [T] to buy insurance from a company, or to provide insurance for someone *I need to get my car insured.* • *The policy insures you against damage and theft.*

**insurmountable** /ˌɪnsəˈmaʊntəbl/ *adj* impossible to deal with *an insurmountable problem/ task*

**insurrection** /ˌɪnsᵊrˈekʃ°n/ *noun* [C, U] when a group of people use force to try to get control of a government

**intact** /ɪnˈtækt/ *adj* not damaged or destroyed *Many of the old buildings are still intact.*

**intake** /ˈɪnteɪk/ *noun* [C] **1** the amount of food or drink that you take into your body [usually singular] *Reducing your salt intake can help to lower blood pressure.* **2** *UK* the group of people who start working or studying somewhere at the same time *a new intake of students*

**intangible** /ɪnˈtændʒəbl/ *adj* An intangible feeling or quality exists but you cannot describe or prove it.

**integral** /ˈɪntɪgrəl/ *adj* necessary and important as part of something *The Internet has become an integral part of modern life.*

**integrate** /ˈɪntɪgreɪt/ *verb* **1** [I, T] to become part of a group or society, or to help someone do this *After a few weeks of training he was fully integrated into the team.* **2** [T] to combine two or more things to make something more effective *plans to integrate the two schools* • *an integrated database* • integration /ˌɪntɪˈgreɪʃ°n/ *noun* [U]

**integrity** /ɪnˈtegrəti/ *noun* [U] honesty and the ability to do or know what is morally right *a woman of great integrity*

**intellect** /ˈɪnt°lekt/ *noun* [C, U] the ability to learn and understand something, and to form ideas, judgments, and opinions about what you have learned *His energy and intellect are respected by many people.*

**intellectual¹** /ˌɪnt°lˈektjuəl/ *adj* **1** using or relating to your ability to think and understand things *intellectual work* • *intellectual and physical development* **2** interested in learning and in thinking about complicated ideas *She's very intellectual.* • **intellectually** *adv*

**intellectual²** /ˌɪntəˈlektjuəl/ *noun* [C] someone who enjoys studying and thinking about complicated ideas

o—⚲**intelligence** /ɪnˈtelɪdʒᵊns/ *noun* [U] **1** the ability to learn, understand, and think about things *a child of low intelligence* **2** secret information about the governments of other countries, or the group of people who get this information *military intelligence* ➜ *See also:* **artificial intelligence**.

o—⚲**intelligent** /ɪnˈtelɪdʒᵊnt/ *adj* able to learn and understand things easily *a highly intelligent young woman* • *an intelligent remark* • **intelligently** *adv*

**intelligible** /ɪnˈtelɪdʒəbl/ *adj* able to be understood ➜ *Opposite* **unintelligible**.

o—⚲**intend** /ɪnˈtend/ *verb* **1** [T] to want and plan to do something *Unfortunately the meeting took longer than we intended.* • [+ to do sth] *How long are you intending to stay in Paris?* • [+ doing sth] *I don't intend seeing him again.* **2 be intended for sb; be intended as sth** to be made, designed, or provided for a particular person or purpose *The book is intended for anyone who wants to learn more about the Internet.*

**intense** /ɪnˈtens/ *adj* **1** extreme or very strong *intense heat/pain* **2** Intense people are very serious, and usually have strong emotions or opinions. *He's always been very intense.* • **intensely** *adv Clare disliked him intensely.* • **intensity** *noun* [U]

**intensify** /ɪnˈtensɪfaɪ/ *verb* [I, T] to become greater, more serious, or more extreme, or to make something do this *The fighting has intensified in the past week.*

**intensive** /ɪnˈtensɪv/ *adj* involving a lot of work in a short period of time *ten weeks of intensive training* • **intensively** *adv*

**in,tensive 'care** *noun* [U] the part of a hospital used for treating people who are seriously ill or very badly injured

**intent¹** /ɪnˈtent/ *noun* [U, no plural] *formal* **1** when you want and plan to do something [+ to do sth] *It had not been his intent to hurt anyone.* **2 to/for all intents (and purposes)** in all the most important ways *To all intents and purposes, the project was a disaster.*

**intent²** /ɪnˈtent/ *adj* **1 be intent on sth/doing sth** to be determined to do or achieve something *She seems intent on winning this year's tennis tournament.* **2** giving a lot of attention to something *She had an intent look on her face.* • **intently** *adv*

o—⚲**intention** /ɪnˈtenʃᵊn/ *noun* [C, U] something that you want and plan to do [+ to do sth] *She announced her intention to resign.* • [+ of + doing sth] *I have no intention of seeing him again.*

**intentional** /ɪnˈtenʃᵊnᵊl/ *adj* planned or intended *I'm sorry if I said something that offended you. It really wasn't intentional.* • **intentionally** *adv*

**interact** /ˌɪntərˈækt/ *verb* [I] **1** to talk and do things with other people *At school, teachers say he interacted well with other students.* **2** If two

things interact, they have an effect on each other. *We are looking at how these chemicals interact.*

**interaction** /ˌɪntərˈækʃᵊn/ *noun* [C, U] **1** the activity of talking and doing things with other people, or the way you do this *Our work involves a lot of interaction with the customers.* **2** when two or more things combine and have an effect on each other

**interactive** /ˌɪntərˈæktɪv/ *adj* **1** Interactive computer programs, games, etc involve the person using them by reacting to the way they use them. **2** involving communication between people

**intercept** /ˌɪntəˈsept/ *verb* [T] to stop someone or something before they are able to reach a particular place *Johnson intercepted the pass and went on to score the third goal.* • **interception** /ˌɪntəˈsepʃᵊn/ *noun* [C, U]

**interchangeable** /ˌɪntəˈtʃeɪndʒəbl/ *adj* If things are interchangeable, you can exchange them because they can be used in the same way. *interchangeable words* • **interchangeably** *adv*

**intercom** /ˈɪntəkɒm/ *noun* [C] an electronic system used for communicating with people in different parts of a building, aircraft, ship, etc *A stewardess asked over the intercom if there was a doctor on board.*

**intercontinental** /ˌɪntəˌkɒntɪˈnentᵊl/ *adj* in or between two continents *an intercontinental flight*

**intercourse** /ˈɪntəkɔːs/ (*also* **sexual intercourse**) *noun* [U] *formal* when a man puts his penis into a woman's vagina

o—⚲**interest¹** /ˈɪntrəst/ *noun* **1** FEELING [U, no plural] the feeling of wanting to give attention to something or discover more about it *Mark had an interest in the media and wanted to become a journalist.* • *After a while he simply lost interest in* (= stopped being interested) *his studies.* • *Bindi felt that her father didn't take much of an interest in her* (= he was not very interested). **2** ACTIVITY/SUBJECT [C] something you enjoy doing, studying, or experiencing *We share a lot of the same interests, particularly music and football.* **3** MONEY YOU PAY [U] the extra money that you must pay to a bank, company, etc which has lent you money *low interest rates* **4** MONEY YOU EARN [U] the money you earn from keeping your money in a bank account **5** QUALITY [U] a quality that makes you think something is interesting *Would this book be of any interest to you?* • *The tour offers a chance to visit places of interest.* **6 be in sb's interest(s)** to help someone and give them an advantage *It may not be in your interests to change jobs so soon.* **7 in the interest(s) of sth** in order to achieve a particular situation or quality *In the interest of safety, passengers are advised to wear their seat belts at all times.* **8** LEGAL RIGHT [C] *formal* the legal right to own or receive part of a building, company, profits, etc ➜ *See also:* **self-interest**, **vested interest**.

**interest²** /ˈɪntrəst/ *verb* [T] If someone or something interests you, you want to give them your attention and discover more about them. *History doesn't really interest me.*

o—⚲**interested** /ˈɪntrəstɪd/ *adj* **1** [never before noun] wanting to give your attention to something and discover more about it *Sarah's only interested in boys, CDs, and clothes.* • [+ to do sth] *I'd be interested to find out more about the course.* ➔ *Opposite* **uninterested. 2** [never before noun] wanting to do, get, or achieve something [+ in + doing sth] *Mark said he's interested in buying your bike.* **3 interested parties/groups** people who will be affected by a situation ➔ *Opposite* **disinterested**.

○━**interesting** /ˈɪntrəstɪŋ/ *adj* Someone or something that is interesting keeps your attention because they are unusual, exciting, or have lots of ideas. *an interesting person* • *The museum was really interesting.* • [+ to do sth] *It'll be interesting to see what Mum thinks of John's new girlfriend.*

---

**USAGE**

**interesting** or **interested?**

**Interested** is used to describe how someone feels about a person or thing.

*I'm interested in theatre.*

~~I'm interesting in theatre.~~

If a person or thing is **interesting**, they make you feel interested.

*It was an interesting film.*

---

**interface**[1] /ˈɪntəfeɪs/ *noun* [C] **1** a connection between two pieces of electronic equipment, or between a person and a computer *a simple user interface* **2** a situation, way, or place where two things can come together and have an effect on each other *the interface between technology and tradition*

**interface**[2] /ˈɪntəfeɪs/ *verb* [I, T] to communicate with people or electronic equipment, or to make people or electronic equipment communicate *We use email to interface with our customers.*

○━**interfere** /ˌɪntəˈfɪər/ *verb* [I] to try to control or become involved in a situation, in a way that is annoying *I know he's worried about us, but I wish he wouldn't interfere.* • *You shouldn't interfere in other people's business.*
**interfere with sth 1** to prevent something from working effectively or from developing successfully *I try not to let my dancing classes interfere with my schoolwork.* **2** If something interferes with radio or television signals, it stops you from getting good pictures or sound.

**interference** /ˌɪntəˈfɪərəns/ *noun* [U] **1** when someone tries to interfere in a situation *There have been claims of too much political interference in education.* **2** noise or other electronic signals that stop you from getting good pictures or sound on a television or radio

**interim**[1] /ˈɪntərɪm/ *adj* [always before noun] temporary and intended to be used or accepted until something permanent exists *an interim solution* • *an interim government*

**interim**[2] /ˈɪntərɪm/ *noun* **in the interim** in the time between two particular periods or events

**interior** /ɪnˈtɪəriər/ *noun* [C] the inside part of something *the grand interior of the hotel* ➔ *Opposite* **exterior**.

**in,terior de'sign** *noun* [U] the job of choosing colours, designs, etc for the inside of a house or room • **interior designer** *noun* [C] someone whose job is to do interior design

**interjection** /ˌɪntəˈdʒekʃən/ *noun* [C] an exclamation or sudden expression of your feelings. For example 'Hey' in 'Hey you!' is an interjection.

**interlude** /ˈɪntəluːd/ *noun* [C] a period of time between two events, activities, etc *a brief interlude of peace*

**intermediary** /ˌɪntəˈmiːdiəri/ *noun* [C] someone who works with two people or groups to help them agree on something important

**intermediate** /ˌɪntəˈmiːdiət/ *adj* **1** between the highest and lowest levels of knowledge or skill *intermediate students* **2** between two different stages in a process *intermediate steps towards achieving our goal*

**interminable** /ɪnˈtɜːmɪnəbl/ *adj* lasting a very long time, in a way that is boring *an interminable train journey* • **interminably** *adv*

**intermission** /ˌɪntəˈmɪʃən/ *noun* [C] a short period between the parts of a play, performance, etc

**intermittent** /ˌɪntəˈmɪtənt/ *adj* stopping and starting again for short periods of time *intermittent rain* • **intermittently** *adv*

**intern**[1] /ˈɪntɜːn/ *noun* [C] *US* **1** a young doctor who works in a hospital to finish their medical education **2** a student who learns about a particular job by doing it for a short period of time • **internship** *noun* [C] the time when someone is an intern

**intern**[2] /ɪnˈtɜːn/ *verb* [T] to put someone in prison for political reasons, especially during a war • **internment** *noun* [U] when someone is interned

**internal** /ɪnˈtɜːnəl/ *adj* **1** [INSIDE A PLACE] happening or coming from inside a particular country, group, or organization *an internal report to management* • *internal disputes* **2** [BODY] inside your body *internal injuries* **3** [PLACE] inside a country, building, area, etc *an internal flight* • *internal walls* ➔ *Opposite* **external**. • **internally** *adv*

○━**international**[1] /ˌɪntəˈnæʃənəl/ *adj* relating to or involving two or more countries *international politics* • *an international team of scientists* • **internationally** *adv*

**international**[2] /ˌɪntəˈnæʃənəl/ *noun* [C] *UK* a game of sport involving two or more countries, or a player in one of these games *a one-day international in South Africa*

○━**the Internet** /ˈɪntənet/ *noun* (*also* **the Net**) a system that connects computers around the world so you can share information with other people *You should check out this music website on the Internet.* • *a company that provides cheap Internet access* ➔ *See study section* **the Internet** *on page Centre 27.*

**interplay** /ˈɪntəpleɪ/ *noun* [U] the effect that two or more things have on each other *I'm interested in the interplay between Latin and English.*

**interpret** /ɪnˈtɜːprɪt/ *verb* **1** [T] to explain or decide what you think a particular phrase, performance, action, etc means *His comments*

---

| iː **see** | ɒ **hot** | ɔː **saw** | ʌ **run** | ʊ **put** | uː **too** | aɪ **my** | aʊ **how** | eɪ **day** | əʊ **no** | ɪə **near** | ɔɪ **boy** | ʊə **poor** | aɪə **fire** | aʊə **sour** |

*were **interpreted as** an attack on the government.* **2** [I, T] to change what someone has said into another language *We had to ask the guide to interpret for us.*

**interpretation** /ɪnˌtɜːprɪˈteɪʃən/ *noun* **1** [C, U] an explanation or opinion of what something means *traditional interpretations of the Bible* **2** [C] the way someone performs a particular play, piece of music, etc *a beautiful interpretation of Swan Lake*

**interpreter** /ɪnˈtɜːprɪtər/ *noun* [C] someone whose job is to change what someone else is saying into another language

**interrogate** /ɪnˈterəgeɪt/ *verb* [T] to ask someone a lot of questions, often with great force *Police have arrested and interrogated the two suspects.* ● **interrogation** /ɪnˌterəˈgeɪʃən/ *noun* [C, U] *twelve hours of brutal interrogation* ● **interrogator** *noun* [C]

**interrogative** /ˌɪntəˈrɒgətɪv/ *noun* [C] a word or sentence used when asking a question. For example 'Who' and 'Why' are interrogatives. ● **interrogative** *adj*

o⫶**interrupt** /ˌɪntəˈrʌpt/ *verb* **1** [I, T] to stop someone while they are talking or doing something, by saying or doing something yourself *Sorry to interrupt, but what time is it?* ● *I was trying to work but the children were interrupting me.* **2** [T] to stop an action or activity, usually for a short period of time *In 1998, a leg injury interrupted his sporting career.*

**interruption** /ˌɪntəˈrʌpʃən/ *noun* [C, U] when an action or activity is interrupted, or something that interrupts someone or something *Due to constant interruptions, the meeting finished late.*

**intersect** /ˌɪntəˈsekt/ *verb* [I, T] If two things such as lines or roads intersect, they go across each other at a particular point.

**intersection** /ˌɪntəˈsekʃən/ *noun* [C] US (UK **junction**) the place where two roads meet or cross each other

**interspersed** /ˌɪntəˈspɜːst/ *adj* **interspersed with sth** having something in several places among something else *farmland interspersed with forests and lakes*

**interstate** /ˈɪntəˌsteɪt/ *adj* [always before noun] relating to, or involving two or more US states *interstate commerce/travel* ● *an interstate highway*

**interval** /ˈɪntəvəl/ *noun* **1** [C] a period of time between two actions, activities, or events *After an interval of three days the peace talks resumed.* **2 at intervals** repeated after a particular period of time or particular distance *Patients were injected with the drug at four-hour intervals* (= every four hours). **3** [C] UK (*UK/US* **intermission**) a short period of time between the parts of a play, performance, etc

**intervene** /ˌɪntəˈviːn/ *verb* [I] **1** BECOME INVOLVED to become involved in a situation in order to try to stop a fight, argument, problem, etc *Government officials refused to intervene in the recent disputes.* ● [+ to do sth] *Harris intervened to stop the attack.* **2** INTERRUPT to interrupt someone who is talking *"Mr Lawrence," the judge intervened, "please be silent."* **3** PREVENT If something intervenes, it

stops something or prevents it from happening. *She was going to marry Barratt but tragedy intervened.*

**intervening** /ˌɪntəˈviːnɪŋ/ *adj* **the intervening months/period/years, etc** the time between two events *In the intervening years, his illness had become a lot worse.*

**intervention** /ˌɪntəˈvenʃən/ *noun* [C, U] when someone intervenes, especially to prevent something from happening *Without medical intervention, the child would have died.*

o⫶**interview¹** /ˈɪntəvjuː/ *noun* [C] **1** JOB/COURSE a meeting in which someone asks you questions to see if you are suitable for a job or course *I had an interview last week for a job in London.* **2** NEWS a meeting in which someone is asked questions for a newspaper article, television show, etc *an exclusive interview with Madonna* **3** POLICE a meeting in which the police ask someone questions to see if they have committed a crime

**interview²** /ˈɪntəvjuː/ *verb* [T] to ask someone questions in an interview *Police are interviewing a 43-year-old man in connection with the murder.* ● *So far we've interviewed five applicants for the Managing Director's job.* ● **interviewer** *noun* [C]

**interviewee** /ˌɪntəvjuˈiː/ *noun* [C] someone who is being interviewed

**intestine** /ɪnˈtestɪn/ *noun* [C] a long tube that carries food from your stomach ● **intestinal** /ˌɪntesˈtaɪnəl/ /ɪnˈtestɪnəl/ *adj* relating to your intestine

**intimacy** /ˈɪntɪməsi/ *noun* [U] when you have a very special friendship or sexual relationship with someone

**intimate¹** /ˈɪntɪmət/ *adj* **1** PRIVATE private and personal *intimate details of her family life* ● *intimate conversations* **2** RELATIONSHIP having a special relationship with someone who you like or love very much *an intimate friend* **3** SMALL If a place or event is intimate, it is small in a way that feels comfortable or private. *an intimate hotel* **4** **an intimate knowledge/understanding of sth** when you know all of the facts about something or about how it works ● **intimately** *adv*

**intimate²** /ˈɪntɪmeɪt/ *verb* [T] *formal* to suggest that something is true without saying it directly

**intimidate** /ɪnˈtɪmɪdeɪt/ *verb* [T] to intentionally frighten someone, especially so that they will do what you want ● **intimidation** /ɪnˌtɪmɪˈdeɪʃən/ *noun* [U]

**intimidated** /ɪnˈtɪmɪdeɪtɪd/ *adj* frightened or nervous because you are not confident in a situation *Older people can feel very intimidated by computers.* ● **intimidating** *adj* making you feel intimidated *I find speaking in front of a crowd very intimidating.*

o⫶**into** /ˈɪntə, ˈɪntuː/ *preposition* **1** IN towards the inside or middle of something *Stop running around and get into bed!* ● *He's gone into a shop across the road.* **2** CHANGE used to show when a person or thing changes from one form or condition to another *Peel the cucumber and chop it into small cubes.* ● *We're planning to turn the smallest bedroom into an office.* ● *Her last novel* *was translated into nineteen languages.* **3** ABOUT involving or about something *an investigation into the cause of the fire* **4** TOWARDS in the direction of something or someone *She was looking straight into his eyes.* **5** HIT moving towards something or someone and hitting them *I backed the car into the garden wall.* **6 be into sth** *informal* to be very interested in something *Kate's really into classical music.* **7** DIVIDE used when dividing one number by another *What's 5 into 125?*

**intolerable** /ɪn'tɒlªrªbl/ *adj* too bad or unpleasant to deal with or accept *an intolerable situation* • *The constant fighting made life at home intolerable.* • **intolerably** *adv*

**intolerance** /ɪn'tɒlªrªns/ *noun* [U] when someone is intolerant *religious intolerance*

**intolerant** /ɪn'tɒlªrªnt/ *adj* refusing to accept any opinions, beliefs, customs, etc that are different from your own

**intonation** /ˌɪntəʊ'neɪʃªn/ *noun* [C, U] the way your voice goes up and down when you speak

**intoxicated** /ɪn'tɒksɪkeɪtɪd/ *adj* **1** *formal* drunk **2** *literary* very excited or enthusiastic about someone or something • **intoxicating** *adj* making you intoxicated • **intoxication** /ɪn,tɒksɪ'keɪʃªn/ *noun* [U]

**intranet** /'ɪntrənet/ *noun* [C] a system that connects the computers in a company or organization so that people can share information and send messages

**intransitive** /ɪn'trænsətɪv/ *adj* An intransitive verb does not have an object. In the sentence 'John arrived first.', 'arrived' is an intransitive verb. ⊃ *Compare* **transitive**.

**intravenous** /ˌɪntrə'viːnəs/ *adj* Intravenous medicines or drugs are put directly into your veins (= tubes that carry your blood). • **intravenously** *adv*

**in-tray** /'ɪntreɪ/ *noun* [C] a container where you keep letters and documents that need to be dealt with

**intrepid** /ɪn'trepɪd/ *adj* brave and willing to do dangerous things *intrepid travellers*

**intricacy** /'ɪntrɪkəsi/ *noun* **1 the intricacies of sth** the complicated details of something *a booklet explaining the intricacies of the game's rules* **2** [U] the quality of being intricate *the intricacy of the stone carvings*

**intricate** /'ɪntrɪkət/ *adj* having many small or complicated parts and details *an intricate pattern* • **intricately** *adv*

**intrigue¹** /ɪn'triːg/ *verb* [T] **intriguing,** *past* **intrigued** If someone or something intrigues you, they interest you very much. *Ancient Egyptian art has always intrigued me.*

**intrigue²** /'ɪntriːg/ *noun* [C, U] a secret, clever plan to deceive someone or do something bad *a tale of romance, intrigue, and betrayal*

**intriguing** /ɪn'triːgɪŋ/ *adj* very interesting *an intriguing story*

**intrinsic** /ɪn'trɪnsɪk/ *adj* [always before noun] An intrinsic quality or thing forms part of the basic character of something or someone. *Drama is an intrinsic part of the school's curriculum.* • **intrinsically** *adv*

o→**introduce** /ˌɪntrə'djuːs/ *verb* [T] **1** SOMETHING NEW to make something exist, happen, or be used for the first time *CD players were first introduced in 1983.* • *We have introduced a new training schedule for employees.* **2** MEETING PEOPLE to tell someone another person's name the first time that they meet *He took me round the room and **introduced** me **to** everyone.* • [often reflexive] *Emma introduced herself and they shook hands.* **3** TO AN AUDIENCE to tell an audience who is going to speak to them or perform for them *I'd like to introduce Rachel Elliott who is our speaker this evening.*

**introduce sb to sth** to help someone experience something for the first time *His father introduced him to the pleasures of good food.*

o→**introduction** /ˌɪntrə'dʌkʃªn/ *noun* **1** SOMETHING NEW [U] when you make something exist, happen, or be used for the first time *the introduction of a minimum wage* **2** BOOK [C] the first part of a book or speech **3** BASIC KNOWLEDGE [C] a book or course which provides basic knowledge about a subject *an introduction to psychology* **4** FIRST EXPERIENCE [no plural] the first time someone experiences something *It was our first **introduction to** great poetry.* **5** FIRST MEETING [C] when you tell someone another person's name the first time that they meet [usually plural] *Can you do the introductions?* **6** TO AN AUDIENCE [C, U] when you tell an audience who is going to speak to them or perform for them *My next guest **needs no introduction.***

**introductory** /ˌɪntrə'dʌktªri/ *adj* **1 an introductory chapter/essay/message, etc** a part that comes at the beginning of a piece of writing or a speech and explains what will come later **2 an introductory book/course/lesson, etc** something that provides basic information about a subject *an introductory course in economics* **3 an introductory discount/fare/offer, etc** something that you get when you start buying something or using a service

**introspective** /ˌɪntrəʊ'spektɪv/ *adj* thinking a lot about your own thoughts and feelings, in a way that is not always good for you • **introspection** /ˌɪntrəʊ'spekʃªn/ *noun* [U]

**introvert** /'ɪntrəʊvɜːt/ *noun* [C] someone who is quiet and shy and prefers to be alone • **introverted** *adj* *an introverted child* ⊃ *Opposite* **extrovert**.

**intrude** /ɪn'truːd/ *verb* [I] to become involved in a situation which people want to be private *I don't mean to intrude, but are you okay?* • *They should not have **intruded on** the family's grief.*

**intruder** /ɪn'truːdªr/ *noun* [C] someone who enters a place where they are not allowed to be, often to commit a crime

**intrusion** /ɪn'truːʒªn/ *noun* [C, U] when someone becomes involved in a situation which people want to be private *She could not bear the intrusion into her private life.*

**intrusive** /ɪn'truːsɪv/ *adj* If something or someone is intrusive, they become involved in things which should be private. *The magazine published intrusive pictures of the princess's family.*

**intuition** /ˌɪntjuː'ɪʃªn/ *noun* [C, U] the feeling that you know something without being able to explain why *Her approach to childcare is based on intuition.*

**intuitive** /ɪn'tjuːɪtɪv/ *adj* using intuition *He has an intuitive understanding of animals.* • **intuitively** *adv*

**Inuit** /'ɪnuɪt/ *noun* [C, U] *plural* **Inuit** or **Inuits** a group of people who live in the cold, northern areas of North America, Russia, and Greenland, or a member of this group *the Inuit people*

**inundate** /'ɪnʌndeɪt/ *verb* **be inundated with/by sth** to receive so much of something that you cannot deal with it *Laura was inundated with flowers, cards, and other gifts.*

**invade** /ɪn'veɪd/ *verb* **1** [I, T] to enter a country by force in order to take control of it *Portugal was invaded by the French in 1807.* **2** [T] to enter a place in large numbers *Every summer the town is invaded by tourists.* **3 invade sb's privacy** to become involved in someone's private life when they do not want you to

**invader** /ɪn'veɪdə'/ *noun* [C] someone who enters a country by force in order to take control of it

**invalid**[1] /'ɪnvəlɪd/ *noun* [C] someone who is so ill that they have to be looked after by other people

**invalid**[2] /ɪn'vælɪd/ *adj* **1** An invalid document, ticket, law, etc is not legally or officially acceptable. **2** An invalid argument is not correct.

**invaluable** /ɪn'væljuəbl/ *adj* extremely useful *Her contacts in government proved invaluable to the company.*

**invariably** /ɪn'veəriəbli/ *adv* always *The train is invariably packed.*

**invasion** /ɪn'veɪʒ³n/ *noun* **1** [C, U] when an army enters a country by force in order to take control of it **2 an invasion of privacy** becoming involved in someone's private life when they do not want you to

o━**invent** /ɪn'vent/ *verb* [T] **1** to design or create something that has never existed before *We've invented a new game.* **2** to think of a story or explanation in order to deceive someone *She invented an excuse to leave.*

o━**invention** /ɪn'venʃ³n/ *noun* **1** [C] something that has been designed or created for the first time *A lot of great inventions have come from America.* **2** [U] when someone designs or creates something new *the invention of printing*

**inventive** /ɪn'ventɪv/ *adj* full of clever and interesting ideas *an inventive person/mind* • **inventive designs** • **inventively** *adv* • **inventiveness** *noun* [U]

**inventor** /ɪn'ventə'/ *noun* [C] someone who designs and makes new things

**inventory** /'ɪnv³ntri, ɪn'vent³ri/ *noun* [C] a list of all the things that are in a place

**invert** /ɪn'vɜːt/ *verb* [T] *formal* to turn something upside-down, or put something in the opposite order from how it usually is

**inverted commas** /ɪn,vɜːtɪd'kɒməz/ *noun* [plural] *UK* a pair of marks (" ") or (' ') used before and after a group of words to show that they are spoken or that someone else originally wrote them

**invest** /ɪn'vest/ *verb* **1** [I, T] to give money to a bank, business, etc, or buy something, because you hope to get a profit *He's invested over a million pounds in the city's waterfront restoration project.* **2** [T] to use a lot of time, effort, or emotions because you want to succeed *I think she invests too much time and energy in her career.*

**invest in sth** to buy something because you think it will be useful *Dad's decided to invest in a computer.*

**investigate** /ɪn'vestɪgeɪt/ *verb* [I, T] to try to discover all the facts about something, especially a crime or accident *He has been questioned by detectives investigating Jenkins' murder.*

**investigation** /ɪn,vestɪ'geɪʃ³n/ *noun* [C, U] when officials try to discover all the facts about something, especially a crime or an accident *Police have begun an investigation into his death.* • *The cause of the fire is still under investigation* (= being investigated).

**investigative** /ɪn'vestɪgətɪv *US* ɪn'vestɪgeɪtɪv/ *adj* trying to discover all the facts about something *investigative journalists*

**investigator** /ɪn'vestɪgeɪtə'/ *noun* [C] someone who tries to discover all the facts about something, especially as their job

**investment** /ɪn'vestmənt/ *noun* **1** [C, U] the money that you put in a bank, business, etc in order to make a profit, or the act of doing this *Businesses need to increase their investment in new technology.* **2** [C] something that you do or have, in order to have more in the future *Going to college is an investment in the future.*

**investor** /ɪn'vestə'/ *noun* [C] someone who puts money in a bank, business, etc in order to make a profit

**inveterate** /ɪn'vet³rət/ *adj* **an inveterate liar/gambler/reader, etc** someone who does something very often

**invigorating** /ɪn'vɪgəreɪtɪŋ/ *adj* making you feel very healthy and energetic *a long, invigorating walk* • **invigorate** *verb* [T] to make you feel very healthy and energetic

**invincible** /ɪn'vɪnsəbl/ *adj* If someone or something is invincible, it is impossible to defeat or destroy them. *The French army seemed invincible.*

**invisible** /ɪn'vɪzəbl/ *adj* Someone or something that is invisible cannot be seen. *invisible particles called electrons* • *The house was invisible from the road.* • **invisibility** /ɪn,vɪzə'bɪləti/ *noun* [U]

o━**invitation** /,ɪnvɪ'teɪʃ³n/ *noun* **1** INVITING SOMEONE [C, U] when someone invites you to do something or go somewhere *an invitation to dinner* • [+ to do sth] *He has accepted their invitation to visit China.* **2** PIECE OF PAPER [C] a piece of paper or card that invites someone to an event **3** CAUSE RESULT [no plural] something that is likely to cause a particular result, especially a bad one *It is an invitation to violence.*

o━**invite**[1] /ɪn'vaɪt/ *verb* [T] **1** SOCIAL EVENT to ask someone to come to a social event *They've invited us to the wedding.* **2** ASK OFFICIALLY to officially ask someone to do something [+ to do sth] *I was invited to appear on television.* **3** REACTION to do something that is likely to cause a particular reaction or result, especially a bad one *Unconventional ideas often invite attack.*

**invite** someone **to** something

Remember to use the preposition **to** with this expression.

*She invited me to the party.*

~~She invited me for the party.~~

~~She invited me at the party.~~

**invite sb in** to ask someone to come into your house *The neighbours **invited** us **in** for coffee.*

**invite sb over** (*also UK* **invite sb round**) to invite someone to come to your house *Let's invite some people over.*

**invite²** /'ɪnvaɪt/ *noun* [C] *informal* an invitation

**inviting** /ɪn'vaɪtɪŋ/ *adj* pleasant and attractive *an inviting smile* ● *The room looked cosy and inviting.* ● invitingly *adv*

**invoice¹** /'ɪnvɔɪs/ *noun* [C] a list that shows you how much you owe someone for work they have done or for goods they have supplied

**invoice²** /'ɪnvɔɪs/ *verb* [T] to send someone an invoice

**invoke** /ɪn'vəʊk/ *verb* [T] *formal* to use a law, rule, etc to support what you are saying or doing *The President may invoke federal law to stop the strike.*

**involuntary** /ɪn'vɒləntᵊri/ *adj* An involuntary movement or action is something you do but cannot control. *an involuntary shudder* ● involuntarily *adv*

o━**involve** /ɪn'vɒlv/ *verb* [T] **1** NECESSARY PART If a situation or activity involves something, that thing is a necessary part of it. *The trips often involve a lot of walking.* ● *There are a lot of risks involved.* **2** AFFECT/INCLUDE to affect or include someone or something in an activity *an event involving hundreds of people* **3** TAKE PART to make someone be part of an activity or process *I prefer teaching methods that actively **involve** students **in** learning.*

o━**involved** /ɪn'vɒlvd/ *adj* **1** be/get involved **(in/with sth)** to do things and be part of an activity or event *How did you get involved in acting?* **2** be/get involved with sb to have a sexual or romantic relationship with someone *She got involved with a boy from college.* **3** complicated *a long and involved story*

o━**involvement** /ɪn'vɒlvmənt/ *noun* [U] when someone or something is involved in an activity or event *He denies any **involvement in** the attack.*

**inward¹** /'ɪnwəd/ *adj* **1** [always before noun] towards the centre or the inside of something *UK* **2** inward investment *UK* money from foreign companies that is put into businesses in your own country **3** [always before noun] inside your mind and not shown to other people *inward feelings* ⊃ Opposite **outward**.

**inward²** /'ɪnwəd/ (*mainly UK* **inwards**) *adv* towards the inside or the centre *The door slowly opened inward.*

**inwardly** /'ɪnwədli/ *adv* in your mind without anyone else seeing or knowing *She smiled inwardly.* ⊃ Opposite **outwardly**.

**iodine** /'aɪədiːn/ *noun* [U] a chemical element found in sea water, and used in some medicines

**IOU** /,aɪəʊ'juː/ *noun* [C] *abbreviation for* I owe you: a piece of paper saying that you will pay back money you owe

**IPA** /,aɪpiː'eɪ/ *noun* [U] *abbreviation for* International Phonetic Alphabet: a system of symbols for showing how words are spoken

**IQ** /,aɪ'kjuː/ *noun* [C, U] *abbreviation for* intelligence quotient: a person's intelligence when measured by a special test *a high/low IQ*

**irate** /aɪ'reɪt/ *adj* extremely angry *Hundreds of irate passengers have complained to the airline.*

**iris** /'aɪərɪs/ *noun* [C] **1** a tall plant with purple, yellow, or white flowers **2** the coloured part of your eye

**Irish** /'aɪərɪʃ/ *adj* relating to Ireland *Irish music/culture* ● *Irish whisky*

**Irish²** /'aɪərɪʃ/ *noun* **1** [U] the language that is spoken in some parts of Ireland **2** the Irish [plural] the people of Ireland

o━**iron¹** /aɪən/ *noun* **1** [U] a dark grey metal used to make steel (= very strong metal) and found in small amounts in blood and food *an iron bar/gate* ● *Most women need more iron in their diet.* **2** [C] a piece of electrical equipment that you use for making clothes flat and smooth ⊃ See also: **cast iron**, **wrought iron**.

**iron²** /aɪən/ *verb* [I, T] to make clothes flat and smooth using an iron *I need to iron a shirt to wear tomorrow.*

**iron sth out** to solve a problem or difficulty *We're still trying to iron out a few problems with the computer system.*

**iron³** /aɪən/ *adj* [always before noun] extremely strong and determined *a man of iron will* ⊃ See also: **cast-iron**.

**ironic** /aɪə'rɒnɪk/ *adj* **1** saying something that you do not mean, as a joke *ironic comments* **2** An ironic situation is strange because it is the opposite of what you expected. [+ that] *It's ironic that she was hurt by the very person she's trying to help.* ● ironically *adv*

**ironing** /'aɪənɪŋ/ *noun* [U] **1** the activity of making clothes flat and smooth using an iron (= a piece of electrical equipment) *John was doing the ironing.* **2** the clothes that are waiting to be ironed, or those that have just been ironed *a basket full of ironing*

**'ironing ,board** *noun* [C] a narrow table that you use for ironing

**irony** /'aɪərᵊni/ *noun* **1** [C, U] a situation that is strange because it is the opposite of what you expected *The irony is that now he's retired, he's busier than ever.* **2** [U] a type of humour in which people say something they do not mean

**irrational** /ɪ'ræʃᵊnᵊl/ *adj* Irrational feelings and actions are based on your emotions and not on good reasons. *irrational behaviour* ● *an irrational fear of flying* ● irrationality /ɪ,ræʃᵊn'æləti/ *noun* [U] ● irrationally *adv*

**irreconcilable** /ɪ,rekᵊn'saɪləbl/ *adj formal* Irreconcilable beliefs, opinions, etc are so different that no agreement is possible. *Irreconcilable differences led to their divorce.*

**irregular** /ɪ'regjələʳ/ *adj* **1** TIME Irregular actions or events happen with a different amount of time between each one. *an irregular heartbeat* ● *They met at irregular intervals.*

**2** [SHAPE] not smooth or straight, or having parts that are different sizes *an irregular coastline* **3** [GRAMMAR] not following the general rules in grammar *irregular verbs/plurals* **4** [BEHAVIOUR] *UK formal* slightly illegal, or not done in the usual and acceptable way *He led a very irregular life.* • irregularity /ɪˌregjəˈlærəti/ *noun* [C, U] • irregularly *adv*

**irrelevant** /ɪˈreləvᵊnt/ *adj* not important in a particular situation *The car had faults but these were **irrelevant** to the crash.* • irrelevance /ɪˈreləvᵊns/ *noun* [C, U] something that is irrelevant, or the quality of being irrelevant • irrelevantly *adv*

**irreparable** /ɪˈrepᵊrəbl/ *adj* Irreparable damage, harm, injury, etc is so bad that it can never be repaired. • irreparably *adv*

**irreplaceable** /ˌɪrɪˈpleɪsəbl/ *adj* Someone or something that is irreplaceable is so valuable or special that you could not get another one like them.

**irrepressible** /ˌɪrɪˈpresəbl/ *adj* **1** always happy and energetic **2** An irrepressible feeling is impossible to control. *an irrepressible urge to travel* • irrepressibly *adv*

**irresistible** /ˌɪrɪˈzɪstəbl/ *adj* **1** extremely attractive and impossible not to like or want *an irresistible smile* **2** too powerful to control or ignore *irresistible pressure* • *an irresistible desire to run away* • irresistibly *adv*

**irrespective** /ˌɪrɪˈspektɪv/ *adv* **irrespective of sth** used to say that something does not affect a situation *Everyone should be treated equally, irrespective of skin colour.*

**irresponsible** /ˌɪrɪˈspɒnsəbl/ *adj* not thinking about the possible bad results of what you are doing *an irresponsible attitude* • irresponsibility /ˌɪrɪˌspɒnsəˈbɪləti/ *noun* [U] • irresponsibly *adv*

**irreverent** /ɪˈrevᵊrᵊnt/ *adj* not showing any respect for people or traditions that are usually respected *irreverent humour* • irreverence /ɪˈrevᵊrᵊns/ *noun* [U] when someone or something is irreverent • irreverently *adv*

**irreversible** /ˌɪrɪˈvɜːsəbl/ *adj* Something that is irreversible cannot be changed back to how it was before. *Smoking has caused irreversible damage to his lungs.* • irreversibly *adv*

**irrevocable** /ɪˈrevəkəbl/ *adj formal* impossible to change or stop *irrevocable decisions* • irrevocably *adv*

**irrigate** /ˈɪrɪgeɪt/ *verb* [T] to provide water for an area of land so that crops can be grown • irrigation /ˌɪrɪˈgeɪʃᵊn/ *noun* [U]

**irritable** /ˈɪrɪtəbl/ *adj* becoming annoyed very easily *Jack's been irritable all day.* • irritability /ˌɪrɪtəˈbɪləti/ *noun* [U] • irritably *adv*

**irritant** /ˈɪrɪtᵊnt/ *noun* [C] **1** someone or something that makes you feel annoyed **2** a substance that makes part of your body hurt

**irritate** /ˈɪrɪteɪt/ *verb* [T] **1** to annoy someone *His comments really irritated me.* **2** to make a part of your body hurt *The smoke irritated her eyes.* • irritation /ˌɪrɪˈteɪʃᵊn/ *noun* [C, U]

**irritated** /ˈɪrɪteɪtɪd/ *adj* annoyed *Ben began to get increasingly **irritated by/at** her questions.* • [+ that] *I was irritated that he didn't thank me.*

**irritating** /ˈɪrɪteɪtɪŋ/ *adj* making you feel annoyed *an irritating habit* • irritatingly *adv*

**is** *strong form* /ɪz/ *weak form* /z/ present simple *he/she/it of* be

**Islam** /ˈɪzlɑːm/ *noun* [U] a religion based on belief in Allah, on the Koran, and on the teachings of Mohammed *The followers of Islam are called Muslims.*

**Islamic** /ɪzˈlæmɪk/ *adj* related to Islam *Islamic art* • *an Islamic country*

o—**island** /ˈaɪlənd/ *noun* [C] an area of land that has water around it *the Caribbean island of Grenada* • *the Hawaiian Islands* • islander *noun* [C] someone who lives on an island ➲ *See also:* **desert island**.

**isle** /aɪl/ *noun* [C] an island, often used in the name of a particular island *the British Isles*

**isn't** /ˈɪzᵊnt/ *short for* is not *Mike isn't coming with us.*

**isolate** /ˈaɪsəleɪt/ *verb* [T] to separate someone or something from other people or things *Scientists have been able to isolate the gene responsible for causing the illness.* • *He had been **isolated from** other prisoners.*

**isolated** /ˈaɪsəleɪtɪd/ *adj* **1** a long way from other places *an isolated village in the mountains* **2** alone and not having help or support from other people *Kazuo felt very isolated at his new school.* **3 an isolated case/example/incident, etc** an event, action, etc that happens only once *This robbery was not an isolated incident.*

**isolation** /ˌaɪsᵊlˈeɪʃᵊn/ *noun* **1** [U] the state of being separate from other people, places, or things *the country's economic isolation from the rest of the world* **2 in isolation** alone, or separately from other people, places, or things *These poems cannot be considered in isolation.* **3** [U] a feeling of being lonely *I had this awful sense of isolation.*

**ISP** /ˌaɪesˈpiː/ *noun* [C] *abbreviation for* Internet service provider: a company that connects your computer to the Internet, and lets you use email and other services

o—**issue¹** /ˈɪʃuː/ *noun* **1** [C] an important subject or problem that people are discussing *the issues of race and social class* • *political issues* • *Chris has raised a very important issue.* **2** [C] the newspaper, magazine, etc that is produced on a particular day *Have you seen the latest issue of Computer World?* **3 at issue** most important in what is being discussed *The point at issue is what is best for the child.* **4 take issue (with sb/sth)** to disagree with what someone says or writes *I would take issue with you on that.*

**issue²** /ˈɪʃuː/ *verb* [T] **issuing**, *past* **issued** **1** to say something officially *The Prime Minister will issue a statement tomorrow.* • *Police issued a warning about the dangers of playing near water.* **2** to officially give something to someone *to issue a passport/ticket/invitation* • *All members will be **issued with** a membership card.*

**IT** /ˌaɪˈtiː/ *noun* [U] *abbreviation for* information technology: the use of computers and other electronic equipment to store and send information

o⊸**it** /ɪt/ *pronoun* **1** THING used to refer to the thing, situation, or idea that has already been talked about *"Have you seen my bag?" "It's in the hall."* • *It was a horrible argument and I don't want to talk about it.* **2** DESCRIPTION used before certain adjectives, nouns, or verbs to introduce an opinion or description of a situation *It's unlikely that she'll arrive on time.* • *It's a pity you can't come with us.* **3** SUBJECT/OBJECT used with certain verbs that need a subject or object but do not refer to a particular noun *It costs less if you travel at the weekend.* • *I liked it in Scotland.* **4** TIME/WEATHER used with the verb 'be' in sentences giving the time, date, weather or distances *It rained all day.* • *What time is it?* **5** SEEM used as the subject of verbs such as 'seem', 'appear' and 'look' *It seemed unfair to leave her at home.* **6** EMPHASIZE used to emphasize one part of a sentence *It's the children I'm concerned about, not me.* **7 it's sb/sth** used to say the name of a person or thing when the person you are speaking to does not know *It's your Dad on the phone.*

**italics** /ɪ'tælɪks/ *noun* [plural] a style of writing or printing in which the letters slope to the right • **italic** *adj* written in italics

**itch**¹ /ɪtʃ/ *verb* **1** [I] If a part of your body itches, it feels uncomfortable and you want to rub it with your nails. *Woollen sweaters make my arms itch.* **2 be itching to do sth** *informal* to want to do something very much *You could tell that they were itching to leave.*

**itch**² /ɪtʃ/ *noun* [C] an uncomfortable feeling on your skin that makes you want to rub it with your nails *I've got an itch in the middle of my back.*

**itching** /'ɪtʃɪŋ/ *noun* [U] when a part of your body itches *a lotion to stop itching*

**itchy** /'ɪtʃi/ *adj* If a part of your body is itchy, it feels uncomfortable and you want to rub it with your nails. *an itchy nose* • **itchiness** *noun* [U]

**it'd** /'ɪtəd/ **1** *short for* it would *It'd be great if we could meet next week.* **2** *short for* it had *It'd taken us an hour to find Bruce's house.*

o⊸**item** /'aɪtəm/ *noun* [C] **1** a single thing in a set or on a list *the last item on the list* • *Various stolen items were found.* **2** a piece of news on television or radio, or in a newspaper *a small item on the back page of the local newspaper*

**itemize** (*also UK* **-ise**) /'aɪtəmaɪz/ *verb* [T] to list things separately, often including details about each thing *an itemized phone bill*

**itinerant** /aɪ'tɪnᵊrᵊnt/ *adj* [always before noun] *formal* travelling from one place to another *an itinerant preacher*

**itinerary** /aɪ'tɪnᵊrᵊri/ *noun* [C] a list of places that you plan to visit on a journey *The President's itinerary includes visits to Boston and New York.*

**it'll** /'ɪtᵊl/ *short for* it will *It'll take about twenty minutes to get there.*

**it's** /ɪts/ **1** *short for* it is *"What time is it?" "It's one o'clock."* **2** *short for* it has *It's been a long day and I'm tired.*

o⊸**its** /ɪts/ *determiner* belonging to or relating to the thing that has already been talked about *The house has its own swimming pool.*

o⊸**itself** /ɪt'self/ *pronoun* **1** the reflexive form of the pronoun 'it' *The cat licked itself clean.* **2** used to emphasize the particular thing you are referring to *The garden is enormous but the house itself is very small.* **3 (all) by itself a** alone *The dog was in the house by itself for several days.* **b** automatically *The heating comes on by itself.* **4 in itself** only the thing being talked about and nothing else *You've managed to complete the course – that in itself is an achievement.*

**ITV** /ˌaɪtiː'viː/ *noun abbreviation for* Independent Television: one of the main television companies in the United Kingdom *There's a good film on ITV tonight.*

**IV** /ˌaɪ'viː/ *US* (*UK* **drip**) *noun* [C] a piece of medical equipment used for putting liquids into your body *He was unconscious and on an IV.*

ivy

**I've** /aɪv/ *short for* I have *I've decided not to go.*

**ivory** /'aɪvᵊri/ *noun* [U] a hard, white substance from the tusks (= long teeth) of some animals, such as elephants (= large, grey animals)

**ivy** /'aɪvi/ *noun* [U] a dark green plant that often grows up walls

# J

**J, j** /dʒeɪ/ the tenth letter of the alphabet

**jab¹** /dʒæb/ *verb* [I, T] **jabbing**, *past* **jabbed** to push something quickly and hard into or towards another thing *He jabbed a finger into her back.*

**jab²** /dʒæb/ *noun* [C] **1** a quick, hard push into or towards something **2** *UK informal* an injection (= when a drug is put in your body with a needle) *a flu jab*

**jack¹** /dʒæk/ *noun* [C] **1** a piece of equipment for lifting a heavy object such as a car **2** a playing card that comes between a ten and a queen *the jack of diamonds*

**jack²** /dʒæk/ *verb*

**jack sth in** *UK informal* to stop doing something, especially a job *She's jacked in her job.*

**jack sth up** *informal* to increase a price or rate suddenly and by a large amount

**jackal** /dʒækᵊl/ *noun* [C] a wild dog that hunts in groups

**jacket** /dʒækɪt/ *noun* [C] a short coat *a leather jacket* ➔ *See colour picture* **Clothes** *on page Centre 5.* ➔ *See also:* **dinner jacket, life jacket, straitjacket.**

**jacket**

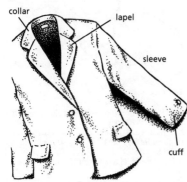

collar

lapel

sleeve

cuff

**jacket po'tato** *noun* [C] *plural* **jacket potatoes** *UK* a potato that has been baked in the oven with its skin on

**jack-knife¹** /dʒæknaɪf/ *noun* [C] *plural* **jack-knives** a knife with a blade that can be folded away into the handle

**jack-knife²** /dʒæk,naɪf/ *verb* [I] If a large truck jack-knifes, the front part turns round to face the back in a way that is not controlled.

**jackpot** /dʒækpɒt/ *noun* **1** [C] an amount of money that is the largest prize anyone can win in a competition **2** **hit the jackpot** to be very successful, especially by winning or earning a lot of money

**Jacuzzi** /dʒəˈkuːzi/ *noun* [C] *trademark* a bath or pool that produces bubbles in the water

**jade** /dʒeɪd/ *noun* [U] a green stone used in making jewellery

**jaded** /dʒeɪdɪd/ *adj* tired or bored with something, especially because you have done it too much

**jagged** /dʒægɪd/ *adj* very rough and sharp *jagged rocks*

**jaguar** /dʒægjuəʳ/ *noun* [C] a large, wild cat that lives in Central and South America

**jail¹** (*also UK* **gaol**) /dʒeɪl/ *noun* [C, U] a place where criminals are kept as a punishment *He ended up in jail.*

**jail²** /dʒeɪl/ *verb* [T] to put someone in a jail [often passive] *He was jailed for two years.*

**jailer** /dʒeɪləʳ/ *noun* [C] someone who guards prisoners in a jail

**jam¹** /dʒæm/ *noun* **1** [C, U] (*also US* **jelly**) a sweet food made from fruit that you spread on bread *a jar of strawberry jam* ➔ *See colour picture* **Food** *on page Centre 7.* **2** [C] (*also* **traffic jam**) a line of cars, trucks, etc that are moving slowly or not moving *We were stuck in a jam for hours.*

**jam²** /dʒæm/ *verb* **jamming**, *past* **jammed** **1 jam sth in/into/on, etc** to push something somewhere firmly and tightly *She jammed her hands into her pockets.* **2** [STUCK] [I, T] to get stuck or make something get stuck *The machine keeps jamming.* **3** [FILL] [T] to fill a place completely [often passive] *The streets were jammed with cars.* **4** [STOP RADIO] [T] to send a signal that stops a radio being able to broadcast

**jamboree** /,dʒæmbᵊrˈiː/ *noun* [C] a big celebration or party

**Jan** *written abbreviation for* January

**jangle** /dʒæŋgl/ *verb* [I, T] If small metal objects jangle, they hit together making a ringing noise, and if you jangle them, you make them make this noise. *He was jangling his keys.* ● **jangle** *noun* [C]

**janitor** /dʒænɪtəʳ/ *noun* [C] *US* someone whose job is to look after a building *the school janitor*

**January** /dʒænjuᵊri/ (*written abbreviation* **Jan**) *noun* [C, U] the first month of the year

**jar¹** /dʒɑːʳ/ *noun* [C] a glass container used for storing food *a jar of jam* ➔ *See picture at* **container.**

**jar²** /dʒɑːʳ/ *verb* **jarring**, *past* **jarred 1** [I, T] to move suddenly, hitting something and causing pain or damage *The movement jarred his injured leg.* **2** [T] If a situation, event, or noise jars you, it shocks you. *The murders jarred both US and Mexican officials.*

**jar on sb** *UK* to annoy someone *Her voice jars on me.*

**jargon** /dʒɑːgən/ *noun* [U] words and phrases used by particular groups of people that are difficult for other people to understand *legal jargon*

**jaundice** /dʒɔːndɪs/ *noun* [U] a disease that makes your eyes and skin yellow

**jaundiced** /dʒɔːndɪst/ *adj* having a negative opinion of something because of bad things that have happened to you *a jaundiced view of marriage*

**jaunt** /dʒɔːnt/ *noun* [C] a short, enjoyable journey

**jaunty** /dʒɔːnti/ *adj* happy and confident *a jaunty smile*

**javelin** /ˈdʒævəlɪn/ *noun* **1** [C] a long, pointed stick that you throw as a sport **2 the javelin** a sport in which you throw a javelin as far as you can ⊃ *See colour picture* **Sports 1** *on page Centre 15.*

**jaw** /dʒɔː/ *noun* [C] **1** either of the two bones in your mouth that contain your teeth ⊃ *See colour picture* **The Body** *on page Centre 2.* **2 sb's jaw drops** If someone's jaw drops, their mouth opens because they are very surprised.

**jazz** /dʒæz/ *noun* [U] music with a strong beat that is often played without written music *a jazz band*

**jealous** /ˈdʒeləs/ *adj* **1** unhappy and angry because you want something that someone else has *His new bike was **making his friends jealous**.* • *Steve has always **been jealous of** his brother's good looks.* **2** upset and angry because someone you love seems too interested in another person *a jealous husband* • jealously *adv*

**jealousy** /ˈdʒeləsi/ *noun* [U] jealous feelings

**jeans** /dʒiːnz/ *noun* [plural] trousers made from denim (= a strong, usually blue, material) *a pair of jeans* ⊃ *See colour picture* **Clothes** *on page Centre 5.*

**Jeep** /dʒiːp/ *noun* [C] *trademark* a strongly built vehicle with big wheels that is used for driving over rough ground

**jeer** /dʒɪər/ *verb* [I, T] to laugh and shout insults at someone *The crowd outside his house jeered as he left.* • jeer *noun* [C]

**Jell-O** /ˈdʒeləʊ/ *noun* [U] *US trademark* jelly

**jelly¹** /ˈdʒeli/ *noun* [C, U] **1** *UK* (*US* **Jell-O**) a soft but solid sweet food that shakes when you move it *jelly and ice cream* **2** *US* (*UK/US* **jam**) a sweet food made from fruit that you spread on bread

**jellyfish** /ˈdʒelifɪʃ/ *noun* [C] *plural* **jellyfish** a sea creature with a clear body that may sting you (= put poison into your skin)

**jeopardize** (*also UK* **-ise**) /ˈdʒepədaɪz/ *verb* [T] to put something in a situation where there is a risk of failing or being harmed *Bad weather could jeopardize all our plans.*

**jeopardy** /ˈdʒepədi/ *noun* **in jeopardy** in danger of failing or being harmed *If the factory closes, local jobs will be in jeopardy.*

**jerk¹** /dʒɜːk/ *verb* [I, T] to move very quickly and suddenly, or to make something move like this *The truck jerked forward.*

**jerk²** /dʒɜːk/ *noun* [C] **1** a quick, sudden movement *a sudden jerk of the head* **2** *mainly US informal* a stupid or annoying person

**jerky** /ˈdʒɜːki/ *adj* Jerky movements are quick and sudden. • jerkily *adv*

**jersey** /ˈdʒɜːzi/ *noun* **1** [C] a piece of clothing which covers the top of your body and is pulled on over your head **2** [U] soft wool or cotton cloth used for making clothes

**jest** /dʒest/ *noun* **in jest** said as a joke

**Jesus Christ** /ˌdʒiːzəsˈkraɪst/ *noun* the Jewish holy man believed by Christians to be the Son of God, and on whose life and teachings Christianity is based

**jet¹** /dʒet/ *noun* [C] **1** an aircraft that flies very fast **2** water or gas that is forced out of something in a thin, strong line ⊃ *See also:* **jumbo jet**.

**jet²** /dʒet/ *verb* [I] **jetting,** *past* **jetted** **jet in/off, etc** to fly somewhere in an aircraft *She jetted off to Athens for a week.*

**jet-black** /ˌdʒetˈblæk/ *noun* [U] a very dark black colour • jet-black *adj* *jet-black hair*

**jet 'engine** *noun* [C] an engine that makes an aircraft fly very fast

**'jet ,lag** *noun* [U] when you feel tired because you have just travelled a long distance on an aircraft

**jettison** /ˈdʒetɪsən/ *verb* [T] **1** to get rid of something you do not want or need *The station has jettisoned educational broadcasts.* **2** If an aircraft or a ship jettisons something, it throws it off to make itself lighter.

**jetty** /ˈdʒeti/ *noun* [C] a wooden structure at the edge of the sea or a lake where people can get on and off boats

**Jew** /dʒuː/ *noun* [C] someone whose religion is Judaism, or who is related to the ancient people of Israel

**jewel** /ˈdʒuːəl/ *noun* [C] a valuable stone that is used to make jewellery

**jeweller** *UK* (*US* **jeweler**) /ˈdʒuːələr/ *noun* [C] someone whose job is to sell or make jewellery

**jewellery** *UK* (*US* **jewelry**) /ˈdʒuːəlri/ *noun* [U] objects made from gold, silver, and valuable stones that you wear for decoration

**jewellery** *UK,* **jewelry** *US*

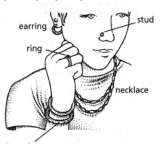

earring • stud • ring • necklace • bracelet

**Jewish** /ˈdʒuːɪʃ/ *adj* relating or belonging to the Jews *Jewish history/law*

**jibe** (*also* **gibe**) /dʒaɪb/ *noun* [C] an insulting remark *He kept making **jibes at** me about my weight.*

**jig** /dʒɪɡ/ *noun* [C] a traditional, quick dance, or the music it is danced to

**jiggle** /ˈdʒɪɡl/ *verb* [I, T] to make quick, short movements from side to side or to make something else move like this

**jigsaw** /ˈdʒɪɡsɔː/ (*also* **'jigsaw ,puzzle**) *noun* [C] a picture in many small pieces that you put together as a game

**jingle¹** /ˈdʒɪŋɡl/ *noun* [C] **1** a short song that is used to advertise a product on the radio or television **2** a sound made when small metal objects hit against each other

**jingle²** /ˈdʒɪŋɡl/ *verb* [I, T] to make the sound of small metal objects hitting against each other *a pocket full of jingling coins*

**jinx** /dʒɪŋks/ *noun* [C] someone or something that brings bad luck *There seems to be **a jinx on** the school.* • jinx *verb* [T]

**jitters** /ˈdʒɪtəz/ *noun* [plural] a nervous feeling *Hospitals give me **the jitters**.*

**jittery** /'dʒɪtəri/ adj nervous *She gets quite jittery about exams.*

**Jnr** UK (UK/US **Jr**) written abbreviation for junior (= the younger of two men in a family with the same name)

o━**job** /dʒɒb/ noun [C] **1** [PAID EMPLOYMENT] the regular work that you do in order to earn money *She got a job in publishing.* • *Hundreds of workers could lose their jobs.* • *Why don't you apply for a part-time job?* ➔ *See usage note at* **work.** **2** [PIECE OF WORK] a piece of work that you have to do *cooking, cleaning and other household jobs* **3** [RESPONSIBILITY] something that is your responsibility *It's my job to water the plants.* **4 make a bad/good, etc job of sth** UK to do sth badly/well, etc **5 do an excellent/good, etc job** to do something very well/well, etc *She did a great job of organizing the event.* **6 out of a job** without a job *How long have you been out of a job?* **7 do the job** If something does the job, it is suitable for a particular purpose. *Here, this knife should do the job.* **8 it's a good job** UK informal If it is a good job that something happened, it is lucky that it happened. [+ (that)] *It's a good job that Jo was.* **9 just the job** UK If something is just the job, it is exactly what you want or need.

**jobless** /'dʒɒbləs/ adj without a job *young jobless people*

**jockey** /'dʒɒki/ noun [C] someone who rides horses in races ➔ *See also:* **disc jockey.**

**jog** /dʒɒg/ verb jogging, past jogged **1** [I] to run slowly for exercise *I jog through the park every morning.* **2** [T] to hit something gently by mistake *He jogged her arm.* **3 jog sb's memory** to cause someone to remember something *They hoped the photographs would jog his memory.* • jog noun [no plural] *Let's go for a jog.* • jogging noun [U]

**jogger** /'dʒɒgər/ noun [C] someone who runs for exercise

o━**join¹** /dʒɔɪn/ verb **1** [BECOME MEMBER] [T] to become a member of a group or organization *He joined the army when he was eighteen.* **2** [DO WITH OTHERS] [T] to do something or go somewhere with someone *Would you like to join us for dinner?* **3** [FASTEN] [T] to fasten or connect things together *Join the ends together with strong glue.* • *A suspension bridge joins the two islands.* **4** [MEET] [I, T] to meet at a particular point *The Mississippi River and the Missouri join near St Louis.* **5 join a line** (*also* UK **join a queue**) to go and stand at the end of a row of people waiting for something ➔ *See also:* join forces (**force¹**).

**join**

Join is not followed by a preposition when it is used in expressions such as 'join a company'.

*He joined the team in 1998.*

~~He joined to the team in 1998.~~

**join in (sth)** to become involved in an activity with other people *We're playing cards. Would you like to join in?*

**join up** to become a member of the army or other military group

**join²** /dʒɔɪn/ noun [C] UK the place where two or more things are fastened together

**joined-up** /,dʒɔɪn'dʌp/ adj UK **1 joined-up writing** a style of writing where each letter in a word is connected to the next one **2 joined-up thinking** thinking about a complicated problem in an intelligent and original way, and considering everything that is connected to it

**joint¹** /dʒɔɪnt/ adj [always before noun] belonging to or done by two or more people *a joint statement* • *The project was a joint effort by all the children in the class.* • jointly adv

**joint²** /dʒɔɪnt/ noun [C] **1** [BODY PART] a place in your body where two bones meet *the knee joint* **2** [MEAT] UK a large piece of meat, usually cooked in the oven *a joint of beef* **3** [CONNECTION] a place where parts of a structure or machine are connected **4** [PLACE]

**joint**

informal a place where something is sold, especially a restaurant or bar *a pizza joint*

,**joint 'venture** noun [C] a business activity that involves two or more companies working together

o━**joke¹** /dʒəʊk/ noun **1** [C] something which someone says to make people laugh, usually a short story with a funny ending *to tell/make a joke* • *a good joke about dogs* **2 be a joke** informal to not be serious or not deserve respect *The investigation was a joke.* **3 be no joke** to be serious or difficult *It's no joke driving on icy roads.* **4 take a joke** to understand and accept a trick without becoming angry or upset ➔ *See also:* **practical joke.**

**joke²** /dʒəʊk/ verb **1** [I] to say funny things, or not be serious *She always jokes about her husband's cooking.* **2 You must be joking!; You're joking!** informal something you say to show that you are surprised by what someone has said, or do not believe it is true • jokingly adv

**joker** /'dʒəʊkər/ noun [C] **1** someone who likes saying or doing funny things **2** one of a set of playing cards which can be used instead of another card in some games

**jolly¹** /'dʒɒli/ adj happy or enjoyable *We had a jolly evening.*

**jolly²** /'dʒɒli/ adv UK very *a jolly good idea*

**jolt¹** /dʒəʊlt/ noun [C] **1** a sudden, violent movement *With a sudden jolt the train started moving again.* **2** an unpleasant shock or surprise *The reminder that he was dead gave her a jolt.*

**jolt²** /dʒəʊlt/ verb [I, T] to move suddenly and forcefully, or to make someone or something do this *The bus stopped suddenly and the passengers were jolted forward.*

**jostle** /'dʒɒsl/ verb [I, T] to push other people in order to get somewhere in a crowd

**jostle for sth** to try hard to get something *Thousands of companies are jostling for business on the Internet.*

**jot** /dʒɒt/ *verb* [T] *jotting, past* **jotted** to write something quickly *She jotted a note to Sue.*

**jot sth down** to write something quickly on a piece of paper so that you remember it *I jotted down some notes during his speech.*

**journal** /'dʒɜːnªl/ *noun* [C] **1** a magazine containing articles about a particular subject *a medical journal* **2** a book in which you regularly write about what has happened to you

**journalism** /'dʒɜːnªlɪzªm/ *noun* [U] the work of writing articles for newspapers, magazines, television, or radio

○━**journalist** /'dʒɜːnªlɪst/ *noun* [C] someone whose job is journalism

**journalistic** /,dʒɜːnªl'ɪstɪk/ *adj* relating to journalism or typical of journalism

○━**journey** /'dʒɜːni/ *noun* [C] when you travel from one place to another *a car/train journey* • *We take games for the children when we go on long journeys.* ➔ *See usage note at* **travel**.

**jovial** /'dʒəʊviªl/ *adj* happy and

**joy** /dʒɔɪ/ *noun* **1** [HAPPINESS] [U] a feeling of great happiness *the joy of winning* **2** [PLEASURE] [C] something or someone that makes you feel very happy *She's a joy to work with.* **3** [SUCCESS] [U] *UK informal* success *I tried ringing for a plumber, but had no joy.*

**joyful** /'dʒɔɪfªl/ *adj* very happy, or making people feel very happy *joyful news* • joyfully *adv*

**joyous** /'dʒɔɪəs/ *adj literary* extremely happy, or making people extremely happy • joyously *adv*

**joyriding** /'dʒɔɪ,raɪdɪŋ/ *noun* [U] stealing cars and driving them fast and dangerously • joyride /'dʒɔɪraɪd/ *noun* [C] *They took the car for a joyride.* • joyrider *noun* [C]

**joystick** /'dʒɔɪstɪk/ *noun* [C] a vertical handle you move to control a computer game, machine, or aircraft

**JP** /,dʒeɪ'piː/ *noun* [C] *abbreviation for* Justice of the Peace: a judge in a small or local court of law

**Jr** (*also UK* **Jnr**) *written abbreviation for* junior (= the younger of two men in a family with the same name) *John F. Kennedy, Jr.*

**jubilant** /'dʒuːbɪlənt/ *adj* feeling or showing great happiness, usually because of a success *jubilant United supporters* • jubilation /,dʒuːbɪ'leɪʃªn/ *noun* [U] a feeling of great happiness and success

**jubilee** /'dʒuːbɪliː/ *noun* [C] a celebration of an important event in the past, usually one which happened 25 or 50 years ago *a golden jubilee* (= 50 years) • *a silver jubilee* (= 25 years)

**Judaism** /'dʒuːdeɪɪzªm/ *noun* [U] the religion of the Jewish people, based on belief in one God and on the laws contained in the Torah

**judge¹** /dʒʌdʒ/ *noun* [C] **1** someone who controls a trial in court, decides how criminals should be punished, and makes decisions about legal things *Judge Moylan* • *The judge ruled that they had acted correctly.* **2** someone who decides which person or thing wins a competition *the Olympic judges* **3** a **bad/good, etc**

**judge of sth** someone who is usually wrong, usually right, etc when they judge something *a good judge of character*

○━**judge²** /dʒʌdʒ/ *verb* **1** [DEVELOP OPINION] [I, T] to have or develop an opinion about something or someone, usually after thinking carefully *The meeting was judged to be a great success.* • [+ question word] *I can't judge whether he's telling the truth or not.* • *You shouldn't judge people on their appearances.* • *He was judged guilty/insane.* **2** judging by/from used to express the reasons why you have a particular opinion *She must be popular judging by the number of letters that she receives.* **3** [COMPETITION] [I, T] to decide the winner or results of a competition *I've been asked to judge the art contest.* **4** [BAD OPINION] [I, T] to have a bad opinion of someone's behaviour, often because you think you are better than them *What gives you the right to judge people?* **5** [GUESS] [T] to try to guess something, especially a measurement *I find it difficult to judge distances.*

○━**judgment** (*also* **judgement**) /'dʒʌdʒmənt/ *noun* **1** [OPINION] [C, U] an opinion about someone or something that you decide on after thinking carefully *The inspector needs to make a judgment about how the school is performing.* **2** [ABILITY] [U] the ability to make good decisions or to be right in your opinions *to have good/bad judgment* **3** [LEGAL DECISION] [C, U] an official legal decision, usually made by a judge

**judgmental** (*also UK* **judgemental**) /dʒʌdʒ'mentªl/ *adj* quick to criticize people

**judicial** /dʒuː'dɪʃªl/ *adj* relating to a court of law or the legal system *a judicial inquiry*

**the judiciary** /dʒuː'dɪʃªri/ *noun* all the judges in a country

**judicious** /dʒuː'dɪʃəs/ *adj* done or decided carefully and with good judgment

**judo** /'dʒuːdəʊ/ *noun* [U] a sport from Japan in which two people try to throw each other to the ground

**jug** /dʒʌɡ/ *noun* [C] a container with a handle used for pouring out liquids *a jug of water*

jug

**juggle** /'dʒʌɡl/ *verb* **1** [T] to try to do several things at once, when it is difficult to have enough time *Many women have to juggle work and family.* **2** [I, T] to keep two or more objects such as balls in the air by throwing them repeatedly, usually in order to entertain people

**juggler** /'dʒʌɡlə³/ *noun* [C] someone who juggles objects to entertain people

○━**juice** /dʒuːs/ *noun* [C, U] the liquid that comes from fruit or vegetables ➔ *See also:* **orange juice.**

**juices** /'dʒuːsɪz/ *noun* [plural] the liquid that comes from cooked meat

**juicy** /'dʒuːsi/ *adj* **1** full of juice *juicy apples* **2** interesting because of shocking or personal information *juicy gossip*

**jukebox** /'dʒuːkbɒks/ *noun* [C] a machine, usually in a bar, which plays a song when you put money into it

**July** /dʒʊ'laɪ/ *noun* [C, U] the seventh month of the year ➔ *See also:* **Fourth of July**.

**jumble¹** /'dʒʌmbl/ *noun* [no plural] a confused mixture or group of things *Her handbag is a jumble of pens, make-up, and keys.*

**jumble²** /'dʒʌmbl/ (*also* **jumble up**) *verb* [T] to mix things together in an untidy way [often passive] *Her clothes were all jumbled up in the suitcase.*

**jumble sale** *UK* (*US* **rummage sale**) *noun* [C] a sale of old items, especially clothes, usually to make money for an organization

**jumbo** /'dʒʌmbəʊ/ *adj* [always before noun] extra large *a jumbo bag of sweets*

**jumbo 'jet** *noun* [C] a very large aircraft for carrying passengers

o-=**jump¹** /dʒʌmp/ *verb* **1** [INTO AIR] [I] to push your body up and away from the ground using your feet and legs *The children were jumping up and down with excitement.* • *I jumped over the log.* • *They jumped into the water.* **2 jump into/up, etc** to move somewhere suddenly and quickly *She jumped into a taxi and rushed to the station.* **3** [GO OVER] [T] to move over something by moving up into the air *The horse jumped the last fence.* **4** [INCREASE] [I, T] to suddenly increase by a large amount *House prices have jumped by 20%.* **5** [FEAR] [I] to make a sudden movement because you are frightened or surprised *Her scream made me jump.* ➔ *See also:* jump on the **bandwagon**, jump to conclusions (**conclusion**), jump the **gun¹**, jump the **queue**.
**jump at sth** to take an opportunity to have or do something in a very willing and excited way *He jumped at the chance to join the band.*

**jump²** /dʒʌmp/ *noun* [C] **1** when you push your body up into the air using your feet and legs *He won with a jump of 8.5 metres.* **2** a sudden increase in the amount of something *a jump in profits* ➔ *See also:* **the high jump**, **the long jump**.

**jumper** /'dʒʌmpə'/ *noun* [C] **1** *UK* (*UK/US* **sweater**) a warm piece of clothing which covers the top of your body and is pulled on over your head ➔ *See colour picture* **Clothes** *on page Centre 5.* **2** *US* (*UK* **pinafore**) a loose dress with no sleeves that is worn over other clothes such as a shirt

**jump rope** *US* (*UK* **skipping rope**) *noun* [C] a rope that you move over your head and then jump over as you move it under your feet

**jumpy** /'dʒʌmpi/ *adj* nervous or anxious

**junction** /'dʒʌŋkʃən/ *noun* [C] *UK* the place where two roads or railway lines meet or cross each other *The accident happened at a busy road junction.* ➔ *See also:* **T-junction**.

**juncture** /'dʒʌŋktʃə'/ *noun* [C] *formal* a particular point in an event or period of time

**June** /dʒuːn/ *noun* [C, U] the sixth month of the year

**jungle** /'dʒʌŋgl/ *noun* [C, U] an area of land, usually in tropical countries, where trees and plants grow close together

**junior¹** /'dʒuːniə'/ *adj* **1** [LOW RANK] low or lower in rank *a junior minister/senator* **2** [YOUNG PEOPLE] for or relating to young people *a junior tennis tournament* **3** [NAME] *mainly US* (*written abbreviation* **Jr**) used at the end of a man's name to show that he is the younger of two men in the same family who have the same name *Hello, I'd like to speak to Mr Anderson Junior, please.*

**junior²** /'dʒuːniə'/ *noun* **1** **be 10/20, etc years sb's junior** to be 10, 20, etc years younger than someone *My wife is 8 years my junior.* **2** [C] a student in their third year of study at an American college or high school (= school for 15–18 year olds) **3** [C] *UK* a child who goes to a junior school

**junior college** *noun* [C, U] a two-year college in the US where students can learn a skill or prepare to enter a university

**junior 'high school** (*also* **junior 'high**) *noun* [C, U] a school in the US or Canada for children who are 12 to 15 years old

**junior school** *noun* [C, U] a school in the UK for children who are 7 to 11 years old

**junk** /dʒʌŋk/ *noun* [U] *informal* old things which have little value

**junk food** *noun* [U] food which is unhealthy but is quick and easy to eat

**junkie** /'dʒʌŋki/ *noun* [C] *informal* **1** someone who cannot stop taking illegal drugs **2** someone who wants something or wants to do something very much *a publicity/computer game junkie*

**junk mail** *noun* [U] letters sent by companies to advertise their goods and services

**junta** /'dʒʌntə/ *noun* [C] a military government that has taken power in a country by force

**Jupiter** /'dʒuːpɪtə'/ *noun* [no plural] the planet that is fifth from the Sun, after Mars and before Saturn

**jurisdiction** /ˌdʒʊərɪs'dɪkʃən/ *noun* [U] the legal power to make decisions and judgments *The school is under the jurisdiction of the local council.*

**juror** /'dʒʊərə'/ *noun* [C] a member of a jury

o-=**jury** /'dʒʊəri/ *noun* [group] **1** a group of people in a court of law who decide if someone is guilty or not **2** a group of people who decide the winner of a competition

o-=**just¹** (*strong form*) /dʒʌst/ (*weak form*) /dʒəst/ *adv* **1** [ONLY] only *I'll just have a small piece. I'm not very hungry.* • *He just wants to win.* • *The film is not just about love.* **2** [RECENTLY] a very short time ago *I've just been on a trip to France.* • *We've only just begun.* **3** [EMPHASIS] used to emphasize something you say *I just can't bear it!* **4** [ALMOST NOT] *UK* almost not *This dress only just fits.* **5** [EXACTLY] exactly *Tim looks just like his father.* • *This carpet would be just right for my bedroom.* **6** [ALMOST NOW] now or very soon *The film is just beginning.* • *I'm just coming!* **7 just before/over/under, etc** a little before/over/under, etc something else *It costs just over $10.* • *She left just before Michael.* **8 just about** almost *I think I've remembered just about everything.* **9 be just about to do sth** to be going to do something very soon *I was just about to phone you.* **10 just as bad/good/ tall, etc (as sb/sth)** equally bad/good/tall, etc *He's just as talented as his brother.* **11 I/you/ we, etc will just have to do sth** used to say that there is nothing else someone can do *You'll just have to wait.* **12 just as** at the same time as *She woke up just as we got there.* **13 it's just as well** used to say that it is lucky that something happened *It's just as well we brought an umbrella.* ➔ *See also:* just the **job**.

**just²** /dʒʌst/ *adj* fair or morally right *a just society* ➔ *Opposite* **unjust**. • **justly** *adv*

**justice** /'dʒʌstɪs/ *noun* **1** [FAIR BEHAVIOUR] [U] behaviour or treatment that is fair and morally correct *She tried to bring about fairness and justice for all.* ➔ *Opposite* **injustice**. **2** [LAW] [U] the system of laws which judges or punishes people *the criminal justice system* **3** [JUDGE] [C] US someone who judges in a court of law **4 bring sb to justice** to catch a criminal and decide if they are guilty or not **5 do sb/sth justice; do justice to sb/sth** to show the best or real qualities of something or someone *This postcard doesn't do justice to the wonderful scenery.*

**Justice of the Peace** *noun* [C] someone who acts as a judge in a small or local court of law

**justifiable** /'dʒʌstɪfaɪəbl/ *adj* having a good reason *justifiable anger* • **justifiably** *adv*

**justification** /ˌdʒʌstɪfɪ'keɪʃⁿn/ *noun* [C, U] a reason for something *There's no **justification for** treating her so badly.*

**justified** /'dʒʌstɪfaɪd/ *adj* fair or having a good reason *justified criticism* • *He's perfectly **justified in** asking for a larger salary.* ➔ *Opposite* **unjustified**.

**justify** /'dʒʌstɪfaɪ/ *verb* [T] to give a good enough reason to make something seem acceptable *I don't know how they can justify those ticket prices.*

**jut** /dʒʌt/ *verb* **jutting**, *past* **jutted jut into/out, etc** If something juts out, it comes out further than the edge or surface around it. *The rocks jutted out into the sea.*

**juvenile¹** /'dʒuːvⁿnaɪl/ *adj* **1** [always before noun] by, for, or relating to young people *juvenile crime* **2** behaving in a silly way as if you were a young child

**juvenile²** /'dʒuːvⁿnaɪl/ *noun* [C] especially in law, a young person

**juvenile de'linquent** *noun* [C] a young criminal

**juxtapose** /ˌdʒʌkstə'pəʊz/ *verb* [T] *formal* to place very different things or people close to each other *The exhibition **juxtaposes** paintings **with** black and white photographs.* • **juxtaposition** /ˌdʒʌkstəpə'zɪʃⁿn/ *noun* [C, U]

# K

**K, k** /keɪ/ the eleventh letter of the alphabet

**K** /keɪ/ *abbreviation for* kilobyte: a unit for measuring the amount of information a computer can store

**kaleidoscope** /kə'laɪdəskəʊp/ *noun* **1** [C] a tube-shaped toy you look through which contains mirrors and pieces of coloured glass that make patterns **2** [no plural] a mixture of different things *The fashion show was a kaleidoscope of colours.*

**kangaroo** /,kæŋgə'ruː/ *noun* [C] a large Australian animal that moves by jumping on its back legs

**karat** /'kærət/ *noun* [C] *another US spelling of* carat (= a unit for measuring how pure gold is, or how much valuable stones weigh)

**karate** /kə'rɑːti/ *noun* [U] a sport from Japan in which people fight using fast, hard hits with the hands or feet

**karma** /'kɑːmə/ *noun* [U] in some religions, the actions of a person in this life or earlier lives, which influence their future

**kayak** /'kaɪæk/ *noun* [C] a light, narrow boat, usually for one person, which you move using a paddle (= stick with a wide, flat part) • **kayaking** *noun* [U] the activity of travelling in a kayak

**kebab** /kɪ'bæb/ (*also* **shish kebab**) *noun* [C] small pieces of meat or vegetables cooked on a long, thin stick

**keel¹** /kiːl/ *noun* [C] a long piece of wood or metal at the bottom of a boat that helps it to balance

**keel²** /kiːl/ *verb*
  **keel over** to fall over suddenly *He said he felt dizzy and then just keeled over.*

O━**keen** /kiːn/ *adj* **1** INTERESTED very interested or enthusiastic *a keen golfer/photographer* • *He's very keen on travelling.* **2** WANTING TO DO wanting to do something very much [+ to do sth] *The shop is keen to attract new customers.* **3** VERY GOOD very good or well developed *a keen sense of smell* • **keenness** *noun* [U] • **keenly** *adv*

O━**keep¹** /kiːp/ *verb past* **kept** **1** HAVE [T] to have something permanently or for the whole of a period of time *You can keep that dress if you like it.* • *He borrowed my bike and kept it all week.* • *I kept my last car for two years.* **2** **keep sth in/on, etc** to regularly store something in a particular place *I think he keeps his keys in the desk drawer.* • *We'll keep your application on file.* **3** **keep doing sth** to continue to do something, or to do something repeatedly *My diets never work, but I keep trying.* • *I keep telling her not to leave her clothes on the floor.* • *He keeps hitting me.* **4** **keep (sb/sth) awake/clean/safe, etc** to remain in a particular state or make someone or something remain in a particular state *Thick socks help me keep warm.* • *He goes jogging twice a week to keep fit.* • *He keeps his car spotlessly clean.* **5** **keep sb/sth in/inside,**

**etc** to make someone or something stay in the same place *They will keep her at home for a few more days.* **6** MAKE DO STH [T] to make someone do something that stops them doing something else [+ doing sth] *She kept me talking for ages.* • *Sorry to **keep you waiting**.* • *Don't let me **keep you** from your work.* **7 keep a secret** to not tell anyone a secret **8 keep a promise/ your word, etc** to do what you have promised to do **9 keep an appointment** to meet someone when you have arranged to meet them **10** MAKE LATE [T] to make someone arrive later than they planned *I was expecting you at six – what kept you?* **11** WRITE [T] to write down something in order to remember it *to keep records/notes* **12** FOOD [I] If food or drink keeps, it remains fresh. **13** PROVIDE MONEY [T] to provide enough money for someone to live *I can't keep a family on that salary.* **14** ANIMALS [T] to have and look after animals *Our neighbours keep pigs.* **15 keep sb going** to provide what someone needs for a short period of time *Dinner is at eight, but I had an apple to keep me going.* ➔ *See also:* keep your **cool³**, keep a straight **face¹**, keep your fingers (**finger¹**) crossed, keep sb in the **picture¹**, keep a low **profile¹**, keep a tight **rein** on sb/sth, keep tabs (**tab**) on sb/sth, keep sb on their toes (**toe¹**).

**keep at sth** to continue working hard at something difficult *Learning a language is hard but you've just got to keep at it.*

**keep (sb/sth) away** to not go somewhere or near something, or to prevent someone from going somewhere or near something *I told them to keep away from the edge of the cliff.*

**keep (sb/sth) back** to not go near something, or to prevent someone or something from going past a particular place *Barriers were built to keep back the flood water.*

**keep sth back** to not tell someone everything you know about a situation or an event *I was sure she was keeping something back.*

**keep sth down** **1** to stop the number, level, or size of something from increasing *I have to exercise to keep my weight down.* **2** to be able to eat or drink without vomiting *I had food poisoning and couldn't keep anything down.*

**keep sb/sth from doing sth** to prevent someone or something from doing something *Try to keep the children from throwing food all over the floor.*

**keep sth from sb** to not tell someone about something *Is there something you're keeping from me?*

**keep sb in** to make a child stay inside as a punishment, or to make someone stay in hospital

**keep (sb/sth) off sth** to not go onto an area, or to stop someone or something going onto an area *Keep off the grass.*

**keep sth off (sb/sth)** to stop something touching or harming someone or something *He put a cloth over the salad to keep the flies off.*

**keep on doing sth** to continue to do something, or to do something again and again *She kept on asking me questions the whole time.*

**keep on** UK to continue to talk in an annoying way about something *I wish he wouldn't keep on about how much he earns.*

---

| j yes | k cat | ʃ she | ʒ decision | θ thin | ð this | ŋ ring | tʃ chip | dʒ jar | æ cat | ɑː arm | e bed | eə hair | ə ago | ɜː her | ɪ sit | i cosy |

**keep (sb/sth) out** to not go into a place, or to stop someone or something from going into a place *He locked the room and put up a sign asking people to keep out.*

**keep to sth 1** to stay in one particular area *We kept to main roads all the way.* **2** to do what you have promised or planned to do *I think we should keep to our original plan.*

**keep sth to sth** If you keep something to a particular number or amount, you make sure it does not become larger than that. *I'm trying to keep costs to a minimum.*

**keep sth to yourself** to keep something secret and not tell anyone else about it

**keep 1** SAME SPEED to move at the same speed as someone or something that is moving forward so that you stay level with them *She was walking so fast I couldn't **keep up with** her.* **2** MAKE PROGRESS to increase or make progress at the same speed as something or someone else so that you stay at the same level as them *Prices have been rising very fast and wages haven't kept up.* **3** UNDERSTAND to be able to understand or deal with something that is happening or changing very fast *I feel it's important to **keep up with** current events.*

**keep sth up** to not allow something that is at a high level to fall to a lower level *Make sure you eat properly – you've got to keep your strength up.*

**keep (sth) up** to continue without stopping or changing or to continue without something allowing it to stop or change *People are having difficulties keeping up the repayments on their loans.*

**keep²** /kiːp/ *noun* [no plural] the money needed to pay for someone to eat and live in a place *He **earns** his **keep** working in a garage.*

**keeper** /ˈkiːpəʳ/ *noun* [C] **1** someone who looks after a place and the things, people, or animals there *a park keeper* **2** *informal* short for goalkeeper (= the player in a sport such as football who tries to stop the ball going into the goal)

**keeping** /ˈkiːpɪŋ/ *noun* **1 for safe keeping** in order to keep something safe *She put the money into a bank for safe keeping.* **2 in keeping with sth** suitable or right for a situation, style, or tradition *The antique desk was in keeping with the rest of the furniture in the room.*

**keg** /keg/ *noun* [C] a large, round container used for storing beer

**kennel** /ˈken³l/ *noun* [C] **1** a small building for a dog to sleep in **2** *US* (*UK* **kennels**) a place where dogs are cared for while their owners are away

**kept** /kept/ *past of* keep

**kerb** *UK* (*US* **curb**) /kɜːb/ *noun* [C] the line of stones at the edge of a pavement (= raised path that people walk on) next to the road

**kernel** /ˈkɜːn³l/ *noun* [C] the part of a nut or seed inside the hard shell which you can usually eat

**kerosene** /ˈkerəsiːn/ *US* (*UK* **paraffin**) *noun* [U] oil used for heating and in lamps (= equipment that produces light)

**ketchup** /ˈketʃʌp/ *noun* [U] a thick sauce made from tomatoes (= round, red fruit) that is eaten cold with food

**kettle** /ˈketl/ *noun* [C] a metal or plastic container with a lid, used for boiling water *Charlotte **put the kettle on** to make some tea.* ➔ *See colour picture* **Kitchen** *on page Centre 10.*

○━**key¹** /kiː/ *noun* [C] **1** FOR LOCKS a piece of metal cut into a particular shape and used for locking things such as doors, or for starting an engine *I've lost my car keys.* **2** METHOD a way of explaining or achieving something *Hard work is the key to success.* **3** KEYBOARD one of the parts you press with your fingers on a keyboard or musical instrument to produce letters, numbers, or to make a sound **4** MUSIC a set of musical notes based on one particular note *the key of D major* **5** SYMBOLS a list which explains the symbols on a map or picture **6** ANSWERS a list of answers to an exercise or game ➔ *See also:* under **lock²** and key.

key

key

**key²** /kiː/ *adj* very important in influencing or achieving something *a key factor/player*

**key³** /kiː/ *verb*

**key sth in** to put information into a computer or machine using a keyboard *You need to key this data in.*

**keyboard** /ˈkiːbɔːd/ *noun* [C] **1** a set of keys on a computer, which you press to make it work, or the rows of keys on a piano ➔ *See colour picture* **The Office** *on page Centre 12.* **2** an electrical musical instrument similar to a piano

**keyhole** /ˈkiːhəʊl/ *noun* [C] a hole in a lock where you put a key

**keynote** /ˈkiːnəʊt/ *noun* [C] the most important part of an event, idea, or speech, or something that is emphasized strongly *the keynote speech/speaker*

**'key ˌring** *noun* [C] a metal ring used for keeping keys together

**kg** *written abbreviation for* kilogram (= a unit for measuring weight)

**khaki** /ˈkɑːki/ *noun* [U] a pale green-brown colour, often worn by soldiers • khaki *adj* ➔ *See colour picture* **Colours** *on page Centre 6.*

**kibbutz** /kɪˈbʊts/ *noun* [C] *plural* **kibbutzim** a place in Israel where people live and work together, often a farm or a factory

○━**kick¹** /kɪk/ *verb* **1** [I, T] to hit or move something or someone with your foot *The boys were kicking a ball back and forth.* • *She kicked me in the stomach.* • *They tried to kick the door down.* **2** [I] to move your feet and legs forwards or backwards quickly and with force *I kicked at them and screamed for help.* **3 kick yourself** *informal* to be very annoyed with yourself for doing something stupid or wrong *I could have kicked myself for saying that.* ➔ *See also:* be **alive** and kicking.

**be kicking about/around** *informal* If something is kicking about, it is in a particular place, but nobody is using it or paying attention to it. *We've probably got a copy of the document kicking around the office.*

**kick in** *informal* to start to be effective or to

happen *The new tax rate kicks in next month.*
**kick off** When a football match or other event kicks off, it starts.
**kick (sth) off** *informal* When you kick off a discussion or activity, you start it.
**kick sb out** *informal* to force someone to leave a place or organization *His wife kicked him out.*
**kick²** /kɪk/ *noun* **1** [C] when you kick something with your foot *He gave her a kick in the ribs.* **2** [C] *informal* a special feeling of excitement and energy *She gets a kick out of performing live.* **3 a kick in the teeth** used when someone treats you badly or unfairly, especially when you need or expect support *This latest pay award amounts to a kick in the teeth.* ⊃ *See also:* **free kick**.

**kickback** /ˈkɪkbæk/ *noun* [C] *US* money given to someone, especially illegally, for providing help, a job, or a piece of business

**kick-off** /ˈkɪkɒf/ *noun* [C, U] the time when a football match begins

O⚬ **kid¹** /kɪd/ *noun* [C] **1** *informal* a child or young person *school kids* **2** a young goat

**kid²** /kɪd/ *verb* [I, T] **kidding**, *past* **kidded 1** to make a joke, or to trick someone with a joke **2** to deceive or trick someone into believing something [**often reflexive**] *You've got to stop kidding yourself. She's not coming back.*

**kiddie** /ˈkɪdi/ *noun* [C] *informal* a child

**kidnap** /ˈkɪdnæp/ *verb* [T] **kidnapping**, *past* **kidnapped** to take someone away using force, usually to obtain money in exchange for releasing them • **kidnap** *noun* [C] *a kidnap victim/attempt* • **kidnapper** *noun* [C]

**kidnapping** /ˈkɪdnæpɪŋ/ *noun* [C, U] when someone is kidnapped

**kidney** /ˈkɪdni/ *noun* [C] one of the two organs in your body which remove waste from the blood and produce urine

O⚬ **kill** /kɪl/ *verb* **1** [DEATH] [I, T] to cause someone or something to die *Sunday's bomb killed 19 people.* • *Their son was killed in a road accident.* **2 sb will kill sb** *informal* used to say that someone will be very angry with someone else *Dad will kill me for being late.* **3** [END] [T] to stop an activity or experience completely *His remark killed the conversation.* **4** [CAUSE PAIN] [T] *informal* to cause you a lot of pain or effort *My feet are killing me.* • *It wouldn't kill you to tidy up occasionally.* ⊃ *See also:* kill **time¹**.
**kill sth/sb off** to stop something or someone from existing any more *Lack of funding is killing off local theatres.*

**kill²** /kɪl/ *noun* **1** [no plural] when an animal is killed **2 go/move in for the kill** to prepare to defeat someone completely or to kill them

**killer** /ˈkɪlə/ *noun* [C] someone who kills, or a disease, substance, or animal that kills *Cancer and heart disease are the UK's biggest killers.* ⊃ *See also:* **serial killer**.

**killing** /ˈkɪlɪŋ/ *noun* **1** [C] a murder, or when someone or something is killed *the killing of civilians* **2 make a killing** *informal* to make a lot of money very quickly

**kiln** /kɪln/ *noun* [C] a large oven for baking bricks and other clay objects until they are hard

**kilo** /ˈkiːləʊ/ *noun* [C] *short for* kilogram

**kilobyte** /ˈkɪləʊbaɪt/ (*written abbreviation* **K**) *noun* [C] a unit for measuring the amount of information a computer can store, equal to 1024 bytes

**kilogram** (*also UK* **kilogramme**) (*written abbreviation* **kg**) /ˈkɪləʊgræm/ *noun* [C] a unit for measuring weight, equal to 1000 grams

**kilometre** *UK* (*US* **kilometer**) (*written abbreviation* **km**) /kɪˈlɒmɪtə/ *noun* [C] a unit for measuring distance, equal to 1000 metres

**kilowatt** /ˈkɪləʊwɒt/ (*written abbreviation* **kW**) *noun* [C] a unit for measuring electrical power, equal to 1000 watts

**kilt** /kɪlt/ *noun* [C] a traditional Scottish skirt for men, made of heavy material with close vertical folds at the back

**kin** /kɪn/ *noun* [**plural**] *formal* the members of your family ⊃ *See also:* **next of kin**.

O⚬ **kind¹** /kaɪnd/ *noun* **1** [C] a type of thing or person *What kind of music do you like?* • *All kinds of people come to our church.* • *Older kids like board games and that kind of thing.* • *Her travel company was the first of its kind* (= the first one like it). **2 some kind of** used to talk about something when you are not sure of its exact type *She has some kind of disability.* **3 kind of** *informal* used when you are trying to explain or describe something, but you cannot be exact *It's kind of unusual.* **4 of a kind** used to describe something that exists but is not very good *The school had a swimming pool of a kind, but it was too small for most classes to use.*

O⚬ **kind²** /kaɪnd/ *adj* Kind people do things to help others and show that they care about them. *Your mother was very kind to us.* • *It was very kind of you to come and see me.* • *Thank you for those kind words.* ⊃ *Opposite* **unkind**.

**kinda** /ˈkaɪndə/ *mainly US informal short for* kind of *I'm kinda busy right now.*

**kindergarten** /ˈkɪndəˌgɑːtᵊn/ *noun* [C, U] **1** in the UK, a school for children under five **2** in the US, a class in school for children aged five

**kind-hearted** /ˌkaɪndˈhɑːtɪd/ *adj* having a kind character *a kind-hearted family man*

**kindly¹** /ˈkaɪndli/ *adv* **1** in a kind or generous way *He smiled at her kindly.* • *She kindly offered to cook me lunch.* **2** *formal* used in instructions to mean 'please', usually when you are annoyed *Would you kindly get out of my car?* **3 not take kindly to sth** to not like something that someone says or does *He doesn't take kindly to criticism.*

**kindly²** /ˈkaɪndli/ *adj old-fashioned* kind *a kindly old gentleman*

**kindness** /ˈkaɪndnəs/ *noun* [C, U] when someone is kind *Thanks for all your kindness this morning.*

**king** /kɪŋ/ *noun* [C] **1** [RULER] a male ruler in some countries *King Richard II* • *the kings and queens of England* **2** [BEST PERSON] the best or most important person in a particular activity *He's the new king of pop music.* **3** [PLAYING CARD] a playing card with a picture of a king on it *the king of spades*

**kingdom** /ˈkɪŋdəm/ *noun* **1** [C] a country with a king or queen *the Kingdom of Belgium* **2 the animal/plant kingdom** all animals or plants considered together

**K**

**kingfisher** /'kɪŋ,fɪʃəʳ/ *noun* [C] a small, brightly coloured bird which catches fish from rivers and lakes

**king-size** (*also* **king-sized**) /'kɪŋsaɪz/ *adj* very big *a king-size bed*

**kink** /kɪŋk/ *noun* [C] a bend in something long and thin *There was a kink in the cassette tape.*

**kinky** /'kɪŋki/ *adj informal* involving strange or unusual sexual behaviour

**kiosk** /'kiːɒsk/ *noun* [C] a small building with a window where things like tickets or newspapers are sold

**kip** /kɪp/ *noun* [C, U] *UK informal* a short period of sleep *He just had time for a kip and a shower.*
● kip *verb* [I] **kipping**, *past* **kipped**

**kipper** /'kɪpəʳ/ *noun* [C] *UK* a type of fish that has been cut open and dried over smoke

⊶**kiss¹** /kɪs/ *verb* [I, T] to press your lips against another person's lips or skin to show love or affection *He kissed her cheek.* ● *Len kissed Samantha goodbye at the front gate.*

⊶**kiss²** /kɪs/ *noun* [C] **1** an act of kissing someone *She ran up and gave me a big kiss.* **2 give sb the kiss of life** *UK* to help to keep someone who has stopped breathing alive by blowing into their mouth

**kit** /kɪt/ *noun* **1** COLLECTION [C] a collection of things kept in a container ready for a particular use *a first-aid/tool kit* **2** CLOTHES [C, U] *UK* a set of clothes worn for sport or military service *a football kit* **3** PARTS [C] a set of parts which you put together to make something *He's making a model car from a kit.*

⊶**kitchen** /'kɪtʃɪn/ *noun* [C] a room used to prepare and cook food in ➔ *See colour picture* **Kitchen** *on page Centre 10.*

**kite** /kaɪt/ *noun* [C] a toy made of paper or cloth which flies in the air on the end of a long string

**kitsch** /kɪtʃ/ *noun* [U] decorative objects or pieces of art that are ugly, silly, or have little value

**kitten** /'kɪtᵊn/ *noun* [C] a young cat

**kitty** /'kɪti/ *noun* [C] an amount of money consisting of a share from everyone in a group, used for a special purpose [usually singular] *We all put money into a kitty to pay for drinks.*

**kiwi** /'kiːwiː/ (*also* '**kiwi ,fruit**) *noun* [C] a small, green fruit with black seeds and brown, hairy skin

**km** *written abbreviation for* kilometre (= a unit for measuring distance)

**knack** /næk/ *noun* [no plural] a special skill, or the ability to use or do something easily *a knack for remembering faces* ● *She has the knack of making people feel comfortable.*

**knackered** /'nækəd/ *adj UK informal* extremely tired

**knead** /niːd/ *verb* [T] to press and shape the mixture for making bread firmly and repeatedly with your hands

⊶**knee** /niː/ *noun* [C] **1** the middle part of your leg where it bends *a knee injury* ➔ *See colour picture* **The Body** *on page Centre 2.* **2** the part of a pair of trousers that covers the knee **3 bring sb/sth to their knees** to destroy or defeat someone or something *The war brought the country to its knees.*

**kneecap** /'niːkæp/ *noun* [C] the round bone at the front of your knee

**knee-deep** /,niː'diːp/ *adj* **1** reaching as high as someone's knees *knee-deep in cold water* **2 be knee-deep in sth** to have a lot of something to deal with *I'm knee-deep in paperwork.*

**knee-jerk** /'niːdʒɜːk/ *adj* **a knee-jerk reaction/response, etc** an immediate reaction that does not allow you time to consider something carefully

**kneel** /niːl/ *verb* [I] *past* **knelt** or **kneeled** to go down into or stay in a position where one or both of your knees are on the ground *She knelt down beside the child.*

**kneel**

**knew** /njuː/ *past tense of* know

**knickers** /'nɪkəz/ *UK* (*US* **panties**) *noun* [plural] women's underwear that covers the bottom ➔ *See usage note at* **underwear**.

⊶**knife¹** /naɪf/ *noun* [C] *plural* **knives** a sharp tool or weapon for cutting, usually with a metal blade and a handle *a knife and fork*

**knife²** /naɪf/ *verb* [T] to attack someone using a knife ➔ *See also:* **jack-knife**.

**knight¹** /naɪt/ *noun* [C] **1** a man of high social rank who fought as a soldier on a horse in the past **2** a man who has been given the title 'Sir' by the King or Queen in the UK

**knight²** /naɪt/ *verb* **be knighted** to be given a knighthood

**knighthood** /'naɪthʊd/ *noun* [C] the title of 'Sir' given to someone by the King or Queen in the UK

**knit** /nɪt/ *verb* [I, T] **knitting**, *past t* **knitted**, *past p also US* **knit** to make clothes using wool and two long needles to join the wool into rows *She was knitting him a jumper.*

**knitting** /'nɪtɪŋ/ *noun* [U] when something is being knitted or the thing that is being knitted *She put down her knitting.*

**knitwear** /'nɪtweəʳ/ *noun* [U] knitted clothes

**knob** /nɒb/ *noun* **1** [C] a round handle, or a round button on a machine *a door knob* ● **Turn**

K

the black **knob** to switch on the radio. **2 a knob of butter** *UK* a small lump of butter

o—**knock¹** /nɒk/ *verb* **1** MAKE NOISE [I] to make a noise by hitting something, especially a door, with your closed hand in order to attract someone's attention *There's someone knocking at/on the door.* • *Please knock before entering.* **2** HIT [T] to hit something or someone and make them move or fall down *He accidentally knocked the vase off the table.* • *I knocked over the mug.* • *He was knocked unconscious by the blast.* **3** CRITICIZE [T] *informal* to criticize someone or something, often unfairly *She knocks every suggestion I make.* **4 Knock it off!** *informal* something you say when you want someone to stop doing something that is annoying you ➜ *See also:* knock the (living) **daylights** out of sb.

---

**USAGE**

**knock**

Be careful to use the correct prepositions. You do not always need one.

*The policeman* **knocked on** *the door.*

*Listen! There's someone* **knocking at** *the door.*

~~Listen! There's someone knocking to the door.~~

---

**knock sth back** *UK informal* to drink alcohol very quickly *He knocked back his beer and left the bar.*

**knock sb down** *UK* to hit someone with a vehicle and injure or kill them [often passive] *She was knocked down by a bus.*

**knock sb/sth down** *US* to cause someone or something to fall to the ground by hitting them

**knock sth down** to destroy a building or part of a building *They are knocking down the old factory to build a cinema.*

**knock off** *informal* to stop working, usually at the end of a day *I don't knock off until six.*

**knock sth off (sth)** to take a particular amount away from something, usually a price *The manager knocked $5 off because it was damaged.*

**knock sb out 1** to make someone become unconscious, usually by hitting them on the head *He was knocked out halfway through the fight.* **2** to defeat a person or team in a competition so they cannot take part any more [often passive] *The French team were knocked out in the semifinal.*

**knock²** /nɒk/ *noun* [C] **1** a sudden short noise made when something or someone hits a surface *a knock at/on the door* **2** when someone or something is hit, sometimes causing damage or injury *a knock on the head*

**knocker** /'nɒkə/ *noun* [C] a metal object fixed to the outside of a door which visitors use to knock

**knock-on** /ˌnɒk'ɒn/ *adj UK* **a knock-on effect** When an event or situation has a knock-on effect, it causes another event or situation. *Cutting schools' budgets will have a knock-on effect on teachers' jobs.*

**knockout** /'nɒkaʊt/ *noun* [C] in boxing, when

one person hits the other hard and they become unconscious

**knot¹** /nɒt/ *noun* **1** [C] a place where pieces of string, rope, etc have been tied together **2** [C] a unit for measuring the speed of the wind, ships, or aircraft **3 tie the knot** *informal* to get married

**knot²** /nɒt/ *verb* [T] **knotting**, *past* **knotted** to tie knots in pieces of string, rope, etc

o—**know¹** /nəʊ/ *verb past t* **knew**, *past p* **known** **1** HAVE INFORMATION [I, T] to have knowledge or information about something in your mind *"How old is she?" "I don't know."* • *Andrew knows a lot about computers.* • [+ question word] *Do you know where the station is?* • [+ (that)] *He knew that she was lying.* • *Do your parents know you smoke?* **2** BE FAMILIAR WITH [T] to be familiar with a person, place, or thing because you have met them, been there, used it, etc before *I've known Tim since primary school.* • *I grew up in Brussels so I know it well.* • *Since moving to London, I've got to know* (= become familiar with) *some nice people.* **3** BE ABLE [T] to be able to do something [+ question word] *Do you know how to ski?* • *I only know* (= understand and speak) *a little Spanish.* **4 let sb know** to tell someone something *Let me know if you're going to the party.* **5** GUESS CORRECTLY [T] to guess something correctly *I knew she'd arrive late.* • *I should have known he wouldn't come.* **6** UNDERSTAND [I, T] to understand and agree with someone *I know what you mean about Pete – I wouldn't trust him at all.* **7 be known as sth** to be called *California is also known as the Golden State.* **8 have known sth** to have had experience of something *I've never known the weather to be so hot.* **9 know better (than to do sth)** to have the intelligence or judgment not to do something *She should have known better than to eat so much. No wonder she feels sick now.* **10 I know a** used when you agree with something someone has just said *"It's a lovely day, isn't it?" "I know – let's hope it lasts."* **b** used when you have an idea *I know – let's go to Helen's house.* **11 you know a** used to emphasize that someone does know what you are referring to *You know, he's the one with curly hair.* **b** something that you say while you are thinking what to say next *It's, you know, supposed to be a surprise.* **c** used to emphasize what you are saying *I'm not an idiot, you know.* **12 as far as I know** used to say that you think something is true, but cannot be sure *As far as I know, he's never been in prison.* **13 you never know** used to say that something could be possible although it does not seem likely *You never know – you might win the lottery.* **14 before you know it** very soon *We'll be there before you know it.* ➜ *See also:* know sth **inside¹** out, know the ropes (**rope¹**), know your **stuff¹**.

---

**USAGE**

**meet, get to know** and **know**

When you **meet someone**, you see or speak to them for the first time. When you **get to know** someone, you

**K**

learn more about them and after this you can say that you know them.

*I met Nick on holiday.*

~~I know Nick on holiday.~~

*We got to know each other and became good friends.*

~~We knew each other and became friends.~~

*How long have you known Nick?*

~~How long have you got to know Nick?~~

---

**know** or **find out?**

To **know** something means to already have information about something.

*Kelly knows what time the train leaves.*

*His parents already know about the problem.*

To **find out** something means to learn new information for the first time.

*Can you find out what time the train leaves?*

*His parents were angry when they found out about the problem.*

**know of sth/sb** to have heard of something or someone and have a little information about them *I know of a good restaurant near the station.*

**know²** /nəʊ/ *noun* **be in the know** to have knowledge about something which not everyone knows *People in the know were sure the film would win an Oscar.*

**know-how** /ˈnəʊhaʊ/ *noun* [U] practical skill and knowledge *technical know-how*

**knowing** /ˈnəʊɪŋ/ *adj* A knowing smile, look, etc shows that you know what another person is really thinking. *He gave me a knowing wink.*

**knowingly** /ˈnəʊɪŋli/ *adv* **1** If you knowingly do something, you mean to do it although it is wrong. **2** showing that you know what another person is really thinking *He smiled knowingly.*

○━**knowledge** /ˈnɒlɪdʒ/ *noun* **1** [U, no plural] information and understanding that you have in

your mind *He will easily find a job with his knowledge and skills.* ● *He has a detailed knowledge of naval history.* ● *He took the car without my knowledge* (= I did not know). **2 to (the best of) sb's knowledge** used to say that someone thinks that something is true, but cannot be sure *To the best of my knowledge, she's never worked abroad.*

**knowledgeable** /ˈnɒlɪdʒəbl/ *adj* knowing a lot *He's very knowledgeable about art.*

**known¹** /nəʊn/ *adj* recognized or known about by most people *He's a member of a known terrorist organization.* ➔ *Opposite* **unknown** ➔ *See also:* **well-known**.

**known²** /nəʊn/ *past participle of* know

**knuckle¹** /ˈnʌkl/ *noun* [C] one of the parts of your finger where it bends ➔ *See also:* a **rap¹** on/across/over the knuckles.

**knuckle²** /ˈnʌkl/ *verb*
**knuckle down** to start to work or study hard

**koala** /kəʊˈɑːlə/ (*also* **ko'ala ,bear**) *noun* [C] an Australian animal like a small bear with grey fur which lives in trees and eats leaves

koala

**the Koran** /kɒrˈɑːn* ⑩ kəˈræn/ *noun* the holy book of Islam

**kosher** /ˈkəʊʃəʳ/ *adj* Kosher food is prepared according to Jewish law.

**kph** *written abbreviation for* kilometres per hour: a unit for measuring speed *a car travelling at 100 kph*

**kudos** /ˈkjuːdɒs/ *noun* [U] praise and respect for what you have done

**kung fu** /kʌŋˈfuː/ *noun* [U] a sport from China in which people fight using their hands and feet

**Kurdish** /ˈkɜːdɪʃ/ *adj* belonging or relating to a Muslim people living in parts of Turkey, Iran, Iraq, etc ● **Kurd** /kɜːd/ *noun* [C] a Kurdish person

**kW** (*also* **kw**) *written abbreviation for* kilowatt (= a unit for measuring electrical power)

K

**L, l** /el/ the twelfth letter of the alphabet

**l** *written abbreviation for* litre (= a unit for measuring liquid)

**lab** /læb/ *noun* [C] *short for* laboratory (= a room used for scientific work)

**label¹** /'leɪbᵊl/ *noun* [C] **1** [INFORMATION] a small piece of paper or other material which gives information about the thing it is fixed to *There should be washing instructions on the label.* **2** [WORD] a word or phrase that is used to describe the qualities of someone or something, usually in a way that is not fair *He seems to be stuck with the label of 'troublemaker'.* **3** [MUSIC] (*also* **record label**) a company that records and sells music *They've just signed a deal with a major record label.*

**label²** /'leɪbᵊl/ *verb* [T] *UK* **labelling**, *past* **labelled**, *US* **labeling**, *past* **labeled 1** to fix a small piece of paper or other material to something which gives information about it *All food has to be labelled with 'best before' or 'use by' dates.* **2** to describe the qualities of someone or something using a word or phrase, usually in a way that is not fair [often passive] *They've been unfairly labelled as criminals.*

**labor** /'leɪbər/ *noun, verb US spelling of* labour

**laboratory** /lə'bɒrətᵊri US 'læbrətɔːri/ *noun* [C] a room used for scientific work *research laboratories* • *a computer laboratory* ➔ *See also:* **language laboratory**.

**laborer** /'leɪbᵊrər/ *noun* [C] *US spelling of* labourer

**laborious** /lə'bɔːriəs/ *adj* Laborious work is very difficult and needs a lot of effort. *a laborious task*

**labors** /'leɪbəz/ *noun* [plural] *US spelling of* labours

**'labor ,union** *US* (*UK/US* **trade union**) *noun* [C] an organization that represents people who do a particular job

**labour¹** *UK* (*US* **labor**) /'leɪbər/ *noun* **1** [WORK] [U] work, especially the type of work that needs a lot of physical effort *manual labour* **2** [WORKERS] [U] people who work *cheap/skilled labour* **3** [BIRTH] [C, U] the stage of pregnancy when a woman has pain in her stomach because the baby is coming out *to be in labour/go into labour* • *labour pains* **4 Labour** [group] *short for* the Labour Party *I voted Labour* (= for the Labour party) *at the last election.* • *a Labour MP* **5 a labour of love** work that you do because you like it, not because you are paid for it

**labour²** *UK formal* (*US* **labor**) /'leɪbər/ *verb* [I] to work hard *He laboured night and day to get the house finished on time.*

**labourer** *UK* (*US* **laborer**) /'leɪbᵊrər/ *noun* [C] a worker who uses a lot of physical effort in their job *a farm labourer*

**the 'Labour ,Party** *noun* [group] one of the three main political parties in the UK

**labours** (*US* **labors**) /'leɪbəz/ *noun* [plural] **sb's**

**labours** work done with a lot of effort *He earned a mere $15 for his labours.*

**lace¹** /leɪs/ *noun* **1** [U] a delicate cloth with patterns of holes *a lace curtain* • *a white lace handkerchief* **2** [C] a string used to tie shoes *to tie/untie your laces*

**lace²** /leɪs/ *verb*

**lace sth up** to fasten something with laces *He laced up his boots.*

**be laced with sth** If food or drink is laced with alcohol or a drug, a small amount has been added to it. *coffee laced with brandy*

**lacerate** /'læsᵊreɪt/ *verb* [T] *formal* to make deep cuts in someone's skin *a lacerated arm* • lacera-tion /,læsᵊr'eɪʃᵊn/ *noun* [C] *formal* a cut

o-⊷ **lack¹** /læk/ *noun* **lack of sth** not having something, or not having enough of something *a lack of food/money* • *a lack of facilities for young people*

o-⊷ **lack²** /læk/ *verb* **1** [T] to not have something, or not have enough of something *She really lacks confidence.* **2 be lacking** If something that you need is lacking, you do not have enough of it. *Enthusiasm has been sadly lacking these past few months at work.* **3 be lacking in sth** to not have a quality *He's totally lacking in charm of any sort.* ➔ *See usage note at* **miss**.

**lacklustre** *UK* (*US* **lackluster**) /'læk,lʌstər/ *adj* without energy or excitement *a lacklustre performance*

**laconic** /lə'kɒnɪk/ *adj formal* using very few words to express yourself *laconic humour/wit*

**lacquer** /'lækər/ *noun* [U] a clear, hard substance which is painted on wood or metal to protect it

**lad** /læd/ *noun* [C] *UK* a boy or young man *a nice young lad* • (*UK informal*) *He's having a night out with the lads* (= his male friends).

**ladder** /'lædər/ *noun* [C] a piece of equipment which is used to reach high places, consisting of short steps fixed between two long sides ➔ *See also:* the first/highest/ next, etc **rung¹** of the ladder.

ladder

**laden** /'leɪdᵊn/ *adj* **be laden with sth** to be holding a lot of something *She staggered home, laden with shopping.*

**the ladies** /'leɪdiz/ *noun* [group] *UK* a toilet in a public place for women *Where's the ladies?* ➔ *See usage note at* **toilet**.

**'ladies' ,room** *noun* [C] *US* a room in a public place where there are women's toilets ➔ *See usage note at* **toilet**.

**ladle** /'leɪdl/ *noun* [C] a large, deep spoon, used to serve soup ➔ *See colour picture* **Kitchen** *on page Centre 10.*

o-⊷ **lady** /'leɪdi/ *noun* **1** [C] a polite way of saying 'woman' *There's a young lady here to see you.*

• *Ladies and gentlemen, can I have your attention please?* **2 Lady** a title used before the name of some women of high social rank in the UK *Lady Alison Weir*

**ladybird** /'leɪdibɜːd/ *UK* (*US* **ladybug** /'leɪdibʌɡ/) *noun* [C] a small flying insect which is usually red with black spots

**lag¹** /læɡ/ (*also* **time lag**) *noun* [C] a period of time between two things happening *You have to allow for a time lag between order and delivery.* ➔ *See also:* **jet lag**.

**lag²** /læɡ/ *verb* **lagging**, *past* **lagged**
**lag behind (sb/sth) 1** to move more slowly than someone or something else so that you are behind them **2** to achieve less than someone or something else *Britain is lagging far behind the rest of Europe on this issue.*

**lager** /'lɑːɡəʳ/ *noun* [C, U] a pale yellow beer *A pint of lager, please.*

**lagoon** /lə'ɡuːn/ *noun* [C] a lake that contains sea water

**laid** /leɪd/ *past of* lay

**laid-back** /,leɪd'bæk/ *adj informal* very relaxed and not seeming worried about anything *a laid-back style of teaching* • *He's very laid-back.*

**lain** /leɪn/ *past participle of* lie

**laissez-faire** /,leɪseɪ'feəʳ/ *adj* allowing things to happen and not trying to control them *laissez-faire capitalism* • *a laissez-faire attitude*

○━**lake** /leɪk/ *noun* [C] a large area of water which has land all around it *to go boating on the lake* • *Lake Windermere*

**lamb** /læm/ *noun* **1** [C] a young sheep *a newborn lamb* • *a lamb's-wool sweater* **2** [U] meat from a young sheep *grilled lamb chops* • *roast leg of lamb* ➔ *See also:* **mutton** dressed as lamb.

**lame** /leɪm/ *adj* **1** A lame excuse or explanation is one that you cannot believe. *He said he didn't go because it was raining, which is a pretty lame excuse if you ask me.* **2** A lame animal or person cannot walk because they have an injured foot or leg. *a lame horse*

**lament** /lə'ment/ *verb* [I, T] *formal* to say that you are disappointed about a situation *He was lamenting the fact that so few people read fiction nowadays.*

**lamentable** /'læməntəbl/ *adj formal* extremely bad *a lamentable performance*

**lamp** /læmp/ *noun* [C] a piece of equipment that produces light *a table lamp* • *an oil lamp* ➔ *See colour picture* **The Living Room** *on page Centre 11.*

**lamppost** /'læmppəʊst/ *noun* [C] a tall post with a light at the top, which you see on roads where there are houses

**lampshade** /'læmpʃeɪd/ *noun* [C] a decorative cover for an electric light ➔ *See colour picture* **The Living Room** *on page Centre 11.*

○━**land¹** /lænd/ *noun* **1** [AREA] [U] an area of ground *agricultural land* • *undeveloped land* • *Many farmers have been forced to sell their land.* ➔ *See usage note at* **country. 2** [NOT SEA] [U] the surface of the Earth that is not sea *to travel over land and sea* **3** [COUNTRY] [C] *literary* a country *a land of ice and snow* ➔ *See also:* **no-man's land**.

○━**land²** /lænd/ *verb* **1** [I, T] If an aircraft lands, it arrives on the ground after a journey, and if you land it, you make it arrive on the ground. *We should land in Madrid at 7 a.m.* • *He*

managed to **land** the helicopter **on** the cliff.
**2 land in/on, etc** If an object or person lands somewhere, they fall to the ground there. *The ball landed in the neighbour's garden.* • *She landed flat on her back.* **3** [T] to get something, usually something good *He's just landed a new job at an agency in London.*
**land sb in sth** to cause someone to be in a difficult situation *His remarks have landed him in a lot of trouble with the association.*
**land sb with sth** If something lands you with problems, it causes problems for you. *The project's failure has landed him with debts of over £50,000.*

**landfill** /'lændfɪl/ *noun* [C] a place where waste is buried in the ground *Local residents are campaigning against the new landfill.* • *a landfill site*

**landing** /'lændɪŋ/ *noun* [C] **1** an arrival on the ground, usually of an aircraft or boat *They had to make an emergency landing in Chicago.* **2** the area of floor at the top of a set of stairs

**landlady** /'lænd,leɪdi/ *noun* [C] a woman who you rent a room or house from

**landlord** /'lændlɔːd/ *noun* [C] a man who you rent a room or house from

**landmark** /'lændmɑːk/ *noun* [C] **1** a building that you can easily recognize, especially one that helps you to know where you are *a historic landmark* **2** an event which is famous or important in the history of something *His speech was a landmark in the history of civil rights.*

**landmine** /'lændmaɪn/ *noun* [C] a bomb which is hidden in the ground

**landowner** /'lænd,əʊnəʳ/ *noun* [C] someone who owns a lot of land *a wealthy landowner*

**landscape** /'lændskeɪp/ *noun* [C] the appearance of an area of land, especially in the countryside *The cathedral dominates the landscape for miles around.*

**landslide** /'lændslaɪd/ *noun* [C] **1** when rocks and soil slide down a mountain or hill **2** an easy victory in an election *a landslide defeat/victory* • *He was re-elected by a landslide in 1972.*

**lane** /leɪn/ *noun* [C] **1** [PART] part of a road or track that is separated from the other parts, usually by a painted line *the inside/middle/outside lane* • *the fast/slow lane* • *They're widening the road from two to three lanes.* **2** [ROAD] a narrow road, usually in the countryside *We drove down a winding country lane.* **3** [BOATS/AIRCRAFT] a route that is regularly used by boats or aircraft *It's one of the world's busiest shipping lanes.*

○━**language** /'læŋɡwɪdʒ/ *noun* **1** [COMMUNICATION] [U] communication between people, usually using words *She has done research into how children acquire language.* **2** [ENGLISH/SPANISH/JAPANESE ETC] [C] a type of communication used by the people of a particular country *How many languages do you speak?* **3** [TYPE OF WORDS] [U] words of a particular type, especially the words used by people in a particular job *legal language* • *the language of business* **4** [COMPUTERS] [C, U] a system of instructions that is used to write computer programs ➔ *See* *also:* **body language**, **modern languages**, **second language**, **sign language**.

**'language la,boratory** *UK* (*US* **'language ,laboratory**) *noun* [C] a room in a college or school where you can use equipment to help you practise listening to and speaking a foreign language

**languid** /'læŋgwɪd/ *adj literary* moving or speaking slowly and with little energy, often in an attractive way *a languid manner/voice*

**languish** /'læŋgwɪʃ/ *verb* [I] *formal* **languish at/in, etc sth** to stay in an unpleasant or difficult situation for a long time *to languish in jail*

**lanky** /'læŋki/ *adj informal* A lanky person is very tall and thin.

**lantern** /'læntən/ *noun* [C] a light that can be carried, usually with a candle inside it *a paper lantern*

**lap¹** /læp/ *noun* [C] **1** Your lap is the top part of your legs when you are sitting down. *Sit on my lap and I'll read you a story.* **2** one journey around a circular race track *He's two laps behind the leaders.*

**lap²** /læp/ *verb* **lapping**, *past* **lapped lap against/ on, etc sth** If water laps against something, it touches it gently in waves. *The sea was lapping round his ankles.*

**lap sth up** *informal* to enjoy something very much *He loved all the attention – he was lapping it up!*

**lapel** /lə'pel/ *noun* [C] the part of a collar that is folded against the front of a shirt or jacket *wide lapels* ➔ *See picture at* **jacket**.

**lapse¹** /læps/ *noun* [C] **1** a period of time when something fails to happen as it should *a memory lapse* • *It is thought that the accident was caused by a **lapse of** concentration.* **2** a period of time passing between two things happening *a time lapse/a lapse of time* • *He turned up again after a lapse of two years.*

**lapse²** /læps/ *verb* [I] If an arrangement lapses, it stops existing because of the amount of time that has passed. *The guarantee lapsed after two years.* • *I've allowed my membership to lapse.*

**lapse into sth** If you lapse into something, you change to a different, and usually bad, condition. *to lapse into silence* • *He suffered a heart attack and then lapsed into a coma.*

**laptop** /'læptɒp/ *noun* [C] a computer that is small enough to be carried around and used where you are sitting

o━**large** /lɑːdʒ/ *adj* **1** big in size or amount *a large number of people* • *a large amount of money* • *Police discovered a large quantity of drugs in the van.* • *She comes from quite a large family.* • *The shirt was a bit too large.* ➔ *Opposite* **small**. **2 be at large** If someone dangerous is at large, they are not in prison. **3 sb/sth at large** people or things in general *This group is not representative of the population at large.* **4 by and large** in most situations *By and large, people have welcomed the changes.*

**largely** /'lɑːdʒli/ *adv* mainly *a largely residential suburb* • *Their complaints have been largely ignored.*

**large-scale** /,lɑːdʒ'skeɪl/ *adj* involving a lot of people or happening in big numbers *a large-scale development* • *large-scale redundancies*

**lark** /lɑːk/ *noun* [C] a small brown bird that is known for its beautiful singing

**larva** /'lɑːvə/ *noun* [C] *plural* **larvae** /'lɑːviː/ the form of some creatures, for example insects, before they develop into a different form *insect larvae*

**lasagne** *UK* (*US* **lasagna**) /lə'zænjə/ US /lə'zɑːnjə/ *noun* [U] a type of Italian food consisting of flat pieces of pasta with layers of meat and sauce in between

**laser** /'leɪzər/ *noun* [C] a strong beam of light that has medical and technical uses *a laser beam* • *laser surgery* • *a laser printer* • *We saw a laser show with fireworks.*

**lash¹** /læʃ/ *verb* **1** [I, T] If wind or rain lashes against something, the wind or rain is very strong and hits or blows hard against it. *Rain lashed against the window.* • *Wind and heavy rain lashed the palm trees.* **2 lash sth down/together, etc** to tie something firmly to something else *The boxes had been lashed together with ropes.*

**lash out 1** to suddenly hit someone *He lashed out and caught her on the side of the face.* **2** to criticize someone angrily *He **lashed out at** the government for refusing to take action.*

**lash²** /læʃ/ *noun* [C] a hit with a whip (= long, thin piece of leather) *He was given forty lashes.*

**lashes** /'læʃɪz/ *noun* [plural] the small hairs on the edges of your eye *She's got lovely long lashes.*

**lass** /læs/ *noun* [C] *UK informal* a girl or a young woman *a young lass*

**last¹** /lɑːst/ *adj, determiner* **1** MOST RECENT [always before noun] the most recent *What was the last film you saw?* • *It's rained for the last three days.* **2** ONE BEFORE PRESENT [always before noun] Your last book, house, job, etc is the one before your present one. *My last house was half this size.* • *I liked his last book but I'm not so keen on this latest one.* **3** FINAL happening or coming at the end *It's the last room on the left.* • *That's the last programme of the series.* • *I was the last one to arrive.* • *"How did she get on in her race?" "She was last."* **4** REMAINING [always before noun] only remaining *Who wants the last piece of cake?* **5 the last person/thing, etc** the least expected or wanted person or thing *Three extra people to feed – that's the last thing I need!* • *He's the last person you'd expect to see at an aerobics class.* ➔ *Opposite* **first** ➔ *See also:* be on its last legs (**leg**), the last **straw**, have the last **word¹**.

o━**last²** /lɑːst/ *adv* **1** after everything or everyone else *I wasn't expecting to win the race but I didn't think I'd come last!* • *We've still got to check the figures but we'll do that last.* **2** used to talk about the most recent time you did something *When did you last see her?* • *I think it was July when I last spoke to him.* **3 last but not least** something that you say to introduce the last person or thing on a list *This is Jeremy, this is Cath and, last but not least, this is Eva.* ➔ *Opposite* **first**.

**last³** /lɑːst/ *noun, pronoun* **1 the last** a person or thing that comes after all the others [+ to do sth] *We were the last to get there.* **2 the last of sth** the only part of something that remains

*We've just finished the last of the wine.* **3 the day/week/year before last** the day, week, or year before the one that has just finished **4 at (long) last** finally *At last, I've found a pair of jeans that actually fit.* **5 the last I heard** used before saying a piece of information about someone that you previously heard *The last I heard, they were selling their house.*

⚬⚊**last⁴** /lɑːst/ *verb* [I, T] **1** to continue to happen, exist, or be useful *How long will the meeting last?* ● *We don't get much sun – enjoy it while it lasts!* ● *Most sessions last about an hour.* ● *The batteries only last about five hours.* **2** to be enough for a period of time *I've only got £30 to last me till the end of the month.* ● *We've got enough food to last another week.*

**last-ditch** /ˌlɑːstˈdɪtʃ/ *adj* **a last-ditch attempt/effort** a final attempt to solve a problem that you have failed to solve several times before *a last-ditch effort to prevent war*

**lasting** /ˈlɑːstɪŋ/ *adj* continuing to exist for a long time *lasting damage* ● *a lasting friendship*

**lastly** /ˈlɑːstli/ *adv* finally *And lastly, I'd like to thank everyone who took part in the event.*

**last-minute** /ˌlɑːstˈmɪnɪt/ *adj* done at the last possible time *I was just doing some last-minute preparations.*

**last 'name** *noun* [C] the name that you and other members of your family all have

**latch¹** /lætʃ/ *noun* [C] **1** a small piece of metal on a door that you move down so that the door will stay closed **2** a type of lock for a door that you need a key to open from the outside

**latch²** /lætʃ/ *verb*
**latch on** *informal* to begin to understand something *It took me ages to latch on to what she was saying.*

⚬⚊**late** /leɪt/ *adj, adv* **1** AFTER THE USUAL TIME after the usual time or the time that was arranged *I was late for work this morning.* ● *We got there too late and all the tickets had been sold.* ● *You're late – you were supposed to be here an hour ago!* ● *We had a late lunch.* **2** NEAR END OF PERIOD near the end of a period of time *It was built in the late nineteenth century.* ● *It was late at night.* ● *Marsha is in her late twenties.* **3** **it's late** something that you say when it is near the end of a day *It's late – I really should be going.* ● *It's getting late and I'm a bit tired.* **4** DEAD [always before noun] not now alive *the late Mrs Walker* **5 of late** *formal* recently *We've scarcely seen him of late.*

**lately** /ˈleɪtli/ *adv* recently *I haven't been feeling so well lately.* ● *Lately, I've been walking to work.*

**latent** /ˈleɪtᵊnt/ *adj* A feeling or quality that is latent exists now but is hidden or not yet developed. *latent hostility/racism*

**later** /ˈleɪtə/ *adj* **1** after some time *I might arrange it for a later date.* **2** more recent *I'm not so familiar with his later work.*

**later (on)** *adv* after some time *I'm off now – see you later.* ● *If you're busy now we could do it later on.* ● *He arrived later that night.*

**latest¹** /ˈleɪtɪst/ *adj* [always before noun] most recent *the latest fashions/news/technology*

**latest²** /ˈleɪtɪst/ *noun* **1 the latest in sth** the most recent of its type *This is the latest in a*

series of terrorist attacks in the region. **2 at the latest** If you tell someone to do something by a particular time at the latest, you mean they must do it before that time. *She said to be there by 8 o'clock at the latest.*

**lather** /ˈlɑːðə/ *noun* **1** [U] small white bubbles that are produced when soap is used with water **2 get into a lather** *informal* to become anxious or upset about something *She'd got into a lather over the arrangements for the party.*

**Latin** /ˈlætɪn/ *noun* [U] the language used by ancient Romans ● Latin *adj*

**Latin A'merican** *adj* relating or belonging to the countries of South and Central America, and Mexico ● Latin American *noun* [C] a Latin American person

**Latino** /ləˈtiːnəʊ/ *noun* [C] *US* someone who lives in the US whose family came from Latin America

**latitude** /ˈlætɪtjuːd/ *noun* **1** [C, U] the distance of a place north or south of the Equator (= imaginary line around the Earth's middle), measured in degrees *The latitude of Helsinki is approximately 60 degrees north.* **2** [U] *formal* freedom to do what you want *She should be allowed the latitude to choose the people she wants.*

**latter** /ˈlætə/ *adj* [always before noun] *formal* near the end of a period *the latter half of the twentieth century*

**the latter** /ˈlætə/ *noun* the second of two people or things that have just been talked about *She offered me more money or a car, and I chose the latter.*

**latterly** /ˈlætəli/ *adv UK formal* recently *She started her career in radio, but latterly she has been working in television.*

**laudable** /ˈlɔːdəbl/ *adj formal* A laudable idea or action deserves admiration, even if it is not successful. *a laudable aim/ambition* ● *His intentions are entirely laudable.*

⚬⚊**laugh¹** /lɑːf/ *verb* [I] to smile while making sounds with your voice that show you are happy or think something is funny *You never laugh at my jokes.* ● *She really makes me laugh.* ● *It's very rare that a book is so good you laugh out loud.* ● *It was so funny, we burst out laughing* (= laughed suddenly and loudly). ⟳ *See also:* be no laughing **matter¹**.

---

**USAGE**

**laugh**

Be careful to choose the correct preposition when one is necessary.

*All the other children **laughed at** him.*

~~All the other children laughed after him.~~

*It wasn't funny at the time, but we **laughed about** it later.*

~~It wasn't funny at the time, but we laughed of it later.~~

---

**laugh at sb/sth** to show that you think someone or something is stupid *I can't go into work looking like this – everyone will laugh at me.* **laugh sth off** to laugh about something unpleasant so that it seems less important *He was upset by the criticism though he tried to laugh it off at the time.*

**laugh²** /lɑːf/ *noun* [C] **1** the act or sound of laughing *a loud/nervous laugh • At the time, I was embarrassed, but I **had a good laugh** (= laughed a lot) about it later.* **2 be a (good) laugh** *UK informal* to be funny *You'd like David – he's a good laugh. • "How was the party?" "Oh, it was a real laugh."* **3 for a laugh** *informal* If you do something for a laugh, you do it because you think it will be funny. *Just for a laugh, I pretended that I'd forgotten it was his birthday.*

**laughable** /ˈlɑːfəbl/ *adj* If something is laughable, it is stupid and you cannot believe it or respect it. *Most people thought his suggestions were laughable.*

**'laughing ˌstock** *noun* [no plural] someone who does something very stupid which makes other people laugh at them *If I wear this hat, I'll be the laughing stock of the party!*

o⚹**laughter** /ˈlɑːftəʳ/ *noun* [U] the sound or act of laughing *I heard the sound of laughter in the room next door. • The crowd **roared with laughter** (= laughed very loudly).*

**launch¹** /lɔːnʃ/ *verb* [T] **1** SEND to send a spacecraft or bomb into the sky, or a ship into the water *to launch a rocket/satellite • to launch a boat/fleet* **2** BEGIN to begin an important activity *to launch an attack/inquiry/investigation* **3** NEW PRODUCT If a company launches a product or service, it makes it available for the first time. *The book was launched last February. • The airline will launch its new transatlantic service next month.*

**launch into sth** to start saying or criticizing something with a lot of anger or energy *Then he launched into a verbal attack on her management of the situation.*

**launch²** /lɔːnʃ/ *noun* [C] **1** SENDING the launching of a spacecraft, ship, or weapon *Poor weather delayed the space shuttle's launch.* **2** BEGINNING the beginning of an activity *The campaign's launch was a well-publicized event.* **3** NEW PRODUCT the time when a new product or service becomes available *The film's launch attracted a lot of Hollywood stars.* **4** BOAT a large boat with a motor *a police launch*

**launder** /ˈlɔːndəʳ/ *verb* [T] to hide the fact that an amount of money has been made illegally by putting the money into legal bank accounts or businesses *to launder drug money •* **laundering** *noun* [U] *money laundering*

**launderette** /ˌlɔːndʳˈret/ *UK* (*US* **laundromat** /ˈlɔːndrəmæt/ *trademark*) *noun* [C] a place where you pay to use machines that wash and dry your clothes

**laundry** /ˈlɔːndri/ *noun* [U] clothes, sheets, etc that need to be washed *to do the laundry •* a *laundry basket*

**laurels** /ˈlɒrʳlz/ *noun* [plural] **rest on your laurels** to be so satisfied with what you have achieved that you make no effort to improve *Just because you've passed your exams, that's no reason to rest on your laurels.*

**lava** /ˈlɑːvə/ *noun* [U] hot melted rock that comes out of a volcano

**lavatory** /ˈlævətʳri/ *noun* [C] *formal mainly UK* a toilet *to go to the lavatory • public lavatories* ➔ *See usage note at* **toilet**.

**lavender** /ˈlævʳndəʳ/ *noun* [U] a plant with purple flowers and a strong, pleasant smell *lavender oil*

**lavish¹** /ˈlævɪʃ/ *adj* showing that a lot of money has been spent *a lavish meal/party •* **lavishly** *adv a lavishly illustrated book*

**lavish²** /ˈlævɪʃ/ *verb*

**lavish sth on sb/sth** to give a large amount of money, presents, attention, etc to someone or something *They have lavished more than £6 million on the new stadium.*

o⚹**law** /lɔː/ *noun* **1 the law** the system of official rules in a country *You're breaking the law. • It's **against the law** (= illegal) not to wear seat belts. • It's their job to enforce the law.* **2 by law** If you have to do something by law, it is illegal not to do it. *They have to provide a contract by law.* **3** RULE [C] an official rule in a country *There are **laws against** drinking in the street. • They led the fight to impose **laws on** smoking.* **4 law and order** the obeying of laws in society *a breakdown in law and order* **5** SUBJECT [U] the subject or job of understanding and dealing with the official laws of a country *to study/practise law • a law school/ firm • a specialist in civil/criminal law* **6** ALWAYS TRUE [C] something that is always true in science, mathematics, etc *the laws of nature/physics • the law of averages/gravity* **7 lay down the law** to repeatedly tell people what they should do, without caring about how they feel *People are fed up with him laying down the law the whole time.* ➔ *See also:* **brother-in-law, common-law, daughter-in-law, father-in-law, in-laws, martial law, mother-in-law, sister-in-law, son-in-law.**

**law-abiding** /ˈlɔːəˌbaɪdɪŋ/ *adj* A law-abiding person always obeys the law. *a law-abiding citizen*

**lawful** /ˈlɔːfʳl/ *adj* allowed by the law *He was going about his lawful business as a press photographer.*

**lawmaker** /ˈlɔːˌmeɪkəʳ/ *noun* [C] *US* someone who makes laws *state lawmakers*

**lawn** /lɔːn/ *noun* [C] an area of grass that is cut *to mow the lawn • There's a cat on the front lawn.*

**'lawn ˌmower** *noun* [C] a machine that you use to cut grass

**lawsuit** /ˈlɔːsuːt/ *noun* [C] a legal complaint against someone that does not usually involve the police *The tenants have **filed a lawsuit** against their landlord.*

o⚹**lawyer** /ˈlɔɪəʳ/ *noun* [C] someone whose job is to understand the law and deal with legal situations *I want to see my lawyer before I say anything.*

**USAGE**

**lawyer, solicitor, barrister, attorney**

In Britain, **lawyers** are divided into two types, **solicitors** and **barristers**. **Solicitors** give advice on legal subjects and work in the lower courts of law. **Barristers** can

L

represent people in the higher courts of law. In America, there is only one type of lawyer, who is sometimes called an **attorney**.

**lax** /læks/ *adj* not careful enough or not well controlled *They seem to have a very lax attitude towards security.*

o⁻ᵏ**lay**¹ /leɪ/ *verb past* **laid** **1 lay sth down/in/on, etc** to put something down somewhere carefully *She laid the baby on the bed.* • *He laid the tray down on the table.* **2** [T] to put something into its correct position *to lay a carpet* • *to lay bricks* **3 lay eggs** If an animal lays eggs, it produces them out of its body. **4 lay the blame on sb** to blame someone, usually when this is not fair *You always lay the blame on me!* **5 lay the table** *UK* to put plates, knives, forks, etc on the table to prepare for a meal ➔ *See also:* lay your cards (**card**) on the table, get/lay your hands (**hand**¹) on sth, lay down the **law**, lay the **foundation(s)** for/of sth.

### USAGE

**lay** and **lie**

Be careful not to confuse these verbs.

**Lay** means 'put down carefully' or 'put down flat'. This verb is always followed by an object. **Laying** is the present participle. **Laid** is the past simple and the past participle.

*She laid the papers on the desk.*

**Lie** means 'be in a horizontal position' or 'be in a particular place'. This verb is irregular and is never followed by an object. **Lying** is the present participle. **Lay** is the past simple and **lain** is the past participle.

*The papers were lying on the desk.*

~~The papers were laying on the desk.~~

*I lay down and went to sleep.*

~~I laid down and went to sleep.~~

The regular verb **lie** means 'not say the truth'.

*He lied to me about his age.*

**lay sth down 1** to officially make new rules, or to officially say how something must be done *The committee has laid down guidelines for future cases.* **2** If someone lays down their weapons, they stop fighting. *It is hoped the two sides will lay down their arms and return to peace.*

**lay into sb** *informal* to attack or criticize someone *They started laying into me for no reason.*

**lay sb off** to stop employing someone, usually because there is no more work for them [often passive] *Thirty more people were laid off last week.*

**lay sth on** to provide something for a group of people *They're laying on free buses to and from the concert.*

**lay sth out 1** to arrange something on a surface *He'd laid his tools out all over the kitchen floor.* **2** to explain something clearly, usually in writing *I've just laid out some proposals.*

**lay²** /leɪ/ *adj* [always before noun] **1** involved in religious activities, but not trained as a priest *a lay preacher* **2** not having special or detailed knowledge of a subject *a lay person/audience*

**lay³** /leɪ/ *past tense of* lie¹

**lay-by** /'leɪbaɪ/ *noun* [C] *UK* a small area where cars can stop at the side of a road

o⁻ᵏ**layer** /leɪəʳ/ *noun* [C] an amount of a substance covering a surface, or one of several amounts of substance, each on top of the other *the outer/top layer* • *Place alternate layers of pasta and meat sauce in a shallow dish.* • *The shelf was covered in a thick layer of dust.* • layer *verb* [T] [often passive] *The potatoes are layered with onion.* ➔ *See also:* **the ozone layer**.

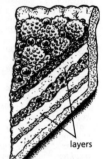

**layer**

**layers**

**layman** /'leɪmən/ (*also* **layperson**) *noun* [C] *plural* **laymen** someone who does not have special knowledge of a subject *Could you please explain that in layman's terms* (= in a simple way) *?*

**layoff** /'leɪɒf/ *noun* [C] the ending of someone's job by an employer, usually because there is no more work [usually plural] *Several hundred more layoffs are planned next month.*

**layout** /'leɪaʊt/ *noun* [C] the way that something is arranged *Do you like the layout of the kitchen?*

o⁻ᵏ**lazy** /'leɪzi/ *adj* **1** Someone who is lazy does not like working or using any effort. *You lazy thing!* • *He's too lazy to make his bed in the morning.* **2** slow and relaxed *a lazy morning/weekend* • lazily *adv* • laziness *noun* [U]

**lb** *written abbreviation for* pound (= a unit for measuring weight)

o⁻ᵏ**lead**¹ /liːd/ *verb past* **led** /led/ *formal* **1** TAKE SOMEONE [I, T] to show someone where to go, usually by taking them to a place or by going in front of them *She led them down the hall.* • *We followed a path that led us up the mountain.* • *You lead and we'll follow.* • *I'll* **lead the way** (= go first to show the route). **2 lead into/to/towards, etc** If a path or road leads somewhere, it goes there. *That path leads to the beach.* **3** BE WINNING [I, T] to be winning a game *They were leading by 11 points at half-time.* • *The Lions lead the Hawks 28–9.* **4** BE THE BEST [T] to be better than anyone else *I still believe that we lead the world in acting talent.* **5** CONTROL [T] to be in control of a group, country, or situation *to lead a discussion* • *Is this man really capable of leading the country?* • *Shearer led his team to victory.* **6 lead sb to do sth** to cause someone to do or think something *What led you to think that?* • *I was led to believe that breakfast was included.* **7 lead a busy/normal/quiet, etc life** to live in a particular way *He was able to lead a normal life* *despite his illness.* **8 lead sb to a conclusion** to cause you to think that something is probably true *So you thought I was leaving, did you? What led you to that conclusion?*

**lead to sth** to cause something to happen or exist *A poor diet can lead to health problems in later life.*

**lead up to sth** to happen before an event *The shops are always busy in the weeks leading up to Christmas.*

o⟶**lead²** /liːd/ *noun* **1** WINNING [no plural] a winning position during a race or other situation where people are competing *She's in the lead* (= winning). • *France has just taken the lead* (= started to win). • *a three-goal lead* **2** FILMS/PLAYS [C] the main person in a film or play *She plays the lead in both films.* **3** DOG [C] *UK* (*US* **leash**) a chain or piece of leather fixed to a dog's collar so that it can be controlled *Dogs must be kept on a lead at all times.* **4** ELECTRICITY [C] *UK* (*US* **cord**) the wire that connects a piece of electrical equipment to the electricity supply **5** INFORMATION [C] information about a crime that police are trying to solve *Police are chasing up a new lead.*

**lead³** /liːd/ *adj* [always before noun] The lead performer or lead part in a performance is the main performer or part. *the lead singer* • *Who played the lead role?*

**lead⁴** /led/ *noun* **1** [U] a soft, heavy, grey, poisonous metal used for roofs, pipes, etc *a lead pipe* • *lead-free petrol/gasoline* **2** [C, U] the black part inside a pencil

o⟶**leader** /ˈliːdəʳ/ *noun* [C] **1** a person in control of a group, country, or situation *a religious leader* • *Who's the leader of the Democratic Party in the Senate?* **2** someone or something that is winning during a race or other situation where people are competing *He's fallen two laps behind the leaders.* • *Microsoft is a world leader in software design.*

**leadership** /ˈliːdəʃɪp/ *noun* **1** [U] the job of being in control of a group, country, or situation *the leadership of the Conservative party* • *leadership skills/qualities* • *a leadership contest* **2** [group] the people in control of a group, country, or situation *There is growing discontent with the leadership.*

**leading** /ˈliːdɪŋ/ *adj* [always before noun] very important or most important *They're the world's leading manufacturer of audio equipment.* • *He's a leading Hollywood producer.*

o⟶**leaf¹** /liːf/ *noun* [C] *plural* **leaves** /liːvz/ **1** a flat, green part of a plant that grows from a stem or branch *an oak leaf* • *a lettuce leaf* • *the falling leaves* **2 take a leaf out of sb's book** *mainly UK* to copy something good that someone else does **3 turn over a new leaf** to start to behave in a better way *I'm not drinking any more – I've turned over a new leaf.*

**leaf²** /liːf/ *verb*

**leaf through sth** to turn the pages of a book or magazine and look at them quickly *She lay on the sofa, leafing through glossy magazines.*

**leaflet** /ˈliːflət/ *noun* [C] a piece of folded paper or a small book which contains information *I picked up a useful leaflet on how to fill in tax forms.*

**leafy** /ˈliːfi/ *adj* [always before noun] A leafy place is pleasant and quiet with a lot of trees. *a leafy lane/suburb*

**league** /liːg/ *noun* **1** [C] a group of teams which compete against each other in a sport *top/bottom of the league* • *major/minor league baseball* • *Who won the league championship this year?* **2 be in league with sb** to be secretly working or planning something with someone, usually to do something bad **3 not be in the same league as sb/sth** *informal* to not be as good as someone or something *It's a nice enough restaurant but it's not in the same league as Rossi's.*

**leak¹** /liːk/ *verb* **1** [I, T] If a liquid or gas leaks, it comes out of a hole by accident, and if a container leaks, it allows liquid or gas to come out when it should not. *Water had leaked all over the floor.* • *The bottle must have leaked because the bag's all wet.* **2** [T] If someone leaks secret information, they intentionally tell people about it. *Details of the report had been leaked to the press.*

**leak out** If secret information leaks out, people find out about it.

**leak²** /liːk/ *noun* [C] **1** a hole in something that a liquid or gas comes out of, or the liquid or gas that comes out *I think we may have a leak in the roof.* • *a gas leak* **2** the act of intentionally telling people a secret

**leakage** /ˈliːkɪdʒ/ *noun* [U] the problem of a liquid or gas coming out of something when it should not *Water companies have been told that they must reduce leakage.*

**leaky** /ˈliːki/ *adj informal* Something that is leaky has a hole in it and liquid and gas can get through. *a leaky boat/roof*

o⟶**lean¹** /liːn/ *verb* *past* **leaned** *also UK* **leant** /lent/ **lean (sth) back/forward/out, etc** to move the top part of your body in a particular direction *She leaned forward and whispered in my ear.* • *He was leaning out of the window.* • *Lean your head back a bit.*

**lean (sth) against/on sth** to sit or stand with part of your body touching something as a support *He leaned against the wall.* • *She leaned her head on his shoulder.*

**lean sth against/on sth** to put something against a wall or other surface so that it is supported *Lean the ladder against the wall.*

**lean on sb/sth** to use someone or something to help you, especially in a difficult situation *Her mother had always leaned on her for support.*

**lean²** /liːn/ *adj* **1** thin and healthy *lean and fit* **2** Lean meat has very little fat on it.

**leaning** /ˈliːnɪŋ/ *noun* [C] a belief or idea [usually plural] *I don't know what his political leanings are.*

**leap¹** /liːp/ *verb past* **leapt** /lept/ *or* **leaped 1 leap into/out of/up, etc** to suddenly move somewhere *He leapt out of his car and ran towards the house.* • *I leapt up to answer the phone.* **2 leap off/over/into, etc** to jump somewhere *She leapt over the wall and disappeared down the alley.*

**leap at sth** to accept the chance to have or do something with enthusiasm *I'd leap at the opportunity to work in Japan.*

L

**leap²** /li:p/ *noun* [C] **1** a sudden improvement or increase *There was a big leap in profits last year.* ● *This represents a great leap forward in technology.* **2** a big jump *He finished third in the long jump with a leap of 26 feet.* **3 by/in leaps and bounds** If progress or growth happens in leaps and bounds, it happens very quickly. *Her reading has improved by leaps and bounds since she started her new school.* ➔ See also: **quantum leap**.

**'leap ,year** *noun* [C] a year that happens every four years, in which February has 29 days instead of 28

○⇤**learn** /lɜ:n/ *verb past* **learned** *also UK* **learnt** /lɜ:nt/ **1** GET SKILL [I, T] to get knowledge or skill in a new subject or activity *I learned Russian at school.* ● *"Can you drive?" "I'm learning."* ● *She's learned a lot about computers in the last three months.* ● [+ to do sth] *I'm learning to play the piano.* ● *Cheese goes in the fridge – will he never learn?* **2** REMEMBER [T] to make yourself remember a piece of writing by reading or repeating it many times *I don't know how actors learn all those lines.* **3** UNDERSTAND [I, T] to start to understand that you must change the way you behave [+ (that)] *She'll have to learn that she can't have everything she wants.* ● *The good thing is, he's not afraid to learn from his mistakes.* ➔ See also: learn your **lesson**, learn the ropes (**rope¹**).

**USAGE**

**learn, teach,** or **study**?

To **learn** is to get new knowledge or skills.

*I want to learn how to drive.*

When you **teach** someone, you give them new knowledge or skills.

*My dad taught me how to drive.*

~~My dad learnt me how to drive.~~

When you **study**, you go to classes, read books, etc to try to understand new ideas and facts.

*He is studying biology at university.*

**learn about/of sth** to hear facts or information that you did not know *We only learned about the accident later.*

**learned** /'lɜ:nɪd/ *adj formal* Someone who is learned has a lot of knowledge from reading and studying. *He was a very learned man.*

**learner** /'lɜ:nə'/ *noun* [C] someone who is getting knowledge or a new skill *learners of English* ● *You have to be patient with her – she's a slow learner.*

**learning** /'lɜ:nɪŋ/ *noun* [U] the process of getting knowledge or a new skill *language learning*

**lease¹** /li:s/ *noun* [C] **1** a legal agreement in which you pay money in order to use a building or a piece of land for a period of time *We signed a three-year lease when we moved into the house.* **2 give sb/sth a new lease of life** *UK (also US* **give sb/sth a new lease on life)** **a** to make someone feel happy or healthy after a period of illness or sadness *The operation has*

given her a new lease of life. **b** to improve something that was old so that it works much better

**lease²** /li:s/ *verb* [T] to use a building or piece of land, or to allow someone to use a building or piece of land, in exchange for money *We want to lease some office space in the centre of town.* ● *The council eventually leased the land to a local company.*

**leash** /li:ʃ/ *(also UK* **lead**) *noun* [C] a chain or piece of leather fixed to a dog's collar so that it can be controlled

○⇤**least¹** /li:st/ *adv* **1** less than anyone or anything else *Which car costs least?* ● *I chose the least expensive dish on the menu.* ● *No one, least of all* (= especially not) *James, is going to be angry with you.* **2 at least a** as much as, or more than, a number or amount *You'll have to wait at least an hour.* **b** something that you say when you are telling someone about an advantage in a bad situation *It's a small house but at least there's a garden.* **c** used to say that someone should give a small amount of help although they do not intend to give a lot *Even if you didn't want to send a present, you could at least have sent a card.* **d** something that you say in order to correct something you said that was wrong *I've seen that film. At least, I saw the beginning then I fell asleep.* **3 not least** *formal* especially *The whole trip was fascinating, not least because of the people I met.* **4 not in the least** not at all *I don't mind staying at home, not in the least.* ➔ See also: **last²** but not least.

**least²** /li:st/ *quantifier* **1** the smallest amount *She earns the least money of all of us.* ● *Jake had more experience than anyone else and I probably had the least.* **2 to say the least** used to emphasize that you could have said something in a much stronger way *We were surprised, to say the least.*

**leather** /'leðə'/ *noun* [U] the skin of animals that is used to make things such as shoes and bags *a leather jacket*

○⇤**leave¹** /li:v/ *verb past* **left** /left/ **1** GO AWAY [I, T] to go away from a place or a situation, either permanently or for a temporary period *I'm leaving work early this afternoon.* ● *What time does the bus leave?* ● *They left for Paris last night.* ● *"Does Trevor still work there?" "No, he left"* (= he does not work there now). ● *She left school at 16.* **2** END RELATIONSHIP [I, T] to end a relationship with a husband, wife, or partner and stop living with them *I'll never leave you.* ● *She left him for a younger man.* **3** NOT TAKE [T] to not take something with you when you go away from a place, either intentionally or by accident *Why don't you leave your jacket in the car?* ● *She'd left a note for him in the kitchen.* ● *That's the second umbrella I've left on the train!* **4** NOT USE ALL [T] to not use all of something *They'd drunk all the wine but they'd left some food.* ● *Are there any biscuits left?* **5** REMAIN [T] to make a permanent mark *The operation may leave a scar.* **6 leave sth open/ on/off, etc** to cause something to stay in a particular condition *Who left the window open?* **7** DO LATER [T] to do something later that you could do immediately *Don't leave your packing till the night before you go.* **8** GIVE [T] to arrange for someone to receive something after you die *His aunt left him a lot of money.* • *He left the house to Julia.* **9 leave sb alone** to stop speaking to or annoying someone *Leave me alone! I'm trying to work.* **10 leave sth alone** to stop touching something *Leave your hair alone!* ➔ *See also:* leave someone to their own devices (**device**), leave your **mark¹**.

**leave sb/sth behind** to leave a place without taking something or someone with you *We were in a hurry and I think I must have left my keys behind.*

**leave behind sth** or **leave sth behind (sb)** to cause a situation to exist after you have left a place *The army left a trail of destruction behind them.*

**leave sth for/to sb** to give someone the responsibility for dealing with something *I've left the paperwork for you.*

**leave sb/sth out** to not include someone or something *I've made a list of names – I hope I haven't left anyone out.*

**be left out** If someone feels left out, they are unhappy because they have not been included in an activity. *The older children had gone upstairs to play and she felt left out.*

**be left over** If an amount of money or food is left over, it remains when the rest has been used or eaten. *There was a lot of food left over from the party.*

**leave²** /liːv/ *noun* [U] a period of time when you do not go to work *She's on maternity/sick leave.*

**leaves** /liːvz/ *plural of* leaf

**lecherous** /ˈletʃⁱrəs/ *adj* A lecherous man shows too much interest in sex, in a way that is unpleasant.

**lecture¹** /ˈlektʃər/ *noun* [C] **1** a formal talk given to a group of people in order to teach them about a subject *We went to a lecture on Italian art.* • *Do you know who's giving the lecture this afternoon?* **2** an angry or serious talk given to someone in order to criticize their behaviour *My dad gave me a lecture on smoking last night.*

**lecture²** /ˈlektʃər/ *verb* **1** [I] to give a formal talk to a group of people, often at a university *She travelled widely throughout North America lecturing on women's rights.* • *For ten years she lectured in law.* **2** [T] to talk angrily to someone in order to criticize their behaviour *Stop lecturing me!* • *His parents used to lecture him on his table manners.*

**lecturer** /ˈlektʃⁱrər/ *noun* [C] *mainly UK* someone who teaches at a university or college *a lecturer in psychology* • *a senior lecturer*

**USAGE**

**lecturer** or **teacher**?

In American English, **lecturer** is formal, and **teacher** or **professor** is usually used instead.

**led** /led/ *past of* lead

**ledge** /ledʒ/ *noun* [C] a long, flat surface that comes out under a window or from the side of a mountain *The birds landed on a ledge about halfway up the cliff.*

**leek** /liːk/ *noun* [C, U] a long white and green vegetable that smells and tastes similar to an onion

**leer** /lɪər/ *verb* [I] to look at someone in an unpleasant and sexually interested way *He was always leering at female members of staff.* • leer *noun* [C]

**leery** /ˈlɪəri/ *adj US* worried and not able to trust someone *I've gotten more leery of the media.*

**leeway** /ˈliːweɪ/ *noun* [U] freedom to do what you want *My current boss gives me much more leeway.*

o-**left¹** /left/ *adj, adv* on or towards the side of your body that is to the west when you are facing north [always before noun] *Step forward on your left leg.* • *She had a diamond earring in her left ear.* • *Turn left at the end of the corridor.* ➔ *Opposite* **right**.

o-**left²** /left/ *noun* **1** [no plural] the left side *Ned's the man sitting on my left in that photo.* • *Jean's house is last on the left.* **2 the Left/left** political groups which believe that power and money should be shared more equally among people *The proposals were sharply criticized by the Left.* ➔ *Opposite* **right**.

**left³** /left/ *past of* leave

**left 'field** *adj US informal* **in/from/out of left field** strange and not expected *His question came out of left field, and I didn't know what to say.*

**left-hand** /ˌleftˈhænd/ *adj* [always before noun] on the left *a left-hand drive car* (= car which you drive sitting on the left-hand side) • *The swimming pool is on the left-hand side of the road.*

**left-handed** /ˌleftˈhændɪd/ *adj* Someone who is left-handed uses their left hand to do most things. *Are you left-handed?*

**leftist** /ˈleftɪst/ *adj* supporting the ideas of parties on the political left *leftist politics/ideas*

**leftover** /ˈleftˌəʊvər/ *adj* [always before noun] Leftover food remains after a meal. *If there's any leftover food we can take it home with us.* • leftovers *noun* [plural] food which remains after a meal *We've been eating up the leftovers from the party all week.*

**left-wing** /ˌleftˈwɪŋ/ *adj* supporting the ideas of parties on the political left *a left-wing newspaper* • left-winger *noun* [C]

o-**leg** /leg/ *noun* [C] **1** PART OF BODY one of the parts of the body of a human or animal that is used for standing and walking *My legs are tired after so much walking.* • *He broke his leg in the accident.* • *There were cuts on her arms and legs.* • *She had bare legs and wore only a light summer dress.* ➔ *See colour picture* **The Body** *on page Centre 2.* **2** FOOD the meat of an animal's leg eaten as food *a chicken leg* **3** FURNITURE one of the vertical parts of a chair, table, etc that is on the floor *a chair/table leg* **4** CLOTHES the part of a pair of trousers that covers one of your legs *He rolled up his trouser legs and waded into the water.* **5** PART OF JOURNEY one part of a journey or competition *the first/ second/third leg of the journey* **6 not have a leg to stand on** to have no chance of proving that something is true *If you don't have a witness, you don't have a leg to stand on.* **7 be on its last legs** *informal* If a machine is on its last legs, it will stop working soon because it is so old. *We've had the same oven for twenty years now and it really is on its last legs.* **8 stretch your legs** *informal* to go for a walk

**leg**

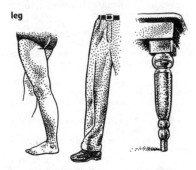

**legacy** /'legəsi/ *noun* [C] **1** a situation that was caused by something from an earlier time *The war has left a **legacy** of hatred.* **2** money or buildings, etc that you receive after someone dies *On the death of his father, he received a small legacy.*

o⟶**legal** /'li:gªl/ *adj* **1** relating to the law *legal action/advice • the legal profession/system* **2** allowed by law *Is it legal to carry a handgun?* ⊃ *Opposite* **illegal**. • **legally** *adv Children under sixteen are not legally allowed to buy cigarettes.*

**legality** /li:'gæləti/ *noun* [U] the legal quality of a situation or action *Some board members have questioned the legality of the proposal.*

**legalize** /'li:gªlaɪz/ *verb* [T] to make something legal *How many Americans want to legalize drugs?* • **legalization** /ˌli:gªlaɪˈzeɪʃªn/ *noun* [U] *the legalization of abortion* ⊃ *See usage note at* **law**.

**legend** /'ledʒənd/ *noun* **1** [C, U] an old story or set of stories from ancient times *the legends of King Arthur • She's writing a book on Greek legend.* **2** [C] a famous person *a living legend • Jazz legend, Ella Fitzgerald, once sang in this bar.*

**legendary** /'ledʒəndªri/ *adj* **1** from a legend (= old story) *a legendary Greek hero* **2** very famous *He became editor of the legendary Irish journal, 'The Bell'.*

**leggings** /'legɪnz/ *noun* [plural] tight trousers that are made of soft material that stretches and are worn mainly by women *a pair of leggings* ⊃ *See colour picture* **Clothes** *on page Centre 5.*

**legible** /'ledʒəbl/ *adj* If writing is legible, you can read it easily. *Her handwriting is barely legible.* ⊃ *Opposite* **illegible**.

**legion** /'li:dʒən/ *noun* [C] a large group of soldiers that forms part of an army

**legions** /'li:dʒənz/ *noun* [plural] **legions of sb** large numbers of people *He failed to turn up for the concert, disappointing the legions of fans waiting outside.*

**legislate** /'ledʒɪsleɪt/ *verb* [I] If a government legislates, it makes a new law. *We believe it is possible to **legislate against** racism. • It's hard to **legislate for** (= make a law that will protect) the ownership of an idea.*

**legislation** /ˌledʒɪ'sleɪʃªn/ *noun* [U] a law or a set of laws *Most people want tougher environmental legislation but large corporations continue to oppose it.*

**legit** /lə'dʒɪt/ *adj informal short for* legitimate

**legitimate** /lɪ'dʒɪtəmət/ *adj* **1** allowed by law *Sales of illegal CDs now exceed those of legitimate recordings.* ⊃ *Opposite* **illegitimate**. **2** A legitimate complaint or fear can be understood or believed. *People have expressed legitimate fears about the spread of the disease.* • **legitimately** *adv He insisted the money had been earned legitimately* (= legally).

**leisure** /'leʒəʳ/ ⓤⓢ /'li:ʒər/ *noun* [U] **1** the time when you are not working *leisure activities • Try to spend your leisure time doing activities you really enjoy.* **2** **at your leisure** If you do something at your leisure, you do it when you have the time. *Take it home and read it at your leisure.*

**leisurely** /'leʒəli/ ⓤⓢ /'li:ʒərli/ *adj* in a relaxed way without hurrying *a leisurely stroll*

**lemon** /'lemən/ *noun* [C, U] an oval, yellow fruit that has sour juice *a slice of lemon • lemon juice* ⊃ *See colour picture* **Fruit and Vegetables** *on page Centre 8.*

**lemonade** /ˌlemə'neɪd/ *noun* [C, U] **1** *UK* a cold drink with a lemon flavour that is sweet and has bubbles **2** *mainly US* a cold drink that is made from lemon juice, water, and sugar

o⟶**lend** /lend/ *verb past* **lent** /lent/ **1** [+ two objects] to give something to someone for a period of time, expecting that they will then give it back to you *She lent me her car for the weekend. • I do have a bike but I've lent it to Sara.* **2** [I, T] If a bank lends money, it gives money to someone who then pays the money back in small amounts over a period. *The bank refused to lend us money for another mortgage.*

**USAGE**

**lend** and **borrow**

Be careful not to confuse these two verbs.

**Lend** means to give something to someone for a period of time.

*It was raining so she lent me her umbrella.*

**Borrow** means to use something which belongs to someone else and give it back later.

*Can I borrow your umbrella? It's raining.*

~~Can I lend your umbrella? It's raining.~~

**lend itself to sth** *formal* to be suitable for a particular purpose *The old system doesn't lend itself to mass production.*

**lend sth to sb/sth** *formal* to add a quality to something or someone *We will continue to lend support to our allies.*

**lender** /'lendəʳ/ *noun* [C] a person or organization that lends money to people *mortgage lenders*

o⟶**length** /leŋθ/ *noun* **1** DISTANCE [C, U] the measurement or distance of something from one end to the other *The carpet is over three metres in length.* • *The length of the bay is roughly 200 miles.* • *The village is so small that its entire* *length could be walked in 15 minutes.* ➔ *See study section* **measurement** *on page Centre 29.* **2** TIME [C, U] the amount of time something takes *the length of a film/play/speech* • *Sitting still for any length of time is quite hard for most children.* **3** WRITING [C, U] the amount of writing in a book or document *He's written books of various lengths on the subject.* • *All of your essays will be about the same length.* **4 at length** If you talk about something at length, you talk for a long time. *We discussed both topics at length.* **5** PIECE [C] a long piece of something *a length of cloth/cord/rope* **6 go to great lengths to do sth** to try very hard to achieve something *He'll go to great lengths to get what he wants.* **7 the length and breadth of sth** in every part of a place *They travelled the length and breadth of Scotland together.*

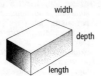
width
depth
length

**lengthen** /'leŋθən/ *verb* [I, T] to become longer or to make something longer *There are plans to lengthen the school day.* • *lengthening waiting lists*

**lengthy** /'leŋθi/ *adj* continuing for a long time *a lengthy discussion/interview/process*

**lenient** /'liːniənt/ *adj* A lenient punishment is not severe.

**lens** /lenz/ *noun* [C] a curved piece of glass in cameras, glasses, and scientific equipment used for looking at things ➔ *See also:* **contact lens**, **zoom lens**.

**lent** /lent/ *past of* lend

**Lent** /lent/ *noun* [U] the religious period before Easter (= a Christian holiday), in which some Christians do not allow themselves something that they usually enjoy *She's given up chocolate for Lent.*

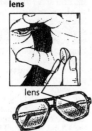
lens
lens

**lentil** /'lentᵊl/ *noun* [C] a very small dried bean which is cooked and eaten *lentil soup*

**Leo** /'liːəʊ/ *noun* [C, U] the sign of the zodiac which relates to the period of 23 July – 22 August, or a person born during this period ➔ *See picture at* **zodiac**.

**leopard** /'lepəd/ *noun* [C] a large, wild animal of the cat family, with yellow fur and dark spots

**leper** /'lepəʳ/ *noun* [C] a person who has leprosy

**leprosy** /'leprəsi/ *noun* [U] a serious skin disease which can destroy parts of the body

**lesbian** /'lezbiən/ *noun* [C] a woman who is sexually attracted to other women *a lesbian affair*

o-᛬**less**¹ /les/ *adv* **1** not as much *I'm trying to exercise more and eat less.* • *Plastic bottles are less expensive to produce.* **2 less and less** If something happens less and less, it gradually becomes smaller in amount or not so frequent. *I find I'm eating less and less red meat.*

o-᛬**less**² /les/ *quantifier* a smaller amount *She gets about £50 a week or less.* • *I was driving at less than 20 miles per hour.* • *Tuberculosis is less of a threat these days.* • *I prefer my coffee with a little less sugar.*

**lessen** /'lesᵊn/ *verb* [I, T] to become less, or to make something less *Exercise and a healthy diet lessen the chance of heart disease.* • *Strengthen the legs and it lessens the strain on the knees.*

**lesser** /'lesəʳ/ *adj* **1** not as large, important, or of such good quality *The price increase was due to labour shortages and, to a lesser extent, the recent earthquake.* • *He faces the lesser charge of assault.* **2 the lesser of two evils** the less bad of two bad things *I suppose I regard the Democratic candidate as the lesser of two evils.*

**lesser-known** /ˌlesəˈnəʊn/ *adj* not as popular or famous as something else *We stayed on one of the lesser-known Greek islands.*

o-᛬**lesson** /'lesᵊn/ *noun* [C] **1** a period of time when a teacher teaches people *The best way to improve your game is to take lessons.* • *She gives French lessons.* • *Lessons start at 9 a.m.* **2** an experience which teaches you how to behave better in a similar situation in the future *My parents made me pay back all the money, and it was a lesson I never forgot.* **3 learn your lesson** to decide not to do something again because it has caused you problems in the past *I'm not going out without my umbrella again – I've learnt my lesson!* **4 teach sb a lesson** to punish someone so that they will not behave badly again *The next time she's late, go without her. That should teach her a lesson.*

o-᛬**let** /let/ *verb* [T] **letting**, *past* let **1** to allow someone to do something, or to allow something to happen *Let them play outside.* • *Don't let the camera get wet.* • *It's best to let nature take its course.* • *We let a whole year go by before we tried again. Don't let me leave without giving you my address.* ➔ *See usage note at* **allow**. **2 let sb/sth in/past/through, etc** to allow someone or something to move to a particular place *They won't let us past the gate.* • *I won't let him near my children.* • *The roof lets in a lot of rain.* **3 let's** something that you say when you are making a suggestion *Let's eat out tonight.* • *Let's not bother with the washing up.* **4 let me/us** something that you say when you are offering to help someone *Let me carry your cases.* **5** If you let a building or part of a building, you allow someone to live there and they give you money. *I let the top floor of my house to a student.* **6 Let's see/Let me see** something that you say when you are trying to remember something or calculate something *Let's see – there are five people and only three beds.* ● *It must have been – let me see – three years ago.* **7 Let's say** something that you say when you are suggesting a possible situation or action *Let's say you manage to sell half the books.* ● *Let's say we'll meet back here in an hour.* **8 let sb know (sth)** to tell someone something [+ question word] *I'll let you know when we've fixed a date for the meeting.* **9 let (sth) go** to stop holding something *I let go of the rope.* ● *You have to let the handle go.* **10 let yourself go** to allow yourself to become less attractive or healthy *It's easy to let yourself go when you're pregnant.* **b** to relax completely and enjoy yourself *It's a party – let yourself go!* **11 let's face it** something that you say when the truth is unpleasant but must be accepted *Let's face it, we're not getting any younger.* **12 let alone** used to emphasize that something is more impossible than another thing *You couldn't trust her to look after your dog, let alone your child.* ⊃ *See also:* let the **cat** out of the bag, let your **hair** down, let sb off the **hook**[1], let off **steam**[1].

**let sb down** to disappoint someone by failing to do what you agreed to do *I promised to go to the party with Jane and I can't let her down.*

**let sb in** to allow someone to enter a room or building, often by opening the door *Could you go down and let Darren in?*

**let yourself in for sth** to become involved in an unpleasant situation without intending to *Do you realize how much work you're letting yourself in for?*

**let sb off** to not punish someone who has done something wrong, or to not punish them severely *I'll let you off this time, but don't ever lie to me again.* ● *The judge let her off with* (= only punished her with) *a fine.*

**let on** to tell someone about something secret *She let on to a friend that he'd lied in court.*

**let sb/sth out** to allow a person or animal to leave somewhere, especially by opening a locked or closed door

**let up** If bad weather or an unpleasant situation lets up, it stops or improves. *I hope the rain lets up for the weekend.*

**letdown** /ˈletdaʊn/ *noun* [no plural] *informal* a disappointment *After all I'd heard about the film it was a bit of a letdown when I finally saw it.*

**lethal** /ˈliːθəl/ *adj* able to cause death *a lethal injection/weapon*

**lethargic** /ləˈθɑːdʒɪk/ *adj* When you feel lethargic, you have no energy and you do not want to do anything. ● **lethargy** /ˈleθədʒi/ *noun* [U] the feeling of being tired and having no energy

⊸**letter** /ˈletəʳ/ *noun* [C] **1** a written message that you send to someone, usually by post *I got a letter from Paul this morning.* **2** a symbol that is used in written language and that represents a sound in that language *the letter K* ⊃ *See also:* **covering letter**.

**letterbox** /ˈletəbɒks/ *noun* [C] *UK* **1** a small hole in a door that letters are put through **2** (*US* **mailbox**) a large, metal container in a public place where you can post letters

**letter carrier** *US* (*UK* **postman**) *noun* [C] someone who takes and brings letters and parcels as a job

**lettuce** /ˈletɪs/ *noun* [C] a plant with green leaves, which is eaten in salads ⊃ *See colour picture* **Fruit and Vegetables** *on page Centre 8.*

**leukaemia** *UK* (*US* **leukemia**) /luːˈkiːmiə/ *noun* [U] a serious disease in which a person's body produces too many white blood cells

⊸**level**[1] /ˈlevəl/ *noun* [C] **1** HEIGHT the height of something *the water level* **2** AMOUNT the amount or number of something *The level of iron in her blood was too low.* ● *Chess requires a high level of concentration.* **3** ABILITY someone's ability compared to other people *Students at this level need a lot of help.* **4** FLOOR a floor in a building *The store had three levels.* ⊃ *See also:* **A level**, a level **playing field**, **sea level**.

**level**[2] /ˈlevəl/ *adj* **1** [never before noun] at the same height *I got down till my face was level with his.* **2** flat or horizontal *Make sure the camera is level before you take the picture.*

**level**[3] /ˈlevəl/ *verb* [T] *UK* **levelling**, *past* **levelled**, *US* **leveling**, *past* **leveled** **1** to make something flat *He levelled the wet cement before it set.* **2** to completely destroy a building *Artillery fire levelled the town.*

**level sth against/at sb** to aim a gun at someone or something *He levelled the gun at my head.*

**level sth at sb** to say that someone has done something wrong [often passive] *Charges of corruption have been levelled against him.*

**level off/out** to stop rising or falling and stay at the same level *Road deaths have levelled off since the speed limit was lowered.*

**level crossing** *UK* (*US* **grade crossing**) *noun* [C] a place where a railway crosses a road

**lever** /ˈliːvəʳ/ *US* /ˈlevər/ *noun* [C] **1** a handle that you push or pull to make a machine work **2** a long bar that you use to lift or move something by pressing one end

**leverage** /ˈliːvərɪdʒ/ *US* /ˈlevərɪdʒ/ *noun* [U] the power to influence people in order to get what you want

**levy** /ˈlevi/ *verb* **levy a charge/fine/tax, etc** to officially demand money [often passive] *A new tax was levied on consumers of luxury goods.*

**lewd** /luːd/ *adj* sexual in a way that is unpleasant *lewd comments/gestures*

**liability** /ˌlaɪəˈbɪləti/ *noun* **1** [U] when you are legally responsible for something *They have admitted liability for the damage caused.* **2** [no plural] someone or something that is likely to cause you a lot of trouble *Wherever we go she upsets someone – she's a real liability.*

**liable** /ˈlaɪəbl/ *adj* **1 be liable to do sth** to be likely to do something *He's liable to make a fuss if you wake him.* **2** legally responsible *Corporate officials are liable for the safety of their employees.*

**liaise** /liˈeɪz/ *verb* [I] to speak to other people at work in order to exchange information with them *Our head office will liaise with the suppliers to ensure delivery.*

**liaison** /liˈeɪzɒn/ *noun* **1** COMMUNICATION [U] communication between people or groups that work with each other **2** PERSON [C] *US* someone who helps groups to communicate effectively with each another *She served as an informal liaison between employees and management.* **3** RELATIONSHIP [C] a short sexual relationship between people who are not married

**liar** /'laɪəʳ/ *noun* [C] someone who tells lies

**Lib Dem** /lɪb'dem/ *noun* [C] *short for* Liberal Democrat

**libel** /'laɪbəl/ *noun* [U] writing which contains bad information about someone which is not true *Tabloid magazines are often sued for libel.*

**liberal** /'lɪbəʳrəl/ *adj* **1** accepting beliefs and behaviour that are new or different from your own *a liberal attitude* • *Her parents were very liberal.* **2** Liberal political ideas emphasize the need to make new laws as society changes and the need for government to provide social services. • **liberal** *noun* [C] someone who is liberal

**liberal arts** US (*UK/US* **arts**) *noun* [plural] subjects of study which are not science, such as history, languages, etc

**Liberal Democrat** *noun* [C] **1 the Liberal Democrats** one of the three main political parties in the UK *He's the leader of the Liberal Democrats.* **2** someone who supports the Liberal Democrats

**liberally** /'lɪbəʳrəli/ *adv* in large amounts *fruit liberally sprinkled with sugar*

**liberate** /'lɪbəreɪt/ *verb* [T] to help someone or something to be free *Troops liberated the city.* • **liberation** /ˌlɪbəʳ'eɪʃən/ *noun* [U] *the invasion and liberation of France*

**liberated** /'lɪbəreɪtɪd/ *adj* not following traditional ways of behaving or old ideas *a liberated woman*

**liberating** /'lɪbəreɪtɪŋ/ *adj* making you feel that you can behave in exactly the way that you want to *Taking all your clothes off can be a very liberating experience.*

**liberty** /'lɪbəti/ *noun* [C, U] **1** the freedom to live, work, and travel as you want to *Many would willingly fight to preserve their liberty.* **2 be at liberty to do sth** *formal* to be allowed to do something *I'm not at liberty to discuss the matter at present.* **3 take the liberty of doing sth** *formal* to do something that will have an effect on someone else, without asking their permission *I took the liberty of booking theatre seats for us.* ⊃ *See also:* **civil liberties**.

**Libra** /'liːbrə/ *noun* [C, U] the sign of the zodiac which relates to the period of 23 September – 22 October, or a person born during this period ⊃ *See picture at* **zodiac**.

**librarian** /laɪ'breəriən/ *noun* [C] someone who works in a library

o—ᴌ**library** /'laɪbrəʳri/ *noun* [C] a room or building that contains a collection of books and other written material that you can read or borrow

**lice** /laɪs/ *plural of* **louse**

**licence** *UK* (*US* **license**) /'laɪsəns/ *noun* [C] an official document that allows you to do or have something *a hunting licence* • *a marriage licence* ⊃ *See also:* **driving licence**, **off-licence**.

**license** /'laɪsəns/ *verb* [T] to give someone official permission to do or have something [often passive, + to do sth] *Undercover agents are licensed to carry guns.*

**licensed** /'laɪsənst/ *adj* **1** *mainly US* officially approved *a licensed physician* **2** A licensed bar or restaurant is officially allowed to serve alcoholic drinks.

**'license ˌplate** *US* (*UK* **number plate**) *noun* [C] an official metal sign with numbers and letters on the front and back of a car ⊃ *See colour picture* **Car** *on page Centre 3.*

**lick¹** /lɪk/ *verb* [T] to move your tongue across the surface of something *to lick your lips* • *We licked the chocolate off our fingers.*

**lick²** /lɪk/ *noun* **1** [C] when you lick something [usually singular] *Here, have a lick of my ice cream.* **2 a lick of paint** *UK informal* If you give a wall or other surface a lick of paint, you paint it.

**lid** /lɪd/ *noun* [C] the top part of a container that can be removed in order to put something in or take something out

o—ᴌ**lie¹** /laɪ/ *verb* [I] **lying**, *past t* **lay**, *past p* **lain 1 lie in/on, etc** to be in a horizontal or flat position on a surface *to lie in bed* • *to lie on a beach* • *to lie on your side* • *The pen lay on the desk.* • *She had lain where she fell until morning.* **2 lie below/in/on/to, etc** to be in a particular place *The river lies 30 km to the south of the city.* ⊃ *See usage note at* **lay**.

**lie around 1** *informal* to spend time lying down and doing very little *We spent a week by the sea, lying around on the beach.* **2** If things are lying around, they are left in an untidy way in places where they should not be. *He's always leaving money lying around.*

**lie back** to lower the top half of your body from a sitting position to a lying position *Lie back and relax.*

**lie down** to move into a position in which your body is flat, usually in order to sleep or rest *I'm not feeling well – I'm going to lie down.* ⊃ *See colour picture* **Phrasal Verbs** *on page Centre 13.*

**lie in** *UK* to stay in bed in the morning later than usual *I lay in till eleven o'clock this morning.*

**lie in sth** to exist or be found in something *Her strength lies in her faith.*

**lie with sb** If the responsibility or blame for something lies with someone, it is their responsibility. *The final decision lies with me.*

o—ᴌ**lie²** /laɪ/ *verb* [I] **lying**, *past* **lied** to say or write something that is not true in order to deceive someone *Are you lying to me?* • *He lied about his qualifications for the job.*

o—ᴌ**lie³** /laɪ/ *noun* [C] something that you say or write which you know is not true *I told a lie when I said I liked her haircut.* ⊃ *See also:* **white lie**.

**lie-in** /'laɪˌɪn/ *noun* [no plural] *UK* when you stay in bed in the morning longer than usual *I had a long lie-in this morning.*

**lieu** /luː/ *noun* **in lieu of sth** *formal* instead of something *She took the money in lieu of the prize.*

**lieutenant** /lef'tenənt ᴜ︠ˢ︡ luː'tenənt/ *noun* [C] an officer of middle rank in the army, navy, or air force *first/second lieutenant*

o—ᴌ**life** /laɪf/ *noun plural* **lives** /laɪvz/ **1** ANIMALS/PLANTS [U] living things and their activities *human/marine life* • *Is there life in outer space?* **2** PERSON'S EXISTENCE [C] the existence of a person *How many lives will be lost to AIDS?* **3** TIME [C, U] the time between a person's birth and their death *I'm not sure I want to spend the rest of my life with him.* • *Life's too short to worry about stuff like that.* • *Unfortunately, accidents are part of life.* • *He had a happy life.* **4** WAY OF LIVING [C, U] a way of living *You lead an exciting life.* **5 family/private/sex, etc life** one part of someone's existence *My private life is nobody's business but mine.* **6** ACTIVITY [U] energy and activity *She was always bubbly and full of life.* • *I looked through the window but couldn't see any signs of life* (= people moving). **7** ACTIVE PERIOD [no plural] the amount of time that a machine, system, etc exists or can be used *Careful use will prolong the life of your machine.* **8 bring sth to life/come to life** to make something more real or exciting, or to become more real or exciting **9 That's life.** something you say which means bad things happen and you cannot prevent them *You don't get everything you want but that's life, isn't it?* **10 Get a life!** *informal* something you say to a boring person when you want them to do more exciting things *Surely you're not cleaning the house on Saturday night? Get a life!* ➔ *See also:* the facts **(fact)** of life, give sb the **kiss²** of life, give sb/sth a new **lease¹** of life, **shelf life**, **walk²** of life.

**lifeboat** /'laɪfbəʊt/ *noun* [C] a small boat that is used to help people who are in danger at sea

**'life ˌcycle** *noun* [C] the changes that happen in the life of an animal or plant

**'life exˌpectancy** *noun* [C, U] the number of years that someone is likely to live

**lifeguard** /'laɪfɡɑːd/ *noun* [C] someone at a swimming pool or beach whose job is to help people who are in danger in the water

**'life ˌjacket** *noun* [C] a piece of equipment that you wear on the upper part of your body to help you float if you fall into water

**life jacket**

**lifeless** /'laɪfləs/ *adj* **1** without life *his lifeless body* **2** without energy or feeling *a lifeless performance*

**lifelike** /'laɪflaɪk/ *adj* If something is lifelike, it looks real. *a lifelike portrait/sculpture*

**lifeline** /'laɪflaɪn/ *noun* [C] something that helps you when you are in a difficult or dangerous situation *For a lot of old people who live on their own, the telephone is a lifeline.*

**lifelong** /ˌlaɪf'lɒŋ/ *adj* [always before noun] for all of your life *a lifelong friend/interest*

**ˌlife 'peer** *noun* [C] someone who has been officially respected in the UK by being given an important title, for example 'Lord' or 'Baroness'

**lifespan** /'laɪfspæn/ *noun* [C] the amount of time that a person lives or a thing exists

**lifestyle** /'laɪfstaɪl/ *noun* [C] the way that you live *a healthy lifestyle* • *She needs a large income to support her lifestyle.*

**life-threatening** /'laɪfθretⁿnɪŋ/ *adj* likely to cause death *life-threatening conditions/diseases*

**lifetime** /'laɪftaɪm/ *noun* [C] the period of time that someone is alive [usually singular] *We'll see such huge changes in our lifetime.*

o⚬**lift¹** /lɪft/ *verb* **1** UP [T] to put something or someone in a higher position *Could you help me lift this table, please?* • *She lifted the baby up and put him in his chair.* • *He lifted his glass to his lips.* **2** WEATHER [I] If fog lifts, it disappears. *By noon the fog had lifted and the day turned hot.* **3** RULES [T] to stop a rule *The government had already lifted the ban on beef imports.* **4** STEAL [T] *informal* to steal or copy something *Entire paragraphs of his thesis were lifted from other sources.* ➔ *See also:* not lift a **finger¹**.

o⚬**lift²** /lɪft/ *noun* [C] **1** MACHINE *UK* (*US* **elevator**) a machine that carries people up and down in tall buildings *Shall we use the stairs or take the lift?* **2** RIDE a free ride somewhere, usually in a car [usually singular] *Can you give me a lift to the airport?* **3** MOVE when you move someone or something up to a higher position

**lift-off** /'lɪftɒf/ *noun* [C] the moment when a spacecraft leaves the ground

**ligament** /'lɪɡəmənt/ *noun* [C] a piece of strong tissue in the body that holds bones together *ankle/knee ligaments* • *torn ligaments*

o⚬**light¹** /laɪt/ *noun* **1** [U] the brightness that shines from the sun, from fire, or from electrical equipment, allowing you to see things *bright/dim light* • *fluorescent/ultraviolet light* • *a beam/ray of light* • *Light was streaming in through the open door.* **2** [C] a device which produces light *car lights* • *to switch/turn the light on* • *They must be in bed – I can't see any lights on anywhere.* **3 a light** a flame from a match, etc used to make a cigarette start burning *Have you got a light, please?* **4 set light to sth** *UK* to make something start burning **5 in the light of sth** (*also US* **in light of sth**) If something is done or happens in the light of facts, it is done or happens because of those facts. *The drug has been withdrawn in the light of new research.* **6 bring sth to light** If information about something bad is brought to light, it is discovered. *The trial brought to light numerous contradictions in his story.* **7 cast/shed light on sth** to help people understand a situation *We were hoping you might be able to shed some light* *on the matter.* **8 come to light** If information about something bad comes to light, it is discovered. **9 light at the end of the tunnel** something which makes you believe that an unpleasant situation will soon end **⊃** *See also:* **green light**, **street light**, **tail light**, **traffic light**.

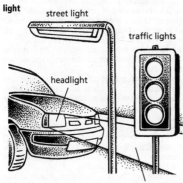

light

street light

traffic lights

headlight

beam of light

o‑**light²** /laɪt/ *adj* **1** [NOT HEAVY] not heavy *light clothing/machinery • I can carry both bags – they're quite light.* **2** [NOT MUCH] small in amount *light rain/snow • The traffic's much lighter than I expected. • I only had a light lunch.* **3** [NOT STRONG] not strong or not forceful *a light breeze • a light embrace* **4** [PALE] Light colours are pale. *light brown/green • a light blue cardigan* **5** [NOT SERIOUS] easy to understand and not serious *light entertainment • I'm taking some light reading on holiday.* **6 make light of sth** to talk or behave as if you do not think a problem is serious *I just laughed and tried to make light of it.* **7 it is light** bright from the sun *Let's go now while it's still light.* • lightness *noun* [U]

**light³** /laɪt/ *verb past* **lit** or **lighted 1** [I, T] to start to burn, or to make something start to burn *to light a candle/cigarette/fire • The wood was damp and wouldn't light.* **2** [T] to produce light somewhere so that you can see things [often passive] *The room was lit by a single light bulb.* • *Burning buildings* **lit up** *the sky.*

**light up** If your face or your eyes light up, you suddenly look happy or excited. *His eyes lit up when you mentioned her name.*

**light (sth) up** to make a cigarette, etc start burning *He made himself a coffee and lit up a cigarette.*

'**light ,bulb** *noun* [C] a glass object containing a wire which produces light from electricity

**lighten** /ˈlaɪtᵊn/ *verb* **1** [I, T] If a serious situation lightens, it becomes less serious, and if something or someone lightens it, they make it less serious. *Her* **mood lightened** *a bit when I asked about her holiday. • He tried to lighten the atmosphere by telling a joke.* **2 lighten the burden/load** to reduce the amount of work or trouble someone has to deal with **3** [I, T] to become less dark, or to make something less dark *The sun had lightened her hair.*

**lighten up** *informal* to become more relaxed and less serious *I wish she'd lighten up a bit.*

**lighter** /ˈlaɪtə<sup>r</sup>/ *noun* [C] a small object that produces a flame and is used to make cigarettes start burning

**light-hearted** /ˌlaɪtˈhɑːtɪd/ *adj* not serious *a light-hearted remark*

**lighthouse** /ˈlaɪthaʊs/ *noun* [C] *plural* **lighthouses** /ˈlaɪthaʊzɪz/ a tall building on the coast containing a large light which warns ships that there are rocks

**lighting** /ˈlaɪtɪŋ/ *noun* [U] the light created by electrical equipment, candles, etc *soft lighting • fluorescent lighting*

**lightly** /ˈlaɪtli/ *adv* **1** gently *He kissed her lightly on the cheek.* **2** not much *lightly cooked vegetables* **3 not do sth lightly** to think carefully about something before you do it, knowing that it is serious *It's not a decision that I take lightly.* **4 get off lightly** (*also UK* **escape lightly**) to have less trouble or punishment than you expected

**lightning** /ˈlaɪtnɪŋ/ *noun* [U] a sudden flash of light in the sky during a storm *thunder and lightning • He was* **struck by lightning** *and killed.*

**lights** /laɪts/ (*also* '**traffic ,lights**) *noun* [plural] a set of red, green, and yellow lights that is used to stop and start traffic *Turn right at the lights.*

**lightweight** /ˈlaɪtweɪt/ *adj* not weighing much *a lightweight jacket for the summer* • lightweight *noun* [C] a sportsman such as a boxer who is not in the heaviest weight group

o‑**like¹** /laɪk/ *preposition* **1** [SIMILAR] similar to or in the same way as someone or something *I wish I were slim like you. • They were acting like children. • He looks like his father. • It sounded like Harry.* **2 What is sb/sth like?** something you say when you want someone to describe someone or something *I haven't met him – what's he like? • So what's your new dress like?* **3** [TYPICAL] If behaviour is like someone, it is typical of the way that they behave. *It's just like Anita to miss her train. • It's not like Tim to be late.* **4** [FOR EXAMPLE] for example *She looks best in bright colours, like red and pink.*

o‑**like²** /laɪk/ *verb* [T] **1** to enjoy something or feel that someone or something is pleasant [+ doing sth] *I just like playing with my computer.* • [+ to do sth] *I like to paint in my spare time. • He really likes her. • What do you* **like** *about him?* **⊃** *Opposite* **dislike**. **2 not like to do sth/not like doing sth** to not usually do something because you think it is wrong *I don't like to criticize her too much.* **3 would like sth** to want something [+ to do sth] *I'd like to think about it. • I'd like some chips with that, please.* **4 Would you like...?** used to offer someone something *Would you like a drink?* • [+ to do sth] *Would you like to eat now?* **5 if you like** **a** used to say 'yes' when someone suggests a plan *"Shall I come?" "If you like."* **b** used when you offer someone something *If you like I could drive you there.* **6 How do you like sb/sth?** used to ask someone for their opinion *How do you like my new shoes?*

o‑**like³** /laɪk/ *conjunction* **1** *informal* in the same way as *Do it exactly like I told you to.* **2** *US informal* as if *He acted like he didn't hear me.*

**like⁴** /laɪk/ noun **1** [no plural] formal someone or something that is similar to someone or something else Economists are predicting a depression, the like of which the world has never seen. **2 and the like** informal and similar things There's a gym that they use for dance and aerobics and the like. **3 sb's likes and dislikes** the things that someone thinks are pleasant and not pleasant

**likeable** /ˈlaɪkəbl/ adj If you are likeable, you are pleasant and easy to like. a likeable character

**likelihood** /ˈlaɪklihʊd/ noun [U] the chance that something will happen There's not much likelihood of that happening.

o—**likely¹** /ˈlaɪkli/ adj **1** expected [+ to do sth] Do remind me because I'm likely to forget. • [+ (that)] It's likely that he'll say no. **2** probably true the most likely explanation ⊃ Opposite unlikely.

**likely²** /ˈlaɪkli/ adv **1** probably She'll most likely come without him. **2 Not likely!** UK informal used to say that you will certainly not do something "So are you coming running with me?" "Not likely!"

**liken** /ˈlaɪkⁿn/ verb
**liken sth/sb to sth/sb** formal to say that two people are similar or two things are similar She's been likened to a young Elizabeth Taylor.

**likeness** /ˈlaɪknəs/ noun [C, U] being similar in appearance There's a definite family likeness around the eyes.

**likewise** /ˈlaɪkwaɪz/ adv formal in the same way Water these plants twice a week and likewise the ones in the bedroom. • Watch what she does and then **do likewise**.

**liking** /ˈlaɪkɪŋ/ noun **1** [no plural] a feeling that you like someone or something He has a **liking for young women**. **2 take a liking to sb** to like someone immediately He obviously took a liking to her. **3 be too bright/sweet, etc for your liking** to be brighter/sweeter, etc than you like **4 be to sb's liking** formal to be the way that someone prefers something Is the wine to your liking, sir?

**lilac** /ˈlaɪlək/ noun [C, U] a small tree that has sweet-smelling purple, pink, or white flowers

**lily** /ˈlɪli/ noun [C] a plant with large, bell-shaped flowers that are often white

**limb** /lɪm/ noun [C] **1** a leg or an arm of a person **2** a large branch of a tree

**lime** /laɪm/ noun **1** FRUIT [C, U] a small, green fruit that is sour like a lemon **2** TREE [C] (also **'lime ,tree**) a large tree that has pale green leaves and yellow flowers **3** SUBSTANCE [U] a white substance that is found in water and soil and is used to improve the quality of soil **4** COLOUR [U] (also **,lime 'green**) a bright colour that is a mixture of yellow and green ⊃ See colour picture **Colours** on page Centre 6. • lime (also **lime-green**) adj

**the limelight** /ˈlaɪmlaɪt/ noun attention from the public She's been **in the limelight** for most of her career.

o—**limit¹** /ˈlɪmɪt/ noun [C] **1** the largest amount of something that is possible or allowed a time limit • a legal limit • Is there a limit on the amount of money you can claim? • There's a limit to how much time we can spend on this.

**2 be over the limit** UK to have more alcohol in your blood than is legally allowed while driving **3 within limits** avoiding behaviour that is extreme or silly You can wear what you want, within limits. **4 off limits** If an area is off limits, you are not allowed to enter it. Most of the palace is off limits to the public. ⊃ See also: **speed limit**.

o—**limit²** /ˈlɪmɪt/ verb [T] to control something so that it is less than a particular amount or number I try to limit the amount of fat that I eat. • We'll have to limit the number of guests.

**be limited to sth** to only exist in a particular area Racial problems are certainly not limited to the south.

**limit sb to sth** to only allow someone a particular amount or number of something [often passive] We're limited to two pieces of luggage each. • [often reflexive] I try to limit myself to two glasses of wine a day.

**limitation** /ˌlɪmɪˈteɪʃⁿn/ noun [C, U] when something is controlled so that it is less than a particular amount or number the limitation of free speech • You can't write everything you want because of space limitations.

**limitations** /ˌlɪmɪˈteɪʃⁿnz/ noun [plural] things that someone is not good at doing Both films show her limitations as an actress.

**limited** /ˈlɪmɪtɪd/ adj small in amount or number a limited choice • limited resources ⊃ Opposite unlimited.

**,limited 'company** noun [C] a company, especially one in the UK, whose owners only have to pay part of the money they owe if the company fails financially

**limousine** /ˌlɪməˈziːn/ (also **limo** /ˈlɪməʊ/) noun [C] a large, expensive car, usually for rich or important people a chauffeur-driven limousine

**limp¹** /lɪmp/ adj soft and weak a limp handshake • a limp lettuce

**limp²** /lɪmp/ verb [I] to walk with difficulty because one of your legs or feet is hurt • limp noun [no plural] She walks with a limp.

o—**line¹** /laɪn/ noun **1** MARK [C] a long, thin mark a horizontal/straight/vertical line • Sign your name on the dotted line. • Draw a line around your hand. **2** ROW [C] a row of people or things a line of trees • We formed two lines, men on one side and women on the other. **3** ROPE ETC [C] a piece of rope or wire with a particular purpose a clothes/fishing line **4** TELEPHONE [C] the connection between two telephones I've got Neil **on the line** for you (= waiting to speak to you). • I'll be with you in a moment – could you **hold the line**, please (= wait)? **5** WAITING [C, U] US (UK queue) a row of people waiting for something, one behind the other We were **standing in line** for hours to get tickets. **6** SONG/POEM [C] a row of words on a page, for example in a song or poem The same line is repeated throughout the poem. **7 lines** the words spoken by an actor in a performance I don't know how actors remember all their lines. **8** OPINION [C] the official opinion of an organization [usually singular] the government's line on immigration **9 along the lines of sth** based on and similar to something He gave a talk along the lines of the one he gave in Oxford. **10 sb's line of reasoning/**

**thinking, etc** your reasons for believing that something is true or right **11** PRODUCT [C] a type of product that a company sells *They're advertising a new* **line** *in garden furniture.* **12** DIRECTION [C] the direction that something moves in *He can't kick the ball in a straight line.* **13 lines** the marks that older people have on their faces, when the skin is loose **14** BORDER [C] *US* a border between two areas *the New York state line* **15 be on the line** If someone's job is on the line, they may lose it. **16 be in line for sth** to be likely to get something good, especially a job **17 be in line with sth** to be similar to and suitable for something *a pay increase in line with inflation* **18 draw the line at sth** to never do something because you think it is wrong *I swear a lot but even I draw the line at certain words.* **19 toe the (party) line** to do what someone in authority tells you to do although you do not agree with it ⊃ *See also:* **the bottom line, dotted line, front line, hard line.**

**line²** /laɪn/ *verb* [T] **1** to form a row along the side of something *Trees and cafes lined the street.* **2 be lined with sth** If a piece of clothing is lined with a material, its inside is covered with it. *a jacket lined with fur*
**line (sb/sth) up** to stand in a row, or to arrange people or things in a row *Books were neatly lined up on the shelves.*
**line sb/sth up** to plan for something to happen *What future projects have you lined up?*

**linen** /ˈlɪnɪn/ *noun* [U] **1** an expensive cloth that is like rough cotton *a linen jacket* **2** pieces of cloth that you use to cover tables and beds *bed linen*

**liner** /ˈlaɪnəʳ/ *noun* [C] a large ship like a hotel, which people travel on for pleasure *a cruise/ocean liner*

**linesman** /ˈlaɪnzmən/ *noun* [C] *plural* **linesmen** in a sport, someone who watches to see if a ball goes into areas where it is not allowed

**linger** /ˈlɪŋgəʳ/ *verb* [I] to stay somewhere for a long time *The smell from the fire still lingered hours later.*

**lingerie** /ˈlɒnʒªri ⓤ ˌlɑːnʒəˈreɪ/ *noun* [U] women's underwear

**lingering** /ˈlɪŋgªrɪŋ/ *adj* [always before noun] lasting a long time *lingering doubts/fears*

**linguist** /ˈlɪŋgwɪst/ *noun* [C] someone who is good at learning foreign languages, or someone who studies or teaches linguistics

**linguistic** /lɪŋˈgwɪstɪk/ *adj* [always before noun] relating to language or linguistics

**linguistics** /lɪŋˈgwɪstɪks/ *noun* [U] the scientific study of languages

**lining** /ˈlaɪnɪŋ/ *noun* [C, U] a material or substance that covers the inside of something *a coat/jacket lining* ● *the lining of the stomach*

o━**link¹** /lɪŋk/ *noun* [C] **1** CONNECTION a connection between two people, things, or ideas *There's a direct* **link** *between diet and heart disease.* ● *Their* **links with** *Britain are still strong.* **2** CHAIN one ring of a chain **3** INTERNET (*also* **hyperlink**) a connection between documents or areas on the Internet *Click on this link to visit our online bookstore.*

o━**link²** /lɪŋk/ *verb* [T] to make a connection

between two or more people, things, or ideas [often passive] *Both men have been* **linked with** *the robberies.* ● *The drug has been* **linked to** *the deaths of several athletes.* ● *The two offices will be linked by computer.*
**link (sb/sth) up** If two or more things or people link up, or if you link them up, they form a connection so that they can operate or work together. *Each house will be linked up with the new communications network.*

**lion** /ˈlaɪən/ *noun* [C] a large, wild animal of the cat family, with light brown fur ⊃ *See also:* **sea lion.**

**lip** /lɪp/ *noun* [C] **1** one of the two soft, red edges of the mouth *He licked his lips.* ● *See colour picture* **The Body** *on page Centre 2.* **2** the edge of a container that liquid is poured from

**lip-read** /ˈlɪpriːd/ *verb* [I, T] *past* **lip-read** to understand what someone is saying by looking at the way their mouth moves ● **lip-reading** *noun* [U]

**lip-service** /ˈlɪpsɜːvɪs/ *noun* [no plural] **give/pay lip-service to sth** *informal* to say that you support an idea or plan, but not do anything to help it succeed *Although everyone pays lip-service to it, nobody talks seriously about cleaning up the environment.*

**lipstick** /ˈlɪpstɪk/ *noun* [C, U] a coloured substance that women put on their lips ⊃ *See picture at* **make up.**

o━**liquid** /ˈlɪkwɪd/ *noun* [C, U] a substance, for example water, that is not solid and that can be poured easily ● **liquid** *adj liquid fuel/nitrogen*

**liquidate** /ˈlɪkwɪdeɪt/ *verb* [T] to close a business because it has no money left ● **liquidation** /ˌlɪkwɪˈdeɪʃªn/ *noun* [C, U] *The store* **went into liquidation.**

**liquor** /ˈlɪkəʳ/ *noun* [U] *US* a strong alcoholic drink

**ˈliquor ˌstore** *US* (*UK* **off-licence**) *noun* [C] a shop that sells alcoholic drink

**lisp** /lɪsp/ *noun* [C] a way of speaking where 's' and 'z' sound like 'th' *She has a slight lisp.* ● **lisp** *verb* [I]

o━**list¹** /lɪst/ *noun* [C] a series of names, numbers, or items that are written one below the other *a shopping list* ● *Is your name* **on the list?** ● *Make a list of everything you need.* ⊃ *See also:* **mailing list, waiting list.**

**list²** /lɪst/ *verb* [T] to make a list, or to include something in a list *The directory lists only small businesses.* ● *All names are listed alphabetically.*

o━**listen** /ˈlɪsªn/ *verb* [I] **1** to give attention to someone or something in order to hear them *What kind of music do you* **listen to?** ● *I listen to the radio while I have breakfast.* ● *She does all the talking – I just sit and listen.* ● *You haven't listened to a word I've said.* ● *Listen, if you need money, I'm happy to lend you some.* **2** to accept someone's advice *I told you she wouldn't like it but you wouldn't* **listen to me!**

### USAGE

**listen, listen to,** or **hear?**

Use **hear** when you want to say that sounds, music, etc come to your ears. You can **hear** something without wanting to.

*I could hear his music through the wall.*

Use **listen** to say that you pay attention to sounds or try to hear something.

*The audience listened carefully.*

*Ssh! I'm listening!*

Use **listen to** when you want to say what it is that you are trying to hear.

*The audience listened to the speaker.*

*Ssh! I'm listening to the radio!*

**listen in** to secretly listen to a conversation, especially a telephone conversation
**listen (out) for sth** to try to hear something *Could you listen out for the phone while I'm upstairs?*
**Listen up** *mainly US* something you say to tell people to listen to you *Okay, everyone, listen up! I have an announcement to make.*

**listener** /'lɪsᵊnəʳ/ *noun* [C] someone who listens *The new radio station already has twelve million listeners.* ● *She's a good listener* (= she gives you all her attention when you speak).
**lit** /lɪt/ *past of* light
**liter** /'liːtəʳ/ *noun* [C] *US spelling of* litre
**literacy** /'lɪtᵊrəsi/ *noun* [U] the ability to read and write
**literal** /'lɪtᵊrᵊl/ *adj* The literal meaning of a word or phrase is its real or original meaning. *the literal meaning/sense*
**literally** /'lɪtᵊrᵊli/ *adv* **1** having the real or original meaning of a word or phrase *They were responsible for literally millions of deaths.* **2** *informal* used to emphasize what you are saying *He missed that kick literally by miles!*
**literary** /'lɪtᵊrᵊri/ *adj* relating to literature, or typical of the type of language that is used in literature *literary criticism*
**literate** /'lɪtᵊrət/ *adj* able to read and write ⊃ *Opposite* **illiterate**.
o⟶**literature** /'lɪtrətʃəʳ/ *noun* [U] **1** books, poems, etc that are considered to be art *classical/modern literature* **2** written information about a subject *There is very little literature on the disease.*
**litre** UK (US **liter**) (*written abbreviation* l) /'liːtəʳ/ *noun* [C] a unit for measuring liquid
**litter**[1] /'lɪtəʳ/ *noun* **1** [U] pieces of paper and other waste that are left in public places **2** [C] a group of baby animals that are from the same mother and born at the same time *a litter of kittens/puppies*
**litter**[2] /'lɪtəʳ/ *verb* [T] If things litter an area, they cover parts of it in an untidy way. *Clothes littered the floor.*
**be littered with sth** to contain a lot of something *The whole book is littered with errors.*
o⟶**little**[1] /'lɪtl/ *adj* **1** SMALL small in size or amount *a little bag/box/town* ● *She's so little.* ● *It costs as little as one dollar.* ● *I might have a little bit of cake.* **2** SHORT [always before noun] short in time or distance *Sit down for a little while.* ● *Let's have a little break.* **3** NOT IMPORTANT [always before noun] not important *It's only a little problem.* ● *I'm having a little trouble with my back.* **4** YOUNG [always before noun] young

and small *She was my little sister and I looked after her.* ⊃ *See usage note at* **small**.
o⟶**little**[2] /'lɪtl/ *quantifier* **1** not much or not enough *He has little chance of winning.* ● *There's so little choice.* **2** **a little sth** a small amount of something *It just needs a little effort.*

USAGE

**little**

When **little** is used as a quantifier, it can only be used with uncountable nouns.

**little**[3] /'lɪtl/ *pronoun* **1** not much, or not enough *We did very little on Sunday.* **2** **a little** a small amount *I only know a little about my grandparents.* ● *"More dessert?" "Just a little, please."*
o⟶**little**[4] /'lɪtl/ *adv* not much or not enough *She ate very little at dinner.* ● *a little-known fact*
o⟶**live**[1] /lɪv/ *verb* **1** [I] to be alive *She only lived a few days after the accident.* ● *I hope I live to see my grandchildren.* **2** **live at/in/near, etc** to have your home somewhere *I still remember the house we lived in.* ● *They live in New York.* ● *We live near each other.* ● *Where do you live?* **3** [I, T] to spend your life in a particular way *Many people are living in poverty.* ● *She lived a full life.* **4** **I'll never live it down!** *humorous* something you say about an embarrassing experience that other people will not forget
**live for sth/sb** to have something or someone as the most important thing in your life *I love dancing – I just live for it.*
**live on** to continue to live *She lived on well into her nineties.*
**live on sth 1** Money that you live on is the money you use to buy the things that you need. *We lived on very little when we were students.* **2** to only eat a particular type of food *All summer we live on hamburgers and hot dogs.*
**live together** If two people live together, they live in the same home and have a sexual relationship, but are not married.
**live up to sth** to be as good as someone hopes *Did the trip live up to your expectations?*
**live with sb** to live in the same home as someone and have a sexual relationship with them although you are not married
**live with sth** to accept a difficult or unpleasant situation *It's a problem she's going to have to live with.*
o⟶**live**[2] /laɪv/ *adj* **1** LIFE having life *Millions of live animals are shipped around the world each year.* **2** ELECTRICITY A live wire has electricity in it. **3** BROADCAST A live radio or television programme is seen or heard as it happens. *live coverage* ● *a live broadcast* **4** AUDIENCE A live performance or recording of a performance is done with an audience. *a live concert* ● *live music* **5** BOMB A live bomb has not yet exploded.
**live**[3] /laɪv/ *adv* broadcast at the same time that something happens *We'll be bringing you the match to you live on Wednesday.*
**livelihood** /'laɪvlihʊd/ *noun* [C, U] the way that you earn the money you need for living *The farm is his livelihood.*
**lively** /'laɪvli/ *adj* full of energy and interest *a lively conversation/debate* ● *a lively child*

**liver** /'lɪvəʳ/ noun 1 [C] a large organ in your body that cleans your blood 2 [U] the liver of an animal that is eaten by people

**lives** /lɪvz/ plural of life

**livestock** /'laɪvstɒk/ noun [U] animals that are kept on a farm

**livid** /'lɪvɪd/ adj very angry

**living¹** /'lɪvɪŋ/ noun 1 [C] the money that you earn from your job [usually singular] to earn/make a living • What does he do for a living (= how does he earn money)? 2 country/healthy, etc living the way in which you live your life ⊃ See also: **standard of living**.

**living²** /'lɪvɪŋ/ adj [always before noun] 1 alive now He's probably the best known living photographer. 2 alive living organisms • living things ⊃ See also: beat/knock the living **daylights** out of sb, scare/frighten the living **daylights** out of sb.

**'living ,room** (also UK **sitting room**) noun [C] the room in a house where people sit to relax and, for example, watch television ⊃ See colour picture **The Living Room** on page Centre 11.

**lizard** /'lɪzəd/ noun [C] a small animal with thick skin, a long tail and four short legs

**load¹** /ləʊd/ noun 1 [C] something that is carried, often by a vehicle We were behind a truck carrying a load of coal. 2 **a load/loads** informal a lot of something There were loads of people there. • Have some more food – there's loads. 3 **a load of rubbish/nonsense, etc** UK informal nonsense

**load²** /ləʊd/ verb 1 [I, T] (also **load up**) to put a lot of things into a vehicle or machine Bring the car up to the door and I'll start loading up. • to load the dishwasher/washing machine ⊃ Opposite **unload**. 2 [T] to put film in a camera or bullets in a gun

**be loaded down with sth** to have too much to carry, or too much work to do I was loaded down with shopping.

**be loaded with sth** to contain a lot of something Most fast foods are loaded with fat.

**-load** /ləʊd/ suffix used at the end of a word to describe an amount of something that is being carried a truckload of soldiers • a busload of schoolchildren

**loaded** /'ləʊdɪd/ adj 1 A loaded gun, or similar weapon, has a bullet in it. 2 [never before noun] informal very rich

**,loaded 'question** noun [C] a question which makes you answer in a particular way

**loaf** /ləʊf/ noun [C] plural **loaves** /ləʊvz/ bread that has been baked in one large piece so that it can be cut into smaller pieces a loaf of bread ⊃ See picture at **bread**.

o-**loan¹** /ləʊn/ noun 1 [C] money that someone has borrowed a bank loan • a student loan • He repaid the loan within two years. 2 **be on loan** If something is on loan, someone is borrowing it. Both paintings are on loan from the city museum.

**loan²** /ləʊn/ verb [+ two objects] to lend something to someone I was glad to **loan** my old books to her. • My dad loaned me the money.

**loath** /ləʊθ/ adj **be loath to do sth** formal to not want to do something because it will cause problems I'm loath to spend it all.

**loathe** /ləʊð/ verb [T] to hate someone or something • **loathing** noun [U] a feeling of hating someone or something

**loaves** /ləʊvz/ plural of loaf

**lobby¹** /'lɒbi/ noun [C] 1 a room at the main entrance of a building, often with doors and stairs that lead to other parts of the building a hotel lobby 2 a group of people who try to persuade the government to do something the anti-smoking lobby

**lobby²** /'lɒbi/ verb [I, T] to try to persuade the government to do something They're **lobbying** for changes to the law.

**lobster** /'lɒbstəʳ/ noun [C, U] a sea creature that has two claws (= sharp, curved parts) and eight legs, or the meat of this animal

o-**local¹** /'ləʊkᵊl/ adj relating to an area near you the local school/newspaper/radio station • **locally** adv locally grown vegetables

**local²** /'ləʊkᵊl/ noun [C] 1 someone who lives in the area you are talking about The locals are very upset about the new law. 2 **sb's local** UK informal a bar that is near someone's home

**,local anaes'thetic** UK (US **local anesthetic**) noun [C, U] a substance that is put into a part of your body so that you do not feel pain there The procedure is carried out **under local anaesthetic**.

**,local au'thority** noun [group] the group of people who govern a small area of a country Local authorities are looking for new ways to promote investment.

**,local 'time** noun [U] the official time in an area or country We will shortly be landing in London, where the local time is 3.15.

**locate** /ləʊ'keɪt/ verb [T] formal 1 to find the exact position of someone or something Police are still trying to locate the suspect. 2 **be located in/near/on, etc** to be in a particular place Both schools are located in the town.

**location** /ləʊ'keɪʃᵊn/ noun 1 [C] a place or position They haven't yet decided on **the location of** the new store. 2 **on location** If a film or television programme is made on location, it is made at a place suitable to the story.

**loch** /lɒk, lɒx/ noun [C] a lake in Scotland Loch Lomond

o-**lock¹** /lɒk/ verb 1 [I, T] to fasten something with a key, or to be fastened with a key Did you lock the door? • If you shut the door it will lock automatically. ⊃ Opposite **unlock**. 2 **lock sth/sb away/in, etc** to put something or someone in a place or container that is fastened with a key She locked herself in her bedroom. • Most of my jewellery is locked away in a safe. 3 [I] to become fixed in one position I tried to move forward but the wheels had locked.

**lock sb in/out** to prevent someone from entering/leaving a room or building by locking the door

**lock (sth) up** to lock all the doors and windows of a building when you leave it Don't forget to lock up when you leave.

**lock sb up** to put someone in prison or a hospital for people who are mentally ill The suspect remained locked up while awaiting trial.

o-**lock²** /lɒk/ noun [C] 1 the thing that is used to close a door, window, etc, and that needs a key

to open it *I heard someone turn a key in the lock.*
• *safety locks* **2** a place on a river with gates to allow boats to move to a different water level **3 under lock and key** kept safely in a room or container that is locked *I tend to keep medicines under lock and key because of the kids.*

**locker** /'lɒkə<sup>r</sup>/ *noun* [C] a small cupboard in a public area where your personal possessions can be kept *a gym/luggage/school locker*

**'locker ,room** *noun* [C] a room where you change your clothes and leave those and other personal possessions in a locker

**locomotive** /,ləʊkə'məʊtɪv/ *noun* [C] the part of a train that makes it move *a steam locomotive*

**lodge**¹ /lɒdʒ/ *noun* [C] a small house in the country that is used especially by people on holiday *a hunting/mountain/ski lodge*

**lodge**² /lɒdʒ/ *verb* **1 lodge in/on, etc** to become stuck somewhere *The bullet had lodged near his heart.* ➔ *Compare* **dislodge**. **2 lodge at/with, etc** to live in someone's home and give them money for it **3 lodge a claim/complaint/ protest, etc** to officially complain about something *He lodged an official complaint against the officers responsible.*

**lodger** /'lɒdʒə<sup>r</sup>/ *UK* (*US* **boarder**) *noun* [C] someone who pays for a place to sleep and meals in someone else's house

**lodgings** /'lɒdʒɪŋz/ *noun* [plural] *mainly UK* a room in someone's home that you pay money to live in *temporary lodgings*

**loft** /lɒft/ *noun* [C] **1** the space under the roof of a house or other building **2** *US* space where someone lives or works in a building that used to be a factory

**log**¹ /lɒg/ *noun* [C] **1** a thick piece of wood that has been cut from a tree *We need more logs for the fire.* **2** a written record of events, often on a ship or aircraft

**log**² /lɒg/ *verb* [T] *logging, past* **logged** to make a written record of events, often on a ship or aircraft

**log in/on** to connect a computer to a system of computers by typing your name, usually so that you can start working

**log off/out** to stop a computer being connected to a computer system, usually when you want to stop working

**loggerheads** /'lɒgəhedz/ *noun* **be at logger- heads (with sb)** If two people or groups are at loggerheads, they disagree strongly about something. *He is at loggerheads with the Prime Minister over public spending.*

**logic** /'lɒdʒɪk/ *noun* [U] the use of reason, or the science of using reason *It was difficult to understand the logic behind his argument.*

**logical** /'lɒdʒɪk<sup>ə</sup>l/ *adj* using reason *a logical choice/conclusion* ➔ *Opposite* **illogical**. • logi- cally *adv Her ideas were clear and logically pre- sented.*

**logistics** /lə'dʒɪstɪks/ *noun* **the logistics of sth/doing sth** the practical arrangements for something *We could all use the one car but I'm not sure about the logistics of it.*

**logo** /'ləʊgəʊ/ *noun* [C] a design or symbol used by a company to advertise its products *a corpo- rate logo*

**loiter** /'lɔɪtə<sup>r</sup>/ *verb* [I] to stand in a place or walk

slowly around without any purpose *A gang of youths were loitering outside the cinema.*

**lollipop** /'lɒlipɒp/ (*also UK* **lolly** /'lɒli/) *noun* [C] a large, hard sweet on a stick

**lone** /ləʊn/ *adj* [always before noun] alone *lone parents* • *the lone survivor*

o⊸**lonely** /'ləʊnli/ *adj* **1** unhappy because you are not with other people *She gets lonely now that the kids have all left home.* ➔ *See usage note at* **alone**. **2** A lonely place is a long way from where people live. • **loneliness** *noun* [U]

**loner** /'ləʊnə<sup>r</sup>/ *noun* [C] someone who likes to be alone *He was always a bit of a loner at school.*

**lonesome** /'ləʊnsəm/ *adj US* lonely

o⊸**long**¹ /lɒŋ/ *adj* **1** DISTANCE having a large dis- tance from one end to the other *long, brown hair* • *long legs* • *a long dress* • *It's a long way to travel to work.* **2** TIME continuing for a large amount of time *a long film/meeting* • *Have you been waiting a long time?* **3** HOW LONG used when asking for or giving information about the distance or time of something *It's about three metres long.* • *Most of the concerts are over three hours long.* • *How long do you want the skirt?* • *Do you know how long the film is?* **4** BOOK A long book or other piece of writing has a lot of pages or words. *a long article/letter* ➔ *See also:* in the long **run**².

o⊸**long**² /lɒŋ/ *adv* **1** for a long time *We didn't have to wait long for the train.* • *The band played long into the night.* **2 as long as** used when you are talking about something that must happen before something else can happen *You can play football as long as you do your homework first.* **3 before long** soon *He'll be home before long.* **4 long ago** If something happened long ago, it happened a great amount of time ago. **5 no longer/not any longer** not now *He no longer works here.*

**long**³ /lɒŋ/ *noun* [U] a large amount of time *She won't be away for long.*

**long**⁴ /lɒŋ/ *verb formal* **long for sth; long to do sth** to want something very much *She longed to see him again.*

**long-distance** /,lɒŋ'dɪst<sup>ə</sup>ns/ *adj* travelling or communicating between two places that are a long way apart *a long-distance race* • *a long- distance phone call*

**long-haul** /,lɒŋ'hɔːl/ *adj* [always before noun] trav- elling a long distance *a long-haul flight*

**longing** /'lɒŋɪŋ/ *noun* [U, no plural] a feeling of wanting something or someone very much *He gazed at her, his eyes full of longing.* • *a longing for his homeland* • **longingly** *adv She looked longingly at the silk dresses.*

**longitude** /'lɒndʒɪtjuːd/ *noun* [U] the distance of a place east or west of an imaginary line from the top to the bottom of the Earth, meas- ured in degrees

**the 'long ,jump** *noun* a sports event where people try to jump as far as possible

**long-life** /,lɒŋ'laɪf/ *adj UK* Long-life drink or food has been treated so that it will last a long time. *long-life milk*

**long-lost** /'lɒŋ,lɒst/ *adj* **long-lost friend/ cousin, etc** a friend or relative that you have not seen for a long time

**long-range** /,lɒŋ'reɪndʒ/ *adj* [always before noun]

**1** relating to a time in the future *a long-range weather forecast* **2** able to be sent long distances *a long-range bomber/missile*

'long ,shot *noun* [C] *informal* something that is not likely to succeed *It's a long shot, but you could try phoning him at home.*

long-sighted /ˌlɒŋˈsaɪtɪd/ UK (US **farsighted**) *adj* able to see objects which are far away but not things which are near to you

long-standing /ˌlɒŋˈstændɪŋ/ *adj* having existed for a long time *a long-standing relationship*

long-suffering /ˌlɒŋˈsʌfᵊrɪŋ/ *adj* A long-suffering person has been very patient for a long time about all the trouble that someone has caused them. *Bill and his long-suffering wife*

long-term /ˌlɒŋˈtɜːm/ *adj* continuing a long time into the future *long-term unemployment*

long-winded /ˌlɒŋˈwɪndɪd/ *adj* If what someone says or writes is long-winded, it is boring because it is too long. *a long-winded explanation*

loo /luː/ *noun* [C] UK *informal* toilet *I'll just go to the loo.* ➲ *See usage note at* **toilet**.

o━**look¹** /lʊk/ *verb* **1** [I] to turn your eyes in the direction of something or someone so that you can see them *Look at the picture on page two.* • *Look at me, Daddy!* • *He was looking out of the window.* • *I looked around and there she was.* **2** [I] to try to find someone or something *I'm looking for my keys.* • *I've looked everywhere but I can't find my bag.* **3 look nice/ strange, etc; look like/as if** used to describe the appearance of a person or thing *That food looks nice.* • *You look tired, my love.* • *Do I look silly in this hat?* • *She looks Italian or Spanish.* • *He looked like a drug addict.* **4 it looks like; it looks as if** used to say that something is likely to happen *It looks like there'll be three of us.* • *It looks as if he isn't coming.* **5 be looking to do sth** to plan to do something *I'm looking to start my own business.* **6 Look!** something you say when you are annoyed and you want people to know that what you are saying is important *Look, I've had enough of your complaints.* ➲ *See also:* look the **part¹**.

USAGE

**look, see,** or **watch?**

See means to notice people and things with your eyes.

*She saw a big spider and screamed.*

*Did you see anyone you knew at the party?*

Look (at) is used when you are trying to see something or someone. Look cannot be followed by an object.

*I've looked everywhere, but can't find my keys.*

*He looked at the map to find the road.*

~~He looked the photographs.~~

Watch means to look at something for a period of time, usually something which moves or changes.

*He watched television all evening.*

*I watched them playing football.*

**look after sb/sth** to take care of someone or something by keeping them healthy or in a good condition *Could you look after the children while I'm out?*

**look ahead** to think about something that will happen in the future and plan for it

**look at sth 1** THINK to think about a subject carefully so that you can make a decision about it *Management is looking at ways of cutting costs.* **2** READ to read something *Can you look at my essay sometime?* **3** EXPERT If an expert looks at something, they examine it. *Did you get the doctor to look at your knee?* **4** OPINION to consider something in a particular way *If I'd been a mother I might have looked at things differently.*

**look back** to remember something in the past *I look back and realize how lucky I was.* • *He looked back on his childhood with affection.*

**look down on sb** to think that someone is less important than you

**look forward to sth/doing sth** to feel happy and excited about something that is going to happen *I'm really looking forward to seeing him.*

**look into sth** to examine the facts about a situation *They are looking into the causes of the accident.*

**look on** to watch something happen but not become involved in it

**look on sb/sth** to think about someone or something in a particular way *We look on him almost as our own son.*

**Look out!** something you say when someone is in danger *Look out – there's a car coming!*

**look out for sb/sth** to try to notice someone or something *Look out for Anna while you're there.*

**look over sth** to examine something quickly *I'm just looking over what you've written.*

**look through sth** to read something quickly *I've looked through a few catalogues.*

**look up** to become better *Our financial situation is looking up.*

**look sth up** to look at a book or computer in order to find information *I looked it up in the dictionary.*

**look up to sb** to respect and admire someone

o━**look²** /lʊk/ *noun* **1** SEE [C] when you look at someone or something [usually singular] *Take a look at these pictures.* • *You've got your photos back – can I have a look?* **2 have/take a look** when you try to find something *I've had a look in the drawer but I can't find my passport.* **3** FACE [C] an expression on someone's face *She had a worried look about her.* • *She gave me a questioning look.* **4** FASHION [no plural] a style or fashion *the new look for the summer* **5 the look of sb/sth** the appearance of someone or something *I like the look of that new music programme they're advertising.* **6 sb's looks** a person's appearance, especially how attractive they are ➲ *See also:* **good looks**.

lookalike /ˈlʊkəlaɪk/ *noun* [C] *informal* someone who looks very similar to a famous person *an Elvis lookalike*

look-in /ˈlʊkɪn/ *noun* UK *informal* **not get a look-in** to get no chance to achieve what you want or to succeed in something *He played so well, nobody else got a look-in.*

**lookout** /'lʊkaʊt/ *noun* **1** [C] a person who watches for danger and warns other people **2 be on the lookout** to be continuing to search for something or someone *I'm always on the lookout for interesting new recipes.*

**loom¹** /luːm/ *verb* [I] **1** to appear as a large, sometimes frightening shape *Dark storm clouds loomed on the horizon.* **2** If an unpleasant event looms, it is likely to happen soon. *The threat of closure looms over the workforce.*

**loom²** /luːm/ *noun* [C] a machine for making cloth by weaving together (= crossing over) threads

**loony** /'luːni/ *noun* [C] *informal* someone who behaves in a crazy way *The man's a complete loony.* • **loony** *adj informal* crazy *loony ideas*

**loop¹** /luːp/ *noun* [C] a circle of something long and thin, such as a piece of string or wire

**loop²** /luːp/ *verb* **loop sth around/over, etc sth** to make something into the shape of a loop *Loop the rope around your waist.*

**loophole** /'luːphəʊl/ *noun* [C] a mistake in an agreement or law which gives someone the chance to avoid having to do something

o━**loose** /luːs/ *adj* **1** NOT FIXED not firmly fixed *There were some loose wires hanging out of the wall.* • *One of my buttons is loose.* **2** CLOTHES large and not fitting tightly *a loose dress/ sweater* **3** FREE An animal that is loose is free to move around. *Two lions escaped and are still loose.* **4** NOT EXACT not exact *It's only a loose translation of the poem.* • **loosely** *adv The film is based very loosely* (= not exactly) *on the novel.* ➔ *See also:* be at a loose **end¹**.

**loose** or **lose**?

Be careful, these two words look and sound similar but have completely different meanings.

**Loose** is an adjective, meaning not fixed or not tight.

*These trousers are a bit loose.*

Be careful not to use **loose** when you really mean the verb **lose**.

*I hope he doesn't lose his job.*

~~I hope he doesn't loose his job.~~

**loosen** /'luːsᵊn/ *verb* [I, T] to become loose or make something loose *He loosened his tie.*
**loosen up** to become more relaxed with other people *After a while he loosened up.*

**loot¹** /luːt/ *verb* [I, T] to steal from shops and houses during a war or period of fighting *Rioters looted the capital.*

**loot²** /luːt/ *noun* [U] goods which have been stolen

**lop** /lɒp/ *verb* **lopping**, *past* **lopped**
**lop sth off** to cut off something in one quick movement *I lopped off the biggest branches.*

**lopsided** /ˌlɒp'saɪdɪd ⑤ 'lɒpsaɪdɪd/ *adj* with one side lower than the other *a lopsided grin*

**loquacious** /ləʊ'kweɪʃəs/ *adj formal* talking a lot

**lord** /lɔːd/ *noun* **1** [C, U] (*also* **Lord**) a man of high social rank, or a title given to a man who has earned official respect, in the UK *Lord Lichfield.* • *The lords and ladies assembled in the hall.* **2 the Lord** God or Christ **3 Good Lord!** *informal* something you say when you are surprised or angry *Good Lord! Is that the time?* ➔ *See also:* **House of Lords**.

**the Lords** /lɔːdz/ (*also* **House of Lords**) *noun* [group] one of the two parts of the British parliament, with members who are chosen by the government

**lorry** /'lɒri/ *UK* (*UK/US* **truck**) *noun* [C] a large road vehicle for carrying goods from place to place ➔ *See picture at* **vehicle**.

o━**lose** /luːz/ *verb past* **lost 1** NOT FIND [T] to not be able to find someone or something *I've lost my passport.* • *She's always losing her car keys.* **2** NOT HAVE [T] to stop having someone or something that you had before *She lost a leg in a car accident.* • *I hope he doesn't lose his job.* • *He lost his mother* (= his mother died) *last year.* **3** HAVE LESS [T] to have less of something than you had before *She's lost a lot of weight.* • *He's losing his hair.* • *to lose your memory/sight* **4** NOT WIN [I, T] If you lose a game, the team or person that you are playing against wins. *Chelsea lost by a goal.* • *They're losing 3–1.* • *They hadn't lost an election in 15 years.* **5 lose faith/interest/patience, etc** to stop feeling something good *I'm rapidly losing interest in the whole subject.* • *He kept on crying and I lost my patience.* • *I've lost faith in doctors.* **6** TIME [T] If you lose a number of hours or days, you cannot work during this time. *Four million hours were lost last year through stress-related illnesses.* **7** CLOCK [T] If a clock loses time, it goes slower than it should. *My watch loses ten minutes every day.* **8** CONFUSE [T] *informal* to confuse someone so that they do not understand something *No, you've lost me there – can you explain that again?* **9 lose your balance** to fall because you are leaning too much to one side **10 lose count of sth** to forget the exact number *I've lost count of how many times I've called her.* **11 lose your life** to die *Millions of young men lost their lives in the war.* ➔ *See also:* fight a losing **battle¹**, lose your **cool³**, lose **face¹**, lose **ground¹** ➔ *See usage note at* **loose**. ➔ *See also:* lose **sight¹** of sth, lose **sleep²** over sth.

**miss** or **lose**?

Usually you **miss** something which happens, such as an event, a train leaving, or an opportunity.

*I'm sorry I'm late, I missed the bus.*

~~I'm sorry I'm late, I lost the bus.~~

Usually you **lose** a thing.

*I've lost my umbrella.*

**lose out** to not have an advantage that someone else has

**loser** /'luːzəʳ/ *noun* [C] **1** someone who does not win a game or competition *The losers of both games will play each other for third place.* **2** *informal* someone who is not successful in anything they do o━**loss** /lɒs/ *noun* **1** NOT HAVING [C, U] when you do not have someone or something that you had before, or when you have less of something than before *loss of income/memory* • *blood/ hair/weight loss* • *job losses* **2** MONEY [C, U] when a company spends more money than it earns *Both companies suffered losses this year.* **3** DISADVANTAGE [no plural] a disadvantage caused by someone leaving an organization *It would be a great loss to the department if you left.* **4 be at a loss** to not know what to do or say [+ to do sth] *I'm at a loss to explain his disappearance.* **5 a sense of loss** sadness because someone has died or left **6** DEATH [C, U] the death of a person *They never got over the loss of their son.*

o━**lost**[1] /lɒst/ *adj* **1** PERSON not knowing where you are or where you should go *I got lost on the way.* **2** OBJECT If something is lost, no one knows where it is. *Things tend to get lost when you move house.* • *Lost: black cat with white paws.* **3** NEW SITUATION not knowing what to do in a new situation *It was his first day in the office and he seemed a bit lost.* **4 be lost without sb/sth** *informal* to be unable to live or work without someone or something *She's lost without her computer.* **5 be lost on sb** If a joke or remark is lost on someone, they do not understand it. **6 Get lost!** *informal* an impolite way of telling someone to go away ⊃ *See also:* **long-lost**.

**lost**[2] /lɒst/ *past of* lose

,lost 'property *noun* [U] *UK* things that people have left in public places which are kept somewhere until the owners can collect them

o━**lot** /lɒt/ *noun* **1 a lot; lots** a large number or amount of people or things *There were a lot of people outside the building.* • *He earns lots of money.* • *I've got a lot to do this morning.* ⊃ *See usage note at* **many**. **2 a lot better/older/ quicker, etc** much better/older/quicker, etc *It's a lot better than the old system.* • *It's a lot quicker by train.* **3 the lot** *UK informal* all of an amount or number *I made enough curry for three people and he ate the lot.* • *I'm sick of the lot of them.* **4** GROUP [C] *UK* a group of people or things that you deal with together *I've already done one lot of washing.* • *I'll recycle the next lot of newspaper.* **5** AREA [C] *US* an area of land *a parking lot* • *an empty lot* **6** SALE [C] something being sold at an auction (= sale where things are sold to the people who pay the most) *Lot 3: a Victorian chest.* **7 sb's lot** the quality of someone's life and the type of experiences they have *They've done much to improve the lot of working people.*

**lotion** /ˈləʊʃ⁰n/ *noun* [C, U] a liquid that you put on your skin to make it soft or healthy *suntan lotion* • *body lotion*

**lottery** /ˈlɒt⁰ri/ *noun* [C] a way of making money by selling numbered tickets to people who then have a chance of winning a prize if their number is chosen *the national lottery*

o━**loud**[1] /laʊd/ *adj* **1** making a lot of noise *a loud noise* • *a loud voice* • *a loud explosion* **2** Loud clothes are too bright or have too many colours. *You shouldn't wear anything too loud to a job interview.* • **loudly** *adv* *She was speaking very loudly.*

**loud**[2] /laʊd/ *adv* **1** loudly *Can you speak a bit louder?* **2 out loud** If you say or read something out loud, you say or read it so that other people can hear you.

**loudspeaker** /ˌlaʊdˈspiːkəʳ/ US ˈlaʊdˌspiːkəʳ/ *noun* [C] a piece of equipment used for making voices or sounds louder

**lounge**[1] /laʊndʒ/ *noun* [C] **1** *UK* the room in a home where you sit and relax **2** *US* a room in a hotel, theatre, airport, etc where people can relax or wait

**lounge**[2] /laʊndʒ/ *verb*

**lounge about/around (sth)** to spend your time in a relaxed way, doing very little *Most days were spent lounging around the pool.*

**louse** /laʊs/ *noun* [C] *plural* **lice** /laɪs/ a very small insect that lives on the bodies or in the hair of people or animals

**lousy** /ˈlaʊzi/ *adj informal* very bad *lousy food/service* • *I felt lousy when I woke up this morning.*

**lout** /laʊt/ *noun* [C] a man who behaves in a rude or violent way

**lovable** (*also* **loveable**) /ˈlʌvəbl/ *adj* A person or animal that is lovable has qualities which make them easy to love.

o━**love**[1] /lʌv/ *verb* [T] **1** ROMANCE/SEX to like someone very much and have romantic or sexual feelings for them *Last night he told me he loved me.* • *I've only ever loved one woman.* **2** FRIENDS/FAMILY to like a friend or a person in your family very much *I'm sure he loves his kids.* **3** ENJOY to enjoy something very much or have a strong interest in something *He loves his music.* • *Like any child, Josh loved toys.* • *She loves animals.* • [+ doing sth] *I love eating out.* **4 I'd love to** used to say that you would very much like to do something that someone is offering *"I wondered if you'd like to meet up sometime?" "I'd love to."*

o━**love**[2] /lʌv/ *noun* **1** ROMANCE/SEX [U] when you like someone very much and have romantic or sexual feelings for them *He's madly in love with* (= he loves) *her.* • *I was 20 when I first fell in love* (= started to love someone). • *a love song/story* **2 make love** to have sex **3** PERSON [C] someone who you like very much and have a romantic or sexual relationship with *He was my first love.* **4** FRIENDS/FAMILY [U] when you like a friend or person in your family very much *Nothing is as strong as the love you have for your kids.* **5** INTEREST [C, U] something that interests you a lot *his love of books* **6 Love from; All my love** something you write at the end of a letter to a friend or someone in your family *Love from Mum.* • *All my love, Louise.* **7** SPEAKING TO SOMEONE *mainly UK* You call someone 'love' to show affection or to be friendly. *"Margot?" "Yes, love."* • *Two portions of chips please, love.* **8** SPORTS [U] in games such as tennis, a score of zero *She's leading by two sets to love.* ⊃ *See also:* a **labour**[1] of love.

'love af,fair *noun* [C] a romantic or sexual relationship

o━**lovely** /ˈlʌvli/ *adj* **1** pleasant or enjoyable *We had a lovely day together.* • *What lovely weather.* **2** very attractive *a lovely dress/house/village* • *You look lovely!*

**lover** /'lʌvə<sup>r</sup>/ *noun* **1** [C] If two people are lovers, they have a sexual relationship but they are not married. *She had a string of lovers before her marriage finally broke up.* **2 a book/cat/dog, etc lover** someone who is very interested in books/cats/dogs, etc *She's a real cat lover.*

**loving** /'lʌvɪŋ/ *adj* showing a lot of affection and kindness towards someone *a loving relationship* • *a loving father* • **lovingly** *adv*

○**low**<sup>1</sup> /ləʊ/ *adj* **1** NOT HIGH near the ground, not high *low aircraft* • *a low fence* • *low ceilings* **2** LEVEL below the usual level *a low income* • *low temperatures/prices* • *low energy levels* • *a low number* • *Fish is very low in* (= contains little) *fat.* **3** SOUND deep or quiet *a low voice* • *a low note* **4** LIGHTS If lights are low, they are not bright. *We have very low lighting in the main room.* **5** UNHAPPY unhappy and without energy *Illness of any sort can leave you feeling low.* ➔ *See also:* be at a low **ebb**<sup>1</sup>, keep a low **profile**<sup>1</sup>.

**low**<sup>2</sup> /ləʊ/ *adv* **1** in or to a low position or level *low-paid workers* • *Turn the oven on low.* **2** with deep notes *You can sing lower than me.*

**low**<sup>3</sup> /ləʊ/ *noun* **a new/record/all-time, etc low** the lowest level *Temperatures in the region hit a record low yesterday.*

**the lowdown** /'ləʊdaʊn/ *noun informal* the most important information about something *Jenny will give you the lowdown on what happened at yesterday's meeting.*

**lower**<sup>1</sup> /'ləʊə<sup>r</sup>/ *adj* being the bottom part of something *I've got a pain in my lower back.* • *She bit her lower lip.*

**lower**<sup>2</sup> /'ləʊə<sup>r</sup>/ *verb* [T] **1** to move something to a low position *They lowered the coffin into the grave.* **2** to reduce the amount of something *I'll join if they lower the entrance fee.*

**lower 'case** *noun* [U] letters of the alphabet which are not written as capital letters, for example a, b, c

**low-fat** /,ləʊ'fæt/ *adj* Low-fat foods do not contain much fat. *low-fat cheese* • *a low-fat diet*

**low-key** /,ləʊ'kiː/ *adj* not attracting attention *The reception itself was surprisingly low-key.*

**lowly** /'ləʊli/ *adj* not important or respected *He took a lowly job in an insurance firm.*

**loyal** /ˈlɔɪəl/ *adj* always liking and supporting someone or something, sometimes when other people do not *a loyal supporter* • *She's very loyal to her friends.* ➔ *Opposite* **disloyal**. • **loyally** *adv*

**loyalties** /'lɔɪəltiz/ *noun* [plural] a feeling of support for someone *My loyalties to my family come before work.*

**loyalty** /'lɔɪəlti/ *noun* [U] the quality of being loyal *Your loyalty to the company is impressive.* ➔ *Opposite* **disloyalty**.

**lozenge** /'lɒzɪndʒ/ *noun* [C] a sweet which you suck to make your throat feel better

**LP** /,el'piː/ *noun* [C] a record that has about 25 minutes of music on each side

**L-plate** /'elpleɪt/ *noun* [C] UK a red and white 'L' symbol on the car of someone learning to drive

**Ltd** *written abbreviation for* limited company (= used after the name of some companies) *Pinewood Supplies Ltd.*

**lubricant** /'luːbrɪkənt/ *noun* [C, U] a liquid, such as oil, which is used to make the parts of an engine move smoothly together

**lubricate** /'luːbrɪkeɪt/ *verb* [T] to put a lubricant on something • **lubrication** /,luːbrɪ'keɪʃ°n/ *noun* [U]

**lucid** /'luːsɪd/ *adj* **1** clear and easy to understand *a lucid account* **2** able to think and speak clearly *In a lucid moment, she spoke about her son.* • **lucidly** *adv*

○**luck** /lʌk/ *noun* [U] **1** good and bad things caused by chance and not by your own actions *It was just luck that I asked for a job at the right time.* • *Then I met this gorgeous woman and I couldn't believe my luck.* • *He seems to have had a lot of bad luck in his life.* **2** success *Have you had any luck* (= succeeded in) *finding your bag? • He's been trying to find work but with no luck so far.* **3 be in luck** *informal* to be able to have or do what you want *"Do you have any tuna sandwiches?" "You're in luck – there's one left."* **4 Good luck!** something you say to someone when you hope that they will be successful *Good luck with your exam!* **5 Bad/Hard luck!** used to show sympathy when someone is unsuccessful or unlucky *"They've run out of tickets." "Oh, bad luck!"* **6 the luck of the draw** If something is the luck of the draw, it is the result of chance and you have no control over it. ➔ *See also:* a **stroke**<sup>1</sup> of luck.

○**lucky** /'lʌki/ *adj* **1** having good things happen to you *"I'm going on holiday." "Lucky you!"* • *The lucky winner will be able to choose from three different holidays.* • *If you're lucky, they might still be serving lunch.* • [+ to do sth] *You're lucky to have such a nice office to work in.* **2** If an object is lucky, some people believe that it gives you luck. *I chose six – it's my lucky number.* ➔ *Opposite* **unlucky**. • **luckily** *adv Luckily I had some money with me.* ➔ *See also:* **happy-go-lucky**.

**lucrative** /'luːkrətɪv/ *adj* If something is lucrative, it makes a lot of money. *a lucrative contract/job/offer*

**ludicrous** /'luːdɪkrəs/ *adj* stupid *a ludicrous idea/suggestion* • **ludicrously** *adv*

**lug** /lʌg/ *verb* [T] **lugging**, *past* **lugged** *informal* to carry or pull a heavy object *You don't want to lug your suitcase across London.*

**luggage** /'lʌgɪdʒ/ *noun* [U] bags and cases that you carry with you when you are travelling ➔ *See also:* **hand luggage**.

**luggage**

backpack

holdall *UK*, carryall *US*

suitcase

**lukewarm** /ˌluːkˈwɔːm/ *adj* **1** A liquid which is lukewarm is only slightly warm. *Dissolve yeast and one tablespoon of sugar in lukewarm water.* **2** showing little interest or enthusiasm *She seemed rather lukewarm about the idea.* • *a lukewarm response*

**lull¹** /lʌl/ *verb* [T] to make someone feel calm and make them want to sleep *Soft music **lulled** him **to sleep**.*

**lull sb into sth/doing sth** to make someone feel safe so that you can then trick them

**lull²** /lʌl/ *noun* [C] a short period of calm in which little happens *a lull in the conversation/traffic*

**lullaby** /ˈlʌləbaɪ/ *noun* [C] a song which you sing to children to make them sleep

**lumber¹** /ˈlʌmbə<sup>r</sup>/ *verb* **lumber along/around/off, etc** to move slowly with heavy steps *The bear lumbered off into the forest.*

**be lumbered with sth/sb** *mainly UK* to have to deal with something or someone that you do not want to *I've been lumbered with my neighbours' cat while they're away.*

**lumber²** /ˈlʌmbə<sup>r</sup>/ *US* (*UK* **timber**) *noun* [U] wood that is used for building

**lumberjack** /ˈlʌmbədʒæk/ *noun* [C] a person whose job is to cut down trees in a forest

**luminary** /ˈluːmɪn<sup>ə</sup>ri/ *noun* [C] *formal* a famous person who is respected for their skills or knowledge

**luminous** /ˈluːmɪnəs/ *adj* Something that is luminous shines in the dark.

**lump¹** /lʌmp/ *noun* [C] **1** a piece of a solid substance with no particular shape *a lump of coal* • *You don't want lumps in the sauce.* **2** a hard piece of tissue under the skin caused by injury or illness *She found a lump in her breast.*

**lump²** /lʌmp/ *verb*

**lump sth/sb together** to put different groups together and think about them or deal with them in the same way *American and Canadian authors tend to be lumped together.*

**ˌlump ˈsum** *noun* [C] a large amount of money given as a single payment *She received a tax-free lump sum on leaving the company.*

**lumpy** /ˈlʌmpi/ *adj* covered with or containing lumps (= bits of solid substance) *a lumpy sauce*

**lunacy** /ˈluːnəsi/ *noun* [U] stupid behaviour that will have bad results *It was lunacy spending all that money.*

**lunar** /ˈluːnə<sup>r</sup>/ *adj* [always before noun] relating to the moon

**lunatic** /ˈluːnətɪk/ *noun* [C] someone who behaves in a crazy way *He drives like a lunatic.*

○━**lunch¹** /lʌnʃ/ *noun* [C, U] a meal that you eat in the middle of the day **➲** *See also:* **packed lunch**.

**lunch²** /lʌnʃ/ *verb* [I] to eat lunch

**luncheon** /ˈlʌnʃən/ *noun* [C] *formal* lunch

**lunchtime** /ˈlʌnʃtaɪm/ *noun* [C, U] the time when lunch is eaten

**lung** /lʌŋ/ *noun* [C] one of the two organs inside your chest that are used for breathing *lung cancer*

**lurch** /lɜːtʃ/ *verb* **lurch forward/towards, etc** to suddenly move in a way that is not controlled *The car lurched forward before hitting the tree.*

**lure¹** /lʊə<sup>r</sup>/ *verb* [T] to persuade someone to go somewhere or do something by offering them something exciting *It seems that he was **lured into** a trap.* • *They had been **lured to** the big city by the promise of high wages.*

**lure²** /lʊə<sup>r</sup>/ *noun* [U] the power to attract people *the lure of fame/power/money*

**lurid** /ˈlʊərɪd/ *adj* **1** shocking in a way that involves sex or violence *lurid details/stories* **2** too brightly coloured *a lurid green miniskirt*

**lurk** /lɜːk/ *verb* [I] to wait somewhere secretly, especially before doing something bad *Someone was lurking in the shadows.*

**lush** /lʌʃ/ *adj* A lush area has a lot of healthy grass, plants, or trees.

**lust¹** /lʌst/ *noun* [U] **1** a strong feeling of sexual attraction to someone **2** when you want something very much *a lust for power*

**lust²** /lʌst/ *verb*

**lust after sb** to feel strong sexual attraction for someone

**lust after sth** to want something very much *to lust after fame/power*

**Lutheran** /ˈluːθ<sup>ə</sup>r<sup>ə</sup>n/ *adj* belonging or relating to a Christian group based on the teachings of Martin Luther *the Lutheran Church* • Lutheran *noun* [C]

**luxurious** /lʌɡˈʒʊəriəs/ *adj* very comfortable and expensive *a luxurious hotel* • *luxurious fabrics*

**luxury** /ˈlʌkʃ<sup>ə</sup>ri/ *noun* **1** COMFORT/PLEASURE [U] great comfort or pleasure from expensive or beautiful things *to live in luxury* • *a luxury apartment/car* **2** NOT NECESSARY [C] something expensive that you enjoy but do not need *It's nice to buy people the little luxuries that they wouldn't buy themselves.* **3** RARE PLEASURE [U, no plural] something which gives you a lot of pleasure but which you cannot often do *A day off work is such a luxury.*

**lying** /ˈlaɪɪŋ/ *present participle of* lie¹,²

**lyrical** /ˈlɪrɪk<sup>ə</sup>l/ *adj* expressing the writer's emotions in a beautiful way *lyrical poetry/verse*

**lyrics** /ˈlɪrɪks/ *noun* [plural] the words of a song

**M, m** /em/ the thirteenth letter of the alphabet

**m** *written abbreviation for* metre (= a unit of length)

**MA** /ˌemˈeɪ/ *noun* [C] *abbreviation for* Master of Arts: a higher university qualification in an arts (= not science) subject

**ma'am** /mæm, mɑːm/ *US short for* madam *Can I help you, Ma'am?*

**mac** /mæk/ *noun* [C] *UK* a coat that you wear in the rain

**macabre** /məˈkɑːbrə/ *adj* strange and frightening, and often connected with death *a macabre story*

**macaroni** /ˌmæk°rˈəʊni/ *noun* [U] pasta that is shaped like small tubes

**machete** /məˈʃeti/ *noun* [C] a large knife with a wide blade

**machinations** /ˌmæʃɪˈneɪʃ°nz/ *noun* [plural] complicated and secret plans and activities *political machinations*

⊶**machine** /məˈʃiːn/ *noun* [C] **1** [EQUIPMENT] a piece of equipment with moving parts that uses power to do a particular job *a fax machine ● a coffee machine ● Clothes are generally sewn by machine these days.* **2** [GROUP] a group of people all working together to achieve the same result *a political/war machine* **3** [COMPUTER] a computer ⊃ *See also:* **answering machine, cash machine, sewing machine, slot machine, vending machine, washing machine.**

**ma'chine ˌgun** *noun* [C] a gun that fires a lot of bullets very quickly

**machinery** /məˈʃiːn°ri/ *noun* [U] **1** machines, often large machines *industrial/farm machinery* **2** the system that a group of people uses to achieve something *the machinery of government*

**macho** /ˈmætʃəʊ ⑤ ˈmɑːtʃəʊ/ *adj informal* Men who are macho emphasize their traditional male qualities, such as physical strength, and do not show emotion.

**mackerel** /ˈmæk°l/ *noun* [C, U] *plural* **mackerel** or **mackerels** a type of sea fish, or the meat from this fish

**mackintosh** /ˈmækɪntɒʃ/ *noun* [C] *old-fashioned* a mac

⊶**mad** /mæd/ *adj* **1** [CRAZY] *informal* stupid or crazy [+ to do sth] *You're mad to walk home alone at night.* **2** [ANGRY] *mainly US* angry *Were your parents mad at you when you came home late?* **3** **go mad** *UK informal* **a** [ANGRY] to become very angry *Dad'll go mad when he finds out you took the car.* **b** [EXCITED] to suddenly become very excited *When the band arrived on stage, the crowd went mad.* **4** [ILL] mentally ill **5** [NOT CONTROLLED] not controlled *We made a mad dash for the exit.* **6** **be mad about sb/sth** *informal* to love someone or something *She's mad about Hugh Grant. ● Jo's mad about skiing.* **7** **like mad** *informal* **a** [QUICKLY] If you run, work, etc like mad, you do it very quickly and

with a lot of energy. **b** [PAIN] If something hurts like mad, it hurts a lot.

**mad** or **mentally ill**?

If someone has mental health problems, it is not polite to say that they are **mad**, use **mentally ill** instead.

**madam** /ˈmædəm/ *noun formal* **1** (*also* **Madam**) You call a woman 'madam' when you are speaking to her politely. *This way, madam.* **2** **Madam** You write 'Madam' at the beginning of a formal letter to a woman when you do not know her name. *Dear Madam, I am writing to...*

**made** /meɪd/ *past of* make

**-made** /meɪd/ *suffix* ⊃ *See* **man-made, ready-made, self-made, tailor-made.**

**madhouse** /ˈmædhaʊs/ *noun* [C] *plural* **madhouses** *informal* a place where there is a lot of uncontrolled noise and activity *With five of us trying to get ready for the party at the same time, the place was a madhouse.*

**madly** /ˈmædli/ *adv* **1** with a lot of energy and enthusiasm *We cheered madly as the team came out onto the field.* **2** **be madly in love** to love someone very much *He's madly in love with Denise.*

**madman, madwoman** /ˈmædmən, ˈmædˌwʊmən/ *noun* [C] *plural* **madmen, madwomen** a crazy person *Was he a madman or a genius? ● He was running around like a madman.*

**madness** /ˈmædnəs/ *noun* [U] **1** stupid or dangerous behaviour *It would be madness to give up your job when you've just bought a house.* **2** mental illness

**maestro** /ˈmaɪstrəʊ/ *noun* [C] someone who is very good at something, especially playing music

**the mafia** /ˈmæfiə ⑤ ˈmɑːfiə/ *noun* a large group of organized criminals *Drug-smuggling activities have been linked to the Mafia.*

⊶**magazine** /ˌmægəˈziːn/ *noun* [C] a thin book published every week or month, that has shiny, colourful pages with articles and pictures *a fashion/news magazine*

**maggot** /ˈmægət/ *noun* [C] a small insect with a soft body and no legs that often lives in decaying food

⊶**magic¹** /ˈmædʒɪk/ *noun* [U] **1** [SPECIAL POWERS] special powers that can make things happen that seem impossible *Do you believe in magic?* **2** [ENTERTAINMENT] clever actions intended to entertain people, often making objects appear and disappear **3** [SPECIAL QUALITY] a quality that makes something or someone seem special or exciting *No one could fail to be charmed by the magic of this beautiful city.* **4** **as if by magic** in a way that is surprising and impossible to explain *Food would appear on the table every day, as if by magic.* ⊃ *See also:* **black magic.**

**magic²** /ˈmædʒɪk/ *adj* **1** with special powers *a magic spell/wand* **2** relating to magic [ENTERTAINMENT] *a magic trick* **3** **magic moments** special and exciting experiences *There were some magic moments on that trip.*

**magical** /ˈmædʒɪk°l/ *adj* **1** with special powers

*Diamonds were once thought to have **magical powers**.* **2** special or exciting *It was a magical night.* • magically *adv I knew my problems would not just magically disappear.*

magician /mə'dʒɪʃ°n/ *noun* [C] **1** someone who entertains people by performing magic tricks **2** a character in old stories who has magic powers

magistrate /'mædʒɪstreɪt/ *noun* [C] a type of judge (= person who decides what punishments should be given) who deals with less serious crimes *Two men are due to appear before a magistrate next week.*

magnate /'mægneɪt/ *noun* [C] someone who is rich and successful in business *a media magnate*

magnesium /mæg'niːziəm/ *noun* [U] a metallic element that burns very brightly, used to make fireworks (= explosives used to entertain people)

magnet /'mægnət/ *noun* **1** [C] an iron object that makes pieces of iron or steel (= metal made with iron) move towards it **2 be a magnet for sb** If a place or event is a magnet for people, a lot of people go there. *Airports are a magnet for thieves.*

**magnet**

magnetic /mæg'netɪk/ *adj* **1** with the power of a magnet *a magnetic field* **2 magnetic tape/disk/storage, etc** equipment for storing information from a computer **3** having a character that attracts people to you

magnificent /mæg'nɪfɪs°nt/ *adj* very good or very beautiful *a magnificent view* • magnificently *adv*

magnify /'mægnɪfaɪ/ *verb* [T] **1** to make an object look larger than it is by looking through special equipment *The cells are first magnified under a microscope.* **2** to make a bad situation worse *All your problems are magnified when you're ill.*

'magnifying ,glass *noun* [C] a piece of curved glass which makes objects look larger than they are

magnitude /'mægnɪtjuːd/ *noun* [U] *formal* the large size or importance of something *People were still unaware of **the magnitude of** the problem.*

mahogany /mə'hɒg°ni/ *noun* [U] a dark, red-brown wood used to make furniture

maid /meɪd/ *noun* [C] a woman who works as a servant in a hotel or in someone's home

maiden¹ /'meɪd°n/ *noun* [C] *literary old-fashioned* a young woman who is not married

maiden² /'meɪd°n/ *adj* **a maiden flight/ voyage** the first journey of a new aircraft or ship

,maiden 'name *noun* [C] the family name that a woman has before she gets married

o⟶mail¹ /meɪl/ *noun* [U] **1** letters and parcels that are brought by post *We got loads of mail this morning.* **2** *mainly US* the system by which letters and parcels are taken and brought *Send it by mail.* • *The letter is in the mail.* ➔ *See also:* **email, junk mail, snail mail, surface mail, voice mail.**

mail² /meɪl/ *verb* [T] *mainly US* to send a letter or parcel or email something *Could you mail it to me?*

mailbox /'meɪlbɒks/ *noun* [C] *US* **1** a small box outside your home where letters are delivered **2** (*UK* **letterbox, post box**) a large, metal container in a public place where you can post letters

'mailing ,list *noun* [C] a list of names and addresses that an organization uses in order to send information to people

mailman /'meɪlmæn/ *US* (*UK* **postman**) *noun* [C] *plural* **mailmen** a man who takes and brings letters and parcels as a job

'mail ,order *noun* [U] a way of buying goods by ordering them from a catalogue (= book) and receiving them by post

maim /meɪm/ *verb* [T] to injure someone permanently *Thousands of innocent people have been killed or maimed by landmines.*

o⟶main¹ /meɪn/ *adj* [always before noun] **1** most important or largest *the main problem/reason* • *The main airport is 15 miles from the capital.* **2 the main thing** the most important fact in a situation *You're happy and that's the main thing.* **3 in the main** generally or mostly *Her friends are teachers in the main.*

main² /meɪn/ *noun* [C] **gas/water main** a pipe that carries gas or water to a building

mainframe /'meɪnfreɪm/ *noun* [C] a large, powerful computer which many people can use at the same time

mainland /'meɪnlənd/ *noun* **the mainland** the main part of a country, not including the islands around it *A daily ferry links the islands to the mainland.* • mainland *adj* [always before noun] *mainland Britain*

o⟶mainly /'meɪnli/ *adv* mostly or to a large degree *The waitresses are mainly French.*

the mains /meɪnz/ *noun* [group] *UK* **1** the system of pipes or wires that carries gas, water, or electricity to a building *The house isn't connected to the mains yet.* **2** the place inside a building where you can connect a machine to a supply of electricity *Is the cooker turned off at the mains?*

mainstay /'meɪnsteɪ/ *noun* **a/the mainstay of sth** the most important thing or activity *Cattle farming is the mainstay of the country's economy.*

mainstream /'meɪnstriːm/ *noun* **the mainstream** the beliefs or way of living accepted by most people *The party is now in the mainstream of politics.* • mainstream *adj* [always before noun] *mainstream culture/politics*

o⟶maintain /meɪn'teɪn/ *verb* [T] **1** NOT CHANGE to make a situation or activity continue in the same way *The army has been brought in to maintain order in the region.* **2** CONDITION to keep a building or area in good condition *A large house is very expensive to maintain.*

**M**

**3** SPEAK TRUTH *formal* to say that you are certain something is true [+ (that)] *He has always maintained that he is innocent.*

**maintenance** /'meɪntᵊnəns/ *noun* [U] **1** the work that is done to keep something in good condition *car maintenance* • *I want a garden that's very low maintenance* (= easy to look after). **2** *UK* regular amounts of money that someone must pay after they have left their family so that the family still has money to live *child maintenance*

**maize** /meɪz/ *UK* (*US* **corn**) *noun* [U] a tall plant with yellow seeds that are eaten as food

**majestic** /mə'dʒestɪk/ *adj* very beautiful or powerful in a way that people admire *majestic scenery*

**majesty** /'mædʒəsti/ *noun* **1** [U] the quality of being majestic *the majesty of the pyramids* **2 His/Her/Your Majesty** used when you are speaking to or about a king or queen *His Majesty King Edward VII*

o–**major**¹ /'meɪdʒəʳ/ *adj* **1** [always before noun] more important or more serious than other things or people of a similar type *a major problem/issue* • *a major city* • *America has played a major role in the peace process.* **2** in music, belonging to a key (= set of musical notes) which often produces a happy sound ⊃ *Opposite* **minor**.

**major**² /'meɪdʒəʳ/ *noun* [C] **1** *US* the most important subject that a college or university student studies, or the student who is studying *What's your major?* • *Diane's an English major.* **2** an officer of middle rank in the army or air force

**major**³ /'meɪdʒəʳ/ *verb*

**major in sth** If you major in a subject, it is the most important part of your course at a college or university.

o–**majority** /mə'dʒɒrəti/ *noun* **1** [no plural] more than half of a group of people or things *The majority of people in this country own their houses.* • *The vast majority of smokers claim they would like to give up.* **2 be in a/the majority** to be larger than other similar groups *Women are in the majority in the publishing world.* **3** [C] in an election, the difference between the number of votes for the winner, and the votes for the party that came second *Labour has a strong majority.* ⊃ *Opposite* **minority**.

o–**make**¹ /meɪk/ *verb* [T] *past* **made 1** CREATE to produce or create something *Shall I make some coffee?* • *They've made a film about her life.* • *My mother made the curtains.* ⊃ *See usage note at* **do**. **2 make a promise/remark/mistake, etc** to promise something, to say something, to do something wrong, etc *We have to make a decision today.* • *You're making a big mistake.* • *She made some useful suggestions.* **3 make sb do sth** to force someone to do something *You can't make me go.* **4 make sb/sth happy/sad/ difficult, etc** to cause someone or something to become happy, sad, difficult, etc *You've made me very happy.* • *This is the song that made her a star.* • *You're making things difficult for yourself.* **5** GO TO to be able to go to an event *I'm afraid I can't make the meeting this afternoon.* **6** EARN MONEY If you make an amount of money, you earn it. *He makes £20,000 a year.* **7** NUMBERS If two or more numbers make a

particular amount, that is the amount when they are added together. *That makes $40 altogether.* **8** PERSONAL QUALITIES [T] to have the right qualities to become a father or mother or to do a particular job *Andy would make a good teacher.* **9** GIVE A JOB [+ **two objects**] to give someone a particular job *They made her a director of the company.* **10 make an appointment** to arrange to do something at a particular time *I've made an appointment with the doctor.* **11 make the bed** to make the sheets and covers on a bed tidy **12 make time** to leave enough time to do something although you are busy [+ to do sth] *You must make time to do your homework.* • **13 make do (with)** to accept that something is less good than you would like *If we can't get a bigger room we'll have to make do with this.* **14 make it** *informal* **a** ARRIVE to manage to arrive at a place *Will we make it in time for the film?* **b** SUCCEED to be successful *Very few actors actually make it.*

**make for sth** to move towards a place *He got up and made for the exit.*

**make sth into sth** to change something into something else *We're going to make the spare room into an office.*

**make of sb/sth** If you ask someone what they make of someone or something, you want to know their opinion about that person or thing. *What do you make of this letter?* • *I don't know what to make of him.*

**make off with sth** *informal* to steal something *Somebody broke into the shop and made off with several TVs and videos.*

**make sth/sb out** to be able to see, hear, or understand something or someone *We could just make out a building through the trees.*

**make out sth** to say something that is not true [+ (that)] *He made out that he'd been living in Boston all year.*

**make out** *US informal* **1** to deal with a situation, usually in a successful way *How is Jake making out in his new school?* **2** to kiss and touch someone in a sexual way

**make sth up** to say or write something that is not true *I made up some story about having to go and see my sick mother.*

**make up sth** to form the whole of an amount *Women make up nearly 50% of medical school entrants.*

**make up** to become friendly with someone again after you have argued with them *Have you made up with Daryl yet?*

**make up for sth** to reduce the bad effect of something, or make something bad become something good *I hope this money will make up for the inconvenience.*

**make it up to sb** to do something good for someone because you have done something bad to them in the past *I'm sorry I missed your birthday. I'll make it up to you, I promise.*

**make**² /meɪk/ *noun* [C] the name of a company that makes a particular product *I like your stereo. What make is it?*

**make-believe** /'meɪkbɪ,liːv/ *noun* [U] when you pretend that something is real *Disneyland creates a world of make-believe.*

**makeover** /'meɪk,əʊvəʳ/ *noun* [C] when you

suddenly improve your appearance by wearing better clothes, cutting your hair, etc *to have a makeover*

**maker** /'meɪkə'/ *noun* [C] the person or company that makes a product *makers of top quality electrical products*

**makeshift** /'meɪkʃɪft/ *adj* [always before noun] temporary and low quality *makeshift shelters*

**make-up, makeup** /'meɪkʌp/ *noun* [U] coloured substances that a woman puts on her face in order to make herself more attractive *to put on/take off make-up* • *She doesn't wear much make-up.*

**make-up**

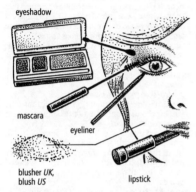

eyeshadow

mascara

eyeliner

blusher *UK*, blush *US*

lipstick

**making** /'meɪkɪŋ/ *noun* [U] **1** the process of making or producing something *There's an article on **the making of** a television series.* • *the art of film making* **2** be a sth/sb in the making to be likely to develop into a particular thing or type of person *What we're seeing is a disaster in the making.* **3** have the makings of sth to seem likely to develop into something *She has the makings of a great violinist.*

**malaria** /mə'leəriə/ *noun* [U] a serious disease that you can get in hot countries if a mosquito (= small insect) bites you

o–**male**[1] /meɪl/ *adj* belonging to or relating to the sex that cannot have babies *a male colleague* ↗ *Opposite* **female**.

**male**[2] /meɪl/ *noun* [C] a male person or animal *In 1987, 27 percent of adult males smoked.*

**male 'chauvinist** *noun* [C] a man who believes that men are better or more important than women

**malice** /'mælɪs/ *noun* [U] when you want to harm or upset someone *There was no malice in her comments.*

**malicious** /mə'lɪʃəs/ *adj* intended to harm or upset someone *malicious gossip*

**malignant** /mə'lɪɡnənt/ *adj* A malignant tumour (= group of diseased cells) is one that could cause death.

**mall** /mɔːl/ *noun* (*also* **shopping mall**) *noun* [C] a large, covered shopping area

**malleable** /'mæliəbl/ *adj* **1** easy to bend or make into a different shape **2** *formal* easily influenced and controlled

**mallet** /'mælɪt/ *noun* [C] a tool like a hammer with a large, flat end made of wood or rubber ↗ *See picture at* **tool**.

**malnutrition** /,mælnju:'trɪʃ°n/ *noun* [U] a serious illness caused by too little food

**malpractice** /,mæl'præktɪs/ *noun* [U] when a doctor, lawyer, etc does not do one of their duties or makes a mistake at work *medical malpractice*

**malt** /mɔːlt/ *noun* [U] a substance made from grain that is used to make drinks, for example beer and whisky (= strong alcoholic drink)

**mama** /mə'mɑː/ *noun* [C] *mainly US* a child's word for 'mother'

**mammal** /'mæm°l/ *noun* [C] an animal that feeds its babies on milk from its body

**mammoth** /'mæməθ/ *adj* very large *a mammoth task/project*

o–**man**[1] /mæn/ *noun plural* **men 1** [C] an adult male human *a young/tall man* • *men and women* **2** [U] used to refer to both men and women *Man is still more intelligent than the cleverest robot.* ↗ *See also:* **best man, garbage man, no-man's land**, the man in the **street**.

**man**[2] /mæn/ *verb* [T] **manning**, *past* **manned** to be present somewhere, especially in order to operate a machine *The emergency room is manned 24 hours a day.*

o–**manage** /'mænɪdʒ/ *verb* **1** DO SUCCESSFULLY [I, T] to do something or deal with something successfully *Will you be able to manage on your own?* • [+ to do sth] *Anyway, we managed to get there on time.* **2** CONTROL [T] to be in control of an office, shop, team, etc *He used to manage the bookshop on King Street.* **3** USE TIME/MONEY [T] to use or organize your time or money *He's no good at managing his money.* **4** HAVE ENOUGH MONEY [I] to have enough money to live *How can anyone **manage on** such a low income?*

**manageable** /'mænɪdʒəbl/ *adj* easy to control *Are they going to reduce classes to a more manageable size?*

o–**management** /'mænɪdʒmənt/ *noun* **1** [U] being in control of an office, shop, team, etc *management skills/training* **2** [group] the people who are in control of an office, shop, team, etc *Management is considering your proposals.* • *middle/senior management*

**manager** /'mænɪdʒə'/ *noun* [C] someone in control of an office, shop, team, etc *a sales manager* • *She's the manager of the local sports club.*

**managerial** /,mænə'dʒɪəriəl/ *adj* relating to a manager or management *managerial experience/skills*

,**managing di'rector** *noun* [C] *mainly UK* the main person in control of a company

**mandate** /'mændeɪt/ *noun* [C] *formal* support for action given to someone by the people voting for them *The electorate have given them a clear **mandate for** social reform.*

**mandatory** /'mændət°ri/ *adj formal* If something is mandatory, it must be done.

**mane** /meɪn/ *noun* [C] the long, thick hair that grows on the necks of animals such as horses or lions

**maneuver**[1] *US* (*UK* **manoeuvre**) /mə'nu:və'/ *noun* [C] **1** a movement that needs care or skill

**2** a clever action, usually done to trick someone *a political/tactical maneuver*

**maneuver²** *US* (*UK* **manoeuvre**) /məˈnuːvəʳ/ *verb* [I, T] to move with care or skill *I find big cars difficult to maneuver.*

**mangled** /ˈmæŋɡld/ *adj* badly crushed and damaged *a mangled body*

**mango** /ˈmæŋɡəʊ/ *noun* [C] *plural* **mangoes** or **mangos** a tropical fruit that has a green skin and is orange inside

**manhood** /ˈmænhʊd/ *noun* [U] the qualities related to being a man and not a boy

**mania** /ˈmeɪniə/ *noun* [U] extreme enthusiasm or interest *football mania*

**maniac** /ˈmeɪniæk/ *noun* [C] *informal* someone who behaves in an extreme or uncontrolled way *a sex maniac* • *He drives like a maniac.*

**manic** /ˈmænɪk/ *adj* behaving in an excited and uncontrolled way

**manicure** /ˈmænɪkjʊəʳ/ *noun* [C, U] when someone makes your hands look attractive by cleaning and cutting your nails, etc *to have a manicure*

**manifest¹** /ˈmænɪfest/ *verb* [T] *formal* to show a quality or condition [**often reflexive**] *Grief manifests itself in a number of different ways.*

**manifest²** /ˈmænɪfest/ *adj* [**always before noun**] *formal* obvious *her manifest lack of interest*

**manifestation** /ˌmænɪfesˈteɪʃən/ *noun* [C, U] *formal* something which shows that a quality or condition exists *one of the manifestations of the disease*

**manifesto** /ˌmænɪˈfestəʊ/ *noun* [C] when a political group says publicly what it intends to do

**manipulate** /məˈnɪpjəleɪt/ *verb* [T] to control someone or something in a clever way so that they do what you want them to do *She knows how to manipulate the press.* • manipulation /məˌnɪpjəˈleɪʃən/ *noun* [U] *the manipulation of language*

**manipulative** /məˈnɪpjələtɪv/ *adj* A manipulative person controls people in a clever and unpleasant way. *a devious, manipulative little boy*

**mankind** /mænˈkaɪnd/ *noun* [U] all people, considered as a group *the history of mankind*

**manly** /ˈmænli/ *adj* having the qualities and appearance that people think a man should have *a deep, manly voice*

**man-made** /ˌmænˈmeɪd/ *adj* not natural, but made by people *man-made fibres* • *a man-made lake*

**manned** /mænd/ *adj* A place or vehicle that is manned has people working in it. *a manned space flight*

○━**manner** /ˈmænəʳ/ *noun* [**no plural**] **1** the way in which a person talks and behaves with other people *an aggressive/friendly manner* **2** the way something happens or something is done *They dealt with the problem in a very efficient manner.*

**mannerism** /ˈmænərɪzəm/ *noun* [C] something strange that someone often does with their face, hands, or voice, and that is part of their personality

**manners** /ˈmænəz/ *noun* [**plural**] polite ways of behaving with other people *bad/good manners* • *table manners* • *He needs to be taught some manners.*

**manoeuvre¹** *UK* (*US* **maneuver**) /məˈnuːvəʳ/ *noun* [C] **1** a movement that needs care or skill **2** a clever action, usually done to trick someone *a political/tactical manoeuvre*

**manoeuvre²** *UK* (*US* **maneuver**) /məˈnuːvəʳ/ *verb* [I, T] to move with care or skill *I find big cars difficult to manoeuvre.*

**manpower** /ˈmænˌpaʊəʳ/ *noun* [U] the people needed or available to do a job *a manpower shortage*

**mansion** /ˈmænʃən/ *noun* [C] a very large house

**manslaughter** /ˈmænˌslɔːtəʳ/ *noun* [U] the crime of killing someone without intending to kill them

**mantelpiece** /ˈmæntəlpiːs/ (*also US* **mantel**) *noun* [C] the shelf above a fireplace (= place in a room where wood, etc is burned) *There was an old family photo on the mantelpiece.* ➔ *See colour picture* **The Living Room** *on page Centre 11.*

**mantra** /ˈmæntrə/ *noun* [C] an idea or belief that people often say but do not think about *the mantra of 'democratic reform'*

**manual¹** /ˈmænjuəl/ *adj* using your hands *manual labour/work* • *a manual control/gearbox* • manually *adv*

**manual²** /ˈmænjuəl/ *noun* [C] a book that tells you how to use something or do something *an instruction manual*

**manufacture** /ˌmænjəˈfæktʃəʳ/ *verb* [T] to produce something, usually in large numbers in a factory *Local industries manufacture plastic products, boats, and clothing.* • manufacture *noun* [U] *the manufacture of computers/margarine*

**manufacturer** /ˌmænjəˈfæktʃərəʳ/ *noun* [C] a company that manufactures something *a shoe manufacturer*

**manufacturing** /ˌmænjəˈfæktʃərɪŋ/ *noun* [U] the production of something, usually in large numbers in a factory *car/food manufacturing* • *manufacturing industry*

**manure** /məˈnjʊəʳ/ *noun* [U] solid waste from animals that is used to make plants grow well *cow/horse manure*

**manuscript** /ˈmænjəskrɪpt/ *noun* [C] a piece of writing or music that has been written, but not published

○━**many** /ˈmeni/ *pronoun, quantifier* **1** used mainly in negative sentences and questions to mean 'a large number of' *I don't have many clothes.* • *Were there many cars on the road?* • *I've got so many things to do this morning.* • *You've given me too many potatoes* (= more than I want). • *There aren't as many people here as last year.* **2 how many** used in questions to ask about the number of something *How many hours a week do you work?* • *How many do you want?* **3 as many as** used before a number or amount to show that the number or amount is large *As many as 6000 people may have been infected with the disease.*

**USAGE**

**many, much,** or **a lot of**?

Many is used with countable nouns in negative sentences and questions. Much is used with uncountable nouns in negative sentences and questions.

*Do you have many friends?*

*I don't earn much money.*

**A lot of** can be used to mean **much** or **many**. In positive sentences it sounds formal to use **much** or **many**. You use **a lot of** instead.

*There was much enthusiasm for the project.*

*There was a lot of enthusiasm for the project.*

---

**Maori** /'mauəri/ *adj* relating or belonging to the original group of people who lived in New Zealand *Maori culture* • **Maori** *noun* [C] a Maori person

**map** /mæp/ *noun* [C] a picture that shows where countries, towns, roads, rivers, etc are *a road/town map* • *a large-scale map of Europe*

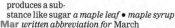
map

**maple** /'meɪpl/ *noun* [C, U] a tree that has colourful leaves in the autumn and that produces a substance like sugar *a maple leaf* • *maple syrup*

**Mar** *written abbreviation for* March

**mar** /mɑːʳ/ *verb* [T] **marring**, *past* **marred** *formal* to spoil something [often passive] *The evening was marred by Meg's appalling behaviour.*

**marathon** /'mærəθ³n/ *noun* [C] **1** a race in which people run for about 26 miles/42 km *the London marathon* • *a marathon runner* **2** a very long event *a dance marathon*

**marble** /'mɑːbl/ *noun* [U] hard, smooth stone which is often used for decoration *green/pink marble* • *a marble statue*

**march¹** /mɑːtʃ/ *noun* [C] **1** an organized walk by a group to show that they disagree with something *to go on a march* **2** the special type of walking that soldiers do

**march²** /mɑːtʃ/ *verb* [I] **1** to walk somewhere as a group to show that you disagree with something *They marched to London to protest against health cuts.* **2** When soldiers march, they walk together with regular steps. **3** **march off/up/down, etc** to walk somewhere fast, often because you are angry *She marched off angrily.*

**March** /mɑːtʃ/ *(written abbreviation* **Mar)** *noun* [C, U] the third month of the year

**mare** /meəʳ/ *noun* [C] a female horse

**margarine** /ˌmɑːdʒə'riːn ⑤ 'mɑːrdʒərɪn/ *noun* [U] a yellow substance made from vegetable oil which you put on bread and use in cooking *Do you prefer margarine or butter?*

**margin** /'mɑːdʒɪn/ *noun* [C] **1** the difference between two amounts of time, money, etc, usually between people in a competition *to win by a narrow/wide margin* • *He took third place by a margin of seven minutes.* **2** an empty space down the side of a page of writing *You can make notes in the margin.* **3** **a margin of error** the amount by which a calculation can be wrong but still produce a good result *a margin of error of 5 percent*

**marginal** /'mɑːdʒɪn³l/ *adj* small and not important *a marginal effect/improvement*

**marginalize** *(also UK* **-ise)** /'mɑːdʒɪn³laɪz/ *verb* [T] to treat someone or something as if they are not important [often passive] *The poorest countries are increasingly marginalized from the world economy.*

**marginally** /'mɑːdʒɪn³li/ *adv* by a small amount *marginally more expensive*

**marijuana** /ˌmærɪ'wɑːnə/ *mainly US (mainly UK* **cannabis)** *noun* [U] a drug that some people smoke for pleasure and that is illegal in many countries

**marina** /mə'riːnə/ *noun* [C] an area of water where people keep their boats

**marinate** /'mærɪneɪt/ *(also* **marinade** /ˌmærɪ'neɪd/) *verb* [T] to add a mixture of oil, wine, herbs, etc to food before cooking it • **marinade** /ˌmærɪ'neɪd/ *noun* [C, U]

**marine¹** /mə'riːn/ *adj* [always before noun] found in the sea, or relating to the sea *marine creatures/life* • *marine biology*

**marine²** /mə'riːn/ *noun* [C] a soldier who has been trained to fight at sea and on land *the Marine Corps*

**marital** /'mærɪt³l/ *adj* [always before noun] relating to marriage *marital problems*

**maritime** /'mærɪtaɪm/ *adj* [always before noun] relating to ships and sea travel *a maritime museum*

O─**mark¹** /mɑːk/ *noun* **1** [AREA] [C] an area of dirt, damage, etc that is left on something *You've got a black mark on your nose.* • *He's left dirty marks all over the carpet.* **2** [SCORE] [C] a number or letter that is written on a piece of work, saying how good the work is *She always gets good marks in English.* **3** [LEVEL] [no plural] a particular level, degree, distance, etc *They've just passed the 5000m mark.* • *Interest rates are somewhere around the seven percent mark.* **4** **a mark of sth** a sign or proof that something exists *a mark of genius* • *There was a minute's silence everywhere as a mark of respect.* **5** **leave/make your mark** to do something that makes you successful or makes people notice you **6** **On your marks. Get set. Go!** something that you say to start a running race **7** **be wide of the mark** to not be correct or accurate ➔ *See also:* **punctuation mark, quotation marks.**

O─**mark²** /mɑːk/ *verb* **1** [HAPPEN] [T] If an event marks the beginning, end, etc of something, it causes it, or happens at the same time as it. *His death marks the end of an era in television.* **2** [CELEBRATE] [T] If you mark an occasion, you do something to celebrate it. *They've declared Tuesday a national holiday to mark the 10th anniversary of Independence.* **3** [SHOW A PLACE] [T] to show where something is by drawing or putting something somewhere *I've marked my street on the map for you.* **4** [GIVE RESULTS] [I, T] to check a piece of work or an exam, showing mistakes and giving a letter or number to say how good it is *to mark essays* **5** [DIRTY] [T] to leave an area of dirt on something

**mark sth out** to show the shape or position of something by drawing a line around it

**marked** /mɑːkt/ *adj* very noticeable *There has been a marked improvement since last year.* • **markedly** *adv*

---

**marker** /'mɑːkə/ *noun* [C] **1** (*also* '**marker ,pen**) a thick pen used especially for writing on boards *a black felt marker* ➔ *See colour picture* **Classroom** *on page Centre 4.* **2** a sign that shows where something is

o━**market¹** /'mɑːkɪt/ *noun* [C] **1** [SELLING PLACE] a place where people go to buy or sell things, often outside *a cattle/fish/flower market* • *a market stall* **2** [SHOP] *US* a supermarket (= large shop that sells food) **3** [BUSINESS] the buying and selling of something *the insurance/personal computer market* **4** [BUYING GROUP] all the people who want to buy a particular product, or the area where they live *South America is our largest market.* • *Is there a market for (= will people buy) second-hand jewellery?* **5 on the market** available to buy *His house has been on the market for over a year.* • *They've put their house on the market.* ➔ *See also:* **black market, flea market, free market, niche market, the stock market.**

**market**

**market²** /'mɑːkɪt/ *verb* [T] to try to sell products using advertising or other ways of making people want to buy them *Their products are very cleverly marketed.* • **marketing** *noun* [U] *a marketing campaign* • *the marketing department*

**marketable** /'mɑːkɪtəbl/ *adj* Marketable products or skills are easy to sell because people want them.

,**market** '**forces** *noun* [plural] the way that prices and wages are influenced by how many people want to buy a particular product and how much is available

**marketplace** /'mɑːkɪtpleɪs/ *noun* **1 the marketplace** in business, the buying and selling of products *We have to learn to compete in the international marketplace.* **2** [C] an area in a town where there is a market

,**market re'search** *noun* [U] the activity of finding out what people like about products and what new things they want to buy *a market research company*

**markings** /'mɑːkɪŋz/ *noun* [plural] the shapes and colours on an animal or bird

**mark-up** /'mɑːkʌp/ *noun* [C] the amount by which the price of something is increased before it is sold again *The usual mark-up on clothes is around 20%.*

**marmalade** /'mɑːmˀleɪd/ *noun* [U] a sweet, soft food made with oranges or lemons and often eaten on toast (= cooked bread)

**maroon¹** /mə'ruːn/ *noun* [U] a dark red-purple colour • maroon *adj* ➔ *See colour picture* **Colours** *on page Centre 6.*

**maroon²** /mə'ruːn/ *verb* **be marooned** to be left somewhere where you cannot get away

**marquee** /mɑː'kiː/ *noun* [C] *UK* **1** a large tent used for parties, shows, etc **2** *US* a large sign over a cinema or theatre that says what films or shows are playing

o━**marriage** /'mærɪdʒ/ *noun* **1** [C, U] the legal relationship of a man and a woman being a husband and a wife *a happy marriage* **2** [C] the ceremony where people become a husband and a wife *a marriage ceremony/certificate*

o━**married** /'mærɪd/ *adj* **1** A married man or woman has a wife or husband. *a married couple* • *She's been married to David for nearly ten years.* ➔ *Opposite* **unmarried.** **2 get married** to begin a legal relationship with someone as their husband or wife *We got married last year.*

**USAGE**

**married**

If you are **married**, you have a husband or wife.

If you are **separated**, you have stopped living with your husband or wife.

If you are **divorced**, you have officially stopped being married.

If you are not married, you are **single**.

**marrow** /'mærəʊ/ *noun* *UK* **1** [C, U] a large vegetable which has dark green skin and is white on the inside **2** [U] (*also* **bone marrow**) the soft substance inside bones

o━**marry** /'mæri/ *verb* **1** [I, T] to begin a legal relationship with someone as their husband or wife *Will you marry me?* • *He never married.* **2** [T] to officially make people become a husband and a wife in a ceremony *We were married by our local vicar.*

**Mars** /mɑːz/ *noun* [no plural] the planet that is fourth from the Sun, after the Earth and before Jupiter

**marsh** /mɑːʃ/ *noun* [C, U] an area of soft, wet land

**marshal** /'mɑːʃˀl/ *noun* [C] **1** someone who helps to organize or control a large public event *race marshals* **2** an important officer in police or fire departments in the US ➔ *See also:* **field marshal.**

**marshmallow** /ˌmɑːʃ'mæləʊ ⑮ 'mɑːrʃˌmæləʊ/ *noun* [C, U] a soft, white food made from sugar

**martial art** /ˌmɑːʃˀl'ɑːt/ *noun* [C] traditional Japanese or Chinese skills of fighting, done as sports in western countries *a martial arts expert*

**martial law** /ˌmɑːʃˀl'lɔː/ *noun* [U] the control of a country by its army instead of by its usual leaders *to declare martial law*

**Martian** /'mɑːʃˀn/ *noun* [C] someone from the planet Mars in stories

**martyr** /ˈmɑːtəʳ/ *noun* [C] someone who dies for their beliefs *a Catholic martyr* • martyrdom *noun* [U]

**marvel¹** /ˈmɑːvᵊl/ *noun* [C] something really surprising, exciting, or good *a marvel of modern technology*

**marvel²** /ˈmɑːvᵊl/ *verb* [I] *UK* **marvelling**, *past* **marvelled**, *US* **marveling**, *past* **marveled** to admire something very much *I'm just **marvelling at** your skills.*

**marvellous** *UK* (*US* **marvelous**) /ˈmɑːvᵊləs/ *adj* extremely good *What a marvellous idea!* • marvellously *UK* (*US* **marvelously**) *adv*

**Marxism** /ˈmɑːksɪzᵊm/ *noun* [U] the political and economic ideas of Karl Marx

**Marxist** /ˈmɑːksɪst/ *adj* relating to Marxism *Marxist ideology* • Marxist *noun* [C] someone who supports Marxism

**mascara** /mæsˈkɑːrə/ *noun* [U] a dark substance that you put on your eyelashes (= hairs that grow above and below your eyes) to make them look longer and thicker ➔ *See picture at* **make-up**.

**mascot** /ˈmæskɒt/ *noun* [C] a toy or a child that a person or a team takes with them to bring them luck *He's our **lucky mascot**.*

**masculine** /ˈmæskjəlɪn/ *adj* **1** having qualities that are typical of men *a masculine appearance/voice* **2** in some languages, belonging to a group of nouns or adjectives that have the same grammatical behaviour. The other groups are 'feminine' and 'neuter'.

**masculinity** /ˌmæskjəˈlɪnəti/ *noun* [U] the qualities that are typical of men

**mash** /mæʃ/ *verb* [T] to crush food until it is soft *(UK) mashed potato/(US) mashed potatoes*

**mask¹** /mɑːsk/ *noun* [C] a covering for the face that protects, hides, or decorates the person wearing it ➔ *See also:* **gas mask**.

**mask²** /mɑːsk/ *verb* [T] to prevent something

**mask**

from being noticed *I've had to put some flowers in there to mask the smell.*

**masked** /mɑːskt/ *adj* wearing a mask *a masked gunman/robber*

**masochism** /ˈmæsəkɪzᵊm/ *noun* [U] when people get pleasure from being hurt • masochist *noun* [C] someone who gets pleasure from being hurt

**masochistic** /ˌmæsəˈkɪstɪk/ *adj* getting pleasure from being hurt *masochistic behaviour*

**masonry** /ˈmeɪsᵊnri/ *noun* [U] the parts of a building that are made of bricks or stone

**masquerade** /ˌmæskᵊrˈeɪd/ *verb*

**masquerade as sb/sth** to pretend to be someone or something *She's just a teacher masquerading as an academic.*

**mass¹** /mæs/ *noun* **1** [C] a solid lump with no clear shape *The sauce was now a sticky mass in the bottom of the pan.* **2 a mass of sth** a large amount or number of something *The garden was a mass of flowers.* • *She had a mass of blond curls.* **3** [U] in physics, the amount of substance that something contains *One litre of water has a mass of one kilogram.* **4 masses** *informal* a large amount or number of something *I've got **masses** of work to do.* • *Take some of our paper – we've got masses.* **5 the masses** the ordinary people who form the largest part of society *He failed to win the support of the masses.*

**mass²** /mæs/ *adj* [always before noun] involving a lot of people *mass destruction/unemployment* • *a mass murderer*

**mass³** /mæs/ *verb* [I, T] *formal* to come together somewhere in large numbers, or make people or things do this *Over 20,000 demonstrators massed in the town's main square.*

**Mass, mass** /mæs/ *noun* [C, U] a religious ceremony in some Christian churches in which people eat bread and drink wine *to go to Mass*

**massacre** /ˈmæsəkəʳ/ *noun* [C] the killing of a lot of people *He ordered the massacre of over 2,000 women and children.* • massacre *verb* [T] *Hundreds of civilians were massacred in the raid.*

**massage** /ˈmæsɑːdʒ ⓤⓢ məˈsɑːdʒ/ *noun* [C, U] the activity of rubbing or pressing parts of someone's body in order to make them relax or to stop their muscles hurting *to have a massage* • *She gave me a foot massage.* • massage *verb* [T] *Would you massage my shoulders?*

**massive** /ˈmæsɪv/ *adj* very big *a massive building* • *massive debts*

**the ˌmass ˈmedia** *noun* [group] newspapers, television, and radio

**mass-produce** /ˌmæsprəˈdjuːs/ *verb* [T] to make a large number of the same thing using machines *Clothes are mass-produced in factories.* • *mass-produced furniture*

**mast** /mɑːst/ *noun* [C] **1** a tall pole on a boat that supports its sails **2** a tall metal pole that sends out television and radio signals

**master¹** /ˈmɑːstəʳ/ *noun* [C] **1** [IN CHARGE] In the past, a servant's master was the man that they worked for. **2** [TEACHER] *old-fashioned* a male teacher *the Latin master* **3** [SKILL] someone who does something very well *He was a **master** of disguise.* **4** [FOR COPYING] a document or recording from which copies can be made **5 Master of Arts/Science, etc** a higher university qualification which usually takes 1 or 2 more years of study after your first qualification, or a person who has this qualification **6 Master's (degree)** a higher university qualification *to study for a Master's degree* **7 Master** *formal* a title for a boy, used before his family name or full name *Master Thomas Mills*

**master²** /ˈmɑːstəʳ/ *verb* [T] to learn how to do something well *to master a technique* • *He lived for several years in Italy but never quite mastered the language.*

**master³** /ˈmɑːstəʳ/ *adj* [always before noun] having

the skills for a particular job *a master chef/craftsman*

**masterful** /ˈmɑːstəfəl/ *adj* done with great skill *a masterful display of golf*

**mastermind** /ˈmɑːstəmaɪnd/ *verb* [T] to plan every detail of a complicated event or activity and make sure that it happens *He allegedly masterminded both bomb attacks in the region.* • **mastermind** *noun* [C] *It is thought he was the mastermind behind* (= the person who planned) *last year's bombing campaign.*

**masterpiece** /ˈmɑːstəpiːs/ *noun* [C] a painting, book, or film that is generally considered to be of excellent quality *'Mona Lisa' is widely regarded as Leonardo da Vinci's masterpiece.*

**mastery** /ˈmɑːstəri/ *noun* **1** **mastery of sth** great skill or understanding of something *his mastery of the Japanese language* **2** **mastery of/over sth** control over something *The two countries battled for mastery over the region.*

**masturbate** /ˈmæstəbeɪt/ *verb* [I] to make yourself feel sexually excited by touching your sexual organs • **masturbation** /ˌmæstəˈbeɪʃən/ *noun* [U]

**mat** /mæt/ *noun* [C] **1** a piece of thick material that you put on the floor, often in order to protect it *There's a mat by the door for you to wipe your feet on.* **2** a small piece of plastic or other material that you put on a table so that hot plates and liquid will not damage it

◦━**match¹** /mætʃ/ *noun* **1** GAME [C] a sports competition in which two people or teams compete against each other *a football/tennis match* **2** FIRE [C] a thin, wooden stick which produces a flame when you rub one end of it against a rough surface *a box of matches* **3** ATTRACTIVE [no plural] If something is a good match for something else, it looks attractive next to it, usually because it is the right colour. *The curtains look nice – they're a perfect match for the sofa.* **4** RELATIONSHIP [no plural] If two people who are having a relationship are a good match, they are very suitable for each other. **5** **be no match for sb/sth** to not be as good as someone or something else *Gibson ran well but was no match for the young Italian.*

◦━**match²** /mætʃ/ *verb* **1** BE THE SAME [I, T] If two things match, they are the same colour or type. *I can't find anything to match my green shirt.* • *Your socks don't match.* • *Traces of blood found on Walker's clothing matched the victim's blood type.* **2** CHOOSE [T] to choose someone or something that is suitable for a particular person, activity, or purpose *In the first exercise, you have to match the famous person to their country of origin.* **3** BE AS GOOD AS [T] to be as good as someone or something else *It would be difficult to match the service this airline gives to its customers.*

**match up** If two pieces of information match up, they are the same. *Their accounts of what happened that evening didn't match up.*

**match sb/sth up** to choose someone or something that is suitable for a particular person, activity, or purpose *They look at your interests and try to match you up with someone suitable.*

**match up to sth** to be as good as something else

*Nothing that he wrote after this point ever matched up to his early work.*

**matchbox** /ˈmætʃbɒks/ *noun* [C] a small box containing matches

**matching** /ˈmætʃɪŋ/ *adj* [always before noun] having the same colour or pattern as something else *She wore purple shorts and a matching T-shirt.*

**mate¹** /meɪt/ *noun* [C] **1** FRIEND UK informal a friend *She's my best mate.* • *Pete was there with a couple of mates.* **2** TALKING TO A MAN UK informal You call a man 'mate' when you are speaking to him informally. *Thanks, mate.* **3** ANIMAL an animal's sexual partner *Swans keep the same mate throughout their life.*

**mate²** /meɪt/ *verb* [I] When animals mate, they have sex in order to produce babies.

◦━**material¹** /məˈtɪəriəl/ *noun* **1** SUBSTANCE [C, U] a solid substance from which things can be made *building materials* • *Crude oil is used as the raw material for making plastics.* **2** CLOTH [C, U] cloth for making clothes, curtains, etc *Her dress was made of a soft, silky material.* **3** INFORMATION [U] the facts or ideas in a piece of writing *I'm collecting material for an article that I'm writing.*

**material²** /məˈtɪəriəl/ *adj* relating to money and possessions and not emotions or thoughts *Material wealth never interested her.* • *the material world*

**materialism** /məˈtɪəriəlɪzəm/ *noun* [U] the belief that having money and possessions is the most important thing in life • **materialistic** /məˌtɪəriəˈlɪstɪk/ *adj* believing in materialism

**materialize** (*also UK* -**ise**) /məˈtɪəriəlaɪz/ *verb* [I] If something does not materialize, it does not happen. *She was promised a promotion but it never materialized.*

**materials** /məˈtɪəriəlz/ *noun* [plural] the equipment that you need for a particular activity *teaching/writing materials*

**maternal** /məˈtɜːnəl/ *adj* **1** like a mother *I've never had much of a maternal instinct* (= wish to have children). **2** [always before noun] A maternal relation is part of your mother's family. *He's my maternal grandfather.*

**maternity** /məˈtɜːnəti/ *adj* [always before noun] related to pregnancy and birth *maternity clothes* • *maternity leave*

**math** /mæθ/ *noun* [U] US short for mathematics

**mathematical** /ˌmæθəˈmætɪkəl/ *adj* relating to mathematics *a mathematical formula/equation* • **mathematically** *adv*

**mathematician** /ˌmæθəməˈtɪʃən/ *noun* [C] someone who studies mathematics

**mathematics** /ˌmæθəˈmætɪks/ *noun* [U] formal the study or science of numbers and shapes

**maths** /mæθs/ *noun* [U] UK short for mathematics

**matinée** /ˈmætɪneɪ US mætəˈneɪ/ *noun* [C] an afternoon performance of a play or film

**matrimony** /ˈmætrɪməni/ *noun* [U] formal the state of being married

**matron** /ˈmeɪtrən/ *noun* [C] **1** NURSE UK old-fashioned a female nurse in a school, or a female nurse who is in charge of other nurses in a hospital **2** WOMAN US a married woman, especially one who is old or a widow (= woman

M

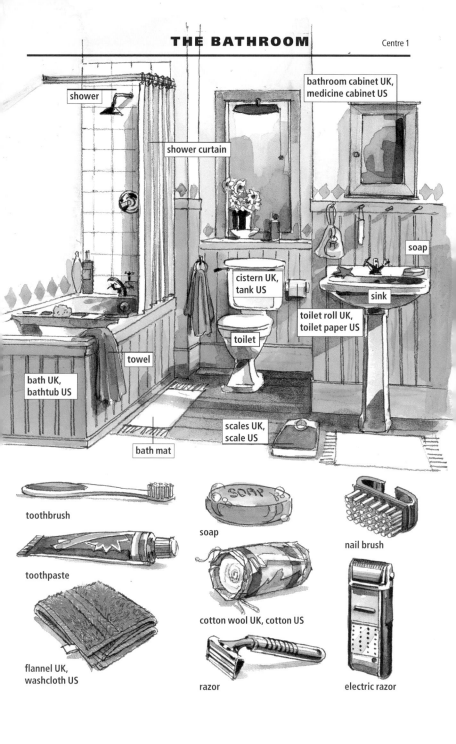

# THE BATHROOM

shower

bathroom cabinet UK, medicine cabinet US

shower curtain

soap

cistern UK, tank US

sink

toilet roll UK, toilet paper US

toilet

towel

bath UK, bathtub US

scales UK, scale US

bath mat

toothbrush

soap

nail brush

toothpaste

cotton wool UK, cotton US

flannel UK, washcloth US

razor

electric razor

# THE BODY

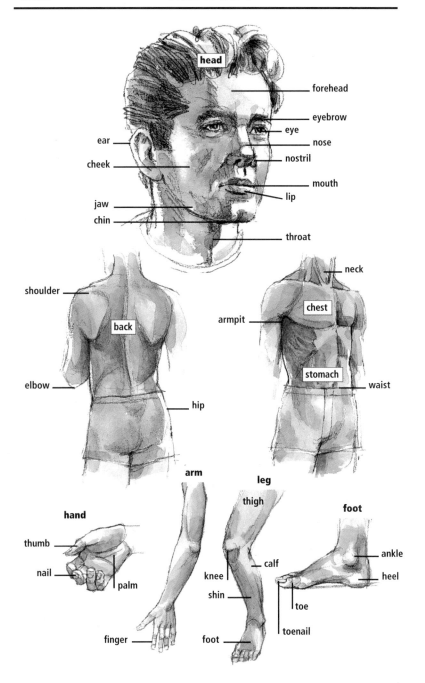

head

forehead

eyebrow

eye

ear

nose

nostril

cheek

mouth

lip

jaw

chin

throat

neck

shoulder

chest

armpit

back

stomach

waist

elbow

hip

arm

leg

thigh

hand

foot

thumb

calf

ankle

nail

knee

heel

palm

shin

toe

finger

foot

toenail

# CAR

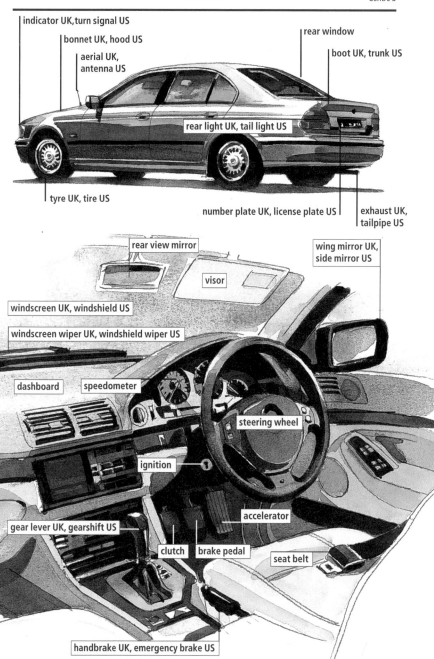

indicator UK, turn signal US

bonnet UK, hood US

aerial UK, antenna US

rear window

boot UK, trunk US

rear light UK, tail light US

tyre UK, tire US

number plate UK, license plate US

exhaust UK, tailpipe US

rear view mirror

wing mirror UK, side mirror US

visor

windscreen UK, windshield US

windscreen wiper UK, windshield wiper US

dashboard

speedometer

steering wheel

ignition

accelerator

gear lever UK, gearshift US

clutch

brake pedal

seat belt

handbrake UK, emergency brake US

# THE CLASSROOM

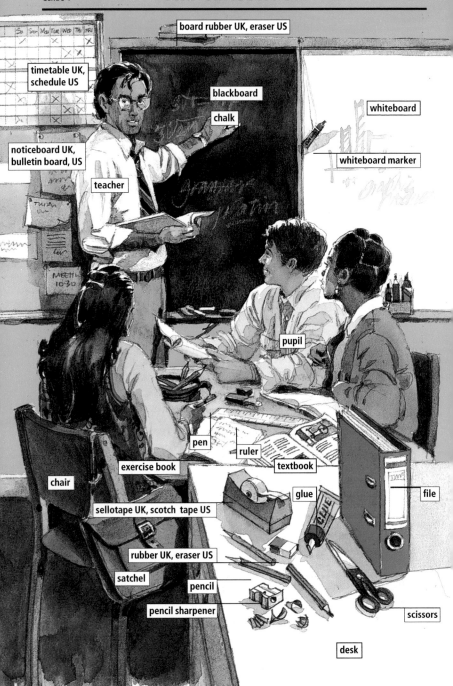

board rubber UK, eraser US

timetable UK, schedule US

blackboard

chalk

whiteboard

noticeboard UK, bulletin board, US

whiteboard marker

teacher

pupil

pen

ruler

exercise book

textbook

chair

glue

file

sellotape UK, scotch tape US

rubber UK, eraser US

satchel

pencil

pencil sharpener

scissors

desk

# CLOTHES

shirt

T-shirt

dress

evening dress

miniskirt

sweatshirt

jumper UK, sweater US

cardigan

skirt

jacket

waterproof jacket

coat

waistcoat UK, vest US

bow tie

tie

scarf    scarf

belt

boots

sandals

buckle

shoes

trainers UK, sneakers US

trousers    jeans

shorts

cycling shorts    leggings

bra

pants UK, panties US

boxer shorts

underpants

vest UK, undershirt US

stockings

tights UK, pantyhose US

socks

bikini

sunglasses

trunks

beret

hat

cap

# COLOURS

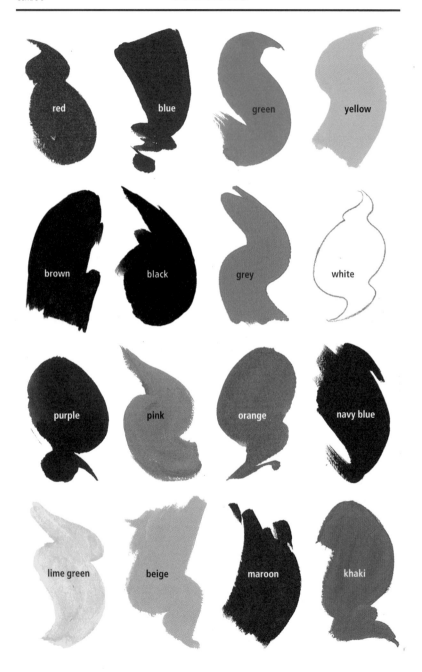

red

blue

green

yellow

brown

black

grey

white

purple

pink

orange

navy blue

lime green

beige

maroon

khaki

roll UK,
sandwich US

sandwich UK & US

soup

biscuits UK,
cookies US

cake

salad

vegetables

pizza

rice

chips UK,
french fries US

cereal

pasta

honey

jam

crisps UK,
chips US

peanuts

egg

butter

fish

yoghurt

cheese

meat

# FRUIT AND VEGETABLES

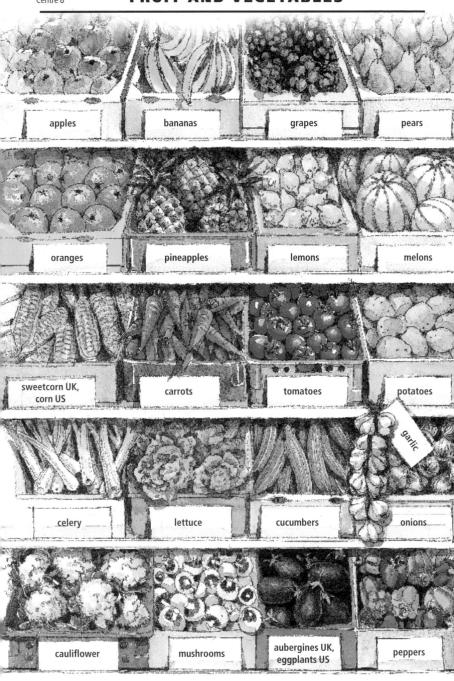

apples

bananas

grapes

pears

oranges

pineapples

lemons

melons

sweetcorn UK,
corn US

carrots

tomatoes

potatoes

garlic

celery

lettuce

cucumbers

onions

cauliflower

mushrooms

aubergines UK,
eggplants US

peppers

blonde/fair

mousy

dark

red

grey

straight

curly

wavy

spiky

moustache

beard

stubble

fringe UK, bangs US

plait UK, braid US

ponytail

shoulder-length

long

short

bald

# THE KITCHEN

chopping board

toaster

bread bin UK,
bread box US

tin opener UK,
can opener US

food processor

grater

oven glove

kettle

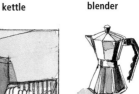

blender

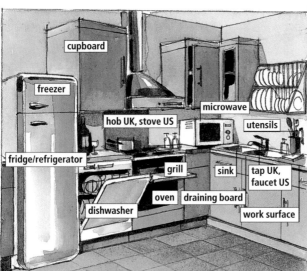

cupboard

freezer

microwave

hob UK, stove US

utensils

fridge/refrigerator

grill

sink

tap UK,
faucet US

oven draining board

dishwasher

work surface

coffee maker

teapot

sieve

colander

scales UK, scale US

measuring spoons

cake tin UK,
cake pan US

rolling pin

saucepan

frying pan

flan dish

whisk

ladle

fish slice UK,
spatula US

# THE LIVING ROOM

picture

mirror

ornaments

window

curtain

mantelpiece

windowsill

radiator

TV

bookcase

cushion

sofa

fireplace

coffee table

vase

rug

armchair

remote control

video UK, VCR US

candles

lampshade

speaker   stereo

clock

lamp

# THE OFFICE

fax

photocopier

monitor

screen

desk tidy UK
desk organizer US

in-tray

paper clips

envelope

file

telephone

mouse

CD

keyboard

disk

folder

desk

filing cabinet

highlighter

bin UK, trash can US

hanging files

chair

wake up

get up

put on

take off

lie down

sit down

stand up

put down

pick up

throw away

put away

wash up

tell off

eat out

turn on

turn off

get on

get off

fall over

work out

# QUANTITIES

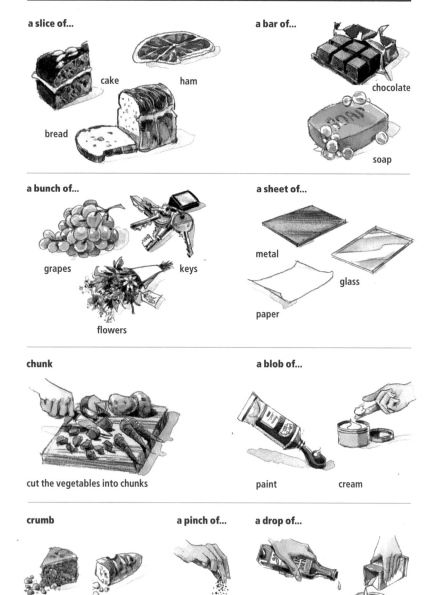

**a slice of...**

cake

ham

bread

**a bar of...**

chocolate

soap

**a bunch of...**

grapes

keys

flowers

**a sheet of...**

metal

glass

paper

**chunk**

cut the vegetables into chunks

**a blob of...**

paint

cream

**crumb**

cake crumbs

breadcrumbs

**a pinch of...**

salt

**a drop of...**

oil

milk

# SPORTS (1)

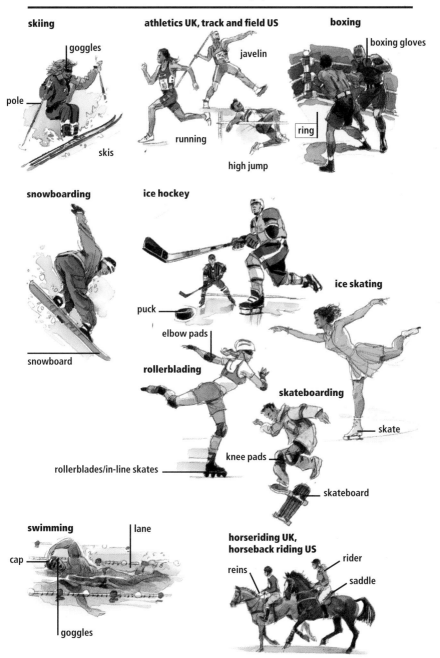

**skiing**

goggles

pole

skis

**athletics UK, track and field US**

javelin

running

high jump

**boxing**

boxing gloves

ring

**snowboarding**

snowboard

**ice hockey**

puck

elbow pads

**rollerblading**

rollerblades/in-line skates

knee pads

**skateboarding**

skateboard

**ice skating**

skate

**swimming**

cap

lane

goggles

**horseriding UK,
horseback riding US**

reins

rider

saddle

# SPORTS (2)

**football UK, soccer US**
- referee
- goal
- goalkeeper

**American football UK, football US**
- helmet
- goal post

**rugby**

**golf**
- cup
- club
- caddie

**basketball**
- backboard
- basket

**cricket**
- bowler
- stumps
- batsman

**baseball**
- cap
- pitcher
- glove/mitt
- batter

**tennis**
- racket
- net

**cycling**
- helmet
- bicycle

**volleyball**
- net

# Study pages

## Adjectives

### Order of adjectives

When you put more than one adjective together, the order of
the adjectives is important.

The order of the adjectives is usually like this:

1 opinion (= what you think about something)
2 size
3 age
4 shape
5 colour
6 origin (= where something comes from)
7 material (= what something is made of)
8 purpose (= what something is used for)

*long, curly hair*

**1** Put the adjectives in the correct order in these phrases:

1 a black old big cat      3 a dirty ski old jacket
2 a Nigerian large drum      4 a leather beautiful briefcase

We do not usually put more than three adjectives together.
Here are some other ways of adding more information:
▶ *She had a shiny, red sports car,* **which** *was brand-new.*
▶ *A long, flowing wedding dress,* **made** *of silk.*

### Gradable and limit adjectives

| awful | | | | wonderful |
|---|---|---|---|---|
| terrible | bad | good | | great |

| | |
|---|---|
| The adjectives in the middle of the diagram are called 'gradable' adjectives – they give a general description of something. We can use *very* with this type of adjective: very/good/bad | The adjectives at the ends of the diagram are called 'limit' adjectives – they express an extreme description of something. We can use *absolutely* with this type of adjective: absolutely wonderful |

**2** Which of these words are limit adjectives and which are gradable adjectives?
Use the dictionary to match each limit adjective with a gradable adjective.

| tiny | starving | exhausted | hot | interesting |
|---|---|---|---|---|
| small | boiling | hungry | tired | fascinating |

## Checking your work

There are many ways that this dictionary can help you avoid common mistakes.

## Usage notes

Words which often cause difficulty for learners of English have special usage notes explaining how to use them correctly.

**1** Correct the following sentences by looking at the usage notes:

1 The new rule <u>affects</u> to everyone.
2 What <u>hour</u> is it?
3 It's <u>quiet</u> hot in here.
4 He did an interesting <u>speech</u>.

## Grammar

Always check the grammar of the words you want to use. There is an explanation of all the grammar codes on p.8, and the Study sections on **Countable and uncountable nouns** and **Verb patterns** will help you too.

## Using the right words

Look carefully at the example sentences, which will show you typical ways of using words. When a word is used with another word extremely often, they are shown in dark type.

**2** Fill in the gaps in these sentences by looking at examples at the entry for the <u>underlined</u> word:

1 You must ___ your <u>homework</u> before you go out.
2 Shall we ___ a <u>taxi</u> to the station?
3 He has no <u>chance</u> ___ getting there on time.
4 I'm ___ rather <u>ill</u> this morning.

➔ See also Study sections
**Spelling** on p. Centre 31,
**Punctuation** on p. Centre 37,
**Collocations** on p. Centre 21

**3** There are 10 mistakes in this essay. Can you find them and correct them?

> My name is Dida and I'm Italian.
> I am 22 year old. When I left the university, my father suggested me to go to London for one year to study english.
>
> When I arrived everything fell very strange. The weather was very cold. In Italy I was used to go out without a coat. I have good accommodations and I have made many new friends. I am studying hard, but I still do many mistakes. When I finish my course here I will go back to Italy to find a work.

## Classroom language

### Asking about words

What does 'fierce' mean?

How do you say ___ in English?

How do you spell 'castle'?

How do you pronounce this word?

What's the past tense/past participle of 'lie'?

Can you give me an example?

Could you say that again, please?

### Asking about activities

I'm sorry, I don't understand what we have to do.

Can you repeat the instructions please?

Could you repeat that, please?

Could you speak more slowly, please?

Could I borrow a pen/pencil, etc, please?

Can you lend me a pen/pencil, please?

How long do we have to do this?

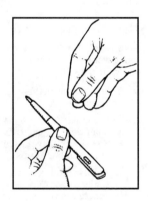

### Classroom instructions

Open your books at page 40.

Turn to page 6.

Close your books.

Work in pairs/groups of three, four etc.

Listen to the tape, then try to answer the questions.

Write the answers on a piece of paper.

Work with your partner.

Look up these words in your dictionary.

No talking, please.

Hand in your homework as you leave.

# Collocations

Collocations are words that are frequently used together. These word combinations are often difficult to guess, so you need to learn them in order to sound natural in English. Important collocations are included in the example sentences in this dictionary.

## Verbs and nouns

Some examples of common verb + noun collocations:

| | | | |
|---|---|---|---|
| make friends | take a photo | make a speech | play the piano |
| make a noise | surf the Web | have fun | write a letter |

**1** Match the verbs on the left with the nouns on the right.
Use your dictionary to help you if you need to.

1 make    4 watch        a a question    d a mistake
2 tell     5 ask          b a train      e a joke
3 catch                 c TV

## Adjectives and nouns

Some examples of common adjective + noun collocations:

| | | | |
|---|---|---|---|
| a great success | a narrow escape | heavy traffic | fresh fruit |
| broad shoulders | a serious illness | a steep hill | a sunny day |

**2** Fill in the gaps with a suitable adjective:

1 I used to be a ___ smoker.
2 He has a ___ Scottish accent.
3 She was late, but at least she had a ___ excuse.
4 The plane could not take off because of ___ cloud.

## Prepositions

**3** Complete the following sentences by adding the missing preposition:

1 I'm worried ___ Jane. She's usually home by now.
2 You have to apply ___ a visa before you go.
3 Can you describe the man ___ me?
4 That girl over there keeps smiling ___ me.

# Countable and uncountable nouns

**Nouns can be countable or uncountable.**

Countable nouns can have *a/an* or *the* before them and can be used both in the singular and the plural:
▶ *There's a **plate**, three **spoons** and a **cup** on the **table**.*

Uncountable nouns cannot have *a/an* before them and cannot be used in the plural:
▶ *The **furniture** in the **accommodation** was ugly but practical. They gave us some **money** to buy more.*

In this dictionary, countable nouns have the symbol [C], and uncountable nouns have the symbol [U].

**1** Are these sentences correct? Look up the noun that is in <u>underlined</u>

1 We get a lot of English <u>homeworks</u>.
2 I've got some <u>sands</u> in my shoe.
3 Did you hear the <u>news</u> about Sara?
4 We need more <u>chairs</u> in this room.
5 Can I have some more <u>pasta</u>?
6 She carried my <u>luggages</u> to the taxi.

**2** Some of these sentences need 'a' or 'an' in the gaps.
Put them in where they are necessary.

1 Why are you taking ___ umbrella? It's not raining.
2 I had ___ soup and ___ bread roll for lunch.
3 It was ___ good idea to have a party.
4 She's looking for ___ work in Madrid.
5 I often go to her for ___ advice.

## *Some* and *any*

You can use **some** and **any** with plural countable nouns:
▶ *There are **some cakes** left. Are there **any biscuits**?*

You can use **some** and **any** with uncountable nouns:
▶ *I'd like **some sugar** in my coffee. Is there **any water** in the jug?*

**3** Fill in the gaps with a noun from the box:

| | | | | |
|---|---|---|---|---|
| chair | suitcase | fly | rice | furniture |
| day | weather | accidents | luggage | |

1 There's a ___ in my soup.
2 I have to buy some ___ for my new house.
3 I haven't got much ___ with me. Just this bag.
4 It's a sunny ___ today.
5 There weren't any ___ on the roads yesterday.

## Much, many, a lot of, a few

| | |
|---|---|
| You can use **many** and **a few** with plural countable nouns:<br>▶ *Did you take many photographs?*<br>▶ *I've got a few friends who live in London.* | You can use **much** with uncountable nouns:<br>▶ *I haven't got **much news** to tell you.* |

You can use **a lot** of with both plural countable nouns and with uncountable nouns:
▶ *Did you take **a lot of photographs**?*
▶ *I haven't **got a lot of news** to tell you.*

**4** Which of the <u>underlined</u> words in parts of these sentences is right?
Put a circle around the correct part.

1 Hurry up! We haven't got <u>many</u>/<u>a lot of</u> time.
2 I don't eat <u>much</u>/<u>many</u> chocolate.
3 I didn't take <u>much</u>/<u>many</u> photographs.
4 I don't listen to <u>much</u>/<u>many</u> classical music.

## Nouns which can be both countable and uncountable

Some nouns can be used both countably and uncountably:
▶ *a fish/fish, a glass/glass, a hair/hair, a chocolate/chocolate*

| | |
|---|---|
| When we use these nouns countably we refer to particular things:<br>▶ *There are **some glasses** on the table.*<br>▶ *I caught **a fish** at the lake.* | When we use these nouns uncountably we refer to the thing in general:<br>▶ *Careful. There's broken glass on the floor.*<br>▶ *I'd like fish and chips for dinner.* |

**5** Look at the items below. How many of them can be used both countably and uncountably?

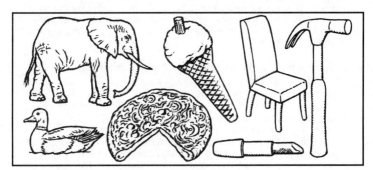

# Family

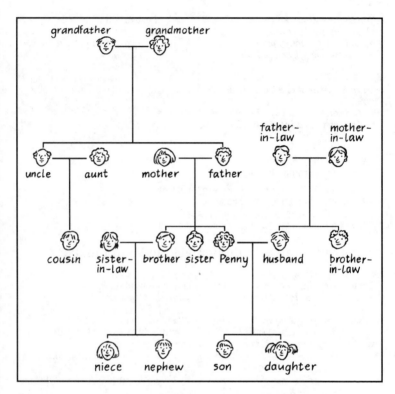

**1** Find a word in the diagram above that fits each definition:

  1  the child of your aunt or uncle
  2  the mother of your mother or father
  3  the brother of your mother or father, or the husband of your aunt
  4  the woman married to your brother, or the sister of your husband or wife
  5  the son of your brother or sister, or the son of your husband's or wife's
     brother or sister

**2** Choose a word from the box below to match each definition:

> partner  boyfriend  stepfather  half-sister  an only child

  1  someone who has no brothers or sisters
  2  a sister who is the daughter of only one of your parents
  3  someone that you are married to or having a sexual relationship with
  4  the man who is married to your mother but is not your father
  5  a man or boy that you have a romantic relationship with

# Food and eating

Here are some sentences that you might say or hear when you go to a restaurant:

▶ *Are you ready to order?*
▶ *Could we have the bill, please?*
▶ *Do you take credit cards?*

▶ *Is the service charge included?*
▶ *Smoking or non-smoking?*

**1** Use the sentences to fill the gaps in the conversation below:

### Before the meal

HARRY: A table for two, please.
WAITER: ___?
HARRY: Non-smoking, please.
WAITER: Come this way. I'll get you some menus.

(*Five minutes later.*)
WAITER: ___?
SYLVIA: Yes, I'd like the duck please.
HARRY: I'll have the pasta.
SYLVIA: And could we have a bottle of red wine, please?
WAITER: Certainly.

### After the meal

WAITER: Would you like any desserts or coffees?
SYLVIA: No, thank you. ___?
WAITER: Certainly. Was everything okay with your meal?
SYLVIA: Yes, it was delicious.
WAITER: Here's your bill.
HARRY: Thank you. ___?
WAITER: Yes we do.
HARRY: ___?
WAITER: No
HARRY: OK, I'll leave the tip separately.

## Giving praise for food

▶ *This is delicious.*
▶ *It's great.*
▶ *The sauce is lovely.*

## Complaining about food

▶ *This food is cold.*
▶ *The meat isn't cooked in the middle.*
▶ *It's a bit too salty/sweet for me.*

## Other things you might ask for

▶ *Could we have some water, please?*
▶ *Could we have some more bread, please?*
▶ *I'd like to see the wine list.*
▶ *Do you do children's portions?*

# Idioms

Idioms are groups of words that have a meaning which is different from
the usual meanings of the words in them. It is often impossible to guess what
they mean. They are used in all types of language, but especially in informal
situations. Idioms often have a stronger meaning than ordinary words.
For example, 'be at loggerheads with someone' has more emphasis than
'be arguing with someone', but they mean the same thing.

## Finding idioms in this dictionary

Most idioms are found at the entry for the first noun in the idiom.
(A noun is a word that is the name of a thing, person, or place.)

**1**   Underline the first noun in each idiom on the left.
Then match each idiom with its meaning on the right.

| | | | |
|---|---|---|---|
| 1 | be up to your neck in sth | a | try to do something you cannot achieve |
| 2 | the final nail in the coffin | b | be very busy |
| 3 | fight a losing battle | c | have nothing to do |
| 4 | be at a loose end | d | not laugh |
| 5 | keep a straight face | e | something that causes failure |

If the idiom does not contain a
noun, try the first verb (word for
doing things) or adjective (word
for describing things). But don't
worry if you do not know where to
look for an idiom. If you look in
the wrong place, you will find an
arrow telling you where to go.

---

∘‣**breathe** /briːð/ *verb* [I, T] to take air
into and out of your lungs *breathe
in/out* • *breathe deeply* • *Doctors gave
him oxygen to help him breathe.* ➲ *See
also:* be breathing down sb's **neck**,
not breathe a **word¹**.

---

**2**   The following sentences all use idioms that contain a part of the body. Choose
a body part from the box below to complete each sentence.

| | | | | |
|---|---|---|---|---|
| head | face | arm | leg | ear |

1   The accident was clearly his fault – he doesn't have a ___ to stand on.
2   Most of her lecture went over my ___ .
3   Dad might lend you his camera if you twist his ___ .
4   I've never taught this class before, so I'll have to play it by ___ .
5   When I saw his hat, I could hardly keep a straight ___ .

# The Internet

### What is the Internet?

The Internet is the system that connects millions of computers all over the world. To **go online** (= connect your computer to the Internet) you need a computer with a **modem**.

### What is a modem?

A modem is a piece of equipment that sends information along telephone lines.

### Is the Internet the same as the World Wide Web?

The **World Wide Web** (**www**) is part of the Internet. It is a system of electronic documents called **websites** that are linked together.

### How can I move around quickly on the www?

You can use your mouse to click on **links** (= connections between the documents or areas on the Internet) to go to a different website, or to move from one part of a website to another. You could also use a **WAP phone**, which is a telephone with a small screen which you can carry around and which allows you to use the Internet.

### What kind of information is there on a website?

Websites can contain almost any kind of information, such as text, pictures, or sound. Usually they consist of a series of **web pages**. The main page on a website is called the **home page**.

### How do I find the website I want?

If you know the **web address** you can type it in at the top of the screen. Otherwise, you can use a **search engine** (= software which searches for information) to surf the Web.

### What does surf the Web mean?

It means 'look at information in a lot of different places, either because you are not sure what you are looking for, or in order to find something'.

### What can I do with the information when I find it?

You can read text or print it out. If there is music you can listen to it. For games or other activities you can sometimes **download** software (= copy computer programs to your computer).

**1** Match the words on the left with the meanings on the right:

| | | | |
|---|---|---|---|
| 1 | browser | a | a connection between documents or areas on the Internet |
| 2 | web page | | |
| 3 | home page | b | the first page that you see when you look at a website |
| 4 | modem | c | a piece of equipment that is used to send information from a computer through a telephone system |
| 5 | download | | |
| 6 | link/hyperlink | d | a computer program which allows you to look at pages on the Internet |
| | | e | a part of a website that can be read on a computer screen |
| | | f | to copy computer programs or information electronically |

## Email

Email addresses usually look like this:   `djones@hotmail.com`

When we tell someone an email address we say: 'D Jones at hotmail dot com'.

## Writing emails

- write the email address of the person you are writing to
  `To: djones@hotmail.com`
- your email address
  `From: pgreen@pippin.org`
- a few words to say what the email is about
  `Subject: party`
- the email address of anyone you want to copy the message to
  `Cc: andy@sedgwick.co.uk`
- attach other computer files which you are sending with the email
  `Attached: H:\Reunion\addresses`

```
 ⬅        ➡       🖅        🖅       🗐      🗑       📎▾
Previous  Next    Reply   Reply All  Forward  Delete  Attachments

To:        djones@hotmail.com
From:      pgreen@pippin.org
Subject:   party
Cc:        andy@sedgwick.co.uk
Attached:  H:\Reunion\addresses

Debbie,
Andy and I are trying to
organize a surprise party for
Cath, as it's her birthday next
week. Could you make it next
Friday, at our place? BTW, I've
attached that list of addresses
you wanted.
Penny :-)
```

Emails are usually shorter and more informal than letters and people sometimes use abbreviations and 'smileys' in them. **Smileys** (also called **emoticons**) are images which look like faces when you see them from the side. They are made using keyboard symbols and are used to express emotions.

| **Abbreviations** | | **Smileys** | |
|---|---|---|---|
| AFAIK | as far as I know | :-) | I'm happy |
| BTW | by the way | :-( | I'm angry/unhappy |
| FYI | for your information | >:-( | I'm very angry/unhappy |
| HTH | hope that helps | :-o | I am very surprised/I'm shouting loudly |
| IMO | in my opinion | :-@ | I'm screaming |
| IOW | in other words | :-* | I'm sending you a kiss |
| TAFN | that's all for now | :-{) | I have a moustache |
| TIA | thanks in advance | 8-) | I wear glasses |

## Measurements

### Metric and imperial measurements

The international system of metric units of measurement is not used in the US. It is used in Britain, but many people still use the older system of imperial units such as pounds, feet, and gallons.

Some units have the same name but mean different amounts in Britain and the US.

| IMPERIAL | METRIC | IMPERIAL | METRIC |
|---|---|---|---|
| 1 inch (in) | 2.5 centimetres (cm) | 1 ounce (oz) | 28 gram (g) |
| 1 foot (ft) | 30 centimetres | 1 pound (lb) | 450 gram |
| | (100 cm = 1 metre (m)) | | |
| 1 yard (yd) | 90 centimetres | 1 pint | UK 0.6 litres US 0.5 litres |
| 5 miles (m) | 8 kilometres (km) | 1 gallon | UK 4.5 litres US 3.8 litres |

### Saying how tall you are

Most people in Britain and the US say their height in imperial units.
▶ *I'm six feet tall.*　　　　　　▶ *I'm five foot seven. (Often written 5' 7".)*

### Saying how much you weigh

In Britain, people usually say their weight in stones and pounds.
There are fourteen pounds in a stone.
▶ *I weigh nine stone three.* (Note that you do not have to say 'pounds'.)
▶ *I weigh seven and a half stone.*

In the US, people usually say their weight in pounds.
▶ *I weigh 160 pounds.*

### Talking about measurements

We normally use adjectives to talk or ask about measurements:
▶ *The box is 30cm long.*　　　　▶ *How tall is David?*

We can also use nouns, but they are more formal:
▶ *The length of the box is 30cm.*　　▶ *What is David's height?*

| height | deep | length | width | depth | high | long | wide |
|---|---|---|---|---|---|---|---|

**1** Look at the words in the box. Decide which are adjectives and which are nouns. Use them to complete the table below.

| | QUESTION | ANSWER | FORMAL |
|---|---|---|---|
| 1 | How wide is it? | It's 5m ___. | The ___ of the x is 5m. |
| 2 | How ___ is it? | It's 50m long. | The length of the x is 50m. |
| 3 | How deep is it? | It's 10m deep. | The ___ of the x is 10m. |
| 4 | How ___ is it? | It's 70m ___. | The height of the x is 70m. |

## The media

### TV and radio

1 Match the programme types on the left with their definitions on the right:

1 documentary
2 soap or soap opera
3 game show
4 cartoon
5 the news

a  a programme in which people play games in order to win money or prizes
b  a film made using characters that are drawn rather than real
c  a programme that gives facts about a real situation or real people
d  the announcement of important events that have happened in the world
e  a programme about the lives of a group of people that is broadcast several times every week

2 Look at the information on the list of TV programmes. What kind of programmes can you watch tonight? Use words from exercise 1.

1  At 7.00 there's a ___ .
2  At 7.30 there's a ___ .
3  At 8.00 there's a ___ .
4  At 8.30 it's the ___ .

> **Tonight's TV**
>
> **Channel 1**
>
> **7.00  Great winged travellers** Migratory birds from Africa. A two-part series.
> **7.30  Hooper Street** Will Eric discover Sonia's secret?
> **8.00  Glittering Prizes** 3 new contestants in this week's show.
> **8.30  News and weather**

---

**Useful phrases**

Be careful to use the correct verbs and prepositions

**watch** programmes on TV
**watch** TV
**listen to** programmes on the radio
**listen to** the radio
**turn up** the TV (= make it louder)

What's **on TV** tonight?
Which channel is the film **on**?
I saw that film **on video**.
**turn over** (= change the channel)
**turn** the radio **down** (= make it quieter)

---

### Newspapers and magazines

Most newspapers come out **daily** (= every day). Some newspapers and magazines come out **weekly** (= every week). Most magazines come out **monthly** (= every month).

3 Name the parts of the newspaper using the words in the box.

| picture   column   headline   caption |
|---|

1 ___     2 ___     3 ___     4 ___

## Modal verbs

Here are some of the uses and meanings of modal verbs.
For a more detailed description, use a good grammar book.

> Here are the main modal verbs of English:
>
> **can   could   may   might   must   ought   shall   will   would**
>
> We also use *need* and *have to* as modal verbs.

### Same word, different use

Each modal verb has more than one use. For example, look at these two
sentences with **can**. The use is explained in brackets.
- ▶ *I **can** swim.* (ability)
- ▶ ***Can** you carry this bag for me?* (request)

**1**  The dictionary helps you decide which meaning of the verb is used.
Look at the modal verb 'can'. How many meanings can you find?

### Expressing instructions, advice, permission, and necessity

> to give instructions or to say that something is necessary
> - ▶ *You **must** wear a helmet when riding a bike.*
> - ▶ *You **mustn't** smoke in here.*
> - ▶ *I **have to** be at the dentist at 3 o'clock.*
> - ▶ *I **need** to fix this door.*
>
> to give advice or to express a strong opinion
> - ▶ *You **should/ought** to go to bed if you're tired.*
> - ▶ *She **shouldn't** worry about me.*
>
> to give and ask for permission
> - ▶ *She **can** borrow my dress.*
> - ▶ ***Can/May/Could** I open the window?*

**2**  Match the sentences on the left with the use on the right:

| | | |
|---|---|---|
| 1  You can borrow my camera if you like. | a | instructions |
| 2  If you feel very ill you should go to the doctor. | b | permission |
| 3  You must lock the door. | c | necessary |
| 4  You don't need to bring food – just something to drink. | d | advice |
| 5  I need to make a phone call before I go out. | e | not necessary |

continued on next page

# Expressing degrees of certainty

In the speaker's opinion, John has the car:
▶ *The car's not here – John **must** have taken it.*

The speaker thinks this is Clare's sister but is not sure:
▶ *She **might / could** be Clare's sister. She looks very like her.*

The speaker thinks this is not possible:
▶ *She **can't** be his mother – she's younger than me.*

The speaker is sure she will do it:
▶ *If she's promised to do it **she'll** do it.*

The speaker is not sure if it will rain:
▶ *It **might / could** rain. It's getting cloudy.*

3  Fill in the gaps in these sentences with a word from the list on the right:

| | |
|---|---|
| 1  He ___ be a hairdresser. His hair's a mess. | a  may |
| 2  'Do you think Joanna will call?' | b  won't |
|    'Who knows? She ___ do.' | c  must |
| 3  She ___ ever come back – I know she won't. | d  can't |
| 4  Her hair's all wet – it ___ be raining. | e  might |
| 5  'It's 1–1 and there are five minutes to play. | |
|    We ___ still win.' | |

# Forming modal verbs

Modal verbs are very different from other verbs of English:

The forms of the verbs do not change, for example there is no -s in the third person of the present tense.
▶ *I can speak Spanish and she can speak Portuguese.*

They are always followed by a main verb and cannot be used as a main verb by themselves.
▶ *I must make a phone call. / We won't wait for you.*

They do not use *do* and *did* to form questions, negatives, and short answers.
▶ *'He wouldn't steal anything, would he?' 'Oh yes he would.'*

| MODAL VERB | SHORT FORM | NEGATIVE | SHORT FORM |
|---|---|---|---|
| can | | cannot | can't |
| could | | could not | couldn't |
| may | | may not | |
| might | | might not | mightn't |
| must | | must not | mustn't |
| ought to | | ought not to | oughtn't to |
| shall | | shall not | shan't |
| will | 'll | will not | won't |
| would | 'd | would not | wouldn't |

## Numbers

### Saying numbers

Don't forget to say 'and' after hundreds:
- ▶ *569*        *five hundred and sixty nine*
- ▶ *7,892*      *seven thousand, eight hundred and ninety two*
- ▶ *4,680,022 four million, six hundred and eighty thousand and twenty two*

### Parts of numbers: decimals and fractions

For decimals we say each number separately after the point (.)
- ▶ *2.5*   *two point five*            ▶ *3.65*   *three point six five*
- ▶ *22.33 twenty two point three three*

For fractions we say:
- ▶ *2¼*   *two and a quarter*          ▶ *⅕*   *one fifth*
- ▶ *5¾*   *five and three quarters*

Remember we use ordinal numbers for most fractions but not for ½, ¼, ¾
- ▶ *⅜*   *three eighths*               ▶ *⅓*   *a third or one third*
- ▶ *1/12*   *a twelfth or one twelfth*

### Percentages and other symbols

Here are some other symbols used with numbers:

| % | percent | 45% | *forty five percent* |
|---|---------|-----|----------------------|
| ° | degree | 22°C | *twenty two degrees Celsius* |
|   |        | 70°F | *seventy degrees Fahrenheit* |
| + | addition | $6 + 2 = 8$ | *six plus two is/equals eight* |
| − | subtraction | $6 - 2 = 4$ | *six minus two is/equals four* |
| × | multiplication | $6 \times 3 = 18$ | *six times three/six multiplied by three is/equals eighteen* |
| ÷ | division | $24 \div 4 = 6$ | *twenty four divided by four is/equals six* |

### Saying 0

'0' can be said in different ways. It is usually said as 'oh' or 'zero' ('zero' is especially used in American English). Here are some ways of saying '0':

MATHS: 0.65 UK: *nought point six five*, US: *zero point six five*
FOOTBALL: 6–0 UK: *six nil*, US: *six to zero*
TENNIS: 15–0 *fifteen love*
TELEPHONE NUMBER: 965703 *nine six five seven oh three*
(also US English *seven zero three*)

## Phrasal verbs

### What are phrasal verbs?

A phrasal verb is a verb followed by one or two adverbs or prepositions.
Here are some examples:

*get up break down look after run out look forward to*

It is usually impossible to guess the meaning of phrasal verbs just
from knowing the meaning of the verb and the adverb or preposition.
For example, 'give up something' means to stop doing or using something.
It has nothing to do with giving things.

### Finding phrasal verbs

In this dictionary, phrasal verbs follow the entry for the main verb, and are in
alphabetical order. For instance, the phrasal verb 'lose out' comes after all the
meanings of the verb 'lose'.

Many verbs are part of several phrasal verbs. The phrasal verbs are shown in
alphabetical order after the main verb.

**1** How many phrasal verbs can you find in the dictionary formed with the
following verbs?

 1 drag  2 hand  3 pack  4 make

**2** Use the dictionary to help you fill in the gaps in the sentences below to make
phrasal verbs.

 1 If you carry ____ spending like that you'll have no money left.
 2 I nodded ____ after lunch.
 3 The brakes suddenly seized ____ .
 4 It took him a long time to get ____ her death.

Of course, verbs are often used with their normal meanings with adverbs and
prepositions too, e.g.:
▶ *I went into the room.*
▶ *He put the book on the shelf.*

These are not phrasal verbs. They are just the normal meanings explained at
the entries for the verbs, adverbs, and prepositions.

### Phrasal verbs with more than one meaning

One phrasal verb can have more than one meaning.
Often, the meanings are not related:
▶ *Just pick up the phone and ring her!*
▶ *She picks up languages really easily.*

3 Write two sentences for each of these phrasal verbs, using different meanings for each sentence:

turn out     catch on     come under sth     fall apart

## The grammar of phrasal verbs

Some phrasal verbs have objects, some do not, and some sometimes have objects and sometimes do not. This is shown in the way the phrasal verb is written in the dictionary. The way the phrasal verb is written also shows you whether the object is a person, a thing, or an action.

Phrasal verbs that do not need an object are shown like this:

**check in**     ► *You need to check in three hours before the flight.*
**drift off**    ► *The room was so hot I could feel myself beginning to drift off.*

Phrasal verbs that need an object are shown like this:

**pack sth in**   ► *I packed in my job to go travelling.*
**pack sb off**   ► *They packed him off to school in Paris.*

Note that **sth** means 'something', and **sb** means 'someone'.

Phrasal verbs where an object is sometimes used and sometimes not used are shown like this:

**pack (sth) up**  ► *I packed up all my belongings and left the house.*
                   ► *Could you help me pack up?*

## Prepositions following phrasal verbs

Many phrasal verbs are often followed by particular prepositions.
These are shown in bold letters in the dictionary.
► *He **dressed up as** a ghost.*

4 Fill in the gaps in these sentences with the correct prepositions.

1 She stood in ___ her boss while he was sick.
2 Just carry on ___ your work.
3 She looked back ___ her days as a student with nostalgia.
4 He's always going on ___ his car.
5 We will have to cut back ___ our spending.

## Pronunciation

Pronouncing words in English is very difficult. Often, words are not written the way they are pronounced. The phonetic symbols after each word in the dictionary show you how to say each word. There is an explanation of all these symbols inside the back cover, and more information about the pronunciation system on page 11.

Some of the symbols are pronounced in the same way as the letter they look like, e.g. /b/ sounds like 'b' in 'bad'. All the others are explained at the bottom of every page in the dictionary.

**1** Look at these words and match them with their pronunciations.

| | | | |
|---|---|---|---|
| 1 | cough | a | /'sɪnəmə/ |
| 2 | throw | b | /θruː/ |
| 3 | through | c | /sɪŋ/ |
| 4 | cup | d | /kɒf/ |
| 5 | cinema | e | /θrəʊ/ |
| 6 | sing | f | /kʌp/ |

**2** All these words are names of animals. Write the name of the animal next to the phonetic symbols.

| | | | | | |
|---|---|---|---|---|---|
| 1 | /məʊl/ | 3 | /hɔːs/ | 5 | /laɪən/ |
| 2 | /dʒɪˈrɑːf/ | 4 | /ʃiːp/ | 6 | /tʃɪmp/ |

## Silent letters

Many words in English contain letters that are not pronounced, for example the 't' in 'listen' /lɪsn/.

**3** Which is the silent letter in each of these words?

| | | | | | |
|---|---|---|---|---|---|
| 1 | know | 3 | island | 5 | two |
| 2 | honest | 4 | wrong | 6 | talk |

## Word stress

In English, it is very important to put the stress on the right part of the word. The symbol / ' / shows you where to put the main stress. (Some words have another, less important stress too.)

| **purple** /'pɜːpl/ | **important** /ɪmˈpɔːtənt/ | **difficult** /'dɪfɪkəlt/ |
|---|---|---|

**4** Put a circle around the part of each word that has the main stress.

| | | | | | |
|---|---|---|---|---|---|
| 1 | brother | 3 | photographer | 5 | computer |
| 2 | education | 4 | below | 6 | necessary |

# Punctuation

|  | Uses | Examples |
|---|---|---|
| capital letter | ■ the first letter of a sentence | *Fishing is popular in Britain.* |
|  | ■ for countries, nationalities, languages, religions, names of people, places, events, organizations, trademarks, days, months, titles | Portugal, Africa, Russian, Moslem, Joanne, John, Dubai, Geneva, the World Trade Fair, Jaguar, the Internet, Sunday, February, Mr. / Mrs. / Ms. / Dr./ Professor |
|  | ■ for titles of books, films, etc. | *Silence of the Lambs* |
|  | ■ for abbreviations | OPEC, AIDS, WWF |
| full stop UK/ period US | ■ the end of a sentence | *I'm going for a walk.* |
|  | ■ sometimes after an abbreviation | Marton Rd./Mrs. White/Dr. Evans |
| question mark | ■ after a direct question | *What's your name?* |
| exclamation mark | ■ at the end of a sentence to express surprise/ shock, etc. | *I can't believe it!* |
|  | ■ to indicate a loud sound | Ouch! Yes! |
| comma | ■ between items in a list | *I need some peas, butter, sugar and eggs.* |
|  | ■ to show a pause in a long sentence | *They didn't want to eat before I'd arrived, but I was an hour late.* |
|  | ■ when you want to add extra information | *The woman, who I'd met last week, waved as she went past.* |
| apostrophe | ■ for missing letters | don't, I'll, it's (it is) |
|  | ■ for possessives | Paul's bike |
|  | Note: words ending in 's' don't need another 's' added | James' house |
| colon | ■ to introduce a list or a quotation in a sentence | *You need the following: paint, brushes, water, cloths.* |
| semi-colon | ■ to separate two parts of a sentence | *I spoke to Linda on Monday; she can't come to the meeting tomorrow.* |
| hyphen | ■ to join two words together | blue-black |
|  | ■ to show that a word has been divided and continues on the next line | *Everyone in the room was horrified by the news,* |
| dash | ■ to separate parts of sentences | *The car – the one with the broken window – was parked outside our house.* |
| quotation marks/UK also inverted commas | ■ to show that words are spoken | *'I'm tired,' she said. 'Let's go,' he suggested.* |
|  | ■ to show that someone else originally wrote the words | *She had described the school as 'not attracting the best pupils'.* |

## Spelling

Because of its history, the English language does not have simple spelling rules. Often words are not written exactly as they sound, so it is important to check the spelling of any new word and to copy it down correctly.

### Top 10 learner spelling errors

(taken from the Cambridge Learners' Corpus)

| 1 | accommodation | double **c** and double **m** |
|---|---|---|
| 2 | centre | **-re** in UK English, **-er** in US English. Be careful not to mix UK and US spellings |
| 3 | too | be careful not to confuse **too** and **to**. |
| 4 | writing | only one **t** |
| 5 | completely | don't forget the second **e** |
| 6 | successful | double **c**, double **s**, but only one **l** |
| 7 | which | don't forget the silent **h** |
| 8 | advertisement | don't forget the **e** in the middle -isement |
| 9 | beautiful | vowel combination **eau**, only one **l** |
| 10 | course | don't forget the ending - **rse** |

Which words do you make the most mistakes with?
Why not make a list which you can use to check your written work?

### Regular inflections

There are many rules you can learn which will help a lot with your spelling. Look at page 12, which explains the rules for regular inflections (e.g. plurals, past tenses).

**1** Write the plural of these nouns.

   1  house  2  watch    3  brick    4  minute    5  fax    6  loss

### Word beginnings

Even the first letter of a word can sometimes be difficult to guess.

**c**  Some words beginning with **c** sound as though they begin with **s**,
  ▶ *cell, centre, circle*

**ps** Words beginning with **ps** sound as though they start with **s**,
  ▶ *pseudonym, psychiatrist*

**ph** Words beginning with **ph** sound as though they start with **f**,
  ▶ *philosophy, phone, physical*

## Same or similar sound, different spelling

Some words in English have the same or very similar sounds, but are spelled differently.

2   Choose the correct word from the pair on the right to fill in the gaps.

1 Stir the ___ into the cake mixture.              flour/flower
2 It's ___ a long way to my brother's house.       quiet/quite
3 A bird sat on the ___ of the tree.               bow/bough
4 The new regulations will not ___ us.             affect/effect
5 I need to ___ up this tear in my shirt.          sow/sew

## Doubling consonants

Some adjectives have a double consonant at the end when they make the comparative form with **-er** and the superlative form with **-est**. When this happens, it is clearly shown in the entry for those adjectives.

> ○—**sad** /sæd/ *adj* **sadder, saddest**
> **1** NOT HAPPY unhappy or making you feel unhappy *I was very sad when our cat died.* • *a sad book/movie* • [+ that] *It's a bit sad that you'll miss our wedding.* • [+ to do sth] *I was sad to see him go.*

Some verbs have a double consonant when they make the present participle or the past tense and past participle. This is also shown clearly in the entry for those verbs.

> **pop**[1] /pɒp/ *verb* **popping,** *past* **popped**
> **1** [I, T] to make a short sound like a small explosion, or to make something do this by breaking it *The music played and champagne corks popped.*

A lot of verbs ending in **l** (e.g. travel, level) have a double consonant in UK English, and a single consonant in US English. This is also shown in the entry for those verbs.

3   Fill in the gaps in the sentences below with the correct inflection of the word on the right. Be careful not to double the consonant where it is not correct to do so.

1 It's usually ___ than this in the summer.       (hot)
2 The use of mobile phones is ___ on aircraft.    (ban)
3 The concert was the ___ I've ever been to.      (loud)
4 I'm ___ to find my way around the city.         (begin)
5 I'm tired of ___ ten hours a day.               (work)

British and American children learn this rhyme to help them with their spelling:

'**I** before **E**, except after **C**.'

▶ *friend, receive*

# Transport and travel

## Talking about travelling

*We went by* 
- car
- train
- plane
- bus
- coach
- bicycle
- boat
- ferry

*We went **on the*** 
- ferry · underground UK
- bus · subway US
- coach · train

*He is **riding** a* 
- motorbike/motorcycle
- bike
- horse

*She is **driving** a* 
- car
- bus
- coach
- lorry UK
- truck US

*She **got in/got out of** the* car.

*He **got on/got off** the* 
- coach
- train
- boat
- bus
- bicycle
- plane
- ferry

## At the train station

— *I'd like a ticket from London to Brighton for next Thursday, please.*
— *Would you like a single UK/one-way ticket US or a return UK/round trip ticket US?*
— *Return please.*
— *And would you like to reserve a seat?*
— *Yes, please. Non-smoking if possible.*
— *Fine. That'll be £20.*

## At the airport

Chris is going to Berlin **by plane**. His parents take him to the **airport terminal**. They go to the **departure area** and find the **check-in desk** for his **flight**. He shows his **ticket** and **passport** and **checks in** his **luggage**. He gets his **boarding card** which he needs to **board the plane**.

He says goodbye to his parents and **goes through passport control** into the **departure lounge**. His flight is leaving from **gate** 7. He has an hour until **take-off**. That's just enough time to look around the **duty-free shops**. His flight is **called** over the **loudspeaker**, "Flight BA134 departing for Berlin is now **ready for boarding**. Would passengers please board at gate 7." The plane **touches down** on time. He gets his luggage from the **baggage collection point** and goes through **customs**. His friend is waiting for him in the **arrivals hall**.

# UK and US English

Although English in the UK and the US is very similar, there are a lot of differences in vocabulary, spelling, grammar, and pronunciation.

This dictionary shows you when there are differences.
For a full explanation of the UK and US labels, see page 10.

## Vocabulary

Many common words for items we see or use every day are different in UK and US English.

1 The words on the left are UK English. Match each one with a
  US word from the list on the right.

| | | | | | |
|---|---|---|---|---|---|
| 1 aubergine | 4 windscreen | | a elevator | d eggplant |
| 2 wardrobe | 5 queue | | b truck | e closet |
| 3 lift | 6 lorry | | c windshield | f line |

In informal language there are lots of differences between UK and US English.

2 The underlined word in each sentence is used in UK English only.
  Replace it with a word from the list on the right which would be understood in
  both UK and US English.

| | |
|---|---|
| 1 I got it from a bloke at work. | a complaining |
| 2 I'm feeling rather poorly today. | b man |
| 3 I wish he'd stop whingeing and do some work. | c weak |
| 4 I was gutted when I heard I hadn't got the job. | d disappointed |
| 5 My brother's too weedy to climb that tree. | e ill |

## Spelling

3 Look at these pairs of words. Which is the UK spelling and which is the US
  spelling?

| | | |
|---|---|---|
| 1 labour/labor | 3 offence/offense | 5 metre/meter |
| 2 center/centre | 4 color/colour | 6 traveller/traveler |

## Pronunciation

In this dictionary, words which are pronounced very differently
in UK and US English have both pronunciations shown at the word.
The US pronunciation follows the symbol ⑤.

4 Which of these words have
  different pronunciations in
  UK and US English?

| | |
|---|---|
| 1 peach | 4 ballet |
| 2 schedule | 5 zebra |
| 3 colour | 6 bicycle |

> **tomato** /təˈmɑːtəʊ ⑤ təˈmeɪtəʊ/ *noun* [C, U]
> *plural* **tomatoes** a soft, round, red fruit
> eaten in salad or as a vegetable ➲ *See colour
> picture* **Fruit and Vegetables** *on page
> Centre 8.*

## Verb patterns

| | |
|---|---|
| Some verbs must have something (an object) after them:<br>▶ *She put **the cup** on the table.*<br>▶ *Did you **bring any** money?*<br><br>These verbs are 'transitive' verbs. They are marked in the dictionary with a [T]. | Other verbs don't need anything after them:<br>▶ *He **fell**.*<br>▶ *They don't want to **stay**.*<br><br>These verbs are 'intransitive' verbs. They are marked in the dictionary with an [I]. |

Some verbs can be both transitive and intransitive:
▶ *Did you **see the moon** last night?* [T]     ▶ *Can you move, please?*
                                                    *I can't **see**.* [I]
▶ *Did you **pay the bill**?* [T]                ▶ *Have you **paid**?* [I]

**1** Look up these verbs in the dictionary to find out if they are transitive or intransitive or both.

| | | | | |
|---|---|---|---|---|
| 1 like | 3 drive | 5 tell | 7 hate | 9 fall |
| 2 hear | 4 smoke | 6 explain | 8 play | 10 hit |

Sometimes a verb has to be followed by other grammar words or grammar patterns, for example a preposition, an infinitive verb, or a verb ending '-ing':

|  |  |
|---|---|
| | *I **apologized to** her.* |
| [+to do sth] | *I **promise to help** you.* |
| [+ -ing] | *Have you **finished reading** the newspaper?* |
| [+ to do sth] | *She **asked us to talk** quietly.* |
| [+ (that)] | *He **told me (that)** it was safe.* |

If you are not sure what type of grammar to use after a verb, look up the word in the dictionary. There is a full explanation of all the grammar codes on page 8.

**2** Can you describe what follows these verbs? Match the underlined parts on the left with a description from the list on the right.

| | |
|---|---|
| 1 He's always **complaining** <u>that</u> nobody listens to him | a  + to do sth |
| 2 Did she **say** <u>where</u> she was going? | b  + two objects |
| 3 He doesn't **like** <u>watching</u> TV. | c  + that |
| 4 They **want** <u>to go</u> shopping. | d  + doing sth |
| 5 He **brought** <u>me some flowers</u>. | e  + question word |

**3** Write a sentence using each of these verbs and the patterns that are shown in the following grammar codes.

| | | | | |
|---|---|---|---|---|
| 1 forget | + [that] | | 4 start | + to do sth |
| 2 tell | + question word | | 5 sell | + two objects |
| 3 like | + doing sth | | | |

## Word Formation

Here are some ways of building words in English.

## Prefixes

Prefixes are added to the beginning of words to change their meaning. There is a list of common prefixes on page 751.

Here are some common prefixes that are used before adjectives to give opposite and often negative meanings:

| | | |
|---|---|---|
| dis- | dissimilar | When you learn a new adjective try to find out |
| il- | illegal | if its opposite is formed with a prefix and write |
| im- | impossible | down the two words together, |
| in- | inexpensive | e.g. happy ≠ unhappy. |
| ir- | irregular | |
| un- | unhappy | |

The prefixes **un-** and **dis-** combine with verbs to form the opposite of the action of the verb.

► *She appeared from behind a door.*

► *He disappeared through the window.*

► *I covered the food with a cloth.*

► *They brushed away the dirt to uncover a box.*

**1** Match the prefixes on the left to the adjectives and verbs on the right to make new words.

| 1 un- | 4 im- | lock | legal |
|---|---|---|---|
| 2 dis- | 5 ir- | responsible | agree |
| 3 il- | | possible | |

**2** Now use the words you have made to fill in the gaps in the sentences below.

1 Which key do I need to ____ this door?
2 The tide is so strong it's ____ to swim against it.
3 It is ____ to drive without a licence.
4 I ____ with her views on immigration.
5 Leaving the children alone was a very ____ thing to do.

**3** There are many other prefixes used in English. Match the prefix on the left with the meaning on the right. Then form new words by choosing a suitable word from the box to combine with each prefix.

| 1 multi- | a half |
|---|---|
| 2 semi- | b in favour of |
| 3 anti- | c former (not now) |
| 4 pro- | d not enough |
| 5 ex- | e many |
| 6 post- | f against |
| 7 over- | g after |
| 8 under- | h too much |

| | |
|---|---|
| president | war |
| cooked | racial |
| graduate | worked |
| circle | democracy |

continued on next page

## Suffixes

Suffixes are used at the ends of words. Here are some common ones:

| -er<br>-or | ■ for people who do activities and for things that have a particular function | worker, swimmer, golfer, driver, actor, sailor, conductor tin opener, screwdriver, hanger, projector |
|---|---|---|
| -ist | ■ for people with certain beliefs<br>■ who play musical instruments<br>■ for some professions | Buddhist, socialist<br><br>violinist, pianist, guitarist<br><br>journalist, pharmacist, artist |
| -ness | to make nouns from adjectives | happiness, sadness, rudeness |
| -(t)ion | to make nouns from verbs | education, television, pollution |
| -ment | to make nouns from verbs | improvement, government |

Note: Adding a suffix to a word sometimes changes its pronunciation. Look at how the stress changes in these words:

**pho**tograph → phot**og**rapher          **ed**ucate → edu**ca**tion

## Noun, verb, adjective?

Most suffixes can tell you whether a word is a noun, adjective or verb. This table shows some common ones:

| adjectives | -able, -al, -ful, -ible, -ive, -less, -ous, -y | washable, natural, beautiful, flexible, active, helpless, adventurous, happy |
|---|---|---|
| nouns | -ance, -(t)ion, -ence, -hood, -ity, -ment, -ness, -ship | performance, reduction, independence, parenthood, similarity, enjoyment, politeness, friendship |
| verb | -en, -ify, -ize | harden, solidify, modernize |

Note: -al can be used to make nouns, e.g. arrival and adjectives, e.g. comical

4 Use suffixes to change the following adjectives and verbs into nouns.

|   |   |   |   |
|---|---|---|---|
| 1 | rude | 4 | ignorant |
| 2 | create | 5 | hilarious |
| 3 | prefer | 6 | develop |

## Writing letters

### Formal letters

> 47 Abrahams Rd
> Cambridge
> CB4 3AL
>
> 21 February 2001
>
> Ms R Perry
> Evening News
> 107 Wolfs Way
> Newtown
> NT7 0PE
>
> Dear Ms Perry ❶
>
> I am ❸ writing to enquire about ❷ the possibility of holiday work with your company this summer. I am very interested in gaining some experience working for a newspaper.
>
> For the last two years I have been editor of the student magazine at my school. Next year I am planning to do a one-year course in newspaper journalism.
>
> I have good computer skills and accurate written English.
>
> I very much hope you have a vacancy for me. I enclose a copy of my CV and look forward to hearing from you soon. ❹
>
> Yours sincerely, ❶
>
> *Anna Thompson*

❶ If you know the name of the person you are writing to, but the letter is formal, end the letter: *Yours sincerely.*

If you do not know the name of the person you are writing to, begin the letter: *Dear Sir/Madam* and end it: *Yours faithfully.*

❷ Other ways of beginning a formal letter:
  ▶ *I am writing to inform you of/that ...*
  ▶ *I am writing to complain about ...*
  ▶ *I am writing regarding your advertisement*
  ▶ *Please send me ...*
  ▶ *Further to my letter of June 1st ...*

❸ You should not use contractions (e.g. I'm, I'd) in a formal letter.

❹ Other ways of ending a formal letter:
  ▶ *Thank you in advance for your help.*
  ▶ *Wishing you all the best for the future.*

continued on next page

## Informal letters

47 Abrahams Rd
Cambridge
CB4 3AL

21 February 2001

Dear Julia,

It was lovely to chat to you the other day. **❶** It seems ages since we last met. We're so excited that you're finally coming over to see us. In fact, John's going to take those two weeks off work so he can spend more time with us.

By the way, could you bring some photos of your family? I'd love to see them.

We're both really looking forward to seeing you. **❷**

Love, **❸**
Anna

**❶** Other ways of starting an informal letter:
  ▶ *Thanks for your letter.*
  ▶ *How are you?*
  ▶ *I hope you're well.*
  ▶ *Sorry it's been so long since I last wrote.*
  ▶ *It was lovely to hear from you.*

**❷** Other ways of ending an informal letter:
  ▶ *Drop me a line soon.*
  ▶ *Write soon.*
  ▶ *Take care.*
  ▶ *Do keep in touch.*
  ▶ *Give my love to Paul.*
  ▶ *Hope to hear from you soon.*

**❸** Before your name, you write:

to close friends:
  ▶ *love from*
  ▶ *all my love*
  ▶ *lots of love*

to less close friends:
  ▶ *best wishes*
  ▶ *all the best*
  ▶ *yours*
  ▶ *kind regards*

# Answer key

### Adjectives

**1** **1** a big old black cat
  **2** a large Nigerian drum
  **3** a dirty old ski jacket
  **4** a beautiful leather briefcase
**2** the gradable adjective comes first in each pair:
  small, tiny; hungry, starving; tired, exhausted;
  hot, boiling; interesting, fascinating

### Checking your work

**1** **1** The new rule affects everyone
  **2** What time is it?
  **3** It's quite hot in here.
  **4** He made an interesting speech.
**2** **1** do **2** take **3** of **4** feeling
**3** My name is Dida and I'm Italian. I am 22 years
  old. When I left university, my father suggested
  going to London for a year to study English.
  When I arrived everything felt very strange.
  The weather was very cold. In Italy I was used
  to going out without a coat. I have good
  accommodation and I have made many new
  friends. I am studying hard, but I still make many
  mistakes. When I finish my course here
  I will go back to Italy to find a job.

### Collocations

**1** **1** d **2** e **3** b **4** c **5** a
**2** **1** heavy **2** strong or broad **3** good
  **4** thick
**3** **1** about **2** for **3** to **4** at

### Countable and uncountable nouns

**1** **1** homework **2** sand **3** ✓ **4** ✓ **5** ✓
  **6** luggage
**2** **1** an **2** –, a **3** a **4** — **5** —
**3** **1** fly **2** furniture **3** luggage **4** day
  **5** accidents
**4** **1** a lot of **2** much **3** many **4** much
**5** duck, ice cream, lipstick, pizza

### Family

**1** **1** cousin **2** grandmother **3** uncle
  **4** sister-in-law **5** nephew
**2** **1** an only child **2** half-sister **3** partner
  **4** stepfather **5** boyfriend

### Idioms

**1** **1** neck: b **2** nail: e **3** battle: a **4** end: c
  **5** face: d
**2** **1** leg **2** head **3** arm **4** ear **5** face

### Measurements

**1** wide, width **2** long **3** depth
**4** high, high

### The media

**1** **1** c **2** e **3** a **4** b **5** d
**2** **1** documentary **2** soap (opera)
  **3** game show **4** news
**3** **1** headline **2** picture **3** columns
  **4** caption

### Modal verbs

**1** 7
**2** **1** b **2** d **3** a **4** e **5** c
**3** **1** d **2** e **3** b **4** c **5** a

### Phrasal verbs

**1** **1** drag: 3 **2** hand: 5 **3** pack: 3
  **4** make: 12
**2** **1** on **2** off **3** up **4** over
**3** your own answers
**4** **1** for **2** with **3** on **4** about **5** on

### Pronunciation

**1** **1** d **2** e **3** b **4** f **5** a **6** c
**2** **1** mole **2** giraffe **3** horse **4** sheep
  **5** lion **6** chimp
**3** **1** k **2** h **3** s **4** w **5** w **6** l
**4** **1** **bro**ther **2** edu**ca**tion **3** pho**tog**rapher
  **4** be**low** **5** com**pu**ter **6** **ne**cessary

## Spelling

1 1 houses   2 watches   3 bricks
   4 minutes   5 faxes   6 losses
2 1 flour   2 quite   3 bough   4 affect
   5 sew
3 1 hotter   2 banned   3 loudest
   4 beginning   5 working

## UK and US English

1 1 d   2 e   3 a   4 c   5 f   6 b
2 1 man   2 ill   3 complaining
   4 disappointed   5 weak
3 (in each case, UK comes first)   1 labour/labor
   2 centre/center   3 offence/offense
   4 colour/color   5 metre/meter
   6 traveller/traveler
4 schedule, ballet, zebra

## Verb patterns

1 1 [T]   2 [I, T]   3 [I, T]   4 [I, T]   5 [T]
   6 [I, T]   7 [T]   8 [I, T]   9 [I]   10 [T]
2 1 c   2 e   3 d   4 a   5 b
3 your own answers

## Word Formation

1 1 unlock   2 disagree   3 illegal
   4 impossible   5 disagre
2 1 unlock   2 iimpossible   3 illegal
   4 disagree   5 irresponsible
3 1 multiracial   2 semicircle   3 anti-war
   4 pro-democracy   5 (ex-p      resident)
   6 (postgraduate)
   7 (overworked)   8 (under-cooked)
4 1 rudeness   2 creation   3 preference
   4 ignorance   5 hilarity   6 development

whose husband has died) **3** PRISON/SCHOOL US a woman who is a manager at some hospitals, schools, prisons, etc

**matt** *UK* (*US* **matte**) /mæt/ *adj* not shiny *a matt photograph* • *matt paint*

○ᵈ **matter¹** /'mætəʳ/ *noun* **1** SUBJECT [C] a subject or situation that you need to think about, discuss, or deal with *I've been thinking about this matter for a long time.* • *He denied any knowledge of the matter.* • **To make matters worse,** *our car broke down!* **2** SUBSTANCE [U] In science, matter is the physical substances that exist in the universe. **3** TYPE OF THING [U] a particular type of substance or thing *vegetable matter* • *printed matter* **4 what's the matter** used to ask or talk about the reason for a problem *What's the matter with your leg?* • *I can't help you if you won't tell me what the matter is.* **5 there's something/nothing the matter** used to say that there is/is not a problem *There's something the matter with the washing machine.* **6 a matter of days/ weeks/feet, etc** used in expressions describing how small an amount or period of time is *The aircraft missed each other by a matter of feet.* **7 a matter of confidence/luck/waiting, etc** If something is a matter of confidence/ luck/waiting, etc, that is what you need for it to happen. *Learning languages is just a matter of hard work.* **8 no matter how/what/when, etc** used to emphasize that something cannot be changed *I never manage to lose any weight, no matter how hard I try.* **9 as a matter of fact** used to emphasize that something is true, especially when it is surprising *As a matter of fact, I used to live next door to him.* **10 a matter of course** If something happens as a matter of course, it always happens as part of the normal process or system. *Babies were tested for the disease as a matter of course.* **11 a matter of life and/or death** a serious situation where people could die *Getting water to these people is a matter of life and death.* **12 it's only a matter of time** If you say that it is only a matter of time before something happens, you are sure it will happen but you do not know when. **13 be no laughing matter** If a subject is no laughing matter, it is serious and not something that people should joke about. ➔ See also: **subject matter**.

○ᵈ **matter²** /'mætəʳ/ *verb* [I] to be important, or to affect what happens *We were late, but it didn't seem to matter.* • *It doesn't matter to me whether he comes or not.* • *"I've forgotten to bring your book back." "It doesn't matter – there's no hurry."*

**matter-of-fact** /,mætərəv'fækt/ *adj* not showing emotion when you talk about something *a matter-of-fact tone/manner* • **matter-of-factly** *adv*

**matting** /'mætɪŋ/ *noun* [U] strong, rough material for covering floors

**mattress** /'mætrəs/ *noun* [C] the soft, comfortable part of a bed that you lie on

**mature¹** /mə'tjʊəʳ/ *adj* **1** completely grown or developed *sexually mature* • *mature trees* **2** Mature people behave like adults in a way which shows they are well developed emotion-

ally. *She seems very mature for thirteen.* ➔ *Opposite* **immature**.

**mature²** /mə'tjʊəʳ/ *verb* [I] **1** AGE to become completely grown or developed **2** BEHAVIOUR to start to behave in a more mature way *Girls mature sooner than boys.* **3** MONEY If an investment (= money you have given to a bank or a company in order to make a profit) matures, you receive the money you have made from it.

**ma,ture 'student** *noun* [C] a college or university student who is older than the usual age

**maturity** /mə'tjʊərəti/ *noun* [U] **1** the quality of behaving like an adult, in a way which shows that you are well developed emotionally *She shows remarkable maturity for a child of 13.* **2** when someone or something is completely grown or developed *Penguins reach maturity in late summer.*

**maul** /mɔːl/ *verb* [T] **1** If you are mauled by an animal, you are injured by its teeth or claws (= the sharp parts of its feet). [often passive] *He was mauled by a lion.* **2** to criticize someone very badly [often passive] *His film was mauled by critics.*

**mausoleum** /,mɔːsə'liːəm/ *noun* [C] a building where dead people are buried

**mauve** /məʊv/ *noun* [U] a pale purple colour • *mauve adj*

**maverick** /'mævərɪk/ *noun* [C] someone who thinks and behaves in an unusual way *a maverick cop/politician*

**max** /mæks/ *adj informal* **1** *abbreviation for* maximum (= the largest amount allowed or possible) **2** *informal* used with numbers or amounts to mean 'at the most' *The trip should take 30 minutes max.* **3 to the max** *informal* as much as possible *He lived life to the max.*

**maxim** /'mæksɪm/ *noun* [C] a phrase which gives advice *Our company works on the maxim that small is beautiful.*

**maximize** (*also UK* **-ise**) /'mæksɪmaɪz/ *verb* [T] to increase something as much as you can *to maximize profits*

○ᵈ **maximum¹** /'mæksɪməm/ *adj* [always before noun] The maximum amount of something is the largest amount that is allowed or possible. *the maximum temperature/speed* ➔ *Opposite* **minimum**.

**maximum²** /'mæksɪməm/ *noun* [no plural] the largest amount that is allowed or possible *The school has a maximum of 30 students per class.*

○ᵈ **may** /meɪ/ *modal verb* **1** used to talk about what is possibly true or will possibly happen *There may be other problems that we don't know about.* • *I think I may have a cold.* **2** *formal* used to ask or give permission *May I be excused, please?* • *You may begin.* **3 may (well) ... but** used to show that the first thing you say is not important when compared to another fact *It may be cheap but it's not very good.* ➔ *See study section* **Modal verbs** *on page Centre 31.*

---

**USAGE**

**may be** or **maybe**?

**May be** is written as two separate words when **be** is used as a verb. Here **may** is being used as a modal verb.

---

*I may be late this evening.*

~~I maybe late this evening.~~

**Maybe** is an adverb, and is written as one word.

*Maybe we should do it tomorrow.*

~~May be we should do it tomorrow.~~

---

**May** /meɪ/ *noun* [C, U] the fifth month of the year

o╼**maybe** /'meɪbi/ *adv* **1** possibly *Maybe we're too early. • It could take a month, or maybe more, to complete.* **2** used to suggest something *Maybe Ted would like to go.*

**mayhem** /'meɪhem/ *noun* [U] a situation in which there is no order or control *With five kids running around, it was complete mayhem.*

**mayonnaise** /ˌmeɪə'neɪz/ *noun* [U] a thick, cold, white sauce that is made from eggs and oil

**mayor** /meəʳ/ *noun* [C] the person who is elected to be the leader of the group that governs a town or city

**maze** /meɪz/ *noun* [C] a complicated system of paths where you can easily become lost

**MB** *written abbreviation for* megabyte (= a unit for measuring the amount of information a computer can store) *This program needs 8 MB of hard-disk space.*

**McCoy** /mə'kɔɪ/ *noun* **the real McCoy** *informal* the real thing, and not a copy or something similar *Cheap sparkling wines cannot be labelled 'champagne' – it has to be the real McCoy.*

**MD** /ˌem'diː/ *abbreviation for* Doctor of Medicine

o╼**me** /miː/ *pronoun* used after a verb or preposition to refer to the person who is speaking or writing *She gave me some money. • She never gave it to me. • Lydia is three years younger than me. • It wasn't me!*

---

**USAGE**

**me** or **I**?

**Me** is used after 'than', 'as', or 'be'. It would sound very formal if you used **I**.

*She's taller than me.*

*David is not as tall as me.*

*"Who's there?" "It's me."*

~~"Who's there?" "It's I."~~

Sometimes **me** is used with another noun as the subject of a sentence, especially in informal English.

*Jane and me went to the cinema yesterday. (informal)*

*Jane and I went to the cinema yesterday.*

---

**meadow** /'medəʊ/ *noun* [C] a field of grass, often with flowers

**meagre** UK (US **meager**) /'miːgəʳ/ *adj* not enough in amount *a meagre ration/salary*

o╼**meal** /miːl/ *noun* [C] **1** when you eat, or the food that you eat at that time *a three-course meal • You should come round for a meal sometime.* **2 make a meal of sth** UK to spend more time and energy doing something than is necessary *A simple apology will do. There's no need to make a meal of it!* ⊃ See also: a **square²** meal.

**mealtime** /'miːltaɪm/ *noun* [C] when you eat *These days I only see him at mealtimes.*

o╼**mean¹** /miːn/ *verb* [T] *past* **meant** /ment/ **1** MEANING to have a particular meaning *What does 'perpendicular' mean? • The red light means stop.* **2** EXPRESS to intend to express a fact or opinion *I didn't mean that as a criticism. • That's what I meant when I said he's been acting oddly. • What exactly do you mean by 'old-fashioned'?* **3 mean to do sth** to intend to do something *I didn't mean to hurt her.* **4** RESULT to have a particular result *These changes will mean better health care for everyone. • [+ (that)] It doesn't mean that you can stop working.* **5** SERIOUS to be serious about something that you have said *I'll take that sandwich away if you don't eat it properly – I mean it!* **6** IMPORTANT to have an important emotional effect on someone *You don't know what it means to me to get this letter. • Their support has meant a lot to us.* **7 have been meaning to do sth** to have been wanting and planning to do something *I've been meaning to call you for weeks.* **8 be meant to do sth** If you are meant to do something, that is what you should do in order to behave correctly. *You're meant to shake the bottle first. • He's not meant to drive any more.* **9 mean well** to intend to behave in a kind way *I know my parents mean well, but I wish they wouldn't interfere.* **10 I mean a** something that people often say before they continue their sentence *I mean, I don't dislike her.* **b** something that you say in order to correct yourself *We went there in May – I mean June.*

**mean²** /miːn/ *adj* **1** UNKIND unkind and unpleasant *I thought my sister was being mean to me.* **2** NOT GENEROUS *mainly UK* A mean person does not like spending money, especially on other people. *He's too mean to buy her a ring.* **3** VIOLENT *mainly US* A mean person or animal is strong and violent, and makes people frightened. *He's a big, mean guy.* **4** GOOD [always before noun] *informal* very good *I make a mean spaghetti.* **5** AVERAGE [always before noun] In mathematics, a mean number is an average number. *Their mean age at death was 84.6.* **6 no mean** used to describe something very difficult *Setting up a business in two days was no mean feat* (= was a difficult thing to do).

**mean³** /miːn/ *noun* [no plural] *formal* the average

**meander** /mi'ændəʳ/ *verb* **1 meander along/ around/through, etc** If a river, a road, or a line of something meanders, it has many curves. *The coast road meanders along the beach for miles.* **2 meander around/from/off, etc** to move around with no clear purpose *We meandered around town for a couple of hours.*

o╼**meaning** /'miːnɪŋ/ *noun* **1** [C, U] The meaning of words, signs, or actions is what they express or represent. *The word 'squash' has several meanings. • The meaning of her gesture was clear.* **2** [U, no plural] purpose or emotional importance *She felt that her life had no meaning.*

**meaningful** /'miːnɪŋfəl/ *adj* **1** USEFUL useful, serious, or important *a meaningful discussion* **2** WITH MEANING having a clear meaning which people can understand *a meaningful compari-*

---

*son/conclusion* **3** LOOK intended to show a meaning, often secretly *a meaningful look* • meaningfully *adv*

**meaningless** /ˈmiːnɪŋləs/ *adj* without any meaning or purpose *He produced yet another set of meaningless statistics.*

o⌐**means** /miːnz/ *noun* **1** [C] *plural* **means** a way of doing something *We had no means of communication.* • *It was a means of making money.* **2** [plural] money *We don't have the means to buy the house.* **3 by no means; not by any means** not at all *I'm not an expert by any means.* • *This is by no means the end of the matter.* **4 by all means** something that you say when you are agreeing to let someone do something *I have a copy of the report on my desk. By all means have a look at it.*

**means-tested** /ˈmiːnztestɪd/ *adj mainly UK* If an amount of money or an activity such as education is means-tested, it is only given to people who are poor enough. *means-tested benefits*

**meant** /ment/ *past of* mean

**meantime** /ˈmiːnˌtaɪm/ *noun* **in the meantime** in the time between two things happening, or while something else is happening *Your computer won't be arriving till Friday. In the meantime, you can use Julie's.*

o⌐**meanwhile** /ˈmiːnˌwaɪl/ *adv* in the time between two things happening, or while something else is happening *The mother is ill. The child, meanwhile, is living with foster parents.*

**measles** /ˈmiːzlz/ *noun* [U] an infectious disease which covers your skin in small, red spots ⊃ *See also:* **German measles**.

**measurable** /ˈmeʒ°rəbl/ *adj* If something is measurable, it is big enough to be measured. *Extra training has led to measurable improvements in performance.* ⊃ *Opposite* **immeasurable**.

o⌐**measure**[1] /ˈmeʒəʳ/ *verb* **1** JUDGE [T] to judge the quality, effect, importance, or value of something *We will soon be able to measure the results of these policy changes.* • *They measured the performance of three different engines.* **2** FIND SIZE [T] to find the size, weight, amount, or speed of something *I've measured all the windows.* • *The distances were measured in kilometres.* **3** BE SIZE [I] to be a certain size *a whale measuring around 60 feet in length*

**measure sth out** to weigh or measure a small amount of something and remove it from a larger amount *Use a hot spoon to measure out honey into a bowl.*

**measure up** to be good enough, or as good as something or someone else *He did not measure up to the requirements of the job.*

**measure**[2] /ˈmeʒəʳ/ *noun* **1** [C] a way of achieving something or dealing with a situation *This arrangement is only a temporary measure.* • *We must take preventative measures to stop the spread of the disease.* • *security measures* **2 a measure of sth** a good way of judging something *Ticket sales are not necessarily a measure of the show's popularity.* **3 a/some measure of sth** *formal* an amount of something *Bulletproof vests give some measure of protection.* **4** [U] a way of measuring something *The basic units of measure we use are distance, time, and mass.*

**5 for good measure** as well as something you have already done or given to someone *They stole his passport and wallet, and for good measure beat him unconscious.* ⊃ *See also:* **tape measure**.

o⌐**measurement** /ˈmeʒəmənt/ *noun* **1** PROCESS [U] the process of measuring something **2** SIZE [C] the size and shape of something *I've taken measurements of all the rooms.* **3** WAY OF MEASURING [U] a way of measuring something *SI units are the standard units of measurement used all over the world.*

o⌐**meat** /miːt/ *noun* [U] muscles and other soft parts of animals, used as food *I don't eat meat.* • *red/white meat* ⊃ *See colour picture* **Food** on *page Centre 7*.

**mecca** /ˈmekə/ *noun* [no plural] a place where particular groups of people like to go because they feel happy there *His Indiana bookstore became a mecca for writers and artists.*

**mechanic** /mɪˈkænɪk/ *noun* [C] someone whose job is to repair machines *a car mechanic*

**mechanical** /mɪˈkænɪk°l/ *adj* **1** relating to or operated by machines *a mechanical engineer* • *a mechanical device* **2** If you do something in a mechanical way, you do it without emotion or without thinking about it. *a mechanical performance* • mechanically *adv*

**mechanics** /mɪˈkænɪks/ *noun* [U] the study of physical forces on objects and their movement

**mechanism** /ˈmekənɪz°m/ *noun* [C] **1** a part of a piece of equipment that does a particular job *The clock's winding mechanism had broken.* **2** a system for achieving something, or the way that a system works *We need a mechanism for resolving this sort of dispute.*

**mechanized** (*also UK* **-ised**) /ˈmekənaɪzd/ *adj* A mechanized organization or activity uses machines. *mechanized farming/production*

**medal** /ˈmed°l/ *noun* [C] a metal disc given as a prize in a competition or given to someone who has been very brave *a bronze medal* • *an Olympic medal* ⊃ *See also:* **gold medal**, **silver medal**.

**medallist** *UK* (*US* **medalist**) /ˈmed°lɪst/ *noun* [C] someone who has received a medal in a sports event *an Olympic medallist*

**meddle** /ˈmedl/ *verb* [I] to try to influence people or change things that are not your responsibility *He's always meddling in other people's business.*

**the media** /ˈmiːdiə/ *noun* [group] television, newspapers, magazines, and radio considered as a group *media coverage/attention* • *The issue has been much discussed in the media.* ⊃ *See also:* **the mass media**.

**mediaeval** /medi'iːv°l/ *adj* another spelling of medieval (= relating to the period in Europe between about AD 500 and AD 1500)

**median** /ˈmiːdiən/ *adj* [always before noun] in mathematics, relating to the middle number or amount in a series *the median age/income*

**mediate** /ˈmiːdieɪt/ *verb* [I, T] to try to find a solution between two or more people who disagree about something *Negotiators were called in to mediate between the two sides.* • mediation /ˌmiːdiˈeɪʃ°n/ *noun* [U]

**mediator** /ˈmiːdieɪtəʳ/ *noun* [C] someone who

M

mediates between people who disagree about something

**medic** /'medɪk/ *noun* [C] *informal* **1** a medical student or doctor **2** *US* someone who does medical work in a military organization

o⁻**medical¹** /'medɪkˀl/ *adj* relating to medicine and different ways of curing illness *medical treatment* • *a medical student* • *She has a **medical condition** that makes it hard for her to work.* • **medically** *adv*

**medical²** /'medɪkˀl/ *UK* (*US* **physical**) *noun* [C] an examination of your body by a doctor to find out if you are healthy

**medicated** /'medɪkeɪtɪd/ *adj* A medicated substance contains medicine. *medicated soap*

**medication** /,medɪ'keɪʃˀn/ *noun* [C, U] medicine that is used to treat an illness *He's **on medication** to control his depression.*

**medicinal** /məˈdɪsɪnˀl/ *adj* Medicinal substances are used to cure illnesses. *I keep some brandy for medicinal purposes.*

o⁻**medicine** /'medsˀn/ *noun* **1** [C, U] a substance used to cure an illness or injury *cough medicine* • *Have you **taken** your **medicine** today?* • *The government appealed for food and medicines after the earthquake.* **2** [U] the science of curing and preventing illness and injury *to study medicine* • *western/Chinese medicine*

**medicine**

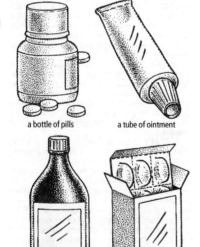

a bottle of pills      a tube of ointment

a bottle of medicine      a box of tablets

**medieval** (*also* **mediaeval**) /,medi'iːvˀl/ *adj* relating to the period in Europe between about AD 500 and 1500 *medieval literature/art*

**mediocre** /,miːdi'əʊkəʳ/ *adj* not good in quality *The acting was mediocre.* • **mediocrity** /,miːdi'ɒkrəti/ *noun* [U]

**meditate** /'medɪteɪt/ *verb* [I] **1** to think calm thoughts for a long period in order to relax or as a religious activity *I meditate twice a day.* **2** *formal* to think seriously about something *He **meditated on** the consequences of his decision.* • **meditation** /,medɪ'teɪʃˀn/ *noun* [U] *Let's spend a few moments in quiet meditation.*

**the Mediterranean** /,medɪtˀr'eɪniən/ *noun* the sea that has southern Europe, northern Africa, and the Middle East around it, or the countries around this sea • **Mediterranean** *adj a Mediterranean climate/island*

o⁻**medium¹** /'miːdiəm/ *adj* in the middle of a group of different amounts or sizes *people of medium weight* • *She bought a **medium-sized** car.* • *The shirt comes in small, medium, and large.*

**medium²** /'miːdiəm/ *noun* [C] *plural* **media** *or* **mediums** a way of communicating or expressing something *the medium of television/radio* • *The Internet has become yet another **medium** for marketing.*

**medium-term** /'miːdiəm,tɜːm/ *adj* continuing into the future for a time that is neither short nor long *The medium-term outlook remains favourable.*

**medley** /'medli/ *noun* [C] a mixture of different items, especially songs *She sang a **medley** of show tunes.*

**meek** /miːk/ *adj* Someone who is meek is quiet and does not argue with others. • **meekly** *adv*

o⁻**meet¹** /miːt/ *verb* past **met** /met/ **1** [COME TOGETHER] [I, T] to come to the same place as someone else by arrangement or by chance *We met for coffee last Sunday.* • *I met my old English teacher while trekking in the Alps.* • *Each student **meets with** an adviser at the start of the school year.* **2** [INTRODUCE] [I, T] to see and speak to someone for the first time *I've always wanted to meet a movie star.* • *"This is Helen." "Pleased to meet you."* ➔ *See usage note at* **know.** **3** [GROUP] [I] If a group of people meet, they come to a place in order to do something. *The shareholders meet once a year to discuss profits.* **4** [PLACE] [T] to wait at a place for someone or something to arrive *They met me at the airport.* **5** [ENOUGH] [T] to be a big enough amount or of a good enough quality for something *This old building will never meet the new fire regulations.* • *Can your product meet the needs of a wide range of consumers?* **6** [ACHIEVE] [T] to be able to achieve something *He met every goal he set for himself.* • *to meet a deadline* **7** [JOIN] [I, T] to join something *There's a large crack where the ceiling meets the wall.* ➔ *See also:* make ends (**end¹**) meet.

**meet** or **visit**?

You **meet** a person, but not a place or thing.

*I met John's parents for the first time last week.*

You **visit** a person, place, or thing.

*I visited my aunt today.*

*We visited Paris and the Eiffel Tower.*

**meet up 1** to meet another person in order to do something together *I met up with a few friends yesterday.* **2** If roads or paths meet up, they join at a particular place. *This path meets up with the main road.*

**meet with sth** to cause a particular reaction or result *Both proposals have met with fierce opposition.* • *(formal) I trust the arrangements meet with your approval* (= I hope that you like them).

**meet²** /miːt/ *noun* [C] *US* a sports competition *a swim/track meet* • *His final jump set a new meet record.*

○⸱**meeting** /ˈmiːtɪŋ/ *noun* [C] **1** an event where people come together for a reason, usually to discuss something *We're having a meeting on Thursday to discuss the problem.* • *He's in a meeting – I'll ask him to call you back later.* **2** *UK* a sporting competition *an international meeting*

**megabyte** /ˈmegəbaɪt/ (*written abbreviation* **MB**) *noun* [C] a unit for measuring the amount of information a computer can store, equal to 1,000,000 bytes

**megaphone** /ˈmegəfəʊn/ *noun* [C] a thing that you hold in your hand and speak into to make your voice louder

**megawatt** /ˈmegəwɒt/ *noun* [C] a unit for measuring electrical power, equal to 1,000,000 watts

**melancholy** /ˈmelənkɒli/ *adj formal* sad • **melancholy** *noun* [U] *formal* a feeling of sadness

**melee** /ˈmeleɪ/ *noun* [C] a situation where many people are behaving in a noisy, confused, and sometimes violent way *In the melee his jaw was broken.*

**mellow¹** /ˈmeləʊ/ *adj* **1** pleasant and soft *a mellow voice* • *a mellow flavour/wine* **2** calm and relaxed *After a few drinks, he became very mellow.*

**mellow²** /ˈmeləʊ/ *verb* [I, T] to become more relaxed and gentle, or to make someone become more relaxed and gentle *Age has mellowed him.*

**melodic** /məˈlɒdɪk/ *adj* Melodic music has a pleasant tune, and melodic sounds are pleasant and like music.

**melodrama** /ˈmeləʊˌdrɑːmə/ *noun* [C, U] a story in which the characters show much stronger emotions than in real life

**melodramatic** /ˌmeləʊdrəˈmætɪk/ *adj* showing much stronger emotions than are necessary for a situation *Don't be so melodramatic! It's only a scratch.*

**melody** /ˈmelədi/ *noun* [C] a song or tune

**melon** /ˈmelən/ *noun* [C, U] a large, round, sweet fruit with a thick, green or yellow skin and a lot of seeds ➔ *See colour picture* **Fruit and Vegetables** *on page Centre 8.*

○⸱**melt** /melt/ *verb* **1** [I, T] If something melts, it changes from a solid into a liquid because of heat and if you melt something, you heat it until it becomes liquid. *The sun soon melted the ice on the pond.* • *The chocolate had melted in my pocket.* • *melted cheese* **2** [I] to start to feel love or sympathy, especially after feeling angry *When he smiles at me, I just melt.* ➔ *See also:* **butter¹** wouldn't melt in sb's mouth.

**melt away** to disappear *Then I saw her and all my fears just melted away.*

**melt sth down** If you melt something down, especially a metal object, you heat it until it changes to liquid.

**meltdown** /ˈmeltdaʊn/ *noun* [C, U] **1** *informal* a situation of complete failure and no control *economic meltdown* **2** a serious accident in which nuclear fuel melts through its container and escapes into the environment

**'melting ˌpot** *noun* [C] a place where people of many different races and from different countries live together

○⸱**member** /ˈmembəʳ/ *noun* [C] a person who belongs to a group or an organization *family/staff members* • *He was a member of the university rowing club.*

**ˌMember of 'Parliament** *noun* [C] *plural* **Members of Parliament** a person who has been elected to represent people in their country's parliament

**membership** /ˈmembəʃɪp/ *noun* **1** [C, U] the state of belonging to a group or an organization *I've applied for membership of the union.* • *a membership card/fee* **2** [group] the people who belong to a group or an organization *Union membership is now over three million and rising.*

**membrane** /ˈmembreɪn/ *noun* [C] a thin sheet of tissue that covers some parts inside the body

**memento** /mɪˈmentəʊ/ *noun* [C] *plural* **mementos** or **mementoes** an object that you keep to remember a person, place, or event

**memo** /ˈmeməʊ/ *noun* [C] a written message sent from one member of an organization to another

**memoirs** /ˈmemwɑːz/ *noun* [plural] a written story of a person's own life and experiences

**memorabilia** /ˌmemᵊrəˈbɪliə/ *noun* [plural] objects relating to famous people or events that people collect *an auction of pop memorabilia*

**memorable** /ˈmemᵊrəbl/ *adj* If an occasion is memorable, you will remember it for a long time because it is so good. *a memorable performance* • *a memorable evening* • **memorably** *adv*

**memorandum** /ˌmemᵊrˈændəm/ *noun plural* **memoranda** *formal* a memo

**memorial** /məˈmɔːriəl/ *noun* [C] an object, often made of stone, that is built to help people remember an important person or event *a war memorial* • *a memorial service*

**memorize** (*also UK* **-ise**) /ˈmemᵊraɪz/ *verb* [T] to learn something so that you remember it exactly *I've memorized all my friends' birthdays.*

○⸱**memory** /ˈmemᵊri/ *noun* **1** ⏤ABILITY⏤ [C, U] your ability to remember *John has an amazing memory for historical facts.* • *She had a photographic memory* (= was able to remember every detail). • *After the accident, he started to suffer from loss of memory.* **2** ⏤THOUGHT⏤ [C] something that you remember [usually plural] *I have fond memories of my childhood.* ➔ *See usage note at* **remember**. **3** ⏤MIND⏤ [C, U] the part of your mind that stores what you remember *He recited the poem from memory.* **4 in memory of sb** If you do something in memory of a dead person, you

**M**

do it to show your respect or love for them. *They built a statue in memory of those who died in the fire.* **5** COMPUTING [C, U] the part of a computer where information and instructions are stored, or the amount of information that can be stored there *You need 32 megabytes of memory to run this software.*

**men** /men/ *plural of* man

**menace¹** /'menɪs/ *noun* **1** [C] something that is likely to cause harm [usually singular] *Drunk drivers are a menace to everyone.* • *the menace of industrial pollution* **2** [U] a dangerous quality that makes you think someone is going to do something bad *His eyes were cold and filled with menace.*

**menace²** /'menɪs/ *verb* [T] *formal* to cause harm to someone or something, or be likely to cause harm *Hurricane Bonnie continues to menace the east coast.*

**menacing** /'menɪsɪŋ/ *adj* making you think that someone is going to do something bad *a menacing gesture/voice*

**mend¹** /mend/ *verb* [T] to repair something that is broken, torn, or not working correctly *I've mended that hole in your skirt for you.* • *We need to get the TV mended.*

**mend²** /mend/ *noun* **be on the mend** *informal* If you are on the mend, your health is improving after an illness.

**mendacious** /men'deɪʃəs/ *adj formal* not telling the truth

**menial** /'miːniəl/ *adj* Menial work is boring, and not well paid or respected. *a menial job/task*

**meningitis** /ˌmenɪn'dʒaɪtɪs/ *noun* [U] a serious infectious disease that affects a person's brain and spinal cord (= the nerves in your back)

**menopause** /'menəʊpɔːz/ *noun* [U] the time, usually between the ages of 45 and 55, when a woman gradually stops having periods (= monthly blood from the uterus)

**'men's ˌroom** *noun* [C] *US* a room in a public place where there are men's toilets ⊃ *See usage note at* **toilet.**

**menstrual** /'menstruəl/ *adj* [always before noun] *formal* relating to menstruating *a menstrual cycle/period*

**menstruate** /'menstrueɪt/ *verb* [I] *formal* to have a monthly flow of blood from the uterus • menstruation /ˌmenstru'eɪʃən/ *noun* [U]

○━**mental** /'mentəl/ *adj* [always before noun] relating to the mind, or involving the process of thinking *mental health/illness* • *a mental disorder/hospital* • mentally *adv a mentally ill person*

**mentality** /men'tæləti/ *noun* [C] a person's opinions or way of thinking *I can't understand the mentality of people who hunt animals for fun.*

○━**mention¹** /'menʃən/ *verb* [T] **1** to briefly speak or write about something or someone *I'll mention your ideas to Caroline.* • *She didn't mention her daughter.* • [+ (that)] *He mentioned that he liked skydiving.* **2 not to mention** used to emphasize the importance of something that you are adding to a list *The resort has great hotels and restaurants, not to mention some of the best skiing in the region.*

**mention²** /'menʃən/ *noun* [C] a brief remark *The report made no mention of the problem.*

**mentor** /'mentɔːr/ *noun* [C] *formal* an experienced person who gives help and advice to someone with less experience

○━**menu** /'menjuː/ *noun* **1** a list of food and drinks that you can order in a restaurant *a lunch/dinner menu* • *I ordered the most expensive thing on the menu* (= available in the restaurant). **2** a list that appears on a computer screen of the choices available in a computer program *a pop-up menu*

**meow** /miːˈaʊ/ *noun* [C] *US spelling of* miaow (= the sound that a cat makes)

**mercenary¹** /'mɜːsənəri/ *noun* [C] a soldier who fights for any country or organization who pays them

**mercenary²** /'mɜːsənəri/ *adj* interested only in getting money or an advantage from a situation

**merchandise** /'mɜːtʃəndaɪz/ *noun* [U] *formal* goods that are traded, or sold in shops *We stock a broad range of merchandise.*

**merchandising** /'mɜːtʃəndaɪzɪŋ/ *noun* [U] the selling of products relating to films, television programmes, and famous people

**merchant¹** /'mɜːtʃənt/ *noun* [C] *formal* someone whose job is buying and selling goods, usually in large amounts *a wine/grain merchant*

**merchant²** /'mɜːtʃənt/ *adj* [always before noun] relating to trading of large amounts of goods *a merchant ship/seaman*

**ˌmerchant 'bank** *noun* [C] a bank that organizes investments in companies or lends money to them • merchant banker *noun* [C]

**mercifully** /'mɜːsɪfli/ *adv informal* used to show that you are pleased that something unpleasant has been avoided *Her illness was mercifully short.*

**merciless** /'mɜːsɪləs/ *adj* cruel, or showing no kindness *a merciless attack* • *She was merciless in her criticism of his work.* • mercilessly *adv He was mercilessly bullied by the older boys.*

**Mercury** /'mɜːkjəri/ *noun* [no plural] the planet that is closest to the Sun, before Venus

**mercury** /'mɜːkjəri/ *noun* [U] a heavy, silver-coloured metal that is liquid at ordinary temperatures

**mercy** /'mɜːsi/ *noun* [U] **1** kindness that makes you forgive someone, usually someone that you have authority over *The prisoners pleaded for mercy.* • *The judge showed no mercy.* **2 be at the mercy of sth/sb** to not be able to protect yourself from something or someone that you cannot control *Farmers are often at the mercy of the weather.*

**mere** /mɪər/ *adj* [always before noun] **1** used to emphasize that something is not large or important *It costs a mere twenty dollars.* • *The mere thought of* (= Just thinking about) *eating octopus makes me feel sick.* **2 the merest** used to emphasize that something is small, often when it has an important effect *She's upset by the merest hint of criticism.*

**merely** /'mɪəli/ *adv* **1** used to emphasize that you mean exactly what you are saying and nothing more *I'm not arguing with you – I'm merely explaining the problem.* **2** used to emphasize that something is not large, important, or effective when compared to something else *The medicine doesn't make you better, it merely stops the pain.*

**merge** /mɜːdʒ/ *verb* [I, T] If two or more things merge, they combine or join, and if you merge two or more things, you combine or join them. *The two companies merged, forming the largest brewery in Canada.* • *The city's smaller libraries will be merged into a large, central one.*

**merger** /'mɜːdʒəʳ/ *noun* [C, U] when two or more companies or organizations join together

**meringue** /mə'ræŋ/ *noun* [C, U] a light, sweet food that is made by baking the white part of an egg mixed with sugar

**merit**[1] /'merɪt/ *noun* [C, U] *formal* good qualities which deserve praise *His ideas have merit.* • *We debated the merits of using television in the classroom.* • *Every application has to be judged on its own merits* (= judged by considering the qualities of each).

**merit**[2] /'merɪt/ *verb* [T] *formal* to be important enough to receive attention or punishment *Her crimes were serious enough to merit a prison sentence.*

**mermaid** /'mɜːmeɪd/ *noun* [C] an imaginary creature that lives in the sea and has the upper body of a woman and the tail of a fish

**merry** /'meri/ *adj* showing enjoyment and happiness *a merry laugh* • *Merry Christmas!* • **merrily** *adv*

**mesh**[1] /meʃ/ *noun* [C, U] material that is like a net and is made of wire, plastic, or thread *a wire mesh fence*

**mesh**[2] /meʃ/ *verb* [I] If two or more things mesh, they are suitable for each other. *Her ideas mesh well with our plans for the future.*

O⊷**mess**[1] /mes/ *noun* [C] **1** UNTIDY Someone or something that is a mess, or is in a mess, is dirty or untidy. [usually singular] *My hair's such a mess!* • *The house is in a mess.* • *Don't make a mess in the kitchen!* **2** DIFFICULT a confused or difficult situation [usually singular] *She told me that her life was a mess.* • *If he hadn't lied, he wouldn't be in this mess now.* **3 make a mess of sth** to damage or spoil something *He made a mess of his first marriage.* **4** MILITARY a place where members of the armed forces eat [usually singular] *the officers' mess*

**mess**[2] /mes/ *verb*

**mess about/around** *informal* **1** to waste time, often by doing things that are not important *Stop messing around and do your homework!* **2** to spend time playing and doing things with no particular purpose *I can spend hours messing around with my computer.*

**mess sb about/around** *UK informal* to treat someone badly, often by not doing something that you have promised *They keep changing their minds about what they want and generally messing us around.*

**mess about/around with sth** *informal* to use or treat something in a careless or harmful way *Who's been messing around with my computer?*

**mess sth up 1** to make something untidy or dirty *I hate wearing hats – they always mess up my hair.* **2** to spoil something, or to do something badly *Don't try to cook lunch by yourself – you'll only mess it up.*

**mess with sb/sth** *informal* to become involved with someone or something dangerous *If you mess with drugs, you're asking for trouble.*

O⊷**message** /'mesɪdʒ/ *noun* [C] **1** a piece of written or spoken information which one person gives to another *Did you get my message?* • *I left her several messages, but she hasn't returned my call.* **2** the most important idea of a film, book, etc *The book conveys a complex message.* **3 get the message** *informal* to understand what someone wants you to do by their actions *Don't return any of his calls – he'll soon get the message and leave you alone.*

**messenger** /'mesɪndʒəʳ/ *noun* [C] someone who takes a message between two people

**the Messiah** /mə'saɪə/ *noun* **1** Jesus Christ **2** the leader that Jews believe God will send them

**Messrs** /'mesəz/ *noun formal* a title used before the names of two or more men *Messrs Davis and Dixon led the discussion on tax reform.*

**messy** /'mesi/ *adj* **1** untidy or dirty *messy hair* • *a messy house/car* • *My son's bedroom is always messy.* **2** unpleasant and complicated *Ian's just gone through a messy divorce.*

**met** /met/ *past of* meet

O⊷**metal** /'metˀl/ *noun* [C, U] a usually hard, shiny material such as iron, gold, or silver which heat and electricity can travel through *scrap metal* • *Metals are used for making machinery and tools.* • *a metal sheet/bar* • **metallic** /mə'tælɪk/ *adj* having a quality that is similar to metal *a metallic paint/taste* • *Our new car is metallic blue.* ➔ *See also:* **heavy metal**.

**metamorphosis** /ˌmetə'mɔːfəsɪs/ *noun plural* **metamorphoses** /metə'mɔːfəsiːz/ **1** [C] a gradual change into something very different *The past year has seen a complete metamorphosis of the country's economy.* **2** [U] in biology, the process by which the young forms of some animals, such as insects, develop into very different adult forms *Caterpillars changing into butterflies is an example of metamorphosis.*

**metaphor** /'metəfəʳ/ *noun* [C, U] a way of describing something by comparing it with something else which has some of the same qualities *She used a computer metaphor to explain how the human brain works.* • **metaphorical** /ˌmetə'fɒrɪkəl/ *adj* using a metaphor

**mete** /miːt/ *verb*

**mete sth out** *formal* to punish someone [often passive] *Long jail sentences are meted out to drug smugglers.*

**meteor** /'miːtiəʳ/ *noun* [C] a rock from outer space which becomes very hot and burns brightly in the sky at night as it enters Earth's atmosphere (= air surrounding Earth)

**meteoric** /ˌmiːtiˈɒrɪk/ *adj* If the development of something is meteoric, it happens very quickly or causes great success. *a meteoric career* • *The band's rise to fame was meteoric.*

**meteorite** /ˈmiːtiəraɪt/ *noun* [C] a piece of rock from outer space which has fallen on Earth's surface

**meteorological** /ˌmiːtiərəˈlɒdʒɪkəl/ *adj* [always before noun] relating to the scientific study of weather

**meteorologist** /ˌmiːtiəˈrɒlədʒɪst/ *noun* [C] someone who studies weather, especially to say how it will be in the near future • **meteorology** *noun* [U] the scientific study of weather

**meter** /ˈmiːtəʳ/ *noun* [C] **1** a piece of equipment for measuring the amount of something such as electricity, time, or light *a gas/water meter* • *a parking/taxi meter* **2** *US spelling of* metre

**methadone** /ˈmeθədəʊn/ *noun* [U] a drug for treating people who want to stop using heroin (= an illegal drug)

**methane** /ˈmiːθeɪn (US) ˈmeθeɪn/ *noun* [U] a gas that has no colour or smell, used for cooking and heating

⊶**method** /ˈmeθəd/ *noun* [C] a way of doing something, often one that involves a system or plan *What's the best method of/for solving this problem?* • *traditional teaching methods*

**methodical** /məˈθɒdɪkəl/ *adj* careful and well organized, using a plan or system *a methodical researcher* • **methodically** *adv*

**Methodist** /ˈmeθədɪst/ *adj* belonging to or relating to a Christian group that was started by John Wesley *the Methodist Church* • **Methodist** *noun* [C]

**methodological** /ˌmeθədəˈlɒdʒɪkəl/ *adj* relating to a methodology *methodological problems*

**methodology** /ˌmeθəˈdɒlədʒi/ *noun* [C, U] the system of methods used for doing, teaching, or studying something

**meticulous** /məˈtɪkjələs/ *adj* very careful, and giving great attention to detail *This book is the result of meticulous research.* • **meticulously** *adv*

**metre** UK (US **meter**) /ˈmiːtəʳ/ *noun* **1** [C] (*written abbreviation* m) a unit for measuring length, equal to 100 centimetres *Our bedroom is five metres wide.* • *She finished third in the women's 400 metres* (= running race). **2** [C, U] a pattern of rhythm in poetry

**metric** /ˈmetrɪk/ *adj* The metric system of measurement uses units based on the gram, metre, and litre.

**metric 'ton** *noun* [C] a unit for measuring weight, equal to 1000 kilograms

**metro¹** /ˈmetrəʊ/ *noun* [C] an underground railway system in a large city *the Paris metro* • *a metro station*

*the Paris metro*

*the London underground*

*the New York subway*

**metro²** /ˈmetrəʊ/ *adj* [always before noun] US *informal* relating to a large city and the towns around it *the New York metro area*

**metropolis** /məˈtrɒpəlɪs/ *noun* [C] a very large city, often the capital of a country or region

**metropolitan** /ˌmetrəˈpɒlɪtən/ *adj* [always before noun] relating to a large city *a metropolitan area/council*

**mg** *written abbreviation for* milligram (= a unit for measuring weight)

**miaow** UK (US **meow**) /miːˈaʊ/ *noun* [C] the sound that a cat makes

**mice** /maɪs/ *plural of* mouse

**mickey** /ˈmɪki/ **take the mickey (out of sb)** UK *informal* to laugh at someone and make them seem silly *She's always taking the mickey out of student teachers.*

**microbe** /ˈmaɪkrəʊb/ *noun* [C] a very small organism, often a bacterium that causes disease

**microchip** /ˈmaɪkrəʊtʃɪp/ *noun* [C] a very small part of a computer or machine which does calculations or stores information

**microcosm** /ˈmaɪkrəʊˌkɒzəm/ *noun* [C] *formal* a place, group of people, or situation that has the same characteristics as a larger one *The town is a microcosm of French culture.*

**microphone** /ˈmaɪkrəfəʊn/ *noun* [C] a piece of electrical equipment for recording or broadcasting sounds, or for making sounds louder

**microprocessor** /ˌmaɪkrəʊˈprəʊsesəʳ (US) ˈmaɪkrəʊˌprɑːsesər/ *noun* [C] the part of a computer that controls all the other parts

**microscope** /ˈmaɪkrəskəʊp/ *noun* [C] a piece of scientific equipment which uses lenses (= pieces of curved glass) to make very small objects look bigger

**microscopic** /ˌmaɪkrəˈskɒpɪk/ *adj* extremely small and needing a microscope to be seen, or using a microscope to see something *microscopic organisms/particles* • *a microscopic analysis/examination*

**microwave¹** /ˈmaɪkrəʊweɪv/ *noun* [C] **1** (*also* **micro,wave 'oven**) an electric oven that uses waves of energy to cook or heat food ➾ *See colour picture* **Kitchen** *on page Centre 10.* **2** a very short wave similar to a radio wave that is used for sending information and cooking

**microwave²** /ˈmaɪkrəʊweɪv/ *verb* [T] to cook or heat food using a microwave oven

**mid-air** /ˌmɪdˈeəʳ/ *noun* **in mid-air** in the air or sky *She jumped up and caught the ball in mid-air.* • **mid-air** *adj* [always before noun] *a mid-air collision*

**midday** /ˌmɪdˈdeɪ/ *noun* [U] 12 o'clock in the middle of the day, or the period around this time *I usually go for a walk at midday.* • *the heat of the midday sun*

⊶**middle¹** /ˈmɪdl/ *noun* **1 the middle** the central part, position, or point in time *We used to live just outside Boston but now we live right* (= exactly) *in the middle.* • *The letter should arrive by the middle of next week.* **2 be in the**

**middle of doing sth** to be busy *I can't talk now – I'm in the middle of cooking a meal.* **3 your middle** *informal* your waist, or your waist and stomach *He wrapped the towel round his middle.* **4 in the middle of nowhere** a long way from places where people live *His car broke down in the middle of nowhere.*

○━**middle**² /'mɪdl/ *adj* [always before noun] **1** in a central position *The middle layer is made of plastic.* ● *Our company rents the middle warehouse.* **2** neither high nor low in importance or amount *middle managers*

**middle-aged** /,mɪdl'eɪdʒd/ *adj* in the middle of your life before you are old *a middle-aged couple/man/woman*

**the ,Middle 'Ages** *noun* the period in European history between the end of the Roman Empire and the start of the Renaissance

**,middle 'class** *noun* [group] a social group that consists of well-educated people, such as doctors, lawyers, and teachers, who have good jobs and are neither very rich nor very poor ● middle-class /,mɪdl'klɑːs/ *adj* belonging or relating to the middle class *a middle-class suburb*

**the ,Middle 'East** *noun* a group of countries in the area where Africa, Asia, and Europe meet *the Middle East peace process* ● Middle Eastern *adj* relating to the Middle East *Middle Eastern cuisine*

**middleman** /'mɪdlmæn/ *noun* [C] *plural* **middlemen** someone who buys goods from one person and sells them to someone else for a higher price *Selling direct from the factory cuts out the middleman.*

**,middle 'name** *noun* [C] an extra name between someone's first and family names

**'middle ,school** *noun* [C] a school in the US for children usually between the ages of 11 and 14

**midget** /'mɪdʒɪt/ *noun* [C] someone who is very small

**the Midlands** /'mɪdləndz/ *noun* the central area of England which includes several large industrial cities

**,mid-life 'crisis** *noun* [C] *plural* **mid-life crises** a period in the middle of your life when you lose confidence in your abilities and worry about the future

**midnight** /'mɪdnaɪt/ *noun* [U] 12 o'clock at night *He died shortly after midnight.*

**midriff** /'mɪdrɪf/ *noun* [C] the front of your body between your chest and waist *Sarah has a butterfly tattooed on her midriff.*

**midst** /mɪdst/ *noun* **1 in the midst of sth** in the middle of something, usually an event or activity *We are currently in the midst of an economic boom.* ● [+ of + doing sth] *Can I phone you back? I'm in the midst of cooking dinner.* **2 in your midst** among the group of people that you belong to *Residents are protesting about a convicted murderer living in their midst.*

**midsummer** /,mɪd'sʌmə'/ *noun* [U] the longest day of the year, or the period around this

**midway** /,mɪd'weɪ/ *adv* **1 midway between sth and sth** at the middle point between two places or things *Leeds is midway between London and Edinburgh.* **2 midway through**

**sth** at the middle point of an activity or a period of time *He scored the third goal midway through the second half.*

**midweek** /,mɪd'wiːk/ *noun* [U] the middle of the week, usually from Tuesday to Thursday ● midweek *adj, adv* [always before noun] in the middle of the week *a midweek game/match* ● *Flights are cheaper if you travel midweek.*

**the Midwest** /,mɪd'west/ *noun* the northern central area of the United States ● Midwestern *adj* [always before noun] relating to the Midwest *a Midwestern city/state*

**midwife** /'mɪdwaɪf/ *noun* [C] *plural* **midwives** /'mɪdwaɪvz/ a nurse who has had special training to help women give birth

**midwifery** /mɪd'wɪf°ri/ *noun* [U] the work of a midwife

**midwinter** /,mɪd'wɪntə'/ *noun* [U] the shortest day of the year, or the period around this

○━**might**¹ /maɪt/ *modal verb* **1** used to talk about what will possibly happen *It might be finished by Thursday.* ● *She might not come.* **2** used to talk about what is possibly true *I think Isabel might be pregnant.* ● *The rain might have stopped by now.* **3 you might like/want to** *UK formal* used to politely suggest something *You might want to try a different approach next time.* ⟳ See study section **Modal verbs** on page *Centre 31.*

**might**² /maɪt/ *noun* [U] *formal* great strength or power *economic/military might* ● *She pushed the door **with all her might** (= with as much force as possible).*

**mightn't** /'maɪt°nt/ *mainly UK formal short for* might not *It mightn't be true.*

**might've** /'maɪtəv/ *short for* might have *The children might've seen her in the park.*

**mighty**¹ /'maɪti/ *adj* very powerful or successful *In their next game they're playing the mighty Redskins.*

**mighty**² /'maɪti/ *adv mainly US informal* very *It's mighty tempting to stay in bed on a rainy morning.*

**migraine** /'maɪgreɪn/ *noun* [C, U] a very bad pain in the head, often one that makes you vomit

**migrant** /'maɪgr°nt/ *noun* [C] someone who goes to live in a different place in order to find work *migrant labour/workers*

**migrate** /maɪ'greɪt ⓤⓢ 'maɪgreɪt/ *verb* [I] **1** When birds, fish, or animals migrate, they travel from one place to another at the same time each year. *Many birds migrate from Europe to African forests for the winter.* **2** When people migrate, they move to another place, often a different country, in order to find work and a better life. *Between 1900 and 1914, 3.1 million people **migrated** to the US from central Europe.* ● migration /maɪ'greɪʃ°n/ *noun* [C, U]

**migratory** /'maɪgreɪt°ri ⓤⓢ 'maɪgrətɔːri/ *adj* [always before noun] relating to birds, fish, or animals that migrate

**mike** /maɪk/ *noun* [C] *informal short for* microphone

**mild** /maɪld/ *adj* **1** WEATHER When weather is mild, it is less cold than you would expect. *a mild winter* ILLNESS When an illness is mild, it is not as serious as it could be. *My doctor said I had a mild form of pneumonia.* **3** WEAK not

M

having a strong effect *a mild taste* • *a mild detergent* **4** KIND calm and gentle *He has a very mild manner.*

**mildly** /'maɪldli/ *adv* **1** slightly *I find his films mildly amusing.* **2 to put it mildly** something you say when an opinion is not expressed as strongly as it should be *The building is unsafe, to put it mildly.*

○━**mile** /maɪl/ *noun* [C] **1** a unit for measuring distance, equal to 1609 metres or 1760 yards *The nearest station is two miles from here.* • *It's a five-mile walk to the next village.* • *The latest high-speed trains can travel at 140 miles per hour.* **2 miles** a very long distance *We drove for miles along dusty roads.* • *Her cottage is miles from the nearest village.*

**mileage** /'maɪlɪdʒ/ *noun* **1** DISTANCE [C, U] the number of miles that a vehicle has travelled since it was new *low mileage* **2** FUEL [C, U] the number of miles a vehicle can travel using a particular amount of fuel **3** ADVANTAGE [U] *informal* an advantage got from something *There's no mileage in taking your employer to court.*

**milestone** /'maɪlstəʊn/ *noun* [C] an important event in the history or development of something or someone *Passing my driving test was an important milestone for me.*

**militant**[1] /'mɪlɪt³nt/ *adj* expressing strong support for a political or social idea, and willing to use extreme or violent methods to achieve it *a militant group/organization* • militancy /'mɪlɪt³nsi/ *noun* [U] when someone is militant

**militant**[2] /'mɪlɪt³nt/ *noun* [C] a militant person

○━**military**[1] /'mɪlɪtri/ *adj* relating to the army, navy, or air force *military action/service*

**the military**[2] /'mɪlɪtri/ *noun* a country's army, navy, and air force

**militia** /mɪ'lɪʃə/ *noun* [C] a group of people who have been trained as soldiers but are not part of a country's official army • militiaman *noun* [C] *plural* **militiamen** a member of a militia

○━**milk**[1] /mɪlk/ *noun* [U] a white liquid produced by women and other female animals, such as cows, for feeding their babies *a carton of milk* • *a milk bottle* • *breast milk* ⊃ See also: **skimmed milk**.

**milk**[2] /mɪlk/ *verb* [T] **1** to get as much money or as many advantages as possible from a person or situation *She milked her grandfather for all his savings.* **2** to take milk from a cow using your hands or a machine

**milkman** /'mɪlkmən/ *noun* [C] *plural* **milkmen** a man whose job is bringing milk to people's homes early in the morning

**milkshake** /'mɪlkʃeɪk/ *noun* [C, U] a sweet drink made of milk and chocolate or fruit *a banana milkshake*

**milky** /'mɪlki/ *adj* **1** containing milk, often a lot of it *milky coffee/tea* **2** similar to milk *a milky liquid*

**the Milky Way** /ˌmɪlki'weɪ/ *noun* the group of very many stars which includes the sun *The Milky Way is visible as a faint band of light across the night sky.*

**mill**[1] /mɪl/ *noun* [C] **1** FLOUR a machine for crushing grain into flour, or a building with

this machine *a flour mill* **2** POWDER a small machine used in the kitchen for crushing things such as coffee beans into a powder *a coffee/pepper mill* **3** MATERIAL a factory where one material or substance is made *a cotton/woollen mill* • *a paper/steel mill*

**mill**[2] /mɪl/ *verb* [T] to use a machine to crush something into a powder *freshly milled black pepper*

**mill about/around (sth)** When people mill around, they come together in a place, usually to wait for someone or something. *A huge crowd was milling around the entrance to the theatre.*

**millennium** /mɪ'leniəm/ *noun* [C] *plural* **millennia 1** a period of 1000 years, often calculated from the date when Christ is thought to have been born **2 the Millennium** the change from the year 1999 to 2000 in the Western calendar *Where did you celebrate the Millennium?*

**milligram** /'mɪlɪgræm/ *noun* (*written abbreviation* **mg**) *noun* [C] a unit for measuring weight, equal to 0.001 grams

**millilitre** *UK* (*US* **milliliter**) (*written abbreviation* **ml**) /'mɪlɪˌliːtə²/ *noun* [C] a unit for measuring liquid, equal to 0.001 litres

**millimetre** *UK* (*US* **millimeter**) (*written abbreviation* **mm**) /'mɪlɪˌmiːtə²/ *noun* [C] a unit for measuring length, equal to 0.001 metres

○━**million** /'mɪljən/ **1** the number 1,000,000 **2 millions** *informal* a lot *I've seen that film millions of times.*

**millionaire** /ˌmɪljə'neə²/ *noun* [C] a very rich person who has money and possessions to the value of at least one million pounds or dollars

**millionth**[1] /'mɪljənθ/ 1,000,000th written as a word

**millionth**[2] /'mɪljənθ/ *noun* [C] one of a million equal parts of something; 1/1,000,000; .000001

**mime** /maɪm/ *verb* [I, T] to act or tell a story without speaking, using movements of your hands and body, and expressions on your face *Pop stars often mime* (= pretend to sing while their song is played) *on TV.* • mime *noun* [C, U] *a mime artist*

**mimic**[1] /'mɪmɪk/ *verb* [T] **mimicking**, *past* **mimicked 1** to copy the way someone talks and behaves, usually to make people laugh *He's always getting into trouble for mimicking his teachers.* **2** to have the same behaviour or qualities as something else *The drug mimics the effects of a natural hormone.*

**mimic**[2] /'mɪmɪk/ *noun* [C] someone who is good at mimicking other people

**mince**[1] /mɪns/ *UK* (*US* **ground beef**) *noun* [U] meat, usually from a cow, which has been cut into very small pieces by a machine

**mince**[2] /mɪns/ *verb* [T] to cut food into small pieces in a machine *Mince the garlic and add it to the onions.* • *minced beef/onions*

**mincemeat** /'mɪnsmiːt/ *noun* [U] **1** a spicy, sweet mixture of apples, dried fruit, and nuts, which have been cut into small pieces **2 make mincemeat of sb** *informal* to defeat someone very easily *A good lawyer could make mincemeat of the company in court.*

**mince 'pie** *noun* [C] a small pastry filled with mincemeat that is eaten mainly at Christmas o━**mind**[1] /maɪnd/ *noun* [C] **1** someone's memory or their ability to think, feel emotions, and be aware of things *For some reason her words stuck in my mind.* ● *She has a very logical mind.* **2 have sth on your mind** to think or worry about something *Jim has a lot on his mind at the moment.* **3 bear/keep sb/sth in mind** to remember someone or something that may be useful in the future *I'll keep you in mind if another job comes up.* ● [+ (that)] *Bear in mind that there's a bank holiday next week.* **4 make your mind up** to make a decision [+ question word] *I haven't made up my mind whether to go yet.* **5 change your mind** to change a decision or opinion *We've changed our minds about selling the house.* **6 come/spring to mind** If an idea comes to mind, it is the first thing you think of. *I was thinking about who might be suitable for this job, and your name came to mind.* **7 put your mind to sth** to give your full attention to something *You could win if you put your mind to it.* **8 be out of your mind** *informal* to be crazy or very stupid *You must be out of your mind going running on a night like this!* **9 be out of your mind with worry/ grief, etc** to be very worried or upset **10 blow your mind** *informal* If something blows your mind, you are very excited or surprised by it. *There was one scene in the film that really blew my mind.* **11 cross your mind** If an idea crosses your mind, you think about it for a short time. *What was the first thing that crossed your mind when you won the prize?* ● [+ (that)] *It never crossed my mind* (= I never thought) *that she might be married.* **12 be in two minds** *UK* (*US* **be of two minds**) to have difficulty making a decision *I'm in two minds about accepting his offer.* **13 put/set sb's mind at rest** to say something to someone to stop them worrying *I was really worried about the tests, but talking to the doctor put my mind at rest.* **14 slip your mind** If something slips your mind, you forget it. *I'm sorry I forgot your birthday – it just slipped my mind.* **15 speak your mind** to say exactly what you think without worrying if it will upset anyone *She has very strong opinions and she's not afraid to speak her mind.* **⊃** *See also:* at/in the **back**[2] of your mind, **frame**[1] of mind, give sb a **piece**[1] of your mind, a **weight** off your mind.

o━**mind**[2] /maɪnd/ *verb* **1** BE ANNOYED [I, T, used in questions and negatives] to be annoyed or worried by something *Do you think he'd mind if I borrowed his book?* ● [+ doing sth] *Tim won't mind lending you his car.* ● *He doesn't seem to mind doing all the driving.* ● *I don't mind taking her* (= I am willing to take her) *if you're too busy.* **2** LOOK AFTER [T] to look after someone or something *Could you mind my suitcase while I go to the toilet?* ● *Who's minding the baby?* **3 do you mind/would you mind** something you say when politely asking someone to do something *Do you mind not smoking in here, please?* ● *Would you mind if I borrowed your phone?* **4** BE CAREFUL [T] something you say when telling someone to be careful with something dangerous *Mind the iron – it's still very hot!* **5 never mind a** something that you say to tell

someone that something is not important *"I forgot to bring any money." "Never mind, you can pay me next week."* **b** something you say to emphasize that something is impossible *I can't afford to buy a bike, never mind a car!* **6 mind you** something you say before saying the opposite of what you have just said *We had a lovely holiday in France, but the weather was appalling.*

**Mind out!** *UK* something you say to warn someone about a danger or to tell them to move *Mind out – this plate's very hot!*

**mind-boggling** /'maɪnd,bɒɡlɪŋ/ *adj informal* difficult to accept, imagine, or understand *The amount of information available on the Internet is mind-boggling.*

**-minded** /'maɪndɪd/ **⊃** *See* **absent-minded**, **narrow-minded**, **open-minded**, **single-minded**.

**minder** /'maɪndər/ *noun* [C] *UK* someone who physically protects a famous, important, or very rich person

**mindless** /'maɪndləs/ *adj* stupid and done without a good reason *mindless violence*

o━**mine**[1] /maɪn/ *pronoun* the things that belong or relate to the person who is speaking or writing *I borrowed them from a friend of mine.* ● *"Whose book is this?" "It's mine."* ● *Can I use your pen? Mine's not working.*

**mine**[2] /maɪn/ *noun* [C] **1** an underground system of holes and passages where people dig out coal or other minerals **2** a bomb hidden in the ground or water which explodes when it is touched *He was killed when he drove over a mine.* **⊃** *See also:* **gold mine**.

**mine**[3] /maɪn/ *verb* **1** [I, T] to dig out of the ground minerals such as coal, metals, and valuable stones *Tin was mined in this area for hundreds of years.* ● *He made his fortune mining for gold and diamonds.* **2** [T] to put mines (= bombs) in the ground or water *The southern coast was heavily mined during the war.*

**minefield** /'maɪnfiːld/ *noun* [C] **1** a situation with many complicated problems *a legal/political minefield* **2** an area of land or sea where bombs have been hidden

**miner** /'maɪnər/ *noun* [C] someone who works in a mine *a coal miner*

**mineral** /'mɪnərəl/ *noun* [C] **1** a valuable or useful substance that is dug out of the ground *The region's rich mineral deposits include oil, gold, and aluminium.* **2** a chemical that your body needs to stay healthy

**'mineral ,water** *noun* [C, U] water which is taken from the ground and contains chemicals that are good for your health *fizzy/sparkling mineral water*

**mingle** /'mɪŋɡl/ *verb* **1** [I, T] to mix, or be mixed *The smell of fresh coffee mingled with cigarette smoke.* **2** [I] to meet and talk to a lot of people at a party or similar event *The party will be a good opportunity to **mingle with** the other students.*

**miniature**[1] /'mɪnətʃər/ *adj* [always before noun] extremely small *a miniature camera*

**miniature**[2] /'mɪnətʃər/ *noun* **1** [C] a very small copy of an object *You can buy miniatures of the statue in the museum shop.* **2 in miniature** If something is in miniature, it is a very small copy of something else. *a model of the ship in miniature*

**minibus** /'mɪnɪbʌs/ *noun* [C] a small bus with seats for about ten people

**minimal** /'mɪnɪm*ə*l/ *adj* very small in amount *Damage to the building was minimal.* • **minimally** *adv*

**minimize** (*also UK* **-ise**) /'mɪnɪmaɪz/ *verb* [T] to make the amount of something that is unpleasant or not wanted as small as possible *Airport staff are trying to minimize the inconvenience caused to passengers.*

o━**minimum¹** /'mɪnɪməm/ *adj* [always before noun] The minimum amount of something is the smallest amount that is allowed, needed, or possible. *How much is the minimum wage?* • *There is a minimum charge of $5 for postage.* ➲ *Opposite* **maximum**.

o━**minimum²** /'mɪnɪməm/ *noun* [no plural] the smallest amount that is allowed, needed, or possible *The judge sentenced him to a minimum of five years in prison.* • *Please keep noise to an absolute minimum.*

**mining** /'maɪnɪŋ/ *noun* [U] the industrial process of digging coal or other minerals out of the ground

**miniscule** /'mɪnɪskjuːl/ *adj* a common spelling of 'minuscule' that is not correct

**miniskirt** /'mɪnɪˌskɜːt/ *noun* [C] a very short skirt ➲ *See colour picture* **Clothes** *on page Centre 5.*

**minister** /'mɪnɪstəʳ/ *noun* [C] **1** a politician who is responsible for a government department or has an important position in it *a finance/ health minister* **2** a priest in some Christian churches *a Baptist/Methodist minister* ➲ *See also:* **prime minister**.

**ministerial** /ˌmɪnɪ'stɪəriəl/ *adj* relating to a government minister *a ministerial job/post*

**ministry** /'mɪnɪstri/ *noun* **1** [C] a government department which is responsible for a particular subject *the Ministry of Defence* • *a Foreign Ministry spokesman* **2 the ministry** the job of being a priest *What made you decide to enter the ministry* (= become a priest)*?*

**mink** /mɪŋk/ *noun* [C, U] a small animal with valuable fur which is used to make expensive coats, or the fur from this animal *a mink coat*

**minor¹** /'maɪnəʳ/ *adj* **1** not important or serious *a minor offence* • *Most of the passengers suffered only minor injuries.* **2** [always before noun] in music, belonging to a key (= set of musical notes) that often produces a sad sound ➲ *Opposite* **major**.

**minor²** /'maɪnəʳ/ *noun* [C] *formal* someone who is too young to have the legal responsibilities of an adult

o━**minority** /maɪ'nɒrəti/ *noun* **1** [no plural] a part of a group which is less than half of the whole group, often much less *The violence was caused by a small minority of football supporters.* • *I voted to accept the proposal, but I was in the minority.* ➲ *Opposite* **majority**. **2** [C] a group of people whose race is different from the race of most of the people where they live [usually plural] *ethnic minorities*

**mint¹** /mɪnt/ *noun* **1** SWEET [C] a sweet with a fresh, strong taste **2** HERB [U] a plant whose

leaves are used to add flavour to food and drinks **3** FACTORY [C] a factory which produces coins for the government

**mint²** /mɪnt/ *verb* [T] to produce a coin for the government

**minus¹** /'maɪnəs/ *preposition* **1** used when the second of two numbers should be taken away from the first *Five minus three is two.* **2** *informal* without something that should be there *She arrived at the meeting minus her briefcase.*

**minus²** /'maɪnəs/ *adj* **1** [always before noun] A minus number is less than zero. *The temperature last night was minus ten.* **2 A minus/B minus, etc** used with scores given to written work meaning 'slightly lower than' *I got an A minus for my last essay.*

**minus³** /'maɪnəs/ *noun* [C] **1** (*also* 'minus ,sign) the sign which shows that the second of two numbers should be taken away from the first, or that a number is less than zero, shown by the symbol (–) **2** a problem or difficulty *It isn't easy having a child but the pluses outweigh the minuses.*

**minuscule** /'mɪnəskjuːl/ *adj* extremely small *The cost of vaccination is minuscule compared to the cost of treating the disease.*

o━**minute¹** /'mɪnɪt/ *noun* [C] **1** a period of time equal to 60 seconds *It'll take you thirty minutes to get to the airport.* • *She was ten minutes late for her interview.* • *"Did you have a good holiday?" "Yes, thanks. I enjoyed every minute of it."* • *a thirty-minute journey* **2** a very short period of time *It'll only take a minute to call him.* • *I'll be with you in a minute.* • *She died within minutes of* (= very soon after) *the attack.* **3 (at) any minute** very soon *Her train should be arriving any minute.* **4 the last minute** the latest time possible *The concert was cancelled at the last minute.* **5 the minute (that)** as soon as *I'll tell you the minute we hear any news.* **6 Wait/Just a minute; Hold on a minute. a** used when asking someone to wait for a short time *Just a minute – I've left my coat in the restaurant.* **b** used when you disagree with something that someone has said or done *Hold on a minute, Pete! I never said you could borrow my car.*

**minute²** /maɪ'njuːt/ *adj* **1** extremely small *a minute amount/quantity* **2** [always before noun] done in great detail *He explained everything in minute detail.*

**the minutes** /'mɪnɪts/ *noun* [plural] an official record of what is said and decided during a meeting *Michael has kindly agreed to take the minutes* (= write them down).

**miracle** /'mɪrəkl/ *noun* [C] **1** something that is very surprising or difficult to believe *an economic miracle* • [+ (that)] *It's a miracle that he's still alive.* • *a miracle cure* **2** an event which should be impossible and cannot be explained by science *One of Christ's miracles was turning water into wine.*

**miraculous** /mɪ'rækjələs/ *adj* very surprising or difficult to believe *John's made a miraculous recovery from his illness.* • **miraculously** *adv*

**mirage** /'mɪrɑːʒ ⓤⓢ mɪ'rɑːʒ/ *noun* [C] when hot air produces an image of water in a desert or on a road

**mirror¹** /'mɪrəʳ/ noun [C] a piece of glass with a shiny metallic material on one side which produces an image of anything that is in front of it *a bathroom mirror* • *He looked at his reflection in the mirror.* ⊃ *See colour picture* **The Living Room** *on page Centre 11* ⊃ *See also:* **rear-view mirror, wing mirror.**

**mirror²** /'mɪrəʳ/ verb [T] to be similar to or represent something *Our newspaper mirrors the opinions of ordinary people.*

**mirth** /mɜːθ/ noun [U] *formal* laughter or happiness

**misadventure** /,mɪsəd'ventʃəʳ/ noun **1** [U] *UK formal* when someone is killed by accident and no one is legally responsible for the death *The coroner recorded a verdict of* **death by misadventure.** **2** [C] an unlucky event

**misanthrope** /'mɪsⁿnθrəʊp/ noun [C] *formal* someone who hates people in general and avoids being with them

**misapprehension** /,mɪsæprɪ'henʃⁿn/ noun [C] *formal* a idea or opinion about someone or something that is wrong [+ that] *He was labouring under the misapprehension* (= wrongly believed) *that she loved him.*

**misbehave** /,mɪsbɪ'heɪv/ verb [I] to behave badly • **misbehaviour** *UK* (*US* **misbehavior**) noun [U] bad behaviour

**misc** *written abbreviation for* miscellaneous

**miscalculate** /,mɪs'kælkjəleɪt/ verb [I, T] **1** to make a mistake when calculating something *I think I've miscalculated how much wine we'll need for the party.* **2** to make a bad decision because you do not completely understand a situation *If she thinks Mike will support her plan, then she's seriously miscalculated.* • **miscalculation** /,mɪskælkjə'leɪʃⁿn/ noun [C, U]

**miscarriage** /mɪ'skærɪdʒ/ noun [C, U] **1** when a baby is born too early and dies because it has not developed enough *She had a miscarriage after her car accident.* **2 miscarriage of justice** when a court makes a wrong or unfair decision

**miscarry** /mɪ'skæri/ verb [I, T] to give birth to a baby too early so that it dies *She miscarried eight weeks into her pregnancy.*

**miscellaneous** /,mɪsⁿl'eɪniəs/ adj [always before noun] consisting of a mixture of several different things *The plumber tried to charge me fifty pounds for miscellaneous items.*

**mischief** /'mɪstʃɪf/ noun [U] behaviour, usually of a child, which is slightly bad but not serious

**mischievous** /'mɪstʃɪvəs/ adj behaving in a way that is slightly bad but not serious *a mischievous grin* • *a mischievous five-year-old* • **mischievously** adv

**misconceived** /,mɪskən'siːvd/ adj If a plan is misconceived, it is not suitable or has not been thought about carefully.

**misconception** /,mɪskən'sepʃⁿn/ noun [C] when your understanding of something is wrong [+ that] *It's a common misconception that older workers cannot learn to use new technology.*

**misconduct** /mɪ'skɒndʌkt/ noun [U] *formal* when someone in a position of responsibility behaves in a way that is morally wrong or breaks rules while doing their job *professional misconduct*

**misdemeanour** *UK* (*US* **misdemeanor**)

/,mɪsdɪ'miːnəʳ/ noun [C] **1** behaviour that is bad or not moral *political/sexual misdemeanours* **2** *US* a crime which is not serious

**misdirect** /,mɪsdɪ'rekt/ verb [T] to use money or people's skills in a way that is not suitable [often passive] *Large quantities of money and expertise have been misdirected.*

**miserable** /'mɪzⁿrəbl/ adj **1** SAD unhappy *I just woke up feeling miserable.* **2** NOT PLEASANT very unpleasant or bad, and causing someone to feel unhappy *Some families are living in miserable conditions.* **3** NOT ENOUGH *informal* A miserable amount is too small to be acceptable. *She offered me a miserable £50 for my old computer.*

**miserably** /'mɪzⁿrəbli/ adv **1** in a way that causes disappointment or suffering *miserably low wages* • *Every job application that I've made has* **failed miserably** (= has been extremely unsuccessful). **2** in a very unhappy way *"I feel so ill," said Rachel miserably.*

**misery** /'mɪzⁿri/ noun [C, U] **1** great suffering or unhappiness *The war brought misery to millions of people.* • *Her husband's drinking is* **making her life a misery. 2 put sb out of their misery** to stop someone worrying by telling them what they want to know

**misfire** /mɪs'faɪəʳ/ verb [I] When something that you do misfires, it does not have the result that you intended. *His joke misfired badly, and he was forced to make a public apology.*

**misfit** /'mɪsfɪt/ noun [C] someone with strange or unusual behaviour who is not accepted by other people *a social misfit*

**misfortune** /mɪs'fɔːtʃuːn/ noun [C, U] bad luck, or an unlucky event [+ to do sth] *He had the misfortune to fall in love with a married woman.*

**misgiving** /mɪs'gɪvɪŋ/ noun [C] a feeling of doubt or worry about a future event [usually plural] *She has serious misgivings about giving birth at home.*

**misguided** /mɪs'gaɪdɪd/ adj not likely to succeed because of a bad judgment or understanding of a situation *The government's policy seems to me completely misguided.*

**mishandle** /mɪs'hændl/ verb [T] to deal with a problem or situation badly *The murder investigation was mishandled from the beginning.*

**mishap** /'mɪshæp/ noun [C, U] an accident or unlucky event which usually is not serious *They suffered a series of mishaps during the trip.*

**misinform** /,mɪsɪn'fɔːm/ verb [T] to give someone false information [often passive] *I'm afraid you've been misinformed about your exam results.*

**misinterpret** /,mɪsɪn'tɜːprɪt/ verb [T] to understand something in the wrong way [often passive] *He claims his speech was deliberately misinterpreted by journalists.*

**misjudge** /mɪs'dʒʌdʒ/ verb [T] **1** to form a wrong opinion about a person or situation *We believe that the government has seriously misjudged the public mood.* **2** to guess an amount or distance wrongly

**misjudgment** (*also UK* **misjudgement**) /mɪs'dʒʌdʒmənt/ noun [C, U] when you form a wrong opinion or make a wrong guess *Her out-*

**M**

*spoken criticism of her boss was a serious mis-judgment.*

**mislay** /mɪˈsleɪ/ *verb* [T] *past* **mislaid** /mɪˈsleɪd/ *formal* to lose something for a short time by forgetting where you put it *I seem to have mislaid my car keys.*

**mislead** /mɪˈsliːd/ *verb* [T] *past* **misled** /mɪˈsled/ to make someone believe something that is untrue by giving them information that is wrong or not complete [**often passive**] *She claims the public was misled by the government.*

**misleading** /mɪˈsliːdɪŋ/ *adj* making someone believe something that is untrue *misleading information/statements*

**mismanage** /ˌmɪsˈmænɪdʒ/ *verb* [T] to control or organize something badly *He accused the government of mismanaging the crisis.* ● mismanagement *noun* [U] when something is badly organized and controlled

**misnomer** /mɪˈsnəʊməʳ/ *noun* [C] a name which is not suitable for the person or thing that it refers to [**usually singular**] *It's a misnomer to call young car thieves 'joyriders'.*

**misogynist** /mɪˈsɒdʒ³nɪst/ *noun* [C] a man who dislikes women very much ● misogynistic /mɪˌsɒdʒ³nˈɪstɪk/ (*also* **misogynist**) *adj* expressing a great dislike of women *a misogynistic attitude/writer*

**misogyny** /mɪˈsɒdʒɪni/ *noun* [U] a great dislike of women

**misplaced** /mɪˈspleɪst/ *adj* If you have a misplaced feeling or belief, it is wrong because you have not understood the situation correctly. *misplaced loyalty/trust*

**misprint** /ˈmɪsprɪnt/ *noun* [C] a mistake made in the printing of a newspaper or book *The article is full of misprints.*

**misread** /mɪsˈriːd/ *verb* [T] *past* **misread** /mɪsˈred/ **1** to make a mistake when you are reading something *He misread the cooking instructions on the packet.* **2** to not understand something correctly *She completely misread the situation.*

**misrepresent** /ˌmɪsreprɪˈzent/ *verb* [T] to say things that are not true about someone or something *He claims that the article misrepresented his views.* ● misrepresentation /ˌmɪsreprɪzenˈteɪʃ³n/ *noun* [C, U]

o→**miss**[1] /mɪs/ *verb* **1** [FEEL SAD] [T] to feel sad about someone that you do not see now or something that you do not have or do now *I'll miss you when you go.* ● [+ doing sth] *He misses having a room of his own.* **2** [NOT GO TO] [T] to not go to something *I missed my class this morning.* **3** [NOT SEE/HEAR] [T] to not see or hear something or someone *Sorry, I missed that, could you repeat it please?* ● *We missed the first five minutes of the film.* **4** [NOT HIT] [I, T] to not hit or catch something as you intended *It should have been such an easy goal and he missed.* **5** [TOO LATE] [T] to arrive too late to get on a bus, train, or aircraft *If I don't leave now, I'll miss my train.* ⊃ *See usage note at* **lose**. **6** [NOT NOTICE] [T] to not notice someone or something *It's the big house on the corner – you can't miss it.* **7 miss a chance/opportunity** to not use an opportunity to do something *You can't afford to miss a chance like this.* **8 miss the point** to not

understand something correctly *He seems to be missing the point completely.* ⊃ *See also:* miss the **boat**.

**miss** or **lack**?

Be careful not to confuse the verb **lack** with **miss**. **Lack** means to not have something, or to not have enough of something.

*Our town lacks a cinema.*

~~Our town misses a cinema.~~

**miss sb/sth out** *UK* to not include someone or something

**miss out** to not do or have something that you would enjoy or something that other people do or have *I got there late and missed out on all the fun.*

**miss**[2] /mɪs/ *noun* **1** [C] when you do not hit or catch something as you intended **2 give sth a miss** *UK informal* to not do an activity *I think I'll give aerobics a miss this evening.* **3 a near miss** something bad which does not happen but almost happens

o→**Miss** /mɪs/ *noun* a title for a girl or woman who is not married, used before her family name or full name *Miss Olivia Allenby* ● *Tell Miss Russell I'm here.* ⊃ *See usage note at* **Mr.**

**misshapen** /mɪsˈʃeɪp³n/ *adj* not the correct or normal shape

**missile** /ˈmɪsaɪl (US) ˈmɪsəl/ *noun* [C] **1** an explosive weapon which can travel long distances through the air *nuclear missiles* ● *a missile attack* **2** an object which is thrown through the air to hit someone or something

o→**missing** /ˈmɪsɪŋ/ *adj* **1** If someone or something is missing, you cannot find them because they are not in their usual place. *Have you found those missing documents?* ● *Her daughter went missing a week ago.* **2** not included in something *There are a couple of things missing from the list.*

**mission** /ˈmɪʃ³n/ *noun* [C] **1** [JOB] an important job, usually travelling somewhere *I'll be going on a fact-finding mission to Paris next week.* **2** [GROUP] an official group of people who are sent somewhere, usually to discover information about something *a trade mission* **3** [JOURNEY] an important journey which a spacecraft or military aircraft goes on **4** [PURPOSE] someone's duty or purpose in life *Her mission in life was to help the poor.*

**missionary** /ˈmɪʃ³n³ri/ *noun* [C] someone who travels to another country to teach people about the Christian religion

**missive** /ˈmɪsɪv/ *noun* [C] *literary* a letter or message

**misspell** /mɪsˈspel/ *verb* [T] *past* **misspelled** (*also* *UK*) **misspelt** to spell something wrongly

**mist**[1] /mɪst/ *noun* [C, U] small drops of water in the air which makes it difficult to see objects which are not near *Gradually the mist cleared and the sun began to shine.*

**mist**[2] /mɪst/ *verb*

**mist over/up** If a glass surface mists over, it becomes covered with very small drops of water so that you cannot see through it easily. *My windscreen is always misting over.*

○▪**mistake¹** /mɪˈsteɪk/ *noun* [C] **1** something that you do or think which is wrong *a spelling mistake* • *He made a lot of mistakes in his written test.* • [+ to do sth] *It would be a big mistake to leave school.* • [+ of + doing sth] *She made the mistake of giving him her phone number.* ➔ *See usage note at* **fault.** **2 by mistake** If you do something by mistake, you do it without intending to. *I picked up someone else's book by mistake.*

---
**USAGE**

**mistake**

Remember to use the correct verb with this word.

*I always* make mistakes *in my essays.*

~~I always do mistakes in my essays.~~

---

**mistake²** /mɪˈsteɪk/ *verb* [T] *past t* **mistook,** *past p* **mistaken** to not understand something correctly *I think you mistook my meaning.*

**mistake sb/sth for sb/sth** to confuse someone or something with someone or something else *People sometimes mistake him for a girl.*

**mistaken** /mɪˈsteɪkən/ *adj* If you are mistaken, or you have a mistaken belief, you are wrong about something. *If you think you can behave like that, you are mistaken.* • **mistakenly** *adv I mistakenly* (= wrongly) *thought he had left.*

**Mister** /ˈmɪstər/ *noun* [U] *US informal* used when calling or talking to a man that you do not know *Hey Mister, you forgot your suitcase!*

**mistletoe** /ˈmɪsltəʊ/ *noun* [U] a plant with white berries (= small, round fruit) which is often used as a decoration at Christmas

**mistook** /mɪˈstʊk/ *past tense of* mistake

**mistreat** /mɪsˈtriːt/ *verb* [T] to treat a person or animal in a bad or cruel way *A local farmer has been accused of mistreating horses.* • **mistreatment** *noun* [U] when people or animals are badly or cruelly treated

**mistress** /ˈmɪstrəs/ *noun* [C] a woman who has a sexual relationship with a man who is married to someone else

**mistrust** /mɪsˈtrʌst/ *noun* [U] when you do not believe or have confidence in someone or something *They have a deep mistrust of strangers.* • **mistrust** *verb* [T]

**misty** /ˈmɪsti/ *adj* If the weather is misty, there is a cloud of small drops of water in the air, which makes it difficult to see objects which are not near. *a cold and misty morning*

**misunderstand** /ˌmɪsʌndəˈstænd/ *verb* [T] *past* **misunderstood 1** to not understand someone or something correctly *He misunderstood the question completely.* **2 be misunderstood** If someone is misunderstood, other people do not understand that they have good qualities.

**misunderstanding** /ˌmɪsʌndəˈstændɪŋ/ *noun* **1** [C, U] when someone does not understand something correctly *There must have been a misunderstanding.* **2** [C] a slight disagreement

**misuse** /ˌmɪsˈjuːz/ *verb* [T] to use something in the wrong way or for the wrong purpose *He misused his position to obtain money dishon-*

*estly.* • **misuse** /ˌmɪsˈjuːs/ *noun* [C, U] *the misuse of drugs/power*

**mite** /maɪt/ *noun* [C] **1** an extremely small insect with eight legs *dust mites* **2** *informal* a small child *You're so cold, you poor little mite!* **3 a mite** *mainly UK informal* slightly *He seemed a mite embarrassed.*

**mitigate** /ˈmɪtɪɡeɪt/ *verb* [T] to reduce the harmful effects of something • **mitigation** /ˌmɪtɪˈɡeɪʃən/ *noun* [U]

**mitigating** /ˈmɪtɪɡeɪtɪŋ/ *adj* **mitigating circumstances/factors** facts that make something bad that someone has done seem less bad or less serious

**mitt** /mɪt/ *noun* [C] a thick leather glove (= cover for the hand) used for catching a baseball ➔ *See colour picture* **Sports 2** *on page Centre 16.*

○▪**mix¹** /mɪks/ *verb* **1** COMBINE SUBSTANCES [I, T] If two or more substances mix, they combine to make one substance, and if you mix two or more substances, you combine them to make one substance. *Mix the powder with water to form a paste.* • *Put the chocolate, butter, and egg in a bowl and mix them all together.* • *Oil and water don't mix.* **2** COMBINE QUALITIES ETC [I, T] to have or do two or more qualities, styles, activities, etc at the same time *a feeling of anger mixed with sadness* **3** MEET [I] to meet and talk to people *She enjoys going to parties and mixing with people.*

**mix sth/sb up** to confuse two people or things by thinking that one person or thing is the other person or thing *People often mix them up because they look so similar.*

**mix sth up** to cause a group of things to be untidy or badly organized *The books were all mixed up in a box.*

**mix²** /mɪks/ *noun* **1** [C] a combination of things or people, often in a group [usually singular] *There's a good mix of nationalities in the class.* **2** [C, U] a powder to which you add liquid in order to make something *cake mix*

**mixed** /mɪkst/ *adj* **1** made of a combination of different people or things *a racially mixed area* • *a mixed salad* • *The study produced mixed results.* **2 mixed feelings** If you have mixed feelings about something, you are pleased and not pleased at the same time. ➔ *See also:* a mixed **blessing.**

**mixed up** *adj informal* **1** confused *I got a bit mixed up and thought we were supposed to be there at eight.* **2 be mixed up in sth** to be involved in an activity that is bad or illegal **3 be mixed up with sb** to be involved with someone who has a bad influence on you *Her son got mixed up with the wrong people.*

**mixer** /ˈmɪksər/ *noun* [C] a machine that mixes things *an electric mixer*

○▪**mixture** /ˈmɪkstʃər/ *noun* **1** [C, U] a substance made of other substances that have been combined *Add milk to the mixture and stir until smooth.* **2** [no plural] when there is a combination of two or more ideas, qualities, styles, etc *Their house is decorated in a mixture of styles.*

**mix-up** /ˈmɪksʌp/ *noun* [C] *informal* when there is a mistake because things are confused [usually singular] *There was a mix-up with the bags at the airport.*

M

---

| j **yes** | k **cat** | ʃ **she** | ʒ **decision** | θ **thin** | ð **this** | ŋ **ring** | tʃ **chip** | dʒ **jar** | æ **cat** | ɑː **arm** | e **bed** | eə **hair** | ə **ago** | ɜː **her** | ɪ **sit** | i **cosy** |

**ml** *written abbreviation for* millilitre (= a unit for measuring liquid)

**mm** *written abbreviation for* millimetre (= a unit for measuring length)

**moan**[1] /məʊn/ *verb* [I] **1** to complain or speak in a way that shows you are unhappy *She's always moaning about something.* **2** to make a low sound, especially because you are in pain *He lay on the floor moaning.* • **moan** *noun* [C]

**mob**[1] /mɒb/ *noun* [C] a large group of people that is often violent or not organized *an angry mob*

**mob**[2] /mɒb/ *verb* [T] **mobbing**, *past* **mobbed** If a group of people mob someone, they get close to them, often to get their photograph or signature. [often passive] *She was mobbed by photographers.*

**mobile**[1] /ˈməʊbaɪl US ˈməʊbəl/ *adj* able to move or be moved easily *a mobile home* ➜ *Opposite* **immobile**.

**mobile**[2] /ˈməʊbaɪl US ˈməʊbiːl/ *noun* [C] **1** a decoration made of objects on threads that hang down and move in the air **2** a mobile phone

,**mobile 'phone** *noun* [C] a telephone that you can carry everywhere with you ➜ *See picture at* **telephone**.

**mobilize** (*also UK* **-ise**) /ˈməʊbɪlaɪz/ *verb* **1** [T] to organize a group of people so that they support or oppose something or someone *He's trying to mobilize support for the strike.* **2** [I, T] *formal* to prepare for a war *The forces were fully mobilized for action.* • **mobilization** /,məʊbɪlaɪˈzeɪʃᵊn/ *noun* [U]

**mock**[1] /mɒk/ *verb* [I, T] to laugh at someone or something in an unkind way *The older kids mocked him whenever he made a mistake.*

**mock**[2] /mɒk/ *adj* [always before noun] not real but appearing or pretending to be exactly like something *a mock exam* • *mock surprise*

**mockery** /ˈmɒkᵊri/ *noun* [U] **1** when someone laughs at someone or something in an unkind way **2 make a mockery of sth** to make something seem stupid *The latest outbreak of fighting makes a mockery of the peace process.*

**modal verb** /ˈməʊdəl,vɜːb/ (*also* **modal**) *noun* [C] a verb, for example 'can', 'might', or 'must', that is used before another verb to show that something is possible, necessary, etc ➜ *See study section* **Modal verbs** *on page Centre 31.*

**mode** /məʊd/ *noun* [C] *formal* a way of doing something *a mode of transport*

○━**model**[1] /ˈmɒdᵊl/ *noun* [C] **1** PERSON someone whose job is to wear fashionable clothes, be in photographs, etc in order to advertise things *a fashion model* **2** COPY a smaller copy of a real object, often used to show how something works or what it looks like *He makes models as a hobby.* **3** EXAMPLE someone or something that is an example for others to copy *a model of good behaviour* **4** DESIGN a design of machine or car that is made by a particular company *I think her car is a slightly older model.* ➜ *See also:* **role model**.

**model**[2] /ˈmɒdᵊl/ *verb* [I, T] *(UK)* **modelling**, *past* **modelled**, *(US)* **modeling**, *past* **modeled** to wear clothes in fashion shows, magazines, etc as a model *She's been modelling for the same designer for years.*

**be modelled on sth** to be based on the design of something else *The house is modelled on a 16th century castle.*

**model yourself on sb** to try to make yourself very similar to someone else *He models himself on Mohammed Ali.*

**modem** /ˈməʊdem/ *noun* [C] a piece of equipment that is used to send information from a computer through a telephone system

**moderate**[1] /ˈmɒdᵊrət/ *adj* **1** average in size or amount and not too much *Eating a moderate amount of fat is healthy.* **2** not extreme, especially relating to political opinions *a moderate political group* • **moderately** *adv*

**moderate**[2] /ˈmɒdᵊrət/ *noun* [C] someone who does not have extreme political opinions

**moderate**[3] /ˈmɒdᵊreɪt/ *verb* [T] to make something less extreme *He's trying to moderate his drinking.*

**moderation** /,mɒdᵊrˈeɪʃᵊn/ *noun* **1 in moderation** If you do something in moderation, you do not do it too much. *I only drink alcohol in moderation now.* **2** [U] when you control your feelings or actions and stop them from becoming extreme

○━**modern** /ˈmɒdᵊn/ *adj* **1** relating to the present time and not to the past *modern society* • *the stresses of modern life* **2** using the newest ideas, design, technology, etc and not traditional *modern art/architecture* • *modern medicine* • **modernity** /mɒdˈɜːnəti/ [U] *formal* when something is modern

**modern-day** /ˈmɒdᵊndeɪ/ *adj* [always before noun] relating to the present time and not to the past *a modern-day version of Shakespeare*

**modernize** (*also UK* **-ise**) /ˈmɒdᵊnaɪz/ *verb* [I, T] to make something more modern or to become more modern *We really need to modernize our image.* • **modernization** /,mɒdᵊnaɪˈzeɪʃᵊn/ *noun* [U]

,**modern 'languages** *noun* [plural] languages that are spoken now such as Spanish or German

**modest** /ˈmɒdɪst/ *adj* **1** not large in size or amount, or not expensive *a modest amount of money* • *Their house is quite modest in size.* **2** If you are modest, you do not talk in a proud way about your skills or successes. *He's very modest about his achievements.* • **modestly** *adv*

**modesty** /ˈmɒdɪsti/ *noun* [U] when you do not talk in a proud way about your skills or successes

**modicum** /ˈmɒdɪkəm/ *noun formal* **a modicum of sth** a small amount of something *a modicum of success*

**modification** /,mɒdɪfɪˈkeɪʃᵊn/ *noun* [C, U] a small change to something *We've made a few modifications to the system.*

**modifier** /ˈmɒdɪfaɪᵊ/ *noun* [C] in grammar, a word that describes or limits the meaning of another word

**modify** /ˈmɒdɪfaɪ/ *verb* [T] **1** to change something in order to improve it [often passive] *The plans will have to be modified to reduce costs.* • *genetically modified food* **2** In grammar, a word that modifies another word describes or limits the meaning of that word. *Adjectives modify nouns.*

**module** /ˈmɒdjuːl/ *noun* [C] **1** *UK* a part of a university or college course **2** a part of an object that can operate alone, especially a part of a spacecraft

**mogul** /ˈməʊgəl/ *noun* [C] an important, powerful person *media/movie moguls*

**Mohammed** /məˈhæmɪd/ *noun* the Arab holy man on whose life and teachings Islam is based

**moist** /mɔɪst/ *adj* slightly wet *Keep the soil moist but not wet.* • *It was a lovely, moist cake.* • **moisten** /ˈmɔɪsən/ *verb* [I, T] to make something slightly wet, or to become slightly wet

**moisture** /ˈmɔɪstʃər/ *noun* [U] very small drops of water in the air or on a surface

**moisturizer** (*also UK* **-iser**) /ˈmɔɪstʃəraɪzər/ *noun* [C, U] a substance which you put on your skin to make it less dry • **moisturize** (*also UK* **-ise**) /ˈmɔɪstʃəraɪz/ *verb* [T] to put moisturizer on your skin

**molasses** /məˈlæsɪz/ (*also UK* **treacle**) *noun* [U] a sweet, thick, dark liquid used in sweet dishes

**mold** /məʊld/ *noun, verb US spelling of* mould

**moldy** /ˈməʊldi/ *adj US spelling of* mouldy

**mole** /məʊl/ *noun* [C] **1** [SKIN] a small, dark mark on the skin **2** [ANIMAL] a small animal with black fur that digs holes in the soil and lives under the ground **3** [PERSON] *informal* someone who gives other organizations or governments secret information about the organization where they work

**molecule** /ˈmɒlɪkjuːl/ *noun* [C] the smallest unit of a substance, consisting of one or more atoms

**molehill** /ˈməʊlhɪl/ *noun* [C] ➲ *See* make a **mountain** out of a molehill.

**molest** /məˈlest/ *verb* [T] to hurt or attack someone in a sexual way *He was accused of molesting children.* • **molestation** /ˌməʊlesˈteɪʃən/ *noun* [U]

**mom** /mɒm/ *US* (*UK* **mum**) *noun* [C] *informal* mother *My mom phoned last night.* • *Can we go now, Mom?*

o━**moment** /ˈməʊmənt/ *noun* **1** [C] a very short period of time *I'll be back in a moment.* • *For a moment I thought it was Anna.* • *Could you wait a moment?* **2** [C] a point in time *Just at that moment, the phone rang.* **3 at the moment** now *I'm afraid she's not here at the moment.* **4 for the moment** If you do something for the moment, you are doing it now but might do something different in the future. *For the moment, let's do what we agreed to.* **5 the moment (that)** as soon as *I'll call you the moment I hear anything.* ➲ *See also:* on the **spur²** of the moment.

**momentarily** /ˈməʊməntərəli/ *adv* for a very short time *I momentarily forgot his name.*

**momentary** /ˈməʊməntəri/ *adj* lasting for a very short time *a momentary lapse of memory*

**momentous** /məʊˈmentəs/ *adj* A momentous decision, event, etc is very important because it has a big effect on the future.

**momentum** /məʊˈmentəm/ *noun* [U] **1** when something continues to move, increase, or develop *to gain/gather momentum* • *The players seemed to lose momentum halfway through the game.* **2** in science, the force that makes something continue to move

**momma** /ˈmɒmə/ *noun* [C] *US another word for* mommy

**mommy** /ˈmɒmi/ *US* (*UK* **mummy**) *noun* [C] *informal* a word for 'mother', used especially by children *I want my mommy!* • *Can I have some candy, Mommy?*

**Mon** *written abbreviation for* Monday

**monarch** /ˈmɒnək/ *noun* [C] a king or queen

**monarchy** /ˈmɒnəki/ *noun* **1** [U, no plural] when a country is ruled by a king or queen *Do you think the monarchy should be abolished?* **2** [C] a country that is ruled by a king or queen

**monastery** /ˈmɒnəstəri/ *noun* [C] a building where men live as a religious group

**monastic** /məˈnæstɪk/ *adj* relating to a monk (= religious man) or a monastery

**Monday** /ˈmʌndeɪ/ (*written abbreviation* **Mon**) *noun* [C, U] the day of the week after Sunday and before Tuesday

**monetary** /ˈmʌnɪtəri/ *adj* relating to money *European monetary union*

o━**money** /ˈmʌni/ *noun* [U] the coins or banknotes (= pieces of paper with values) that are used to buy things *How much money have you got?* • *It costs a lot of money to buy a house.* • *He **spends** all his **money** on clothes and CDs.* • *The company's not **making** (= earning) any money at the moment.* ➲ *See also:* **pocket money**.

**'money ˌorder** *US* (*UK* **postal order**) *noun* [C] an official piece of paper bought at a post office that you can send instead of money

**mongrel** /ˈmʌŋgrəl/ *noun* [C] a dog that is a mix of different breeds

**monies** /ˈmʌniz/ *noun* [plural] *formal* amounts of money

**monitor¹** /ˈmɒnɪtər/ *noun* [C] **1** [SCREEN] a screen that shows information or pictures, usually connected to a computer *a colour monitor* ➲ *See colour picture* **The Office** *on page Centre 12.* **2** [MACHINE] a machine, often in a hospital, that measures something such as the rate that your heart beats *a heart monitor* **3** [PERSON] someone who watches something to make certain that it is done correctly or fairly *a human rights monitor*

**monitor²** /ˈmɒnɪtər/ *verb* [T] to watch something carefully and record your results *to monitor progress*

**monk** /mʌŋk/ *noun* [C] a member of a group of religious men living apart from other people

**monkey** /ˈmʌŋki/ *noun* [C] a hairy animal with a long tail that lives in hot countries and climbs trees

**monochrome** /ˈmɒnəkrəʊm/ *adj* A monochrome image is only in black, white, and grey and not in colour.

**monogamy** /məˈnɒgəmi/ *noun* [U] when someone has a sexual relationship with only one person • **monogamous** *adj* relating to monogamy *a monogamous relationship*

**monolingual** /ˌmɒnəʊˈlɪŋgwəl/ *adj* using only one language *monolingual and bilingual dictionaries*

**monolithic** /ˌmɒnəʊˈlɪθɪk/ *adj* large and powerful

**monologue** (*also US* **monolog**) /ˈmɒnəlɒg/ *noun* [C] a long speech by one person, often in a performance

M

**mononucleosis** /ˌmɒnəʊˌnjuːkli'əʊsɪs/ *US* (*UK* **glandular fever**) *noun* [U] an infectious disease that makes your glands (= small organs in your body) swell and makes you feel tired

**monopolize** (*also UK* **-ise**) /məˈnɒpᵊlaɪz/ *verb* [T] to control a situation by being the only person or organization involved in it

**monopoly** /məˈnɒpᵊli/ *noun* [C] **1** when a company or organization is the only one in an area of business or activity and has complete control of it *They **have a monopoly on** the postal service.* **2** a company or other organization that has a monopoly in a particular industry

**monosyllabic** /ˌmɒnəʊsɪ'læbɪk/ *adj* using only short words such as 'yes' or 'no', usually because you do not want to talk

**monotonous** /məˈnɒtᵊnəs/ *adj* If something is monotonous, it is boring because it stays the same. *a monotonous voice* • *monotonous work* • monotonously *adv*

**monsoon** /mɒnˈsuːn/ *noun* [C] the season when there is heavy rain in Southern Asia

**monster** /ˈmɒnstəʳ/ *noun* [C] an imaginary creature that is large, ugly, and frightening

**monstrous** /ˈmɒnstrəs/ *adj* **1** very bad or cruel *a monstrous crime* **2** like a monster *a monstrous size*

o⚞ **month** /mʌnθ/ *noun* [C] **1** one of the twelve periods of time that a year is divided into *last/next month* • *Your birthday's this month, isn't it?* **2** a period of approximately four weeks *She'll be working here for six months.* • *I saw him about three months ago.*

**monthly** /ˈmʌnθli/ *adj, adv* happening or produced once a month *a monthly meeting* • *a monthly magazine*

**monument** /ˈmɒnjəmənt/ *noun* [C] **1** a building or other structure that is built to make people remember an event in history or a famous person *a national monument* • *They built the statue as **a monument to** all the soldiers who died.* **2** an old building or place that is important in history *an ancient monument*

**monumental** /ˌmɒnjə'mentᵊl/ *adj* very large *a monumental task*

**moo** /muː/ *noun* [C] the sound that a cow makes • moo *verb* [I] mooing, *past* mooed

o⚞ **mood** /muːd/ *noun* **1** [C, U] the way someone feels at a particular time *to be in a good/bad mood* • *What sort of mood is he in today?* • *The public mood changed dramatically after the bombing.* **2 be in a mood** to not be friendly to other people because you are feeling angry *Ignore him – he's in a mood.* **3 be in the mood for sth/to do sth** to want to do or have something *I'm not really in the mood for shopping at the moment.* **4 be in no mood for sth/to do sth** to not want to do something with someone else, often because you are angry with them **5** [C] in grammar, one of the different ways a sentence is being used, for example to give an order, express a fact, etc *the indicative/imperative mood*

**moody** /ˈmuːdi/ *adj* If someone is moody, they are often unfriendly because they feel angry or unhappy. *He can be very moody and rude.* • moodily *adv* • moodiness *noun* [U]

o⚞ **moon** /muːn/ *noun* **1 the moon** the round object that shines in the sky at night and moves around the Earth (= crescent/full/ **new moon** the shape made by the amount of the moon that you can see at a particular time **3** [C] a round object like the moon that moves around another planet *The planet Saturn has eighteen moons.* **4 once in a blue moon** rarely *We only go out once in a blue moon.* **5 be over the moon** *UK* to be very pleased about something *"I bet she was pleased with her results." "She was over the moon."*

**moonlight** /ˈmuːnlaɪt/ *noun* [U] light that comes from the moon *In the moonlight she looked even more beautiful.* • moonlit *adj* [always before noun] with light from the moon

**moor** /mɔːʳ/ *noun* [C] an open area in the countryside that is covered with rough grass and bushes [usually plural] *the Yorkshire Moors*

**moose** /muːs/ *noun* [C] *plural* **moose** a large deer that comes from North America

**moot point** /ˌmuːt'pɔɪnt/ *noun* [C] a subject that people cannot agree about

**mop**¹ /mɒp/ *noun* [C] a piece of equipment used for cleaning floors that has a long handle and thick strings at one end

**mop**² /mɒp/ *verb* [T] **mopping**, *past* **mopped** to use a mop *to mop the floor*

**mop sth up** to use a cloth or mop to remove liquid from a surface

o⚞ **moral**¹ /ˈmɒrᵊl/ *adj* **1** [always before noun] relating to beliefs about what is right or wrong *moral standards/values* • *a moral issue* **2** behaving in a way that most people think is correct and honest *He's a very moral person.* ⊃ Compare **amoral**. ⊃ Opposite **immoral**. • morally *adv* *morally wrong*

**moral**² /ˈmɒrᵊl/ *noun* [C] something you learn from a story or event about how to behave *The moral of the story is never lie.*

**morale** /məˈrɑːl/ *noun* [U] the amount of confidence or hope for the future that people feel *The pay increase should help to improve staff morale.*

**morality** /məˈrælɪti/ *noun* [U] ideas and beliefs about what is right or wrong

**morals** /ˈmɒrᵊlz/ *noun* [plural] principles of good behaviour *He doesn't care what he does, he has no morals at all.*

**moral su'pport** *noun* [U] help and encouragement *Roz has said she'll come with me for moral support.*

**morbid** /ˈmɔːbɪd/ *adj* showing too much interest in unpleasant things such as death *a morbid fascination with death*

o⚞ **more**¹ /mɔːʳ/ *quantifier* **1** something in addition to what you already have *Is there any more soup?* • *Would anyone like some more food?* • *I need a bit more money.* **2** a greater number or amount of people or things *There are a lot more people here today than there were yesterday.* • *He knows more about computers than I do.* **3 more and more** an increasing number *More and more people are choosing not to get married.* ⊃ See also: **any more**.

**more**

The opposite of more is **fewer** for countable nouns and **less** for uncountable nouns.

*He takes more exercise now.*

*He takes less exercise now.*

*He smokes fewer cigarettes.*

o━**more²** /mɔːʳ/ *adv* **1 more beautiful/ difficult/ interesting, etc** used to show that someone or something has a greater amount of a quality than someone or something else *It's more expensive than the others.* • *She's far more intelligent than her sister.* **2** used to show that something happens a greater number of times than before *We eat out a lot more than we used to.* **3 more or less** almost *We've more or less finished work on the house.* **4 more and more** more as time passes *It's becoming more and more difficult to pass the exam.* ➲ *See also:* **any more**.

**more**

More is used to form the comparative of many adjectives and adverbs that have two or more syllables.

*a more expensive hotel*

~~an expensiver hotel~~

*Could you drive more slowly please?*

The opposite of the adverb more is **less**.

*a less expensive hotel*

**moreover** /mɔːrˈəʊvəʳ/ *adv formal* also *It is a cheap and, moreover, effective way of dealing with the problem.*

**morgue** /mɔːg/ *noun* [C] a building or room where dead bodies are prepared and kept before a funeral

**Mormon** /ˈmɔːmən/ *adj* belonging or relating to a Christian group that was started in the US by Joseph Smith *the Mormon Church* • Mormon *noun* [C]

o━**morning** /ˈmɔːnɪŋ/ *noun* [C, U] **1** the first half of the day, from the time when the sun rises or you wake up until the middle of the day *Friday morning* • *tomorrow morning* • *I got up late this morning.* **2 in the morning a** during the early part of the day *I listen to the radio in the morning.* **b** tomorrow morning *I'll pack my bags in the morning.* **3 3/4, etc o'clock in the morning** 3/4, etc o'clock in the night *My car alarm went off at 3 o'clock in the morning.* **4 (Good) morning.** used to say hello to someone in the morning

**moron** /ˈmɔːrɒn/ *noun* [C] *informal* a very stupid person • moronic /mɔːˈrɒnɪk/ *adj informal* stupid

**morose** /məˈrəʊs/ *adj* If someone is morose, they are not friendly or happy and they talk very little.

**morphine** /ˈmɔːfiːn/ *noun* [U] a powerful drug that is used to reduce pain

**morsel** /ˈmɔːsəl/ *noun* [C] a small piece of something *a morsel of food*

**mortal¹** /ˈmɔːtəl/ *adj* **1** not living forever ➲ *Opposite* **immortal**. **2 mortal danger/fear/ terror, etc** extreme danger/fear/terror, etc, because you could die • mortally *adv mortally wounded*

**mortal²** /ˈmɔːtəl/ *noun* [C] *literary* a human being

**mortality** /mɔːˈtæləti/ *noun* [U] **1** the number of deaths at a particular time or in a particular place *infant mortality* • *the mortality rate* **2** the way that people do not live forever *Her death made him more aware of his own mortality.*

**mortar** /ˈmɔːtəʳ/ *noun* **1** [C] a heavy gun that fires explosives high into the air *a mortar attack/bomb* **2** [U] a mixture of substances, for example sand and water, that is used between bricks or stones to keep them together

**mortgage** /ˈmɔːgɪdʒ/ *noun* [C] money that you borrow to buy a home *a monthly mortgage payment*

**mortify** /ˈmɔːtɪfaɪ/ *verb* **be mortified** to feel very embarrassed or upset about something *I told her she'd upset John and she was mortified.*

**mortuary** /ˈmɔːtʃuˁri/ *noun* [C] a building or room where dead bodies are prepared and kept before a funeral

**mosaic** /məʊˈzeɪɪk/ *noun* [C, U] a picture or pattern that is made with small pieces of coloured stone, glass, etc

mosaic

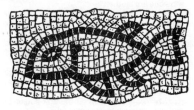

**Moslem** /ˈmɒzləm/ *noun* [C] *another spelling of* Muslim (= someone who believes in Islam) • Moslem *adj*

**mosque** /mɒsk/ *noun* [C] a building where Muslims say their prayers

**mosquito** /məˈskiːtəʊ/ *noun* [C] *plural* **mosquitoes** a small flying insect that sucks your blood, sometimes causing malaria (= a serious disease)

**moss** /mɒs/ *noun* [C, U] a very small, green plant that grows on the surface of rocks, trees, etc

o━**most¹** /məʊst/ *adv* **1 the most attractive/ important/popular, etc** used to show that someone or something has the greatest amount of a quality *She's the most beautiful girl I've ever seen.* • *There are various reasons but this is the most important.* **2** more than anyone or anything else *Which subject do you like most?* • *Sam enjoyed the swings most of all.*

o━**most²** /məʊst/ *quantifier* **1** almost all of a group of people or things *Most people think he's guilty.* • *Most of our students walk to school.*

**most**

The adverb **most** is used to form the superlative of many adjectives and adverbs.

*the most beautiful actress in the world*

• *She wears jeans most of the time.* **2** a larger amount than anyone or anything else *This one costs the most.* • *Which of you earns most?* **3 the most** the largest number or amount possible *That's the most I can pay you.* **4 make the most of sth** to take full advantage of something because it may not last long *We should make the most of this good weather.* **5 at (the) most** not more than a particular amount or number *The journey will take an hour at the most.*

⚬⤙**mostly** /ˈməʊstli/ *adv* mainly or most of the time *She reads mostly romantic novels.*

**motel** /məʊˈtel/ *noun* [C] a hotel for people who are travelling by car

**moth** /mɒθ/ *noun* [C] an insect with large wings that often flies at night and is attracted to light ➜ *See picture at* **insect**.

⚬⤙**mother** /ˈmʌðər/ *noun* [C] **1** your female parent *a single mother* • *My mother and father are divorced.* **2 Mother** The title of an important nun (= woman who lives in a female religious group) *Mother Teresa* ➜ *See also:* **surrogate mother**.

**motherhood** /ˈmʌðəhʊd/ *noun* [U] when someone is a mother

**mother-in-law** /ˈmʌðərɪnˌlɔː/ *noun* [C] *plural* **mothers-in-law** the mother of your husband or wife

**motherly** /ˈmʌðəli/ *adj* A motherly woman is like a mother, usually because she is kind and looks after people.

**'Mother's ˌDay** *noun* [C, U] a Sunday in the spring when people give their mothers presents to show their love

**ˌmother 'tongue** *noun* [C] the first language that you learn when you are a child

**motif** /məʊˈtiːf/ *noun* [C] a small design used as a decoration on something *a floral motif*

**motion¹** /ˈməʊʃən/ *noun* **1** ⌈MOVEMENT⌉ [U] when or how something moves *The motion of the boat made him feel sick.* **2** ⌈ACTION⌉ [C] a single action or movement *She made a motion with her hand.* **3** ⌈SUGGESTION⌉ [C] a suggestion that you make in a formal meeting or court of law *to propose/oppose a motion* **4 set sth in motion** to make something start to happen **5 go through the motions** to do something that you have to do without enthusiasm ➜ *See also:* **slow motion**.

**motion²** /ˈməʊʃən/ *verb* **motion (for/to) sb to do sth** to make a movement as a sign for someone to do something *She motioned him to sit down.*

**motionless** /ˈməʊʃənləs/ *adj* not moving *He stood motionless in the middle of the road.*

**motivate** /ˈməʊtɪveɪt/ *verb* [T] **1** to make someone enthusiastic about doing something [+ to do sth] *Teaching is all about motivating people to learn.* **2** to cause someone to behave in a particular way [often passive] *Some people are motivated by greed.* • motivated *adj a racially motivated crime* • *a very motivated student* (= one who works hard and wants to succeed)

**motivation** /ˌməʊtɪˈveɪʃən/ *noun* [U] **1** enthusiasm for doing something *There is a lack of motivation among the staff.* **2** the need or reason for doing something *What was the motivation for the attack?*

**motivational** /ˌməʊtɪˈveɪʃənəl/ *adj* [always before noun] giving you encouragement to do something *a motivational speaker*

**motive** /ˈməʊtɪv/ *noun* [C] a reason for doing something *The police don't yet know the motive for the killing.*

**motor¹** /ˈməʊtər/ *noun* [C] the part of a machine or vehicle that changes electricity or fuel into movement and makes it work *an electric motor*

**motor²** /ˈməʊtər/ *adj* [always before noun] relating to cars *motor racing*

**motorcycle** /ˈməʊtəˌsaɪkl/ (*also* **motorbike** /ˈməʊtəbaɪk/) *noun* [C] a vehicle with two wheels and an engine

**motoring** /ˈməʊtərɪŋ/ *adj* [always before noun] UK relating to driving *a motoring offence*

**motorist** /ˈməʊtərɪst/ *noun* [C] someone who drives a car

**motorway** /ˈməʊtəweɪ/ UK (US **freeway, expressway**) *noun* [C] a long, wide road, usually used by traffic travelling fast over long distances

**mottled** /ˈmɒtld/ *adj* A mottled pattern has a mixture of dark and light areas. *mottled skin*

**motto** /ˈmɒtəʊ/ *noun* [C] a short phrase that expresses someone's purpose or beliefs *Her motto is, "Work hard, play hard".*

**mould¹** UK (US **mold**) /məʊld/ *noun* **1** [U] a green or black substance that grows in wet places or on old food **2** [C] a container that is used to make something in a particular shape *a chocolate mould* **3 break the mould** to do something differently after it has been done in the same way for a long time

**mould²** UK (US **mold**) /məʊld/ *verb* [T] to make a soft substance a particular shape *moulded plastic*

**mouldy** UK (US **moldy**) /ˈməʊldi/ *adj* covered with mould *mouldy cheese*

**mound** /maʊnd/ *noun* [C] **1** a large pile of something *a mound of clothes waiting to be ironed* **2** a higher area of soil, like a small hill *an ancient burial mound*

**Mount** /maʊnt/ *noun* [C] used in the names of mountains *Mount Everest*

**mount** /maʊnt/ *verb* **1 mount a campaign/ challenge/protest, etc** to arrange a series of organized activities that will achieve a particular result **2** ⌈INCREASE⌉ [I] to increase in amount or level *Tension in the room was mounting.* • *mounting problems* **3 mount sth on/to, etc** to fix an object onto something *They've mounted a camera on the wall by the door.* **4** ⌈GO UP⌉ [T] to go up something *to mount the stairs* **5** ⌈RIDE⌉ [T] to get on a horse or bicycle ➜ *Opposite* **dismount**.

**mount up** to gradually become a large amount *My homework is really mounting up this week.*

o﹣ᴹ**mountain** /'maʊntɪn/ *noun* [C] **1** a very high hill *to climb a mountain* • *a mountain range* **2** *informal* a large pile of something *There's a mountain of papers on my desk.* **3 make a mountain out of a molehill** to deal with a small problem as if it were a big problem

**mountainous** /'maʊntɪnəs/ *adj* A mountainous area has a lot of mountains.

**mourn** /mɔːn/ *verb* [I, T] to feel very sad because someone has died *He mourned for his dead son every day.*

**mourner** /'mɔːnər/ *noun* [C] someone at a funeral

**mournful** /'mɔːnfəl/ *adj* very sad *a mournful voice* • mournfully *adv*

**mourning** /'mɔːnɪŋ/ *noun* [U] when someone mourns the death of someone else *a period of mourning* • *She's in mourning for her husband.*

**mouse** /maʊs/ *noun* [C] *plural* **mice 1** a small piece of equipment connected to a computer that you move with your hand to control what the computer does **2** a small animal with fur and a long, thin tail

mouse

**mousse** /muːs/ *noun* [C, U] **1** a soft, cold food that is often sweet and usually has eggs or cream in it *chocolate mousse* **2** a substance that you put in your hair so that it stays in a particular shape

**moustache** (*also US* **mustache**) /məˈstɑːʃ ⓤⓈ ˈmʌstæʃ/ *noun* [C] a line of hair that some men grow above their mouths ➡ *See colour picture* **Hair** *on page Centre 9.*

**mousy** (*also* **mousey**) /'maʊsi/ *adj* **1** Mousy hair is light brown. ➡ *See colour picture* **Hair** *on page Centre 9.* **2** A mousy person is shy and not very interesting.

o﹣ᴹ**mouth** /maʊθ/ *noun* [C] **1** the part of the face that is used for eating and speaking ➡ *See colour picture* **The Body** *on page Centre 2.* **2 mouth of a cave/tunnel, etc** the opening or entrance of a cave/tunnel, etc **3 mouth of a river** where a river goes into the sea ➡ *See also:* **butter¹** *wouldn't melt in sb's mouth.*

**mouthful** /'maʊθfʊl/ *noun* [C] the amount of food or drink that you can put into your mouth at one time

**mouthpiece** /'maʊθpiːs/ *noun* [C] a person,

newspaper, etc that expresses the opinions of the government or a political group

**mouthwash** /'maʊθwɒʃ/ *noun* [U] a liquid used to make your mouth clean and fresh

**movable** /'muːvəbl/ *adj* able to be moved

o﹣ᴹ**move¹** /muːv/ *verb* **1** CHANGE PLACE [I] If a person or an organization moves, they go to a different place to live or work. *Eventually, he moved to Germany.* • *She's moving into a new apartment.* • *Our children have all moved away.* **2** POSITION [I, T] to change place or position, or to make something change place or position *We moved the chairs to another room.* • *I can't cut your hair if you keep moving.* • *Someone was moving around upstairs.* **3 move ahead/along/forward, etc** to make progress with something that you have planned to do *The department is moving ahead with changes to its teaching programme.* **4** ACTION [I] to take action [+ to do sth] *The company moved swiftly to find new products.* **5** TIME [T] to change the time or order of something *We need to move the meeting back a few days.* **6** FEELING [T] to make someone have strong feelings of sadness or sympathy [often passive] *I was deeply moved by his speech.* • *Many people were moved to tears* (= were so sad they cried). ➡ *Compare* **unmoved.** **7 move house** *UK* to leave your home in order to live in a new one **8 get moving** *informal* to hurry *We're leaving in five minutes, so get moving!*

**USAGE**

**move** or **travel**?

Move means to change position or put something in a different position.

*Could you move back a bit, please?*

*Why don't you move the table over there?*

Travel means to go from one place to another, usually in a vehicle.

*Most people travel to work by car.*

**move in** to begin living in a new home *We're moving in next week.* • *She's just moved in with her boyfriend.* • *They want to move in together before they get married.*

**move out** to stop living in a particular home *He moved out when he was only eighteen.*

**move on 1** NEW PLACE to leave the place where you are staying and go somewhere else *After three days in Madrid we thought we'd move on.* **2** NEW ACTIVITY to start doing a new activity *I'd done the same job for ten years and felt it was time to move on.* **3** NEW SUBJECT to change from one subject to another when you are talking or writing *Let's move on to the next topic.*

**move over** to change the place where you are sitting or standing so that there is space for someone else to sit or stand

**move²** /muːv/ *noun* [C] **1** something that you do in order to achieve something or to make progress in a situation *"I've told her she's got to find somewhere else to live." "Good move!"* • *The latest policies are clearly a move towards democracy.* • *a good career move* **2** when you go to live or work in a different place *The move will cost us a lot of money.* **3 make a move a** to change from one place or position to another *He made a move as if to leave.* **b** *UK informal* to leave somewhere *I'd better make a move or I'll be late.* **4 get a move on** *informal* to hurry *Come on, get a move on!*

⊶**movement** /'muːvmənt/ *noun* **1** GROUP [C] a group of people with the same beliefs who work together to achieve something *the women's movement* • *the labour movement* **2** CHANGE [C] a change or development in the way people think or behave *a movement towards democracy* **3** POSITION [C, U] a change of position or place *His movements were rather clumsy.* **4** MUSIC [C] a part of a piece of music *The symphony opens with a slow movement.* **5 sb's movements** what someone is doing during a particular period of time *I don't know his movements this week.*

⊶**movie** /'muːvi/ *noun* [C] *US* **1** a film **2 the movies** *US* (*UK* **the cinema**) a cinema, or group of cinemas *What's playing at the movies?* • *Why don't we go to the movies tonight?*

'**movie** ,**star** *noun* [C] a famous movie actor or actress

'**movie** ,**theater** *US* (*UK* **cinema**) *noun* [C] a building where you go to watch films

**moving** /'muːvɪŋ/ *adj* **1** causing strong feelings of sadness or sympathy *a moving story/tribute* **2** [always before noun] A moving object is one that moves. *a moving target*

**mow** /məʊ/ *verb* [T] *past t* **mowed**, *past p* **mown** or **mowed** to cut grass using a machine *to mow the lawn*

**mower** /'məʊəʳ/ (*also* **lawn mower**) *noun* [C] a machine that you use to cut grass

**MP** /,em'piː/ *noun* [C] *abbreviation for* Member of Parliament: someone who has been elected to the government of the United Kingdom

**mph** *written abbreviation for* miles per hour: a unit for measuring speed *a 30 mph speed limit*

⊶**Mr** /'mɪstəʳ/ *noun* a title for a man, used before his family name or full name *Good morning, Mr Smith.* • *This package is addressed to Mr Gordon Harper.*

---

**USAGE**

**Mr, Mrs, Ms, Miss**

All these titles are used before someone's name.

**Mr** is used for men.

**Mrs** is used for women who are married.

**Miss** is used for girls or for women who are not married.

**Ms** is used for women and does not show if a woman is married. Many women prefer to use this title to **Miss** or **Mrs**.

When you do not know someone's last name, it is polite to use **sir** or **madam**.

*Can I help you, madam?*

~~Can I help you, Mrs?~~

---

⊶**Mrs** /'mɪsɪz/ *noun* a title for a married woman, used before her family name or full name

*Hello, Mrs. Jones.* • *Please send your application to the finance director, Mrs Laura Fox.*

**Ms** /mɪz/ *noun* a title for a woman, used before her family name or full name *Ms Holly Fox*

**MS** /,em'es/ *noun* [U] *abbreviation for* multiple sclerosis (= a serious disease that gradually makes it difficult for a person to see, speak, or move)

**MSc** *UK* (*US* **MS**) /,emes'siː/ *noun* [C] *abbreviation for* Master of Science: a higher university qualification in a science subject

⊶**much¹** /mʌtʃ/ *quantifier* **1** QUESTION In questions, 'much' is used to ask about the amount of something. *Was there much food there?* • *How much money will I need for the taxi?* **2** NEGATIVE In negative sentences, 'much' is used to say that there is not a large amount of something. *She doesn't earn much money.* • *Pete didn't say much at dinner.* • *I don't eat very much before a performance.* • *"Is there any coffee left?" "Not much."* • *There's nothing much to do here in the evenings.* **3 too much/so much** a large amount of something, often more than you want *I'd love to come, but I've got too much work.* • *We were having so much fun, I didn't want to go home.* **4** A LOT OF *formal* a lot of *Much work remains to be done.* • *Much of his evidence was unreliable.* **5 not much of a sth** used when you want to say that a person or thing is a bad example of something *I'm not much of a cook.* • *It's not much of a job, but it pays the bills.* **6 not be up to much** *UK informal* to be of bad quality *Her latest novel isn't up to much.* ➲ *See usage note at* **many**.

⊶**much²** /mʌtʃ/ *adv* **more**, **most 1** [used in questions and negatives] often or a lot *Do you go to London much?* • *I don't like curry very much.* **2** used before comparative adjectives (= adjectives like 'better' and 'smaller', that are used to compare things) to mean 'a lot' *Their old house was much bigger.* • *That's a much more sensible idea.* • *"Is her new car faster than her old one?" "Oh yes, much."*

**muck¹** /mʌk/ *noun* [U] *informal* dirt *You've got muck on your shoes.*

**muck²** /mʌk/ *verb*
**muck about/around** *mainly UK informal* to behave stupidly and waste time *Stop mucking around, will you!*
**muck sth up** *informal* to do something badly, or to spoil something *I mucked up the interview.* • *She lost her car keys and that mucked up the whole weekend.*

**mucus** /'mjuːkəs/ *noun* [U] a thick liquid produced inside the nose and other parts of the body

⊶**mud** /mʌd/ *noun* [U] a thick liquid mixture of soil and water, or this mixture after it has dried *He'd been playing football and was covered in mud.*

**muddle¹** /'mʌdl/ *noun* [C, U] a situation of confusion or bad organization *There was a big muddle over who was buying the tickets.* • *I'm in such a muddle with these bills.* • *Dad got into a muddle over* (= was confused about) *the plans for Christmas.*

**muddle²** /'mʌdl/ *verb* **get sb/sth muddled up** to think that a person or thing is someone or something else *I often get Jonathan and his brother muddled up.*

**muddle through (sth)** to manage to do something although you do not know how to do it well *None of us has any formal training but somehow we muddle through.*

**muddle sth up** to arrange things in the wrong order *Please don't muddle up those books – I've just sorted them out.*

**muddled** /'mʌdld/ *adj* **1** A person who is muddled is confused. *He became increasingly muddled as he grew older.* **2** Things that are muddled are badly organized. *He left his clothes in a muddled pile in the corner.*

**muddy** /'mʌdi/ *adj* covered by or containing mud (= mixture of soil and water) *a muddy stream* • *Don't you bring those muddy boots into the kitchen!*

**mudguard** /'mʌdgɑːd/ *UK* (*US* **fender**) *noun* [C] a curved piece of metal or plastic fixed above a wheel of a bicycle or motorcycle to prevent water or dirt from hitting the person's legs

**muffin** /'mʌfɪn/ *noun* [C] **1** a small, sweet cake *a blueberry muffin* **2** *UK* (*US* **English muffin**) a small, round, flat bread that is often eaten hot with butter *toasted muffins*

**muffin**

muffin *UK*,
English muffin *US*

muffin

**muffle** /'mʌfl/ *verb* [T] to make a noise quieter and less clear *The pillow muffled her screams.* • **muffled** *adj* Muffled sounds cannot be heard clearly. *a muffled sound/voice* • *a muffled scream/cry*

**muffler** /'mʌflər/ *US* (*UK* **silencer**) *noun* [C] a part of a vehicle that reduces noise

**mug**[1] /mʌg/ *noun* [C] **1** a large cup with straight sides usually used for hot drinks *a coffee mug* • *a steaming mug of tea* **2** *informal* someone who is stupid and easily deceived *I was such a mug to think he'd pay me back.*

**mug**[2] /mʌg/ *verb* [T] **mugging**, *past* **mugged** to attack and rob someone in a public place [often passive] *He was mugged as he walked across the park.* • **mugger** *noun* [C] someone who mugs people

**mugging** /'mʌgɪŋ/ *noun* [C, U] when someone is attacked in a public place and money, etc stolen from them

**muggy** /'mʌgi/ *adj* When the weather is muggy, it is unpleasantly warm and the air contains a lot of water. *a muggy afternoon*

**Muhammad** /mə'hæmɪd/ *noun* another

spelling of Mohammed (= the Arab holy man on whose life and teachings Islam is based)

**mule** /mjuːl/ *noun* [C] an animal whose mother is a horse and whose father is a donkey (= animal like a small horse)

**mull** /mʌl/ *verb*

**mull sth over** to think carefully about something for a long time, often before you make a decision *I need time to mull things over before I decide what to do.*

**mullah** /'mʌlə/ *noun* [C] a Muslim religious teacher or leader

**multilingual** /ˌmʌlti'lɪŋgwəl/ *adj* using or speaking more than two languages

**multimedia** /ˌmʌlti'miːdiə/ *adj* [always before noun] Multimedia computers and programs use sound, pictures, film, and text. *multimedia software/technology*

**multinational**[1] /ˌmʌlti'næʃənəl/ *adj* active in several countries, or involving people from several countries *a multinational company/corporation*

**multinational**[2] /ˌmʌlti'næʃənəl/ *noun* [C] a large company that produces goods or services in several countries

**multiple**[1] /'mʌltɪpl/ *adj* with several parts *multiple injuries*

**multiple**[2] /'mʌltɪpl/ *noun* [C] a number that can be divided by another number an exact number of times *Nine is a multiple of three.*

**ˌmultiple 'choice** *adj* A multiple choice exam or question gives you different answers and you choose the correct one.

**multiple sclerosis** /ˌmʌltɪplsklə'rəʊsɪs/ *noun* [U] a serious disease that gradually makes it difficult for a person to see, speak, or move

**multiplex** /'mʌltɪpleks/ *noun* [C] a cinema which has separate screens and shows different films at the same time

**multiplication** /ˌmʌltɪplɪ'keɪʃən/ *noun* [U] the process of multiplying a number with other numbers

**multiply** /'mʌltɪplaɪ/ *verb* **1** [I, T] to increase by a large number, or to cause something to increase by a large number *In warm weather, germs multiply rapidly.* **2** [T] to add one number to itself a particular number of times *Three multiplied by six equals eighteen.*

**multiracial** /ˌmʌlti'reɪʃəl/ *adj* involving people from different races *a multiracial society*

**multitude** /'mʌltɪtjuːd/ *noun* [C] *formal* a large number of people or things *a multitude of problems/questions*

o━ **mum** /mʌm/ *UK* (*US* **mom**) *noun* [C] *informal* mother *I asked my mum but she said no.* • *Can we go now, Mum?*

**mumble** /'mʌmbl/ *verb* [I, T] to speak too quietly and not clearly enough for someone to understand you *He mumbled something about it being a waste of time.*

**mummy** /'mʌmi/ *noun* [C] **1** *UK informal* (*US* **mommy**) a word for 'mother', used especially by children *Come here, Mummy!* • *My mummy and daddy came too.* **2** a dead body covered in cloth, especially from ancient Egypt *an ancient/Egyptian mummy*

**mumps** /mʌmps/ *noun* [U] an illness that chil-

M

# munch

dren get which makes the throat and neck swell *to have mumps*

**munch** /mʌnʃ/ *verb* [I, T] to eat something in a noisy way *She was sitting on the lawn munching an apple.*

**mundane** /mʌn'deɪn/ *adj* ordinary, or not interesting *a mundane task/life*

**municipal** /mju:'nɪsɪpᵊl/ *adj* [always before noun] relating to the government of a town or city *a municipal council/election*

**munitions** /mju:'nɪʃᵊnz/ *noun* [plural] bombs, guns, and other military equipment *a munitions factory*

**mural** /'mjʊərᵊl/ *noun* [C] a picture that is painted on a wall

o⚊**murder**[1] /'mɜːdəʳ/ *noun* [C, U] **1** the crime of intentionally killing someone *to commit murder* • *She was charged with attempted murder.* • *a murder charge/trial* **2 be murder** *informal* to be unpleasant or cause difficulty *Driving in Chicago at rush hour is murder.*

o⚊**murder**[2] /'mɜːdəʳ/ *verb* [T] to kill someone intentionally and illegally [often passive] *He was murdered by a former employee.* • *She was accused of/convicted of murdering her husband.*

**murderer** /'mɜːdᵊrəʳ/ *noun* [C] someone who has committed murder *a convicted murderer*

**murderous** /'mɜːdᵊrəs/ *adj* [always before noun] likely to kill someone, or wanting to kill them *a murderous dictator/regime* • *murderous thoughts*

**murky** /'mɜːki/ *adj* **1** secret, and involving dishonest or illegal activities *He has a **murky** past as an arms dealer.* • *the murky world of drug dealing* **2** dirty and dark *murky water*

**murmur**[1] /'mɜːməʳ/ *verb* [I, T] to speak quietly so that you can only be heard by someone near you *"Go to sleep now," she murmured.* • *He murmured a few words of sympathy.*

**murmur**[2] /'mɜːməʳ/ *noun* [C] the sound of something being said quietly *I could hear the low murmur of voices from behind the door.*

o⚊**muscle**[1] /'mʌsl/ *noun* **1** [C, U] one of many pieces of tissue in the body that are connected to bones and which produce movement by becoming longer or shorter *aching joints and muscles* • *stomach/thigh muscles* • *I think I may have pulled* (= injured) *a muscle.* **2** [U] the ability to control or influence people *political/military muscle*

**muscle**[2] /'mʌsl/ *verb*

**muscle in** to force yourself into an activity in which other people do not want you to be involved *How can we stop him **muscling in on** this project?*

**muscular** /'mʌskjələʳ/ *adj* **1** having firm, strong muscles *muscular legs/arms* **2** relating to muscles *muscular aches/pains*

**muse** /mju:z/ *verb* [I] *formal* to think carefully about something for a long time *I was just **musing about** relationships.*

**museum** /mju:'zi:əm/ *noun* [C] a building where you can look at important objects connected with art, history, or science *a museum of modern art*

**mush** /mʌʃ/ *noun* [U] *informal* food that is unpleasantly soft and wet, usually because it has been cooked for too long

**mushroom**[1] /'mʌʃruːm/ *noun* [C] a type of fungus (= organism like a plant) with a short stem and a round top, some types of which can be eaten *pasta with wild mushrooms* • *mushroom pizza/soup*

**mushroom**

**mushroom**[2] /'mʌʃruːm/ *verb* [I] to increase or develop very quickly *Crime in the city has mushroomed during the past decade.* • *mushrooming costs*

o⚊**music** /'mju:zɪk/ *noun* [U] **1** a pattern of sounds that is made by playing instruments or singing, or a recording of this *pop/rock/dance music* • *classical music* • *He likes listening to music.* • *Could you put on some music?* • *a music festival* • *a music lesson/teacher* **2** written signs which represent sounds that can be sung or played with instruments *I never learnt to **read music*** (= understand written music). **3 face the music** to accept punishment or criticism for something bad that you have done ➚ *See also:* **chamber music**, **country music**, **folk music**.

**musical**[1] /'mju:zɪkᵊl/ *adj* **1** [always before noun] relating to music *a musical instrument* **2** good at playing music *She comes from a very musical family.* • **musically** *adv*

**musical**[2] /'mju:zɪkᵊl/ *noun* [C] a play or film in which singing and dancing tell part of the story *a Broadway/Hollywood musical*

**musician** /mju:'zɪʃᵊn/ *noun* [C] someone who plays a musical instrument, often as a job *a talented jazz/classical musician*

**Muslim** (*also* **Moslem**) /'mʊzlɪm ⓤⓢ 'mʌzləm/ *noun* [C] someone who believes in Islam • **Muslim** *adj a Muslim family*

**muslin** /'mʌzlɪn/ *noun* [U] a very thin cotton cloth

**mussel** /'mʌsᵊl/ *noun* [C] a small sea creature that has a black shell in two parts and that can be eaten

o⚊**must**[1] *strong form* /mʌst/ *weak forms* /məst, məs/ *modal verb* **1** [NECESSARY] used to say that it is necessary that something happens or is done *The meat must be cooked thoroughly.* • *You mustn't show this letter to anyone else.* • *I must get some sleep.* **2** [LIKELY] used to show that you think something is very likely or certain to be true *It must have been very upsetting for her.* • *You must be exhausted.* • *She must be very wealthy.* **3** [SUGGEST] used to show that you think it is a good idea for someone to do something *You must come and stay with us some time.* ➚ *See study section* **Modal verbs** *on page Centre 31.*

**must**[2] /mʌst/ *noun* **be a must** *informal* If something is a must, it is very important to have or do it. *The restaurant has become so popular that reservations are a must.*

**mustache** /mə'stɑːʃ ⓤⓢ 'mʌstæʃ/ *noun* [C]

*another US spelling of* moustache (= a line of hair above the mouth)

**mustard** /'mʌstəd/ *noun* [U] a thick, spicy, yellow or brown sauce often eaten in small amounts with meat *a teaspoon of mustard*

**muster** /'mʌstər/ (*also* **muster up**) *verb* [T] to get enough support, bravery, or energy to do something difficult *I hope she musters the courage to invite him for dinner.*

**mustn't** /'mʌsⁿnt/ *short for* must not *You mustn't let her know I'm coming.*

**musty** /'mʌsti/ *adj* smelling old and slightly wet in an unpleasant way *a musty room* • *the musty smell of old books*

**mutant** /'mju:tⁿnt/ *noun* [C] an organism or cell that is different from others of the same type because of a change in its genes *a mutant virus*

**mutation** /mju:'teɪʃⁿn/ *noun* [C, U] a permanent change in the genes of an organism, or an organism with such a change *The disease is caused by a mutation in a single gene.*

**mute** /mju:t/ *adj* **1** expressed in thoughts but not in speech or writing *The president has remained mute about whether he will resign.* • *I gazed at her in mute admiration.* **2** unable to speak for physical or mental reasons *a school for deaf and mute children*

**muted** /'mju:tɪd/ *adj* **1** [FEELING] not strongly expressed *a muted response/reaction* • *muted criticism* **2** [SOUND] A muted sound is quieter than usual. *muted voices* **3** [COLOUR] [always before noun] A muted colour is not bright or easily noticed. *He was dressed in muted shades of grey and brown.*

**mutilate** /'mju:tɪleɪt/ *verb* [T] to damage someone's body violently and severely, often by cutting off a part of it *a mutilated body/corpse* • mutilation /,mju:tɪ'leɪʃⁿn/ *noun* [C, U]

**mutiny** /'mju:tɪni/ *noun* [C, U] when a group of people, usually soldiers or sailors, refuse to obey orders, often because they want to be in control themselves • mutiny *verb* [I] to take part in a mutiny

**mutt** /mʌt/ *noun* [C] *informal* a dog that is a mixture of different breeds (= types)

**mutter** /'mʌtər/ *verb* [I, T] to speak quietly so that your voice is difficult to hear, often when complaining about something *She walked past me, muttering to herself.* • *He muttered something about the restaurant being too expensive.* • mutter *noun* [C]

**mutton** /'mʌtⁿn/ *noun* [U] **1** meat from an adult sheep *a leg/shoulder of mutton* **2** **mutton dressed as lamb** *UK informal* an older woman who wears clothes that would be more suitable for a young woman

**mutual** /'mju:tʃuəl/ *adj* **1** When two or more people have a mutual feeling, they have the same opinion about each other. *mutual admiration/respect* • *He doesn't like her, and I suspect the feeling's mutual.* **2** When two or more people have a mutual friend or interest, they have the same one. *Andrew and Jean were introduced to each other by a **mutual friend.***

**mutually** /'mju:tʃuəli/ *adv* You use mutually before an adjective when the adjective describes all sides of a situation. *a mutually dependent relationship* • *Being attractive and intelligent are not **mutually exclusive** (= someone can be attractive and intelligent).*

**muzzle¹** /'mʌzl/ *noun* [C] **1** the mouth and nose of a dog, or a covering put over these to prevent the dog biting **2** the open end of the long cylindrical part of a gun

**muzzle²** /'mʌzl/ *verb* [T] **1** to put a muzzle on a dog *Dangerous dogs must be muzzled in public places.* **2** to prevent someone expressing their own opinions

o-= **my** /maɪ/ *determiner* belonging to or relating to the person who is speaking or writing *Tom's my older son.* • *It's not my fault.* • *My house is near the station.*

**myriad** /'mɪriəd/ *adj literary* very many *myriad problems* • myriad *noun* [C] *literary Digital technology resulted in **a myriad of** (= many) new TV channels.*

o-= **myself** /maɪ'self/ *pronoun* **1** the reflexive form of the pronouns 'me' or 'I' *I've bought myself a new coat.* • *I looked at myself in the mirror.* **2** used to emphasize the pronoun 'I', especially when the speaker wants to talk about their actions and not someone else's *I'll tell her myself.* • *Jack always drinks red wine but I prefer white myself.* **3 (all) by myself** alone or without anyone else's help *I live by myself in a small flat.* • *Mummy, I got dressed all by myself.* **4 (all) to myself** for my use only *I'll have the flat all to myself this weekend.* • *I need a couple of hours to myself.*

**mysterious** /mɪ'stɪəriəs/ *adj* **1** strange or unknown, and not explained or understood *a mysterious stranger* • *the mysterious death of her son* **2** refusing to talk about something and behaving in a secretive way *Nick is being very **mysterious about** where he's going on holiday.* • mysteriously *adv to disappear/vanish mysteriously*

**mystery¹** /'mɪstⁿri/ *noun* **1** [C, U] something strange or unknown that cannot be explained or understood *an unsolved mystery* • *He never gave up hope that he would solve the mystery of his son's disappearance.* • *He's out of work, so how he pays his rent is **a mystery to me** (= I cannot explain it).* **2** [C] a story, often about a crime, in which the strange events that happen are explained at the end *a murder mystery*

**mystery²** /'mɪstⁿri/ *adj* [always before noun] A mystery person or thing is one who is unknown. *I saw her with a mystery man in a restaurant last night.*

**mystic** /'mɪstɪk/ *noun* [C] someone who attempts to be united with God through prayer

**mystical** /'mɪstɪkⁿl/ (*also* **mystic**) *adj* **1** relating to the religious beliefs and activities of mystics **2** involving magical or spiritual powers that are not understood

**mysticism** /'mɪstɪsɪzⁿm/ *noun* [U] the religious beliefs and activities of mystics

**mystify** /'mɪstɪfaɪ/ *verb* [T] If something mystifies someone, they cannot understand or explain it because it is confusing or complicated. [often passive] *I was mystified by the decision.*

**mystique** /mɪ'sti:k/ *noun* [U] a mysterious quality that makes a person or thing seem

M

interesting or special *the mystique of the princess*

myth /mɪθ/ *noun* [C] **1** an ancient story about gods and brave people, often one that explains an event in history or the natural world *a Greek myth* **2** an idea that is not true but is believed by many people *It's a myth that men are better drivers than women.*

mythical /'mɪθɪkᵊl/ (*also* **mythic**) *adj* **1** existing in a myth *a mythical character* **2** imaginary or not true

mythology /mɪ'θɒlədʒi/ *noun* [U] myths, often those relating to a single religion or culture *classical mythology* • *the mythology of the ancient Greeks* • mythological /ˌmɪθᵊl'ɒdʒɪkᵊl/ *adj*

# N

**N, n** /en/ the fourteenth letter of the alphabet

**N/A** (*also US* **NA**) *abbreviation for* not applicable: used on official forms to show that you do not need to answer a question

**naff** /næf/ *adj UK informal* silly and not fashionable *naff lyrics*

**nag** /næg/ *verb* [I, T] **nagging**, *past* **nagged** to keep criticizing or giving advice to someone in an annoying way *They keep nagging me about going to university.*

**nag (away) at sb** If doubts or worries nag at you, you think about them all the time. *The same thought has been nagging away at me since last week.*

**nagging** /ˈnægɪŋ/ *adj* [always before noun] Nagging doubts or worries make you worried and you cannot forget them. *a nagging doubt/suspicion*

o⌐**nail¹** /neɪl/ *noun* [C] **1** a thin piece of metal with a sharp end, used to join pieces of wood together *a hammer and nails* **2** the hard surface at the end of your fingers and toes *fingernails/toenails* • *to cut your nails* • *nail clippers/scissors*

nail

• *Stop biting your nails.* **3 hit the nail on the head** to describe exactly what is causing a situation or problem **4 the final nail in the coffin** an event which causes the failure of something that had already started to fail *This latest evidence could be the final nail in the coffin for Jackson's case.*

**nail²** /neɪl/ *verb* **1 nail sth down/on/to, etc** to fasten something with nails *There was a 'private property' sign nailed to the tree.* **2** [T] *mainly US informal* to catch someone who has committed a crime *They eventually **nailed** him for handling stolen goods.*

**nail sb down** to make someone give you exact details or a decision about something *I haven't managed to nail him down to a date yet.*

**nail sth down** *US* to understand something completely, or to describe something correctly *We haven't been able to nail down the cause of the fire yet.*

ˈnail ˌbrush *noun* [C] a small brush, used for cleaning your nails ➔ *See colour picture* **The Bathroom** *on page Centre 1.*

ˈnail ˌpolish (*also UK* ˈnail ˌvarnish) *noun* [U] paint that you put on your nails

**naive** /naɪˈiːv/ *adj* If someone is naive, they believe things too easily and do not have enough experience of the world. *I was much younger then, and very naive.* • **naively** *adv I naively believed that we would be treated as equals.* • **naivety** /naɪˈiːvəti/ *noun* [U] the quality of being naive

o⌐**naked** /ˈneɪkɪd/ *adj* **1** not wearing clothes or not covered by anything *a naked thigh/shoulder* • *He was stark naked* (= completely naked). **2** [always before noun] A naked feeling or quality is not hidden, although it is bad. *naked aggression/greed* **3 the naked eye** If something can be seen by the naked eye, it is big enough to be seen without special equipment.

o⌐**name¹** /neɪm/ *noun* **1** [C] the word or group of words that is used to refer to a person, thing, or place *What's your name?* • *My name's Alexis.* • *I can't remember the name of the street he lives on.* • *He didn't mention her by name* (= he did not say her name). **2 in the name of sth** If bad things are done in the name of something, they are done in order to help that thing succeed. *So much blood has been spilt in the name of religion.* **3 a bad/good name** If things or people have a bad/good name, people have a bad/good opinion of them. *Their behaviour gives us all a bad name.* • *They are trying to restore the good name of the school.* **4 call sb names** to use impolite or unpleasant words to describe someone **5 make a name for yourself** to become famous or respected by a lot of people *He's been trying to make a name for himself in the music business.* **6 the name of the game** the main purpose or most important part of an activity *Popularity is the name of the game in television.* ➔ *See also:* **Christian name, brand name, family name, first name, last name, maiden name, middle name.**

o⌐**name²** /neɪm/ *verb* [T] **1** GIVE A NAME ▸ to give someone or something a name [+ two objects] *We named our first son Mike.* • *A young boy named Peter answered the phone.* **2** SAY NAME ▸ to say what the name of someone or something is [often passive] *The dead man has been **named as** John Kramer.* • *She cannot be named for legal reasons.* **3** ANNOUNCE ▸ to announce who has got a new job or won a prize [+ two objects] *She has been named manager of the new Edinburgh branch.* **4 you name it** something that you say which means anything you say or choose *I've never seen such a wide selection. You name it, they've got it.*

**name sb after sb** to give someone the same name as someone else *We named him after my wife's brother.*

**nameless** /ˈneɪmləs/ *adj* If someone or something is nameless, they have no name or their name is not known. *a nameless soldier* ➔ *Compare* **unnamed**.

**namely** /ˈneɪmli/ *adv* a word used when you are going to give more detail about something you have just said *She learned an important lesson from failing that exam, namely that nothing is ever certain.*

**namesake** /ˈneɪmseɪk/ *noun* [C] **your namesake** someone who has the same name as you

**nan** /nɑːn/ *noun* [C] *UK informal* grandmother *My nan lives just down the road.*

**nanny** /ˈnæni/ *noun* [C] someone whose job is to look after a family's children *They have a full-time nanny.*

**nap** /næp/ *noun* [C] a short sleep *He likes to **have/ take a nap** after lunch.* • **nap** *verb* [I] **napping**, *past* **napped**

**nape** /neɪp/ noun [C] the back of your neck

**napkin** /ˈnæpkɪn/ (also UK **serviette**) noun [C] a piece of cloth or paper used when you eat to keep your clothes clean and to clean your mouth and hands *a paper napkin*

**nappy** /ˈnæpi/ UK (US **diaper**) noun [C] a thick piece of paper or cloth worn by a baby on its bottom *disposable nappies* • *to change a nappy*

**narcissism** /ˈnɑːsɪsɪzᵊm/ noun [U] formal great interest in and pleasure at your own appearance and qualities • **narcissistic** /ˌnɑːsɪˈsɪstɪk/ adj If people or their actions are narcissistic, they show narcissism.

**narcotic** /nɑːˈkɒtɪk/ noun [C] a drug that stops you feeling pain or makes you sleep, and that is addictive (= difficult to stop using)

**narrate** /nəˈreɪt/ verb [T] formal to tell the story in a book, film, play, etc *'Peter and the Wolf,' narrated by actress Glenn Close* • **narration** /nəˈreɪʃᵊn/ noun [U] formal

**narrative** /ˈnærətɪv/ noun [C] formal a story or description of a series of events

**narrator** /nəˈreɪtəʳ/ noun [C] the person who tells the story in a book, film, play, etc

⊶**narrow¹** /ˈnærəʊ/ adj **1** Narrow things measure a small distance from one side to the other. *a narrow lane/street* • *a narrow tie* **2** including only a small number *He has very narrow interests.* **3 a narrow defeat/victory** If you have a narrow defeat/victory, you only just lose/win. **4 a narrow escape** If you have a narrow escape, you only just avoid danger.

**narrow**

**wide**

**narrow²** /ˈnærəʊ/ verb [I, T] **1** to become less wide or to make something less wide *The road has been narrowed to one lane.* • *His eyes narrowed angrily.* **2** to become less or to make something become less *to narrow the gap between rich and poor*

**narrow sth down** to make something, for example a list or a choice, smaller and clearer by removing the things that are less important *We've managed to narrow the list down to four.*

**narrowly** /ˈnærəʊli/ adv only by a small amount *A tile fell off the roof, narrowly missing my head.*

**narrow-minded** /ˌnærəʊˈmaɪndɪd/ adj not willing to accept new ideas or opinions different from your own

**nasal** /ˈneɪzᵊl/ adj relating to the nose *the nasal passages*

**nascent** /ˈnæsᵊnt, ˈneɪsᵊnt/ adj formal starting to develop *a nascent democracy*

**nasty** /ˈnɑːsti/ adj **1** [BAD] very bad *a nasty shock/surprise* • *a nasty smell/taste* • *a nasty cut/burn* **2** [UNKIND] unkind *She's always being nasty to her little brother.* **3** [ANGRY] very angry or violent *When I asked for the money, he turned really nasty.* • **nastiness** noun [U]

⊶**nation** /ˈneɪʃᵊn/ noun [C] a country or the people living in a country *African/Asian nations* • *industrial/oil-producing nations* • *The entire nation mourned her death.* • *They are a nation of dog lovers.* ➜ See also: **the United Nations**. ➜ See usage note at **country**.

⊶**national¹** /ˈnæʃᵊnᵊl/ adj **1** relating to the whole of a country *to threaten national security* • *a sense of national identity/unity* • *a national newspaper* • *national elections* • *His income is way above the national average.* • *Gambling is a national pastime* (= many people do it) *here.* **2** [always before noun] connected with the traditions of a particular nation *national dress/customs* • **nationally** adv *He's a nationally known sports figure.*

**national²** /ˈnæʃᵊnᵊl/ noun [C] someone who officially belongs to a particular country *a British/Chinese national*

**ˌnational ˈanthem** noun [C] the official song of a country, played at public events

**the ˌNational ˈHealth Service** noun the system providing free medical services in the UK

**ˌnational ˈholiday** (also US **federal holiday**) noun [C] a day when most people in a country do not have to work

**ˌNational Inˈsurance** noun [U] the system in the UK in which people regularly pay money to the government in order to help people who are ill or have no work

**nationalism** /ˈnæʃᵊnᵊlɪzᵊm/ noun [U] **1** a feeling of pride in your own country **2** the belief that a particular area should have its own government *Welsh nationalism*

**nationalist** /ˈnæʃᵊnᵊlɪst/ noun [C] someone who wants a particular area to have its own government

**nationalistic** /ˌnæʃᵊnᵊlˈɪstɪk/ adj having a lot of pride, often too much pride, in your own country *nationalistic fervour*

**nationality** /ˌnæʃᵊnˈæləti/ noun [C, U] If you have American/British/Swiss, etc nationality, you are legally a member of that country. *What nationality is she?* • *She has dual nationality* (= nationality of two countries). • *workers of many different nationalities*

**nationalize** /ˈnæʃᵊnᵊlaɪz/ verb [T] If private companies are nationalized, the government takes control of them. [often passive] *British Aerospace was nationalized in 1977 by the Labour Party.* • **nationalization** /ˌnæʃᵊnᵊlaɪˈzeɪʃᵊn/ noun [U] the nationalization of diamond mines

**ˌnational ˈpark** noun [C] a large area of park for use by the public, usually an area of special beauty *In the US, national parks are owned and managed by the government.*

**ˌnational ˈservice** noun [U] the period of time

young people in some countries have to spend in the army

**nationwide** /ˌneɪʃᵊnˈwaɪd/ *adj, adv* including all parts of a country *a nationwide campaign/ tour* • *Surveys have been carried out nationwide.*

**native**¹ /ˈneɪtɪv/ *adj* **1** BORN IN [always before noun] Your native town or country is the place where you were born. *It was a custom in his native Algeria.* • *She is a native-born Texan.* **2** LANGUAGE [always before noun] Your native language is the first language you learn. *a native speaker of English* (= someone who learned English as their first language) **3** PEOPLE [always before noun] relating to the people who lived in a country first, before other people took control of it *the native inhabitants/population* **4** ANIMALS AND PLANTS Native animals or plants live or grow naturally in a place, and have not been brought from somewhere else. *a large bird native to Europe*

**native**² /ˈneɪtɪv/ *noun* [C] **1** someone who was born in a particular place *He's **a native of** Texas.* **2** an old-fashioned and often offensive word for a person who lived in a country, for example an African country, before Europeans went there

**Native A'merican** *adj* relating or belonging to the original group of people who lived in North America *Native American art/culture* • Native American *noun* [C]

**NATO** (*also UK* **Nato**) /ˈneɪtəʊ/ *noun abbreviation for* North Atlantic Treaty Organization: an international military organization formed in 1949 to improve the defence of Western Europe

**natter** /ˈnætəʳ/ *verb* [I] *mainly UK informal* to talk about things that are not important • natter *noun* [no plural] *(UK) to have a natter*

o─**natural** /ˈnætʃᵊrᵊl/ *adj* **1** NATURE Something that is natural exists or happens because of nature, not because it was made or done by people. *natural gas/resources* • *natural beauty* • *to die of natural causes* (= because you are ill or old) • *This product contains only natural ingredients.* **2** NORMAL normal or expected *a natural impulse/instinct* • *It's perfectly natural to feel nervous.* ⊃ *Opposite* **unnatural**. **3** FROM BIRTH If you have a natural characteristic, it is something you have been born with. *a natural talent* • *She's a natural athlete/blonde.* • naturalness *noun* [U]

ˌnatural 'gas *noun* [U] a gas that is found under the ground and is used for cooking and heating

ˌnatural 'history *noun* [U] the study of animals and plants

**naturalist** /ˈnætʃᵊrᵊlɪst/ *noun* [C] someone who studies animals and plants

**naturalistic** /ˌnætʃᵊrᵊlˈɪstɪk/ *adj* Naturalistic art, writing, or acting tries to show things as they really are.

**naturalize** /ˈnætʃᵊrᵊlaɪz/ *verb* **be naturalized** to officially become a member of another country *a naturalized US citizen* • naturalization /ˌnætʃᵊrᵊlaɪˈzeɪʃᵊn/ *noun* [U]

**naturally** /ˈnætʃᵊrᵊli/ *adv* **1** AS EXPECTED as you would expect *Well, naturally, he was very disap-*

pointed, but he's determined to try again. **2** NORMALLY in a normal way *Relax and try to behave naturally.* **3** FROM BIRTH having been born with a characteristic *naturally aggressive/funny/slim* **4** NATURE Something that exists or happens naturally is part of nature and not made or done by people. *Organic tomatoes are grown naturally without chemical fertilizers.* • *I hope I'll die naturally in my sleep.*

ˌnatural 'sciences *noun* [plural] sciences that relate to the physical world such as biology, chemistry, and physics

ˌnatural se'lection *noun* [U] the way that plants and animals die when they are weak or not suitable for the place where they live, while stronger ones continue to exist

o─**nature** /ˈneɪtʃəʳ/ *noun* **1** PLANTS AND ANIMALS [U] all the plants, creatures, substances, and forces that exist in the universe, which are not made by people *the laws of nature* • *I like to get out and enjoy nature.* • *a nature trail* **2** CHARACTER [no plural] someone's character *I didn't think it was in his nature to behave like that.* **3** TYPE [no plural] *formal* type *What exactly is the nature of your business?* • *I don't like hunting and things of that nature.* ⊃ *See also:* **human nature, second nature.**

─────────────────────────────

**USAGE**

**nature, the environment** and **countryside**

Nature means all the things in the world which exist naturally and were not created by people.

*He's interested in wildlife and anything to do with nature.*

The environment means the land, water, and air that animals and plants live in. It is usually used when talking about the way people use or damage the natural world.

*The government has introduced new policies to protect the environment.*

Countryside means land where there are no towns or cities.

*I love walking in the countryside.*

─────────────────────────────

'nature re,serve *noun* [C] a place where animals and plants live and are protected

**naught** *old-fashioned* (*also UK* **nought**) /nɔːt/ *noun* [U] nothing

**naughty** /ˈnɔːti/ *adj* **1** If a child is naughty, they behave badly. *a naughty little boy/girl* **2** a word used humorously to describe things that are sexual *naughty films/magazines*

**nausea** /ˈnɔːziə/ *noun* [U] the unpleasant feeling of wanting to vomit *She was hit by a sudden wave of nausea.*

**nauseating** /ˈnɔːsieɪtɪŋ/ *adj* If something is nauseating, it makes you want to vomit. *a nauseating smell*

**nauseous** /ˈnɔːsiəs/ *adj* If you feel nauseous, you feel like you might vomit, and if something is nauseous, it makes you want to vomit.

**nautical** /ˈnɔːtɪkᵊl/ *adj* relating to boats or sailing *a nautical mile*

**N**

**naval** /ˈneɪvᵊl/ *adj* [always before noun] relating to the navy *a naval base/officer*

**navel** /ˈneɪvᵊl/ *noun* [C] the small, round, and usually hollow place on your stomach, where you were connected to your mother before birth

**navigable** /ˈnævɪɡəbl/ *adj* If an area of water is navigable, it is wide, deep, and safe enough to sail a boat on.

**navigate** /ˈnævɪɡeɪt/ *verb* **1** [WITH MAP] [I, T] to find the right direction to travel by using maps or other equipment *He navigated the ship back to Plymouth.* • *We navigated using a map and compass.* • *I drive and he navigates.* **2** [BOAT] to successfully sail along an area of water **3** [DIFFICULT JOURNEY] [T] to find your way through a difficult place *We had to navigate several flights of stairs.* **4** [SYSTEM] [T] to successfully use a complicated system *to navigate the Internet* • navigation /ˌnævɪˈɡeɪʃᵊn/ *noun* [U] • navigator *noun* [C] a person who navigates

**navy** /ˈneɪvi/ *noun* **1 the Navy** ships and soldiers used for fighting wars at sea *to be in the navy* • *to join the navy* **2** [U] (*also* **navy 'blue**) a very dark blue colour ⊃ *See colour picture* **Colours** *on page Centre 6.*

**Nazi** /ˈnɑːtsi/ *noun* [C] someone who supported the ideas of Hitler in Germany in the 1930s and 1940s *Nazi propaganda*

**nb, NB** /ˌenˈbiː/ used to tell the reader that a particular piece of information is very important

o━**near**[1] /nɪəʳ/ *adv, preposition* **1** [DISTANCE] not far away in distance *Could you come a bit nearer, please?* • *I stood near the window.* • *They live in a small village near the Danish border.* • *Are you going anywhere near the post office?* **2 be/ come near to doing sth** to almost achieve or do something *This is the nearest I've ever got to winning anything.* • *He came near to punching him.* **3** [STATE] If something or someone is near a particular state, they are almost in that state. *She looked near exhaustion.* • *Climbing that mountain is near impossible without ropes.* • *She was near to tears* (= almost crying) *when I told her.* **4** [TIME] not far away in time *We shouldn't be partying so near her exams.* • *We can decide nearer the time.* **5** [SIMILAR] similar *The feelings I had were near hysteria.* • *He is Russia's nearest thing to a rock legend.* **6 nowhere near** not close in distance, amount, time, or quality *It wasn't me – I was nowhere near him.* • *That's nowhere near enough for six people.* • *It was nowhere near as difficult as I thought it would be.* **7 near enough** almost *The books were ordered near enough alphabetically.*

o━**near**[2] /nɪəʳ/ *adj* **1** not far away in distance or time *The school's very near.* • *The nearest garage is 10 miles away.* • *The baby's due date was getting nearer.* **2 in the near future** at a time that is not far away *Space travel may become very common in the near future.* ⊃ *See also: a near* **miss**[2].

**near**[3] /nɪəʳ/ *verb* [T] to get close to something in distance or time *The building work is nearing completion at last.* • *It started raining just as we neared home.*

**nearby** /ˌnɪəˈbaɪ/ *adj, adv* not far away *a nearby town/village* • *An old friend of mine has just moved nearby.*

o━**nearly** /ˈnɪəli/ *adv* **1** almost *It's nearly three weeks since I last saw her.* • *Nearly all the food had gone when I arrived.* • *She nearly drowned when she was eight.* • *I'll be with you in a minute – I've nearly finished.* **2 not nearly (as/so)** a lot less *It's not nearly as expensive as I thought.* • *There are not nearly enough jobs to go round.*

**nearsighted** /ˌnɪəˈsaɪtɪd/ *US* (*UK* **short-sighted**) *adj* If you are nearsighted, you cannot see things very well if they are too far away.

**neat** /niːt/ *adj* **1** [TIDY] tidy and clean *He always looks very neat and tidy.* **2** [GOOD] *US informal* good *That's really neat.* • *What a neat idea.* **3** [ALCOHOL] A neat alcoholic drink is drunk on its own, and not mixed with any other liquid. • **neatly** /ˈniːtli/ *adv* in a tidy way *neatly dressed* • *a neatly folded pile of clothes*

**necessarily** /ˌnesəˈserᵊli/ *adv* **not necessarily** not for certain *That's not necessarily true.* • *I know she doesn't say much, but it doesn't necessarily mean she's not interested.*

o━**necessary** /ˈnesəsᵊri/ *adj* needed in order to achieve something [+ to do sth] *Is it really necessary to give so much detail?* • *Does he have the necessary skills and experience?* • *The police are prepared to use force, if necessary.* ⊃ *Opposite* **unnecessary**.

**necessitate** /nəˈsesɪteɪt/ *verb* [T] *formal* to make something necessary

**necessity** /nəˈsesəti/ *noun* **1** [U] the need for something *There's no financial necessity for her to work.* • *Sewing is something I do out of necessity, not for pleasure.* **2** [C] something you need *Most people seem to consider a car a necessity, not a luxury.*

o━**neck** /nek/ *noun* [C] **1** the part of the body between your head and your shoulders *He was wearing a gold chain around his neck.* • *She fell off a horse and broke her neck.* ⊃ *See colour picture* **The Body** *on page Centre 2.* **2** the part of a piece of clothing that goes around your neck *a polo-neck/V-neck jumper* **3 be breathing down sb's neck** to watch what someone does all the time in a way that annoys them *The last thing I want is a boss breathing down my neck.* **4 neck and neck** If two people who are competing are neck and neck, they are very close and either of them could win. **5 be up to your neck (in sth)** to be very busy *I'd like to help, but I'm up to my neck at the moment.* ⊃ *See also:* **polo neck**, by the **scruff** of the/your neck.

**necklace** /ˈnekləs/ *noun* [C] a piece of jewellery that you wear around your neck *a pearl necklace* ⊃ *See picture at* **jewellery**.

**nectar** /ˈnektəʳ/ *noun* [U] a sweet liquid produced by plants and collected by bees

**nectarine** /ˈnektᵊriːn/ *noun* [C] a soft, round fruit which is sweet and juicy and has a smooth red and yellow skin

**née** /neɪ/ *adj* [always before noun] a word used to introduce the family name that a woman had before she got married *Margaret Hughes, née Johnson*

o━**need**[1] /niːd/ *verb* [T] **1** If you need something, you must have it, and if you need to do something, you must do it. *I need some new shoes.* • *The country still desperately needs help.* • [+ to do sth] *The doctor said I might need to have an operation.* • [+ to do sth] *If there's anything else you need to know, just give me a call.* • *We need you to look after the children for us.* **2 don't need to do sth/ needn't do sth** used in order to say that someone does not have to do something or should not do something *You didn't need to come all this way.* • *You don't need to be frightened.* • *She needn't have taken him to the hospital.* **3** If something needs something to be done to it, that thing should be done in order to improve it. *Do the clothes on this chair need washing?* • *The car needs to be serviced.* **4 There needs to be sth** used to say that something is necessary *There needs to be more funding for education in this country.*

o--**need**[2] /niːd/ *noun* **1** [no plural] something that is necessary to have or do *There's an urgent need for more medical supplies.* • [+ to do sth] *Is there any need to change the current system?* • *There's really no need for that sort of behaviour.* **2 be in need of sth** to need something *My car's in desperate need of repair.*

**needle** /niːdl/ *noun* [C] **1** MEDICAL the thin, sharp, metal part of a piece of medical equipment used to take blood out of the body, or to put medicine or drugs in **2** SEWING a thin, pointed metal object with a small hole at one end for thread, used in sewing *a needle and thread* **3** MEASURING a thin, pointed piece of metal or plastic that moves to point to numbers on equipment used for measuring things ➔ See also: **pins and needles**.

**needless** /niːdləs/ *adj* not necessary *a needless expense* • **Needless to say** (= as you would expect), *it rained the whole time we were there.* • **needlessly** *adv*

**needn't** /niːdᵊnt/ *short for* need not *You needn't have come.*

**needs** /niːdz/ *noun* [plural] the things you need in order to have a good life *her emotional/social needs* • *The city is struggling to* **meet the needs** *of its homeless people.*

**needy** /niːdi/ *adj* Needy people do not have enough money. *The mayor wants to establish permanent housing for* **the needy**.

**negate** /nɪˈɡeɪt/ *verb* [T] *formal* to make something lose its effect or value • **negation** /nɪˈɡeɪʃᵊn/ *noun* [U] *formal*

o--**negative**[1] /ˈneɡətɪv/ *adj* **1** NO ENTHUSIASM not having enthusiasm or positive opinions about something *negative feelings* • *Many people have a negative attitude towards ageing.* **2** BAD A negative effect is bad and causes damage to something. *Terrorist threats have had a very negative impact on tourism.* **3** MEDICINE If the result of a test to prove if someone is pregnant or ill is negative, that person is not pregnant or ill. **4** NUMBERS A negative number is less than zero. **5** GRAMMAR In language, a negative word or phrase expresses the meaning 'no' or 'not'.

**negative**[2] /ˈneɡətɪv/ *noun* [C] **1** a piece of film from which a photograph can be produced, where dark areas look light and light areas look dark **2** a word or phrase which expresses the meaning 'no' or 'not'

**negatively** /ˈneɡətɪvli/ *adv* **1** without enthusiasm or positive opinions *to react/respond negatively* **2** with a bad effect *negatively affected*

**negativity** /ˌneɡəˈtɪvəti/ *noun* [U] when you do not feel enthusiastic or positive about things

**neglect**[1] /nɪˈɡlekt/ *verb* [T] **1** to not give enough care or attention to something or someone *to neglect your appearance/the garden* • [often passive] *Some of these kids have been badly neglected in the past.* • *neglected children* **2 neglect to do sth** to not do something, often intentionally *He neglected to mention the fact that we could lose money on the deal.*

**neglect**[2] /nɪˈɡlekt/ *noun* [U] when you do not give enough care or attention to something or someone *to suffer years of neglect*

**negligence** /ˈneɡlɪdʒəns/ *noun* [U] when you are not careful enough in something you do, especially in a job where your actions affect other people *Her parents plan to sue the surgeon for medical negligence.*

**negligent** /ˈneɡlɪdʒənt/ *adj* not giving enough care or attention to a job or activity, especially where your actions affect someone else *The report found him negligent in his duties.*

**negligible** /ˈneɡlɪdʒəbl/ *adj* small and not important *a negligible effect/result*

**negotiable** /nɪˈɡəʊʃiəbl/ *adj* If something is negotiable, it is not completely fixed, and can be changed after discussion. *The January deadline is not negotiable.*

**negotiate** /nɪˈɡəʊʃieɪt/ *verb* **1** [I, T] to try to make or change an agreement by discussion *to negotiate with employers about working conditions* **2** [T] to successfully move around, through, or past something *to negotiate your way around/through a city* • **negotiation** /nɪˌɡəʊʃiˈeɪʃᵊn/ *noun* [C, U] *peace negotiations* • **negotiator** *noun* [C] *a peace negotiator*

**Negro** /ˈniːɡrəʊ/ *noun* [C] *plural* **Negroes** *old-fashioned* a word that means a black person, which some people think is offensive

o--**neighbour** *UK* (*US* **neighbor**) /ˈneɪbəʳ/ *noun* [C] **1** someone who lives very near you, especially in the next house *Our next-door neighbours are always arguing.* **2** someone or something that is near or next to someone or something else *The French make more films than their European neighbours.*

**neighbourhood** *UK* (*US* **neighborhood**) /ˈneɪbəhʊd/ *noun* [C] an area of a town or city that people live in *I grew up in a very poor neighbourhood.* • *Are there any good restaurants in the neighbourhood* (= in this area)?

**neighbouring** *UK* (*US* **neighboring**) /ˈneɪbᵊrɪŋ/ *adj* [always before noun] near or next to somewhere *neighbouring countries/villages*

o--**neither**[1] /ˈnaɪðəʳ, ˈniːðəʳ/ *adv* used to say that a negative fact is also true of someone or something else *Jerry doesn't like it, and neither do I.* • *Her family wouldn't help her and neither would anyone else.* • *She's not very tall and neither is her husband.*

o--**neither**[2] /ˈnaɪðəʳ, ˈniːðəʳ/ *pronoun, determiner* not either of two people or things *Luckily, neither child was hurt in the accident.* • *Neither of us had ever been to London before.* • *They gave us two keys, but neither worked.*

N

**neither³** /'naɪðəʳ, 'niːðəʳ/ *conjunction* **neither ... nor** used when a negative fact is true of two people or things or when someone or something does not have either of two qualities *Neither he nor his mother would talk to the police.* • *Their performance was neither entertaining nor educational.*

---

**USAGE**

**Neither...nor**

This expression can be used with a singular or plural verb.

*Neither Jack nor Philip likes/like football.*

---

**neon** /'niːɒn/ *noun* [U] a gas that produces bright, colourful light when electricity passes through it, often used in signs *neon lights/signs*

**nephew** /'nefjuː/ *noun* [C] the son of your brother or sister, or the son of your husband's or wife's brother or sister

**Neptune** /'neptjuːn/ *noun* [no plural] the planet that is eighth from the Sun, after Uranus and before Pluto

**nerd** /nɜːd/ *noun* [C] *informal* someone, especially a man, who is not fashionable and who is interested in boring things • **nerdy** *adj informal* boring and not fashionable

**nerve** /nɜːv/ *noun* 1 [PART OF THE BODY] [C] one of the threads in your body which carry messages between your brain and other parts of the body *the optic nerve* • *nerve cells/endings* 2 [BEING BRAVE] [no plural] the quality of being brave [+ to do sth] *I haven't got the nerve to tell him I'm leaving.* • *He lost his nerve and couldn't go through with it.* 3 [RUDENESS] [no plural] the rudeness necessary to do something you know will upset someone *You've got a nerve, coming here!* • [+ to do sth] *I can't believe she had the nerve to talk to me after what happened.* 4 **hit/touch a (raw) nerve** to upset someone by talking about a particular subject *By the look on her face, he really hit a nerve with that last remark.*

**nerve-racking** /'nɜːv,rækɪŋ/ *adj* If an experience is nerve-racking, it makes you very nervous.

**nerves** /nɜːvz/ *noun* [plural] 1 the state of being nervous *I need something to calm my nerves.* • *I always suffer from nerves before a match.* 2 **steady/strong nerves** the ability to be calm in difficult situations *You need a cool head and steady nerves for this job.* 3 **get on sb's nerves** to annoy someone, especially by doing something again and again *If we spend too much time together we end up getting on each other's nerves.*

○━**nervous** /'nɜːvəs/ *adj* 1 worried and anxious *a nervous cough/laugh* • *She's very nervous about her driving test.* 2 [always before noun] relating to the nerves in the body *a nervous disorder*

**nervous breakdown** *noun* [C] a short period of mental illness when people are too ill to continue with their normal lives

**nervously** /'nɜːvəsli/ *adv* in a worried and anxious way *to giggle/laugh nervously* • **nervousness** *noun* [U]

**nervous system** *noun* [C] your brain and all the nerves in your body which control your feelings and actions *a disease of the central nervous system*

**nest¹** /nest/ *noun* [C] a home built by birds for their eggs and by some other creatures to live in *a birds'/wasps' nest*

**nest²** /nest/ *verb* [I] to live in a nest or build a nest

**nestle** /'nesl/ *verb* 1 **nestle (sth) against/in/on, etc** to rest yourself or part of your body in a comfortable, protected position *The cat was nestling in her lap.* 2 **nestle beneath/between/in, etc** If a building, town, or object nestles somewhere, it is in a protected position, with bigger things around it. *a village nestled in the Carpathian mountains*

**net¹** /net/ *noun* 1 [U] material made of crossed threads with holes between them 2 [C] something made with a piece of net, for example for catching fish or insects, or for sports *a fishing net* • *a tennis/basketball net* 3 **the Net** short for the Internet ➔ *See also:* **safety net**.

**net**

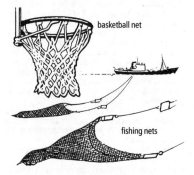

basketball net

fishing nets

**net²** (*also* UK **nett**) /net/ *adj* A net amount of money has had costs such as tax taken away from it. *a net income/profit of £10,000*

**net³** /net/ *verb* [T] **netting**, *past* **netted** 1 to get an amount of money as profit *One trader netted a bonus of £1 million.* 2 to hit, throw, or kick a ball into a net *He netted a great penalty.*

**netball** /'netbɔːl/ *noun* [U] a game usually played by teams of women, where a ball is thrown from player to player and goals are scored by throwing the ball through a high net

**netting** /'netɪŋ/ *noun* [U] material made of crossed threads or wires with holes between them *wire netting*

**nettle** /'netl/ *noun* [C] a wild plant whose leaves hurt you if you touch them

**network¹** /'netwɜːk/ *noun* [C] 1 [SYSTEM] a system or group of connected parts *a rail/road network* • *a network of cables/tunnels* 2 [PEOPLE] a group of people who know each other or who work together *a large network of friends* 3 [COMPANY] a large television or radio company that broadcasts programmes in many areas

---

**network²** /'netwɜ:k/ verb **1** [I] to use social events to meet people who might be useful for your business **2** [T] to connect computers together so that they can share information and programs

**networking** /'netwɜ:kɪŋ/ noun [U] **1** when you use social events to meet people who might be useful for your business **2** when you connect computers together so that they can share programs and information

**neural** /'njʊərəl/ adj [always before noun] relating to the nerves in your body *neural activity/development*

**neurology** /njʊə'rɒlədʒi/ noun [U] the study of the system of nerves in people's bodies ● **neurological** /ˌnjʊərə'lɒdʒɪkəl/ adj *Neurological illnesses affect the nerves in people's bodies.* ● **neurologist** /njʊə'rɒlədʒɪst/ noun [C] a doctor who deals with neurological illnesses

**neuron** /'njʊərɒn/ noun [C] a nerve cell which carries messages between your brain and other parts of your body

**neurosis** /njʊə'rəʊsɪs/ noun [C] plural **neuroses** /njʊə'rəʊsiːz/ a mental illness, often causing you to worry too much about something

**neurotic** /njʊə'rɒtɪk/ adj If you are neurotic, you worry about things too much.

**neuter** /'njuːtər/ adj in some languages, belonging to a group of nouns or adjectives that have the same grammatical behaviour. The other groups are 'masculine' and 'feminine'.

**neutral¹** /'njuːtrəl/ adj **1** independent and not supporting any side in an argument, fight, or competition *neutral ground/territory* ● *He decided to remain neutral on the issue.* **2** Neutral colours are not strong or bright.

**neutral²** /'njuːtrəl/ noun [U] In driving, neutral is the position of the gears (= parts of a vehicle that control how fast the wheels turn) when they are not connected. *to be in neutral*

**neutrality** /njuː'træləti/ noun [U] the state of being independent and not supporting any side in an argument, war, etc *political neutrality*

**neutron** /'njuːtrɒn/ noun [C] a part of an atom which has no electrical charge (= the electricity something stores or carries)

o⌐**never** /'nevər/ adv **1** not ever, not one time *"Have you ever been to Australia?" "No, never."* ● *I've never even thought about that before.* ● *She'll never be able to have children.* ● *He just walked out of the door one day and never came back.* **2** used to emphasize something negative *I never knew you lived around here.*

### USAGE

**never**

Never has a negative meaning so you do not need 'not' in the same sentence.

*I'll never do that again.*

~~I'll not never do that again.~~

**never-ending** /ˌnevər'endɪŋ/ adj If something is never-ending, it continues for ever. *The housework in this place is just never-ending.*

**nevertheless** /ˌnevəðə'les/ adv despite that *I*

knew a lot about the subject already, but her talk was interesting nevertheless.

o⌐**new** /njuː/ adj **1** DIFFERENT different from before *I need some new shoes.* ● *Have you met Fiona's new boyfriend?* ● *He's starting his new job on Monday.* ● *We're always looking for new ways to improve our services.* **2** RECENTLY MADE recently made *Their house is quite new – it's about five years old.* ● *The factory will provide hundreds of new jobs for the area.* **3** NOT KNOWN BEFORE not known before *to discover a new gene/star* **4 be new to sb** If a situation or activity is new to you, you have not had experience of it before. *You'll have to be patient, this is all new to me.* **5 be new to sth** If you are new to a situation or activity, you have only recently started experiencing it. *I'm new to the job.* ● *They're new to the area.* ⊃See also: a whole new **ball game**, new **blood**, **brand new**, break new **ground¹**, new **heights**, turn over a new **leaf¹**, give sb/sth a new **lease¹** of life.

**newborn** /ˌnjuː'bɔːn/ adj [always before noun] A newborn baby has just been born. ● **newborn** noun [C] a newborn baby

**newcomer** /'njuːˌkʌmər/ noun [C] someone who has only recently arrived or started doing something *He's a relative newcomer to the area.*

**new-found** /'njuːˌfaʊnd/ adj [always before noun] A new-found quality or ability has started recently. *This success is a reflection of their new-found confidence.*

**newly** /'njuːli/ adv recently *a newly married couple* ● *newly-built houses*

o⌐**news** /njuːz/ noun [U] **1 the news** the announcement of important events on television, radio, and in newspapers *the local/national news* ● *to watch the 6 o'clock news* ● *Did you see that report about child labour on the news last night?* ● *a news bulletin/report* **2** new information *Have you had any news about your job yet?* ● *I've got some good news for you.* ● *Any news from John?* **3 be news to sb** informal to be a surprise to someone *He's leaving? Well that's certainly news to me.* **4 be bad/good news for sb** to affect someone badly/well *This weather is bad news for farmers.*

**newsagent** /'njuːzˌeɪdʒənt/ noun [C] UK **1 newsagent's** a shop that sells newspapers, magazines, and things like sweets and cigarettes **2** someone who owns or works in a newsagent's

**newscast** /'njuːzkɑːst/ noun [C] US a television or radio broadcast of the news *the evening newscast*

**newscaster** /'njuːzkɑːstər/ noun [C] someone who reads the news on the radio or television

**newsgroup** /'njuːzgruːp/ noun [group] a group of people who use the Internet to exchange emails about a particular subject

**newsletter** /'njuːzˌletər/ noun [C] a regular report with information for people who belong to an organization or who are interested in a particular subject *a monthly newsletter about business and the environment*

o⌐**newspaper** /'njuːsˌpeɪpər/ noun **1** [C] large, folded sheets of paper which are printed with

**N**

the news and sold every day or every week *a local/national newspaper* • *I read about his death in the newspaper.* • *a newspaper article/headline* **2** [U] paper from newspapers *The cups were wrapped in newspaper.*

**newsprint** /'njuːzprɪnt/ *noun* [U] cheap, low quality paper used to print newspapers

**newsreader** /'njuːzˌriːdə'/ *noun* [C] *UK* someone who reads the news on the radio or television

**newsstand** /'njuːzstænd/ *noun* [C] *US* a small shop in a public area of a building or station, or part of a bigger shop, where newspapers and magazines are sold

**newsworthy** /'njuːzˌwɜːði/ *adj* interesting or important enough to be included in the news

**the ˌNew 'Testament** *noun* the part of the Bible (= holy book) written after the birth of Jesus Christ

**ˌnew 'wave** *noun* [U] people who are doing activities in a new and different way *the new wave of wine producers*

**ˌnew 'year** (*also* **New Year**) *noun* [C] the period in January when another year begins *Happy New Year!* • *We're going away in the new year.*

**ˌNew ˌYear's 'Day** *noun* [C, U] 1 January, the first day of the year and a public holiday in many countries

**ˌNew ˌYear's 'Eve** *noun* [C, U] 31 December, the last day of the year

**next¹** /nekst/ *adj* **1 next week/year/Monday, etc** the week/year/Monday, etc that follows the present one *I'm planning to visit California next year.* • *Are you doing anything next Wednesday?* • *Next time, ask my permission before you borrow the car.* **2** The next time, event, person, or thing is the one nearest to now or the one that follows the present one. *What time's the next train to London?* • *We're going to be very busy for the next few months.* **3** The next place is the one nearest to the present one. *She only lives in the next village.* • *Turn left at the next roundabout.* **4 the next best thing** the thing that is best, if you cannot have or do the thing you really want *Coaching football is the next best thing to playing.* **5 the next thing I knew** used to talk about part of a story that happens in a sudden and surprising way *A car came speeding round the corner, and the next thing I knew I was lying on the ground.*

**next²** /nekst/ *adv* **1** immediately after *You'll never guess what happened next.* • *Where shall we go next?* **2** The time when you next do something is the first time you do it again. *Could you get some coffee when you next go to the supermarket?*

⚬ᴹ**next³** /nekst/ *preposition* **next to sth/sb** very close to something or someone, with nothing in between *Come and sit next to me.* • *The factory is right next to a residential area.*

**next⁴** /nekst/ *pronoun* **1** the person or thing that follows the present person or thing *Who's next to see the nurse?* • *Blue roses? Whatever/what next?* (= What other strange things might happen?) **2 the weekend/week/Thursday, etc after next** the weekend/week/Thursday, etc that follows the next one

**ˌnext 'door** *adj, adv* in the next room, house,

or building *What are your next-door neighbours like?* • *That's the old man who lives next door to Paul.*

**ˌnext of 'kin** *noun* [C] *plural* **next of kin** *formal* the person you are most closely related to *The names of the dead cannot be released until their next of kin have been notified.*

**the NHS** /ˌeneɪtʃ'es/ *noun abbreviation for* the National Health Service: the system providing free medical services in the UK *Did she get it done privately or* **on the NHS**?

**nib** /nɪb/ *noun* [C] the pointed end of a pen, where the ink comes out

**nibble** /'nɪbl/ *verb* [I, T] to eat something by taking very small bites or to bite something gently *He was nibbling a biscuit.* • *She nibbled playfully at his ear.*

⚬ᴹ**nice** /naɪs/ *adj* **1** pleasant *They live in a nice old house on Market Street.* • *We could go to the coast tomorrow, if the weather's nice.* • [+ to do sth] *It was very nice to meet you.* • [+ doing sth] *Nice talking to you.* **2** kind and friendly *He seems like a really nice guy.* • *She's always been very nice to me.* **3 nice and sth** *informal* used to emphasize a positive quality *nice and clean* • *This chair's nice and comfy.*

**nicely** /'naɪsli/ *adv* **1** well *That table would fit nicely in the bedroom.* • *His business is doing very nicely.* **2** in a pleasant way *nicely dressed* • *They spoke to us very nicely.*

**niche** /niːʃ ⑤ nɪtʃ/ *noun* [C] **1** a job or activity that is very suitable for someone *After years of job dissatisfaction, he's at last* **found his niche** *in financial services.* **2** a hollow space cut into a wall

**ˌniche 'market** *noun* [C] when a product or service is only sold to a small number of people

**nick¹** /nɪk/ *verb* [T] **1** STEAL *UK, informal informal* to steal something *She got caught nicking CDs from Woolworth's.* **2** CATCH *UK informal* If the police nick someone, they catch that person because they have committed a crime. [often passive] *He got nicked for handling stolen goods.* **3** CUT to make a small cut in something without intending to *He nicked himself shaving.*

**nick²** /nɪk/ *noun* **1** [C] *mainly UK, informal* a prison or police station *They spent the night in the nick.* **2** [C] a small cut *He has a little nick on his cheek.* **3 in bad/good nick** *UK informal* in bad/good condition **4 in the nick of time** just before it was too late *The ambulance arrived in the nick of time.*

**nickel** /'nɪkl/ *noun* **1** [C] a US or Canadian coin with a value of 5 cents **2** [U] a silver-white metal that is often mixed with other metals

**nickname** /'nɪkneɪm/ *noun* [C] a name used informally instead of your real name *His behaviour has earned him the nickname 'Mad Dog'.* • nickname *verb* [+ two objects] *They nicknamed her 'The Iron Lady'.*

**nicotine** /'nɪkətiːn/ *noun* [U] a poisonous chemical substance in tobacco

**niece** /niːs/ *noun* [C] the daughter of your brother or sister, or the daughter of your husband's or wife's brother or sister

**nifty** /'nɪfti/ *adj informal* well-designed and effective *a nifty piece of software*

**nigger** /'nɪgəʳ/ *noun* [C] a very offensive word for a black person

**niggle** /'nɪgl/ *verb* **1** [I, T] to worry or annoy someone slightly for a long time *a niggling injury* **2 niggle about/over, etc** *UK* to complain about things which are not very important *She kept niggling about the extra work.* • niggle *noun* [C]

**nigh** /naɪ/ *adv literary* **1** near *The end of the world is nigh.* **2 well nigh/nigh on** *old-fashioned* almost *Our family has lived here well nigh two hundred years.*

O🔑**night** /naɪt/ *noun* [C, U] **1** ⟦DARK⟧ the time in every 24 hours when it is dark and people usually sleep *I didn't get any sleep last night – the baby just wouldn't stop crying.* • *It's warm during the day, but it can get quite cold at night.* • *The phone rang in the middle of the night.* • *Did you hear that storm during the night?* • *We stayed up almost all night talking.* • *Tim's working nights this week.* **2** ⟦EVENING⟧ the period from the evening to the time when you go to sleep *Did you have a good time last night?* • *Are you doing anything on Friday night?* **3** ⟦SAYING THE TIME⟧ used to describe the hours from the evening until just after 12 midnight *They're open from 7 in the morning until 10 o'clock at night.* **4 have an early/a late night** to go to bed early/late *We had a bit of a late night last night.* **5 a night out** an evening spent away from home doing something enjoyable *a night out at the theatre* **6 Good night.** You say 'Good night' to someone who is going to bed *Good night, sleep well.* ➔ *See also:* at/in the **dead³** of night.

**nightclub** /'naɪtklʌb/ *noun* [C] a place where you can dance and drink at night *to go to a nightclub*

**nightdress** /'naɪtdres/ *noun* [C] *mainly UK* a loose dress that women wear in bed

**nightfall** /'naɪtfɔːl/ *noun* [U] the time in the evening when it gets dark

**nightgown** /'naɪtgaʊn/ *noun* [C] a loose dress that women wear in bed

**nightie** /'naɪti/ *noun* [C] a loose dress that women wear in bed

**nightingale** /'naɪtɪŋgeɪl/ *noun* [C] a small brown bird which sings very well

**nightlife** /'naɪtlaɪf/ *noun* [U] entertainment for the night such as bars, restaurants, and theatres *What's the nightlife like around here?*

**nightly** /'naɪtli/ *adv* happening every night *the nightly news*

**nightmare** /'naɪtmeəʳ/ *noun* [C] **1** a very unpleasant experience *The traffic can be a real nightmare after 4.30.* **2** a frightening dream

'**night ˌschool** *noun* [U] classes for adults that are taught in the evening

**nightstick** /'naɪtstɪk/ *US* (*UK* **truncheon**) *noun* [C] a short stick that police officers carry to use as a weapon

**night-time** /'naɪttaɪm/ *noun* [U] the period of time when it is dark at night

**nil** /nɪl/ *noun* [U] **1** *UK* In sports results, nil means 'zero'. *Germany beat England three nil* (= 3 – 0). **2** not existing *The chances of that happening are virtually nil.*

**nimble** /'nɪmbl/ *adj* able to move quickly and easily *nimble fingers*

**nine** /naɪn/ the number 9

**nineteen** /ˌnaɪn'tiːn/ the number 19 • nineteenth 19th written as a word

**ninety** /'naɪnti/ **1** the number 90 **2 the nineties** the years from 1990 to 1999 **3 be in your nineties** to be aged between 90 and 99 • ninetieth 90th written as a word

**ninth¹** /naɪnθ/ 9th written as a word

**ninth²** /naɪnθ/ *noun* [C] one of nine equal parts of something; 1/9

**nip** /nɪp/ *verb* nipping, *past* nipped **1 nip down/ out/up, etc** *UK informal* to go somewhere quickly and for a short time *I'm just nipping down the road to get a paper.* **2** [T] If something nips you, it gives you a small, sharp bite. *His parrot nipped him on the nose.* ➔ *See also:* nip sth in the **bud**.

**nipple** /'nɪpl/ *noun* [C] the small, circular area of slightly darker, harder skin in the centre of each breast in women, or on each side of the chest in men

**nitrate** /'naɪtreɪt/ *noun* [C, U] a chemical that is used on crops to make them grow better

**nitrogen** /'naɪtrədʒən/ *noun* [U] a gas that has no colour or smell and is the main part of air

**the nitty-gritty** /ˌnɪti'grɪti/ *noun* the important details of a subject or activity *English teachers should concentrate on the nitty-gritty of teaching grammar.*

**no.** *written abbreviation for* number

O🔑**no¹** /nəʊ/ *exclamation* **1** something that you say in order to disagree, give a negative answer, or say that something is not true *"Have you seen Louise?" "No, I haven't."* • *"Have you ever been to Ireland?" "No."* • *"Can I have some more cake?" "No, you'll be sick."* • *"He's really ugly." "No he isn't!"* **2** something that you say to agree with something that is negative *"He's not very bright, is he?" "No, I'm afraid not."* **3 Oh no!** something that you say when you are shocked and upset *Oh no! It's gone all over the carpet!*

O🔑**no²** /nəʊ/ *determiner* **1** not any *There were no signposts anywhere.* • *I had no difficulty getting work.* • *There was no mention of money.* **2** a word used to say that something is forbidden *No smoking.* • *There was no talking in her classes.* **3 There's no doing sth** something that you say when an action is impossible *There's no pleasing some people* (= nothing that you do will make them happy).

O🔑**no³** /nəʊ/ *adv* **no ... than** not any *The work should be done no later than Friday.* • *There were no more than ten people there.*

**nobility** /nəʊ'bɪləti/ *noun* **1 the nobility** [group] the people from the highest social group in a society **2** [U] the quality of being noble

**noble¹** /'nəʊbl/ *adj* **1** honest, brave, and kind *a noble gesture* • *He was a generous, noble man.* **2** belonging to the highest social group of a society *She was born into an ancient, noble family.*

**noble²** /'nəʊbl/ *noun* [C] a person of the highest social group in some countries

**nobleman, noblewoman** /'nəʊblmən, 'nəʊbl,wʊmən/ *noun* [C] *plural* **noblemen, noblewomen** someone belonging to the highest social group in some countries

**N**

**nobly** /ˈnəʊbli/ adv in a brave or generous way *She nobly offered to sell her jewellery.*

o━**nobody** /ˈnəʊbədi/ pronoun no person *There was nobody I could talk to.* • *Nobody else agreed with her.* • *Nobody's listening.* • *Sally helped me, but nobody else bothered.*

**nocturnal** /nɒkˈtɜːnəl/ adj **1** Nocturnal animals and birds are active at night. **2** happening at night *nocturnal activities/excursions/habits*

**nod** /nɒd/ verb [I], past **nodded** to move your head up and down as a way of agreeing, to give someone a sign, or to point to something *They nodded enthusiastically at the proposal.* • *Barbara nodded in approval.* • *She nodded towards Hugh.* • **nod** noun [C] *He gave a nod of approval.*

**nod off** informal to start sleeping *I must have nodded off after lunch.*

**nodule** /ˈnɒdjuːl/ noun [C] a small lump, especially on a plant or someone's body

**no-fault** /ˈnəʊfɔːlt/ adj [always before noun] US No-fault laws or systems are ones where it is not important who is responsible for what has happened. *no-fault insurance*

**no-go 'area** noun [C] mainly UK an area, usually in a city, where it is too dangerous to go because there is a lot of violent crime there

o━**noise** /nɔɪz/ noun [C, U] a sound, often a loud, unpleasant sound *a deafening/loud noise* • *Stop making so much noise!* • *I could hear a hissing noise.* • *The engine's making funny noises.* • *There is some background noise on the recording.* • *I had to shout above the noise of the party.*

o━**noisy** /ˈnɔɪzi/ adj Noisy people or things make a lot of noise. *A crowd of noisy protesters gathered in the square.* • *We've had problems with noisy neighbours.* • **noisily** adv *He revved the engine noisily.*

**nomad** /ˈnəʊmæd/ noun [C] a member of a group of people who move from one place to another instead of living in the same place all the time • **nomadic** /nəʊˈmædɪk/ adj Nomadic people move from place to place.

**'no-man's ˌland** noun [U, no plural] an area of land which no one owns or controls, especially in a war

**nominal** /ˈnɒmɪnəl/ adj **1** existing officially, but not in reality *a nominal leader* • *Their review procedures were fairly nominal.* **2** A nominal sum of money is a small amount of money. *a nominal charge/fee*

**nominally** /ˈnɒmɪnəli/ adv officially but not in reality *nominally Catholic areas*

**nominate** /ˈnɒmɪneɪt/ verb [T] **1** to officially suggest a person for a job or a position in an organization, or to suggest a person or their work for a prize [often passive] *Judges are nominated by the governor.* • *The film was nominated for an Academy Award.* • *He was nominated as best actor.* **2** to choose someone for a job or to do something *He has nominated his brother as his heir.* • [+ to do sth] *Two colleagues were nominated to attend the conference.*

**nomination** /ˌnɒmɪˈneɪʃən/ noun [C, U] **1** the act of officially suggesting a person for a job or their work for a prize *to seek/win a nomination* • *the presidential nomination* • *He won the*

Democratic/Republican nomination • *He won the Democratic **nomination** for mayor of Chicago.* • *She has just received her fourth Oscar **nomination**.* **2** the choice of someone for a job or to do something *They did everything they could to defeat his nomination to be surgeon general.*

**nominee** /ˌnɒmɪˈniː/ noun [C] a person or a piece of work which has been nominated

**nonchalant** /ˈnɒnʃələnt/ US /ˌnɑːnʃəˈlɑːnt/ adj calm and not worried *a nonchalant shrug* • **nonchalantly** adv

**noncommittal** /ˌnɒnkəˈmɪtəl/ adj not showing your opinion about something *a noncommittal expression/response*

**nondescript** /ˈnɒndɪskrɪpt/ adj not interesting *a nondescript building/man*

o━**none** /nʌn/ quantifier **1** not any *None of them smoke.* • *In 1992, the company had 2,700 part-time workers. Today it has none.* • *There were only three births here in March and none at all in April.* • *Of the Democratic candidates, none has an obvious lead.* • *He asked if there was any hope. I told him frankly that there was none.* **2 none too clean/clever/pleased, etc** not at all clean/clever/pleased, etc *His handkerchief was none too clean.* **3 none the happier/poorer/wiser, etc** not any happier/poorer/wiser, etc than before *She must have explained the theory three times, but I'm still none the wiser.*

**nonetheless** /ˌnʌnðəˈles/ adv despite what has just been said *He was extremely rude in meetings. Nonetheless, his arguments found some support.*

**non-event** /ˌnɒnɪˈvent/ noun [no plural] informal an event that was not as exciting or interesting as you expected it to be *Her party was a bit of a non-event.*

**non-existent** /ˌnɒnɪɡˈzɪstənt/ adj not existing *We knew our chances of success were non-existent.*

**nonfiction** /ˌnɒnˈfɪkʃən/ noun [U] writing about things which are true *nonfiction books/titles*

**no-no** /ˈnəʊnəʊ/ noun [C] informal something that is forbidden or not socially acceptable *Cardigans are a fashion no-no this season.*

**no-nonsense** /ˌnəʊˈnɒnsəns/ adj [always before noun] not having or allowing others to have any silly ideas or behaviour *a no-nonsense approach to child rearing*

**nonplussed** /ˌnɒnˈplʌst/ adj extremely surprised

**non-profit-making** /ˌnɒnˈprɒfɪtˌmeɪkɪŋ/ UK (US **nonprofit**) adj A non-profit-making organization does not make money from its activities.

**nonsense** /ˈnɒnsəns/ noun [U] **1** If something someone has said or written is nonsense, it is silly and not true. *She talks such nonsense sometimes.* • *That's a load of nonsense.* • *These claims are utter nonsense.* • *It's nonsense to suggest they could have cheated.* **2** silly behaviour *Will you stop this childish nonsense!* **3 make a nonsense of sth** UK to spoil something or make it seem stupid *Cuts to the text made a nonsense of the play.*

**non-smoker** /ˌnɒnˈsməʊkəʳ/ noun [C] a person who does not smoke

**non-smoking** /ˌnɒnˈsməʊkɪŋ/ adj A non-smoking area is one where people are not allowed to smoke.

**non-starter** /ˌnɒnˈstɑːtəʳ/ *noun* [C] *informal* something that will not be successful *The amount of money needed makes his project a non-starter.*

**non-stop** /ˌnɒnˈstɒp/ *adj, adv* without stopping or resting *non-stop flights from Britain to the West Indies* • *We've been talking non-stop the whole way.* • *She is on stage for three hours non-stop.*

**non-violent** /ˌnɒnˈvaɪələnt/ *adj* not using violent methods *non-violent action/protests* • *non-violent crimes/offenders*

**noodles** /ˈnuːdlz/ *noun* [plural] thin pieces of pasta (= food made from flour, eggs, and water)

**nook** /nʊk/ *noun* **every nook and cranny** every part of a place *I know every nook and cranny of this place.*

**noon** /nuːn/ *noun* [U] 12 o'clock in the middle of the day *He has until noon to act.* • *The service will be held at 12 noon.*

o━**'no ˌone** *pronoun* no person *No one bothered to read the report.* • *No one knows where he is now.* • *There was no one there.* • **No one else** *makes puddings like my Mum.*

**noose** /nuːs/ *noun* [C] a piece of rope tied in a circle, used to catch animals or to hang (= kill) people

o━**nor** /nɔːʳ/ *adv, conjunction* **1 neither...nor...** used after 'neither' to introduce the second thing in a negative sentence *Strangely, neither James nor Emma saw what happened.* • *He neither spoke nor moved.* **2 nor can I/nor do you, etc** *mainly UK* used after something negative to say that the same thing is true for someone or something else *"I don't like cats." "Nor do I."* • *"I won't get to see him tomorrow." "Nor will Tom."* • *She couldn't speak a word of Italian and nor could I.*

**Nordic** /ˈnɔːdɪk/ *adj* from or relating to the North European countries of Sweden, Denmark, Norway, Finland, and Iceland

**norm** /nɔːm/ *noun* **1 the norm** the usual way that something happens *Short-term job contracts are the norm nowadays.* **2** [C] an accepted way of behaving in a particular society [usually plural] *cultural/social norms*

o━**normal** /ˈnɔːməl/ *adj* usual, ordinary, and expected *to lead a normal life* • *It's perfectly normal to feel some degree of stress at work.* • *It's normal for couples to argue now and then.* • *That's a fairly normal weight for someone of your height.* • *Now that trains are running again things are back to normal.*

**normality** /nɔːˈmæləti/ (*also US* **normalcy** /ˈnɔːməlsi/) *noun* [U] a situation in which everything is happening normally *a return to normality*

o━**normally** /ˈnɔːməli/ *adv* **1** usually *Normally, I start work around nine o'clock.* **2** in the ordinary way that you would expect *Both lungs are now functioning normally.*

o━**north, North** /nɔːθ/ *noun* [U] **1** the direction that is on your left when you face towards the rising sun *The stadium is to the north of the city.* **2 the north** the part of an area that is further towards the north than the rest *She's from the*

north of England. • **north** *adj a north wind* • **north** *adv towards the north I live north of the river.* • *We're going to visit Paul's family up north.*

**north**

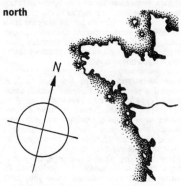

**northbound** /ˈnɔːθbaʊnd/ *adj* going or leading towards the north

**northeast, Northeast** /ˌnɔːθˈiːst/ *noun* [U] **1** the direction between north and east **2 the northeast** the northeast part of a country • *northeast, Northeast adj, adv*

**northeastern, Northeastern** /ˌnɔːθˈiːstən/ *adj* in or from the northeast

**northerly** /ˈnɔːðəli/ *adj* **1** towards or in the north *Canada's most northerly point* **2** A northerly wind comes from the north.

**northern, Northern** /ˈnɔːðən/ *adj* in or from the north part of an area *Northern England* • *a northern accent*

**northerner, Northerner** /ˈnɔːðənəʳ/ *noun* [C] someone from the north part of a country

**northernmost** /ˈnɔːðənməʊst/ *adj* The northernmost part of an area is the part furthest to the north.

**north-facing** /ˈnɔːθˌfeɪsɪŋ/ *adj* [always before noun] positioned towards the north *a north-facing slope*

**the ˌNorth 'Pole** *noun* the point on the Earth's surface which is furthest north

**northward, northwards** /ˈnɔːθwəd, ˈnɔːθwədz/ *adv* towards the north • **northward** *adj a northward direction*

**northwest, Northwest** /ˌnɔːθˈwest/ *noun* [U] **1** the direction between north and west **2 the northwest** the northwest part of a country • *northwest, Northwest adj, adv*

**northwestern, Northwestern** /ˌnɔːθˈwestən/ *adj* in or from the northwest

o━**nose[1]** /nəʊz/ *noun* [C] **1** the part of your face through which you breathe and smell *a big/broken nose* • *She paused to blow her nose* (= breathe out hard to empty it into a piece of cloth). ➔ *See colour picture* **The Body** *on page Centre 2.* **2 get up sb's nose** *UK informal* to annoy someone *I prefer not to have to deal with him – he gets up my nose.* **3 poke/stick your nose into sth** *informal* to show too much interest in a situation that does not involve you *You shouldn't go sticking your nose into other*

**N**

*people's business!* **4 thumb your nose at sth/sb** to show that you do not respect rules, laws, or powerful people *The rebels thumbed their noses at the international community.*

**5 turn your nose up at sth** *informal* to not accept something because you do not think it is good enough for you *He turned his nose up at my offer of soup, saying he wanted a proper meal.* **6 under your nose** If something bad happens under your nose, it happens close to you but you do not notice it.

**nose²** /nəʊz/ *verb*
  **nose about/around (sth)** *informal* to look around a place, often in order to find something *I caught him nosing around in my office.*

**nosebleed** /ˈnəʊzbliːd/ *noun* [C] **have a nosebleed** to have blood coming from your nose

**nosedive** /ˈnəʊzdaɪv/ *verb* [I] to fall very quickly in value *The economy nosedived after the war.* • **nosedive** *noun* [C]

**nosey** /ˈnəʊzi/ *adj another spelling of* nosy

**nostalgia** /nɒsˈtældʒə/ *noun* [U] a feeling of happiness mixed with sadness when you think about things that happened in the past *his nostalgia for his college days*

**nostalgic** /nɒsˈtældʒɪk/ *adj* feeling both happy and sad when you think about things that happened in the past *Talking about those holidays has made me feel quite nostalgic.*

**nostril** /ˈnɒstrəl/ *noun* [C] one of the two holes at the end of your nose ➔ *See colour picture* **The Body** *on page Centre 2.*

**nosy** /ˈnəʊzi/ *adj* always trying to find out private things about other people *nosy neighbours* • *Don't be so nosy!*

ᵒ⁻**not** /nɒt/ *adv* **1** used to form a negative phrase after verbs like 'be', 'can', 'have', 'will', 'must', etc, usually used in the short form 'n't' in speech *I won't tell her.* • *I can't go.* • *He hasn't eaten yet.* • *Don't you like her?* • *It isn't difficult* (= It is easy). • *The service isn't very good* (= it is bad). • *You're coming, aren't you?* • *I will not tolerate laziness.* **2** used to give the next word or group of words a negative meaning *I told you not to do that.* • *I like most vegetables but not cabbage.* • *"Come and play football, Dad." "Not now, Jamie."* • *"Whose are these?" "Not mine."* **3** used after verbs like 'be afraid', 'hope', 'suspect', etc in short, negative replies *"Do you think it's going to rain?" "I hope not."* • *"Have you finished?" "I'm afraid not."* **4 certainly/ hopefully not** used after an adverb in short, negative replies *"She's not exactly poor, is she?" "Certainly not."* • *"We won't need much money, will we?" "Hopefully not."* **5 not at all** used instead of 'no' or 'not' to emphasize what you are saying *"I hope this won't cause you any trouble." "No, not at all."* • *I'm not at all happy about it.* **6 Not at all.** used as a polite reply after someone has thanked you *"Thanks for all your help." "Not at all."* **7 if not** used to say what the situation will be if something does not happen *I hope to see you there but, if not, I'll call you.* **8 or not** used to express the possibility that something might not happen *Are you coming or not?* **9 not a/one** used to emphasize that there is nothing of what you are talking about *Not one person came to hear him talk.*

• *"You haven't heard from Nick, have you?" "Not a word."*

**not ... either**
The words **not ... either** are used to add another piece of negative information.

*I'd forgotten my credit card and I didn't have any cash either.*

~~I'd forgotten my credit card and I didn't have any cash neither.~~

*Helen didn't enjoy it either.*

~~Helen didn't enjoy it too.~~

**notable** /ˈnəʊtəbl/ *adj* If someone or something is notable, they are important or interesting. *a notable exception/feature*

**notably** /ˈnəʊtəbli/ *adv* used to emphasize an important example of something *Florida is well known for many of its fruits, notably oranges and avocados.*

**notation** /nəʊˈteɪʃ³n/ *noun* [U] a system of written symbols used especially in mathematics or to represent musical notes

**notch¹** /nɒtʃ/ *noun* [C] **1** a level of quality or amount *His game is a notch above any other player's.* • *Interest rates have moved up another notch.* **2** a cut in the shape of the letter V on the edge or surface of something

**notch²** /nɒtʃ/ *verb*
  **notch up sth** to achieve something *He has notched up a total of 34 goals this season.*

ᵒ⁻**note¹** /nəʊt/ *noun* **1** ⌈LETTER⌉ [C] a short letter *He left a note on her desk.* • *Did you get my note?* **2** ⌈INFORMATION⌉ [C] words that you write down to help you remember something *She studied her notes before the exam.* • *Let me make a note of* (= write) *your phone number.* • *The doctor took notes* (= wrote information) *while I described my symptoms.* **3** ⌈EXPLANATION⌉ [C] a short explanation or an extra piece of information that is given at the bottom of a page or at the back of a book *See note 3, page 37.* **4** ⌈FEELING⌉ [no plural] a particular feeling or mood *a sad/serious/positive note* • *His speech had just the right note of sympathy.* **5** ⌈MUSIC⌉ [C] a single musical sound or the symbol that represents it **6** ⌈MONEY⌉ [C] *UK* (*US* **bill**) a piece of paper money *a ten-pound note* **7 take note (of sth)** to pay careful attention to something *Make sure you take note of what she says.* • *Safety standards are being tightened. Employers, take note.* **8 sb/sth of note** *formal* someone or something famous or important *A medieval church is the only monument of note in the town.* **9 compare notes** If two people compare notes, they tell each other what they think about something that they have both done. *We compared notes about our experiences in China.*

**note²** /nəʊt/ *verb* [T] **1** to notice something *She noted a distinct chill in the air.* • [+ (that)] *We noted that their idea had never been tried.* **2** to say or write something *In the article, she notes several cases of medical incompetence.*

● [+ (that)] *The senator noted that almost no one had been prepared for a recession.*

**note down sth** to write something so that you do not forget it *I noted down the telephone number for the police.*

notebook /'nəʊtbʊk/ *noun* [C] **1** a book with empty pages that you can write in **2** a small computer that can be carried around and used anywhere

noted /'nəʊtɪd/ *adj* important or famous *a noted artist* ● *He was noted for his modern approach to architecture.*

notepaper /'nəʊt,peɪpəʳ/ *noun* [U] paper that you write letters on

noteworthy /'nəʊt,wɜːði/ *adj* If someone or something is noteworthy, they are important or interesting. *a noteworthy example*

o━nothing /'nʌθɪŋ/ *pronoun* **1** not anything *I've had nothing to eat since breakfast.* ● *He claimed that he did nothing wrong.* ● *He had nothing in his pockets.* ● *There was **nothing else** (= no other thing) I could do to help.* ● *She did **nothing but** criticize* (= criticized a lot). **2** not something important or of value *He's a dangerous person – human life means nothing to him.* ● *A thousand pounds is nothing to a woman of her wealth.* **3 for nothing** without a successful result *I've come all this way for nothing.* **4 be nothing to do with sb** If something is or has nothing to do with you, you have no good reason to know about it or be involved with it. *I wish he wouldn't offer advice on my marriage – it's nothing to do with him.* **5 have nothing to do with sb/sth** to have no connection or influence with someone or something *He made his own decision – I had nothing to do with it.* **6 to say nothing of sth** used to emphasize other problems you have not talked about *Most wild otters have disappeared from populated areas, to say nothing of wilderness areas.* **7 nothing of the sort** used to emphasize that something is not true *He said that he was a legitimate businessman – in fact, he was nothing of the sort.* **8 It was nothing.** a polite reply to someone who has thanked you for doing something **9 be nothing if not sth** used to emphasize a quality *The senator was nothing if not honest* (= he was very honest). **10 stop at nothing** to be willing to do anything in order to achieve something *He will stop at nothing to get what he wants.*

nothingness /'nʌθɪŋnəs/ *noun* [U] a state where nothing exists

o━notice¹ /'nəʊtɪs/ *verb* [I, T] to see something and be aware of it *If the sign's too small, no one will notice it.* ● *Do you think he'll notice my new hair style?* ● [+ (that)] *I noticed that he walked with a limp.*

notice² /'nəʊtɪs/ *noun* **1** SIGN [C] a sign giving information about something *The notice said that the pool was closed for repairs.* ● *Have you seen any notices about the new sports club?* **2** WARNING [U] a warning that something will happen *I had to give my landlord a month's notice before moving.* **3 at short notice** UK (US **on short notice**) only a short time before something happens **4** ATTENTION [U] attention *I didn't **take** any **notice of** (= give attention to)*

his advice. ● *It has **come to** our **notice*** (= we became aware) *that you are being overcharged for your insurance.* **5 hand/give in your notice** to tell your employer that you are going to stop working for them *I handed in my notice yesterday.*

noticeable /'nəʊtɪsəbl/ *adj* easy to see or be aware of *There was a noticeable difference in his behaviour after the injury.* ● noticeably *adv As summer approaches, the days get noticeably longer.*

noticeboard /'nəʊtɪsbɔːd/ UK (US **bulletin board**) *noun* [C] a board on a wall where you put advertisements and announcements *I saw the ad on the noticeboard.* ᕙ *See colour picture* **Classroom** *on page Centre 4.*

notify /'nəʊtɪfaɪ/ *verb* [T] *formal* to officially tell someone about something *You should notify the police if you are involved in a road accident.* ● [+ (that)] *The court notified her that her trial date had been postponed.* ● notification /,nəʊtɪfɪ'keɪʃ°n/ *noun* [C, U] *She claimed that the bank had closed her account without prior notification.*

notion /'nəʊʃ°n/ *noun* [C] an idea or belief *The notion of sharing is unknown to most two-year-olds.*

notoriety /,nəʊt°r'aɪəti/ *noun* [U] when someone is famous for something bad *He gained notoriety for his racist speeches.*

notorious /nəʊ'tɔːriəs/ *adj* famous for something bad *a notorious criminal* ● *She was notorious for her bad temper.* ● notoriously *adv Mount Everest is a notoriously difficult mountain to climb.*

notwithstanding /,nɒtwɪθ'stændɪŋ/ *adv, preposition formal* despite *Injuries notwithstanding, he won the semi-final match.*

nought /nɔːt/ *noun* [C, U] **1** UK the number 0 **2** *old-fashioned* (*mainly US* **naught**) nothing

o━noun /naʊn/ *noun* [C] a word that refers to a person, place, object, event, substance, idea, feeling, or quality. For example the words 'teacher', 'book', 'development', and 'beauty' are nouns. ᕙ *See also:* **countable noun, proper noun, uncountable noun.**

nourish /'nʌrɪʃ/ *verb* [T] *formal* to provide living things with food in order to make them grow or stay healthy *Mammals provide milk to nourish their young.*

nourishing /'nʌrɪʃɪŋ/ *adj* Nourishing food makes you healthy.

nourishment /'nʌrɪʃmənt/ *noun* [U] *formal* the food that you need to stay alive and healthy

Nov *written abbreviation for* November

novel¹ /'nɒv°l/ *noun* [C] a book that tells a story about imaginary people and events *Have you read any good novels lately?* ● novelist *noun* [C] someone who writes novels

novel² /'nɒv°l/ *adj* new or different from anything else *a novel idea/approach*

novelty /'nɒv°lti/ *noun* **1** QUALITY [U] the quality of being new or unusual *The fashion industry relies on novelty, and photographers are always looking for new faces.* **2** NEW THING [C] an object, event, or experience that is new or unusual *Tourists are still a novelty on this remote island.* **3** CHEAP TOY [C] a cheap toy or unusual object, often given as a present

N

**November** /nəʊ'vembə'/ (written abbreviation **Nov**) noun [C, U] the eleventh month of the year

**novice** /'nɒvɪs/ noun [C] someone who is beginning to learn how to do something *I've never used a computer before – I'm a complete novice.* ● *a novice driver*

o⟶**now**[1] /naʊ/ adv **1** [AT PRESENT] at the present time *She's finished her degree and now she teaches English.* ● *Do you know where Eva is* **right now** (= at this moment)? **2** [IMMEDIATELY] immediately *Come on, Andreas, we're going home now.* ● *I don't want to wait – I want it now!* **3** [LENGTH OF TIME] used to show the length of time that something has been happening, from the time it began until the present *I've lived in Cambridge for two years now.* **4** [IN SPEECH] used when you start to tell someone something *Now, I have been to Glasgow many times before.* ● *Now then, would anyone else like to ask a question?* **5 just now** a very short time ago *When I came in just now, everyone was laughing.* ● *Who was that woman who was speaking just now?* **6 (every) now and then/again** If something happens now and then, it happens sometimes but not very often. *I love chocolate, but I only eat it now and then.* **7 any day/ minute/time, etc now** used to say that something will happen very soon *We're expecting our second child any day now.*

o⟶**now**[2] /naʊ/ (also **now that**) conjunction as a result of a new situation *Now that I've got a car I can visit her more often.* ● *You should help in the house more, now you're older.*

**now**[3] /naʊ/ pronoun the present time or moment *Now isn't a good time to speak to him.* ● *She'd kept calm until now.* ● *I'll be more careful* **from now on** (= from this moment and always in the future).

**nowadays** /'naʊədeɪz/ adv at the present time, especially when compared to the past *Everything seems more expensive nowadays.*

o⟶**nowhere** /'nəʊweə'/ adv **1** not anywhere *The room was very crowded – there was nowhere to sit.* ● *We had nowhere else to go.* ● *Nowhere was the lack of skilled workers more apparent than in the engineering section.* **2 out of nowhere** If someone or something appears out of nowhere, they appear suddenly or unexpectedly. *The car came out of nowhere and we had to swerve to miss it.* **3 get/go nowhere** informal to fail to make any progress or achieve anything *They're getting nowhere on this project.* ● *He and I dated for a while, but it went nowhere.* **4 get you nowhere** If something gets you nowhere, it does not help you to succeed. *Bad manners will get you nowhere.*

**noxious** /'nɒkʃəs/ adj [always before noun] formal poisonous or harmful *noxious fumes/gases*

**nozzle** /'nɒzl/ noun [C] a narrow, hollow object which is fixed to a tube and which helps you to control the liquid or air that comes out

**n't** /ənt/ short for not *She isn't* (= is not) *going.* ● *I can't* (= cannot) *hear you.* ● *They didn't* (= did not) *believe me.*

**nuance** /'njuːɑːns/ noun [C] a very slight difference in meaning, appearance, sound, etc ● *a subtle nuance* ● *Linguists explore the nuances of language.*

o⟶**nuclear** /'njuːkliə'/ adj [always before noun] **1** relating to the energy that is released when the nucleus (= central part) of an atom is divided *nuclear weapons/waste* ● *a nuclear power plant* **2** relating to the nucleus (= central part) of an atom *nuclear physics*

,**nuclear re'actor** noun [C] a large machine which uses nuclear fuel to produce power

**nucleus** /'njuːkliəs/ noun [C] plural **nuclei** /'njuːkliaɪ/ **1** the central part of an atom or cell **2** the central or most important part of a group or idea *Senior coaches picked the nucleus of the team.*

**nude**[1] /njuːd/ adj not wearing any clothes *Our children were running around the garden in the nude* (= not wearing any clothes).

**nude**[2] /njuːd/ noun [C] a painting or other piece of art that shows a nude person

**nudge** /nʌdʒ/ verb [T] to gently push someone or something *She nudged me towards the door.* ● nudge noun [C] *I gave him a nudge.*

**nudity** /'njuːdəti/ noun [U] when you are wearing no clothes *Some people are easily offended by nudity.*

**nugget** /'nʌgɪt/ noun [C] **1** a small amount of something good *nuggets of wisdom* **2** a small, round piece of a solid substance *gold nuggets*

**nuisance** /'njuːsᵊns/ noun [C] **1** a person, thing, or situation that annoys you or causes problems for you *Not being able to use my computer is a real nuisance.* **2 make a nuisance of yourself** to annoy someone or cause problems for them

**nullify** /'nʌlɪfaɪ/ verb [T] formal **1** to make something lose its effect *Advances in medicine have nullified the disease's effect.* **2** to say officially that something has no legal power *The judge could nullify the entire trial.*

**numb** /nʌm/ adj **1** If a part of your body is numb, you cannot feel it. *My fingers and toes were numb with cold.* **2** If you are numb with a bad emotion, you are so shocked that you are not able to think clearly. *I was numb with grief after his death.*

o⟶**number**[1] /'nʌmbə'/ noun **1** [SYMBOL] [C] a symbol or word used in a counting system or used to show the position or order of something *Think of a number smaller than 100.* ● *Pablo's favourite number is seven.* ● *The Prime Minister lives at number 10, Downing Street.* ● *Look at item number three on your agenda.* **2** [GROUP OF NUMBERS] [C] a group of numbers that represents something *What's your phone number?* ● *Each person receives a membership number when they join.* **3** [AMOUNT] [C] an amount *a small number of* (= a few) ● *a large number of* (= many) ● *There were a number of* (= several) *soldiers present at the rally.* ● *Scientists have noticed a drop in the number of song birds in Britain.* ⟳ See usage note at **amount**. ⟳ See also: **cardinal number, ordinal number, phone number, telephone number**.

**number**[2] /'nʌmbə'/ verb [T] **1** to give something a number [often passive] *Each volume was numbered and indexed.* **2** If people or things number a particular amount, there are that many of them. *Our company's sales force numbered over 5,000.*

'**number ,plate** UK (US **license plate**) noun [C]

an official metal sign with numbers and letters on the front and back of a car ➲ *See colour picture* **Car** *on page Centre 3.*

**numeral** /ˈnjuːmᵊrᵊl/ *noun* [C] a symbol used to represent a number ➲ *See also:* **Roman numeral.**

**numerical** /njuːˈmerɪkl/ *adj* [always before noun] relating to or expressed by numbers *a numerical calculation/value* ● *The exams were filed in numerical order.*

**numerous** /ˈnjuːmᵊrəs/ *adj formal* many *He is the author of numerous articles.*

**nun** /nʌn/ *noun* [C] a member of a group of religious women living apart from other people

o─**nurse¹** /nɜːs/ *noun* [C] someone whose job is to care for ill and injured people

**nurse²** /nɜːs/ *verb* [T] **1** [CARE FOR] to care for a person or animal that is ill *We nursed the injured sparrow back to health.* **2** [FEED] *US* to feed a baby milk from its mother's breast *She nursed her son until he was a year old.* **3** [INJURY] to try to cure an illness or injury by resting *He was nursing a broken nose.* **4** [EMOTION] to think about an idea or an emotion for a long time *She nursed a great hatred towards her older sister.*

**nursery** /ˈnɜːsᵊri/ *noun* [C] **1** a place where babies and young children are looked after without their parents **2** a place where plants are grown and sold

**'nursery ˌrhyme** *noun* [C] a short poem or song for young children

**'nursery ˌschool** *noun* [C] a school for very young children

**nursing** /ˈnɜːsɪŋ/ *noun* [U] the job of being a nurse

**'nursing ˌhome** *noun* [C] a place where old people live to receive medical care

**nurture** /ˈnɜːtʃəʳ/ *verb* [T] *formal* **1** to encourage or support the development of someone or something *He was an inspiring leader who nurtured the talents of his colleagues.* **2** to look after, feed, and protect young children, animals, or plants *The rains nurtured the newly planted crops.*

o─**nut** /nʌt/ *noun* [C] **1** [FOOD] the dry fruit of some trees which grows in a hard shell, and can often be eaten *a brazil/cashew nut* **2** [METAL] a piece of metal with a hole in it through which you put a bolt (= metal pin) to hold pieces of wood or metal together ➲ *See picture at* **tool. 3** [KEEN] *informal* a person who is keen on a particular subject or hobby *She's a real sports nut.* **4 the nuts and bolts** the basic parts of a job or an activity *Law school can teach you theory, but it can't teach you the nuts and bolts of the profession.*

**nutrient** /ˈnjuːtriənt/ *noun* [C] *formal* any substance that animals need to eat and plants need from the soil in order to live and grow *A healthy diet should provide all your essential nutrients.*

**nutrition** /njuːˈtrɪʃᵊn/ *noun* [U] the food that you eat and the way that it affects your health *Good nutrition is essential for growing children.* ● **nutritional** *adj* relating to nutrition *Some snacks have little nutritional value.*

**nutritious** /njuːˈtrɪʃəs/ *adj* Nutritious food contains substances that your body needs to stay healthy. *a nutritious meal*

**nuts** /nʌts/ *adj informal* **1** crazy *They thought I was nuts to go parachuting.* **2 go nuts** to become very excited, angry, or upset *If I don't have a holiday soon, I'll go nuts.*

**nutshell** /ˈnʌtʃel/ *noun* **in a nutshell** something that you say when you are describing something using as few words as possible *The answer, in a nutshell, is yes.*

**nutty** /ˈnʌti/ *adj* **1** *informal* crazy *nutty ideas* **2** Something nutty tastes of nuts.

**nylon** /ˈnaɪlɒn/ *noun* [U] a strong, artificial material used to make clothes, ropes, etc *nylon stockings* ● *a nylon shirt/bag*

**nymph** /nɪmf/ *noun* [C] in Greek and Roman stories, a spirit in the form of a young girl who lives in trees, rivers, mountains, etc

**N**

**O, o** /əʊ/ the fifteenth letter of the alphabet

**oak** /əʊk/ noun [C, U] a large tree found in northern countries, or the wood of this tree

**OAP** /ˌəʊeɪˈpiː/ noun [C] UK abbreviation for old-age pensioner: a person who regularly receives money from the state because they are too old to work

**oar** /ɔːʳ/ noun [C] **1** a long pole with a wide, flat end that you use to move a boat through water **2 stick/put your oar in** UK informal to involve yourself in a discussion or situation when other people do not want you to We'd just reached a decision when Jack came along and stuck his oar in.

**oasis** /əʊˈeɪsɪs/ noun [C] plural **oases** /əʊˈeɪsiːz/ **1** a place in the desert where there is water and where plants grow **2** a place that is much calmer and more pleasant than what is around it The cafe was an oasis in the busy, noisy city.

**oath** /əʊθ/ noun **1** [C] a formal promise an oath of allegiance • They refused to **take an oath** (= to promise) loyalty to the king. **2 under oath** If someone is under oath, they have promised to tell the truth in a law court. He denied under oath that he was involved in the crime.

**oats** /əʊts/ noun [plural] grain which people eat or feed to animals

**obedience** /əʊˈbiːdiəns/ noun [U] when someone is willing to do what they are told to do He demanded complete obedience from his soldiers. ⊃ Opposite **disobedience**. • obedient /əʊˈbiːdiənt/ adj willing to do what you are told to do an obedient child/dog ⊃ Opposite **disobedient**.

**obese** /əʊˈbiːs/ adj extremely fat Obese people are more likely to suffer heart attacks. • obesity noun [U] when someone is obese Obesity is rising steadily in Europe and North America.

o-ᵏ **obey** /əʊˈbeɪ/ verb [I, T] to do what you are told to do by a person, rule, or instruction If you refuse to obey the law, you'll be arrested. • He gave the command, and we obeyed. ⊃ Opposite **disobey**.

**obfuscate** /ˈɒbfʌskeɪt/ verb [T] formal to make something harder to understand or less clear

**obituary** /əʊˈbɪtʃʊəri/ noun [C] a report in a newspaper that gives details about a person who has recently died

o-ᵏ **object¹** /ˈɒbdʒɪkt/ noun **1** [C] a thing that you can see or touch but that is usually not alive a bright, shiny object **2 the object of sth** the purpose of something The object of the game is to score more points than the opposing team. **3 the object of sb's affection/desire, etc** the cause of someone's feelings He's the object of my affection. **4** [C] in grammar, the person or thing that is affected by the action of the verb ⊃ See also: **direct object**, **indirect object**.

**object²** /əbˈdʒekt/ verb [I] to feel or say that you do not like or do not approve of something or someone We **objected to** his unreasonable demands. • Would anyone object if I were to leave early? ⊃ See also: **conscientious objector**.

**objection** /əbˈdʒekʃ°n/ noun [C, U] when someone says that they do not like or approve of something or someone Our main **objection to** the new factory is that it's noisy. • I **have** no **objections**, if you want to stay an extra day.

**objectionable** /əbˈdʒekʃ°nəbl/ adj formal very unpleasant

**objective¹** /əbˈdʒektɪv/ noun [C] something that you are trying to achieve His main objective was to increase profits.

**objective²** /əbˈdʒektɪv/ adj only influenced by facts and not by feelings I try to be objective when I criticize someone's work.

**obligation** /ˌɒblɪˈgeɪʃ°n/ noun [C, U] something that you do because it is your duty or because you feel you have to a moral/legal obligation • to fulfil an obligation • He was **under no obligation** to answer any questions. • [+ to do sth] Parents have an obligation to make sure their children receive a proper education.

**obligatory** /əˈblɪgət°ri/ adj If something is obligatory, you must do it because of a rule, or because everyone else does it. obligatory military service • a salesman with the obligatory mobile phone

**oblige** /əˈblaɪdʒ/ verb **1 be obliged to do sth** to be forced to do something Sellers are not legally obliged to accept the highest offer. **2** [I, T] formal to be helpful The manager was only too happy to oblige.

**obliged** /əˈblaɪdʒd/ adj **1 feel obliged to do sth** to think that you must do something They helped us when we moved so I feel obliged to do the same. **2** formal old-fashioned grateful or pleased Thank you, I'm much obliged to you.

**oblique** /əʊˈbliːk/ adj formal not expressed in a direct way an oblique comment • obliquely adv formal

**obliterate** /əˈblɪt°reɪt/ verb [T] to destroy something completely [often passive] The town was obliterated by bombs.

**oblivion** /əˈblɪviən/ noun [U] **1** when someone or something is not remembered to disappear into oblivion **2** when you are not aware of what is happening around you He drank himself **into oblivion**.

**oblivious** /əˈblɪviəs/ adj not aware of something She seemed completely **oblivious to** what was happening around her.

**obnoxious** /əbˈnɒkʃəs/ adj very unpleasant or rude He was loud and obnoxious.

**obscene** /əbˈsiːn/ adj **1** relating to sex in a way that is unpleasant or shocking an obscene gesture • obscene language **2** An obscene amount of something is morally wrong because it is too large. obscene profits • The house is so big it's obscene.

**obscenity** /əbˈsenəti/ noun **1** [U] when something is sexually shocking obscenity laws/trials **2** [C] a sexually shocking word or expression [usually plural] He was shouting obscenities at people walking by.

**obscure¹** /əbˈskjʊəʳ/ adj **1** not known by many people an obscure figure/writer **2** difficult to understand His answers were obscure and confusing.

**obscure**[2] /əb'skjʊəʳ/ *verb* [T] **1** to prevent something from being seen or heard [often passive] *The moon was partially obscured by clouds.* **2** to make something difficult to understand *He deliberately obscured details of his career in the army.*

**obscurity** /əb'skjʊərəti/ *noun* [U] when something or someone is not known by many people *to fade into obscurity* ● *He rose from relative obscurity to worldwide recognition.*

**obsequious** /əb'si:kwiəs/ *adj formal* too willing to praise or obey someone

**observance** /əb'zɜː.vᵊns/ *noun* [C, U] *formal* when someone obeys a law or follows a religious custom *strict observance of the law* ● *religious observances*

**observant** /əb'zɜː.vᵊnt/ *adj* good or quick at noticing things *He's very observant.*

**observation** /ˌɒb.zə'veɪ.ʃᵊn/ *noun* **1** [U] when someone watches someone or something carefully *The doctor wants to keep him **under observation** for a week.* ● *to have good powers of observation* (= to be good at noticing things) **2** [C] a remark about something that you have noticed *He **made an** interesting **observation**.*

**observatory** /əb'zɜː.vətri/ *noun* [C] a building that is used by scientists to look at stars and planets

**observe** /əb'zɜːv/ *verb* [T] **1** WATCH to watch someone or something carefully *Children learn by observing adults.* **2** NOTICE *formal* to notice something **3** SAY *formal* to make a remark about something you have noticed *"It's still raining," he observed.* **4** OBEY to obey a law, rule, or religious custom *to observe the law*

**observer** /əb'zɜː.vəʳ/ *noun* [C] **1** someone who watches people and events as a job *a UN observer* ● *a political observer* **2** someone who sees something *a casual observer*

**obsess** /əb'ses/ *verb* [I, T] If something or someone obsesses you, or if you obsess about something or someone, you think about them all the time. *She used to obsess about her weight.* ● *He married a woman whose young daughter obsessed him.*

**obsessed** /əb'sest/ *adj* **be obsessed by/with sb/sth** to think about someone or something all the time *to be obsessed with money/sex*

**obsession** /əb'seʃᵊn/ *noun* [C, U] someone or something that you think about all the time *an unhealthy obsession with death* ● *a lifelong/national obsession*

**obsessive** /əb'sesɪv/ *adj* thinking too much about something, or doing something too much *obsessive behaviour* ● *He's obsessive about his health.* ● obsessively *adv obsessively tidy*

**obsolete** /ˈɒb.sə.liːt/ *adj* not used now *obsolete equipment* ● *Will books become obsolete because of computers?*

**obstacle** /ˈɒb.stə.kl/ *noun* [C] something that makes it difficult for you to go somewhere or to succeed at something *to overcome an obstacle* ● *His refusal to talk is the main **obstacle** to peace.*

**obstetrician** /ˌɒb.stə'trɪʃᵊn/ *noun* [C] a doctor who looks after pregnant women and helps in the birth of children

**obstinate** /ˈɒb.stɪnət/ *adj* not willing to change your ideas or behaviour although you are wrong *He's a very rude and obstinate man.*

**obstruct** /əb'strʌkt/ *verb* [T] **1** to be in a place that stops someone or something from moving or stops someone from seeing something *to obstruct the traffic* ● *There was a pillar obstructing our view.* **2** to try to stop something from happening or developing *to obstruct a police investigation* ● obstruction /əb'strʌkʃᵊn/ *noun* [C, U] *Your car's causing an obstruction.* ● *the obstruction of justice*

**obtain** /əb'teɪn/ *verb* [T] *formal* to get something *to obtain permission* ● *He obtained a law degree from the University of California.* ● obtainable *adj* If something is obtainable, you can get it. *This information is easily obtainable on the Internet.*

o▬**obvious** /ˈɒb.viəs/ *adj* easy to understand or see *an obvious choice/answer* ● [+ (that)] *It's obvious that he doesn't really care about her.*

o▬**obviously** /ˈɒb.viəsli/ *adv* in a way that is easy to understand or see *They're obviously in love.* ● *Obviously we want to start as soon as possible.*

o▬**occasion** /ə'keɪʒᵊn/ *noun* **1** [C] a time when something happens *a previous/separate occasion* ● *We met on several occasions to discuss the issue.* ➔ *See usage note at* **possibility. 2** [C] an important event or ceremony *a special occasion* ● *She bought a new dress for the occasion.* **3 on occasion(s)** sometimes, but not often *I only drink alcohol on occasion.*

**occasional** /ə'keɪʒᵊnᵊl/ *adj* not happening often *He still plays the occasional game of football.* ● occasionally *adv They only meet occasionally.*

**the occult** /ˈɒk.ʌlt/ *noun* the study of magic or mysterious powers

**occupant** /ˈɒk.jəpᵊnt/ *noun* [C] *formal* someone who lives or works in a room or building *the occupant of No. 46*

**occupation** /ˌɒk.jə'peɪʃᵊn/ *noun* **1** JOB [C] *formal* your job *You have to give your name, age, and occupation on the application form.* ➔ *See usage note at* **work. 2** CONTROL [U] when an army moves into a place and takes control of it *a military occupation* **3** HOBBY [C] *formal* something that you do in your free time

**occupational** /ˌɒk.jə'peɪʃᵊnᵊl/ *adj* relating to your job *an occupational hazard*

**occupied** /ˈɒk.jəpaɪd/ *adj* **1** being used by someone *All of these seats are occupied.* ➔ *Opposite* **unoccupied. 2** busy doing something or thinking about something *There was enough **to keep** us **occupied**.*

**occupier** /ˈɒk.jəpaɪəʳ/ *noun* [C] *UK* someone who lives or works in a room or building

**occupy** /ˈɒk.jəpaɪ/ *verb* [T] **1** FILL to fill a place or period of time *His book collection occupies most of the room.* ● *The baby seems to occupy all our time.* **2** LIVE to live or work in a room or building *They occupy the second floor of the building.* **3** CONTROL to move into a place and take control of it *The troops eventually occupied most of the island.*

o▬**occur** /ə'kɜːʳ/ *verb* [I] **occurring,** *past* **occurred 1** *formal* to happen, often without being planned *According to the police, the shooting occurred at about 12.30 a.m.* **2 occur in/among,**

O

**etc sth/sb** to exist or be present in a particular place or group of people *Minerals occur naturally in the Earth's crust.* • *The disease mainly occurs in women over 40.*

**occur to sb** to suddenly think of something [+ (that)] *It had never occurred to me that he might be lying.*

**occurrence** /ə'kʌrəns/ *noun* [C] something that happens *a common/everyday occurrence*

**ocean** /'əʊʃən/ *noun* **1** [no plural] the sea *to swim in the ocean* **2** [C] one of the five main areas that the sea is divided into *the Pacific Ocean*

o━**o'clock** /ə'klɒk/ *adv* **one/two/three, etc o'clock** used after the numbers one to twelve to mean exactly that hour when you tell the time *It was ten o'clock when we got home.*

**Oct** *written abbreviation for* October

**octagon** /'ɒktəgən/ *noun* [C] a flat shape with eight equal sides

**octave** /'ɒktɪv/ *noun* [C] the space between two musical notes that are eight notes apart

**October** /ɒk'təʊbə'/ *(written abbreviation* **Oct)** *noun* [C, U] the tenth month of the year

**octopus** /'ɒktəpəs/ *noun* [C] a sea creature with eight long arms

**octopus**

**odd** /ɒd/ *adj*
**1** STRANGE strange or unusual *I always thought there was something odd about her.* • *It's a bit odd that he didn't come.* **2** NOT OFTEN [always before noun] not happening often *He does odd jobs here and there.* **3** SEPARATED [always before noun] being one of a pair when the other item is missing *an odd sock* **4** APPROXIMATELY used after a number to mean approximately *There are thirty odd kids in the class.* **5** NUMBER An odd number does not produce a whole number when it is divided by two.

**oddity** /'ɒdɪti/ *noun* [C] someone or something that is strange or unusual

**oddly** /'ɒdli/ *adv* in a strange way *He's been behaving very oddly lately.* • *Oddly enough, business was good during the bad weather months.*

**odds** /ɒdz/ *noun* [plural] **1** the probability that something will happen *What are the odds of winning the top prizes?* • *I'm afraid the odds are against us.* **2 against all (the) odds** If you do or achieve something against all the odds, you succeed although you were not likely to. *We won the game against all odds.* **3 be at odds with sb/sth** to not agree with someone or something *His remark was at odds with our report.* **4 odds and ends** *informal* a group of small objects of different types which are not valuable or important

**odious** /'əʊdiəs/ *adj formal* very unpleasant *an odious little man*

**odour** UK *(US* **odor)** /'əʊdə'/ *noun* [C] a smell, often one that is unpleasant *body odour*

**odyssey** /'ɒdɪsi/ *noun* [C] *literary* a long, exciting journey

**oestrogen** UK *(US* **estrogen)** /'iːstrəʊdʒ³n* US 'estrədʒən/ *noun* [U] a chemical substance in a woman's body

o━**of** *strong form* /ɒv/ *weak form* /əv/ *preposition* **1** BELONG belonging or relating to someone or something *a friend of mine* • *the colour of her hair* • *part of the problem* **2** AMOUNT used after words which show an amount *a kilo of apples* • *both of us* • *a handful of raisins* **3** NUMBER used with numbers, ages, and dates *a boy of six* • *a decrease of 10%* • *the 14th of February 1995* **4** CONTAIN containing *a glass of milk* • *sacks of rubbish* **5** MADE made or consisting of *dresses of lace and silk* **6** ADJECTIVE/ VERB used to connect particular adjectives and verbs with nouns *frightened of spiders* • *smelling of garlic* **7** SHOW showing someone or something *a map of the city centre* **8** CAUSE showing a reason or cause *He died of a heart attack.* **9** POSITION showing position or direction *the front of the queue* • *a small town north of Edinburgh* **10** ACTION/FEELING used after nouns describing actions or feelings to mean 'done to' or 'experienced by' *the destruction of the rain forest* • *the suffering of millions* **11** WRITTEN written or made by *the collected works of William Shakespeare*

o━**off¹** /ɒf/ *adv, preposition* **1** NOT TOUCHING not touching or connected to something or not on a surface *Keep off the grass!* • *A button came off my coat.* **2** AWAY away from a place or position *He ran off to find his friend.* • *I'll be off* (= will go) *soon.* **3** NOT OPERATING not operating or being used *Make sure you switch your computer off.* **4** NEAR near to a building or place *An island off the coast of Spain.* **5** PRICE If a price has a certain amount of money off, it costs that much less than the usual price. *These jeans were $10 off.* **6** DISTANCE/TIME far in distance or time *You can see the village off in the distance.* • *My holidays seem a long way off.* **7 go off sth/sb** UK to stop liking something or someone *I've gone off meat.* **8** NOT AT WORK not at work *I had 6 months off when my son was born.* ⊃ *See also:* off the **cuff**, **on²** and off.

**off²** /ɒf/ *adj* [never before noun] **1** NOT CORRECT not correct *Our sales figures were off by ten percent.* **2** FOOD If food or drink is off, it is not now fresh and good to eat or drink. *This milk smells off.* **3** NOT AT WORK not at work *He's off today – I think he's ill.* ⊃ *See also:* **off-chance**.

**offal** /'ɒf³l/ *noun* [U] organs from the inside of animals that are killed for food

,**off 'balance** *adj, adv* If someone or something is off balance, they are in a position where they are likely to fall or be knocked down. *to knock/throw someone off balance*

**off-chance** /'ɒftʃɑːns/ *noun* UK *informal* **on the off-chance** hoping that something may be possible, although it is not likely *I went to the station on the off-chance that she'd be there, but she wasn't on any of the trains from London.*

,**off 'duty** *adj* When an official such as a police officer is off duty, they are not working.

o━**offence** UK *(US* **offense)** /ə'fens/ *noun* **1** [U] when something rude makes someone upset or angry *to cause/give offence* • *Many people take offence at swearing.* • *I'm sure she meant no*

---

*offence by her remarks.* **2** [C] a crime *a criminal/drug-related offence* • *He committed several serious offences.*

o-**offend** /ə'fend/ *verb* **1** [T] to make someone upset or angry [often passive] *I was deeply offended by her comments.* **2** [I] *formal* to commit a crime *If she offends again, she'll go to prison.*

**offender** /ə'fendə<sup>r</sup>/ *noun* [C] someone who has committed a crime *a sex offender* • *a young offender*

o-**offense** /ə'fens/ *noun* US spelling of offence

**offensive<sup>1</sup>** /ə'fensɪv/ *adj* **1** likely to make people angry or upset *an offensive remark* **2** used for attacking *an offensive weapon*

**offensive<sup>2</sup>** /ə'fensɪv/ *noun* [C] an attack *It's time to launch a major offensive against terrorism.*

o-**offer<sup>1</sup>** /'ɒfə<sup>r</sup>/ *verb* **1** ASK [+ two objects] to ask someone if they would like something *They offered me a job.* • *Someone should offer that old lady a seat.* **2** SAY YOU WILL DO [I, T] to say that you are willing to do something [+ to do sth] *He offered to get me a cab.* **3** AGREE TO PAY [T] to say that you will pay a particular amount of money [+ two objects] *I offered him £500 for the car.* • *Police have offered a $1,000 reward for information.* **4** PROVIDE [T] to give or provide something *to offer advice* • *The hotel offers a wide range of facilities.*

o-**offer<sup>2</sup>** /'ɒfə<sup>r</sup>/ *noun* [C] **1** ASK when you ask someone if they would like something *an offer of help* • *a job offer* • *to accept/refuse an offer* **2** PAYMENT an amount of money that you say you will pay for something *The highest offer anyone has made so far is £150.* **3** CHEAP a cheap price or special arrangement for something *This special offer ends on Friday.* **4** **on offer** UK **a** at a cheaper price than usual *Are these jeans still on offer?* **b** available to do or have *We were amazed at the range of products on offer.*

**offering** /'ɒf<sup>ə</sup>rɪŋ/ *noun* [C] something that you give to someone *a peace offering*

**offhand<sup>1</sup>** /,ɒf'hænd/ *adj* not friendly or polite *He was a bit offhand with me.*

**offhand<sup>2</sup>** /,ɒf'hænd/ *adv* [used in questions and negatives] immediately, without thinking about something *I don't know offhand how much it will cost.*

o-**office** /'ɒfɪs/ *noun* **1** PLACE [C] a room or building where people work *an office worker* • *office block* • *I never get to the office before nine.* ⊃ *See colour picture* **The Office** *on page Centre 12.* **2** INFORMATION [C] a room or building where you can get information, tickets, or a particular service *a ticket office* • *the tourist office* **3** JOB [U] an important job in an organization *Some people think he has been **in** office for too long.* • *She **held** the office of mayor for eight years.* ⊃ *See also:* **the Oval Office, box office, post office, register office, registry office.**

**officer** /'ɒfɪsə<sup>r</sup>/ *noun* [C] **1** MILITARY someone with an important job in a military organization *an army/naval officer* **2** GOVERNMENT someone who works for a government department *a customs officer* • *a prison officer* **3** POLICE a police officer *a uniformed officer* ⊃ *See also:* **probation officer.**

o-**official<sup>1</sup>** /ə'fɪʃ<sup>ə</sup>l/ *adj* **1** APPROVED approved by the government or someone in authority *the official language of Singapore* • *an official document/report* **2** JOB [always before noun] relating to the duties of someone in a position of authority *the official residence of the ambassador* • *an official visit* **3** KNOWN known by the public *It's official – they're getting married!* **4** NOT TRUE [always before noun] An official explanation or statement is one that is given, but which may not be true. *The official reason for the delay is bad weather.* ⊃ *Opposite* **unofficial.** • **officially** *adv The new hospital was officially opened yesterday.*

**official<sup>2</sup>** /ə'fɪʃ<sup>ə</sup>l/ *noun* [C] someone who has an important position in an organization such as the government *a senior official* • *a UN official*

**offing** /'ɒfɪŋ/ *noun* **be in the offing** If something is in the offing, it will happen or be offered soon. *He thinks there might be a promotion in the offing.*

**off-licence** /'ɒf,laɪs<sup>ə</sup>ns/ *UK (US* **liquor store)** *noun* [C] a shop that sells alcoholic drink

**off-peak** /,ɒf'piːk/ *adj* not at the most popular and expensive time *an off-peak phone call*

**offset** /,ɒf'set/ *verb* [T] **offsetting,** *past* **offset** If one thing offsets another thing, it has the opposite effect and so creates a more balanced situation. [often passive] *The costs have been offset by savings in other areas.*

**offshore** /,ɒf'ʃɔː<sup>r</sup>/ *adj* [always before noun] **1** in the sea and away from the coast *an offshore island* **2** An offshore bank or bank account is based in another country and so less tax has to be paid. *an offshore account/trust*

**offside** /,ɒf'saɪd/ *(also US* **offsides)** *adj* [always before noun] In sports such as football, a player who is offside is in a position that is not allowed.

**offspring** /'ɒfsprɪŋ/ *noun* [C] *plural* **offspring** *formal* the child of a person or animal *to produce offspring*

**off-the-cuff** /,ɒfðə'kʌf/ *adj* An off-the-cuff remark is one that is not planned.

o-**often** /'ɒf<sup>ə</sup>n, 'ɒft<sup>ə</sup>n/ *adv* **1** many times or regularly *I often see her there.* • *He said I could visit as often as I liked.* • **How often** (= How many times) *do you go to the gym?* • *I don't see her very often.* **2** If something often happens or is often true, it is normal for it to happen or it is usually true. *Headaches are often caused by stress.* • *Brothers and sisters often argue.* • *December is often mild.*

**ogre** /'əʊgə<sup>r</sup>/ *noun* [C] an unpleasant, frightening person

**oh** /əʊ/ *exclamation* **1** used before you say something, often before replying to what someone has said *"Ian's going." "Oh, I didn't realize."* • *"I'm so sorry." "Oh, don't worry."* **2** used to show an emotion or to emphasize your opinion about something *Oh, no! I don't believe it!* • *"I don't think I can come." "Oh, that's a shame."* • *Oh, how sweet of you!*

o-**oil** /ɔɪl/ *noun* [U] **1** a thick liquid that comes from under the Earth's surface that is used as a fuel and for making parts of machines move smoothly *an oil company* • *an oil well* **2** a thick liquid produced from plants or animals that is used in cooking *vegetable oil* ➲ *See also:* **crude oil**, **olive oil**.

**oilfield** /'ɔɪlˌfiːld/ *noun* [C] an area under the ground where oil is found *an offshore oilfield*

**'oil ˌpainting** *noun* [C] a picture made using paint which contains oil

**'oil ˌspill** *noun* [C] when oil has come out of a ship and caused pollution

**oily** /'ɔɪli/ *adj* containing a lot of oil or covered with oil *oily fish* • *oily hands*

**oink** /ɔɪŋk/ *noun* [C] the sound that a pig makes

**ointment** /'ɔɪntmənt/ *noun* [C, U] a smooth, thick substance that is used on painful or damaged skin

**okay¹** (*also* **OK**) /əʊ'keɪ/ *exclamation* **1** used when agreeing to do something or when allowing someone to do something *"Let's meet this afternoon." "Okay."* • *"Can I use the car?" "Okay."* **2** used before you start speaking, especially to a group of people *Okay, I'm going to start by showing you a few figures.*

⚬**okay²** (*also* **OK**) /əʊ'keɪ/ *adj, adv informal* **1** GOOD good or good enough *Is your food okay?* • *It was okay, but it wasn't as good as his last film.* **2** SAFE safe or healthy *Is your grandmother okay now?* **3** ALLOWED allowed or acceptable *Is it okay if I leave early today?* • [+ to do sth] *Is it okay to smoke in here?*

⚬**old** /əʊld/ *adj* **1** LIVED LONG having lived or existed for a long time *an old man/woman* • *an old house* • *We're all getting older.* • *Children should show some respect for* **the old**. **2** USED A LOT having been used or owned for a long time *You might get dirty so wear some old clothes.* **3** AGE used to describe or ask about someone's age *How old are you?* • *She'll be 3 years old this month.* ➲ *See usage note at* **year.** **4 an old friend/enemy, etc** someone who has been your friend/enemy, etc for a long time *I met an old friend who I was at college with.* **5** BEFORE [always before noun] used before or in the past *I think the old system was better in many ways.* • *When he visits his mother, he sleeps in his old room.*

**older, oldest, elder, eldest**

Older and oldest are the comparative and superlative forms of the adjective 'old'.

*I'm four years older than my sister.*

*Pedro is the oldest student in the class.*

The adjectives **elder** and **eldest** are only used before nouns. They are usually used when you are comparing members of a family.

*My elder brother is a doctor.*

*Mary has three sons. Her eldest boy is called Mark.*

**ˌold 'age** *noun* [U] the period of time when you are old

**ˌold-age 'pension** *noun* [U] *UK* money that people receive regularly from the government when they are old and have stopped working

**ˌold-age 'pensioner** *noun* [C] *UK* someone who gets an old-age pension

**olden** /'əʊldᵊn/ *adj* **in the olden days/in olden times** a long time ago

⚬**old-fashioned** /ˌəʊld'fæʃᵊnd/ *adj* not modern *old-fashioned clothes/furniture*

**oldie** /'əʊldi/ *noun* [C] *informal* an old song or film, or an old person *a golden oldie*

**old-style** /'əʊldstaɪl/ *adj* [always before noun] used or done in the past *old-style politics*

**the ˌOld 'Testament** *noun* the part of the Bible (= holy book) written before the birth of Jesus Christ

**the 'Old ˌWorld** *noun* Asia, Africa, and Europe

**olive** /'ɒlɪv/ *noun* **1** [C] a small green or black fruit with a bitter taste that is eaten or used to produce oil **2** [U] (*also* ˌolive **'green**) a colour that is a mixture of green and yellow • olive (*also* **olive-green**) *adj*

**ˌolive 'oil** *UK* (*US* **'olive ˌoil**) *noun* [U] oil produced from olives, used for cooking or on salads

**the Olympic Games** /ðiːə'lɪmpɪkˌgeɪmz/ (*also* **the Olympics**) *noun* [plural] an international sports competition that happens every four years • Olympic *adj* [always before noun] relating to the Olympic Games *She broke the Olympic record.*

**ombudsman** /'ɒmbʊdzmən/ *noun* [C] *plural* **ombudsmen** someone who deals with complaints that people make against the government or public organizations

**omelette** /'ɒmlət/ (*also US* **omelet**) *noun* [C] a food made with eggs that have been mixed and fried, often with other foods added *a cheese omelette*

**omen** /'əʊmən/ *noun* [C] a sign of what will happen in the future *a good/bad omen*

**ominous** /'ɒmɪnəs/ *adj* making you think that something bad is going to happen *an ominous sign* • *ominous clouds*

**omission** /əʊ'mɪʃᵊn/ *noun* [C, U] when something has not been included but should have been *There are some serious omissions in the book.*

**omit** /əʊ'mɪt/ *verb* **omitting**, *past* **omitted 1** [T] to not include something [often passive] *He was omitted from the team because of his behaviour.* **2 omit to do sth** *mainly UK formal* to not do something *She omitted to mention where she was going.*

⚬**on¹** /ɒn/ *preposition* **1** SURFACE on a surface of something *We put all of our medicine on a high shelf.* • *Ouch, you're standing on my foot!* **2** PLACE in a particular place *the diagram on page 22* • *I met her on a ship.* **3** RECORDING/PERFORMANCE used to show the way in which something is recorded or performed *What's on television tonight?* • *I bought the CD but you can buy it on cassette.* **4** TOUCHING used to show what happens as a result of touching something *I cut myself on a knife.* **5** SUBJECT about *a book on pregnancy* **6** MONEY/TIME used to show what money or time is used for *I've wasted too much time on this already.* • *She refuses to spend more than £20 on a pair of shoes.* **7** NEXT TO next to or along the side of *The post office is on Bateman Street.* **8** DATE/DAY used to show the date or day when something happens

*He's due to arrive on 14 February.* ● *I'm working on my birthday.* **9** USING *using something I spoke to Mum on the phone.* ● *I wrote it on my word processor.* **10** AFTER *happening after something and often because of it The Prince was informed on his return to the UK.* **11** TRANSPORT *used to show some methods of travelling Did you go over on the ferry?* ● *Sam loves travelling on buses.* **12** FOOD/FUEL/DRUGS *used to show something that is used as food, fuel, or a drug This radio runs on batteries.* ● *I can't drink wine because I'm on antibiotics.* **13 be on a committee/panel, etc** *to be a member of a group or organization She's on the playgroup committee.* **14 have/carry sth on you** *to have something with you Do you have your driving licence on you?* **15 be on me/him, etc** *informal used to show who is paying for something This meal is on me.*

o⟶ **on²** /ɒn/ *adv* **1** CONTINUE *used to show that an action or event continues The old tradition lives on.* ● *It was a complicated situation that dragged on for weeks.* **2** WEAR *If you have something on, you are wearing it. She's got a black coat on.* ● *Why don't you put your new dress on?* **3** WORKING *working or being used The heating has been on all day.* **4** TRAVEL *into a bus, train, plane, etc Amy got on at Stamford.* **5** HAPPENING *happening or planned I've got a lot on at the moment.* ● *Have you checked what's on at the cinema?* **6 on and off** (*also* **off and on**) *If something happens on and off during a period of time, it happens sometimes. They've been seeing each other on and off since Christmas.*

o⟶ **once¹** /wʌns/ *adv* **1** *one time It's only snowed once or twice this year.* ● *I go swimming* ***once a week*** (= one time every week). **2** *in the past, but not now This house once belonged to my grandfather.* **3 once again** *again Once again I'm left with all the washing up.* **4 all at once** *suddenly All at once he stood up and walked out of the room.* **5 at once** *immediately I knew at once that I would like it here.* **b** *at the same time They all started talking at once.* **6 once in a while** *sometimes but not often He plays tennis once in a while.* **7 once and for all** *If you do something once and for all, you do it now so that it does not have to be dealt with again. Let's get to the bottom of this matter once and for all!* **8 once more** *one more time If you say that once more, I'm going to leave.* **9 for once** *used to mean that something is happening that does not usually happen For once, I think I have good news for him.* **10 once upon a time** *used at the beginning of a children's story to mean that something happened a long time ago* ➔ *See also:* once in a blue **moon**.

o⟶ **once²** /wʌns/ *conjunction as soon as Once I've found somewhere to live, I'll send you my new address.*

**oncoming** /'ɒn,kʌmɪŋ/ *adj* [always before noun] Oncoming vehicles are coming towards you.

**one¹** /wʌn/ *the number 1* ➔ *See also:* back to **square¹** one.

o⟶ **one²** /wʌn/ *pronoun* **1** *used to refer to a particular person or thing in a group that has already been talked about I've just made some scones,*

*do you want one?* ● *Throw those gloves away and get some new ones.* ● *Chris is* ***the one*** *with glasses.* **2** *formal any person in general One ought to respect one's parents.* **3 one at a time** *separately Eat them one at a time.* **4 one by one** *separately, with one thing happening after another One by one the old buildings have been demolished.* **5 one another** *each other How can they reach an agreement if they won't talk to one another?* **6 (all) in one** *combined into a single thing It's a CD player and cassette deck all in one.*

o⟶ **one³** /wʌn/ *determiner* **1** PARTICULAR PERSON/THING *used to refer to a particular person or thing in a group One drawback is the cost of housing in the area.* ● *One of our daughters has just got married.* **2** FUTURE TIME *used to refer to a time in the future which is not yet decided We must have a drink together one evening.* **3** TIME IN PAST *at a particular time in the past I first met him one day in the park.* **4** ONLY *only He's the one person you can rely on in this place.* **5** WITH ADJECTIVE *mainly US used to emphasize an adjective That's one big ice cream you've got there!* **6 one or two** *a few I'd like to make one or two suggestions.* ➔ *See also:* put sth to one **side¹**, be one **step¹** ahead (of sb).

**one-man** /,wʌn'mæn/ *adj* [always before noun] with only one person doing something *a one-man show*

**one-off** /,wʌn'ɒf/ *adj* [always before noun] *UK only happening once a one-off payment* ● **one-off** *noun* [C] *UK something that only happens once His Olympic victory was not just a one-off.*

**one-on-one** /,wʌnɒn'wʌn/ *adj, adv mainly US only including two people*

**onerous** /'ɔʊnᵊrəs/ *adj formal difficult and needing a lot of effort an onerous task*

**oneself** /wʌn'self/ *pronoun formal the reflexive form of the pronoun 'one' when it refers to the person speaking or people in general How else should one protect oneself and one's family?*

**one-sided** /,wʌn'saɪdɪd/ *adj* **1** *If a competition is one-sided, one team or player is much better than the other. a one-sided contest/game* **2** *only considering one opinion in an argument in a way that is unfair a one-sided view*

**one-time** /'wʌntaɪm/ *adj* [always before noun] A one-time position or job is one that you had or did in the past, but not now. *a one-time friend/minister*

**one-to-one** /,wʌntə'wʌn/ *adj, adv mainly UK only including two people She's having private lessons on a one-to-one basis.*

**one-way** /,wʌn'weɪ/ *adj* If a road is one-way, you can only drive on it in one direction. *a one-way street*

,one-way 'ticket *US* (*UK* single) *noun* [C] A one-way ticket for a journey can only be used to travel in one direction and not for returning.

**ongoing** /'ɒn,gəʊɪŋ/ *adj* [always before noun] still happening *an ongoing process/investigation*

**onion** /'ʌnjən/ *noun* [C, U] a round vegetable with layers that has a strong taste and smell ➔ *See colour picture* **Fruit and Vegetables** *on page Centre 8.* ➔ *See also:* **spring onion**.

**online** /,ɒn'laɪn/ *adj, adv connected to a system of computers, especially the Internet online* services • to go online (= start using the Internet) • Most newspapers are now available online.

**onlooker** /ˈɒnˌlʊkəʳ/ noun [C] someone who watches something happening without becoming involved in it a crowd of onlookers

o—**only¹** /ˈəʊnli/ adv 1 [NOT MORE] not more than a particular size or amount • It'll only take a few minutes. • She's only fifteen. 2 [NO ONE/ NOTHING ELSE] not anyone or anything else The offer is available to UK residents only. • 3 [RECENTLY] used to mean that something happened very recently She's only just finished writing it. 4 **not only ... (but) also** used to say that one thing is true and another thing is true too, especially a surprising thing Not only did he turn up late, he also forgot his books.

o—**only²** /ˈəʊnli/ adj [always before noun] used to mean that there are not any others This could be our only chance. • You're the only person here I know.

**only³** /ˈəʊnli/ conjunction used to introduce a statement which explains why something you have just said cannot happen or is not completely true I'd phone him myself only I know he's not there at the moment.

ˈ**only ˌchild** noun [C] plural **only children** someone who has no brothers or sisters

**onset** /ˈɒnset/ noun **the onset of sth** the beginning of something, usually something unpleasant the onset of cancer

**onslaught** /ˈɒnslɔːt/ noun [C] when someone attacks or criticizes someone or something

o—**onto** (also **on to**) /ˈɒntuː/ preposition 1 used to show movement into or on a particular place The sheep were loaded onto trucks. • Can you get back onto the path? 2 **hold/grip, etc onto sth** to hold something Hold onto my hand before we cross the road. 3 used to show that you are starting to talk about a different subject Can we move onto the next item on the agenda? 4 **be onto sb** to know that someone has done something wrong or illegal She knows we're onto her and she's trying to get away. • Who **put** the police **onto** (= told the police about) her? 5 **be onto sth** to know or discover something useful or important Researchers think they may be onto something big. • Can you **put** me **onto** (= tell me about) a good dentist?

**the onus** /ˈəʊnəs/ noun formal the responsibility for doing something The **onus is on** parents to make sure their children attend school.

**onward** /ˈɒnwəd/ (also **onwards**) adv 1 **from the 1870s/March/6.30 pm, etc onwards** beginning at a time and continuing after it 2 If you move onwards, you continue to go forwards.

**oops** /uːps/ exclamation something you say when you make a mistake or have a slight accident Oops! I've spilled my coffee.

**ooze** /uːz/ verb 1 [I, T] If a liquid oozes from something or if something oozes a liquid, the liquid comes out slowly. Blood was oozing out of the wound. 2 [T] informal to show a lot of a quality to ooze charm/confidence

**opaque** /əʊˈpeɪk/ adj 1 If an object or substance is opaque, you cannot see through it. 2 formal difficult to understand

o—**open¹** /ˈəʊpᵊn/ adj 1 [NOT CLOSED] not closed or fastened an open door/window • Someone had left the gate **wide** open. • Is there a bottle of wine already open? • I threw all the doors open (= opened them quickly). • A magazine was lying open on her lap. • The kids were so tired they could hardly keep their eyes open. 2 [DOING BUSINESS] A shop or business is open during the time it is available for business or serving customers. Most shops are open on Sundays now. 3 [WITHOUT BUILDINGS] [always before noun] An open area of land has no buildings on it or near it. large open spaces • open fields 4 [NOT COVERED] [always before noun] without a roof or cover an open courtyard 5 [FOR EVERYONE] If a place or event is open, everyone can go to it or become involved in it. an open debate • Are the gardens **open to the public? 6 [HONEST] An open person is honest and does not hide their feelings. He's very open and friendly. 7 [NOT HIDDEN] [always before noun] Open feelings, usually negative ones, are not hidden. open hostility/rivalry 8 [NOT DECIDED] If a decision or question is open, it has not yet been decided. We don't have to make a firm arrangement now. Let's **leave it open. 9 have/ keep an open mind** to wait until you know all the facts before you form an opinion about something or judge someone The cause of the fire is still unclear and we are keeping an open mind. 10 **open to discussion/suggestions, etc** willing to consider a discussion/suggestions, etc This is only a proposal. I'm open to suggestions. 11 **open to abuse/criticism, etc** likely to be abused/criticized, etc The system is wide open to abuse. ⟳ See also: with your eyes (**eye¹**) open.

**open**

The window is open.

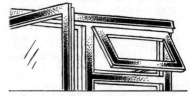

The book is open.

**USAGE**

**open and close**

Be careful not to confuse the adjective and verb forms of these words.

The adjectives are **open** and **closed**.

*Is the supermarket open on Sunday?*

*The museum is closed today.*

The verbs are **open** and **close**.

*The supermarket opens at 8 a.m.*

*The museum closes at 5 p.m. today.*

o—**open**[2] /'əʊpᵊn/ *verb* **1** NOT CLOSED [I, T] If something opens, it changes to a position that is not closed, and if you open it, you make it change to a position that is not closed. *to open a door/window* • *The gate won't open.* • *Don't open your eyes yet.* **2** REMOVE COVER [T] to remove part of a container or parcel so that you can see or use what it contains *Karen opened the box and looked inside.* • *Why don't you open the envelope?* • *I can't open this bottle.* **3** PREPARE FOR USE [I, T] If an object opens, the parts that are folded together move apart, and if you open it, you make the parts that are folded together move apart. *Shall I open the umbrella?* • *Open your books at page 22.* **4** START WORK [I] If a shop or office opens at a particular time of day, it starts to do business at that time. *What time does the bank open?* **5** START OFFICIALLY [I, T] If a business or activity opens, it starts officially for the first time, and if you open it, you make it start officially for the first time. *That restaurant's new – it only opened last month.* • *Several shops have opened up in the last year.* **6** MAKE AVAILABLE [T] to allow people to use a road or area *They opened up the roads again the day after the flooding.* **7 open an account** to make an arrangement to keep your money with a bank *Have you opened a bank account yet?* ➲ *See also:* open the **floodgates**.

**open (sth) up 1** to create a new opportunity or possibility *A teaching qualification can open up many more career opportunities.* **2** to open the lock on the door of a building *The caretaker opens up the school every morning at seven.*

**open up** to start to talk more about yourself and your feelings *I've tried to get him to open up to me, but with no success.*

**the open** /'əʊpᵊn/ *noun* **1 in the open** outside *We spent the night in the open.* **2 bring sth out into the open** to tell people information that was secret [often passive] *It's time this issue was brought out into the open.*

**open-air** /ˌəʊpən'eəʳ/ *adj* [always before noun] An open-air place does not have a roof. *an open-air swimming pool* • *an open-air theatre*

**'open ˌday** *noun* [C] *UK* a day when people can visit a school or organization to see what happens there

**open-ended** /ˌəʊpən'endɪd/ *adj* An open-ended activity or situation does not have a planned ending. *We are not willing to enter into open-ended discussions.*

**opener** /'əʊpᵊnəʳ/ *noun* [C] **1 bottle/can/tin, etc opener** a piece of kitchen equipment used to open bottles/cans, etc **2** someone or something that begins a series of events, usually in sports ➲ *See also:* **eye-opener.**

**opening**[1] /'əʊpᵊnɪŋ/ *noun* [C] **1** HOLE a hole or space that something or someone can pass

through *We found an opening in the fence and climbed through.* **2** START the beginning of something *The opening of the opera is quite dramatic.* **3** CEREMONY a ceremony at the beginning of an event or activity *I've been invited to the opening of the new exhibition on Tuesday.* **4** OPPORTUNITY a job or an opportunity to do something *There's **an opening for** an editorial assistant in our department.*

**opening**[2] /'əʊpᵊnɪŋ/ *adj* [always before noun] happening at the beginning of an event or activity *the opening night* • *her opening remarks*

**openly** /'əʊpᵊnli/ *adv* without hiding any of your thoughts or feelings *He talks quite openly about his feelings.*

**open-minded** /ˌəʊpən'maɪndɪd/ *adj* willing to consider ideas and opinions that are new or different to your own *Luckily, both my parents were very open-minded.*

**openness** /'əʊpᵊnnəs/ *noun* [U] when someone is honest about their thoughts and feelings *I appreciated his openness.*

**opera** /'ɒpᵊrə/ *noun* [C, U] a musical play in which most of the words are sung *to go to the opera* • *opera singers* • *an opera house* (= building for opera) • **operatic** /ˌɒpᵊr'ætɪk/ *adj* relating to opera *an operatic society*

o—**operate** /'ɒpᵊreɪt/ *verb* **1** ORGANIZATION [I, T] If an organization or business operates, it is working, and if you operate it, you manage it and make it work. *Our company is operating under very difficult conditions at present.* **2** MACHINE [I, T] If a machine operates, it does what it is designed to do, and if you operate it, you make it do what it is designed to do. *You have to be trained to operate the machinery.* • *These new sewing machines are easy to operate.* **3** TREATMENT [I] to treat an illness or injury by cutting someone's body and removing or repairing part of it *I don't think they're going to operate.* • *Did they have to **operate on** him?*

**'operating ˌroom** *US* (*UK* **operating theatre**) *noun* [C] a room in a hospital where doctors do operations

**'operating ˌsystem** *noun* [C] computer software that controls how different parts of a computer work together

**'operating ˌtheatre** *UK* (*US* **operating room**) *noun* [C] a room in a hospital where doctors do operations

o—**operation** /ˌɒpᵊr'eɪʃᵊn/ *noun* [C] **1** MEDICAL TREATMENT when a doctor cuts someone's body to remove or repair part of it *a heart/lung operation* • *a major/minor operation* • *My son's got to **have an operation.*** **2** ORGANIZATION an organization or business *a large commercial operation* **3** ACTIVITY an activity that is intended to achieve a particular purpose *a military/peacekeeping operation* • *a joint operation by French and Spanish police* • *an operation to smuggle drugs into Britain* **4 in operation** If a machine or system is in operation, it is working or being used. *The new rail link is now in operation.* • *Most of the machines are now back in operation.*

**operational** /ˌɒpᵊr'eɪʃᵊnᵊl/ *adj* **1** If a system is operational, it is working. *The service becomes* *fully operational next June.* **2** [always before noun] relating to a particular acvtivity *operational control/responsibility*

**operative**[1] /ˈɒpˈrətɪv/ *adj formal* working or being used *The agreement will not become operative until all members have signed.*

**operative**[2] /ˈɒpˈrətɪv/ *noun* [C] *mainly US* someone who does secret work for a government or other organization *a former CIA operative*

**operator** /ˈɒpəreɪtəʳ/ *noun* [C] TELEPHONE someone who helps to connect people on a telephone system *Why don't you call the operator?* **2** MACHINE someone whose job is to use and control a machine or vehicle *a computer operator* **3** BUSINESS a company that does a particular type of business *a tour operator*

☞**opinion** /əˈpɪnjən/ *noun* **1** [C] a thought or belief about something or someone *What's your opinion about/on the matter?* • *He has fairly strong opinions on most subjects.* • *Why don't we ask Daniel's opinion?* • *In my opinion* (= I think) *he's the best football player we have in this country.* **2 public opinion** the thoughts and beliefs that most people have about a subject *Eventually, the government will have to take notice of public opinion.* **3 have a high/low opinion of sb/sth** to think that someone or something is good/bad *He has a low opinion of doctors.*

**opinionated** /əˈpɪnjəneɪtɪd/ *adj* being too certain that your strong opinions are correct

**oˈpinion ˌpoll** *noun* [C] when people are asked questions to discover what they think about a subject *The latest opinion poll shows that the president's popularity has improved.*

**opium** /ˈəʊpiəm/ *noun* [U] a drug made from the seeds of a poppy (= a red flower)

**opponent** /əˈpəʊnənt/ *noun* [C] **1** someone who you compete against in a game or competition *He beat his opponent six games to two.* **2** someone who disagrees with an action or belief and tries to change it *an opponent of slavery* • *a political opponent*

**opportune** /ˈɒpətjuːn/ *adj formal* **an opportune moment/time** a good time for something to happen *His letter arrived at an opportune moment.*

**opportunist** /ˌɒpəˈtjuːnɪst/ *noun* [C] someone who tries to get power or an advantage in every situation • **opportunistic** /ˌɒpətjuːˈnɪstɪk/ *adj* using a situation to get power or an advantage

☞**opportunity** /ˌɒpəˈtjuːnəti/ *noun* **1** [C, U] a situation in which it is possible for you to do something, or a possibility of doing something *a good/wonderful/unique opportunity* • *a golden* (= very good) *opportunity* • [+ to do sth] *Everyone will have an opportunity to comment.* • *There are plenty of opportunities for research.* • *Don't miss this opportunity to win a million pounds.* • *She talks about her boyfriend at every opportunity.* • *We don't get much opportunity to go dancing these days.* **2** [C] the chance to get a job [usually plural] *opportunities for young graduates* • *job/employment opportunities* **3 take the opportunity to do sth** to use an occasion to do or say something *I'd like to take this opportunity to thank all of you.* ➔ *See usage note at* **possibility**.

☞**oppose** /əˈpəʊz/ *verb* [T] to disagree with a plan

or activity and to try to change or stop it *The committee opposed a proposal to allow women to join the club.*

**opposed** /əˈpəʊzd/ *adj* **1 be opposed to sth** to disagree with a plan or activity *We're not opposed to tax increases.* **2 as opposed to** used to say that two things are very different *I'm talking about English football, as opposed to European football.*

**opposing** /əˈpəʊzɪŋ/ *adj* **1 opposing teams/players, etc** Opposing teams/players, etc are competing against each other. **2 opposing ideas/beliefs, etc** Opposing ideas/beliefs, etc are completely different. *The book presents two opposing views.*

☞**opposite**[1] /ˈɒpəzɪt/ *adj* **1** in a position facing something or someone but on the other side *on the opposite page* • *in the opposite corner* • *We live on opposite sides of the city.* • *I noticed a gate at the opposite end of the courtyard.* **2** completely different *Police attempts to calm the violence had completely the opposite effect.*

**opposite**[2] /ˈɒpəzɪt/ *adv, preposition* in a position facing something or someone but on the other side *The couple sat down opposite her.* • *(UK) She lives opposite* (= on the other side of the road). • *Is there a bakery opposite your house?*

**opposite**[3] /ˈɒpəzɪt/ *noun* [C] someone or something that is completely different from another person or thing *They're complete opposites.* • *He's the exact opposite of my father.*

**the ˌopposite ˈsex** *noun* someone who is male if you are female, or female if you are male *It's not always easy to meet members of the opposite sex.*

☞**opposition** /ˌɒpəˈzɪʃˈn/ *noun* **1** [U] strong disagreement *Is there much opposition to the proposed changes?* • *There has been strong opposition from local residents.* **2 the Opposition/opposition** political parties that are not in power

**oppress** /əˈpres/ *verb* [T] **1** to treat a group of people in an unfair way, often by limiting their freedom [often passive] *Women were oppressed by a society which considered them inferior.* **2** to make someone feel anxious *The thought of tomorrow's interview oppressed him.*

**oppressed** /əˈprest/ *adj* treated in an unfair way *oppressed minorities* • *the poor and the oppressed*

**oppression** /əˈpreʃˈn/ *noun* [U] when people are treated in a way that is unfair and that limits their freedom *political oppression* • *the oppression of women*

**oppressive** /əˈpresɪv/ *adj* **1** UNFAIR cruel and unfair *an oppressive government/regime* **2** HOT If the weather or heat is oppressive, it is too hot and there is no wind. *oppressive heat* **3** NOT RELAXING not relaxing or pleasant *an oppressive silence*

**oppressor** /əˈpresəʳ/ *noun* [C] someone who treats people in an unfair way, often by limiting their freedom

**opt** /ɒpt/ *verb* **opt for sth; opt to do sth** to choose something or to decide to do something *Mike opted for early retirement.* • *Most people opt to have the operation.*

**opt out** to choose not to be part of an activity or

to stop being involved in it *He's decided to* **opt out of** *the company's pension scheme.*

**optical** /'ɒptɪkᵊl/ *adj* relating to light or the ability to see *optical equipment/instruments* • *an optical telescope*

,**optical i'llusion** *noun* [C] something that you think you see, but which is not really there

**optician** /ɒp'tɪʃᵊn/ *noun* [C] **1** *UK* someone whose job is to test people's eyes **2 optician's** *UK* a shop where you can have your eyes tested and have your glasses made **3** *US* someone whose job is to make eye glasses

**optimism** /'ɒptɪmɪzᵊm/ *noun* [U] when you believe good things will happen *a mood/spirit of optimism* • *There is* **cause/reason for** *optimism.* • *He expressed cautious* **optimism about** *the future.* ⊃ *Opposite* **pessimism**.

**optimist** /'ɒptɪmɪst/ *noun* [C] someone who always believes that good things will happen

**optimistic** /,ɒptɪ'mɪstɪk/ *adj* always believing that good things will happen *We're* **optimistic about** *our chances of success.* • [+ (that)] *I'm not optimistic that we'll reach an agreement.* ⊃ *Opposite* **pessimistic**.

**optimum** /'ɒptɪməm/ *adj* [always before noun] *formal* best or most suitable *the optimum temperature*

o━**option** /'ɒpʃᵊn/ *noun* **1** [C] a choice *That's an option you might like to consider.* • *We don't have many options.* • [+ of + doing sth] *You always have the option of not attending.* **2 have no option (but to do sth)** to not have the possibility of doing something else *We didn't want to dismiss him, but we had no option.* **3 keep/leave your options open** to wait and not make a decision or choice yet ⊃ *See also:* **soft option**.

**optional** /'ɒpʃᵊnᵊl/ *adj* If something is optional, it is available but you do not have to have it. *an optional extra*

**opulent** /'ɒpjələnt/ *adj* Opulent things are expensive and give a feeling of luxury. *an opulent bathroom*

o━**or** *strong form* /ɔːr/ *weak form* /ər/ *conjunction* **1** BETWEEN POSSIBILITIES used between possibilities, or before the last in a list of possibilities *Would you like toast or cereal?* • *Is that a boy or a girl?* • *You can have beer, wine, or mineral water.* • *The house will take two or three years to complete.* **2** CHANGE used to change or correct something you have said *We told the truth, or most of it.* **3** REASON used to give a reason for something you have said *She must love him or she wouldn't have stayed with him all these years.* **4** NOT EITHER used after a negative verb between a list of things to mean not any of those things or people *Tim doesn't eat meat or fish.* • *She doesn't have a telephone or a fax machine.*

**oral¹** /'ɔːrᵊl/ *adj* **1** spoken *an oral examination* • *an oral agreement* **2** relating to or using the mouth *an oral vaccine* • *oral medication* • **orally** *adv*

**oral²** /'ɔːrᵊl/ *noun* [C] an examination that is spoken, usually in a foreign language *a French/Spanish oral*

o━**orange¹** /'ɒrɪndʒ/ *adj* being a colour that is a mixture of red and yellow *a deep orange sunset* ⊃ *See colour picture* **Colours** *on page Centre 6.*

**orange²** /'ɒrɪndʒ/ *noun* **1** FRUIT [C] a round, sweet fruit with a thick skin and a centre that is divided into many equal parts *orange juice* ⊃ *See colour picture* **Fruit and Vegetables** *on page Centre 8.* **2** COLOUR [C, U] a colour that is a mixture of red and yellow ⊃ *See colour picture* **Colours** *on page Centre 6.* **3** DRINK [U] *UK* a drink made with oranges *Would you like some orange?*

'**orange ,juice** *noun* [U] a drink made from the juice of oranges

**orator** /'ɒrətər/ *noun* [C] *formal* someone who gives good speeches *a brilliant orator*

**oratory** /'ɒrətᵊri/ *noun* [U] *formal* when people give good speeches *powerful oratory* • *political oratory*

**orbit** /'ɔːbɪt/ *noun* [C, U] the circular journey that a spacecraft or planet makes around the sun, the moon, or another planet *the Earth's orbit* • *Two satellites are already* **in orbit**. • *It was the first spacecraft to* **go into orbit** *around Jupiter.* • **orbit** *verb* [I, T] *The moon orbits the Earth.*

**orchard** /'ɔːtʃəd/ *noun* [C] a piece of land where fruit trees are grown *an apple/cherry orchard*

**orchestra** /'ɔːkɪstrə/ *noun* [C] **1** a large group of musicians who play different instruments together *a symphony orchestra* • *a youth orchestra* **2** *US* (*UK* **the stalls**) the seats on the main floor near the front of a theatre or cinema • **orchestral** /ɔː'kestrᵊl/ *adj* [always before noun] Orchestral music is played by or written for an orchestra.

**orchestrate** /'ɔːkɪstreɪt/ *verb* [T] to intentionally organize something in order to achieve what you want *a carefully orchestrated demonstration of support*

**orchid** /'ɔːkɪd/ *noun* [C] a plant with flowers which are an unusual shape and beautiful colours

orchid

**ordain** /ɔː'deɪn/ *verb* [T] to officially make someone a Christian priest *[often passive] Dr Coker was ordained by the Bishop of London in 1986.*

**ordeal** /ɔː'diːl/ *noun* [C] a very unpleasant experience *a terrible ordeal* • *They feared he would not survive the ordeal.* • *She* **went through the ordeal** *of being interviewed by a panel of ten people.*

o━**order¹** /'ɔːdər/ *noun* **1** ARRANGEMENT [C, U] the arrangement of a group of people or things in a list from first to last *in alphabetical order* • *in the right/wrong order* • *We ranked the tasks* **in order of** *importance.* **2** INSTRUCTION [C] an instruction that someone must obey *to obey orders* • *to give orders* **3 under orders** If you are under orders, someone has told you to do something. *[+ to do sth] Team members are under orders to behave well.* • *They claimed*

*they were under orders from the president.*
**4** [REQUEST] [C] a request for food or goods in return for payment *Can I take your order now?* **5** [TIDINESS] [U] a situation in which everything is in its correct place *It's nice to see some order around here for a change.* • *I want to put all my things in order before I go away.* ⊃ *Opposite* **disorder**. **6 out of order a** [MACHINE] If a machine or system is out of order, it is not working as it should. *The coffee machine's out of order:* **b** [BEHAVIOUR] If someone's behaviour is out of order, it is not acceptable. *What he did was completely out of order.* **7 in order to do/ for sth to do sth** with the purpose of achieving something *She worked all summer in order to save enough money for a holiday.* • *In order for our relationship to continue, we need to talk about our problems.* **8** [NO TROUBLE] [U] a situation in which people obey laws and there is no trouble *The army was brought in to* **restore order** *to the troubled province.* • *How long can the police maintain* (= keep) *order?* ⊃ *Opposite* **disorder**. **9 economic/political/social order** the way that the economy, politics, or society is organized *a threat to the established social order* **10** [GROUP] [C] a religious group who live together and have the same rules *an order of nuns* • *a monastic order* ⊃ *See also:* **mail order**, **postal order**, **standing order**.

o━**order²** /ˈɔːdəʳ/ *verb* **1** [TELL] [T] to give someone an instruction that they must obey [+ **to do sth**] *He ordered them to leave.* **2** [REQUEST] [I, T] to ask for food, goods, etc *to order a drink/pizza* • *to order tickets* • *Shall we order? I'm starving.* • *We've ordered new lights for the kitchen.* • [+ two objects] *Can I order you a drink?* **3** [ARRANGE] [T] to arrange a group of people or things in a list from first to last *Have you ordered the pages correctly?*
**order sb about/around** to tell someone what they should do all the time *You can't just come in here and start ordering people around.*

**orderly¹** /ˈɔːdəli/ *adj* tidy or organized *an orderly pile* • *Please form an orderly queue.* ⊃ *Opposite* **disorderly**.

**orderly²** /ˈɔːdəli/ *noun* [C] a hospital worker who has no special skills or training

**ordinal number** /ˌɔːdɪnəlˈnʌmbəʳ/ *(also* **ordinal)** *noun* [C] a number such as 1st, 2nd, 3rd, etc that shows the order of things in a list

**ordinance** /ˈɔːdɪnəns/ *noun* [C] *mainly US* a law or rule which limits or controls something *a tax ordinance*

**ordinarily** /ˈɔːdənərɪli/ *adv* usually *people who would not ordinarily carry guns*

o━**ordinary** /ˈɔːdənri/ *adj* **1** not special, different, or unusual in any way *ordinary life* • *an ordinary day* • *I had a very ordinary childhood.* **2** Ordinary people are not rich or famous and do not have special skills. *ordinary people/citizens* • *an ordinary man/woman* **3 out of the ordinary** unusual or different *Their relationship was a little out of the ordinary.* • *The investigation revealed* **nothing out of the ordinary**.

**ore** /ɔːʳ/ *noun* [U] rock or soil from which metal can be obtained *iron ore*

**organ** /ˈɔːgən/ *noun* [C] **1** a part of an animal or plant that has a special purpose *reproductive/*

sexual organs • *The liver is a* **vital organ** (= you need it to stay alive). • *an organ donor/transplant* **2** a large musical instrument that has keys like a piano and produces different notes when air is blown through pipes of different lengths *a church organ*

**organic** /ɔːˈgænɪk/ *adj* **1** [FARMING] not using artificial chemicals when keeping animals or growing plants for food *organic farming/ farmers* • *organic food/vegetables* **2** [CHEMISTRY] In chemistry, 'organic' describes chemicals that contain carbon. *organic compounds* **3** [LIVING] from a living organism *organic matter/material* ⊃ *Opposite* **inorganic**. • *organically adv organically grown vegetables*

**organism** /ˈɔːgənɪzəm/ *noun* [C] a living thing, often one that is extremely small *Plants, animals, bacteria, and viruses are organisms.*

**organist** /ˈɔːgənɪst/ *noun* [C] someone who plays the organ (= an instrument like a piano)

o━**organization** *(also UK* **-isation)** /ˌɔːgənaɪˈzeɪʃən/ *noun* **1** [GROUP] [C] an official group of people who work together for the same purpose *a charitable/voluntary organization* **2** [ARRANGEMENT] [U] the way that parts of something are arranged *Better organization of the office would improve efficiency.* **3** [PLAN] [U] the planning of an activity or event *Who was responsible for the organization of the conference?* • *organizational adj organizational skills*

o━**organize** *(also UK* **-ise)** /ˈɔːgənaɪz/ *verb* [T] to plan or arrange something *to organize a meeting/wedding*

**organized** *(also UK* **-ised)** /ˈɔːgənaɪzd/ *adj* **1** An organized person plans things well and does not waste time or effort. ⊃ *Opposite* **disorganized**. **2** [always before noun] involving a group of people who have planned to do something together *organized crime/religion* ⊃ *See also:* **well-organized**.

**organizer** *(also UK* **-iser)** /ˈɔːgənaɪzəʳ/ *noun* [C] someone who plans an event or activity *conference/exhibition organizers*

**orgasm** /ˈɔːgæzəm/ *noun* [C, U] the time of greatest pleasure and excitement during sex *to have an orgasm*

**orgy** /ˈɔːdʒi/ *noun* [C] **1** a noisy party at which people have a lot of sex, alcohol, or illegal drugs **2 an orgy of sth** a period when there is too much of an often bad activity *an orgy of destruction*

**the Orient** /ˈɔːriənt/ *noun* *old-fashioned* the countries of east Asia

**Oriental** /ˌɔːriˈentəl/ *adj* relating or belonging to the countries of east Asia *Oriental art*

**orientated** /ˈɔːriənteɪtɪd/ *UK (UK/US* **oriented)** *adj* directed towards or interested in something

**orientation** /ˌɔːriənˈteɪʃən/ *noun* **1** [C, U] the type of beliefs that a person has *He's very secretive about his political orientation.* **2** [U] training or preparation for a new job or activity *an orientation session*

**oriented** /ˈɔːriəntɪd/ *(also UK* **orientated)** *adj* directed towards or interested in something *His new TV series is* **oriented towards** *teenage viewers.* • *He's very family oriented.*

**origin** /ˈɒrɪdʒɪn/ *noun* [C, U] **1** the cause of something, or where something begins or comes from *the origin of the universe* • *This dish is Greek in origin.* **2** the country, race, or social class of a person's family *ethnic origin* • *She's of Irish origin.*

o─**original**¹ /əˈrɪdʒ³n³l/ *adj* **1** special and interesting because of not being the same as others *Her essay was full of original ideas.* • *He's a highly original thinker.* **2** [always before noun] existing since the beginning, or being the earliest form of something *His original plan was to stay for a week, but he ended up staying for a month.* • *Do you still have the original version of this document?*

**original**² /əˈrɪdʒ³n³l/ *noun* [C] something that is in the form in which it was first created and has not been copied or changed *The latest version of the software is much more reliable than the original.* • *If the painting were an original, it would be very valuable.*

**originality** /əˌrɪdʒ³nˈæləti/ *noun* [U] the quality of being interesting and different from everyone or everything else *The judges were impressed by the originality of his work.*

o─**originally** /əˈrɪdʒ³n³li/ *adv* at the beginning or before any changes *Despite the accident, she intends to complete her tour as originally planned.* • *The bathroom was originally a bedroom.*

**originate** /əˈrɪdʒ³neɪt/ *verb* [I] **originate from/in/with, etc** to come from a particular place or person, or to begin during a particular period *Citrus fruits originated in China and Southeast Asia.*

**originator** /əˈrɪdʒ³neɪtər/ *noun* [C] *formal* The originator of an idea is the person who first thought of it.

**ornament** /ˈɔːnəmənt/ *noun* [C] an attractive object that is used as a decoration in a home or garden ➔ *See colour picture* **The Living Room** *on page Centre 11.*

**ornamental** /ˌɔːnəˈment³l/ *adj* used for decoration and having no other purpose

**ornate** /ɔːˈneɪt/ *adj* decorated with a lot of complicated patterns *ornate wooden doors*

**ornithology** /ˌɔːnɪˈθɒlədʒi/ *noun* [U] the scientific study of birds • **ornithologist** *noun* [C] a scientist who studies birds

**orphan**¹ /ˈɔːf³n/ *noun* [C] a child whose parents are dead

**orphan**² /ˈɔːf³n/ *verb* **be orphaned** When a child is orphaned, both their parents die. *She was orphaned at the age of six.* • *orphaned children*

**orphanage** /ˈɔːf³nɪdʒ/ *noun* [C] a home for children whose parents are dead

**orthodox** /ˈɔːθədɒks/ *adj* **1** keeping the traditional beliefs and customs of Judaism or some types of Christianity *an orthodox Jewish family* • *the Russian/Greek Orthodox Church* **2** If ideas or methods are orthodox, most people think they are correct, usually because they have existed for a long time. *orthodox medicine* ➔ *Opposite* **unorthodox**.

**orthodoxy** /ˈɔːθədɒksi/ *noun* [C, U] *formal* an idea of a society, religion, political party, or subject that most people believe is correct, or a set of such ideas

**orthopaedic** UK (US **orthopedic**) /ˌɔːθəˈpiːdɪk/ *adj* [always before noun] relating to the treatment or study of bones that have been injured or have not grown correctly *an orthopaedic surgeon*

**Oscar** /ˈɒskər/ *noun* [C] *trademark* one of several prizes given to actors and people who make films every year in Hollywood in the US *Who won the Oscar for best actress this year?* • *The film received twelve Oscar nominations.*

**oscillate** /ˈɒsɪleɪt/ *verb* [I] *formal* to move repeatedly between two positions or opinions *an oscillating fan* • *The story oscillates between comedy and tragedy.* • **oscillation** /ˌɒsɪˈleɪʃ³n/ *noun* [C, U]

**ostensibly** /ɒsˈtensɪbli/ *adv* If something is ostensibly the reason for something else, people say it is the reason, although you do not believe it. *He was discharged from the army, ostensibly for medical reasons.*

**ostentatious** /ˌɒstenˈteɪʃəs/ *adj* intended to attract attention or admiration, often by showing money or power *an ostentatious display of wealth* • **ostentatiously** *adv*

**osteopath** /ˈɒstiəυpæθ/ *noun* [C] someone who treats injuries to bones and muscles by moving and rubbing them

**osteoporosis** /ˌɒstiəυpəˈrəυsɪs/ *noun* [U] a disease which makes bones weak and makes them break easily

**ostracize** (*also UK* **-ise**) /ˈɒstrəsaɪz/ *verb* [T] When a group of people ostracizes someone, they refuse to talk to or do things with that person. [often passive] *He was ostracized by the other children at school.*

**ostrich** /ˈɒstrɪtʃ/ *noun* [C] a very large bird from Africa which cannot fly but can run very fast

o─**other**¹ /ˈʌðər/ *adj, determiner* **1** MORE used to refer to people or things which are similar to or in addition to those you have talked about *I don't like custard – do you have any other desserts?* • *The crops were damaged by rats and other pests.* • *I don't think he's funny, but other people do.* **2** PART OF SET used to talk about the remaining members of a group or items in a set *Mario and Anna sat down to watch the other dancers.* • *I found one shoe – have you seen the other one?* **3** DIFFERENT different from a thing or person which you have talked about *Our train was delayed, so we had to make other arrangements.* • *Ask me some other time, when I'm not so busy.* ➔ *See usage note at* **another**. **4 the other side/end (of sth)** the opposite side/end of something *Our house is on the other side of town.* • *Go around to the other side and push!* **5 the other day/week, etc** used to mean recently, without giving a particular date *I asked Kevin about it just the other day.* **6 every other day/week, etc** happening one day/week, etc but not the next *Alice goes to the gym every other day.* **7 other than** except *The form cannot be signed by anyone other than the child's parent.* • [+ to do sth] *They had no choice other than to surrender.* **8 other than that** *informal* except for the thing you have just said *My arm was a bit sore – other than that I was fine.*

o─**other**² /ˈʌðər/ *pronoun* **1** used to refer to a person or thing which belongs to a group or set that you have already talked about *Mario and Anna sat down to watch the others dance.* • *Hold the racket in one hand, and the ball in the other.* • *Some of the pieces were damaged, others were missing.* **2 others** used to refer to people or things that are similar to people or things you have already talked about *This is broken – do you have any others?* ➔ *See also:* **each other**.

**others** /ˈʌðəz/ *pronoun* [plural] other people *Don't expect others to do your work for you.*

o▬**otherwise**¹ /ˈʌðəwaɪz/ *adv* **1** except for what has just been referred to *She hurt her arm in the accident, but otherwise she was fine.* **2** different to what has just been stated *It's obvious they're in love, so it's silly of them to pretend otherwise.* • *I'll meet you there at 6 o'clock unless I hear otherwise.* • *I'd like to help you with any problems, financial or otherwise.*

**otherwise**² /ˈʌðəwaɪz/ *conjunction* used when saying what will happen if someone does not obey an order or do what has been suggested *You'd better phone home, otherwise your parents will start to worry.* • *He ought to pay the fine, otherwise he might go to prison.*

**otter** /ˈɒtə<sup>r</sup>/ *noun* [C] a small animal with short, brown fur and a long body that swims well and eats fish

**ouch** /aʊtʃ/ *exclamation* something you say when you experience sudden physical pain *Ouch! This radiator's really hot.*

o▬**ought** /ɔːt/ *modal verb* **1 ought to do sth** used to say or ask what is the correct or best thing to do *We ought to tidy up before we go.* • *You ought to see a doctor.* • *He ought to have told her the truth.* • *Ought I to phone her?* **2 ought to be/do sth** used to say that you expect something to be true or that you expect something to happen *She ought to be home by seven.* • *He ought to pass the exam this time.* ➔ *See study section* **Modal verbs** *on page Centre 31.*

**oughtn't** /ˈɔːt<sup>ə</sup>nt/ *formal short for* ought not *He oughtn't to have shouted at us.*

**ounce** /aʊns/ *noun* **1** [C] (*written abbreviation* **oz**) a unit for measuring weight, equal to 28.35 grams ➔ *See also:* **fluid ounce**. **2 not have an ounce of sth** to not have any of a quality or emotion *His new novel doesn't have an ounce of originality.* **3 every ounce of sth** all of a quality or emotion that is available *He deserves every ounce of support that we can give him.*

o▬**our** /aʊə<sup>r</sup>/ *determiner* belonging to or relating to the person who is speaking and one or more other people *Janice is our youngest daughter.*

o▬**ours** /aʊəz/ *pronoun* the things that belong or relate to the person who is speaking and one or more other people *Matt's a friend of ours.* • *That's their problem – not ours.*

o▬**ourselves** /ˌaʊəˈselvz/ *pronoun* **1** the reflexive form of the pronoun 'we' *We've promised ourselves a holiday abroad this year.* **2** used for emphasis with the pronoun 'we' or when referring to yourself and at least one other person *John and I arranged the wedding reception ourselves.* **3 (all) by ourselves** alone or without anyone else's help *It's a big garden but we manage to look after it by ourselves.* **4 (all) to ourselves** for our use only *We arrived early and had the swimming pool all to ourselves.*

**oust** /aʊst/ *verb* [T] to force someone to leave a position of power or responsibility [often passive] *He was ousted from power by a military coup.*

o▬**out**¹ /aʊt/ *adj, adv* **1** [AWAY FROM] used to show movement away from the inside of a place or container *He dropped the bag and all the apples fell out.* • *She opened the window and stuck her head out.* **2** [OUTSIDE] outside a building or room *Would you like to wait out here?* • *It's bitterly cold out today.* **3** [NOT THERE] not in the place where you usually live or work, especially for a short time *I came round to see you this morning but you were out.* **4** [FIRE/LIGHT] A fire or light that is out is not burning or shining. *Bring some more wood, the fire's gone out.* **5** [AVAILABLE] available to buy or see *When's the new Spielberg film out?* **6** [FASHION] no longer fashionable or popular *Trousers like that went out years ago.* **7** [NOT ACCURATE] not accurate *Your figures are out by £300.* **8** [GAME] no longer able to play or take part in a game or competition *Two of the best players were out after ten minutes.* **9** [APPEAR] able to be seen *After a few minutes the sun came out.* • *The daffodils aren't out yet.* **10** [NOT POSSIBLE] not possible or not acceptable *Next weekend is out because we're going away.* **11 be out of sth** to have no more of something left *We're nearly out of money.* **12 be out for sth; be out to do sth** to intend to do something, especially for an unpleasant reason *He's only out to impress the boss.* ➔ *See also:* **out of**.

**out**² /aʊt/ *verb* [T] to report to the public the secret that someone is homosexual [often passive] *He was outed by a tabloid newspaper.*

**out-and-out** /ˌaʊtnˈaʊt/ *adj* [always before noun] complete or in every way *an out-and-out lie* • *He's an out-and-out racist.*

**the outback** /ˈaʊtbæk/ *noun* the areas of Australia where few people live, especially the central desert areas

**outbid** /ˌaʊtˈbɪd/ *verb* [T] **outbidding**, *past* **outbid** to offer to pay more for something than someone else *She had to outbid two rivals to buy the business.*

**outbreak** /ˈaʊtbreɪk/ *noun* [C] when something unpleasant and difficult to control starts, such as a war or disease *an outbreak of flu/fighting*

**outburst** /ˈaʊtbɜːst/ *noun* [C] a sudden, forceful expression of emotion in words or actions *an angry outburst*

**outcast** /ˈaʊtkɑːst/ *noun* [C] someone who is not accepted by society because they are different to most other people *a social outcast*

**outcome** /ˈaʊtkʌm/ *noun* [C] the final result of an activity or process *the outcome of an election*

**outcrop** /ˈaʊtkrɒp/ (*also US* **outcropping**) *noun* [C] a rock or group of rocks that sticks out above the surface of the ground

**outcry** /ˈaʊtkraɪ/ *noun* [C] a strong public expression of anger and disapproval about a recent event or decision *There has been a public outcry against the new road.*

**outdated** /ˌaʊtˈdeɪtɪd/ *adj* not modern enough *outdated equipment* • *an outdated idea*

**outdo** /ˌaʊtˈduː/ *verb* [T] *past* **outdid**, *past p*

**outdone** to do something better than someone else *They are always trying to outdo each other with their jokes and funny stories.*

**outdoor** /ˌaʊt'dɔːʳ/ *adj* [always before noun] happening, used, or in a place that is outside and not inside a building *outdoor activities* • *an outdoor concert* • *an outdoor swimming pool* • *outdoor clothing* ⊃ *Opposite* **indoor**.

**outdoors** /ˌaʊt'dɔːz/ *adv* not inside a building *If it's warm this evening, we could eat outdoors.* ⊃ *Opposite* **indoors**.

**the outdoors** /ˌaʊt'dɔːz/ *noun* countryside *He enjoys hunting, fishing, and the outdoors.*

**outer** /'aʊtəʳ/ *adj* [always before noun] on the edge or surface of something *Remove the outer layers of the onion.* ⊃ *Opposite* **inner**.

**outer 'space** *noun* [U] the universe outside the Earth and its gases where other planets and stars are

**the outfield** /'aʊtfiːld/ *noun* the outer area of the playing field in sports such as cricket and baseball • **outfielder** *noun* [C] a baseball player who stands in the outfield

**outfit**[1] /'aʊtfɪt/ *noun* [C] **1** a set of clothes for a particular event or activity *a cowboy outfit* • *I need a new outfit for the party.* **2** *informal* an organization, company, or any group of people who work together

**outfit**[2] /'aʊtfɪt/ *verb* [T] **outfitting**, *past* **outfitted** *US* to provide equipment for something [often passive] *My hotel room was small and outfitted with cheap wooden furniture.*

**outgoing** /ˌaʊt'gəʊɪŋ/ ⓤⓢ /'aʊtgəʊɪŋ/ *adj* **1** FRIENDLY Someone who is outgoing is friendly, talks a lot, and enjoys meeting people. *Anne is very outgoing, but her sister's quite shy.* **2** LEAVING POWER [always before noun] leaving a position of power or responsibility *the outgoing president* **3** LEAVING A PLACE [always before noun] going to another place *outgoing calls/messages*

**outgoings** /'aʊtˌgəʊɪŋz/ *noun* [plural] *UK* money that you have to spend on rent, food, etc

**outgrow** /ˌaʊt'grəʊ/ *verb* [T] *past t* **outgrew**, *past p* **outgrown** **1** to grow too big for something *He's already outgrown these shoes.* • *The company has outgrown this building.* **2** to develop so that something is not now suitable *She's outgrown her current job and needs a new challenge.*

**outing** /'aʊtɪŋ/ *noun* **1** [C] when a group of people go on a short journey for pleasure or education *a family/school outing* • *to go on an outing* **2** [U] when someone says publicly that someone else is homosexual *Do you think the outing of politicians is in the public interest?*

**outlandish** /ˌaʊt'lændɪʃ/ *adj* very strange and unusual *an outlandish story/idea* • *outlandish behaviour/clothes*

**outlast** /ˌaʊt'lɑːst/ *verb* [T] to continue for longer than someone or something else

**outlaw**[1] /'aʊtlɔː/ *verb* [T] to make something officially illegal *I think all handguns should be outlawed.*

**outlaw**[2] /'aʊtlɔː/ *noun* [C] *old-fashioned* a criminal *a dangerous outlaw*

**outlay** /'aʊtleɪ/ *noun* [C] an amount of money spent by a business or government *The project requires an initial outlay of $450,000.*

**outlet** /'aʊtlet/ *noun* [C] **1** SHOP In business, an outlet is a shop that sells one type of product or the products of one company. **2** CHEAP SHOP *US* a shop that sells goods for a lower price than usual **3** EXPRESS a way for someone to express an emotion, idea, or ability *She needs a job that will provide* **an outlet for** *her creative talent.* **4** WAY OUT a place where a liquid or gas can flow out of something **5** CONNECTION *US* a place where you can connect a wire on a piece of electrical equipment *an electrical outlet*

**outline**[1] /'aʊtlaɪn/ *verb* [T] to describe only the most important ideas or facts about something *He outlined the department's plans for next year.*

**outline**[2] /'aʊtlaɪn/ *noun* [C] **1** a short description of the most important ideas or facts about something *He gave us a brief outline of the town's history.* **2** the shape made by the outside edge of something

**outlive** /ˌaʊt'lɪv/ *verb* [T] to continue living or existing after someone or something else has died or stopped existing *She outlived both her children.*

**outlook** /'aʊtlʊk/ *noun* **1** [no plural] the likely future situation *The* **outlook for** *the economy next year is bleak.* **2** [C] the way a person thinks about something *Despite her illness, she has a very positive* **outlook on** *life.*

**outlying** /'aʊtˌlaɪɪŋ/ *adj* [always before noun] far from towns and cities, or far from the centre of a place *outlying farms/villages* • *outlying areas/districts*

**outmanoeuvre** *UK* (*US* **outmaneuver**) /ˌaʊtmə'nuːvəʳ/ *verb* [T] to do something clever that gives you an advantage over someone you are competing against *She outmanoeuvred her opponents throughout the election campaign.*

**outmoded** /ˌaʊt'məʊdɪd/ *adj* not modern enough *outmoded equipment*

**outnumber** /ˌaʊt'nʌmbəʳ/ *verb* [T] to be larger in number than another group *Women now far outnumber men on language courses.*

**out of** *preposition* **1** AWAY FROM used to show movement away from the inside of a place or container *A bunch of keys fell out of her bag.* • *She stepped out of the car and walked towards me.* **2** NO LONGER IN no longer in a place or situation *He's out of the country until next month.* • *I've been out of work for the past year.* **3** MADE FROM used to show what something is made from *The statue was carved out of a single block of stone.* **4** BECAUSE OF used to show the reason why someone does something *I only gave her the job out of pity.* **5** FROM AMONG from among an amount or number *Nine out of ten people said they preferred it.* **6** NOT INVOLVED no longer involved in something *He missed the practice session and now he's out of the team.*

**out-of-court** /ˌaʊtəv'kɔːt/ *adj* [always before noun] agreed without involving a law court *an out-of-court settlement*

**out-of-date** /ˌaʊtəv'deɪt/ *adj* old and not useful or correct any more *I do have a road map but I think it's out-of-date.*

**out-of-town** /ˌaʊtəv'taʊn/ *adj* [always before noun] positioned or happening in the countryside or on the edge of a town *an out-of-town supermarket*

**O**

**outpace** /ˌaʊtˈpeɪs/ *verb* [T] to move or develop more quickly than someone or something else

**outpatient** /ˈaʊtˌpeɪʃ³nt/ *noun* [C] someone who is treated in a hospital but does not sleep there at night

**outperform** /ˌaʊtpəˈfɔːm/ *verb* [T] to do something better than someone or something else *Girls are consistently outperforming boys at school.*

**outplay** /ˌaʊtˈpleɪ/ *verb* [T] to play a game or sport better than another player or team

**outpost** /ˈaʊtpəʊst/ *noun* [C] a small place that is far from large towns or cities, often where a government or company is represented

**outpouring** /ˈaʊtˌpɔːrɪŋ/ *noun* [C] when an emotion is expressed a lot in public *His death provoked a national **outpouring of** grief.*

**output¹** /ˈaʊtpʊt/ *noun* [U] **1** [AMOUNT] the amount of something that is produced *Over the past year the factory's output has fallen by 15%.* **2** [INFORMATION] information produced by a computer *You can look at the output on screen before you print it out.* **3** [POWER] the power or energy produced by an electrical or electronic system *The maximum output of the amplifier is 35 watts.*

**outrage¹** /ˈaʊtreɪdʒ/ *noun* **1** [U] a strong feeling of anger or shock *moral outrage* • *The scandal caused public outrage.* • *These murders have provoked outrage across the country.* **2** [C] something that causes great anger or shock *a terrorist outrage* • [+ (that)] *It's an outrage that these children don't have enough to eat.*

**outrage²** /ˈaʊtreɪdʒ/ *verb* [T] to make someone feel very angry or shocked [often passive] *The audience was outraged by his racist comments.* • *Local people were **outraged at** the bombing.*

**outrageous** /ˌaʊtˈreɪdʒəs/ *adj* shocking or extreme *outrageous behaviour/clothes* • *The prices in that restaurant were outrageous.* • **outrageously** *adv outrageously expensive*

**outran** /ˌaʊtˈræn/ *past tense of* outrun

**outreach** /ˈaʊtriːtʃ/ *noun* [U] mainly US when an organization helps people with their social, medical, or educational problems *an outreach programme* • *an outreach worker*

**outright¹** /ˈaʊtraɪt/ *adj* [always before noun] total, clear, and certain *an outright ban on smoking* • *an outright lie* • *an outright victory* • **outright** /ˌaʊtˈraɪt/ *adv She needs 51% of the vote to win outright.* • *He was killed outright* (= immediately) *when the car hit him.*

**outrun** /ˌaʊtˈrʌn/ *verb* [T] **outrunning**, *past t* **outran**, *past p* **outrun** to move or develop faster or further than someone or something

**outscore** /ˌaʊtˈskɔːr/ *verb* [T] mainly US to score more points than another player or team

**outset** /ˈaʊtset/ *noun* **at/from the outset** at or from the beginning of something *I made my views clear at the outset.* • *We knew from the outset that we were unlikely to win.*

**outshine** /ˌaʊtˈʃaɪn/ *verb* [T] *past* **outshone** to be much better than someone else *She easily outshone the other students on the course.*

○━**outside¹** /ˌaʊtˈsaɪd/ (*mainly US* **outside of**) *preposition* **1** not in a particular building or room, but near it *She waited outside his room for nearly two hours.* **2** not in a flat just outside *Blackpool* • *You have to phone a different number outside office hours.*

○━**outside²** /ˌaʊtˈsaɪd/ *adv* **1** not inside a building *Go and play outside for a while.* • *It's cold outside today.* **2** not in a particular building or room, but near it *She knocked on his bedroom door and left the tray outside.*

○━**outside³** /ˈaʊtsaɪd/ *adj* [always before noun] **1** not in a building *an outside light* • *outside activities* **2** from a different organization or group of people *outside help* • *outside influences* ➜ *See also:* **the outside world**.

**the outside⁴** /ˌaʊtˈsaɪd/ *noun* the outer part or surface of something *The pie was cooked on the outside but cold in the middle.*

**outside ˈchance** *noun* [no plural] when something is not likely to happen *She has an outside chance of reaching the final.*

**outsider** /ˌaʊtˈsaɪdər/ *noun* [C] someone who does not belong to a particular group, organization, or place *The villagers are very suspicious of outsiders.* ➜ *Compare* **insider**.

**the ˌoutside ˈworld** *noun* other people in other places *When he was in prison, his radio was his only contact with the outside world.*

**outsize** /ˌaʊtˈsaɪz/ (*also* **outsized**) *adj* [always before noun] larger than usual *an outsize jumper*

**the outskirts** /ˈaʊtskɜːts/ *noun* the outer area of a city, town, or village *There are plans to build a new stadium **on the outskirts of** Liverpool.*

**outspoken** /ˌaʊtˈspəʊk³n/ *adj* expressing an opinion forcefully and not worrying about what other people think *outspoken comments* • *He's an outspoken critic of nuclear energy.*

**outstanding** /ˌaʊtˈstændɪŋ/ *adj* **1** excellent and much better than most *an outstanding achievement* • *an outstanding player* **2** waiting to be paid or dealt with *an outstanding debt* • *an outstanding issue*

**outstandingly** /ˌaʊtˈstændɪŋli/ *adv* used to emphasize how good something is *outstandingly successful*

**outstay** /ˌaʊtˈsteɪ/ *verb* ➜ *See* **outstay your welcome⁴**.

**outstretched** /ˌaʊtˈstretʃt/ *adj* When a part of your body is outstretched, it is reaching out as far as possible. *He ran towards me with his arms outstretched.*

**outstrip** /ˌaʊtˈstrɪp/ *verb* [T] **outstripping**, *past* **outstripped** When one amount outstrips another amount, it is much greater than it. *Demand for the toys far outstrips supply.*

**outta** /ˈaʊtə/ *informal short for* out of *Let's get outta here!*

**outward** /ˈaʊtwəd/ *adj* [always before noun] **1** showing on the outside *He had a serious illness, but there was no outward sign of it.* **2** **outward flight/journey, etc** when you travel away from a place that you will return to ➜ *Opposite* **inward**.

**outwardly** /ˈaʊtwədli/ *adv* If someone is outwardly calm, confident, etc, they seem to be calm, confident, etc, although they may not feel that way. *She was very nervous, but she remained outwardly calm.* ➜ *Opposite* **inwardly**.

**outwards** /ˈaʊtwədz/ *mainly UK* (*mainly US* **outward**) *adv* towards the outside or away from the centre *This door opens outwards.*

**outweigh** /ˌaʊtˈweɪ/ *verb* [T] to be greater or more important than something else *The benefits of this treatment far outweigh the risks.*

**outwit** /ˌaʊtˈwɪt/ *verb* [T] **outwitting**, *past* **outwitted** to get an advantage over someone by doing something clever and deceiving them *She outwitted her kidnappers and managed to escape.*

**oval** /ˈəʊvᵊl/ *adj* in the shape of an egg or a slightly flat circle *an oval face* • *an oval table* • oval *noun* [C] an oval shape ➔ *See picture at* **shape**.

**the 'Oval ,Office** *noun* the office of the president of the United States

**ovary** /ˈəʊvᵊri/ *noun* [C] the part of a woman or female animal that produces eggs • ovarian /əʊˈveəriən/ *adj* [always before noun] relating to the ovaries *ovarian cancer*

**ovation** /əʊˈveɪʃᵊn/ *noun* [C] when a group of people clap for a long time to show that they approve of someone or something ➔ *See also:* **standing ovation**.

**oven** /ˈʌvᵊn/ *noun* [C] a piece of kitchen equipment with a door, which is used for cooking food *an electric oven* • *a microwave oven* • *Place the cake in a preheated oven at 190°C and bake for 45 minutes.* ➔ *See colour picture* **Kitchen** *on page Centre 10*.

**o-●over¹** /ˈəʊvᵊʳ/ *adv, preposition* **1** ABOVE above or higher than something *The sign over the door said "Private, No Entry".* • *A fighter plane flew over.* **2** SIDE TO SIDE If you walk, jump, climb, etc over an object or place, you go from one side of it to the other side. *We had to climb over large rocks to get to the beach.* **3** AMOUNT more than a particular amount, number, or age *Over 5,000 Internet users contact our website every year.* • *Suitable for children aged 5 and over.* **4** OPPOSITE SIDE on or to the opposite side of a road, bridge, path, etc *The station is over the bridge.* **5** COVER covering someone or something *She placed the quilt over the bed.* **6** DOWN down from a higher to a lower position *The little boy fell over and started to cry.* • *She tripped over the rug.* **7** PLACE to a particular place *Could you bring the plates over here* (= bring them to this place). • *Why don't you come over* (= come to my home) *on Friday evening?* • *He was sent over there during the war.* **8** TIME during a particular period of time *I was in Seattle over the summer.* **9** ABOUT connected with or about *It's stupid arguing over something so trivial.* **10** NOT USED not used *There's some food left over from the party.* **11** USING using the radio or telephone *I made the booking over the phone.* **12** be/get over sth to feel better after being ill or feeling unhappy about something *It took him months to get over splitting up with his girlfriend.* **13** do sth over *US* to do something again from the beginning because you did not do it well the first time *You've ruined it! - Now I'll have to do it over.* **14** (all) over again again from the beginning *It looks all messy. I'm going to have to do it all over again.* **15** over and over (again) repeatedly *He was whistling the same tune over and over.* **16** roll/turn, etc (sth) over to move so that a different part is showing, or to make

something do this *She turned the page over.* **17** CONTROL in control of someone or something *Her husband has a lot of influence over her.* • *She manages three people and has a sales director over her* (= with a higher rank than her).

**o-●over²** /ˈəʊvᵊʳ/ *adj* **1** [never before noun] finished *The exams will be over next week.* • *It was all over very quickly.* **2** get sth over (and done) with to do something difficult or unpleasant as soon as you can so that you do not have to worry about it any more

**overall** /ˈəʊvᵊrɔːl/ *adj* [always before noun] considering everything or everyone *the overall cost of the holiday* • *the overall effect* • overall /ˌəʊvᵊrˈɔːl/ *adv How would you rate the school overall?* • *We lost the first game, but won overall.*

**overalls** /ˈəʊvᵊrɔːlz/ *noun* [plural] **1** *UK* (*US* **coveralls**) a piece of clothing that you wear over your clothes to keep them clean while you are working **2** *US* (*UK* **dungarees**) trousers with a part that covers your chest and straps that go over your shoulders

**overbearing** /ˌəʊvəˈbeərɪŋ/ *adj* trying to have too much control over other people *an overbearing mother*

**overblown** /ˌəʊvəˈbləʊn/ *adj* If something is overblown, it is made to seem more important or serious than it really is.

**overboard** /ˈəʊvəbɔːd/ *adv* **1** over the side of a boat and into the water *to fall overboard* **2** go overboard *informal* to do something too much, or to be too excited about something *I think people go overboard at Christmas.*

**overburdened** /ˌəʊvəˈbɜːdᵊnd/ *adj* having too much to deal with *overburdened with work*

**overcame** /ˌəʊvəˈkeɪm/ *past tense of* overcome

**overcast** /ˈəʊvəkɑːst/ *adj* cloudy and dark *an overcast sky/day*

**overcharge** /ˌəʊvəˈtʃɑːdʒ/ *verb* [I, T] to charge someone too much money for something *The shop overcharged me by £5.*

**overcoat** /ˈəʊvəkəʊt/ *noun* [C] a long, warm coat

**overcome** /ˌəʊvəˈkʌm/ *verb past t* **overcame**, *past p* **overcome 1** [T] to deal with and control a problem or feeling *He's trying to overcome his drug addiction and find a job.* • *Let's hope she overcomes her shyness.* **2** be overcome by excitement/fear/sadness, etc to suddenly have too much of a feeling *She was overcome by emotion.* **3** be overcome by smoke/fumes, etc to become ill or weak because you have been breathing smoke or poisonous gas *One worker died when he was overcome by chemical fumes.*

**overcrowded** /ˌəʊvəˈkraʊdɪd/ *adj* containing too many people or things *an overcrowded classroom/prison* • overcrowding *noun* [U]

**overdo** /ˌəʊvəˈduː/ *verb* [T] *past t* **overdid**, *past p* **overdone** to do or use too much of something *I went to the gym yesterday, but I think I overdid it a bit.*

**overdone** /ˌəʊvəˈdʌn/ *adj* cooked for too long

**overdose** /ˈəʊvədəʊs/ *noun* [C] too much of a drug taken at one time *Her daughter died of a drug overdose.* • overdose /ˌəʊvəˈdəʊs/ *verb* [I]

**overdraft** /'əʊvədrɑːft/ *noun* [C] If you have an overdraft, you have taken more money out of your bank account than you had in it. *a £250 overdraft*

**overdrawn** /,əʊvə'drɔːn/ *adj* If you are overdrawn, you have taken more money out of your bank account than you had in it. *We've gone £200 overdrawn!*

**overdue** /,əʊvə'djuː/ *adj* happening later than expected *This decision is long overdue.*

**overestimate** /,əʊvə'restɪmeɪt/ *verb* [I, T] to guess or think that something is bigger or better than it really is *They overestimated her ability to do the job.* ⊃ Opposite **underestimate**.

**overflow** /,əʊvə'fləʊ/ *verb* **1** [I] If a container or a place overflows, the thing that is inside it starts coming out because it is too full. *The bath overflowed, and there's water all over the floor!* • *The bin was overflowing with rubbish.* **2** [I, T] to come out of a container or a place because it is too full *The river overflowed its banks after the heavy rainfall.* **3 overflow with confidence/happiness/love, etc** to have a lot of a quality or emotion • overflow /'əʊvəfləʊ/ *noun* [C, U]

**overflow**

**overgrown** /,əʊvə'grəʊn/ *adj* covered with plants that have become too big *an overgrown garden*

**overhang** /,əʊvə'hæŋ/ *verb* [T] *past* **overhung** to hang over something *overhanging branches*

**overhaul** /,əʊvə'hɔːl/ *verb* [T] to examine a machine or a system carefully and improve it or repair it *to overhaul an engine* • overhaul /'əʊvəhɔːl/ *noun* [C]

**overhead** /,əʊvə'hed/ *adj, adv* above you, usually in the sky *overhead power cables* • *A police helicopter was hovering overhead.*

**overheads** /'əʊvəhedz/ *UK* (*US* **overhead**) *noun* [plural] money that a company spends on its regular and necessary costs, for example rent and heating

**overhear** /,əʊvə'hɪər/ *verb* [T] *past* **overheard** to hear what someone is saying when they are not talking to you [+ doing sth] *I overheard him telling her he was leaving.*

**overheat** /,əʊvə'hiːt/ *verb* [I] to become too hot *The engine keeps overheating.*

**overhung** /,əʊvə'hʌŋ/ *past of* overhang

**overjoyed** /,əʊvə'dʒɔɪd/ *adj* very happy [+ to do sth] *He was overjoyed to hear from his old friend.*

**overkill** /'əʊvəkɪl/ *noun* [U] when something is done too much *Should I add an explanation or would that be overkill?*

**overlap¹** /,əʊvə'læp/ *verb* [I, T] **overlapping**, *past* **overlapped 1** If two subjects or activities overlap, they are the same in some way. *Although our job titles are different, our responsibilities overlap quite a lot.* **2** If two objects overlap, part of one covers part of the other. • overlap /'əʊvəlæp/ *noun* [C, U]

**overload** /,əʊvə'ləʊd/ *verb* [T] **1** to put too many people or things into or onto a vehicle [often passive] *The coach was overloaded with passengers.* **2** to give someone more work or problems than they can deal with

**overlook** /,əʊvə'lʊk/ *verb* [T] **1** VIEW to have a view of something from above *a balcony overlooking the sea* **2** NOT NOTICE to not notice or consider something *Two important facts have been overlooked in this case.* **3** FORGIVE to forgive or ignore someone's bad behaviour

**overly** /'əʊvəli/ *adv* in a way that is extreme or too much *overly optimistic* • *It wasn't overly expensive.*

**overnight** /,əʊvə'naɪt/ *adv* **1** for or during the night *Sometimes we would stay overnight at my grandmother's house.* **2** very quickly or suddenly *Change does not happen overnight.* • overnight *adj* [always before noun] *overnight rain* • *an overnight* (= sudden) *success*

**overpass** /'əʊvəpɑːs/ *US* (*UK* **flyover**) *noun* [C] a bridge that carries a road over another road

**overpower** /,əʊvə'paʊər/ *verb* [T] **1** to defeat someone by being stronger than they are [often passive] *The gunman was overpowered by two security guards.* **2** If a feeling, smell, etc overpowers you, it is very strong and makes you feel weak.

**overpowering** /,əʊvə'paʊərɪŋ/ *adj* unpleasantly strong or powerful *an overpowering smell*

**overpriced** /,əʊvə'praɪst/ *adj* too expensive

**overran** /,əʊvə'ræn/ *past tense of* overrun

**overrated** /,əʊvə'reɪtɪd/ *adj* If something is overrated, it is considered to be better or more important than it really is.

**overreact** /,əʊvəri'ækt/ *verb* [I] to react in a way that is more extreme than you should *She tends to overreact to criticism.*

**override** /,əʊvə'raɪd/ *verb* [T] *past t* **overrode**, *past p* **overridden 1** If someone in authority overrides a decision or order, they officially decide that it is wrong. *I don't have the power to override his decision.* **2** to be more important than something else *His desire for money seems to override anything else.*

**overriding** /,əʊvə'raɪdɪŋ/ *adj* [always before noun] more important than others *an overriding concern/reason*

**overrule** /,əʊvə'ruːl/ *verb* [T] If someone in authority overrules a decision or order, they officially decide that it is wrong. *Does the judge have the power to overrule the jury?*

**overrun** /,əʊvə'rʌn/ *verb* **overrunning**, *past t* **overran**, *past p* **overrun 1** [T] If something unpleasant overruns a place, it fills it in large numbers. [often passive] *The house was overrun by rats.* • *Troops overran the city.* **2** [I] *UK* to continue for a longer time than planned *Sorry I'm late, but the meeting overran by 20 minutes.*

**overseas** /ˌəʊvəˈsiːz/ *adj* [always before noun] in, to, or from another country *an overseas student* • overseas *adv to live/work overseas*

**oversee** /ˌəʊvəˈsiː/ *verb* [T] **overseeing**, *past t* **oversaw**, *past p* **overseen** to watch work as it is done in order to make certain that it is done correctly *A committee has been set up to oversee the project.*

**overshadow** /ˌəʊvəˈʃædəʊ/ *verb* [T] **1** to cause something to be less enjoyable [often passive] *The party was overshadowed by a family argument.* **2** to cause someone or something to seem less important or successful

**oversight** /ˈəʊvəsaɪt/ *noun* [C, U] a mistake that you make by not noticing something or by forgetting to do something

**oversleep** /ˌəʊvəˈsliːp/ *verb* [I] *past* **overslept** to sleep longer than you had intended

**overstate** /ˌəʊvəˈsteɪt/ *verb* [T] to talk about something in a way that makes it seem more important than it really is

**overstep** /ˌəʊvəˈstep/ *verb* **overstepping**, *past* **overstepped overstep the mark** to behave in a way that is not allowed or not acceptable

**overt** /əʊˈvɜːt/ *adj* done or shown publicly and not hidden *overt criticism* • overtly *adv overtly racist remarks*

**overtake** /ˌəʊvəˈteɪk/ *verb past t* **overtook**, *past p* **overtaken 1** [T] to become more successful than someone or something else *Tobacco has overtaken coffee to become the country's leading export.* **2** [I, T] to go past a vehicle or person that is going in the same direction *It's dangerous to overtake on a bend.*

**over-the-counter** /ˌəʊvəðəˈkaʊntəʳ/ *adj* [always before noun] Over-the-counter medicines can be bought in a shop without first visiting a doctor. • over-the-counter *adv Most of these tablets can be bought over-the-counter.*

**overthrow** /ˌəʊvəˈθrəʊ/ *verb* [T] *past t* **overthrew**, *past p* **overthrown** to remove someone from power by using force *They were accused of plotting to overthrow the government.* • overthrow /ˈəʊvəθrəʊ/ *noun* [no plural] *the overthrow of the government*

**overtime** /ˈəʊvətaɪm/ *noun* [U] extra time that you work after your usual working hours *unpaid overtime* • overtime *adv I have to work overtime tonight.*

**overtones** /ˈəʊvətəʊnz/ *noun* [plural] ideas that seem to be expressed but that are not stated directly *His speech had political overtones.*

**overtook** /ˌəʊvəˈtʊk/ *past tense of* overtake

**overture** /ˈəʊvətjʊəʳ/ *noun* [C] a piece of classical music that introduces another longer piece such as an opera

**overturn** /ˌəʊvəˈtɜːn/ *verb* **1 overturn a conviction/ruling/verdict, etc** to officially change a legal decision **2** [I, T] If something overturns or if you overturn something, it turns over onto its top or onto its side. *She overturned her car in the accident.*

**overview** /ˈəʊvəvjuː/ *noun* [C] a short descrip-

tion giving the most important facts about something *I'll just give you an overview of the job.*

**overweight** /ˌəʊvəˈweɪt/ *adj* too heavy or too fat *He's still a few pounds overweight.* ➲ *Opposite* **underweight**.

**overwhelm** /ˌəʊvəˈwelm/ *verb* [T] If a feeling or situation overwhelms someone, it has an effect that is too strong or extreme. [often passive] *She was overwhelmed by the excitement of it all.*

**overwhelming** /ˌəʊvəˈwelmɪŋ/ *adj* very strong in effect or large in amount *an overwhelming feeling of sadness* • *They won by an overwhelming majority.* • overwhelmingly *adv*

**overworked** /ˌəʊvəˈwɜːkt/ *adj* Someone who is overworked has to work too much. *We're overworked and underpaid.*

**ovulate** /ˈɒvjəleɪt/ *verb* [I] When a woman ovulates, her body produces eggs.

○━**owe** /əʊ/ *verb* [T] **1** to have to pay money back to someone [+ two objects] *You still owe me money.* • *He owes about £5000 to the bank.* **2 owe sb an apology/favour/drink, etc** to have to give something to someone because they deserve it *I think I owe you an apology.* • *Thanks, I owe you a drink for that.* **3 owe your existence/ success, etc to sb/sth** to have something or achieve something because of someone or something else *The museum owes much of its success to the present generation of young British artists.*

**owing to** *preposition* because of *The concert has been cancelled owing to lack of support.*

**owl** /aʊl/ *noun* [C] a bird that has large eyes and hunts small animals at night

○━**own**¹ /əʊn/ *adj, pronoun, determiner* **1** belonging to or done by a particular person or thing *It was my own idea.* • *Each student has their own dictionary.* • *Petra makes all her own clothes.* • *"Is that your mum's car?" "No, it's my own (= it belongs to me)."* **2 of your own** belonging to someone or something *I'll have a home of my own (= home belonging only to me) someday.* **3 (all) on your own a** alone *Jessica lives on her own.* **b** If you do something on your own, you do it without any help from other people. *She's raised three kids on her own.* **4 come into your/its own** to be very useful or successful *By the 1970s, Abrams was starting to come into his own as a soloist.* **5 get your own back (on sb)** *UK* to do something unpleasant to someone because they have done something unpleasant to you *He made me cry, but I got my own back when I stamped on his toy cars.* **6 hold your own** to be as successful as other people or things *She could always hold her own in political debates.*

○━**own**² /əʊn/ *verb* [T] to have something that legally belongs to you *The University owns a lot of the land around here.*

**own up** to admit that you have done something wrong [+ to + doing sth] *No one has owned up to breaking that window.*

**owner** /ˈəʊnəʳ/ *noun* [C] someone who legally owns something *a property owner* • ownership *noun* [U] when you own something

**ox** /ɒks/ *noun* [C] *plural* **oxen** a large, male cow, used especially in the past to pull farm vehicles

**oxygen** /ˈɒksɪdʒən/ *noun* [U] a gas that is in the air and that animals need to live

**oxymoron** /ˌɒksɪˈmɔːrɒn/ *noun* [C] two words used together, which mean two different or opposite things, such as 'bitter-sweet' or 'smart casual'

**oyster** /ˈɔɪstə/ *noun* [C] a sea creature that lives in a flat shell and is eaten as food

**oz** *written abbreviation for* ounce (= a unit for measuring weight) *an 8 oz steak*

**ozone** /ˈəʊzəʊn/ *noun* [U] a form of oxygen that has a powerful smell

**the 'ozone ,layer** *noun* the layer of ozone high above the Earth's surface that prevents the sun from harming the Earth

# P

**P, p** /piː/ the sixteenth letter of the alphabet

**p 1** *written abbreviation for* page *See diagram on p.135.* **2** *abbreviation for* penny or pence (= units of British money) *a 20p coin* ➔ *See usage note at* **pence.**

**pace¹** /peɪs/ *noun* **1** [no plural] the speed at which someone or something moves or does something *We started to walk at a much faster pace.* • the pace of life **2** [C] a step *Every few paces I stopped to listen.* **3 keep pace with sb/sth** to move or develop at the same speed as someone or something else *We have to keep pace with the changing times.* ➔ *See also:* at a **snail's** pace.

**pace²** /peɪs/ *verb* **1 pace about/up and down, etc** to walk around because you are worried or excited about something *He kept pacing up and down, glancing at his watch.* **2 pace yourself** to be careful not to do something too quickly so that you do not get too tired to finish it *You must learn to pace yourself if you want to win.*

**pacemaker** /'peɪsˌmeɪkəʳ/ *noun* [C] a small piece of medical equipment in someone's heart that makes it work at the correct speed

**pacifier** /'pæsɪfaɪəʳ/ *US* (*UK* **dummy**) *noun* [C] a small rubber object that you give to a baby to suck in order to make it calm

**pacifism** /'pæsɪfɪzᵊm/ *noun* [U] the belief that war or fighting of any type is wrong • **pacifist** /'pæsɪfɪst/ *noun* [C] someone who believes in pacifism

**pacify** /'pæsɪfaɪ/ *verb* [T] to do something in order to make someone less angry or upset *She smiled at Jamie to pacify him.*

o⟶**pack¹** /pæk/ *verb* **1** [I, T] to put your things into bags or boxes when you are going on holiday or leaving the place where you live *I've got to go home and pack.* • to pack your bags ➔ *Opposite* **unpack.** **2** [T] If people pack a place, there are so many of them in it that it is very crowded. *Thousands of fans packed the club.*

**pack sth in** *informal* to stop doing something *If this job doesn't get any better I'm going to pack it in.* **2** to manage to do a lot of things in a short period of time *We were only there four days but we packed so much in.*

**pack sb off** *informal* to send someone away *We were packed off to our grandparents' for the summer holidays.*

**pack (sth) up** to collect all your things together when you have finished doing something *I'm about to pack my things up and go home.*

**pack²** /pæk/ *noun* [C] **1** BOX *mainly US* a small box that contains several of the same thing *a pack of cigarettes* **2** BAG *mainly US* a bag that you carry on your back **3** ANIMALS a group of animals that live together, especially those of the dog family *a pack of wolves* **4** CARDS (*also US* **deck**) a set of playing cards ➔ *See also:* **fanny pack.**

**package¹** /'pækɪdʒ/ *noun* [C] **1** PARCEL an object that is covered in paper, inside a box, etc, espe-

cially so that it can be sent somewhere *He was carrying a package under his arm.* **2** GROUP OF THINGS a group of objects, plans, or arrangements that are sold or considered together *a computer package* • *This ski package includes hotel, transportation, and four days of skiing.* **3** BOX *US* a box or container in which something is put to be sold *a package of raisins/cookies*

**package**

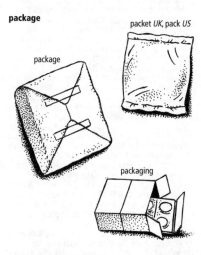

packet *UK*, pack *US*

package

packaging

**package²** /'pækɪdʒ/ *verb* [T] **1** to put something into a box or container so that it can be sold *It's neatly packaged in a blue and white box.* **2** to show someone or something in an attractive way so that people will like or buy them *What's important is the way we package the programme.*

**package holiday** *UK* (*UK/US* **package tour**) *noun* [C] a holiday that is arranged for you by a travel company and for which you pay a fixed price before you go *Package tours often offer the best value for money.*

**packaging** /'pækɪdʒɪŋ/ *noun* [U] the paper, box, etc that something is inside so that it can be sold or sent somewhere

**packed** /pækt/ (*also UK* **packed out**) *adj* very crowded *The hall was packed.*

**packed lunch** *noun* [C] *UK* food that you put in a bag or box and take to eat at work, school, etc

**packet** /'pækɪt/ *UK* (*US* **pack**) *noun* [C] a small container that contains several of the same thing *a packet of cigarettes/sweets*

**packing** /'pækɪŋ/ *noun* [U] **1** when you put things into bags or boxes in order to take them somewhere *I've got to do my packing because I'm going tomorrow.* **2** paper, material, etc that you put around an object in a box so that it does not get damaged

**pact** /pækt/ *noun* [C] an agreement between two people or groups *We have a pact never to talk about each other.*

**pad**[1] /pæd/ *noun* [C] **1** (*also US* **tablet**) sheets of paper that have been fastened together at one edge, used for writing or drawing *There's a pad and pencil by the phone.* **2** a small piece of soft material used to protect something or to make something comfortable *knee/shin pads*

**pad**[2] /pæd/ *verb* **padding**, *past* **padded 1 pad about/around/down, etc** to walk somewhere with small, quiet steps *He padded downstairs and out of the front door.* **2** [T] to protect something or make something more comfortable by filling or surrounding it with soft material

**pad sth out** to make a piece of writing or a speech longer by adding more information to it

**padding** /'pædɪŋ/ *noun* [U] soft material that is used to fill or cover something to protect it or make it more comfortable

**paddle**[1] /'pædl/ *noun* **1** [C] a short pole with one flat end that you use to make a small boat move through the water **2** [no plural] *UK* when you walk in water that is not deep *to go for a paddle*

**paddle**[2] /'pædl/ *verb* **1** BOAT [I, T] to move a small boat through water with a paddle **2** WALK [I] *UK* (*US* **wade**) to walk in water that is not deep **3** SWIM [I] *US* to swim using short, quick movements with your arms and legs

**paddock** /'pædək/ *noun* [C] a small field where animals are kept, especially horses

**paddy field** /'pædi,fiːld/ *UK* (*UK/US* **rice paddy**) *noun* [C] a field in which rice is grown

**padlock** /'pædlɒk/ *noun* [C] a metal lock with a U-shaped part that is used for fastening bicycles, doors, etc • padlock *verb* [T]

**paediatrician** *UK* (*US* **pediatrician**) /,piːdiə'trɪʃᵊn/ *noun* [C] a children's doctor

**paedophile** *UK* (*US* **pedophile**) /'piːdəʊfaɪl/ *noun* [C] someone who is sexually interested in children

**pagan** /'peɪɡᵊn/ *adj* relating to religious beliefs that do not belong to any of the main religions of the world *a pagan festival* • pagan *noun* [C] someone who has pagan religious beliefs

o-**page**[1] /peɪdʒ/ *noun* [C] **1** a piece of paper in a book, magazine, etc, or one side of a piece of paper *The article is on page 36.* • *I've only read 50 pages so far.* **2** (*also* **web page**) one part of a website (= area of information on the Internet) that you can view or print separately ➔ *See also:* **the Yellow Pages, home page.**

**page**[2] /peɪdʒ/ *verb* [T] **1** to call someone using a sound system in a public place **2** to send a message to someone's pager (= small piece of electronic equipment)

**pageant** /'pædʒənt/ *noun* [C] a show that happens outside in which people dress and act as if they are from a time in history

**pageantry** /'pædʒəntri/ *noun* [U] ceremonies in which there are a lot of people in special clothes

**pager** /'peɪdʒəʳ/ *noun* [C] a small piece of electronic equipment that you carry which makes a noise or movement when someone sends a message

**pagoda** /pə'ɡəʊdə/ *noun* [C] a tall religious building in Asia with many levels, each of which has a curved roof

**paid** /peɪd/ *past of* pay

**pail** /peɪl/ *noun* [C] a container with an open top and a handle used for carrying liquids

o-**pain**[1] /peɪn/ *noun* **1** [C, U] an unpleasant physical feeling caused by an illness or injury *chest/stomach pains* • *Are you in pain?* • *I felt a sharp pain in my foot.* • *She was given some medicine to ease the pain.* **2** [U] sadness or mental suffering caused by an unpleasant event *I can't describe the pain I suffered when he died.* **3 be a pain (in the neck)** *informal* to be annoying *My brother can be a real pain in the neck sometimes.* **4 be at pains to do sth; take pains to do sth** to make a lot of effort to do something *He was at great pains to explain the reasons for his decision.*

**pain**[2] /peɪn/ *verb* [T] *formal* If something pains you, it makes you feel sad or upset. [+ to do sth] *It pained him to see animals being treated so cruelly.*

**pained** /peɪnd/ *adj* appearing to be sad or upset *a pained expression*

o-**painful** /'peɪnfᵊl/ *adj* **1** causing physical pain *Recovery from the operation is a slow and painful process.* **2** making you feel sad or upset *a painful memory*

**painfully** /'peɪnfᵊli/ *adv* **1** in a painful way *He landed painfully on his elbow.* **2 painfully clear/obvious, etc** If a problem is painfully clear/obvious, etc, it is embarrassing because it is so clear/obvious, etc. *It was painfully obvious that she didn't like him.* **3** used to emphasize an unpleasant situation or quality *She's painfully thin.* • *Progress has been painfully slow.*

**painkiller** /'peɪn,kɪləʳ/ *noun* [C] a drug which reduces pain

**painless** /'peɪnləs/ *adj* **1** causing no physical pain *a painless death* **2** causing no problems or difficulties *There is no painless way of learning a language.* • painlessly *adv*

**painstaking** /'peɪnz,teɪkɪŋ/ *adj* done with a lot of care *It took months of painstaking research to write the book.* • painstakingly *adv*

o-**paint**[1] /peɪnt/ *noun* [C, U] a coloured liquid that you put on a surface to decorate it *a gallon of blue paint* • *The door needs another coat* (= layer) *of paint.*

o-**paint**[2] /peɪnt/ *verb* **1** [T] to cover a surface with paint in order to decorate it *We've painted the kitchen yellow.* **2** [I, T] to produce a picture of something or someone using paint *I learned to paint in Italy.* • *These pictures were all painted by local artists.* ➔ *See also:* paint a bleak/rosy, etc **picture**[1] of sth.

**paintbrush** /'peɪntbrʌʃ/ *noun* [C] a brush that is used for painting pictures or for painting surfaces such as walls and doors ➔ *See picture at* **brush.**

**painter** /'peɪntəʳ/ *noun* [C] **1** someone who paints pictures **2** someone whose job is to paint surfaces, such as walls and doors *a painter and decorator*

o-**painting** /'peɪntɪŋ/ *noun* **1** [C] a picture that someone has painted **2** [U] the activity of painting pictures or painting surfaces ➔ *See also:* **oil painting.**

o-**pair**[1] /peəʳ/ *noun* [C] **1** TWO THINGS two things that look the same and that are used together *a pair of socks/shoes* **2** TWO PARTS something that is made of two parts that are joined together *a pair of scissors* • *a new pair of jeans/trousers* **3** [TWO PEOPLE] two people who are doing something together *For the next exercise, you'll need to work in pairs.*

**pair**

a pair of trousers

a pair of scissors

a pair of gloves

**pair²** /peə<sup>r</sup>/ *verb*
**pair off** If two people pair off, they begin a romantic or sexual relationship. *By the end of the party, most people had paired off.*
**pair sb off with sb** to introduce one person to another because you hope they will begin a romantic relationship *Caroline tried to pair me off with her sister.*
**pair up** to join another person for a short time in order to do something *I paired up with Chris for the last dance.*

**pajamas** /pə'dʒɑːməz/ *noun* [plural] US spelling of pyjamas (= shirt and trousers that you wear in bed)

**pal** /pæl/ *noun* [C] informal a friend *He's an old pal of mine.*

**palace** /'pælɪs/ *noun* [C] a large house where a king or queen lives *Buckingham Palace* • *the presidential palace*

**palatable** /'pælətəbl/ *adj formal* **1** If food or drink is palatable, it has a pleasant taste. *a very palatable local wine* **2** If an idea or plan is palatable, it is acceptable. *They need to make the project more palatable to local people.* ⊃ *Opposite* **unpalatable.**

**palate** /'pælət/ *noun* [C] **1** the top part of the inside of your mouth **2** your ability to judge and enjoy good food and drink *For less sophisticated palates, the restaurant also serves burgers and fries.*

o━ᴵ**pale** /peɪl/ *adj* **1** pale blue/green/red, etc light blue/green/red, etc *a pale yellow dress* **2** If your face is pale, it has less colour than usual because you are ill or frightened. *You're looking a bit pale – are you all right?*

**pall¹** /pɔːl/ *verb* [I] to become less interesting and enjoyable *The pleasure of not having to work soon began to pall.*

**pall²** /pɔːl/ *noun* **1 a pall of dust/smoke, etc** a thick cloud of dust/smoke, etc **2 cast a pall over sth** If an unpleasant situation or piece of news casts a pall over an event, it spoils it. *The*

news of Nick's accident cast a pall over the celebrations.

**palm¹** /pɑːm/ *noun* [C] **1** the inside surface of your hand ⊃ *See colour picture* **The Body** *on page Centre 2.* **2** a palm tree

**palm²** /pɑːm/ *verb*
**palm sb off** to tell someone something that is not true so that they will stop asking questions *He palmed me off with an excuse about why he couldn't pay.*
**palm sth off as sth** to deceive people by saying that something has a particular quality or value that it does not have
**palm sth off on sb** to give or sell something to someone because you want to get rid of it *He palmed his old computer off on me.*

**'palm ,tree** *noun* [C] a tall tree with long leaves at the top which grows in hot countries

**palpable** /'pælpəbl/ *adj* very obvious *There was a palpable sense of tension in the crowd.*

**paltry** /'pɔːltri/ *adj* A paltry amount of something, especially money, is very small. *a paltry sum of money*

**pamper** /'pæmpə<sup>r</sup>/ *verb* [T] to treat someone in a kind way and give them everything they want *She pampered herself with a trip to the beauty salon.*

**pamphlet** /'pæmflɪt/ *noun* [C] a very thin book with a paper cover that gives information about something *The tourist office gave me a pamphlet about places to visit in the city.*

**pan¹** /pæn/ *noun* [C] a metal container with a handle that is used for cooking food in ⊃ *See also:* a **flash²** in the pan, **frying pan.**

**pan²** /pæn/ *verb* [T] **panning,** past **panned** *informal* to criticize something severely [often passive] *His last novel was panned by the critics.*
**pan out** to develop in a particular way *Not all his ideas had panned out in the way he would have liked.*

**panacea** /ˌpænə'siːə/ *noun* [C] something that people believe can solve all their problems

**panache** /pə'næʃ/ *noun* [U] a confident and attractive way of doing things *The orchestra played with great panache.*

**pancake** /'pænkeɪk/ *noun* [C] a thin, flat food made from flour, milk, and egg mixed together and cooked in a pan

**panda** /'pændə/ *noun* [C] a large, black and white animal that lives in forests in China

**pandemonium** /ˌpændə'məʊniəm/ *noun* [U] when there is a lot of noise and confusion because people are angry or excited about something that has happened *Pandemonium broke out in the courtroom as they took him away.*

**pander** /'pændə<sup>r</sup>/ *verb*
**pander to sb/sth** to do what someone wants although it is wrong *He said he would not pander to public pressure.*

**pane** /peɪn/ *noun* [C] a flat piece of glass in a window or door

**panel** /'pænªl/ *noun* [C] **1** [PIECE] a flat, rectangular piece of wood, metal, etc that forms the surface of a door, wall, etc **2** [PEOPLE] a group of people who are chosen to discuss something or make a decision about something *a panel of experts* **3** [CONTROLS] the part of a car, aircraft, etc that the controls are fixed to ➔ *See also:* **solar panel.**

**panelling** UK (US **paneling**) /'pænəlɪŋ/ *noun* [U] flat, rectangular pieces of wood that form the surface of walls, doors, etc *carved oak panelling*

**panellist** UK (US **panelist**) /'pænəlɪst/ *noun* [C] one of a group of people who are chosen to discuss something or make a decision about something

**pang** /pæŋ/ *noun* [C] a sudden, strong feeling of an unpleasant emotion *Bernard felt a sharp pang of jealousy.*

**panhandle** /'pæn,hændl/ *verb* [I] US to ask people for money in a public place ● panhandler *noun* [C] US

**panic¹** /'pænɪk/ *noun* [C, U] a sudden, strong feeling of worry or fear that makes you unable to think or behave calmly *He was in a panic about his exams.* ● *She had a panic attack* (= suddenly felt extreme panic) *in the supermarket.*

**panic²** /'pænɪk/ *verb* [I, T] **panicking,** *past* **panicked** to suddenly feel so worried or frightened that you cannot think or behave calmly, or to make someone feel this way *Don't panic, we've got plenty of time.* ● *You panicked me by telling me I was late.*

**panic-stricken** /'pænɪk,strɪkən/ *adj* extremely frightened

**panorama** /,pænər'ɑːmə/ *noun* [C] a view of a wide area

**panoramic** /,pænər'æmɪk/ *adj* A panoramic view is very wide. *a panoramic view of the city*

**pansy** /'pænzi/ *noun* [C] a small garden flower with round petals which can be many different colours

**pant** /pænt/ *verb* [I] to breathe quickly and loudly because it is hot or because you have been running, etc

**panther** /'pænθər/ *noun* [C] a large, black, wild cat

**panties** /'pæntiz/ *mainly US* (UK **knickers**) *noun* [plural] women's underwear that covers the bottom ➔ *See usage note at* **underwear.**

**pantomime** /'pæntəmaɪm/ *noun* [C, U] a funny play performed in the UK around Christmas, based on traditional children's stories

**pantry** /'pæntri/ *noun* [C] a small room where food is kept

**pants** /pænts/ *noun* [plural] **1** US (UK/US **trousers**) a piece of clothing that covers the legs and has a separate part for each leg **2** UK (US **underpants**) underwear that covers the bottom ➔ *See colour picture* **Clothes** *on page Centre 5.* ➔ *See usage note at* **underwear.**

**'pant ,suit** US (UK **trouser suit**) *noun* [C] a woman's jacket and trousers made of the same material

**pantyhose** /'pæntihəʊz/ US (UK **tights**) *noun* [plural] a piece of women's clothing made of very thin material that covers the legs and bottom ➔ *See colour picture* **Clothes** *on page Centre 5.*

**papa** /pə'pɑː/ *noun* [C] *old-fashioned another word* for father

**the papacy** /'peɪpəsi/ *noun* the position or authority of the Pope (= leader of the Roman Catholic Church)

**papal** /'peɪpl/ *adj* relating to the Pope (= leader of the Roman Catholic Church)

○━ **paper¹** /'peɪpər/ *noun* **1** [MATERIAL] [U] thin, flat material used for writing on, covering things in, etc *a piece/sheet of paper* **2** [NEWSPAPER] [C] a newspaper *I buy a paper every morning.* **3** [EXAM] [C] UK an examination *Candidates must answer two questions from each paper.* **4** [WRITING] [C] a piece of writing about a particular subject written by someone who has been studying that subject *She's just published a paper on language acquisition.* ➔ *See also:* **White Paper, blotting paper, carbon paper, toilet paper, wrapping paper.**

**paper²** /'peɪpər/ *verb* [T] to decorate the walls of a room by covering them with paper

**paperback** /'peɪpəbæk/ *noun* [C] a book that has a soft paper cover

**'paper ,clip** *noun* [C] a small piece of metal used to hold several pieces of paper together ➔ *See colour picture* **The Office** *on page Centre 12.*

**papers** /'peɪpəz/ *noun* [plural] official documents *I keep all my papers safely locked away.*

**'paper ,weight** *noun* [C] a small, heavy object that you put on top of pieces of paper to stop them from moving

**paperwork** /'peɪpəwɜːk/ *noun* [U] the part of a job that involves writing letters, organizing information, etc

**par** /pɑːr/ *noun* **1 be on a par with sb/sth** to be the same as or equal to someone or something **2 below par** not as good as usual *I'm feeling a bit below par today.* **3 be par for the course** If a type of behaviour, event, or situation is par for the course, it not good but it is normal or as you would expect. *"Simon was late." "That's just par for the course, isn't it?"*

**parable** /'pærəbl/ *noun* [C] a short story, especially in the Bible, that shows you how you should behave

**parachute** /'pærəʃuːt/ *noun* [C] a large piece of cloth which is fixed to your body by strings and helps you to drop safely from an aircraft ● parachute *verb* [I] to jump from an aircraft using a parachute

parachute

**parade¹** /pə'reɪd/ *noun* [C] a line of people or vehicles that moves through a public place as a way of celebrating an occasion *a victory parade*

**parade²** /pə'reɪd/ *verb* **1 parade down/ past/through sth** to walk as a group, usually to show disagreement about something *Thousands of workers paraded through the streets.* **2 parade around/up and down, etc** to walk somewhere so that people will see and admire you *The kids were parading around in their new clothes.* **3** [T] to try to make someone notice something that you are proud of, especially how rich you are or how much you know

**paradigm** /'pærədaɪm/ *noun* [C] *formal* a typical example or model of something *Career women are establishing a new paradigm of work and family life.*

**paradise** /'pærədaɪs/ *noun* **1** [no plural] in some religions, a place where good people go after they die **2** [C, U] a perfect place or situation *a tropical paradise* • *a shoppers' paradise*

**paradox** /'pærədɒks/ *noun* [C] a situation that seems very strange or impossible because of two opposite qualities or facts • paradoxical /ˌpærə'dɒksɪkᵊl/ *adj* involving a paradox *It seems paradoxical to me but if you drink hot tea, it seems to cool you down.* • paradoxically *adv*

**paraffin** /'pærəfɪn/ *UK* (*US* **kerosene**) *noun* [U] oil used for heating and lights

**paragraph** /'pærəɡrɑːf/ *noun* [C] a part of a text that contains at least one sentence and starts on a new line

**parallel¹** /'pærəlel/ *adj* **1** If two or more lines are parallel, the distance between them is the same along all their length. *The streets are parallel.* **2** similar and happening at the same time *Parallel experiments are being conducted in both countries.*

**parallel²** /'pærəlel/ *noun* [C] a similarity *There are a number of* **parallels between** *our two situations.* • *People are* **drawing parallels** (= describing similarities) *between the two cases.*

**paralyse** *UK* (*US* **paralyze**) /'pærᵊlaɪz/ *verb* [T] **1** to make someone unable to move all or part of their body [often passive] *He was paralysed from the waist down by polio.* **2** to make something stop working *Rail strikes have paralysed the city's transport system.*

**paralysed** *UK* (*US* **paralyzed**) /'pærᵊlaɪzd/ *adj* **1** unable to move all or part of your body because of an injury or illness **2** unable to move or speak because you are so frightened *to be paralysed with fear*

**paralysis** /pə'ræləsɪs/ *noun* [U] **1** being unable to move all or part of your body because of injury or illness *muscular paralysis* **2** not being able to take action *political paralysis*

**paralyze** /'pærᵊlaɪz/ *verb* [T] *US spelling of* paralyse

**paramedic** /ˌpærə'medɪk/ *noun* [C] someone who is trained to give medical treatment to people who are injured or very ill, but who is not a doctor or nurse

**parameter** /pə'ræmɪtər/ *noun* [C] a limit that controls the way you can do something [usually plural] *Before we can start the research we need to* **set** *some* **parameters** (= decide some limits).

**paramilitaries** /ˌpærə'mɪlɪtᵊriz/ *noun* [plural] people who belong to paramilitary organizations

**paramilitary** /ˌpærə'mɪlɪtᵊri/ *adj* [always before noun] organized like an army, but not belonging to an official army *a paramilitary organization/group*

**paramount** /'pærəmaʊnt/ *adj formal* more important than anything else *Safety, of course,*

is paramount. • *Communication is of* **paramount importance**.

**paranoia** /ˌpærə'nɔɪə/ *noun* [U] **1** when you wrongly think that other people do not like you and are always criticizing you *Do you think his boss really hates him or is it just paranoia?* **2** a mental illness that makes people wrongly think that other people are trying to harm them • paranoid /'pærᵊnɔɪd/ *adj* when you have paranoia *Stop being so paranoid – no one's talking about you.*

**paraphernalia** /ˌpærəfə'neɪliə/ *noun* [U] all the objects used in a particular activity *the painter's paraphernalia of brushes, paints, and pencils*

**paraphrase** /'pærəfreɪz/ *verb* [I, T] to express something that has been said or written in a different way, usually so that it is clearer • paraphrase *noun* [C]

**parasite** /'pærəsaɪt/ *noun* [C] **1** a plant or animal that lives on or inside another plant or animal in order to get food **2** a lazy person who expects other people to give them money and food

**paratrooper** /'pærətruːpər/ *noun* [C] a soldier who is trained to be dropped from an aircraft using a parachute (= large piece of cloth fixed to the body by strings)

○⚊**parcel** /'pɑːsᵊl/ *noun* [C] something that is covered in paper so that it can be sent by post ⊃ *See also:* **part¹** and parcel.

**parched** /pɑːtʃt/ *adj* **1 be parched** *informal* to be very thirsty *I'm going to get a drink – I'm parched.* **2** very dry *a parched desert/land*

**pardon¹** /'pɑːdᵊn/ *exclamation* **1** (*also US* **pardon me**) a polite way of asking someone to repeat what they have just said *"You'll need an umbrella." "Pardon?" "I said you'll need an umbrella."* **2 Pardon me.** used to say 'sorry' after you have done something rude, for example after burping (= letting air from your stomach out of your mouth)

**pardon²** /'pɑːdᵊn/ *noun* **1** [C] when someone who has committed a crime is officially forgiven and allowed to be free **2 I beg your pardon.** *formal spoken* **a** used for saying 'sorry' when you have made a mistake or done something wrong *I beg your pardon – I thought you were speaking to me.* **b** used to show that you strongly disagree or that you are angry about something that someone has said *I beg your pardon young man – I don't want to hear you speak like that again!*

**pardon³** /'pɑːdᵊn/ *verb* [T] to officially forgive someone who has committed a crime and allow them to be free

○⚊**parent** /'peᵊrᵊnt/ *noun* [C] your mother or father *Her parents live in Oxford.* • parental /pə'rentᵊl/ *adj* relating to a parent *parental responsibility*

**parentheses** /pə'renθəsiːz/ (*also UK* **brackets**) *noun* [plural] two curved lines ( ) used around extra information or information that should be considered as separate from the main part *The age of each student is listed* **in parentheses**.

**parenthood** /'peᵊrᵊnthʊd/ *noun* [U] being a parent *the demands of parenthood* • *single parenthood*

**parish** /'pærɪʃ/ *noun* [C] an area that has its own church

P

**parishioner** /pəˈrɪʃ°nə°/ noun [C] someone who lives in a parish and often goes to church

**parity** /ˈpærəti/ noun [U] formal equality, usually relating to the money people earn or their position *The union has also asked for wage parity with similar public-sector workers.* ⊃ Opposite **disparity**.

O▪**park¹** /pɑːk/ noun [C] a large area of grass, often in a town, where people can walk and enjoy themselves *We went for a walk in the park.* ⊃ See also: **amusement park**, **car park**, **industrial park**, **national park**, **theme park**, **trailer park**.

O▪**park²** /pɑːk/ verb [I, T] to leave a vehicle in a particular place for a period of time *I parked the car near the old bridge.* • *You can park outside the school.*

**parking** /ˈpɑːkɪŋ/ noun [U] leaving a vehicle in a particular place for a period of time *free/underground parking*

ˈ**parking ˌlot** US (UK **car park**) noun [C] a place where vehicles can be parked

O▪**parliament** /ˈpɑːləmənt/ noun [C, U] in some countries, a group of people who make the laws for the country *the Russian parliament* • parliamentary /ˌpɑːləˈment°ri/ adj [always before noun] relating to a parliament *a parliamentary candidate/election* ⊃ See also: **Houses of Parliament**, **Member of Parliament**.

**parlour** UK (US **parlor**) /ˈpɑːlə°/ noun [C] a shop that provides a particular type of goods or services *a beauty/pizza parlour*

**parody** /ˈpærədi/ noun [C, U] a film, book, etc that copies someone else's style in a way that is funny *It's a parody of a low-budget 1950's horror movie.* • parody verb [T]

**parole** /pəˈrəʊl/ noun [U] when someone is allowed to leave prison early but is only allowed to remain free if they behave well *He's hoping to get released on parole.*

**parrot** /ˈpærət/ noun [C] a tropical bird with a curved beak and colourful feathers that can be taught to copy what people say

**parsimonious** /ˌpɑːsɪˈməʊniəs/ adj formal not willing to spend money or give something

**parsley** /ˈpɑːsli/ noun [U] a herb that is added to food to give it flavour

**parsnip** /ˈpɑːsnɪp/ noun [C] a long, cream-coloured root that is eaten as a vegetable

O▪**part¹** /pɑːt/ noun 1 NOT ALL [C, U] one of the things that, with other things, makes the whole of something *Part of this form seems to be missing.* • *That's only part of the problem.* • *I did French as part of my degree course.* • *It's all part of growing up.* • *You're part of the family.* 2 **take part (in sth)** to be involved in an activity with other people *She doesn't usually take part in any of the class activities.* 3 FILM/PLAY [C] a person in a film or play *He writes good parts for women.* • *He plays the part of the father.* 4 **have/play a part in sth** to be one of the people or things that are involved in an event or situation *Did you have any part in this production?* • *Alcohol plays a part in 60 percent of violent crime.* 5 MACHINE [C] a piece of a machine or vehicle *aircraft parts* • *spare parts* 6 HAIR [C] US (UK **parting**) the line on your head made by brushing your hair in two

different directions 7 **the best/better part of sth** most of a period of time *It took the better part of the afternoon to put those shelves up.* 8 **in part** formal partly *He is in part to blame for the accident.* 9 **for the most part** mostly or usually *I enjoyed it for the most part.* 10 **look the part** to look suitable for a particular situation *If you're going to be a successful business-woman, you've got to look the part.* 11 **part and parcel** If something is part and parcel of an experience, it is a necessary part of that experience and cannot be avoided. *Stress is part and parcel of the job.*

**part²** /pɑːt/ adv not completely *She's part Irish and part English.*

**part³** /pɑːt/ verb 1 SEPARATE [I, T] If two sides of something part, they become separated, and if you part them, you make them separate. *Slowly her lips parted and she smiled.* 2 LEAVE [I, T] formal If two people part, or if one person parts from another, they leave each other. *That summer, after six years of marriage, we parted.* • *Even after we parted company, we remained in contact.* 3 HAIR [T] to brush your hair in two directions so that there is a straight line showing on your head *In my school days, I had long hair parted in the middle.*

**part with sth** to give something to someone else, often when you do not want to *You know how hard it is to get Simon to part with his money.*

**partial** /ˈpɑːʃ°l/ adj 1 not complete *He made a partial recovery.* 2 **be partial to sth** If you are partial to something, you like it. *I'm rather partial to red wine myself.*

**partially** /ˈpɑːʃ°li/ adv not completely *partially cooked*

**participant** /pɑːˈtɪsɪp°nt/ noun [C] someone who is involved in an activity *All participants finishing the race will receive a medal.*

**participate** /pɑːˈtɪsɪpeɪt/ verb [I] to be involved with other people in an activity *She rarely participates in any of the discussions.* • participation /pɑːˌtɪsɪˈpeɪʃ°n/ noun [U] *Both shows encourage audience participation.*

**participle** /pɑːˈtɪsɪpl/ (US) /ˈpɑːtɪsɪpl/ noun [C] the form of a verb that usually ends with '-ed' or '-ing' and is used in some verb tenses or as an adjective ⊃ See also: **past participle**, **present participle**.

**particle** /ˈpɑːtɪkl/ noun [C] a very small piece of something *particles of dust*

O▪**particular** /pəˈtɪkjələ°/ adj 1 ONE PERSON/THING [always before noun] used to talk about one thing or person and not others *Is there any particular restaurant you'd like to go to?* • *"Why did you ask?" "No particular reason."* • *I can't remember what he said on that particular occasion.* 2 SPECIAL [always before noun] special *"Was anything important said at the meeting?" "Nothing of particular interest."* 3 NOT EASILY SATISFIED [never before noun] choosing things carefully and not easily satisfied *Teenagers are very particular about the clothes they'll wear.* 4 **in particular** especially *For Hilary in particular it was interesting.* • *Are you looking for anything in particular?*

O▪**particularly** /pəˈtɪkjələli/ adv especially *She*

*didn't seem particularly interested.* • *"Was the food good?" "Not particularly."*

**particulars** /pəˈtɪkjələz/ *noun* [plural] *formal* details about something or someone *There's a form for you to note down all your particulars.*

**parting**[1] /ˈpɑːtɪŋ/ *noun* **1** [C, U] *formal* when you are separated from another person, often for a long time *The pain of parting gradually lessened over the years.* **2** [C] *UK* (*US* **part**) the line on your head made by brushing your hair in two different directions

**parting**[2] /ˈpɑːtɪŋ/ *adj* **parting glance/words, etc** something that you do or say as you leave

**partisan**[1] /ˌpɑːtɪˈzæn/ ⓤⓢ /ˈpɑːrtɪzən/ *adj* showing support for a particular political system or leader *partisan politics* • *a partisan crowd*

**partisan**[2] /ˌpɑːtɪˈzæn/ ⓤⓢ /ˈpɑːrtɪzən/ *noun* [C] **1** someone who supports a particular political system or leader **2** a member of a group that secretly fights against soldiers who are controlling their country

**partition** /pɑːˈtɪʃᵊn/ *noun* **1** [C] a wall that divides a room into two parts **2** [U] when a country divides into two or more countries or areas of government • **partition** *verb* [T]

o-**partly** /ˈpɑːtli/ *adv* used to show that something is true to some degree but not completely *The house is partly owned by her father.* • *He was partly responsible.*

o-**partner**[1] /ˈpɑːtnəʳ/ *noun* [C] **1** RELATIONSHIP someone that you are married to or having a sexual relationship with *sexual partners* • *Are partners invited to the office dinner?* **2** SPORTS/ DANCING someone that you are dancing or playing a sport or game with **3** BUSINESS someone who owns a business with another person *a junior/senior partner* • *He's a* **partner in** *a law firm.* **4** COUNTRY a country that has an agreement with another country *a trading partner* • *Britain and its European partners*

**partner**[2] /ˈpɑːtnəʳ/ *verb* [T] to be someone's partner in a dance, sport, or game *He looks certain to partner him again in the finals.*

**partnership** /ˈpɑːtnəʃɪp/ *noun* **1** [C, U] when two people or organizations work together to achieve something *She's* **gone into partnership** (= started to work together) *with an ex-colleague.* **2** [C] a company which is owned by two or more people

**part-time** /ˌpɑːtˈtaɪm/ *adj, adv* working or studying only for part of the day or the week *a part-time job/student* • *He works part-time as a waiter.*

o-**party**[1] /ˈpɑːti/ *noun* [C] **1** EVENT an event where people enjoy themselves by talking, eating, drinking, and dancing *a birthday party* • *We're* **having** *a* **party** *to celebrate the occasion.* **2** POL- ITICS an organization that shares the same political beliefs and tries to win elections *a political party* **3** GROUP a group of people who are working or travelling together *a party of tourists* **4** LEGAL one of the sides in a legal agreement or disagreement *the guilty party* • *We hope to provide a solution that is acceptable to both parties.* ⊃ *See also:* **the Conservative Party**, **the Democratic Party**, **the Green Party**, **the Labour Party**, **the**

**Republican Party**, toe the party **line**[1], **search party**, **slumber party**, **third party**.

**party**[2] /ˈpɑːti/ *verb* [I] to enjoy yourself by talking, eating, drinking, and dancing with a group of people *They were out partying till five o'clock in the morning.*

o-**pass**[1] /pɑːs/ *verb* **1** GO PAST [I, T] (*also* **pass by**) to go past something or someone *She passed me this morning in the corridor.* • *I was just passing by so I thought I'd stop and say hello.* • *Cars kept passing us on the motorway.* **2** **pass (sth) over/through, etc** to go in a particular direction, or to cause something to go in a particular direction *Another plane passed over our heads.* • *We pass through your village on the way home.* **3** GIVE [T] to give something to someone *Could you pass the salt, please?* • *He* **passed** *a note* **to** *her in the meeting.* **4** TIME [I] If a period of time passes, it happens. *Four years have passed since that day.* **5** **pass (the) time** to spend time doing something *She was eating only to pass the time.* **6** EXAM [I, T] to succeed at a test or an exam, or to decide that someone has been successful *I passed my driving test the first time.* • *The examiner passed her because her spoken English was so good.* **7** BE MORE THAN [T] to be more than a particular level *Donations have passed the one million mark.* **8** SPORTS [I, T] in sports, to throw or kick a ball to someone else *Edwards* **passes to** *Brinkworth.* **9** **pass a law/motion, etc** to officially approve of something and make it into a law or rule *They passed a law banning the sale of alcohol.* **10** GO AWAY [I] If a feeling passes, it goes away. *I know he's angry now but it'll pass.* **11** **pass judgment** to judge someone's behaviour **12** **pass sentence** If a judge passes sentence, they state what the criminal's punishment will be. **13** **let sth pass** to decide not to criticize someone when they say something unpleasant or they make a mistake ⊃ *See also:* pass the **buck**[1].

**pass sth around/round** to offer something to each person in a group of people *Take a copy for yourself and pass the rest around.*

**pass as/for sth/sb** If someone or something passes as or for someone or something else, they appear like that person or thing. *She's fifteen but could easily pass for eighteen.*

**pass away** to die *She passed away peacefully in her sleep.*

**pass sth down** to teach or give something to someone who will be alive after you have died [often passive] *Folk tales have been passed down from generation to generation.*

**pass sth/sb off as sth/sb** to pretend that something or someone is different from what they really are *He tried to pass himself off as some sort of expert.*

**pass on** to die *He passed on almost ten years ago.*

**pass sth on 1** TELL to tell someone something that someone else has told you *Did you pass on my message to him?* **2** GIVE to give something to someone else *Could you pass it on to Laura when you've finished reading it?* **3** DISEASE to give a disease to another person *The virus can be passed on through physical contact.*

**pass out** to become unconscious *I don't remem-*

*ber any more because I passed out at that point.*
**pass sth up** to not use an opportunity to do something interesting *It's a great opportunity – you'd be a fool to pass it up.*

**pass²** /pɑːs/ *noun* [C] **1** TEST a successful result in a test or a course *A pass is above 60%.* **2** DOCUMENT an official document that allows you to do something *a bus/rail pass* • *You need a pass to get into the building.* **3** SPORTS in sports, when you throw or kick a ball to someone else **4** PATH a narrow path between two mountains *a mountain pass* ➔ See also: **boarding pass.**

**passage** /'pæsɪdʒ/ *noun* **1** SPACE [C] (*also* **passageway** /'pæsɪdʒweɪ/) a long, narrow space that connects one place to another *There's a passage to the side of the house, leading to the garden.* **2** WRITING/MUSIC [C] a short part of a book, speech, or piece of music *She can quote whole passages from the novel.* **3** TUBE [C] a tube in your body that allows air, liquid, etc to pass through it *the nasal/respiratory passages* **4** PROGRESS [U, no plural] the movement or progress from one stage or place to another *It's a difficult passage from boyhood to manhood.* **5 the passage of time** *literary* the way that time passes *Love changes with the passage of time.*

**passenger** /'pæsᵊndʒəʳ/ *noun* [C] someone who is travelling in a vehicle, but not controlling the vehicle *a front-seat passenger* • *a passenger seat/train*

**passer-by** /ˌpɑːsə'baɪ/ *noun* [C] *plural* **passers-by** someone who is walking past something by chance *Police were alerted by a passer-by who saw the accident.*

**passing¹** /'pɑːsɪŋ/ *adj* [always before noun] lasting only for a short time and not important *a passing interest/thought*

**passing²** /'pɑːsɪŋ/ *noun* **1 the passing of time/years** the way that time passes *With the passing of time their love had changed.* **2 in passing** If you say something in passing, you talk about one thing briefly while talking mainly about something else. *She mentioned in passing that she'd seen Stuart.*

**passion** /'pæʃᵊn/ *noun* **1** [U] a strong, sexual feeling for someone *She saw the passion in his eyes.* **2** [C, U] a strong belief in something or a strong feeling about a subject *She spoke with passion about the injustice.* **3 a passion for sth** when you like something very much *a passion for football*

**passionate** /'pæʃᵊnət/ *adj* **1** having a strong, sexual feeling for someone *a passionate affair/lover* **2** showing a strong belief in something or a strong feeling about a subject *a passionate speaker* • **passionately** *adv*

**passive** /'pæsɪv/ *adj* **1** letting things happen to you and not taking action *Women at that time were expected to be passive.* **2** A passive verb or sentence is one in which the subject does not do or cause the action but is affected by it. For example 'He was released from prison.' is a passive sentence.

**the passive** /'pæsɪv/ (*also* **the ˌpassive 'voice**) *noun* the passive form of a verb

**ˌpassive 'smoking** *noun* [U] breathing in smoke from other people's cigarettes

**Passover** /'pɑːsˌəʊvəʳ/ *noun* [U] the Jewish period of religious celebration held in March or April

**passport** /'pɑːspɔːt/ *noun* **1** [C] an official document, often a small book, that you need to enter or leave a country *a British passport* **2 a passport to sth** something that allows you to achieve something else *Education is a passport to a better life.*

**password** /'pɑːswɜːd/ *noun* [C] a secret word that allows you to do something, such as use your computer

o━ᴬ**past¹** /pɑːst/ *adj* **1** BEFORE NOW [always before noun] having happened or existed before now *past relationships* • *I know this from past experience.* **2** UNTIL NOW [always before noun] used to refer to a period of time before and until the present *I've spent the past ten years in and out of jobs.* • *It's been raining for the past three days.* **3** FINISHED [never before noun] Something that is past has now finished. *My student days are past.* **4 past tense** the form of the verb which is used to show what happened in the past

o━ᴬ**past²** /pɑːst/ *noun* **1 the past a** the time before the present and all the things that happened then *the distant/recent past* • *In the past people would bathe once a month.* **b** the form of the verb which is used to show what happened in the past **2 sb's past** all of the things that someone has done in their life *I knew nothing about his past.*

o━ᴬ**past³** /pɑːst/ *adv, preposition* **1** FURTHER further than *I live on Station Road, just past the Post Office.* **2** UP TO AND FURTHER up to and further than someone or something *Three boys went past us on mountain bikes.* • *I've just seen the bus go past.* **3** AFTER HOUR used to say 'after' the hour when you are saying what time it is *It's five past three.* **4** AFTER LIMIT after a particular time or age limit *This bacon is past its sell-by date.* **5 past it** *informal* too old to do something **6 I wouldn't put it past sb (to do sth)** *informal* used to say that you would not be surprised if someone did something, especially something bad, because it is a typical thing for them to do *I wouldn't put it past him to sell her jewellery.*

**pasta** /'pæstə ⑤ 'pɑːstə/ *noun* [U] a food that is made from flour, water, and sometimes eggs and is made in many different shapes *Spaghetti's my favourite pasta.* ➔ See colour picture **Food** on page Centre 7.

**paste¹** /peɪst/ *noun* [C, U] **1** a soft, wet, sticky substance that is used to stick things together *wallpaper paste* **2** a soft food that spreads easily *tomato/almond paste*

**paste²** /peɪst/ *verb* [T] to stick a piece of paper to another piece of paper *The cuttings had been pasted into a scrapbook.* ➔ See also: **cut and paste.**

**pastel** /'pæstᵊl ⑤ pæs'tel/ *adj* A pastel colour is light. *pastel colours/shades* • *pastel pink* • **pastel** *noun* [C] *The bedroom is decorated in pastels* (= pale colours).

**pastime** /'pɑːstaɪm/ *noun* [C] an activity that you enjoy doing when you are not working *Shopping is one of her favourite pastimes.*

**pastor** /'pɑːstəʳ/ *noun* [C] a priest in some Protestant churches

**pastoral** /'pɑːstᵊrᵊl/ adj **1** related to giving advice and looking after people *the teacher's pastoral role* **2** [always before noun] *literary* relating to life in the country *a pastoral song/tradition*

,**past par'ticiple** UK (US ,**past 'participle**) noun [C] the form of a verb that usually ends with '-ed' and can be used in the perfect tense, the passive tense, or as an adjective. For example 'baked' is the past participle of 'bake'.

**the ,past 'perfect** (also **the pluperfect**) noun the form of a verb that is used to show that an action had already finished when another action happened. In English, the past perfect is made with 'had' and a past participle.

**pastry** /'peɪstri/ noun **1** [U] a mixture of flour, fat, and water that is cooked, usually used to cover or contain other food **2** [C] a small cake that is made with pastry

**pasture** /'pɑːstʃər/ noun [C] an area of land with grass where animals can feed

**pat**[1] /pæt/ verb [T] **patting**, *past* **patted** to touch a person or animal with a flat hand in a gentle, friendly way *She stopped to pat the dog.*

**pat**[2] /pæt/ noun **1** [C] when you pat a person or animal *He gave her an encouraging **pat on** the shoulder.* **2 a pat on the back** praise for something good that someone has done *I got a pat on the back for all my hard work.*

**patch**[1] /pætʃ/ noun [C] **1** AREA a small area that is different from the area around it *a bald patch.* • *There are icy patches on the road.* **2** MATERIAL a piece of material that you use to cover a hole in your clothes or in other material *He had leather patches sewn on the elbows of his jacket.* **3** EYE a small piece of material used to cover an injured eye **4** LAND a small area of land used for a particular purpose *a cabbage/vegetable patch* **5 a bad/rough, etc patch** a difficult time *I think their marriage is going through a bad patch.* **6 not be a patch on sb/sth** UK *informal* to not be as good as someone or something else *Her cooking is okay but it's not a patch on yours.*

**patch**[2] /pætʃ/ verb [T] to repair a hole in a piece of clothing or other material by sewing a piece of material over it *to patch your trousers*

**patch sth up** to try to improve your relationship with someone after you have had an argument *Has he managed to patch things up with her?*

**patchwork** /'pætʃwɜːk/ noun **1** [U] a type of sewing in which a lot of small pieces of different material are sewn together *a patchwork quilt* **2 a patchwork of sth** something that seems to be made of many different pieces *We flew over a patchwork of fields.*

**patchy** /'pætʃi/ adj **1** not complete or not good in every way *a patchy knowledge of Spanish* **2** existing only in some areas *patchy clouds/fog*

**pâté** /'pæteɪ ⓤ pætˈeɪ/ noun [U] a soft food, usually made of meat or fish, that you spread on bread, etc *liver pâté*

**patent**[1] /'peɪtᵊnt, 'pætᵊnt/ noun [C] a legal right that a person or company receives to make or sell a particular product so that others cannot copy it • **patent** verb [T] to get a patent for something

**patent**[2] /'peɪtᵊnt, 'pætᵊnt/ adj *formal* **patent**

**lie/nonsense** something that is obviously false *The explanation he gave – that was patent nonsense.* • **patently** adv *formal* Her claims are patently (= obviously) false.

**paternal** /pə'tɜːnᵊl/ adj **1** like a father *paternal affection* **2** [always before noun] A paternal relative is part of your father's family. *He was my paternal grandfather.*

**paternity** /pə'tɜːnəti/ noun [U] the state of being a father *paternity leave*

**path** /pɑːθ/ noun [C] **1** GROUND a long, narrow area of ground for people to walk along *There's a path through the forest.* • *a garden path* **2** DIRECTION the direction that a person or vehicle moves in *a flight path* **3** CHOOSING a particular way of doing something over a period of time *a career path* • *Whichever path we choose, we'll have difficulties.*

**pathetic** /pə'θetɪk/ adj **1** *informal* showing no skill, effort, or bravery *He made a rather pathetic attempt to apologize.* • *You're too frightened to speak to her? Come on, that's pathetic!* • *It was a pathetic performance.* **2** sad and weak *Four times the pathetic little creature fell to the ground.* • **pathetically** adv *a pathetically small amount of money*

**pathological** /,pæθə'lɒdʒɪkᵊl/ adj **1** Pathological behaviour or feelings are extreme and cannot be controlled. *a pathological liar* • *pathological hatred* **2** relating to pathology (= the study of disease)

**pathologist** /pə'θɒlədʒɪst/ noun [C] a doctor who has studied pathology, especially one who tries to find out why people have died

**pathology** /pə'θɒlədʒi/ noun [U] the scientific study of disease and causes of death

**pathos** /'peɪθɒs/ noun [U] *literary* a quality in a situation that makes you feel sympathy and sadness

o—**patience** /'peɪʃᵊns/ noun [U] **1** the quality of being able to stay calm and not get angry, especially when something takes a long time *Finally, I lost my patience and shouted at her.* • *Making small scale models takes a lot of patience.* ➔ Opposite **impatience**. **2** UK (US **solitaire**) a card game for one person

o—**patient**[1] /'peɪʃᵊnt/ adj having patience *You need to be patient with children.* • **patiently** adv ➔ Opposite **impatient**.

o—**patient**[2] /'peɪʃᵊnt/ noun [C] someone who is being treated by a doctor, nurse, etc *a cancer patient*

**patio** /'pætiəʊ/ noun [C] an outside area with a stone floor next to a house, where people can sit to eat and relax

**patriot** /'peɪtriət/ noun [C] someone who loves their country and is proud of it

**patriotic** /,peɪtri'ɒtɪk/ adj showing love for your country and pride in it *patriotic duty* • *a patriotic song* • **patriotism** /'peɪtriətɪzm/ noun [U] when you love your country and are proud of it

**patrol**[1] /pə'trəʊl/ noun **1** [C, U] the act of looking for trouble or danger around an area or building *We passed a group of soldiers on patrol.* • *a patrol boat/car* **2** [C] a group of soldiers or vehicles that patrol an area or building *a border patrol* • *an armed patrol*

**P**

**patrol²** /pə'trəʊl/ *verb* [I, T] **patrolling**, *past* **patrolled** to look for trouble or danger in an area or around a building *Police patrol the streets night and day.*

**patron** /'peɪtrən/ *noun* [C] **1** someone who supports and gives money to artists, writers, musicians, etc *a generous patron* • *a patron of the arts* **2** a customer at a bar, restaurant, or hotel

**patronize** (*also UK* **-ise**) /'pætrənaɪz/ *verb* [T] **1** to speak or behave towards someone as if you were better than them *Don't patronize me! I know what I'm doing.* • *a patronizing attitude/tone* **2** *formal* to go to a store, business, etc, especially if you go regularly

**ˌpatron ˈsaint** *noun* [C] a saint (= a special, famous Christian) who is believed to help a particular place, person, or activity *St. Christopher is the patron saint of travellers.*

○━**pattern** /'pætən/ *noun* [C] **1** WAY a particular way that something is often done or repeated *behaviour patterns* **2** DESIGN a design of lines, shapes, colours, etc **3** SHAPE a drawing or shape that helps you to make something *a dress pattern*

○━**pause** /pɔːz/ *verb* [I] to stop doing something for a short time *She paused for a moment and looked around her.* • **pause** *noun* [C] *There was a short pause before he spoke.*

**pave** /peɪv/ *verb* [T] to cover a path or road with flat stones, bricks, concrete, etc

**pavement** /'peɪvmənt/ *noun* [C] **1** *UK* (*US* **sidewalk**) a path by the side of a road that people walk on *It's illegal to park on the pavement.* **2** *US* the hard surface of a road

**pavilion** /pə'vɪljən/ *noun* [C] **1** TENT a large tent that is used for outside events **2** SPORTS *UK* a building next to a sports field where players can change their clothes **3** BUILDING *US* one of a group of related buildings, such as a hospital

**paw** /pɔː/ *noun* [C] the foot of certain animals, such as cats and dogs • **paw** (*also* **paw at**) *verb* [T] to touch something with a paw *I could hear the dog pawing at the door.*

**pawn¹** /pɔːn/ *noun* [C] **1** in the game of chess, the smallest piece and the one that has the lowest value **2** someone who does not have power and is used by other people

**pawn²** /pɔːn/ *verb* [T] to leave something with a pawnbroker, who gives you money for it and will sell it if you do not pay the money back *She pawned her wedding ring to pay the rent.*

**pawnbroker** /'pɔːnˌbrəʊkəʳ/ *noun* [C] someone who lends you money in exchange for items that they will sell if you cannot pay the money back

○━**pay¹** /peɪ/ *verb past* **paid 1** BUY [I, T] to give money to someone because you are buying something from them, or because you owe them money *Helen paid for the tickets.* • *Did you pay the telephone bill?* • *You can pay by cash or credit card.* **2** WORK [I, T] to give someone money for the work that they do *She gets paid twice a month.* • *People work for them because they pay well.* • [+ two objects] *We paid them £600 for the work.* • *a paid job* **3** ADVANTAGE [I] to be a good thing to do because it gives you money or an advantage *Crime doesn't pay.* **4** SUFFER [I, T] to suffer because of something bad you have done *He's*

*certainly paying for his mistakes.* **5** **pay attention** to look at or listen to someone or something carefully *I missed what she was saying because I wasn't paying attention.* **6** **pay sb a compliment** to tell someone that you admire something about them **7** **pay tribute to sb/sth** to thank someone or say that you admire someone or something, especially in public *He paid tribute to his former teacher.* **8** **pay sb/sth a visit; pay a visit to sb/sth** to visit a place or a person, usually for a short time

**pay for** something

Remember that when **pay** means give money to buy something, it is usually followed by the preposition **for**.

*Rachel paid for the meal.*

~~Rachel paid the meal.~~

**pay sb/sth back** to pay someone the money that you owe them *Only borrow money if you're sure you can pay it back.* • *I lent him £10 last month and he still hasn't paid me back.*

**pay sth off** to pay all of the money that you owe *I'm planning to pay off my bank loan in five years.*

**pay (sth) out** to spend a lot of money on something, or to pay a lot of money to someone *I've just paid out £700 to get the car fixed.*

**pay up** *informal* to give someone all of the money that you owe them, especially when you do not want to *Come on, pay up!*

**pay²** /peɪ/ *noun* [U] the money you receive from your employer for doing your job (*UK*) *a pay rise/*(*US*) *a pay raise* • *good rates of pay*

**pay, wage, salary,** or **income?**

**Pay** is a general word which means the money that you receive for working.

*Doctors usually get more pay than teachers.*

A **wage** is an amount of money you receive each day or week. It is often paid in cash (= notes and coins).

*His weekly wage was $400.*

A **salary** is the money you receive each month. A person's **salary** is often expressed as the total amount in a year.

*His salary is £20,000.*

Your **income** is the total amount of money that you earn by working or investing money.

*She has a monthly income of £1,300.*

○━**payment** /'peɪmənt/ *noun* **1** [U] the act of paying *They will accept payment by credit card.* **2** [C] the amount of money that is paid *monthly payments* ➲ *See also:* **balance of payments, down payment.**

**ˈpay ˌphone** *noun* [C] a telephone in a public place that you pay to use

**PC¹** /ˌpiː'siː/ *noun* [C] **1** a personal computer **2** *UK abbreviation for* police constable (= a police officer of the lowest rank)

**PC²** /ˌpiːˈsiː/ *adj abbreviation for* politically correct (= careful to speak or behave in a way which is not offensive to women, people of a particular race, or people who have physical or mental problems)

**PE** /ˌpiːˈiː/ *noun* [U] *abbreviation for* physical education: classes at school where children do exercise and play sport

**pea** /piː/ *noun* [C] a small, round, green seed that people eat as a vegetable

○⇥**peace** /piːs/ *noun* [U] **1** when there is no war, violence, or arguing *peace talks* • *a peace agreement/treaty* • *There seems little hope for world peace.* • *The UN sent troops to the region to keep the peace.* **2** when there is quiet and calm *a feeling of peace* • *After a busy day, all I want is peace and quiet.* • *I wish you'd stop complaining and leave me in peace!* **3 peace of mind** a feeling that you do not need to worry about anything *We lock our doors and windows at night for peace of mind.* ➜ *See also:* **Justice of the Peace**.

○⇥**peaceful** /ˈpiːsfəl/ *adj* **1** without violence *a peaceful protest* **2** quiet and calm *The churchyard was empty and peaceful.* • peacefully *adv He died peacefully at home.*

**peacekeeping** /ˈpiːsˌkiːpɪŋ/ *adj* [always before noun] relating to the activity of preventing war and violence *peacekeeping forces/troops* • *a peacekeeping effort/operation* • peacekeeper /ˈpiːsˌkiːpər/ *noun* [C] someone, usually a soldier, who tries to prevent war and violence in countries where there is trouble *UN peacekeepers*

**peacetime** /ˈpiːstaɪm/ *noun* [U] a time when a country is not at war

**peach** /piːtʃ/ *noun* [C] a soft, sweet, round fruit with red and yellow skin

**peacock** /ˈpiːkɒk/ *noun* [C] a large, male bird with long tail feathers that it can lift up to show a lot of colours

**peak¹** /piːk/ *noun* [C] **1** the highest level or value of something *Here we see an athlete at the peak of fitness.* • *The price of gold reached its peak during the last recession.* • *peak travel times* **2** the top of a mountain, or the mountain itself *snow-covered/mountain peaks*

**peak**

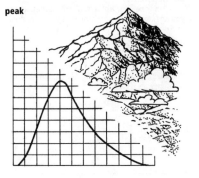

**peak²** /piːk/ *verb* [I] to reach the highest level or value of something *Her singing career peaked in the 1990s.*

**peanut** /ˈpiːnʌt/ *noun* [C] an oval-shaped nut with a soft, brown shell *salted peanuts* • *peanut oil* ➜ *See colour picture* **Food** *on page Centre 7.*

**ˌpeanut ˈbutter** *UK* (*US* **ˈpeanut ˌbutter**) *noun* [U] a pale brown food made by crushing peanuts *a peanut butter and jelly sandwich*

**pear** /peər/ *noun* [C] an oval-shaped, pale green or yellow fruit ➜ *See colour picture* **Fruit and Vegetables** *on page Centre 8.*

**pearl** /pɜːl/ *noun* [C] a hard, white, round object that is made inside the shell of an oyster (= a sea creature) and that is used to make jewellery *a string of pearls* • *a pearl necklace* • *pearl earrings*

**pear-shaped** /ˈpeəʃeɪpt/ *adj* **go pear-shaped** *UK informal* If a plan goes pear-shaped, it fails.

**peasant** /ˈpezənt/ *noun* [C] a poor person who works on the land, usually in a poor country *a peasant farmer*

**peat** /piːt/ *noun* [U] a dark brown soil made from decaying plants that you can burn as fuel or that you can put around living plants to help them grow

**pebble** /ˈpebl/ *noun* [C] a small stone

**pecan** /ˈpiːkæn/ ⓤⓈ /pɪˈkɑːn/ *noun* [C] a nut that grows on a tree, or the tree itself *chopped pecans* • *pecan pie*

**peck¹** /pek/ (*also* **peck at**) *verb* [T] If a bird pecks something, it lifts or hits it with its beak. *chickens pecking at corn*

**peck²** /pek/ *noun* [C] **1 give sb a peck on the cheek** to give someone a quick, gentle kiss on the face **2** when a bird pecks something

**peculiar** /pɪˈkjuːliər/ *adj* **1** strange, often in an unpleasant way *The wine had a peculiar, musty smell.* **2 peculiar to sb/sth** belonging to or relating to a particular person or thing *Her accent is peculiar to the region.*

**peculiarity** /pɪˌkjuːliˈærəti/ *noun* [C] **1** something that is typical of a person, place, or thing *Each college has its own traditions and peculiarities.* **2** a strange or unusual characteristic *My mother always hummed – it was one of her little peculiarities.*

**peculiarly** /pɪˈkjuːliəli/ *adv* **1** in a way that is typical of someone or something *a peculiarly American sense of humour* **2** in a strange way *The birds were peculiarly quiet just before the earthquake.*

**pedagogue** /ˈpedəgɒg/ *noun* [C] *formal* a teacher, usually a very strict one

**pedal** /ˈpedəl/ *noun* [C] a part of a machine that you press with your foot to operate or move the machine *bicycle pedals* • *a gas/brake pedal*

**pedant** /ˈpedənt/ *noun* [C] someone who thinks too much about details and rules • pedantic /pɪˈdæntɪk/ *adj* thinking too much about details and rules *I hate to be pedantic, but Freud was actually Austrian, not German.*

**peddle** /ˈpedl/ *verb* [T] to sell things, especially drugs or things of bad quality *The shops on the pier peddled cheap souvenirs to the tourists.* • *He was arrested for peddling drugs.*

**pedestal** /ˈpedɪstəl/ *noun* [C] **1** the base for a statue (= model of a person or animal) **2 put sb on a pedestal** to believe that someone is perfect

**pedestrian¹** /pɪˈdestriən/ *noun* [C] a person who

**P**

is walking and not travelling in a vehicle *Many streets are reserved for cyclists and pedestrians.* • *a pedestrian precinct/crossing*

**pedestrian²** /pɪ'destriən/ *adj formal* ordinary or not interesting *pedestrian ideas* • *a pedestrian speech*

pe,destrian 'crossing *UK* (*US* **crosswalk**) *noun* [C] a special place on a road where traffic must stop if people want to cross

**pediatrician** /ˌpiːdiə'trɪʃən/ *noun* [C] *US spelling of* paediatrician

**pedigree¹** /'pedɪɡriː/ *noun* [C] **1** a list of the parents and other relatives of an animal **2** someone's family history, or their education and experience

**pedigree²** /'pedɪɡriː/ *adj* [always before noun] A pedigree animal has parents and other relatives all from the same breed and is thought to be of high quality. *a pedigree dog*

**pedophile** /'piːdəʊfaɪl/ *noun* [C] *US spelling of* paedophile

**pee¹** /piː/ *verb* [I] **peeing**, *past* **peed** *informal* to urinate • **pee** *noun* [no plural] *informal Do I have time for a pee before we go?*

**peek¹** /piːk/ *verb* [I] to look at something for a short time, often when you do not want other people to see you *I peeked out the window to see who was there.*

**peek²** /piːk/ *noun* **have/take a peek** to look at something for a short time

**peel¹** /piːl/ *verb* **1** [T] to remove the skin of fruit or vegetables *Peel and chop the onions.* **2** [I, T] If you peel something from a surface, you remove it and if something peels, it comes away from a surface. *The paint is starting to **peel off** where the wall is damp.* ➔ *See also:* keep your eyes (**eye¹**) peeled for sb/sth.

**peel sth off** to take off clothes, especially wet or tight clothes *We peeled off our muddy socks and left them outside.*

**peel²** /piːl/ *noun* [U] the skin of fruit or vegetables, especially after it has been removed *Combine nuts, sugar, and orange peel in a small bowl.*

**peep** /piːp/ *verb* **1 peep at/ through/out, etc** to look at something for a short time, often when you do not want other people to see you *She peeped at them through the fence.* **2 peep through/over/out from, etc** to appear but not be seen completely *The sun peeped out from behind the clouds.* • **peep** *noun* [no plural] *She took a peep at herself in the mirror.*

**peer¹** /pɪər/ *noun* [C] **1** someone who is the same age, or who has the same social position or abilities as other members of a group *Most teenagers want to be accepted by their peers.* **2** in the UK, a person who has a title and a high social position

**peer²** /pɪər/ *verb* **peer at/into/through, etc** to look carefully or with difficulty *She peered at me over her glasses.*

'peer ,group *noun* [C] a group of people of about the same age, social position, etc *He was the first of his peer group to get married.*

'peer ,pressure *noun* [U] strong influence on a member of a group to behave in the same way as other members in the group, although that behaviour is not good *Many teenagers take drugs because of boredom or peer pressure.*

**peg¹** /peɡ/ *noun* [C] **1** [ON WALL] an object on a wall or door that you hang things on **2** [ON ROPE] (*also* **clothes peg**) *UK* a short piece of wood, plastic, etc that is used to hold clothes on a rope while they dry **3** [STICK] a stick made of metal or wood that has a sharp end and which is used to fix something somewhere *a tent peg*

**peg²** /peɡ/ *verb* [T] **pegging**, *past* **pegged** to fix the cost of borrowing money or the value of a country's money at a particular level [often passive] *Interest rates were **pegged at** 8.2 %.*

**pellet** /'pelɪt/ *noun* [C] a small, hard ball of metal, grain, etc *shotgun/feed pellets*

**pelvic** /'pelvɪk/ *adj* [always before noun] relating to the area below your waist and above your legs

**pelvis** /'pelvɪs/ *noun* [C] the group of bones that forms the area below your waist and above your legs and to which your leg bones are joined

○→**pen¹** /pen/ *noun* [C] **1** a long, thin object that you use to write or draw in ink ➔ *See colour picture* **Classroom** *on page Centre 4.* **2** a small area with a fence around it that you keep animals in *a pig/sheep pen* ➔ *See also:* **ballpoint pen, felt-tip pen, fountain pen**.

**pen²** /pen/ *verb* [T] **penning**, *past* **penned** *literary* to write something *sonnets penned by Shakespeare*

**pen sb/sth in/up** to keep people or animals in a small area [often passive] *The soldiers were penned up in their barracks.*

**penal** /'piːnəl/ *adj* [always before noun] relating to the punishment of criminals *a penal code/system*

**penalize** (*also UK* -**ise**) /'piːnəlaɪz/ *verb* [T] **1** to cause someone a disadvantage *The present tax system penalizes poor people.* **2** to punish someone for breaking a law or a rule *He was penalized early in the match for dangerous play.*

**penalty** /'penəlti/ *noun* [C] **1** a punishment for doing something which is against a law or rule *There's a £50 penalty for late cancellation of tickets.* **2** in sports, an advantage given to a team when the opposing team has broken a rule *They won a penalty in the first five minutes of the game.* • *a penalty goal/kick* ➔ *See also:* **death penalty**.

**penance** /'penəns/ *noun* [C, U] an act that shows you are sorry for something that you have done

**pence** /pens/ *noun* plural of British penny; p

**USAGE**

**pence, pennies, or p?**

Pence is the usual plural of penny *(UK)* and is used to talk about amounts of money. In informal *(UK)* English you can also say p.

*Can you lend me 50 pence?*

*Can you lend me 50p?*

The plural form **pennies** is only used to talk about the coins as objects.

*He found some pennies in his pocket.*

**penchant** /'pɒnʃɒŋ/ ⓊⓈ /'pentʃənt/ *noun* **have a penchant for sth** *formal* to like something very much *Miguel has a penchant for fast cars.*

○┅**pencil** /'pensəl/ *noun* [C, U] a long, thin wooden object with a black or coloured point that you write or draw with ➲ *See colour picture* **Classroom** *on page Centre 4.*

'**pencil ,sharpener** *noun* [C] a tool that you use to make pencils sharp ➲ *See colour picture* **Classroom** *on page Centre 4.*

**pendant** /'pendənt/ *noun* [C] a piece of jewellery on a chain that you wear around your neck

**pending**[1] /'pendɪŋ/ *preposition formal* used to say that one thing must wait until another thing happens *Several employees have been suspended pending an investigation.*

**pending**[2] /'pendɪŋ/ *adj formal* not decided or finished *Their court case is still pending.*

**pendulum** /'pendjələm/ *noun* [C] a heavy object on a chain or stick that moves from side to side, especially inside a large clock

**penetrate** /'penɪtreɪt/ *verb* **1** [I, T] If something penetrates an object, it moves into that object. *The bullet penetrated his skull.* **2** [T] If someone penetrates a place or a group, they succeed in moving into or joining it. *No one in our industry has successfully penetrated the Asian market.* ● penetration /,penɪ'treɪʃᵊn/ *noun* [U]

**penetrating** /'penɪtreɪtɪŋ/ *adj* **1** intelligent and full of careful thought *a penetrating discussion/mind* ● *She wrote a penetrating analysis of Shakespeare's Hamlet.* **2 a penetrating gaze/look/stare, etc** If someone gives you a penetrating look, you feel as if they know what you are thinking. **3** If a sound is penetrating, it is very strong and unpleasant. *a penetrating voice/scream*

**penguin** /'peŋgwɪn/ *noun* [C] a large, black and white sea bird that swims and cannot fly

**penicillin** /,penɪ'sɪlɪn/ *noun* [U] a type of medicine that kills bacteria and is used to treat illness

**peninsula** /pə'nɪnsjələ/ *noun* [C] a long, thin piece of land which has water around most of it *the Korean peninsula*

**peninsula**

**penis** /'piːnɪs/ *noun* [C] the part of a man's or male animal's body that is used for urinating and having sex

**penitentiary** /,penɪ'tenʃᵊri/ *noun* [C] a prison in the US

**pennant** /'penənt/ *noun* [C] a long, pointed flag

**penniless** /'penɪləs/ *adj* having no money

**penny** /'peni/ *noun* [C] *plural* **pence** or **p** or **pennies 1** a coin or unit of money with a value of 1/100 of a pound (= UK unit of money); p *There are 100 pence in a pound.* ● *fifty pence/50p* ➲ *See usage note at* **pence**. **2** a coin with a value of one cent (= 1/100 of a dollar) *My dad always let us have his pennies to buy candy.* **3 every penny** all of an amount of money *He seemed intent on spending every penny of his salary.*

**pension**[1] /'penʃᵊn/ *noun* [C] money that is paid regularly by the government or a private company to a person who has stopped working because they are old or ill *a state/private pension* ● *a pension plan/scheme* ● pensioner *noun* [C] *mainly UK* someone who receives a pension ➲ *See also:* **old-age pension**, **old-age pensioner**

**pension**[2] /'penʃᵊn/ *verb*
**pension sb off** *mainly UK* If an organization pensions someone off, it forces that person to leave their job but pays them a pension.

**the Pentagon** /'pentəgɒn/ *noun* the department of the US government that controls the army, navy, etc, or the building where it is *The Pentagon refused to comment on potential military targets.*

**penthouse** /'penthaʊs/ *noun* [C] *plural* **penthouses** /'penthaʊzɪz/ an expensive apartment at the top of a building

**pent-up** /,pent'ʌp/ *adj* [always before noun] Pent-up feelings are feelings that you have not expressed for a long time. *pent-up anger*

**penultimate** /pə'nʌltɪmət/ *adj* [always before noun] *formal* next to the last *Y is the penultimate letter of the alphabet.*

○┅**people**[1] /'piːpl/ *noun* **1** [plural] more than one person *Our company employs over 400 people.* ● *People live much longer than they used to.* **2 the people** all the ordinary people in a country *The rebels have gained the support of the people.* **3** [C] *formal* all the people of a race *Europe is made up of many different peoples.*

**people**[2] /'piːpl/ *verb*
**be peopled by/with sb** *literary* to be filled with a particular kind of person *His novels are peopled with angry young men.*

**pepper**[1] /'pepər/ *noun* **1** [U] a black, grey, or red powder that is made from crushed seeds, used to give food a slightly spicy flavour *salt and pepper* **2** [C] a hollow green, red, or yellow vegetable *green/red pepper* ➲ *See colour picture* **Fruit and Vegetables** *on page Centre 8.*

**pepper**[2] /'pepər/ *verb*
**pepper sth with sth** to include a lot of something [often passive] *His speech was peppered with quotations.*

**peppermint** /'pepəmɪnt/ *noun* **1** [U] oil from a plant that is added to food to give it a strong, fresh taste, or the taste itself *peppermint tea* **2** [C] a small, hard sweet that tastes like peppermint

**per** *strong form* /pɜː/ *weak form* /pər/ *preposition* for each *Our hotel room costs $60 per night.* ● *The speed limit is 100 kilometres per hour.* ● *The wedding dinner will cost £30 per head* (= for each person).

**per annum** /pɜːr'ænʌm/ *adv formal* every year *a salary of $19,000 per annum*

**per capita** /pɜː'kæpɪtə/ *adj, adv formal* for each person *This county has the lowest per capita income in the country.* ● *Belgians eat more chocolate per capita than any other nation in Europe.*

**perceive** /pə'siːv/ *verb* [T] *formal* **1** to think of something or someone in a particular way [often passive] *The British are often perceived as being very formal.* **2** to notice something that is

**P**

not easy to notice *We perceived a faint light in the distance.*

O━**percent** (*also* **per cent**) /pə'sent/ *adj, adv* for or out of every 100, shown by the symbol % *a 40 percent increase in prices* ● percent (*also* **per cent**) *noun* [C] *Nearly 70 percent of all cars in the UK are less than five years old.*

**percentage** /pə'sentɪdʒ/ *noun* [C] an amount of something, often expressed as a number out of 100 *The percentage of women who work has risen steadily.* ● *The percentage of people who are left-handed is small – only about 10%.*

**perceptible** /pə'septəbl/ *adj formal* just able to be noticed *a perceptible difference in colour* ● *His pulse was barely perceptible.*

**perception** /pə'sepʃ°n/ *noun* **1** [C] what you think or believe about someone or something *The public perception of him as a hero is surprising.* **2** [U] the ability to notice something *Alcohol reduces your perception of pain.*

**perceptive** /pə'septɪv/ *adj* quick to notice or understand things *a perceptive writer*

**perch**[1] /pɜːtʃ/ *verb* **1 perch (sth) on/in/above, etc** to be in a high position or in a position near the edge of something, or to put something in this position [often passive] *The village was perched on the side of a mountain.* ● *She wore glasses perched on the end of her nose.* **2 perch on/in, etc** to sit near the edge of something *The children perched on the edges of their seats.*

**perch**[2] /pɜːtʃ/ *noun* [C] a place where a bird sits, especially a stick inside a cage

**percussion** /pə'kʌʃ°n/ *noun* [U] musical instruments that make a sound when you hit them with a stick or your hand *Drums, tambourines, and cymbals are percussion instruments.*

**perennial**[1] /p°'reniəl/ *adj* happening again and again, or continuing for a long time *the perennial problem of unemployment*

**perennial**[2] /p°'reniəl/ *noun* [C] a plant that lives for several years

O━**perfect**[1] /'pɜːfɪkt/ *adj* **1** [WITHOUT FAULT] without fault, or as good as possible *James is a perfect husband and father.* ● *Her performance was perfect.* **2** [SUITABLE] exactly right for someone or something *You'd be perfect for the job.* ● *The weather's just perfect for a picnic.* **3** [TO EMPHASIZE] [always before noun] used to emphasize a noun *His suggestion makes perfect sense.*

**perfect**[2] /pə'fekt/ *verb* [T] to make something as good as it can be *I've spent hours perfecting my speech.*

**the perfect** /'pɜːfɪkt/ (*also* **the ,perfect 'tense**) *noun* the form of the verb that is used to show an action that has happened in the past or before another time or event. In English, the perfect is made with 'have' and a past participle. ➔ *See also:* **the future perfect**, **the past perfect**, **the present perfect**.

**perfection** /pə'fekʃ°n/ *noun* [U] when someone or something is perfect *She strives for perfection in everything she does.* ● *chicken legs cooked to perfection*

**perfectionist** /pə'fekʃ°nɪst/ *noun* [C] someone who wants everything to be perfect

O━**perfectly** /'pɜːfɪktli/ *adv* **1** used to emphasize the word that follows it *To be perfectly honest, I*

*don't care any more.* ● *I made it perfectly clear to him what I meant.* **2** in a perfect way *The jacket fits perfectly, the skirt not so well.*

**perforated** /'pɜːfəreɪtɪd/ *adj* **1** Perforated materials such as paper have small holes in them so that they can be torn or liquid can pass through them. **2** If an organ of your body is perforated, it has a hole in it. *a perforated eardrum* ● perforate *verb* [T]

O━**perform** /pə'fɔːm/ *verb* **1** [I, T] to entertain people by acting, singing, dancing, etc *She has performed all over the world.* ● *The orchestra will perform music by Mozart.* **2** [T] *formal* to do a job or a piece of work *In the future, many tasks will be performed by robots.* ● *Surgeons performed the operation in less than two hours.* **3 perform well/badly, etc** If something performs well, badly, etc, it works that way. *These cars perform poorly at high speeds.*

O━**performance** /pə'fɔːməns/ *noun* **1** [C] acting, singing, dancing, or playing music to entertain people *a performance of Shakespeare's Hamlet* **2** [U] how successful someone or something is *The company's performance was poor for the first two years.* ● *Some athletes take drugs to improve their performance.*

**performer** /pə'fɔːmə°/ *noun* [C] someone who entertains people

**the per,forming 'arts** *noun* [plural] types of entertainment that are performed in front of people, such as dancing, singing, and acting

**perfume** /'pɜːfjuːm/ *noun* [C, U] a liquid with a pleasant smell that women put on their skin ● perfumed *adj* containing perfume

O━**perhaps** /pə'hæps/ *adv* **1** possibly *Perhaps I'll go to the gym after work.* ● *Ben won't be coming but perhaps it's better that way.* **2** used when you want to suggest or ask someone something *Perhaps you should leave now.*

**peril** /'per°l/ *noun* [C, U] *formal* extreme danger *A shortage of firefighters is putting lives in peril.* ● *His book describes the perils of war.*

**perilous** /'per°ləs/ *adj formal* very dangerous *a perilous journey* ● perilously *adv*

**perimeter** /pə'rɪmɪtə°/ *noun* [C] the outer edge of an area *the perimeter of the airport*

O━**period** /'pɪəriəd/ *noun* [C] **1** [TIME] a length of time *a 24-hour period* ● *a period of four months* **2** [SCHOOL/SPORTS] one of the equal parts of time that a school day or sports game is divided into **3** [WOMEN] when blood comes out of a woman's uterus each month **4** [MARK] *US* (*UK* **full stop**) a mark (.) used at the end of a sentence, or to show that the letters before it are an abbreviation ➔ *See study section* **Punctuation** *on page Centre 37.*

**periodic** /ˌpɪəri'ɒdɪk/ *adj* happening regularly *Our sales team makes periodic trips to Asia.* ● periodically *adv*

**periodical** /ˌpɪəri'ɒdɪk°l/ *noun* [C] a magazine about a particular subject

**peripheral** /pə'rɪf°r°l/ *adj* not as important as someone or something else

**periphery** /pə'rɪf°ri/ *noun* [C] the outer edge of an area *The soldiers were camped on the periphery of the village.*

**perish** /'perɪʃ/ *verb* [I] *literary* to die *Hundreds of people perished in the flood.*

**perishable** /ˈperɪʃəbl/ adj Food that is perishable goes bad very quickly.

**perjury** /ˈpɜːdʒˀri/ noun [U] the crime of telling a lie in a court of law *The witness was accused of committing perjury.*

**perk¹** /pɜːk/ noun [C] an advantage, such as money or a car, that you are given because of your job [usually plural] *A mobile phone is one of the perks of the job.*

**perk²** /pɜːk/ verb

**perk (sb) up** to start to feel happier, or to make someone feel happier *A cup of coffee always perks me up in the morning.*

**perm** /pɜːm/ noun [C] the use of chemicals on someone's hair to make it have curls for several months, or the hair style that is made in this way *I'm thinking of having a perm.* • perm verb [T]

**permanence** /ˈpɜːmˀnəns/ noun [U] when something continues forever or for a long time

o─╼**permanent** /ˈpɜːmˀnənt/ adj continuing forever or for a long time *permanent damage* • *a permanent job* • permanently adv *He moved here permanently in 1992.*

**permeate** /ˈpɜːmieɪt/ verb [T] formal to move gradually into every part of something *The pungent smell of vinegar permeated the air.* • *Drug dealers have permeated every level of society.*

**permissible** /pəˈmɪsəbl/ adj formal allowed by the rules [+ to do sth] *It is not permissible to smoke inside the building.*

o─╼**permission** /pəˈmɪʃˀn/ noun [U] when you allow someone to do something *She gave him permission without asking any questions.* • [+ to do sth] *He has permission to stay in the country for one more year.* • *They even have to ask permission before they go to the toilet.* • *He took the car without permission.*

**permissive** /pəˈmɪsɪv/ adj allowing people to behave in ways which other people may not approve of *permissive attitudes*

**permit¹** /pəˈmɪt/ verb **permitting,** past **permitted 1** [T] formal to allow something [often passive] *Photography is not permitted inside the museum.* • [+ to do sth] *He permitted them to leave.* **2** [I] to make something possible *The match starts at 3 p.m., weather permitting.*

**permit²** /ˈpɜːmɪt/ noun [C] an official document that allows you to do something *a work permit* • *You need a permit to park your car here.*

**pernicious** /pəˈnɪʃəs/ adj formal very harmful

**perpendicular** /ˌpɜːpˀnˈdɪkjʊləʳ/ adj at an angle of 90 degrees to something

**perpetrate** /ˈpɜːpɪtreɪt/ verb [T] formal to do something very bad [often passive] *They heard of torture perpetrated by the army.*

**perpetrator** /ˈpɜːpɪtreɪtəʳ/ noun [C] formal someone who has done something very bad *There is great public pressure to bring the perpetrators of these crimes to justice.*

**perpetual** /pəˈpetʃuəl/ adj never ending *He seems to be in a perpetual state of confusion.* • perpetually adv

**perpetuate** /pəˈpetʃueɪt/ verb [T] formal to make something continue, especially something bad *People think of him as a cruel man, an image perpetuated by the media.*

**perplexed** /pəˈplekst/ adj confused *He seemed a little perplexed by the question.* • perplex verb [T]

**perplexing** /pəˈpleksɪŋ/ adj confusing *a perplexing problem*

**persecute** /ˈpɜːsɪkjuːt/ verb [T] to treat someone unfairly or cruelly because of their race, religion, or beliefs [often passive] *He was persecuted for his religious beliefs.* • persecution /ˌpɜːsɪˈkjuːʃˀn/ noun [U] *political/religious persecution*

**persecutor** /ˈpɜːsɪkjuːtəʳ/ noun [C] someone who persecutes people

**perseverance** /ˌpɜːsɪˈvɪərˀns/ noun [U] when you persevere *Hard work and perseverance do pay off in the end.*

**persevere** /ˌpɜːsɪˈvɪəʳ/ verb [I] to continue to try to do something although it is difficult *Despite the difficulties, I decided to persevere with the project.*

**persist** /pəˈsɪst/ verb [I] **1** If an unpleasant feeling or situation persists, it continues to exist. *If symptoms persist, consult a doctor.* **2** to continue to do something although it is annoying other people *He persists in calling me Jane, even though I've corrected him twice.*

**persistence** /pəˈsɪstˀns/ noun [U] when someone or something persists

**persistent** /pəˈsɪstˀnt/ adj **1** Something unpleasant that is persistent continues for a long time and is difficult to get rid of. *a persistent cough* **2** A persistent person continues to do something although other people do not want them to. *He can be very persistent sometimes.* • persistently adv *He has persistently lied to us.*

o─╼**person** /ˈpɜːsˀn/ noun plural **people 1** [C] a human being *You're the only person I know here.* • *He is a very dangerous person.* **2** in **person** If you do something in person, you go somewhere to do it yourself. *If you can't be there in person the next best thing is watching it on TV.* ⊃ See also: **the first person, the second person, the third person.**

**persona** /pəˈsəʊnə/ noun [C] plural **personae** or **personas** the way your character seems to other people *He's trying to improve his public persona.*

o─╼**personal** /ˈpɜːsˀnˀl/ adj **1** RELATING TO A PERSON [always before noun] relating to or belonging to a particular person *I can only speak from my own personal experience.* • *Please ensure you take all personal belongings with you when you leave the train.* • *This is a personal view and not that of the government.* **2** PRIVATE relating to the private parts of someone's life, including their relationships and feelings *He's got a few personal problems at the moment.* • *She prefers to keep her personal and professional lives separate.* **3** FOR ONE PERSON [always before noun] designed for or used by one person *a personal computer/stereo* • *a personal loan/pension* **4** RUDE rude about or offensive towards someone *I know you're upset, but there's no need to get personal* (= start making offensive remarks). **5** BODY [always before noun] relating to your body *personal hygiene*

o─╼**personality** /ˌpɜːsˀnˈælɪti/ noun **1** CHARACTER [C] the way you are as a person *She's got a lovely, bubbly personality.* **2** FAMOUS [C] a

famous person *a well-known TV personality*
**3** [INTERESTING] [U] the quality of having a very strong or interesting character *Sales people need a lot of personality.*

**personalized** (*also UK* **-ised**) /'pɜːsənəlaɪzd/ *adj* A personalized object has someone's name on it, or has been made for a particular person. *a personalized fitness plan* • personalize *verb* [T]

**personally** /'pɜːsənəli/ *adv* **1** done by you and not someone else *I'd like to personally apologize for the delay.* **2** used when you are going to give your opinion *Personally, I'd rather stay at home and watch TV.* **3 take sth personally** to think that someone is criticizing you when they are not *You mustn't take everything so personally.*

**personal 'pronoun** *noun* [C] a word that is used to refer to a person in speech or in writing. For example the words 'I', 'you', and 'they' are personal pronouns.

**personify** /pə'sɒnɪfaɪ/ *verb* [T] If someone personifies a particular quality, they are a perfect example of that quality. *She seems to personify honesty and goodness.* • personified *adj* [always after noun] *Tom has always been laziness personified.* • personification /pə,sɒnɪfɪ'keɪʃʰn/ *noun* [U]

**personnel** /,pɜːsʰn'el/ *noun* **1** [plural] the people who work for an organization *military personnel* **2** [U] the department of an organization that deals with finding people to work there, keeping records about them, etc *I need to speak to someone in Personnel.* • *the personnel manager*

**perspective** /pə'spektɪv/ *noun* **1** [C] the way you think about something *Being unemployed has made me see things from a different perspective.* **2** [U] when things are drawn so that they appear to be a realistic size and in a realistic position **3 put sth in/into perspective** If something puts a problem into perspective, it makes you understand how unimportant that problem is.

**perspicacious** /,pɜːspɪ'keɪʃəs/ *adj formal* quick in noticing, understanding, or judging things accurately

**perspiration** /,pɜːspʰr'eɪʃʰn/ *noun* [U] *formal* the liquid that comes out of your skin when you get hot

**perspire** /pə'spaɪəʳ/ *verb* [I] *formal* to produce liquid through your skin because you are hot or nervous

o⃯**persuade** /pə'sweɪd/ *verb* [T] to make someone agree to do something by talking to them a lot about it [+ to do sth] *We managed to persuade him to come with us.* • [+ (that)] *I persuaded her that it was the right thing to do.* ⊃ *Opposite* **dissuade**.

**persuasion** /pə'sweɪʒʰn/ *noun* **1** [U] when you persuade someone *I'm sure she'll agree, she just needs a little gentle persuasion.* **2** [C] *formal* a political, religious, or moral belief *There were people of all persuasions there.*

**persuasive** /pə'sweɪsɪv/ *adj* able to make people agree to do something *It's a very persuasive argument.* • persuasively *adv*

**pertain** /pə'teɪn/ *verb*
**pertain to sth** *formal* to relate to something *Some important evidence pertaining to the case has been overlooked.*

**pertinent** /'pɜːtɪnənt/ *adj formal* relating directly to a subject *a pertinent question*

**perturbed** /pə'tɜːbd/ *adj* worried or upset *He seemed slightly perturbed by the news.* • perturb *verb* [T]

**peruse** /pə'ruːz/ *verb* [T] *formal* to look at or read something in order to find what interests you

**pervade** /pə'veɪd/ *verb* [T] *formal* to move gradually through every part of something *Cheap perfume and tobacco pervaded the room.*

**pervasive** /pə'veɪsɪv/ *adj formal* moving into or through everywhere or everything *a pervasive smell* • *the pervasive influence of television*

**perverse** /pə'vɜːs/ *adj* strange and not what most people would expect or enjoy *In a perverse way, I enjoy going to the dentist.* • perversely *adv*

**perversion** /pə'vɜːʃʰn/ *noun* [C, U] **1** getting sexual pleasure in a way that seems strange or unpleasant **2** when something that is right is changed into something that is wrong *the perversion of justice*

**pervert¹** /'pɜːvɜːt/ *noun* [C] someone who gets sexual pleasure in a strange or unpleasant way

**pervert²** /pə'vɜːt/ *verb* [T] to change something that is right into something that is wrong *They were charged with conspiracy to pervert the course of justice.*

**perverted** /pə'vɜːtɪd/ *adj* relating to getting sexual pleasure in a strange or unpleasant way

**pessimism** /'pesɪmɪzʰm/ *noun* [U] when you believe bad things will happen ⊃ *Opposite* **optimism**.

**pessimist** /'pesɪmɪst/ *noun* [C] someone who always believes that bad things will happen *Don't be such a pessimist!*

**pessimistic** /,pesɪ'mɪstɪk/ *adj* always believing that bad things will happen *He was feeling pessimistic about the future.* ⊃ *Opposite* **optimistic**.

**pest** /pest/ *noun* [C] **1** an animal that causes damage to plants, food, etc *Most farmers think foxes are pests.* **2** *informal* an annoying person

**pester** /'pestəʳ/ *verb* [T] to annoy someone by asking them something again and again [+ to do sth] *He's been pestering me to go out with him all week.*

**pesticide** /'pestɪsaɪd/ *noun* [C, U] a chemical that is used to kill insects which damage plants

**pet¹** /pet/ *noun* [C] an animal that someone keeps in their home *my pet rabbit*

**pet²** /pet/ *verb* [T] **petting**, *past* **petted** **1** to touch an animal because you feel affection for them **2** to touch someone in a sexual way

**petal** /'petʰl/ *noun* [C] one of the thin, flat, coloured parts on the outside of a flower *rose petals*

**peter** /'piːtəʳ/ *verb*
**peter out** to gradually stop or disappear *The track petered out after a mile or so.*

**pet 'hate** *UK* (*US* ,pet 'peeve) *noun* [C] something that annoys you a lot *That's one of my pet hates – people who smoke while other people are eating.*

**petite** /pə'tiːt/ *adj* A petite woman is small and thin in an attractive way.

**petition¹** /pə'tɪʃʰn/ *verb* [I, T] to officially ask someone in authority to do something [+ to do sth] *They are petitioning the government to increase funding for the project.*

**petition²** /pə'tɪʃ°n/ *noun* [C] a document that has been signed by a lot of people officially asking someone in authority to do something *Will you sign this petition against experiments on animals?*

**petrified** /'petrɪfaɪd/ *adj* extremely frightened *I'm petrified of spiders.*

**petrol** /'petr°l/ *UK* (*US* **gas**) *noun* [U] a liquid fuel used in cars *unleaded petrol*

**petroleum** /pə'trəʊliəm/ *noun* [U] thick oil found under the Earth's surface which is used to produce petrol and other substances

**'petrol ,station** *UK* (*US* **gas station**) *noun* [C] a place where you can buy petrol

**petticoat** /'petɪkəʊt/ *noun* [C] a thin piece of women's clothing worn under a dress or skirt

**petty** /'peti/ *adj* **1** [always before noun] unimportant or not serious *petty details* • *petty crime* **2** [never before noun] complaining too much about unimportant things *You can be so petty sometimes!*

**petulant** /'petʃələnt/ *adj* behaving in an angry, silly way like a child

**pew** /pjuː/ *noun* [C] a long seat in a church

**pewter** /'pjuːtə°/ *noun* [U] a blue-grey metal

**phantom¹** /'fæntəm/ *noun* [C] the spirit of a dead person

**phantom²** /'fæntəm/ *adj* [always before noun] imagined, not real *phantom pains*

**pharaoh** /'feərəʊ/ *noun* [C] a king of ancient Egypt

**pharmaceutical** /ˌfɑːmə'sjuːtɪk°l/ *adj* relating to the production of medicines *a pharmaceutical company* • *the pharmaceutical industry* • **pharmaceuticals** *noun* [plural] medicines

**pharmacist** /'fɑːməsɪst/ *noun* [C] someone who is trained to prepare or sell medicines

**pharmacy** /'fɑːməsi/ *noun* **1** [C] a shop or part of a shop that prepares and sells medicines **2** [U] the study of the preparation of medicines

**phase¹** /feɪz/ *noun* [C] a stage or period which is part of a longer period *The first phase of the project is scheduled for completion next year.* • *My younger daughter is going through a phase of only wearing black.*

**phase²** /feɪz/ *verb*

**phase sth in** to gradually start using a new system, process, or law *The new tax will be phased in over five years.*

**phase sth out** to gradually stop using something

**PhD** /ˌpiːeɪtʃ'diː/ *noun* [C] an advanced university qualification, or a person who has this qualification *a PhD course/programme* • *Maria has a PhD in mathematics.*

**pheasant** /'fez°nt/ *noun* [C] *plural* **pheasants** or **pheasant** a bird with a long tail that is shot for food

**phenomenal** /fɪ'nɒmɪn°l/ *adj* extremely successful or showing great qualities or abilities *The film has been a phenomenal success.* • **phenomenally** *adv*

**phenomenon** /fɪ'nɒmɪnən/ *noun* [C] *plural* **phenomena** something that exists or happens, usually something unusual *storms, lightning, and other natural phenomena* • *Road rage seems to be a fairly recent phenomenon.*

**phew** (*also* **whew**) /fjuː/ *exclamation* used when you are happy that something is not going to happen, or when you are tired or hot

**philanthropist** /fɪ'lænθrəpɪst/ *noun* [C] someone who gives money to people who need help

**philosopher** /fɪ'lɒsəfə°/ *noun* [C] someone who studies or writes about the meaning of life

**philosophical** /ˌfɪlə'sɒfɪk°l/ *adj* **1** relating to the study or writing of philosophy *a philosophical problem/question* **2** accepting unpleasant situations in a calm and wise way *She seems fairly philosophical about the failure of her marriage.* • **philosophically** *adv*

**philosophy** /fɪ'lɒsəfi/ *noun* **1** [C, U] the study or writing of ideas about the meaning of life, or a particular set of ideas about the meaning of life *Descartes is considered by many to be the father of modern philosophy.* **2** [C] a way of thinking about what you should do in life *My philosophy has always been to give those with ability the chance to progress.*

**phlegm** /flem/ *noun* [U] a thick liquid produced in your lungs, throat, and nose when you have a cold (= common illness that makes you sneeze)

**phlegmatic** /fleg'mætɪk/ *adj formal* Someone who is phlegmatic is calm and does not get excited easily.

**phobia** /'fəʊbiə/ *noun* [C] an extreme fear of something *My mum's got a phobia about birds.*

o→**phone¹** /fəʊn/ (*also* **telephone**) *noun* **1** [U] a communication system that is used to talk to someone who is in another place *We'll contact you by phone when we get the results.* **2** [C] a piece of equipment that is used to talk to someone who is in another place *Would someone please answer the phone?* • *I could hear the phone ringing.* **3 on the phone a** using the phone *She's been on the phone all night.* **b** *UK* when you have a phone *Is he on the phone?* ⊃ *See also:* **cellular phone, mobile phone, pay phone.**

o→**phone²** /fəʊn/ (*also* **phone up**) *verb* [I, T] to communicate with someone by telephone *I tried to phone her last night, but she was out.* • *I'm going to phone for a taxi.* ⊃ *See usage note at* **telephone.**

P

'phone ,book noun [C] a book that contains the telephone numbers of people who live in a particular area

'phone ,box UK (US 'phone ,booth) noun [C] a small structure containing a public telephone ⊃ See picture at **telephone**.

'phone ,call noun [C] when you use the telephone Will you excuse me, I've got to **make a phone call**.

'phone ,card noun [C] a small piece of plastic used to pay for the use of some telephones

phone-in /'fəʊnɪn/ UK (US **call-in**) noun [C] a television or radio programme in which the public can ask questions or give opinions over the telephone

'phone ,number noun [C] the number of a particular telephone

phonetic /fəʊ'netɪk/ adj relating to the sounds you make when you speak the international phonetic alphabet • phonetically adv

phoney[1] UK (US **phony**) /'fəʊni/ adj informal not real He gave the police a phoney number.

phoney[2] UK (US **phony**) /'fəʊni/ noun [C] informal someone who is not sincere • phoney UK (US **phony**) adj (informal) a phoney smile

phosphate /'fɒsfeɪt/ noun [C, U] a chemical that is used in cleaning products and to help plants grow

○━photo /'fəʊtəʊ/ noun [C] a picture produced with a camera a black-and-white/colour photo • I took a photo of Jack lying on the beach. • a photo album

photocopier /'fəʊtəʊˌkɒpiər/ noun [C] a machine which produces copies of documents by photographing them ⊃ See colour picture **The Office** on page Centre 12.

photocopy /'fəʊtəʊˌkɒpi/ noun [C] a copy of a document made with a photocopier I made a **photocopy** of my letter before sending it. • photocopy verb [T]

photogenic /ˌfəʊtəʊ'dʒenɪk/ adj Someone who is photogenic has the type of face that looks attractive in a photograph.

○━photograph[1] /'fəʊtəgrɑːf/ noun [C] a picture produced with a camera a black-and-white/ colour photograph • He took a lovely **photograph of** the children in the garden.

photograph[2] /'fəʊtəgrɑːf/ verb [T] to take a photograph of someone or something They were photographed leaving a nightclub together.

photographer /fə'tɒgrəfər/ noun [C] someone whose job is to take photographs

photographic /ˌfəʊtə'græfɪk/ adj [always before noun] relating to photographs photographic equipment/film • photographic evidence

photography /fə'tɒgrəfi/ noun [U] the activity or job of taking photographs

phrasal verb /ˌfreɪzəl'vɜːb/ noun [C] a verb together with an adverb or preposition which has a different meaning to the meaning of its separate parts. For example 'look up' and 'carry on' are phrasal verbs. ⊃ See colour picture **Phrasal Verbs** on page Centre 13.

phrase[1] /freɪz/ noun [C] a group of words which are often used together and have a particular meaning

phrase[2] /freɪz/ verb [T] to express something by

choosing to use particular words It might have been better if he had phrased it differently.

○━physical[1] /'fɪzɪkəl/ adj **1** relating to the body physical fitness/strength • People put too much emphasis on physical appearance (= what you look like). • He has a severe physical disability. **2** [always before noun] relating to real things that you can see and touch a physical object • There was no physical evidence linking Jones to Shaw's murder.

physical[2] /'fɪzɪkəl/ US (UK **medical**) noun [C] an examination of your body by a doctor to find out if you are healthy

physically /'fɪzɪkəli/ adv in a way that relates to the body physically attractive/fit

,physical 'therapist US (UK/US **physiotherapist**) noun [C] someone whose job is to give people physical therapy

,physical 'therapy US (UK/US **physiotherapy**) noun [U] treatment for illness or injury in which you practise moving parts of your body

physician /fɪ'zɪʃən/ noun [C] formal a doctor

physicist /'fɪzɪsɪst/ noun [C] someone who studies physics

physics /'fɪzɪks/ noun [U] the scientific study of natural forces, such as energy, heat, light, etc

physio /'fɪziəʊ/ noun [C, U] UK informal short for physiotherapy or physiotherapist

physiological /ˌfɪziə'lɒdʒɪkəl/ adj relating to how the bodies of living things work

physiology /ˌfɪzi'ɒlədʒi/ noun [U] the scientific study of how the bodies of living things work

physiotherapist /ˌfɪziəʊ'θerəpɪst/ (also US **physical therapist**) noun [C] someone whose job is to give people physiotherapy

physiotherapy /ˌfɪziəʊ'θerəpi/ (also US **physical therapy**) noun [U] treatment for illness or injury in which you practise moving parts of your body

physique /fɪ'ziːk/ noun [C] the shape and size of your body He has a very muscular physique.

pianist /'piːənɪst/ noun [C] someone who plays the piano

piano /pi'ænəʊ/ noun [C] a large wooden musical instrument with strings inside and black and white bars that produce sounds when you press them ⊃ See also: **grand piano**.

○━pick[1] /pɪk/ verb [T] **1** CHOOSE to choose something or someone Do you want to help me pick some numbers for my lottery ticket? • I was never picked for the school football team. **2** FLOWERS/ FRUIT ETC If you pick flowers, fruit, etc, you take them off a tree or out of the ground. I picked some apples this morning. **3** REMOVE to remove small pieces from something with your fingers You'll have to let the glue dry and then you can pick it off. **4** pick a fight/argument to start a fight or argument with someone **5** pick sb's pocket to steal something from someone's pocket ⊃ See also: have a **bone[1]** to pick with sb.

pick at sth **1** to only eat a small amount of your food because you are worried or ill He picked at his food but had no appetite. **2** to remove small pieces from something with your fingers If you keep picking at that scab it'll never heal.

pick on sb to choose a person and criticize or treat them unfairly He just started picking on me for no reason.

**pick sth/sb out** to choose someone or something from a group of people or things *She picked out a red shirt for me to try on.*

**pick sth/sb up 1** to lift something or someone by using your hands *He picked his coat up off the floor.* • *Just pick up the phone and call him.* ➔ *See colour picture* **Phrasal Verbs** *on page Centre 13.* **2** to collect someone who is waiting for you, or to collect something that you have left somewhere *Can you pick me up from the airport?* • *I've got to pick up those books I ordered.*

**pick sth up 1** GET to get something *I picked up a leaflet on mortgages while I was at the bank.* • *She picked up some real bargains in the sale.* **2** LEARN to learn a new skill or language by practising it and not by being taught it *He hadn't done any skiing before the holiday, but he picked it up really quickly.* **3** ILLNESS to get an illness from someone or something *She picked up a nasty stomach bug while she was on holiday.* **4** SIGNAL If a piece of equipment picks up a signal, it receives it. *Antennas around the top of the ship picked up the radar signals.* **5** NOTICE to notice something *Police dogs picked up the scent of the two men from clothes they had left behind.*

**pick sb up 1** to start talking to someone in order to try to begin a romantic relationship with them **2** If the police pick someone up, they take that person to the police station.

**pick up 1** If a business or social situation picks up, it improves. *Business is really starting to pick up now.* **2** If the wind picks up, it becomes stronger.

**pick up sth** If a vehicle picks up speed, it starts to go faster.

pick² /pɪk/ *noun* **1** [C] a sharp metal stick used to break hard ground or rocks **2 the pick of sth** the best of a group of things or people **3 have/take your pick** to choose what you want *We've got tea, coffee, or hot chocolate – take your pick.*

picket /'pɪkɪt/ (*also* **'picket ˌline**) *noun* [C] a group of people who stand outside a building in order to show their anger about something and to try to stop people going inside • picket *verb* [I, T] *Protesters picketed cinemas across the whole country.*

ˌpicket 'fence *noun* [C] *US* a low fence made from a row of flat sticks that are pointed at the top

pickle /'pɪkl/ *noun* **1** [C, U] *UK* food which has been put into vinegar or salt water for a long time and has a sour taste *a cheese and pickle sandwich* • *cold meat and pickles* **2** [C] *US* a small cucumber (= a green, cylindrical vegetable) that has been put in vinegar or in a liquid containing salt and spices • pickled *adj pickled onions*

pickpocket /'pɪkˌpɒkɪt/ *noun* [C] someone who steals things from people's pockets

pickup /'pɪkʌp/ (*also* **'pickup ˌtruck**) *noun* [C] *US* a small, open truck

picky /'pɪki/ *adj informal* Someone who is picky does not like many things. *a picky eater* • *He's very **picky about** his clothes.*

picnic /'pɪknɪk/ *noun* [C] a meal that you make and take with you somewhere to eat outside

*We're going to **have a picnic** down by the lake.* • picnic *verb* [I] **picnicking**, *past* **picnicked**

pictorial /pɪk'tɔːriəl/ *adj* relating to pictures or shown using pictures

o--**picture¹** /'pɪktʃər/ *noun* [C] **1** DRAWING ETC a drawing, painting, or photograph of something or someone *to draw/paint a picture* • *She's got pictures of pop stars all over her bedroom wall.* • *Did you **take many pictures** (= photograph many things) while you were in Sydney?* ➔ *See colour picture* **The Living Room** *on page Centre 11.* **2** IDEA an idea of what something is like [usually singular] *I've got a much clearer picture of what's happening now.* **3** TV the image on a television screen *I'm afraid it's not a very good picture.* **4** FILM *Could this be the first animated film to win a best picture award?* **5 the pictures** *mainly UK* the cinema *I really fancy going to the pictures tonight.* **6 get the picture** *informal* used to say that someone understands a situation *Oh right, I get the picture.* **7 paint a bleak/rosy, etc picture of sth** to describe something in a particular way *She paints a rosy* (= happy) *picture of family life.* **8 put/keep sb in the picture** *informal* to explain to someone what is happening *Jim had no idea what was going on till I put him in the picture.*

picture² /'pɪktʃər/ *verb* [T] **1** to imagine something in a particular way *The house isn't at all how I had pictured it.* **2** to show someone or something in a picture [often passive] *They were pictured holding hands on the beach.*

picturesque /ˌpɪktʃə'resk/ *adj* A picturesque place is attractive to look at. *a picturesque cottage on the edge of the Yorkshire Moors*

pie /paɪ/ *noun* [C, U] a type of food made with meat, vegetables, or fruit which is covered in pastry and baked *apple/meat pie* ➔ *See also:* **mince pie**.

o--**piece¹** /piːs/ *noun* [C] **1** AMOUNT/PART an amount of something, or a part of something *a piece of paper/wood* • *She cut the flan into eight pieces.* • *Some of the pieces seem to be missing.* • *These shoes are **falling to pieces*** (= breaking into pieces). **2** ONE one of a particular type of thing *a useful piece of equipment/software* • *It's a beautiful piece of furniture.* **3** SOME some of a particular type of thing *a piece of news/information* • *Can I give you a piece of advice?* **4** ART/WRITING ETC an example of artistic, musical, or written work *There was an interesting piece on alternative medicine in the paper yesterday.* • *He's got two pieces on show in the Summer exhibition.* **5 ten-/twenty-, etc pence piece** a coin with a value of ten/twenty, etc pence (= British money) *Have you got any twenty-pence pieces for the parking meter?* **6 be a piece of cake** *informal* to be very easy *The test was a piece of cake.* **7 give sb a piece of your mind** *informal* to speak angrily to someone because they have done something wrong *If he does that again I'm going to give him a piece of my mind.* **8 go/fall to pieces** If someone goes to pieces, they become so upset that they cannot control their feelings or think clearly. *He went to pieces when his mother died.* ➔ *See also:* **set-piece**.

**piece²** /piːs/ *verb*
  **piece sth together** to try to understand something or discover the truth by collecting different pieces of information *Police are trying to piece together a profile of the murderer.*

**piecemeal** /ˈpiːsmiːl/ *adj, adv* happening very gradually *The land is being sold in a piecemeal fashion over a number of years.*

**pier** /pɪə/ *noun* [C] a long structure that is built from the land out over the sea and sometimes has entertainments, restaurants, etc on it *We went for a walk along the pier.*

**pier**

**pierce** /pɪəs/ *verb* [T] **1** to make a hole in something using a sharp point *I'd like to have my ears pierced.* **2** *literary* If a light or a sound pierces something, it is suddenly seen or heard. *A few rays of sunlight pierced the bedroom shutters.*

**piercing** /ˈpɪəsɪŋ/ *adj* **1** A piercing noise, light, etc is very strong and unpleasant. *I heard a loud, piercing scream.* **2** Piercing eyes seem to look at you very closely.

**piety** /ˈpaɪəti/ *noun* [U] a strong belief in religious morals

**pig¹** /pɪɡ/ *noun* [C] **1** a large pink, brown, or black farm animal that is kept for its meat **2** *informal* someone who is very unpleasant, or someone who eats a lot *He's an ignorant pig.* ⊃ *See also:* **guinea pig**.

**pig²** /pɪɡ/ *verb* **pigging**, *past* **pigged**
  **pig out** *informal* to eat too much *We pigged out on the cakes and pastries.*

**pigeon** /ˈpɪdʒən/ *noun* [C] a grey bird which often lives on buildings in towns

**pigeonhole¹** /ˈpɪdʒənhəʊl/ *noun* [C] one of a set of small open boxes in which letters or messages are left, especially in an office or hotel

**pigeonhole²** /ˈpɪdʒənhəʊl/ *verb* [T] If you pigeonhole someone, you unfairly decide what type of person they are.

**piggyback** /ˈpɪɡibæk/ (*also* **'piggyback ,ride**) *noun* [C] a way of carrying someone on your back in which they put their arms and legs around you

**piggy bank** /ˈpɪɡi,bæŋk/ *noun* [C] a small container, often in the shape of a pig, used by children to keep money in

**pigheaded** /ˌpɪɡˈhedɪd/ *adj* refusing to change

your opinion or the way you are doing something although it would be better if you did

**piglet** /ˈpɪɡlət/ *noun* [C] a baby pig

**pigment** /ˈpɪɡmənt/ *noun* [C, U] a substance that gives something colour *What is the name of the pigment contained in green plants?* ● **pigmentation** /ˌpɪɡmənˈteɪʃən/ *noun* [U] the natural colour of a living thing

**pigsty** /ˈpɪɡstaɪ/ (*also US* **pigpen** /ˈpɪɡpen/) *noun* [C] a place where pigs are kept

**pigtail** /ˈpɪɡteɪl/ *noun* [C] a hairstyle in which the hair is twisted together and tied [usually plural] *A little girl in pigtails presented the flowers.*

**pike** /paɪk/ *noun* [C, U] *plural* **pike** a large river fish with sharp teeth, or the meat of this fish

**pile¹** /paɪl/ *noun* **1** [C] an amount of a substance in the shape of a small hill or a number of objects on top of each other *a pile of books/ bricks* ● *a pile of sand/rubbish* ● *The clothes were arranged in piles on the floor.* **2 a pile of sth/piles of sth** *informal* a lot of something *It's all right for him, he's got piles of money.*

**pile²** /paɪl/ *verb*
  **pile in/out** *informal* to enter/leave a place quickly and not in an organized way *She opened the door and we all piled in.*
  **pile sth up** to make a lot of things into a pile by putting them on top of each other *Just pile those books up over there.*
  **pile up** If something unpleasant piles up, you get more of it. *My work's really starting to pile up.*

**pile-up** /ˈpaɪlʌp/ *noun* [C] an accident involving several cars

**pilfer** /ˈpɪlfə/ *verb* [I, T] to steal things that do not have much value

**pilgrim** /ˈpɪlɡrɪm/ *noun* [C] someone who travels to a place which is important in their religion

**pilgrimage** /ˈpɪlɡrɪmɪdʒ/ *noun* [C, U] a journey to a place which has religious importance *to go on a pilgrimage to Mecca*

**pill** /pɪl/ *noun* **1** [C] a small, hard piece of medicine that you swallow *a vitamin pill* ● *I've taken a couple of pills, but my headache still hasn't gone.* ⊃ *See picture at* **medicine**. **2 the pill** a pill which prevents a woman from becoming pregnant ⊃ *See also:* **sleeping pill**.

**pillar** /ˈpɪlə/ *noun* **1** [C] a tall structure made of stone, wood, etc which supports something above it *The new bridge will be supported by 100 concrete pillars.* **2 a pillar of sth** someone or something who is very important to a place, organization, etc *He was a pillar of the local community.*

**pillow** /ˈpɪləʊ/ *noun* [C] a soft object which you rest your head on in bed

**pillowcase** /ˈpɪləʊkeɪs/ *noun* [C] a cloth cover for a pillow

**pilot** /ˈpaɪlət/ *noun* [C] someone who flies an aircraft ● **pilot** *verb* [T]

**pimp** /pɪmp/ *noun* [C] someone who controls the work and money of a prostitute (= person who has sex for money)

**pimple** /ˈpɪmpl/ *noun* [C] a small spot on your skin ● **pimply** *adj* ⊃ *See also:* **goose pimples**.

**pin¹** /pɪn/ *noun* [C] **1** a thin piece of metal with a sharp point used to fasten pieces of cloth, etc together *She pricked her finger on a pin.* **2** a thin piece of metal, wood, plastic, etc that holds or fastens things together *He's had a metal pin put in his leg so that the bones heal properly.* ⊃ *See also:* **drawing pin, pins and needles, rolling pin, safety pin.**

**pin²** /pɪn/ *verb* [T] **pinning,** *past* **pinned 1** to fasten something with a pin *We're not allowed to pin anything on these walls.* • *She had a red ribbon pinned to her collar.* **2 pin sb to/against/under, etc** to force someone to stay in a position by holding them *They pinned him to the ground.* ⊃ *See also:* pin your hopes (**hope²**) on sb/sth.

**pin sb down 1** to make someone give you details or a decision about something *I've been trying to get a decision from Jim, but he's very difficult to pin down.* **2** to force someone to stay in a horizontal position by holding them *They pinned him down on the floor.*

**pin sth down** to discover exact details about something *Investigators are trying to pin down the cause of the fire.*

**pin sth on sb** *informal* to blame someone for something they did not do *They tried to pin the murder on the dead woman's husband.*

**pin sth up** to fasten something to a wall using a pin *The exam results have been pinned up on the noticeboard.*

**PIN** /pɪn/ (*also* '**PIN ,number**) *noun* [C] *abbreviation for* Personal Identification Number: the secret number that allows you to use a bank card in a machine

**pinafore** /'pɪnəfɔːʳ/ *UK* (*US* **jumper**) *noun* [C] a loose dress with no sleeves that is worn over other clothes such as a shirt

**pincer** /'pɪnsəʳ/ *noun* [C] one of a pair of curved hand-like parts of an animal such as a crab (= round, flat sea animal with ten legs)

**pinch¹** /pɪnʃ/ *verb* [T] **1** to press someone's skin tightly between your thumb and first finger, sometimes causing pain *One of the kids had been pinching her and she was crying.* **2** *mainly UK informal* to steal something that does not have much value *Who's pinched my ruler?*

**pinch²** /pɪnʃ/ *noun* [C] **1** a small amount of a substance that you pick up between your thumb and your first finger *a pinch of salt/ pepper* ⊃ *See colour picture* **Quantities** *on page Centre 14.* **2** when you press part of the body or an area of skin tightly between your thumb and first finger **3 at a pinch** *UK* (*US* **in a pinch**) If something can be done at a pinch, it is possible but it is difficult. *We can fit ten round the table, at a pinch.* **4 feel the pinch** to have problems because you do not have enough money ⊃ *See also:* take sth with a pinch of **salt¹**.

**pinched** /pɪnʃt/ *adj* A pinched face looks thin and ill.

**pine¹** /paɪn/ *noun* **1** [C, U] (*also* '**pine ,tree**) a tall tree with long, thin leaves shaped like needles **2** [U] the pale coloured wood from this tree

**pine²** /paɪn/ (*also* **pine away**) *verb* [I] to be sad because you want someone or something that has gone away *He's pining for his ex-girlfriend.*

**pineapple** /'paɪnæpl/ *noun* [C, U] a large fruit with thick skin and sharp leaves sticking out of the top which is sweet and yellow inside

**pinecone** /'paɪn,kəʊn/ *noun* [C] a hard, brown, oval object that grows on pine and fir trees (= tall trees which stay green all winter)

**ping** /pɪŋ/ *verb* [I] to make a short, high noise like a bell *They could hear the microwave pinging in the kitchen.* • ping *noun* [C]

**pink** /pɪŋk/ *adj* being a pale red colour *pretty, pink flowers* • pink *noun* [C, U] ⊃ *See colour picture* **Colours** *on page Centre 6.*

**pinnacle** /'pɪnəkl/ *noun* [no plural] the highest or best part of something *At 35, she is at the pinnacle of her career.*

**pinpoint** /'pɪnpɔɪnt/ *verb* [T] to say exactly what or where something is *It is difficult to pinpoint the exact time of death.*

,**pins and 'needles** *noun* **have pins and needles** to feel slight sharp pains in a part of your body when you move it after keeping it still for a period of time

**pint** /paɪnt/ *noun* [C] **1** (*written abbreviation* **pt**) a unit for measuring liquid, equal to 0.568 litres in the UK and 0.473 litres in the US **2** *UK informal* a pint of beer

**pin-up** /'pɪnʌp/ *noun* [C] an attractive, famous person who is often in big photographs which people stick to their walls, or the photograph of that person

**pioneer** /,paɪə'nɪəʳ/ *noun* [C] someone who is one of the first people to do something *one of the pioneers of modern science* • pioneer *verb* [T] *He pioneered the use of lasers in surgery.*

**pioneering** /,paɪə'nɪərɪŋ/ *adj* [always before noun] starting the development of something important *pioneering work/research on atomic energy*

**pious** /'paɪəs/ *adj* having strong religious beliefs and living or behaving in a way which shows these beliefs

**pip¹** /pɪp/ *noun* [C] *UK* a small seed inside fruit such as apples and oranges

**pip²** /pɪp/ *verb* [T] **pipping,** *past* **pipped** *UK informal* to beat someone by a very small amount

**pipe¹** /paɪp/ *noun* [C] **1** a long tube which liquid or gas can move through *A water pipe had burst, flooding the basement.* **2** a tube with a bowl-shaped part at one end, used to smoke tobacco *to smoke a pipe* ⊃ *See also:* **exhaust pipe.**

**pipe²** /paɪp/ *verb* [T] to send something through a pipe *Water is piped from a spring to houses in the local area.*

**pipe down** *informal* to stop making noise and become quieter *You kids better pipe down in there!*

**pipe up** *informal* to suddenly say something *Then Lydia piped up with her view of things.*

**pipeline** /'paɪplaɪn/ *noun* [C] **1** a series of pipes

**pineapple**

that carry liquid or gas over a long distance **2 be in the pipeline** If a plan is in the pipeline, it is being developed and will happen in the future. *We have several projects in the pipeline.*

**piping** /'paɪpɪŋ/ *noun* [U] a piece of pipe *copper piping*

**piping 'hot** *adj* Piping hot food is very hot.

**piquant** /'piːkənt/ *adj formal* having a pleasant, spicy taste

**pique**[1] /piːk/ *noun* [U] *formal* when someone is annoyed

**pique**[2] /piːk/ *verb* piquing, *past* piqued **pique sb's curiosity/interest, etc** to make someone interested in something

**piqued** /piːkt/ *adj* annoyed

**piracy** /'paɪrəsi/ *noun* [U] **1** attacking and stealing from ships **2** the illegal activity of copying and selling music, films, etc *software/video piracy*

**pirate**[1] /'paɪrət/ *noun* [C] **1** someone who attacks ships and steals from them **2** someone who illegally copies and sells music, films, etc

**pirate**[2] /'paɪrət/ *verb* [T] to illegally copy and sell music, films, etc

**pirate**[3] /'paɪrət/ *adj* [always before noun] illegally copied *a pirate CD/video*

**Pisces** /'paɪsiːz/ *noun* [C, U] the sign of the zodiac which relates to the period of 20 February – 20 March, or a person born during this period ➔ *See picture at* **zodiac**.

**piss**[1] /pɪs/ *verb* [I] *very informal* a very impolite word meaning to pass urine from the body **piss sb off** *very informal* to annoy someone

**piss**[2] /pɪs/ *noun* **take the piss** *UK very informal* an impolite phrase meaning to make jokes about someone

**pissed** /pɪst/ *adj very informal* **1** *mainly UK* an impolite way of describing someone who has drunk too much alcohol **2** *US* an impolite way of describing someone who is angry

**pissed 'off** *adj very informal* an impolite way of describing someone who is angry

**pistol** /'pɪstəl/ *noun* [C] a small gun

**piston** /'pɪstən/ *noun* [C] a part of an engine that moves up and down and makes other parts of the engine move

**pit**[1] /pɪt/ *noun* [C] **1** HOLE a large hole which has been dug in the ground **2** SEED *US* (*UK* stone) a large, hard seed that grows inside some types of fruit and vegetables **3** COAL (*also US* 'pit ,mine) a place where coal is dug out from under the ground *Thousands of jobs were lost as more pits closed.* **4 the pits** *UK* (*US* the pit) the place where racing cars stop to be repaired or filled with fuel during a race **5 be the pits** *informal* to be very bad *Our hotel was the absolute pits.*

**pit**[2] /pɪt/ *verb* pitting, *past* pitted **pit sb/sth against sb/sth** to make someone or something compete against someone or something else *Chelsea will be pitted against Manchester United in the fourth round of the tournament.*

**pitch**[1] /pɪtʃ/ *verb* **1** LEVEL [T] to make something suitable for a particular level or group of people [often passive] *His talk was pitched at slightly too high a level for the audience.* **2** PERSUADE [I, T] *mainly US* to try to persuade someone to do

something *She pitched the idea to me over lunch.* ● *They are* **pitching for** *new business at the moment.* **3 pitch (sb/sth) forward/into, etc** to suddenly move in a particular direction, or to make someone or something suddenly move in a particular direction *He braked too hard and the car pitched forward.* ● *She pitched the stone into the river.* **4 pitch a tent** to choose a place for a tent and put it there **5** BALL [I, T] in baseball, to throw the ball towards the person who is going to hit it *He used to pitch for the Chicago White Sox.* **6** SOUND [T] to make sound at a particular level *The tune was pitched much too high for me.*

**pitch in** *informal* to help a group of people to do some work that needs to be done *If we all pitch in, we'll get this kitchen cleaned up in no time.*

**pitch**[2] /pɪtʃ/ *noun* **1** SPORT [C] *UK* an area of ground where a sport is played *a cricket/football pitch* **2** THROW [C] in baseball, a throw towards the person who is going to hit the ball *He struck out two batters with six pitches.* **3** SOUND [U] how high or low a sound is **4** PERSUADING [C, U] the things someone says in order to persuade you to do something *I wasn't very impressed by his sales pitch.* ➔ *See also:* **fever pitch**.

**pitch-black** /ˌpɪtʃ'blæk/ (*also* **pitch-dark**) *adj* very dark *Outside it was pitch-black.*

**pitcher** /'pɪtʃər/ *noun* [C] **1** in baseball, someone who throws the ball at the person who is going to hit it ➔ *See colour picture* **Sports 2** *on page Centre 16.* **2** *US* a container for holding and pouring out liquids *a pitcher of water*

**pitfall** /'pɪtfɔːl/ *noun* [C] a likely mistake or problem in a situation *the pitfalls of buying a house*

**pithy** /'pɪθi/ *adj* A pithy remark expresses something in a very clear and direct way.

**pitiful** /'pɪtɪfəl/ *adj* **1** making you feel pity *I didn't recognize him, he looked so pitiful.* **2** very bad *a pitiful excuse* ● *pitiful wages* ● **pitifully** *adv*

**pittance** /'pɪtəns/ *noun* [no plural] a very small amount of money *She works very long hours and yet she earns a pittance.*

◐─ **pity**[1] /'pɪti/ *noun* **1 It's a pity...** used to say that something is disappointing *It's a pity you're not staying longer.* **2** [U] a feeling of sympathy for someone *It's not pity she needs, it's practical help.* ● *I was hoping someone would* **take pity on me** (= help me in a difficult situation) *and give me a lift home.* ➔ *See also:* **self-pity**.

**pity**[2] /'pɪti/ *verb* [T] to feel sorry for someone *She doesn't want people to pity her.*

**pivot** /'pɪvət/ *noun* [C] **1** a fixed point on which something balances or turns **2** the most important part of something ● **pivot** *verb* [I, T]

**pivotal** /'pɪvətəl/ *adj* having a very important influence on something *He has played a pivotal role in the negotiations.*

**pixel** /'pɪksəl/ *noun* [C] a small point that forms part of the image on a computer screen

**pixie** /'pɪksi/ *noun* [C] a small imaginary person who can do magic things

**pizza** /'piːtsə/ *noun* [C, U] a food made from a flat, round piece of bread covered with cheese, vegetables, etc and cooked in an oven ➔ *See colour picture* **Food** *on page Centre 7.*

**placard** /'plækɑːd/ noun [C] a large sign with writing that someone carries, often to show that they disagree with something

**placate** /plə'keɪt/ ⓤⓢ 'pleɪkeɪt/ verb [T] formal to make someone less angry about something

o─**place¹** /pleɪs/ noun **1** [SOMEWHERE] [C] a position, building, town, area, etc His leg's broken in two places. • Is there a place where we can talk privately? • Edinburgh would be a nice place to live. • What a stupid place to park. **2 take place** to happen The meeting will take place next week. **3 in place a** in the correct position The chairs are all in place. **b** If a rule, system, etc is in place, it has started to exist. There are now laws in place to prevent this from happening. **4 out of place a** not in the correct position Why are my files all out of place? **b** not right or suitable for a particular situation Everyone else was wearing jeans and I felt completely out of place in my office clothes. **5 all over the place** in or to many different places There was blood all over the place. • I ran all over the place looking for them. **6 in place of sth** instead of something Try adding fruit to your breakfast cereal in place of sugar. **7** [HOME] [C] informal someone's home Do you want to come over to my place tonight? • They've just bought a place in Spain. **8** [OPPORTUNITY] [C] an opportunity to take part in something Are there any places left on the theatre trip? • She's got a place at Liverpool University to do Spanish. **9 in first/second/third, etc place** If you are in first/second, etc place in a race or competition, that is your position. He finished in fifth place. **10 fall into place** When events or details that you did not understand before fall into place, they become easy to understand. When Jo told me she had a twin sister, everything fell into place. **11 in the first place** used to refer to the time when something started How did this error happen in the first place? **12 put sb in their place** to let someone know that they are not as important as they think they are ➔ See also: **decimal place**, have/take **pride¹** of place.

**place²** /pleɪs/ verb **1 place sth in/on, etc** to put something somewhere carefully She placed a large dish in front of me. **2** [T] to cause someone to be in a situation One stupid action has placed us all at risk. **3 can't place sb** to not be able to remember who someone is or where you have met them I recognize her face, but I can't quite place her. **4 place an advertisement/bet/order, etc** to arrange to have an advertisement, bet, order, etc **5 place emphasis/importance, etc on sth** to give something emphasis, importance, etc They place a lot of importance on qualifications.

**placement** /'pleɪsmənt/ noun **1** [C] UK a position that someone has with an organization for a short time in order to learn about the work that is done there He got a month's placement on a national newspaper. **2** [U, no plural] when you put something or someone somewhere the placement of additional police on the streets

**placid** /'plæsɪd/ adj A placid person is calm and does not often get angry or excited. • placidly adv

**plagiarism** /'pleɪdʒ°rɪz°m/ noun [U] when someone copies someone else's work or ideas He was accused of plagiarism.

**plagiarize** (also UK **-ise**) /'pleɪdʒ°raɪz/ verb [I, T] to copy someone else's work or ideas • plagiarist /'pleɪdʒ°rɪst/ noun [C] someone who plagiarizes

**plague¹** /pleɪg/ noun [C] **1** a serious disease that spreads quickly and kills a lot of people **2 a plague of sth** a large number of something unpleasant that causes a lot of damage a plague of rats

**plague²** /pleɪg/ verb [T] **plaguing**, past **plagued** to make someone suffer for a long time [often passive] He's been plagued by bad luck ever since he bought that house.

**plaid** /plæd/ noun [C, U] US cloth with a pattern of different coloured squares and crossing lines a plaid dress

o─**plain¹** /pleɪn/ adj **1** [SIMPLE] simple and not complicated plain food **2** [NOT MIXED] not mixed with other colours, substances, etc a plain blue carpet • plain yoghurt **3** [PERSON] A plain person is not attractive to look at. **4** [OBVIOUS] obvious and clear [+ (that)] It's quite plain that she doesn't want to talk to me about it. ➔ See also: be plain **sailing**.

**plain²** /pleɪn/ adv informal **plain stupid/wrong, etc** completely stupid/wrong, etc That's just plain stupid!

**plain³** /pleɪn/ noun [C] a large area of flat land

**plainclothes** /'pleɪn,kləʊðz/ adj [always before noun] Plainclothes police wear normal clothes and not a uniform.

**plainly** /'pleɪnli/ adv **1** in a simple way that is not complicated plainly dressed **2** in a clear and obvious way This is plainly wrong.

**plaintiff** /'pleɪntɪf/ noun [C] someone who takes legal action against someone else in a court of law

**plaintive** /'pleɪntɪv/ adj sounding sad a plaintive cry

**plait** /plæt/ UK (US **braid**) verb [T] to twist three pieces of hair, rope, etc together so that they form one long piece • plait UK (US **braid**) noun [C] She wore her hair in plaits. ➔ See colour picture **Hair** on page Centre 9.

o─**plan¹** /plæn/ noun [C] **1** an arrangement for what you intend to do or how you intend to do something the country's economic plan • Do you have any plans for the weekend? • The plan is that we'll buy a car once we're there. • There's been a **change of plan** and we're going on Wednesday instead. • Luckily, everything went **according to plan** (= happened the way it was planned). **2** a drawing that shows how something appears from above or will appear from above when it is built a street plan. • We had a designer draw up a plan for the yard.

o─**plan²** /plæn/ verb **planning**, past **planned** **1** [I, T] to think about and decide what you are going to do or how you are going to do something We're just planning our holidays. • As a manager, you've got to **plan ahead**. • I'd **planned** the meeting for Friday. **2 plan to do sth** to intend to do something He plans to go to college next year. **3** [T] to decide how something will be built We got an architect to help us plan our new kitchen.

P

**plan on doing sth** to intend to do something *We're planning on catching the early train.*

**plan sth out** to think about and decide what you are going to do or how you are going to do something *Have you planned out your journey?* ● *I'm just planning out my day.*

☞**plane**[1] /pleɪn/ *noun* [C] **1** [FLYING] a vehicle that flies and has an engine and wings *What time does her plane get in (= arrive)?* ● *He likes to watch the planes taking off and landing.* ● *a plane crash* **2** [TOOL] a tool that you use to make wood smooth **3** [SURFACE] in mathematics, a flat surface

**plane**[2] /pleɪn/ *verb* [T] to make a piece of wood smooth using a tool called a plane

**planet** /'plænɪt/ *noun* [C] a large, round object in space that moves around the sun or another star *Jupiter is the largest planet of our solar system.* ● **planetary** *adj* relating to planets

**planetarium** /ˌplænɪ'teəriəm/ *noun* [C] *plural* **planetariums** or **planetaria** a building that has a machine for showing the positions and movements of the stars and planets

**plank** /plæŋk/ *noun* [C] a long, flat piece of wood *wooden planks*

**plankton** /'plæŋktən/ *noun* [U] very small plants and animals in the sea that are eaten by fish

**planner** /'plænə/ *noun* [C] someone whose job is to plan things, especially which buildings are built in towns *urban planners*

**planning** /'plænɪŋ/ *noun* [U] **1** the activity of thinking about and deciding what you are going to do or how you are going to do something *Events like these take months of careful planning.* **2** control over which buildings are built in an area *town planning* ➔ *See also:* **family planning**.

☞**plant**[1] /plɑːnt/ *noun* [C] **1** a living thing that grows in the soil or water and has leaves and roots, especially one that is smaller than a tree *Have you watered the plants?* ● *tomato plants* **2** a large factory where an industrial process happens *a nuclear power plant* ➔ *See also:* **potted plant**.

**plant**[2] /plɑːnt/ *verb* [T] **1** [SEEDS/PLANTS] to put seeds or plants in the ground so that they will grow *to plant bulbs/seeds/trees* **2** [SECRETLY] to secretly put something in a place that will make someone seem guilty *She insisted that the drugs had been **planted on** her without her knowledge.* **3 plant a bomb** to put a bomb somewhere so that it will explode there **4 plant sth in/next/on, etc** to put something firmly in a particular place *He planted himself next to me on the sofa.* **5** [IDEA/DOUBTS] to make someone start thinking something *I was confident till you planted doubts in my mind.*

**plantation** /plæn'teɪʃən/ *noun* [C] **1** an area of land in a hot country where a crop is grown *a banana/cotton/sugar plantation* **2** an area of land where trees are grown to produce wood

**plaque** /plɑːk/ *noun* **1** [C] a flat piece of metal or stone with writing on it which is fixed to a wall, often in order to make people remember a dead person *There's a commemorative plaque outside the house where he was born.* **2** [U] a harmful substance that forms on your teeth

**plasma** /'plæzmə/ *noun* [U] the clear liquid part of blood which contains the blood cells

**plaster**[1] /'plɑːstə/ *noun* **1** [U] a substance that is spread on walls in order to make them smooth **2** [C] *UK* (*US* **Band-Aid** *trademark*) a small piece of sticky material that you put on cuts on your body **3 be in plaster** *UK* (*US* **be in a cast**) If your arm or leg is in plaster, it is covered in a hard, white substance to protect a broken bone. *She had her leg in plaster for three months after the accident.*

**plaster**[2] /'plɑːstə/ *verb* [T] **1** to cover most of a surface with something *My boots were **plastered with** mud.* ● *She had plastered posters all over her bedroom wall.* **2** to cover a wall with a substance in order to make it smooth

**plastered** /'plɑːstəd/ *adj informal* very drunk

☞**plastic** /'plæstɪk/ *noun* [C, U] a light, artificial substance that can be made into different shapes when it is soft and is used in a lot of different ways *Most children's toys are made of plastic.* ● **plastic** *adj a plastic bag/container/raincoat*

**plasticity** /plæs'tɪsəti/ *noun* [U] *formal* the quality of being soft enough to make into many different shapes

**plastic 'surgery** *noun* [U] operations on someone's face or body to make them more attractive *to have plastic surgery*

**'plastic ˌwrap** *US* (*UK* **clingfilm**) *noun* [U] thin, transparent plastic used for wrapping or covering food

☞**plate** /pleɪt/ *noun* **1** [FOOD] [C] a flat, round object which is used for putting food on *a dinner plate* ● *a plate of biscuits* **2** [METAL/GLASS] [C] a flat piece of metal or glass *I had a metal plate put in my knee after the accident.* **3 gold/silver plate** metal with a thin layer of gold or silver on top **4** [PICTURE] [C] a picture in a book ➔ *See also:* **L-plate, license plate, number plate**.

**plateau** /'plætəʊ/ ⓤⓢ plæ'təʊ/ *noun* [C] *plural* (*UK*) **plateaux** (*also US*) **plateaus 1** a large area of high, flat land **2** a period when the level of something stays the same [usually singular] *Sales are still good but they've reached a plateau.*

**platform** /'plætfɔːm/ *noun* [C] **1** [RAISED SURFACE] a raised surface for people to stand on, especially when they are speaking to a lot of people *The speakers all stood on a platform.* **2** [TRAIN] the area in a railway station where you get on and off the train *The train for London, Paddington, will depart from platform 12.* **3** [POLITICS] all the things that a political party promises to do if they are elected *They campaigned on a platform of low taxation.* **4** [FOR OPINIONS] a way of telling the public about your opinions *Basically, he uses the newspaper as a platform for airing his political views.*

**platinum** /'plætɪnəm/ ⓤⓢ 'plætnəm/ *noun* [U] a silver-coloured metal that is very valuable

**platitude** /'plætɪtjuːd/ *noun* [C] something that is boring because it has been said many times before

**platonic** /plə'tɒnɪk/ *adj* A platonic relationship is friendly and not sexual.

**platoon** /plə'tuːn/ *noun* [C] a small group of soldiers

**platter** /'plætər/ noun [C] a large plate used for serving food

**plaudit** /'plɔːdɪt/ noun [C] formal praise [usually plural] *He has **earned/won** plaudits* (= been praised) *for his latest novel.*

**plausible** /'plɔːzɪbl/ adj If something that someone says or writes is plausible, it could be true. *a plausible excuse/explanation* • plausibility /ˌplɔːzɪ'bɪləti/ noun [U] when something is plausible ↗ *Opposite* **implausible**.

o-x**play**¹ /pleɪ/ verb **1** SPORTS/GAMES [I, T] When you play a sport or game, you take part in it. *You play tennis, don't you Sam?* • *We often used to play cards.* • *I used to **play** netball **for** my school.* • *I'm playing Tony* (= playing against Tony) *at squash tonight.* • *Two of the team weren't playing because they were injured.* • *Newcastle are **playing against** Arsenal tonight.* **2** CHILDREN [I, T] When children play, they enjoy themselves with toys and games. *She likes playing with her dolls.* • *Emma won't play with me.* **3** MUSIC [I, T] to make music with a musical instrument *Tim was playing the piano.* **4** RECORD/RADIO [I, T] If a radio, record, etc plays, it produces sounds, or if you play a radio, record, etc you make it produce sounds. *A radio was playing in the background.* • *He plays his records late into the night.* **5** ACTING [T] to be a character in a film or play *Morgan played the father in the film version.* **6 play a joke/trick on sb** to deceive someone as a joke *I played a trick on her and pretended we'd eaten all the food.* ↗ *See also:* play it by **ear**, play sth by **ear**, play games (**game**¹), play (it) **safe**¹, play for **time**¹, play **truant**.

**play about/around** to behave in a silly way *Stop playing around and get on with your homework!*

**be playing at sth** UK If you ask what someone is playing at, you are angry because they are doing something silly. *What do you think you're playing at!*

**play sth back** to listen to sounds or watch pictures that you have just recorded *When I played back our conversation, I realized I hadn't made myself clear.*

**play sth down** to try to make people think that something is less important or bad than it really is *The government have tried to play down the seriousness of the incident.*

**play on sth** to use someone's fears in order to make that person do or believe what you want *A lot of marketing strategies just play on your fears and insecurities.*

**play up** UK **1** If a child plays up, he or she behaves badly. **2** If a machine plays up, it does not work as it should.

**play (about/around) with sth 1** to think about or try different ways of doing something *We've been playing around with ideas for a new TV show.* **2** to keep touching or moving something, often when you are bored or nervous *Stop playing with your hair!*

**play**² /pleɪ/ noun **1** THEATRE [C] a story that is written for actors to perform, usually in a theatre *We saw a play at the National Theatre.* • *Most schools usually **put on a play** (= perform a play) at Christmas.* **2** SPORTS/ GAMES [U] the activity of taking part in a sport or a game *Rain stopped play in the Hingis-Davenport match.* **3** CHILDREN [U] when children enjoy themselves with toys and games *a play area* **4 fair play** behaviour that is fair, honest, and does not take advantage of people **5 a play on words** a joke using a word or phrase that has two meanings ↗ *See also:* **foul play**, **role-play**.

**playboy** /'pleɪbɔɪ/ noun [C] a rich man who spends his time enjoying himself and has relationships with a lot of beautiful women

o-x**player** /'pleɪər/ noun [C] **1** someone who plays a sport or game *football/tennis players* **2** someone who plays a musical instrument *a piano player* ↗ *See also:* **CD player**, **cassette player**, **record player**.

**playful** /'pleɪfəl/ adj funny and not serious *a playful mood/remark* • playfulness noun [U] • playfully adv

**playground** /'pleɪgraʊnd/ noun [C] an area of land where children can play, especially at school

**playgroup** /'pleɪgruːp/ noun [C] a place where small children go during the day when they are too young to go to school

**'playing ,card** noun [C] one of a set of 52 small pieces of stiff paper with numbers and pictures on, used for playing games

**'playing ,field** noun [C] **1** an area of land used for sports such as football **2 a level playing field** a situation in which everyone has the same chance of succeeding

**playoff** /'pleɪɒf/ noun [C] a game between two teams that have equal points in order to decide which is the winner

**playpen** /'pleɪpen/ noun [C] a small structure with net or bars around the sides that young children are put into so that they can play safely

**playroom** /'pleɪruːm/ noun [C] a room in a house for children to play in

**plaything** /'pleɪθɪŋ/ noun [C] someone who is treated without respect and is forced to do things for someone else's enjoyment

**playtime** /'pleɪtaɪm/ noun [C, U] UK a period of time when children at school can play outside

**playwright** /'pleɪraɪt/ noun [C] someone who writes plays

**plaza** /'plɑːzə/ noun [C] US **1** an open, public area in a city or town *Mexico City's main plaza is called the Zocalo.* **2** a group of buildings with shops, often including an open, public area *a shopping plaza*

**plc, PLC** /ˌpiːel'siː/ noun [C] abbreviation for Public Limited Company: used after the name of a large company in Britain whose shares (= equal parts of its total value) can be bought and sold by the public

**plea** /pliː/ noun [C] **1** when someone says in a court of law if they are guilty or not guilty of the crime they have been accused of *a plea of guilty/not guilty* **2** a strong request *an emotional plea for forgiveness*

**plead** /pliːd/ verb past **pleaded** (also US) **pled 1** LEGAL [T] to say in a court of law if you are guilty or not guilty of the crime you have been accused of *He **pleaded** not guilty **to** five felony*

**P**

*charges.* **2** ASK [I] to ask for something in a strong and emotional way *"You must believe me!" she pleaded.* • *He pleaded with her to come back.* • *She pleaded for mercy.* **3** EXCUSE [T] to say something as an excuse *You'll just have to plead ignorance* (= say you did not know). **4 plead sb's case/cause** to say something to try to help someone get what they want or avoid punishment

⚬⁻**pleasant** /'plezⁿnt/ *adj* **1** enjoyable or attractive *pleasant weather/surroundings* • *We had a very pleasant evening.* **2** A pleasant person has a friendly character. ➲ *Opposite* **unpleasant**.
• pleasantly *adv I was pleasantly surprised.*

**pleasantry** /'plezⁿntri/ *noun* [C] a polite thing that you say when you meet someone [usually plural] *They exchanged pleasantries about the weather.*

⚬⁻**please**¹ /pliːz/ *exclamation* **1** something that you say to be polite when you are asking for something or asking someone to do something *Could you fill in the form, please?* • *I'll have the curry, please.* • *Please may I use your telephone?* **2 Yes, please.** used to accept something politely *"Would you like a lift home?" "Oh yes, please."*

**please**² /pliːz/ *verb* **1** [I, T] to make someone happy *the desire to please* • *I only got married to please my parents.* ➲ *Opposite* **displease**. **2 anything/as/what/whatever, etc you please** used to say that someone can have or do anything they want *Feel free to talk about anything you please.* • *He can come and go as he pleases.* **3 Please yourself.** a slightly rude way of telling someone that you do not care what they choose to do *"I don't want anything to eat." "Please yourself."*

⚬⁻**pleased** /pliːzd/ *adj* **1** happy or satisfied *I wasn't very pleased about having to pay.* • [+ to do sth] *I'm pleased to be back in England.* • [+ (that)] *He was pleased that she had come back.* • *I'm really pleased with the quality of his work.* **2 Pleased to meet you.** a polite way of greeting someone you are meeting for the first time

**pleasing** /'pliːzɪŋ/ *adj* Something that is pleasing gives pleasure. *the most pleasing aspect of her work* • *These buildings are very pleasing to the eye.*

**pleasurable** /'pleʒᵊrəbl/ *adj* enjoyable *a pleasurable experience*

⚬⁻**pleasure** /'pleʒəʳ/ *noun* **1** HAPPINESS [U] a feeling of happiness or enjoyment *His visits used to give us such pleasure.* • *She seemed to take pleasure in* (= enjoy) *humiliating people.* • *It gives me great pleasure to introduce our next guest.* ➲ *Opposite* **displeasure**. **2** ENJOYABLE EXPERIENCE [C, U] an enjoyable activity or experience *Food is one of life's great pleasures.* • *It was a pleasure to do business with you.* • *I once had the pleasure of sharing a taxi with her.* **3** NOT WORK [U] If you do something for pleasure, you do it because you enjoy it and not because it is your job. *reading for pleasure* • *I never mix business and pleasure.* **4 It's a pleasure.; My pleasure.** a polite way of replying to someone who has thanked you *"Thank you for a wonderful evening." "My pleasure."*

**pleated** /'pliːtɪd/ *adj* A pleated piece of clothing or piece of cloth has regular, vertical folds in it. *a pleated skirt*

**pled** /pled/ *US past of* plead

**pledge**¹ /pledʒ/ *noun* [C] a serious promise [+ to do sth] *a pledge to create jobs* • *He made a solemn pledge to the American people.*

**pledge**² /pledʒ/ *verb* [T] to promise seriously to do something or give something *Foreign donors have pledged $550 million.* • *He pledged his support to Mandela.* • [+ to do sth] *He pledged to cut government salaries.*

**plentiful** /'plentɪfᵊl/ *adj* If something is plentiful, there is a lot of it available. *a plentiful supply of meat*

⚬⁻**plenty** /'plenti/ *quantifier* **1** easily as much or as many as you need *Don't bring any food – we've got plenty.* • *There is plenty of evidence to support her claims.* • *There's plenty of room.* • *Help yourself to food – there's plenty more.* **2 plenty big/large/wide, etc enough** easily as big/large/wide, etc as you need something to be *This house is plenty big enough for two families.* **3** a lot *I know plenty of unemployed musicians.* • *There's plenty for you to do.* • *He has plenty to say on the subject.*

**plethora** /'pleθᵊrə/ *noun* **a plethora of sth** *formal* a large number of something *There is a confusing plethora of pension plans.*

**pliers** /plaɪəz/ *noun* [plural] a tool for holding or pulling small things like nails or for cutting wire *a pair of pliers* ➲ *See picture at* **tool**.

**plight** /plaɪt/ *noun* [no plural] *formal* an unpleasant or difficult situation *the plight of the sick and the poor*

**plod** /plɒd/ *verb* **plodding**, *past* **plodded** **plod along/on/through, etc** to walk with slow, heavy steps *We plodded through the mud.*

**plonk**¹ /plɒŋk/ *verb* *UK informal* **plonk sth down/in/on, etc** to put something somewhere quickly and without care *She plonked her bag on the floor.*
**plonk yourself down** to sit down quickly and without care

**plonk**² /plɒŋk/ *noun* [U] *UK informal* cheap wine

**plop**¹ /plɒp/ *noun* [C] the sound made by an object when it falls into water

**plop**² /plɒp/ *verb* **plopping**, *past* **plopped** *US informal* **plop (sth) down/onto, etc** to put something somewhere quickly and without care *She plopped down next to me.*

**plot**¹ /plɒt/ *noun* [C] **1** STORY the things that

happen in a story *I don't like movies with complicated plots.* **2** PLAN a plan to do something bad [+ to do sth] *a plot to blow up the embassy* **3** LAND a piece of land, often for growing food or for building on *a building plot*

**plot²** /plɒt/ *verb* **plotting**, *past* **plotted 1** [I, T] to plan to do something bad [+ to do sth] *They plotted to bring down the government.* • *He fired all those accused of **plotting against** him.* **2** [T] to make marks on a map, picture, etc to show the position or development of something *This chart plots the position of all aircraft.*

**plough¹** *UK* (*US* **plow**) /plaʊ/ *noun* [C] a large tool used by farmers to turn over the soil before planting crops

plough *UK*, plow *US*

**plough²** *UK* (*US* **plow**) /plaʊ/ *verb* [I, T] to turn over soil with a plough
**plough sth back** to spend the money that a business had earned on improving that business *All profits are **ploughed back into** the company.*
**plough into sth** to hit something with great force *My car ploughed straight into the car in front.*
**plough on** to continue doing something, although it is difficult or boring
**plough through sth** to finish what you are reading, eating, or working on, although there is a lot of it *I had to plough through the whole report.*

**plow** /plaʊ/ *noun, verb US spelling of* plough
**ploy** /plɔɪ/ *noun* [C] a slightly dishonest method used to try to achieve something [+ to do sth] *The phone call was just a ploy to get rid of her.*

**pluck** /plʌk/ *verb* **1 pluck sth/sb from/out, etc** to quickly pull something or someone from the place where they are *He plucked a £50 note out of his wallet.* • *A helicopter plucked him from the sea.* **2** BIRD [T] to pull all the feathers out of a bird before cooking it **3** MUSIC [T] If you pluck the strings of a musical instrument, you pull them with your fingers to make a sound. **4** PLANT [T] *literary* to pick a flower or part of a plant **5 pluck your eyebrows** to pull hairs out of your eyebrows (= lines of hair above your eyes) to make them look tidy ⊃ *See also:* pluck up the **courage** (to do sth).

**plug¹** /plʌg/ *noun* [C] **1** ELECTRICITY a plastic or rubber object with metal pins, used to connect electrical equipment to an electricity supply *I*

need to change the plug on my hairdryer. **2** HOLE something you put in a hole to block it *a bath plug* **3** ADVERTISEMENT when someone talks about a new book, film, etc in public to advertise it *She managed to get in a plug for her new book.* **4 pull the plug** to prevent an activity from continuing *They have pulled the plug on jazz broadcasts.* ⊃ *See also:* **spark plug**.

**plug**

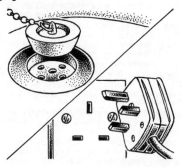

**plug²** /plʌg/ *verb* [T] **plugging**, *past* **plugged 1 plug a gap/hole** *mainly UK* to solve a problem by supplying something that is needed *The new computer system will help to plug the gap in the county's ability to collect taxes.* **2** to talk about a new book, film, etc in public to advertise it *He was on TV, plugging his new book.* **3** to block a hole
**plug away** *informal* to work hard at something for a long time *I'm still plugging away at my article.*
**plug sth in** to connect a piece of electrical equipment to an electricity supply *Could you plug the iron in for me?* ⊃ *Opposite* unplug.
**plug sth into sth** to connect one piece of electrical equipment to another *You need to plug the speakers into the stereo.*

**plughole** /'plʌghəʊl/ (*also US* **drain**) *noun* [C] the hole in a bath or sink (= place in a kitchen where dishes are washed) where the water flows away

**plum** /plʌm/ *noun* [C] a soft, round fruit with red, yellow, or purple skin and a stone in the middle

**plumage** /'pluːmɪdʒ/ *noun* [U] a bird's feathers
**plumber** /'plʌməʳ/ *noun* [C] someone whose job is to repair or connect water pipes and things like toilets and baths
**plumbing** /'plʌmɪŋ/ *noun* [U] the water pipes in a building
**plume** /pluːm/ *noun* **1 a plume of dust/ smoke, etc** a tall, thin amount of dust/smoke, etc rising into the air. **2** [C] a large feather, often worn for decoration
**plummet** /'plʌmɪt/ *verb* [I] to fall very quickly in amount or value *Temperatures plummeted to minus 20.*
**plump¹** /plʌmp/ *adj* **1** quite fat *a plump child* **2** pleasantly round or full *nice plump cloves of garlic*

P

**plump²** /plʌmp/ *verb*
  **plump for sth** *UK* to choose something, especially after thinking about it for a time *I plumped for the salmon.*

**plunder** /'plʌndəʳ/ *verb* [I, T] to steal, especially during a war *Many of the region's churches had been plundered.* • plunder *noun* [U] *They lived mainly by plunder.*

**plunge¹** /plʌndʒ/ *verb* **1 plunge down/into, etc** to fall or move down very quickly and with force *The car came off the road and plunged down the hillside.* • *He plunged into the water.* **2** [I] to become lower in temperature, value, etc very suddenly and quickly *Temperatures plunged below zero.*

  **plunge sth into sth** to push something very hard into something else *He plunged the knife into the man's stomach.*

  **plunge sb/sth into sth** to make someone or something suddenly be unhappy or in an unpleasant situation [often passive] *The country had been plunged into chaos.*

  **plunge into sth** to start doing something with a lot of energy *Trying to forget about her, he plunged into his work.*

**plunge²** /plʌndʒ/ *noun* **1** [C] a sudden and quick decrease in the value, amount, or level of something *Prices have taken a plunge* (= suddenly become less). **2 take the plunge** to do something important or difficult, especially after thinking about it for a long time *We're finally going to take the plunge and buy a house.*

**the pluperfect** /ˌpluː'pɜːfɪkt/ (*also* **the past perfect**) *noun* the form of the verb that is used to show that an action had already finished when another action happened. In English, the pluperfect is made with 'had' and a past participle.

**plural** /'plʊərəl/ *noun* [C] a word or part of a word which shows that you are talking about more than one person or thing. For example 'babies' is the plural of 'baby'. • plural *adj* 'Cattle' and 'trousers' are plural nouns.

**pluralism** /'plʊərəlɪzºm/ *noun* [U] the existence in a society of many different types of people with many different beliefs and opinions *political pluralism* • pluralist (*also* **pluralistic** /ˌplʊərəl'ɪstɪk/) *adj* relating to pluralism *a pluralist society*

o→ **plus¹** /plʌs/ *preposition* **1** added to *Five plus three is eight.* **2** and also *You've won their latest CD plus two tickets for their concert.*

**plus²** /plʌs/ *adj* **40 plus, 150 plus, etc** more than the amount stated *temperatures of 40 plus*

**plus³** /plʌs/ *conjunction informal* and also *Don't go there in August. It'll be too hot, plus it'll be really expensive.*

**plus⁴** /plʌs/ *noun* [C] **1** *informal* an advantage *Well, the apartment has a garden so that's a plus.* **2** (*also* **'plus ˌsign**) the symbol +, used between two numbers to show that they are being added together

**plush** /plʌʃ/ *adj* Plush furniture, buildings, rooms, etc are very expensive and comfortable. *a plush red carpet*

**Pluto** /'pluːtəʊ/ *noun* [no plural] the planet that is furthest from the Sun, after Neptune

**plutonium** /pluː'təʊniəm/ *noun* [U] a chemical element that is used in the production of nuclear power and nuclear weapons

**ply** /plaɪ/ *verb* **1 ply across/between, etc** *old-fashioned* to often make a particular journey *fishing boats plying across the harbour* **2 ply your trade** to work at your job, especially selling things

  **ply sb with sth 1** to give someone a lot of something again and again *They plied me with food and drink.* **2** to ask someone a lot of questions *They plied him with questions about where he had been.*

**plywood** /'plaɪwʊd/ *noun* [U] wood that is made by sticking several thin layers of wood together

o→ **p.m.** (*also* **pm**) /ˌpiː'em/ used when you are referring to a time after 12 o'clock in the middle of the day, but before 12 o'clock in the middle of the night *Opening hours: 9 a.m. - 6 p.m.*

**PM** /ˌpiː'em/ *noun* [C] *abbreviation for* prime minister: the leader of an elected government in some countries

**pneumatic** /nju:'mætɪk/ *adj* filled with air, or operated using air *pneumatic tyres* • *a pneumatic drill*

**pneumonia** /njuː'məʊniə/ *noun* [U] a serious illness in which your lungs fill with liquid and it is difficult to breathe

**poach** /pəʊtʃ/ *verb* **1** COOK [T] to cook something, especially an egg without its shell, by putting it into liquid that is gently boiling **2** ANIMALS [I, T] to illegally catch or kill animals, especially by going onto land without the permission of the person who owns it **3** PERSON [I, T] to persuade someone to leave a company or team in order to work or play for yours *They can poach experienced people easily because they offer higher salaries.*

**poacher** /'pəʊtʃəʳ/ *noun* [C] someone who illegally catches or kills animals

o→ **pocket¹** /'pɒkɪt/ *noun* [C] **1** BAG a small bag that is sewn or fixed onto or into a piece of clothing, a bag, the back of a seat, etc *a coat/shirt/trouser pocket* • *He was asked to empty his pockets.* • *Safety instructions are in the pocket on the seat in front of you.* **2** SMALL AREA/AMOUNT a small area or small amount of something that is different from what is around it *There was real poverty in some pockets of the country.* • *small pockets of air trapped inside the glass* **3** MONEY the amount of money that you have for spending *I shouldn't have to pay for travel out of my own pocket* (= with my own money). **4 be out of pocket** to have less money than you should have because you have paid for something *The holiday company cancelled our trip and we were left hundreds of pounds out of pocket.*

**pocket²** /'pɒkɪt/ *verb* [T] **1** to take something, especially money, which does not belong to you *His plan was to pocket the money from the sale of the business and leave the country.* **2** to put something in your pocket *Juan pocketed the knife and walked away.*

**pocket³** /'pɒkɪt/ *adj* [always before noun] small enough to fit in your pocket *a pocket dictionary*

**pocketbook** /'pɒkɪtbʊk/ *noun* [C] *US* **1** a woman's bag **2** Someone's pocketbook is their ability to pay for something. *The sales tax hits consumers in the pocketbook.*

**pocketful** /'pɒkɪtfʊl/ *noun* [C] the amount you can fit in a pocket *a pocketful of coins*

**pocketknife** /'pɒkɪtnaɪf/ *noun* [C] *plural* **pocketknives** a small knife that folds into a case

'**pocket ,money** *noun* [U] an amount of money given regularly to a child by its parents *Kevin spent his pocket money on ice cream and sweets.*

**pod** /pɒd/ *noun* [C] the long, flat part of some plants that has seeds in it *a pea pod*

**podiatrist** /pə'daɪətrɪst/ *US* (*UK* **chiropodist**) *noun* [C] someone whose job is to treat problems with people's feet

**podium** /'pəʊdiəm/ *noun* [C] a small, raised area, sometimes with a tall table on it, that someone stands on when they are performing or speaking

o-ᴗ**poem** /'pəʊɪm/ *noun* [C] a piece of writing, especially one that has short lines and uses words that sound the same *love poems*

**poet** /'pəʊɪt/ *noun* [C] someone who writes poems

**poetic** /pəʊ'etɪk/ *adj* **1** Something that is poetic makes you feel strong emotions because it is so beautiful. *To him, life seemed poetic.* **2** relating to poetry *poetic language*

o-ᴗ**poetry** /'pəʊɪtri/ *noun* [U] poems in general, or the writing of poetry *I enjoy all kinds of poetry, especially love poetry.* • *In her spare time she would write poetry.*

**poignant** /'pɔɪnjənt/ *adj* making you feel sad *It's a poignant story about a poor family's struggle to survive.* • poignancy /'pɔɪnjənsi/ *noun* [U] when something is poignant • poignantly *adv*

o-ᴗ**point**[1] /pɔɪnt/ *noun* **1** OPINION [C] an opinion, idea, or fact which someone says or writes *Could I make a point about noise levels? • He explained his point by drawing a diagram. • I take your point (= I agree with you) about cycling, but I still prefer to walk.* **2** IMPORTANT OPINION [no plural] an opinion or fact that deserves to be considered seriously, or which other people agree is true *"She's always complaining that the office is cold." "Well, she's got a point." • "How are we going to get there if there are no trains?" "That's a point."* **3** the point the most important part of what has been said or written *I thought he was never going to get to the point. • The point is, if you don't claim the money now you might never get it. • To say his art is simplistic is missing the point (= not understanding the most important thing about it).* **4** SHARP [C] the thin, sharp end of something *the point of a needle* **5** PLACE [C] a particular place *a stopping/fuelling point • the point where the pipes enter the building* **6** TIME [C] a particular time in an event or process *At this point, people started to leave. • It has got to the point where I can hardly bear to speak to him. • That was a particularly low point in race relations.* **7** be at/on the point of doing sth to be going to do something very soon *Amy was on the point of crying.* **8** REASON [no plural] the reason for or purpose of something *What's the point of studying if you*

can't get a job afterwards? • *There's no point inviting her – she never comes to parties.* **9** beside the point not important or not connected with what you are talking about *The fact that he doesn't want to come is beside the point – he should have been invited.* **10** make a point of doing sth to be certain that you always do a particular thing *He made a point of learning all the names of his staff.* **11** to the point If something someone says or writes is to the point, it expresses the most important things without extra details. *His report was short and to the point.* **12** up to a point partly *What he says is true up to a point.* **13** GAME [C] a unit used for showing who is winning in a game or competition *With 3 games still to play, Manchester United are 5 points ahead.* **14** MEASUREMENT [C] a unit used in some systems of measuring and comparing things *The stock exchange fell by five points.* **15** boiling/freezing/melting point the temperature at which a substance boils, freezes, or melts **16** QUALITY [C] a quality which someone has *I know she's bossy, but she has lots of good points too.* • *Chemistry never was my strong point (= I was never good at it).* **17** MATHEMATICS [C] (*also* decimal point) the mark (.) that is used to separate the two parts of a decimal *One mile equals one point six (= 1.6) kilometres.* **18** DIRECTION [C] one of the marks on a compass (= object used for showing directions) ⊃ *See also:* breaking point, a case in point, decimal point, focal point, moot point, point of view, starting-point, turning point, vantage point.

**point**

A **point** (.) is used to separate a whole number from a fraction (= number less than 1).

*Normal body temperature is 36.9° celsius.*

A **comma** (,) is used to divide large numbers into groups of three so that they are easier to read.

*28,071,973*

*1,378*

o-ᴗ**point**[2] /pɔɪnt/ *verb* **1** SHOW [I] to show where someone or something is by holding your finger or a thin object towards it *She pointed at/to a bird flying overhead.* **2** AIM [T] to hold something so that it faces towards something else *She pointed her camera at them.* **3** FACE [I] to face towards a particular direction *The solar panels were pointing away from the sun.*

**point sb/sth out** to make a person notice someone or something *I didn't think about the disadvantages until you pointed them out to me.*

**point sth out** to tell someone a fact *If he makes a mistake I always think it's best to point it out immediately.*

**point to/towards sth** to show that something probably exists, is happening, or is true *All the evidence points to suicide.*

**point-blank** /ˌpɔɪnt'blæŋk/ *adj, adv* **1** If you refuse point-blank, you refuse completely and

will not change your decision. **2 at point-
blank range** If someone is shot at point-blank
range, they are shot from a very short distance
away.

**pointed** /'pɔɪntɪd/ *adj* **1** If someone says something in a pointed way, they intend to criticize
someone. *He made some pointed references to
her history of drug problems.* **2** A pointed object
has a thin, sharp end. *a pointed chin/ beard*

**pointer** /'pɔɪntə'/ *noun* [C] **1** a piece of information which can help you understand a situation
or do something better *I asked for some point-
ers on applying for jobs.* **2** an object that you
use to point at something

**pointless** /'pɔɪntləs/ *adj* Something that is
pointless has no purpose. *pointless argu-
ments/conflict* ● [+ to do sth] *It would be pointless
to argue with him.* ● **pointlessly** *adv*

**,point of 'view** *noun* [C] *plural* **points of view**
**1** a way of thinking about a situation *From a
medical point of view, there was no need for the
operation.* **2** an opinion *You have to be willing
to see other people's points of view.*

**poise** /pɔɪz/ *noun* [U] **1** when you behave in a
calm and confident way *Recovering his poise,
he congratulated his opponent.* **2** when you
move or stand in a careful, pleasant way

**poised** /pɔɪzd/ *adj* **1** READY [never before noun]
ready to do something [+ to do sth] *They
have three hundred ships, all poised to attack.*
**2** POSITION [never before noun] in a particular
position or situation, ready to move or
change *a helicopter poised above the crowd*
**3** CALM calm and confident *a poised performance*

**poison¹** /'pɔɪz²n/ *noun* [C, U] a substance that
can make you ill or kill you if you eat or drink
it *Someone had put poison in her drink.*

**poison²** /'pɔɪz²n/ *verb* [T] **1** KILL to try to kill
someone by giving them a dangerous sub-
stance to drink or eat *He tried to poison his wife.*
**2** MAKE DANGEROUS to put poison or a dangerous substance in something *They poisoned the
city's water supply.* **3** SPOIL to make something
very unpleasant *These arguments were poisoning his life.* **4 poison sb's mind** to make
someone think bad things about someone or
something *Her father had **poisoned her mind
against** me.* ● **poisoned** *adj*

**poisoning** /'pɔɪz²nɪŋ/ *noun* [U] an illness caused
by eating, drinking, or breathing a dangerous
substance *alcohol/lead poisoning* ⊃ See also:
**food poisoning**.

**poisonous** /'pɔɪz²nəs/ *adj* **1** containing poison
*poisonous gas* **2** A poisonous animal uses
poison in order to defend itself. *a poisonous
snake*

**poke¹** /pəʊk/ *verb* **1** [T] to quickly push your
finger or other pointed object into someone or
something *Nell kept poking me in the arm.* ● *He
poked the fire with his stick.* **2 poke (sth)
round/out/through, etc** to appear through or
from behind something, or to make something
do this *Grace poked her head round the door.*
● *I thought I saw a bicycle wheel poking out
of the water.* ⊃ See also: poke your **nose¹** into
sth.

**poke about/around** *informal* to look for

**poke**

She poked her head out of
the window.

She poked him.

something by moving other things *I was
poking around in the garage, looking for a paint
brush.*

**poke²** /pəʊk/ *noun* [C] when you quickly push
your finger or other pointed object into
someone or something *I gave him a poke in the
back.*

**poker** /'pəʊkə'/ *noun* **1** [U] a game played with
cards in which people try to win money from
each other **2** [C] a long, metal stick used for
moving the coal or wood in a fire so that it
burns better

**poker-faced** /'pəʊkə,feɪst/ *adj* not showing on
your face what you are really thinking or
feeling

**poky** *informal* (*also* **pokey**) /'pəʊki/ *adj* **1** A
room or house that is poky is unpleasant
because it is too small. **2** *US* too slow

**polar** /'pəʊlə'/ *adj* relating to the North or South
Pole

**,polar 'bear** *UK* (*US* **'polar ,bear**) *noun* [C] a
large, white bear that lives in the North Pole
(= most northern part of the Earth)

**Polaroid** /'pəʊl²rɔɪd/ *noun* [C] *trademark* a
camera that prints a photograph immediately
after you have taken it, or a picture taken with
this type of camera

**pole** /pəʊl/ *noun* **1** [C] a long, thin stick made of
wood or metal, often used to hold something up
*tent poles* **2 the North/South Pole** the part of
the Earth that is furthest North/South **3 be
poles apart** to be complete opposites

**polemic** /pə'lemɪk/ *noun* [C, U] *formal* writing or
speech that strongly criticizes or defends an
idea, a belief, etc

**'pole ,vault** *noun* [no plural] a sport in which
you use a very long stick to jump over a high
bar

○⨯**police¹** /pə'liːs/ *noun* [plural] the official organization that makes people obey the law and that
protects people and places against crime, or
the people who work for this organization
*I heard a gun shot and decided to call **the
police**.* ● *A 30-year-old taxi driver is being interviewed by police.* ● *a police helicopter* ● *a police
investigation*

**police**[2] /pə'li:s/ *verb* [T] to make sure that people obey the law in a particular place or when they are doing a particular activity *Clubs have to pay for the cost of policing matches.*

po,lice 'constable *noun* [C] in the UK, a police officer of the lowest rank

po'lice de,partment *noun* [C] in the US, the police force in an area or city

po'lice ,force *noun* [C] the police in a country or area

**policeman, policewoman** /pə'li:smən, pə'li:s,wumən/ *noun* [C] *plural* **policemen, policewomen** a man/woman who is a member of the police

po'lice ,officer *noun* [C] someone who is a member of the police

po,lice 'state *UK* (*US* po'lice ,state) *noun* [C] a country in which the people are not free to do what they want because the government controls them

po'lice ,station *noun* [C] the office of the police in a town or part of a city

**policy** /'pɒləsi/ *noun* **1** [C, U] a set of ideas or a plan of what to do in particular situations that has been agreed by a government, business, etc *economic policy* • *It is company policy to help staff progress in their careers.* **2** [C] an agreement that you have with an insurance company (= company that pays the costs if you are injured, etc)

**polio** /'pəʊliəʊ/ *noun* [U] a serious disease that sometimes makes it impossible for you to move your muscles

**polish**[1] /'pɒlɪʃ/ *noun* **1** [C, U] a substance that you rub on something in order to make it clean and shiny **2** [no plural] when you rub something in order to make it clean and shiny *Just give the table a polish.* ➔ *See also:* **nail polish**.

**polish**[2] /'pɒlɪʃ/ *verb* [T] to rub something with a cloth in order to make it clean or to make it shine *to polish your shoes*

**polish sth off** *informal* to finish something quickly *I gave him a bowl of ice cream which he soon polished off.*

**polished** /'pɒlɪʃt/ *adj* **1** clean and shiny after polishing *a polished floor* **2** done with skill and style *He gave a highly polished performance.*

o━**polite** /pə'laɪt/ *adj* behaving in a way that is not rude and shows that you do not only think about yourself *I'm afraid I wasn't very polite to her.* • *She was too polite to point out my mistake.* • politely *adv He thanked them politely.* • politeness *noun* [U]

o━**political** /pə'lɪtɪkəl/ *adj* relating to or involved in politics *There are two main political parties in my country.* • *The church has a strong political influence.* • politically *adv*

po,litical a'sylum *noun* [U] protection given by a government to someone whose political activities have made it too dangerous for them to live in their own country

po,litically co'rrect *adj* careful to speak or behave in a way which is not offensive to women, people of a particular race, or people who have physical or mental problems *It's not politically correct to call women 'girls'.* • political correctness *noun* [U]

po,litical 'prisoner *noun* [C] someone who is in prison because their political activities or opinions oppose the government

o━**politician** /,pɒlɪ'tɪʃən/ *noun* [C] someone who works in politics, especially a member of the government *Churchill was a distinguished politician.*

**politicize** (*also UK* -ise) /pə'lɪtɪsaɪz/ *verb* [T] to make something or someone become more involved with politics [often passive] *The whole issue has been politicized.* • *a highly politicized debate*

o━**politics** /'pɒlɪtɪks/ *noun* **1** [ACTIVITIES] [U] ideas and activities relating to how a country or area is governed *He has little interest in local politics.* **2** [JOB] [U] a job in politics *She's planning to retire from politics next year.* **3** sb's politics someone's opinions about how a country or area should be governed *I don't know what his politics are, but he strongly disagreed with the decision.* **4** [RELATIONSHIPS] [plural] the relationships in a group which allow particular people to have power over others *I try not to get involved in office politics.*

**polka** /'pɒlkə/ *noun* [C] a type of dance, or a piece of music used for this type of dance

**polka-dot** /'pɒlkə,dɒt/ *adj* [always before noun] having a regular pattern of small, round spots *a polka-dot bikini*

**poll**[1] /pəʊl/ (*also* **opinion poll**) *noun* [C] when people are asked questions to discover what they think about a subject *A recent poll indicated that 77 percent of Americans supported the president.*

**poll**[2] /pəʊl/ *verb* [T] **1** to ask someone's opinion as part of a study on what people think about a subject [often passive] *Most students polled said they preferred the new system.* **2** to receive a particular number of votes in an election *Labour polled only 45 percent of the Scottish vote.*

**pollen** /'pɒlən/ *noun* [U] a powder produced by flowers, which is carried by insects or the wind and makes other flowers produce seeds

'pollen ,count *noun* [C] the measurement of the amount of pollen in the air

'polling ,day *UK* (*US* **election day**) *noun* [C] the day when people vote in an election

'polling ,station *UK* (*US* 'polling ,place) *noun* [C] a building where people go to vote in an election

the polls /pəʊlz/ *noun* [plural] voting in an election *The country will go to the polls* (= vote) *on 13 September.*

**pollster** /'pəʊlstər/ *noun* [C] someone who tries to discover what most people think about a subject by asking questions

**pollute** /pə'lu:t/ *verb* [T] to make water, air, soil, etc dirty or harmful *We need a fuel that won't pollute the environment.* • pollutant *noun* [C] a substance that pollutes water, air, etc

**pollution** /pə'lu:ʃən/ *noun* [U] damage caused to water, air, etc by harmful substances or waste *The book shows simple things you can do to reduce pollution from your car.*

**polo** /'pəʊləʊ/ *noun* [U] a game played between two teams who ride horses and hit a ball with long, wooden hammers

'polo ,neck *UK* (*US* **turtleneck**) *noun* [C] a piece

P

of clothing that covers the top part of the body and has a tube-like part covering the neck *a black polo neck sweater*

polo neck *UK*, turtleneck *US*

**'polo ,shirt** *noun* [C] a cotton shirt with short sleeves, a collar, and buttons at the front

**polyester** /ˌpɒli'estəʳ/ *noun* [U] a type of artificial cloth used for making clothes *a polyester shirt/skirt*

**polytechnic** /ˌpɒli'teknɪk/ *noun* [C] a college where students study scientific and technical subjects

**polythene** /'pɒliθiːn/ *UK* (*US* **polyethylene** /ˌpɒli'eθəliːn/) *noun* [U] a thin, soft plastic often used for making bags

**pomp** /pɒmp/ *noun* [U] *formal* special clothes, decorations, and music at an official ceremony

**pompous** /'pɒmpəs/ *adj* Someone who is pompous is too serious and thinks they are more important than they really are. • **pompously** *adv* • **pomposity** /pɒm'pɒsəti/ *noun* [U] when someone is pompous

**pond** /pɒnd/ *noun* [C] a small area of water, especially one that has been made artificially in a park or garden

**ponder** /'pɒndəʳ/ *verb* [I, T] *literary* to think carefully about something [+ question word] *He pondered what might have happened if he hadn't gone home.*

**ponderous** /'pɒndᵊrəs/ *adj* **1** Ponderous speech or writing is boring or too serious. **2** slow because of being very heavy or large • **ponderously** *adv*

**pony** /'pəʊni/ *noun* [C] a small horse

**ponytail** /'pəʊniteɪl/ *noun* [C] hair tied at the back of your head so that it hangs down like a horse's tail ➔ *See colour picture* **Hair** *on page Centre 9.*

**poodle** /'puːdl̩/ *noun* [C] a type of dog with thick, curly hair

**pool¹** /puːl/ *noun* **1** SWIM [C] (*also* **swimming pool**) an area of water that has been made for people to swim in *The hotel has two outdoor pools.* **2** LIQUID [C] a small area of water or a small amount of liquid on a surface *We dipped our feet in a shallow pool by the rocks.* • *a pool of blood* **3** GAME [U] a game in which two people use long, thin sticks to hit coloured balls into holes around the edge of a table **4** COLLECTION [C] a collection of money, people, or equipment which is shared by a group of people *a car pool for company business*

**pool²** /puːl/ *verb* [T] If a group of people pool their money, knowledge, or equipment, they collect it together so that it can be shared or used for a particular purpose. *Several villages pooled their resources to set up a building project.*

**the pools** /puːlz/ *noun* [plural] in Britain, a game in which people try to win a lot of money by guessing the results of football matches

o⚡**poor** /pɔːʳ/ US pʊr/ *adj* **1** NO MONEY having very little money or few possessions *Most of these people are desperately poor.* • *Modern fertilizers are too expensive for poorer countries to afford.* • *housing for the poor* **2** BAD of very low quality *poor health* • *Last year's exam results were poor.* • *a poor harvest* • *The meeting went smoothly but attendance was poor* (= not many people came). **3** NO SKILL not having much skill at a particular activity *She's always been poor at spelling.* • *Sam's a poor swimmer.* **4** SYMPATHY [always before noun] used to show sympathy for someone *That cold sounds terrible, you poor thing.* **5 be poor in sth** If something is poor in a particular substance, it has very little of the substance. *Avoid foods which are high in calories but poor in nutrients.*

**poorly¹** /'pɔːli/ *adv* badly *poorly educated*

**poorly²** /'pɔːli/ *adj UK informal* ill *Rosie was feeling poorly so I put her to bed.*

**pop¹** /pɒp/ *verb* **popping**, *past* **popped 1** [I, T] to make a short sound like a small explosion, or to make something do this by breaking it *The music played and champagne corks popped.* **2 pop in/out/over, etc** *informal* to go to a particular place *Doug's just popped out for a few minutes.* • *I'll pop in to the supermarket on my way home.* **3 pop sth in/into/on, etc** *informal* to quickly put something in a particular place *Can you pop the pizza in the oven?* **4 pop out/up** to move quickly and suddenly, especially out of something

**pop up** *informal* to suddenly appear or happen, often unexpectedly *A message just popped up on my screen.*

**pop²** /pɒp/ *noun* **1** MUSIC [U] (*also* '**pop ,music**) modern music with a strong beat which is popular with young people **2** SOUND [C] a short sound like a small explosion **3** DRINK [U] *informal* (*also US* **soda**) a sweet drink with bubbles **4** FATHER [no plural] *US informal* father

**popcorn** /'pɒpkɔːn/ *noun* [U] yellow seeds of grain that break open when heated and are eaten with salt, sugar, or butter *We sat in front of the TV with a huge bowl of popcorn.*

**Pope** /pəʊp/ *noun* [C] the leader of the Roman Catholic Church *Pope John Paul II* • *The Pope was due to visit Paraguay in May.*

**poplar** /'pɒpləʳ/ *noun* [C, U] a tall tree with branches that grow up to form a thin, pointed shape

**popper** /'pɒpəʳ/ *noun* [C] *UK* (*US* **snap**) a metal or plastic object used to fasten clothing, made of two parts which fit together with a short, loud sound

**poppy** /'pɒpi/ *noun* [C] a red flower with small, black seeds

**populace** /'pɒpjələs/ *noun* [group] *formal* all the people who live in a particular country or place

o⚡**popular** /'pɒpjələʳ/ *adj* **1** LIKED liked by many people *'Jack' was the most popular boy's name.* • *The North African coast is becoming increasingly popular with British tourists.* ➔ *Opposite* **unpopular. 2** GENERAL [always before noun] for or involving ordinary people and not specialists or people who are very educated *The issue was given full coverage in the popular press.* **3** MANY PEOPLE [always before noun] A popular belief, opinion, etc is one that many people have. *The allegations are false, contrary to popular belief.*

**popularity** /ˌpɒpjəˈlærəti/ *noun* [U] the quality of being liked by many people *the increasing popularity of organic produce* ➲ *Opposite* **unpopularity**.

**popularize** (*also UK* -**ise**) /ˈpɒpjəlˀraɪz/ *verb* [T] to make something become known or liked by many people *It was the World Cup which popularized professional soccer in the United States.*
• popularization /ˌpɒpjəlˀraɪˈzeɪʃˀn/ *noun* [U]

**popularly** /ˈpɒpjələli/ *adv* **popularly believed/ called/known, etc** believed, called, etc by most people *Los Angeles is popularly known as 'LA'.*

**populate** /ˈpɒpjəleɪt/ *verb* **be populated** If an area is populated by people or animals, they live in that area. *The countryside is densely/ sparsely populated* (= there are many/few people). • *The forest was populated by rare and colourful birds.*

o━**population** /ˌpɒpjəˈleɪʃˀn/ *noun* **1** [C, U] the number of people living in a particular area *What's the population of Brazil?* **2** [group] all the people living in a particular area, or all the people or animals of a particular type *a 9% rise in the prison population*

**populous** /ˈpɒpjələs/ *adj formal* A populous area has a lot of people living in it. *It's one of the world's most populous cities.*

**pop-up** /ˈpɒpʌp/ *adj* [always before noun] **1** A pop-up book is a book which has pictures that stand up from the pages when the book is opened. **2** A pop-up menu is a list of choices which can appear or disappear on a computer screen as you want it to. *Select the option you want from the pop-up menu.*

**porcelain** /ˈpɔːsˀlɪn/ *noun* [U] a hard, shiny, white substance used to make cups, plates, etc, or the cups and plates themselves *a porcelain dish* • *a fine collection of porcelain*

**porch** /pɔːtʃ/ *noun* [C] a covered area built onto the entrance to a house

**pore¹** /pɔːʳ/ *noun* [C] a very small hole in your skin that sweat (= salty liquid) can pass through

**pore²** /pɔːʳ/ *verb*
**pore over sth** to study or look carefully at something, especially a book or document *Jeremy spent the afternoon poring over his exam notes.*

**pork** /pɔːk/ *noun* [U] meat from a pig *roast pork*
• *pork chops*

**pornography** /pɔːˈnɒgrəfi/ (*also* **porn** *informal*) *noun* [U] magazines and films showing naked people or sexual acts that are intended to make people feel sexually excited
• pornographic /ˌpɔːnəˈgræfɪk/ *adj* relating to pornography *pornographic images/videos*

**porous** /ˈpɔːrəs/ *adj* allowing liquid or air to pass through *porous rock*

**porridge** /ˈpɒrɪdʒ/ *noun* [U] a soft, white food made of oats (= type of grain) and water or milk

**port** /pɔːt/ *noun* **1** [SHIPS] [C] a town or an area of a town next to water where ships arrive and leave from *a fishing port* • *the Belgian port of Zeebrugge* **2** [DRINK] [U] a sweet, strong, red wine

which is made in Portugal **3** [LEFT] [U] the left side of a ship or aircraft *the port side*

**portable** /ˈpɔːtəbl/ *adj* able to be carried *a portable computer/phone*

**portal** /ˈpɔːtˀl/ *noun* [C] a page on the Internet that people use to start searching the World Wide Web

**porter** /ˈpɔːtəʳ/ *noun* [C] someone whose job is to carry other people's bags in hotels, stations, etc

**portfolio** /ˌpɔːtˈfəʊliəʊ/ *noun* [C] **1** a collection of designs, pictures, documents, etc that represents a person's work, or the large, flat container that it is carried in **2** a collection of accounts, money, etc that is owned by a person or organization *a stock portfolio*

**porthole** /ˈpɔːthəʊl/ *noun* [C] a small, round window in the side of a ship or aircraft

**portion** /ˈpɔːʃˀn/ *noun* [C] **1** a part of something *A large portion of their profits go straight back into new projects.* **2** the amount of food served to one person, especially in a restaurant *Breakfast was delicious – and the portions were huge!*

**portly** /ˈpɔːtli/ *adj humorous* quite fat *a portly gentleman*

**portrait** /ˈpɔːtrɪt/ *noun* **1** [C] a painting, drawing, or photograph of someone *a portrait of the princess* • *a portrait gallery/painter* **2** a **portrait of sb/sth** a film or book which describes someone or something in detail *His latest film is a portrait of life in the 1920s.* ➲ *See also:* **self-portrait**.

**portray** /pɔːˈtreɪ/ *verb* [T] **1** If a book or film portrays someone or something, it describes or shows them. *Both novels portray the lives of professional athletes.* • *In the film he's portrayed as a hero.* **2** to act the part of a character in a film or play • portrayal *noun* [C, U] when you portray someone or something *He won several awards for his portrayal of the dictator.*

**pose¹** /pəʊz/ *verb* **1 pose a danger/problem/ threat, etc** to cause a problem *A lot of these chemicals pose very real threats to our health.* **2** [I] to stay in a particular position so that someone can paint or photograph you *The two leaders posed for photographs outside the White House.* **3** [I] *mainly UK* to try to make people notice and admire you, especially by looking fashionable *Pascal was posing in his new sunglasses.* **4 pose a question** *formal* to ask a question

**pose as sb** to pretend that you are someone else *He got into her house by posing as an electrician.*

**pose²** /pəʊz/ *noun* **1** [C] the position that you stay in while someone photographs or paints you *an elegant pose* **2** [no plural] when someone pretends to be more clever or interesting than they really are *She's not really interested in art, it's just a pose.*

**posh** /pɒʃ/ *adj* **1** expensive and used or owned by rich people *a posh hotel/restaurant* **2** *UK* from a high social class *a posh voice*

o━**position¹** /pəˈzɪʃˀn/ *noun* **1** [SITTING/STANDING] [C, U] the way someone is sitting, standing, or lying, or if something is pointing up or down, etc *a kneeling position* • *I go to sleep on my back but I always wake up in a different position.*

**P**

• *Make sure your chair is in the upright* *position.* **2** SITUATION [C] the situation that someone is in [usually singular] *She's in a very difficult position.* **3 be in a position to do sth** to be able to do something because of your situation *I'm not in a position to talk about this at the moment.* **4** PLACE [C] the place where someone or something is *I'm trying to find our position on the map.* • *You're in a good position next to the window.* **5 be in position** If someone or something is in position, they are in the place that they should be in. **6 in first/second/third, etc position** in first/second/third, etc place in a race or other competition *She finished the race in third position.* **7** JOB [C] a job *to apply for a position in a company* **8** OPINION [C] *formal* a way of thinking about a subject *What's the company's position on recycling?* **9** GAME [C] the part that someone plays in a game such as football *What position does he play?* **10** IMPORTANCE [C] your level of importance in society *the position of women in society*

**position²** /pəˈzɪʃən/ *verb* [T] to put someone or something in a place for a reason [often reflexive] *I positioned myself as far away from her as possible.*

o━**positive** /ˈpɒzətɪv/ *adj* **1** HAPPY feeling happy about your life and your future *a positive attitude* • *I'm feeling much more positive about things now.* **2** ENCOURAGING Something that is positive makes you feel better about a situation. *We've shown people samples of the product and had a very positive response.* **3** CERTAIN [never before noun] certain that something is true *"Are you sure you saw him?" "Absolutely positive."* • [+ (that)] *I'm positive that I switched it off.* **4** PROOF [always before noun] showing without any doubt that something is true *positive proof* **5** MEDICAL TEST If a medical test is positive, it shows that the person being tested has a disease or condition. *She did a pregnancy test and it was positive.* **6** NUMBER In mathematics, a positive number is greater than zero. **7 positive charge** the electrical charge that is carried by protons (= parts of atoms)

**positively** /ˈpɒzətɪvli/ *adv* **1** in a good way that makes you feel happier *Most children respond positively to praise and encouragement.* **2** used to emphasize something that you say, especially when it is surprising *Our waiter was positively rude.*

**possess** /pəˈzes/ *verb* **1** [T] *formal* to have or own something *Certainly, he possesses the skills for the job.* • *He was found guilty of possessing an illegal weapon.* **2 what possessed her/him/you, etc?** something that you say when someone has done something stupid [+ to do sth] *What possessed you to tell him?*

**possessed** /pəˈzest/ *adj* controlled by evil spirits

**possession** /pəˈzeʃən/ *noun* **1** [C] a thing that you own [usually plural] *personal possessions* • *He woke up to discover that all his possessions had been stolen.* **2** [U] *formal* when you have or own something *I have in my possession a photograph which may be of interest to you.* • *He was caught in possession of explosives.*

**possessive** /pəˈzesɪv/ *adj* **1** wanting someone to love and spend time with you and no one else

*She stopped seeing him because he was becoming too possessive.* **2** In grammar, a possessive word or form of a word shows who or what something belongs to. For example the words 'mine' and 'yours' are possessive pronouns.

o━**possibility** /ˌpɒsəˈbɪləti/ *noun* **1** [C, U] a chance that something may happen or be true *a distinct/real possibility* • *Is there any possibility of changing this ticket?* • [+ (that)] *There is a strong possibility that she was lying.* **2** [C] something that you can choose to do *"We could go by car." "Yes, that's a possibility."* • *Have you considered the possibility of flying?* ⊃ Opposite **impossibility**.

### USAGE

**possibility, occasion,** or **opportunity?**

A **possibility** is a chance that something may happen or be true. Possibility cannot be followed by an infinitive.

*Is there a possibility of finding a cure for AIDS?*

~~Is there a possibility to find a cure for AIDS?~~

An **occasion** is an event, or a time when something happens. Occasion does not mean 'chance' or 'opportunity'.

*Birthdays are always special occasions.*

An **opportunity** is a possibility of doing something, or a situation which gives you the possibility of doing something.

*The trip to Paris gave me an opportunity to speak French.*

*Students had the opportunity to ask questions during the lecture.*

*I have more opportunity to travel than my parents did.*

~~I have more possibility to travel than my parents did.~~

o━**possible** /ˈpɒsəbl/ *adj* **1** If something is possible, it can happen or be done. [+ to do sth] *Is it possible to speak to the manager please?* • *The operation will make it possible for her to walk without crutches.* • *I'll send it today, if possible.* ⊃ Opposite **impossible**. **2** If something is possible, it might or might not exist or be true. *possible safety problems* • [+ (that)] *It's possible that the tapes were stolen.* **3 as much/quickly/soon, etc as possible** as much/quickly/soon, etc as something can happen or be done *I'll go as soon as possible.* **4 the best/cheapest/worst, etc possible** the best/cheapest/worst, etc that can happen or exist *the shortest possible time*

o━**possibly** /ˈpɒsəbli/ *adv* **1** NOT CERTAIN used when something is not certain *Someone, possibly Tom, had left the window open.* **2** EMPHASIS used with 'can' or 'could' for emphasis *We'll do everything we possibly can to help.* • *I couldn't possibly ask you to do that.* **3** QUESTIONS used in polite questions *Could I possibly borrow your bike?*

o━**post¹** /pəʊst/ *noun* **1** SYSTEM [no plural] UK (US **mail**) the system for sending letters, parcels, etc *Your letter is in the post.* • *I'm sending the documents by post.* **2** LETTERS [U] UK (US **mail**) letters, parcels, etc that you send or receive

*Has the post arrived yet?* • *Did I get any post today?* **3** JOB [C] *formal* a job *a part-time post* • *a teaching post* **4** POLE [C] a long, vertical piece of wood or metal fixed into the ground at one end *I found the dog tied to a post.* **5** PLACE [C] a place where someone stands to guard something

o⇥**post²** /pəʊst/ *verb* [T] **1** *UK* (*US* **mail**) to send a letter or parcel by post *Did you post my letter?* **2 be posted to France/London/Singapore, etc** to be sent to France/London/Singapore, etc to work, usually for the government or army **3 post a notice/sign, etc** to put a notice/sign, etc somewhere *He posted the message on the noticeboard.* **4 keep sb posted** to make certain that someone always knows what is happening *Keep me posted on anything that happens while I'm away.*

**postage** /ˈpəʊstɪdʒ/ *noun* [U] money that you pay to send a letter or parcel *first-class postage* • *postage and packing*

ˈpostage ˌstamp *noun* [C] a small, official piece of paper that you buy and stick onto a letter or parcel before you post it

**postal** /ˈpəʊstəl/ *adj* [always before noun] relating to the system of sending letters and parcels *the postal service/system*

ˈpostal ˌorder *UK* (*US* **money order**) *noun* [C] an official piece of paper bought at a post office that you can send instead of money

ˈpost ˌbox *UK* (*US* **mailbox**) *noun* [C] a large, metal container in a public place where you can post letters

**postcard** /ˈpəʊstkɑːd/ *noun* [C] a card with a picture on one side that you send without an envelope *Send me a postcard.*

**postcode** /ˈpəʊstkəʊd/ *noun* [C] a group of letters and numbers that comes at the end of someone's address in the UK ⊃ *Compare* **zip code**.

**poster** /ˈpəʊstə/ *noun* [C] a large, printed picture or notice that you put on a wall, in order to decorate a place or to advertise something

**posterity** /pɒsˈterəti/ *noun* [U] the people who will be alive in the future *These works of art should be preserved for posterity.*

**postgraduate** /ˌpəʊstˈɡrædʒuət/ *noun* [C] a student who has one degree and is studying for a more advanced qualification *a postgraduate degree*

**posthumous** /ˈpɒstjəməs/ *adj* happening after someone's death *the posthumous publication of her letters* • **posthumously** *adv*

**posting** /ˈpəʊstɪŋ/ *noun* [C] *mainly UK* when you are sent to work in another place *a posting to Madrid*

**postman** /ˈpəʊstmən/ *UK* (*US* **mailman, letter carrier**) *noun* [C] *plural* **postmen** a man who takes and brings letters and parcels as a job

**postmark** /ˈpəʊstmɑːk/ *noun* [C] an official mark on a letter or parcel, showing the place and time it was sent

**post-mortem** /ˌpəʊstˈmɔːtəm/ *noun* [C] a medical examination of a dead body to find out why the person died

ˈpost ˌoffice *noun* [C] a place where you can buy stamps and send letters and parcels

**postpone** /pəʊstˈpəʊn/ *verb* [T] to arrange for

something to happen at a later time *The trip to the museum has been postponed until next week.*

**postscript** /ˈpəʊstskrɪpt/ *noun* [C] extra information at the end of a letter or email, usually added after writing the letters 'PS'

**posture** /ˈpɒstʃə/ *noun* [U] the position of your back, shoulders, etc when you are standing or sitting *She has very good posture.*

**postwar** /ˈpəʊstwɔːr/ *adj* happening or existing in the period after a war *postwar Europe*

**pot¹** /pɒt/ *noun* **1** [C] a round container, usually used for storing things or cooking *a flower pot* • *a pot of coffee/tea* • *pots and pans* **2 go to pot** to be damaged or spoilt because no effort has been made *My diet's gone to pot since the holidays.* ⊃ *See also:* **melting pot**.

**pot²** /pɒt/ *verb* [T] **potting**, *past* **potted** to put a plant into a pot filled with soil

**potassium** /pəˈtæsiəm/ *noun* [U] a chemical element that combines easily with other elements, often used to help plants grow well

o⇥**potato** /pəˈteɪtəʊ/ *noun* [C, U] *plural* **potatoes** a round vegetable with a brown, yellow, or red skin that grows in the ground *boiled/fried potatoes* • *mashed potato* ⊃ *See colour picture* **Fruit and Vegetables** *on page Centre 8.* ⊃ *See also:* **couch potato, jacket potato, sweet potato.**

poˈtato ˌchip *US* (*UK* **crisp**) *noun* [C] a very thin, dry, fried slice of potato *a bag of potato chips*

**potent** /ˈpəʊtᵊnt/ *adj* very powerful or very effective *a potent drug/weapon* • **potency** /ˈpəʊtᵊnsi/ *noun* [U] when something is potent

**potential¹** /pəˈtenʃᵊl/ *adj* [always before noun] A potential problem, employer, partner, etc may become one in the future, although they are not one now. *a potential danger/threat* • *a potential customer* • *A number of potential buyers have expressed interest in the building.* • **potentially** *adv a potentially fatal condition*

**potential²** /pəˈtenʃᵊl/ *noun* **1** [U] qualities or abilities that may develop and allow someone or something to succeed *to achieve your full potential* • *She has a lot of potential as a writer.* **2 potential for sth/doing sth** the possibility that something may happen *There is the potential for some really interesting research.*

**pothole** /ˈpɒthəʊl/ *noun* [C] a hole in the surface of a road

**potted** /ˈpɒtɪd/ *adj* **1** planted in a container *potted plants/flowers* • *a potted palm* **2 potted history/version, etc of sth** *UK* a story or report that has been changed to make it shorter and more simple *a potted version of Shakespeare*

ˌpotted ˈplant (*also UK* ˈpot ˌplant) *noun* [C] a plant that is grown in a container, and usually kept inside

**potter¹** /ˈpɒtə/ *noun* [C] a person who makes plates, bowls, etc from clay

**potter²** /ˈpɒtə/ *verb*
**potter about/around (sth)** *mainly UK* to spend time in a pleasant, relaxed way, often doing small jobs in your house *Sunday is usually spent pottering around the house.*

**pottery** /ˈpɒtᵊri/ *noun* **1** OBJECTS [U] plates, bowls, etc that are made from clay **2** ACTIVITY [U] the activity of making plates, bowls, etc from clay **3** PLACE [C] a place where plates, bowls, etc made from clay are made or sold

**potty¹** /'pɒti/ *noun* [C] a small toilet that young children use

**potty²** /'pɒti/ *adj UK informal* crazy or stupid *to go potty*

**pouch** /pautʃ/ *noun* [C] **1** a small, soft bag made of leather or cloth **2** a pocket of skin in which some female animals carry their babies

**poultry** /'pəultri/ *noun* **1** [plural] chickens and other birds that people breed for meat and eggs **2** [U] the meat of chickens and other birds eaten as food

**pounce** /pauns/ *verb* [I] to suddenly move towards a person or animal that you want to catch *The police were waiting to pounce when he arrived at the airport.*

**pounce on sth/sb** to immediately criticize a mistake *His critics are waiting to pounce on any mistakes.*

o&#42;**pound¹** /paund/ *noun* [C] **1** the unit of money used in the UK and Ireland; £ *a hundred pounds/£100* • *a pound coin* **2** (*written abbreviation* **lb**) a unit for measuring weight, equal to 453.6 grams or 16 ounces *a pound of potatoes* • *The baby weighed just four pounds when she was born.*

**pound²** /paund/ *verb* **1** [I, T] to hit something many times using a lot of force *Someone was pounding on the door.* **2** [I] If your heart pounds, it beats very quickly. *My heart was pounding as I walked out onto the stage.* **3 pound along/down/up, etc** to run somewhere with quick, loud steps *He pounded up the stairs.*

o&#42;**pour** /pɔː/ *verb* **1** [T] to make a liquid flow from or into a container *I poured the milk into a jug.* • [+ two objects] *Can I pour you a drink?* **2** [I] (*also UK* **pour down**) to rain, producing a lot of water *We can't go out in this weather – it's pouring!* **3 pour into/out/from, etc a** to flow quickly and in large amounts *Blood was pouring from my leg.* **b** to enter or leave a place in large numbers *The crowd poured out into the street.*

**pour**

**pour sth out** If you pour out your feelings or thoughts, you talk very honestly about what is making you sad. *She listened quietly while he poured out his troubles.*

**pout** /paut/ *verb* [I] to push your lips forward because you are annoyed or because you want to look sexually attractive • pout *noun* [C]

**poverty** /'pɒvəti/ *noun* [U] when you are very poor *to live in poverty*

**poverty-stricken** /'pɒvəti,strik³n/ *adj* A poverty-stricken area or person is very poor.

**POW** /,piːəu'dʌblju:/ *noun* [C] *abbreviation for* prisoner of war: a soldier who is caught by enemy soldiers during a war

**powder** /'paudə/ *noun* [C, U] a dry substance made of many small, loose grains *curry powder* • *face powder* • powdered *adj* in the form of a

powder *powdered milk/sugar* ⊃ *See also:* **talcum powder**.

o&#42;**power¹** /paʊə/ *noun* **1** CONTROL [U] control or influence over people and events *He likes to have power over people.* **2** POLITICS [U] political control in a country *They have been in power too long.* • *When did this government come to power* (= start to control the country)? **3** ENERGY [U] energy, usually electricity, that is used to provide light, heat, etc *nuclear power* • *Turn off the power at the main switch.* **4** COUNTRY [C] a country that has a lot of influence over others *a major world power* **5** OFFICIAL RIGHT [C, U] an official or legal right to do something [+ to do sth] *It's not in my power to stop him publishing this book.* **6** STRENGTH [U] strength or force *economic/military power* **7** ABILITY [U] a natural ability *to lose the power of speech* **8 do everything in your power to do sth** to do everything that you are able and allowed to do *I've done everything in my power to help him.* **9 the powers that be** important people who have authority over others ⊃ *See also:* **balance of power**.

**power²** /paʊə/ *verb* [T] to supply energy to a machine and make it work [often passive] *The clock is powered by two small batteries.*

'**power ,cut** (*also US* **power outage**) *noun* [C] when the supply of electricity suddenly stops

o&#42;**powerful** /'paʊəf³l/ *adj* **1** CONTROL A powerful person is able to control and influence people and events. *a powerful man/woman* **2** STRENGTH having a lot of strength or force *a powerful engine/weapon* **3** EFFECT having a strong effect on people *a powerful effect/influence* • *a powerful image* • powerfully *adv*

**powerless** /'paʊələs/ *adj* not able to control events [+ to do sth] *The police were powerless to stop the fighting.*

**power outage** /'paʊər,autidʒ/ *US* (*UK/US* **power cut**) *noun* [C] when the supply of electricity suddenly stops

'**power ,station** (*also US* '**power ,plant**) *noun* [C] a place where electricity is produced

'**power ,tool** *noun* [C] a tool that uses electricity

**pp** *written abbreviation for* pages *See pp 10 – 12 for more information.*

**PR** /,piː'ɑː/ *noun* [U] *abbreviation for* public relations: writing and activities that are intended to make a person, company, or product more popular *good/bad PR* • *a PR campaign*

**practicable** /'præktikəbl/ *adj formal* able to be done successfully *It's just not practicable to travel in this weather.*

o&#42;**practical¹** /'præktik³l/ *adj* **1** REAL relating to real situations or actions and not to thoughts or ideas *practical experience/problems* • *They can offer practical help.* **2** SUITABLE suitable or useful for a situation which may involve some difficulty *practical clothes/shoes* • *Pale carpets just aren't practical if you have kids.* **3** POSSIBLE able to be done successfully *a practical solution* • *The plan is simply not practical.* **4** GOOD AT PLANNING Someone who is practical is good at planning things and dealing with problems. *She has a lot of interesting ideas but she's not very practical.* **5** GOOD WITH HANDS good at repairing and making things

**practical²** /'præktɪkªl/ *noun* [C] a lesson or examination in which you do or make something instead of only writing

**practicalities** /ˌpræktɪ'kælətiz/ *noun* [plural] real situations or facts *the practicalities of running your own business*

**practicality** /ˌpræktɪ'kæləti/ *noun* [U] **1** the possibility that something can be done successfully *I like the idea but I'm not sure about the practicality of it.* **2** how suitable or useful something is for a situation which may involve some difficulty

**ˌpractical 'joke** *noun* [C] a trick using actions and not words to make people laugh *to play a practical joke on someone*

**practically** /'præktɪkªli/ *adv* **1** almost *It's practically impossible to get there.* • *We see her practically every day.* **2** in a suitable or useful way *We need to think practically.*

**practice** /'præktɪs/ *noun* **1** [REPEATING] [U] when you repeat an activity to improve your ability *We need a bit more practice before the concert.* • *I've got basketball practice tonight.* **2** [ACTIVITY] [C, U] what people do or how they do it *business/working practices* • [+ of + doing sth] *the illegal practice of copying CDs* • [+ to do sth] *It is common practice to bury waste in landfills.* **3** [WORK] [C] a business in which several doctors or lawyers work together, or the work that they do *a legal/medical practice* **4 in practice** If something is true in practice, this is the real situation. *In practice, the new laws have had little effect.* **5 be out of practice** to not do something well because you have not done it recently *I didn't play very well today – I'm out of practice.* **6 put something into practice** to try a plan or idea *Next month we will have a chance to put these ideas into practice.*

**practise** *UK* (*US* **practice**) /'præktɪs/ *verb* **1** [REPEAT] [I, T] to repeat something regularly in order to improve your ability *How often do you practise?* • *You need to practise your pronunciation.* • *They're practising for tomorrow's concert.* **2** [WORK] [I, T] to work as a doctor or a lawyer *to practise medicine/law* **3** [CUSTOM/RELIGION] [T] to do something regularly according to a custom, religion, or a set of rules *to practise a religion* **4 practise what you preach** to behave as well as you often tell other people they should behave *I'd have more respect for him if he practised what he preached.*

**practised** *UK* (*US* **practiced**) /'præktɪst/ *adj* very good at doing something because you have done it so often *She answered the questions with practised ease.*

**practising** *UK* (*US* **practicing**) /'præktɪsɪŋ/ *adj* a **practising Catholic/Jew/Muslim, etc** someone who follows the rules of a religion

**practitioner** /præk'tɪʃªnªr/ *noun* [C] *formal* someone who works as a doctor or a lawyer *a medical practitioner* ➲ *See also:* **general practitioner**.

**pragmatic** /præg'mætɪk/ *adj* doing things in a practical and realistic way and not using only ideas *a pragmatic approach to a problem*

**pragmatism** /'prægmətɪzªm/ *noun* [U] when someone is pragmatic • **pragmatist** *noun* [C] someone who is pragmatic

**prairie** /'preªri/ *noun* [C] a large, flat area of land in North America that is usually covered in grass

**praise¹** /preɪz/ *verb* [T] **1** to say that you admire someone or something, or that they are very good *He praised the team's performance.* • *Residents praised the firemen for their swift action.* **2** to give respect and thanks to a god *Praise God, no one was hurt.*

**praise²** /preɪz/ *noun* [U] words you say to show that you admire someone or something *They deserve praise for their achievements.* • *Her first novel won a lot of praise from the critics.*

**praiseworthy** /'preɪzˌwɜːði/ *adj formal* deserving praise

**pram** /præm/ *noun* [C] *mainly UK* a small vehicle with four wheels for carrying a baby

**prance** /prɑːns/ *verb* [I] to walk or dance in a proud way, often because you want people to look at you *She was prancing around in a bikini.*

**prank** /præŋk/ *noun* [C] a trick that is intended to be funny

**prat** /præt/ *noun* [C] *UK very informal* a stupid person

**prawn** /prɔːn/ *noun* [C] a small sea animal which you can eat, and which has a shell and ten legs

**pray** /preɪ/ *verb* [I, T] **1** to speak to a god in order to show your feelings or to ask for something *Let us pray for all the sick children.* • [+ that] *She prayed that God would forgive her.* **2** to hope very much that something will happen *We're just praying for rain.*

**prayer** /preªr/ *noun* **1** [C] the words you say to a god *Shall we say a prayer for him?* **2** [U] when you say words to a god *They knelt in prayer.*

**preach** /priːtʃ/ *verb* **1** [I, T] to talk to a group of people about a religious subject, usually as a priest in a church *to preach the gospel* • *Many people had come to hear him preach.* **2** [I] to try to persuade people to believe or support something, often in an annoying way ➲ *See also:* **practise** what you preach.

**preacher** /'priːtʃªr/ *noun* [C] someone who speaks in public about a religious subject, especially someone whose job is to do this

**preamble** /'priːæmbl/ *noun* [C] *formal* an introduction to a speech or piece of writing

**precarious** /prɪ'keªriªs/ *adj* **1** A precarious situation is likely to become worse. *Many illegal immigrants are in a precarious position.* **2** not fixed and likely to fall *That shelf looks a bit precarious.* • **precariously** *adv Her cup was balanced precariously on the arm of the chair.*

**precaution** /prɪ'kɔːʃªn/ *noun* [C] something that you do to prevent bad things happening in the future *Driving alone at night can be dangerous, so always take precautions.* • *They called the doctor as a precaution.* • [+ of + doing sth] *He took the precaution of locking the door.* • **precautionary** *adj* a **precautionary measure/step** something that you do in order to prevent something bad from happening

**precede** /prɪ'siːd/ *verb* [T] *formal* to happen or exist before something else [often passive] *The formal ceremony was preceded by a parade.* • **preceding** *adj* [always before noun] happening or coming before *the preceding months • the preceding chapter*

**precedence** /'presɪdᵊns/ *noun* [U] when someone or something is considered more important than another person or thing *to give precedence to something • Quality should take precedence over cost.*

**precedent** /'presɪdᵊnt/ *noun* [C, U] an action or decision that is used as an example when someone wants to do a similar thing in the future *This decision has set an important legal precedent for other countries.*

**precinct** /'priːsɪŋkt/ *noun* **1 a pedestrian/ shopping precinct** *UK* an area in a town where there are shops and no cars are allowed **2** [C] *US* an area in a city that a particular group of police are responsible for, or the building in which they work *the 45th precinct*

**precincts** /'priːsɪŋkts/ *noun* [plural] the area of land around a building, especially a large church *the cathedral precincts*

**precious**¹ /'preʃəs/ *adj* **1** very important to you *His books are his most precious possessions.* **2** rare and very valuable *a precious vase • a precious metal/stone*

**precious**² /'preʃəs/ *adv* **precious few/little** very little or very few of something *We have precious little money at present.*

**precipice** /'presɪpɪs/ *noun* [C] **1** a dangerous situation that could lead to failure or harm *The two countries stood on the precipice of war.* **2** a steep side of a mountain or high area of land

**precipitate** /prɪ'sɪpɪteɪt/ *verb* [T] *formal* to make something happen [often passive] *The war was precipitated by an invasion.*

**precipitation** /prɪˌsɪpɪ'teɪʃᵊn/ *noun* [U] In science, precipitation is rain or snow that falls on the ground.

**precis** /'preɪsiː/ *noun* [C, U] *formal* a report giving the main ideas of a piece of writing or speech

o‑**precise** /prɪ'saɪs/ *adj* **1** exact and accurate *precise details/instructions • Their calendars were more precise than the one we use today.* ⊃ *Opposite* **imprecise. 2 to be precise** used to give exact details about something *We met in 1994 – October first to be precise.* **3** [always before noun] used to emphasize something that you are referring to *At that precise moment, the door opened.*

**precisely** /prɪ'saɪsli/ *adv* **1** EXACTLY exactly *at 6 o'clock precisely* **2** EMPHASIS used to emphasize something *This is precisely the kind of thing I was hoping to avoid.* **3** AGREEMENT used to agree with what someone else says *"It's not the shape I dislike, it's the colour." "Precisely!"*

**precision** /prɪ'sɪʒᵊn/ *noun* [U] when something is very exact and accurate *She parked the car with great precision.*

**preclude** /prɪ'kluːd/ *verb* [T] *formal* to prevent something from happening [+ from + doing sth] *His illness precludes him from taking part in any sports.*

**precocious** /prɪ'kəʊʃəs/ *adj* Children who are precocious have the confidence or skill of an adult. *A precocious child, she went to university at the age of 15.*

**preconceived** /ˌpriːkən'siːvd/ *adj* Preconceived

ideas are decided before the facts of a situation are known. *preconceived ideas/notions*

**preconception** /ˌpriːkən'sepʃᵊn/ *noun* [C] what you believe before you know the facts of a situation *People have so many preconceptions about unmarried mothers.*

**precondition** /ˌpriːkən'dɪʃᵊn/ *noun* [C] *formal* what must happen before something else can happen *The ceasefire is a precondition for peace talks.*

**precursor** /ˌpriː'kɜːsəʳ/ *noun* [C] *formal* something which happens or exists before something else and influences its development *The European Coal and Steel Community was a precursor of the European Union. • Infection with HIV is a precursor to AIDS.*

**predate** /ˌpriː'deɪt/ *verb* [T] to exist or happen before something else *The drinking of alcohol predates the Greeks and Romans.*

**predator** /'predətəʳ/ *noun* [C] an animal that kills and eats other animals

**predatory** /'predətᵊri/ *adj* **1** A predatory person tries to get things from other people in a way that is unfair. **2** A predatory animal kills and eats other animals.

**predecessor** /'priːdɪˌsesəʳ/ ⓊⓈ /'predəsesəʳ/ *noun* [C] **1** the person who was in a job or position before *He seems a lot better than his predecessor.* **2** something that existed before another, similar thing *The predecessors to these computers were much larger and heavier.*

**predetermined** /ˌpriːdɪ'tɜːmɪnd/ *adj* *formal* decided before *They met at a predetermined time and place.*

**predeterminer** /ˌpriːdɪ'tɜːmɪnəʳ/ *noun* [C] a word that is used before a determiner to give more information about a noun. For example 'all' in 'all these children' is a predeterminer.

**predicament** /prɪ'dɪkəmənt/ *noun* [C] a problem or a difficult situation *I sympathize with your predicament.*

**predicate** /'predɪkət/ *noun* [C] the part of a sentence which gives information about the subject. In the sentence 'We went to the airport.', 'went to the airport' is the predicate.

**predicative** /prɪ'dɪkətɪv/ *adj* A predicative adjective comes after a verb. In the sentence 'She is happy.', 'happy' is a predicative adjective. ⊃ *Compare* **attributive**.

**predict** /prɪ'dɪkt/ *verb* [T] to say what you think will happen in the future *Companies are predicting massive profits. •* [+ (that)] *They predicted that the temperature would reach 80 degrees today.*

**predictable** /prɪ'dɪktəbl/ *adj* happening or behaving in a way that you expect and not unusual or interesting *a predictable result • She's so predictable.* ⊃ *Opposite* **unpredictable. •** *predictably adv*

**prediction** /prɪ'dɪkʃᵊn/ *noun* [C, U] when you say what you think will happen in the future *I wouldn't like to make any predictions about the result of this match.*

**predilection** /ˌpriːdɪ'lekʃᵊn/ *noun* [C] *formal* when you like something very much *She has a predilection for chocolate.*

**predisposed** /ˌpriːdɪ'spəʊzd/ *adj* **be predisposed to sth** to be more likely than other people to have a medical problem or to behave in a particular way *Some people are predisposed to addiction.* • predisposition /ˌpriːdɪspəˈzɪʃᵊn/ *noun* [C] when you are likely to have a medical problem or to behave in a particular way *people with a predisposition to heart disease*

**predominant** /prɪˈdɒmɪnənt/ *adj* more important or noticeable than others *He has played a predominant role in these talks.* • predominance /prɪˈdɒmɪnəns/ *noun* [U] when something is more important or noticeable than others *the predominance of English on the Internet*

**predominantly** /prɪˈdɒmɪnəntli/ *adv* mostly or mainly *a predominantly Asian community*

**predominate** /prɪˈdɒmɪneɪt/ *verb* [I] to be the largest in number or the most important *Olive trees predominate in this area.*

**pre-eminent** /ˌpriːˈemɪnənt/ *adj* more important or better than others *a pre-eminent artist/scholar* • pre-eminence /ˌpriːˈemɪnəns/ *noun* [U] when someone or something is much more important or better than others

**pre-empt** /ˌpriːˈempt/ *verb* [T] to do something before something else happens in order to prevent it or reduce its effect • pre-emptive *adj* preventing something else from happening *to take pre-emptive action*

**preen** /priːn/ *verb* [I, T] **1** If a bird preens or preens itself, it makes its feathers clean and tidy. **2** to try to look attractive *When you've finished preening, perhaps we can go out.* • [often reflexive] *The actors preened themselves in the dressing room.*

**pre-existing** /ˌpriːɪɡˈzɪstɪŋ/ *adj* existing before something else *a pre-existing medical condition*

**prefabricated** /ˌpriːˈfæbrɪkeɪtɪd/ *adj* **a prefabricated building/home/house, etc** a building that has already been partly built when it is put together

**preface** /ˈprefɪs/ *noun* [C] a piece of writing at the beginning of a book that explains why it was written

**prefect** /ˈpriːfekt/ *noun* [C] in the UK, an older student in a school who has special duties and some authority

○▪**prefer** /prɪˈfɜːʳ/ *verb* [T] **preferring**, *past* **preferred** **1** to like someone or something more than another person or thing *I prefer dogs to cats.* • [+ doing sth] *She prefers watching tennis to playing.* **2** **would prefer** used to say what you want or ask someone what they want [+ to do sth] *I'd prefer to go alone.* • *Would you prefer red or white wine?*

---

**USAGE**

**prefer**

Remember that **prefer** is often followed by **to do sth** or **doing sth**.

*I prefer to walk.*

*I prefer walking.*

~~I prefer walk.~~

---

**preferable** /ˈprefᵊrəbl/ *adj* better or more suitable *Staying at home is **preferable to** going out with someone you don't like.*

**preferably** /ˈprefᵊrəbli/ *adv* if possible *Serve the pudding with ice cream, preferably vanilla.*

**preference** /ˈprefᵊrᵊns/ *noun* **1** [C, U] when you like something or someone more than another person or thing *personal preferences* • *We have white and brown bread. Do you **have a preference**?* • *I have a **preference for** dark-haired men.* **2** **give preference to sb** to give special treatment to someone *Hospitals must give preference to urgent cases.*

**preferential** /ˌprefᵊrˈenʃᵊl/ *adj* **preferential treatment** If you are given preferential treatment, you are treated in a better way than other people. *There were complaints that some guests had been given preferential treatment.*

**prefix** /ˈpriːfɪks/ *noun* [C] a group of letters that you add to the beginning of a word to make another word. In the word 'unimportant', 'un-' is a prefix. ⊃ *Compare* **suffix**.

**pregnancy** /ˈpreɡnᵊnsi/ *noun* [C, U] when a woman is pregnant *a teenage pregnancy*

○▪**pregnant** /ˈpreɡnᵊnt/ *adj* **1** A pregnant woman has a baby developing inside her uterus. *to get pregnant* • *She's five months pregnant.* **2 a pregnant pause/silence** a pause or silence full of meaning that is not said in words

**prehistoric** /ˌpriːhɪˈstɒrɪk/ *adj* relating to a time in the past before there were written records of events *prehistoric remains* • *prehistoric cave paintings*

**prejudice¹** /ˈpredʒədɪs/ *noun* [C, U] when someone dislikes a group of people or treats them unfairly because they are a different race, sex, religion, etc *racial prejudice* • *prejudice against women*

**prejudice²** /ˈpredʒədɪs/ *verb* [T] **1** to influence someone in an unfair way so that they have a bad opinion of someone or something *Her comments may have **prejudiced** the voters **against** him.* **2** to have a harmful effect on a situation *Newspaper reports have prejudiced the trial.*

**prejudiced** /ˈpredʒədɪst/ *adj* feeling dislike for a group of people or treating them unfairly because they are a different race, sex, religion, etc *Are the police **prejudiced against** black people?*

**preliminary** /prɪˈlɪmɪnᵊri/ *adj* [always before noun] done or happening in order to prepare for the main event or activity *a preliminary discussion/meeting* • preliminary *noun* [C] something that you do at the start of an event or activity

**prelude** /ˈpreljuːd/ *noun* **1 a prelude to sth** something that happens before another event or activity, usually as an introduction to it *There are hopes that the talks are a prelude to an agreement.* **2** [C] a short piece of music that introduces the main piece

**premature** /ˈpremətʃəʳ (US) ˌpriːməˈtʊr/ *adj* happening too soon or before the usual time *premature ageing/death* • *a premature baby* • [+ to do sth] *It seems a bit premature to start talking about it already.* • prematurely *He died prematurely of cancer.*

**premeditated** /ˌpriːˈmedɪteɪtɪd/ *adj* If a crime is premeditated, it is planned. *premeditated murder* • *a premeditated attack*

**premenstrual** /ˌpriːˈmenstruəl/ *adj* related to the time just before a woman's period

(= monthly blood from the uterus) *premenstrual syndrome/tension*

**premier**¹ /'premiə' US prɪ'mɪr/ *noun* [C] the leader of a government *the Chinese premier* • **premiership** *noun* [U] the period in which someone is premier

**premier**² /'premiə' US prɪ'mɪr/ *adj* [always before noun] best or most important *the city's premier hotel* •

**premiere** /'premiə' US prɪ'mɪr/ *noun* [C] the first public performance of a film, play, etc *a film premiere* • *the world premiere* • **premiere** *verb* [I, T] [often passive] *The opera was premiered in Paris.*

**premise** /'premɪs/ *noun* [C] *formal* an idea that you use to support another theory

**premises** /'premɪsɪz/ *noun* [plural] the land or buildings used by an organization *We're moving to new premises.* • *Smoking is not allowed anywhere* **on the premises**.

**premium**¹ /'priːmiəm/ *noun* **1** [C] an amount of money you pay for insurance (= payments for an accident or illness) *How much is the monthly premium?* **2** [C] an amount or rate that is higher than average *You pay a premium for apartments in the city centre.* **3** **be at a premium** If something useful is at a premium, there is not enough of it. *Time is at a premium just before the start of exams.* **4** **place/put a premium on sth** to consider a quality or achievement as very important *She puts a premium on honesty.*

**premium**² /'priːmiəm/ *adj* [always before noun] A premium product is of a higher quality or value than others. *premium beer/cigars* • *premium gasoline*

**premonition** /,premə'nɪʃᵊn/ *noun* [C] a feeling that something, especially something unpleasant, is going to happen *to have a premonition* • *a premonition of disaster*

**prenatal** /,priː'neɪtᵊl/ US (UK **antenatal**) *adj* relating to pregnant women before their babies are born *prenatal care*

**preoccupation** /priː,ɒkjə'peɪʃᵊn/ *noun* **1** [C, U] when you think or worry about something so much that you do not think about other things *a preoccupation with death/food* **2** [C] something that you think or worry about a lot *His main preoccupations are football and women.*

**preoccupied** /,priː'ɒkjəpaɪd/ *adj* thinking or worrying about something a lot *She's been very preoccupied recently.* • *He's far too* **preoccupied with** *his own problems to notice mine.* • **preoccupy** /,priː'ɒkjəpaɪ/ *verb* [T] If something preoccupies you, you think or worry about it a lot.

o-**preparation** /,prepᵊr'eɪʃᵊn/ *noun* [U] the things that you do or the time that you spend preparing for something *Did you do much preparation for your interview?* • *He's been painting the outside of the house in preparation for winter.* • *the preparation of the document*

**preparations** /,prepər'eɪʃᵊnz/ *noun* [plural] things that you do to get ready for something *wedding preparations* • *We've been* **making preparations** *for the journey.*

**preparatory** /prɪ'pærətᵊri/ *adj* done in order to get ready for something *preparatory work*

**pre'paratory ˌschool** *noun formal* a prep school

o-**prepare** /prɪ'peə'/ *verb* **1** [I, T] to get someone or something ready for something that will happen in the future *I haven't prepared my speech yet.* • *They're* **preparing for** *the big match.* • *We're preparing the students for their end-of-year exam.* • [+ to do sth] *I was busy preparing to go on holiday.* **2** **prepare yourself** to make yourself ready to deal with a difficult situation *Prepare yourself for a shock.* • *You should prepare yourself for a long wait.* **3** [T] to make food ready to be eaten *to prepare lunch*

**prepared** /prɪ'peəd/ *adj* **1** ready to deal with a situation *It's best to be prepared.* • *I wasn't* **prepared for** *the cold.* **2** **be prepared to do sth** to be willing to do something *You must be prepared to work hard.*

**preponderance** /prɪ'pɒndᵊrᵊns/ *noun formal* **a preponderance of sth** when there is a larger amount of one thing than of others *There is a preponderance of older people in this area.*

**preposition** /,prepə'zɪʃᵊn/ *noun* [C] a word or group of words that is used before a noun or pronoun to show place, direction, time, etc. For example 'on' in 'Your keys are on the table.' is a preposition.

**preposterous** /prɪ'pɒstᵊrəs/ *adj* extremely stupid *That's a preposterous idea!*

**prep school** /'prepskuːl/ *noun* [C] **1** in the UK, a private school for children aged between 8 and 13 **2** in the US, a private school which prepares students for college

**prerequisite** /,priː'rekwɪzɪt/ *noun* [C] *formal* something that is necessary in order for something else to happen or exist *Trust is a* **prerequisite for** *any sort of relationship.*

**prerogative** /prɪ'rɒgətɪv/ *noun* [C] *formal* something that you have the right to do because of who you are *Alex makes the decisions – that's his prerogative as company director.*

**Presbyterian** /,prezbɪ'tɪəriən/ *adj* belonging or relating to a type of Christian church with elected groups of local members involved in the official organization of local churches • **Presbyterian** *noun* [C]

**pre-school** /'priːskuːl/ *adj* [always before noun] relating to children who are too young to go to school *pre-school children/education* • **preschool** *noun* [C] US a school for children younger than five years old

**prescribe** /prɪ'skraɪb/ *verb* [T] **1** to say what medical treatment someone needs [often passive] *Painkillers are the most common drugs prescribed by doctors in Britain.* **2** *formal* to say officially what people must do *rules prescribed by law*

**prescription** /prɪ'skrɪpʃᵊn/ *noun* **1** [C] a piece of paper saying what medicine someone needs or the medicine itself *a doctor's prescription* **2 on prescription** UK (US **by prescription**) If you get a medicine on prescription, you only get it if you have a written instruction from your doctor.

**prescriptive** /prɪ'skrɪptɪv/ *adj formal* saying exactly what must happen *The government's homework guidelines are too prescriptive.*

**presence** /'prezᵊns/ *noun* **1** [IN A PLACE] [U] when someone or something is in a place *I didn't notice her presence.* • *She signed the document* *in the presence of two witnesses.* **2** POLICE/ SOLDIERS [no plural] a group of police or soldiers who are watching or controlling a situation *a strong police presence* **3** QUALITY [U] a quality that makes people notice and admire you **4 presence of mind** the ability to deal with a difficult situation quickly and effectively *She had the presence of mind to press the alarm.* **5 make your presence felt** to have a strong effect on other people *The new police chief has really made his presence felt.*

o⁻**present**¹ /'prezᵊnt/ *adj* **1 be present** to be in a particular place *The whole family was present.* **2** [always before noun] happening or existing now *the present situation* • *What is your present occupation?* **3 present tense** the form of the verb which is used to show what happens or exists now

o⁻**present**² /'prezᵊnt/ *noun* **1 the present a** the period of time that is happening now *Let's talk about the present.* • *The play is set in the present.* **b** the form of the verb which is used to show what happens or exists now **2** [C] something that you give to someone, usually for a particular occasion *a birthday/wedding present* • *to give someone a present* • *Did you get many presents?* **3 at present** now *At present she's working abroad.*

**present**³ /prɪ'zent/ *verb* **1** GIVE to give something to someone, often at a formal ceremony *to present a prize* • *They **presented** her with a bouquet.* **2** INFORMATION to give people information in a formal way *He **presented** the report to his colleagues.* **3 present a danger/threat/ problem, etc** to cause a danger/threat/ problem, etc *The final exam may present some problems.* **4** TV/RADIO *UK* (*US* **host**) to introduce a television or radio programme *He presents a weekly sports quiz.* **5** PLAY/FILM to show a play or film *The school is presenting 'West Side Story' this term.* **6** INTRODUCE to introduce someone formally *May I present my daughters?* **7** OPPORTUNITY If an opportunity presents itself, it becomes possible. *I'd be happy to go to New York, if the opportunity presented itself.*

**presentable** /prɪ'zentəbl/ *adj* looking clean and tidy enough *He was looking quite presentable in his jacket and tie.*

**presentation** /ˌprezᵊn'teɪʃᵊn/ *noun* **1** SHOW [U] the way something is arranged or shown to people *Presentation is important if you want people to buy your products.* **2** TALK [C] a talk giving information about something *a sales presentation* • *She **gave** an excellent **presentation**.* **3** CEREMONY [C] a formal ceremony at which you give someone something *a presentation ceremony*

**present-day** /ˌprezᵊnt'deɪ/ *adj* existing now *present-day attitudes*

**presenter** /prɪ'zentəʳ/ *UK* (*US* **host**) *noun* [C] someone who introduces a radio or television programme

**presently** /'prezᵊntli/ *adv* **1** *formal* now *He's presently living with his parents.* **2** *old-fashioned* soon or after a short time *I'll be back presently.*

ˌ**present par'ticiple** *UK* (*US* ˌ**present 'participle**) *noun* [C] the form of a verb that ends with '-ing'

the ˌ**present 'perfect** *noun* the form of the verb that is used to show actions or events that have happened in a period of time up to now. The sentence 'I have never been to Australia.' is in the present perfect.

**preservation** /ˌprezə'veɪʃᵊn/ *noun* [U] when you keep something the same or prevent it from being damaged or destroyed *the preservation of peace* • *the preservation of wildlife*

**preservative** /prɪ'zɜːvətɪv/ *noun* [C, U] a substance used to prevent decay in food or in wood

**preserve**¹ /prɪ'zɜːv/ *verb* [T] **1** to keep something the same or prevent it from being damaged or destroyed *to preserve peace* • *to preserve the environment* **2** to add substances to something so that it stays in good condition for a long time *to preserve food/wood*

**preserve**² /prɪ'zɜːv/ *noun* **1** FOOD [C, U] *UK* (*US* **preserves**) a sweet food made from fruit, sugar, and water *apricot/strawberry preserve* **2** ACTIV- ITY [no plural] an activity which only a particular group of people can do *Sport used to be a male preserve.* • *Owning racehorses is the preserve of the rich.* **3** AREA [C] *mainly US* an area where wild animals and plants are protected

**preside** /prɪ'zaɪd/ *verb* [I] to be officially responsible for a formal meeting or ceremony *An elderly priest **presided** at the marriage ceremony.*

**preside over sth** to be in charge of a situation, especially a formal meeting or legal trial *The case was **presided** over by a senior judge.*

**presidency** /'prezɪdᵊnsi/ *noun* **1** [C] the period when someone is president *Her presidency lasted seven years.* **2 the presidency** the job of being president *He won the presidency by a wide margin.*

o⁻**president** /'prezɪdᵊnt/ *noun* [C] **1** the highest political position in some countries, usually the leader of the government *to be elected president* • *President Clinton* **2** the person in charge of a company or organization ➔ *See also:* **vice president**.

**presidential** /ˌprezɪ'denʃᵊl/ *adj* relating to the president of a country *a presidential campaign* • *a presidential candidate*

o⁻**press**¹ /pres/ *verb* **1** PUSH [I, T] to push something firmly *Press the button to start the machine.* • *Can you press a bit harder on my shoulders, please?* • *He pressed his face against the window.* **2** PERSUADE [T] to try hard to persuade someone to do something [+ to do sth] *The committee pressed him to reveal more information.* • *We **pressed** him for an answer but he refused.* **3 press charges** to complain officially about someone in a court of law *The family decided not to **press charges against** him.* **4** MAKE SMOOTH [T] to make clothes smooth by ironing them *I need to press these trousers.* **5** MAKE FLAT [T] to make something flat by putting something heavy on it for a long time *to press fruit/flowers* **6 press a case/claim** to try to make people accept your demands

**press ahead/forward/on** to continue to do something in a determined way *They're determined to press ahead with their plans despite opposition.*

**press**² /pres/ *noun* **1 the press** newspapers and

**P**

magazines, or the people who write them *the local/national press* • *press reports/coverage* **2 good/bad press** praise or criticism from newspapers, magazines, television, etc *She's had a lot of bad press recently.* **3** BUSINESS [C] a business that prints and sells books *Cambridge University Press* **4** PRINT [C] (*also* **printing press**) a machine used to print books, newspapers, and magazines **5** MAKE FLAT [no plural] when you make cloth flat and smooth with a piece of equipment *Can you give these trousers a press?*

'press ,conference *noun* [C] a meeting at which someone officially gives information to the newspapers, television, etc *to call/hold a press conference*

**pressed** /prest/ *adj* **be pressed for time/money** to not have much time/money *I can't stop – I'm a bit pressed for time.*

**pressing** /'presɪŋ/ *adj* A pressing problem or situation needs to be dealt with immediately. *a pressing need for housing*

'press re,lease *noun* [C] an official piece of information that is given to newspapers, television, etc

**press-up** /'presʌp/ *UK* (*US* **push-up**) *noun* [C] a physical exercise in which you lie facing the floor and use your hands to push your body up *I did forty press-ups yesterday.*

o-**pressure**[1] /'preʃə'/ *noun* **1** MAKE SOMEONE DO [U] when someone tries to make someone else do something by arguing, persuading, etc *public/political pressure* • [+ to do sth] *Teachers are under increasing pressure to work longer hours.* • *The government is facing pressure from environmental campaigners.* **2** PROBLEMS [C, U] difficult situations that make you feel worried or unhappy *the pressures of work* • *Be nice to him – he's been under a lot of pressure recently.* **3** LIQUID/GAS [C, U] the force that a liquid or gas produces when it presses against an area *water pressure* **4** PUSH [U] the force that you produce when you push something **5 put pressure on sb** to try to force someone to do something [+ to do sth] *They're putting pressure on me to make a decision.* ⊃ *See also:* **blood pressure, peer pressure**.

**pressure**[2] /'preʃə'/ (*also UK* **pressurize, -ise** /'preʃ³raɪz/) *verb* [T] to try to force someone to do something [often passive + into + doing sth] *We will not be pressured into making a decision.*

'pressure ,cooker *noun* [C] a pan with a lid which you use to cook food quickly in steam

'pressure ,group *noun* [C] a group of people who try to influence what the public or the government think about something

**pressurize** *UK* (*also* **-ise**) /'preʃ³raɪz/ *verb* [T] to try to force someone to do something [often passive + into + doing sth] *He was pressurized into signing the agreement.*

**pressurized** (*also UK* **-ised**) /'preʃəraɪzd/ *adj* containing air or gas that is kept at a controlled pressure *a pressurized container*

**prestige** /pres'tiːʒ/ *noun* [U] when people feel respect and admiration for you, often because you are successful *His company has gained international prestige.* • **prestigious** /pres'tɪdʒəs/ *adj* respected and admired, usually because of

being important *a prestigious award* • *a prestigious university*

**presumably** /prɪ'zjuːməbli/ *adv* used to say what you think is the likely situation *Presumably he just forgot to send the letter.*

**presume** /prɪ'zjuːm/ *verb* **1** [T] to think that something is likely to be true, although you are not certain [+ (that)] *I presume that you've done your homework.* **2 be presumed dead/ innocent, etc** If someone is presumed dead/ innocent, etc, it seems very likely that they are dead/innocent, etc. **3 presume to do sth** *formal* to do something that you do not have the right or the skills to do *I certainly wouldn't presume to tell you how to do your job.*

**presumption** /prɪ'zʌmpʃ°n/ *noun* **1** [C] when you believe that something is true without any proof [+ (that)] *I object to the presumption that young people are only interested in pop music.* **2** [U] behaviour that is rude and does not show respect

**presumptuous** /prɪ'zʌmptʃuəs/ *adj* Someone who is presumptuous confidently does things that they have no right to do. *It was a bit presumptuous of her to take the car without asking.*

**presuppose** /,priːsə'pəuz/ *verb* [T] *formal* If an idea or situation presupposes something, that thing must be true for the idea or situation to work.

**pretence** *UK* (*US* **pretense**) /prɪ'tens/ *noun* **1** [U] when you make someone believe something that is not true *I can't keep up the pretence any longer.* • *They made absolutely no pretence of being interested.* **2 under false pretences** If you do something under false pretences, you do it when you have lied about who you are or what you are doing. *The police charged him with obtaining money under false pretences.*

o-**pretend** /prɪ'tend/ *verb* [I, T] to behave as if something is true when it is not [+ (that)] *I can't pretend that I like him.* • [+ to do sth] *Were you just pretending to be interested?* • *She's not really hurt – she's only pretending.*

**pretense** /prɪ'tens/ *noun US spelling of* pretence

**pretension** /prɪ'tenʃ°n/ *noun* [C, U] when you try to seem better or more important than you really are [usually plural] *He seems to be without pretensions of any sort.*

**pretentious** /prɪ'tenʃəs/ *adj* trying to seem more important or clever than you really are *a pretentious film* • *Many art critics are extremely pretentious.*

**pretext** /'priːtekst/ *noun* [C] a false reason that you use to explain why you are doing something *I called her on the pretext of needing some information.*

o-**pretty**[1] /'prɪti/ *adv informal* **1** quite, but not extremely *The traffic was pretty bad.* • *I'm pretty sure they'll accept.* **2 pretty much/well** almost *We've pretty much finished here.*

o-**pretty**[2] /'prɪti/ *adj* **1** If a woman or girl is pretty, she is attractive. *Your daughter is very pretty.* **2** If a place or an object is pretty, it is pleasant to look at. *a pretty little village*

**prevail** /prɪ'veɪl/ *verb* [I] *formal* **1** to get control or influence *We can only hope that common* *sense will prevail.* **2** to be common among a group of people *The use of guns prevails among the gangs in this area.*

**prevail on/upon sb to do sth** *formal* to persuade someone to do something that they do not want to do *He was eventually prevailed upon to accept the appointment.*

**prevailing** /prɪˈveɪlɪŋ/ *adj* [always before noun] **1** existing a lot in a particular group, area, or at a particular time *a prevailing attitude/mood* **2 a prevailing wind** a wind that usually blows in a particular place

**prevalent** /ˈprevələnt/ *adj* existing a lot in a particular group, area, or at a particular time *These diseases are more prevalent among young children.* ● prevalence /ˈprevələns/ *noun* [U] when something exists a lot in a particular group, area, or at a particular time *the prevalence of smoking among teenagers*

O─**prevent** /prɪˈvent/ *verb* [T] to stop something happening or to stop someone doing something *to prevent accidents/crime* ● [+ from + doing sth] *Members of the public were prevented from entering the building.* ● preventable *adj* If something is preventable, it can be prevented.

**protect** or **prevent**?

Protect means to keep someone or something safe from bad things.

*You should wear sunscreen to protect your skin.*

Prevent means to stop something from happening.

*Wearing sunscreen can help prevent skin cancer.*

**preventative** /prɪˈventətɪv/ *adj another word for* preventive

**prevention** /prɪˈvenʃən/ *noun* [U] when you stop something happening or stop someone doing something *crime prevention* ● *the prevention of diseases*

**preventive** /prɪˈventɪv/ (*also* **preventative**) *adj* Preventive action is intended to stop something before it happens. *preventive measures* ● *preventive medicine*

**preview** /ˈpriːvjuː/ *noun* [C] **1** an opportunity to see a film, play, etc before it is shown to the public **2** a short film that advertises a film or television programme ● preview *verb* [T]

O─**previous** /ˈpriːviəs/ *adj* existing or happening before something or someone else *the previous day/year* ● *a previous attempt* ● *his previous marriage* ● previously *adv He previously worked as a teacher.*

**prey¹** /preɪ/ *noun* **1** [U] an animal that is hunted and killed by another animal **2 fall prey to sth** to be hurt or deceived by something or someone bad ⊃ *See also:* **bird of prey**.

**prey²** /preɪ/ *verb*

**prey on sth** If an animal preys on another animal, it catches it and eats it. *Spiders prey on flies and other small insects.*

**prey on/upon sb** to hurt or deceive people who are weak and easy to deceive *These young thieves prey on the elderly.*

O─**price¹** /praɪs/ *noun* **1** [C] the amount of money that you pay to buy something *high/low prices* ● *House prices are falling/rising.* ● *The price of fuel has gone up again.* **2** [no plural] the unpleasant results that you must accept or experience for getting or doing something *Suspension from the club was a high/small price to pay* (= very bad/not very bad thing to experience) *for his mistake.* ● *The price of this peace will be perpetual vigilance.* **3 at a price** If you can get something at a price, you have to pay a lot of money for it. *False passports are available, at a price.* **4 at any price** If you want something at any price, you will do anything to get it. *She wanted the job at any price.*

**price** or **prize**?

These two words sound very similar but have different spellings and very different meanings – be careful not to confuse them.

Price means 'the amount of money that you pay to buy something'.

*The price of oil has risen by 20%.*

Prize means 'something valuable that is given to someone who wins a competition or who has done good work'.

*She won first prize in the competition.*

**price²** /praɪs/ *verb* [T] to say what the price of something is [often passive] *The book is **priced** at $40.*

**priceless** /ˈpraɪsləs/ *adj* **1** very valuable *a priceless antique/painting* **2** very important or useful *A trip round the world is a priceless opportunity.*

**pricey** (*also* **pricy**) /ˈpraɪsi/ *adj informal* expensive *That jacket's a bit pricey!*

**prick** /prɪk/ *verb* [T] to make a very small hole in something with a sharp object *Prick the potatoes all over before baking.* ● *I pricked my finger on a pin.* ● prick *noun* [C] *The injection won't hurt – you'll just feel a slight prick.*

**prickle¹** /ˈprɪkl/ *noun* [C] a sharp point on the surface of some plants or the skin of some animals

**prickle²** /ˈprɪkl/ *verb* [I] If part of your body prickles, it feels as if a lot of sharp points are touching it because you are frightened or excited. *a prickling sensation*

**prickly** /ˈprɪkli/ *adj* **1** covered with prickles *a prickly bush* **2** *informal* A prickly person or relationship is unfriendly or difficult to deal with. *She gets very prickly if you ask her questions about her private life.*

**pricy** /ˈpraɪsi/ *adj another spelling of* pricey

O─**pride¹** /praɪd/ *noun* [U] **1** SATISFACTION a feeling of satisfaction at your achievements or the achievements of your family or friends *She felt a great sense of pride as she watched him accept the award.* ● *The whole community **takes pride in** (= feels proud about) the school.* **2** RESPECT the respect that you feel for yourself *Defeat in the World Cup has badly damaged national pride.* **3** IMPORTANCE the belief that you are better or more important than other people *His*

P

*pride prevented him from asking for help.* **4 sb's pride and joy** something or someone that is very important to you *He spends hours cleaning that motorcycle – it's his pride and joy.* **5 have/take pride of place** If something takes pride of place, you put it in the best position so that it can be seen easily. *A photo of her grandchildren took pride of place on the wall.* **6 swallow your pride** to decide to do something although it will embarrass you *He swallowed his pride and asked if he could have his old job back.*

**pride²** /praɪd/ *verb*
**pride yourself on sth/doing sth** to feel satisfaction at a quality or skill that you have *The company prides itself on having the latest technology.*

**priest** /priːst/ *noun* [C] someone who performs religious duties and ceremonies

**the priesthood** /ˈpriːsthʊd/ *noun* the job of being a priest *After university, he spent three years training for the priesthood.*

**prim** /prɪm/ *adj* Someone who is prim behaves in a very formal way and is easily shocked by anything rude. *Sarah wouldn't find that funny – she's far too prim and proper* (= shocked by anything rude). • **primly** *adv*

**prima donna** /ˌpriːmə ˈdɒnə/ *noun* [C] someone who behaves badly and expects to get everything they want because they think that they are very important

**primal** /ˈpraɪmᵊl/ *adj formal* very basic, or relating to the time when human life on Earth began *primal instincts*

**primarily** /praɪˈmerᵊli/ *adv* mainly *She's known primarily as a novelist but she also writes poetry.*

**primary¹** /ˈpraɪmᵊri/ *adj* [always before noun] most important *Her primary responsibility is to train new employees.*

**primary²** /ˈpraɪmᵊri/ *noun* [C] a vote in which people in a political party in the US choose the person who will represent them in an election

**primary 'colour** *UK* (*US* **primary ˌcolor**) *noun* [C] one of the three colours, which in paint, etc are red, blue, and yellow, that can be mixed together to make any other colour

**'primary ˌschool** (*also US* **elementary school**) *noun* [C] a school for children aged 5 to 11

**primate** /ˈpraɪmeɪt/ *noun* [C] a member of the group of animals which includes monkeys and people, which have large brains and hands and feet developed for climbing

**prime¹** /praɪm/ *adj* [always before noun] **1** main, or most important *the prime suspect in a murder investigation* **2** of the best quality *The hotel is in a prime location in the city centre.* **3 a prime example** a very good example of something

**prime²** /praɪm/ *noun* [no plural] the period in your life when you are most active or successful *At 35, she's in her prime.* • *the prime of life*

**prime³** /praɪm/ *verb* [T] to prepare someone for an event or situation, often by giving them the information that they need *The president had been well primed before the debate.*

**ˌprime 'minister** *noun* [C] the leader of an elected government in some countries

**ˌprime 'time** *noun* [U] the time in the evening when the largest number of people watch television *The show's so popular that it's been moved to prime time.* • *prime-time television*

**primeval** /praɪˈmiːvᵊl/ *adj* belonging to a very early period in the history of the world *primeval forest*

**primitive** /ˈprɪmɪtɪv/ *adj* **1** relating to human society at a very early stage of development, with people living in a simple way without machines or a writing system *primitive man* • *primitive societies* **2** very basic or old-fashioned *The conditions at the campsite were rather primitive.*

**primrose** /ˈprɪmrəʊz/ *noun* [C] a wild plant with pale yellow flowers

**prince** /prɪns/ *noun* [C] **1** the son of a king or queen, or one of their close male relatives *Prince Edward* **2** the male ruler of a small country

**princely** /ˈprɪnsli/ *adj* **a princely sum** a large amount of money *It cost the princely sum of £2 million.*

**princess** /prɪnˈses* ⓤⓢ *ˈprɪnsəs/ *noun* [C] **1** the daughter of a king or queen, or one of their close female relatives **2** the wife of a prince

**principal¹** /ˈprɪnsəpᵊl/ *adj* [always before noun] main, or most important *Her principal reason for moving is to be nearer her mother.*

**principal²** /ˈprɪnsəpᵊl/ *noun* [C] the person in charge of a school or college *She was caught smoking and sent to see the principal.*

**principality** /ˌprɪnsɪˈpæləti/ *noun* [C] a country ruled by a prince

**principally** /ˈprɪnsəpᵊli/ *adv* mainly *The advertising campaign is aimed principally at women.*

○━**principle** /ˈprɪnsəpl/ *noun* **1** [C, U] a rule or belief which influences your behaviour and which is based on what you think is right *He must be punished – it's a matter of principle.* **2** [C] a basic idea or rule which explains how something happens or works *The organization works on the principle that all members have the same rights.* **3 in principle** If you agree with something in principle, you agree with the idea or plan although you do not know the details or you do not know if it will be possible. *They have approved the changes in principle.* **4 on principle** If you refuse to do something on principle, you refuse to do it because you think it is morally wrong. *She doesn't wear fur on principle.*

**principled** /ˈprɪnsəpld/ *adj* showing strong beliefs about what is right and wrong

○━**print¹** /prɪnt/ *verb* **1** ⬚WRITING/IMAGES⬚ [T] to produce writing or images on paper or other material with a machine *The instructions are printed on the side of the box.* **2** ⬚BOOKS/NEWSPAPERS⬚ [T] to produce books, newspapers, magazines, etc, usually in large quantities, using machines *Fifty thousand booklets have been printed for the exhibition.* **3** ⬚INCLUDE⬚ [T] to include a piece of writing in a newspaper or magazine *They printed his letter in Tuesday's paper.* **4** ⬚WRITE⬚ [I, T] to write words without joining the letters together *Please print your name and address clearly using capitals.* **5** ⬚PATTERN⬚ [T] to produce a pattern on material or paper

**print sth out** to produce a printed copy of a document that has been written on a computer *Can you print out a copy of that letter for me?*

**print²** /prɪnt/ *noun* **1** [WORDS] [U] words, letters, or numbers that are produced on paper by a machine *The print's so small in this book that I can hardly read it.* **2 in/out of print** If a book is in print, it is possible to buy a new copy of it, and if it is out of print, it is not now possible. *The novel was first published in 1880 and has been in print ever since.* **3** [PICTURE] [C] a copy of a picture made using photography or by pressing paper onto a design covered in ink *a print of Van Gogh's 'Sunflowers'* **4** [PHOTOGRAPH] [C] a photograph that is produced on paper **5** [PATTERN] [C] a pattern that is produced on material or paper *a floral print* **6** [HAND] [C] (*also* **fingerprint**) a mark that is left on a surface where someone has touched it *His prints were found all over the house and he was arrested the next day.* **7** [MARK] [C] a mark that is left on a surface where someone has walked *The dog left prints all over the kitchen floor.* ➔ *See also:* **small print**.

**printer** /ˈprɪntəʳ/ *noun* [C] **1** a machine which is connected to a computer and which produces writing or images on paper *a laser printer* **2** a person or company that prints books, newspapers, magazines, etc

**printing** /ˈprɪntɪŋ/ *noun* [U] when writing or images are produced on paper or other material using a machine

**'printing ,press** *noun* [C] a machine that prints books, newspapers, magazines, etc

**printout** /ˈprɪntaʊt/ *noun* [C] information or a document that is printed from a computer *He asked for a printout of the year's sales figures.*

**prior** /praɪəʳ/ *adj formal* **1** [always before noun] existing or happening before something else *The course requires no prior knowledge of Spanish.* **2 prior to sth** before a particular time or event *the weeks prior to her death*

**prioritize** (*also UK* **-ise**) /praɪˈɒrɪtaɪz/ *verb* [I, T] to decide which of a group of things are the most important so that you can deal with them first *You must learn to prioritize your work.*

**priority** /praɪˈɒrəti/ *noun* [C] **1** something that is very important and that must be dealt with before other things *My first/top priority is to find somewhere to live.* **2 give priority to sth** to consider that something is more important than other things and deal with it first **3 have/take priority (over sth)** to be more important than other things and to be dealt with first *His job seems to take priority over everything else.*

**prise** /praɪz/ *verb UK* **prise sth apart/off/open, etc** to use force to move, remove, or open something *I prised the lid off with a spoon.*

**prism** /ˈprɪzᵊm/ *noun* [C] an object made of clear glass which separates the light that passes through it into different colours

o━**prison** /ˈprɪzᵊn/ *noun* [C, U] a place where criminals are kept as a punishment *He's spent most of his life in prison.* ● *She was sent to prison for two years.*

o━**prisoner** /ˈprɪzᵊnəʳ/ *noun* **1** [C] someone who is being kept in prison as a punishment, or because they have been caught by an enemy

**2 hold/keep/take sb prisoner** to catch someone and guard them so that they cannot escape ➔ *See also:* **political prisoner**.

**,prisoner of 'war** *noun* [C] *plural* **prisoners of war** a soldier who is caught by enemy soldiers during a war *a prisoner of war camp*

**pristine** /ˈprɪstiːn/ *adj* in very good condition, as if new *Her car is in pristine condition.*

**privacy** /ˈprɪvəsi ⓤⓢ ˈpraɪvəsi/ *noun* [U] when you are alone and people cannot see or hear what you are doing *I hate sharing a bedroom – I never get any privacy.*

o━**private¹** /ˈpraɪvɪt/ *adj* **1** [NOT EVERYONE] only for one person or group and not for everyone *Each room has a balcony and a private bathroom.* ● *You can't park here – this is private property.* **2** [NOT GOVERNMENT] controlled by or paid for by a person or company and not by the government *Charles went to a private school.* **3** [SECRET] If information or an emotion is private, you do not want other people to know about it. *This is a private matter – it doesn't concern you.* **4 in private** If you do something in private, you do it where other people cannot see or hear you. *I need to talk to you in private.* **5 sb's private life** someone's personal relationships and activities and not their work **6** [QUIET] A place which is private is quiet and there are no other people there to see or hear what you are doing. *Is there somewhere private where we can talk?* ● **privately** *adv*

**private²** /ˈpraɪvɪt/ *noun* [C] a soldier of the lowest rank in the army

**privatize** (*also UK* **-ise**) /ˈpraɪvɪtaɪz/ *verb* [T] If an industry or organization owned by the government is privatized, it is sold to private companies. ● **privatization** /ˌpraɪvɪtaɪˈzeɪʃᵊn/ *noun* [U]

**privilege** /ˈprɪvᵊlɪdʒ/ *noun* **1** [C, U] an advantage that only one person or group has, usually because of their position or because they are rich **2** [no plural] an opportunity to do something special or enjoyable [+ of + doing sth] *I had the privilege of meeting the Queen.* ● **privileged** *adj* having a privilege *to be in a privileged position*

**privy** /ˈprɪvi/ *adj formal* **privy to sth** knowing information that is not known by many people

o━**prize¹** /praɪz/ *noun* [C] something valuable that is given to someone who wins a competition or who has done good work *to win a prize* ● *first/second prize* ● *the Nobel Prize for Literature* ➔ *See also:* **booby prize**. ➔ *See usage note at* **price**.

**prize²** /praɪz/ *adj* [always before noun] A prize animal or vegetable is good enough to win a competition.

**prize³** /praɪz/ *verb* [T] to think that something is very valuable or important [often passive] *The ability to speak English is a skill prized by many employers.* ● *His car is his prized possession.*

**prize-winning** /ˈpraɪzˌwɪnɪŋ/ *adj* [always before noun] having won a prize *a prize-winning author*

**pro** /prəʊ/ *noun* **1** [C] *informal* someone who earns money for playing a sport *a golf/tennis pro* **2 the pros and cons** the advantages and disadvantages of something [+ of + doing sth] *We* *discussed the pros and cons of buying a bigger house.*

**proactive** /ˌprəʊˈæktɪv/ *adj* taking action by causing change and not only reacting to change when it happens

**probability** /ˌprɒbəˈbɪləti/ *noun* **1** [C, U] how likely it is that something will happen [+ of + doing sth] *What's the probability of winning?* ● [+ (that)] *There's a high probability that he'll get the job.* **2 in all probability** used to mean that something is very likely *She will, in all probability, have left before we arrive.*

**probable** /ˈprɒbəbl/ *adj* likely to be true or to happen *The probable cause of death was heart failure.* ● [+ (that)] *It's highly probable that he'll lose his job.*

o─⚫**probably** /ˈprɒbəbli/ *adv* used to mean that something is very likely *I'll probably be home by midnight.*

**probation** /prəʊˈbeɪʃᵊn/ *noun* [U] **1** a period of time when a criminal must behave well and not commit any more crimes in order to avoid being sent to prison *to be on probation* **2** a period of time at the start of a new job when you are watched and tested to see if you are suitable for the job ● **probationary** *adj* relating to probation *a probationary period*

**pro'bation ,officer** *noun* [C] someone whose job is to watch and help criminals who have been put on probation

**probe**¹ /prəʊb/ *verb* [I, T] to ask a lot of questions in order to discover information about something or someone *The interviewer probed deep into her private life.* ● *probing questions*

**probe**² /prəʊb/ *noun* [C] **1** when you try to discover information about something by asking a lot of questions *an FBI probe into corruption* **2** a long, thin, metal tool used by doctors to examine parts of the body

o─⚫**problem** /ˈprɒbləm/ *noun* **1** [C] a situation that causes difficulties and that needs to be dealt with *financial/health problems* ● *I'm having problems with my computer.* ● *Drugs have become a serious problem in the area.* ➲ *See usage note at* **trouble**. **2** [C] a question that you use mathematics to solve **3 No problem.** *informal* **a** something that you say to mean you can or will do what someone has asked you to do *"Can you get me to the airport by 11.30?" "No problem."* **b** something that you say when someone has thanked you for something *"Thanks for taking me home." "No problem."*

**problematic** /ˌprɒbləˈmætɪk/ *adj* full of problems or difficulties *He has a very problematic relationship with his father.*

**procedure** /prəʊˈsiːdʒəʳ/ *noun* [C, U] the official or usual way of doing something *The company has new procedures for dealing with complaints.* ● *You must follow correct procedure at all times.*

**proceed** /prəʊˈsiːd/ *verb* [I] *formal* **1** to continue as planned *His lawyers have decided not to proceed with the case.* **2 proceed to do sth** to do something after you have done something else *She sat down and proceeded to tell me about her skiing trip.* **3 proceed along/down/to, etc** *formal* to move or travel in a particular direction *Passengers for Sydney should proceed to gate 21.*

**proceedings** /prəˈsiːdɪŋz/ *noun* [plural] **1** legal action against someone *The bank is threatening to start legal proceedings against him.* **2** a series of organized events or actions *The chairman opened the proceedings with a short speech.*

**proceeds** /ˈprəʊsiːdz/ *noun* [plural] the money that is earned from an event or activity *All proceeds from the concert will go to charity.*

o─⚫**process**¹ /ˈprəʊses/ (US) /ˈprɑːses/ *noun* **1** [C] a series of actions that you take in order to achieve a result *Buying a house can be a long and complicated process.* **2** [C] a series of changes that happen naturally *the ageing process* **3 in the process** If you are doing something, and you do something else in the process, the second thing happens as a result of doing the first thing. *She stood up to say hello and spilled her drink in the process.* **4 be in the process of doing sth** to have started doing something *We're in the process of painting our apartment.*

**process**² /ˈprəʊses/ (US) /ˈprɑːses/ *verb* [T] **1** to add chemicals to a substance, especially food, in order to change it or make it last longer *processed food* **2** to deal with information or documents in an official way or by using a computer *Visa applications take 28 days to process.* ● **processing** *noun* [U] *data processing*

**procession** /prəˈseʃᵊn/ *noun* [C] a line of people or vehicles that moves forward slowly as part of a ceremony or public event *a funeral procession*

**processor** /ˈprəʊsesəʳ/ *noun* [C] the main part of a computer that controls all the other parts ➲ *See also:* **food processor, word processor**.

**proclaim** /prəʊˈkleɪm/ *verb* [T] *formal* to announce something officially or in public ● **proclamation** /ˌprɒkləˈmeɪʃᵊn/ *noun* [C] an official announcement about something important

**procrastinate** /prəʊˈkræstɪneɪt/ *verb* [I] *formal* to wait a long time before doing something that you must do *I know I've got to deal with the problem at some point – I'm just procrastinating.*

**procure** /prəˈkjʊəʳ/ *verb* [T] *formal* to obtain something that is difficult to get

**prod** /prɒd/ *verb* **prodding**, *past* **prodded 1** [I, T] to push someone or something with your finger or with a pointed object *He prodded me in the back and told me to hurry up.* **2** [T] to encourage someone to do something [+ into + doing sth] *We need to prod him into making a decision.* ● **prod** *noun* [C] [usually singular] *to give someone a prod*

**prodigious** /prəˈdɪdʒəs/ *adj formal* extremely great in size or ability *a prodigious talent* ● *a prodigious appetite*

**prodigy** /ˈprɒdɪdʒi/ *noun* [C] a young person who is very good at something *A child prodigy, she entered university at the age of eleven.*

o─⚫**produce**¹ /prəˈdjuːs/ *verb* [T] **1** MAKE to make or grow something *The factory produces about 900 cars a year.* ● *This plant will produce small yellow flowers in the spring.* **2** CAUSE to cause a particular reaction or result *Nuts produce an allergic reaction in some people.* **3** SHOW to take an object from somewhere so that people can see it *One of the men suddenly produced a gun from his pocket.* **4** FILM/PLAY to control how a film, play, programme, or musical recording is made *He's produced some of the top Broadway shows.* ➔ *See also:* **mass-produce**.

**produce²** /'prɒdjuːs/ *noun* [U] food that is grown or made in large quantities to be sold *dairy produce*

**producer** /prə'djuːsə²/ *noun* [C] **1** a company, country, or person that makes goods or grows food *Australia is one of the world's main producers of wool.* **2** someone who controls how a film, play, programme, or musical recording is made *a film/record producer*

◐**product** /'prɒdʌkt/ *noun* [C] **1** something that is made or grown to be sold *a whole new range of skin-care products.* • *Does she eat* **dairy products** (= things made from milk)? **2 product of sth** someone or something that is the result of a particular experience or process *His lack of confidence is the product of an unhappy childhood.* ➔ *See also:* **by-product**, **end-product**.

◐**production** /prə'dʌkʃən/ *noun* **1** MAKING [U] when you make or grow something *Sand is used in the production of glass.* • *The new model* **goes into production** (= starts being made) *next year.* **2** AMOUNT [U] the amount of something that is made or grown *We need to increase production by 20%.* **3** PERFORMANCE [C] a performance or series of performances of a play or show *a school production of 'Romeo and Juliet'* **4** ORGANIZING FILM/PLAY [U] when someone controls how a film, play, programme, or musical recording is made *She wants a career in TV production.*

**productive** /prə'dʌktɪv/ *adj* **1** producing a good or useful result *We had a very productive meeting and sorted out a lot of problems.* **2** producing a large amount of goods, food, work, etc *productive land* • *a productive worker*

**productivity** /ˌprɒdʌk'tɪvəti/ *noun* [U] the rate at which goods are produced *high/low productivity* • *We need to increase productivity by 50%.*

**Prof** /prɒf/ *noun* [C] short for professor *Prof Susan Nishio*

**profane** /prə'feɪn/ *adj formal* showing no respect for God or for religious or moral rules *profane language* • **profanity** /prə'fænəti/ *noun* [U] *formal*

**profess** /prə'fes/ *verb* [T] *formal* to express a quality or belief, often when it is not true [+ **to do sth**] *She professes to hate shopping, but she's always buying new things.*

**profession** /prə'feʃən/ *noun* [C] **1** a type of work that needs special training or education *What's your profession?* • *He's working in a restaurant, but he's a teacher* **by profession** (= he trained to be a teacher). ➔ *See usage note at* **work**. **2** [group] the people who do a type of work considered as a group *The medical profession has expressed concern about the new drug.*

◐**professional¹** /prə'feʃənəl/ *adj* **1** JOB [always before noun] relating to a job that needs special training or education *You should get some professional advice about your finances.* **2** EARNING MONEY Someone is professional if they earn money for a sport or activity which most

people do as a hobby. *a professional athlete/ musician* • *a professional golf championship* ➔ *Opposite* **amateur**. **3** SKILL showing skill and careful attention *a professional attitude* • *He looks very professional in that suit.* ➔ *Opposite* **unprofessional**.

**professional²** /prə'feʃənəl/ *noun* [C] **1** TRAINED someone who does a job that needs special training or education **2** WITH EXPERIENCE someone who has done a job for a long time and who does it with a lot of skill *She dealt with the problem like a true professional.* **3** SPORTS someone who earns money for doing a sport or activity which most other people do as a hobby *a rugby professional* ➔ *Opposite* **amateur**.

**professionalism** /prə'feʃənəlɪzəm/ *noun* [U] the skill and careful attention which trained people are expected to have *He complained about the lack of professionalism in the company.*

**professionally** /prə'feʃənəli/ *adv* **1** WORK in a way that relates to your work *I know him professionally, but he's not a close friend.* **2** WITH TRAINING Work that is done professionally is done by someone who has had special training. *Their house has been professionally decorated.* **3** HIGH STANDARDS in a way that shows high standards or skill *He dealt with the situation very professionally.* **4** SPORT If someone does an activity or sport professionally, they earn money for doing it. *He's good enough at football to play professionally.*

**professor** /prə'fesə²/ *noun* [C] the highest rank of teacher in a British university, or a teacher in an American university or college *a professor of history at Oxford* • *My tutor is Professor Blackman.*

**proffer** /'prɒfə²/ *verb* [T] *formal* to offer something to someone *to proffer advice*

**proficiency** /prə'fɪʃənsi/ *noun* [U] when you can do something very well *The job requires* **proficiency** *in written and spoken English.*

**proficient** /prə'fɪʃənt/ *adj* very good at something *She's* **proficient in** *two languages.* • *I've become quite* **proficient at** *repairing bicycles.*

**profile¹** /'prəʊfaɪl/ *noun* [C] **1** DESCRIPTION a short description of someone's life, character, work, etc **2** HEAD a side view of someone's face or head *The picture shows him* **in profile**. **3** ATTENTION the amount of attention that something receives *We need to increase our company's profile in Asia.* **4 high profile** important and noticeable *a high profile job* **5 keep a low profile** to try not to be noticed

profile

**profile²** /'prəʊfaɪl/ *verb* [T] to describe someone's life, character, work, etc

◐**profit¹** /'prɒfɪt/ *noun* [C, U] money that you get from selling goods or services for more than they cost to produce or provide *a profit of $4.5* million • *It's very hard for a new business to* **make a profit** *in its first year.*

**profit²** /'prɒfɪt/ *verb*

**profit from sth** to earn a profit or get an advantage from something *Investors have profited from a rise in interest rates.*

**profitable** /'prɒfɪtəbl/ *adj* **1** making or likely to make a profit *a profitable business* **2** useful or likely to give you an advantage *a profitable discussion* • profitability /ˌprɒfɪtə'bɪlɪti/ *noun* [U] • profitably *adv*

**profound** /prə'faʊnd/ *adj* **1** EFFECT If an effect is profound, it is extreme. *The war had a profound impact on people's lives.* **2** FEELING If a feeling is profound, you feel it very strongly. *a profound sense of sadness* **3** UNDERSTANDING If an idea or piece of work is profound, it shows intelligence or a great ability to understand. *a profound question* • *His theories were simple, but profound.* • profoundly *adv*

**profusely** /prə'fjuːsli/ *adv* a lot *He apologized profusely for being late.*

**profusion** /prə'fjuːʒən/ *noun* [U, no plural] *formal* an extremely large amount of something *a profusion of wild flowers* • *Bacteria grow in profusion in the warm, wet soil.*

**prognosis** /prɒg'nəʊsɪs/ *noun* [C] *plural* **prognoses** /prɒg'nəʊsiːz/ *formal* **1** a judgment that a doctor makes about an ill person's chance of becoming healthy **2** an opinion about the future of someone or something *The prognosis for economic growth is good.*

o-**program¹** /'prəʊgræm/ *noun* [C] **1** a set of instructions that you put into a computer to make it do something *to write a computer program* **2** *US spelling of* programme

**program²** /'prəʊgræm/ *verb* [T] **programming**, *past* **programmed 1** If you program a computer, you give it a set of instructions to do something. **2** *US spelling of* programme

o-**programme¹** *UK* (*US* **program**) /'prəʊgræm/ *noun* [C] **1** TELEVISION/RADIO a show on television or radio *a TV programme* • *Did you see that programme about spiders last night?* **2** PLAN a plan of events or activities with a particular purpose *a health education programme* **3** THIN BOOK a thin book that you buy at a theatre, sports event, etc which tells you who or what you are going to see

**programme²** *UK* (*US* **program**) /'prəʊgræm/ *verb* [T] If you programme a machine, you give it a set of instructions to do something. [+ to do sth] *I've programmed the video to start recording at 10 o'clock.*

**programmer** /'prəʊgræməʳ/ *noun* [C] someone who writes computer programs as a job • programming *noun* [U] when someone writes computer programs

o-**progress¹** /'prəʊgres/ (US) /'prɒgres/ *noun* [U] **1** development and improvement of skills, knowledge, etc *slow/rapid progress* • *technological progress* • *He has made good progress in French this year.* **2 in progress** *formal* happening or being done now *Quiet please – Exams in progress.* **3** movement towards a place

**progress²** /prəʊ'gres/ *verb* [I] **1** to improve or develop in skills, knowledge, etc *Technology has progressed rapidly in the last 100 years.* **2** to continue gradually *I began to feel more relaxed as the evening progressed.*

**progression** /prəʊ'greʃən/ *noun* [C, U] when something or someone changes to the next stage of development *a logical/natural progression* • *Drugs can stop the progression of the disease.*

**progressive** /prəʊ'gresɪv/ *adj* **1** thinking or behaving in a new or modern way *progressive ideas/attitudes* **2** developing or happening gradually *a progressive disease* • progressively *adv* gradually *My headaches are getting progressively worse.*

**the progressive** /prəʊ'gresɪv/ *noun* the form of the verb that is used to show that an action is continuing. In English, the progressive is made with 'be' and the present participle.

**prohibit** /prəʊ'hɪbɪt/ *verb* [T] *formal* to officially forbid something [often passive] *Smoking is prohibited on most international flights.* • [+ from + doing sth] *The new law prohibits people from drinking alcohol in the street.* • *a prohibited substance* • prohibition /ˌprəʊhɪ'bɪʃən/ *noun* [U] when something is prohibited *the prohibition of drugs*

**prohibitive** /prəʊ'hɪbətɪv/ *adj* If the cost of something is prohibitive, it is too expensive for many people. *The cost of flying first class is prohibitive for most people.* • prohibitively *adv* prohibitively expensive

o-**project¹** /'prɒdʒekt/ *noun* [C] **1** a carefully planned piece of work that has a particular purpose *a research project* • *The new building project will cost $45 million.* • *My next project will be to paint the bedrooms.* **2** a piece of school work that involves detailed study of a subject *We're doing a class project on the environment.*

**project²** /prə'dʒekt/ *verb* **1** CALCULATE [T] to calculate an amount or make a guess about the future based on information that you have [often passive + to do sth] *As people live longer, the demand for health care is projected to increase dramatically.* • *projected costs/growth* **2** IMAGE [T] to show a film or other image on a screen or a wall *Laser images were projected onto a screen.* **3** QUALITY [T] If you project a particular quality, that quality is what most people notice about you. *She projected an image of strong leadership.* **4** **project from/into/out, etc** *formal* to stick out

**projection** /prə'dʒekʃən/ *noun* **1** [C] a calculation or guess about the future based on information that you have *government projections of population growth* **2** [U] when a film or an image is projected onto a screen or wall

**projector** /prəʊˈdʒektər/ *noun* [C] a machine that projects films or pictures onto a screen or a wall

**proliferate** /prəʊˈlɪfəreɪt/ *verb* [I] *formal* to increase in number very quickly

**proliferation** /prəʊˌlɪfəˈreɪʃən/ *noun* [U] when something increases in number very quickly *the proliferation of new TV channels*

**prolific** /prəʊˈlɪfɪk/ *adj* producing a lot of something *a prolific writer/composer*

**prologue** /ˈprəʊlɒg/ *noun* [C] an introduction to a book, film, or play

**prolong** /prəʊˈlɒŋ/ *verb* [T] to make something last longer *Eating a good diet can prolong your life.*

**prolonged** /prəʊˈlɒŋd/ *adj* continuing for a long time *a prolonged illness* • *Avoid prolonged exposure to the sun.*

**prom** /prɒm/ *noun* [C] in the US, a formal dance party for older students held at the end of the school year *a school prom*

**promenade** /ˌprɒməˈnɑːd/ *noun* [C] a wide path by the sea

**prominence** /ˈprɒmɪnəns/ *noun* [U] when someone or something is important or famous *He first came to prominence as a singer in the 1980s.*

**prominent** /ˈprɒmɪnənt/ *adj* **1** important or famous *a prominent figure/businessman* **2** very easy to see or notice *a prominent feature* • *prominent eyes* • prominently *adv*

**promiscuous** /prəˈmɪskjuəs/ *adj* Someone who is promiscuous has sex with a lot of people. • promiscuity /ˌprɒmɪˈskjuːəti/ *noun* [U] when someone is promiscuous

o-***promise**[1] /ˈprɒmɪs/ *verb* **1** [I, T] to say that you will certainly do something or that something will certainly happen [+ to do sth] *She promised to write to me every week.* • [+ (that)] *Paul promised me that he'd cook dinner tonight.* **2** [+ two objects] to say that you will certainly give something to someone *They promised us a reward.* • *Grandma's ring was promised to me.* **3 promise to be sth** If something promises to be good, exciting, etc, people expect that it will be good, exciting, etc. *It promises to be a really exciting game.*

**promise**

When you use the expression promise someone something, no preposition is needed after the verb.

*He promised his mum that he would clean his room.*

*He promised to his mum that he would clean his room.*

o-***promise**[2] /ˈprɒmɪs/ *noun* **1** [C] when you say that you will certainly do something *I'm not sure I can do it so I won't make any promises.* **2 keep/break a promise** to do/not do what you said that you would do **3 show promise** If someone or something shows promise, they are likely to be successful. *As a child, he showed great promise as an athlete.*

**promising** /ˈprɒmɪsɪŋ/ *adj* likely to be very good or successful in the future *a promising student* • *a promising start to the game*

**promo** /ˈprəʊməʊ/ *noun* [C] *informal* an advertisement, especially a short film

**promote** /prəˈməʊt/ *verb* [T] **1** ENCOURAGE to encourage something to happen or develop to promote good health/peace **2** ADVERTISE to advertise something *The band is promoting their new album.* **3** JOB to give someone a more important job in the same organization [often passive] *She's just been promoted to manager.*

**promoter** /prəˈməʊtər/ *noun* [C] **1** someone who organizes a large event *a concert promoter* **2** someone who tries to encourage something to happen or develop *a promoter of sexual equality*

**promotion** /prəˈməʊʃən/ *noun* **1** ADVERTISEMENT [C, U] activities to advertise something *a sales promotion* • *They're giving away free T-shirts as a special promotion.* **2** JOB [C, U] when someone is given a more important job in the same organization *She was given a promotion in her first month with the company.* **3** ENCOURAGE [U] when you encourage something to happen or develop *the promotion of a healthy lifestyle*

**promotional** /prəˈməʊʃənəl/ *adj* Promotional items or activities are used to advertise something. *a promotional campaign/video* • *promotional material*

**prompt**[1] /prɒmpt/ *verb* [T] **1** to cause something *His remarks prompted a lot of discussion.* **2 prompt sb to do sth** to cause someone to do sth *What prompted him to leave?* **3** to help someone, often an actor, remember what they were going to say or do

**prompt**[2] /prɒmpt/ *adj* done or acting quickly and without waiting, or arriving at the correct time *a prompt reply* • prompt payment • promptly *adv*

**prone** /prəʊn/ *adj* **1 be prone to sth/doing sth** to often do something or suffer from something, especially something bad *I'm prone to headaches.* • *He's prone to forgetting things.* **2 accident/injury, etc prone** often having accidents/injuries, etc ⊃ *See also:* **accident-prone.**

o-***pronoun** /ˈprəʊnaʊn/ *noun* [C] a word that is used instead of a noun which has usually already been talked about. For example the words 'she', 'it', and 'mine' are pronouns. ⊃ *See also:* **personal pronoun, relative pronoun.**

**pronounce** /prəˈnaʊns/ *verb* [T] **1** to make the sound of a letter or word *How do you pronounce his name?* **2 pronounce sb/sth dead/a success, etc** *formal* to state that something is true in an official or formal way *Doctors pronounced him dead at 12.23 a.m.*

**pronounced** /prəˈnaʊnst/ *adj* very easy to notice *She spoke with a pronounced American accent.*

**pronouncement** /prəˈnaʊnsmənt/ *noun* [C] *formal* an official announcement *to make a pronouncement*

**pronunciation** /prəˌnʌnsiˈeɪʃən/ *noun* [C, U] how words are pronounced *Mario's English pronunciation is excellent.* • *There are two different pronunciations of this word.*

o-***proof** /pruːf/ *noun* [U] a fact or a piece of information that shows something exists or is true *She showed us her passport as proof of her identity.* • [+ (that)] *My landlord has asked for proof that I'm employed.*

**-proof** /pruːf/ *suffix* used at the end of words to mean 'protecting against' or 'not damaged by' *a bulletproof vest • a waterproof jacket*

**prop¹** /prɒp/ *verb* **propping,** *past* **propped prop sth against/on, etc** to put something somewhere so that it is supported on or against something *He propped the ladder against the wall.* **prop sth up 1** to lift and give support to something by putting something under it *We had to prop up the bed with some bricks.* **2** to help something to continue *For years the industry was propped up by the government.*

**prop²** /prɒp/ *noun* [C] an object used in a film or play *a stage prop*

**propaganda** /ˌprɒpəˈgændə/ *noun* [U] information or ideas, which are often false, that an organization prints or broadcasts to make people agree with what it is saying *political propaganda* • **propagandist** *noun* [C] someone who creates, prints, or broadcasts propaganda

**propagate** /ˈprɒpəgeɪt/ *verb formal* **1** [I, T] If you propagate plants, you help them to produce new plants, and if plants propagate, they produce new plants. *Plants are propagated from small cuttings.* **2** [T] to tell your ideas or opinions to a lot of people in order to make them agree with what you are saying *to propagate lies/rumours* • propagation /ˌprɒpəˈgeɪʃᵃn/ *noun* [U] *formal.*

**propel** /prəˈpel/ *verb* [T] **propelling,** *past* **propelled 1 propel sb into/to sth** to cause someone to do an activity or be in a situation *The film propelled him to international stardom.* **2** to push or move something somewhere, often with a lot of force *a rocket propelled through space*

**propeller** /prəˈpelə/ *noun* [C] a piece of equipment made of two or more flat metal pieces that turn around and cause a ship or aircraft to move

**propensity**

/prəˈpensəti/ *noun* [C] *formal* If someone has a propensity for something or to do something, they often do it. *to have a propensity for violence • a propensity to talk too much*

o→**proper** /ˈprɒpə/ *adj* **1** CORRECT [always before noun] correct or suitable *the proper way to do something • Please put those books back in their proper place.* **2** REAL [always before noun] *mainly UK* real and satisfactory *his first proper job • You should eat some proper food instead of just sweets.* **3** ACCEPTABLE socially acceptable *It's not proper to interrupt someone when they're speaking.* **4** MAIN [always after noun] referring to the main or most important part of something *I live outside Cambridge – I don't live in the city proper.*

o→**properly** /ˈprɒpəli/ *adv* correctly, or in a satisfactory way *The TV doesn't work properly. • She doesn't eat properly.*

**propeller**

,**proper 'noun** *noun* [C] a word or group of words that is the name of a person or place and always begins with a capital letter. For example 'Tony' and 'London' are proper nouns.

o→**property** /ˈprɒpəti/ *noun* **1** BUILDING [C, U] a building or area of land *There are several properties for sale in this area. • Private property – no parking.* • *a property developer/owner* **2** OBJECT [U] objects that belong to someone *The police recovered a large amount of stolen property.* **3** QUALITY [C] a quality of something *the medicinal properties of wild plants* ⊃ *See also:* **lost property.**

**prophecy** /ˈprɒfəsi/ *noun* [C, U] when someone says that something will happen in the future • **prophesy** /ˈprɒfəsaɪ/ *verb* [I, T] to say that you believe something will happen in the future

**prophet** /ˈprɒfɪt/ *noun* [C] someone sent by God to tell people what to do, or to say what will happen in the future

**prophetic** /prəˈfetɪk/ *adj* saying what will happen in the future *a prophetic dream/vision • Her warnings proved prophetic.*

**proponent** /prəˈpəʊnənt/ *noun* [C] *formal* someone who supports a particular idea or plan of action *a proponent of nuclear energy*

**proportion** /prəˈpɔːʃᵃn/ *noun* **1** [C] a part of a total number or amount *Children make up a large proportion of the world's population. • The class consists of both men and women in roughly equal proportions.* **2 out of proportion** If something is out of proportion, it is much bigger or smaller than it should be, when compared to other things. *The punishment is completely out of proportion to the crime.* **3 in proportion** If something is in proportion, it is the right size or shape when compared to other things. **4 in proportion to** If something changes in proportion to another thing, it changes to the same degree as that thing. *Your tax payment increases in proportion to your salary.* **5 blow/get sth out of proportion** to behave as if something that has happened is much worse than it really is

**proportional** /prəˈpɔːʃᵃnᵃl/ *adj* If two amounts are proportional, they change at the same rate so that the relationship between them does not change. *Weight is proportional to size.*

**pro,portional ,represen'tation** *noun* [U] a system of voting in which the number of a political party's elected representatives is related to the number of votes the party gets

**proportionate** /prəˈpɔːʃᵃnət/ *adj* If two amounts are proportionate, they change at the same rate so that the relationship between them does not change. *His success was proportionate to his efforts.* ⊃ *Opposite* **disproportionate.** • **proportionately** *adv*

**proportions** /prəˈpɔːʃᵃnz/ *noun* [plural] the size, shape, or level of something *a building of pleasing proportions • Crime has increased to alarming proportions.*

**proposal** /prəˈpəʊzᵃl/ *noun* [C] **1** a suggestion for a plan [+ to do sth] *a proposal to raise taxes • The proposal for a new sports hall has been rejected.* **2** when someone asks someone to marry them

**propose** /prəˈpəʊz/ *verb* **1** [T] to suggest a plan

or action [+ (that)] *I propose that we delay our decision until we have more information.* • *proposed changes* **2 propose to do sth** to intend to do something *They propose to cycle across Europe.* **3** [I] to ask someone to marry you *He proposed to me on my birthday.*

**proposition** /ˌprɒpəˈzɪʃᵊn/ *noun* [C] **1** OFFER an offer or suggestion, usually in business *an attractive/interesting proposition* **2** IDEA an idea or opinion [+ that] *the proposition that all people are created equal* **3** PLAN in the US, a formal plan that people accept or refuse by voting

**proprietary** /prəˈpraɪətᵊri/ *adj* [always before noun] *formal* owned or controlled by a company

**proprietor** /prəˈpraɪətəʳ/ *noun* [C] *formal* the owner of a business such as a hotel, shop, newspaper, etc

**propriety** /prəˈpraɪəti/ *noun* [U] *formal* socially acceptable behaviour

**propulsion** /prəˈpʌlʃᵊn/ *noun* [U] a force that pushes something forward *jet propulsion*

**prosaic** /prəʊˈzeɪɪk/ *adj formal* ordinary and not interesting

**prose** /prəʊz/ *noun* [U] ordinary written language that is not poetry *He's a wonderful writer – readers love his clear and lively prose.*

**prosecute** /ˈprɒsɪkjuːt/ *verb* [I, T] to accuse someone of a crime in a law court *No one has been prosecuted for the murders.*

**prosecution** /ˌprɒsɪˈkjuːʃᵊn/ *noun* **1 the prosecution** [group] the lawyers who are prosecuting someone in a court of law *The prosecution will begin presenting evidence today.* **2** [C, U] when someone is prosecuted

**prosecutor** /ˈprɒsɪkjuːtəʳ/ *noun* [C] a lawyer who prosecutes people

**prospect** /ˈprɒspekt/ *noun* **1** [C, U] the possibility that something good might happen in the future *Is there any prospect of the weather improving?* **2** [no plural] the idea of something that will happen in the future [+ of + doing sth] *We face the prospect of having to start all over again.* • *I'm very excited at the prospect of seeing her again.* **3 sb's prospects** the possibility of being successful at work *He's hoping the course will improve his career prospects.*

**prospective** /prəˈspektɪv/ *adj* **prospective buyers/employers/parents, etc** Prospective buyers, employers, parents, etc are not yet buyers, employers, parents, etc but are expected to be in the future.

**prospectus** /prəˈspektəs/ *noun* [C] a book or magazine which gives information about a school, college, or business for future students or customers

**prosper** /ˈprɒspəʳ/ *verb* [I] to be successful, usually by earning a lot of money

**prosperity** /prɒsˈperəti/ *noun* [U] when someone is successful, usually by earning a lot of money

**prosperous** /ˈprɒspᵊrəs/ *adj* successful, usually by earning a lot of money

**prostitute** /ˈprɒstɪtjuːt/ *noun* [C] someone whose job is having sex with people • **prostitution** /ˌprɒstɪˈtjuːʃᵊn/ *noun* [U]

**prostrate** /ˈprɒstreɪt/ *adj* lying flat on the ground with your face pointing down

**protagonist** /prəʊˈtægᵊnɪst/ *noun* [C] *formal* the main character in a play, film, or story

o⍪**protect** /prəˈtekt/ *verb* [I, T] to keep someone or something safe from something dangerous or bad *It's important to protect your skin from the harmful effects of the sun.* • *Vitamin C may help protect against cancer.* ⊃ *See usage note at* **prevent.** • **protection** /prəˈtekʃᵊn/ *noun* [U] *This coat doesn't provide any protection against the rain.*

**protective** /prəˈtektɪv/ *adj* **1** giving protection *protective clothing* • *a protective mask* **2** wanting to protect someone from criticism, hurt, danger, etc because you like them *She's fiercely protective of her children.*

**protector** /prəˈtektəʳ/ *noun* [C] someone or something that protects

**protégé** /ˈprɒtəʒeɪ/ *noun* [C] a young person who is helped and taught by an older and usually famous person

**protein** /ˈprəʊtiːn/ *noun* [U] food such as meat, cheese, fish, or eggs that is necessary for the body to grow and be strong

**protest¹** /ˈprəʊtest/ *noun* [C, U] when people show that they disagree with something by standing somewhere, shouting, carrying signs, etc *a protest against the war* • *a peaceful/ violent protest*

**protest²** /prəʊˈtest/ *verb* **1 protest (about/ against/at sth)** to show that you disagree with something by standing somewhere, shouting, carrying signs, etc *They're on strike to protest against job losses.* • *Students were protesting about cuts to the education budget.* **2 protest sth** US to show that you disagree with something by standing somewhere, shouting, carrying signs, etc *Thousands gathered to protest the plan.* **3** [I, T] to say something forcefully or complain about something [+ that] *The girl was crying, protesting that she didn't want to leave her mother.*

**Protestant** /ˈprɒtɪstᵊnt/ *adj* belonging or relating to the part of the Christian religion that separated from the Roman Catholic Church in the 1500s • **Protestant** *noun* [C] *His mother was a Protestant.* • **Protestantism** *noun* [U] the beliefs of the Protestant Churches

**protestation** /ˌprɒtesˈteɪʃᵊn/ *noun* [C] *formal* when someone says something forcefully or complains about something *He was arrested despite his protestations of innocence.*

**protester** (*also* **protestor**) /prəˈtestəʳ/ *noun* [C] someone who shows that they disagree with something by standing somewhere, shouting, carrying signs, etc

**protocol** /ˈprəʊtəkɒl/ *noun* [C, U] the rules about what you must do and how you must behave in official or very formal situations *royal protocol*

**proton** /ˈprəʊtɒn/ *noun* [C] a part of an atom with a positive electrical charge

**prototype** /ˈprəʊtəʊtaɪp/ *noun* [C] the first model or example of something new that can be developed or copied in the future *a prototype for a new car*

**protracted** /prəˈtræktɪd/ *adj formal* If an unpleasant situation is protracted, it lasts a long time. *a protracted dispute/struggle*

**protrude** /prəʊˈtruːd/ *verb* [I] If something such

P

as a part of the body protrudes, it comes out from the surface more than usual. *protruding ears/teeth*

o━**proud** /praʊd/ *adj* **1** feeling very pleased about something you have done, something you own, or someone you know *She was so proud of her son.* ● [+ to do sth] *I'm very proud to be involved in this project.* **2 be too proud to do sth** to not be able to do something, especially ask for help, because you are too embarrassed *He's too proud to ask you for any money.* **3** feeling that you are more important than you really are

**proudly** /'praʊdli/ *adv* in a way that shows you are pleased about something you have done, something you own, or someone you know *He proudly showed us a photo of his grandchildren.*

o━**prove** /pruːv/ *verb* [T] *past* **proved**, *past p* (*esp. US*) **proven** **1** to show that something is true *They knew who had stolen the money, but they couldn't prove it.* ● [+ (that)] *Can you prove that you weren't there?* ● *He's desperately trying to prove his innocence.* ⊃ *Opposite* **disprove**. **2 prove sth/to be sth** to show a particular quality after a period of time *The new treatment has proved to be very effective.* **3 prove yourself** to show that you are good at something *I wish he'd stop trying to prove himself all the time.*

**proven** /'pruːvᵊn/ *adj* If something is proven, it has been shown to be true. *proven ability/skills*

**proverb** /'prɒvɜːb/ *noun* [C] a famous phrase or sentence which gives you advice *an ancient Chinese proverb* ● **proverbial** /prəʊ'vɜːbiəl/ *adj* relating to a proverb

o━**provide** /prə'vaɪd/ *verb* [T] to supply something to someone *This booklet provides useful information about local services.* ● *It's a new scheme to provide schools with free computers.* ● **provider** *noun* [C] someone who provides something *an Internet service provider*

**provide for sb** to give someone the things they need such as money, food, or clothes *He has a wife and two young children to provide for.*

**provided (that)** (*also* **providing (that)**) *conjunction* only if *He's welcome to come along, provided that he behaves himself.*

**province** /'prɒvɪns/ *noun* **1** [C] one of the large areas which some countries are divided into because of the type of government they have *the Canadian province of Alberta* **2 the provinces** the areas of a country that are not the capital city and so are not considered exciting or fashionable

**provincial** /prə'vɪnʃᵊl/ *adj* **1** relating to a province **2** relating to or typical of the provinces *a provincial town* ● *provincial attitudes*

**provision** /prə'vɪʒᵊn/ *noun* **1** [U] when something is provided for someone *We need to increase the provision of health care for the elderly.* **2 make provision for sth** to make arrangements to deal with something *He hasn't made any provision for his retirement yet.* **3** [C] a rule that is part of a law or an agreement

**provisional** /prə'vɪʒᵊnᵊl/ *adj* If a situation or arrangement is provisional, it is not certain and might change in the future. *These dates are*

*only provisional at the moment.* ● **provisionally** *adv*

**provisions** /prə'vɪʒᵊnz/ *noun* [**plural**] supplies of food and other necessary items

**proviso** /prə'vaɪzəʊ/ *noun* [C] *formal* something that must happen as part of an agreement *He was released from prison with the proviso that he doesn't leave the country.*

**provocation** /ˌprɒvə'keɪʃᵊn/ *noun* [C, U] when someone makes you angry *He'll start a fight at the slightest provocation.*

**provocative** /prə'vɒkətɪv/ *adj* **1** causing an angry reaction, usually intentionally *a provocative question/remark* **2** Provocative clothes, images, etc are sexually exciting. ● **provocatively** *adv She dresses very provocatively.*

**provoke** /prə'vəʊk/ *verb* [T] **1** to cause a strong and usually angry reaction *to provoke an argument/attack* ● *Her statement has provoked a public outcry.* **2** to intentionally make someone angry so that they react in an angry or violent way *He claimed he was provoked by the victim.*

**prowess** /'praʊɪs/ *noun* [U] *formal* when you are good at doing something *athletic/sporting prowess*

**prowl**[1] /praʊl/ *verb* [I, T] to walk around somewhere slowly as if hunting someone or something *to prowl the streets*

**prowl**[2] /praʊl/ *noun* **be on the prowl** to be hunting for someone or something

**proximity** /prɒk'sɪməti/ *noun* [U] *formal* when something is near to something else *What's good about this hotel is its proximity to the airport.*

**proxy** /'prɒksi/ *noun* **by proxy** using another person to do something instead of doing something yourself *to vote by proxy*

**prude** /pruːd/ *noun* [C] someone who does not like to hear or see things relating to sex *Don't be such a prude.* ● **prudish** *adj a prudish woman*

**prudent** /'pruːdᵊnt/ *adj formal* wise and careful [+ to do sth] *I think it would be prudent to leave now before it starts raining.* ● **prudence** /'pruːdᵊns/ *noun* [U] *formal* ● **prudently** *adv*

**prune**[1] /pruːn/ *verb* [T] If you prune a tree or bush, you cut off some of the branches or flowers to help it grow better.

**prune**[2] /pruːn/ *noun* [C] a dried plum (= type of fruit)

**pry** /praɪ/ *verb* **1** [I] to try to discover private things about people *to pry into someone's personal life.* ● *She wanted a private holiday away from prying eyes.* **2 pry sth apart/loose/open, etc** to open something with difficulty *She managed to pry open a window and escape.*

**PS** /ˌpiː'es/ used when you want to add extra information at the end of a letter or email *PS Give my love to Emma.*

**psalm** /sɑːm/ *noun* [C] a song or poem from the Bible (= holy book)

**pseudonym** /'sjuːdənɪm/ *noun* [C] a name used by a writer instead of their own name *He writes under a pseudonym.*

**psych** /saɪk/ *verb*

**psych yourself up** *informal* to try to make yourself feel confident and ready to do something difficult

**psyche** /'saɪki/ *noun* [C] the human mind and feelings *the male psyche*

**psychedelic** /ˌsaɪkɪ'delɪk/ *adj* **1** Psychedelic drugs make you see things that are not really there. **2** Psychedelic colours or patterns are very strong, bright, and strange.

**psychiatrist** /saɪ'kaɪətrɪst/ *noun* [C] a doctor who is trained in psychiatry

**psychiatry** /saɪ'kaɪətri/ *noun* [U] the study and treatment of mental illness • psychiatric /ˌsaɪki'ætrɪk/ *adj* relating to psychiatry *a psychiatric disorder* • *a psychiatric nurse*

**psychic** /'saɪkɪk/ *adj* having a special mental ability, for example so that you are able to know what will happen in the future or know what people are thinking *psychic powers*

**psycho** /'saɪkəʊ/ *noun* [C] *informal* someone who is crazy and frightening

**psychoanalysis** /ˌsaɪkəʊə'næləsɪs/ *noun* [U] the treatment of mental problems by studying and talking about people's dreams, fears, and experiences • psychoanalytic /ˌsaɪkəʊˌænə'lɪtɪk/ *adj* relating to psychoanalysis

**psychoanalyst** /ˌsaɪkəʊ'ænəlɪst/ *noun* [C] someone who treats people using psychoanalysis

**psychological** /ˌsaɪkəl'ɒdʒɪkəl/ *adj* relating to the human mind and feelings *psychological problems* • psychologically *adv*

**psychologist** /saɪ'kɒlədʒɪst/ *noun* [C] someone who has studied the human mind and feelings

**psychology** /saɪ'kɒlədʒi/ *noun* [U] **1** the study of the human mind and feelings *child psychology* • *He's studying psychology and philosophy.* **2** the way someone thinks and behaves *the psychology of serial killers*

**psychopath** /'saɪkəʊpæθ/ *noun* [C] someone who is very mentally ill and usually dangerous • psychopathic /ˌsaɪkəʊ'pæθɪk/ *adj a psychopathic killer*

**psychosis** /saɪ'kəʊsɪs/ *noun* [C] *plural* **psychoses** /saɪ'kəʊsiːz/ a mental illness that makes you believe things that are not real

**psychotherapy** /ˌsaɪkəʊ'θerəpi/ *noun* [U] the treatment of mental problems by talking about your feelings instead of taking medicine • psychotherapist *noun* [C] someone who gives people psychotherapy

**psychotic** /saɪ'kɒtɪk/ *adj* suffering from a mental illness that makes you believe things that are not true

**pt** *noun* [C] **1** *written abbreviation for* point (= a unit used for showing who is winning in a game or competition) *Hill 81 pts, Villeneuve 68 pts* **2** *written abbreviation for* pint (= a unit for measuring liquid)

**PTO** /ˌpiːtiː'əʊ/ *UK abbreviation for* please turn over: used at the bottom of a page of writing to show that there is more information on the other side

**pub** /pʌb/ *noun* [C] a place where you can get drinks such as beer and usually food *We're all going to the pub after work.*

**puberty** /'pjuːbəti/ *noun* [U] the time when children's bodies change and become like adults' bodies *to reach puberty*

**pubic hair** /ˌpjuːbɪk'heəʳ/ *noun* [U] the hair that grows around the sexual organs

O─**public**[1] /'pʌblɪk/ *adj* **1** **public awareness/health/support, etc** the awareness/health/support, etc of all ordinary people *Public opinion has turned against him.* • *Is it really in the public interest* (= useful for people) *to publish this information?* **2** **public parks/toilets/transport, etc** parks/toilets/transport, etc that are for everyone to use and are not private *Smoking should be banned in public places.* **3** **a public announcement/appearance/statement, etc** an announcement/appearance/statement, etc that can be seen or heard or known by everyone *The Prime Minister is due to make a public statement later today.* **4** **make sth public** to allow everyone to know about something *The government does not plan to make its findings public.* **5** **public funds/services/spending, etc** funds/services/spending, etc controlled or supplied by the government and not by a private company

O─**public**[2] /'pʌblɪk/ *noun* [group] **1** **the (general) public** all ordinary people *a member of the public* • *The public has a right to know about this.* • *The house is only open to the general public on Sundays.* **2** **in public** where everyone can see you *He shouldn't behave like that in public.*

**public ad'dress system** (*also UK* **tannoy**) *noun* [C] a system of equipment used in public places that someone speaks into in order to make their voice loud enough to hear

**publication** /ˌpʌblɪ'keɪʃən/ *noun* **1** [U] when a book, newspaper, etc is printed and sold **2** [C] a book, newspaper, or magazine *a monthly/weekly publication*

**publicist** /'pʌblɪsɪst/ *noun* [C] someone whose job is to make people know about someone or something by advertising or giving information in the newspaper, on television, etc

**publicity** /pʌb'lɪsəti/ *noun* [U] advertising or information about someone or something in the newspaper, on television, etc *a publicity campaign* • *to get bad/good publicity*

**publicize** (*also UK* **-ise**) /'pʌblɪsaɪz/ *verb* [T] to make people know about something by advertising or giving information in newspapers, on television, etc *a highly/widely publicized event*

**publicly** /'pʌblɪkli/ *adv* If you do something publicly, everyone can see it, hear it, or know about it.

**public re'lations** *noun formal* PR (=writing and activities that are intended to make a person, company, or product more popular)

**public 'school** *UK* (*US* **public ˌschool**) *noun* [C] **1** in the UK, a school that you pay to go to **2** (*UK* **state school**) in the US, a school that is free to go to because the government provides the money for it

**public u'tility** *noun* [C] an organization that supplies the public with water, gas, or electricity

O─**publish** /'pʌblɪʃ/ *verb* [T] **1** PRINT to prepare and print a book, newspaper, magazine, article, etc so that people can buy it [often passive] *This book is published by Cambridge University Press.* **2** WRITE to write something that is then printed in a book, newspaper, magazine, etc *He's published several short stories in national*

P

*magazines.* **3** [MAKE PUBLIC] to make information available to the public

**publisher** /'pʌblɪʃəʳ/ *noun* [C] a company or person who prepares and prints books, newspapers, magazines, etc

**publishing** /'pʌblɪʃɪŋ/ *noun* [U] the business of preparing and printing books, newspapers, magazines, etc *a career in publishing*

**puck** /pʌk/ *noun* [C] in ice hockey (= a sport), a small, hard disc that players hit with a stick ➔ *See colour picture* **Sports 1** *on page Centre 15.*

**pudding** /'pʊdɪŋ/ *noun* **1** [C, U] in the UK, a sweet dish that is usually eaten as the last part of a meal *We've got apple pie for pudding.* **2** [U] in the US, a soft, sweet food made from milk, sugar, eggs, and sometimes flour *chocolate/ vanilla pudding*

**puddle** /'pʌdl/ *noun* [C] a pool of liquid on the ground, usually from rain

**puerile** /'pjʊəraɪl ⓤⓈ 'pjuːərɪl/ *adj formal* behaving in a silly way like a child

**puff¹** /pʌf/ *verb* **1** [I] to breathe fast and with difficulty, usually because you have been doing exercise **2** [I, T] to smoke something *to puff on a cigarette*

**puff sth out** to make your chest or your face become bigger by filling them with air

**puff up** If part of your body puffs up, it becomes larger because it is infected or injured.

**puff²** /pʌf/ *noun* [C] **1** a small amount of smoke, gas, powder, etc *a puff of smoke/air* **2** when someone breathes in smoke from a cigarette *to take a puff on a cigarette*

**puffin** /'pʌfɪn/ *noun* [C] a black and white sea bird with a large head and brightly coloured beak

**puffy** /'pʌfi/ *adj* If the skin around your eyes is puffy, it is slightly swollen. *His eyes were still puffy with sleep.*

**puke** /pjuːk/ (*also* **puke up**) *verb* [I, T] *informal* to vomit

⚬╼**pull¹** /pʊl/ *verb* **1** [I, T] to take hold of something and move it somewhere *If you keep pulling his tail, he'll bite you.* • *No wonder it's not working, someone's* **pulled** *the plug* **out.** • *He* **pulled off** *his boots.* • *She bent down and* **pulled up** *her socks.* **2 pull a muscle** to injure a muscle by stretching it too much **3 pull a gun/knife, etc on sb** to suddenly take out a weapon *He pulled a gun on us and demanded money.* ➔ *See also:* pull your **hair** out, pull the **plug¹**, not pull any punches (**punch²**), pull out all the stops (**stop²**), pull strings (**string¹**), pull your **weight**.

**pull sth apart 1** to destroy something by tearing it into pieces **2** to say that something, usually a piece of work, is very bad

**pull sb/sth apart** to separate two things or people

**pull at sth** to pull something several times, usually with quick, light movements *Stop pulling at my sleeve.*

**pull away 1** If a vehicle pulls away, it starts moving. *I just managed to get on the bus before it pulled away.* **2** If you pull away from someone who is holding you, you suddenly move your body backwards, away from them.

**pull sth down** to destroy a building because it is

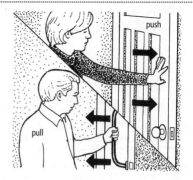

not wanted any more *They've started pulling down the old cinema.*

**pull in/into sth** If a vehicle pulls in or pulls into somewhere, it moves in that direction and stops there. *They pulled in at the side of the road.*

**pull sth off** to succeed in doing or achieving something difficult *He is about to pull off his biggest deal yet.*

**pull off** *UK* If a vehicle pulls off, it starts moving. *The car pulled off and sped up the road.*

**pull on sth** to put on clothes quickly *I pulled on my jeans and ran downstairs.*

**pull out** If a vehicle pulls out, it starts moving onto a road or onto a different part of the road. *That car pulled out right in front of me.*

**pull over** If a vehicle pulls over, it moves to the side of the road and stops.

**pull through** to continue to live after you have been badly injured or very ill

**pull yourself together** *informal* to become calm and behave normally again after being angry or upset

**pull up 1** If a vehicle pulls up, it stops, often for a short time. *A car pulled up outside the bank and two men got out.* **2 pull up a chair** to move a chair nearer to something or someone *Why don't you pull up a chair and join us?*

**pull²** /pʊl/ *noun* [no plural] a strong force that causes something to move somewhere or be attracted to something

**pulley** /'pʊli/ *noun* [C] a wheel with a rope going round it which is used to lift things

pulley

**pullover** /'pʊləʊvəʳ/ *noun* [C] a warm piece of clothing which covers the top of your body and is pulled on over your head *a black woolly pullover*

**pulp** /pʌlp/ *noun* [U] **1** a soft, wet substance made from wood, which is used to make paper **2** the soft part inside a fruit or vegetable

**pulpit** /'pʊlpɪt/ *noun* [C] the raised structure in a church where the priest stands when he speaks to everyone

**pulsate** /pʌl'seɪt ⓤⓢ 'pʌlseɪt/ *verb* [I] to beat or move with a strong, regular rhythm *The whole room was pulsating with music.*

**pulse** /pʌls/ *noun* [C] the regular movement of blood through your body when your heart is beating *She put her fingers on his wrist to **take my pulse*** (= count the number of beats per minute). • *My **pulse rate** is 70.*

**pulses** /'pʌlsɪz/ *noun* [plural] *UK* seeds such as beans or peas which are cooked and eaten as food

**pump¹** /pʌmp/ *noun* [C] a piece of equipment which forces liquid or gas to move somewhere *a gas/petrol pump* • *a water pump*

**pump**

bicycle pump

petrol pump *UK*, gas pump *US*

**pump²** /pʌmp/ *verb* [T] to force liquid or gas to move somewhere *Your heart pumps blood around your body.* • *Firemen used powerful hoses to **pump** water **into** the building.*

**pump sth into sth** to give a lot of money to a plan or organization *They've pumped millions of pounds into the economy.*

**pump sth out** *informal* to continuously produce a lot of something *a radio pumping out music*

**pump sth up** to fill something with air using a pump *You should pump your tyres up.*

**pumpkin** /'pʌmpkɪn/ *noun* [C, U] a large, round vegetable with thick, orange skin

**pun** /pʌn/ *noun* [C] a joke that you make by using a word that has two meanings

**punch¹** /pʌnʃ/ *verb* [T] **1** to hit someone or something with your fist (= closed hand) *He punched me twice in the stomach.* **2 punch a hole in sth** to make a hole in something with a special piece of equipment

**punch²** /pʌnʃ/ *noun* **1** HIT [C] when you hit someone or something with your fist (= closed hand) *a punch on the nose* **2** DRINK [U] a sweet, mixed drink made from fruit juice, spices, and usually alcohol **3** HOLE [C] a piece of equipment that makes a hole in something **4 not pull any punches** to speak in an honest way without trying to be kind

**punchline** /'pʌntʃlaɪn/ *noun* [C] the last part of a joke that makes it funny

**punch-up** /'pʌntʃʌp/ *noun* [C] *UK informal* a fight in which people hit each other with their fists (= closed hands)

**punctual** /'pʌŋktʃuəl/ *adj* arriving at the right time and not too late • **punctuality** /ˌpʌŋktʃu'æləti/ *noun* [U] when you are punctual • **punctually** *adv*

**punctuate** /'pʌŋktʃueɪt/ *verb* [T] to add punctuation marks to written words so that people can see when a sentence begins and finishes, that something is a question, etc

**punctuation** /ˌpʌŋktʃu'eɪʃⁿn/ *noun* [C] the use of punctuation marks in writing so that people can see when a sentence begins and finishes, that something is a question, etc

**punctu'ation ˌmark** *noun* [C] a symbol used in punctuation

**puncture¹** /'pʌŋktʃəʳ/ *noun* [C] **1** a small hole made by a sharp object **2** *UK* a hole in a tyre that makes the air come out *to have a puncture*

**puncture²** /'pʌŋktʃəʳ/ *verb* [T] to make a hole in something *The knife went through his ribs and punctured his lung.*

**pundit** /'pʌndɪt/ *noun* [C] someone who is an expert in a subject and often gives their opinions on television, radio, etc *a political pundit*

**pungent** /'pʌndʒⁿnt/ *adj* A pungent smell is very strong. *the pungent smell of vinegar*

o⊶**punish** /'pʌnɪʃ/ *verb* [T] to make someone suffer because they have done something bad [often passive] *They must be severely **punished for** these crimes.*

**punishable** /'pʌnɪʃəbl/ *adj* A crime that is punishable is one that you can be punished for. *Drug dealing is **punishable by** death in some countries.*

**punishing** /'pʌnɪʃɪŋ/ *adj* very difficult and making you tired *a punishing schedule*

o⊶**punishment** /'pʌnɪʃmənt/ *noun* [C, U] when someone is punished *He had to stay in his bedroom as a punishment for fighting.* ➔ *See also:* **capital punishment, corporal punishment,** be a **glutton** for punishment.

**punitive** /'pjuːnətɪv/ *adj formal* given as a punishment or seeming like a punishment *punitive action*

**punk** /pʌŋk/ *noun* **1** STYLE [U] (*also* ˌpunk 'rock) a style of music and fashion in the 1970s which was wild, loud, and violent **2** PERSON [C] someone who wears punk clothes and likes punk music **3** BAD MAN [C] *US informal* a bad young man

**punt¹** /pʌnt/ *noun* [C] **1** a long boat with a flat bottom that you push along the river with a long pole **2** in some sports, a powerful kick which causes the ball to go very far

**punt²** /pʌnt/ *verb* **1** [I, T] to go or take someone along a river in a punt **2** [T] in some sports, to kick a ball after you have dropped it from your hands and before it touches the ground

**punter** /'pʌntəʳ/ *noun* [C] *UK informal* someone who is buying something or making a bet (= risking money on a competition)

**puny** /'pjuːni/ *adj* very small and weak

**pup** /pʌp/ *noun* [C] a young dog or other particular type of baby mammal *a seal pup*

**pupil** /'pjuːpⁿl/ *noun* [C] **1** a student at school

P

*The school has 1,100 pupils aged 11 to 18.* ➲ *See colour picture* **Classroom** *on page Centre 4.* **2** the black, round part in the centre of your eye

**puppet** /'pʌpɪt/ *noun* [C] **1** a toy in the shape of a person or animal that you can move with strings or by putting your hand inside *a glove puppet* **2** someone who is controlled by someone else *a political puppet*

**puppy** /'pʌpi/ *noun* [C] a young dog *a litter of puppies*

**purchase¹** /'pɜːtʃəs/ *verb* [T] *formal* to buy something *Tickets must be purchased two weeks in advance.*

**purchase²** /'pɜːtʃəs/ *noun formal* **1** [C, U] when you buy something *the illegal purchase of guns* **2** [C] something that you buy *a major purchase*

○⊷**pure** /pjʊəʳ/ *adj* **1** NOT MIXED A pure substance is not mixed with anything else. *pure gold* • *pure wool* **2** EMPHASIS [always before noun] used to emphasize a feeling, quality, or state is completely and only that thing *pure coincidence* • *Her face had a look of pure delight.* **3** CLEAN clean and healthy *pure air/water* **4 pure mathematics/physics, etc** the study of mathematics/physics, etc based only on ideas and not on practical use **5** GOOD completely good and not having any bad qualities or bad morals

**puree** /'pjʊəreɪ/ US pjʊə'reɪ/ *noun* [U] a thick, smooth, liquid food made by crushing and mixing fruit or vegetables *tomato puree*

**purely** /'pjʊəli/ *adv* only *She married him purely for his money.*

**purgatory** /'pɜːgətʳri/ *noun* [U] **1** in the Catholic religion, a very unpleasant place where you have to go and suffer before you go to heaven **2** a very unpleasant situation *This diet is purgatory.*

**purge** /pɜːdʒ/ *verb* [T] **1** to get rid of bad feelings that you do not want [often reflexive] *She wanted to **purge** herself **of** guilt.* **2** to get rid of people from an organization because you do not agree with them • **purge** *noun* [C]

**purify** /'pjʊərɪfaɪ/ *verb* [T] to remove bad substances from something to make it pure *Plants help to purify the air.* • *purified water* • purification /ˌpjʊərɪfɪ'keɪʃʳn/ *noun* [U]

**purist** /'pjʊərɪst/ *noun* [C] someone who believes in and follows very traditional rules or ideas in a subject

**puritanical** /ˌpjʊərɪ'tænɪkʳl/ *adj* having severe religious morals and not wanting people to enjoy themselves • puritan /'pjʊərɪtʳn/ *noun* [C] *a puritanical person*

**purity** /'pjʊərəti/ *noun* [U] the quality of being pure *air purity*

**purple** /'pɜːpl/ *adj* being a colour that is a mixture of red and blue *purple pansies* • purple *noun* [C, U] ➲ *See colour picture* **Colours** *on page Centre 6.*

**purport** /pə'pɔːt/ *verb*
**purport to be/do sth** *formal* to pretend to be or do something *a man purporting to be a police officer*

○⊷**purpose** /'pɜːpəs/ *noun* **1** [C] why you do something or why something exists *The main **purpose of** the meeting is to discuss the future of the company.* • *The drug may be legalized for*

medical purposes. **2** [U] the feeling of knowing what you want to do *He seems to have lost all **sense of purpose**.* **3 on purpose** intentionally *I didn't do it on purpose, it was an accident.* **4 serve a purpose** to have a use *These small village shops serve a very useful purpose.* ➲ *See also:* **cross purposes**, *to all intents* (**intent¹**) and purposes.

**purpose-built** /ˌpɜːpəs'bɪlt/ *adj mainly UK* A purpose-built building has been specially designed for the way it will be used.

**purposeful** /'pɜːpəsfʳl/ *adj* showing that you know what you want to do *He has a quiet, purposeful air.* • purposefully *adv*

**purposely** /'pɜːpəsli/ *adv* intentionally *I wasn't purposely trying to hurt you.*

**purr** /pɜːʳ/ *verb* [I] **1** CAT If a cat purrs, it makes a soft sound in its throat to show pleasure. **2** PERSON to talk in a soft, low voice **3** CAR If a car purrs, its engine is very smooth and makes a soft sound.

**purse¹** /pɜːs/ *noun* [C] **1** *UK* a small container for money, usually used by a woman *a leather purse* **2** *mainly US* (*mainly UK* **handbag**) a bag, usually carried by a woman *I always carry aspirin in my purse.*

**purse²** /pɜːs/ *verb* **purse your lips** to press your lips tightly together, often to show that you are angry

**pursue** /pə'sjuː/ US pərˈsuː/ *verb* [T] **pursuing**, *past* **pursued 1** If you pursue a plan, activity, or situation, you try to do it or achieve it, usually over a long period of time. *She decided to pursue a career in television.* **2** to follow someone or something, usually to try to catch them *The car was pursued by helicopters.* **3 pursue a matter** to try to discover information about something *We will not be pursuing this matter any further.*

**pursuit** /pə'sjuːt/ US pərˈsuːt/ *noun* [U] **1** when you try to achieve a plan, activity, or situation, usually over a long period of time *the pursuit of pleasure* • *He left his native country in pursuit of freedom.* **2** when you follow someone or something to try to catch them *The police are in pursuit of a 25-year-old murder suspect.*

**pursuits** /pə'sjuːts/ *noun* [plural] *formal* activities or hobbies *He enjoys climbing and other outdoor pursuits.*

**purveyor** /pə'veɪəʳ/ *noun* [C] *formal* someone who sells or provides something *a purveyor of antiques*

**pus** /pʌs/ *noun* [U] a yellow substance that is produced when part of your body is infected

○⊷**push¹** /pʊʃ/ *verb* **1** MOVE SOMETHING [I, T] to move someone or something by pressing them with your hands or body *She **pushed** the books **aside** and sat down on my desk.* • *We **pushed** the children **down** the slide.* • *He **pushed** me violently **out** of the door.* • *Someone **pushed** him **into** the river.* ➲ *See picture at* **pull**. **2** MOVE YOURSELF [I, T] to move somewhere by moving someone or something away from you [+ into + doing sth] *He pushed past me.* • *He **pushed his way** to the front of the crowd.* **3** PRESS [T] to press something *If you push this button, your seat goes back.* **4 push (sb) for sth/to do sth** to try hard to achieve something or to make someone else do something *Local residents are pushing for the road to be made safer.* **5** ENCOURAGE [T] to try to make someone do something that they do not want to do [+ into + doing sth] *My mother pushed me into having ballet lessons.* **6 push yourself** to make yourself work very hard to achieve something ➔ *See also:* push the **boat** out.

**push sb about/around** to tell someone what to do in a rude way *I'm fed up with being pushed around.*

**push ahead/forward** to continue doing something, especially when this is difficult *They have decided to* **push ahead** *with legal action.*

**push sth/sb aside** to decide to forget about or ignore something or someone *We can't just push these problems aside – we have to deal with them.*

**push in** *UK informal* to rudely join a line of people who are waiting for something by moving in front of some of the people who are already there

**push on** to continue doing something, especially when this is difficult

**push sb/sth over** to push someone or something so that they fall to the ground

**push sth through** to make a plan or suggestion be officially accepted *We're trying to push this deal through as quickly as possible.*

**push sth up** to increase the amount, number, or value of something *If you want to travel on Saturday, it will push the price up a bit.*

push² /pʊʃ/ noun **1 a push for sth/to do sth** a big effort to achieve something or make someone do something *a push for higher standards in education* **2** [C] when you move someone or something by pressing them with your hands or body [usually singular] *She gave him a little push towards the door.* **3 give sb the push** *UK informal* to get rid of someone from a job or relationship **4** [C] encouragement to make someone do something [usually singular] *I'm sure he'll go, he just needs a little push that's all.* **5 at a push** *UK If you can do something at a push, you can do it but it will be difficult.* **6 if/when push comes to shove** If you say that something can be done if push comes to shove, you mean that it can be done if the situation becomes so bad that you have to do it. *If push comes to shove, we'll just have to sell the car.*

pushchair /'pʊʃtʃeəʳ/ *UK* (*US* **stroller**) *noun* [C] a chair on wheels which is used to move small children

pushed /pʊʃt/ *adj UK* **be pushed for sth** *informal* to not have much of something *I can't stop, I'm a bit pushed for time.*

pusher /'pʊʃəʳ/ *noun* [C] someone who sells illegal drugs

push-up /'pʊʃʌp/ *US* (*UK* **press-up**) *noun* [C] a physical exercise in which you lie facing the floor and use your hands to push your body up *I did forty push-ups yesterday.*

pushy /'pʊʃi/ *adj* behaving in an unpleasant way by trying too much to get something or to make someone do something *a pushy salesman*

o─put /pʊt/ *verb* [T] **putting**, *past* put **1 put sth down/in/on**, etc to move something to a place or position *Where have you put the keys?* ● *She*

put her bag on the floor. ● *You can put your coat in the car.* ● *He put his arm around her.* **2 put sb in a mood/position, etc** to cause someone or something to be in a particular situation *They'd had an argument and it had put her in a bad mood.* ● *This puts me in a very difficult position.* **3** to say something using particular words *I don't know quite how to put this, but I'm leaving.* **4** to write something *Please put your name on the list by Monday evening.*

**put sth across** to explain or express something clearly so that people understand it easily

**put sth aside** to save something so that you can use it later *I've been putting a bit of money aside every month.*

**put sth away** to put something in the place where you usually keep it *She folded the towels and put them away in the cupboard.* ➔ *See colour picture* **Phrasal Verbs** *on page Centre 13.*

**put sth back** to put something where it was before it was moved *I put the book back on the shelf.*

**put sth down 1** STOP HOLDING to put something that you are holding onto the floor or onto another surface *I'll just put my bag down for a minute, it's rather heavy.* ➔ *See colour picture* **Phrasal Verbs** *on page Centre 13.* **2** TELEPHONE *UK If you put the phone down, you put the part of the telephone that you speak into back to its usual position.* **3** ANIMAL to kill an animal, usually because it is suffering

**put sb down 1** to make someone feel stupid or unimportant by criticizing them *I'm tired of him putting me down all the time.* **2** to write someone's name on a list or document, usually in order to arrange for them to do something *I've put you down for the trip to Rome next week.*

**put sth down to sth** *UK* to think that a problem or situation is caused by a particular thing

**put sth forward** to state an idea or opinion, or to suggest a plan, so that it can be considered or discussed

**put sb/sth in sth** to arrange for someone or something to go somewhere *to put someone in prison* ● *to put some money in the bank* ● *I'd never put my mother in an old people's home.*

**put sth in** to fix something into a room or building *I've just had a new kitchen put in.*

**put sth into sth/doing sth** If you put time, work, or effort into something, you spend a lot of time or effort doing it. *We've put a lot of effort into this project and we want it to succeed.*

**put sth off** to decide or arrange to do something at a later time *I must talk to her about this, I can't put it off any longer.*

**put sb off (sth)** to make someone not like someone or something, or not want to do something *Jan was talking about her operation and it put me off my food.*

**put sth on 1** CLOTHES to put clothes or shoes onto your body *You'd better put your coat on, it's cold outside.* ➔ *See colour picture* **Phrasal Verbs** *on page Centre 13.* **2** EQUIPMENT *mainly UK* to make a piece of equipment work by pressing a switch *Can you put the light on please?* **3** BEHAVIOUR to pretend to have a particular feeling, or to behave in a way which is not real or natural for you *He's not really upset, he's just*

**P**

*putting it on.* **4** MUSIC/FILM to put a CD or other
recording into a machine so that you can see or
hear it *Why don't you put on some music?* **5 put
on weight** *UK* to become fatter and heavier

**put sth out 1** STOP SHINING *mainly UK* to make
a light stop shining by pressing a switch *Please
put the lights out when you leave.* **2** STOP
BURNING to make something that is burning
stop burning *to put out a fire* **3** PUT OUTSIDE to
put something outside the house *to put out the
rubbish/trash*

**put sb out** to cause trouble or extra work for
someone *It would be great if you could help, but
I don't want to put you out.*

**be put out** to be annoyed, often because of
something that someone has done or said to
you *He seemed a bit **put out at** not having been
invited.*

**put sb through sth** to make someone experience or do something unpleasant or difficult
*Why did they put themselves through this
ordeal?*

**put sb through** to connect someone using a telephone to the person they want to speak to *Can
you put me through to customer services, please?*

**put sth to sb 1** to suggest an idea or plan to
someone so that they can consider it or discuss
it **2** to ask someone a question *to put a question
to someone*

**put sth together 1** to put the parts of something in the correct place and join them to each
other *You buy it in a kit and then put it together
yourself.* **2** to prepare a piece of work by collecting several ideas and suggestions and organizing them *to put together a plan/proposal*

**put sth up 1** BUILD to build something *to put up
a tent* ● *We spent the weekend putting up a fence
in the backyard.* **2** FASTEN to fasten something
to a wall or ceiling *to put up shelves* ● *I need to
put up some curtains in the back bedroom.*
**3** INCREASE *mainly UK* to increase the price or
value of something *They're going to put up the
price of fuel.*

**put sb up** to let someone stay in your home for a
short period *If you need somewhere to stay, we
can put you up for the night.*

**put up with sb/sth** to accept unpleasant behav-

iour or an unpleasant situation, although you
do not like it *He's so rude, I don't know how you
put up with him.*

**putrid** /'pjuːtrɪd/ *adj* decaying and smelling bad
*a putrid smell*

**putt** /pʌt/ *verb* [I, T] in golf, to hit the ball gently
when you are near the hole ● **putt** *noun* [C]

**putty** /'pʌti/ *noun* [U] a soft, grey substance that
becomes hard when it is dry and is used to
fasten glass into windows or to fill small holes
in wood

**puzzle¹** /'pʌzl/ *noun* [C] **1** a game or activity in
which you have to put pieces together or
answer questions using skill *to do/solve a
puzzle* ● *a crossword puzzle* ● *a jigsaw puzzle*
**2** a situation which is very difficult to understand *Scientists have been trying to **solve** this
**puzzle** for years.*

**puzzle²** /'pʌzl/ *verb* [T] to make someone confused because they do not understand something [often passive] *I was puzzled by what he
said.*

**puzzle over sth** to try to solve a problem or
understand a situation by thinking carefully
about it

**puzzled** /'pʌzld/ *adj* confused because you do
not understand something *He had a puzzled
look on his face.*

**puzzling** /'pʌzlɪŋ/ *adj* If something is puzzling,
it confuses you because you do not understand
it.

**PVC** /ˌpiːviːˈsiː/ *noun* [U] a strong material
similar to thick plastic

**pyjamas** *UK* (*US* **pajamas**) /pɪ'dʒɑːməz/ *noun*
[plural] shirt and trousers that you wear in bed *a
pair of blue pyjamas*

**pylon** /'paɪlɒn/ *noun* [C] a tall structure which
supports electrical wires above the ground

**pyramid** /'pɪrəmɪd/ *noun* [C] a shape with a
square base and four triangular sides that
meet to form a point at the top ➝ *See picture at*
**shape**.

**pyre** /paɪəʳ/ *noun* [C] a pile of wood on which a
dead person is burned in some countries

**python** /'paɪθ°n/ *noun* [C] a large snake that kills
other animals by putting itself tightly around
them

**P**

**Q, q** /kjuː/ the seventeenth letter of the alphabet

**QC** /ˌkjuːˈsiː/ noun [C] abbreviation for Queen's Counsel: a lawyer of high rank in the UK Adam Lewis is a QC specializing in child law. • Horace Rumpole QC

**qt** written abbreviation for quart (= a unit for measuring liquid)

**quack** /kwæk/ noun [C] the sound made by a duck (= water bird) • quack verb [I]

**quadruple** /ˈkwɒdrʊpl/ verb [I, T] If an amount quadruples, it becomes multiplied by four, or if you quadruple it, you multiply it by four. The number of visitors to the town has quadrupled in the last two years.

**quagmire** /ˈkwɒɡmaɪəʳ/ noun [C] **1** a difficult and unpleasant situation a legal quagmire **2** an area of wet ground that you can sink into

**quail** /kweɪl/ noun [C] plural quail or quails a small bird which is shot for food

**quaint** /kweɪnt/ adj attractive or unusual in an old-fashioned way a quaint little village

**quake**[1] /kweɪk/ noun [C] US short for earthquake (= when the Earth shakes)

**quake**[2] /kweɪk/ verb [I] to shake because you are frightened

o⤴**qualification** /ˌkwɒlɪfɪˈkeɪʃᵊn/ noun **1** EXAMS [C] mainly UK what you get when you pass an exam or a course [usually plural] legal/medical qualifications • I want to go to college and get some qualifications so that I can get a good job. • What qualifications do you need to be a nanny? **2** SKILLS [C] the skills, qualities, or experience that you need in order to do something The only qualification needed for this job is an eye for detail. **3** COMPETITION [U] success in getting into a competition England's qualification for the World Cup **4** ADDITION [C, U] an addition to something that is said that makes its meaning less certain

**qualified** /ˈkwɒlɪfaɪd/ adj **1** having passed exams or courses a newly qualified teacher • a highly qualified accountant **2 qualified to do sth** having the skills, qualities, or experience that you need in order to do something I think John is the best qualified to make that decision. **3** If something someone says is qualified, they have added something to it to make it less certain. The answer was a qualified yes. ⊃ Opposite **unqualified**.

**qualifier** /ˈkwɒlɪfaɪəʳ/ noun [C] **1** a game or competition which decides whether you can enter another competition **2** someone who has succeeded in getting into a competition

**qualify** /ˈkwɒlɪfaɪ/ verb **1** BE ALLOWED [I, T] If you qualify for something, you are allowed to do it or have it, and if something qualifies you for something, it allows you to do it or have it. Foreign students no longer qualify for grants in the UK. • To qualify for the competition, you must be over 18. • His disability qualifies him for extra benefits. ⊃ Opposite **disqualify**.

**2** PASS EXAMS [I] mainly UK to pass exams so that you are able to do a job He's recently qualified as a doctor. **3** GET INTO COMPETITION [I] to succeed in getting into a competition Nigeria were the first team to qualify for the World Cup. **4** ADD [T] to add something to what you say to make its meaning less certain

**qualitative** /ˈkwɒlɪtətɪv/ ⓤⓢ /ˈkwɑːlɪteɪtɪv/ adj formal relating to how good something is and not how much of it there is • qualitatively adv

o⤴**quality**[1] /ˈkwɒləti/ noun **1** GOOD OR BAD [U] how good or bad something is good/high quality • poor/low quality • The air quality in this area is terrible. • All we are asking for is a decent **quality of life**. • The spokeswoman says a **quality control** system is being developed for next year. **2** GOOD [U] when something is very good or well made A designer label isn't necessarily a guarantee of quality. **3** CHARACTER [C] part of the character or personality of someone or something leadership qualities • Joe has a lot of good qualities, but I don't think he has the ability to discipline the team.

**quality**[2] /ˈkwɒləti/ adj [always before noun] very good We only sell quality products in this store. • She wants to spend more **quality time** (= time spent well) with her children.

**qualm** /kwɑːm/ noun [C] a worry or doubt about something She **has no qualms about** taking her clothes off in public.

**quandary** /ˈkwɒndᵊri/ noun [no plural] a situation in which you are trying to make a difficult choice We're **in a quandary over** which school to send her to.

**quantifier** /ˈkwɒntɪfaɪəʳ/ noun [C] a word or group of words that is used before a noun to show an amount of that noun. For example the words 'many', 'some', and 'a lot of' are quantifiers.

**quantify** /ˈkwɒntɪfaɪ/ verb [T] to measure or state the amount of something It is difficult to quantify the damage that this storm has caused.

**quantitative** /ˈkwɒntɪtətɪv/ ⓤⓢ /ˈkwɑːntəteɪtɪv/ adj relating to quantity

o⤴**quantity** /ˈkwɒntəti/ noun **1** [C, U] the amount or number of something Food has improved in quality and quantity thanks to modern farming methods. • A vast quantity of information is available on the Internet. • They are now developing ways to produce the vaccine **in large quantities** and cheaply. **2 an unknown quantity** someone or something that you do not know and so you cannot be certain about

**quantum leap** /ˌkwɒntʌmˈliːp/ noun [C] a sudden, large increase or improvement in something [usually singular] a quantum leap in information technology

**quarantine** /ˈkwɒrᵊntiːn/ noun [U] If an animal or person is put into quarantine, they are kept away from other animals or people because they have or might have a disease.

**quarrel**[1] /ˈkwɒrᵊl/ noun **1** [C] an argument She walked out after **having a quarrel with** her boss. **2 have no quarrel with sb/sth** to not disagree with someone or something We have no quarrel with either of those ideas.

**quarrel**[2] /ˈkwɒrᵊl/ verb [I] (UK) **quarrelling**, past **quarrelled**, (US) **quarreling**, past **quarreled** to have an argument with someone *She'd been **quarrelling with** her mother all morning.*

**quarry** /'kwɒri/ *noun* [C] a place where stone is dug out of a large hole in the ground *a marble quarry* • quarry *verb* [T] to dig stone out of a quarry

**quart** /kwɔːt/ (*written abbreviation* **qt**) *noun* [C] a unit for measuring liquid, equal to 1.14 litres in the UK and 0.95 litres in the US

o→**quarter** /'kwɔːtəʳ/ *noun* **1** EQUAL PART [C] (*also US* **fourth**) one of four equal parts of something; 1/4 *Three quarters of the island's residents speak English.* • *My house is one and three-quarter miles/a mile and three-quarters from here.* • *I waited a quarter of an hour for her.* **2** BEFORE/AFTER HOUR [no plural] a period of 15 minutes before or after the hour *It's (a)* ***quarter to three*** (= 2.45). • (*also US*) *It's* ***a quarter of three*** (= 2.45). • *We're leaving at (a)* ***quarter past six*** (= 6.15). • (*also US*) *We're leaving at (a)* ***quarter after six*** (= 6.15). **3** BUSINESS [C] one of four periods of time into which a year is divided for financial calculations such as profits or bills (= orders for payment) *I get an electricity bill every quarter.* **4** SCHOOL [C] *US* one of four periods of time into which a year at college or university is divided **5** SPORT [C] *US* one of four periods of time into which some sports games are divided **6** PART OF TOWN [C] a part of a town, often where people from a particular country or religion live *the Jewish quarter* **7** COIN [C] a US or Canadian coin with a value of 25 cents, which is a quarter of a dollar

quarter

**quarterback** /'kwɔːtəbæk/ *noun* [C] a player in American football who controls the attack

**quarter-final** /ˌkwɔːtəˈfaɪnᵊl/ *noun* [C] the part of a competition when eight people or teams are left and there are four games to decide who will reach the semi-final (= when only four people or teams are left) *She was knocked out of the competition* ***in the quarter-finals.***

**quarterly** /'kwɔːtəli/ *adj, adv* produced or happening every three months *Water and electricity bills are paid quarterly.* • *a quarterly magazine/report*

**quarters** /'kwɔːtəz/ *noun* [plural] rooms to live in or sleep in, usually for people in a military organization

**quartet** /kwɔːˈtet/ *noun* [C] four people singing or playing music in a group

**quartz** /'kwɔːts/ *noun* [U] a mineral used to make watches and clocks accurate

**quash** /kwɒʃ/ *verb* [T] **1** *formal* to officially change a legal decision so that it stops existing *His conviction was quashed last month.* **2** to stop something that you do not want to happen *He appeared on television to quash rumours that he was seriously ill.*

**quay** /kiː/ *noun* [C] a structure built next to water where ships stop and goods are taken on and off

**queasy** /'kwiːzi/ *adj* If you feel queasy, you feel slightly ill as if you might vomit.

**queen** /kwiːn/ *noun* [C] **1** FEMALE RULER a female ruler in some countries *Queen Elizabeth II* • *God save the Queen!* **2** KING'S WIFE the wife of a king when he is the main ruler in a country **3** PLAYING CARD a playing card with a picture of a queen on it *the Queen of diamonds* **4** INSECT a large female insect which is the most important in a group and which produces all the eggs *queen bee*

**queer** /kwɪəʳ/ *adj* **1** *informal* homosexual **2** strange

**quell** /kwel/ *verb* [T] *formal* to stop something that you do not want to happen *to quell a riot* • *to quell rumours*

**quench** /kwenʃ/ *verb* **quench your thirst** to drink liquid so that you stop being thirsty

**query**[1] /'kwɪəri/ *noun* [C] a question *His job is to answer telephone* ***queries about*** *airline schedules.*

**query**[2] /'kwɪəri/ *verb* [T] to ask questions in order to check that something is true or correct [+ question word] *A few students have queried whether exam marks were added up correctly.*

**quest** /kwest/ *noun* [C] *formal* an attempt to get something or do something difficult *the* ***quest for truth*** • [+ to do sth] *He has begun his quest to become the Conservative Party's first Asian MP.*

o→**question**[1] /'kwestʃən/ *noun* **1** SENTENCE [C] a sentence or phrase that asks you for information *Is it OK if I* ***ask*** *you a few* ***questions?*** • *He refused to* ***answer*** *my* ***question.*** • *If you have any* ***questions about*** *the scheme, do ask me.* • *"So where's the money coming from?" "That's* ***a good question"*** (= I do not know). **2** SITUATION [C] a situation or problem that needs to be considered *This documentary* ***raises*** *important* ***questions*** *about the American legal system.* • *Two important* ***questions arise*** *from this debate.* **3** DOUBT [U] doubt [+ that] *There is* ***no question*** *that this was an accidental fire.* • *His ability as a chef has never been* ***in question.*** • *"So you agree she's the right person for the job." "Yes, absolutely,* ***without question."*** • *The report* ***brings/calls into question*** (= causes doubts about) *the safety of this drug.* **4** **sb/sth in question** the person or thing that is being discussed *He claims that he was in the pub with his girlfriend on the night in question.* **5** **be out of the question** If something is out of the question, it is not possible or not allowed. ⊃ *See also:* **loaded question, rhetorical question.**

---

**USAGE**

**ask a question**

Remember to use the verb **ask** with **question**.

*We weren't allowed to ask any questions.*

~~We weren't allowed to make any questions.~~

---

**question**[2] /'kwestʃən/ *verb* [T] **1** to ask someone questions *Detectives were* ***questioning*** *a boy* ***about*** *the murder.* • [often passive] *Two out of three people questioned in the survey were non-smokers.* **2** to show or feel doubt about some-

**Q**

thing *I'm not for a moment questioning your decision.* • [+ question word] *I'm just questioning whether we need the extra staff.*

**questionable** /'kwestʃənəbl/ *adj* **1** not certainly true or correct [+ question word] *It is highly questionable whether this drug has any benefits at all.* **2** not honest or not legal *He's being investigated for questionable business practices.*

**questioning** /'kwestʃənɪŋ/ *noun* [U] when the police ask someone questions about a crime *She was taken in for questioning by police yesterday morning.*

**'question ,mark** *noun* [C] a mark (?) used at the end of a question ➔ *See study section* **Punctuation** *on page Centre 37.*

**questionnaire** /ˌkwestʃə'neəʳ/ *noun* [C] a set of questions asked of a large number of people to discover information about a subject *Residents have been sent questionnaires about their homes and energy use.*

**'question ,tag** *noun* [C] a short phrase such as 'isn't it' or 'don't you' that is added to the end of a sentence to check information or to ask if someone agrees with you. In the sentence, 'It's hot, isn't it?', 'isn't it' is a question tag.

**queue** /kjuː/ *UK* (*US* **line**) *noun* [C] **1** a row of people waiting for something, one behind the other *to join the queue* • *Are you in the queue?* **2 jump the queue** to move in front of people who have been waiting longer for something than you • **queue (up)** *UK* (*US* **line up**) *verb* [I] to stand in a row in order to wait for something [+ to do sth] *They're queueing up to get tickets.*

**quibble** /'kwɪbl/ *verb* **quibble about/over/with sth** to argue about something that is not important *They spend far too much time quibbling over detail.* • **quibble** *noun* [C]

**quiche** /kiːʃ/ *noun* [C, U] a dish made of a pastry base filled with a mixture of egg and milk and usually cheese, vegetables, or meat

○⊸**quick¹** /kwɪk/ *adj* **1** doing something fast or taking only a short time *I tried to catch him but he was too quick for me.* • [+ to do sth] *Publishers were quick to realize that a profit could be made.* **2** lasting a short time *Can I ask you a quick question?*

**quick²** /kwɪk/ *adv informal* fast *Come here, quick!*

**quicken** /'kwɪkən/ *verb* [I, T] to become faster or to cause something to become faster *His breathing quickened.*

○⊸**quickly** /'kwɪkli/ *adv* fast or in a short time *I quickly shut the door.* • *These people need to be treated as quickly as possible.*

**quid** /kwɪd/ *noun* [C] *plural* **quid** *UK informal* a pound (= UK unit of money) *This bike's not bad for twenty quid.*

○⊸**quiet¹** /kwaɪət/ *adj* **1** NOT NOISY making little or no noise *Can you be quiet, please? We're trying to work.* • *The children are very quiet. I wonder what they're doing.* **2** NOT BUSY without much noise or activity *I fancy a quiet night in tonight.* • *They found a table in a quiet corner of the restaurant.* **3** NOT TALKING MUCH If someone is quiet, they do not talk very much. *He was a shy, quiet man.* **4 keep (sth) quiet** to

not talk about something that is secret *It might be wise to keep this quiet for a while.*

USAGE

**quiet** or **quite**?

Be careful, these two words look very similar, but they are spelled differently and have completely different meanings.

Quiet means making little or no noise.

*The house was very quiet without the children around.*

Quite means a little or a lot but not completely.

*It's quite cold today.*

**quiet²** /kwaɪət/ *noun* [U] when there is little or no noise *She needs a bit of peace and quiet.*

**quieten** /'kwaɪətən/ *UK* (*US* **quiet**) *verb* [T] to make someone or something quiet **quieten (sb/sth) down** *UK* (*US* **quiet (sb/sth) down**) to become quieter or calmer, or to make a person or animal become quieter or calmer

**quietly** /'kwaɪətli/ *adv* **1** making little or no noise *"Don't worry," she said quietly.* **2** doing something without much noise or activity *He sat quietly on the sofa, waiting for her to come home.*

**quilt** /kwɪlt/ *noun* [C] a cover for a bed which is filled with feathers or other warm material

**quip** /kwɪp/ *verb* [I, T] **quipping**, *past* **quipped** to say something in a funny and clever way • **quip** *noun* [C]

**quirk** /kwɜːk/ *noun* **1** [C] a strange habit *My aunt has a few odd quirks.* **2 quirk of fate** a strange and unexpected event *By some quirk of fate, we came to live in the same town.* • **quirky** *adj* strange *a quirky sense of humour*

**quit** /kwɪt/ *verb* **quitting**, *past* **quit 1** [I, T] to leave your job or school permanently *She recently quit her job to spend more time with her family.* **2** [T] to stop doing something *I quit smoking and put on weight.*

○⊸**quite¹** /kwaɪt/ *adv* **1** *UK* a little or a lot but not completely *I'm quite tired, but I'm happy to walk a little further.* • *He's quite attractive but not what I'd call gorgeous.* **2** completely *The two situations are quite different.* • *Are you quite sure you want to go?* **3 not quite** almost but not completely *I'm not quite sure that I understand this.* • *He didn't get quite enough votes to win.* **4 quite a bit/a few/a lot, etc** a large amount or number *There are quite a few letters for you here.* • *He's changed quite a bit.*

**quiver** /'kwɪvəʳ/ *verb* [I] to shake slightly *Her lower lip was quivering.* • **quiver** *noun* [C]

**quiz¹** /kwɪz/ *noun* [C] *plural* **quizzes 1** a game in which you answer questions *a television quiz show* **2** *US* a short test on a subject in school

**quiz²** /kwɪz/ *verb* [T] **quizzing**, *past* **quizzed** to ask someone questions about something *A group of journalists quizzed them about/on the day's events.*

**quizzical** /'kwɪzɪkəl/ *adj* A quizzical expression or look seems to ask a question without words. *She gave me a quizzical look.*

**quota** /'kwəʊtə/ *noun* [C] a limited amount of something that is officially allowed *an import quota*

Q

**quotation** /kwəʊˈteɪʃᵊn/ *noun* [C] **1** a sentence or phrase that is taken out of a book, poem, or play *a quotation from Shakespeare/the Bible* **2** the amount that a piece of work will probably cost *Make sure you get a quotation for all the work before they start.*

**quot'ation ˌmarks** *noun* [plural] a pair of marks (" ") or (' ') used before and after a group of words to show that they are spoken or that someone else originally wrote them

**quote¹** /kwəʊt/ *verb* **1** REPEAT [I, T] to repeat what someone has said or written *I was quoting from Marx.* • *Witnesses were quoted as saying there were two gunmen.* **2** GIVE EXAMPLE [T] to give a fact or example in order to support what you are saying *The minister quoted recent unemployment figures.* **3** COST [T] to say how much a piece of work will cost before you do it

**quote²** /kwəʊt/ *noun* [C] *short for* quotation

**quotes** /kwəʊts/ *noun* [plural] *short for* quotation marks

**the Qur'an** /kɒrˈɑːn/ *noun another spelling of* the Koran (= the holy book of Islam)

**R, r** /ɑːʳ/ the eighteenth letter of the alphabet

**rabbi** /'ræbaɪ/ *noun* [C] a leader and teacher in the Jewish religion *Rabbi Hugo Gryn*

**rabbit** /'ræbɪt/ *noun* [C] a small animal with fur and long ears that lives in a hole in the ground

**rabble** /'ræbl/ *noun* [no plural] a group of noisy, uncontrolled people

**rabies** /'reɪbiːz/ *noun* [U] a serious disease that people can get if they are bitten by an infected animal

o⸺**race¹** /reɪs/ *noun* 1 COMPETITION [C] a competition in which people run, ride, drive, etc against each other in order to see who is the fastest *a horse race* 2 PEOPLE [C, U] one of the groups that people are divided into according to their physical characteristics *people of many different races* 3 FOR POWER [C] a situation in which people compete against each other for power or control *the race for governor* 4 **the races** an event when horses race against each other 5 **a race against time/the clock** a situation in which something has to be done very quickly *It's a race against time to get the building finished before the rainy season sets in.* ➜ *See also:* **the human race, the rat race.**

---

**USAGE**

**race** or **species**?

Race is used to talk about one of the groups that people are divided into according to their physical characteristics.

*the human race*

*People of all races and religions live in America.*

Species is used to talk about types of animals and plants.

*eagles, vultures, and other species of bird*

---

**race²** /reɪs/ *verb* 1 [I, T] to compete in a race *I'll race you to the end of the road.* • *I used to* **race against** him at school. 2 **race along/down/over, etc** to move somewhere very quickly *I raced over to see what was the matter.* 3 **race sb to/back, etc** to take someone somewhere very quickly *Ambulances raced the injured to a nearby hospital.* 4 [T] to put a horse, dog, etc in a race

**racecourse** /'reɪskɔːs/ *noun* [C] *UK* the place where horses, cars, etc race

**racehorse** /'reɪshɔːs/ *noun* [C] a horse that has been trained to run in races

**race re'lations** *noun* [plural] the relationship between people from different races who live together in the same place

**racetrack** /'reɪstræk/ *noun* [C] the place where horses, cars, etc race

**racial** /'reɪʃəl/ *adj* relating to people's race *a racial minority* • *racial discrimination/tension* • **racially** *adv a racially motivated crime*

**racing** /'reɪsɪŋ/ *noun* [U] the activity or sport in which people, animals, or vehicles race against each other *motor racing* ➜ *See also:* **horse racing.**

**racism** /'reɪsɪzᵊm/ *noun* [U] the belief that other races of people are not as good as your own, or the unfair treatment of people because they belong to a particular race

**racist** /'reɪsɪst/ *noun* [C] someone who believes that other races of people are not as good as their own *Four of the named killers are known to be racists.* • **racist** *adj a racist attack/comment*

**rack¹** /ræk/ *noun* [C] a type of shelf that you can put things on or hang things from *a magazine/luggage/vegetable rack*

**rack²** /ræk/ *verb* 1 **be racked with pain/guilt, etc** If someone is racked with pain or an emotion, they suffer a lot because of it. 2 **rack your brain/brains** *informal* to think very hard, usually to try to remember something or solve a problem

**rack up sth** *informal* to get or achieve a lot of something *He's racked up debts of over thirty thousand pounds.*

**racket** /'rækɪt/ *noun* 1 SPORT [C] (*also* **racquet**) a piece of equipment that you use to hit a ball in sports such as tennis ➜ *See colour picture* **Sports 2** *on page Centre 16.* 2 ILLEGAL [C] *informal* an illegal activity that is used to make money *a drugs smuggling racket* 3 NOISE [no plural] *informal* a loud noise *The neighbours were making such a racket.*

**radar** /'reɪdɑːʳ/ *noun* [U] a system that uses radio waves to find out the position of something you cannot see

**radiant** /'reɪdiənt/ *adj* 1 showing that you are very happy *a radiant smile* 2 very bright • **radiance** /'reɪdiəns/ *noun* [U]

**radiate** /'reɪdieɪt/ *verb* 1 **radiate from/out, etc** to spread out in all directions from a particular point *A number of roads radiate out from the centre.* 2 [T] to show an emotion or quality in your face or behaviour *His face just radiates happiness.* 3 [T] to send out heat or light

**radiation** /ˌreɪdi'eɪʃᵊn/ *noun* [U] 1 a form of energy that comes from a nuclear reaction and that in large amounts can be very dangerous *dangerously high levels of radiation* • *radiation sickness* 2 energy from heat or light that you cannot see *solar/microwave radiation*

**radiator** /'reɪdieɪtəʳ/ *noun* [C] 1 a metal piece of equipment that is filled with hot water and is used to heat a room ➜ *See colour picture* **The Living Room** *on page Centre 11.* 2 a part of a vehicle engine that is used to make the engine cool

**radical¹** /'rædɪkᵊl/ *adj* 1 A radical change is very big and important. *a radical reform* 2 believing that there should be big social and political changes *a radical group/movement* • *radical politics* • **radically** *adv The company has changed radically in recent years.*

**radical²** /'rædɪkᵊl/ *noun* [C] someone who supports the idea that there should be big social and political changes

o⸺**radio¹** /'reɪdiəʊ/ *noun* 1 BROADCASTS [C] a piece of equipment used for listening to radio broadcasts *a car radio* 2 **the radio** the programmes that you hear when you listen to the radio *We heard him speaking on the radio this morning.* • *I listen to the radio in the evening.* **3** SYSTEM [U] a system of sending and receiving sound through the air *local radio* • *a radio station* **4** MESSAGES [C] a piece of equipment for sending and receiving messages by sound

**radio²** /'reɪdiəʊ/ *verb* [I, T] **radioing**, *past* **radioed** to send a message to someone by radio *They radioed for help.*

**radioactive** /ˌreɪdiəʊ'æktɪv/ *adj* containing harmful radiation (= energy from a nuclear reaction) *radioactive waste*

**radioactivity** /ˌreɪdiəʊæk'tɪvəti/ *noun* [U] when something is radioactive *The site was found to be contaminated by radioactivity.*

**radish** /'rædɪʃ/ *noun* [C] a small, round, white or red vegetable with a slightly hot taste that you eat in salad

**radius** /'reɪdiəs/ *noun* [C] *plural* **radii** **1** a certain distance from a particular point in any direction *Most facilities lie within a two-mile radius of the house.* **2** the distance from the centre of a circle to its edge

radius

**raffle** /'ræfl/ *noun* [C] a competition in which people buy tickets with numbers on them and win a prize if any of their numbers are chosen *raffle tickets* • **raffle** *verb* [T] to offer something as a prize in a raffle

**raft** /rɑːft/ *noun* **1** [C] a small, flat boat made by tying pieces of wood together **2 a raft of sth/sb** a lot of things or people *a raft of data*

**rafter** /'rɑːftəʳ/ *noun* [C] one of the long pieces of wood that supports a roof

**rag** /ræg/ *noun* [C] **1** a piece of old cloth that you use to clean things **2 be like a red rag to a bull** *UK* If a particular subject is like a red rag to a bull, it always makes someone angry.

**rage¹** /reɪdʒ/ *noun* **1** [C, U] strong anger that you cannot control *a jealous rage* • *He flew into a rage* (= suddenly became angry) *over the smallest mistake.* **2 be all the rage** *informal* to be very popular ➔ *See also:* **road rage**.

**rage²** /reɪdʒ/ *verb* [I] **1** to continue with great force or violence *The battle raged well into the night.* **2** to speak or behave in a very angry way

**ragged** /'rægɪd/ *adj* **1** CLOTHES old and torn *ragged jeans* **2** PERSON wearing clothes that are old and torn *a ragged child* **3** ROUGH rough and not smooth *a ragged edge*

ragged

**rags** /rægz/ *noun* [plural] **1** clothes that are old and torn *an old man dressed in rags* **2 go from rags to riches** to start your life very poor and then later in life become very rich

**raid¹** /reɪd/ *noun* [C] **1** SOLDIERS a sudden attack on a place by soldiers *an air raid* • *a dawn raid* **2** POLICE a sudden visit to a place by police in order to find someone or something *a police raid to recover illegal weapons* **3** STEAL when people enter a place by force in order to steal from it *a bank raid* ➔ *See also:* **air raid**.

**raid²** /reɪd/ *verb* [T] **1** SOLDIERS If soldiers raid a place, they suddenly attack it. **2** POLICE If the police raid a place, they suddenly visit it in order to find someone or something. *Police raided nine properties in search of the documents.* **3** STEAL to steal many things from somewhere *to raid the fridge*

**rail** /reɪl/ *noun* **1** FOR HANGING [C] *UK* a horizontal bar on the wall that you hang things on *a curtain rail* **2** FOR SUPPORTING [C] a bar around or along something which you can hold to stop you from falling *a hand rail* **3** TRAIN SYSTEM [U] trains as a method of transport *rail travel* • *a rail link* • *They sent the shipment by rail.* **4** TRAIN [C] the metal tracks that trains run on ➔ *See also:* **towel rail**.

rail

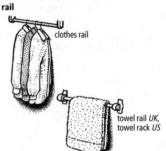

clothes rail

towel rail *UK*,
towel rack *US*

**railing** /'reɪlɪŋ/ *noun* [C] a fence made from posts and bars *an iron railing*

**'railroad ˌtie** *US* (*UK* **sleeper**) *noun* [C] a piece of wood that is used to support a railway track

**railway** /'reɪlweɪ/ *noun* **1** [C] (*also US* **railroad** /'reɪlrəʊd/) the metal tracks that trains travel on *Repairs are being carried out on the railway.* **2 the railway(s)** (*also US* **the railroad(s)**) the organizations connected with trains *He worked on the railways all his life.*

○━**rain¹** /reɪn/ *noun* **1** [U] water that falls from the sky in small drops *heavy rain* • *It looks like rain* (= as if it will rain). **2 the rains** in tropical countries, the time of year when there is a lot of rain *They were waiting for the rains to come.* ➔ *See also:* **acid rain**.

○━**rain²** /reɪn/ *verb* **it rains** If it rains, water falls from the sky in small drops. *It was raining all weekend.* • *If it rains, we'll have to come inside.* **be rained off** *UK* (*US* **be rained out**) If a sport or outside activity is rained off, it cannot start or continue because it is raining. *Most of today's matches were rained off.*

**rainbow** /'reɪnbəʊ/ *noun* [C] a half circle with

seven colours that sometimes appears in the sky when the sun shines through rain

**'rain ,check** noun [C] **1** US a piece of paper which allows you to buy something at a low price although that thing is now being sold at a higher price **2** US a ticket that allows you to see an event at a later time if bad weather stops that event from happening **3 take a rain check on sth** something you say when you cannot accept someone's invitation, but would like to do it at a later time *I'm busy now, but can I take a rain check on that cup of coffee?*

**raincoat** /'reɪnkəʊt/ noun [C] a coat that you wear when it is raining

**raindrop** /'reɪndrɒp/ noun [C] a single drop of rain

**rainfall** /'reɪnfɔːl/ noun [U] the amount of rain that falls in a particular place at a particular time *monthly rainfall* • *heavy rainfall*

**rainforest** /'reɪnˌfɒrɪst/ noun [C] a forest with a lot of tall trees where it rains a lot *a tropical rainforest*

**rainy** /'reɪni/ adj raining a lot *a rainy afternoon*

o→ **raise**[1] /reɪz/ verb [T] **1** LIFT to lift something to a higher position *to raise your hand* **2** INCREASE to increase an amount or level *to raise prices/taxes* **3** IMPROVE to improve something *to raise standards* **4** MONEY to collect money from other people *They're raising money for charity.* **5 raise your voice** to speak loudly and angrily to someone **6 raise hopes/fears/doubts, etc** to cause emotions or thoughts *Her answers raised doubts in my mind.* **7 raise a question/subject, etc** to start talking about a subject that you want other people to consider **8** CHILD to look after and educate a child until they have become an adult *Their ideas on how to raise children didn't always agree.* **9** ANIMALS/CROPS to make an animal or crop grow *to raise chickens/sheep* ⊃ *See also:* raise the **alarm**[1]. ⊃ *See usage note at* **rise.**

**raise**[2] /reɪz/ US (UK **rise**) noun [C] an increase in the amount of money that you earn *We usually get a raise at the start of a year.*

**raisin** /'reɪzᵊn/ noun [C] a dried grape (= small round fruit)

**rake**[1] /reɪk/ noun [C] a garden tool with a long handle that is used for moving dead leaves, grass, etc

**rake**[2] /reɪk/ verb [I, T] to use a rake to move dead leaves, grass, etc
**rake sth in** informal to earn a large amount of money. *He's raking it in.*

**rally**[1] /'ræli/ noun [C] **1** a large public meeting in support of something *an election/campaign rally* **2** a car or motorcycle race *a rally driver*

**rally**[2] /'ræli/ verb **1** [I, T] to come together or bring people together to support something *Her fans rallied behind her from the start.* **2** [I] to get stronger or better after being weak *The stock market rallied late in the day.*
**rally around/round (sb)** to help or give support to someone *If one of the family has a crisis we rally round them.*

**ram**[1] /ræm/ verb [T] **ramming,** past **rammed** to hit something or push something into something with great force *He had to stop suddenly and a car rammed into him.*

**ram**[2] /ræm/ noun [C] a male sheep

**RAM** /ræm/ noun [U] abbreviation for random access memory: a computer's ability to immediately store information

**Ramadan** /'ræmədæn/ noun [U] the Muslim religious period in which Muslims do not eat or drink during the part of the day when it is light

**ramble**[1] /'ræmbl/ verb **1 ramble along/through, etc** to walk for a long time, especially in the countryside *We rambled through fields and woods.* **2 ramble** (also **ramble on**) to talk for a long time in a boring and often confused way *He rambled on for hours about his time in the army.*

**ramble**[2] /'ræmbl/ noun [C] a long walk in the countryside

**rambler** /'ræmbləʳ/ noun [C] someone who walks in the countryside

**rambling** /'ræmblɪŋ/ adj **1** A rambling speech, letter, etc is very long and confused. **2** A rambling building is big and without a regular shape.

**ramifications** /,ræmɪfɪ'keɪʃᵊnz/ noun [plural] the possible results of an action

**ramp** /ræmp/ noun [C] **1** a sloping surface that joins two places that are at different heights *a wheelchair ramp* **2** US (UK **slip road**) a short road that is used to drive onto or off a large, fast road

**rampage**[1] /ræm'peɪdʒ/ verb [I] to run around or through an area, making a lot of noise and causing damage *Angry citizens rampaged through the city.*

**rampage**[2] /'ræmpeɪdʒ/ noun [no plural] when a group of people rampage *Rioters went on a rampage through the city.*

**rampant** /'ræmpənt/ adj growing or spreading quickly, in a way that cannot be controlled *rampant corruption/inflation*

**ramshackle** /'ræmˌʃækl/ adj A ramshackle building is in very bad condition.

**ran** /ræn/ past tense of run

**ranch** /rɑːnʃ/ noun [C] a large farm where animals are kept *a cattle/sheep ranch*

**rancher** /'rɑːnʃəʳ/ noun [C] someone who owns or works on a ranch

**rancid** /'rænsɪd/ adj Rancid fat, such as oil or butter, smells and tastes bad because it is not fresh.

**random** /'rændəm/ adj **1** done or chosen without any plan or system *random testing* • *a random selection* **2 at random** chosen by chance *Winners will be chosen at random.* • **randomly** adv

**rang** /ræŋ/ past tense of ring[2]

**range**[1] /reɪndʒ/ noun **1** OF THINGS [C] a group of different things of the same general type *a range of colours/patterns* • *We discussed a wide range of subjects.* **2** AMOUNT [C] the amount or number between a particular set of limits [usually singular] *The price range is from $100 to $200.* • *The product is aimed at young people in the 18–25 age range.* **3** DISTANCE [U] the distance from which things can be seen, heard, or reached *The soldiers came within firing range.* • *He was shot at close range* (= from very near). **4** MOUNTAINS [C] a line of hills or mountains **5** SHOOTING [C] a place where you can practise shooting a gun *a rifle/shooting range*

R

**range²** /reɪndʒ/ *verb* **1 range from sth to sth** to have several different amounts or types *Tickets range from $12 to $35.* • *Choose from 13 colours, ranging from classic white to antique blue.* **2** [I] to deal with a large number of subjects *The discussion ranged over many topics.*

**ranger** /'reɪndʒə'/ *noun* [C] someone whose job is to look after a forest or a park *a forest ranger*

**rank¹** /ræŋk/ *noun* **1** [C, U] a position in society or in an organization, for example the army *He holds the rank of colonel.* **2 the ranks** the ordinary members of an organization, especially the army **3 break ranks** to publicly show that you disagree with a group that you belong to **4 the rank and file** the ordinary members of an organization and not its leaders ⊃ *See also:* **taxi rank**.

**rank²** /ræŋk/ *verb* [I, T] to have a position in a list which shows things or people in order of importance, or to give someone or something a position on such a list *He ranked number one in the world at the start of the competition.* • *The city's canals now rank among the world's dirtiest.*

**ransom** /'ræns³m/ *noun* [C, U] the money that is demanded for the return of someone who is being kept as a prisoner *a ransom note/letter*

**rant** /rænt/ *verb* [I] to talk a lot about something in an excited or angry way *He was ranting and raving about the injustice of the situation.*

**rap¹** /ræp/ *noun* **1** [U] a type of music in which the words are spoken and there is a strong beat *a rap artist* **2** [C] a sudden, short sound made when someone or something hits a hard surface *There was a rap on the window.* **3 a rap on/across/over the knuckles** a punishment that is not severe

**rap²** /ræp/ *verb* **rapping, past rapped 1** [I, T] to hit a hard surface to make a sudden, short noise *He rapped on the door.* **2** [I] to perform rap music

**rape** /reɪp/ *verb* [T] to force someone to have sex when they do not want to • **rape** *noun* [C, U]

**rapid** /'ræpɪd/ *adj* happening or moving very quickly *rapid change/growth* • **rapidity** /rə'pɪdəti/ *noun* [U] • **rapidly** *adv*

**rapids** /'ræpɪdz/ *noun* [plural] a part of a river where the water moves very fast

**rapist** /'reɪpɪst/ *noun* [C] someone who forces another person to have sex when they do not want to

**rapport** /ræp'ɔːʳ/ *noun* [U, no plural] a good understanding of someone and ability to communicate with them *She has a good rapport with her staff.*

**rapture** /'ræptʃə'/ *noun* [U] a feeling of extreme pleasure and excitement

○⁻**rare** /reə'/ *adj* **1** very unusual *a rare disease/species* • [+ to do sth] *It's very rare to see these birds in England.* **2** If meat is rare, it is still red because it has only been cooked for a short time. *a rare steak*

**rarely** /'reəli/ *adv* not often *I rarely see her these days.*

**raring** /'reərɪŋ/ *adj* **be raring to do sth** *informal* to be very enthusiastic about starting something

**rarity** /'reərəti/ *noun* **1 be a rarity** to be unusual *Genuine enthusiasm is a rarity.* **2** [U] the fact that something is not common *Precious stones are valued for their rarity.*

**rascal** /'rɑːskəl/ *noun* **1** [C] *humorous* a person who behaves badly, but who you still like **2** *old-fashioned* a dishonest man

**rash¹** /ræʃ/ *noun* [C] **1** a group of small, red spots on the skin *an itchy rash* • *Certain foods give him a rash.* **2 a rash of sth** a group of unpleasant events of the same type, happening at the same time *There has been a rash of burglaries in the area.*

**rash²** /ræʃ/ *adj* done suddenly and without thinking carefully *a rash decision/promise*

**rasher** /'ræʃə'/ *noun* [C] *UK* a slice of bacon (= meat from a pig)

**raspberry** /'rɑːzbʰri/ *noun* [C] a small, soft, red fruit that grows on bushes

**rat** /ræt/ *noun* [C] **1** an animal that looks like a large mouse and has a long tail *Rats carry disease.* **2** *informal* an unpleasant, dishonest person

○⁻**rate¹** /reɪt/ *noun* [C] **1** HOW MANY how often something happens, or how many people something happens to *the birth rate* • *the rate of unemployment* **2** MONEY a fixed amount of money given for something *the interest/exchange rate* • *rates of pay* **3** SPEED the speed at which something happens *the rate of progress* **4 at this rate** used before saying what will happen if a situation continues in the same way *At this rate we're not going to be there till midnight.* **5 at any rate** used before saying one fact that is certain in a situation that you are generally not certain about *Well, at any rate we need her to be there.* **6 first-/second-/third-rate** very good, bad, or very bad *a first-rate hotel* ⊃ *See also:* **birth rate**, **exchange rate**.

**rate²** /reɪt/ *verb* [T] **1** to judge the quality or ability of someone or something *How do you rate her as a singer?* **2** to deserve something *The incident didn't even rate a mention* (= was not written about) *in the local newspaper.*

○⁻**rather** /'rɑːðə'/ *adv* **1** slightly or to a degree *I rather like it.* • *I find her books rather dull.* **2 rather than** instead of *I thought we could go to the cinema this evening rather than stay at home.* • *He saw his music as a hobby rather than a career.* **3 would rather** If you would rather do something, you would prefer to do that thing. *I'd much rather go out for a meal than stay in and watch TV.* **4** used to change something you have just said and make it more correct *I tried writing some drama, or rather comedy-drama, but it wasn't very good.*

**ratify** /'rætɪfaɪ/ *verb* [T] to make an agreement official *Sixty-five nations need to ratify the treaty.*

**rating** /'reɪtɪŋ/ *noun* **1** [C] a measurement of how good or popular something or someone is *A high percentage of Americans gave the President a positive rating.* **2 the ratings** a list of television and radio programmes showing how popular they are

**ratio** /'reɪʃiəʊ/ *noun* [C] the relationship between two things expressed in numbers to show how much bigger one is than the other *The female to male ratio at the college is 2 to 1.*

**ration¹** /'ræʃʰn/ *noun* [C] the amount of some-

**R**

thing that you are allowed to have when there is little of it available *a food/petrol ration*

**ration²** /'ræʃ³n/ *verb* [T] to give people only a small amount of something because there is little of it available *They might have to start rationing water.*

**rational** /'ræʃ³n³l/ *adj* **1** based on facts and not affected by someone's emotions or imagination *a rational argument/debate/explanation* **2** able to make decisions based on facts and not be influenced by your emotions or imagination *Look, we've got to try to be rational about this.* ⊃ *Opposite* **irrational.** • **rationally** *adv*

**rationale** /ˌræʃə'nɑːl/ *noun* [C] a group of reasons for a decision or belief *I don't understand the rationale behind the policy.*

**rationalize** (*also UK* **-ise**) /'ræʃ³n³laɪz/ *verb* **1** [I, T] to try to find reasons to explain your behaviour or emotions *I can't rationalize the way I feel towards him.* **2** [T] *mainly UK* to improve the way a business is organized, usually by getting rid of people • **rationalization** /ˌræʃ³n³laɪ'zeɪʃ³n/ *noun* [C, U]

**the ˈrat ˌrace** *noun informal* the unpleasant way that people compete against each other at work in order to succeed

**rattle¹** /'rætl/ *verb* **1** [I, T] to make a noise like something knocking repeatedly, or to cause something to make this noise *Her cup rattled on its saucer.* • *The wind blew hard, rattling the doors and windows.* **2** [T] to make someone nervous [often passive] *He was clearly rattled by their angry reaction.*

**rattle sth off** to quickly say a list or something that you have learned *She can rattle off the names of all the players.*

**rattle²** /'rætl/ *noun* [C] a toy that a baby shakes to make a noise

**raucous** /'rɔːkəs/ *adj* loud and unpleasant *raucous behaviour/laughter*

**ravage** /'rævɪdʒ/ *verb* [T] to damage or destroy something [often passive] *The whole area has been ravaged by war.*

**ravages** /'rævɪdʒɪz/ *noun* **the ravages of disease/time/war, etc** the damaging effects of disease/time/war, etc

**rave¹** /reɪv/ *verb* [I] **1** to talk about something that you think is very good in an excited way *He went there last year and he's been raving about it ever since.* **2** to talk in an angry, uncontrolled way

**rave²** /reɪv/ *noun* [C] an event where people dance to modern, electronic music

**raven** /'reɪv³n/ *noun* [C] a large, black bird

**ravenous** /'ræv³nəs/ *adj* very hungry • **ravenously** *adv*

**ravine** /rə'viːn/ *noun* [C] a narrow, deep valley with very steep sides

*ravine*

**raving** /'reɪvɪŋ/ *adj informal* completely uncontrolled *He was acting like a raving lunatic.*

**ravings** /'reɪvɪŋz/ *noun* [plural] the strange things that a crazy person says *the ravings of a madman*

**ravishing** /'rævɪʃɪŋ/ *adj* very beautiful

o—**raw** /rɔː/ *adj* **1** [FOOD] not cooked *raw meat/vegetables* **2** [NATURAL] in the natural state *raw materials* • *raw sugar* **3** [INJURY] If a part of the body is raw, the skin has come off and it is red and painful. • **rawness** *noun* [U] ⊃ *See also:* hit/touch a raw **nerve**.

**ray** /reɪ/ *noun* [C] **1** a narrow beam of light, heat, or energy *an ultraviolet ray* • *the rays of the sun* **2** **a ray of hope/comfort, etc** a small amount of hope, etc ⊃ *See also:* **X-ray.**

**razor** /'reɪzə'/ *noun* [C] a piece of equipment with a sharp blade used for removing hair from the face, legs, etc ⊃ *See colour picture* **The Bathroom** *on page Centre 1.*

**ˈrazor ˌblade** *noun* [C] a very thin, sharp blade that you put in a razor

**Rd** *written abbreviation for* road *17, Lynton Rd*

o—**reach¹** /riːtʃ/ *verb* **1** [ARRIVE] [T] to arrive somewhere *We won't reach Miami till five or six o'clock.* **2** [STRETCH] [I, T] to stretch your arm and hand to touch or take something *Our little girl isn't tall enough to reach the light switches.* • *She reached for a cigarette.* • *She reached down to stroke the dog's head.* • *He reached out and grabbed her arm.* **3** **can reach (sth)** to be able to touch or take something with your hand *Could you get that book down for me – I can't reach.* **4** [BE LONG ENOUGH] [I, T] If something reaches, or reaches something, it is long enough to touch something. *The rope won't be long enough to reach the ground.* **5** [LEVEL] [T] to get to a particular level, situation, etc *We hope to reach our goal by May next year.* • *I've reached the point where I'm about to give up.* **6** **reach a decision/agreement/conclusion, etc** to make a decision, agreement, etc about something **7** [TELEPHONE] [T] to speak to someone on the telephone *You can reach him at home.*

**USAGE**

**reach**

When **reach** means 'arrive somewhere' or 'get to a particular level' it is not normally followed by a preposition.

*We finally reached the hotel just after midnight.*

*The project has now reached the final stage.*

~~The project has now reached to the final stage.~~

**reach²** /riːtʃ/ *noun* **1** **out of/beyond (sb's) reach** too far away for someone to take hold of *I keep the medicines up here, out of the kids' reach.* **2** **beyond (sb's) reach** not possible for someone to have *With all this money we can buy things previously beyond our reach.* **3** **be within reach (of sth)** to be close enough to travel to *You'll be within easy reach of London.* **4** **be within (sb's) reach** a to be close enough for someone to take hold of *The gun lay within*

**R**

*reach.* **b** possible for someone to achieve *Winning the championship suddenly seemed within their reach.*

o→**react** /ri'ækt/ *verb* [I] **1** SAY/DO to say, do, or feel something because of something else that has been said or done *He reacted angrily to her comments.* **2** BAD EFFECT to become ill because something that you have eaten or used on your body has had a bad effect on you *My skin reacts to most perfumes.* **3** SUBSTANCES In science, if a substance reacts with another substance, it changes. *Carbon reacts with oxygen to produce carbon dioxide.*

**react against sth** to do the opposite of what someone wants you to do because you do not like their rules or ideas

o→**reaction** /ri'ækʃ°n/ *noun* **1** CAUSED BY SOMETHING [C, U] something you say, feel, or do because of something that has happened *What was his reaction to the news?* **2** **reactions** *mainly UK* the ability to move quickly when something suddenly happens *Drivers need to have quick reactions.* **3** CHANGE [no plural] a change in the way people behave or think because they do not agree with the way people behaved or thought in the past *In art, there was a reaction against Realism.* **4** BAD EFFECT [C] an unpleasant feeling or illness caused by something you have eaten or used on your body *A number of people have had a bad reaction to this drug.* **5** SUBSTANCES [C] a change which happens when two substances are put together *a chemical reaction* ➔ *See also:* **chain reaction.**

**reactionary** /ri'ækʃ°n°ri/ *adj* being against political or social progress • **reactionary** *noun* [C] someone who is against political or social progress

**reactor** /ri'æktə°/ (*also* **nuclear reactor**) *noun* [C] a large machine which uses nuclear fuel to produce power

o→**read¹** /ri:d/ *verb past* **read** /red/ **1** WORDS [I, T] to look at words and understand what they mean *What was the last book you read?* • *I've been reading about John F Kennedy.* • [+ that] *I've read that the economy is going to improve by the end of the year.* **2** SAY [I, T] to look at words that are written and say them aloud for other people to listen to *Do you want me to read it to you?* • [+ two objects] *I read him a story at bedtime.* **3** SIGNS [T] to look at signs and be able to understand them *Can you read music?* **4** MEASUREMENT [T] to show the temperature, time, etc on a piece of measuring equipment *The thermometer read 20 degrees this morning.* ➔ *See also:* **lip-read.**

**read sth into sth** to believe that an action, remark, etc has a particular meaning when it has not *Don't read too much into anything he says.*

**read sth out** to read something and say the words aloud so that other people can hear *He read out the names of all the winners.*

**read sth over/through** to read something from the beginning to the end, especially to find mistakes *I read over my essay to check for errors.*

**read²** /ri:d/ *noun* [no plural] **1** the act of reading something *It's not brilliant but it's worth a read.* **2 a good/easy, etc read** something that is enjoyable, easy, etc to read

**readable** /'ri:dəbl/ *adj* enjoyable and easy to read

**reader** /'ri:də°/ *noun* [C] someone who reads *She's a slow reader.*

**readership** /'ri:dəʃɪp/ *noun* [no plural] the number and type of people who read a particular newspaper, magazine, etc *These magazines have a very young readership.*

**readily** /'redɪli/ *adv* **1** quickly and easily *Information is readily available on the Internet.* **2** willingly and without stopping to think *He readily admits to having problems himself.*

**readiness** /'redɪnəs/ *noun* [U] **1** when someone is willing to do something [+ to do sth] *They expressed a readiness to accept our demands.* **2** when someone is prepared for something *It was time to repair their shelters in readiness for the winter.*

o→**reading** /'ri:dɪŋ/ *noun* **1** ACTIVITY [U] the activity or skill of reading books *I did a lot of reading on holiday.* **2** EVENT [C] an event at which someone reads something to an audience *a poetry reading* **3** MEASUREMENT [C] the measurement that is shown on a piece of measuring equipment *It's best to take a meter reading as soon as you move in.*

**readjust** /ˌri:ə'dʒʌst/ *verb* **1** [I] to change in order to deal with a new situation, such as a new job or home *The children will have to readjust to a new school.* **2** [T] to move something slightly or make a small change to something *He readjusted his tie.*

o→**ready** /'redi/ *adj* **1** [never before noun] prepared for doing something *Give me a call when you're ready.* • [+ to do sth] *Are you ready to go yet?* • *We're going at eight, so you've got an hour to get ready.* • *The army was ready for action.* **2** [never before noun] prepared and available to be eaten, drunk, used, etc *Is dinner ready?* • *They're building new offices, but they won't be ready till next year.* • *When will the book be ready for publication?* **3 be ready to do sth** to be willing to do something *We are ready to die for our country.* ➔ *See also:* **rough¹** and ready.

**ready-made** /ˌredi'meɪd/ *adj* made and ready to use *ready-made meals*

o→**real¹** /rɪəl/ *adj* **1** NOT IMAGINED existing and not imagined *He's not real you know, he's just a character in a book.* • *Romance is never like that in real life.* **2** TRUE true and not pretended *What was the real reason she didn't come?* • *Is that your real name?* **3** NOT ARTIFICIAL not artificial or false *real fur/leather* • *It's not a toy gun, it's the real thing.* **4** FOR EMPHASIS [always before noun] used to emphasize a noun *She was a real help.* **5 Get real!** *informal* used to tell someone that they are hoping for something that will never happen, or that they believe something that is not true ➔ *See also:* the real **McCoy.**

**real²** /rɪəl/ *adv* *US informal* very *It's real easy to get there from here.*

**'real es,tate** *noun* [U] *US* buildings and land

**'real estate ,agent** *US* (*UK* **estate agent**) *noun* [C] someone who sells buildings and land as their job

**realism** /'rɪəlɪz°m/ *noun* [U] **1** when things and people in art, literature, etc are shown as they are in real life **2** when you accept and deal with the true facts of a situation and do not hope for things that will not happen

**realist** /'rɪəlɪst/ *noun* [C] **1** someone who accepts the true facts of a situation and does not hope for things that will not happen **2** an artist or writer who shows people and things in their work as they are in real life

**realistic** /,rɪə'lɪstɪk/ *adj* **1** accepting the true facts of a situation and not basing decisions on things that will not happen *Let's be realistic – we're not going to finish this by Friday.* **2** showing things and people as they really are, or making them seem to be real *realistic special effects in a film* ⊃ *Opposite* **unrealistic.** • realistically *adv*

**reality** /rɪ'ælɪti/ *noun* **1** [U] the way things or situations really are and not the way you would like them to be *Listening to music is my escape from reality.* • *Sooner or later you have to face up to reality.* • *He may seem charming but in reality he's actually quite unpleasant.* **2 the reality/realities of sth** the truth about an unpleasant situation *the harsh realities of life* **3 become a reality** to start to happen or exist *New jobs could become a reality by next month.* ⊃ *See also:* **virtual reality.**

**realization** (*also UK* **-isation**) /,rɪəlaɪ'zeɪʃⁿn/ *noun* **1** [U, no plural] when you notice or understand something that you did not notice or understand before [+ that] *There is a growing realization that education has benefits at many levels.* **2** [U] when you achieve something that you wanted *the realization of an ambition*

o⌐**realize** (*also UK* **-ise**) /'rɪəlaɪz/ *verb* [T] **1** to notice or understand something that you did not notice or understand before [+ question word] *I didn't realize how unhappy she was.* • *I suddenly realized I'd met him before.* • [+ (that)] *Some people just don't seem to realize that the world has changed.* **2 realize an ambition/dream/goal, etc** to achieve something that you have wanted for a long time *He had realized all his ambitions by the age of 30.*

o⌐**really** /'rɪəli/ *adv* **1** very or very much *She's really nice.* • *I really don't want to go.* • *That's really interesting.* • *"Did you like it then?" Er, not really"* (= no). **2** used when you are saying what is the truth of a situation *She tried to hide what she was really thinking.* • *They didn't really say anything important.* **3 Really?** used when you are surprised at what someone has just said *"Apparently, he's leaving." "Really?"*

**realm** /relm/ *noun* [C] **1** *formal* an area of knowledge or activity *successes in the realm of foreign policy* **2** *literary* a country that has a king or queen

**realtor** /'riːltər/ *US* (*UK* **estate agent**) *noun* [C] someone who sells buildings or land as their job

**reap** /riːp/ *verb* **1 reap the benefits/profits/rewards** to get something good by working hard for it *Sometimes, this approach can reap tremendous rewards.* **2** [I, T] to cut and collect a crop of grain

**reappear** /,riːə'pɪər/ *verb* [I] to appear again or return after a period of time *He reappeared later that day.* • reappearance /,riːə'pɪərⁿns/ *noun* [C, U]

**rear¹** /rɪər/ *noun* **1 the rear** the back part of something *First class accommodation is towards the rear of the train.* **2 bring up the rear** to be at the back of a group of people who are walking or running • rear *adj* [always before noun] *a rear window/wheel*

**rear²** /rɪər/ *verb* **1** [T] If you rear children or young animals, you care for them until they are adults. *In these waters they breed and rear their young.* **2** [I] (*also* **rear up**) If a horse rears, it stands on its back legs. ⊃ *See also:* raise/rear its ugly **head¹.**

**rearrange** /,riːə'reɪndʒ/ *verb* [T] **1** to change the order or position of things *I've rearranged the furniture.* **2** to change the time of an event or meeting *I've rearranged the meeting for Monday.*

**rear-view mirror** *noun* [C] a small mirror inside a car which the driver looks in to see what is happening behind the car ⊃ *See colour picture* **Car** *on page Centre 3.*

o⌐**reason¹** /'riːzⁿn/ *noun* **1** WHY [C] the facts about why something happens or why someone does something *I knew Sam was going – that was the reason I went there.* • *Is there any particular reason why he doesn't want to come?* • *He left without giving a reason.* • *That was the reason for telling her.* **2** RIGHT [C, U] something that makes it right for you to do something [+ to do sth] *There is every reason to believe the project will be finished on time.* • *I think we have reason to be concerned.* **3** ABILITY [U] the ability to think and make good decisions *By this time he'd lost his powers of reason.* **4 within reason** If something is within reason, it is acceptable and possible. *You can have as much as you like, within reason.* **5 it stands to reason** If it stands to reason that something happens or is true, it is what you would expect. *It stands to reason that a child who is constantly criticized will have little self-confidence.*

**USAGE**

**reason**

Be careful to choose the correct preposition.

*That was the main* **reason for** *the trip.*

~~That was the main reason of the trip.~~

**reason²** /'riːzⁿn/ *verb* [T] to decide that something is true after considering the facts [+ that] *We reasoned that it was unlikely he would be a serious threat to the public.*

**reason with sb** to persuade someone not to do something stupid by giving them good reasons not to *I've tried reasoning with her but it's hopeless.*

**reasonable** /'riːzⁿnəbl/ *adj* **1** FAIR fair and showing good judgment [+ to do sth] *It's not reasonable to expect people to work those hours.* ⊃ *Opposite* **unreasonable.** **2** BIG ENOUGH big enough or large enough in number, although not big or not many *There were a reasonable number of people there.* • *It's a reasonable amount of cash.* **3** GOOD ENOUGH good enough but not the best *I'd say her work is of a reason-*

R

*able standard.* **4** CHEAP not expensive *reasonable prices*

**reasonably** /'riːzªnəbli/ *adv* **1** in a fair way, showing good judgment *Why can't we discuss this reasonably, like adults?* **2** **reasonably good/successful/well, etc** good/successful/well, etc enough but not very good or very well *I did reasonably well at school but not as well as my sister.* **3** **reasonably priced** not expensive

**reasoning** /'riːzªnɪŋ/ *noun* [U] the process of thinking about something in order to make a decision *I don't understand the **reasoning** **behind** this decision.*

**reassure** /ˌriːə'ʃʊəʳ/ *verb* [T] to say something to stop someone from worrying [+ that] *He reassured me that I would be paid soon.* ● reassurance /ˌriːə'ʃʊəʳns/ *noun* [C, U] something that you say to make someone stop worrying *Despite my repeated reassurances that she was welcome, she wouldn't come.*

**reassuring** /ˌriːə'ʃʊərɪŋ/ *adj* making you feel less worried *a reassuring smile/voice* ● reassuringly *adv*

**rebate** /'riːbeɪt/ *noun* [C] an amount of money that is given back to you because you have paid too much *a tax/rent rebate*

**rebel**[1] /'rebªl/ *noun* [C] **1** someone who fights against the government in their country, especially a soldier *Rebels seized control of the airport.* **2** someone who does not like authority and refuses to obey rules

**rebel**[2] /rɪ'bel/ *verb* [I] **rebelling**, *past* **rebelled** **1** to fight against the government **2** to refuse to obey rules because you do not like authority *She **rebelled against** her family.*

**rebellion** /rɪ'beliən/ *noun* [C, U] when people fight against the government in their country

**rebellious** /rɪ'beliəs/ *adj* refusing to obey rules because you do not like authority *a rebellious teenager*

**rebirth** /ˌriː'bɜːθ/ *noun* [no plural] when something becomes popular or active for the second time *the rebirth of the women's movement*

**rebound**[1] /rɪ'baʊnd/ *verb* [I] to move back through the air after hitting something *The ball rebounded off the post.*

**rebound**[2] /'riːbaʊnd/ *noun* **be on the rebound** to be unhappy because your romantic relationship has ended *She was on the rebound when she met her second husband.*

**rebuff** /rɪ'bʌf/ *verb* [T] *formal* to refuse someone's suggestion or offer, especially in an unfriendly way *The company has rebuffed several buyout offers.* ● rebuff *noun* [C]

**rebuild** /ˌriː'bɪld/ *verb* [T] *past* **rebuilt** **1** to build something again after it has been damaged *The cathedral was rebuilt after being destroyed by fire.* **2** to make a situation succeed again after something bad caused it to fail *The country is still struggling to rebuild its economy.*

**rebuke** /rɪ'bjuːk/ *verb* [T] *formal* to speak angrily to someone because they have done something wrong ● rebuke *noun* [C] *formal*

**recalcitrant** /rɪ'kælsɪtrənt/ *adj formal* not willing to obey or help someone *recalcitrant schoolchildren*

**recall** /rɪ'kɔːl/ *verb* [T] **1** to remember something *I don't recall arranging a time to meet.* **2** to

order the return of someone or something [often passive] *The ambassador was recalled to London.* ● *The manufacturer has recalled the computers because of faulty wiring.* ● recall /'riːkɔːl/ *noun* [U]

**recap** /'riːkæp/ *verb* [I] **recapping**, *past* **recapped** to repeat the most important parts of what you have just said ● recap /'riːkæp/ *noun* [C]

**recapture** /ˌriː'kæptʃəʳ/ *verb* [T] **1** to catch a person or animal that has escaped **2** to experience or feel something from the past again *Some men try to recapture their youth by going out with younger women.*

**recede** /rɪ'siːd/ *verb* [I] **1** MOVE AWAY to become further and further away *The coastline receded into the distance.* **2** LESS STRONG If a memory or feeling recedes, it becomes less clear or strong. *Even painful memories recede with time.* **3** HAIR If a man's hair recedes, it stops growing at the front of his head. *a receding hairline*

**receipt** /rɪ'siːt/ *noun* **1** [C] a piece of paper that proves that you have received goods or money *Could I have a receipt?* ● *Remember to keep receipts for any work done.* **2** [U] *formal* the act of receiving something *Items must be returned within fourteen days of receipt.*

**receipts** /rɪ'siːts/ *US* (*UK* **takings**) *noun* [plural] the amount of money that a business gets from selling things *box-office receipts*

o━**receive** /rɪ'siːv/ *verb* [T] **1** GET to get something that someone has given or sent to you *Occasionally, he receives letters from fans.* ● *She received a number of awards during her lifetime.* **2** REACT to react to a suggestion or piece of work in a particular way [often passive] *His first book was not well received* (= people did not like it). **3** WELCOME to formally welcome guests ⊃ *See also:* be on/at the receiving **end**[1] of sth.

**receiver** /rɪ'siːvəʳ/ *noun* [C] **1** TELEPHONE the part of a telephone that you hold in your hand and use for listening and speaking **2** RADIO/TV the part of a radio or television that receives signals from the air **3** PERSON someone who officially deals with a company when it has to stop business because it cannot pay the money it owes

o━**recent** /'riːsªnt/ *adj* happening or starting from a short time ago *a recent photo* ● *a recent survey* ● *In recent years, sales have decreased quite markedly.*

o━**recently** /'riːsªntli/ *adv* not long ago *Have you seen any good films recently?* ● *Until recently he worked as a teacher.*

**reception** /rɪ'sepʃªn/ *noun* **1** HOTEL/OFFICE [no plural] the place in a hotel or office building where people go when they arrive *Ask for me at reception.* ● *a reception area/desk* **2** PARTY [C] a formal party that is given to celebrate a special event or to welcome someone *a wedding reception* **3** REACTION [no plural] the way people react to something or someone *We were given a very warm reception.* **4** RADIO/TV [U] the quality of a radio or television signal

**receptionist** /rɪ'sepʃªnɪst/ *noun* [C] someone who works in a hotel or office building, answering the telephone and dealing with guests *a hotel receptionist*

**receptive** /rɪ'septɪv/ adj willing to think about and accept new ideas *She's generally very receptive to ideas and suggestions.*

**recess** /rɪ'ses/ noun 1 NOT WORKING [C, U] a time in the day or in the year when a parliament or law court is not working *a parliamentary/congressional recess* • *The court is in recess for thirty minutes.* 2 SCHOOL [C, U] US (UK break) a period of free time between classes at school *At recess the boys would fight.* 3 WALL [C] a part of a wall in a room that is further back than the rest of the wall

**recession** /rɪ'seʃ°n/ noun [C, U] a time when the economy of a country is not successful *The latest report confirms that the economy is in recession.*

**recharge** /ˌriː'tʃɑːdʒ/ verb [T] to fill a battery (= object that provides a machine with power) with electricity so that it can work again

**recipe** /'resɪpi/ noun 1 [C] a list of foods and a set of instructions telling you how to cook something *a recipe for carrot cake* 2 **be a recipe for disaster/trouble/success, etc** to be likely to become a disaster, a success, etc

**recipient** /rɪ'sɪpiənt/ noun [C] someone who receives something *a recipient of an award*

**reciprocal** /rɪ'sɪprək°l/ adj involving two people or groups that agree to help each other in a similar way *a reciprocal arrangement*

**reciprocate** /rɪ'sɪprəkeɪt/ verb [I, T] to do something for someone because they have done something similar for you

**recital** /rɪ'saɪt°l/ noun [C] a performance of music or poetry *a piano recital*

**recite** /rɪ'saɪt/ verb [I, T] to say something aloud from memory *She can recite the whole poem.*

**reckless** /'rekləs/ adj doing something dangerous and not caring about what might happen *reckless driving* • **recklessly** adv

**reckon** /'rek°n/ verb [T] 1 to think that something is probably true *I reckon he likes her.* • [+ (that)] *He reckons that he earns more in a week than I do in a month.* 2 to guess that a particular number is correct *His fortune is reckoned at $5 million.* ⊃ *See also: a force¹ to be reckoned with.*

**reckon on sth/doing sth** to think that something is going to happen and make it part of your plans

**reckon with sb/sth** to deal with someone or something difficult

**reclaim** /rɪ'kleɪm/ verb [T] 1 to get something back from someone *You can reclaim the tax at the airport.* 2 to make land good enough to be used for growing crops

**recline** /rɪ'klaɪn/ verb 1 [I] to lie back with the upper part of your body in a horizontal position *I found him reclining on the sofa.* 2 [I, T] If a chair reclines, you can lower the back part so that you can lie in it, and if you recline a chair, you put it in this position. *a reclining chair/seat*

**recluse** /rɪ'kluːs/ noun [C] someone who lives alone and does not like being with other people • **reclusive** adj living alone and avoiding other people

**recognition** /ˌrekəg'nɪʃ°n/ noun 1 ACCEPT [U, no plural] when you accept that something is true or real *There is a growing recognition of the scale of the problem.* • [+ that] *There is a general recognition that she's the best person for the job.* 2 HONOUR [U] when someone is publicly thanked for something good that they have done *Ellen gained recognition for her outstanding work.* • *He was given a medal in recognition of his bravery.* 3 KNOW [U] when you know something or someone because you have seen or experienced them before *I waved at her, but she showed no sign of recognition.*

**recognizable** (also UK -**isable**) /'rekəgnaɪzəbl/ adj able to be recognized (= able to be known) *Megan's voice is instantly recognizable.* • **recognizably** adv

o--**recognize** (also UK -**ise**) /'rekəgnaɪz/ verb [T] 1 KNOW to know someone or something because you have seen or experienced them before *I recognized her from her picture.* • *Doctors are trained to recognize the symptoms of disease.* 2 ACCEPT to accept that something is true or real [+ (that)] *She recognized that she had been partly to blame.* • *Smoking is recognized as a leading cause of lung cancer.* 3 SHOW RESPECT to officially show respect for someone for an achievement *He was recognized by the governor for his work with teenagers.*

**recoil** /rɪ'kɔɪl/ verb [I] to react to something with fear or hate *She recoiled in horror at the thought of touching a snake.*

**recollect** /ˌrekəl'ekt/ verb [T] to remember something *I didn't recollect having seen him.*

**recollection** /ˌrekəl'ekʃ°n/ noun [C, U] when you remember something *He had no recollection of the incident.*

o--**recommend** /ˌrekə'mend/ verb [T] 1 to say that someone or something is good or suitable for a particular purpose *Can you recommend a good wine to go with this dish?* • *She has been recommended for promotion.* 2 to advise someone that something should be done *The judge is likely to recommend a long jail sentence.* • [+ that] *The report recommended that tourists avoid the region.* • *The recommended dose is two tablets every four hours.*

**recommendation** /ˌrekəmen'deɪʃ°n/ noun 1 [C] a piece of advice about what to do in a particular situation *The marketing department made several recommendations to improve sales.* • [+ that] *It's my recommendation that this factory be closed immediately.* 2 [C, U] a suggestion that someone or something is good or suitable for a particular purpose *I bought this book on Andy's recommendation.*

**recompense** /'rekəmpens/ noun [U] formal payment that you give to someone when you have caused them difficulty or an injury *Angry soccer fans sought recompense for the cancelled match.* • **recompense** verb [T] formal *He was recompensed for loss of earnings.*

**reconcile** /'rek°nsaɪl/ verb [T] 1 to make two different ideas, beliefs, or situations agree or able to exist together *It is sometimes difficult to reconcile science and religion.* • *How can you reconcile your love of animals with your habit of eating them?* 2 **be reconciled (with sb)** to become friendly with someone after you have

R

argued with them *I doubt that I'll ever be reconciled with my ex-husband.*

**reconcile yourself to sth** to accept a situation although you do not like it *Eventually he reconciled himself to living without her.*

**reconciliation** /ˌrekˀn.sɪliˈeɪʃˀn/ *noun* **1** [C, U] when two people or groups become friendly again after they have argued *to seek a reconciliation* **2** [U, no plural] the process of making two opposite ideas, beliefs, or situations agree *the reconciliation of facts with theory*

**reconnaissance** /rɪˈkɒnɪsˀns/ *noun* [U] the process of getting information about a place or an area for military use

**reconsider** /ˌriːkˀnˈsɪdəʳ/ *verb* [I, T] to think again about a decision or opinion and decide if you want to change it *We've been asked to reconsider the proposal.* • reconsideration /ˌriːkˀn.sɪdˀrˈeɪʃˀn/ *noun* [U]

**reconstruct** /ˌriːkˀnˈstrʌkt/ *verb* [T] **1** to create a description of a past event using all the information that you have *The police tried to reconstruct the crime using evidence found at the scene.* **2** to build something again after it has been damaged or destroyed

**reconstruction** /ˌriːkˀnˈstrʌkʃˀn/ *noun* [C, U] **1** when you create a description of a past event using all the information that you have *A reconstruction of the crime was shown on TV.* **2** when you build something again after it has been damaged or destroyed

o-**record**[1] /ˈrekɔːd/ *noun* **1** STORED INFORMATION [C, U] information that is written on paper or stored on computer so that it can be used in the future *medical/dental records* • *My teacher* **keeps** *a* **record** *of my absences.* • *This has been the hottest summer* **on record** (= the hottest summer known about). **2** BEHAVIOUR [C] A person's or company's record is their behaviour or achievements. [usually singular] *She has an outstanding academic record* (= has done very well in school). • *Of all airlines they have the best safety record.* **3** BEST [C] the best, biggest, longest, tallest, etc *to set/break a record* • *He* **holds** *the world* **record** *for 100 metres.* **4** MUSIC [C] a flat, round, plastic disc that music is stored on, used especially in the past *to play a record* **5** **off the record** If you say something off the record, you do not want the public to know about it. **6** **put/set the record straight** to tell people the true facts about a situation ➔ *See also:* **track record**.

o-**record**[2] /rɪˈkɔːd/ *verb* **1** [T] to write down information or store it on a computer so that it can be used in the future *He recorded details of their conversation in his diary.* **2** [I, T] to store sounds or pictures using electronic equipment, a camera, etc so that you can listen to them or see them again *to record a new album* • *I recorded that programme for you.* • *a recorded message*

**record-breaking** /ˈrekɔːdˌbreɪkɪŋ/ *adj* [always before noun] better, bigger, longer, etc than anything else before *record-breaking sales of the new video*

**recorder** /rɪˈkɔːdəʳ/ *noun* [C] **1** a machine for storing sounds or pictures *a video recorder* **2** a long, thin, hollow instrument that you play by blowing into it ➔ *See also:* **cassette recorder**, **tape recorder**.

**recording** /rɪˈkɔːdɪŋ/ *noun* [C, U] sounds or moving pictures that have been recorded, or the process of recording *a recording of classical music* • *a new system of digital recording*

**'record ˌlabel** *noun* [C] a company that records and sells music

**'record ˌplayer** *noun* [C] a machine that makes it possible to hear the music on a record (= a flat, round disc used especially in the past)

**recount**[1] /rɪˈkaʊnt/ *verb* [T] *formal* to tell a story or describe an event *He was recounting a story about a woman he'd met on a train.*

**recount**[2] /ˌriːˈkaʊnt/ *verb* [T] to count something again

**recount**[3] /ˈriːkaʊnt/ *noun* [C] a second count of votes in an election *They demanded a recount.*

**recoup** /rɪˈkuːp/ *verb* [T] to get back money that you have lost or spent *to recoup your losses*

**recourse** /rɪˈkɔːs/ *noun* [U] *formal* someone or something that can help you in a difficult situation *For many cancer patients, surgery is the only recourse.* • *They solved their problem* **without recourse to** (= without using) *violence.*

o-**recover** /rɪˈkʌvəʳ/ *verb* **1** HEALTH [I] to become healthy or happy again after an illness, injury, or period of sadness *It takes a long time to* **recover from** *surgery.* • *She never* **recovered from** *the death of her husband.* **2** SITUATION [I] If a system or situation recovers, it returns to the way it was before something bad happened. *The economy was quick to recover after the election.* **3** BODY [T] to be able to use or feel again part of your body which has been damaged *He never fully recovered the use of his legs.* **4** GET BACK [T] to get something back that has been lost or stolen *Police recovered the stolen money.*

**recovery** /rɪˈkʌvˀri/ *noun* **1** HEALTH [U, no plural] when you feel better or happier again after an illness, injury, or period of sadness *She only had the operation last month but she's* **made a** **good recovery.** **2** SITUATION [U, no plural] when a system or situation returns to the way it was before something bad happened *economic recovery* • *The housing industry has* **made a** **remarkable recovery.** **3** GET BACK [U] when you get back something that was lost or stolen *the recovery of stolen jewels*

**recreate** /ˌriːkriˈeɪt/ *verb* [T] to make something exist or happen again *They plan to recreate a typical English village in Japan.*

**recreation** /ˌrekriˈeɪʃˀn/ *noun* [C, U] activities that you do for enjoyment when you are not working *Shopping seems to be her only form of recreation.* • *a recreation area/centre* • recreational *adj*

**recrimination** /rɪˌkrɪmɪˈneɪʃˀn/ *noun* [C, U] *formal* the things you say when you blame someone for something, or the act of blaming someone for something

**recruit**[1] /rɪˈkruːt/ *verb* [I, T] to try to persuade someone to work for a company or to join an organization • recruitment *noun* [U] when you recruit people *graduate recruitment*

**recruit**[2] /rɪˈkruːt/ *noun* [C] someone who has recently joined an organization *a new recruit*

**rectangle** /ˈrɛktæŋgl/ *noun* [C] a shape with four 90° angles and four sides, with opposite sides of equal length and two sides longer than the other two ➲ *See picture at* **shape**. • rectangular /rekˈtæŋgjələ<sup>r</sup>/ *adj* shaped like a rectangle *a rectangular room*

**rectify** /ˈrektɪfaɪ/ *verb* [T] *formal* to correct something or change it so that it is acceptable *The government has promised to rectify the situation.*

**rector** /ˈrektə<sup>r</sup>/ *noun* [C] a priest in some Christian churches

**rectum** /ˈrektəm/ *noun* [C] the last part of the body that solid waste travels through before coming out of the bottom

**recuperate** /rɪˈkuːpˀreɪt/ *verb* [I] to become healthy again after an illness or injury *She's still recuperating from her injuries.* • recuperation /rɪˌkjuːpˀrˈeɪʃˀn/ *noun* [U]

**recur** /rɪˈkɜː<sup>r</sup>/ *verb* [I] recurring, *past* recurred to happen again or many times *The same ideas recur throughout her books.* • recurrence /rɪˈkʌrˀns/ *noun* [C, U] when something recurs *a recurrence of the disease*

**recurring** /rɪˈkɜːrɪŋ/ (*also* **recurrent**) *adj* happening again or many times *a recurring dream*

**recycle** /ˌriːˈsaɪkl/ *verb* [I, T] to put used paper, glass, plastic, etc through a process so that it can be used again *We recycle all our newspapers and bottles.* • recyclable /ˌriːˈsaɪkləbl/ *adj* able to be recycled *Glass is recyclable.*

**recycled** /ˌriːˈsaɪkld/ *adj* Recycled paper, glass, plastic, etc has been used before and put through a process so that it can be used again.

**recycling** /ˌriːˈsaɪklɪŋ/ *noun* [U] when paper, glass, plastic, etc is put through a process so that it can be used again *ways to encourage recycling* • *a recycling centre*

o━**red**¹ /red/ *adj* redder, reddest **1** COLOUR being the same colour as blood *a red shirt* ➲ *See colour picture* **Colours** *on page Centre 6.* **2** HAIR Red hair is an orange-brown colour. *Rosie's got red hair and freckles.* ➲ *See colour picture* **Hair** *on page Centre 9.* **3 go red** *UK* (*US* **turn red**) If someone goes red, their face becomes red because they are embarrassed or angry. *He kissed her on the cheek and she went bright red.* **4** WINE Red wine is made from black grapes (= small, round, purple fruits). ➲ *See also:* be like a red **rag** to a bull.

o━**red**² /red/ *noun* **1** [C, U] the colour of blood ➲ *See colour picture* **Colours** *on page Centre 6.* **2 in the red** If your bank account is in the red, you have spent more money than there was in it. **3 see red** to become very angry

**the ˌred ˈcarpet** *noun* special treatment that is given to an important person when they go somewhere *She's given the red carpet treatment wherever she goes.*

**redden** /ˈredˀn/ *verb* [I, T] to become red or to make something become red *His face reddened with anger.*

**redeem** /rɪˈdiːm/ *verb* [T] **1** IMPROVE to make something seem less bad *He tried to redeem his reputation by working extra hard.* • *a redeeming feature* **2 redeem yourself** to do something that makes people have a better opinion of you after you have done something bad *He*

*was two hours late, but he redeemed himself by bringing presents.* **3** GET SOMETHING to exchange something for something else **4** RELIGION to save someone from evil, especially according to the Christian religion

**redemption** /rɪˈdemʃˀn/ *noun* **1** [U] when someone is saved from evil, especially according to the Christian religion **2 be beyond redemption** to be too bad to be improved or saved

**redeploy** /ˌriːdɪˈplɔɪ/ *verb* [T] to move employees, soldiers, equipment, etc to a different place or use them in a more effective way • redeployment *noun* [C, U] when you redeploy someone or something

**redevelop** /ˌriːdɪˈveləp/ *verb* [T] to make a place more modern by improving old buildings or building new ones *There are plans to redevelop the city's waterfront area.* • redevelopment *noun* [C, U] when a place is redeveloped

**red-handed** /ˌredˈhændɪd/ *adv* **catch sb red-handed** *informal* to discover someone doing something wrong *He was caught red-handed trying to steal a car.*

**redhead** /ˈredhed/ *noun* [C] someone who has red hair

**ˌred ˈherring** *noun* [C] a fact or idea that takes your attention away from something that is important

**red-hot** /ˌredˈhɒt/ *adj* extremely hot

**redirect** /ˌriːdɪˈrekt/ *verb* [T] **1** to send something in a different direction *Traffic should be redirected away from the city centre.* **2** to use money, energy, etc for a different purpose *Money spent on weapons could be redirected to hospitals and schools.*

**redistribute** /ˌriːdɪˈstrɪbjuːt/ *verb* [T] to share money, land, power, etc between people in a different way from before *to redistribute wealth* • redistribution /ˌriːdɪstrɪˈbjuːʃˀn/ *noun* [U] the process of redistributing something

**redo** /ˌriːˈduː/ *verb* [T] to do something again *I'm going to have to redo that report.*

**redress**¹ /rɪˈdres/ *verb* [T] *formal* to correct something that is wrong, unfair, or not equal *laws aimed at redressing racial inequality*

**redress**² /rɪˈdres/ (US) /ˈriːdres/ *noun* [U] *formal* payment for an action or situation that is wrong or unfair

**ˌred ˈtape** *noun* [U] official rules that do not seem necessary and make things happen very slowly

o━**reduce** /rɪˈdjuːs/ *verb* [T] to make something less *to reduce air pollution* • *Prices have been reduced by almost 50 percent.* • *The number of employees was reduced from 500 to 300.*

**reduce sb to sth/doing sth** to make someone unhappy or cause them to be in a bad situation *She was reduced to tears by his comments.* • *I lost my job and was reduced to borrowing money from friends.*

**reduce sth to sth** to destroy something, especially something that has been built *The earthquake reduced the city to rubble.*

**reduction** /rɪˈdʌkʃˀn/ *noun* [C, U] when something is reduced *She refused to accept a reduction in wages.* • *price reductions*

**redundancy** /rɪˈdʌndˀnsi/ *noun* **1** [C, U] *UK*

R

when your employer makes you stop working because there is not enough work *There have been a lot of redundancies in the mining industry.* **2** [U] when something is not needed or used because there are other similar or more modern things

**redundant** /rɪ'dʌndənt/ *adj* **1** NOT WORKING *UK* not working because your employer has told you there is not enough work *Eight thousand people have been made redundant in Britain this year.* **2** NOT NEEDED *UK* not needed or used any more because there are other similar or more modern things *redundant weapons* **3** TOO MUCH more than is needed, especially extra words that mean the same thing

**redwood** /'redwʊd/ *noun* [C, U] a very tall tree that grows on the west coast of the US, or the wood of this tree

**reed** /riːd/ *noun* [C] a tall, stiff plant like grass that grows near water

**reef** /riːf/ *noun* [C] a line of rocks or sand near the surface of the sea *a coral reef*

**reek** /riːk/ *verb* [I] to have a very unpleasant smell *The whole room reeked of sweat.* ● reek *noun* [no plural]

**reel**[1] /riːl/ *verb* [I] **1** to feel very shocked *She was still reeling from the news of his death.* **2** to walk in a way that looks as if you are going to fall over *He came reeling down the street like a drunk.*

**reel sth off** to say a long list of things quickly and without stopping *She reeled off a list of all the countries she'd been to.*

**reel**[2] /riːl/ *noun* [C] an object shaped like a wheel that you can roll film, thread, etc around

**re-elect** /,riːɪ'lekt/ *verb* [T] to elect someone again to a particular position

**re-election** /,riːɪ'lekʃ°n/ *noun* [C, U] when someone is elected again to the same position *She's (UK) standing for/(US) running for re-election* (= she wants to be re-elected).

**ref** /ref/ *noun* [C] *informal short for* referee

o━**refer** /rɪ'fɜːʳ/ *verb* referring, *past* referred

**refer to sb/sth 1** to talk or write about someone or something, especially briefly *She didn't once refer to her son.* ● *He always referred to his father as 'the old man'.* **2** If writing or information refers to someone or something, it relates to that person or thing. *The sales figures refer to UK sales only.*

**refer to sth** to read something in order to get information *Please refer to your owner's manual for more information.*

**refer sb/sth to sb/sth** to send someone or something to a different place or person for information or help *My doctor referred me to a specialist.* ● *All customer complaints are referred to the main office.*

**referee**[1] /,ref°r'iː/ *noun* [C] someone who makes sure that players follow the rules during a sports game ➔ *See colour picture* **Sports 2** *on page Centre 16.*

**referee**[2] /,ref°r'iː/ *verb* [I, T] refereeing, *past* refereed to be the referee in a sports game

**reference** /'ref°r°ns/ *noun* **1** SAY [C, U] when you briefly talk or write about someone or something *In his book, he makes several references to his time in France.* **2** with/in reference to

**sth** *formal* relating to something *I am writing to you with reference to the job advertised in yesterday's newspaper.* **3** LOOK AT [C, U] when you look at information, or the thing that you look at for information *Please keep this handout for future reference* (= to look at in the future). **4** LETTER [C] a letter that is written by someone who knows you, to say if you are suitable for a job or course ➔ *See also:* **cross reference.**

**'reference ,book** *noun* [C] a book that you look at in order to find information

**referendum** /,ref°r'endəm/ *noun* [C] an occasion when all the people in a country can vote in order to show their opinion about a political question

**referral** /rɪ'fɜːr°l/ *noun* [C, U] when someone or something is sent to a different place or person for information or help

**refill** /,riː'fɪl/ *verb* [T] to fill something again *He got up and refilled their glasses.* ● refill /'riːfɪl/ *noun* [C] *I finished my drink and asked for a refill.*

**refine** /rɪ'faɪn/ *verb* [T] **1** to make a substance pure by removing other substances from it **2** to improve an idea, method, system, etc by making small changes *The engineers spent months refining the software.*

**refined** /rɪ'faɪnd/ *adj* **1** PURE A refined substance has been made more pure by removing other substances from it. *refined sugar* **2** POLITE very polite and showing knowledge of social rules **3** IMPROVED improved by many small changes *a refined method*

**refinement** /rɪ'faɪnmənt/ *noun* **1** IMPROVEMENT [C, U] a small change that improves something *Several refinements have been made to improve the car's performance.* **2** POLITE [U] polite behaviour and knowledge of social rules *a woman of refinement* **3** PURE [U] the process of making a substance pure

**refinery** /rɪ'faɪn°ri/ *noun* [C] a factory where substances, such as sugar, oil, etc are made pure

o━**reflect** /rɪ'flekt/ *verb* **1** SHOW [T] to show or be a sign of something *The statistics reflect a change in people's spending habits.* **2** SEND BACK [T] If a surface reflects heat, light, sound, etc, it sends the light, etc back and does not absorb it. **3** IMAGE [I, T] If a surface such as a mirror or water reflects something, you can see the image of that thing in the mirror, water, etc. *He saw himself reflected in the shop window.* **4** THINK [I] *formal* to think in a serious and careful way *In prison, he had plenty of time to reflect on the crimes he had committed.*

**reflect on sb/sth** If something reflects on someone or something, it affects other people's opinion of them, especially in a bad way. *The whole affair reflects badly on the government.*

**reflection** /rɪ'flekʃ°n/ *noun* **1** [C] the image of something in a mirror, on a shiny surface, etc *I saw my reflection in the window.* **2** [C, U] *formal* when you think in a serious and careful way *He paused for reflection before answering my question.* ● **On reflection** (= after thinking again), *I think I was wrong.* **3 a reflection of sth** something that is a sign or result of a particular situation *His poor job performance is a* *reflection of his lack of training.* **4 a reflection on sb/sth** something that makes people have a particular opinion about someone or something, especially a bad opinion *Low test scores are a sad reflection on our school system.*

**reflection**

**reflective** /rɪˈflektɪv/ *adj* **1** thinking carefully and quietly *a reflective mood* **2** A reflective surface is one that you can see easily when a light shines on it. *a jacket made of reflective material*

**reflex** /ˈriːfleks/ *noun* [C] a physical reaction that you cannot control *Shivering and blushing are reflexes.* • *a reflex action*

**reflexes** /ˈriːfleksɪz/ *noun* [plural] your ability to react quickly *A boxer needs to have good reflexes.*

**reflexive** /rɪˈfleksɪv/ *adj* A reflexive verb or pronoun is used to show that the person who does the action is also the person who is affected by it. In the sentence 'I looked at myself in the mirror.', 'myself' is a reflexive pronoun.

**reform**[1] /rɪˈfɔːm/ *noun* [C, U] when changes are made to improve a system, organization, or law, or a change that is made *economic/political reform* • *Students have called for reforms in the admission process.*

**reform**[2] /rɪˈfɔːm/ *verb* **1** [T] to change a system, organization, or law in order to improve it *efforts to reform the education system* **2** [I, T] to change your behaviour and stop doing bad things, or to make someone else do this *a programme to reform criminals* • *a reformed drug addict*

**reformer** /rɪˈfɔːmə/ *noun* [C] someone who tries to improve a system or law by changing it *a social reformer*

**refrain**[1] /rɪˈfreɪn/ *verb* [I] *formal* to stop yourself from doing something [+ from + doing sth] *Please refrain from talking during the performance.*

**refrain**[2] /rɪˈfreɪn/ *noun* [C] **1** *formal* a phrase or idea that you repeat often *'Every vote counts' is a familiar refrain in politics.* **2** a part of a song that you repeat

**refresh** /rɪˈfreʃ/ *verb* [T] **1** to make you feel less hot or tired *A cool drink should refresh you.* **2 refresh sb's memory** to help someone remember something

**refreshing** /rɪˈfreʃɪŋ/ *adj* **1** different and interesting *a refreshing change* • [+ to do sth] *It's refreshing to see a film that's so original.*

**2** making you feel less hot or tired *a refreshing shower/swim* • **refreshingly** *adv*

**refreshments** /rɪˈfreʃmənts/ *noun* [plural] food and drinks that are available at a meeting, event, on a journey, etc *Refreshments are available in the lobby.*

**refrigerate** /rɪˈfrɪdʒəreɪt/ *verb* [T] to make or keep food cold so that it stays fresh *You should refrigerate any leftover food immediately.* • **refrigeration** /rɪˌfrɪdʒəˈreɪʃən/ *noun* [U]

**refrigerated** /rɪˈfrɪdʒəreɪtɪd/ *adj* **1** A refrigerated container or vehicle keeps the things inside it cold. **2** Refrigerated food or drink is cold because it has been kept in a refrigerator.

**refrigerator** /rɪˈfrɪdʒəreɪtə/ *noun* [C] a large container that uses electricity to keep food cold ➔ *See colour picture* **Kitchen** *on page Centre 10.*

**refuel** /ˌriːˈfjuːəl/ *verb* [I, T] to put more fuel into an aircraft, ship, etc so that it can continue its journey

**refuge** /ˈrefjuːdʒ/ *noun* **1** [U] protection from danger or unpleasant conditions *We took refuge from the storm in an old barn.* **2** [C] a place where you are protected from danger *a refuge for homeless people*

**refugee** /ˌrefjuˈdʒiː/ *noun* [C] someone who has been forced to leave their country, especially because of a war *a refugee camp*

**refund**[1] /ˈriːfʌnd/ *noun* [C] an amount of money that is given back to you, especially because you are not happy with something you have bought *The holiday company apologized and gave us a full refund.*

**refund**[2] /ˌriːˈfʌnd/ *verb* [T] to give back money that someone has paid to you

**refurbish** /ˌriːˈfɜːbɪʃ/ *verb* [T] *formal* to repair or improve a building • **refurbishment** *noun* [C, U] the process of refurbishing a building *The library was closed for refurbishment.*

**refusal** /rɪˈfjuːzəl/ *noun* [C, U] when someone refuses to do or accept something [+ to do sth] *his refusal to admit his mistake*

o⸺**refuse**[1] /rɪˈfjuːz/ *verb* [I, T] to say that you will not do or accept something *I asked him to leave but he refused.* • [+ to do sth] *Cathy refuses to admit that she was wrong.*

**refuse**[2] /ˈrefjuːs/ *noun* [U] *formal* waste *a pile of refuse*

**refute** /rɪˈfjuːt/ *verb* [T] *formal* to say or prove that something is not true or correct *attempts to refute his theory* • *She angrily refuted their claims.*

**regain** /rɪˈɡeɪn/ *verb* [T] to get something back again *Armed troops have regained control of the capital.* • *It was several hours before he regained consciousness.*

**regal** /ˈriːɡəl/ *adj* very special and suitable for a king or queen *a regal dress*

**regard**[1] /rɪˈɡɑːd/ *verb* [T] **1** to think of someone or something in a particular way *She is generally regarded as one of the greatest singers this century.* • *The plans were regarded with suspicion.* **2** *formal* to look carefully at someone or something

**regard**[2] /rɪˈɡɑːd/ *noun* **1** [U] respect or admiration for someone or something *I have the greatest regard for her.* ➔ *Opposite* **disregard**. **2 in/with regard to sth** *formal* relating to

R

something *I am writing in regard to your letter of 24 June.*

**regarding** /rɪˈgɑːdɪŋ/ *preposition formal* about or relating to *I am writing to you regarding your application dated 29 April.*

**regardless** /rɪˈgɑːdləs/ *adv* **1 regardless of sth** despite something *She'll make a decision regardless of what we think.* **2** without thinking about problems or difficulties *Mr Redwood claimed he would carry on with his campaign regardless.*

**regards** /rɪˈgɑːdz/ *noun* [plural] friendly greetings *Give/send my regards to your mother when you see her.*

**regeneration** /rɪˌdʒenəˈreɪʃᵊn/ *noun* [U] the process of improving a place or system, especially to make it more active or successful *a programme of urban regeneration* • regenerate /rɪˈdʒenəreɪt/ *verb* [T] to improve a place or system

**reggae** /ˈregeɪ/ *noun* [U] a type of popular music from Jamaica with a strong beat

**regime** /reɪˈʒiːm/ *noun* [C] a system of government or other control, especially one that people do not approve of *the former Communist regime*

**regiment** /ˈredʒɪmənt/ *noun* [group] a large group of soldiers • regimental /ˌredʒɪˈmentᵊl/ *adj* relating to a regiment

**regimented** /ˈredʒɪmentɪd/ *adj* too controlled or organized *a regimented lifestyle*

o─**region** /ˈriːdʒᵊn/ *noun* **1** [C] a particular area in a country or the world *China's coastal region* **2** [C] an area of the body *pain in the lower abdominal region* **3 in the region of sth** approximately *It probably cost somewhere in the region of £900.*

**regional** /ˈriːdʒᵊnᵊl/ *adj* relating to a region (= particular area in a country) *a regional dialect/newspaper*

**register**[1] /ˈredʒɪstəʳ/ *noun* **1** [C] an official list of names *a register of approved builders* • *the electoral register* **2** [C, U] the style of language, grammar, and words used in particular situations *a formal/informal register* ⊃ *See also:* **cash register**.

**register**[2] /ˈredʒɪstəʳ/ *verb* **1** ON A LIST [I, T] to put information about someone or something, especially a name, on an official list *Is he registered with the authorities to sell alcohol?* • *Students need to register for the course by the end of April.* • *a registered nurse* **2** SHOW A FEELING [T] to show an opinion or feeling *People gathered to register their opposition to the plans.* **3** SHOW AMOUNT [I, T] to show an amount on an instrument that measures something *The earthquake registered 7.3 on the Richter scale.*

**registered** /ˈredʒɪstəd/ *adj* **registered mail/post** a special service that records when a letter or parcel is sent and received

ˈ**register ˌoffice** *noun* [C] in Britain, a place where births, deaths, and marriages are officially recorded and where you can get married

**registrar** /ˌredʒɪˈstrɑːʳ/ *noun* [C] **1** someone whose job is to keep official records, especially of births, deaths, and marriages, or of students at a university **2** UK a type of hospital doctor

**registration** /ˌredʒɪˈstreɪʃᵊn/ *noun* **1** [U] when a name or information is recorded on an official list **2** [C] (*also* regis'tration ˌnumber) *mainly UK* the official set of numbers and letters on the front and back of a vehicle *a car with the registration M148 VVH*

**registry** /ˈredʒɪstri/ *noun* [C] a place where official records are kept *the land registry*

ˈ**registry ˌoffice** *noun* [C] in Britain, a place where births, deaths, and marriages are officially recorded and where you can get married

**regress** /rɪˈgres/ *verb* [I] *formal* to go back to an earlier, less advanced state • regression /rɪˈgreʃᵊn/ *noun* [U] *formal* when someone or something regresses

o─**regret**[1] /rɪˈgret/ *verb* [T] **regretting**, *past* **regretted 1** to feel sorry about a situation, especially something that you wish you had not done *If you don't tell her the truth you'll regret it later.* • [+ doing sth] *I really regret leaving school so young.* • [+ (that)] *He began to regret that he hadn't paid more attention in class.* **2** *formal* used to say that you are sorry that you have to tell someone about a situation [+ to do sth] *We regret to inform you that the application has been refused.* • [+ (that)] *The council regrets that the money is no longer available.*

**regret**[2] /rɪˈgret/ *noun* [C, U] a feeling of sadness about a situation, especially something that you wish you had not done *We married very young but we've been really happy and I've no regrets.* • *It is with great regret that I announce Steve Adam's resignation.* • regretful *adj* expressing regret • regretfully *adv*

**regrettable** /rɪˈgretəbl/ *adj* If something is regrettable, you wish it had not happened and you feel sorry about it. *a deeply regrettable incident* • regrettably *adv*

o─**regular**[1] /ˈregjələʳ/ *adj* **1** SAME TIME/SPACE repeated with the same amount of time or space between one thing and the next *a regular pulse* • *Plant the seedlings at regular intervals.* **2** OFTEN happening or doing something often, especially at the same time every week, year, etc *a regular occurrence* • *a regular visitor to Brussels* • *We arranged to meet on a regular basis.* **3** USUAL *US* usual or normal *I couldn't see my regular dentist.* **4** SIZE *informal* being a standard size *a burger and regular fries* **5** SHAPE Something that has a regular shape is the same on both or all sides. *She's got lovely, regular teeth.* **6** GRAMMAR following the usual rules or patterns in grammar *'Talk' is a regular verb but 'go' is not.* ⊃ *Opposite* **irregular**. • regularity /ˌregjəˈlærəti/ *noun* [U] when something is regular

**regular**[2] /ˈregjələʳ/ *noun* [C] *informal* someone who often goes to a particular shop, restaurant, etc *Mick was one of the regulars at the local pub.*

o─**regularly** /ˈregjələli/ *adv* **1** often *Accidents occur regularly on this stretch of the road.* **2** at the same time each day, week, month, etc *They meet regularly – usually once a week.*

**regulate** /ˈregjəleɪt/ *verb* [T] **1** to control an activity or process, especially by using rules *laws regulating advertising* **2** to control the speed, temperature, etc of something *Babies find it difficult to regulate their body temperature.*

**regulation** /,regjə'leɪʃ°n/ noun **1** [C] an official rule that controls how something is done [usually plural] *building regulations* **2** [U] when a process or activity is controlled *government regulation of interest rates*

**regulator** /'regjəleɪtə°/ noun [C] **1** someone whose job is to make sure that a system works in a fair way *the water industry regulator* **2** a piece of equipment that is used to control the temperature, speed, etc of something

**regulatory** /'regjələt°ri/ adj controlling an activity or process, especially by using rules

**rehab** /'ri:hæb/ noun [U] informal treatment to help someone stop drinking too much alcohol or taking drugs *He spent six months in rehab.*
• *a rehab clinic*

**rehabilitate** /,ri:hə'bɪlɪteɪt/ verb [T] to help someone live a normal life again after they have had a serious illness or been in prison *a programme to rehabilitate young offenders*
• rehabilitation /,ri:hə,bɪlɪ'teɪʃ°n/ noun [U]

**rehearsal** /rɪ'hɜːs°l/ noun [C, U] a time when all the people involved in a play, dance, etc practise in order to prepare for a performance

**rehearse** /rɪ'hɜːs/ verb [I, T] to practise a play, dance, etc in order to prepare for a performance

**reign**[1] /reɪn/ noun **1** [C] a period of time when a king or queen rules a country *the reign of Henry VIII* **2** [no plural] a period of time when someone controls a sports team, an organization, etc *Christie's reign as captain of the British athletics team* **3 reign of terror** a period of time when someone uses violence to control people

**reign**[2] /reɪn/ verb [I] **1** to be the king or queen of a country *Queen Victoria reigned for 64 years.* **2** formal to be the main feeling or quality in a situation *Chaos reigned as angry protesters hammered on the doors.*

**,reigning 'champion** noun [C] the most recent winner of a competition

**reimburse** /,ri:ɪm'bɜːs/ verb [T] formal to pay money back to someone, especially money that they have spent because of their work *Employees will no longer be reimbursed for taxi fares.* • reimbursement /,ri:ɪm'bɜːsmənt/ noun [U] formal when you reimburse someone

**rein** /reɪn/ noun **1** [C] a long, thin piece of leather that helps you to control a horse [usually plural] *Hold the reins in your left hand.* ➜ *See colour picture* **Sports 1** *on page Centre 15.* **2 free rein** the freedom to do or say what you want [+ to do sth] *The school gives teachers free rein to try out new teaching methods.* **3 keep a tight rein on sb/sth** to have a lot of control over someone or something *We've been told to keep a tight rein on spending.*

**reincarnation** /,ri:ɪnkɑː'neɪʃ°n/ noun [U] the belief that a dead person's spirit returns to life in another body

**reindeer** /'reɪndɪə°/ noun [C] plural reindeer a type of deer with large horns that lives in northern parts of Europe, Asia, and America

**reinforce** /,ri:ɪn'fɔːs/ verb [T] **1** to make an existing opinion or idea stronger *to reinforce a view/feeling* **2** to make something stronger *a security door reinforced by steel bars* • reinforced

concrete • reinforcement noun [C, U] when you reinforce something

**reinforcements** /,ri:ɪn'fɔːsmənts/ noun [plural] soldiers who are sent to make an army stronger

**reinstate** /,ri:ɪn'steɪt/ verb [T] **1** to give someone the job or position that they had before *He was unfairly dismissed and reinstated two months later.* **2** to cause a rule, law, etc to exist again • reinstatement noun [C, U] when you reinstate someone or something

**reinvent** /,ri:ɪn'vent/ verb **1** [T] to produce something new that is based on something that already exists *The story of Romeo and Juliet was reinvented as a Los Angeles gangster movie.* **2 reinvent yourself** to change the way you look and behave so that you seem very different ➜ *See also:* reinvent the **wheel**[1].

**reiterate** /ri'ɪt°reɪt/ verb [T] formal to say something again so that people take notice of it [+ that] *I must reiterate that we have no intention of signing this contract.* • reiteration /ri,ɪt°r'eɪʃ°n/ noun [C, U]

o━**reject**[1] /rɪ'dʒekt/ verb [T] **1** NOT ACCEPT to refuse to accept or agree with something *The United States government rejected the proposal.* **2** JOB/COURSE to refuse to accept someone for a job, course, etc *I applied to Cambridge University but I was rejected.* **3** PERSON to not give someone the love or attention they were expecting *She felt rejected by her husband.*

**reject**[2] /'ri:dʒekt/ noun [C] a product that is damaged or not perfect in some way

**rejection** /rɪ'dʒekʃ°n/ noun **1** NOT ACCEPT [C, U] when you refuse to accept or agree with something *Their rejection of the peace plan is very disappointing for the government.* **2** JOB/COLLEGE [C] a letter that says you have not been successful in getting a job, a place at college, etc *I've sent off ten applications but I've only had rejections so far.* **3** PERSON [U] when someone does not give someone else the love or attention they were expecting *a feeling of rejection*

**rejoice** /rɪ'dʒɔɪs/ verb [I] literary to feel very happy because something good has happened

**rejoicing** /rɪ'dʒɔɪsɪŋ/ noun [U] when people show that they are very happy because something good has happened

**rejoin** /rɪ'dʒɔɪn/ verb [T] to return to a person or place *I was feeling better, so I rejoined the party.*

**rejuvenate** /rɪ'dʒuːv°neɪt/ verb [T] to make someone look or feel young and energetic again *You're supposed to come back from a holiday feeling rejuvenated.* • rejuvenation /rɪ,dʒuːv°n'eɪʃ°n/ noun [U]

**rekindle** /,ri:'kɪndl/ verb [T] to make someone have a feeling that they had in the past *The trip seemed to rekindle their love for each other.*

**relapse** /rɪ'læps, 'ri:læps/ noun [C, U] **1** when someone becomes ill again after a period of feeling better *I had a relapse last year and was off work for a month.* **2** when something or someone gets worse again after being better *The company's share prices have suffered a relapse this week.* • relapse /rɪ'læps/ verb [I]

**relate** /rɪ'leɪt/ verb **1** [I, T] to be connected, or to find or show the connection between two or

more things *How do the two proposals relate?*
**2** [T] *formal* to tell a story or describe a series of
events

**relate to sb/sth** to be connected to, or to be
about someone or something *Please provide all
information relating to the claim.*

**relate to sb** to understand how someone feels
*Most teenagers find it hard to relate to their
parents.*

o━**related** /rɪ'leɪtɪd/ *adj* **1** connected *There's been
an increase in criminal activity **related to**
drugs.* **2** If two or more people are related, they
belong to the same family. *Did you know that
I'm **related to** Jackie?* ◐ *Opposite* **unrelated**.

o━**relation** /rɪ'leɪʃ³n/ *noun* **1** [C, U] a connection
between two or more things *the relation between
smoking and lung cancer* **2** [C] someone who
belongs to the same family as you *He's called Ken
Russell, no relation to* (= he is not from the same
family as) *the film director.* **3 in relation to sth
a** when compared with something *Salaries are
low in relation to the cost of living.* **b** about or
relating to something *I'd like to ask you something in relation to what you said earlier.*

**relations** /rɪ'leɪʃ³nz/ *noun* [plural] the way two
people or groups feel and behave towards each
other *It was an attempt to restore diplomatic
relations between the two countries.* ◐ *See also:*
**public relations**, **race relations**.

o━**relationship** /rɪ'leɪʃ³nʃɪp/ *noun* **1** BEHAVIOUR
[C] the way two people or groups feel and
behave towards each other *He has a very good
relationship with his older sister.* **2** ROMANTIC
[C] a sexual or romantic friendship *I don't
feel ready for a relationship at the moment.*
**3** CONNECTION [C, U] a connection between two
or more things *the relationship between
sunburn and skin cancer*

**USAGE**

**have a relationship with** someone

Be careful to use the correct preposition in this
expression.

*I have a good relationship with my parents.*

~~I have a good relationship to my parents.~~

o━**relative¹** /'relətɪv/ *noun* [C] a member of your
family *a party for friends and relatives*

**relative²** /'relətɪv/ *adj* **1** [always before noun] compared to other similar things or people *the relative prosperity of the West* **2 relative to sth**
when compared to something else *The economy
has been declining relative to other countries.*

,**relative 'clause** *noun* [C] a part of a sentence
that is used to describe the noun which comes
just before it. In the sentence, 'The woman who
I saw yesterday wasn't his wife.', 'who I saw
yesterday' is a relative clause.

**relatively** /'relətɪvli/ *adv* quite, when compared
to other things or people *Eating out is relatively cheap.* ● *Students will find the course relatively easy.*

,**relative 'pronoun** *noun* [C] a word such as
'that', 'which', or 'who' that is used to begin a
relative clause

o━**relax** /rɪ'læks/ *verb* **1** PERSON [I, T] to become

happy and comfortable because nothing is worrying you, or to make someone do this *I find it
difficult to relax.* ● *The wine had relaxed him
and he began to talk.* **2** LESS STIFF [I, T] If a part
of your body relaxes, it becomes less stiff, and
if you relax it, you make it become less stiff.
*Try these exercises to relax your neck muscles.*
**3** RULES [T] to make laws or rules less severe
*The government has recently relaxed laws on
bringing animals into Britain.* ● relaxation
/ˌriːlæk'seɪʃ³n/ *noun* [U]

o━**relaxed** /rɪ'lækst/ *adj* **1** feeling happy and comfortable because nothing is worrying you *She
seemed relaxed and in control of the situation.*
**2** A relaxed situation is comfortable and informal. *There was a very relaxed atmosphere at the
party.*

**relaxing** /rɪ'læksɪŋ/ *adj* making you feel relaxed
*a relaxing bath*

**relay¹** /ˌriː'leɪ/ *verb* [T] **1** to send a message from
one person to another *Cory had an idea which
he relayed to his friend immediately.* **2** to broadcast radio or television signals

**relay²** /'riːleɪ/ (*also* '**relay ,race**) *noun* [C] a race in
which each member of a team runs or swims
part of the race

o━**release¹** /rɪ'liːs/ *verb* [T] **1** PRISONER to allow a
prisoner to be free *Six hostages were released
shortly before midday.* **2** STOP HOLDING to stop
holding someone or something *Release the
handle.* **3** INFORMATION to let the public have
news or information about something *Police
have not released the dead woman's name.*
**4** RECORD/FILM to make a record or film available for people to buy or see *The album is due to
be released in time for Christmas.* **5** SUBSTANCE
to let a substance flow out from somewhere
*Dangerous chemicals were accidentally released
into the river.*

**release²** /rɪ'liːs/ *noun* **1** FROM PRISON [C] when
someone is allowed to leave prison *After his
release from jail, Jackson found it difficult to
find work.* **2** FILM/RECORD [C] a new film or
record that you can buy *Have you heard the
group's latest release?* **3** SUBSTANCE [C, U] when
a substance is allowed to flow out of somewhere *a release of toxic gas from the factory*
◐ *See also:* **press release**.

**relegate** /'relɪgeɪt/ *verb* [T] to put someone or
something in a less important position [often
passive] *He'd been relegated to the B team.* ● rel-
egation /ˌrelɪ'geɪʃ³n/ *noun* [U]

**relent** /rɪ'lent/ *verb* [I] to allow something that
you refused to allow before *The security guard
relented and let them through.*

**relentless** /rɪ'lentləs/ *adj* never stopping or
getting any less extreme *relentless criticism*
● relentlessly *adv* *He searched for her relentlessly.*

**relevance** /'reləvəns/ (*also US* **relevancy**
/'reləvəntsi/) *noun* [U] the degree to which something is related or useful to what is happening
or being talked about *This point has no relevance to the discussion.*

**relevant** /'reləvənt/ *adj* related or useful to what
is happening or being talked about *relevant
information* ● *Education should be relevant to
children's needs.* ◐ *Opposite* **irrelevant**.

**R**

**reliable** /rɪˈlaɪəbl/ *adj* able to be trusted or believed *a reliable car* • *reliable information* • *Andy's very reliable – if he says he'll do something, he'll do it.* ➔ *Opposite* **unreliable**. • reliability /rɪˌlaɪəˈbɪləti/ *noun* [U] how reliable someone or something is *I'm not sure about the reliability of those statistics.* • **reliably** *adv I am reliably informed that the concert has been cancelled.*

**reliance** /rɪˈlaɪəns/ *noun* **reliance on sb/sth** when someone or something depends on someone or something else *our increasing reliance on computers*

**reliant** /rɪˈlaɪənt/ *adj* **be reliant on sb/sth** to depend on someone or something *I don't want to be reliant on anybody.* ➔ *See also:* **self-reliant**.

**relic** /ˈrelɪk/ *noun* [C] a very old thing from the past *an Egyptian relic*

**relief** /rɪˈliːf/ *noun* **1** EMOTION [U, no plural] the good feeling that you have when something unpleasant stops or does not happen *It'll be such a relief when these exams are over.* • *"James can't come tonight." "Well, that's a relief!"* **2** HELP [U] money, food, or clothes that are given to people because they need help *an international relief operation* **3** PHYSICAL FEELING [U] when something stops hurting you *I'd been trying to sleep to find relief from the pain.*

**relieve** /rɪˈliːv/ *verb* [T] **1** to make pain or a bad feeling less severe *Breathing exercises can help to relieve stress.* **2** to allow someone to stop working by taking their place *The 7 a.m. team arrived to relieve the night workers.*
**relieve sb of sth** *formal* to take something away from someone *Let me relieve you of your luggage.*

**relieved** /rɪˈliːvd/ *adj* feeling happy because something unpleasant did not happen or you are not worried about something any more [+ (that)] *I'm just relieved that she's safe and well.* • [+ to do sth] *I heard a noise and was relieved to find that it was only a cat.*

**religion** /rɪˈlɪdʒən/ *noun* [C, U] the belief in a god or gods, or a particular system of belief in a god or gods *the Christian religion*

**religious** /rɪˈlɪdʒəs/ *adj* **1** relating to religion *religious paintings* **2** having a strong belief in a religion *He's a very religious man.*

**religiously** /rɪˈlɪdʒəsli/ *adv* **1** regularly *He visited the old woman religiously every weekend.* **2** in a religious way

**relinquish** /rɪˈlɪŋkwɪʃ/ *verb* [T] *formal* to allow something to be taken away from you *At 80 he still refuses to relinquish control of the company.*

**relish**[1] /ˈrelɪʃ/ *verb* [T] to enjoy something *I don't relish the thought of a twelve-hour flight.*

**relish**[2] /ˈrelɪʃ/ *noun* **1** [U] enjoyment *He had baked a cake which the children now ate with relish.* **2** [C] a sauce that you put on your food to give it more taste

**relive** /ˌriːˈlɪv/ *verb* [T] to remember something so clearly that you feel as if it is happening now

**relocate** /ˌriːləʊˈkeɪt/ US /riːˈləʊˌkeɪt/ *verb* [I, T] to move to another place *The company relocated to Tokyo.* • relocation /ˌriːləʊˈkeɪʃən/ *noun* [U] *relocation costs*

**reluctant** /rɪˈlʌktənt/ *adj* not wanting to do something [+ to do sth] *Many victims of crime are reluctant to go to the police.* • reluctance /rɪˈlʌktəns/ *noun* [U] when someone does not want to do something [+ to do sth] *a reluctance to accept changes* • **reluctantly** *adv*

**rely** /rɪˈlaɪ/ *verb*
**rely on sb/sth 1** to need someone or something in order to be successful, work correctly, etc *Families rely more on wives' earnings than before.* **2** to trust someone or something [+ to do sth] *I know I can rely on you to help me.*

**remain** /rɪˈmeɪn/ *verb* **1** [I] to continue to exist when everything or everyone else has gone *Only a few hundred of these animals remain today.* ➔ *See usage note at* **rest**. **2 remain calm/open, etc; remain a secret/mystery/ prisoner, etc** to continue to be in the same state *Despite the chaos around him, he remained calm.* • *The exact date of the wedding remains a secret.* **3 remain at/in/with, etc** *formal* to stay in the same place *She will remain at her mother's until I return.*

**the remainder** /rɪˈmeɪndər/ *noun* the things or people that are left when everything or everyone else has gone or been dealt with *He drank the remainder of his coffee and got up to leave.*

**remaining** /rɪˈmeɪnɪŋ/ *adj* [always before noun] continuing to exist when everything or everyone else has gone or been dealt with *Mix in half the butter and keep the remaining 50g for later.*

**remains** /rɪˈmeɪnz/ *noun* [plural] **1** the parts of something, especially a building, that continue to exist when the rest of it has been destroyed *the remains of a Buddhist temple* **2** *formal* someone's body after they have died *Three months after he disappeared, his remains were found in a cave.*

**remake** /ˈriːmeɪk/ *noun* [C] a film that is the same as one that has been made before *a remake of 'King Kong'* • remake /ˌriːˈmeɪk/ *verb* [T] *past* **remade**

**remand**[1] /rɪˈmɑːnd/ *noun* **on remand** UK in prison before your trial (= when a law court decides if you are guilty or not) *He spent two weeks on remand in Bullingdon prison.*

**remand**[2] /rɪˈmɑːnd/ *verb* **be remanded in custody** UK to be kept in prison on remand *He was charged with murder and remanded in custody.*

**remark**[1] /rɪˈmɑːk/ *noun* [C] something that you say *He made a remark about her clothes.*

**remark**[2] /rɪˈmɑːk/ *verb* [I] to say something [+ that] *He remarked that she was looking thin.*
**remark on/upon sth** to say something about something that you have just noticed *He remarked on how well you were looking.*

**remarkable** /rɪˈmɑːkəbl/ *adj* very unusual or noticeable in a way that you admire *a remarkable woman* • *He has a remarkable memory.* ➔ *Opposite* **unremarkable**.

**remarkably** /rɪˈmɑːkəbli/ *adv* in a way that makes you feel surprised *She has remarkably good skin for her age.*

**remarry** /ˌriːˈmæri/ *verb* [I] to get married again *His wife died in 1970 and he never remarried.*

**remedial** /rɪˈmiːdiəl/ *adj* [always before noun] **1** intended to help people who are having difficulty learning something *remedial English classes* **2** *formal* intended to improve something *Remedial action is needed.*

**remedy**[1] /'remədi/ *noun* [C] **1** something that makes you better when you are ill *a flu remedy* **2** something that solves a problem *The remedy for the traffic problem is to encourage people to use public transport.*

**remedy**[2] /'remədi/ *verb* [T] to solve a problem, or to improve a bad situation *They were able to remedy the problem very easily.*

o‑**remember** /rɪ'membər/ *verb* [I, T] **1** If you remember a fact or something from the past, you keep it in your mind, or bring it back into your mind. *I can't remember his name.* • [+ doing sth] *I don't remember signing a contract.* • [+ (that)] *Just as the door closed he remembered that his keys were inside the room.* **2** to not forget to do something [+ to do sth] *I must remember to send Carol a birthday card.*

### USAGE

**remember** or **memory**?

Remember is a verb. Use remember when you think about or bring thoughts into your mind about a person, place, or event from the past.

*I can remember when I was at school.*

Memory is a noun. Use memory to talk about the person, place, or event from the past that you think about.

*I have good memories of when I was at school.*

**remembrance** /rɪ'membrəns/ *noun* [U] when you remember and show respect for someone who has died *They erected a statue in remembrance of him.*

o‑**remind** /rɪ'maɪnd/ *verb* [T] to make someone remember something, or remember to do something *Every time we meet he reminds me about the money he lent me.* • [+ to do sth] *Will you remind me to buy some eggs?*

### USAGE

**remind** or **remember**?

If you remember a fact or something from the past, you keep it in your mind, or bring it back into your mind.

*I can't remember the name of the film.*

*Did you remember to bring your passport?*

When you remind someone to do something, you make them remember it.

*Can you remind me to phone Anna tomorrow?*

~~Can you remember me to phone Anna tomorrow?~~

**remind sb of sth/sb** to make someone think of something or someone else *Harry reminds me of my father.* • *This song reminds me of our trip to Spain.*

**reminder** /rɪ'maɪndər/ *noun* [C] something that makes you remember something else *For me, ice cream is a reminder of happy childhood holidays at the seaside.*

**reminisce** /,remɪ'nɪs/ *verb* [I] to talk about pleasant things that happened in the past *We were just reminiscing about our school days.* • remi-

niscence *noun* [C, U] when you reminisce

**reminiscent** /,remɪ'nɪsᵊnt/ *adj* **reminiscent of sth/sb** making you think of someone or something that is similar *a smell reminiscent of an old church*

**remission** /rɪ'mɪʃᵊn/ *noun* **be in remission** to be in a period of time when a serious illness is better *He is in remission at the moment.* • *The disease seems to be in remission.*

**remit**[1] /'ri:mɪt/ *noun* [no plural] *UK* the things that you are responsible for in your job

**remit**[2] /rɪ'mɪt/ *verb* [T] **remitting**, *past* **remitted** *formal* to send money to someone

**remnant** /'remnənt/ *noun* [C] a piece of something that continues to exist when the rest of that thing has gone *the remnants of last night's meal*

**remorse** /rɪ'mɔːs/ *noun* [U] the feeling that you are sorry for something bad that you have done *He has shown no remorse for his actions.* • remorseful *adj* feeling remorse

**remorseless** /rɪ'mɔːsləs/ *adj* **1** *UK* never stopping *remorseless pressure to succeed* **2** cruel • remorselessly *adv*

**remote** /rɪ'məʊt/ *adj* **1** PLACE far away *It was a remote mountain village with no electricity supply.* • *His voice sounded remote.* **2** TIME far in time *in the remote past* **3** SLIGHT slight *There is a remote possibility that it could be cancer.* • remoteness *noun* [U]

**re,mote con'trol** *noun* **1** [C] (*also* **remote**) a piece of equipment that is used to control something such as a television from a distance ➲ See colour picture **The Living Room** on page Centre 11. **2** [U] the use of radio waves to control something such as a television from a distance

**remotely** /rɪ'məʊtli/ *adv* **not remotely interested/surprised/possible, etc** not at all interested, surprised, etc *I'm not remotely interested in football.*

**removal** /rɪ'muːvᵊl/ *noun* **1** [U] when you remove something *stain removal* **2** [C, U] *UK* when you remove everything from one house to take to another *a removals firm*

o‑**remove** /rɪ'muːv/ *verb* [T] **1** TAKE AWAY to take something away *An operation was needed to remove the bullets from his chest.* **2** TAKE OFF to take something off *Liz removed her jacket and hung it on a chair.* • *Carefully remove the lid, then stir the paint.* **3** JOB *formal* to make someone stop doing their job [often passive] *He had been removed from his job on medical grounds.* **4 be far removed from sth** to be very different from something *The princess's world was far removed from reality.*

**remuneration** /rɪ,mjuːnᵊr'eɪʃᵊn/ *noun* [U] *formal* when someone is paid for work they have done

**the Renaissance** /rə'neɪsᵊns (US) ,renə'sɑːns/ *noun* the period during the 14th, 15th, and 16th centuries in Europe when there was a lot of interest and activity in art, literature, ideas, etc

**renaissance** /rə'neɪsᵊns (US) ,renə'sɑːns/ *noun* [no plural] a time when something becomes popular or fashionable again *The British film industry* *is enjoying a renaissance.*

**rename** /ˌriːˈneɪm/ *verb* [T] to give something a new name [+ **two objects**] *Siam was renamed Thailand in 1939.*

**render** /ˈrendəʳ/ *verb* [T] *formal* **1** to cause something or someone to be in a particular state or condition *The trees rendered the road as dark as a tunnel.* • *She was rendered speechless upon hearing the news.* **2** to give someone a decision, opinion, help, etc *payment for services rendered*

**rendering** /ˈrendᵊrɪŋ/ *noun* [C] the way that something is performed, written, drawn, etc *a child's rendering of a house*

**rendezvous** /ˈrɒndɪvuː/ *noun* [C] *plural* **rendezvous** an arrangement to meet someone, or the place you have arranged to meet them • rendezvous *verb* [I]

**rendition** /renˈdɪʃᵊn/ *noun* [C] the way in which a song, piece of music, etc is performed

**renegade** /ˈrenɪɡeɪd/ *noun* [C] someone who changes and joins a group that is against their own group *a group of renegade soldiers*

**renege** /rəˈneɪɡ/ (US) rəˈnɪɡ/ *verb*
**renege on sth** *formal* to not do what you said you were going to do *to renege on a promise/agreement*

**renew** /rɪˈnjuː/ *verb* [T] **1** OFFICIAL AGREEMENT to arrange to continue an official agreement that was going to end soon *I've decided not to renew my golf club membership this year.* **2** BUY UK to get a new one of something that is old *A car isn't the sort of thing you renew every year.* **3** DO AGAIN to start to do something again *The next morning enemy war planes renewed their bombing.* • renewal *noun* [C, U] when you renew something

**renewable** /rɪˈnjuːəbl/ *adj* **1** A renewable form of energy can be produced as quickly as it is used. *a renewable energy source such as wind power* **2** A renewable official agreement is one that you can arrange to continue when the time limit is reached. *a 6-month renewable contract*

**renewed** /rɪˈnjuːd/ *adj* starting again in a stronger way than before *He sang now with renewed confidence.*

**renounce** /rɪˈnaʊns/ *verb* [T] to officially say that you do not have the right to something any more, or that you do not want to be involved in something any more *They had renounced all rights to ownership of the land.*

**renovate** /ˈrenəveɪt/ *verb* [T] to repair and decorate a building that is old and in bad condition • renovation /ˌrenəˈveɪʃᵊn/ *noun* [C, U]

**renowned** /rɪˈnaʊnd/ *adj* famous *The Lake District is **renowned for** its beauty.*

o──**rent¹** /rent/ *verb* **1** HOME [I, T] to pay money to live in a building that someone else owns *He'll be renting an apartment until he can find a house to buy.* **2** PAY TO USE [T] *US* (*UK* **hire**) to pay money to use something for a short time *We could rent a car for the weekend.* **3** RECEIVE MONEY [T] (*also* **rent out**) to allow someone to pay you money to live in your building *I rented out my house and went travelling for a year.*

**USAGE**

**rent** and **hire**

In British English you **rent** something for a long time.

*I rent a 2-bedroom flat.*

In British English you **hire** something for a short time.

*We hired a car for the weekend.*

In American English the word **rent** is used in both situations.

*I rent a 2-bedroom apartment.*

*We rented a car for the weekend.*

**rent²** /rent/ *noun* [C, U] the amount of money that you pay to live in a building that someone else owns *They couldn't afford the rent.*

**rental** /ˈrentᵊl/ *noun* [C, U] an arrangement to rent something, or the amount of money that you pay to rent something • *The price includes flights and car rental.* • *Skate rental costs $3.25.*

**renter** /ˈrentəʳ/ *noun* [C] *US* someone who pays money to live in a house or an apartment that someone else owns

**renunciation** /rɪˌnʌnsiˈeɪʃᵊn/ *noun* [U, no plural] when you say that you do not want something or believe in something any more *a renunciation of violence*

**reorganize** (*also* UK **-ise**) /ˌriːˈɔːɡənaɪz/ *verb* [I, T] to organize something again in order to improve it *He's completely reorganized his schedule for the week.* • reorganization /riːˌɔːɡʳnaɪˈzeɪʃᵊn/ *noun* [C, U]

**rep** /rep/ *noun* [C] *informal* someone whose job is to sell things for a company *the UK sales rep*

**repaid** /ˌriːˈpeɪd/ *past of* repay

o──**repair¹** /rɪˈpeəʳ/ *verb* [T] **1** to fix something that is broken or damaged *I must **get my bike repaired**.* **2** to improve a bad situation *It will take a long time to repair relations between the two countries.*

**repair²** /rɪˈpeəʳ/ *noun* **1** [C, U] something that you do to fix something that is broken or damaged [usually plural] *The repairs cost me £150.* **2 be in good/bad repair** to be in good/bad condition *Most of the building is in very bad repair.*

**repatriate** /riːˈpætrieɪt/ (US) riːˈpeɪtrieɪt/ *verb* [T] to send someone back to their own country • repatriation /ˌriːpætriˈeɪʃᵊn/ (US) riːˌpeɪtriˈeɪʃᵊn/ *noun* [U]

**repay** /ˌriːˈpeɪ/ *verb* [T] *past* **repaid 1** to pay back money that you have borrowed *to repay a loan* **2** to do something kind for someone who has done something to help you *What can I do to repay you for your kindness?* • repayment /rɪˈpeɪmənt/ *noun* [C, U] when you repay someone or the money that you pay back

**repeal** /rɪˈpiːl/ *verb* [T] to officially make a law end

o──**repeat¹** /rɪˈpiːt/ *verb* [T] **1** to say or do something more than once *He repeated the number.* • *The test must be repeated several times.* • *"I don't know!" he repeated.* **2** to tell someone something that someone else has told you *I've got some news for you but you mustn't **repeat** it **to** anyone.*

**repeat**² /rɪˈpiːt/ *noun* **1** [no plural] when something happens or is done more than once *Everything is being done to avoid a repeat of the tragedy.* **2** [C] *UK* (*US* **rerun**) a television or radio programme that is broadcast again

**repeated** /rɪˈpiːtɪd/ *adj* [always before noun] done or happening more than once *He has refused repeated requests to be interviewed.* • **repeatedly** *adv The victim was stabbed repeatedly with a knife.*

**repel** /rɪˈpel/ *verb* [T] **repelling**, *past* **repelled 1** to make someone or something move away or stop attacking you *a smell that repels insects* **2** If someone or something repels you, they think they are extremely unpleasant.

**repellent**¹ /rɪˈpelənt/ *adj* extremely unpleasant *I find his views utterly repellent.*

**repellent**² /rɪˈpelənt/ *noun* [C, U] **insect/mosquito repellent** a substance that you use to keep insects away

**repent** /rɪˈpent/ *verb* [I, T] *formal* to say that you are sorry for doing something bad • **repentance** *noun* [U] *formal* when someone repents

**repentant** /rɪˈpentənt/ *adj formal* feeling sorry about something bad that you have done ➌ *Opposite* **unrepentant.**

**repercussions** /ˌriːpəˈkʌʃ³nz/ *noun* [plural] the effects that an action or event has on something, especially bad effects *Any decrease in tourism could have serious repercussions for the local economy.*

**repertoire** /ˈrepətwɑː/ *noun* [C] all the songs, plays, etc that someone can perform

**repertory** /ˈrepət³ri/ *noun* **1** [C, U] when a group of actors performs several different plays during a period of time *They have four plays in repertory this season.* • *a repertory company/theatre* **2** [C] all the songs, plays, etc that someone can perform

**repetition** /ˌrepɪˈtɪʃ³n/ *noun* [C, U] when something is repeated *We don't want a repetition of last year's disaster.*

**repetitive** /rɪˈpetətɪv/ (*also* **repetitious** /ˌrepɪˈtɪʃəs/) *adj* doing or saying the same thing several times, especially in a way that is boring *a repetitive job* • **repetitively** *adv*

o⁻**replace** /rɪˈpleɪs/ *verb* [T] **1** USE INSTEAD to start using another thing or person instead of the one that you are using now *We're thinking of replacing our old TV with a fancy new one.* **2** BE USED INSTEAD to start to be used instead of the thing or person that is being used now *This system will replace the old one.* **3** GET SOMETHING NEW to get something new because the one you had before has been lost or damaged *We'll have to replace this carpet soon.* **4** PUT BACK *formal* to put something back in the place where it usually is *She picked up the books and carefully replaced them on the shelf.*

**replacement** /rɪˈpleɪsmənt/ *noun* **1** [C] the thing or person that replaces something or someone *It's not going to be easy to find a replacement for you.* **2** [U] when something or someone is replaced

**replay** /ˈriːpleɪ/ *noun* [C] **1** an important part of a sports game or other event on television that is shown again immediately after it has happened **2** *UK* a game of sport that is played

again • **replay** /ˌriːˈpleɪ/ *verb* [T] ➌ *See also:* **action replay** *UK*, **instant replay** *US*.

**replenish** /rɪˈplenɪʃ/ *verb* [T] *formal* to fill something or make it complete again *to replenish supplies* • **replenishment** *noun* [U] *formal* when you fill something or make it complete again

**replica** /ˈreplɪkə/ *noun* [C] something that is made to look almost exactly the same as something else *a replica of the White House*

**replicate** /ˈreplɪkeɪt/ *verb* [T] *formal* to make or do something again in exactly the same way • **replication** /ˌreplɪˈkeɪʃ³n/ *noun* [C, U]

o⁻**reply**¹ /rɪˈplaɪ/ *verb* [I, T] to answer *"I don't understand," she replied.* • *He didn't reply to my e-mail.* • [+ that] *Henry replied that he had no idea what I was talking about.*

o⁻**reply**² /rɪˈplaɪ/ *noun* [C, U] an answer *Her reply was short and unfriendly.* • *Have you had a reply to your letter?* • *She sent me an e-mail in reply* (= as an answer).

o⁻**report**¹ /rɪˈpɔːt/ *noun* [C] **1** a description of an event or situation *a police report* • *an annual report on the economy* **2** *UK* (*US* **re′port ,card**) when teachers write about a child's progress at school for their parents

o⁻**report**² /rɪˈpɔːt/ *verb* **1** DESCRIBE [I, T] to describe a recent event or situation, especially on television, radio, or in a newspaper *Jo Smith reports on recent developments.* • [+ that] *She reported that the situation had changed dramatically.* • [+ doing sth] *A woman outside the shop reported seeing the gun.* **2** TELL [T] to tell someone in authority that something has happened, especially an accident or crime *He should have reported the accident immediately.* • *Have you reported the fault to a technician?* **3** COMPLAIN [T] to complain about someone's behaviour to someone in authority. *I'm going to report him to the police.* • *Duncan's been reported for smoking.*

**report to sb/sth** to go to someone or a place and say that you have arrived *All visitors please report to reception.*

**reportedly** /rɪˈpɔːtɪdli/ *adv* If something has reportedly happened or is reportedly a fact, people say it has happened or is true. *Two students were reportedly killed and several wounded.*

**re,ported 'speech** *noun* [U] speech or writing that is used to report what someone has said, but not using exactly the same words

**reporter** /rɪˈpɔːtə/ *noun* [C] someone whose job is to discover information about news events and describe them on television, radio, or in a newspaper

**repossess** /ˌriːpəˈzes/ *verb* [T] to take back someone's house, car, furniture, etc because they cannot finish paying for them • **repossession** /ˌriːpəˈzeʃ³n/ *noun* [C, U] when someone repossesses something, or the thing that is repossessed

**reprehensible** /ˌreprɪˈhensəbl/ *adj formal* Reprehensible behaviour is extremely bad.

o⁻**represent** /ˌreprɪˈzent/ *verb* [T] **1** BE to be equal to something *In practice the figure represents a 10% pay cut.* • *The cancellation of the new road project represents a victory for protesters.* **2** SPEAK FOR to officially speak or do something for someone else because they have asked you to *The union represents over 200 employees.* **3** [COMPETITION] to be the person from a country, school, etc that is in a competition **4** [SIGN] to be a sign or symbol of something *The crosses on the map represent churches.* **5** [SHOW] to show someone or something in a particular way

**representation** /ˌreprɪzenˈteɪʃ³n/ *noun* **1** [U] speaking or doing something officially for another person *Can he afford legal representation?* **2** [C, U] the way someone or something is shown *an accurate representation of country life* ➔ *See also:* **proportional representation**.

**representative¹** /ˌreprɪˈzentətɪv/ *noun* [C] someone who speaks or does something officially for another person ➔ *See also:* **House of Representatives**.

**representative²** /ˌreprɪˈzentətɪv/ *adj* the same as other people or things in a particular group *Are his views representative of the rest of the department?*

**repress** /rɪˈpres/ *verb* [T] **1** to stop yourself from showing your true feelings *Brigitta repressed a sudden desire to cry.* **2** to control what people do, especially by using force ● repression /rɪˈpreʃ³n/ *noun* [U] when you repress someone or something

**repressed** /rɪˈprest/ *adj* **1** unable to show your true feelings and emotions *a lonely, repressed man* **2** A repressed feeling or emotion is one that you do not show. *repressed anger*

**repressive** /rɪˈpresɪv/ *adj* cruel and not allowing people to have freedom *a repressive military regime*

**reprieve** /rɪˈpriːv/ *noun* [C] **1** an official order that stops a prisoner from being killed as a punishment **2** when something happens to stop a bad situation ● reprieve *verb* [T]

**reprimand** /ˈreprɪmɑːnd/ *verb* [T] to tell someone in an official way that they have done something wrong [+ for + doing sth] *Watts has already been reprimanded for disclosing confidential information.* ● reprimand *noun* [C]

**reprisal** /rɪˈpraɪz³l/ *noun* [C, U] something violent or unpleasant that is done to punish an enemy for something they have done *The attack was in reprisal for police raids.* ● *He did not wish to be filmed because he feared reprisals.*

**reproach¹** /rɪˈprəʊtʃ/ *noun* [C, U] criticism of someone, especially for not being successful or not doing what is expected *There was a hint of reproach in his voice.* ● *The article gave the impression that the teachers were above/beyond reproach* (= could not be criticized). ● reproachful *adj* showing criticism *a reproachful look* ● reproachfully *adv*

**reproach²** /rɪˈprəʊtʃ/ *verb* [T] to criticize someone for not being successful or not doing what is expected [often reflexive] *You've no reason to reproach yourself.*

**reproduce** /ˌriːprəˈdjuːs/ *verb* **1** [T] to make a copy of something *The diagram is reproduced by permission of the original author.* **2** [I] *formal* If people, animals, or plants reproduce, they produce babies or young animals or plants.

**reproduction** /ˌriːprəˈdʌkʃ³n/ *noun* **1** [U] the process of producing babies or young animals and plants **2** [C] a copy of something, especially a painting

**reproductive** /ˌriːprəˈdʌktɪv/ *adj* [always before noun] relating to the process of producing babies or young animals and plants *the reproductive organs*

**reptile** /ˈreptaɪl/ *noun* [C] an animal whose body is covered with scales (= pieces of hard skin), and whose blood changes temperature, for example a snake ● reptilian /repˈtɪliən/ *adj* like a reptile, or relating to reptiles

**republic** /rɪˈpʌblɪk/ *noun* [C] a country with no king or queen but with an elected government *France is a republic.*

**republican** /rɪˈpʌblɪkən/ *noun* [C] **1** someone who supports the principles of a republic **2** **Republican** someone who supports the Republican Party in the US *the Republican candidate* ● republican *adj* relating to a republic *a republican government*

**the Republican Party** *noun* [group] one of the two main political parties in the US

**repudiate** /rɪˈpjuːdieɪt/ *verb* [T] *formal* to refuse to accept or agree with something *Cousteau repudiated all criticism.* ● repudiation /rɪˌpjuːdiˈeɪʃ³n/ *noun* [U] *formal*

**repugnant** /rɪˈpʌɡnənt/ *adj* *formal* extremely unpleasant *She thought the idea morally repugnant.* ● repugnance /rɪˈpʌɡnəns/ *noun* [U] *formal* when something or someone is repugnant

**repulse** /rɪˈpʌls/ *verb* [T] **1** If someone or something repulses you, you think they are extremely unpleasant. *The smell of him repulsed her.* **2** to successfully stop a military attack [often passive] *The enemy attack was quickly repulsed.*

**repulsion** /rɪˈpʌlʃ³n/ *noun* [U, no plural] a strong feeling that someone or something is extremely unpleasant

**repulsive** /rɪˈpʌlsɪv/ *adj* extremely unpleasant, especially to look at *a repulsive man with long, greasy hair*

**reputable** /ˈrepjətəbl/ *adj* known to be good and honest *a reputable organization*

o-m **reputation** /ˌrepjəˈteɪʃ³n/ *noun* [C] the opinion that people have about someone or something based on their behaviour or character in the past *Both hotels have a good reputation.* ● *He has a reputation for efficiency.*

**reputed** /rɪˈpjuːtɪd/ *adj* *formal* believed by most people to be true *She earns a reputed one million dollars a year.* ● [+ to do sth] *The ghost of a young woman is reputed to haunt the building.* ● reputedly *adv*

**request¹** /rɪˈkwest/ *noun* [C, U] when you politely or officially ask for something *His doctor made an urgent request for a copy of the report.* ● *An application form is available on request* (= if you ask for it). ● *A clause was added to the contract at his request* (= because he asked).

**request²** /rɪˈkwest/ *verb* [T] to politely or officially ask for something *We've requested a further two computers.* ● [+ that] *They requested that no photographs be taken in the church.*

**requiem** /ˈrekwiəm/ *noun* [C] a Christian ceremony where people pray for someone who has died, or a piece of music written for this ceremony

○━**require** /rɪ'kwaɪəʳ/ *verb* [T] **1** to need or demand something *Training to be a doctor requires a lot of hard work.* ● [+ that] *A recent law requires that all programmes are censored.* **2 require sb to do sth** to officially demand that someone does something [often passive] *You are required by law to produce a valid passport.*

---

**USAGE**

**require** or **request**?

The main meaning of **require** is 'need'.

*Learning a language requires time and effort.*

**Request** means 'ask for'.

*I wrote a letter to request more information.*

~~I wrote a letter to require more information.~~

---

**requirement** /rɪ'kwaɪəmənt/ *noun* [C] something that is needed or demanded *college entrance requirements* ● *Valid insurance is a legal requirement.*

**requisite** /'rekwɪzɪt/ *adj* [always before noun] *formal* needed for a particular purpose *I felt that he lacked the requisite skills for the job.*

**rerun** /'riːrʌn/ *US* (*UK* **repeat**) *noun* [C] a television or radio programme or film that is broadcast again

○━**rescue**[1] /'reskjuː/ *verb* [T] **rescuing**, *past* **rescued** to save someone from a dangerous or unpleasant situation *Fifty passengers had to be rescued from a sinking ship.* ● **rescuer** *noun* [C]

**rescue**[2] /'reskjuː/ *noun* **1** [C, U] when someone is saved from a dangerous or unpleasant situation *an unsuccessful rescue attempt* **2 come to the/sb's rescue** to help someone who is in a difficult situation *I forgot my purse but Anna came to the rescue and lent me some money.*

○━**research**[1] /rɪ'sɜːtʃ/ *noun* [U] when someone studies a subject in detail in order to discover new information *research into language development* ● *They are doing research into the effects of passive smoking.* ● *a research project* ⊃ *See also:* **market research**.

**research**[2] /rɪ'sɜːtʃ/ *verb* [I, T] to study a subject in detail in order to discover new information about it *He spent several years researching a rare African dialect.* ● **researcher** *noun* [C]

**resemblance** /rɪ'zembləns/ *noun* [C, U] a similarity between two people or things, especially in their appearance *There's a striking resemblance between Diane and her mother.* ● *He bears a resemblance to* (= looks like) *someone I used to know.*

**resemble** /rɪ'zembl/ *verb* [T] to look like or be like someone or something *She resembles her father.*

**resent** /rɪ'zent/ *verb* [T] to feel angry and upset about a situation or about something that someone has done [+ doing sth] *I resent having to work late.* ● *He resents the fact that she gets more money than he does.*

**resentful** /rɪ'zentfʰl/ *adj* angry and upset about a situation that you think is unfair *He was bit-*

terly *resentful of his brother's success.* ● resentfully *adv* ● resentfulness *noun* [U]

**resentment** /rɪ'zentmənt/ *noun* [U] a feeling of anger about a situation that you think is unfair

**reservation** /ˌrezə'veɪʃʰn/ *noun* **1** [C] an arrangement that you make to have a seat on an aircraft, a room in a hotel, etc *I'd like to make a reservation for Friday evening.* **2** [C, U] a doubt or a feeling that you do not agree with something completely *I still have reservations about her ability to do the job.*

**reserve**[1] /rɪ'zɜːv/ *verb* [T] **1** to arrange to have a seat on an aircraft, a room in a hotel, etc *I'd like to reserve two seats on the 9:15 to Birmingham.* **2** to not allow people to use something because it is only for a particular person or for a particular purpose *This seat is reserved for elderly or disabled passengers.*

**reserve**[2] /rɪ'zɜːv/ *noun* **1** SUPPLY [C] a supply of something that you keep until it is needed *emergency cash reserves* **2 in reserve** ready to be used if you need it *I always keep a little money in reserve.* **3** QUALITY [U] when someone does not show what they are thinking or feeling **4** SPORT [C] in sport, an extra player who is ready to play if one of the other players has an injury **5** AREA [C] an area of land where animals and plants are protected ⊃ *See also:* **nature reserve**.

**reserved** /rɪ'zɜːvd/ *adj* not wanting to show what you are thinking or feeling *a quiet, reserved woman*

**reservoir** /'rezəvwɑːʳ/ *noun* [C] an artificial lake where water is stored before it goes to people's houses

**reshuffle** /ˌriː'ʃʌfl/ *noun* [C] when people in an organization, especially a government are given different jobs to do *a government reshuffle* ● **reshuffle** *verb* [T]

**reside** /rɪ'zaɪd/ *verb* formal **reside in/with, etc** to live somewhere *My sister currently resides in Seattle.*

**residence** /'rezɪdʰns/ *noun* formal **1** [C] a building where someone lives *the Queen's official residence* **2** [U] when someone lives somewhere *He took up residence* (= started to live) *in St. Louis.* **3 in residence** living or working somewhere *He was writer in residence with a professional theatre company.* ⊃ *See also:* **hall of residence**.

**resident**[1] /'rezɪdʰnt/ *noun* [C] **1** someone who lives in a particular place *complaints from local residents* **2** *US* a doctor who is working in a hospital to get extra training in a particular area of medicine

**resident**[2] /'rezɪdʰnt/ *adj* living in a place *She has been resident in Britain for most of her life.*

**residential** /ˌrezɪ'denʃʰl/ *adj* **1** A residential area has only houses and not offices or factories. **2** *UK* A residential job or course is one where you live at the same place as you work or study.

**residual** /rɪ'zɪdjuəl/ *adj* remaining after most of something has gone *residual guilt*

**residue** /'rezɪdjuː/ *noun* [C] something that remains after most of a substance has gone or been removed *The machine sucks up the water but leaves a muddy residue.*

**resign** /rɪ'zaɪn/ *verb* [I, T] to officially tell your employer that you are leaving your job *She*

R

**resigned as** headteacher. • Mr Aitken has **resigned from** the company.

**resign yourself to sth** to make yourself accept something that you do not like because you cannot easily change it He resigned himself to living alone.

resignation /ˌrezɪgˈneɪʃ°n/ noun **1** [C, U] when someone tells their employer that they are leaving their job a letter of resignation • I **handed in my resignation** yesterday. **2** [U] when you accept something that you do not like because you cannot easily change it

resilient /rɪˈzɪliənt/ adj strong enough to get better quickly after damage, illness, shock, etc Growth figures show that the economy is still fairly resilient. • resilience /rɪˈzɪliəns/ noun [U]

resin /ˈrezɪn/ noun [C, U] **1** a thick, sticky substance that is produced by some trees **2** a substance that is used for making plastics

resist /rɪˈzɪst/ verb [I, T] **1** AVOID to stop yourself from doing something that you want to do I can't resist chocolate. • [+ doing sth] I just can't resist reading other people's mail. **2** NOT ACCEPT to refuse to accept something and try to stop it from happening The President is resisting calls for him to resign. **3** FIGHT to fight against someone or something that is attacking you British troops resisted the attack for two days.

resistance /rɪˈzɪst°ns/ noun [U, no plural] **1** DISAGREE when people disagree with a change, idea, etc and refuse to accept it resistance to political change **2** FIGHT when someone fights against someone who is attacking them She didn't **put up** much **resistance** (= fight). **3** ILLNESS the ability of your body to not be affected by illnesses Cold weather may lower the body's **resistance to** infection.

resistant /rɪˈzɪst°nt/ adj **1** not wanting to accept something, especially changes or new ideas They're **resistant to** change. **2** not harmed or affected by something a water-resistant cover • Bacteria can become **resistant to** antibiotics.

resolute /ˈrez°luːt/ adj formal determined not to change what you do or believe because you think that you are right a resolute opponent of the war • resolutely adv

resolution /ˌrez°ˈluːʃ°n/ noun **1** DECISION [C] an official decision that is made after a group or organization have voted Congress **passed a resolution** in support of the plan (= voted to support it). **2** PROMISE [C] a promise to yourself to do something My New Year's **resolution is** to do more exercise. **3** SOLUTION [U, no plural] formal the solution to a problem a successful resolution to the crisis **4** DETERMINATION [U] formal the quality of being determined

resolve¹ /rɪˈzɒlv/ verb **1** [T] to solve or end a problem or difficulty an attempt to resolve the dispute **2** [I, T] formal to decide that you will do something and be determined to do it [+ to do sth] I have resolved to keep my bedroom tidy.

resolve² /rɪˈzɒlv/ noun [U] formal when you are very determined to do something

resonant /ˈrez°nənt/ adj A resonant sound is loud and clear. a deep, resonant voice • resonance /ˈrez°nəns/ noun [U]

resonate /ˈrez°neɪt/ verb [I] to make a loud, clear sound

resort¹ /rɪˈzɔːt/ noun **1** [C] a place where many people go for a holiday a ski resort **2** **a last resort** something that you do because everything else has failed Soldiers were given the authority to shoot, but only as a last resort.

resort² /rɪˈzɔːt/ verb

**resort to sth/doing sth** to do something that you do not want to do because you cannot find any other way of achieving something They should be able to control the riots without resorting to violence.

resound /rɪˈzaʊnd/ verb [I] to make a loud sound, or to be filled with a loud sound The whole hall **resounded with** applause.

resounding /rɪˈzaʊndɪŋ/ adj [always before noun] **1** very loud resounding applause **2** **a resounding success/victory/failure, etc** a very great success, victory, etc

resource /rɪˈzɔːs, ˈriːsɔːrs/ noun [C] something that a country, person, or organization has which they can use [usually plural] financial/natural resources ➔ See also: **human resources**.

resourceful /rɪˈzɔːsf°l/ adj good at finding ways to solve problems • resourcefulness noun [U]

respect¹ /rɪˈspekt/ noun **1** POLITE [U] when you are polite to someone, especially because they are older or more important than you You should show more **respect for** your parents. **2** ADMIRATION [U] when you admire someone because of their knowledge, skill, or achievements She's an excellent teacher and I have the greatest **respect for** her. **3** SHOW IMPORTANCE [U] when you show by your behaviour that you think something is important or needs to be dealt with carefully Electricity can be dangerous and should always be **treated with respect**. **4** **in this respect/many respects** in a particular way, or in many ways The school has changed in many respects. **5** **with respect to sth; in respect of sth** formal relating to a particular thing I am writing with respect to your letter of 24 June. **6** **pay your respects a** formal to visit someone or go to talk to them **b** (also **pay your last respects**) to go to someone's funeral ➔ See also: **self-respect**.

o-➔respect² /rɪˈspekt/ verb [T] **1** to admire someone because of their knowledge, achievements, etc I respect him for his honesty. **2** If you respect someone's rights, customs, wishes, etc you accept their importance and are careful not to do anything they would not want.

respectable /rɪˈspektəbl/ adj **1** behaving in a socially acceptable way or looking socially acceptable a respectable family • a respectable hotel **2** large enough or good enough a respectable income • respectably adv • respectability /rɪˌspektəˈbɪləti/ noun [U]

respected /rɪˈspektɪd/ adj admired by people because of your knowledge, achievements, etc a highly respected doctor

respectful /rɪˈspektf°l/ adj showing respect for someone or something • respectfully adv

respective /rɪˈspektɪv/ adj [always before noun] relating to each of the people or things that you have just talked about members of staff and their respective partners

respectively /rɪˈspektɪvli/ adv in the same order as the people or things you have just

R

talked about *Mr Ewing and Mr Campbell gave £2000 and £250 respectively.*

**respiration** /ˌrespəˈreɪʃ³ri/ *noun* [U] *formal* the process of breathing

**respiratory** /rɪˈspɪrət³ri US ˈrespərətɔːri/ *adj* [always before noun] relating to the process of breathing *respiratory illnesses*

**respite** /ˈrespaɪt US ˈrespɪt/ *noun* [U, no plural] a short period of rest from something difficult or unpleasant *The weekend was a brief respite from the pressures of work.*

o⁻**respond** /rɪˈspɒnd/ *verb* [I] **1** to say or do something as an answer or reaction to something that has been said or done [+ by + doing sth] *The government has responded by sending food and medical supplies to the region.* • *How quickly did the police respond to the call?* **2** to improve as the result of a particular medical treatment *She's responding well to drug treatment.*

**respondent** /rɪˈspɒndənt/ *noun* [C] someone who has answered a request for information [usually plural] *More than half the respondents were opposed to the new tax.*

o⁻**response** /rɪˈspɒns/ *noun* [C, U] an answer or reaction to something that has been said or done *The President's comments provoked an angry response from students.* • *I'm writing in response to your letter of 14 February.*

o⁻**responsibility** /rɪˌspɒnsəˈbɪləti/ *noun* **1** [C, U] something that it is your job or duty to deal with *The head of the department has various additional responsibilities.* • [+ to do sth] *It is your responsibility to make sure that your homework is done on time.* **2** **take/accept/claim responsibility for sth** to say that you have done something or caused something to happen, especially something bad *No one has yet claimed responsibility for yesterday's bomb attack.*

o⁻**responsible** /rɪˈspɒnsəbl/ *adj* **1** **be responsible for sb/sth/doing sth** to be the person whose duty is to deal with someone or something *I'm responsible for looking after the children in the evenings.* **2** **be responsible for sth/doing sth** to be the person who caused something to happen, especially something bad *Who was responsible for the accident?* **3** showing good judgment and able to be trusted *a hard-working and responsible employee* • *a responsible attitude* ⊃ *Opposite* **irresponsible**. **4** A responsible job is important because you have to make decisions that affect other people. **5** **be responsible to sb** If you are responsible to someone at work, they are in a higher position than you and you have to tell them what you have done.

**responsibly** /rɪˈspɒnsəbli/ *adv* in a way that shows you have good judgment and can be trusted *to behave responsibly*

**responsive** /rɪˈspɒnsɪv/ *adj* listening to someone or something and having a positive and quick reaction to them *a wonderfully responsive audience* • *They have not been very responsive to the needs of disabled customers.* • **responsiveness** *noun* [U]

o⁻**rest¹** /rest/ *noun* **1** **the rest** the part of something that remains, or the others that remain

*I'm not sure I want to spend the rest of my life with him.* • *She was slightly older than the rest of us.* • *The rest were all found not guilty.* **2** [C, U] a period of time when you relax or sleep *Why don't you have a rest?* • *I must get some rest.* **3** **come to rest** to stop moving *The car came to rest at the edge of the road.* ⊃ *See also:* put/set sb's **mind¹** at rest.

o⁻**rest²** /rest/ *verb* **1** [I] to relax or sleep because you are tired after doing an activity or because you are ill *Pete's resting after his long drive.* **2** **rest your eyes/feet/legs, etc** to stop using your eyes/feet, etc for a while because they are tired **3** **rest (sth) on/against, etc** If something rests somewhere, or if you rest it somewhere, it is supported by something else. *She rested her elbows on the table.* ⊃ *See also:* rest on your **laurels**.

**rest, stay,** or **remain**?

Rest means to relax or sleep because you are tired or ill.

*The doctor told him to rest.*

Stay means to continue to be in the same place, job, or particular state.

*It was raining, so we stayed at home.*

~~It was raining, so we rested at home.~~

Remain means to continue to be in the same state, or to continue to exist when everything or everyone else has gone.

*He remained unconscious for a week after the accident.*

*After the earthquake, nothing remained of the village.*

**rest on/upon sth** *formal* to depend on something *The whole future of the team rests on his decision.*

**restart** /ˌriːˈstɑːt/ *verb* [T] to start something again that had stopped *They want to restart the talks.*

o⁻**restaurant** /ˈrest³rɒnt/ *noun* [C] a place where you can buy and eat a meal *an Italian/vegetarian restaurant* • *We had lunch at/in a restaurant near the station.*

**restaurateur** /ˌrestɒrəˈtɜːʳ/ *noun* [C] someone who owns a restaurant

**restive** /ˈrestɪv/ *adj formal* unable to be quiet and calm

**restless** /ˈrestləs/ *adj* **1** unable to be still or relax because you are bored or nervous *The audience was getting restless.* **2** not satisfied with what you are doing now and wanting something new *After a while in the same relationship I start to get restless.* • **restlessly** *adv* • **restlessness** *noun* [U]

**restore** /rɪˈstɔːʳ/ *verb* [T] **1** MAKE EXIST to make something good exist again *Three wins in a row helped restore the team's confidence.* • *Peace has now been restored in the region.* **2** REPAIR to repair something old *to restore antiques* **3** RETURN *formal* to give something back to the person it was stolen from or who lost it *The painting was restored to its rightful owner.* • **restoration** /ˌrest³rˈeɪʃ³n/ *noun* [C, U] *The build-*

*ing is now closed for restoration* (= repair work).
• *the restoration* (= return) *of the former government*

**restrain** /rɪ'streɪn/ *verb* [T] **1** to stop someone doing something, sometimes by using force *He became violent and had to be physically restrained.* • [+ from + doing sth] *I had to restrain myself from shouting at him.* **2** to limit something *to restrain arms sales*

**restrained** /rɪ'streɪnd/ *adj* calm and not showing emotions *I was expecting him to be furious but he was very restrained.* ➔ *Opposite* **unrestrained**.

**restraint** /rɪ'streɪnt/ *noun* **1** [U] showing control over your feelings **2** [C] control over something *wage restraints*

**restrict** /rɪ'strɪkt/ *verb* [T] to limit something *They've brought in new laws to restrict the sale of cigarettes.* • *I restrict myself to two glasses of wine most evenings.*

**restricted** /rɪ'strɪktɪd/ *adj* controlled or limited *They do good food but the choice is fairly restricted.*

**restriction** /rɪ'strɪkʃᵊn/ *noun* [C, U] a rule or law that limits what people can do *There are restrictions on how many goods you can bring into the country.* • *parking restrictions*

**restrictive** /rɪ'strɪktɪv/ *adj* limiting activities too much *restrictive practices*

**restroom** /'restruːm/ *noun* [C] US a room with toilets that is in a public place, for example in a restaurant ➔ *See usage note at* **toilet**.

**restructure** /ˌriː'strʌktʃəʳ/ *verb* [I, T] to organize a system or organization in a new way • **restructuring** *noun* [U]

o—ˣ **result¹** /rɪ'zʌlt/ *noun* **1** HAPPEN [C, U] something that happens or exists because something else has happened *Unemployment has risen as a direct result of new economic policies.* • *Most accidents are the result of human error.* **2** COMPETITION [C] the score or number of votes at the end of a competition or election *The election results will be known by Sunday.* • *What was the result of this afternoon's match?* **3** INFORMATION [C] information that you get from something such as an exam, a scientific experiment, or a medical test *She's waiting for the results of a blood test.* • *the results of a survey*

**result²** /rɪ'zʌlt/ *verb* [I] to happen or exist because something else has happened *There was a food shortage resulting from the lack of rainfall.*
**result in sth** to be the reason something happens *The improvements in training resulted in increased wins.*

**resultant** /rɪ'zʌltᵊnt/ *adj formal* happening as a result of something else

**résumé** /'rezəmeɪ/ US (UK **CV**) *noun* [C] a document which describes your qualifications and the jobs that you have done, which you send to an employer that you want to work for

**resume** /rɪ'zjuːm/ *verb* [I, T] *formal* If an activity resumes, or if you resume it, it starts again. *The talks are due to resume today.* • **resumption** /rɪ'zʌmpʃᵊn/ *noun* [no plural] *the resumption of peace talks*

**resurface** /ˌriː'sɜːfɪs/ *verb* [I] to appear again after having been lost or forgotten *The story resurfaced in the news again last week.*

**resurgence** /rɪ'sɜːdʒᵊns/ *noun* [no plural] when something starts to happen again or people become interested in something again *There has been a resurgence of interest in the game.*
• **resurgent** /rɪ'sɜːdʒᵊnt/ *adj* happening again

**resurrect** /ˌrezᵊr'ekt/ *verb* [T] to make something exist again which has not existed for a long time *With this film Dykes hopes to resurrect his career.*

**resurrection** /ˌrezᵊr'ekʃᵊn/ *noun* [U] **1** when something starts to exist again which has not existed for a long period *the resurrection of a fashion* **2** in the Christian religion, Jesus Christ's return to life after he was killed

**resuscitate** /rɪ'sʌsɪteɪt/ *verb* [T] to make someone breathe again when they have stopped breathing • **resuscitation** /rɪ,sʌsɪ'teɪʃᵊn/ *noun* [U]

**retail¹** /'riːteɪl/ *noun* [U] when products are sold to customers from shops *jobs in retail*

**retail²** /'riːteɪl/ *verb* **retail at/for £50/$100, etc** to be sold to the public for a particular price *This computer retails at $2,000.*

**retailer** /'riːteɪləʳ/ *noun* [C] someone who sells products to the public

**retailing** /'riːteɪlɪŋ/ *noun* [U] the business of selling products to customers in shops

**retain** /rɪ'teɪn/ *verb* [T] to continue to keep something *The council will retain control of the school.*

**retaliate** /rɪ'tælieɪt/ *verb* [I] to do something bad to someone because they have done something bad to you *They have threatened to retaliate against any troops that attack.* • **retaliation** /rɪ,tæli'eɪʃᵊn/ *noun* [U] *They bombed the hotel in retaliation for the arrests.* • **retaliatory** /rɪ'tæliətᵊri/ *adj retaliatory measures*

**retarded** /rɪ'tɑːdɪd/ *adj* less mentally developed than other people of the same age

**retention** /rɪ'tenʃᵊn/ *noun* [U] when something continues to be kept

**rethink** /ˌriː'θɪŋk/ *verb* [I, T] *past* **rethought** to change what you think about something or what you plan to do *We've had to rethink our strategy.* • **rethink** /'riːθɪŋk/ *noun* [no plural] *The whole issue needs a fundamental rethink.*

**reticent** /'retɪsᵊnt/ *adj* saying little about what you think or feel *He was reticent about his private life.* • **reticence** /'retɪsᵊns/ *noun* [U]

**retina** /'retɪnə/ *noun* [C] a part at the back of the eye, which is affected by light and sends messages to the brain

o—ˣ **retire** /rɪ'taɪəʳ/ *verb* [I] **1** to leave your job and stop working, usually because you are old *She retired from the company in 1990.* **2** *formal* to go to another place where you can be alone or more private *After dinner, he retired to his bedroom.*

**retired** /rɪ'taɪəd/ *adj* having stopped working, often because you are old *a retired farmer/teacher*

**retiree** /rɪ'taɪriː/ *noun* [C] US someone who has stopped working, usually because they are old

**retirement** /rɪ'taɪəmənt/ *noun* **1** [C, U] when you leave your job and stop working, usually because you are old *He's taking early retirement.* **2** [U] the period of your life after you have stopped working *We wish you a long and happy retirement.*

**R**

**retiring** /rɪ'taɪərɪŋ/ *adj* shy and quiet

**retort** /rɪ'tɔːt/ *verb* [T] *formal* to answer someone quickly in an angry or funny way *"That doesn't concern you," she retorted sharply.* • **retort** *noun* [C] *formal*

**retrace** /rɪ'treɪs/ *verb* **retrace your steps** to go back somewhere the same way that you came *I was lost so I retraced my steps.*

**retract** /rɪ'trækt/ *verb* [I, T] *formal* to admit that something you said before was not true *Several key witnesses have retracted their statements.*

**retraining** /ˌriː'treɪnɪŋ/ *noun* [U] when someone learns new skills so they can do a different job

**retreat**[1] /rɪ'triːt/ *verb* [I] **1** When soldiers retreat, they move away from the enemy, especially to avoid fighting. *The army was forced to retreat.* **2 retreat to/into, etc** to go away to a place or situation which is safer or quieter *She retreated into the bathroom for some peace and quiet.*

**retreat**[2] /rɪ'triːt/ *noun* **1** MOVE [U, no plural] a move away, especially to a place or situation which is safer or quieter *He saw the dog coming towards him and beat a hasty retreat* (= moved quickly away). **2** MILITARY [C, U] a move back by soldiers or an army, especially to avoid fighting *a strategic retreat* **3** PLACE [C] a quiet place where you can go to rest or be alone *a mountain retreat*

**retrial** /ˌriː'traɪəl/ *noun* [C] a new trial for a crime that has already been judged in a law court *The judge ordered a retrial.*

**retribution** /ˌretrɪ'bjuːʃən/ *noun* [U] *formal* punishment for something morally wrong that was done *They're seeking retribution for the killings.*

**retrieve** /rɪ'triːv/ *verb* [T] to get something after first finding it *I've just retrieved the ball from the bottom of the pond.* • *computer tools for retrieving information* • **retrieval** *noun* [U] when something is retrieved *the storage and retrieval of information*

**retriever** /rɪ'triːvə/ *noun* [C] a large dog with thick black or light brown hair

**retro** /'retrəʊ/ *adj* looking or sounding like something from the past *His clothes had a retro look.*

**retrospect** /'retrəʊspekt/ *noun* **in retrospect** thinking now about something in the past *In retrospect, I should probably have told her.*

**retrospective**[1] /ˌretrəʊ'spektɪv/ *noun* [C] a show of work done by an artist over many years

**retrospective**[2] /ˌretrəʊ'spektɪv/ *adj* If a law or decision is retrospective, it affects situations in the past as well as in the future. • **retrospectively** *adv*

o⚞**return**[1] /rɪ'tɜːn/ *verb* **1** GO BACK [I] to go or come back to a place where you were before *She returned to America in 1954.* • *I won't return from my holiday till May.* **2** GIVE BACK [T] to give, send, or put something back where it came from *I have to return the book by Friday.* • *He immediately returned the records to the files.* **3 return to sth** to start doing an activity again or talking about something again *I returned to work three months after Susie was born.* • *We keep returning to the same subject.*

**b** to go back to a previous condition *Life has begun to return to normal now that the war is over.* **4** HAPPEN AGAIN [I] If something returns, it happens again. *If the pains return phone the doctor.* **5** DO THE SAME [T] to react to something that someone does or says by doing or saying the same *I returned his smile.* • *I must return Michael's call* (= telephone him because he telephoned me earlier). **6 return a verdict/ sentence** to announce if someone is guilty or not guilty or what punishment the person will be given in a law court *The jury returned a verdict of guilty.* **7** SPORTS [T] to hit or throw a ball back to someone when playing a sport

**return**[2] /rɪ'tɜːn/ *noun* **1** GOING BACK [no plural] when someone goes or comes back to a place where they were before *On his return to Sydney, he started up a business.* **2** GIVING BACK [no plural] when something is given back, put back, or sent back *the return of the stolen goods* **3** ACTIVITY [no plural] when someone starts an activity again *This film marks his return to acting.* **4** HAPPENING AGAIN [no plural] when something starts to happen or be present again *the return of the platform shoe* • *What we are seeing here is a return to traditional values.* **5** TICKET [C] *UK* (*US* **round-trip ticket**) a ticket that lets you travel to a place and back again, for example on a train *Could I have two returns to Birmingham?* **6** PROFIT [C, U] the profit that you get from an investment *This fund has shown high returns for the last five years.* **7 in return** in exchange for something or as a reaction to something *I'd like to give them something in return for everything they've done for us.* **8** SPORTS [C] when a ball is thrown or hit back to another player in a sports match *She hit an excellent return.* **9** COMPUTER [U] a key on a computer keyboard that is used to make the computer accept information or to start a new line in a document *Type in the password and press return.* ➔ *See also:* **day return**.

**returnable** /rɪ'tɜːnəbl/ *adj* If something is returnable, it can be taken or given back. *a returnable deposit*

**reunification** /ˌriːjuːnɪfɪ'keɪʃən/ *noun* [U] when a country that was divided into smaller countries is joined together again as one country *the reunification of Germany*

**reunion** /ˌriː'juːniən/ *noun* [C] an occasion when people who have not met each other for a long time meet again *a family/school reunion*

**reunite** /ˌriːjuː'naɪt/ *verb* [I, T] to meet again after being apart for a long time, or to bring people together who have been apart for a long time [often passive] *Years later, he was reunited with his brother.*

**reuse** /ˌriː'juːz/ *verb* [T] to find a new use for something so that it does not have to be thrown away *Businesses are finding new ways to reuse materials.* • **reusable** *adj*

**Rev** written abbreviation for Reverend (= title of Christian official) *Rev Jo Harding*

**rev** /rev/ (*also* **rev up**) *verb* [I, T] **revving**, *past* **revved** to increase the engine speed of a vehicle *He revved the engine and drove off.*

**revamp** /ˌriː'væmp/ *verb* [T] to change something in order to make it better *They're revamping the restaurant.*

**Revd** *written abbreviation for* Reverend (= title of Christian official) *the Revd Laurie Clow*

**reveal** /rɪ'viːl/ *verb* [T] **1** to give someone a piece of information that is surprising or that was previously secret [+ that] *It was revealed in this morning's papers that the couple intend to marry.* **2** to allow something to be seen that, until then, had been hidden *His shirt came up at the back, revealing an expanse of white skin.*

**revealing** /rɪ'viːlɪŋ/ *adj* **1** showing someone's true character or the true facts about someone or something *a revealing biography/remark* **2** If clothes are revealing, they show a lot of your body.

**revel** /'rev°l/ *verb* (UK) **revelling**, *past* **revelled**, (US) **reveling**, *past* **reveled**
**revel in sth** to enjoy a situation or activity very much *He revelled in his role as team manager.*

**revelation** /ˌrev°l'eɪʃ°n/ *noun* **1** [C] a piece of information that is discovered although it was intended to be kept secret *He resigned following revelations about his private life.* **2 be a revelation** to be an extremely pleasant surprise *Anna's boyfriend was a revelation.*

**revenge** /rɪ'vendʒ/ *noun* [U] something that you do to punish someone who has done something bad to you *He's made life very difficult for me but I'll get/take my revenge.* • *He was shot in revenge for the murder.*

**revenue** /'rev°njuː/ (*also* **revenues**) *noun* [U] large amounts of money received by a government as tax, or by a company

**reverberate** /rɪ'vɜːb°reɪt/ *verb* [I] If a sound reverberates, it is heard for a long time as it is sent back from different surfaces. *The sound of the shots reverberated around the building.*

**revere** /rɪ'vɪəʳ/ *verb* [T] *formal* to respect and admire someone very much *a revered religious leader*

**reverence** /'rev°r°ns/ *noun* [U] *formal* a strong feeling of respect and admiration

**Reverend** /'rev°r°nd/ *adj* used as a title before the name of some Christian officials *the Reverend Alan Pringle*

**reverie** /'rev°ri/ *noun* [C] *formal* a pleasant state in which you are thinking of something else, not what is happening around you

**reversal** /rɪ'vɜːs°l/ *noun* [C] when something changes to its opposite *In a reversal of traditional roles, Paul stayed at home to look after the baby and Clare went out to work.*

**reverse**[1] /rɪ'vɜːs/ *verb* **1** [I, T] to drive a vehicle backwards *I hate reversing into parking spaces.* **2** [T] to change a situation or change the order of things so that it becomes the opposite *It is unlikely that the judge will reverse his decision.* • *Let's reverse the order – I'll give the first talk and you the second.*

**reverse**[2] /rɪ'vɜːs/ *noun* **1 the reverse** the opposite of what has been suggested *"So, is he happier?" "Quite the reverse – I've never seen him look so miserable."* **2** [U] (*also* **re,verse 'gear**) the method of controlling a vehicle that makes it go backwards *Put the car into reverse.* **3 in reverse** in the opposite order or way *Do the same steps but this time in reverse.*

**reverse**[3] /rɪ'vɜːs/ *adj* [always before noun] opposite to the usual way or to the way you have just

described *I'm going to read out the names of the winners in reverse order.*

**reversible** /rɪ'vɜːsəbl/ *adj* **1** If something is reversible, it can be changed back to what it was before. *Most of the damage done to the cells is reversible.* ⊃ *Opposite* **irreversible.** **2** Reversible clothes can be worn so that the inside is the outside. *a reversible jacket*

**revert** /rɪ'vɜːt/ *verb*
**revert to sth/doing sth** to go back to how something was before *For a while I ate low-fat food but then I reverted to my old eating habits.* • reversion /rɪ'vɜːʃ°n/ *noun* [U, no plural]

**review**[1] /rɪ'vjuː/ *noun* **1** [C, U] the process of considering something again in order to make changes to it *a review of teachers' pay* • *The policy is now under review* (= being considered). **2** [C] a report in a newspaper, magazine, or programme that gives an opinion about a new book, film, etc *a book review* • *The film has had mixed reviews* (= some good, some bad).

**review**[2] /rɪ'vjuː/ *verb* **1** CONSIDER [T] to consider something again in order to decide if changes should be made *The courts will review her case.* **2** REPORT [T] to give your opinion in a report about a film, book, television programme, etc *He reviews films for The Times.* **3** STUDY [I, T] US (UK **revise**) to study a subject before you take a test

**reviewer** /rɪ'vjuːəʳ/ *noun* [C] someone who writes reviews of a book, film, etc

**reviled** /rɪ'vaɪld/ *adj* hated *He is possibly the most reviled man in Britain.*

**revise** /rɪ'vaɪz/ *verb* **1** [T] to change something so that it is more accurate *a revised edition of the book* **2** [I, T] US (UK **review**) to study a subject before you take a test

**revision** /rɪ'vɪʒ°n/ *noun* **1** [C, U] when you change something so that it is more accurate *a downward revision of prices* **2** [U] UK when you study a subject before taking a test

**revitalize** (*also* UK **-ise**) /ˌriː'vaɪt°laɪz/ *verb* [T] to make something more active or exciting *attempts to revitalize the city*

**revival** /rɪ'vaɪv°l/ *noun* **1** [C, U] when something becomes more active or popular again *a revival in folk music* • *Yoga is enjoying a revival.* **2** [C] a performance of a play, opera, etc that has not been performed for a long time

**revive** /rɪ'vaɪv/ *verb* **1** EXIST AGAIN [T] to make something from the past exist again *to revive memories* • *A lot of traditional skills are currently being revived.* **2** CONSCIOUS [I, T] to become conscious again or make someone conscious again *A police officer tried unsuccessfully to revive her.* **3** FEEL BETTER [I, T] to start to feel healthier and more active again, or to make someone feel this way *A cup of tea and something to eat might revive you.*

**revoke** /rɪ'vəʊk/ *verb* [T] *formal* to stop someone having official permission to do something, or to change an official decision *His work permit was revoked after six months.*

**revolt**[1] /rɪ'vəʊlt/ *noun* [C, U] when people try to change a government, often using violence, or when they refuse to accept someone's authority *a slave/peasant revolt*

**revolt**[2] /rɪ'vəʊlt/ *verb* **1** [I] to try to change a gov-

R

ernment, often using violence, or to refuse to accept someone's authority *Many were killed when nationalists revolted against the new government.* **2 be revolted by sth** to think that something is extremely unpleasant

**revolting** /rɪˈvəʊltɪŋ/ *adj* extremely unpleasant

**revolution** /ˌrevəˈluːʃ³n/ *noun* **1** POLITICS [C, U] a change in the way a country is governed, usually to a different political system and often using violence or war *the French Revolution* **2** CHANGE [C] a very important change in the way people think or do things *the technological revolution* • *This discovery caused a revolution in medicine.* **3** CIRCLE [C, U] one whole circular movement around a central point, for example one whole movement of a wheel

**revolutionary¹** /ˌrevəˈluːʃ³n³ri/ *adj* **1** completely different from what was done before *The twentieth century has brought about revolutionary changes in our lifestyles.* **2** relating to a political revolution *a revolutionary movement*

**revolutionary²** /ˌrevəˈluːʃ³n³ri/ *noun* [C] someone who tries to cause or take part in a political revolution

**revolutionize** (*also UK* **-ise**) /ˌrevəˈluːʃ³naɪz/ *verb* [T] to change something in every way so that it is much better *This will revolutionize the way we do business.*

**revolve** /rɪˈvɒlv/ *verb* [I] to move in a circle around a central point *A fan was revolving slowly.* • **revolving** *adj* [always before noun] *a revolving door*

**revolve around/round sth/sb** to have as the only interest or subject *Her whole life revolves around her children.*

**revolver** /rɪˈvɒlvə³/ *noun* [C] a small gun

**revue** /rɪˈvjuː/ *noun* [C] a show in a theatre with jokes, songs, and dancing

**revulsion** /rɪˈvʌlʃ³n/ *noun* [U] a strong feeling that something is very unpleasant

⊶**reward¹** /rɪˈwɔːd/ *noun* **1** [C, U] something good that you get or experience because you have worked hard, behaved well, etc *There'll be a reward for whoever finishes first.* **2** [C] money that the police give to someone who gives them information about a crime

**reward²** /rɪˈwɔːd/ *verb* [T] to give a reward to someone *She was rewarded for her bravery.*

**rewarding** /rɪˈwɔːdɪŋ/ *adj* making you feel satisfied that you have done something well *Teaching is hard work but it's very rewarding.*

**rewind** /ˌriːˈwaɪnd/ *verb* [I, T] *past* rewound /ˌriːˈwaʊnd/ to make a sound or television recording go back to the beginning

**rework** /ˌriːˈwɜːk/ *verb* [T] to change a piece of music or writing in order to improve it or make it more suitable *Elton John reworked his 1974 hit, 'Candle in the Wind', for Princess Diana's funeral.*

**rewrite** /ˌriːˈraɪt/ *verb* [T] *past t* rewrote, *past p* rewritten to write something again in order to improve it *I had to rewrite my essay.*

**rhapsody** /ˈræpsədi/ *noun* [C] a piece of music for instruments

**rhetoric** /ˈret³rɪk/ *noun* [U] language that is intended to make people believe things, often language that is not sincere *It was the usual*

*political speech, full of empty rhetoric.* • **rhetorical** /rɪˈtɒrɪk³l/ *adj* • **rhetorically** *adv*

**rhe‚torical 'question** *noun* [C] a question that is not intended as a real question because you do not expect anyone to answer it

**rheumatism** /ˈruːmətɪz³m/ *noun* [U] a disease in which there is swelling and pain in the joints (= parts of the body where bones join)

**rhino** /ˈraɪnəʊ/ *noun* [C] *short for* rhinoceros

**rhinoceros** /raɪˈnɒs³rəs/ *noun* [C] a large animal from Africa or Asia that has thick skin and one or two horns on its nose

**rhubarb** /ˈruːbɑːb/ *noun* [U] a plant that has long, red stems that can be cooked and eaten as a fruit

**rhyme¹** /raɪm/ *verb* [I] If a word rhymes with another word, the end part of the words sound the same. *'Moon' rhymes with 'June.'*

**rhyme²** /raɪm/ *noun* **1** POEM [C] a short poem that has words that rhyme at the end of each line **2** STYLE [U] a style of writing or speaking that uses words which rhyme *The story was written entirely in rhyme.* **3** WORD [C] a word that rhymes with another word ⊃ *See also:* **nursery rhyme.**

**rhythm** /ˈrɪð³m/ *noun* [C, U] a regular, repeating pattern of sound *You need a sense of rhythm to be a good dancer.* • **rhythmic** /ˈrɪðmɪk/ *adj* with rhythm • **rhythmically** *adv*

**rib** /rɪb/ *noun* [C] one of the curved bones in the chest

**ribbon** /ˈrɪb³n/ *noun* [C] a long, narrow piece of cloth that is used for tying things or used for decoration

**'rib ‚cage** *noun* [C] the structure of ribs (= curved bones) in the chest

⊶**rice** /raɪs/ *noun* [U] small grains from a plant that are cooked and eaten ⊃ *See colour picture* **Food** *on page Centre 9.*

**'rice ‚paddy** (*also UK* **paddy field**) *noun* [C] a field in which rice is grown

⊶**rich** /rɪtʃ/ *adj* **1** MONEY having much more money than most people, or owning things that could be sold for a lot of money *She's the third richest woman in Britain.* • *These cars are only for the rich.* **2** CONTAINING A LOT containing a lot of something that is important or valuable *rich soil* • *Both foods are rich in Vitamin C.* **3** FOOD Rich food has a lot of butter, cream, or eggs in it. *a rich sauce* **4** STRONG A rich sound is low and strong, and a rich colour is bright and strong. • **richness** *noun* [U]

**riches** /ˈrɪtʃɪz/ *noun* [plural] *literary* a lot of money or valuable objects ⊃ *See also:* go from **rags to riches.**

**richly** /ˈrɪtʃli/ *adv* **1 be richly decorated/furnished, etc** to have a lot of beautiful or expensive decoration, furniture, etc *a richly decorated church* **2 be richly rewarded** to be paid a lot of money **3 richly deserve** to very much deserve something *Later that year he received the award he so richly deserved.*

**rickety** /ˈrɪkəti/ *adj* likely to break soon *a rickety wooden chair*

**ricochet** /ˈrɪkəʃeɪ/ *verb* [I] to hit a surface and then be sent back through the air *The bullet ricocheted off the wall.*

⊶**rid¹** /rɪd/ *adj* **1 get rid of sth a** to throw something away or give something to someone because you do not want it now *We must get rid of some of those old books.* **b** to end something unpleasant *I can't seem to get rid of this headache.* **2 get rid of sb** to make someone leave *She was useless at her job so we had to get rid of her.* **3 be rid of sb/sth** to be without someone or something that you do not like or want *I'd do anything to be rid of him.*

**rid²** /rɪd/ *verb* ridding, *past* rid
**rid sth of sth** to remove something unpleasant from somewhere *to rid the world of nuclear weapons*
**rid yourself of sth** to remove something that you do not want *to rid yourself of a reputation*

**riddance** /ˈrɪdᵊns/ *noun* **Good riddance!** used to express pleasure when you have got rid of something or someone that you do not want

**ridden** /ˈrɪdᵊn/ *past participle of* ride

**riddle** /ˈrɪdl/ *noun* [C] **1** a strange and difficult question that has a clever and often funny answer **2** a situation or event that you cannot understand *Scientists may have solved the riddle of Saturn's rings.*

**riddled** /ˈrɪdld/ *adj* **be riddled with sth** to contain a large number of something bad *The wall was riddled with bullets.*

o━**ride¹** /raɪd/ *verb past t* rode, *past p* ridden **1** [I, T] to travel by sitting on a horse, bicycle, or motorcycle and controlling it *I ride my bike to work.* • *She taught me to ride* (= to ride a horse). ➔ *See usage note at* **drive**. **2** [T] *US* to travel in a vehicle as a passenger *I've told her not to ride the subway at night.*
**ride on sth** If something important rides on a situation, it will succeed or fail depending on the situation. *There was $600,000 riding on the outcome of the deal.*
**ride out sth** to continue to exist during a bad situation *to ride out a recession*

**ride²** /raɪd/ *noun* [C] **1** VEHICLE a journey in a vehicle or train *Can I give you a ride to the station?* **2** BICYCLE a journey riding a bicycle, motorcycle, or horse *He's gone out for a ride on his bike.* **3** PLAYING a machine at a fair (= event outdoors) which moves people up and down, round in circles, etc as they sit in it

**rider** /ˈraɪdə/ *noun* [C] someone who rides a horse, bicycle, or motorcycle

**ridge** /rɪdʒ/ *noun* [C] **1** a long, narrow piece of high land, especially along the top of a mountain *a mountain ridge* **2** a narrow, raised line on a flat surface

**ridicule¹** /ˈrɪdɪkjuːl/ *verb* [T] to make people laugh at someone in an unkind way *I was ridiculed for saying they might win.*

**ridicule²** /ˈrɪdɪkjuːl/ *noun* [U] when people laugh at someone in an unkind way *I don't want to become an object of ridicule* (= to be laughed at).

**ridiculous** /rɪˈdɪkjələs/ *adj* very silly *I've never heard anything so ridiculous.* • *a ridiculous suggestion* • **ridiculously** *adv* ridiculously expensive

**riding** /ˈraɪdɪŋ/ *noun* [U] the sport or activity of riding horses

**rife** /raɪf/ *adj* [never before noun] Something unpleasant that is rife is very common. *Rumours were rife that the band would split up.*

**rifle¹** /ˈraɪfl/ *noun* [C] a long gun that you hold against your shoulder when you shoot

**rifle²** /ˈraɪfl/ (*also* **rifle through**) *verb* [T] to quickly search through things, often in order to steal something *I caught him rifling through my drawers.*

**rift** /rɪft/ *noun* [C] **1** a serious disagreement *the deepening rift between the government and the unions* **2** a very large hole that separates parts of the Earth's surface

**rig¹** /rɪg/ *verb* [T] rigging, *past* rigged to arrange an election, competition, etc so that the results are not fair or true *He accused the government of rigging the elections.*
**rig sth up** to quickly make a piece of equipment from any materials you can find

**rig²** /rɪg/ *noun* [C] a large structure for removing gas or oil from the ground or the sea *an oil rig*

**rigging** /ˈrɪgɪŋ/ *noun* [U] a system of ropes and chains used to support a ship's masts (= poles)

o━**right¹** /raɪt/ *adj* **1** CORRECT correct or true *He only got half the answers right.* • *You're right about Alison – she's incredible!* • *"You came here in 1979, didn't you?" "That's right."* **2** DIRECTION [always before noun] on or towards the side of your body that is to the east when you are facing north *your right hand* • *There's a tree on the right side of the house.* **3** SUITABLE suitable or best in a particular situation *I'm not sure she's the right person for the job.* • *Are we going in the right direction?* **4** ACCEPTABLE fair or morally acceptable *It's not right to criticize him behind his back.* **5 put sth right** to solve a problem **6** COMPLETE [always before noun] *UK informal* used for emphasizing when something is bad *His house is a right mess.* ➔ *See also:* **all right.** ➔ *See usage note at* **correct.**

**right** or **true**?

Right is usually used to say something is correct or to agree with something someone has said.

*He gave the right answer.*

*"That's right, they live in central London."*

True is usually used to say something is based on facts.

*Is it true that she's leaving?*

*Everything I've told you is true.*

o━**right²** /raɪt/ *adv* **1** EXACTLY exactly in a place or time *He's right here with me.* • *I fell asleep right in the middle of her speech.* **2** CORRECTLY correctly *Nothing was going right.* • *He guessed right most of the time.* **3** DIRECTION to the right side *Turn right after the bridge.* **4 right away/ now/after** immediately *Do you want to start right away?* • *We'll be able to meet them right after lunch.* **5** ALL all the way *Did you read it right through to the end?* **6** IN SPEECH *UK* used at the beginning of a sentence to get someone's attention or to show you have understood someone *Right, who's turn is it to tidy up?* • *Right, so Helen's coming tomorrow and Trevor on Thursday.* **7 Right** used in the UK as part of the title of some politicians and

Christian officials *Right Honourable/Reverend*
**8 It serves her/him/you right!** *informal*
something you say about a bad thing which has
happened to a person and which they deserve
*So she left him, did she? Serves him right!*
• rightness *noun* [U] ➔ *See also:* **be right up sb's**
**alley**, be right up sb's **street**.

&#9900;**right³** /raɪt/ *noun* **1** LAW [C] something that the
law allows you to do *the right to free speech*
• [+ to do sth] *the right to vote* **2** DIRECTION [U]
the right side of your body, or the direction
towards this side *You'll find her in the second*
*room* **on the right. 3** BEHAVIOUR [U] morally
correct behaviour *I've tried to teach them the*
*difference between right and wrong.* **4 have**
**a/no right to do sth** to have, or not have, a
good reason for something *He has a right to be*
*angry.* • *She had no right to speak to me like*
*that.* **5 the Right/right** political groups which
support capitalism (= a system in which
industries and companies are owned by people
and not the government) *The right cam-*
*paigned against the president.*

**right⁴** /raɪt/ *verb* [T] **1** to put something back in a
vertical position, or to return to a vertical position [often reflexive] *The boat righted itself and I*
*rowed us back to the shore.* **2 right a wrong** to
do something good to make an unfair situation
seem better *How can we right the wrongs of the*
*past?*

'**right ˌangle** *noun* [C] an angle of the type that
is in a square

**righteous** /'raɪtʃəs/ *adj* morally right and for
good moral reasons *righteous anger/indigna-*
*tion* • righteousness *noun* [U] ➔ *See also:* **self-**
**righteous.**

**rightful** /'raɪtf°l/ *adj* [always before noun] legally
or morally correct *The wallet was returned to*
*its rightful owner.*

**right-hand** /ˌraɪt'hænd/ *adj* [always before noun]
**1** on the right of something *On* **the right-hand**
**side** *you'll see a sign.* **2 sb's right-hand**
**man/woman** the person that you most trust
and depend on, especially at work

**right-handed** /ˌraɪt'hændɪd/ *adj* Someone who
is right-handed uses their right hand to do
most things.

**rightly** /'raɪtli/ *adv* in a correct way *Most*
*people quite rightly regard this information as*
*private.*

**rights** /raɪts/ *noun* [plural] freedom to do and say
things without fear of punishment ➔ *See also:*
**civil rights, human rights.**

**right-wing** /ˌraɪt'wɪŋ/ *adj* supporting the ideas
of parties on the political right *a right-wing*
*newspaper* • right-winger *noun* [C]

**rigid** /'rɪdʒɪd/ *adj* **1** not able to change or be
changed easily *I found the rules a little too*
*rigid.* **2** not able to bend or move easily *a rigid*
*structure* • *She sat rigid with fear.* • rigidly *adv*
• rigidity /rɪ'dʒɪdəti/ *noun* [U] being unable to
bend or change easily

**rigorous** /'rɪɡ°rəs/ *adj* careful to look at or consider every part of something to make sure it is
correct or safe *rigorous testing* • *a rigorous*
*medical examination* • rigorously *adv*

**rigour** *UK* (*US* **rigor**) /'rɪɡəʳ/ *noun* [U] when you
look at or consider every part of something to

make sure it is correct or safe *His arguments*
*lack intellectual rigour.*

**rigours** *UK* (*US* **rigors**) /'rɪɡəz/ *noun* **the**
**rigours of sth** the difficult conditions of a particular situation *the rigours of a harsh winter*

**rim** /rɪm/ *noun* [C] the edge of something round
*the rim of a wheel*

**rind** /raɪnd/ *noun* [C, U] the thick skin of fruits
such as oranges and lemons and other foods,
for example cheese

&#9900;**ring¹** /rɪŋ/ *noun* [C] **1** JEWELLERY a round piece
of jewellery that you wear on your finger *a*
*wedding ring* • *a gold ring* ➔ *See picture at* **jew-**
**ellery. 2** CIRCLE something that is the shape of
a circle *The children sat in a ring around the*
*teacher.* **3** SOUND the sound a bell makes *The*
*ring of the doorbell woke him up.* **4 a crime/**
**drug/spy, etc ring** a group of people who are
involved in an illegal activity *5* **a**
**boxing/circus ring** an area with seats around
it where boxers (= people fighting) or people in
a circus (= show) perform **6 give sb a ring** to
telephone someone *If you want anything just*
*give me a ring.* ➔ *See also:* **key ring.**

&#9900;**ring²** /rɪŋ/ *verb past t* **rang**, *past p* **rung 1** SOUND
[I, T] If something rings, it makes the sound of a
bell, and if you ring a bell, you cause it to make
a sound. *The phone's ringing.* • *I rang the door-*
*bell.* **2** TELEPHONE [I, T] *UK* (*UK/US* **call**) to telephone someone *Have you rung your mother?*
• *I've rung for a taxi.* **3** EARS [I] If your ears are
ringing, you can hear a loud sound after the
sound has stopped. ➔ *See also:* ring a **bell**, ring
**true.**

**ring (sb) back** *UK* (*UK/US* **call (sb) back**) to telephone someone a second time, or to telephone
someone who rang you earlier *I'm a bit busy –*
*can I ring you back later?*

**ring off** *UK* (*UK/US* **hang up**) to end a telephone
conversation and put down the part of the telephone that you speak into *She'd rung off before*
*I could say goodbye.*

**ring³** /rɪŋ/ *verb* [T] *past* **ringed** to make a circle
around something *Dozens of armed police*
*ringed the building.*

**ringleader** /'rɪŋˌliːdəʳ/ *noun* [C] the leader of a
group who are doing something harmful or
illegal *the ringleader of a gang of drug smug-*
*glers*

'**ring ˌroad** *noun* [C] *UK* a road built to
take traffic around the outside of a city

**rink** /rɪŋk/ *noun* [C] a large, flat surface made of
ice or wood where you can skate (= move
wearing boots with wheels or a piece of metal )
*a roller skating rink* ➔ *See also:* **ice rink.**

**rinse¹** /rɪns/ *verb* [T] to wash something in clean
water in order to remove dirt or soap *Rinse the*
*beans with cold water.*

**rinse sth out** to quickly wash the inside of
something with clean water *I'll just rinse these*
*glasses out and leave them to dry.*

**rinse²** /rɪns/ *noun* [C] **1** when you wash something in clean water to remove dirt or soap
*Give it a quick rinse, then squeeze it dry.* **2** a
liquid that is used for changing the colour of
someone's hair *a dark brown rinse*

**riot¹** /raɪət/ *noun* **1** [C] angry, violent behaviour
by a crowd of people *a race riot* • *Riots started*

*in several cities.* **2 run riot** to behave in a noisy, violent, or wild way without being controlled *They allow their kids to run riot.*

**riot²** /raɪət/ *verb* [I] to take part in a riot *People were rioting in the streets.* • **rioter** *noun* [C]

**rioting** /'raɪətɪŋ/ *noun* [U] when a crowd of people riots *There was widespread rioting.*

**riotous** /'raɪətəs/ *adj* **1** wild and not controlled by anyone *a riotous party* **2** *formal* violent and not controlled *He was charged with riotous behaviour and jailed for six months.*

**rip¹** /rɪp/ *verb* **ripping**, *past* **ripped 1** [I, T] to tear quickly and suddenly, or to tear something quickly and suddenly *She ripped her dress getting off her bike.* • *He ripped open the parcel.* **2 rip sth out/off/from, etc** to remove something by pulling it away quickly *Hedges had been ripped out to make larger fields.*

**rip sb off** *informal* to cheat someone by making them pay too much money for something *We were ripped off by the first taxi driver.*

**rip sth off** to remove a piece of clothing very quickly and carelessly *I ripped off my clothes and jumped in the shower.*

**rip through sth** to move through a place or building, destroying it quickly *The bomb ripped through the building, killing six people.*

**rip sth up** to tear something into small pieces *He ripped up all her letters.*

**rip²** /rɪp/ *noun* [C] a hole in the shape of a line when cloth or paper has been torn

**ripe** /raɪp/ *adj* **1** developed enough and ready to be eaten *ripe bananas* **2 ripe for sth** developed enough to be ready for something *The country is ripe for change.* • *The time is ripe for* (= It is the right time for) *investing in new technology.*

**ripen** /'raɪpᵊn/ *verb* [I, T] to become ripe, or to make something become ripe *The peaches had ripened in the sun.*

**rip-off** /'rɪpɒf/ *noun* [C] *informal* something that costs far too much money *The drinks here are a complete rip-off.*

**ripple¹** /'rɪpl/ *verb* [I, T] to move in small waves, or to make something move in small waves *A field of wheat rippled in the breeze.*

**ripple²** /'rɪpl/ *noun* [C] **1** a small wave or series of small waves on the surface of water *She dived in, sending ripples across the pool.* **2** something that spreads through a place in a gentle way *a ripple of applause/laughter*

o━**rise¹** /raɪz/ *verb* [I] *past t* **rose**, *past p* **risen 1** INCREASE to increase in level *rising temperatures* • *Prices rose by 10 percent.* **2** GO UP to move up *The balloon rose slowly into the air.* **3** STAND to stand, especially after sitting *He rose from his seat.* **4 rise to/through, etc** to become more important, successful, or rich *He quickly rose to stardom.* **5** STRENGTH to become stronger or louder *The wind is rising.* • *Her voice rose to a scream.* **6** HIGH to be high above something *The bridge rose almost 600 feet above the water.* **7** APPEAR When the sun or moon rises, it appears in the sky. *The sun rises in the East.* **8 rise to the occasion/challenge, etc** to deal with a difficult job or opportunity successfully

**rise** or **raise**?

Be careful not to confuse these two verbs. **Rise** means to increase or move up. This verb cannot be followed by an object.

*The price of petrol is rising.*

~~The price of petrol is raising.~~

**Raise** means to lift something to a higher position or to increase an amount or level. This verb must always be followed by an object.

*The government has raised the price of petrol.*

~~The government has rised the price of petrol.~~

**rise above sth** to succeed in not allowing something harmful or bad to affect or hurt you

**rise up** to try to defeat and change a government

o━**rise²** /raɪz/ *noun* **1** [C] an increase in the level of something *a tax rise* • *a rise in interest rates* **2 sb's rise to fame/power, etc** when someone becomes very famous or powerful **3 give rise to sth** to cause something *The bacteria live in the human body but do not give rise to any symptoms.* **4** [C] *UK* (*US* **raise**) an increase in the amount of money that you earn *a pay rise* • *She's asked for a two percent rise.*

o━**risk¹** /rɪsk/ *noun* **1** [C, U] the possibility of something bad happening *the risk of heart disease* • *People in the Northeast face the **highest risk** of being burgled.* • [+ (that)] *There is a slight risk that the blood could have become infected.* **2** [C] something bad that might happen *There are more **health risks** when older women get pregnant.* **3 at risk** being in a situation where something bad is likely to happen *Releasing these prisoners into the community puts the public **at risk**.* • *If you've got asthma, you're more **at risk of** having eczema.* **4 at your own risk** If you do something at your own risk, you are completely responsible for anything bad that might happen because of it. **5 run the risk of sth** to do something although something bad might happen because of it *I think I'll run the risk of hurting her feelings, and tell her the truth.* **6 take a risk** to do something although something bad might happen because of it *This time I'm not taking any risks – I'm going to get insured.*

o━**risk²** /rɪsk/ *verb* [T] **1** If you risk something bad, you do something although that bad thing might happen. [+ doing sth] *I'd like to help you, but I can't risk losing my job.* **2** If you risk something important, you cause it to be in a dangerous situation where you might lose it. *He risked his life to save me.*

**risky** /'rɪski/ *adj* dangerous because something bad might happen *Investing in shares is always a risky business.*

**rite** /raɪt/ *noun* [C] a traditional ceremony in a particular religion or culture *initiation/funeral rites*

**ritual** /'rɪtʃuəl/ *noun* [C] an activity or a set of actions that are always done in the same way or at the same time, sometimes as part of a religion

*Coffee and the paper are part of my morning ritual.* • **ritualistic** /ˌrɪtjuˈəlˈɪstɪk/ *adj* done as a ritual

**rival¹** /ˈraɪvəl/ *noun* [C] someone or something that is competing with another person or thing *business/political rivals* • **rival** *adj* [always before noun] *a rival company/gang* • **rivalry** *noun* [C, U] when two people or things are rivals *There is intense **rivalry between** the two teams.*

**rival²** /ˈraɪvəl/ *verb* [T] *(UK)* **rivalling**, *past* **rivalled**, *(US)* **rivaling**, *past* **rivaled** to be good enough to compete with someone or something else *Australian wine can now rival the best from France.*

o-- **river** /ˈrɪvər/ *noun* [C] a long, natural area of water that flows across the land and into a sea, lake, or another river *the River Thames* • *Two major rivers flow through the town.*

**riverside** /ˈrɪvəsaɪd/ *noun* [no plural] the area of land at the side of a river *a riverside path*

**rivet¹** /ˈrɪvɪt/ *verb* **be riveted** to give something all of your attention because it is so interesting or important *Her eyes were **riveted on/to** his face.*

**rivet²** /ˈrɪvɪt/ *noun* [C] a metal pin used to fasten pieces of metal together

**riveting** /ˈrɪvɪtɪŋ/ *adj* extremely interesting or exciting *I found the film absolutely riveting.*

**roach** /rəʊtʃ/ *noun* [C] *plural* **roach** or **roaches** US a cockroach (= large insect that sometimes breeds in houses)

o-- **road** /rəʊd/ *noun* **1** [C, U] a long, hard surface built for vehicles to drive on *Be careful when you cross the road.* • *The journey takes about three hours **by road** (= in a car, bus, etc).* • *Follow the **main road** (= large road) till you come to a church.* • *a road accident* **2 Road** (written abbreviation **Rd**) used in the name of a road as part of an address *142 Park Road* **3 along/down/up the road** a distance away on the same road *There's a supermarket just down the road.* **4 over the road** UK *(UK/US* **across the road***)* on the other side of the road *Who lives in that big house over the road?* **5 on the road** driving or travelling, usually over a long distance *We'd been on the road for 48 hours and we were exhausted.* **6 down the road** If an event is a particular period of time down the road, it will not happen until that period has passed. *Why worry about something that's 10 years down the road?* **7 go down that road** to decide to do something in a particular way *I don't think we want to go down that road.* ➔ See *also:* **ring road, slip road, trunk road.**

**roadblock** /ˈrəʊdblɒk/ *noun* [C] something that is put across a road to stop people who are driving down it *The police had set up a road-block and were checking identity papers.*

**road rage** *noun* [U] anger and violence between drivers *a road rage incident*

**roadshow** /ˈrəʊdʃəʊ/ *noun* [C] a radio or television programme broadcast from a public place

**roadside** /ˈrəʊdsaɪd/ *noun* [C] the area next to a road [usually singular] *They found an injured cat lying **by the roadside**.*

**roadway** /ˈrəʊdweɪ/ *noun* [C] the part of the road that the traffic drives on

**roadworks** /ˈrəʊdwɜːks/ *noun* [plural] UK repairs being done to the road

**roadworthy** /ˈrəʊd,wɜːði/ *adj* If a car is road-worthy, it is in good enough condition to be safe to drive.

**roam** /rəʊm/ *verb* [I, T] to move around a place without any purpose *gangs of youths roaming the street at night* • *They let their hens roam around free and happy.*

**roar¹** /rɔːr/ *verb* **1** [I] to make a loud, deep sound *We could hear a **lion roaring** from the other side of the zoo.* • *She roared with laughter.* **2 roar past/down, etc** If a vehicle roars somewhere, it moves fast making a loud noise. *A huge motorcycle roared past.* **3** [I, T] to say something in a very loud voice *"Stop that!" he roared.*

**roar²** /rɔːr/ *noun* [C] a loud, deep sound *a lion's roar* • *the roar of a jet engine*

**roaring** /ˈrɔːrɪŋ/ *adj* [always before noun] **1** A roaring fire or wind is very powerful. **2** *informal* used to emphasize a situation or state *The party was a roaring success.*

**roast¹** /rəʊst/ *verb* [I, T] If you roast food, you cook it in an oven or over a fire, and if food roasts, it is cooked in an oven or over a fire. *Roast the lamb in a hot oven for 35 minutes.* • **roast** *adj* [always before noun] *roast beef/pork* ➔ See picture at **cook.**

**roast²** /rəʊst/ *noun* [C] a piece of roasted meat *We usually have a roast for lunch on Sunday.*

**rob** /rɒb/ *verb* [T] **robbing**, *past* **robbed 1** to steal from someone or somewhere, often using violence *to rob a bank* • *Two tourists were robbed at gunpoint in the city centre last night.* **2 rob sb of sth** to take something important away from someone *The war had robbed them of their innocence.*

**robber** /ˈrɒbər/ *noun* [C] someone who steals *a bank robber* • *a gang of armed robbers*

**robbery** /ˈrɒbəri/ *noun* [C] the crime of stealing from someone or somewhere *a bank robbery* • *an armed robbery* • *to commit a robbery*

**robe** /rəʊb/ *noun* [C] a long, loose piece of clothing, often something that is worn for ceremonies or special occasions

**robin** /ˈrɒbɪn/ *noun* [C] a small, brown bird with a red chest

**robot** /ˈrəʊbɒt/ *noun* [C] a machine controlled by a computer, which can move and do other things that people can do • **robotic** /rəʊˈbɒtɪk/ *adj* relating to or like a robot

**robust** /rəʊˈbʌst/ *adj* strong and healthy *He looks robust enough.* • *a robust economy*

o-- **rock¹** /rɒk/ *noun* **1** [SUBSTANCE] [U] the hard, natural substance which forms part of the Earth's surface *a layer of volcanic rock* **2** [LARGE PIECE] [C] a large piece of rock or stone *Huge waves were crashing against the rocks.* **3** [MUSIC] [U] loud, modern music with a strong beat, often played with electric guitars and drums *hard/soft rock* • *rock music* • *a rock band/singer* **4 on the rocks a** If a relationship is on the rocks, it has problems and is likely to end soon. **b** If a drink is on the rocks, it is served with ice in it.

**rock²** /rɒk/ *verb* **1** [I, T] to move backwards and forwards or from side to side, or to make someone or something do this *She rocked back and forth on her chair.* • *He gently rocked the baby to sleep.* **2** [T] to shock a large number of people [often passive] *The country has been rocked by a series of drug scandals.* ➔ *See also:* rock the **boat**.

**ˌrock ˈbottom** *noun informal* **hit/reach rock bottom** to reach the lowest level possible *The president's popularity has hit rock bottom.*

**rocket¹** /ˈrɒkɪt/ *noun* [C] **1** a tube-shaped vehicle for travelling in space **2** a tube-shaped weapon that carries a bomb

**rocket²** /ˈrɒkɪt/ *verb* [I] **1** to quickly increase in value or amount *House prices have rocketed this year.* **2** to make quick progress *She rocketed to stardom after modelling for Vogue last year.*

**rock 'n' roll** /ˌrɒkənˈrəʊl/ (*also* ˌrock and ˈroll) *noun* [U] a type of dance music that was especially popular in the 1950s

**ˈrock ˌstar** *noun* [C] a famous rock musician

**rocky** /ˈrɒki/ *adj* with lots of rocks *a rocky beach*

**rod** /rɒd/ *noun* [C] a thin, straight pole *a fishing rod* • *The concrete is strengthened with steel rods.*

**rode** /rəʊd/ *past tense of* ride

**rodent** /ˈrəʊdᵊnt/ *noun* [C] an animal with long, sharp teeth, such as a mouse or rabbit

**rodeo** /ˈrəʊdiəʊ/ *noun* [C] a competition in which people show their skill at riding wild horses and catching cows

**roe** /rəʊ/ *noun* [U] fish eggs

**rogue** /rəʊɡ/ *adj* [always before noun] not behaving in the way that is expected or wanted *a rogue state* • *rogue cells*

o⟶**role** /rəʊl/ *noun* [C] **1** the job someone or something has in a particular situation *This part of the brain **plays an** important **role in** learning.* **2** a part in a play or film *In his latest film, he **plays the role of** a violent gangster.* ➔ *See also:* title **role**.

**ˈrole ˌmodel** *noun* [C] someone you try to behave like because you admire them *Jane is such a good role model for her younger sister.*

**role-play** /ˈrəʊlˌpleɪ/ *noun* [C, U] pretending to be someone else, especially as part of learning a new skill

o⟶**roll¹** /rəʊl/ *verb* **1** roll (sth) **across/around/over, etc** to move somewhere by turning in a circular direction, or to make something move this way *The ball rolled through the goalkeeper's legs.* • *She rolled over onto her side.* **2 roll down/in/off, etc** to move somewhere smoothly *Tears rolled down her face.* • *His car started rolling down the drive.* **3** [T] to turn something around itself to make the shape of a ball or tube *to roll a cigarette* **4 roll your eyes** to move your eyes so that they are looking up, usually to show surprise or disapproval **5 be rolling in it** *informal* to be very rich ➔ *See also:* set/start the **ball** rolling.

**roll in** to arrive in large numbers *She only set up the business last year and already the money's rolling in.*

**roll sth up** to fold something around itself to make the shape of a ball or tube, or to make a piece of clothing shorter *to roll up your sleeves/trouser legs* • *to roll up a carpet* ➔ *Opposite* **unroll**.

**roll**

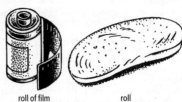

roll of film            roll

**roll up** *informal* to arrive somewhere, usually late *By the time Jim rolled up, the party had almost finished.*

o⟶**roll²** /rəʊl/ *noun* [C] **1** ROUND OBJECT something that has been turned around itself into a round shape like a tube *a roll of film* • *a roll of toilet paper* **2** BREAD a small loaf of bread for one person *Would you like a roll and butter with your soup?* **3** LIST a list of names *the electoral roll* **4** SOUND a long, deep sound *a roll of thunder* • *a drum roll* **5 be on a roll** *informal* to be having a successful period *We were on a roll, winning our fourth game in a row.* ➔ *See also:* rock 'n' **roll**, toilet **roll**.

**roller** /ˈrəʊlə/ *noun* [C] a piece of equipment in the shape of a tube which is rolled around or over something *She uses rollers to curl her hair.* • *Logs are stripped of their bark and crushed between huge rollers.*

**Rollerblades** /ˈrəʊləbleɪdz/ *noun* [plural] *trademark* (*also* **in-line skates**) boots with a single line of wheels on the bottom, used for moving across the ground *a teenager on rollerblades* • **rollerblading** *noun* [U] *Lots of people go rollerblading in Central Park.* ➔ *See colour picture* **Sports 1** *on page Centre 15.*

**roller coaster** /ˈrəʊləˌkəʊstə/ *noun* [C] an exciting entertainment which is like a fast train that goes up and down very steep slopes

**ˈroller ˌskate** *noun* [C] a boot with wheels on the bottom, used for moving across the ground • **roller skating** *noun* [U]

**ˈrolling ˌpin** *noun* [C] a kitchen tool shaped like a tube that you roll over pastry to make it thinner before cooking ➔ *See colour picture* **Kitchen** *on page Centre 10.*

**Roman¹** /ˈrəʊmən/ *adj* relating to ancient Rome or its empire *Roman remains*

**Roman²** /ˈrəʊmən/ *noun* [C] someone who lived in ancient Rome or its empire

**ˌRoman ˈCatholic** *adj* related to the part of the Christian religion that has the Pope (= a very important priest) as its leader • **Roman Catholic** *noun* [C] *He is a Roman Catholic.* • **Roman Catholicism** *noun* [U] the beliefs of the Roman Catholic religion

**romance** /rəʊˈmæns/ *noun* **1** LOVE [C, U] an exciting relationship of love between two people, often a short one *They got married last September after a whirlwind romance.* **2** STORY [C] a story about love **3** EXCITEMENT [U] a feeling of excitement or exciting danger *the romance of the sea*

**ˌRoman ˈnumeral** *noun* [C] a letter that represents a number in the Roman system in which I

R

is 1, II is 2, V is 5, etc *My watch has Roman numerals.*

○━**romantic¹** /rəʊˈmæntɪk/ *adj* **1** LOVE relating to exciting feelings of love *a romantic dinner for two* **2** STORY relating to a story about love *romantic fiction* ● *a romantic comedy* **3** IDEAS thinking that things are better than they really are, and that things are possible which are not *a romantic view of the world* ● romantically *adv*

**romantic²** /rəʊˈmæntɪk/ *noun* [C] someone who thinks that things are better than they really are, and that things are possible which are not

**romanticize** (*also UK* **-ise**) /rəʊˈmæntɪsaɪz/ *verb* [T] to make something seem much better or exciting than it really is *a romanticized image of married life*

**romp** /rɒmp/ *verb* **romp around/in/through, etc** to run around in a happy, energetic way *The children were romping around in the garden.* ● romp *noun* [C]

○━**roof** /ruːf/ *noun* **1** [C] the surface that covers the top of a building or vehicle *a flat/sloping roof* ● *He climbed onto the roof.* **2** **the roof of your mouth** the top part of the inside of your mouth **3** **a roof over your head** somewhere to live **4** **go through the roof** If the level of something, especially a price, goes through the roof, it increases very quickly. **5** **hit the roof** *informal* to become very angry and start shouting *If I'm late again he'll hit the roof.*

**roofing** /ˈruːfɪŋ/ *noun* [U] material used to make a roof

**rooftop** /ˈruːftɒp/ *noun* [C] the top of a roof *a view across the city rooftops*

**rook** /rʊk/ *noun* [C] a large, black bird that lives in Europe

**rookie** /ˈrʊki/ *noun* [C] *mainly US* someone who has only recently started doing a job or activity and so has no experience *a rookie cop*

○━**room¹** /ruːm, rʊm/ *noun* **1** [C] a part of the inside of a building, which is separated from other parts by walls, floors, and ceilings *a hotel room* **2** [U] space for things to fit into *Is there enough* **room** *for all of us in your car?* ● *Can everyone move up a bit to* **make room** *for these people?* ● [+ to do sth] *There's hardly enough room to move in here.* **3** **room for sth** a possibility for something to happen *His work isn't bad but there's still some room for improvement.* ➲ *See also:* **changing room, chat room, dining room, drawing room, dressing room, elbow room, emergency room, living room, locker room, men's room, operating room, sitting room, waiting room.**

**room²** /ruːm, rʊm/ *verb* **room with sb** *US* to share a bedroom with someone, usually at college

**roommate** /ˈruːmmeɪt/ *noun* [C] **1** someone who you share a room with **2** *US* (*UK* **housemate/flatmate**) someone who you share your home with

**roomy** /ˈruːmi/ *adj* having a lot of space *It looks small, but it's really quite roomy inside.*

**roost** /ruːst/ *noun* [C] **1** a place where birds go to rest or sleep **2** **rule the roost** to be the person who makes all the decisions in a group

**rooster** /ˈruːstər/ *noun* [C] a male chicken

○━**root¹** /ruːt/ *noun* **1** [C] the part of a plant that grows under the ground and gets water and food from the soil **2** [C] the part of a hair or tooth that is under the skin **3** **the root of sth** the cause of something, usually something bad *the root of all evil* ➲ *See also:* **grass roots.**

**root²** /ruːt/ *verb*

**root about/around (sth)** to search for something, especially by looking through other things *She was rooting around in her drawer for a pencil.*

**root for sb** *informal* to show support for someone who is in a competition or who is doing something difficult *Good luck! We're all rooting for you.*

**be rooted in sth** to be based on something or caused by something *Most prejudices are rooted in ignorance.*

**root sth/sb out** to find and get rid of the thing or person that is causing a problem *It is our aim to root out corruption.*

**roots** /ruːts/ *noun* [plural] where someone or something originally comes from *the roots of modern jazz* ● *He lives in London but his roots are in Edinburgh.*

**rope¹** /rəʊp/ *noun* [C, U] **1** very thick string made from twisted thread **2** **be on the ropes** *mainly US* to be doing badly and likely to fail *His career is on the ropes.* **3** **learn/know the ropes** to learn/know how to do a job or activity ➲ *See also:* at the **end¹** of your rope, **jump rope, skipping rope.**

**rope²** /rəʊp/ *verb* [T] to tie things together with rope

**rope sb in** *informal* to persuade someone to help you with something, especially when they do not want to

**rosary** /ˈrəʊzəri/ *noun* [C] a string of beads (= small, round balls) that is used to count prayers in the Catholic religion

**rose¹** /rəʊz/ *noun* [C] a flower with a pleasant smell and thorns (= sharp points on the stem), that grows on a bush *He gave me a bunch of red roses.*

**rose²** /rəʊz/ *past tense of* rise

**rosé** /ˈrəʊzeɪ (*US*) rəʊˈzeɪ/ *noun* [U] pink wine

**rosemary** /ˈrəʊzməri/ *noun* [U] a herb that grows as a bush with thin, pointed leaves

**rosette** /rəʊˈzet/ *noun* [C] **1** *UK* (*US* **ribbon**) a decoration made of coloured cloth, which is given as a prize **2** *UK* a decoration made of coloured cloth in the shape of a rose, worn to show political support for someone

**roster** /ˈrɒstər/ *noun* [C] **1** a plan which shows who must do which jobs and when they must do them *a duty roster* **2** a list of names of people who belong to a team or organization

**rostrum** /ˈrɒstrəm/ *noun* [C] a raised surface which someone stands on to make a speech or receive a prize

**rosy** /ˈrəʊzi/ *adj* **1** Rosy faces are a healthy pink colour. *rosy cheeks* **2** very positive and happy *The future looks rosy.*

**rot¹** /rɒt/ *verb* [I, T] **rotting**, *past* **rotted** If vegetable or animal substances rot, they decay, and if something rots them, it makes them decay. *The fruit had been left to rot on the trees.* ● *Sugar rots your teeth.* ● *the smell of rotting fish*

**R**

**rot²** /rɒt/ *noun* [U] **1** decay *There was rot in the woodwork.* **2 the rot sets in** *UK* If the rot sets in, a situation starts to get worse. **3 stop the rot** *UK* to do something to prevent a situation from continuing to get worse

**rota** /'rəʊtə/ *noun* [C] *UK* (*UK/US* **roster**) a plan which shows who must do which jobs and when they must do them

**rotary** /'rəʊt³ri/ *adj* [always before noun] moving in a circular direction

**rotate** /rəʊ'teɪt/ *verb* [I, T] **1** to turn in a circular direction, or to make something turn in a circular direction *The television rotates for viewing at any angle.* **2** to change from one person or thing to another in a regular order *Farmers usually rotate their crops to improve the soil.* • rotation /rəʊ'teɪʃ³n/ *noun* [C, U] *the rotation of the Earth* • *crop rotation*

**rotten** /'rɒt³n/ *adj* **1** Rotten vegetable or animal substances are decaying. *rotten eggs* **2** *informal* very bad *rotten weather*

**rottweiler** /'rɒtwaɪlə³/ *noun* [C] a type of large, powerful dog

o━**rough¹** /rʌf/ *adj* **1** NOT SMOOTH A rough surface is not smooth. *rough hands* • *rough ground* **2** APPROXIMATE approximate *a rough estimate* • *Can you give me a rough idea of the cost?* **3** FORCEFUL If the sea or weather is rough, there is a lot of strong wind and sometimes rain. *The boat sank in rough seas off the Swedish coast.* **4** ILL [never before noun] *UK* ill *I feel a bit rough after last night.* **5** DIFFICULT difficult or unpleasant *She's having a rough time at work.* **6** DANGEROUS dangerous or violent *a rough part of town* • *Hockey can be quite a rough game.* **7** NOT PERFECT quickly done and not perfect *These are just rough sketches.* **8 rough and ready a** produced quickly without preparation **b** not very polite or well-educated • roughness *noun* [U]

**rough²** /rʌf/ *noun* **take the rough with the smooth** *UK* to accept the unpleasant parts of a situation as well as the pleasant parts

**rough³** /rʌf/ *adv* **live/sleep rough** *UK* to live and sleep outside because you have nowhere else to live

**rough⁴** /rʌf/ *verb* **rough it** to live in a way that is simple and not comfortable

**roughage** /'rʌfɪdʒ/ *noun* [U] a substance in fruit and vegetables that helps you to get rid of waste from the body

**roughen** /'rʌf³n/ *verb* [I, T] to become rough or make something become rough *Years of housework had roughened her hands.*

o━**roughly** /'rʌfli/ *adv* **1** approximately *There's been an increase of roughly 30% since last year.* **2** forcefully or violently *He pushed us roughly out of the door.*

**roulette** /ru:'let/ *noun* [U] a game in which a small ball moves around a dish with numbers on it, and people try to win money by guessing where the ball will stop

o━**round¹** /raʊnd/ *adj* **1** in the shape of a circle or ball *a round table/window* • *round eyes* • *a round face* ➔ *See picture at* **flat**. **2 round figures/numbers** numbers given to the nearest 10, 100, 1000, etc and not as the exact amounts

o━**round²** /raʊnd/ *UK* (*UK/US* **around**) *adv, preposition* **1** IN A CIRCLE on all sides of something *We sat round the table.* • *She had a scarf round her neck.* **2** DIRECTION to the opposite direction *She looked round.* • *Turn the car round and let's go home.* **3** TO A PLACE to or in different parts of a place *He showed me round the flat.* **4** SEVERAL PLACES from one place or person to another *He went round the room asking people individually.* • *Could you pass these forms round, please?* **5** VISIT to someone's home *Wendy's coming round this afternoon.* **6** NEAR near an area *Do you live round here?* **7 round about** at approximately a time or approximately an amount *We'll be there round about 10 o'clock.* **8 round and round** moving in a circle without stopping *We drove round and round trying to find the hotel.*

**round³** /raʊnd/ *noun* [C] **1 first/second/third/ etc, round** a part of a competition *He was beaten in the first round.* **2** EVENTS a group of events that is part of a series *a round of interviews* • *a new round of talks between the two countries* **3** VISITS *UK* regular visits to a group of people or houses to give them something or to see them *a milk/newspaper round* **4** DRINKS drinks that you buy for a group of people *It's your turn to buy the next round.* **5 round of applause** when people clap *The crowd gave him a huge round of applause.* **6** BULLETS a bullet or a set of bullets to be fired at one time from a gun **7 round of golf** a game of golf

**round⁴** /raʊnd/ *verb* [T] to go around something *They rounded the corner at high speed.*

**round sth down** to reduce a number to the nearest whole or simple number

**round sth off** to end an activity in a pleasant way *We rounded off the lesson with a quiz.*

**round sb/sth up** to find and bring together a group of people or animals *The police are rounding up the usual suspects.*

**round sth up** to increase a number to the nearest whole or simple number

**roundabout¹** /'raʊndə,baʊt/ *noun* [C] **1** *UK* (*US* **traffic circle**) a circular place where roads meet and where cars drive around until they arrive at the road that they want to turn into *to go round a roundabout* **2** *UK* an entertainment which goes round and round while children sit on it

roundabout *UK*, traffic circle *US*

roundabout

**roundabout²** /ˈraʊndəˌbaʊt/ *adj* [always before noun] A roundabout way of doing something or going somewhere is not the direct way.

**rounded** /ˈraʊndɪd/ *adj* smooth and curved *a table with rounded corners*

**rounders** /ˈraʊndəz/ *noun* [U] a British game in which you try to hit a small ball and then run round all four sides of a large square

**roundly** /ˈraʊndli/ *adv* If you criticize someone or something roundly, you do it very strongly. *The action was roundly condemned by French and German leaders.*

**round ˈtrip** *noun* [C] a journey from one place to another and back to where you started

**round-trip ˈticket** US (UK **return**) *noun* [C] a ticket that lets you travel to a place and back again, for example on a train

**round-up** /ˈraʊndʌp/ *noun* [C] **1** when a group of people or animals are found and brought together *a police round-up* **2** a short report of all the facts or events relating to a subject *a news round-up*

**rouse** /raʊz/ *verb* [T] **1** to cause a feeling or emotion in someone *This issue is rousing a lot of public interest.* **2** *formal* to wake someone up *He was roused from a deep sleep.*

**rousing** /ˈraʊzɪŋ/ *adj* making people feel excited and proud or ready to take action *a rousing performance/speech*

**rout** /raʊt/ *verb* [T] to defeat someone completely • **rout** *noun* [C] *an election rout*

o━**route** /ruːt ⑤ ruːt, raʊt/ *noun* [C] **1** the roads or paths you follow to get from one place to another place *an escape route* • *Crowds gathered all **along the route** to watch the race.* **2** a method of achieving something *A university education is seen by many as the best route to a good job.* ⊃ See also: **en route**.

**routine¹** /ruːˈtiːn/ *noun* **1** [C, U] the things you regularly do and how and when you do them *a daily routine* • *He longed to escape the routine of an office job.* **2** [C] a regular series of movements, jokes, etc used in a performance *a dance routine*

**routine²** /ruːˈtiːn/ *adj* **1** done regularly and not unusual *a routine procedure* • *routine checks* **2** done regularly and very boring *His job is very routine.*

**routinely** /ruːˈtiːnli/ *adv* regularly or often

**roving** /ˈrəʊvɪŋ/ *adj* [always before noun] moving around from one place to another place *a roving reporter*

o━**row¹** /rəʊ/ *noun* **1** [C] a straight line of people or things *a row of chairs/houses* • *My students sit at desks in rows for most of the time.* **2** [C] a line of seats *to sit on the back/front row* • *Isn't that Sophie sitting in the row behind us?* **3** **in a row** one after another without a break *He's just won the tournament for the fifth year in a row.* ⊃ See also: **death row**.

**row²** /rəʊ/ *verb* [I, T] to move a boat or move someone in a boat through the water using oars (= poles with flat ends) *They rowed out to an island in the centre of the lake.* • **rowing** *noun* [U]

**row³** /raʊ/ *noun* UK **1** [LOUD ARGUMENT] [C] a loud, angry argument *a blazing row* • *The couple next door are always **having rows**.*

**2** [DISAGREEMENT] [C] a disagreement about a political or public situation *A row has erupted over defence policy.* **3** [NOISE] [no plural] very loud noise *The kids were making a terrible row upstairs.*

**rowdy** /ˈraʊdi/ *adj* loud and uncontrolled *rowdy behaviour* • *rowdy football fans*

**ˈrow ˌhouse** US (UK **terraced house**) *noun* [C] one of a row of houses that are joined together

**ˈrowing ˌboat** UK (US **rowboat** /ˈrəʊbəʊt/) *noun* [C] a small boat moved by oars (= poles with flat ends)

o━**royal¹** /ˈrɔɪəl/ *adj* **1** relating to a queen or king and their family *the British royal family* • *a royal visit* **2** **Royal** used in the UK as part of the title of a royal person *His Royal Highness, the Duke of York*

**royal²** /ˈrɔɪəl/ *noun* [C] *informal* a member of a royal family *a book about the royals*

**royalist** /ˈrɔɪəlɪst/ *noun* [C] someone who supports the principle of having a King or Queen • **royalist** *adj*

**royalties** /ˈrɔɪəltiz/ *noun* [plural] money that is paid to a writer, actor, etc each time their work is sold or performed *He could receive as much as $1 million **in royalties** over the next six years.*

**royalty** /ˈrɔɪəlti/ *noun* [U] the members of the royal family

**RSVP** /ˌɑːresviːˈpiː/ used at the end of a written invitation to mean 'please answer' *RSVP by October 9th*

**rub¹** /rʌb/ *verb* **rubbing**, *past* **rubbed** **1** [T] to press your hand or a cloth on a surface and move it backwards and forwards *She rubbed her hands together to warm them.* • *He rubbed himself dry with a towel.* • *Rub the stain with a damp cloth.* **2** **rub sth into/on, etc** to move a substance backwards and forwards over a surface so that it covers it and goes into it *I rubbed some suntan oil on her back.* • *Rub the butter into the flour.* **3** [I, T] to touch and move against something, often causing pain or damage *My new boots are rubbing against my toes.* **4** **rub it in** *informal* to upset someone by talking to them about something which you know they want to forget ⊃ See also: rub shoulders (**shoulder¹**) with sb, rub sb up the wrong **way¹**.

**rub off** If a quality or characteristic of a particular person rubs off, other people begin to have it because they have been with that person. *His enthusiasm is starting to **rub off on** the rest of us.*

**rub sth out** UK to remove writing from something by rubbing it with a piece of rubber or a cloth

**rub²** /rʌb/ *noun* [C] when you rub something [usually singular] *Give it a rub and it'll feel better.*

**rubber** /ˈrʌbəʳ/ *noun* **1** [U] a strong material that bends easily, originally produced from the juice of a tropical tree, and used to make tyres, boots, etc **2** [C] UK (US **eraser**) a small object which is used to remove pencil marks from paper ⊃ See colour picture **Classroom** on page Centre 4.

**ˌrubber ˈband** (*also* UK **elastic band**) *noun* [C] a thin circle of rubber used to hold things together

,rubber 'boot noun [C] US (UK **wellies** [plural]) a large shoe made of rubber that covers your foot and part of your leg

rubber-stamp /ˌrʌbəˈstæmp/ verb [T] to officially approve a decision or plan without thinking very much about it

rubbery /ˈrʌbəri/ adj feeling or bending like rubber a rubbery piece of meat

rubbish /ˈrʌbɪʃ/ noun [U] mainly UK 1 WASTE things that you throw away because you do not want them Our rubbish gets collected on Thursdays. • a rubbish dump/bin 2 NONSENSE something that is nonsense or stupid Ignore him, he's talking rubbish. 3 BAD QUALITY informal something that is of bad quality There's so much rubbish on TV.

rubble /ˈrʌbl/ noun [U] pieces of broken bricks from a building that has been destroyed a pile of rubble

rubella /ruːˈbelə/ (also German measles) noun [U] a disease which causes red spots on your skin

rubric /ˈruːbrɪk/ noun [C] a set of instructions or an explanation, especially in an examination paper or book

ruby /ˈruːbi/ noun [C] a valuable red stone which is used in jewellery

rucksack /ˈrʌksæk/ noun [C] UK a bag that you carry on your back ⊃ See picture at **bag**.

rudder /ˈrʌdəʳ/ noun [C] a piece of equipment that changes the direction of a boat or aircraft

ruddy /ˈrʌdi/ adj A ruddy face is red. ruddy cheeks

o–⚬rude /ruːd/ adj 1 behaving in a way which is not polite and upsets other people a rude remark • He complained that a member of staff had been **rude** to him. • [+ to do sth] It would be rude to leave without saying goodbye. 2 Rude words or jokes relate to sex or going to the toilet. • rudely adv • rudeness noun [U] ⊃ See also: a rude **awakening**.

rudiments /ˈruːdɪmənts/ noun formal **the rudiments of sth** the most basic parts or principles of something • rudimentary /ˌruːdɪˈmentʳri/ adj formal very basic

rueful /ˈruːfʳl/ adj showing slight sadness about something but not in a serious way a rueful smile • ruefully adv

ruffle /ˈrʌfl/ verb [T] If someone ruffles your hair, they rub it gently. He ruffled my hair and kissed me.

rug /rʌg/ noun [C] 1 a soft piece of material used to cover the floor The dog was lying on the rug in front of the fire. ⊃ See colour picture **The Living Room** on page Centre 11. 2 UK a soft cover that keeps you warm or comfortable

rugby /ˈrʌgbi/ noun [U] a sport played by two teams with an oval ball and H-shaped goals a rugby player ⊃ See colour picture **Sports 2** on page Centre 16.

rugged /ˈrʌgɪd/ adj 1 If an area of land is rugged, it looks rough and has lots of rocks. a rugged coastline 2 If a man looks rugged, his face looks strong and attractive. a rugged face

o–⚬ruin¹ /ˈruːɪn/ verb [T] 1 to spoil or destroy something [often passive] They were late and the dinner was ruined. • It's ruining his health living in that damp house. 2 to cause someone

to lose all their money or their job If the newspapers get hold of this story they'll ruin him.

ruin² /ˈruːɪn/ noun 1 DESTRUCTION [U] the destruction of something Fonthill Abbey fell **into ruin** 10 years after it was built. 2 BROKEN BUILDING [C] the broken parts that are left from an old building or town Thousand of tourists wander around these ancient ruins every year. 3 LOSING EVERYTHING [U] when someone loses everything such as all their money or their job The collapse of the bank has left many people **in** financial **ruin**. 4 **be/lie in ruins** to be in a very bad state The war left one million people dead and the country in ruins.

o–⚬rule¹ /ruːl/ noun 1 INSTRUCTION [C] an official instruction about what you must or must not do to break (= not obey) the rules. • to obey/follow the rules • You can't smoke at school, it's **against** the rules (= not allowed). 2 LEADER [U] when someone is in control of a country military rule • There have been reports of immense human suffering **under his rule**. 3 USUAL WAY [no plural] the usual way something is an exception to the rule • Workers in the North are, **as a rule**, paid less than those in the South. 4 PRINCIPLE [C] a principle of a system, such as a language or science the rules of grammar 5 **a rule of thumb** a way of calculating something, which is not exact but which will help you to be correct enough 6 **bend/stretch the rules** to allow someone to do something which is not usually allowed We don't usually let students take books home, but I'll bend the rules on this occasion. ⊃ See also: **ground rules**.

rule² /ruːl/ verb [I, T] 1 to make an official legal decision [+ (that)] The judge ruled that it was wrong for a 16-year-old girl to be held in an adult prison. 2 to be in control of somewhere, usually a country [often passive] They were ruled for many years by a dictator. • the ruling party ⊃ See also: rule the **roost**.

rule sb/sth out to decide that something or someone is not suitable for a particular purpose, or to decide that something is impossible The police have not ruled him out as a suspect.

ruler /ˈruːləʳ/ noun [C] 1 the leader of a country 2 a flat, straight stick which is used to measure things ⊃ See colour picture **Classroom** on page Centre 4.

ruling /ˈruːlɪŋ/ noun [C] an official legal decision, usually made by a judge

rum /rʌm/ noun [C, U] a strong, alcoholic drink made from sugar

rumble /ˈrʌmbl/ verb [I] to make a deep, long sound The smell of cooking made his stomach rumble. • rumble noun [no plural] the distant rumble of thunder

rumbling /ˈrʌmblɪŋ/ noun [C] a deep, long sound the rumbling of a train passing by

rumblings /ˈrʌmblɪŋz/ noun [plural] signs that people are angry about something rumblings of discontent

rummage /ˈrʌmɪdʒ/ verb **rummage around/ in/through, etc** to search inside something and move things around I found him rummaging through my drawers.

'rummage ˌsale US (UK **jumble sale**) noun [C]

R

a sale of old items, especially clothes, usually to make money for an organization

**rumour**¹ *UK* (*US* **rumor**) /'ruːmər/ *noun* [C] a fact that a lot of people are talking about although they do not know if it is true *to spread rumours* • *to deny rumours* • [+ (that)] *I heard a rumour that you were leaving.*

**rumour**² *UK* (*US* **rumor**) /'ruːmər/ *verb* **be rumoured** If a fact is rumoured, people are talking about it although they do not know if it is true. [+ (that)] *It's rumoured that the company director is about to resign.* • [+ to do sth] *The company is rumoured to be in financial difficulty.*

**rump** /rʌmp/ *noun* [C] the area above an animal's back legs

**rumpled** /'rʌmpld/ *adj* Rumpled clothes or sheets are untidy because they have folds in them.

⊶**run**¹ /rʌn/ *verb* **running**, *past t* **ran**, *past p* **run 1** MOVE FAST [I, T] to move on your feet at a faster speed than walking *He can run very fast.* • *He ran away when I tried to pick him up.* • [+ to do sth] *We had to run to catch up with him.* • *I run about three miles every morning.* **2** ORGANIZE [T] to organize or control something *She ran her own restaurant for five years.* **3** **run sb/sth to/down, etc** to take someone or something somewhere, usually by car *Could you run me to the station this afternoon?* **4** WORKING [T] If a piece of equipment is running, it is switched on and working, and if you run it, you switch it on and make it work. *The engine is running more smoothly now.* **5** USE COMPUTER [T] If you run a computer program, you use it on your computer. *Did you run a virus check this morning?* **6** TRAVELLING [I] If trains or buses are running, they are available to travel on. *The buses only run until 11 p.m.* **7** LIQUID [I] If liquid runs somewhere, it flows. *Tears ran down her face.* • *Have you got a tissue? My nose is running* (= liquid is coming out of it). **8** PUBLISH [T] to publish something in a newspaper or magazine *All the papers are running this story on the front page.* **9 run a bath** *UK* to fill a bath with water so that it is ready to use **10 run sth along/over/ through, etc sth** to move something along, over, or through something else *She ran her fingers through her hair.* **11 run through/down/along, etc** If something long and narrow runs somewhere, it is in that position. *There are wires running across the floor.* • *The road runs parallel to the railway line.* **12** CONTINUE [I] If a play, film, etc runs for a period of time, it continues that long. *The play ran for five months before moving to the West End.* **13 run in the/sb's family** If a quality, ability, disease, etc runs in the family, many members of the family have it. *A love of animals runs in our family.* **14** COLOUR [I] If a colour runs, it comes out of some material when it is washed. **15 be running at sth** to be at a particular level *Inflation is now running at 5.8%.* ⊃ *See also:* run your/an **eye**¹ over sth, run the **gauntlet**, run **riot**¹, run out of **steam**¹, run **wild**¹.

**run across sb** to meet someone you know when you are not expecting to *I ran across Jim in town the other day.*

**run after sb/sth** to chase someone or something that is moving away from you

**run around** to be very busy doing a lot of different things *I'm exhausted, I've been running around all morning.*

**run away** to secretly leave a place because you are unhappy there *to run away from home*

**run sth by sb** to tell someone about something so that they can give their opinion about it *Can I run something by you, Sam?*

**run sb/sth down** *informal* to criticize someone or something, often unfairly

**run for sth** to compete in an election *He's running for mayor again this year.*

**run into sb** to meet someone you know when you are not expecting to *I ran into Emma on my way home.*

**run into sth 1** HIT to hit something while you are driving a vehicle *He skidded and ran into a tree.* **2** REACH A LEVEL If an amount runs into thousands, millions, etc, it reaches that level. **3** PROBLEMS If you run into difficulties, you begin to experience them. *to run into trouble*

**run off** *informal* to leave somewhere unexpectedly *He ran off with all my money.*

**run on sth** If a machine runs on a supply of power, it uses that power to work. *The scanner runs on mains electricity and batteries.*

**run out 1** to use all of something so that there is none left *I've nearly run out of money.* **2** If a supply of something runs out, there is none left because it has all been used. *Come on, time is running out.*

**run sb/sth over** to hit someone or something with a vehicle and drive over them, injuring or killing them *He was run over by a bus as he crossed the road.*

**run through sth** to repeat something in order to practise it or to make sure that it is correct *I just need to run through my speech one more time.*

**run sth up** If you run up a debt, you do things which cause you to owe a large amount of money.

**run up against sth** If you run up against problems or difficulties, you begin to experience them.

⊶**run²** /rʌn/ *noun* **1** MOVING [C] when you move on your feet at a speed faster than walking as a sport [usually singular] *to go for a run* **2** SCORING [C] in cricket or baseball, a single point *to score a run* **3 a dummy/practice/trial run** when you do something to practise it before the real time **4 a run of sth** when something happens several times without something different happening during that period *a run of 10 games without a win* • *a run of good/bad luck* **5** PERFORMANCES [C] a period of performances of a play, film, etc **6 be on the run** to be trying to avoid being caught, especially by the police **7 make a run for it** *informal* to suddenly run fast in order to escape from somewhere **8 in the long/short run** at a time that is far away or near in the future

**runaway**¹ /'rʌnəweɪ/ *adj* [always before noun] **1 a runaway success/victory/winner, etc** something good that happens very quickly or easily **2** A runaway vehicle is moving away from

**R**

somewhere without anyone controlling it. *a runaway car/train*

**runaway²** /'rʌnə,weɪ/ *noun* [C] someone who has secretly left a place because they are unhappy there *teenage runaways*

**run-down** /,rʌn'daʊn/ *adj* Run-down buildings or areas are in very bad condition. *a run-down housing estate*

**rundown** /'rʌndaʊn/ *noun* [no plural] a report of the main facts relating to a subject *He gave us a rundown on what happened at the meeting.*

**rung¹** /rʌŋ/ *noun* **1** [C] one of the horizontal parts across a ladder (= structure for climbing up) **2 the first/highest/next, etc rung of the ladder** the first, highest, next, etc position, especially in society or in a job *She's on the bottom rung of the management ladder.*

**rung²** /rʌŋ/ *past participle of* ring²

**run-in** /'rʌnɪn/ *noun* [C] *informal* an argument *to have a run-in with someone*

**runner** /'rʌnəʳ/ *noun* **1** [C] someone who runs, usually in competitions *a long-distance runner* **2 drug/gun runner** someone who takes drugs or guns illegally from one place to another ⊃ *See also:* **front-runner.**

**,runner 'bean** *UK* (*US* **'runner ,bean**) *noun* [C] a long, flat, green bean

**runner-up** /,rʌnər'ʌp/ *noun* [C] *plural* **runners-up** someone who finishes in second position in a competition

**running¹** /'rʌnɪŋ/ *noun* [U] **1** the sport of moving on your feet at a speed faster than walking *I go running three times a week.* • *running shoes* ⊃ *See colour picture* **Sports 1** on *page Centre 15.* **2** the activity of controlling or looking after something *He has recently handed over the day-to-day running of the museum to his daughter.* • *running costs*

**running²** /'rʌnɪŋ/ *adj* **1** [always before noun] continuing for a long time *a running battle* • *a running joke* **2 second/third, etc day/week, etc running** If something happens for the second/third, etc day/week, etc running, it happens on that number of regular occasions without changing. *He's won the Championship for the fifth year running.* **3 running water** If a place has running water, it has a working water system. *They bought an old house with no electricity or running water.*

**runny** /'rʌni/ *adj* **1** A runny substance is more liquid than usual. *runny egg* **2 runny nose** If you have a runny nose, your nose is producing liquid all the time.

**run-of-the-mill** /,rʌnəvðə'mɪl/ *adj* ordinary and not special or exciting in any way *He gave a fairly run-of-the-mill speech.*

**run-up** /'rʌnʌp/ *noun* **the run-up to sth** *UK* the period of time before an event *Sales increased by 15% in the run-up to Christmas.*

**runway** /'rʌnweɪ/ *noun* [C] a large road that aircraft use to land on or to start flying from

**rupture** /'rʌptʃəʳ/ *verb* [I, T] If you rupture something, you break or tear it, and if something ruptures, it breaks or tears. *He fell and ruptured a*

*ligament in his knee.* • *a ruptured pipeline*
• rupture *noun* [C]

**rural** /'rʊərəl/ *adj* relating to the countryside and not to towns *a rural area*

**ruse** /ruːz/ *noun* [C] a way of deceiving someone so that they do something that you want them to do [+ to do sth] *The story was just a ruse to get her out of the house.*

o━**rush¹** /rʌʃ/ *verb* **1** [I, T] to hurry or move quickly somewhere, or to make someone or something hurry or move quickly somewhere *We rushed out into the street to see what all the noise was.* • *The UN has rushed medical supplies to the war zone.* • [+ to do sth] *We had to rush to catch the bus.* **2 rush to do sth** to do something quickly and enthusiastically *His friends rushed to congratulate him after the ceremony.* **3** [T] to make someone do something more quickly than they want to do it [+ into + doing sth] *I refuse to be rushed into making a decision.*

o━**rush²** /rʌʃ/ *noun* [no plural] **1** MOVEMENT when something suddenly moves somewhere quickly *a rush of air* • *She felt a sudden rush of blood to her face.* **2** ACTIVITY a lot of things happening or a lot of people trying to do something [+ to do sth] *There was a mad rush to get tickets for the concert.* **3** HURRY when you have to hurry or move somewhere quickly *I'm sorry I can't talk now, I'm in a rush.*

**rushes** /rʌʃɪz/ *noun* [plural] tall plants that grow near water

**'rush ,hour** *noun* [C, U] the time when a lot of people are travelling to or from work and so roads and trains are very busy *the morning/evening rush hour* • *I hate driving during the rush hour.*

**rust** /rʌst/ *noun* [U] a dark orange substance that you get on metal when it has been damaged by air and water • rust *verb* [I, T]

**rustic** /'rʌstɪk/ *adj* simple and old-fashioned in style in a way that is typical of the countryside

**rustle** /'rʌsl/ *verb* [I, T] If things such as paper or leaves rustle, or if you rustle them, they move about and make a soft, dry sound. *Outside, the trees rustled in the wind.*

**rustle up sth** to produce something very quickly *I managed to rustle up a meal from the bits and pieces I found in his fridge.*

**rusty** /'rʌsti/ *adj* **1** Rusty metal has rust (= an orange substance) on its surface. *rusty nails* **2** If a skill you had is now rusty, it is not now good because you have forgotten it. *My French is a bit rusty.*

**rut** /rʌt/ *noun* **1 in a rut** in a bad situation where you do the same things all the time, or where it is impossible to make progress *He seems to be stuck in a rut at the moment.* **2** [C] a deep, narrow mark in the ground made by a wheel

**ruthless** /'ruːθləs/ *adj* not caring if you hurt or upset other people when you try to get what you want *ruthless ambition* • *a ruthless dictator* • ruthlessly *adv* • ruthlessness *noun* [U]

**rye** /raɪ/ *noun* [U] a plant that has grains which are used to make things such as bread and whisky (= strong alcoholic drink) *rye bread*

**R**

# S

**S, s** /es/ the nineteenth letter of the alphabet

**the Sabbath** /'sæbəθ/ *noun* a day of the week that many religious groups use for prayer and rest

**sabbatical** /sə'bætɪkəl/ *noun* [C, U] a period when a university teacher does not do their usual work and instead travels or studies *He was **on sabbatical** last year.*

**sabotage** /'sæbətɑːʒ/ *verb* [T] **1** to damage or destroy something in order to prevent an enemy from using it *Rebels sabotaged the roads and bridges.* **2** to spoil someone's plans or efforts in order to prevent them from being successful *She tried to sabotage my chances of getting the job.* • sabotage *noun* [U] *an act of sabotage*

**saccharin** /'sækərɪn/ *noun* [U] a sweet, chemical substance that is used in food instead of sugar

**sachet** /'sæʃeɪ ⓤⓈ sæ'ʃeɪ/ *noun* [C] a small bag containing a small amount of something *sachets of sugar and coffee powder*

**sack¹** /sæk/ *noun* **1** [C] a large bag made of paper, plastic, or cloth and used to carry or store things **2 the sack** *UK* When someone gets the sack or is given the sack, they are told to leave their job. *He got the sack from his last job.*

**sack²** /sæk/ *verb* [T] *UK* to tell someone to leave their job, usually because they have done something wrong *He was sacked for being late.*

**sacrament** /'sækrəmənt/ *noun* [C] an important religious ceremony in the Christian Church *the sacrament of marriage*

**sacred** /'seɪkrɪd/ *adj* **1** relating to a religion or considered to be holy *sacred music* • *a sacred object* **2** too important to be changed or destroyed *I don't work at weekends – my private time is sacred.*

**sacrifice¹** /'sækrɪfaɪs/ *noun* [C, U] **1** something valuable that you give up in order to achieve something, or the act of giving it up *Sometimes you have to **make sacrifices** to succeed.* **2** something offered to a god in a religious ceremony, especially an animal that is killed, or the act of offering it ⊃ *See also:* **self-sacrifice**.

**sacrifice²** /'sækrɪfaɪs/ *verb* [T] **1** to give up something that is valuable to you in order to achieve something *There are thousands of men ready to **sacrifice** their lives **for** their country.* **2** to kill an animal and offer it to a god in a religious ceremony

**sacrilege** /'sækrɪlɪdʒ/ *noun* [U, no plural] when you treat something that is holy or important without respect

**sacrosanct** /'sækrəʊsæŋkt/ *adj formal* too important to be changed or destroyed *Human life is sacrosanct.*

○⚡**sad** /sæd/ *adj* **sadder, saddest 1** NOT HAPPY unhappy or making you feel unhappy *I was very sad when our cat died.* • *a sad book/movie* • [+ that] *It's a bit sad that you'll miss our wedding.* • [+ to do sth] *I was sad to see him go.*

**2** NOT SATISFACTORY [always before noun] not pleasant or satisfactory *The sad truth is that we've failed.* **3** NOT FASHIONABLE *UK informal* boring or not fashionable *You enjoy reading timetables? You sad man!* • sadness *noun* [U] *We could see the sadness in their faces.*

**sadden** /'sædən/ *verb* [T] *formal* to make someone feel sad or disappointed [often passive] *We were saddened by his death.*

**saddle¹** /'sædl/ *noun* [C] **1** a leather seat that you put on a horse so that you can ride it ⊃ *See colour picture* **Sports 1** *on page Centre 15.* **2** a seat on a bicycle or motorcycle

**saddle²** /'sædl/ (*also* **saddle up**) *verb* [I, T] to put a saddle on a horse

**saddle sb with sth** to give someone a job or problem which will cause them a lot of work or difficulty

**sadistic** /sə'dɪstɪk/ *adj* getting pleasure from being cruel or violent *sadistic behaviour* • *a sadistic murderer* • sadist /'seɪdɪst/ *noun* [C] someone who gets pleasure from being cruel or violent • sadism /'seɪdɪzᵊm/ *noun* [U]

**sadly** /'sædli/ *adv* **1** NOT HAPPY in a sad way *She shook her head sadly.* **2** NOT SATISFACTORY in a way that is not satisfactory *Enthusiasm has been sadly lacking these past few months at work.* **3** SORRY used to say that you are sorry something is true *Sadly, the marriage did not last.*

**sae, SAE** /ˌeseɪ'iː/ *noun* [C] *UK abbreviation for* stamped addressed envelope or self-addressed envelope: an envelope that you put a stamp and your own address on and send to someone so that they can send you something back *Send an SAE for further information.*

**safari** /sə'fɑːri/ *noun* [C, U] a journey, usually to Africa, to see or hunt wild animals *She is **on safari** in Kenya.*

○⚡**safe¹** /seɪf/ *adj* **1** NOT DANGEROUS not dangerous or likely to cause harm *a safe driver* • *a safe and cheap source of energy* • *Air travel is generally quite safe.* • *We live in a safe neighbourhood.* • [+ to do sth] *Is it safe to drink the water here?* ⊃ *Opposite* **unsafe**. **2** NOT HARMED not harmed or damaged *She said that all the hostages were safe.* • *She returned **safe and sound** (= not harmed in any way).* **3** NOT IN DANGER not in danger or likely to be harmed *I feel safe when I'm with you.* • *During the daylight hours we're **safe from** attack.* **4 safe to say** If it is safe to say something, you are sure it is correct. *I think it's safe to say that he'll be the next president.* **5 a safe place; somewhere safe** a place where something will not be lost or stolen *It's very valuable so put it somewhere safe.* **6 play (it) safe** *informal* to be careful and not take risks *There was fresh crab on the menu, but I played safe and ordered the lasagne.* • safely *adv Make sure you drive safely.* • *I can safely say (= I am certain) I have never met anyone as rude as him.* ⊃ *See also:* a safe **bet²**.

**safe²** /seɪf/ *noun* [C] a strong metal box or cupboard with locks where you keep money, jewellery, and other valuable things

**safeguard¹** /'seɪfgɑːd/ *verb* [T] to protect something from harm *a plan to safeguard public health*

**safeguard against sth** to do things that you hope will stop something unpleasant from happening *A good diet will safeguard against disease.*

**safeguard²** /'seɪfɡɑːd/ *noun* [C] a law, rule, or system that protects people or things from being harmed or lost *The disk has built-in safeguards to prevent certain errors.*

,safe 'haven *noun* [C] a place where someone is safe from danger

o▬**safety** /'seɪfti/ *noun* [U] **1** when you are safe *food/road safety* • *The hostages were led to safety* (= to a safe place). • *a safety valve* **2** how safe something is *Safety at the factory has been improved.* ➔ *See usage note at* **security**.

'safety ,belt *noun* [C] a piece of equipment that keeps you fastened to your seat when you are travelling in a vehicle *Please fasten your safety belt for take-off.*

'safety ,net *noun* [C] **1** a plan or system that will help you if you get into a difficult situation *Legal aid provides a safety net for people who can't afford a lawyer.* **2** a net that will catch someone if they fall from a high place

'safety ,pin *noun* [C] a pin with a round cover that fits over the sharp end

**saffron** /'sæfrən/ *noun* [U] a yellow powder that is used as a spice

**sag** /sæɡ/ *verb* [I] **sagging,** *past* **sagged 1** to sink or bend down *Our mattress sags in the middle.* **2** *informal* to become weaker or less successful *a sagging economy*

**saga** /'sɑːɡə/ *noun* [C] a long story about a lot of people or events

**sagacious** /sə'ɡeɪʃəs/ *adj literary* having or showing understanding and the ability to make good decisions and judgments

**sage** /seɪdʒ/ *noun* **1** [U] a herb whose leaves are used to give flavour to food **2** [C] *literary* a wise person

**Sagittarius** /ˌsædʒɪ'teəriəs/ *noun* [C, U] the sign of the zodiac which relates to the period of 22 November – 22 December, or a person born during this period ➔ *See picture at* **zodiac**.

**said** /sed/ *past of* say

**sail¹** /seɪl/ *verb* **1** TRAVEL [I] to travel in a boat or a ship *We sailed to Malta.* **2** CONTROL BOAT [I, T] to control a boat that has no engine and is pushed by the wind *I learned to sail when I was a child.* • *to make a sale* **2 (up) for sale** available through the storm. **3** START JOURNEY [I] When a ship sails, it starts its journey, and if people sail from a particular place or at a particular time, they start their journey. *This ship sails weekly from Florida to the Bahamas.* **4 sail over/past/through, etc** to move quickly through the air *The ball sailed past me.*

**sail through (sth)** to succeed very easily, especially in a test or competition *She sailed through her exams.*

**sail²** /seɪl/ *noun* **1** [C] a large piece of material that is fixed to a pole on a boat to catch the wind and make the boat move **2 set sail** to start a journey by boat or ship

**sailboat** /'seɪlbəʊt/ *noun* [C] *US* a small boat with sails

**sailing** /'seɪlɪŋ/ *noun* **1** [U] a sport using boats with sails *(UK) a sailing boat* **2 be plain sailing** to be very easy

**sailor** /'seɪlər/ *noun* [C] someone who sails ships or boats as their job or as a sport

**saint** /seɪnt/ *noun* [C] **1** a dead person who has been officially respected by the Christian Church for living their life in a holy way *Catherine of Siena was **made a saint** in 1461.* **2** a very kind or helpful person ➔ *See also:* **patron saint**.

**saintly** /'seɪntli/ *adj* very good and kind

o▬**sake** /seɪk/ *noun* **1 for the sake of sth** for this reason or purpose *For the sake of convenience, they combined the two departments.* • *For safety's sake, you shouldn't swim alone.* **2 for the sake of sb** in order to help or please someone *He begged her to stay for the sake of the children.* **3 for God's/goodness/heaven's, etc sake!** something you say when you are angry about something *For heaven's sake, stop moaning!*

o▬**salad** /'sæləd/ *noun* [C, U] a cold mixture of vegetables that have not been cooked, usually eaten with meat, cheese, etc *I made a big salad for lunch.* ➔ *See colour picture* **Food** *on page Centre 7.*

**salami** /sə'lɑːmi/ *noun* [C, U] a spicy sausage (= tube of meat and spices) that is usually eaten cold in slices

**salaried** /'sælərid/ *adj* receiving a fixed amount of money from your employer, usually every month

o▬**salary** /'sæləri/ *noun* [C, U] a fixed amount of money that you receive from your employer, usually every month ➔ *See usage note at* **pay**.

o▬**sale** /seɪl/ *noun* **1** SELLING THINGS [U, no plural] the act of selling something, or the time when something is sold *The sale of alcohol is now banned.* • *to make a sale* **2 (up) for sale** available to buy *For sale: ladies bicycle – good condition.* • *The house next to mine is up for sale.* **3 on sale a** AVAILABLE *UK* available to buy in a shop *The video and book are now on sale.* **b** CHEAP available for a lower price than usual *This album was on sale for half price.* **4** EVENT [C] an event where things are sold *We organized a sale of used books to raise money for charity.* **5** CHEAP PRICE [C] a time when a shop sells goods at a lower price than usual *UK) I bought this dress in the sale.* ➔ *See also:* **car boot sale, jumble sale**.

**saleable** /'seɪləbl/ *adj* Something that is saleable can be sold easily. *He's painted some very saleable landscapes.*

**sales** /seɪlz/ *noun* [plural] **1** the number of items sold *Our sales have doubled this year.* **2** the part of a company that deals with selling things *I used to work in sales.* • *a sales department*

'sales as,sistant *(also US* 'sales ,clerk*) noun* [C] someone whose job is selling things in a shop

**salesman,**    **saleswoman**    /'seɪlzmən, 'seɪlz,wʊmən/ *noun* [C] *plural* **salesmen, saleswomen** someone whose job is selling things

**salesperson** /'seɪlz,pɜːsⁿn/ *noun* [C] *plural* **salespeople** someone whose job is selling things

**salient** /'seɪliənt/ *adj formal* The salient facts about something or qualities of something are the most important things about them.

**saline** /'seɪlaɪn ⑤ 'seɪliːn/ *adj formal* containing salt *saline solution*

**saliva** /sə'laɪvə/ noun [U] the liquid that is made in your mouth

**sallow** /'sæləʊ/ adj Sallow skin is slightly yellow and does not look healthy.

**salmon** /'sæmən/ noun [C, U] plural **salmon** a large, silver fish, or the pink meat of this fish *fresh/smoked salmon*

**salmonella** /ˌsælmə'nelə/ noun [U] a type of bacteria which can make you very ill, sometimes found in food that is not cooked enough

**salon** /'sælɒn/ noun [C] a shop where you can have your hair cut or have your appearance improved *a hair salon* ➔ See also: **beauty salon**.

**saloon** /sə'luːn/ noun [C] **1** *UK* (*US* **sedan**) a large car with a separate, closed area for bags **2** *US old-fashioned* a public bar

**salsa** /'sælsə/ noun [U] **1** a cold, spicy sauce **2** a type of dance and music from Latin America *a salsa club*

○⃛**salt**[1] /sɔːlt, sɒlt/ noun [U] **1** a white substance used to add flavour to food *salt and pepper • Pass the salt, please.* **2 take sth with a pinch of salt** *UK* (*US* **take sth with a grain of salt**) to not completely believe something that someone tells you

**salt**[2] /sɔːlt, sɒlt/ verb [T] to add salt to food

**salt cellar** *UK* (*US* **'salt ,shaker**) noun [C] a small container with holes in for shaking salt on food

**saltwater** /'sɔːlt,wɔːtəʳ/ adj [always before noun] living in or containing water that has salt in it *a saltwater fish*

**salty** /'sɔːlti/ adj tasting of or containing salt *Is the soup too salty?*

**salute**[1] /sə'luːt/ noun [C] a sign of respect to someone of a higher rank in a military organization, often made by raising the right hand to the side of the head *to give a salute*

**salute**[2] /sə'luːt/ verb [I, T] to give a salute to someone of a higher rank in a military organization

**salvage**[1] /'sælvɪdʒ/ verb [T] **1** to save things from a place where other things have been damaged or lost *gold coins salvaged from a shipwreck* **2** to try to make a bad situation better *an attempt to salvage her reputation*

**salvage**[2] /'sælvɪdʒ/ noun [U] when things are saved from being damaged, or the things that are saved *a salvage company*

**salvation** /sæl'veɪʃᵊn/ noun [U] **1** in the Christian religion, when God saves someone from the bad effects of evil **2** something or someone that saves you from harm or a very unpleasant situation *Getting a dog was Dad's salvation after Mum died.*

○⃛**same**[1] /seɪm/ adj, pronoun **1 the same a** exactly alike *He's the same age as me. • We work at the same speed. • Cars cost the same here as they do in Europe.* **b** not another different thing or situation *They met at the same place every week. • You meet the same people at all these events.* **c** not changed *She's the same lively person she's always been. • He looks exactly the same as he did ten years ago.* **2 all/just the same** despite what has just been said *He doesn't earn much. All the same, he ought to pay for some of his own drinks.* **3 the**

**same old arguments/faces/story, etc** *informal* something or someone you have seen or heard many times before **4 Same here.** *informal* something that you say when something another person has said is also true for you *"I think she's awful." "Same here."* ➔ See also: be in the same **boat**, in the same **vein**, be on the same **wavelength**.

○⃛**same**[2] /seɪm/ adv **the same** in the same way *We treat all our children the same.*

**sample**[1] /'sɑːmpl/ noun [C] **1** SHOW a small amount of something that shows you what it is like *a free sample of chocolate • She brought in some samples of her work.* **2** EXAMINE a small amount of a substance that a doctor or scientist collects in order to examine it *a blood/urine sample* **3** NUMBER a small number of people from a larger group that is being tested *a representative sample • a sample of 500 male drivers*

**sample**[2] /'sɑːmpl/ verb [T] **1** to taste a small amount of food or drink to decide if you like it *We sampled eight different cheeses.* **2** to experience a place or an activity, often for the first time *an opportunity to sample the local night life*

**sanatorium** (*also US* **sanitarium**) /ˌsænə'tɔːriəm/ noun [C] plural **sanatoriums** or **sanatoria** a hospital where people go to rest and get well after a long illness

**sanction**[1] /'sæŋkʃᵊn/ noun **1** [C] a punishment for not obeying a rule or a law *economic/trade sanctions against a country* **2** [U] official approval or permission

**sanction**[2] /'sæŋkʃᵊn/ verb [T] to formally approve of something *He refused to sanction the publication of his private letters.*

**sanctity** /'sæŋktəti/ noun formal **the sanctity of life/marriage, etc** when something is very important and deserves respect

**sanctuary** /'sæŋktʃʊəri/ noun **1** QUIET [C, U] a quiet and peaceful place *After a busy day, I like to escape to the sanctuary of my garden.* **2** PROTECTION [C, U] a place that provides protection *to seek sanctuary* **3** ANIMALS [C] a place where animals are protected and cannot be hunted *a bird/wildlife sanctuary*

○⃛**sand**[1] /sænd/ noun [U] a substance that is found on beaches and in deserts, which is made from very small grains of rock *a grain of sand*

**sand**[2] /sænd/ verb [T] to make wood smooth by rubbing it with sandpaper (= strong paper with a rough surface)

**sandal** /'sændᵊl/ noun [C] a light shoe with straps that you wear in warm weather. ➔ See colour picture **Clothes** on page Centre 5.

**sandcastle** /'sænd,kɑːsl/ noun [C] a model of a castle made of wet sand, usually built by children on a beach

**'sand ,dune** noun [C] a hill of sand in the desert or on the coast

**sandpaper** /'sænd,peɪpəʳ/ noun [U] strong paper with a rough surface that is rubbed against wood to make it smooth

**sands** /sændz/ noun [plural] a large area of sand

**sandstone** /'sændstəʊn/ noun [U] rock made of sand

○⃛**sandwich**[1] /'sænwɪdʒ/ noun [C] two slices of

bread with meat, cheese, etc between them *a cheese/tuna sandwich* ➲ *See colour picture* **Food** *on page Centre 7.*

**sandwich²** /'sænwɪdʒ/ *verb*
**be sandwiched between sth/sb** *informal* to be in a small space between two people or things *Andorra is a small country sandwiched between Spain and France.*

**sandy** /'sændi/ *adj* covered with or containing sand *a sandy beach*

**sane** /seɪn/ *adj* **1** not suffering from mental illness **2** [always before noun] showing good judgment *a sane attitude/decision* ➲ *Opposite* **insane.**

**sang** /sæŋ/ *past tense of* sing

**sanguine** /'sæŋgwɪn/ *adj formal* positive and full of hope *The director is sanguine about the company's prospects.*

**sanitarium** /,sænɪ'teərɪəm/ *noun* [C] *plural* **sanitariums** or **sanitaria** *another US spelling of* sanatorium (= a hospital where people rest and get well after a long illness)

**sanitary** /'sænɪt²ri/ *adj* relating to preventing disease by removing dirt and waste *sanitary conditions* • *His kitchen wasn't very sanitary* (= was not clean).

**'sanitary ,towel** *UK* (*US* ,sanitary 'napkin) *noun* [C] a thick piece of soft paper that a woman wears to absorb blood from her period (= monthly blood from the uterus)

**sanitation** /,sænɪ'teɪʃ²n/ *noun* [U] a system for protecting people's health by removing dirt and waste

**sanity** /'sænəti/ *noun* [U] **1** the quality of behaving calmly and showing good judgment *Jogging helps me keep my sanity.* **2** when you have a healthy mind and are not mentally ill ➲ *Opposite* **insanity.**

**sank** /sæŋk/ *past tense of* sink

**Santa** /'sæntə/ (*also* **Santa Claus** /'sæntəklɔːz/) *noun* [no plural] a kind, fat, old man in red clothes who people say brings presents to children at Christmas

**sap¹** /sæp/ *verb* [T] **sapping,** *past* **sapped** to gradually make something weak *Ten years of war had sapped the country's strength.*

**sap²** /sæp/ *noun* [U] the liquid inside plants and trees

**sapling** /'sæplɪŋ/ *noun* [C] a young tree

**sapphire** /'sæfaɪə'/ *noun* [C] a bright blue, transparent stone

**sarcasm** /'sɑːkæz²m/ *noun* [U] when you say the opposite of what you mean to insult someone or show them that you are annoyed *"Oh, I am sorry," she said, her voice heavy with sarcasm.*

**sarcastic** /sɑː'kæstɪk/ *adj* using sarcasm *a sarcastic comment/remark* • *Are you being sarcastic?* • sarcastically *adv*

**sardine** /sɑː'diːn/ *noun* [C] a small sea fish that you can eat

**SASE** /,eseɪes'iː/ *noun* [C] *US abbreviation for* self-addressed stamped envelope: an envelope that you put a stamp and your own address on and send to someone so that they can send you something back *Please enclose a SASE with your payment.*

**sash** /sæʃ/ *noun* [C] a long, narrow piece of cloth that is worn around the waist or over the shoulder, often as part of a uniform

**sassy** /'sæsi/ *adj US informal* **1** very energetic and confident *a smart, sassy young woman* **2** slightly rude, but not offensive *a sassy remark*

**sat** /sæt/ *past of* sit

**Sat** *written abbreviation for* Saturday

**Satan** /'seɪt²n/ *noun* [no plural] the Devil (= the enemy of God)

**satanic** /sə'tænɪk/ *adj* relating to the Devil (= the enemy of God) *a satanic cult/ritual*

**satchel** /'sætʃ²l/ *noun* [C] a large bag with a strap that goes over your shoulder, often used for carrying school books ➲ *See colour picture* **Classroom** *on page Centre 4.*

**satellite** /'sæt²laɪt/ *noun* [C] **1** a piece of equipment that is sent into space around the Earth, to receive and send signals or to collect information *a spy/weather satellite* **2** a natural object that moves around a planet in space *The moon is the Earth's satellite.*

**,satellite 'television** (*also* ,satellite T'V) *noun* [U] television programmes that are broadcast using a satellite

**satin** /'sætɪn/ *noun* [U] a smooth, shiny cloth

**satire** /'sætaɪə'/ *noun* **1** [U] when you use jokes and humour to criticize people or ideas *political satire* **2** [C] a story, film, etc that uses satire • satirist /'sæt²rɪst/ *noun* [C] someone who uses satire

**satirical** /sə'tɪrɪk²l/ *adj* using satire *a satirical magazine/novel*

**satisfaction** /,sætɪs'fækʃ²n/ *noun* [U] **1** the pleasant feeling you have when you get something that you wanted or do something that you wanted to do *job satisfaction* • *She smiled with satisfaction.* • [+ of + doing sth] *I had the satisfaction of knowing that I'd done everything I could.* **2 to sb's satisfaction** as well as someone wants *He won't get paid until he completes the job to my satisfaction.* ➲ *Opposite* **dissatisfaction.**

○ⁱ**satisfactory** /,sætɪs'fækt²ri/ *adj* good enough *We hope very much to find a satisfactory solution to the problem.* ➲ *Opposite* **unsatisfactory.** • satisfactorily *adv*

○ⁱ**satisfied** /'sætɪsfaɪd/ *adj* **1** pleased because you have got what you wanted, or because something has happened in the way that you wanted *Are you satisfied with the new arrangement?* ➲ *Opposite* **dissatisfied.** **2 be satisfied that** If you are satisfied that something is true, you believe it. *The judge was satisfied that she was telling the truth.* ➲ *See also:* **self-satisfied.**

**satisfy** /'sætɪsfaɪ/ *verb* **1** [T] to please someone by giving them what they want or need *They sell 31 flavours of ice cream – enough to satisfy everyone!* **2 satisfy conditions/needs/requirements, etc** to have or provide something that is needed or wanted *She satisfies all the requirements for the job.* **3 satisfy sb that** to make someone believe that something is true *I satisfied myself that I had locked the door.*

**satisfying** /'sætɪsfaɪɪŋ/ *adj* making you feel pleased by providing what you need or want *a satisfying meal* • *My work is very satisfying.*

**saturate** /'sætʃ²reɪt/ *verb* **1 be saturated with sth** to be filled with a lot or too much of something *The city is saturated with cheap*

**S**

*restaurants.* **2** [T] to make something completely wet *Heavy rain had saturated the playing field.* • saturation /ˌsætʃʳˈreɪʃᵊn/ *noun* [U]

,**saturated 'fat** *noun* [C, U] a fat found in meat, milk, and eggs, which is thought to be bad for your health

**Saturday** /ˈsætədeɪ/ (*written abbreviation* **Sat**) *noun* [C, U] the day of the week after Friday and before Sunday

**Saturn** /ˈsætən/ *noun* [no plural] the planet that is sixth from the Sun, after Jupiter and before Uranus

➝**sauce** /sɔːs/ *noun* [C, U] a hot or cold liquid that you put on food to add flavour *mint sauce* • *pasta with tomato sauce* ➔ *See also:* **soy sauce**.

**saucepan** /ˈsɔːspən/ *noun* [C] a deep, metal pan, usually with a long handle and a lid, that is used to cook food in ➔ *See colour picture* **Kitchen** *on page Centre 10.*

**saucer** /ˈsɔːsəʳ/ *noun* [C] a small plate that you put under a cup *a cup and saucer*

**saucy** /ˈsɔːsi/ *adj* slightly rude, or referring to sex in a funny way *a saucy postcard/joke*

**sauna** /ˈsɔːnə/ *noun* [C] **1** a room that is hot and filled with steam where people sit to relax or feel healthy *a gym with a pool and a sauna* **2 have a sauna** to spend time inside a sauna

**saunter** /ˈsɔːntəʳ/ *verb* **saunter into/over/ through, etc** to walk in a slow and relaxed way *He sauntered through the door two hours late.*

**sausage** /ˈsɒsɪdʒ/ *noun* [C, U] a mixture of meat and spices pressed into a long tube

**sauté** /ˈsəʊteɪ/ /səʊˈteɪ/ *verb* [T] to fry food quickly in a small amount of hot oil

**savage**[1] /ˈsævɪdʒ/ *adj* **1** extremely violent *a savage attack* **2** severe *savage criticism* • savagely *adv*

**savage**[2] /ˈsævɪdʒ/ *verb* [T] **1** to attack violently [often passive] *A sheep had been savaged by a dog.* **2** to severely criticize someone or something [often passive] *Her performance was savaged by the critics.*

**savage**[3] /ˈsævɪdʒ/ *noun* [C] *old-fashioned* an offensive word for a person from a country at an early stage of development

➝**save**[1] /seɪv/ *verb* **1** MAKE SAFE [T] to stop someone or something from being killed or destroyed *He was badly injured, but the doctors saved his life.* • *She saved the children from drowning.* • *He had to borrow money to save his business.* **2** MONEY [I, T] (*also* **save up**) to keep money so that you can buy something with it in the future *We've saved almost $900 for our wedding.* • *Michael's saving up for a new computer.* **3** KEEP [T] to keep something to use in the future *I've saved some food for you.* • *She saved her black dress for special occasions.* **4 save money/space/time, etc** to reduce the amount of money/space/time, etc that you have to use *You'll save time by doing it yourself.* **5 save sb (from) doing sth** to help someone avoid having to do something *We'll eat in a restaurant – it'll save you having to cook.* **6 save files/work, etc** to store work or information electronically on or from a computer **7 save a goal** to prevent a player from scoring a goal *He saved two goals in the last minute of the game.* ➔ *See also:* save the **day**, save **face**[1].

**save on sth** to avoid using something so that you do not have to pay for it *She walks to work to save on bus fares.*

**save**[2] /seɪv/ *noun* [C] when someone prevents a goal from being scored in a sport *The goalkeeper made a great save.*

**saver** /ˈseɪvəʳ/ *noun* [C] someone who saves money in a bank

**saving** /ˈseɪvɪŋ/ *noun* [C] *UK* (*US* **savings**) when you pay less money than you would usually have to use [usually singular] *a saving of £20.*

**savings** /ˈseɪvɪŋz/ *noun* [plural] money that you have saved, usually in a bank *I spent all my savings on a new kitchen.* • *a savings account*

**savings and 'loan associ,ation** *US* (*UK* **building society**) *noun* [C] a bank that is owned by the people who keep their money in it and that lets them borrow money to buy a house

**saviour** *UK* (*US* **savior**) /ˈseɪvjəʳ/ *noun* **1** [C] someone who saves someone or something from harm or difficulty **2 the Saviour** in Christianity, Jesus Christ

**savour** *UK* (*US* **savor**) /ˈseɪvəʳ/ *verb* [T] to enjoy food or a pleasant experience as much and as slowly as possible *to savour a meal* • *We savoured our moment of victory.*

**savoury** *UK* (*US* **savory**) /ˈseɪvᵊri/ *adj* Savoury food is not sweet. *savoury biscuits*

**savvy** /ˈsævi/ *noun* [U] *informal* practical knowledge and ability *business/political savvy* • savvy *adj informal* having knowledge and ability *a savvy consumer*

**saw**[1] /sɔː/ *noun* [C] a tool with a sharp edge that you use to cut wood or other hard material ➔ *See picture at* **tool.** • saw *verb* [I, T] *past t* **sawed**, *past p* **sawn** *esp. US* **sawed** to use a saw *They sawed the door in half.* • *He sawed through the pipe.*

**saw**[2] /sɔː/ *past tense of* see

**sawdust** /ˈsɔːdʌst/ *noun* [U] very small pieces of wood and powder that are produced when you cut wood with a saw

**saxophone** /ˈsæksəfəʊn/ (*also* **sax** *informal*) *noun* [C] a metal musical instrument that you play by blowing into it and pressing keys to produce different notes • saxophonist /sækˈsɒfᵊnɪst/ (US) /ˈsæksəfəʊnɪst/ *noun* [C] someone who plays the saxophone

➝**say**[1] /seɪ/ *verb* [T] *says, past said* **1** WORDS to speak words *"I'd like to go home," she said.* • *I couldn't hear what they were saying.* • *How do you say this word?* **2** TELL to tell someone about a fact, thought, or opinion [+ question word] *Did she say where she was going?* • *Officials refused to say what had happened.* • [+ (that)] *The jury said that he was guilty.* **3** INFORMATION to give information in writing, numbers, or signs *My watch says one o'clock.* • *The recipe said to use four ounces of butter.* • *What do the papers say about the election?* **4 say sth to yourself** to think something but not speak *"I hope she likes me," he said to himself.* **5** SHOW to show what you think without using words *His smile seemed to say that I was forgiven.* **6 (let's) say...** used to introduce a suggestion or possible example of something *More women study languages than, say, engineering or science.* • *Say you were offered a better job in another city –*

*would you take it?* **7 You can say that again!**
*informal* used to show that you completely
agree with something that someone has just
said *"That was a very bad movie!" "You can say
that again!"* **8 it goes without saying** If
something goes without saying, it is generally
accepted or understood. *It goes without saying
that smoking is harmful to your health.* ➔ *See
also:* Say **cheese**!, easier (**easy²**) said than done.

**say** or **tell**?

Say can refer to any type of speech.

*"Good night," she said.*

*She said she was unhappy.*

*Jim said to meet him here.*

Tell is used to report that someone has given information
or an order. The verb **tell** is always followed by the person
that the information or order is given to.

*Simon told me about his new job.*

*He told us to stay here.*

**say²** /seɪ/ *noun* **1** [U, no plural] when you are
involved in making a decision about something *We had some say in how our jobs would
develop.* **2 have your say** to give your opinion
about something *We can't vote yet – Christina
hasn't had her say.*

**saying** /'seɪɪŋ/ *noun* [C] a famous phrase that
people use to give advice about life *Have you
heard the saying, "misery loves company"?*

**scab** /skæb/ *noun* [C] a layer of dried blood that
forms to cover a cut in the skin

**scaffolding** /'skæfᵊldɪŋ/ *noun* [U] a temporary
structure made of flat boards and metal poles,
used to work on a tall building *to erect scaffolding*

**scald** /skɔːld/ *verb* [T] to burn something or
someone with very hot liquid or steam *She
scalded her mouth on the hot soup.*

**scale¹** /skeɪl/ *noun* **1** [SIZE] [no plural] the size or
level of something *We don't yet know the scale of
the problem.* • *Nuclear weapons cause destruction on a massive scale* (= cause a lot of
destruction). **2 large-/small-scale** A large-
/small-scale event or activity is large/small in
size. *a large-scale investigation* **3** [MEASURING
SYSTEM] [C] the set of numbers, amounts, etc
used to measure or compare the level of something *How would you rate her work on a scale
of 1–10?* **4** [EQUIPMENT] [C] *US* (*UK* **scales** [plural])
a piece of equipment for measuring weight
*a bathroom/kitchen scale* ➔ *See colour picture*
**Kitchen** *on page Centre 10,* **The Bathroom** *on
page Centre 1.* **5** [COMPARISON] [C, U] how the size of
things on a map, model, etc relates to the same
things in real life *a map with a scale of one
centimetre per ten kilometres* **6** [MUSIC] [C] a
series of musical notes that is always played
in order and that rises gradually from the
first note **7** [SKIN] [C] one of the flat pieces of hard
material that covers the skin of fish and snakes

**scale²** /skeɪl/ *verb* [T] to climb something that is
high or steep *to scale a wall*

**scale sth back** *mainly US* (*UK/US* **scale sth
down**) to make something smaller than it was
or smaller than it was planned to be *A shortage
of money has forced them to scale back their
plans.*

**scales** /skeɪlz/ *noun* [plural] *UK* (*US* **scale** [C]) a
piece of equipment for measuring weight
*bathroom/kitchen scales* ➔ *See colour picture*
**Kitchen** *on page Centre 10,* **The Bathroom** *on
page Centre 1.*

**scallion** /'skæliən/ *US* (*UK* **spring onion**) *noun* [C]
a small onion with a white part at the bottom
and long, green leaves, which is eaten in salads

**scallop** /'skæləp/ *noun* [C] a small sea creature
that lives in a shell and is eaten as food

**scalp** /skælp/ *noun* [C] the skin on the top of your
head under your hair

**scalpel** /'skælpᵊl/ *noun* [C] a small, sharp knife
that doctors use to cut through skin during an
operation

**scalper** /'skælpəʳ/ *US* (*UK* **tout**) *noun* [C]
someone who unofficially sells tickets outside
theatres, sports grounds, etc

**scaly** /'skeɪli/ *adj* If your skin is scaly, it is rough
and falls off in small, dry pieces.

**scam** /skæm/ *noun* [C] *informal* an illegal plan
for making money

**scamper** /'skæmpəʳ/ *verb* **scamper away/
down/off, etc** to run quickly and with small
steps, like a child or a small animal *I shouted
and the dog scampered off.*

**scampi** /'skæmpi/ *noun* [U] prawns (= small sea
creatures) that have been fried *scampi and
chips*

**scan¹** /skæn/ *verb* [T] **scanning**, *past* **scanned**
**1** [EXAMINE] to examine something with a
machine that can see inside an object or body
*Airports use X-ray machines to scan luggage for
weapons.* **2** [COMPUTER] to use a piece of equipment that copies words or pictures from paper
into a computer *to scan photos into a computer*
**3** [LOOK] to look around an area quickly to try to
find a person or thing *She scanned the crowd
for a familiar face.* **4** [READ] (*also* **scan
through**) to quickly read a piece of writing to
understand the main meaning or to find a
particular piece of information *I scanned
the travel brochures looking for a cheap holiday.*

**scan²** /skæn/ *noun* [C] a medical examination in
which an image of the inside of the body is
made using a special machine *a brain scan*

**scandal** /'skændᵊl/ *noun* [C, U] something that
shocks people because they think it is morally
wrong *a sex scandal* • *His speech caused a
scandal.*

**scandalous** /'skændᵊləs/ *adj* shocking or
morally wrong *a scandalous waste of money*

**Scandinavian** /ˌskændɪ'neɪviən/ *adj* from or
relating to the countries of Sweden, Denmark,
Norway, and sometimes Finland and Iceland
• Scandinavian *noun* [C] *The tourists we met were
mainly Scandinavians and other Europeans.*

**scanner** /'skænəʳ/ *noun* [C] **1** a piece of equipment that copies words or pictures from paper
into a computer **2** a piece of medical equipment used to examine images of the inside of
someone's body

**S**

**scant** /skænt/ adj [always before noun] very little and not enough *His work has received only scant attention outside this country.*

**scantily** /'skæntɪli/ adv **scantily clad/dressed** not wearing many clothes and showing a lot of the body

**scanty** /'skænti/ adj very small in size or quantity *scanty clothing*

**scapegoat** /'skeɪpgəʊt/ noun [C] someone who is blamed for a bad situation, although they have not caused it *He was made a scapegoat for the disaster.*

**scar** /skɑːʳ/ noun [C] **1** a permanent mark left on the body from a cut or other injury **2** damage done to a person's mind by a very unpleasant event or situation *a psychological scar* • scar verb [T] **scarring**, *past* **scarred** to cause a scar [often passive] *He was scarred for life by the accident.*

**scarce** /skeəs/ adj rare or not available in large amounts *scarce resources*

**scarcely** /'skeəsli/ adv **1** only just *They had scarcely finished eating when the doorbell rang.* **2 can scarcely do sth** If you say you can scarcely do something, you mean it would be wrong to do it. *He's only two – you can scarcely blame him for behaving badly.*

**scarcity** /'skeəsəti/ noun [C, U] when there is not enough of something *a scarcity of food/affordable housing*

**scare¹** /skeəʳ/ verb [T] **1** to frighten a person or animal *Sudden, loud noises scare me.* **2 scare the hell/life/living daylights, etc out of sb** *informal* to make someone feel very frightened ➔ See also: scare sb out of their **wits**.
**scare sb/sth away/off** to make a person or an animal so frightened that they go away *She scared off her attacker by screaming.*
**scare sb away/off** to make someone worried about doing something so that they decide not to do it *The recent bomb attacks have scared away the tourists.*

**scare²** /skeəʳ/ noun [C] **1** a sudden feeling of fear or worry *The earthquake gave us a scare.* **2** a situation that worries or frightens people *a food/health scare*

**scarecrow** /'skeəkrəʊ/ noun [C] a model of a person that is put in a field to frighten birds and stop them from eating the plants

◦━**scared** /skeəd/ adj frightened or worried *Robert's scared of heights.* • *I was scared to death* (= very frightened). • [+ (that)] *We were scared that we'd be killed.*

**scarf¹** /skɑːf/ noun [C] plural **scarves** /skɑːvz/ or **scarfs** a piece of cloth that you wear around your neck, head, or shoulders to keep warm or for decoration ➔ See colour picture **Clothes** on page Centre 5.

**scarf²** /skɑːf/ (also **scarf down**) verb [T] *US informal* (*UK* **scoff**) to eat a lot of something quickly *Who scarfed all the cookies?* • *Dan scarfed down three hamburgers!*

**scarlet** /'skɑːlət/ noun [U] a bright red colour • scarlet adj

**scary** /'skeəri/ adj *informal* frightening *a scary place/woman*

**scathing** /'skeɪðɪŋ/ adj criticizing very strongly *He was scathing about the report.*

**scatter** /'skætəʳ/ verb **1** [T] to throw objects over an area so that they land apart from each other *He scattered some flower seeds in the garden.* **2** [I] to suddenly move apart in different directions *The crowd scattered at the sound of gunshots.*

**scatter**

**scattered** /'skætəd/ adj covering a wide area *His toys were scattered all over the floor.* • *There will be scattered showers* (= separate areas of rain) today.

**scattering** /'skætərɪŋ/ noun [no plural] a small number of separate things, especially in a large area *a scattering of houses*

**scavenge** /'skævɪndʒ/ verb [I, T] to search for food or for useful things that have been thrown away • scavenger noun [C] a person or animal who scavenges

**scenario** /sɪ'nɑːriəʊ/ noun **1** [C] a description of a situation, or of a situation that may develop in the future **2 worst-case scenario** the worst situation that you can imagine

**scene** /siːn/ noun **1** PART OF FILM [C] a short part of a film, play, or book in which the events happen in one place *a love scene* • *the final scene* **2** VIEW [C] a view or picture of a place, event, or activity *scenes of everyday life* **3** PLACE [C] a place where an unpleasant event has happened *the scene of the crime* • *The police soon arrived at the scene.* **4 the club/gay/music, etc scene** all the things connected with a particular way of life or activity **5** ARGUMENT [C] when people have a loud argument or show strong emotions in a public place [usually singular] *She made a scene when I told her she couldn't come with us.* **6 behind the scenes** If something happens behind the scenes, it happens secretly. **7 set the scene for sth** to make an event or situation possible or likely to happen

**scenery** /'siːnəri/ noun [U] **1** the attractive, natural things that you see in the countryside *The Grand Canyon is famous for its spectacular scenery.* **2** the large pictures of buildings, countryside, etc used on a theatre stage

**scenic** /'siːnɪk/ adj having views of the attractive, natural things in the countryside *a scenic route* • *an area of great scenic beauty*

**scent** /sent/ noun **1** SMELL [C] a pleasant smell *the sweet scent of orange blossoms* **2** LIQUID [C, U] a pleasant smelling liquid that people put on their skin **3** ANIMAL [C, U] the smell of an animal or a person that is left somewhere

**scented** /'sentɪd/ adj having a pleasant smell *a scented candle*

**sceptic** *UK* (*US* **skeptic**) /'skeptɪk/ noun [C] someone who doubts that a belief or an idea is true or useful

**sceptical** *UK* (*US* **skeptical**) /'skeptɪkᵊl/ adj doubting that something is true or useful

*Scientists remain **sceptical about** astrology.*
* *She was **sceptical of** the new arrangement.*

**scepticism** UK (US **skepticism**) /'skeptɪsɪz²m/
*noun* [U] when you doubt that something is true
or useful *There was some **scepticism about** her
ability to do the job.*

**schedule¹** /'ʃedjuːl ⑤ 'skedʒuːl/ *noun* **1** [C, U] a
plan that gives events or activities and the
times that they will happen or be done *I have a
very busy schedule today.* • *Will the work be
completed **on schedule** (= at the expected
time)?* • *The project was finished **ahead of
schedule** (= earlier than planned).* **2** [C] *mainly
US* a list of times when buses, trains, etc
arrive and leave

**schedule²** /'ʃedjuːl ⑤ 'skedʒuːl/ *verb* [T] to
arrange that an event or an activity will
happen at a particular time [often passive] *Your
appointment has been **scheduled for** next
Tuesday.* • *a scheduled flight*

o─ᴹ**scheme¹** /skiːm/ *noun* [C] **1** *mainly UK* an official plan or system *an insurance/savings
scheme* • *a training scheme for teenagers* **2** [C]
a plan for making money, especially in a dishonest way *a scheme to steal money from investors*

**scheme²** /skiːm/ *verb* [I] to make a secret plan in
order to get an advantage, usually by deceiving
people

**schizophrenia** /ˌskɪtsəʊ'friːniə/ *noun* [U] a
serious mental illness in which someone
cannot understand what is real and what is
imaginary • schizophrenic /ˌskɪtsəʊ'frenɪk/ *noun*
[C] someone who suffers from schizophrenia

**schizophrenic** /ˌskɪtsəʊ'frenɪk/ *adj* relating to
schizophrenia *schizophrenic patients/symp-
toms*

**scholar** /'skɒlər/ *noun* [C] someone who has
studied a subject and knows a lot about it *a
legal scholar*

**scholarly** /'skɒləli/ *adj* **1** A scholarly article or
book is a formal piece of writing by a scholar
about a particular subject. **2** If someone is
scholarly, they study a lot and know a lot about
what they study.

**scholarship** /'skɒləʃɪp/ *noun* **1** [C] an amount of
money given to a person by an organization to
pay for their education, usually at a college or
university **2** [U] when you study a subject for a
long time

**scholastic** /skə'læstɪk/ *adj* [always before noun]
relating to school and education *scholastic
achievements*

o─ᴹ**school** /skuːl/ *noun* **1** [PLACE] [C] a place where
children go to be educated *Which school do you
go to?* • *I ride my bike to school.* **2** [TIME] [U] the
time that you spend at school *I like school.*
• *We're going shopping after school.* • *I started
school when I was five.* **3** [PEOPLE] [no plural] all
the students and teachers at a school *The whole
school took part in the project.* **4** **a dance/
language/riding, etc school** a place where
you can study a particular subject **5** [PART] [C] a
part of a college or university *the University of
Cambridge Medical School* **6** [UNIVERSITY] [C, U]
*US informal* in the US, any college or university, or the time you spend there *Which schools
did you apply for?* **7** [FISH] [C] a group of fish or
other sea animals **8** **school of thought** the

ideas and beliefs shared by a group of people
*There are several schools of thought about how
the universe began.* ⊃ *See also:* **boarding
school**, **elementary school**, **grade school**,
**grammar school**, **high school**, **junior high
school**, **junior school**, **middle school**,
**night school**, **nursery school**, **prep school**,
**preparatory school**, **primary school**,
**public school**, **secondary school**, **state
school**.

**schoolboy** /'skuːlbɔɪ/ *noun* [C] a boy who goes
to school

**schoolchild** /'skuːltʃaɪld/ *noun* [C] *plural*
**schoolchildren** a child who goes to school

**schooldays** /'skuːldeɪz/ *noun* [plural] *UK* the
period in your life when you go to school

**schoolgirl** /'skuːlgɜːl/ *noun* [C] a girl who goes
to school

**schooling** /'skuːlɪŋ/ *noun* [U] education at
school

**schoolteacher** /'skuːlˌtiːtʃər/ *noun* [C] someone
who teaches children in a school

o─ᴹ**science** /saɪəns/ *noun* **1** [U] the study and knowledge of the structure and behaviour of natural
things in an organized way **2** [C, U] a particular
type of science *computer science* • *Chemistry,
physics, and biology are all sciences.* ⊃ *See also:*
**natural sciences**, **social science**.

**ˌscience 'fiction** *noun* [U] stories about life in
the future or in other parts of the universe

o─ᴹ**scientific** /ˌsaɪən'tɪfɪk/ *adj* relating to science,
or using the organized methods of science
*scientific experiments/research* • scientifically
*adv a scientifically proven fact*

o─ᴹ**scientist** /'saɪəntɪst/ *noun* [C] someone who
studies science or works in science

**sci-fi** /'saɪ.faɪ/ *noun* [U] *informal short for*
science fiction

**scintillating** /'sɪntɪleɪtɪŋ/ *adj* very interesting
or exciting *a scintillating performance*

**scissors** /'sɪzəz/
*noun* [plural] a tool
for cutting paper,
hair, cloth, etc that
you hold in your
hand and that has
two blades that
move against each
other *a pair of
scissors*

**scissors**

**scoff** /skɒf/ *verb* **1** [I]
to laugh at someone
or something, or
criticize them in a
way that shows you
do not respect them
*The critics **scoffed
at** his work.* **2** [I, T]
*UK informal* (US **scarf**) to eat a lot of something
quickly *Who scoffed all the chocolates?*

**scold** /skəʊld/ *verb* [T] *old-fashioned* to speak
angrily to someone because they have done
something wrong

**scone** /skɒn, skəʊn/ *noun* [C] a small, round cake
*tea and buttered scones*

**scoop¹** /skuːp/ *verb* [T] to remove something from
a container using a spoon, your curved hands,
etc *She scooped the ice cream into the dishes.*

**scoop sth/sb up** to lift something or someone with your hands

**scoop**[2] /skuːp/ *noun* [C] **1** a large, deep spoon for lifting and moving an amount of something, or the amount that can be held in it *an ice cream scoop* • *a scoop of ice cream* **2** a piece of news discovered and printed by one newspaper before it appears anywhere else

**scoot** /skuːt/ *verb informal* **scoot along/down/ over, etc** to go somewhere quickly

**scooter** /ˈskuːtəʳ/ *noun* [C] **1** a small motorcycle **2** a child's vehicle that has two wheels fixed to the ends of a long board and a long handle

**scope** /skəʊp/ *noun* **1** [no plural] how much a subject or situation relates to *Do we know the full scope of the problem yet?* **2** [U] the opportunity to do something *There is plenty of scope for improvement.*

**scorch** /skɔːtʃ/ *verb* [T] to damage something with fire or heat *The fire destroyed the house and scorched the surrounding trees.*

**scorched** /skɔːtʃt/ *adj* slightly burnt, or damaged by fire or heat *scorched earth/fields*

**scorching** /ˈskɔːtʃɪŋ/ *adj* very hot *a scorching hot day*

○━**score**[1] /skɔːʳ/ *noun* **1** [C] the number of points someone gets in a game or test *a high/low score* • *What's the score?* **2** **scores of sth** a large number of people or things *Scores of teenage girls were waiting to get his autograph.* **3** [C] a printed piece of music **4** **on that/this score** about the thing or subject which you have just discussed *The company will pay your travel expenses, so don't worry on that score.*

○━**score**[2] /skɔːʳ/ *verb* [I, T] to get points in a game or test *He scored just before half-time to put Liverpool 2–1 ahead.*

**scoreboard** /ˈskɔːbɔːd/ *noun* [C] a large board which shows the score of a game

**scorer** /ˈskɔːrəʳ/ *noun* [C] a player who scores points in a game *Domingo was Italy's top scorer.*

**scorn** /skɔːn/ *noun* [U] *formal* the feeling that something is stupid and does not deserve your respect • **scorn** *verb* [T] *formal* to show scorn for someone or something *You scorned all my suggestions.*

**scornful** /ˈskɔːnfᵊl/ *adj formal* showing that you think something is stupid and does not deserve your respect *I'm very scornful of any findings that lack proper scientific data.* • **scornfully** *adv*

**Scorpio** /ˈskɔːpiəʊ/ *noun* [C, U] the sign of the zodiac which relates to the period of 23 October – 21 November, or a person born during this period ⊃ *See picture at* **zodiac**.

**scorpion** /ˈskɔːpiən/ *noun* [C] a small, insect-like creature with a curved, poisonous tail

**Scotch** /skɒtʃ/ (*also* ˌScotch ˈwhisky) *noun* [C, U] a type of whisky (= strong alcoholic drink)

ˌScotch ˈtape *US trademark* (*UK* **Sellotape** *trademark*) *noun* [U] clear, thin tape used for sticking things, especially paper, together ⊃ *See colour picture* **Classroom** *on page Centre 4.*

**the Scots** /skɒts/ *noun* [plural] the people of Scotland

**Scottish** /ˈskɒtɪʃ/ *adj* relating to Scotland *the Scottish Parliament* • *Scottish history*

**scour** /skaʊəʳ/ *verb* [T] **1** to search for something very carefully, often over a large area *The*

*police scoured the surrounding countryside for possible clues.* **2** to clean something by rubbing it with something rough

**scourge** /skɜːdʒ/ *noun formal* **the scourge of sth** something which causes a lot of suffering or trouble *Drug-related crime is the scourge of modern society.*

**scout**[1] /skaʊt/ *noun* **1** [C] (*also* **Boy Scout**) a member of an organization for young people which teaches them practical skills and encourages them to be good members of society **2** **the Scouts** an organization for young people which teaches them practical skills and encourages them to be good members of society **3** [C] someone whose job is to find good musicians, sports people, etc to join an organization *a talent scout*

**scout**[2] /skaʊt/ (*also* **scout around**) *verb* [I] to try to find something by looking in different places *I'm scouting around for somewhere to park.*

**scowl** /skaʊl/ *verb* [I] to look at someone angrily *He scowled at me from behind his paper.* • **scowl** *noun* [C]

**scrabble** /ˈskræbl/ *verb*

**scrabble about/around** to use your fingers to quickly find something that you cannot see *She scrabbled around in her bag, trying to find her keys.*

**scramble** /ˈskræmbl/ *verb* **1** **scramble down/ out/up, etc** to move or climb quickly but with difficulty, often using your hands *We scrambled up the hill.* **2** [I] to compete with other people for something which there is very little of [+ to do sth] *New teachers scramble to get jobs in the best schools.* • **scramble** *noun* [no plural] *There was a mad scramble for places near the front.*

ˌscrambled ˈeggs *noun* [plural] eggs which are mixed together and then cooked

**scrap**[1] /skræp/ *noun* **1** [SMALL PIECE] [C] a small piece or amount of something *He wrote his phone number on a scrap of paper.* • *I've read every scrap of information I can find on the subject.* **2** [OLD] [U] old cars and machines that are not now needed but have parts which can be used to make other things *scrap metal* • *The car was so badly damaged we could only sell it as scrap.* **3** [FIGHT] [C] *informal* a fight or an argument, usually not very serious *He was always getting into scraps at school.*

**scrap**[2] /skræp/ *verb* [T] **scrapping**, *past* **scrapped** **1** *informal* to not continue with a plan or idea *That project has now been scrapped.* **2** to get rid of something which you do not now want

**scrapbook** /ˈskræpbʊk/ *noun* [C] a book with empty pages where you can stick newspaper articles, pictures, etc, that you have collected and want to keep

**scrape**[1] /skreɪp/ *verb* [T] **1** to damage the surface of something by rubbing it against something rough *Jamie fell over and scraped his knee.* **2** to remove something from a surface using a sharp edge *The next morning I had to scrape the ice off the car.* **3** **scrape a win/draw/pass** *UK* to succeed in a test or competition but with difficulty *France scraped a 3–2 win over Norway.*

**scrape by** to manage to live when you do not

have enough money *He has to scrape by on $100 a month.*

**scrape through (sth)** to succeed in something but with a lot of difficulty *I scraped through my exams* (= just passed).

**scrape sth together** to manage with a lot of difficulty to get enough of something, often money *I finally scraped together enough money for a flight home.*

scrape² /skreɪp/ *noun* [C] **1** the slight damage caused when you rub a surface with something rough *He suffered a few cuts and scrapes but nothing serious.* **2** *informal* a difficult or dangerous situation which you cause yourself *She's always getting into scrapes.*

scrappy /'skræpi/ *adj* **1** *UK* untidy or organized badly *They won but it was a scrappy match.* **2** *US* determined to win or achieve something *a scrappy competitor*

scratch¹ /skrætʃ/ *verb* **1** RUB SKIN [I, T] to rub your skin with your nails, often to stop it itching (= feeling unpleasant) *My skin was so itchy, I was scratching all night.* • *He scratched his head.* **2** HURT/DAMAGE [T] to make a slight cut or long, thin mark with a sharp object *The surface was all scratched.* • *I scratched myself on the roses.* **3** RUB SURFACE [I, T] to rub a hard surface with a sharp object, often making a noise *I could hear the cat scratching at the door.*

scratch² /skrætʃ/ *noun* **1** [C] a slight cut or a long, thin mark made with a sharp object *I've got all these scratches on my arm from the cat.* **2** [no plural] when you rub your skin with your nails, often to stop it itching (= feeling unpleasant) *Could you give my back a scratch?* **3 from scratch** If you do something from scratch, you do it from the beginning. *We didn't have any furniture of our own so we had to start from scratch.* **4 not be/come up to scratch** *informal* to not be good enough *She told me my work wasn't up to scratch.*

scrawl /skrɔːl/ *verb* [T] to write something quickly so that it is untidy *She scrawled a note, but I couldn't read it.* • scrawl *noun* [C, U]

scrawny /'skrɔːni/ *adj* too thin *a scrawny neck*

o⟶scream¹ /skriːm/ *verb* [I, T] to make a loud, high noise with your voice, or to shout something in a loud, high voice because you are afraid, hurt, or angry *Someone was screaming in the street.* • *She screamed for help.* • *I could hear a woman screaming, "Get me out of here!"*

scream² /skriːm/ *noun* **1** [C] when someone screams *We heard screams coming from their apartment.* **2 be a scream** *informal* to be very funny *You'd love Amanda – she's a scream.*

screech /skriːtʃ/ *verb* **1** [I, T] to make an unpleasant, high, loud sound *A car came screeching around the corner.* • *She was screeching at him at the top of her voice.* **2 screech to a halt/stop** If a vehicle screeches to a halt, it suddenly stops, making an unpleasant, high sound. • screech *noun* [C] *We could hear the screech of brakes.*

o⟶screen¹ /skriːn/ *noun* **1** COMPUTER/TV [C] the part of a television or computer which shows images or writing *I spend most of my day working in front of a computer screen.* **2 on**

**screen** using a computer *Do you work on screen?* **3** FILM SURFACE [C] a large, flat surface where a film or an image is shown **4** CINEMA [U, no plural] cinema films *an actor of stage and screen* (= theatre and films) • *She first appeared on screen in 1965.* **5** NET [C] a wire net which covers a window or door and is used to stop insects coming in **6** SEPARATE [C] a vertical structure which is used to separate one area from another

**screen**

cinema screen *UK,*
movie screen *US*

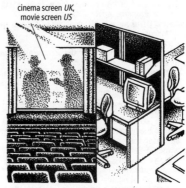

computer screen

screen² /skriːn/ *verb* [T] **1** MEDICAL to find out if people have an illness by doing medical tests on them *Babies are routinely screened for the condition.* **2** GET INFORMATION to find out information about someone in order to decide if they are suitable for a particular job *Applicants are screened to ensure that none of them is a security risk.* **3** SHOW to show something on television or at a cinema [often passive] *The first episode will be screened tonight.*

**screen sth off** to separate one area from another using a vertical structure *Part of the room is screened off and used as an office.*

screenplay /'skriːnpleɪ/ *noun* [C] a story that is written for television or for a film

screw¹ /skruː/ *noun* [C] a small, pointed piece of metal that you turn round and round to fix things together, especially pieces of wood ⊃ See picture at **tool**.

screw² /skruː/ *verb* **1 screw sth down/to/onto, etc** to fasten something with a screw *You need to screw the cabinet to the wall.* **2 screw sth on/ down/together, etc** to fasten something by turning it round until it is tight, or to be fastened this way *The lid is screwed on so tight I can't get it off.* ⊃ Opposite **unscrew**. **3 screw up your eyes/face** to move the muscles of your face so that your eyes become narrow *He screwed up his eyes in the bright sunlight.*

**screw (sth) up** *informal* to make a mistake, or to spoil something *I screwed up my exams last year.*

**screw sth up** to twist and crush a piece of paper with your hands *She screwed the letter up and threw it in the bin.*

**screwdriver** /'skru:,draɪvəʳ/ *noun* [C] a tool for turning screws ⮕ *See picture at* **tool**.

**screwed-up** /,skru:d'ʌp/ *adj informal* If someone is screwed-up, they are unhappy and anxious because they have had a lot of bad experiences.

**scribble** /'skrɪbl/ *verb* [I, T] to write or draw something quickly and carelessly *She scribbled some notes in her book.* • **scribble** *noun* [C, U] something that has been scribbled

**script** /skrɪpt/ *noun* **1** [C] the words in a film, play, etc *He wrote a number of film scripts.* **2** [C, U] a set of letters used for writing a particular language *Arabic/Roman script*

**scripted** /'skrɪptɪd/ *adj* A scripted speech or broadcast has been written before it is read or performed.

**scripture** /'skrɪptʃəʳ/ (*also* **the scriptures**) *noun* [U] the holy books of a religion

**scriptwriter** /'skrɪpt,raɪtəʳ/ *noun* [C] someone who writes the words for films or radio or television programmes

**scroll¹** /skrəʊl/ *noun* [C] a long roll of paper with writing on it, used especially in the past

**scroll²** /skrəʊl/ *verb* **scroll up/down/through, etc** to move text or an image on a computer screen so that you can look at the part that you want

**scrooge** /skru:dʒ/ *noun* [C] *informal* someone who spends very little money

**scrounge** /skraʊndʒ/ *verb* [I, T] *informal* to get something from someone else instead of paying for it yourself *He's always scrounging money off you.*

**scrub¹** /skrʌb/ *verb* [I, T] **scrubbing**, *past* **scrubbed** to clean something by rubbing it hard with a brush *to scrub the floor*

**scrub²** /skrʌb/ *noun* **1** [U] bushes and small trees that grow in a dry area **2** [no plural] when you clean something by rubbing it with a brush *I gave my hands a good scrub.*

**scruff** /skrʌf/ *noun* **by the scruff of the/your neck** by the back of the neck *She picked the cat up by the scruff of its neck.*

**scruffy** /'skrʌfi/ *adj* dirty and untidy *scruffy jeans* • *I don't like to look scruffy.*

**scruple** /'skru:pl/ *noun* [C] a belief that something is wrong which stops you from doing that thing [usually plural] *She* **has no scruples** *about accepting bribes.*

**scrupulous** /'skru:pjələs/ *adj* **1** very careful and giving great attention to details *He's very scrupulous about making sure that all the facts are checked.* **2** always honest and fair ⮕ *Opposite* **unscrupulous**.

**scrutinize** (*also UK* **-ise**) /'skru:tɪnaɪz/ *verb* [T] to examine something very carefully *The evidence was carefully scrutinized.*

**scrutiny** /'skru:tɪni/ *noun* [U] when you examine something carefully *Every aspect of her life came* **under** *public scrutiny.*

**scuba diving** /'sku:bə,daɪvɪŋ/ *noun* [U] a sport in which you swim under water using special equipment for breathing

**scuff** /skʌf/ *verb* [T] to make a mark on your shoes by rubbing them against something rough

**scuffle** /'skʌfl/ *noun* [C] a short fight in which people push each other *A scuffle broke out* (= started) *behind the courtroom.*

**sculptor** /'skʌlptəʳ/ *noun* [C] someone who makes sculpture

**sculpture** /'skʌlptʃəʳ/ *noun* **1** [C, U] a piece of art that is made from stone, wood, clay, etc *a wooden sculpture* • *modern sculpture* **2** [U] the art of making objects from stone, wood, clay, etc *She teaches sculpture at an art school.*

**scum** /skʌm/ *noun* **1** [U, no plural] an unpleasant, thick substance on the surface of a liquid *There was a thick layer of scum on the water.* **2** [U] *informal* an offensive way of referring to a very bad person

**scurry** /'skʌri/ *verb* **scurry along/around/away, etc** to walk quickly or run because you are in a hurry *I saw Gina scurrying around, getting everything ready.*

**scuttle** /'skʌtl/ *verb* **scuttle across/along/away, etc** to run quickly using short steps *A beetle scuttled across the floor.*

**scythe** /saɪð/ *noun* [C] a tool with a long handle and a curved blade that is used to cut tall grass and crops

○⟶**sea** /si:/ *noun* **1** [C, U] a large area of salt water *I'd like to live by the sea.* • *We went swimming in the sea.* • *It was our third day at sea* (= travelling on the sea). • *It's cheaper to send parcels by sea* (= on a ship). **2** a particular area of salt water *the North Sea* • *the Black Sea* **3** **a sea of sth** a large number of something *He looked across the room and saw a sea of faces.*

**seabed** /'si:bed/ *noun* [no plural] the floor of the sea

**seafood** /'si:fu:d/ *noun* [U] animals from the sea that are eaten as food, especially animals that live in shells

**seafront** /'si:frʌnt/ *noun* [C] *UK* a part of a town that is next to the sea [usually singular] *We walked along the seafront.*

**seagull** /'si:gʌl/ *noun* [C] a grey and white bird that lives near the sea

**seahorse** /'si:hɔ:s/ *noun* [C] a small fish that has a head and neck the same shape as a horse's

**seal¹** /si:l/ *noun* [C] **1** ANIMAL an animal with smooth fur that eats fish and lives near the sea **2** ON A CONTAINER a piece of paper or plastic on a container that you break in order to open it **3** OFFICIAL MARK an official mark made of wax, paper, or metal that is put on important documents **4** STOP LIQUID/AIR an object or substance that stops liquid or air from leaving or entering a container

**seal²** /si:l/ *verb* [T] **1** (*also* **seal up**) to close an entrance or container so that air or liquid cannot enter or leave it *She quickly sealed up the bottle.* **2** to close a letter or parcel by sticking the edges together *to seal an envelope*

**seal sth off** to prevent people from entering an area or building, often because it is dangerous *Police immediately sealed off the streets.*

**'sea ,level** *noun* [U] the level of the sea's surface, used to measure the height of an area of land

**'sea ,lion** *noun* [C] a large seal (= sea animal)

**seam** /si:m/ *noun* [C] **1** a line of sewing where two pieces of cloth have been joined together **2** a long, thin layer of coal under the ground

---

**seaman** /'si:mən/ *noun* [C] *plural* **seamen** a sailor

**seance** /'seɪɒns/ *noun* [C] a meeting at which people try to communicate with spirits of dead people

o─**search¹** /sɜːtʃ/ *verb* **1** [TRY TO FIND] [I, T] to try to find someone or something *I've searched my bedroom but I can't find my watch.* • *He searched in his pockets for some change.* • *Police are still **searching** the woods **for** the missing girl.* **2** [POLICE] [T] If the police search someone, they look in their clothes and bags to see if they are hiding anything illegal, such as drugs. *They were searched at the airport.* **3** [FIND ANSWER] [I] to try to find an answer to a problem *Doctors are still **searching for** a cure.*

**USAGE**

**search** or **search for**?

If you **search** a place or person, you are looking for something in that place or on that person.

*The police searched the man* (= looked in his clothes) *for drugs.*

*I searched the kitchen* (= looked in the kitchen) *for my watch.*

If you **search for** something or someone, you are looking for that thing or that person.

*I searched for my watch.*

~~I searched my watch.~~

o─**search²** /sɜːtʃ/ *noun* **1** [C] when you try to find someone or something [usually singular] *Police are continuing their **search for** the missing girl.* • *They went off **in search of** (= to find) a bar.* **2** [no plural] when you try to find an answer to a problem *the search for happiness*

'**search ,engine** *noun* [C] a computer program which finds information on the Internet by looking for words which you have typed in

**searching** /sɜːtʃɪŋ/ *adj* A searching question or look is intended to discover the truth about something.

'**search ,party** *noun* [C] a group of people who look for someone who is lost

'**search ,warrant** *noun* [C] an official document that allows the police to search a building

**searing** /sɪərɪŋ/ *adj* [always before noun] extreme and unpleasant *searing pain/heat*

'**sea ,shell** *noun* [C] the empty shell of some types of sea animals

**the seashore** /'si:ʃɔːʳ/ *noun* the area of land along the edge of the sea

**seasick** /'si:sɪk/ *adj* feeling ill because of the way a boat is moving

**the seaside** /'si:saɪd/ *noun* an area or town next to the sea *We had a picnic **at the seaside**.* • *a seaside resort/community*

o─**season¹** /'si:zᵊn/ *noun* [C] **1** one of the four periods of the year; winter, spring, summer, or autumn **2** a period of the year when a particular thing happens [usually singular] *the holiday season* • *the rainy/dry season* • *the football season* **3 in season a** If vegetables or fruit are in season, they are available and ready to eat.

**b** If a female animal is in season, she is ready to mate. **4 out of season a** If vegetables or fruit are out of season, they are not usually available at that time. **b** If you go somewhere out of season, you go during a period of the year when few people are there.

**season²** /'si:zᵊn/ *verb* [T] to add salt or spices to food that you are cooking

**seasonal** /'si:zᵊnᵊl/ *adj* happening or existing only at a particular time of the year *a seasonal worker* • *the seasonal migration of birds*

**seasoned** /'si:zᵊnd/ *adj* [always before noun] having a lot of experience of doing something *a seasoned traveller*

**seasoning** /'si:zᵊnɪŋ/ *noun* [C, U] salt or spices that you add to food

'**season ,ticket** *UK* (*US* ,**season** '**ticket**) *noun* [C] a ticket that you can use many times without having to pay each time

o─**seat¹** /si:t/ *noun* [C] **1** [SIT] something that you sit on *Please, **have/take a seat*** (= sit down). • *I've booked three seats for the cinema tonight.* • *the back/front seat of a car* **2** [PART] the flat part of a chair, bicycle, etc that you sit on **3** [POLITICS] a position in a parliament or other group that makes official decisions *a seat in parliament* • *a congressional seat*

**seat²** /si:t/ *verb* **1 seat yourself in/on/next to, etc** to sit somewhere *I seated myself next to the fire.* **2 be seated a** to be sitting down *The director was seated on his right.* **b** used to politely ask a group of people to sit down *Would the people at the back please be seated.* **3 seat 4/12/200, etc** If a building, room, or vehicle seats a particular number of people, that many people can sit in it. *The new concert hall seats 1500 people.*

'**seat ,belt** *noun* [C] a strap that you fasten across your body when travelling in a vehicle *to fasten your seat belt* ➔ *See colour picture* **Car** *on page Centre 3.*

**seating** /'si:tɪŋ/ *noun* [U] the seats in a public place, or the way that they are arranged

**seaweed** /'si:wi:d/ *noun* [U] a plant that you find on the beach and that grows in the sea

**sec** /sek/ *noun* [C] *informal* a very short time *Just a sec – I'm nearly ready.*

**secluded** /sɪ'klu:dɪd/ *adj* If a place is secluded, it is quiet and not near people. *a secluded beach/garden*

**seclusion** /sɪ'klu:ʒᵊn/ *noun* [U] when someone lives alone, away from other people *He lived **in seclusion** for the rest of his life.*

**second¹** /'sekᵊnd/ *adj, pronoun* **1** referring to the person, thing, or event that comes immediately after the first *You're second on the list.* • *This is my second piece of chocolate cake.* • *She didn't win but she did **come second*** (= was the one after the winner) *in one race.* **2** 2nd written as a word ➔ *See also:* **second best**, **second-hand**, **second language**, **second nature**, **the second person**, **second-rate**, **second thought**, **second wind**.

o─**second²** /'sekᵊnd/ *noun* [C] **1** [TIME] one of the 60 parts a minute is divided into **2** [SHORT TIME] *informal* a very short period of time *I'll be back in just a second.* • *It only took a few seconds.* **3** [PRODUCT] something that is sold

S

cheaply because it is damaged or not in perfect condition [usually plural] *Some of those towels are seconds.*

**second³** /'sekᵊnd/ *verb* [T] to formally support an idea at a meeting [often passive] *The chairperson's proposal was seconded by Ms Jones.*

**second⁴** /sɪ'kɒnd/ *verb* [T] *UK* to send someone to another job for a fixed period of time [often passive] *He was seconded from the police to the Department of Transport.*

**secondary** /'sekᵊndᵊri/ *adj* **1** relating to the education of students aged between 11 and 18 *secondary education* **2** less important than something else *What matters is the size of the office. The location is of secondary importance.*

**secondary school** *noun* [C] *mainly UK* a school for students aged between 11 and 18

**second best** *adj* not the best but the next best *the second best candidate* ● **second best** *noun* [U]

**second-class** /ˌsekənd'klɑːs/ *adj* **1** TRAVEL relating to the less expensive way of travelling in a train, aircraft, etc, that most people use *a second-class carriage/ticket* **2** NOT IMPORTANT less important than other people *Women are still treated as second-class citizens.* **3** UNIVERSITY a second-class university degree is a good degree but not the best possible ● **second class** *adv We always travel second class.*

**second-hand** /ˌsekᵊnd'hænd/ *adj, adv* If something is second-hand, someone else owned or used it before you. *second-hand books/clothes* ● *She buys a lot of clothes second-hand.*

**second language** *noun* [C] a language that you speak that is not the first language you learned as a child

**secondly** /'sekᵊndli/ *adv* used for introducing the second reason, idea, etc *I want two things: firstly, more money, and secondly, better working hours.*

**second nature** *noun* [U] something that you can do easily because you have done it many times before *After a few years, teaching became second nature to me.*

**the second person** *noun* the form of a verb or pronoun that is used when referring to the person being spoken or written to. For example 'you' is a second person pronoun

**second-rate** /ˌsekᵊnd'reɪt/ *adj* of bad quality *a second-rate writer*

**second thought** *noun* **1 on second thoughts** *UK* used when you want to change a decision you have made *I'll have tea, please – on second thoughts, make that coffee.* **2 without a second thought** If you do something without a second thought, you do it without first considering if you should do it or not. *She'll spend a hundred pounds on a dress without a second thought.* **3 have second thoughts** to change your opinion about something or start to doubt it [+ about + doing sth] *I've been having second thoughts about doing the course.*

**second wind** *noun* [no plural] a return of energy that makes it possible to continue an activity *I was feeling tired, but I got my second wind after lunch.*

**secrecy** /'siːkrəsi/ *noun* [U] when something is kept secret *Politicians criticized the secrecy surrounding the air attack.*

o⊸**secret¹** /'siːkrət/ *adj* **1** If something is secret, other people are not allowed to know about it. *a secret affair/meeting* ● *I'll tell you but you must keep it secret.* **2 secret admirer/drinker, etc** someone who does something or feels something without telling other people about it ● *secretly adv He secretly taped their conversation.* ⊃ *See also:* **top-secret**.

o⊸**secret²** /'siːkrət/ *noun* [C] **1** something that you tell no one about or only a few people *I'm having a party for him but it's a secret.* ● *Can you keep a secret?* **2 the secret** the best way of achieving something *That's the secret to making a good cocktail.* ● *So what's the secret of your success?* **3 in secret** without telling other people *For years they met in secret.*

**secret agent** *noun* [C] someone who tries to find out secret information, especially about another country

**secretarial** /ˌsekrə'teəriəl/ *adj* relating to the work of a secretary (= office worker who types letters, etc) *secretarial skills*

o⊸**secretary** /'sekrətᵊri/ *noun* [C] **1** someone who works in an office, typing letters, answering the telephone, and arranging meetings, etc **2** (*also* **Secretary**) an official who is in charge of a large department of the government *the Secretary of State*

**secrete** /sɪ'kriːt/ *verb* [T] to produce a substance *A mixture of substances are secreted by cells within the stomach.* ● **secretion** /sɪ'kriːʃᵊn/ *noun* [C, U]

**secretive** /'siːkrətɪv/ *adj* not willing to tell people what you know or what you are doing *He's very secretive about his relationships.* ● **secretively** *adv*

**secret service** *noun* [no plural] **1** in the UK, a department of the government that tries to find out secret information about foreign countries **2** in the US, a government organization that protects the president

**sect** /sekt/ *noun* [C] a group of people with a set of religious or political beliefs, often extreme beliefs

**sectarian** /sek'teəriən/ *adj* relating to the differences between religious groups *sectarian violence*

o⊸**section** /'sekʃᵊn/ *noun* [C] **1** one of the parts that something is divided into *a non-smoking section in a restaurant* ● *the business section of a newspaper* ● *the tail section of an aircraft* **2** a model or drawing of something that shows how it would look if it were cut from top to bottom and seen from the side ⊃ *See also:* **cross-section**.

**sector** /'sektə/ *noun* [C] **1** one part of a country's economy *the private/public sector* ● *the financial/manufacturing sector* **2** one of the parts that an area is divided into *the British sector of the North Sea*

**secular** /'sekjələ/ *adj* not religious or not controlled by a religious group *secular education* ● *a secular state*

**secure¹** /sɪ'kjʊə/ *adj* **1** NOT FAIL not likely to fail or be lost *a secure investment/job* **2** SAFE safe from danger *I don't feel that the house is secure.* **3** CONFIDENT confident about yourself and the situation that you are in *I need to feel* secure in a relationship. **4** FIXED firmly fastened and not likely to fall or break *Check that all windows and doors are secure.* ⊃ *Opposite* **insecure.**

**secure²** /sɪˈkjʊəʳ/ *verb* [T] **1** ACHIEVE to achieve something, after a lot of effort *to secure the release of hostages* **2** FASTEN to fasten something firmly *He secured the bike to the gate.* **3** MAKE SAFE to make something safe

**securely** /sɪˈkjʊəli/ *adv* If something is securely fastened, it will not fall or become loose.

**security** /sɪˈkjʊərəti/ *noun* [U] **1** BEING SAFE the things that are done to keep someone or something safe *airport/national security* • *a security alarm* **2** SAFE SITUATION when something is not likely to fail or be lost *financial security* • *job security* **3** CONFIDENCE confidence about yourself and the situation that you are in *the security of a long-term relationship* **4** BORROWING something valuable that you offer to give someone when you borrow money if you cannot pay the money back ⊃ *Opposite* **insecurity** ⊃ *See also:* **social security.**

**security** or **safety**?

Security means activities or people that protect you from harm, or that try to stop crime.

*He works as a security guard.*

*airport security*

Safety is when you are safe or how safe something is.

*Remember to wear your safety belt in the car.*

*Children should have lessons in road safety.*

**sedan** /sɪˈdæn/ *US* (*UK* **saloon**) *noun* [C] a large car with a separate, closed area for bags

**sedate¹** /sɪˈdeɪt/ *adj* calm and slow *walking at a sedate pace*

**sedate²** /sɪˈdeɪt/ *verb* [T] to give a person or animal a drug to make them feel calm • **sedation** /sɪˈdeɪʃᵊn/ *noun* [U] *She had to be put under sedation.*

**sedative** /ˈsedətɪv/ *noun* [C] a drug used to sedate a person or an animal

**sedentary** /ˈsedᵊntᵊri/ *adj* spending a lot of time sitting down or not being active *a sedentary job/lifestyle*

**sediment** /ˈsedɪmənt/ *noun* [C, U] a solid substance that forms a layer at the bottom of a liquid

**seduce** /sɪˈdjuːs/ *verb* [T] **1** to persuade someone to have sex with you, especially someone young **2** to persuade someone to do something they would not normally do *I wouldn't have bought it but I was seduced by the low prices.*

**seductive** /sɪˈdʌktɪv/ *adj* **1** sexually attractive *a seductive smile/voice* **2** making you want to have or do something *the seductive power of money*

o—⸚ **see** /siː/ *verb* **seeing,** *past t* **saw,** *past p* **seen** **1** EYES [I, T] to notice people and things with your eyes *Have you seen Jo?* • *Turn the light on so I can see.* ⊃ *See usage note at* **look. 2** UNDERSTAND [I, T] to understand something *I see what*

you mean. • *I don't see why I should go.* **3** MEET [T] to meet or visit someone *I'm seeing Peter tonight.* • *You should see a doctor.* **4** WATCH [T] to watch a film, television programme, etc *Did you see that film last night?* **5** INFORMATION [T] to find out information [+ question word] *I'll just see what time the train gets in.* **6** IMAGINE [T] to imagine or think about something or someone in a particular way *I just can't see him as a father.* **7** BELIEVE [T, used in questions and negatives] to believe that something will happen *I can't see us finishing on time.* **8** HAPPEN [T] to be the time or place where something happens *This decade has seen huge technological advances.* **9 see that** If you ask someone to see that something happens, you want them to make sure it happens. *Could you see that everyone gets a copy of this letter?* **10 see sb home/to the station, etc** to go somewhere with someone, especially to make sure they are safe *Let me see you home.* **11 I'll/we'll see** used to say that you will make a decision about something later *"Dad, can I have a guitar?" "We'll see."* **12 see you** *informal* used for saying goodbye ⊃ *See also:* be glad/happy, etc to see the **back²** of sb/sth, see **eye¹** to eye (with sb), see **red².**

**see about sth/doing sth** to deal with something, or arrange for something to be done *You should see about getting your hair cut.*

**see sth in sb/sth** to believe that someone or something has a particular quality *I can't understand what you see in her* (= why you like her).

**see sb off** to go to the place that someone is leaving from in order to say goodbye to them *My parents came to the airport to see me off.*

**see sb out** to take someone to the door of a room or building when they are leaving *Don't worry, I'll see myself out* (= leave the room/building by myself).

**see through sb/sth** to understand that someone is trying to deceive you *I saw through him at once.*

**see to sth** to deal with something *Don't worry, I'll see to everything while you're away.*

**seed¹** /siːd/ *noun* **1** [C, U] a small round or oval object produced by a plant that a new plant can grow from *Sow the seeds* (= plant them) *near the surface.* **2** (the) **seeds of sth** the beginning of something *the seeds of hope/change* ⊃ *See also:* **sesame seed.**

**seed²** /siːd/ *verb* **1** [T] to plant seeds in the ground **2 be seeded first/second, etc** in tennis, to be the first/second, etc on a list of players expected to succeed in a competition

**seedless** /ˈsiːdləs/ *adj* without seeds *seedless grapes*

**seedling** /ˈsiːdlɪŋ/ *noun* [C] a young plant that has been grown from a seed

**seedy** /ˈsiːdi/ *adj informal* looking dirty or in bad condition and likely to be involved in immoral activities *a seedy bar/hotel*

**ˌseeing ˈeye dog** *US* (*UK/US* **guide dog**) *noun* [C] a dog that is trained to help blind people

**seek** /siːk/ *verb* [T] *past* **sought 1** to try to find or get something *to seek advice/a solution* **2** to try to do something [+ to do sth] *They are seeking to* *change the rules.* ● *to seek re-election* ➔ *See also:* **hide-and-seek**.

○━**seem** /siːm/ *verb* **seem happy/a nice person, etc; seem like/as if, etc** to appear to be a particular thing or to have a particular quality *She seemed happy enough.* ● *It seemed like a good idea at the time.* ● *There doesn't seem to be any real solution.* ● [+ (that)] *It seems that the bars close early here.* ● *It seems to me* (= I think) *that she's in the wrong job.*

**seemingly** /ˈsiːmɪŋli/ *adv* appearing to be something without really being that thing *a seemingly harmless comment*

**seen** /siːn/ *past participle of* see

**seep** /siːp/ *verb* **seep from/into/through, etc** to flow very slowly through something *Water was seeping through the walls.*

**seesaw** /ˈsiːsɔː/ (*also US* **teeter-totter**) *noun* [C] a long board that children play on by sitting at each end and using their feet on the ground to push the board up and down

**seesaw**

**seethe** /siːð/ *verb* [I] to be very angry, often without showing it *I left him **seething with** anger.*

**segment** /ˈsegmənt/ *noun* [C] one of the parts that something can be divided into *a segment of the population/market* ● *an orange segment*

**segregate** /ˈsegrɪgeɪt/ *verb* [T] to separate one group of people from another, especially one sex or race from another *At school the girls were segregated from the boys.* ● segregation /ˌsegrɪˈgeɪʃən/ *noun* [U] *racial segregation*

**seismic** /ˈsaɪzmɪk/ *adj* relating to or caused by an earthquake (= when the earth shakes) *seismic activity*

**seize** /siːz/ *verb* [T] **1** [HOLD] to take hold of something quickly and firmly *She seized my arm and pulled me towards her.* **2** [OPPORTUNITY] to do something quickly when you have the opportunity *You need to seize every opportunity.* **3** [PLACE] to take control of a place suddenly by using military force *Troops seized control in the early hours of the morning.* **4** [DRUGS ETC] to take away something that is illegal, for example drugs *Officials seized 2.7 tons of cocaine from the ship.*

**seize on/upon sth** to quickly use something that will give you an advantage *Her story was seized upon by the press.*

**seize up** If part of your body or a machine seizes up, it stops moving or working in the normal way. *His right leg suddenly seized up during the race.*

**seizure** /ˈsiːʒər/ *noun* **1** [CONTROL] [U] when someone takes control of a country, government, etc *a seizure of power* **2** [DRUGS ETC] [C] when someone in authority takes away something that is illegal, for example drugs *a seizure of heroin* **3** [ILLNESS] [C] a sudden attack of an illness *an epileptic seizure*

**seldom** /ˈseldəm/ *adv* not often *We seldom go out in the evenings.*

**select¹** /sɪˈlekt/ *verb* [T] to choose someone or something *We've selected three candidates.*

**select²** /sɪˈlekt/ *adj* consisting of only a small group of people who have been specially chosen *a select group*

**selection** /sɪˈlekʃən/ *noun* **1** [U] when someone or something is chosen *the selection process* **2** [C] a group of people or things that has been chosen *We have a wide selection of imported furniture.* ➔ *See also:* **natural selection**.

**selective** /sɪˈlektɪv/ *adj* **1** careful about what you choose *He's very selective about the people he spends time with.* **2** involving only people or things that have been specially chosen *selective breeding*

**self** /self/ *noun* [C, U] *plural* **selves** /selvz/ your characteristics, including your personality, your abilities, etc *our sense of self* ● *his true self*

**self-assured** /ˌselfəˈʃʊəd/ *adj* confident about yourself

**self-centred** *UK* (*US* **self-centered**) /ˌselfˈsentəd/ *adj* interested only in yourself

**self-confident** /ˌselfˈkɒnfɪdənt/ *adj* feeling sure about yourself and your abilities ● self-confidence *noun* [U] being self-confident

**self-conscious** /ˌselfˈkɒnʃəs/ *adj* too aware of what other people are thinking about you and your appearance ● self-consciously *adv* ● self-consciousness *noun* [U]

**self-contained** /ˌselfkənˈteɪnd/ *adj* *UK* If a flat is self-contained, it has its own kitchen, bathroom, and entrance.

**self-control** /ˌselfkənˈtrəʊl/ *noun* [U] the ability to control your emotions and actions although you are very angry, upset, etc

**self-defence** *UK* (*US* **self-defense**) /ˌselfdɪˈfens/ *noun* [U] when you protect yourself from someone who is attacking you by fighting *He claimed he had acted in self-defence.*

**self-destructive** /ˌselfdɪˈstrʌktɪv/ *adj* A self-destructive action harms the person who is doing it.

**self-discipline** /ˌselfˈdɪsɪplɪn/ *noun* [U] the ability to make yourself do things that you do not want to do

**self-employed** /ˌselfɪmˈplɔɪd/ *adj* working for yourself and not for a company or other organization

**self-esteem** /ˌselfɪˈstiːm/ *noun* [U] confidence in yourself and a belief in your qualities and abilities *She suffers from low self-esteem.*

**self-evident** /ˌselfˈevɪdənt/ *adj* obviously true and not needing to be explained

**self-explanatory** /ˌselfɪkˈsplænətəri/ *adj* easy to understand and not needing to be explained

**self-help** /ˌselfˈhelp/ *adj* A self-help book, activity, organization, etc is designed to help you deal with your problems on your own. *a self-help group for alcoholics*

**self-indulgent** /ˌselfɪnˈdʌldʒ°nt/ *adj* doing or having things that you like although they are not necessary or are bad for you ● self-indulgence /ˌselfɪnˈdʌldʒ°ns/ *noun* [C, U]

**self-inflicted** /ˌselfɪnˈflɪktɪd/ *adj* If an injury or a problem is self-inflicted, you have caused it yourself.

**self-interest** /ˌselfˈɪntrəst/ *noun* [U] interest in what will help you and not what will help other people

**selfish** /ˈselfɪʃ/ *adj* caring only about yourself and not other people *It's very selfish of him.* ● selfishly *adv* ● selfishness *noun* [U]

**selfless** /ˈselfləs/ *adj* caring about other people and not about yourself

**self-made** /ˌselfˈmeɪd/ *adj* rich because you have earned a lot of money yourself *a self-made millionaire*

**self-pity** /ˌselfˈpɪti/ *noun* [U] sadness for yourself because you think you have suffered so much, especially when this is not true

**self-portrait** /ˌselfˈpɔːtreɪt/ *noun* [C] a picture that you draw or paint of yourself

**self-reliant** /ˌselfrɪˈlaɪənt/ *adj* able to do things yourself without depending on other people

**self-respect** /ˌselfrɪˈspekt/ *noun* [U] the feeling of pride in yourself and your character ● self-respecting *adj*

**self-righteous** /ˌselfˈraɪtʃəs/ *adj* believing that you are morally better than other people

**self-sacrifice** /ˌselfˈsækrɪfaɪs/ *noun* [U] when you do not have or do something so that you can help other people

**self-satisfied** /ˌselfˈsætɪsfaɪd/ *adj* too pleased with yourself and what you have achieved

**self-service** /ˌselfˈsɜːvɪs/ *adj* A self-service restaurant or shop is one in which you serve yourself and are not served by the people who work there.

**self-sufficient** /ˌselfsəˈfɪʃ°nt/ *adj* having everything that you need yourself and not needing help from others

o--**sell** /sel/ *verb past* **sold 1** FOR MONEY [I, T] to give something to someone who gives you money for it *He sold his guitar for £50.* ● *I sold my bike to Claire.* ● [+ two objects] *I'm hoping she'll sell me her car.* **2** OFFER [T] to offer something for people to buy *Excuse me, do you sell newspapers?* **3** sell for/at sth to be available for sale at a particular price *The shirts are selling for £30 each.* **4** A LOT [I, T] to be bought in large numbers *His last book sold eight million copies.* **5** MAKE YOU WANT [T] to make someone want to buy something *Scandal sells newspapers.* **6** IDEA/PLAN [T] to persuade someone that an idea or plan is good *I'm currently trying to sell the idea to my boss.*

**sell sth off** to sell all or part of a business *The company announced that it would be selling off its hotels.*

**sell out** If a shop sells out of something, it sells all of that thing. *They'd sold out of bread by the time I got there.*

**sell up** *UK* to sell your house or company in order to go somewhere else or do something else

'**sell-by ˌdate** *noun* [C] *UK* the date printed on a food or drink container after which it should not be sold

**seller** /ˈselə°/ *noun* [C] **1** someone who sells something *a flower seller* **2** a product that a company sells *Our biggest sellers are the calendars.*

**Sellotape** /ˈseləuteɪp/ *UK trademark* (*US* **Scotch tape** *trademark*) *noun* [U] clear, thin material with glue on it, used to stick things together, especially paper ➔ *See colour picture* **Classroom** *on page Centre 4.*

**sellout** /ˈselaut/ *noun* [no plural] **1** a performance or event where all of the tickets have been sold **2** *informal* when someone does something that is against their beliefs in order to get money or power

**selves** /selvz/ *plural of* self

**semantic** /sɪˈmæntɪk/ *adj* connected with the meaning of language

**semblance** /ˈsembləns/ *noun* **a semblance of normality/order, etc** a small amount of a quality, but not as much as you would like *Our lives have now returned to some semblance of normality.*

**semen** /ˈsiːmən/ *noun* [U] the liquid that is produced by the male sex organs, that contains sperm (= cells that join with female eggs to make new life)

**semester** /sɪˈmestə°/ *noun* [C] *mainly US* one of the two time periods that a school or college year is divided into

**semicircle** /ˈsemɪˌsɜːkl/ *noun* [C] half a circle

**semicircle**

**semicolon** /ˌsemɪˈkəʊlən ⑥ ˈsemɪˌkəʊlən/ *noun* [C] a mark (;) used to separate parts of a sentence, or items in a list which already has commas ➔ *See study section* **Punctuation** *on page Centre 37.*

**semi-detached** /ˌsemɪdɪˈtætʃt/ *adj UK* A semi-detached house has one wall that is joined to another house.

**semifinal** /ˌsemɪˈfaɪn°l/ *noun* [C] one of the two games in a sports competition that are played to decide who will play in the final game

**seminar** /ˈsemɪnɑː°/ *noun* [C] a meeting of a group of people with a teacher or expert for training, discussion, or study of a subject

**Semitic** /sɪˈmɪtɪk/ *adj* relating to the Jewish or Arab races, or their languages

**the Senate** /ˈsenɪt/ *noun* [group] a part of a government in some countries

**senator** /ˈsenətə°/ *noun* [C] someone who has been elected to the Senate *Senator Moynihan*

S

o-**send** /send/ *verb* [T] *past* **sent 1** to arrange for something to go or be taken somewhere, especially by post [+ **two objects**] *I sent him a letter last week.* • *Do you think we should send flowers?* **2** to make someone go somewhere *I sent him into the house to fetch some glasses.* **3 send sb to sleep** to cause someone to start sleeping *Reading usually sends me to sleep.* ⊃ *See also:* send sb round the **bend²**.

**send sth back** to return something to the person who sent it to you, especially because it is damaged or not suitable *I had to send the shirt back because it didn't fit me.*

**send for sb** to send someone a message asking them to come to see you *Do you think we should send for a doctor?*

**send sth in** to send something to an organization *Viewers were asked to send in photographs of their pets.*

**send sb in** to send soldiers, police, etc to a place in order to deal with a dangerous situation

**send (off/away) for sth** to write to an organization to ask them to send you something *I've sent off for a catalogue.*

**send sth off** to send a letter, document, or parcel by post *Have you sent off your application form yet?*

**send sb off** *UK* to order a sports player to leave the playing area because they have done something wrong

**send sth out 1** to send something to a lot of different people *to send out invitations* **2** to produce light, sound, etc

**send sb/sth up** *UK* to make someone or something seem stupid by copying them in a funny way

**send-off** /'sendɒf/ *noun* [C] when a group of people say goodbye to someone at the same time *I got a good send-off at the station.*

**senile** /'siːnaɪl/ *adj* confused and unable to remember things because of old age • senility /sɪ'nɪləti/ *noun* [U] the state of being senile

**senior¹** /'siːniəʳ/ *adj* [MORE IMPORTANT] having a more important job or position than someone else *a senior officer/executive* • *We work in the same team but she's senior to me.* **2** [OLDER] older *senior students* **3** [NAME] *mainly US* (*written abbreviation* **Sr**) used at the end of a man's name to show that he is the older of two men in the same family who have the same name *Hello, may I speak to Ken Griffey Senior, please?*

**senior²** /'siːniəʳ/ *noun* **1 be 20/30, etc years sb's senior** to be 20/30, etc years older than someone *She married a man 20 years her senior.* **2** [C] *US* a student who is in the last year of high school or college

,**senior 'citizen** *noun* [C] an old person

**seniority** /ˌsiːni'ɒrəti/ *noun* [U] the state of being older or of having a more important position in an organization

**sensation** /sen'seɪʃᵊn/ *noun* **1** [PHYSICAL] [C, U] a physical feeling, or the ability to physically feel things *a burning sensation* • *Three months after the accident she still has no sensation in her right foot.* **2** [FEELING] [C] a strange feeling or idea that you can not explain *I had the strangest sensation that I had met him before.*

**3** [EXCITEMENT] [no plural] a lot of excitement, surprise, or interest, or the person or event that causes these feelings *Their affair* **caused** *a sensation.*

**sensational** /sen'seɪʃᵊnᵊl/ *adj* **1** done in a way that is intended to shock people *sensational journalism* **2** very exciting or extremely good *a sensational performance*

**sensationalism** /sen'seɪʃᵊnᵊlɪzᵊm/ *noun* [U] when a story is told in a way that is intended to shock people

o-**sense¹** /sens/ *noun* **1** [GOOD JUDGMENT] [U] good judgment, especially about practical things *He had the good sense to book a seat in advance.* **2** [ABILITY] [no plural] the ability to do something *a sense of direction* • *good business sense* **3** [NATURAL ABILITY] [C] one of the five natural abilities of sight, hearing, touch, smell, and taste *I have a very poor sense of smell.* **4 a sense of humour** *UK* (*US* **sense of humor**) the ability to understand funny things and to be funny yourself **5 a sense of loyalty/responsibility/security, etc** the quality or feeling of being loyal, responsible, safe, etc *He has absolutely no sense of loyalty.* • *Driving along in a comfortable car can give you a false sense of security.* **6** [MEANING] [C] the meaning of a word, phrase, or sentence **7 in a sense/in some senses** thinking about something in a particular way *In a sense, he's right.* **8 make sense a** to have a meaning or reason that you can understand *He's written me this note but it doesn't make any sense.* **b** to be a good thing to do [+ to do sth] *It makes sense to buy now while prices are low.* **9 make sense of sth** to understand something that is difficult to understand *I'm trying to make sense of this document.* **10 come to your senses** to start to understand that you have been behaving stupidly ⊃ *See also:* **common sense**.

**sense²** /sens/ *verb* [T] to understand what someone is thinking or feeling without being told about it [+ (that)] *I sensed that you weren't happy about this.*

**senseless** /'sensləs/ *adj* **1** happening or done without a good reason *senseless violence* **2** not conscious *He was beaten senseless.*

**sensibility** /ˌsensɪ'bɪləti/ *noun* [C, U] *formal* someone's feelings, or the ability to understand what other people feel

o-**sensible** /'sensɪbl/ *adj* **1** showing good judgment *a sensible decision* • [+ to do sth] *Wouldn't it be more sensible to leave before the traffic gets bad?* • *She's only thirteen but she's very sensible.* **2** having a practical purpose *sensible shoes/clothes* • sensibly *adv* *to eat/behave sensibly* • *sensibly dressed for the weather*

**sensitive** /'sensɪtɪv/ *adj* **1** [KIND] able to understand what people are feeling and deal with them in a way that does not upset them *I want a man who's kind and sensitive.* **2** [EASILY UPSET] easily upset by the things people say or do *He was always sensitive to criticism.* • *She's very sensitive about her weight.* **3** [SUBJECT] A sensitive subject or situation needs to be dealt with carefully in order to avoid upsetting people. *Gender is a very sensitive subject.* **4** [EASILY DAMAGED] easily damaged or hurt *sensitive* *eyes/skin* **5** EQUIPMENT Sensitive equipment is able to measure very small changes. ➔ *Opposite* **insensitive.** • sensitively *adv I think she dealt with the problem very sensitively.* • sensitivity /ˌsensɪˈtɪvəti/ *noun* [U] when someone or something is sensitive

**sensitive** or **sensible**?

Remember that **sensible** does not mean 'easily upset' or 'able to understand what people are feeling'. The word you need to express that is **sensitive**.

*Don't criticize her too much. She's very sensitive.*

**sensor** /ˈsensəʳ/ *noun* [C] a piece of equipment that can find heat, light, etc *Sensors detect movement in the room.*

**sensual** /ˈsensjuəl/ *adj* relating to physical pleasure, often sexual pleasure *a sensual experience* • *a sensual mouth* • sensuality /ˌsensjuˈæləti/ *noun* [U] being sensual

**sensuous** /ˈsensjuəs/ *adj* giving physical pleasure *the sensuous feel of silk sheets*

**sent** /sent/ *past of* send

o-ᴝ**sentence¹** /ˈsentəns/ *noun* **1** [C] a group of words, usually containing a verb, that expresses a complete idea **2** [C, U] a punishment that a judge gives to someone who has committed a crime *a 30-year sentence*

**sentence²** /ˈsentəns/ *verb* [T] to give a punishment to someone who has committed a crime [often passive] *She was sentenced to six months in prison.*

**sentiment** /ˈsentɪmənt/ *noun* **1** [C, U] an opinion that you have because of the way you feel about something *nationalist/religious sentiments* **2** [U] emotional feelings such as sympathy, love, etc, especially when they are not considered to be suitable for a situation *I find her writing full of sentiment.*

**sentimental** /ˌsentɪˈment°l/ *adj* **1** showing kind feelings such as sympathy, love, etc, especially in a silly way *a sentimental song* • *The British are very sentimental about animals.* **2** related to feelings and memories and not related to how much money something costs *It wasn't an expensive ring but it had great sentimental value.* • sentimentality /ˌsentɪmenˈtæləti/ *noun* [U]

**sentry** /ˈsentri/ *noun* [C] a soldier who stands outside a building in order to guard it

**separable** /ˈsep°rəbl/ *adj* able to be separated ➔ *Opposite* **inseparable.**

o-ᴝ**separate¹** /ˈsep°rət/ *adj* **1** NOT JOINED not joined or touching anything else *a separate compartment* • *I try to keep meat separate from other food.* **2** NOT AFFECTING not affecting or related to each other *I've asked him to turn his music down on three separate occasions.* • *I have my professional life and my private life and I try to keep them separate.* **3** DIFFERENT *Use a separate sheet of paper.* • separately *adv*

o-ᴝ**separate²** /ˈsep°reɪt/ *verb* **1** DIVIDE [I, T] to divide into parts, or to make something divide into parts *I separated the class into three groups.* **2** MOVE APART [I, T] to move apart, or to make

people move apart *I shall separate you two if you don't stop talking.* **3** HUSBAND/WIFE [I] to start to live in a different place from your husband or wife because the relationship has ended *My parents separated when I was four.* ➔ *See usage note at* **married.**

**separation** /ˌsep°rˈeɪʃ°n/ *noun* **1** [C, U] when people or things are separate or become separate from other people or things *the separation of church and state* • *Their working in different countries meant long periods of separation.* **2** [C] a legal agreement when two people stay married but stop living together

**September** /sepˈtembəʳ/ (*written abbreviation* **Sept**) *noun* [C, U] the ninth month of the year

**septic** /ˈseptɪk/ *adj* infected by poisonous bacteria (= small living things which cause disease)

**sequel** /ˈsiːkw°l/ *noun* [C] a film, book, etc that continues the story from an earlier one

**sequence** /ˈsiːkwəns/ *noun* **1** [C] a series of related events or things that have a particular order *the sequence of events that led to his death* **2** [U] the order that events or things should happen or be arranged in *I got my slides mixed up and they appeared out of sequence.*

**sequin** /ˈsiːkwɪn/ *noun* [C] a small, flat, shiny circle that is sewn onto clothes for decoration

**serenade** /ˌserəˈneɪd/ *noun* [C] a song, usually about love

**serendipity** /ˌser°nˈdɪpəti/ *noun* [U] when you are lucky and find something interesting or valuable by chance *The scientist's discovery was a real case of serendipity.*

**serene** /sɪˈriːn/ *adj* calm and quiet *a serene face/smile* • serenely *adv*

**sergeant** /ˈsɑːdʒ°nt/ *noun* [C] **1** an officer of low rank in the police **2** a soldier of middle rank in the army or air force

**serial** /ˈsɪəriəl/ *noun* [C] a story in a magazine or on television or radio that is told in separate parts over a period of time

**'serial ˌkiller** *noun* [C] someone who has murdered several people over a period of time

o-ᴝ**series** /ˈsɪəriːz/ *noun* [C] *plural* **series 1** several things or events of the same type that come one after the other *a series of lectures* **2** a group of television or radio programmes that have the same main characters or deal with the same subject *a four-part drama series*

o-ᴝ**serious** /ˈsɪəriəs/ *adj* **1** BAD A serious problem or situation is bad and makes people worry. *a serious accident/illness* • *This is a serious matter.* **2** NOT JOKING thinking or speaking sincerely about something and not joking *I'm being serious now – this is a very real problem.* • *Are you serious about changing your job?* **3** QUIET A serious person is quiet and does not laugh often. *a serious child* • *You look very serious – is something wrong?* • seriousness *noun* [U]

o-ᴝ**seriously** /ˈsɪəriəsli/ *adv* **1** in a serious way *seriously injured* • *Smoking can seriously damage your health.* **2** used to show that what you are going to say is not a joke *Seriously though, you mustn't say that.* **3** **take sb/sth seriously** to believe that someone or something is important and that you should pay attention to them *The police have to take any terrorist threat seriously.*

**sermon** /'sɜːmən/ noun [C] a religious speech given by a priest in church *to deliver/give a sermon*

**serotonin** /ˌserə'təʊnɪn/ noun [U] a chemical in your brain which controls your moods

**serpent** /'sɜːpᵊnt/ noun [C] *literary* a snake

**serrated** /sɪ'reɪtɪd/ adj A serrated edge, usually of a knife, has sharp triangular points along it.

**serrated**

**serum** /'sɪərəm/ noun [U] a clear liquid in blood that contains substances that stop infection

**servant** /'sɜːvᵊnt/ noun [C] someone who works and lives in someone else's house doing their cooking and cleaning, especially in the past つ *See also:* **civil servant**.

○<sup>■</sup>**serve**¹ /sɜːv/ verb

**1** FOOD/DRINK [I, T] to give someone food or drink, especially guests or customers in a restaurant or bar *We're not allowed to serve alcohol to anyone under 18.* **2** SHOP [I, T] to help customers and sell things to them in a shop *Are you being served?* **3** WORK [I, T] to do work that helps society, for example in an organization such as the army or the government *to serve in the army* • *to serve on a committee/jury* • *He served as mayor for 5 years.* **4** BE USEFUL [I, T] to be useful as something *It's a very entertaining film but it also serves an educational purpose.* • *The spare bedroom also serves as a study.* • [+ to do sth] *He hopes his son's death will serve to warn others about the dangers of owning a gun.* **5** PRISON [T] to be in prison for a period of time *Williams, 42, is serving a four-year jail sentence.* **6** SPORT [I] in a sport such as tennis, to throw the ball up into the air and then hit it towards the other player **7** **serves one/two/four, etc** If an amount of food serves a particular number, it is enough for that number of people. つ *See also:* It serves her/him/you **right²!**.

**serve**² /sɜːv/ noun [C] in sports such as tennis, when you throw the ball up into the air and hit it towards the other player

**server** /'sɜːvəʳ/ noun [C] a computer that is used only for storing and managing programs and information used by other computers *an email/Internet server*

○<sup>■</sup>**service**¹ /'sɜːvɪs/ noun **1** SHOP [U] when people help you and bring you things in a place such as a shop, restaurant, or hotel *The food was nice, but the service wasn't very good.* **2** SYSTEM [C] a system that supplies something that people need *financial/medical services* • *electricity/water services* • *They **provide** a free bus **service** from the station.* **3** WORK [U] the time you spend working for an organization *He retired last week after 25 years' service.* **4** CEREMONY [C] a religious ceremony *They held a memorial **service** for the victims of the*

*bombing.* **5** CAR/MACHINE [C] when a car or machine is examined for faults and repaired **6** SPORT [C] when you throw a ball up into the air and hit it towards the other player in sports such as tennis つ *See also:* **the Civil Service**, **community service**, **lip-service**, **the National Health Service**, **national service**, **secret service**.

**service**² /'sɜːvɪs/ verb [T] to examine and repair a car or machine

**serviceable** /'sɜːvɪsəbl/ adj able to be used, but not very good or attractive *I have some old but serviceable chairs.*

**'service ˌcharge** noun [C] an amount of money that is added to what you pay in a restaurant for being helped and brought things *a 10% service charge*

**serviceman** /'sɜːvɪsmən/ noun [C] *plural* **servicemen** a man who is in the army or navy

**the services** /'sɜːvɪsɪz/ noun [plural] the military forces such as the army or navy

**'service ˌstation** noun [C] a place at the side of a road where you can buy fuel for cars and food

**serviette** /ˌsɜːvi'et/ *UK* (*UK/US* **napkin**) noun [C] a piece of cloth or paper used when you eat, to keep your clothes clean and to clean your mouth and hands

**servile** /'sɜːvaɪl/ ⑤ /'sɜːrvᵊl/ adj too willing to do things for other people

**serving** /'sɜːvɪŋ/ noun [C] an amount of food for one person to eat *a large serving of rice*

**sesame seed** /'sesəmiˌsiːd/ noun [C] a small seed that is used to add a taste to food

**session** /'seʃᵊn/ noun **1** [C] a period during which you do one activity *a weekly aerobics session* • *We're having a training session this afternoon.* **2** [C, U] a meeting of an official group of people such as in a court or in the government *The court is now in session.*

○<sup>■</sup>**set**¹ /set/ verb **setting**, *past* **set** **1** A TIME [T] to arrange a time when something will happen [often passive] *The next meeting is set for 6 February.* **2** LEVEL [T] to decide the level of something *The interest rate has been set at 5%.* **3** MACHINE [T] to press switches on a machine so that it will start when you want it to *I've set the alarm for 6.30.* • [+ to do sth] *Can you set the video to record 'Neighbours' please?* **4** **set an example/a record/a standard, etc** to do something in a way that people will copy or try to improve on *Try to set a good example to the children.* • *She's set a new world record with that jump.* **5** **set fire to sth; set sth on fire** to make something start burning **6** **set sb free** to allow someone to leave prison, or to allow a person or animal to escape **7** **set sth alight** to make something start burning **8** **set the table** to put plates, knives, forks, etc on the table before you have a meal **9** SUN [I] When the sun sets, it moves down in the sky so that it cannot be seen. *The sun rises in the East and sets in the West.* **10** BECOME SOLID [I] If a liquid substance sets, it becomes solid. *How long does cement take to set?* **11** SCHOOL WORK [T] *UK* If you set work or an exam at a school or college, you ask the students to do it. [+ two objects] *Mr Harley forgot to set us any maths homework.* **12** **set sth down/on, etc** to put something somewhere

*She set the vase down on the table.* **13** BOOK/ FILM/PLAY [T] If a book, play, or film is set in a place or period of time, the story happens there or at that time. [often passive] *It's a historical adventure set in India in the 1940s.* **14 set to work** to start working

**set about sth/doing sth** to start doing something, especially something that uses a lot of time or energy *I got home and immediately set about cleaning the house.*

**be set against sth/doing sth** to not want to do or have something *He is dead set against the move.*

**set sb/sth apart** If a quality sets someone or something apart, it makes them different from and usually better than others of the same type. *It's their intelligence which sets them apart from other rock bands.*

**set sth aside** to save something, usually time or money, for a special purpose

**set sb/sth back** to make something happen more slowly or later than it should *The heavy traffic set us back about half an hour.*

**set sb back (sth)** *informal* to cost someone a large amount of money *A car like that will probably set you back about £12,000.*

**set in** If something unpleasant sets in, it begins and seems likely to continue. *This rain looks as if it has set in for the rest of the day.*

**set off** to start a journey *What time are you setting off tomorrow morning?*

**set sth off** to cause something to begin or happen, especially a loud noise or a lot of activity *He's always burning the toast and setting off the smoke alarm.*

**set sb/sth on/upon sb** to make a person or animal attack someone *If you come any closer, I'll set the dog on you.*

**set out 1** to start doing something when you have already decided what you want to achieve [+ to do sth] *I'd done what I set out to do.* **2** to start a journey

**set sth out** to give all the details of something, or to explain something clearly, especially in writing *Your contract will set out the terms of your employment.*

**set sth up 1** to start a company or organization *A committee has been set up to investigate the problem.* **2** to arrange for something to happen *I've set up a meeting with him for next week.*

**set sb up** to trick someone in order to make them do something, or in order to make them seem guilty of something that they have not done

**set (sth) up** to get all the necessary equipment ready for an activity *I need one or two people to help me set up the display.*

O━ᵐ**set²** /set/ *noun* [C] **1** GROUP a group of things which belong together *a set of instructions/ rules • a set of keys/tools* **2** FILM/PLAY the place where a film or play is performed or recorded, and the pictures, furniture, etc that are used *They first met on the set of 'Star Wars'.* **3** TENNIS one part of a tennis match *Agassi is leading by four games to one in the third set.* **4** TV/RADIO a television or radio *a TV set* **5** MUSIC a group of songs or tunes that go together to make a musical performance

**set³** /set/ *adj* **1** fixed and never changing *Most people work for a set number of hours each week.* • *I have no set routine.* **2 be all set** to be ready [+ to do sth] *We were all set to go when the phone rang.* ➔ *See also:* On your marks. (**mark¹**) Get set. Go!

**setback** /'setbæk/ *noun* [C] a problem that makes something happen later or more slowly than it should *The project has suffered a series of setbacks this year.*

**set-piece** /ˌset'piːs/ *noun* [C] a speech or set of actions that has been carefully planned and practised

**settee** /set'iː/ *UK (UK/US* **sofa**) *noun* [C] a large, comfortable seat for more than one person

**setting** /'setɪŋ/ *noun* [C] **1** the place where something is or where something happens, often in a book, play, or film *The house provided the setting for the TV series 'Pride and Prejudice'.* **2** a position on the controls of a piece of equipment *Set the oven at the lowest setting.*

**settle** /'setl/ *verb* **1** ARGUMENT [T] If you settle an argument, you solve the problem and stop arguing. *to settle a dispute* **2** LIVE [I] to start living somewhere that you are going to live for a long time *He travelled around Europe for years before finally settling in Vienna.* **3** DECIDE [T] to decide or arrange something [often passive] *Right, that's settled. We're going to Spain.* **4** RELAX [I, T] to relax into a comfortable position *I yawned, and settled back on the sofa.* • [often reflexive] *She settled herself into the chair opposite.* **5** PAY [T] If you settle a bill or a debt, you pay the money that you owe. *I've got some bills to settle.* **6** MOVE DOWN [I] to move down towards the ground or the bottom of something and then stay there *Do you think the snow will settle?* ➔ *See also:* the **dust¹** settles.

**settle down 1** to start living in a place where you intend to stay for a long time, usually with a partner *Do you think he'll ever settle down and have a family?* **2** to start to feel happy and confident with a new situation *Has she settled down in her new job?*

**settle (sb) down** to become quiet and calm, or to make someone become quiet and calm *Come on children, stop chatting and settle down please!*

**settle for sth** to accept something, especially something that is not exactly what you want *He wants a full refund and he won't settle for anything less.*

**settle in** to begin to feel relaxed and happy in a new home or job *Are you settling in OK?*

**settle on/upon sth** to agree on a decision *We still haven't settled on a place to meet.*

**settle up** to pay someone the money that you owe them *I need to settle up with you for the tickets.*

**settled** /'setld/ *adj* **1 be settled** to feel happy and relaxed in a place or situation *He seems quite settled now.* **2** regular and not often changing *The weather's a lot more settled at this time of year.* ➔ *Opposite* **unsettled**.

**settlement** /'setlmənt/ *noun* [C] **1** an official agreement that finishes an argument *a peace settlement* **2** a town or village which people built to live in after arriving from somewhere else *a Jewish settlement*

**settler** /'setlə<sup>r</sup>/ *noun* [C] someone who moves to a new place where there were not many people before *The first European settlers arrived in Virginia in 1607.*

**set-up** /'setʌp/ *noun* [C] *informal* **1** the way that something is arranged or organized *It took me a while to get used to the set-up in my new job.* **2** a plan that is dishonest and is intended to trick someone

**seven** /'sev<sup>ə</sup>n/ the number 7

**seventeen** /,sev<sup>ə</sup>n'ti:n/ the number 17 • seventeenth 17th written as a word

**seventh**[1] /'sev<sup>ə</sup>nθ/ 7th written as a word

**seventh**[2] /'sev<sup>ə</sup>nθ/ *noun* [C] one of seven equal parts of something; 1/7

**seventy** /'sev<sup>ə</sup>nti/ **1** the number 70 **2 the seventies** the years from 1970 to 1979 **3 be in your seventies** to be aged between 70 and 79 • seventieth 70th written as a word

**sever** /'sevə<sup>r</sup>/ *verb* [T] **1** to cut through something, especially a part of the body *to sever an artery* • [often passive] *Two of her fingers were severed in the accident.* **2 sever links/ties, etc with sb** to end a relationship with someone

o━**several** /'sev<sup>ə</sup>r<sup>ə</sup>l/ *pronoun, determiner* some, but not a lot *Several people have complained about the scheme.* • *Several of my friends studied in Manchester.* • *Do you want to take one? – We've got several.*

**severance** /'sev<sup>ə</sup>rəns/ *noun* [U] when an employer forces an employee to leave a job *severance pay*

**severe** /sɪ'vɪə<sup>r</sup>/ *adj* **1** BAD extremely bad *a severe headache* • *severe weather conditions* **2** NOT KIND not kind or gentle *a severe punishment* **3** PERSON A severe person looks unfriendly or very strict. • severely *adv to be severely injured* • *She has been severely criticized for the speech.*

**severity** /sɪ'verəti/ *noun* [U] how severe something is

**sew** /səʊ/ *verb* [I, T] *past t* sewed, *past p* sewn or sewed to join things together with a needle and thread *I need to sew a button on my shirt.*

**sew sth up 1** to close or repair something by sewing the edges together **2 have sth sewn up** *informal* to be certain to win or succeed at something *They had the game sewn up after the first twenty minutes.*

**sewage** /'su:ɪdʒ/ *noun* [U] waste water and waste from toilets *a sewage treatment plant*

**sewer** /sʊə<sup>r</sup>/ *noun* [C] a large underground system of pipes that carries away sewage

**sewing** /'səʊɪŋ/ *noun* [U] **1** the activity of joining pieces of cloth together or repairing them with a needle and thread **2** the pieces of cloth that you are joining together or repairing with a needle and thread

**'sewing ma,chine** *noun* [C] a machine that joins pieces of cloth together with a needle and thread

**sewn** /səʊn/ *past participle of* sew

o━**sex** /seks/ *noun* **1** [U] sexual activity between people *to have sex with someone* • *sex education* **2** [U] the fact of being male or female *Do you know what sex the baby is?* • *sex discrimination*

**3 the female/male/opposite, etc sex** people who are female/male/the other sex from you, etc

**sexism** /'seksɪz<sup>ə</sup>m/ *noun* [U] when someone is treated unfairly because they are a woman or because they are a man • sexist *adj sexist attitudes/jokes*

o━**sexual** /'sekʃʊəl/ *adj* **1** relating to the activity of sex *sexual experiences* • *sexual organs* **2** relating to being male or female *sexual discrimination* • *sexual equality*

**,sexual 'intercourse** *noun* [U] *formal* when a man puts his penis into a woman's vagina

**sexuality** /,sekʃu'æləti/ *noun* [U] the way you feel about sexual activity and the type of sex you prefer

**sexually** /'sekʃʊəli/ *adv* in a way that relates to the activity of sex *sexually attractive* • *a sexually transmitted disease*

**sexy** /'seksi/ *adj* attractive or exciting in a sexual way *sexy underwear* • *He's very sexy.*

**sh** (*also* **shh**) /ʃ/ *exclamation* used to tell someone to be quiet

**shabby** /'ʃæbi/ *adj* **1** looking untidy and in bad condition *shabby clothes/furniture* **2** Shabby behaviour or treatment is bad and unfair. • shabbily *adv shabbily dressed* • *shabbily treated*

**shack**[1] /ʃæk/ *noun* [C] a small simple building that has been badly built

**shack**[2] /ʃæk/ *verb*

**shack up with sb** *very informal* to start living in the same house as someone you are having a romantic relationship with

**shackle** /'ʃækl/ *verb* [T] **1** to fasten a prisoner's arms or legs together with chains **2 be shackled by sth** to be prevented from doing what you want to do by something

**shackles** /'ʃæklz/ *noun* [plural] chains used to fasten together prisoners' arms or legs

**shade**[1] /ʃeɪd/ *noun* **1** NO SUN [U] an area where there is no light from the sun and so it is darker and not as hot *I'd prefer to sit in the shade.* **2** COLOUR [C] a colour, especially when referring to how dark or light it is *a pale/dark shade of grey* • *pastel shades* **3** COVER [C] a cover that stops too much light coming from the sun or from an electric light *a lamp shade* **4 a shade** a small amount *He's perhaps a shade taller* **5 a shade of meaning/opinion, etc** a slight difference in the meaning of something

shade          shadow

---

**shade²** /ʃeɪd/ verb [T] to cover something in order to protect it from the sun *He shaded his eyes with his hand.*

**shades** /ʃeɪdz/ noun [plural] informal sunglasses (= dark glasses that protect your eyes from the sun)

o⅄**shadow¹** /'ʃædəʊ/ noun **1** [C, U] a dark area made by something that is stopping the light *The tree had cast* (= made) *a long shadow.* ➔ See picture at **shade**. **2 beyond/without a shadow of a doubt** If something is true beyond a shadow of a doubt, it is certainly true. **3 cast a shadow over sth** to spoil a good situation with something unpleasant *The bombing has cast a shadow over the Queen's visit.*

**shadow²** /'ʃædəʊ/ verb [T] to follow someone secretly in order to see where they go and what they do [often passive] *He was being shadowed by a private detective.*

**shadowy** /'ʃædəʊi/ adj **1** dark and full of shadows *in a shadowy corner* **2** secret and mysterious *the shadowy world of espionage*

**shady** /'ʃeɪdi/ adj **1** A shady place is protected from the sun and so it is darker and cooler. *We found a shady spot to sit in.* **2** informal dishonest and illegal *a shady businessman* • *shady deals*

**shaft** /ʃɑːft/ noun [C] **1** a long, vertical hole that people or things can move through, either inside a building or in the ground *a mine shaft* • *a ventilation shaft* **2** the handle of a tool or weapon **3 a shaft of light** a beam of light

o⅄**shake¹** /ʃeɪk/ verb past t **shook**, past p **shaken** **1** MOVE [I, T] to make quick, short movements from side to side or up and down, or to make something or someone do this *He was shaking with nerves.* • *We heard a loud bang, and then the house began to shake.* • *Shake the bottle.* **2 shake hands** to hold someone's hand and move it up and down when you meet them for the first time, or when you make an agreement with them *The two leaders smiled and shook hands for the photographers.* • *I shook hands with him.* **3 shake your head** to move your head from side to side to mean 'no' **4** SHOCK [T] to shock or upset someone [often passive] *No one was injured in the crash, but the driver was badly shaken.* **5** VOICE [I] If your voice shakes, you sound very nervous or frightened.

**shake sth off** to get rid of an illness or something that is causing you problems *I hope I can shake off this cold before the weekend.*
**shake sb off** to succeed in escaping from someone who is following you
**shake sth out** to hold something that is made of cloth at one end and move it up and down in order to get rid of dirt
**shake sb up** If an unpleasant experience shakes

**shake**

someone up, it makes them feel shocked and upset. *The accident really shook him up.*

**shake²** /ʃeɪk/ noun [C] **1** when you shake something *Give it a good shake before you open it.* **2** (also **milkshake**) a sweet drink made of milk and chocolate or fruit

**shake-up** /'ʃeɪkʌp/ noun [C] when big changes are made to a system or an organization *This is the biggest shake-up in the legal system for fifty years.*

**shaky** /'ʃeɪki/ adj **1** MOVING making quick, short movements from side to side or up and down *shaky hands* **2** NOT STRONG not physically strong because you are nervous, old, or ill *I felt a bit shaky when I stood up.* **3** LIKELY TO FAIL not working well and likely to fail *They managed to win the game, despite a very shaky start.*

o⅄**shall** strong form /ʃæl/ weak form /ʃəl/ modal verb **1 shall I/we...? a** used to make an offer or suggestion *Shall I cook dinner tonight?* • *We'll ask him later, shall we?* **b** used to ask someone what to do *What restaurant shall we go to?* • *Who shall I ask?* **2 I/we shall...** formal used to say what you are going to do in the future *I shall be talking to her tomorrow.* • *I shan't forget to tell them.* ➔ See study section **Modal verbs** *on page Centre 31.*

**USAGE**

**shall and will**

Shall and will are both used to talk about what you are going to do in the future. Shall is usually used with 'I' or 'we' and is more formal than will.

**shallot** /ʃə'lɒt/ noun [C] a vegetable like a small onion

o⅄**shallow** /'ʃæləʊ/ adj **1** not deep *shallow water* • *a shallow dish* ➔ See picture at **deep**. **2** not showing any interest in serious ideas

**the shallows** /'ʃæləʊz/ noun [plural] areas of shallow water

**sham** /ʃæm/ noun [no plural] something that is not what it seems to be and is intended to deceive people *Newspapers have described their marriage as a sham.*

**shambles** /'ʃæmblz/ noun **be a shambles** informal to be very badly organized *The performance was a complete shambles.*

**shame¹** /ʃeɪm/ noun **1 a shame** If you describe something as a shame, you are disappointed that it has happened. [+ to do sth] *It's a real shame to waste all this food.* • [+ (that)] *What a shame that they had to destroy such a beautiful building.* **2** [U] when you feel embarrassed and guilty about something bad that you have done *to be filled with shame* **3 have no shame** to not feel embarrassed or guilty about doing bad or embarrassing things **4 put sb/sth to shame** to be much better than someone or something else *Your cooking puts mine to shame.*

**shame²** /ʃeɪm/ verb [T] to make someone feel embarrassed and guilty about something [+ into + doing sth] *His children are trying to shame him into giving up smoking.*

**shameful** /'ʃeɪmfᵊl/ adj Something shameful is bad and should make you feel embarrassed and guilty. *a shameful secret* • shamefully adv

**S**

**shameless** /'ʃeɪmləs/ *adj* without feeling embarrassed or guilty although you should *shameless behaviour/lies* • shamelessly *adv*

**shampoo** /ʃæm'puː/ *noun* [C, U] a liquid substance that you use to wash your hair *a bottle of shampoo* • shampoo *verb* [T] **shampooing**, *past* **shampooed**

**shan't** /ʃɑːnt/ *mainly UK short for* shall not *I was invited to the party, but I shan't be going.*

**shanty town** /'ʃænti,taʊn/ *noun* [C] an area on the edge of a town where poor people live in very simply built houses

○⚹**shape**[1] /ʃeɪp/ *noun* **1** [C, U] the physical form of something made by the line around its outer edge *a circular/rectangular/triangular shape* • *You can recognize trees by the shape of their leaves.* • *Very few people are really happy with their body shape.* **2 in good/bad/great, etc shape** in good/bad, etc health or condition *She runs every day so she's in pretty good shape.* **3 out of shape** not healthy or physically strong **4 keep in shape** to stay healthy and physically strong **5 take shape** to start to develop and become more clear or certain *The project is slowly beginning to take shape.* **6 all shapes and sizes** many different types of people or things *We saw people there of all shapes and sizes.*

**shapes**

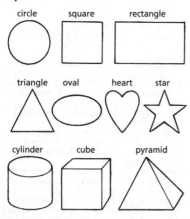

circle    square    rectangle

triangle    oval    heart    star

cylinder    cube    pyramid

**shape**[2] /ʃeɪp/ *verb* [T] **1** to influence the way that something develops [often passive] *Their attitudes were shaped during the war.* **2** to make something become a particular shape *Combine the meat and egg and shape the mixture into small balls.*

**shape up** *informal* to develop or improve *Things at work seem to be shaping up quite nicely.*

**-shaped** /ʃeɪpt/ *suffix* used after nouns to mean 'having a particular shape' *a heart-shaped cake* ➔ *See also:* **pear-shaped**.

**shapeless** /'ʃeɪpləs/ *adj* not having a clear or well designed shape *a shapeless dress*

**shapely** /'ʃeɪpli/ *adj* having an attractive shape *shapely legs*

○⚹**share**[1] /ʃeər/ *verb* **1** [I, T] to have or use something at the same time as someone else *She shares a house with Paul.* **2** [I, T] to divide something between two or more people *We shared a pizza and a bottle of wine.* • *We shared the cost of the wedding between us.* **3 share an interest/opinion, etc** to have the same interest/opinion, etc as someone else *They share a love of gardening.* • *I don't share your views on this subject.* **4 share your problems/thoughts/ideas, etc** to tell someone your problems/thoughts, etc

**share sth out** to divide something into smaller amounts and give one amount to each person in a group *Profits are shared out equally among members of the group.*

**share**[2] /ʃeər/ *noun* [C] **1** one of the equal parts that the value of a company is divided into when it is owned by a group of people *to buy/sell shares* • *We own shares in a number of companies.* • *Share prices have fallen for the third day running.* **2** a part of something that has been divided [usually singular] *When am I going to get my share of the money?* **3 have your (fair) share of sth** to have a lot of something and enough of it, usually something bad *We've had our fair share of rain already this summer.*

**shareholder** /'ʃeə,həʊldər/ *noun* [C] someone who owns shares in a company *a shareholders' meeting*

**shareware** /'ʃeəweər/ *noun* [U] software that can be used by anyone without having to pay for it

**Sharia** /ʃə'riːə/ *noun* [U] the holy law of Islam

**shark** /ʃɑːk/ *noun* [C] a large fish with very sharp teeth

○⚹**sharp**[1] /ʃɑːp/ *adj* **1** ABLE TO CUT having a very thin or pointed edge that can cut things *a sharp knife* • *sharp claws/teeth* **2 a sharp rise/increase/drop, etc** a sudden and very large increase or reduction in something **3 a sharp contrast/difference/distinction, etc** a very big and noticeable difference between two things **4** QUICK quick to notice and understand things *a sharp mind* **5 a sharp pain** a sudden, short, strong pain **6** SEVERE severe and not gentle *sharp criticism* • *She can be a bit sharp with people sometimes.* **7 a sharp bend/turn, etc** a sudden large change in the direction you are travelling **8** SOUR A sharp taste is slightly sour. **9** CLEAR A sharp image is very clear. *a photograph in sharp focus* **10 a sharp wit** the ability to say things that are funny and clever **11 a sharp tongue** If you have a sharp tongue, you often upset people by saying unkind things to them. **12** FASHIONABLE If a piece of clothing or a style is sharp, it is fashionable and tidy. *young men in sharp suits* **13 C sharp/F sharp, etc** the musical note that is between the note C, F, etc and the note above it **14** TOO HIGH A sharp musical note sounds unpleasant because it is slightly higher than it should be. • sharply *adv* • sharpness *noun* [U]

**sharp**[2] /ʃɑːp/ *adv* **3 o'clock/8.30 p.m., etc sharp** at exactly 3 o'clock, 8.30 p.m., etc

**sharp**[3] /ʃɑːp/ *noun* [C] a musical note that is between one note and the note above it

**sharpen** /'ʃɑːpᵊn/ verb [T] to make something sharper to sharpen a knife/pencil

**shatter** /'ʃætəʳ/ verb **1** [I, T] to break into very small pieces, or to make something break into very small pieces Someone threw a stone at the car, shattering the windscreen. **2** [T] to destroy something good, such as your confidence, hopes, or belief in something The accident completely shattered her confidence.

**shattered** /'ʃætəd/ adj **1** very upset **2** UK informal very tired By the time I got home I was absolutely shattered.

**shave¹** /ʃeɪv/ verb [I, T] to cut hair off your face or body to shave your head/legs • shaving cream/foam

**shave sth off** to cut a very thin piece off a surface

**shave²** /ʃeɪv/ noun **1** [C] when a man shaves the hair growing on his face **2 a close shave** a situation when something unpleasant or dangerous almost happens

**shaven** /'ʃeɪvᵊn/ adj A shaven part of the body has had the hair cut off it. a gang of youths with shaven heads

**shaver** /'ʃeɪvəʳ/ noun [C] a piece of electrical equipment used to cut hair off the head or body

**shavings** /'ʃeɪvɪŋz/ noun [plural] very thin pieces that have been cut off something wood shavings

**shawl** /ʃɔːl/ noun [C] a piece of cloth that is worn by a woman around her shoulders or used to cover a baby

o—⊶ **she** strong form /ʃiː/ weak form /ʃi/ pronoun used as the subject of the verb when referring to someone female who has already been talked about "When is Ruth coming?" "She'll be here soon."

**sheaf** /ʃiːf/ noun [C] plural **sheaves** /ʃiːvz/ **1** several pieces of paper held together a sheaf of papers **2** several pieces of wheat or corn (= plant for grain) tied together

**shear** /ʃɪəʳ/ verb [T] past t **sheared**, past p **sheared** or **shorn** to cut the wool off a sheep

**shears** /ʃɪəz/ noun [plural] a cutting tool with two large blades, like a large pair of scissors a pair of garden shears

**sheath** /ʃiːθ/ noun [C] a cover for the sharp blade of a knife

**she'd** /ʃiːd/ **1** short for she had By the time I got there, she'd fallen asleep. **2** short for she would She knew that she'd be late.

**shed¹** /ʃed/ noun [C] a small building used to store things such as tools a garden shed

**shed²** /ʃed/ verb [T] **shedding**, past **shed 1 shed leaves/skin/hair, etc** to lose something because it falls off A lot of trees shed their leaves in the autumn. **2** to get rid of something that you do not want or need A lot of companies are shedding jobs. • He's shed a lot of weight. **3 shed tears** to cry **4 shed blood** to kill or injure someone ⊃ See also: shed **light¹** on sth.

**sheen** /ʃiːn/ noun [no plural] a smooth shine on a surface

**sheep** /ʃiːp/ noun [C] plural **sheep** a farm animal whose skin is covered with wool a flock of sheep

**sheepish** /'ʃiːpɪʃ/ adj slightly embarrassed,

usually because you have done something stupid a sheepish grin/look • **sheepishly** adv

**sheer** /ʃɪəʳ/ adj **1** EXTREME [always before noun] used to emphasize how strong a feeling or quality is a look of sheer delight/joy • sheer determination/hard work **2** LARGE [always before noun] used to emphasize the large size or amount of something The delays are due to the sheer volume of traffic. **3** STEEP very steep a sheer cliff face **4** CLOTH Sheer cloth is very thin and you can see through it. sheer tights/nylons

**sheet** /ʃiːt/ noun [C] **1** a large piece of cloth put on a bed to lie on or under a double fitted sheet • to change the sheets **2 a sheet of paper/glass/metal, etc** a flat piece of paper/glass, etc a sheet of yellow paper ⊃ See colour picture **Quantities** on page Centre 14. ⊃ See also: balance **sheet**.

**sheet**

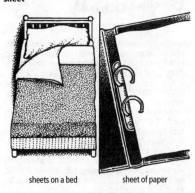

sheets on a bed              sheet of paper

**sheeting** /'ʃiːtɪŋ/ noun [U] a large flat piece of material, usually used as a cover plastic sheeting

**Sheikh** (also **Sheik**) /ʃeɪk/ noun [C] an Arab leader

**shelf** /ʃelf/ noun [C] plural **shelves** /ʃelvz/ a flat, horizontal board used to put things on, often fixed to a wall or inside a cupboard a book shelf • on the top/bottom shelf

**'shelf ˌlife** noun [C] plural **shelf lives** A product's shelf life is the length of time it stays in good condition and can be used. [usually singular] Fresh fruit has a very short shelf life.

**she'll** /ʃiːl/ short for she will She'll be away until Tuesday.

**shell¹** /ʃel/ noun [C] **1** the hard outer covering of some creatures and of eggs, nuts, or seeds a snail's shell • an egg shell **2** a bomb fired from a large gun ⊃ See also: sea shell.

**shell²** /ʃel/ verb [T] to attack a place with bombs

**shell out (sth)** informal to pay or give money for something, especially when you do not want to

**shellfish** /'ʃelfɪʃ/ noun [U] sea creatures that live in shells and are eaten as food

**shelter¹** /'ʃeltəʳ/ noun **1** [C] a place that protects you from bad weather or danger a bomb shelter **2** [U] protection from bad weather or danger We took shelter from the rain in a doorway.

**shell**

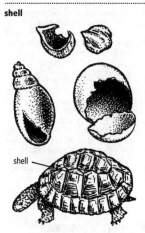

shell

shell

**shelter²** /ˈʃeltər/ *verb* **1 shelter from/in/under, etc** to go under a cover or inside a building to be protected from bad weather or danger *They went under a tree to shelter from the rain.* **2** [T] to provide cover or protection for someone *Many households are already sheltering refugees.*

**sheltered** /ˈʃeltəd/ *adj* **1** covered or protected from bad weather or danger *a sheltered spot by the wall* **2 a sheltered existence/life/upbringing, etc** If you have a sheltered life, you are protected too much and experience very little danger or excitement. **3 sheltered accommodation/housing** *UK* houses for old and ill people in a place where help can be given if it is needed

**shelve** /ʃelv/ *verb* [T] to decide not to continue with a plan [often passive] *The project had to be shelved when they ran out of money.*

**shelves** /ʃelvz/ *plural of* shelf

**shenanigans** /ʃɪˈnænɪɡənz/ *noun* [plural] *informal* secret or dishonest behaviour *political shenanigans*

**shepherd¹** /ˈʃepəd/ *noun* [C] someone whose job is to look after sheep

**shepherd²** /ˈʃepəd/ *verb* [T] to go somewhere with someone in order to guide them or protect them *children shepherded to school by their parents*

**sheriff** /ˈʃerɪf/ *noun* [C] an elected law officer in the US

**sherry** /ˈʃeri/ *noun* [C, U] a strong Spanish wine that is drunk before a meal

**she's** /ʃiːz/ **1** *short for* she is *She's a very good student.* **2** *short for* she has *She's been working very hard.*

**shh** /ʃ/ *exclamation* used to tell someone to be quiet

**shield¹** /ʃiːld/ *noun* [C] **1** a large, flat object that police officers and soldiers hold in front of their bodies to protect themselves **2** a person or thing used as protection *The hostages are being used as human shields.*

**shield²** /ʃiːld/ *verb* [T] to protect someone or

something from something dangerous or unpleasant *to shield your eyes from the sun*

**shift¹** /ʃɪft/ *noun* [C] **1** a change in something *There has been a dramatic **shift in** public opinion on this matter.* **2** a period of work in a place such as a factory or hospital *afternoon/night shift* • *He works an eight-hour shift.*

**shift²** /ʃɪft/ *verb* **1** [CHANGE] [I, T] to change something *We are trying to **shift** the emphasis **from** curing illness **to** preventing it.* **2** [MOVE STH] [T] to move something to another place *We need to shift all these boxes into the other room.* **3** [MOVE YOURSELF] [I, T] to move into a different position *He shifted uncomfortably in his seat.* **4** [CHANGE SPEED] [T] (*also* **shift into**) *US* to change the position of the gears (= parts that control how fast the wheels turn) in a vehicle *to shift gears* • *She shifted into neutral and turned off the engine.*

**shifty** /ˈʃɪfti/ *adj informal* Someone who looks shifty looks dishonest.

**shilling** /ˈʃɪlɪŋ/ *noun* [C] a unit of money used in the past in the UK

**shimmer** /ˈʃɪmər/ *verb* [I] to shine gently and seem to be moving slightly *The trees shimmered in the moonlight.*

**shin** /ʃɪn/ *noun* [C] the front part of a leg between the knee and the foot ⊃ *See colour picture* **The Body** *on page Centre 2.*

◦ᐟ**shine¹** /ʃaɪn/ *verb past* **shone** *or* **shined** **1** [PRODUCE LIGHT] [I] to produce bright light *The sun was shining brightly through the window.* **2** [POINT LIGHT] [I, T] to point a light somewhere *The car's headlights shone right into my eyes.* **3** [REFLECT] [I, T] If a surface shines, it reflects light, and if you shine it, you make it reflect light. *She polished her shoes until they shone.* **4** [EYES/FACE] [I] If your eyes or face shine, you look happy, healthy, or excited. *His eyes were shining with excitement.* **5** [DO WELL] [I] to do something very well, usually better than other people.

**shine²** /ʃaɪn/ *noun* **1** [no plural] when something is bright from reflected light on its surface *hair with body and shine* **2 take a shine to sb** *informal* to like someone immediately *I think he's taken a bit of a shine to you.* **3 take the shine off sth** to spoil something pleasant

**shingle** /ˈʃɪŋɡl/ *noun* [U] *UK* a lot of very small pieces of stone on a beach

**shiny** /ˈʃaɪni/ *adj* A shiny surface is bright because it reflects light. *shiny, black shoes* • *shiny hair*

◦ᐟ**ship¹** /ʃɪp/ *noun* [C] a large boat that carries people or goods by sea *a cruise ship* • *a cargo ship*

**ship²** /ʃɪp/ *verb* [T] **shipping**, *past* **shipped** to send something from one place to another [often passive] *These vegetables have been shipped halfway around the world.*

**shipment** /ˈʃɪpmənt/ *noun* **1** [C] an amount of goods sent from one place to another *The first shipments of food arrived this month.* **2** [U] when something is sent from one place to another *the shipment of nuclear waste*

**shipwreck¹** /ˈʃɪprek/ *noun* [C] an accident in which a ship is destroyed at sea

**shipwreck²** /ˈʃɪprek/ *verb* **be shipwrecked** If

S

someone is shipwrecked, the ship they are in is destroyed in an accident.

**shipyard** /'ʃɪpjɑːd/ noun [C] a place where ships are built or repaired

**shirk** /ʃɜːk/ verb [I, T] to avoid doing something because it is difficult or unpleasant *to shirk your duties/responsibilities*

○━**shirt** /ʃɜːt/ noun [C] a piece of clothing worn on the top part of the body, often made of thin material like cotton and fastened with buttons down the front ⊃ *See colour picture* **Clothes** on *page Centre 5.* ⊃ *See also:* **polo shirt**, **T-shirt**.

**shish kebab** /'ʃɪʃkəˌbæb/ noun [C] small pieces of meat or vegetables cooked on a long, thin stick

**shit¹** /ʃɪt/ exclamation very informal a very impolite word used to show surprise, anger, disappointment, etc

**shit²** /ʃɪt/ noun [U] very informal a very impolite word for waste from the body of a person or animal that comes out of their bottom

**shiver** /'ʃɪvəʳ/ verb [I] to shake because you are cold or frightened *She shivered with cold.* • shiver noun [C] *He felt a shiver run down his spine* (= He felt afraid).

**shoal** /ʃəʊl/ noun [C] a large group of fish swimming together

○━**shock¹** /ʃɒk/ noun 1 SURPRISE [C, U] a big, unpleasant surprise *We got a nasty shock when he gave us the bill.* • *Her death came as a terrible shock to him.* • *They are still in shock* (= feeling the effect of a shock) *from the accident.* 2 ILLNESS [U] a medical condition when someone is extremely weak because of damage to their body *He went into shock and nearly died.* 3 ELECTRICITY [C] (also **electric shock**) a sudden, painful feeling that you get when electricity flows through your body 4 MOVEMENT [C] a sudden movement caused by an explosion, accident, etc ⊃ *See also:* **culture shock**.

○━**shock²** /ʃɒk/ verb [I, T] to surprise and upset someone [often passive] *Many people were shocked by the violent scenes in the film.* • shocked adj [+ to do sth] *We were shocked to find rat poison in our hotel room.*

**shocking** /'ʃɒkɪŋ/ adj 1 very surprising and upsetting or immoral *shocking news* • *This report contains scenes that some people may find shocking.* 2 UK very bad *My memory is shocking.* • shockingly adv

**shoddy** /'ʃɒdi/ adj very bad quality *shoddy goods* • *shoddy work*

○━**shoe** /ʃuː/ noun [C] 1 a strong covering for the foot, often made of leather *a pair of shoes* • *training shoes* • *to put your shoes on/take your shoes off* ⊃ *See colour picture* **Clothes** on *page Centre 5.* 2 **be in sb's shoes** informal to be in the same situation as someone else, especially an unpleasant situation *What would you do if you were in my shoes?*

**shoelace** /'ʃuːleɪs/ noun [C] a long, thin piece of material used to fasten shoes

**shoestring** /'ʃuːstrɪŋ/ noun **on a shoestring** If you do something on a shoestring, you do it using very little money.

**shone** /ʃɒn/ ⓤⓢ /ʃəʊn/ past of shine

**shoo** /ʃuː/ verb **shooing**, past **shooed shoo sb away/off/out, etc** to make a person or animal

leave a place by chasing them or shouting 'shoo' at them • shoo exclamation

**shook** /ʃʊk/ past tense of shake

○━**shoot¹** /ʃuːt/ verb past **shot** 1 INJURE [T] to injure or kill a person or animal by firing a bullet from a gun at them [often passive] *He was robbed and then shot in the stomach.* • *An innocent bystander was shot dead in the incident.* 2 FIRE BULLET [I, T] to fire a bullet from a gun *Don't shoot!* 3 SPORT [I] to try to score points in sports such as football by hitting, kicking, or throwing the ball towards the goal 4 **shoot across/out/up, etc** to move somewhere very quickly *She shot across the road without looking.* 5 FILM [T] to use a camera to record a film or take a photograph [often passive] *Most of the film was shot in Italy.*

**shoot sb/sth down** to destroy an aircraft or make it fall to the ground by firing bullets or weapons at it *The plane was shot down over enemy territory.*

**shoot up** If a number or amount shoots up, it increases very quickly. *Prices have shot up by 25%.*

**shoot²** /ʃuːt/ noun [C] 1 a new branch or stem growing on a plant *bamboo shoots* 2 when someone takes photographs or makes a film *a fashion shoot*

**shooting** /'ʃuːtɪŋ/ noun 1 [C] when someone is injured or killed by a bullet from a gun *a fatal shooting* 2 [U] the sport of firing bullets from guns, sometimes to kill animals

○━**shop¹** /ʃɒp/ (also US **store**) noun [C] a building or part of a building where you can buy things *a book shop* • *a shoe shop* • *to go to the shops* • *a shop window* ⊃ *See also:* **charity shop**.

---

**USAGE**

**shop** or **store**?

In American English the usual word for shop is **store**.

*He went to the store to buy some cookies.*

In British English the word **store** is only used to mean a very large shop where you can buy many different things.

*Harrods is a famous department store.*

---

**shop²** /ʃɒp/ verb [I] **shopping**, past **shopped** to buy things in shops *I'm shopping for baby clothes.* • *I usually go shopping on Saturday.*

**shop around** to compare the price and quality of the same thing from different places before deciding which one to buy *to shop around for a computer*

**shop as,sistant** UK (US **sales clerk**) noun [C] someone whose job is selling things in a shop

**shop 'floor** noun [no plural] the part of a factory where things are made and not the part where the managers' offices are

**shopkeeper** /'ʃɒpˌkiːpəʳ/ noun [C] someone who owns or manages a small shop

**shoplifting** /'ʃɒplɪftɪŋ/ noun [U] stealing things from a shop • shoplifter noun [C] • shoplift verb [I]

**shopper** /'ʃɒpəʳ/ noun [C] someone who is buying things from shops

○━**shopping** /'ʃɒpɪŋ/ noun [U] 1 when you buy

**S**

things from shops *I love shopping.* • *a shopping basket/trolley* **2** the things that you buy from a shop or shops *Can you help me unpack the shopping?* • *a shopping bag* ⊃ *See also:* **window shopping**.

'**shopping ,centre** *UK* (*US* **shopping center**) *noun* [C] a place where a lot of shops have been built close together

'**shopping ,mall** *noun* [C] a large, covered shopping area

**shore¹** /ʃɔːʳ/ *noun* [C, U] the area of land along the edge of the sea or a lake *They had to abandon the boat and swim back to shore.*

**shore²** /ʃɔːʳ/ *verb*
**shore sth up** to help or improve something that is likely to fail

**shorn** /ʃɔːn/ *past participle of* shear

o⟶**short¹** /ʃɔːt/ *adj* **1** DISTANCE having a small distance from one end to the other *short, brown hair* • *short legs* • *a short skirt* **2** TIME continuing for a small amount of time *a short visit* • *There's a short break for coffee between classes.* **3** BOOK A short book or other piece of writing has few pages or words. *a short article/story* **4** PERSON A short person is not as tall as most people. *She's short and slim with dark hair.* **5** NOT HAVING ENOUGH not having enough of something *I'm a bit **short of money** at the moment.* • *Would you like to play? We're a couple of people short.* • *He seemed a bit **short of breath** (= having difficulty breathing).* **6 be short for sth** to be a shorter way of saying the same thing *'Mick' is short for 'Michael'.* **7 be short with sb** to talk to someone quickly in an angry or rude way • shortness *noun* [U] ⊃ *See also:* in the short **run²**.

**short²** /ʃɔːt/ *adv* **1 short of doing sth** without doing something *He did everything he could to get the money, short of robbing a bank.* **2 stop short of sth/doing sth** to almost do something but decide not to do it *She stopped short of accusing him of lying.* **3 fall short of sth** to not reach a particular level, but only by a small amount *Sales for the first half of this year fell just short of the target.* **4 cut sth short** to have to stop doing something before it is finished *They had to cut the holiday short when her mother was taken ill.*

**short³** /ʃɔːt/ *noun* **1 in short** in a few words *In short, we need more staff.* **2** [C] a short film **3** [C] *UK* a small amount of a strong alcoholic drink like whisky

**shortage** /'ʃɔːtɪdʒ/ *noun* [C] when there is not enough of something *a shortage of nurses* • *food shortages*

**shortbread** /'ʃɔːtbred/ *noun* [U] a hard, sweet cake

**short-circuit** /,ʃɔːt'sɜːkɪt/ *noun* [C] a fault in an electrical connection • short-circuit *verb* [I, T]

**shortcoming** /'ʃɔːt,kʌmɪŋ/ *noun* [C] a fault [usually plural] *I like him despite his shortcomings.*

**shortcut** (*also UK* ,**short 'cut**) /'ʃɔːtkʌt/ *noun* [C] **1** a quicker and more direct way of getting somewhere or doing something *I took a **shortcut** through the car park.* **2** In computing, a shortcut is a quick way to start or use a computer program. *a shortcut key*

**shorten** /'ʃɔːtᵊn/ *verb* [I, T] to become shorter or to make something shorter *Smoking shortens your life.*

**shortfall** /'ʃɔːtfɔːl/ *noun* [C] the difference between the amount that is needed and the smaller amount that is available *a shortfall in government spending*

**shorthand** /'ʃɔːthænd/ *noun* [U] a fast way of writing using abbreviations and symbols

**shortlist** /'ʃɔːtlɪst/ *noun* [C] *UK* a list of people who are competing for a prize, job, etc, who have already been chosen from a larger list *to be on the shortlist* • shortlist *verb* [T] *UK short-listed candidates*

**short-lived** /,ʃɔːt'lɪvd/ *adj* only lasting for a short time

**shortly** /'ʃɔːtli/ *adv* **1** If something is going to happen shortly, it will happen soon. *Our plans for the next year will be announced shortly.* **2 shortly after/before sth** a short time after or before something *He left here shortly after midnight.*

**short-range** /,ʃɔːt'reɪndʒ/ *adj* intended to go a short distance *a short-range missile*

**shorts** /ʃɔːts/ *noun* [plural] **1** a very short pair of trousers that stop above the knees *T-shirt and shorts* • *cycling shorts* **2** *US* men's underwear to wear under trousers ⊃ *See colour picture* **Clothes** *on page Centre 5.* ⊃ *See also:* **boxer shorts.**

**short-sighted** /,ʃɔːt'saɪtɪd/ *adj* **1** not able to see far without wearing glasses **2** not thinking enough about how an action will affect the future *a short-sighted policy*

**short-term** /,ʃɔːt'tɜːm/ *adj* lasting a short time *short-term memory*

**short-wave** /'ʃɔːtweɪv/ *noun* [U] a system used to broadcast radio signals around the world *short-wave radio*

**shot¹** /ʃɒt/ *noun* [C] **1** GUN when a bullet is fired from a gun *Three **shots** were fired.* **2** SPORT when someone tries to score points in sports such as football by hitting or throwing the ball *Good shot!* **3** PHOTOGRAPH a photograph *I got a good shot of them leaving the hotel together.* **4 give sth a shot; have/take a shot at sth** *informal* to try to do something, often for the first time *I've never played football, but I'll give it a shot.* • *They might have a shot at the World Championships next year.* **5** MEDICINE an amount of medicine put into the body with a special needle *I took the dog to the vet for his shots.* **6** DRINK a small amount of a strong alcoholic drink *a shot of whisky* **7 like a shot** If someone does something like a shot, they do it quickly and enthusiastically. *If I had the chance to go to Paris, I'd be there like a shot.* **8 a shot in the dark** an attempt to guess something when you have no information or knowledge about it ⊃ *See also:* **long shot**.

**shot²** /ʃɒt/ *past of* shoot

**shotgun** /'ʃɒtgʌn/ *noun* [C] a long gun that fires small, metal balls

o⟶**should** *strong form* /ʃʊd/ *weak form* /ʃəd/ *modal verb* **1** BEST used to say or ask what is the correct or best thing to do *He should have gone to the doctor.* • *Should I apologize to her?* • *You shouldn't be so angry with him.* **2** EXPECT used

---

| iː **see** | ɒ **hot** | ɔː **saw** | ʌ **run** | ʊ **put** | uː **too** | aɪ **my** | aʊ **how** | eɪ **day** | əʊ **no** | ɪə **near** | ɔɪ **boy** | ʊə **poor** | aɪə **fire** | aʊə **sour** |

to say that you expect something to be true or that you expect something to happen *She should be feeling better by now.* • *The letter should arrive by Friday.* **3** POSSIBLE *formal* used to refer to a possible event in the future *Should you have any further queries, please do not hesitate to contact me.* • *I'll be in my office, if anyone should ask.* **4 why should/shouldn't...?** used to ask or give the reason for something, especially when you are surprised or angry about it *He told me to forgive her, but why should I?* ➔ *See study section* **Modal verbs** *on page Centre 31.*

⊶**shoulder¹** /'ʃəʊldəʳ/ *noun* **1** [C] where your arm joins your body next to your neck *She looked over her shoulder.* • *He put his arm around my shoulder.* **2** [C] *US* (*UK* **hard shoulder**) the area on the edge of a main road, where a car can stop in an emergency **3 rub shoulders with sb** to spend time with famous people **4 a shoulder to cry on** someone who gives you sympathy when you are upset ➔ *See also:* have a **chip¹** on your shoulder.

shoulder
shoulder
shoulder
shoulder blade

**shoulder²** /'ʃəʊldəʳ/ *verb* **shoulder the blame/burden/responsibility, etc** to accept that you are responsible for something difficult or bad

'**shoulder ,bag** *noun* [C] a bag with a long strap that you hang from your shoulder

'**shoulder ,blade** *noun* [C] a large, flat bone on each side of your back below your shoulder

**shoulder-length** /'ʃəʊldəleŋθ/ *adj* If your hair is shoulder-length, it goes down as far as your shoulders. ➔ *See colour picture* **Hair** *on page Centre 9.*

**shouldn't** /'ʃʊdˀnt/ *short for* should not *I shouldn't have said that.*

**should've** /'ʃʊdəv/ *short for* should have *She should've finished by now.*

⊶**shout¹** /ʃaʊt/ *verb* [I, T] to say something very loudly *"Look out!" she shouted.* • *I was angry and I shouted at him.* • *I shouted out her name but she didn't hear me.*

**shout²** /ʃaʊt/ *noun* [C] when you say something very loudly or make a very loud sound with your voice *He was woken by a loud shout.*

**shove** /ʃʌv/ *verb* [I, T] **1** to push someone or something in a rough way *He wouldn't move, so I shoved him out of the way.* **2 shove sth into/in/under, etc** to put something somewhere in a quick, careless way *She shoved the suitcase under the bed.* • **shove** *noun* [C] *to give someone a shove* ➔ *See also:* if/when **push²** comes to shove.

**shovel** /'ʃʌvˀl/ *noun* [C] a tool with a long handle, used for digging or moving things such as soil or snow • **shovel** *verb* [I, T] *UK*

**shovelling**, *past* **shovelled**, *US* **shoveling**, *past* **shoveled**

⊶**show¹** /ʃəʊ/ *verb past t* **showed**, *past p* **shown** **1** PROVE [T] If numbers, results, facts, etc show something, they prove that it is true. [+ (that)] *Research shows that 40% of the programme's viewers are aged over 55.* • *Sales figures show a significant increase last month.* **2** LET SOMEONE SEE [T] to let someone look at something [+ two objects] *Show me your photos.* • *Show your passport to the officer.* **3 show sb what to do/how to do sth** to teach someone how to do something by explaining it or by doing it yourself while they watch *She showed me how to use the new computer system.* • *Have you shown him what to do?* **4** EXPRESS [T] to express a feeling so that other people are able to notice it *He hasn't shown any interest so far.* • *If she was upset, she certainly didn't show it.* **5** EASY TO SEE [I, T] to be easy to see, or to make something easy to see *The sadness really shows on her face.* • *Light-coloured carpets show the dirt.* **6 show sb into/around/round, etc** to take someone to or round a place *He showed us into a big room full of books.* • *She showed me round the factory.* **7** IMAGE [T] If a picture, film, map, etc shows something, that thing can be seen in the picture, film, etc. *A diagram shows the levels of rainfall in different parts of the country.* **8** FILM [I, T] If a cinema shows a film or a film is showing somewhere, you can go and see it there.

**show off** to try to make people admire your abilities or achievements in a way which other people find annoying *He was the kind of kid who was always showing off to his classmates.*

**show sb/sth off** to show something or someone you are proud of to other people *I couldn't wait to show off my new ring.*

**show up** *informal* to arrive somewhere *I waited for nearly half an hour, but he didn't show up.*

**show sb up** to behave in a way that makes someone you are with feel embarrassed *I didn't want my parents there, showing me up in front of all my friends.*

**show²** /ʃəʊ/ *noun* **1** [C] a television or radio programme or a theatre performance *He's got his own show on Channel 5.* **2** [C] an event at which a group of similar things are brought together for the public to see *a fashion show* • *a flower show* **3 a show of sth** an expression of a feeling which can be clearly seen by other people *Crowds gathered in the central square in a show of support for the government.* **4 for show** for looking at only, and not for using *The cakes are just for show – you can't eat them.* **5 on show** being shown to the public *Her designs are currently on show at the Museum of Modern Art.* ➔ *See also:* **chat show**, **game show**, **talk show**.

'**show ,business** (*also* **show biz** *informal*) *noun* [U] the entertainment industry, including films, television, theatre, etc

**showcase** /'ʃəʊkeɪs/ *noun* [C] an event which is intended to show the best qualities of something *The exhibition acts as a showcase for British design.*

**showdown** /'ʃəʊdaʊn/ *noun* [C] an argument or

fight that is intended to end a period of disagreement *Opponents of the changes are heading for a showdown with party leaders.*

**shower**[1] /ʃaʊəʳ/ *noun* [C] **1** WASH If you have or take a shower, you wash your whole body while standing under a flow of water. *I got up, had a shower and got dressed.* **2** BATHROOM EQUIPMENT a piece of bathroom equipment that you stand under to wash your whole body *He likes to sing in the shower.* ➔ *See colour picture* **The Bathroom** *on page Centre 1.* **3** RAIN a short period of rain **4 a shower of sth** a lot of small things in the air, especially falling through the air *a shower of glass*

**shower**[2] /ʃaʊəʳ/ *verb* [I] to wash standing under a shower

**shower sb with sth** to give a lot of something to someone *I was showered with gifts.*

**showing** /ˈʃəʊɪŋ/ *noun* **1** [C] a broadcast of a television programme at a particular time or of a film at a cinema *There's a repeat showing of Wednesday's episode on Saturday morning.* **2 a good/poor/strong, etc showing** how successful someone is in a competition, election, etc *She made a good showing in the world championships.*

**showman** /ˈʃəʊmən/ *noun* [C] *plural* **showmen** someone who is very good at entertaining people

**shown** /ʃəʊn/ *past participle of* show

**show-off** /ˈʃəʊɒf/ *noun* [C] someone who tries to make other people admire their abilities or achievements in a way which is annoying

**showroom** /ˈʃəʊruːm/ *noun* [C] a large room where you can look at large items for sale, such as cars or furniture

**shrank** /ʃræŋk/ *past tense of* shrink

**shrapnel** /ˈʃræpnəl/ *noun* [U] small, sharp pieces of metal which fly through the air when a bomb explodes

**shred**[1] /ʃred/ *noun* [C] **1** a very small piece that has been torn from something [usually plural] *She tore the letter to shreds.* **2 not a shred of sth** not the smallest amount of something *There is not a shred of evidence to support his story.*

**shred**[2] /ʃred/ *verb* [T] **shredding**, *past* **shredded** to tear or cut something into small, thin pieces *shredded cabbage*

**shrewd** /ʃruːd/ *adj* good at judging situations and making decisions which give you an advantage *a shrewd businessman* • *a shrewd investment* • shrewdly *adv*

**shriek** /ʃriːk/ *verb* [I, T] to make a sudden, loud, high noise because you are afraid, surprised, excited, etc *to shriek with laughter* • *"It's about to explode!" she shrieked.* • shriek *noun* [C]

**shrill** /ʃrɪl/ *adj* A shrill sound is very high, loud, and often unpleasant. *a shrill voice/laugh*

**shrimp** /ʃrɪmp/ *noun* [C] a small, pink, sea animal that you can eat, with a curved body and a shell

**shrine** /ʃraɪn/ *noun* [C] a place where people go to pray because it is connected with a holy person or event

**shrink**[1] /ʃrɪŋk/ *verb* [I, T] *past t* **shrank**, *past p* **shrunk** to become smaller, or to make something smaller *My shirt shrank in the wash.* • *Its forests have shrunk to almost half the size they were 10 years ago.*

**shrink from sth/doing sth** to avoid doing something that is difficult or unpleasant *We will not shrink from using force.*

**shrink**[2] /ʃrɪŋk/ *noun* [C] *informal* a doctor trained to help people with mental or emotional problems

**shrivel** /ˈʃrɪvəl/ *verb* [I] *UK* **shrivelling**, *past* **shrivelled**, *US* **shriveling**, *past* **shriveled** If something shrivels, it becomes smaller, dryer, and covered in lines, often because it is old. • shrivelled *adj There were a few shrivelled apples at the bottom of the bowl.*

**shroud**[1] /ʃraʊd/ *noun* [C] a cloth used to cover the body of a dead person

**shroud**[2] /ʃraʊd/ *verb* **1 be shrouded in darkness/fog/mist** to be hidden or covered by the dark/fog, etc *The island was shrouded in sea mist.* **2 be shrouded in mystery/secrecy** to be difficult to find out about or to know the truth about *Details of the president's trip remain shrouded in secrecy.*

**shrub** /ʃrʌb/ *noun* [C] a large plant, smaller than a tree, that has several main stems

**shrubbery** /ˈʃrʌbəri/ *noun* **1** [C, U] an area of a garden with shrubs in it **2** [U] *US* shrubs considered as a group

**shrug** /ʃrʌg/ *verb* [I, T] **shrugging**, *past* **shrugged** to move your shoulders up and down to show that you do not care about something or that you do not know something *I told him we weren't happy with it but he just shrugged his shoulders.* • shrug *noun* [C]

**shrug sth off** to not worry about something and treat it as not important *The team manager shrugged off criticism.*

**shrunk** /ʃrʌŋk/ *past participle of* shrink

**shrunken** /ˈʃrʌŋkən/ *adj* having become smaller or having been made smaller *a shrunken old man*

**shudder** /ˈʃʌdəʳ/ *verb* [I] to shake, usually because you are thinking of something unpleasant *I still shudder at the thought of the risks we took.* • *She shuddered with horror.* • shudder *noun* [C]

**shuffle** /ˈʃʌfl/ *verb* **1** WALK [I] to walk slowly without lifting your feet off the floor *I heard him shuffling around downstairs.* **2** ARRANGE [I, T] If you shuffle papers or cards, you mix them or arrange them in a different order. **3** MOVE [I, T] to move your body or feet a little because you feel nervous or uncomfortable. *People starting shuffling their feet and looking at their watches.*

**shun** /ʃʌn/ *verb* [T] **shunning**, *past* **shunned** to avoid or ignore someone or something *He was shunned by colleagues and family alike.* • *She has always shunned publicity.*

**shunt** /ʃʌnt/ *verb* [T] to move someone or something from one place to another, usually because they are not wanted *As a teenager he was shunted between different children's homes.*

⊶ **shut**[1] /ʃʌt/ *verb* [I, T] **shutting**, *past* **shut 1** to close something, or to become closed *Shut the door.* • *He lay back and shut his eyes.* • *The lid shut with a bang.* **2** *UK* (*UK/US* **close**) When a shop, restaurant, etc shuts, it stops serving customers and does not allow them to enter. *The museum shuts at 4 o'clock on a Friday.*

• *Several schools were shut because of the bad weather.*

**shut sb/sth away** to put someone or something in a place from which they cannot leave or be taken away

**shut (sth) down** If a business or a large piece of equipment shuts down or someone shuts it down, it stops operating. *Many factories have been forced to shut down.* • *We shut the whole computer system down for 24 hours.*

**shut sth/sb in (sth)** to prevent someone or something from leaving a place by shutting a door or gate *We normally shut the dog in the kitchen when we go out.*

**shut sth off** to stop a machine working, or to stop the supply of something *Shut the engine off.* • *Oil supplies have been shut off.*

**shut sth/sb out** to stop someone or something from entering a place or from being included in something *The curtains shut out most of the light from the street.*

**shut (sb) up** *informal* to stop talking or making a noise, or to make someone do this *Just shut up and get on with your work!*

**shut sb/sth up** to keep a person or animal somewhere and prevent them from leaving *You can't keep it shut up in a cage all day.*

**shut²** /ʃʌt/ *adj* [never before noun] **1** closed *Her eyes were shut and I thought she was asleep.* **2** *UK* (*UK/US* **closed**) When a shop, restaurant, etc is shut, it has stopped serving customers and does not allow people to enter it.

**shutdown** /'ʃʌtdaʊn/ *noun* [C] when a business or a large piece of equipment stops operating, usually for a temporary period

**shutter** /'ʃʌtər/ *noun* [C] **1** a wooden or metal cover on the outside of a window **2** the part at the front of a camera which opens quickly to let in light when you take a photograph

**shuttle¹** /'ʃʌtl/ *noun* [C] **1** a bus, train, plane etc which travels regularly between two places, usually a short distance *the London-Glasgow shuttle* • *There's a shuttle service between the airport and the city centre.* **2** (*also* '**space ,shuttle**) a spacecraft which can go into space and return to Earth more than once

**shuttle²** /'ʃʌtl/ *verb* [I, T] to travel or take people regularly between the same two places *He shuttles between Ireland and England.*

**shuttlecock** /'ʃʌtlkɒk/ *noun* [C] (*also US* **birdie**) a small object with feathers that is used like a ball in badminton (= sport like tennis)

o-∞ **shy¹** /ʃaɪ/ *adj* **shyer**, **shyest** not confident, especially about meeting or talking to new people *He was too shy to say anything to her.* • **shyly** *adv* *She smiled shyly.* • **shyness** *noun* [U]

**shy²** /ʃaɪ/ *verb* [I] If a horse shies, it moves backwards suddenly because it has been frightened by something.

**shy away from sth** to avoid doing something, usually because you are not confident enough to do it *He tends to shy away from public speaking.*

**sibling** /'sɪblɪŋ/ *noun* [C] *formal* a sister or brother

**sic** /sɪk/ *adv* (**sic**) used in writing after a word that you have copied to show that you know it has been spelt or used wrongly

o-∞ **sick¹** /sɪk/ *adj* **1** ill *He was off work sick for most of last week.* • *They provide care for the sick.* **2 be sick** If you are sick, food and drink comes up from your stomach and out of your mouth. *The baby was sick all down his shirt.* **3 feel sick** to feel that the food or drink in your stomach might soon come up through your mouth *I was so nervous I felt quite sick.* **4 be sick of sth** *informal* to be bored with or annoyed about something that has been happening for a long time *I'm sick of people telling me how to run my life.* **5 It makes me sick.** *informal* something you say when you are jealous of someone *She looks fantastic whatever she wears – it makes me sick.* **6** cruel and unpleasant *He's got a sick mind.* • *a sick joke*

**USAGE**

**sick, ill, and be sick**

In British English **ill** is the word that is usually used to mean 'not well'. In American English the word for this is **sick**.

*He went home early because he felt ill/sick.*

In British English to **be sick** is to bring food up from the stomach. Another way of saying this is the word **vomit**, which is used both in British and American English.

**sick²** /sɪk/ *noun* [U] *UK informal* food or liquid that has come up from someone's stomach and out of their mouth

**sicken** /'sɪkən/ *verb* [T] to shock someone and make them very angry *Sickened by the violence, she left.*

**sickening** /'sɪkənɪŋ/ *adj* causing shock and anger *a sickening act of violence*

**sickle** /'sɪkl/ *noun* [C] a tool with a round blade used to cut long grass or grain crops

**sickly** /'sɪkli/ *adj* **1** weak and often ill *a sickly child* **2** unpleasant and making you feel slightly ill *a sickly smell*

**sickness** /'sɪknəs/ *noun* **1** [ILL] [U] when you are ill *She's had three weeks off for sickness this year.* **2** [VOMIT] [U] when the food or drink in your stomach come up through your mouth, or a feeling that this might happen *morning/travel sickness* **3** [ILLNESS] [C, U] a particular illness *radiation sickness*

o-∞ **side¹** /saɪd/ *noun* [C] **1** [PART OF SOMETHING] one of the two parts that something would divide into if you drew a line down the middle *In most countries people drive on the right side of the road.* • *Which side of the bed do you sleep on?* • *They were on the other side of the room.* **2** [SURFACE] a flat, outer surface of an object, especially one that is not its top, bottom, front, or back *The ingredients are listed on the side of the box.* • *The side of the car was badly scratched.* **3** [EDGE] one edge of something *A square has four sides.* • *There were chairs round the sides of the room.* **4** [NEXT TO SOMETHING] the area next to something *trees growing by the side of the road* • *There were flowers in pots on either side of the front door.* **5** [PAPER/COIN ETC] either of the two surfaces of a thin, flat object such as a piece of paper or a coin *Write on both sides of the paper.* **6** [ARGUMENT] one of the people or

S

groups who are arguing, fighting, or competing *Whose **side** is he on?* • *Whenever we argue he always takes Alice's **side*** (= gives support to Alice). **7** TEAM *UK* the players in a sports team *He's been selected for the national **side**.* **8** PART OF A SITUATION part of a situation that can be considered or dealt with separately *She looks after the financial **side** of things.* **9** CHARACTER a part of someone's character *She has a very practical **side**.* **10** BODY the two areas of your body from under your arms to the tops of your legs *Stand with your arms by your **sides**.* • *She lay on her **side**.* **11** STORY Someone's **side** of a story is the way in which they explain how something happened. *I thought I'd better listen to Clare's **side** of the story.* • *So far they'd only heard the story from the wife's **side**.* **12** TELEVISION/RADIO *UK* a number on a television or radio that you can choose in order to receive a broadcast *Which **side** is the film on?* **13 from side to side** If something moves from side to side, it moves from left to right and back again repeatedly *swinging from side to side* **14 side-by-side** If two things or people are side-by-side, they are next to each other. *sitting side-by-side on the sofa* • *Alex laid them down side-by-side on the table.* **15** RELATIVES the part of your family who are either your mother's relatives or your father's relatives *They tend to be tall on my mother's **side** of the family.* **16 err on the side of caution** to be very careful instead of taking a risk or making a mistake **17 on the side** in addition to your main job *She does a bit of bar work on the side.* **18 put sth to one side** to not use or deal with something now, but keep it for a later time ⊃ *See also:* **the flip side**.

**side²** /saɪd/ *verb*
**side with sb** to support one person or group in an argument *If ever there was any sort of argument, she'd always side with my father.*

**sideboard** /ˈsaɪdbɔːd/ *noun* [C] a piece of furniture with a flat top and low cupboards and drawers, used for storing dishes and glasses, etc in the room you eat in

**sideburns** /ˈsaɪdbɜːnz/ *noun* [plural] hair that grows on the sides of a man's face in front of the ear

**side-effect** /ˈsaɪdɪfekt/ *noun* [C] **1** another effect that a drug has on your body in addition to the main effect for which the doctor has given you the drug *Headaches are one side effect of this drug.* **2** an unexpected result of a situation

**sidekick** /ˈsaɪdkɪk/ *noun* [C] someone who helps, or is friends with, a more powerful and important person

**sideline¹** /ˈsaɪdlaɪn/ *noun* [C] a job or business in addition to your main job or business *He works in a bank but teaches English **as a sideline**.*

**sideline²** /ˈsaɪdlaɪn/ *verb* [T] to stop someone from being included in an activity that they usually do, especially a sport [often passive] *He's broken his ankle and could be sidelined for weeks.*

**sidelines** /ˈsaɪdlaɪnz/ *noun* [plural] **1** the outside edge of the playing area of a sport such as football *The coach was shouting instructions from*

*the sidelines.* **2 on the sidelines** not really involved in something

**sidelong** /ˈsaɪdlɒŋ/ *adj* **a sidelong glance/look** a very short look at someone, moving your eyes to the side, and not looking at them directly

**'side ˌmirror** *US* (*UK* **wing mirror**) *noun* [C] a small mirror on the side of a car or truck

**sideshow** /ˈsaɪdʃəʊ/ *noun* [C] an event or activity that is considered less important than another event or activity

**sidestep** /ˈsaɪdstep/ *verb* [T] **sidestepping**, *past* **sidestepped** to avoid talking about a subject, especially by starting to talk about something else *She neatly sidestepped questions about her recent divorce.*

**sidetrack** /ˈsaɪdtræk/ *verb* [T] to make someone forget what they were doing or speaking about and start doing or speaking about something different [often passive] *Sorry, I was talking about staffing and I got sidetracked.*

**sidewalk** /ˈsaɪdwɔːk/ *US* (*UK* **pavement**) *noun* [C] a path with a hard surface by the side of a road that people walk on

**sideways** /ˈsaɪdweɪz/ *adv* in a direction to the left or right, not forwards or backwards *He glanced sideways.*

**siding** /ˈsaɪdɪŋ/ *noun* **1** [C] a short railway track, connected to a main track, where trains are kept when they are not being used **2** [U] *US* material which covers the outside walls of a building, usually in layers

**sidle** /ˈsaɪdl/ *verb* **sidle along/over/up, etc** to walk towards someone, trying not to be noticed *He sidled up to her and whispered something in her ear.*

**siege** /siːdʒ/ *noun* [C, U] when an army or the police stand around a building or city to stop supplies from entering it, in order to force the people inside to stop fighting *The city is **under siege** from rebel forces.*

**siesta** /siˈestə/ *noun* [C] a short period of rest or sleep in the afternoon

**sieve** /sɪv/ *noun* [C] a piece of kitchen equipment with a wire or plastic net which separates large pieces of food from liquids or powders *Pass the sauce through a sieve to remove any lumps.* • **sieve** *verb* [T] ⊃ *See colour picture* **Kitchen** *on page Centre 10.*

**sift** /sɪft/ *verb* [T] **1** to put flour, sugar, etc through a sieve (= wire net shaped like a bowl) to break up large pieces *Sift the flour into a large bowl.* **2** (*also* **sift through**) to carefully look at every part of something in order to find something *to sift through evidence/papers*

**sigh** /saɪ/ *verb* [I, T] to breathe out slowly and noisily, often because you are annoyed or unhappy *He sighed deeply and sat down.* • *'I'm all alone now,' she sighed.* • **sigh** *noun* [C] *a sigh of relief*

⟶**sight¹** /saɪt/ *noun* **1** ABILITY [U] the ability to use your eyes to see *Doctors managed to save his sight.* **2 the sight of sb/sth** when you see someone or something *The sight of so much blood had shocked him.* • *(informal)* *I **can't stand the sight of** her* (= I hate her). ⊃ *See usage note at* **view**. **3** AREA SEEN [U] the area that it is possible for you to see *Eventually he disappeared from sight.* • *I looked for her but she was* *nowhere in sight.* ● *I was able to park within sight of the house.* ● *Security guards were waiting out of sight* (= where they could not be seen). **4** VIEW [C] something which you see, especially something interesting *the sights and sounds of the market* **5 at first sight** when you first see or hear about something or someone *It may, at first sight, seem a surprising choice.* **6 the sights** the beautiful or interesting places in a city or country, that a lot of people visit *He took me around New York and showed me the sights.* **7 lose sight of sth** to forget about an important idea or fact because you are thinking too much about other, less important things *We mustn't lose sight of the original aims of this project.* **8 set your sights on sth** to decide to achieve something *She's set her sights on becoming an actress.*

---

**USAGE**

**sights** or **sightseeing**?

Sights are all the interesting or beautiful places which you can visit in a city or country.

*We visited the sights of Paris.*

Sightseeing is the activity of visiting places which are famous or historical.

*We did some sightseeing in Paris.*

---

**sight²** /saɪt/ *verb* [T] to see something that it is difficult to see or that you have been looking for [often passive] *The ship was last sighted off the French coast at 8 o'clock yesterday evening.*

**-sighted**/'saɪtɪd/ used after a word describing a person's ability to see *long-/short-sighted* ● *partially-sighted*

**sighted** /'saɪtɪd/ *adj* A sighted person is able to see. *the differences between blind and sighted children*

**sighting** /'saɪtɪŋ/ *noun* [C] when you see something that is rare or unusual *UFO sightings* ● *Several sightings of dolphins have been reported.*

**sightseeing** /'saɪtsiːɪŋ/ *noun* [U] the activity of visiting places which are interesting because they are historical, famous, etc *a sightseeing tour of London* ● **sightseer** /'saɪtˌsiːəʳ/ *noun* [C] a person who goes sightseeing

**sign¹** /saɪn/ *noun* [C] **1** PROOF something which shows that something is happening *Flowers are the first sign of Spring.* ● [+ (that)] *It's a sign that things are improving.* ● *Staff are showing signs of strain.* **2** NOTICE a symbol or message in a public place which gives information or instructions *a road sign* ● *a 'no-smoking' sign* **3** SYMBOL a symbol which has a particular meaning *a dollar/pound sign* ● *the sign of the cross* **4** MOVEMENT a movement you make to give someone information or tell them what to do ➡ *See also:* **star sign**.

**sign²** /saɪn/ *verb* [I, T] to write your name on something to show that you wrote/painted, etc it or to show that you agree to it *He signs his letters 'Prof. James D. Nelson'.* ● *to sign a contract/treaty*

**sign for sth** UK If a player signs for a football

team, he signs a formal agreement saying that he will play for that team. *It was announced today that Williams has signed for the Italian club Inter Milan.*

**sign (sb) in** to write your name or someone else's name in a book when you arrive at a building such as an office or hotel

**sign on 1** to sign a document saying that you will work for someone *She's signed on with a temp agency.* **2** UK to sign a form at a government office to say that you do not have a job and that you want to receive money from the government

**sign (sb) out** to write your name or someone else's name in a book when leaving a building such as an office or factory

**sign up** to arrange to do an organized activity *I've signed up for evening classes at the local college.*

**signal¹** /'sɪɡnəl/ *noun* [C] **1** ACTION a movement, light, or sound which gives information, or tells people what to do *At a signal from their teacher, the children all held up their flags.* ● *Don't move until I give the signal.* **2** WAVE a series of light waves or sound waves which are sent to a radio or television **3** TRAINS a piece of equipment which tells trains to stop or to continue **4** VEHICLES/PEOPLE US a piece of equipment that shows people or vehicles when to stop, go, or move carefully *a traffic signal*

**signal²** /'sɪɡnəl/ *verb* [I, T] UK **signalling**, *past* **signalled**, US **signaling**, *past* **signaled** **1** to make a movement which gives information or tells people what to do *He signalled for them to be quiet.* ● [+ to do sth] *He signalled the driver to stop.* **2** to show that you intend or are ready to do something [+ (that)] *The US signalled that they were ready to enter talks.*

**signatory** /'sɪɡnətəri/ *noun* [C] *formal* a person or country that signs an official document

**signature** /'sɪɡnətʃəʳ/ *noun* [C] your name written in your own way which is difficult for someone else to copy

**significance** /sɪɡ'nɪfɪkəns/ *noun* [U] the importance or meaning of something *I still don't understand the significance of his remark.* ● *This is a development which has great economic significance for the region.*

**significant** /sɪɡ'nɪfɪkənt/ *adj* important or noticeable *These measures will save a significant amount of money.* ● *It is significant that Falkner did not attend the meeting himself.* ➡ *Opposite* **insignificant**. ● **significantly***adv*

**signify** /'sɪɡnɪfaɪ/ *verb* [T] to be a sign of something *Red signifies danger.* ● *These lines on the road – what do they signify?*

**signing** /'saɪnɪŋ/ *noun* [C] **1** UK a player who has joined a sports team or a musician who has joined a record company **2** the act of signing something [usually singular] *the signing of the declaration*

**'sign ˌlanguage** *noun* [C, U] a system of communication using hand movements, used by people who are deaf (= cannot hear)

**signpost**/'saɪnpəʊst/ *noun* [C] a sign by the side of the road that gives information about routes and distances

**Sikh** /siːk/ *noun* [C] someone who believes in an

Indian religion based on belief in a single god and on the teachings of Guru Nanak • **Sikh** *adj a Sikh temple* • **Sikhism** *noun* [U]

○━**silence**[1] /'saɪləns/ *noun* **1** NO SOUND [U] when there is no sound *The three men ate **in silence**.* • *No sound broke the silence of the wintry landscape.* **2** NO TALKING [U] when someone says nothing about a particular subject *She ended her silence yesterday and spoke to a TV reporter about the affair.* **3** PERIOD OF TIME [C] a period of time when there is no sound or no talking *an awkward/embarrassed silence* • *There was a short silence while she thought about it.*

**silence**[2] /'saɪləns/ *verb* [T] **1** to stop something making a sound or stop someone from talking, often about a particular subject *He silenced the alarm.* • *Opponents of the government would be silenced or thrown into prison.* **2** to stop people from criticizing you by giving a good argument to support your opinion *He seems to have silenced his critics.*

**silencer** /'saɪlənsər/ *noun* [C] **1** *UK* (*US* **muffler**) a part of a vehicle that reduces noise **2** a piece of equipment that you use on a gun to reduce the sound of it firing

○━**silent** /'saɪlənt/ *adj* **1** NO SOUND without any sound *The building was dark and silent.* • *At last the guns fell silent.* **2** NO TALKING without talking *He remains silent about his plans.* **3** LETTER If a letter in a word is silent, it is not pronounced. *The 'p' in 'receipt' is silent.* • **silently** *adv The snow fell silently all around them.*

**silhouette** /ˌsɪlu'et/ *noun* [C, U] the shape of something when the light is behind it so that you cannot see any details *He saw a woman **in silhouette**.* • **silhouetted** *adj the roofs silhouetted against the night sky*

**silicon** /'sɪlɪkən/ *noun* [U] a chemical element used in making electronic equipment such as computers, and materials such as glass and concrete *a silicon chip*

**silk** /sɪlk/ *noun* [U] a type of cloth which is light and smooth *a silk dress/shirt*

**silken** /'sɪlkən/ *adj literary* soft and smooth, like silk *her silken skin*

**silky** /'sɪlki/ *adj* soft and smooth, like silk *a large, silky, grey cat*

○━**silly** /'sɪli/ *adj* **1** stupid *silly games/hats* • *I feel silly in this hat.* • *It's a bit silly spending all that money on something we don't need.* **2** small and not important *She gets upset over such silly things.* • **silliness** *noun* [U]

**silt** /sɪlt/ *noun* [U] sand and clay that has been carried along by a river and is left on land

**silver**[1] /'sɪlvər/ *noun* **1** METAL [U] a valuable, shiny, grey-white metal used to make coins and jewellery *silver and gold* • *a solid silver ring* **2** OBJECTS [U] objects made of silver **3** PRIZE [C] a silver medal (= a small, round disc given to someone for finishing second in a race or competition)

**silver**[2] /'sɪlvər/ *adj* **1** made of silver *a silver coin* • *a silver necklace* **2** being the colour of silver *a silver sports car* • *red, green, and silver Christmas decorations*

,**silver** '**medal** *noun* [C] a small, round disc given to someone for finishing second in a race or competition

**silverware** /'sɪlvəweər/ *noun* [U] *US* (*UK* **cutlery**) knives, forks, spoons, etc that are used for eating

,**silver** '**wedding anniversary** *noun* [C] the date that is 25 years after the day that two people married

**silvery** /'sɪlvəri/ *adj* shiny and pale like silver *a silvery light*

○━**similar** /'sɪmɪlər/ *adj* Something which is similar to something else has many things the same, although it is not exactly the same. *The two houses are remarkably similar.* • *The style of cooking is **similar to** that of Northern India.* ⊃ *Opposite* **dissimilar**.

**similarity** /ˌsɪmɪ'lærəti/ *noun* [C, U] when two things or people are similar, or a way in which they are similar *There are a number of **similarities between** the two systems.* • *He bears a striking **similarity to** his grandfather.*

**similarly** /'sɪmɪləli/ *adv* in a similar way

**simile** /'sɪmɪli/ *noun* [C] a phrase which compares one thing to something else, using the words 'like' or 'as', for example 'as white as snow'

**simmer** /'sɪmər/ *verb* [I, T] to gently cook a liquid or something with liquid in it so that it is very hot, but does not boil

○━**simple** /'sɪmpl/ *adj* **1** EASY not difficult to do or to understand [+ to do sth] *It's very simple to use.* • *Just mix all the ingredients together – it's as simple as that.* **2** NOT COMPLICATED not complicated or containing details which are not necessary *a simple life* • *a simple black dress* (= dress without decoration) **3** IMPORTANT used to describe the one important fact, truth, etc *We chose her for the simple reason that she's the best person for the job.*

**simplicity** /sɪm'plɪsəti/ *noun* [U] **1** when something is not complicated and has few details or little decoration *I admire the simplicity of his designs.* **2** when something is easy to understand

**simplify** /'sɪmplɪfaɪ/ *verb* [T] to make something less complicated or easier to do or to understand *We need to simplify the instructions.* • **simplification** /ˌsɪmplɪfɪ'keɪʃən/ *noun* [C, U]

**simplistic** /sɪm'plɪstɪk/ *adj* making something complicated seem simple by ignoring many of the details *a simplistic explanation*

**simply** /'sɪmpli/ *adv* **1** EMPHASIS used to emphasize what you are saying *We simply don't have the time.* **2** ONLY only *A lot of people miss out on this opportunity simply because they don't know about it.* **3** NOT COMPLICATED in a way which is not complicated or difficult to understand *simply prepared food* • *He explained it as simply as he could.*

**simulate** /'sɪmjəleɪt/ *verb* [T] to do or make something which behaves or looks like something real but which is not real *The company uses a computer to simulate crash tests of its new cars.* • **simulation** /ˌsɪmjə'leɪʃən/ *noun* [C, U]

**simulator** /'sɪmjəleɪtər/ *noun* [C] a machine on which people can practise operating a vehicle or an aircraft without having to drive or fly *a flight simulator*

**simultaneous** /ˌsɪmˀlˈteɪnɪəs/ *adj* If two or more things are simultaneous, they happen or exist at the same time. *simultaneous translation* • simultaneously *adv* *It was broadcast simultaneously in Britain and France.*

**sin¹** /sɪn/ *noun* **1** [C, U] something which is against the rules of a religion *the sin of pride* **2** [no plural] *informal* something that you should not do because it is morally wrong *You've only got one life and it's a sin to waste it.*

**sin²** /sɪn/ *verb* [I] **sinning**, *past* **sinned** to do something that is against the rules of a religion • **sinner** *noun* [C] someone who does something against the rules of a religion

o—►**since¹** /sɪns/ *adv, preposition* from a time in the past until a later time or until now *The country has been independent since 1948.* • *They've been waiting since March.* • *The factory had been closed since the explosion.* • *I've felt fine ever since.*

o—►**since²** /sɪns/ *conjunction* **1** from a time in the past until a later time or until now *He's been much happier since he started his new job.* • *I've known Tim since he was seven.* **2** because *He drove quite slowly since we had plenty of time.*

**sincere** /sɪnˈsɪəʳ/ *adj* **1** honest and saying or showing what you really feel or believe *He seems to be sincere.* ➔ *Opposite* **insincere**. **2** sincere apologies/thanks, etc *formal* used to add emphasis when you are expressing a feeling *The family wishes to express their sincere thanks to all the staff at the hospital.* • **sincerity** /sɪnˈserəti/ *noun* [U] *No one doubted his sincerity.*

**sincerely** /sɪnˈsɪəli/ *adv* **1** in a sincere way *I sincerely hope that this never happens again.* **2** Yours sincerely *formal* used at the end of formal letters where you know the name of the person you are writing to

**sinful** /ˈsɪnfˀl/ *adj* against the rules of a religion or morally wrong *a sinful waste of money*

o—►**sing** /sɪŋ/ *verb* [I, T] *past* **sang**, *past p* **sung** to make musical sounds with your voice *They all sang 'Happy Birthday' to him.* • *She sings in the church choir.*

**singer** /ˈsɪŋəʳ/ *noun* [C] someone who sings *a jazz singer*

**singing** /ˈsɪŋɪŋ/ *noun* [U] the activity of singing

o—►**single¹** /ˈsɪŋgl/ *adj* **1** ONE [always before noun] only one *There was a single light in the corner of the room.* **2** every single used to emphasize that you are talking about each one of a group or series *I call him every single day.* • *He could hear every single word we said.* **3** MARRIAGE not married *He's young and single, without any responsibilities.* ➔ *See usage note at* **married**. **4** PARENT [always before noun] looking after your children alone without a partner or the children's other parent *a single mother* • *a single-parent family* **5** FOR ONE [always before noun] for only one person *a single bed*

**single²** /ˈsɪŋgl/ *noun* [C] **1** a record or CD which includes only one main song **2** *UK* (*US* **one-way ticket**) a ticket for a journey that is from one place to another but not back again *Could I have a single to London, please?*

**single³** /ˈsɪŋgl/ *verb*

**single sb/sth out** to choose one person or thing from a group to criticize or praise them *The report singled him out for special criticism.* • *The whole team played well – I don't want to single out any one player.*

**single-handedly** /ˌsɪŋglˈhændɪdli/ (*also* **single-handed**) *adv* on your own, without anyone's help *After his partner left, he kept the business going single-handedly.* • **single-handed** /ˌsɪŋglˈhændɪd/ *adj* [always before noun] *a single-handed round-the-world yacht race*

**single-minded** /ˌsɪŋglˈmaɪndɪd/ *adj* very determined to achieve something *She had a single-minded determination to succeed in her career.*

**singles** /ˈsɪŋglz/ *noun* [U] a game in sports such as tennis, in which one person plays against another *He won the men's singles title two years running.*

**singly** /ˈsɪŋgli/ *adv* separately or one at a time *We don't sell them singly, only in packs of four or ten.*

**singular** /ˈsɪŋgjələʳ/ *adj* **1** The singular form of a word is used to talk about one person or thing. For example 'woman' is the singular form of 'women'. **2** *formal* very special, or found only in one person or situation *a landscape of singular beauty*

**the singular** /ˈsɪŋgjələʳ/ *noun* the singular form of a word

**singularly** /ˈsɪŋgjələli/ *adv* *formal* very *Fulbright was singularly uninterested in his comments.*

**sinister** /ˈsɪnɪstəʳ/ *adj* making you feel that something bad or evil might happen *a sinister figure dressed in black*

o—►**sink¹** /sɪŋk/ *verb past t* **sank** (*also US*) **sunk**, *past p* **sunk 1** WATER [I, T] to go down or make something go down below the surface of water and not come back up *The Titanic sank after hitting an iceberg.* • *During the first wave of attacks, they sank three enemy ships.* ➔ *See picture at* **float**. **2** SOFT SUBSTANCE [I, T] to go down, or make something go down, into something soft *My feet keep sinking into the sand.* • *It sank its teeth into his arm.* **3** MOVE DOWN [I] to move down slowly *The sun sank below the horizon.*

**sink in** If an unpleasant or surprising fact sinks in, you gradually start to believe it and understand what effect it will have on you. *It still hasn't sunk in that I'll never see her again.*

**sink sth into sth** to spend a large amount of money in a business or other piece of work *Millisat has already sunk $25 million into the Hong Kong project.*

**sink into sth** to slowly move into a sitting or lying position, in a relaxed or tired way *I just want to go home and sink into a hot bath.*

**sink²** /sɪŋk/ *noun* [C] a bowl that is fixed to the wall in a kitchen or bathroom that you wash dishes or your hands, etc in ➔ *See colour picture* **The Bathroom** *on page Centre 1.*

**sinus** /ˈsaɪnəs/ *noun* [C] one of the spaces inside the head that are connected to the back of the nose

**sip** /sɪp/ *verb* [I, T] **sipping**, *past* **sipped** to drink, taking only a small amount at a time *She sipped her champagne.* • **sip** *noun* [C] *He took a sip of his coffee and then continued.*

S

**siphon¹** /'saɪfᵊn/ *noun* [C] a piece of equipment for moving liquid from one place to another

**siphon²** /'saɪfᵊn/ *verb* [T] **1** to remove liquid from a container using a siphon **2** (*also* **siphon off**) to dishonestly take money from an organization or other supply over a period of time

**sir** /sɜːʳ/ *noun* **1** (*also* **Sir**) You call a man 'sir' when you are speaking to him politely. *Excuse me, sir, is this seat taken?* **2** You write 'Sir' at the beginning of a formal letter to a man when you do not know his name. *Dear Sir, I am writing to...* **3 Sir** a title used in the UK before the name of a man who has been officially respected or who has a high social rank *Sir Cliff Richard*

**siren** /'saɪərən/ *noun* [C] a piece of equipment that makes a loud sound as a warning *a police siren*

O-ᴍ**sister** /'sɪstəʳ/ *noun* [C] **1** RELATIVE a girl or woman who has the same parents as you *an older/younger sister* • *my big/little sister* **2** RELIGION (*also* **Sister**) a nun (= woman who lives in a female religious group) *Sister Bridget* **3** NURSE (*also* **Sister**) a female nurse in the UK who is responsible for a hospital ward (= an area of a hospital containing beds for ill people) *I asked Sister if he would be able to go home soon.* **4** MEMBER a woman who is a member of the same race, religious group, organization, etc

**sister-in-law** /'sɪstᵊrɪnlɔː/ *noun* [C] *plural* **sisters-in-law** the woman married to your brother, or the sister of your husband or wife

**sisterly** /'sɪstəli/ *adj* experienced by or for a sister *sisterly love*

O-ᴍ**sit** /sɪt/ *verb* **sitting**, *past* **sat 1** BODY POSITION [I] to be in a position with the weight of your body on your bottom and the top part of your body up, for example, on a chair *Emma was sitting on a stool.* • *The children sat at the table by the window.* • *We sat by the river and had a picnic.* **2** MOVE BODY [I] (*also* **sit down**) to move your body into a sitting position after you have been standing *She came over and sat beside him.* • *She sat down on the grass.* ➔ *See colour picture* **Phrasal Verbs** *on page Centre 13.* **3 sit sb down/at/in, etc** to make someone sit somewhere *She sat me down and told me the bad news.* • *I thought we'd sit the children at the end of the table.* **4** STAY [I] to stay in one place for a long time and not be used *He hardly ever drives the car. It just sits in the garage.* **5** MEETING [I] If a court, parliament, etc sits, it has a meeting to do its work. *The board will be sitting next week.* **6** TEST/EXAM [T] *UK* to take a test or exam *The changes will affect many students sitting their exams this summer.* ➔ *See also:* sit on the **fence¹**.

**sit about/around** to spend time sitting down and doing very little [+ doing sth] *He just sits around all day watching television.*

**sit back 1** to relax in a chair so that your back is against the back of the chair *Just sit back and enjoy the show.* **2** to wait for something to happen without making any effort to do anything yourself *You can't just sit back and expect someone else to deal with the problem.*

**sit in** to go to a meeting or class to watch *I sat in on a couple of classes before choosing a course.*

**sit sth out 1** to not do an activity such as a game

or dance because you are tired or have an injury *I think I'll sit out the next dance.* **2** to wait for something unpleasant to finish before you do anything *The government is prepared to sit out the strike rather than agree to union demands.*

**sit through sth** to stay until the end of a meeting, performance, etc that is very long or boring *We had to sit through two hours of speeches.*

**sit up 1** to move your body to a sitting position after you have been lying down *I sat up and opened my eyes.* **2** to stay awake and not go to bed although it is late [+ doing sth] *We sat up talking all night.*

**sitcom** /'sɪtkɒm/ *noun* [C, U] a funny television programme that is about the same group of people every week in different situations

**site¹** /saɪt/ *noun* **1** HISTORY [C] the place where something important happened in the past *a historic site* • *the site of a battle* **2** AREA [C] an area that is used for something or where something happens *a building site* **3 on site** inside a factory, office building, etc *There are two restaurants on site.* • *They provide on-site childcare facilities for employees.* **4** INTERNET [C] *short for* website (= an area on the Internet where information about a particular subject, organization, etc can be found)

**site²** /saɪt/ *verb formal* **site sth in/on, etc** to build something in a particular place [often passive] *The company's head office is sited in Geneva.*

**sitter** /'sɪtəʳ/ *noun* [C] *mainly US* a babysitter (= someone who looks after children when their parents go out)

**sitting** /'sɪtɪŋ/ *noun* [C] **1** a meeting of a parliament, court, etc *a late-night sitting of parliament* **2** one of the times when a meal is served to a large group of people who cannot all eat at the same time

**'sitting ,room** *noun* [C] *UK* the room in a house where people sit to relax and, for example, watch television

**situated** /'sɪtjueɪtɪd/ *adj formal* **be situated in/on/by, etc** to be in a particular place *a hotel situated by Lake Garda*

O-ᴍ**situation** /ˌsɪtjuˈeɪʃᵊn/ *noun* [C] **1** the set of things that are happening and the conditions that exist at a particular time and place *the economic/political situation* • *He's in a difficult situation.* **2** *formal* the position of a town, building, etc *The park's situation was perfect.*

**six** /sɪks/ the number 6

**sixteen** /ˌsɪkˈstiːn/ the number 16 • **sixteenth** 16th written as a word

**sixth¹** /sɪksθ/ 6th written as a word

**sixth²** /sɪksθ/ *noun* [C] one of six equal parts of something; 1/6

**'sixth ,form** *noun* [C] in Britain, the part of a school for students between the ages of 16 and 18

**sixty** /'sɪksti/ **1** the number 60 **2 the sixties** the years from 1960 to 1969 **3 be in your sixties** to be aged between 60 and 69 • **sixtieth** 60th written as a word

**sizable** /'saɪzəbl/ *adj another spelling of* sizeable

o⅃**size¹** /saɪz/ noun **1** [C, U] how big or small something is *It's an area about the size of Oxford.*
• *The size of some of those trees is incredible* (= they are very large). **2** [C] one of the different measurements in which things, for example clothes, food containers, etc are made *a size 10 skirt* • *What size shoes do you take?* • *I usually buy the 1.5 litre size.* ⤷ *See also:* all shapes (**shape¹**) and sizes.

**size²** /saɪz/ verb
**size sb/sth up** to look at someone or think about something carefully before making a judgment *I could see her trying to size me up.*

**sizeable** (*also* **sizable**) /'saɪzəbl/ adj quite large *a sizeable crowd*

**-sized** /saɪzd/ suffix used at the end of a word to mean 'of a particular size' *a medium-sized pizza* • *a good-sized bedroom*

**sizzle** /'sɪzl/ verb [I] to make the sound of food cooking in hot oil

**skate¹** /skeɪt/ noun [C] **1** (*also* **roller skate**) a boot with wheels on the bottom, used for moving across the ground *a pair of skates* **2** (*also* **ice skate**) a boot with a metal part on the bottom, used for moving across ice ⤷ *See colour picture* **Sports 1** *on page Centre 15.* **3 get/put your skates on** *UK informal* used to tell someone to hurry

**skate²** /skeɪt/ verb [I] to move using skates
• **skater** noun [C] • **skating** noun [U]

**skateboard** /'skeɪtbɔːd/ noun [C] a board with wheels on the bottom, that you stand on and move forward by pushing one foot on the ground ⤷ *See colour picture* **Sports 1** *on page Centre 15.*

**skateboarding** /'skeɪtbɔːdɪŋ/ noun [U] the activity of moving using a skateboard ⤷ *See colour picture* **Sports 1** *on page Centre 15.*

**skeletal** /'skelɪtl/ adj like a skeleton, or relating to skeletons

**skeleton** /'skelɪtⁿn/ noun **1** [C] the structure made of all the bones in the body of a person or animal *the skeleton of a dog* **2 a skeleton crew/staff/service** the smallest number of people that you need to keep an organization working *The Red Cross has withdrawn all but a skeleton staff from the country.* **3 have a skeleton in the cupboard** *UK* (*US* **have a skeleton in the closet**) to have an embarrassing or unpleasant secret about something that happened in the past *Most people have a few skeletons in the cupboard.*

**skeptic** /'skeptɪk/ noun [C] *US spelling of* sceptic

**skeptical** /'skeptɪkⁿl/ adj *US spelling of* sceptical

**skepticism** /'skeptɪsɪzⁿm/ noun [U] *US spelling of* scepticism

**sketch¹** /sketʃ/ noun [C] **1** PICTURE a picture that you draw quickly and with few details *He did a quick sketch of the cat.* **2** ACTING a short piece of acting about a funny situation **3** DESCRIPTION a short description of something without many details

**sketch²** /sketʃ/ verb [T] to draw a sketch *I sketched a map for him on a scrap of paper.*
**sketch sth out** to give a short description with few details, especially of an idea or plan *I've sketched out some ideas for my new book.*

**sketchy** /'sketʃi/ adj with few details *Reports about the accident are still sketchy.*

**ski¹** /skiː/ noun [C] one of a pair of long, thin pieces of wood or plastic that you wear on the bottom of boots to move over snow ⤷ *See colour picture* **Sports 1** *on page Centre 15.*

**ski²** /skiː/ verb [I] **skiing**, *past* **skied** to move over snow wearing skis • **skier** noun [C] • **skiing** noun [U] *I'd like to go skiing in Switzerland.* ⤷ *See also:* **water-skiing**.

**skid** /skɪd/ verb [I] **skidding**, *past* **skidded** If a vehicle skids, it slides along a surface and you cannot control it. *The car skidded on ice and hit a tree.* • **skid** noun [C]

**skies** /skaɪz/ noun [plural] the sky in a particular place or in a particular state *beautiful, clear, blue skies*

**skilful** *UK* (*US* **skillful**) /'skɪlfⁿl/ adj **1** good at doing something *a skilful artist* **2** done or made very well *skilful use of language* • **skilfully** *UK* adv

o⅃**skill** /skɪl/ noun [C, U] the ability to do an activity or job well, especially because you have practised it *You need good communication skills to be a teacher.*

**skilled** /skɪld/ adj **1** having the abilities needed to do an activity or job well *a highly skilled* (= very skilled) *photographer* • *He has become skilled in dealing with the media.* **2** Skilled work needs someone who has had special training to do it. ⤷ *Opposite* **unskilled**.

**skillet** /'skɪlɪt/ noun [C] *mainly US* a large, heavy pan with a long handle, used for frying food

**skillful** /'skɪlfⁿl/ adj *US spelling of* skilful

**skim** /skɪm/ verb **skimming**, *past* **skimmed** **1** MOVE OVER [I, T] to move quickly, and almost or just touch the surface of something *Birds skimmed the surface of the pond.* **2** REMOVE [T] (*also* **skim off**) to remove something from the surface of a liquid *Skim off any excess fat before serving.* **3** READ QUICKLY [T] (*also* **skim through**) to read or look at something quickly without looking at the details *She began skimming through the reports on her desk.*

**skimmed 'milk** (*also US* **'skim ,milk**) noun [U] milk that has had the fat removed from it

**skimp** /skɪmp/ verb
**skimp on sth** to not spend enough time or money on something, or not use enough of something *We've got plenty of cheese so don't skimp on it.*

**skimpy** /'skɪmpi/ adj Skimpy clothes show a lot of your body. *a skimpy bikini/dress*

o⅃**skin¹** /skɪn/ noun [C, U] **1** BODY the outer layer of a person or animal's body *dark/fair/olive skin* • *skin cancer* **2** ANIMAL the outer layer of a dead animal used as leather, fur, etc *a leopard skin rug* **3** FRUIT the outer layer of a fruit or vegetable *a banana/potato skin* **4** LIQUID a thin, solid layer that forms on the top of a liquid *A skin had formed on the top of the milk.* **5 do sth by the skin of your teeth** *informal* to only just succeed in doing something *They held on by the skin of their teeth to win 1–0.* **6 have (a) thick skin** to not care if someone criticizes you

**skin²** /skɪn/ verb [T] **skinning**, *past* **skinned 1** to remove the skin from something **2** (*also UK*

S

graze) to injure your skin by rubbing it against something rough *Mary fell and skinned her knees.*

**skinhead** /ˈskɪnhed/ *noun* [C] a man who has extremely short hair, especially one who behaves in a violent way

**skinny** /ˈskɪni/ *adj* Someone who is skinny is too thin.

**skip¹** /skɪp/ *verb* **skipping**, *past* **skipped** 1 MOVE FORWARD [I] to move forward, jumping quickly from one foot to the other *She watched her daughter skipping down the street.* 2 JUMP [I] (*US* ,**skip** ˈ**rope**) to jump over a rope while you or two other people move it over and then under your body again and again *I skip for ten minutes every day to keep fit.* 3 NOT DO [T] to not do something that you usually do or that you should do *I think I'll skip lunch today – I'm not very hungry.* 4 AVOID [T] (*also* **skip over**) to avoid reading or talking about something by starting to read or talk about the next thing instead *I usually skip the boring bits.*

**skip²** /skɪp/ *noun* [C] 1 *UK* (*US* **Dumpster** *trademark*) a very large, metal container for big pieces of rubbish 2 when you jump quickly from one foot to the other

**skipper** /ˈskɪpəʳ/ *noun* [C] *informal* the leader of a team, an aircraft, a ship, etc

ˈ**skipping** ,**rope** *UK* (*US* **jump rope**) *noun* [C] a rope that you move over your head and then jump over as you move it under your feet

**skirmish** /ˈskɜːmɪʃ/ *noun* [C] a small fight

**skirt¹** /skɜːt/ *noun* [C] a piece of women's clothing that hangs from the waist and has no legs
❍ *See colour picture* **Clothes** *on page Centre 5.*

**skirt²** /skɜːt/ *verb* (*also* **skirt around**) 1 to avoid talking about something *I deliberately skirted the question of money.* 2 to move around the edge of something *We skirted around the edge of the field.*

**skittle** /ˈskɪtl/ *noun* 1 [C] one of a set of bottle-shaped objects that you try to knock down with a ball as a game 2 **skittles** [U] a game in which you try to knock down bottle-shaped objects with a ball

**skive** /skaɪv/ (*also* **skive off**) *verb* [I, T] *UK* to not go to school or work when you should, or to leave school or work earlier than you should • **skiver** *noun* [C] *UK informal* someone who skives

**skulk** /skʌlk/ *verb* **skulk about/behind/in, etc** to hide somewhere or move around quietly in a way that makes people think you are going to do something bad *I saw a man skulking behind the shed.*

**skull** /skʌl/ *noun* [C] the part of your head that is made of bone and which protects your brain

ˈ**skull** ,**cap** *noun* [C] a small round hat worn especially by some religious men

**skunk** /skʌŋk/ *noun* [C] a black and white animal that produces a very unpleasant smell in order to defend itself

०⚊**sky** /skaɪ/ *noun* [U, no plural] the area above the Earth where you can see clouds, the sun, the moon, etc *a beautiful, blue sky* • *The sky suddenly went dark.* ❍ *See also:* **skies.**

**skydiving** /ˈskaɪ,daɪvɪŋ/ *noun* [U] the sport of jumping out of an aircraft with a parachute (=

large piece of cloth that allows you to fall slowly to the ground)

**skylight** /ˈskaɪlaɪt/ *noun* [C] a window in the roof of a building

**skyline** /ˈskaɪlaɪn/ *noun* [C] the pattern that is made against the sky by tall buildings *the New York skyline*

skyline

**skyscraper** /ˈskaɪ,skreɪpəʳ/ *noun* [C] a very tall building

**slab** /slæb/ *noun* [C] a thick, flat piece of something, especially stone *a slab of concrete*

**slack¹** /slæk/ *adj* 1 LOOSE loose or not tight *Suddenly the rope became slack.* 2 BUSINESS If business is slack, there are not many customers. 3 LAZY not trying hard enough in your work *slack management*

**slack²** /slæk/ *informal* (*also US* **slack off**) *verb* [I] to work less hard than usual *I'm afraid I haven't been to the gym recently – I've been slacking.*

**slacken** /ˈslækən/ *verb* [I, T] 1 to become slower or less active, or to make something become slower or less active *Economic growth is slackening.* 2 to become loose, or to make something become loose *As you get older your muscles slacken.*

**slacks** /slæks/ *noun* [plural] *mainly US* trousers

**slag** /slæg/ *verb* **slagging**, *past* **slagged**
**slag sb/sth off** *UK informal* to criticize someone or something in an unpleasant way

**slain** /sleɪn/ *past participle of* slay

**slalom** /ˈslɑːləm/ *noun* [C] a race in which you go forwards by moving from side to side between poles

**slam** /slæm/ *verb* **slamming**, *past* **slammed** 1 [I, T] to close with great force, or to make something close with great force *Kate heard the front door slam.* • *Don't slam the gate.* 2 **slam sth down/ onto/into, etc** to put something somewhere with great force *She slammed the phone down.*
• slam *noun* [C] [usually singular] *the slam of a car door*

**slander** /ˈslɑːndəʳ/ *noun* [C, U] the crime of saying bad things about someone that are not true • slander *verb* [T] • **slanderous** /ˈslɑːndərəs/ *adj* saying bad things about someone that are not true

**slang** /slæŋ/ *noun* [U] informal language, often language that is only used by people who belong to a particular group *prison slang*

**slant¹** /slɑːnt/ *verb* [I, T] to slope in a particular direction, or to make something slope in a particular direction *Pale sunlight slanted through the curtain.*

**slant²** /slɑːnt/ *noun* [no plural] 1 a position that is sloping *The road is on/at a slant.* 2 a way of writing about something that shows who or what you support *a political slant* • *It's certainly a new slant on the subject.*

**slap¹** /slæp/ *verb* [T] **slapping**, *past* **slapped** to hit someone with the flat, inside part of your hand *She slapped him across the face.*

**slap sth on** to quickly put or spread something on a surface *I'll just slap some make-up on.*

**slap²** /slæp/ *noun* [C] **1** a hit with the flat, inside part of your hand **2 a slap in the face** something someone does that insults or upsets you *After all that hard work, losing my job was a real slap in the face.*

**slapdash** /'slæpdæʃ/ *adj* done quickly and without being careful *Her work has been a bit slapdash recently.*

**slapstick** /'slæpstɪk/ *noun* [U] when actors do funny things like falling down, hitting each other, etc to make people laugh

**slap-up** /'slæp,ʌp/ *adj* **slap-up meal/dinner, etc** *UK informal* a large and very good meal

**slash¹** /slæʃ/ *verb* [T] **1** to cut something by making a quick, long cut with something very sharp *His throat had been slashed.* **2** to reduce the amount of something by a lot *to slash prices*

**slash²** /slæʃ/ *noun* [C] **1** a long, deep cut **2** a mark (/) used in writing to separate words or numbers, often to show a choice or connection

**slate¹** /sleɪt/ *noun* [C, U] a dark grey rock that can easily be cut into thin pieces, or a small, flat piece of this used to cover a roof

**slate²** /sleɪt/ *verb* [T] *UK* **1** to criticize someone or something severely [often passive] *The film had been slated by critics.* **2 be slated** *US* to be expected to happen in the future, or to be expected to be or do something in the future [+ to do sth] *Filming is slated to begin next spring.* • *The game is slated for next week.*

**slaughter¹** /'slɔːtəʳ/ *verb* [T] **1** ANIMAL to kill an animal for meat **2** PEOPLE to kill a lot of people in a very cruel way **3** DEFEAT *informal* to defeat someone very easily

**slaughter²** /'slɔːtəʳ/ *noun* [U] when a lot of people or animals are killed in a cruel way

**slaughterhouse** /'slɔːtəhaʊs/ *noun* [C] *plural* **slaughterhouses** /'slɔːtəhaʊzɪz/ a place where animals are killed for meat

**slave¹** /sleɪv/ *noun* **1** [C] someone who is owned by someone else and has to work for them *He treats his mother like a slave.* **2 be a slave to sth** to be completely controlled or influenced by something *You're a slave to fashion.*

**slave²** /sleɪv/ (*also* **slave away**) *verb* [I] *informal* to work very hard *Giorgio was slaving away at his homework.*

**slavery** /'sleɪvʳri/ *noun* [U] the system of owning slaves, or the condition of being a slave

**slay** /sleɪ/ *verb* [T] *past t* **slew**, *past p* **slain** *literary* to kill someone in a very violent way

**sleaze** /sliːz/ *noun* [U] political or business activities that are morally wrong

**sleazy** /'sliːzi/ *adj* unpleasant and morally wrong, often in a way that relates to sex *He spent the night drinking in a sleazy bar.*

**sledge¹** /sledʒ/ *UK* (*US* **sled** /sled/) *noun* [C] a vehicle that is used for travelling on snow

**sledge²** /sledʒ/ *UK* (*US* **sled** /sled/) *verb* [I] to travel on snow using a sledge

**sleek** /sliːk/ *adj* **1** Sleek hair is smooth and very shiny. **2** A sleek car is attractive and looks expensive.

**o—¤sleep¹** /sliːp/ *verb* *past* **slept** **1** [I] to be in the state of rest when your eyes are closed, your body is not active, and your mind is unconscious *We had to sleep in the car that night.* • *Did you sleep well?* **2 sleep four/six, etc** If a place sleeps four, six, etc, it is big enough for that number of people to sleep in. **3 sleep on it** to wait until the next day before making a decision about something important so that you can think about it carefully ➔ *See also:* not sleep a **wink²**.

**sleep in** to sleep longer in the morning than you usually do

**sleep sth off** to sleep until you feel better, especially after drinking too much alcohol

**sleep over** to sleep in someone else's home for a night *After the party, I slept over at Tom's house.*

**sleep through sth** to continue to sleep although there is noise *I don't know how you slept through the storm.*

**sleep with sb** *informal* to have sex with someone

**o—¤sleep²** /sliːp/ *noun* **1** [U, no plural] the state you are in when you are sleeping, or a period of time when you are sleeping *I haven't had **a good night's sleep** (= a long sleep at night) for weeks.* • *You need to go home and **get some sleep**.* • *It took me ages to **get to sleep** (= to succeed in sleeping).* • *He died peacefully in his sleep.* **2 go to sleep a** to begin to sleep *Babies often go to sleep after a feed.* **b** *informal* If part of your body goes to sleep, you cannot feel it. *I'd been sitting on my feet and they'd gone to sleep.* **3 put sth to sleep** to kill an animal that is very old or ill **4 could do sth in your sleep** to be able to do something very easily **5 lose sleep over sth** to worry about something *Everyone makes mistakes so I wouldn't lose any sleep over it if I was you.*

**sleeper** /'sliːpəʳ/ *noun* **1 a light/heavy sleeper** someone who wakes up easily/does not wake up easily **2** TRAIN [C] a train or a part of a train that has beds in it **3** SUPPORT [C] *UK* (*US* **railroad tie**) a piece of wood that is used to support a railway track (= the thing a train moves along on) **4** JEWELLERY [C] *UK* a small gold or silver ring worn in the ear

**'sleeping ˌbag** *noun* [C] a long bag made of thick material that you sleep inside

**'sleeping ˌpill** *noun* [C] a medicine that you take to help you sleep

**sleepless** /'sliːpləs/ *adj* **sleepless night** a night when you are not able to sleep *He'd spent a sleepless night worrying about his exam.* • **sleepless-ness** *noun* [U]

**sleep-over** /'sliːpəʊvəʳ/ *noun* [C] a party when a group of young people stay at a friend's house for the night

**sleepwalk** /'sliːp,wɔːk/ *verb* [I] to get out of bed

**sleeping bag**

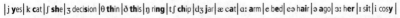

and walk around while you are sleeping • sleepwalker *noun* [C]

**sleepy** /'sli:pi/ *adj* **1** feeling tired and wanting to go to sleep *The heat had made me sleepy.* **2** quiet and with little activity *a sleepy little town* • sleepily *adv* • sleepiness *noun* [U]

**sleet** /sli:t/ *noun* [U] a mixture of snow and rain • sleet *verb* [I] *It was sleeting when I looked outside.*

**sleeve** /sli:v/ *noun* **1** [C] the part of a jacket, shirt, etc that covers your arm *He rolled up his sleeves to do the dishes.* ➜ *See picture at* **jacket.** **2 have sth up your sleeve** *informal* to have a secret plan *They were worried he might have another nasty surprise up his sleeve.*

**-sleeved** /sli:vd/ *suffix* **short-sleeved/long-sleeved** having short/long sleeves *a short-sleeved shirt*

**sleigh** /sleɪ/ *noun* [C] a large vehicle that is pulled by animals and used for travelling on snow

**slender** /'slendə'/ *adj* thin in an attractive way *a slender woman with long, red hair*

**slept** /slept/ *past of* sleep

**sleuth** /slu:θ/ *noun* [C] *old-fashioned* a police officer whose job is to discover who has committed a crime

**slew** /slu:/ *past tense of* slay

**slice¹** /slaɪs/ *noun* **1** [C] a flat piece of food that has been cut from a larger piece *a slice of bread/cake/meat* ➜ *See colour picture* **Quantities** *on page Centre 14.* **2 a slice of sth** a part of something that is being divided *a large slice of the profits* ➜ *See also:* **fish slice.**

**slice²** /slaɪs/ *verb* [T] **1** (*also* **slice up**) to cut food into flat pieces *Could you slice the tomatoes?* **2** (*also* **slice into/through**) to cut into or through something with a knife *I almost sliced my finger off.* ➜ *See also:* the best/greatest **thing** since sliced bread.

**slick** /slɪk/ *adj* **1** done with a lot of skill *a slick performance* **2** attractive but in a way that is not sincere or honest *He was a bit slick – I didn't trust him.*

o-**slide¹** /slaɪd/ *verb past* **slid 1 slide (sth) across/down/along, etc** to move smoothly over a surface, or to make something move smoothly over a surface *He likes sliding on the ice.* • *He slid the letter into his pocket.* **2 slide (sth) into/out of/through, etc** to move somewhere quietly, or to make something move quietly *She slid out of the room, being careful not to wake Alan.*

**slide²** /slaɪd/ *noun* **1** [PHOTOGRAPH] [C] a small piece of film that you shine light through in order to see a photograph **2** [GAME] [C] a large object that children climb and slide down as a game **3** [GLASS] [C] a small piece of glass that you put something on when you want to look at it under a microscope (= equipment used to make things look bigger) **4** [LESS/WORSE] [no plural] when the level or quality of something gets less or worse *a price slide*

o-**slight¹** /slaɪt/ *adj* **1** small and not important *slight differences in colour* • *We're having a slight problem with our computer system.* **2** Someone who is slight is thin.

**slight²** /slaɪt/ *noun* [C] an action or remark that insults someone

**slighted** /'slaɪtɪd/ *adj* **be/feel slighted** to feel insulted because someone has done or said something which shows that they think you are not important *Annie felt slighted because she hadn't been invited to the meeting.*

**slightest** /'slaɪtɪst/ *adj* **1 the slightest** [always before noun] the smallest *She doesn't have the slightest chance of succeeding.* • *The slightest movement will disturb these shy animals.* **2 not in the slightest** not at all *"Do you mind if I open the window?" "Not in the slightest."*

o-**slightly** /'slaɪtli/ *adv* a little *I think I did slightly better in my exams this time.* • *I find it slightly worrying.*

**slim¹** /slɪm/ *adj* **slimmer, slimmest 1** Someone who is slim is thin in an attractive way. **2** small and not as much as you would like *There's a slim chance he'll succeed.*

**slim²** /slɪm/ *verb* [I] **slimming,** *past* **slimmed** *UK* to eat less in order to become thinner

**slim down** to become thinner

**slim sth down** to reduce the size of something *It is not our intention to slim down the workforce.*

**slime** /slaɪm/ *noun* [U] a thick, sticky liquid that is unpleasant to touch

**slimy** /'slaɪmi/ *adj* **1** covered in slime **2** *informal* too friendly in a way that is not sincere

**sling¹** /slɪŋ/ *noun* [C] **1** a piece of cloth that you wear around your neck and put your arm into to support it when it is injured **2** a piece of cloth or a strap that you tie around your body to carry things in *She had her baby in a sling.*

**sling²** /slɪŋ/ *verb past* **slung 1 sling sth over/around/on, etc** to put something in a position where it hangs loosely *He slung his bag over his shoulder.* **2 sling sth into/onto/under, etc** to throw something somewhere in a careless way *She slung her coat onto the bed.*

**slingshot** /'slɪŋʃɒt/ *US* (*UK* **catapult**) *noun* [C] a Y-shaped object with a piece of elastic across it used by children to shoot small stones

**slink** /slɪŋk/ *verb past* **slunk slink away/off/out, etc** to move somewhere quietly so that no one will notice you *I caught him slinking out of the meeting.*

o-**slip¹** /slɪp/ *verb* **slipping,** *past* **slipped 1** [FALL] [I] to slide by accident and fall or almost fall *She slipped on the ice and broke her ankle.* **2** [OUT OF POSITION] [I] to slide out of the correct position *The photo had slipped from the frame.* **3 slip away/out/through, etc** to go somewhere quietly or quickly *I'll slip out of the room if I get bored.* **4 slip sth into/through, etc** to put something somewhere quickly or secretly *She slipped the letter into an envelope and sealed it.* **5** [GIVE SECRETLY] [+ two objects] *informal* to give something to someone secretly *I slipped her a five pound note.* **6** [GET LESS/WORSE] [I] to get less or worse in level or quality *His school grades have slipped recently.* **7 let sth slip** to forget that something is a secret and tell someone about it ➜ *See also:* slip your **mind¹.**

**slip into sth** to quickly put on a piece of clothing

**slip sth off** to quickly take off a piece of clothing *Slip your shirt off and I'll listen to your heart.*

**slip sth on** to quickly put on a piece of clothing *I'll just slip my shoes on.*

**slip out** If a remark slips out, you say it without intending to. *I didn't mean to tell anyone you were getting married – it just slipped out.*

**slip out of sth** to quickly take off a piece of clothing

**slip up** to make a mistake

**slip²** /slɪp/ *noun* [C] **1** PAPER a small piece of paper *He wrote the number on a slip of paper.* **2** FALL when you slide by accident and fall or almost fall **3** WOMEN'S CLOTHING a piece of clothing that a woman wears under a dress or skirt **4** MISTAKE a small mistake **5 give sb the slip** *informal* to escape from someone you do not want to be with **6 a slip of the tongue** a mistake made by using the wrong word

**slipper** /'slɪpəʳ/ *noun* [C] a soft, comfortable shoe that you wear in the house

**slippery** /'slɪpəri/ *adj* **1** smooth and wet and difficult to hold or walk on *Be careful – the floor's slippery.* **2 a slippery slope** a bad situation that is likely to get worse

**'slip ˌroad** UK (US **ramp**) *noun* [C] a short road that is used to drive onto or off a motorway (= wide, fast road)

**slit¹** /slɪt/ *noun* [C] a long, narrow cut or hole in something *Make a slit in the pastry to allow the steam to escape.*

**slit²** /slɪt/ *verb* [T] **slitting**, *past* **slit** to make a long, narrow cut in something *She slit her wrists.*

**slither** /'slɪðəʳ/ *verb* [I] to move smoothly by twisting and sliding

**sliver** /'slɪvəʳ/ *noun* [C] a thin piece of something that has come off a larger piece *slivers of glass*

**slob** /slɒb/ *noun* [C] *informal* a lazy or dirty person

**slog¹** /slɒg/ *verb* **slogging**, *past* **slogged** *informal* **slog up/down/through, etc** to move forward with difficulty *We slogged up the hill in silence.*

**slog away** *informal* to work very hard for a long time *I've been slogging away at this for hours and I'm exhausted.*

**slog²** /slɒg/ *noun* [U, no plural] *UK informal* a period of hard work *Studying for all the exams was a hard slog.*

**slogan** /'sləʊgən/ *noun* [C] a short phrase that is easy to remember and is used to make people notice something *an advertising slogan*

**slop** /slɒp/ *verb* **slopping**, *past* **slopped slop (sth) about/around/into, etc** If liquid slops about, it moves around or over the edge of its container, and if you slop it about, you make it move around or over the edge of its container. *Her hand shook, making her tea slop into the saucer.*

**slope¹** /sləʊp/ *noun* [C] a surface or piece of land that is high at one end and low at the other *There's a steep slope to climb before we're at the top.* ➔ *See also:* **a slippery** slope.

**slope²** /sləʊp/ *verb* [I] to be high at one end and low at the other *The field slopes down to the river.*

**sloppy** /'slɒpi/ *adj* **1** CARELESS not done carefully *His work was sloppy and full of spelling mistakes.* **2** CLOTHES Sloppy clothes are loose and untidy. *a girl wearing a sloppy sweater and torn jeans* **3** TOO WET A sloppy substance has too much liquid in it. • **sloppily** *adv* • **sloppiness** *noun* [U]

**slosh** /slɒʃ/ *verb* **slosh against/over/around, etc** If liquid sloshes, it moves against or over the edge of its container. *Water sloshed over the edge of the pool as the swimmers dived in.*

**sloshed** /slɒʃt/ *adj informal* drunk

**slot¹** /slɒt/ *noun* [C] **1** a long, narrow hole that you put something into, especially money **2** a period of time that you allow for something in a plan *The programme is being moved to a later slot.*

**slot²** /slɒt/ *verb* [I, T] **slotting**, *past* **slotted** to fit into a slot, or to make something fit into a slot **slot sb/sth in** to find time for someone or something in a period of time that has already been planned *Dr O'Neil can slot you in around 9.30.*

**sloth** /sləʊθ/ *noun* **1** [C] an animal that moves very slowly and lives in Central and South America **2** [U] *literary* when someone is lazy

**'slot maˌchine** *noun* [C] a machine that you put money into in order to try to win money

**slouch¹** /slaʊtʃ/ *verb* [I] to stand, sit, or walk with your shoulders forward so that your body is not straight *Stop slouching and stand up straight.*

slouch

**slouch²** /slaʊtʃ/ *noun* **1** [no plural] the position your body is in when you slouch **2 be no slouch** *informal* to work very hard and be good at something *He's no slouch when it comes to cooking.*

**slovenly** /'slʌv(ə)nli/ *adj* lazy, untidy, and dirty *slovenly habits* • **slovenliness** *noun* [U]

**o— slow¹** /sləʊ/ *adj* **1** NOT FAST moving, happening, or doing something without much speed *I'm making slow progress with the painting.* • *He's a very slow reader.* **2 be slow to do sth; be slow in doing sth** to take a long time to do something *The government has been slow to react to the problem.* • *The ambulance was very slow in coming.* **3** CLOCK If a clock is slow, it shows a time that is earlier than the correct time. **4** BUSINESS If business is slow, there are few customers. **5** NOT CLEVER not quick at learning and understanding things **6** NOT EXCITING not exciting *I find his films very slow.*

**slow²** /sləʊ/ *verb* [I, T] to become slower or to make something become slower *The car slowed to a halt* (= moved more and more slowly until it stopped).

**slow (sth) down** to become slower or to make something become slower *Slow down, Claire, you're walking too fast!* • *High interest rates have slowed down the rise in house prices.*

**slow down** If someone slows down, they become less active. *The doctor told me I should slow down and not work so hard.*

**slowdown** /ˈsləʊdaʊn/ *noun* [C] when business activity becomes slower *an economic slowdown*
• *The figures show a slowdown in retail sales.*

○━**slowly** /ˈsləʊli/ *adv* at a slow speed *Could you speak more slowly, please?*

ˌ**slow ˈmotion** *noun* [U] a way of showing pictures from a film or television programme at a slower speed than normal *They showed a replay of the goal in slow motion.*

**sludge** /slʌdʒ/ *noun* [U] soft, wet soil, or a substance that looks like this

**slug**¹ /slʌg/ *noun* [C] **1** a small, soft creature with no legs, that moves slowly and eats plants ➲ *See picture at* **snail. 2** a small amount of a drink, especially an alcoholic drink *He took a slug of whisky from the bottle.*

**slug**² /slʌg/ *verb* [T] **slugging,** *past* **slugged** *informal* to hit someone with your fist (= closed hand)

**slug it out** *informal* to fight, argue, or compete with someone until one person wins *Sampras and Rafter slugged it out for a place in the final.*

**sluggish** /ˈslʌgɪʃ/ *adj* moving or working more slowly than usual *a sluggish economy* • *I felt really sluggish after lunch.*

**slum** /slʌm/ *noun* [C] a poor and crowded area of a city where the buildings are in a very bad condition *He grew up in the slums of Mexico City.* • *slum areas*

**slumber** /ˈslʌmbə/ *noun* [C, U] *literary* sleep *She lay down on the bed and fell into a deep slumber.*
• **slumber** *verb* [I] *literary*

ˈ**slumber ˌparty** *noun* [C] *US* a party when a group of children spend the night at one child's house

**slump**¹ /slʌmp/ *verb* **1** [I] If a price, value, or amount slumps, it goes down suddenly. *Sales have slumped by 50%.* **2 slump back/down/over,** *etc* to fall or sit down suddenly because you feel tired or weak *She slumped back in her chair, exhausted.*

**slump**² /slʌmp/ *noun* [C] **1** a sudden fall in prices or sales *a slump in world oil prices* **2** a period when there is very little business activity and not many jobs *It's been the worst economic slump for 25 years.*

**slung** /slʌŋ/ *past of* sling

**slunk** /slʌŋk/ *past of* slink

**slur**¹ /slɜːʳ/ *verb* [I, T] **slurring,** *past* **slurred** to speak without separating your words clearly, often because you are tired or drunk *He'd drunk too much and was slurring his words.*

**slur**² /slɜːʳ/ *noun* [C] a criticism that will make people have a bad opinion of someone or something *a racial slur* • *She regarded it as a slur on her character.*

**slurp** /slɜːp/ *verb* [I, T] *informal* to drink in a noisy way *He slurped his tea.* • **slurp** *noun* [C] *informal*

**slush** /slʌʃ/ *noun* [U] snow that has started to melt

**sly** /slaɪ/ *adj* **slyer, slyest 1** deceiving people in a clever way to get what you want **2 sly smile** a smile that shows you know something that other people do not *"I know why Chris didn't come home yesterday," she said with a sly smile.*
• **slyly** *adv*

**smack**¹ /smæk/ *verb* **1** [T] to hit someone with

the flat, inside part of your hand *Do you think it's right to smack children when they're naughty?* **2 smack sth against/onto/down, etc** to hit something hard against something else *Ray smacked the ball into the net.*

**smack of sth** If something smacks of an unpleasant quality, it seems to have that quality. *a policy that smacks of racism*

**smack**² /smæk/ *noun* [C] a hit with the flat, inside part of your hand *Stop shouting or I'll give you a smack !*

**smack**³ /smæk/ *informal* (*also UK* ˈ**smack ˌbang**) (*also US* ˌ**smack ˈdab**) *adv* **1** exactly in a particular place *She lives smack in the middle of Edinburgh.* **2** suddenly and with a lot of force *He braked too late and ran smack into the car in front.*

○━**small** /smɔːl/ *adj* **1** [LITTLE] little in size or amount *They live in a small apartment near Times Square.* • *We teach the children in small groups.* **2** [YOUNG] A small child is very young. *a woman with three small children* **3** [NOT IMPORTANT] not important or serious *a small mistake* • *Jenny's got a small part in the school play.* **4 feel small** to feel stupid or unimportant *Simon was always trying to make me feel small.*

**USAGE**

**small** or **little**?

Small refers to size and is the usual opposite of 'big' or 'large'.

*Could I have a hamburger and a small Coke please?*

*Our house is quite small.*

Little refers to size but also expresses the speaker's feelings. For example, it can suggest that the speaker likes or dislikes something.

*They live in a beautiful little village.*

*Rats are horrible little animals.*

The comparative and superlative forms of **little** are not usually used in British English. Use **smaller** or **smallest** instead.

*My car is smaller than yours.*

~~My car is littler than yours.~~

**small**² /smɔːl/ *adv* in a small size *Emma knitted the sweater far too small.*

ˌ**small ˈchange** *noun* [U] coins that have little value

ˈ**small ˌfry** *noun* [U] *informal* people or activities that are not considered important *Compared to companies that size we're just small fry.*

ˌ**small ˈprint** *noun* [U] the part of a written agreement that is printed smaller than the rest and that contains important information *Make sure you read the small print before you sign.*

**small-scale** /ˌsmɔːlˈskeɪl/ *adj* A small-scale activity or organization is not big and involves few people.

ˈ**small ˌtalk** *noun* [U] polite conversation between people at social events *He's not very good at making small talk.*

**small-time** /'smɔːl,taɪm/ *adj* [always before noun] *informal* not important or successful *a small-time criminal*

**smart**[1] /smɑːt/ *adj* **1** INTELLIGENT intelligent *Rachel's one of the smartest kids in the class.* **2** TIDY If you look smart or your clothes are smart, you look clean and tidy. *a smart, blue suit* • *I need to look a bit smarter for my interview.* **3** FASHIONABLE fashionable and expensive *a smart, new restaurant* • *smart riverside apartments* **4** MACHINE/WEAPON A smart machine, weapon, etc uses computers to make it work. *smart bombs* • **smartly** *adv*

**smart**[2] /smɑːt/ *verb* [I] **1** to feel upset because someone has said or done something unpleasant to you *The team are still smarting from last week's defeat.* **2** If part of your body smarts, it hurts with a sharp, burning pain. *The smoke from the fire made her eyes smart.*

'**smart ,card** *noun* [C] a small, plastic card that contains a very small computer and can be used to pay for things or to store personal information

**smarten** /'smɑːt³n/ *verb*
**smarten (sb/sth) up** to make a person or place look more clean and tidy *plans to smarten up the city centre*

**smash**[1] /smæʃ/ *verb* **1** [I, T] to break into a lot of pieces with a loud noise, or to make something break into a lot of pieces with a loud noise *Thieves smashed the shop window and stole $50,000 worth of computer equipment.* **2 smash (sth) against/into/through, etc** to hit a hard object or surface with a lot of force, or to make something do this *The car skidded and smashed into a tree.* • *He smashed the glass against the wall.* **3** [T] to destroy a political or criminal organization *attempts to smash a drug smuggling ring* **smash sth up** to damage or destroy something *They were arrested for smashing up a hotel bar.*

**smash**[2] /smæʃ/ (*also* ,**smash 'hit**) *noun* [C] a very successful film, song, play, etc *the smash hit movie 'Titanic'*

**smashing** /'smæʃɪŋ/ *adj UK old-fashioned* extremely good or attractive *We had a smashing time at Bob and Vera's party.*

**smear**[1] /smɪəʳ/ *verb* [T] **1** to spread a thick liquid or sticky substance over something *His shirt was smeared with paint.* • *He smeared sun cream over his face and neck.* **2** to say unpleasant and untrue things about someone in order to harm them, especially in politics

**smear**[2] /smɪəʳ/ *noun* [C] **1** a dirty mark *There was a smear of oil on his cheek.* **2** an unpleasant and untrue story about someone that is meant to harm them, especially in politics *She dismissed the story as a smear.* • *a smear campaign*

o—**smell**[1] /smel/ *verb past* **smelled** (*also UK*) **smelt**
**1 smell of/like; smell delicious/horrible, etc** to have a particular quality that people notice by using their nose *I've been cooking, so my hands smell of garlic.* • *That soup smells delicious – what's in it?* **2** NOTICE [T] to notice something by using your nose *I think I can smell something burning.* **3** UNPLEASANT [I] to have an unpleasant smell *Your running shoes really smell!* **4** PUT YOUR NOSE NEAR [T] to put your nose near something and breathe in so that you can notice its smell *Come and smell these flowers.* **5** ABILITY [I] to have the ability to notice smells *Dogs can smell much better than humans.*

o—**smell**[2] /smel/ *noun* **1** QUALITY [C] the quality that something has which you notice by using your nose *The smell of roses filled the room.* • *There was a delicious smell coming from the kitchen.* **2** UNPLEASANT [C] an unpleasant smell *I wish I could get rid of that smell in the bathroom.* **3** ABILITY [U] the ability to notice smells *Smoking can affect your sense of smell.*

**smelly** /'smeli/ *adj* having an unpleasant smell *smelly feet*

**smelt** /smelt/ *UK past of* smell

o—**smile**[1] /smaɪl/ *verb* [I] to make a happy or friendly expression in which the corners of your mouth curve up *She smiled at me.*

### USAGE

**smile at** someone/something

Be careful to choose the right preposition after the verb smile.

She smiled at *the little girl.*

~~She smiled to the little girl.~~

o—**smile**[2] /smaɪl/ *noun* [C] a happy or friendly expression in which the corners of your mouth curve up *He gave me a big smile and wished me good luck.* • *"I passed my driving test," she said with a smile.*

**smiley** /'smaɪli/ *noun* [C] an image such as :-) which looks like a face when you look at it from the side, made using keyboard symbols and used in emails to express emotions

**smirk** /smɜːk/ *verb* [I] to smile in an annoying or unkind way *What are you smirking at?* • **smirk** *noun* [C]

**smitten** /'smɪt³n/ *adj* [never before noun] loving someone or liking something very much *He's absolutely smitten with this Carla woman.*

**smog** /smɒg/ *noun* [U] air pollution in a city that is a mixture of smoke, gases, and chemicals

o—**smoke**[1] /sməʊk/ *noun* **1** [U] the grey or black gas that is produced when something burns **2** [no plural] when someone smokes a cigarette *I'm just going outside for a smoke.*

o—**smoke**[2] /sməʊk/ *verb* **1** CIGARETTE [I, T] to breathe smoke into your mouth from a cigarette *Do you mind if I smoke?* • *She smokes thirty cigarettes a day.* **2** MEAT/FISH [T] to give meat or fish a special taste by hanging it over burning wood *smoked ham/salmon* **3** PRODUCE SMOKE [I] to produce or send out smoke *smoking chimneys* ➔ *See also:* **chain-smoke**.

**smoker** /'sməʊkəʳ/ noun [C] someone who smokes cigarettes regularly *He used to be a* **heavy smoker** (= someone who smokes a lot). ⊃ *Opposite* **non-smoker**.

**smoking** /'sməʊkɪŋ/ noun [U] when someone smokes a cigarette or regularly smokes cigarettes *The new law will restrict smoking in public places.* ⊃ *See also:* **passive smoking**.

**smoky** /'sməʊki/ adj **1** filled with smoke *a smoky bar/room* **2** having the smell, taste, or appearance of smoke *That ham has a delicious, smoky flavour.*

**smolder** /'sməʊldəʳ/ verb [I] *US spelling of* smoulder

◦⊸**smooth¹** /smuːð/ adj **1** SURFACE having a regular surface that has no holes or lumps in it *soft, smooth skin* • *a smooth wooden table* **2** SUBSTANCE A substance that is smooth has no lumps in it. *Mix the butter and sugar together until smooth.* **3** MOVEMENT happening without any sudden movements or changes *The plane made a smooth landing.* **4** PROCESS happening without problems or difficulties *Her job is to help students make a smooth transition from high school to college.* **5** PERSON too polite and confident in a way that people do not trust *a smooth salesman* • smoothness noun [U] ⊃ *See also:* take the **rough²** with the smooth.

**smooth²** /smuːð/ (*also* **smooth down/out, etc**) verb [T] to move your hands across something in order to make it flat *He straightened his tie and smoothed down his hair.*

**smooth sth over** to make a disagreement or problem seem less serious, especially by talking to the people involved in it *Would you like me to smooth things over between you and Nick?*

**smoothly** /'smuːðli/ adv **1** **go smoothly** to happen without any problems or difficulties *Everything was going smoothly until Darren arrived.* **2** without any sudden movements or changes *The car accelerated smoothly.*

**smother** /'smʌðəʳ/ verb [T] **1** KILL to kill someone by covering their face with something so that they cannot breathe **2** LOVE to give someone too much love and attention so that they feel they have lost their freedom *I try not to smother him.* **3** PREVENT to prevent something from happening *I tried to smother my cough.* **4** FIRE to make a fire stop burning by covering it with something

**smother sth in/with sth** to cover something completely with a substance *She took a slice of chocolate cake and smothered it in cream.*

**smoulder** UK (*US* **smolder**) /'sməʊldəʳ/ verb [I] **1** to burn slowly, producing smoke but no flames *The fire was still smouldering the next morning.* • smouldering bonfire **2** to have a strong feeling, especially anger, but not express it *I could see he was smouldering with anger.*

**smudge¹** /smʌdʒ/ noun [C] a dirty mark *a smudge of ink*

**smudge²** /smʌdʒ/ verb [I, T] If ink, paint, etc smudges, or if it is smudged, it becomes dirty or not clear because someone has touched it. *Be careful you don't smudge the drawing.*

**smug** /smʌɡ/ adj too pleased with your skill or success in a way that annoys other people *a*

**smug smile** • smugly adv *"I've never lost a match yet," she said smugly.*

**smuggle** /'smʌɡl/ verb [T] to take something into or out of a place in an illegal or secret way *He was arrested for smuggling cocaine into Britain.* • smuggler noun [C] *drug smugglers* • smuggling noun [U]

**snack¹** /snæk/ noun [C] a small amount of food that you eat between meals *Do you want a quick snack before you go out?* • snack food

**snack²** /snæk/ verb [I] *informal* to eat a snack *I've been snacking on chocolate and biscuits all afternoon.*

**snag¹** /snæɡ/ noun [C] *informal* a problem or difficulty *I'd love to come – the only snag is I have to be home by 3 o'clock.*

**snag²** /snæɡ/ verb [T] **snagging**, *past* **snagged 1** If you snag something, it becomes stuck on a sharp object and tears. *I snagged my coat on the wire.* **2** *US informal* to get, catch, or win something *She managed to snag a seat in the front row.*

**snail** /sneɪl/ noun [C] **1** a small creature with a long, soft body and a round shell **2 at a snail's pace** very slowly *There was so much traffic that we were travelling at a snail's pace.*

snail

slug

**snail mail** noun [U] humorous informal letters or messages that are not sent by email but by post

**snake¹** /sneɪk/ noun [C] a long, thin creature with no legs that slides along the ground

**snake²** /sneɪk/ verb **snake across/around/ through, etc** to follow a route that has a lot of bends *The river snakes through some of the most spectacular countryside in France.*

**snap¹** /snæp/ verb **snapping**, *past* **snapped 1** BREAK [I, T] If something long and thin snaps, it breaks making a short, loud sound, and if you snap it, you break it, making a short, loud sound. *The twigs snapped as we walked on them.* • *She snapped the carrot in half* (= into two pieces). **2 snap (sth) open/shut/together, etc** to suddenly move to a particular position, making a short, loud noise, or to make something do this *She snapped the book shut.* • *The suitcase snapped open and everything fell out.* **3** SPEAK ANGRILY [I, T] to say something suddenly in an angry way *"I don't know what you mean," he snapped.* • *I was snapping at the children because I was tired.* **4** LOSE CONTROL [I] to suddenly be unable to control a strong feeling, especially anger *She asked me to do the work again and I just snapped.* **5** PHOTOGRAPH [T] *informal* to take a photograph of someone or something *Photographers snapped the Princess everywhere she went.* **6** ANIMAL [I] If an animal snaps, it tries to bite someone. *The dog was barking and snapping at my ankles.* ⊃ *See also:* snap your fingers (**finger¹**).

**snap out of sth** *informal* to force yourself to stop feeling sad, angry, upset etc *He's in a bad mood now but he'll soon snap out of it.*

**snap sth up** *informal* to buy or get something quickly because it is cheap or exactly what you want *The dress was perfect, so I snapped it up.*

**snap sb up** *informal* to immediately accept someone's offer to join your company or team because you want them very much *She was snapped up by a large law firm.*

**snap²** /snæp/ *noun* **1** [SOUND] [no plural] a sudden, short, loud sound like something breaking or closing *I heard a snap as I sat on the pencil.* **2** [PHOTOGRAPH] [C] *UK informal* (*UK/US* **snapshot**) a photograph *holiday snaps* **3** [FASTENING] [C] *US* (*UK* **popper**) a metal or plastic object made of two parts which fit together with a short, loud sound, used to fasten clothing **4** [GAME] [U] a card game in which you say "snap" when you see two cards that are the same **5 be a snap** *US informal* to be very easy *The French test was a snap.*

**snap³** /snæp/ *adj* **snap decision/judgment** A snap decision or judgment is made very quickly and without careful thought.

**snappy** /'snæpi/ *adj* **1** written or spoken in a short and interesting way *a snappy title* **2** Snappy clothes are fashionable. *a snappy new suit* **3 make it snappy** *informal* used to tell someone to hurry

**snapshot** /'snæpʃɒt/ *noun* [C] a photograph that you take quickly without thinking

**snare¹** /sneəʳ/ *noun* [C] a piece of equipment used to catch animals

**snare²** /sneəʳ/ *verb* [T] **1** to catch an animal using a snare **2** to trick someone so that they cannot escape from a situation *She's trying to snare a rich husband.*

**snarl** /snɑːl/ *verb* **1** [I, T] to speak angrily *"Go away!" he snarled.* • *She snarled at me.* **2** [I] If an animal snarls, it shows its teeth and makes an angry sound. • snarl *noun* [C]

**snatch¹** /snætʃ/ *verb* [T] **1** to take something or someone quickly and suddenly *Bill snatched the telephone from my hand.* • *The child was snatched from his bed.* **2** to do or get something quickly because you only have a short amount of time *I managed to snatch some lunch.*

**snatch²** /snætʃ/ *noun* [C] a short part of a conversation, song, etc that you hear *I keep hearing snatches of that song on the radio.*

**sneak¹** /sniːk/ *verb past* **sneaked** (*also US*) **snuck 1 sneak into/out/around, etc** to go somewhere quietly because you do not want anyone to hear you *I sneaked into his bedroom while he was asleep.* **2 sneak sth into/out of/through, etc** to take something somewhere without anyone seeing you *We tried to sneak the dog into the hotel.* **3 sneak a look/glance at sb/sth** to look at someone or something quickly and secretly *I sneaked a look at the answers.*

**sneak up** to move close to someone without them seeing or hearing you *Don't sneak up on me like that – you scared me!*

**sneak²** /sniːk/ *noun* [C] *informal UK* someone who you do not like because they tell people when someone else has done something bad

**sneaker** /'sniːkəʳ/ *US* (*UK* **trainer**) *noun* [C] a soft

sports shoe ⊃ *See colour picture* **Clothes** *on page Centre 5.*

**sneaking** /'sniːkɪŋ/ *adj* **1 have a sneaking feeling/suspicion** to think that something is true but not be sure [+ (that)] *I have a sneaking feeling that the English test is going to be very difficult.* **2 have a sneaking admiration/fondness for sb** *UK* to like someone secretly, especially when you do not want to

**sneaky** /'sniːki/ *adj* doing things in a secret and unfair way

**sneer** /snɪəʳ/ *verb* [I] to talk about, or look at someone or something in a way that shows you do not approve of them *Carlos sneered at my attempts to put the tent up.* • sneer *noun* [C]

**sneeze** /sniːz/ *verb* [I] When you sneeze, air suddenly comes out through your nose and mouth. *He had a cold and was sneezing a lot.* • sneeze *noun* [C]

**snicker** /'snɪkəʳ/ *US* (*UK* **snigger**) *verb* [I] to laugh quietly in a rude way • snicker *noun* [C]

**snide** /snaɪd/ *adj* A snide remark criticizes someone in an unpleasant way.

**sniff** /snɪf/ *verb* **1** [I] to breathe air in through your nose in a way that makes a noise *Sam had a cold and she kept sniffing.* **2** [I, T] to breathe air in through your nose in order to smell something *She sniffed the flowers.* • sniff *noun* [C]

**snigger** /'snɪɡəʳ/ *UK* (*US* **snicker**) *verb* [I] to laugh quietly in a rude way *The boys were sniggering at the teacher.* • snigger *noun* [C]

**snip¹** /snɪp/ *verb* [I, T] **snipping**, *past* **snipped** to cut something using scissors (= tool with two flat blades) with quick, small cuts *She snipped the article out of the magazine.*

**snip²** /snɪp/ *noun* **1** a small, quick cut with scissors (= tool with two flat blades) **2 be a snip** *UK informal* to be very cheap

**snipe** /snaɪp/ *verb* [I] **1** to criticize someone in an unpleasant way *I hate the way politicians snipe at each other.* **2** to shoot people from a place that they cannot see *Rebels were indiscriminately sniping at civilians.* • sniping *noun* [U]

**sniper** /'snaɪpəʳ/ *noun* [C] someone who shoots at people from a place they cannot see

**snippet** /'snɪpɪt/ *noun* [C] a small piece of information, news, conversation, etc *I kept hearing snippets of conversation.*

**snob** /snɒb/ *noun* [C] someone who thinks they are better than other people because they are in a higher social position • snobbery /'snɒbʳri/ *noun* [U] behaviour and opinions that are typical of a snob

**snobbish** /'snɒbɪʃ/ (*also* **snobby**) *adj* like a snob *a snobbish attitude*

**snog** /snɒɡ/ *verb* [I, T] **snogging**, *past* **snogged** *UK informal* If two people snog, they kiss each other for a long time. • snog *noun* [C] *UK informal*

**snooker** /'snuːkəʳ/ *noun* [U] a game in which two people use long sticks to hit coloured balls into holes at the edge of a table

**snoop** /snuːp/ *verb* [I] to look around a place secretly in order to find out information about someone *I found her snooping around in my bedroom.* • snoop *noun* [no plural]

**snooty** /'snuːti/ *adj* Someone who is snooty

behaves in an unfriendly way because they think they are better than other people.

**snooze** /snuːz/ *verb* [I] *informal* to sleep for a short time, especially during the day *Grandpa was snoozing in his chair.* • snooze *noun* [C] *informal Why don't you have a snooze?*

**snore** /snɔːʳ/ *verb* [I] to breathe in a very noisy way while you are sleeping *I couldn't sleep because my brother was snoring.* • snore *noun* [C]

**snorkel**¹ /'snɔːkəl/ *noun* [C] a tube that you use to help you breathe if you are swimming with your face under water

**snorkel**² /'snɔːkəl/ *verb* [I] (*UK*) **snorkelling**, *past* **snorkelled**, (*US*) **snorkeling**, *past* **snorkeled** to swim using a snorkel

**snort** /snɔːt/ *verb* [I, T] to breathe out noisily through your nose, especially to show that you are annoyed or think something is funny *"Stupid man!" he snorted.* • *Rosie started snorting with laughter.* • snort *noun* [C]

**snot** /snɒt/ *noun* [U] *informal* the thick liquid that is produced in your nose

**snout** /snaʊt/ *noun* [C] the long nose of some animals, such as pigs

o⟶**snow**¹ /snəʊ/ *noun* [U] soft white pieces of frozen water that fall from the sky when the weather is cold *children playing in the snow*

**snow**² /snəʊ/ *verb* If it snows, snow falls from the sky. *It snowed all day yesterday.* **2 be snowed in** to be unable to leave a place because there is too much snow *We were snowed in for two days.* **3 be snowed under** to have too much work *I'm snowed under with homework.*

**snowball**¹ /'snəʊbɔːl/ *noun* [C] a ball made from snow that children throw at each other

**snowball**² /'snəʊbɔːl/ *verb* [I] If a problem, idea, or situation snowballs, it quickly grows bigger or more important. *The whole business idea snowballed from one phone call.*

**snowboard** /'snəʊbɔːd/ *noun* [C] a large board that you stand on to move over snow ➋ *See colour picture* **Sports 1** *on page Centre 15.*

**snowboarding** /'snəʊbɔːdɪŋ/ *noun* [U] a sport in which you stand on a large board and move over snow • snowboarder *noun* [C] ➋ *See colour picture* **Sports 1** *on page Centre 15.*

**snowdrift** /'snəʊdrɪft/ *noun* [C] a deep pile of snow that the wind has blown

**snowdrop** /'snəʊdrɒp/ *noun* [C] a small, white flower that you can see at the end of winter

**snowfall** /'snəʊfɔːl/ *noun* [C, U] the snow that falls at one time, or the amount of snow that falls *a heavy snowfall* (= a lot of snow)

**snowflake** /'snəʊfleɪk/ *noun* [C] a small piece of snow that falls from the sky

**snowman** /'snəʊmæn/ *noun* [C] *plural* **snowmen** something that looks like a person and is made from snow *The kids made a snowman in the garden.*

**snowplough** *UK* (*US* **snowplow**) /'snəʊplaʊ/ *noun* [C] a vehicle used for moving snow off roads and railways

**snowstorm** /'snəʊstɔːm/ *noun* [C] a storm when a lot of snow falls

**snowy** /'snəʊi/ *adj* snowing or covered with snow *a cold, snowy day*

**Snr** *UK* (*UK/US* **Sr**) *written abbreviation for* senior (= the older of two men in a family with the same name) *Thomas Smith, Snr*

**snub** /snʌb/ *verb* [T] **snubbing**, *past* **snubbed** to be rude to someone, especially by not speaking to them • snub *noun* [C]

**snuck** /snʌk/ *US past of* sneak

**snuff**¹ /snʌf/ *noun* [U] tobacco powder that people breathe in through their noses, especially in the past

**snuff**² /snʌf/ *verb*
**snuff sth out 1** *informal* to suddenly end something *England's chances were snuffed out by three brilliant goals from the Italians.* **2** to stop a candle flame from burning by covering it or pressing it with your fingers

**snug** /snʌg/ *adj* **1** warm and comfortable *a snug little house* **2** Snug clothes fit tightly. *a pair of snug brown shoes* • snugly *adv*

**snuggle** /'snʌgl/ *verb* **snuggle up/down/into, etc** to move into a warm, comfortable position *I snuggled up to him on the sofa.*

o⟶**so**¹ /səʊ/ *adv* **1** VERY used before an adjective or adverb to emphasize what you are saying, especially when there is a particular result *I was so tired when I got home.* • *I love her so much.* • [+ (that)] *I was so upset that I couldn't speak.* **2** ANSWER used to give a short answer to a question to avoid repeating a phrase *"Is Ben coming to the party?" "I hope so."* **3** **so did we/so have I/so is mine, etc** used to say that someone else also does something or that the same thing is true about someone or something else *"We saw the new Star Trek movie last night." "Oh, so did we."* **4** GET ATTENTION used to get someone's attention when you are going to ask them a question or when you are going to start talking *So, when are you two going to get married?* **5** SHOW SOMETHING used with a movement of your hand to show someone how to do something or show them the size of something *The box was so big.* • *For this exercise, you have to put your hands like so.* **6** **so it is/so they are, etc** used to agree with something that you had not noticed before *"The cat's hiding under the chair." "So it is."* **7** **or so** used after a number or amount to show that it is not exact *"How many people were at the party?" "Fifty or so, I guess."* **8** **I told you so** used to say that you were right and that someone should have believed you **9** **So (what)?** used to say that you do not think something is important, especially in a rude way *"She might tell Emily." "So what?"* **10** **and so on/forth** used after a list of things to show that you could have added other similar things *She plays a lot of tennis and squash and so on.* **11** **so as (not) to do sth** used to give the reason for doing something *He went in very quietly so as not to wake the baby.* **12** **only so much/many** used to say that there are limits to something *There's only so much help you can give someone.* **13** **so much for...** *informal* used to say that something has not been useful or successful *"The computer's crashed again." "So much for new technology."*

o⟶**so**² /səʊ/ *conjunction* **1** used to say that something is the reason why something else happens *I was tired so I went to bed.* • *Greg had* *some money so he bought a bike.* **2 so (that)** in order to make something happen or be possible *He put his glasses on so that he could see the television better.* **3** used at the beginning of a sentence to connect it with something that was said or happened previously *So we're not going away this weekend after all?*

**so³** /səʊ/ *adj* **be so** to be correct or true *"Apparently, she's moving to Canada." " Is that so?"*

**soak** /səʊk/ *verb* [I, T] **1** If you soak something, or let it soak, you put it in a liquid for a period of time. *He left the pan in the sink to soak.* • *Soak the bread in the milk.* **2** If liquid soaks somewhere or soaks something, it makes something very wet. *The rain soaked my clothes.* • *The ink soaked through the paper onto the table.*
**soak sth up** If a dry substance soaks up a liquid, the liquid goes into the substance. *Fry the potatoes until they soak up all the oil.*

**soaked** /səʊkt/ *adj* completely wet *My shirt was soaked.*

**soaking** /'səʊkɪŋ/ *adj* completely wet *You're soaking – why didn't you take an umbrella?* • *The dog was soaking wet.*

**so-and-so** /'səʊəndsəʊ/ *noun* [C] **1** used to talk about someone or something without saying a particular name *It was the usual village news – so-and-so got married to so-and-so, and so-and-so's having a baby.* **2** *informal* someone who you do not like *He's a lazy so-and-so.*

o-**soap** /səʊp/ *noun* **1** [U] a substance that you use for washing *a bar of soap* • *soap powder* ➔ *See colour picture* **The Bathroom** *on page Centre 1.* **2** [C] (*also* '**soap** ,**opera**) a television programme about the lives of a group of people that is broadcast several times every week

**soapy** /'səʊpi/ *adj* containing soap, or covered with soap *soapy hands*

**soar** /sɔːʳ/ *verb* [I] **1** to increase to a high level very quickly *House prices have soared.* **2** to move quickly and smoothly in the sky, or to move quickly up into the sky *The birds were soaring high above.* • *soaring adj*

**sob** /sɒb/ *verb* [I] **sobbing**, *past* **sobbed** to cry in a noisy way • *sob noun* [C]

**sober¹** /'səʊbəʳ/ *adj* **1** NOT DRUNK Someone who is sober is not drunk. **2** SERIOUS Someone who is sober is serious and thinks a lot. *He was in a sober mood.* **3** NOT BRIGHT *UK* Clothes or colours that are sober are plain and not bright. *a sober, grey dress* • *soberly adv*

**sober²** /'səʊbəʳ/ *verb*
**sober (sb) up** to become less drunk or to make someone become less drunk *You'd better sober up before you go home.*

**sobering** /'səʊbərɪŋ/ *adj* making you feel serious *a sobering thought*

**so-called** /,səʊ'kɔːld/ *adj* [always before noun] used to show that you think a word that is used to describe someone or something is wrong *My so-called friend has stolen my girlfriend.*

**soccer** /'sɒkəʳ/ (*also UK* **football**) *noun* [U] a game in which two teams of eleven people kick a ball and try to score goals

**sociable** /'səʊʃəbl/ *adj* Someone who is sociable enjoys being with people and meeting new people.

o-**social** /'səʊʃəl/ *adj* **1** relating to society and the way people live *social problems* • *social and political changes* **2** relating to the things you do with other people for enjoyment when you are not working *I have a very good social life.* • *socially adv* ➔ *Compare* **anti-social**.

**socialism** /'səʊʃəlɪzəm/ *noun* [U] a political system in which the government owns important businesses and industries, and which allows the people to share the money and opportunities equally

**socialist** /'səʊʃəlɪst/ *noun* [C] someone who supports socialism • *socialist adj socialist principles*

**socialize** (*also UK* **-ise**) /'səʊʃəlaɪz/ *verb* [I] to spend time enjoying yourself with other people *The cafe is a place where students can socialize with teachers.*

,**social 'science** *noun* [C, U] the study of society and the way people live

,**social se'curity** *noun* [U] money that the government gives to people who are old, ill, or not working

'**social ,worker** *noun* [C] someone whose job is to help people who have problems because they are poor, old, have difficulties with their family, etc • *social work noun* [U]

o-**society** /sə'saɪəti/ *noun* **1** [C, U] a large group of people who live in the same country or area and have the same laws, traditions, etc *Unemployment is a problem for society.* • *The US is a multicultural society.* **2** [C] an organization for people who have the same interest or aim *the London Zoological Society* ➔ *See also:* **building society**.

**sociology** /,səʊʃi'ɒlədʒi/ *noun* [U] the study of society and the relationship between people in society • *sociologist* /,səʊʃi'ɒlədʒɪst/ *noun* [C] someone who studies sociology

**sociopath** /'səʊʃiəʊpæθ/ *noun* [C] someone who is completely unable to behave in a way that is acceptable to society

**sock** /sɒk/ *noun* [C] something that you wear on your foot inside your shoe [usually plural] *a pair of black socks* ➔ *See colour picture* **Clothes** *on page Centre 5.*

**socket** /'sɒkɪt/ *noun* [C] **1** the place on a wall where you connect electrical equipment to the electricity supply **2** a hollow place where one thing fits inside another thing *Your eyeball is in your eye socket.*

**soda** /'səʊdə/ *noun* **1** [U] (*also* '**soda** ,**water**) water with bubbles in it that you mix with other drinks **2** [C, U] *US* (*also* '**soda** ,**pop** *old-fashioned*) a sweet drink with bubbles *a can of soda*

**sodden** /'sɒdən/ *adj* extremely wet *Your shoes are sodden!*

**sodium** /'səʊdiəm/ *noun* [U] a chemical element that is found in salt and food *a low-sodium diet*

o-**sofa** /'səʊfə/ *noun* [C] a large, comfortable seat for more than one person ➔ *See colour picture* **The Living Room** *on page Centre 11.*

o-**soft** /sɒft/ *adj* **1** NOT HARD not hard, and easy to press *a soft cushion* • *Cook the onion until it's soft.* **2** SMOOTH smooth and pleasant to touch *soft hair/skin* **3** SOUND A soft sound is very quiet. *He spoke in a soft voice.* **4** COLOUR/LIGHT

A soft colour or light is not bright. *soft lilac paint* **5** PERSON too kind and not angry enough when someone does something wrong *The kids are naughty because she's too soft on them.* **6** DRUGS Soft drugs are illegal drugs that some people think are not dangerous. ● **softness** *noun* [U] ⊃ *See also:* have a soft **spot**¹ for sb.

**softball** /'sɒftbɔːl/ *noun* [U] a game that is like baseball but played with a larger and softer ball

,**soft 'drink** UK (US '**soft ,drink**) *noun* [C] a cold, sweet drink that does not have alcohol in it

**soften** /'sɒfⁿn/ *verb* [I, T] **1** to become softer or to make something become softer *Heat the butter until it softens.* **2** to become more gentle or to make someone or something become more gentle *Her voice softened.*

**softly** /'sɒftli/ *adv* in a quiet or gentle way *"Are you OK?" she said softly.*

,**soft 'option** *noun* [C] UK a choice that is easier than other choices *The cookery course is not a soft option.*

**soft-spoken** /,sɒft'spəʊkⁿn/ *adj* having a quiet, gentle voice *a small, soft-spoken man*

**software** /'sɒftweəʳ/ *noun* [U] programs that you use to make a computer do different things *educational software*

**soggy** /'sɒgi/ *adj* very wet and soft *soggy ground*

**soil**¹ /sɔɪl/ *noun* [C, U] the top layer of earth that plants grow in *clay/sandy soil*

**soil**² /sɔɪl/ *verb* [T] *formal* to make something dirty ● **soiled** *adj* dirty *soiled clothes*

**solace** /'sɒləs/ *noun* [U, no plural] *formal* comfort when you are feeling sad *Music was a great solace to me.*

**solar** /'səʊləʳ/ *adj* relating to, or involving the sun *a solar eclipse* ● *solar energy*

,**solar 'panel** *noun* [C] a piece of equipment that changes light from the sun into electricity

**the 'solar ,system** *noun* the sun and planets that move around it

**sold** /səʊld/ *past of* sell

o➜**soldier** /'səʊldʒəʳ/ *noun* [C] a member of an army

**sole**¹ /səʊl/ *adj* [always before noun] **1** only *the sole survivor* **2** not shared with anyone else *She has sole responsibility for the project.*

**sole**² /səʊl/ *noun* **1** FOOT [C] the bottom part of your foot that you walk on **2** SHOE [C] the part of a shoe that is under your foot **3** FISH [C, U] a small, flat fish that you can eat

**solely** /'səʊlli/ *adv* only, and not involving anyone or anything else *I bought it solely for that purpose.*

**solemn** /'sɒləm/ *adj* **1** serious or sad *solemn music* ● *Everyone looked very solemn.* **2** A solemn promise, warning, etc is serious and sincere. ● **solemnly** *adv* ● **solemnity** /sə'lemnəti/ *noun* [U]

**solicit** /sə'lɪsɪt/ *verb* **1** [T] *formal* to ask someone for money, information, or help *to solicit donations for a charity* **2** [I] to offer sex for money, usually in a public place

**soliciting** /sə'lɪsɪtɪŋ/ *noun* [U] when someone offers to have sex for money

**solicitor** /sə'lɪsɪtəʳ/ *noun* [C] in Britain, a lawyer who gives legal advice and help, and who works

in the lower courts of law ⊃ *See usage note at* **lawyer**.

o➜**solid**¹ /'sɒlɪd/ *adj* **1** HARD/FIRM hard and firm without holes or spaces, and not liquid or gas *solid ground* ● *solid food* **2** STRONG strong and not easily broken or damaged *solid furniture* **3** **solid gold/silver/wood, etc** gold/silver/wood, etc with nothing added *a solid silver bracelet* **4** TIME continuing for a period of time without stopping *The noise continued for two solid hours/two hours solid.* **5** INFORMATION [always before noun] Solid information, proof, etc is based on facts and you are certain that it is correct. *This provides solid evidence that he committed the crime.* **6** PERSON honest and able to be trusted ● **solidity** /sə'lɪdəti/ *noun* [U] ● **solidly** *adv*

**solid**² /'sɒlɪd/ *noun* [C] **1** a substance or object that is not a liquid or a gas **2** a shape that has length, width, and height, and is not flat

**solidarity** /,sɒlɪ'dærəti/ *noun* [U] agreement and support between people in a group who have similar aims or beliefs

**solidify** /sə'lɪdɪfaɪ/ *verb* [I] If a liquid solidifies, it becomes solid.

**solids** /'sɒlɪdz/ *noun* [plural] food that is not liquid *Three weeks after the operation he still couldn't eat solids.*

**solipsism** /'sɒlɪpsɪzⁿm/ *noun* [U] the belief that in life you can only really know yourself and your own experiences

**solitaire** /,sɒlɪ'teəʳ US 'sɒləteər/ US (UK **patience**) *noun* [U] a card game for one person

**solitary** /'sɒlɪtⁿri/ *adj* **1** A solitary person or thing is the only person or thing in a place. *a solitary figure/walker* **2** A solitary activity is done alone. *solitary walks*

,**solitary con'finement** *noun* [U] when a prisoner is kept in a room alone as a punishment *He was kept in solitary confinement for ten days.*

**solitude** /'sɒlɪtjuːd/ *noun* [U] being alone *He went upstairs to read the letter in solitude.*

**solo**¹ /'səʊləʊ/ *adj, adv* done alone by one person only *a solo performance* ● *to perform solo*

**solo**² /'səʊləʊ/ *noun* [C] a piece of music for one person or one instrument

**soloist** /'səʊləʊɪst/ *noun* [C] a musician who performs a solo

**solstice** /'sɒlstɪs/ *noun* [C] the longest day or the longest night of the year *the summer/winter solstice*

**soluble** /'sɒljəbl/ *adj* If a substance is soluble, it will dissolve in water. *soluble vitamins* ● *These tablets are soluble in water.*

o➜**solution** /sə'luːʃⁿn/ *noun* [C] **1** the answer to a problem *There's no easy solution to this problem.* **2** a liquid which a substance has been dissolved into

---

**USAGE**

**solution** to a problem

Be careful to choose the correct preposition after solution.

*This could be one solution to the problem.*

~~This could be one solution of the problem.~~

~~This could be one solution for the problem.~~

---

o━**solve** /sɒlv/ *verb* [T] to find the answer to something *to solve a problem* • *to solve a mystery/puzzle* • *Police are still no nearer to solving the crime.*

**solvent¹** /'sɒlvənt/ *noun* [C] a liquid which is used to dissolve other substances

**solvent²** /'sɒlvənt/ *adj* having enough money to pay your debts

**sombre** *UK* (*US* **somber**) /'sɒmbəʳ/ *adj* **1** sad and serious *a sombre expression/mood* **2** dark and without bright colours *a sombre colour/room*

o━**some¹** *strong form* /sʌm/ *weak form* /sʰm/ *pronoun, quantifier* **1** UNKNOWN AMOUNT used to refer to an amount of something without saying exactly how much or how many *You'll need a pair of scissors and some glue.* • *I can't eat all this chocolate, would you like some?* • *Could I have some more* (= an extra amount of) *paper, please?*

---

**USAGE**

**some** or **any**?

Be careful not to confuse these two words. **Any** is used in questions and negative sentences.

*Have you got any friends in America?*

*I haven't got any money.*

**Some** is used in positive sentences.

*I've got some friends in America.*

Sometimes **some** is used in questions, especially when the speaker thinks that the answer will be 'yes'.

*Have you got some money I could borrow?*

The same rules are true for 'something/anything' and 'someone/anyone'.

*I didn't see anyone I knew.*

*I saw someone I knew at the party.*

---

**2** NOT ALL used to refer to part of a larger amount or number of something and not all of it *In some cases it's possible to fix the problem right away.* • *Some of the children were frightened.* **3** UNKNOWN NAME used to refer to someone or something when you do not know the name of it or exact details about it *Some girl phoned for you, but she didn't leave a message.* **4** **some time/distance, etc** a large amount of time, distance, etc *I'm afraid it'll be some time before it's ready.*

**some²** *strong form* /sʌm/ *weak form* /sʰm/ *adv* used before a number to show that it is not the exact amount *He died some ten years ago.*

o━**somebody** /'sʌmbədi/ *pronoun* another word for **someone**

**someday** /'sʌmdeɪ/ *adv US* at an unknown time in the future *We plan to get married someday.* • *I know someday soon I'll have to make a decision.*

o━**somehow** /'sʌmhaʊ/ *adv* in a way which you do not know or do not understand *Don't worry, we'll fix it somehow.* • **Somehow or other** (= I do not know how) *they managed to get in.* • *Somehow he reminds me of my brother.*

o━**someone** /'sʌmwʌn/ (*also* **somebody**) *pronoun* **1** used to refer to a person when you do not

know who they are or when it is not important who they are *There's someone at the door.* • *Will someone please answer the phone?* **2 someone else** a different person *Sorry, I thought you were talking to someone else.*

**someplace** /'sʌmpleɪs/ *adv US* used to refer to a place when you do not know where it is or when it is not important where it is *They live someplace in the South.* • *If they don't like it here, they can go someplace else* (= to a different place).

**somersault** /'sʌməsɔːlt/ *noun* [C] when you roll your body forwards or backwards so that your feet go over your head and come back down to the ground again • **somersault** *verb* [I]

o━**something** /'sʌmθɪŋ/ *pronoun* **1** used to refer to a thing when you do not know what it is or when it is not important what it is *As soon as I walked in, I noticed that something was missing.* • *We know about the problem and we're trying to do something about it.* • *It's not something that will be easy to change.* • *There's something else* (= another thing) *I wanted to tell you.* **2 or something (like that)** used to show that what you have just said is only an example or you are not certain about it *Why don't you go to a movie or something?* **3 something like** similar to or approximately *He paid something like $2000 for his car.* **4 be something** *informal* to be a thing which is important, special, or useful *The President visiting our hotel – that would really be something.* • *It's not much but it's something* (= better than nothing). **5 something of a sth** used to describe a person or thing in a way which is partly true but not completely or exactly *It came as something of a surprise.* • *He has a reputation as something of a troublemaker.* **6 be/have something to do with sth/sb** to be related to something or a cause of something but not in a way which you know about or understand exactly *It might have something to do with the way it's made.*

**sometime** /'sʌmtaɪm/ *adv* used to refer to a time when you do not know exactly what it is or when it is not important what it is *sometime before June* • *sometime in the next couple of days/months* • *You must come over and visit sometime.*

o━**sometimes** /'sʌmtaɪmz/ *adv* on some occasions but not always or often *He does cook sometimes, but not very often.* • *Sometimes I feel like no one understands me.*

**somewhat** /'sʌmwɒt/ *adv formal* slightly *We were somewhat disappointed with the food.*

o━**somewhere** /'sʌmweəʳ/ *adv* **1** used to refer to a place when you do not know exactly where it is or when it is not important exactly where it is *They had difficulties finding somewhere to live.* • *He comes from somewhere near London.* • *Can you think of somewhere else* (= a different place) *we could go?* **2 somewhere around/between, etc** approximately *He earns somewhere around £50,000 a year.* **3 get somewhere** to achieve something or to make progress *Right, that's the printer working. Now we're getting somewhere!*

o━**son** /sʌn/ *noun* [C] your male child

S

**sonar** /'səʊnɑːr/ noun [U] a system, used especially on ships, which uses sound waves to find the position of things in the water

**sonata** /sə'nɑːtə/ noun [C] a piece of music written to be played on a piano or on another instrument and the piano together

⚬ᴹ **song** /sɒŋ/ noun [C] words that go with a short piece of music a folk/love song • to sing a song

**songwriter** /'sɒŋˌraɪtər/ noun [C] someone who writes songs

**sonic** /'sɒnɪk/ adj relating to sound

**son-in-law** /'sʌnɪnlɔː/ noun [C] plural sons-in-law your daughter's husband

**sonnet** /'sɒnɪt/ noun [C] a poem with 14 lines, written in a particular pattern Shakespeare's sonnets

⚬ᴹ **soon** /suːn/ adv **1** after a short period of time I've got to leave quite soon. • It's too soon to make a decision. • He joined the company soon after leaving college. **2 as soon as** at the same time or a very short time after As soon as I saw her, I knew there was something wrong. • They want it as soon as possible. **3 sooner or later** used to say that you do not know exactly when something will happen, but you are sure that it will happen Sooner or later they'll realize that it's not going to work. **4 would sooner** would prefer I'd sooner spend a bit more money than take chances with safety. **5 no sooner … than** used to show that something happens immediately after something else No sooner had we got home than the phone rang.

**soot** /sʊt/ noun [U] a black powder produced when coal, wood, etc is burnt

**soothe** /suːð/ verb [T] **1** to make something feel less painful I had a long, hot bath to soothe my aching muscles. **2** to make someone feel calm or less worried to soothe a crying baby • soothing adj making you feel calm or in less pain soothing music • a soothing effect/voice

**sophisticated** /sə'fɪstɪkeɪtɪd/ adj **1** well-educated and having experience of the world or knowledge of culture **2** A sophisticated machine or system is very advanced and works in a clever way. a sophisticated computer system • sophistication /sə,fɪstɪ'keɪʃən/ noun [U]

**sophomore** /'sɒfəmɔːr/ noun [C] US a student studying in the second year of a course at a US university or high school (= school for students aged 15 to 18)

**soprano** /sə'prɑːnəʊ/ noun [C] a female singer who sings the highest notes

**sordid** /'sɔːdɪd/ adj unpleasant, dirty, or immoral a sordid affair

**sore**[1] /sɔːr/ adj **1** painful, especially when touched a sore throat/knee • Her eyes were red and sore. **2 sore point/spot/subject** a subject which causes disagreement or makes people angry when it is discussed Money is a bit of a sore point with him at the moment. ➔ See also: stick/stand out like a sore **thumb**[1].

**sore**[2] /sɔːr/ noun [C] an area of skin which is red and painful because of an infection

**sorely** /'sɔːli/ adv formal very much to be sorely disappointed/tempted • He will be sorely missed by everyone.

**sorrow** /'sɒrəʊ/ noun [C, U] formal when someone feels very sad • sorrowful adj formal

⚬ᴹ **sorry** /'sɒri/ adj **1 (I'm) sorry** something that you say to be polite when you have done something wrong, or when you cannot agree with someone or accept something Sorry I'm late. • Oh, I'm sorry. I didn't see you there. • Tom, I'm so **sorry about** last night – it was all my fault. • I'm sorry, but I just don't think it's a good idea. **2** used to show sympathy or sadness for a person or situation I **feel sorry for** the children – it must be very hard for them. • I was **sorry to hear** about your brother's accident. • [+ (that)] I'm sorry that things didn't work out for you. **3 Sorry?** mainly UK used as a polite way to say that you did not hear what someone has just said Sorry? What was that? **4** used to say that you wish something in the past had not happened or had been different [+ (that)] I'm sorry that I ever met him. **5 a sorry sight/state/tale** a bad condition or situation Her car was in a sorry state after the accident.

⚬ᴹ **sort**[1] /sɔːt/ noun **1** [C] a type of something We both like the same **sort of** music. • What sort of shoes does she wear? • I'm going to have a salad of some sort. **2 all sorts of sth** many different types of something **3 sort of** informal used to describe a situation approximately It's a sort of pale orange colour. **4 (and) that sort of thing** informal used to show that what you have just said is only an example from a larger group of things They sell souvenirs, postcards, that sort of thing. **5 of sorts** informal used to describe something which is not a typical example He managed to make a curtain of sorts out of an old sheet.

⚬ᴹ **sort**[2] /sɔːt/ verb **1** [T] to arrange things into different groups or types or into an order They **sort** the paper **into** white and coloured for recycling. • The names are sorted alphabetically. **2 be sorted/get sth sorted** UK informal If something is sorted or you get something sorted, you successfully deal with it and find a solution or agreement. I think that's more or less sorted now. • Did you manage to get everything sorted?

**sort sth out** to successfully deal with something, such as a problem or difficult situation Have you sorted out your schedule yet?

**sort through sth** to look at a number of things to organize them or to find something I had the sad task of sorting through her papers after she died.

**so-so** /'səʊsəʊ/ adj informal not very good, but not bad "Are you feeling better today?" "So-so."

**soufflé** /'suːfleɪ ᴜˢ suːf'leɪ/ noun [C, U] a light food made by baking the white part of eggs chocolate/cheese soufflé

**sought** /sɔːt/ past of seek

**sought-after** /'sɔːtˌɑːftər/ adj wanted by lots of people, but difficult to get a house in a sought-after location

**soul** /səʊl/ noun **1** SPIRIT [C] the part of a person which is not their body, which some people believe continues to exist after they die **2** MUSIC [U] (also 'soul ,music) popular music which expresses deep feelings, originally performed by Black Americans **3** PERSON [C] informal a person I didn't see a soul when I went out. ➔ See also: **heart** and soul.

**soulful** /'səʊlfəl/ adj expressing deep feelings, often sadness soulful eyes

**soulless** /'səʊlləs/ adj without any interesting or attractive characteristics a soulless housing estate

**soul-searching** /'səʊl‚sɜ:tʃɪŋ/ noun [U] when you think very carefully about something to decide if it is the right thing to do After much soul-searching, he decided to leave his job.

o▪**sound**[1] /saʊnd/ noun 1 [C, U] something that you hear or that can be heard I could **hear** the **sounds** of the city through the open window. • She stood completely still, not **making a sound**. • Can you turn the sound up (= make a radio, television, etc louder)? 2 **the sound of sth** informal how something seems to be, from what you have been told or heard I like the sound of the beef in red wine sauce. • He's really enjoying college, **by the sound of it**.

o▪**sound**[2] /saʊnd/ verb 1 **sound good/interesting/strange, etc** to seem good/interesting/strange, etc, from what you have heard or read Your plans sound really interesting. 2 **sound like/as if/as though** to seem like something, from what you have heard or read That sounds like a really good idea. • I don't want to sound as if I'm trying to create extra problems. 3 **sound angry/happy/rude, etc** to seem angry/happy/rude, etc when you speak You don't sound too sure about it. 4 [I, T] to make a noise It looks and **sounds like** a real bird. • If the alarm sounds, you must leave the building immediately.

**sound**[3] /saʊnd/ adj good or safe and able to be trusted sound advice/judgment • The building is quite old, but still structurally sound. ⊃ Opposite **unsound**.

**sound**[4] /saʊnd/ adv **sound asleep** in a deep sleep

**soundbite** /'saʊndbaɪt/ noun [C] a short statement which is easy to remember, usually used by a politician to get attention on television, in newspapers, etc

**soundly** /'saʊndli/ adv 1 **sleep soundly** to sleep well 2 **soundly beaten/defeated** beaten/defeated easily and by a large amount

**soundtrack** /'saʊndtræk/ noun [C] the music used in a film

o▪**soup** /su:p/ noun [U] a hot, liquid food, made from vegetables, meat, or fish chicken/tomato soup ⊃ See colour picture **Food** on page Centre 7.

**sour**[1] /saʊər/ adj 1 having a sharp, sometimes unpleasant, taste or smell, like a lemon, and not sweet These plums are a bit sour. 2 very unfriendly or unpleasant Their relationship suddenly **turned sour**.

**sour**[2] /saʊər/ verb [T] to make something unpleasant or unfriendly This affair has soured relations between the two countries.

**source** /sɔ:s/ noun [C] 1 where something comes from a source of income/information • Oranges are a good **source of** vitamin C. 2 someone who gives information to the police, newspapers, etc

o▪**south, South** /saʊθ/ noun [U] 1 the direction that is on your right when you face towards the rising sun 2 **the south** the part of an area that is further towards the south than the rest • south adj the south side of the house • south adv towards the south Birds fly south in winter.

**southbound** /'saʊθbaʊnd/ adj going or leading towards the south

**southeast, Southeast** /‚saʊθ'i:st/ noun [U] 1 the direction between south and east 2 **the southeast** the southeast part of a country • southeast, Southeast adj, adv

**southeastern, Southeastern** /‚saʊθ'i:stən/ adj in or from the southeast

**southerly** /'sʌðəli/ adj 1 towards or in the south We continued in a southerly direction. 2 A southerly wind comes from the south.

**southern, Southern** /'sʌðən/ adj in or from the south part of an area the southern half of the country

**southerner, Southerner** /'sʌðənər/ noun [C] someone from the south part of a country

**southernmost** /'sʌðənməʊst/ adj The southernmost part of an area is the part furthest to the south.

**south-facing** /'saʊθ‚feɪsɪŋ/ adj [always before noun] positioned towards the south a south-facing garden/window

**the ‚South 'Pole** noun a point on the Earth's surface which is furthest south

**southward, southwards** /'saʊθwəd, 'saʊθwədz/ adv towards the south • southward adj a southward direction

**southwest, Southwest** /‚saʊθ'west/ noun [U] 1 the direction between south and west 2 **the southwest** the southwest part of the country • southwest, Southwest adj, adv

**southwestern, Southwestern** /‚saʊθ'westən/ adj in or from the southwest

**souvenir** /‚su:vən'ɪər/ noun [C] something which you buy or keep to remember a special event or holiday a souvenir shop • I kept the ticket as a **souvenir** of my trip.

**sovereign**[1] /'sɒvrɪn/ adj A sovereign country or state is completely independent. • sovereignty /'sɒvrənti/ noun [U] the power of a country to control its own government

**sovereign, Sovereign**[2] /'sɒvrɪn/ noun [C] formal a king or queen

**sow**[1] /səʊ/ verb [T] past t sowed, past p sown or **sowed** to put seeds into the ground to sow seeds/crops

**sow**[2] /saʊ/ noun [C] a female pig

**soya bean** /'sɔɪə‚bi:n/ UK (US **soybean** /'sɔɪbi:n/) noun [C] a bean used to produce oil, and which is used in many foods

**soy sauce** /‚sɔɪ'sɔ:s/ noun [U] a dark brown sauce made from soya beans, used in Chinese and Japanese cooking

**spa** /spɑ:/ noun [C] a place where people go to improve their health by exercising or by having baths in special water a health spa • a spa town

o▪**space**[1] /speɪs/ noun 1 [C, U] an empty area which is available to be used a parking space • We need more open spaces for children to play in. • There wasn't enough **space for** everyone. • [+ to do sth] We don't have the space to store it all. 2 [U] the area outside the Earth They plan to send another satellite into space. • space travel 3 **in the space of six weeks/three hours, etc** during a period of six weeks/three hours, etc It all happened in the space of 10 minutes. ⊃ See also: **breathing space, outer space**.

**space²** /speɪs/ *verb* [T] to arrange things so that there is some distance or time between them [often passive] *They will have to be spaced at least two metres apart.*

**spacecraft** /'speɪskrɑːft/ *noun* [C] *plural* **spacecraft** a vehicle which can travel outside the Earth and into space

**spaceship** /'speɪsʃɪp/ *noun* [C] a vehicle which can travel outside the Earth and into space, especially one which is carrying people

**spacious** /'speɪʃəs/ *adj* large and with a lot of space *a spacious apartment/office*

**spade** /speɪd/ *noun* [C] **1** a tool with a long handle and a flat, metal part at one end used for digging **2 spades** playing cards with black leaf shapes on them *the ace of spades*

**spaghetti** /spə'geti/ *noun* [U] long, thin pieces of pasta

**spam** /spæm/ *noun* [U] emails that you do not want, usually advertisements

**span** /spæn/ *noun* [C] **1** the period of time that something exists or happens *a short attention span* • *an average life span of seventy years* **2** the length of something from one end to the other *a wing span of five metres* • span *verb* [T] **spanning**, *past* **spanned** to exist or continue for a particular distance or length of time *Her acting career spanned almost forty years.*

**spaniel** /'spænjəl/ *noun* [C] a dog with long hair and long ears

**spank** /spæŋk/ *verb* [T] to hit someone, usually a child, on their bottom

**spanner** /'spænər/ *UK* (*US* **wrench**) *noun* [C] a tool with a round end that is used to turn nuts and bolts (= metal objects used to fasten things together) ➜ *See picture at* **tool**.

**spar** /spɑːr/ *verb* [I] **sparring**, *past* **sparred** to fight or argue with someone in a friendly way

o—•**spare¹** /speər/ *adj* **1** If something is spare, it is available to use, because it is extra and not being used. *a spare bedroom* • *spare cash* • *spare parts* **2 spare time** time when you are not working *I enjoy gardening in my spare time.*

**spare²** /speər/ *noun* [C] an extra thing which is not being used and which can be used instead of a part which is broken, lost, etc

**spare³** /speər/ *verb* **1** [T] to give time or money to someone *I have to go soon, but I can spare a few minutes.* • [+ two objects] *Can you spare me some change?* **2** [+ two objects] to prevent someone from having to experience something unpleasant [often passive] *I was spared the embarrassment of having to sing in front of everybody.* **3 to spare** If you have time, money, etc to spare, you have more than you need. *I arrived at the station with more than an hour to spare.* **4 spare no effort/expense, etc** to use a lot of effort/expense, etc to do something [+ to do sth] *We will spare no effort to find out who did this.* **5 spare sb's life** to not kill someone ➜ *See also:* spare a **thought¹** for sb.

**sparingly** /'speərɪŋli/ *adv* carefully using only a very small amount of something *to eat/drink sparingly* • **sparing** *adj*

**spark¹** /spɑːk/ *noun* [C] **1** [FIRE] a very small, bright piece of burning material *The fire was caused by a spark from a cigarette.*

**2** [ELECTRICITY] a small flash of light caused by electricity **3** [START] a small idea or event which causes something bigger to start *a spark of hope/inspiration*

**spark²** /spɑːk/ (*also* **spark off**) *verb* [T] to cause an argument, fight, etc to start happening *to spark a debate/protest* • *to spark criticism/fears*

**sparkle¹** /'spɑːkl/ *verb* [I] **1** to shine brightly because of reflected light *water sparkling in the sun* • *Her eyes sparkled with excitement.* **2** to do something in a special or exciting way *The concert gave her an opportunity to sparkle.*

**sparkle²** /'spɑːkl/ *noun* **1** [C, U] the light from something reflecting on a shiny surface **2** [U] the quality of being special or exciting *The performance lacked a bit of sparkle.*

**sparkling** /'spɑːklɪŋ/ *adj* **1** shining brightly because of reflected light **2** special or exciting *a sparkling performance* • *sparkling conversation* **3 sparkling water/wine** water/wine with bubbles in it

**'spark ,plug** *noun* [C] a part in an engine that makes the fuel burn

**sparrow** /'spærəʊ/ *noun* [C] a small, brown bird which is common in towns and cities

**sparse** /spɑːs/ *adj* **1** existing only in small amounts over a large area *sparse population/vegetation* **2** A room that is sparse contains little furniture and does not seem very comfortable. • **sparsely** *adv sparsely populated/furnished*

**spartan** /'spɑːtən/ *adj* very simple and not comfortable or luxurious *The rooms were clean but spartan.*

**spasm** /'spæzᵊm/ *noun* [C, U] when a muscle suddenly gets tight in a way that you cannot control *a back/muscle spasm* • *to go into spasm*

**spasmodic** /spæz'mɒdɪk/ *adj* happening suddenly for short periods of time and not in a regular way

**spat** /spæt/ *past of* spit

**spate** /speɪt/ *noun* **a spate of accidents/crimes/thefts, etc** a large number of bad things which happen at about the same time

**spatial** /'speɪʃᵊl/ *adj* relating to the position, area, and size of things • **spatially** *adv*

**spatter** /'spætər/ *verb* [T] to cover someone or something with small drops of liquid without intending to [often passive] *His shirt was spattered with blood.*

**spatula** /'spætjələ/ *noun* [C] a tool with a wide flat blade, used in cooking for mixing, spreading, or lifting food ➜ *See colour picture* **Kitchen** *on page Centre 10.*

**spawn** /spɔːn/ *verb* [T] to cause a lot of other things to be produced or to exist *Her death spawned several films and books.*

o—•**speak** /spiːk/ *verb* *past t* **spoke**, *past p* **spoken** **1** [I] to say something using your voice *to speak loudly/quietly* • *There was complete silence – nobody spoke.* **2 speak to sb** *mainly UK* (*mainly US* **speak with sb**) to talk to someone *Could I speak to Mr Davis, please?* • *Have you spoken with your new neighbors yet?* **3 speak about/of sth** to talk about something *He refused to speak about the matter in public.* • *In the interview she spoke of her sadness at her*

S

*mother's death.* **4 speak English/French/ German, etc** to be able to communicate in English/French/German, etc *Do you speak English?* • *He speaks very good French.* **5** [I] to make a speech to a large group of people *She was invited to speak at a conference in Madrid.* **6 speak for/on behalf of sb** to express the feelings, opinions, etc of another person or of a group of people *I've been chosen to speak on behalf of the whole class.* **7 generally/personally, etc speaking** used to explain that you are talking about something in a general/personal, etc way *Personally speaking, I don't like cats.* **8 so to speak** used to explain that the words you are using do not have their usual meaning ➔ *See also:* speak of the **devil**, speak your **mind**[1].

**speak** or **talk**?

Remember that you **speak** a language. You do not **talk** it.

*She speaks French.*

~~She talks French.~~

**speak out** to give your opinion about something in public, especially on a subject which you have strong feelings about *He decided to speak out against the bombing.*
**speak up 1** to say something in a louder voice so that people can hear you *Could you speak up a bit? I can't hear you.* **2** to give your opinion about something, especially about a problem or to support someone else *It's getting bad – it's time someone spoke up about it.*
**speaker** /'spiːkə<sup>r</sup>/ *noun* [C] **1** the part of a radio, CD player, etc which the sound comes out of ➔ *See colour picture* **The Living Room** *on page Centre 11.* **2 an English/French/German, etc speaker** someone who can speak English/French, etc **3** someone who makes a speech to a group of people *a guest speaker*
**spear** /spɪə<sup>r</sup>/ *noun* [C] a long weapon with a sharp point at one end used for hunting
**spearhead** /'spɪəhed/ *verb* [T] to lead an attack or series of actions *to spearhead a campaign*
**spearmint** /'spɪəmɪnt/ *noun* [U] a type of mint (= a herb used as a flavour for sweets) *spearmint chewing gum*
o--◄ **special**[1] /'speʃ<sup>ə</sup>l/ *adj* **1** better or more important than usual things *a special friend* • *I'm cooking something special for her birthday.* **2 special attention/care/treatment** treatment that is better than usual **3 special offer** *UK* a price which is lower than usual *I bought them because they were on special offer.* **4** different from normal things, or used for a particular purpose *You need to use a special kind of paint.* • *Some of the children have special educational needs.*
**special**[2] /'speʃ<sup>ə</sup>l/ *noun* [C] **1** a television programme made for a particular reason or occasion and not part of a series *The Christmas special had 24.3 million viewers.* **2** a dish in a restaurant which is not usually available *Today's specials are written on the board.*
**specialist** /'speʃ<sup>ə</sup>lɪst/ *noun* [C] someone who has

a lot of experience, knowledge, or skill in a particular subject *a cancer/software specialist* • *He's a specialist in childhood illnesses.* • *specialist advice/help*
**speciality** /ˌspeʃi'æləti/ *UK* (*US* **specialty** /'speʃ<sup>ə</sup>lti/) *noun* [C] a product, skill, etc that a person or place is especially known for *We tasted a local speciality made from goat's cheese.*
**specialize** (*also UK* **-ise**) /'speʃ<sup>ə</sup>laɪz/ *verb* [I] to spend most of your time studying one particular subject or doing one type of business *She works for a company specializing in business law.* • specialization /ˌspeʃ<sup>ə</sup>laɪ'zeɪʃ<sup>ə</sup>n/ *noun* [U]
**specialized** (*also UK* **-ised**) /'speʃ<sup>ə</sup>laɪzd/ *adj* relating to a particular subject or activity and not general *specialized equipment/language*
o--◄ **specially** /'speʃ<sup>ə</sup>li/ *adv* for a particular purpose *They searched the building with specially trained dogs.* • *I made this specially for you.*

**specially** or **especially**?

Sometimes these two words both mean 'for a particular purpose'.

*I cooked this meal specially/especially for you.*

**Specially** is often used before an adjective made from a past participle, e.g. specially prepared, specially trained.

*He uses a specially adapted wheelchair.*

**Especially** is used to give emphasis to a person or thing. This word is not usually used at the beginning of a sentence.

*I like all kinds of films, especially horror films.*

**species** /'spiːʃiːz/ *noun* [C] *plural* **species** a group of plants or animals which share similar characteristics *a rare species of bird* ➔ *See usage note at* **race**.
**specific** /spə'sɪfɪk/ *adj* **1** used to refer to a particular thing and not something general *a specific purpose/reason* • *Could we arrange a specific time to meet?* **2** exact or containing details *Could you be more specific about the problem?*
**specifically** /spə'sɪfɪk<sup>ə</sup>li/ *adv* **1** for a particular reason, purpose, etc *They're designed specifically for children.* • [+ to do sth] *She bought it specifically to wear at the wedding.* **2** exactly or in detail *I specifically told them that she doesn't eat meat.*
**specification** /ˌspesɪfɪ'keɪʃ<sup>ə</sup>n/ *noun* [C] *formal* a detailed description of how something should be done, made, etc *They are made exactly to the customer's specifications.*
**specifics** /spə'sɪfɪks/ *noun* [plural] exact details about something *I can't comment on the specifics of the case.*
**specify** /'spesɪfaɪ/ *verb* [T] to say or describe something in a detailed way [+ question word] *They didn't specify what colour they wanted.*
**specimen** /'spesəmɪn/ *noun* [C] **1** an animal, plant, etc used as an example of its type, especially for scientific study *This is one of the museum's finest specimens.* **2** a small amount of a substance, such as blood, that is used for a test

S

**speck** /spek/ *noun* [C] a very small spot or a very small amount of something *a speck of dirt/dust* • *I watched the car until it was just a tiny speck in the distance.*

**speckled** /'spekld/ *adj* covered in a pattern of very small spots *a speckled egg*

**specs** /speks/ *noun* [plural] *informal short for* spectacles

**spectacle** /'spektəkl/ *noun* [C] **1** an event that is exciting or unusual to watch **2 make a spectacle of yourself** to do something that makes you look stupid and that makes other people look at you *He got drunk and made a real spectacle of himself.*

**spectacles** /'spektəklz/ *noun* [plural] *old-fashioned* glasses *a pair of spectacles*

**spectacular** /spek'tækjələʳ/ *adj* extremely good, exciting, or surprising *a spectacular success* • *a spectacular view* • **spectacularly** *adv a spectacularly beautiful country*

**spectator** /spek'teɪtəʳ/ *noun* [C] someone who watches an event, sport, etc *They won 4–0 in front of over 40,000 cheering spectators.* • **spectate** /spek'teɪt/ *verb* [I] to watch an event, sport, etc

**spectre** UK (US **specter**) /'spektəʳ/ *noun* **1 the spectre of sth** the idea of something unpleasant that might happen in the future *This attack raises the spectre of a return to racial violence.* **2** [C] *literary* a ghost (= dead person's spirit)

**spectrum** /'spektrəm/ *noun* [C] *plural* **spectra** **1** all the different ideas, opinions, possibilities, etc that exist *He has support from across the whole political spectrum.* **2** the set of colours into which light can be separated

**speculate** /'spekjəleɪt/ *verb* [I, T] to guess possible answers to a question when you do not have enough information to be certain *The police refused to speculate about the cause of the accident.* • [+ that] *The newspapers have speculated that they will get married next year.*

**speculation** /ˌspekjə'leɪʃᵊn/ *noun* [U] when people guess about something without having enough information to be certain [+ that] *He has strongly denied speculation that he is planning to leave.*

**speculative** /'spekjələtɪv/ *adj* based on a guess and not on information *The article was dismissed as highly speculative.* • **speculatively** *adv*

**sped** /sped/ *past of* speed

O━**speech** /spiːtʃ/ *noun* **1** [U] someone's ability to talk, or an example of someone talking *His speech was very slow and difficult to understand.* • *These changes can be seen in both speech and writing.* **2** [C] a formal talk that someone gives to a group of people *I had to make a speech at my brother's wedding.* **3 free speech/freedom of speech** the right to say or write what you want ➔ *See also:* **figure of speech, reported speech.**

USAGE

**make/give a speech**

Be careful to choose the correct verb.

*I have to make a speech.*

~~I have to do a speech.~~

*He gave a speech at the conference.*

~~He said a speech at the conference.~~

**speechless** /'spiːtʃləs/ *adj* unable to speak because you are so angry, shocked, surprised, etc *I couldn't believe what he was telling me – I was speechless.*

O━**speed**¹ /spiːd/ *noun* **1** [C, U] how fast something moves or happens *high/low speed* • *He was travelling at a speed of 90 mph.* **2** [U] very fast movement *He put on a sudden burst of speed.* **3 up to speed** having all the most recent information about a subject or activity *The course should bring you up to speed with the latest techniques.*

**speed**² /spiːd/ *verb past* **sped** or **speeded** **1 speed along/down/past, etc** to move somewhere or happen very fast *The three men jumped into a car and sped away.* **2 be speeding** to be driving faster than you are allowed to **speed (sth) up** to move or happen faster, or to make something move or happen faster *Can you try to speed up a bit please?*

**speedboat** /'spiːdbəʊt/ *noun* [C] a small, fast boat with an engine

**speeding** /'spiːdɪŋ/ *noun* [U] driving faster than you are allowed to *They were stopped by the police for speeding.*

**'speed ˌlimit** *noun* [C] the fastest speed that a vehicle is allowed to travel on a particular road *to break the speed limit*

**speedometer** /spiː'dɒmɪtəʳ/ *noun* [C] a piece of equipment in a vehicle that shows how fast it is moving ➔ *See colour picture* **Car** *on page Centre 3.*

**speedy** /'spiːdi/ *adj* done quickly *a speedy decision/recovery* • **speedily** *adv*

O━**spell**¹ /spel/ *verb past* **spelled** (*also UK*) **spelt** **1** [T] to write down or tell someone the letters which are used to make a word *How do you spell that?* • *Her name's spelt S-I-A-N.* **2** [I] If you can spell, you know how to write the words of a language correctly. *My grammar's all right, but I can't spell.* **3 spell disaster/trouble, etc** If something spells disaster, trouble, etc, you think it will cause something bad to happen in the future. *The new regulations could spell disaster for small businesses.* **spell sth out** to explain something in a very clear way with details *They sent me a letter, spelling out the details of the agreement.*

**spell**² /spel/ *noun* [C] **1** a period of time *a short spell in Australia* • *a spell of dry weather* **2** a magic instruction *The witch cast a spell over him and he turned into a frog.*

**spelling** /'spelɪŋ/ *noun* **1** [C] how a particular word is spelt *Use a dictionary to check the spelling of difficult words.* • *There are two possible spellings of this word.* • *spelling mistakes* **2** [U] someone's ability to spell words *My spelling is terrible.*

**spelt** /spelt/ *UK past of* spell

O━**spend** /spend/ *verb* [T] *past* **spent** **1** to use money to buy or pay for something *The company has spent £1.9 million on improving its computer network.* • *She spends too much money on clothes.* • *How much did you spend?* **2** to use time doing something or being somewhere *He spent 18 months working on the project.* • *He's planning to* **spend** *some* **time** *at home with his family.* • *How long did you spend in Edinburgh?*

**spending** /'spendɪŋ/ *noun* [U] the money which is used for a particular purpose, especially by a government or organization *government spending on health* • *spending cuts*

**spent¹** /spent/ *adj* already used, so not useful or effective any more *spent bullets*

**spent²** /spent/ *past of* spend

**sperm** /spɜːm/ *noun* [C] *plural* **sperm** a small cell produced by a male animal which joins an egg from a female animal to create a baby

**spew** /spjuː/ (*also* **spew out**) *verb* [I, T] If something spews liquid or gas, or liquid or gas spews from something, it flows out in large amounts. *The factory spews out clouds of black smoke.*

**sphere** /sfɪəʳ/ *noun* [C] **1** a subject or area of knowledge, work, etc *the political sphere* **2** a round object shaped like a ball

**spice¹** /spaɪs/ *noun* **1** [C, U] a substance made from a plant, which is used to give a special taste to food *herbs and spices* **2** [U] something that makes something else more exciting *A scandal or two adds a little spice to office life.*

**spice²** /spaɪs/ *verb* [T] to add spice to something [often passive] *The apples were* **spiced with** *nutmeg and cinnamon.*

**spice sth up** to make something more interesting or exciting *You can always spice up a talk with a few pictures.*

**spicy** /'spaɪsi/ *adj* containing strong flavours from spice *spicy food* • *a spicy sauce*

**spider** /'spaɪdəʳ/ *noun* [C] an insect with eight long legs which catches insects in a web (= structure like a net)

**spidery** /'spaɪdəri/ *adj* thin and often untidy, looking like a spider *spidery handwriting*

**spike** /spaɪk/ *noun* [C] a long, thin piece of metal, wood, etc with a sharp point at one end • **spiky** *adj* covered with spikes or having that appearance *spiky hair* ➔ *See colour picture* **Hair** *on page Centre 9.*

○━ **spill** /spɪl/ *verb* [T] *past* **spilled** (*also UK*) **spilt** to pour liquid somewhere without intending to *Someone at the party spilled red wine on the carpet.* • spill *noun* [C] *an oil spill*

**spill out** to flow or fall out of a container *The contents of the truck spilled out across the road.* **2** If people spill out of a place, large numbers of them move out of it. *The crowd spilled out onto the street.*

**spill over** If a bad situation spills over, it begins to have an unpleasant effect on another situation or group of people. *There are fears that the war could spill over into neighbouring countries.*

○━ **spin¹** /spɪn/ *verb* [I, T] **spinning**, *past* **spun 1** If something spins or you spin something, it turns around and around quickly. *The car* **spun across** *the road.* **2** to make thread by twisting together cotton, wool, etc

**spin (sb) around/round** If you spin around, or someone spins you around, your body turns quickly to face the opposite direction. *She spun round to see what had happened.*

**spin sth out** to make something such as a story

or an activity last as long as possible

**spin²** /spɪn/ *noun* **1** TURN [C, U] the movement of something turning round very quickly *The skater did a series of amazing spins and jumps.* **2** IDEA [no plural] when an idea is expressed in a clever way that makes it seem better than it really is, especially in politics *This report* **puts** *a different* **spin on** *the issue.* **3** CAR [no plural] *informal* a short journey by car *Why don't you take it for a quick spin and see what you think?*

**spinach** /'spɪnɪtʃ/ *noun* [U] a vegetable with large, dark green leaves and a strong taste

**spinal** /'spaɪnəl/ *adj* relating to the spine *a spinal injury*

'**spin ,doctor** *noun* [C] *informal* someone whose job is to make ideas, events, etc seem better than they really are, especially in politics

**spine** /spaɪn/ *noun* [C] **1** the long structure of bones down the centre of your back, which supports your body **2** the narrow part of a book cover where the pages are joined together and which you can see when it is on a shelf

**spineless** /'spaɪnləs/ *adj* A spineless person has a weak personality and is frightened easily.

**spin-off** /'spɪnɒf/ *noun* [C] a product that develops from another more important product

**spinster** /'spɪnstəʳ/ *noun* [C] *old-fashioned* a woman who has never married

**spiral** /'spaɪərəl/ *noun* [C] **1** a shape made by a curve turning around and around a central point *a spiral staircase* **2 a downward spiral** a situation which is getting worse very quickly, and which is difficult to control

**spire** /spaɪəʳ/ *noun* [C] a tall, pointed tower on the top of a building such as a church

**spirit¹** /'spɪrɪt/ *noun* **1** FEELING [no plural] the way people think and feel about something *a spirit of optimism* • *Everyone soon* **got into the spirit of** (= started to enjoy) *the carnival – singing, dancing, and having fun.* **2 community/team, etc spirit** when you feel enthusiasm about being part of a group **3 in good/high/low spirits** feeling good/excited/ unhappy **4** NOT BODY [C] the part of a person which is not their body, which some people believe continues to exist after they die **5** NOT ALIVE [C] something which people believe exists but does not have a physical body, such as a ghost *evil spirits* **6** the spirit of the law/an agreement, etc the intended meaning of the law/an agreement, etc and not just the written details **7** DRINK [C] a strong alcoholic drink, such as whisky or vodka [usually plural] *I don't often drink spirits.*

**spirit²** /'spɪrɪt/ *verb* **be spirited away/out/to, etc** to be moved somewhere secretly *He was spirited away to a secret hide-out in Mexico.*

**spirited** /'spɪrɪtɪd/ *adj* enthusiastic and determined, often in a difficult situation *a spirited performance*

**spiritual** /'spɪrɪtʃuəl/ *adj* relating to deep feelings and beliefs, especially religious beliefs *a spiritual leader*

**spiritualism** /'spɪrɪtʃuəlɪzəm/ *noun* [U] the belief that living people can communicate with people who are dead • **spiritualist** *noun* [C] someone who is involved with spiritualism

**spit**[1] /spɪt/ *verb* [I, T] **spitting**, *past* **spat** *(also US)* **spit** **1** to force out the liquid in your mouth *I don't like to see people spitting in public.* • *He took a mouthful of coffee and then spat it out.* **2 Spit it out!** *informal* used to tell someone to say more quickly what it is they want to say *Come on, spit it out!*

**spit**[2] /spɪt/ *noun* **1** [U] *informal* the liquid that is made in your mouth **2** [C] a long, thin stick used for cooking meat over a fire

**spite** /spaɪt/ *noun* **1 in spite of sth** although something exists or happens *He still smokes, in spite of all the health warnings.* • *In spite of a bad storm, the plane landed safely.* **2** [U] a feeling of anger towards someone which makes you want to hurt or upset them *He hid my new jacket out of spite.*

**spiteful** /'spaɪtfəl/ *adj* intentionally hurting or upsetting someone *That was a very spiteful thing to do.* • **spitefully** *adv*

**splash**[1] /splæʃ/ *verb* [I, T] **1** If a liquid splashes or you splash a liquid, drops of it hit or fall on something. *The paint splashed onto his new shirt.* • *She splashed some cold water on her face.* **2 splash about/around/through, etc** to move in water so that drops of it go in all directions *The children splashed about in the puddles.* **3 be splashed across/all over sth** to be the main story in a newspaper, usually on the front page, which many people will see *His picture was splashed across the front pages of all the newspapers the next morning.*

**splash out (sth)** *UK* to spend a lot of money on something which you want but do not need *He splashed out on the best champagne for the party.* • *They splashed out over a thousand pounds on a new kitchen.*

**splash**[2] /splæʃ/ *noun* [C] **1** a drop of liquid which has fallen on something, or the mark made by it *There were several small splashes of paint on the carpet.* • *Add a splash of lemon juice.* **2** the sound of something falling into or moving in water *They sat listening to the splash of raindrops on the lake.* **3 a splash of colour** a small area of colour which makes something look brighter *The flowers added a splash of colour to the room.* **4 make a splash** *informal* to get a lot of public attention *The film made quite a splash in the US.*

**splatter** /'splætə[r]/ *verb* [I, T] If a liquid splatters or you splatter it, it falls onto a surface, often in many small drops. [often passive] *His clothes were splattered with blood.*

**splendid** /'splendɪd/ *adj* very good or very beautiful, special, etc *a splendid idea* • *a splendid view* • **splendidly** *adv*

**splendour** *UK* (*US* **splendor**) /'splendə[r]/ *noun* [C, U] when something is extremely beautiful or luxurious *Tourists marvelled at the splendour of the medieval cathedral.*

**splinter** /'splɪntə[r]/ *noun* [C] **1** a small, sharp piece of wood, glass, etc which has broken from a large piece *I've got a splinter in my finger.* **2 a splinter group** a small group of people that forms after leaving a larger organization, such as a political party • **splinter** *verb* [I] to break into small, sharp pieces

○ **split**[1] /splɪt/ *verb* **splitting**, *past* **split** **1** [BREAK] [I,

T] If something splits or if you split it, it tears so that there is a long, thin hole in it. *He split his trousers when he bent over.* • *Her shoes were splitting apart at the sides.* **2** [DIVIDE] [I, T] (*also* **split up**) to divide into smaller parts or groups, or to divide something into smaller parts or groups *The children split up into three groups.* **3** [SHARE] [T] to share something by dividing it into smaller parts *The cost of the wedding will be split between the two families.* **4** [DISAGREE] [I, T] If a group of people splits, or something splits them, they disagree and form smaller groups. *This issue could split the Conservative Party.* • [often passive] *The government is split on the issue of hunting.* ⊃ *See also:* split hairs (**hair**).

**split up** If two people split up, they end their relationship. *She split up with her boyfriend.*

**split**[2] /splɪt/ *noun* [C] **1** a long, thin hole in something where it has broken apart *There's a split in my trousers.* **2** when a group of people divides into smaller groups because they disagree about something *This issue is likely to cause a major split in the party.*

**split**[3] /splɪt/ *adj* **a split second** a very short period of time *It was all over in a split second.* • *a split second decision*

**,splitting 'headache** *noun* [C] a very bad pain in your head *I've got a splitting headache.*

**splurge** /splɜːdʒ/ *verb* [I, T] to spend a lot of money on something which you want but do not need *We could either save the money or splurge on a new car.* • **splurge** *noun* [C] *Their biggest splurge each year is a five-day skiing vacation.*

○ **spoil** /spɔɪl/ *verb* *past* **spoiled** or **spoilt** **1** [MAKE BAD] [T] to stop something from being enjoyable or successful *The picnic was spoiled by the bad weather.* • *I don't want to spoil the fun, but could you turn the music down a bit?* **2** [CHILD] [T] If you spoil a child, you let them have anything they want or do anything they want, usually making them badly behaved. **3** [TREAT WELL] [T] to treat someone very well, buying them things or doing things for them *He's always sending flowers – he absolutely spoils me!* **4** [FOOD] [I] *formal* If food spoils, it starts to decay and you cannot eat it.

**spoils** /spɔɪlz/ *noun* [plural] *formal* things which are taken by the winners of a war *the spoils of victory/war*

**spoilt** /spɔɪlt/ *UK* (*US* **spoiled** /spɔɪld/) *adj* badly behaved because you are always given what you want or allowed to do what you want *He was behaving like a spoilt child.*

**spoke**[1] /spəʊk/ *noun* [C] one of the thin pieces of metal which connects the middle of a wheel to the outside edge, for example, on a bicycle

**spoke**[2] /spəʊk/ *past tense of* speak

**spoken** /'spəʊkən/ *past participle of* speak

**spokesman, spokeswoman** /'spəʊksmən, 'spəʊks,wʊmən/ *noun* [C] *plural* **spokesmen, spokeswomen** a man/woman who is chosen to speak officially for a group or organization *A spokesman for the company refused to comment on the reports.*

**spokesperson** /'spəʊks,pɜːs⁰n/ *noun* [C] *plural* **spokespeople** someone who is chosen to speak officially for a group or organization

**sponge** /spʌndʒ/ *noun* [C, U] **1** a soft substance full of small holes, which absorbs liquid very easily and is used for washing things **2** (*also* **'sponge ,cake**) a soft, light cake • **spongy** *adj* soft, like a sponge

**sponsor**[1] /'spɒnsə/ *verb* [T] to give money to someone to support an activity, event, or organization, sometimes as a way to advertise your company or product *The event is sponsored by First National Bank.* • (*UK*) *a sponsored walk* (= a walk for charity) • **sponsorship** *noun* [U] when someone gives money to support something

**sponsor**[2] /'spɒnsə/ *noun* [C] a person or organization that gives money to support an activity, event, etc

**spontaneous** /spɒn'teɪniəs/ *adj* happening naturally and suddenly and without being planned *a spontaneous reaction* • *The crowd broke into spontaneous applause.* • **spontaneity** /ˌspɒntə'neɪəti/ *noun* [U] when something is spontaneous *The performance was boring and lacked spontaneity.* • **spontaneously** *adv*

**spoof** /spuːf/ *noun* [C] a funny television programme, film, article, etc that copies the style of a real programme, film, article, etc *They did a spoof of the Oscars, giving awards for the worst films of the year.*

**spooky** /'spuːki/ *adj informal* strange and frightening *There's something spooky about that place.*

o— **spoon** /spuːn/ *noun* [C] an object with a handle and a round, curved part at one end, used for eating and serving food *knives, forks, and spoons* • *Mix the butter and sugar together with a wooden spoon.* • **spoon** *verb* [T] to move or serve food using a spoon *Spoon the sauce over the fish.*

**spoonful** /'spuːnfʊl/ *noun* [C] the amount of something which can be held on a spoon *Then add a spoonful of yoghurt.*

**sporadic** /spə'rædɪk/ *adj* not happening regularly or happening in different places *sporadic violence* • **sporadically** *adv*

o— **sport**[1] /spɔːt/ *noun* **1** [C] a game or activity which people do to keep healthy or for enjoyment, often competing against each other *winter sports* • *team sports* • *a sports centre* ⊃ *See colour picture* **Sports 1 & 2** *on page Centre 15 & 16.* **2** [U] *UK* all types of physical activity which people do to keep healthy or for enjoyment *I always enjoyed sport when I was at school.* ⊃ *See also:* **blood sport**.

**sport**[2] /spɔːt/ *verb* [T] *humorous* to wear something, especially something which people notice *He turned up sporting a bright red baseball cap and sunglasses.*

**sporting** /'spɔːtɪŋ/ *adj* relating to sports *a sporting hero* • *sporting goods*

**'sports ,car** *noun* [C] a car designed to go very fast, often with only two seats and an open roof

**sportsman, sportswoman** /'spɔːtsmən, 'spɔːtsˌwʊmən/ *noun* [C] *plural* **sportsmen, sportswomen** a man/woman who is good at sport

**sportsmanship** /'spɔːtsmənʃɪp/ *noun* [U] behaviour in sport which is fair and shows respect for other players *We hope to teach children good sportsmanship.*

**sportswear** /'spɔːtsweər/ *noun* [U] clothes, shoes, etc for people to wear when they play sports *a sportswear shop*

**sporty** /'spɔːti/ *adj* **1** Sporty cars, clothes, etc are attractive, comfortable, and stylish. **2** Sporty people are good at sports.

o— **spot**[1] /spɒt/ *noun* [C] **1** [ROUND MARK] a small, round mark which is a different colour to the surface it is on *a blue shirt with white spots* • *I noticed a small spot of oil on my jacket.* **2** [SKIN] *UK* (*US* **pimple**) an unpleasant, small, red mark on your skin *He suffered badly with spots as a teenager.* **3** [PLACE] a place *We found a good spot to sit and have our picnic.* • *The town is a popular tourist spot.* **4 a spot of sth** *UK old-fashioned* a small amount of something *a spot of lunch/shopping* **5 on the spot a** [TIME] immediately *I accepted the job on the spot.* **b** [PLACE] in the place where something happens *The police were called and they were on the spot within three minutes.* **6 have a soft spot for sb** to like someone a lot *I've always had a soft spot for her.* **7 put sb on the spot** to ask someone a question which is difficult or embarrassing to answer at that time ⊃ *See also:* **beauty spot**, **blind spot**.

**spot**[2] /spɒt/ *verb* [T] **spotting**, *past* **spotted** to see or notice something or someone *They were spotted together in London last week.* • *She soon spotted the mistake.*

**spotless** /'spɒtləs/ *adj* completely clean *By the time I'd finished, the whole room was spotless.*

**spotlight** /'spɒtlaɪt/ *noun* **1** [C] a strong light which can be pointed in different directions **2 the spotlight** when someone gets public attention by being on television, in the newspapers, etc *to be in the spotlight* • *She's rarely out of the media spotlight these days.* • **spotlight** *verb* [T] *past* **spotlighted** *or* **spotlit**

**,spot 'on** *adj* [never before noun] *UK* exactly correct *Her imitation of Ann was spot on.*

**spotty** /'spɒti/ *adj* **1** [SKIN] *UK* having a lot of unpleasant, small, red marks on your skin *a spotty young man with greasy hair* **2** [PATTERN] *UK* with a pattern of round marks *a spotty dress* **3** [NOT GOOD/REGULAR] *US* (*UK* **patchy**) If an action, quality, supply, etc is spotty, it is not all good or regular. *Sales of tickets for the concert have been spotty.*

**spouse** /spaʊs/ *noun* [C] *formal* your husband or wife

**spout**[1] /spaʊt/ *noun* [C] an opening of a container, in the shape of a tube which liquid flows out through *the spout of a teapot*

**spout**[2] /spaʊt/ *verb* [I, T] **1** If a liquid spouts or if something makes it spout, it flows out of something with force. **2** *informal* to talk a lot about something, often when other people are not interested *He was spouting his usual rubbish about politics.*

**sprain** /spreɪn/ *verb* [T] to injure part of your body by twisting it, but not so badly that it breaks *I slipped on the ice and sprained my ankle.* • **sprain** *noun* [C]

**sprang** /spræŋ/ *past tense of* spring

**sprawl** /sprɔːl/ *verb* [I] **1** (*also* **sprawl out**) to sit or lie in a relaxed, untidy position with your arms and legs stretched out *He sprawled out on* *the sofa.* **2** to cover a large area, often in a way which is not tidy or not planned *sprawling suburbs* • *sprawl* noun [U] *urban sprawl*

**spray**¹ /spreɪ/ noun **1** [C, U] liquid in a container which forces it out in small drops *hair spray* • *spray paint* **2** [U] many small drops of liquid blown through the air *sea spray*

**spray**² /spreɪ/ verb **1** [T] to force liquid out of a container in many small drops *The fields are sprayed with pesticides.* • *She sprayed a little perfume on her wrists.* **2** [I, T] If small pieces of something spray somewhere or if something sprays them, they are sent through the air in all directions. *A brick shattered the window,* **spraying** *the room* **with** *pieces of broken glass.*

o━**spread**¹ /spred/ verb past **spread** **1 spread sth across/over/through, etc** to arrange something so that it covers a large area *He* **spread** *the cards* **out** *on the table.* **2** TIME [T] (*also* **spread out**) to arrange for something to happen over a period of time and not at once *The payments will be spread over two years.* **3** INCREASE [I] to increase, or move to cover a larger area or affect a larger number of people *The smoke soon spread into all the rooms in the house.* • *The virus is spread by rats.* **4** SURFACE [T] to move a soft substance across a surface so that it covers it *What I really like is hot buttered toast* **spread with** *strawberry jam.* • *He* **spread** *a thin layer of glue on the paper.* **5** INFORMATION [I, T] If information spreads or if someone spreads it, it is communicated from one person to another. *News of his death spread quickly.*

**spread out** If people spread out, they move from being close together in a group to being in different places across a larger area. *They spread out to search the whole area.*

**spread**² /spred/ noun **1** MOVEMENT [U] when something moves to cover a larger area or affect a larger number of people *They are looking for ways to slow down* **the spread of** *the disease.* **2** FOOD [C, U] a soft food which you put on bread *The children love cheese spread in their sandwiches.* **3** NEWSPAPER [C] an article which covers one or more pages of a newspaper or magazine *a double-page spread*

**spreadsheet** /'spredʃiːt/ noun [C] a computer program which helps you to do business calculations and planning

**spree** /spriː/ noun **a shopping/spending, etc spree** a short period when someone does a lot of shopping/spending, etc *We went on a spending spree.*

**sprig** /sprɪg/ noun [C] a small piece of a plant with leaves *a sprig of parsley*

**sprightly** /'spraɪtli/ adj A sprightly person is able to move about easily and quickly although they are old.

o━**spring**¹ /sprɪŋ/ noun **1** SEASON [C, U] the season of the year between winter and summer, when the weather becomes warmer and plants start to grow again *I'm starting a new course in the* **spring**. • *spring flowers/weather* **2** METAL [C] a piece of metal which curves round and round and which returns to its original shape after being pushed or pulled *bed springs* **3** WATER [C] a place where water comes out of the ground *hot springs* **4** MOVEMENT [C, U] when someone or

something suddenly moves or jumps somewhere

**spring**² /sprɪŋ/ verb past t **sprang** (*also US*) **sprung**, past p **sprung** **1 spring back/forward/ out, etc** to jump or move somewhere suddenly *The cat sprang onto the sofa.* • *I tried to shut the door, but it kept springing open.* **2 spring to life** to suddenly become very active *After about 8 o'clock, the city springs to life.* **3 spring to mind** If a word or idea springs to mind, you suddenly think of it. *He asked if I knew any good places to go, but nothing sprang to mind.*

**spring from sth** to come from or be the result of something *Many of his problems spring from his strict religious upbringing.*

**spring sth on sb** to suddenly tell or ask someone something when they do not expect it *I'm sorry to spring this on you, but could you give a talk at tomorrow's meeting?*

**spring up** to appear suddenly *A lot of new hotels have sprung up along the coast recently.*

,**spring 'clean** UK (*UK/US* ,**spring 'cleaning**) noun [no plural] when you clean a place more carefully and using more effort than usual *I gave the kitchen a spring clean at the weekend.* • **spring clean** verb [I, T] UK

,**spring 'onion** UK (*US* **scallion**) noun [C, U] a small onion with a white part at the bottom and long, green leaves, which is eaten in salads

**sprinkle** /'sprɪŋkl/ verb [T] to gently drop small pieces of something over a surface *Sprinkle the cake with sugar before serving.* • **sprinkling** noun [no plural] a small amount of a powder or liquid that has been sprinkled on a surface *a sprinkling of pepper/snow*

**sprinkler** /'sprɪŋklə/ noun [C] a piece of garden equipment which automatically spreads drops of water over grass and plants

**sprint** /sprɪnt/ verb [I] to run very fast for a short distance *She sprinted along the road to the bus stop.* • **sprinter** noun [C] someone who runs short distances in competitions • **sprint** noun [C] *a 100m sprint*

**sprout**¹ /spraʊt/ verb [I, T] If a plant sprouts, or if it sprouts something, it begins to produce leaves, flowers, etc. *The seeds I planted are just beginning to sprout.*

**sprout up** If a large number of things sprout up, they suddenly appear or begin to exist. *New buildings are sprouting up all over the city.*

**sprout**² /spraʊt/ noun [C] **1** (*also* **brussel sprout**) a small, green vegetable which is round and made of leaves **2** a part of a plant that is just beginning to grow

**spruce** /spruːs/ verb

**spruce sb/sth up** to make someone or something cleaner or more tidy [often reflexive] *I'd like to spruce myself up a bit before we go out.*

**sprung** /sprʌŋ/ **1** past participle of spring **2** US past tense of spring

**spun** /spʌn/ past tense of spin

**spur**¹ /spɜː/ (*also* **spur on**) verb [T] **spurring**, past **spurred** to encourage someone to do something or something to happen *Spurred on by his fans, he won the next three games easily.*

**spur**² /spɜː/ noun [C] **1** a sharp, pointed piece of metal fixed to the boot of someone riding a horse **2 on the spur of the moment** If you do something on the spur of the moment, you do it suddenly, without planning it.

**spurious** /'spjʊəriəs/ *adj formal* false and not based on the truth

**spurn** /spɜːn/ *verb* [T] *formal* to not accept someone or something *to spurn an opportunity* • *a spurned lover*

**spurt**[1] /spɜːt/ *verb* **1** [I, T] (*also* **spurt out**) If something spurts liquid or fire, or if liquid or fire spurts from somewhere, it flows out suddenly with force. *Blood was spurting out of his stomach.* **2 spurt ahead/into/past, etc** to increase your speed, effort, or activity *She spurted ahead in the final lap.*

**spurt**[2] /spɜːt/ *noun* [C] **1** a sudden, short increase in speed, effort, or activity *He works in short spurts.* **2** a sudden, powerful flow of liquid *The water came out of the tap* **in spurts.**

**sputter** /'spʌtər/ *verb* [I] to make several quick, explosive sounds *The car sputtered to a halt.*

**spy**[1] /spaɪ/ *noun* [C] someone who secretly tries to discover information about a person, country, etc

**spy**[2] /spaɪ/ *verb* **1** [I] to secretly try to discover information about a person, country, etc **2** [T] *literary* to see someone or something, often from a distance *I spied him on the dance floor.*
**spy on sb** to secretly watch someone *He spied on her through the keyhole.*

**sq** *written abbreviation for* square in measurements *an area of 70 sq km* (= square kilometres)

**squabble** /'skwɒbl/ *verb* [I] to argue about something that is not important *They're always squabbling over money.* • squabble *noun* [C]

**squad** /skwɒd/ *noun* [C] **1 bomb/drug/fraud, etc squad** a group of police officers who have special skills to deal with particular problems **2 death/firing/hit, etc squad** a group of people who are trained to kill, usually with guns **3** a sports team *the England rugby squad*

**squadron** /'skwɒdrən/ *noun* [C] a group of soldiers, ships, aircraft, etc in a military organization *a squadron of fighter jets*

**squalid** /'skwɒlɪd/ *adj* **1** very dirty and unpleasant *squalid conditions* **2** morally bad *a squalid affair*

**squall** /skwɔːl/ *noun* [C] a sudden storm with strong winds

**squalor** /'skwɒlər/ *noun* [U] extremely dirty and unpleasant conditions *They were found living in absolute squalor.*

**squander** /'skwɒndər/ *verb* [T] to waste time, money, etc *He* **squandered** *all his money* **on** *alcohol and drugs.*

o—ᴴ**square**[1] /skweər/ *noun* [C] **1** [SHAPE] a shape with four equal sides and four 90° angles ⊃ *See picture at* **shape.** **2** [PLACE] an open area with buildings around it, often in the centre of a town *Trafalgar Square* **3** [NUMBER] in mathematics, a number that results from multiplying a number by itself *The square of 3 is 9.* **4 back to square one** back to the beginning of a long process or piece of work *None of the applicants were suitable, so we had to go back to square one and advertise the job again.* ⊃ *See also:* **fair**[3] and square.

o—ᴴ**square**[2] /skweər/ *adj* **1** having the shape of a square *a square room* • *He has broad shoulders and a square jaw.* **2 square centimetre/metre/mile, etc** the area of a square with sides that are a centimetre/metre/mile, etc long *3000 square feet of office space* **3 a square meal** a big, healthy meal *You need three square meals a day.*

**square**[3] /skweər/ *verb* **2/3/4, etc squared** 2/3/4, etc multiplied by itself *Four squared is sixteen.*
**square off** *US* to prepare to fight, compete, or argue with someone *The two teams will square off in the finals next Saturday.*
**square up** *UK* **1** to prepare to fight, compete, or argue with someone *The players squared up to each other and started shouting.* **2** *informal* to pay someone the money that you owe them *If you pay for it now, I'll* **square up with** *you later.*
**square with sth** to match or to agree with something *Her story doesn't quite square with the evidence.*

**squarely** /'skweəli/ *adv* directly *I looked him squarely in the eye.* • *The report put the blame squarely on the police.*

,**square 'root** *noun* **the square root of 16/64/144, etc** the number you multiply by itself to get 16/64/144, etc *The square root of 144 is 12.*

**squash**[1] /skwɒʃ/ *noun* **1** [SPORT] [U] a sport in which two people hit a small rubber ball against the four walls of a room *a game of squash* • *a squash court/racket* **2 it's a squash** *UK* used to say that there are too many people or things in a small space *We managed to get in but it was a squash.* **3** [DRINK] [U] *UK* a sweet drink that tastes like fruit **4** [VEGETABLE] [C, U] a fruit with hard skin, a soft inside, and large seeds, that you cook and eat as a vegetable

**squash**[2] /skwɒʃ/ *verb* **1** [T] to crush something into a flat shape *I stepped on a spider and squashed it.* **2** [I, T] to push someone or something into a small space [often passive] *The kids were all squashed into the back seat.*

**squat**[1] /skwɒt/ *verb* [I] **squatting,** *past* **squatted 1** (*also* **squat down**) to bend your legs so that you are sitting with your bottom very close to the ground *He squatted down beside me.* **2** to live in an empty building without the owner's permission

**squat**[2] /skwɒt/ *adj* short and wide *a squat little man*

**squat**[3] /skwɒt/ *noun* [C] a building that people are living in without the owner's permission

**squatter** /'skwɒtər/ *noun* [C] someone who lives in a building without the owner's permission

**squawk** /skwɔːk/ *verb* [I] If a bird squawks, it makes a loud, unpleasant noise. • squawk *noun* [C]

**squeak** /skwiːk/ *verb* [I] to make a short, high sound *His shoes squeaked loudly as he walked.* • squeak *noun* [C]

**squeaky** /'skwiːki/ *adj* **1** making short, high sounds *a squeaky voice* **2 squeaky clean** very clean

**squeal** /skwiːl/ *verb* [I] to make a loud, high sound, often because of fear or excitement *She* **squealed with** *delight.* • squeal *noun* [C] *squeals of laughter*

**squeamish** /ˈskwiːmɪʃ/ *adj* If you are squeamish about something such as blood, you find it very unpleasant and it makes you feel ill.

⊶**squeeze**[1] /skwiːz/ *verb* **1** [T] to press something firmly *She squeezed his hand and said goodbye.* **2 squeeze into/through/past, etc** to move somewhere where there is very little space *She squeezed through a narrow gap in the wall.* **3 squeeze a lemon/orange, etc** to press a lemon/orange, etc to get juice from it

**squeeze sth/sb in** to manage to do something or see someone when you are very busy *The doctor will try to squeeze you in this afternoon.*

**squeeze**[2] /skwiːz/ *noun* **1** [C] when you press something firmly *He gave her hand a little squeeze.* **2 it's a squeeze** used to say that there are too many people or things in a small space *We all got in, but it was a tight squeeze.* **3 a squeeze of lemon/orange, etc** a small amount of juice from a lemon/orange, etc

**squid** /skwɪd/ *noun* [C] *plural* **squid** or **squids** a sea creature with a long body and ten long arms

**squiggle** /ˈskwɪɡl/ *noun* [C] *informal* a short, curly line *Her signature just looks like a squiggle.*

**squint** /skwɪnt/ *verb* [I] to look at something with your eyes partly closed *She was squinting at her computer screen.*

**squirm** /skwɜːm/ *verb* [I] to twist your body because you are embarrassed, nervous, etc

**squirrel** /ˈskwɪrəl/ ⓊⓈ /ˈskwɜːrəl/ *noun* [C] a small animal with a big, fur tail that climbs trees and eats nuts

**squirt** /skwɜːt/ *verb* [I, T] **1** If liquid squirts, it comes out suddenly and with force, and if you squirt liquid, you make it come out suddenly and with force. *Water squirted out all over the floor.* **2 squirt sb with sth** to hit someone with a liquid

**Sr** (*also UK* **Snr**) *written abbreviation for* senior (= the older of two men in a family with the same name) *Joseph Kennedy, Sr.*

**St 1** *written abbreviation for* street (= a road in a town or city that has houses or other buildings) *42 Oxford St* **2** *written abbreviation for* saint (= a dead person who has been officially respected by the Christian Church for living their life in a holy way) *St Patrick*

**stab**[1] /stæb/ *verb* [T] **stabbing**, *past* **stabbed** to push a knife into someone *He was stabbed several times in the chest.*

**stab**[2] /stæb/ *noun* [C] **1** the act of pushing a knife into someone *He had a deep stab wound in his neck.* **2 a stab of guilt/jealousy/regret, etc** a sudden, unpleasant emotion *She felt a stab of guilt.* **3 have a stab at sth/doing sth** *informal* to try to do something, or to try an activity that you have not done before *She had a stab at solving the problem.*

**stabbing** /ˈstæbɪŋ/ *noun* [C] when someone stabs someone *Where were you on the night of the stabbing?* • (*US*) *a stabbing death*

**'stabbing ˌpain** *noun* [C] a sudden, strong pain

**stability** /stəˈbɪləti/ *noun* [U] when something is not likely to change or move *political/financial stability* • *Our country has enjoyed a long* period of peace and stability. ⊃ *Opposite* **instability.**

**stabilize** (*also UK* **-ise**) /ˈsteɪbəlaɪz/ *verb* [I, T] If you stabilize something, or if something stabilizes, it stops changing or moving. *The economy has finally stabilized.* • *The medication helps to stabilize his heart rate.* • **stabilization** /ˌsteɪbəlaɪˈzeɪʃən/ *noun* [U]

**stable**[1] /ˈsteɪbl/ *adj* **1** SITUATION not likely to change or end suddenly *a stable relationship* • *The doctor said his condition was stable.* **2** OBJECT fixed or safe and not likely to move *Be careful! That chair isn't very stable.* **3** PERSON mentally calm and not easily upset ⊃ *Opposite* **unstable.**

**stable**[2] /ˈsteɪbl/ *noun* [C] a building where horses are kept

**stack**[1] /stæk/ *noun* [C] **1** a tidy pile of things *a stack of books/CDs* **2 stacks of sth** *informal* a lot of something *There are stacks of studies linking salt to high blood pressure.*

**stack**[2] /stæk/ (*also* **stack up**) *verb* [T] to arrange things in a tidy pile *Can you help me stack these chairs?*

**stadium** /ˈsteɪdiəm/ *noun* [C] a large, open area with seats around it, used for playing and watching sports *a football/baseball stadium*

⊶**staff**[1] /stɑːf/ *noun* [group] the people who work for an organization *The report includes doctors, nurses, and other hospital staff.* • *The company has a staff of over 500 employees.* • *Please talk to a member of staff.*

**staff**[2] /stɑːf/ *verb* [T] to provide workers for an organization [often passive] *The charity was staffed by volunteers.*

**stag** /stæɡ/ *noun* [C] a male deer

⊶**stage**[1] /steɪdʒ/ *noun* **1** [C] a period of development, or a particular time in a process *an early stage in his career* • *Our project is in its final stages.* • *I'm not prepared to comment at this stage.* **2** [C] the raised area in a theatre where actors perform *He's on stage for most of the play.* **3 the stage** performances in theatres *He's written plays for television and the stage.* **4 set the stage for sth** to make something possible or likely to happen *The meeting set the stage for future cooperation between the companies.*

**stage**[2] /steɪdʒ/ *verb* **1 stage a demonstration/protest, etc** to organize and take part in a public meeting to complain about something **2 stage a concert/show, etc** to organize and produce a performance of music or a play, etc *They staged a free concert in Central Park.*

**stagger** /ˈstæɡər/ *verb* **1** [I] to walk as if you might fall *He staggered drunkenly towards the door.* **2** [T] to arrange events so that they do not happen at the same time *We stagger our lunch breaks at work.*

**staggered** /ˈstæɡəd/ *adj* [never before noun] very shocked or surprised *I was staggered at the prices.*

**staggering** /ˈstæɡərɪŋ/ *adj* very shocking and surprising *He earns a staggering amount of money.*

**stagnant** /ˈstæɡnənt/ *adj* **1** Stagnant water or air does not flow and becomes dirty and smells unpleasant. *a stagnant pond* **2** A stagnant economy, society, or organization does not develop or grow.

**stagnate** /stæg'neɪt/ ⓤ⟨ˈstægneɪt/ *verb* [I] to stay the same and not grow or develop *He expects the economy to stagnate and unemployment to rise.* • stagnation /stæg'neɪʃᵊn/ *noun* [U]

**'stag ˌnight** *noun* [C] a night when a group of men go out just before one of them gets married

**staid** /steɪd/ *adj* serious and old-fashioned *a staid, middle-aged man*

**stain**[1] /steɪn/ *noun* **1** [C] a dirty mark on something that is difficult to remove *a blood/grass stain* • *a stain on the carpet* **2** [C, U] a thin, clear paint that you put on wood to make it darker *wood stain*

**stain**[2] /steɪn/ *verb* **1** [I, T] to leave a dirty mark on something which is difficult to remove, or to become dirty in this way *That wine I spilt has stained my shirt.* • *Avoid light carpets because they stain easily.* **2** [T] to paint a wooden surface with a thin paint in order to change its colour *She stained the bookcase to match the desk.*

**ˌstained ˈglass** *noun* [U] coloured glass that is used to make pictures in windows *a stained-glass window*

**stainless steel** /ˌsteɪnləsˈstiːl/ *noun* [U] a type of steel (= strong metal) that is not damaged by water

**stair** /steə**r**/ *noun* [C] one of the steps in a set of steps

**staircase** /'steəkeɪs/ *noun* [C] a set of stairs and the structure around them *a spiral staircase*

o⟶**stairs** /steəz/ *noun* [plural] a set of steps from one level in a building to another *to go up/down the stairs* • *to climb the stairs* • *a flight* (= set) *of stairs*

**stairway** /'steəweɪ/ *noun* [C] a set of stairs and the structure around them

**stake**[1] /steɪk/ *noun* **1 be at stake** If something is at stake, it is in a situation where it might be lost or damaged. *We have to act quickly – people's lives are at stake.* **2** [C] a part of a business that you own, or an amount of money that you have invested in a business *He has a 30 percent stake in the company.* **3** [C] a strong stick with a pointed end that you push into the ground *a wooden stake*

**stake**[2] /steɪk/ *verb* **stake a/your claim** to say that you want something and that you should have it

**stake sth on sth** to risk something on the result of a competition or situation *He has staked his reputation on the film's success.*

**stake sth out** to watch a place in order to catch criminals or to see a famous person *The police are staking out the house where the terrorists are hiding.*

**stakes** /steɪks/ *noun* [plural] money or other advantages that you may get or lose in a competition or situation *People get very competitive because the stakes are so high.*

**stale** /steɪl/ *adj* **1** old and not fresh *stale bread* • *Cake goes stale quickly if it's not covered.* **2** boring or bored, and not producing or feeling excitement or enthusiasm like before *After 21 years their marriage had begun to go stale.* • *I'd been too long in the same job and was getting stale.*

**stalemate** /'steɪlmeɪt/ *noun* [C, U] a situation in which neither side in an argument can win *The talks ended in a stalemate.*

**stalk**[1] /stɔːk/ *verb* **1** [T] to follow a person or animal closely and secretly, often to try to catch or attack them *She claimed that the man had been stalking her for a month.* **2 stalk out/off, etc** to walk in an angry or proud way *She stalked out of the restaurant.*

**stalk**[2] /stɔːk/ *noun* [C] the main stem of a plant

**stalker** /'stɔːkə**r**/ *noun* [C] someone who follows a person or animal closely and secretly, often to try to catch or attack them

**stall**[1] /stɔːl/ *noun* [C] **1** mainly UK a small shop with an open front or a table from which goods are sold *a market stall* **2** US a small area in a room for washing or using the toilet *a shower stall*

**stall**[2] /stɔːl/ *verb* **1** [ENGINE] [I, T] If an engine stalls, or if you stall it, it stops working suddenly. *The car stalled when I stopped at the traffic lights.* **2** [STOP] [I] to stop making progress *The peace talks have stalled over the issue of nuclear weapons.* **3** [MORE TIME] [T] to intentionally make someone wait or make something happen later so that you have more time *She wanted an answer immediately, but I managed to stall her.*

**stallion** /'stæljən/ *noun* [C] an adult male horse

**the stalls** /stɔːlz/ *UK* (*US* **orchestra**) *noun* [plural] the seats on the main floor near the front of a theatre or cinema *a seat in the stalls*

**stalwart** /'stɔːlwət/ *noun* [C] someone who supports an organization, team, etc in a very loyal way • stalwart *adj*

**stamina** /'stæmɪnə/ *noun* [U] the physical or mental energy that allows you to do something for a long time *Marathon runners need a lot of stamina.*

**stammer** /'stæmə**r**/ *verb* [I] to pause a lot and repeat sounds because of a speech problem or because you are nervous *He blushed and began to stammer.* • stammer *noun* [C] *He has a stammer.*

o⟶**stamp**[1] /stæmp/ *noun* [C] **1** (*also* **postage stamp**) a small, official piece of paper that you buy and stick onto a letter or parcel before you post it **2** a tool for putting a special ink mark on something, or the mark made by it *a stamp in a passport* **3 stamp of approval** official, public approval *The president has put his stamp of approval on the proposal.*

**stamp**[2] /stæmp/ *verb* **1** [T] to make a mark on something with a tool that you put ink on and press down *She stamped the date on the invoice.* **2** [I, T] to put your foot down on the ground hard and quickly, often to show anger *"No!" she shouted, stamping her foot.* ➲ *See also:* **rubber-stamp**.

**stamp sth out** to get rid of something that is wrong or harmful *a campaign to stamp out racism*

**stampede** /stæm'piːd/ *noun* [C] when a large group of animals or people suddenly move in an uncontrolled way, often in the same direction *Gunfire caused a stampede in the marketplace.* • stampede *verb* [I]

**stance** /stæns/ *noun* [C] **1** an opinion or belief

about something, especially if you say it in public [usually singular] *What's their **stance** on nuclear energy?* • *They are taking a very tough stance against drugs.* **2** *formal* the way that someone stands [usually singular] *an awkward stance*

○━**stand¹** /stænd/ *verb past* **stood 1** ON FEET [I] to be in a vertical position on your feet *We'd been standing for hours.* • *He's standing over there, next to Karen.* **2** RISE [I] (*also* **stand up**) to rise to a vertical position on your feet from sitting or lying down *I get dizzy if I stand up too quickly.* • *Please stand when the bride arrives.* ➔ *See colour picture* **Phrasal Verbs** *on page Centre 13.* **3 stand in line** *US* (*UK* **queue**) to wait for something as part of a line of people *We stood in line all afternoon.* **4 stand (sth) in/against/by, etc sth** to be in or to put something in a particular place or position *His walking stick stood by the door.* • *You'll have to stand the sofa on its end to get it through the door.* **5 can't stand sb/sth** *informal* to hate someone or something *I can't stand him.* • [+ doing sth] *She can't stand doing housework.* **6** ACCEPT [T] to be able to accept or deal with a difficult situation *She couldn't stand the pressures of the job.* • *The pain was more than he could stand.* **7 stand at sth** to be at a particular level, amount, height, etc *Inflation currently stands at 3 percent.* **8 where you stand on sth** what your opinion is about something *We asked the senator where she stood on gun control.* **9 where you stand (with sb)** what someone thinks about you, how they expect you to behave, and how they are likely to behave *She said she will never leave her husband, so now at least I know where I stand.* **10** OFFER [I] If an offer still stands, it still exists. *You're welcome to visit any time – my invitation still stands.* **11 as it stands** as something is now, without changes in it *The law as it stands is very unclear.* **12 stand trial** If someone stands trial, they appear in a law court where people decide if they are guilty of a crime. *to stand trial for murder* **13 stand to gain/lose sth** to be in a situation where you can get/lose money or an advantage *He stands to gain a fortune if the company is sold.* **14** ELECTION [I] *UK* (*US* **run**) to compete in an election for an official position *to stand for office* ➔ *See also:* stand on your own two feet (**foot¹**), stand your **ground¹**, not have a **leg** to stand on, it stands to **reason¹**, stand sb in good **stead**.

**stand about/around** to spend time standing somewhere and doing very little *They stood around waiting for the store to open.*

**stand aside** to leave a job or position so that someone else can do it instead *It's time he stood aside and let a more experienced person do it.*

**stand back** to move a short distance away from something or someone *Stand back while I light the fire.*

**stand by 1** to be ready to do something or to help *Doctors were standing by to treat the injured passengers.* **2** to do nothing to prevent something unpleasant from happening *We can't stand by while millions of people starve.*

**stand by sb** to continue to support someone when they are in a difficult situation *She stood by him throughout his troubled career.*

**stand by sth** If you stand by an agreement, decision, etc, you do not change it. *The government stood by its promise to improve education.*

**stand down** *UK* to leave a job or position so that someone else can do it instead *He stood down as party leader.*

**stand for sth 1** If a letter stands for a word, it is used to represent it. *UFO stands for 'unidentified flying object'.* **2** If a group of people stand for a set of ideas, they support those ideas. *The party stands for low taxes and individual freedom.* **3 not stand for sth** If you will not stand for something, you will not accept a situation or someone's behaviour. *He can't speak to me like that – I won't stand for it!*

**stand in** to do something that someone else was going to do because they cannot be there *She stood in for me when I was sick.*

**stand out 1** to be very easy to see or notice *The bright blue letters really stand out on the page.* **2** to be better than other similar things or people *His application stood out from all the rest.* ➔ *See also:* stand out like a sore **thumb¹**.

**stand up** If an idea or some information stands up, it is proved to be correct.

**stand sb up** to fail to meet someone when you said you would *He's stood me up twice now.*

**stand up for sth/sb** to support an idea or a person who is being criticized [often reflexive] *Never be afraid to stand up for yourself.*

**stand²** /stænd/ *noun* **1** SHOP [C] a small shop with an open front or a table from which goods are sold *a hot dog stand* • *Visit our stand at the trade fair.* **2** SPORT [C] *UK* (*US* **stands**) a structure in a sports ground where people can stand or sit to watch an event **3** FURNITURE [C] a piece of furniture for holding things *a music/hat stand* **4 the (witness) stand** (*UK* **the dock**) the place in a law court where people sit or stand when they are being asked questions *The judge asked her to **take the stand** (= go into the witness stand).* **5** OPINION [C] an opinion or belief about something, especially if you say it in public [usually singular] *What's the President's **stand** on gun control?* **6 take a stand** to express your opinion about something publicly *He refuses to take a stand on this issue.* **7 make a stand** to publicly defend something or stop something from happening *It's about time someone made a stand.*

○━**standard¹** /'stændəd/ *noun* [C] **1** a level of quality, especially a level that is acceptable *a high standard of service* • *low safety standards* • *His work was below standard* (= not acceptable). • *She sets very high standards for herself.* **2** a level of behaviour, especially a level that is acceptable [usually plural] *high moral standards* ➔ *See also:* double standard.

**standard²** /'stændəd/ *adj* usual and not special *standard procedure/practice*

**standardize** (*also UK* **-ise**) /'stændədaɪz/ *verb* [T] to change things so that they are all the same *I wish someone would standardize clothing sizes.* • standardization /ˌstændədaɪˈzeɪʃən/ *noun* [U] *the standardization of computer terms*

,**standard of 'living** noun [C] plural **standards of living** how much money and comfort someone has *a high standard of living*

**standby** /'stændbaɪ/ noun [C] plural **standbys** **1** someone or something extra that is ready to be used if needed *We kept our old TV as a standby in case the new one broke.* **2 be on standby** to be ready to do something or to be used if needed *Police were on standby in case there was any trouble after the game.*

**stand-in** /'stændɪn/ noun [C] someone who does what another person was going to do because the other person cannot be there

**standing**[1] /'stændɪŋ/ noun [U] Your standing is the opinion that other people have of you. *Last week's speech has improved the Prime Minister's standing in the polls.*

**standing**[2] /'stændɪŋ/ adj [always before noun] **1** permanent and not only created when necessary *a standing committee* ● *He has a standing invitation to stay at our house.* **2 a standing joke** a situation that a group of people often make jokes about *The poor quality of his work has become a standing joke in the office.* ⊃ See also: **long-standing**.

,**standing 'order** noun [C] UK an instruction to a bank to pay someone a fixed amount of money at regular times from your account

,**standing o'vation** noun [C] when people stand while clapping to show that they have enjoyed a performance very much *She got a standing ovation for her speech.*

**stand-off** (UK (US **standoff**) /'stændɒf/ noun [C] when an argument or fight stops for a period of time because no one can win or get an advantage

**standpoint** /'stændpɔɪnt/ noun [C] a particular way of thinking about a situation or problem *to look at something from a political/religious standpoint*

**standstill** /'stændstɪl/ noun [no plural] a situation in which all movement or activity has stopped *The traffic came to a standstill in the thick fog.*

**stand-up** /'stændʌp/ adj [always before noun] A stand-up comedian is someone who stands in front of a group of people and tells jokes as a performance. *stand-up comedy*

**stank** /stæŋk/ past tense of stink

**staple**[1] /'steɪpl/ adj [always before noun] A staple food, product, etc is basic and very important. *a staple diet of rice and fish*

**staple**[2] /'steɪpl/ noun [C] a small piece of wire that you put through pieces of paper to join them together ● **staple** verb [T] to join pieces of paper together with staples

**stapler** /'steɪplər/ noun [C] a piece of equipment used for putting staples through paper

∘⧟**star**[1] /stɑːr/ noun [C] **1** ⟨SKY⟩ a ball of burning gases that you see as a small point of light in the sky at night **2** ⟨FAMOUS PERSON⟩ a famous singer, actor, sports person, etc *a pop star* **3** ⟨BEST PERSON⟩ someone in a group of people who is the best at doing something *Baggio is one of our star players.* **4** ⟨SHAPE⟩ a shape that has five or more points ⊃ See picture at **shape**. **5 two-star/three-star, etc** used to show how good a restaurant or hotel is *a five-star hotel*

**6 sb's stars/the stars** UK informal something you read that tells you what will happen to you based on the position of the stars in the sky *My stars said it would be a good month for romance.* ⊃ See also: **co-star, film star, rock star**.

**star**[2] /stɑːr/ verb [I, T] **starring**, past **starred** If a film, play, etc stars someone, or if someone stars in a film, play, etc, they are the main person in it. *a film starring Meg Ryan* ● *Tom Hanks starred in 'Sleepless in Seattle'.* ⊃ See also: **co-star**.

**starboard** /'stɑːbəd/ noun [U] the right side of a ship or aircraft

**starch** /stɑːtʃ/ noun **1** [C, U] a substance in foods such as rice, bread, and potatoes **2** [U] a substance used to make cloth stiff ● **starchy** adj containing a lot of starch

**stardom** /'stɑːdəm/ noun [U] when someone is very famous for acting, singing, etc

**stare** /steər/ verb [I] to look at someone or something for a long time and not move your eyes *Sean was staring at me.* ● **stare** noun [C]

**stark**[1] /stɑːk/ adj **1** unpleasantly clear and obvious *His death is a stark warning to other people about the dangers of drugs.* **2 stark difference/contrast** a total difference *Jerry is very lazy, in stark contrast to his sister who works very hard.* **3** with a very plain and simple appearance and not very attractive *a stark, snowy landscape* ● **starkly** adv

**stark**[2] /stɑːk/ adv **stark naked** wearing no clothes

**starry** /'stɑːri/ adj A starry sky or night is one in which you can see a lot of stars.

'**star ,sign** UK (US **sign**) noun [C] one of the twelve signs that are based on star positions when you are born, which some people believe shows what type of person you are *"What star sign are you?" "I'm Capricorn."*

∘⧟**start**[1] /stɑːt/ verb **1** ⟨BEGIN DOING⟩ [I, T] to begin doing something [+ doing sth] *He started smoking when he was eighteen.* ● [+ to do sth] *Maria started to laugh.* ● *We start work at nine o'clock.* **2** ⟨BEGIN HAPPENING⟩ [I, T] to begin to happen or to make something begin to happen *The programme starts at seven o'clock.* ● *Police believe the fire started in the kitchen.* **3** ⟨BUSINESS⟩ [I, T] (also **start up**) If a business, organization, etc starts, it begins to exist, and if you start it, you make it begin to exist. *She started her own computer business.* ● *A lot of new restaurants have started up in the area.* **4** ⟨CAR⟩ [I, T] (also **start up**) If a car or engine starts, it begins to work, and if you start it, you make it begin to work. *The car won't start.* ● *Start up the engine.* **5 to start with a** used to talk about what a situation was like at the beginning before it changed *I was happy at school to start with, but later I hated it.* **b** used before saying the first thing in a list of things *To start with, we need better computers. Then we need more training.* **6** ⟨MOVE SUDDENLY⟩ [I] to move suddenly because you are frightened or surprised ⊃ See also: start the **ball** rolling, start off on the wrong **foot**[1].

**start (sth) off** to begin by doing something, or to make something begin by doing something *She started off the meeting with the monthly sales report.*

**start on sth** to begin doing something *Have you started on your homework yet?*

**start out** to begin your life or the part of your life when you work, in a particular way *My dad started out as a sales assistant in a shop.*

**start over** *US* to begin something again *If you make a mistake, you'll have to start over.*

o⤹**start²** /stɑːt/ *noun* **1** BEGINNING [C] the beginning of something [usually singular] *Our teacher checks who is in class at the start of each day.* • *Ivan has been involved in the project from the start.* • *The meeting got off to a bad start* (= began badly). **2 make a start** *mainly UK* to begin doing something *I'll make a start on the washing-up.* **3 for a start** *UK* used when you are giving the first in a list of reasons or things *I won't be going – I've got too much homework for a start.* **4** ADVANTAGE [C] an advantage that you have over someone else when you begin something [usually singular] *I'm grateful for the start I had in life.* **5 the start** the place where a race begins **6** SUDDEN MOVEMENT [no plural] a sudden movement that you make because you are frightened or surprised *Kate sat up with a start.* ➔ *See also:* **false start.**

**starter** /'stɑːtəʳ/ *noun* **1** [C] *UK* (*US* **appetizer**) something that you eat as the first part of a meal **2** [C] *US* in sports, a member of a team who is involved in a competition from the beginning *At only 20, he's the team's youngest starter.* **3 for starters** *informal* used to say that something is the first in a list of things *Try this exercise for starters.* ➔ *See also:* **non-starter.**

**starting-point** /'stɑːtɪŋˌpɔɪnt/ *noun* [C] an idea, subject, etc that you use to begin a discussion or process

**startle** /'stɑːtl/ *verb* [T] to suddenly surprise or frighten someone *The sound startled me.* • **startled** *adj a startled expression*

**startling** /'stɑːtlɪŋ/ *adj* making you feel very surprised *startling news*

**start-up** /'stɑːtʌp/ *adj* [always before noun] relating to starting a business *start-up costs*

**starve** /stɑːv/ *verb* [I, T] to become ill or die because you do not have enough food, or to make someone ill or die because they do not have enough food *Many people have starved to death in parts of Africa.* • **starvation** /stɑː'veɪʃᵊn/ *noun* [U] *Children were dying of starvation.*

**starved** /stɑːvd/ *adj* **1 be starved of sth** *UK* (*US* **be starved for sth**) to not have enough of something that you need very much *a child starved of love* • *a school starved for money* **2** *mainly US informal* very hungry

**starving** /'stɑːvɪŋ/ *adj* **1** dying because there is not enough food *starving people* **2** *informal* very hungry *I'm absolutely starving.*

**stash¹** /stæʃ/ (*also* **stash away**) *verb* [T] *informal* to keep a lot of something in a safe, secret place *His money was stashed away in a cupboard.*

**stash²** /stæʃ/ *noun* [C] *informal* a lot of something that you keep in a safe, secret place *He had a stash of whisky under the bed.*

o⤹**state¹** /steɪt/ *noun* **1** CONDITION [C] the condition that something or someone is in *the state of the economy* • *The building is in a terrible state.* **2 in/into a state** *informal* very upset or nervous *Ben was in a real state before the exam.*

**3** PART OF COUNTRY [C] (*also* **State**) one of the parts that some countries such as the US are divided into *Washington State* • *Alaska is the largest state in the US.* **4** COUNTRY [C] a country *a union of European states* ➔ *See usage note at* **country. 5 the state** the government of a country *financial help from the state* **6 state visit/occasion, etc** an important visit/occasion, etc involving the leader of a government **7 the States** the United States of America ➔ *See also:* **police state, welfare state.**

**state²** /steɪt/ *verb* [T] to officially say or write something [+ (that)] *Two medical reports stated that he was mentally ill.*

**stately** /'steɪtli/ *adj* formal and slow *a stately procession through the streets*

**stately 'home** *noun* [C] a big, old house in the countryside that people pay to visit in Britain

o⤹**statement** /'steɪtmənt/ *noun* [C] **1** something that someone says or writes officially *The pop star is expected to make a statement about his involvement with drugs.* **2** (*also* **bank statement**) a piece of paper that shows how much money you have put into your bank account and how much you have taken out

**state of a'ffairs** *noun* [no plural] a situation *a sad state of affairs*

**state of 'mind** *noun* [C] *plural* **states of mind** how you are feeling at a particular time *to be in a positive state of mind*

**state-of-the-art** /ˌsteɪtəvðiˈɑːt/ *adj* using the newest ideas, designs, and materials *a computer system that uses state-of-the-art technology*

**state 'school** *UK* (*US* **public school**) *noun* [C] a school that is free to go to because the government provides the money for it

**statesman** /'steɪtsmən/ *noun* [C] *plural* **statesmen** an important politician, especially one who people respect

**static¹** /'stætɪk/ *adj* not moving or changing *The number of students on the course has remained static.*

**static²** /'stætɪk/ *noun* [U] **1** (*also* **static elec'tricity**) electricity that you get when two surfaces rub together **2** noise on a radio or television that is caused by electricity in the air

o⤹**station¹** /'steɪʃᵊn/ *noun* [C] **1** TRAINS a building where trains stop so that you can get on or off them *Dad met me at the station.* **2 bus station** (*also UK* **coach station**) a building where a bus starts or ends its journey **3** SERVICE a building where a particular service is based *(UK) a petrol station/(US) a gas station* **4** RADIO/TV a company that broadcasts television or radio programmes *a classical music station* ➔ *See also:* **filling station, fire station, police station, polling station, power station, service station.**

**station** or **stop**?

Station is used for trains.

*the train/railway station*

*the underground/tube station*

Stop or bus stop is used for buses.

*I stood at the bus stop for over half an hour.*

---

| iː **see** | ɒ **hot** | ɔː **saw** | ʌ **run** | ʊ **put** | uː **too** | aɪ **my** | aʊ **how** | eɪ **day** | əʊ **no** | ɪə **near** | ɔɪ **boy** | ʊə **poor** | aɪə **fire** | aʊə **sour** |

*Get off at the third stop.*

A **bus station** is a place where many buses start or end their journeys.

**station²** /'steɪʃⁿn/ *verb* **be stationed at/in, etc** If someone such as a soldier is stationed somewhere, they are sent there to work for a period of time. *US soldiers stationed in Germany*

**stationary** /'steɪʃⁿnᵊri/ *adj* not moving *stationary cars*

**stationer's** /'steɪʃənəz/ *noun* [C] *UK* a shop where you can buy pens, paper, and other things for writing

**stationery** /'steɪʃⁿnᵊri/ *noun* [U] things that you use for writing, such as pens and paper

**'station ,wagon** *US* (*UK* **estate car**) *noun* [C] a big car with a large space for bags behind the back seat

**statistic** /stə'tɪstɪk/ *noun* [C] a fact in the form of a number that shows information about something [**usually plural**] *Statistics show that skin cancer is becoming more common.* • **statistical** *adj* relating to statistics *statistical evidence* • **statistically** *adv*

**statistics** /stə'tɪstɪks/ *noun* [U] the subject that involves collecting and studying numbers to show information about something

**statue** /'stætʃuː/ *noun* [C] a model that looks like a person or animal, usually made from stone or metal

**stature** /'stætʃəʳ/ *noun* [U] *formal* **1** the importance that someone has because of their work *a scientist of international stature* **2** your height *a man of small stature*

**status** /'steɪtəs/ *noun* [U] **1** the position that you have in relation to other people because of your job or social position *The pay and status of nurses has improved.* **2** the legal position of someone or something *What's your **marital status** (= are you married or not)?*

**the status quo** /,steɪtəs'kwəʊ/ *noun formal* the situation that exists now, without any changes *They only want to maintain the status quo.*

**'status ,symbol** *noun* [C] something that someone owns that shows they have a high position in society

**statute** /'stætʃuːt/ *noun* [C] *formal* a law or rule

**statutory** /'stætjətᵊri/ *adj formal* decided or controlled by law *a statutory minimum wage*

**staunch** /stɔːnʃ/ *adj* [**always before noun**] very loyal in your support for someone or your belief in something *a staunch supporter of the Communist party*

**stave** /steɪv/ *verb*
**stave sth off** to stop something bad from happening now although it may happen later *He had a bar of chocolate to stave off his hunger.*

o-*stay¹** /steɪ/ *verb* **1** NOT LEAVE [I] to continue to be in a place, job, etc and not leave *The weather was bad so we stayed at home.* • *Do you want to stay in teaching?* **2** IN A STATE [T] to continue to be in a particular state *The supermarket stays open late.* • *I was tired and couldn't stay awake.* **3** VISIT [I, T] to spend a short period of time in a place *We stayed in a hotel.* • *We're going to stay with my grandmother.* **4 stay put** *informal* to continue to

be in the same place *He told me to stay put while he fetched the car.* ➔ *See usage note at* **rest**.

**stay behind** to not leave a place when other people leave *I stayed behind after class to speak to the teacher.*

**stay in** to stay in your home *Let's stay in tonight and watch a video.*

**stay on** to continue to be in a place, job, or school after other people have left *I stayed on an extra two years at school.*

**stay out** to not go home at night, or to go home late *He stayed out all night.*

**stay out of sth** to not become involved in an argument or discussion *It's better to stay out of their arguments.*

**stay up** to go to bed later than usual [+ **to do sth**] *She stayed up to watch a film.*

**stay²** /steɪ/ *noun* [C] a period of time that you spend in a place *Did you enjoy your stay in Tokyo?*

**stead** /sted/ *noun* **stand sb in good stead** to be useful to someone in the future *The course will stand you in good stead.*

**steadfast** /'stedfɑːst/ *adj formal* refusing to change your beliefs or what you are doing *He is steadfast in his support for political change.* • **steadfastly** *adv*

**steady¹** /'stedi/ *adj* **1** GRADUAL happening at a gradual, regular rate *steady economic growth* • *a steady improvement* **2** STILL still and not shaking *You need steady hands to be a dentist.* ➔ *Opposite* **unsteady.** **3** NOT CHANGING not changing *She drove at a steady speed.* **4 steady job/work** a job that is likely to continue for a long time and pay you regular money • **steadily** *adv* • **steadiness** *noun* [U]

**steady²** /'stedi/ *verb* **1** [T] to make something stop shaking or moving *He managed to steady the plane.* **2 steady yourself** to stop yourself from falling *She grabbed hold of the rail to steady herself.*

**steak** /steɪk/ *noun* [C, U] a thick, flat piece of meat or fish *steak and chips*

o-*steal** /stiːl/ *verb past t* **stole**, *past p* **stolen 1** [I, T] to secretly take something that does not belong to you, without intending to return it *Burglars broke into the house and stole a computer.* • *stolen cars* **2 steal away/in/out, etc** to move somewhere quietly and secretly

**stealth** /stelθ/ *noun* [U] secret, quiet behaviour • **stealthy** *adj* behaving in a secret, quiet way • **stealthily** *adv*

o-*steam¹** /stiːm/ *noun* **1** [U] the gas that water produces when you heat it **2 let off steam** to get rid of your anger, excitement, etc by being noisy or using a lot of energy **3 run out of steam** to not have enough energy to finish doing something

**steam²** /stiːm/ *verb*

**steam**

S

**1** [T] to cook something using steam *steamed rice*
**2** [I] to produce steam *a steaming bowl of soup*
**steam (sth) up** If glass steams up, or if you
steam it up, it becomes covered in steam. *The
mirror in the bathroom steamed up.*

**steamer** /'stiːmə<sup>r</sup>/ *noun* [C] **1** a pan used for
cooking food using steam **2** a ship that uses
steam power

**steamy** /'stiːmi/ *adj* **1** hot and full of steam *a
steamy kitchen* **2** sexually exciting *a steamy
love story*

**steel<sup>1</sup>** /stiːl/ *noun* [U] a very strong metal made
from iron, used for making knives, machines,
etc ⊃ *See also:* **stainless steel**.

**steel<sup>2</sup>** /stiːl/ *verb* **steel yourself** to prepare
yourself to do something difficult or unpleas-
ant *He was steeling himself for an argument.*

**steely** /'stiːli/ *adj* [always before noun] very strong
and determined *a steely determination to
succeed*

o⎯**steep<sup>1</sup>** /stiːp/ *adj* **1** SLOPE A steep slope, hill, etc
goes up or down very quickly. *The hill was too
steep to cycle up.* **2** CHANGE A steep increase or
fall in something is very big and quick. *a steep
rise in prices* **3** PRICE *informal* very expensive
*Hotel prices are steep at $300 for a room.*
● **steeply** *adv Food prices have risen steeply.*
● **steepness** *noun* [U]

**steep<sup>2</sup>** /stiːp/ *verb* **be steeped in sth** to have a
lot of something around or to be strongly influ-
enced by something *The town is steeped in
history.*

**steeple** /'stiːpl/ *noun* [C] a church tower that has
a point at the top

**steer** /stɪə<sup>r</sup>/ *verb* **1** [I, T] to control the direction
of a vehicle *I tried to steer the boat away from
the bank.* **2** [T] to influence the way a situation
develops *I managed to **steer the conversation**
away from my exam results.* **3 steer sb into/
out of/towards, etc** to guide someone somewhere, especially by putting your hand on
their back *He steered me towards the door.* ⊃ *See
also:* steer **clear<sup>3</sup>** of sb/sth.

**steering** /'stɪərɪŋ/ *noun* [U] the parts of a vehicle
that control its direction

'**steering ,wheel** *noun* [C] a wheel that you
turn to control the direction of a vehicle

**stem<sup>1</sup>** /stem/ *noun* [C] the long, thin part of a
plant that the leaves and flowers grow on

**stem<sup>2</sup>** /stem/ *verb* [T] **stemming**, *past* **stemmed** to
stop something from continuing or increasing
*The new procedures are intended to **stem the
flow** of drugs into the country.*
**stem from sth** to develop as the result of something *Her problems stem from childhood.*

**stench** /stenʃ/ *noun* [C] a very unpleasant smell
*the stench of rotten fruit*

**stencil** /'stensəl/ *noun* [C] a piece of paper or
plastic with patterns cut into it, that you use to
paint patterns onto a surface ● stencil *verb* [I, T]
*(UK)* stencilling, *past* stencilled, *(US)* stenciling,
*past* stenciled to use a stencil to paint patterns
onto a surface

o⎯**step<sup>1</sup>** /step/ *noun* [C] **1** MOVEMENT one of the
movements you make with your feet when you
walk *She **took** a few **steps** forward and then
started to speak.* **2** METHOD one of the things
that you do to achieve something *This meeting

*is the first **step** towards a peace agreement.*
● *The company has **taken steps** to improve its
customer service.* **3** STAIR one of the surfaces
that you walk on when you go up or down stairs
**4 in step (with sb/sth)** having the same ideas,
opinions, etc as other people *This time, Britain
is in step with the rest of Europe.* **5 out of step
(with sb/sth)** having different ideas, opinions,
etc from other people *Her views are out of
step with government policy.* **6 be one step
ahead (of sb)** to have done something before
someone else **7 watch your step a** used to tell
someone to be careful about where they are
walking **b** to be careful about what you say and
do

**step<sup>2</sup>** /step/ *verb* **stepping**, *past* **stepped 1 step
back/forward/over, etc** to move somewhere
by lifting your foot and putting it down in a different place *She stepped carefully over the dog.*
**2 step on/in sth** to put your foot on or in something *I accidentally stepped on her foot.*
**step down** to leave an important job *He stepped
down as manager of the Italian team.*
**step in** to become involved in a difficult situation in order to help [+ **to do sth**] *A Japanese
bank stepped in to provide financial help.*
**step sth up** to increase what you are doing to
try to achieve something *Police have stepped up
their efforts to find the man.*

**stepbrother** /'step,brʌðə<sup>r</sup>/ *noun* [C] not your
parent's son but the son of the person your
parent has married

**step-by-step** /,stepbaɪ'step/ *adj* [always before
noun] A step-by-step method, plan, etc, deals
with one thing and then another thing in a
fixed order. *a step-by-step guide to buying a
house*

**stepchild** /'steptʃaɪld/ *noun* [C] *plural* **stepchil-
dren** the child of your husband or wife from an
earlier marriage

**stepdaughter** /'step,dɔːtə<sup>r</sup>/ *noun* [C] the
daughter of your husband or wife from an
earlier marriage

**stepfather** /'step,fɑːðə<sup>r</sup>/ *noun* [C] the man who
has married your mother but is not your father

**stepmother** /'step,mʌðə<sup>r</sup>/ *noun* [C] the woman
who has married your father but is not your
mother

**stepping-stone** /'stepɪŋstəʊn/ *noun* [C] **1** an
event or experience that helps you achieve
something else *Education is a stepping-stone to
a good job.* **2** one of several stones that you
walk on to cross a stream

**stepsister** /'step,sɪstə<sup>r</sup>/ *noun* [C] not your
parent's daughter but the daughter of the
person your parent has married

**stepson** /'stepsʌn/ *noun* [C] the son of your
husband or wife from an earlier marriage

**stereo** /'steriəʊ/ *noun* **1** [C] a piece of equipment for playing CDs, listening to the radio, etc that
has two speakers (= parts where sound comes
out) *a car stereo* ⊃ *See colour picture* **The Living
Room** *on page Centre 11.* **2** [U] a system for
hearing music, speech, etc through two speakers (= parts where sound comes out) *The
concert was broadcast **in stereo.*** ● *stereo sound*

**stereotype<sup>1</sup>** /'steriətaɪp/ *noun* [C] a fixed idea
that people have about what a particular type

of person is like, especially an idea that is wrong *racial stereotypes* • stereotypical /ˌsteriəʊ'tɪpɪkᵊl/ *adj* having the qualities that you expect a particular type of person to have *a stereotypical student*

**stereotype²** /'steriəʊtaɪp/ *verb* [T] to have a fixed idea about what a particular type of person is like, especially an idea that is wrong [often passive] *Young people are often stereotyped as being lazy.*

**sterile** /'steraɪl/ *adj* **1** CLEAN completely clean and without any bacteria *a sterile needle* **2** NO CHILDREN unable to produce children **3** NO IDEAS not having enough new ideas *a sterile discussion* • sterility /stə'rɪləti/ *noun* [U]

**sterilize** (*also UK* **-ise**) /'sterᵊlaɪz/ *verb* [T] **1** to make something clean and without bacteria *a sterilized needle* **2** to perform a medical operation on someone to make them unable to have children • sterilization /ˌsterᵊlaɪ'zeɪʃᵊn/ *noun* [U]

**sterling** /'stɜːlɪŋ/ *noun* [U] British money *I'd like to change my dollars into pounds sterling, please.*

**stern¹** /stɜːn/ *adj* very serious and without any humour *a stern expression/face* • *stern criticism* • sternly *adv*

**stern²** /stɜːn/ *noun* [C] the back part of a ship

**steroid** /'sterɔɪd/ *noun* [C] a drug for treating injuries that some people use illegally in sport to make their muscles stronger

**stethoscope** /'steθəskəʊp/ *noun* [C] a piece of equipment that a doctor uses to listen to your heart and breathing

**stew** /stjuː/ *noun* [C, U] a dish made of vegetables and meat cooked together slowly in liquid *beef/lamb stew* • stew *verb* [T] to cook food slowly in liquid *stewed fruit*

**steward** /'stjuːəd/ *noun* [C] **1** a man who looks after people on an aircraft, boat, or train *an air steward* **2** someone who helps to organize a race or big event

**stewardess** /'stjuːədɪs/ *noun* [C] a woman who looks after people on an aircraft, boat, or train *air stewardess*

o-**stick¹** /stɪk/ *verb past* **stuck 1** JOIN [I, T] to become joined to something else or to make something become joined to something else, usually with a substance like glue *Anne stuck a picture of her boyfriend on the wall.* • *The stamp wouldn't stick to the envelope.* **2** PUT **stick sth in/on/under, etc** *informal* to put something somewhere *Just stick your bag under the table.* **3** SOMETHING SHARP **stick (sth) in/into/through, etc** If something sharp sticks into something, it goes into it, and if you stick something sharp somewhere, you push it into something. *She stuck the needle into his arm.* **4** NOT MOVE [I] to become fixed in one position and not be able to move *This drawer has stuck – I can't open it.* **5 can't stick sb/sth** *UK informal* to not like someone or something *I can't stick her.* ➔ *See also:* stick to your guns (**gun¹**), stick your **nose¹** into sth, stick your **oar** in.

**stick around** *informal* to stay somewhere for a period of time *Stick around after the concert and you might meet the band.*

**stick at sth** to continue trying hard to do something difficult *I know it's hard learning to drive but stick at it.*

**stick by sb** to continue to support someone when they are having problems

**stick out 1** If part of something sticks out, it comes out further than the edge or surface. *His ears stick out a bit.* **2** to be very easy to notice *She certainly sticks out in a crowd.* ➔ *See also:* stick out like a sore **thumb¹**.

**stick sth out** to make part of your body come forward from the rest of your body *The little boy stuck his tongue out.*

**stick it out** *informal* to continue doing something that is boring, difficult, or unpleasant *It's a difficult course but I'm determined to stick it out.*

**stick to sth** to continue doing or using something and not change to anything else *I'll stick to lemonade – I'm driving.*

**stick together** If people stick together, they support and help each other.

**stick up** to point up above a surface and not lie flat *I can't go out with my hair sticking up like this.*

**stick up for sb/sth** *informal* to support someone or something when they are being criticized

**stick with sb/sth** to continue using someone or doing something and not change to anyone or anything else *He's a good builder – I think we should stick with him.*

o-**stick²** /stɪk/ *noun* [C] **1** a long, thin piece of wood, usually broken or fallen from a tree **2 walking/hockey, etc stick** a long, thin piece of wood that you use when you are walking/playing hockey, etc **3** a long, thin piece of something *a stick of candy/celery* ➔ *See also:* **carrot** and stick, get (hold of) the wrong **end¹** of the stick.

**sticker** /'stɪkəʳ/ *noun* [C] a piece of paper or plastic with writing or a picture on it that you stick onto a surface *a car sticker* ➔ *See also:* **bumper sticker**.

**sticky** /'stɪki/ *adj* **1** made of or covered with a substance that can stick to other things *sticky fingers* • *sticky tape* **2** Sticky weather is unpleasantly hot. *a sticky August afternoon* **3** a **sticky moment/problem/situation, etc** *informal* a moment/problem/situation, etc that is difficult or embarrassing you

o-**stiff¹** /stɪf/ *adj* **1** HARD hard and difficult to bend *stiff material* **2** NOT MOVING A door, drawer, etc that is stiff does not move as easily as it should. **3** HURTING If a part of your body is stiff, it hurts and is difficult to move. *I've got a stiff neck.* **4** SEVERE very severe or difficult *stiff competition/opposition* • *We need stiffer penalties for drink driving.* **5** FORMAL behaving in a way that is formal and not relaxed **6** THICK A stiff substance is thick and does not move around easily. *Whip the cream until it is stiff.* **7 stiff drink/whisky/vodka, etc** a strong alcoholic drink *I need a stiff brandy.* **8 stiff wind/breeze** a wind that is quite strong • stiffly *adv* • stiffness *noun* [U]

**stiff²** /stɪf/ *adv* **bored/scared/worried, etc stiff** extremely bored, worried, etc *The lecture was awful – I was bored stiff.*

**stiffen** /'stɪfᵊn/ *verb* **1** [I, T] to become stiff or to make something become stiff **2** [I] to suddenly stop moving because you are frightened or angry *She stiffened at the sound of the doorbell.*

**stifle** /'staɪfl/ *verb* [T] to stop something from happening or continuing *to stifle a sneeze/ yawn* • *Large supermarkets stifle competition.*

**stifling** /'staɪflɪŋ/ *adj* extremely hot *a stifling summer in Rome*

**stigma** /'stɪɡmə/ *noun* [C, U] when people disapprove of something, especially when this is unfair *There is still **a stigma attached** to being mentally ill.* • **stigmatize** (*also UK* **-ise**) *verb* [T] to treat someone or something unfairly by disapproving of them [often passive] *Unmarried mothers are stigmatized by society.*

**stiletto** /stɪ'letəʊ/ *noun* [C] a shoe with a very high, pointed heel (= part at the bottom and back of a shoe) *a pair of stilettos*

○━**still¹** /stɪl/ *adv* **1** CONTINUING used to say that something is continuing to happen now or that someone is continuing to do something now *He's still here if you want to speak to him.* • *Do you still play basketball?* **2** POSSIBLE used to say that something continues to be possible *We could still catch the train if we leave now.* **3** EMPHASIS used to emphasize that you did not expect something to happen because something else makes it surprising *He didn't do much work but still came top of the class.* • *The weather was terrible. Still, we had a good holiday.* **4** **better/harder/worse, etc still** better/harder/worse, etc than something else

○━**still²** /stɪl/ *adj* **1** **stand/stay/sit, etc still** to stand, stay, sit, etc without moving *Sit still so I can brush your hair.* **2** A still place is calm and quiet. *It was night and the whole village was still.* **3** *UK* A still drink does not have any bubbles in it. • **stillness** *noun* [U]

**still³** /stɪl/ *noun* [C] a photograph from one moment in a film

**stillborn** /,stɪl'bɔːn ⓤ⑤ 'stɪl,bɔːn/ *adj* born dead *a stillborn baby*

**stilt** /stɪlt/ *noun* [C] **1** one of two long poles that you can stand on and use to walk above the ground [usually plural] *a clown on stilts* **2** one of several poles that support a building above the ground [usually plural] *a house on stilts*

**stilted** /'stɪltɪd/ *adj* talking or writing in a formal way that does not sound natural *a stilted conversation*

**stimulant** /'stɪmjələnt/ *noun* [C] a drug that makes you feel more active and awake *Coffee contains caffeine which is a stimulant.*

**stimulate** /'stɪmjəleɪt/ *verb* [T] **1** to make something happen or develop more *It stimulates the production of red blood cells.* **2** to make someone feel interested and excited *Colourful pictures can stimulate a child.* • **stimulation** /,stɪmjə'leɪʃ⁰n/ *noun* [U]

**stimulating** /'stɪmjəleɪtɪŋ/ *adj* interesting and making you think *a stimulating discussion*

**stimulus** /'stɪmjələs/ *noun* [C, U] *plural* **stimuli** /'stɪmjəlaɪ/ something that makes something else happen, grow, or develop more *The report provided the stimulus for more studies.*

**sting¹** /stɪŋ/ *verb past* **stung 1** CAUSE PAIN [T] If an insect, plant, etc stings you, it causes pain by putting poison into your skin. *He was stung*

by a wasp. **2** FEEL PAIN [I, T] If your eyes, skin, etc sting, or if something makes them sting, you feel a sudden, burning pain. *That shampoo really made my eyes sting.* **3** UPSET [T] to upset someone [often passive] *She was clearly stung by his criticism.*

**sting²** /stɪŋ/ *noun* **1** WOUND [C] a painful wound that you get when an insect, plant, etc puts poison into your skin *a wasp/bee sting* **2** PAIN [no plural] a sudden, burning pain in your eyes, skin, etc **3** UPSET [no plural] the feeling of being upset by something *the sting of defeat*

**stingy** /'stɪndʒi/ *adj informal* not generous *He's too stingy to buy any drinks.*

**stink¹** /stɪŋk/ *verb* [I] *past t* **stank** (*also US*) **stunk**, *past p* **stunk 1** to smell very bad *The kitchen stinks of fish.* **2** *informal* to be very bad and dishonest *If you ask me, the whole affair stinks.*

**stink²** /stɪŋk/ *noun* **1** **make/cause/create, etc a stink** *informal* to complain about something in a forceful way *He caused a real stink about his hotel room.* **2** [no plural] a very bad smell

**stint** /stɪnt/ *noun* [C] a period of time spent doing something *He had a two-year stint as a teacher in Spain.*

**stipulate** /'stɪpjəleɪt/ *verb* [T] *formal* to say exactly what must be done [+ **(that)**] *The rules stipulate that smoking is not allowed.* • **stipulation** /,stɪpjə'leɪʃ⁰n/ *noun* [C]

○━**stir¹** /stɜːʳ/ *verb* **stirring**, *past* **stirred 1** MIX [T] to mix food or liquid by moving a spoon round and round in it *Stir the mixture until it is smooth.* **2** MOVE [I, T] to move slightly or make someone move slightly *The baby stirred in its sleep.* **3** FEEL [T] to make someone feel a strong emotion *The case has stirred great anger among the public.*
**stir sth up 1** to cause arguments or bad feelings between people, often intentionally *I think she just likes to stir up trouble.* **2** If something stirs up memories, it makes you remember events in the past. *The photographs stirred up some painful memories.*

**stir²** /stɜːʳ/ *noun* **1** **cause/create a stir** to make people excited or surprised *Her new book has caused quite a stir.* **2** [no plural] when you mix food or liquid with a spoon *Could you give the soup a stir?*

**stir-fry** /'stɜː,fraɪ/ *verb* [T] to fry small pieces of vegetable, meat, etc very quickly while mixing them around • **stir-fry** *noun* [C]

**stirring** /'stɜːrɪŋ/ *adj* making people feel excitement or other strong emotions *a stirring performance/speech*

**stirrup** /'stɪrəp/ *noun* [C] one of the two metal parts that support your feet when you are riding a horse

**stitch¹** /stɪtʃ/ *noun* **1** THREAD [C] a short line of thread that is sewn through a piece of material **2** WOUND [C] one of the small pieces of thread that is used to sew together a cut *She needed 50 stitches in her head.* **3** WOOL [C] one of the small circles of wool that you make when you are knitting (= making something from wool) **4** PAIN [no plural] a sudden pain that you get in the side of your body when you exercise too much *to get a stitch* **5** **in stitches** laughing a lot *He had the whole audience in stitches.*

**stitch²** /stɪtʃ/ *verb* [I, T] to sew two things

together or to repair something by sewing *I need to get my shoes stitched.*

**stitch sth up** to sew together the two parts of something that have come apart *The nurse stitched up my finger.*

**stock¹** /stɒk/ *noun* **1** SHOP [U] all the goods that are available in a shop *We're expecting some new stock in this afternoon.* **2 be in stock/out of stock** to be available/not available in a shop **3** SUPPLY [C] a supply of something that is ready to be used [usually plural] *stocks of food/weapons* **4** COMPANY [C, U] the value of a company, or a share in its value *to buy/sell stock • falling/rising stock prices* **5** LIQUID [U] a liquid made by boiling meat, bones, or vegetables and used to make soups, sauces, etc *chicken/vegetable stock* **6 take stock (of sth)** to think carefully about a situation before making a decision ⊃ *See also:* **laughing stock.**

**stock²** /stɒk/ *verb* [T] to have something available for people to buy *They stock a wide range of books and magazines.*

**stock up** to buy a lot of something *We'd better stock up on food for the holiday.*

**stock³** /stɒk/ *adj* **stock answer/phrase, etc** an answer/phrase, etc that is always used and so is not really useful

**stockbroker** /'stɒk,brəʊkəʳ/ *noun* [C] someone whose job is to buy and sell stocks and shares in companies for other people

**the 'stock ex,change** (*also* **the 'stock ,market**) *noun* **1** the place where stocks and shares in companies are bought and sold **2** the value of stocks and shares being bought and sold

**stocking** /'stɒkɪŋ/ *noun* [C] a very thin piece of clothing that covers a woman's foot and leg *a pair of stockings* ⊃ *See colour picture* **Clothes** *on page Centre 5.*

**stockpile** /'stɒkpaɪl/ *verb* [T] to collect a lot of something, usually so that it can be used in the future *to stockpile food • stockpile noun* [C] *a stockpile of weapons*

**stocky** /'stɒki/ *adj* having a wide, strong, body *a short, stocky man*

**stoic** /'stəʊɪk/ *adj formal* dealing with pain, problems, etc, but never complaining • **stoically** *adv* • **stoicism** /'stəʊɪsɪzᵊm/ *noun* [U]

**stole** /stəʊl/ *past tense of* steal

**stolen** /'stəʊlᵊn/ *past participle of* steal

**stolid** /'stɒlɪd/ *adj* calm and not showing emotion or excitement

**stomach¹** /'stʌmək/ *noun* [C] *plural* **stomachs** **1** the organ inside your body where food is digested **2** the front part of your body just below your chest *He punched me in the stomach.* ⊃ *See colour picture* **The Body** *on page Centre 2.* **3 have no stomach for sth** to not feel brave enough to do something unpleasant ⊃ *See also:* have butterflies (**butterfly**) (in your stomach).

**stomach²** /'stʌmək/ *verb informal* **can't stomach sth** to be unable to deal with, watch, etc something unpleasant *I can't stomach horror movies.*

**'stomach ,ache** *noun* [C, U] pain in your stomach *I've got terrible stomach ache.*

**stomp** /stɒmp/ *verb* [I] to put your foot down on the ground hard and quickly, or to walk with

heavy steps, usually because you are angry *He stomped off to his room.*

o─**stone¹** /stəʊn/ *noun* **1** SUBSTANCE [U] a hard, natural substance that is found in the ground *a stone wall* **2** ROCK [C] a small rock or piece of rock **3** JEWEL [C] a hard, valuable substance that is often used in jewellery *precious stones* **4** WEIGHT [C] *plural* **stone** *UK* a unit for measuring weight, equal to 6.35 kilograms or 14 pounds *I gained two stone when I was pregnant.* **5** SEED [C] the hard seed that is at the centre of some fruits *a cherry stone* ⊃ *See also:* **stepping-stone.**

**stone²** /stəʊn/ *verb* [T] to kill or hurt someone by throwing stones (= small rocks) at them, usually as a punishment [often passive] *Two men were stoned to death by the crowd.*

**stoned** /stəʊnd/ *adj informal* **1** relaxed or excited because of the effect of drugs **2** drunk

**stonemason** /'stəʊn,meɪsᵊn/ *noun* [C] someone who makes things from stone

**stony** /'stəʊni/ *adj* **1** covered with or containing stones (= small rocks) *a stony path/road* **2** not friendly, usually because you are angry *a stony silence*

**stood** /stʊd/ *past of* stand

**stool** /stuːl/ *noun* [C] a seat that does not have a back or arms *a piano/bar stool*

**stoop¹** /stuːp/ *verb* [I] to bend the top half of your body forward and down *He stooped to pick up the letter.*

**stoop to sth/doing sth** to do something bad that will give you an advantage *I can't believe he would stoop to blackmail.*

**stoop²** /stuːp/ *noun* **1** [no plural] when the upper part of your body is bent forwards *He has a slight stoop.* **2** [C] *US* a raised area in front of the door of a house, with steps leading up to it

o─**stop¹** /stɒp/ *verb* **stopping**, *past* **stopped** **1** FINISH [I, T] to finish doing something that you were doing [+ doing sth] *Stop laughing – it's not funny.* • *He started to say something and then stopped.* • *I'm trying to work but I keep having to stop to answer the phone* (= stop so that I can answer the telephone). **2** FOR A SHORT TIME [I] to stop a journey or an activity for a short time *He stopped at a pub for lunch.* **3** NOT OPERATE [I, T] to not continue to operate, or to make something not continue to operate *My watch has stopped.* • *Can you stop the video for a minute?* **4** FINISH MOVING [I, T] to not move any more, or make someone or something not move any more *A car stopped outside the house.* • *I stopped someone in the street to ask for directions.* **5** BUS/TRAIN [I] If a bus, train, etc stops at a particular place, it pauses at that place so that people can get on and off. *Does this train stop at Cambridge?* **6** END [T] to make something end *We must find a way to stop the war.* **7** PREVENT [T] to prevent something from happening or someone from doing something [+ from + doing sth] *Health workers are trying to stop the disease from spreading.* **8 Stop it/that!** used to tell someone to finish doing something, usually something annoying *Stop it! I can't concentrate if you keep making a noise.* **9 stop a cheque** *UK* (*US* **stop a check**) to prevent money from being paid from a cheque (= a piece of paper that you sign to pay for things) ➔ *See also:* stop at **nothing**, stop the **rot²**.

**stop doing something** or **stop to do something**?

Stop doing something means 'not continue with an activity'.

*Suddenly, everyone stopped talking.*

~~Suddenly, everyone stopped to talk.~~

Stop to do something means 'stop one activity so that you can do something else'.

*We stopped to look at the map.*

**stop by (sth)** to visit a person or place for a short time *If you're passing our house, why don't you stop by sometime?*

**stop off** to visit a place for a short time when you are going somewhere else *We stopped off in Paris for a couple of days before heading south.*

**stop²** /stɒp/ *noun* [C] **1** a place where a bus or train stops so that people can get on or off *We need to get off at the next stop.* ➔ *See usage note at* **station.** **2 put a stop to sth** to end something unpleasant *We must put a stop to the violence.* **3** a place where you stop on a journey, or the time that you spend there *We had an overnight stop in Singapore.* **4 come to a stop** to stop moving *The car came to a stop in front of an old cottage.* **5 pull out all the stops** to do everything you can to make something succeed *They pulled out all the stops for their daughter's wedding.* ➔ *See also:* **bus stop, full stop.**

**stoplight** /'stɒplaɪt/ *US noun* [C] a set of red, green, and yellow lights that is used to stop and start traffic

**stopover** /'stɒp,əʊvə<sup>r</sup>/ *noun* [C] a short stop between parts of a journey, especially a plane journey

**stoppage** /'stɒpɪdʒ/ *noun* [C] when people stop working because they are angry about something their employers have done

**stopwatch** /'stɒpwɒtʃ/ *noun* [C] a watch that can measure exactly how long it takes to do something and is often used in sports activities

**storage** /'stɔːrɪdʒ/ *noun* [U] when you put things in a safe place until they are needed *We had to put our furniture into storage.*

○<sup>—</sup>**store¹** /stɔː<sup>r</sup>/ *noun* [C] **1** *mainly US* a shop *a book store* • *She works at a men's clothing store.* ➔ *See usage note at* **shop. 2** a supply of something that you are keeping to use later *a store of grain* **3 be in store (for sb)** If something is in store for you, it will happen to you in the future. *There's a surprise in store for you!* **4 set great store by sth** *UK* to believe that something is very important *Martina sets great store by physical strength and fitness.* ➔ *See also:* **chain store, convenience store, department store, liquor store.**

○<sup>—</sup>**store²** /stɔː<sup>r</sup>/ *verb* [T] **1** (*also* **store away**) to put something somewhere and not use it until you need it *We have a lot of old clothes stored in the attic.* **2** to keep information on a computer *All the data is stored on diskettes.*

**storeroom** /'stɔːruːm/ *noun* [C] a room where goods are kept until they are needed

**storey** *UK* (*US* **story**) /'stɔːri/ *noun* [C] a level of a building *a three-storey house*

**stork** /stɔːk/ *noun* [C] a large, white bird with very long legs which walks around in water to find its food

○<sup>—</sup>**storm¹** /stɔːm/ *noun* [C] **1** very bad weather with a lot of rain, snow, wind, etc *a snow/thunder storm* **2 a storm of controversy/protest, etc** a strong, negative reaction to something that has been said or done

**storm²** /stɔːm/ *verb* **1** [T] to attack a building, town, etc, using violence *Armed police stormed the embassy and arrested hundreds of protesters.* **2 storm into/out of, etc** to enter or leave a place in a very noisy way because you are angry *He stormed out of the meeting.*

**stormy** /'stɔːmi/ *adj* **1** If it is stormy, the weather is bad with a lot of wind and rain. *a stormy night* **2** A stormy relationship or situation involves a lot of anger and arguments. *a stormy relationship* • *a stormy meeting/debate*

○<sup>—</sup>**story** /'stɔːri/ *noun* [C] **1** DESCRIPTION a description of a series of real or imaginary events which is intended to entertain people *a horror/detective story* • *the story of the revolution* • *Tell us a story, Mum.* • *She reads stories to the children every night.* **2** REPORT a report in a newspaper, magazine, or news programme *Today's main story is the hurricane in Texas.* **3** EXPLANATION an explanation of why something happened, which may not be true *Did he tell you the same story about why he was late?* **4** BUILDING *US spelling of* storey

**stout¹** /staʊt/ *adj* **1** quite fat *a short, stout man* **2** If shoes or other objects are stout, they are strong and thick.

**stout²** /staʊt/ *noun* [C, U] a very dark beer

**stove** /stəʊv/ *noun* [C] **1** a piece of equipment that you cook on *I've left some soup on the stove for you.* ➔ *See colour picture* **Kitchen** *on page Centre 10.* **2** a piece of equipment that burns coal, gas, wood, etc and is used for heating a room

**stow** /stəʊ/ (*also* **stow away**) *verb* [T] to put something in a particular place until it is needed *Our camping equipment is stowed away in the loft.*

**stowaway** /'stəʊə,weɪ/ *noun* [C] someone who hides on a ship or aircraft so that they can travel without paying

**straddle** /'strædl/ *verb* [T] **1** to sit or stand with one leg on either side of something *He straddled the chair.* **2** to be on both sides of a place *Niagara Falls straddles the Canadian border.*

**straggle** /'strægl/ *verb* [I] **1** to move more slowly than other members of a group *Some runners are straggling a long way behind.* **2** to grow or spread out in an untidy way *I could see a line of straggling bushes.*

**straggly** /'strægli/ *adj* growing or spreading out in an untidy way *a straggly beard*

○<sup>—</sup>**straight¹** /streɪt/ *adj* **1** NOT CURVED not curved or bent *a straight road* • *straight hair* ➔ *See colour picture* **Hair** *on page Centre 9.* **2** LEVEL in a position that is level or vertical *That shelf's not straight.* **3** IN A SERIES [always before noun] one after another *They've won five straight games* *so far.* **4** HONEST *honest a straight answer* • *I don't think he was being straight with me.* **5** DRINK An alcoholic drink that is straight is not mixed with water, ice, etc. **6 get sth straight** to make sure that you completely understand a situation *Let me get this straight – am I paying for this?* **7** NOT HOMOSEXUAL *informal* not homosexual ⊃ *See also:* keep a straight face¹.

o⫶**straight²** /streɪt/ *adv* **1** in a straight line *It's straight ahead.* • *He was looking straight at me.* **2** immediately *I went straight back to sleep.* **3 sit up/stand up straight** to sit or stand with your body vertical **4 not think straight** If you cannot think straight, you are not thinking clearly about something. *I was so tired, I couldn't think straight.* **5 tell sb straight (out)** to tell someone the truth in a clear way *I told him straight that he wasn't getting a pay increase.* **6 straight away** immediately *Go there straight away.*

straighten /'streɪtᵊn/ *verb* [I, T] to become straight or to make something straight

**straighten sth out** to successfully deal with a problem or a confusing situation *We need to straighten a few things out.*

**straighten sth up** to make a place tidy *Could you straighten up your room?*

**straighten up** to stand so that your back is straight

straightforward /ˌstreɪt'fɔːwəd/ *adj* **1** easy to do or understand *The task looked fairly straightforward.* **2** saying clearly and honestly what you think *She's very straightforward.*

strain¹ /streɪn/ *noun* **1** FEELING [C, U] when you feel worried and nervous about something *The strain of the last few months had exhausted her.* **2 put a strain on sb/sth** to cause problems for someone or to make a situation difficult *Children put tremendous strains on a marriage.* **3** INJURY [C, U] an injury to part of your body that is caused by using it too much *back strain* **4** STRETCH [U] when something is pulled or stretched too tightly *The rope broke under the strain.* **5** DISEASE/PLANT [C] a type of disease or plant *a new strain of virus*

strain² /streɪn/ *verb* **1** TRY HARD [I, T] to try hard to do something, usually to see or hear something [+ to do sth] *I had to strain to hear the music.* **2** INJURE [T] to injure part of your body by using it too much *I think I've strained a muscle.* **3** CAUSE PROBLEMS [T] to cause problems for a situation or relationship *The incident has strained relations between the two countries.* **4** MONEY [T] to cause too much of something to be used, especially money *The war is straining the defence budget.* **5** SEPARATE [T] to separate solids from a liquid by pouring the mixture into a container with small holes in it *Strain the sauce to remove the seeds and skins.*

strained /streɪnd/ *adj* **1** showing that someone is nervous or anxious *We had a rather strained conversation.* **2** If a relationship is strained, problems are spoiling that relationship. *Relations are still strained between the two countries.*

strait /streɪt/ *noun* [C] a narrow area of sea that connects two large areas of sea [usually plural] *the straits of Florida*

strait-jacket /'streɪtˌdʒækɪt/ *noun* [C] a special jacket used for mentally ill people that prevents them from moving their arms

strand /strænd/ *noun* [C] **1** a thin piece of hair, thread, rope, etc *She tucked a strand of hair behind her ear.* **2** one part of a story, situation, idea, etc *There are a number of different strands to the plot.*

stranded /'strændɪd/ *adj* unable to leave a place *We were stranded at the airport for ten hours.*

o⫶**strange** /streɪndʒ/ *adj* **1** If something is strange, it is surprising because it is unusual or unexpected. [+ (that)] *It's strange that she hasn't called.* • *It's midnight and he's still at work – that's strange.* • *What a strange-looking man.* **2** A strange person or place is one that you are not familiar with. *I was stuck in a strange town with no money.* • strangely *adv She's been behaving very strangely (= in an unusual way) recently.*

stranger /'streɪndʒəʳ/ *noun* [C] **1** someone you have never met before *I can't just walk up to a complete stranger and start speaking to them.* **2 be no stranger to sth** to have a lot of experience of something *He's no stranger to hard work himself.*

strangle /'stræŋgl/ *verb* [T] **1** to kill someone by pressing their throat with your hands, a rope, wire, etc [often passive] *Police believe the victim was strangled.* **2** to prevent something from developing *High-level corruption is strangling the economy.*

stranglehold /'stræŋglhəʊld/ *noun* [no plural] a position of complete control that prevents something from developing *Two major companies have a stranglehold on the market.*

strap /stræp/ *noun* [C] a narrow piece of material used to fasten two things together or to carry something *a watch strap* • *a bra strap* • *I want a bag with a shoulder strap.* • strap *verb* [T] **strapping**, *past* **strapped** to fasten something using a strap

strategic /strə'tiːdʒɪk/ *adj* **1** PLAN helping to achieve a plan, usually in business or politics *strategic planning* **2** WAR related to fighting a war *strategic weapons* **3** POSITION If something is in a strategic position, it is in a useful place for achieving something. • strategically *adv*

strategy /'strætədʒi/ *noun* **1** [C] a plan that you use to achieve something *a sales strategy* **2** [U] the act of planning how to achieve something *military strategy*

straw /strɔː/ *noun* **1** [U] the long, dried stems of plants such as wheat (= plant for grain), often

**S**

given to animals for sleeping on and eating *a straw hat* **2** [C] a thin plastic or paper tube that you use for drinking through **3 the final/last straw** the last in a series of unpleasant events which finally makes you stop accepting a bad situation *Last week he came home drunk at five in the morning, and that was the last straw.*

**strawberry** /'strɔːbºri/ *noun* [C] a small, red fruit with a green leaf at the top and small, brown seeds on its surface

**stray¹** /streɪ/ *verb* [I] **1** to move away from the place where you should be, without intending to *I suddenly realized that I had strayed far from the village.* **2** to start thinking or talking about a different subject from the one you should be giving attention to *We seem to have strayed from the original subject.*

**stray²** /streɪ/ *adj* [always before noun] **1** A stray animal is lost or has no home. *a stray dog* **2** A stray piece of something has become separated from the main part. *a stray hair*

**stray³** /streɪ/ *noun* [C] an animal that is lost or has no home

**streak¹** /striːk/ *noun* [C] **1** a thin line or mark *She has a streak of white hair.* **2** a quality in someone's character, especially a bad one *Tom has a stubborn streak.* **3 a winning/losing streak** a period of always winning/losing a game *I'm on a winning streak.*

**streak²** /striːk/ *verb* **1 streak across/down/ through, etc** to move quickly *The plane streaked across the sky.* **2 be streaked with sth** to have thin lines of a different colour *His dark hair was lightly streaked with grey.*

**stream¹** /striːm/ *noun* [C] **1** a small river **2 a stream of sth a** a line of people or vehicles moving in the same direction *a constant stream of traffic* **b** a large number of similar things that happen or appear one after another *He has produced a steady stream of books.* **c** a moving line of liquid, gas, smoke, etc *A stream of smoke was coming from the chimney.*

**stream**

stream          stream of water

**stream²** /striːm/ *verb* **stream down/in/ through, etc** to move or flow continuously in one direction *Tears were streaming down her face.*

**streamer** /'striːmºr/ *noun* [C] a long, narrow piece of coloured paper that you use to decorate a room or place for a party

**streamline** /'striːmlaɪn/ *verb* [T] **1** to make an organization or process simpler and more effective *We need to streamline our production procedures.* **2** to give a vehicle a smooth shape so that it moves easily through air or water

◦━**street** /striːt/ *noun* [C] **1** a road in a town or city that has houses or other buildings *We live on the same street.* • *a street map* **2 the man/ person, etc in the street** a typical, ordinary person **3 be right up sb's street** *UK informal* (*US* **be right up sb's alley**) to be exactly the type of thing that someone knows about or likes to do *I've got a little job here which should be right up your street.* **4 be streets ahead (of sb/sth)** *UK* to be much better or more advanced than someone or something else *American film companies are streets ahead of their European rivals.* ➔ *See also:* **high street**, **Wall Street**.

**streetcar** /'striːtkɑːʳ/ *US* (*UK/US* **tram**) *noun* [C] an electric vehicle for carrying passengers, mostly in cities, which runs along metal tracks in the road

**'street ˌlight** (*also* **'street ˌlamp**) *noun* [C] a light on a tall post next to a street ➔ *See picture at* **light**.

◦━**strength** /streŋθ/ *noun* **1** [STRONG] [U] when someone or something is strong *upper-body strength* • *A good boxer needs skill as well as strength.* **2** [INFLUENCE] [U] the power or influence that an organization, country, etc has *economic strength* **3** [BEING BRAVE] [U] when you are brave or determined in difficult situations *I think she showed great strength of character.* • *He has a great deal of inner strength.* **4** [GOOD QUALITIES] [C] a good quality or ability that makes someone or something effective *We all have our strengths and weaknesses.* • *The great strength of this arrangement is its simplicity.* **5** [STRONG FEELING] [U] how strong a feeling or opinion is *There is great strength of feeling against tax increases.* **6** [VALUE] [U] the value of a country's money *The strength of the dollar has traders worried.* **7 at full strength** with the necessary number of people *Our team is now at full strength.* **8 on the strength of sth** If you do something on the strength of facts or advice, you do it because of them. *On the strength of this year's sales figures, we've decided to expand the business.* **9 go from strength to strength** *UK* to continue to become more successful ➔ *See also:* **a tower¹ of strength**.

**strengthen** /'streŋθºn/ *verb* [I, T] to become stronger or make something become stronger *exercises to strengthen the leg muscles*

**strenuous** /'strenjuəs/ *adj* using or needing a lot of effort *strenuous exercise*

◦━**stress¹** /stres/ *noun* **1** [WORRY] [C, U] feelings of worry caused by difficult situations such as problems at work *work-related stress* • *Regular exercise can help reduce stress.* • *She's been under a lot of stress recently.* **2** [IMPORTANCE] [U] special importance that you give to something *At school, they laid great stress on academic achievement.* **3** [PHYSICAL FORCE] [C, U] physical force on something *Jogging puts a lot of stress* *on your knee joints.* **4** STRONG PART [U] when you say one part of a word more strongly *In the word 'blanket', the stress is on the first syllable.*

**stress²** /stres/ *verb* **1** [T] to emphasize something in order to show that it is important [+ (that)] *I stressed that this was our policy.* **2** [I] *US informal* to be worried *Stop stressing about tonight – it'll be fine.*

**stressed** /strest/ (*also* **stressed out**) *adj* worried and not able to relax *Tanya's really stressed out about her exams.*

**stressful** /'stresfəl/ *adj* making you stressed *a stressful job*

o→**stretch¹** /stretʃ/ *verb* **1** [I, T] to become longer or wider, or to pull something so that it becomes longer or wider *Don't pull my sweater – you'll stretch it.* **2** [I, T] to make your body or part of your body straighter and longer *Stretch your arms above your head.* **3 stretch away/into, etc** to cover a large area *The fields stretched away into the distance.* **4 stretch into/over, etc** to continue for a long period of time *The discussions will probably stretch into next month.* ➔ *See also:* stretch your legs (**leg**), stretch the rules (**rule¹**). **stretch out** to lie with your legs and arms spread out in a relaxed way

**stretch²** /stretʃ/ *noun* [C] **1** LAND/WATER an area of land or water *a stretch of coastline* **2** TIME a continuous period of time *He often worked ten hours at a stretch.* **3** BODY when you stretch part of your body *I always do a few stretches before I go jogging.* **4 not by any stretch of the imagination** used to say that something, often a description, is certainly not true *She was never a great player, not by any stretch of the imagination.*

**stretcher** /'stretʃər/ *noun* [C] a flat structure covered with cloth which is used to carry someone who is ill or injured

**stricken** /'strɪkən/ *adj* suffering from the effects of something bad, such as illness, sadness, etc *a child stricken by fear* ➔ *See also:* **panic-stricken**, **poverty-stricken**.

o→**strict** /strɪkt/ *adj* **1** PERSON A strict person makes sure that children or people working for them behave well and does not allow them to break any rules. *a strict teacher* • *My parents were very strict with us.* **2** RULE If a rule, law, etc is strict, it must be obeyed. *She gave me strict instructions to be there by ten.* **3** BEHAVIOUR [always before noun] always behaving in a particular way because of your beliefs *a strict Muslim* **4** EXACT exactly correct *a strict translation of a text*

**strictly** /'strɪktli/ *adv* **1** exactly or correctly *That's not strictly true.* • ***Strictly speaking*** (= The rules say), *we're not allowed to give you any advice.* **2** done or existing for a particular person or purpose *Her visit is strictly business.* **3 strictly forbidden/prohibited** used to emphasize that something is not allowed

**stride¹** /straɪd/ *verb past t* **strode stride across/ down/into, etc** to walk somewhere with long steps *She strode across the stage.*

**stride²** /straɪd/ *noun* [C] **1** a long step when walking or running **2 get into your stride** *UK* (*US* **hit your stride**) to start to do something well and with confidence because you have been doing it for a period *Once I get into my stride,*

*I'm sure I'll work much faster.* **3 take sth in your stride** *UK* (*US* **take sth in stride**) to calmly deal with something that is unpleasant and not let it affect what you are doing *There are often problems at work but she seems to take it all in her stride.*

**strident** /'straɪdənt/ *adj* **1** expressed in a strong way *strident criticism* **2** loud and unpleasant *a strident voice*

**strife** /straɪf/ *noun* [U] *formal* trouble or disagreement between people

o→**strike¹** /straɪk/ *verb past* **struck 1** HIT [T] to hit someone or something *Two climbers were struck by falling rocks.* • *His car went out of control and struck a tree.* • *I've never heard of anyone being struck by lightning.* **2** THINK [T] If a thought or idea strikes you, you suddenly think of it. [+ (that)] *It struck me that I'd forgotten to order the champagne.* **3 strike sb as sth** If someone strikes you as having a particular quality, they seem to have that quality. *He didn't strike me as a passionate man.* **4** NOT WORK [I] to stop working for a period of time because you want more money, etc *Bus drivers are threatening to strike.* **5** EFFECT [T] If something bad strikes something or someone, it affects them strongly and quickly. *The hurricane struck the coast at about eight in the morning.* **6** ATTACK [I] to attack suddenly *The marines will strike at dawn.* **7** CLOCK [I, T] If a clock strikes, a bell rings to show what the time is. **8 strike gold, oil, etc** to find a supply of gold, oil, etc in the ground **9 strike a match** to light a match in order to produce fire **10 strike a balance** to give two things the same amount of attention *It's important to strike a balance between spending and saving.* **11 strike a deal** If two people strike a deal, they promise to do something for each other which will give them both an advantage. *The book's author has struck a deal with a major film company.* ➔ *See also:* strike a **chord** (with sb), be struck **dumb**.

**strike back** to attack someone who has attacked you

**strike out 1** to start moving towards somewhere in a determined way *She struck out for the opposite bank.* **2** *US informal* to fail at something *I really struck out with her – she wouldn't even let me kiss her goodbye.*

**strike sth out** to draw a line through something wrong that you have written

**strike up sth** to start a conversation or relationship with someone *I struck up a conversation with a guy who worked behind the bar.*

**strike²** /straɪk/ *noun* **1** [C, U] a period of time when people are not working because they want more money, etc *Teachers are planning to go on strike next month.* **2** [C] a sudden military attack *an air strike* ➔ *See also:* **hunger strike**.

**striker** /'straɪkər/ *noun* [C] **1** someone who is on strike **2** a football player whose job is to try to score goals

**striking** /'straɪkɪŋ/ *adj* **1** easily noticed *There's a striking resemblance between them.* **2** very attractive *She's very striking.*

**string¹** /strɪŋ/ *noun* **1** [C, U] very thin rope used for tying things *a ball of string* **2** [C] a piece of wire that is part of a musical instrument *guitar strings* **3 a string of beads/pearls** a set of decorative things joined together on a thread, worn as jewellery **4 a string of sth** a number of similar things *a string of questions* • *As a writer, she's enjoyed a string of successes.* **5 no strings (attached)** If there are no strings attached to an offer or arrangement, there is nothing that is unpleasant that you have to accept. *I'll drive you home – no strings attached.* **6 pull strings** to secretly use the influence that you have over important people to get something or to help someone *I may be able to pull a few strings, if you need the money urgently.*

**string²** /strɪŋ/ *verb* [T] *past* **strung** to hang something somewhere with string *They had strung flags across the entrance to welcome us home.*

**string sb along** to deceive someone for a long time about what you are intending to do

**be strung out** If a group of things or people are strung out somewhere, they are in a line with spaces between them. *There were chairs strung out across the room.*

**stringent** /'strɪndʒənt/ *adj* Stringent controls, rules, etc are very strict or extreme.

**the strings** /strɪŋz/ *noun* [plural] the people in a musical group who play instruments with strings on them such as the violin

**strip¹** /strɪp/ *verb* **stripping**, *past* **stripped 1** [I, T] (*also UK* **strip off**) to remove all your clothes, or to remove all someone else's clothes *She was stripped and searched by the guards.* • *He stripped off his clothes and ran into the sea.* **2** [T] (*also* **strip off**) to remove a covering from the surface of something *to strip paint/wallpaper off the wall*

**strip sb of sth** to take something important away from someone as a punishment *He was stripped of his gold medal.*

**strip²** /strɪp/ *noun* [C] **1** PIECE a long, narrow piece of something *a strip of paper/plastic* **2** AREA a long, narrow area of land or water **3** REMOVING CLOTHES entertainment in which someone takes off their clothes in a sexually exciting way *a strip club/show* ➭ *See also:* **comic strip**.

**stripe** /straɪp/ *noun* [C] a long, straight area of colour *white with blue stripes* ➭ *See picture at* **horizontal**.

**striped** /straɪpt/ *adj* with a pattern of stripes *a striped shirt*

**stripey** /'straɪpi/ *adj another spelling of* stripy

**stripper** /'strɪpər/ *noun* [C] someone who takes off their clothes in a sexually exciting way to entertain people

**striptease** /'strɪptiːz/ *noun* [C, U] entertainment in which someone takes off their clothes in a sexually exciting way

**stripy** (*also* **stripey**) /'straɪpi/ *adj* with a pattern of stripes *stripy trousers*

**strive** /straɪv/ *verb* [I] *past t* **strove** or **strived**, *past p* **striven** or **strived** *formal* to try very hard to do or achieve something *to strive for happiness/peace* • [+ to do sth] *We are constantly striving to improve our service.*

**strode** /strəʊd/ *past of* stride

**stroke¹** /strəʊk/ *noun* **1** ILLNESS [C] a sudden problem in your brain that changes the flow of blood and makes you unable to move part of

your body *to have/suffer a stroke* **2** MOVEMENT [C] a movement that you make against something with your hand, a pen, brush, etc *a brush stroke* **3** SWIMMING [C] a style of swimming **4** SPORT [C] when you move your arm and hit the ball in sports such as tennis, golf, etc **5 a stroke of luck** something good that happens to you by chance *He had exactly the part that I needed so that was a stroke of luck.*

**stroke²** /strəʊk/ *verb* [T] to gently move your hand over a surface *to stroke a cat/dog* • *He stroked her hair.*

**stroll** /strəʊl/ *verb* **stroll along/down/through, etc** to walk somewhere in a slow and relaxed way *They strolled along the beach.* • **stroll** *noun* [C] *Shall we go for a stroll around the garden?*

**stroller** /'strəʊlər/ *US* (*UK* **pushchair**) *noun* [C] a chair on wheels which is used to move small children

⊶**strong** /strɒŋ/ *adj* **1** PHYSICALLY POWERFUL A strong person or animal is physically powerful. *Are you strong enough to lift this table on your own?* **2** NOT BREAK A strong object does not break easily or can support heavy things. *a strong box/chair* **3** QUALITY of a good quality or level and likely to be successful *a strong competitor/team* • *a strong economy* **4** FEELING A strong feeling, belief, or opinion is felt in a very deep and serious way. *a strong sense of pride* **5** NOTICEABLE If a taste, smell, etc is strong, it is very noticeable. *There's a strong smell of burning.* **6** PERSONALITY If a person or their personality is strong, they are confident and able to deal with problems well. **7** ALCOHOL containing a lot of alcohol *a strong drink* **8** RELATIONSHIP If a friendship, relationship, etc is strong, it is likely to last for a long time. **9 strong chance/possibility, etc** something that is very likely to happen *There's a strong possibility of rain this afternoon.* **10 strong opposition/support, etc** a lot of opposition/support, etc **11 strong language** words that some people might consider to be offensive **12 sb's strong point** something that someone is very good at *Cooking is not my strong point.* **13 be still going strong** continuing to be successful after a long time

**strongly** /'strɒŋli/ *adv* very much or in a very serious way *He is strongly opposed to violence of any sort.*

**strong-willed** /ˌstrɒŋ'wɪld/ *adj* very determined to do what you want to do

**stroppy** /'strɒpi/ *adj UK informal* angry or arguing a lot *a stroppy teenager*

**strove** /strəʊv/ *past tense of* strive

**struck** /strʌk/ *past of* strike

**structural** /'strʌktʃərəl/ *adj* relating to the structure of something *structural damage*

⊶**structure¹** /'strʌktʃər/ *noun* **1** [C, U] the way that parts of something are arranged or put together *cell structure* • *grammatical structure* **2** [C] a building or something that has been built

**structure²** /'strʌktʃər/ *verb* [T] to arrange something in an organized way *How is the course structured?*

⊶**struggle¹** /'strʌgl/ *verb* [I] **1** to try very hard to do something difficult [+ to do sth] *He's struggling to pay off his debts.* **2** to fight someone when they are holding you *She struggled but couldn't break free.*

**struggle on** to continue doing something that is difficult

o-ᴹ**struggle**² /ˈstrʌgl/ *noun* [C] **1** when you try very hard to do something difficult *It was a real struggle to stay awake during the film.* **2** a fight between people

**strum** /strʌm/ *verb* [I, T] **strumming**, *past* **strummed** to move your fingers across the strings of a guitar

**strung** /strʌŋ/ *past of* string

**strut** /strʌt/ *verb* **strutting**, *past* **strutted** **strut along/around/down, etc** to walk somewhere with big steps in a proud way ➔ *See also:* strut your **stuff**¹.

**stub**¹ /stʌb/ *noun* [C] the short, end piece of something such as a cigarette or pencil that is left after it has been used *There were cigarette stubs all over the floor.*

**stub**² /stʌb/ *verb* **stubbing**, *past* **stubbed stub your toe** to hit your toe against a hard surface by accident

**stub sth out** to stop a cigarette from burning by pressing the burning end against a hard surface

**stubble** /ˈstʌbl/ *noun* [U] **1** very short, stiff hairs, usually on a man's face ➔ *See colour picture* **Hair** *on page Centre 9.* **2** the short bits of dried plant stems left in a field after it has been cut

**stubborn** /ˈstʌbən/ *adj* determined not to change your ideas, plans, etc, although other people want you to • **stubbornly** *adv* • **stubbornness** *noun* [U]

**stubby** /ˈstʌbi/ *adj* short and thick *stubby legs/fingers*

**stuck**¹ /stʌk/ *adj* [never before noun] **1** not able to move anywhere *My car got stuck in a ditch.* • *We were stuck at the airport for twelve hours.* **2** not able to continue reading, answering questions, etc because something is too difficult *I keep getting stuck on difficult words.* **3** **be stuck with sb/sth** to have to deal with someone or something unpleasant because no one else wants to *Whenever we eat out, I always get stuck with the bill.*

**stuck**² /stʌk/ *past of* stick

**stud** /stʌd/ *noun* [C] **1** JEWELLERY a small, metal piece of jewellery that is put through a part of your body such as your ear or nose ➔ *See picture at* **jewellery. 2** DECORATION a small piece of metal that is fixed to the surface of something, usually for decoration **3** ANIMALS (*also* **'stud ,farm**) a place where horses are kept for breeding

o-ᴹ**student** /ˈstjuːdⁿnt/ *noun* [C] someone who is studying at a school or university *a law student* • *a foreign student* ➔ *See also:* **mature student.**

**studio** /ˈstjuːdiəʊ/ *noun* [C] **1** ART a room where an artist or photographer works **2** TV/RADIO a room where television/radio programmes or musical recordings are made **3** FILMS a film company or a place where films are made

**studious** /ˈstjuːdiəs/ *adj* spending a lot of time studying • **studiously** *adv*

o-ᴹ**study**¹ /ˈstʌdi/ *verb* **1** [I, T] to learn about a subject, usually at school or university *I studied biology while going into medicine.* ➔ *See usage note at* **learn. 2** [T] to look at something very carefully *He studied his face in the mirror.*

o-ᴹ**study**² /ˈstʌdi/ *noun* **1** FINDING OUT INFORMATION [C] when someone studies a subject in detail in order to discover new information *For years, studies have shown the link between smoking and cancer.* **2** LEARNING [U] when you learn about a subject, usually at school or university *the study of English literature* **3** ROOM [C] a room in a house where you can read, write, etc ➔ *See also:* **case study.**

o-ᴹ**stuff**¹ /stʌf/ *noun* [U] *informal* **1** used to refer to a substance or a group of things or ideas, etc without saying exactly what they are *There's some sticky stuff on the carpet.* • *They sell bread and cakes and stuff like that.* • *What sort of stuff are you interested in?* • *Can I leave my stuff at your house?* **2** **know your stuff** *informal* to know a lot about a subject, or to be very good at doing something *She's an excellent teacher – she really knows her stuff.* **3** **strut your stuff** *humorous informal* to dance

**stuff**² /stʌf/ *verb* [T] **1 stuff sth in/into/behind, etc** to push something into a small space, often quickly or in a careless way *He stuffed the papers into his briefcase and left.* **2** FILL to completely fill a container with something *an envelope stuffed with money* **3** FOOD to fill meat, vegetables, etc with a mixture of food before you cook them *stuffed peppers* **4** DEAD ANIMAL to fill the body of a dead animal with special material so that it looks as if it is still alive

**stuffing** /ˈstʌfɪŋ/ *noun* [U] **1** a mixture of food which is put into meat, vegetables, etc before they are cooked **2** material which is used to fill the inside of things such as soft chairs, beds, toys, etc

**stuffy** /ˈstʌfi/ *adj* **1** If a room or a building is stuffy, it is hot and unpleasant and the air is not fresh. **2** old-fashioned, formal and boring *a stuffy club for wealthy old men*

**stumble** /ˈstʌmbl/ *verb* [I] **1** to step badly and almost fall over *Mary stumbled on the loose rocks.* **2** to make a mistake, such as pausing or repeating a word, while speaking or performing *He kept **stumbling** over the same word.*

**stumble across/upon sth/sb** to discover something by chance, or to meet someone by chance *I stumbled across these photographs while I was cleaning out my desk.*

**'stumbling ,block** *noun* [C] a problem which makes it very difficult to do something *Lack of money has been the main stumbling block.*

**stump**¹ /stʌmp/ *noun* [C] **1** the short part of something that is left after most of it has been removed *a tree stump* **2** one of the three vertical wooden sticks that you throw a ball at in the game of cricket ➔ *See colour picture* **Sports 2** *on page Centre 16.*

**stump**² /stʌmp/ *verb* **1 be stumped by sth** *informal* to not be able to answer a question or solve a problem because it is too difficult *Scientists are completely stumped by this virus.* **2** [I] *US* to travel to different places to get political support

**stump (sth) up** *UK informal* to provide money for something, especially when you do not want to

**stun** /stʌn/ *verb* [T] **stunning**, *past* **stunned 1** to shock or surprise someone very much [often passive] *Friends and family were stunned by her sudden death.* **2** to make a person or animal unconscious, usually by hitting them on the head

**stung** /stʌŋ/ *past of* sting

**stunk** /stʌŋk/ **1** *past participle of* stink **2** *US past tense of* stink

**stunning** /'stʌnɪŋ/ *adj* very beautiful *stunning views over the city* • *She's stunning.* • stunningly *adv a stunningly beautiful woman*

**stunt¹** /stʌnt/ *noun* [C] **1** when someone does something dangerous that needs great skill, usually in a film *He always does his own stunts.* **2** something that is done to get people's attention *Their marriage was just a cheap publicity stunt.*

**stunt²** /stʌnt/ *verb* [T] to stop the normal growth or development of something *They say that smoking stunts your growth.*

**stupefied** /'stjuːpɪfaɪd/ *adj* so shocked, tired, etc that you cannot think • stupefying *adj* making you stupefied • stupefy *verb* [T]

**stupendous** /stjuː'pendəs/ *adj* extremely good or large *a stupendous performance* • stupendously *adv stupendously successful*

o-★**stupid** /'stjuːpɪd/ *adj* **1** silly or not intelligent *That was a really stupid thing to do.* • *How could you be so stupid?* **2** [always before noun] *informal* used to show that you are annoyed about something which is causing a problem *I can never get this stupid machine to work!* • stupidity /stjuː'pɪdəti/ *noun* [U] • stupidly *adv*

**stupor** /'stjuːpə'/ *noun* [no plural] when someone is almost unconscious and cannot think clearly, especially because they have drunk too much alcohol *He staggered into the room in a drunken stupor.*

**sturdy** /'stɜːdi/ *adj* very strong and solid *sturdy walking boots*

**stutter** /'stʌtə'/ *verb* [I, T] to repeat the first sound of a word several times when you talk, usually because you have a speech problem *"C-c-can we g-go now?" she stuttered.* • stutter *noun* [no plural] *He has a really bad stutter.*

o-★**style** /staɪl/ *noun* **1** WAY [C, U] a way of doing something that is typical of a particular person, group, place, or period *a style of painting/writing* **2** DESIGN [C, U] a way of designing hair, clothes, furniture, etc *She's had her hair cut in a really nice style.* **3** QUALITY [U] the quality of being attractive and fashionable or behaving in a way which makes people admire you *She's got style.* **4 do sth in style** to do something in a way that people admire, usually because it involves spending a lot of money *If we ever get married we'll do it in style.* **5 cramp sb's style** to prevent someone from enjoying themselves, especially by going somewhere with them *Are you sure you don't mind me coming with you? I'd hate to cramp your style.*

**style²** /staɪl/ *verb* [T] to shape or design hair, clothes, furniture, etc in a particular way *He spends hours in the bathroom styling his hair.*

**-style** /staɪl/ *suffix* used at the end of words to mean 'looking or behaving like something or someone' *antique-style furniture* • *Japanese-style management* ⊃ *See also:* **old-style**.

**stylish** /'staɪlɪʃ/ *adj* fashionable and attractive *a stylish, black suit* • stylishly *adv stylishly dressed*

**suave** /swɑːv/ *adj* If someone, especially a man, is suave, they are polite and confident in a way that is attractive but may be false. *suave and sophisticated*

**subconscious¹** /sʌb'kɒnʃəs/ *adj* Subconscious thoughts and feelings influence your behaviour without you being aware of them. *a subconscious fear* • subconsciously *adv*

**subconscious²** /sʌb'kɒnʃəs/ *noun* [no plural] the part of your mind which contains thoughts and feelings that you are not aware of but which influence your behaviour *The memory was buried deep within my subconscious.*

**subculture** /'sʌb,kʌltʃə'/ *noun* [C] a group of people with beliefs, interests, etc that are different from the rest of society

**subdivide** /,sʌbdɪ'vaɪd/ *verb* [T] to divide something into smaller parts [often passive] *Each chapter is subdivided into smaller sections.* • subdivision /,sʌbdɪ'vɪʒ³n/ *noun* [C, U]

**subdue** /səb'djuː/ *verb* [T] **subduing**, *past* **subdued** to start to control someone or something, especially by using force

**subdued** /səb'djuːd/ *adj* **1** quiet because you are feeling sad or worried *She seemed a bit subdued.* **2** Subdued lights or colours are not bright. *subdued lighting*

o-★**subject¹** /'sʌbdʒɪkt/ *noun* [C] **1** WHAT what someone is writing or talking about *a series of programmes on the subject of homelessness* **2** STUDY an area of knowledge studied in school or university *Chemistry is my favourite subject.* **3** GRAMMAR the person or thing which performs the action described by the verb. In the sentence 'Bob phoned me yesterday.', 'Bob' is the subject. **4** PERSON someone who is from a particular country, especially a country with a king or queen *a British subject*

**subject²** /'sʌbdʒɪkt/ *adj* **subject to sth 1** often affected by something, especially something unpleasant *Departure times are subject to alteration.* **2** only able to happen if something else happens *The pay rise is subject to approval by management.*

**subject³** /səb'dʒekt/ *verb* **subject sb/sth to sth** to make someone or something experience something unpleasant *In prison, he was subjected to beatings and interrogations.*

**subjective** /səb'dʒektɪv/ *adj* influenced by someone's beliefs or feelings, instead of facts *a subjective judgment* • subjectively *adv* • subjectivity /,sʌbdʒek'tɪvəti/ *noun* [U] when someone or something is influenced by beliefs or feelings instead of facts

**'subject ,matter** *noun* [U] what is being talked or written about *I'm not sure whether the subject matter is suitable for children.*

**subjunctive** /səb'dʒʌŋktɪv/ *noun* [no plural] the form of the verb which is used to express doubt, possibility, or wish. In the sentence 'I wish I were rich.', 'were' is in the subjunctive. • subjunctive *adj*

**sublime** /sə'blaɪm/ *adj* extremely good, beautiful, or enjoyable *sublime scenery* • sublimely *adv*

**submarine** /ˌsʌbmˈrɪːn/ *noun* [C] a boat that travels under water

**submerge** /səbˈmɜːdʒ/ *verb* [I, T] to cause something to be under the surface of water, or to move below the surface of water *The floods destroyed farmland and submerged whole villages.* • submerged *adj*

**submission** /səbˈmɪʃ²n/ *noun* **1** [U] when you accept that someone has complete control over you *They tried to starve her into submission.* **2** [C, U] when you send a document, plan, etc to someone so that they can consider it, or the document, plan, etc that you send *The deadline for submissions is 29 April.*

**submissive** /səbˈmɪsɪv/ *adj* always doing what other people tell you to do *a quiet, submissive wife*

**submit** /səbˈmɪt/ *verb* **submitting**, *past* **submitted** **1** [T] to send a document, plan, etc to someone so that they can consider it *Applications must be submitted before 31 January.* **2** [I] to accept that someone has control over you and do what they tell you to do *He was forced to submit to a full body search.*

**subordinate**[1] /səˈbɔːd²nət/ *adj* less important or lower in rank *a subordinate position/role* • *An individual's needs are subordinate to those of the group.*

**subordinate**[2] /səˈbɔːd²nət/ *noun* [C] someone who has a less important position than someone else in an organization

**subordinate**[3] /səˈbɔːdɪneɪt/ *verb* [T] *formal* to put someone or something into a less important position • subordination /səˌbɔːdɪˈneɪʃ²n/ *noun* [U]

**sub,ordinate 'clause** *noun* [C] in grammar, a clause which cannot form a separate sentence but adds information to the main clause

**subpoena** /səbˈpiːnə/ *noun* [C] a legal document ordering someone to go to court • subpoena *verb* [T] to give someone a subpoena

**subscribe** /səbˈskraɪb/ *verb* [I] to pay money to an organization so that you regularly receive a service or product, such as a magazine or newspaper *to subscribe to a magazine/an internet service* • subscriber *noun* [C]

**subscribe to sth** *formal* to agree with an opinion, belief, etc *I certainly don't subscribe to the view that women are morally superior to men.*

**subscription** /səbˈskrɪpʃ²n/ *noun* [C] an amount of money that you pay regularly to receive a product or service or to be a member of an organization *an annual subscription*

**subsequent** /ˈsʌbsɪkwənt/ *adj* [always before noun] happening after something else *The mistakes were corrected in a subsequent edition of the book.* • subsequently *adv*

**subservient** /səbˈsɜːviənt/ *adj* always doing what other people want you to do

**subside** /səbˈsaɪd/ *verb* [I] **1** to become less strong or extreme *The violence seems to be subsiding at last.* **2** If a building subsides, it sinks down to a lower level.

**subsidence** /səbˈsaɪd²ns/ *noun* [U] when buildings or land sink down to a lower level

**subsidiary** /səbˈsɪdi²ri/ *noun* [C] a company which is owned by another larger company

**subsidize** (*also* UK **-ise**) /ˈsʌbsɪdaɪz/ *verb* [T] If a government or other organization subsidizes something, it pays part of the cost of it, so that prices are reduced. *We have a subsidized restaurant at work.*

**subsidy** /ˈsʌbsɪdi/ *noun* [C] money given by a government or other organization to pay part of the cost of something *housing subsidies for the poor*

**subsist** /səbˈsɪst/ *verb* [I] to manage to live when you only have a very small amount of food or money • subsistence *noun* [U]

○━**substance** /ˈsʌbst²ns/ *noun* **1** [C] a solid, liquid, or gas *a dangerous substance* • *illegal substances* (= illegal drugs) **2** [U] truth or importance *There's no substance to the allegations.* **3 the substance of sth** the most important part of what someone has said or written

**substandard** /sʌbˈstændəd/ *adj* Something that is substandard is not as good as it should be. *substandard conditions/housing*

**substantial** /səbˈstænʃ²l/ *adj* **1** large in amount *a substantial change/increase* • *a substantial amount of money/time* **2** large and strong *a substantial building* ⊃ *Opposite* **insubstantial**.

**substantially** /səbˈstænʃ²li/ *adv* by a large amount *House prices are substantially higher in the south.*

**substantiate** /səbˈstænʃieɪt/ *verb* [T] *formal* to provide facts which prove that something is true *His claims have never been substantiated.*

**substantive** /ˈsʌbst²ntɪv/ *adj* *formal* important or serious *a substantive issue/problem*

**substitute**[1] /ˈsʌbstɪtjuːt/ *noun* [C] someone or something that is used instead of another person or thing *Margarine can be used as a substitute for butter.* • *a substitute teacher*

**substitute**[2] /ˈsʌbstɪtjuːt/ *verb* **1** [T] to use someone or something instead of another person or thing *You can substitute pasta for the rice, if you prefer.* **2 substitute for sb** to do someone's job because they are not there *I'm substituting for her while she's on holiday.* • substitution /ˌsʌbstɪˈtjuːʃ²n/ *noun* [C, U]

**subsume** /səbˈsjuːm/ *verb* [T] *formal* to include someone or something as part of a larger group [often passive] *The company has been subsumed by a large US bank.*

**subterfuge** /ˈsʌbtəfjuːdʒ/ *noun* [C, U] *formal* a trick or a dishonest way of achieving something *They obtained the information by subterfuge.*

**subterranean** /ˌsʌbt²rˈeɪniən/ *adj* under the ground *subterranean passages*

**subtitles** /ˈsʌbˌtaɪtlz/ *noun* [plural] words shown at the bottom of a cinema or television screen to explain what is being said *It's a French film with English subtitles.*

**subtle** /ˈsʌtl/ *adj* **1** NOT OBVIOUS not obvious or easy to notice *a subtle change/difference* • *a subtle hint* **2** NOT STRONG A subtle flavour, colour, etc is delicate and not strong or bright. **3** CLEVER clever in a way that does not attract attention *a subtle way of solving the problem* • subtly *adv*

**subtlety** /ˈsʌtlti/ *noun* **1** [U] the quality of being subtle **2** [C] something that is subtle

**subtract** /səbˈtrækt/ *verb* [T] to take a number or

amount away from another number or amount *You need to* **subtract** *25% from the final figure.*
• subtraction /səb'trækʃən/ *noun* [C, U]

**suburb** /'sʌbɜːb/ *noun* [C] an area where people live outside the centre of a city *a suburb of New York* • suburban /sə'bɜːbən/ *adj* relating to a suburb *a suburban area/home*

**suburbia** /sə'bɜːbiə/ *noun* [U] the suburbs of towns and cities generally

**subversive** /səb'vɜːsɪv/ *adj* trying to destroy the authority of a government, religion, etc *subversive literature* • subversive *noun* [C] someone who is subversive

**subvert** /sʌb'vɜːt/ *verb* [T] *formal* to try to destroy the authority of a government, religion, etc *a plot to subvert the government* • subversion /səb'vɜːʃən/ *noun* [U] *formal*

**subway** /'sʌbweɪ/ *noun* [C] **1** *UK* (*UK/US* **underpass**) a passage under a road or railway for people to walk through **2** *US* (*UK* **underground**) a system of trains that travel underground *We can take the subway to Grand Central Station.* ➔ *See usage note at* **metro**.

○╌**succeed** /sək'siːd/ *verb* **1** [I] to achieve what you are trying to achieve *She has the skill and determination to succeed.* • [+ in + doing sth] *He has finally succeeded in passing his exams.* **2** [T] to take an official job or position after someone else *The Queen was succeeded by her eldest son when she died.*

**USAGE**

**succeed**

Remember that succeed is often followed by the preposition in + doing sth.

*Two prisoners succeeded in escaping.*

~~Two prisoners succeeded to escape.~~

○╌**success** /sək'ses/ *noun* **1** [U] when you achieve what you want to achieve *Her success is due to hard work and determination.* **2** [C] something that has a good result or that is very popular *His first film was a great success.*

**USAGE**

**success**

Be careful to choose the correct verb with this noun.

*The evening was a great success.*

*They tried for weeks but had little success.*

*They are determined to make a success of the scheme.*

~~She reached success as a writer.~~

○╌**successful** /sək'sesfəl/ *adj* **1** [ACHIEVEMENT] achieving what you want to achieve *If the operation is successful, she should be walking within a few months.* **2** [WORK] having achieved a lot or made a lot of money through your work *a successful businessman* **3** [POPULAR] very popular *a successful book/film* ➔ *Opposite* **unsuccessful**. • successfully *adv*

**succession** /sək'seʃən/ *noun* **1** [no plural] a number of similar events or people that happen, exist, etc after each other *to suffer a succession of*

injuries • *a succession of boyfriends* **2 in quick/rapid succession** If several things happen in quick/rapid succession, they happen very quickly after each other. *She had her first three children in quick succession.* **3** [U] when someone takes an official position or job after someone else

**successive** /sək'sesɪv/ *adj* happening after each other *He has just won the World Championship for the third successive year.*

**successor** /sək'sesə'/ *noun* [C] **1** someone who has a position or job after someone else *He is her most likely successor.* **2** an organization, product, etc that follows and takes the place of an earlier one

**succinct** /sək'sɪŋkt/ *adj* said in a very clear way using only a few words *a succinct explanation* • succinctly *adv*

**succulent** /'sʌkjələnt/ *adj* If food is succulent, it is good to eat because it has a lot of juice. *a succulent piece of meat*

**succumb** /sə'kʌm/ *verb* [I] *formal* **1** to not be able to stop yourself doing something *I succumbed to temptation and had some cheesecake.* **2** to die or suffer badly from an illness

○╌**such** /sʌtʃ/ *pronoun, determiner* **1** used to refer to something or someone that you were just talking about, or something or someone of that type *It's difficult to know how to treat such cases.* **2** used to emphasize a quality of someone or something *She's such a nice person.* • *It's such a shame that he's leaving.* **3 such as** for example *She can't eat dairy products, such as milk and cheese.* **4 as such** used after a word or phrase in negative statements to mean in the exact meaning of that word or phrase *There are no rules as such, just a few guidelines.* **5 such ... that** used to talk about the result of something *The whole thing was such a worry that I began to lose sleep over it.* **6 there's no such thing/person (as) ...** used to say that something or someone does not exist *There's no such thing as ghosts.*

**such-and-such** /'sʌtʃənsʌtʃ/ *determiner informal* used instead of referring to a particular or exact thing *If they tell you to arrive at such-and-such a time, get there a couple of minutes before.*

**suck** /sʌk/ *verb* **1** [I, T] to have something in your mouth and use your tongue, lips, etc to pull on it or to get liquid, air, etc out of it *to suck a sweet/lollipop* • *to suck your thumb* **2 suck sth in/under/up, etc** to pull something somewhere using the force of moving air, water, etc *He was sucked under the boat and drowned.* **3 be sucked into sth** to become involved in something bad when you do not want to **4 he/it/this, etc sucks!** *US very informal* If someone or something sucks, they are bad or unpleasant. **suck up to sb** *very informal* to try to make someone who is in authority like you by doing and saying things that will please them

**sucker** /'sʌkə'/ *noun* [C] **1** *informal* someone who believes everything that you tell them and is easy to deceive **2** something that helps an animal or object stick to a surface

**suction** /'sʌkʃən/ *noun* [U] when something is forced into a container or space by removing air

---

○▪**sudden** /'sʌdᵊn/ adj **1** done or happening quickly and unexpectedly *a sudden change/increase* • *His sudden death was a great shock to us all.* **2 all of a sudden** unexpectedly *All of a sudden she got up and walked out.* • suddenness *noun* [U]

○▪**suddenly** /'sʌdᵊnli/ adv quickly and unexpectedly *I suddenly realized who she was.* • *It all happened so suddenly that I can't remember much about it.*

**suds** /sʌdz/ noun [plural] small bubbles made from soap and water

**sue** /suː/ verb [I, T] **suing**, past **sued** to take legal action against someone and try to get money from them because they have harmed you *He's threatening to sue the newspaper for slander.*

**suede** /sweɪd/ noun [U] leather that has a slightly rough surface

○▪**suffer** /'sʌfə'/ verb **1** [I, T] to experience pain or unpleasant emotions *I can't bear to see animals suffering.* **2 suffer from sth** to have an illness or other health problem *She suffers from severe depression.* **3 suffer a broken leg/a heart attack, etc** to experience an injury or other sudden health problem *He suffered a serious neck injury in the accident.* **4 suffer damage/defeat/loss, etc** to experience something bad such as damage/defeat/loss, etc **5** [I] to become worse in quality *If you're tired all the time your work tends to suffer.*

**sufferer** /'sʌfərə'/ noun [C] someone who suffers from an illness or other health problem *AIDS/cancer sufferers*

**suffering** /'sʌfərɪŋ/ noun [U] when someone experiences pain or unpleasant emotions *human suffering*

**suffice** /sə'faɪs/ verb [I] formal to be enough *You don't need to give a long speech – a few sentences will suffice.*

**sufficient** /sə'fɪʃᵊnt/ adj as much as is necessary *She didn't have sufficient time to answer all the questions.* ➔ Opposite **insufficient**. • sufficiently adv *I was sufficiently close to hear what they were saying.* ➔ See also: **self-sufficient**.

**suffix** /'sʌfɪks/ noun [C] a group of letters that you add to the end of a word to make another word. In the word 'slowly', '-ly' is a suffix. ➔ Compare **prefix**.

**suffocate** /'sʌfəkeɪt/ verb [I, T] to die because you cannot breathe or to kill someone by stopping them from breathing *He suffocated her with a pillow.* • suffocation /ˌsʌfə'keɪʃᵊn/ noun [U]

○▪**sugar** /'ʃʊgə'/ noun **1** [U] a very sweet substance used to give flavour to food and drinks *coffee with milk and sugar* **2** [C] a spoon of sugar in a cup of tea or coffee *He likes two sugars in his tea.*

○▪**suggest** /sə'dʒest/ verb [T] **1** [IDEA] to express an idea or plan for someone to consider [+ (that)] *I suggest that we park the car here and walk into town.* • [+ doing sth] *He suggested having the meeting at his house.* **2** [ADVICE] to say that someone or something is suitable for something *to suggest someone for a job* • *Can you suggest a good hotel?* **3** [SEEM TRUE] to make something seem likely to be true *All the evidence suggests that she did it.*

○▪**suggestion** /sə'dʒestʃᵊn/ noun **1** [C] an idea or plan that someone suggests *to make a suggestion* • *Have you got any suggestions for improvements?* **2 a suggestion of/that sth** something that makes something seem likely to be true *There's no suggestion of any connection between the two men.* **3 at sb's suggestion** following the advice that someone has given you *We went to that restaurant at Paul's suggestion.*

**suggestive** /sə'dʒestɪv/ adj **1** making you think about sex *suggestive comments/remarks* **2 suggestive of sth** formal similar to something and making you think about it *The shapes are suggestive of human forms.* • suggestively adv

**suicidal** /ˌsuːɪ'saɪdᵊl/ adj **1** so unhappy that you want to kill yourself *to feel suicidal* **2** likely to have an extremely bad result *a suicidal decision*

**suicide** /'suːɪsaɪd/ noun **1** [C, U] when you intentionally kill yourself *He committed suicide after a long period of depression.* **2** [U] when you do something that will have an extremely bad result for you *political suicide*

○▪**suit¹** /suːt/ noun [C] **1** a jacket and trousers or a jacket and skirt that are made from the same material *She wore a dark blue suit.* **2** one of the four types of cards with different shapes on them in a set of playing cards **3 follow suit** to do the same as someone else has just done *If other shops lower their prices, we will have to follow suit.* ➔ See also: **bathing suit**, **pant suit**, **trouser suit**, **wet suit**.

○▪**suit²** /suːt/ verb [T] **1** to make someone look more attractive *Green really suits you.* **2** to be acceptable or right for someone *It would suit me better if we left a bit earlier.* ➔ See usage note at **fit**. **3 be suited to/for sth** to be right for someone or something *These plants are better suited to a warm climate.* ➔ See also: suit sb down to the **ground¹**.

○▪**suitable** /'suːtəbl/ adj acceptable or right for someone or something *a suitable time to call* • *This film is suitable for children.* ➔ Opposite **unsuitable**. • suitably adv *suitably dressed*

**suitcase** /'suːtkeɪs/ noun [C] a rectangular case with a handle that you use to carry clothes when you are travelling *to pack your suitcase* ➔ See picture at **luggage**.

**suite** /swiːt/ noun [C] **1** several pieces of furniture which go together *a bedroom suite* **2** a set of hotel rooms which are used together ➔ See also: en **suite**.

**suitor** /'suːtə'/ noun [C] old-fashioned a man who wants to marry a particular woman

**sulfur** /'sʌlfə'/ noun [U] US spelling of sulphur

**sulk** /sʌlk/ verb [I] to look unhappy and not speak to anyone because you are angry about something *He's upstairs sulking in his bedroom.* • sulky adj *a sulky teenager*

**sullen** /'sʌlən/ adj in an unpleasant mood and not smiling or speaking to anyone

**sulphur** UK (US **sulfur**) /'sʌlfə'/ noun [U] a yellow chemical element that has an unpleasant smell

**sultan** /'sʌltᵊn/ noun [C] a ruler in some Muslim countries

**sultana** /sʌl'tɑːnə/ noun [C] UK a dried grape (= small round fruit) often used in cakes

S

**sultry** /'sʌltri/ *adj* **1** If a woman is sultry, she behaves in a sexually attractive way. *a sultry voice* **2** If the weather is sultry, it is hot and wet. *a sultry summer night*

**sum¹** /sʌm/ *noun* [C] **1** MONEY an amount of money *a large/small sum of money* **2** MATHS *UK* a simple mathematical calculation such as adding two numbers together *Kids these days can't do sums without a calculator.* **3** TOTAL the total amount that you get when you add two or more numbers together *The sum of six and seven is thirteen.* ⊃ *See also:* **lump sum**.

**sum²** /sʌm/ *verb* **summing,** *past* **summed**
**sum (sth/sb) up** to describe briefly the important facts or characteristics of something or someone *The purpose of a conclusion is to sum up the main points of an essay.*
**sum sth/sb up** to quickly decide what you think about something or someone *I think she summed up the situation very quickly.*

**summarize** (*also UK* **-ise**) /'sʌmᵊraɪz/ *verb* [I, T] to describe briefly the main facts or ideas of something

**summary¹** /'sʌmᵊri/ *noun* [C] a short description that gives the main facts or ideas about something *He gave a brief summary of what happened.*

**summary²** /'sʌmᵊri/ *adj* [always before noun] *formal* decided or done quickly, without the usual discussions or legal arrangements *a summary arrest/execution*

o━**summer** /'sʌmᵊ/ *noun* [C, U] the season of the year between spring and autumn, when the weather is warmest *We usually go away in the summer.* • *a long, hot summer* • **summery** *adj* typical of or suitable for summer *You look very summery in that dress.*

**summertime** /'sʌmətaɪm/ *noun* [U] when it is summer *In the summertime, we often eat outside.*

**summit** /'sʌmɪt/ *noun* [C] **1** an important meeting between the leaders of two or more governments *a two-day summit* • *a summit meeting* **2** the top of a mountain *The climbers hope to reach the summit before nightfall.*

**summon** /'sʌmən/ *verb* [T] **1** *formal* to officially order someone to come to a place *He was summoned to a meeting.* **2** **summon (up) the courage/strength, etc** to make a great effort to do something [+ to do sth] *He tried to summon up the courage to speak to her.*

**summons** /'sʌmənz/ *noun* [C] an official order saying that you must go to a court of law

**Sun** *written abbreviation for* Sunday

o━**sun¹** /sʌn/ *noun* **1 the sun** the large, bright star that shines in the sky during the day and provides light and heat for the Earth *The sun rises in the East and sets in the West.* **2** [U, no plural] the light and heat that comes from the sun *I can't sit in the sun for too long.*

**sun²** /sʌn/ *verb* **sunning,** *past* **sunned sun yourself** to sit or lie in the sun *She was sitting on the deck sunning herself.*

**sunbathe** /'sʌnbeɪð/ *verb* [I] to sit or lie in the sun so that your skin becomes brown • **sunbathing** *noun* [U]

**sunburn** /'sʌnbɜːn/ *noun* [U] when your skin becomes painful and red from being in the sun

too long • **sunburnt** (*also* **sunburned**) *adj a sunburnt nose*

**sundae** /'sʌndeɪ/ *noun* [C] a sweet dish made of ice cream with fruit and nuts

**Sunday** /'sʌndeɪ/ (*written abbreviation* **Sun**) *noun* [C, U] the day of the week after Saturday and before Monday

**sundry** /'sʌndri/ *adj* **1** [always before noun] of different types *sundry items* **2 all and sundry** *UK informal* (*US* **various and sundry**) everyone *I don't want all and sundry knowing about my problems.*

**sunflower** /'sʌnflaʊə'/ *noun* [C] a tall, yellow flower with a large, black centre full of seeds

**sung** /sʌŋ/ *past participle of* sing

**sunglasses** /'sʌn,glɑːsɪz/ *noun* [plural] dark glasses that you wear to protect your eyes from the sun ⊃ *See colour picture* **Clothes** *on page Centre 5.*

**sunk** /sʌŋk/ **1** *past participle of* sink **2** *US past tense of* sink

**sunken** /'sʌŋkən/ *adj* [always before noun] **1** at a lower level than the surrounding area *a sunken bath* **2** having fallen down to the bottom of the sea *a sunken ship* **3 sunken eyes/cheeks** eyes or cheeks that make you look ill because they go too far into your face

**sunlight** /'sʌnlaɪt/ *noun* [U] the light from the sun

**sunlit** /'sʌnlɪt/ *adj* [always before noun] A sunlit place is bright because of light from the sun. *a sunlit room*

**sunny** /'sʌni/ *adj* **1** bright because of light from the sun *a lovely sunny day* **2** behaving in a happy way *a sunny smile/personality*

**sunrise** /'sʌnraɪz/ *noun* [C, U] when the sun appears in the morning and the sky becomes light

**sunscreen** /'sʌnskriːn/ *noun* [U] a substance that protects your skin in the sun

**sunset** /'sʌnset/ *noun* [C, U] when the sun disappears in the evening and the sky becomes dark

**sunshine** /'sʌnʃaɪn/ *noun* [U] the light from the sun *Let's sit over there in the sunshine.*

**sunstroke** /'sʌnstrəʊk/ *noun* [U] an illness caused by spending too much time in the sun

**suntan** /'sʌntæn/ (*also* **tan**) *noun* [C] when your skin is brown from being in the sun *He was determined to get a good suntan on holiday.* • **suntan oil** • **suntanned** (*also* **tanned**) *adj*

**super** /'suːpə'/ *adj, adv informal* very good *We had a super time.*

**superb** /suː'pɜːb/ *adj* excellent *a superb performance/restaurant* • **superbly** *adv*

**superficial** /,suːpə'fɪʃᵊl/ *adj* **1** NOT SERIOUS If someone is superficial, they never think about things that are serious or important. **2** NOT COMPLETE not complete and involving only the most obvious things *superficial knowledge* • *a superficial resemblance* **3** NOT DEEP only on the surface of something *superficial damage* • **superficially** *adv*

**superfluous** /suː'pɜːfluəs/ *adj* not needed, or more than is needed *superfluous details/information*

**superhuman** /,suːpə'hjuːmən/ *adj* **superhuman effort/strength, etc** more effort/strength, etc than a normal human being

**superimpose** /,suːpᵊrɪm'pəʊz/ *verb* [T] to put an

image, text, etc over something so that the thing under it can still be seen

**superintendent** /ˌsuːpⁿrɪnˈtendənt/ *noun* [C] **1** in Britain, a police officer of high rank **2** in the US, an official responsible for a place, event, etc

**superior¹** /suːˈpɪəriəʳ/ *adj* **1** better than other things *superior quality* • *This car is far superior to the others.* **2** thinking that you are better than other people *She has a very superior manner.*

**superior²** /suːˈpɪəriəʳ/ *noun* [C] someone in a higher position than you at work *I will have to report this to my superiors.*

**superiority** /suːˌpɪəriˈɒrəti/ *noun* [U] **1** when something is better than other things *the superiority of modern design* **2** when you think that you are better than other people *She has an air of superiority.*

**superlative** /suːˈpɜːlətɪv/ *noun* [C] the form of an adjective or adverb that is used to show that someone or something has more of a particular quality than anyone or anything else. For example 'best' is the superlative of 'good' and 'slowest' is the superlative of 'slow'. ⊃ *Compare* **comparative**.

o-*   **supermarket** /ˈsuːpəˌmɑːkɪt/ *noun* [C] a large shop that sells food, drink, products for the home, etc

**supermodel** /ˈsuːpəˌmɒdⁿl/ *noun* [C] a very famous model (= someone whose job is to wear fashionable clothes for photographs)

**the supernatural** /ˌsuːpəˈnætʃⁿrⁿl/ *noun* things that cannot be explained by our knowledge of science or nature • supernatural *adj supernatural forces/powers*

**superpower** /ˈsuːpəˌpaʊəʳ/ *noun* [C] a country that has great military and political power in the world

**supersede** /ˌsuːpəˈsiːd/ *verb* [T] to take the place of someone or something that went before [often passive] *Records were superseded by CDs.*

**supersonic** /ˌsuːpəˈsɒnɪk/ *adj* faster than the speed of sound *supersonic aircraft*

**superstar** /ˈsuːpəstɑːʳ/ *noun* [C] a very famous singer, performer, etc

**superstition** /ˌsuːpəˈstɪʃⁿn/ *noun* [C, U] when someone believes that particular actions or objects are lucky or unlucky

**superstitious** /ˌsuːpəˈstɪʃəs/ *adj* believing that particular objects or events are lucky or unlucky *Are you superstitious about the number 13?*

**superstore** /ˈsuːpəstɔːʳ/ *noun* [C] a very large shop that sells many different things, often outside a town

**supervise** /ˈsuːpəvaɪz/ *verb* [I, T] to watch a person or activity and make certain that everything is done correctly, safely, etc *Students must be supervised by a teacher at all times.* • supervisor *noun* [C] someone who supervises

**supervision** /ˌsuːpəˈvɪʒⁿn/ *noun* [U] when you supervise someone or something *He needs constant supervision.*

**supper** /ˈsʌpəʳ/ *noun* [C] a meal that you eat in the evening *What are we having for supper?*

**supplant** /səˈplɑːnt/ *verb* [T] *formal* to take the place of someone or something

**supple** /ˈsʌpl/ *adj* able to bend or move easily *a supple body*

**supplement** /ˈsʌplɪmənt/ *noun* [C] an extra amount or part added to something *to take a vitamin supplement* • *a newspaper with a colour supplement* • supplement /ˈsʌplɪment/ *verb* [T] *She works part-time to supplement her pension.*

**supplementary** /ˌsʌplɪˈmentⁿri/ (*also US* **supplemental**) *adj* added to something *supplementary pages/materials*

**supplier** /səˈplaɪəʳ/ *noun* [C] someone who provides things that people want or need, often over a long period of time

**supplies** /səˈplaɪz/ *noun* [plural] the food, equipment, etc that is needed for a particular activity, holiday, etc

o-*   **supply¹** /səˈplaɪ/ *verb* [T] to provide things that people want or need, often over a long period of time *to supply food/drugs to people* • *This lake* **supplies** *the whole town* **with** *water.*

o-*   **supply²** /səˈplaɪ/ *noun* **1** [C] an amount of something that is ready to be used *a supply of water* • *food supplies* **2 in short supply** If something is in short supply, there is little of it available. **3** [C] the system of supplying something to people *Someone has turned off the electricity supply.*

o-*   **support¹** /səˈpɔːt/ *verb* [T] **1** AGREE to agree with an idea, group, or person *Do you support their views on nuclear weapons?* **2** PROVE to help to show that something is true *There's no evidence to support his story.* **3** HOLD to hold the weight of someone or something *Is this ladder strong enough to support me?* **4** PAY to look after someone by paying for their food, clothes, etc *She has three children to support.* **5** SPORT mainly *UK* to like a particular sports team and want them to win *Who do you support?*

o-*   **support²** /səˈpɔːt/ *noun* **1** AGREEMENT [U] agreement with an idea, group or person *Is there much public* **support** *for the death penalty?* **2 in support of sth/sb** agreeing with someone or something *The minister spoke in support of military action.* **3** HELP [U] help or encouragement *emotional/financial support* • *She needs all the love and support we can give her.* **4** OBJECT [C] an object that can hold the weight of something ⊃ *See also:* **child support**, **income support**, **moral support**.

**supporter** /səˈpɔːtəʳ/ *noun* [C] **1** someone who supports a particular idea, group, or person *a strong supporter of the government* **2** *mainly UK* someone who likes a particular sports team and wants them to win *English football supporters*

**supportive** /səˈpɔːtɪv/ *adj* giving help or encouragement *a very supportive friend*

o-*   **suppose** /səˈpəʊz/ *verb* **1 be supposed to do sth a** to be expected or intended to do something, especially when this does not happen *These drugs are supposed to reduce the pain.* • *He was supposed to be here by nine.* **b** If you are supposed to do something, the rules say that you should do it. *You're supposed to pay by the end of the month.* • *You're not supposed to smoke in here.* **2 be supposed to be sth** to be considered by many people to be something *The scenery is supposed to be fantastic.* **3** [T] to think that something is likely to be true [+ (that)] *I suppose that you've already heard the news?* **4 suppose/supposing (that)** used to introduce an idea for someone to consider *Suppose he phones tonight. What should I say?* **5 I suppose** used to show that you are not certain or not completely happy about something *It was quite interesting, I suppose.* **6 I suppose so** used to show agreement to something when you do not really want to *"Can I come with you?" "I suppose so."*

**supposed** /sə'pəʊzɪd/ *adj* [always before noun] used to show that you do not believe that someone or something really is what many people consider them to be *a supposed genius* • supposedly /sə'pəʊzɪdli/ *adv The building is supposedly in good condition.*

**supposition** /ˌsʌpə'zɪʃən/ *noun* [C, U] *formal* when someone believes that something is true although there is no proof

**suppress** /sə'pres/ *verb* [T] **1** [FEELINGS] to control feelings so that they do not show *I could barely suppress my anger.* **2** [INFORMATION] to prevent information from being known *to suppress evidence/news* **3** [FIGHT] to stop someone or something by using force [often passive] *The rebellion was suppressed by government forces.* • suppression /sə'preʃən/ *noun* [U]

**supremacy** /suː'preməsi/ *noun* [U] when a country or group of people is more powerful, successful, etc than anyone else *a battle/struggle for supremacy*

**supreme** /suː'priːm/ *adj* **1** of the highest rank or greatest importance *the supreme ruler* **2** very great *supreme confidence/effort* • supremely *adv* very *supremely confident*

**the su,preme 'court** *noun* the court of law that has the most authority in a state or country

**surcharge** /'sɜːtʃɑːdʒ/ *noun* [C] an extra amount of money that you have to pay for something *There is a surcharge for single rooms.*

⚬⊶**sure¹** /ʃɔːʳ/ *adj* **1** [never before noun] certain [+ (that)] *I'm sure that he won't mind.* • [+ question word] *She's not sure what she's going to do next.* • *I'm quite sure about the second answer.* ⊃ *Opposite* **unsure**. **2 make sure (that)** to take action so that you are certain that something happens, is true, etc *Make sure that you close all the windows before you leave.* **3 be sure of sth** to be confident that something is true *He'll win, I'm sure of it.* **4 for sure** without any doubts *I think he's from Korea but don't know for sure.* **5 be sure of yourself** to be confident of your own abilities, qualities, etc *She's always been very sure of herself.* **6 be sure to do sth a** If you are sure to do something, it is certain that you will do it. *He's sure to go back there again.* **b** used to tell someone what they must remember to do *Be sure to tell her I called.* **7 a sure sign of/that sth** something that makes something seem certain to be true **8 sure thing** something that is certain to happen *Death is the one sure thing about life.* **9 sure** (*also US* **sure thing**) used to show agreement *"Can I borrow your pen please?" "Sure."*

**10 sure enough** as expected *He said the book was on his desk, and sure enough, there it was.*

⚬⊶**surely** /'ʃɔːli/ *adv* used to express surprise that something has happened or is going to happen *You surely didn't tell him, did you?* • *Surely you're not going to go out dressed like that?*

**surf¹** /sɜːf/ *verb* **1** [I] to ride on a wave in the sea using a special board **2 surf the Internet/Net/Web** to look at information on the Internet by moving from one page to another using electronic links (= connections) • surfer *noun* [C] someone who surfs • surfing *noun* [U]

**surf²** /sɜːf/ *noun* [U] the top of the waves in the sea as it moves onto the coast

⚬⊶**surface¹** /'sɜːfɪs/ *noun* **1** [C] the top or outside part of something *the Earth's surface* • *The sun was reflected on the surface of the water.* **2** [no plural] what someone or something seems to be like when you do not know much about them *On the surface he seemed very pleasant.* ⊃ *See also:* **work surface**.

**surface²** /'sɜːfɪs/ *verb* **1** [APPEAR] [I] to appear or become public, often after being hidden *This problem first surfaced about two weeks ago.* **2** [RISE] [I] to rise to the surface of water *The submarine surfaced a few miles off the coast.* **3** [COVER] [T] to cover a road with a hard substance

**'surface ,mail** *noun* [U] letters, parcels, etc that are sent by road, sea, or train and not by aircraft

**surfboard** /'sɜːfbɔːd/ *noun* [C] a long piece of wood or plastic that you use to ride on waves in the sea

**surfeit** /'sɜːfɪt/ *noun* [no plural] *formal* too much of something *We've had a surfeit of applications from women for this job.*

**surge¹** /sɜːdʒ/ *verb* **1 surge forward/into/through, etc** to move somewhere with great strength *The crowd surged against the barriers.* **2** [I] to increase very quickly *Prices surged on the stock exchange.*

**surge²** /sɜːdʒ/ *noun* [C] **1** a large increase in something *a surge in spending* **2** a sudden movement forward

**surgeon** /'sɜːdʒən/ *noun* [C] a doctor who does medical operations ⊃ *See also:* **veterinary surgeon**.

**surgery** /'sɜːdʒəri/ *noun* **1** [U] when a doctor cuts your body open and repairs or removes something *to have surgery* • *heart/knee surgery* **2** [C] *UK* a place where doctors or other medical workers treat people ⊃ *See also:* **plastic surgery**.

**surgical** /'sɜːdʒɪkəl/ *adj* relating to medical operations *surgical instruments/gloves* • surgically *adv*

**surly** /'sɜːli/ *adj* unfriendly and rude *a surly teenager*

**surmount** /sə'maʊnt/ *verb* [T] *formal* to deal successfully with a problem

**surname** /'sɜːneɪm/ *noun* [C] the name that you and other members of your family all have *His surname is Walker.*

**surpass** /sə'pɑːs/ *verb* [T] *formal* to be or do better than someone or something else *The book's success surpassed everyone's expectations.*

**surplus** /'sɜːpləs/ *noun* [C, U] an amount of something that is more than you need *Every year we produce a huge **surplus of** meat.* ● surplus *adj surplus wheat*

o━**surprise**[1] /sə'praɪz/ *noun* **1** [C] an event that you did not expect to happen *I didn't know that my parents were coming – it was a lovely surprise.* ● *Her resignation **came as a** complete **surprise*** (= was very surprising). ● *a surprise party* **2** [U] the feeling that you get when something happens that you did not expect *He agreed to everything, much **to my surprise**.* **3 take/catch sb by surprise** to be unexpected and make someone feel surprise *I wasn't expecting her to be so angry – it took me by surprise.*

**surprise**[2] /sə'praɪz/ *verb* [T] **1** to make someone feel surprise *I didn't tell her I was coming home early – I thought I'd surprise her.* **2** to find or attack someone when they are not expecting it

o━**surprised** /sə'praɪzd/ *adj* feeling surprise because something has happened that you did not expect [+ to do sth] *I'm surprised to see you here.* ● *She wasn't **surprised at** his decision.* ● [+ (that)] *I'm surprised that you've decided to leave.*

o━**surprising** /sə'praɪzɪŋ/ *adj* not expected and making someone feel surprised *It's not surprising you're putting on weight, the amount you're eating!* ● surprisingly *adv surprisingly good*

**surreal** /sə'rɪəl/ (*also* **surrealistic** /sə,rɪə'lɪstɪk/) *adj* strange and not real, like something in a dream *His paintings have a surreal quality.*

**surrender** /sᵊr'endəʳ/ *verb* **1** [I] to stop fighting and admit that you have been beaten *Rebel troops are refusing to surrender.* **2** [T] *formal* to give something to someone else because you have been forced or officially asked to give it to them *He was released on the condition that he surrendered his passport.* ● surrender *noun* [C, U]

**surreptitious** /,sʌrəp'tɪʃəs/ *adj* done secretly so that other people do not see *surreptitious glances at the clock* ● surreptitiously *adv*

**surrogate** /'sʌrəgɪt/ *adj* [always before noun] used instead of someone or something else *Twenty years older than her, he effectively became a surrogate father.* ● surrogate *noun* [C] someone or something that is used instead of someone or something else *He seemed to regard her as a surrogate for his dead mother.*

,surrogate 'mother *noun* [C] a woman who has a baby for a woman who is not able to have a baby herself

o━**surround** /sə'raʊnd/ *verb* [T] **1** to be or go everywhere around something or someone *The house is surrounded by a large garden.* ● *The police have surrounded the building.* ● *the surrounding countryside* **2 be surrounded by sb/sth** to have a lot of people or things near you *She's surrounded by the people she loves.* **3** If a feeling or situation surrounds an event, it is closely connected with it. *Mystery still surrounds the exact circumstances of his death.*

**surroundings** /sə'raʊndɪŋz/ *noun* [plural] the place where someone or something is and the things that are in it *Have you got used to your new surroundings?*

**surveillance** /sɜː'veɪləns/ *noun* [U] when someone is watched carefully, especially by the police or army, because they are expected to do something wrong *The police have **kept** the man **under** strict **surveillance**.*

**survey**[1] /'sɜːveɪ/ *noun* [C] **1** QUESTIONS an examination of people's opinions or behaviour made by asking people questions *Holidays in the UK are becoming more popular, according to a recent survey.* **2** BUILDING *UK* an examination of the structure of a building in order to find out if there is anything wrong with it *The bank have refused a loan until we've had a survey done on the property.* **3** LAND when an area of land is looked at, and its measurements and details recorded, especially in order to make a map

**survey**[2] /sə'veɪ/ *verb* [T] **1** EXAMINE to look at or examine something carefully *I got out of the car to survey the damage.* **2** QUESTION to ask people questions in order to find out about their opinions or behaviour *75% of midwives surveyed were in favour of home births.* **3** LAND to measure and record the details of an area of land **4** BUILDING *UK* to examine the structure of a building in order to find out if there is anything wrong with it

**surveyor** /sə'veɪəʳ/ *noun* [C] **1** *UK* someone whose job is to examine the structure of buildings **2** someone whose job is to measure and record the details of an area of land

**survival** /sə'vaɪvᵊl/ *noun* [U] when someone or something continues to live or exist, especially after a difficult or dangerous situation *Flood victims had to fight for survival.*

o━**survive** /sə'vaɪv/ *verb* **1** NOT DIE [I, T] to continue to live after almost dying because of an accident, illness, etc *He was born with a heart problem and only survived ten days.* ● *No one survived the plane crash.* **2** EXIST [I, T] to continue to exist after being in a difficult or dangerous situation *Only two buildings survived the earthquake.* **3** LIVE LONGER [T] If you survive someone, you continue to live after they have died.

**survivor** /sə'vaɪvəʳ/ *noun* [C] someone who continues to live after almost dying because of an accident, illness, etc *Rescuers have given up hope of finding any more survivors.*

**susceptible** /sə'septəbl/ *adj* easily influenced or harmed by something *Older people are more **susceptible to** the virus.* ● *a susceptible young teenager* ● susceptibility /sə,septə'bɪləti/ *noun* [U] when someone is susceptible

**sushi** /'suːʃi/ *noun* [U] Japanese food made of cold rice and fish which has not been cooked *a sushi bar*

**suspect**[1] /'sʌspekt/ *noun* [C] someone who may have committed a crime *He's the **prime suspect*** (= the most likely suspect) *in the murder case.*

o━**suspect**[2] /sə'spekt/ *verb* [T] **1** CRIME to think that someone may have committed a crime or done something bad *He was **suspected of** drug dealing.* ● *suspected terrorists* **2** THINK LIKELY to think that something is probably true, or is likely to happen [+ (that)] *They suspected that he was lying.* **3** NOT TRUST to not trust someone or something *She suspected his motives for offering to help.*

**suspect**[3] /'sʌspekt/ *adj* difficult to trust or believe *His explanation was highly suspect.*

**suspend** /səˈspend/ *verb* [T] **1** to stop something happening for a short time *The semi-final was suspended because of bad weather.* **2 suspend sth from/between, etc** to hang something from somewhere [often passive] *A light bulb was suspended from the ceiling.* **3** to not allow someone to go to work or school for a period of time because they have done something wrong [often passive] *She was suspended from school for fighting.*

**suspenders** /səˈspendəz/ *noun* [plural] **1** UK (US **garters**) pieces of elastic fixed to a belt that hold up a woman's stockings (= very thin pieces of clothing that cover a woman's foot and leg) **2** US (UK **braces**) two straps fixed to a pair of trousers that go over your shoulders and stop the trousers from falling down

**suspense** /səˈspens/ *noun* [U] the feeling of excitement that you have when you are waiting for something to happen *What's your answer then? Don't keep me in suspense.*

**suspension** /səˈspenʃən/ *noun* **1** STOP [U] when someone stops something happening for a period of time *an immediate suspension of all imports and exports* **2** JOB/SCHOOL [C, U] when someone is not allowed to go to work or school for a period of time **3** VEHICLE [C, U] equipment which is fixed to the wheels of a vehicle in order to make it move more smoothly

**suspicion** /səˈspɪʃən/ *noun* **1** [C, U] a feeling or belief that someone has done something wrong *They were arrested on suspicion of drug dealing.* • *Several members of staff are under suspicion of stealing money.* **2** [C] an idea that something may be true [+ (that)] *I had a vague suspicion that the two events might be connected.*

**suspicious** /səˈspɪʃəs/ *adj* **1** making you feel that something is wrong or that something bad or illegal is happening *suspicious behaviour/circumstances* • *I called airport security after noticing a suspicious-looking package.* **2** not trusting someone *Many of them remain suspicious of journalists.* • **suspiciously** *adv She's been acting very suspiciously lately.*

**sustain** /səˈsteɪn/ *verb* [T] **1** to cause or allow something to continue for a period of time *The team may not be able to sustain this level of performance.* **2** to support someone or something so that they can live or exist *The money he received was hardly enough to sustain a wife and five children.* **3 sustain damage/injuries/losses** *formal* If someone or something sustains injuries, damage, losses, etc, they are injured, damaged, etc. *She later died in hospital of the injuries sustained in the accident.*

**sustainable** /səˈsteɪnəbl/ *adj* able to continue over a period of time *sustainable development/growth*

**sustained** /səˈsteɪnd/ *adj* continuing for a period of time without getting weaker *a sustained attack* • *sustained pressure*

**svelte** /svelt/ *adj* thin in an attractive way

**swab** /swɒb/ *noun* [C] a small piece of material used for cleaning an injury or for taking a small amount of a substance from someone's body so that it can be tested

**swagger** /ˈswægər/ *verb* [I] to walk in a way that shows that you are confident and think that you are important *A group of young men swaggered around in leather jackets.* • **swagger** *noun* [no plural]

○ᴹ**swallow**[1] /ˈswɒləʊ/ *verb* **1** FOOD OR DRINK [T] to move your throat in order to make food or drink go down *These tablets are too big to swallow.* • *The snake swallowed the bird whole.* **2** THROAT [I] to make a movement with your throat as if you are eating, sometimes because you are nervous *It hurts when I swallow.* • *Claire swallowed hard, opened the door and stepped inside.* **3** ACCEPT [T] to accept something unpleasant *They found the final decision hard to swallow.* **4** BELIEVE [T] *informal* to believe something, usually something which is not true *I told him we were journalists and he seemed to swallow it.* ⊃ *See also:* swallow your **pride**[1].

**swallow sth up** to make something disappear *Many small businesses are being swallowed up by large international companies.*

**swallow**[2] /ˈswɒləʊ/ *noun* [C] **1** a small bird with long, pointed wings and a tail with two points **2** the movement of swallowing

**swam** /swæm/ *past tense of* swim

**swamp**[1] /swɒmp/ *noun* [C, U] an area of very wet, soft land

**swamp**[2] /swɒmp/ *verb* [T] **1** to give someone more of something than they can deal with [often passive] *The company was swamped with calls about its new service.* • *The market has been swamped by cheap imports.* **2** If an area is swamped, it becomes covered with water. *Heavy rain has swamped many villages in the region.*

**swan** /swɒn/ *noun* [C] a large, white bird with a long neck which lives on lakes and rivers

**swap** /swɒp/ *verb* [I, T] **swapping**, *past* **swapped** to give something to someone and get something from them in return *Would you mind if Dave swapped places with you for a bit?* • **swap** *noun* [C] *We'll do a swap.*

**swarm**[1] /swɔːm/ *noun* [C] a large group of things, usually insects, moving together *a swarm of bees*

**swarm**[2] /swɔːm/ *verb* [I] to move in a large group *TV reporters swarmed outside the pop star's home.*

**swarm with sb/sth** If a place is swarming with people, insects, etc, there are a lot of them moving around in it. *The house was swarming with police.*

**swarthy** /ˈswɔːði/ *adj* having dark skin

**swat** /swɒt/ *verb* [T] **swatting**, *past* **swatted** to hit something, especially an insect, with a flat object *He swatted a fly with his newspaper.*

**sway** /sweɪ/ *verb* **1** [I] to move slowly from one side to the other *The trees swayed gently in the wind.* **2** [T] to persuade someone to change their opinion or decision *I think I was swayed by what James said.*

○ᴹ**swear** /sweər/ *verb past t* **swore**, *past p* **sworn** **1** BAD LANGUAGE [I] to use language which people think is rude or offensive *He was sent home because he swore at the teacher.* • *She swore loudly and threw the box on the floor.* **2** PROMISE [I, T] to make a serious promise [+ to do sth] *I swear to tell the truth.* • [+ (that)] *She swore that she was at home at the time of the accident.* **3** TRUE [T] used to say that you are sure something is true [+ (that)] *I could have sworn that she said she lived in Canterbury* (= I was sure she lived in Canterbury, but now I have found that it is not true).

**swear by sth** to believe strongly that something is useful or effective *Have you tried using vinegar to clean windows? My Mum swears by it.*

**swear sb in** to make someone such as a president, judge, etc officially promise to be honest and responsible when they start their job [often passive] *Mr Stein was sworn in as City Council president yesterday.*

swearing /'sweərɪŋ/ *noun* [U] using rude or offensive language *He was always getting into trouble for swearing.*

'swear ,word *noun* [C] a word which people think is rude or offensive

sweat /swet/ *verb* [I] to produce liquid through your skin because you are hot or nervous *I'd been running and I was sweating.* • sweat *noun* [U] *The sweat was running down his face.*

**sweat it out** *informal* to wait nervously for an unpleasant situation to improve or end *I don't get my exam results till the end of June so I'll just have to sweat it out till then.*

**sweat over sth** to work hard at something *She's been sweating over the preparations for the party all weekend.*

sweater /'swetə<sup>r</sup>/ (*also UK* jumper) *noun* [C] a warm piece of clothing which covers the top of your body and is pulled on over your head ➷ *See colour picture* **Clothes** *on page Centre 5.*

sweats /swets/ *noun* [plural] *US* a sweatshirt and sweatpants (= loose, comfortable trousers), often worn for exercising

sweatshirt /'swetʃɜːt/ *noun* [C] a piece of clothing made of soft cotton which covers the top of your body and is pulled on over your head ➷ *See colour picture* **Clothes** *on page Centre 5.*

sweaty /'sweti/ *adj* covered in sweat *He was hot and sweaty from working in the garden.*

swede /swiːd/ *UK noun* [C, U] a round, yellow vegetable which grows in the ground

sweep¹ /swiːp/ *verb past* swept **1** [I, T] (*also* sweep up) to clean the floor using a brush *She's just swept the floor.* • *He swept up the pieces of broken glass* (= removed them with a brush). **2 be swept along/away, etc** to be pushed or carried along, often by something strong which you cannot control *Many trees were swept away in the flood.* • *They got swept along by the crowd.* **3** [I, T] to quickly affect a large area *The disease is sweeping the country.* • *Panic swept through the crowd.* **4 sweep along/into/past, etc** to move quickly, especially in a way that shows you think you are important *She swept past me in the corridor.*

sweep² /swiːp/ *noun* [C] **1** a long movement [usually singular] *With a sweep of his arm, he gestured towards the garden.* **2** something shaped in a long curve *a long sweep of sandy beach* ➷ *See also:* **chimney sweep**.

sweeping /'swiːpɪŋ/ *adj* **1** [always before noun] affecting many things or people *sweeping changes/reforms* **2 sweeping statement/generalization** when someone says something that is very general and has not been carefully thought about

sweepstake /'swiːpsteɪk/ *UK* (*US* sweepstakes) *noun* [C] a type of betting (= risking money on a competition) in which the winner receives all the money

o━sweet¹ /swiːt/ *adj* **1** TASTE with a taste like sugar *It was covered in a very sweet chocolate sauce.* **2** ATTRACTIVE attractive, often because of being small *Look at that kitten – isn't she sweet?* **3** KIND kind and friendly *It was really sweet of you to come.* **4** SMELL/SOUND A sweet smell or sound is pleasant. • sweetness *noun* [U]

sweet² /swiːt/ *UK* (*US* candy) *noun* [C] a small piece of sweet food, often made of sugar or chocolate *You shouldn't eat so many sweets – they're bad for your teeth.*

sweetcorn /'swiːtkɔːn/ *UK* (*US* corn) *noun* [U] the sweet, yellow seeds of maize (= a plant) which are eaten as a vegetable ➷ *See colour picture* **Fruit and Vegetables** *on page Centre 8.*

sweeten /'swiːt<sup>ə</sup>n/ *verb* [T] to make something sweeter, for example, by adding more sugar *She gave me a hot lemon drink, sweetened with honey.*

sweetener /'swiːt<sup>ə</sup>nə<sup>r</sup>/ *noun* [C] **1** something which is used to make something taste sweeter *an artificial sweetener* **2** something that is used to persuade someone to do something

sweetheart /'swiːthɑːt/ *noun* [C] You call someone 'sweetheart' to show affection or to be friendly. *Come here, sweetheart.*

sweetly /'swiːtli/ *adv* in an attractive or kind way *She smiled sweetly.*

,sweet po'tato *UK* (*US* 'sweet po,tato) *noun* [C, U] *plural* sweet potatoes a long, red vegetable like a potato but that tastes slightly sweet

swell¹ /swel/ *verb past t* swelled, *past p* swollen *or* swelled **1** [I] (*also* swell up) to increase in size *One side of his face had swollen up where he'd been stung.* **2** [I, T] to increase in amount because more things are added *The population of the region was swollen by refugees from across the border.*

swell² /swel/ *noun* **1** [C, U] the movement of waves in the sea, or the waves themselves *ocean swells* **2** [C] an increase

swell³ /swel/ *adj* *US old-fashioned* good or pleasant *Everyone's having a swell time.*

swelling /'swelɪŋ/ *noun* [C, U] a part of your body which has become bigger because of illness or injury *The doctor gave me drugs to reduce the swelling in my ankle.*

sweltering /'sweltərɪŋ/ *adj* so hot that you feel uncomfortable *It was a sweltering afternoon in August.*

swept /swept/ *past of* sweep

swerve /swɜːv/ *verb* [I] to change direction suddenly, especially when you are driving a vehicle *He swerved to avoid a cyclist and hit another car.*

swift /swɪft/ *adj* happening or moving quickly *a swift response* • swiftly *adv*

swig /swɪg/ *verb* [T] swigging, *past* swigged *informal* to drink something, taking a lot of

liquid into your mouth at a time • **swig** *noun* [C]
*He **took a swig of** his beer and carried on with
the story.*

**swill¹** /swɪl/ *verb* [T] **1** (*also* **swill out**) to clean
something by making liquid move around it
*The dentist handed me a glass of water to swill
my mouth out.* **2** to quickly drink a large
amount of something, especially alcohol

**swill²** /swɪl/ *noun* [U] waste food that is fed to
pigs

○━**swim¹** /swɪm/ *verb* **swimming**, *past t* **swam**, *past
p* **swum** **1** THROUGH WATER [I, T] to move
through water by moving your body *I learnt to
swim when I was about 5 years old.* • *I swim
thirty lengths of the pool most mornings.* ➔ See
*colour picture* **Sports 1** *on page Centre 15.* **2** HEAD [I]
If your head swims, you feel confused and are
unable to see or think clearly. *Just the thought
of all that work makes my head swim.* **3** SEEM
TO MOVE [I] to seem to move about *I got up suddenly and the room started swimming.* • **swimming** *noun* [U] *I usually **go swimming** about
twice a week.* • **swimmer** *noun* [C] *I'm not a very
strong swimmer.*

**swim²** /swɪm/ *noun* [C] a time when you swim *I
went for a swim before breakfast.*

**swimming costume** UK (US **bathing suit**)
*noun* [C] a piece of clothing that you wear to go
swimming

**swimming pool** *noun* [C] an area of water
that has been made for people to swim in

**swimming trunks** *noun* [plural] a piece of
clothing that boys and men wear when they
swim

**swimsuit** /'swɪmsuːt/ *noun* [C] a piece of clothing that girls and women wear to go swimming

**swindle** /'swɪndl/ *verb* [T] to get money from
someone by cheating or deceiving them [often
passive] *She was swindled out of thousands of
dollars.* • **swindle** *noun* [C] *a multi-million-
pound swindle* • **swindler** *noun* [C]

**swine** /swaɪn/ *noun* **1** [plural] *formal* pigs **2** [C]
*informal* an unpleasant person

**swing¹** /swɪŋ/ *verb past* **swung** **1** BACKWARDS/
FORWARDS [I, T] to move smoothly backwards
and forwards, or to make something do this
*She really swings her arms when she walks.*
**2** CURVE [I, T] to move smoothly in a curve, or to
make something do this *The door swung shut.*
• *Watch the ball as you swing the bat.* **3** CHANGE
[I] If someone's opinion or their feelings swing,
they suddenly change. *Her moods swing with
absolutely no warning.*

**swing around/round** to turn around quickly
*She suddenly heard a voice behind her and
swung round.*

**swing at sb** *informal* to try to hit someone

**swing²** /swɪŋ/ *noun* [C] **1** FOR CHILDREN a chair
hanging on two ropes that children sit on and
swing backwards and forwards **2** HIT an
attempt to hit someone *Isn't that the boy Mark
**took a swing at** (= tried to hit)?* **3** CHANGE a
sudden change *He suffered terrible mood
swings.* **4 be in full swing** If an event is in full
swing, everything has started and there is a lot
of activity. *By ten o'clock, the party was in full
swing.*

**swipe¹** /swaɪp/ *verb* [T] **1** (*also* **swipe at**) to move

your arm in order to try to hit someone or
something **2** *informal* to steal something

**swipe²** /swaɪp/ *noun* [C] an attempt to hit
someone

**swipe card** *noun* [C] *UK* a small piece of
plastic that contains electronic information,
used to open doors, etc

**swirl** /swɜːl/ *verb* [I, T] to move around and around
quickly, or to make something do this *The mist
swirled round the castle.* • **swirl** *noun* [C]

**swish** /swɪʃ/ *verb* [I, T] to move quickly through
the air making a soft sound, or to make something do this • **swish** *noun* [C] *the swish of curtains closing*

○━**switch¹** /swɪtʃ/ *verb* [I, T] **1** to change from one
thing to another *We're trying to encourage
people to **switch from** cars **to** bicycles.* • *He's
just switched jobs.* **2** to exchange something
with someone else *After a couple of months we
switched roles.*

**switch (sth) off** to turn off a light, television,
etc by using a switch *Have you switched the
computer off?*

**switch off** *UK* to stop giving your attention
to someone or something *I'm afraid I just
switch off when she starts telling me about her
problems.*

**switch (sth) on** to turn on a light, television, etc
by using a switch *Could you switch on the light?*

**switch over 1** *UK* to change from one television
or radio station to another **2** to change from
doing one thing to another *We've decided to
switch over to low fat milk.*

○━**switch²** /swɪtʃ/ *noun* [C] **1** a small object that
you push up or down with your finger to turn
something electrical on or off **2** a change *There
has been a switch in policy.*

**switchboard** /'swɪtʃbɔːd/ *noun* [C] a piece of
equipment that is used to direct all the telephone calls made from and to a building

**swivel** /'swɪvəl/ (*also* **swivel around**) *verb* [I, T]
(*UK*) **swivelling**, *past* **swivelled**, (*US*) **swiveling**,
*past* **swiveled** to turn round, or to make something turn round

**swollen¹** /'swəʊlən/ *adj* bigger than usual *a
swollen wrist/ankle* • *swollen rivers*

**swollen²** /'swəʊlən/ *past participle of* swell

**swoop** /swuːp/ *verb* [I] **1** to suddenly move very
quickly down through the air *Huge birds
**swoop down** from the sky.* **2** to suddenly attack
*The day before police had **swooped on** his home.*
• **swoop** *noun* [C]

**swop** /swɒp/ *verb* [I, T] **swopping**, *past* **swopped**
*another UK spelling of* swap (= to give something to someone and get something from them
in return)

**sword** /sɔːd/ *noun* [C] a weapon with a long,
metal blade and a handle, used especially in
the past

**swordfish** /'sɔːdfɪʃ/ *noun* [C, U] *plural* **swordfish**
a large fish with a long, pointed part at the
front of its head, that can be eaten as food

**swore** /swɔː/ *past tense of* swear

**sworn¹** /swɔːn/ *adj* **1 sworn statement/testi-
mony, etc** something that you have officially
said is true **2 sworn enemies** two people, or
two groups of people who are completely
against each other

**sworn**[2] /swɔːn/ *past participle of* swear

**swot**[1] /swɒt/ *noun* [C] *UK informal* someone who studies too much

**swot**[2] /swɒt/ *UK informal* (*US* **cram**) *verb* [I] **swotting**, *past* **swotted** to study a lot *I'm swotting for tomorrow's exam.*

**swot up (on sth)** to learn as much as you can about a subject, especially before an examination

**swum** /swʌm/ *past participle of* swim

**swung** /swʌŋ/ *past of* swing

**sycamore** /ˈsɪkəmɔːʳ/ *noun* [C, U] a tree with leaves that are divided into five parts and with seeds that turn around as they fall

**sycophantic** /ˌsɪkəʊˈfæntɪk/ *adj formal* Someone who is sycophantic praises people in authority in a way that is not sincere, especially in order to get an advantage for themselves. ● sycophant /ˈsɪkəfænt/ *noun* [C]

**syllable** /ˈsɪləbl/ *noun* [C] a word or part of a word that has one vowel sound *'But' has one syllable and 'apple' has two syllables.*

**syllabus** /ˈsɪləbəs/ *noun* [C] *plural* **syllabuses** or **syllabi** a list of the subjects that are included in a course of study

o━**symbol** /ˈsɪmbʲl/ *noun* [C] **1** a sign or object that is used to represent something *A heart shape is the symbol of love.* **2** a number, letter, or sign that is used instead of the name of a chemical substance, another number, etc *The symbol for oxygen is O.* ⊃ *See also:* **status symbol**.

**symbolic** /sɪmˈbɒlɪk/ *adj* representing something else *The blue, white and red of the French flag are symbolic of liberty, equality and fraternity.* ● symbolically *adv*

**symbolism** /ˈsɪmbʲlɪzʲm/ *noun* [U] the use of signs and objects in art, films, etc to represent ideas

**symbolize** (*also UK* **-ise**) /ˈsɪmbʲlaɪz/ *verb* [T] to represent something *The lighting of the Olympic torch symbolizes peace and friendship among the nations of the world.*

**symmetrical** /sɪˈmetrɪkʲl/ (*also* **symmetric**) *adj* having the same shape or size on both halves *Faces are roughly symmetrical.*

**symmetry** /ˈsɪmətri/ *noun* [U] when something is symmetrical

o━**sympathetic** /ˌsɪmpəˈθetɪk/ *adj* **1** showing that you understand and care about someone's problems *My boss is very sympathetic about my situation.* **2** agreeing with or supporting someone's ideas or actions *He was sympathetic to their views.* ⊃ *Opposite* **unsympathetic**. ● sympathetically *adv*

**USAGE**

**sympathetic**

Be careful not to use **sympathetic** when you simply want to say that someone is **nice**, **friendly**, or **kind**. Remember that if someone is **sympathetic**, they understand your problems.

**sympathize** (*also UK* **-ise**) /ˈsɪmpəθaɪz/ *verb* [I] **1** to understand and care about someone's problems *It's a really bad situation – I do sympathize with her.* **2** to agree with or support

someone's ideas or actions *I sympathize with the general aims of the party.*

**sympathizer** (*also UK* **-iser**) /ˈsɪmpəθaɪzəʳ/ *noun* [C] someone who supports a particular political organization, or believes in a particular set of ideas *a communist sympathizer*

o━**sympathy** /ˈsɪmpəθi/ *noun* [U] **1** when you show that you understand and care about someone's problems *I have no sympathy for people who say they can't find work but are really just too lazy to look.* ● *It's not money she wants, it's just a little sympathy.* **2** agreement with or support for someone's ideas or actions *Scott was in sympathy with this view.*

**symphony** /ˈsɪmfəni/ *noun* [C] a long piece of music for an orchestra (= large group of different musicians)

**symptom** /ˈsɪmptəm/ *noun* [C] **1** a physical feeling or problem which shows that you have a particular illness *The inability to sleep is often a symptom of some other illness.* **2** a problem that is caused by and shows a more serious problem *The drinking was just a symptom of his general unhappiness.* ● symptomatic /ˌsɪmptəˈmætɪk/ *adj* relating to a symptom

**synagogue** /ˈsɪnəgɒg/ *noun* [C] a building in which Jewish people pray

**sync** /sɪŋk/ *noun informal* **1** **be in sync** to be happening at the same time **2** **be out of sync** to not be happening at the same time

**synchronize** (*also UK* **-ise**) /ˈsɪŋkrənaɪz/ *verb* [T] **1** to make something happen at the same time as something else *We had a problem synchronizing the music and the images.* **2** **synchronize watches** to make two or more watches show exactly the same time ● synchronization /ˌsɪŋkrənaɪˈzeɪʲn/ *noun* [U]

**syndicate** /ˈsɪndɪkət/ *noun* [C] a group of people or companies who join together in order to achieve something *a bank syndicate* ● *a crime syndicate*

**syndrome** /ˈsɪndrəʊm/ *noun* [C] a combination of physical problems that often go together in a particular illness

**synergy** /ˈsɪnədʒi/ *noun* [C, U] when two companies or groups work together and achieve more success than they would separately *a synergy between the two software companies*

**synonym** /ˈsɪnənɪm/ *noun* [C] a word or phrase that means the same as another word or phrase

**synonymous** /sɪˈnɒnɪməs/ *adj* **1** If one thing is synonymous with another, they are very closely connected with each other in people's minds. *It is a country where wealth is synonymous with corruption.* **2** If one word is synonymous with another, they have the same meaning.

**synopsis** /sɪˈnɒpsɪs/ *noun* [C] *plural* **synopses** a short description of a book, film, etc

**syntax** /ˈsɪntæks/ *noun* [U] the grammatical arrangement of words in a sentence

**synthesis** /ˈsɪnθəsɪs/ *noun* [C, U] *plural* **syntheses** /ˈsɪnθəsiːz/ *formal* the mixing of several things to make another whole new thing

**synthesize** (*also UK* **-ise**) /ˈsɪnθəsaɪz/ *verb* [T] to mix several things in order to make something else

**synthesizer** (*also UK* **-iser**) /ˈsɪnθəsaɪzəʳ/ *noun*

**S**

[C] an electronic musical instrument that can copy the sounds made by other musical instruments

**synthetic** /sɪn'θetɪk/ *adj* not made from natural substances *synthetic rubber* • synthetically *adv*

**syphilis** /'sɪfɪlɪs/ *noun* [U] a serious disease caught during sex that spreads slowly from the sex organs to all parts of the body

**syringe** /sɪ'rɪndʒ/ *noun* [C] a piece of medical equipment used to push liquid into or take liquid out of someone's body

**syrup** /'sɪrəp/ *noun* [U] a very sweet liquid made from sugar and water

o⚹**system** /'sɪstəm/ *noun* [C] **1** METHOD a way or method of doing things *the American legal system* • *the public transport system* **2** EQUIPMENT a set of connected pieces of equipment that operate together *They've had an alarm system installed at their home.* **3** BODY parts of the body that work together in order to make something happen *the body's immune system* **4 the system** the laws and rules of a society **5 get sth out of your system** to get rid of a strong feeling or a need to do something, especially by expressing that feeling or doing the thing you want to do *It's not a bad idea to travel before getting a job – that way you get it out of your system.* ➷ *See also:* **immune system, nervous system, operating system, public address system, the solar system.**

**systematic** /ˌsɪstə'mætɪk/ *adj* done using a fixed and organized plan *the systematic collection and analysis of information* • systematically *adv*

**S**

| iː **see** | ɒ **hot** | ɔː **saw** | ʌ **run** | ʊ **put** | uː **too** | aɪ **my** | aʊ **how** | eɪ **day** | əʊ **no** | ɪə **near** | ɔɪ **boy** | ʊə **poor** | aɪə **fire** | aʊə **sour** |

# T

**T, t** /tiː/ the twentieth letter of the alphabet

**ta** /tɑː/ *exclamation UK informal* thank you

**tab** /tæb/ *noun* [C] **1** a small piece of paper, metal, etc that is fixed to something and that you use to open it or find out information about it *Pull tab to open.* **2** an amount of money that you owe for something you have bought or for a service you have used *Officials said the tab for the new bridge would be $8 million.* **3 pick up the tab** to pay for something, especially a meal in a restaurant **4 keep tabs on sb/sth** *informal* to watch someone or something carefully to check they do nothing wrong

**tabby** /'tæbi/ *noun* [C] a cat that has stripes in its fur

o━**table**[1] /'teɪbl/ *noun* [C] **1** a piece of furniture with four legs, used for eating off, putting things on, etc *the kitchen table* **2 lay the table** *UK* (*UK/US* **set the table**) to put plates, knives, forks, etc on the table to prepare for a meal **3** a set of numbers or words written in rows that go across and down the page *The table below shows the results of the experiment.* **4 turn the tables on sb** to change a situation so that you have an advantage over someone who before had an advantage over you ➔ *See also:* put/lay your cards (**card**) on the table, **coffee table**, **dressing table**.

**table**[2] /'teɪbl/ *verb* [T] **1** *UK* to formally suggest that a particular subject is discussed **2** *US* to decide to discuss something later

**tablecloth** /'teɪblklɒθ/ *noun* [C] a piece of material that covers a table, especially during a meal

**tablespoon** /'teɪblspuːn/ *noun* [C] a large spoon used for measuring or serving food, or the amount this spoon can hold

**tablet** /'tæblət/ *noun* [C] **1** MEDICINE a small, round object containing medicine that you swallow ➔ *See picture at* **medicine**. **2** STONE a square piece of stone that has words cut into it **3** PAPER *US* (*UK/US* **pad**) sheets of paper that have been fastened together at one edge, used for writing or drawing

'table ,tennis *noun* [U] a game in which two or four people hit a small ball over a low net on a large table

**tabloid** /'tæblɔɪd/ *noun* [C] a small newspaper with a lot of pictures and short, simple news stories

**taboo** /tə'buː/ *noun* [C, U] something that you should not say or do because people generally think it is morally wrong, unpleasant, or embarrassing *Sex is a taboo in this country.* • *taboo adj Suicide is a taboo subject.*

**tacit** /'tæsɪt/ *adj formal* understood without being said *a tacit agreement*

**taciturn** /'tæsɪtɜːn/ *adj formal* saying very little and not seeming friendly

**tack**[1] /tæk/ *noun* **1 take/try a different tack** to try to deal with a problem in a different way *I've tried being nice to her and it doesn't work so I might take a different tack.* **2** [C] a small, sharp nail with a flat top *carpet tacks* **3** [C] *US* (*UK* **drawing pin**) a short pin with a flat, round top, used for fastening pieces of paper to the wall

**tack**[2] /tæk/ *verb* [T] **1** to fasten something to a wall with a tack **2** to sew something loosely **tack sth on** to add something that you had not planned to add

**tackle**[1] /'tækl/ *verb* [T] **1** DEAL WITH to try to deal with a problem *new ways to tackle crime* **2** SPEAK TO *UK* to speak to someone about something bad that they have done *I decided to tackle him about his absences.* **3** BALL to try to get the ball from someone in a game such as football

**tackle**[2] /'tækl/ *noun* **1** [C] an attempt to get the ball from someone in a game such as football **2** [U] all the things you need for a particular activity *fishing tackle*

**tacky** /'tæki/ *adj* **1** *informal* cheap and of bad quality *tacky holiday souvenirs* **2** slightly sticky

**tact** /tækt/ *noun* [U] the ability to talk to people about difficult subjects without upsetting them

**tactful** /'tæktfᵊl/ *adj* careful not to say or do anything that could upset someone • *tactfully adv*

**tactic** /'tæktɪk/ *noun* [C] a way of doing something that you plan in order to achieve what you want [usually plural] *These bomb attacks represent a change of tactics by the terrorists.*

**tactical** /'tæktɪkᵊl/ *adj* relating to tactics, or done in order to achieve something *a tactical vote* • *tactically adv*

**tactless** /'tæktləs/ *adj* not being careful about saying or doing something that could upset someone

**tad** /tæd/ *noun informal* **a tad** a little *It was a tad expensive, I thought.*

**tadpole** /'tædpəʊl/ *noun* [C] a small, black animal that lives in water and will become a frog (= green jumping animal)

**taffeta** /'tæfɪtə/ *noun* [U] a stiff, shiny cloth used in women's formal dresses

**tag**[1] /tæg/ *noun* [C] a small piece of paper or plastic with information on it that is fixed to something *a price tag*

**tag**[2] /tæg/ *verb* [T] **tagging**, *past* **tagged** to put a tag on something

**tag along** *informal* to go somewhere with someone, especially when they have not asked you to *If you're going to town do you mind if I tag along?*

**tail**[1] /teɪl/ *noun* [C] **1** the long, narrow part that sticks out at the back of an animal's body *The dog's pleased to see you – he's wagging his tail.* **2** the back part of something long, such as a plane **3 the tail end of sth** the last part of something *the tail end of the eighties*

**tail**[2] /teɪl/ *verb* [T] to secretly follow someone, especially because you think they have done something wrong

**tail off** to gradually become quieter, smaller, less frequent, etc *His voice tailed off.*

**tailback** /'teɪlbæk/ *noun* [C] *UK* a line of cars that have stopped or are moving very slowly because of an accident or other problem on the road in front of them

---

| j yes | k cat | ʃ she | ʒ decision | θ thin | ð this | ŋ ring | tʃ chip | dʒ jar | æ cat | ɑː arm | e bed | eə hair | ə ago | ɜː her | ɪ sit | i cosy |

**tailcoat** /'teɪl,kəʊt/ *noun* [C] a formal coat that has a short front part and a long back part that is divided in two

**tailgate** /'teɪlgeɪt/ *verb* [I, T] to drive too closely to the car in front of you • **tailgating** *noun* [U]

**'tail ,light** *noun* [C] *US* one of the two red lights on the back of a car ➔ *See colour picture* **Car** *on page Centre 3.*

**tailor**[1] /'teɪlə<sup>r</sup>/ *noun* [C] someone whose job is to make or repair clothes, especially men's clothes

**tailor**[2] /'teɪlə<sup>r</sup>/ *verb* [T] to make or change something so that it is suitable *The kitchen can then be **tailored** exactly to the customer's needs.*

**tailor-made** /ˌteɪlə'meɪd/ *adj* **1** perfect for a particular person or purpose *It sounds as if you're tailor-made for the job.* **2** Tailor-made clothes are made by a tailor.

**tailpipe** /'teɪlpaɪp/ *US* (*UK* **exhaust pipe**) *noun* [C] the pipe that waste gas from a vehicle's engine flows through ➔ *See colour picture* **Car** *on page Centre 3.*

**tails** /teɪlz/ *noun* [plural] **1** the side of a coin that does not have someone's head on it *Let's toss a coin – **heads or tails?*** **2** a formal coat that has a short front part and a long back part that is divided in two

**taint** /teɪnt/ *verb* [T] **1** to spoil people's opinion of someone [often passive] *a government tainted by scandal* **2** to spoil something, especially food or blood, by adding a harmful substance

○━**take** /teɪk/ *verb* [T] *past t* **took**, *past p* **taken** **1** CARRY to get and carry something with you when you go somewhere *I always **take** my mobile phone **with** me.* **2** GO to go somewhere with someone, often paying for them or being responsible for them *I **took** the kids **to** the park.* • *I'm taking my wife to Florence for the weekend.* ➔ *See usage note at* **bring**. **3** WITHOUT PERMISSION to remove something without permission *Someone's taken my coat.* **4** GET HOLD to get hold of something and move it *He reached across and took the glass from her.* **5** ACCEPT to accept something *So, are you going to take the job?* • *Do you take credit cards?* **6** NEED If something takes a particular amount of time, or a particular quality, you need that amount of time or that quality in order to be able to do it. [+ to do sth] *It's taken me three days to get here.* • *It takes a lot of courage to stand up and talk in front of so many people.* **7** MEDICINE to swallow or use medicine *Take two tablets, three times a day.* **8** MEASURE to measure something *Have you taken her temperature?* **9** CLOTHES to wear a particular size of clothes *I take a size 12 in trousers.* **10** SPACE to have enough space for a particular number of people or things *There's six of us and the car only takes five.* **11** TRAVEL to travel somewhere by using a bus, train, car, etc, or by using a particular road *Are you taking the train to Edinburgh?* • *Take the A316 towards Richmond.* **12** take a break/rest, etc to stop working for a period *If you're tired, take a rest.* **13** take pleasure/pride/an interest, etc to have a particular, good feeling about something that you do *I take great pleasure in cooking.* • *These women take their jobs very seriously* (= think their jobs are very important). **14** take a

**look** to look at something *Take a look at these photos.* **15** UNDERSTAND to understand something in a particular way *Whatever I say she'll take it the wrong way.* **16 I take it (that)** used when you think that what you say is probably true *I take it you're not coming with us.* **17 can't take sth** to not be able to deal with an unpleasant situation *We argue all the time – I really can't take it any more.* **18 take it from me** accept that what I say is true, because I know or have experienced it *You could be doing a much less interesting job, take it from me.* **19 take sth as it comes** to deal with something as it happens, without planning for it *With an illness like this you just have to take every day as it comes.* **20** BY FORCE to get control of something by force *By morning they had taken the city.*

---

**USAGE**

**take part in** or **take place?**

If someone **takes part in** something, they join other people in doing it.

*All the children took part in the competition.*

If something **takes place**, it happens.

*The festival takes place every summer in the castle gardens.*

---

**take after sb** to be similar to an older member of your family *Peter's very tall – he takes after his father.*

**take sth apart** to separate something into its different parts *He spent the whole afternoon taking his bike apart.*

**take sth away 1** to remove something *The waitress took our plates away.* • *Supermarkets are taking business away from small local shops.* **2** to subtract a number *Take 3 away from 20.*

**take sb away** to make someone leave a place and go with you *Police came in the night and took him away.*

**take sth back 1** to return something to the place you borrowed or bought it from **2** to admit that your opinion was wrong *You're right, he's nice – I take back everything I said about him.*

**take sth down 1** to write something *Did you take down the telephone number?* **2** to remove something that is on a wall or something that is temporary *I've taken the pictures down.* • *We took the tent down.*

**take sth in 1** UNDERSTAND to understand something *It was an interesting lecture but there was just too much to take in.* **2** FILM/BUILDING ETC to go to see a film, visit an interesting building, etc for enjoyment *I thought we might get something to eat and then take in a movie.* **3** CLOTHES to make a piece of clothing narrower

**take sb in 1** If the police take someone in, they take that person to the police station. **2** to let someone stay in your house *You could earn some extra cash by taking in foreign students.* **3 be taken in** to be deceived by someone

**take sth off 1** to remove something *If you're hot, take your jacket off.* • *Take your feet off the* chair. ➔ *See colour picture* **Phrasal Verbs** *on page Centre 13.* **2** to spend time away from your work *I'm taking Friday off to get some things done around the house.*

**take off 1** AIRCRAFT If an aircraft takes off, it begins to fly. **2** SUCCESSFUL to suddenly become successful *Her career had just taken off.* **3** LEAVE to suddenly leave without telling anyone where you are going *He took off in the middle of the night.*

**take sth on** to accept a responsibility *I don't want to take on too much work.*

**take sb on 1** to begin to employ someone *We'll be taking on two new members of staff.* **2** to compete against someone *I might take you on at tennis sometime.*

**take on sth** to begin to have a particular quality *Her voice took on a tone of authority.*

**take sth out** to remove something from somewhere *He reached into his bag and took out a book.*

**take sb out** to go somewhere with someone and pay for them *Are you taking her out for her birthday?*

**take sth out on sb** to unfairly treat someone badly because you are upset *Don't take it out on me!*

**take (sth) over** to get control of or responsibility for something *They've recently been taken over by a larger company.* • *Who'll be taking over from Cynthia when she retires?*

**take sb through sth** to explain something to someone *I'll take you through it one more time then you can try it yourself.*

**take to sb/sth** to start to like someone or something *For some reason, I just didn't take to him.*

**take to sth/doing sth** to start doing something *Dad's taken to swimming every morning.*

**take sth up 1** to start doing a particular job or activity *I thought I might take up cycling.* **2** to use an amount of time or space *This desk takes up too much space.*

**take sb up on sth** to accept an offer *Could I take you up on your offer of a ride home?*

**take sth up with sb** to discuss something with someone *You'll have to take the matter up with your manager.*

**takeaway** /ˈteɪkəweɪ/ UK (US **takeout** /ˈteɪkaʊt/) *noun* [C] a meal that you buy in a restaurant but eat at home, or a shop that sells this type of meal

**take-off** /ˈteɪkɒf/ *noun* **1** [C, U] when an aircraft leaves the ground and begins to fly **2** [C] a film, book, etc that copies someone else's style in a way that is funny

**takeover** /ˈteɪkˌəʊvəʳ/ *noun* [C] when a company gets control of another company

**takings** /ˈteɪkɪŋz/ UK (US **receipts**) *noun* [plural] all the money that a business gets from selling things

**talcum powder** /ˈtælkəmˌpaʊdəʳ/ (*also* **talc**) *noun* [U] white powder that you put on your skin after a bath

**tale** /teɪl/ *noun* [C] a story, especially one which is not true or is difficult to believe *My grandfather used to tell us tales of his time as a pilot during the war.* ➔ *See also:* **fairy tale.**

∘⚹**talent** /ˈtælənt/ *noun* [C, U] a natural ability to do

something *She showed an early talent for drawing.* • **talented** *adj* showing natural ability in a particular area *a talented young musician*

**talisman** /ˈtælɪzmən/ *noun* [C] *plural* **talismans** an object that people think will make them lucky

∘⚹**talk¹** /tɔːk/ *verb* **1** [I] to say things to someone *We were just talking about Simon's new girlfriend.* • *The teacher's always telling him to stop talking.* • *It was nice talking to you.* • *(US) It was nice talking with you.* ➔ *See usage note at* **speak. 2** [I] to discuss something with someone, often to try to find a solution to a disagreement *The two sides have agreed to talk.* **3 talk about sth/doing sth** to think about or make plans to do something in the future *They're talking about building a new fire station just up the road.* **4 talk business/politics, etc** to discuss a particular subject *I don't like to talk business over lunch.* **5 talking of sth** UK (US **speaking of sth**) used when you are going to start talking about something that is related to what has just been said *Talking of holidays, did you hear about Lesley's skiing trip?* ➔ *See also:* talk of the **devil.**

**talk at sb** to talk to someone without letting them say anything or without listening to them

**talk back** If a child talks back to an adult, they answer them rudely.

**talk down to sb** to talk to someone in a way that shows you think they are not intelligent or not important

**talk sb into/out of (doing) sth** to persuade someone to do or not do something *We managed to talk Lisa into doing the cooking.* • *Jeff talked me out of painting the room pink.*

**talk sth over** to discuss something with someone, often to find out their opinion or to get advice before making a decision *Why don't you talk it over with your parents first?*

∘⚹**talk²** /tɔːk/ *noun* **1** CONVERSATION [C] a conversation between two people, often about a particular subject *I had a long talk with Chris at the weekend about going to university.* **2** PEOPLE [U] when people talk about what might happen or be true *There's been some talk of possible job losses.* • *There's been a lot of talk about green issues lately.* **3** TO A GROUP [C] when someone speaks to a group of people about a particular subject *Someone's coming to the school to give a talk about road safety.* **4 be all talk (and no action)** If someone is all talk, they never do the brave or exciting things they often say they will do. ➔ *See also:* **small talk.**

**talkative** /ˈtɔːkətɪv/ *adj* A talkative person talks a lot.

**talks** /tɔːks/ *noun* [plural] formal meetings, especially between political leaders, to discuss a problem and to try to reach an agreement *peace talks* • *US officials are holding talks with EU leaders over trade.*

**ˈtalk ˌshow** US (UK **chat show**) *noun* [C] an informal television or radio programme where people are asked questions about themselves and their lives

∘⚹**tall** /tɔːl/ *adj* **1** having a greater than average height. *He's tall and thin.* • *It's one of the tallest* *buildings in the city.* **2** used to describe or ask about the height of someone or something *How tall is she?* • *He's almost 2 metres tall.*

**tally**¹ /'tæli/ *noun* [C] the number of things you have achieved, used, won, etc until now *This adds to his* ***tally*** *of 12 race wins so far this year.*

**tally**² /'tæli/ *verb* **1** [I] If two numbers or stories tally, they are the same. **2** [T] (*also* **tally up**) to find out the total number

**the Talmud** /'tælmʊd/ *noun* the ancient Jewish written laws and traditions

**talon** /'tælən/ *noun* [C] a sharp nail on the foot of a bird that it uses to catch animals

**tambourine** /ˌtæmbᵊr'iːn/ *noun* [C] a musical instrument with a wooden ring and small metal discs loosely fixed to it which you play by shaking or hitting

**tame**¹ /teɪm/ *adj* **1** If an animal is tame, it is not wild and not frightened of people. **2** too controlled and not exciting *His TV show is very tame in comparison with his live performances.*

**tame**² /teɪm/ *verb* [T] to make a wild animal tame

**tamper** /'tæmpəʳ/ *verb*
**tamper with sth** to touch or make changes to something which you should not, often in order to damage it *The files had been tampered with and there were some documents missing.*

**tampon** /'tæmpɒn/ *noun* [C] a small roll of cotton which a woman puts in her vagina to absorb her monthly flow of blood

**tan**¹ /tæn/ (*also* **suntan**) *noun* [C] when your skin is brown from being in the sun • tan *verb* [I, T] **tanning**, *past* **tanned** *I tan quite easily.*

**tan**² /tæn/ *adj* **1** being a pale yellow-brown colour *a tan jacket* **2** (*UK/US* **tanned**) having darker skin because you have been in the sun

**tandem** /'tændəm/ *noun* **1 in tandem (with sb)** If someone does something in tandem with someone else, they do it together or at the same time. *The police are working in tandem with local charity groups.* **2** [C] a bicycle for two people

**tangent** /'tændʒᵊnt/ *noun* [C] **1** a straight line which touches but does not cross a curve **2 go off at/on a tangent** to suddenly start talking about a different subject

**tangerine** /ˌtændʒᵊr'iːn/ *noun* [C] a fruit like a small orange

**tangible** /'tændʒəbl/ *adj* Something which is tangible is real and can be seen, touched, or measured. *tangible benefits/evidence* ⊃ *Opposite* **intangible**.

**tangle**¹ /'tæŋgl/ *noun* [C] several things which have become twisted together in an untidy way *a tangle of hair/wires*

**tangle**² /'tæŋgl/ *verb* [I, T] to become twisted together, or to make things become twisted together ⊃ *Opposite* **disentangle**, **untangle**.

**tangled** /'tæŋgld/ *adj* **1** (*also* **tangled up**) twisted together in an untidy way *The wires are all tangled.* **2** confused and difficult to understand *tangled finances* **3 be tangled up in/with sth** to be involved in something unpleasant or complicated that is difficult to escape from *He doesn't want to get tangled up in office politics.*

**tango** /'tæŋgəʊ/ *noun* [C] a South American dance

**tangy** /'tæŋi/ *adj* having a strong, sharp but pleasant taste or smell *a tangy lemon drink* • **tang** *noun* [no plural]

**tank** /tæŋk/ *noun* [C] **1** a large container for storing liquid or gas (*UK*) *a petrol tank*/(*US*) *a gas tank* • *a hot-water tank* **2** a large, strong military vehicle with a gun on it which moves on wheels inside large metal belts ⊃ *See also:* **think tank**.

**tanker** /'tæŋkəʳ/ *noun* [C] a ship or truck used to carry large amounts of liquid or gas *an oil tanker*

**tanned** /tænd/ (*also US* **tan**) *adj* having darker skin because you have been in the sun

**tannoy** /'tænɔɪ/ *UK trademark* (*UK/US* **public address system**) *noun* [no plural] a system of equipment used in public places that someone speaks into in order to make their voice loud enough to hear

**tantalizing** (*also UK* **-ising**) /'tæntəlaɪzɪŋ/ *adj* Something that is tantalizing is very attractive and makes you want it, although often you cannot have it. *a tantalizing glimpse of blue sea*

**tantamount** /'tæntəmaʊnt/ *adj* **be tantamount to sth** to be almost as bad as something else *Resignation would be tantamount to admitting he was guilty.*

**tantrum** /'tæntrəm/ *noun* [C] when someone, especially a child, suddenly shows that they are very angry, usually because they cannot have something *Tim* ***threw a tantrum*** *in the middle of the supermarket.*

**tap**¹ /tæp/ *noun* [C] **1** WATER mainly *UK* (*also US* **faucet**) the part at the end of a pipe which controls the flow of water *the cold/hot tap* • *to turn a tap on/off* • *She rinsed the cup under the tap.* **2** KNOCK a gentle knock or touch, or the noise made by knocking something gently *I felt a tap on my shoulder.* • *There was a tap at the door.* **3** TELEPHONE a small piece of equipment that can be fixed to someone's telephone in order to listen to their telephone calls **4 on tap** easily available *They have all that sort of information on tap.*

tap *UK*, faucet *US*

**tap**² /tæp/ *verb* **tapping**, *past* **tapped 1** KNOCK [I, T] to knock or touch something gently *She tapped her fingers nervously on the table.* • *I tapped on the window to try and get her attention.* **2** A SUPPLY [T] If you tap a supply of something, you use what is available. *There are immense natural resources waiting to be tapped.* **3** TELEPHONE [T] to use a special piece of equipment to listen to someone's telephone calls [often passive] *I think the phone's been tapped.*

**tap into sth** to use part of a large supply of something for your own advantage *We're hoping to be able to tap into this rich store of data.*

'**tap ,dancing** *noun* [U] a type of dancing where the dancer wears special shoes with pieces of metal on the bottom which make a noise • tap dance *verb* [I] • tap dancer *noun* [C]

**tape**[1] /teɪp/ *noun* **1** [RECORDING] [C, U] a long, thin piece of plastic which is used to store sound, pictures, or information, or a plastic box containing it *Can you turn the tape over?* • *I've got the match on tape.* **2** [STICKY] [U] a thin piece of plastic which has glue on one side and is used for sticking things together *adhesive/sticky tape* **3** [MATERIAL] [C, U] a long, thin piece of material used, for example, in sewing or to tie things together ⊃ *See also:* **Scotch tape, red tape.**

**tape**[2] /teɪp/ *verb* **1** [T] to record something onto tape *Their conversations were taped by the police.* • *I often tape programmes and watch them later.* **2 tape sth to/onto, etc** to stick something somewhere using tape *There was a message taped to the door.*

'**tape ,measure** *noun* [C] a long, thin piece of cloth, metal, or plastic used to measure lengths

**taper** /'teɪpə'/ *verb* [I, T] to become gradually narrower at one end • tapered *adj*

**taper off** to become gradually smaller or less frequent *Sales have gradually tapered off.*

'**tape re,corder** *noun* [C] a machine used to record sound onto tape • tape recording *noun* [C] something which has been recorded on tape

**tapestry** /'tæpɪstri/ *noun* [C] a picture or pattern created by sewing different coloured threads onto heavy cloth

'**tap ,water** *noun* [U] water which comes out of a tap (= part at the end of a pipe)

**tar** /tɑː'/ *noun* [U] **1** a thick, black substance that is sticky when hot and is used to cover roads **2** a black, sticky substance that is produced when tobacco burns • tar *verb* [T] **tarring,** *past* **tarred** to cover something with tar

**tarantula** /tə'ræntjələ/ *noun* [C] a large, hairy spider that is often poisonous

o-ª**target**[1] /'tɑːgɪt/ *noun* [C] **1** [ATTACK] something or someone that you attack, shoot at, try to hit, etc *It's very difficult to hit a moving target.* • *Foreign businesses in the region have become a target for terrorist attacks.* **2** [ACHIEVE] something that you intend to achieve *I'm hoping to save £3,000 by June – that's my target.* • *If you want to lose weight, you have to set yourself* (= decide) *a target.* **3** [BLAME] the person or thing that people are criticizing or blaming for something *Such extreme views have recently made him the target of criticism.* **4 be on target** to have made enough progress in order to achieve something that you intended to achieve [+ **to** **sth**] *We're on target to finish the project in June.* **5 target audience/market, etc** the group of people that a programme, product, etc is aimed at

**target**[2] /'tɑːgɪt/ *verb* [T] **1** to aim an attack at a particular person or place *They mostly targeted military bases.* **2** to aim advertising, criticism, or a product at someone [often passive] *The*

*products are targeted at people in their late twenties.*

**tariff** /'tærɪf/ *noun* [C] **1** an amount of money that has to be paid for goods that are brought into a country *import tariffs* **2** a list of prices

**tarmac** /'tɑːmæk/ *noun trademark* **1** [U] *UK (US* **asphalt)** a thick, black substance that is sticky when hot and is used to cover roads **2 the tarmac** the area at an airport where aircraft land and take off

**tarnish** /'tɑːnɪʃ/ *verb* **1** [T] to spoil the way in which people think of someone so that they do not respect them *to tarnish someone's image/ reputation* **2** [I, T] If a metal tarnishes or something tarnishes it, it becomes less bright and shiny.

**tarpaulin** /tɑː'pɔːlɪn/ *(also US* **tarp)** *noun* [C, U] a large piece of plastic or cloth that water cannot go through which is used to cover and protect things

**tart**[1] /tɑːt/ *noun* [C] **1** an open pastry case with a sweet filling, often of fruit *an apple tart* **2** *UK very informal* a woman who dresses or behaves in a way to attract a lot of attention from men

**tart**[2] /tɑːt/ *adj* having a sour, bitter taste *You might need some sugar on the fruit – it's a bit tart.*

**tartan** /'tɑːtᵊn/ *noun* [C, U] cloth with a pattern of different coloured squares and crossing lines *a tartan kilt*

**task** /tɑːsk/ *noun* [C] a piece of work, especially something unpleasant or difficult [+ **of** + **doing** sth] *I was given the task of sorting out all the stuff in the garage.*

'**task ,force** *noun* [C] a group of people, often a military group, who are brought together in order to do a particular job

**tassel** /'tæsᵊl/ *noun* [C] a decoration made of a group of short threads tied together which is hung on curtains, furniture, etc

o-ª**taste**[1] /teɪst/ *noun* **1** [FOOD] [C, U] the flavour of a particular food in your mouth *a sweet/bitter taste* • *It's got quite a strong taste.* **2** [ABILITY] [U] the ability to feel different flavours in your mouth *When you've got a cold you often lose your sense of taste.* **3 a taste** a small amount of food that you have in order to try it *Could I have just a taste of the sauce?* **4** [WHAT YOU LIKE] [C, U] the particular things you like, such as styles of music, clothes, decoration, etc *I don't like his taste in music.* • *It's okay, but it's not really to my taste.* **5** [ART/STYLE ETC] [U] the ability to judge what is attractive or suitable, especially in things related to art, style, beauty, etc *Everything in his house is beautiful – he's got very good taste.* **6 be in good taste** to be acceptable in a way that will not upset or anger people **7 be in bad/poor taste** to be unacceptable in a way that will upset or anger people *He told a joke about a plane crash which I thought was in rather poor taste.* **8 a taste for sth** when you like or enjoy something *I've developed a bit of a taste for opera.* • *Over the years I've lost my taste for travel.* **9 taste of sth** when you do or experience something new for a short time *That was my first taste of Mexican culture.*

o-ª**taste**[2] /teɪst/ *verb* **1 taste funny/nice/sweet, etc** If food tastes a particular way, it has that flavour. *This sauce tastes strange.* • *It tastes of chocolate.* **2 can taste sth** to be able to experience a particular flavour in a food *You can really taste the garlic in it.* **3** [T] to put food or drink in your mouth to find out what its flavour is like *I always taste food while I'm cooking it.*

**'taste ,buds** *noun* [plural] the cells on your tongue that allow you to taste different foods

**tasteful** /'teɪstfəl/ *adj* attractive and chosen for style and quality *a tasteful beige suit* • **tastefully** *adv tastefully dressed/decorated*

**tasteless** /'teɪstləs/ *adj* **1** UGLY ugly or without style **2** OFFENSIVE likely to upset or anger people *a tasteless joke* **3** FOOD having no flavour *The meat was dry and tasteless.*

**tasty** /'teɪsti/ *adj* Food which is tasty has a good flavour and is nice to eat. *They do a really tasty chicken and mushroom soup.*

**tattered** /'tætəd/ *adj* old and badly torn *tattered clothes*

**tatters** /'tætəz/ *noun* **in tatters** badly torn, damaged, or spoilt *The yacht finally made it to the harbour, its sails in tatters.* • *His reputation is in tatters.*

**tattoo** /tæt'uː/ *noun* [C] a design on someone's skin that is put on using ink and a needle • **tattoo** *verb* [T]

**tatty** /'tæti/ *adj UK informal* untidy and in bad condition *He turned up wearing a pair of tatty old jeans.*

**taught** /tɔːt/ *past of* teach

**taunt** /tɔːnt/ *verb* [T] to repeatedly say unkind things to someone in order to upset them or make them angry *He was taunted by his classmates because of his size.* • **taunt** *noun* [C]

**Taurus** /'tɔːrəs/ *noun* [C, U] the sign of the zodiac which relates to the period of 21 April – 22 May, or a person born during this period ➔ *See picture at* **zodiac.**

**taut** /tɔːt/ *adj* stretched very tight *My skin feels taut.*

**tavern** /'tævən/ *noun* [C] *mainly US* a place where people go to drink alcohol

**tawdry** /'tɔːdri/ *adj* **1** unpleasant and immoral **2** cheap and of bad quality

**tawny** /'tɔːni/ *adj* being a light yellow-brown colour

o⁻**tax**¹ /tæks/ *noun* [C, U] money that you have to pay to the government from what you earn or when you buy things *They're putting up the tax on cigarettes.* • *Do you have to pay tax on that?* ➔ *See also:* **income tax.**

**tax**² /tæks/ *verb* [T] **1** to make someone pay a tax *Goods such as clothes are taxed at 15%.* **2** to need a lot of effort *It's only a short report – it shouldn't tax me too much.*

**taxable** /'tæksəbl/ *adj* If something is taxable, you have to pay tax on it. *taxable income*

**taxation** /tæk'seɪʃən/ *noun* [U] the system of making people pay taxes

**tax-free** /,tæks'friː/ *adj* If something is tax-free, you do not pay tax on it.

o⁻**taxi** /'tæksi/ *noun* [C] a car with a driver who you pay to take you somewhere *a taxi driver* • *I'll take a taxi to the airport.*

**taxing** /'tæksɪŋ/ *adj* difficult and needing a lot of thought or effort to do or understand

**'taxi ,rank** *UK* (*US* **'taxi ,stand**) *noun* [C] a place where you can go to get a taxi

**TB** /,tiː'biː/ *noun* [U] *abbreviation for* tuberculosis (= a serious infectious disease of the lungs)

**tbsp** *written abbreviation for* tablespoonful: the amount that can be held by a large spoon used for measuring food

o⁻**tea** /tiː/ *noun* [C, U] **1** DRINK a hot drink that you make by pouring water onto dried leaves, or the leaves that you use to make this drink *herbal teas* • *Would you like a cup of tea or coffee?* **2** AFTERNOON MEAL *UK* a small afternoon meal of cakes, biscuits, etc and tea to drink *They invited us for afternoon tea.* **3** EVENING MEAL *UK* a word used by some people for the meal that is eaten in the evening

**teabag** /'tiːbæg/ *noun* [C] a small paper bag with dried leaves inside, used for making tea

o⁻**teach** /tiːtʃ/ *verb past* **taught 1** GIVE LESSONS [I, T] to give lessons in a particular subject at a school, university, etc *She taught at Harvard University for several years.* • *He teaches history.* **2** SHOW HOW TO [T] to show or explain to someone how to do something [+ to do sth] *My dad taught me to drive.* • *Can you teach me how to knit?* **3** GET KNOWLEDGE [T] If a situation teaches you something, it gives you new knowledge or helps you to understand something. [+ to do sth] *The whole experience taught him to be more careful with money.* ➔ *See usage note at* **learn** ➔ *See also:* teach sb a **lesson.**

o⁻**teacher** /'tiːtʃəʳ/ *noun* [C] someone whose job is to teach in a school, college, etc *a history/science teacher* ➔ *See colour picture* **Classroom** *on page Centre 4* ➔ *See usage note at* **lecturer.**

**teaching** /'tiːtʃɪŋ/ *noun* [U] the job of being a teacher *He decided to go into teaching* (= become a teacher).

**teachings** /'tiːtʃɪŋz/ *noun* [plural] the ideas or beliefs of someone, such as a political or religious leader *the teachings of Martin Luther King*

**teacup** /'tiːkʌp/ *noun* [C] a cup that you drink tea from

o⁻**team**¹ /tiːm/ *noun* [group] **1** a group of people who play a sport or game together against another group of players *a basketball/football team* • *Which team are you on?* **2** a group of people who work together to do something *a management team* • *a team of advisers*

**team**² /tiːm/ *verb*

**team up** to join someone else and work together with them to do something *I teamed up with Brendan for the doubles tournament.*

**teammate** /'tiːmmeɪt/ *noun* [C] a member of your team

**teamwork** /'tiːmwɜːk/ *noun* [U] when a group of people work well together

**teapot** /'tiːpɒt/ *noun* [C] a container used for making and serving tea, which has a lid, a handle, and a spout (= tube that liquid comes out of) ➔ *See colour picture* **Kitchen** *on page Centre 10.*

o⁻**tear**¹ /teəʳ/ *verb past t* **tore**, *past p* **torn 1** [T] to pull paper, cloth, etc into pieces, or to make a hole in it by accident *The nail had torn a hole in my skirt.* **2** [I] If paper, cloth, etc tears, it becomes damaged because it has been pulled.

*The paper is very thin and tears easily.* **tear**

**3 tear sth out of/off/down, etc** to remove something by pulling it quickly and violently *She tore his picture down from the wall.*

**4 tear along/about/past, etc** *informal* to move somewhere very quickly *The kids were tearing around the house.* **5 be torn between**

**sth and sth** to be unable to decide between two choices *I'm torn between the apple pie and the chocolate mousse.* ➔ *See also:* tear your **hair** out.

**tear sth apart 1** to make a group of people argue or fight with each other *The country was torn apart by 12 years of civil war.* **2** to destroy something *The building was torn apart by the bomb blast.*

**tear sb apart** to make someone very unhappy *Seeing the children suffer really tears me apart.*

**tear sb away** to make someone stop doing something that they enjoy, in order to do something else *I'll bring Ian, if I can tear him away from his computer games.*

**tear sth down** to intentionally destroy a building or structure *They tore down the old hospital and built some offices.*

**tear sth off** to quickly remove your clothes *He tore off his shirt and jumped into the stream.*

**tear sth up** to tear paper into a lot of small pieces *He tore up her photograph.*

o⇥**tear²** /teəʳ/ *noun* [C] a hole in a piece of cloth, paper, etc where it has been torn

o⇥**tear³** /tɪəʳ/ *noun* [C] a drop of water that comes from your eye when you cry *Suddenly he burst into tears* (= started crying). *• There were tears in her eyes as she watched him go. • I was in tears* (= crying) *by the end of the film.* **• tearful** *adj* crying *a tearful goodbye* **• tearfully** *adv* ➔ *See also:* in floods (**flood²**) of tears.

'tear ˌgas *noun* [U] a gas that makes people's eyes hurt, used by the police or army to control violent crowds

**tease** /tiːz/ *verb* [I, T] to laugh at someone or say unkind things to them, either because you are joking or because you want to upset them *They were teasing Dara about her new haircut. • Don't get upset, I'm only teasing.*

**teaspoon** /'tiːspuːn/ *noun* [C] a small spoon that is used for mixing drinks and measuring small amounts of food, or the amount this spoon can hold

**teatime** /'tiːtaɪm/ *noun* [C, U] *UK* the time in the evening when people have a meal

'tea ˌtowel *noun UK* (*US* **dishtowel**) *noun* [C] a cloth that is used for drying plates, dishes, etc

**tech¹** /tek/ *adj mainly US short for* technical (**1**) *online tech support*

**tech²** /tek/ *noun mainly US* **1** [U] *short for* technology *high/low tech • tech stocks* **2** [C] *informal short for* technician *Bill was a lab tech at NYU.*

o⇥**technical** /'teknɪkəl/ *adj* **1** SCIENCE/INDUSTRY relating to the knowledge, machines, or methods used in science and industry *We're having a few technical problems.* **2** SPECIALIZED relating to the knowledge and methods of a particular subject or job *There are a few technical terms here that I don't understand.* **3** PRACTICAL SKILL relating to practical skills and methods that are used in a particular activity *As a dancer she had great technical skill.*

**technicalities** /ˌteknɪ'kælətiz/ *noun* [plural] the exact details of a system or process *the technicalities of photography*

**technicality** /ˌteknɪ'kæləti/ *noun* [C] a small detail of a law or rule

**technically** /'teknɪkəli/ *adv* **1** relating to the knowledge, machines, or methods used in science and industry *technically advanced weapons* **2** according to the exact details of a rule, law, or fact *Irvine is technically British but lives in Dublin and races for the Irish team.*

**technician** /tek'nɪʃən/ *noun* [C] someone whose job involves practical work with scientific or electrical equipment *a computer/lab technician*

**technique** /tek'niːk/ *noun* [C, U] a particular or special way of doing something [+ for + doing sth] *Scientists have developed a new technique for taking blood samples.*

o⇥**technology** /tek'nɒlədʒi/ *noun* [C, U] knowledge, equipment, and methods that are used in science and industry *computer technology* **• technological** /ˌteknə'lɒdʒɪkəl/ *adj* relating to, or involving technology *technological developments* **• technologically** *adv* ➔ *See also:* **information technology**.

**teddy bear** /'tedi,beəʳ/ (*also UK* **teddy**) *noun* [C] a soft, toy bear

**tedious** /'tiːdiəs/ *adj* boring *a tedious job* **• tediously** *adv*

**tee** /tiː/ *noun* [C] a small stick that is used for holding a golf ball

**teem** /tiːm/ *verb* **be teeming with sb/sth** to contain large numbers of people or animals *The town centre was teeming with tourists.*

**teeming** /'tiːmɪŋ/ *adj* full of people *the teeming city*

**teen¹** /tiːn/ *noun* [C] *mainly US short for* teenager

**teen²** /tiːn/ *adj* [always before noun] *informal* relating to, or popular with people who are between 13 and 19 years old *a teen idol • a teen magazine*

**teenage** /'tiːneɪdʒ/ *adj* [always before noun] aged between 13 and 19 or suitable for people of that age *a teenage daughter • a teenage disco*

**teenager** /'tiːnˌeɪdʒəʳ/ *noun* [C] someone who is between 13 and 19 years old

**teens** /tiːnz/ *noun* [plural] the part of your life between the age of 13 and 19 *Her youngest daughter is still in her teens.*

'tee ˌshirt *noun* [C] *another spelling of* T-shirt (= a piece of cotton clothing for the top part of the body with short sleeves and no collar)

**teeter** /'tiːtəʳ/ *verb* **1** **be teetering on the brink/edge of sth** to be in a situation where

T

something bad might happen very soon *The economy is teetering on the brink of collapse.* **2 teeter about/across/around, etc** to look as if you are going to fall *She teetered around the room in six-inch heels.*

**teeter-totter** /ˌtiːtəˈtɒtəʳ/ *US* (*UK/US* **seesaw**) *noun* [C] a long board that children play on by sitting at each end and using their feet on the ground to push the board up and down

**teeth** /tiːθ/ *plural of* tooth

**teethe** /tiːð/ *verb* **1 be teething** If a baby is teething, it is getting its first teeth. **2 teething problems/troubles** problems that happen because something is new and has not been done before *As with all projects, there were a few teething troubles.*

**teetotal** /ˌtiːˈtəʊtᵊl/ *adj* never drinking any alcohol • teetotaller *UK* (*US* **teetotaler**) *noun* [C] someone who never drinks alcohol

**tel** *abbreviation for* telephone number *Tel 0113 246369*

**telecommunications** /ˌtelɪkəˌmjuːnɪˈkeɪʃᵊnz/ *noun* [U, group] the process or business of sending information or messages by telephone, radio, etc

**telecommuting** /ˌtelɪkəˈmjuːtɪŋ/ ⓤⓢ ˈtelɪkəˌmjuːtɪŋ/ *US* (*UK* **teleworking**) *noun* [U] working at home, while communicating with your office by computer and telephone • telecommuter *noun* [C] *US*

**telecoms** /ˈtelɪkɒmz/ *noun* [U] *short for* telecommunications

**telegram** /ˈtelɪgræm/ *noun* [C] a message that is sent by telegraph and printed on paper

**telegraph** /ˈtelɪgrɑːf/ *noun* [U] an old-fashioned system of sending messages using radio or electrical signals

**telemarketing** /ˈtelɪˌmɑːkɪtɪŋ/ (*also UK* **telesales**) *noun* [U] the selling of goods or services by telephone

**telepathy** /tɪˈlepəθi/ *noun* [U] the ability to know what someone is thinking or to communicate thoughts without speaking or writing • telepathic /ˌtelɪˈpæθɪk/ *adj* having or involving telepathy

o─**telephone¹** /ˈtelɪfəʊn/ (*also* **phone**) *noun* **1** [U] a

telephone box *UK*, telephone booth *US*

telephone

mobile phone

communication system that is used to talk to someone who is in another place *a telephone call* • *I'm sorry, he's on the telephone* (= using the telephone) *at the moment.* **2** [C] a piece of equipment that is used to talk to someone who is in another place *The telephone rang and she hurried to pick it up.* • *Could you answer the telephone?*

**telephone²** /ˈtelɪfəʊn/ (*also* **phone**) *verb* [I, T] *formal* to communicate with someone by telephone

**telephone** and **phone**

Telephone and phone mean the same thing, but we usually use **phone** for both the noun and the verb.

*I'll phone you this evening.*

*Can I use your phone, please?*

When the phone rings or when you want to make a phone call, you **pick** it **up**.

*I picked up the phone and dialled his number.*

When you finish a phone call, you **put** the phone **down** or you **hang up**.

*Don't hang up – I can explain everything!*

*She thanked him and put the phone down.*

~~She thanked him and hung up the phone.~~

**ˈtelephone diˌrectory** *noun* [C] a book that contains the telephone numbers of people who live in a particular area

**ˈtelephone ˌnumber** (*also* **phone number**) *noun* [C] the number of a particular telephone

**telesales** /ˈtelɪseɪlz/ *UK* (*UK/US* **telemarketing**) *noun* [U] the selling of goods or services by telephone

**telescope** /ˈtelɪskəʊp/ *noun* [C] a piece of equipment, in the shape of a tube, that makes things which are far away look bigger or nearer

**televise** /ˈtelɪvaɪz/ *verb* [T] to show something on television *The concert will be televised live around the world.*

o─**television** /ˈtelɪvɪʒᵊn/ *noun* **1** EQUIPMENT [C] a piece of equipment in the shape of a box, with a screen on the front, used for watching programmes *Richard switched the television on.* **2** PROGRAMMES [U] the programmes that are shown on a television *I mostly watch television in the evening.* • *I saw it on television.* • *a television programme* **3** SYSTEM [U] the system or business of making and broadcasting programmes for television *She works in television.* • *a television company/network* ➔ See also: **closed-circuit television, satellite television.**

**on television**

Be careful to use the correct preposition.

*What's on television tonight?*

~~What's in television tonight?~~

USAGE

**watch television**

Be careful to choose the correct verb with television.

*My children watch too much television.*

~~My children look too much television.~~

**teleworking** /'telɪ,wɜːkɪŋ/ *UK* (*US* **telecommuting**) *noun* [U] working at home, while communicating with your office by computer and telephone • **teleworker** *noun* [C] *UK*

⊶**tell** /tel/ *verb past* **told 1** SAY [T] to say something to someone, usually giving them information *He told me about his new school.* • [+ (that)] *Sally told me that the play didn't last until 9 o'clock.* • [+ question word] *Can you tell me what time the next bus leaves?* ➋ *See usage note at* **say**. **2 tell sb to do sth** to order someone to do something *I told you to stay here.* **3 can tell** to know or recognize something from what you hear, see, etc [+ (that)] *You could tell that he was tired.* • [+ question word] *You can never tell whether Hajime's being serious or not.* • *I can't tell the difference between them.* **4** UNDERSTAND FROM [T] If something tells you something, it gives you information. *What does the survey tell us about the lives of teenagers?* **5 (I'll) tell you what** used to suggest a plan *Tell you what, let's go swimming and then get a pizza.* **6** EFFECT [I] to have a bad effect on someone *The worry of the last few months was starting to tell on him.* **7 (I) told you so!** *informal* used when someone has caused problems for themselves by doing something that you told them not to ➋ *See also:* tell sb's **fortune**.

**tell sb/sth apart** to be able to see the difference between two things or people that are very similar *It's impossible to tell the twins apart.*

**tell sb off** to tell someone that they have done something wrong and that you are angry about it [+ **for** + doing sth] *Darren got told off for talking in class.* ➋ *See colour picture* **Phrasal Verbs** *on page Centre 13.*

**teller** /'telə/ *noun* [C] *US* someone who works in a bank and gives out or takes in money ➋ *See also:* **fortune-teller**.

**telling** /'telɪŋ/ *adj* showing the truth about a situation, or showing what someone really thinks *a telling comment*

**telltale** /'telteɪl/ *adj* [always before noun] showing something that someone is trying to keep secret *She was showing all the telltale signs of pregnancy.*

**telly** /'teli/ *noun* [C, U] *UK informal short for* television

**temp** /temp/ *noun* [C] someone who works in an office for a short time while someone else is away, ill, etc • **temp** *verb* [I] to work as a temp in an office

**temper¹** /'tempə/ *noun* **1** [C, U] when someone becomes angry very easily *He's got a really bad temper.* **2 be in a bad/foul, etc temper** to be feeling angry *I'd avoid her if I were you – she's in a foul temper.* **3 lose your temper (with sb)** to suddenly become very angry *I lost my temper with the children this morning.* **4 keep**

**your temper** to succeed in staying calm and not becoming angry

**temper²** /'tempə/ *verb* [T] *formal* to make something less strong, extreme, etc *I learnt to temper my criticism.*

**temperament** /'tempᵊrəmənt/ *noun* [C, U] the part of your character that affects your moods and the way you behave *I don't think he's got the right temperament to be a teacher.*

**temperamental** /,tempᵊrə'mentᵊl/ *adj* **1** becoming angry or upset very often and suddenly **2** A machine, vehicle, etc that is temperamental does not always work correctly.

**temperate** /'tempᵊrət/ *adj formal* having weather that is not very hot and not very cold *a temperate climate*

⊶**temperature** /'temprətʃə/ *noun* **1** [C, U] how hot or cold something is *The room's kept at a temperature of around 20°C.* • *Last night the temperature dropped to below freezing.* **2 sb's temperature** how hot or cold someone's body is *The doctor examined him and took his temperature* (= measured his temperature). **3 have a temperature** to be hotter than usual because you are ill

**template** /'templət/ *noun* [C] **1** a metal, plastic, etc pattern that is used for making many copies of a shape **2** a system that helps you arrange information on a computer screen

**temple** /'templ/ *noun* [C] **1** a building where people in some religions go to pray or worship *a Buddhist/Hindu temple* **2** the area on each side of your head in front of the top of your ear

**tempo** /'tempəʊ/ *noun* **1** [U, no plural] the speed at which an activity happens *The tempo of the game increased in the second half.* **2** [C, U] *formal* the speed of a piece of music

⊶**temporary** /'tempᵊrᵊri/ *adj* existing or happening for only a short or limited time *a temporary job* • *temporary accommodation/housing* • **temporarily** *adv*

**tempt** /tempt/ *verb* [T] to make someone want to have or do something, especially something that they do not need or something that is wrong [+ **to do sth**] *She's trying to tempt me to go shopping with her.* • *I'm tempted not to go to my next class.*

**temptation** /temp'teɪʃᵊn/ *noun* **1** [C, U] a feeling that you want to do or have something, although you know you should not [+ **to do sth**] *I resisted the temptation to* (= I did not) *have another piece of chocolate cake.* **2** [C] something that makes you want to do or have something although you know you should not *He knew crime was wrong but the money was too great a temptation.*

**tempting** /'temptɪŋ/ *adj* Something that is tempting makes you want to have or do it. *a tempting invitation/offer*

**ten** /ten/ *the number* 10

**tenacious** /tɪ'neɪʃəs/ *adj* very determined to do something and not wanting to stop • **tenaciously** *adv* • **tenacity** /tɪ'næsəti/ *noun* [U]

**tenancy** /'tenənsi/ *noun* [C, U] the period of time when someone rents a room, house, etc

**tenant** /'tenənt/ *noun* [C] someone who pays rent to live in a room, house, etc

⊶**tend** /tend/ *verb* **1 tend to do sth** to often do a

T

particular thing or be likely to do a particular thing *I tend to wear dark colours.* • *July and August tend to be our busiest months.* **2** [T] (*also* **tend to**) *formal* to look after someone or something *He spends most afternoons tending his vegetable garden.*

**tendency** /'tendənsi/ *noun* [C] something that someone often does, or something that often happens [+ to do sth] *She* **has a tendency** *to talk for too long.* • *There is a growing* **tendency for** *companies to employ people on short contracts.*

**tender¹** /'tendər/ *adj* **1** GENTLE kind and gentle *a tender kiss/look* **2** FOOD Tender meat or vegetables are soft and easy to cut. **3** PAINFUL If part of your body is tender, it is painful when you touch it. **4 at the tender age of 8/17/25 etc** *literary* at the young age of 8/17, etc *She first appeared on stage at the tender age of 14.* • tenderness *noun* [U]

**tender²** /'tendər/ *verb formal* **1** [I] to make a formal offer to do a job or to provide a service **2** [T] *formal* to formally offer a suggestion, idea, money etc *He tendered his resignation* (= offered to leave his job).

**tender³** /'tendər/ *noun* [C, U] a formal offer to do some work *The work has been* **put out to tender** (= people have been asked to make offers to do the work).

**tenderly** /'tendəli/ *adv* in a kind and gentle way *He looked at her tenderly.*

**tendon** /'tendən/ *noun* [C] a strong piece of tissue in your body that connects a muscle to a bone

**tenement** /'tenəmənt/ *noun* [C] a large building that is divided into apartments, usually in a poor area of a city

**tenet** /'tenɪt/ *noun* [C] a principle or belief of a theory or religion *one of the basic tenets of Islam*

**tenner** /'tenər/ *noun* [C] *UK informal* a piece of paper money that has a value of £10

**tennis** /'tenɪs/ *noun* [U] a sport in which two or four people hit a small ball to each other over a net ➔ *See colour picture* **Sports 2** *on page Centre 16.* ➔ *See also:* **table tennis**.

**tenor** /'tenər/ *noun* [C] a male singer with a high voice

**tense¹** /tens/ *adj* **1** FEELING nervous, worried, and not able to relax *The students looked tense as they waited for their exam results.* **2** SITUATION A tense situation makes you feel nervous and worried. *There were some tense moments in the second half of the game.* **3** MUSCLE A tense muscle feels tight and stiff.

**tense²** /tens/ (*also* **tense up**) *verb* [I, T] If your muscles tense, they become tight and stiff, and if you tense them, you make them do this. *Don't tense your shoulders, just relax.*

**tense³** /tens/ *noun* [C, U] the form of a verb which shows the time at which an action happened. For example 'I sing' is in the present tense and 'I will sing' is in the future tense.

**tension** /'tenʃən/ *noun* **1** NO TRUST [C, U] a feeling of fear or anger between two groups of people who do not trust each other *ethnic/racial tension* • *There are growing* **tensions** *between the two countries.* **2** BEING NERVOUS [U] a feeling that you are nervous,

worried, and not relaxed *You could feel the tension in the room as we waited for her to arrive.* **3** TIGHT [U] when a muscle, rope, etc, is tight or stiff

**tent** /tent/ *noun* [C] a structure made of metal poles and cloth which is fixed to the ground with ropes and used as a cover or to sleep under *It only took twenty minutes to* **put the tent up** (= make it ready to use).

**tentacle** /'tentəkl/ *noun* [C] one of the long, arm-like parts of some sea creatures

**tentative** /'tentətɪv/ *adj* **1** A tentative idea, plan, agreement, etc is not certain. *The two companies have announced a tentative deal.* **2** doing something in a way that shows you are not confident *a child's tentative first steps* • tentatively *adv*

**tenth¹** /tenθ/ 10th written as a word

**tenth²** /tenθ/ *noun* [C] one of ten equal parts of something; 1/10; 0.1

**tenuous** /'tenjuəs/ *adj* A tenuous connection, idea, or situation is weak and possibly does not exist. *The court is* **unlikely** *to accept such tenuous evidence.* • tenuously *adv*

**tenure** /'tenjər/ *noun* [U] **1** BUILDING/LAND the legal right to live in a building or use a piece of land for a period **2** TIME the period of time when someone has an important job *his tenure as president* **3** PERMANENT If you have tenure in your job, your job is permanent.

**tepid** /'tepɪd/ *adj* A tepid liquid is slightly warm.

**term¹** /tɜːm/ *noun* **1** WORD [C] a word or phrase that is used to refer to a particular thing, especially in a technical or scientific subject *a legal/technical term* **2** TIME [C] the fixed period of time when someone does an important job or is in a particular place *a prison term* • *The government has been elected for another four-year term.* **3** SCHOOL [C] one of the periods of time that the school or university year is divided into *We've got a test at the end of term.* **4 in the long/short, etc term** a long/short, etc period of time from now *The situation should improve in the long term.* ➔ *See also:* **half-term**.

**term²** /tɜːm/ *verb* [T] *formal* to use a particular word or phrase to describe something *Critics termed the movie a 'disaster'.*

**terminal¹** /'tɜːmɪnəl/ *noun* [C] **1** a building where you can get onto an aircraft, bus, or ship *a terminal building* **2** a screen and keyboard with which you can use a computer *an office with several terminals*

**terminal²** /'tɜːmɪnəl/ *adj* A terminal illness will cause death. *terminal cancer* • terminally *adv terminally ill*

**terminate** /'tɜːmɪneɪt/ *verb* [I, T] *formal* If something terminates, it ends, and if you terminate something, you make it end. *His contract has been terminated.* • termination /ˌtɜːmɪˈneɪʃən/ *noun* [C, U]

**terminology** /ˌtɜːmɪˈnɒlədʒi/ *noun* [C, U] the special words and phrases that are used in a particular subject *medical/scientific terminology*

**terminus** /'tɜːmɪnəs/ *noun* [C] the place where a train or bus finishes its journey

**terms** /tɜːmz/ *noun* [plural] **1** the rules of an agreement *Under the terms of their contract,* *employees must give 3 months notice if they want to leave.* **2 be on good/bad/friendly, etc terms** to have a good/bad, etc relationship with someone **3 not be on speaking terms** to not speak to someone because you have argued with them **4 in ... terms** (*also* **in terms of sth**) used to explain which part of a problem or situation you are referring to *In financial terms, the project was not a success.* **5 in no uncertain terms** in a direct and often angry way *I told him to go away in no uncertain terms.* **6 come to terms with sth** to accept a sad situation *He still hasn't come to terms with his brother's death.* ➔ *See also:* a **contradiction** in terms.

**terrace** /'terɪs/ *noun* [C] **1** a flat area outside a house, restaurant, etc where you can sit **2** *UK* a row of houses that are joined together

**,terraced 'house** *UK* (*US* **row house**) *noun* [C] one of a row of houses that are joined together

**the terraces** /'terɪsɪz/ *noun* [plural] in the UK, wide, concrete steps where people stand to watch a football game

**terrain** /tə'reɪn/ *noun* [C, U] a particular type of land *rough terrain*

**terrestrial** /tə'restriəl/ *adj formal* relating to the Earth, not space

o—**terrible** /'terəbl/ *adj* very bad, of low quality, or unpleasant *a terrible accident* • *The weather was terrible.*

**terribly** /'terəbli/ *adv* **1** very *She seemed terribly upset.* **2** very badly *I slept terribly last night.*

**terrier** /'teriəʳ/ *noun* [C] a type of small dog

**terrific** /tə'rɪfɪk/ *adj* **1** excellent *a terrific opportunity* • *I thought she looked terrific.* **2** [always before noun] very large, great, or serious *a terrific increase in prices* • *a terrific storm* • **terrifically** *adv*

**terrified** /'terəfaɪd/ *adj* very frightened *I'm terrified of flying.* • [+ (that)] *Maggie was terrified that her parents would discover the truth.*

**terrify** /'terəfaɪ/ *verb* [T] to make someone feel very frightened *The idea of parachuting out of an aircraft terrifies me.* • **terrifying** *adj a terrifying experience*

**territorial** /,terɪ'tɔːriəl/ *adj* relating to the land that is owned or controlled by a particular country *a territorial dispute*

**territory** /'terɪtʳri/ *noun* **1** LAND [C, U] land that is owned or controlled by a particular country *Spanish territory* **2** PERSON/ANIMAL [C, U] an area that an animal or person thinks belongs to them *Cats like to protect their territory.* **3** AREA OF KNOWLEDGE [U] an area of knowledge or experience *With this project we'll be moving into unknown territory.*

**terror** /'terəʳ/ *noun* [U] a feeling of being very frightened *There was a look of terror on his face.* ➔ *See also:* **reign¹** of terror.

**terrorism** /'terəʳɪzʳm/ *noun* [U] the use of violence for political purposes, for example putting bombs in public places *an act of terrorism*

**terrorist** /'terərɪst/ *noun* [C] someone who is involved in terrorism *a terrorist attack*

**terrorize** (*also UK* **-ise**) /'terəraɪz/ *verb* [T] to make someone feel very frightened by saying that you will hurt or kill them *A gang of young men with knives have been terrorizing local people.*

**terse** /tɜːs/ *adj* said or written in a few words, often showing that you are annoyed • **tersely** *adv*

**tertiary** /'tɜːʃʳri/ *adj UK formal* Tertiary education is education at university or college level. *a tertiary institution*

o—**test¹** /test/ *noun* [C] **1** EXAM a set of questions to measure someone's knowledge or ability *a driving test* • *You have to take a test.* • *Only two students in the class failed the test.* • *Did you pass the biology test?* **2** MEDICAL a short medical examination of part of your body *an eye test* • *a pregnancy test* **3** EXPERIMENT something that you do to discover if something is safe, works correctly, etc *a safety test* **4** SITUATION a situation that shows how good something is *This will be a real test of his ability.*

o—**test²** /test/ *verb* [T] **1** EXPERIMENT to do something in order to discover if something is safe, works correctly, etc *None of our products are tested on animals.* **2** MEDICAL to do a medical examination of part of someone's body *I'm going to get my hearing tested.* **3** EXAM to give someone a set of questions, in order to measure their knowledge or ability *an exam designed to test writing skills* • *You'll be tested on all the things we've studied this term.* **4** SITUATION If a situation tests someone, it proves how good, strong, etc they are.

**testament** /'testəmənt/ *noun formal* **a testament to sth** *formal* proof of something good *It's a testament to Jane's popularity that so many people are celebrating with her today.* ➔ *See also:* **the New Testament**, **the Old Testament**.

**testicle** /'testɪkl/ *noun* [C] one of the two round, male sex organs that produce sperm

**testify** /'testɪfaɪ/ *verb* [I] to say what you know or believe is true in a law court [+ that] *Elliott testified that he had met the men in a bar.*

**testimony** /'testɪməni/ *noun* **1** [C, U] a formal statement about what someone knows or believes is true, especially in a law court *the testimony of a witness* **2** **testimony to sth** *formal* proof of something good *The book's continued popularity is testimony to the power of clever marketing.*

**'test ‚ tube** *noun* [C] a glass tube that is open at one end and used in scientific experiments

**tetanus** /'tetʳnəs/ *noun* [U] a serious disease that makes your muscles stiff and is caused by an infection that gets into the body through a cut

**tether** /'teðəʳ/ *verb* [T] to tie an animal to something so that it cannot move away • **tether** *noun* [C] ➔ *See also:* at the **end¹** of your tether.

o—**text** /tekst/ *noun* **1** [C, U] the written words in a book, magazine, etc, not the pictures *a page of text* **2** [C] a book or piece of writing that you study as part of a course

**textbook** /'tekstbʊk/ *noun* [C] a book about a particular subject, written for students *a chemistry/French textbook* ➔ *See colour picture* **Classroom** *on page Centre 4.*

**textile** /'tekstaɪl/ *noun* [C] any type of cloth that is made by weaving (= crossing threads under and over each other)

**texture** /'tekstʃəˀ/ *noun* [C, U] the way that something feels when you touch it *wood with a rough texture*

○ᆨ**than** *strong form* /ðæn/ *weak form* /ðᵊn/ *preposition, conjunction* used to compare two different things or amounts *Susannah's car is bigger than mine.* • *Tom's a bit taller than Sam.* • *It cost less than I expected.*

○ᆨ**thank** /θæŋk/ *verb* [T] **1** to tell someone that you are grateful for something they have done or given you *I'd like to thank everyone who's helped me.* • *I haven't thanked her for her present yet.* • [+ for + doing sth] *Yu Yin thanked the boys for helping her.* **2 thank God/goodness/ Heavens, etc** something that you say when you are happy because something bad did not happen *Thank goodness you're okay – I was really worried.*

**thankful** /'θæŋkfᵊl/ *adj* pleased or grateful about something [+ (that)] *We were thankful that none of the children saw the accident.*

**thankfully** /'θæŋkfᵊli/ *adv* used at the beginning of a sentence to show that you are pleased or grateful about something *Thankfully, nobody was hurt.*

**thankless** /'θæŋkləs/ *adj* A thankless job is difficult or unpleasant and no one thanks you for doing it. *Nursing can be a thankless job.*

**thanks**[1] /θæŋks/ *exclamation informal* **1** used to tell someone that you are grateful because they have given you something or done something for you *Can you pass me the book? Thanks very much.* • *Thanks for all your help.* **2 thanks/no, thanks** used to accept or refuse someone's offer *"Would you like a cup of coffee?" "No, thanks."*

○ᆨ**thanks**[2] /θæŋks/ *noun* [plural] **1** words that show you are grateful for something someone has given to you or done for you *He sent a message of thanks.* **2 thanks to sb/sth** because of someone or something *I passed my driving test, thanks to the extra help my Dad gave me.* • *Thanks to John, we missed the train.*

**Thanksgiving** /ˌθæŋks'gɪvɪŋ/ *noun* [C, U] a holiday in the autumn in the US and Canada, when families have a big meal together

○ᆨ**'thank ˌyou** *exclamation* **1** used to tell someone that you are grateful because they have given you something or done something for you *Thank you very much for the birthday card.* • *"Here's the money I promised you." "Thank you."* **2 thank you/no, thank you** used to accept or refuse someone's offer *"Would you like something to eat?" "No, thank you."*

**thank-you** /'θæŋkjuː/ *noun* [C] something that you say or do to thank someone for doing something [+ for + doing sth] *I bought Emma some chocolates as a thank-you for looking after the dog.* • *a thank-you present*

○ᆨ**that**[1] /ðæt/ *determiner plural* **those 1** used to refer to something or someone that has already been talked about or seen *Did you know that woman in the post office?* • *How much are those shoes?* **2** used to refer to something or someone that is not near you *He went through that door.* • *Have you seen that man over there?* ➔ *See usage note at* **this**.

**that**[2] /ðæt/ *pronoun plural* **those 1** used to refer

to something that has already been talked about or seen *That looks heavy.* • *You can't possibly wear those!* **2** used to refer to something that is not near you *What's that in the corner?* **3 that's it a** used to say that something is correct *You need to push the two pieces together. That's it.* **b** used to say that something has ended *Well that's it then, we've finished.* **4 that's that** used to say that something has happened or a decision has been made and there is nothing more to say or do *I won't agree to it and that's that.* **5 that is (to say)** used to correct something you have said or give more information about something *Everybody was at the meeting, well everyone except Jeanne, that is.*

**USAGE**

**this/these** or **that/those** ?

Use **this** or **these** to talk about people and things which are close to the speaker.

*This is my sister Sarah.*

*Do you like these earrings I'm wearing?*

Use **that** or **those** to talk about people and things which are further away from the speaker.

*That girl over there is called Sarah.*

*I liked those earrings you wore last night.*

○ᆨ**that**[3] *strong form* /ðæt/ *weak form* /ðət/ *conjunction* **1** used after some verbs, nouns, and adjectives to introduce a new part of a sentence *He said that he'd collect it later.* • *Is it true that she's pregnant?* **2** used instead of 'who' or 'which' at the beginning of a relative clause *Have you eaten all the cake that I made yesterday?*

○ᆨ**that**[4] /ðæt/ *adv* **1** used when describing the size, amount, or state of something or someone *I've never seen a fish that big before.* **2 not (all) that big/good/warm, etc** not very big, good, warm, etc *It hasn't been all that cold this winter.*

**thatched** /θætʃt/ *adj* A thatched building has a roof that is made of straw (= dried grass-like stems). *a thatched cottage*

**thaw** /θɔː/ *verb* **1** [I, T] (*also* **thaw out**) If something that is frozen thaws, it becomes warmer and softer or changes to liquid, and if you thaw something that is frozen, you make it do this. *Allow the meat to thaw before cooking it.* • *The sun came out and thawed the ice.* **2** [I] If a relationship between people thaws, it becomes more friendly after being bad. • **thaw** *noun* [C] *a spring thaw* • *a thaw in relations*

○ᆨ**the** *strong form* /ðiː/ *weak forms* /ði, ðə/ *determiner* **1** ALREADY KNOWN used before nouns to refer to particular things or people that have already been talked about or are already known *Can you pass the salt?* • *I'll pick you up at the station.* • *That's the new restaurant I told you about.* **2** ONLY ONE used before nouns when only one of something exists *Have you seen the Eiffel Tower?* • *I'd love to travel round the world.* **3** SINGULAR NOUN used before a singular noun to refer to all the things or people described by that noun *The tiger has become extinct in many countries.* **4** ADJECTIVE used before some adjectives to make them into nouns *a home for the elderly* • *relatives of the deceased* **5** COMPARE used before each of two adjectives or adverbs to show how one thing changes depending on another *The longer we live here, the more we like it.* **6** EACH used with units or measurements to mean each or every *How many Belgian francs to the pound?* **7** BODY used when referring to a part of the body *He held her tightly by the arm.* **8** TIME used before numbers which refer to dates or periods of time *the sixties* • *Thursday the 29th of April* **9** MUSIC used with the names of musical instruments or dances to mean the type of instrument or dance in general *Can you play the violin?*

o— **theatre** UK (US **theater**) /ˈθɪətəʳ/ noun **1** BUILDING WITH STAGE [C] a building with a stage where people go to watch plays *the Arts Theatre* **2** BUILDING FOR FILMS [C] US a building where people go to watch films *a movie theater* **3** WORK [U] the work of writing, acting in, and producing plays *I want to work in theatre.* **4** MEDICAL [C, U] UK a room in a hospital where doctors do operations

**theatrical** /θiˈætrɪkəl/ adj **1** [always before noun] relating to the theatre *theatrical make-up* **2** doing and saying things in a very obvious way that is intended to make people notice you

**theft** /θeft/ noun [C, U] the action or crime of stealing something *car theft* • *There have been several thefts in the area recently.*

o— **their** /ðeəʳ/ determiner **1** belonging to or relating to a group of people, animals, or things that have already been talked about *It was their problem, not mine.* **2** used to refer to what belongs to or relates to a person when you want to avoid saying 'his' or 'her' or when you do not know if the person is male or female *Did this person give their name?*

o— **theirs** /ðeəz/ pronoun the things that belong or relate to a group of people, animals, or things that have already been talked about *I think she's a relation of theirs.*

o— **them** strong form /ðem/ weak form /ðəm/ pronoun **1** used after a verb or preposition to refer to a group of people, animals, or things that have already been talked about *I'm looking for my keys – have you seen them?* **2** used after a verb or preposition to refer to a person when you want to avoid saying 'him' or 'her' or when you do not know if the person is male or female *When each passenger arrives we ask them to fill in a form.*

o— **theme** /θiːm/ noun **1** [C] the subject of a book, film, speech, etc *The theme of loss runs through most of his novels.* **2 theme music/song/tune** the music that is played at the beginning and end of a particular television or radio programme

'**theme** ,**park** noun [C] a park with entertainments, such as games, machines to ride on, restaurants, etc, that are all based on one idea *a Disney theme park*

o— **themselves** /ðəmˈselvz/ pronoun **1** the reflexive form of the pronoun 'they' *They're both 16 –*

they're old enough to look after themselves. **2** used to emphasize the pronoun 'they' or the particular group of people you are referring to *The staff themselves were unhappy with the decision.* • *They've decided to run the club themselves.* **3 (all) by themselves** alone or without anyone else's help *The kids arranged the party all by themselves.* **4 (all) to themselves** for their use only *They had the whole campsite to themselves.*

o— **then**[1] /ðen/ adv **1** TIME at that time *Call me tomorrow – I'll have time to speak then.* • *Tim and I were at school together, but I haven't seen him since then.* **2** NEXT next, or after something has happened *She trained as a teacher and then became a lawyer.* • *Let me finish my drink, then we'll go.* **3** SO so or because of that *Have a rest now, then you won't be tired this evening.* • *"My interview's at 9 o'clock." "You'll be catching an early train, then?"* **4** IN ADDITION used in order to add something to what you have just said *I've got two essays to write and then my science project to finish.* **5 now then/ right then/okay then** used to introduce a question or a suggestion *Right then, what do you want to drink?* • *Now then, shall we make a start?*

**then**[2] /ðen/ adj [always before noun] used to refer to something which was true in the past but which is not true now *the then Prime Minister Margaret Thatcher*

**thence** /ðens/ adv formal from there *The oil is shipped to Panama and thence to Texan refineries.*

**theology** /θiˈɒlədʒi/ noun [U] the study of religion and religious belief • **theological** /ˌθiːəˈlɒdʒɪkəl/ adj *theological college*

**theoretical** /θɪəˈretɪkəl/ adj **1** based on the ideas that relate to a subject, not the practical uses of that subject *theoretical physics* **2** related to an explanation that has not been proved

**theoretically** /θɪəˈretɪkəli/ adv in a way that obeys some rules but is not likely *It is theoretically possible.*

**theorist** /ˈθɪərɪst/ noun [C] someone who develops ideas about the explanation for events *a political theorist*

**theorize** (also UK **-ise**) /ˈθɪəraɪz/ verb [I, T] to develop a set of ideas about something [+ that] *Investigators theorized that the crash was caused by engine failure.*

o— **theory** /ˈθɪəri/ noun **1** [C] an idea or set of ideas that is intended to explain something *Darwin's theory of evolution* **2** [U] the set of principles on which a subject is based *economic theory* **3 in theory** If something is possible in theory, it should be possible but often it does not happen this way. *In theory, the journey should be shorter but in practice, the roadworks slow you down.*

**therapeutic** /ˌθerəˈpjuːtɪk/ adj **1** helping to cure a disease or improve your health *the therapeutic benefits of massage* **2** helping you to feel happier and more relaxed *I find gardening very therapeutic.*

**therapist** /ˈθerəpɪst/ noun [C] someone whose job is to treat a particular type of mental or physical illness *a speech therapist*

T

**therapy** /ˈθerəpi/ *noun* [C, U] the work of treating mental or physical illness without using an operation *cancer therapy* • *She's now in therapy to help her deal with her alcohol problem.* ➔ *See also:* **physical therapy**.

**there¹** *strong form* /ðeəʳ/ *weak form* /ðəʳ/ *pronoun* **There is/are/was, etc** used to show that something exists or happens *There are three pubs in the village.* • *There's not much room in the back of the car.* • *There have been a lot of accidents on this road.* • *Is there any milk?*

○━**there²** /ðeəʳ/ *adv* **1** PLACE in or at a particular place *We live in York because my wife works there.* • *I went to the party but I didn't know anyone there.* • *We'll never get there* (= arrive) *in time!* **2** DIRECTION used when you are pointing or looking at something in order to make someone look in the same direction *Put them in that box there.* • *Your bag's over there by the door.* **3** AVAILABLE present or available *They were all there – Mark, Jill, and the three kids.* • *That money is there for you if you need it.* **4** POINT at a particular point in a process or activity *Do you want to play another game or do you want to stop there?* • *Keep on trying – you'll get there* (= succeed) *in the end.* **5 there and then** If you do something there and then, you do it immediately. *I showed James the ring I liked and he bought it there and then.* **6 There you are/go. a** used when you are giving something to someone *Do you want a tissue? There you are.* **b** used to emphasize that you were right *There you go – I told you you'd win!*

**thereabouts** /ˈðeərəbaʊts/ *adv mainly UK* near the number, amount, or time that has just been given *For this recipe you'll need 1kg of tomatoes, or thereabouts.*

**thereafter** /ˌðeəˈrɑːftəʳ/ *adv formal* after a particular amount, time, or event *Faxes cost $1.20 for the first page, and 60 cents for each page thereafter.*

**thereby** /ˌðeəˈbaɪ/ *adv formal* as a result of a particular action or event *The new dam will improve the water supply and thereby reduce hunger and disease.*

○━**therefore** /ˈðeəfɔːʳ/ *adv* for that reason *The region has suffered severe flooding and tourists are therefore advised not to travel there.*

**therein** /ˌðeəˈrɪn/ *adv formal* **1** in a particular document or place *We recommend that you study the report and the proposals contained therein.* **2 therein lies sth** because of the reason that has just been given *But the medicines are expensive, and therein lies the problem.*

**thereof** /ˌðeəˈrɒv/ *adv formal* relating to what has just been said *It's gospel music, traditional country, jazz and some strange combinations thereof.*

**thermal** /ˈθɜːməl/ *adj* [always before noun] **1** relating to heat *thermal energy* • **2** Thermal clothes are made to keep you warm. *thermal underwear*

**thermometer** /θəˈmɒmɪtəʳ/ *noun* [C] a piece of equipment that measures the temperature of the air or of your body

**Thermos** /ˈθɜːmɒs/ *noun* [C] *trademark* a container that keeps hot liquids hot or cold liquids

cold *(UK) a Thermos flask/(US) a Thermos bottle* ➔ *See picture at* **flask**.

**thermostat** /ˈθɜːməstæt/ *noun* [C] a piece of equipment that controls the temperature of something or of a place

**thesaurus** /θɪˈsɔːrəs/ *noun* [C] a book in which words with similar meanings are put together in groups

○━**these** /ðiːz/ *pronoun, determiner plural of* this ➔ *See usage note at* **that, this**.

**thesis** /ˈθiːsɪs/ *noun* [C] *plural* **theses** /ˈθiːsiːz/ **1** a long piece of writing that you do as part of an advanced university course *a master's/PhD thesis* **2** *formal* a theory that is suggested and can then be argued with or agreed with *That is the central thesis of the book.*

○━**they** /ðeɪ/ *pronoun* **1** GROUP used as the subject of the verb when referring to a group of people, animals, or things that have already been talked about *I saw Kate and Nigel yesterday – they came over for dinner.* • *"Have you seen my car keys?" "They're on the kitchen table."* **2** PERSON used to refer to a person when you want to avoid saying 'he' or 'she' or when you do not know if the person is male or female *Someone I met at a party said they knew you.* **3** PEOPLE people in general *They say that breaking a mirror brings you seven years' bad luck.*

**they'd** /ðeɪd/ **1** *short for* they had *They'd just moved in when I saw them.* **2** *short for* they would *They'd like to take us out to dinner.*

**they'll** /ðeɪl/ *short for* they will *They'll be in Scotland next week.*

**they're** /ðeəʳ/ *short for* they are *They're both from Washington.*

**they've** /ðeɪv/ *short for* they have *They've got three children – two girls and a boy.*

○━**thick¹** /θɪk/ *adj*

**1** DISTANCE Something that is thick is larger than usual between its opposite sides. *a thick slice of meat* • *a thick layer of snow* **2 10cm/2m, etc thick** being 10cm/2m, etc thick *a piece of wood 2cm*

thick          thin

*thick* **3** LARGE AMOUNT growing very close together and in large amounts *thick, dark hair* **4** SMOKE Thick smoke, cloud, or fog is difficult to see through. *Thick, black smoke was pouring out of the chimney.* **5** LIQUID A thick substance or liquid has very little water in it and does not flow easily. *Stir the sauce over a low heat until thick.* **6** STUPID *UK informal* not intelligent **7 be thick with sth** If something is thick with a particular substance, it is covered in or full of that substance. *The air was thick with petrol fumes.* **8 thick and fast** quickly and in large numbers *Calls were coming in thick and fast by the end of the programme.* ➔ *See also:* have (a) thick **skin¹**.

**thick²** /θɪk/ *noun* **1 be in the thick of sth** to be involved in a situation at the point where there is most activity *He loves being in the thick of the*

**T**

*action.* **2 through thick and thin** If you support or stay with someone through thick and thin, you always support or stay with them in easy and difficult situations. *She'd stuck by* (= stayed with) *Neil through thick and thin.*

**thicken** /'θɪkᵊn/ *verb* [I, T] to become thicker, or to make something thicker *Boil the sauce until it thickens.*

**thickly** /'θɪkli/ *adv* in thick pieces, or in a thick layer *toast thickly spread with butter*

**thickness** /'θɪknəs/ *noun* [C, U] the distance between the opposite sides of something *Fry the steak for 3–5 minutes, depending on the thickness.*

**thick-skinned** /ˌθɪk'skɪnd/ *adj* If someone is thick-skinned, they do not get upset when other people criticize them.

**thief** /θiːf/ *noun* [C] *plural* **thieves** /θiːvz/ someone who steals things *a car thief* • *Thieves stole $500,000 worth of computer equipment.*

**thigh** /θaɪ/ *noun* [C] the top part of your leg above your knee ⊃ *See colour picture* **The Body** *on page Centre 2.*

**thimble** /'θɪmbl/ *noun* [C] a small metal or plastic object that you use to protect your finger when you are sewing

o-ᴙ **thin¹** /θɪn/ *adj* **thinner, thinnest 1** [DISTANCE] Something that is thin is smaller than usual between its opposite sides. *a thin slice of ham* • *The walls are very thin.* ⊃ *See picture at* **thick. 2** [PERSON] A thin person or animal has very little fat on their body. **3** [LIQUID] A thin substance or liquid has a lot of water in it and flows easily. *thin soup* **4** [AMOUNT] having only a small number of people or a small amount of something *Government troops were very thin along the border.* • *His hair is going thin on top.* **5** [AIR] Thin air does not have enough oxygen in it. **6 wear thin a** If your patience wears thin, you become less and less patient with someone who is annoying you. **b** If a joke or explanation wears thin, it becomes less effective because it has been used too much. ⊃ *See also:* disappear/ vanish into thin **air¹**, be thin on the **ground¹**, through **thick²** and thin.

**thin²** /θɪn/ *verb* [T] **thinning,** *past* **thinned** to make a substance less thick, often by adding a liquid to it

**thin out** If a large number of people or things thin out, they become fewer in number.

o-ᴙ **thing** /θɪŋ/ *noun* **1** [OBJECT] [C] used to refer to an object without saying its name *How do I switch this thing off?* • *I need to get a few things in town.* **2** [PERSON] [C] used to refer to a person or animal when you are expressing your feelings towards them *You look tired, you poor thing.* • *He's spending three months in Barbados, lucky thing!* **3** [IDEA] [C] used to refer to an idea, event, or activity • *I can't believe Nick would say such a thing!* • *Meeting Nina was the best thing that's ever happened to me.* **4 for one thing** used to give a reason for something *You can't wear Amy that shirt – for one thing it's too small for her.* **5 the thing is** *informal* used to introduce a problem which relates to something that you have just said *I'd love to go out tonight, but the thing is, I've got to finish my report.* **6 a thing** used instead of 'anything' in

order to emphasize what you are saying *I haven't got a thing to wear!* **7 have a thing about sth/sb** *informal* to like or dislike something or someone very much *He's got a thing about blonde women.* **8 it's a good thing** *informal* If it is a good thing that something happened, it is lucky that it happened. [+ (that)] *It's a good thing that Jo was there to help you.* **9 first/last thing** *informal* at the beginning/ end of the day *I'll phone him first thing and tell him I can't come.* • *She likes a glass of milk last thing at night.* **10 be sb's thing** *informal* If an activity or subject is someone's thing, they are very interested in it and like doing it. *Jogging's just not my thing – I prefer team sports.* **11 the best/greatest thing since sliced bread** *humorous* extremely good *When I first got this computer I thought it was the best thing since sliced bread.*

**things** /θɪŋz/ *noun* [plural] **1** what is happening in your life *Don't worry – things will get better soon.* **2** the objects that you own *I'll just gather my things and then I'll be ready.* **3 be hearing/ seeing things** to imagine that you can hear or see things that do not exist

**thingy** /'θɪŋi/ *noun* [C] *UK informal* used to refer to something or someone when you cannot remember their name *We ate that beef thingy for lunch.*

o-ᴙ **think¹** /θɪŋk/ *verb past* **thought 1** [OPINION] [I, T] to have an opinion about something or someone *Do you think it's going to rain?* • [+ (that)] *I don't think that Emma will get the job* (= I believe she will not get it). • *What did you think of the film?* • *What do you think about modern art?* **2** [CONSIDER] [I] to consider an idea or a problem *He thought for a few seconds before answering.* • *You should think about where you want to live.* **3** [EXPECT] [I, T] to believe that something is true, or to expect that something will happen, although you are not sure *I think she's called Joanna.* • *"Does this train stop at Oxford?" "Yes, I think so."* • [+ (that)] *I never thought that I would see Steven again.* **4 think about/of doing sth** to consider doing something *I'm thinking of moving to Sydney.* • *We thought about getting married, but decided not to.* **5 think about/of sb/sth** to use your mind to imagine a situation *I'm sorry I can't be at the wedding, but I'll be thinking of you.* **6 think of sth** to use your imagination and intelligence to produce an idea, a solution to a problem, or an answer to a question *When did you first think of the idea?* • *I need to think of a suitable response to this letter.* **7 think a lot of sb/sth** to admire someone, or to believe that something is good quality *Simon thinks a lot of you, you know.* **8 not think much of sb/sth** to not like someone, or to believe that something is not good quality *I don't think much of the food here.* **9 I think** used to introduce a suggestion or explanation in order to be polite [+ (that)] *It's getting late – I think that we should go.* **10 Who would have thought...?** used to express how surprising something is [+ (that)] *Who would have thought that buying a house could take so long?* ⊃ *See also:* think the **world¹** of sb.

**think about** or **think of**?

Think about someone/something means to have thoughts in your mind about a person or thing, or to consider them.

*I was thinking about my mother.*

*I thought about the question before answering.*

~~I thought the question before answering.~~

Think of/about something/someone also means to have an opinion about something or someone.

*What do you think of/about the colour?*

~~What do you think the colour?~~

Think of doing something means to consider the possibility of doing something.

*We are thinking of having a party.*

~~We are thinking to have a party.~~

**think back** to remember something that happened in the past *I **thought back to** the time when I was living in Toronto.*
**think sth out** to consider all the possible details of something *The scheme was well thought out.*
**think sth over** to consider an idea or plan carefully before making a decision
**think sth through** to carefully consider the possible results of doing something *It sounds like a good idea but we need to think it through.*
**think sth up** to produce a new idea or plan *I don't want to go tonight and I'm trying to think up an excuse.*
**think²** /θɪŋk/ *noun UK* **have a think** to consider something carefully *Have a think about it and then tell me what you've decided.*
**thinker** /ˈθɪŋkəʳ/ *noun* [C] someone who considers important subjects or produces new ideas *a political/religious thinker*
**thinking** /ˈθɪŋkɪŋ/ *noun* [U] **1** when you use your mind to consider something *This problem requires careful thinking.* **2** someone's ideas or opinions *The book discusses the impact of Christian thinking on western society.* ➔ *See also:* **wishful thinking**.
**'think ˌtank** *noun* [C] a group of people who advise the government or an organization about particular subjects and who suggest new ideas
**thinly** /ˈθɪnli/ *adv* **1** in thin pieces, or in a thin layer *She sliced the bread thinly.* **2** with only a small number of people or things *thinly populated areas*
**third¹** /θɜːd/ 3rd written as a word
**third²** /θɜːd/ *noun* [C] **1** one of three equal parts of something; 1/3 **2 a third** in the UK, one of the lowest exam results you can achieve at the end of a university course
**thirdly** /ˈθɜːdli/ *adv* used in order to introduce the third thing in a list *There are three factors to take into account: firstly cost, secondly time, and thirdly staff.*
**ˌthird 'party** *noun* [C] someone who is not one of the two main people or groups that are involved in a situation

**the, third 'person** *noun* the form of a verb or pronoun that is used when referring to the person or thing being spoken about or described. For example 'she' and 'they' are third person pronouns.
**the ˌThird 'World** *noun* the countries in Africa, Asia, and South America, which do not have well-developed economies
**thirst** /θɜːst/ *noun* **1** [U, no plural] the feeling that you want to drink something *Many of the refugees collapsed from thirst and hunger.* • *I had a long, cold drink to **quench** my **thirst** (= stop me feeling thirsty).* **2 a thirst for sth** a strong wish for something *a thirst for adventure*
o-ʌ**thirsty** /ˈθɜːsti/ *adj* wanting or needing a drink *I felt really hot and thirsty after my run.* • thirstily *adv*
**thirteen** /ˌθɜːˈtiːn/ the number 13 • thirteenth 13th written as a word
**thirty** /ˈθɜːti/ **1** the number 30 **2 the thirties** the years from 1930 to 1939 **3 be in your thirties** to be between the ages of 30 and 39 • thirtieth 30th written as a word
o-ʌ**this¹** /ðɪs/ *determiner plural* **these 1** ALREADY TALKED ABOUT used to refer to something that you have already talked about *Most people don't agree with this decision.* • *How did you hear about this course?* **2** NEAR used to refer to something or someone that is near you or that you are pointing to *How much does this CD cost?* • *David gave me these earrings for my birthday.* **3** TIME used to refer to the present week, month, year, etc or the one that comes next *I'll see you this evening.* • *Kate and Nigel are getting married this June.* **4** NOW TALKING ABOUT *informal* used to refer to a particular person or thing that you are going to talk about *I met this guy at a party who knows your sister.* • *We went to this really great club last night.* ➔ *See usage note at* **that** ➔ *See also:* be out of this **world¹**.
**this²** /ðɪs/ *pronoun plural* **these 1** ALREADY TALKED ABOUT used to refer to something that you have already talked about *When did this happen?* • *This is the best news I've heard all week!* **2** NEAR used to refer to something or someone that is near you or that you are pointing to *Try some of this – it's delicious.* • *Are these your keys?* • *This is my girlfriend, Beth.* **3** SAY/ASK WHO used to say or ask who someone is when speaking on the telephone, radio, etc *"Hello, is this Julie Hawkins?" "Yes, who's this?"* **4 this and that** different things which are not very important *"What are you doing today?" "Oh, just this and that."*

**this/that** or **these/those**?

Remember this and that are used before a singular noun. These and those are used before a plural noun.

*Look at this photo.*

*Look at these photos.*

*Can you pass me that book please?*

*Can you pass me those books please?*

**this³** /ðɪs/ *adv* used when describing the size, amount, or state of something or someone *I need a piece of wood this big.* • *I've never seen her this angry.*

**thistle** /ˈθɪsl/ *noun* [C] a wild plant with purple flowers and sharp points

**thorn** /θɔːn/ *noun* [C] a small, sharp point on the stem of a plant

**thorny** /ˈθɔːni/ *adj* **1** covered in thorns **2** A thorny problem, question, subject, etc is difficult to deal with.

**thorough** /ˈθʌrə ⓤ ˈθɜːrəʊ/ *adj* careful and covering every detail *The government has promised a thorough investigation of the matter.* • thoroughness *noun* [U]

**thoroughbred** /ˈθʌrəbred/ *noun* [C] a horse especially bred for racing

**thoroughly** /ˈθʌrəli/ *adv* **1** very carefully *Wash the spinach thoroughly before cooking.* **2** very, or very much *We thoroughly enjoyed ourselves.*

○─ **those** /ðəʊz/ *pronoun, determiner plural of* that ➔ *See usage note at* **that, this.**

○─ **though¹** /ðəʊ/ *conjunction* **1** used to introduce a fact or opinion that makes the other part of the sentence seem surprising *And though she's quite small, she's very strong.* • *Nina didn't phone, even though she said she would.* **2** but *They're coming next week, though I don't know when.* • *The restaurant serves good, though extremely expensive, food.*

○─ **though²** /ðəʊ/ *adv* used to add a new fact or opinion which changes what you have just said *Okay, I'll come to the party – I'm not staying late though.*

○─ **thought¹** /θɔːt/ *noun* **1** IDEA [C] an idea or opinion *Do you have any thoughts about/on where you want to spend Christmas?* • [+ of + doing sth] *The thought of seeing her again filled him with happiness.* • *(informal) "Why don't we invite Ben?" "That's a thought* (= That's a good idea)." **2** THINKING [U] the activity of thinking, or when you think about something carefully *She sat staring at the picture, deep in thought.* • *You'll need to give the matter some thought.* **3** CARE [no plural] when you do something that shows you care about someone *Thanks for the card – it was a really kind thought.* **4** SET OF IDEAS [U] a set of ideas about a particular subject *The book examines his influence on recent political thought.* **5 spare a thought for sb** to think about someone who is in a bad situation *Spare a thought for all the people who have lost their homes.* ➔ *See also:* **school** of thought, **second thought.**

**thought²** /θɔːt/ *past of* think

**thoughtful** /ˈθɔːtfᵊl/ *adj* **1** quiet because you are thinking about something *You look thoughtful.* **2** kind and always thinking about how you can help other people *Thank you for the card – it was very thoughtful of you.* • thoughtfully *adv* She gazed thoughtfully into the distance. • thoughtfulness *noun* [U]

**thoughtless** /ˈθɔːtləs/ *adj* not considering how your actions and words might upset someone else *I should have called her to say we'd be late – it was a bit thoughtless of me.* • thoughtlessly *adv*

**thought-provoking** /ˈθɔːtprəˌvəʊkɪŋ/ *adj*

making you think a lot about a subject *a thought-provoking book/film*

○─ **thousand** /ˈθaʊzᵊnd/ **1** the number 1000 **2 thousands** *informal* a lot *She tried on thousands of dresses but didn't like any of them.*

**thousandth¹** /ˈθaʊzᵊndθ/ 1000th written as a word

**thousandth²** /ˈθaʊzᵊndθ/ *noun* [C] one of a thousand equal parts of something; 1/1000; .001 *a thousandth of a second*

**thrash** /θræʃ/ *verb* **1** HIT [T] to hit a person or animal several times as a punishment **2** MOVE [I] to move from side to side in a violent way *He was screaming in pain and thrashing around on the floor.* **3** DEFEAT [T] *informal* to win against someone very easily

**thrash sth out** to discuss a plan or problem in detail until you reach an agreement or find a solution

**thrashing** /ˈθræʃɪŋ/ *noun* [C] **1** *informal* when you win against someone very easily *Their hopes of victory ended with a 7–2 thrashing by Germany.* **2** *old-fashioned* when someone hits a person or animal several times as a punishment

**thread¹** /θred/ *noun* **1** [C, U] a long, thin piece of cotton, wool, etc that is used for sewing *a needle and thread* **2** [C] the connection between different events or different parts of a story or discussion *By that point I'd lost the thread of the conversation.*

**thread²** /θred/ *verb* [T] **1 thread a needle** to push thread through the hole in a needle **2 thread your way through, between, etc** to move carefully through a crowded place, changing direction in order to avoid people or things

**threadbare** /ˈθredbeəʳ/ *adj* Threadbare material or clothes are very thin because they have been used too much. *a threadbare carpet*

○─ **threat** /θret/ *noun* **1** HARM [C] when someone says they will kill or hurt you, or cause problems for you if you do not do what they want *a death threat* • *I was scared he would carry out his threat* (= do what he said he would do). **2** DAMAGE [C] someone or something that is likely to cause harm or damage [usually singular] *a threat to the environment* • *Smoking poses* (= is) *a serious threat to your health.* **3** POSSIBILITY [no plural] the possibility that something bad will happen *the threat of invasion*

○─ **threaten** /ˈθretᵊn/ *verb* **1** HARM [T] to tell someone that you will kill or hurt them, or cause problems for them if they do not do what you want *He threatened the staff with a gun and demanded money.* • [+ to do sth] *He threatened to report her to the police.* **2** DAMAGE [T] to be likely to cause harm or damage to something or someone *His knee problem is threatening his cycling career.* **3** HAPPEN [I] If something bad threatens to happen, it is likely to happen. [+ to do sth] *The conflict threatened to spread to neighbouring countries.* • threatening *adj* threatening behaviour • threateningly *adv*

**three** /θriː/ the number 3

**three-dimensional** /ˌθriːdɪˈmenʃᵊnᵊl/ *(also* **3-D** /ˌθriːˈdiː/*) adj* having length, depth, and height *three-dimensional computer graphics*

**threshold** /'θreʃhəʊld/ *noun* **1** [C] the level at which something starts to happen *He had a low boredom threshold.* **2 on the threshold of sth** at the start of a new and important time or development *We're on the threshold of a new era in European relations.* **3** [C] the floor of an entrance

**threw** /θruː/ *past tense of* throw

**thrift** /θrɪft/ *noun* [U] careful use of money so that you do not spend too much ● **thrifty** *adj*

'**thrift** ,**shop** *US* (*UK* **charity shop**) *noun* [C] a shop which sells goods given by the public, especially clothes, to make money for a particular charity

**thrill**[1] /θrɪl/ *noun* [C] a strong feeling of excitement and pleasure *It was a big thrill meeting the stars of the show.* ● [+ of + doing sth] *the thrill of winning a competition*

**thrill**[2] /θrɪl/ *verb* [T] to make someone feel excited and happy *Ballesteros thrilled the golf world with his performance.*

**thrilled** /θrɪld/ *adj* very excited and pleased *She was thrilled with your present.*

**thriller** /'θrɪlər/ *noun* [C] a book or film with an exciting story, often about crime

**thrilling** /'θrɪlɪŋ/ *adj* very exciting *a thrilling game*

**thrive** /θraɪv/ *verb* [I] to grow very well, or to become very healthy or successful *The business is thriving.* ● *He seems to thrive on hard work.* ● **thriving** *adj a thriving economy*

**throat** /θrəʊt/ *noun* [C] **1** the back part of your mouth and the passages inside your neck *a sore throat* **2** the front of your neck *He grabbed her round the throat.* ○ *See colour picture* **The Body** *on page Centre 2.* **3 clear your throat** to cough once so that you can speak more clearly

**throb** /θrɒb/ *verb* [I] **throbbing**, *past* **throbbed** **1** If a part of your body throbs, you feel pain in it in a series of regular beats. *My head was throbbing.* **2** to make a strong, regular sound or movement *The whole house throbbed with the music.* ● **throb** *noun* [C] *the throb of the engine*

**throes** /θrəʊz/ *noun* **in the throes of sth** in a difficult or unpleasant situation *a country in the throes of war*

**throne** /θrəʊn/ *noun* **1** [C] the special chair that a king or queen sits on **2 the throne** the position of being king or queen *He came to the throne in 1936.*

**throng**[1] /θrɒŋ/ *noun* [C] *literary* a large group of people

**throng**[2] /θrɒŋ/ *verb* [I, T] to be or go somewhere in very large numbers *drunken people thronging the streets* ● *The street was thronged with shoppers and tourists.*

**throttle**[1] /'θrɒtl/ *verb* [T] to press someone's throat tightly so they cannot breathe

**throttle**[2] /'θrɒtl/ *noun* [C] the part of a vehicle that controls how much fuel or power goes to the engine

○ᐟ**through**[1] /θruː/ *preposition* **1** ONE SIDE TO ANOTHER from one end or side of something to the other *The River Seine flows through Paris.* ● *The sun was shining through the window.* ● *She cut through the wire.* **2** START TO END from the start to the end of something *He*

worked through the night. ● *The phone rang halfway through the programme.* **3** BECAUSE OF because of someone or something, or with someone's help *I got the job through my mum's friend.* ● *He became ill through eating undercooked meat.* **4** UNTIL *US* (*UK* **to**) from a particular time until and including another time *The store is open Monday through Friday.* ● *I worked there from May through September.*

○ᐟ**through**[2] /θruː/ *adv* **1** from one end or side to another *He opened the door and walked through.* **2 read/think/talk, etc sth through** to read, think, talk to someone, etc very carefully about something from the start to the end *I've thought it through and decided not to take the job.* **3** connected to someone by telephone *I tried to phone David but I couldn't get through.* ● *Can you put me through to the manager, please?*

**through**[3] /θruː/ *adj* **1 be through with sth** *informal* to have finished using something or doing something *Let me know when you're through with the iron.* **2 be through (with sb)** *informal* to not have a relationship with someone any more **3** [always before noun] *UK* A through train goes all the way from one place to another place without the passenger having to change trains.

○ᐟ**throughout** /θruː'aʊt/ *adv, preposition* **1** in every part of a place *The same laws apply throughout much of Europe.* ● *The house was painted pink throughout.* **2** during the whole of a period of time *He yawned throughout the performance.* ● *We spent a week in London and it rained throughout.*

○ᐟ**throw**[1] /θrəʊ/ *verb* [T] *past t* **threw**, *past p* **thrown** **1** THROUGH THE AIR to make something move through the air by pushing it out of your hand *Amy threw the ball to the dog.* ● *He threw the book at the wall.* ● [+ two objects] *Throw me a chocolate.* ● *How far can you throw?* **2 throw sth in/on, etc** to put something somewhere quickly and without thinking about it *He threw his clothes on the floor and got into bed.* **3 throw sth around/down/on, etc** to suddenly and quickly move your body or a part of your body *She threw her arms around the child.* ● *Gabriela threw herself onto the bed and started to cry.* **4 throw sb from/forward, etc** to make someone move somewhere suddenly or fall down [often passive] *The bus suddenly stopped and we were thrown forward.* **5** CONFUSE to make someone feel shocked or confused *It threw me completely when he asked me to marry him.* **6** LIGHT to make light or shadows (= dark shapes) appear on something *The trees threw shadows across the road.* ○ *See also:* throw **caution**[1] to the wind, throw sb in at the deep **end**[1], throw down the **gauntlet**, throw in the **towel**, throw your **weight** around.

**throw sth away 1** to get rid of something that you do not want any more *He read the magazine and then threw it away.* ○ *See colour picture* **Phrasal Verbs** *on page Centre 13.* **2** to waste a skill or opportunity *You've spent three years studying – don't throw it all away.*

**throw sth in** to add something extra when you

sell something and not increase the price *They're selling computers with a free printer thrown in.*

**throw sth out** to get rid of something that you do not want any more *I must throw some of my old clothes out.*

**throw sb out** to force someone to leave *He was thrown out of school for taking drugs.*

**throw (sth) up** *informal* to vomit

**throw sth up** to produce new problems or ideas *The meeting threw up some interesting ideas.*

**throw²** /θrəʊ/ *noun* [C] when you throw something *a throw of the dice*

**throwback** /'θrəʊbæk/ *noun* [C] something that is like something of the same type in the past *Her style of playing is a throwback to the early days of jazz.*

**thru** /θruː/ *adv mainly US informal* another spelling of through, used in signs and advertisements

**thrust¹** /θrʌst/ *verb past* **thrust**

**thrust sth behind/into/through, etc** to push something somewhere suddenly and with force *She thrust a letter into my hand and told me to read it.*

**thrust sth on/upon sb** to force someone to accept or deal with something [often passive] *Fatherhood had been thrust on him.*

**thrust²** /θrʌst/ *noun* **1** [C, U] a strong push or the power used to push something forward **2 the thrust of sth** the main part or ideas of what someone says or does *The main thrust of our work involves helping victims of crime.*

**thud** /θʌd/ *noun* [C] the sound that is made when something heavy falls or hits something else *There was a thud as he fell on the floor.* • **thud** *verb* [I] **thudding**, *past* **thudded**

**thug** /θʌg/ *noun* [C] an unpleasant person who behaves violently

**thumb¹** /θʌm/ *noun* [C] **1** the short, thick finger on the side of your hand that can touch the top of all your other fingers **⊃** *See colour picture* **The Body** *on page Centre 2.* **2 have a green thumb** *US* (*UK* **have green fingers**) to be good at gardening and making plants grow well **3 be under sb's thumb** If you are under someone's thumb, they control you completely. **4 stick/ stand out like a sore thumb** to be very different from all the other people or things around *I was the only one in uniform and I stuck out like a sore thumb.* **⊃** *See also:* a **rule¹** of thumb.

**thumb²** /θʌm/ *verb* **⊃** *See* thumb your **nose¹** at sth/sb.

**thumb through sth** to quickly turn the pages of a book or magazine

**thumbtack** /'θʌmtæk/ *US* (*UK* **drawing pin**) *noun* [C] a pin with a wide, flat top, used for fastening pieces of paper to a wall

**throw**

**thump** /θʌmp/ *verb* **1** HIT [T] *UK* to hit someone with your fist (= closed hand) **2** NOISE [I, T] to hit something and make a noise *She thumped the tambourine.* **3** HEART [I] If your heart thumps, it beats very quickly because you are excited or frightened. *She stood outside the room, her heart thumping.* • **thump** *noun* [C]

**thunder¹** /'θʌndəʳ/ *noun* [U] the loud noise in the sky that you hear during a storm *thunder and lightning*

**thunder²** /'θʌndəʳ/ *verb* **1 it thunders** When it thunders during a storm, a loud noise comes from the sky. **2 thunder along/down/ through, etc** to move in a way that makes a deep, loud, continuous sound *Traffic thunders through the village all day.*

**thunderous** /'θʌndərəs/ *adj* extremely loud *the thunderous roar of the aircraft's engine*

**thunderstorm** /'θʌndəstɔːm/ *noun* [C] a storm that has thunder (= loud noise) and lightning (= sudden flashes of light in the sky)

**Thursday** /'θɜːzdeɪ/ (*written abbreviation* **Thur, Thurs**) *noun* [C, U] the day of the week after Wednesday and before Friday

**thus** /ðʌs/ *adv formal* **1** used after saying a fact to introduce what then happened as a result *The guard fell asleep, thus allowing Bates to escape.* **2** in this way *They limit the number of people allowed into the forest, thus preventing damage to the trails.*

**thwart** /θwɔːt/ *verb* [T] to prevent someone from doing what they have planned to do

**thyme** /taɪm/ *noun* [U] a herb used in cooking

**thyroid** /'θaɪrɔɪd/ *noun* [C] an organ in the neck that produces a substance that helps your body to grow and develop

**tick¹** /tɪk/ *noun* [C] **1** CLOCK the sound that some clocks or watches make every second **2** MARK *UK* (*US* **check**) a mark (✓) that shows something is correct or has been done **3** INSECT a small insect that sucks the blood of animals **4** TIME *UK informal* a short time *Wait a tick!*

**tick²** /tɪk/ *verb* **1** [I] If a clock or watch ticks, it makes a sound every second. **2** [T] *UK* to mark something with a tick **3 what makes sb tick** *informal* the reasons for someone's behaviour

**tick away/by** If seconds or minutes tick away or by, they pass. *With the final seconds ticking away, Milan scored a goal.*

**tick sth off** *UK* (*US* **check sth off**) to put a small mark next to something on a list to show that you have dealt with it

**tick sb off 1** *UK informal* to tell someone that they have done something wrong and that you are angry about it *I got ticked off for not going to the meeting.* **2** *US informal* to annoy someone

**tick over** *UK* If a business or system ticks over, it continues to work but makes little progress. *Carlton managed to keep the business ticking over.*

o-* **ticket** /'tɪkɪt/ *noun* [C] **1** a small piece of paper that shows you have paid to do something, for example travel on a bus, watch a film, etc *a lottery ticket* • *plane tickets* **2** a piece of paper that orders you to pay money because you have put your car in an illegal place, driven too fast, etc *a parking ticket* **⊃** *See also:* **round-trip ticket**, **season ticket**.

**T**

**tickle** /'tɪkl/ *verb* **1** TOUCH LIGHTLY [T] to touch someone lightly with your fingers, in order to make them laugh **2** PART OF THE BODY [I, T] If a part of your body tickles, or if something tickles it, it feels uncomfortable and you want to rub it. *My nose is tickling.* **3** AMUSE [T] to make someone smile or laugh *I was very tickled by his comments.* • tickle *noun* [C]

**tidal** /'taɪdᵊl/ *adj* relating to the regular rising and falling of the sea

**'tidal ,wave** *noun* [C] a very large wave that destroys things, often caused by an earthquake (= when the Earth shakes)

**tidbit** *US* (*UK* **titbit**) /'tɪdbɪt/ *noun* [C] a small piece of nice food, or an interesting piece of information

**tide¹** /taɪd/ *noun* **1** [C] the regular rise and fall in the level of the sea *high/low tide* **2** [no plural] an increase in something that is developing *the rising tide of drug-related deaths*

**tide²** /taɪd/ *verb*
**tide sb over (sth)** to help someone through a difficult time, especially by giving them money *I lent him some cash to tide him over the weekend.*

**tidy¹** /'taɪdi/ *adj* **1** having everything in the right place and arranged in a good order *Her room was clean and tidy.* **2** liking to keep things in the correct place and arranged in a good order *I'm afraid I'm not very tidy.* ➔ *Opposite* **untidy.** • tidily *adv* • tidiness *noun* [U]

**tidy²** /'taɪdi/ (*also* **tidy up**) *verb* [I, T] *UK* to make a place tidy *I'm tidying up before our guests arrive.*
**tidy sth away** *UK* to put things back in drawers, cupboards, etc after you have used them

○━**tie¹** /taɪ/ *verb* tying, *past* tied **1** **tie sth to/ together/around, etc** to fasten something with string, rope, etc *a pretty box tied with a red ribbon* • *The dog was tied to a tree.* **2** [T] to make a knot in a piece of string, rope, etc *She tied the scarf.* ➔ *Opposite* **untie.** **3** [I] to have the same score as someone else at the end of a competition or game *Sweden tied with France in the winter sports competition.* ➔ *See also:* tie the **knot¹.**
**tie sb down** to limit someone's freedom *I don't want to be tied down by having children.*
**tie in** If one idea or statement ties in with

**tie**

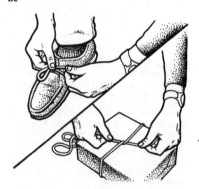

another one, they have some of the same information in them. *His story ties in with what Gemma told me.*
**tie sb/sth up** to tie a part of someone's body with a rope or something similar so they cannot move ➔ *Opposite* **untie.**
**tie sth up** to fasten something together using string, rope, etc
**be tied up** to be very busy and unable to speak to anyone, go anywhere, etc *Mrs Moran is tied up in a meeting at the moment but I'll ask her to call you later.*

**tie²** /taɪ/ *noun* [C] **1** CLOTHES a long, thin piece of cloth that a man wears around his neck with a shirt ➔ *See colour picture* **Clothes** *on page Centre 5.* **2** CONNECTION a relationship that connects you with a place, person, etc [usually plural] *The two countries have close ties with each other.* **3** GAME/ COMPETITION when a game or competition ends with two people or teams having the same score ➔ *See also:* **bow tie.**

**tie-break** /'taɪbreɪk/ *noun* [C] an extra part that is played when a game or competition ends in a tie, to decide who is the winner

**tier** /tɪə/ *noun* [C] one of several rows or layers *the upper tier of seats in a stadium*

**tiger** /'taɪgə/ *noun* [C] a large wild cat that has yellow fur with black lines on it

○━**tight¹** /taɪt/ *adj* **1** FIRM firm and difficult to move *Make sure the knot is tight.* **2** CLOTHES fitting your body very closely *a tight skirt* **3** CONTROLLED controlled and obeying all rules completely *tight security* • *They kept tight control of the school budget.* **4** STRAIGHT If cloth, wire, skin, etc is tight, it has been pulled so that it is straight or smooth. **5** NOT MUCH If money, time, or space is tight, there is only just enough of it. *We should get six people into the car but it will be tight.* • tightly *adv* • tightness *noun* [U] ➔ *See also:* keep a tight **rein** on sb/sth.

**tight²** /taɪt/ *adv* very firmly or closely *He held her tight.*

**tighten** /'taɪtᵊn/ *verb* [I, T] to become tighter or to make something become tighter *His hand tightened around her arm.* ➔ *See also:* tighten your **belt¹.**
**tighten sth up** to make something become firmer and less easy to move *Tighten up the screws.*
**tighten (sth) up** to make a rule, system, or law more difficult to avoid *I think they should tighten up the laws on gun ownership.*

**tightrope** /'taɪtrəup/ *noun* [C] a rope high above the ground that a performer walks along at a circus (= show)

**tights** /taɪts/ *UK* (*US* **pantyhose**) *noun* [plural] a piece of women's clothing made of very thin material that covers the legs and bottom *a pair of black tights* ➔ *See colour picture* **Clothes** *on page Centre 5.*

**tile** /taɪl/ *noun* [C] one of the flat, square pieces that are used for covering roofs, floors, or walls • tile *verb* [T] *a tiled kitchen*

○━**till¹** /tɪl/ *preposition, conjunction* until *The supermarket is open till midnight.* • *I lived with my parents till I was twenty.*

**till²** /tɪl/ *noun* [C] **1** *UK* a machine that holds the money in a shop and shows how much you have to pay **2** *US* a drawer where money is kept in a store

**tilt** /tɪlt/ *verb* [I, T] to move into a position where one end or side is higher than the other, or to make something move into this position *He tilted backwards on his chair.* • **tilt** *noun* [no plural]

**timber** /'tɪmbəʳ/ *noun* **1** WOOD [U] *UK* (*US* **lumber**) wood that is used for building **2** TREE [U] *US* trees that are grown to provide wood for building **3** PIECE OF WOOD [C] *UK* a large piece of wood *The roof was supported by timbers.*

o🔤**time¹** /taɪm/ *noun* **1** HOURS/YEARS ETC [U] Time is what we measure in minutes, hours, days, etc. *He wants to spend more time with his family.* • *Time seems to pass so slowly when you're unhappy.* **2** PARTICULAR POINT [C, U] a particular point in the day or night *What time is it?* • *What time do you leave for school in the mornings?* • *Can you tell me the times of the trains to London, please?* ➔ *See usage note at* **hour**. **3 it's time (for/to do sth)** used to say that something should happen or be done now *It's time to get up.* **4 in (good) time** early or at the right time *We arrived in time to catch the train.* **5 on time** not early or late *I got to school on time.* **6 can tell the time** to be able to know what time it is by looking at a clock or watch **7** PERIOD [no plural] a period of minutes, hours, years, etc *I lived in Switzerland for a long time.* • *It takes time* (= takes a long time) *to make friends at a new school.* **8 have time** to have enough time to do something *Do you have time for a cup of coffee?* • [+ to do sth] *I never have time to eat breakfast.* **9 in no time** very soon *We'll be home in no time.* **10** OCCASION [C] an occasion when something happens *Give me a call the next time you're in Seattle.* • *I can't remember the last time we went away.* • *How many times have you been to Germany?* **11 at the same time** If two things happen at the same time, they happen together. *We arrived at the same time.* **12 one, two, six, etc at a time** one, two, six, etc on one occasion *He carried the chairs, three at a time.* **13 time after time** again and again on repeated occasions **14 all the time a** very often *"She's been late twice this week." "It happens all the time."* **b** during the whole of a period of time *He was ill all the time we were in Spain.* **15 three/eight/nine, etc times** used to say how much bigger, better, worse, etc one thing is than another thing *Ben earns three times more than me.* **16 in a day's/two months', etc time** a week, two months, etc from now *I have to go to the doctor again in a month's time.* **17 at times** sometimes *At times, I wish I didn't have to go to school.* **18 for the time being** for now but not permanently *I'm living with my parents for the time being.* **19** IN THE PAST [C] a period of time in the past *Did you enjoy your time in Japan?* **20 at one time** at a time in the past *At one time, you could drive without taking a driving test.* **21 before sb's time** before someone was born **22 from time to time** sometimes, but not often *I still see my ex-boyfriend from time to time.* **23** RACE [C] the amount of time that someone takes in a race *a winning time of three*

*minutes* **24** IN A PLACE [U] the time in a particular place *The plane arrives at 20.50, New York time.* **25 be ahead of your time** to have new ideas a long time before other people think that way **26 behind the times** not fashionable or modern *Dad's a bit behind the times.* **27 bide your time** to wait for an opportunity to do something *She was biding her time until she could get her revenge.* **28 give sb a hard time** to criticize someone and make them feel guilty about something they have done *Ever since I missed the goal, the other players have been giving me a hard time.* **29 have no time for sb/sth** to have no respect for someone or something *I have no time for people who are racist.* **30 kill time** to do something while you are waiting for something else *I went shopping to kill some time before my job interview.* **31 play for time** *UK* to try to make something happen more slowly because you want more time or because you do not want it to happen **32 take your time** to do something without hurrying ➔ *See also:* **half-time, local time**, in the **nick²** of time, **night-time, prime time**, a **race¹** against time.

**time²** /taɪm/ *verb* [T] **1** to decide that something will happen at a particular time *They timed production of the CD so it was in the shops just before Christmas.* • *Her comment was well timed.* **2** to measure how long it takes for something to happen or for someone to do something *It's a good idea to time yourself while you do the exercises.* ➔ *See also:* **two-time**.

**time-consuming** /'taɪmkən‚sjuːmɪŋ/ *adj* needing a lot of time *The legal process was time-consuming and expensive.*

**time-honoured** *UK* (*US* **time-honored**) /'taɪm‚ɒnəd/ *adj* [always before noun] A time-honoured tradition or way of doing things is one that has been used for a long time.

**'time ‚lag** *noun* [C] a period of time between two things happening

**timeless** /'taɪmləs/ *adj* not changing because of time or fashion *Her clothes have a timeless quality.*

**timely** /'taɪmli/ *adj* happening or done at exactly the right time ➔ *Opposite* **untimely**.

**time-out** /‚taɪm'aʊt/ *noun* [C] a short period during a sports game in which players can rest

**timer** /'taɪməʳ/ *noun* [C] a piece of equipment that measures time

**times** /taɪmz/ *preposition* used to say that one number is multiplied by another number *Two times three is six.*

**timescale** /'taɪmskeɪl/ *noun* [C] the amount of time that something takes or during which something happens

**timetable** /'taɪm‚teɪbl/ *noun* [C] **1** (*also US* **schedule**) a list of times when buses, trains, etc arrive and leave **2** a list of dates and times that shows when things will happen ➔ *See colour picture* **Classroom** *on page Centre 4.*

**timid** /'tɪmɪd/ *adj* shy and easily frightened *a timid little boy* • **timidly** *adv* • **timidity** /tɪ'mɪdəti/ *noun* [U]

**timing** /'taɪmɪŋ/ *noun* [U] **1** the time when something happens *the timing of the announcement* **2** the ability to do something at exactly the right time *You need great timing to be a good football player.*

**tin** /tɪn/ *noun* **1** METAL CONTAINER [C] *UK* (*UK/US* **can**) a metal container in which food is sold *a tin of beans/soup* ➲ *See picture at* **container**. **2** CONTAINER WITH LID [C] *UK* a metal container with a lid that you keep food or other substances in *a biscuit tin • a paint tin* **3** COOKING EQUIPMENT [C] (*US* **pan**) a flat pan that you cook food in *a roasting tin* **4** METAL [U] a soft, silver metal that is often combined with other metals or used to cover them

**tinfoil** /'tɪnfɔɪl/ *noun* [U] metal made into very thin sheets like paper and used mainly for covering food

**tinge** /tɪndʒ/ *noun* [C] a small amount of a sad feeling or colour *"Goodbye," he said, with a tinge of sadness.* • **tinged** *adj Her dark hair is now tinged with grey.*

**tingle** /'tɪŋgl/ *verb* [I] If a part of your body tingles, the skin feels slightly uncomfortable. *My hands are starting to tingle with the cold.* • **tingle** *noun* [C]

**tinker** /'tɪŋkə/ *verb* [I] to make small changes to something in order to improve or repair it *Tim loves tinkering with car engines.*

**tinkle** /'tɪŋkl/ *verb* [I] to make a soft, high, ringing sound • **tinkle** *noun* [C]

**tinned** /tɪnd/ *UK* (*UK/US* **canned**) *adj* Tinned food is sold in metal containers.

**'tin ,opener** *UK* (*UK/US* **can opener**) *noun* [C] a piece of kitchen equipment for opening metal food containers ➲ *See colour picture* **Kitchen** *on page Centre 10.*

**tinsel** /'tɪnsəl/ *noun* [U] long, shiny, coloured string, used as a decoration at Christmas (= a Christian holiday)

**tint¹** /tɪnt/ *noun* [C] a particular colour *the yellow and red tints of autumn*

**tint²** /tɪnt/ *verb* [T] to add a small amount of a colour to something *Do you think he tints his hair?*

**tinted** /'tɪntɪd/ *adj* Tinted glass has colour added to it. *tinted sunglasses*

**tiny** /'taɪni/ *adj* extremely small *a tiny baby • a tiny little room*

**tip¹** /tɪp/ *noun* [C] **1** END the end of something long and narrow *the tips of your fingers* **2** ADVICE a piece of useful advice *gardening tips • Emma was giving me some tips on how to grow tomatoes.* **3** MONEY an extra amount of money that you give to a driver, someone working in a restaurant, etc to thank them *We left a tip because the waiter was so friendly.* **4** WASTE *UK* (*UK/US* **dump**) a place where people take things that they want to get rid of *We took our old fridge to the tip.* **5** UNTIDY PLACE *UK informal* (*UK/US* **dump**) a place that is dirty and untidy *His bedroom is an absolute tip.* **6 be on the tip of your tongue** If a word is on the tip of your tongue, you want to say it but cannot remember it. **7 be the tip of the iceberg** to be a small part of a very big problem

**tip²** /tɪp/ *verb* **tipping**, *past* **tipped** [I, T] to move so that one side is higher than the other side, or to make something move in this way *The table tipped and all the drinks fell on the floor.* **2 tip sth into/onto/out of sth** to make the contents

of a container fall out by holding the container in a position where this happens *She tipped the contents of her purse onto the table.* **3** [I, T] to give an extra amount of money to a driver, someone working in a restaurant, etc to thank them **4 be tipped as/to do/for sth** *UK* If someone is tipped to achieve something, most people say it will happen. *Christie was tipped to win the race.*

**tip sb off** to warn someone secretly about something so that they can take action or prevent it happening • **tip-off** /'tɪpɒf/ *noun* [C] a piece of information that you give someone secretly, so that they can take action or prevent something happening

**tip (sth) over** If something tips over, or if you tip it over, it falls onto its side.

**tiptoe¹** /'tɪptəʊ/ *noun* **on tiptoe** standing on your toes with the rest of your feet off the ground

**tiptoe²** /'tɪptəʊ/ *verb* **tiptoe across/down/through, etc** to walk quietly on your toes

**tire¹** /taɪə/ *noun* [C] *US spelling of* tyre ➲ *See colour picture* **Car** *on page Centre 3.*

**tire²** /taɪə/ *verb* [I, T] to become tired or to make someone become tired *He tires easily.*

**tire of sth/doing sth** to become bored with something *He never tires of playing games on his computer.*

**tire sb out** to make someone very tired

○⌐**tired** /taɪəd/ *adj* **1** feeling that you want to rest or sleep *I'm too tired to go out tonight.* • *He was tired out* (= very tired) *by the end of the day.* • *She never seems to get tired.* **2 tired of doing sth** bored or annoyed by something that has happened too often *I'm tired of listening to her problems.* • **tiredness** *noun* [U]

**USAGE**

**tired of** or **tired from?**

If you are **tired of** something or **of doing** something, you are bored or annoyed by it.

*I'm tired of hearing his awful jokes.*

If you are **tired from** something, you want to rest because of it.

*I'm tired from the long journey.*

**tireless** /'taɪələs/ *adj* working very hard at something and not stopping *He was a tireless worker for children's organizations.*

**tiresome** /'taɪəsəm/ *adj formal* making you feel annoyed or bored *a tiresome little boy*

**tiring** /taɪərɪŋ/ *adj* making you feel tired *a long and tiring day*

**tissue** /'tɪʃuː/ *noun* **1** ANIMAL/PLANT [C, U] the material that animals and plants are made of *human brain tissue* **2** FOR YOUR NOSE [C] a soft piece of paper that you use for cleaning your nose **3** FOR WRAPPING [U] (*also* **'tissue ,paper**) soft, thin paper that you cover things with in order to protect them

**tit** /tɪt/ *noun* [C] **1** *very informal* a woman's breast **2 tit for tat** *informal* when you do something bad to someone because they have done something bad to you

**titbit** *UK* (*US* **tidbit**) /'tɪtbɪt/ *noun* [C] a small piece of nice food, or an interesting piece of information

o⚹**title** /'taɪtl/ *noun* [C] **1** BOOK/FILM ETC the name of a book, film, etc **2** SPORTS what you get if you win an important sports competition *He won the 1999 world motor racing title.* **3** SOMEONE'S NAME a word such as 'Lord', 'Dr', etc that is used before someone's name

**titled** /'taɪtld/ *adj* having a title such as 'Lord', 'Lady', or 'Duke' that shows you have a high social position

**title-holder** /'taɪtl,həʊldəʳ/ *noun* [C] someone who has won a sports competition *the World Grand Prix title-holder*

'**title ,role** *noun* [C] the person in a play or film who has the same name as the play's or film's title

**titter** /'tɪtəʳ/ *verb* [I] to laugh in a nervous way
• **titter** *noun* [C]

**T-junction** /'tiː,dʒʌŋkʃ°n/ *UK* (*US* **intersection**) *noun* [C] a place where two roads join and make the shape of the letter 'T'

o⚹**to**[1] **1** used with a verb to make the infinitive *I want to learn Spanish.* • *He forgot to feed the cat.* • *Do you know how to make a cake?* **2** used to give the reason for doing something *I'm just going out to get some milk.*

o⚹**to**[2] *strong form* /tuː/ *weak forms* /tʊ, tə/ *preposition* **1** DIRECTION in the direction of somewhere *Dimitri is going to Germany next week.* • *I ran to the door.* **2** ANOTHER PERSON used to show who receives something or experiences an action *Could you give these keys to Pete?* • *Anna was speaking to her mother on the phone.* • *I lent my bike to Tom.* **3** POSITION almost touching or facing something *She stood with her back to the window.* **4** from ... to ... **a** used to give information about periods of time and distances *The museum is open from Monday to Saturday.* • *The bus goes from London to Cambridge.* **b** including *The book deals with everything from childhood to old age.* **5** BEFORE used to say 'before' the hour when you are saying what time it is *It's five to three.* **6** COMPARE used to compare two things *I prefer football to cricket.* **7** UNTIL until a particular time or state *It's only two weeks to my birthday.* • *She nursed him back to health.* **8** SOMEONE'S OPINION used to say what someone's opinion is *Fifty pounds is nothing to Matthew* (= he would not think it was a lot of money). **9** *to sb's* **disappointment/relief/surprise, etc** used to say that someone feels surprised, disappointed, etc by something *To Pierre's disappointment, Monique wasn't at the party.* **10** MEASUREMENT used to say how many parts make up a whole unit of measurement or money *There are 100 pence to the British pound.* **11** BELONGING belonging to or connected with *Can you give me the keys to the car?*

**to**[3] /tuː/ *adv* **1** *UK* If you push or pull a door to, you close it. **2** *to and fro* backwards and forwards *The sign was swinging to and fro in the wind.*

**toad** /təʊd/ *noun* [C] a small, brown animal with long back legs for swimming and jumping

**toadstool** /'təʊdstuːl/ *noun* [C] a poisonous fungus (= organism like a plant) with a short

stem and a round top

**toast**[1] /təʊst/ *noun* **1** [U] bread that has been heated to make it brown *a slice of toast* **2** [C] a time when people lift their glasses and drink because they want someone to be successful, happy, etc *At the wedding, there was a toast to the happy couple.*

**toast**[2] /təʊst/ *verb* [T] **1** to lift your glass and drink with other people because you want someone to be successful, happy, etc **2** to heat bread so that it becomes brown

**toaster** /'təʊstəʳ/ *noun* [C] a machine that heats bread so that it becomes brown ⊃ *See colour picture* **Kitchen** *on page Centre 10.*

**toasty** /'təʊsti/ *adj* warm and comfortable *It's nice and toasty near the fire.*

**tobacco** /tə'bækəʊ/ *noun* [U] dried leaves that are inside cigarettes

**toboggan** /tə'bɒɡ°n/ *noun* [C] a board that you sit or lie on, used for going down a hill on a surface of snow

o⚹**today** /tə'deɪ/ *noun, adv* [U] **1** this day, or on this day *It's Johann's birthday today.* • *Today is Friday.* **2** the period of time that is happening now or in this period of time *More young people smoke today than in the past.*

**toddle** /'tɒdl/ *verb* **toddle down/off/to, etc** *informal* to walk somewhere *Sophie said goodbye and toddled off towards the station.*

**toddler** /'tɒdləʳ/ *noun* [C] a child who has just learned to walk

**toe**[1] /təʊ/ *noun* [C] **1** one of the five separate parts at the end of your foot *your big toe* (= largest toe) • *your little toe* (= smallest toe) ⊃ *See colour picture* **The Body** *on page Centre 2.* **2** the part of a shoe or sock that covers your toes **3** *keep sb on their toes* to make sure that someone gives all their attention to what they are doing and is ready for anything that might happen

**toe**[2] /təʊ/ *verb* ⊃ *See* toe the (party) **line**[1].

**toenail** /'təʊneɪl/ *noun* [C] one of the hard, flat parts on top of the end of your toes ⊃ *See colour picture* **The Body** *on page Centre 2.*

**toffee** /'tɒfi/ *noun* [C, U] a sticky sweet, made by boiling sugar and butter together

o⚹**together**[1] /tə'ɡeðəʳ/ *adv* **1** WITH SOMEONE with each other *We went shopping together.* • *They live together.* **2** CONNECTED used to say that two or more things are joined to each other, mixed with each other, etc *She tied the two pieces of rope together.* **3** SAME PLACE in the same place or close to each other *We all sat together.* **4** SAME TIME at the same time *We'll deal with the next two items on the list together.* **5** *together with sth* in addition to something *She sent some flowers together with a card.* ⊃ *See also:* get your **act**[2] together, **get-together**.

**together**[2] /tə'ɡeðəʳ/ *adj informal* Someone who is together thinks clearly and organizes their life well.

**togetherness** /tə'ɡeðənəs/ *noun* [U] a feeling of friendship

**toil** /tɔɪl/ *verb* [I] *literary* to do difficult work for a long time • **toil** *noun* [U] *literary*

o⚹**toilet** /'tɔɪlɪt/ *noun* [C] **1** a bowl that you sit on or stand near when you get rid of waste substances from your body ⊃ *See colour picture* **The**

**T**

**Bathroom** *on page Centre 1.* **2** *UK* (*US* **bathroom**) a room with a toilet in it

USAGE

**toilet**

Toilet is the most general word. In British English the informal word **loo** is often used. In American English the word **bathroom** is often used to mean toilet, especially in the home.

In public places toilets are usually called **the ladies** or **the gents** in Britain and the **men's room**, **ladies' room**, or **restroom** in America.

The **lavatory** is slightly formal and **WC** is only used in British English. These two words are not used much today.

'**toilet ,paper** *noun* [U] paper used for cleaning your body after you have used the toilet

**toiletries** /'tɔɪlɪtriz/ *noun* [plural] things such as soap, toothpaste (= substance for cleaning teeth), etc that you use for making yourself clean

'**toilet ,roll** *noun* [C] *UK* paper for cleaning your body after using the toilet that is folded around a tube ➔ *See colour picture* **The Bathroom** *on page Centre 1.*

**token**[1] /'təʊkⁿn/ *noun* [C] **1** LOVE/THANKS something that you give to someone in order to show them love, to thank them, etc *I gave Helen some chocolates as a token of thanks for all her help.* **2** INSTEAD OF MONEY a round piece of metal or plastic that you put in some machines instead of money *You need a token to get out of the car park.* **3** PAPER *UK* (*US* **gift certificate**) a piece of paper that you give someone which they can exchange for a book, CD, etc *a book/record/gift token*

**token**[2] /'təʊkⁿn/ *adj* [always before noun] **1** A token person is chosen so that an organization can pretend that they care about that type of person. *a token woman* • *The club has two token black members.* **2** A token action is small or unimportant and may show your future intentions or may only pretend to. *He made a token effort to find a job.*

**told** /təʊld/ *past of* tell

**tolerable** /'tɒlⁿrəbl/ *adj* acceptable but not excellent *The food was just about tolerable but the service was terrible.* ➔ *Opposite* **intolerable**. • **tolerably** *adv*

**tolerance** /'tɒlⁿrⁿns/ *noun* [U] the quality of allowing people to do or believe what they want although you do not agree with it *religious/racial tolerance* ➔ *See also:* **zero tolerance**.

**tolerant** /'tɒlⁿrⁿnt/ *adj* allowing people to do what they want especially when you do not agree with it *a tolerant attitude* • *I think we're becoming more tolerant of children in public places.* ➔ *Opposite* **intolerant**.

**tolerate** /'tɒlⁿreɪt/ *verb* [T] **1** to accept or allow something although you do not like it *We will not tolerate racism of any sort.* **2** to be able to deal with something unpleasant and not be harmed by it *These plants can tolerate very low temperatures.* • **toleration** /,tɒlⁿr'eɪʃⁿn/ *noun* [U]

**toll**[1] /təʊl/ *noun* **1** [C] money that you pay to use

a bridge, road, etc **2** [no plural] the number of people who are killed or injured **3 take its toll** to have a bad effect on someone or something, especially over a long period of time *The stress was starting to take its toll on him.* ➔ *See also:* **death toll**.

**toll**[2] /təʊl/ *verb* [I] When a bell tolls, it rings slowly, especially because someone has died.

**toll-free** /,təʊl'friː/ *US* (*UK* **freephone**) *adj* A toll-free number is a telephone number that you can connect to without paying.

**tomato** /tə'mɑːtəʊ US tə'meɪtəʊ/ *noun* [C, U] *plural* **tomatoes** a soft, round, red fruit eaten in salad or as a vegetable ➔ *See colour picture* **Fruit and Vegetables** *on page Centre 8.*

**tomb** /tuːm/ *noun* [C] a place where a dead person is buried, usually with a monument (= stone structure)

**tomboy** /'tɒmbɔɪ/ *noun* [C] a young girl who behaves and dresses like a boy

**tombstone** /'tuːmstəʊn/ *noun* [C] a stone that shows the name of a dead person who is buried under it

**tomcat** /'tɒmkæt/ *noun* [C] a male cat

○⚬**tomorrow** /tə'mɒrəʊ/ *noun, adv* [U] **1** the day after today or on the day after today *It's my birthday tomorrow.* • *Tomorrow is Friday.* **2** the future, or in the future *the children of tomorrow*

**ton** /tʌn/ *noun* [C] *plural* **tons** or **ton 1** a unit for measuring weight, equal to 1016 kilograms in the UK and 907 kilograms in the US ➔ *Compare* **tonne**. **2 tons of sth** *informal* a lot of something *We've got tons of cheese left.* **3 weigh a ton** *informal* to be very heavy

**tone**[1] /təʊn/ *noun* **1** SOUND QUALITY [C, U] the quality of a sound, especially of someone's voice *I knew by her tone of voice that she was serious.* **2** FEELING/STYLE [U, no plural] the general feeling or style that something has *Then the director arrived and the whole tone of the meeting changed.* **3** TELEPHONE [C] an electronic sound made by a telephone *a dialling tone/an engaged tone* **4** COLOUR [C] one of the many types of a particular colour

**tone**[2] /təʊn/ (*also* **tone up**) *verb* [T] to make your muscles or skin firmer and stronger *Try these exercises to tone up your stomach muscles.*

**tone sth down** to make a piece of writing, a speech, etc less offensive or rude *The show was toned down for television.*

**tone-deaf** /,təʊn'def US 'təʊndef/ *adj* unable to sing the correct musical notes or hear the difference between musical notes

**tongs** /tɒŋz/ *noun* [plural] a tool used for picking things up, that has two pieces joined together at one end

○⚬**tongue** /tʌŋ/ *noun* **1** MOUTH [C] the soft thing inside your mouth that you move and use for tasting and speaking **2** FOOD [C, U] the tongue of some animals that you can eat as meat **3** LANGUAGE [C] *formal* a language *Japanese is her native tongue* (= the language she learnt to speak as a child). ➔ *See also:* **mother tongue**, a **slip**[2] of the tongue, be on the **tip**[1] of your tongue.

**tongue-in-cheek** /,tʌŋɪn'tʃiːk/ *adj, adv* said or done as a joke

**tongue-tied** /'tʌŋtaɪd/ *adj* unable to say anything because you are nervous

'tongue ,twister noun [C] a phrase or sentence that is difficult to say quickly because it has many similar sounds in it

tonic /'tɒnɪk/ noun 1 [C, U] (also 'tonic ,water) a drink with bubbles in it that has a bitter taste and is often added to alcoholic drinks 2 [no plural] something that makes you feel better *Spending time with Leo is always a tonic.*

o-᷼tonight /tə'naɪt/ noun, adv [U] the night of this day, or during the night of this day *What are you doing tonight?* • *I'm looking forward to tonight.*

tonne /tʌn/ noun [C] plural tonnes or tonne UK a metric ton (= unit for measuring weight, equal to 1000 kilograms) ➔ Compare ton.

tonsil /'tɒns²l/ noun [C] one of the two small, soft parts at the back of your mouth

tonsillitis /,tɒnsəl'aɪtɪs/ noun [U] an illness that makes your tonsils very painful

o-᷼too /tuː/ adv 1 too small/heavy/much, etc used before adjectives and adverbs to mean 'more than is allowed, necessary, possible, etc' *The film is also far too long.* • *There are too many cars on the roads these days.* • [+ to do sth] *I decided it was too early to get up and went back to sleep.* 2 also *Do you know Jason too?* • *I'll probably go there next year too.* 3 not too used before adjectives and adverbs to mean 'not very' *"How was your exam?" "Not too bad, I suppose." • I didn't play too well today.*

took /tʊk/ past tense of take

o-᷼tool /tuːl/ noun [C] 1 a piece of equipment that you use with your hands in order to help you do something 2 something that helps you to do a particular activity *Computers are an essential tool for modern scientists.* ➔ See also: power tool.

toot /tuːt/ UK (UK/US honk) verb toot your

**tools**

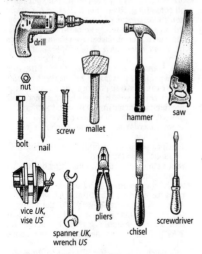

drill

nut

screw

bolt   nail

mallet

hammer

saw

vice UK,
vise US

pliers

spanner UK,
wrench US

chisel

screwdriver

**horn** If a driver toots their horn, they make a short sound with the horn (= thing you press to

make a warning noise). • toot noun [C]

o-᷼tooth /tuːθ/ noun [C] plural teeth 1 one of the hard, white objects in your mouth that you use for biting and crushing food *You should brush your teeth twice a day.* 2 one of the row of metal or plastic points that stick out from a tool such as a comb (= thing used to make your hair tidy), or saw (= thing used to cut wood) 3 grit your teeth to accept a difficult situation and deal with it in a determined way ➔ See also: a kick² in the teeth, do sth by the skin¹ of your teeth, wisdom tooth.

toothache /'tuːθeɪk/ noun [U] a pain in one of your teeth

toothbrush /'tuːθbrʌʃ/ noun [C] a small brush that you use to clean your teeth ➔ See picture at brush.

toothpaste /'tuːθpeɪst/ noun [U] a substance that you use to clean your teeth ➔ See colour picture **The Bathroom** on page Centre 1.

toothpick /'tuːθpɪk/ noun [C] a small, thin stick that you use to remove pieces of food from between your teeth

o-᷼top¹ /tɒp/ noun 1 HIGHEST PART [C] the highest part of something *They were waiting for him at the top of the stairs.* • *I want a cake with cherries on top.* 2 SURFACE [C] the flat, upper surface of something *the table top* 3 LID [C] the lid or cover of a container, pen, etc *Put the top back on the bottle.* 4 CLOTHING [C] a piece of women's clothing worn on the upper part of the body 5 TOY [C] a toy that turns round and round when you move its handle up and down 6 the top the most important position in a company, team, etc *At forty he was already at the top of his profession.* 7 at the top of your voice UK (US at the top of your lungs) shouting very loudly 8 from top to bottom completely *I've searched the house from top to bottom and still can't find it.* 9 get on top of sb If a difficult situation gets on top of someone, it upsets them. 10 off the top of your head informal If you say a fact off the top of your head, you say it immediately, from memory. *"What date is their wedding?" "I couldn't tell you off the top of my head."* 11 on top of sth a in addition to something else that is bad *And then, on top of everything else, her car was stolen.* b able to deal with or in control of something *I'm not at all sure that he's on top of the situation.* 12 be on top of the world informal to be very happy 13 over the top mainly UK informal too extreme and not suitable *I thought her performance was way over the top.*

o-᷼top² /tɒp/ adj [always before noun] 1 the best, most important, or most successful *He's one of the country's top athletes.* 2 at the highest part of something *I can't reach the top shelf.* • *I had to undo the top button of my jeans.*

top³ /tɒp/ verb [T] topping, past topped 1 to be better or more than something *I don't think film makers will ever top 'Gone With The Wind'.* 2 be topped with sth to be covered with something *lemon tart topped with cream*

top sth off informal to finish something in an enjoyable or successful way

top sth up UK (US top sth off) to add more

T

liquid to a container in order to make it full

,top 'hat *UK* (*US* 'top ,hat) *noun* [C] a tall, black or grey hat worn by men on some formal occasions

topic /'tɒpɪk/ *noun* [C] a subject that you talk or write about

topical /'tɒpɪkəl/ *adj* relating to things that are happening now

topless /'tɒpləs/ *adj* without clothes on the upper part of your body

topmost /'tɒpməʊst/ *adj* [always before noun] highest *the topmost branches of a tree*

topography /tə'pɒgrəfi/ *noun* [U] the shape and other physical characteristics of a piece of land

topping /'tɒpɪŋ/ *noun* [C, U] food that is put on top of other food in order to give it more flavour, or to make it look attractive

topple /'tɒpl/ *verb* **1** [I, T] to fall, or to make something or someone fall **2** [T] to make a leader lose their position of power

top-secret /,tɒp'si:krət/ *adj* Top-secret information is very important and must not be told to anyone.

topsy-turvy /,tɒpsi'tɜ:vi/ *adj informal* confused or badly organized

the Torah /'tɔ:rə/ *noun* the holy books of the Jewish religion, especially the first five books of the Bible

torch¹ /tɔ:tʃ/ *noun* [C] **1** *UK* (*US* **flashlight**) a small electric light that you hold in your hand **2** a long stick with material that burns tied to the top of it

torch² /tɔ:tʃ/ *verb* [T] *informal* to destroy something by burning it *A number of houses were torched.*

tore /tɔ:r/ *past tense of* tear

torment¹ /tɔ:'ment/ *verb* [T] to make someone suffer or worry a lot *All evening the question tormented her.* • tormentor *noun* [C]

torment² /'tɔ:ment/ *noun* [C, U] extreme unhappiness or pain

torn /tɔ:n/ *past participle of* tear

tornado /tɔ:'neɪdəʊ/ (*also US* **twister**) *noun* [C] *plural* **tornados** or **tornadoes** an extremely strong and dangerous wind that blows in a circle and destroys buildings as it moves along

torpedo /tɔ:'pi:dəʊ/ *noun* [C] *plural* **torpedoes** a long, thin bomb that is fired from a ship and moves under water to destroy another ship

torrent /'tɒrənt/ *noun* [C] **1 a torrent of sth** a lot of something unpleasant *a torrent of abuse* **2** a large amount of water that is moving very fast

torrential /tə'renʃəl/ *adj* Torrential rain is very heavy rain.

torso /'tɔ:səʊ/ *noun* [C] the main part of a human body without its arms, legs, or head

tortoise /'tɔ:təs/ *noun* [C] an animal with a thick, hard shell that it can move its head and legs into for protection

tortuous /'tɔ:tʃuəs/ *adj formal* **1** very complicated or difficult *Gaining permission to build was a long and tortuous process.* **2** A tortuous road has many turns in it.

torture¹ /'tɔ:tʃər/ *verb* [T] to cause someone severe pain, often in order to make them tell you something • torturer *noun* [C]

torture² /'tɔ:tʃər/ *noun* [C, U] **1** when someone is

tortured **2** a very unpleasant experience *I had to sit there listening to her for two whole hours – it was torture!*

Tory /'tɔ:ri/ *noun* [C] someone who supports the Conservative Party in the UK *a Tory voter*

toss¹ /tɒs/ *verb* **1 toss sth away/into/on, etc** to throw something somewhere carelessly *He read the letter quickly, then tossed it into the bin.* **2** [I, T] (*also* **toss up**) to throw a coin in the air and guess which side will land facing upwards as a way of deciding something

toss² /tɒs/ *noun* **1 a toss of a coin** when you throw a coin in the air and guess which side will land facing upwards as a way of deciding something **2 a toss of your head/hair** when you move your head quickly backwards

tot /tɒt/ *noun* [C] *informal* **1** a small child **2** *UK* a small amount of strong alcohol

◯⊶total¹ /'təʊtəl/ *adj* [always before noun] **1** including everything *The total cost of the work was $800.* **2** extreme or complete *The whole evening was a total disaster.*

◯⊶total² /'təʊtəl/ *noun* [C] the amount you get when you add several smaller amounts together *In total we made over £3,000.*

total³ /'təʊtəl/ *verb* [T] (*UK*) **totalling**, *past* **totalled**, (*US*) **totaling**, *past* **totaled** to add up to a particular amount

totalitarian /təʊ,tælɪ'teəriən/ *adj* belonging to a political system in which the people in power have complete control and do not allow anyone to oppose them • totalitarianism *noun* [U]

◯⊶totally /'təʊtəli/ *adv* completely *They look totally different.* • *I totally disagree.*

tote bag /'təʊt,bæg/ *noun* [C] *US* a large bag with handles and an open top

totter /'tɒtər/ *verb* [I] to walk in a way that looks as if you are going to fall *She tottered around the dance floor.*

◯⊶touch¹ /tʌtʃ/ *verb* **1** [HAND] [T] to put your hand on something *You can look at them but please don't touch them.* **2** [GET CLOSE] [I, T] If two things touch, they are so close to each other that there is no space between them. *These two wires must not touch.* **3** [EMOTION] [T] If something kind that someone says or does touches you, it makes you feel pleased or a little sad. [often passive] *I was deeply touched by her letter.* **4 not touch sth** to not eat or drink something **5 not touch sb/sth** to not harm someone or not damage something ➲ *See also:* touch all the bases (**base¹**), touch a (raw) **nerve**.

touch down When a plane touches down, it lands.

touch on sth to briefly talk about something *We only touched on the subject.*

touch sth up to improve something by making small changes

touch² /tʌtʃ/ *noun* **1** [HAND] [no plural] when you put your hand on something *I felt the touch of his hand on my face.* **2** [ABILITY] [U] the ability to feel things by putting your hand on them *It was cold to the touch* (= when I touched it). **3** [DETAIL] [C] a small detail that makes something better *Having flowers on the tables was a nice touch.* **4 a touch** a little *Add a little olive oil and a touch of vinegar.* **5 be/get/keep, etc in touch** to communicate or continue to communicate with someone by telephoning, or writing to them **6 lose touch** to stop communicating with someone, usually because they do not live near you now *We've lost touch over the years.* **7 be out of touch** to know little about what has recently happened

**touchdown** /ˈtʌtʃdaʊn/ *noun* **1** [C, U] when an aircraft lands **2** [C] when the ball is carried or thrown over a line in order to score points in rugby or American football

**touched** /tʌtʃt/ *adj* pleased or a little sad because someone has done something kind *She was touched that he had remembered her birthday.*

**touching** /ˈtʌtʃɪŋ/ *adj* making you feel sadness or sympathy *a touching performance*

**touchstone** /ˈtʌtʃstəʊn/ *noun* [no plural] something that other things can be judged against

**touchy** /ˈtʌtʃi/ *adj* **1** easily upset *Why are you so touchy today?* **2 touchy subject/issue, etc** a subject that you have to talk about carefully because it is likely to upset someone

○—**tough** /tʌf/ *adj* **1** DIFFICULT difficult *Starting a new job can be tough.* ● *We've had to make some tough decisions.* **2** SEVERE Tough rules are severe. *tough new laws on noise pollution* **3** STRONG THING not easily damaged, cut, etc *Children's shoes have to be tough.* ● *This meat's very tough.* **4** STRONG PERSON physically strong and not afraid of violence *a tough guy* **5** DETERMINED determined and not easily upset *You have to be tough to survive in politics.* **6** UNFAIR unfair or unlucky *It can be tough on kids when parents get divorced.*

**toughen** /ˈtʌfᵊn/ (*also* **toughen up**) *verb* [I, T] to become stronger, or to make something or someone stronger *School tends to toughen kids up.*

**toupee** /ˈtuːpeɪ/ /tuːˈpeɪ/ *noun* [C] a piece of artificial (= not natural) hair worn by a man to cover part of his head where there is no hair

**tour¹** /tʊər/ *noun* [C, U] a visit to and around a place, area, or country *a tour of Europe* ● *We went on a guided tour of the cathedral.* ● *The band are on tour* (= travelling and performing in different places).

**tour²** /tʊər/ *verb* [I, T] to travel around a place for pleasure *to tour the States*

**tourism** /ˈtʊərɪzᵊm/ *noun* [U] the business of providing services for tourists, including organizing their travel, hotels, entertainment, etc

○—**tourist** /ˈtʊərɪst/ *noun* [C] someone who visits a place for pleasure and does not live there

**tournament** /ˈtʊənəmənt/ *noun* [C] a competition with a series of games between many teams or players, with one winner at the end *a golf/tennis tournament*

**tourniquet** /ˈtʊənɪkeɪ ⓤⓢ ˈtɜːrnɪkɪt/ *noun* [C] a long piece of cloth that you tie tightly around an injured arm or leg to stop the blood coming out

**tousled** /ˈtaʊsld/ *adj* Tousled hair is untidy.

**tout¹** /taʊt/ *verb* **1** [T] to praise someone or something in order to make people think that they are important [often passive] *He is being touted as the next big star.* **2** [I, T] mainly UK to try to persuade people to buy something *Drug dealers*

*were seen touting for business outside schools.*

**tout²** /taʊt/ UK (US **scalper**) *noun* [C] someone who unofficially sells tickets outside theatres, sporting events, etc

**tow¹** /təʊ/ *verb* [T] to pull a car, boat, etc, using a rope or chain connected to another vehicle *His car was towed away by the police.*

**tow²** /təʊ/ *noun* **in tow** *informal* If you have someone in tow, you have them with you. *Shopping can be very stressful with young children in tow.*

○—**towards** /təˈwɔːdz/ *mainly UK* (*mainly US* **toward**) *preposition* **1** DIRECTION in the direction of someone or something *She stood up and walked towards him.* ● *He kept glancing towards the telephone.* **2** POSITION near to a time or place *Your seats are towards the back of the theatre.* ● *He only became successful towards the end of his life.* **3** FEELING used when talking about feelings about something or someone *His attitude towards work needs to improve.* **4** PURPOSE for the purpose of buying or achieving something *We're asking people for a contribution towards the cost.* ● *This piece of work counts towards your final mark.*

○—**towel** /ˈtaʊəl/ *noun* [C] **1** a soft piece of cloth or paper that you use for drying yourself or for drying something *a bath/beach towel* ● *a paper towel* ⊃ *See colour picture* **The Bathroom** *on page Centre 1.* **2 throw in the towel** to stop trying to do something because you do not think you can succeed *Their candidate should just throw in the towel and admit defeat.* ⊃ *See also:* **sanitary towel, tea towel.**

**'towel ˌrail** UK (US **'towel ˌrack**) *noun* [C] a horizontal bar on the wall that you hang towels on ⊃ *See picture at* **rail.**

**tower¹** /taʊər/ *noun* [C] **1** a very tall, narrow building, or part of a building *a church tower* ● *the Eiffel Tower* **2 a tower of strength** someone who helps you a lot during a difficult time

**tower²** /taʊər/ *verb* **tower over/above sb/sth** to be much taller or higher than someone or something else *David towers over his mother.*

**'tower ˌblock** *noun* [C] UK a very tall building divided into apartments or offices

**towering** /ˈtaʊərɪŋ/ *adj* [always before noun] very tall *towering mountains/trees*

○—**town** /taʊn/ *noun* **1** [C] a place where people live and work, usually larger than a village but smaller than a city *It's a small town in the north of England.* **2** [U] the central area of a town where the shops are *I usually go into town on a Saturday.* ● *Shall I meet you in town?* **3 go to town (on sth)** to spend a lot of money or time doing something in order to make it special *They've really gone to town on the decorations.* **4 out on the town** *informal* enjoying yourself in bars, restaurants, etc in the evening ⊃ *See also:* **ghost town, shanty town.**

**ˌtown 'hall** *noun* [C] a large building where local government is based

**township** /ˈtaʊnʃɪp/ *noun* [C] in South Africa, an area where only black people live

**toxic** /ˈtɒksɪk/ *adj* poisonous *toxic chemicals/ fumes* ● *toxic waste* (= poisonous waste materials produced by industry) ● *toxicity*

/tɒkˈsɪsəti/ *noun* [U] *formal* how poisonous a substance is

**toxin** /ˈtɒksɪn/ *noun* [C] *formal* a poisonous substance

o━**toy¹** /tɔɪ/ *noun* [C] an object for children to play with *a toy car/train* • *He was happily playing with his toys.*

**toy²** /tɔɪ/ *verb*
**toy with sth 1** to briefly think about doing something, but not really intend to do it *I've toyed with the idea of going to work abroad.* **2** to move something around in your hands without any clear purpose *He sat toying with his empty glass.*

**trace¹** /treɪs/ *verb* [T] **1** FIND to find someone or something that was lost *Police have so far failed to trace the missing woman.* **2** ORIGIN to find the origin of something *She's traced her family back to the sixteenth century.* • *They were able to trace the call* (= find out the number of the telephone used). **3** DEVELOPMENT to describe the way something has developed over time *The book traces the development of women's art since the start of the century.* **4** COPY to copy a picture by putting transparent paper on top and following the outer line of the picture with a pen *tracing paper*

**trace²** /treɪs/ *noun* **1** [C, U] proof that someone or something was in a place *There was no trace of her anywhere.* • *Ships have disappeared without trace* (= completely). **2** [C] a small amount of something *They found traces of blood on his clothing.*

**track¹** /træk/ *noun* **1** PATH [C] a narrow path or road *We followed a dirt track off the main road.* **2** RAILWAY [C] the long metal lines which a train travels along *(UK) a railway track/(US) a railroad track* **3** RACE [C] a path, often circular, used for races *a race track* • *track events* **4** SPORT [U] *US* the sport of running in races around a wide circular path made for this sport **5** MUSIC [C] one song or piece of music on a CD, record, etc **6 keep track** to continue to know what is happening to someone or something *He changes jobs so often – I find it hard to keep track of what he's doing.* **7 lose track** to not know what is happening to someone or something any more *I've lost track of how much we've spent.* **8 on track** making progress and likely to succeed [+ to do sth] *A fighter from Edinburgh is on track to become world heavyweight boxing champion.* • *We've got a lot of work to do but we're on the right track.* **9 a fast track (to sth)** a very quick way of achieving or dealing with something *These intensive courses claim to offer a fast track to wealth and success.* **10 off the beaten track** in a place where few people go

**track²** /træk/ *verb* [T] **1** to follow a person or animal by looking for proof that they have been somewhere, or by using electronic equipment *The wolves are tracked by using radio collars.* **2** to record the progress or development of something over a period *The project tracks the effects of population growth on the area.*
**track sth/sb down** to find something or someone after looking for them in a lot of different places *The man was finally tracked down by French police.*

,**track and 'field** *US* (*UK* **athletics**) *noun* [U] the sports which include running, jumping, and throwing ⟳ *See colour picture* **Sports 1** *on page Centre 15.*

,**track 'record** *UK* (*US* '**track ,record**) *noun* [C] how well or badly you have done in the past *This company has an impressive track record in completing projects on time.*

**tracks** /træks/ *noun* [plural] the marks left on the ground by a person, animal, or vehicle *We followed their tracks in the snow.*

**tracksuit** /ˈtræksuːt/ *noun* [C] *UK* loose, comfortable clothes, usually trousers and a top, especially worn for exercising

**tract** /trækt/ *noun* [C] **1** a system of connected tubes in someone's body which has a particular purpose *the digestive/respiratory tract* **2** a large area of land

**tractor** /ˈtræktəʳ/ *noun* [C] a strong vehicle with large back wheels used on farms for pulling things

o━**trade¹** /treɪd/ *noun* **1** BUYING AND SELLING [U] the buying and selling of large numbers of goods or services, especially between countries *a trade agreement/dispute* • *They rely heavily on trade with Europe.* • *The laws ban the international trade in ivory.* **2** BUSINESS [C] a particular area of business or industry *the building/ tourist trade* **3** JOB [C] someone's job, especially one which needs skill in using their hands *He's a builder by trade.*

**trade²** /treɪd/ *verb* **1** [I] to buy and sell goods or services, especially between countries *This will increase costs for companies trading with Asia.* **2** [T] *mainly US* to give something to someone and receive something else in exchange *He traded his guitar for a leather jacket.* • *trading noun* [U]
**trade sth in** to give something as part of your payment for something else *He traded his old car in for a new model.*

**trademark** /ˈtreɪdmɑːk/ *noun* [C] the name of a particular company or product which cannot be used by anyone else

**trade-off** /ˈtreɪdɒf/ *noun* [C] a situation where you accept something bad in order to have something good *There's always a trade-off between speed and quality.*

**tradesman** /ˈtreɪdzmən/ *noun* [C] *plural* **tradesmen** *UK* someone who works in trade or in a trade which needs skill in using their hands, usually in the building industry

,**trade 'union** (*also US* **labor union**) *noun* [C] an organization that represents people who do a particular job

o━**tradition** /trəˈdɪʃən/ *noun* [C, U] a custom or way of behaving that has continued for a long time in a group of people or a society *There is a great tradition of dance in St Petersburg.* • *We decided to break with tradition* (= not behave as usual) *this year and go away for Christmas.*

o━**traditional** /trəˈdɪʃən³l/ *adj* following the customs or ways of behaving that have continued in a group of people or society for a long time *traditional Hungarian dress* • *traditional farming methods* • **traditionally** *adv*

**traditionalist** /trəˈdɪʃən³lɪst/ *noun* [C] someone

---

| i: **see** | ɒ **hot** | ɔ: **saw** | ʌ **run** | ʊ **put** | u: **too** | aɪ **my** | aʊ **how** | eɪ **day** | əʊ **no** | ɪə **near** | ɔɪ **boy** | ʊə **poor** | aɪə **fire** | aʊə **sour** |

who believes in traditional ideas and ways of doing things

o━**traffic** /'træfɪk/ *noun* [U] **1** CARS ETC the cars, trucks, etc using a road *Traffic is heavy* (= there are a lot of cars, etc) *in both directions.* • *a traffic accident* • *Sorry we're late – we got stuck in traffic.* **2** PLANES/SHIPS the planes or ships moving around an area *air traffic control* **3** ILLEGAL the illegal buying and selling of goods, such as drugs, weapons, etc *the traffic in illegal drugs*

'**traffic ,circle** *US* (*UK* **roundabout**) *noun* [C] a circular place where roads meet and where cars drive around until they arrive at the road that they want to turn into ➲ *See picture at* **roundabout**.

'**traffic ,jam** *noun* [C] a line of cars, trucks, etc that are moving slowly or not moving at all *They got stuck in a traffic jam.*

**trafficking** /'træfɪkɪŋ/ *noun* [U] the activity of illegally buying and selling goods, such as drugs or weapons *arms/drug trafficking* • trafficker *noun* [C]

'**traffic ,light** *noun* [C] (*also* **lights** [plural]) a set of red, green, and yellow lights that is used to stop and start traffic [usually plural] *Turn left at the traffic lights.* ➲ *See picture at* **light**.

'**traffic ,warden** *noun* [C] *UK* someone whose job is to make sure that people do not leave their cars in illegal places

**tragedy** /'trædʒədi/ *noun* **1** [C, U] an event or situation which is very sad, often involving death *the tragedy of their daughter's death* **2** [C] a play with a sad end *a Greek tragedy*

**tragic** /'trædʒɪk/ *adj* very sad, often relating to death and suffering *a tragic accident/death* • tragically *adv He was tragically killed in a flying accident at the age of 25.*

**trail**[1] /treɪl/ *noun* [C] **1** a line of marks that someone or something leaves behind as they move *He left a trail of muddy footprints across the kitchen floor.* **2** a path through the countryside, often where people walk *a nature trail*

**trail**[2] /treɪl/ *verb* **1** FOLLOW [T] to follow someone, especially without knowing it, in order to watch or catch them *He suspected he was being trailed by undercover police.* **2** HANG DOWN [I, T] *UK* to hang down and touch the ground, or to make something do this *Your coat's trailing in the mud.* **3** LOWER SCORE [I, T] to have a lower score than someone else, especially in a sporting event *City were trailing United 2–1 at half time.*

**trail away/off** If someone's voice trails away or off, it gradually becomes quieter until it stops.

**trailer** /'treɪlə'/ *noun* [C] **1** CONTAINER a container with wheels that can be pulled by a car or a truck **2** HOUSE *mainly US* a house on wheels which can be pulled by a car **3** FILM short parts of a film or television programme which are shown in order to advertise it

'**trailer ,park** *noun* [C] *US* a place where trailers (= vehicles that people live in) can park

o━**train**[1] /treɪn/ *noun* **1** [C] a long, thin vehicle which travels along metal tracks and carries people or goods *a train journey* • *We could go by train.* • *You'll have to catch/get the next*

*train.* **2 train of thought/events** a series of connected thoughts, ideas, or events which come or happen one after the other *I was interrupted and lost my train of thought.*

o━**train**[2] /treɪn/ *verb* **1** TEACH [T] to teach someone how to do something, usually a skill that is needed for a job *We are training all our staff in how to use the new computer system.* • [+ to do sth] *The aid workers trained local people to give the injections.* **2** LEARN [I] to learn the skills you need to do a job *He trained as a lawyer in Vienna.* • *I'm trained in basic first aid.* **3** SPORT [I, T] to practise a sport or exercise, often in order to prepare for a sporting event, or to help someone to do this *He's been training hard for the race for several weeks now.*

**trainee** /ˌtreɪ'niː/ *noun* [C] someone who is learning how to do something, especially a job *a trainee accountant/teacher*

**trainer** /'treɪnə'/ *noun* [C] **1** PERSON someone who trains people *a fitness trainer* **2** ANIMALS a person who trains animals *a racehorse trainer* **3** SHOE *UK* (*US* **sneaker**) a soft sports shoe *a pair of trainers* ➲ *See colour picture* **Clothes** on *page Centre 5.*

o━**training** /'treɪnɪŋ/ *noun* [U] **1** the process of learning the skills you need to do a particular job or activity *a training course* • *computer/management training* **2** preparation for a sport or competition *weight training* • *He's in training for the big match next month.*

**trait** /treɪt/ *noun* [C] a quality, good or bad, in someone's character *a family trait*

**traitor** /'treɪtə'/ *noun* [C] someone who is not loyal to their country or to a group which they are a member of

**trajectory** /trə'dʒektəri/ *noun* [C] *formal* the curved line that something follows as it moves through the air

**tram** /træm/ *noun* [C] an electric vehicle for carrying passengers, mostly in cities, which moves along metal lines in the road

**tramp**[1] /træmp/ *noun* [C] someone who has no home, job, or money and who lives outside

**tramp**[2] /træmp/ *verb* [I, T] to walk a long way, or to walk with heavy steps because you are tired *We spent all day tramping around the city looking for somewhere cheap to stay.*

**trample** /'træmpl/ (*also* **trample on**) *verb* [T] to walk on something, usually damaging or hurting it *She shouted at the boys for trampling on her flowers.* • *Two people were trampled to death in the panic.*

**trampoline** /'træmpəliːn/ *noun* [C] a piece of sports equipment that you jump up and down on, made of a metal structure with a piece of strong material fixed to it

**trance** /trɑːns/ *noun* [C] a condition in which you are not completely conscious of what is happening around you or able to control what you are doing *He sat staring out of the window as if in a trance.*

**tranquil** /'træŋkwɪl/ *adj* calm and quiet *a tranquil garden* • tranquility (*also* **tranquillity**) /træŋ'kwɪləti/ *noun* [U] *I love the tranquility of the woods.*

**tranquilizer** (*also UK* **-iser**) /'træŋkwɪˌlaɪzə'/ *noun* [C] a drug which is used to make people or

T

animals sleep or to make them calm

**transaction** /træn'zækʃⁿn/ *noun* [C] *formal* when someone buys or sells something, or when money is exchanged *a business/financial transaction*

**transatlantic** /ˌtrænzət'læntɪk/ *adj* crossing the Atlantic *a transatlantic flight/phone call*

**transcend** /træn'send/ *verb* [T] *formal* to be better or more important than something else *Somehow her appeal transcends class barriers.*

**transcribe** /træn'skraɪb/ *verb* [T] to make a written record of something you hear, such as speech or music *I later transcribed the tapes of the interviews.* • transcription /træn'skrɪpʃⁿn/ *noun* [C, U] a written record of speech, music, etc, or the process of making it

**transcript** /'trænskrɪpt/ *noun* [C] an exact written record of speech, music, etc

**transfer** /træns'fɜːʳ/ *verb* **transferring**, *past* **transferred 1** MOVE [T] to move someone or something from one place to another *She was later transferred to a different hospital.* • *I'll transfer some money into my other account.* **2** CHANGE JOB/TEAM ETC [I, T] to change to a different job, team, place of work, etc, or to make someone do this *After a year he transferred to University College, Dublin.* **3** CHANGE OWNER [T] to change who owns or controls something *We had all the documents transferred to my name.* • transfer /'trænsfɜːʳ/ *noun* [C, U] *It speeds up the transfer of information from one office to another.* • *I'm hoping for a transfer to the Brussels office.*

**transfixed** /træns'fɪkst/ *adj* unable to move or stop looking at something because you are so interested, surprised, or frightened *We all sat in silence, transfixed by what we saw on the screen.*

**transform** /træns'fɔːm/ *verb* [T] to change something completely, usually to improve it *Within weeks they had transformed the area into a beautiful garden.* • transformation /ˌtrænsfə'meɪʃⁿn/ *noun* [C, U] a complete change *The company has undergone a dramatic transformation in the past five years.*

**transformer** /træns'fɔːməʳ/ *noun* [C] a piece of equipment that changes the strength of an electrical current

**transfusion** /træns'fjuːʒⁿn/ (*also* **blood transfusion**) *noun* [C] when blood is put into someone's body

**transgress** /trænz'gres/ *verb* [I, T] *formal* to do something which is against a law or rule • transgression /trænz'greʃⁿn/ *noun* [C]

**transient¹** /'trænziənt/ *adj* *formal* **1** lasting only for a short time *transient pleasures* **2** staying in one place only for a short time

**transient²** /'trænziənt/ *noun* [C] *US* someone who has no home and stays in a place for only a short time

**transistor** /træn'zɪstəʳ/ *noun* [C] a small piece of electrical equipment used in radios, televisions, etc

**transit** /'trænsɪt/ *noun* [U] *formal* the movement of goods or people from one place to another *Some things got damaged in transit* (= while they were being moved).

**transition** /træn'zɪʃⁿn/ *noun* [C, U] *formal* when something changes from one system or method to another, often gradually *The country is in the process of making the transition from military rule to democracy.* • transitional *adj* *a transitional period*

**transitive** /'trænsətɪv/ *adj* A transitive verb always has an object. In the sentence 'I'll make a drink.', 'make' is a transitive verb. ⊃ *Compare* **intransitive**.

**transitory** /'trænsɪtⁿri/ *adj* *formal* lasting only for a short time *the transitory nature of life*

**translate** /trænz'leɪt/ *verb* [I, T] **1** to change written or spoken words from one language to another *We were asked to translate a list of sentences.* • *The book has now been translated from Spanish into more than ten languages.* **2** *formal* If an idea or plan translates into an action, it makes it happen. *So how does this theory translate into practical policy?*

**translation** /trænz'leɪʃⁿn/ *noun* [C, U] something which has been translated from one language to another, or the process of translating

**translator** /trænz'leɪtəʳ/ *noun* [C] someone whose job is to change written or spoken words from one language to another

**translucent** /trænz'luːsⁿnt/ *adj* If something is translucent, light can pass through it and you can almost see through it. *translucent fabric/plastic*

**transmission** /trænz'mɪʃⁿn/ *noun* **1** BROADCAST [C, U] the process of broadcasting something by radio, television, etc, or something which is broadcast *radio/satellite transmission* **2** SPREADING [U] *formal* the process of passing something from one person or place to another *There is still a risk of transmission of the virus through infected water.* **3** CAR [U] the system in a car that moves power from its engine to its wheels *automatic/manual transmission*

**transmit** /trænz'mɪt/ *verb* [T] **transmitting**, *past* **transmitted 1** to broadcast something, or to send out signals using radio, television, etc [often passive] *The information is transmitted electronically to the central computer.* **2** *formal* to pass something from one person or place to another *The disease is transmitted by mosquitoes.* • transmitter *noun* [C] *a radio/satellite transmitter*

**transparency** /træn'spærⁿnsi/ *noun* [C] a photograph or picture printed on plastic which you can see on a screen by shining a light through it

**transparent** /træn'spærⁿnt/ *adj* If a substance or material is transparent, you can see through it. *transparent plastic*

**transpire** /træn'spaɪəʳ/ *verb* *formal* **1** **It transpires that** If it transpires that something has happened, this fact becomes known. *It later transpired that he had known about the plan from the beginning.* **2** [I] to happen

**transplant** /'trænsplɑːnt/ *noun* [C] an operation in which a new organ is put into someone's body *a heart/kidney transplant* • transplant /træn'splɑːnt/ *verb* [T] to remove an organ or other body part from one person and put it into someone else's body

o⁻ᵘ**transport¹** /'trænspɔːt/ *noun* [U] **1** a vehicle or system of vehicles, such as buses, trains, aircraft, etc for getting from one place to another *He can't drive so he has to rely on **public transport**.* • *the city's transport system* **2** when people or goods are moved from one place to another *the transport of live animals*

**transport²** /træn'spɔːt/ *verb* [T] to move people or goods from one place to another

**transportation** /ˌtrænspɔː'teɪʃºn/ *noun* [U] **1** *US* (*UK* **transport**) a vehicle or system of vehicles, such as buses, trains, etc for getting from one place to another *Bicycles are an efficient and cheap form of transportation.* **2** when people or goods are moved from one place to another *transportation costs*

**transvestite** /trænz'vestaɪt/ *noun* [C] someone, especially a man, who likes to wear the clothes of someone of the opposite sex

**trap¹** /træp/ *noun* [C] **1** a piece of equipment for catching animals *a mouse trap* **2** a dangerous or unpleasant situation which is difficult to escape from [usually singular] *Such families get caught in the poverty trap.* ➔ *See also:* **booby trap**.

**trap²** /træp/ *verb* [T] **trapping**, *past* **trapped 1** CANNOT ESCAPE If someone or something is trapped, they cannot move or escape from a place or situation. *The car turned over, trapping the driver underneath.* • *Five years into the marriage he felt trapped.* **2** ANIMAL to catch an animal using a trap **3** TRICK to trick someone into doing or saying something that they do not want to

**ˌtrap 'door** *noun* [C] a small door that you cannot see in a floor or ceiling

**trappings** /'træpɪŋz/ *noun* [plural] things that you usually get when you are rich and successful, such as a big house and car *the trappings of success/power*

**trash¹** /træʃ/ *noun* [U] **1** *US* (*UK* **rubbish**) things that you throw away because you do not want them **2** *informal* something that is of bad quality *It's better than the trash she usually reads.*

**trash²** /træʃ/ *verb* [T] *informal* to destroy something *Vandals broke in and trashed the place.*

**ˈtrash ˌcan** *noun* [C] *US* a container for waste, often one that is kept outdoors ➔ *See colour picture* **The Office** *on page Centre 12.*

**trashy** /'træʃi/ *adj informal* of very bad quality *a trashy novel/movie*

**trauma** /'trɔːmə/ *noun* [C, U] severe shock caused by an unpleasant experience, or the experience which causes this feeling *the trauma of marriage breakdown*

**traumatic** /trɔː'mætɪk/ *adj* If an experience is traumatic, it makes you feel very shocked and upset. *His parents split up when he was eight, which he found very traumatic.*

**traumatized** (*also UK* **-ised**) /'trɔːmətaɪzd/ *adj* very shocked and upset for a long time *The violence that he witnessed left him traumatized.*

○━**travel¹** /'trævºl/ *verb* (*UK*) **travelling**, *past* **travelled**, (*US*) **traveling**, *past* **traveled 1** [I, T] to make a journey *I spent a year travelling around Asia.* • *He travelled over 100 miles to be at the wedding.* • *He has to travel abroad a lot on business.* **2** [I] If light, sound, or news travels, it moves from one place to another.

*News of the accident travelled fast.* ➔ *See usage note at* **move**.

**travel²** /'trævºl/ *noun* **1** [U] the activity of travelling *air/rail travel* • *travel expenses/insurance* **2** *sb's* **travels** someone's journey *I meet all kinds of interesting people on my travels.*

USAGE

**travel, journey,** or **trip?**

The noun **travel** is a general word which means the activity of travelling.

*Air travel has become much cheaper.*

Use **journey** to talk about when you travel from one place to another.

*He fell asleep during the train journey.*

*Did you have a good journey?*

~~Did you have a good travel?~~

A **trip** is a journey in which you visit a place for a short time and come back again.

*a business trip*

*a 3-day trip to Spain*

**ˈtravel ˌagency** (*also* **ˈtravel ˌagent's**) *noun* [C] a company or shop that makes travel arrangements for people

**ˈtravel ˌagent** *noun* [C] someone whose job is making travel arrangements for people

**traveller** /'trævºləʳ/ *noun* [C] **1** (*also US* **traveler**) someone who is travelling or who often travels *We're doing a survey of business travellers.* **2** *UK* another word for gypsy (= a member of a race of people who travel from place to place, especially in Europe)

**ˈtraveller's ˌcheque** *UK* (*US* **traveler's check**) *noun* [C] a special piece of paper which you buy at a bank and exchange for local money when you are in another country

**traverse** /trə'vɜːs/ *verb* [T] *formal* to move across something

**travesty** /'trævəsti/ *noun* [C] *formal* If something is a travesty, it is very badly done or unfair and does not represent how that thing should be. *She described the trial as a travesty of justice.*

**trawl** /trɔːl/ *verb*

**trawl through sth** *mainly UK* to look through a lot of things in order to find something *to trawl through data*

**trawler** /'trɔːləʳ/ *noun* [C] a large ship which is used for catching fish by pulling a large net through the sea behind it

**tray** /treɪ/ *noun* [C] a flat object with higher edges, used for carrying food and drinks *She came back carrying a tray of drinks.*

**treacherous** /'tretʃºrəs/ *adj* **1** very dangerous, especially because of bad weather conditions *Ice had made the roads treacherous.* **2** *formal* If someone is treacherous, they deceive people who trust them.

**treachery** /'tretʃºri/ *noun* [U] *formal* when a person deceives someone who trusts them

**treacle** /'triːkl/ *UK* (*UK/US* **molasses**) *noun* [U] a sweet, thick, dark liquid used in sweet dishes

**tread¹** /tred/ *verb past t* **trod,** *past p* **trodden 1** [I, T] *mainly UK* to put your foot on something or to press something down with your foot *I trod on a piece of broken glass.* • *David trod in some paint.* • *The kids were treading cake crumbs into the carpet.* **2 tread carefully/gently/ lightly, etc** to be careful what you say so that you do not upset someone **3 tread water** to float vertically in the water by moving your arms and legs up and down

**tread²** /tred/ *noun* **1** [C, U] the pattern of lines on the surface of a tyre **2** [no plural] the sound of someone putting their feet down when walking

**treadmill** /'tredmɪl/ *noun* [C] **1** a machine with a moving part which you walk or run on for exercise **2** a job which is boring because you have to repeat the same thing again and again

**treason** /'triːzⁿn/ *noun* [U] the crime of doing something that harms your country or government, especially by helping its enemies

**treasure¹** /'treʒəʳ/ *noun* **1** [U] a collection of gold, silver, jewellery and valuable objects, especially in children's stories *buried treasure* **2** [C] a very valuable object [usually plural] *art treasures*

**treasure²** /'treʒəʳ/ *verb* [T] If you treasure something, it is very important to you and gives you a lot of pleasure. *I shall treasure those memories of her.*

**treasurer** /'treʒəʳəʳ/ *noun* [C] someone who is responsible for the money of an organization

**treasury** /'treʒəʳri/ *noun* [C] the government department which controls a country's money supply and economy

o━**treat¹** /triːt/ *verb* [T] **1** DEAL WITH to behave towards or deal with someone in a particular way *He treats her really badly.* • *She felt she'd been unfairly treated by her employer.* • *They treat her like one of their own children.* **2** CONSIDER to consider something in a particular way *He treated my suggestion as a joke.* **3** ILLNESS/INJURY to give medical care to someone for an illness or injury *He's being treated for cancer at a hospital in Manchester.* **4** SPECIAL to do or buy something special for someone *I'm going to treat her to dinner at that nice Italian restaurant.* **5** PROTECT to put a substance on something in order to protect it *The wood is then treated with a special chemical to protect it from the rain.*

**treat²** /triːt/ *noun* [C] something special which you buy or do for someone else *a birthday treat* • *As a special treat I'm taking him out for dinner.* • *Annie, put your money away, this is my treat* (= I am paying). ➔ *See also:* **Trick or treat!**.

**treatise** /'triːtɪz/ *noun* [C] a formal piece of writing that examines a particular subject

o━**treatment** /'triːtmənt/ *noun* **1** [C, U] something which you do to try to cure an illness or injury, especially something suggested or done by a doctor *She's receiving treatment for a lung infection.* **2** [U] the way you deal with or behave towards someone or something *There have been complaints about the treatment of prisoners.*

**treaty** /'triːti/ *noun* [C] a written agreement between two or more countries *a peace treaty*

**treble** /'trebl/ *verb* [I, T] to increase three times

in size or amount, or to make something do this

o━**tree** /triː/ *noun* [C] a tall plant with a thick stem which has branches coming from it and leaves ➔ *See also:* **Christmas tree, family tree, palm tree**.

**trek** /trek/ *noun* [C] a long, difficult journey that

**tree**

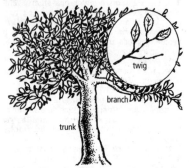

you make by walking *They started out on the long trek across the mountains.* • *trek verb* [I] **trekking,** *past* **trekked**

**trellis** /'trelɪs/ *noun* [C] a wooden structure fixed to a wall for plants to grow up

**tremble** /'trembl/ *verb* [I] to shake slightly, especially because you are nervous, frightened, or cold *My hands were trembling so much I could hardly hold the pen.* • *Her voice trembled with emotion.*

**tremendous** /trɪ'mendəs/ *adj* **1** extremely good *I think she's doing a tremendous job.* **2** very large, great, strong, etc *a tremendous amount of money* • *tremendously adv* very much

**tremor** /'treməʳ/ *noun* [C] **1** a slight earthquake (= when the Earth shakes) **2** a slight shaking of part of your body which you cannot control

**trench** /trenʃ/ *noun* [C] a long, narrow hole dug into the ground

**trenchant** /'trenʃənt/ *adj formal* expressing strong criticism *trenchant criticism/views*

**trenchcoat** /'trentʃˌkəʊt/ *noun* [C] a long coat that does not let water through, similar in style to a military coat

o━**trend** /trend/ *noun* [C] a general development or change in a situation *There's a trend towards more locally produced television programmes.* • *I'm not familiar with the latest trends in teaching methodology.*

**trendy** /'trendi/ *adj informal* fashionable at the moment *Have you seen Rickmer's trendy new glasses?*

**trepidation** /ˌtrepɪ'deɪʃⁿn/ *noun* [U] *formal* fear or worry about something you are going to do *It was with trepidation that I accepted Klein's invitation.*

**trespass** /'trespəs/ *verb* [I] to go on someone's land without their permission • *trespasser noun* [C]

o━**trial** /traɪəl/ *noun* [C, U] **1** a legal process to

decide if someone is guilty of a crime *The two men are now on trial for attempted murder.* • *He will be taken to the US to stand trial.* **2** a test of something new to find out if it is safe, works correctly, etc *The drug is currently undergoing clinical trials.* **3 trial and error** a way of learning the best way to do something by trying different methods *There aren't any instructions with it – it's just a matter of trial and error.*

**trials** /traɪəlz/ *noun* [plural] **1** a sports competition to find out how good a player is **2 trials and tribulations** problems and suffering *the trials and tribulations of growing up*

**triangle** /'traɪæŋgl/ *noun* [C] **1** a flat shape with three sides ⊃ *See picture at* **shape**. **2** a small musical instrument made of a piece of metal with three sides which you hit with a metal bar • **triangular** /traɪ'æŋgjələʳ/ *adj* shaped like a triangle

**tribe** /traɪb/ *noun* [C] a group of people who live together, usually in areas far away from cities, and who share the same culture and language and still have a traditional way of life *Native American tribes* • **tribal** *adj* relating to a tribe *a tribal dance*

**tribulations** /ˌtrɪbjə'leɪʃ°nz/ *noun* [plural] ⊃ *See* **trials** and tribulations.

**tribunal** /traɪ'bjuːn°l/ *noun* [C] an official court or group of people whose job is to deal with a particular problem or disagreement ⊃ *See also:* **industrial tribunal**.

**tributary** /'trɪbjət°ri/ *noun* [C] a river or stream which flows into a larger river

**tribute** /'trɪbjuːt/ *noun* [C, U] **1** something which you do or say to show that you respect and admire someone, especially in a formal situation *The concert was organized as a tribute to the singer who died last year.* • *The President paid tribute to* (= expressed his admiration for) *the brave soldiers who had defended the country.* **2 be a tribute to sb/sth** to show how good someone or something is *It's a tribute to Mark's hard work that the project is finished.*

o─**trick¹** /trɪk/ *noun* [C] **1** [DECEIVE] something you do to deceive or cheat someone, or to make someone look stupid as a joke *a trick question* • *I wasn't really ill – it was just a trick.* • *My little brother liked to **play tricks on** me* (= do things to deceive me as a joke). **2** [METHOD] an effective way of doing something *What's the trick to pulling out this sofa bed?* **3** [MAGIC] something that is done to entertain people and that seems to be magic *a card trick* **4 do the trick** If something does the trick, it solves a problem or has the result you want. *If I've got a headache, a couple of aspirins usually do the trick.* ⊃ *See also:* **hat trick**.

**trick²** /trɪk/ *verb* [T] to deceive someone [+ into + doing sth] *They tricked him into signing the papers.*

**trickery** /'trɪk°ri/ *noun* [U] the use of tricks to deceive or cheat people

**trickle** /'trɪkl/ *verb* **1 trickle down/from/out of, etc** If liquid trickles somewhere, it flows slowly and in a thin line. *She could feel the sweat trickling down her back.* **2 trickle in/into/out, etc** to go somewhere slowly in

small numbers *People began to trickle into the classroom.* • **trickle** *noun* [C] *a trickle of blood*

**Trick or 'treat!** **1** something that children say on Halloween (= a holiday on 31 October), when they dress to look frightening and visit people's houses to ask for sweets **2 go trick or treating** If children go trick or treating, they visit people's houses on Halloween to ask for sweets.

**tricky** /'trɪki/ *adj* difficult to deal with or do *a tricky question/situation*

**tricycle** /'traɪsɪkl/ *noun* [C] a bicycle with one wheel at the front and two at the back

**trifle** /'traɪfl/ *noun* **1 a trifle** *formal* slightly *It does seem a trifle odd.* **2** [C, U] *UK* a cold, sweet dish that has layers of cake, fruit, custard (= sweet, yellow sauce), and cream **3** [C] *formal* something silly or unimportant

**trigger¹** /'trɪgəʳ/ (*also* **trigger off**) *verb* [T] to make something begin to happen *His arrest triggered mass protests.*

**trigger²** /'trɪgəʳ/ *noun* [C] **1** the part of a gun that you pull when you shoot **2** an event or situation that makes something else happen *Stress can be a **trigger for** many illnesses.*

**trillion** /'trɪljən/ the number 1,000,000,000,000

**trilogy** /'trɪlədʒi/ *noun* [C] a series of three books, plays, etc with the same characters or subject

**trim¹** /trɪm/ *verb* [T] **trimming**, *past* **trimmed** **1** (*also* **trim off**) to cut a small amount from something to make it tidy or to remove parts that you do not need *I've had my hair trimmed.* • *Trim the fat off the meat.* **2** to reduce something *to trim costs* **3 be trimmed with sth** to be decorated with something around the edges *a silk dress trimmed with lace*

**trim²** /trɪm/ *noun* **1** [no plural] when you cut something to make it tidy *The hedge needs a trim.* **2** [U, no plural] decoration that is added to something such as clothes or a car *The car has a stereo, sunroof, and leather trim.*

**trim³** /trɪm/ *adj* looking thin and healthy

**trimester** /trɪ'mestəʳ (US) traɪ'mestər/ *noun* [C] *mainly US* one of the periods of time that the school or university year is divided into

**trimming** /'trɪmɪŋ/ *noun* [C, U] decoration on the edge of something such as a piece of clothing

**trimmings** /'trɪmɪŋz/ *noun* [plural] extra dishes that are often eaten with a main dish *a roast dinner with all the trimmings*

**the Trinity** /'trɪnəti/ *noun* the existence of God in three forms, Father, Son, and Holy Spirit, in the Christian religion

**trio** /'triːəʊ/ *noun* [C] a group of three things or people, especially three musicians who play together

o─**trip¹** /trɪp/ *noun* [C] a journey in which you visit a place for a short time and come back again *a business trip* • *a day trip to Paris* • *We might **take a trip** to Spain later in the summer.* ⊃ *See also:* **round trip** ⊃ *See usage note at* **travel**.

**trip²** /trɪp/ *verb* **tripping**, *past* **tripped** **1** [I] to fall or almost fall because you hit your foot on something when you are walking or running *Careful you don't **trip over** the cat!* • *He **tripped on** a stone and hurt his ankle.* **2** [T] to make someone fall by putting your foot in front of their foot

**trip (sb) up 1** *UK* to fall because you hit

your foot on something, or to make someone fall by putting your foot in front of their foot **2** to make a mistake, or to cause someone to make a mistake *I tripped up on the last question.*

**triple¹** /'trɪpl/ *adj* having three parts of the same type, or happening three times *a triple world champion*

**triple²** /'trɪpl/ *verb* [I, T] to increase three times in size or amount, or to make something do this *Sales have tripled in the past five years.*

**triplet** /'trɪplət/ *noun* [C] one of three children who are born to the same mother at the same time

**tripod** /'traɪpɒd/ *noun* [C] a piece of equipment with three legs, used for supporting a camera

**trite** /traɪt/ *adj* A trite remark, idea, etc does not seem sincere or true because it has been used so much before or is too simple.

**triumph¹** /'traɪəmf/ *noun* **1** [C] an important success, achievement, or victory *Barcelona's 2–0 triumph over Manchester United* **2** [U] the feeling of happiness that you have when you win something or succeed

**triumph²** /'traɪəmf/ *verb* [I] to win or succeed *The Democrats once again triumphed in recent elections.*

**triumphant** /traɪˈʌmfənt/ *adj* feeling very pleased because you have won something or succeeded *the President's triumphant return to the White House* • **triumphantly** *adv*

**trivia** /'trɪviə/ *noun* [U] small facts or details that are not important

**trivial** /'trɪviəl/ *adj* small and not important *a trivial matter/offence*

**trivialize** (*also UK* -**ise**) /'trɪviˈəlaɪz/ *verb* [T] to make something seem less important or serious than it really is *I don't mean to trivialize the problem.*

**trod** /trɒd/ *past tense of* tread

**trodden** /'trɒdⁿn/ *past participle of* tread

**trolley** /'trɒli/ *noun* [C] **1** *UK* (*US* **cart**) a metal structure on wheels that is used for carrying things *a supermarket trolley* • *a luggage trolley* **2** *US* (*UK/US* **tram**) an electric vehicle for carrying passengers, mostly in cities, which runs along metal tracks in the road

**trombone** /trɒmˈbəʊn/ *noun* [C] a metal musical instrument that you play by blowing into it and sliding a tube up and down

**troop¹** /truːp/ *noun* [C] a group of people or animals

**troop²** /truːp/ *verb informal* **troop into/through/out of, etc** to walk somewhere in a large group *We all trooped into the hall in silence.*

**trooper** /'truːpəʳ/ *noun* [C] a police officer in the US state police force

**troops** /truːps/ *noun* [plural] soldiers *UN troops have been sent to help in the rescue effort.*

**trophy** /'trəʊfi/ *noun* [C] a prize, such as a silver cup, that you get for winning a race or competition

**tropical** /'trɒpɪkᵊl/ *adj* from or in the hottest parts of the world *a tropical climate* • *tropical diseases*

**the tropics** /'trɒpɪks/ *noun* [plural] the hottest parts of the world, near to the Equator (= imaginary line around the Earth's middle)

**trot¹** /trɒt/ *verb* **trotting**, *past* **trotted** **1** [I] If a horse trots, it runs slowly with short steps. **2 trot down/up/along, etc** to walk with quick, short steps *The little boy trotted along behind his father.*

**trot sth out** *informal* to say something that has been said many times before and does not seem sincere *They always trot out the same old statistics.*

**trot²** /trɒt/ *noun* **1** [no plural] the speed that a horse moves when it trots **2 on the trot** If you do several things on the trot, you do them one after the other. *They won three games on the trot.*

**trouble¹** /'trʌbl/ *noun* **1** PROBLEMS [C, U] problems, difficulties, or worries [+ doing sth] *We had trouble finding somewhere to park.* • *She's been having a lot of trouble with her boss recently.* • *I'd like to go to the party, but the trouble is my parents won't let me.* **2 the trouble with sb/sth** used to say what is wrong with someone or something *The trouble with a white floor is that it gets dirty so quickly.* • *The trouble with John is that he doesn't think before he speaks.* **3** NOT WORKING [U] a problem that you have with a machine or part of your body *back trouble* • *car trouble* **4** FIGHTING [U] a situation in which people are fighting or arguing *The trouble started after a group of drunken football fans started to throw bottles.* **5** DIFFICULT SITUATION [U] a difficult or dangerous situation *The company was in trouble and had huge debts.* **6** PUNISHMENT [U] when you have done something wrong and are likely to be punished *Her children are always in trouble.* • *They got into trouble with the police.* **7** EXTRA WORK [U] when you use extra time or energy to do something [+ to do sth] *He took the trouble to write to each of them personally.* • *"Would you like to have a meal with us?" "Only if it's not too much trouble."*

**trolley**

supermarket trolley *UK*, shopping cart *US*

luggage trolley *UK*, luggage cart *US*

**USAGE**

**trouble** or **problem**?

Problem means 'a situation that causes difficulties and that needs to be dealt with'. You can talk about a

**problem** or **problems**.

*Tell me what the problem is.*

*There's a problem with the engine.*

*He's having a few problems at work.*

**Trouble** means 'problems, difficulties, or worries' and is used to talk about problems in a more general way. **Trouble** is almost always uncountable so do not use the determiner 'a' before it.

*We had some trouble while we were on holiday.*

*He helped me when I was in trouble.*

*I had trouble with the car last night.*

~~I had a trouble with the car last night.~~

**trouble²** /'trʌbl/ *verb* [T] **1** If something troubles you, you think about it a lot and it makes you worry. *The situation has been troubling me for a while.* • *a troubled expression* **2** *formal* used to ask someone politely to help you *I'm sorry to trouble you, but could you tell me how to get to the station?*

**troublemaker** /'trʌbl,meɪkəʳ/ *noun* [C] someone who intentionally causes problems

**troublesome** /'trʌblsəm/ *adj* causing a lot of problems, especially over a long period of time *a troublesome knee injury*

**trough** /trɒf/ *noun* [C] **1** a long, narrow container that animals eat or drink from **2** *formal* a low point in a series of high and low points *peaks and troughs*

**troupe** /tru:p/ *noun* [C] a group of singers, dancers, etc who perform together

o⤴**trousers** /'traʊzəz/ (*also US* **pants**) *noun* [plural] a piece of clothing that covers the legs and has a separate part for each leg *a pair of trousers* ➔ *See colour picture* **Clothes** *on page Centre 5.*

'**trouser ,suit** *UK* (*US* **pant suit**) *noun* [C] a woman's jacket and trousers made of the same material

**trout** /traʊt/ *noun* [C, U] *plural* **trout** a type of river fish, or the meat from this fish

**truant** /'tru:ənt/ *noun* [C] **1** a child who stays away from school without permission **2 play truant** *UK* to stay away from school without permission • truancy /'tru:ənsi/ *noun* [U] when children are truants

**truce** /tru:s/ *noun* [C] an agreement between two enemies to stop fighting for a period of time

o⤴**truck** /trʌk/ (*also UK* **lorry**) *noun* [C] a large road vehicle for carrying goods from place to place ➔ *See picture at* **vehicle**.

**trucker** /'trʌkəʳ/ *noun* [C] *mainly US* someone whose job is driving trucks

**trudge** /trʌdʒ/ *verb* **trudge along/through/up, etc** to walk slowly with heavy steps, especially because you are tired *We trudged back up the hill.*

o⤴**true** /tru:/ *adj* **1** based on facts and not imagined *a true story* • [+ (that)] *Is it true that Martin and Sue are getting married?* ➔ *See usage note at* **right** ➔ *Opposite* **untrue**. **2** [always before noun] real *a true friend* • *true love* **3 come true** If a dream or hope comes true, it really happens. *I always dreamt of winning money but I never thought it would come true.* **4 be true to sb/sth**

to be loyal and sincere even in a difficult situation *It's important to be true to your principles.* **5 ring true** to seem to be the truth *Something about the story didn't ring true.*

**truffle** /'trʌfl/ *noun* [C] **1** a soft sweet that is made with chocolate **2** a fungus (= organism like a plant) that you can eat, which grows under the ground

**truly** /'tru:li/ *adv* **1** NOT FALSE used to emphasize that something is true in every way *The project was truly a team effort.* **2** VERY used to emphasize a description of something *It's truly amazing to watch a baby being born.* **3** SINCERE used to emphasize that something is sincere or honest *I truly believe that he is innocent.*

**trump** /trʌmp/ *noun* **1** [C] a card that has a higher value than other cards in some card games **2 come/turn up trumps** *UK* to be successful, or provide something that is needed, especially when people do not expect you to *He's really come up trumps with this latest book.*

'**trump ,card** *noun* [C] an advantage that will help you succeed, especially one that other people do not know about

**trumpet** /'trʌmpɪt/ *noun* [C] a metal musical instrument that you play by blowing into it and pressing buttons to make different notes • trumpeter *noun* [C]

**truncheon** /'trʌnʃⁿn/ *UK* (*US* **nightstick**) *noun* [C] a short stick that police officers carry to use as a weapon

**trundle** /'trʌndl/ *verb* **trundle (sth) along/down/up, etc** to move slowly on wheels, or to push something slowly on wheels *The bus trundled along the lane.*

**trunk** /trʌŋk/ *noun* [C] **1** TREE the thick stem of a tree that the branches grow from ➔ *See picture at* **tree**. **2** CAR *US* (*UK* **boot**) a closed space at the back of a car for storing things in ➔ *See colour picture* **Car** *on page Centre 3.* **3** NOSE the long nose of an elephant (= large, grey animal) **4** CONTAINER a large box with a lid that you store things in **5** BODY the main part of your body, not your head, legs, or arms

'**trunk ,road** *noun* [C] *UK* a main road across a country or area

**trunks** /trʌŋks/ (*also* **swimming trunks**) *noun* [plural] a piece of clothing that boys and men wear when they swim ➔ *See colour picture* **Clothes** *on page Centre 5.*

o⤴**trust¹** /trʌst/ *verb* **1** [T] to believe that someone is good and honest and will not harm you *My sister warned me not to trust him.* ➔ *Opposite* **distrust, mistrust. 2 trust sb to do sth** to be sure that someone will do the right thing or what they should do *I trust them to make the right decision.* **3 trust sb with sb/sth** to allow someone to look after someone or something because you believe they will be careful *I wouldn't trust him with my car.* **4 Trust sb (to do sth)!** *mainly UK informal* used to say that it is typical of someone to do something stupid *Trust Chris to leave the tickets at home!* **5 I trust (that)** *formal* used to say that you hope something is true *I trust that you had an enjoyable stay.*

o⤴**trust²** /trʌst/ *noun* **1** [U] the belief that you can

**T**

trust someone or something *a marriage based on love and trust* • *They **showed** a lot of **trust** in me right from the beginning.* ➲ *Opposite* **distrust, mistrust**. **2** [C, U] a legal arrangement that allows a person or organization to control someone else's money

**trustee** /trʌsˈtiː/ *noun* [C] someone who has legal control over someone else's money or possessions

**trusting** /ˈtrʌstɪŋ/ *adj* always believing that other people are good or honest and will not harm or deceive you

**trustworthy** /ˈtrʌst,wɜːði/ *adj* Someone who is trustworthy can be trusted.

o⚊**truth** /truːθ/ *noun plural* **truths** /truːðz/ **1** **the truth** the real facts about a situation *Do you think he was **telling the truth**? • I don't think we'll ever know **the truth about** what really happened.* **2** [U] the quality of being true *There may be some truth in their claim.* **3** [C] a fact or idea that people accept is true *moral/religious truths* ➲ *Opposite* **untruth**.

**truthful** /ˈtruːθfᵊl/ *adj* honest and not containing or telling any lies *a truthful answer* • truthfully *adv* • truthfulness *noun* [U]

o⚊**try**¹ /traɪ/ *verb* **1** [ATTEMPT] [I] to attempt to do something [+ **to do sth**] *I tried to open the window but couldn't.* • *Try not to drop anything this time.* **2** [TEST] [T] to do, test, taste, etc something to discover if it works or if you like it *I tried that recipe you gave me last night.* • *He tried the door, but the handle was broken.* **3** [+ **doing sth**] *Why don't you try using a different shampoo?* **3** [LAW] [T] to examine facts in a court of law to decide if someone is guilty of a crime [often passive] *He was **tried for** attempted murder.*

**try sth on** to put on a piece of clothing to discover if it fits you or if you like it *Could I try this dress on, please?*

**try sth out** to use something to discover if it works or if you like it *We're going to try out that new restaurant tonight.*

**try**² /traɪ/ *noun* **1** [C] an attempt to do something *She suggested I should **have a try**.* **2** **give sth a try** to do something in order to find out if it works or if you like it **3** [C] when a team scores points in rugby (= game played with an oval ball) by putting the ball on the ground behind the other team's goal line

**trying** /ˈtraɪɪŋ/ *adj* annoying and difficult *I've had a very trying day.*

**tsar** *UK* (*UK/US* **czar**) /zɑːʳ/ *noun* [C] **1** a male Russian ruler before 1917 **2** a powerful official who makes important decisions for the government about a particular activity

**T-shirt** (*also* **tee shirt**) /ˈtiːʃɜːt/ *noun* [C] a piece of cotton clothing for the top part of the body with short sleeves and no collar ➲ *See colour picture* **Clothes** *on page Centre 5*.

**tsp** *written abbreviation for* teaspoonful: the amount that can be held by a small spoon used for measuring food

**tub** /tʌb/ *noun* [C] **1** [LARGE CONTAINER] a large, round container with a flat base and an open top *Outside was a stone patio with tubs of flowering plants.* **2** [FOOD CONTAINER] a small, plastic container with a lid, used for storing food *a tub of ice cream/margarine* ➲ *See picture at*

**container**. **3** [BATH] *US* (*UK* **bath**) a large container that you fill with water and sit in to wash ➲ *See colour picture* **The bathroom** *on page Centre 1*.

**tuba** /ˈtjuːbə/ *noun* [C] a large, metal musical instrument that produces low notes, and is played by blowing into it

**tube** /tjuːb/ *noun* **1** [C] a pipe made of glass, plastic, metal, etc, especially for liquids or gases to flow through **2** [C] a long, thin container for a soft substance, that you press to get the substance out *a tube of toothpaste* ➲ *See picture at* **container**. **3** **the Tube** the system of railways under the ground in London *I got the Tube to Oxford Circus.* ➲ *See also:* **test tube**.

**tuberculosis** /tjuː,bɜːkjəˈləʊsɪs/ *noun* [U] a serious infectious disease of the lungs

**tubing** /ˈtjuːbɪŋ/ *noun* [U] a long piece of metal, plastic, etc in the shape of a tube *steel tubing*

**tubular** /ˈtjuːbjələʳ/ *adj* in the shape of a tube

**tuck** /tʌk/ *verb* **1 tuck sth into/behind/under, etc** to push a loose piece of clothing or material somewhere to make it tidy *Tuck your shirt in.* • *I tucked the sheet under the mattress.* **2 tuck sth behind/under/in, etc** to put something in a small place so that it is safe and cannot move *I found an old letter tucked in the back of the book.*

**tuck sth away** to put something in a safe place *Helen tucked the money away in her purse.*

**be tucked away** to be in a place that is hidden, or in a place that few people go to *He lives in a cottage tucked away in the Suffolk countryside.*

**tuck in/tuck into sth** *UK informal* to start eating something, especially with enthusiasm *I was just about to tuck into a huge bowl of pasta.*

**tuck sb in/up** to make someone, especially a child, comfortable in bed by putting the covers around them

**Tuesday** /ˈtjuːzdeɪ/ (*written abbreviation* **Tue, Tues**) *noun* [C, U] the day of the week after Monday and before Wednesday

**tuft** /tʌft/ *noun* [C] a small group of hairs, grass, etc

**tug**¹ /tʌg/ *verb* [T] **tugging**, *past* **tugged** to pull something suddenly and strongly *Tom tugged at his mother's arm.*

**tug**² /tʌg/ *noun* [C] **1** a sudden, strong pull on something **2** (*also* **tugboat** /ˈtʌgbəʊt/) a boat used for pulling larger ships

**tuition** /tjuˈɪʃᵊn/ *noun* [U] **1** the teaching of one person or of a small group of people *French tuition* **2** *mainly US* money that you pay for being taught, especially at college or university

**tulip** /ˈtjuːlɪp/ *noun* [C] a brightly coloured spring flower in the shape of a cup

**tumble** /ˈtʌmbl/ *verb* [I] **1** to suddenly fall *He tumbled down the stairs.* **2** If the price or value of something tumbles, it suddenly becomes lower. *Share prices tumbled by 20%.* • tumble *noun* [C]

**tumble dryer** *UK* (*US* **dryer**) *noun* [C] a machine that dries clothes

**tumbler** /ˈtʌmbləʳ/ *noun* [C] a glass that you drink out of, that has straight sides and no handle

**tummy** /ˈtʌmi/ *noun* [C] *informal* stomach

**tumour** *UK* (*US* **tumor**) /ˈtjuːməʳ/ *noun* [C] a

group of cells in someone's body which are not growing normally

**tumultuous** /tjuːˈmʌltjuəs/ *adj* full of noise and excitement *tumultuous applause*

**tuna** /ˈtjuːnə/ *noun* [C, U] *plural* **tuna** a large sea fish, or the meat from this fish

**tune¹** /tjuːn/ *noun* **1** [C] a series of musical notes that are pleasant to listen to *He was humming a tune as he dried the dishes.* **2 in tune** singing or playing the right notes **3 out of tune** singing or playing the wrong notes *The piano is out of tune.* **4 change your tune** to suddenly change your opinion about something **5 be in tune with sb** to be able to understand what someone wants or needs *The government is not in tune with the voters.*

**tune²** /tjuːn/ *verb* [T] **1** to make slight changes to a musical instrument so that it plays the right notes **2** to make changes to a television or radio so that it receives programmes from a particular company *Stay tuned for* (= continue watching or listening for) *more details.* • *The radio is tuned to Radio 5.*

**tune in** to watch or listen to a particular television or radio programme *Be sure to tune in to next week's show.*

**tune (sth) up** to make slight changes to a musical instrument before you play it so that it produces the right notes *The orchestra were tuning up.*

**tunic** /ˈtjuːnɪk/ *noun* [C] a loose piece of clothing that covers the top part of your body

o-**tunnel¹** /ˈtʌnᵊl/ *noun* [C] a long passage under the ground or through a mountain *The train went into the tunnel.* ⊃ *See also:* **light¹** at the end of the tunnel.

**tunnel²** /ˈtʌnᵊl/ *verb* [I, T] *(UK)* **tunnelling**, *past* **tunnelled**, *(US)* **tunneling**, *past* **tunneled** to dig a tunnel

**turban** /ˈtɜːbən/ *noun* [C] a long piece of cloth that men from some religions fold around their heads

**turbine** /ˈtɜːbaɪn/ *noun* [C] a large machine that produces power by using gas, steam, etc to turn a wheel

**turbulent** /ˈtɜːbjələnt/ *adj* **1** A turbulent situation, time, etc is one in which there are a lot of sudden changes, arguments, or violence. *a turbulent relationship* **2** Turbulent air or water moves very strongly and suddenly. • **turbulence** /ˈtɜːbjələns/ *noun* [U]

**turf¹** /tɜːf/ *noun* [U] short, thick grass and the soil it is growing in

**turf²** /tɜːf/ *verb*

**turf sb out** *UK informal* to make someone leave

**turkey** /ˈtɜːki/ *noun* [C, U] a bird that looks like a large chicken, or the meat of this bird

**turmoil** /ˈtɜːmɔɪl/ *noun* [U, no plural] a situation in which there is a lot of trouble, confusion, or noise *The whole region is in turmoil.*

o-**turn¹** /tɜːn/ *verb* **1** MOVE YOUR BODY [I] to move your body so that you are facing a different direction *Ricky turned and saw Sue standing in the doorway.* **2** CHANGE DIRECTION [I, T] to change direction when you are moving, or to make a car do this *Turn left at the traffic lights.* • *I turned the car into the drive.* **3** CHANGE POSITION [T] to move something round so that it

faces a different direction *Ella turned the cup to hide the crack in it.* **4** GO ROUND [I, T] to move around a central point in a circle, or to make something do this *Turn the steering wheel as quickly as you can.* **5 turn blue/cold/sour, etc** to become blue, cold, etc *The sky turned black and it started to rain.* **6 turn 16/21, etc** to become a particular age or time *He turned 18 last May.* **7 turn a page** to move a page in a book or magazine in order to see the next one ⊃ *See also:* turn your **back²** on sb/sth, turn the **clock¹** back, turn a blind **eye¹** (to sth), turn over a new **leaf¹**, turn your **nose¹** up at sth, turn the tables (**table¹**) on sb, turn up trumps (**trump**), turn sth **upside down¹**.

**turn sb away** to not allow someone to enter a place *By 10 o'clock the club was already full and they were turning people away.*

**turn (sb) back** to return in the direction you have come from, or to make someone do this *They had to turn back because of the bad weather.*

**turn sb/sth down** to refuse an offer or request *They did offer me the job, but I turned it down.*

**turn sth down** to reduce the level of sound or heat that a machine produces *Could you turn the radio down, please?*

**turn (sb/sth) into sb/sth** to change and become someone or something different, or to make someone or something do this *There are plans to turn his latest book into a film.* • *They've turned an old factory into a nightclub.*

**turn off (sth)** to leave the road you are driving along and drive on a different road

**turn sth off** to move the switch on a machine, light, etc so that it stops working, or to stop the supply of water, electricity, etc *How do you turn the computer off?* • *She turned off the lights and went to sleep.* ⊃ *See colour picture* **Phrasal Verbs** *on page Centre 13.*

**turn sth on** to move the switch on a machine, light, etc so that it starts working, or to start the supply of water, electricity, etc *Ben turned the TV on.* ⊃ *See colour picture* **Phrasal Verbs** *on page Centre 13.*

**turn out 1** to happen in a particular way, or to have a particular result *The bomb warning turned out to be a false alarm.* • [+ (that)] *I got talking to her and it turned out that we'd been to the same school.* **2** If people turn out for an event, they go to be there or watch. *Over 800 people turned out for the protest.*

**turn sth out 1** to produce something *The factory turns out more than 600 vehicles a month.* **2** to move the switch on a light so that it stops working

**turn (sth) over** *UK* to change to a different television station *Are you watching this or can I turn over?*

**turn to sb** to ask someone for help or advice *Eventually she turned to her aunt for help.*

**turn to sth 1** to find a page in a book *Turn to page 105.* **2** to start to do something bad, especially because you are unhappy *She turned to drugs after the break-up of her marriage.*

**turn up 1** *informal* to arrive *Fred turned up late again.* **2** If something that you have been looking for turns up, you find it.

**turn sth up** to increase the level of sound or heat that a machine produces *I'm cold, could you turn the heating up please?*

o━**turn²** /tɜːn/ *noun* **1** [TIME] [C] the time when you can or must do something, usually before or after someone else [+ to do sth] *It's your turn to feed the rabbit – I did it yesterday.* • *You'll have to be patient and wait your turn.* **2 take turns** (*also UK* **take it in turns**) If two or more people take turns, one person does something, then another person does something, etc. [+ doing sth] *They all took turns carrying the suitcase.* • [+ to do sth] *The children took it in turns to hold the baby.* **3 in turn** one after another *He spoke to the three boys in turn.* **4** [CHANGE DIRECTION] [C] a change in the direction in which you are moving or facing *a right/left turn* **5** [BEND] [C] a bend or corner in a road, river, etc *Take the next turn on the right.* **6 turn of events** the way in which a situation develops, especially a sudden or unexpected change **7 take a turn for the better/worse** to become better or worse suddenly **8 do sb a good turn** to do something to help someone **9 the turn of the century** the start of a new century ⊃ *See also:* **U-turn,** turn over a new **leaf¹**.

**turnaround** /'tɜːnˀraʊnd/ *noun* [C] when a bad situation changes into a good one

**turning** /'tɜːnɪŋ/ *noun* [C] *UK* a corner where one road meets another *Take the second turning on the left.*

'**turning ,point** *noun* [C] a time when an important change begins to happen *This event marked a turning point in the country's history.*

**turnip** /'tɜːnɪp/ *noun* [C, U] a large, round, pale yellow vegetable that grows under the ground

**turn-off** /'tɜːnɒf/ *noun* **1** [C] a place where you can leave a main road to go onto another road **2** [no plural] *informal* something which you dislike or which makes you feel less interested, especially sexually *Greasy hair is a real turn-off.*

**turnout** /'tɜːnaʊt/ *noun* [C] the number of people at an event, such as a meeting or election [usually singular] *They blamed the low turnout on the bad weather.*

**turnover** /'tɜːn,əʊvəʳ/ *noun* **1** [no plural] how much money a business earns in a period of time **2** [U, no plural] the rate at which workers leave an organization and new workers join it *a high turnover of staff*

'**turn ,signal** *US* (*UK* **indicator**) *noun* [C] a light that flashes on a vehicle to show that the driver intends to turn right or left ⊃ *See colour picture* **Car** *on page Centre 3.*

**turnstile** /'tɜːnstaɪl/ *noun* [C] a gate that only allows one person to go through it at a time

**turpentine** /'tɜːpˀntaɪn/ (*also UK* **turps** /tɜːps/) *noun* [U] a clear liquid that has a strong smell and is used for removing paint

**turquoise** /'tɜːkwɔɪz/ *noun* [U] a blue-green colour • **turquoise** *adj*

**turret** /'tʌrɪt/ *noun* [C] a small tower that is part of a building

**turtle** /'tɜːtl/ *noun* [C] an animal with four legs and a hard shell that lives mainly in water

**turtleneck** /'tɜːtlnek/ *US* (*UK* **polo neck**) *noun*

[C] a piece of clothing that covers the top part of the body and has a tube-like part covering the neck *a turtleneck sweater* ⊃ *See picture at* **polo neck.**

**tusk** /tʌsk/ *noun* [C] one of the two long, pointed teeth that come out of the mouth of some animals

**tussle** /'tʌsl/ *noun* [C] a fight or argument, especially between two people who want the same thing

**tut** /tʌt/ (*also* **tut-tut**) *exclamation* a sound you make when you do not approve of something

**tutor** /'tjuːtəʳ/ *noun* **1** someone who teaches one person or a very small group of people *a private tutor* **2** *UK* a university teacher who is responsible for a small group of students • **tutor** *verb* [T]

**tutorial** /tjuː'tɔːriəl/ *noun* [C] **1** a class in which a small group of students talks about a subject with their tutor, especially at a British university **2** a set of instructions and exercises that teaches you how to use a computer program

**tux** /tʌks/ *noun* [C] *US short for* tuxedo

**tuxedo** /tʌk'siːdəʊ/ *US* (*UK* **dinner jacket**) *noun* [C] a black or white jacket that a man wears on a very formal occasion ⊃ *See picture at* **dinner jacket.**

o━**TV** (*also* **tv**) /,tiː'viː/ *noun* [C, U] *abbreviation for* television *What's on TV tonight?* • *We could stay in and watch TV.* ⊃ *See colour picture* **The Living Room** *on page Centre 11.*

**twang** /twæŋ/ *noun* [C] the sound that is made by pulling a tight string or wire • **twang** *verb* [I, T]

**tweak** /twiːk/ *verb* [T] **1** to change something slightly to try to improve it **2** to pull or twist something quickly and suddenly *Dad sat there tweaking his beard.* • **tweak** *noun* [C]

**tweed** /twiːd/ *noun* [U] a thick, rough cloth made of wool

**tweezers** /'twiːzəz/ *noun* [plural] a small tool with two narrow pieces of metal joined at one end, used for picking up or pulling out very small things

**twelfth¹** /twelfθ/ 12th written as a word

**twelfth²** /twelfθ/ *noun* [C] one of twelve equal parts of something; 1/12

**twelve** /twelv/ the number 12

**twenty** /'twenti/ **1** the number 20 **2 the twenties** the years from 1920 to 1929 **3 be in your twenties** to be aged between 20 and 29 • **twenti-eth** 20th written as a word

o━**twice** /twaɪs/ *adv* two times *I've been there twice.* • *I have to take the tablets twice a day.*

**twiddle** /'twɪdl/ *verb* [I, T] to move your fingers around, or turn something around many times, especially because you are bored *Karen just sat there twiddling with her hair.*

**twig** /twɪg/ *noun* [C] a small, thin branch on a tree ⊃ *See picture at* **tree.**

**twilight** /'twaɪlaɪt/ *noun* [U] the time just before it becomes completely dark in the evening

o━**twin¹** /twɪn/ *noun* [C] one of two children who are born to the same mother at the same time ⊃ *See also:* **identical twin.**

**twin²** /twɪn/ *adj* [always before noun] used to describe two similar things that are a pair *twin beds*

**twin³** /twɪn/ *verb past* **twinned** *UK* **be twinned**

**with sth** If a town in one country is twinned with a town in another country, the two towns have a special relationship. *Leeds in England is twinned with Dortmund in Germany.*

**twinge** /twɪndʒ/ *noun* [C] **1** a sudden, slight emotion *a twinge of guilt* **2** a sudden, slight pain

**twinkle** /'twɪŋkl/ *verb* [I] **1** If light twinkles, it shines and seems to be quickly flashing on and off. *The lights of the town twinkled in the distance.* **2** If someone's eyes twinkle, they look bright and happy. • **twinkle** *noun* [C]

**twirl** /twɜːl/ *verb* [I, T] to turn around and around quickly, or to make something do this • **twirl** *noun* [C]

o⤴**twist¹** /twɪst/ *verb* **1** TURN [T] to turn something using your hand *She sat there nervously twisting the ring around on her finger.* **2** BEND [T] to bend and turn something many times and change its shape *The wheels of the bike had been twisted in the accident.*

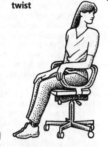

twist

**3** TURN YOUR BODY [I, T] to turn part of your body to face a different direction *She twisted her head so she could see what was happening.* **4** CHANGE DIRECTION [I] If a road, river, etc twists, it has a lot of bends in it. *The path twisted and turned up the side of the mountain.* **5** INJURE [T] If you twist a part of your body, such as your knee, you injure it by turning it suddenly. **6** CHANGE MEANING [T] to unfairly change the meaning of something that someone has said *Journalists had twisted his remarks.* ➜ *See also:* twist sb's **arm¹**.

**twist²** /twɪst/ *noun* **1** UNEXPECTED CHANGE a sudden change in a story or situation that you do not expect *The story has an unusual twist at the end.* **2** MOVEMENT when you twist something **3** PART a part of something that is twisted *There's a twist in the wire.* **4** SHAPE a shape that is made by twisting something *Finally, add a twist of lemon for decoration.* **5** RIVER/ROAD a bend in a river, road, etc

**twisted** /'twɪstɪd/ *adj* **1** Something that is twisted is bent a lot of times and does not have its usual shape. **2** strange and slightly unpleasant or cruel *He'd become bitter and twisted.*

**twister** /'twɪstər/ *noun* [C] *US* another word for tornado (= an extremely strong and dangerous wind that blows in a circle) ➜ *See also:* **tongue twister**.

**twit** /twɪt/ *noun* [C] *informal* a silly person

**twitch** /twɪtʃ/ *verb* [I] If a part of your body twitches, it suddenly makes a slight movement in a way that you cannot control. *His face twitched nervously.* • **twitch** *noun* [C]

**twitter** /'twɪtər/ *verb* [I] If a bird twitters, it makes a series of short, high sounds.

**two** /tuː/ **1** the number 2 **2** in **two** into two

pieces *She broke the chocolate in two.* **3** put **two and two together** to guess the truth from details that you notice about a situation *She didn't tell me she was pregnant – I just put two and two together.* ➜ *See also:* stand on your own two feet (**foot¹**), the **lesser** of two evils, be in two minds (**mind¹**).

**two-time** /ˌtuːˈtaɪm/ *verb* [T] *informal* If someone two-times their partner, they secretly have a romantic relationship with someone else.

**two-way** /'tuːˌweɪ/ *adj* moving, or allowing something to move or work in two directions *a two-way street*

**tycoon** /taɪˈkuːn/ *noun* [C] someone who is very successful and powerful in business and has a lot of money *a media tycoon*

**tying** /'taɪɪŋ/ *present participle of* tie

o⤴**type¹** /taɪp/ *noun* [C] **1** a person or thing that is part of a group of people or things that have similar qualities, or a group of people or things that have similar qualities *They sell over 20 different types of cheese.* • *Illnesses of this type are very common in children.* **2** someone who has particular qualities or interests *He's the outdoor type* (= enjoys being outside). **3** not be **sb's type** *informal* to not be the type of person that someone thinks is attractive *I like Bertrand but he's not really my type.* ➜ *See also:* **blood type**.

**type²** /taɪp/ *verb* [I, T] to write something using a keyboard • **typing** *noun* [U]

**typewriter** /'taɪpˌraɪtər/ *noun* [C] a machine with keys that you press to produce letters and numbers on paper • **typewritten** /'taɪpˌrɪtᵊn/ *adj* printed using a typewriter *a typewritten letter*

**typhoid** /'taɪfɔɪd/ *noun* [U] a serious infectious disease that is caused by dirty water or food

**typhoon** /taɪˈfuːn/ *noun* [C] a violent storm with very strong winds

o⤴**typical** /'tɪpɪkᵊl/ *adj* having all the qualities you expect a particular person, object, place, etc to have *typical German food* • *This style of painting is typical of Monet.*

**typically** /'tɪpɪkᵊli/ *adv* **1** used for saying that something is typical of a person, thing, place, etc *behaviour that is typically English* **2** used for saying what usually happens *Schools in the area typically start at 8.30.*

**typify** /'tɪpɪfaɪ/ *verb* [T] to be a typical example or quality of something *Emma's opinions typify the attitude of many young people.*

**typist** /'taɪpɪst/ *noun* [C] someone who types (= writes using a machine), especially as their job

**tyranny** /'tɪrᵊni/ *noun* [U] when a leader or government has too much power and uses that power in a cruel and unfair way • **tyrannical** /tɪˈrænɪkᵊl/ *adj* using or involving tyranny

**tyrant** /'taɪərᵊnt/ *noun* [C] someone who has total power and uses it in a cruel and unfair way

**tyre** *UK* (*US* **tire**) /taɪər/ *noun* [C] a thick, round piece of rubber filled with air, that fits around a wheel *It's got a flat tyre* (= tyre with no air in it). ➜ *See colour picture* Car *on page Centre 3.*

# U, u

**U, u** /juː/ the twenty-first letter of the alphabet

**ubiquitous** /juːˈbɪkwɪtəs/ *adj formal* seeming to be in all places *the ubiquitous security cameras*

**udder** /ˈʌdər/ *noun* [C] the part of a female cow, goat, etc that hangs under its body and produces milk

**UFO** /ˌjuːefˈəʊ/ *noun* [C] *abbreviation for* unidentified flying object: something strange that you see in the sky that could be from another part of the universe

**ugh** /ʌɡ/ *exclamation* used to show that you think something is very unpleasant *Ugh! What a smell!*

o⁻**ugly** /ˈʌɡli/ *adj* **1** unpleasant to look at *an ugly city* **2** An ugly situation is very unpleasant, usually because it involves violence. *There were ugly scenes outside the stadium.* • ugliness *noun* [U] **Ɔ** *See also:* raise/rear its ugly **head¹**.

**uh** *US* (*UK* **er**) /ə/ *exclamation* something that you say when you are thinking what to say next *It's not too far – it's about, uh, five miles from here.*

**UK** /ˌjuːˈkeɪ/ *noun abbreviation for* United Kingdom

**ulcer** /ˈʌlsər/ *noun* [C] a painful, infected area on your skin or inside your body *a mouth/stomach ulcer*

**ulterior** /ʌlˈtɪəriər/ *adj* **ulterior motive/purpose, etc** a secret purpose or reason for doing something

**ultimate¹** /ˈʌltɪmət/ *adj* [always before noun] **1** better, worse, or greater than all similar things *Climbing Mount Everest is the ultimate challenge.* • *the ultimate insult* **2** final or most important *the ultimate aim/solution*

**ultimate²** /ˈʌltɪmət/ *noun* **the ultimate in sth** the best or greatest example of something *It describes the hotel as 'the ultimate in luxury'.*

**ultimately** /ˈʌltɪmətli/ *adv* **1** finally, after a series of things have happened *a disease that ultimately killed him* **2** used to emphasize the most important fact in a situation *Ultimately, he'll have to decide.*

**ultimatum** /ˌʌltɪˈmeɪtəm/ *noun* [C] when someone says they will do something that will affect you badly if you do not do what they want *The children were given an ultimatum – finish their work quietly or stay behind after class.*

**ultrasonic** /ˌʌltrəˈsɒnɪk/ *adj* involving ultrasound

**ultrasound** /ˈʌltrəsaʊnd/ *noun* [U] very high sound waves that are used in medical tests to produce a picture of something inside your body *an ultrasound scan*

**ultraviolet** /ˌʌltrəˈvaɪələt/ *adj* Ultraviolet light makes your skin become darker.

**umbilical cord** /ʌmˈbɪlɪklˌkɔːd/ *noun* [C] the tube that connects a baby to its mother before it is born

**umbrella** /ʌmˈbrelə/ *noun* [C] **1** a thing that you hold above your head to keep yourself dry when it is raining **2 umbrella group/organization, etc** a large organization that is made of many smaller organizations

**umpire** /ˈʌmpaɪər/ *noun* [C] someone whose job is to watch a sports game and make sure that the players obey the rules *a tennis/cricket umpire* • umpire *verb* [I, T]

**umpteen** /ʌmˈtiːn/ *quantifier informal* very many *I've been there umpteen times and I still can't remember the way.* • umpteenth *I drank my umpteenth cup of coffee.*

**the UN** /ˌjuːˈen/ *noun abbreviation for* the United Nations: an international organization that tries to solve world problems in a peaceful way

o⁻**unable** /ʌnˈeɪbl/ *adj* **be unable to do sth** to not be able to do something *Some days he is unable to get out of bed.*

**unabridged** /ˌʌnəˈbrɪdʒd/ *adj* An unabridged book, play, etc is in its original form and has not been made shorter.

**unacceptable** /ˌʌnəkˈseptəbl/ *adj* too bad to be allowed to continue *The water contains unacceptable levels of pollution.* • *I find that sort of behaviour completely unacceptable.* • unacceptably *adv*

**unaccompanied** /ˌʌnəˈkʌmpənid/ *adj* not having anyone with you when you go somewhere *Unaccompanied children are not allowed in the museum.*

**unaccountable** /ˌʌnəˈkaʊntəbl/ *adj* **1** impossible to explain *For some unaccountable reason, I've got three copies of the same book.* **2** not having to give reasons for your actions or decisions • unaccountably *adv*

**unaffected** /ˌʌnəˈfektɪd/ *adj* not changed by something *Smaller colleges will be unaffected by the new regulations.*

**unaided** /ʌnˈeɪdɪd/ *adj, adv* without help *He's now well enough to walk unaided.*

**unanimous** /juːˈnænɪməs/ *adj* agreed by everyone *The jury was unanimous in finding Simpson guilty.* • unanimity /ˌjuːnəˈnɪməti/ *noun* [U] when everyone agrees about something • unanimously *adv* *The members unanimously agreed to the proposal.*

**unannounced** /ˌʌnəˈnaʊnst/ *adj, adv* without telling anyone first *an unannounced visit* • *They arrived unannounced on Saturday.*

**unarmed** /ʌnˈɑːmd/ *adj* not carrying a weapon

**unashamedly** /ˌʌnəˈʃeɪmɪdli/ *adv* in a way that shows you are not embarrassed or worried about what other people think of you *Galliano is unashamedly romantic.*

**unassuming** /ˌʌnəˈsjuːmɪŋ/ *adj* not wanting to be noticed *a shy, unassuming man*

**unattached** /ˌʌnəˈtætʃt/ *adj* not married or having a romantic relationship

**unattended** /ˌʌnəˈtendɪd/ *adj* not being watched or looked after *Passengers should not leave bags unattended.*

**unattractive** /ˌʌnəˈtræktɪv/ *adj* **1** not beautiful or nice to look at *I felt old and unattractive.* **2** not interesting or useful *an unattractive proposition*

**unauthorized** (*also UK* -**ised**) /ʌnˈɔːθəraɪzd/ *adj* done without official permission *an unauthorized use of company money*

**unavailable** /ˌʌnəˈveɪləbl/ *adj* **1** not able to talk to someone or meet them, especially because you are doing other things *The manager was unavailable for comment.* **2** impossible to buy or get *The book is unavailable in Britain.*

**unavoidable** /ˌʌnəˈvɔɪdəbl/ *adj* impossible to avoid or prevent *an unavoidable delay*

**unaware** /ˌʌnəˈweəʳ/ *adj* [never before noun] not knowing about something *He seems totally unaware of the problem.*

**unawares** /ˌʌnəˈweəz/ *adv* **catch/take sb unawares** If something catches or takes you unawares, it happens when you do not expect it to. *The rain caught me unawares and I didn't have my umbrella.*

**unbalanced** /ʌnˈbælənst/ *adj* **1** slightly mentally ill **2** false and not fair *He gave an unbalanced view of the situation.*

**unbearable** /ʌnˈbeərəbl/ *adj* too painful or unpleasant for you to continue to experience *The heat was almost unbearable.* ● **unbearably** *adv*

**unbeatable** /ʌnˈbiːtəbl/ *adj* much better than everyone or everything else *We aim to sell the best products at unbeatable prices.*

**unbeaten** /ʌnˈbiːtʰn/ *adj* in sports, having won every game *Manchester United remain unbeaten this season.*

**unbelievable** /ˌʌnbɪˈliːvəbl/ *adj* **1** extremely bad or good and making you feel surprised *It's unbelievable how lucky she's been.* **2** not probable and difficult to believe ● **unbelievably** *adv*

**unborn** /ʌnˈbɔːn/ *adj* not yet born *the unborn child*

**unbridled** /ʌnˈbraɪdld/ *adj* An unbridled feeling is one that you do not try to hide or control. *unbridled enthusiasm*

**unbroken** /ʌnˈbrəʊkʰn/ *adj* continuous and with no pauses *unbroken sunshine*

**unbutton** /ʌnˈbʌtʰn/ *verb* [T] to open the buttons on a piece of clothing *He unbuttoned his jacket.*

**uncalled for** /ʌnˈkɔːldfɔːʳ/ *adj* If an action or remark is uncalled for, it is unfair or unkind. *That was uncalled for, Tess – apologize to your brother.*

**uncanny** /ʌnˈkæni/ *adj* strange and impossible to explain *an uncanny resemblance* ● **uncannily** *adv*

**uncertain** /ʌnˈsɜːtʰn/ *adj* **1** not sure or not able to decide about something *Bridie was uncertain about meeting him.* **2** not known, or not completely certain *The museum faces an uncertain future.* ● **uncertainly** *adv* **uncertainty** *noun* [C, U]

**unchanged** /ʌnˈtʃeɪndʒd/ *adj* staying the same *The area has remained virtually unchanged in fifty years.*

**uncharacteristic** /ˌʌnkærəktərˈɪstɪk/ *adj* not typical ● **uncharacteristically** *adv*

**unchecked** /ʌnˈtʃekt/ *adj* If something bad continues unchecked, it is not stopped.

o━**uncle** /ˈʌŋkl/ *noun* [C] the brother of your mother or father, or the husband of your aunt

**unclean** /ʌnˈkliːn/ *adj* morally bad, as described by the rules of a religion

**unclear** /ʌnˈklɪəʳ/ *adj* **1** not easy to understand *The situation at the moment is unclear.* ● [+ question word] *It's unclear what actually happened that night.* **2** If you are unclear about something, you do not understand it exactly. *I'm unclear about exactly who's doing what.*

**uncomfortable** /ʌnˈkʌmftəbl/ *adj* **1** not feeling comfortable and pleasant, or not making you feel comfortable and pleasant *I've eaten so much, I'm really quite uncomfortable.* ● *These shoes are really uncomfortable.* **2** slightly embarrassed, or making you feel slightly embarrassed *an uncomfortable silence* ● **uncomfortably** *adv*

**uncommon** /ʌnˈkɒmən/ *adj* unusual [+ for + to do sth] *It's not uncommon for people to become ill* (= they often become ill) *when they travel.* ● **uncommonly** *adv*

**uncompromising** /ʌnˈkɒmprəmaɪzɪŋ/ *adj* determined not to change your ideas or decisions *an uncompromising attitude*

**unconcerned** /ˌʌnkənˈsɜːnd/ *adj* not worried by something *The baby seemed unconcerned by all the noise.*

**unconditional** /ˌʌnkənˈdɪʃʰnʰl/ *adj* done or given without any limits and without asking for anything for yourself *unconditional love* ● **unconditionally** *adv*

**unconfirmed** /ˌʌnkənˈfɜːmd/ *adj* An unconfirmed report or story may not be true because there is no proof yet.

**unconnected** /ˌʌnkəˈnektɪd/ *adj* If two or more things are unconnected, there is no connection between them. *a series of unconnected events* ● *The stomach ailment was unconnected with his cancer.*

**unconscious**[1] /ʌnˈkɒnʃəs/ *adj* **1** in a state as though you are sleeping, for example because you have been hit on the head *She was knocked unconscious.* **2** An unconscious thought or feeling is one that you do not know you have. *an unconscious fear* ● **unconsciousness** *noun* [U]

**unconscious**[2] /ʌnˈkɒnʃəs/ *noun* [no plural] the part of your mind that contains feelings and thoughts that you do not know about, and that influences the way you behave

**unconsciously** /ʌnˈkɒnʃəsli/ *adv* If you do something unconsciously, you do it without knowing that you are doing it.

**unconstitutional** /ˌʌnˌkɒnstɪˈtjuːʃʰnʰl/ *adj* not allowed by the rules of an organization or political system

**uncontrollable** /ˌʌnkənˈtrəʊləbl/ *adj* unable to be controlled *uncontrollable anger* ● *an uncontrollable desire to cry* ● **uncontrollably** *adv*

**unconventional** /ˌʌnkənˈvenʃʰnʰl/ *adj* doing things in a way that is different from most people *an unconventional lifestyle*

**uncountable noun** /ˌʌnˌkaʊntəbʰlˈnaʊn/ (*also* **uncount noun**) *noun* [C] a noun which does not have a plural form and cannot be used with 'a' or 'one'. For example 'music' and 'furniture' are uncountable nouns. ➜ *See study section* **Countable and uncountable nouns** *on page Centre 22.*

**uncouth** /ʌn'kuːθ/ *adj* behaving in a rude, unpleasant way

**uncover** /ʌn'kʌvəʳ/ *verb* [T] **1** to discover something that had been secret or hidden *The inspectors uncovered evidence of corruption.* **2** to remove a cover from something

**undaunted** /ʌn'dɔːntɪd/ *adj* not frightened to do something that is difficult or dangerous *Keiko spoke, undaunted by the crowd.*

**undecided** /ˌʌndɪ'saɪdɪd/ *adj* If you are undecided about something, you have not made a decision yet. *I'm still undecided about whether to apply for the job.*

**undeniable** /ˌʌndɪ'naɪəbl/ *adj* certainly true *an undeniable fact* • **undeniably** *adv*

o--⬝**under**¹ /'ʌndəʳ/ *preposition* **1** BELOW below something *She pushed her bag under the table.* • *The children were sitting under a tree.* **2** BELOW THE SURFACE below the surface of something *He could only keep his head under the water for a few seconds.* **3** LESS THAN less than a number, amount, or age *You can buy the whole system for just under $2000.* • *We don't serve alcohol to anyone under 18.* **4** CONTROLLED BY controlled or governed by a particular person, organization, etc *a country under military rule* • *The restaurant is under new management.* • *I'm managing the project and have three people under me.* **5** RULE/LAW according to a rule, law, etc *Under the new law, all new buildings must be approved by the local government.* **6** IN A PARTICULAR STATE in a particular state or condition *The President is under pressure to resign.* • *Students are allowed to miss school under certain circumstances.* **7** IN PROGRESS used to say that something is happening at the moment but is not finished *A new 16-screen cinema is under construction.* • *Several different plans are under discussion.* **8** NAME using a particular name, especially one that is not your usual name *He also wrote several detective novels under the name, Edgar Sandys.* **9** PLACE IN LIST used to say which part of a list, book, library, etc you should look in to find something *Books about health problems are under 'Medicine'.*

o--⬝**under**² /'ʌndəʳ/ *adv* **1** below the surface of something *The child was swimming and suddenly started to go under.* **2** less than a particular number, amount, or age *I want a computer that is £2000 or under.*

**under-age** /ˌʌndər'eɪdʒ/ *adj* younger than the legal age when you are allowed to do something *under-age drinking*

**undercover** /ˌʌndə'kʌvəʳ/ *adj, adv* working secretly in order to get information for the police or government *an undercover police officer*

**undercut** /ˌʌndə'kʌt/ *verb* [T] **undercutting**, *past* **undercut** to sell something at a lower price than someone else

**the underdog** /'ʌndədɒg/ *noun* the person or team that is expected to lose a race or competition

**underestimate** /ˌʌndəʳr'estɪmeɪt/ *verb* [T] **1** to not understand how large, strong, or important something is *Many people underestimate the cost of owning a car.* **2** to not understand how powerful or clever someone is *I thought it would be an easy game but I had underestimated my opponent.* ➜ *Opposite* **overestimate**.

**underfoot** /ˌʌndə'fʊt/ *adv* under your feet as you walk *It's slippery underfoot.*

**undergo** /ˌʌndə'gəʊ/ *verb* [T] **undergoing**, *past t* **underwent**, *past p* **undergone** to experience something, especially a change or medical treatment *The country is currently undergoing major political change.* • *He is undergoing surgery for a heart problem.*

**undergraduate** /ˌʌndə'grædʒuət/ (*also* **undergrad** /'ʌndəgræd/ *informal*) *noun* [C] a student who is studying for their first university degree (= qualification)

**underground**¹ /'ʌndəgraʊnd/ *adj, adv* **1** under the surface of the ground *underground caves* • *an animal that lives underground* **2** Underground political activities are secret and illegal. *an underground political organization*

**underground**² /'ʌndəgraʊnd/ *UK* (*US* **subway**) *noun* [no plural] a system of trains that is built under a city *the London Underground* ➜ *See usage note at* **metro**.

**undergrowth** /'ʌndəgrəʊθ/ *noun* [U] short plants and bushes that grow around trees

**underhand** /ˌʌndə'hænd/ (*also* **underhanded**) *adj* secret and not honest *underhand business deals*

**underline** /ˌʌndə'laɪn/ *verb* [T] **1** to draw a line under a word or sentence **2** to emphasize the importance or truth of something *The report underlines the need for more teachers in schools.*

**underlying** /ˌʌndə'laɪɪŋ/ *adj* [always before noun] An underlying reason or problem is the real reason or problem, although it is not obvious. *We need to look at the underlying reasons for ill health.*

**undermine** /ˌʌndə'maɪn/ *verb* [T] to make someone less confident or make something weaker *A series of scandals have undermined people's confidence in the government.*

**underneath**¹ /ˌʌndə'niːθ/ *adv, preposition* under something *Florian was wearing a jacket with a red shirt underneath.* • *Deborah pushed her shoes underneath the bed.*

**the underneath**² /ˌʌndə'niːθ/ *noun* the bottom part of something

**underpaid** /ˌʌndə'peɪd/ *adj* not earning enough for your work

**underpants** /'ʌndəpænts/ *noun* [plural] a piece of underwear that covers the area between your waist and the top of your legs ➜ *See colour picture* **Clothes** *on page Centre 5* ➜ *See usage note at* **underwear**.

**underpass** /'ʌndəpɑːs/ *noun* [C] a road or path that goes under another road

**underprivileged** /ˌʌndə'prɪvᵊlɪdʒd/ *adj* poor and having fewer opportunities than most people *underprivileged families*

**underrate** /ˌʌndə'reɪt/ *verb* [T] to think that someone or something is not as good as they really are *Critics have continued to underrate*

*Sampras.* • **underrated** *adj I think he's really underrated as an actor.* ➜ *Opposite* **overrated**.

**underscore** /ˌʌndəˈskɔːʳ/ *verb* [T] *mainly US* to emphasize the importance of something

**undershirt** /ˈʌndəʃɜːt/ *US* (*UK* **vest**) *noun* [C] a piece of underwear that you wear under a shirt ➜ *See colour picture* **Clothes** *on page Centre 5.*

**the underside** /ˈʌndəsaɪd/ *noun* the bottom surface of something *There was some damage to the underside of the car.*

o┅**understand** /ˌʌndəˈstænd/ *verb* [I, T] *past* **understood 1** [KNOW MEANING] to know the meaning of something that someone says *I don't understand half of what he says.* • *She didn't understand so I explained it again.* • *I understand written French but I don't speak it very well.* **2** [KNOW WHY/HOW] to know why or how something happens or works [+ question word] *We still don't fully understand how the brain works.* **3** [KNOW FEELINGS] to know how someone feels or why they behave in a particular way *I don't understand James sometimes.* • [+ question word] *I understand why she's so angry.* **4 I/we understand (that)...** *formal* used to say that you believe something is true because someone has told you it is *I understand that the school is due to close next year.* **5 make yourself understood** to say something to someone in a way that they understand *I had a little difficulty making myself understood.*

**understandable** /ˌʌndəˈstændəbl/ *adj* An understandable feeling or action is one that you would expect in that particular situation. *It's understandable that he's angry.* • **understandably** *adv She's understandably upset.*

**understanding**[1] /ˌʌndəˈstændɪŋ/ *noun* **1** [KNOWLEDGE] [U, no plural] knowledge about a subject, situation, etc or about how something works *We now have a better understanding of this disease.* **2** [AGREEMENT] [C] an informal agreement between two people [usually singular, + that] *We **have an understanding** that we don't discuss the subject in front of his mother.* **3** [SYMPATHY] [U] sympathy *Thank you for your understanding.* **4 my/her/his, etc understanding** what you thought to be true *It was my understanding that she was coming alone.* **5** [ABILITY] [U] the ability to learn or think about something *The computer side of the course was way beyond my understanding* (= was too difficult for me).

**understanding**[2] /ˌʌndəˈstændɪŋ/ *adj* showing sympathy for someone's problems *Fortunately, my girlfriend is very understanding.*

**understated** /ˌʌndəˈsteɪtɪd/ *adj* simple and attractive in style *an understated black dress* • *understated elegance*

**understatement** /ˌʌndəˈsteɪtmənt/ *noun* [C, U] when you say that something is less extreme than it really is *'Quite big', did you say? That's an understatement – he's enormous!*

**understood** /ˌʌndəˈstʊd/ *past of* understand

**understudy** /ˈʌndəˌstʌdi/ *noun* [C] an actor in the theatre who learns the words and actions of another character so that they can perform if the usual actor is ill

**undertake** /ˌʌndəˈteɪk/ *verb past t* **undertook**, *past p* **undertaken** *formal* **1** [T] to start work on

something that will take a long time or be difficult *Max has undertaken the task of restoring an old houseboat.* **2 undertake to do sth** to promise to do something

**undertaker** /ˈʌndəˌteɪkəʳ/ *noun* [C] someone whose job is to organize funerals and prepare dead bodies to be buried or burned

**undertaking** /ˈʌndəˌteɪkɪŋ/ *noun* [C] **1** a difficult or important piece of work, especially one that takes a long time [usually singular] *Building your own house is a major undertaking.* **2** *UK* a legal or official promise to do something [usually singular] *The newspaper has **given an undertaking** not to print the story.*

**undertone** /ˈʌndətəʊn/ *noun* [C] a feeling or quality that exists but is not obvious *an article with worrying political undertones*

**undertook** /ˌʌndəˈtʊk/ *past tense of* undertake

**undervalued** /ˌʌndəˈvæljuːd/ *adj* If someone or something is undervalued, they are more important or useful than people think they are.

**underwater** /ˌʌndəˈwɔːtəʳ/ *adj, adv* under the surface of water *an underwater camera* • *Seals can hear very well underwater.*

**underwear** /ˈʌndəweəʳ/ *noun* [U] the clothes that you wear next to your skin, under your other clothes

**types of underwear**

Underpants are a piece of underwear that cover the bottom. In British English **underpants** are only worn by men or boys, but in American English they can also be worn by women and girls.

The American English word **panties** is a piece of underwear for women or girls that covers the bottom. The British English word for **panties** is **knickers** or **pants**.

**underweight** /ˌʌndəˈweɪt/ *adj* too light

**underwent** /ˌʌndəˈwent/ *past tense of* undergo

**underworld** /ˈʌndəwɜːld/ *noun* [no plural] criminals and their activities *the criminal/London underworld*

**undesirable** /ˌʌndɪˈzaɪərəbl/ *adj formal* Something that is undesirable is not wanted because it is bad or unpleasant. *an undesirable influence*

**undeveloped** /ˌʌndɪˈveləpt/ *adj* Undeveloped land has no buildings on it and is not used for anything.

**undid** /ʌnˈdɪd/ *past tense of* undo

**undisclosed** /ˌʌndɪsˈkləʊzd/ *adj* If official information is undisclosed, it is secret. *The meeting is taking place at an undisclosed location.*

**undisputed** /ˌʌndɪˈspjuːtɪd/ *adj* If something is undisputed, everyone agrees about it. *an undisputed fact* • *the undisputed champion/winner*

**undisturbed** /ˌʌndɪˈstɜːbd/ *adj* not interrupted or changed in any way *undisturbed sleep*

**undivided** /ˌʌndɪˈvaɪdɪd/ *adj* **undivided attention/loyalty/support, etc** complete attention, support, etc *There, now you can have my undivided attention.*

**undo** /ʌnˈduː/ *verb* [T] **undoing**, *past t* **undid**, *past*

**U**

*p* **undone 1** to open something that is tied or fastened *I took off my hat and undid my coat.* • *Can you undo this knot for me?* **2** to get rid of the effects of something that has been done before *Some of the damage caused by pollution cannot be undone.*

**undoing** /ʌn'duːɪŋ/ *noun* **be sb's undoing** to be the thing that makes someone fail *It was a policy that proved to be the President's undoing.*

**undone** /ʌn'dʌn/ *adj* **1** not fastened or tied *Her coat was undone.* **2** not done *I don't think I've left anything undone.*

**undoubted** /ʌn'daʊtɪd/ *adj* [always before noun] used to emphasize that something is true *The project was an undoubted success.*

**undoubtedly** /ʌn'daʊtɪdli/ *adv* used to emphasize that something is true *Stress has undoubtedly contributed to her illness.*

**undress** /ʌn'dres/ *verb* [I, T] to remove your clothes or someone else's clothes • **undressed** *adj I got undressed and went to bed.*

**undue** /ʌn'djuː/ *adj* [always before noun] *formal* more than is necessary *I don't want to cause undue alarm.*

**undulating** /'ʌndjəleɪtɪŋ/ *adj formal* having slight slopes or curves, or moving slightly up and down *undulating roads* • *undulating waves*

**unduly** /ʌn'djuːli/ *adv formal* more than necessary *She didn't seem unduly concerned.*

**unearth** /ʌn'ɜːθ/ *verb* [T] **1** to find something in the ground [often passive] *Thousands of dinosaur bones have been unearthed in China.* **2** to find something that has been secret or hidden *Reporters unearthed evidence of criminal activity.*

**unearthly** /ʌn'ɜːθli/ *adj* strange and frightening *an unearthly light/silence*

**unease** /ʌn'iːz/ *noun* [U] when you feel worried because you think something bad might happen

**uneasy** /ʌn'iːzi/ *adj* worried because you think something bad might happen *I feel a bit **uneasy about** her travelling alone.*

**uneconomic** /ʌn,iːkə'nɒmɪk/ (*also* **uneconomical**) *adj* **1** using too much money, fuel, time, etc *a car that is uneconomic to run* **2** not making enough profit *plans to close uneconomic factories*

o━**unemployed** /,ʌnɪm'plɔɪd/ *adj* not having a job *I've been unemployed for six months.* • *the government is helping to create jobs for the **unemployed**.*

o━**unemployment** /,ʌnɪm'plɔɪmənt/ *noun* [U] **1** the number of people who are unemployed *a rise/fall in unemployment* • *The **unemployment rate** has increased to 20 percent.* **2** when you do not have a job

**unending** /ʌn'endɪŋ/ *adj* seeming to continue forever *an unending series of problems*

**unequal** /ʌn'iːkwəl/ *adj* **1** different in size, level, amount, etc **2** unfair *the unequal distribution of wealth* • **unequally** *adv*

**unequivocal** /,ʌnɪ'kwɪvəkəl/ *adj formal* clear and certain *an unequivocal answer* • **unequivocally** *adv*

**unethical** /ʌn'eθɪkəl/ *adj* morally bad *unethical business methods*

**uneven** /ʌn'iːvən/ *adj* not level or smooth *an uneven floor* • **unevenly** *adv*

**unexpected** /,ʌnɪk'spektɪd/ *adj* Something that is unexpected surprises you because you did not know it was going to happen. *His death was completely unexpected.* • **unexpectedly** *adv*

**unfailing** /ʌn'feɪlɪŋ/ *adj* An unfailing quality or ability is one that someone always has. *unfailing love and support* • **unfailingly** *adv*

o━**unfair** /ʌn'feəʳ/ *adj* **1** not treating people in an equal way *an unfair system* • *The test was unfair because some people had seen it before.* **2** not true and morally wrong [+ to do sth] *It's unfair to blame Frank for everything.* • **unfairly** *adv* • **unfairness** *noun* [U]

**unfaithful** /ʌn'feɪθfəl/ *adj* having sex with someone who is not your wife, husband, or usual sexual partner *She was **unfaithful to** me.*

**unfamiliar** /,ʌnfə'mɪljəʳ/ *adj* **1** not known to you *an unfamiliar face* • *His name was **unfamiliar to** me.* **2** **be unfamiliar with sth** to not have any knowledge or experience of something *Many older people are unfamiliar with computers.*

**unfashionable** /ʌn'fæʃⁿəbl/ *adj* not fashionable or popular at a particular time

**unfasten** /ʌn'fɑːsⁿn/ *verb* [T] to open something that is closed or fixed together *to unfasten a seat belt*

**unfavourable** UK (US **unfavorable**) /ʌn'feɪvⁿrəbl/ *adj* **1** negative and showing that you do not like something *unfavourable publicity* **2** not good and likely to cause problems *unfavourable weather conditions* • **unfavourably** *adv*

**unfeeling** /ʌn'fiːlɪŋ/ *adj* not having sympathy for other people

**unfettered** /ʌn'fetəd/ *adj formal* not limited by rules *The UN inspectors were given unfettered access to all nuclear sites.*

**unfinished** /ʌn'fɪnɪʃt/ *adj* not completed *an unfinished novel/portrait*

**unfit** /ʌn'fɪt/ *adj* **1** not suitable or good enough *The food was judged **unfit for** human consumption.* **2** UK not healthy because you do too little exercise

**unfold** /ʌn'fəʊld/ *verb* **1** [I] If a situation or story unfolds, it develops or becomes known. *The nation watched on TV as the tragic events unfolded.* **2** [I, T] to become open and flat, or to make something become open and flat *I unfolded the map.*

**unforeseen** /,ʌnfɔː'siːn/ *adj* not expected *The concert was cancelled due to **unforeseen circumstances.***

**unforgettable** /,ʌnfə'getəbl/ *adj* Something that is unforgettable is so good, interesting, etc that you remember it for a long time. *Seeing Niagara Falls was an unforgettable experience.*

**unfortunate** /ʌn'fɔːtʃⁿət/ *adj* **1** used to show that you wish something was not true or had not happened *an unfortunate mistake* • [+ (that)] *It was unfortunate that she lost her job just as her husband became ill.* **2** unlucky *One unfortunate person failed to see the hole and fell straight into it.*

o━**unfortunately** /ʌn'fɔːtʃⁿənətli/ *adv* used to say that you wish something was not true or that something had not happened *I'd love to come, but unfortunately I have to work.*

**unfounded** /ʌnˈfaʊndɪd/ *adj* not based on facts *unfounded allegations/rumours*

**unfriendly** /ʌnˈfrendli/ *adj* not friendly

**unfulfilled** /ˌʌnfʊlˈfɪld/ *adj* **1** An unfulfilled wish, hope, promise, etc is one that has not happened or not been achieved. *an unfulfilled ambition/dream* **2** unhappy because you think you should be achieving more in your life

**ungainly** /ʌnˈɡeɪnli/ *adj* moving in a way that is not attractive *an ungainly walk*

**ungrateful** /ʌnˈɡreɪtfªl/ *adj* not thanking or showing that you are pleased with someone who has done something for you

o‑**unhappy** /ʌnˈhæpi/ *adj* **1** sad *an unhappy childhood* **2** not satisfied *Giorgio was unhappy with his test results.* • *I'm unhappy about the situation.* • unhappily *adv* • unhappiness *noun* [U]

**unharmed** /ʌnˈhɑːmd/ *adj* [never before noun] not harmed or damaged *Both children escaped unharmed from the burning building.*

**unhealthy** /ʌnˈhelθi/ *adj* **1** CAUSE ILLNESS likely to damage your health *Eating too much is unhealthy.* **2** ILL not strong, and likely to become ill *She looks pale and unhealthy.* **3** NOT NORMAL not normal and slightly unpleasant *an unhealthy interest in weapons*

**unheard** /ʌnˈhɜːd/ *adj* not listened to or considered *Her cries went unheard.*

**un'heard ˌof** *adj* [never before noun] never having happened before *Thirty years ago the disease was unheard of.*

**unhelpful** /ʌnˈhelpfʊl/ *adj* **1** not improving a situation *an unhelpful remark* **2** not wanting to help someone, in a way that seems unfriendly *The taxi driver was rude and unhelpful.*

**unhurt** /ʌnˈhɜːt/ *adj* not harmed

**unicorn** /ˈjuːnɪkɔːn/ *noun* [C] an imaginary white horse with a horn growing from the front of its head

**unidentified** /ˌʌnaɪˈdentɪfaɪd/ *adj* not recognized *The body of an unidentified woman was found in a field last night.*

**unification** /ˌjuːnɪfɪˈkeɪʃªn/ *noun* [U] when two or more countries join together and become one country *the unification of East and West Germany*

**uniform**[1] /ˈjuːnɪfɔːm/ *noun* [C, U] a special set of clothes that are worn by people who do a particular job or people who go to a particular school *a school uniform* • *a nurse's uniform* • *Tom looks completely different in uniform* (= wearing a uniform). • uniformed *adj* uniformed police officers

**uniform**[2] /ˈjuːnɪfɔːm/ *adj* being the same size, shape, amount, etc *a row of houses of uniform height* • uniformity /ˌjuːnɪˈfɔːməti/ *noun* [U] • uniformly *adv*

**unify** /ˈjuːnɪfaɪ/ *verb* [T] to join together two or more countries or groups to make a single one *We need a leader who can unify the party.* • unified *adj* Many people want a more unified Europe.

**unilateral** /ˌjuːnɪˈlætªrªl/ *adj* A unilateral action or decision is done or made by one country, group, etc without waiting for others to agree. *unilateral nuclear disarmament* • unilaterally *adv*

**unimaginable** /ˌʌnɪˈmædʒɪnəbl/ *adj* Something that is unimaginable is difficult to imagine because it is so bad, good, big, etc. *unimaginable pain/wealth* • unimaginably *adv*

**unimportant** /ˌʌnɪmˈpɔːtªnt/ *adj* not important

**uninhabitable** /ˌʌnɪnˈhæbɪtəbl/ *adj* too cold, dangerous, etc to live in

**uninhabited** /ˌʌnɪnˈhæbɪtɪd/ *adj* If a place is uninhabited, no one lives there. *an uninhabited island*

**uninhibited** /ˌʌnɪnˈhɪbɪtɪd/ *adj* feeling free to behave in any way that you want without worrying about other people's opinions

**unintelligible** /ˌʌnɪnˈtelɪdʒəbl/ *adj* impossible to understand

**uninterested** /ʌnˈɪntrəstɪd/ *adj* not interested *He's completely uninterested in politics.*

**uninterrupted** /ˌʌnˌɪntªrˈʌptɪd/ *adj* continuous *I want a radio station that offers uninterrupted music.*

**union** /ˈjuːnjən/ *noun* **1** [C] (*also* **trade union**) (*also US* **labor union**) an organization that represents people who do a particular job *a teachers'/firefighters' union* **2** [U, no plural] when two or more countries, groups, etc join together to make one country, group, etc *a move towards full economic union of EU countries* ➜ *See also:* **the European Union.**

o‑**unique** /juːˈniːk/ *adj* **1** different from everyone and everything else *Everyone's fingerprints are unique.* **2** unusual and special *a unique opportunity* **3** **be unique to sb/sth** to exist in only one place, or be connected with only one person or thing *It's a method of education that is unique to this school.* • uniquely *adv* • uniqueness *noun* [U]

**unisex** /ˈjuːnɪseks/ *adj* for both men and women *unisex clothes* • *a unisex hairdresser*

**unison** /ˈjuːnɪsªn/ *noun* **in unison** If people do something in unison, they all do it at the same time.

**unit** /ˈjuːnɪt/ *noun* [C] **1** GROUP a group of people who are responsible for a particular part of an organization *an anti-terrorist unit* **2** MEASURE a measure used to express an amount or quantity *The kilogram is a unit of weight.* **3** SINGLE a single, complete thing that may be part of a larger thing *a French course book with ten units* **4** FURNITURE a piece of furniture that fits together with other pieces *kitchen units* **5** MACHINE a small machine, or part of a machine, that has a particular purpose *a computer's central processing unit* **6** BUILDING a single apartment, office, etc in a larger building

**unite** /juːˈnaɪt/ *verb* [I, T] to join together as a group, or to make people join together as a group *We need a leader who can unite the party.*

**united** /juːˈnaɪtɪd/ *adj* **1** If people are united, they all agree about something. *On the issue of education the party is united.* **2** joined together *a united Germany*

**the Unˌited 'Nations** *noun* [group] an international organization that tries to solve world problems in a peaceful way

**unity** /ˈjuːnəti/ *noun* [U] when everyone agrees with each other or wants to stay together *national unity* • *family unity*

**universal** /ˌjuːnɪˈvɜːsəl/ adj relating to everyone in the world, or to everyone in a particular group *Kittens and puppies have an almost universal appeal.* ● **universally** adv *It's a style of music that is universally popular.*

**the universe** /ˈjuːnɪvɜːs/ noun everything that exists, including stars, space, etc *Many people believe that there is life elsewhere in the universe.*

o—**university** /ˌjuːnɪˈvɜːsəti/ noun [C, U] a place where students study at a high level to get a degree (= type of qualification) *the University of Cambridge* ● *I applied to three universities.* ● *(mainly UK) Sarah studied chemistry at university.* ● *(mainly UK) I want to go to university when I finish school.*

**unjust** /ʌnˈdʒʌst/ adj not fair *unjust treatment* ● **unjustly** adv

**unjustified** /ʌnˈdʒʌstɪfaɪd/ adj done without a reason and not deserved *unjustified criticism*

**unkempt** /ʌnˈkempt/ adj untidy *Her hair was long and unkempt.*

**unkind** /ʌnˈkaɪnd/ adj slightly cruel *I didn't tell her the truth because I thought it would be unkind.* ● **unkindly** adv ● **unkindness** noun [U]

**unknown¹** /ʌnˈnəʊn/ adj **1** not known *The cause of his death is still unknown.* **2** not famous *an unknown actor* ⊃ See also: an unknown **quantity**.

**unknown²** /ʌnˈnəʊn/ noun **1 the unknown** things that you have not experienced and know nothing about *It's normal to fear the unknown.* **2** [C] someone who is not famous *The game was won by a complete unknown.*

**unlawful** /ʌnˈlɔːfəl/ adj formal illegal *unlawful possession of guns* ● **unlawfully** adv

**unleaded** /ʌnˈledɪd/ adj Unleaded fuel does not contain lead (= a metal).

**unleash** /ʌnˈliːʃ/ verb [T] to suddenly cause a strong reaction *The newspaper report unleashed a storm of protest from readers.*

o—**unless** /ənˈles, nnˈles/ conjunction except if *I won't call you unless there are any problems.*

**unlike** /ʌnˈlaɪk/ preposition **1** different from someone or something *Jackie's really clever, unlike her sister.* ● *The furniture was unlike anything she had ever seen.* **2** not typical of someone or something *It's unlike her to be quiet – was there something wrong?*

o—**unlikely** /ʌnˈlaɪkli/ adj **1** not expected to happen [+ (that)] *It's unlikely that I'll be able to come to the party.* ● [+ to do sth] *He's unlikely to arrive before midday.* **2** probably not true *an unlikely explanation*

**unlimited** /ʌnˈlɪmɪtɪd/ adj without any limits *a service that offers unlimited Internet access*

**unload** /ʌnˈləʊd/ verb **1** [I, T] to remove things from a vehicle *Can you help me unload the car?* **2** [I] If a ship, aircraft, etc unloads, goods are taken off it.

**unlock** /ʌnˈlɒk/ verb [T] to open something which is locked using a key

**unlucky** /ʌnˈlʌki/ adj having or causing bad luck [+ to do sth] *The team played well and was unlucky to lose.* ● *Some people think it's unlucky to walk under ladders.* ● **unluckily** adv

**unmarked** /ʌnˈmɑːkt/ adj having no signs or words that show what something is *an unmarked grave*

**unmarried** /ʌnˈmærɪd/ adj not married

**unmatched** /ʌnˈmætʃt/ adj better than anyone or anything else *Horses have an athletic beauty unmatched by any other animal.*

**unmistakable** /ˌʌnmɪˈsteɪkəbl/ adj Something that is unmistakable is very obvious and cannot be confused with anything else. *an unmistakable look of disappointment* ● **unmistakably** adv

**unmoved** /ʌnˈmuːvd/ adj not feeling any emotion *It's impossible to remain unmoved by pictures of starving children.*

**unnamed** /ʌnˈneɪmd/ adj An unnamed person or thing is talked about but their name is not said. *The money was given by an unnamed businessman.*

**unnatural** /ʌnˈnætʃərəl/ adj not normal or right *an unnatural interest in death* ● **unnaturally** adv *unnaturally thin*

o—**unnecessary** /ʌnˈnesəsəri/ adj **1** not needed *You don't want to make any unnecessary car journeys in this weather.* **2** unkind *Why did she say that? That was unnecessary.* ● **unnecessarily** /ʌnˈnesəsərəli/ adv

**unnerve** /ʌnˈnɜːv/ verb [T] to make someone feel nervous or frightened

**unnerving** /ʌnˈnɜːvɪŋ/ adj making you feel nervous or frightened *He kept looking at me which I found unnerving.*

**unnoticed** /ʌnˈnəʊtɪst/ adj without being seen or noticed *We managed to slip away unnoticed.*

**unobtrusive** /ˌʌnəbˈtruːsɪv/ adj not attracting attention *He was quiet and unobtrusive.* ● **unobtrusively** adv

**unoccupied** /ʌnˈɒkjəpaɪd/ adj An unoccupied building, room, seat, etc has no one in it.

**unofficial** /ˌʌnəˈfɪʃəl/ adj not said or done by the government or someone in authority *Unofficial reports suggest the death toll from the earthquake is around 600.* ● **unofficially** adv

**unorthodox** /ʌnˈɔːθədɒks/ adj unusual and different from most people's opinions, methods, etc *unorthodox ideas* ● *an unorthodox style of teaching*

**unpack** /ʌnˈpæk/ verb [I, T] to take things out of a bag, box, etc *Bella unpacked her suitcase.* ● *I haven't had time to unpack yet.*

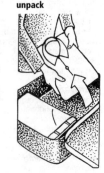
**unpack**

**unpaid** /ʌnˈpeɪd/ adj **1** An unpaid debt, tax, etc has not been paid. **2** working without getting any money *unpaid work*

**unpalatable** /ʌnˈpælətəbl/ adj formal shocking and difficult to accept *an unpalatable fact*

**unparalleled** /ʌnˈpærəleld/ adj formal better, greater, worse, etc than anything else *an act of unparalleled cruelty*

**unplanned** /ʌnˈplænd/ adj not planned or expected *an unplanned pregnancy*

**unpleasant** /ʌnˈplezᵊnt/ *adj* **1** not enjoyable or pleasant *an unpleasant experience/smell* **2** rude and angry *The waiter got quite unpleasant with us.* • unpleasantly *adv*

**unplug** /ʌnˈplʌg/ *verb* [T] to stop a piece of electrical equipment being connected to an electricity supply by pulling its plug (= object with pins) out of the wall

**unpopular** /ʌnˈpɒpjələʳ/ *adj* disliked by most people *an unpopular idea* • *an unpopular teacher* • unpopularity /ʌnˌpɒpjəˈlærəti/ *noun* [U]

**unprecedented** /ʌnˈpresɪdᵊntɪd/ *adj* never having happened before *The Internet has given people unprecedented access to information.*

**unpredictable** /ˌʌnprɪˈdɪktəbl̩/ *adj* changing so much that you do not know what will happen next *unpredictable weather conditions* • unpredictability /ˌʌnprɪˌdɪktəˈbɪlɪti/ *noun* [U]

**unprofessional** /ˌʌnprəˈfeʃᵊnᵊl/ *adj* behaving badly at work *an unprofessional attitude*

**unprovoked** /ˌʌnprəˈvəʊkt/ *adj* An unprovoked attack is one in which the person who is attacked has done nothing to cause it.

**unqualified** /ʌnˈkwɒlɪfaɪd/ *adj* **1** without the qualifications or knowledge to do something [+ to do sth] *She was totally unqualified to look after children.* **2** [always before noun] *formal* total and not limited in any way *an unqualified success*

**unquestionably** /ʌnˈkwestʃᵊnəbli/ *adv* in a way that is obvious and causes no doubt *She is unquestionably the best person for the job.*

**unravel** /ʌnˈrævᵊl/ *verb* [I, T] *(UK)* **unravelling**, *past* **unravelled**, *(US)* **unraveling**, *past* **unraveled** **1** If you unravel a difficult situation or story, or if it unravels, it becomes clear and easier to understand. *No one has yet unravelled the mystery of his death.* **2** to stop being twisted together, or to move pieces of string, etc so that they are not twisted together

**unreal** /ʌnˈrɪəl/ *adj* Something that is unreal seems so strange that it is difficult to believe. *For a while I couldn't believe she was dead – it all seemed unreal.* • unreality /ˌʌnriˈæləti/ *noun* [U]

**unrealistic** /ˌʌnrɪəˈlɪstɪk/ *adj* not thinking about what is likely to happen or what you can really do *She has a totally unrealistic view of life.* • [+ to do sth] *It's unrealistic to expect their decision before Tuesday.*

**unreasonable** /ʌnˈriːzᵊnəbl̩/ *adj* not fair *unreasonable demands* • [+ to do sth] *It seems unreasonable to expect one person to do both jobs.* • unreasonably *adv*

**unrelated** /ˌʌnrɪˈleɪtɪd/ *adj* having no connection *Police said his death was **unrelated** to the attack.*

**unrelenting** /ˌʌnrɪˈlentɪŋ/ *adj* *formal* never stopping or getting any less extreme *unrelenting pressure* • *The heat was unrelenting.*

**unreliable** /ˌʌnrɪˈlaɪəbl̩/ *adj* not able to be trusted or depended on *an unreliable witness* • *The trains were noisy, dirty, and unreliable.*

**unremarkable** /ˌʌnrɪˈmɑːkəbl̩/ *adj* ordinary and not interesting *an unremarkable town*

**unremitting** /ˌʌnrɪˈmɪtɪŋ/ *adj* *formal* never stopping or getting any less extreme *unremitting pain* • *unremitting efforts*

**unrepentant** /ˌʌnrɪˈpentənt/ *adj* not feeling sorry about something bad that you have done

**unreservedly** /ˌʌnrɪˈzɜːvɪdli/ *adv* completely *The minister has apologized unreservedly.*

**unresolved** /ˌʌnrɪˈzɒlvd/ *adj* *formal* If a problem or question is unresolved, there is still no solution or answer. *The question of who owns the land **remains unresolved**.*

**unrest** /ʌnˈrest/ *noun* [U] when a lot of people are angry about something and are likely to become violent *political/social unrest*

**unrestrained** /ˌʌnrɪˈstreɪnd/ *adj* not limited or controlled *unrestrained anger*

**unrivalled** UK (US **unrivaled**) /ʌnˈraɪvᵊld/ *adj* better than any other of the same type *The museum has an unrivalled collection of modern American paintings.*

**unroll** /ʌnˈrəʊl/ *verb* [T] to open something that was rolled into a tube shape and make it flat *He unrolled the carpet.*

**unruly** /ʌnˈruːli/ *adj* **1** behaving badly and difficult to control *unruly children* **2** Unruly hair is difficult to keep tidy.

**unsafe** /ʌnˈseɪf/ *adj* **1** dangerous *The building is unsafe.* • [+ to do sth] *The water was dirty and unsafe to drink.* **2** If you feel unsafe, you feel that you are in danger. *Many women feel unsafe on the streets at night.*

**unsatisfactory** /ʌnˌsætɪsˈfæktᵊri/ *adj* not good enough to be acceptable *Many school buildings are in an unsatisfactory condition.*

**unsavoury** UK (US **unsavory**) /ʌnˈseɪvᵊri/ *adj* unpleasant and morally offensive *He had a rather unsavoury reputation.*

**unscathed** /ʌnˈskeɪðd/ *adj* [never before noun] not harmed *The driver of the car was killed but both passengers escaped unscathed.*

**unscrew** /ʌnˈskruː/ *verb* [T] **1** to remove something by twisting it *I can't unscrew the lid.* **2** to remove something by taking the screws (= small, metal pieces) out of it

**unscrupulous** /ʌnˈskruːpjələs/ *adj* behaving in a way that is dishonest or unfair in order to get what you want *an unscrupulous financial adviser*

**unseat** /ʌnˈsiːt/ *verb* [T] to remove someone from a powerful position *Kennedy has a good chance of unseating the President at the next election.*

**unseen** /ʌnˈsiːn/ *adj, adv* not seen or noticed *an exhibition of previously unseen photographs*

**unsettled** /ʌnˈsetld/ *adj* **1** changing often *The weather continues to be unsettled.* **2** anxious and not able to relax or feel happy in a situation *Children tend to get unsettled if you keep changing their routine.*

**unsettling** /ʌnˈsetlɪŋ/ *adj* making you feel anxious *an unsettling experience*

**unsightly** /ʌnˈsaɪtli/ *adj* unpleasant to look at *unsightly piles of litter*

**unskilled** /ʌnˈskɪld/ *adj* **1** without special skills or qualifications *an unskilled labourer/worker* **2** Unskilled work does not need people with special skills or qualifications.

**unsolicited** /ˌʌnsəˈlɪsɪtɪd/ *adj* not asked for and often not wanted *unsolicited advice*

**unsolved** /ʌnˈsɒlvd/ *adj* having no answer or solution *an unsolved mystery*

U

**unsound** /ʌnˈsaʊnd/ *adj* **1** based on ideas, facts, and reasons that are wrong *an unsound argument* **2** in a bad condition *The bridge was structurally unsound.*

**unspeakable** /ʌnˈspiːkəbl/ *adj* extremely bad or shocking *unspeakable crimes/suffering* • **unspeakably** *adv*

**unspecified** /ʌnˈspesɪfaɪd/ *adj* If something is unspecified, you are not told what it is. *The court awarded her an unspecified amount of money.*

**unspoiled** (*also UK* **unspoilt** /ʌnˈspɔɪlt/) /ʌnˈspɔɪlt/ *adj* An unspoiled place is beautiful because it has not been changed or damaged by people. *an island with clean, unspoiled beaches*

**unspoken** /ʌnˈspəʊkᵊn/ *adj* not said, but thought or felt *unspoken doubts*

**unstable** /ʌnˈsteɪbl/ *adj* **1** CHANGE likely to change or end suddenly *an unstable relationship* • *an unstable economy* **2** PERSON If someone is unstable, their moods and behaviour change suddenly, especially because they are mentally ill. **3** MOVE not fixed or safe and likely to move *That chair looks a bit unstable.*

**unsteady** /ʌnˈstedi/ *adj* moving slightly from side to side, as if you might fall *The alcohol had made her unsteady on her feet.*

**unstuck** /ʌnˈstʌk/ *adj* **1 come unstuck** *UK* If something comes unstuck, it stops being fixed to something. *One of the photos has come unstuck.* **2 come unstuck** *UK informal* to experience difficulties and fail *The negotiations came unstuck at a crucial stage.*

**unsuccessful** /ˌʌnsəkˈsesfᵊl/ *adj* not achieving what was wanted or intended *an unsuccessful attempt/effort* • **unsuccessfully** *adv*

**unsuitable** /ʌnˈsuːtəbl/ *adj* not acceptable or right for someone or something *My parents considered the programme unsuitable for children.*

**unsung** /ʌnˈsʌŋ/ *adj* not famous or praised although you have done something very well *He was the **unsung hero** of the match.*

**unsure** /ʌnˈʃʊəʳ/ *adj* **1** not certain or having doubts *I'm a bit **unsure about** what to do.* **2 unsure of yourself** without confidence

**unsuspecting** /ˌʌnsəˈspektɪŋ/ *adj* [always before noun] not aware that something bad is happening *In each case the unsuspecting victim had been invited into Cooper's home.*

**unsympathetic** /ˌʌnsɪmpəˈθetɪk/ *adj* **1** showing that you do not understand or care about someone's problems *I told him I'd got a cold but he was completely unsympathetic.* **2** not agreeing with or supporting someone's ideas or actions

**untangle** /ʌnˈtæŋgl/ *verb* [T] **1** to separate pieces of string, hair, wire, etc that have become twisted together *I'm trying to untangle these wires.* **2** to understand the different parts of a situation that has become confused or very complicated *Historians have tried to untangle the complex issues behind the events.*

**untapped** /ʌnˈtæpt/ *adj* not yet used *untapped potential*

**untenable** /ʌnˈtenəbl/ *adj formal* If an argument, action, or situation is untenable, it cannot be supported or defended from criticism. *an untenable position*

**unthinkable** /ʌnˈθɪŋkəbl/ *adj* If something is unthinkable, it is so strange that you can not imagine it will ever happen. *Thirty years ago a no-smoking restaurant would have been unthinkable.*

**untidy** /ʌnˈtaɪdi/ *adj* not tidy *an untidy room* • *She's really untidy at home.*

**untidy**

**untie** /ʌnˈtaɪ/ *verb* [T] **untying**, *past* **untied** to open a knot or something that has been tied with a knot *I untied my shoelaces and kicked off my shoes.*

**untie**

○━**until** /ᵊnˈtɪl/ (*also* **till**) *preposition, conjunction* **1** continuing to happen before a particular time or event and then stopping *The show will be on until the end of the month.* • *Whisk the egg whites until they look white and fluffy.* **2** as far as *Carry on until you reach the traffic lights and turn right.* **3 not until** not before a particular time or event *It doesn't open until 7.* • *We won't start until Jeanne arrives.*

**untimely** /ʌnˈtaɪmli/ *adj* happening too soon *her untimely death from cancer*

**untold** /ʌnˈtəʊld/ *adj* [always before noun] too much to be measured or counted *untold riches* • *untold damage*

**untouched** /ʌnˈtʌtʃt/ *adj* **1** not changed or damaged in any way *Most of the island remains **untouched by** tourism.* **2** If food is untouched, it has not been eaten.

**untoward** /ˌʌntəˈwɔːd/ *adj formal* unexpected and causing problems *If nothing **untoward** happens we should be there by midday.*

**untrained** /ʌnˈtreɪnd/ *adj* **1** never having been taught the skills for a particular job *untrained staff* **2 the untrained eye** someone without the skill or knowledge to judge what they see *To the untrained eye, most fake diamonds look real.*

**untried** /ʌn'traɪd/ *adj* not yet used or tested *new and untried technology*

**untrue** /ʌn'truː/ *adj* false

**untruth** /ʌn'truːθ/ *noun* [C] *formal* a lie, or something that is not true

**unused¹** /ʌn'juːzd/ *adj* not used now or not used before now *an unused room*

**unused²** /ʌn'juːst/ *adj* **be unused to sth** to not have experience of something *I was unused to city life.*

**unusual** /ʌn'juːʒuəl/ *adj* different and not ordinary, often in a way that is interesting or exciting *an unusual name* • [+ to do sth] *It's fairly unusual to keep insects as pets.*

**unusually** /ʌn'juːʒuəli/ *adv* **1 unusually big/strong/good, etc** bigger, stronger, better, etc than is normal *unusually warm weather* **2 unusually for sb** in a way that is not usual for someone *Unusually for me, I actually couldn't finish my meal.*

**unveil** /ʌn'veɪl/ *verb* [T] **1** to tell the public about an idea or plan that was secret before *The new policy is due to be unveiled later this month.* **2** to remove the cover from an object as part of an official ceremony

**unwanted** /ʌn'wɒntɪd/ *adj* not wanted *an unwanted pregnancy*

**unwarranted** /ʌn'wɒr²ntɪd/ *adj formal* without a good reason *unwarranted accusations* • *His fears proved to be unwarranted.*

**unwelcome** /ʌn'welkəm/ *adj* not wanted *unwelcome publicity* • *an unwelcome visitor*

**unwell** /ʌn'wel/ *adj* [never before noun] *formal* ill *to feel/look unwell*

**unwieldy** /ʌn'wiːldi/ *adj* An unwieldy object is difficult to carry because it is heavy, large, or a strange shape.

**unwilling** /ʌn'wɪlɪŋ/ *adj* not wanting to do something [+ to do sth] *A lot of people are unwilling to accept change.* • **unwillingly** *adv* • **unwillingness** *noun* [U]

**unwind** /ʌn'waɪnd/ *verb past* **unwound 1** [I] *informal* to relax, especially after working *Music helps me to unwind.* **2** [I, T] If you unwind something, or if something unwinds, it stops being curled round or twisted round something else and is made straight. *He unwound the bandage.*

**unwise** /ʌn'waɪz/ *adj* stupid and likely to cause problems *an unwise decision* • **unwisely** *adv*

**unwittingly** /ʌn'wɪtɪŋli/ *adv* without intending to do something *I apologized for the chaos I had unwittingly caused.*

**unworkable** /ʌn'wɜːkəbl/ *adj* A plan that is unworkable is impossible. *The policy has been described as unworkable.*

**unwrap** /ʌn'ræp/ *verb* [T] to remove the paper, cloth, etc that is covering something *She carefully unwrapped the present.*

**unwrap**

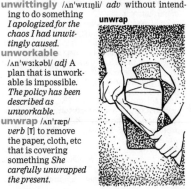

**unwritten** /ʌn'rɪt²n/ *adj* **an unwritten agreement/law/rule** an agreement, law, etc that is accepted and obeyed by most people but is not formally written

**unzip** /ʌn'zɪp/ *verb* [T] **unzipping**, *past* **unzipped** to open something by using its zip (= two rows of metal or plastic points that fasten two sides together) *He unzipped his trousers.*

o–**up¹** /ʌp/ *adv, preposition* **1** [HIGHER PLACE] towards or in a higher place *He ran up the stairs.* • *Pick up your clothes and put them away.* • *She looked up and smiled at me.* **2** [VERTICAL] vertical or as straight as possible *He stood up.* • *She opened her eyes and sat up.* **3** [INCREASE] to a greater degree, amount, volume, etc *Inflation keeps pushing prices up.* • *Can you turn up the heat? I'm freezing!* • *Please speak up* (= speak louder), *I can't hear you.* **4** [COMPLETELY] used to emphasize that someone completes an action or uses all of something *I used up all my money.* • *Eat up the rest of your dinner.* **5 up the road/street, etc** along or further along the street/road, etc *My best friend lives up the street from me.* • *He ran up the path and hugged her.* **6 go/walk, etc up to sb/sth** to walk directly towards someone or something until you are next to them *He walked straight up to me and introduced himself.* **7** [DIRECTION] in or towards a particular direction, usually north *We moved from London up to Scotland.* • *Chris lives up north.* **8 up and down** If something or someone moves up and down, they move repeatedly in one direction and then in the opposite direction. *The children were constantly running up and down the stairs.* **9 up to 10, 20, etc** any amount under 10, 20, etc *We can invite up to 65 people.* **10 up to** until a particular time *You can call me up to midnight.* **11 up to sth** equal in quality or achievement *His work wasn't up to his usual standard.* **12 up to sth/doing sth** able to do something *It'll be a while before I feel up to walking again.* **13 be up to (sth)** *informal* to be doing or planning something, often something secret and bad *Joe, what are you up to?* **14 be up to sb** If an action or decision is up to someone, they are responsible for doing or making it. *I can't decide for you Jack, it's up to you.* • [+ to do sth] *It's up to her to decide whether she wants to enter the competition.* **15 be up against sb/sth** If you are up against a situation or a person, they make it very difficult for you to achieve what you want to achieve. *We were up against some of the best players in the world.*

**up²** /ʌp/ *adj* [never before noun] **1** [NOT IN BED] not in bed *I was up all night with the baby.* • *Is she up yet?* **2 be up and around/about** to be well enough after an illness to get out of bed and move around **3** [FINISHED] If a period of time is up, it has ended. *My health club membership is up.* **4** [INCREASE] If a level or amount is up, it has increased. *Profits are up by 26%.* **5** [ROAD] *UK* If a road is up, it is being repaired. **6** [OPERATING] If a computer system is up, it is operating. **7** [SPORT] *US* In baseball and similar sports, if a player is up, they are taking a turn to play. **8 be up and running** If a system, organization, or machine is up and running, it is operating.

U

**up³** /ʌp/ *verb* [T] **upping**, *past* **upped** to increase something *Dad's upped my allowance by fifty cents a week.*

**up-and-coming** /ˌʌpᵊŋ'kʌmɪŋ/ *adj* [always before noun] becoming popular and likely to achieve success *He's a young, up-and-coming DJ.*

**upbeat** /'ʌp,biːt/ *adj informal* positive and expecting a situation to be good or successful *He remains upbeat about the future.*

**upbringing** /'ʌp,brɪŋɪŋ/ *noun* [no plural] the way your parents treat you when you are growing up *a middle-class/religious upbringing*

**upcoming** /'ʌp,kʌmɪŋ/ *adj* [always before noun] An upcoming event will happen soon. *the upcoming elections*

**update¹** /ʌp'deɪt/ *verb* [T] **1** to add new information *We've just updated our website.* • *I'll update you on* (= tell you about) *any developments.* **2** to make something more modern *They need to update their image.*

**update²** /'ʌpdeɪt/ *noun* [C] **1** new information *I'll need regular updates on your progress.* **2** a new form of something which existed at an earlier time *It's an update of an old 60's movie.*

**upfront¹** /ˌʌp'frʌnt/ *adj* **1** paid or obtained before work starts *an upfront payment/fee* **2** behaving in a way that makes your beliefs and intentions obvious to other people *She's very upfront about her dislike of men.*

**upfront²** /ˌʌp'frʌnt/ *adv* If you pay someone upfront, you pay them before they work for you.

**upgrade** /ʌp'ɡreɪd/ *verb* [T] to improve something so that it is of a higher quality or a newer model *to upgrade a computer* • upgrade /'ʌpɡreɪd/ *noun* [C]

**upheaval** /ʌp'hiːvᵊl/ *noun* [C, U] a very big change that causes difficulty or confusion *political/social upheaval*

**uphill¹** /ʌp'hɪl/ *adj* **an uphill battle/struggle/task** something that is difficult to do and needs a lot of effort *I can lose weight but it's a real uphill struggle.*

**uphill²** /ʌp'hɪl/ *adv* towards the top of a hill *We'd walked half a mile uphill.*

**uphold** /ʌp'həʊld/ *verb* [T] *past* **upheld 1** to agree with a decision, especially a legal one, and say it was correct *The court upheld the ruling.* **2** to support a decision, principle, or law *Police officers are expected to uphold the law.*

**upholstery** /ʌp'həʊlstᵊri/ *noun* [U] the material that covers chairs and other types of seats

**upkeep** /'ʌpkiːp/ *noun* [U] the process of keeping something in good condition, or of keeping a person or animal healthy

**upland** /'ʌplənd/ *adj* [always before noun] existing on a hill or mountain *upland areas*

**uplands** /'ʌpləndz/ *noun* [plural] high areas of land *the uplands of Nepal*

**uplifting** /ʌp'lɪftɪŋ/ *adj* making you feel happy and full of good feelings *an uplifting film*

**upmarket** /ˌʌp'mɑːkɪt/ *UK* (*US* **upscale**) *adj* expensive and used by people who are rich and from a high social class *an upmarket hotel/restaurant*

**upon** /ə'pɒn/ *preposition formal* on

**upper** /'ʌpəʳ/ *adj* [always before noun] **1** at a higher position *an upper floor* • *the upper lip* • *the upper body* **2** of a higher social class **3** **the upper limit** the highest amount or level, or the longest time that something is allowed ⇒ *See also:* get/gain the upper **hand¹**.

**upper case** *noun* [U] letters written as capitals

**upper class** *noun* [C] the highest social class of people *members of the upper classes* • upper-class *adj an upper-class accent*

**uppermost** /'ʌpəməʊst/ *adj* **1** highest *the building's uppermost floors* **2** **be uppermost in sb's mind** to be the most important thing someone is thinking about *The safety of her children was uppermost in her mind.*

**upright¹** /'ʌpraɪt/ *adv* vertical and as straight as possible *to sit/stand upright* ⇒ *See also:* **bolt upright**.

**upright²** /'ʌpraɪt/ *adj* **1** straight up or vertical *Please return your seat to an upright position and fasten your seat belt.* **2** honest and morally good *an upright citizen*

**uprising** /'ʌp,raɪzɪŋ/ *noun* [C] when a large group of people try to make political changes or change the government by fighting [usually singular] *a general/popular uprising*

**uproar** /'ʌprɔːʳ/ *noun* [U, no plural] when many people complain about something angrily *The book caused an uproar in the United States.* • *Local residents are (UK) in uproar/(US) in an uproar over plans for the new road.*

**uproot** /ʌp'ruːt/ *verb* [T] **1** to pull a tree or plant out of the ground *Hundreds of trees were uprooted in the storm.* **2** to make someone leave a place where they have been living for a long time *The war has uprooted nearly half the country's population.*

**ups and downs** *noun* [plural] the mixture of good and bad things that happen to people *Like most married couples, we've had our ups and downs.*

**upscale** /'ʌp,skeɪl/ *US* (*UK* **upmarket**) *adj* expensive and used by people who are rich and from a high social class *an upscale restaurant/neighbourhood*

○⚹ **upset¹** /ʌp'set/ *adj* **1** unhappy or worried because something unpleasant has happened *They'd had an argument and she was still upset about it.* • *Mike got very upset when I told him the news.* **2** **upset stomach/tummy** an illness in the stomach

**upset²** /ʌp'set/ *verb* [T] **upsetting**, *past* **upset 1** to make someone feel unhappy or worried *The phone call had clearly upset her.* **2** to cause problems for something *If I arrived later would that upset your plans?* **3** **upset sb's stomach** to make someone feel ill in the stomach

**upset³** /'ʌpset/ *noun* [C] **1** when someone beats the player or team that was expected to win *After Harding won the second set, a major upset seemed likely.* **2** **a stomach/tummy upset** *UK* an illness in the stomach **3** a difficulty or problem *We had the usual upsets but overall the day went well.*

**upsetting** /ʌp'setɪŋ/ *adj* making you feel unhappy or worried *I found the programme very upsetting.*

**the upshot** /'ʌpʃɒt/ *noun* the final result of a

discussion or series of events *The upshot is that we've decided to move to Sydney.*

**ˌupside 'down[1]** *adv* **1** turned so that the part that is usually at the top is now at the bottom *One of the pictures had been hung upside down.* • *Turn the jar* ***upside down*** *and shake it.* **2 turn sth upside down a** to make a place very untidy while looking for something **b** to change someone's life or a system completely *Their lives were turned upside down when their son was arrested.*

**ˌupside 'down[2]** *adj* turned so that the part that is usually at the top is now at the bottom *Why is this box upside down?*

**upside down**

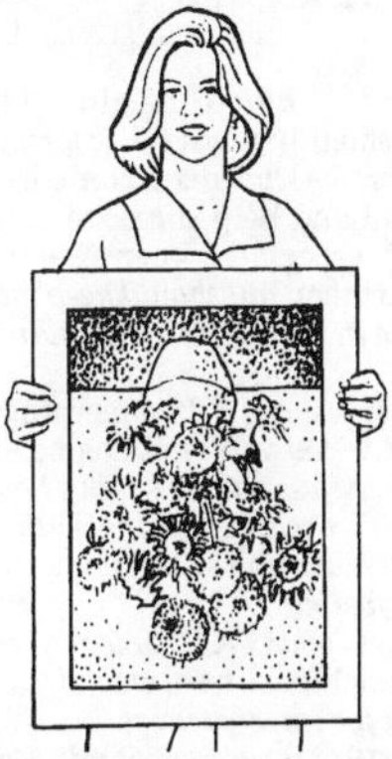

**upstage** /ʌp'steɪdʒ/ *verb* [T] to do something that takes people's attention away from someone or something and gives it to you instead *You mustn't upstage the bride.*

**upstairs** /ʌp'steəz/ *adv* on or to a higher level of a building *He ran upstairs to answer the phone.* • *The people who live upstairs are very noisy.* • **upstairs** *adj an upstairs bedroom*

**upstart** /'ʌpstɑːt/ *noun* [C] someone who has just started a job but already thinks they are very important

**upstate** /ˌʌp'steɪt/ *adj US* in the northern part of a US state (= one of the parts into which the country is divided) *upstate New York* • **upstate** *adv She's taken a trip upstate with some friends.*

**upstream** /ʌp'striːm/ *adv* along a river in the opposite direction to the way that the water is moving

**upsurge** /'ʌpsɜːdʒ/ *noun* [C] a sudden increase *an upsurge in violent crime*

**uptake** /'ʌpteɪk/ *noun informal* **be slow/quick on the uptake** to be slow/quick to understand something

**uptight** /ʌp'taɪt/ *adj informal* worried or nervous and not able to relax

**up-to-date** /ˌʌptə'deɪt/ *adj* **1** modern, and using the most recent technology or knowledge **2** having the most recent information *The Internet keeps us up-to-date.*

**up-to-the-minute** /ˌʌptəðə'mɪnɪt/ *adj* most recent *up-to-the-minute news*

**uptown** /ʌp'taʊn/ *adj, adv US* in or to the northern part of a city *She lives uptown.*

**upturn** /'ʌptɜːn/ *noun* [C] an improvement, especially in economic conditions or a business *There's been a sharp* ***upturn in*** *sales.*

**upturned** /ʌp'tɜːnd/ *adj* pointing up, or turned so the under side faces up *an upturned collar* • *an upturned boat*

**upward** /'ʌpwəd/ *adj* [always before noun] moving towards a higher place or level *an upward glance* • *an upward trend in sales*

**upwards** /'ʌpwədz/ *mainly UK* (*mainly US* **upward**) *adv* **1** towards a higher place or level *House prices have started moving upwards again.* **2 upwards of sth** more than a particular amount *Double rooms cost upwards of £70 a night.*

**uranium** /jʊə'reɪniəm/ *noun* [U] a heavy, grey metal that is used in the production of nuclear power

**Uranus** /'jʊərᵊnəs/ *noun* [no plural] the planet that is seventh from the Sun, after Saturn and before Neptune

**urban** /'ɜːbᵊn/ *adj* belonging or relating to a town or city *urban areas* • *urban development*

**urbane** /ɜː'beɪn/ *adj* confident, relaxed, and polite *With his good looks and urbane manner, he was very popular.*

**urge[1]** /ɜːdʒ/ *verb* [T] **1 urge sb to do sth** to try to persuade someone to do something *His parents urged him to go to university.* **2** *formal* to strongly advise an action *Financial experts are* ***urging caution.***

**urge sb on** to encourage someone to do or achieve something *The crowd was cheering and urging her on.*

**urge[2]** /ɜːdʒ/ *noun* [C] a strong wish or need [+ to do sth] *I resisted a powerful urge to slap him.*

**urgency** /'ɜːdʒᵊnsi/ *noun* [U] when something is very important and needs you to take action immediately *a matter of great urgency*

o-ᵆ**urgent** /'ɜːdʒᵊnt/ *adj* very important and needing you to take action immediately *an urgent message* • *The refugees were in urgent need of food and water.* • **urgently** *adv I need to speak to you urgently.*

**urinate** /'jʊərɪneɪt/ *verb* [I] to get rid of urine from your body

**urine** /'jʊərɪn/ *noun* [U] the liquid that comes out of your body when you go to the toilet

**urn** /ɜːn/ *noun* [C] **1** a round container that is used for plants or to store someone's ashes (= the powder that is left after a dead body has been burned) **2** a metal container that is used to make a large amount of coffee or tea and to keep it hot

o-ᵆ**us** *strong form* /ʌs/ *weak forms* /əs, s/ *pronoun* used after a verb or preposition to refer to the person who is speaking or writing and one or more other people *She gave us all a present.* • *Would you like to have dinner with us next Saturday?*

**USA** /ˌjuːes'eɪ/ *noun abbreviation for* United States of America

**usage** /'juːsɪdʒ/ *noun* **1** [C, U] the way that words are used *a guide to English grammar and usage* **2** [U] the amount of something that is used, or the way that something is used *restrictions on water usage*

o⊶**use**[1] /juːz/ *verb* [T] *past* **used 1** PURPOSE If you use something, you do something with it for a particular purpose. *Can I use your pen?* • *I paid for the tickets using my credit card.* • *She uses her car for work.* • [+ to do sth] *Nick used the money to buy a CD player.* **2** MAKE LESS to take an amount from a supply of something *A shower uses less water than a bath.* **3** PERSON to treat someone badly in order to get what you want *He was just using me to make his girlfriend jealous.* **4** WORD to say or write a particular word or phrase *'Autumn' is used in British English and 'fall' in American English.* **5 could use sth** *mainly US informal* something that you say when you want or need something *I could use some help with these packages, please.*

**use sth up** to finish a supply of something *Someone's used up all the milk.*

o⊶**use**[2] /juːs/ *noun* **1** USING [U] when you use something, or when something is being used *an increase in the use of mobile phones* • *Guests have free use of the hotel swimming pool.* • *Turn the machine off when it's not in use* (= being used). **2** PURPOSE [C] a purpose for which something is used *A food processor has a variety of uses in the kitchen.* • *Can you find a use for this box?* **3 be (of) any/some use** to be useful *Is this book of any use to you?* **4 be (of) no use** to not be useful *His advice was no use at all.* **5 be no use; be no use doing sth** used to say that trying to do something has no effect *It was no use talking to him – he wouldn't listen.* • *It's no use! I just can't get this lid off.* **6** WORD [C] one of the meanings of a word, or the way that a particular word is used *Can you list all the uses of the verb 'go'?* **7 the use of sth** permission to use something, or the ability to use something *Martin has offered me the use of his car.* • *She lost the use of both legs in the accident.* **8 make use of sth** to use something that is available *We were encouraged to make use of all the facilities.*

o⊶**used**[1] /juːst/ *adj* **used to sth/doing sth** If you are used to something, you have done it or experienced it many times before. *He's used to working long hours.* • *We've been living here for two years and we've (UK) got used to/(US) gotten used to the heat.* ⊃ *Opposite* **unused**.

**used**[2] /juːzd/ *adj* Something that is used is not new and has been owned by someone else. *a used car* ⊃ *Opposite* **unused**.

o⊶**used to** /'juːstuː/ *modal verb* **used to do/be sth** If something used to happen or a situation used to exist, it happened regularly or existed in the past but it does not exist now. *I used to go out every night when I was a student.* • *Monica used to live in Glasgow.* • *He used to be a lot fatter.* ⊃ *See study section* **Modal verbs** *on page Centre 31.*

**used to** and **be used to**

Used to + verb is for talking about a situation or regular activity in the past.

*My dad used to smoke when he was younger.*

*I used to live in Italy, but now I live in England.*

When you make used to + verb into a question or negative using the verb do, the correct form is use to.

*My dad didn't use to smoke.*

*Where did you use to live?*

~~Where did you used to live?~~

The expression be used to something/doing something is for talking about something which you have done or experienced a lot before.

*I don't mind the heat. I'm used to hot weather.*

*He's not used to working long hours.*

~~He's not use to working long hours.~~

o⊶**useful** /'juːsfəl/ *adj* **1** helping you to do or achieve something *useful information* • *a useful course for students* **2 come in useful** *UK* to be useful and help someone do or achieve something, especially when there is nothing else to help them *You should keep that paint – it might come in useful.* • **usefully** *adv* • **usefulness** *noun* [U]

o⊶**useless** /'juːsləs/ *adj* **1** If something is useless, it does not work well or it has no effect. *This umbrella's useless – there's a big hole in it.* • [+ doing sth] *It's useless arguing with her.* **2** *UK informal* having no skill in an activity *Dave's useless at football.*

**user** /'juːzər/ *noun* [C] someone who uses a product, machine, or service *drug users* • *a new service for Internet users*

**user-friendly** /ˌjuːzə'frendli/ *adj* A machine or system that is user-friendly is easy to use or understand. *user-friendly software*

**usher**[1] /'ʌʃər/ *verb* **usher sb into/to/across, etc** to show someone where to go or sit *She ushered me into her office.*

**usher in sth** *formal* to be at the start of a period when important changes happen, or to cause important changes to start happening *His presidency ushered in a new era of democracy.*

**usher**[2] /'ʌʃər/ *noun* [C] someone who shows people where to sit in a theatre or at a formal event

o⊶**usual** /'juːʒuəl/ *adj* **1** normal and happening most often *I went to bed at my usual time.* • *This winter has been much colder than usual.* ⊃ *Opposite* **unusual**. **2 as usual** in the way that happens most of the time *As usual, Ben was the last to arrive.*

o⊶**usually** /'juːʒəli/ *adv* in the way that most often happens *I usually get home at about six o'clock.* • *Usually I just have a sandwich.*

**usurp** /juː'zɜːp/ *verb* [T] *formal* to take someone else's job or power when you should not

**utensil** /juː'tensəl/ *noun* [C] a tool that you use for doing jobs in the house, especially cooking *wooden cooking utensils* ⊃ *See colour picture* **Kitchen** *on page Centre 10.*

**uterus** /'juːtərəs/ *noun* [C] the organ inside a woman's body where a baby grows

**utilitarian** /ˌjuːtɪlɪ'teəriən/ *adj* designed to be useful and not beautiful *utilitarian furniture*

**utility** /juː'tɪləti/ (*also* **public utility**) *noun* [C] an

U

organization that supplies the public with water, gas, or electricity

**utilize** *formal (also UK* **-ise**) /ˈjuːtɪlaɪz/ *verb* [T] to use something in an effective way *The vitamins come in a form that is easily utilized by the body.*

**utmost¹** /ˈʌtməʊst/ *adj* [always before noun] *formal* used to emphasize how important or serious something is *a matter of the utmost importance* • *The situation needs to be handled* **with** *the* **utmost** *care.*

**utmost²** /ˈʌtməʊst/ *noun* **do your utmost** to try as hard as you can to do something [+ to do sth] *We did our utmost to finish the project on time.*

**utopia** /juːˈtəʊpiə/ *noun* [C, U] an imaginary place where everything is perfect

**utopian** /juːˈtəʊpiən/ *adj* A utopian idea or plan is based on the belief that things can be made perfect. *a utopian vision of society*

**utter¹** /ˈʌtə/ *adj* [always before noun] used to emphasize something *She dismissed the article as utter nonsense.* • *To my utter amazement, Richard appeared with a bottle of champagne.*

**utter²** /ˈʌtə/ *verb* [T] *formal* to say something *She left without uttering a word.*

**utterance** /ˈʌtərəns/ *noun* [C] *formal* something that you say

**utterly** /ˈʌtəli/ *adv* completely *It's utterly ridiculous.*

**U-turn** /ˈjuːtɜːn/ *noun* [C] **1** a change of direction that you make when driving in order to travel in the opposite direction **2** a complete change from one opinion or plan to an opposite one *the government's U-turn on economic policy*

U

**V**

**V, v** /viː/ the twenty-second letter of the alphabet

**V** *written abbreviation for* volt (= a unit for measuring an electric current) *a 9V battery*

**v** *UK* (*UK/US* **vs**) *preposition abbreviation for* versus (= used to say that one team or person is competing against another) *Germany v France*

**vacancy** /'veɪkᵊnsi/ *noun* [C] **1** a room that is not being used in a hotel *Do you have any vacancies?* **2** a job that is available for someone to do *Tell me if you hear of any vacancies for secretaries.*

**vacant** /'veɪkᵊnt/ *adj* **1** EMPTY Somewhere that is vacant is available because it is not being used. *a vacant building* **2** JOB A vacant job is available for someone to do. **3** EXPRESSION A vacant expression on someone's face shows they are not thinking about anything. ● **vacantly** *adv*

**vacate** /və'keɪt US 'veɪkeɪt/ *verb* [T] *formal* to leave a room, building, chair, etc so that someone else can use it

○⊷**vacation**[1] /və'keɪʃᵊn US veɪ'keɪʃᵊn/ *noun* [C, U] **1** *US* (*UK* **holiday**) a period of time when you are not at home but are staying somewhere else for enjoyment *We're taking a vacation in Florida.* ● *We met Bob and Wendi on vacation.* **2** *mainly US* a period of the year when schools or colleges are closed *the summer vacation* ● *He's on vacation for three months.*

**vacation**[2] /və'keɪʃᵊn US veɪ'keɪʃᵊn/ *US* (*UK* **holiday**) *verb* **vacation in/on/by, etc** to go on vacation *Sam was vacationing in Guatemala.*

**vaccinate** /'væksɪneɪt/ *verb* [T] to give someone a vaccine to stop them from getting a disease *Have you been vaccinated against polio?* ● **vaccination** /ˌvæksɪ'neɪʃᵊn/ *noun* [C, U]

**vaccine** /'væksiːn/ *noun* [C, U] a substance that is given to people to stop them from getting a particular disease

**vacuum**[1] /'vækjuːm/ *noun* **1** [C] a space that has no air or other gas in it **2** [no plural] when someone or something important is not now in your life and you are unhappy *When her husband died, it left a big vacuum in her life.*

**vacuum**[2] /'vækjuːm/ *verb* [I, T] to clean somewhere using a vacuum cleaner

**'vacuum ˌcleaner** (*also UK* **Hoover**) *noun* [C] an electric machine that cleans floors by sucking up dirt

**vagaries** /'veɪgəriz/ *noun* [plural] sudden changes that are not expected or known about before they happen *the vagaries of the English weather*

**vagina** /və'dʒaɪnə/ *noun* [C] the part of a woman's body that connects her outer sex organs to the place where a baby grows

**vagrant** /'veɪgrᵊnt/ *noun* [C] *formal* someone who has no job and no home and who lives outside

**vague** /veɪg/ *adj* **1** not clear or certain *I have a vague idea of where the hotel is.* ● *He was a bit vague about directions.* **2** showing that someone is not thinking clearly or does not understand *a vague expression* ● **vaguely** *adv I vaguely* (= slightly) *remember meeting her.* ● **vagueness** *noun* [U]

**vain** /veɪn/ *adj* **1 in vain** without any success *I tried in vain to start a conversation.* **2 vain attempt/effort/hope** A vain attempt, effort, etc does not have the result you want. **3** too interested in your own appearance and thinking you are very attractive ● **vainly** *adv*

**Valentine** /'væləntaɪn/ (*also* '**Valentine ˌcard**) *noun* [C] a card (= stiff, folded paper with a message inside) that you give someone on Valentine's Day

**Valentine's Day** /'væləntaɪnz,deɪ/ *noun* [C, U] 14 February, a day when you give a Valentine to someone you have a romantic relationship with or would like a romantic relationship with

**valet** /'væleɪ/ *noun* [C] **1** *US* someone who parks your car when you arrive at a restaurant, hotel, or airport **2** a male servant who looks after a man's clothes and helps him to dress

**valiant** /'væliənt/ *adj formal* very brave *a valiant effort* ● **valiantly** *adv*

**valid** /'vælɪd/ *adj* **1** based on good reasons or facts that are true *a valid argument* **2** A valid ticket or document is legally acceptable. *The ticket is valid for three months.* ⊃ *Opposite* **invalid.** ● **validity** /və'lɪdəti/ *noun* [U]

**validate** /'vælɪdeɪt/ *verb* [T] *formal* to prove that something is true ● **validation** /ˌvælɪ'deɪʃᵊn/ *noun* [C, U]

**valley** /'væli/ *noun* [C] an area of low land between hills or mountains

**valley**

**valour** *UK literary* (*US* **valor**) /'vælə/ *noun* [U] when someone is very brave, especially during a war

○⊷**valuable** /'væljuəbl/ *adj* **1** Valuable objects could be sold for a lot of money. *valuable paintings and antiques* **2** Valuable information, help, advice, etc is very helpful.

**valuables** /'væljuəblz/ *noun* [plural] small things that you own which could be sold for a lot of money *valuables such as jewellery and watches*

**valuation** /ˌvælju'eɪʃᵊn/ *noun* [C, U] when someone judges how much money something could be sold for

○⊷**value**[1] /'væljuː/ *noun* **1** [C, U] how much money something could be sold for *The new road has affected the value of these houses.* ● *Cars quickly go down in value.* **2** [U] how useful or important something is *a document of great historical value* **3 good value (for money)** If something is good value it is of good quality or there is a lot of it so you think the amount of money you spent on it was right. *The meal was very good value.* ➔ *See also:* **face value**.

**value²** /'vælju:/ *verb* [T] **valuing,** *past* **valued 1** If you value something or someone, they are very important to you. *I always value his opinion.* **2** to judge how much money something could be sold for *The ring was valued at $1000.*

**values** /'vælju:z/ *noun* [plural] your beliefs about what is morally right and wrong and what is most important in life

**valve** /vælv/ *noun* [C] something that opens and closes to control the flow of liquid or gas

**vampire** /'væmpaɪə'/ *noun* [C] in stories, a dead person who bites people's necks and drinks their blood

**van** /væn/ *noun* [C] a vehicle that is used for carrying things but which is smaller than a truck ➔ *See picture at* **vehicle**.

**vandal** /'vænd³l/ *noun* [C] someone who intentionally damages things in public places *Vandals had smashed the shop window.*

**vandalism** /'vænd³lɪz³m/ *noun* [U] the crime of intentionally damaging things in public places

**vandalize** (*also UK* **-ise**) /'vænd³laɪz/ *verb* [T] to intentionally damage things in public places

**vanguard** /'vænɡɑːd/ *noun* **in the vanguard of sth** involved in the most recent changes in technology and understanding *Libraries are in the vanguard of the electronic revolution.*

**vanilla** /və'nɪlə/ *noun* [U] a substance that is used to give flavour to some sweet foods *vanilla ice cream*

**vanish** /'vænɪʃ/ *verb* [I] to disappear suddenly *The sun vanished behind the trees.* • *The report mysteriously vanished from the files.* ➔ *See also:* vanish into thin **air¹**.

**vanity** /'vænəti/ *noun* [U] when someone thinks they are very attractive and is too interested in their own appearance

**vantage point** /'vɑːntɪdʒ,pɔɪnt/ *noun* [C] **1** the way you think about a subject when you are in a particular situation *From my vantage point, it is difficult to see how things can improve.* **2** a place from which you can see something very well

**vapour** *UK* (*US* **vapor**) /'veɪpə'/ *noun* [U] many small drops of liquid in the air which look like a cloud

**variable¹** /'veəriəbl/ *adj* changing often *The sound quality on the recording is variable.* • **variability** /,veəriə'bɪləti/ *noun* [U]

**variable²** /'veəriəbl/ *noun* [C] something that changes in different situations

**variance** /'veəriəns/ *noun formal* **at variance with sb/sth** If two things or people are at variance with each other, they do not agree or are very different. *The statement seems to be at variance with government policy.*

**variant** /'veəriənt/ *noun* [C] something that is a slightly different form from the usual one *There are several variants of the virus.* • *spelling variants*

**variation** /,veəri'eɪʃ³n/ *noun* **1** [C, U] a difference in amount or quality *variations in price* **2** [C] something that is slightly different from the usual form *It's a variation on the standard apple pie.*

**varied** /'veərɪd/ *adj* consisting of many different types of things *a long and varied career*

o⅃**variety** /və'raɪəti/ *noun* **1 a variety of sth/sb** many different types of things or people *Ben has done a variety of jobs.* **2** [C] a different type of something *a new variety of potato* **3** [U] a lot of different activities, situations, people, etc *I need more variety in my life.*

o⅃**various** /'veəriəs/ *adj* many different *They have offices in various parts of the country.* • *I started learning Spanish for various reasons.*

**variously** /'veəriəsli/ *adv* in many different ways *The event was variously described as "terrible", "shocking", and "unbelievable".*

**varnish¹** /'vɑːnɪʃ/ *noun* [C, U] a clear liquid that you paint onto wood to protect it and make it shine ➔ *See also:* **nail varnish**.

**varnish²** /'vɑːnɪʃ/ *verb* [T] to put varnish on a surface

**vary** /'veəri/ *verb* **1** ⎡BE DIFFERENT⎤ [I] If things of the same type vary, they are different from each other. *Car prices vary greatly across Europe.* • *Roses vary widely in size and shape.* **2** ⎡CHANGE⎤ [I] to change *Temperatures vary depending on the time of year.* **3** ⎡INTENTIONALLY CHANGE⎤ [T] to often change something that you do *I try to vary what I eat.*

**vase** /vɑːz ⑤ veɪs/ *noun* [C] a container that you put flowers in

**vasectomy** /və'sektəmi/ *noun* [C] a medical operation that is done to stop a man having children

**vast** /vɑːst/ *adj* extremely big *a vast amount of money* • *vast forest areas*

**vastly** /'vɑːstli/ *adv* very much *Life now is vastly different from 100 years ago.*

**VAT** /,viːeɪ'tiː/ *noun* [U] *abbreviation for* value added tax: a tax on goods and services in the UK

**vault¹** /vɔːlt/ *noun* [C] **1** a special room in a bank where money, jewellery, and other valuable objects are kept **2** a room under a church where people are buried

**vault²** /vɔːlt/ *verb* [I, T] to jump over something by first putting your hands on it *Rick vaulted the gate and ran off.* ➔ *See also:* **pole vault**.

**VCR** /,viːsiː'ɑː'/ *mainly US* (*UK* **video**) *noun* [C] *abbreviation for* video cassette recorder: a machine that you use for recording television programmes and playing videos (= recorded films or programmes)

**VDU** /,viːdiː'juː/ *noun* [C] *UK abbreviation for* visual display unit: a machine with a screen that shows information from a computer

**'ve** /v/ *short for* have *I've already eaten.*

**veal** /viːl/ *noun* [U] meat from a very young cow

**veer** /vɪə'/ *verb* **veer across/off/towards, etc** to suddenly change direction *The car veered off the road and hit a tree.*

vase

V

**veg** /vedʒ/ *noun* [C, U] *plural* **veg** *UK informal short for* vegetables *fruit and veg*

**vegan** /'viːɡən/ *noun* [C] someone who does not eat meat, fish, eggs, milk, or cheese • **vegan** *adj*

o—★**vegetable** /'vedʒtəbl/ *noun* [C] a plant that you eat, for example potatoes, onions, beans, etc ⊃ *See colour picture* **Fruit and Vegetables** *on page Centre 8.*

**vegetarian**[1] /ˌvedʒɪ'teəriən/ *noun* [C] someone who does not eat meat or fish

**vegetarian**[2] /ˌvedʒɪ'teəriən/ *adj* not eating, containing, or using meat or fish *All her children are vegetarian.* • *a vegetarian restaurant/pizza*

**vegetation** /ˌvedʒɪ'teɪʃən/ *noun* [U] the plants and trees that grow in a particular area

**veggie** /'vedʒi/ *noun* [C] *UK informal* a vegetarian • **veggie** *adj*

**vehement** /'viːəmənt/ *adj* showing strong, often negative, feelings about something *vehement criticism/opposition* • **vehemently** *adv*

o—★**vehicle** /'viːɪkl/ *noun* **1** [C] *formal* something such as a car or bus that takes people from one place to another, especially using roads **2 a vehicle for sth/doing sth** something that you use as a way of telling people your ideas or opinions *The paper was merely a vehicle for his political beliefs.*

**vehicles**

bus
van
car
lorry *UK*, truck *US*

**veil** /veɪl/ *noun* **1** [C] a thin piece of material that covers a woman's face **2 draw a veil over sth** *UK* to not talk any more about a subject because it could cause trouble or embarrassment

**veiled** /veɪld/ *adj* said so that the true meaning or purpose is not clear *veiled criticism*

**vein** /veɪn/ *noun* [C] **1** one of the tubes in your body that carries blood to your heart **2** one of the thin lines on a leaf **3 in the same vein** in the same style of speaking or writing

**Velcro** /'velkrəʊ/ *noun* [U] *trademark* material that consists of two pieces of cloth that stick together, used to fasten clothes

**velocity** /vɪ'lɒsəti/ *noun* [C, U] in science, the speed at which something moves

**velvet** /'velvɪt/ *noun* [U] cloth that has a thick, soft surface on one side *a black velvet jacket*

**vendetta** /ven'detə/ *noun* [C] when someone tries to do something bad to someone over a period of time because they have been treated badly by them *He had a vendetta against the company after he lost his job.*

**vending machine** /'vendɪŋmə,ʃiːn/ *noun* [C] a machine that sells drinks, cigarettes, chocolate, etc

**vendor** /'vendɔːr/ *noun* [C] **1** someone who sells something outside *an ice cream vendor* **2** *formal* a company that sells goods or services

**veneer** /və'nɪər/ *noun* **1** [C, U] a thin layer of wood that covers a piece of furniture that is made of a cheaper material **2 a veneer of sth** *formal* a way of behaving that is not sincere and hides someone's real character or emotions *a thin veneer of calm/respectability*

**venerable** /'venərəbl/ *adj* old and very much respected *a venerable institution/tradition*

**venetian blind** /vənˌiːʃən'blaɪnd/ *noun* [C] a covering for a window that is made from long, flat, horizontal pieces of metal or wood which you can move to let in light

**vengeance** /'vendʒəns/ *noun* **1** [U] when you do something bad to someone who has done something bad to you, or the feeling of wanting to do this *an act of vengeance* **2 with a vengeance** If something happens with a vengeance, it happens a lot or in a very strong way. *The disease swept across the country with a vengeance.*

**vengeful** /'vendʒfəl/ *adj formal* wanting vengeance

**venison** /'venɪsən/ *noun* [U] meat from a deer

**venom** /'venəm/ *noun* [U] **1** poison that some snakes and insects produce **2** a feeling of extreme anger or hate *Much of his venom was directed at his boss.* • **venomous** *adj* containing or involving venom

**vent**[1] /vent/ *noun* [C] a hole in a wall or machine that lets air in and allows smoke or smells to go out

**vent**[2] /vent/ *verb* **vent your anger/frustration, etc** to do or say something to show your anger or another strong, bad feeling

**ventilate** /'ventɪleɪt/ *verb* [T] to let air come into and go out of a room or building • **ventilation** /ˌventɪ'leɪʃən/ *noun* [U] *a ventilation system*

**venture**[1] /'ventʃər/ *noun* [C] a new activity that may not be successful *a business venture* ⊃ *See also:* **joint venture**.

**venture**[2] /'ventʃər/ *verb formal* **1 venture into/out/outside, etc** to leave a safe place and go somewhere that may involve risks *If the snow stops I might venture out.* **2** [T] to be brave enough to say something that might be criticized *I didn't dare venture an opinion.*

**venue** /'venjuː/ *noun* [C] a place where a sports game, musical performance, or special event happens

**Venus** /'viːnəs/ *noun* [no plural] the planet that is second from the Sun, after Mercury and before the Earth

**veranda** (*also* **verandah**) /ve'rændə/ *noun* [C] a room that is joined to the outside of a house and has a roof and floor but no outside wall

o—★**verb** /vɜːb/ *noun* [C] a word or group of words that refers to an action, state, or experience. For example the words 'arrive', 'make', 'be', and 'feel' are verbs. ⊃ *See also:* **auxiliary verb**, **modal verb**, **phrasal verb**.

**verbal** /'vɜːbəl/ adj 1 spoken and not written a verbal promise 2 relating to words or the use of words verbal ability/skills • **verbally** adv

**verbatim** /vɜːˈbeɪtɪm/ adj, adv using the exact words that were originally used

**verdict** /'vɜːdɪkt/ noun [C] 1 a decision in a court of law saying if someone is guilty or not a guilty verdict • The jury took nine hours to reach a verdict. 2 someone's opinion about something after experiencing it, often for the first time You tried out that Italian restaurant? What was the verdict?

**verge**[1] /vɜːdʒ/ noun [C] 1 UK the edge of a road or path that is usually covered in grass 2 **be on the verge of sth/doing sth** to be going to happen or to do something very soon a company on the verge of financial disaster

**verge**[2] /vɜːdʒ/ verb

**verge on sth** to almost be a particular state or quality His constant questions verged on rudeness.

**verify** /'verɪfaɪ/ verb [T] to prove that something is true, or do something to discover if it is true It was impossible to verify her statement. • **verification** /ˌverɪfɪˈkeɪʃən/ noun [U]

**veritable** /'verɪtəbl/ adj [always before noun] formal used to emphasize how extreme something is Their house was a veritable palace (= was very large).

**vermin** /'vɜːmɪn/ noun [plural] small animals that damage crops and can give people diseases

**versatile** /'vɜːsətaɪl ⓤⓈ 'vɜːrsətəl/ adj 1 having many different skills a versatile player/performer 2 useful for doing a lot of different things a versatile tool • **versatility** /ˌvɜːsəˈtɪləti/ noun [U]

**verse** /vɜːs/ noun 1 [C] one of the parts that a song or poem is divided into I only know the first verse. 2 [U] words that are in the form of poetry The story was told in verse.

o—**version** /'vɜːʃən/ noun [C] 1 one form of something that is slightly different to other forms of the same thing I saw the original version of the film. 2 someone's description of what has happened Bates gave his version of events to the police.

**versus** /'vɜːsəs/ preposition 1 used to say that one team or person is competing against another Tomorrow's game is Newcastle versus Arsenal. 2 used to compare two things or ideas, especially when you have to choose between them private education versus state education

**vertical** /'vɜːtɪkəl/ adj pointing straight up from a surface a vertical line • **vertically** adv ⊃ See picture at **horizontal**.

**vertigo** /'vɜːtɪɡəʊ/ noun [U] when you feel slightly ill because you are in a high place and feel as if you might fall

**verve** /vɜːv/ noun [U] formal energy and enthusiasm

o—**very**[1] /'veri/ adv 1 used to emphasize an adjective or adverb She was very pleased. • Marie speaks very slowly. • Thank you very much. 2 **not very good/tall/happy, etc** not good, happy, etc The film wasn't very good.

**very**[2] /'veri/ adj [always before noun] used to emphasize a noun This is the very house where we stayed.

**vessel** /'vesəl/ noun [C] 1 formal a ship or large boat 2 old-fashioned a container for liquids ⊃ See also: **blood vessel**.

**vest** /vest/ noun [C] 1 UK (US **undershirt**) a piece of underwear that you wear under a shirt 2 US (UK **waistcoat**) a piece of clothing with buttons at the front and no sleeves, that you wear over a shirt ⊃ See colour picture **Clothes** on page Centre 5.

**vested interest** /ˌvestɪdˈɪntrest/ noun [C] If you have a vested interest in something, you want it to happen because it will give you advantages.

**vestige** /'vestɪdʒ/ noun [C] a very small amount of something that still exists after most of it has gone There is still a vestige of hope that she might be found alive.

**vet**[1] /vet/ noun [C] someone whose job is to give medical care to animals that are ill or hurt

**vet**[2] /vet/ verb [T] **vetting**, past **vetted** to look at details of someone's life, in order to make sure that they are suitable for a particular job [often passive] Applicants for the job are carefully vetted.

**veteran** /'vetərən/ noun [C] 1 someone who has been in an army or navy during a war a veteran of World War Two 2 someone who has done a job or activity for a long time a 20-year veteran of BBC news

**veterinarian** /ˌvetərɪˈneəriən/ noun [C] US a vet

**veterinary** /'vetərɪnəri/ adj formal relating to medical care given to animals that are ill or hurt

**veterinary surgeon** noun [C] UK formal a vet

**veto**[1] /'viːtəʊ/ verb [T] **vetoing**, past **vetoed** If someone in authority vetoes something, they do not allow it to happen, although other people have agreed to it. The plan was vetoed by the President.

**veto**[2] /'viːtəʊ/ noun [C, U] plural **vetoes** when someone in authority does not allow something to happen

**vexed** /vekst/ adj **vexed question/issue, etc** a situation that causes problems and is difficult to deal with the vexed issue of unemployment

**via** /vaɪə/ preposition 1 going through or stopping at a place on the way to another place The train to Utrecht goes via Amsterdam. 2 using a particular machine, system, or person to send or receive something I receive all my work via e-mail.

**viable** /'vaɪəbl/ adj effective and able to be successful a viable alternative to nuclear power • an economically viable plan • **viability** /ˌvaɪəˈbɪləti/ noun [U]

**viaduct** /'vaɪədʌkt/ noun [C] a long, high bridge across a valley

**vibes** /vaɪbz/ noun [plural] informal the way a person or place makes you feel I get bad vibes from her.

**vibrant** /'vaɪbrənt/ adj 1 full of excitement and energy a vibrant city • a vibrant, young performer 2 A vibrant colour is very bright.

**vibrate** /vaɪˈbreɪt ⓤⓈ 'vaɪbreɪt/ verb [I, T] to shake with small, quick movements or to make something shake this way The music was so loud that the floor was vibrating. • **vibration** /vaɪˈbreɪʃən/ noun [C, U]

**vicar** /'vɪkəʳ/ *noun* [C] a priest in some Christian churches

**vicarage** /'vɪkərɪdʒ/ *noun* [C] the house where a vicar lives

**vicarious** /vɪ'keəriəs/ *adj* [always before noun] A vicarious feeling is one you get from seeing or hearing about another person's experiences. *It gives me vicarious pleasure to watch him eat.*

**vice** /vaɪs/ *noun* 1 [BAD HABIT] [C] something bad that someone often does *Smoking is his only vice.* 2 [CRIME] [U] crime that involves sex or drugs 3 [TOOL] [C] *UK* (*US* **vise**) a tool used for holding something tightly while you cut it, make it smooth, etc ➜ *See picture at* **tool**.

,**vice 'president** *noun* [C] 1 the person who is a rank lower than the president of a country 2 *US* someone who is responsible for part of a company *She's vice president of sales and marketing.*

**vice versa** /ˌvaɪs'vɜːsə/ *adv* used for referring to the opposite of what you have just said *Never use indoor lights outside and vice versa.*

**vicinity** /vɪ'sɪnəti/ *noun* **in the vicinity (of sth)** *formal* in the area near a place *A number of buildings in the vicinity of the fire were damaged.*

**vicious** /'vɪʃəs/ *adj* 1 violent and dangerous *a vicious attack on a child* • *a vicious dog* 2 intended to upset someone *a vicious rumour* • **viciously** *adv*

,**vicious 'circle** (*also* ,**vicious 'cycle**) *noun* [no plural] when one problem causes another problem which then makes the first problem worse

o┅**victim** /'vɪktɪm/ *noun* [C] someone who has suffered the effects of violence, illness, or bad luck *victims of crime* • *hurricane/flood victims*

**victimize** (*also UK* **-ise**) /'vɪktɪmaɪz/ *verb* [T] to treat someone unfairly because you do not like or approve of them *Ben feels he has been victimized by his teacher.*

**victor** /'vɪktəʳ/ *noun* [C] *formal* the person who wins a fight or competition

**Victorian** /vɪk'tɔːriən/ *adj* from or relating to the period between 1837 and 1901 in Britain *a Victorian house*

**victorious** /vɪk'tɔːriəs/ *adj* having won a fight or competition *a victorious army*

**victory** /'vɪktəri/ *noun* [C, U] when you win a fight or competition *Phoenix managed a 135–114 victory over Denver.*

o┅**video¹** /'vɪdiəʊ/ *noun* 1 [C, U] a plastic box that you put into a machine in order to record a television programme or watch a programme that is already recorded *The children were watching a video of 'The Lion King'.* • *You can get the film on video.* 2 [C] *UK* (*also UK* **video recorder**) (*US* **VCR**) a machine that you use for recording a television programme or watching a video ➜ *See colour picture* **The Living Room** *on page Centre 11.*

**video²** /'vɪdiəʊ/ *verb* [T] **videoing**, *past* **videoed** to record something using a camera or video machine

'**video ,game** *noun* [C] a game in which you make pictures move on a screen

'**video rec,order** *noun* [C] a video machine

**videotape** /'vɪdiəʊteɪp/ *noun* [C, U] a thin strip of material inside a plastic box that is used

for recording television programmes and films

**vie** /vaɪ/ *verb* [I] **vying**, *past* **vied** to try hard to do something more successfully than someone else *The children were vying for attention.* • [+ to do sth] *Film crews were vying with each other to get the best pictures.*

o┅**view¹** /vjuː/ *noun* 1 [OPINION] [C] your opinion *We have different views about/on education.* • *In her view this is wrong.* 2 [THINGS YOU SEE] [C] the things that you can see from a place *There was a lovely view of the lake from the bedroom window.* 3 [ABILITY TO SEE] [no plural] how well you can see something from a particular place *We had a great view of the procession.* 4 [POSITION] [U] a position from which something can be seen *The house was hidden from view behind a wall.* • *He turned the corner and the harbour came into view.* 5 **in full view of sb** happening where someone can easily see *All this happened in full view of the cameras.* 6 **in view of sth** *formal* because of *In view of recent events, we have decided to cancel the meeting.* 7 **with a view to doing sth** *formal* so that you can do something *He's doing some improvements on the house with a view to selling it.* ➜ *See also:* **point of view.**

---

**USAGE**

**view** or **sight**?

**View** means the countryside, buildings, things, etc which you can see from a place, or how well you can see something. A **view** is usually pleasant.

*We had a wonderful view from the aircraft.*

~~We had a wonderful sight from the aircraft.~~

**Sight** means when you see something, or the ability to see.

*The sight of blood makes me feel sick.*

~~The view of blood makes me feel sick.~~

*He lost his sight in an accident.*

~~He lost his view in an accident.~~

---

**view²** /vjuː/ *verb* [T] *formal* 1 to have a particular opinion about someone or something *In all three countries he is viewed as a terrorist.* 2 to watch something *They were able to view the city from a helicopter.*

**viewer** /'vjuːəʳ/ *noun* [C] someone who watches a television programme

**viewpoint** /'vjuːpɔɪnt/ *noun* [C] a way of thinking about a situation *From his viewpoint the action seemed entirely justified.*

**vigil** /'vɪdʒɪl/ *noun* [C, U] when people stay somewhere quietly in order to show that they support someone, disagree with someone, etc *an all-night vigil for peace*

**vigilant** /'vɪdʒɪlənt/ *adj* watching carefully and always ready to notice anything dangerous or illegal *Police have asked people to be vigilant after yesterday's bomb attack.* • **vigilance** /'vɪdʒɪləns/ *noun* [U]

**vigilante** /ˌvɪdʒɪ'lænti/ *noun* [C] a member of a group of people who try to catch criminals and punish them without having any legal authority

**vigor** /'vɪgəʳ/ noun [U] *US spelling of* vigour

**vigorous** /'vɪgᵊrəs/ adj **1** showing or needing a lot of physical energy *vigorous exercise* **2** showing strong, often negative, feelings about something *a vigorous debate* ● *He was a vigorous opponent of the government.* ● **vigorously** adv *Bates vigorously* (= strongly) *denies murdering his wife.*

**vigour** UK (US **vigor**) /'vɪgəʳ/ noun [U] strength and energy *She set about her work **with** great **vigour**.*

**vile** /vaɪl/ adj extremely unpleasant *a vile attack* ● *The bathroom was vile.*

**vilify** /'vɪlɪfaɪ/ verb [T] *formal* to say bad things about someone so that other people will not like or approve of them

**villa** /'vɪlə/ noun [C] a large house, especially one used for holidays in a warm country

o─ᵃ**village** /'vɪlɪdʒ/ noun [C] a place where people live in the countryside that includes buildings such as shops and a school but which is smaller than a town *She lives in a small village outside Oxford.* ● *a village shop*

**villager** /'vɪlɪdʒəʳ/ noun [C] someone who lives in a village

**villain** /'vɪlən/ noun [C] a bad person in a film, book, etc

**vindicate** /'vɪndɪkeɪt/ verb [T] *formal* to prove that what someone said or did was right after people generally thought it was wrong ● **vindication** /,vɪndɪ'keɪʃᵊn/ noun [C, U] *formal*

**vindictive** /vɪn'dɪktɪv/ adj intending to harm or upset someone who has harmed or upset you

**vine** /vaɪn/ noun [C] a plant that grapes (= small, green or purple fruit used for making wine) grow on

**vinegar** /'vɪnɪgəʳ/ noun [U] a sour liquid that is used in cooking, often made from wine

**vineyard** /'vɪnjəd/ noun [C] an area of land where someone grows grapes (= small, green or purple fruit) for making wine

**vintage¹** /'vɪntɪdʒ/ adj **1** WINE Vintage wine is wine of a good quality that was made in a particular year. **2** VERY GOOD having all the best or most typical qualities of something, especially from the past *a vintage Hollywood movie* **3** CAR A vintage car was made between 1919 and 1930.

**vintage²** /'vɪntɪdʒ/ noun [C] the wine that was made in a particular year *The 1993 vintage is one of the best.*

**vinyl** /'vaɪnᵊl/ noun [U] a type of very strong plastic

**viola** /vi'əʊlə/ noun [C] a wooden instrument, larger than a violin, that you hold against your neck and play by moving a special stick across strings

**violate** /'vaɪəleɪt/ verb [T] *formal* **1** to not obey a law, rule, or agreement *Countries that violate international law will be dealt with severely.* **2** to not allow someone something that they should morally be allowed to have *They were accused of violating human rights.* ● **violation** /,vaɪə'leɪʃᵊn/ noun [C, U] *a violation of privacy*

o─ᵃ**violence** /'vaɪəlᵊns/ noun [U] **1** when someone

tries to hurt or kill someone else *an act of violence* ● *A number of people were killed in the violence.* ● **Violence against** women has increased in recent years. **2** extreme force and energy, especially of something causing damage *Such was the violence of the explosion that three buildings collapsed.*

o─ᵃ**violent** /'vaɪəlᵊnt/ adj **1** ACTION involving violence *a victim of violent crime* ● *a violent protest* ● *I don't like violent films* (= films that show violence). **2** PERSON likely to hurt or kill someone else *a violent criminal* **3** DAMAGE sudden and causing damage *a violent explosion/storm* **4** EMOTIONS showing very strong feelings, especially anger *violent emotions* ● **violently** adv ⊃ *See also:* **non-violent**.

**violet** /'vaɪələt/ noun **1** [C] a small plant with a small, purple flower **2** [U] a pale purple colour

**violin** /,vaɪə'lɪn/ noun [C] a wooden musical instrument that you hold against your neck and play by moving a bow (= special stick) across strings ● **violinist** /vaɪə'lɪnɪst/ noun [C] someone who plays a violin

**VIP** /,viːaɪ'piː/ noun [C] *abbreviation for* very important person: someone who is famous or powerful and is treated in a special way *The airport has a separate lounge for VIPs.*

**viper** /'vaɪpəʳ/ noun [C] a small, poisonous snake

**viral** /'vaɪrᵊl/ adj caused by or relating to a virus (= infectious organism) *a viral infection*

**virgin¹** /'vɜːdʒɪn/ noun [C] someone who has never had sex

**virgin²** /'vɜːdʒɪn/ adj Virgin land, forest, etc has not been used or damaged by people.

**virginity** /və'dʒɪnəti/ noun [U] when someone has never had sex *Emma lost her virginity* (= had sex for the first time) *at sixteen.*

**Virgo** /'vɜːgəʊ/ noun [C, U] the sign of the zodiac which relates to the period of 23 August – 22 September, or a person born during this period ⊃ *See picture at* **zodiac**.

**virile** /'vɪraɪl ᵁˢ 'vɪrᵊl/ adj A virile man is strong and has sexual energy. ● **virility** /vɪ'rɪləti/ noun [U]

**virtual** /'vɜːtʃuəl/ adj [always before noun] **1** almost a particular thing or quality *They played the game in virtual silence.* **2** using computer images and sounds that make you think an imagined situation is real *a virtual art gallery*

**virtually** /'vɜːtʃuəli/ adv almost *They're virtually the same.* ● *I've virtually finished.*

**virtual re'ality** noun [U] when a computer produces images and sounds that make you feel an imagined situation is real

**virtue** /'vɜːtjuː/ noun **1** ADVANTAGE [C, U] an advantage or useful quality *The great virtue of having a small car is that you can park it easily.* **2** GOOD QUALITY [C] a good quality that someone has *Patience is not among his virtues.* **3** MORAL BEHAVIOUR [U] behaviour that is morally good **4** **by virtue of sth** *formal* because of something *She succeeded by virtue of hard work rather than talent.*

**virtuoso** /,vɜːtju'əʊsəʊ/ noun [C] someone who is extremely good at doing something, especially playing a musical instrument

**virtuous** /'vɜːtʃuəs/ adj behaving in a good and moral way ● **virtuously** adv

**virulent** /'vɪrʊlᵊnt/ adj **1** A virulent disease or poison causes severe illness very quickly. **2** formal criticizing or hating someone or something very much *a virulent attack on the government*

o-ᴗ**virus** /'vaɪərəs/ noun [C] **1** an infectious organism too small to be seen that causes disease, or an illness that it causes *The doctor says I've got a virus.* **2** a program that is secretly put onto a computer in order to destroy the information that is stored on it

**visa** /'viːzə/ noun [C] an official mark in your passport (= document which proves your nationality) that allows you to enter or leave a particular country *She went to Miami on a tourist visa.*

**vis-à-vis** /ˌviːzɑː'viː/ preposition relating to something, or in comparison with something *I have to speak to James vis-à-vis the conference arrangements.*

**vise** /vaɪs/ noun [C] US spelling of vice (= a tool used for holding something tightly while you cut it, make it smooth, etc) ➔ See picture at **tool**.

**visibility** /ˌvɪzə'bɪləti/ noun [U] how far or how well you can see because of weather conditions *good/poor visibility* • *It was foggy and visibility was down to 50 metres.*

**visible** /'vɪzəbl/ adj able to be seen *The fire was visible from five kilometres away.* ➔ Opposite **invisible**. • **visibly** adv *She was visibly upset.*

**vision** /'vɪʒᵊn/ noun **1** IDEA [C] an idea or image in your mind of what something could be like in the future *a vision of a better society* **2** SEE [U] the ability to see *He has poor vision in his left eye.* **3** ABILITY TO PLAN [U] the ability to make plans for the future that are imaginative and wise *As a leader, he lacked vision.* **4** RELIGION [C] when you see someone or something that no one else can see as part of a religious experience

**visionary** /'vɪʒᵊnᵊri/ adj able to make plans for the future that are imaginative and wise *a visionary leader* • **visionary** noun [C]

o-ᴗ**visit¹** /'vɪzɪt/ verb [I, T] **1** to go to someone's home and spend time with them *We have friends coming to visit this weekend.* **2** to go to a place and spend a short amount of time there *Did you visit St Petersburg while you were in Russia?* ➔ See usage note at **meet**.

**visit with sb** US to spend time talking with someone who you know *Mom was visiting with our neighbor.*

o-ᴗ**visit²** /'vɪzɪt/ noun [C] when you visit a place or a person *the President's visit to Hong Kong* • *Why don't you pay him a visit (= visit him)?*

o-ᴗ**visitor** /'vɪzɪtəʳ/ noun [C] someone who visits a person or place *The museum attracts large numbers of visitors.*

**visor** /'vaɪzəʳ/ noun [C] **1** PART OF HAT the part of a helmet (= hard hat that protects your head) that you can pull down to cover your face **2** HAT a hat that has a curved part above your eyes to protect them from the sun **3** CAR the parts in the front window of a car that you pull down to protect your eyes from the sun ➔ See colour picture **Car** on page Centre 3.

**vista** /'vɪstə/ noun [C] a view, especially a beautiful view that you look at from a high place

**visual** /'vɪʒuəl/ adj relating to seeing *The film has some powerful visual effects.* • **visually** adv *visually appealing*

**visual 'aid** noun [C] something that helps you understand or remember information, such as a picture or film

**visualize** (also UK -ise) /'vɪʒuᵊlaɪz/ verb [T] to create a picture in your mind of someone or something *I was very surprised when I met Geoff – I'd visualized someone much older.* • **visualization** /ˌvɪʒuᵊlaɪ'zeɪʃᵊn/ noun [U]

**vital** /'vaɪtᵊl/ adj **1** necessary *Tourism is vital to the country's economy.* • [+ (that)] *It's vital that you send off this form today.* **2** formal full of energy

**vitality** /vaɪ'tæləti/ noun [U] energy and strength *At 48, he still projects an image of youth and vitality.*

**vitally** /'vaɪtᵊli/ adv in a very important way *Safety at work is vitally important.*

**vitamin** /'vɪtəmɪn US 'vaɪtəmɪn/ noun [C] one of a group of natural substances in food that you need to be healthy *Oranges are full of vitamin C.*

**vitriolic** /ˌvɪtri'ɒlɪk/ adj formal criticizing someone in a very severe and unpleasant way

**viva** /'vaɪvə/ noun [C] UK a spoken examination at university

**vivacious** /vɪ'veɪʃəs/ adj A vivacious person, especially a woman, is full of energy and enthusiasm.

**vivid** /'vɪvɪd/ adj **1** Vivid descriptions or memories produce strong, clear images in your mind. *He gave a very vivid description of life in Caracas.* **2** A vivid colour is very bright. • **vividly** adv *I remember my first day at school very vividly.*

**vivisection** /ˌvɪvɪ'sekʃᵊn/ noun [U] when living animals are used in scientific experiments, especially in order to discover the effects of new drugs

**vixen** /'vɪksᵊn/ noun [C] a female fox (= wild dog with red-brown fur)

**vocabulary** /vəʊ'kæbjᵊri/ noun **1** WORDS [C, U] all the words you know in a particular language *Reading helps to widen your vocabulary.* **2** LANGUAGE [no plural] all the words that exist in a language, or that are used when discussing a particular subject *Computing has its own specialist vocabulary.* **3** LIST [no plural] a list of words and their meanings

**vocal** /'vəʊkᵊl/ adj **1** expressing your opinions in a strong way *She is a vocal supporter of women's rights.* **2** involving or relating to the voice, especially singing *vocal music*

**'vocal ˌchords** noun [plural] folds of skin at the top of your throat that make sounds when air from your lungs moves over them

**vocalist** /'vəʊkᵊlɪst/ noun [C] the person who sings in a group of people who play popular music

**vocals** /'vəʊkᵊlz/ noun [plural] the part of a piece of music that is sung

**vocation** /vəʊ'keɪʃᵊn/ noun [C, U] a strong feeling that you are right for a particular type of work, or a job that gives you this feeling *He knew that teaching was his true vocation.*

**vocational** /vəʊ'keɪʃᵊnᵊl/ adj Vocational education and skills prepare you for a particular type of work. *The college offers both vocational and academic courses.*

**vociferous** /vəʊˈsɪfᵊrəs/ *adj formal* expressing your opinions in a loud and strong way *She has become increasingly **vociferous in** her opposition to the scheme.*

**vodka** /ˈvɒdkə/ *noun* [C, U] a strong alcoholic drink that is popular in Russia and Poland

**vogue** /vəʊg/ *noun* [U, no plural] If there is a vogue for something, it is very fashionable. *This period saw a **vogue for** Japanese painting.* • *Flat shoes are **in vogue** (= fashionable) this spring.*

o━**voice¹** /vɔɪs/ *noun* 1 SOUNDS [C] the sounds that you make when you speak or sing *I could hear voices in the next room.* • *Jessie has a beautiful singing voice.* • *Could you please **keep your voices down** (= speak more quietly)?* • *He **raised his voice** (= spoke more loudly) so that everyone could hear.* 2 **lose your voice** to become unable to speak, often because of an illness *She had a bad cold and was losing her voice.* 3 OPINION [C] someone's opinion about a particular subject *The programme gives people the opportunity to make their voices heard.* 4 PERSON [no plural] someone who expresses the opinions or wishes of a group of people *It's important that students have a voice on the committee.* ➔ *See also:* **the passive** voice.

**voice²** /vɔɪs/ *verb* [T] to say what you think about a particular subject *He has voiced concern about the new proposals.*

'**voice ,mail** *noun* [U] an electronic telephone answering system

**void¹** /vɔɪd/ *adj* 1 [never before noun] not legally or officially acceptable *The contracts were declared void.* 2 **be void of sth** *formal* to be without something *His last statement was entirely void of meaning.*

**void²** /vɔɪd/ *noun* [no plural] 1 when someone or something important is not now in your life and you are unhappy *Her husband's death **left a void** in her life.* 2 a large hole or empty space

**vol** *written abbreviation for* volume

**volatile** /ˈvɒlətaɪl/ US /ˈvɑːlətᵊl/ *adj* 1 A volatile person can suddenly become angry or violent. 2 A volatile situation might suddenly change. *a volatile political situation* • **volatility** /ˌvɒləˈtɪləti/ *noun* [U]

**volcano** /vɒlˈkeɪnəʊ/ *noun* [C] *plural* **volcanoes** or **volcanos** a mountain with a large hole at the top which sometimes explodes and produces hot, melted rock and smoke • **volcanic** /vɒlˈkænɪk/ *adj* relating to a volcano *volcanic ash*

volcano

**vole** /vəʊl/ *noun* [C] a small animal like a mouse

**volition** /vəʊˈlɪʃᵊn/ *noun* [U] *formal* the power to make your own decisions *He left the firm **of his own volition** (= because he decided to).*

**volley¹** /ˈvɒli/ *noun* 1 [C] in sports, a kick or hit in which a player returns a ball before it touches the ground 2 **a volley of shots/gunfire, etc** when a lot of bullets are shot at the same time *A volley of bullets ripped through the floorboards.* 3 **a volley of abuse/complaints, etc** a lot of insults/complaints, etc said at the same time

**volley²** /ˈvɒli/ *verb* [I, T] in sports, to return a ball by kicking or hitting it before it touches the ground

**volleyball** /ˈvɒlibɔːl/ *noun* [U] a game in which two teams use their hands to hit a ball over a net without allowing it to touch the ground ➔ *See colour picture* **Sports 2** *on page Centre 16.*

**volt** /vəʊlt/ *(written abbreviation* **V)** *noun* [C] a unit for measuring the force of an electric current

**voltage** /ˈvəʊltɪdʒ/ *noun* [C, U] the force of an electric current, measured in volts

**volume** /ˈvɒljuːm/ *noun* 1 SOUND [U] the level of sound produced by a television, radio, etc *to turn the volume up/down* 2 AMOUNT [U] the number or amount of something, especially when it is large *the volume of work involved* 3 SPACE [U] the amount of space inside an object *Which of the bottles has the larger volume?* 4 BOOK [C] a book, especially one of a set *a new dictionary in two volumes*

**voluminous** /vəˈluːmɪnəs/ *adj formal* very large *voluminous trousers*

**voluntary** /ˈvɒləntᵊri/ *adj* 1 Voluntary work is done without being paid and usually involves helping people. *She does voluntary work for the Red Cross.* • *voluntary organizations* 2 done or given because you want to and not because you have been forced to *voluntary contributions* ➔ *Opposite* **involuntary**. • **voluntarily** /ˌvɒlənˈteᵊrᵊli/ *adv She left voluntarily.*

**volunteer¹** /ˌvɒlənˈtɪəʳ/ *verb* 1 OFFER [I, T] to offer to do something without being asked or told to do it [+ to do sth] *Rob volunteered to look after the kids.* 2 ARMY [I] to join the army, navy, etc without being officially told to join *In 1939 he **volunteered for** active service.* 3 INFORMATION [T] to give information without being asked *No one volunteered the truth.*

**volunteer²** /ˌvɒlənˈtɪəʳ/ *noun* [C] 1 someone who does work without being paid, especially work that involves helping people *a Red Cross volunteer* 2 someone who does or gives something because they want to and not because they have been forced to *Any volunteers to help me move these books?*

**voluptuous** /vəˈlʌptʃuəs/ *adj* A voluptuous woman has a sexually attractive body, often with large breasts.

**vomit¹** /ˈvɒmɪt/ *verb* [I, T] If someone vomits, the food or liquid that was in their stomach comes up and out of their mouth. *She was vomiting blood.*

**vomit²** /ˈvɒmɪt/ *noun* [U] the food or liquid that comes from your mouth when you vomit

**voodoo** /ˈvuːduː/ *noun* [U] a religion involving magic and praying to spirits

**voracious** /vəˈreɪʃəs/ *adj* wanting to do something a lot, especially wanting to eat a lot of food *She has a voracious appetite.* • *a voracious* reader of historical novels • **voraciously** adv • **voracity** /vəˈræsəti/ noun [U]

◦▲**vote¹** /vəʊt/ verb [I, T] to show your choice or opinion in an election or meeting by writing a cross on an official piece of paper or putting your hand up *Who did you vote for?* • *The unions voted against strike action.* • [+ **to do sth**] *Staff have voted to accept the pay offer.*

◦▲**vote²** /vəʊt/ noun [C] **1** when someone shows their choice or opinion in an election or meeting by writing a cross on an official piece of paper or putting their hand up *He lost the election by twenty votes.* **2** a way of making a decision by asking a group of people to vote *We called a meeting in order to take a vote on the proposal.* **3** **the vote a** the total number of votes given or received in an election *The Green party got 10% of the vote.* **b** when someone is officially allowed to vote *In some countries women still don't have the vote.*

**voter** /ˈvəʊtəʳ/ noun [C] someone who votes or who is officially allowed to vote

**vouch** /vaʊtʃ/ verb
**vouch for sb/sth** to say that you know from experience that something is true or good, or that someone has a good character

**voucher** /ˈvaʊtʃəʳ/ noun [C] a piece of paper that can be used instead of money to pay for goods or services *a discount voucher*

**vow¹** /vaʊ/ verb [T] to make a serious promise or decision [+ (**that**)] *She vowed that she would* never leave the children again. • [+ **to do sth**] *I've vowed never to go there again.*

**vow²** /vaʊ/ noun [C] a serious promise or decision *marriage vows* • *I made a vow that I would write to him once a week.*

**vowel** /vaʊəl/ noun [C] a speech sound that you make with your lips and teeth open, shown in English by the letters 'a', 'e', 'i', 'o' or 'u'

**voyage** /ˈvɔɪdʒ/ noun [C] a long journey, especially by ship, or in space *The ship sank on its maiden voyage* (= first journey).

**vs** (also UK **v**) preposition written abbreviation for versus (= used to say that one team or person is competing against another)

**vulgar** /ˈvʌlgəʳ/ adj **1** rude and likely to upset or anger people, especially by referring to sex and the body in an unpleasant way *vulgar jokes/language* **2** not showing good judgment about what is suitable or pleasant to look at *a vulgar shade of yellow* • **vulgarity** /vʌlˈgærəti/ noun [U]

**vulnerable** /ˈvʌlnᵊrəbl/ adj easy to hurt or attack physically or emotionally *She was a vulnerable sixteen-year-old.* • *The troops are in a vulnerable position.* • *He's more vulnerable to infection because of his injuries.* • **vulnerability** /ˌvʌlnᵊrəˈbɪləti/ noun [U]

**vulture** /ˈvʌltʃəʳ/ noun [C] a large bird with no feathers on its head or neck that eats dead animals

**vying** /ˈvaɪɪŋ/ present participle of vie

**V**

**W, w** /'dʌblju:/ the twenty-third letter of the alphabet

**W** *written abbreviation for* watt (= a unit for measuring electrical power) *a 40W light bulb*

**wacky** /'wæki/ *adj informal* unusual in a funny or surprising way *a wacky sense of humour*

**wad** /wɒd/ *noun* [C] **1** a thick pile of pieces of paper, especially paper money *a wad of cash* **2** a piece of soft material in the shape of a ball *a wad of (UK) cotton wool/(US) cotton*

**waddle** /'wɒdl/ *verb* [I] A duck (= water bird) or fat person that waddles walks with short steps, moving from side to side.

**wade** /weɪd/ *verb* **wade across/through, etc** to walk through water *He waded across the river.* **wade through sth** to read a lot of boring or difficult information

**wafer** /'weɪfəʳ/ *noun* [C] a light, thin biscuit

**waffle¹** /'wɒfl/ *noun* **1** [U] *informal* speech or writing that says nothing important **2** [C] a square, flat cake with a pattern of holes in it, eaten especially in the US

**waffle²** /'wɒfl/ *(also* **waffle on**) *verb* [I] *informal* to talk or write a lot and say nothing important

**waft** /wɒft/ *verb* **waft from/through, etc** to gradually move through the air *The smell of coffee wafted through the room.*

**wag** /wæg/ *verb* [I, T] **wagging,** *past* **wagged 1** If a dog wags its tail, it moves it from side to side. **2** If you wag your finger, you move it from side to side, often to tell someone not to do something.

**wage¹** /weɪdʒ/ *noun* [no plural] *(also* **wages** the amount of money a person regularly receives for their job *weekly wages* ● *the minimum wage* ⊃ *See usage note at* **pay.**

**wage²** /weɪdʒ/ *verb* **wage a battle/campaign/ war, etc** to fight or organize a series of activities in order to achieve something *They're currently waging a campaign to change the law.*

**wager** /'weɪdʒəʳ/ *verb* [T] to risk money on the result of a game, race, competition, etc ● **wager** *noun* [C]

**wagon** /'wægən/ *noun* [C] a large vehicle with four large wheels pulled by horses

**wail** /weɪl/ *verb* [I, T] **1** to cry loudly because you are very unhappy *"I've lost my mummy," she wailed.* **2** If a siren (= loud noise to warn of danger) wails, it makes a noise. *Somewhere in the distance a police siren was wailing.* ● **wail** *noun* [C]

**waist** /weɪst/ *noun* [C] **1** the part around the middle of your body where you wear a belt *She had a 26 inch waist.* ⊃ *See colour picture* **The Body** *on page Centre 2.* **2** the part of a piece of clothing that fits round the waist

**waistcoat** /'weɪstkəʊt/ *UK (US* **vest)** *noun* [C] a piece of clothing with buttons at the front and no sleeves, that you wear over a shirt ⊃ *See colour picture* **Clothes** *on page Centre 5.*

**waistline** /'weɪstlaɪn/ *noun* [C] how big or small

your waist is, or the part of a piece of clothing that goes around the waist

o-ᴗ**wait¹** /weɪt/ *verb* [I] **1** to stay in a place until someone or something arrives or someone or something is ready for you *I'm waiting for Clive.* ● *How long did you wait for a taxi?* ● [+ to do sth] *I'm still waiting to use the phone.* **2** to not do something until something else happens *We'll wait till Jane gets here before we start eating.* **3 can't wait** *informal* used to say how excited you are about something that you are going to do [+ to do sth] *I can't wait to see him.* **4 keep sb waiting** to be late so that someone has to wait for you *I'm sorry to have kept you waiting.* **5 wait and see** to wait to discover what will happen *We'll wait and see what she says.* ⊃ *See also:* be waiting in **the wings.**

USAGE

**wait** or **expect?**

When you **wait**, you stay somewhere until a person or thing arrives or is ready.

*I waited twenty minutes for the bus.*

*She's waiting for her exam results.*

When you **expect** something, you think that it will happen.

*I'm expecting the bus to arrive in about 5 minutes.*

*She expected to do well in the exam.*

~~She waited to do well in the exam.~~

**wait about/around** to stay in a place and do nothing while you wait for someone to arrive or something to happen

**wait in** *UK* to stay at home because you are expecting someone to visit or telephone you

**wait on sb** to bring a meal to someone, especially in a restaurant

**wait up** to not go to bed at night until someone has come home *I'll be quite late, so don't wait up for me.*

**wait²** /weɪt/ *noun* [no plural] when you stay in a place until someone or something arrives or someone or something is ready for you *We had a long wait at the airport.*

**waiter** /'weɪtəʳ/ *noun* [C] a man who works in a restaurant, bringing food to customers

**waiting list** *noun* [C] a list of people who are waiting until it is their time to have or do something *a hospital waiting list*

**waiting room** *noun* [C] a room in which people wait for something, for example to see a doctor or take a train

**waitress** /'weɪtrəs/ *noun* [C] a woman who works in a restaurant, bringing food to customers

**waive** /weɪv/ *verb* [T] **1** to allow someone not to obey the usual rule or not to pay the usual amount of money *He agreed to waive his fee to help us.* **2** to decide not to have something that you are allowed by law to have *She waived her right to have a lawyer representing her.*

o-ᴗ**wake¹** /weɪk/ *(also* **wake up)** *verb* [I, T] *past t* **woke,** *past p* **woken** to stop sleeping or to make someone else stop sleeping *I've only just woken* up. • *Could you wake me up before you go?* • *You woke me up making so much noise.* ⊃ *See colour picture* **Phrasal Verbs** *on page Centre 13.*

**wake up to sth** to start to understand something that is important *We need to wake up to the fact that the Earth's resources are limited.*

**wake²** /weɪk/ *noun* **1 in the wake of sth** after something has happened, and often because it has happened *Airport security was extra tight in the wake of last week's bomb attacks.* **2** [C] the waves behind a moving ship **3** [C] when people come together to remember someone who has recently died

'**wake-up ,call** *noun* [C] a telephone call to wake you in the morning, especially when you are staying in a hotel

○ᴿ**walk¹** /wɔːk/ *verb* **1** [I, T] to move forward by putting one foot in front of the other and then repeating the action *She walks to school.* • *We walked twenty miles in all.* **2 walk sb home/to sth** to walk with someone in order to guide them or keep them safe *He walked me to my house.* **3 walk the dog** to walk with a dog to give the dog exercise **4 walk all over sb** *informal* to treat someone badly

---

**USAGE**

**walk** or **go on foot**?

The expression **go on foot** means **walk**, usually when you are describing how you get somewhere.

*How do you get to school? I go on foot/I walk.*

---

**walk into sth** to get a job easily
**walk off with sth** to win something easily *She walked off with the top prize.*
**walk out** to leave a job, meeting, or performance because you are angry or do not approve of something *He was so disgusted by the film he walked out.*
**walk out on sb** to suddenly leave your husband, wife, or partner and end your relationship with them *He walked out on his wife and kids.*

○ᴿ**walk²** /wɔːk/ *noun* **1** [C] a journey that you make by walking, often for enjoyment *We usually go for a walk on Sunday afternoons.* • *He took the dog for a walk.* **2 a short/ten-minute, etc walk** a journey that takes a short time/ten minutes, etc when you walk *The station is just a five-minute walk from the house.* **3** [C] a path or route where people can walk for enjoyment *There are some lovely walks in the forest.* **4 walk of life** People from different walks of life have different jobs and different experiences in life.

**walker** /ˈwɔːkə⁾/ *noun* [C] someone who walks for exercise or enjoyment

**walkie talkie** /ˌwɔːkiˈtɔːki/ *noun* [C] a radio that you carry with you and that lets you talk to someone else with a similar radio

○ᴿ**wall** /wɔːl/ *noun* [C] **1** one of the vertical sides of a room or building *There were several large paintings on the wall.* **2** a vertical structure made of brick or stone that divides areas that are owned by different people *a garden wall* **3 drive sb up the wall** *informal* to make someone very angry *She drives me up the*

*wall.* ⊃ *See also:* **fly²** on the wall, be banging your **head¹** against a brick wall.

**walled** /wɔːld/ *adj* **walled garden/city** a garden/city with walls around it

**wallet** /ˈwɒlɪt/ (*also US* **billfold**) *noun* [C] a small, flat container for paper money and credit cards (= plastic cards used for paying with), usually used by a man

**wallop** /ˈwɒləp/ *verb* [T] *informal* to hit someone or something hard • **wallop** *noun* [no plural] *informal*

**wallow** /ˈwɒləʊ/ *verb* [I] **1** to allow yourself to feel too much sadness in a way that stops people respecting you *There's no use wallowing in self-pity.* **2** to lie or move around in soil or water, especially for pleasure

**wallpaper** /ˈwɔːlˌpeɪpə⁾/ *noun* [U] paper, usually with a pattern, that you decorate walls with • **wallpaper** *verb* [T]

'**Wall ,Street** *noun* the financial area of New York where shares (= small, equal parts of the value of a company) are bought and sold *The company's shares rose on Wall Street yesterday.*

**wally** /ˈwɒli/ *noun* [C] *UK informal* a silly person

**walnut** /ˈwɔːlnʌt/ *noun* **1** [C] a nut that is in two halves inside a brown shell, and whose surface has curves and folds in it **2** [U] the hard wood of the tree that produces walnuts, used to make furniture

**walrus** /ˈwɔːlrəs/ *noun* [C] a large sea animal that has two tusks (= long, pointed teeth that come out of the mouth)

**waltz¹** /wɒls/ *noun* [C] a dance for two partners performed to music that has a rhythm of three beats, or the music for the dance

**waltz²** /wɒls/ *verb* [I] **1** to dance a waltz **2 waltz in/off, etc** to walk somewhere quickly and confidently, often in a way that annoys other people *You can't just waltz into my bedroom – it's private!*

**wan** /wɒn/ *adj* pale and looking ill or tired

**wand** /wɒnd/ *noun* [C] a thin stick that someone who performs magic tricks holds in their hand

**wander** /ˈwɒndə⁾/ *verb* **1** [I, T] to walk slowly about a place without any purpose *They wandered aimlessly around the town.* **2** [I] (*also* **wander off**) to walk away from the place where you should be *He was here a moment ago – he must have wandered off.* **3 sb's attention/mind/thoughts, etc wander** If someone's attention/mind, etc wanders, they start thinking about one subject when they should be thinking about a different subject. *I was bored and my thoughts started to wander.*

**wane** /weɪn/ *verb* [I] to become less powerful, important, or popular *Interest in the product is starting to wane.*

**wangle** /ˈwæŋgl/ *verb* [T] *informal* to succeed in getting something that a lot of people want, by being clever or tricking someone *He managed to wangle an invitation to the party.*

○ᴿ**want¹** /wɒnt/ *verb* [T] **1** to hope to have or do something, or to wish for something *He wants a new car.* • [+ to do sth] *I don't want to talk about it.* • *You can't always do what you want.* • *We can go later if you want.* • *I want him to explain why.* **2** to need something *This soup wants* more salt. **3 want to do sth** *UK informal* used to give advice to someone *You want to go to bed earlier and then you won't be so tired.* **4 be wanted** to be needed for a particular activity or in a particular place *You're wanted on the phone.*

---

**USAGE**

**want something/someone to do something**

Be careful to use the correct form after this expression. You cannot say 'that' after **want**.

*I just want him to enjoy himself.*

~~I just want that he enjoy himself.~~

*They don't want the school holidays to end.*

~~They don't want that the school holidays end.~~

---

**want²** /wɒnt/ *noun* **want of sth** when there is not enough of something *If we fail, it won't be* **for want of** *effort* (= it is not because we have not tried).

**wanted** /'wɒntɪd/ *adj* If someone is wanted, the police think they have committed a serious crime and are trying to find them. *He is wanted for murder.*

**wanton** /'wɒntən/ *adj formal* done in order to cause suffering or destruction but with no other reason *wanton cruelty/violence*

**wants** /wɒnts/ *noun* [plural] the things you want or need

o—* **war** /wɔːʳ/ *noun* **1** FIGHTING [C, U] fighting, using soldiers and weapons, between two or more countries, or two or more groups inside a country *They've been* **at war** *for the past five years.* • *He was only a child when the war* **broke out** (= started). • *If this country* **goes to war** (= starts to fight in a war), *thousands of people will die.* **2** COMPETING [C, U] when two or more groups are trying to be more successful than each other *a price war between supermarkets* **3** TO STOP [no plural] an attempt to stop something bad or illegal *the war against crime/drugs* ➔ *See also:* **civil war, prisoner of war, world war**.

**'war ,crime** *noun* [C] a crime during a war that breaks the international rules of war • **war criminal** *noun* [C] someone who is guilty of a war crime

**ward¹** /wɔːd/ *noun* [C] a room in a hospital where people receiving medical treatment stay, often for the same type of illness *the maternity ward*

**ward²** /wɔːd/ *verb*
**ward sth off** to prevent something unpleasant happening *I take vitamin C to ward off colds.*

**warden** /'wɔːdⁿn/ *noun* [C] **1** *US* (*UK* **governor**) someone who is responsible for controlling a prison **2** *UK* someone who is responsible for looking after a particular building or the people in it ➔ *See also:* **traffic warden**.

**warder** /'wɔːdəʳ/ *noun* [C] *UK* a prison guard

**wardrobe** /'wɔːdrəʊb/ *noun* **1** [C] *UK* (*US* **closet**) a large cupboard for keeping clothes in **2** [no plural] all the clothes that you own

**warehouse** /'weəhaʊs/ *noun* [C] *plural* **warehouses** /'weəhaʊzɪz/ a large building for storing goods that are going to be sold

**wares** /weəz/ *noun* [plural] *literary* goods that are for sale, especially not in a shop *People were selling their wares at the side of the road.*

**warfare** /'wɔːfeəʳ/ *noun* [U] fighting in a war, especially using a particular type of weapon *chemical/modern warfare*

**warhead** /'wɔːhed/ *noun* [C] the part of a missile (= weapon) that explodes when it reaches the place it is aimed at *a nuclear warhead*

**warlord** /'wɔːlɔːd/ *noun* [C] a military leader who controls a particular area of a country

o—* **warm¹** /wɔːm/ *adj* **1** TEMPERATURE having a temperature between cool and hot *It's nice and warm in here.* • *Are you warm enough?* • *Make sure you* **keep warm**. **2** CLOTHES Warm clothes or covers keep your body warm. *a warm sweater* **3** FRIENDLY friendly and showing affection *a warm smile/welcome*

**warm²** /wɔːm/ *verb* [I, T] to become warm or to make something become warm *She warmed her feet against his.* • *I'll warm the soup.*
**warm to sb/sth** to start to like a person or idea
**warm up** to do gentle exercises in order to prepare yourself for more energetic exercise *They were warming up before the match.* • **warm-up** /'wɔːmʌp/ *noun* [C]
**warm (sb/sth) up** to become warmer or to make someone or something warmer *The house soon warms up with the heating on.* • *A hot drink will warm you up.*

**warmly** /'wɔːmli/ *adv* in a friendly way

**warmth** /wɔːmθ/ *noun* [U] **1** the heat that is produced by something *the warmth of the fire* **2** when someone is friendly and shows affection *There was no warmth in his eyes.*

o—* **warn** /wɔːn/ *verb* [T] **1** to tell someone that something bad may happen in the future, so that they can prevent it [+ that] *I warned you that it would be cold but you still wouldn't wear a coat.* • *I've been warning him for months.* **2** to advise someone not to do something that could cause danger or trouble [+ to do sth] *I warned you* **not** *to tell her.*

o—* **warning** /'wɔːnɪŋ/ *noun* [C, U] something that tells or shows you that something bad may happen *All cigarette packets carry a warning.* • *The bombs fell completely without warning.*

**warp** /wɔːp/ *verb* **1** [I, T] to become bent into the wrong shape or to make something do this *The window frames had warped.* **2** [T] If something warps your mind, it makes you strange and cruel.

**warpath** /'wɔːpɑːθ/ *noun* **be on the warpath** *informal* to be trying to find someone in order to be angry with them

**warped** /wɔːpt/ *adj* strange and cruel *You've got a warped mind!*

**warplane** /'wɔːˌpleɪn/ *noun* [C] an aircraft for carrying bombs

**warrant¹** /'wɒrⁿnt/ *noun* [C] an official document that allows someone to do something, for example that allows a police officer to search a building *The police have a warrant for his arrest.* ➔ *See also:* **search warrant**.

**warrant²** /'wɒrⁿnt/ *verb* [T] to make something necessary *None of her crimes is serious enough to warrant punishment.*

**W**

**warranty** /ˈwɒrᵊnti/ *noun* [C, U] a written promise made by a company to change or repair one of its products if it has a fault *a five-year warranty*

**warren** /ˈwɒrᵊn/ (*also* '**rabbit ˌwarren**) *noun* [C] a group of connected underground holes where rabbits live

**warring** /ˈwɔːrɪŋ/ *adj* **warring factions/ parties/sides, etc** groups that are fighting against each other

**warrior** /ˈwɒriəʳ/ *noun* [C] a person who has experience and skill in fighting in a war, especially in the past

**warship** /ˈwɔːʃɪp/ *noun* [C] a ship with weapons, used in war

**wart** /wɔːt/ *noun* [C] a small, hard lump that grows on the skin

**wartime** /ˈwɔːtaɪm/ *noun* [U] a period when a country is fighting a war

**war-torn** /ˈwɔːˌtɔːn/ *adj* damaged by war *a war-torn country*

**wary** /ˈweəri/ *adj* If you are wary of someone or something, you do not trust them completely. *She's still wary of strangers.* • **warily** *adv* • **wariness** *noun* [U]

⊶**wash¹** /wɒʃ/ *verb* **1** [T] to make something clean using water, or water and soap *Dad was washing the dishes.* **2** [I, T] to clean part of your body with water and soap *Have you washed your hands?* • *I got washed and dressed.* **3 be washed away/out/up, etc** If something is washed away/out, etc, it is moved there by water. *A lot of the waste is washed out to sea.* **4 wash against/on, etc** If water washes somewhere, it flows there. *Waves washed against the base of the cliff.*

**wash sth away** If water washes something away, it removes that thing. *Floods washed away much of the soil.*

**wash sth down** to drink something with food or medicine to make it easier to swallow *I had a plate of sandwiches, washed down with a glass of cool beer.*

**wash out** If a colour or dirty mark washes out, it disappears when you wash something. *Most hair dye washes out after a few weeks.*

**wash (sth) up** *UK* to wash the dishes, pans, and other things you have used for cooking and eating a meal ⊃ *See colour picture* **Phrasal Verbs** *on page Centre 13.*

**wash up** *US* to wash your hands, especially before a meal *Go and wash up – your dinner's ready.*

**wash²** /wɒʃ/ *noun* **1 a wash a** when you wash a part of your body *Have you had a wash?* **b** *mainly UK* when you wash something *Could you give the car a wash?* **2** [C, U] clothes, sheets, etc that are being washed together *Your jeans are in the wash.*

**washable** /ˈwɒʃəbl/ *adj* Something that is washable will not be damaged by being washed.

**washbasin** /ˈwɒʃˌbeɪsᵊn/ *UK* (*UK/US* **sink**) *noun* [C] a bowl in a bathroom that water can flow into, used for washing your face or hands

**washcloth** /ˈwɒʃklɒθ/ *US* (*UK* **flannel**) *noun* [C] a small cloth that you use to wash your face and body ⊃ *See colour picture* **The Bathroom** *on page Centre 1.*

**washed-out** /ˌwɒʃtˈaʊt/ *adj* looking pale and tired

**washer** /ˈwɒʃəʳ/ *noun* [C] **1** a thin, flat ring that is put between a nut and a bolt (= metal objects used to fasten things together) **2** a machine that washes clothes

**washing** /ˈwɒʃɪŋ/ *noun* [U] clothes, sheets, and similar things that are being washed or have been washed, or when you wash these *I'm doing the washing this morning.* • *He does his own washing and ironing.*

'**washing ma,chine** *noun* [C] a machine that washes clothes

**washing-up** /ˌwɒʃɪŋˈʌp/ *noun* [U] *UK* when you wash the dishes, pans, and other things you have used for cooking and eating a meal *He was doing the washing-up.*

**washout** /ˈwɒʃaʊt/ *noun* [no plural] *informal* an event that fails badly *No one came to the fete – it was a complete washout.*

**washroom** /ˈwɒʃruːm/ *noun* [C] *mainly US* a room where you can go to the toilet or wash your hands and face

**wasn't** /ˈwɒzᵊnt/ *short for* was not *I wasn't hungry this morning.*

**wasp** /wɒsp/ *noun* [C] a flying insect with a thin, black and yellow body a wasp sting

**wasp**

**wastage** /ˈweɪstɪdʒ/ *noun* [U] when you waste something *fuel wastage*

⊶**waste¹** /weɪst/ *noun* **1** [U, no plural] a bad use of something useful, such as time or money, when there is a limited amount of it *Meetings are **a waste of** time.* • *They throw away loads of food – it's such a waste.* • *a waste of energy/resources* **2** [U] things that are not wanted, especially what remains after you have used something *household/nuclear waste* **3 go to waste** to not be used *I hate to see good food go to waste.*

⊶**waste²** /weɪst/ *verb* [T] **1** to use too much of something or use something badly when there is a limited amount of it *I don't want to waste any more time so let's start.* • *Why waste your money on things you don't need?* **2 be wasted on sb** to be clever or of high quality in a way that someone will not understand or enjoy *Good coffee is wasted on Joe – he prefers instant.* **waste away** to become thinner and weaker

**waste³** /weɪst/ *adj* [always before noun] Waste material is not now needed and can be got rid of. *waste paper*

**wasteful** /ˈweɪstfᵊl/ *adj* using too much of something, or using something badly when there is a limited amount of it

**wasteland** /ˈweɪstlænd/ *noun* [C, U] an area of land that cannot be used in any way

'**wastepaper ˌbasket** *UK* (*US* **wastebasket**) *noun* [C] a container that is used inside buildings for putting rubbish such as paper into

⊶**watch¹** /wɒtʃ/ *verb* **1** ⎣LOOK AT⎦ [I, T] to look at something for a period of time *I watched him*

W

*as he arrived.* • *The kids are watching TV.* • *I want to watch the news* (= programme on television). ⟳ *See usage note at* **look. 2** [BE CAREFUL] [T] to be careful about something *She has to watch what she eats.* • *Watch how you cross the road!* **3** [GIVE ATTENTION TO] [T] to give attention to a situation which is changing *We'll be watching the case with interest.* ⟳ *See also:* **birdwatching,** watch your **step**[1].

**watch out** used to tell someone to be careful because they are in danger *Watch out! There's a car coming!* • *Drivers were told to watch out for black ice on the road.*

**watch over sb** to look after someone and protect them if it is necessary

o━**watch**[2] /wɒtʃ/ *noun* **1** [C] a small clock on a strap that you fasten round your wrist (= lower arm) *I don't wear a watch.* **2** [U, no plural] when you watch or give attention to something or someone, especially to make sure nothing bad happens *We're keeping a close watch on the situation.*

**watchdog** /'wɒtʃdɒg/ *noun* [C] an organization whose job is to make sure that companies behave legally and provide good services

**watchful** /'wɒtʃfəl/ *adj* careful to notice things and ready to deal with problems *They were playing outside under the watchful eye of a teacher.*

**watchword** /'wɒtʃwɜːd/ *noun* [no plural] a word or phrase that describes the main ideas or most important part of something *As regards fashion, the watchword this season is simplicity.*

o━**water**[1] /'wɔːtəʳ/ *noun* [U] **1** the clear liquid that falls from the sky as rain and that is in seas, lakes, and rivers *hot/cold water* • *a drink of water* **2** (*also* **waters**) an area in the sea or in a river or lake *coastal waters* **3** **be in deep water** to be in a difficult situation which is hard to deal with *They tried to adopt a baby illegally and ended up in very deep water.* **4** **be (like) water off a duck's back** If criticisms, insults, etc are like water off a duck's back to you, they do not affect you at all. *She calls him lazy and useless, but it's like water off a duck's back.* ⟳ *See also:* **drinking water, mineral water, tap water.**

**water**[2] /'wɔːtəʳ/ *verb* **1** [PLANTS] [T] to pour water over plants **2** [MOUTH] [I] If food makes your mouth water, it makes you want to eat it, sometimes making your mouth produce liquid. *The smells from the kitchen are making my mouth water.* **3** [EYES] [I] If your eyes water, they produce liquid because something is hurting them. *The smoke was making my eyes water.*

**water sth down** to add water to a drink, especially an alcoholic drink **2** to make a plan or idea less extreme, usually so that people will accept it

**watercolour** *UK* (*US* **watercolor**) /'wɔːtəˌkʌləʳ/ *noun* [C] a type of paint that is mixed with water, or a picture made with this paint

**watercress** /'wɔːtəkres/ *noun* [U] a small, strong-tasting plant that is eaten in salads

**waterfall** /'wɔːtəfɔːl/ *noun* [C] a stream of water that flows from a high place, often to a pool below

**waterfront** /'wɔːtəfrʌnt/ *noun* [C] a part of a town which is next to the sea, a lake, or a river *waterfront restaurants*

**waterhole** /'wɔːtəhəʊl/ *noun* [C] a small pool of water in a dry area where animals go to drink

'**watering ˌcan** *noun* [C] a container used for watering plants in the garden

**waterlogged** /'wɔːtəlɒgd/ *adj* Waterlogged land is too wet.

**watermark** /'wɔːtəmɑːk/ *noun* [C] a pattern or picture on paper, especially paper money, which you can only see when a strong light is behind it

**watermelon** /'wɔːtəˌmelən/ *noun* [C, U] a large, round, green fruit that is pink inside with a lot of black seeds

**waterproof** /'wɔːtəpruːf/ *adj* Waterproof material or clothing does not let water through. *a waterproof sleeping bag*

**waters** /'wɔːtəz/ *noun* [plural] the part of a sea around the coast of a country that legally belongs to that country

**watershed** /'wɔːtəʃed/ *noun* [no plural] an important event after which a situation completely changes *The discovery marked a watershed in the history of medicine.*

**water-skiing** /'wɔːtəˌskiːɪŋ/ *noun* [U] a sport in which someone is pulled behind a boat while standing on skis (= long, narrow pieces of wood or plastic fastened to the feet)

**watertight** /'wɔːtətaɪt/ *adj* **1** Something that is watertight prevents any water from entering it. **2** A watertight reason or excuse is one that no one can prove is false. *a watertight alibi*

**waterway** /'wɔːtəweɪ/ *noun* [C] a river or canal (= river made by people, not nature) which people can use to travel along

**watery** /'wɔːtəri/ *adj* **1** made with too much water *watery soup* **2** Watery eyes are wet with tears.

**watt** /wɒt/ (*written abbreviation* **W**) *noun* [C] a unit for measuring electrical power *a 60 watt light bulb*

o━**wave**[3] /weɪv/ *verb* **1** [I] to raise your hand and move it from side to side in order to attract someone's attention or to say goodbye *Wave goodbye to Grandma.* • *She waved at him.* **2** **wave sb in/on/through, etc** to show which way you want someone to go by moving your hand in that direction *The police waved him on.* **3** [I, T] (*also* **wave about/around**) to move from side to side in the air or make something move this way *The long grass waved in the breeze.* • *He started waving his arms about wildly.*

**wave**

a wave        She's waving.

**wave sth aside** to refuse to consider what someone says *She waved aside all my objections.*
**wave sb off** to wave your hand to someone as they are leaving in order to say goodbye *We went to the station to wave him off.*

○⚫**wave²** /weɪv/ *noun* [C] **1** WATER a line of higher water that moves across the surface of the sea or a lake *I could hear the waves crashing against the rocks.* **2** GROUP a group of people or things that arrive or happen together or in a short period of time *There has been a wave of kidnappings in the region.* • *Another wave of refugees is arriving at the border.* **3 a wave of hatred/enthusiasm/sadness, etc** when you suddenly feel an emotion *She felt a sudden wave of sadness.* **4** HAND when you raise your hand and move it from side to side in order to attract someone's attention or say goodbye *She gave a little wave as the train left.* **5** ENERGY a piece of sound, light, or other energy that travels up and down in a curved pattern *a radio wave* ➔ *See also:* **new wave, tidal wave.**

**wavelength** /ˈweɪvleŋθ/ *noun* [C] **1** the length of radio wave used by a radio company for broadcasting its programmes **2** the distance between one sound or light wave, etc and the next **3 be on the same wavelength** If two people are on the same wavelength, they have the same way of thinking and it is easy for them to understand each other.

**waver** /ˈweɪvəʳ/ *verb* [I] **1** to start to be uncertain about a belief or decision *Her support for him never wavered.* • *I'm wavering between the blue shirt and the red.* **2** to shake slightly or lose strength *His voice wavered and I thought he was going to cry.*

**wavy** /ˈweɪvi/ *adj* with slight curves *wavy hair* ➔ *See colour picture* **Hair** *on page Centre 9.*

**wax¹** /wæks/ *noun* [U] a solid substance that becomes soft when warm and melts easily, often used to make candles

**wax²** /wæks/ *verb* [T] **1** to put wax on something, especially to make it shiny *They cleaned and waxed my car.* **2** If you wax your legs, you remove the hair from them by using wax.

○⚫**way¹** /weɪ/ *noun* **1** METHOD [C] how you do something [+ to do sth] *I must find a way to help him.* • [+ of + doing sth] *We looked at various ways of solving the problem.* • [+ (that)] *It was the way that she told me that I didn't like.* **2** ROUTE [C] the route you take to get from one place to another [usually singular] *Is there another way out of here?* • *I must buy a paper on the way home.* • *Can you find your way back to my house?* • *I took the wrong road and lost my way* (= got lost). **3 make your way to/through/towards, etc** to move somewhere, often with difficulty *We made our way through the shop to the main entrance.* **4 be on her/my/its, etc way** to be arriving soon *Apparently she's on her way.* **5 in/out of the/sb's way** in/not in the area in front of someone that they need to pass or see through *I couldn't see because Bill was in the way.* • *Sorry, am I in your way?* • *Could you move out of the way, please?* **6 a third of the way/most of the way, etc** used to say how much of something is completed *A third of the way through the film she dies.* **7 get in the way**

**of sth/sb** to prevent someone from doing or continuing with something *Don't let your new friends get in the way of your studies.* **8 be under way** to be already happening *Building work is already under way.* **9 give way (to sb/ sth) a** ALLOW to allow someone to get what they want, or to allow something to happen after trying to prevent it *The boss finally gave way when they threatened to stop work.* **b** TRAFFIC *(US yield) UK* to allow other vehicles to go past before you move onto a road **10 give way to sth** to change into something else *Her excitement quickly gave way to horror.* **11 give way** If something gives way, it falls because it is not strong enough to support the weight on top of it. *Suddenly the ground gave way under me.* **12 get sth out of the way** to finish something *I'll go shopping when I've got this essay out of the way.* **13** DIRECTION [C] a direction something faces or travels *This bus is going the wrong way.* • *Which way up does this picture go* (= which side should be at the top)? • *(UK) He always wears his baseball cap the wrong way round* (= backwards). **14** SPACE/TIME [no plural] an amount of space or time *We're a long way from home.* • *The exams are still a long way away/off.* **15 make way** to move away so that someone or something can pass **16 make way for sth** If you move or get rid of something to make way for something new, you do so in order to make a space for the new thing. *They knocked down the old houses to make way for a new hotel.* **17 in a way/in many ways** used to say that you think something is partly true *In a way his behaviour is understandable.* **18 in no way** not at all *This is in no way your fault.* **19 there's no way** *informal* If there is no way that something will happen, it is certainly not allowed or not possible. *There's no way that dog's coming in the house.* **20 No way!** *informal* certainly not *"Would you invite him to a party?" "No way!"* **21 get/have your (own) way** to get what you want, although it might upset other people *She always gets her own way in the end.* **22 in a big/small way** *informal* used to describe how much or little you do a particular thing *They celebrate birthdays in a big way.* **23 a/sb's way of life** the way someone lives *Violence has become a way of life there.* **24 by the way** used when you say something that does not relate to what is being discussed *Oh, by the way, my name's Julie.* **25 go out of your way to do sth** to try very hard to do something pleasant for someone *He went out of his way to make us feel welcome.* **26 rub sb up the wrong way** *UK (US rub sb the wrong way) informal* to annoy someone without intending to ➔ *See also:* **the Milky Way.**

**way²** /weɪ/ *adv informal* used to emphasize how extreme something is *The room was way too hot.* • *He's in second place but he's way behind/ off.*

**way 'out** *noun* [C] **1** *UK (UK/US exit)* a door that takes you out of a building **2** a way of avoiding doing something unpleasant *I'm supposed to be going to this meeting at 2.00 and I'm looking for a way out.*

**wayside** /ˈweɪsaɪd/ *noun* **fall by the wayside**

**W**

to fail to complete something or be completed *Many students fall by the wayside during their first year at college.*

**wayward** /'weɪwəd/ *adj literary* behaving badly in a way that causes trouble for other people

**WC** /,dʌblju:'si:/ *noun* [C] *UK abbreviation for* water closet: a toilet, especially in a public place ⊃ *See usage note at* **toilet**.

o→**we** *strong form* /wi:/ *weak form* /wi/ *pronoun* **1** used as the subject of the verb when the person speaking or writing is referring to themselves and one or more other people *My wife and I both play golf and we love it.* **2** people generally *The world in which we live is very different.*

o→**weak** /wi:k/ *adj* **1** [BODY] not physically strong *He felt too weak to sit up.* • *The children were weak with/from hunger.* **2** [CHARACTER] not powerful, or not having a strong character *a weak government/leader* **3** [LIKELY TO FAIL] likely to fail *a weak economy* • *a weak team* **4** [LIKELY TO BREAK] likely to break and not able to support heavy things *a weak bridge* **5** [TASTE] A weak drink has little taste or contains little alcohol. *weak coffee/beer* **6** [REASON] A weak reason or excuse is one that you cannot believe because there is not enough proof to support it. **7** [NOT GOOD] not good at something *She reads well but her spelling is weak.* **8** [SLIGHT] difficult to see or hear *He spoke in a weak voice.* • *a weak light* • **weakly** *adv*

**weaken** /'wi:kᵊn/ *verb* [I, T] **1** to become less strong or powerful, or to make someone or something less strong or powerful *A number of factors have weakened the economy.* **2** to become less certain or determined about a decision, or to make someone less determined *I told him he wasn't having any more money but then I weakened.*

**weakling** /'wi:klɪŋ/ *noun* [C] someone who is physically weak

**weakness** /'wi:knəs/ *noun* **1** [U] when someone or something is not strong or powerful *Asking for help is not a sign of weakness.* **2** [C] a particular part or quality of something or someone that is not good *What do you think are your weaknesses as a manager?* • *There are a number of weaknesses in this proposal.* **3 have a weakness for sth/sb** to like a particular thing or person very much *She has a real weakness for ice cream.*

**wealth** /welθ/ *noun* **1** [U] when someone has a lot of money or valuable possessions *He enjoyed his new wealth and status.* **2 a wealth of sth** a large amount of something good *a wealth of experience/information*

**wealthy** /'welθi/ *adj* rich *a wealthy businessman/nation* • *Only the very wealthy can afford to live here.*

**wean** /wi:n/ *verb* [T] to start to give a baby food to eat instead of its mother's milk

**wean sb off sth** to make someone gradually stop using something that is bad for them *I'm trying to wean myself off fatty food generally.*

o→**weapon** /'wepən/ *noun* [C] a gun, knife, or other object used to kill or hurt someone *nuclear weapons* • *Police have found the murder weapon.* • **weaponry** *noun* [U] weapons

o→**wear¹** /weəʳ/ *verb past t* **wore**, *past p* **worn** **1** [DRESS] [T] to have a piece of clothing, jewellery, etc on your body *I wear jeans a lot of the time.* • *She wears glasses.* • *I don't usually wear make-up for work.* **2** [FACE] [T] to show a particular emotion on your face *He was wearing a smile/frown.* **3** [HAIR] [T] to arrange or grow your hair in a particular way *She usually wears her hair in a ponytail.* **4** [SPOIL] [I, T] to become thin and damaged after being used a lot, or to make this happen *The carpet is already starting to wear in places.* • *He keeps wearing holes in his socks.* ⊃ *See also:* wear **thin¹**.

**wear (sth) away** to disappear after a lot of time or use, or to make something disappear in this way *The words on the gravestone had worn away completely.*

**wear sb down** to make someone feel tired and less able to argue *Their continual nagging just wears me down.*

**wear off** If a feeling or the effect of something wears off, it gradually disappears. *The anaesthetic is starting to wear off.*

**wear on** If a period of time wears on, it passes, especially slowly. *As time wore on she became more and more unhappy.*

**wear sb out** to make someone extremely tired *All this walking is wearing me out.*

**wear (sth) out** to use something so much that it is damaged and cannot be used any more, or to become damaged in this way *He's already worn out two pairs of shoes this year.*

**wear²** /weəʳ/ *noun* [U] **1** (*also* **wear and tear**) damage that happens to something when it is used a lot *The furniture is already showing signs of wear.* **2** how much you wear a piece of clothing *These clothes are not for everyday wear.* **3 be the worse for wear** *informal* to be in a bad state or condition *He looked a little the worse for wear this morning.*

**-wear** /weəʳ/ *suffix* used at the end of words that describe a particular type of clothes *menswear/swimwear*

**wearing** /'weərɪŋ/ *adj* making you tired or annoyed

**weary** /'wɪəri/ *adj* **1** tired *You look weary, my love.* **2 weary of sth/sb** bored with something or someone *She grew weary of the children and their games.* • **wearily** *adv* • **weariness** *noun* [U]

**weasel** /'wi:zᵊl/ *noun* [C] a small animal with a long body that kills and eats other small animals

o→**weather¹** /'weðəʳ/ *noun* [U] **1** the temperature or conditions outside, for example if it is hot, cold, sunny, etc *The flight was delayed because of bad weather.* **2 be/feel under the weather** to feel ill

**weather²** /'weðəʳ/ *verb* [T] to deal with a difficult situation or difficult conditions *to weather criticism/a recession*

**weathered** /'weðəd/ *adj* looking rough and old *a weathered face*

**'weather ,forecast** *noun* [C] a description of what the weather will be like

**weave** /wi:v/ *verb* **1 weave in and out; weave through** *past* **weaved** to go somewhere by moving around a lot of things *to weave in and*

**W**

out of the traffic • to weave through the crowd **2** [I, T] past t **wove**, past p **woven** to make cloth on a machine by crossing threads under and over each other

**web** /web/ noun [C] **1** a type of net made by a spider (= insect with eight legs) to catch other insects *a spider's web* **2 the Web** (also **the World Wide Web**) part of the Internet that consists of all the connected websites (= pages of text and pictures)

**webmaster** /ˈwebmɑːstəʳ/ noun [C] someone who creates a website ( = area on the Internet) and checks that it continues to work correctly and shows recent information

**ˈweb ˌpage** noun [C] a part of a website that can be read on a computer screen

**website** /ˈwebsaɪt/ noun [C] an area on the Web (= computer information system) where information about a particular subject, organization, etc can be found

**we'd** /wiːd/ **1** short for we had *By the time she arrived we'd eaten.* **2** short for we would *We'd like two tickets for the three o'clock show, please.*

**Wed** (also **Weds**) written abbreviation for Wednesday

○⚬**wedding** /ˈwedɪŋ/ noun [C] an official ceremony at which a man and woman get married *We're going to a wedding on Saturday.* • *a wedding dress/ring* ➣ See also: **golden wedding**.

**wedge¹** /wedʒ/ noun [C] a piece of something that is thin at one end and thicker at the other *a big wedge of cheese*

**wedge²** /wedʒ/ verb [T] **1 wedge sth open/shut** to use a wedge or similar shaped object to keep a door or window firmly open or closed *The room was hot so I wedged the door open.* **2** to push something into a narrow space *I was wedged between Andy and Pete in the back of the car.*

**Wednesday** /ˈwenzdeɪ/ (written abbreviation **Wed, Weds**) noun [C, U] the day of the week after Tuesday and before Thursday

**wee¹** /wiː/ noun [no plural] mainly UK informal when you urinate *to have a wee* • *I need a wee.* • **wee** verb [I] **weeing**, past **wee**

**wee²** /wiː/ adj small, usually used by Scottish speakers *a wee girl*

**weed¹** /wiːd/ noun [C] a wild plant that you do not want to grow in your garden *Dandelions are common weeds.*

**weed²** /wiːd/ verb [I, T] to remove wild plants from a garden where they are not wanted

**weed sb/sth out** to get rid of people or things that you do not want from a group *The government plans to weed out bad teachers.*

**weedy** /ˈwiːdi/ adj UK informal thin and weak *He looks too weedy to be an athlete.*

○⚬**week** /wiːk/ noun **1** [C] a period of seven days *last week/next week* • *I've got three exams this week.* • *We get paid every week.* **2 the week** the five days from Monday to Friday when people usually go to work or school *I don't go out much during the week.*

**weekday** /ˈwiːkdeɪ/ noun [C] one of the five days from Monday to Friday, when people usually go to work or school *This road is very busy on weekdays.*

○⚬**weekend** /ˌwiːkˈend/ ⓤⓢ /ˈwiːkend/ noun [C] **1** Saturday and Sunday, the two days in the week when many people do not work *Are you doing anything this weekend?* • *I'm going home for the weekend.* **2 at the weekend** UK (US **on the weekend**) on Saturday or Sunday *He's going to a football match at the weekend.*

**weekly** /ˈwiːkli/ adj, adv happening once a week or every week *a weekly newspaper* • *We're paid weekly.*

**weep** /wiːp/ verb [I, T] past **wept** literary to cry, usually because you are sad

○⚬**weigh** /weɪ/ verb **1 weigh 200g/75 kg/10 stone, etc** to have a weight of 200g/75 kg/10 stone, etc *How much do you weigh?* **2** [T] to measure how heavy someone or something is *Can you weigh that piece of cheese for me?* • *She weighs herself every day.* **3** [T] (also UK **weigh up**) to consider something carefully, especially in order to make a decision *The jury must weigh the evidence.* • *He needs to weigh up the pros and cons of going to college.*

**weigh sth against sth** to judge which of two things is more important before making a decision *The advantages have to be weighed against the possible disadvantages.*

**be weighed down by/with sth 1** to be carrying or holding too much *She was weighed down with shopping bags.* **2** to be very worried about something *be weighed down by problems/debts*

**weigh on/upon sb/sth** If a problem or responsibility weighs on you, it makes you worried or unhappy. *Problems at work are weighing on me.*

**weigh sth out** to measure an amount of something *Weigh out 8 ounces of flour.*

○⚬**weight** /weɪt/ noun **1** AMOUNT [U] how heavy someone or something is *He's about average height and weight.* **2 lose weight** If someone loses weight, they become lighter and thinner. *I need to lose a bit of weight.* **3 put on/gain weight** If someone puts on weight or gains weight, they become heavier and fatter. **4** HEAVINESS [U] the quality of being heavy *The shelf collapsed under the weight of the books.* **5** OBJECT [C] something that is heavy *You're not supposed to lift heavy weights after an operation.* **6 carry weight** to be considered important and effective in influencing someone *His opinions carry a lot of weight with the scientific community.* **7 pull your weight** to work as hard as other people in a group *The rest of the team complained that Sarah wasn't pulling her weight.* **8 throw your weight around** to behave as if you are more important or powerful than other people **9 a weight off your mind** when a problem which has been worrying you stops or is dealt with *Finally selling that house was a weight off my mind.* ➣ See also: **paper weight**.

**weighted** /ˈweɪtɪd/ adj **be weighted in favour of/towards/against sth** to give one group an advantage or disadvantage over other people *The system is weighted in favour of families with young children.*

**weights** /weɪts/ noun [plural] heavy pieces of metal that you lift up and down to make your muscles stronger

**weighty** /ˈweɪti/ adj very serious and impor-

**W**

tant *The film deals with the weighty issues of religion and morality.*

**weir** /wɪə/ *noun* [C] *UK* a low wall built across a river to control the flow of water

**weird** /wɪəd/ *adj* very strange *I had a really weird dream last night.*

**welcome¹** /'welkəm/ *exclamation* used to greet someone who has just arrived somewhere *Welcome home!* • *Welcome to the UK.*

o━ **welcome²** /'welkəm/ *verb* [T] **1** to greet someone who has arrived in a place *Both families were there to welcome us.* **2** to be pleased about something and want it to happen *The decision was welcomed by everybody.* • *I would welcome your advice.*

**welcome³** /'welkəm/ *adj* **1** If something is welcome, people are pleased about it and want it to happen. *a welcome change* • *Your comments are very welcome.* ➔ *Opposite* **unwelcome. 2 You're welcome.** used to be polite to someone who has thanked you *"Thank you." "You're welcome."* **3 make sb (feel) welcome** to make a visitor feel happy and comfortable in a place by being kind and friendly to them *They made me very welcome in their home.* **4 be welcome to do sth** used to tell someone that they can certainly do something, if they want to *Anyone who is interested is welcome to come along.* **5 be welcome to sth** used to tell someone that they can certainly have something, if they want it, because you do not

**welcome⁴** /'welkəm/ *noun* [no plural] **1** when someone is greeted when they arrive somewhere *He was given a warm* (= friendly) *welcome by his fans.* **2 outstay/overstay your welcome** to stay somewhere too long so that people want you to leave

**weld** /weld/ *verb* [T] to join pieces of metal together by heating them until they almost melt and then pressing them together

**welfare** /'welfeə/ *noun* [U] **1** Someone's welfare is their health and happiness. *He is concerned about the welfare of young men in prison.* **2** *US* (*UK* **social security**) money paid by a government to people who are poor, ill, or who do not have jobs *to be on welfare* (= getting welfare)

**welfare 'state** *UK* (*US* **'welfare ˌstate**) *noun* [no plural] a system in which the government looks after and pays for people who are ill, old, or who cannot get a job

**we'll** /wiːl/ *short for* we shall or we will *We'll be home on Friday.*

o━ **well¹** /wel/ *adj* [never before noun] **better, best 1** healthy *to feel/look well* • *I'm not very well.* • *Are you feeling better now?* ➔ *Opposite* **unwell. 2 all is well** everything is in a good or acceptable state *I hope all is well with Jack.* **3 be all very well** used to show that you do not agree with something or that you are annoyed about something *It's all very well for her to say everything's fine, she doesn't have to live here.* **4 be (just) as well** used to say that something might be a good thing to do or happen [+ **(that)**] *It was just as well that you left when you did.* ➔ *See also:* be **alive** and well.

o━ **well²** /wel/ *adv* **better, best 1** in a successful or satisfactory way *I thought they played well.* • *He's doing well at school/work.* **2** in a

complete way or as much as possible *I know him quite well.* • *Stir the mixture well.* ➔ *See usage note at* **good. 3 as well** also *Are you going to invite Steve as well?* **4 as well as sth** in addition to something *They have lived in the United States as well as Britain.* **5 may/might as well do sth** If you may/might as well do something, it will not spoil the situation if you do that thing. *If we're not waiting for Karen, we might as well go now.* **6 may/might/could well** used to say that something is likely to be true *He could well be at Michelle's house.* **7 well above/ahead/below, etc** above/ahead/below, etc by a large amount *It was well after seven o'clock when we got home.* **8 can't/couldn't very well do sth** used to say that something is not a suitable or practical thing to do *I couldn't very well tell her while he was there.* **9 Well done.** used to tell someone how pleased you are about their success *"I passed my exams." "Well done!"*

o━ **well³** /wel/ *exclamation* **1** used at the beginning of a sentence to pause slightly or to express doubt or disagreement *"You'll go, won't you?" "Well, I'm not sure."* • *"You said the food was bad." "Well, I didn't exactly say that."* **2** (*also* **well, well**) used to express surprise *Well, well, I never expected that to happen.* **3 oh well** used to say that a situation cannot be changed although it might be disappointing *Oh well, it doesn't matter, I can always buy another one.*

**well⁴** /wel/ *noun* [C] a deep hole in the ground from which you can get water, oil, or gas

**well-balanced** /ˌwel'bælənst/ *adj* **1 a well-balanced diet/meal** food which includes all the different types of food that the body needs to be healthy **2** Well-balanced people are calm and have good judgment.

**well-behaved** /ˌwelbɪ'heɪvd/ *adj* behaving in a polite and quiet way *a well-behaved child*

**well-being** /'wel,biːɪŋ/ *noun* [U] when someone is healthy, happy, and comfortable

**well-built** /ˌwel'bɪlt/ *adj* having a large, strong body

**well-connected** /ˌwelkə'nektɪd/ *adj* having important or powerful friends

**well-done** /ˌwel'dʌn/ *adj* Meat that is well-done has been cooked completely and is not pink inside.

**well-dressed** /ˌwel'drest/ *adj* wearing attractive, good quality clothes

**well-earned** /ˌwel'ɜːnd/ *adj* **well-earned break/holiday/rest, etc** a rest that you deserve because you have been working hard

**well-educated** /ˌwel'edʒʊkeɪtɪd/ *adj* having had a good education

**well-established** /ˌwelɪ'stæblɪʃt/ *adj* having existed for a long time *a well-established tradition*

**well-fed** /ˌwel'fed/ *adj* having eaten enough good food *a well-fed cat*

**well-heeled** /ˌwel'hiːld/ *adj* having a lot of money, expensive clothes, etc

**wellies** /'weliz/ *UK informal* (*US* **rubber boots**) *noun* [plural] large rubber boots that you wear outside when the ground is wet and dirty *a pair of wellies*

**well-informed** /ˌwelɪn'fɔːmd/ *adj* knowing a lot of useful information

W

# wellingtons

**wellingtons** /'welɪŋtənz/ *UK noun* [plural] wellies

**well-intentioned** /ˌwelɪn'tenʃᵊnd/ *adj* trying to be helpful and kind but not improving a situation

**well-kept** /ˌwel'kept/ *adj* **1 a well-kept secret** something that has been carefully and successfully kept secret *The recipe is a well-kept secret.* **2** tidy and organized *a well-kept kitchen*

**well-known** /ˌwel'nəʊn/ *adj* famous *a well-known actor*

**well-meaning** /ˌwel'miːnɪŋ/ *adj* trying to be helpful and kind but not improving a situation *well-meaning friends*

**well-off** /ˌwel'ɒf/ *adj* having a lot of money *His parents are very well-off.*

**well-organized** (*also UK* **-ised**) /ˌwel'ɔːgᵊnaɪzd/ *adj* working in an effective and successful way because of good organization

**well-paid** /ˌwel'peɪd/ *adj* earning a lot of money

**well-placed** /ˌwel'pleɪst/ *adj* in a very convenient position or in a position that gives someone an advantage [+ to do sth] *She's very well-placed to find out what's going on.*

**well-read** /ˌwel'red/ *adj* having read a lot of books on different subjects

**well-to-do** /ˌweltə'duː/ *adj* old-fashioned having a lot of money *a well-to-do family*

**well-wisher** /'welˌwɪʃəʳ/ *noun* [C] someone who wants another person to be happy, successful, or healthy *A crowd of well-wishers gathered outside the hospital.*

**Welsh** /welʃ/ *noun* [U] **1** a language that is spoken in some parts of Wales **2 the Welsh** the people of Wales

**went** /went/ *past tense of* go

**wept** /wept/ *past of* weep

**we're** /wɪəʳ/ *short for* we are *Hurry! We're late!*

**weren't** /wɜːnt/ *short for* were not *They weren't there.*

o⟶**west**¹ /west/ *noun* [U] **1** the direction that you face to see the sun go down **2 the west** the part of an area that is further towards the west than the rest **3 the West** the countries of North America and western Europe ● west *adj the west coast of Ireland* ● west *adv* towards the west *They lived in a village four miles west of Oxford.*

**the ˌWest 'End** *noun* a part of central London that has a lot of shops, theatres, restaurants, etc

**westerly** /'westᵊli/ *adj* **1** towards or in the west *Senegal is the most westerly country in Africa.* **2** A westerly wind comes from the west. *westerly breezes*

**western, Western**¹ /'westən/ *adj* [always before noun] **1** in or from the west part of an area *western France* **2** related to the countries of North America and western Europe *a Western diplomat*

**western**² /'westən/ *noun* [C] a film or story that happens in the west of the US at the time when Europeans started living there

**westerner, Westerner** /'westənəʳ/ *noun* [C] someone who is from a country in North America or western Europe

**westernized** (*also UK* **-ised**) /'westənaɪzd/ *adj* having a culture like North America and western Europe *Some Asian countries are becoming increasingly westernized.*

**ˌWest 'Indian** *adj* belonging or relating to the West Indies *a West Indian island* ● West Indian *noun* [C] someone from the West Indies

**the ˌWest 'Indies** *noun* [plural] a group of islands in the Caribbean Sea

**westward, westwards** /'westwəd, 'westwədz/ *adv* towards the west *They were travelling westward.* ● westward *adj*

o⟶**wet**¹ /wet/ *adj* **wetter, wettest 1** [WATER] covered in water or another liquid *a wet towel* ● *We got soaking wet in the rain.* ● *(UK) Look at you – you're wet through* (= very wet)*!* **2** [RAIN] raining *a wet and windy day* **3** [NOT DRY] not dry yet *wet paint* **4** [PERSON] *UK informal* Someone who is wet has a weak personality.

**wet**² /wet/ *verb* [T] **wetting**, *past* **wet** *or* **wetted 1 wet the bed/your pants/yourself, etc** to urinate in your bed or in your underwear without intending to **2** to make something wet

**'wet ˌsuit** *noun* [C] a piece of clothing covering the whole body that keeps you warm and dry when you are under water

**we've** /wiːv/ *short for* we have *We've bought a house.*

**whack** /wæk/ *verb* [T] *informal* to hit someone or something in a quick, strong way *She whacked him on the head with her book.* ● whack *noun* [C] *informal*

**whale** /weɪl/ *noun* [C] a very large animal that looks like a large fish, lives in the sea and breathes air through a hole at the top of its head

**whaling** /'weɪlɪŋ/ *noun* [U] hunting whales

**wharf** /wɔːf/ *noun* [C] *plural* **wharves** /wɔːvz/ an area next to the sea or a river where goods can be put on or taken off ships

o⟶**what** /wɒt/ *pronoun, determiner* **1** [INFORMATION] used to ask for information about something *What's this?* ● *What time is it?* ● *What happened?* ⊃ *See usage note at* **how.** **2** [THE THING] used to refer to something without naming it *I heard what he said.* ● *Do you know what I mean?* ● *What I like most about her is her honesty.* **3** [NOT HEARD] *informal* used when you have not heard what someone has said and you want them to repeat it. Some people think this use is not polite. *"Do you want a drink Tom?" "What?"* **4** [REPLY] *informal* used to ask what someone wants when they call you *"Hey Jenny?" "Yes, what?"* **5 what a/an ...** used to give your opinion, especially when you have strong feelings about something *What a mess!* ● *What an awful day!* **6 what about...?** used to suggest something *What about asking Martin to help?* **7 what ... for?** used to ask about the reason for something *What are you doing that for?* ● *"We really need a bigger car." "What for?"* **8 what if...?** used to ask about something that could happen in the future, especially something bad *What if I don't pass my exams?* **9 what's up (with sb)** *informal* used to ask why someone is unhappy or angry *What's up, Angie? You look troubled.* **10 what with** *informal* used to talk about the reasons for a particular situation, especially a bad or

W

difficult situation *I'm tired, what with travelling all day yesterday and sleeping badly.* **11 what's more** used to add something surprising or interesting to what you have just said

o─**whatever** /wɒt'evəʳ/ *adv, pronoun, determiner*
**1** ANYTHING anything or everything *Do whatever you want.* ● *He eats whatever I put in front of him.* **2** NO DIFFERENCE used to say that what happens is not important because it does not change a situation *Whatever happens I'll still love you.* ● *We'll support you, whatever you decide.* **3** QUESTION used to ask for information when you are surprised or angry about something *Whatever do you mean?* **4 or whatever** or something similar *The children are usually outside playing football or whatever.*

**whatnot** /'wɒtnɒt/ **and whatnot** *informal* and other things of a similar type *They sell cards and wrapping paper and whatnot.*

**whatsoever** /ˌwɒtsəʊ'evəʳ/ (*also* **whatever**) *adv* **no...whatsoever** none at all *There's no evidence whatsoever that she was involved.*

**wheat** /wiːt/ *noun* [U] a plant whose grain is used for making flour, or the grain itself

o─**wheel**[1] /wiːl/ *noun* **1** [C] a circular object fixed under a vehicle so that it moves smoothly over the ground *My bike needs a new front wheel.* **2 the wheel** a steering wheel (= circular object you turn to direct a vehicle) *You should drive with both hands on the wheel.* ● *He fell asleep at the wheel* (= while driving). **3 reinvent the wheel** to waste time trying to create something that has been done before **◑** *See also:* **Ferris wheel**.

**wheel**[2] /wiːl/ *verb* **wheel sth around/into/to, etc** to push something that has wheels somewhere *He wheeled his bicycle into the garden.* **wheel around/round** to quickly turn around *She wheeled around to face him.*

**wheelbarrow** /'wiːlˌbærəʊ/ *noun* [C] a big, open container with a wheel at the front and handles that is used to move things, especially around in a garden

**wheelchair** /'wiːltʃeəʳ/ *noun* [C] a chair with wheels used by someone who cannot walk

**wheeze** /wiːz/ *verb* [I] to make a noisy sound when breathing because of a problem in your lungs

o─**when**[1] /wen/ *adv* used to ask at what time something happened or will happen *When's your birthday?* ● *When did he leave?* ● *When are you going away?*

o─**when**[2] /wen/ *conjunction* **1** used to say at what time something happened or will happen *I found it when I was cleaning out the cupboards.* ● *We'll go when you're ready.* **2** although *Why are you doing this when I've asked you not to?*

**whenever** /wen'evəʳ/ *conjunction* every time or at any time *You can go whenever you want.* ● *I try to help them out whenever possible.*

o─**where**[1] /weəʳ/ *adv* used to ask about the place or position of someone or something *Where does she live?* ● *Where are my car keys?*

o─**where**[2] /weəʳ/ *conjunction* **1** at, in, or to a place or position *He's not sure where they are.* ● *I know where to go.* **2** relating to a particular part of a process or situation *We've now reached the point where we can make a decision.*

**whereabouts**[1] /ˌweərə'baʊts/ *adv* used to ask in what place or area someone or something is *Whereabouts does he live?*

**whereabouts**[2] /'weərəbaʊts/ *noun* **sb's whereabouts** the place where someone or something is *His whereabouts are unknown.*

**whereas** /weə'ræz/ *conjunction* compared with the fact that *His parents were rich, whereas mine had to struggle.*

**whereby** /weə'baɪ/ *adv formal* by which *They've introduced a system whereby people share cars.*

**wherein** /weə'rɪn/ *adv formal* in which

**whereupon** /'weərəpɒn/ *conjunction formal* after which *We decided to have a picnic, whereupon it started to rain.*

**wherever**[1] /weə'revəʳ/ *conjunction* **1** in or to any place or every place *You can sit wherever you like.* **2 wherever possible** every time it is possible *We try to use natural fabrics wherever possible.*

**wherever**[2] /weə'revəʳ/ *adv* used to ask in what situation or place something happened, especially when the person asking feels surprised *Wherever did you get that idea?*

**wherewithal** /'weəwɪðɔːl/ *noun* **the wherewithal to do sth** the money, skills, or other things that are needed to do something

o─**whether** /'weðəʳ/ *conjunction* **1** used to talk about a choice between two or more possibilities *Someone's got to tell her, whether it's you or me.* ● *I didn't know whether or not to go.* **2** if *I wasn't sure whether you'd like it.*

**whew** /fjuː/ *exclamation* used when you are happy that something is not going to happen, or when you are tired or hot

o─**which** /wɪtʃ/ *pronoun, determiner* **1** CHOICE used to ask or talk about a choice between two or more things *Which of these do you like best?* ● *Which way is it to the station?* ● *I just don't know which one to choose.* **2** REFERRING TO SOMETHING used at the beginning of a relative clause to show what thing is being referred to *These are principles which we all believe in.* **3** EXTRA INFORMATION used to give more information about something *The book, which includes a map, gives you all the information you need about Venice.* **4** GIVING OPINION used when you give an opinion about what you have just said *He took us both out for lunch, which I thought was very kind of him.*

W

~~The restaurant who is next to the pub is good.~~

Use who to refer to a person.

*The boy who is wearing the red coat is called Paul.*

~~The boy which is wearing the red coat is called Paul.~~

Sometimes it is possible to use 'that' or no word instead of which or who.

*He's the man (that) I saw in the bar.*

*This is the shirt (that) I bought yesterday.*

---

**whichever** /wɪ'tʃevəʳ/ *pronoun, determiner*
**1** used to say that what happens is not important because it does not change a situation *Whichever option we choose there'll be disadvantages.* • *It's a sad situation whichever way you look at it.* **2** any of a group of similar things *Choose whichever bedroom you want.*

**whiff** /wɪf/ *noun* [no plural] a smell which you only smell for a short time *I just caught a whiff of garlic from the kitchen.*

o━**while¹** /waɪl/ (*also UK* **whilst** /waɪlst/) *conjunction* **1** [DURING] during the time that *I read a magazine while I was waiting.* • *I can't talk to anyone while I'm driving.* • *While you're away, I might decorate the bathroom.* **2** [ALTHOUGH] although *And while I like my job, I wouldn't want to do it forever.* **3** [COMPARING] used to compare two different facts or situations *Tom is very confident while Katy is shy and quiet.*

o━**while²** /waɪl/ *noun* **a while** a period of time *a long/short while* • *I'm going out for a while.*

**while³** /waɪl/ *verb*
**while sth away** to spend time in a relaxed way because you are waiting for something or because you have nothing to do *We played a few games to while away the time.*

**whim** /wɪm/ *noun* [C] when you suddenly want to do something without having a reason *We booked the holiday on a whim.*

**whimper** /'wɪmpəʳ/ *verb* [I] to make quiet crying sounds because of fear or pain *The dog was whimpering with pain.*

**whimsical** /'wɪmzɪkəl/ *adj* unusual in a way that is slightly funny *a whimsical tale*

**whine** /waɪn/ *verb* [I] **1** to complain in an annoying way *She's always whining about something.* **2** to make a long, high, sad sound *The dog whined and scratched at the door.* • whine *noun* [C]

**whinge** /wɪndʒ/ *verb* [I] **whingeing** or **whinging** *UK informal* to complain in an annoying way *Oh, stop whingeing!* • whinge *noun* [C] *UK He was just having a whinge.*

**whip¹** /wɪp/ *noun* [C] a long piece of leather fixed to a handle and used to hit an animal or person

**whip²** /wɪp/ *verb* **whipping**, *past* **whipped 1** [T] to hit a person or animal with a whip **2** [T] to make a food such as cream more solid by mixing it hard with a kitchen tool **3 whip (sth) away/off/out, etc** *informal* to move or make something move in a fast, sudden way *She opened the bag and whipped out her camera.*
**whip up sth 1** to try to make people have strong feelings about something *to whip up*

enthusiasm/hatred **2** to prepare food very quickly *I could whip up a risotto if you like.*

**whir** /wɜːʳ/ *noun, verb* **whirring**, *past* **whirred** *US spelling of* whirr

**whirl¹** /wɜːl/ *verb* [I, T] to move or make something move quickly round and round

**whirl²** /wɜːl/ *noun* [no plural] **1** when a lot of exciting or confusing things happen at the same time *a whirl of activity* **2** a sudden turning movement **3 give sth a whirl** *informal* to try to do something, often for the first time *I've never danced salsa before but I'll give it a whirl.*

**whirlpool** /'wɜːlpuːl/ *noun* [C] an area of water that moves round and round very quickly

**whirlwind¹** /'wɜːlwɪnd/ *adj* **a whirlwind romance/visit/tour, etc** a relationship/visit, etc that only lasts a short time

**whirlwind²** /'wɜːlwɪnd/ *noun* **1 a whirlwind of sth** a lot of sudden activity, emotion, etc *a whirlwind of activity* **2** [C] a strong wind that moves round and round very quickly

**whirr** *UK* (*US* **whir**) /wɜːʳ/ *noun* [no plural] a low, continuous sound *the whirr of machinery* • whirr *UK* (*US* **whir**) *verb* [I]

**whisk¹** /wɪsk/ *verb* [T] **1 whisk sb away/off/ into, etc** *informal* to take someone somewhere quickly *They whisked him off to the police station.* **2** to mix food such as eggs, cream, etc very quickly using a fork or whisk *Whisk the mixture until smooth.*

**whisk²** /wɪsk/ *noun* [C] a kitchen tool made of wire that is used to mix eggs, cream, etc, or to make such food thicker ➔ *See colour picture* **Kitchen** *on page Centre 10.*

**whisker** /'wɪskəʳ/ *noun* [C] one of the long, stiff hairs that grows around the mouths of animals such as cats

**whiskers** /'wɪskəz/ *noun* [plural] *old-fashioned* hairs growing on a man's face

**whiskey** /'wɪski/ *noun* [C, U] whisky in Ireland or the United States

**whisky** /'wɪski/ *noun* [C, U] a strong, alcoholic drink made from grain

o━**whisper** /'wɪspəʳ/ *verb* [I, T] to speak extremely quietly so that other people cannot hear *She whispered something to the girl sitting next to her.* • whisper *noun* [C]

**whistle¹** /'wɪsl/ *verb* **1** [I, T] to make a sound by breathing air out through a small hole made with your lips or through a whistle *Someone whistled at her as she walked past.* **2** [I] to produce a sound when air passes through a narrow space *He could hear the wind whistling through the trees.*

**whistle²** /'wɪsl/ *noun* [C] **1** a small, simple instrument that makes a high sound when you blow through it *The referee blew the whistle to end the game.* **2** the sound made by someone or something whistling

o━**white¹** /waɪt/ *adj* **1** [COLOUR] being the colour of snow or milk *a white T-shirt* • *white walls* ➔ *See colour picture* **Colours** *on page Centre 6.* **2** [PERSON] Someone who is white has skin that is pale in colour. *He's described as a white man in his early thirties.* **3** [OF WHITE PEOPLE] relating to white people *the white community* **4** [FACE] having a pale face because you are ill or you are

W

feeling shocked *He was white with shock.*
**5** COFFEE UK White coffee has milk or cream
added to it. *Two coffees please, one black and
one white.* **6** WINE White wine is a pale yellow
colour. • whiteness *noun* [U] ➔ *See also:* **black¹**
and white.

**white²** /waɪt/ *noun* **1** COLOUR [C, U] the colour of
snow or milk ➔ *See colour picture* **Colours** *on page
Centre 6.* **2** PERSON [C] a white person *For a long
time, whites controlled the economy here.* **3** EGG
[C] the part of an egg that is white when it is
cooked *Mix the egg whites with the sugar.* ➔ *See
also:* in **black²** and white.

**whiteboard** /'waɪtbɔːd/ *noun* [C] a large board
with a white surface that teachers write on
➔ *See colour picture* **Classroom** *on page Centre 4.*

**white-collar** /ˌwaɪt'kɒləʳ/ *adj* relating to work
in an office or in a job that needs special knowledge and education *white-collar jobs/workers*

**the ˌWhite ˈHouse** *noun* **1** the US president
and government **2** the building that is the
official home and offices of the US president
• White House *adj a White House spokesman*

**ˌwhite ˈlie** *noun* [C] a lie which is not important
and is usually said to avoid upsetting someone

**whiten** /'waɪtⁿn/ *verb* [I, T] to become white or to
make something become white

**ˌWhite ˈPaper** *noun* [C] a government report in
the UK giving information or suggestions on a
subject *a White Paper on employment*

**whitewash** /'waɪtwɒʃ/ *noun* [no plural] when the
truth about a serious mistake, crime, etc is
hidden from the public *The newspaper accused
the government of a whitewash.* • whitewash
*verb* [T]

**whizz** (*also* whiz) /wɪz/ *verb* **whizz by/past/
through, etc** *informal* to move somewhere
very quickly *She whizzed down the street in her
new sports car.*

**whizzkid** (*also* whizkid) /'wɪz,kɪd/ *noun* [C] a
young person who is very successful or good at
doing something *a computer whizzkid*

**o━who** /huː/ *pronoun* **1** NAME used to ask about
someone's name or which person or group
someone is talking about *Who told you?*
• *Who's that?* **2** WHICH PERSON used at the
beginning of a relative clause to show which
person or group of people you are talking
about *That's the man who I saw in the bank.*
**3** ADD INFORMATION used to give more information about someone *My brother, who's only just
seventeen, has already passed his driving test.*
➔ *See usage note at* **which**.

**who'd** /huːd/ **1** *short for* who had *I was reading
about a man who'd sailed around the world.*
**2** *short for* who would *Who'd have thought
we'd still be friends?*

**whoever** /huː'evəʳ/ *pronoun* **1** WHICH PERSON
the person who *Whoever broke the window will
have to pay for it.* • *Could I speak to whoever is
in charge please?* **2** ANY PERSON used to say
that it is not important which person or group
does something *Can whoever leaves last lock
up, please?* **3** SURPRISE used to ask who a
person is when expressing surprise *Whoever
could that be phoning at this time?* • *Whoever
would believe such a ridiculous story?*

**o━whole¹** /həʊl/ *adj* **1** [always before noun] complete,

including every part *She spent the whole afternoon studying.* • *The whole family went to the
show.* **2** [never before noun] as a single object and
not in pieces *The chick swallowed the worm
whole.* ➔ *See also:* a whole new **ball game**, the
whole **world¹**.

**o━whole²** /həʊl/ *noun* **1 the whole of sth** all of
something *His behaviour affects the whole of
the class.* **2 as a whole** when considered as a
group and not in parts *The population as a
whole is getting healthier.* **3 on the whole** generally *We've had a few problems, but on the
whole we're very happy.*

**wholefood** /'həʊlfuːd/ *noun* [U] UK food that is
as natural as possible, without artificial things
added to it *a wholefood shop*

**wholehearted** /ˌhəʊl'hɑːtɪd/ *adj* **wholehearted agreement/approval/support, etc**
complete agreement/approval/support, etc
without any doubts • wholeheartedly *adv
I agree wholeheartedly.*

**wholemeal** /'həʊlmiːl/ *UK* (*UK/US* **whole
wheat**) *adj* made using whole grains, or made
from flour that contains whole grains *wholemeal bread/flour*

**wholesale** /'həʊlseɪl/ *adj* **1** relating to products
which are sold in large amounts, usually at a
cheaper price *wholesale prices* **2** [always before
noun] complete or affecting a lot of things,
people, places, etc *wholesale changes* • wholesale *adv*

**wholesaler** /'həʊl,seɪləʳ/ *noun* [C] a company
that sells products in large amounts to shops
which then sell them to customers

**wholesome** /'həʊlsəm/ *adj* **1** Wholesome food
is good for your health. **2** morally good *wholesome family entertainment*

**ˌwhole ˌwheat** (*also UK* **wholemeal**) *adj* made
using whole grains, or made from flour that
contains whole grains *whole wheat bread/flour*

**who'll** /huːl/ *short for* who will *Who'll be at your
party?*

**wholly** /'həʊlli/ *adv* completely *His behaviour is
wholly unacceptable.*

**o━whom** /huːm/ *pronoun formal* used instead of
'who' as the object of a verb or preposition
*I met a man with whom I used to work.*

**USAGE**

**whom** or **who**?

Whom is very formal and most people use **who** instead.

*Whom did you see at the party?*

*Who did you see at the party?*

Whom should be used after a preposition but most
people avoid this by putting the preposition at the end of
the sentence and using **who**.

*With whom did you go to the party?*

*Who did you go to the party with?*

**whoop** /wuːp/ *noun* [C] a loud, excited shout *He
gave a loud whoop of delight.*

**whooping cough** /'huːpɪŋ,kɒf/ *noun* [U] a
serious children's disease in which a cough is
followed by a 'whoop' noise

---

| j **y**es | k **c**at | ʃ **sh**e | ʒ deci**s**ion | θ **th**in | ð **th**is | ŋ ri**ng** | tʃ **ch**ip | dʒ **j**ar | æ **c**at | ɑː **ar**m | e b**e**d | eə h**air** | ə **a**go | ɜː h**er** | ɪ s**i**t | i cos**y** |

**whoops** /wups/ *exclamation* used when you make a mistake or have a small accident

**whopping** /'wɒpɪŋ/ *adj* [always before noun] *informal* extremely large *a whopping 50 percent increase*

**who're** /'huːə/ *short for* who are *Who're the people we're going to see?*

**whore** /hɔːʳ/ *noun* [C] an offensive word for someone whose job is having sex with people

**who's** /huːz/ **1** *short for* who is *Who's your new friend?* **2** *short for* who has *Who's been using my computer?*

○━**whose** /huːz/ *pronoun, determiner* **1** used to ask who something belongs to or who someone or something is connected with *Whose gloves are these?* • *Whose car shall we use?* **2** used to say that something or someone is connected with or belongs to a person *She has a brother whose name I can't remember.*

**who've** /huːv/ *short for* who have *I know people who've bought their homes on the Internet.*

○━**why** /waɪ/ *adv* **1** used to ask or talk about the reasons for something *Why didn't you call me?* • *I wonder why he didn't come.* • *So that's the reason why he asked her!* **2 Why don't you?/ why not do sth?** used to make a suggestion *Why don't you come with us?* • *Why not give it a try?* **3 why not?** *informal* used to agree with something that someone has suggested *"Let's have an ice cream." "Yes, why not?"*

**wicked** /'wɪkɪd/ *adj* **1** BAD extremely bad and morally wrong *a wicked man* **2** AMUSING funny or enjoyable in a way that is slightly bad or unkind *a wicked sense of humour* **3** GOOD *very informal* extremely good *They sell some wicked clothes.*

**wicker** /'wɪkəʳ/ *adj* made from thin branches crossed over and under each other *a wicker basket*

**wicket** /'wɪkɪt/ *noun* [C] in cricket, an arrangement of three long, vertical poles with two short poles across the top

○━**wide¹** /waɪd/ *adj* **1** LONG DISTANCE measuring a long distance or longer than usual from one side to the other *a wide river/road* • *I have very wide feet.* ➲ *See picture at* **narrow**. **2 5 miles/3 inches/6 metres, etc wide** having a distance of 5 miles/3 inches/6 metres, from one side to the other *The swimming pool is five metres wide.* **3 a wide range/selection/variety, etc** a lot of different types of thing *The library is a good source of a wide range of information.* **4** EYES If your eyes are wide, they are completely open. *Her eyes were wide with fear.* **5** BALL If a ball, shot, etc is wide, it does not go near enough to where it was intended to go. ➲ *See also:* be wide of the **mark¹**.

**wide²** /waɪd/ *adv* **1 wide apart/open** as far apart/open as possible *The window was wide open.* **2 wide awake** completely awake

**wide-eyed** /ˌwaɪd'aɪd/ *adj* with your eyes completely open because of surprise, fear, happiness, etc *The children looked on, wide-eyed with wonder.*

○━**widely** /'waɪdli/ *adv* **1** including a lot of different places, people, subjects, etc *widely known* • *He has travelled widely in Europe.* **2 differ/**

**vary widely** to be very different *Prices vary widely from shop to shop.*

**widen** /'waɪdᵊn/ *verb* [I, T] **1** to become wider or make something become wider *The road is being widened to two lanes.* **2** to increase or make something increase in number or degree *to widen choice*

**wide-ranging** /ˌwaɪd'reɪndʒɪŋ/ *adj* including a lot of subjects *a wide-ranging discussion/interview*

**widespread** /'waɪdspred/ *adj* affecting or including a lot of places, people, etc *a widespread problem* • *widespread support*

**widow** /'wɪdəʊ/ *noun* [C] a woman whose husband has died

**widowed** /'wɪdəʊd/ *adj* If someone is widowed, their husband or wife has died.

**widower** /'wɪdəʊəʳ/ *noun* [C] a man whose wife has died

**width** /wɪtθ/ *noun* **1** [C, U] the distance from one side of something to the other side *a width of 2 metres* • *height, length, and width* ➲ *See picture at* **length**. **2** [C] the distance across the shorter side of a swimming pool when you swim across it

**wield** /wiːld/ *verb* [T] **1** to hold a weapon or tool and look as if you are going to use it *They were confronted by a man wielding a knife.* **2 wield influence/power, etc** to have a lot of influence or power over other people

**wiener** /'wiːnəʳ/ *noun* [C] *US* a long thin sausage (= tube of meat and spices) that is usually eaten in bread

○━**wife** /waɪf/ *noun* [C] *plural* **wives** /waɪvz/ the woman that a man is married to *I've never met William's wife.*

**wig** /wɪg/ *noun* [C] a covering of real or artificial hair that you wear on your head *She was wearing a blonde wig.*

**wiggle** /'wɪgl/ *verb* [I, T] to make small movements from side to side or to make something else move from side to side *He was wiggling his hips to the music.* • wiggle *noun* [no plural]

○━**wild¹** /waɪld/ *adj* **1** ANIMAL A wild animal or plant lives or grows in its natural environment and not where people live. *a wild dog* • *wild flowers* **2** LAND Wild land is in a completely natural state. *a wild garden* **3** ENERGETIC very energetic and not controlled *a wild party* • *wild dancing* **4** WEATHER with a lot of wind, rain, etc *a wild and stormy night* **5 a wild accusation/guess/rumour, etc** something that you say which is not based on facts and is probably wrong **6 be wild about sth** *informal* to be very enthusiastic about something *He's wild about jazz.* **7 run wild** If someone, especially a child, runs wild, they behave as they want to and no one controls them. *Their nine-year-old son is left to run wild.* • wildness *noun* [U] ➲ *See also:* beyond your wildest dreams (**dream¹**).

**wild²** /waɪld/ *noun* **1 in the wild** in a natural environment *Animals are better off in the wild than in a zoo.* **2 the wilds** an area which is far from where people usually live *the wilds of Alaska*

**wild boar** *noun* [C] a wild pig

**wild card** *noun* [C] someone or something

W

that you know nothing about *a wild-card candidate in the election*

**wildcard** /'waɪld,kɑːd/ *noun* [C] in computing, a sign that is used to represent any letter or series of letters *a wildcard search*

**wilderness** /'wɪldənəs/ *noun* [C] a place that is in a completely natural state without houses, industry, roads, etc [usually singular] *a beautiful mountain wilderness*

**wildlife** /'waɪldlaɪf/ *noun* [U] animals, birds, and plants living in their natural environment *a wildlife park*

**wildly** /'waɪldli/ *adv* **1** in a very energetic way and without control *They cheered wildly.* **2** extremely *It hasn't been wildly successful.*

**wiles** /waɪlz/ *noun* [plural] tricks or clever ways of making other people do what you want *I'll use my womanly wiles.*

**wilful** *UK* (*US* **willful**) /'wɪlfəl/ *adj* doing what you want to do, although you are not allowed to or other people tell you not to *wilful disobedience* • **wilfully** *adv*

O—★**will**[1] *strong form* /wɪl/ *weak forms* /wəl, əl/ *modal verb* **1** FUTURE used to talk about what is going to happen in the future, especially things that you are certain about *Claire will be five next month.* • *I'll see him on Saturday.* • *She'll have a great time.* ➔ *See usage note at* **shall**. **2** ABLE/WILLING used to talk about what someone or something is willing or able to do *Ask Susie if she'll take them.* • *I've asked her but she won't come.* • *The car won't start.* **3** ASK used to ask someone to do something or to politely offer something to someone *Will you give me her address?* • *Will you have a drink with us, Phil?* **4** IF used in conditional sentences that start with 'if' and use the present tense *If he's late again I'll be very angry.* **5** HAPPENING OFTEN used to talk about something that often happens, especially something annoying *Accidents will happen.* • *He will keep talking when I'm trying to concentrate.* **6** it/that will be *mainly UK* used to talk about what is probably true *That will be Helen at the front door.* • *That will be his mother with him.* ➔ *See study section* **Modal verbs** *on page Centre 31.*

**will**[2] /wɪl/ *noun* **1** MENTAL POWER [C, U] the mental power to control your thoughts and actions or to succeed in doing something difficult *She has a very strong will.* • [+ to do sth] *He lacks the will to win.* **2** WANT [no plural] what someone wants *She was forced to marry him against her will.* **3** DOCUMENT [C] a legal document that gives instructions about what should happen to your money and possessions after you die *She left me some money in her will.* ➔ *See also:* **free will, ill will.**

**willful** /'wɪlfəl/ *adj US* spelling of wilful

O—★**willing** /'wɪlɪŋ/ *adj* **1 be willing to do sth** to be happy to do something, if you need to *He's willing to pay a lot of money for that house.* **2** wanting to do something *He is a very willing assistant.* ➔ *Opposite* **unwilling.** • **willingly** *adv He would willingly risk his life for her.* • **willingness** *noun* [U]

**willow** /'wɪləʊ/ *noun* [C] a tree with long, thin leaves that grows near water

**willowy** /'wɪləʊi/ *adj* tall and attractively thin *a willowy blonde*

**willpower** /'wɪlpaʊəʳ/ *noun* [U] the ability to make yourself do difficult things or to stop yourself from doing enjoyable things that are bad for you *It takes great willpower to lose weight.*

**wilt** /wɪlt/ *verb* [I] If a plant wilts, it starts to bend because it is dying or needs water.

**wily** /'waɪli/ *adj* good at getting what you want, especially by deceiving people

**wimp** /wɪmp/ *noun* [C] *informal* someone who is not brave and tries to avoid dangerous or difficult situations *I'm too much of a wimp to go rock climbing.* • **wimpy** *adj informal*

O—★**win**[1] /wɪn/ *verb* **winning**, *past* **won 1** COMPETITION [I, T] to get the most points in a competition or game, or the most votes in an election *Barcelona won the game 6–0.* • *Who do you think will win the election?* **2** ARGUMENT [I, T] to be successful in a war, fight, or argument *Protesters have won their battle to stop the road being built.* **3** PRIZE [T] to get a prize in a game or competition *He won $500.* • *She won a gold medal at the Olympics.* **4 win approval/respect/support, etc** to get approval/respect/support, etc because of your skill and hard work *Her plans have won the support of many local people.* **5 sb can't win** *informal* used to say that nothing someone does in a situation will succeed or please people *Whatever I do seems to annoy her – I just can't win.*

## USAGE

**win** or **beat**?

You **win** a game or competition.

*Who do you think will win the football game?*

You **beat** someone, or a team you are playing against.

*We beat both teams.*

~~We won both teams.~~

**win sb over** to persuade someone to support you or agree with you

**win**[2] /wɪn/ *noun* [C] when someone wins a game or competition *The Jets have only had three wins this season.*

**wince** /wɪns/ *verb* [I] to suddenly look as if you are suffering because you feel pain or because you see or think about something unpleasant *It makes me wince just to think about eye operations.*

**winch** /wɪnʃ/ *noun* [C] a machine with a thick chain, used for lifting heavy things • **winch** *verb* [T] to lift someone or something with a winch *The injured climber was winched to safety by a helicopter.*

O—★**wind**[1] /wɪnd/ *noun* **1** [C, U] a natural, fast movement of air *The weather forecast said there would be strong winds and rain.* **2** [U] *UK* (*US* **gas**) gas or air in your stomach that makes you feel uncomfortable and sometimes makes noises **3 get wind of sth** to discover something that is intended to be a secret *Dad got wind of our plans for a party.* **4 get your wind (back)** to breathe easily again, for example after you have been running ➔ *See also:* throw **caution**[1] to the wind, **second wind.**

**W**

**wind²** /wɪnd/ *verb* [T] to make someone have difficulty breathing, often by hitting them in the stomach

**wind³** /waɪnd/ *verb past* **wound 1 wind sth around/round, etc sth** to turn or twist something long and thin around something else several times *She wound the rope around the tree.* ⊃ *Opposite* **unwind. 2 wind (up) a clock/toy/watch, etc** to make a clock/toy/watch, etc work by turning a small handle or button several times *Did you remember to wind the alarm clock?* **3 wind along/down/through, etc** If a river, road, etc winds somewhere, it bends a lot and is not straight. *The path winds along the edge of the bay.*

**wind (sth) down** to gradually end, or to make something gradually end *to wind down a business*

**wind down** (*also* **unwind**) to gradually relax after doing something that has made you tired or worried

**wind up** to finally be somewhere or do something, especially without having planned it *If he carries on like this, he'll wind up in prison.* • [+ doing sth] *I wound up having to start the course from the beginning again.*

**wind (sth) up** to end, or to make something end *It's time to wind up the game now.*

**wind sb up** *UK informal* **1** to tell someone something that is not true, as a joke *Have I really won or are you winding me up?* **2** to annoy someone *He keeps complaining and it really winds me up.*

**windfall** /'wɪndfɔːl/ *noun* [C] an amount of money that you get that you did not expect *Investors each received a windfall of £1000.*

**winding** /'waɪndɪŋ/ *adj* **a winding path/road/street, etc** a path/road, etc that bends a lot and is not straight

**'wind ,instrument** *noun* [C] a musical instrument that you play by blowing into it *A flute is a wind instrument.*

**windmill** /'wɪndmɪl/ *noun* [C] a building with long parts at the top that turn in the wind, used for producing power or crushing grain

**windmill**

○━**window** /'wɪndəʊ/ *noun* [C] **1** a space in the wall of a building or vehicle that has glass in it, used for letting light and air inside and for looking through *Open the window if you're too hot.* • *a window frame/ledge* ⊃ *See colour picture* **The Living Room** *on page Centre 11.* **2** a separate area on a computer screen showing information and which you can move around *to minimize/maximize a window* ⊃ *See also:* **French windows.**

**windowpane** /'wɪndəʊpeɪn/ *noun* [C] a piece of glass in a window

**'window ,shopping** *noun* [U] when you look at things in shops but do not buy anything

**windowsill** /'wɪndəʊsɪl/ *noun* [C] a shelf at the bottom of a window ⊃ *See colour picture* **The Living Room** *on page Centre 11.*

**windpipe** /'wɪndpaɪp/ *noun* [C] the tube that carries air from your throat to your lungs

**windscreen** /'wɪndskriːn/ *UK* (*US* **windshield** /'wɪndʃiːld/) *noun* [C] the window at the front end of a car, bus, etc ⊃ *See colour picture* **Car** *on page Centre 3.*

**'windscreen ,wiper** *UK* (*US* **'windshield ,wiper**) *noun* [C] one of two long, metal and rubber parts that move against a windscreen to remove rain ⊃ *See colour picture* **Car** *on page Centre 3.*

**windsurfing** /'wɪndsɜːfɪŋ/ *noun* [U] a sport in which you sail across water by standing on a board and holding onto a large sail • **windsurfer** *noun* [C]

**windswept** /'wɪndswept/ *adj* **1** A windswept place often has strong winds. *a remote, windswept hill* **2** looking untidy because you have been in the wind *windswept hair*

**windy** /'wɪndi/ *adj* with a lot of wind *a windy day* • *Outside it was cold and windy.*

○━**wine** /waɪn/ *noun* [C, U] an alcoholic drink that is made from the juice of grapes (= small, green or purple fruit), or sometimes other fruit *a glass of wine* • *red/white wine*

**wing**

wing

○━**wing** /wɪŋ/ *noun* [C] **1** CREATURE one of the two parts that a bird or insect uses to fly **2** AIRCRAFT one of the two long, flat parts at the sides of an aircraft that make it stay in the sky **3** CAR *UK* (*US* **fender**) one of the parts at each corner of a car above the wheels **4** BUILDING a part of a large building that is joined to the side of the main part *Their offices are in the West wing.* **5** POLITICS a group of people in an organization or political party who have the same beliefs *the nationalist wing of the party* **6 take sb under your wing** to help and protect someone who is younger than you or who has less experience than you

**winged** /wɪŋd/ *adj* with wings *a winged insect*

**'wing ,mirror** *UK* (*US* **side mirror**) *noun* [C] a small mirror on the side of a car or truck ⊃ *See colour picture* **Car** *on page Centre 3.*

**the wings** /wɪŋz/ *noun* [plural] **1** the area behind the sides of a stage where actors wait just before they perform **2 be waiting in the wings** to be ready to do something or be used at any time

**wink¹** /wɪŋk/ *verb* [I] to quickly close and then open one eye, in order to be friendly or to show that something is a joke *She smiled and winked at me.*

**wink**

**wink²** /wɪŋk/ *noun* [C] **1** when you wink at someone *He gave me a friendly wink.* **2 not sleep a wink** to not have any sleep *I was so excited last night – I didn't sleep a wink.*

o<sup>—</sup>**winner** /'wɪnər/ *noun* [C] someone who wins a game, competition, or election *the winners of the World Cup*

**winnings** /'wɪnɪŋz/ *noun* [plural] money that you win in a competition

o<sup>—</sup>**winter** /'wɪntər/ *noun* [C, U] the coldest season of the year, between autumn and spring *We went skiing last winter.* • *a mild winter* • **wintry** /'wɪntri/ *adj* cold and typical of winter *wintry showers* (= snow mixed with rain) ⊃ *See also:* at/in the **dead³** of winter.

**wipe¹** /waɪp/ *verb* [T] **1** to clean or dry something by moving a cloth across it *I had a job wiping tables in a cafe.* • *She wiped her hands on the towel.* **2 wipe sth from/away/off, etc** to remove dirt, water, a mark, etc from something with a cloth or your hand *He wiped a tear from his eye.*

**wipe sth out** to destroy something completely *The earthquake wiped out many villages.*

**wipe sth up** to remove a substance, usually liquid, with a cloth *Have you got something I could wipe this mess up with?*

**wipe²** /waɪp/ *noun* [C] **1** when you clean or dry something with a cloth *I'll give the table a wipe.* **2** a thin cloth or piece of paper used for cleaning *baby wipes*

**wiper** /'waɪpər/ (*also* **windscreen wiper**) *noun* [C] a long, metal and rubber part that removes rain from the front window of a vehicle

o<sup>—</sup>**wire¹** /waɪər/ *noun* **1** [C, U] thin, metal thread, used to fasten things or to make fences, cages, etc **2** [C] a long, thin piece of metal thread, usually covered in plastic, that carries electricity *electrical wires* ⊃ *See also:* **barbed wire**.

**wire²** /waɪər/ *verb* [T] **1** [ELECTRICITY] (*also* **wire**

up**) to connect wires so that a piece of electrical equipment will work *Do you know how to wire a burglar alarm?* **2** [JOIN] to join two things together using wire **3** [SEND] *US* to send a message or money using an electrical communication system

**wireless** /'waɪələs/ *noun* [C] *old-fashioned* a radio

**wiring** /'waɪərɪŋ/ *noun* [U] the system of wires that carry electricity around a building *The fire was caused by faulty wiring.*

**wiry** /'waɪəri/ *adj* **1** Someone who is wiry is strong but quite thin. **2** Wiry hair is thick and stiff, like wire. *a wiry beard*

**wisdom** /'wɪzdəm/ *noun* **1** [U] the ability to use your knowledge and experience to make good decisions and judgments **2 the wisdom of sth/doing sth** If you doubt the wisdom of something, you think it is probably not a good plan. *Many people have questioned the wisdom of spending so much money on weapons.*

**'wisdom ,tooth** *noun* [C] *plural* **wisdom teeth** one of the four teeth at the back of your mouth that are the last to grow

**wise¹** /waɪz/ *adj* **1** A wise decision or action shows good judgment and is the right thing to do. *I think we've made a wise choice.* • [+ to do sth] *It's always wise to see a doctor if you're worried about your health.* ⊃ *Opposite* **unwise**. **2** A wise person is able to use their knowledge and experience to make good decisions and give good advice. **3 be none the wiser** *informal* to still not understand something after someone has tried to explain it to you • **wisely** *adv*

**wise²** /waɪz/ *verb*

**wise up** *informal* to start to understand the truth about a situation *Employers are starting to wise up to the fact that people want flexible working hours.*

o<sup>—</sup>**wish¹** /wɪʃ/ *verb* **1 wish (that)** to want a situation that is different from the one that exists *I wish that I didn't have to go to work.* • *I wish he would leave.* • *I wish I had been there.* **2 wish to do sth** *formal* to want to do something *I wish to speak to the manager.* **3 wish sb luck/success, etc** to say that you hope someone will be lucky, successful, etc *I wished him luck for his test.* **4 I/you wish!** *informal* used to say that you would like something to be true although you know it is not true *"Have your exams finished yet?" "I wish!"*

o<sup>—</sup>**wish²** /wɪʃ/ *noun* [C] **1** what you want to do or what you want to happen *The hospital always tries to respect the wishes of its patients.* • *I have no wish to travel the world.* **2** something that you say secretly to yourself about what you want to have or happen *She closed her eyes and made a wish.* **3 best wishes** something you say or write at the end of a letter, to show that you hope someone is happy and has good luck *Please give her my best wishes when you see her.*

**wishful thinking** /ˌwɪʃfəl'θɪŋkɪŋ/ *noun* [U] when you want something to happen or be true but it is impossible

**wisp** /wɪsp/ *noun* [C] **1 a wisp of cloud/smoke/ steam** a small, thin line of cloud/smoke/

W

steam **2 a wisp of hair/grass, etc** a thin piece of hair/grass, etc • **wispy** *adj* in the form of wisps *wispy hair* • *a wispy cloud*

**wistful** /'wɪstfᵊl/ *adj* slightly sad because you are thinking about something you cannot have *a wistful look/smile* • **wistfully** *adv*

**wit** /wɪt/ *noun* [U] the ability to say things that are funny and clever *a woman of great intelligence and wit*

**witch** /wɪtʃ/ *noun* [C] in stories, a woman who has magical powers that she uses to do bad or strange things

**witchcraft** /'wɪtʃkrɑːft/ *noun* [U] the use of magic to make bad or strange things happen

**witch-hunt** /'wɪtʃhʌnt/ *noun* [C] when a group of people try to blame someone and punish them for something, in a way that is unfair

○━**with** /wɪð/ *preposition* **1** TOGETHER used to say that people or things are in a place together or are doing something together *Emma lives with her boyfriend.* • *Hang your coat with the others.* **2** HAVING having or including something *a house with a swimming pool* • *a woman with brown eyes* **3** USING using something *She hit him over the head with a tennis racket.* **4** HOW used to describe the way someone does something *He plays with great enthusiasm.* • *She shut the drawer with a bang.* **5** WHAT used to say what fills, covers, etc something *a bucket filled with water* • *shoes covered with mud* **6** CAUSE because of something *She was trembling with fear.* **7** RELATING TO relating to something or someone *There's something wrong with the car.* • *The doctors are very pleased with his progress.* **8** POSITION used to describe the position of someone's body *She sat with her legs crossed.* **9 be with me/you** *informal* to understand what someone is saying *Sorry, I'm not with you – can you say that again?*

**withdraw** /wɪð'drɔː/ *verb past t* **withdrew**, *past p* **withdrawn 1** MONEY [T] to take money out of a bank account *She withdrew $50.* **2** REMOVE [T] to remove something, especially because of an official decision *This product has been withdrawn from sale.* • *He has threatened to withdraw his support.* **3** MILITARY [I, T] If a military force withdraws, or if someone withdraws it, it leaves the place where it is fighting. *The President has ordered troops to be withdrawn from the area.* **4** COMPETITION [I] to decide that you will not now be in a race, competition, etc *Christie was forced to withdraw from the race because of injury.* **5** SOMETHING SAID [T] *formal* to say that you want people to ignore something you said before because it was not true *He admitted taking the money, but later withdrew his confession.*

**withdrawal** /wɪð'drɔːᵊl/ *noun* **1** MONEY [C] when you take money out of a bank account *This account allows you to make withdrawals whenever you want to.* **2** STOP [C, U] when someone stops doing something, for example helping someone or giving money [usually singular] *the withdrawal of financial support* **3** MILITARY [C, U] when a military force moves out of an area [usually singular] *the withdrawal of troops* **4** DRUGS [U] the unpleasant feelings that someone gets when they stop taking a drug

that they have taken for a long time *withdrawal symptoms* **5** ALONE [U] when someone prefers to be alone and does not want to talk to other people *Withdrawal can be a symptom of depression.*

**withdrawn** /wɪð'drɔːn/ *adj* [never before noun] quiet and not talking to other people

**wither** /'wɪðə'/ (*also* **wither away**) *verb* [I] If a plant withers, it becomes dry and starts to die.

**withering** /'wɪðərɪŋ/ *adj* **withering attack/ contempt/look** criticism or an expression that shows that someone strongly disapproves of someone or something *He published a withering attack on the government's policies.*

**withhold** /wɪð'həʊld/ *verb* [T] *past* **withheld** to not give someone the information, money, etc that they want *The company has decided to withhold payment until the job has been finished.*

○━**within**[1] /wɪˈðɪn/ *preposition* **1** TIME before a particular period of time has finished *The ambulance arrived within 10 minutes.* • *Consume within two days of purchase.* **2** DISTANCE less than a particular distance from something *She was born within 20 miles of New York.* • *The hotel is within easy reach of* (= near) *the airport.* **3** INSIDE inside an area, group or system *a dispute within the department* • *There's a pharmacy within the hospital building.* **4** LIMIT not outside the limits of something *The project was completed well within budget.* **5 within the law/ the rules/your rights, etc** allowed according to the law/the rules/your rights, etc *You're perfectly within your rights to complain.*

**within**[2] /wɪˈðɪn/ *adv* inside someone or something *The organization needs to change from within.*

○━**without** /wɪˈðaʊt/ *preposition* **1** not having, using, or doing something *I did the test without any problems.* • *I can't see without my glasses.* • *He went to school without eating any breakfast.* **2** when someone is not with someone else *You can start the meeting without me.* **3 go/do without (sth)** to not have something important *They went without sleep for three days.*

**withstand** /wɪð'stænd/ *verb* [T] *past* **withstood** to not be damaged or broken by something *a bridge designed to withstand earthquakes*

○━**witness**[1] /'wɪtnəs/ *noun* [C] **1** COURT someone in a court of law who says what they have seen and what they know about a crime *The witness was called to the stand.* **2** SEE someone who sees an accident or crime *Police are appealing for witnesses to the shooting.* **3** DOCUMENT someone who signs their name on an official document to say that they were present when someone else signed it

**witness**[2] /'wɪtnəs/ *verb* [T] **1** to see something happen, especially in an accident or crime *Did anyone witness the attack?* **2** to sign your name on an official document to say that you were present when someone else signed it

**'witness ˌbox** *UK* (*UK/US* **'witness ˌstand**) *noun* [C] the place in a court of law where a witness stands or sits when they are answering questions

**wits** /wɪts/ *noun* [plural] **1** intelligence and the ability to think quickly **2 keep/have your**

**W**

**wits about you** to be ready to think quickly in a situation and react to things that you are not expecting *You have to keep your wits about you when you're cycling.* **3 be at your wits' end** to be very worried about something and not know what you should do next **4 scare/frighten sb out of their wits** to make someone very frightened

**witty** /'wɪti/ *adj* using words in a funny and clever way *a witty comment* • *He was witty and charming.*

**wives** /waɪvz/ *plural of* wife

**wizard** /'wɪzəd/ *noun* [C] **1** in stories, a man who has magical powers **2** *informal* someone who is very good at something or knows a lot about something *a computer wizard*

**wobble** /'wɒbl/ *verb* [I, T] If something wobbles or you make something wobble, it moves from side to side, often because it is not on a flat surface. *The ladder started to wobble.* • *Stop wobbling the table.* • **wobbly** *adj* likely to wobble *a wobbly chair*

**woe** /wəʊ/ *noun* [U] *literary* sadness *full of woe*

**woeful** /'wəʊfᵊl/ *adj* very bad and showing no skill *a woeful attempt/performance* • **woefully** *adv*

**woes** /wəʊz/ *noun* [plural] *formal* **your woes** your problems and worries

**wok** /wɒk/ *noun* [C] a large, bowl-shaped pan that is used for frying Chinese food

**woke** /wəʊk/ *past tense of* wake

**woken** /'wəʊkᵊn/ *past participle of* wake

**wolf**[1] /wʊlf/ *noun* [C] *plural* **wolves** /wʊlvz/ a wild animal like a large dog

**wolf**[2] /wʊlf/ (*also* **wolf down**) *verb* [T] *informal* to eat something very quickly *I gave her a plate of pasta and she wolfed it down.*

o—**woman** /'wʊmən/ *noun* [C] *plural* **women** /'wɪmɪn/ an adult female person *a 30-year-old woman* • *There are two women at the bus stop.* • **womanhood** *noun* [U] the state of being a woman

**womanly** /'wʊmənli/ *adj* having the qualities and appearance that people think a woman should have *womanly charms*

**womb** /wuːm/ *noun* [C] the organ inside a woman's body where a baby grows

**women** /'wɪmɪn/ *plural of* woman

**won** /wʌn/ *past of* win

o—**wonder**[1] /'wʌndə²/ *verb* **1** [I, T] to want to know something or to try to understand the reason for something [+ question word] *I wonder what he's making for dinner.* • *I wonder why she left so suddenly.* **2 I/we wonder if/whether ...** used to politely ask someone for something or to suggest something *I wonder if you could help me?* • *We were wondering if you'd like to come over for a meal sometime.*

**wonder**[2] /'wʌndə²/ *noun* **1** [U] surprise and admiration *The boys gazed in wonder at the shiny, red Ferrari.* **2** [C] something that makes you feel surprise or admiration [usually plural] *the wonders of modern medicine* **3 no wonder** used to say that you are not surprised about something *No wonder she failed the test if she didn't do any work.* **4 it's a wonder (that)** used to say that you are surprised about something *It's a wonder he's still alive.*

o—**wonderful** /'wʌndəfᵊl/ *adj* very good *a wonderful idea* • *We had a wonderful time in Spain.* • **wonderfully** *adv*

**won't** /wəʊnt/ *short for* will not *I won't be home before midnight.*

**woo** /wuː/ *verb* [T] **wooing**, *past* **wooed** to try to persuade someone to support you or to use your business *a political party trying to woo young voters*

o—**wood** /wʊd/ *noun* **1** [C, U] the hard material that trees are made of *a piece of wood* **2** [C] (*also* **woods**) a large area of trees growing near each other *We went for a walk in the woods.*

**wooded** /'wʊdɪd/ *adj* covered with trees *a wooded area*

**wooden** /'wʊdᵊn/ *adj* made of wood *a wooden chair*

**woodland** /'wʊdlənd/ *noun* [C, U] an area of land with a lot of trees

**woodwind** /'wʊdwɪnd/ *noun* [U] the group of musical instruments that you play by blowing into them *woodwind instruments*

**woodwork** /'wʊdwɜːk/ *noun* [U] **1** the parts of a building that are made from wood **2** the activity of making things from wood

**woof** /wʊf/ *noun* [C] the sound made by a dog

o—**wool** /wʊl/ *noun* [U] **1** the soft, thick hair on a sheep **2** thick thread or material that is made from the hair of a sheep *a wool suit* • *a ball of wool* ⊃ *See also:* **cotton wool.**

**woollen** UK (US **woolen**) /'wʊlən/ *adj* made of wool *woollen gloves*

**woolly** UK (US **wooly**) /'wʊli/ *adj* made of wool, or made of something that looks like wool *a green woolly hat*

o—**word**[1] /wɜːd/ *noun* **1** [C] a group of letters or sounds that mean something, or a single letter or sound that means something *'Hund' is the German word for 'dog'.* • *He has difficulty spelling long words.* **2 not believe/understand/hear, etc a word** to not believe/understand/hear, etc anything *I don't believe a word he says.* **3 a word of warning/advice/thanks, etc** something that you say to warn someone, give them advice, thank them, etc *Just a word of warning – he doesn't like people being late.* **4 have a word with sb** to talk to someone for a short time *I'll have a word with Ted and see if he wants to come.* **5 put in a good word for sb** to praise someone, often to someone who might be able to employ them **6 give sb your word** to promise someone something *He gave me his word that he wouldn't tell anyone.* **7 take sb's word for it** to believe what someone says without any proof **8 in other words** used to explain what something means in a different way *He said he's too busy, in other words, he isn't interested.* **9 in sb's words** used when you repeat what someone said *In the manager's words, the game was 'a total disaster'.* **10 word for word** using the exact words that were originally used *She repeated word for word what he had told her.* **11 have the last word** to say the last thing in a discussion or argument or make the final decision about something **12 not breathe a word** to not tell people a secret *Don't breathe a word about this to anyone.* **13 not get a word in edgeways** UK (US **not**

**W**

**get a word in edgewise)** to be unable to say anything because someone else is talking so much ➔ *See also:* a **play²** on words, **swear word**.

**word²** /wɜːd/ *verb* [T] to choose the words you use when you are saying or writing something *How should I word this letter?*

**wording** /'wɜːdɪŋ/ *noun* [U] the words that are used when someone says or writes something

**word 'processor** *noun* [C] a computer or computer program that you use for writing letters, reports, etc • word processing *noun* [U]

**wore** /wɔːʳ/ *past tense of* wear

○━**work¹** /wɜːk/ *verb* **1** JOB [I, T] to do a job, especially the job you do to earn money *Helen **works** for a computer company. • He **works as** a waiter in an Italian restaurant. • My Dad works very long hours* (= he works a lot of hours). **2** MACHINE [I] If a machine or piece of equipment works, it is not broken. *Does this radio work? • The washing machine isn't working.* **3** SUCCEED [I] If something works, it is effective and successful. *Her plan to get rid of me didn't work.* **4 can work sth; know how to work sth** to know how to use a machine or piece of equipment *Do you know how to work the video recorder?* **5** EFFORT [I, T] to do something that needs a lot of time or effort, or to make someone do this [+ to do sth] *He's been working to improve his speed. • Our teacher works us very hard.* **6 work your way around/through/up, etc sth** to achieve something gradually *I have a pile of homework to work my way through.*

**work against sb** to make it more difficult for someone to achieve something *Age can work against you when you are looking for a job.*

**work at sth** to try hard to achieve something [+ doing sth] *You need to work at improving your writing.*

**work on sth** to spend time repairing or improving something *Tim loves working on old cars.*

**work sth out 1** to calculate an amount *I'm trying to work out the total cost.* **2** to understand something or decide something after thinking very carefully [+ question word] *I haven't worked out what to do yet.*

**work out 1** If a problem or difficult situation works out, it gradually becomes better. *Don't worry – everything will work out in the end.* **2** to do exercises to make your body stronger ➔ *See colour picture* **Phrasal Verbs** *on page Centre 13.* **3 work out badly/well, etc** to happen or develop in a particular way *Changing schools worked out really well for me.* **4 work out at sth** to be the result when you calculate something *If we share the costs, it works out at $10 per person.*

**work sb out** *UK* to understand the reasons for someone's behaviour *I can't work him out at all.*

**work up to sth** to gradually prepare yourself for something difficult

○━**work²** /wɜːk/ *noun* **1** EFFORT [U] when you use physical or mental effort to do something *Decorating that room was hard work.* **2** PLACE [U] the place where you go to do your job *He had an accident at work.* **3** JOB [U] something you do as a job to earn money *Has she got any work yet? • Many young people are out of work*

(= they do not have a job). **4** ACTIVITY [U] the activities that you have to do at school, for your job, etc *Have you got a lot of work to do?* • *The teacher said she was pleased with my work.* **5 get/set to work (on sth)** to start doing something **6** ART/MUSIC ETC [C, U] a painting, book, piece of music, etc *The exhibition includes works by Picasso and Klee.* • *the complete works of Shakespeare* **7 do sb's dirty work** to do something unpleasant or difficult for someone else because they do not want to do it themselves **8 have your work cut out** to have something very difficult to do *It's a demanding job – she's going to have her work cut out for her.* ➔ *See also:* **donkey work**, **work of art**.

---

### USAGE

**work** or **job**?

Work is something you do to earn money. Remember that this noun is uncountable.

*She enjoys her work in the hospital.*

*He's looking for work.*

~~He's looking for a work.~~

Job is used to talk about the particular work activity which you do.

*He's looking for a job in computer programming.*

*Teaching must be an interesting job.*

~~Teaching must be an interesting work.~~

Occupation is a formal word which means the job that you do. It is often used on forms. See also: **career** and **profession**.

---

**workable** /'wɜːkəbl/ *adj* A workable plan or system can be used or done easily and is effective. ➔ *Opposite* **unworkable**.

**workaholic** /ˌwɜːkə'hɒlɪk/ *noun* [C] *informal* someone who works too much and does not have time to do anything else

**workbook** /'wɜːkbʊk/ *noun* [C] a book with questions and exercises in it that you use when you are learning something

**worked 'up** *adj* very nervous, angry, or excited

**worker** /'wɜːkəʳ/ *noun* **1** [C] someone who works for a company or organization but does not have a powerful position *an office worker* **2 a quick/slow/good, etc worker** someone who works quickly/slowly/well, etc ➔ *See also:* **social worker**.

**workforce** /'wɜːkfɔːs/ *noun* [group] **1** all the people who work for a company or organization **2** all the people in a country who are able to do a job *10% of the workforce are unemployed.*

**working** /'wɜːkɪŋ/ *adj* [always before noun] **1** relating to your job *good working conditions* **2 a working man/woman, etc** someone who has a job *a working mother* **3 a working knowledge of sth** knowledge about something which is good enough to be useful *She has a working knowledge of German and Russian.* ➔ *See also:* **hard-working**.

---

,**working** '**class** *noun* [C] the social class of
people who have little money and who usually
do physical work • working-class /,wɜːkɪŋ'klɑːs/
*adj* a working-class family

**workings** /'wɜːkɪŋz/ *noun* **the workings of
sth** how something works *the workings of the
mind*

**workload** /'wɜːkləʊd/ *noun* [C] the amount of
work that you have to do *Nurses have a very
**heavy workload** (= they work hard).*

**workman** /'wɜːkmən/ *noun* [C] *plural* **workmen**
someone who does a physical job such as building

**workmanship** /'wɜːkmənʃɪp/ *noun* [U] the skill
that is used in making something

,**work of** '**art** *noun* [C] *plural* **works of art 1** a
very beautiful and important painting,
drawing, etc *They stole several valuable works
of art.* **2 be a work of art** to be something
which is beautiful or needed a lot of skill to
create *Have you seen the wedding cake? It's a
work of art.*

**workout** /'wɜːkaʊt/ *noun* [C] when you do a
series of exercises to make your body strong
and healthy *a daily workout at the gym*

**workplace** /'wɜːkpleɪs/ *noun* [C] the place
where you work *We are trying to get rid of bullying in the workplace.*

**worksheet** /'wɜːkˌʃiːt/ *noun* [C] a piece of paper
with questions and exercises for students

**workshop** /'wɜːkʃɒp/ *noun* [C] **1** when a group
of people meet to learn more about something
by discussing it and doing practical exercises *a
workshop on crime prevention* **2** a place where
people use tools and machines to make or
repair things

**workstation** /'wɜːkˌsteɪʃ°n/ *noun* [C] a computer and the area around it where you work in
an office

'**work** ,**surface** (*also* **worktop** /'wɜːktɒp/) *noun*
[C] a flat surface for preparing food in a kitchen

o-x**world**[1] /wɜːld/ *noun* **1 the world** the Earth and
all the people, places, and things on it *Everest is
the highest mountain in the world.* • *She's travelled all over the world.* **2** [C] the people and
things that are involved in a particular activity
or subject [usually singular] *the entertainment
world* • *the world of politics* **3 the developing/
industrialized/Western, etc world** a particular area of the Earth **4 the plant/animal, etc
world** plants/animals, etc as a group **5 your
world** your life and experiences *His whole
world fell apart when she left.* **6 do sb a/the
world of good** *informal* to make someone feel
much happier or healthier *That swim has done
me a world of good.* **7 be out of this world**
*informal* to be of extremely good quality *Their
chocolate cake is just out of this world!* **8 think
the world of sb** to like and admire someone
very much **9 the whole world** *informal*
everyone *The whole world knew she was getting
married before I did.* ⟳ *See also:* **the Old World,
the Third World,** have the **best**[3] of both
worlds, not be the **end**[1] of the world, **the
outside world,** be on **top**[1] of the world.

**world**[2] /wɜːld/ *adj* [always before noun] relating
to the whole world *world peace* • *the world
championships*

**world-class** /,wɜːld'klɑːs/ *adj* one of the best in
the world *a world-class swimmer*

**world-famous** /,wɜːld'feɪməs/ *adj* known by
people everywhere in the world *The Eiffel
Tower is a world-famous landmark.*

**worldly** /'wɜːldli/ *adj* **1 sb's worldly goods/
possessions** everything that someone owns
*She lost all her worldly possessions in a fire.*
**2** having had a lot of experience of life *a
worldly woman*

,**world** '**war** *noun* [C] a war in which several
large or important countries fight

**worldwide** /,wɜːld'waɪd/ *adj, adv* in all parts of
the world *10 million copies have been sold
worldwide.*

the ,**World Wide** '**Web** *noun* part of the
Internet that consists of all the connected websites (= pages of text and pictures)

**worm**[1] /wɜːm/ *noun* [C] a small creature with a
long, thin, soft body and no legs ⟳ *See also:* a
**can**[2] of worms.

**worm**[2] /wɜːm/ *verb* **worm your way into sth**
to gradually get into a situation by making
people like you and trust you, especially by
deceiving them *He wormed his way into the
family.*

**worn**[1] /wɔːn/ *adj* Worn clothing or objects have
been used a lot and
show damage. *a
worn leather chair*

**worn** *noun*

**worn**[2] /wɔːn/ *past
participle of* wear

**worn-out** /,wɔːn'aʊt/
*adj* **1** extremely
tired *I was absolutely
worn out after all
that dancing.*
**2** Something that is
worn-out is so old or
has been used so
much that it is
damaged too much
to repair. *a worn-out
carpet*

o-x**worried** /'wʌrid/ *adj*
anxious because you are thinking about problems or unpleasant things that might happen
*She's really **worried about** her son.* • [+ (that)]
*I'm worried that she'll tell Maria.*

o-x**worry**[1] /'wʌri/ *verb* **1** [I] to think about problems or unpleasant things that might happen
in a way that makes you feel anxious *Don't
worry – she'll be all right.* • *She's always worrying about something.* • [+ (that)] *I worry that
he might run away.* **2** [T] to make someone feel
anxious because of problems or unpleasant
things that might happen *It worries me that he
hasn't phoned yet.*

---

**USAGE**

**worry about something** or **someone**

Be careful to use the correct preposition after this verb.

*They were all worried about their jobs.*

~~They were all worried for their jobs.~~

---

**worry**[2] /'wʌri/ *noun* **1** [C] a problem that makes

you feel anxious *health worries* **2** [U] when you are anxious about something *She's been sick with worry.*

**worrying** /ˈwʌriɪŋ/ *adj* making you feel anxious *a worrying situation* • **worryingly** *adv* *She's worryingly thin.*

**worse¹** /wɜːs/ *adj (comparative of bad)* **1** more unpleasant or difficult than something else that is also bad *The exam was worse than I expected.* • *We'll have to stop the game if the rain gets any worse.* **2** more ill *The drugs aren't working, he just seems to be getting worse.* **3** be none the worse for sth to not be harmed or damaged by something *He seemed none the worse for the experience.* **4** worse luck *UK informal* used to show that you are annoyed or unhappy about something *I've got to work on Saturday, worse luck!*

**worse²** /wɜːs/ *noun* [U] **1** something that is more unpleasant or difficult *It was a nasty accident, although I've seen worse.* **2** for the worse If a situation changes for the worse, it becomes worse.

**worse³** /wɜːs/ *adv (comparative of bad)* less well *He was treated much worse than I was.*

**worsen** /ˈwɜːsᵊn/ *verb* [I, T] to become worse or to make something become worse *His condition suddenly worsened last week.*

**worse 'off** *adj* [never before noun] poorer or in a more difficult situation *If Rick loses his job we'll be even worse off.*

**worship** /ˈwɜːʃɪp/ *verb* **worshipping**, *past worshipped*, *(also US)* **worshiping**, *past worshiped* **1** [I, T] to show respect for a god by saying prayers or performing religious ceremonies **2** [T] to love and respect someone very much *She worshipped her mother.* • **worship** *noun* [U] *a place of worship* (= a religious building) • **worshipper** *noun* [C]

**worst¹** /wɜːst/ *adj (superlative of bad)* **the worst** the most unpleasant or difficult *What's the worst job you've ever had?*

**worst²** /wɜːst/ *noun* **1** the worst the most unpleasant or difficult thing, person, or situation *I've made some mistakes in the past, but this is definitely the worst.* **2** at worst used to say what the most unpleasant or difficult situation could possibly be *At worst, we might lose our money.* **3** if the worst comes to the worst *UK (US if worse/worst comes to worst)* if a situation develops in the most unpleasant or difficult way

**worst³** /wɜːst/ *adv (superlative of bad)* the most badly *the worst affected area*

○⚬**worth¹** /wɜːθ/ *adj* **1** be worth sth to have a particular value, especially in money *Our house is worth about £60,000.* **2** be worth doing/ seeing/trying, etc to be useful or enjoyable to do/see/try, etc *It's not as good as his last book but it's definitely worth reading.* **3** be worth it to be useful or enjoyable despite needing a lot of effort *It was a long climb up the mountain but the view was worth it.* • *Don't bother complaining – it's really not worth it.* **4** be worth your while If it is worth your while doing something, it is useful or enjoyable despite needing a lot of effort. *It isn't worth my while going all that way just for one day.*

○⚬**worth²** /wɜːθ/ *noun* **1** £20/$100, etc worth of sth the amount of something that you can buy for £20/$100, etc *I've put £2 worth of stamps on the letter.* **2** a month's/ year's, etc worth of sth the amount of something that can be done or used in a month/year, etc *an hour's worth of free phone calls* **3** [U] how important or useful someone or something is *She's finally proved her worth.*

**worthless** /ˈwɜːθləs/ *adj* **1** not important or useful *He made me feel stupid and worthless.* **2** having no value in money *The painting's a fake – it's completely worthless.*

**worthwhile** /ˌwɜːθˈwaɪl/ *adj* useful and enjoyable, despite needing a lot of effort *It's a difficult course but it's very worthwhile.*

**worthy** /ˈwɜːði/ *adj* **1** deserving respect, admiration, or support *a worthy cause* • *a worthy champion* **2** be worthy of attention/respect, etc to deserve attention/respect, etc

○⚬**would** *strong form* /wʊd/ *weak form* /wəd/ *modal verb* **1** [IF] used to say what might happen if something else happened *What would you do if you lost your job?* **2** [SAID/THOUGHT] used as the past form of 'will' to talk about what someone has said or thought *Sue promised that she would help.* • *They thought that she would never recover.* **3** [WILLING] used as the past form of 'will' to talk about what someone was willing to do or what something was able to do *I asked her to talk to him, but she wouldn't.* • *The car wouldn't start this morning.* **4** would like/love sth used to say politely that you want something *I'd* (= I would) *like a cup of coffee, please.* **5** would you used to politely ask someone something *Would you like a drink?* • *Would you come with me, please?* **6** [IMAGINE] used to talk about a situation that you can imagine happening *It would be lovely to go to New York.* **7** I would imagine/think, etc used to give an opinion in a polite way *I would imagine she'll discuss it with her husband first.* **8** [OFTEN] used to talk about things that happened often in the past *He would always turn and wave at the end of the street.* **9** She/he/you would! *mainly UK* used to show that you are not surprised by someone's annoying behaviour *Margot spent £200 on a dress for the occasion but she would, wouldn't she?* ➪ *See study section* **Modal verbs** *on page Centre 31.*

**wouldn't** /ˈwʊdᵊnt/ *short for* would not *She wouldn't let us watch TV.*

**wound¹** /wuːnd/ *noun* [C] an injury, especially one that is made by a knife or bullet

**wound²** /wuːnd/ *verb* [T] **1** to injure someone, especially with a knife or gun [often passive] *He was badly wounded in the attack.* • *wounded* *soldiers* **2** to upset someone [often passive] *She was deeply wounded by his rejection.*

**wound³** /waʊnd/ *part of* wind³

**wound 'up** *adj* very nervous, worried, or angry *He gets very wound up before an important match.*

**wove** /wəʊv/ *past tense of* weave²

**woven** /'wəʊvən/ *past participle of* weave²

**wow** /waʊ/ *exclamation* informal something that you say to show surprise, excitement, admiration, etc *Wow! Look at that car!*

**wrangle¹** /'ræŋgl/ *noun* [C] a long and complicated argument *a legal wrangle*

**wrangle²** /'ræŋgl/ *verb* [I] to argue with someone for a long time *They're still wrangling over money.*

**wrap** /ræp/ *verb* [T] **wrapping**, *past* **wrapped** **1** (*also* **wrap up**) to cover something or someone with paper, cloth, etc *to wrap a present* • *They wrapped him in a blanket.* ➔ *Opposite* **unwrap**. **2 wrap sth around sb/sth** to fold paper, cloth, etc around something to cover it *He wrapped a towel around his waist.* **3 wrap your arms/ fingers, etc around sb/sth** to put your arms/ fingers, etc around someone or something *She wrapped her arms around my neck.*

**wrap sth up 1** to fold paper, cloth, etc around something to cover it *Have you wrapped up Jenny's present?* **2** to finish an activity successfully *We hope to have this deal wrapped up by Monday.*

**wrap up** to dress in warm clothes *Wrap up well – it's cold outside.*

**be wrapped up in sth** to give so much of your attention to something that you do not have time for other things or people

**wrapper** /'ræpə⁰/ *noun* [C] a piece of paper or plastic that covers something that you buy, especially food *(UK) sweet wrappers/(US) candy wrappers*

**wrapping** /'ræpɪŋ/ *noun* [C, U] paper or plastic that is used to cover and protect something

**'wrapping ,paper** *noun* [U] decorated paper that is used to cover presents

**wrath** /rɒθ/ *noun* [U] *literary* extreme anger

**wreak** /ri:k/ *verb past* **wrought** or **wreaked** **wreak havoc** to cause a lot of damage or harm *Floods have wreaked havoc in central Europe.*

**wreath** /ri:θ/ *noun* [C] *plural* **wreaths** /ri:ðz/ a large ring of leaves and flowers used as a decoration or to show respect for someone who has died

**wreck¹** /rek/ *verb* [T] to destroy something completely *The explosion wrecked several cars.*

**wreck²** /rek/ *noun* [C] **1** VEHICLE a car, ship, or aircraft that has been very badly damaged **2** PERSON *informal* someone who is in a bad physical or mental condition [usually singular] *I was a complete wreck by the end of my exams.* **3** ACCIDENT *mainly US* a bad accident involving a car or train *a car/train wreck*

**wreckage** /'rekɪdʒ/ *noun* [U] the parts that remain of a car, ship, or aircraft that has been destroyed *Two survivors were pulled from the wreckage.*

**wren** /ren/ *noun* [C] a very small, brown bird

**wrench¹** /renʃ/ *verb* [T] **1 wrench sth from/off, etc sb/sth** to pull something violently away

from a fixed position *The phone had been wrenched off the wall.* **2** to injure part of your body by turning it suddenly *I wrenched my right shoulder playing tennis.*

**wrench²** /renʃ/ *noun* **1** [no plural] when you are very sad because you have to leave someone or something *She found leaving home a real wrench.* **2** [C] *US* (*UK* **spanner**) a tool with a round end that is used to turn nuts and bolts (= metal objects used to fasten things together) ➔ *See picture at* **tool**.

**wrestle** /'resl/ *verb* [I] to fight with someone by holding them and trying to push them to the ground

**wrestle with sth** to try very hard to deal with a difficult problem or decision *He's still wrestling with his conscience.*

**wrestling** /'reslɪŋ/ *noun* [U] a sport in which two people fight and try to push each other to the ground • **wrestler** *noun* [C]

**wretched** /'retʃɪd/ *adj* **1** UNHAPPY very unhappy or ill *I'd been feeling wretched all day so I went to bed early.* **2** BAD very bad or of poor quality *The refugees were living in wretched conditions.* **3** ANNOYED [always before noun] used to show that something or someone makes you angry *This wretched phone won't work!*

**wriggle** /'rɪgl/ *verb* [I, T] **1** to twist your body or move part of your body with short, quick movements *She wriggled her toes in the warm sand.* **2 wriggle out of sth/doing sth** to avoid doing something that you have agreed to do *Are you trying to wriggle out of going to the meeting?*

**wring** /rɪŋ/ (*also* **wring out**) *verb* [T] *past* **wrung** to twist a cloth or piece of clothing with your hands to remove water from it *He wrung out his socks and hung them up to dry.* ➔ *See also:* **wring your hands** (**hand¹**).

**wrinkle** /'rɪŋkl/ *noun* [C] **1** a small line on your face that you get when you grow old **2** a small fold in a piece of cloth • **wrinkle** *verb* [I, T] *a wrinkled face*

**wrinkles**

**wrist** /rɪst/ *noun* [C] the part of your body between your hand and your arm

**writ** /rɪt/ *noun* [C] a legal document that orders someone to do something

o━**write** /raɪt/ *verb past t* **wrote**, *past p* **written 1** WORDS [I, T] to produce words, letters, or numbers on a surface using a pen or pencil *Write your name at the top of the page.* • *She can't read or write.* **2** BOOK [I, T] to create a book, story, article, etc or a piece of music *He's writing a book on Russian literature.* • *She writes for Time magazine.* **3** LETTER [I, T] to send someone a letter [+ two objects] *I wrote her a letter last week.* • *Has Bill written to you recently?* **4** DOCUMENT [T] (*also* **write out**) to put all the information that is needed on a document *He wrote out a cheque for £250.*

W

USAGE

**write**

Remember to use the correct grammar after **write**.

write **to** someone

*Rachel wrote to me last week.*

write someone **a letter**

*Rachel wrote me a letter last week.*

write someone (American English) *US*

*Rachel wrote me last week.*

**write back** to reply to someone's letter
**write sth down** to write something on a piece of paper so that you do not forget it *Did you write Jo's phone number down?*
**write in** to write a letter to a newspaper, television company, etc *Lots of people have written in to complain about the show.*
**write off** to write a letter to an organization asking them to send you something *I've written off for an information pack.*
**write sth off 1** to accept that an amount of money has been lost or will never be paid to you *to write off debts* **2** *UK* to damage a vehicle so badly that it cannot be repaired
**write sb/sth off** to decide that someone or something is not useful or important *They had written him off before they even met him.*
**write sth up** to write something in a complete form, usually using notes that you made earlier *Have you written up that report yet?*
**write-off** /'raɪtɒf/ *noun* [C] *UK* a vehicle that is damaged so badly in an accident that it cannot be repaired *I wasn't hurt, but the car was a complete write-off.*
o⤳**writer** /'raɪtə'/ *noun* [C] someone whose job is writing books, stories, articles, etc
**write-up** /'raɪtʌp/ *noun* [C] an article in a newspaper or magazine in which someone gives their opinion about a performance, product, etc *The film got a very good write-up in yesterday's paper.*
**writhe** /raɪð/ *verb* [I] to twist your body in a violent way, often because you are in pain *She lay on her bed, writhing in agony.*
o⤳**writing** /'raɪtɪŋ/ *noun* [U] **1** SKILL the skill or activity of producing words on a surface *Teachers focus on reading and writing in the first year.* **2** WORDS words that have been written or printed *The writing was too small to read.* **3** STYLE the way that someone writes *You've got very neat writing.* **4** BOOKS the books, stories, articles, etc written by a particular person or group of people *She's studying women's writing of the 1930s.* **5** JOB the activity or job of creating books, stories, or articles **6 in writing** An agreement that is in writing is official because it has been written and not

only spoken. *Please confirm your reservation in writing.*
**written¹** /'rɪtᵊn/ *adj* [always before noun] presented as a document on paper *a written statement/warning*
**written²** /'rɪtᵊn/ *past participle of* write
o⤳**wrong¹** /rɒŋ/ *adj* **1** NOT CORRECT not correct *the wrong answer* ● *We're going the wrong way.* **2 be wrong** to think or say something that is not correct *You were wrong about the party – it's today, not tomorrow.* **3 get sth wrong** to produce an answer or result that is not correct *I got most of the answers wrong.* **4** PROBLEM [never before noun] If something is wrong, there is a problem. *There's something wrong with my computer.* ● *What's wrong?* **5** NOT MORAL [never before noun] morally bad [+ to do sth] *It's wrong to tell lies.* **6** NOT SUITABLE not suitable *I think she's wrong for this job.* ⊃ See also: get (hold of) the wrong **end¹** of the stick, get/start off on the wrong **foot¹**, not put a **foot¹** wrong, rub sb up the wrong **way¹**.
o⤳**wrong²** /rɒŋ/ *adv* **1** in a way that is not correct *He always says my name wrong.* **2 go wrong** to develop problems *Something's gone wrong with my computer.* **3 Don't get me wrong.** *informal* used when you do not want someone to think that you do not like someone or something *Don't get me wrong, I like her, but she can be very annoying.*
**wrong³** /rɒŋ/ *noun* **1** [C, U] when something is not morally right *She's old enough to know the difference between right and wrong.* **2 be in the wrong** to be responsible for a mistake or something bad that has happened
**wrong⁴** /rɒŋ/ *verb* [T] *formal* to treat someone unfairly *a wronged man*
**wrongdoing** /'rɒŋˌduːɪŋ/ *noun* [C, U] *formal* when someone does something that is illegal or not honest
**wrongful** /'rɒŋfᵊl/ *adj* **wrongful arrest/conviction/imprisonment, etc** when someone is accused of something or punished for something unfairly or illegally ● wrongfully *adv* *wrongfully arrested*
**wrongly** /'rɒŋli/ *adv* **1** in a way that is not correct *The letter was wrongly addressed.* **2 wrongly accused/convicted/imprisoned, etc** accused or punished unfairly or illegally *She was wrongly convicted of drug smuggling.*
**wrote** /rəʊt/ *past tense of* write
**wrought** /rɔːt/ *past of* wreak
**wrought 'iron** *noun* [U] iron that can be bent into shapes and used to make gates, furniture, etc
**wrung** /rʌŋ/ *past of* wring
**wry** /raɪ/ *adj* A wry expression or remark shows your humour despite being in a difficult or disappointing situation. *a wry smile* ● wryly *adv*
**www** /ˌdʌblju:ˈdʌblju:ˈdʌblju:/ *noun abbreviation for* World Wide Web (= part of the Internet that consists of all the connected websites)

W

**X, x** /eks/ LETTER **1** the twenty-fourth letter of the alphabet **2** WRONG used to show that an answer is wrong **3** KISS used to represent a kiss at the end of a letter **4** UNKNOWN used to represent an unknown person or thing

**xenophobia** /ˌzenəʊˈfəʊbiə/ *noun* [U] extreme dislike or fear of people from other countries
● xenophobic /ˌzenəʊˈfəʊbɪk/ *adj*

**XL** /ˌeksˈel/ *abbreviation for* extra large: the largest size of clothes

**Xmas** /ˈkrɪstməs/ *noun* [U] *informal* used as a short way of writing 'Christmas' (= a Christian holiday), mainly on signs or cards *Happy Xmas!*

**X-ray** /ˈeksreɪ/ *noun* [C] **1** a photograph that shows the inside of your body *They **took an X-ray of** his leg.* **2** a wave of energy that can pass through solid materials ● X-ray *verb* [T] to take a photograph that shows the inside of something

**xylophone** /ˈzaɪləfəʊn/ *noun* [C] a musical instrument consisting of a row of flat, metal bars that you hit with sticks

**Y, y** /waɪ/ the twenty-fifth letter of the alphabet

**ya** /jə/ *pronoun informal* you *See ya later.*

**yacht** /jɒt/ *noun* [C] a large boat with sails used for pleasure or in races *a luxury yacht*

**Yank** /jæŋk/ *noun* [C] *informal* someone from the US, sometimes considered an offensive word

**yank** /jæŋk/ *verb* [T] *informal* to pull something with a strong, sudden movement *She yanked the drawer open.* ● *He yanked at the rope.*

**yap** /jæp/ *verb* [I] **yapping**, *past* **yapped** If a small dog yaps, it makes a lot of short, high sounds.

○━**yard** /jɑːd/ *noun* [C] **1** UNIT (*written abbreviation* **yd**) a unit for measuring length, equal to 0.9144 metres or 3 feet *There's a bus stop a few hundred yards up the road.* **2** HOUSE *US (UK* **garden**) an area of land in front of or behind a house **3** AREA a small area of ground next to a building, often with a fence or wall around it *a school yard*

**yardstick** /'jɑːdstɪk/ *noun* [C] something that you use to judge how good or successful something else is *If popularity is the yardstick of success, he's done very well.*

**yarn** /jɑːn/ *noun* **1** [U] thread used for making cloth **2** [C] *informal* a long story that is probably not true

**yawn** /jɔːn/ *verb* [I] to take a deep breath with your mouth wide open, because you are tired or bored *She yawned and looked at her watch.* ● yawn *noun* [C]

**yawn**

**yawning** /'jɔːnɪŋ/ *adj* **a yawning gap** a very big gap (= space or difference)

**yd** *written abbreviation for* yard (= a unit for measuring length)

**yeah** /jeə/ *exclamation informal spoken* yes *Yeah, I agree.*

○━**year** /jɪəʳ/ *noun* [C] **1** a period of 12 months, or 365 or 366 days, especially from 1 January to 31 December *last year/next year* ● *He joined the company a year ago.* **2 the academic/financial, etc year** the period of a year that is used by universities/businesses, etc to organize their activities **3 be two/twelve/37, etc years old** to be a particular age *Her son is six years old.* **4 a two/twelve-/37-, etc year-old** someone who is a particular age **5** *UK* a group of students who start college or a course together *He was in my year at school.* **6 years** a long time *I haven't seen Linda for years.* ➔ *See also:* for **donkey**'s **years**, **leap year**, **new year**.

**yearbook** /'jɪəbʊk/ *noun* [C] a book produced every year by a school or organization, containing information about its activities, members, etc

**yearly** /'jɪəli/ *adj, adv* happening once a year or every year *a yearly fee* ● *Interest is paid yearly.*

**yearn** /jɜːn/ *verb* **yearn for sth; yearn to do sth** to want something very much with a feeling of sadness *They yearned for peace.* ● *She yearned to get away.* ● yearning *noun* [C, U]

**yeast** /jiːst/ *noun* [U] a substance used to make bread rise and to make beer and wine

**yell** /jel/ *verb* [I, T] to shout something very loudly *The policeman yelled at them to stop.* ● yell *noun* [C]

○━**yellow** /'jeləʊ/ *adj* being the same colour as a lemon or the sun *a bright yellow tablecloth* ● yellow *noun* [C, U] the colour yellow ➔ *See colour picture* **Colours** *on page Centre 6.*

**the ˌYellow ˈPages** *UK trademark* (*US* **the ˈYellow ˌPages**) *noun* [plural] a big, yellow book containing telephone numbers of shops and businesses

**yelp** /jelp/ *verb* [I] If a dog yelps, it gives a sudden cry because of pain or shock.

**yep** /jep/ *exclamation informal spoken* yes

○━**yes¹** /jes/ *exclamation* **1** AGREE used to agree with something, or to give a positive answer to something *"Can I borrow your pencil?" "Yes, of course."* ● *"Are you feeling better?" "Yes, thanks."* ● *"Coffee?" " Yes, please."* **2** ANSWER used as an answer when someone calls you *"Jack!" "Yes?"* **3** DISAGREE used to disagree with a negative announcement *"He's not here yet." "Yes he is, I've just seen him."*

**yes²** /jes/ *noun* [C] a positive reaction or agreement with something *Was that a yes or a no?*

○━**yesterday** /'jestədeɪ/ *noun, adv* [U] the day before today *I went to see the doctor yesterday.* ● *yesterday morning/afternoon*

○━**yet¹** /jet/ *adv* **1** [used in questions and negatives] before now or before that time *Have you read his book yet?* ● *"Has he called?" "No, not yet."* **2** now or as early as this time *I don't want to go home yet.* **3 the best/worst, etc yet** the best or worst, etc until now *That was my worst exam yet.* **4 be/have yet to do sth** to not have done something that was expected before this time

*They have yet to make a decision.* **5 yet again/ another/more, etc** used to show that you are surprised or annoyed that something is being repeated or increased *He's given us yet more work to do.* **6 could/may/might, etc yet** used to say there is still a possibility that something will happen *He may win yet.*

**yet²** /jet/ *conjunction* used to add something that seems surprising because of what you have just said *simple yet effective*

**yew** /juː/ *noun* [C, U] a tree with dark, needle-shaped leaves, or the wood of this tree

**yield¹** /jiːld/ *verb* **1** [T] to produce or provide something *to yield a profit* • *The investigation yielded some unexpected results.* **2 yield to demands/pressure, etc** to be forced to do something **3** [I] *US* (*UK* **give way**) to stop in order to allow other vehicles to go past before you drive onto a bigger road

**yield²** /jiːld/ *noun* [C] the amount of something that is produced

**yo** /jəʊ/ *exclamation mainly US informal* used as a greeting

**yob** /jɒb/ *noun* [C] *UK informal* a rude or violent young man

**yoga** /ˈjəʊɡə/ *noun* [U] a set of exercises for the mind and body, based on the Hindu religion *She does yoga three times a week.*

**yoghurt** (*also* **yogurt**) /ˈjɒɡət ⑤ ˈjəʊɡərt/ *noun* [C, U] a thick, liquid food with a slightly sour taste which is made from milk *a low-fat strawberry yoghurt* ➲ *See colour picture* **Food** *on page Centre 7.*

**yolk** /jəʊk/ *noun* [C] the round, yellow part in the middle of an egg

**Yom Kippur** /ˌjɒmkɪˈpʊəʳ/ *noun* [U] a Jewish holy day in September or October

**yonder** /ˈjɒndəʳ/ *adv, determiner literary* in that place or direction

o-* **you** *strong form* /juː/ *weak form* /ju, jə/ *pronoun* **1** used to refer to the person or people you are talking to *I love you.* • *You said I could go with you.* **2** people generally *You learn to accept these things as you get older.*

**you'd** /juːd/ **1** *short for* you had *You'd better go home now.* **2** *short for* you would *I expect you'd like some lunch.*

**you'll** /juːl/ *short for* you will *I hope you'll come again.*

o-* **young¹** /jʌŋ/ *adj* having lived or existed for only a short time and not old *young children/ people* • *We were very young when we met.*

**young²** /jʌŋ/ *noun* [plural] **1 the young** young people generally *It's the sort of music that*

*appeals mainly to the young.* **2 sth's young** an animal's babies

**youngster** /ˈjʌŋstəʳ/ *noun* [C] a young person, especially an older child *He talked to the youngsters about the dangers of drugs.*

o-* **your** *strong form* /jɔːʳ/ *weak form* /jəʳ/ *determiner* **1** belonging or relating to the person or people you are talking to *Can I borrow your pen?* • *It's not your fault.* **2** belonging or relating to people in general *You never stop loving your children.*

**you're** /jɔːʳ/ *short for* you are *You're my best friend.*

o-* **yours** /jɔːz/ *pronoun* **1** the things that belong or relate to the person or people you are talking to *Is this pen yours?* • *Our tent's smaller than yours.* **2 Yours faithfully/sincerely, etc** used just before your name at the end of a polite or formal letter **3 yours truly** *humorous* I or me

o-* **yourself** /jɔːˈself/ *pronoun plural* **yourselves** **1** the reflexive form of the pronoun 'you' *Don't cut yourself with that sharp knife.* **2** used to emphasize the pronoun 'you' when talking about the actions of the person you are speaking to *Did you make the dress yourself?* **3 (all) by yourself/yourselves** alone or without anyone else's help *I'm amazed you managed to move those boxes all by yourself.* **4 (all) to yourself** for your use only *So you've got the whole house to yourself this weekend?*

**youth** /juːθ/ *noun formal* **1** YOUNG MAN [C] a young man *gangs of youths* **2** YOUNG PEOPLE [group] young people generally *the youth of today* • *a youth club* **3 sb's youth** the period of time when someone is young *I was very shy in my youth.* **4** QUALITY [U] the quality of being young

**youthful** /ˈjuːθfəl/ *adj* typical of a young person *youthful energy/good looks*

**'youth ˌhostel** *noun* [C] a cheap, simple hotel, especially for young people who are travelling around

**you've** /juːv/ *short for* you have *If you've finished your work, you can go.*

**yo-yo** /ˈjəʊjəʊ/ *noun* [C] a small, round toy that you make go up and down on a string that you hang from your finger

**yuck** /jʌk/ *exclamation informal* used to say that something looks or tastes very unpleasant

**yum** /jʌm/ (*also* ˌyum ˈyum) *exclamation informal* used to say that something tastes very good

**yummy** /ˈjʌmi/ *adj informal* If food or drink is yummy, it tastes very good.

**yuppie** /ˈjʌpi/ *noun* [C] a young person who earns a lot of money and likes expensive things

# Z

**Z, z** /zed/ the twenty-sixth and last letter of the alphabet

**zany** /'zeɪni/ *adj* funny in a strange way *zany humour*

**zap** /zæp/ *verb* [T] **zapping**, *past* **zapped** *informal* to attack or destroy something in a fast and powerful way

**zeal** /ziːl/ *noun* [U] extreme enthusiasm *religious zeal*

**zealous** /'zeləs/ *adj* extremely enthusiastic ● **zealously** *adv*

**zebra** /'zebrə ⓤⓢ 'ziːbrə/ *noun* [C] an animal like a horse with black and white lines

**,zebra 'crossing** *noun* [C] *UK* a part of the road painted with black and white lines where people can cross over safely

**Zen** /zen/ *noun* [U] a religion that developed from Buddhism

**zenith** /'zenɪθ ⓤⓢ 'ziːnɪθ/ *noun* [no plural] *literary* the highest or most successful point of something *The city reached its zenith in the 1980s.*

**zero** /'zɪərəʊ/ the number 0

**,zero 'tolerance** *noun* [U] when you do not accept any bad behaviour, often by using laws to prevent it *zero tolerance of crime*

**zest** /zest/ *noun* [U] **1** excitement and enthusiasm *a zest for life* **2** the outer skin of a lemon or orange used to give flavour to food

**zigzag** /'zɪgzæg/ *noun* [C] a line that changes direction from left to right and back again at sharp angles ● **zigzag** *verb* [I] **zigzagging**, *past* **zigzagged** to make a movement or pattern like a zigzag

**zillion** /'zɪljən/ *quantifier informal* a very large number *a zillion times* ● *zillions of things to look at*

**zinc** /zɪŋk/ *noun* [U] a blue-white metal that is used to make or cover other metals

**zip¹** /zɪp/ *noun* [C] *UK* (*US* **zipper**) *noun* [C] a thing for fastening clothes, bags, etc consisting of two rows of very small parts that connect together *Your zip's undone.*

**zip²** /zɪp/ *verb* **zipping**, *past* **zipped 1** [T] (*also* **zip up**) to fasten something with a zip *He zipped up his jacket.* **2 zip along/around/past, etc** *informal* to move somewhere very quickly

**'zip ,code** *noun* [C] a set of numbers that go after someone's address in the US ➔ *Compare* **postcode**.

**zipper** /'zɪpə/ *noun* [C] *US* a zip

**the zodiac** /'zəʊdiæk/ *noun* the twelve signs representing groups of stars which are thought by some people to influence your life and personality *What sign of the zodiac are you?*

**zodiac**

Capricorn     Aquarius     Pisces

Aries     Taurus     Gemini

Cancer     Leo     Virgo

Libra     Scorpio     Sagittarius

**zombie** /'zɒmbi/ *noun* [C] **1** a dead body that walks around because of magic **2 like a zombie** *informal* in a very tired, slow way *The day after the party I was walking around like a zombie.*

**zone** /zəʊn/ *noun* [C] an area where a particular thing happens *a war zone* ● *a nuclear-free zone* ➔ *See also:* **buffer zone**.

**zoo** /zuː/ *noun* [C] a place where wild animals are kept and people come to look at them

**zoological** /,zəʊə'lɒdʒɪkªl/ *adj* relating to the scientific study of animals

**zoology** /zu'ɒlədʒi ⓤⓢ zəʊ'ɒlədʒi/ *noun* [U] the scientific study of animals and how they behave ● **zoologist** *noun* [C] someone who studies zoology

**zoom** /zuːm/ *verb informal* **zoom along/down/ past, etc** to travel somewhere very fast, especially with a loud noise
**zoom in** to make something appear much closer and larger when using a camera or computer *The TV cameras zoomed in on her face.*

**'zoom ,lens** *noun* [C] a lens (= part of a camera) that can make something appear much closer and larger

**zucchini** /zu'kiːni/ *US* (*UK* **courgette**) *noun* [C, U] *plural* **zucchini** or **zucchinis** a long, green vegetable which is white inside

---

| iː **see** | ɒ **hot** | ɔː **saw** | ʌ **run** | ʊ **put** | uː **too** | aɪ **my** | aʊ **how** | eɪ **day** | əʊ **no** | ɪə **near** | ɔɪ **boy** | ʊə **poor** | aɪə **fire** | aʊə **sour** |

# Appendices

# Common first names

The names in brackets are short, informal forms of the names.

## Male names

Adam /'ædəm/
Alan /'ælən/
Alexander /ˌælɪg'zɑːndər/
 (Alex) /'ælɪks/
Andrew /'ændruː/
 (Andy) /'ændi/
Anthony
 UK /'æntəni/
 US /'ænθəni/
 (Tony) /'təuni/
Benjamin /'bendʒəmɪn/
 (Ben) /ben/
Charles /tʃɑːlz/
 (Charlie) /'tʃɑːli/
Christopher /'krɪstəfər/
 (Chris) /krɪs/
Daniel /'dænjəl/
 (Dan) /dæn/
Darren /'dærən/
David /'deɪvɪd/
 (Dave) /deɪv/
Edward /'edwəd/
 (Ed) /ed/
 (Ted) /ted/

Geoffrey /'dʒefri/
 (Geoff) /dʒef/
George /dʒɔːdʒ/
Harry /'hæri/
Jack /dʒæk/
James /dʒeɪmz/
 (Jim) /dʒɪm/
John /dʒɒn/
Jonathan /'dʒɒnəθən/
Joseph /'dʒəuzɪf/
 (Joe) /dʒəu/
Joshua /'dʒɒʃjuə/
 (Josh) /dʒɒʃ/
Ian /'iːən/
Kevin /'kevɪn/
Liam /'liːəm/
Mark /mɑːk/
Martin /'mɑːtɪn/
Matthew /'mæθjuː/
 (Matt) /mæt/
Michael /'maɪkəl/
 (Mike) /maɪk/
 (Mick) /mɪk/

Nicholas /'nɪkələs/
 (Nick) /nɪk/
Patrick /'pætrɪk/
Paul /pɔːl/
Peter /'piːtər/
 (Pete) /piːt/
Philip /'fɪlɪp/
 (Phil) /fɪl/
Richard /'rɪtʃəd/
 (Ricky) /'rɪki/
 (Dick) /dɪk/
Robert /'rɒbət/
 (Bob) /bɒb/
 (Rob) /rɒb/
Samuel /'sæmjuəl/
 (Sam) /sæm/
Simon /'saɪmən/
Thomas /'tɒməs/
 (Tom) /tɒm/
Timothy /'tɪməθi/
 (Tim) /tɪm/
William /'wɪljəm/
 (Billy) /'bɪli/
 (Will) /wɪl/

## Female names

Alice /'ælɪs/
Alison /'ælɪsən/
Amanda /ə'mændə/
 (Mandy) /'mændi/
Amy /'eɪmi/
Ann/Anne /æn/
Bridget /'brɪdʒɪt/
Carol /'kærəl/
Caroline /'kærəlaɪn/
Catherine/Kathryn
/'kæθərɪn/
 (Kate) /keɪt/
 (Katie) /'keɪti/
 (Cath) /kæθ/
Charlotte /'ʃɑːlət/
Chloe /'kləui/
Christine /'krɪstiːn/
 (Chris) /krɪs/

Clare/Claire /kleər/
Deborah /'debərə/
 (Debbie) /'debi/
Diane /daɪ'æn/
Elizabeth /ɪ'lɪzəbəθ/
 (Beth) /beθ/
 (Liz) /lɪz/
Emily /'emɪli/
Emma /'emə/
Hannah /'hænə/
Helen /'helən/
Jane /dʒeɪn/
Jennifer /'dʒenɪfər/
 (Jenny) /'dʒeni/
Joanne /dʒəu'æn/
 (Jo) /dʒəu/
Julie /'dʒuːli/
Karen /'kærən/

Laura /'lɔːrə/
Linda /'lɪndə/
Lucy /'luːsi/
Margaret /'mɑːgərət/
 (Maggie) /'mægi/
Mary /'meəri/
Rachel /'reɪtʃəl/
Rebecca /rɪ'bekə/
 (Becky) /'beki/
Ruth /ruːθ/
Sarah /'seərə/
Sharon /'ʃærən/
Sophie /'səufi/
Susan /'suːzən/
 (Sue) /suː/
Tracy /'treɪsi/
Valerie /'væləri/

# Geographical names

This list shows the spellings and pronunciations of countries, regions, and continents. Each name is followed by its related adjective. Most of the time you can use the adjective to talk about a person who comes from each place. However, in some cases you must use a special word, which is listed in the column labelled 'Person' (for example, **Finland, Finnish, Finn**).

To talk about more than one person from a particular place, add 's', except for:

- words ending in 'ese' or 's', which remain the same (**Chinese, Swiss**)
- words ending in 'man' or 'woman', which change to 'men' and 'women' (**Irishman**).

This list is for reference only. Inclusion does not imply or suggest status as a sovereign nation.

| Name | Adjective | Person (if different from adj) |
|---|---|---|
| Afghanistan /æfˈgænɪstæn/ | Afghan /ˈæfgæn/ | |
| Africa /ˈæfrɪkə/ | African /ˈæfrɪkən/ | |
| Albania /ælˈbeɪniə/ | Albanian /ælˈbeɪniən/ | |
| Algeria /ælˈdʒɪəriə/ | Algerian /ælˈdʒɪəriən/ | |
| Central America /ˌsentrəl əˈmerɪkə/ | Central American /ˌsentrəl əˈmerɪkən/ | |
| North America /ˌnɔːθ əˈmerɪkə/ | North American /ˌnɔːθ əˈmerɪkən/ | |
| South America /ˌsaʊθ əˈmerɪkə/ | South American /ˌsaʊθ əˈmerɪkən/ | |
| Andorra /ænˈdɔːrə/ | Andorran /ænˈdɔːrən/ | |
| Angola /æŋˈgəʊlə/ | Angolan /æŋˈgəʊlən/ | |
| Antigua and Barbuda /ænˈtiːgə æn bɑːˈbjuːdə/ | Antiguan /ænˈtiːgən/ | |
| Argentina /ˌɑːdʒənˈtiːnə/ | Argentine /ˈɑːdʒəntaɪn/ | |
| Armenia /ɑːˈmiːniə/ | Armenian /ɑːˈmiːniən/ | |
| Asia /ˈeɪʒə/ | Asian /ˈeɪʒən/ | |
| Australia /ɒsˈtreɪliə/ | Australian /ɒsˈtreɪliən/ | |
| Austria /ˈɒstriə/ | Austrian /ˈɒstriən/ | |
| Azerbaijan /ˌæzəbaɪˈdʒɑːn/ | Azerbaijani /ˌæzəbaɪˈdʒɑːni/ | Azeri /əˈzeəri/ |
| The Bahamas /ðə bəˈhɑːməz/ | Bahamian /bəˈheɪmiən/ | |
| Bahrain /bɑːˈreɪn/ | Bahraini /bɑːˈreɪni/ | |
| Bangladesh /ˌbæŋgləˈdeʃ/ | Bangladeshi /ˌbæŋgləˈdeʃi/ | |
| Barbados /bɑːˈbeɪdɒs/ | Barbadian /bɑːˈbeɪdiən/ | |
| Belarus /ˌbeləˈruːs/ | Belorussian /ˌbeləˈrʌʃən/ | |
| Belgium /ˈbeldʒəm/ | Belgian /ˈbeldʒən/ | |
| Belize /beˈliːz/ | Belizian /bəˈliːziən/ | |
| Benin /beˈniːn/ | Beninese /ˌbenɪˈniːz/ | |
| Bhutan /buːˈtɑːn/ | Bhutanese /ˌbuːtəˈniːz/ | |
| Bolivia /bəˈlɪviə/ | Bolivian /bəˈlɪviən/ | |
| Bosnia-Herzegovina /ˌbɒzniəˌhɜːzəgɒˈvɪnə/ | Bosnian /ˈbɒzniən/ | |
| Botswana /bɒtˈswɑːnə/ | Botswanan /bɒtˈswɑːnən/ | Motswana /mɒtˈswɑːnə/ |
| Brazil /brəˈzɪl/ | Brazilian /brəˈzɪliən/ | |
| Brunei /bruːˈnaɪ/ | Bruneian /bruːˈnaɪən/ | |
| Bulgaria /bʌlˈgeəriə/ | Bulgarian /bʌlˈgeəriən/ | |

| Name | Adjective | Person |
|---|---|---|
| Burkina Faso /bɜːˈkiːnə ˈfæseʊ/ | Burkinabe /bɜːˈkiːnəˌbei/ | |
| Burundi /bʊˈrʊndi/ | Burundi /bʊˈrʊndi/ | Burundian /bʊˈrʊndiən/ |
| Cambodia /ˌkæmˈbəʊdiə/ | Cambodian /ˌkæmˈbəʊdiən/ | |
| Cameroon /ˌkæməˈruːn/ | Cameroonian /ˌkæməˈruːniən/ | |
| Canada /ˈkænədə/ | Canadian /kəˈneidiən/ | |
| Cape Verde /ˌkeip ˈvɜːd/ | Cape Verdean /ˌkeip ˈvɜːdiən/ | |
| The Central African Republic /ðə ˈsentrəl ˈæfrɪkən rɪˈpʌblɪk/ | Central African /ˌsentrəl ˈæfrɪkən/ | |
| Chad /tʃæd/ | Chadian /ˈtʃædiən/ | |
| Chile /ˈtʃɪli/ | Chilean /ˈtʃɪliən/ | |
| China /ˈtʃaɪnə/ | Chinese /tʃaɪˈniːz/ | |
| Colombia /kəˈlʌmbiə/ | Colombian /kəˈlʌmbiən/ | |
| Comoros /ˈkɒmərəʊz/ | Comoran /kəˈmɔːrən/ | |
| The Democratic Republic of Congo /ðə ˌdeməˈkrætɪk rɪˈpʌblɪk əv ˈkɒngəʊ/ | Congolese /ˌkɒŋgəˈliːz/ | |
| The Republic of Congo /ðə rɪˈpʌblɪk əv ˈkɒngəʊ/ | Congolese /ˌkɒŋgəˈliːz/ | |
| Costa Rica /ˌkɒstəˈriːkə/ | Costa Rican /ˌkɒstəˈriːkən/ | |
| Côte d'Ivoire /ˌkəʊt diːˈvwɑː/ | Ivorian /aɪˈvɔːriən/ | |
| Croatia /krəʊˈeɪʃə/ | Croatian /krəʊˈeɪʃən/ | Croat /ˈkrəʊæt/ |
| Cuba /ˈkjuːbə/ | Cuban /ˈkjuːbən/ | |
| Cyprus /ˈsaɪprəs/ | Cypriot /ˈsɪpriət/ | |
| The Czech Republic /ðə tʃek rɪˈpʌblɪk/ | Czech /tʃek/ | |
| Denmark /ˈdenmɑːk/ | Danish /ˈdeɪnɪʃ/ | Dane /deɪn/ |
| Djibouti /dʒɪˈbuːti/ | Djiboutian /dʒɪˈbuːtiən/ | |
| Dominica /ˌdəˈmɪnɪkə/ | Dominican /dəˈmɪnɪkən/ | |
| The Dominican Republic /ðə dəˈmɪnɪkən rɪˈpʌblɪk/ | Dominican /dəˈmɪnɪkən/ | |
| East Timor /iːst ˈtiːmɔːʳ/ | East Timorese /iːst ˌtiːmɔːˈriːz/ | |
| Ecuador /ˈekwədɔːʳ/ | Ecuadorian /ˌekwəˈdɔːriən/ | |
| Egypt /ˈiːdʒɪpt/ | Egyptian /ɪˈdʒɪpʃən/ | |
| El Salvador /ˌel ˈsælvədɔːʳ/ | Salvadoran /ˌsælvəˈdɔːrən/ | |
| Equatorial Guinea /ˌekwətɔːriəl ˈgɪni/ | Equatorial Guinean /ˌekwətɔːriəl ˈgɪniən/ | |
| Eritrea /ˌerɪˈtreɪə/ | Eritrean /ˌerɪˈtreɪən/ | |
| Estonia /esˈtəʊniə/ | Estonian /esˈtəʊniən/ | |
| Ethiopia /ˌiːθiˈəʊpiə/ | Ethiopian /ˌiːθiˈəʊpiən/ | |
| Europe /ˈjʊərəp/ | European /ˌjʊərəˈpiːən/ | |
| Fiji /ˈfiːdʒiː/ | Fijian /fɪˈdʒiːən/ | |
| Finland /ˈfɪnlənd/ | Finnish /ˈfɪnɪʃ/ | Finn /fɪn/ |
| France /frɑːnts/ | French /frentʃ/ | Frenchman /ˈfrentʃmən/ |
| Gabon /gæbˈɒn/ | Gabonese /ˌgæbənˈiːz/ | |
| Gambia /ˈgæmbiə/ | Gambian /ˈgæmbiən/ | |
| Georgia /ˈdʒɔːdʒə/ | Georgian /ˈdʒɔːdʒən/ | |
| Germany /ˈdʒɜːməni/ | German /ˈdʒɜːmən/ | |
| Ghana /ˈgɑːnə/ | Ghanaian /gɑːˈneɪən/ | |
| Greece /griːs/ | Greek /griːk/ | |
| Greenland /ˈgriːnlənd/ | Greenland /ˈgriːnlənd/ | Greenlander /ˈgriːnləndəʳ/ |
| Grenada /grəˈneɪdə/ | Grenadian /grəˈneɪdiən/ | |
| Guatemala /ˌgwɑːtəˈmɑːlə/ | Guatemalan /ˌgwɑːtəˈmɑːlən/ | |
| Guinea /ˈgɪni/ | Guinean /ˈgɪniən/ | |

| Name | Adjective | Person |
|------|-----------|--------|
| Guinea-Bissau /ˌgɪnibɪˈsaʊ/ | Guinea-Bissauan /ˌgɪnibɪˈsaʊən/ | |
| Guyana /gaɪˈænə/ | Guyanese /ˌgaɪəˈniːz/ | |
| Haiti /ˈheɪti/ | Haitian /ˈheɪʃən/ | |
| Honduras /hɒnˈdjʊərəs/ | Honduran /hɒnˈdjʊərən/ | |
| Hungary /ˈhʌŋgəri/ | Hungarian /hʌŋˈgeəriən/ | |
| Iceland /ˈaɪslənd/ | Icelandic /aɪsˈlændɪk/ | Icelander /ˈaɪsləndər/ |
| India /ˈɪndiə/ | Indian /ˈɪndiən/ | |
| Indonesia /ˌɪndəˈniːʒə/ | Indonesian /ˌɪndəˈniːʒən/ | |
| Iran /ɪˈrɑːn/ | Iranian /ɪˈreɪniən/ | |
| Iraq /ɪˈrɑːk/ | Iraqi /ɪˈrɑːki/ | |
| Ireland /ˈaɪələnd/ | Irish /ˈaɪrɪʃ/ | Irishman /ˈaɪrɪʃmən/ |
| Israel /ˈɪzreɪl/ | Israeli /ɪzˈreɪli/ | |
| Italy /ˈɪtəli/ | Italian /ɪˈtæliən/ | |
| Jamaica /dʒəˈmeɪkə/ | Jamaican /dʒəˈmeɪkən/ | |
| Japan /dʒəˈpæn/ | Japanese /ˌdʒæpəˈniːz/ | |
| Jordan /ˈdʒɔːdn/ | Jordanian /dʒɔːˈdeɪniən/ | |
| Kazakhstan /ˌkæzækˈstɑːn/ | Kazakh /kæˈzæk/ | |
| Kenya /ˈkenjə/ | Kenyan /ˈkenjən/ | |
| Kiribati /ˌkɪrəˈbæs/ | Kiribati /ˌkɪrəˈbæs/ | |
| North Korea /ˌnɔːθ kəˈriːə/ | North Korean /ˌnɔːθ kəˈriːən/ | |
| South Korea /ˌsaʊθ kəˈriːə/ | South Korean /ˌsaʊθ kəˈriːən/ | |
| Kuwait /kuːˈweɪt/ | Kuwaiti /kuːˈweɪti/ | |
| Kyrgyzstan /ˌkɜːgɪˈstɑːn/ | Kyrgyz /ˈkɜːgɪz/ | |
| Laos /laʊs/ | Laotian /ˈlaʊʃən/ | |
| Latvia /ˈlætviə/ | Latvian /ˈlætviən/ | |
| Lebanon /ˈlebənən/ | Lebanese /ˌlebəˈniːz/ | |
| Lesotho /ləˈsuːtuː/ | Basotho /bəˈsuːtuː/ | Mosotho /məˈsuːtuː/ |
| Liberia /laɪˈbɪəriə/ | Liberian /laɪˈbɪəriən/ | |
| Libya /ˈlɪbiə/ | Libyan /ˈlɪbiən/ | |
| Liechtenstein /ˈlɪktənstaɪn/ | Liechtenstein /ˈlɪktənstaɪn/ | Liechtensteiner /ˈlɪktənstaɪnər/ |
| Lithuania /ˌlɪθjuˈeɪniə/ | Lithuanian /ˌlɪθjuˈeɪniən/ | |
| Luxembourg /ˈlʌksəmbɜːg/ | Luxembourg /ˈlʌksəmbɜːg/ | Luxembourger /ˈlʌksəmbɜːgər/ |
| Madagascar /ˌmædəˈgæskər/ | Malagasy /ˌmæləˈgæsi/ | |
| Malawi /məˈlɑːwi/ | Malawian /məˈlɑːwiən/ | |
| Malaysia /məˈleɪziə/ | Malaysian /məˈleɪziən/ | |
| The Maldives /ðə ˈmɔːldiːvz/ | Maldivian /mɔːlˈdɪviən/ | |
| Mali /ˈmɑːli/ | Malian /ˈmɑːliən/ | |
| Malta /ˈmɔːltə/ | Maltese /mɔːlˈtiːz/ | |
| The Marshall Islands /ðə ˈmɑːʃəl ˈaɪləndz/ | Marshallese /ˌmɑːʃəˈliːz/ | |
| Mauritania /ˌmɒrɪˈteɪniə/ | Mauritanian /ˈmɒrɪˈteɪniən/ | |
| Mauritius /məˈrɪʃəs/ | Mauritian /məˈrɪʃən/ | |
| Mexico /ˈmeksɪkəʊ/ | Mexican /ˈmeksɪkən/ | |
| Micronesia /ˌmaɪkrəˈniːziə/ | Micronesian /ˌmaɪkrəˈniːziən/ | |
| Moldova /mɒlˈdəʊvə/ | Moldovan /mɒlˈdəʊvən/ | |
| Monaco /ˈmɒnəkəʊ/ | Monégasque /mɒneɪˈgæsk/ | |
| Mongolia /mɒŋˈgəʊliə/ | Mongolian /mɒŋˈgəʊliən/ | |
| Morocco /məˈrɒkəʊ/ | Moroccan /məˈrɒkən/ | |
| Mozambique /ˌməʊzæmˈbiːk/ | Mozambican /ˌməʊzæmˈbiːkən/ | |

| Name | Adjective | Person |
|------|-----------|--------|
| Myanmar /'mjænmɑːʳ/ | Burmese /bɜː'miːz/ | |
| Namibia /nə'mɪbiə/ | Namibian /nə'mɪbiən/ | |
| Nauru /nɑː'uːruː/ | Nauruan /nɑːuː'ruːən/ | |
| Nepal /nə'pɔːl/ | Nepalese /ˌnepəl'iːz/ | |
| The Netherlands /ðə 'neðələnz/ | Dutch /dʌtʃ/ | Dutchman /'dʌtʃmən/ |
| New Zealand /ˌnjuː'ziːlənd/ | New Zealand /ˌnjuː'ziːlənd/ | New Zealander /ˌnjuː'ziːləndəʳ/ |
| Nicaragua /ˌnɪkə'rɑːgwə/ | Nicuraguan /ˌnɪkə'rɑːgwən/ | |
| Niger /niː'ʒeə/ | Nigerien /niː'ʒeəriən/ | |
| Nigeria /naɪ'dʒɪəriə/ | Nigerian /naɪ'dʒɪəriən/ | |
| Norway /'nɔːweɪ/ | Norwegian /nɔː'wiːdʒən/ | |
| Oman /əʊ'mɑːn/ | Omani /əʊ'mɑːni/ | |
| Pakistan /ˌpɑːkɪ'stɑːn/ | Pakistani /ˌpɑːkɪ'stɑːni/ | |
| Palestine /'pæləstaɪn/ | Palestinian /ˌpælə'stɪniən/ | |
| Panama /'pænəmɑː/ | Panamanian /ˌpænə'meɪniən/ | |
| Papua New Guinea /'pæpuə njuː 'gɪni/ | Papua New Guinean /'pæpuə njuː 'gɪniən/ | |
| Paraguay /'pærəgwaɪ/ | Paraguayan /ˌpærə'gwaɪən/ | |
| Peru /pə'ruː/ | Peruvian /pə'ruːviən/ | |
| The Philippines /ðə 'fɪlipiːnz/ | Philippine /'fɪlipiːn/ | Filipino /ˌfɪlɪ'piːnəʊ/ |
| Poland /'pəʊlənd/ | Polish /'pəʊlɪʃ/ | Pole /pəʊl/ |
| Portugal /'pɔːtʃəgəl/ | Portuguese /ˌpɔːtʃə'giːz/ | |
| Qatar /'kʌtɑːʳ/ | Qatari /kʌ'tɑːri/ | |
| Romania /rʊ'meɪniə/ | Romanian /rʊ'meɪniən/ | |
| Russia /'rʌʃə/ | Russian /'rʌʃən/ | |
| Rwanda /ru'ændə/ | Rwandan /ru'ændən/ | |
| Saint Kitts and Nevis /seɪnt kɪts ən 'nevɪs / | Kittsian /'kɪtsiən/ | |
| Saint Lucia /seɪnt 'luːʃə/ | Saint Lucian /seɪnt 'luːʃən/ | |
| Saint Vincent and the Grenadines /seɪnt 'vɪntsənt ən ðə ˌgrenə'diːnz/ | Vincentian /vɪn'sɪntiən/ | |
| Samoa /sə'məʊə/ | Samoan /sə'məʊən/ | |
| San Marino /ˌsænmə'riːnəʊ/ | Sanmarinese /ˌsænmærɪ'niːz/ | |
| São Tomé and Príncipe /ˌsaʊ tə'meɪ ən 'prɪnsɪpeɪ/ | Sao Tomean /ˌsaʊ tə'meɪən/ | |
| Saudi Arabia /ˌsaʊdi ə'reɪbiə/ | Saudi /'saʊdi/ | |
| Scandinavia /ˌskændɪˌneɪviə/ | Scandinavian /ˌskændɪˌneɪviən/ | |
| Senegal /ˌsenɪ'gɔːl/ | Senegalese /ˌsenɪgə'liːz/ | |
| The Seychelles /ðə seɪ'ʃelz/ | Seychelles /seɪ'ʃelz/ | Seychellois /seɪʃel'wɑː/ |
| Sierra Leone /siˌerəli'əʊn/ | Sierra Leonean /si'erə li'əʊniən/ | |
| Singapore /ˌsɪŋə'pɔːʳ/ | Singaporean /ˌsɪŋə'pɔːriən/ | |
| Slovakia /slə'vækiə/ | Slovak /'sləʊvæk/ | |
| Slovenia /slə'viːniə/ | Slovenian /slə'viːniən/ | Slovene /'sləʊviːn/ |
| The Solomon Islands /ðə 'sɒləmən 'aɪləndz/ | Solomon Islander /'sɒləmən 'aɪləndəʳ/ | |
| Somalia /sə'mɑːliə/ | Somali /sə'mɑːli/ | |
| South Africa /ˌsaʊθ 'æfrɪkə/ | South African /ˌsaʊθ 'æfrɪkən/ | |
| Spain /speɪn/ | Spanish /'spænɪʃ/ | Spaniard /'spænjəd/ |
| Sri Lanka /ˌsriː'læŋkə/ | Sri Lankan /ˌsriː'læŋkən/ | |

| Name | Adjective | Person |
|------|-----------|--------|
| Sudan /suːˈdɑːn/ | Sudanese /ˌsuːdəˈniːz/ | |
| Suriname /ˌsʊərɪˈnæm/ | Surinamese /ˌsʊərɪnæmˈiːz/ | |
| Swaziland /ˈswɑːzilænd/ | Swazi /ˈswɑːzi/ | |
| Sweden /ˈswiːdn/ | Swedish /ˈswiːdɪʃ/ | Swede /swiːd/ |
| Switzerland /ˈswɪtsələnd/ | Swiss /swɪs/ | |
| Syria /ˈsɪriə/ | Syrian /ˈsɪriən/ | |
| Taiwan /ˌtaɪˈwɑːn/ | Taiwanese /ˌtaɪwəˈniːz/ | |
| Tajikistan /tɑːˈdʒiːkɪˌstɑːn/ | Tajik /tɑːˈdʒiːk/ | |
| Tanzania /ˌtænzəˈniːə/ | Tanzanian /ˌtænzəˈniːən/ | |
| Thailand /ˈtaɪlænd/ | Thai /taɪ/ | |
| Tibet /tɪˈbet/ | Tibetan /tɪˈbetn/ | |
| Togo /ˈtəʊɡəʊ/ | Togolese /ˌtəʊɡəˈliːz/ | |
| Tonga /ˈtɒŋə/ | Tongan /ˈtɒŋən/ | |
| Trinidad and Tobago /ˈtrɪnɪdæd ən təˈbeɪɡəʊ/ | Trinidadian /ˌtrɪnɪˈdædiən/ | |
| Tunisia /tjuːˈnɪziə/ | Tunisian /tjuːˈnɪziən/ | |
| Turkey /ˈtɜːki/ | Turkish /ˈtɜːkɪʃ/ | Turk /tɜːk/ |
| Turkmenistan /tɜːkˌmenɪˈstɑːn/ | Turkmen /ˈtɜːkmen/ | |
| Tuvalu /tuːˈvɑːluː/ | Tuvaluan /ˌtuːvɑːˈluːən/ | |
| Uganda /juːˈgændə/ | Ugandan /juːˈgændən/ | |
| Ukraine /juːˈkreɪn/ | Ukrainian /juːˈkreɪniən/ | |
| The United Arab Emirates /ðə juːˈnaɪtɪd ˈærəb ˈemɪrəts/ | Emirian /eˈmɪriən/ | |
| The United Kingdom /ðə juːˈnaɪtɪd ˈkɪŋdəm/ | British /ˈbrɪtɪʃ/ | Briton /ˈbrɪtən/ |
| The United States of America /ðə juːˈnaɪtɪd steɪts əv əˈmerɪkə/ | American /əˈmerɪkən/ | |
| Uruguay /ˈjʊərəgwaɪ/ | Uruguayan /ˌjʊərəˈgwaɪən/ | |
| Uzbekistan /ʊzˌbekɪˈstɑːn/ | Uzbek /ˈʊzbek/ | |
| Vanuatu /ˌvænuˈɑːtuː/ | Vanuatuan /ˌvænuɑːˈtuːən/ | |
| Vatican City /ˈvætɪkən ˈsɪti/ | Vatican /ˈvætɪkən/ | |
| Venezuela /ˌvenɪˈzweɪlə/ | Venezuelan /ˌvenɪˈzweɪlən/ | |
| Vietnam /ˌviːetˈnæm/ | Vietnamese /ˌviːetnəˈmiːz/ | |
| Western Sahara /ˌwestən ˌsəˈhɑːrə/ | Sahrawian /saɪˈrɑːwiən/ | |
| Yemen /ˈjemən/ | Yemeni /ˈjeməni/ | |
| Yugoslavia /ˌjuːɡəʊˈslɑːviə/ | Yugoslav /ˈjuːɡəʊslɑːv/ | |
| Zambia /ˈzæmbiə/ | Zambian /ˈzæmbiən/ | |
| Zimbabwe /zɪmˈbɑːbweɪ/ | Zimbabwean /zɪmˈbɑːbwiən/ | |

# Regular verb tenses: The simple tenses

## Present Simple

used for action in the present, for things that are always true or that happen regularly, and for opinions and beliefs

I/we/you/they   arrive (**do not** arrive)
he/she/it          arrives (**does not** arrive)

## Past Simple

used for completed actions and events in the past

I/we/you/they   arrive**d** (**did not** arrive)
he/she/it          arrive**d** (**did not** arrive)

## Future Simple

used for actions and events in the future

I/we/you/they   **will** arrive (**will not** arrive)
he/she/it          **will** arrive (**will not** arrive)

## Present Perfect

used to show that an event happened or an action was completed at some time before the present

I/we/you/they   **have** arrive**d** (**have not** arrive**d**)
he/she/it          **has** arrive**d** (**has not** arrive**d**)

## Past Perfect

used to show that an event happened or an action was completed before a particular time in the past

I/we/you/they   **had** arrive**d** (**had not** arrive**d**)
he/she/it          **had** arrive**d** (**had not** arrive**d**)

## Future Perfect

used to show that something will be completed before a particular time in the future

I/we/you/they   **will have** arrive**d** (**will not have** arrive**d**)
he/she/it          **will have** arrive**d** (**will not have** arrive**d**)

# Regular verb tenses:
# The continuous/progressive tenses

### Present Continuous/Progressive

used for actions or events that are happening or developing now, for future plans, or to show that an event is repeated

| | |
|---|---|
| I | **am** arriving (**am not** arriving) |
| we/you/they | **are** arriving (**are not** arriving) |
| he/she/it | **is** arriving (**is not** arriving) |

### Past Continuous/Progressive

used for actions or events in the past that were not yet finished or that were interrupted

| | |
|---|---|
| I | **was** arriving (**was not** arriving) |
| we/you/they | **were** arriving (**were not** arriving) |
| he/she/it | **was** arriving (**was not** arriving) |

### Future Continuous/Progressive

used for actions or events in the future that will continue into the future

| | |
|---|---|
| I/we/you/they | **will be** arriving (**will not be** arriving) |
| he/she/it | **will be** arriving (**will not be** arriving) |

### Present Perfect Continuous/Progressive

used for actions or events that started in the past but are still happening now, or for past actions which only recently finished and their effects are seen now

| | |
|---|---|
| I/we/you/they | **have been** arriving (**have not been** arriving) |
| he/she/it | **has been** arriving (**has not been** arriving) |

### Past Perfect Continuous/Progressive

used for actions or events that happened for a period of time but were completed before a particular time in the past

| | |
|---|---|
| I/we/you/they | **had been** arriving (**had not been** arriving) |
| he/she/it | **had been** arriving (**had not been** arriving) |

### Future Perfect Continuous/Progressive

used for actions or events that will already be happening at a particular time in the future

| | |
|---|---|
| I/we/you/they | **will have been** arriving (**will not have been** arriving) |
| he/she/it | **will have been** arriving (**will not have been** arriving) |

# Irregular Verbs

This list gives the infinitive form of the verb, its past tense, and then the past participle. If two forms are given, look the verb up in the dictionary to see whether they have a different meaning.

| Infinitive | Past Tense | Past Participle | Infinitive | Past Tense | Past Participle |
|---|---|---|---|---|---|
| arise | arose | arisen | dream | dreamed, dreamt | dreamed, dreamt |
| awake | awoke | awoken | drink | drank | drunk |
| be | was/were | been | drive | drove | driven |
| bear | bore | borne | dwell | dwelt, dwelled | dwelt, dwelled |
| beat | beat | beaten, (also US) beat | eat | ate | eaten |
| become | became | become | fall | fell | fallen |
| befall | befell | befallen | feed | fed | fed |
| begin | began | begun | feel | felt | felt |
| bend | bent | bent | fight | fought | fought |
| bet | bet, betted | bet, betted | find | found | found |
| bid | bid, bade | bid, bidden | flee | fled | fled |
| bind | bound | bound | fling | flung | flung |
| bite | bit | bitten | fly | flew | flown |
| bleed | bled | bled | forbid | forbade | forbidden |
| blow | blew | blown | forecast | forecast, forecasted | forecast, forecasted |
| break | broke | broken | foresee | foresaw | foreseen |
| breed | bred | bred | forget | forgot | forgotten |
| bring | brought | brought | forgive | forgave | forgiven |
| broadcast | broadcast, (also US) broadcasted | broadcast, (also US) broadcasted | forgo | forwent | forgone |
| | | | forsake | forsook | forsaken |
| build | built | built | freeze | froze | frozen |
| burn | burnt, burned | burnt, burned | get | got | got, (also US) gotten |
| burst | burst | burst | | | |
| bust | (UK) bust, (US) busted | (UK) bust, (US) busted | give | gave | given |
| | | | go | went | gone |
| buy | bought | bought | grind | ground | ground |
| cast | cast | cast | grow | grew | grown |
| catch | caught | caught | hang | hung, hanged | hung, hanged |
| choose | chose | chosen | have | had | had |
| cling | clung | clung | hear | heard | heard |
| come | came | come | hide | hid | hidden |
| cost | cost | cost | hit | hit | hit |
| creep | crept | crept | hold | held | held |
| cut | cut | cut | hurt | hurt | hurt |
| deal | dealt | dealt | input | inputted, input | inputted, input |
| dig | dug | dug | | | |
| dive | dived, (also US) dove | dived | keep | kept | kept |
| | | | kneel | knelt, kneeled | knelt, kneeled |
| draw | drew | drawn | know | knew | known |
| | | | lay | laid | laid |

| Infinitive | Past Tense | Past Participle | Infinitive | Past Tense | Past Participle |
|---|---|---|---|---|---|
| lead | led | led | rewrite | rewrote | rewritten |
| lean | leaned, (also UK) leant | leaned, (also UK) leant | rid | rid | rid |
| | | | ride | rode | ridden |
| leap | leapt, leaped | leapt, leaped | ring | rang | rung |
| learn | learned, (also UK) learnt | learned, (also UK) learnt | rise | rose | risen |
| | | | run | ran | run |
| leave | left | left | saw | sawed | sawn, (also US) sawed |
| lend | lent | lent | | | |
| let | let | let | say | said | said |
| lie | lay, lied | lain, lied | see | saw | seen |
| light | lit, lighted | lit, lighted | seek | sought | sought |
| lose | lost | lost | sell | sold | sold |
| make | made | made | send | sent | sent |
| mean | meant | meant | set | set | set |
| meet | met | met | sew | sewed | sewn, sewed |
| mislay | mislaid | mislaid | shake | shook | shaken |
| mislead | misled | misled | shear | sheared | sheared, shorn |
| misread | misread | misread | shed | shed | shed |
| misspell | misspelled, (also UK) misspelt | misspelled, (also UK) misspelt | shine | shone | shone |
| | | | shoot | shot | shot |
| | | | show | showed | shown, showed |
| mistake | mistook | mistaken | shrink | shrank | shrunk |
| misunderstand | misunderstood | misunderstood | shut | shut | shut |
| mow | mowed | mown, mowed | sing | sang | sung |
| outdo | outdid | outdone | sink | sank | sunk |
| outgrow | outgrew | outgrown | sit | sat | sat |
| overcome | overcame | overcome | slay | slew | slain |
| overdo | overdid | overdone | sleep | slept | slept |
| overhang | overhung | overhung | slide | slid | slid |
| overhear | overheard | overheard | sling | slung | slung |
| override | overrode | overridden | slink | slunk | slunk |
| overrun | overran | overrun | slit | slit | slit |
| oversee | oversaw | overseen | smell | smelled, (also UK) smelt | smelled, (also UK) smelt |
| oversleep | overslept | overslept | | | |
| overtake | overtook | overtaken | sow | sowed | sown, sowed |
| overthrow | overthrew | overthrown | speak | spoke | spoken |
| pay | paid | paid | speed | sped, speeded | sped, speeded |
| plead | pleaded, (also US) pled | pleaded, (also US) pled | spell | spelled, (also UK) spelt | spelled, (also UK) spelt |
| | | | spend | spent | spent |
| prove | proved | proved, (also US) proven | spill | spilled, (also UK) spilt | spilled, (also UK) spilt |
| put | put | put | spin | spun | spun |
| quit | quit | quit | spit | spat, (also US) spit | spat, (also US) spit |
| read | read | read | | | |
| rebuild | rebuilt | rebuilt | split | split | split |
| repay | repaid | repaid | spoil | spoiled, spoilt | spoiled, spoilt |
| rethink | rethought | rethought | spread | spread | spread |
| rewind | rewound | rewound | | | |

| Infinitive | Past Tense | Past Participle | Infinitive | Past Tense | Past Participle |
|---|---|---|---|---|---|
| spring | sprang | sprung | thrust | thrust | thrust |
| stand | stood | stood | tread | trod | trodden |
| steal | stole | stolen | undercut | undercut | undercut |
| stick | stuck | stuck | undergo | underwent | undergone |
| sting | stung | stung | understand | understood | understood |
| stink | stank, (also US) stunk | stunk | undertake | undertook | undertaken |
|  |  |  | undo | undid | undone |
| stride | strode | strode | unwind | unwound | unwound |
| strike | struck | struck | uphold | upheld | upheld |
| string | strung | strung | upset | upset | upset |
| strive | strove, strived | striven, strived | wake | woke | woken |
| swear | swore | sworn | wear | wore | worn |
| sweep | swept | swept | weave | wove, weaved | woven, weaved |
| swell | swelled | swollen, swelled | weep | wept | wept |
| swim | swam | swum | wet | wet, wetted | wet, wetted |
| swing | swung | swung | win | won | won |
| take | took | taken | wind | wound | wound |
| teach | taught | taught | withdraw | withdrew | withdrawn |
| tear | tore | torn | withhold | withheld | withheld |
| tell | told | told | withstand | withstood | withstood |
| think | thought | thought | wring | wrung | wrung |
| throw | threw | thrown | write | wrote | written |

# Word beginnings and endings

You can change the meaning of many English words simply by adding a group of letters to the beginning or the ending of a word.

## Prefixes

A group of letters added to the beginning of a word is called **prefix**. Here is a list of the most common prefixes and examples of how they are used.

**Anglo-** relating to the UK or England *an Anglophile* (= someone who loves England)

**anti- 1** opposed to or against *anti-racist laws* **2** preventing or destroying *an anti-aircraft missile*

**auto- 1** operating without being controlled by humans *autopilot* (= a computer that directs an aircraft) **2** self *an autobiography* (= a book that someone writes about their own life)

**bi-** two *bilingual* (= speaking two languages) • *bimonthly* (= happening twice in a month or once every two months)

**centi-, cent-** hundred *a centimetre* • *a century*

**co-** with or together *a co-author* • *to coexist*

**contra-** against or opposite *to contradict* (= say the opposite) • *contraception* (= something that is used to prevent pregnancy)

**counter-** opposing or as a reaction to *a counter-attack* (= an attack on someone who has attacked you)

**cross- 1** across *cross-border* **2** including different groups or subjects *a cross-party committee* (= one formed from many political parties) • *cross-cultural*

**de-** to take something away *deforestation* (= when the trees in an area are cut down)

**dis-** not or the opposite of *dishonest* • *disbelief* • *to disagree*

**e-** electronic, usually relating to the Internet *email* • *e-commerce*

**eco-** relating to the environment *eco-friendly tourism* (= tourism which does not damage the environment)

**Euro-** relating to Europe *Europop* (= modern, young people's music from Europe)

**ex-** from before *an ex-boyfriend* • *an ex-boss*

**extra-** outside of or in addition to *extracurricular activities* (= activities that are in addition to the usual school work)

**hyper-** having a lot of or too much of a quality *hyperactive* • *hypersensitive* (= more than normally sensitive)

**ill-** in a way which is bad or not suitable *ill-prepared* • *an ill-judged remark*

**in-, il-, im-, ir-** not *incorrect* • *illegal* • *impossible* • *irregular*

**inter-** between or among *international* • *an interdepartmental meeting*

**intra-** within *an intranet*

**kilo-** a thousand *a kilometre* • *a kilogram*

**mega- 1** informal extremely *megarich* (= extremely rich) **2** one million *40 megabytes*

**micro-** very small *a microchip* • *microscopic* (= extremely small)

**mid-** in the middle of *mid-July*. • *a man in his mid-forties* • *mid-afternoon/-morning*

**milli-** a thousandth *a millisecond*

**mini-** small *a miniskirt* (= very short skirt) • *a minibus*

**mis-** not or badly *mistrust* • *to misbehave*

**mono-** one or single *monolingual* • *a monologue*

**multi-** many *a multi-millionaire* • *a multi-storey car park*

**neo-** new *neo-fascists*

**non-** not or the opposite of *non-alcoholic drinks* • *non-smokers*

**out-** more than or better than *to outgrow* • *to outnumber* • *to outdo someone* (= to show that you are better than someone)

**over-** too much *to overeat* • *overpopulated*

**poly-** many *polygamy* (= having more than one husband or wife at the same time) • *a polygon* (= shape with many sides)

**post-** after or later than *postwar* • *a postgraduate*

**pre-** before or earlier than *pre-tax profits* • *pre-school*

**pro-** supporting *pro-democracy demonstrations*

**pseudo-** false *a pseudonym* (= false name used especially by a writer) • *pseudo-academic*

**quasi-** partly *quasi-religious ideas*

**re-** again *to remarry* • *a reusable container*

**semi-** half or partly *a semicircle* • *semi-frozen*

**socio-** relating to society *socio-economic*

**sub- 1** under or below *subzero temperatures* **2** less important or a smaller part of a larger whole *a subsection*

**super-** extremely or more than usual *a supermodel* • *super-rich*

**thermo-** relating to heat or temperature *a thermostat* (= piece of equipment that controls temperature) • *a thermometer*

**trans- 1** across *transatlantic flights* **2** showing a change *to transform* • *to translate*

**tri-** three *a triangle* • *a tripod*

**ultra-** extremely *ultra-modern architecture* • *ultra-careful*

**un-** not or the opposite of *unhappy* • *unfair* • *to unfasten*

**under- 1** not enough *undercooked potatoes* • *underprivileged children* **2** below *underwear* • *an underpass*

## Suffixes

A **suffix** is a group of letters at the end of a word which changes the word's meaning and often its part of speech. Here is a list of the most common suffixes and examples of how they are used.

**-able/-ible** changes a verb into an adjective meaning 'able to be' *avoid → avoidable* • *admire → admirable* • *like → likeable*

**-age** changes a verb into a noun meaning 'the action described by the verb or the result of that action' *marry → marriage* • *break → breakage* • *spill → spillage*

**-al 1** changes a noun into an adjective meaning 'relating to' *culture → cultural* • *nation → national* • *nature → natural* **2** changes a verb into a noun meaning 'the action described by the verb' *approve → approval* • *remove → removal*

**-an, -ian 1** makes a noun meaning 'a person who does something' *historian* • *politician* **2** makes an adjective meaning 'belonging somewhere' *American*

**-ance, -ence, -ancy, -ency** makes a noun meaning 'an action, state, or quality' *performance* • *independence* • *preference*

**-ation, -ion** changes a verb into a noun meaning 'the process of the action described by the verb, or the result of that action' *educate → education* • *explain → explanation* • *connect → connection*

**-ed** makes an adjective meaning, 'having this thing or quality' *bearded* • *coloured* • *surprised*

**-ee** changes a verb into a noun meaning 'someone that something is done to' *employ → employee* • *interview → interviewee* • *train → trainee*

**-en** changes an adjective into a verb meaning 'to become or make something become' *thick → thicken* • *fat → fatten* • *soft → soften*

**-ence, -ency** See **-ance**

**-er, -or** changes a verb into a noun meaning 'the person or thing that does the activity' *dance → dancer* • *employ → employer* • *act → actor* • *cook → cooker* (= a machine for cooking) • *time → timer*

**-ful** changes a noun into an adjective meaning, 'having a particular quality' *beauty → beautiful* • *power → powerful* • *use → useful*

**-hood** makes a noun meaning 'the state of being something and the time when someone is something' *childhood* • *motherhood*

**-ian** See **-an**

**-ible** See **-able**

**-ical** changes a noun ending in **-y** or **-ics** into an adjective meaning 'relating to' *history → historical* • *politics → political*

**-ing** makes an adjective meaning 'making someone feel something' *interest → interesting* • *surprise → surprising* • *shock → shocking*

**-ion** See **-ation**

**-ise** See **-ize**

**-ish** makes an adjective meaning **1** slightly *a greyish colour* • *a smallish* (= quite small) *house* **2** typical of or similar to *a childish remark* **3** approximately *fiftyish* (= about fifty)

**-ist 1** makes a noun meaning 'a person who does a particular activity' *artist* • *novelist* • *scientist* **2** makes a noun and an adjective meaning 'someone with a particular set of beliefs' *communist* • *feminist*

**-ive** changes a verb into an adjective meaning 'having a particular quality or effect' *attract → attractive* • *create → creative* • *explode → explosive*

**-ize, -ise** changes an adjective into a verb meaning 'to make something become' *modern → modernize* • *commercial → commercialize*

**-less** changes a noun into an adjective meaning 'without' *homeless people* • *a meaningless statement* • *a hopeless situation*

**-like** changes a noun into an adjective meaning 'typical of or similar to' *childlike trust* • *a cabbage-like vegetable*

**-ly 1** changes an adjective into an adverb describing the way that something is done *She spoke slowly.* • *Drive safely.* **2** makes an adjective and an adverb meaning 'happening every day, night, week, etc' *a daily newspaper* • *We hold the meeting weekly.* **3** changes a noun into an adjective meaning 'like that person or thing' *mother → motherly* • *coward → cowardly*

**-ment** changes a verb into a noun meaning 'the action or process described by a verb, or its result' *develop → development* • *disappoint → disappointment*

**-ness** changes an adjective into a noun meaning 'the quality or condition described by the adjective' *sweet → sweetness* • *happy → happiness* • *dark → darkness* • *ill → illness* •

**-ology** makes a noun meaning 'the study of something' *psychology* (= the study of the mind) • *sociology* (= the study of society)

**-or** See **-er**

**-ous** changes a noun into an adjective meaning 'having that quality' *danger → dangerous* • *ambition → ambitious*

**-phile** makes a noun meaning 'enjoying or liking something' *a Francophile* (= someone who loves France) • *a bibliophile* (= someone who loves books)

**-ship** makes a noun showing involvement between people • *friendship* • *a relationship* • *partnership*

**-ward, -wards** makes an adverb meaning 'towards a direction or place' *inward* • *forward* • *homeward*

**-wise** changes a noun into an adverb meaning 'relating to this subject' *Weather-wise, the holiday was great.* • *How are we doing time-wise?*

**-y** changes a noun into an adjective meaning 'having a lot of something (often something bad)' *noise → noisy* • *dirt → dirty* • *smell → smelly*

# Word building

It is useful to know how to build up word families using the prefixes and suffixes listed on pages 751–752, and for some exams you need to know these word families. In the list below, words in heavy type are words which have the symbol ⌐ by them in the dictionary, meaning that they are very common and important to learn. The other words on each line are words in the same family, often formed with prefixes and suffixes, or sometimes just a different part of speech (e.g. anger, which is a noun and a verb). All the words in this list have entries in the dictionary except for some beginning with 'un-', 'im-', 'in-' or 'ir-', or ending with '-ly' or '-ily', where the meaning is always regular. Sometimes words in a word family can have meanings which are quite different from others in the group, so you should always check in the dictionary if you are not sure of the meaning.

| Nouns | Adjectives | Verbs | Adverbs |
|---|---|---|---|
| **ability**, disability, inability | **able**, unable, disabled | enable, disable | ably |
| acceptance | **acceptable**, unacceptable, accepted | **accept** | acceptably, unacceptably |
| **accident** | accidental | | accidentally |
| accuracy, inaccuracy | **accurate**, inaccurate | | accurately, inaccurately |
| accusation, the accused, accuser | accusing | **accuse** | accusingly |
| **achievement**, achiever | achievable | **achieve** | |
| **act**, **action**, inaction, interaction, reaction, transaction | acting | **act** | |
| **activity**, inactivity | **active**, inactive, interactive, proactive | activate | actively |
| addition | additional | **add** | additionally |
| admiration, admirer | admirable | **admire** | admirably |
| **advantage**, disadvantage | advantageous, disadvantaged | | advantageously |
| advertisement, advertiser, **advertising** | | advertise | |
| **advice**, adviser | advisable, inadvisable, advisory | **advise** | |
| **agreement**, disagreement | agreeable | **agree**, disagree | agreeably |
| **aim** | aimless | **aim** | aimlessly |
| amazement | amazed, **amazing** | amaze | amazingly |
| **anger** | **angry** | anger | angrily |
| announcement, announcer | unannounced | **announce** | unannounced |
| **appearance**, disappearance, reappearance | | **appear**, disappear, reappear | |
| applicant, application | applicable, applied | **apply** | |
| appreciation | appreciable, appreciative | **appreciate** | appreciatively |
| approval, disapproval | approving, disapproving | **approve**, disapprove | approvingly |
| approximation | approximate | approximate | **approximately** |
| **argument** | arguable, argumentative | **argue** | arguably |
| arrangement | | **arrange**, rearrange | |
| **art**, **artist**, artistry | artistic | | artistically |
| shame | **ashamed**, unashamed, shameful, shameless | shame | shamefully, shamelessly |
| attachment | attached, unattached, detachable, detached | **attach**, detach | |
| **attack**, counter-attack, attacker | | **attack**, counter-attack | |
| **attention** | attentive, inattentive | attend | attentively |

| Nouns | Adjectives | Verbs | Adverbs |
|---|---|---|---|
| attraction, attractiveness | **attractive**, unattractive | attract | attractively |
| **authority**, authorization | authoritarian, authoritative, unauthorized | authorize | |
| availability | **available**, unavailable | | |
| avoidance | avoidable, unavoidable | **avoid** | |
| awareness | **aware**, unaware | | unawares |
| base, the basics, basis | baseless, **basic** | **base** | **basically** |
| bearer | bearable, unbearable | **bear** | |
| beat, beating | unbeatable, unbeaten | **beat** | |
| beautician, **beauty** | **beautiful** | | beautifully |
| beginner, **beginning** | | **begin** | |
| **behaviour**/US **behavior**, misbehaviour/US misbehavior | behavioural/US behavioral | **behave**, misbehave | |
| **belief**, disbelief | believable, unbelievable | **believe**, disbelieve | unbelievably |
| block, blockage | blocked, unblocked | **block**, unblock | |
| **blood**, bleeding | bloodless, bloody | bleed | |
| the boil, boiler | boiling | **boil** | |
| bore, boredom | **bored**, **boring** | bore | boringly |
| **break**, outbreak, breakage | unbreakable, **broken**, unbroken | **break** | |
| breath, breather, breathing | breathless | **breathe** | breathlessly |
| **brother**, brotherhood | brotherly | | |
| build, builder, **building** | | **build**, rebuild | |
| burn, burner | burning, burnt | **burn** | |
| burial | buried | **bury** | |
| **calculation**, calculator | incalculable, calculated, calculating | **calculate** | |
| calm, calmness | **calm** | calm | calmly |
| capability | **capable**, incapable | | capably |
| **care**, carer | careful, careless, caring, uncaring | **care** | carefully, carelessly |
| celebration, celebrity | celebrated, celebratory | **celebrate** | |
| **centre**/US **center**, centralization, decentralization | **central**, centralized | centre/US center, centralize, decentralize | centrally |
| certainty, uncertainty | **certain**, uncertain | | certainly, uncertainly |
| **challenge**, challenger | challenging | challenge | |
| change | changeable, interchangeable, unchanged, changing | **change** | |
| **character**, characteristic, characterization | characteristic, uncharacteristic | characterize | characteristically |
| **chemical**, chemist, chemistry | chemical | | chemically |
| **circle**, semicircle, circulation | circular | circle, circulate | |
| cleaner, cleaning, cleanliness | **clean**, unclean | **clean** | clean, cleanly |
| clarity, clearance, clearing | **clear**, unclear | **clear** | clear, **clearly** |
| close, closure | closed, closing | **close** | |
| closeness | **close** | | **close**, closely |
| **clothes**, clothing | clothed, unclothed | clothe | |
| **collection**, collector | collected, collective | **collect** | collectively |
| **colour**/US **color**, colouring/US coloring | coloured/US colored, discoloured/US discolored, colourful/US colorful, colourless/US colorless | colour/US color | colourfully/US colorfully |
| **combination** | combined | **combine** | |
| comfort, discomfort | **comfortable**, uncomfortable, comforting | comfort | comfortably |
| **commitment** | noncommittal, committed | **commit** | |
| **communication**, communicator | communicative, uncommunicative | **communicate** | |

| Nouns | Adjectives | Verbs | Adverbs |
|---|---|---|---|
| **comparison** | comparable, incomparable, comparative | **compare** | comparatively |
| **competition**, competitor | competitive, uncompetitive | **compete** | competitively |
| completion, incompleteness | **complete**, incomplete | **complete** | **completely**, incompletely |
| complication | **complicated**, uncomplicated | complicate | |
| **computer**, computing, computerization | | computerize | |
| concentration | concentrated | **concentrate** | |
| concern | **concerned**, unconcerned | **concern** | |
| **conclusion** | concluding, conclusive, inconclusive | conclude | conclusively |
| **condition**, precondition, conditioner, conditioning | conditional, unconditional | condition | conditionally, unconditionally |
| **confidence** | **confident**, confidential | confide | confidently, confidentially |
| confirmation | confirmed, unconfirmed | **confirm** | |
| **confusion** | confused, confusing | **confuse** | confusingly |
| **connection** | connected, disconnected, unconnected | **connect**, disconnect | |
| subconscious, unconscious, consciousness, unconsciousness | **conscious**, subconscious, unconscious | | consciously, unconsciously |
| **consequence** | consequent, inconsequential | | consequently |
| consideration | considerable, considerate, inconsiderate, considered | **consider**, reconsider | considerably, considerately |
| **continent** | continental, intercontinental | | |
| continuation, continuity | continual, continued, **continuous** | **continue**, discontinue | continually, continuously |
| **contribution**, contributor | contributory | **contribute** | |
| **control**, controller | controlling, uncontrollable | **control** | uncontrollably |
| convenience, inconvenience | **convenient**, inconvenient | inconvenience | conveniently |
| | convinced, convincing, unconvincing | **convince** | convincingly |
| cook, cooker, cookery, **cooking** | cooked, uncooked | **cook** | |
| cool, coolness | **cool** | cool | coolly |
| **correction**, correctness | **correct**, incorrect, corrective | **correct** | correctly, incorrectly |
| count, recount | countable, uncountable, countless | **count**, recount | |
| **cover**, coverage, covering | undercover, uncovered | **cover**, uncover | undercover |
| creation, creativity, creator | creative, uncreative | **create**, recreate | creatively |
| **crime**, **criminal**, criminologist | criminal, incriminating | incriminate | criminally |
| critic, **criticism** | **critical**, uncritical | **criticize** | critically |
| **crowd**, overcrowding | **crowded**, overcrowded | crowd | |
| cruelty | **cruel** | | cruelly |
| **cry**, outcry | crying | cry | |
| **culture**, subculture | cultural, cultured | | culturally |
| cure | cured, incurable | **cure** | |
| **custom**, **customer**, customs | customary | accustom | customarily |
| cut, cutting | cutting | **cut**, undercut | |
| **damage**, damages | damaging | **damage** | |
| **danger** | endangered, **dangerous** | endanger | dangerously |
| dare, daring | daring | **dare** | daringly |
| **dark**, darkness | **dark**, darkened, darkening | darken | darkly |
| **date** | dated, outdated | date, predate | |
| **day**, midday | daily | | daily |
| **dead**, **death** | **dead**, deadly, deathly | deaden | deadly, deathly |
| deal, dealer, dealings | | **deal** | |
| deceit, deceiver, deception | deceitful, deceptive | **deceive** | deceptively |

| Nouns | Adjectives | Verbs | Adverbs |
|-------|-----------|-------|---------|
| **decision**, indecision | decided, undecided, decisive, indecisive | **decide** | decidedly, decisively, indecisively |
| decoration, decorator | decorative | **decorate** | decoratively |
| deep, **depth** | **deep**, deepening | deepen | deeply |
| **defeat**, defeatism, defeatist | undefeated, defeatist | **defeat** | |
| **defence**/US **defense**, defendant, defender | defenceless/US defenseless, indefensible, defensive | **defend** | defensively |
| definition | **definite**, indefinite | define | **definitely**, indefinitely |
| **demand**, demands | demanding, undemanding | **demand** | |
| **democracy**, democrat | democratic, undemocratic | | democratically |
| demonstration, demonstrator | demonstrable, demonstrative | **demonstrate** | demonstrably |
| denial | undeniable | **deny** | undeniably |
| dependant, dependence, independence, dependency | dependable, dependent, independent | **depend** | dependably, independently |
| **description** | describable, indescribable, nondescript, descriptive | **describe** | descriptively |
| **desire** | desirable, undesirable, desired, undesired | desire | |
| destroyer, destruction | indestructible, destructive | **destroy** | destructively |
| determination, determiner | **determined**, predetermined indeterminate | determine | determinedly |
| developer, **development**, redevelopment | developed, undeveloped, developing | **develop**, redevelop | |
| **difference**, indifference, differentiation | **different**, indifferent | differ, differentiate | differently |
| directness, **direction**, directions, **director** | **direct**, indirect | **direct**, redirect | directly, indirectly |
| disagreement | disagreeable | **disagree** | disagreeably |
| disappointment | **disappointed**, disappointing | disappoint | disappointingly |
| **disaster** | disastrous | | disastrously |
| disciplinarian, **discipline** | disciplinary, disciplined, undisciplined | discipline | |
| discoverer, **discovery** | | **discover** | |
| **distance** | **distant** | distance | distantly |
| disturbance | disturbed, undisturbed, disturbing | **disturb** | disturbingly |
| divide, division, subdivision | divided, undivided, divisible, divisive | **divide**, subdivide | |
| **divorce**, divorcee | divorced | divorce | |
| do, doing | done, overdone, undone | **do**, outdo, overdo, redo, undo | |
| **doubt**, doubter | undoubted, doubtful, doubtless | **doubt** | undoubtedly, doubtfully |
| **dream**, dreamer | dream, dreamless, dreamy | **dream** | dreamily |
| **dress**, dresser, dressing | dressed, undressed, dressy | **dress**, redress, undress | |
| **drink**, drinker, drinking, drunk, drunkenness | **drunk**, drunken | **drink** | drunkenly |
| drive, **driver**, driving | driving | **drive** | |
| due, dues | **due**, undue | | due, duly, unduly |
| earner, earnings | | **earn** | |
| **earth** | earthy, earthly, unearthly | unearth | |
| ease, unease, easiness | **easy**, uneasy | ease | **easily**, uneasily, easy |
| **east**, easterner | east, easterly, eastern | | east, eastward(s) |
| economics, economist, **economy** | **economic**, economical, uneconomic(al) | economize | economically |
| **education** | educated, uneducated, educational | educate | educationally |
| **effect**, effectiveness, ineffectiveness | **effective**, ineffective, ineffectual | effect | effectively, ineffectively |
| **effort** | effortless | | effortlessly |
| **election**, re-election, elector, electorate | unelected, electoral | elect, re-elect | |

| Nouns | Adjectives | Verbs | Adverbs |
|-------|-----------|-------|---------|
| electrician, **electricity** | **electric, electrical** | electrify | electrically |
| electronics | **electronic** | | electronically |
| embarrassment | **embarrassed, embarrassing** | embarrass | embarrassingly |
| **emotion** | emotional, emotive | | emotionally |
| **emphasis** | emphatic | **emphasize** | emphatically |
| employee, **employer, employment,** unemployment | unemployed | **employ** | |
| encouragement, discouragement | encouraged, encouraging, discouraging | **encourage**, discourage | encouragingly |
| **end**, ending | unending, endless | **end** | endlessly |
| **energy** | energetic | energize | energetically |
| enjoyment | enjoyable | **enjoy** | enjoyably |
| enormity | **enormous** | | enormously |
| **entrance**, entrant, **entry** | | **enter** | |
| entertainer, **entertainment** | entertaining | entertain | entertainingly |
| enthusiasm, enthusiast | **enthusiastic**, unenthusiastic | enthuse | enthusiastically, unenthusiastically |
| **environment**, environmentalist | environmental | | environmentally |
| equality, inequality | **equal**, unequal | equalize | **equally**, unequally |
| escape, escapism | escaped, inescapable | **escape** | inescapably |
| essence, essentials | **essential** | | essentially |
| estimate, estimation | estimated | **estimate**, overestimate, underestimate | |
| **event**, non-event | eventful, uneventful, eventual | | eventfully, eventually |
| **exam**, examination, cross-examination, examiner | | examine, cross-examine | |
| excellence | **excellent** | excel | excellently |
| **excitement** | excitable, **excited, exciting**, unexciting | excite | excitedly, excitingly |
| **excuse** | excusable, inexcusable | **excuse** | inexcusably |
| existence | non-existent, existing, pre-existing | **exist**, coexist | |
| expectancy, expectation | expectant, unexpected | **expect** | expectantly, unexpectedly |
| expenditure, **expense**, expenses | **expensive**, inexpensive | expend | expensively, inexpensively |
| **experience**, inexperience | **experienced**, inexperienced | experience | |
| **experiment** | experimental | experiment | experimentally |
| **expert**, expertise | expert, inexpert | | expertly |
| explaining, **explanation** | unexplained, explanatory, explicable, inexplicable | **explain** | inexplicably |
| explosion, explosive | exploding, explosive | **explode** | explosively |
| exploration, explorer | exploratory | **explore** | |
| **expression** | expressive | **express** | expressively |
| extreme, extremism, extremist, extremity | **extreme**, extremist | | **extremely** |
| **fact** | factual | | factually |
| fail, failure | unfailing | **fail** | unfailingly |
| fairness | **fair**, unfair | | **fairly**, unfairly |
| **faith**, faithfulness | faithful, unfaithful | | faithfully |
| familiarity, **family** | **familiar**, unfamiliar | familiarize | familiarly |
| fame | famed, **famous**, infamous | | famously, infamously |
| **fashion** | fashionable, unfashionable | fashion | fashionably, unfashionably |
| fat | **fat**, fattening, fatty | fatten | |
| fastener | | **fasten**, unfasten | |
| **fault** | faultless, faulty | fault | faultlessly |
| **fear** | fearful, fearless, fearsome | fear | fearfully, fearlessly |
| feel, **feeling**, feelings | unfeeling | **feel** | |

| Nouns | Adjectives | Verbs | Adverbs |
|---|---|---|---|
| **fiction**, nonfiction | fictional | | |
| fill, refill, filling | filling | **fill**, refill | |
| final, semifinal, finalist | **final** | finalize | **finally** |
| finish | finished, unfinished | **finish** | |
| firmness, infirmity | **firm**, infirm | | firmly |
| **fish**, fishing | fishy | fish | fishily |
| fit, fittings | fitted, fitting | **fit** | fittingly |
| fix, fixation, fixture | fixed, transfixed, unfixed | **fix** | |
| **flat** | **flat** | flatten | flat, flatly |
| **flower** | flowered/flowery, flowering | flower | |
| fold, folder | folded, folding | **fold**, unfold | |
| follower, following | following | **follow** | |
| **force** | forceful, forcible | **force** | forcefully, forcibly |
| **forest**, deforestation, forestry | forested | | |
| forgetfulness | forgetful, unforgettable | **forget** | forgetfully |
| forgiveness | forgiving, unforgiving | **forgive** | |
| **form**, formation, transformation, reformer, transformer | reformed | **form**, reform, transform | |
| formality | **formal**, informal | formalize | formally, informally |
| fortune | fortunate, unfortunate | | **fortunately**, unfortunately |
| freebie, **freedom** | **free** | **free** | free, freely |
| freeze, freezer, freezing | freezing, frozen | **freeze** | |
| frequency, infrequency | **frequent**, infrequent | frequent | **frequently**, infrequently |
| freshness, refreshments | **fresh**, refreshing | freshen, refresh | freshly, refreshingly |
| **friend**, friendliness | friendly, unfriendly | befriend | |
| fright | **frightened**, **frightening**, frightful | **frighten** | frighteningly, frightfully |
| **fruit**, fruition | fruitful, fruitless, fruity | | fruitfully, fruitlessly |
| **fund**, refund, funding | funded | fund, refund | |
| furnishings, **furniture** | furnished, unfurnished | furnish | |
| **garden**, gardener, gardening | | garden | |
| generalization | **general** | generalize | **generally** |
| generosity | **generous** | | generously |
| gentleness | **gentle** | | gently |
| gladness | **glad** | gladden | gladly |
| **glass**, glasses | glassy | | |
| good, goodies, goodness, goods | **good** | | |
| **government**, governor | governmental, governing | govern | governmentally |
| gratitude, ingratitude | **grateful**, ungrateful | | gratefully |
| greatness | **great** | | greatly |
| **green**, greenery, greens | **green** | | |
| **ground**, underground, grounding, grounds | groundless, underground | ground | underground |
| grower, **growth**, undergrowth | growing, grown, overgrown | **grow**, outgrow | |
| guilt, guiltiness | **guilty** | | guiltily |
| **habit** | habitual | | habitually |
| **hair**, hairiness | hairless, hairy | | |
| **hand**, handful | underhand, handy | **hand** | |
| handle, handler, handling | | **handle** | |
| hanger | hanging | **hang**, overhang | |
| happiness, unhappiness | **happy**, unhappy | | happily, unhappily |
| hardship | **hard** | harden | **hard**, hardly |
| **harm** | unharmed, harmful, harmless | **harm** | harmlessly |
| **head**, heading | overhead, heady | head, behead | overhead |
| **health** | **healthy**, unhealthy | | healthily, unhealthily |
| hearing | unheard, unheard of | **hear**, overhear | • |

| Nouns | Adjectives | Verbs | Adverbs |
|---|---|---|---|
| **heart** | heartened, heartening, heartless, hearty | | heartily, heartlessly |
| **heat**, heater, heating | heated, unheated | heat, overheat | heatedly |
| **height**, heights | heightened | heighten | |
| **help**, helper, helpfulness, helping | helpful, unhelpful, helpless | **help** | helpfully, helplessly |
| Highness | **high** | | high, highly |
| historian, **history** | historic, prehistoric, historical | | historically |
| hold, holder, holding | | **hold** | |
| **home** | homeless, homely | home | **home** |
| honesty, dishonesty | **honest**, dishonest | | honestly, dishonestly |
| **hope**, hopefulness, hopelessness | hopeful, hopeless | **hope** | **hopefully**, hopelessly |
| human, humanism, humanity, inhumanity | **human**, inhuman, superhuman, humane | | humanly, humanely |
| hunger | **hungry** | | hungrily |
| hurry | hurried, unhurried | **hurry** | hurriedly |
| hurt | unhurt, hurtful | **hurt** | hurtfully |
| **ice**, icicle, icing | icy | ice | icily |
| identification, identity | identifiable, unidentified | **identify** | |
| **imagination** | imaginable, unimaginable, imaginary, imaginative | **imagine** | unimaginably, imaginatively |
| **importance** | **important**, unimportant | | importantly |
| **impression** | impressionable, impressive | impress | impressively |
| **improvement** | improved | **improve** | |
| **increase** | increased | **increase** | increasingly |
| credibility, incredulity | **incredible**, credible, incredulous | | incredibly, incredulously |
| **independence**, independent | **independent** | | independently |
| industrialist, industrialization, **industry** | **industrial**, industrialized, industrious | | industrially, industriously |
| **infection**, disinfectant | infectious | infect, disinfect | infectiously |
| **inflation** | inflatable, inflated, inflationary | inflate, deflate | |
| informant, **information**, informer | informative, uninformative, informed, uninformed | inform, misinform | |
| **injury** | injured, uninjured | **injure** | |
| innocence | **innocent** | | innocently |
| insistence | insistent | **insist** | insistently |
| instance, instant | **instant**, instantaneous | | instantly, instantaneously |
| **instruction**, instructor | instructive | instruct | instructively |
| **intelligence** | **intelligent**, unintelligent, intelligible, unintelligible | | intelligently |
| intent, **intention** | intended, unintended, intentional, unintentional | **intend** | intentionally, unintentionally |
| **interest** | **interested**, disinterested, uninterested, **interesting** | interest | interestingly |
| interruption | uninterrupted | **interrupt** | |
| **interview**, interviewee | | interview | |
| **introduction** | introductory | **introduce** | |
| **invention**, inventiveness, inventor | inventive | **invent**, reinvent | inventively |
| **invitation**, invite | uninvited, inviting | **invite** | invitingly |
| **involvement** | **involved**, uninvolved | **involve** | |
| **item** | itemized | itemize | |
| **joke**, joker | | joke | jokingly |
| journal, journalism, **journalist** | journalistic | | |
| judge, **judg(e)ment** | judgmental | **judge** | |
| **juice**, juices | juicy | | |
| keenness | **keen** | | keenly |

| Nouns | Adjectives | Verbs | Adverbs |
|---|---|---|---|
| keep, keeper, keeping | kept | **keep** | |
| kill, overkill, killer, killing | | **kill** | |
| kindness, unkindness | **kind**, unkind | | kindly, unkindly |
| **knowledge** | knowing, knowledgeable, known, unknown | **know** | knowingly, unknowingly, knowledgeably |
| enlargement | **large** | enlarge | largely |
| laugh, **laughter** | laughable | **laugh** | laughably |
| **law, lawyer**, outlaw | lawful, unlawful | outlaw | lawfully, unlawfully |
| laziness | **lazy** | | lazily |
| **lead, leader**, leadership | lead, leading | **lead** | |
| learner, learning | learned, unlearned | **learn** | |
| legality, illegality, legalization | **legal**, illegal | legalize | legally, illegally |
| **length** | lengthening, lengthy | lengthen | lengthily |
| liar, **lie** | lying | lie | |
| **life** | lifeless, lifelike, lifelong | | lifelessly |
| **light**, lighter, lighting, lightness | **light** | light, lighten | lightly |
| dislike, liking | likeable | **like**, dislike | |
| likelihood | **likely**, unlikely | | likely |
| **limit**, limitation, limitations | limited, unlimited | **limit** | |
| **literature**, literacy | literary, literate, illiterate | | |
| liveliness, living | **live**, lively, living | **live**, outlive, relive | live |
| local, location, relocation | **local** | dislocate, relocate | locally |
| loser, **loss** | lost | **lose** | |
| | loud | | aloud, loud/loudly |
| **love**, lover | lovable, unlovable, loveless, lovely, loving | **love** | lovingly |
| low | **low**, lower, lowly | lower | low |
| **luck** | **lucky**, unlucky | | luckily, unluckily |
| **machine**, machinery, mechanic, mechanics, mechanism | mechanical, mechanized | | mechanically |
| **magic**, magician | magic, magical | | magically |
| make, remake, maker, making | unmade | **make**, remake | |
| **man**, manhood, mankind | manly, manned, unmanned | man | |
| **management**, manager | manageable, unmanageable, managerial | **manage** | |
| **mark**, marker, markings | marked, unmarked | **mark** | markedly |
| **market**, marketing | marketable | market | |
| **marriage** | **married**, unmarried | **marry**, remarry | |
| **match** | matching, unmatched | **match** | |
| **material**, materialism, materialist, materials | material, immaterial, materialistic | materialize | |
| **meaning** | meaningful, meaningless | **mean** | meaningfully |
| measure, **measurement** | measurable, immeasurable | **measure** | immeasurably |
| medical, medication, **medicine** | **medical**, medicated, medicinal | | medically |
| memorial, **memory** | memorable | memorize | memorably |
| mentality | **mental** | | mentally |
| **method**, methodology | methodical, methodological | | methodically |
| militancy, militant, the military, militia | **military**, militant | | militantly, militarily |
| **mind**, minder, reminder | mindless | **mind**, remind | mindlessly |
| minimum | minimal, **minimum** | minimize | minimally |
| miss | **missing** | **miss** | |
| **mistake** | mistaken, unmistakable | mistake | unmistakably, mistakenly |
| mix, mixer, **mixture** | mixed | **mix** | |
| modernity, modernization | **modern** | modernize | |
| **moment** | momentary, momentous | | momentarily |
| **mood**, moodiness | moody | | moodily |

| Nouns | Adjectives | Verbs | Adverbs |
|---|---|---|---|
| moral, morals, morality, immorality | **moral**, amoral, immoral | | morally |
| **mother**, motherhood | motherly | | |
| move, **movement**, removal, remover | movable, unmoved, moving | **move**, remove | movingly |
| **murder**, murderer | murderous | **murder** | murderously |
| **music**, musical, musician | musical, unmusical | | musically |
| name | named, unnamed, nameless | **name**, rename | namely |
| **nation**, national, multinational, nationalism, nationalist, nationality, nationalization | **national**, international, multinational, nationalistic | nationalize | nationally, internationally |
| **nature**, naturalist, naturalization, naturalness the supernatural | **natural**, supernatural, unnatural, naturalistic | naturalize | naturally, unnaturally |
| necessity | **necessary**, unnecessary | necessitate | necessarily, unnecessarily |
| **need**, needs | needless, needy | **need** | needlessly |
| nerve, nerves, nervousness | **nervous** | | nervously |
| **news**, renewal | **new**, renewable, renewed | renew | newly |
| **night**, midnight | | | overnight, nightly |
| **noise** | noisy | | noisily |
| normality/US normalcy, abnormality | **normal**, abnormal | | **normally**, abnormally |
| **north**, northerner | north, northerly, northern | | north, northward(s) |
| notice | noticeable, unnoticed | **notice** | noticeably |
| **number**, numeral | innumerable, numerical, numerous | number, outnumber | |
| **nurse**, nursery, nursing | | nurse | |
| obedience, disobedience | obedient, disobedient | **obey**, disobey | obediently, disobediently |
| **occasion** | occasional | | occasionally |
| **offence**/US **offense**, offender, offensive | offensive, inoffensive | **offend** | offensively |
| **office**, officer, official | **official**, unofficial | | officially, unofficially |
| the open, opener, opening, openness | **open**, opening | **open** | openly |
| **operation**, cooperation, operative, cooperative operator | operational, operative, cooperative | **operate**, cooperate | operationally |
| **opposition**, opposite | opposed, opposing, **opposite** | **oppose** | opposite |
| **option** | optional | opt | optionally |
| **order**, disorder | disordered, orderly, disorderly | **order** | |
| **organization**, disorganization, reorganization, organizer | organizational, organized, disorganized | **organize**, disorganize, reorganize | |
| origin, original, originality, originator | **original**, unoriginal | originate | **originally** |
| owner, ownership | | **own**, disown | |
| pack, package, packaging, packet, packing | packed | **pack**, unpack, package | |
| **pain** | pained, **painful**, painless | pain | painfully, painlessly |
| **paint**, painter, **painting** | | **paint** | |
| **part**, counterpart, parting, partition | partial, parting | part, partition | part, partially, **partly** |
| pass, overpass, underpass, passage, passing | passing | **pass** | |
| **patience**, impatience, **patient** | **patient**, impatient | | patiently, impatiently |
| pay, **payment**, repayment | unpaid, underpaid | **pay**, repay | |
| **peace** | **peaceful** | | peacefully |
| perfection, imperfection, perfectionist | **perfect**, imperfect | perfect | **perfectly** |

| Nouns | Adjectives | Verbs | Adverbs |
|---|---|---|---|
| **performance**, performer | | **perform** | |
| **permission**, permit | permissible, impermissible, permissive | permit | |
| **person**, **personality** | **personal**, impersonal, personalized | personalize, personify | personally |
| persuasion | persuasive | **persuade**, dissuade | persuasively |
| **photo**, **photograph**, photographer, photography | photogenic, photographic | photograph | |
| **picture** | pictorial, picturesque | picture | |
| **place**, placement, displacement, replacement | misplaced | place, displace, replace | |
| **plan**, planner, planning | unplanned | **plan** | |
| **plant**, transplant, plantation | | plant, transplant | |
| play, interplay, replay, **player**, playfulness | playful | **play**, outplay, replay | playfully |
| pleasantry, **pleasure**, displeasure | **pleasant**, unpleasant, **pleased**, displeased, pleasing, pleasurable | please, displease | pleasantly, unpleasantly |
| **poem**, poet, **poetry** | poetic | | |
| **point**, pointer | pointed, pointless | **point** | pointlessly |
| politeness | **polite**, impolite | | politely, impolitely |
| **politician**, **politics** | **political**, politicized | politicize | politically |
| popularity, unpopularity, popularization | **popular**, unpopular | popularize | popularly |
| **population** | populated, unpopulated, populous | populate | |
| **possibility**, impossibility, the impossible | **possible**, impossible | | **possibly**, impossibly |
| **post**, postage | postal | **post** | |
| **power**, superpower | **powerful**, overpowering, powerless | power, empower, overpower | powerfully |
| practical, practicalities, practicality | practicable, **practical**, impractical | | practically |
| **practice**, practitioner | practised/*US* practiced, practising/*US* practicing | **practise/*US* practice** | |
| precision | **precise**, imprecise | | precisely |
| preference | preferable, preferential | **prefer** | preferably |
| **preparation**, preparations | prepared, unprepared, preparatory | **prepare** | |
| presence, **present**, presentation, presenter | **present**, presentable | present, represent | presently |
| press, **pressure** | pressed, pressing, pressurized | **press**, pressure/pressurize | |
| prevention | preventable, preventive/preventative | **prevent** | |
| **price** | overpriced, priceless, pricey/pricy | price | |
| print, printer, printing | printed | **print** | |
| **prison**, **prisoner**, imprisonment | | imprison | |
| privacy, private, privatization | **private** | privatize | privately |
| probability | probable, improbable | | **probably**, improbably |
| **process**, processing, procession, processor | processed | process | |
| produce, producer, **product**, **production**, reproduction, productivity | productive, counterproductive, reproductive, unproductive | **produce**, reproduce | |
| profession, professional, professionalism | **professional**, unprofessional | | professionally |
| **profit**, profitability | profitable, unprofitable | profit | profitably |
| **progress**, progression | progressive | progress | progressively |
| **proof** | proven, unproven | prove, disprove | |

| Nouns | Adjectives | Verbs | Adverbs |
|---|---|---|---|
| protection, protector | protected, unprotected, protective | **protect** | protectively |
| provider, provision, provisions | provisional | **provide** | provisionally |
| public, publication, publicist, publicity | **public** | publicize | publicly |
| publisher, publishing | published, unpublished | **publish** | |
| **punishment** | punishable, punishing | **punish** | |
| purification, purist, purity, impurity | **pure**, impure | purify | purely |
| **purpose** | purposeful | | purposefully, purposely |
| push, pusher | pushed, pushy | **push** | |
| **qualification**, disqualification, qualifier | qualified, unqualified | qualify, disqualify | |
| **quarter**, quarters | quarterly | quarter | quarterly |
| **question**, questioning | questionable, unquestionable | question | unquestionably |
| quiet, disquiet | **quiet** | quieten/quiet | quietly |
| **race**, racism, racist | racial, multiracial, racist | | racially |
| rarity | **rare** | | rarely |
| **rate**, rating | overrated, underrated | rate, underrate | |
| **reaction**, reactor | reactionary | **react**, overreact | |
| read, reader, readership, **reading** | readable, unreadable | **read** | |
| readiness | **ready** | | readily |
| realism, realist, reality, unreality, realization | **real**, unreal, realistic, unrealistic | **realize** | real, **really**, realistically |
| **reason**, reasoning | reasonable, unreasonable | reason | reasonably, unreasonably |
| receipt, receipts, receiver, reception | receptive | **receive** | |
| recognition | recognizable, unrecognizable | **recognize** | recognizably |
| **record**, recorder, recording | recorded, unrecorded | **record** | |
| referee, reference, referral | | **refer**, referee | |
| reflection | reflective | **reflect** | |
| regret | regrettable, regretful | **regret** | regrettably, regretfully |
| regular, regularity, irregularity | **regular**, irregular | | **regularly**, irregularly |
| **relation**, relations, **relationship, relative** | **related**, unrelated, relative | relate | relatively |
| relaxation | **relaxed**, relaxing | **relax** | |
| reliability, reliance | **reliable**, unreliable, reliant | **rely** | reliably |
| **religion** | **religious**, irreligious | | religiously |
| the remainder, remains | remaining | **remain** | |
| **remark** | remarkable, unremarkable | remark | remarkably |
| repair, disrepair | irreparable | **repair** | irreparably |
| repeat, repetition | repeated, repetitive/repetitious | **repeat** | repeatedly, repetitively |
| **report**, reporter | unreported | **report** | reportedly |
| representation, representative | representative, unrepresentative | **represent** | |
| **reputation**, disrepute | reputable, disreputable, reputed | | reputedly |
| respect, disrespect, respectability | respectable, respected, respectful, disrespectful, respective | **respect** | respectably, respectfully, disrespectfully, respectively |
| respondent, **response**, responsiveness | responsive, unresponsive | **respond** | |
| **responsibility**, irresponsibility | **responsible**, irresponsible | | responsibly, irresponsibly |
| **rest**, unrest, restlessness | restless | **rest** | restlessly |
| retiree, retirement | retired, retiring | **retire** | |
| **reward** | rewarding, unrewarding | reward | |
| riches, richness, enrichment | **rich** | enrich | richly |
| ride, rider, riding | overriding | **ride**, override | |

| Nouns | Adjectives | Verbs | Adverbs |
|---|---|---|---|
| **right**, rightness, rights, righteousness | right, righteous, rightful | right | **right**, rightly, rightfully |
| **roll**, roller | | **roll**, unroll | |
| romance, romantic | **romantic**, unromantic, romanticized | romance, romanticize | romantically |
| rough, roughage, roughness | **rough** | rough, roughen | rough, **roughly** |
| round, rounders, roundness | **round**, rounded | round | **round**, roundly |
| royal, royalist, royalty | **royal**, royalist | | royally |
| rudeness | **rude** | | rudely |
| **rule**, ruler, ruling | ruling, unruly | rule, overrule | |
| **run**, rerun, runner, running | running, runny | **run**, outrun, overrun | |
| sadness | **sad** | sadden | sadly |
| safe, **safety** | **safe**, unsafe | | safely |
| satisfaction, dissatisfaction | **satisfactory**, unsatisfactory, **satisfied**, dissatisfied, unsatisfied, satisfying | satisfy | satisfactorily, unsatisfactorily |
| save, saver, saving, savings, saviour/*US* savior | | **save** | |
| | **scared**, scary | scare | |
| **school**, pre-school, schooling | pre-school | | |
| **science**, **scientist** | **scientific**, unscientific | | scientifically |
| **score**, scorer | | **score**, outscore, underscore | |
| **search**, research, researcher | searching | **search**, research | |
| **seat**, seating | seated | seat, unseat | |
| secrecy, secret | **secret**, secretive | | secretly, secretively |
| **sense**, nonsense, sensibility, sensitivity, insensitivity | **sensible**, senseless, sensitive, insensitive | sense | sensibly, sensitively, insensitively |
| separation | separable, inseparable, **separate** | **separate** | inseparably, separately |
| seriousness | **serious** | | **seriously** |
| servant, serve, server, **service**, disservice, the services, serving | serviceable, servile | **serve**, service | |
| **sex**, sexism, sexuality | sexist, **sexual**, bisexual, sexy | | sexually |
| **shadow** | shadowy | shadow, overshadow | |
| shake | shaky | **shake** | shakily |
| **shape** | shapeless, shapely | shape | |
| (pencil) sharpener, sharpness | **sharp** | sharpen | sharp, sharply |
| shine | shiny | **shine**, outshine | |
| **shock** | shocked, shocking | **shock** | shockingly |
| **shop**, shopper, **shopping** | | shop | |
| short, shortage, shortness, shorts | **short** | shorten | short, shortly |
| shyness | **shy** | shy | shyly |
| sick, sickness | **sick**, sickening, sickly | sicken | sickeningly |
| **sight**, insight, oversight, sighting | sighted, unsightly | sight | |
| **sign**, **signal**, signatory, signature, signing | signed, unsigned | **sign**, signal | |
| significance, insignificance | **significant**, insignificant | signify | significantly, insignificantly |
| **silence**, silencer | **silent** | silence | silently |
| similarity | **similar**, dissimilar | | similarly |
| simplicity, simplification | **simple**, simplistic | simplify | simply |
| singer, singing | unsung | **sing** | |
| single, singles | **single**, singular | single | singly |
| **skill** | skilful/*US* skillful, skilled, unskilled | | skilfully/*US* skillfully |
| **sleep**, sleeper, sleepiness, sleeplessness | asleep, sleepless, sleepy | **sleep** | sleepily |
| slight | **slight**, slighted, slightest | | **slightly** |

| Nouns | Adjectives | Verbs | Adverbs |
|---|---|---|---|
| slip, slipper | slippery | **slip** | |
| **smoke**, smoker, non-smoker, smoking | smoked, smoking, non-smoking, smoky | **smoke** | |
| smoothness | **smooth** | smooth | smoothly |
| **society**, sociologist, sociology | sociable, unsociable, **social**, anti-social, unsocial | socialize | socially |
| softness | **soft** | soften | softly |
| solid, solidarity, solidity, solids | **solid** | solidify | solidly |
| **solution**, solvent | soluble, insoluble, unsolved, solvent | **solve** | |
| **south**, southerner | south, southerly, southern | | south, southward(s) |
| speaker, **speech** | unspeakable, speechless, outspoken, unspoken | **speak** | unspeakably |
| special, specialist, speciality/*US* specialty specialization | **special**, specialized | specialize | **specially** |
| **speed**, speeding | speedy | speed | speedily |
| spelling | | **spell**, misspell | |
| spoils | spoilt/spoiled, unspoiled/unspoilt | **spoil** | |
| **sport** | sporting, sporty | sport | |
| **spot** | spotted, spotless, spotty | spot | spotlessly |
| stand, standing | standing, outstanding | **stand** | outstandingly |
| **standard**, standardization | standard, substandard | standardize | |
| **start**, starter, non-starter | | **start**, restart | |
| **statement**, understatement | understated | state, overstate | |
| **steam**, steamer | steamy | steam | |
| steepness | **steep** | | steeply |
| sticker | sticky, stuck, unstuck | **stick** | |
| stiffness | **stiff** | stiffen | stiff, stiffly |
| **stone** | stoned, stony | stone | |
| stop, stoppage | non-stop | **stop** | non-stop |
| **storm** | stormy | storm | |
| | **straight** | straighten | **straight** |
| stranger | **strange** | | strangely |
| **strength** | **strong** | strengthen | strongly |
| **stress** | stressed, stressful | stress | |
| strike, striker | striking | **strike** | |
| **structure**, restructuring | structural | structure, restructure | structurally |
| **student**, **study** | studious | **study** | studiously |
| stupidity | **stupid** | | stupidly |
| **style** | stylish | style | stylishly |
| **substance** | substantial, insubstantial, substantive | substantiate | substantially |
| **success**, succession, successor | **successful**, unsuccessful, successive | **succeed** | successfully, unsuccessfully |
| suddenness | **sudden** | | **suddenly** |
| sufferer, suffering | insufferable | **suffer** | insufferably |
| **suggestion** | suggestive | **suggest** | suggestively |
| **summer**, midsummer | summery | | |
| supplier, supplies, **supply** | | **supply** | |
| **support**, supporter | supportive | **support** | |
| supposition | supposed | **suppose**, presuppose | supposedly |
| **surface** | | surface, resurface | |
| **surprise** | **surprised**, surprising | surprise | surprisingly |
| surroundings | surrounding | **surround** | |
| survival, survivor | | **survive** | |
| suspect, suspicion | suspect, suspected, unsuspecting, suspicious | **suspect** | suspiciously |
| swearing | sworn | **swear** | |

| Nouns | Adjectives | Verbs | Adverbs |
|---|---|---|---|
| sweet, sweetener, sweetness | **sweet** | sweeten | sweetly |
| swim, swimmer, swimming | | **swim** | |
| **symbol**, symbolism | symbolic | symbolize | symbolically |
| **sympathy**, sympathizer | **sympathetic**, unsympathetic | sympathize | sympathetically |
| **system** | systematic | | systematically |
| takings, undertaking | | **take**, overtake, undertake | |
| **talk**, talks | talkative | **talk** | |
| **taste**, distaste | tasteful, distasteful, tasteless, tasty | **taste** | tastefully, distastefully |
| **tax**, taxation | taxable, taxing | tax | |
| **teacher**, teaching, teachings | | **teach** | |
| **tear** | tearful | | tearfully |
| technicalities, technicality, technician, technique | **technical** | | technically |
| **technology** | technological | | technologically |
| **thanks** | thankful, thankless | **thank** | thankfully |
| theorist, **theory** | theoretical | theorize | theoretically |
| thick, thickness | **thick** | thicken | thickly |
| thinness | **thin** | thin | thinly |
| think, rethink, thinker, thinking | unthinkable | **think**, rethink | |
| thirst | **thirsty** | | thirstily |
| **thought**, thoughtfulness | thoughtful, thoughtless | | thoughtfully, thoughtlessly |
| **threat** | threatening | **threaten** | threateningly |
| tightness | **tight** | tighten | tight, tightly |
| **time**, overtime, timer, timing | timeless, timely, untimely | time | |
| tiredness | **tired**, tireless, tiresome, tiring | tire | tirelessly |
| **title**, subtitles | titled | entitle | |
| **top**, topping | **top**, topless, topmost | top | |
| touch | touched, untouched, touching, touchy | **touch** | touchingly |
| | **tough** | toughen | toughly |
| **trade**, trader, trading | | trade | |
| **tradition**, traditionalist | **traditional** | | traditionally |
| trainee, trainer, **training**, retraining | untrained | **train** | |
| **transport**, transportation | | transport | |
| treat, **treatment**, mistreatment | untreated | **treat**, mistreat | |
| **trick**, trickery | tricky | trick | |
| **trouble** | troubled, troublesome | trouble | |
| **trust**, distrust, mistrust, trustee | trusting, trustworthy | **trust**, distrust, mistrust | |
| **truth**, untruth, truthfulness | **true**, untrue, truthful | | truly, truthfully |
| try | trying, untried | **try** | |
| **turn**, upturn, turning | upturned | **turn**, overturn | |
| twist, twister | twisted | **twist** | |
| **type** | **typical** | typify | typically |
| understanding, misunderstanding | understandable, understanding, misunderstood | **understand**, misunderstand | understandably |
| upset | **upset**, upsetting | upset | |
| urgency | **urgent** | | urgently |
| usage, **use**, disuse, misuse, usefulness, user | reusable, **used**, disused, unused, **useful**, **useless** | **use**, misuse, reuse | usefully |
| valuables, **value**, values | **valuable**, invaluable, undervalued | value, devalue | |
| variable, variance, variant, **variety** | variable, varied, **various** | vary | invariably, variously |
| **view**, overview, preview, review, viewer | | view, preview, review | |

| Nouns | Adjectives | Verbs | Adverbs |
|---|---|---|---|
| **violence** | **violent**, non-violent | violate | violently |
| **visit**, **visitor** | | **visit**, revisit | |
| **vote**, voter | | **vote** | |
| want, wants | wanted, unwanted | **want** | |
| **war**, warfare, warrior | postwar, warring | | |
| warmth | **warm** | warm | warmly |
| wash, washer, washing | washable, unwashed | **wash** | |
| wastage, **waste** | waste, wasteful | **waste** | wastefully |
| **watch** | watchful | **watch** | |
| **water**, waters | underwater, waterproof, watery | water | underwater |
| **way**, subway | | | midway |
| weakling, weakness | **weak** | weaken | weakly |
| wear, underwear | wearing, worn | **wear** | |
| **week**, midweek | weekly, midweek | | weekly, midweek |
| **weight**, weights | overweight, underweight, weighted, weighty | **weigh**, outweigh | |
| welcome | welcome, unwelcome | **welcome** | |
| **west**, western, westerner | westerly, western | | west, westward(s) |
| **white**, whiteness | **white** | whiten | |
| **whole** | **whole**, wholesome, unwholesome | | |
| width | **wide** | widen | **wide**, **widely** |
| wild, wildness | **wild** | | wildly |
| willingness, unwillingness | **willing**, unwilling | | willingly, unwillingly |
| win, **winner**, winnings | | **win** | |
| **winter**, midwinter | wintry | | |
| **wire**, wireless, wiring | wiry | wire | |
| **woman**, womanhood | womanly | | |
| wonder | **wonderful** | **wonder** | wonderfully |
| **wood** | wooded, wooden | | |
| **wool** | woollen/*US* woolen, woolly/*US* wooly | | |
| **word**, wording | | word | |
| **work**, workaholic, worker, workings | workable, unworkable, overworked, working | **work**, rework | |
| **world**, underworld | world, worldly, unworldly, worldwide | | worldwide |
| worry | **worried**, unworried, worrying | **worry** | worryingly |
| **worth** | **worth**, worthless, worthwhile, worthy, unworthy | | |
| **writer**, **writing** | written, unwritten | **write**, rewrite | |
| wrong | **wrong**, wrongful | wrong | **wrong**, wrongly, wrongfully |
| **year** | yearly | | yearly |
| young, youngster, youth | **young**, youthful | | |